McDougal Littell

CLASSZONE

Visit classzone.com and get connected.

ClassZone resources provide instruction, practice and learning support for students and parents.

Activity Center

- Create games with the Activity Maker
- Interactive NetExplorations offer project ideas and links to related topics

Review Center

- Provides a unique way to review key concepts and events
- Chapter quizzes and instant feedback

Current Events

- Takes you beyond the text and keeps you up-to-date on world events
- Reflects the most recent political, economic, and social issues
- Provides weekly current events quizzes to help check comprehension

Research and Writing

- Includes links to primary sources, chapter resources, biographies, and state-specific resources
- Provides support for your writing assignments through complete writing models, rubrics, and research guides

Access the online version of your textbook at classzone.com

Your complete text, along with animated maps, charts and infographics, is available for immediate use!

McDougal Littell
Where Great Lessons Begin

New York EDITION

WORLD HISTORY

PATTERNS OF INTERACTION

Roger B. Beck

Linda Black

Larry S. Krieger

Phillip C. Naylor

Dahia Ibo Shabaka

Senior Consultants

Roger B. Beck, Ph.D.

Roger B. Beck is a professor of African History, World History, History of the Third World, and Social Studies Methods at Eastern Illinois University. He is also a social studies student teacher supervisor at that university. Dr. Beck recently served as associate dean of the Graduate School and International Programs at Eastern Illinois University. In addition to his distinguished teaching career at high school, college, and graduate school levels, Dr. Beck is a contributing author to several books and has written numerous articles, reviews, and papers. He is also an active member of the National Council for the Social Studies, the World History Association, and the African Studies Association. Dr. Beck was a key contributor to the National Standards for World History.

Linda Black, B.A., M.Ed.

Linda Black teaches World History at Cypress Falls High School in Houston, Texas, and has had a distinguished career in education as a teacher of world history, American history, and Texas history. In 1993–1994, Mrs. Black was named an Outstanding Secondary Social Studies Teacher in the United States by the National Council for the Social Studies. In 1996, she was elected to the Board of Directors of the National Council for the Social Studies. She is an active member of that council, the Texas Council for the Social Studies, and the World History Association. She served on the College Board Test Development for Advanced Placement World History from 1995 to 2003.

Larry S. Krieger, B.A., M.A., M.A.T.

Larry S. Krieger is the social studies supervisor for grades K-12 in Montgomery Township Public Schools in New Jersey. For 26 years he has taught world history in public schools. He has also introduced many innovative in-service programs, such as "Putting the Story Back in History," and has co-authored several successful history textbooks. Mr. Krieger earned his B.A. and M.A.T. from the University of North Carolina and his M.A. from Wake Forest University.

Phillip C. Naylor, Ph.D.

Phillip C. Naylor is an associate professor of history at Marquette University and teaches European, North African, and West Asian undergraduate and graduate courses. He was the director of the Western Civilization program for nine years where he inaugurated a "transcultural approach" to the teaching of the traditional survey. He has authored *France and Algeria: A History of Decolonization and Transformation*, coauthored *The Historical Dictionary of Algeria*, and coedited *State and Society in Algeria*. He has published numerous articles, papers, and reviews, and produced CD-ROM projects. In 1996, Dr. Naylor received the Reverend John P. Raynor, S.J., Faculty Award for Teaching Excellence at Marquette University. In 1992, he received the Edward G. Roddy Teaching Award at Merrimack College.

Dahia Ibo Shabaka, B.A., M.A., Ed.S.

Dahia Ibo Shabaka is the director of Social Studies and African-Centered Education in the Detroit Public Schools system. She has an extensive educational and scholarly background in the disciplines of history, political science, economics, law, and reading, and in secondary education, curriculum development, and school administration and supervision. Ms. Shabaka has been a teacher, a curriculum coordinator, and a supervisor of social studies in the Detroit Secondary Schools. In 1991 she was named Social Studies Educator of the Year by the Michigan Council for the Social Studies. Ms. Shabaka is the recipient of a Fulbright Fellowship at the Hebrew University in Israel and has served as an executive board member of the National Social Studies Supervisors Association.

Acknowledgments begin on page R135.
ISBN-13 978-0-618-91330-5 ISBN-10 0-618-91330-0
Printed in the United States of America.
4 5 6 7 8 9–DWO–12 11 10 09 08

This text contains material that appeared originally in *World History: Perspectives on the Past* (D.C. Heath and Company) by Larry S. Krieger, Kenneth Neill, and Dr. Edward Reynolds.

NEW YORK REVIEWERS

Mark Chenault
West Side High School
New York, NY

Michael Harnick
Williamsville East High School
East Amherst, NY

Bryant Harris
Thurgood Marshall Academy
New York, NY

Amy R. Kantz
Williamsville East High School
East Amherst, NY

Lisa Kissinger
Shenendehowa High School
Clifton Park, NY

Paul Lampe
Rochester City Schools
Rochester, NY

Nick Petraccione
Bethlehem Central Schools
Delmar, NY

Mark F. Whitworth
Bronx Regional High School
New York, NY

Content Consultants

The content consultants reviewed the content for historical depth and accuracy and for clarity of presentation.

Jerry Bentley
Department of History
University of Hawaii
Honolulu, Hawaii

Marc Brettler
Department of Near Eastern and Judaic Studies
Brandeis University
Waltham, Massachusetts

Steve Gosch
Department of History
University of Wisconsin at Eau Claire
Eau Claire, Wisconsin

Don Holsinger
Department of History
Seattle Pacific University
Seattle, Washington

Patrick Manning
World History Center
Department of History
Northeastern University
Boston, Massachusetts

Richard Saller
Department of History
University of Chicago
Chicago, Illinois

Wolfgang Schlauch
Department of History
Eastern Illinois University
Charleston, Illinois

Susan Schroeder
Department of History
Loyola University of Chicago
Chicago, Illinois

Scott Waugh
Department of History
University of California, Los Angeles
Los Angeles, California

Multicultural Advisory Board Consultants

The multicultural advisers reviewed the manuscript for appropriate historical content.

Pat A. Brown
Director of the Indianapolis Public Schools Office of African Centered Multicultural Education
Indianapolis Public Schools
Indianapolis, Indiana

Ogle B. Duff
Associate Professor of English
University of Pittsburgh
Pittsburgh, Pennsylvania

Mary Ellen Maddox
Black Education Commission Director
Los Angeles Unified School District
Los Angeles, California

Jon Reyhner
Associate Professor and Coordinator of the Bilingual Multicultural Education Program
Northern Arizona University
Flagstaff, Arizona

Ysidro Valenzuela
Fresno High School
Fresno, California

Consultants and Reviewers (continued)

Teacher Review Panels

The following educators provided ongoing review during the development of prototypes, the table of contents, and key components of the program.

Patrick Adams
Pasadena High School
Pasadena, Texas

Bruce Bekemeyer
Marquette High School
Chesterfield, Missouri

Ellen Bell
Bellaire High School
Bellaire, Texas

Margaret Campbell
Central High School
St. Louis, Missouri

Nancy Coates
Belleville East High School
Belleville, Illinois

Kim Coil
Francis Howell North High School
St. Charles, Missouri

Craig T. Grace
Lanier High School
West Austin, Texas

Katie Ivey
Dimmitt High School
Dimmitt, Texas

Gary Kasprovich
Granite City High School
Granite City, Illinois

Pat Knapp
Burgess High School
El Paso, Texas

Eric R. Larson
Clark High School
Plano, Texas

Linda Marrs
Naaman Forest High School
Garland, Texas

Harry McCown
Hazelwood West High School
Hazelwood, Missouri

Terry McRae
Robert E. Lee High School
Tyler, Texas

Joseph Naumann (retired)
McCluer North High School
Florissant, Missouri

Sherrie Prahl
The Woodlands High School
The Woodlands, Texas

Dorothy Schulze
Health Careers High School
San Antonio, Texas

Liz Silva
Townview Magnet Center
Dallas, Texas

Linda Stevens
Central High School
San Angelo, Texas

Leonard Sullivan
Pattonville High School
Maryland Hts., Missouri

Carole Weeden
Fort Zumwalt South High School
St. Peters, Missouri

Rita Wylie
Parkway West Sr. High School
Ballwin, Missouri

Teacher Consultants

Glenn Bird
Springville High School
Springville, Utah

Michael Cady
North High School
Phoenix, Arizona

William Canter
Guilford High School
Rockford, Illinois

Nancy Coates
Belleville East High School
Belleville, Illinois

Paul Fitzgerald
Estancia High School
Costa Mesa, California

Craig T. Grace
Lanier High School
West Austin, Texas

Joy McKee
Lamar High School
Arlington, Texas

Terry McRae
Robert E. Lee High School
Tyler, Texas

Myra Osman
Homewood Flossmoor High School
Flossmoor, Illinois

Dorothy Schulze
Health Careers High School
Dallas, Texas

Linda Stevens
Central High School
San Angelo, Texas

The following educators wrote activities for the program.

Charlotte Albaugh
Grand Prairie High School
Grand Prairie, Texas

Mark Aguirre
Scripps Ranch High School
San Diego, California

Sharon Ballard
L.D. Bell High School
Hurst, Texas

Bryon Borgelt
St. John's Jesuit High School
Toledo, Ohio

William Brown (retired)
Northeast High School
Philadelphia, Pennsylvania

Haley Brice Clark
DeBakey Health Prof. High School
Houston, Texas

John Devine
Elgin High School
Elgin, Illinois

Karen Dingeldein
Cudahy High School
Cudahy, Wisconsin

Joanne Dodd
Scarborough High School
Houston, Texas

Jan Ellersieck
Ft. Zummalt South High School
St. Peters, Missouri

Craig T. Grace
Lanier High School
West Austin, Texas

Korri Kinney
Meridian High School
Meridian, Idaho

Jerome Love
Beaumont High School
St. Louis, Missouri

Melissa Mack
St. Margaret's High School
San Juan Capistrano, California

Harry McCown
Hazelwood West High School
Hazelwood, Missouri

Terry McRae
Robert E. Lee High School
Tyler, Texas

Joseph Naumann (retired)
McCluer North High School
Florissant, Missouri

Theresa C. Noonan
West Irondequoit High School
Rochester, New York

Robert Parker
St. Margaret's High School
San Juan Capistrano, California

Janet Rogolsky
Sylvania Southview High School
Sylvania, Ohio

Dorothy Schulze
Health Careers High School
San Antonio, Texas

Evelyn Sims
Skyline Center High School
Dallas, Texas

Brenda Smith
Colorado Springs School District 11
Colorado Springs, Colorado

Linda Stevens
Central High School
San Angelo, Texas

Leonard Sullivan
Pattonville High School
Maryland Heights, Missouri

Linda Tillis
South Oak Cliff High School
Dallas, Texas

Andrew White
Morrow High School
Clayton, Georgia

Student Board

The following students reviewed prototype materials for the textbook.

LaShaunda Allen
Weston High School
Greenville, MS

Brandy Andreas
Rayburn High School
Pasadena, TX

Adam Bishop
Jordan High School
Sandy, UT

Jennifer Bragg
Midlothian High School
Midlothian, VA

Nicole Fevry
Midwood High School
Brooklyn, NY

Phillip Gallegos
Hilltop High School
Chula Vista, CA

Matt Gave
Stevenson Senior High School
Sterling Heights, MI

Blair Hogan
Leesville Road High School
Raleigh, NC

Ngoc Hong
Watkins Mill Senior High School
Gaithersburg, MD

Iman Jalali
Glenbrook North High School
Northbrook, IL

Vivek Makhijani
Durfee High School
Fall River, MA

Todd McDavitt
Derby High School
Derby, KS

Teniqua Mitchell
Linden-McKinley High School
Columbus, OH

Cicely Nash
Edmond Memorial High School
Edmond, OK

Brian Nebrensky
Hillsboro High School
Hillsboro, OR

Jesse Neumyer
Cumberland Valley High School
Mechanicsburg, PA

Nora Patronas
Alba High School
Bayou La Batre, LA

Lindsey Petersen
Stoughton High School
Stoughton, WI

Nicholas Price
Central Lafourche Senior
High School
Mathews, LA

Ben Richey
Fort Vancouver High School
Vancouver, WA

Karen Ryan
Silver Creek High School
San Jose, CA

Matt Shaver
Weatherford High School
Weatherford, TX

Richie Spitler
Atlantic High School
Port Orange, FL

Jessie Stoneberg
Burnsville High School
Burnsville, MN

Kelly Swick
Ocean Township High School
Oakhurst, NJ

Jason Utzig
Kenmore East High School
Tonawanda, NY

Justin Woodly
North Cobb High School
Kennesaw, GA

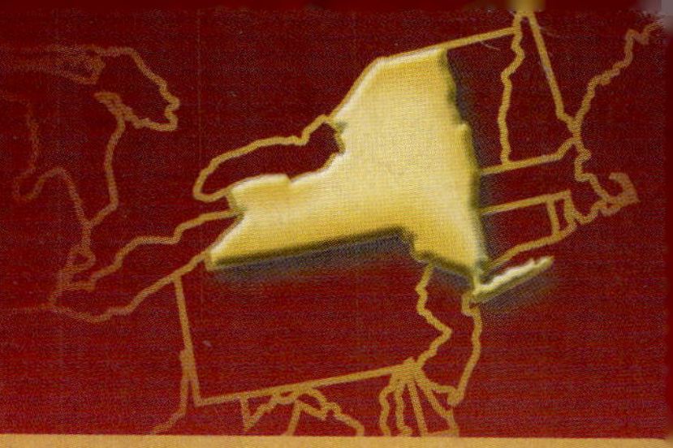

NEW YORK

OVERVIEW
New York Student Edition

New York Edition Table of Contents NY8

New York Steps to Success NY39

- Guide to Understanding New York State's Core Curriculum: Global History and Geography
- Guide to the New York State Regents Exam

Lessons with Embedded New York State Core Curriculum Content

Look for the New York symbol throughout this book. It highlights targeted content to help you succeed on your test.

Complete New York State Core Curriculum: Global History and Geography R149

Liberty Island, New York © Christopher Hill/Alamy

Beginnings of Civilization

4 million B.C.–200 B.C.

Introduction
Guide to the New York State Regents Exam S1
RAND McNALLY World Atlas A1

CHAPTER 1 Prehistory–2500 B.C.
The Peopling of the World 2
1 Human Origins in Africa 5
ANALYZING KEY CONCEPTS: *Culture* 6
HISTORY THROUGH ART: *Cave Paintings* 12
2 Humans Try to Control Nature 14
3 Civilization
CASE STUDY *Ur in Sumer* 19
2 ANALYZING KEY CONCEPTS: *Civilization* 21
New York State Regents Exam Practice 25

CHAPTER 2 3500 B.C.–450 B.C.
Early River Valley Civilizations 26
1 City-States in Mesopotamia 29
2 Pyramids on the Nile 35
HISTORY IN DEPTH: *Pyramids and Mummies* 39
SOCIAL HISTORY: *Work and Play in Ancient Egypt* 42
3 Planned Cities on the Indus 44
SCIENCE & TECHNOLOGY: *Plumbing in Mohenjo-Daro* 47
4 River Dynasties in China 50
New York State Regents Exam Practice 57

CHAPTER 3 2000 B.C.–250 B.C
People and Ideas on the Move 58
1 The Indo-Europeans 61
2 Hinduism and Buddhism Develop 66
3 Seafaring Traders 72
HISTORY IN DEPTH: *Phoenician Trade* 75
4 The Origins of Judaism 77
ANALYZING KEY CONCEPTS: *Judaism* 80
DIFFERENT PERSPECTIVES: *The Flood Story* 83
New York State Regents Exam Practice 85

CHAPTER 4 1570 B.C.–200 B.C.
First Age of Empires 86
1 The Egyptian and Nubian Empires 89
HISTORY IN DEPTH: *Egyptian Influence on Nubian Culture* 92
2 The Assyrian Empire 95
3 The Persian Empire 99
GLOBAL IMPACT: *Empire Building* 102
4 The Unification of China 104
HISTORY IN DEPTH: *The Great Wall of China* 108
New York State Regents Exam Practice 111

COMPARING AND CONTRASTING: *Ancient Civilizations* 112

Tutankhamen death mask
(page 39)

Hebrew Flood Story art
(page 83)

Great Wall of China
(page 108)

New Directions in Government and Society

2000 B.C.–A.D. 700

CHAPTER 5 2000 B.C.–300 B.C.

Classical Greece — 120

1 **Cultures of the Mountains and the Sea** 123
2 **Warring City-States** 127
HISTORY IN DEPTH: *Festivals and Sports* 130
3 **Democracy and Greece's Golden Age** 134
HISTORY THROUGH ART: *Greek Art and Architecture* 140
4 **Alexander's Empire** 142
5 **The Spread of Hellenistic Culture** 146
New York State Regents Exam Practice 151

CHAPTER 6 500 B.C.–A.D. 500

Ancient Rome and Early Christianity — 152

1 **The Roman Republic** 155
2 **The Roman Empire** 160
SOCIAL HISTORY: *Life in a Roman Villa* 166
3 **The Rise of Christianity** 168
4 **The Fall of the Roman Empire** 173
DIFFERENT PERSPECTIVES: *The Fall of the Roman Empire* 177
5 **Rome and the Roots of Western Civilization** 178
ANALYZING KEY CONCEPTS: *Western Civilization* 180
SCIENCE & TECHNOLOGY: *The Colosseum* 182
New York State Regents Exam Practice 185

CHAPTER 7 400 B.C.–A.D. 550

India and China Establish Empires — 186

1 **India's First Empires** 189
2 **Trade Spreads Indian Religions and Culture** 193
HISTORY THROUGH ART: *Hindu and Buddhist Art* 198
3 **Han Emperors in China** 200
GLOBAL IMPACT: *Trade Networks* 204
New York State Regents Exam Practice 209

CHAPTER 8 1500 B.C.–A.D. 700

African Civilizations — 210

1 **Diverse Societies in Africa** 213
SCIENCE & TECHNOLOGY: *African Ironworking* 218
2 **Migration**
CASE STUDY *Bantu-Speaking Peoples* 220
3 **The Kingdom of Aksum** 225
New York State Regents Exam Practice 231

CHAPTER 9 40,000 B.C.–A.D. 700

The Americas: A Separate World — 232

1 **The Earliest Americans** 235
2 **Early Mesoamerican Civilizations** 240
HISTORY THROUGH ART: *Olmec Sculpture* 244
3 **Early Civilizations of the Andes** 246
HISTORY IN DEPTH: *Nazca Lines* 248
New York State Regents Exam Practice 251

COMPARING AND CONTRASTING: *Classical Ages* 252

Roman fresco, Pompeii, Italy (page 167)

Asoka's lions (page 190)

Kuba mask, Africa (page 224)

UNIT 3

NEW YORK

An Age of Exchange and Encounter

500–1500

Dome of the Rock
(page 266)

CHAPTER 10 600–1250

The Muslim World 260

1 **The Rise of Islam** 263
ANALYZING ARCHITECTURE: *The Dome of the Rock* 266
2 **Islam Expands** 269
3 **Muslim Culture** 273
SCIENCE & TECHNOLOGY: *Astronomy* 275
New York State Regents Exam Practice 281

WORLD RELIGIONS AND ETHICAL SYSTEMS 282

Buddhism 284
Christianity 286
Hinduism 288
Islam 290
Judaism 292
Confucianism 294

11th century Byzantine cross
(page 301)

CHAPTER 11 500–1500

Byzantines, Russians, and Turks Interact 298

1 **The Byzantine Empire** 301
ANALYZING KEY CONCEPTS: *Roman Catholicism and Eastern Orthodoxy* 305
2 **The Russian Empire** 307
HISTORY THROUGH ART: *Russian Religious Art and Architecture* 312
3 **Turkish Empires Rise in Anatolia** 314
New York State Regents Exam Practice 319

CHAPTER 12 600–1350

Empires in East Asia 320

1 **Tang and Song China** 323
SOCIAL HISTORY: *Tang and Song China: People and Technology* 328
2 **The Mongol Conquests** 330
HISTORY IN DEPTH: *A Mighty Fighting Force* 332
3 **The Mongol Empire** 335
4 **Feudal Powers in Japan** 339
HISTORY IN DEPTH: *Japanese Samurai* 342
5 **Kingdoms of Southeast Asia and Korea** 344
New York State Regents Exam Practice 349

Tang and Song China,
movable type (page 329)

CHAPTER 13 500–1200

European Middle Ages 350

1 Charlemagne Unites Germanic Kingdoms 353
2 Feudalism in Europe 358
ANALYZING KEY CONCEPTS: *Feudalism* 361
3 The Age of Chivalry 364
SCIENCE & TECHNOLOGY: *Castles and Siege Weapons* 366
4 The Power of the Church 370
New York State Regents Exam Practice 375

CHAPTER 14 800–1500

The Formation of Western Europe 376

1 Church Reform and the Crusades 379
HISTORY IN DEPTH: *Gothic Architecture* 381
DIFFERENT PERSPECTIVES: *The Crusades* 386
2 Changes in Medieval Society 387
3 England and France Develop 393
4 The Hundred Years' War and the Plague 398
GLOBAL IMPACT: *The Spread of Epidemic Disease* 400
New York State Regents Exam Practice 405

CHAPTER 15 800–1500

Societies and Empires of Africa 406

1 North and Central African Societies 409
2 West African Civilizations 413
HISTORY THROUGH ART: *Benin Bronzes* 420
3 Eastern City-States and Southern Empires 422
ANALYZING ARCHITECTURE: *Great Zimbabwe* 426
New York State Regents Exam Practice 429

COMPARING AND CONTRASTING: *Trade Networks* 430

Illuminated manuscript (page 354)

Emperor Charlemagne (page 357)

Benin sculpture (page 421)

UNIT 4

NEW YORK

Connecting Hemispheres

500–1800

Elizabeth I of England (page 493)

Safavid shah (page 506)

Early globe (page 529)

CHAPTER 16 500–1500

People and Empires in the Americas 438

1 North American Societies 441
2 Maya Kings and Cities 446
HISTORY THROUGH ART: *Maya Architecture* 450
3 The Aztecs Control Central Mexico 452
HISTORY IN DEPTH: *The Aztec Calendar* 457
4 The Inca Create a Mountain Empire 459
SOCIAL HISTORY: *Incan Mummies* 464
New York State Regents Exam Practice 467

CHAPTER 17 1300–1600

European Renaissance and Reformation 468

1 Italy: Birthplace of the Renaissance 471
HISTORY THROUGH ART: *Renaissance Ideas Influence Renaissance Art* 478
2 The Northern Renaissance 480
SOCIAL HISTORY: *City Life in Renaissance Europe* 486
3 Luther Leads the Reformation 488
ANALYZING KEY CONCEPTS: *Protestantism* 491
4 The Reformation Continues 495
DIFFERENT PERSPECTIVES: *The Reformation* 501
New York State Regents Exam Practice 503

CHAPTER 18 1300–1700

The Muslim World Expands 504

1 The Ottomans Build a Vast Empire 507
2 Cultural Blending
CASE STUDY *The Safavid Empire* 512
3 The Mughal Empire in India 516
HISTORY THROUGH ART: *Cultural Blending in Mughal India* 522
New York State Regents Exam Practice 525

CHAPTER 19 1400–1800

An Age of Explorations and Isolation 526

1 Europeans Explore the East 529
SCIENCE & TECHNOLOGY: *The Tools of Exploration* 531
2 China Limits European Contacts 536
HISTORY IN DEPTH: *The Forbidden City* 538
3 Japan Returns to Isolation 542
New York State Regents Exam Practice 549

CHAPTER 20 1492–1800

The Atlantic World 550

1 Spain Builds an American Empire 553
DIFFERENT PERSPECTIVES: *The Legacy of Columbus* 560
2 European Nations Settle North America 561
3 The Atlantic Slave Trade 566
4 The Columbian Exchange and Global Trade 571
GLOBAL IMPACT: *Food Exchange* 572
ANALYZING KEY CONCEPTS: *Mercantilism* 574
New York State Regents Exam Practice 577

COMPARING AND CONTRASTING: *Methods of Government* 578

UNIT 5

NEW YORK

Absolutism to Revolution

1500–1900

CHAPTER 21 1500–1800

Absolute Monarchs in Europe 586

1 Spain's Empire and European Absolutism 589
ANALYZING KEY CONCEPTS: *Absolutism* 594
2 The Reign of Louis XIV 596
HISTORY IN DEPTH: *The Palace at Versailles* 600
3 Central European Monarchs Clash 603
4 Absolute Rulers of Russia 608
SOCIAL HISTORY: *Surviving the Russian Winter* 612
5 Parliament Limits the English Monarchy 614
New York State Regents Exam Practice 619

CHAPTER 22 1550–1789

Enlightenment and Revolution 620

1 The Scientific Revolution 623
2 The Enlightenment in Europe 629
DIFFERENT PERSPECTIVES: *European Values During the Enlightenment* 635
3 The Enlightenment Spreads 636
4 The American Revolution 640
ANALYZING KEY CONCEPTS: *Democracy* 643
New York State Regents Exam Practice 647

CHAPTER 23 1789–1815

The French Revolution and Napoleon 648

1 The French Revolution Begins 651
2 Revolution Brings Reform and Terror 656
SCIENCE & TECHNOLOGY: *The Guillotine* 659
DIFFERENT PERSPECTIVES: *The French Revolution* 662
3 Napoleon Forges an Empire 663
4 Napoleon's Empire Collapses 668
5 The Congress of Vienna 672
New York State Regents Exam Practice 677

CHAPTER 24 1789–1900

Nationalist Revolutions Sweep the West 678

1 Latin American Peoples Win Independence 681
GLOBAL IMPACT: *Struggling Toward Democracy* 684
2 Europe Faces Revolutions 687
ANALYZING KEY CONCEPTS: *Nationalism* 688
3 Nationalism
CASE STUDY *Italy and Germany* 692
4 Revolutions in the Arts 698
HISTORY THROUGH ART: *Revolutions in Painting* 702
New York State Regents Exam Practice 705

COMPARING AND CONTRASTING: *Political Revolutions* 706

Louis XIV of France (page 588)

Early telescope (page 626)

Riots in Paris (page 690)

UNIT 6

NEW YORK

Industrialism and the Race for Empire

1700–1914

CHAPTER 25 1700–1900

The Industrial Revolution 714

1 **The Beginnings of Industrialization** 717

GLOBAL IMPACT: *Revolutions in Technology* 719

2 **Industrialization**

CASE STUDY *Manchester* 723

ANALYZING KEY CONCEPTS: *Industrialization* 727

3 **Industrialization Spreads** 729

4 **Reforming the Industrial World** 734

ANALYZING KEY CONCEPTS: *Capitalism vs. Socialism* 737

DIFFERENT PERSPECTIVES: *Industrialization* 741

New York State Regents Exam Practice 743

CHAPTER 26 1815–1914

An Age of Democracy and Progress 744

1 **Democratic Reform and Activism** 747

2 **Self-Rule for British Colonies** 751

SOCIAL HISTORY: *Life in Early Australia* 756

3 **War and Expansion in the United States** 758

4 **Nineteenth-Century Progress** 762

SCIENCE & TECHNOLOGY: *Edison's Inventions* 763

New York State Regents Exam Practice 769

CHAPTER 27 1850–1914

The Age of Imperialism 770

1 **The Scramble for Africa** 773

2 **Imperialism**

CASE STUDY *Nigeria* 779

ANALYZING KEY CONCEPTS: *Imperialism* 780

DIFFERENT PERSPECTIVES: *Views of Imperialism* 785

3 **Europeans Claim Muslim Lands** 786

4 **British Imperialism in India** 791

5 **Imperialism in Southeast Asia** 796

New York State Regents Exam Practice 801

CHAPTER 28 1800–1914

Transformations Around the Globe 802

1 **China Resists Outside Influence** 805

2 **Modernization in Japan** 810

HISTORY THROUGH ART: *Japanese Woodblock Printing* 814

3 **U.S. Economic Imperialism** 816

SCIENCE & TECHNOLOGY: *Panama Canal* 820

4 **Turmoil and Change in Mexico** 822

New York State Regents Exam Practice 829

COMPARING AND CONTRASTING: *Scientific and Technological Changes* 830

Singer sewing machine (page 720)

Marie Curie (page 765)

England as an octopus in an American political cartoon (page 785)

UNIT 7

NEW YORK

The World at War

1900–1945

CHAPTER 29 1914–1918

The Great War 838

1 Marching Toward War 841
2 Europe Plunges into War 845
HISTORY IN DEPTH: *The New Weapons of War* 848
SCIENCE & TECHNOLOGY: *Military Aviation* 850
3 A Global Conflict 851
DIFFERENT PERSPECTIVES: *Views of War* 857
4 A Flawed Peace 858
New York State Regents Exam Practice 863

CHAPTER 30 1900–1939

Revolution and Nationalism 864

1 Revolutions in Russia 867
ANALYZING KEY CONCEPTS: *Communism* 872
2 Totalitarianism
CASE STUDY *Stalinist Russia* 874
ANALYZING KEY CONCEPTS: *Totalitarianism* 875
HISTORY THROUGH ART: *Propaganda* 880
3 Imperial China Collapses 882
HISTORY IN DEPTH: *The Long March* 885
4 Nationalism in India and Southwest Asia 887
New York State Regents Exam Practice 893

CHAPTER 31 1919–1939

Years of Crisis 894

1 Postwar Uncertainty 897
SOCIAL HISTORY: *Labor-Saving Devices in the United States* 902
2 A Worldwide Depression 904
3 Fascism Rises in Europe 910
ANALYZING KEY CONCEPTS: *Fascism* 911
4 Aggressors Invade Nations 915
New York State Regents Exam Practice 921

CHAPTER 32 1939–1945

World War II 922

1 Hitler's Lightning War 925
2 Japan's Pacific Campaign 931
3 The Holocaust 936
4 The Allied Victory 940
GLOBAL IMPACT: *Arming for War* 946
5 Europe and Japan in Ruins 948
New York State Regents Exam Practice 953

COMPARING AND CONTRASTING: *The Changing Nature of Warfare* 954

Machine gun (page 848)

Mohandas K. Gandhi (page 866)

Japanese attack on Pearl Harbor (page 932)

UNIT 8

NEW YORK

Perspectives on the Present

1945–Present

CHAPTER 33 1945–Present

Restructuring the Postwar World 962

1 Cold War: Superpowers Face Off 965
SCIENCE & TECHNOLOGY: *The Space Race* 971
2 Communists Take Power in China 972
3 Wars in Korea and Vietnam 976
4 The Cold War Divides the World 982
HISTORY IN DEPTH: *How the Cold War Was Fought* 983
5 The Cold War Thaws 988
New York State Regents Exam Practice 993

Winston Churchill, Franklin D. Roosevelt, and Joseph Stalin (page 965)

CHAPTER 34 1945–Present

The Colonies Become New Nations 994

1 The Indian Subcontinent Achieves Freedom 997
2 Southeast Asian Nations Gain Independence 1004
SOCIAL HISTORY: *Changing Times in Southeast Asia* 1010
3 New Nations in Africa 1012
4 Conflicts in the Middle East 1017
HISTORY IN DEPTH: *Signs of Hope* 1022
5 Central Asia Struggles 1024
New York State Regents Exam Practice 1029

Nelson Mandela (page 1044)

CHAPTER 35 1945–Present

Struggles for Democracy 1030

1 Democracy
CASE STUDY *Latin American Democracies* 1033
2 The Challenge of Democracy in Africa 1040
3 The Collapse of the Soviet Union 1046
4 Changes in Central and Eastern Europe 1052
HISTORY IN DEPTH: *Ethnic Groups in the Former Yugoslavia* 1057
5 China: Reform and Reaction 1059
HISTORY THROUGH ART: *Photojournalism* 1064
New York State Regents Exam Practice 1067

ISS satellite (page 1072)

CHAPTER 36 1960–Present

Global Interdependence 1068

1 The Impact of Science and Technology 1071
2 Global Economic Development 1075
ANALYZING KEY CONCEPTS: *Globalization* 1078
DIFFERENT PERSPECTIVES: *Economics and the Environment* 1081
3 Global Security Issues 1082
4 Terrorism
CASE STUDY *September 11, 2001* 1087
5 Cultures Blend in a Global Age 1093
GLOBAL IMPACT: *Rock 'n' Roll* 1094
New York State Regents Exam Practice 1099

COMPARING AND CONTRASTING: *Nation Building* 1100

REFERENCE

NEW YORK

Skillbuilder Handbook R1

Section 1: Reading Critically
1.1 Determining Main Ideas R2
1.2 Following Chronological Order R3
1.3 Clarifying; Summarizing R4
1.4 Identifying Problems and Solutions R5
1.5 Analyzing Causes and Recognizing Effects R6
1.6 Comparing and Contrasting R7
1.7 Distinguishing Fact from Opinion R8

Section 2: Higher-Order Critical Thinking
2.1 Categorizing R9
2.2 Making Inferences R10
2.3 Drawing Conclusions R11
2.4 Developing Historical Perspective R12
2.5 Formulating Historical Questions R13
2.6 Making Predictions R14
2.7 Hypothesizing R15
2.8 Analyzing Motives R16
2.9 Analyzing Issues R17
2.10 Analyzing Bias R18
2.11 Evaluating Decisions and Courses of Action R19
2.12 Forming and Supporting Opinions R20
2.13 Synthesizing R21

Section 3: Exploring Evidence: Print, Visual, Technology Sources
3.1 Analyzing Primary and Secondary Sources R22
3.2 Visual, Audio, and Multimedia Sources R23
3.3 Using the Internet R24
3.4 Interpreting Maps R25
3.5 Interpreting Charts R27
3.6 Interpreting Graphs R28
3.7 Analyzing Political Cartoons R29

Section 4: Creating Presentations
4.1 Writing for Social Studies R30
4.2 Creating a Map R31
4.3 Creating Charts and Graphs R32
4.4 Creating and Using a Database R33
4.5 Creating a Model R34
4.6 Creating/Interpreting a Research Outline R35
4.7 Creating Oral Presentations R36
4.8 Creating Written Presentations R37

Primary Source Handbook R39

Rig Veda, *Creation Hymn* R40
Bible, *Psalm 23* R41
Confucius, *Analects* R42
Thucydides, *History of the Peloponnesian War* R43
Plato, *The Apology* R44
Tacitus, *Annals* R45
Qur'an R46
Sei Shōnagon, *The Pillow Book* R47
Magna Carta R48
Popol Vuh R49
Niccolò Machiavelli, *The Prince* R50
Sir Thomas More, *Utopia* R51
James Madison, *The Federalist, "Number 51"* R52
Mary Wollstonecraft, *A Vindication of the Rights of Woman* R53
Élisabeth Vigée-Lebrun, *Memoirs of Madame Vigée-Lebrun* R54
Sadler Committee, *Report on Child Labor* R55
Abraham Lincoln, *Second Inaugural Address* R56
Elizabeth Cady Stanton, *The Natural Rights of Civilized Women* R57
Woodrow Wilson, *The Fourteen Points* R58
Elie Wiesel, *Night* R59
Jeanne Wakatsuki Houston and James D. Houston, *Farewell to Manzanar* R60
Nelson Mandela, *Inaugural Address* R61
Martin Luther King, Jr., *I Have a Dream* R62
Cesar Chavez, *An Open Letter* R63

Economics Handbook R64

Glossary R76

Spanish Glossary R92

New York State Core Curriculum: Global History and Geography R149

Patterns of Interaction Video Series

Each video in the series *Patterns of Interaction* relates to a *Global Impact* feature in the text. These eight exciting videos show how cultural interactions have shaped our world and how patterns in history continue to the present day.

Volume 1

Building Empires

The Rise of the Persians and the Inca

Watch the Persian and Incan empires expand and rule other peoples, with unexpected results for both conquered and conquering cultures.

Trade Connects the World

Silk Roads and the Pacific Rim

Explore the legendary trade routes of the Silk Roads and the modern trade in the Pacific Rim, and notice how both affect much more than economics.

Volume 2

The Spread of Epidemic Disease

Bubonic Plague and Smallpox

Look for sweeping calamities and incredible consequences when interacting peoples bring devastating diseases to one another.

The Geography of Food

The Impact of Potatoes and Sugar

Notice how the introduction of new foods to a region provides security to some and spells disaster for others.

Volume 3

Struggling Toward Democracy

Revolutions in Latin America and South Africa

Examine the impact of democratic ideas that incite people to join revolutions in 19th-century Latin America and 20th-century South Africa.

Technology Transforms an Age

The Industrial and Electronic Revolutions

See how another kind of revolution, caused by innovations in industry and communication, brings change to the modern world.

Volume 4

Arming for War

Modern and Medieval Weapons

Watch how warring peoples' competition in military technology has resulted in a dangerous game of developing bigger, better, and faster weaponry throughout the ages.

Cultural Crossroads

The United States and the World

Observe how universal enjoyments like music, sports, and fashion become instruments of cultural blending worldwide.

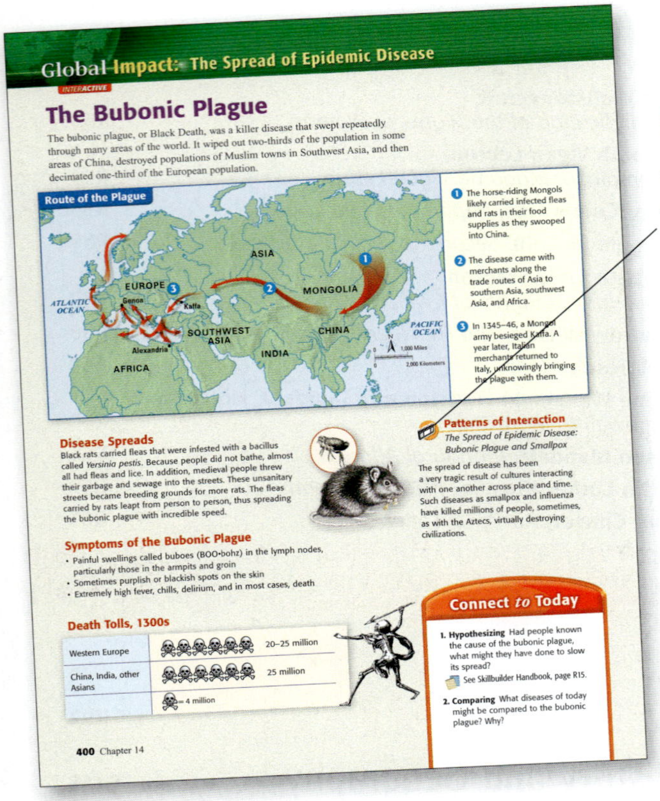

Global Impact: The Spread of Epidemic Disease

INTERACTIVE

The Bubonic Plague

The bubonic plague, or Black Death, was a killer disease that swept repeatedly through many areas of the world. It wiped out two-thirds of the population in some areas of China, destroyed populations of Muslim towns in Southwest Asia, and then decimated one-third of the European population.

1 The horse-riding Mongols likely carried infected fleas and rats in their food supplies as they swooped into China.

2 The disease came with merchants along the trade routes of Asia to southern Asia, southwest Asia, and Africa.

3 In 1345–46, a Mongol army besieged Kaffa. A year later, Italian merchants returned to Italy, unknowingly bringing the plague with them.

Disease Spreads

Black rats carried fleas that were infested with a bacillus called *Yersinia pestis*. Because people did not bathe, almost all had fleas and lice. In addition, medieval people threw their garbage and sewage into the streets. These unsanitary streets became breeding grounds for more rats. The fleas carried by rats leapt from person to person, thus spreading the bubonic plague with incredible speed.

Patterns of Interaction

The Spread of Epidemic Disease: Bubonic Plague and Smallpox

The spread of disease has been a very tragic result of cultures interacting with one another across place and time. Such diseases as smallpox and influenza have killed millions of people, sometimes, as with the Aztecs, virtually destroying civilizations.

Symptoms of the Bubonic Plague

- Painful swellings called buboes (BOO•bohz) in the lymph nodes, particularly those in the armpits and groin
- Sometimes purplish or blackish spots on the skin
- Extremely high fever, chills, delirium, and in most cases, death

Death Tolls, 1300s

Western Europe	20–25 million
China, India, other Asians	25 million
	(skull) = 4 million

Connect *to* Today

1. **Hypothesizing** Had people known the cause of the bubonic plague, what might they have done to slow its spread?
   See Skillbuilder Handbook, page R15.
2. **Comparing** What diseases of today might be compared to the bubonic plague? Why?

400 Chapter 14

The video icon in the *Global Impact* feature provides you with a link to the *Patterns of Interaction* video series.

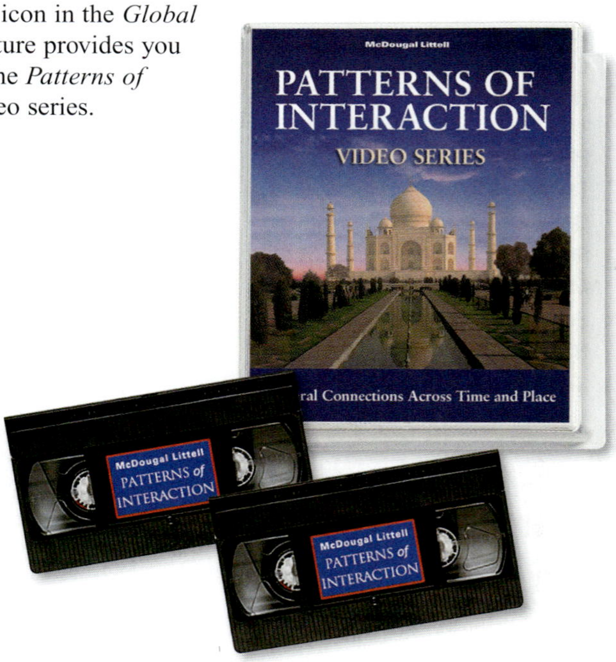

Features

Analyzing Key Concepts

Culture 6
Civilization 21
Judaism 80
Western Civilization 180
Roman Catholicism and Eastern Orthodoxy 305
Feudalism 361
Protestantism 491
Mercantilism 574
Absolutism 594
Democracy 643
Nationalism 688
Industrialization 727
Capitalism vs. Socialism 737
Imperialism 780
Communism 872
Totalitarianism 875
Fascism 911
Globalization 1078

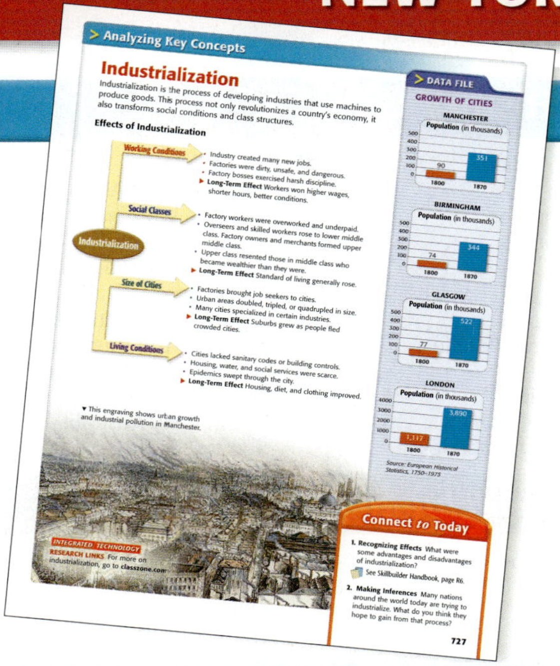

> Analyzing Key Concepts

Industrialization

Industrialization is the process of developing industries that use machines to produce goods. This process not only revolutionizes a country's economy, it also transforms social conditions and class structures.

Effects of Industrialization

Industrialization

Working Conditions
- Industry created many new jobs.
- Factories were dirty, unsafe, and dangerous.
- Factory bosses exercised harsh discipline.
- ▶ **Long-Term Effect** Workers won higher wages, shorter hours, better conditions.

Social Classes
- Factory workers were overworked and underpaid.
- Overseers and skilled workers rose to lower middle class. Factory owners and merchants formed upper middle class.
- Upper class resented those in middle class who became wealthier than they were.
- ▶ **Long-Term Effect** Standard of living generally rose.

Size of Cities
- Factories brought job seekers to cities.
- Urban areas doubled, tripled, or quadrupled in size.
- Many cities specialized in certain industries.
- ▶ **Long-Term Effect** Suburbs grew as people fled crowded cities.

Living Conditions
- Cities lacked sanitary codes or building controls.
- Housing, water, and social services were scarce.
- Epidemics swept through the city.
- ▶ **Long-Term Effect** Housing, diet, and clothing improved.

▼ This engraving shows urban growth and industrial pollution in Manchester.

INTEGRATED TECHNOLOGY
RESEARCH LINKS For more on industrialization, go to classzone.com

> DATA FILE

GROWTH OF CITIES

Source: European Historical Statistics, 1750–1975

Connect *to* Today

1. **Recognizing Effects** What were some advantages and disadvantages of industrialization?
   See Skillbuilder Handbook, page R6.
2. **Making Inferences** Many nations around the world today are trying to industrialize. What do you think they hope to gain from that process?

727

Analyzing Primary Sources

Hammurabi's Code of Laws 33
The Ten Commandments 79
Assyrian Sculpture 97
A Husband's Advice 129
Resisting Mongol Rule 310
Rebelling Against the Mongols 310
Daily Life of a Noblewoman 368
Daily Life of a Peasant Woman 368
The Magna Carta 395
Mansa Musa's Kingdom 416
Islamic Law in Mogadishu 424
The Market at Tlatelolco 455
Tenochtitlán—A Bustling City 455
The Renaissance Man 473
The Renaissance Woman 473
The Conquest of Constantinople 509
The Horrors of the Middle Passage 569
Laws Protect Freedom 631
Laws Ensure Security 631
Starvation in Ireland 754
Allied View of Armistice 855
German Reaction to Armistice 855
Satyagraha 888
Nonviolence 888
Writers of the "Lost Generation" 898
The Palestinian View 1020
The Israeli View 1020
Ken Saro-Wiwa 1042
Training the Chinese Army 1061

Analyzing Art, Artifacts, Architecture, Political Cartoons, Photographs

The Aryan Caste System 64
Nok Sculpture 217
Pillars of Aksum 228
A Bison Kill Site 238
The Dome of the Rock 266
Muslim Art 277
Women of the Heian Court 341
Chivalry 365
Great Zimbabwe 426
Perspective 474
Peasant Life 481
"Right Leg in the Boot at Last" 695
Motion Studies 700
Warlike Japan 812
Juárez: Symbol of Mexican Independence 824
Guernica 918
Military Rule and Democracy 1037
Glasnost 1047

Different Perspectives: Using Primary and Secondary Sources

The Flood Story 83
The Fall of the Roman Empire 177
The Crusades 386
The Reformation 501
The Legacy of Columbus 560
European Values During the Enlightenment 635
The French Revolution 662
Industrialization 741
Views of Imperialism 785
Views of War 857
Economics and the Environment 1081

Features

Social History

Work and Play in Ancient Egypt 42
Bull Leapers of Knossos 73
Life in a Roman Villa 166
Chinese Society 202
Collecting Water 215
Muslim Prayer 268
Tang and Song China: People and Technology 328
An Age of Superstition 371
Surnames 388
Negotiating Conflict in Stateless Societies 410
Islam in West Africa 417
Iroquois Women 445
Incan Mummies 464
City Life in Renaissance Europe 486
China's Population Boom 540
Surviving the Russian Winter 612
Bread 655
Nationalistic Music 689
Life in Early Australia 756
Social Class in India 793
The Frozen Front 849
Ukrainian Kulaks 879
Labor-Saving Devices in the United States 902
Life in the Depression 907
Changing Times in Southeast Asia 1010
The Romanian Language 1055
Molecular Medicine 1074

Science & *Technology*

Plumbing in Mohenjo-Daro 47
The Colosseum 182
African Ironworking 218
Astronomy 275
Castles and Siege Weapons 366
The Tools of Exploration 531
The Guillotine 659
Edison's Inventions 763
Panama Canal 820
Military Aviation 850
The Space Race 971

History *in* Depth

Time Line of Planet Earth 9
The Neolithic Ice Man 15
Pyramids and Mummies 39
The Rosetta Stone 40
Lady Hao's Tomb 52
Phoenician Trade 75
Egyptian Influence on Nubian Culture 92
The Great Wall of China 108
Festivals and Sports 130
Gladiator Games 165
Headhunters 247
Nazca Lines 248
A Mighty Fighting Force 332
Japanese Samurai 342
The Medieval Manor 362
Gothic Architecture 381
Craft Guilds 388
Muslim Scholars 391
The Longbow 402
Queen Amina's Reign 418
The Aztec Calendar 457
Building the Taj Mahal 520
A Ship's Rations 532
The Forbidden City 538
Zen Buddhism 547
Pirates 563
Slavery 567
The Palace at Versailles 600
Emancipation 691
Inventions in America 720
Acadians to Cajuns 752
Social Darwinism 766
Winston Churchill and the Boer War 778
Suez Canal 789
The Armenian Massacre 844
The New Weapons of War 848
The Long March 885
Investing in Stocks 906
Jewish Resistance 938
Berlin Airlift 969
The Red Guards 975
How the Cold War Was Fought 983
Genocide in Rwanda 1016
Signs of Hope 1022
Destroying the Past 1026
Ethnic Groups in the Former Yugoslavia 1057

History *in* Depth

INTERACTIVE

The Aztec Calendar

The Aztec system of tracking the days was very intricate. Archaeologists believe that the Aztec calendar system was derived from the Maya system. The Aztecs followed two main calendars: a sacred one with 13 months of 20 days and an agricultural or solar one with 18 months of 20 days. (Notice that this comes to 360 days. The Aztecs then had an unlucky five-day period known as *nemontemi*, making their solar calendar 365 days long.) Every 52 years, the two calendars would start on the same day, and a great ceremony of fire marked the occasion.

▲ Aztec Gods
The Aztecs worshiped many different gods. They were a vital part of the Aztec calendar and daily life. The Aztecs paid tribute to different gods depending, in part, on the day, week, month, year, and religious cycle of the Aztec calendars. The god shown here is a sun god, Tonatiuh.

◄ Aztec Sunstone
Originally located in the main ceremonial plaza of Tenochtitlán, the Aztec calendar stone measures 13 feet in diameter and weighs 24 tons. It was uncovered in Mexico City in 1790. The Sunstone, as it is called, contains a wealth of information about the days that began and ended the Aztec months, the gods associated with the days, and many other details.

This is an artist's rendition of the inner circle of the Sunstone. In the center is the god Tonatiuh.

The four squares that surround Tonatiuh are glyphs or symbols of the four ages preceding the time of the Aztecs: Tiger, Water, Wind, and Rain.

In the ring just outside the symbols of the previous ages, 20 segments represent the 20 days that made up an Aztec month. Each day had its own symbol and a god who watched over the day. The symbol pointed to here is Ocelotl, the jaguar.

SKILLBUILDER: Interpreting Visual Sources
1. **Hypothesizing** *Why do you think the Aztecs put Tonatiuh, a sun god, in the center of the Sunstone? Explain your reasons.*
2. **Comparing and Contrasting** *How is the Aztec calendar different from the calendar we use today? How is it similar?*

People and Empires in the Americas **457**

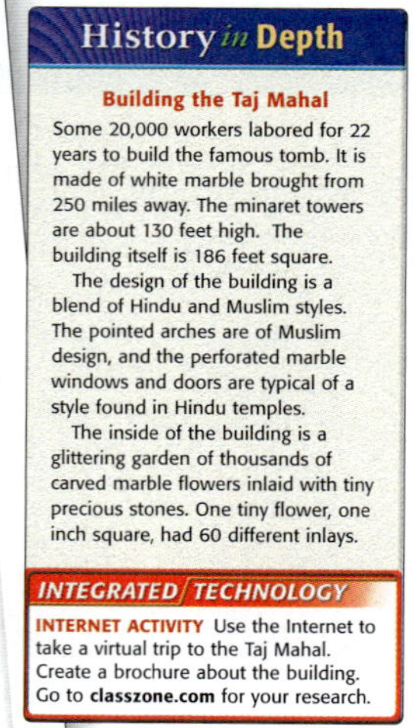

History *in* Depth

Building the Taj Mahal

Some 20,000 workers labored for 22 years to build the famous tomb. It is made of white marble brought from 250 miles away. The minaret towers are about 130 feet high. The building itself is 186 feet square.

The design of the building is a blend of Hindu and Muslim styles. The pointed arches are of Muslim design, and the perforated marble windows and doors are typical of a style found in Hindu temples.

The inside of the building is a glittering garden of thousands of carved marble flowers inlaid with tiny precious stones. One tiny flower, one inch square, had 60 different inlays.

INTEGRATED TECHNOLOGY

INTERNET ACTIVITY Use the Internet to take a virtual trip to the Taj Mahal. Create a brochure about the building. Go to **classzone.com** for your research.

History *through* Art

Cave Paintings 12
Greek Art and Architecture 140
Hindu and Buddhist Art 198
Olmec Sculpture 244
Russian Religious Art and Architecture 312
Benin Bronzes 420
Maya Architecture 450
Renaissance Ideas Influence Renaissance Art 478
Cultural Blending in Mughal India 522
Revolutions in Painting 702
Japanese Woodblock Printing 814
Propaganda 880
Photojournalism 1064

History *through* Art

Renaissance Ideas Influence Renaissance Art

The Renaissance in Italy produced extraordinary achievements in many different forms of art, including painting, architecture, sculpture, and drawing. These art forms were used by talented artists to express important ideas and attitudes of the age.

The value of humanism is shown in Raphael's *School of Athens*, a depiction of the greatest Greek philosophers. The realism of Renaissance art is seen in a portrait such as the *Mona Lisa*, which is an expression of the subject's unique features and personality. And Michelangelo's *David* shares stylistic qualities with ancient Greek and Roman sculpture.

INTEGRATED TECHNOLOGY
RESEARCH LINKS For more on Renaissance art, go to **classzone.com**

▼ **Classical and Renaissance Sculpture**
Michelangelo Influenced by classical statues, Michelangelo sculpted *David* from 1501 to 1504. Michelangelo portrayed the biblical hero in the moments just before battle. David's posture is graceful, yet his figure also displays strength. The statue, which is 18 feet tall, towers over the viewer.

▲ **Portraying Individuals**
Da Vinci The *Mona Lisa* (c. 1504–1506) is thought to be a portrait of Lisa Gherardini, who, at 16, married Francesco del Giocondo, a wealthy merchant of Florence who commissioned the portrait. Mona Lisa is a shortened form of Madonna Lisa (Madam, or My Lady, Lisa). Renaissance artists showed individuals as they really looked.

478 Chapter 17

Connect *to* Today

Chad Discovery 11
Iraq's Ancient Treasures at Risk 23
Scorpion King 37
Buddhism in the West 71
Modern Marathons 133
Entertainment in India: Bollywood 195
Bantu Languages: Swahili 223
Turkey 317
Acupuncture 325
Two Koreas 347
Epic Films 367
Shakespeare's Popularity 483
Women Leaders of the Indian Subcontinent 519
Trading Partners 535
Kabuki Theater 545
U.S. Democracy 617
Cybercafés 637
Left, Right, and Center 657
Congress of Vienna and the United Nations 675
Child Labor Today 728
Communism Today 738
Northern Ireland Today 755
Special Economic Zones 806
Tiananmen Square 883
A New War Crimes Tribunal 950
Vietnam Today 981
The Taliban 987
The Coldest War 999

Global Impact

The Royal Road 102
The Jewish Diaspora 170
The Spread of Buddhism 197
Papermaking 203
Trade Networks: Silk Roads 204
A Road Paved with Gold: Aksum to Rome 227
The Thousand and One Nights 276
The Bubonic Plague 400
Swahili 427
The Printing Press 484
Jesuit Missionaries 500
The Columbian Exchange 572
Tulip Mania 592
The French Revolution 644
Struggling Toward Democracy 684
Revolutions in Technology 719
Industrialization in Japan 732
The Women's Movement 749
Western Views of the East 813
The Influenza Epidemic 853
Fascism in Argentina 914
The Atomic Bomb 946
Rock 'n' Roll 1094

Global Patterns

The Incan System of Record Keeping 20
Pythagorean Theorem 148
The Epic 179
Pyramids 242
Warriors and Animal Symbols 454
Other Renaissances 477
East Meets West 611
International Baseball 1094

Features (continued)

History Makers

The Leakey Family 7
Hammurabi 34
Siddhartha Gautama 68
King Solomon 81
Hatshepsut 90
Confucius, Laozi 105
Pericles 135
Socrates 139
Plato 139
Aristotle 139
Alexander 143
Hannibal 158
Julius Caesar 161
Augustus 162
Asoka 190
Chandragupta Maurya 190
Ibn Rushd 279
Empress Theodora 303
Ivan III 311
Malik Shah 315
Tang Taizong 324
Wu Zhao 324
Genghis Khan 331
Kublai Khan 337
Marco Polo 337
Benedict 355
Scholastica 355
Richard the Lion-Hearted 384
Saladin 384
Eleanor of Aquitaine 394
Joan of Arc 403
Sundiata 415
Mansa Musa 415
Pachacuti 460
Medici Family 472
Leonardo da Vinci 475
Michelangelo Buonarroti 475
Martin Luther 489
Elizabeth I 494
John Calvin 496
Suleyman the Lawgiver 510
Akbar 518
Prince Henry 530
Kangxi 539
Francisco Pizarro, Atahualpa 557

Louis XIV 598
Maria Theresa 606
Frederick the Great 606
Peter the Great 609
Voltaire 630
Mary Wollstonecraft 633
Catherine the Great 639
Thomas Jefferson 641
Louis XVI 653
Marie Antoinette 653
Jean-Paul Marat 658
Napoleon Bonaparte 664
Simón Bolívar 683
José de San Martín 683
Otto von Bismarck 696
Ludwig van Beethoven 699
Adam Smith 735
Karl Marx 736
Jane Addams 740
Queen Victoria and Prince Albert 748
Abraham Lincoln 761
Marie Curie 765
Samori Touré 782
Queen Liliuokalani 799
José Martí 818
Porfirio Díaz 825
Emiliano Zapata 826
Kaiser Wilhelm II 842
Woodrow Wilson 859
Georges Clemenceau 859
V. I. Lenin 868
Joseph Stalin 877
Mustafa Kemal 890
Benito Mussolini 912
Adolf Hitler 912
Winston Churchill 927
General Douglas MacArthur 934
General Dwight D. Eisenhower 944
Mao Zedong 974
Ho Chi Minh 978
Fidel Castro 985
Imre Nagy 989
Alexander Dubček 989
Jawaharlal Nehru 1000
Aung San Suu Kyi 1006
Jomo Kenyatta 1013
Golda Meir 1019
Nelson Mandela 1044
F. W. de Klerk 1044
Mikhail Gorbachev 1048
Boris Yeltsin 1048
Vladimir Putin 1051
Jiang Zemin 1062
Mother Teresa 1084

Comparing & Contrasting

Unit 1
Ancient Civilizations 112

Unit 2
Classical Ages 252

Unit 3
Trade Networks 430

Unit 4
Methods of Government 578

Unit 5
Political Revolutions 706

Unit 6
Scientific and Technological Changes 830

Unit 7
The Changing Nature of Warfare 954

Unit 8
Nation Building 1100

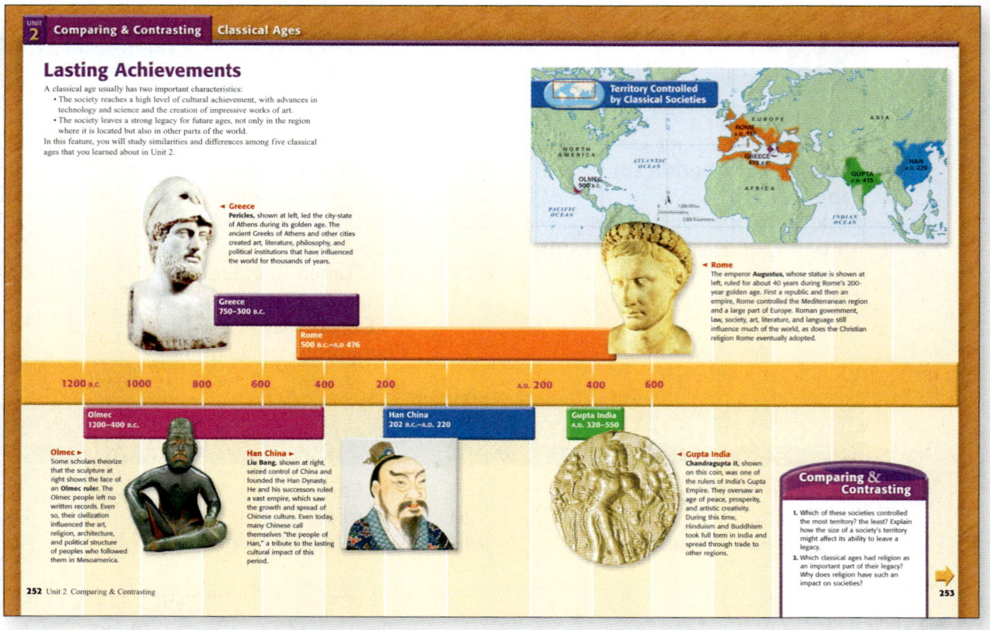

Historical and Political Maps

Unit 1
Prehistoric World to 2500 B.C. 3
Early Human Migration, 1,600,000–10,000 B.C. 10
Agriculture Emerges, 5000–500 B.C. 17
Four River Valley Civilizations 27
The Fertile Crescent, 2500 B.C. 30
Ancient Egypt, 3000–2000 B.C. 36
Ancient India, 2500–1500 B.C. 45
Ancient China, 2000–200 B.C. 51
World Climate Regions 57
The Ancient World, 1500 B.C.–250 B.C. 59
Indo-European Migrations, Starting about 1700 B.C. 62
Aryan Invasions of India, 1500–250 B.C. 65
The Patterns of Ancient Trade, 2000–250 B.C. 75
Canaan, the Crossroads, 2000–600 B.C. 78
Ancient Empires, 700 B.C.–221 B.C. 87
Kush Empire, 700 B.C. 93
Assyrian Empire, 650 B.C. 96
Persian Empire, 500 B.C. 101
A Ride Along the Royal Road 102
The Qin Dynasty, 221–202 B.C. 108
Ancient Civilizations 112

Unit 2
Greek City-States, 750 B.C. 121
Mycenaean Greece, c. 1250 B.C. 124
The Persian Wars, 490–479 B.C. 132
Peloponnesian War, 431–404 B.C. 137
Alexander and His Successors, 336–300 B.C. 144
The Roman World, 265 B.C.–A.D. 117 153
Punic Wars, 264–146 B.C. 159
Trade in the Roman Empire, A.D. 200 163
Spread of Christianity in the Roman World to A.D. 500 171
Invasions into the Roman Empire, A.D. 350–500 175
India and China, 321 B.C.–A.D. 9 187
Indian Empires, 250 B.C.–A.D. 400 191
Asian Trade Routes, A.D. 400 196
Han Dynasty, 200 B.C.–A.D. 220 201
Former Han, 200 B.C. 201
Silk Roads 204
Spread of Iron-Working, 500 B.C.–A.D. 700 211
Vegetation Regions of Africa 214
Bantu Migrations, 3000 B.C.–A.D. 1100 222
Aksum, A.D. 300–700 226
Land Area of Africa 231
American Civilizations, 1200 B.C.–A.D. 700 233
Migration Routes, 40,000–10,000 B.C. 237
Olmec Civilization, 900 B.C. 241
Early Civilizations, 1200 B.C.–A.D. 700 247
Early America, 1200 B.C.–A.D. 700 251
Territory Controlled by Classical Societies 253

Unit 3
Muslim World, 1200 261
Trade Routes, A.D. 570 264
Three Empires: Byzantine, Russian, Seljuk, c. 1100 299
Constantinople, A.D. 550 302
The Viking Invasions of Eastern Europe, 820–941 308
The Khanate of the Golden Horde, 1294 309
East and Southeast Asia, 900–1200 321
The Steppe 330
The Mongol Empire, 1294 334
Japan to 1300 340
Southeast Asia, 900–1200 345
Population Density: Tang Dynasty 349

Europe, c. 500 351
Charlemagne's Empire, 768–843 356
Invasions in Europe, 700–1000 359
The Holy Roman Empire, 1100 372
Europe, 14th Century 377
The Crusades, 1096–1204 383
Route of the Plague 400
Africa, 800–1500 407
Selected African Societies, 800–1500 411
Empire of Ghana, A.D. 1000 414
Empire of Mali, A.D. 1400 414
Empire of Songhai, A.D. 1500 414
East African Trade, 1000 423
Western Africa, 2003 429
Trade Routes: Africa, Asia, Europe, 1500 430

Unit 4
The Americas, 800 B.C.–A.D.1535 439
North American Culture Areas, c. 1400 442
Mesoamerican Civilizations, 200 B.C.–A.D. 1521 447
South American Culture Areas, 100–1535 461
Europe, 1500 469
Religions in Europe, 1560 497
Spread of Protestantism 497
Empire Builders, 1683 505
Ottoman Empire, 1451–1566 508
Safavid Empire, 1683 514
Growth of the Mughal Empire, 1526–1707 517
Early Explorations, 1400s 527
Europeans in the East, 1487–1700 534
Japan in the 17th Century 543
European Claims in America, 1700 551
European Exploration of the Americas, 1492–1682 555
Europeans in North America, 1754 and 1763 564
Triangle Trade System, 1451–1870 568
Four Governments 578

Unit 5
Europe, 1650 587
Defeat of the Spanish Armada, 1588 590
Europe After the Thirty Years' War, 1648 604
The Expansion of Russia, 1500–1800 610
The English Civil War, 1642–1645 616
Modern European Monarchs, 2003 619
Centers of Enlightenment, c.1740 621
North America, 1783 642
Napoleon's Empire, 1810 649
War in Europe, 1805–1813 666
Napoleon's Russian Campaign, 1812 670
Europe, 1810 and 1817 674
Great Britain and France, 1810 677
Revolutions, 1848 679
Enlightenment Ideas Spread to Latin America, 1789–1810 684
Latin America, 1800 and 1830 685
The Unification of Italy, 1858–1870 694
The Unification of Germany, 1865–1871 697

Unit 6
Industry in Europe, 1870 715
The Growth of Railroads in the United States 730
Western Democracies, 1900 745
Australia and New Zealand to 1850 753
U.S. Expansion, 1783–1853 759
Civil War in the United States, 1861–1865 760
Colonial Claims, 1900 771
Imperialism in Africa, 1878 and 1913 777
Traditional Ethnic Boundaries of Africa 777
Nigeria, 1914 781
Resistance Movements in Africa, 1881–1906 783
Ottoman Empire, 1699–1914 787
Suez Canal 789
Western-Held Territories in Asia, 1910 792
Colonies in Southeast Asia, 1895 797
The British Empire, 1900 801
Colonial Powers Carve Up China, 1850–1910 803
China: Spheres of Influence and Treaty Ports, c. 1900 808
The Spanish-American War, 1898: the Caribbean and the Philippines 819
Panama Canal 820

Unit 7
Europe, 1914 839
The Balkan Peninsula, 1914 843
World War I in Europe, 1914–1918 846
Galipoli Campaign, 1915 851
The World at War, 1914–1918 852
Europe Pre-World War I 860
Europe Post-World War I 860
Southwest Asia, 1926 865
Russian Revolution and Civil War, 1905–1922 870
The Long March 885
Oil Fields, 1938 891
Expansion in Europe, 1931–1939 895
Aggression in Africa, 1935–1939 917
Aggression in Asia, 1931–1937 917
European and African Battles, 1939–1945 923
World War II: German Advances, 1939–1941 926
World War II in Asia and the Pacific, 1941–1945 933
Battle of Midway, June 1942 933
World War II: Allied Advances, 1942–1945 942
The D-Day Invasion, June 6, 1944 944
Nazi Labor and Death Camps 953

Unit 8
Cold War Enemies, 1949 963
Superpower Aims in Europe 966
Divided Germany, 1948–1949 969
War in Korea, 1950–1953 977
War in Vietnam, 1957–1973 979
How the Cold War Was Fought 983
Cold War Hot Spots, 1948–1975 984
New Nations, 1946–1991 995
The Indian Subcontinent, 1947 998
Southeast Asia, 1945–1975 1005
Africa, 1955 1014
Africa, 1975 1014
The Middle East, 1947–present 1018
Central Asia 1025
Types of Government, 2003 1031
Latin America, 2003 1035
Africa, 1967 1041
Regions of Nigeria, 1967 1041
The Breakup of the Soviet Union, 1991 1049
Major Industries of Germany, 2003 1054
Ethnic Groups in the Former Yugoslavia 1057
World Migration, 2002 1069
World Trading Blocks, 2003 1077
World AIDS Situation, 2002 1085

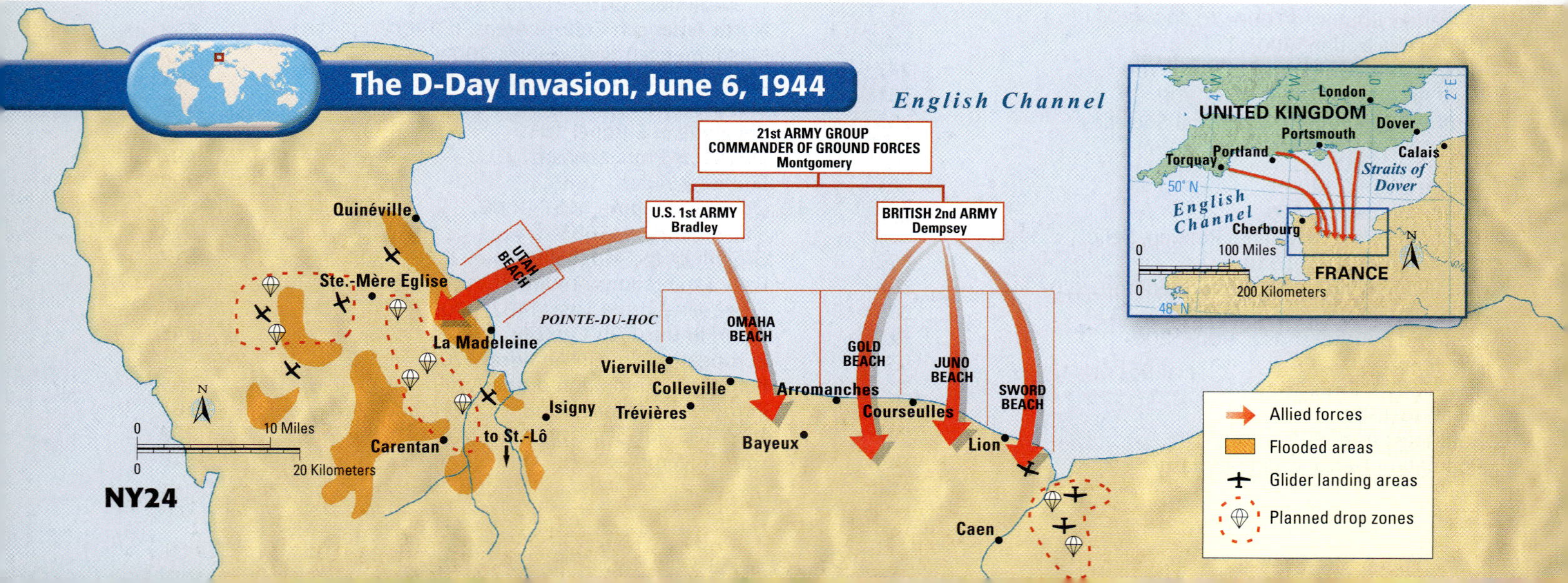

Charts

Chinese Writing 53
Language Family Resemblances 61
The Four Noble Truths 69
Alphabets—Ancient and Modern 74
The Sacred Writings of Judaism 80
Chinese Ethical Systems 106
Characteristics of Civilizations 114
Forms of Government 128
Athenian and United States Democracy 134
Greek Astronomy 147
Comparing Republican Governments 157
Roman Emperors, A.D. 37–A.D. 180 164
Multiple Causes: Fall of the Western Roman Empire 174
Comparing Two Great Empires: Han China and Rome 206
Migration: Push-Pull Factors 221
The Effects of Agriculture 239
Cultural Achievements 254
Basic Differences Between Sunni and Shi'a Muslims 271
Muslim Population, 1990s 281
A Comparison of World Religions and Ethical Systems 296
The 11th Century: Comparing Two Churches 305
Five Empires 319
Inventions of Tang and Song China 328
The Commercial Revolution 390
The Development of England and France 397
If the Plague Struck America Today 401
Population in Europe, 1000–1340 405
Selected African Societies, 800–1500 411
East African Trade Goods 423
Major Trade Networks 432
Rise and Fall of the Maya 449
Rise and Fall of the Aztecs 458
Rise and Fall of the Inca 463
Causes of the Reformation 488
Religious Beliefs and Practices in the 16th Century 491
Cultural Blending 513
Key Characteristics 578
Changing Idea: Scientific Method 626
Changing Idea: The Right to Govern 629
Major Ideas of the Enlightenment 632
Changing Idea: Relationship Between Ruler and State 638
Changing Idea: Colonial Attachment to Britain 642
Enlightenment Ideas and the U.S. Constitution 643
Eligible Voters 643
Population of France, 1787 652
Positive and Negative Results of Nationalism 688
Types of Nationalist Movements 692
Causes of the Revolutions 708
Effects of Revolutions 710
Capitalism vs. Socialism 737
Rise of Mass Culture 767
Forms of Imperialism 780
Imperial Management Methods 780
Reforms of Mexican Constitution of 1917 827
Two Top Fighter Planes: A Comparison 850
The Treaty of Versailles: Major Provisions 861
Causes and Effects of Two Russian Revolutions, 1917 871
Evolution of Communist Thought 872
Key Traits of Totalitarianism 875
Characteristics of Fascism 911
Jews Killed Under Nazi Rule 939
Hiroshima: Day of Fire 946
Costs of World War II: Allies and Axis 949
Superpower Aims in Europe 966
Chinese Political Opponents, 1945 973
Major Strategies of the Cold War 983
U.S.–Soviet Military Power, 1986–1987 993
Making Democracy Work 1033
Differences Among the Ethnic Groups 1057
Mao's Attempts to Change China 1059
Internet Users Worldwide, 2002 1073
Arguments For and Against Economic Globalization 1078
International Casualties of Terrorism, 1997–2002 1089
National Characteristics 1102

Graphs

Agricultural Revolution 17
Topography 121
Major Movie Producers, 2000 195
Cities, A.D. 900 273
World Population's Religious Affiliations 282
Population of Three Roman Cities 375
Death Tolls, 1300s 400
The Division of Christianity 491
Comparison of Empires 525
The Growth of Early Modern China 540
Native Population of Central Mexico, 1500–1620 556
Africans Enslaved in the Americas, 1451–1870 568
Debt of the Royal Family, 1643–1715 602
Average High Temperature for January, Russian Cities 613
Average High Temperature for January, U.S. Cities 613
Voters in the 2000 U.S. Presidential Election 643
Percent of Income Paid in Taxes 652
Beheading by Class 659
The Divisions in Spanish Colonial Society, 1789 681
British Cotton Consumption, 1800–1900 719
Growth of Cities 727
The Growth of Cities, 1700–1900 743
Expansion of Suffrage in Britain 748
The Great Famine, 1845–1851 754
Australia's Population 757
Civil War Deaths 760
Independent African Countries 780
Tolls Collected on the Panama Canal, 1916–1920 829
World War I Statistics 856
The Buildup of the Soviet Economy, 1928–1938 878
Oil Output, 1910–1940 893
Mechanical Washing Machines Shipped 903
Persons Employed as Private Laundress 903
Stock Prices, 1925–1933 906
Unemployment Rate, 1928–1938 908
World Trade, 1929–1933 908
Military Casualties, World War I and World War II 958
Countries Aided by the Marshall Plan, 1948–1951 968
Poverty Levels in Asia 1002
ASEAN Exports, 1990–2001 1011
Brazilian Economy, 1955–2000 1036
Population Living in Poverty, 2001 1038
Some Major Internet Nations 1073
Multinational Corporations, 2002 1076
Total Attacks, 1982–2002 1089
Number of Refugees, 1992–2002 1099

Time Lines, Infographics, and Political Cartoons

Time Lines

Chapter 1 2
Hominid Development 8
Time Line of Planet Earth 9
Chapter 2 26
Chapter 3 58
Chapter 4 86
Civilizations of the Ancient World 113
Chapter 5 120
Alexander's Empire and Its Legacy, 336–306 B.C. 145
Chapter 6 152
Ancient Rome and Early Christianity 184
Chapter 7 186
India and China Establish Empires 208
Chapter 8 210
Chapter 9 232
Classical Ages 252
Chapter 10 260
Chapter 11 298
Byzantines, Russians, and Turks 318
Chapter 12 320
Dynasties of China, 500–1400 338
Chapter 13 350
Chapter 14 376
Chapter 15 406
Chapter 16 438
Chapter 17 468
Henry VIII Causes Religious Turmoil 492
Chapter 18 504
Chapter 19 526
Chapter 20 550
Three Worlds Meet, 1492–1700 573
Chapter 21 586
Chapter 22 620
Major Steps in the Scientific Revolution 626
Chapter 23 648
Chapter 24 678
Political Revolutions 706
Chapter 25 714
Chapter 26 744
Chapter 27 770
Chapter 28 802
Scientific and Technological Changes 830
Chapter 29 838
Chapter 30 864
Chapter 31 894
Aggression in Europe, Asia, and Africa, 1931–1939 916
Chapter 32 922
Technology of War 954
Chapter 33 962
The Space Race 971
Chapter 34 994
A Turbulent History 1001
The Israeli-Palestinian Struggle 1021
Chapter 35 1030
South Africa, 1948–2000 1045
Chapter 36 1068
Five Developing Nations 1100

Infographics

Table of "Components of Culture" 6
How Culture Is Learned 6
Characteristics of Civilization in Sumer 21
The City of Ur 22
The Mighty Nile 36
Pyramids and Mummies 39
Monsoon Winter and Summer 45
Dynastic Cycle in China 54
Merchant Ships 75
The Great Wall of China 108
Greek Astronomy 147
A Roman Villa 166
The Colosseum 182
Chinese Society 202
Hunter-Gatherer Community 212
Vegetation Regions of Africa 214
African Ironworking 218
Mammoth hunt 234
Migration Routes 237
Early Civilizations, 1200 B.C.–A.D. 700 247
Alexandria 262
Major Buddhist Sects 285
Major Christian Sects 287
Major Hindu Sects 289
Major Islamic Sects 291
Major Jewish Sects 293
The Five Relationships 295
Chinese Inventions 322
Japanese Samurai 342
Southeast Asia, 900–1200 345
Western European Peasants, 1100s 352
European Feudalism 361
Japanese Feudalism 361
The Medieval Manor 362
Castles and Siege Weapons 366
Crusade Party 378
Gothic Architecture 381
The Commercial Revolution 390
Route of the Plague 400
If the Plague Struck America Today 401
Trade in the Sahara 408
The Lost-Wax Process 421
Types of Trade Networks 431
The Printing Press 484
The Division of Christianity 491
The Tools of Exploration 531
Zheng He's Treasure Ship 537
The Forbidden City 538
The Columbian Exchange 572
Mercantilism 574
Organization of the Ottoman Government 580
Organization of the Tokugawa Shogunate 580
Absolutism 594
The Palace at Versailles 600
Expansion of U.S. Voting Rights 643
Conquerors of the Bastille Parade 650
The Guillotine 659
Napoleon's Russian Campaign, 1812 670
Bonds That Create a Nation-State 688
Model of a Revolution 707
The Day of a Child Laborer, William Cooper 724
Effects of Industrialization 727
An Age of Inventions 764
China and Japan Confront the West 811
Panama Canal Cross-Section 820
Impact of Technological Change 832
Scientific Change 834
Key Traits of Totalitarianism 875
Characteristics of Fascism 911
Global Corporation 1078
Ozone Levels 1080
International Terrorist Attacks 1089
Destruction in New York City and the Pentagon 1090

Political Cartoons

Seven-Headed Martin Luther 501
The Three Estates 652
"Little Johnny Bull" 668
"Right Leg in the Boot at Last" 695
Political Cartoons, 1789 and 1765 709
Political Cartoon 741
A Court for King Cholera 769
"The Devilfish in Egyptian Waters" 785
Warlike Japan 812
Roosevelt Corollary 821
Czechoslovakia's Iron Curtain 967
Philippine Islands 1029
Military Rule and Democracy 1037
Glasnost 1047
Intensive Communism Unit 1067
Ship of Fools 1081

JEFF STAHLER
Courtesy Cincinnati Post

Primary and Secondary Sources

NEW YORK

Chapter 1
Mary Leakey, quoted in *National Geographic,* 7
Richard E. Leakey, *The Making of Mankind,* 9
Robert Braidwood, quoted in *Scientific American,* 16
Richard E. Leakey, *The Making of Mankind,* 25

Chapter 2
Code of Hammurabi, (trans. L. W. King), 33
Herodotus, *The History of Herodotus,* 38
Duke of Shao, quoted in *The Chinese Heritage,* 54
"Hymn to the Nile," from *Ancient Near Eastern Texts,* 57

Chapter 3
Krishna, speaking in the *Mahabharata,* 65
Svetasvatara Upanishad IV. 3–4, 67
Buddha, from *Samyutta Nikaya,* 69
Herodotus, in *History,* Book IV (5th century B.C.), 74
Genesis 12:1–2, 77
Deuteronomy 5:6–22, 79
From *The Torah,* 83
From *The Epic of Gilgamesh,* 83
From *The Fish Incarnation of Vishnu,* 83
1 Samuel 8:4–8, 85

Chapter 4
Piankhi, monument in Cairo Museum, 93
Nahum 3:7, 3:18, 97
Ezra 1:2–3, 100
Confucius, *Analects,* 2.7, 105
Laozi, *Dao De Ching,* Passage 37, 106
Confucius, *Analects,* 2.3, 111

Chapter 5
Pericles, an Athenian statesman, 122
Edith Hamilton, "Theseus," *Mythology,* 122
Thucydides, a historian, 122
Homer, *Iliad* (tr. Ian Johnston), 126
Xenophon, *The Economist,* Book 10 (tr. H. G. Dakyns), 129
Pericles, "The Funeral Oration," from *The Peloponnesian War,* from Thucydides, 135
Plutarch, *Parallel Lives: Marcellus,* 148
Aristotle, *Politics,* 151

Chapter 6
Livy, *The Early History of Rome,* 155
Tiberius Gracchus, quoted in Plutarch, *The Lives of Noble Greeks and Romans,* 160
Luke, 6:27–31, 169
St. Augustine, *The City of God,* 172
Edward Gibbon, *The History of the Decline and Fall of the Roman Empire,* 177
Arther Ferrill, *The Fall of the Roman Empire,* 177
Finley Hooper, *Roman Realities,* 177
St. Jerome, quoted in *Rome: A Profile of a City, 312–1308,* 177
Virgil, *Aeneid,* 179
Tacitus, *Annals,* 181
Decree from the Roman Province of Asia, 185

Chapter 7
Megasthenes, in *Geography* by Strabo, 190
Quote from *The Wonder That Was India,* 194
Sima Qian, *Records of the Grand Historian,* 202
Ban Gu and **Ban Zhao** in *History of the Former Han Dynasty,* 204
Asoka, in *A History of Modern India,* 209

Chapter 8
Djeli Mamoudou Kouyate, from *Sundiata, an Epic of Old Mali,* 216
Cosmas, quoted in *Travellers in Ethiopia,* 226
King Ezana of Aksum, quoted in *Africa: Past and Present,* 226
From *Travellers in Ethiopia,* 231

Chapter 9
Thomas Canby, "The Search for the First Americans," *National Geographic,* 236
Walter Alva, "Richest Unlooted Tomb of a Moche Lord," *National Geographic,* 249
Brian Fagan, quoted in *The Peru Reader,* 251

Chapter 10
Qur'an sura 96:1–5, 265
Khalid Ibn al-Walid, quoted in *Early Islam,* 270
Muhammad, quoted in *The Sayings of Muhammad,* 274
Ikhwan As-Safa, quoted in *The World of Islam,* 279
Abd Al-Latif, quoted in *A History of the Arab Peoples,* 281

World Religions and Ethical Systems
Dhammapada 365, 285
Acts 16:30–31, 287
From the *Rig Veda* 1.125.5, 289
Qur'an sura 31:20, 291
Deuteronomy 6:4, 293
Confucius, *Analects* 1.16, 295
Karen Armstrong, *A History of God,* 297

Chapter 11
Theodora, quoted by Procopius in *History of the Wars,* 303
Saint Basil, quoted in *The Letters,* 304
From *The Primary Chronicle,* 308
From *Medieval Russia,* 310
Jalaludin Rumi, from *Unseen Rain,* 315
Wassaf, quoted in *The Mongol Empire,* 317
Zenkovsky, *Medieval Russia's Epics, Chronicles, and Tales,* 319

Chapter 12
Tu Fu, "Moonlight Night," 326
Marco Polo, *The Travels of Marco Polo,* 337
Sung Lien, quoted in *The Essence of Chinese Civilization,* 349

PRIMARY SOURCE

The same moon is above Fuzhou tonight;
From the open window she will be watching it alone,
The poor children are too little to be able to remember Ch'ang-an.
Her perfumed hair will be dampened by the dew, the air may be too chilly on her delicate arms.
When can we both lean by the wind-blown curtains and see the tears dry on each other's face?

TU FU, "Moonlight Night"

Chapter 13
Einhard, *Life of Charlemagne,* 356
William Langland, *Piers Plowman,* 363
From *The Song of Roland,* 367
From *Women in Medieval Times,* 368
Pope Gregory, cited in *Basic Documents in Medieval History,* 372
Geoffrey Chaucer, *The Canterbury Tales,* 375

Chapter 14
Emperor Alexius Comnenus, quoted in *The Dream and the Tomb* by Robert Payne, 382
Pope Urban II, quoted in *World Civilizations–Sources, Images, and Interpretations,* 386
William of Tyre, quoted in *The Medieval Reader,* 386
Saladin, quoted in *The Dream and the Tomb,* 386
The Magna Carta, 395
Giovanni Boccaccio, *The Decameron,* 399
Edward I of England, from a letter, 405

Primary and Secondary Sources (continued)

Chapter 15
Al-Bakri, quoted in *Africa in the Days of Exploration,* 414
Ibn Battuta, quoted in *Africa in the Days of Exploration,* 416
From the *Kano Chronicle,* 418
Ibn Batutta, *Travels of Ibn Batutta,* 424

Chapter 16
From the *Popol Vuh,* 448
Crónica Mexicayotl, 454
Hernando Cortés, *Letters of Information,* 455
Bernal Díaz, *The Conquest of New Spain,* 455
From *In the Trail of the Wind,* 467

Chapter 17
Baldassare Castiglione, *The Courtier,* 473
Isabella D'Este, *Letters,* 473
Giovanni Boccaccio, Preface, *Decameron,* 476
Niccolò Machiavelli, *The Prince,* 476
Vittoria Colonna, *Poems,* 477
Thomas More, *Utopia,* 482
Christine de Pizan, *The Book of The City of Ladies,* 482
William Shakespeare, *Hamlet,* 483
Martin Luther, quoted in *The Protestant Reformation* by Lewis W. Spitz, 490
Katherina Zell, quoted in *Women of the Reformation,* 498
Ignatius of Loyola, *Spiritual Exercises,* 498
Martin Luther, quoted in *A World Lit Only By Fire: The Medieval Mind and the Renaissance,* 501
Steven Ozment, *Protestants: The Birth of a Revolution,* 501
G. R. Elton, *Reformation Europe,* 501
Hans Brosamer, "Seven-Headed Martin Luther" (1529), 501
Niccolò Machiavelli, *The Prince,* 503

Chapter 18
Kritovoulos, *History of Mehmed the Conqueror*, 509, 525

Chapter 19
Afonso de Albuquerque, from *The Commentaries of the Great Afonso Dalbuquerque,* 533
Qian-Long, from a letter to King George III of Great Britain, 540
Matsuo Basho, from *Matsuo Basho,* 544
Anonymous Japanese Writer, quoted in *Sources of Japanese Tradition,* 545
Kangxi, quoted in *Emperor of China: Self-Portrait of K'Ang-Hsi,* 549

Chapter 20
Christopher Columbus, *Journal of Columbus,* 553
Samuel Eliot Morison, *Admiral of the Ocean Sea,* 560
Bartolomé de Las Casas, quoted in *Columbus: The Great Adventure,* 560
Suzan Shown Harjo, "I Won't Be Celebrating Columbus Day," *Newseek,* Fall/Winter 1991, 560
Olaudah Equiano, quoted in *Eyewitness: The Negro in American History,* 569
Bernardino de Sahagun, quoted in *Seeds of Change,* 573
Thomas Mun, quoted in *World Civilizations,* 575
John Cotton, quoted in *The Annals of America,* 577

Chapter 21
Miguel de Cervantes, *Don Quixote de la Mancha,* 592
Jean Bodin, *Six Books on the State,* 595
Duke of Saint-Simon, *Memoirs of Louis XIV and the Regency,* 599
Frederick II, *Essay on Forms of Government,* 606
From the English Bill of Rights, 619

PRIMARY SOURCE

Soldiers! I am pleased with you. On the day of Austerlitz, you justified everything that I was expecting of [you]. . . . In less than four hours, an army of 100,000 men, commanded by the emperors of Russia and Austria, was cut up and dispersed. . . . 120 pieces of artillery, 20 generals, and more than 30,000 men taken prisoner—such are the results of this day which will forever be famous. . . . And it will be enough for you to say, "I was at Austerlitz," to hear the reply: "There is a brave man!"

NAPOLEON, quoted in *Napoleon* by André Castelot

Chapter 22
Galileo Galilei, quoted in *The Discoverers,* 625
Jean Jacques Rousseau, *The Social Contract,* 631
Baron de Montesquieu, *The Spirit of Laws,* 631
Voltaire, *Candide,* 635
Jonathan Swift, *Gulliver's Travels,* 635
William Hogarth, *Canvassing for Votes* (painting), 635
Preamble, Constitution of the United States of America, 647

Chapter 23
Comte D'Antraigues, quoted in *Citizens: A Chronicle of the French Revolution,* 652
Maximilien Robespierre, "On the Morals and Political Principles of Domestic Policy," 660
Charles Dickens, *A Tale of Two Cities,* 662
Edmund Burke, quoted in *Burke's Politics,* 662
Thomas Paine, from *The Writings of Thomas Paine,* 662
Napoleon, quoted in *Napoleon* by André Castelot, 665
Simón Bolívar, from *Selected Writings of Bolívar,* 677

Chapter 24
Otto von Bismarck, speech to the German parliament on February 6, 1888, 705

Chapter 25
Edward Bains, *The History of Cotton Manufacture in Great Britain,* 720
Elizabeth Gaskell, *Mary Barton,* 724
Hugh Miller, "Old Red Sandstone," 728
Lucy Larcom, *A New England Girlhood*, 730
Alexis de Tocqueville, 1848 speech, 735
Karl Marx and **Friedrich Engels,** *The Communist Manifesto,* 736
Mary Paul, quoted in *Women and the American Experience,* 741
Andrew Carnegie, *Autobiography of Andrew Carnegie,* 741
Friederich Engels, *The Condition of the Working Class in England in 1844,* 741
Walter Crane (political cartoon), 741
Charles Dickens, *Hard Times,* 743

Chapter 26
Emmeline Pankhurst, *Why We Are Militant,* 749
William Bennett, quoted in *Narrative of a Recent Journey of Six Weeks in Ireland,* 754
William Shorey Coodey, quoted in *The Trail of Tears,* 758
Seneca Falls Convention, "Declaration of Sentiments," 769

Chapter 27
Cecil Rhodes, *Confession of Faith,* 775
Edward Morel, *The Black Man's Burden,* 782
J. A. Hobson, *Imperialism,* 785
Dadabhai Naoroji, speech before Indian National Congress, 1871, 785

Jules Ferry, quoted in *The Human Record: Sources of Global History,* 785
"The Devilfish in Egyptian Waters" (political cartoon), 785
Jamal al-Din al-Afghani, in a letter to Hasan Shirazi, April 1891, 790
Lord Kitchener, quoted in *Asia and Western Dominance,* 794
King Chulalongkorn, "Royal Proclamation in Education," 798
Kwaku Dua III to Frederic M. Hodgson, 1889, 801

Chapter 28

Lin Zexu, quoted in *China's Response to the West,* 806
Ponciano Arriaga, speech to the Constitutional Convention, 1856–1857, 824
From an article in the *Tokyo Times,* 829

Chapter 29

Frédéric Passy, quoted in *Nobel: The Man and His Prizes,* 842
Valentine Fleming, quoted in *The First World War,* 847
Shirley Millard, *I Saw Them Die,* 854
Harry Truman, quoted in *The First World War,* 855
Herbert Sulzbach, *With the German Guns,* 855
Woodrow Wilson, 1917 speech to Congress, 857
Erich Maria Remarque, *All Quiet on the Western Front,* 857
Wilfred Owen, "Dulce et Decorum Est," 857
Maurice Neumont, "They Shall Not Pass, 1914–1918" 857
From an editorial in *Vossische Zeitung,* May 18, 1915, 863

Chapter 30

Mao Zedong, quoted in *Chinese Communism and the Rise of Mao,* 884
Mohandas K. Gandhi, Chapter XVII, *Hind Swaraj,* 888
Mohandas K. Gandhi, *The Origin of Nonviolence,* 888
Mohandas K. Gandhi, Letter to Sir Daniel Hamilton, 893

Chapter 31

F. Scott Fitzgerald, *The Great Gatsby,* 898
Franklin Roosevelt, First Inaugural Address, 909
Erich Ludendorff, letter to President Hindenburg, February 1, 1933, 912
Winston Churchill, speech before the House of Commons, October 5, 1938, 919
William Shirer, quoted in *The Strenuous Decade,* 921

Chapter 32

General Charles de Gaulle, quoted in *Charles de Gaulle: A Biography,* 927
Lieutenant John Spainhower, quoted in *War Diary 1939–1945,* 932
Ralph G. Martin, in *The GI War,* 935
M. I. Libau, quoted in *Never to Forget: The Jews of the Holocaust,* 937
Elie Wiesel, quoted in *Night,* 939
Simon Weisenthal, quoted in *Never to Forget: The Jews of the Holocaust,* 949
From *The Christian Century,* August 29, 1945, 953

Chapter 33

Winston Churchill, "Iron Curtain" speech, March 1946, 967
Harry S. Truman, speech to Congress, March 12, 1947, 968
Fidel Castro, quoted in an interview, October 27, 1962, 985
Robert McNamara, quoted in *Inside the Cold War,* 990
Ho Chi Minh, quoted in *America and Vietnam,* 993

Chapter 34

Zahida Amjad Ali, *Freedom, Trauma, Continuities,* 999
Jawaharlal Nehru, speech before the Constituent Assembly, August 14, 1947, 999
New York Times, June 28, 1998, 1001
Corazón Aquino, inaugural speech, February 24, 1986, 1006
Megawati Sukarnoputri, July 23, 2001, 1008
Fawaz Turki, quoted in *The Arab-Israeli Conflict,* 1020
Abraham Tamir, quoted in *From War to Peace,* 1020
Anwar Sadat, Knesset speech, November 20, 1977, 1020
Arthur James Balfour, in a letter to Lord Rothschild, November 2, 1917, 1029

Chapter 35

Ken Saro-Wiwa, *A Month and a Day: A Detention Diary,* 1042
David M. Kotz, "The Cure That Could Kill," 1050
Xiao Ye, "Tiananmen Square: A Soldier's Story," 1061
Orville Schell, "The Coming of Mao Zedong Chic," 1067

Chapter 36

Lester R. Brown, 1081
The Liberty Institute, 1081
Chris Madden (political cartoon), 1081
Josef Joffe, from "America the Inescapable," 1099

Comparing & Contrasting

Unit 1

Code of Hammurabi, adapted from a translation by James B. Pritchard, 115
From *The Bible,* 115
Confucius, the *Analects,* 115

Unit 2

Edgar Allan Poe, from "To Helen," 255
Fa Xian, from *The Travels of Fa Xian,* 255
Pericles, *Funeral Oration,* 257
Henry C. Boren, *Roman Society,* 257
Rhoads Murphey, *A History of Asia,* 257

Unit 3

Francesco Balducci Pegolotti, *The Discoverers,* 435
Ibn Battuta, *Ibn Battuta in Black Africa,* 435
Fernão Lopes de Castanheda, *History of the Discovery and Conquest of India,* 435

Unit 4

Niccolò Machiavelli, *The Discourses,* 583
Garcilaso de la Vega, *The Incas,* 583

Unit 5

From the English Parliament's Bill of Rights, 1689, 709
Thomas Paine, *Common Sense,* 710
Simón Bolívar, "The Jamaica Letter," 711
Maximilien Robespierre, speech of February 5, 1794, 711

Unit 6

Jared Diamond, *Guns, Germs, and Steel,* 833
John Vaughn, "Thirty Years of the Telephone," 833
Paul Johnson, *The Birth of the Modern,* 835

Unit 7

American Consul General at Beint, letter to the U.S. Secretary of State, 1915, 957
Primo Levi, *Survival in Auschwitz,* 957
Sergeant Major Ernest Shepherd, *A Sergeant-Major's War,* 958
U.S. Marine Corps correspondent, article, 958
Laura de Gozdawa Turczynowicz, *When the Prussians Came to Poland,* 959
Tatsuichiro Akizuki, *Nagasaki,* 1945, 959

Unit 8

David Lamb, *The Africans,* 1103
Ariel Sharon, inauguration speech, March 7, 2001, 1104
Abdul Kalam, inauguration speech, July 25, 2002, 1104
Vicente Fox, inauguration speech, December 1, 2000, 1104
Olusegun Obasanjo, inauguration speech, May 29, 1999, 1105
Gloria Macapagal Arroyo, inauguration speech, January 20, 2001, 1105

While historical events are unique, they often are driven by similar, repeated forces. In telling the history of our world, this book pays special attention to eight significant and recurring themes. These themes are presented to show that from America, to Africa, to Asia, people are more alike than they realize. Throughout history humans have confronted similar obstacles, have struggled to achieve similar goals, and continually have strived to better themselves and the world around them.

Power and Authority

History is often made by the people and institutions in power. As you read about the world's powerful people and governments, try to answer several key questions.

- Who holds the power?
- How did that person or group get power?
- What system of government provides order in this society?
- How does the group or person in power keep or lose power?

Religious and Ethical Systems

Throughout history, humans around the world have been guided by, as much as anything else, their religious and ethical beliefs. As you examine the world's religious and ethical systems, pay attention to several important issues.

- What beliefs are held by a majority of people in a region?
- How do these major religious beliefs differ from one another?
- How do the various religious groups interact with one another?
- How do religious groups react toward nonmembers?

Revolution

Often in history, great change has been achieved only through force. As you read about the continuous overthrow of governments, institutions, and even ideas throughout history, examine several key questions.

- What long-term ideas or institutions are being overthrown?
- What caused people to make this radical change?
- What are the results of the change?

Interaction with Environment

Since the earliest of times, humans have had to deal with their surroundings in order to survive. As you read about our continuous interaction with the environment, keep in mind several important issues.

- How do humans adjust to the climate and terrain where they live?
- How have changes in the natural world forced people to change?
- What positive and negative changes have people made to their environment?

Economics

Economics has proven to be a powerful force in human history. From early times to the present, human cultures have been concerned with how to use their scarce resources to satisfy their needs. As you read about different groups, note several key issues regarding the role of economics in world history.

- What goods and services does a society produce?
- Who controls the wealth and resources of a society?
- How does a society obtain more goods and services?

Cultural Interaction

Today, people around the world share many things, from music, to food, to ideas. Human cultures actually have interacted with each other since ancient times. As you read about how different cultures have interacted, note several significant issues.

- How have cultures interacted (trade, migration, or conquest)?
- What items have cultures passed on to each other?
- What political, economic, and religious ideas have cultures shared?
- What positive and negative effects have resulted from cultural interaction?

Empire Building

Since the beginning of time, human cultures have shared a similar desire to grow more powerful—often by dominating other groups. As you read about empire building through the ages, keep in mind several key issues.

- What motivates groups to conquer other lands and people?
- How does one society gain control of others?
- How does a dominating society control and rule its subjects?

Science and Technology

All humans share an endless desire to know more about their world and to solve whatever problems they encounter. The development of science and technology has played a key role in these quests. As you read about the role of science and technology in world history, try to answer several key questions.

- What tools and methods do people use to solve the various problems they face?
- How do people gain knowledge about their world? How do they use that knowledge?
- How do new discoveries and inventions change the way people live?

Geography Themes

Geography is the study of the earth and its features. It is also an important part of human history. Since the beginning of time, all civilizations have had to control their surroundings in order to survive. In addition, geography has played a vital role in many historical events. Like history itself, geography reflects several key themes. These themes help us to understand the different ways in which geography has helped shape the story of world history.

Location

Location tells us where in the world a certain area is. Geographers describe location in two ways: absolute location and relative location. An area's absolute location is its point of latitude and longitude. Latitude is the distance in degrees north or south of the equator. Longitude is the degree distance east or west of an imaginary vertical line that runs through Greenwich, England, called the prime meridian. An area's relative location describes where it is in terms of other areas.

In absolute terms, the middle of Singapore lies at 1°20' north latitude and 103°50' east longitude. This information allows you to pinpoint Singapore on a map. In relative terms, Singapore is an island country on the southern tip of the Malay Peninsula near where the South China Sea and the Indian Ocean meet. How might Singapore's location on the sea have helped it develop into an economic power?

Human/Environment Interaction

Throughout history, humans have changed and have been changed by their environment. Because they live on an island, the people of Singapore have built a bridge in order to travel more easily to mainland Malaysia. In addition, Singapore residents have carved an inviting harbor out of parts of its coastline in order to accommodate the island's busy ocean traffic.

Singapore is one of the most densely populated countries in the world. Many of its over four million citizens live in the capital city, Singapore. The country's population density is almost 18,000 persons per square mile. In contrast, the United States has a population density of 82 persons per square mile. What environmental challenges does this situation pose?

Region

A region is any area that has common characteristics. These characteristics may include physical factors, such as landforms or climate. They also may include cultural aspects, such as language or religion. Singapore is part of a region known as Southeast Asia. The countries of this region share such characteristics as rich, fertile soil, as well as a strong influence of Buddhism and Islam.

Because regions share similar characteristics, they often share similar concerns. In 1967, Singapore joined with the other countries of Southeast Asia to form the Association of Southeast Asian Nations. This body was created to address the region's concerns. What concerns might Singapore have that are unique?

Place

Place, in geography, indicates what an area looks like in both physical and human terms. The physical setting of an area—its landforms, soil, climate, and resources—are aspects of place. So are the different cultures which inhabit an area.

The physical characteristics of Singapore include a hot, moist climate with numerous rain forests. In human terms, Singapore's population is mostly Chinese. How does Singapore's human characteristic tie it to other countries?

Movement

In geography, movement is the transfer of people, goods, and ideas from one place to another. In many ways, history is the story of movement. Since early times, people have migrated in search of better places to live. They have traded with distant peoples to obtain new goods. And they have spread a wealth of ideas from culture to culture.

Singapore, which is a prosperous center of trade and finance, attracts numerous people in search of greater wealth and new goods. What about Singapore's geography makes it the ideal place for the trading of goods?

Time

While history is the story of people, it is also the examination of when events occurred. Keeping track of the order of historical events will help you to better retain and understand the material. To help you remember the order and dates of important events in history, this book contains numerous time lines. Below is some instruction on how to read a time line, as well as a look at some terms associated with tracking time in history.

How to Read a Time Line

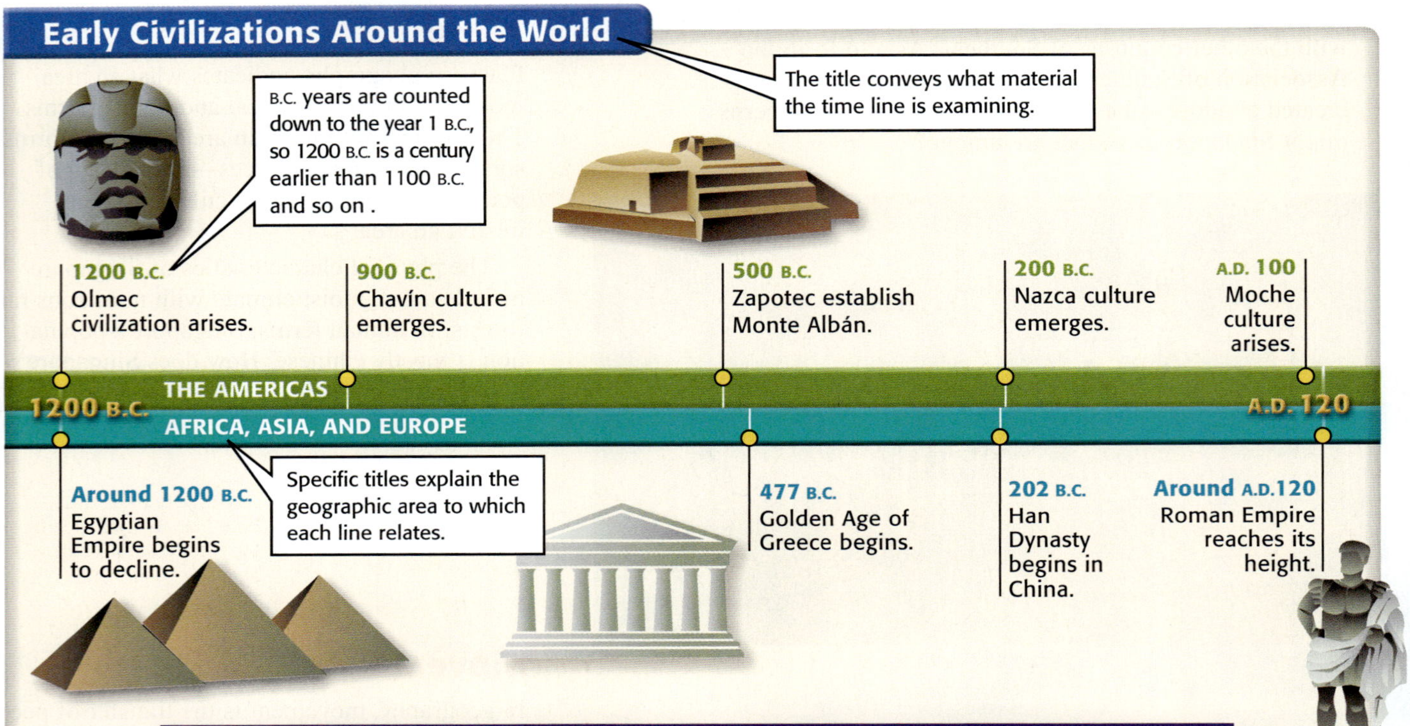

Common Chronological Terms	
B.C.	"Before Christ." Refers to a date so many years before the birth of Jesus Christ.
A.D.	"Anno Domini" ("in the year of the lord"). Refers to a date so many years after the birth of Jesus Christ.
BCE/CE	"Before the Common Era" and "Common Era." These terms correspond to B.C. and A.D., respectively.
decade	10 years. (For example: The 1930s was a decade of economic depression in many parts of the world.)
century	100 years. Note that the first century A.D. refers to the years 1 to 100. So, the twentieth century refers to the years 1901–2000. (For example: The fall of China's Han Empire in A.D. 220 was an important event of the third century.)
millennium	1,000 years. (For example, January 1, 2001, is the start of a new millennium.)
age/era	Broad time period characterized by a shared pattern of life. Ages and eras usually do not have definite starting or ending points. (For example: The Stone Age began around 2 million years ago and lasted until about 3000 B.C. It refers to the period when humans used stone, rather than metal tools.)

You are about to examine not only thousands of years of history, but nearly every region of the globe. To help you visualize the faraway places you read about, this book contains numerous maps. Many of these maps contain several layers of information that provide a better understanding of how and why events in history occurred. Below is a look at how to read a map in order to obtain all of the rich information it offers.

How to Read a Map

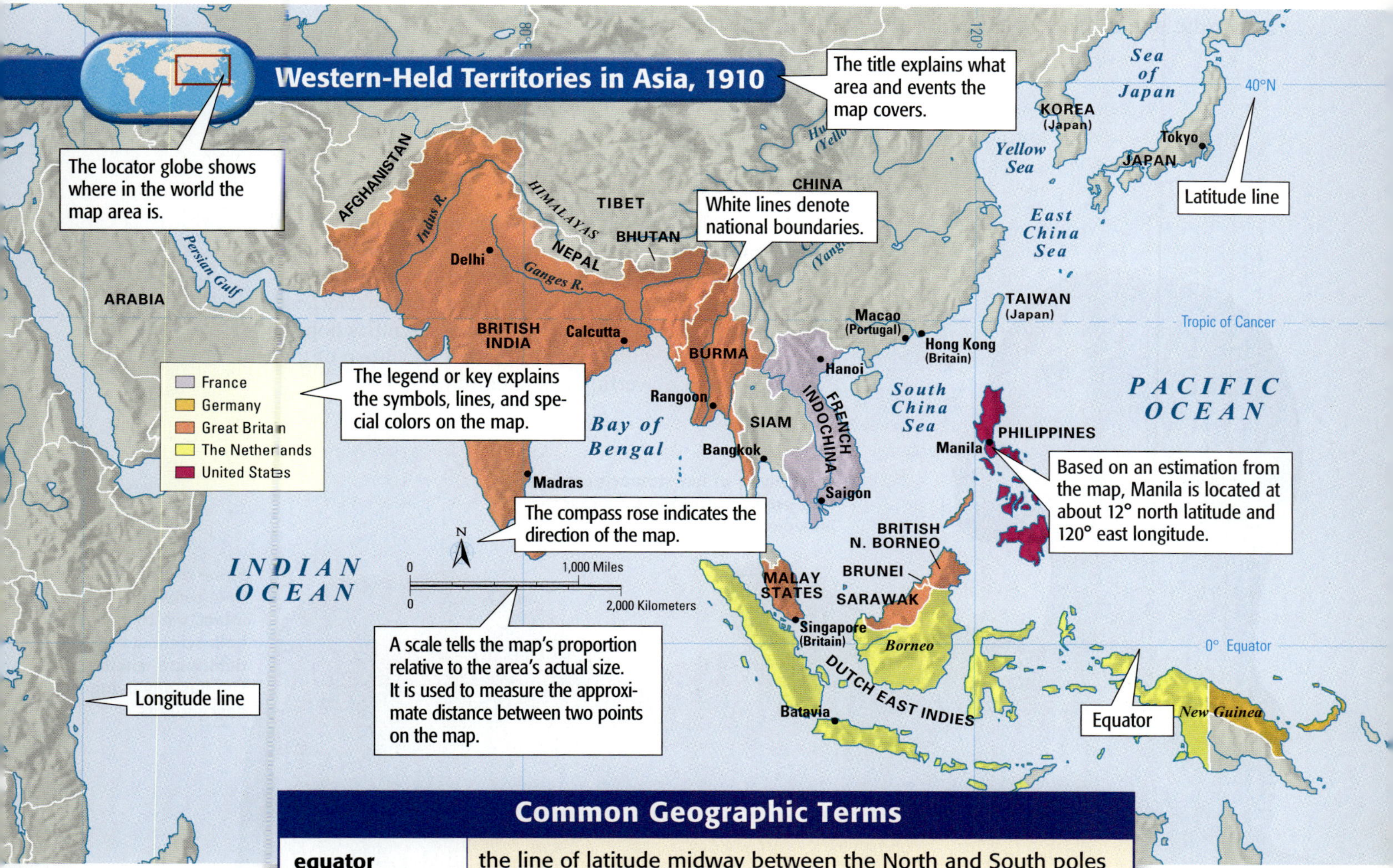

Common Geographic Terms	
equator	the line of latitude midway between the North and South poles
latitude	imaginary lines that circle the globe from east to west, measuring an area's distance north and south of the equator
longitude	imaginary lines that circle the globe from north to south, measuring an area's distance east or west of the prime meridian
prime meridian	the line of longitude at 0° that runs through Greenwich, England
hemisphere	half the globe. The globe can be divided into Northern and Southern hemispheres (separated by the equator) or into Eastern and Western hemispheres (separated by the prime meridian).

How Do We Know?

Do you like puzzles? If so, you are in luck. You are about to encounter the greatest puzzle there is: history. The study of history is much more than the recollection of dates and names. It is an attempt to answer a continuous and puzzling question: what really happened?

In their effort to solve this puzzle, historians and researchers use a variety of methods. From digging up artifacts, to uncovering eyewitness accounts, experts collect and analyze mountains of data in numerous ways. As a result, the history books you read more accurately depict what life was like in a culture 5,000 years ago, or what caused the outbreak of a devastating war. The following two pages examine some of the pieces used to solve the puzzle of history.

Clues from an Ancient Girl

In 1995, an anthropologist discovered the mummified and frozen remains of a teenage girl in the Andes Mountains of South America. Scientists believe that she is about 500 years old and was a member of the Inca Empire. Because much of her remains are well preserved, scientists hope she will provide them with new information about one of the Americas' most powerful ancient cultures.

An analysis of her stomach content may provide information about the Inca diet.

Some of her DNA remains intact, which will help scientists determine whether she has any living descendants.

Her clothing, believed to belong to the upper class, should shed new light on how noble Inca women dressed.

Modern Science

The ever-improving field of science has lent its hand in the search to learn more about the past. Using everything from microscopes to computers, researchers have shed new light on many historical mysteries. Here, a researcher uses computer technology to determine what the owner of a prehistoric human skull may have looked like.

Written Sources

Historians often look to written documents for insight into the past. There are various types of written sources. Documents written during the same time period as an event are known as *primary* sources. They include such things as diaries and newspapers. They also include drawings, such as the one shown here by Italian painter and inventor, Leonardo da Vinci. His rough sketch of a helicopter-type machine tells us that as early as the late 1400s, humans considered mechanical flight. Material written about an event later, such as books, are known as *secondary* sources. Some written sources began as oral tradition—legends, myths, and beliefs passed on by spoken word from generation to generation.

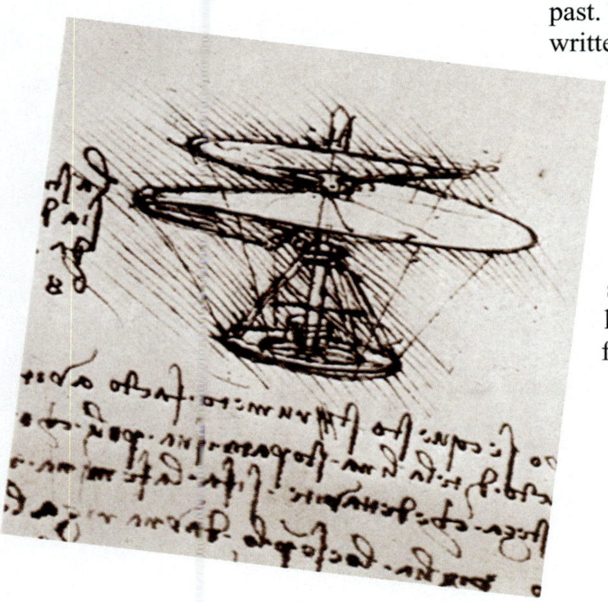

Digging Up History

Researchers have learned much about the past by discovering the remains of ancient societies. Spearheads like these, which date back to around 9,500 B.C., were found throughout North America. They tell us among other things that the early Americans were hunters. These spearheads were once considered to be the earliest evidence of humankind in the Americas. However, as an example of how history continues to change, scientists recently found evidence of human life in South America as early as 10,500 B.C.

NEW YORK

STEPS TO SUCCESS

Guide to Understanding
New York State's Core Curriculum: Global History and Geography NY41

- New York State's Core Curriculum: Global History and Geography is organized into a methodology section and eight historical units. Each unit lists the content that is assessed on the Regents Exam.

Guide to the New York State Regents Exam S1

- The New York State Regents in Global History and Geography is designed to measure your understanding of the core curriculum content.

For a complete list of the New York State Core Curriculum: Global History and Geography, see page R149.

Liberty Island, New York © Christopher Hill/Alamy

Why Study History?

When you study world history, you will see how the past informs your everyday life. Many things, such as the clothes you wear and the music you listen to, have been influenced by past cultures and traditions.

Learn how to think like a historian! Dive into the dramatic events of the world's past and uncover the lives of the people who shaped the world's history.

- **Solve the Puzzle**—Look at history as a puzzle to solve. Your textbook will offer "clues" that will bring history to life, and will show you the impact many events have made on the world today.

  The "History Makers" and "Primary Source" features will introduce you to leaders of the past, and will help bring their perspectives on past events to life.

- **Explore Other Cultures**—Your textbook will allow you to visit other cultures and discover the traditions and beliefs that made those cultures unique.

- **Become a Better Critical Thinker**—Many activities and questions throughout this book will encourage you to think critically about the events and people in world history.

  For example, what would *you* have done if you had ruled England during the Reformation?

  Features like "Different Perspectives" and "Interact with History" will also help to hone your critical thinking skills.

© Corbis

What Will I Learn?

Guide to Understanding

New York State's Core Curriculum: Global History and Geography

New York State's Core Curriculum: Global History and Geography is organized into a methodology section and eight historical units. All of the core content is covered in this book.

Methodology of Global History and Geography

Unit One	**Ancient World—Civilizations and Religions (4000 BC–500 AD)**
Unit Two	**Expanding Zones of Exchange and Encounter (500–1200)**
Unit Three	**Global Interactions (1200–1650)**
Unit Four	**The First Global Age (1450–1770)**
Unit Five	**An Age of Revolution (1750–1914)**
Unit Six	**A Half Century of Crisis and Achievement (1900–1945)**
Unit Seven	**The 20th Century Since 1945**
Unit Eight	**Global Connections and Interactions**

Each unit lists the core content that is assessed on the New York State Regents in Global History and Geography.

Historical Unit	Assessed Core Curriculum Content
Unit Eight Global Connections and Interactions	B. Economic issues 1. North/South dichotomy: issues of development (post-colonialism) a. Africa b. Latin America

CONNECT TO YOUR NEW YORK TEST

At the end of this course, you will take a test called the NEW YORK STATE REGENTS IN GLOBAL HISTORY AND GEOGRAPHY. This graduation test is designed to measure your understanding and mastery of the core curriculum content.

Overview

New York State's Core Curriculum: Global History and Geography

The charts that follow provide a brief overview of the core content in the methodology section and in each historical unit. This content is the knowledge you need to succeed on your New York State Regents in Global History and Geography. Look for the core content references at the beginning of each section.

For a complete list of the New York State Core Curriculum: Global History and Geography, see page R149.

Methodology of Global History and Geography

Core Curriculum Content	Why It Matters Now
A. History 1. Skills of historical analysis a. Investigate differing and competing interpretations of historical theories–multiple perspectives	The ability to analyze evidence and theories is an important skill to master. This and other social studies skills provide the basis to understand and appreciate the knowledge gained through the study of world history.

Unit One Ancient World–Civilizations and Religions (4000 BC–500 AD)

Core Curriculum Content	Why It Matters Now
C. Classical civilizations 2. Greek civilization a. Human and physical geography b. The rise of city-states–Athens/Sparta c. Contributions: art, architecture, philosophy, science–Plato, Socrates, Aristotle d. Growth of democracy in Athens versus Spartan political system e. Alexander the Great and Hellenistic culture–cultural diffusion	Ancient Greece was the birthplace of much of the West's cultural heritage. For example, many political systems today, including our own democracy, mirror the forms of government that evolved in ancient Greece.

Unit Two Expanding Zones of Exchange and Encounter (500–1200)

Core Curriculum Content	Why It Matters Now
E. The spread of Islam to Europe, Asia, and Africa 1. Human and physical geography 2. Organizational structure 3. The development of Islamic law and its impact 4. Social class: women and slavery in Muslim society 5. Position of "people of the book"	Like all major religions, Islam spread from its point of origin to the wider world. As Islam spread to Europe, Asia, and Africa, it produced a cultural blending that has continued into the modern world.

Unit Three Global Interactions (1200–1650)

Core Curriculum Content	Why It Matters Now
F. Renaissance and humanism 1. Human and physical geography 2. Shift in worldview—other-worldly to secular 3. Greco-Roman revival (interest in humanism) 4. Art and architecture (e.g., da Vinci and Michelangelo) 5. Literature (e.g., Dante, Cervantes, Shakespeare) 6. Political science (e.g., Machiavelli) 7. New scientific and technological innovations (Gutenberg's moveable type printing press, cartography, naval engineering, and navigational and nautical devices)	The Renaissance is one of the great turning points in history. Advances in technology, scientific knowledge, and social thought laid the foundation for the modern world. Even today, the influences of Renaissance art and literature can be seen in modern thought, art, and architecture.

Unit Four The First Global Age (1450–1770)

Core Curriculum Content	Why It Matters Now
A. The Ming Dynasty (1368–1644) 1. Human and physical geography 2. Restoration of Chinese rule, Chinese world vision 3. The impact of China on East Asia and Southeast Asia 4. China's relationship with the West 5. Contributions 6. Expansion of trade (Zheng He, 1405–1433)	China emerged as the main economic and political power in Asia during the Ming Dynasty. It did so while maintaining its isolation from the West. Today, China is a major economic and political power in the world. It still maintains its independence from the West. Understanding the roots of this independence will help you understand modern China.

Unit Five An Age of Revolution (1750–1914)

Core Curriculum Content	Why It Matters Now
B. The Enlightenment in Europe 1. The writings of Locke, Voltaire, Rousseau, and Montesquieu 2. The impact of the Enlightenment on nationalism and democracy 3. The Enlightenment despots—Maria Theresa and Catherine the Great	Ideas have always transcended borders. Our own American Revolution was fueled by the ideas of the Enlightenment. Understanding how Enlightenment ideas shaped people's views can help us appreciate the importance of the political freedoms we enjoy today.

Unit Six A Half Century of Crisis and Achievement (1900–1945)

Core Curriculum Content	Why It Matters Now
D. World War II–causes and impact 1. Human and physical geography 2. The Nazi and Japanese states 3. Key individuals–Hitler, Mussolini, Stalin, Churchill, and Roosevelt 4. Key events–Dunkirk, the Blitz, D-Day, Hitler's second front, the war in the Pacific 5. The Nazi Holocaust: the extermination of Jews, Poles, other Slavs, Gypsies, disabled, and others 6. Resistance 7. Japan's role–Nanjing, Bataan, Pearl Harbor 8. War in China–Long March 9. Impacts of technology on total war 10. Hiroshima and Nagasaki 11. War crime trials 12. Global spatial arrangements–post-World War II world	World War II was an important period in the history of the United States. During World War II, the United States assumed a leading role in world affairs. Our nation's military and economic capabilities, which played a deciding factor in winning the war, have continued to influence world affairs ever since. Knowing about this time period will help you understand the United States' role in the world today.

Unit Seven The 20th Century Since 1945

Core Curriculum Content	Why It Matters Now
B. Role of the United Nations 1. Peace keeping 2. Social and economic programs 3. Contemporary social conditions	Much of modern history is the story of nation building and the clash of nations. Since its founding in 1945, the United Nations has played an important role in peace keeping and in assisting nations with economic and social development.

Unit Eight Global Connections and Interactions

Core Curriculum Content	Why It Matters Now
A. Social and political patterns and change 4. Modernization/tradition–finding a balance a. Japan b. Middle East (Saudi Arabia, Egypt, Afghanistan, and Algeria) c. Africa d. Latin America	Continuity and change are important themes in world history. As the world has become increasingly interconnected, many countries have struggled to balance traditional beliefs and modern ideas. Understanding this struggle will help you make sense of cultural clashes in the world today.

NEW YORK

Guide to
The New York State Regents Exam

Find online test practice at www.classzone.com

The chart below provides a guide to the test-taking strategies that will help prepare you for the **New York State Regents in Global History and Geography.**

- **Learn** each strategy by reviewing the numbered steps on the page listed in the column.
- **Practice** the strategy on the following page.
- **Apply** the strategies you learned in the **New York State Regents Exam Practice** at the end of each chapter.

STRATEGY	LEARN	PRACTICE	APPLY
Multiple Choice	p. S2	p. S3	end of every section and chapter
Primary Sources	p. S4	p. S5	p. 25, Chapter 1 p. 583, Unit 4 p. 855, Chapter 29
Secondary Sources	p. S6	p. S7	p. 177, Chapter 6
Political Cartoons	p. S8	p. S9	p. 812, Chapter 28 p. 1029, Chapter 34 p. 1037, Chapter 35
Charts	p. S10	p. S11	p. 147, Chapter 5 p. 281, Chapter 10 p. 317, Chapter 11
Line and Bar Graphs	p. S12	p. S13	p. 17, Chapter 1 p. 375, Chapter 13 p. 829, Chapter 28
Pie Graphs	p. S14	p. S15	p. 681, Chapter 24 p. 748, Chapter 26
Political Maps	p. S16	p. S17	p. 677, Chapter 23 p. 801, Chapter 27
Thematic Maps	p. S18	p. S19	p. 17, Chapter 1 p. 302, Chapter 11
Time Lines	p. S20	p. S21	p. 831, Chapter 28
Reading Visuals	p. S22	p. S23	p. 390, Chapter 14
Document-Based Questions	pp. S24–S25	pp. S26–S27	p. 33, Chapter 2 p. 395, Chapter 14

REGENTS STRATEGIES

Multiple Choice

A multiple-choice question consists of a stem and a set of alternatives. The stem is usually in the form of a question or an incomplete sentence. One of the alternatives correctly answers the question or completes the sentence.

1. Read the stem carefully and try to answer the question or complete the sentence before looking at the alternatives.
2. Look for key words in the stem. They may direct you to the correct answer.
3. Read each alternative with the stem. Don't make your final decision on the correct answer until you have read all of the alternatives.
4. Look for modifiers to help you rule out incorrect alternatives.
5. Eliminate alternatives that you know are wrong.

answers: 1 (1); 2 (2); 3 (3); 4 (4)

stem

1 1 The Sahara is mostly

2 *Mostly* is a key word here. Changing it to *partly* would alter the sentence and call for a different answer.

3 alternatives

(1) scattered with rocks and gravel
(2) made up of sand dunes
(3) located south of the equator
(4) covered with tall grasses and bushes

2 Over hundreds of years, the Bantu people migrated from West Africa to

(1) all of North Africa
(2) East and South Africa
(3) South and Southwest Asia
(4) every continent except Antarctica

4 Absolute words, such as *all, never, always, every,* and *only,* often signal an incorrect alternative.

3 The traditional griots of West Africa passed on the histories of their people by

(1) writing books
(2) painting murals
(3) telling stories
(4) carving statues

5 You can eliminate **(1)** if you remember that few African societies had written languages.

4 Which of the following is one of the trading cities of East Africa?

(1) Mali
(2) Songhai
(3) Ghana
(4) Kilwa

Directions: Read each question carefully and choose the *best* answer from the four alternatives.

1 Which of the following is a reason why the Renaissance began in Italy?

(1) Italy had several thriving cities.
(2) The Black Death did not strike Italy.
(3) Italian merchants lacked political power.
(4) Italy had lost its classical Roman heritage.

2 Reformation teachings were adopted by

(1) the Catholic Church
(2) all the countries in Europe
(3) some countries in Europe
(4) common people, but not rulers

3 Akbar differed from Aurangzeb in that he

(1) extended the boundaries of the Mughal Empire
(2) followed Western ways
(3) defended religious freedom
(4) enforced strict Islamic laws

4 During the 1700s, the Atlantic slave trade was dominated by the

(1) Dutch
(2) English
(3) Portuguese
(4) Spanish

REGENTS STRATEGIES

Primary Sources

Primary sources are written or made by people who were at historical events, either as observers or participants. Primary sources include journals, diaries, letters, speeches, newspaper articles, autobiographies, wills, deeds, and financial records.

1. Look at the source line to learn about the document and its author. Consider the reliability of the information in the document.
2. Skim the document to get an idea of what it is about. (This source includes three paragraphs that are distinct but address a related theme—rulers and moral behavior.)
3. Note any special punctuation. Ellipses, for example, indicate that words or sentences have been removed from the original.
4. Use active reading strategies. For instance, ask and answer questions on the content as you read.
5. Use context clues to help you understand difficult or unfamiliar words. (From the context, you realize that *chastisements* means "punishments.")
6. Before rereading the document, skim the questions. This will help you focus your reading and more easily locate answers.

answers: 1 (2); 2 (3)

Moral Rulers

Book II, 3. The Master said, Govern the people by regulations, keep order among them by chastisements, and they will flee from you, and lose all self-respect. Govern them by moral force, keep order among them by ritual and they will keep their self-respect and come to you of their own accord. . . .

Book XI, 23. . . . The Master said, . . . What I call a great minister is one who will only serve his prince while he can do so without infringement of the Way, and as soon as this is impossible, resigns. . . .

Book XIII, 6. The Master said, If the ruler himself is upright, all will go well even though he does not give orders. But if he himself is not upright, even though he gives orders, they will not be obeyed.

—*The Analects of Confucius*

This is a collection of writings on government, ethics, literature, and other subjects by the ancient Chinese scholar and teacher Confucius.

1 Which sentence best expresses the main idea shared by these paragraphs?

(1) Rules and regulations are hard to live by.
(2) Leaders should act morally in ruling the people.
(3) A leader's goodness is judged by the punishments he administers.
(4) Rulers should expect their people to obey them no matter what they say.

2 This advice from Confucius seems most appropriate for

(1) workers and farmers
(2) merchants and town artisans
(3) rulers and their advisers
(4) soldiers and priests

Directions: Use this passage, written by the traveler Leo Africanus, and your knowledge of world history to answer questions 1 through 4.

Crossing the Desert

In the way which leads from Fez to Timbuktu are certain pits environed either with the hides or bones of camels. Neither do the merchants in summer time pass that way without great danger of their lives: for oftentimes it happens that when the south wind blows all those pits are stopped up with sand. And so the merchants, when they can find neither those pits, nor any sign thereof, must needs perish with extreme thirst; whose carcasses are afterwards found lying scattered here and there, and scorched with the heat of the sun. . . .

For some time being sore athirst we could not find one drop of water, partly because our guide strayed out of the direct course, and partly because our enemies had cut off the springs and channels of the foresaid pits and wells. Insomuch that the small quantity of water which we found was sparingly to be kept: for that which would scarce suffice us for five days, we were constrained to keep for ten.

—Leo Africanus, *History and Description of Africa* (1550)

1 This account most likely describes the dangers of working in the

(1) African rain forest
(2) Savannas of East Africa
(3) Sahara salt trade
(4) Atlantic slave trade

2 What is most likely the purpose of the pits that Africanus describes in the first sentence?

(1) They probably hold water.
(2) They are used to store supplies.
(3) They contain valuable skins and hides.
(4) They can be used to hide from enemies.

3 Which of the following might cause merchant caravans to run short of water?

(1) enemies cutting off water supplies
(2) camels straying off course
(3) merchants not paying guides
(4) summer monsoons coming late

4 Which statement best describes the believability of the passage?

(1) The statements are not credible because they are secondhand.
(2) The author is merely recounting rumors and cannot be believed.
(3) The statements are believable because the author experienced the events.
(4) The author's believability cannot be evaluated without looking at other sources.

REGENTS STRATEGIES

Secondary Sources

Secondary sources are written or made by people who were not at the original events. They often combine information from several primary sources. The most common types of written secondary sources are biographies and history books.

1. Read the title to preview the content of the passage. (The title here signals that the passage is about a person named Malinche who seems to be controversial.)
2. Skim the passage to locate the main idea—the central point that is supported by other details.
3. Notice words and phrases that clarify the sequence of events.
4. Read actively by asking and answering questions about what you read. (You might ask yourself: "Why did opinions of Malinche change over time?")
5. Before rereading the passage, review the questions to identify the information you need to find.

answers: 1 (1); 2 (2)

1 **Malinche, Heroine or Traitor?**

The origins of the Native American woman Malinche are unknown. What is clear is that in 1519—when she was perhaps 15 years old—she was given with 19 other young women to Hernando Cortés, who had recently landed in Mexico. Malinche greatly aided Cortés's conquest of the Aztecs. **2** She spoke both Nahuatl—the language of the Aztecs—and Mayan. Over time, she also learned Spanish and became Cortés's chief translator. She also advised Cortés on the tricky politics of Mexico's Native American peoples.

The Spanish conquistadors reportedly admired and honored Malinche, calling her Doña Marina. And for many centuries, she **3** was seen as a praiseworthy figure. In the 1800s, though, people came to view her harshly. Writers and artists portrayed her as a traitor to her people. This criticism of Malinche began after Mexico won its independence from Spain, and reflected anti-Spanish feeling. Today, however, she is once again seen favorably. **4**

5

1 Which of the following statements about Malinche is a fact?

(1) She spoke three languages.
(2) She was a traitor.
(3) She was a heroine.
(4) She hated the Spanish.

Remember that a fact is a verifiable statement. An opinion is a statement of someone's belief about something.

2 Based on this account, which person or group would be most likely to view Malinche as a traitor?

These words signal that you have to make inferences from information in the passage.

(1) Cortés and the conquistadors
(2) a supporter of Mexican independence in the 1800s
(3) one of the 19 other women who were with her in 1519
(4) a historian writing about her today

Directions: Use the passage and your knowledge of world history to answer questions 1 through 4.

Polynesian Canoes

The Polynesian voyaging canoe, one of the great ocean-going craft of the ancient world, was the means by which generations of adventurous voyagers were able to extend the human frontier far out into the Pacific, discovering and colonizing a vast realm of Oceanic islands. By 1000 B.C., when Mediterranean sailors were sailing in their land-locked sea, the immediate ancestors of the Polynesians had reached the previously uninhabited archipelagoes of Fiji, Tonga, and Samoa, in the middle of the Pacific Ocean. Their descendants went on from there to settle all the habitable islands in a large triangular section of the ocean bounded by the Hawaiian archipelago, tiny Easter Island, and the massive islands of New Zealand—an area equivalent to most of Europe and Asia combined.

The canoes in which people spread into the Pacific were not only humankind's first truly ocean-going craft, but also embodied a unique way of gaining the stability needed to carry sail in rough, open ocean waters. [This involved] adding outrigger floats to one or both sides of a single canoe hull, or by joining two hulls together by means of crossbeams and coconut-fiber lashings to make the so-called double canoe.

—Ben Finney, "The Polynesian Voyaging Canoe," in *New World and Pacific Civilizations: Cultures of America, Asia, and the Pacific*, edited by Goran Burenhult.

1 The Polynesians used voyaging canoes to colonize

(1) a small area of the Pacific

(2) a large area of the Pacific

(3) most of Europe and Asia

(4) Australia and New Guinea

2 What evidence does the author provide to support his claim that the Polynesian voyaging canoe was "one of the great ocean-going craft of the ancient world"?

(1) statistics about its size

(2) comparisons to European craft

(3) statements about its use in exploring and colonizing the Pacific

(4) statements about its use by civilizations beyond the Pacific

3 The Polynesians gave their canoes the stability needed to handle the rough ocean waters by adding

(1) outrigger floats

(2) more sails

(3) ballasted hulls

(4) wooden keels

4 By 1000 B.C., the Pacific voyagers had reached

(1) the Hawaiian archipelago

(2) the islands of New Zealand

(3) Fiji, Tonga, and Samoa

(4) tiny Easter Island

NEW YORK STATE REGENTS

Political Cartoons

Political cartoons use a combination of words and images to express a point of view on political issues. They are useful primary sources, because they reflect the opinions of the time.

1. Identify the subject of the cartoon. Titles and captions often provide clues to the subject matter.
2. Use labels to help identify the people, places, and events represented in the cartoon.
3. Note where and when the cartoon was published for more information on people, places, and events.
4. Identify any important symbols—ideas or images that stand for something else—in the cartoon.
5. Analyze the point of view presented in the cartoon. The use of caricature—the exaggeration of physical features—often signals how the cartoonist feels.
6. Interpret the cartoonist's message.

answers: 1 (1); 2 (4)

(1) "NEXT!"

Daniel Fitzpatrick, *St. Louis Post-Dispatch,* August 24, 1939.

(4) The cartoonist uses the swastika, the symbol of the Nazi Party, to represent Germany.

(5) The swastika looks like a huge, menacing machine, which can easily overrun the Polish landscape.

(2) The label *Poland* indicates the location of the subject addressed in the cartoon.

(3) The date of the publication, 1939, suggests that the cartoon might concern the beginning of World War II.

(6) The cartoonist suggests that Poland will be the German war machine's next victim.

1 The machine-like swastika in the cartoon represents

(1) Nazi Germany
(2) the Soviet Union
(3) Napoleon's empire
(4) the Polish military

2 Which sentence best summarizes the cartoonist's message?

(1) Germany must beware of Poland.
(2) Poland is in danger of civil war.
(3) Germany and Poland are military giants.
(4) Poland will be Germany's next victim.

Directions: Use the cartoon and your knowledge of world history to answer questions 1 through 4.

Steve Sack, *Minneapolis Star-Tribune,* January 1, 1992.

1 What leader from the Middle East does the cartoon show?

(1) Iraq's Saddam Hussein
(2) Egypt's Hosni Mubarak
(3) Syria's Hafez al-Assad
(4) Libya's Muammar al-Qaddafi

2 How has the cartoonist drawn this leader?

(1) as a soldier
(2) as a poor person
(3) as Count Dracula
(4) as Frankenstein's monster

3 The countries identified in the cartoon include

(1) Saudi Arabia and Kuwait
(2) West Germany and China
(3) the United States and the Soviet Union
(4) France and Japan

4 The most appropriate title for this cartoon would be

(1) "A Monster Walks at Night"
(2) "They've Created a Monster"
(3) "The Monster of the Middle East"
(4) "A Monstrous Creation"

REGENTS STRATEGIES

Charts

Charts present information in a visual form. History textbooks use several types of charts, including tables, flow charts, Venn diagrams, and info-graphics. The chart most commonly found in standardized tests is the table. This organizes information in columns and rows for easy viewing.

1. Read the title and identify the broad subject of the chart.
2. Read the column and row headings and any other labels. These will provide more details about the subject of the chart.
3. Note how the information in the chart is organized.
4. Compare and contrast the information from column to column and row to row.
5. Try to draw conclusions from the information in the chart.
6. Read the questions and then study the chart again.

answers: 1 (4); 2 (1)

1 This chart is about the number of people who immigrated to different countries.

4 Notice that the years covered in the table are not the same for all countries.

Immigration to Selected Countries

Country	Period	Number of Immigrants
Argentina	1856-1932	6,405,000
Australia	1861-1932	2,913,000
Brazil	1821-1932	4,431,000
British West Indies	1836-1932	1,587,000
Canada	1821-1932	5,206,000
Cuba	1901-1932	857,000
Mexico	1911-1931	226,000
New Zealand	1851-1932	594,000
South Africa	1881-1932	852,000
United States	1821-1932	34,244,000
Uruguay	1836-1932	713,000

Source: Alfred W. Crosby, Jr., *The Columbian Exchange: Biological and Cultural Consequences of 1492*

3 This chart organizes the countries alphabetically. In some charts, information is organized according to years or the value of the numbers displayed.

5 Think about what the countries with the highest number of immigrants have in common.

6

1 The country that received the vast majority of immigrants was

(1) Argentina
(2) Brazil
(3) Canada
(4) the United States

2 The Latin American country that received the most immigrants was

(1) Argentina
(2) Brazil
(3) Cuba
(4) Uruguay

Directions: Use the chart and your knowledge of world history to answer questions 1 through 4.

Crude Steel Production for Selected Countries (in thousands of metric tons)

Year	China	Germany*	Japan	Korea	Russia/ USSR	United Kingdom	United States
1900	—	6,646	1	—	2,214	4,979	10,351
1910	—	13,699	250	—	3,444	6,476	26,512
1920	—	8,538	845	—	162	9,212	42,807
1930	—	11,511	2,289	—	5,761	7,443	41,351
1940	—	19,141	7,528	—	19,000	13,183	60,765
1950	61	12,121	4,839	—	27,300	16,553	87,848
1960	1,866	34,100	22,138	—	65,292	24,695	91,920
1970	1,779	45,041	93,322	—	115,886	28,314	119,310
1980	3,712	43,838	111,935	8,558	148,000	11,278	101,457
1990	6,535	44,022	110,339	23,125	154,414	17,896	89,276
2000	127,200	46,400	106,400	43,100	59,100	15,200	101,500

* Figures from 1950 through 1990 are West Germany only.

Source: International Iron and Steel Institute; Japan Iron and Steel Federation

1 Which country produced the most crude steel in 1900?

(1) Germany
(2) Russia/USSR
(3) United Kingdom
(4) United States

2 Japanese crude steel production most likely dropped from 1940 to 1950 due to

(1) growing competition from Korea and the USSR
(2) rising production in China
(3) damage to the industry suffered in World War II
(4) mergers with American companies

3 By 2000, the largest share of crude steel was being produced by countries in

(1) Africa
(2) Asia
(3) Europe
(4) North America

4 What country rose from no crude steel production to be the world's largest producer in 50 years?

(1) China
(2) Germany
(3) Korea
(4) United Kingdom

REGENTS STRATEGIES

Line and Bar Graphs

Graphs show statistics in a visual form. Line graphs are particularly useful for showing changes over time. Bar graphs make it easy to compare numbers or sets of numbers.

1. Read the title and identify the broad subject of the graph.
2. Study the labels on the vertical and horizontal axes to see the kinds of information presented in the graph. Note the intervals between amounts and between dates. This will help you read the graph more efficiently.
3. Look at the source line and evaluate the reliability of the information in the graph.
4. If the graph presents information over time, look for trends—generalizations you can make about changes over time.
5. Draw conclusions and make inferences based on information in the graph.
6. Read the questions carefully and then study the graph again.

answers: 1 (3); 2 (2)

1 Exports of English Manufactured Goods, 1699–1774

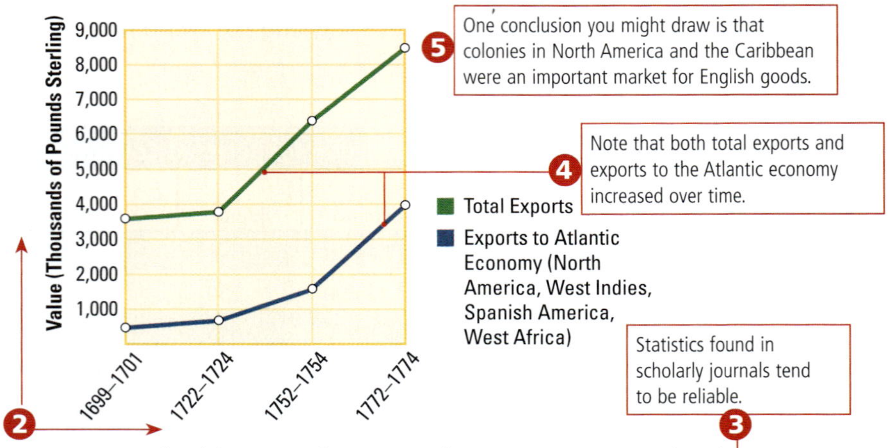

Source: R. Davis, "English Foreign Trade, 1700–1774," *Economic History Review* (1962)

6 1 Which statement best describes the change in proportion of Atlantic economy exports to total exports?

(1) It started small and remained small.
(2) It started large and remained large.
(3) It grew over time.
(4) It decreased over time.

---

1 Nations with High Foreign Debt, 2000

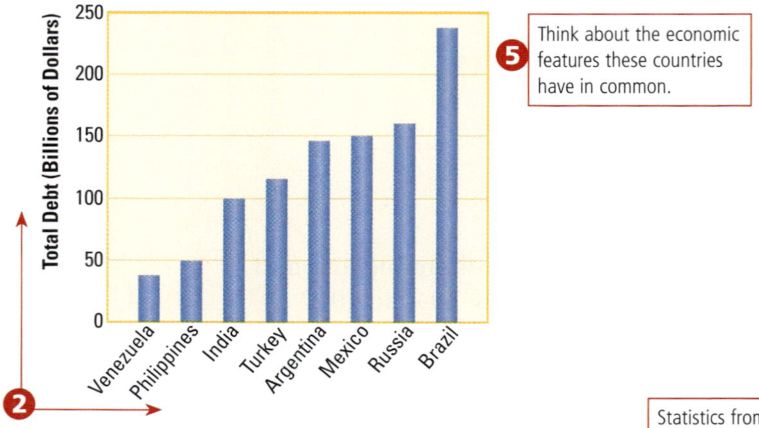

Source: The World Bank

3 Statistics from major organizations, such as the World Bank, tend to be reliable.

6 2 Which nation has the largest foreign debt?

(1) Venezuela
(2) Brazil
(3) Mexico
(4) Russia

Directions: Use the graphs and your knowledge of world history to answer questions 1 through 4.

Japan: Gross Domestic Product, 1984–2000

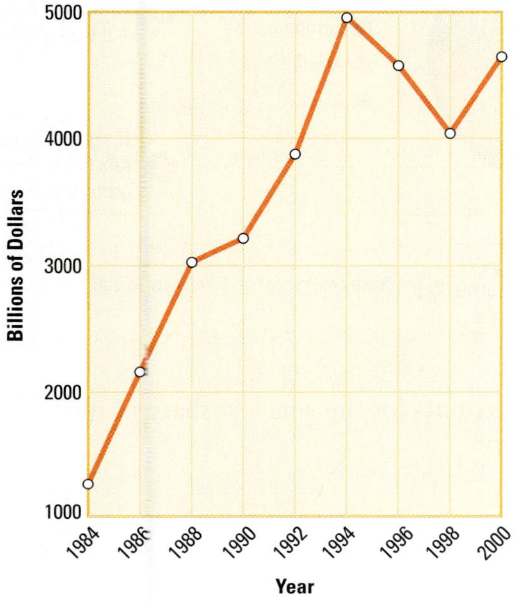

Source: *Annual Report on National Accounts 2002,* Cabinet Office of the Government of Japan

Unemployment Rates for Selected Countries, 2002

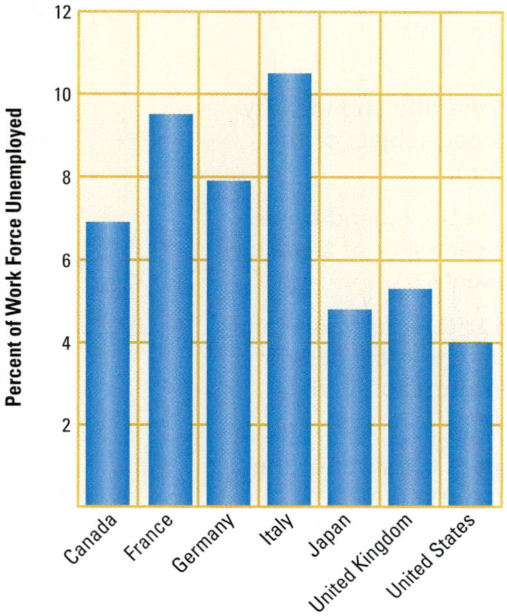

Source: Organization for Economic Cooperation and Development

1 Which of the following periods saw a decline in the gross domestic product of Japan?

(1) 1984 to 1988
(2) 1988 to 1992
(3) 1990 to 1994
(4) 1994 to 1998

2 From 1986 to 1994, Japan's gross domestic product

(1) more than doubled
(2) more than tripled
(3) grew by about five times
(4) grew nearly ten times

3 Which of these countries had the lowest unemployment rate in 2002?

(1) Italy
(2) Japan
(3) United Kingdom
(4) United States

4 In 2002, France's unemployment rate stood at

(1) about 9 percent
(2) well over 9 percent
(3) about 7 percent
(4) less than 7 percent

REGENTS STRATEGIES

Pie Graphs

A pie, or circle, graph shows relationships among the parts of a whole. These parts look like slices of a pie. The size of each slice is proportional to the percentage of the whole that it represents.

1. Read the title and identify the broad subject of the pie graph.
2. Look at the legend to see what each slice of the pie represents.
3. Look at the source line and evaluate the reliability of the information in the graph.
4. Compare the slices of the pie and try to make generalizations and draw conclusions from your comparisons.
5. Read the questions carefully.
6. Eliminate choices that you know are wrong and then select the best answer from the remaining choices.

answers: 1 (4); 2 (3)

1 World Population by Region, 2002

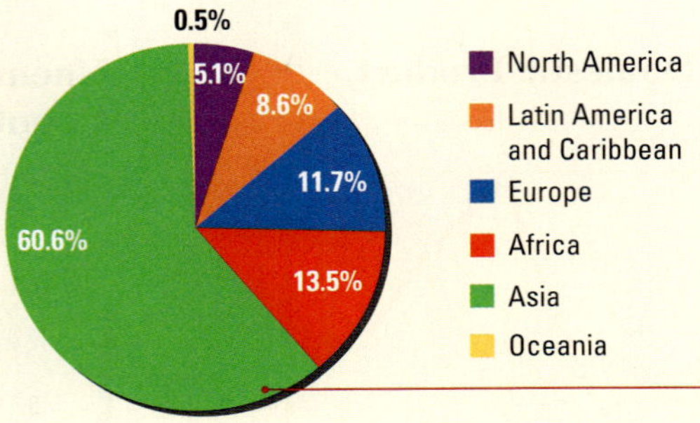

2 Note that each region is shown by a distinct color in the pie graph.

4 The graph shows that Asia has by far the largest population.

The Population Reference Bureau specializes in studies of United States and international population data. 3

Source: Population Reference Bureau

5

1 Which region accounts for the smallest share of the world population?

(1) Africa
(2) North America
(3) Latin America and the Caribbean
(4) Oceania

2 A greater share of the world's population lives in Latin America and the Caribbean than lives in

(1) Africa
(2) Europe
(3) North America
(4) Asia

6 For this question, find the "pie slices" for each of the regions listed in the alternatives. Compare each one to the "pie slice" for Latin America and the Caribbean.

Directions: Use the pie graph and your knowledge of world history to answer questions 1 through 4.

World Energy Consumption by Region

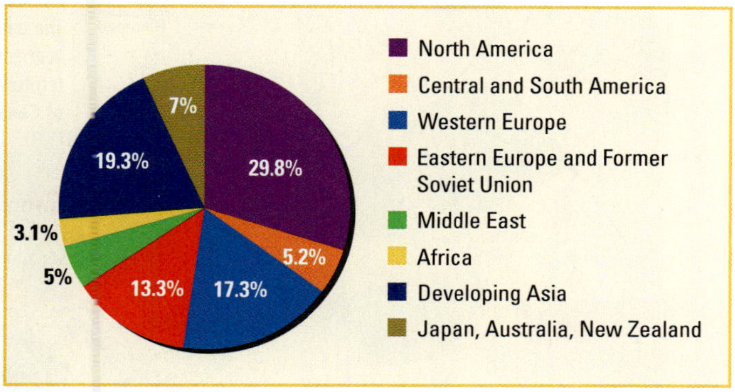

Source: "Earth Pulse," *National Geographic* (March 2001)

1 Energy consumption statistics for Russia are included in the region called

(1) North America
(2) Western Europe
(3) Eastern Europe and former Soviet Union
(4) Developing Asia

2 Which region uses the highest proportion of energy?

(1) North America
(2) Western Europe
(3) Eastern Europe and former Soviet Union
(4) Developing Asia

3 The word *Developing* in the legend refers to countries that are

(1) growing in population
(2) adopting new methods of agriculture
(3) developing nuclear weapons
(4) moving toward industrial economies

4 Japan, Australia, and New Zealand are grouped together because they are in the same part of the world and

(1) have roughly equal populations
(2) have advanced industrial economies
(3) rely on fishing for food
(4) rely on other countries for economic aid

REGENTS STRATEGIES

Political Maps

Political maps show countries and the political divisions within them—states or provinces, for example. They also show the location of major cities. In addition, political maps often show some physical features, such as mountain ranges, oceans, seas, lakes, and rivers.

1. Read the title of the map to identify the subject and purpose of the map.
2. Review the labels on the map. They also will reveal information about the map's subject and purpose.
3. Study the legend to find the meaning of the symbols used on the map.
4. Use the scale to estimate distances between places shown on the map.
5. Use the compass rose to determine the direction on the map.
6. Read the questions and then carefully study the map to determine the answers.

answers: 1 (2); 2 (3)

1 Canada in 1871

6

1 Which of the following became a province of Canada in 1870?

(1) New Brunswick
(2) Manitoba
(3) Ontario
(4) Quebec

2 About how long is the United States-Canada border from western Lake Superior to the Pacific Ocean?

Use the scale to answer questions like this.

(1) 900 miles
(2) 1,200 miles
(3) 1,500 miles
(4) 1,800 miles

Directions: Use the map and your knowledge of world history to answer questions 1 through 4.

The Persian Empire

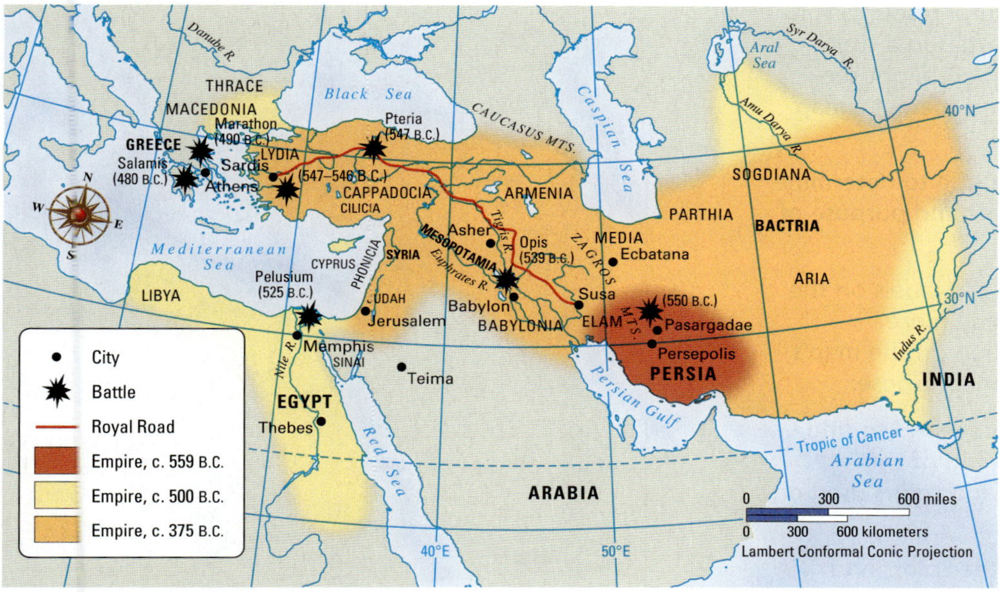

1 The oldest part of the Persian Empire is found

(1) east of the Zagros Mountains
(2) in Arabia
(3) along the Caspian Sea
(4) in the region called Bactria

2 The Persian Empire reached its greatest extent, including Egypt and the Indus River valley, by

(1) 559 B.C.
(2) 500 B.C.
(3) 375 B.C.
(4) 475 B.C.

3 The battles of Marathon and Salamis were fought between the Persians and the

(1) Egyptians
(2) Syrians
(3) Greeks
(4) Phoenicians

4 The Royal Road between Susa and Sardis was most likely used

(1) to bring food and supplies from Bactria to Persia
(2) by Egyptian and Syrian peasants traveling west
(3) to carry riches looted by Persian soldiers
(4) by the Persian army and royal messengers

REGENTS STRATEGIES

Thematic Maps

A thematic map, or special-purpose map, focuses on a particular topic. The movements of peoples, a country's natural resources, and major battles in a war are all topics you might see illustrated on a thematic map.

1. Read the title to determine the subject and purpose of the map.
2. Examine the labels on the map to find more information on the map's subject and purpose.
3. Study the legend to find the meaning of the symbols and colors used on the map.
4. Look at the colors and symbols on the map to try to identify patterns.
5. Read the questions, and then carefully study the map to determine the answers.

answers: 1 (3); 2 (2)

1 The Spread of Buddhism

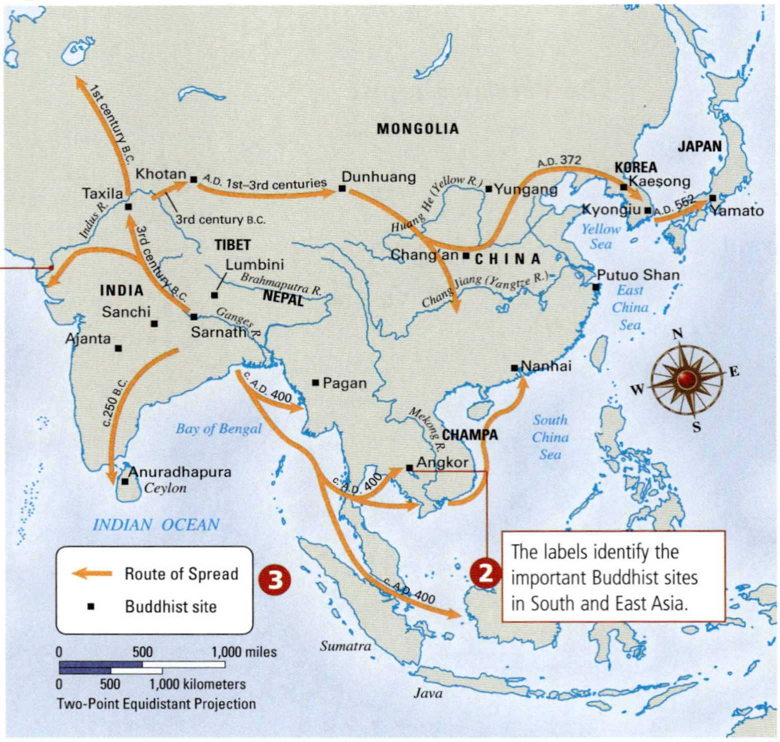

4 Notice that Buddhism began in northern India and next spread to much of the rest of the Indian subcontinent.

5

1 To which area did Buddhism spread after A.D. 550?

(1) Java

(2) China

(3) Japan

(4) Champa

2 The routes tracing the spread of Buddhism show the great cultural influence that China had on

(1) Mongolia and Vietnam

(2) Korea and Japan

(3) Vietnam and Korea

(4) India and Japan

Directions: Use the map and your knowledge of world history to answer questions 1 through 4.

The Christian Conquest of Muslim Spain

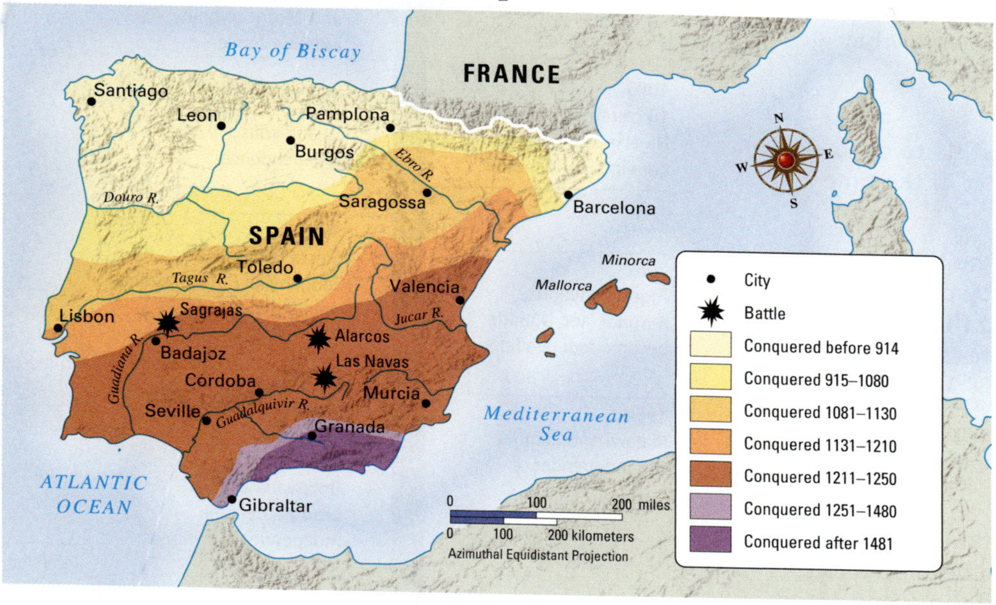

1 The Christian conquest of Muslim lands on the Iberian Peninsula began

(1) in the west
(2) in the north
(3) along the Mediterranean coast
(4) along the entire Atlantic coast

2 By about 1250, Christians held what portion of the Iberian Peninsula?

(1) less than half
(2) about half
(3) slightly more than half
(4) almost the entire peninsula

3 In what time period was the Battle of Las Navas fought?

(1) between 914 and 1080
(2) between 1131 and 1210
(3) between 1211 and 1250
(4) between 1251 and 1480

4 The last major city that the Christians captured was

(1) Barcelona
(2) Granada
(3) Seville
(4) Valencia

REGENTS STRATEGIES

Time Lines

A time line is a type of chart that lists events in the order in which they occurred. In other words, time lines are a visual method of showing what happened when.

1. Read the title to discover the subject of the time line.
2. Identify the time period covered by the time line by noting the earliest and latest dates shown.
3. Read the events and their dates in sequence. Notice the intervals between events.
4. Use your knowledge of history to develop a fuller picture of the events listed in the time line. For example, place the events in a broader context by considering what was happening elsewhere in the world.
5. Use the information you have gathered from these strategies to answer the questions.

answers: 1 (1); 2 (3)

1 The End of Colonialism in Africa

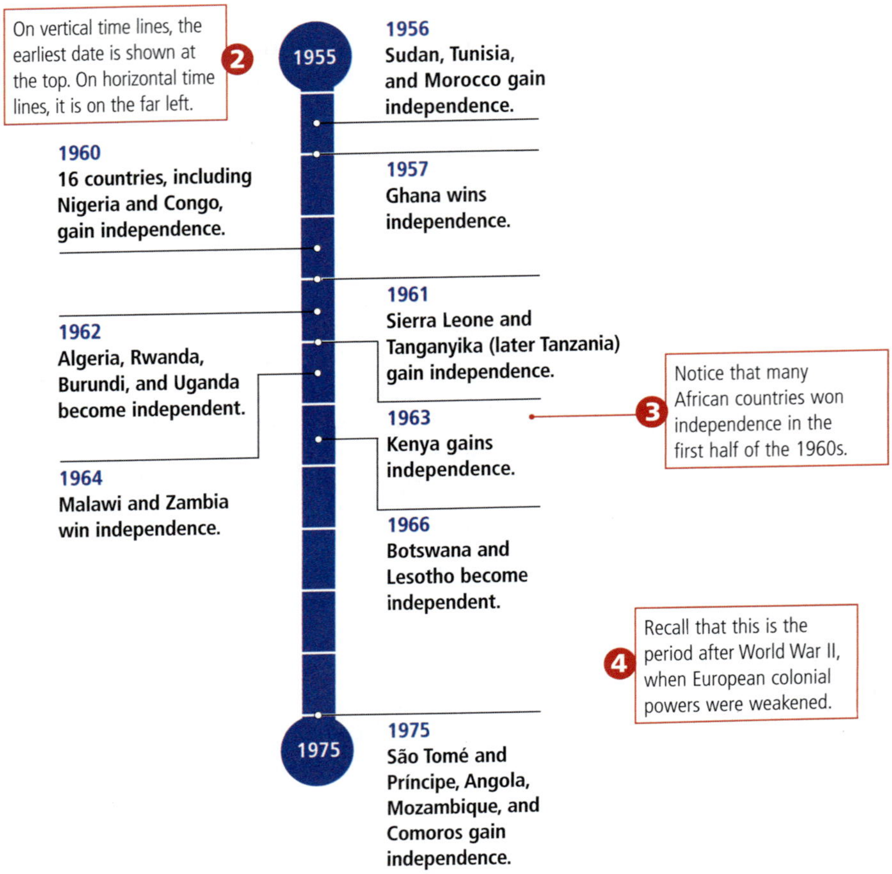

5

1 The first countries to win independence were all located in

(1) North Africa
(2) West Africa
(3) East Africa
(4) Southern Africa

2 Which of the following titles best describes events in the 1960s?

(1) The Rise of Communism
(2) The Rise of Colonialism
(3) The Decade of Independence
(4) The Decade of Suffering

Directions: Use the time line and your knowledge of world history to answer questions 1 through 4.

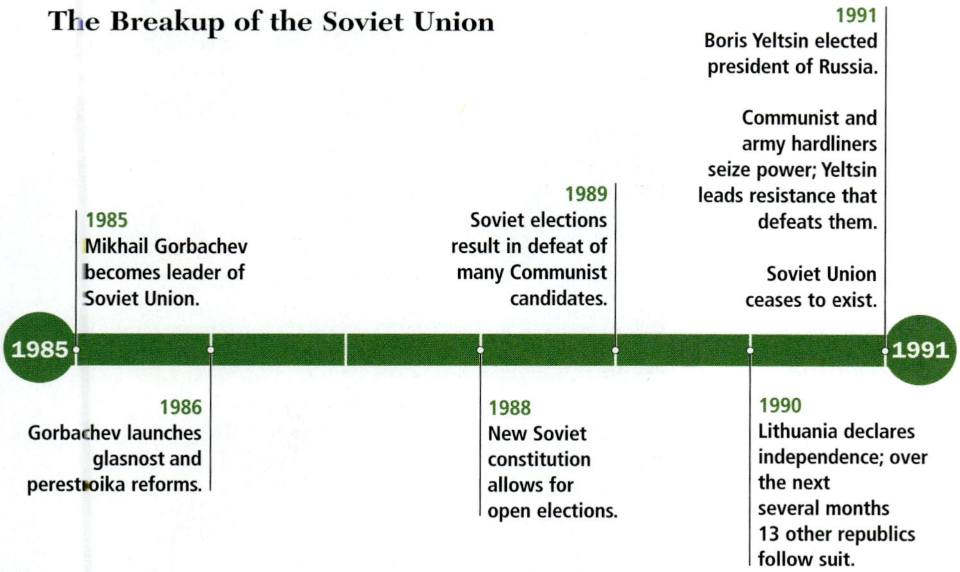

1 What event was a direct result of the new constitution that took effect in 1988?

(1) Gorbachev launched glasnost and perestroika reforms.

(2) Many Communist candidates lost elections.

(3) Communist hardliners seized power.

(4) Several Soviet republics declared independence.

2 When did Lithuania declare its independence from the Soviet Union?

(1) 1988

(2) 1989

(3) 1990

(4) 1991

3 What was the result of the hard-liners' attempt to seize power in 1991?

(1) They prevented the collapse of the Soviet Union.

(2) Leaders in other Communist countries joined their cause.

(3) Gorbachev defeated Yeltsin in a struggle for power.

(4) They failed to gain control, and the country rapidly fell apart.

4 For much of the time it existed, the Soviet Union was engaged with the United States in a long conflict called

(1) World War I

(2) World War II

(3) the Gulf War

(4) the Cold War

Reading Visuals

Written-response questions may focus on various kinds of documents. Each document usually is accompanied by a series of questions. These questions call for short answers that, for the most part, can be found directly in the document. Some answers, however, require knowledge of the subject or time period addressed in the document.

1. Read the title of the document to discover the subject addressed in the questions.
2. Study and analyze the document. Take notes on what you see.
3. Read the questions carefully and then study the document again to locate the answers.
4. Carefully write your answers. Tailor the length of your answers to the directions and the space provided.

2 Written-response questions use a wide range of documents including short passages, cartoons, charts, graphs, maps, time lines, posters, and other visual materials. This document is a photograph showing ruins in Palenque, Mexico. The flat-topped pyramid is typical of the early civilizations of Mesoamerica.

1 **Maya Pyramid in Palenque, Mexico**

3 1 Palenque was one of the city-states of what Mesoamerican civilization?

Maya

2 For what purpose do you think this pyramid was built?

4 *religious purposes*

3 What reasons have been suggested for the decline of this civilization in the late A.D. 800s?

Since the question uses the plural *reasons*, your answer must include more than one explanation.

warfare among Maya city-states, which disrupted trade and caused economic hardship; over-farming and population growth, which caused ecological damage, resulting in food shortages, famine, and disease

Directions: Use the diagram and your knowledge of world history to answer question 1.

Plan of the Great Pyramid at Giza

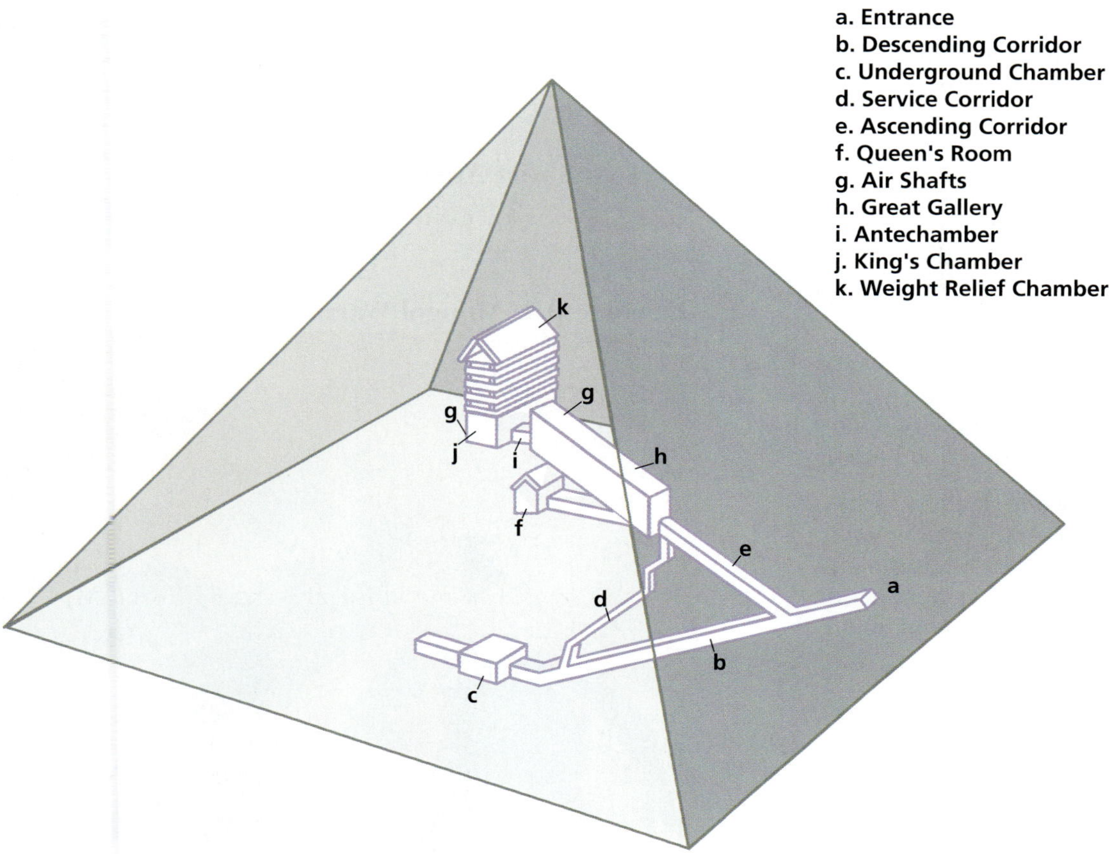

1 How and for what purpose were the pyramids of ancient Egypt built?

Illustration: By permission of Dr. Zahi Hawass.

Document-Based Questions

A document-based question (DBQ) requires you to analyze and interpret a variety of documents. These documents often are accompanied by short-answer questions. You use these answers and information from the documents to write an essay on a specified subject.

1. Read the "Historical Context" section to get a sense of the issue addressed in the question.
2. Read the "Task" section and note the action words. This will help you understand exactly what the essay question requires.
3. Study and analyze each document. Consider what connection the documents have to the essay question. Take notes on your ideas.
4. Read and answer the document-specific questions. Think about how these questions connect to the essay topic.

Introduction

❶ **Historical Context:** For hundreds of years, Mongol nomads lived in separate tribes, sometimes fighting among themselves. In the early 1200s, a new leader—Genghis Khan—united these tribes and turned the Mongols into a powerful fighting force.

❷ **Task:** Discuss how the Mongols achieved their conquest of Central and East Asia and what impact their rule had on Europeans.

Part A: Short Answer

Study each document carefully and answer the questions that follow.

❸ Document 1: Mongol Warrior

❹ 1 What were the characteristics of Mongol warriors?

The Mongol soldiers were excellent horsemen who could travel great distances without rest. They attacked swiftly and without mercy, they used clever psychological warfare to strike fear into their enemies, and they adopted new weapons and technology.

Painting: Victoria & Albert Museum, London/Art Resource, New York.

Document 2: The Mongol Empire

2 What route connected the Mongol Empire to Europe? What was the major purpose of this route?

The Silk Road; it was the major trade route between Asia and Europe.

Document 3: The Great Khan's Wealth

Let me tell you further that several times a year a [command] goes forth through the towns that all those who have gems and pearls and gold and silver must bring them to the Great Khan's mint. This they do, and in such abundance that it is past all reckoning; and they are all paid in paper money. By this means the Great Khan acquires all the gold and silver and pearls and precious stones of all his territories.

—Marco Polo, *The Travels of Marco Polo* (c. 1300)

3 How did Marco Polo's descriptions of his travels encourage European interest in East Asia?

Europeans were attracted by his descriptions of the great wealth.

5 Part B: Essay

Using information from the documents, your answers to the questions in Part A, and your knowledge of world history, write an essay discussing how the Mongols conquered Central and East Asia and what effects their rule had on Europeans. 6

5 Carefully read the essay question. Then write an outline for your essay.

6 Write your essay. Be sure that it has an introductory paragraph that introduces your argument, main body paragraphs that explain it, and a concluding paragraph that restates your position. In your essay, include quotations or details from specific documents to support your ideas. Add other supporting facts or details that you know from your study of world history.

Sample Response The best essays will link the Mongols' tactics, fierce will, and strong military organization to their successful conquest of vast areas in Central and East Asia (Documents 1 and 2). They will also note that rule over these vast lands brought a period of peace and united regions that had before then been separate. Essays should point out that this peace revived trade along the Silk Road (Document 2) and brought new inventions and ideas to Europe. Further, accounts of the immense wealth in Mongol lands (Document 3) spurred Europeans' interest in tapping into that wealth.

Introduction

Historical Context: For many centuries, kings and queens ruled the countries of Europe. Their power was supported by nobles and armies. European society began to change, however, and in the late 1700s, those changes produced a violent upheaval in France.

Task: Discuss how social conflict and intellectual movements contributed to the French Revolution and why the Revolution turned radical.

Part A: Short Answer

Study each document carefully and answer the questions that follow.

Document 1: Social Classes in Pre-Revolutionary France

1 What do the peasant woman, noblewoman, and nun represent? Why is the peasant woman shown carrying the noblewoman and the nun?

 Engraving: *Le Grand Abus.* Engraving of a cartoon held in the collection of M. de baron de Vinck d'Orp of Brussels/Mary Evans Picture Library, London.

Document 2: A Declaration of Rights

1. Men are born and remain free and equal in rights. Social distinctions may be founded only upon the general good.
2. The aim of all political association is the preservation of the natural . . . rights of man. These rights are liberty, property, security, and resistance to oppression. . . .
6. Law is the expression of the general will. Every citizen has a right to participate personally, or through his representative, in its foundation. It must be the same for all, whether it protects or punishes. All citizens, being equal in the eyes of the law, are equally eligible to all dignities and to all public positions and occupations, according to their abilities, and without distinction except that of their virtues and talents.

—*Declaration of the Rights of Man and of the Citizen* (1789)

2 How do these statements reflect the ideals of the Enlightenment?

Document 3: The French Revolution—Major Events

1789

July 1789
Crowd storms the Bastille.
Aug. 1789
National Assembly abolishes feudalism, approves *Declaration of the Rights of Man and of the Citizen.*
Nov. 1789
National Assembly seizes lands of Catholic Church.

July 1790
Church put under control of government; France made a constitutional monarchy.

June 1791
Royal family arrested in escape attempt.

Aug. 1792
Paris mob captures King Louis XVI.
Sep. 1792
Crowds kill priests, nobles in September Massacres; monarchy abolished.

Jan. 1793
King executed by guillotine.
Spring 1793
Robespierre and allies gain control of government, begin to arrest rivals.
1793–1794
Reign of Terror: about 300,000 arrested and 17,000 executed.

July 1794
Robespierre executed, Terror ends.

1794

3 The French Revolution was moderate at first but quickly became radical. How does the information in the time line illustrate this?

Part B: Essay

Using information from the documents, your answers to the questions in Part A, and your knowledge of world history, write an essay discussing how social conflict and intellectual movements contributed to the French Revolution and why the Revolution turned radical.

RAND McNALLY

World Atlas

Contents

World: Political A2
World: Physical A4
North America: Political A6
North America: Physical A7
Mexico, Central America, and the Caribbean: Political A8
South America: Political A10
South America: Physical A11
Europe: Political A12
Europe: Physical A14
Africa: Political A16
Africa: Physical A17
Asia: Political A18
Asia: Physical A20
Australia and Oceania A22
Ancient World in the 7th Century B.C. A23
Roman Empire About A.D. 120 . . . . A24
The Ottoman, Safavid, and Mughal Empires in the 16th and 17th Centuries A26
Revolutions in the Atlantic World 1776–1826 . . . . A28
Latin America 1800–1850 . . . . . A30
Latin America 1850–1900 . . . . . A31
Industrialization of Europe 1815 . . . . A32
Industrialization of Europe 1910 . . . . A33
Europe 1922–1940 . . . . A34
Africa About A.D. 1400 . . . . A36
European Partition of Africa: 19th Century A37
Resistance to Colonialism 1870–1930 . . . . A38
Middle East/Israel Political A40
Eastern Southern Asia A.D. 750 . . . . A42
Asia 1900 . . . . A44
Russia and the Former Soviet Union A46

Complete Legend for Physical and Political Maps

Symbols

Symbol	Meaning
(lake symbol)	Lake
(salt lake symbol)	Salt Lake
(seasonal lake symbol)	Seasonal Lake
(river symbol)	River
\	Waterfall
—	Canal
△	Mountain Peak
▲	Highest Mountain Peak

Cities

■ Los Angeles	City over 1,000,000 population
▣ Calgary	City of 250,000 to 1,000,000 population
• Haifa	City under 250,000 population
⊛ *Paris*	National Capital
★ Vancouver	Secondary Capital (State, Province, or Territory)

Type Styles Used to Name Features

CHINA	Country
O N T A R I O	State, Province, or Territory
PUERTO RICO (U.S.)	Possession
A T L A N T I C O C E A N	Ocean or Sea
A l p s	Physical Feature
Borneo	Island

Boundaries

(boundary line)	International Boundary
(boundary line)	Secondary Boundary

Land Elevation and Water Depths

Land Elevation

Meters	Feet
3,000 and over	9,840 and over
2,000 - 3,000	6,560 - 9,840
500 - 2,000	1,640 - 6,560
200 - 500	656 - 1,640
0 - 200	0 - 656

Water Depth

Meters	Feet
Less than 200	Less than 656
200 - 2,000	656 - 6,560
Over 2,000	Over 6,560

ARCTIC OCEAN
GREENLAND (Den.)
Baffin Bay
Arctic Circle
ICELAND
FAROE IS. (Den.)
RUSSIA
ALASKA
Yukon (U.S.)
Anchorage
Aleutian Islands
Hudson Bay
CANADA
UNITED KINGDOM
IRELAND
London
Vancouver
Newfoundland
Missouri
Montréal
Ottawa
FRANCE
Chicago
Madrid
PORTUGAL
SPAIN
UNITED STATES
New York
Washington D.C.
Azores (Port.)
Colorado
Mississippi
Los Angeles
Casablanca
MOROCCO
Houston
MIDWAY IS. (U.S.)
ATLANTIC
Canary Islands (Sp.)
Gulf of Mexico
W. SAHARA
Tropic of Cancer
MEXICO
BAHAMAS
Hawaiian Islands (U.S.)
CUBA
DOM. REP.
HAITI
PUERTO RICO (U.S.)
CAPE VERDE
MAURITANIA
MALI
Mexico City
BELIZE
JAMAICA
Caribbean Sea
SENEGAL
GUAT.
HOND.
GAMBIA
Niger
BURK. FASO
PACIFIC
EL SAL.
NIC.
GUINEA-BISSAU
GUINEA
Caracas
TRINIDAD AND TOBAGO
COSTA RICA
VENEZUELA
GUYANA
SIERRA LEONE
COTE D'IVOIRE
GHANA
PANAMA
SURINAME
FRENCH GUIANA
LIBERIA
COLOMBIA
Equator
Galapagos Islands (Ecuador)
ECUADOR
Amazon
KIRIBATI
PERU
BRAZIL
Lima
OCEAN
OCEAN
SAMOA
AMERICAN SAMOA
COOK ISLANDS (N.Z.)
ST. HELENA (U.K.)
BOLIVIA
TONGA
FRENCH POLYNESIA
PARAGUAY
Tropic of Capricorn
Rio de Janeiro
Easter Island (Chile)
ARGENTINA
CHILE
URUGUAY
Santiago
Buenos Aires
N
0 1000 2000 Miles
0 1000 2000 3000 Kilometers
Copyright by Rand McNally & Co.
Robinson Projection
FALKLAND IS. (U.K.)
South Georgia (U.K.)
South Orkney Is. (U.K.)
South Shetland Is. (U.K.)
Antarctic Circle
Weddell Sea
180° 165° 150° 135° 120° 105° 90° 75° 60° 45° 30° 15°
75° 60° 45° 30° 15° 0° 15° 30° 45° 60° 75°

ARCTIC OCEAN
Franz Josef Land
Spitsbergen (Nor.)
Novaya Zemlya
R U S S I A
Yenisey
Lena
Ob'
Volga
Moscow
Novosibirsk
NORWAY
FINLAND
SWEDEN
EST.
LAT.
LITH.
North Sea
DEN.
NETH.
BEL.
GERMANY
POLAND
BELARUS
UKRAINE
CZ.
SLVK.
AUS.
HUNG.
SWITZ.
MOLD.
ROM.
CRO.
BOS.
SERB.
ITALY
BUL.
ALB.
MA
Rome
GREECE
Black Sea
GEO.
ARM.
AZER.
Caspian Sea
KAZAKHSTAN
UZBEKISTAN
TURKMENISTAN
KYRG.
TAJIK.
MONGOLIA
TURKEY
Mediterranean Sea
Crete
CYPRUS
LEB.
SYRIA
ISRAEL
JORDAN
IRAQ
IRAN
AFGHANISTAN
PAKISTAN
KUWAIT
QATAR
U.A.E.
OMAN
SAUDI ARABIA
TUNISIA
ALGERIA
LIBYA
EGYPT
Cairo
Red Sea
Nile
NIGER
CHAD
SUDAN
ERITREA
YEMEN
DJIBOUTI
Addis Ababa
ETHIOPIA
SOMALIA
BENIN
NIGERIA
Lagos
CAMEROON
CENTRAL AFRICAN REPUBLIC
EQUATORIAL GUINEA
GABON
Congo
UGANDA
KENYA
RWANDA
REP. OF CONGO
DEM. REP. OF CONGO
BURUNDI
TANZANIA
ANGOLA
ZAMBIA
MALAWI
MOZAMBIQUE
ZIMBABWE
NAMIBIA
BOTSWANA
SWAZILAND
SOUTH AFRICA
LESOTHO
Cape Town
COMOROS
MADAGASCAR
MAURITIUS
REUNION (Fr.)
SEYCHELLES
MALDIVES
Mumbai (Bombay)
Arabian Sea
INDIA
NEPAL
BHU.
BNGL.
Ganges
Kolkata (Calcutta)
Bay of Bengal
SRI LANKA
CHINA
Beijing
Chang Jiang (Yangtze)
Shanghai
Guangzhou
NORTH KOREA
SOUTH KOREA
Sea of Japan
JAPAN
Tokyo
Sea of Okhotsk
Bering Sea
TAIWAN
MYANMAR
LAOS
THAILAND
Bangkok
CAMBODIA
VIETNAM
South China Sea
PHILIPPINES
BRUNEI
MALAYSIA
SINGAPORE
Borneo
Sumatra
Jakarta
Java
INDONESIA
EAST TIMOR
New Guinea
PAPUA NEW GUINEA
PACIFIC OCEAN
Tropic of Cancer
NORTHERN MARIANA ISLANDS (U.S.)
WAKE ISLAND (U.S.)
GUAM (U.S.)
PALAU
FED. STATES OF MICRONESIA
MARSHALL ISLANDS
Equator
SOLOMON ISLANDS
INDIAN OCEAN
Darwin
Coral Sea
VANUATU
FIJI
NEW CALEDONIA (Fr.)
Tropic of Capricorn
AUSTRALIA
Darling
Perth
Sydney
Melbourne
Tasmania
NEW ZEALAND
Wellington
Kerguelen Islands (Fr.)
SOUTHERN OCEAN
Antarctic Circle
ANTARCTICA
15°
30°
45°
60°
75°
90°
105°
120°
135°
150°
165°
180°

RAND McNALLY

ARCTIC OCEAN
Franz Josef Land
Spitsbergen
North Cape
Novaya Zemlya
Scandinavian Peninsula
Yenisey
Lena
Ob'
Ural Mts.
Siberia
North Sea
EUROPE
Volga
Moscow
Don
Alps
Balkan Peninsula
Black Sea
Caucasus
Mt. Elbrus 18,510 Ft. 5,642m
Caspian Sea
Aral Sea
Altai Mts.
ASIA
Sardinia
Sicily
Crete
Cyprus
Mediterranean Sea
Cairo
Zagros Mts.
Pamir
Plateau of Tibet
Himalayas
Indus
Ganges
Mt. Everest 29,035 Ft. 8,850m
Gobi Desert
Beijing
Huang
Yangtze
Sea of Okhotsk
Amur
Bering Sea
Kamchatka Peninsula
Sakhalin
Hokkaidō
Sea of Japan
Honshū
Kyūshū
East China Sea
PACIFIC
Tropic of Cancer
Taiwan
Sahara Desert
Arabian Peninsula
Red Sea
Nile
AFRICA
Sahel
Mumbai (Bombay)
Arabian Sea
Deccan Plateau
Bay of Bengal
Hainan Island
Mekong
South China Sea
Luzon
Mariana Islands
Wake Island
Guam
Socotra
Lakshadweep
Sri Lanka
Mindanao
Palau Islands
OCEAN
Caroline Islands
Marshall Islands
Ethiopian Plateau
Malay Peninsula
Gulf of Guinea
Congo
Congo Basin
Rift Valley
Maldive Islands
Borneo
Celebes
Equator
Kilimanjaro 19,340 Ft. 5,895m
Sumatra
New Guinea
Solomon Islands
Seychelles
Java
Timor
INDIAN
Cocos Island
New Hebrides
Coral Sea
Zambezi
Madagascar
Mauritius
Reunion
Great Sandy Desert
New Caledonia
Fiji Is.
Kalahari Desert
Tropic of Capricorn
AUSTRALIA
Great Dividing Range
OCEAN
Darling
Sydney
Cape Town
Cape of Good Hope
Cape Leeuwin
North Island
Aoraki (Mt. Cook) 12,316 Ft. 3,754m
Tasmania
South Island
Kerguelen Islands
SOUTHERN OCEAN
Antarctic Circle
Enderby Land
Wilkes Land
Queen Maud Land
Victoria Land
ANTARCTICA
15° 30° 45° 60° 75° 90° 105° 120° 135° 150° 165° 180°
75° 60° 45° 30° 15° 0° 15° 30° 45° 60° 75°
Land Elevation
Meters Feet
3,000 9,840
2,000 6,560
500 1,640
200 656
0 0
Water Depth
0 0
200 656
2,000 6,560

ASIA
RUSSIA
Arctic Circle
Bering Strait
Bering Sea
Aleutian Islands
North Pole
ARCTIC OCEAN
Beaufort Sea
Prudhoe Bay
Queen Elizabeth Islands
Ellesmere Island
Banks Island
Devon Island
Victoria Island
Baffin Bay
Baffin Island
GREENLAND (Denmark)
Godthab
ICELAND
Reykjavik
U.S.
Yukon
Fairbanks
Anchorage
Valdez
Gulf of Alaska
Whitehorse
Juneau
Mackenzie
Great Bear Lake
Great Slave Lake
Yellowknife
Hudson Bay
Peace
CANADA
Nelson
Edmonton
Calgary
Saskatoon
Saskatchewan
Regina
Lake Winnipeg
Winnipeg
Victoria
Vancouver
Newfoundland
St. John's
Gulf of St. Lawrence
St. Lawrence
Québec
Saint John
Halifax
Thunder Bay
Lake Superior
Montréal
Ottawa
Toronto
Lake Ontario
Lake Huron
Lake Michigan
Lake Erie
PACIFIC OCEAN
Seattle
Columbia
Spokane
Portland
Missouri
Billings
Great Salt Lake
Minneapolis
Milwaukee
Detroit
Chicago
Cleveland
Boston
New York
Philadelphia
Washington D.C.
Norfolk
Sacramento
San Francisco
UNITED STATES
Omaha
Denver
Colorado
Arkansas
Kansas City
Indianapolis
Cincinnati
St. Louis
Ohio
Las Vegas
Los Angeles
San Diego
Tijuana
Phoenix
Albuquerque
Oklahoma City
Red
Nashville
Memphis
Charlotte
Atlanta
Mississippi
BERMUDA (U.K.)
ATLANTIC OCEAN
Tropic of Cancer
Dallas
Houston
San Antonio
New Orleans
Jacksonville
Tampa
Miami
Ciudad Juárez
Hermosillo
Gulf of California
Chihuahua
Rio Grande
MEXICO
Torreón
Culiacán
Monterrey
GULF OF MEXICO
BAHAMAS
Nassau
Havana
CUBA
DOMINICAN REPUBLIC
PUERTO RICO (U.S.)
HAITI
Port-au-Prince
Santo Domingo
JAMAICA
Kingston
San Luis Potosí
Guadalajara
León
Mérida
Cancún
Mexico City
Puebla
Veracruz
Acapulco
BELIZE
Belmopan
GUATEMALA
Guatemala City
HONDURAS
Tegucigalpa
San Salvador
EL SALVADOR
Lago de Nicaragua
NICARAGUA
Managua
COSTA RICA
San José
PANAMA
Panama City
Golfo de Panamá
CARIBBEAN SEA
Caracas
VENEZUELA
COLOMBIA
Bogotá
SOUTH AMERICA
BRAZIL
Equator
N
National Capital
Secondary Capital (State, Province, or Territory)
City over 1,000,000 population
City of 250,000 to 1,000,000 population
City under 250,000 population
0 200 400 600 800 1000 Miles
0 300 600 900 1200 1500 Kilometers
Copyright by Rand McNally & Co.
Lambert Azimuthal Equal Area Projection

North Pole
ARCTIC OCEAN
ASIA
RUSSIA
Arctic Circle
Bering Sea
Bering Strait
Point Hope
Point Barrow
Prudhoe Bay
Beaufort Sea
Cape Bathurst
Queen Elizabeth Islands
Ellesmere Island
Devon Island
Banks Island
Victoria Island
Baffin Bay
Cape Adair
Baffin Island
GREENLAND (Denmark)
Ice Cap
ICELAND
Norwegian Sea
Cape Farvel
Cape Mercy
Foxe Basin
Aleutian Islands
Alaska Peninsula
Brooks Range
U.S.
Yukon
Kuskokwim
Mt. McKinley 20,320 Ft. 6,194m
Alaska Range
Anchorage
Mt. Logan 19,551 Ft. 5,959m
Gulf of Alaska
Whitehorse
Mackenzie
Great Bear Lake
Great Slave Lake
Coast Mountains
PACIFIC OCEAN
Queen Charlotte Islands
Vancouver Island
Peace
Lake Athabasca
Hudson Bay
Churchill
Péninsule d'Ungava
CANADA
Edmonton
Rocky Mountains
Canadian Shield
Nelson
Saskatchewan
Lake Winnipeg
Albany
James Bay
Newfoundland
Gulf of St. Lawrence
St. Lawrence
Vancouver
Columbia
Cascade Range
Cape Blanco
Cape Mendocino
Great Plains
Great Lakes
Lake Superior
Lake Michigan
Lake Huron
Lake Ontario
Lake Erie
Montréal
Ottawa
Niagara Falls
Cape Cod
New York
Washington D.C.
Snake
Great Salt Lake
Great Basin
Missouri
Chicago
UNITED STATES
Coast Ranges
Sierra Nevada
Mt. Whitney 14,494 Ft. 4,418m
Colorado
Denver
Arkansas
Colorado Plateau
Los Angeles
Ozark Plateau
Ohio
Appalachian Mts.
Coastal Plain
Cape Hatteras
BERMUDA (U.K.)
ATLANTIC OCEAN
Red
Mississippi
Tropic of Cancer
Gulf of California
Baja California
MEXICO
Sierra Madre Occidental
Sierra Madre Oriental
Rio Grande
Houston
GULF OF MEXICO
Cape Canaveral
The Everglades
Miami
BAHAMAS
Havana
CUBA
DOMINICAN REPUBLIC
HAITI
PUERTO RICO (U.S.)
JAMAICA
Cabo San Lucas
Gulf of Campeche
Yucatán Peninsula
Mexico City
BELIZE
GUATEMALA
HONDURAS
CARIBBEAN SEA
NICARAGUA
EL SALVADOR
Lago de Nicaragua
COSTA RICA
PANAMA
Golfo de Panamá
VENEZUELA
COLOMBIA
SOUTH AMERICA
BRAZIL
Equator
Land Elevation
Meters
Feet
3,000 9,840
2,000 6,560
500 1,640
200 656
0 0
Water Depth
0 0
200 656
2,000 6,560
0 200 400 600 800 1000 Miles
0 300 600 900 1200 1500 Kilometers
Copyright by Rand McNally & Co.
Lambert Azimuthal Equal Area Projection

Lambert Conformal Conic Projection

RAND McNALLY

RAND McNALLY

GULF OF MEXICO
NORTH AMERICA
CUBA
Greater Antilles
HAITI
DOMINICAN REPUBLIC
JAMAICA
PUERTO RICO (U.S.)
Lesser Antilles
BELIZE
Gulf of Honduras
HONDURAS
MEXICO
GUATEMALA
EL SALVADOR
NICARAGUA
COSTA RICA
PANAMA
Gulf of Panama
CARIBBEAN SEA
ATLANTIC OCEAN
Cristóbal Colón Peak 18,948 Ft. 5,775m
Caracas
TRINIDAD AND TOBAGO
Orinoco
Llanos
VENEZUELA
GUYANA
SURINAME
FRENCH GUIANA
Cape Orange
Magdalena
Bogotá
COLOMBIA
Galapagos Islands (Ec.)
ECUADOR
Chimborazo 20,703 Ft. 6,310m
Putumayo
Japurá
Negro
Amazon
Manaus
Ilha de Marajó
Belém
Equator
Amazon Basin
Tapajós
Tocantins
Madeira
Juruá
Selvas
BRAZIL
Ucayali
Andes
PERU
Recife
Mt. Huascarán 22,133 Ft. 6,746m
Lima
Mato Grosso Plateau
Mt. Illampu 21,066 Ft. 6,421m
Lake Titicaca
BOLIVIA
Cordillera Oriental
São Francisco
Brasília
Serra do Espinhaço
Mt. Sajama 21,463 Ft. 6,542m
Gran Chaco
Paraná
PARAGUAY
São Paulo
Rio de Janeiro
Tropic of Capricorn
Atacama Desert
Isla San Ambrosio (Chile)
Isla San Felix (Chile)
Mt. Ojos del Salado 22,615 Ft. 6,893m
Paraná
URUGUAY
PACIFIC OCEAN
Archipiélago Juan Fernández (Chile)
Mt. Aconcagua 22,831 Ft. 6,959m
Santiago
Buenos Aires
Río de la Plata
Pampas
CHILE
ARGENTINA
San Matías Gulf
Península Valdés
Chiloé
Patagonia
San Jorge Gulf
Point Medanoso
ATLANTIC OCEAN
Grand Bay
West Falkland
FALKLAND ISLANDS (U.K.)
East Falkland
Strait of Magellan
Tierra del Fuego
Cape Horn
South Georgia (U.K.)
South Sandwich Islands (U.K.)
Drake Passage
South Shetland Islands (U.K.)
South Orkney Islands (U.K.)
Land Elevation
Meters Feet
3,000 9,840
2,000 6,560
500 1,640
200 656
0 0
Water Depth
0 0
200 656
2,000 6,560
0 200 400 600 800 1000 Miles
0 300 600 900 1200 1500 Kilometers
Copyright by Rand McNally & Co.
Lambert Azimuthal Equal Area Projection
N

National Capital
Secondary Capital (State, Province, or Territory)
City over 1,000,000 population
City of 250,000 to 1,000,000 population
City under 250,000 population
0 100 200 300 400 Miles
0 200 400 600 Kilometers
Copyright by Rand McNally & Co.
Lambert Conformal Conic Projection
ATLANTIC OCEAN
ICELAND
Reykjavík
Arctic Circle
NORWEGIAN SEA
FAROE ISLANDS (Den.)
NORWAY
SWEDEN
Trondheim
Bergen
Oslo
Umeå
Gulf of Bothnia
Tampere
Stockholm
Vänern
Vättern
Göteborg
Skagerrak
DENMARK
Copenhagen
BALTIC SEA
LITHUANIA
Kaliningrad
RUSSIA
Gdańsk
POLAND
Szczecin
Warsaw
Wisła
Oder
Wrocław
Kraków
UNITED KINGDOM
SCOTLAND
Aberdeen
Glasgow
Edinburgh
NORTHERN IRELAND
Belfast
IRELAND
Dublin
Cork
Irish Sea
St. George's Channel
Liverpool
Manchester
WALES
Birmingham
ENGLAND
Cardiff
Thames
London
Plymouth
NORTH SEA
NETHERLANDS
Amsterdam
The Hague
Strait of Dover
English Channel
Brussels
BELGIUM
Luxembourg
LUX.
GERMANY
Hamburg
Elbe
Berlin
Rhine
Cologne
Bonn
Frankfurt
Dresden
Prague
CZECH REPUBLIC
Stuttgart
Danube
Munich
SLOVAKIA
Bratislava
Vienna
AUSTRIA
Budapest
HUNGARY
Le Havre
Paris
Seine
Strasbourg
Loire
Nantes
FRANCE
Bay of Biscay
Bordeaux
Lyon
Geneva
Zürich
Bern
SWITZERLAND
LIECH.
Rhône
Toulouse
Marseille
Nice
MONACO
SLOVENIA
Ljubljana
Zagreb
CROATIA
Belgrade
BOSNIA AND HERZEGOVINA
Sarajevo
SERBIA AND MONTENEGRO
Skopje
MACEDONIA
ALBANIA
Tiranë
Turin
Milan
Venice
Po
Genoa
SAN MARINO
Florence
ADRIATIC SEA
ITALY
Corsica (Fr.)
Rome
VATICAN CITY
Sardinia (It.)
Cagliari
Naples
Bari
TYRRHENIAN SEA
Palermo
Sicily
Catania
IONIAN SEA
MEDITERRANEAN SEA
Valletta
MALTA
A Coruña
Gijón
Bilbao
Porto
Valladolid
Ebro
Zaragoza
ANDORRA
Barcelona
PORTUGAL
Lisbon
Tagus
Madrid
SPAIN
Valencia
Palma
Córdoba
Seville
Málaga
Strait of Gibraltar
GIBRALTAR (U.K.)
Rabat
MOROCCO
AFRICA
Algiers
ALGERIA
Tunis
TUNISIA
Hammerfest

RUSSIA
FINLAND
ESTONIA
LATVIA
BELARUS
UKRAINE
MOLDOVA
ROMANIA
BULGARIA
GREECE
KAZAKHSTAN
UZBEKISTAN
TURKMENISTAN
GEORGIA
ARMENIA
AZERBAIJAN
AZER.
TURKEY
IRAN
IRAQ
SYRIA
LEBANON
NORTH CYPRUS
CYPRUS
ASIA
WHITE SEA
BLACK SEA
CASPIAN SEA
Sea of Azov
Aral Sea
AEGEAN SEA
Gulf of Finland
Lake Ladoga
Lake Onega
Lake Peipus
Rybinsk Res.
Murmansk
Arkhangel'sk
Oulu
Northern Dvina
Syktyvkar
Pechora
Ob'
Irtysh
Petrozavodsk
Kirov
Perm'
Helsinki
St. Petersburg
Cherepovets
Izhevsk
Ufa
Tallinn
Nizhniy Novgorod
Kazan'
Yaroslavl'
Tver'
Samara
Riga
Moscow
Oka
Ryazan'
Vitsyebsk
Penza
Vilnius
Tula
Minsk
Bryansk
Lipetsk
Saratov
Don
Ural
Syr Darya
Homyel'
Voronezh
Volgograd
Chernobyl
Kiev
Kharkiv
Volga
Amu Darya
L'viv
Luhans'k
Astrakhan'
Vinnytsya
Dnieper
Dnipro-petrovs'k
Donets'k
Dniester
Rostov
Kryvyy Rih
Zaporizhzhya
Mariupol'
Iași
Chișinău
Stavropol'
Krasnodar
Cluj-Napoca
Odesa
Galați
Simferopol'
Groznyy
Ashgabat
Sevastopol'
Tbilisi
Baku
Craiova
Bucharest
Danube
Yerevan
Varna
Sofia
Plovdiv
Tehran
Istanbul
Thessaloniki
Ankara
Athens
Euphrates
Baghdad
Tigris
Nicosia
Beirut
Crete
70°
40°
50°
60°
80°
30°

ICELAND
Horn
Fontur
Surtsey
Arctic Circle
NORWEGIAN SEA
Lofoten Islands
Kebnekaise 6,926 Ft. 2,111m
Torneälven
Luleälven
Umeälven
Lap
Scandinavian Peninsula
NORWAY
SWEDEN
Galdhøpiggen 8,100 Ft. 2,469m
Glomma
Klarälven
Dalälven
Gulf of Bothnia
Stockholm
Vänern
Vättern
Öland
BALTIC SEA
Skagerrak
ATLANTIC OCEAN
FAROE ISLANDS (Den.)
Hebrides
Orkney Islands
Grampian Mts.
UNITED KINGDOM
Cheviot Hills
NORTH SEA
DENMARK
IRELAND
Irish Sea
St. George's Channel
Great Britain
Thames
London
Bornholm (Den.)
RUSSIA
NETHERLANDS
Elbe
Berlin
Northern Euro
Oder
GERMANY
POLAND
Wisła
BELGIUM
Rhine
LUX.
English Channel
Strait of Dover
Paris
Paris Basin
Seine
Loire
CZECH REPUBLIC
Bohemian Forest
Black Forest
SLOVAKIA
Danube
FRANCE
Saône
Jura
SWITZERLAND
LIECH.
AUSTRIA
HUNGARY
Great Hungarian Plain
Mt. Blanc 15,771 Ft. 4,808m
Alps
SLOVENIA
Drava
CROATIA
Dordogne
Massif Central
Rhône
Po
Bay of Biscay
Cantabrian Mts.
Douro
Duero
Iberian Mts.
Ebro
Pyrenees
ANDORRA
Iberian Peninsula
Lisbon
PORTUGAL
Tagus
SPAIN
Sierra Morena
MONACO
Apennines
SAN MARINO
Dinaric Alps
BOSNIA AND HERZEGOVINA
Balkan
SERBIA AND MONTENEGRO
ADRIATIC SEA
Corsica (Fr.)
Rome
ITALY
ALBANIA
MACEDONIA
Sardinia (It.)
Vesuvius 4,190 Ft. 1,277m
Pindus Mts.
Balearic Islands
Minorca
Majorca
Ibiza
Strait of Gibraltar
GIBRALTAR (U.K.)
TYRRHENIAN SEA
Mt. Etna 10,902 Ft. 3,323m
Sicily
IONIAN SEA
MEDITERRANEAN
Algiers
ALGERIA
AFRICA
MOROCCO
TUNISIA
MALTA
Land Elevation
Meters
Feet
3,000
9,840
2,000
6,560
500
1,640
200
656
0
0
Water Depth
0
0
200
656
2,000
6,560
0
100
200
300
400 Miles
0
200
400
600 Kilometers
Copyright by Rand McNally & Co.
Lambert Conformal Conic Projection

Murmansk
Kola Peninsula
Ponoy
WHITE SEA
Timan Ridge
Pechora
Mezen
Ural Mountains
Ob'
Irtysh
FINLAND
Onega
Northern Dvina
Northern Uvals (Uplands)
Kama
Lake Onega
Sukhona
Lake Ladoga
Helsinki
Gulf of Finland
ESTONIA
Lake Peipus
Rybinsk Res.
RUSSIA
ASIA
LATVIA
Valdai Hills
Moscow
Oka
LITHUANIA
Plain
Central Russian Upland
Khopër
Syr Darya
Neman
Don
Ural
KAZAKHSTAN
BELARUS
Pripyat
Dnieper Lowland
Caspian Depression
Aral Sea
Kiev
Donets Basin
Volga
UZBEKISTAN
UKRAINE
Dnieper
Amu Darya
Dniester
Carpathian Mts.
MOLDOVA
CASPIAN SEA
TURKMENISTAN
ROMANIA
Transylvanian Alps
Sea of Azov
Crimean Peninsula
Caucasus
Mt. Elbrus 18,510 Ft. 5,642m
GEORGIA
Baku
BLACK SEA
Danube
Peninsula
ARMENIA
AZERBAIJAN
AZER.
BULGARIA
Istanbul
Tehran
TURKEY
IRAN
Mt. Olympus 9,570 Ft. 2,917m
GREECE
AEGEAN SEA
IRAQ
SYRIA
Euphrates
Tigris
NORTH CYPRUS
CYPRUS
LEBANON
Rhodes
Crete
SEA

ATLANTIC OCEAN
Azores (Port.)
Madeira Islands (Port.)
Canary Islands (Spain)
Strait of Gibraltar
PORTUGAL
SPAIN
Madrid
FRANCE
EUROPE
ITALY
Rome
MALTA
AUS.
HUN.
BOS.
SERB.
ALB.
GREECE
Athens
ROMANIA
BUL.
UKRAINE
RUSSIA
Black Sea
GEORGIA
ARM.
AZER.
TURKEY
Caspian Sea
KAZ.
Aral Sea
UZBEKISTAN
TURKMENISTAN
ASIA
IRAN
IRAQ
SYRIA
CYPRUS
LEBANON
ISRAEL
JORDAN
KUWAIT
Persian Gulf
QATAR
U.A.E.
Riyadh
SAUDI ARABIA
OMAN
YEMEN
Socotra (Yem.)
Gulf of Aden
Mediterranean Sea
Red Sea
Algiers
Oran
Qacentina
Tunis
TUNISIA
Rabat
Casablanca
MOROCCO
Marrakech
Ghardaia
ALGERIA
In Salah
Tamanrasset
El Aaiún
WESTERN SAHARA (MOROCCO)
Tropic of Cancer
Tripoli
Gulf of Sidra
Banghāzī
Sabhā
LIBYA
Alexandria
Cairo
Suez
Asyut
EGYPT
Aswan
Lake Nasser
MAURITANIA
Nouakchott
CAPE VERDE
Dakar
SENEGAL
Sénégal
GAMBIA
GUINEA-BISSAU
GUINEA
Conakry
Freetown
SIERRA LEONE
Monrovia
LIBERIA
COTE D'IVOIRE
Abidjan
Timbuktu
MALI
Gao
Niger
Bamako
BURKINA FASO
Ouagadougou
GHANA
Lake Volta
TOGO
BENIN
Accra
Cotonou
Lagos
NIGER
Agadez
Niamey
Kano
NIGERIA
Abuja
Benue
CHAD
Lake Chad
Abéché
N'Djamena
SUDAN
Port Sudan
Nile
Omdurman
Khartoum
Blue Nile
Waw
Mountain Nile
ERITREA
Asmara
Lake Tana
ETHIOPIA
Addis Ababa
Dire Dawa
DJIBOUTI
Djibouti
SOMALIA
Mogadishu
CAMEROON
Douala
Yaoundé
Malabo
EQUATORIAL GUINEA
SAO TOME AND PRINCIPE
Libreville
GABON
REP. OF CONGO
Brazzaville
Kinshasa
CENTRAL AFRICAN REPUBLIC
Bangui
Ubangi
Congo
Uele
Kisangani
DEM. REP. OF CONGO
Mbuji-Mayi
Kolwezi
Lubumbashi
UGANDA
Kampala
Lake Victoria
Lake Turkana
KENYA
Nairobi
Mombasa
Kigali
RWANDA
Bujumbura
BURUNDI
Lake Tanganyika
Dodoma
TANZANIA
Dar es Salaam
Equator
INDIAN OCEAN
SEYCHELLES
Ascension (St. Helena)
Luanda
Lobito
ANGOLA
Huambo
Ndola
ZAMBIA
Zambezi
Lusaka
Lake Kariba
MALAWI
Lake Nyasa
Lilongwe
MOZAMBIQUE
COMOROS
Mayotte (Fr.)
Antsiranana
Mozambique Channel
Antananarivo
MADAGASCAR
Fianarantsoa
MAURITIUS
Reunion (Fr.)
Beira
Harare
ZIMBABWE
Okavango
NAMIBIA
Windhoek
BOTSWANA
Gaborone
Limpopo
Pretoria
Johannesburg
Maputo
SWAZILAND
Maseru
LESOTHO
Durban
Orange
SOUTH AFRICA
Cape Town
Port Elizabeth
St. Helena (U.K.)
Tropic of Capricorn
Tristan da Cunha Group (St. Helena)
Prince Edward Islands (S. Af.)
Crozet Islands (Fr.)
National Capital
City over 1,000,000 population
City of 250,000 to 1,000,000 population
City under 250,000 population
0 200 400 600 800 1000 Miles
0 300 600 900 1200 1500 Kilometers
Copyright by Rand McNally & Co.
Lambert Azimuthal Equal Area Projection

RAND McNALLY

ARCTIC OCEAN
ATLANTIC OCEAN
ICELAND
FAROE ISLANDS (Den.)
Arctic Circle
Norwegian Sea
Barents Sea
SVALBARD (Nor.)
Spitsbergen
Franz Josef Land
Severnaya Zemlya
Novaya Zemlya
Kara Sea
IRELAND
UNITED KINGDOM
London
North Sea
DENMARK
NORWAY
SWEDEN
FINLAND
PORTUGAL
SPAIN
Paris
FRANCE
GERMANY
POLAND
ESTONIA
LATVIA
LITH.
BELARUS
Moscow
Kiev
UKRAINE
ROMANIA
BULGARIA
ITALY
Adriatic Sea
GREECE
ALBANIA
MOROCCO
ALGERIA
TUNISIA
LIBYA
Mediterranean Sea
Black Sea
Volga
Pechora
Noril'sk
Ob'
Yenisey
RUS
Yekaterinburg
Chelyabinsk
Omsk
Novosibirsk
Barnaul
Ishim
Irtysh
Astana
Karaganda
Semipalatinsk
Öskemen
KAZAKHSTAN
Aral Sea
Syr Darya
Lake Balkhash
Almaty
Ürümqi
Bishkek
KYRGYZSTAN
UZBEKISTAN
Tashkent
TURKMENISTAN
Dushanbe
TAJIKISTAN
İstanbul
İzmir
Ankara
TURKEY
GEORGIA
Tbilisi
ARM.
Yerevan
AZER.
Baku
Caspian Sea
CYPRUS
N. CYPRUS
LEBANON
SYRIA
Damascus
ISRAEL
Amman
JORDAN
Cairo
EGYPT
Nile
Euphrates
Tigris
Baghdad
IRAQ
Tabrīz
Tehran
Mashhad
IRAN
Eşfahān
Kuwait
KUWAIT
SAUDI ARABIA
Riyadh
Jiddah
Persian Gulf
BAHRAIN
QATAR
Abu Dhabi
U.A.E.
Muscat
OMAN
Gulf of Oman
YEMEN
Sanaa
Red Sea
Gulf of Aden
Socotra (Yem.)
Kabul
AFGHANISTAN
Islamabad
Lahore
Amritsar
PAKISTAN
Indus
Karachi
Hyderābād
Delhi
New Delhi
Ganges
NEPAL
Kathmandu
Brahmaputra
Kānpur
Ahmadābād
INDIA
Nāgpur
Kolkata (Calcutta)
Mumbai (Bombay)
Godavari
Hyderābād
Arabian Sea
Bay of Bengal
Bangalore
Chennai (Madras)
Lakshadweep (India)
SRI LANKA
Colombo
MALDIVES
INDIAN OCEAN
CHAD
SUDAN
Blue Nile
ERITREA
DJIBOUTI
ETHIOPIA
SOMALIA
KENYA
UGANDA
RWANDA
BURUNDI
DEM. REP. OF THE CONGO (ZAIRE)
TANZANIA
ZAMBIA
MALAWI
MOZAMBIQUE
N
0 200 400 600 800 Miles
0 200 400 600 800 1000 Kilometers
Copyright by Rand McNally & Co.
Lambert Azimuthal Equal Area Projection

National Capital
City over 1,000,000 population
City of 250,000 to 1,000,000 population
City under 250,000 population
PACIFIC OCEAN
Laptev Sea
East Siberian Sea
Bering Sea
Sea of Okhotsk
Sea of Japan
Yellow Sea
East China Sea
Philippine Sea
South China Sea
Luzon Strait
Taiwan Strait
Gulf of Tonkin
Gulf of Thailand
Andaman Sea
Sulu Sea
Celebes Sea
Java Sea
Banda Sea
Arafura Sea
Timor Sea
Coral Sea
Gulf of Carpentaria
Tropic of Cancer
Equator
New Siberian Islands
ALEUTIAN ISLANDS (U.S.)
Kamchatka Peninsula
Petropavlovsk-Kamchatskiy
Anadyr
Palana
Magadan
Yakutsk
Yana
Lena
Sakhalin
Kuril Islands
Khabarovsk
Amur
Angara
Lake Baikal
Kraynoyarsk
Irkutsk
Chita
Enisei
SIA
MONGOLIA
Ulaanbaatar
Qiqihar
Harbin
Changchun
Shenyang
Vladivostok
Sapporo
Hokkaido
Honshu
Tokyo
Nagoya
Osaka
Shikoku
Kyushu
JAPAN
NORTH KOREA
SOUTH KOREA
Seoul
Pusan
Beijing
Tianjin
Jinan
Taiyuan
Huang
Lanzhou
Xi'an
Nanjing
Shanghai
Hangzhou
Wuhan
CHINA
Chengdu
Chongqing
Chang (Yangtze)
Lhasa
Guiyang
Fuzhou
Taipei
TAIWAN
Kaohsiung
Guangzhou
Hong Kong
Nanning
Kunming
BHUTAN
Brahmaputra
BNGL.
Dhaka
Chittagong
MYANMAR
Yangon
LAOS
Vientiane
Hanoi
Hainan Island
Mekong
THAILAND
Bangkok
Da Nang
VIETNAM
CAMBODIA
Phnom Penh
Ho Chi Minh City
Andaman Islands (India)
Nicobar Islands (India)
Luzon
PHILIPPINES
Manila
Samar
Cebu
Mindanao
Davao
NORTHERN MARIANA ISLANDS (U.S.)
GUAM (U.S.)
FEDERATED STATES OF MICRONESIA
PALAU
Bandar Seri Begawan
BRUNEI
MALAYSIA
Kuala Lumpur
Singapore
Medan
Sumatra
Palembang
Borneo
Banjarmasin
Manado
Celebes
Ceram
INDONESIA
Jakarta
Bandung
Java
Surabaya
EAST TIMOR
Timor
New Guinea
PAPUA NEW GUINEA
AUSTRALIA
70°
60°
50°
40°
30°
170°
180°
20°
10°
0°
90°
100°
110°
120°
130°
140°
150°

ATLANTIC OCEAN
ARCTIC OCEAN
ICELAND
FAROE ISLANDS (Den.)
IRELAND
UNITED KINGDOM
London
North Sea
DENMARK
NORWAY
SWEDEN
FINLAND
Barents Sea
Novaya Zemlya
Severnaya Zemlya
Kara Sea
Yamal Pen.
Arctic Circle
PORTUGAL
SPAIN
GIBRALTAR (U.K.)
MOROCCO
FRANCE
GERMANY
POLAND
BELARUS
UKRAINE
ROMANIA
BULGARIA
GREECE
ITALY
Moscow
Volga
Ural Mountains
Ob
West Siberian Lowland
Yenisey
Novosibirsk
Irtysh
Ishim
Astana
KAZAKHSTAN
Caspian Depression
Aral Sea
Syr Darya
Lake Balkhash
Ust-Urt Plateau
UZBEKISTAN
Amu Darya
Kara Kum (Desert)
TURKMENISTAN
KYRGYZSTAN
Tian Shan
TAJIKISTAN
Pamirs
Tarim Basin
K2 (Qogir Feng) 28,250 Ft. 8,611m
Altun Shan
Kunlun Mts.
Hindu Kush
AFGHANISTAN
PAKISTAN
Indus
HIMALAYA MTS.
NEPAL
Mt. Everest 29,035 Ft. 8,850m
New Delhi
Ganges
Great Indian Desert
INDIA
Mumbai (Bombay)
Western Ghats
Godavari
Deccan Plateau
Eastern Ghats
Bay of Bengal
SRI LANKA
Lakshadweep (India)
MALDIVES
Arabian Sea
INDIAN OCEAN
ALGERIA
TUNISIA
Mediterranean Sea
Black Sea
Caucasus
GEORGIA
ARM.
AZER.
Ankara
TURKEY
Mount Ararat 16,940 Ft. 5,165m
CYPRUS
N. CYPRUS
LEBANON
ISRAEL
SYRIA
JORDAN
IRAQ
Tigris
Euphrates
Tehran
IRAN
Dasht-e Kavir
Zagros Mts.
Caspian Sea
KUWAIT
Persian Gulf
BAHRAIN
QATAR
U.A.E.
Gulf of Oman
OMAN
An-Nafud
SAUDI ARABIA
Arabian Peninsula
Rub Al-Khali
YEMEN
Gulf of Aden
Socotra (Yem.)
LIBYA
EGYPT
Cairo
Nile
Sinai Pen.
Red Sea
CHAD
SUDAN
ERITREA
DJIBOUTI
ETHIOPIA
SOMALIA
KENYA
UGANDA
RWANDA
BURUNDI
DEM. REP. OF THE CONGO (Zaire)
TANZANIA
ZAMBIA
MALAWI
MOZAMBIQUE
0 200 400 600 800 Miles
0 200 400 600 800 1000 Kilometers
Copyright by Rand McNally & Co.
Lambert Azimuthal Equal Area Projection
N

Land Elevation
Meters
Feet
3,000
9,840
2,000
6,560
500
1,640
200
656
0
0
Water Depth
0
0
200
656
2,000
6,560
RUSSIA
Siberia
Central Siberian Uplands
Taymyr Peninsula
Laptev Sea
New Siberian Islands
East Siberian Sea
Arctic Circle
Indigirka
Kolyma
Verkhoyansk Mts.
Lena
Bering Sea
Aleutian Islands (U.S.)
Kamchatka Peninsula
Sea of Okhotsk
Sakhalin
Kuril Islands
Stanovoy Range
Angara
Lake Baikal
Amur
Tatar Strait
Sikhote-Alin Mts.
Hokkaido
Sayan Mountains
Greater Khingan Range
Sea of Japan
Honshu
Tokyo
Mt. Fuji
12,388 ft.
3,776m
JAPAN
Shikoku
Kyushu
MONGOLIA
Altai Mts.
Gobi Desert
Beijing
NORTH KOREA
SOUTH KOREA
Yellow Sea
Qilian Shan
Huang
Shanghai
East China Sea
CHINA
Qinling Shandi
Chang (Yangtze)
TAIWAN
Taiwan Strait
PACIFIC OCEAN
Tropic of Cancer
NORTHERN MARIANA ISLANDS (U.S.)
GUAM (U.S.)
Philippine Sea
FEDERATED STATES OF MICRONESIA
BHUTAN
Brahmaputra
Irrawaddy
Salween
Xi
Red
Gulf of Tonkin
Hainan Island
Luzon Strait
Luzon
PHILIPPINES
BNGL.
MYANMAR
LAOS
Mekong
South China Sea
Manila
THAILAND
Bangkok
VIETNAM
CAMBODIA
Mindanao
PALAU
Equator
Sulu Sea
Andaman Islands (India)
Andaman Sea
Gulf of Thailand
Celebes Sea
Moluccas
New Guinea
PAPUA NEW GUINEA
Nicobar Islands (India)
MALAY PENINSULA
MALAYSIA
BRUNEI
MALAYSIA
Celebes
Ceram
Str. of Malacca
Singapore
Borneo
Banda Sea
Arafura Sea
Coral Sea
Sumatra
Greater Sunda Islands
INDONESIA
EAST TIMOR
Timor
Gulf of Carpentaria
Java Sea
Timor Sea
AUSTRALIA
Jakarta
Java
70°
60°
50°
40°
30°
170°
180°
20°
10°
0°
10°
20°
90°
100°
110°
120°
130°
140°
150°

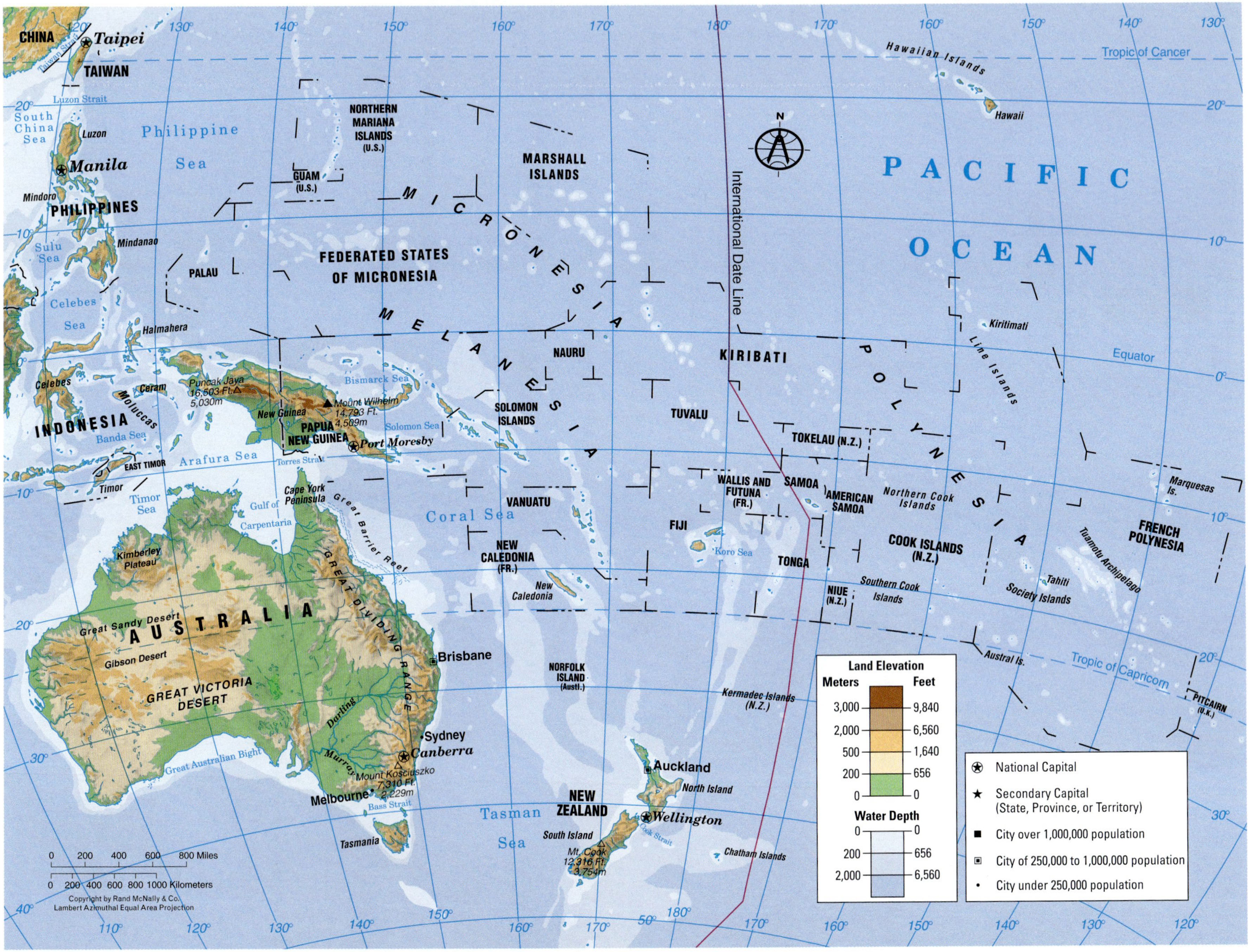
PACIFIC OCEAN
MICRONESIA
MELANESIA
POLYNESIA
CHINA
Taipei
TAIWAN
Taiwan Strait
Luzon Strait
South China Sea
Luzon
Manila
Mindoro
PHILIPPINES
Mindanao
Philippine Sea
Sulu Sea
Celebes Sea
Celebes
Halmahera
Ceram
Moluccas
INDONESIA
Banda Sea
EAST TIMOR
Timor
Timor Sea
Arafura Sea
PALAU
GUAM (U.S.)
NORTHERN MARIANA ISLANDS (U.S.)
FEDERATED STATES OF MICRONESIA
MARSHALL ISLANDS
NAURU
KIRIBATI
TUVALU
SOLOMON ISLANDS
Puncak Jaya 16,503 Ft. 5,030m
New Guinea
Mount Wilhelm 14,793 Ft. 4,509m
PAPUA NEW GUINEA
Port Moresby
Bismarck Sea
Solomon Sea
Torres Strait
Cape York Peninsula
Gulf of Carpentaria
Great Barrier Reef
Coral Sea
VANUATU
NEW CALEDONIA (FR.)
New Caledonia
FIJI
Koro Sea
WALLIS AND FUTUNA (FR.)
SAMOA
AMERICAN SAMOA
TOKELAU (N.Z.)
TONGA
NIUE (N.Z.)
Northern Cook Islands
COOK ISLANDS (N.Z.)
Southern Cook Islands
International Date Line
Hawaiian Islands
Hawaii
Kiritimati
Line Islands
Equator
Tropic of Cancer
Marquesas Is.
FRENCH POLYNESIA
Tuamotu Archipelago
Tahiti
Society Islands
Austral Is.
Tropic of Capricorn
PITCAIRN (U.K.)
Kimberley Plateau
Great Sandy Desert
AUSTRALIA
Gibson Desert
GREAT VICTORIA DESERT
GREAT DIVIDING RANGE
Brisbane
Darling
Murray
Sydney
Canberra
Mount Kosciuszko 7,310 Ft. 2,229m
Melbourne
Bass Strait
Great Australian Bight
Tasmania
NORFOLK ISLAND (Austl.)
Kermadec Islands (N.Z.)
Tasman Sea
NEW ZEALAND
Auckland
North Island
Wellington
Cook Strait
South Island
Mt. Cook 12,316 Ft. 3,754m
Chatham Islands
N
0 200 400 600 800 Miles
0 200 400 600 800 1000 Kilometers
Copyright by Rand McNally & Co.
Lambert Azimuthal Equal Area Projection
Land Elevation
Meters Feet
3,000 9,840
2,000 6,560
500 1,640
200 656
0 0
Water Depth
0 0
200 656
2,000 6,560
National Capital
Secondary Capital (State, Province, or Territory)
City over 1,000,000 population
City of 250,000 to 1,000,000 population
City under 250,000 population

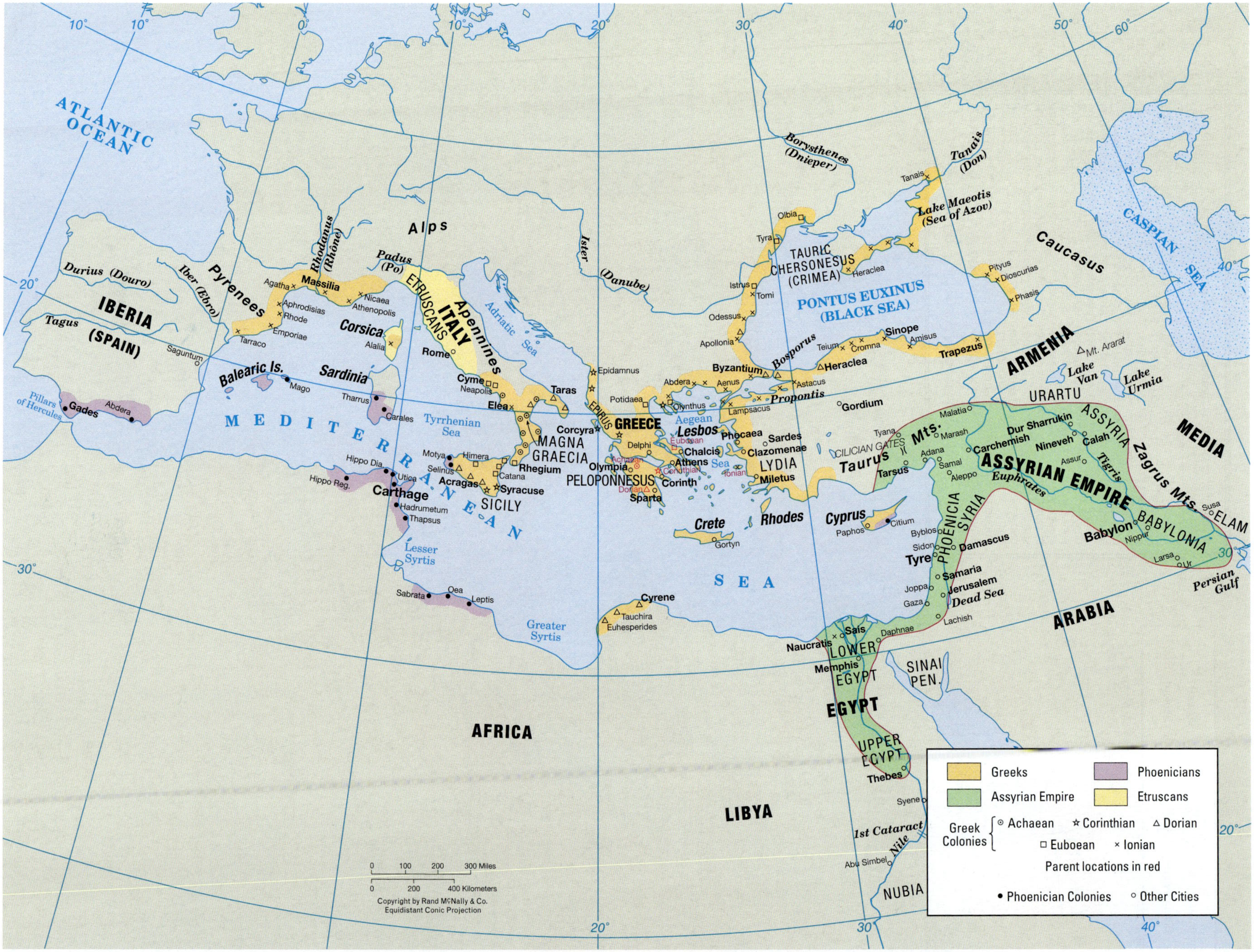
ATLANTIC OCEAN
IBERIA (SPAIN)
Durius (Douro)
Tagus
Iber (Ebro)
Pyrenees
Pillars of Hercules
Gades
Abdera
Saguntum
Tarraco
Emporiae
Rhode
Aphrodisias
Agatha
Massilia
Rhodanus (Rhône)
Nicaea
Athenopolis
Alps
Padus (Po)
ETRUSCANS
ITALY
Apennines
Corsica
Alalia
Sardinia
Tharrus
Carales
Balearic Is.
Mago
Rome
Cyme
Neapolis
Elea
Taras
Adriatic Sea
Tyrrhenian Sea
MEDITERRANEAN SEA
Hippo Dia.
Hippo Reg.
Utica
Carthage
Hadrumetum
Thapsus
Lesser Syrtis
Sabrata
Oea
Leptis
Greater Syrtis
Motya
Selinus
Himera
Acragas
Catana
Syracuse
SICILY
Rhegium
MAGNA GRAECIA
Corcyra
EPIRUS
Epidamnus
Ister
(Danube)
GREECE
Delphi
Olympia
PELOPONNESUS
Corinth
Sparta
Achaean
Corinthian
Dorian
Euboean
Chalcis
Athens
Potidaea
Olynthus
Abdera
Aenus
Aegean Sea
Lesbos
Ionian
Phocaea
Sardes
Clazomenae
LYDIA
Miletus
Crete
Gortyn
Rhodes
Cyrene
Tauchira
Euhesperides
Byzantium
Bosporus
Propontis
Lampsacus
Astacus
Apollonia
Odessus
Istrus
Tomi
Tyra
Olbia
Borysthenes (Dnieper)
TAURIC CHERSONESUS (CRIMEA)
Heraclea
PONTUS EUXINUS (BLACK SEA)
Heraclea
Teium
Cromna
Sinope
Amisus
Trapezus
Tanais
Tanais (Don)
Lake Maeotis (Sea of Azov)
Pityus
Dioscurias
Phasis
Caucasus
CASPIAN SEA
ARMENIA
Mt. Ararat
Lake Van
Lake Urmia
URARTU
Gordium
Tyana
CILICIAN GATES
Taurus Mts.
Tarsus
Adana
Marash
Malatia
Samal
Aleppo
Carchemish
Dur Sharrukin
Nineveh
Calah
Assur
ASSYRIA
Tigris
Euphrates
ASSYRIAN EMPIRE
Zagrus Mts.
MEDIA
Susa
ELAM
Babylon
Nippur
BABYLONIA
Larsa
Ur
Persian Gulf
Cyprus
Paphos
Citium
Byblos
Sidon
Tyre
PHOENICIA
SYRIA
Damascus
Samaria
Joppa
Jerusalem
Dead Sea
Gaza
Lachish
Daphnae
Sais
Naucratis
LOWER EGYPT
Memphis
EGYPT
SINAI PEN.
UPPER EGYPT
Thebes
Syene
1st Cataract
Nile
Abu Simbel
NUBIA
ARABIA
AFRICA
LIBYA
Greeks
Phoenicians
Assyrian Empire
Etruscans
Greek Colonies
Achaean
Corinthian
Dorian
Euboean
Ionian
Parent locations in red
Phoenician Colonies
Other Cities
0 100 200 300 Miles
0 200 400 Kilometers
Copyright by Rand McNally & Co.
Equidistant Conic Projection

Roman City Names and Modern Equivalents

ROMAN NAME	MODERN NAME
Ancyra	Ankara
Aquincum	Budapest
Arelate	Arles
Augusta Treverorum	Trier, Treves
Augusta Vindelicorum	Augsburg
Augustodunum	Autun
Bononia	Bologna
Burdigala	Bordeaux
Caesar Augusta	Saragossa
Camulodunum	Colchester
Carales	Cagliari
Colonia Agrippina	Cologne
Deva	Chester
Eburacum	York
Emerita Augusta	Merida
Gades	Cadiz
Hispalis	Seville
Lindum	Lincoln
Londinium	London
Lugdunum	Lyon
Lugdunum Batavorum	Leiden
Lutetia	Paris
Malaca	Malaga
Massilia	Marseille
Mazaca Caesarea	Kayseri
Mediolanum	Milan
Moguntiacum	Mainz
Nemausus	Nimes
Olisipo	Lisbon
Patavium	Padua
Salmantica	Salamanca
Thessalonica	Salonika
Toletum	Toledo
Tolosa	Toulouse
Valentia	Valencia
Vindobona	Vienna

Bastarnian Mts.
Dnieper
Dniester
SARMATIA
Tanais
Olbia
Lake Maeotis
Panticapeum
Phanagoria
Tomi
Danube
MOESIA
Odessus
BLACK SEA
Dioscurias
CAUCASUS
CASPIAN SEA
Aral Sea
Sinope
Trapezus
THRACE
Byzantium
Heraclea
Amisus
PONTUS
Halys
Nicomedia
BITHYNIA
Nicaea
Prusa
LESSER ARMENIA
ARMENIA
(114-117 A.D.)
Artaxata
L. Thospitis
L. Matianus
Ancyra
GALATIA
Pergamum
ASIA
Smyrna
Sardes
Ephesus
Laodicea
Halicarnassus
Mazaca Caesarea
CAPPADOCIA
Melitene
Amida
SOPHENE
Edessa
Rhesaena
Nisibis
LYCAONIA
Iconium
PISIDIA
PAMPHYLIA
Tyana
COMMAGENE
Adana
Carrhae
OSROENE
ASSYRIA
(115-117 A.D.)
Singara
Tigris
Ecbatana
PARTHIAN EMPIRE
Rhodes
LYCIA
CILICIA
Tarsus
Antioch
Nicephorium
Apamea
SYRIA
Circesium
Dura
MESOPOTAMIA
Euphrates
ZAGRUS MTS.
Seleucia
Ctesiphon
Susa
CYPRUS
Emesa
Palmyra
Damascus
Babylon
(115-117 A.D.)
Sidon
Tyre
Caesarea
PALESTINE
Jerusalem
Gaza
PERSIA
Alexandria
Pelusium
PETRAEA
Petra
ARABIA
Persian Gulf
Memphis
Arsinoe
Arsinoe
Oxyrhynchus
Nile
Antinoopolis
EGYPT
Ptolemais
Coptos
Thebes
Syene
Red Sea
Berenice
30°
40°
50°
0 100 200 300 Miles
0 200 400 Kilometers
Copyright by Rand McNally & Co.
Equidistant Conic Projection

The Ottoman, Safavid, and Mughal Empires in the 16th and 17th Centuries

MUSCOVY
Don
Volga
Ural
Don-Volga Canal Project 1569
Azov
Aral Sea
Syr Darya (Jaxartes)
Caspian Sea
Urganch
Amu Darya (Oxus)
Trabzon 1461
Tiflis
Darband
Bashkent 1473
Erivan
Chaldiran 1514
Ardabil 1501
Tabriz 1501
Bukhara
Samarqand
Ghujduvan 1512
Marj Dabiq 1516
Aleppo 1516
Mosul 1516
Marv
Astarabad
Qazvin
Hamadan 1503
Kirmanshah 1503
Mashhad
Harat 1510
Jam 1528
Balkh
Kabul
Indus
Qum 1503
Kashan 1503
Euphrates
Tigris
Damascus 1516
Baghdad 1534
Isfahan 1503
Yazd 1504
KASHMIR 1586
Lahore
Qandahar
Multan
Panipat 1526, 1556
Delhi
Kirman 1504
Shiraz 1504
Basra 1546
Persian Gulf
Kelat 1595
Kannauj 1540
Bandar 'Abbas
Hurmuz
Fatihpur Sikri
Agra
Lucknow
Chavsa 1539
Jaunpur
Patna
Jodhpur
SIND 1591
Gulf of Oman
Medina
Masqat
Chanderi 1572
Cambay 1572
GONDWANA
Surat
Mecca
Red Sea
Rissa
Daman
Diu 1538
Ahmadnagar 1598
BERAR 1596
Ramgir 1687
Bidar
Golconda 1687
Arabian Sea
Bijapur 1686
Goa
Bay of Bengal
Mangalore
Gulf of Aden
Cochin
Ceylon (Sri Lanka)
Colombo
INDIAN OCEAN
N
40°
50°
60°
70°
80°
50°
40°
30°
20°
10°
0°

Revolutions in the Atlantic World 1776–1826

GREENLAND
ICELAND
SWEDEN-NORWAY
Stockholm
St. Petersburg
Moscow
RUSSIAN EMPIRE
Decembrist Revolt 1825
Copenhagen
DENMARK
UNITED KINGDOM
Ireland 1798
Dublin
London
DUTCH 1784, 1795
BELGIAN 1789
1815
Waterloo
Berlin
GERMAN STATES
Warsaw
Polish Revolutions 1791, 1794
(Kosciusko)
(Ypsilanti) 1821
AUSTRIAN EMPIRE
Vienna
Budapest
Belgrade
Serb Revolt 1804
BLACK SEA
Constantinople
OTTOMAN EMPIRE
Athens
Greek Revolution 1821
Valmy 1792
Paris
Republic 1792-99
Reign of Terror 1793-94
Napoleon 1799-1814
Restoration 1814-1830
SWITZ. 1798
Verona
Venice
Milan
Italian Revolutions 1796-99, 1820
Rome
Naples
FRENCH REVOLUTION 1789
(Franklin in England 1757-62, 1764-75)
(Adams in Holland and England 1780-88)
(Franklin in France 1776-85)
(Jefferson in France 1785-89)
(Miranda in Europe 1785-1805)
(Bolívar in Europe 1799-1802, 1804-07)
(San Martín in Spain 1785-1811)
Madrid
SPAIN 1812, 1820
PORTUGAL 1820
Lisbon
Trafalgar 1805
MEDITERRANEAN SEA
(Bonaparte's French Army 1798)
Cairo
EGYPT
AFRICA
ATLANTIC OCEAN
DOCTRINE 1823
AZIL
N
1825 Dates of successful revolutions or declarations of independence
1820 Dates of unsuccessful or supressed revolutions
Battles
Boundaries and political names as of 1826
Disputed boundaries

ATLANTIC OCEAN
PACIFIC OCEAN
Gulf of Mexico
Caribbean Sea
Gila
TEXAS
U.S. 1846-48
U.S. annexation,1845
Río Grande Bravo
▲1836 from Mex.
Monterrey
MEXICO
▲ 1821 From Sp.
⚔1823
San Luis Potosí
Matamoros
Tampico
U.S., 1848
México
Veracruz
YUCATÁN
⚔1847-53
U.S.,1822-25
Bahamas (Br.)
Havana
⚔1844
CUBA
Santiago
1844-61
U.S.,1800
U.S.,1824
Santo Domingo
PUERTO RICO
Virgin Is.(Den.)
San Juan
⚔1848
Guadeloupe
1815,1822
Br.,1807-14
Martinique
Port-au-Prince
JAMAICA
HAITI
1804 from Fr.▲
1806-20⚔
DOMINICAN REPUBLIC
▲1821 from Sp.
1844 from Haiti
BELIZE
GUATEMALA
HONDURAS
Br., 1846
Guatemala
Tegucigalpa
San Salvador
EL SALVADOR
León
NICARAGUA
Bluefields
MOSQUITIA
(Miskito Indians)
San José
COSTA RICA
⚔1842
(CENTRAL AMERICAN STATES)
▲1821 from Sp.
1823 from Mexico
1838 From United Provinces of Central America
⚔1827-1829
Aruba
Bonaire
Curaçao
St Lucia
Barbados
St Vincent
Grenada
Tobago
Trinidad
Maracaibo
Cartagena
Caracas
Panamá
VENEZUELA
▲1819 from Sp.
1830 from Gran Colombia
Angostura
Georgetown
Paramaribo
Cayenne
BRITISH GUIANA
DUTCH GUIANA
FRENCH GUIANA
Magdalena
Orinoco
Bogotá
NUEVA GRANADA
▲1819 from Sp.
1830 from Gran Colombia
Galápagos Is. (Ec.)
Quito
ECUADOR
▲1822 from Sp.
1830 from Gran Colombia
Guayaquil
Negro
Amazon
Pará
Maranhão
Ceará
Marañón
Ucayali
ACRE
BRAZIL
▲1822 from Port.
Pernambuca
Trujillo
U.S., Br., Fr., 1835-36
PERU
▲1821 from Sp.
Callao
Lima
Pisco
Cuzco
Lake Titicaca
BOLIVIA
▲ 1825 from Sp.
⚔1839
La Paz
Mato Grosso
Xingu
Araguaia
Tocantins
São Francisco
⚔1831-35
Bahia
Minas Novas
Diamantina
Tacna
Arica
Chuquisaca
Potosí
GRAN CHACO
Paraguay
Iquique
1836-39
PARAGUAY
▲1811 from Sp.
Rio de Janeiro
São Paulo
Antofagasta
Jujuy
Salta
Asunción
Copiapó
Tucumán
LA PLATA
▲ 1816 from Sp.
⚔1826,1838-39
⚔ 1835-45
CHILE
▲ 1818 from Sp.
⚔1830
Córdoba
Santa Fé
1825-28
1843-45
Paraná
Pôrto Alegre
1825-28
URUGUAY
▲ 1814 from Sp., 1828 from Brazil
⚔1836-52
Valparaíso
Santiago
Mendoza
Rosario
Montevideo
Br.,1828,1843
Buenos Aires
Río de la Plata
U.S.,1833
Fr.,1806-07,1845
Br.,1838,1845
Concepción
Valdivia
PATAGONIA
(Mapuche Indians)
Br.,1833
U.S.,1831-32
Falkland Islands
South Georgia
0 200 400 600 800 1000 Miles
0 400 800 1200 1600 Kilometers
Copyright by Rand McNally & Co.
Pseudo-Cylindrical Projection
N
Independent state
British colony
Dutch colony
French colony
Spanish colony
U.S. colony
Disputed area
Latin American military forces
U.S. or European intervention
Projected canals
Independence date and colonial power
Civil war

ATLANTIC OCEAN
PACIFIC OCEAN
Gulf of Mexico
Caribbean Sea
Gila
GADSDEN PURCHASE
U.S., 1853
Rio Grande
Bravo
U.S.,1859,1866, 1873,1876
U.S., 1898
Bahamas (Br.)
Sp.,1868-78, 1895-98
Monterrey
MEXICO
Tampico
San Luis Potosí
Sp., Br., 1861-63
Fr.,1861-67
México
1854, 1857-60, 1867, 1876
Veracruz
1871
U.S.,1870
Havana
CUBA
▲1898 from Sp.
U.S., 1891
Santiago
DOMINICAN REPUBLIC
Santo Domingo
Sp.,1868
U.S.,1898
San Juan
PUERTO RICO
Virgin Is. (Den.)
Guadeloupe
Dominica
Martinique
St. Lucia
St. Vincent
Barbados
1876
Grenada
Tobago
Trinidad
Curaçao
HAITI
Port-au-Prince
JAMAICA
1865
Navassa I. (U.S.)
Sp., 1861-65
BRITISH HONDURAS
Br.,1896, 1899
U.S., 1853-54,1857,1894, 1896,1898,1899
U.S.,1856,1860, 1865,1868, 1873,1885, 1895,1898
GUATEMALA
1885
Guatemala
HONDURAS
1857
San Salvador
EL SALVADOR
NICARAGUA
1855-57
1897
Greytown
San Juan del Sur
1857
COSTA RICA
1870
Panamá
PANAMA
Cartagena
Maracaibo
Caracas
VENEZUELA
1858-63
1868-70
Angostura (Ciudad Bolívar)
Georgetown
Paramaribo
Cayenne
BRITISH GUIANA
DUTCH GUIANA
FRENCH GUIANA
Orinoco
Magdalena
COLOMBIA
Bogotá
1863-80,1899-1903
Quito
Galápagos Is. (Ec.)
Guayaquil
ECUADOR
Negro
Manaus
Amazon
Tabatinga
Pará (Belém)
Maranhão
Ceará (Fortaleza)
Pernambuco (Recife)
BRAZIL
Marañón
Ucayali
1867
Trujillo
PERU
ACRE
Xingu
Araguaia
Tocantins
São Francisco
Callao
Lima
Sp.,1864
Pisco
Cuzco
Lake Titicaca
1867,1889-1903
BOLIVIA
1899
Mato Grosso
Bahia (Salvador)
La Paz
Minas Novas
Tacna
Arica
Sucre
GRAN CHACO
Diamantina
Potosí
Iquique
1879-83
Paraguay
Paraná
PARAGUAY
1889
Rio de Janeiro
Antofagasta
Jujuy
1855
São Paulo
Salta
Asunción
Copiapó
Tucumán
1865-70
U.S.,Br.,1858
U.S.,1891
Pôrto Alegre
It.,1868
1851, 1859, 1891
Córdoba
1851-52
1855, 1864-65, 1868
Fr.,Sp.,1855,1868
Br.,1858,1868
Santa Fé
Mendoza
Valparaíso
Rosario
URUGUAY
1865,1892
Sp.,1866
Santiago
Buenos Aires
Montevideo
CHILE
ARGENTINA
Río de la Plata
U.S.,1855,1858,1868
Concepción
1852,1859, 1861,1890
U.S.,1852-53,1890
Valdivia
Br.,Fr.,1852
1879
PATAGONIA
Falkland Islands
South Georgia
N
0 200 400 600 800 1000 Miles
0 400 800 1200 1600 Kilometers
Copyright by Rand McNally & Co.
Pseudo-Cylindrical Projection

Industrialization of Europe 1815

ATLANTIC OCEAN
NORTH SEA
BALTIC SEA
MEDITERRANEAN SEA
UNITED KINGDOM
45,800,000
(530)
10,200,000
Glasgow
Edinburgh
Belfast
Dublin
Newcastle
Leeds
Bradford
Hull
Liverpool
Manchester
Stoke
Sheffield
Nottingham
Birmingham
Leicester
Bristol
London
Portsmouth
138,909,000
31,803,000
30,848,000
49,460,000
10,245,000
NORWAY
2,400,000
(810)
Christiania
SWEDEN
5,500,000
(1580)
604,000
Stockholm
FINLAND
3,100,000
(730)
Saint Petersburg
Riga
Moscow
DENMARK
2,800,000
(770)
Copenhagen
27,814,000
(Includes Black Sea Ports)
Konigsberg
NETHERLANDS
5,900,000
(330)
The Hague
Rotterdam
Amsterdam
Antwerp
Brussels
Lille
BELGIUM
7,424,000
(730)
1,850,000
Hamburg
Kiel
Bremen
Hanover
Dusseldorf
Duisburg
Essen
Dortmund
Wuppertal
Cologne
GERMANY
64,900,000
(600)
13,100,000
Stettin
Berlin
Magdeberg
Leipzig
Dresden
Chemnitz
Breslau
Frankfurt
Nuremberg
Stuttgart
Munich
Prague
Warsaw
Lodz
POLAND
12,100,000
(320)
RUSSIA IN EUROPE
119,000,000
(240)
3,040,000
Kiev
Kharkov
Lemberg
Odessa
Paris
FRANCE
39,600,000
(790)
4,000,000
Lyon
Bordeaux
Marseille
61,362,000
41,403,000
SWITZ.
3,753,000
(770)
Vienna
AUSTRIA-HUNGARY
28,600,000
(490)
1,500,000
Budapest
20,900,000
(620)
502,000
Trieste
Turin
Milan
Genoa
Florence
ITALY
34,700,000
(310)
350,000
Rome
Naples
Palermo
Catania
51,958,000
7,609,000
BOSNIA
SERBIA
MONTENEGRO
RUMANIA
Bucharest
BULGARIA
Constantinople
OTTOMAN EMPIRE
Smyrna
GREECE
2,631,000
(370)
PORTUGAL
5,960,000
(330)
Lisbon
SPAIN
19,200,000
(440)
370,000
Madrid
Valencia
Barcelona
N
20°
60°
10°
0°
20°
30°
40°
50°
60°
50°
40°
0 100 200 300 Miles
0 200 400 Kilometers
Copyright by Rand McNally & Co.
Lambert Conformal Conic Projection
20% or more of population in cities of 100,000 or more
11-20% of population in cities of 100,000 or more
6-10% of population in cities of 100,000 or more
5% or less of population in cities of 100,000 or more
Paris Cities of 1,000,000 or more
Lyon Cities from 500,000 to 1,000,000
Genoa Cities from 200,000 to 500,000
Cities with less than 200,000 not shown
Explanation of Figures
39,600,000 Population in 1910
(790) Railroad mileage per million of population
4,000,000 Pig iron production in long or metric tons
61,362,000 Ship tons in ports

ICELAND
Reykjavik
ATLANTIC
OCEAN
ARCTIC
Faroe Islands (Den.)
Shetland Islands
Orkney Is.
Hebrides
SCOTLAND
Aberdeen
Glasgow
Edinburgh
GREAT BRITAIN
IRISH FREE STATE
Dublin
Belfast
Cork
Liverpool
Manchester
Leeds
Hull
Sheffield
WALES
ENGLAND
Birmingham
Cardiff
Bristol
Oxford
Thames
London
Dover
Plymouth
Portsmouth
North Sea
NORWAY
Occupied by Germany 1940
Bergen
Stavanger
Oslo
SWEDEN
Uppsala
Stockholm
Göteborg
Hälsingborg
Gulf of Bothnia
Vaasa (Vasa)
Aland Is.
Gulf
Baltic Sea
Gotland
Öland
Riga
DENMARK
Occupied by Germany 1940
Aalborg
Copenhagen
Bornholm
Helgoland
LITHUANIA
Annexed
Annexed by USSR 1940
MEMELAND
To Ger. 1939
Memel
Kovno (Kaunas)
Königsberg
Danzig
EAST PRUSSIA
Grodno
NETHERLANDS
Occ. by Ger. 1940
Amsterdam
Rotterdam
Rhine
Weser
Elbe
Bremen
Hamburg
Lübeck
Kiel
Hanover
Stettin
Berlin
Potsdam
Magdeburg
Essen
Cologne
GERMANY
Oder
Tannenberg
Bialystok
Nazi-Soviet Pact Annexed by Germany 1939
Vistula
Posen
Brest-Litovsk
POLAND
Lublin
Channel Is.
English Channel
Brest
Le Havre
Caen
Amiens
Dunkirk
Lille
Brussels
BELGIUM
Occ. by Ger. 1940
LUX.
Seine
Versailles
Reims
LORRAINE
Verdun
Paris
Fontainbleau
Rennes
St. Nazaire
Nantes
Loire
Orléans
Occupied by Germany 1940
Bay of Biscay
La Rochelle
FRANCE
Bordeaux
Limoges
Dijon
Saône
ALSACE
Strassburg
Lyon
VICHY FRANCE 1940
Garonne
Bayonne
Grenoble
Rhône
Montpellier
Avignon
Toulouse
Marseille
Nice
Toulon
Pyrenees
ANDORRA
SAAR
To Germany Plebiscite 1935
Mainz
Frankfurt
Mannheim
Weimar
Leipzig
Dresden
SILESIA
Breslau
Nürnberg
Stuttgart
BAVARIA
Danube
Munich
Prague
Pilsen
To Ger. at Munich 1938
CZECHOSLOVAKIA
Cracow
To Pol. 1938
Tesin
Przemysl
Lemberg (Lwow)
Tarnopol
Basel
Zürich
Berne
SWITZERLAND
Geneva
LIECH.
Innsbruck
Vienna
Bratislava (Pressburg)
AUSTRIA
To Germany Anschluss 1938
Annexed by Hungary 1939
Kosice
RUTHENIA
Budapest
HUNGARY
Oradea
Mohacs
BUKOVINA
Annexed by Hungary 1940
Cluj
TRANSYLVANIA
RUMANIA
Sibiu
WALLACHIA
TRENTINO
Ljubljana
Graz
Drava
Milan
Verona
Trieste
Turin
Po
Venice
Parma
Genoa
Fiume
Zagreb
Bologna
San Remo
Ravenna
SAN MARINO
CROATIA
Florence
Zara
Sava
BOSNIA
Belgrade
Temisoara
DALMATIA
Sarajevo
SERBIA
Morava
Nish
Danube
YUGOSLAVIA
Split
Dubrovnik (Ragusa)
MONTENEGRO
Cattaro
Novi Pazar
Sofia
BULGARIA
Maritsa
Philippopolis
Tiber
Ancona
Adriatic Sea
Lagosta (To Italy)
ITALY
Rome
Naples
Bari
Taranto
Brindisi
Antivari
Durazzo
Tirana
ALBANIA
Valona
Vardar
MACEDONIA
Dede-Agach
Kavala
Salonika
Dardanelles
Yannina
Corfu
GREECE
Lesbos
Aegean Sea
Messolongi
Patras
Athens
Sparta
Crete
Candia
Ionian Islands
Cephallenia
Ionian Sea
Corsica (To France)
Ajaccio
Sardinia (To Italy)
Cagliari
Tyrrhenian Sea
Palermo
Messina
SICILY
Syracuse
Malta (Br.)
MEDITERRANEAN
Corunna
Oporto
Coimbra
PORTUGAL
Lisbon
Duero
Burgos
Santander
Valladolid
Salamanca
Tagus
Madrid
Ebro
Saragossa
Barcelona
SPAIN
Toledo
Guadiana
Cordoba
Guadalquivir
Seville
Granada
Cadiz
Valencia
Balearic Islands (To Spain)
Minorca
Majorca
Cartagena
Almeria
Gibraltar (To Great Britain)
Tangier
SPANISH AREA
Rabat
MOROCCO
To France
Atlas
Mountains
Oran
Algiers
ALGERIA
To France
Tunis
TUNIS
French Protectorate
Tripoli
TRIPOLITANIA
To Italy
LIBYA
Bengazi
Gulf of Sidra
CYRENAICA
To Italy
E
0 100 200 300 Miles
0 200 400 Kilometers
Copyright by Rand McNally & Co.
Equidistant Conic Projection

Principal status quo powers
Principal Revisionist powers
1914 Boundaries
1922 Boundaries
OCEAN
Pechenga
Murmansk
MURMAN COAST
KOLA PENINSULA
White Sea
Archangel
Ceded to USSR 1940
Ternio
FINLAND
Lake Onega
Lake Ladoga
Ceded to USSR 1940
Helsingfors (Helsinki)
Viborg
Kronstadt
Gulf of Finland
Leningrad (Petrograd)
Revel (Tallinn)
ESTONIA
Annexed by USSR 1940
LATVIA
by USSR
Pskov
Novgorod
Vologda
Yaroslavl
Volga
Kalinin (Tver)
Moscow
W. Dvina
Vitebsk
Smolensk
Borisov
Vilna
Minsk
Mogilev
Oka
Tula
Riazan
Tambov
Penza
Briansk
Orel
Kursk
Voronezh
Pinsk
Annexed by USSR 1939 Nazi-Soviet Pact
Pripet
Chernigov
Zhitomir
Kiev
Dnieper
Kharkov
Poltava
Kirovograd (Elizavetgrad)
Dnepropetrovsk (Ekaterinoslav)
Bug
Czernowitz
BESSARABIA
MOLDAVIA
Dniester
Prut
Kishinev
Annexed by USSR 1940
Odessa
Cherson
UKRAINE
Taganrog
Rostov
Sea of Azov
Galatz
Braila
Bucharest
Silistra
DOBRUJA
Constantsa
To Bulgaria 1940
Ruschuk
Varna
Burgas
Sevastopol
Novorossiisk (Anapa)
Krasnodar (Ekaterinodar)
Kuban
Voroshilovsk (Stavropol)
BLACK SEA
Sukhumi
Poti
Batum
Sinope
Samsun
Trebizond
Kars
Bosporus
Adrianople
Midia
Enos
Istanbul (Constantinople)
Skutari
Eregli
Gallipoli
Brusa
Ankara (Angora)
Irmak
Kizil
TURKEY
ASIA MINOR
Smyrna
Aidin
Konia
Adana
Adalia
Makri
DODECANESE (Italian)
Rhodes
ALEXANDRETTA
Annexed by Turkey 1939
Aleppo
Nikosia
Cyprus (Br.)
Limasol
Latakia
Homs
SYRIA
Fr. Mandate
Beirut
Damascus
SEA
Acre
PALESTINE
Br. Mandate
Jaffa
Jerusalem
Amman
TRANSJORDAN
Br. Mandate
Dead Sea
Independent Kingdom with British Protective Rights
Alexandria
Port Said
EGYPT
Nile
Cairo
Red Sea
ARABIA
Boundary of Armenia as arbitrated by President Wilson
Line of the treaty of Sèvres
Bdry. between Syria and Turkey as Established by Agree. Aug. 1921
Bdry. line between Fr. and Br. Mandate Territories as Established by Agree. Dec.
Mosul
Tigris
Baghdad
IRAQ
Independent since 1932
Euphrates
KUWAIT
Kuwait
Persian Gulf
Ordzhonikidze (Vladikavkaz)
Terek
Grozni
Petrovsk
DAGHESTAN
Derbent
REPUBLIC OF GEORGIA
Tiflis
Kura
REPUBLIC OF ARMENIA
REPUBLIC OF AZERBAIJAN
Baku
Erivan
Lenkoran
Tabriz
L. Urmia
Teheran
PERSIA
CASPIAN SEA
Astrakhan
Stalingrad
Don
Volga
Saratov
Uralsk
Ural
Chkalov
Orsk
Kuibyshev
UNION OF SOVIET SOCIALIST REPUBLICS
Krasnovodsk
TURKESTAN
Aral Sea
Gorkii (Nizhni Novgorod)
Kazan
Kama
Kirov
Molotov
Sverdlovsk
Cheliabinsk
Ufa
Belaia
Magnitogorsk
Tobol
Kustanai
Ishim
Akmolinsk
Irtish
Ob
Pechora
Dvina
Vychegda
30°
40°
50°
60°
70°
80°
90°

Africa About A.D. 1400

NORTH ATLANTIC OCEAN
AZORES
Port.
MADEIRA IS.
Port.
CANARY IS.
Sp.
EUROPE
Black Sea
Caspian Sea
Aral Sea
ASIA
Persian Gulf
ARABIA
Red Sea
Mediterranean Sea
Algiers
Tunis
TUNIS
Fr. Prot. since 1881
Fez
SULTANATE OF MOROCCO
FRENCH COLONY OF ALGERIA
1830
Tripoli
Bengazi
Barca
TRIPOLI
A Vilayet of Ottoman Empire until 1911-12
FEZZAN
Alexandria
Cairo
Suez Canal
1869
EGYPT
Tributary of Ottoman Empire Occupied by Great Britain after 1882
Tuat
Spanish Protectorate
RIO DE ORO
Boundaries Modified in 1900
René Caillié 1827
Heinrich Barth 1849-1855
W. Oudney, D. Denham and Clapperton 1822-23
G. Nachtigal 1869
"Northern Limit of Arms and Spiritous Liquors Zone"
Import of arms and spiritous liquors zone. As a result of the Brussels Anti-Slavery Conference of 1889-90, the import of arms was regulated and that of intoxicating drinks prohibited to the regions between 20 N. and 22 S. Latitude.
Nile
Egyptian territory in revolt under the Mahdi. Conquered by Anglo-Egyptian forces, 1898
Omdurman
Khartoum
ITAL. ERITREA
FRENCH COLONY OF SENEGAL
Cape Verde
Tombouctu
FRENCH SUDAN
Niger
Senegal
Barth
Anglo-French Agree. 1893
Sokoto
L. Chad
Kuka
BORNU
G. Nachtigal 1874
DARFUR
KORDOFAN
Aduwa
Gondar
L. Tana
Assab
1882
Obok
1883
Aden
Gulf of Aden
SOCOTRA
(Br.)
Cape Guardafui
FRENCH SOM.
Zeila
BR. SOMALILAND
Protectorate 1888
PORT. GUINEA
ROYAL NIGER CO.
1886
FRENCH UBANGHI
Freetown
SIERRA LEONE
Monrovia
REP. OF LIBERIA
FR. IVORY COAST COLONY
GOLD COAST COL.
TOGO
DAHOMEY
LAGOS COLONY
NIGER COAST (OIL RIVERS) PROT.
1884
GERMAN KAMERUN
J.B. Marchand 1897-98
Fashoda
Addis Abeba
ABYSSINIA
Italian Protectorate, 1889
Protectorate abandoned 1896
Anglo-Italian Agreement 1894
ITALIAN SOMALILAND
L. Rudolf
Jub
FERNANDO PO
Sp.
CORISCO BAY
Rio Muni, Sp.
Gulf of Guinea
Fr.-Congo Agree. 1887
Congo
Stanley II
L. Albert Nyanza
L. Victoria Nyanza
CONGO FREE STATE
Under Sovereignty of Leopold II of Belgium after 1885
Anglo-Ger. Tr. 1890
ANNOBAN
Sp.
COLONY OF FRENCH CONGO
1885
Brazzaville
Leopoldville
CABINDA
Port.
Boma
Ujiji
Stanley I 1871-72
Burton-Speke 1856
L. Tanganyika
GERMAN EAST AFRICA
PEMBA
ZANZIBAR
British Prot. 1890
Leased from Zanzibar 1888
Purchased 1890
INDIAN OCEAN
SOUTH ATLANTIC OCEAN
Luanda
PORTUGUESE
Livingstone II 1854
L. Mweru
L. Bangweolu
Livingstone III 1860
Benguela
WEST
ANGOLA
AFRICA
BRITISH CENTRAL AFRICA PROTECTORATE
1891
L. Nyassa
Livingstone III
EAST AFRICA
Mozambique
Mossamedes
Victoria Falls
Zambezi
Cape Frio
German-Port. Tr.
BRITISH SOUTH AFRICA CO.
Chartered, 1889
Conquered Matabeleland, 1893
PORT.
Quelimane
Mozambique Channel
MADAGASCAR
French Conquest Completed 1896
Tamatave
Antananarive
GERMAN SOUTHWEST AFRICA
"Southern Limit of Arms and Spiritous Liquors Zone"
WALFISH BAY
Br. 1878
BECHUANALAND PROTECTORATE
1885
SOUTH AFRICAN REP. (TRANSVAAL)
Limpopo
Pretoria
Johannesburg
Lourenco Marques
SWAZILAND
Luderitz Bay (Angra Pequena)
Orange
BECHUANALAND
British Colony
1885
ORANGE FREE STATE
Vaal
COLONY OF NATAL
Bloemfontein
Durban
BASUTOLAND
CAPE COLONY
Capetown
Br. 1806
Cape of Good Hope
CONTROL OF TERRITORY
Great Britain 1885
Great Britain 1898
France 1885
France 1898
Turkey
Congo Free State 1885
Congo Free State (Belgium) 1898
Germany 1885
Germany 1898
Spain 1885
Spain 1898
Portugal 1885
Portugal 1898
Italy
0 200 400 600 Miles
0 200 400 600 800 Kilometers
Copyright by Rand McNally & Co.
Lambert Azimuthal Equal Area Projection

ATLANTIC OCEAN
Easter rising, 1916
Ireland
UNITED KINGDOM
Britain
NETHERLANDS
BELGIUM
LUX.
GERMAN EMPIRE
RUSSIAN EMPIRE
FRANCE
SWITZ.
AUSTRIA-HUNGARY
ROMANIA
MONTENEGRO
SERBIA
BULGARIA
Black Sea
Dagestani rebellion, 1877–78
Aral Sea
Caspian Sea
Muslim revolt in Turkestan, 1916
Corsica
ITALY
ALBANIA
SPAIN
PORTUGAL
Azores
Balearic Is.
Sardinia
GREECE
Sicily
Malta
Crete
Dodecanese Is.
Cyprus
OTTOMAN EMPIRE
Mediterranean Sea
Russo-Afghan conflict, 1885
AFGHANISTAN
Anglo-Afghan War, 1878-1880
PERSIA
Jallaz incident, 1911
TUNISIA
Madeira Islands
MOROCCO
Nationalist revolt, 1915-16
Canary Islands
IFNI
ALGERIA
Sanusi revolt, 1912-31
TRIPOLITANIA (LIBYA)
Dinshaway incident, 1906
Urabi uprising, 1881-82
EGYPT
KUWAIT
Persian Gulf
QATAR
RIO DE ORO
NEJD
TRUCIAL STATES
OMAN
Red Sea
Cape Verde Islands
FRENCH WEST AFRICA
Mahdist State, 1881-98
Arabian Sea
Mande revolt under Samori, 1884-98
Sokoto uprising, 1906
Rabih revolt, 1897-1900
ERITREA
Abyssinia defeats Italians at Adowa, 1896
ANGLO-EGYPTIAN SUDAN
GAMBIA
ADEN
Socotra
PORTUGUESE GUINEA
NIGERIA
BRITISH SOMALILAND
FRENCH EQUATORIAL AFRICA
SIERRA LEONE
Ashanti resistance, 1872–74,1900
ABYSSINIA (ETHIOPIA)
Somali resistance, 1891-1920
LIBERIA
Anyang revolt, 1904
GOLD COAST
TOGO-LAND
Fernando Poó
KAMERUN
ITALIAN SOMALILAND
Maldives
Bunyoro resistance, 1890-98
UGANDA
BRITISH EAST AFRICA
RIO MUNI
Equator
Sao Tomé-Príncipe
Tutsi/Hutu resistance, 1911-17
Nandi and Gusli revolt, 1895-1908
BELGIAN CONGO
GERMAN EAST AFRICA
Abushiri revolt, 1888-89
CABINDA
Arab revolt, 1891-94
Hehe revolt, 1891-98
Maji-Maji revolt, 1905-09
Nationalist uprisings, 1913
ANGOLA (PORTUGUESE WEST AFRICA)
Arab revolt, 1887-89
Comoros
NYASALAND
NORTHERN RHODESIA
Revolt under Chilembwe, 1915
MOZAMBIQUE (PORTUGUESE EAST AFRICA)
SOUTHERN RHODESIA
GERMAN SOUTHWEST AFRICA
MADAGASCAR
Nationalist revolt, 1898-1904
Mauritius
Matabele and Mashona insurrections, 1896
Réunion
WALVIS BAY
BECHUANA-LAND
Herrero Hottentot uprisings, 1904-06
SWAZILAND
Zulu resistance, 1879,1906
BASUTOLAND
UNION OF SOUTH AFRICA
N
Belgian
British
Dutch
French
German
Italian
Portuguese
Russian
Spanish
United States
Area of anti-colonial resistance
Spheres of Influence
British
French
German
Russian
Japanese
0 200 400 600 800 1000 Miles
0 400 800 1200 1600 Kilometers
Copyright by Rand McNally & Co.
Times Projection
20°
0°
20°
40°
60°
40°
20°
0°
20°
40°

OUTER MONGOLIA
Russians evicted from Chinese Turkestan, 1877–78
Boxer Rebellion, 1899-1900
WEIHAI
KOREA
CHINA
JAPANESE EMPIRE
Sakhalin
Kuril Islands
Japanese sphere of influence
Aleutian Islands
PACIFIC OCEAN
SIKKIM
BHUTAN
NEPAL
INDIA
Nationalist underground in Bengal, 1905-09
Nationalist underground in Maharashtra, 1905-09
BURMA
Anglo-Burmese War, 1886-91
YANAM
Bay of Bengal
PONDICHERRY
Andaman Islands
Ceylon
Nicobar Islands
Viet revolts in Tonkin, 1883-1913
HONG KONG
MACAO
KWANGCHOWAN
Hainan
Ryukyu Is.
Formosa (Taiwan)
Bonin Islands
Viet revolts in Annam, 1906-08
SIAM
FRENCH INDOCHINA
Cambodian revolt, 1885-87
Viet revolts in Cochin China, 1885-86
Philippine-American War, 1898-1902
PHILIPPINE ISLANDS (U.S)
Moro (Muslim) resistance, 1898-1913
Mariana Islands
Guam
Palau
Caroline Islands
Marshall Islands
BRUNEI
NORTH BORNEO
SARAWAK
MALAYA
Muslim revolt in Atchin, 1881-1908
Singapore
Sumatra
Borneo
Celebes
KAISER-WILHELMSLAND
Bismarck Archipelago
Equator
Moluccas
New Guinea
PAPUA
Saminist peasant uprising, 1914-17
DUTCH EAST INDIES
Java
Bali
Lombok
Nationalist revolts, 1881-94
TIMOR (Port.)
Timor
Solomon Islands
INDIAN OCEAN
New Hebrides (Br.-Fr.)
New Caledonia
AUSTRALIA
NEW ZEALAND
80°
100°
120°
140°
160°
180°
40°
20°
0°
20°
40°

Adriatic Sea
Skopje
Sofia
BLACK SEA
Groznyy
CASPIAN
MACEDONIA
BULGARIA
GEORGIA
RUSSIA
Tirane
ITALY
ALBANIA
Thessaloniki
Istanbul
Samsun
Tbilisi
ARMENIA
AZERBAIJAN
Baku
Bursa
Yerevan
AZER.
GREECE
Aegean Sea
Ankara
Eskişehir
Erzurum
Ionian Sea
Ionian Islands
TURKEY
Izmir
Athens
Kayseri
Lake Urmia
Tabriz
Konya
Diyarbakir
Lake Van
Orumiyeh
Rasht
Antalya
Adana
Gaziantep
Aleppo
Mosul
Arbil
Crete
NORTH CYPRUS
SYRIA
Kirkuk
CYPRUS
Nicosia
Hamadan
Qom
MEDITERRANEAN SEA
Hims
Euphrates
Tigris
Bakhtaran
LEBANON
Beirut
Banghazi
Damascus
Baghdad
IRAQ
Tubruq
ISRAEL
Ar Rutbah
Gulf of Sidra
Tel Aviv-Yafo
Ammān
Karbala
Port Said
Alexandria
Gaza
Jerusalem
An Najaf
Dead Sea
Ahvaz
Suez Canal
JORDAN
Basra
Giza
Suez
KUWAIT
Cairo
Kuwait
El Fayoum
Al 'Aqabah
Sinai Pen.
El Minya
Gulf of Aqaba
LIBYA
Nile
EGYPT
Asyût
Gulf of Suez
Suhag
Buraydah
Ad Dammam
Luxor
Al Hufuf
Tropic of Cancer
Medina
Riyadh
Aswân
Lake Nasser
RED SEA
SAUDI ARABIA
Jiddah
Mecca
At Ta'if
Port Sudan
CHAD
Nile
Khamis Mushayt
SUDAN
ERITREA
Omdurman
Sanaa
YEMEN
Khartoum
Kassala
Asmera
Al Hudaydah
Al Mukalla
Al Fāshir
Wad Madani
Al Ubayyid
Ta'izz
Nyala
Aden
Blue Nile
ETHIOPIA
Lake Tana
Gulf of Aden
DJIBOUTI
Djibouti
White Nile
CENTRAL AFRICAN REP.
Malakal
Addis Ababa
SOMALIA

KAZAKHSTAN
UZBEKISTAN
Amu Darya
TURKMENISTAN
Ashgabat
SEA
Mashhad
Tehrān
IRAN
AFGHAN.
Bīrjand
Eşfahān
Yazd
Daryacheh-ye Hamun
Kermān
Zāhedān
Shīrāz
Bandar-e Būshehr
Bandar-e 'Abbās
Persian Gulf
Strait of Hormuz
BAHRAIN
Manama
QATAR
Doha
OMAN
Dubai
Abu Dhabi
Gulf of Oman
UNITED ARAB EMIRATES
Tropic of Cancer
Muscat
Şūr
OMAN
ARABIAN SEA
N
Socotra (Yem.)
INDIAN OCEAN
0 100 200 300 400 Miles
0 200 400 600 Kilometers
Copyright by Rand McNally & Co.
Lambert Conformal Conic Projection
40°
30°
20°
10°
60°
50°

0 10 20 30 40 50 Miles
0 20 40 60 80 Kilometers
Copyright by Rand McNally & Co.
Lambert Conformal Conic Projection
33°
34°
35°
Beirut
Sidon
LEBANON
Lītanī
Tyre
MEDITERRANEAN SEA
Acre
Haifa
Sea of Galilee
Golan Heights
Tiberia
Nazaret
N
Ⓐ Golan Heights. Occupied and unilaterally annexed by Israel.
Ⓑ West Bank. Controlled by Israel, parts administered by the Palestinian Authority. Permanent status to be determined.
Ⓒ Gaza Strip. Administered by the Palestinian Authority following unilateral withdrawal by Israel in 2005. Permanent status to be determined.
Hadera
Janīn
Irbid
Netanya
Nābulus
Jordan
Tel Aviv-Yafo
West Bank
As Salt
Rehovot
'Ammān
Ashdod
Jericho
Jerusalem
Ashqelon
Bethlehem
Gaza
Gaza Strip
Hebron
Dead Sea
Khan Yunus
Port Said
Pelusium Bay
Beersheba
Al Karak
El Arish
Dimona
Suez Canal
El Qantara el-Sharqîya
Aţ Ţafīlah
ISRAEL
Ismailia
JORDAN
Negev Desert
Great Bitter Lake
Ma'ān
EGYPT
Suez
Gulf of Suez
Sinai Peninsula
Elat
Aqaba
Gulf of Aqaba
32°
31°
30°

ABBASID CALIPHATE
TIEN SHAN
TARIM BASIN
TAKLIMAKAN DESERT
TIBETAN
HIMALAYA MOUNTAINS
GURJARA-PRATIHARAS
SILK ROAD
Baghdad
Merv
Samarkand
Herat
Kabul
Kashi (Kashgar)
Yutian (Khotan)
Multan
Lhasa
Volga
Caspian Sea
Aral Sea
Syr Darya
Amu Darya
Tigris
Persian Gulf
Irtysh
Ob'
Yamuna
Ganges
Arabian Sea
Bay of Bengal
Sri Lanka
INDIAN OCEAN
40°
50°
60°
70°
80°
90°
30°
20°
10°
0°
National Capital
Major Cities
0 200 400 600 800 Miles
0 200 400 600 800 1000 Kilometers
Copyright by Rand McNally & Co.
Lambert Azimuthal Equal Area Projection
N

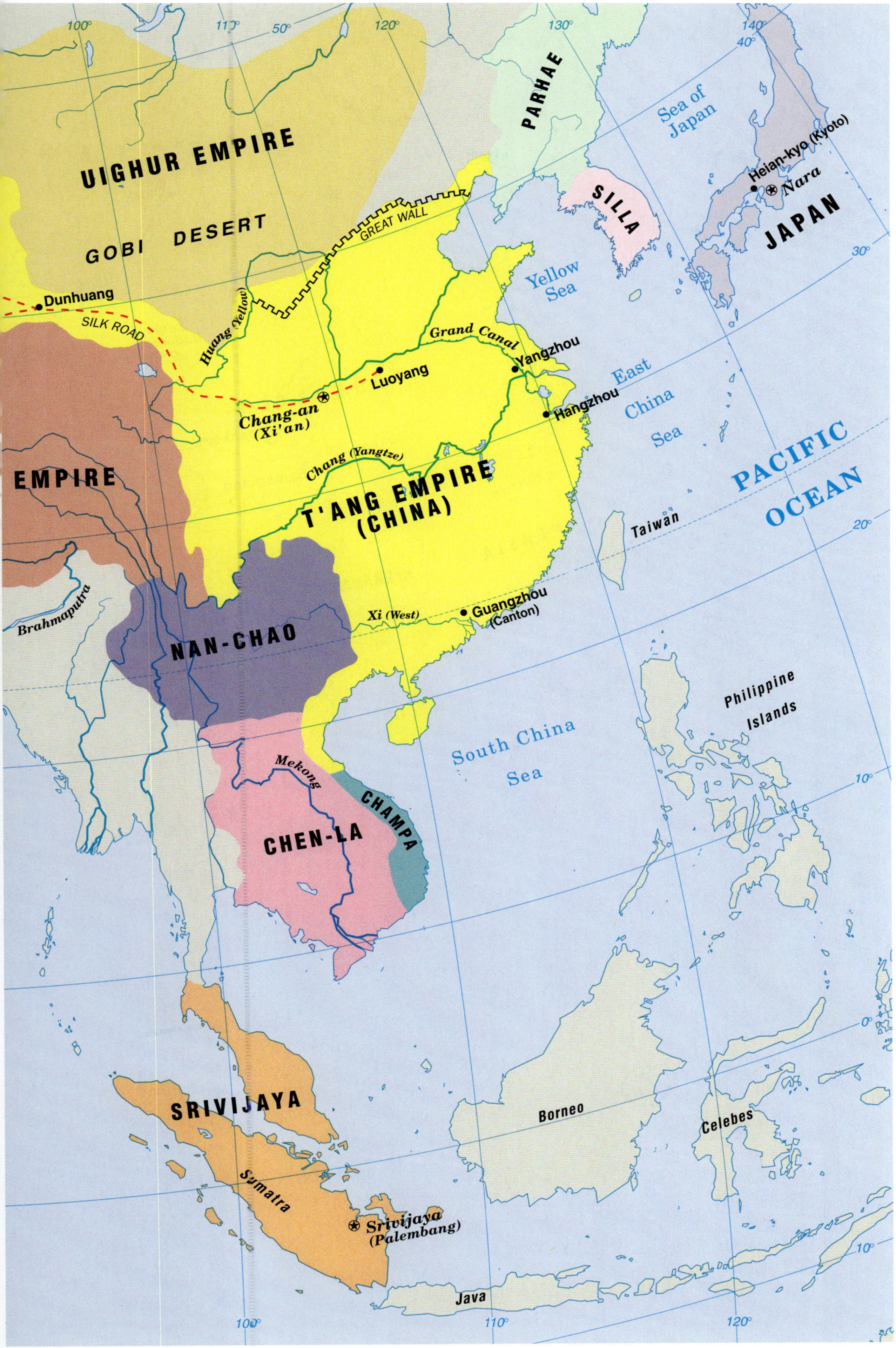
UIGHUR EMPIRE
GOBI DESERT
PARHAE
Sea of Japan
SILLA
Heian-kyo (Kyoto)
Nara
JAPAN
GREAT WALL
Yellow Sea
Dunhuang
SILK ROAD
Huang (Yellow)
Grand Canal
Yangzhou
Luoyang
East China Sea
Hangzhou
Chang-an (Xi'an)
EMPIRE
Chang (Yangtze)
T'ANG EMPIRE (CHINA)
PACIFIC OCEAN
Taiwan
Brahmaputra
Xi (West)
Guangzhou (Canton)
NAN-CHAO
Philippine Islands
South China Sea
Mekong
CHAMPA
CHEN-LA
SRIVIJAYA
Borneo
Celebes
Sumatra
Srivijaya (Palembang)
Java
100°
110°
50°
120°
130°
140°
40°
30°
20°
10°
0°

AUSTRIA-HUNGARY
MONT.
SERB.
ROMANIA
BULGARIA
GREECE
OTTOMAN EMPIRE
Constantinople
Black Sea
Moscow
Dnieper
Volga
Samara
RUSSIAN
Omsk
Ob'
Irtysh
Caspian Sea
Aral Sea
Lake Balkhash
TURKESTAN
Tashkent
Bukhara
Samarkand
TIEN SHAN
TARIM BASIN
TAKLIMAKAN DESERT
Cyprus (Br.)
Mediterranean Sea
Suez Canal
Cairo
Jerusalem
EGYPT
Euphrates
Tigris
Baghdad
Tehran
PERSIA
Kabul
AFGHANISTAN
KASHMIR
PUNJAB
KUWAIT
ARABIA
BAHRAIN
Persian Gulf
QATAR
TRUCIAL OMAN
OMAN
Red Sea
Mecca
BALUCHISTAN
Indus
SIND
RAJPUTANA
Delhi
HIMALAYA MTS.
NEPAL
Yamuna
Ganges
BENGAL
BRITISH
ORISSA
ERITREA
HADRAMAUT
Aden (Br.)
FR. SOM.
ABYSSINIA
BRITISH SOMALILAND
ITALIAN SOMALILAND
Bombay
HYDERABAD
Hyderabad
Arabian Sea
Goa (Port.)
MYSORE
MADRAS
Madras
Ceylon
Colombo
INDIAN OCEAN
N
British
French
Dutch
Italian
Portuguese
United States
0 200 400 600 800 Miles
0 200 400 600 800 1000 Kilometers
Copyright by Rand McNally & Co.
Lambert Azimuthal Equal Area Projection
20°
30°
40°
50°
60°
70°
80°
10°
0°

EMPIRE
Yenisey
Angara
Lena
Lake Baikal
Irkutsk
Chita
Amur
MANCHURIA
Sakhalin
Vladivostok
Hokkaido
Sea of Japan
Honshu
Tokyo
JAPANESE EMPIRE
KOREA
Seoul
MONGOLIA
INNER MONGOLIA
GOBI DESERT
Beijing
Tianjin
Lushun (Rus.)
Weihai (Br.)
Qingdao (Ger.)
Shikoku
Kyushu
Huang (Yellow)
Shanghai
Hangzhou
Ryukyu Islands (Japan)
PACIFIC OCEAN
CHINESE EMPIRE
Wuhan
(Yangtze)
Chang
TIBET
Chongqing
Fuzhou
Taiwan (Japan)
Brahmaputra
BHUTAN
ASSAM
Xi (West)
Canton (Guangzhou)
Hong Kong (Br.)
Macao (Port.)
Luzon
PHILIPPINE ISLANDS (U.S.)
Calcutta
INDIA
BURMA
Kwangchowan (Fr.)
Manila
South China Sea
ANNAM
Mekong
SIAM
FRENCH INDOCHINA
Rangoon
Bay of Bengal
Bangkok
Saigon
Mindanao
Andaman Islands (Br.)
BRITISH NORTH BORNEO
BRUNEI
Nicobar Islands (Br.)
SARAWAK
Moluccas
MALAYA
Singapore
Borneo
Celebes
Sumatra
DUTCH EAST INDIES
Batavia
Java
TIMOR (Port.)
90°
100°
110°
120°
130°
140°
150°
160°
60°
50°
40°
30°
20°
10°

SWEDEN
Gulf of Bothnia
BALTIC SEA
FINLAND
Gulf of Finland
Gulf of Riga
Tallinn
ESTONIA
Riga
LATVIA
LITHUANIA
Vilnius
RUSSIA
GERMANY
Berlin
POLAND
Warsaw
CZECH REP.
AUS.
SLOVAKIA
HUNG.
ROMANIA
BELARUS
Minsk
UKRAINE
Kiev
Dnipropetrovs'k
Kharkiv
Odesa
MOLDOVA
Chişinău
Donets'k
Sea of Azov
BLACK SEA
Krasnodar
Sochi
Rostov-na-Donu
Stavropol'
GEORGIA
Tbilisi
TUR.
ARMENIA
Yerevan
AZERBAIJAN
Baku
Groznyy
CASPIAN SEA
Astrakhan'
Volga
Volgograd
Saint Petersburg
Lake Ladoga
Lake Onega
Petrozavodsk
Murmansk
WHITE SEA
BARENTS SEA
Franz Josef Land
Svalbard (Nor.)
Novaya Zemlya
KARA SEA
Arkhangel'sk
Northern Dvina
Cherepovets
Rybinsk Res.
Yaroslavl'
Tver'
Moscow
Tula
Lipetsk
Ryazan'
Voronezh
Don
Saratov
Penza
Nizhniy Novgorod
Kazan'
Kirov
Izhevsk
Perm'
Samara
Ufa
Yekaterinburg
Nizhniy Tagil
Chelyabinsk
Syktyvkar
Pechora
Arctic Circle
Vorkuta
Amderma
Dikson
Salekard
Berezovo
Ob'
Serov
Tyumen'
Tobol'sk
Irtysh
Kurgan
Surgut
Nizhevartovsk
Dudinka
Noril'sk
Igarka
Novy Urengoy
Yenisey
RUSSIA
Omsk
Novosibirsk
Tomsk
Achinsk
Kemerovo
Krasnoyarsk
Barnaul
Biysk
Novokuznetsk
Rubtsovsk
Kyzyl
Oral
Ural
Aqtöbe
Qostanay
Petropavlovsk
Ishim
Astana (Aqmola)
Pavlodar
Qaraghandy
KAZAKHSTAN
Semey
Öskemen
Aqtau
Aral Sea
Syr Darya
Qyzylorda
Lake Balkhash
Taldyqorghan
Almaty
Zhambyl
Shymkent
Tashkent
Nukus
UZBEKISTAN
Nebitdag
TURKMENISTAN
Ashgabat
Amu Darya
Bukhara
Samarkand
KYRGYZSTAN
Bishkek
Namangan
Andizhan
TAJIKISTAN
Dushanbe
Tehran
Mashad
IRAN
AFGHANISTAN
Kabul
PAKISTAN
CHINA
Ürümqi
10°
20°
30°
40°
50°
60°
70°
80°
90°

ARCTIC OCEAN
UNITED STATES
Bering Strait
Saint Lawrence Island
Wrangell Island
EAST SIBERIAN SEA
BERING SEA
Severnaya Zemlya
New Siberian Islands
Kotelny Island
Novaya Sibir Island
LAPTEV SEA
Arctic Circle
Anadyr'
Srednekolymsk
Indigirka
Tiksi
Kolyma
Seymchan
Komandorskiye Islands
Ust'-Kamchatsk
Verkhoyansk
Kamchatka Peninsula
Zhigansk
Petropavlovsk-Kamchatskiy
Magadan
Lena
Vilyuysk
Yakutsk
Tura
Lower Tunguska
Aldan
SEA OF OKHOTSK
S I A
Olëkminsk
Okha
Angara
Bodaybo
Sakhalin
Kuril Islands
Nikolayevsk-na-Amure
Ust'-Kut
Amur
Bratsk
Zeya
Komsomol'sk-na-Amure
Tulun
Svobodnyy
Yuzhno-Sakhalinsk
Cheremkhovo
Blagoveshchensk
Lake Baikal
La Perouse Strait
Angarsk
Irkutsk
Chita
Khabarovsk
Ulan-Ude
Birobidzhan
Hokkaido
JAPAN
PACIFIC OCEAN
Ulan Bator
Harbin
MONGOLIA
Vladivostok
Nakhodka
National Capital
City over 1,000,000 population
City of 250,000 to 1,000,000 population
City under 250,000 population
0 100 200 300 400 500 Miles
0 200 400 600 800 Kilometers
Copyright by Rand McNally & Co.
Lambert Azimuthal Equal Area Projection
N
Shenyang
NORTH KOREA
P'yŏngyang
SEA OF JAPAN
80° 180° 170° 70° 60° 160° 170° 140° 100° 120° 180° 170° 50° 160° 40° 150° 110° 120° 40° 130° 140°

UNIT 1 Beginnings of Civilization

4 million B.C. – 200 B.C.

Rising out of the sands of Egypt are enduring signs of an ancient civilization. Pictured here are the pyramids of Giza, which were built as tombs for Egyptian rulers.

Comparing & Contrasting

Ancient Civilizations

In Unit 1, you will learn about several ancient civilizations such as in Egypt. At the end of the unit, you will have a chance to compare and contrast the civilizations you studied. (See pages 112–117.)

CHAPTER 1

The Peopling of the World, Prehistory–2500 B.C.

NEW YORK CORE CURRICULUM FOCUS

- Early people used technology to adapt to their environments.
- The Neolithic Revolution, or the beginning of farming, brought far-reaching social changes, such as the rise of cities.

Previewing Main Ideas

INTERACTION WITH ENVIRONMENT As early humans spread out over the world, they adapted to each environment they encountered. As time progressed, they learned to use natural resources.

Geography *Study the time line and the map. Where in Africa did human life begin?*

SCIENCE AND TECHNOLOGY The earliest peoples came up with new ideas and inventions in order to survive. As people began to live in settlements, they continued to develop new technology to control the environment.

Geography *Early humans began to migrate about 1.8 million years ago. What paths did these migrations take?*

ECONOMICS Early humans hunted animals and gathered wild plant foods for 3 to 4 million years. Then about 10,000 years ago, they learned to tame animals and to plant crops. Gradually, more complex economies developed.

Geography *Early settlement sites often were near rivers. Why might they have been located there?*

INTEGRATED TECHNOLOGY

eEdition
- Interactive Maps
- Interactive Visuals
- Interactive Primary Sources

INTERNET RESOURCES

Go to **classzone.com** for:
- Research Links
- Internet Activities
- Primary Sources
- Chapter Quiz
- Maps
- Test Practice
- Current Events

WORLD **4,000,000 B.C.**

4,000,000 B.C. First hominids appear in Africa. (early hominid footprint) ▶

2,500,000 B.C. Paleolithic Age begins. (Paleolithic lunar calendar) ▶

1,600,000 B.C. *Homo erectus* appears.

200,000 B.C. Neanderthals appear.

Prehistoric World to 2500 B.C.

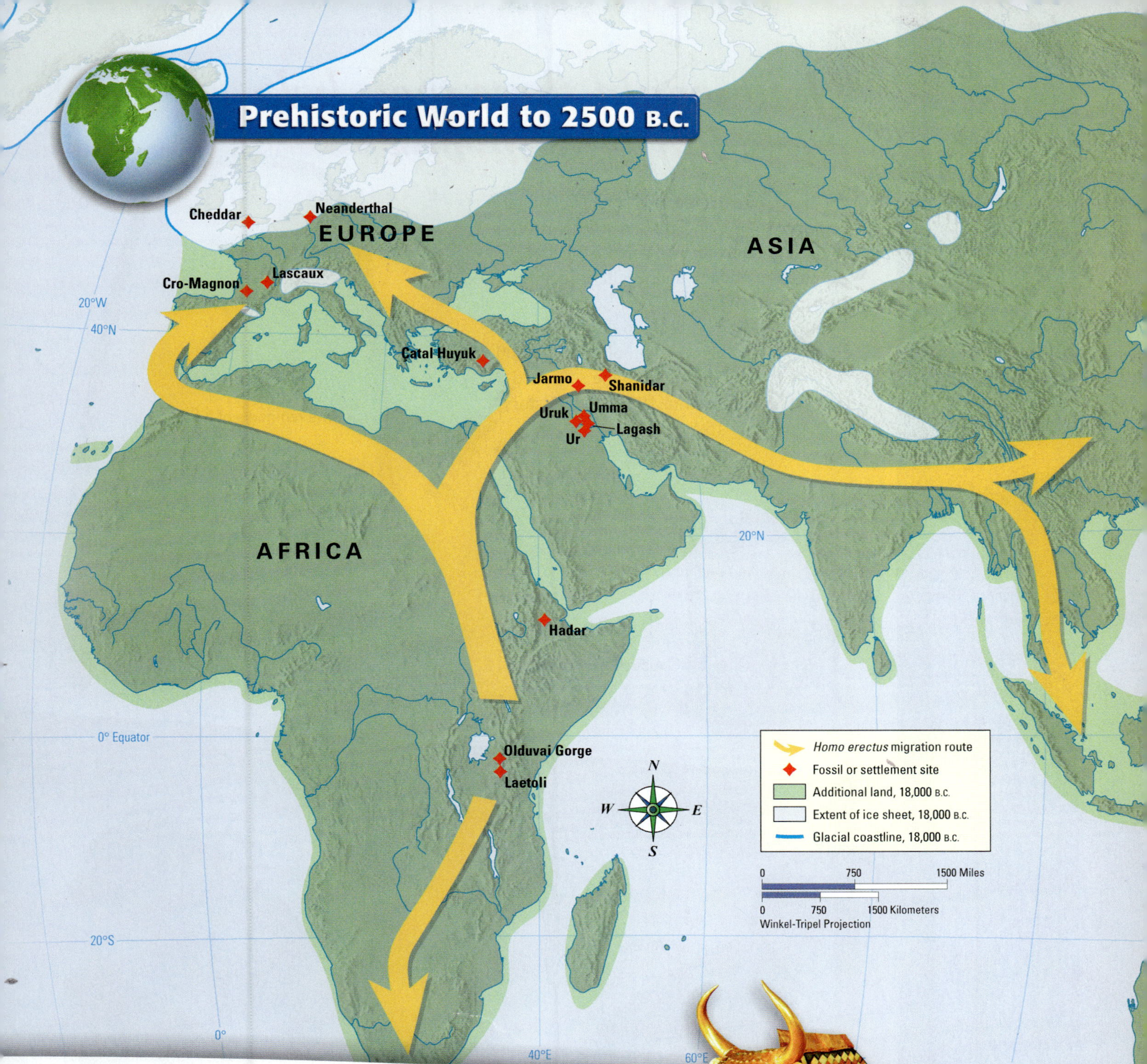

40,000 B.C.
Cro-Magnons emerge.

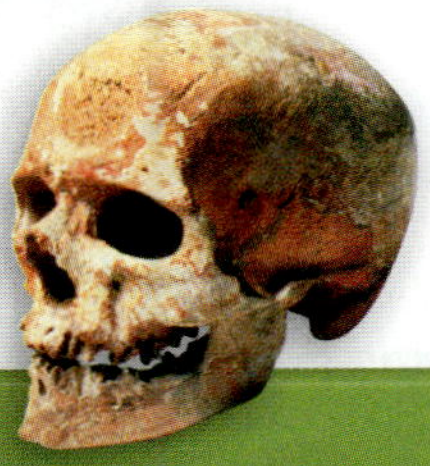

8000 B.C.
Neolithic Age begins; first agriculture takes place.

3000 B.C.
Bronze Age well-established in Mesopotamia.

2600 B.C.
City of Ur flourishes in Sumer.

2500 B.C.

Interact *with* History

How would these tools help early humans survive?

You have joined a team of scientists on an expedition to an ancient site where early humans once lived. The scientists' goal is to search for evidence that might unlock the mysteries of the past.

You're an eyewitness to their astounding discovery—human-made tools about 5,000 years old. They belonged to the so-called Ice Man, discovered in 1991. (See History in Depth, page 15.)

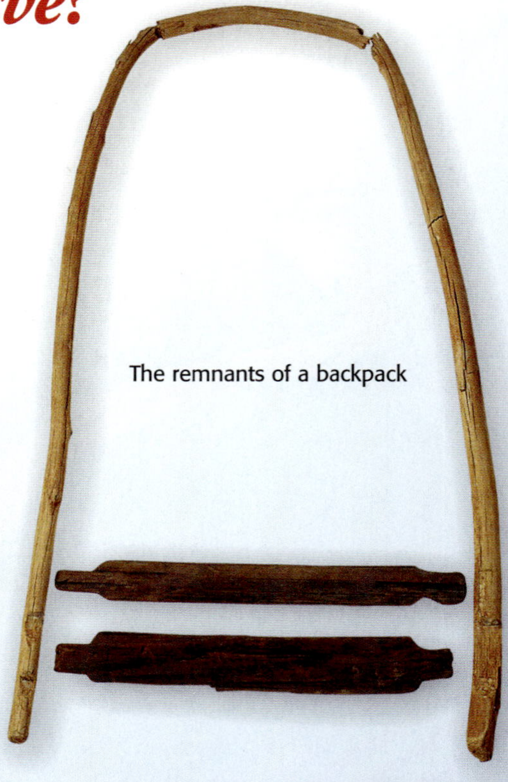
The remnants of a backpack

A birch-bark container

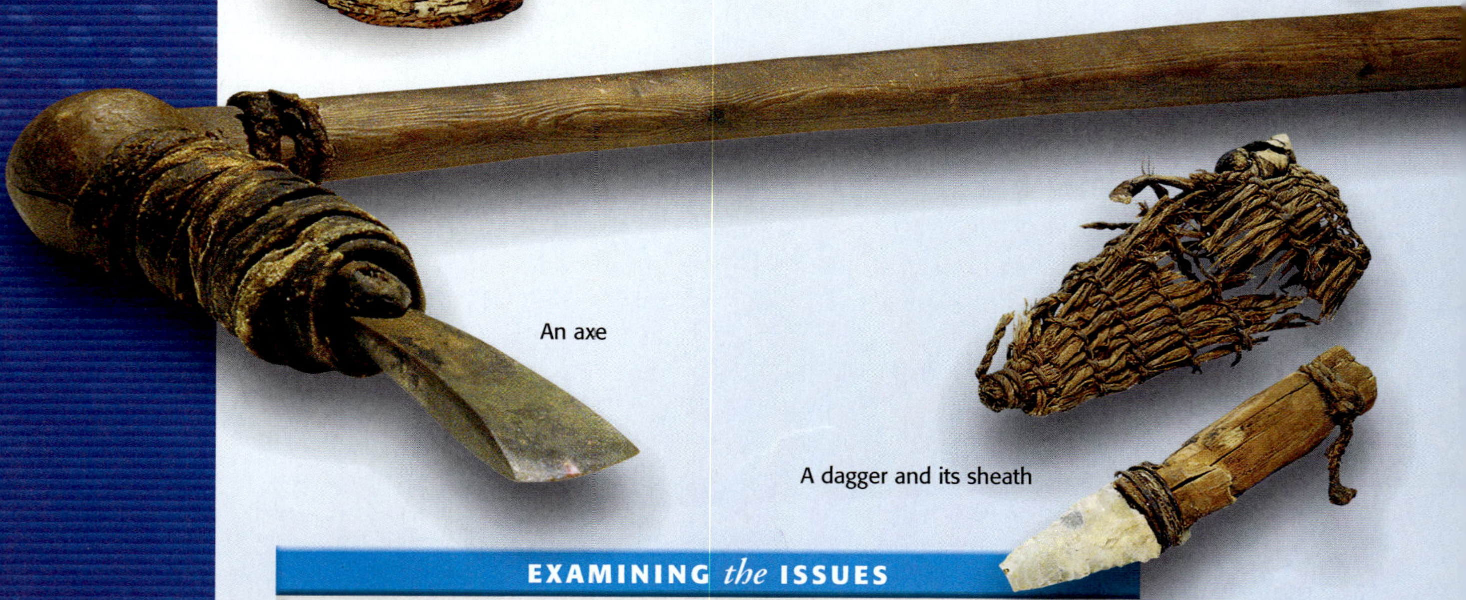
An axe

A dagger and its sheath

EXAMINING *the* ISSUES

- **What did early humans need to do to survive?**
- **What physical actions would these tools help humans do?**

As a class, discuss these questions. In your discussion, think about recent tools and inventions that have changed people's lives. As you read about the ancestors of present-day humans, notice how early toolmakers applied their creativity and problem-solving skills.

Human Origins in Africa

CONNECT TO THE NEW YORK STATE CORE CURRICULUM

Unit 1.A.1. Human and physical geography
Unit 1.A.4.a. Out of Africa

TERMS & NAMES

- artifact
- culture
- hominid
- Paleolithic Age
- Neolithic Age
- technology
- *Homo sapiens*

SETTING THE STAGE What were the earliest humans like? Many people have asked this question. Because there are no written records of prehistoric peoples, scientists have to piece together information about the past. Teams of scientists use a variety of research methods to learn more about how, where, and when early humans developed. Interestingly, recent discoveries provide the most knowledge about human origins and the way prehistoric people lived. Yet, the picture of prehistory is still far from complete.

Scientists Search for Human Origins

Written documents provide a window to the distant past. For several thousand years, people have recorded information about their beliefs, activities, and important events. Prehistory, however, dates back to the time before the invention of writing—roughly 5,000 years ago. Without access to written records, scientists investigating the lives of prehistoric peoples face special challenges.

TAKING NOTES
Categorizing Use a diagram to list advances of each hominid group.

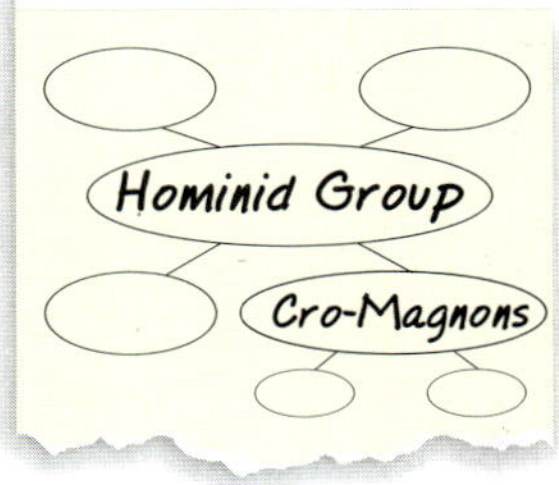

Scientific Clues Archaeologists are specially trained scientists who work like detectives to uncover the story of prehistoric peoples. They learn about early people by excavating and studying the traces of early settlements. An excavated site, called an archaeological dig, provides one of the richest sources of clues to the prehistoric way of life. Archaeologists sift through the dirt in a small plot of land. They analyze all existing evidence, such as bones and artifacts. Bones might reveal what the people looked like, how tall they were, the types of food they ate, diseases they may have had, and how long they lived. **Artifacts** are human-made objects, such as tools and jewelry. These items might hint at how people dressed, what work they did, or how they worshiped.

Scientists called anthropologists study **culture**, or a people's unique way of life. Anthropologists examine the artifacts at archaeological digs. From these, they re-create a picture of early people's cultural behavior. (See Analyzing Key Concepts on culture on the following page.)

Other scientists, called paleontologists, study fossils—evidence of early life preserved in rocks. Human fossils often consist of small fragments of teeth, skulls, or other bones. Paleontologists use complex techniques to date ancient fossil remains and rocks. Archaeologists, anthropologists, paleontologists, and other scientists work as a team to make new discoveries about how prehistoric people lived.

Culture

In prehistoric times, bands of humans that lived near one another began to develop shared ways of doing things: common ways of dressing, similar hunting practices, favorite animals to eat. These shared traits were the first beginnings of what anthropologists and historians call *culture*.

Culture is the way of life of a group of people. Culture includes common practices of a society, its shared understandings, and its social organization. By overcoming individual differences, culture helps to unify the group.

Components of Culture

Common Practices	Shared Understandings	Social Organization
• what people eat	• language	• family
• clothing and adornment	• symbols	• class and caste structure
• sports	• religious beliefs	• relationships between individual and community
• tools and technology	• values	• government
• social customs	• the arts	• economic system
• work	• political beliefs	• view of authority

How Culture Is Learned

People are not born knowing about culture. Instead, they must learn culture. Generally, individuals learn culture in two ways. First, they observe and imitate the behavior of people in their society. Second, people in their society directly teach the culture to them, usually through spoken or written language.

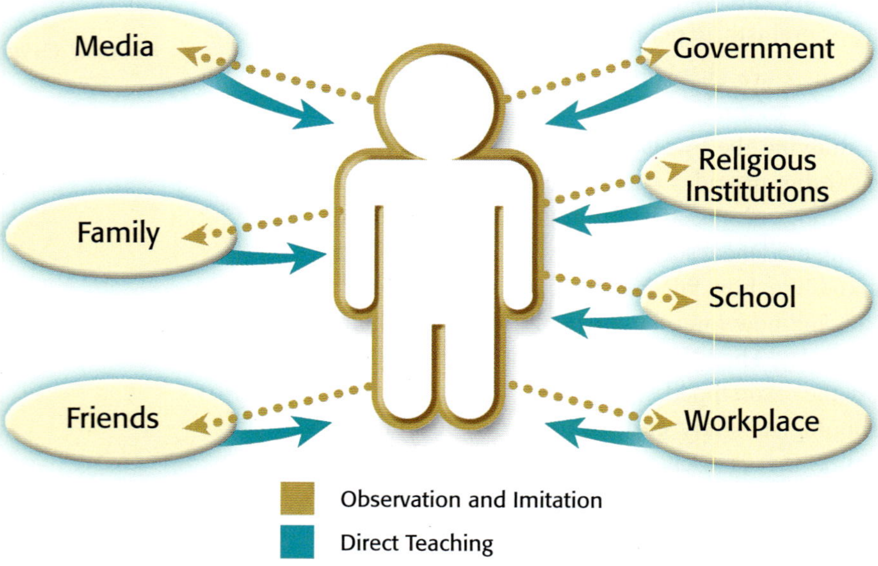

INTEGRATED TECHNOLOGY
RESEARCH LINKS For more on culture, go to **classzone.com**

> DATA FILE

CULTURAL DATA

Annual movie attendance, 1998–2000 (per person)*

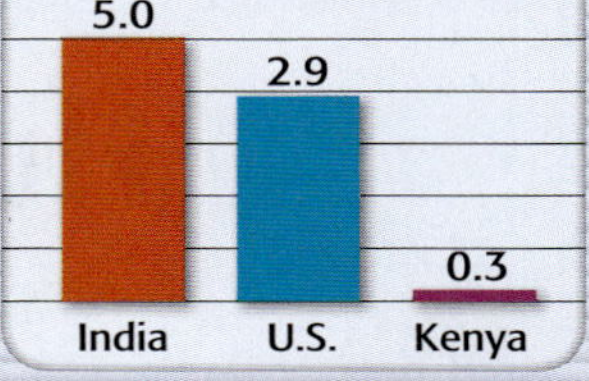

* UNESCO, last update 3/03

Marriage rates, 1999 (per 1,000 population)*

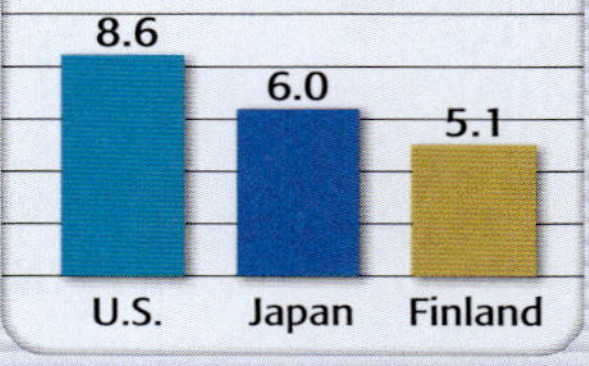

* *Monthly Bulletin of Statistics,* United Nations, October 2001

Divorces, 1996 (as % of marriages)*

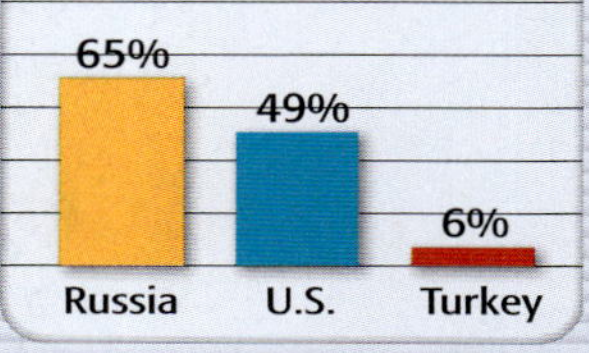

* *Human Development Report,* United Nations, 2000

Average family size, 1980–1990*

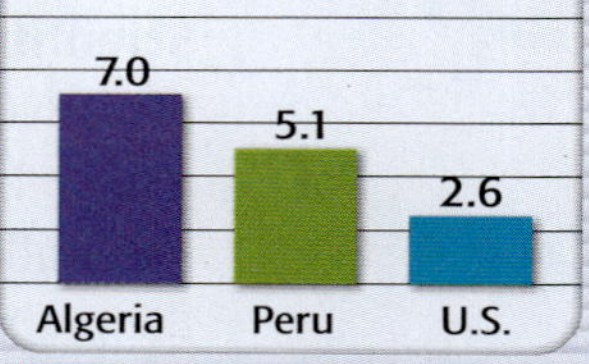

* UNESCO, last update 8/17/01

Connect *to* Today

1. **Forming and Supporting Opinions** In U.S. culture, which shared understanding do you think is the most powerful? Why?

   See Skillbuilder Handbook, page R20.

2. **Making Inferences** Judging from the divorce rate in Turkey, what components of culture do you think are strong in that country? Why?

Early Footprints Found In the 1970s, archaeologist Mary Leakey led a scientific expedition to the region of Laetoli in Tanzania in East Africa. (See map on page 10.) There, she and her team looked for clues about human origins. In 1978, they found prehistoric footprints that resembled those of modern humans preserved in volcanic ash. These footprints were made by humanlike beings now called australopithecines (aw•STRAY•loh•PIHTH•ih•SYNZ). Humans and other creatures that walk upright, such as australopithecines, are called **hominids**. The Laetoli footprints provided striking evidence about human origins:

PRIMARY SOURCE

What do these footprints tell us? First, . . . that at least 3,600,000 years ago, what I believe to be man's direct ancestor walked fully upright. . . . Second, that the form of the foot was exactly the same as ours. . . . [The footprints produced] a kind of poignant time wrench. At one point, . . . she [the female hominid] stops, pauses, turns to the left to glance at some possible threat or irregularity, and then continues to the north. This motion, so intensely human, transcends time.

MARY LEAKEY, quoted in *National Geographic*

The Discovery of "Lucy" While Mary Leakey was working in East Africa, U.S. anthropologist Donald Johanson and his team were also searching for fossils. They were exploring sites in Ethiopia, about 1,000 miles to the north. In 1974, Johanson's team made a remarkable find—an unusually complete skeleton of an adult female hominid. They nicknamed her "Lucy" after the song "Lucy in the Sky with Diamonds." She had lived around 3.5 million years ago—the oldest hominid found to that date. **A**

MAIN IDEA

Drawing Conclusions

A Why were the discoveries of hominid footprints and "Lucy" important?

Hominids Walk Upright Lucy and the hominids who left their footprints in East Africa were species of australopithecines. Walking upright helped them travel distances more easily. They were also able to spot threatening animals and carry food and children.

These early hominids had already developed the opposable thumb. This means that the tip of the thumb can cross the palm of the hand. The opposable thumb was crucial for tasks such as picking up small objects and making tools. (To see its importance, try picking up a coin with just the index and middle fingers. Imagine all of the other things that cannot be done without the opposable thumb.)

History Makers

The Leakey Family

The Leakey family has had a tremendous impact on the study of human origins. British anthropologists Louis S. B. Leakey (1903–1972) and Mary Leakey (1913–1996) began searching for early human remains in East Africa in the 1930s. Their efforts turned what was a sideline of science into a major field of scientific inquiry. Mary became one of the world's renowned hunters of human fossils.

Their son Richard; Richard's wife, Maeve; and Richard and Maeve's daughter Louise have continued the family's fossil-hunting in East Africa into the 21st century.

INTEGRATED TECHNOLOGY

RESEARCH LINKS For more on the Leakey family, go to **classzone.com**

The Old Stone Age Begins

The invention of tools, mastery over fire, and the development of language are some of the most impressive achievements in human history. Scientists believe these occurred during the prehistoric period known as the Stone Age. It spanned a vast length of time. The earlier and longer part of the Stone Age, called the Old Stone Age or **Paleolithic Age**, lasted from about 2.5 million to 8000 B.C. The oldest stone chopping tools date back to this era. The New Stone Age, or **Neolithic Age**, began about 8000 B.C. and ended as early as 3000 B.C. in some areas. People who lived during this second phase of the Stone Age learned to polish stone tools, make pottery, grow crops, and raise animals.

Hominid Development

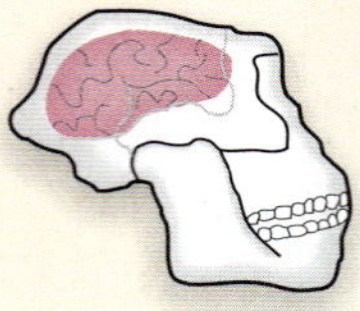

Australopithecines

- 4 million to 1 million B.C.
- found in southern and eastern Africa
- brain size 500 cm^3 (cubic centimeters)
- first humanlike creature to walk upright

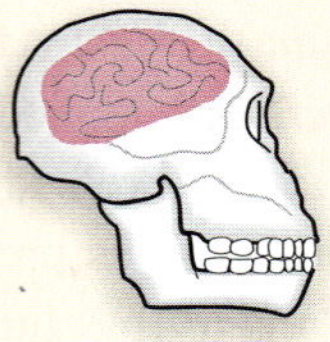

Homo habilis

- 2.5 million to 1.5 million B.C.
- found in East Africa
- brain size 700 cm^3
- first to make stone tools

4 million years ago

3 million years ago

Much of the Paleolithic Age occurred during the period in the earth's history known as the Ice Age. During this time, glaciers alternately advanced and retreated as many as 18 times. The last of these ice ages ended about 10,000 years ago. By the beginning of the Neolithic Age, glaciers had retreated to roughly the same area they now occupy.

***Homo habilis* May Have Used Tools** Before the australopithecines eventually vanished, new hominids appeared in East Africa around 2.5 million years ago. In 1960, archaeologists Louis and Mary Leakey discovered a hominid fossil at Olduvai (OHL•duh•vy) Gorge in northern Tanzania. The Leakeys named the fossil *Homo habilis,* which means "man of skill." The Leakeys and other researchers found tools made of lava rock. They believed *Homo habilis* used these tools to cut meat and crack open bones. Tools made the task of survival easier.

***Homo erectus* Develops Technology** About 1.6 million years ago, before *Homo habilis* left the scene, another species of hominids appeared in East Africa. This species is now known as *Homo erectus,* or "upright man." Some anthropologists believe *Homo erectus* was a more intelligent and adaptable species than *Homo habilis. Homo erectus* people used intelligence to develop **technology**—ways of applying knowledge, tools, and inventions to meet their needs. These hominids gradually became skillful hunters and invented more sophisticated tools for digging, scraping, and cutting. They also eventually became the first hominids to migrate, or move, from Africa. Fossils and stone tools show that bands of *Homo erectus* hunters settled in India, China, Southeast Asia, and Europe.

According to anthropologists, *Homo erectus* was the first to use fire. Fire provided warmth in cold climates, cooked food, and frightened away attacking animals. The control of fire also probably helped *Homo erectus* settle new lands.

Homo erectus may have developed the beginnings of spoken language. Language, like technology, probably gave *Homo erectus* greater control over the environment and boosted chances for survival. The teamwork needed to plan hunts and cooperate in other tasks probably relied on language. *Homo erectus* might have named objects, places, animals, and plants and exchanged ideas. (B)

MAIN IDEA

Recognizing Effects

(B) How did *Homo erectus* use fire to adapt to the environment?

The Dawn of Modern Humans

Many scientists believe *Homo erectus* eventually developed into ***Homo sapiens***—the species name for modern humans. *Homo sapiens* means "wise men." While they physically resembled *Homo erectus, Homo sapiens* had much larger brains.

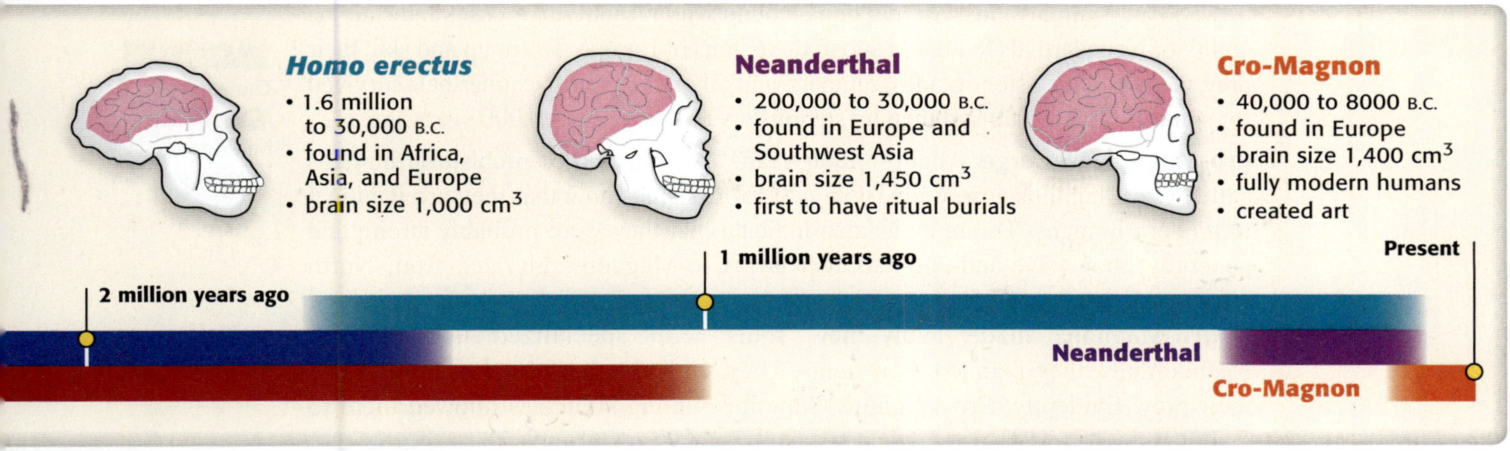

Scientists have traditionally classified Neanderthals and Cro-Magnons as early groups of *Homo sapiens.* However, in 1997, DNA tests on a Neanderthal skeleton indicated that Neanderthals were not ancestors of modern humans. They were, however, affected by the arrival of Cro-Magnons, who may have competed with Neanderthals for land and food.

Neanderthals' Way of Life In 1856, as quarry workers were digging for limestone in the Neander Valley in Germany, they spotted fossilized bone fragments. These were the remains of Neanderthals, whose bones were discovered elsewhere in Europe and Southwest Asia. These people were powerfully built. They had heavy slanted brows, well-developed muscles, and thick bones. To many people, the name "Neanderthal" calls up the comic-strip image of a club-carrying caveman. However, archaeological discoveries reveal a more realistic picture of these early hominids, who lived between 200,000 and 30,000 years ago.

Evidence suggests that Neanderthals tried to explain and control their world. They developed religious beliefs and performed rituals. About 60,000 years ago, Neanderthals held a funeral for a man in Shanidar Cave, located in northeastern Iraq. Some archaeologists theorize that during the funeral, the Neanderthal's family covered his body with flowers. This funeral points to a belief in a world beyond the grave. Fossil hunter Richard Leakey, the son of Louis and Mary Leakey, wrote about the meaning of this Neanderthal burial:

PRIMARY SOURCE

> The Shanidar events . . . speak clearly of a deep feeling for the spiritual quality of life. A concern for the fate of the human soul is universal in human societies today, and it was evidently a theme of Neanderthal society too.
>
> **RICHARD E. LEAKEY,** *The Making of Mankind*

Neanderthals were also resourceful. They survived harsh Ice Age winters by living in caves or temporary shelters made

History *in* Depth

Time Line of Planet Earth

Imagine the 102 stories of the Empire State Building as a scale for a time line of the earth's history. Each story represents about 40 million years. Modern human beings have existed for just a tiny percentage of the life of this planet.

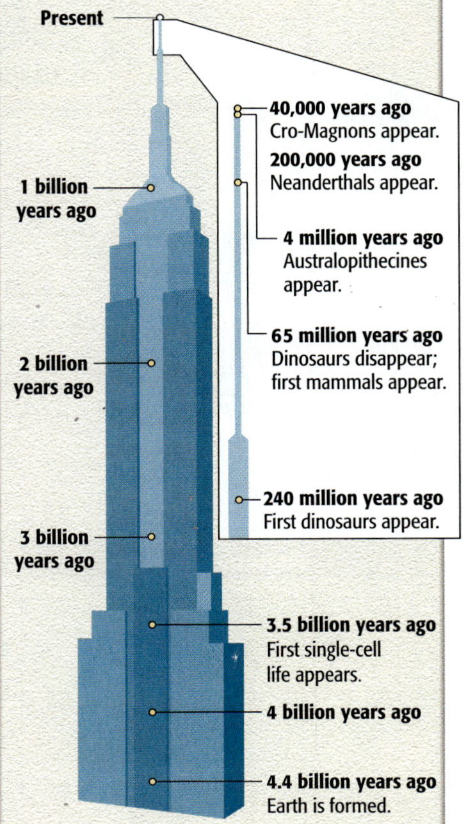

of wood and animal skins. Animal bones found with Neanderthal fossils indicate the ability of Neanderthals to hunt in subarctic regions of Europe. To cut up and skin their prey, they fashioned stone blades, scrapers, and other tools. The Neanderthals survived for some 170,000 years and then mysteriously vanished about 30,000 years ago. C

MAIN IDEA

Comparing

C How were Neanderthals similar to people today?

Cro-Magnons Emerge About 40,000 years ago, a group of prehistoric humans called Cro-Magnons appeared. Their skeletal remains show that they are identical to modern humans. The remains also indicate that they were probably strong and generally about five-and-one-half feet tall. Cro-Magnons migrated from North Africa to Europe and Asia.

Cro-Magnons made many new tools with specialized uses. Unlike Neanderthals, they planned their hunts. They studied animals' habits and stalked their prey. Evidently, Cro-Magnons' superior hunting strategies allowed them to survive more easily. This may have caused Cro-Magnon populations to grow at a slightly faster rate and eventually replace the Neanderthals. Cro-Magnons' advanced skill in spoken language may also have helped them to plan more difficult projects. This cooperation perhaps gave them an edge over the Neanderthals.

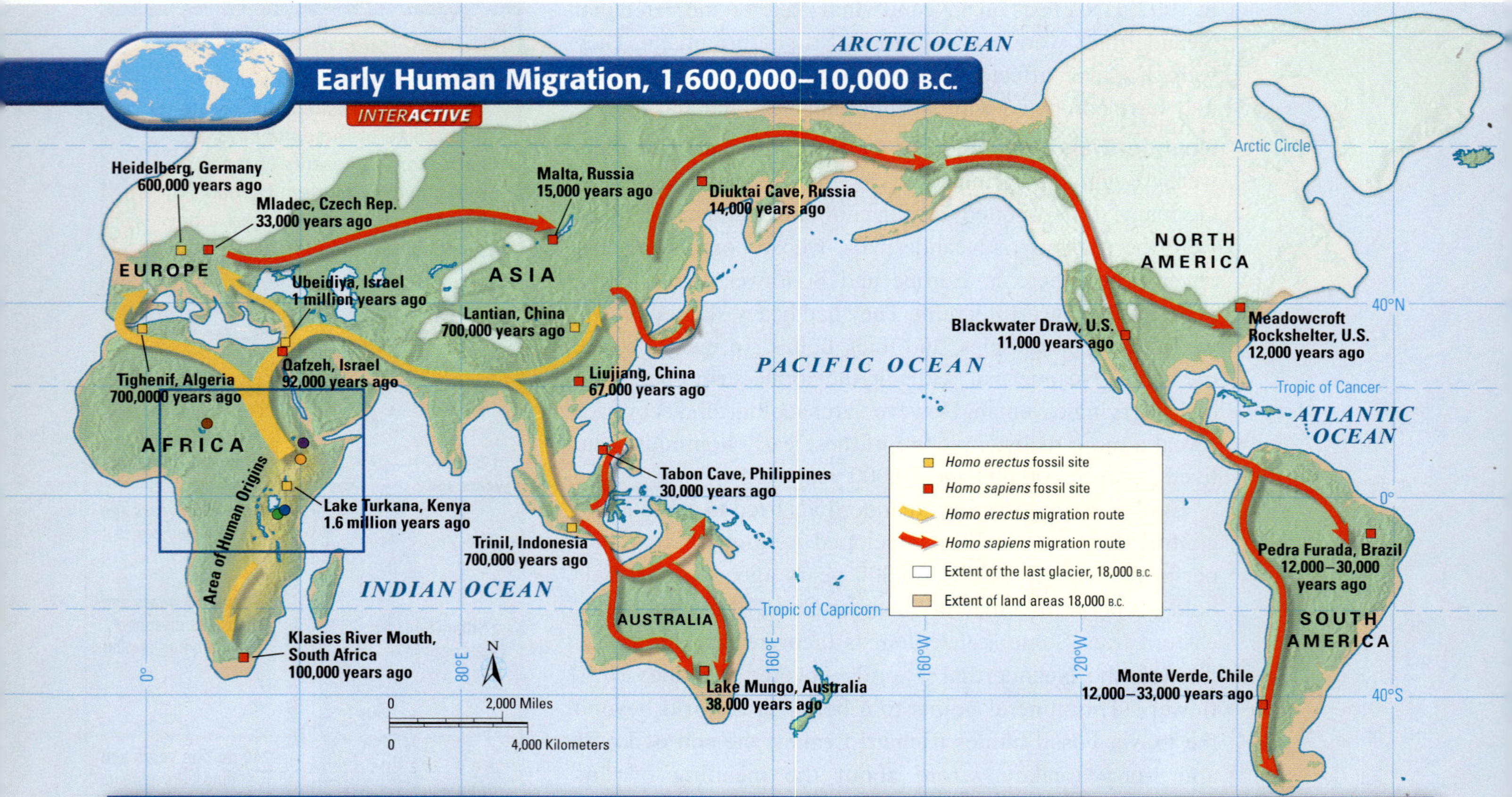

- **1960** At Olduvai Gorge, Tanzania, Louis Leakey finds 2-million-year-old **stone tools.**
- **1974** In Ethiopia, Donald Johanson finds "Lucy," a 3.5-million-year-old **hominid skeleton**.
- **1978** At Laetoli, Tanzania, Mary Leakey finds 3.6-million-year-old **hominid footprints.**
- **1994** In Ethiopia, an international team of scientists finds 2.33-million-year-old **hominid jaw.**
- **2002** In Chad, scientists announce discovery of a possible 6-million-year-old **hominid skull.**

GEOGRAPHY SKILLBUILDER: Interpreting Maps

1. **Movement** *To what continents did* Homo erectus *groups migrate after leaving Africa?*
2. **Human-Environment Interaction** *What do the migration routes of* Homo sapiens *reveal about their survival skills and ability to adapt?*

New Findings Add to Knowledge

Scientists are continuing to work at numerous sites in Africa. Their discoveries change our views of the still sketchy picture of human origins in Africa and of the migration of early humans out of Africa.

Fossils, Tools, and Cave Paintings Newly discovered fossils in Chad and Kenya, dating between 6 and 7 million years old, have some apelike features but also some that resemble hominids. Study of these fossils continues, but evidence suggests that they may be the earliest hominids. A 2.33-million-year-old jaw from Ethiopia is the oldest fossil belonging to the line leading to humans. Stone tools found at the same site suggest that toolmaking may have begun earlier than previously thought.

New discoveries also add to what we already know about prehistoric peoples. For example, in 1996, a team of researchers from Canada and the United States, including a high school student from New York, discovered a Neanderthal bone flute 43,000 to 82,000 years old. This discovery hints at a previously unknown talent of the Neanderthals—the gift of musical expression. The finding on cave walls of drawings of animals and people dating back as early as 35,000 years ago gives information on the daily activities and perhaps even religious practices of these peoples.

Early humans' skills and tools for surviving and adapting to the environment became more sophisticated as time passed. As you will read in Section 2, these technological advances would help launch a revolution in the way people lived.

Connect *to* Today

Chad Discovery

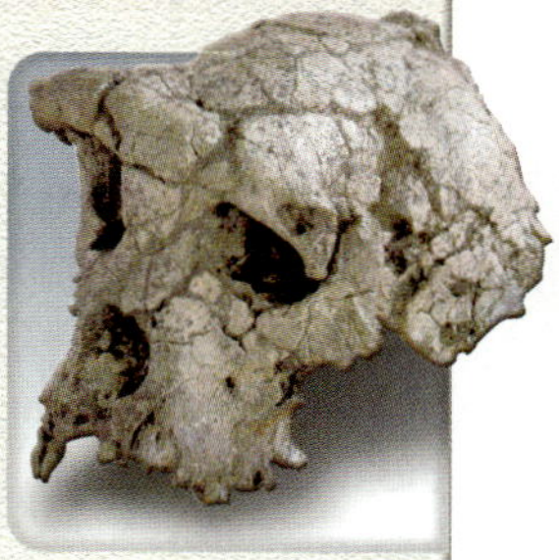

In 2002, an international team of scientists announced the discovery of a 6- to 7-million-year-old skull in northern Chad. The skull is similar in size to a modern chimpanzee, with a similar brain capacity. (See photograph.)

The team reported that the skull, nicknamed *Toumai,* or "hope of life," was the earliest human ancestor so far discovered. Its date is, in fact, millions of years older than the previous oldest-known hominid. The skull dates from the time that scientists believe the ancestors of humans split from the great apes.

Whether the skull is actually human

INTEGRATED TECHNOLOGY

INTERNET ACTIVITY Create a TV news special on the Chad skull. Include conflicting theories on its origin. Go to **classzone.com** for your research.

NEW YORK CORE CURRICULUM REVIEW

TERMS & NAMES 1. For each term or name, write a sentence explaining its significance.

- artifact
- culture
- hominid
- Paleolithic Age
- Neolithic Age
- technology
- *Homo sapiens*

USING YOUR NOTES

2. Which advance by a hominid group do you think was the most significant? Explain.

MAIN IDEAS

3. What clues do bones and artifacts give about early peoples?
4. What were the major achievements in human history during the Old Stone Age?
5. How did Neanderthals and Cro-Magnons differ from earlier peoples?

CRITICAL THINKING & WRITING

6. **RECOGNIZING EFFECTS** Why was the discovery of fire so important?
7. **MAKING INFERENCES** Why will specific details about the physical appearance and the customs of early peoples never be fully known?
8. **SYNTHESIZING** How do recent findings keep revising knowledge of the prehistoric past?
9. **WRITING ACTIVITY** INTERACTION WITH ENVIRONMENT Write a **persuasive essay** explaining which skill—toolmaking, the use of fire, or language—you think gave hominids the most control over their environment.

CONNECT TO TODAY **CREATING AN ILLUSTRATED NEWS ARTICLE**

Research a recent archaeological discovery. Write a two-paragraph **news article** about the find and include an illustration.

Cave Paintings

Cave paintings created by primitive people are found on every continent. The oldest ones were made about 35,000 years ago. Cave paintings in Europe and Africa often show images of hunting and daily activities. In the Americas and Australia, on the other hand, the paintings tend to be more symbolic and less realistic.

Scholars are not sure about the purpose of cave paintings. They may have been part of magical rites, hunting rituals, or an attempt to mark the events during various seasons. Another theory is that cave paintings (especially the more realistic ones) may simply be depictions of the surrounding world.

INTEGRATED TECHNOLOGY

RESEARCH LINKS For more on cave paintings, go to **classzone.com**

▼ Cave Paintings at Tassili n'Ajer, Algeria

These paintings depict women, children, and cattle. Located in Algeria, the Tassili n'Ajer (tah•SEEL•ee nah• ZHEER) site contains more than 15,000 images. They depict shifts in climate, animal migrations, and changes in human life. The oldest paintings date back to about 6000 B.C. Images continued to be painted until around the second century A.D.

▼ Cave Paintings at *Cuevas de las Manos* in Argentina

Cuevas de las Manos (Cave of the Hands) is located in the Rio Pinturas ravine, northeast of Santa Cruz, Argentina. Its rock walls display numerous hand paintings in vivid colors. The Tehuelches (tuh•WEHL•cheez) people created the paintings between 13,000 and 9,500 years ago. The cave is about 78 feet deep and, at the entrance, about 48 feet wide and 32 feet high.

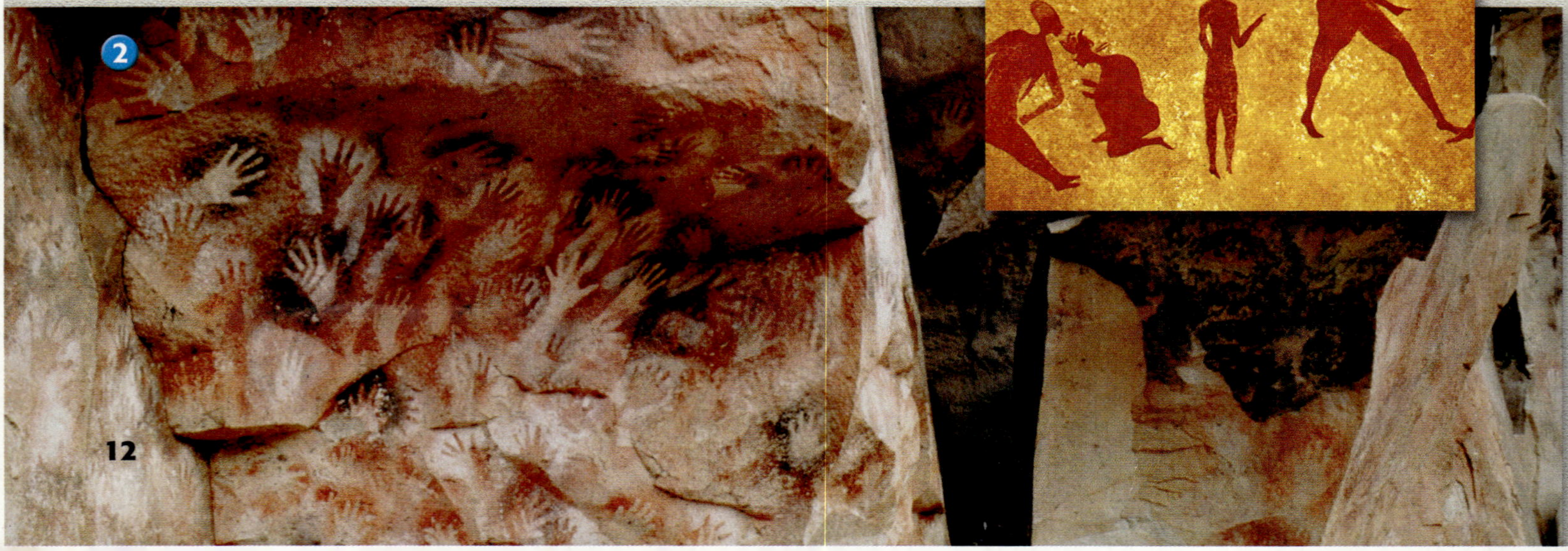

▲ **Replica of Lascaux Cave Painting, France**
Discovered in 1940 , the Lascaux (lah•SKOH) cave contains more than 600 painted animals and symbols. These works were probably created between 15,000 and 13,000 B.C. In 1963, the cave was closed to the public. The high volume of visitors and the use of artificial lighting were damaging the paintings. A partial replica of the cave was created and is visited by about 300,000 people a year.

▲ **Australian Aboriginal Cave Painting**
This Aboriginal cave painting is in Kakadu (KAH•kuh•doo) National Park, Australia. Aboriginal people have lived in this area for at least 25,000 years. The painting depicts a Barramundi (bahr•uh•MUHN•dee) fish and a Dreamtime spirit. In the Aboriginal culture, Dreamtime is a supernatural past in which ancestral beings shaped and humanized the natural world.

Connect *to* Today

1. **Analyzing Motives** Why do you think primitive peoples used the walls of caves for their paintings?
   See Skillbuilder Handbook, page R15.
2. **Comparing and Contrasting** How are these paintings similar to or different from public murals created today?

Humans Try to Control Nature

CONNECT TO THE NEW YORK STATE CORE CURRICULUM

Unit 1.A.1. Human and physical geography
Unit 1.A.3. Relationship to the environment

TERMS & NAMES

- nomad
- hunter-gatherer
- Neolithic Revolution
- slash-and-burn farming
- domestication

SETTING THE STAGE By about 40,000 years ago, human beings had become fully modern in their physical appearance. With a shave, a haircut, and a suit, a Cro-Magnon man would have looked like a modern business executive. However, over the following thousands of years, the way of life of early humans underwent incredible changes. People developed new technology, artistic skills, and most importantly, agriculture.

TAKING NOTES

Outlining Use an outline to organize main ideas and details.

Humans Try to Control Nature

I. Early Advances in Technology and Art
A.
B.
II. The Beginnings of Agriculture

Early Advances in Technology and Art

Early modern humans quickly distinguished themselves from their ancestors, who had spent most of their time just surviving. As inventors and artists, more advanced humans stepped up the pace of cultural changes.

Tools Needed to Survive For tens of thousands of years, men and women of the Old Stone Age were nomads. **Nomads** were highly mobile people who moved from place to place foraging, or searching, for new sources of food. Nomadic groups whose food supply depends on hunting animals and collecting plant foods are called **hunter-gatherers**. Prehistoric hunter-gatherers, such as roving bands of Cro-Magnons, increased their food supply by inventing tools. For example, hunters crafted special spears that enabled them to kill game at greater distances. Digging sticks helped food gatherers pry plants loose at the roots.

Early modern humans had launched a technological revolution. They used stone, bone, and wood to fashion more than 100 different tools. These expanded tool kits included knives to kill and butcher game, and fish hooks and harpoons to catch fish. A chisel-like cutter was designed to make other tools. Cro-Magnons used bone needles to sew clothing made of animal hides.

Artistic Expression in the Paleolithic Age The tools of early modern humans explain how they met their survival needs. Yet their world best springs to life through their artistic creations. Necklaces of seashells, lion teeth, and bear claws adorned both men and women. People ground mammoth tusks into polished beads. They also carved small realistic sculptures of animals that inhabited their world.

As you read in the Cave Paintings feature, Stone Age peoples on all continents created cave paintings. The best-known of these are the paintings on the walls and ceilings of European caves, mainly in France and Spain. Here early artists drew lifelike images of wild animals. Cave artists made colored paints from charcoal, mud, and animal blood. In Africa, early artists engraved pictures on rocks or painted scenes in caves or rock shelters. In Australia, they created paintings on large rocks.

The Beginnings of Agriculture

Vocabulary
Edible means "safe to be eaten."

For thousands upon thousands of years, humans survived by hunting game and gathering edible plants. They lived in bands of 25 to 70 people. The men almost certainly did the hunting. The women gathered fruits, berries, roots, and grasses. Then about 10,000 years ago, some of the women may have scattered seeds near a regular campsite. When they returned the next season, they may have found new crops growing. This discovery would usher in the **Neolithic Revolution**, or the agricultural revolution—the far-reaching changes in human life resulting from the beginnings of farming. The shift from food-gathering to food-producing culture represents one of the great breakthroughs in history.

Causes of the Agricultural Revolution Scientists do not know exactly why the agricultural revolution occurred during this period. Change in climate was probably a key reason. (See chart on page 17.) Rising temperatures worldwide provided longer growing seasons and drier land for cultivating wild grasses. A rich supply of grain helped support a small population boom. As populations slowly rose, hunter-gatherers felt pressure to find new food sources. Farming offered an attractive alternative. Unlike hunting, it provided a steady source of food.

Early Farming Methods Some groups practiced **slash-and-burn farming**, in which they cut trees or grasses and burned them to clear a field. The ashes that remained fertilized the soil. Farmers planted crops for a year or two, then moved to another area of land. After several years, trees and grass grew back, and other farmers repeated the process of slashing and burning.

History *in* Depth

The Neolithic Ice Man

In 1991, two German hikers made an accidental discovery that gave archaeologists a firsthand look at the technology of early toolmakers. Near the border of Austria and Italy, they spotted the mummified body of a prehistoric traveler, preserved in ice for some 5,000 years (upper right).

Nicknamed the "Ice Man," this early human was not empty-handed. The tool kit found near him included a six-foot longbow and a deerskin case with 14 arrows. It also contained a stick with an antler tip for sharpening flint blades, a small flint dagger in a woven sheath, a copper ax, and a medicine bag.

Scientific research on the body (lower right) concluded that the Ice Man was in his 40s when he died in the late spring or early summer from an arrow wound. Scientists also determined that in the hours before his death, he ate wild goat, red deer, and grains. The Ice Man is housed in a special museum in Bolzano, Italy.

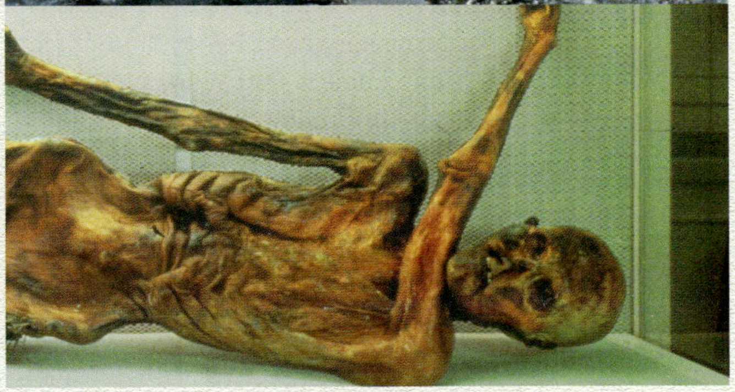

Domestication of Animals Food gatherers' understanding of plants probably spurred the development of farming. Meanwhile, hunters' expert knowledge of wild animals likely played a key role in the **domestication**, or taming, of animals. They tamed horses, dogs, goats, and pigs. Like farming, domestication of animals came slowly. Stone Age hunters may have driven herds of animals into rocky ravines to be slaughtered. It was then a small step to drive herds into human-made enclosures. From there, farmers could keep the animals as a constant source of food and gradually tame them.

Not only farmers domesticated animals. Pastoral nomads, or wandering herders, tended sheep, goats, camels, or other animals. These herders moved their animals to new pastures and watering places.

Agriculture in Jarmo Today, the eroded and barren rolling foothills of the Zagros Mountains in northeastern Iraq seem an unlikely site for the birthplace of agriculture. According to archaeologist Robert Braidwood, thousands of years ago the environmental conditions of this region favored the development of agriculture. Wild wheat and barley, along with wild goats, pigs, sheep, and horses, had once thrived near the Zagros Mountains.

In the 1950s, Braidwood led an archaeological dig at a site called Jarmo. He concluded that an agricultural settlement was built there about 9,000 years ago:

PRIMARY SOURCE (A)

We found weights for digging sticks, hoe-like [tools], flint-sickle blades, and a wide variety of milling stones. . . . We also discovered several pits that were probably used for the storage of grain. Perhaps the most important evidence of all was animal bones and the impressions left in the mud by cereal grains. . . . The people of Jarmo were adjusting themselves to a completely new way of life, just as we are adjusting ourselves to the consequences of such things as the steam engine. What they learned about living in a revolution may be of more than academic interest to us in our troubled times.

ROBERT BRAIDWOOD, quoted in *Scientific American*

MAIN IDEA

Analyzing Primary Sources

(A) Why do you think Braidwood believes that we can learn from early peoples?

The Jarmo farmers, and others like them in places as far apart as Mexico and Thailand, pioneered a new way of life. Villages such as Jarmo marked the beginning of a new era and laid the foundation for modern life.

Villages Grow and Prosper

The changeover from hunting and gathering to farming and herding took place not once but many times. Neolithic people in many parts of the world independently developed agriculture, as the map at the right shows.

Farming Develops in Many Places Within a few thousand years, people in many other regions, especially in fertile river valleys, turned to farming.

- **Africa** The Nile River Valley developed into an important agricultural center for growing wheat, barley, and other crops.
- **China** About 8,000 years ago, farmers along the middle stretches of the Huang He (Yellow River) cultivated a grain called millet. About 1,000 years later, farmers first domesticated wild rice in the Chang Jiang River delta.
- **Mexico and Central America** Farmers cultivated corn, beans, and squash.
- **Peru** Farmers in the Central Andes were the first to grow tomatoes, sweet potatoes, and white potatoes.

From these early and varied centers of agriculture, farming then spread to surrounding regions. (B)

MAIN IDEA

Making Inferences

(B) What advantages might farming and herding have over hunting and gathering?

Agriculture Emerges, 5000–500 B.C.

INTERACTIVE

▲ A Neolithic grindstone and vessel used to grind grain

Agricultural Revolution

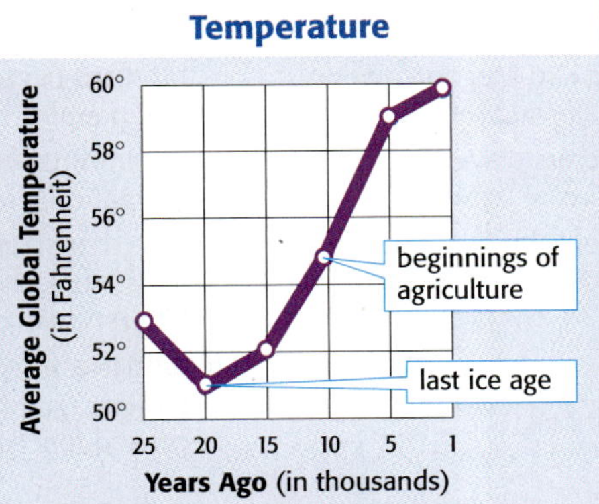

Source: *Ice Ages, Solving the Mystery*

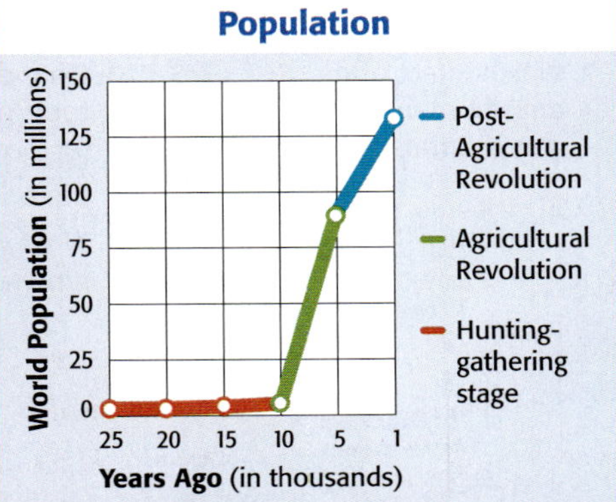

Source: *A Geography of Population: World Patterns*

SKILLBUILDER: Interpreting Maps and Charts

1. **Map** *What geographic feature favored the development of agricultural areas before 5000 B.C.?*
2. **Chart** *What effect did the agricultural revolution have on population growth? Why?*

Catal Huyuk In 1958, archaeologists discovered the agricultural village now known as Catal Huyuk (chuh•TUL-hoo•YOOK), or the "forked mound." It was located on a fertile plain in south-central Turkey (about 30 miles from modern-day Konya), near a twin-coned volcano. Catal Huyuk covered an area of about 32 acres. At its peak 8,000 years ago, the village was home to 5,000 to 6,000 people who lived in about 1,000 dwellings. These rectangular-shaped houses were made of brick and were arranged side-by-side like a honeycomb.

▼ A 9,000-year-old baked-clay figurine found in Catal Huyuk

Catal Huyuk showed the benefits of settled life. Its rich, well-watered soil produced large crops of wheat, barley, and peas. Villagers also raised sheep and cattle. Catal Huyuk's agricultural surpluses supported a number of highly skilled workers, such as potters and weavers. But the village was best known at the time for its obsidian products. This dark volcanic rock, which looks like glass, was plentiful. It was used to make mirrors, jewelry, and knives for trade.

Catal Huyuk's prosperity also supported a varied cultural life. Archaeologists have uncovered colorful wall paintings depicting animals and hunting scenes. Many religious shrines were dedicated to a mother goddess. According to her worshipers, she controlled the supply of grain.

Vocabulary
Shrines are places where sacred relics are kept.

The new settled way of life also had its drawbacks—some of the same that affected hunter-gatherer settlements. Floods, fire, drought, and other natural disasters could destroy a village. Diseases, such as malaria, spread easily among people living closely together. Jealous neighbors and roving nomadic bands might attack and loot a wealthy village like Catal Huyuk.

Despite problems, these permanent settlements provided their residents with opportunities for fulfillment—in work, in art, and in leisure time. As you will learn in Section 3, some early villages expanded into cities. These urban centers would become the setting for more complex cultures in which new tools, art, and crafts were created.

NEW YORK CORE CURRICULUM REVIEW

TERMS & NAMES 1. For each term or name, write a sentence explaining its significance.
• nomad • hunter-gatherer • Neolithic Revolution • slash-and-burn farming • domestication

USING YOUR NOTES

2. Which effect of the development of agriculture was the most significant?

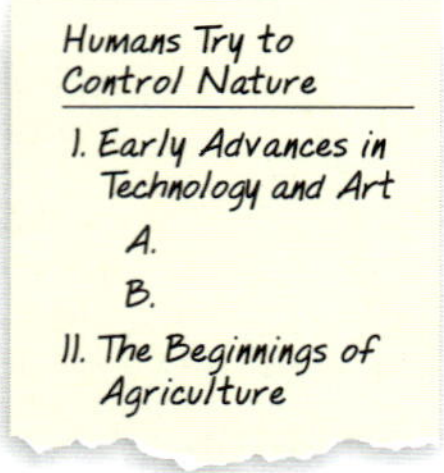

MAIN IDEAS

3. How did Cro-Magnon's new tools make survival easier?
4. What factors played a role in the origins of agriculture?
5. What were the first crops grown in the Americas?

CRITICAL THINKING & WRITING

6. **MAKING INFERENCES** What kinds of problems did Stone Age peoples face?
7. **SUMMARIZING** In what ways did Neolithic peoples dramatically improve their lives?
8. **HYPOTHESIZING** Why do you think the development of agriculture occurred around the same time in several different places?
9. **WRITING ACTIVITY** SCIENCE AND TECHNOLOGY Write a two-paragraph **opinion paper** on the most significant consequences of the Agricultural Revolution.

CONNECT TO TODAY **CREATING A CHART**
Use text information on Jarmo and Catal Huyuk to make a **chart** listing the tools, weapons, and other artifacts that archaeologists today might find at an ancient site of a farming settlement.

3

Civilization

Case Study: Ur in Sumer

CONNECT TO THE NEW YORK STATE CORE CURRICULUM

Unit 1.A.5.c. Move toward more complex government system
Unit 1.B.1.a. Human and physical geography of early river civilizations

TERMS & NAMES

- civilization
- specialization
- artisan
- institution
- scribe
- cuneiform
- Bronze Age
- barter
- ziggurat

SETTING THE STAGE Agriculture marked a dramatic change in how people lived together. They began dwelling in larger, more organized communities, such as farming villages and towns. From some of these settlements, cities gradually emerged, forming the backdrop of a more complex way of life—civilization.

TAKING NOTES
Summarizing Use a chart to summarize characteristics of the civilization at Sumer.

Characteristics
1.
2.
3.
4.
5.

Villages Grow into Cities

Over the centuries, people settled in stable communities that were based on agriculture. Domesticated animals became more common. The invention of new tools—hoes, sickles, and plow sticks—made the task of farming easier. As people gradually developed the technology to control their natural environment, they reaped larger harvests. Settlements with a plentiful supply of food could support larger populations.

As the population of some early farming villages increased, social relationships became more complicated. The change from a nomadic hunting-gathering way of life to settled village life took a long time. Likewise, the change from village life to city life was a gradual process that spanned several generations.

Economic Changes To cultivate more land and to produce extra crops, ancient people in larger villages built elaborate irrigation systems. The resulting food surpluses freed some villagers to pursue other jobs and to develop skills besides farming. Individuals who learned to become craftspeople created valuable new products, such as pottery, metal objects, and woven cloth. In turn, people who became traders profited from a broader range of goods to exchange—craftwork, grains, and many raw materials. Two important inventions—the wheel and the sail—also enabled traders to move more goods over longer distances.

Social Changes A more complex and prosperous economy affected the social structure of village life. For example, building and operating large irrigation systems required the labor of many people. As other special groups of workers formed, social classes with varying wealth, power, and influence began to emerge. A system of social classes would become more clearly defined as cities grew.

Religion also became more organized. During the Old Stone Age, prehistoric people's religious beliefs centered around nature, animal spirits, and some idea of an afterlife. During the New Stone Age, farming peoples worshiped the many gods and goddesses who they believed had power over the rain, wind, and other forces of nature. Early city dwellers developed rituals founded on these earlier religious beliefs. As populations grew, common spiritual values became lasting religious traditions.

How Civilization Develops

Most historians believe that one of the first civilizations arose in Sumer. Sumer was located in Mesopotamia, a region that is part of modern Iraq. A **civilization** is often defined as a complex culture with five characteristics: (1) advanced cities, (2) specialized workers, (3) complex institutions, (4) record keeping, and (5) advanced technology. Just what set the Sumerians apart from their neighbors?

Advanced Cities Cities were the birthplaces of the first civilizations. A city is more than a large group of people living together. The size of the population alone does not distinguish a village from a city. One of the key differences is that a city is a center of trade for a larger area. Like their modern-day counterparts, ancient city dwellers depended on trade. Farmers, merchants, and traders brought goods to market in the cities. The city dwellers themselves produced a variety of goods for exchange.

Specialized Workers As cities grew, so did the need for more specialized workers, such as traders, government officials, and priests. Food surpluses provided the opportunity for **specialization**—the development of skills in a specific kind of work. An abundant food supply allowed some people to become expert at jobs besides farming. Some city dwellers became **artisans**—skilled workers who make goods by hand. Specialization helped artisans develop their skill at designing jewelry, fashioning metal tools and weapons, or making clothing and pottery. The wide range of crafts artisans produced helped cities become centers of trade.

Complex Institutions The soaring populations of early cities made government, or a system of ruling, necessary. In civilizations, leaders emerged to maintain order among people and to establish laws. Government is an example of an **institution**—a long-lasting pattern of organization in a community. Complex institutions, such as government, religion, and the economy, are another characteristic of civilization.

With the growth of cities, religion became a formal institution. Most cities had great temples where dozens of priests took charge of religious duties. Sumerians believed that every city belonged to a god who governed the city's activities. The temple was the hub of both government and religious affairs. It also served as the city's economic center. There food and trade items were distributed. (A)

MAIN IDEA

Drawing Conclusions

(A) Why were cities essential to the growth of civilizations?

Record Keeping As government, religion, and the economy became more complex, people recognized the need to keep records. In early civilizations, government officials had to document tax collections, the passage of laws, and the storage of grain. Priests needed a way to keep track of the calendar and important rituals. Merchants had to record accounts of debts and payments.

Most civilizations developed a system of writing, though some devised other methods of record keeping. Around 3000 B.C., Sumerian **scribes**—or professional record keepers—invented a system of writing called **cuneiform** (KYOO•nee•uh•FAWRM), meaning "wedge-shaped." (Earlier Sumerian writing consisted of pictographs—symbols of the

Global Patterns

The Incan System of Record Keeping

Early civilizations other than Sumer also developed record keeping. The empire of the ancient Incan civilization stretched along the western coast of South America. Though the Inca had no writing system, they kept records using a *quipu*, a set of colored strings tied with different-size knots at various intervals (see photograph). Each knot represented a certain amount or its multiple. The colors of each cord represented the item being counted: people, animals, land, and so on.

The *quipucamayoc*, officials who knew how to use the *quipu*, kept records of births, deaths, marriages, crops, and historical events.

objects or what they represented.) The scribe's tool, called a stylus, was a sharpened reed with a wedge-shaped point. It was pressed into moist clay to create symbols. Scribes baked their clay tablets in the sun to preserve the writing.

People soon began to use writing for other purposes besides record keeping. They also wrote about their cities' dramatic events—wars, natural disasters, the reign of kings. Thus, the beginning of civilization in Sumer also signaled the beginning of written history.

Improved Technology New tools and techniques are always needed to solve problems that emerge when large groups of people live together. In early civilizations, some farmers harnessed the powers of animals and nature. For example, they used ox-drawn plows to turn the soil. They also created irrigation systems to expand planting areas.

Sumerian artisans relied on new technology to make their tasks easier. Around 3500 B.C., they first used the potter's wheel to shape jugs, plates, and bowls. Sumerian metalworkers discovered that melting together certain amounts of copper and tin made bronze. After 2500 B.C., metalworkers in Sumer's cities turned out bronze spearheads by the thousands. The period called the **Bronze Age** refers to the time when people began using bronze, rather than copper and stone, to fashion tools and weapons. The Bronze Age started in Sumer around 3000 B.C., but the date varied in other parts of Asia and in Europe.

▲ The wedge-shaped symbols of cuneiform are visible on this clay tablet.

> Analyzing Key Concepts

Civilization

As the history of Sumer demonstrates, civilization first developed in cities. In fact, the very word *civilization* comes from the Latin word for citizen. However, the development of cities is only one aspect of civilization. Many scholars define civilization as a complex culture with five characteristics. The graphic organizer to the right shows how Sumer displayed these five characteristics.

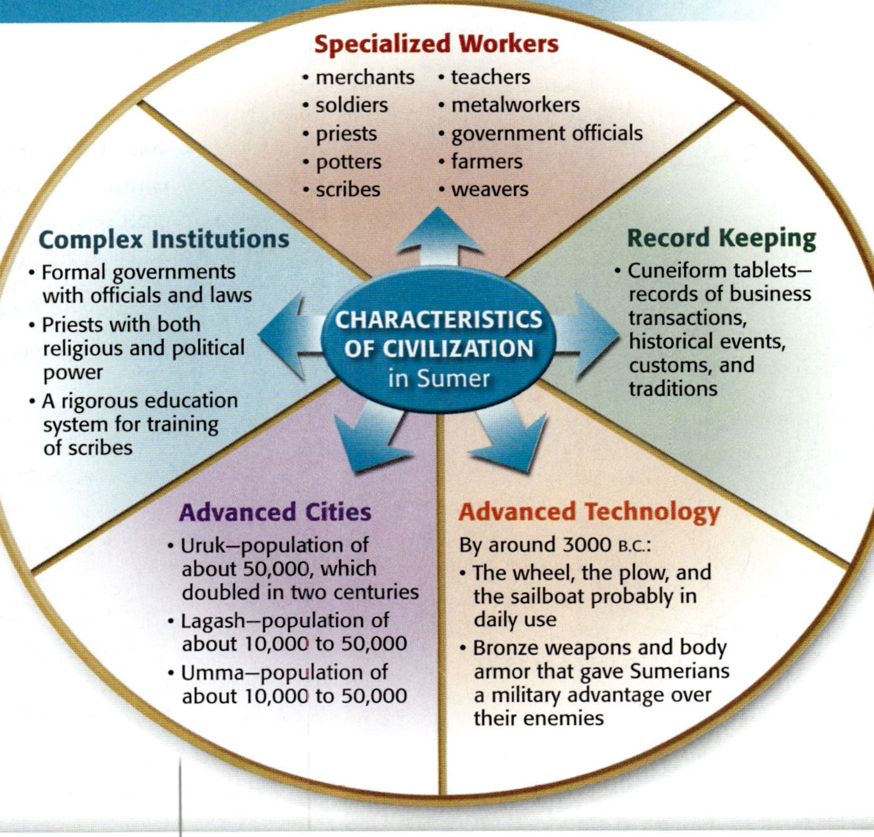

SKILLBUILDER:
Interpreting Graphics

1. **Making Inferences** *Judging from the information on this graphic, what economic activities probably took place in Sumerian cities?*
2. **Drawing Conclusions** *What is the relationship between the development of specialized workers and the development of complex institutions?*

Civilization Emerges in Ur

Ur, one of the earliest cities in Sumer, stood on the banks of the Euphrates River in what is now southern Iraq. Some 30,000 people once lived in this ancient city. Ur was the site of a highly sophisticated civilization.

After excavating from 1922 to 1934, English archaeologist Leonard Woolley and his team unraveled the mystery of this long-lost civilization. From archaeological evidence, Woolley concluded that around 3000 B.C., Ur was a flourishing urban civilization. People in Ur lived in well-defined social classes. Rulers, as well as priests and priestesses, wielded great power. Wealthy merchants profited from foreign trade. Artists and artisans created lavish jewelry, musical instruments, and gold daggers. Woolley's finds have enabled historians to reconstruct Ur's advanced culture.

An Agricultural Economy Imagine a time nearly 5,000 years ago. Outside the mud-brick walls surrounding Ur, ox-driven plows cultivate the fields. People are working barefoot in the irrigation ditches that run between patches of green plants. With stone hoes, the workers widen ditches to carry water into their fields from the reservoir a mile away. This large-scale irrigation system was developed to provide Ur with food surpluses, which keep the economy thriving. The government officials who direct this public works project ensure its smooth operation. **B**

MAIN IDEA

Analyzing Causes

B How did Ur's agricultural way of life foster the development of civilization there?

Life in the City A broad dirt road leads from the fields to the city's wall. Inside, city dwellers go about their daily lives. Most live in windowless, one-story, boxlike houses packed tightly along the street. A few wealthy families live in two-story houses with an inner courtyard.

Down another street, artisans work in their shops. A metalworker makes bronze by mixing molten copper with just the right quantity of tin. Later, he will hammer the bronze to make spearheads—weapons to help Ur's well-organized armies

The City of Ur

INTERACTIVE

▲ Aerial photograph of Ur taken in 1930.

1. **Ziggurat** A massive temple
2. **Court of Nanna** Sacred place of Ur's moon god
3. **Home of the High Priestess** Place where a woman with great religious authority lived
4. **Surrounding Wall** Defense for protecting Ur residents
5. **Temple and Treasury** Administrative centers in Ur
6. **Royal Cemetery** Burial site of the queen and king of Ur

NEW YORK STATE REGENTS EXAM PRACTICE

Use the quotation and your knowledge of world history to answer questions 1 and 2.
Additional Test Practice, pp. S1–S33

PRIMARY SOURCE

Litter of the past is the basis of archaeology. The coins, the pottery, the textiles and the buildings of bygone eras offer us clues as to how our [early ancestors] behaved, how they ran their economy, what they believed in and what was important to them. What archaeologists retrieve from excavations are images of past lives. . . . [These images] are pieced together slowly and painstakingly from the information contained in objects found.

RICHARD LEAKEY in *The Making of Mankind*

1 According to Richard Leakey, what is the job of the archaeologist?
(1) to study coins to learn about an economy
(2) to clean out caves where early ancestors lived
(3) to create images of coins, pottery, and textiles
(4) to examine artifacts found at a location

2 What term applies to the behaviors, economic activities, and beliefs referred to by Richard Leakey?
(1) culture
(2) civilization
(3) case study
(4) artifacts

Use the illustration of the Stone Age cave painting from Argentina and your knowledge of world history to answer question 3.

3 What information might an archaeologist learn from this painting?
(1) the height of the humans living in the region
(2) the names of gods worshiped here
(3) types of animals found in the region
(4) the time of year this cave was visited

INTEGRATED TECHNOLOGY

TEST PRACTICE Go to **classzone.com**
- Diagnostic tests
- Tutorials
- Strategies
- Additional practice

ALTERNATIVE ASSESSMENT

1. Interact *with* History

INTERACTION WITH ENVIRONMENT On page 4, you played the role of an amateur archaeologist as you tried to figure out the uses of some prehistoric tools. Now that you've read the chapter, what new clues have you discovered that would help you unravel the mystery of who made the tool with the wedge-shaped blade, and why? What evidence can you use to support your conclusions about its purpose? Discuss your ideas with a small group.

2. WRITING ABOUT HISTORY

Consider the religious practices of the Neanderthals, the villagers of Catal Huyuk, and the city dwellers of Ur. Write a two-paragraph **essay** analyzing the development of religious beliefs over the course of the Stone Age. In your essay, consider the archaeological evidence that supports the scientific conclusions about beliefs, practices, and organization.

INTEGRATED TECHNOLOGY

NetExplorations: Cave Art

Go to *NetExplorations* at **classzone.com** to learn more about prehistoric cave art. Search the Internet for other examples of cave art—start with the list of sites at *NetExplorations* —and use some of the examples to create an online or classroom exhibit. Create a log and ask visitors to the exhibit to answer questions such as:
- What do you see in each cave art example?
- What do the materials used, the subject matter, and the style of each example suggest about the lives of prehistoric people?
- How does prehistoric art help historians learn about the people who created it?

CHAPTER 2

Early River Valley Civilizations, 3500 B.C.–450 B.C.

Previewing Main Ideas

INTERACTION WITH ENVIRONMENT The earliest civilizations formed on fertile river plains. These lands faced challenges, such as seasonal flooding and a limited growing area.

Geography *What rivers helped sustain the four river valley civilizations?*

POWER AND AUTHORITY Projects such as irrigation systems required leadership and laws—the beginnings of organized government. In some societies, priests controlled the first governments. In others, military leaders and kings ruled.

Geography *Look at the time line and the map. In which empire and river valley area was the first code of laws developed?*

SCIENCE AND TECHNOLOGY Early civilizations developed bronze tools, the wheel, the sail, the plow, writing, and mathematics. These innovations spread through trade, wars, and the movement of peoples.

Geography *Which river valley civilization was the most isolated? What factors contributed to that isolation?*

NEW YORK CORE CURRICULUM FOCUS

- Early civilizations created governments ruled by priests, military leaders, or kings.
- The Babylonians produced the Code of Hammurabi, a list of 282 laws.

INTEGRATED TECHNOLOGY

eEdition
- Interactive Maps
- Interactive Visuals
- Interactive Primary Sources

INTERNET RESOURCES

Go to **classzone.com** for:
- Research Links
- Internet Activities
- Primary Sources
- Chapter Quiz
- Maps
- Test Practice
- Current Events

WORLD 3500 B.C. — 2500 B.C.

3000 B.C. City-states form in Sumer, Mesopotamia. (bronze head of an Akkadian ruler)

2660 B.C. Egypt's Old Kingdom develops. (Egyptian scribe statue)

Four River Valley Civilizations

1792 B.C.
Hammurabi develops code of laws for Babylonian Empire.

1027 B.C.
Zhou Dynasty forms in China. (Zhou bronze vessel) ▶

1500 B.C.

500 B.C.

1750 B.C.
◀ Indus Valley civilization declines. (fragment of a Harappan pot)

Interact *with* History

Why do communities need laws?

The harvest has failed and, like many others, you have little to eat. There are animals in the temple, but they are protected by law. Your cousin decides to steal one of the pigs to feed his family. You believe that laws should not be broken and try to persuade him not to steal the pig. But he steals the pig and is caught.

The law of the Babylonian Empire—Hammurabi's Code—holds people responsible for their actions. Someone who steals from the temple must repay 30 times the cost of the stolen item. Because your cousin is unable to pay this fine, he is sentenced to death. You begin to wonder whether there are times when laws should be broken.

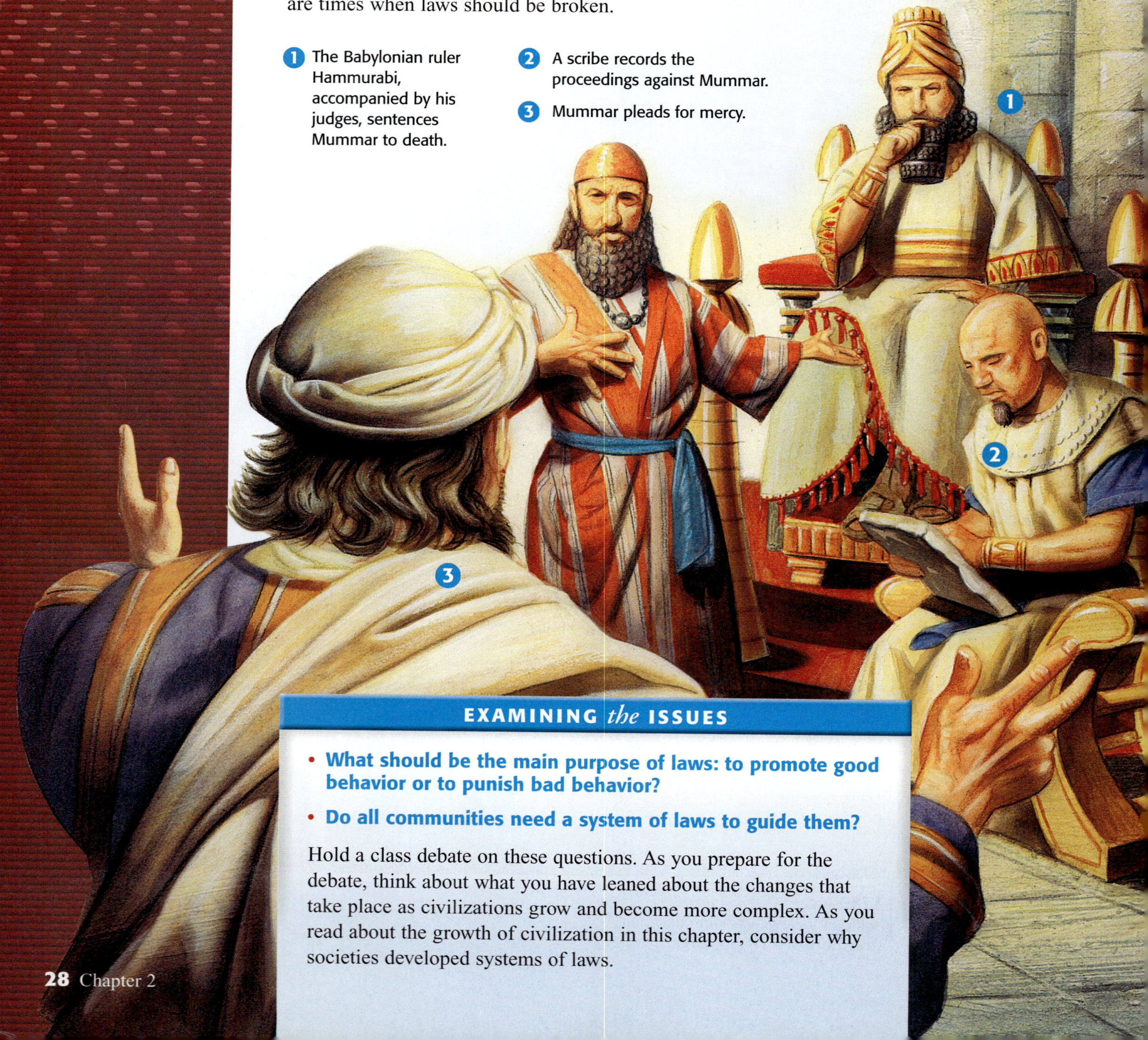

1. The Babylonian ruler Hammurabi, accompanied by his judges, sentences Mummar to death.
2. A scribe records the proceedings against Mummar.
3. Mummar pleads for mercy.

EXAMINING *the* ISSUES

- **What should be the main purpose of laws: to promote good behavior or to punish bad behavior?**
- **Do all communities need a system of laws to guide them?**

Hold a class debate on these questions. As you prepare for the debate, think about what you have leaned about the changes that take place as civilizations grow and become more complex. As you read about the growth of civilization in this chapter, consider why societies developed systems of laws.

City-States in Mesopotamia

CONNECT TO THE NEW YORK STATE CORE CURRICULUM

Unit 1.B.1.a. Human and physical geography of early river civilizations
Unit 1.B.1.e.5. Legal systems–Code of Hammurabi

TERMS & NAMES

- Fertile Crescent
- Mesopotamia
- city-state
- dynasty
- cultural diffusion
- polytheism
- empire
- Hammurabi

SETTING THE STAGE Two rivers flow from the mountains of what is now Turkey, down through Syria and Iraq, and finally to the Persian Gulf. Over six thousand years ago, the waters of these rivers provided the lifeblood that allowed the formation of farming settlements. These grew into villages and then cities.

Geography of the Fertile Crescent

A desert climate dominates the landscape between the Persian Gulf and the Mediterranean Sea in Southwest Asia. Yet within this dry region lies an arc of land that provided some of the best farming in Southwest Asia. The region's curved shape and the richness of its land led scholars to call it the **Fertile Crescent**. It includes the lands facing the Mediterranean Sea and a plain that became known as **Mesopotamia** (MEHS•uh•puh•TAY•mee•uh). The word in Greek means "land between the rivers."

The rivers framing Mesopotamia are the Tigris (TY•grihs) and Euphrates (yoo•FRAY•teez). They flow southeastward to the Persian Gulf. (See the map on page 30.) The Tigris and Euphrates rivers flooded Mesopotamia at least once a year. As the floodwater receded, it left a thick bed of mud called silt. Farmers planted grain in this rich, new soil and irrigated the fields with river water. The results were large quantities of wheat and barley at harvest time. The surpluses from their harvests allowed villages to grow.

TAKING NOTES

Identifying Problems and Solutions Use a chart to identify Sumer's environmental problems and their solutions.

Problems	Solutions
1.	1.
2.	2.
3.	3.

Environmental Challenges People first began to settle and farm the flat, swampy lands in southern Mesopotamia before 4500 B.C. Around 3300 B.C., the people called the Sumerians, whom you read about in Chapter 1, arrived on the scene. Good soil was the advantage that attracted these settlers. However, there were three disadvantages to their new environment.

- Unpredictable flooding combined with a period of little or no rain. The land sometimes became almost a desert.
- With no natural barriers for protection, a Sumerian village was nearly defenseless.
- The natural resources of Sumer were limited. Building materials and other necessary items were scarce.

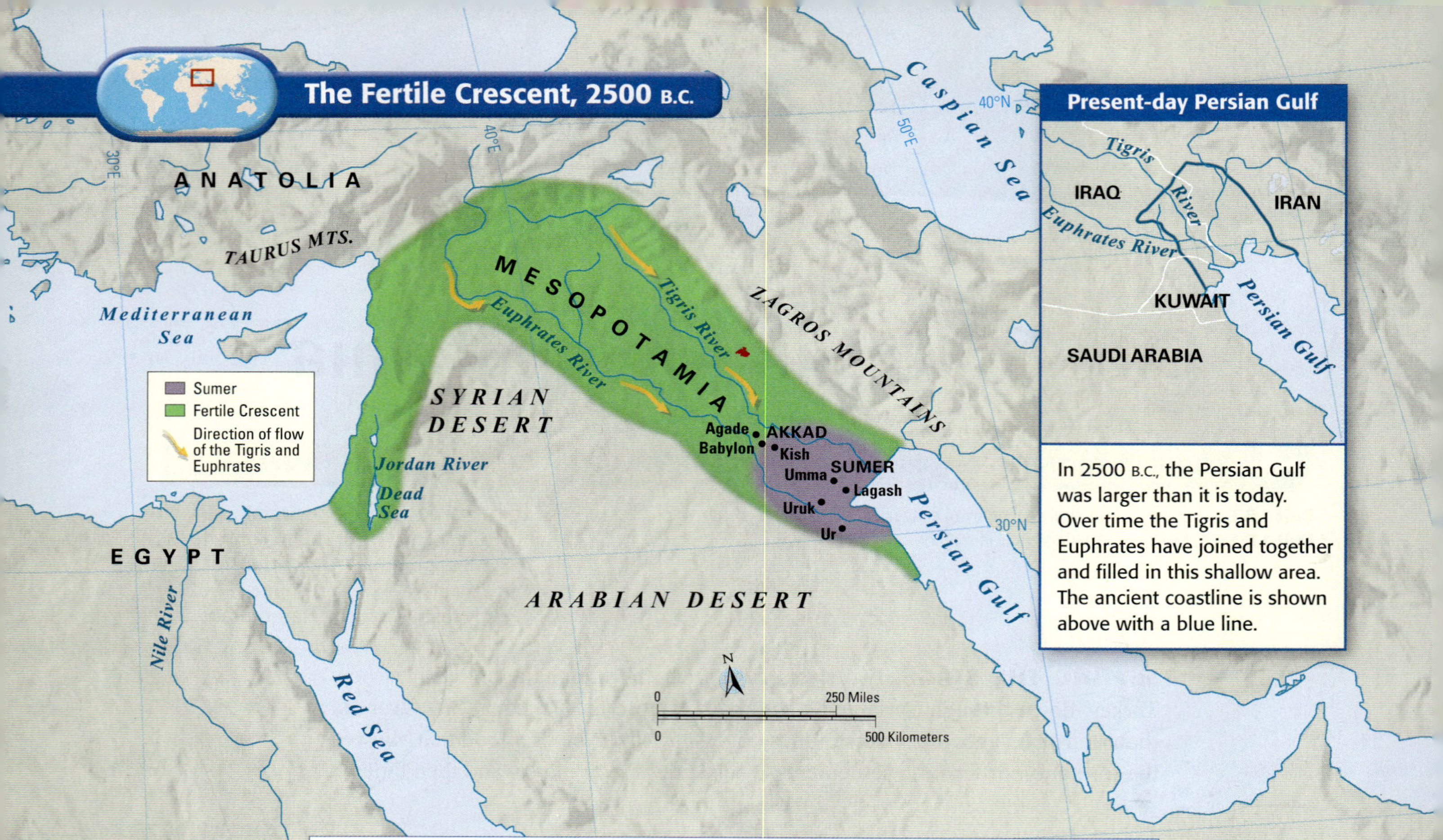

GEOGRAPHY SKILLBUILDER: Interpreting Maps

1. **Location** *Where are the Tigris and Euphrates River valleys found?*
2. **Place** *What is the most likely cause of the change in the Persian Gulf coastline?*

Solving Problems Through Organization Over a long period of time, the people of Sumer created solutions to deal with these problems.

- To provide water, they dug irrigation ditches that carried river water to their fields and allowed them to produce a surplus of crops.
- For defense, they built city walls with mud bricks.
- Sumerians traded their grain, cloth, and crafted tools with the peoples of the mountains and the desert. In exchange, they received raw materials such as stone, wood, and metal.

These activities required organization, cooperation, and leadership. It took many people working together, for example, for the Sumerians to construct their large irrigation systems. Leaders were needed to plan the projects and supervise the digging. These projects also created a need for laws to settle disputes over how land and water would be distributed. These leaders and laws were the beginning of organized government—and eventually of civilization. (A)

MAIN IDEA

Summarizing

(A) What are three solutions to the environmental challenges of Mesopotamia?

Sumerians Create City-States

The Sumerians stand out in history as one of the first groups of people to form a civilization. As you learned in Chapter 1, five key characteristics set Sumer apart from earlier human societies: (1) advanced cities, (2) specialized workers, (3) complex institutions, (4) record keeping, and (5) improved technology. All the later peoples who lived in this region of the world built upon the innovations of Sumerian civilization.

By 3000 B.C., the Sumerians had built a number of cities, each surrounded by fields of barley and wheat. Although these cities shared the same culture, they developed their own governments, each with its own rulers. Each city and the surrounding land it controlled formed a **city-state**. A city-state functioned much as an independent country does today. Sumerian city-states included Uruk, Kish, Lagash, Umma, and Ur. As in Ur, the center of all Sumerian cities was the walled temple with a ziggurat in the middle. There the priests and rulers appealed to the gods for the well-being of the city-state.

Priests and Rulers Share Control Sumer's earliest governments were controlled by the temple priests. The farmers believed that the success of their crops depended upon the blessings of the gods, and the priests acted as go-betweens with the gods. In addition to being a place of worship, the ziggurat was like a city hall. (See page 22 for a ziggurat.) From the ziggurat the priests managed the irrigation system. Priests demanded a portion of every farmer's crop as taxes.

In time of war, however, the priests did not lead the city. Instead, the men of the city chose a tough fighter who could command the city's soldiers. At first, a commander's power ended as soon as the war was over. After 3000 B.C., wars between cities became more and more frequent. Gradually, Sumerian priests and people gave commanders permanent control of standing armies. **B**

MAIN IDEA

Analyzing Causes

B How did military leaders gain power in the city-states?

In time, some military leaders became full-time rulers. These rulers usually passed their power on to their sons, who eventually passed it on to their own heirs. Such a series of rulers from a single family is called a **dynasty**. After 2500 B.C., many Sumerian city-states came under the rule of dynasties.

The Spread of Cities Sumer's city-states grew prosperous from the surplus food produced on their farms. These surpluses allowed Sumerians to increase long-distance trade, exchanging the extra food and other goods for items they needed.

By 2500 B.C., new cities were arising all over the Fertile Crescent, in what is now Syria, northern Iraq, and Turkey. Sumerians exchanged products and ideas, such as living in cities, with neighboring cultures. This process in which a new idea or a product spreads from one culture to another is called **cultural diffusion**.

▼ Iku-Shamagen, King of Mari, a city-state in Sumer, offers prayers to the gods.

Sumerian Culture

The belief systems, social structure, technology, and arts of the Sumerians reflected their civilization's triumph over its dry and harsh environment.

A Religion of Many Gods Like many peoples in the Fertile Crescent, the Sumerians believed that many different gods controlled the various forces in nature. The belief in more than one god is called **polytheism** (PAHL•ee•thee•IHZ•uhm). Enlil, the god of storms and air, was among the most powerful gods. Sumerians feared him as "the raging flood that has no rival." Demons known as Ugallu protected humans from the evil demons who caused disease, misfortune, and misery.

Sumerians described their gods as doing many of the same things humans do—falling in love, having children, quarreling, and so on. Yet the Sumerians also believed that their gods were both immortal and all-powerful. Humans were nothing but their servants. At any moment, the mighty anger of the gods might strike, sending a fire, a flood, or an enemy to destroy a city. To keep the gods happy, the

▲ This gold and lapis ram with a shell fleece was found in a royal burial tomb.

Sumerians built impressive ziggurats for them and offered rich sacrifices of animals, food, and wine.

Sumerians worked hard to earn the gods' protection in this life. Yet they expected little help from the gods after death. The Sumerians believed that the souls of the dead went to the "land of no return," a dismal, gloomy place between the earth's crust and the ancient sea. No joy awaited souls there. A passage in a Sumerian poem describes the fate of dead souls: "Dust is their fare and clay their food."

Some of the richest accounts of Mesopotamian myths and legends appear in a long poem called the *Epic of Gilgamesh*. (See a selection from the Gilgamesh epic on page 83.)

Vocabulary
epic: a long heroic poem that tells the story of a historical or legendary figure

Life in Sumerian Society With civilization came the beginning of what we call social classes. Kings, landholders, and some priests made up the highest level in Sumerian society. Wealthy merchants ranked next. The vast majority of ordinary Sumerian people worked with their hands in fields and workshops. At the lowest level of Sumerian society were the slaves. Some slaves were foreigners who had been captured in war. Others were Sumerians who had been sold into slavery as children to pay the debts of their poor parents. Debt slaves could hope to eventually buy their freedom.

Social class affected the lives of both men and women. Sumerian women could work as merchants, farmers, or artisans. They could hold property in their own names. Women could also join the priesthood. Some upper-class women did learn to read and write, though Sumer's written records mention few female scribes. However, Sumerian women had more rights than women in many later civilizations.

Sumerian Science and Technology Historians believe that Sumerians invented the wheel, the sail, and the plow and that they were among the first to use bronze. Many new ideas and inventions arose from the Sumerians' practical needs.

- **Arithmetic and geometry** In order to erect city walls and buildings, plan irrigation systems, and survey flooded fields, Sumerians needed arithmetic and geometry. They developed a number system in base 60, from which stem the modern units for measuring time (60 seconds = 1 minute) and the 360 degrees of a circle.
- **Architectural innovations** Arches, columns, ramps, and the pyramid shaped the design of the ziggurat and permanently influenced Mesopotamian civilization.
- **Cuneiform** Sumerians created a system of writing. One of the first known maps was made on a clay tablet in about 2300 B.C. Other tablets contain some of the oldest written records of scientific investigations in the areas of astronomy, chemistry, and medicine.

The First Empire Builders

From 3000 to 2000 B.C., the city-states of Sumer were almost constantly at war with one another. The weakened city-states could no longer ward off attacks from the peoples of the surrounding deserts and hills. Although the Sumerians never recovered from the attacks on their cities, their civilization did not die. Succeeding sets of rulers adapted the basic ideas of Sumerian culture to meet their own needs.

Sargon of Akkad About 2350 B.C., a conqueror named Sargon defeated the city-states of Sumer. Sargon led his army from Akkad (AK•ad), a city-state north of Sumer. The Akkadians had long before adopted most aspects of Sumerian culture. Sargon's conquests helped to spread that culture even farther, beyond the Tigris-Euphrates Valley.

By taking control of both northern and southern Mesopotamia, Sargon created the world's first **empire**. An empire brings together several peoples, nations, or previously independent states under the control of one ruler. At its height, the Akkadian Empire loosely controlled land from the Mediterranean Coast in the west to present-day Iran in the east. Sargon's dynasty lasted only about 200 years, after which it declined due to internal fighting, invasions, and a famine. (C)

MAIN IDEA

Contrasting

(C) How does an empire differ from a city-state?

Babylonian Empire In about 2000 B.C., nomadic warriors known as Amorites invaded Mesopotamia. Gradually, the Amorites overwhelmed the Sumerians and established their capital at Babylon, on the Euphrates River. The Babylonian Empire reached its peak during the reign of **Hammurabi**, from 1792 B.C. to 1750 B.C. Hammurabi's most enduring legacy is the code of laws he put together.

Hammurabi's Code Hammurabi recognized that a single, uniform code of laws would help to unify the diverse groups within his empire. He collected existing rules, judgments, and laws into the Code of Hammurabi. Hammurabi had the code engraved in stone, and copies were placed all over his empire.

Analyzing Primary Sources

Hammurabi's Code of Laws

The image at the right shows the top of a pillar that had Hammurabi 's Code engraved on it. Hammurabi's law code prescribed punishments ranging from fines to death. Often the punishments were based on the social class of the victim. Here are some examples of the laws:

PRIMARY SOURCE

8. If a man has stolen an ox, a sheep, a pig, or a boat that belonged to a temple or palace, he shall repay thirty times its cost. If it belonged to a private citizen, he shall repay ten times. If the thief cannot pay, he shall be put to death.

142. If a woman hates her husband and says to him "You cannot be with me," the authorities in her district will investigate the case. If she has been chaste and without fault, even though her husband has neglected or belittled her, she will be held innocent and may return to her father's house.

143. If the woman is at fault, she shall be thrown into the river.

196. If a man put out the eye of another man, his eye shall be put out.

198. If he puts out the eye of freed man or break the bone of a free man, he shall pay one gold mina.

199. If he put out the eye of a man's slave, or break the bone of a man's slave, he shall pay one-half of its value.

CODE OF HAMMURABI, *adapted from a translation by L. W. King*

DOCUMENT-BASED QUESTIONS

1. **Making Inferences** *Why might the punishments for the crimes be based on social class?*
2. **Forming Opinions** *What do you think the value was in making the punishments for the crimes known to all?*

History Makers

Hammurabi
? –1750 B.C.

The noted lawgiver Hammurabi was also an able military leader, diplomat, and administrator of a vast empire. Hammurabi himself described some of his accomplishments:

> *As for the land of Sumer and Akkad, I collected the scattered peoples thereof, and I procured food and drink for them. In abundance and plenty I pastured them, and I caused them to dwell in peaceful habitation.*

INTEGRATED TECHNOLOGY

RESEARCH LINKS For more on Hammurabi, go to **classzone.com**

The code lists 282 specific laws dealing with everything that affected the community, including family relations, business conduct, and crime. Since many people were merchants, traders, or farmers, for example, many of the laws related to property issues. Additionally, the laws sought to protect women and children from unfair treatment. The laws tell us a great deal about the Mesopotamians' beliefs and what they valued.

Although the code applied to everyone, it set different punishments for rich and poor and for men and women. It frequently applied the principle of retaliation (an eye for an eye and a tooth for a tooth) to punish crimes.

The prologue of the code set out the goals for this body of law. It said, "To bring about the rule of righteousness in the land, to destroy the wicked and the evil-doers; so that the strong should not harm the weak." Thus, Hammurabi's Code reinforced the principle that government had a responsibility for what occurred in society. For example, if a man was robbed and the thief was not caught, the government was required to compensate the victim. **D**

MAIN IDEA

Recognizing Effects

D How did Hammurabi's law code advance civilization?

Nearly two centuries after Hammurabi's reign, the Babylonian Empire, which had become much smaller, fell to the neighboring Kassites. Over the years, new groups dominated the Fertile Crescent. Yet the later peoples, including the Assyrians, Phoenicians, and Hebrews, would adopt many ideas of the early Sumerians. Meanwhile, a similar pattern of development, rise, and fall was taking place to the west, along the Nile River in Egypt. Egyptian civilization is described in Section 2.

NEW YORK CORE CURRICULUM REVIEW

TERMS & NAMES **1.** For each term or name, write a sentence explaining its significance.

• Fertile Crescent • Mesopotamia • city-state • dynasty • cultural diffusion • polytheism • empire • Hammurabi

USING YOUR NOTES

2. Which of the problems you listed required the most complex solution? Explain.

Problems	Solutions
1.	1.
2.	2.
3.	3.

MAIN IDEAS

3. What were the three environmental challenges to Sumerians?

4. How did the Sumerians view the gods?

5. What areas of life did Hammurabi's Code cover?

CRITICAL THINKING & WRITING

6. DETERMINING MAIN IDEAS How was Sumerian culture spread throughout Mesopotamia?

7. RECOGNIZING EFFECTS Why is the development of a written code of laws important to a society?

8. ANALYZING CAUSES How did the need to interact with the environment lead to advances in civilization?

9. WRITING ACTIVITY POWER AND AUTHORITY What advantages did living in cities offer the people of ancient Mesopotamia? Do modern cities offer any of the same advantages? Write a **compare-and-contrast essay** supporting your answer with references to the text.

CONNECT TO TODAY **WRITING A STATUS REPORT**

Research the South East Anatolian Water Project in Turkey. The project will place dams on the Tigris and Euphrates rivers. Create a **map** and write a **status report** that summarizes the current status of the project.

Pyramids on the Nile

CONNECT TO THE NEW YORK STATE CORE CURRICULUM

Unit 1.B.1.a. Human and physical geography of early river civilizations
Unit 1.B.1.e.4. Architecture

TERMS & NAMES

- delta
- Narmer
- pharaoh
- theocracy
- pyramid
- mummification
- hieroglyphics
- papyrus

SETTING THE STAGE To the west of the Fertile Crescent in Africa, another river makes its way to the sea. While Sumerian civilization was on the rise, a similar process took place along the banks of this river, the Nile in Egypt. Yet the Egyptian civilization turned out to be very different from the collection of city-states in Mesopotamia. Early on, Egypt was united into a single kingdom, which allowed it to enjoy a high degree of unity, stability, and cultural continuity over a period of 3,000 years.

The Geography of Egypt

From the highlands of East Africa to the Mediterranean Sea, the Nile River flows northward across Africa for over 4,100 miles, making it the longest river in the world. (See the map on page 36.) A thin ribbon of water in a parched desert land, the great river brings its water to Egypt from distant mountains, plateaus, and lakes in present-day Burundi, Tanzania, Uganda, and Ethiopia.

Egypt's settlements arose along the Nile on a narrow strip of land made fertile by the river. The change from fertile soil to desert—from the Black Land to the Red Land—was so abrupt that a person could stand with one foot in each.

The Gift of the Nile As in Mesopotamia, yearly flooding brought the water and rich soil that allowed settlements to grow. Every year in July, rains and melting snow from the mountains of east Africa caused the Nile River to rise and spill over its banks. When the river receded in October, it left behind a rich deposit of fertile black mud called silt.

Before the scorching sun could dry out the soil, the peasants would prepare their wheat and barley fields. All fall and winter they watered their crops from a network of irrigation ditches.

In an otherwise parched land, the abundance brought by the Nile was so great that the Egyptians worshiped it as a god who gave life and seldom turned against them. As the ancient Greek historian Herodotus (hih•RAHD•uh•tuhs) remarked in the fifth century B.C., Egypt was the "gift of the Nile."

Environmental Challenges Egyptian farmers were much more fortunate than the villagers of Mesopotamia. Compared to the unpredictable Tigris and Euphrates rivers, the Nile was as regular as clockwork. Even so, life in Egypt had its risks.

TAKING NOTES

Summarizing Use a web diagram to summarize Egyptian achievements.

The Mighty Nile
The Landsat image (left) shows the Nile flowing into its delta. An outline of the continental United States (below) shows the length of the Nile's course. The actual length of the Nile with all its twists and turns is more than 4,100 miles.

GEOGRAPHY SKILLBUILDER: Interpreting Maps
1. **Movement** *In which direction does the Nile flow?*
2. **Location** *Describe the location of Upper Egypt and Lower Egypt.*

- When the Nile's floodwaters were just a few feet lower than normal, the amount of fresh silt and water for crops was greatly reduced. Thousands of people starved.
- When floodwaters were a few feet higher than usual, the unwanted water destroyed houses, granaries, and the precious seeds that farmers needed for planting.
- The vast and forbidding deserts on either side of the Nile acted as natural barriers between Egypt and other lands. They forced Egyptians to live on a very small portion of the land and reduced interaction with other peoples.

However, the deserts shut out invaders. For much of its early history, Egypt was spared the constant warfare that plagued the Fertile Crescent. (A)

MAIN IDEA
Contrasting
(A) What was the main difference between the flooding of the Nile and that of the rivers in Mesopotamia?

Upper Egypt and Lower Egypt Ancient Egyptians lived along the Nile from the mouth well into the interior of Africa. River travel was common, but it ended at the point in the Nile where boulders turn the river into churning rapids called a cataract (KAT•uh•rakt). This made it impossible for riverboats to pass this spot, known as the First Cataract, to continue upstream south to the interior of Africa.

Between the First Cataract and the Mediterranean lay two very different regions. Because its elevation is higher, the river area in the south is called Upper Egypt. It is a skinny strip of land from the First Cataract to the point where the river starts to fan out into many branches. To the north, near the sea, Lower Egypt includes the Nile **delta** region. The delta begins about 100 miles before the river enters the Mediterranean. The delta is a broad, marshy, triangular area of land formed by deposits of silt at the mouth of the river.

The Nile provided a reliable system of transportation between Upper and Lower Egypt. The Nile flows north, so northbound boats simply drifted with the current. Southbound boats hoisted a wide sail. The prevailing winds of Egypt blow from north to south, carrying sailboats against the river current. The ease of contact made possible by this watery highway helped unify Egypt's villages and promote trade.

Egypt Unites into a Kingdom

Egyptians lived in farming villages as far back as 5000 B.C., perhaps even earlier. Each village had its own rituals, gods, and chieftain. By 3200 B.C., the villages of Egypt were under the rule of two separate kingdoms, Lower Egypt and Upper Egypt. Eventually the two kingdoms were united. There is conflicting historical evidence over who united Upper and Lower Egypt. Some evidence points to a king called Scorpion. More solid evidence points to a king named **Narmer**.

The king of Lower Egypt wore a red crown, and the king of Upper Egypt wore a tall white crown shaped like a bowling pin. A carved piece of slate known as the Narmer Palette shows Narmer wearing the crown of Lower Egypt on one side and the crown of Upper Egypt on the other side. Some scholars believe the palette celebrates the unification of Egypt around 3000 B.C.

Narmer created a double crown from the red and white crowns. It symbolized a united kingdom. He shrewdly settled his capital, Memphis, near the spot where Upper and Lower Egypt met, and established the first Egyptian dynasty. Eventually, the history of ancient Egypt would consist of 31 dynasties, spanning 2,600 years. Historians suggest that the pattern for Egypt's great civilization was set during the period from 3200 to 2700 B.C. The period from 2660 to 2180 B.C., known as the Old Kingdom, marks a time when these patterns became widespread.

Connect *to* Today

Scorpion King

In 1999 Egyptologists discovered a series of carvings on a piece of rock about 18 by 20 inches. The tableau scene has symbols that may refer to a king named Scorpion.

The rock shows a figure carrying a staff. Near the head of the figure is a scorpion. Another artifact, a macehead, also shows a king with the scorpion symbol. Both artifacts suggest that Egyptian history may go back to around 3250 B.C. Some scholars believe the Scorpion is the earliest king to begin unification of Egypt, represented by the double crown shown below.

crown of Upper Egypt | **crown of Lower Egypt** | **crown of Upper and Lower Egypt**

Pharaohs Rule as Gods The role of the king was one striking difference between Egypt and Mesopotamia. In Mesopotamia, kings were considered to be representatives of the gods. To the Egyptians, kings were gods. The Egyptian god-kings, called **pharaohs** (FAIR•ohz), were thought to be almost as splendid and powerful as the gods of the heavens. This type of government in which rule is based on religious authority is called a **theocracy**.

The pharaoh stood at the center of Egypt's religion as well as its government and army. Egyptians believed that the pharaoh bore full responsibility for the kingdom's well-being. It was the pharaoh who caused the sun to rise, the Nile to flood, and the crops to grow. It was the pharaoh's duty to promote truth and justice. **B**

MAIN IDEA

Making Inferences

B Why were Egypt's pharaohs unusually powerful rulers?

Builders of the Pyramids Egyptians believed that their king ruled even after his death. He had an eternal life force, or *ka,* which continued to take part in the governing of Egypt. In the Egyptians' mind, the *ka* remained much like a living king in its needs and pleasures. Since kings expected to reign forever, their tombs were even more important than their palaces. For the kings of the Old Kingdom, the resting place after death was an immense structure called a **pyramid**. The Old Kingdom was the great age of pyramid building in ancient Egypt.

These magnificent monuments were remarkable engineering achievements, built by people who had not even begun to use the wheel. Unlike the Sumerians, however, the Egyptians did have a good supply of stone, both granite and limestone. For the Great Pyramid of Giza, for example, the limestone facing was quarried just across the Nile. Each perfectly cut stone block weighed at least 2 1/2 tons. Some weighed 15 tons. More than 2 million of these blocks were stacked with precision to a height of 481 feet. The entire structure covered more than 13 acres.

The pyramids also reflect the strength of the Egyptian civilization. They show that Old Kingdom dynasties had developed the economic strength and technological means to support massive public works projects, as well as the leadership and government organization to carry them out.

Egyptian Culture

With nature so much in their favor, Egyptians tended to approach life more confidently and optimistically than their neighbors in the Fertile Crescent. Religion played an important role in the lives of Egyptians.

Religion and Life Like the Mesopotamians, the early Egyptians were polytheistic, believing in many gods. The most important gods were Re, the sun god, and Osiris (oh•SY•rihs), god of the dead. The most important goddess was Isis, who represented the ideal mother and wife. In all, Egyptians worshiped more than 2,000 gods and goddesses. They built huge temples to honor the major deities.

Vocabulary
deities: gods or goddesses

In contrast to the Mesopotamians, with their bleak view of death, Egyptians believed in an afterlife, a life that continued after death. Egyptians believed they would be judged for their deeds when they died. Anubis, god and guide of the underworld, would weigh each dead person's heart. To win eternal life, the heart could be no heavier than a feather. If the heart tipped the scale, showing that it was heavy with sin, a fierce beast known as the Devourer of Souls would pounce on the impure heart and gobble it up. But if the soul passed this test for purity and truth, it would live forever in the beautiful Other World.

People of all classes planned for their burials, so that they might safely reach the Other World. Kings and queens built great tombs, such as the pyramids, and other Egyptians built smaller tombs. Royal and elite Egyptians' bodies were preserved by **mummification**, which involves embalming and drying the corpse to prevent it from decaying. Scholars still accept Herodotus's description of the process of mummification as one of the methods used by Egyptians.

PRIMARY SOURCE C

First, they draw out the brains through the nostrils with an iron hook. . . . Then with a sharp stone they make an incision in the side, and take out all the bowels. . . . Then, having filled the belly with pure myrrh, cassia, and other perfumes, they sew it up again; and when they have done this they steep it in natron [a mineral salt], leaving it under for 70 days. . . . At the end of 70 days, they wash the corpse, and wrap the whole body in bandages of waxen cloth.

HERODOTUS, *The History of Herodotus*

MAIN IDEA

Analyzing Primary Sources

C What does this description suggest about the Egyptians' knowledge of the human body?

Attendants placed the mummy in a coffin inside a tomb. Then they filled the tomb with items the dead person could use in the afterlife, such as clothing, food, cosmetics, and jewelry. Many Egyptians purchased scrolls that contained hymns, prayers, and magic spells intended to guide the soul in the afterlife. This collection of texts is known as the *Book of the Dead.*

INTERACTIVE

Pyramids and Mummies

Etched into some of the stones of the pyramids are the nicknames of the teams of workers who built them—"the Vigorous Gang," "the Enduring Gang," and "the Craftsman Gang," for example. Just as construction workers today leave their marks on the skyscrapers they build, the pyramid builders scratched messages for the ages inside the pyramids.

Who were the pyramid builders? Peasants provided most of the labor. They worked for the government when the Nile was in flood and they could not farm. In return for their service, though, the country provided the workers with food and housing during this period.

◄ The ancient Egyptians mummified the body so the soul could return to it later. Egyptian embalmers were so skillful that modern archaeologists have found mummies that still have hair, skin, and teeth.

▼ This solid gold death mask of the pharaoh Tutankhamen covered the head of his mummy. The mask, which weighs 22.04 pounds, is part of a popular exhibit in the Egyptian Museum in Cairo, Egypt.

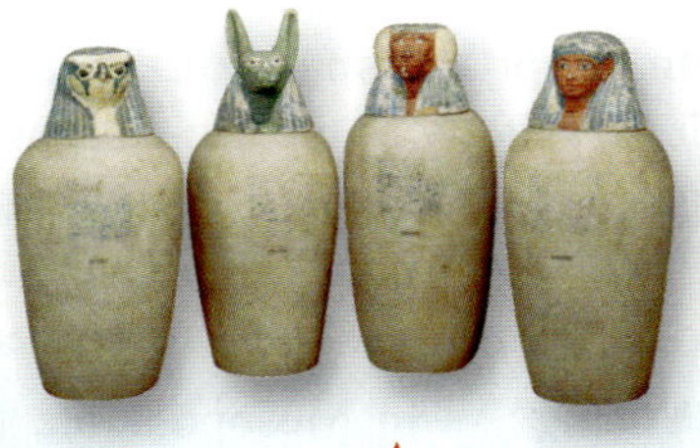

▲ These clay vessels are called Canopic jars. After preparing the mummy, embalmers placed the brain, liver, and other internal organs of the mummy in these jars.

▼ The largest of the pyramids is the Great Pyramid (right background) at Giza, completed about 2556 B.C. The diagram shows how the interior of a pyramid looks.

SKILLBUILDER: Interpreting Visual Sources

1. **Making Inferences** *What does the elaborate nature of Egyptian burials suggest about their culture?*
2. **Comparing and Contrasting** *In what ways are modern burial practices similar to those of the ancient Egyptians? How are they different?*

Life in Egyptian Society

Like the grand monuments to the kings, Egyptian society formed a pyramid. The king, queen, and royal family stood at the top. Below them were the other members of the upper class, which included wealthy landowners, government officials, priests, and army commanders. The next tier of the pyramid was the middle class, which included merchants and artisans. At the base of the pyramid was the lower class, by far the largest class. It consisted of peasant farmers and laborers.

In the later periods of Egyptian history, slavery became a widespread source of labor. Slaves, usually captives from foreign wars, served in the homes of the rich or toiled endlessly in the gold mines of Upper Egypt.

The Egyptians were not locked into their social classes. Lower-and middle-class Egyptians could gain higher status through marriage or success in their jobs. Even some slaves could hope to earn their freedom as a reward for their loyal service. To win the highest positions, people had to be able to read and write. Once a person had these skills, many careers were open in the army, the royal treasury, the priesthood, and the king's court.

Women in Egypt held many of the same rights as men. For example, a wealthy or middle-class woman could own and trade property. She could propose marriage or seek divorce. If she were granted a divorce, she would be entitled to one-third of the couple's property. **D**

MAIN IDEA

Comparing

D How was the status of women similar in Egyptian and Sumerian societies?

Egyptian Writing As in Mesopotamia, the development of writing was one of the keys to the growth of Egyptian civilization. Simple pictographs were the earliest form of writing in Egypt, but scribes quickly developed a more flexible writing system called **hieroglyphics** (HY•uhr•uh•GLIHF•ihks). This term comes from the Greek words *hieros* and *gluph,* meaning "sacred carving."

As with Sumerian cuneiform writing, in the earliest form of hieroglyphic writing, a picture stood for an idea. For instance, a picture of a man stood for the idea of a man. In time, the system changed so that pictures stood for sounds as well as ideas. The owl, for example, stood for an *m* sound or for the bird itself. Hieroglyphs could be used almost like letters of the alphabet.

Although hieroglyphs were first written on stone and clay, as in Mesopotamia, the Egyptians soon invented a better writing surface—**papyrus** (puh•PY•ruhs) reeds. These grew in the marshy delta. The Egyptians split the reeds into narrow strips, placed them crosswise in two layers, dampened them, and then pressed them. As the papyrus dried, the plant's sap glued the strips together into a paperlike sheet.

Egyptian Science and Technology Practical needs led to many Egyptian inventions. For example, the Egyptians developed a calendar to help them keep track of the time between floods and to plan their planting season. Priests observed that the same star—Sirius—appeared above the eastern horizon just before the floods came.

History *in* Depth

The Rosetta Stone

In 1799, near the delta village of Rosetta, some French soldiers found a polished black stone inscribed with a message in three languages. One version was written in hieroglyphics (top inset). A second version was in a simpler form of hieroglyphics, and the third was in Greek (both are shown in the bottom inset).

Since ancient Greek was a well-known language, it provided clues to the meaning of the hieroglyphics. Still, deciphering the Rosetta Stone took many years. In 1822, a French scholar named Jean François Champollion (shahm•paw•LYAWN) finally broke the code of the hieroglyphics.

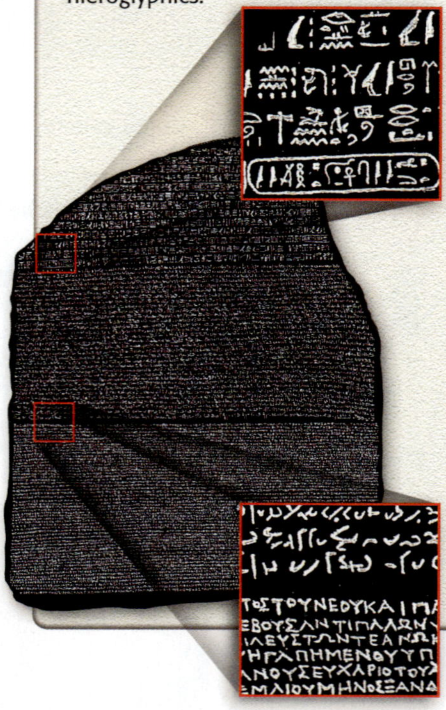

They calculated the number of days between one rising of the star and the next as 365 days—a solar year. They divided this year into 12 months of 30 days each and added five days for holidays and feasting. This calendar was so accurate that it fell short of the true solar year by only six hours.

Egyptians developed a system of written numbers for counting, adding, and subtracting. The system would have helped to assess and collect taxes. Scribes used an early form of geometry to survey and reset property boundaries after the annual floods. Mathematical knowledge helped Egypt's skillful engineers and architects make accurate measurements to construct their remarkable pyramids and palaces. Egyptian architects were the first to use stone columns in homes, palaces, and temples.

MAIN IDEA

Summarizing

E What were the main achievements of the ancient Egyptians?

Egyptian medicine was also famous in the ancient world. Egyptian doctors knew how to check a person's heart rate by feeling for a pulse in different parts of the body. They set broken bones with splints and had effective treatments for wounds and fevers. They also used surgery to treat some conditions. E

Invaders Control Egypt

The power of the pharaohs declined about 2180 B.C., marking the end of the Old Kingdom. Strong pharaohs regained control during the Middle Kingdom (2040–1640 B.C.) and restored law and order. They improved trade and transportation by digging a canal from the Nile to the Red Sea. They built huge dikes to trap and channel the Nile's floodwaters for irrigation. They also created thousands of new acres of farmland by draining the swamps of Lower Egypt.

The prosperity of the Middle Kingdom did not last. In about 1640 B.C., a group from the area of Palestine moved across the Isthmus of Suez into Egypt. These people were the Hyksos (HIHK•sahs), which meant "the rulers of foreign lands." The Hyksos ruled much of Egypt from 1630 to 1523 B.C.

Egypt would rise again for a new period of power and glory, the New Kingdom, which is discussed in Chapter 4. During approximately the same time period as the Old Kingdom and Middle Kingdom existed in Egypt, civilization was emerging in the Indus River Valley.

NEW YORK CORE CURRICULUM REVIEW

TERMS & NAMES 1. For each term or name, write a sentence explaining its significance.

- delta
- Narmer
- pharaoh
- theocracy
- pyramid
- mummification
- hieroglyphic
- papyrus

USING YOUR NOTES

2. Which of the Egyptian achievements do you consider the most important? Explain.

MAIN IDEAS

3. How did being surrounded by deserts benefit Egypt?
4. How did the Egyptians view the pharaoh?
5. Why did Egyptians mummify bodies?

CRITICAL THINKING & WRITING

6. **DRAWING CONCLUSIONS** Which of the three natural features that served as boundaries in ancient Egypt was most important to Egypt's history? Explain.
7. **RECOGNIZING EFFECTS** What impact did Egyptian religious beliefs have on the lives of Egyptians?
8. **COMPARING AND CONTRASTING** How were cuneiform and hieroglyphic writing similar? different?
9. **WRITING ACTIVITY** SCIENCE AND TECHNOLOGY Select an Egyptian invention or achievement. Write a **paragraph** about how your selected achievement changed the Egyptians' life.

CONNECT TO TODAY **CREATING A LANGUAGE**

Devise a **set of symbols** to create a language. Write several sentences and have classmates try to decipher the message.

Work and Play in Ancient Egypt

For ancient Egyptians, life often involved hard work. When the weather was good, most worked in the fields, producing food for their families and for export. During flood season, thousands of these farmers were called upon to help build the pharaohs' temples.

But life was not all about work. Archaeological digs offer evidence that both upper-class Egyptians and the common people found ways to enjoy themselves.

INTEGRATED TECHNOLOGY

RESEARCH LINKS For more on life in ancient Egypt, go to **classzone.com**

▼ Games

Games were popular with all classes of Egyptian society. The board shown below is for the game senet—also depicted in the painting. Players threw sticks or knuckle bones to move their pieces through squares of good or bad fortune. A player won by moving all his or her pieces off the board.

▲ Farmers

This detail from a tomb painting shows Egyptian farmers at work. Egyptians grew enough wheat and barley to have food reserves for themselves and for export to other civilizations. They also grew fruit and vegetables in irrigated fields.

▲ Cosmetics

Ancient Egyptians used cosmetics for both work and play. They protected field workers from sun and heat and were used to enhance beauty. Egyptian men and women applied makeup, called kohl, to their eyes. They made kohl from minerals mixed with water. They also soaked flowers and fragrant woods in oil and rubbed the oil into their skin. The dark eye makeup softened the glare of the sun. The oils protected their skin from the dry air. Egyptians kept their cosmetics in chests such as the one shown above.

▼ Temple Builders

The artist's colorful drawing of what the Karnak Temple Complex might have looked like explains why Egyptian pharaohs needed thousands of laborers to build their temples. Some historians believe the laborers may have been part of a rotating workforce drafted from the agricultural classes around Egypt—a form of community service. The photo at lower left shows the temple as it is today. Although faded and eroded, the temple still inspires awe.

DATA FILE

MORE ON WORK

- **Surgeons** Ancient Egypt had skilled surgeons. Written evidence shows that Egyptian surgeons knew how to stitch cuts and set broken bones. Some Egyptian mummies even show evidence of being operated on. We know the names of about 150 physicians—2 of them were women.
- **Papyrus Growers** A large industry was built around the harvesting of papyrus. Papyrus was used to make the material Egyptians wrote on. Scrolls of various sizes could be made One mathematics papyrus was 15 feet long and 3 inches wide.

MORE ON PLAY

- **Pets** Egyptians kept various animals as pets. Nobles would even have their pets mummified and buried with them. A single pet cemetery was discovered that contained 1,000,000 bird mummies.
- **Royal Dogs** The Pharaoh hound was very popular in ancient Egypt. Artifacts from 4000 B.C. show images of the breed. Today, a Pharaoh hound puppy bred for competition can cost up to $1,500.

Connect *to* Today

1. **Making Inferences** From what you have read here, what inferences can you make about Egyptian society?
   See Skillbuilder Handbook, page R10.
2. **Comparing and Contrasting** How are the work and leisure activities of ancient Egypt different from those in the United States today? How are they similar?

Planned Cities on the Indus

TERMS & NAMES

- subcontinent
- monsoon
- Harappan civilization

SETTING THE STAGE The great civilizations of Mesopotamia and Egypt rose and fell. They left behind much physical evidence about their ways of life. This is the case in what today is the area known as Pakistan and part of India where another civilization arose about 2500 B.C. However, historians know less about its origins and the reasons for its eventual decline than they do about the origins and decline of Mesopotamia and Egypt, because the language of the culture has not been translated.

TAKING NOTES
Drawing Conclusions
Use the graphic organizer to draw conclusions about Indus Valley civilizations.

Indus Valley	
Cities	fact
Language	fact
Trade	fact

The Geography of the Indian Subcontinent

Geographers often refer to the landmass that includes India, Pakistan, and Bangladesh as the Indian **subcontinent**. A wall of the highest mountains in the world—the Hindu Kush, Karakorum, and Himalayan ranges—separates this region from the rest of the Asian continent.

Rivers, Mountains, and Plains The world's tallest mountains to the north and a large desert to the east helped protect the Indus Valley from invasion. The mountains guard an enormous flat and fertile plain formed by two rivers—the Indus and the Ganges (GAN•jeez). Each river is an important link from the interior of the subcontinent to the sea. The Indus River flows southwest from the Himalayas to the Arabian Sea. Much of the lower Indus Valley is occupied by the Thar Desert. Farming is possible only in the areas directly watered by the Indus. The Ganges drops down from the Himalayas and flows eastward across northern India. It joins the Brahmaputra River as it flows to the Bay of Bengal.

The Indus and Ganges and the lands they water make up a large area that stretches 1,700 miles across northern India and is called the Indo-Gangetic Plain. Like the Tigris, the Euphrates, and the Nile, these rivers carry not only water for irrigation, but also silt, which produces rich land for agriculture.

Below the Indo-Gangetic Plain, the southern part of the subcontinent is a peninsula that thrusts south into the Indian Ocean. The center of the peninsula is a high plateau cut by twisting rivers. This region is called the Deccan (DEK•uhn) Plateau. The plateau is framed by low mountain ranges called the Eastern and Western Ghats. These mountains keep moist air from reaching the plateau, making it a dry region. A narrow border of lush, tropical land lies along the coasts of southern India.

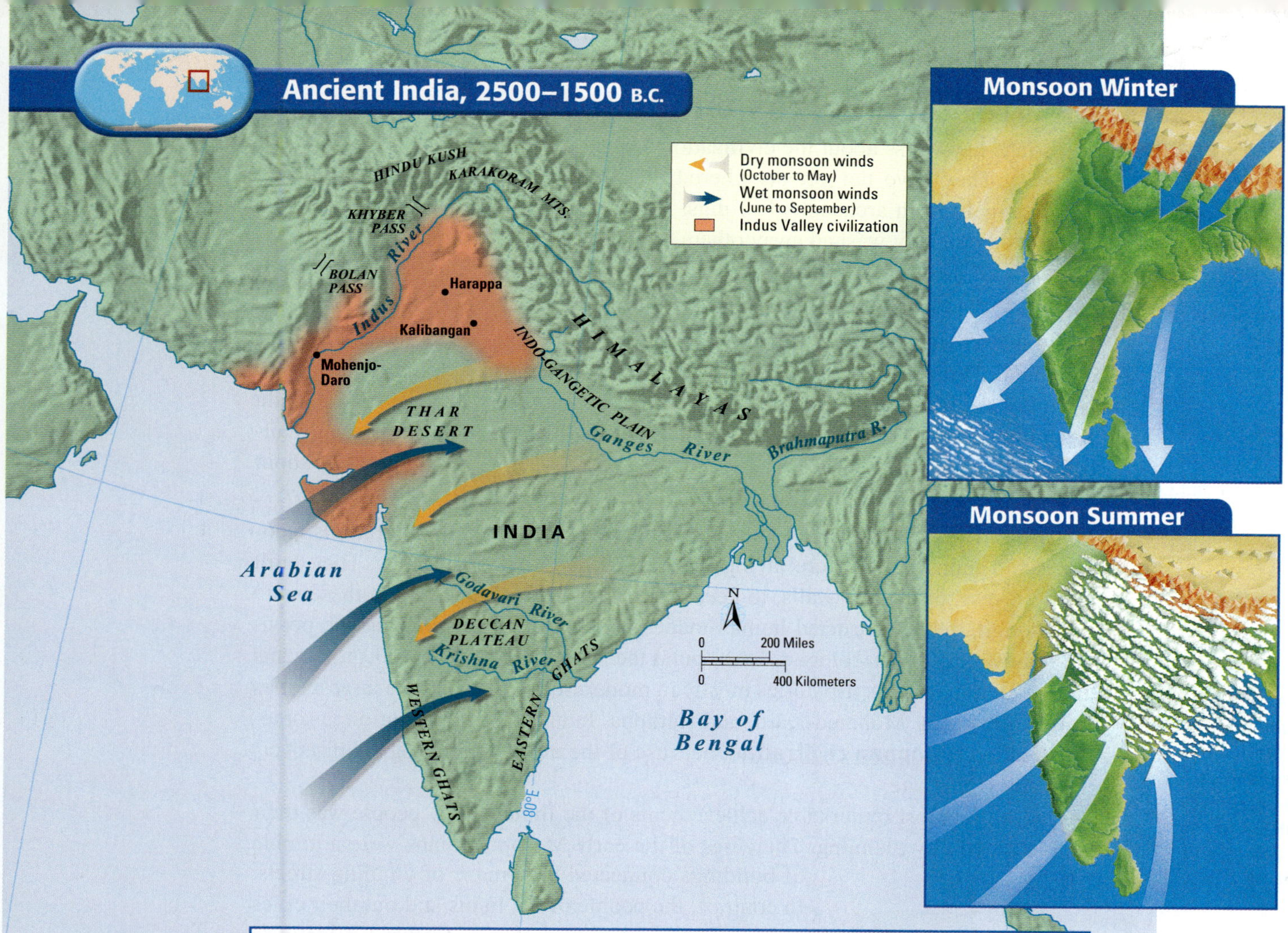

GEOGRAPHY SKILLBUILDER: Interpreting Maps

1. **Human-Environment Interaction** *What landforms presented natural barriers around the Indus Valley?*
2. **Movement** *Why do the winter monsoon winds carry so little moisture?*

Monsoons Seasonal winds called **monsoons** dominate India's climate. From October to February, winter monsoons from the northeast blow dry air westward across the country. Then, from the middle of June through October, the winds shift. These monsoons blow eastward from the southwest, carrying moisture from the ocean in great rain clouds. The powerful storms bring so much moisture that flooding often happens. When the summer monsoons fail to develop, drought often causes crop disasters.

Environmental Challenges The civilization that emerged along the Indus River faced many of the same challenges as the ancient Mesopotamian and Egyptian civilizations.

- Yearly floods spread deposits of rich soil over a wide area. However, the floods along the Indus were unpredictable.
- The rivers sometimes changed course.
- The cycle of wet and dry seasons brought by the monsoon winds was unpredictable. If there was too little rain, plants withered in the fields and people went hungry. If there was too much rain, floods swept away whole villages. (A)

MAIN IDEA

Identifying Problems

(A) What environmental challenge did the farmers of the Indus Valley face that the Sumerians and Egyptians did not?

Civilization Emerges on the Indus

Historians know less about the civilization in the Indus Valley than about those to the west. They have not yet deciphered the Indus system of writing. Evidence comes largely from archaeological digs, although many sites remain unexplored, and floods probably washed away others long ago. At its height, however, the civilization of the Indus Valley influenced an area much larger than did either Mesopotamia or Egypt.

Earliest Arrivals No one is sure how human settlement began in the Indian subcontinent. Perhaps people who arrived by sea from Africa settled the south. Northern migrants may have made their way through the Khyber Pass in the Hindu Kush mountains. Archaeologists have found evidence in the highlands of agriculture and domesticated sheep and goats dating to about 7000 B.C. By about 3200 B.C., people were farming in villages along the Indus River.

Planned Cities Around 2500 B.C., while Egyptians were building pyramids, people in the Indus Valley were laying the bricks for India's first cities. They built strong levees, or earthen walls, to keep water out of their cities. When these were not enough, they constructed human-made islands to raise the cities above possible floodwaters. Archaeologists have found the ruins of more than 100 settlements along the Indus and its tributaries mostly in modern-day Pakistan. The largest cities were Kalibangan, Mohenjo-Daro, and Harappa. Indus Valley civilization is sometimes called **Harappan civilization**, because of the many archaeological discoveries made at that site.

One of the most remarkable achievements of the Indus Valley people was their sophisticated city planning. The cities of the early Mesopotamians were a jumble of buildings connected by a maze of winding streets. In contrast, the people of the Indus laid out their cities on a precise grid system. Cities featured a fortified area called a citadel, which contained the major buildings of the city. Buildings were constructed of oven-baked bricks cut in standard sizes, unlike the simpler, irregular, sun-dried mud bricks of the Mesopotamians.

Early engineers also created sophisticated plumbing and sewage systems. These systems could rival any urban drainage systems built before the 19th century. The uniformity in the cities' planning and construction suggests that the Indus peoples had developed a strong central government.

Harappan Planning Harappa itself is a good example of this city planning. The city was partially built on mud-brick platforms to protect it from flooding. A thick brick wall about three and a half miles long surrounded it. Inside was a citadel, which provided protection for the royal family and also served as a temple.

The streets in its grid system were as wide as 30 feet. Walls divided residential districts from each other. Houses varied in size. Some may have been three stories high. Narrow lanes separated rows of houses, which were laid out in block units. Houses featured bathrooms where wastewater flowed out to the street and then to sewage pits outside the city walls.

▼ A map of the citadel portion of Mohenjo-Daro shows an organized pattern of buildings and streets.

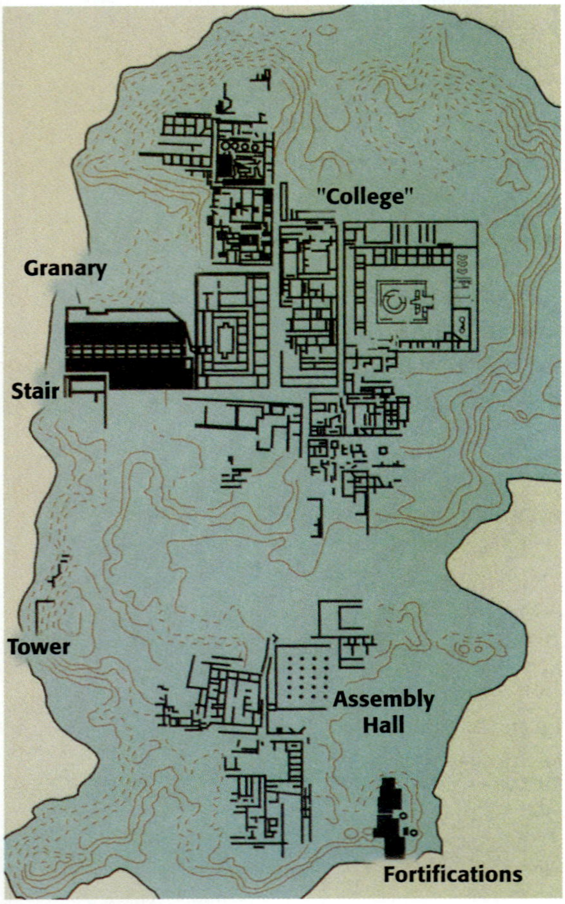

Plumbing in Mohenjo-Daro

From the time people began living in cities, they have faced the problem of plumbing: how to obtain clean water and remove human wastes? In most ancient cities, people retrieved water from a river or a central well. They dumped wastes into open drainage ditches or carted them out of town. Only the rich had separate bathrooms in their homes.

By contrast, the Indus peoples built extensive and modern-looking plumbing systems. In Mohenjo-Daro, almost every house had a private bathroom and toilet. No other civilization achieved this level of convenience until the 19th and 20th centuries. The toilets were neatly built of brick with a wooden seat. Pipes connected to each house carried wastewater into an underground sewer system.

INTEGRATED TECHNOLOGY

RESEARCH LINKS For more on water and waste management go to **classzone.com**

Plumbing Facts

- The ancient Romans also built sophisticated plumbing and sewage systems. Aqueducts supplied Roman cities with water.
- In the 17th century, engineers installed a series of water wheels to pump water for the fountains of Versailles, the palace of French king Louis XIV. The water was pumped from a river three miles away. This was the largest water-supply system powered by machine rather than gravity.
- The flush toilet was patented in 1775 by Alexander Cumming, a British mathematician and watchmaker.

1. In their private baths, people took showers by pouring pitchers of water over their head.

2. Wastes drained through clay pipes into brick sewers running below the streets. These sewers had manholes, through which sanitation workers could inspect the drains and clean out the muck.

Connect *to* Today

1. **Making Inferences** What does the attention the Indus people gave to the plumbing and sewer systems suggest about their culture?
   See Skillbuilder Handbook, Page R10.

2. **Comparing and Contrasting** Find out how water is supplied and wastewater disposed of in your home or community. How does the system in your home or community compare with what was used in Mohenjo-Daro?

Harappan Culture

Harappan culture spread throughout the Indus valley. Like the Egyptian and Mesopotamian civilizations you have studied, the culture was based on agriculture. Artifacts help to explain some aspects of the culture.

▼ Harappan seals show an elephant (top), an Indian rhinoceros (middle), and a zebu bull (bottom).

Language Like the other two river valley civilizations, the Harappan culture developed a written language. In contrast to cuneiform and hieroglyphics, the Harappan language has been impossible to decipher. This is because, unlike the other two languages, linguists have not found any inscriptions that are bilingual. The Harappan language is found on stamps and seals made of carved stone used for trading pottery and tools. About 400 symbols make up the language. Scientists believe the symbols, like hieroglyphs, are used both to depict an object and also as phonetic sounds. Some signs stand alone and others seem to be combined into words. (B)

MAIN IDEA

Clarifying

(B) What is the main reason Harappan language has not been deciphered?

Culture The Harappan cities show a remarkable uniformity in religion and culture. The housing suggests that social divisions in the society were not great. Artifacts such as clay and wooden children's toys suggest a relatively prosperous society that could afford to produce nonessential goods. Few weapons of warfare have been found, suggesting that conflict was limited.

The presence of animal images on many types of artifacts suggests that animals were an important part of the culture. Animals are seen on pottery, small statues, children's toys, and seals used to mark trade items. The images provide archaeologists with information about animals that existed in the region. However, some of the seals portray beasts with parts of several different animals—for example, the head of a man, an elephant trunk and tusks, horns of a bull, and the rump of a tiger. As in the case of the Harappan language, the meaning of these images has remained a mystery.

Role of Religion As with other cultures, the rulers of the Harappan civilization are believed to have close ties to religion. Archaeologists think that the culture was a theocracy. But no site of a temple has been found. Priests likely prayed for good harvests and safety from floods. Religious artifacts reveal links to modern Hindu culture. Figures show what may be early representations of Shiva, a major Hindu god. Other figures relate to a mother goddess, fertility images, and the worship of the bull. All of these became part of later Indian civilization.

Trade The Harappans conducted a thriving trade with peoples in the region. Gold and silver came from the north in Afghanistan. Semiprecious stones from Persia and the Deccan Plateau were crafted into jewelry. The Indus River provided an excellent means of transportation for trade goods. Brightly colored cotton cloth was a desirable trade item since few people at the time knew how to grow cotton. Overland routes moved goods from Persia to the Caspian Sea.

The Indus River provided a link to the sea. This access allowed Indus Valley inhabitants to develop trade with distant peoples, including the Mesopotamians. Seals probably used by Indus merchants to identify their goods have been found in Sumer. Ships used the Persian Gulf trade routes to bring copper, lumber, precious stones, and luxury goods to Sumer. Trading began as early as 2600 B.C. and continued until 1800 B.C.

Indus Valley Culture Ends

Around 1750 B.C., the quality of building in the Indus Valley cities declined. Gradually, the great cities fell into decay. The fate of the cities remained a mystery until the 1970s. Then, satellite images of the subcontinent of India revealed evidence of shifts in tectonic plates. The plate movement probably caused earthquakes and floods and altered the course of the Indus River.

Vocabulary
tectonic plates: moving pieces of the earth's crust

Some cities along the rivers apparently suffered through these disasters and survived. Others were destroyed. The shifts may have caused another river, the Sarswati, to dry up. Trade on this river became impossible, and cities began to die. Harappan agriculture, too, would have been influenced by these events. It is likely that these environmental changes prevented production of large quantities of food. Furthermore, Harappan agriculture may have suffered as a result of soil that was exhausted by overuse. This too, may have forced people to leave the cities in order to survive.

Other factors had an impact on the Indus subcontinent. As Chapter 3 explains, the Aryans, a nomadic people from north of the Hindu Kush mountains, swept into the Indus Valley around 1500 B.C. Indian civilization would grow again under the influence of these nomads. At this same time, farther to the east, another civilization was arising. It was isolated from outside influences, as you will learn in Section 4. (C)

MAIN IDEA
Analyzing Causes
(C) What factors may have contributed to the decline of the Indus Valley civilization?

▲ The bearded figure above might be a Harappan god or perhaps a priest king.

NEW YORK CORE CURRICULUM REVIEW

TERMS & NAMES 1. For each term or name, write a sentence explaining its significance.
- subcontinent
- monsoon
- Harappan civilization

USING YOUR NOTES

2. What is one conclusion you can draw about the Indus Valley civilization?

Indus Valley	
Cities	fact
Language	fact
Trade	fact

MAIN IDEAS

3. What problems can monsoons cause?
4. How were the planned cities of the Indus Valley different from other early cities?
5. What reasons are suggested for the disappearance of the Indus Valley civilization?

CRITICAL THINKING & WRITING

6. **DRAWING CONCLUSIONS** What evidence suggests Indus Valley cities were run by a strong central government?
7. **SYNTHESIZING** What skills would the construction of planned cities require? Explain.
8. **MAKING INFERENCES** How were the people of the Indus Valley connected to Mesopotamia?
9. **WRITING ACTIVITY** INTERACTION WITH ENVIRONMENT
Write a **comparison** of how Sumerians, Egyptians, and the people of the Harappan civilization made use of their environment. Then identify which group you think made better use of what they had.

INTEGRATED TECHNOLOGY **INTERNET ACTIVITY**
Use the Internet to research Harappan seals. Make some sketches of what you see. Then create a **sketch** of a seal that might have been found in a ruin in an Indus Valley civilization.

INTERNET KEYWORD
Harappan seals

River Dynasties in China

CONNECT TO THE NEW YORK STATE CORE CURRICULUM

Unit 1.B.1.a. Human and physical geography of early river civilizations
Unit 1.C.1.d. Mandate of Heaven

TERMS & NAMES

- loess
- oracle bone
- Mandate of Heaven
- dynastic cycle
- feudalism

SETTING THE STAGE The walls of China's first cities were built 4,000 years ago. This was at least 1,000 years after the walls of Ur, the great pyramids of Egypt, and the planned cities of the Indus Valley were built. Unlike the other three river valley civilizations, the civilization that began along one of China's river systems continues to thrive today.

TAKING NOTES
Following Chronological Order On a time line, identify major events in early Chinese dynasties.

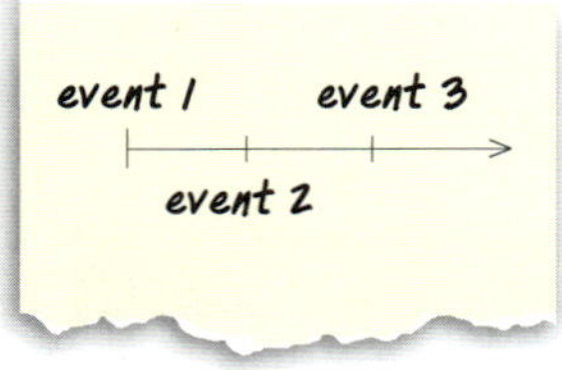

The Geography of China

Natural barriers somewhat isolated ancient China from all other civilizations. To China's east lay the Yellow Sea, the East China Sea, and the Pacific Ocean. Mountain ranges and deserts dominate about two-thirds of China's landmass. In west China lay the Taklimakan (TAH•kluh•muh•KAHN) Desert and the icy 15,000-foot Plateau of Tibet. To the southwest are the Himalayas. And to the north are the desolate Gobi Desert and the Mongolian Plateau.

River Systems Two major river systems flow from the mountainous west to the Pacific Ocean. The Huang He (hwahng HUH), also known as the Yellow River, is found in the north. In central China, the Chang Jiang (chang jyhang), also called Yangtze (yang•SEE), flows east to the Yellow Sea. The Huang He, whose name means "yellow river," deposits huge amounts of yellowish silt when it overflows its banks. This silt is actually fertile soil called **loess** (LOH•uhs), which is blown by the winds from deserts to the west and north.

Environmental Challenges Like the other ancient civilizations in this chapter, China's first civilization developed in a river valley. China, too, faced the dangers of floods—but its geographic isolation posed its own challenges.

- The Huang He's floods could be disastrous. Sometimes floods devoured whole villages, earning the river the nickname "China's Sorrow."
- Because of China's relative geographic isolation, early settlers had to supply their own goods rather than trading with outside peoples.
- China's natural boundaries did not completely protect these settlers from outsiders. Invasions from the west and north occurred again and again in Chinese history.

China's Heartland Only about 10 percent of China's land is suitable for farming. Much of the land lies within the small plain between the Huang He and the

Yellow silt gives the Huang He a distinctive color.

GEOGRAPHY SKILLBUILDER: Interpreting Maps

1. **Location** *Describe the location of the Huang He and Chang Jiang in terms of where they begin and end.*
2. **Region** *What area did the Shang and Zhou dynasties control?*

Chang Jiang in eastern China. This plain, known as the North China Plain, is China's heartland. Throughout China's long history, its political boundaries have expanded and contracted depending on the strength or weakness of its ruling families. Yet the heartland of China remained the center of its civilization.

Civilization Emerges in Shang Times

Fossil remains show that ancestors of modern humans lived in southwest China about 1.7 million years ago. In northern China near Beijing, a *Homo erectus* skeleton was found. Known as Peking man, his remains show that people settled the river valley as much as 500,000 years ago.

The First Dynasties Even before the Sumerians settled in southern Mesopotamia, early Chinese cultures were building farming settlements along the Huang He. Around 2000 B.C., some of these settlements grew into China's first cities. According to legend, the first Chinese dynasty, the Xia (shyah) Dynasty, emerged about this time. Its leader was an engineer and mathematician named Yu. His flood-control and irrigation projects helped tame the Huang He and its tributaries so that settlements could grow. The legend of Yu reflects the level of technology of a society making the transition to civilization.

About the time the civilizations of Mesopotamia, Egypt, and the Indus Valley fell to outside invaders, a people called the Shang rose to power in northern China.

History *in* Depth

Lady Hao's Tomb

Lady Hao was a wife of king Wu Ding, a Shang ruler, during the 1200s B.C. Her relatively small grave contained some 460 bronze artifacts, 750 jade objects, and more than 6,880 cowry shells. Also found in the tomb beside Lady Hao's coffin were the remains of 16 people and 6 dogs.

Writings found in other places reveal a remarkable figure in Lady Hao. On behalf of her husband, she led more than one military campaign, once with a force of 13,000 troops. She also took charge of rituals dedicated to the spirits of Shang ancestors, a duty reserved for the most distinguished members of the royal family.

INTEGRATED TECHNOLOGY

INTERNET ACTIVITY Create a multimedia presentation about Lady Hao's tomb and its contents. Go to **classzone.com** for your research.

The Shang Dynasty lasted from around 1700 B.C. to 1027 B.C. It was the first family of Chinese rulers to leave written records. The Shang kings built elaborate palaces and tombs that have been uncovered by archaeologists.The artifacts reveal much about Shang society.

Early Cities Among the oldest and most important Shang cities was Anyang (ahn•YAHNG), one of the capitals of the Shang Dynasty. Unlike the cities of the Indus Valley or Fertile Crescent, Anyang was built mainly of wood. The city stood in a forest clearing. The higher classes lived in timber-framed houses with walls of clay and straw. These houses lay inside the city walls. The peasants and crafts-people lived in huts outside the city.

The Shang surrounded their cities with massive earthen walls for protection. The archaeological remains of one city include a wall of packed earth 118 feet wide at its base that encircled an area of 1.2 square miles. It likely took 10,000 men more than 12 years to build such a structure. Like the pyramids of Egypt or the cities of the Indus Valley, these walls demonstrate the Shang rulers' ability to raise and control large forces of workers. (A)

MAIN IDEA

Comparing

(A) What did Shang cities have in common with those of Sumer?

Shang peoples needed walled cities because they were constantly waging war. The chariot, one of the major tools of war, was probably first introduced by contact with cultures from western Asia. Professional warriors underwent lengthy training to learn the techniques of driving and shooting from horse-drawn chariots.

The Development of Chinese Culture

In the Chinese view, people who lived outside of Chinese civilization were barbarians. Because the Chinese saw their country as the center of the civilized world, their own name for China was the Middle Kingdom.

The culture that grew up in China had strong unifying bonds. From earliest times, the group seems to have been more important than the individual. A person's chief loyalty throughout life was to the family. Beyond this, people owed obedience and respect to the ruler of the Middle Kingdom, just as they did to the elders in their family.

Family The family was central to Chinese society. The most important virtue was respect for one's parents. The elder men in the family controlled the family's property and made important decisions. Women, on the other hand, were treated as inferiors. They were expected to obey their fathers, their husbands, and later, their own sons. When a girl was between 13 and 16 years old, her marriage was arranged, and she moved into the house of her husband. Only by bearing sons for her husband's family could she hope to improve her status.

Social Classes Shang society was sharply divided between nobles and peasants. A ruling class of warrior-nobles headed by a king governed the Shang. These noble families owned the land. They governed the scattered villages within the Shang lands and sent tribute to the Shang ruler in exchange for local control.

Vocabulary
tribute: payment made to keep peace

Religious Beliefs In China, the family was closely linked to religion. The Chinese believed that the spirits of family ancestors had the power to bring good fortune or disaster to living members of the family. The Chinese did not regard these spirits as mighty gods. Rather, the spirits were more like troublesome or helpful neighbors who demanded attention and respect. Every family paid respect to the father's ancestors and made sacrifices in their honor.

Through the spirits of the ancestors, the Shang consulted the gods. The Shang worshiped a supreme god, Shang Di, as well as many lesser gods. Shang kings consulted the gods through the use of **oracle bones**, animal bones and tortoise shells on which priests had scratched questions for the gods. After inscribing a question on the bone, a priest applied a hot poker to it, which caused it to crack. The priests then interpreted the cracks to see how the gods had answered.

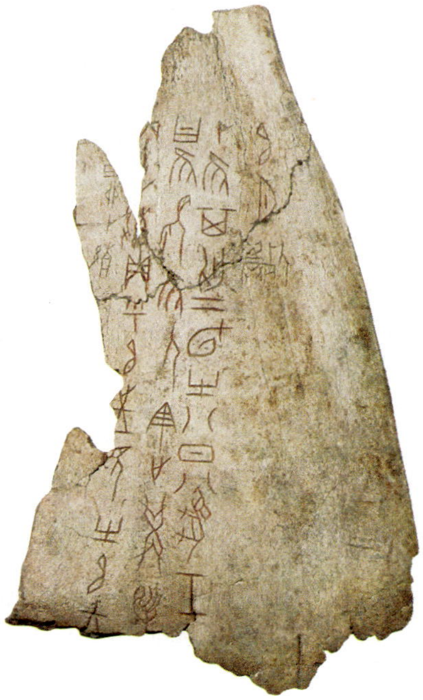

▲ The earliest evidence of Chinese writing is seen on oracle bones like this one found in the city of Anyang.

Development of Writing In the Chinese method of writing, each character generally stands for one syllable or unit of language. Recall that many of the Egyptian hieroglyphs stood for sounds in the spoken language. In contrast, there were practically no links between China's spoken language and its written language. One could read Chinese without being able to speak a word of it. (This seems less strange when you think of our own number system. Both a French person and an American can understand the written equation 2 + 2 = 4. But an American may not understand the spoken statement "Deux et deux font quatre.")

The Chinese system of writing had one major advantage. People in all parts of China could learn the same system of writing, even if their spoken languages were very different. Thus, the Chinese written language helped unify a large and diverse land, and made control much easier.

The disadvantage of the Chinese system was the enormous number of written characters to be memorized—a different one for each unit of language. A person needed to know over 1,500 characters to be barely literate. To be a true scholar, one needed to know at least 10,000 characters. For centuries, this severely limited the number of literate, educated Chinese. As a general rule, a nobleperson's children learned to write, but peasant children did not. B

MAIN IDEA

Recognizing Effects

B How did writing help unite China?

Chinese Writing

The earliest writing systems in the world—including Chinese, Sumerian, and Egyptian—developed from pictographs, or simplified drawings of objects. The writing system used in China today is directly related to the pictographic writing found on Shang oracle bones. As you can see in the chart below, the ancient pictographs can still be recognized in many modern Chinese characters.

	ox	goat, sheep	tree	moon	earth	water	field	heaven	to pray
Ancient symbol									
Modern character	牛	羊	木	月	土	水	田	天	祝

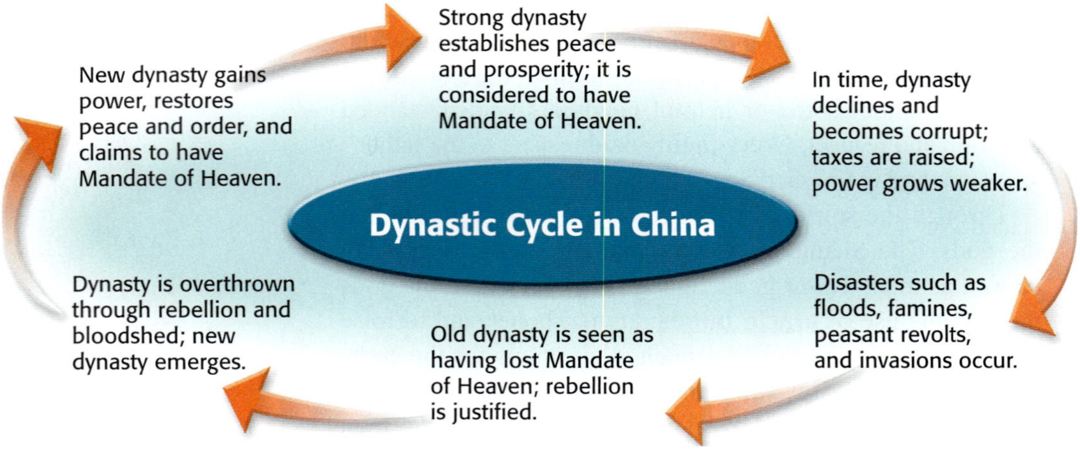

Zhou and the Dynastic Cycle

Around 1027 B.C., a people called the Zhou (joh) overthrew the Shang and established their own dynasty. The Zhou had adopted much of the Shang culture. Therefore, the change in dynasty did not bring sweeping cultural change. Nevertheless, Zhou rule brought new ideas to Chinese civilization.

Mandate of Heaven To justify their conquest, the Zhou leaders declared that the final Shang king had been such a poor ruler that the gods had taken away the Shang's rule and given it to the Zhou. This justification developed over time into a broader view that royal authority came from heaven. A just ruler had divine approval, known as the **Mandate of Heaven**. A wicked or foolish king could lose the Mandate of Heaven and so lose the right to rule. The Duke of Shao, an aide of the Zhou leader who conquered the Shang, described the mandate:

Vocabulary
mandate: a command or instruction from a higher authority

PRIMARY SOURCE

Heaven, unpitying, has sent down ruin on Yin [another name for Shang]. Yin has lost the Mandate, and we Zhou have received it. I dare not say that our fortune would continue to prosper, even though I believe that heaven favors those who are sincere in their intentions. I dare not say, either that it would end in certain disaster. . . .

The Mandate of Heaven is not easy to gain. It will be lost when men fail to live up to the reverent and illustrious virtues of their forefathers.

DUKE OF SHAO, quoted in *The Chinese Heritage*

The Mandate of Heaven became central to the Chinese view of government. Floods, riots, and other calamities might be signs that the ancestral spirits were displeased with a king's rule. In that case, the Mandate of Heaven might pass to another noble family. This was the Chinese explanation for rebellion, civil war, and the rise of a new dynasty. Historians describe the pattern of rise, decline, and replacement of dynasties as the **dynastic cycle**, shown above. C

MAIN IDEA
Synthesizing
C According to Chinese beliefs, what role did the Mandate of Heaven play in the dynastic cycle?

Control Through Feudalism The Zhou Dynasty controlled lands that stretched far beyond the Huang He in the north to the Chang Jiang in the south. To govern this vast area, it gave control over different regions to members of the royal family and other trusted nobles. This established a system called **feudalism**. Feudalism is a political system in which nobles, or lords, are granted the use of lands that legally belong to the king. In return, the nobles owe loyalty and military service to the king and protection to the people who live on their estates. Similar systems would arise centuries later in both Japan and Europe.

At first, the local lords lived in small walled towns and had to submit to the superior strength and control of the Zhou rulers. Gradually, however, the lords grew stronger as the towns grew into cities and expanded into the surrounding territory.

Peoples who had been hostile toward the lords gradually accepted their rule and adopted Zhou ways. As a result, the local lords became less dependent on the king. More and more, they fought among themselves and with neighboring peoples for wealth and territory.

Improvements in Technology and Trade The Zhou Dynasty produced many innovations.

- Roads and canals were built to stimulate trade and agriculture.
- Coined money was introduced, which further improved trade.
- Blast furnaces that produced cast iron were developed.

Zhou cast iron production would not be matched in Europe until the Middle Ages. The Zhou used iron to create weapons, especially dagger-axes and swords. They also used it for common agricultural tools such as sickles, knives, and spades. Iron tools made farm work easier and more productive. The ability to grow more food helped Zhou farmers support thriving cities.

▲ These Chinese coins are made of bronze. Their shape resembles a digging tool such as a hoe or spade.

A Period of Warring States The Zhou ruled from around 1027 to 256 B.C. The Zhou empire was generally peaceful and stable. Gradually, however, Zhou rule weakened. In 771 B.C., nomads from the north and west sacked the Zhou capital and murdered the Zhou monarch. A few members of the royal family escaped and set up a new capital at Luoyang.

However, the Zhou kings at Luoyang were almost powerless, and they could not control the noble families. The lords sought every opportunity to pick fights with neighboring lords. As their power grew, these warlords claimed to be kings in their own territory. As a result, the later years of the Zhou are often called "the time of the warring states."

Amidst the bloodshed, traditional values collapsed. The very heart of Chinese civilization—love of order, harmony, and respect for authority—had been replaced with chaos, arrogance, and defiance. As you will learn in Chapter 4, the dynastic cycle was about to bring a new start to Chinese civilization.

NEW YORK CORE CURRICULUM REVIEW

TERMS & NAMES 1. For each term or name, write a sentence explaining its significance.

- loess
- oracle bone
- Mandate of Heaven
- dynastic cycle
- feudalism

USING YOUR NOTES

2. Which event do you think was a turning point in Chinese history?

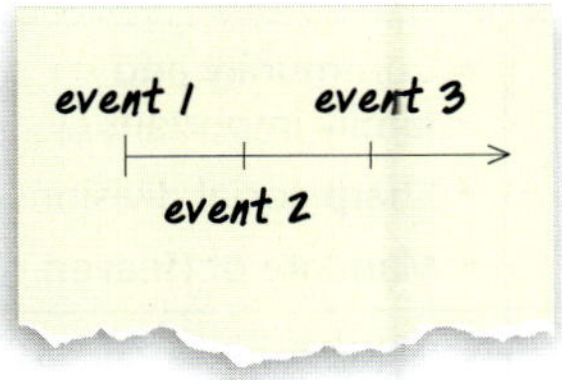

MAIN IDEAS

3. Between which two rivers is the heartland of China found?
4. What family obligations did a Chinese person have?
5. How is the dynastic cycle connected to the Mandate of Heaven?

CRITICAL THINKING & WRITING

6. **RECOGNIZING EFFECTS** In your judgment, what are the benefits and drawbacks of the belief that the group was more important than the individual?
7. **COMPARING** How did the social classes in Shang society differ from those in Egyptian society?
8. **ANALYZING MOTIVES** Do you think that the Zhou Dynasty's downfall resulted from its method of control? Why or why not?
9. **WRITING ACTIVITY** POWER AND AUTHORITY Study the dynastic cycle. Then write a **letter to the editor** suggesting that the current ruler should be replaced.

CONNECT TO TODAY **CREATING A POSTER**

Research the Three Gorges Dam Project in China. The project will place dams on the Chang Jiang. Create a **poster** showing the locations of the dams, some statistics about them, and an explanation of the project's purpose.

Chapter 2 Assessment

TERMS & NAMES

Briefly explain the importance of each of the following to early river valley civilizations from 3500–450 B.C.

1. Fertile Crescent
2. city-state
3. polytheism
4. empire
5. pharaoh
6. hieroglyphics
7. Harappan civilization
8. Mandate of Heaven

MAIN IDEAS

City-States in Mesopotamia Section 1 (pages 29–34)

9. What is the Fertile Crescent and why is it called that?
10. Name three disadvantages of Sumer's natural environment.
11. What circumstances led to the beginning of organized government?

Pyramids on the Nile Section 2 (pages 35–43)

12. Why did the Egyptians build pyramids?
13. Herodotus remarked that Egypt was the "gift of the Nile." What did he mean by this?

Planned Cities on the Indus Section 3 (pages 44–49)

14. What does the uniformity of Indus Valley cities tell us about their government?
15. What evidence exists to show that Indus Valley civilizations traded with Sumer?

River Dynasties in China Section 4 (pages 50–55)

16. What was the great advantage of the Chinese written language?
17. Explain the dynastic cycle in China.

CRITICAL THINKING

1. USING YOUR NOTES
Create a Venn diagram to indicate differences and similarities in religious beliefs among these ancient civilizations.

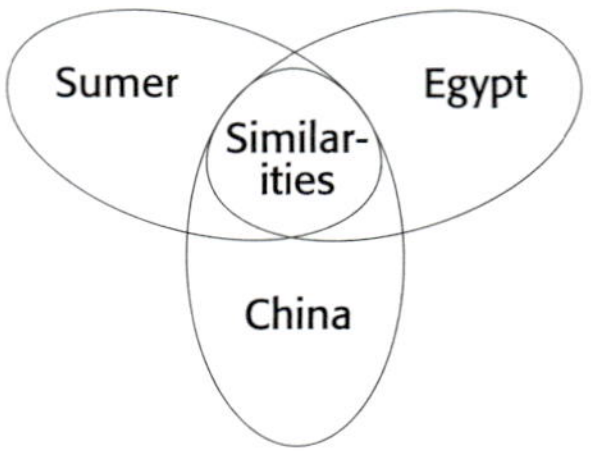

2. HYPOTHESIZING
POWER AND AUTHORITY Think about a massive public project that might be done today, such as building a large dam. In terms of government power and authority, how would this be similar to the building of the pyramids? How would it be different?

3. DRAWING CONCLUSIONS
SCIENCE AND TECHNOLOGY Why was it necessary to develop writing before civilization could advance?

4. MAKING INFERENCES
What reasons might be suggested for the location of civilizations along river valleys?

5. COMPARING
How was a theocracy different from a government run by warrior-kings?

VISUAL SUMMARY

Early River Valley Civilizations

	Sumer	Egypt	Indus Valley	China
Environment	• Tigris and Euphrates flooding unpredictable • No natural barriers • Limited natural resources	• Nile flooding predictable • Natural barriers: deserts • Nile an easy transportation link	• Indus flooding unpredictable • Natural barriers: mountains, deserts • Monsoon winds	• Huang He flooding unpredictable • Natural barriers: mountains, deserts • Geographically isolated
Power and Authority	• Independent city-states governed by monarchs • City-states united into first empires	• Pharaohs rule kingdom as gods • Pharaohs built pyramids	• Strong centralized government • Planned cities	• Community and family important • Sharp social divisions • Mandate of Heaven
Science and Technology	• Cuneiform • Irrigation • Bronze • Wheel, sail, plow	• Hieroglyphics • Pyramids • Mathematics, geometry • Medicine	• Writing (not yet deciphered) • Cities built on precise grid • Plumbing and sewage systems	• Writing • Silk • Coined money • Cast iron

Use the quotation and your knowledge of world history to answer questions 1 and 2.
Additional Test Practice, pp. S1–S33

PRIMARY SOURCE

The Lord of Fishes, He Who Makes the marsh birds to Go Upstream. There are no birds which come down because of the hot winds. He who makes barley and brings emmer [a kind of wheat] into being, that he may make the temples festive. If he is sluggish, then nostrils are stopped up, and everybody is poor. If there be thus a cutting down in the food offerings of the gods, then a million men perish among mortals, covetousness is practiced, the entire land is in a fury, and great and small are on the execution-block. . . . When he rises, then the land is in jubilation, then every belly is in joy, every backbone takes on laughter, and every tooth is exposed.

"Hymn to the Nile," from *Ancient Near Eastern Texts*

1 What natural phenomenon does the Lord of the Fishes represent?
(1) volcanic action
(2) monsoons
(3) the annual flooding of the Nile
(4) a major fish kill

2 Why are the people happy when the Lord of the Fishes comes to them?
(1) The wars they fight will be over.
(2) They will have food to eat.
(3) Corruption will stop.
(4) There will be a new pharaoh.

Use the map and your knowledge of world history to answer question 3.

World Climate Regions

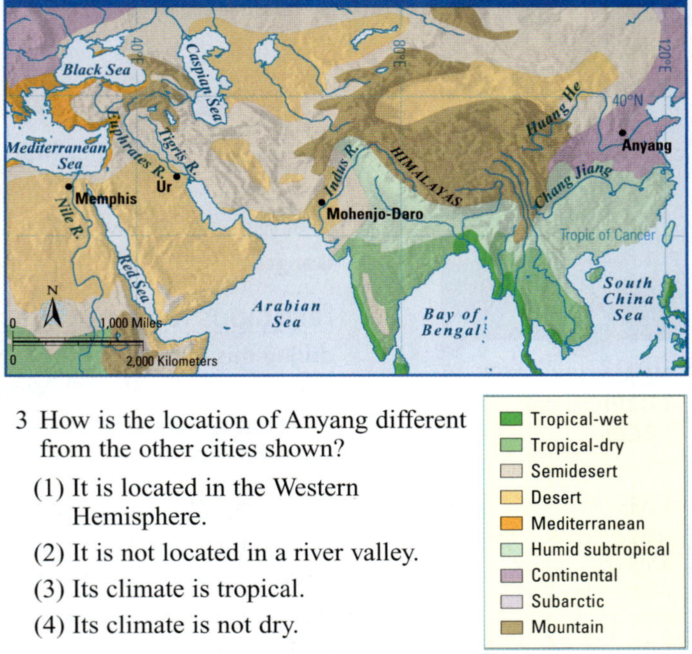

3 How is the location of Anyang different from the other cities shown?
(1) It is located in the Western Hemisphere.
(2) It is not located in a river valley.
(3) Its climate is tropical.
(4) Its climate is not dry.

INTEGRATED TECHNOLOGY

TEST PRACTICE Go to **classzone.com**
- Diagnostic tests
- Tutorials
- Strategies
- Additional practice

ALTERNATIVE ASSESSMENT

1. Interact *with* History

On page 28, you looked at the justice of Hammurabi's Code. Now that you have read about the development of four civilizations, think about how laws differ from place to place. How have they developed and changed over time? What similarities do you see between Hammurabi's Code and the laws you live under today? How are they different? Discuss your opinions with a small group.

2. WRITING ABOUT HISTORY

INTERACTION WITH ENVIRONMENT Write four **poems**, one for each civilization in the chapter. Include some reference to how each civilization interacted with the environment. Consider the following:
- the effect of the environment on life in the area
- responses to the environment by the people

INTEGRATED TECHNOLOGY

Creating a Multimedia Presentation

Using the Internet, the library, or government resources, research the street structure of Washington, D.C., Boston, or the structure of your hometown streets. Identify their similarities and differences. Then research/work with a team to present your findings in a multimedia presentation.
- Which cities have a grid system? Which do not?
- What evidence is there of planning in the cities?
- What are the obvious similarities and differences of the two locations?

CHAPTER 3

People and Ideas on the-Move, 2000 B.C.–250 B.C.

Previewing Main Ideas

INTERACTION WITH ENVIRONMENT Early peoples often migrated from their lands to find new homes that promised a better life. Once they moved, they had to deal with a new environment.

Geography *Why did so many of the ancient trade routes cross the seas?*

RELIGIOUS AND ETHICAL SYSTEMS Three major world religions developed during this time. Hinduism and Buddhism originated in India, while Judaism developed in Southwest Asia.

Geography *What routes of communication existed between the Bay of Bengal near India and Phoenicia and Jerusalem in Southwest Asia?*

ECONOMICS Traders transported their goods to other parts of the world. Among the early trading peoples were the Phoenicians, who dominated the Mediterranean. Sea traders also traveled between India and Arabia.

Geography *How was the Arabian Peninsula well situated to take part in world trade?*

NEW YORK CORE CURRICULUM FOCUS

- Indo-Europeans spread their language and beliefs as they migrated into Europe, India, and Southwest Asia.
- The Phoenicians established trade routes that connected Africa and Europe by sea.

INTEGRATED TECHNOLOGY

eEdition
- Interactive Maps
- Interactive Visuals
- Interactive Primary Sources

INTERNET RESOURCES

Go to classzone.com for:
- Research Links
- Internet Activities
- Primary Sources
- Chapter Quiz
- Maps
- Test Practice
- Current Events

EASTERN HEMISPHERE

2000 B.C. Hittites migrate to Anatolia. (Hittite burial stone) ▶

1500 B.C. Aryans invade India.

2000 B.C. | **1500 B.C.**

WESTERN HEMISPHERE

1200 B.C. ◀ Olmec civilization emerges in southeast Mexico. (Olmec giant stone head)

The Ancient World, 1500 B.C.–250 B.C.

1100 B.C. Phoenicians begin to dominate Mediterranean trade. (Carthaginian glass bead) ▶

814 B.C. Carthage founded as a Phoenician trade center.

586 B.C. Jerusalem captured by Babylonians.

1000 B.C.

250 B.C.

900 B.C. Chavín culture arises in Peru.

500 B.C. Zapotecs found Monte Albán. (Zapotec jade mask) ▶

Interact *with* History

Why might you leave your homeland?

When your family, along with many others, decided to leave its homeland, you wondered whether you should go. It was hard to leave the land you love. Yet life there was becoming increasingly difficult. As your community grew larger, grazing for its many animals had become scarce. And lately, there had been rumors of coming invaders.

You have been walking and riding for days. Now you wonder whether you should have stayed. Will you find a new homeland, a better place in which to live? Will you survive the journey? Will you be welcome in a new land?

EXAMINING *the* ISSUES

- **If you had stayed, would you have been able to adapt to changing conditions?**
- **Will you have to adopt the customs of the people living in a new land? How will you survive there?**

As a class, discuss these questions. In your discussion, weigh the advantages and disadvantages of staying in your homeland and of leaving. As you read about migration in this chapter, see how old and new ways of doing things can blend together when groups of people move.

1

The Indo-Europeans

CONNECT TO THE NEW YORK STATE CORE CURRICULUM

Unit 1.B.1.a. Human and physical geography of early river civilizations
Unit 1.B.1.d. Social structures and urbanization

TERMS & NAMES

- Indo-Europeans
- steppes
- migration
- Hittites
- Anatolia
- Aryans
- Vedas
- Brahmin
- caste
- *Mahabharata*

SETTING THE STAGE In India and in Mesopotamia, civilizations first developed along lush river valleys. Even as large cities such as Mohenjo-Daro and Harappa declined, agriculture and small urban communities flourished. These wealthy river valleys attracted nomadic tribes. These peoples may have left their own homelands because of warfare or changes in the environment.

Indo-Europeans Migrate

The **Indo-Europeans** were a group of nomadic peoples who may have come from the **steppes**—dry grasslands that stretched north of the Caucasus (KAW•kuh•suhs). The Caucasus are the mountains between the Black and Caspian seas. These primarily pastoral people herded cattle, sheep, and goats. The Indo-Europeans also tamed horses and rode into battle in light, two-wheeled chariots. They lived in tribes that spoke forms of a language that we call Indo-European.

TAKING NOTES

Categorizing Use a web diagram to record some of the languages that stem from Indo-European.

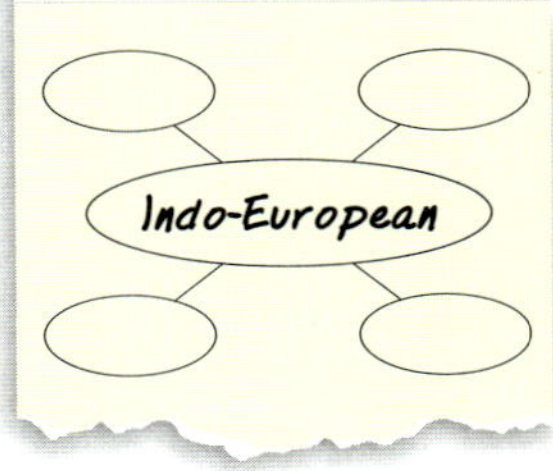

The Indo-European Language Family The languages of the Indo-Europeans were the ancestors of many of the modern languages of Europe, Southwest Asia, and South Asia. English, Spanish, Persian, and Hindi all trace their origins back to different forms of the original Indo-European language.

Historians can tell where Indo-European tribes settled by their languages. Some Slavic speakers moved north and west. Others, who spoke early Celtic, Germanic, and Italic languages, moved west through Europe. Speakers of Greek and Persian went south. The Aryans (AIR•ee•uhnz), who spoke an early form of Sanskrit, located in India.

Notice the similarities of words within the Indo-European family of languages.

Language Family Resemblances

English	Sanskrit	Persian	Spanish	German
mother	mātár	muhdáhr	madre	Mutter
father	pitár	puhdáhr	padre	Vater
daughter	duhitár	dukhtáhr	hija	Tochter
new	návas	now	nuevo	neu
six	sát	shahsh	seis	sechs

Indo-European Migrations, Starting about 1700 B.C.

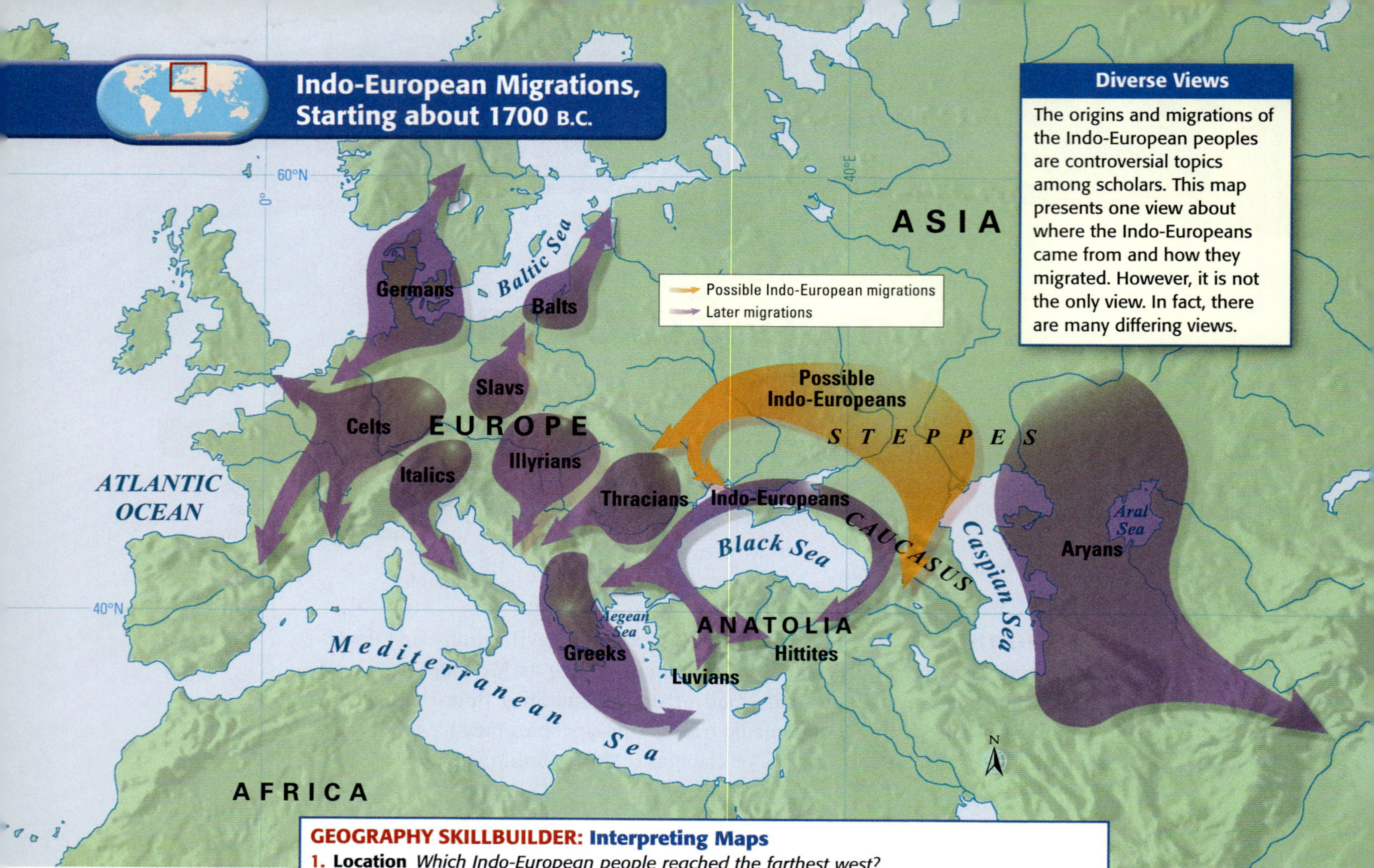

Diverse Views

The origins and migrations of the Indo-European peoples are controversial topics among scholars. This map presents one view about where the Indo-Europeans came from and how they migrated. However, it is not the only view. In fact, there are many differing views.

GEOGRAPHY SKILLBUILDER: Interpreting Maps

1. **Location** *Which Indo-European people reached the farthest west?*
2. **Movement** *Describe the movement of the Indo-Europeans in their earliest migrations.*

An Unexplained Migration No one knows why these people left their homelands in the steppes. Whatever the reason, Indo-European nomads began to migrate outward in all directions between 1700 and 1200 B.C. These **migrations**, movements of a people from one region to another, happened in waves over a long period of time.

The Hittite Empire

By about 2000 B.C., one group of Indo-European speakers, the **Hittites**, occupied **Anatolia** (AN•uh•TOH•lee•uh), also called Asia Minor. Anatolia is a huge peninsula in modern-day Turkey that juts out into the Black and Mediterranean seas. Anatolia is a high, rocky plateau, rich in timber and agriculture. Nearby mountains hold important mineral deposits. Separate Hittite city-states came together to form an empire there in about 1650 B.C. The city of Hattusas (hah•TOO•sahs) was its capital.

The Hittite empire went on to dominate Southwest Asia for 450 years. Hittites occupied Babylon, the chief city in the Tigris-Euphrates Valley, and struggled with Egypt for control of northern Syria. Neither the Hittites nor the Egyptians were able to get the upper hand. So, the two peoples ended their conflicts by signing a peace treaty. They each pledged to help the other fight off future invaders.

Hittites Adopt and Adapt The Hittites used their own Indo-European language with one another. However, for international use, they adopted Akkadian, the language of the Babylonians they had conquered. The Hittites borrowed ideas about literature, art, politics, and law from the Mesopotamians. The Hittites thus blended their own traditions with those of other, more advanced peoples.

Chariots and Iron Technology The Hittites excelled in the technology of war. They conquered an empire against Egyptian opposition—largely through their superior chariots and their iron weapons. The Hittite war chariot was light and easy to maneuver. The chariot had two wheels and a wooden frame covered with leather and was pulled by two or sometimes four horses. The Hittite chariot proved itself a superb fighting machine.

▲ This Hittite relief sculpture shows an archer in a chariot with his charioteer.

The Hittites used iron in their chariots, and they owed many of their military victories to the skill of their ironworkers. Ancient peoples had long known that iron was stronger than bronze. They also knew that it could hold a sharper edge. However, the process of purifying iron ore and working it into weapons and tools is complex. Around 1500 B.C., the Hittites were the first in Southwest Asia to work with iron and harden it into weapons of war. The raw materials they needed—iron ore and wood to make charcoal—were easily available to them in the mountains of Anatolia. Knowledge of iron technology traveled widely with the Hittites—in both their trade and conquests. **A**

MAIN IDEA

Recognizing Effects

A How did environmental features in Anatolia help the Hittites advance technologically?

Despite its military might, the powerful Hittite empire fell quite suddenly around the year 1190 B.C. As part of a great wave of invasions, tribes attacked from the north and burned the Hittite capital city.

Aryans Transform India

Before 2000 B.C., the Hittites began establishing themselves in Anatolia. At the same time some scholars believe, another Indo-European people, the **Aryans**, whose homeland was probably somewhere between the Caspian and Aral seas, crossed over the northwest mountain passes into the Indus River Valley of India. Other scholars believe the Aryans originated in India. There is no archaeological evidence to prove either hypothesis.

Though they left almost no archaeological record, their sacred literature, the **Vedas** (VAY•duhz), left a picture of Aryan life. The Vedas are four collections of prayers, magical spells, and instructions for performing rituals. The most important of the collections is the Rig Veda. The Rig Veda contains 1,028 hymns to Aryan gods. For many years, no written form of the Vedas existed. Instead, elders of one generation passed on this tradition orally to the next generation.

A Caste System Develops The Aryans fought their enemies, a people they called the *dasas*. The Aryans differed from the *dasas* in many ways. Aryans were taller, lighter in skin color, and spoke a different language. Unlike the earlier inhabitants of the Indus Valley, the Aryans had not developed a writing system. They were also a pastoral people and counted their wealth in cows. The *dasas,* on the other hand, were town dwellers who lived in communities protected by walls.

When they first arrived in India, Aryans were organized into four groups based on occupation: 1) **Brahmins** (priests), 2) warriors, 3) traders and landowners, and 4) peasants or traders. The group that an Aryan belonged to determined his or her role in society.

Analyzing Art

The Aryan Caste System

The four major castes emerged from Purusha (the first human being) shown at the right. Purusha is identified with the creator god Brahma. The Brahmins (priests) were his mouth, the warriors were his arms, the landowners and traders were his legs, and the laborers and peasants were his feet.

SKILLBUILDER:
Interpreting Visual Sources
Making Inferences *Why might the caste of Brahmins (priests) have been associated with the mouth?*

were laborers who did work that Aryans did not want to do. *Varna,* or skin color, was a distinguishing feature of this system. So the four major groups came to be known as the *varnas.* Later, in the 15th century A.D., explorers from Portugal encountered this social system and called these groups **castes** (kasts).

As time went on, the four basic castes gradually grew more complex—with hundreds of subdivisions. Classical texts state that caste should not be determined by birth. However, over time, some communities developed a system in which people were born into their caste. Their caste membership determined the work they did, whom they could marry, and the people with whom they could eat. Cleanliness and purity became all-important. Those considered the most impure because of their work (butchers, gravediggers, collectors of trash) lived outside the caste structure. They were known as "untouchables," since even their touch endangered the ritual purity of others. B

MAIN IDEA
Making Inferences
B How were the more physical forms of work viewed by Aryans?

Aryan Kingdoms Arise Over the next few centuries, Aryans extended their settlements east, along the Ganges and Yamuna river valleys. (See map on page 65.) Progress was slow because of difficulties clearing the jungle for farming. This task grew easier when iron came into use in India about 1000 B.C.

When the Aryans first arrived in India, chiefs were elected by the entire tribe. Around 1000 B.C., however, minor kings who wanted to set up territorial kingdoms arose among the Aryans. They struggled with one another for land and power. Out of this strife emerged a major kingdom: Magadha. Under a series of ambitious kings, Magadha began expanding in the sixth century B.C. by taking over surrounding kingdoms. By the second century B.C., Magadha had expanded south to occupy almost all of the Indian subcontinent.

One of the great epics of India, the ***Mahabharata*** (MAH•huh•BAH•ruh•tuh), reflects the struggles that took place in India as the Aryan kings worked to control Indian lands. One part of the *Mahabharata* is the *Bhagavad Gita.* It tells the story of a warrior prince about to go to war. His chariot driver is Krishna, a god in human form.

◀ This painting of Krishna battling with a demon in the form of a snake was created in 1785.

One of the most famous incidents in Indian literature occurs when Krishna instructs the young warrior on the proper way to live, fight, and die:

PRIMARY SOURCE

He who thinks this Self [eternal spirit] to be a slayer, and he who thinks this Self to be slain, are both without discernment; the Soul slays not, neither is it slain. . . . But if you will not wage this lawful battle, then will you fail your own [caste] law and your honor, and incur sin. . . . The people will name you with dishonor; and to a man of fame dishonor is worse than death.

KRISHNA, speaking in the *Bhagavad Gita*

The violence and confusion of the time led many to speculate about the place of the gods and human beings in the world. As a result, religion in India gradually changed. New religions were born, which you will read about in Section 2.

NEW YORK CORE CURRICULUM REVIEW

TERMS & NAMES 1. For each term or name, write a sentence explaining its significance.

• Indo-Europeans • steppes • migration • Hittites • Anatolia • Aryans • Vedas • Brahmin • caste • Mahabharata

USING YOUR NOTES

2. Why did so many languages originate from Indo-European roots?

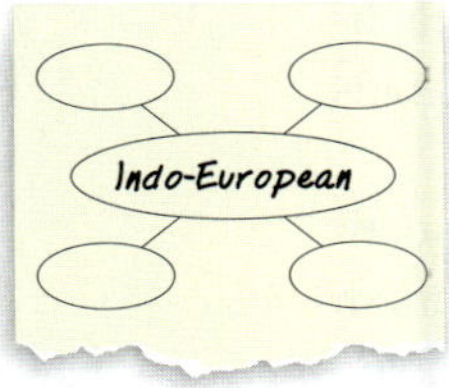

MAIN IDEAS

3. What were some of the technological achievements of the Hittites?
4. What were some of the borrowings of the Hittites?
5. Where do some historians think the Aryans lived before they arrived in India?

CRITICAL THINKING & WRITING

6. **FORMING OPINIONS** What important contributions did the Aryans make to the culture and way of life in India in terms of religion, literature, and roles in society?
7. **DRAWING CONCLUSIONS** Look at the Hittite chariot on page-63. What made it an excellent fighting machine?
8. **COMPARING AND CONTRASTING** What were some of the differences between the Aryans and the *dasas* in India?
9. **WRITING ACTIVITY** INTERACTION WITH ENVIRONMENT Write-an **expository essay** in which you discuss environmental reasons why the Indo-Europeans might have migrated.

INTEGRATED TECHNOLOGY **INTERNET ACTIVITY**

Use the Internet to create a **chart** that shows how a word in English is expressed in other Indo-European languages. Choose languages other than the ones listed on page 61 in this section.

INTERNET KEYWORD
words in Indo-European languages

Hinduism and Buddhism Develop

CONNECT TO THE NEW YORK STATE CORE CURRICULUM

Unit 1.E.1.b. Hinduism
Unit 1.E.1.c. Buddhism

TERMS & NAMES

- reincarnation
- karma
- Jainism
- Siddhartha Gautama
- enlightenment
- nirvana

SETTING THE STAGE At first, the Aryans and non-Aryans followed their own forms of religion. Then as the two groups intermingled, the gods and forms of their religions also tended to blend together. This blending resulted in the worship of thousands of gods. Different ways of living and different beliefs made life more complex for both groups. This complexity led some people to question the world and their place in it. They even questioned the enormous wealth and power held by the Brahmin priests. Out of this turmoil, new religious ideas arose that have continued to influence millions of people today.

TAKING NOTES

Comparing and Contrasting Use a Venn diagram to compare the beliefs and practices of Buddhism and Hinduism.

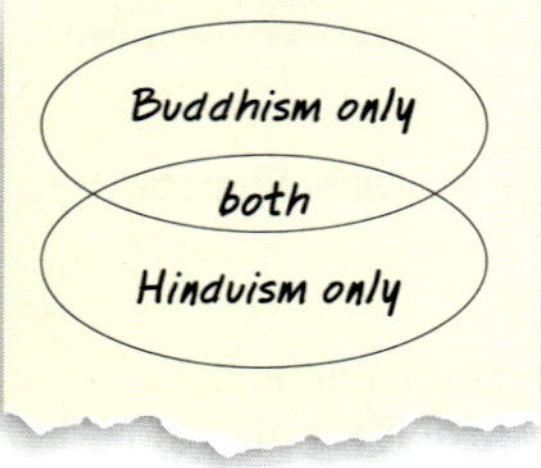

Hinduism Evolves Over Centuries

Hinduism is a collection of religious beliefs that developed slowly over a long period of time. Some aspects of the religion can be traced back to ancient times. In a Hindu marriage today, for example, the bride and groom marry in the presence of the sacred fire as they did centuries ago. The faithful recite daily verses from the Vedas.

From time to time, scholars have tried to organize the many popular cults, gods, and traditions into one grand system of belief. However, Hinduism—unlike religions such as Buddhism, Christianity, or Islam—cannot be traced back to one founder with a single set of ideas.

Origins and Beliefs Hindus share a common worldview. They see religion as a way of liberating the soul from the illusions, disappointments, and mistakes of everyday existence. Sometime between 750 and 550 B.C., Hindu teachers tried to interpret and explain the hidden meaning of the Vedic hymns. The teachers' comments were later written down and became known as the Upanishads (oo•PAHN•ih•shahdz).

The Upanishads are written as dialogues, or discussions, between a student and a teacher. In the course of the dialogues, the two explore how a person can achieve liberation from desires and suffering. This is described as *moksha* (MOHK•shah), a state of perfect understanding of all things. The teacher distinguishes between atman, the individual soul of a living being, and Brahman, the world soul that contains and unites all atmans. Here is how one teacher explains the unifying spirit of Brahman:

PRIMARY SOURCE

Thou art woman, Thou art man, Thou art the lad and the maiden too. Thou art the old man tottering on his staff: Once born thou comest to be, thy face turned every way! A dark-blue moth art Thou, green [parrot] with red eyes. Pregnant with lightning—seasons, seas: Thyself beginningless, all things dost Thou pervade. From Thee all worlds were born.

Svetasvatara Upanishad. IV. 3–4

When a person understands the relationship between atman and Brahman, that person achieves perfect understanding (*moksha*) and a release from life in this world. This understanding does not usually come in one lifetime. By the process of **reincarnation** (rebirth), an individual soul or spirit is born again and again until *moksha* is achieved. A soul's **karma**—good or bad deeds—follows from one reincarnation to another. Karma influences specific life circumstances, such as the caste one is born into, one's state of health, wealth or poverty, and so on.

Hinduism Changes and Develops Hinduism has gone through many changes over the last 2,500 years. The world soul, Brahman, was sometimes seen as having the personalities of three gods: Brahma, the creator; Vishnu, the protector; and Shiva, the destroyer. Vishnu also took on many forms or personalities, for example, as Krishna, the divine cowherder, and as Rama, the perfect king. Over the centuries, Brahma gradually faded into the background, while the many forms of Devi, a great Mother Goddess, grew in importance.

Hindus today are free to choose the deity they worship or to choose none at all. Most, however, follow a family tradition that may go back centuries. They are also free to choose among three different paths for achieving *moksha.* These are the path of right thinking, the path of right action, or the path of religious devotion. (A)

MAIN IDEA

Making Inferences

(A) How might the lack of a single founder result in Hinduism changing more over time than other religions?

Hinduism and Society Hindu ideas about karma and reincarnation strengthened the caste system. If a person was born as an upper-caste male—a Brahmin, warrior, or merchant—his good fortune was said to come from good karma earned in a former life. However, a person who was born as a female, a laborer, or an untouchable might be getting the results of bad deeds in a former life. With some exceptions, only men of the top three varnas could hope to achieve *moksha* in their present life. The laws of karma worked with the same certainty as the world's other natural laws. Good karma brought good fortune and bad karma resulted in bad fortune.

▼ Vishnu grew to become a major Hindu god. He is seen here as the whole Universe in all its variety. He is blue, the color of infinity.

Together, the beliefs of Hinduism and its caste structure dominated every aspect of a person's life. These beliefs determined what one could eat and the way in which one ate it, personal cleanliness, the people one could associate with, how one dressed, and so on. Today, even in the most ordinary activities of daily life, Hindus turn to their religion for guidance.

New Religions Arise The same period of speculation reflected in the Upanishads also led to the rise of two other religions: Jainism (JY•nihz•uhm) and Buddhism. Mahavira, the founder of **Jainism**, was born about 599 B.C. and died in 527 B.C. Mahavira believed that everything in the universe has a soul and so should not be harmed. Jain monks carry the doctrine of nonviolence to its logical conclusion. They sweep ants off their path and wear gauze masks over their mouths to avoid breathing in an insect accidentally. In keeping with this nonviolence, followers of Jainism looked for occupations that would not harm any creature. So they have a tradition of working in trade and commerce. **B**

MAIN IDEA

Synthesizing

B How far might the Jain respect for life extend?

Because of their business activities, Jains today make up one of the wealthiest communities in India. Jains have traditionally preached tolerance of all religions. As a result, they have made few efforts to convert followers of other faiths. Because of this tolerance, Jains have not sent out missionaries. So, almost all of the nearly five million Jains in the world today live in India.

The Buddha Seeks Enlightenment

Buddhism developed out of the same period of religious questioning that shaped modern Hinduism and Jainism. The founder of Buddhism, **Siddhartha Gautama** (sihd•DAHR•tuh GOW•tuh•muh), was born into a noble family that lived in Kapilavastu, in the foothills of the Himalayas in Nepal. According to Buddhist legend, the baby exhibited the marks of a great man. A prophecy indicated that if the child stayed at home he was destined to become a world ruler. If the child left home, however, he would become a universal spiritual leader. To make sure the boy would be a great king and world ruler, his father isolated him in his palace. Separated from the world, Siddhartha married and had a son.

Siddhartha's Quest Siddhartha never ceased thinking about the world that lay outside, which he had never seen. When he was 29, he ventured outside the palace four times. First he saw an old man, next a sick man, then a corpse, and finally a wandering holy man who seemed at peace with himself. Siddhartha understood these events to mean that every living thing experiences old age, sickness, and death and that only a religious life offers a refuge from this inevitable suffering. Siddhartha decided to spend his life searching for religious truth and an end to life's suffering. So, soon after learning of his son's birth, he left the palace.

Siddhartha wandered through the forests of India for six years seeking **enlightenment**, or wisdom. He tried many ways of reaching an enlightened state. He first debated with other religious seekers. Then he fasted, eating only six grains of rice a day. Yet none of these methods brought him to the truth, and he continued to suffer. Finally, he sat in meditation under a large fig tree. After 49 days of meditation, he achieved an understanding of the cause of suffering in this world. From then on, he was known as the Buddha, meaning "the enlightened one."

Vocabulary

fasted: ate very little.

Origins and Beliefs The Buddha preached his first sermon to five companions who had accompanied him on his wanderings. That first sermon became a landmark in the history of the world's religions. In it, he laid out the four main ideas that he had come to understand in his enlightenment. He called those ideas the Four Noble Truths:

History Makers

Siddhartha Gautama

c. 563–483 B.C.

According to Buddhist tradition, Siddhartha Gautama's mother had dreamt of a beautiful elephant that was bright as silver. When asked to interpret the dream, Brahmin priests declared that the child to be born would either be a great monarch or a Buddha (an enlightened one).

Tradition also relates that at Gautama's birth, he exhibited the signs of a child destined for greatness. There were 32 such signs, including golden-tinged skin, webbed fingers and toes, a knob on the top of his skull, a long tongue, a tuft of hair between his eyebrows, and a thousand-spoked wheel on each foot. Some images of the Buddha display these traits.

The Four Noble Truths	
First Noble Truth	Life is filled with suffering and sorrow.
Second Noble Truth	The cause of all suffering is people's selfish desire for the temporary pleasures of this world.
Third Noble Truth	The way to end all suffering is to end all desires.
Fourth Noble Truth	The way to overcome such desires and attain enlightenment is to follow the Eightfold Path, which is called the Middle Way between desires and self-denial.

The Eightfold Path, a guide to behavior, was like a staircase. For the Buddha, those who were seeking enlightenment had to master one step at a time. Most often, this mastery would occur over many lifetimes. Here is how he described the Middle Way and its Eightfold Path:

PRIMARY SOURCE

What is the Middle Way? . . . It is the Noble Eightfold Path—Right Views, Right Resolve, Right Speech, Right Conduct, Right Livelihood, Right Effort, Right Mindfulness, and Right Concentration. This is the Middle Way.

BUDDHA, from *Samyutta Nikaya*

By following the Eightfold Path, anyone could reach **nirvana**, the Buddha's word for release from selfishness and pain.

As in Hinduism, the Buddha accepted the idea of reincarnation. He also accepted a cyclical, or repetitive, view of history, where the world is created and destroyed over and over again. However, the Buddha rejected the many gods of Hinduism. Instead, he taught a way of enlightenment. Like many of his time, the Buddha reacted against the privileges of the Brahmin priests, and thus he rejected the caste system. The final goals of both religions—*moksha* for Hindus and nirvana for Buddhists—are similar. Both involve a perfect state of understanding and a break from the chain of reincarnations. (C)

MAIN IDEA

Comparing

(C) In what ways are Buddhism and Hinduism similar?

▼ Buddhist tradition says that just before he died, the Buddha lay on his right side between two trees. This reclining Buddha is made of bronze.

▲ Buddhist monks view a temple at Angkor Wat in Cambodia.

The Religious Community The five disciples who heard the Buddha's first sermon were the first monks admitted to the *sangha,* or Buddhist religious order. At first, the *sangha* was a community of Buddhist monks and nuns. However, *sangha* eventually referred to the entire religious community. It included Buddhist laity (those who hadn't devoted their entire life to religion). The religious community, together with the Buddha and the *dharma* (Buddhist doctrine or teachings), make up the "Three Jewels" of Buddhism.

Buddhism and Society Because of his rejection of the caste system, many of the Buddha's early followers included laborers and craftspeople. He also gained a large following in northeast India, where the Aryans had less influence. The Buddha reluctantly admitted women to religious orders. He feared, however, that women's presence would distract men from their religious duties.

Monks and nuns took vows (solemn promises) to live a life of poverty, to be nonviolent, and not to marry. They wandered throughout India spreading the Buddha's teachings. Missionaries carried only a begging bowl to receive daily charity offerings from people. During the rainy season, they retreated to caves high up in the hillsides. Gradually, these seasonal retreats became permanent monasteries—some for men, others for women. One monastery, Nalanda, developed into a great university that also attracted non-Buddhists.

The teachings of the Buddha were written down shortly after his death. Buddhist sacred literature also includes commentaries, rules about monastic life, manuals on how to meditate, and legends about the Buddha's previous reincarnations (the *Jatakas*). This sacred literature was first written down in the first century B.C.

Buddhism in India During the centuries following the Buddha's death, missionaries were able to spread his faith over large parts of Asia. Buddhist missionaries went to Sri Lanka and Southeast Asia in the third century B.C. Buddhist ideas also traveled along Central Asian trade routes to China. However, Buddhism never gained a significant foothold in India, the country of its origin. Several theories exist about Buddhism's gradual disappearance in India. One theory states that

Hinduism simply absorbed Buddhism. The two religions constantly influenced each other. Over time, the Buddha came to be identified by Hindus as one of the ten incarnations (reappearances on earth) of the god Vishnu. Hindus, therefore, felt no need to convert to Buddhism.

Vocabulary
pilgrimages:-travels to holy places.

Nonetheless, despite the small number of Buddhists in India, the region has always been an important place of pilgrimages for Buddhists. Today, as they have for centuries, Buddhist pilgrims flock to visit spots associated with the Buddha's life. These sites include his birthplace at Kapilavastu, the fig tree near Gaya, and the site of his first sermon near Varanasi. Buddhists also visit the *stupas,* or sacred mounds, that are said to contain his relics. The pilgrims circle around the sacred object or sanctuary, moving in a clockwise direction. They also lie face down on the ground as a sign of humility and leave flowers. These three actions are important rituals in Buddhist worship.

Trade and the Spread of Buddhism-As important as missionaries were to the spread of Buddhism, traders played an even more crucial role in this process. Along with their products, traders carried Buddhism beyond India to Sri Lanka. Buddhist religion was also brought southeast along trade routes to Burma, Thailand, and the island of Sumatra. Likewise, Buddhism followed the Central Asian trade routes, called the Silk Roads, all the way to China. From China, Buddhism spread to Korea—and from Korea to Japan. The movement of trade thus succeeded in making Buddhism the most widespread religion of East Asia. Throughout human history, trade has been a powerful force for the spread of ideas. Just as trade spread Buddhism in East Asia, it helped spread cultural influences in another major region of the world: the Mediterranean basin, as you will learn in Section 3.

Connect *to* Today

Buddhism in the West

Throughout the 20th century, large numbers of Asians have immigrated to the West, particularly to North America. Many of them brought Buddhism with them. Today, Buddhist temples are a common feature of many large cities in the West.

Since the 1950s, many non-Asians who were dissatisfied with the religions of the West have turned to Buddhism for insight into life's meaning. Today, Buddhism can claim about one million Asian and non-Asian believers in North America.

INTEGRATED TECHNOLOGY

INTERNET ACTIVITY Create a bar graph to show the number of Buddhists in some American cities. Go to **classzone.com** for your research.

NEW YORK CORE CURRICULUM REVIEW

TERMS & NAMES 1. For each term or name, write a sentence explaining its significance.

- reincarnation
- karma
- Jainism
- Siddhartha Gautama
- enlightenment
- nirvana

USING YOUR NOTES

2. What are the terms for enlightenment in each religion?

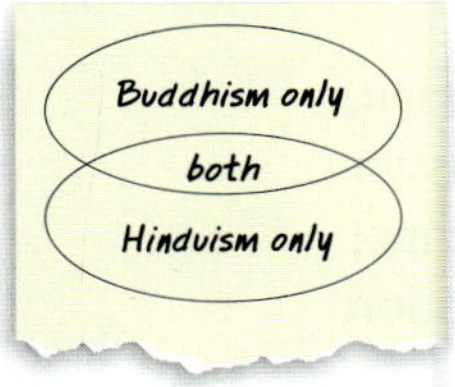

MAIN IDEAS

3. What are the Four Noble Truths of Buddhism?
4. How has Hinduism influenced social structure in India?
5. How did Buddhism spread?

CRITICAL THINKING & WRITING

6. **MAKING INFERENCES** How might the belief in reincarnation provide a form of social control?
7. **COMPARING** How are the Vedas and the Upanishads similar?
8. **MAKING INFERENCES** Look at the image of Vishnu on page-67. Why might blue represent infinity?
9. **WRITING ACTIVITY** RELIGIOUS SYSTEMS How did the experiences of Siddhartha Gautama influence his religious and ethical beliefs? Write a brief **biography** of his life. Include family background, accomplishments, and a list of his beliefs.

CONNECT TO TODAY **CREATING A MAP**

Where in the world is Hinduism the main religion? What about Buddhism? Copy an **outline map** of the world. Then color in those regions of the world where Buddhism and Hinduism are the dominant religions. Use a different color for each religion.

3

Seafaring Traders

CONNECT TO THE NEW YORK STATE CORE CURRICULUM

Unit 1.C.7.a. Phoenician trade routes
Unit 1.C.7.c.1. Linking Africa and Eurasia

TERMS & NAMES

- Minoans
- Aegean Sea
- Knossos
- King Minos
- Phoenicians

SETTING THE STAGE Buddhism spread to Southeast Asia and to East Asia mainly through Buddhist traders. In the Mediterranean, the same process took place: traders in the region carried many new ideas from one society to another. They carried new ways of writing, of governing, and of worshiping their gods.

TAKING NOTES
Comparing Identify accomplishments that were Minoan and those that were Phoenician in the following chart.

Minoan	Phoenician
1.	1.
2.	2.
3.	3.

Minoans Trade in the Mediterranean

A powerful seafaring people, the **Minoans** (mih•NOH•uhnz) dominated trade in the eastern Mediterranean from about 2000 to 1400 B.C. They lived on Crete, a large island on the southern edge of the **Aegean Sea** (ee•JEE•uhn). The Minoans produced some of the finest painted pottery of the time. They traded that pottery, along with swords, figurines, and vessels of precious metals, over a large area.

Along with their goods, Minoans also exported their art and culture. These included a unique architecture, burial customs, and religious rituals. Minoan culture had a major influence on Greece, for example. Trading turned Crete into a "stepping stone" for cultural exchange throughout the Mediterranean world.

Unearthing a Brilliant Civilization Archaeologists in the late 19th and early 20th centuries excavated **Knossos**, the Minoan capital city. There, they found the remains of an advanced and thriving culture. It must have been a peaceful one as well, since Minoan cities did not seem to need fortifications to protect them. The archaeologists named the civilization they found in Crete *Minoa* after **King Minos** (MY•nuhs). According to legend, Minos was a king who owned a half-human, half-bull monster called the Minotaur (MIHN•uh•TAWR). He kept the monster locked inside a labyrinth, a complicated maze from which no one could escape.

The excavation of Knossos and its painted walls produced much information about Minoans. The wall paintings, as well as the official seals and vases, show the Minoans as graceful, athletic people who loved nature and beautiful objects. They also enjoyed sports such as boxing, wrestling, and bull leaping.

Many Minoan artworks depict women and their role in religious ceremonies. The art suggests that women held a higher rank than in most neighboring cultures. A great Mother Earth Goddess seems to have ruled over the other gods of Crete. Also, priestesses took charge of some shrines, aided by male assistants.

Social History

Bull Leapers of Knossos

The wall painting to the right captures the death-defying jump of a Minoan bull leaper in mid-flight. Many works of Minoan art show young men performing incredible acrobatic leaps over the horns of angry bulls. In one case, the gymnast jumps over the bull's horns, makes a somersault off its back, and lands behind its tail.

In another gymnastic feat, some team members hang on to the horns of a bull, using their bodies to cushion its horns and to force its head low, while another team member jumps over its back.

What was the reason for this bull leaping? Was it a sport? Just a "fun" activity? An initiation for young warriors? Or a religious ritual? Most likely it was all of these things.

The Minoans sacrificed bulls and other animals to their gods. In at least one case, a young man was sacrificed. Excavation of a mountain temple revealed the bones of a 17-year-old boy on an altar, along with the skeletons of three priests. The positions of the skeletons suggest that the priests carried out the human sacrifice just before the building collapsed.

Minoan Culture's Mysterious End The Minoan civilization finally ended about 1200 B.C. The reasons for its end are unclear. Could it have been the result of some natural disaster? Did the island become overpopulated? Or was it overrun by invaders?

The civilization had withstood previous disasters. In about 1700 B.C., a great disaster, perhaps an earthquake, destroyed most Minoan towns and cities. The Minoans rebuilt the cities with equal richness. Then in 1470 B.C. a series of earthquakes rocked Crete. The quakes were followed by a violent volcanic eruption on the neighboring island of Thera. Imagine the shaking of the earth, the fiery volcanic blast, then a huge tidal wave, and finally a rain of white volcanic ash.

The disaster of 1470 B.C. was a blow from which the Minoans never fully recovered. This time, the Minoans had trouble rebuilding their cities. Nonetheless, Minoan civilization did linger on for almost 300 years. After that, invaders from Greece may have taken advantage of their weakened condition to destroy them. Some Minoans fled to the mountains to escape the ruin of the kingdom. Crete's influence as a major sea power and cultural force was over. (A)

MAIN IDEA

Summarizing

(A) What adjectives might describe Minoan civilization?

Phoenicians Spread Trade and Civilization

About 1100 B.C., after Crete's decline, the most powerful traders along the Mediterranean were the **Phoenicians** (fih•NIHSH•uhnz). Phoenicia was mainly the area now known as Lebanon. Phoenicians never united into a country. Instead, they founded a number of wealthy city-states around the Mediterranean that sometimes competed with one another. The first cities in Phoenicia, such as Byblos, Tyre, and Sidon, were important trading centers.

The Phoenicians were remarkable shipbuilders and seafarers. They were the first Mediterranean people to venture beyond the Strait of Gibraltar. Some scholars believe that the Phoenicians traded for tin with inhabitants of the southern coast of Britain. Some evidence exists for an even more remarkable feat—sailing around the continent of Africa by way of the Red Sea and back through the Strait of Gibraltar. Such a trip was not repeated again for 2,000 years. The Greek historian Herodotus (hih•RAHD•uh•tuhs) relates the feat:

PRIMARY SOURCE

The Phoenicians set out from the Red Sea and sailed the southern sea [the Indian Ocean]; whenever autumn came they would put in and sow the land, to whatever part of Libya [Africa] they might come, and there await the harvest; then, having gathered in the crop, they sailed on, so that after two years had passed, it was in the third that they rounded the Pillars of Heracles [Strait of Gibraltar] and came to Egypt. There they said (what some may believe, though I do not) that in sailing round Libya they had the sun on their right hand [in reverse position].

HERODOTUS, in *History*, Book IV (5th century B.C.)

Alphabets—Ancient and Modern

Phoenician	Greek	English
𐤀	Α	A
𐤁	Β	B
𐤂	Γ	C
𐤃	Δ	D
𐤄	Ε	E
𐤅		F
		G
	Ζ	
	Η	H
𐤈	Θ	
	Ι	I
		J
𐤊	Κ	K
𐤋	Λ	L
𐤌	Μ	M
𐤍	Ν	N
	Ξ	
𐤏	Ο	O
𐤐	Π	P
𐤑		
𐤒		Q
𐤓	Ρ	R
	Σ	S
𐤎		
𐤕	Τ	T
	Υ	U
	Φ	
		V
		W
	Χ	X
	Ψ	
𐤔		Y
𐤆		Z
	Ω	

SKILLBUILDER: Interpreting Charts

1. **Comparing** *Which letters show the most similarity across the three alphabets?*
2. **Making Inferences** *Why might one language have fewer letters in its alphabet than another?*

Commercial Outposts Around the Mediterranean The Phoenicians' most important city-states in the eastern Mediterranean were Sidon and Tyre, both known for their production of red-purple dye, and Byblos, a trading center for papyrus. (See map on page 59.) Phoenicians built colonies along the northern coast of Africa and the coasts of Sicily, Sardinia, and Spain. The colonies were about 30 miles apart—about the distance a Phoenician ship could sail in a day. The greatest Phoenician colony was at Carthage (KAHR•thihj), in North Africa. Settlers from Tyre founded Carthage in about 814 B.C.

The Phoenicians traded goods they got from other lands—wine, weapons, precious metals, ivory, and slaves. They also were known as superb craftspeople who worked in wood, metal, glass, and ivory. Their red-purple dye was produced from the murex, a kind of snail that lived in the waters off Sidon and Tyre. One snail, when left to rot, produced just a drop or two of a liquid of a deep red-purple color. Some 60,000 snails were needed to produce one pound of dye, which only royalty could afford.

Phoenicia's Great Legacy: The Alphabet As merchants, the Phoenicians needed a way of recording transactions clearly and quickly. So the Phoenicians developed a writing system that used symbols to represent sounds. The Phoenician system was phonetic—that is, one sign was used for one sound. In fact, the word *alphabet* comes directly from the first two letters of the Phoenician alphabet: *aleph* and *beth.* As they traveled around the Mediterranean, the Phoenicians introduced this writing system to their trading partners. The Greeks, for example, adopted the Phoenician alphabet and changed the form of some of the letters.

Phoenician Trade

Phoenicia was located in a great spot for trade because it lay along well-traveled routes between Egypt and Asia. However, the Phoenicians did more than just trade with merchants who happened to pass through their region. The Phoenicians became expert sailors and went looking for opportunities to make money.

The Patterns of Ancient Trade, 2000–250 B.C.

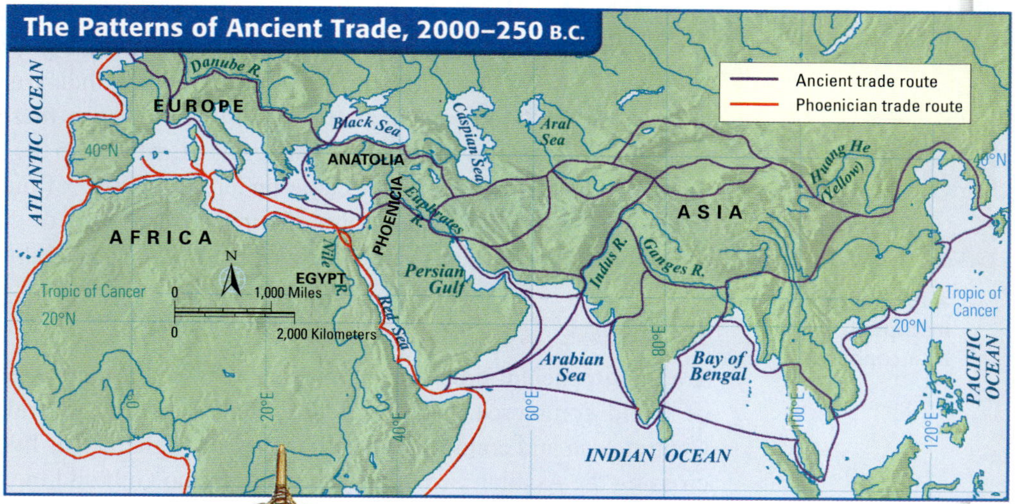

Merchant Ships

Phoenician sailors developed the round boat, a ship that was very wide and had a rounded bottom. This shape created a large space for cargo.

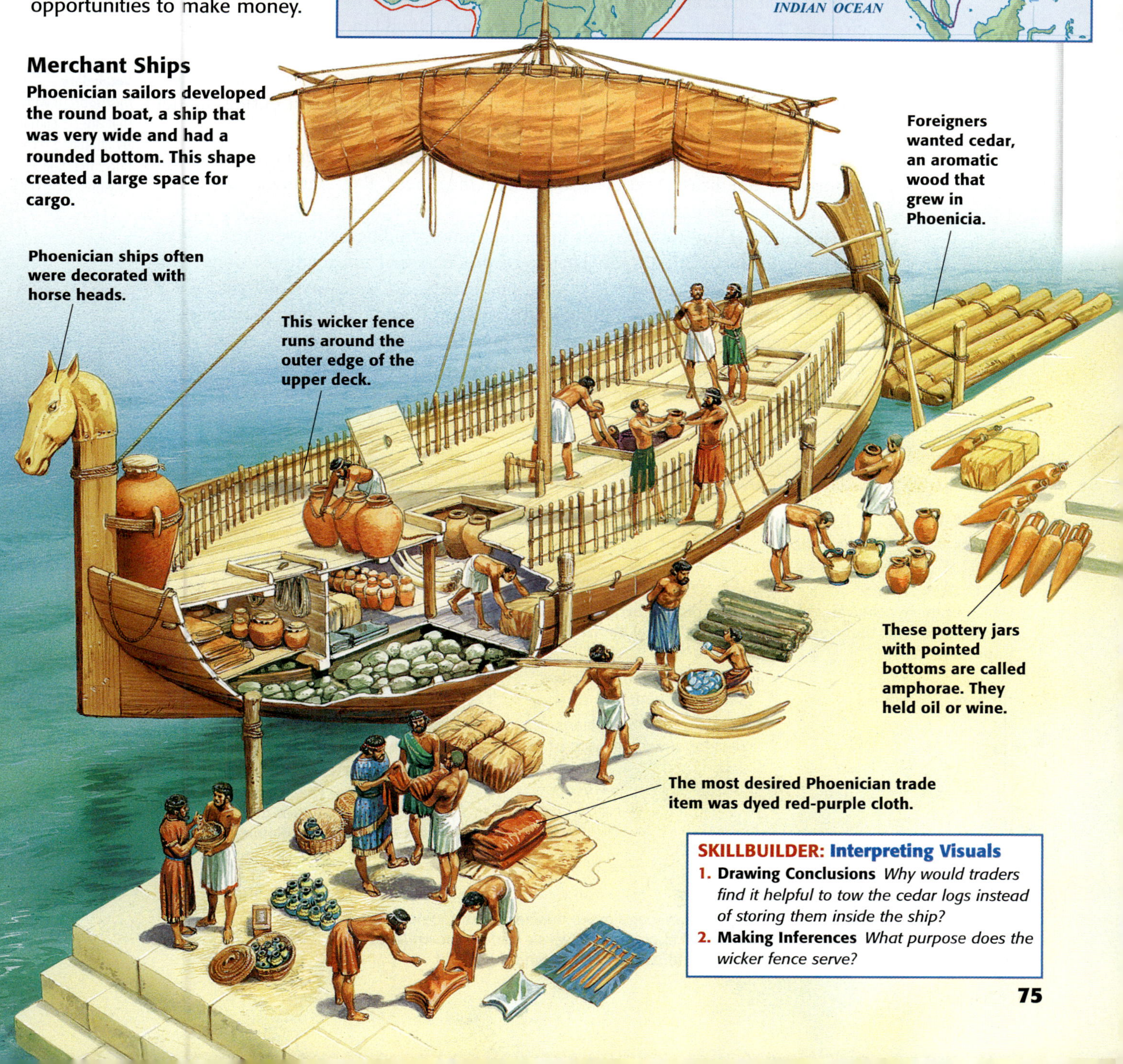

SKILLBUILDER: Interpreting Visuals

1. **Drawing Conclusions** *Why would traders find it helpful to tow the cedar logs instead of storing them inside the ship?*
2. **Making Inferences** *What purpose does the wicker fence serve?*

▲ Phoenician inscription from a sarcophagus

Few examples of Phoenician writing exist. Most writings were on papyrus, which crumbled over time. However, the Phoenician contribution to the world was enormous. With a simplified alphabet, learning was now accessible to more people.

Phoenician trade was upset when their eastern cities were captured by Assyrians in 842 B.C. However, these defeats encouraged exiles to set up city-states like Carthage to the west. The Phoenician homeland later came under the control of the Babylonians and of the Persian empire of King Cyrus I. One of their most lasting contributions remains the spread of the alphabet.

Ancient Trade Routes

Trading in ancient times also connected the Mediterranean Sea with other centers of world commerce, such as South and East Asia. Several land routes crossed Central Asia and connected to India through Afghanistan. Two sea routes began by crossing the Arabian Sea to ports on the Persian Gulf and the Red Sea. From there, traders either went overland to Egypt, Syria, and Mediterranean countries, or they continued to sail up the Red Sea. To cross the Arabian Sea, sailors learned to make use of the monsoon winds. These winds blow from the southwest during the hot months and from the northeast during the cool season.

Vocabulary
monsoon:-a wind that affects climate by changing direction in certain seasons.

To widen the variety of their exports, Indian traders used other monsoon winds to travel to Southeast Asia and Indonesia. Once there, they obtained spices and other products not native to India.

Though traveling was difficult in ancient times, trading networks like those of the Phoenicians ensured the exchange of products and information. Along with their goods, traders carried ideas, religious beliefs, art, and ways of living. They helped with the process of cultural diffusion as well as with moving merchandise.

Phoenician traders made crucial contributions to world civilization. At the same time, another eastern Mediterranean people, the Jews, were creating a religious tradition that has lasted more than 3,000 years. This is discussed in Section 4.

NEW YORK CORE CURRICULUM REVIEW

TERMS & NAMES 1. For each term or name, write a sentence explaining its significance.
• Minoans • Aegean Sea • Knossos • King Minos • Phoenicians

USING YOUR NOTES

2. Which of these achievements do you think was the most important? Why?

Minoan	Phoenician
1.	1.
2.	2.
3.	3.

MAIN IDEAS

3. What did the excavations at Knossos reveal about Minoan culture?
4. Where did the Phoenicians settle and trade?
5. Why did the Phoenicians develop a writing system?

CRITICAL THINKING & WRITING

6. **MAKING INFERENCES** What might have caused the collapse of Minoan culture?
7. **COMPARING** What were some similarities between the Minoans and Phoenicians in terms of trade?
8. **ANALYZING PRIMARY SOURCES** Go back to Herodotus' account of a voyage around Africa on page 74. What words show his doubt? Why was he doubtful?
9. **WRITING ACTIVITY** ECONOMICS The Phoenicians founded many city-states. These city-states often competed. Do you think it would have made more sense to cooperate? Write a brief **essay** explaining your opinion.

CONNECT TO TODAY **MAKING A DATABASE**
How might a commonly or widely accepted language make business and trade easier to transact? Make a **database** of bulleted points showing the ways a widely known language (such as English) would make it easier to conduct business around the world.

4

The Origins of Judaism

CONNECT TO THE NEW YORK STATE CORE CURRICULUM

Unit 1.E.1.e. Judaism
Unit 1.B.1.e.5. Legal systems

TERMS & NAMES

- Palestine
- Canaan
- Torah
- Abraham
- monotheism
- covenant
- Moses
- Israel
- Judah
- tribute

SETTING THE STAGE The Phoenicians lived in a region at the eastern end of the Mediterranean Sea that was later called **Palestine**. The Phoenicians were not the only ancient people to live in Palestine. The Romans had given the area that name after the Philistines, another people who lived in the region. **Canaan** (KAY•nuhn) was the ancient home of the Hebrews, later called the Jews, in this area. Their history, legends, and moral laws are a major influence on Western culture, and they began a tradition also shared by Christianity and Islam.

The Search for a Promised Land

Ancient Palestine's location made it a cultural crossroads of the ancient world. By land, it connected Asia and Africa and two great empires, both eager to expand. To the east lay Assyria and Babylonia and to the west Egypt. Palestine's seaports opened onto the two most important waterways of that time: the Mediterranean and the Red seas. The Hebrews settled in Canaan, which lay between the Jordan River and the Mediterranean Sea. In fact, Hebrews often used the word *Canaan* to refer to all of ancient Palestine. According to the Bible, Canaan was the land God had promised to the Hebrew people.

TAKING NOTES
Following Chronological Order
Use a time line to show major Hebrew leaders and one fact about each.

2000 B.C.

Abraham: father of Jewish people.

From Ur to Egypt Most of what we know about the early history of the Hebrews is contained in the first five books of the Hebrew Bible. Jews call these books the **Torah** (TAWR•uh) and consider them the most sacred writings in their tradition. Christians respect them as part of the Old Testament.

In the Torah, God chose **Abraham** (AY•bruh•HAM) to be the "father" of the Hebrew people. God's words to Abraham expressed a promise of land and a pledge:

PRIMARY SOURCE
Go from your country and your kindred and your father's house to the land that I will show you. I will make of you a great nation, and I will bless you, and make your name great.

Genesis 12:1–2

Abraham was a shepherd who lived in the city of Ur, in Mesopotamia. The Book of Genesis tells that God commanded him to move his people to Canaan. Around 1800 B.C., Abraham, his family, and their herds made their way to Canaan. Then, around 1650 B.C., the descendants of Abraham moved to Egypt.

▲ This statue of Moses was carved by Michelangelo.

The God of Abraham The Bible tells how Abraham and his family roamed for many years from Mesopotamia to Canaan to Egypt and back to Canaan. All the while, their God, whose name was Yahweh, watched over them. Gods worshiped by other people were often local, and were associated with a specific place.

Unlike the other groups around them, who were polytheists, the Hebrews were monotheists. They prayed to only one God. **Monotheism** (MAHN•uh•thee•IHZ•uhm), a belief in a single god, comes from the Greek words *mono*, meaning "one," and *theism*, meaning "god-worship." The Hebrews proclaimed Yahweh as the one and only God. In their eyes, Yahweh had power over all peoples, everywhere. To the Hebrews, God was not a physical being, and no physical images were to be made of him.

The Hebrews asked Yahweh for protection from their enemies, just as other people prayed to their gods to defend them. According to the Bible, Yahweh looked after the Hebrews not so much because of ritual ceremonies and sacrifices but because Abraham had promised to obey him. In return, Yahweh had promised to protect Abraham and his descendants. This mutual promise between God and the founder of the Hebrew people is called a **covenant** (KUHV•uh•nuhnt).

Moses and the Exodus

The Bible says the Hebrews migrated to Egypt because of a drought and threat of a famine. At first, the Hebrews were given places of honor in the Egyptian kingdom. Later, however, they were forced into slavery.

"Let My People Go" The Hebrews fled Egypt—perhaps between 1300 and 1200 B.C. Jews call this event "the Exodus," and they remember it every year during the

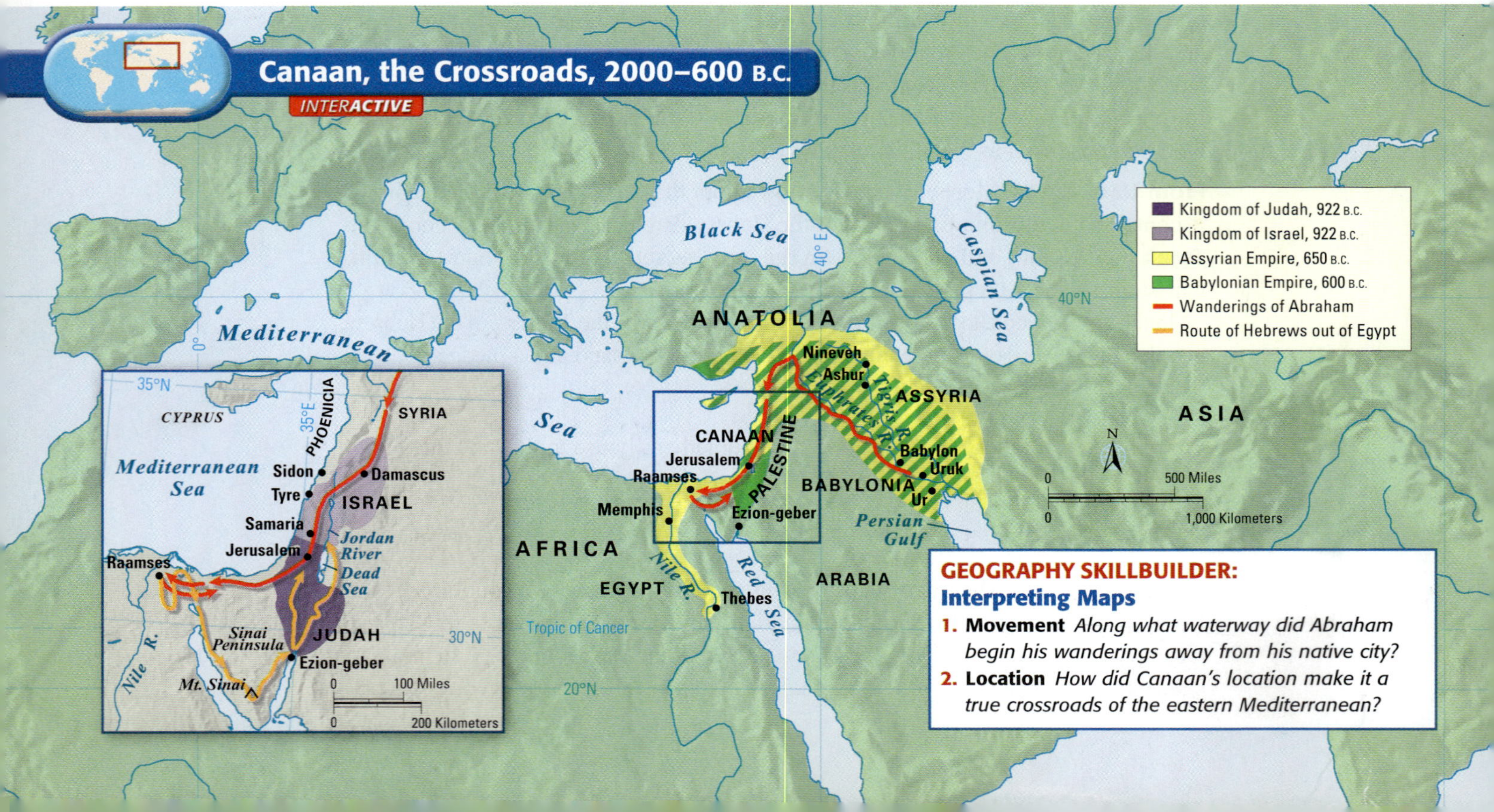

GEOGRAPHY SKILLBUILDER: Interpreting Maps

1. **Movement** *Along what waterway did Abraham begin his wanderings away from his native city?*
2. **Location** *How did Canaan's location make it a true crossroads of the eastern Mediterranean?*

Analyzing Primary Sources

The Ten Commandments

The Ten Commandments are the ten orders or laws given by God to Moses on Mount Sinai. These orders serve as the basis for Jewish laws.

PRIMARY SOURCE

1. I am the Lord your God. . . . You shall have no other gods besides me.
2. You shall not make for yourself a sculptured image.
3. You shall not swear falsely by the name of the Lord your God.
4. Remember the Sabbath day and keep it holy.
5. Honor your father and your mother. . . .
6. You shall not murder.
7. You shall not commit adultery.
8. You shall not steal.
9. You shall not bear false witness against your neighbor.
10. You shall not covet . . . anything that is your neighbor's.

Exodus 20: 2–14

DOCUMENT-BASED QUESTIONS

1. **Comparing** *Do the first four commandments concern themselves more with the Hebrews' relationship with God or with one another?*
2. **Contrasting** *What do the last six commandments have in common that distinguishes them from the first four?*

▲ Tradition dictates that the Torah be written on a scroll and kept at the synagogue in an ornamental chest called an ark.

festival of Passover. The Torah says that the man who led the Hebrews out of slavery was named **Moses**. It is told that at the time of Moses' birth, the Egyptian pharaoh felt threatened by the number of Hebrews in Egypt. He thus ordered all Hebrew male babies to be killed. Moses' mother hid her baby in the reeds along the banks of the Nile. There, an Egyptian princess found and adopted him. Though raised in luxury, he did not forget his Hebrew birth. When God commanded him to lead the Jews out of Egypt, he obeyed.

A New Covenant While the Hebrews were traveling across the Sinai (SY•ny) Peninsula, Moses climbed to the top of Mount Sinai to pray. The Bible says he spoke with God. When Moses came down from Mount Sinai, he brought down two stone tablets on which Yahweh had written the Ten Commandments.

These commandments and the other teachings that Moses delivered to his people became the basis for the civil and religious laws of Judaism. The Hebrews believed that these laws formed a new covenant between God and the Hebrew people. God promised to protect the Hebrews. They promised to keep God's commandments. (A)

MAIN IDEA

Contrasting

(A) How did the religion of the Hebrews differ from many of the religions of their neighbors?

The Land and People of the Bible The Torah reports that the Hebrews wandered for 40 years in the Sinai Desert. Later books of the Bible tell about the history of the Hebrews after their wanderings. After the death of Moses, they returned to Canaan, where Abraham had lived. The Hebrews made a change from a nomadic, tribal society to settled herders, farmers, and city dwellers. They learned new technologies from neighboring peoples in Canaan.

When the Hebrews arrived in Canaan, they were loosely organized into twelve tribes. These tribes lived in separate territories and were self-governing. In times of emergency, the Bible reports that God would raise up judges. They would unite the tribes and provide judicial and military leadership during a crisis. In the course of time, God chose a series of judges, one of the most prominent of whom was a woman, Deborah.

Hebrew Law Deborah's leadership was unusual for a Hebrew woman. The roles of men and women were quite separate in Hebrew society. Women could not officiate at religious ceremonies. In general, a Hebrew woman's most important duty was to raise her children and provide moral leadership for them.

The Ten Commandments were part of a code of laws delivered to Moses. The code included other rules regulating social and religious behavior. In some ways, this code resembled Hammurabi's Code with its attitude of "an eye for an eye and a tooth for a tooth." However, its strict justice was softened by expressions of God's mercy. The code was later interpreted by religious teachers called prophets. These interpretations tended to emphasize greater equality before the law than did other codes of the time. The prophets constantly urged the Hebrews to stay true to their covenant with God.

The prophets taught that the Hebrews had a duty to worship God and live justly with one another. The goal was a moral life lived in accordance with God's laws. In the words of the prophet Micah, "He has told you, O mortal what is good; and what does the Lord require of you but to do justice, and to love kindness, and to walk humbly with your God?" This emphasis on right conduct and the worship of one God is called ethical monotheism—a Hebrew idea that has influenced human behavior for thousands of years through Judaism, Christianity, and Islam. **B**

MAIN IDEA
Summarizing
B What does Hebrew law require of believers?

Analyzing Key Concepts

Judaism

Judaism is the religion of the Jewish people. In Judaism, one of the most important ways for a person to please God is to study the scriptures, or sacred writings, and to live according to what they teach. Many Jews keep a scroll of an important scripture passage in a mezuzah (a holder attached to a doorpost) like the one shown here.

SKILLBUILDER: Interpreting Charts

1. **Contrasting** *What is contained in the Hebrew Bible that is not in the Talmud? What is in the Talmud that is not in the Hebrew Bible?*
2. **Hypothesizing** *What kind of poetry would you expect to find in the Hebrew Bible? Explain what you think the subjects or themes of the poems might be.*

The Sacred Writings of Judaism

Sacred Writings	Contents
Hebrew Bible	**Torah** • first five books of the Bible • recounts origins of humanity and Judaism • contains basic laws of Judaism **Prophets** • stories about and writings by Jewish teachers • divided into Former Prophets and Latter Prophets • recounts Jewish history and calls for repentance and obedience **Writings** • a collection of various other writings • includes poetry, history and stories, and philosophical writings called wisdom literature
Talmud	**Mishnah** • written versions of Jewish oral law **Gemara** • explanations and interpretations of the Mishnah

The Kingdom of Israel

Canaan—the land that the Hebrews believed had been promised them by God—combined largely harsh features such as arid desert, rocky wilderness, grassy hills, and the dry, hot valley of the Jordan River. Water was never plentiful; even the numerous limestone formations soaked up any excess rainfall. After first settling in the south-central area of ancient Palestine, the Hebrews expanded south and north.

Saul and David Establish a Kingdom The judges occasionally pulled together the widely scattered tribes for a united military effort. Nonetheless, the Philistines, another people in the area, threatened the Hebrews' position in ancient Palestine. The Hebrews got along somewhat better with their Canaanite neighbors. Eventually, the only large tribe left of the 12 tribes was the tribe of Judah. As a result, Hebrews came to be called *Jews,* and their religion, *Judaism.*

From about 1020 to 922 B.C., the Hebrews united under three able kings: Saul, David, and Solomon. The new kingdom was called **Israel** (IHZ•ree•uhl). For 100 years, Israel enjoyed its greatest period of power and independence.

Saul, the first of the three kings, was chosen largely because of his success in driving out the Philistines from the central hills of ancient Palestine. Saul is portrayed in the Bible as a tragic man, who was given to bouts of jealousy. After his death, he was succeeded by his son-in-law, David. King David, an extremely popular leader, united the tribes, established Jerusalem as the capital, and founded a dynasty.

Solomon Builds the Kingdom About the year 962 B.C., David was succeeded by his son Solomon, whose mother was Bathsheba. Solomon was the most powerful of the Hebrew kings. He built a trading empire with the help of his friend Hiram, the king of the Phoenician city of Tyre. Solomon also beautified the capital city of Jerusalem. The crowning achievement of his extensive building program in Jerusalem was a great temple, which he built to glorify God. The temple was also to be a permanent home for the Ark of the Covenant, which contained the tablets of Moses' law.

The temple that Solomon built was not large, but it gleamed like a precious gem. Bronze pillars stood at the temple's entrance. The temple was stone on the outside, while its inner walls were made of cedar covered in gold. The main hall was richly decorated with brass and gold. Solomon also built a royal palace even more costly and more magnificent than the temple.

The Kingdom Divides Solomon's building projects required high taxes and badly strained the kingdom's finances. In addition, men were forced to spend one month out of every three working on the temple. The expense and forced labor caused much discontent. As a result, after Solomon's death, the Jews in the northern part of the kingdom, which was located far from the south, revolted. By 922 B.C., the kingdom had divided in two. Israel was in the north and **Judah** (JOO•duh) was in the south. C

MAIN IDEA

Drawing Conclusions

C How might geographical distance make the split of Israel and Judah more likely?

History Makers

King Solomon
962?–922? B.C.

In the Bible, Solomon prays to God for "an understanding mind," which God grants him.

Soon after, the story goes, two women and a baby boy were brought before him. Each woman claimed the baby was hers. After hearing their testimony, Solomon declared, "Divide the living boy in two; then give half to the one and half to the other."

One said: "Please, my lord, give her the living boy; certainly do not kill him!" However, the other woman accepted: "It shall be neither mine nor yours; divide it."

Solomon knew that the woman who would give up the child to save it was the real mother.

INTEGRATED TECHNOLOGY

RESEARCH LINKS For more on King Solomon, go to **classzone.com**

The next 200 years were confusing for the two kingdoms of Israel and Judah. Sometimes they fought each other; sometimes they joined together to fight common enemies. Each of the kingdoms had periods of prosperity, followed by low periods of conflict and decline.

The Babylonian Captivity

Disaster finally struck as the two kingdoms lost their independence. In 738 B.C., both Israel and Judah began paying **tribute**—peace money paid by a weaker power to a stronger—to Assyria. By paying tribute, Israel and Judah hoped to ensure that the mighty Assyrian empire would not attack. But this tribute was not enough and in 725 B.C. the Assyrians began a relentless siege of Samaria, the capital of Israel. By 722 B.C., the whole northern kingdom had fallen to the Assyrians' ferocious assault.

The southern kingdom of Judah resisted for another 150 years before it too was destroyed. The destruction of Judah was to come at the hands of the Babylonians. After conquering Israel, the Assyrians rapidly lost power to a rising Babylonian empire. The great Babylonian king Nebuchadnezzar (nehb•uh•kuhd•NEHZ•uhr) ran the Egyptians out of Syria and ancient Palestine, and he twice attacked Jerusalem. The city finally fell in 586 B.C. Solomon's temple was destroyed in the Babylonian victory. Many of the survivors were exiled to Babylon. During the exile in Babylon, the Bible describes how the prophet Ezekiel urged his people to keep their religion alive in a foreign land.

Then about 50 years after the fall of Judah, another change in fortune occurred: in 539 B.C., the Persian king Cyrus the Great conquered Babylon. The next year, Cyrus allowed some 40,000 exiles to return to Jerusalem to rebuild the temple. Many, however, stayed in Babylonia.

Work on the second temple was completed in 515 B.C. The walls of Jerusalem were rebuilt in 445 B.C. Soon, however, other empires dominated the region—first the Persians, then the Greeks, and then the Romans. These new empires would take control both of ancient Palestine and the destiny of the Jewish people. **D**

MAIN IDEA

Making Inferences

D The temple was rebuilt before the walls of Jerusalem. What does this fact indicate about the Jews after the Babylonian captivity?

NEW YORK CORE CURRICULUM REVIEW

TERMS & NAMES 1. For each term or name, write a sentence explaining its significance.

• Palestine • Canaan • Torah • Abraham • monotheism • covenant • Moses • Israel • Judah • tribute

USING YOUR NOTES

2. Which of these leaders do you think was the most important? Why?

2000 B.C.

Abraham: father of Jewish people

MAIN IDEAS

3. Where did Abraham and his family originally come from?
4. What were some of the achievements of Solomon?
5. What was the Babylonian Captivity?

CRITICAL THINKING & WRITING

6. **DEVELOPING HISTORICAL PERSPECTIVE** What were the main problems faced by the Hebrews between 2000 B.C. and 700 B.C.?
7. **ANALYZING ISSUES** What were some of the factors that made Canaan a good place for the Hebrews to settle?
8. **COMPARING** In what ways are the laws delivered to Moses similar to Hammurabi's Code?
9. **WRITING ACTIVITY** RELIGIOUS AND ETHICAL SYSTEMS What might have been the advantages of monotheism? Write a **paragraph** in which you support your opinions.

CONNECT TO TODAY **CREATING A PIE GRAPH**

What are some of the important monotheistic religions in the world today? Create a **pie graph** in which you show the relative size of various monotheistic religions.

INTERACTIVE

The Flood Story

The tale of a devastating flood appears among the legends of ancient peoples throughout the world. In some versions, the story of the flood serves to explain how the world came to be. In others, the flood is heaven's punishment for evil deeds committed by humans.

A PRIMARY SOURCE

The Torah

Only one man, Noah, found favor in the Hebrew God Yahweh's eyes.

And God said to Noah, "I have determined to make an end of all flesh, for the earth is filled with violence because of them. . . . Make yourself an ark of cypress wood. . . . And of every living thing, of all flesh, you shall bring two of every kind into the ark . . . they shall be male and female. ". . .

The rain fell on the earth forty days and forty nights. . . . At the end of forty days Noah opened the window of the ark . . . and . . . sent out the dove . . . and the dove came back . . . and there in its beak was a freshly plucked olive leaf; so Noah knew that the waters had subsided from the earth. . . .

Then God said to Noah, "Go out of the ark. . . . Bring out with you every living thing that is with you. . . . I establish my covenant with you, that . . . never again shall there be a flood to destroy the earth."

B PRIMARY SOURCE

The Epic of Gilgamesh

In this Mesopotamian legend, Utnapishtim, like Noah, escapes a worldwide flood by building an ark. Ea, the god of wisdom, warns Utnapishtim of the coming catastrophe in a dream.

O man of Shurrupak, son of Ubara-Tutu; tear down your house and build a boat, abandon possessions and look for life. . . .

I loaded into [the boat] all that I had of gold and of living things, my family, my kin, the beast of the field both wild and tame. . . .

For six days and six nights the winds blew, torrent and tempest and flood overwhelmed the world. . . . When the seventh day dawned the storm from the south subsided, the sea grew calm, the flood was stilled; I looked at the face of the world and there was silence, all mankind was turned to clay. . . . I opened a hatch and the light fell on my face. Then I bowed low, I sat down and I wept, the tears streamed down my face, for on every side was the waste of water.

C PRIMARY SOURCE

The Fish Incarnation of Vishnu

The Hindu god Vishnu, in his first earthly incarnation, took the form of Matsya, the fish, and saved humankind.

One day, as the sage Manu was praying at the river Ganges, a small fish asked for his protection. Manu put the fish in an earthen jar, but soon the fish was too big for the jar. So Manu put it into the river, but soon it outgrew the river. So Manu put the fish in the ocean. . . .

The fish told Manu there would be a great deluge [flood]. He advised Manu to build a large boat and take . . . the seeds of various kinds of plants, and one of each type of animal. When the deluge came, the fish said, he would take the ark . . . to safety.

Sure enough, when the deluge occurred, the fish was there. Manu tied the boat to the horns of the fish. . . . The fish then pulled the boat through the waters until it reached a mountain peak.

D PRIMARY SOURCE

Anonymous

This art dates from the fifth century A.D. It shows Noah and his ark in the Hebrew flood story. In the picture, Noah is welcoming back the dove he had sent out from the ark at the end of 40 days. The dove is carrying in its beak an olive leaf.

Document-Based QUESTIONS

1. Based on Source A, what promise does God make to mankind?
2. What are some of the differences among the gods in Sources A, B, and C?
3. What are some of the similarities among the flood stories in Sources A, B, and C?
4. In Source D, what is the dove bringing to Noah and what might it represent?

Chapter 3 Assessment

TERMS & NAMES

For each term or name below, briefly explain its importance in the years 3500 B.C. to 259 B.C.

1. Indo-Europeans
2. caste
3. reincarnation
4. Siddhartha Gautama
5. Minoans
6. Phoenicians
7. monotheism
8. Moses

MAIN IDEAS

The Indo-Europeans Section 1 (pages 61–65)

9. What are three reasons that historians give to explain why Indo-Europeans migrated?
10. What are two technologies that helped the Hittites build their empire?
11. How were the Aryans different from the non-Aryans (*dasas*) that they encountered when migrating to India?

Hinduism and Buddhism Develop Section 2 (pages 66–71)

12. In Hinduism, how are the ideas of karma, reincarnation, and *moksha* connected?
13. Why were lower castes more likely to convert to Buddhism?

Seafaring Traders Section 3 (pages 72–76)

14. What did the Minoans export?
15. What is Phoenicia's greatest legacy to the world?

The Origins of Judaism Section 4 (pages 77–83)

16. What is ethical monotheism and why is it important?
17. What caused the division of Solomon's kingdom?
18. What are two ways in which early Judaism differed from other religions of the time?

CRITICAL THINKING

1. USING YOUR NOTES

RELIGIOUS AND ETHICAL SYSTEMS In a chart, fill in information about three world religions.

Religion	Founder	Time Originated	Area Originated
Hinduism			
Buddhism			
Judaism			

2. DRAWING CONCLUSIONS

INTERACTION WITH ENVIRONMENT How important were the migrations of the Indo-European peoples? How lasting were the changes that they brought? Explain your conclusion.

3. RECOGNIZING EFFECTS

What were some of the effects of King Solomon's reign?

4. COMPARING

ECONOMICS How were the economic foundations of Minoan and Phoenician civilizations similar?

5. DEVELOPING HISTORICAL PERSPECTIVE

Why was monotheism unusual in its time and place?

VISUAL SUMMARY

Three Major Religions

	Hinduism	Buddhism	Judaism
Number of Gods	Many gods, all faces of Brahman	Originally, no gods	One God
Holy Books	Vedas; Upanishads, *Mahabharata*, and others	Books on the teachings and life of the Buddha	The Torah and other books of the Hebrew Bible
Moral Law	Karma	Eightfold Path	Ten Commandments
Leaders	Brahmins	Monks	Priests, judges, kings, prophets
Final Goal	*Moksha*	Enlightenment, Nirvana	A moral life through obedience to God's law

NEW YORK STATE REGENTS EXAM PRACTICE

The following passage tells how the Hebrews asked the prophet Samuel to appoint their king. Use the quotation and your knowledge of world history to answer questions 1 and 2.

Additional Test Practice, pp. S1–S33

PRIMARY SOURCE

Then all the elders of Israel gathered together and came to Samuel at Ramah, and said to him, ". . . appoint for us, then, a king to govern us, like other nations." . . . Samuel prayed to the Lord, and the Lord said to Samuel, "Listen to the voice of the people in all that they say to you; for they have not rejected you, but they have rejected me from being king over them. Just as they have done to me, from the day I brought them up out of Egypt to this day, forsaking me and serving other gods, so also they are doing to you."

1 SAMUEL 8:4–8

1 What seems to be the writer's reaction to the Hebrews' demand for a king?

(1) approval (3) indifference
(2) disapproval (4) amusement

2 Who does this passage say was Israel's real king?

(1) Samuel (3) Moses
(2) The Lord (4) Solomon

Use the statue of a Hittite god and your knowledge of world history to answer question 3.

3 What does the fact that this statue is made of gold tell you about how the owner viewed it?

(1) trivial (3) worthless
(2) valuable (4) disposable

INTEGRATED TECHNOLOGY

TEST PRACTICE Go to **classzone.com**

- Diagnostic tests
- Strategies
- Tutorials
- Additional practice

ALTERNATIVE ASSESSMENT

1. Interact *with* History

On page 60, you considered leaving your homeland before you knew what some of the consequences of your decision might be. Now that you've read the chapter, reconsider your decision. Would you still make the same choice, or have you changed your mind? Discuss the consequences of your decision on your life.

2. WRITING ABOUT HISTORY

Write an **expository essay** describing how ironworking helped the Aryans to carry out their migrations to India, as well as their conquering and settling of territory.

Consider the effect of ironworking technology on the following:

- weapons and tools
- transportation
- conquest
- settlement

INTEGRATED TECHNOLOGY

Participating in a WebQuest

Introduction You are a member of a special committee commissioned by the Indian government to abolish the caste system.

Task Create an electronic presentation of the issues you had to consider and the problems you faced in abolishing the caste system.

Process and Procedures Assume the role of one of these committee members—religious leader, economist, historian, sociologist—to research Indian society and to present the issues. Use this chapter and the Internet as resources for your research.

Evaluation and Conclusion The caste system was officially abolished by the Indian government in 1955. How did this project contribute to your understanding of the caste system? What additional information would you like to know?

CHAPTER 4

First Age of Empires, 1570 B.C.–200 B.C.

Previewing Main Ideas

EMPIRE BUILDING Groups from Africa to China sought to conquer other groups and spread their influence across vast regions. These societies built the world's first great empires.

Geography *On the map, locate the Nile, Tigris, and Euphrates rivers, where many of the early empires arose. Why do you think the empire builders fought over these regions?*

CULTURAL INTERACTION For a long period, Egypt ruled Kush and the two cultures interacted. When the Kush Empire conquered Egypt, therefore, the Kushites adopted many Egyptian cultural values and ideas.

Geography *Study the map and time line. What other cultures might have adopted Egyptian values?*

RELIGIOUS AND ETHICAL SYSTEMS After the warring states period, Chinese philosophers developed different ethical systems to restore China's social order.

Geography *How might China's location have affected the spread of the ethical systems that began there?*

NEW YORK CORE CURRICULUM FOCUS

- Confucian ideas about government led to the creation of a bureaucracy, or trained civil service, in China.
- The Qin Dynasty unified China by force in the third century B.C.

INTEGRATED TECHNOLOGY

eEdition
- Interactive Maps
- Interactive Visuals
- Interactive Primary Sources

VIDEO *Patterns of Interaction: The Rise of the Persians and the Inca*

INTERNET RESOURCES

Go to **classzone.com** for:
- Research Links
- Internet Activities
- Primary Sources
- Chapter Quiz
- Maps
- Test Practice
- Current Events

AFRICA, SOUTHWEST ASIA, CHINA

1570 B.C. Egypt's New Kingdom is established. (temple at Karnak built during era) ▶

1570 B.C. — **1000 B.C.**

WORLD

1500 B.C. ◀ Mycenaean culture thrives on the Greek mainland. (gold death mask of a Mycenaean king)

1200 B.C. Minoan civilization mysteriously ends.

850 B.C. Assyrian Empire begins its rise to power.

751 B.C. Nubian kingdom of Kush conquers Egypt. (Nubian pottery) ▶

750 B.C. Greek city-states begin colonization.

550 B.C. Persian Empire flourishes.

509 B.C. Rome becomes a republic.

500 B.C.

334 B.C. Alexander starts to build his empire. ▶

202 B.C. The Qin Dynasty collapses. Civil war follows.

200 B.C.

Interact *with* History

How will the empire help you or harm you?

As a merchant traveling with your camel caravan, your life has become increasingly difficult. Bandits and thieves roam the roads, attacking traders like you. A new military empire is advancing through your region, putting down the outlaw bands. However, the military empire is also imposing harsh laws and heavy taxes on the regions it conquers.

EXAMINING *the* ISSUES

- **Why might a merchant welcome the expansion of a strong empire?**
- **How might the empire oppress the region?**

In small groups, answer the questions, then report back to the class. In your discussion, remember what you've learned about military conquest and the behavior of such groups as the Sumerians, Egyptians, and Hittites. As you read about the empires in this chapter, consider how the winners treat the people under their power and how the conquered people respond.

The Egyptian and Nubian Empires

CONNECT TO THE NEW YORK STATE CORE CURRICULUM

Unit 1.B.1.a. Human and physical geography of early river civilizations
Unit 1.B.1.b. Traditional economies

TERMS & NAMES

- Hyksos
- New Kingdom
- Hatshepsut
- Thutmose III
- Nubia
- Ramses II
- Kush
- Piankhi
- Meroë

SETTING THE STAGE As you learned in Chapter 2, Egyptian civilization developed along the Nile River and united into a kingdom around 3100 B.C. During the Middle Kingdom (about 2080–1640 B.C.), trade with Mesopotamia and the Indus Valley enriched Egypt. Meanwhile, up the Nile River, less than 600 miles south of the Egyptian city of Thebes, a major kingdom had developed in the region of Nubia. For centuries, the Nubian kingdom of Kush traded with Egypt. The two kingdoms particularly influenced each other culturally.

TAKING NOTES

Following Chronological Order Use a time line to identify important events in the history of Egypt and Nubia.

1570 B.C.	A.D. 350
Egyptian New Kingdom established	Aksum defeats Meroë

Nomadic Invaders Rule Egypt

After the prosperity of the Middle Kingdom, Egypt descended into war and violence. This was caused by a succession of weak pharaohs and power struggles among rival nobles. The weakened country fell to invaders who swept across the Isthmus of Suez in chariots, a weapon of war unknown to the Egyptians. These Asiatic invaders, called **Hyksos** (HIHK•sohs), ruled Egypt from about 1640 to 1570 B.C. The Hyksos invasion shook the Egyptians' confidence in the desert barriers that had protected their kingdom.

Hebrews Migrate to Egypt During the Hyksos rule, some historians believe that another Asiatic group, the Hebrews, settled in Egypt. According to the Bible, Abraham and his family first crossed the Euphrates River and came to Canaan around 1800 B.C. Then, around 1650 B.C., the descendants of Abraham moved again—this time to Egypt. Some historians believe that the Hyksos encouraged the Hebrews to settle there because the two groups were racially similar. The Egyptians resented the presence of the Hyksos in their land but were powerless to remove them.

Expulsion and Slavery Around 1600 B.C., a series of warlike rulers began to restore Egypt's power. Among those who helped drive out the Hyksos was Queen Ahhotep (ah•HOH•tehp). She took over when her husband was killed in battle. The next pharaoh, Kamose (KAH•mohs), won a great victory over the hated Hyksos. His successors drove the Hyksos completely out of Egypt and pursued them across the Sinai Peninsula into Palestine. According to some Biblical scholars, the Hebrews remained in Egypt and were enslaved and forced into hard labor. They would not leave Egypt until sometime between 1500 and 1200 B.C., the time of the Exodus.

The New Kingdom of Egypt

After overthrowing the Hyksos, the pharaohs of the **New Kingdom** (about 1570–1075 B.C.) sought to strengthen Egypt by building an empire. As you may recall, an empire brings together several peoples or states under the control of one ruler. Egypt entered its third period of glory during the New Kingdom era. During this time, it was wealthier and more powerful than ever before.

Equipped with bronze weapons and two-wheeled chariots, the Egyptians became conquerors. The pharaohs of the 18th Dynasty (about 1570–1365 B.C.) set up an army including archers, charioteers, and infantry, or foot soldiers.

Vocabulary
A *dynasty* is a series of rulers from a single family.

Hatshepsut's Prosperous Rule Among the rulers of the New Kingdom, **Hatshepsut** (hat•SHEHP•SOOT), who declared herself pharaoh around 1472 B.C., was unique. She took over because her stepson, the male heir to the throne, was a young child at the time. Unlike other New Kingdom rulers, Hatshepsut spent her reign encouraging trade rather than just waging war.

The trading expedition Hatshepsut ordered to the Land of Punt (poont), near present-day Somalia, was particularly successful. Hatshepsut sent a fleet of five ships down the Red Sea to Punt in search of myrrh, frankincense, and fragrant ointments used for religious ceremonies and in cosmetics. In addition to these goods, Hatshepsut's fleet brought back gold, ivory, and unusual plants and animals.

History Makers

Hatshepsut
reigned 1472–1458 B.C.

Hatshepsut was an excellent ruler of outstanding achievement who made Egypt more prosperous. As male pharaohs had done, Hatshepsut planned a tomb for herself in the Valley of the Kings. Carved reliefs on the walls of the temple reveal the glories of her reign.

The inscription from Hatshepsut's obelisk at Karnak trumpets her glory and her feelings about herself:

> *I swear as Re loves me, as my father Amon favors me, as my nostrils are filled with satisfying life, as I wear the white crown, as I appear in the red crown, . . . as I rule this land like the son of Isis.*

INTEGRATED TECHNOLOGY

INTERNET ACTIVITY Create a photo exhibit on the trading expeditions to Punt ordered by Hatshepsut. Include pictures of murals of goods collected. Go to **classzone.com** for your research.

Thutmose the Empire Builder Hatshepsut's stepson, **Thutmose III** (thoot•MOH•suh), proved to be a much more warlike ruler. In his eagerness to ascend to the throne, Thutmose III may even have murdered Hatshepsut. Between the time he took power and his death around 1425 B.C., Thutmose III led a number of victorious invasions eastward into Palestine and Syria. His armies also pushed farther south into **Nubia**, a region of Africa that straddled the upper Nile River. Egypt had traded with Nubia and influenced the region since the time of the Middle Kingdom.

Egypt was now a mighty empire. It controlled lands around the Nile and far beyond. In addition, it drew boundless wealth from them. Contact with other cultures brought Egypt new ideas as well as material goods. Egypt had never before—nor has it since—commanded such power and wealth as during the reigns of the New Kingdom pharaohs.

The Egyptians and the Hittites The Egyptians' conquest of parts of Syria and Palestine around 1400 B.C. brought them into conflict with the Hittites. The Hittites had moved into Asia Minor around 1900 B.C. and later expanded southward into Palestine.

After several smaller battles, the Egyptians and Hittites clashed at Kadesh around 1285 B.C. The pharaoh **Ramses II** (RAM•SEEZ) and a Hittite king later made a treaty that promised "peace and brotherhood between us forever." Their alliance lasted for the rest of the century. (A)

MAIN IDEA
Recognizing Effects
(A) What were some of the political and economic effects of Egypt's conquests?

An Age of Builders Like the rulers of the Old Kingdom, who built the towering pyramids, rulers of the New Kingdom

▲ Four statues of Ramses II guarded the entrance to the Great Temple at Abu Simbel.

erected grand buildings. In search of security in the afterlife—and protection from grave robbers—they hid their splendid tombs beneath desert cliffs. The site they chose was the remote Valley of the Kings near Thebes. Besides royal tombs, the pharaohs of this period also built great palaces and magnificent temples. Indeed, the royal title *pharaoh* means "great house" and comes from this time period.

Ramses II, whose reign extended from approximately 1290 to 1224 B.C., stood out among the great builders of the New Kingdom. At Karnak, he added to a monumental temple to Amon-Re (AH•muhn•RAY), Egypt's chief god. Ramses also ordered a temple to be carved into the red sandstone cliffs above the Nile River at Abu Simbel (AH•boo SIHM•buhl). He had these temples decorated with enormous statues of himself. The ears of these statues alone measured more than three feet.

The Empire Declines

The empire that Thutmose III had built and Ramses II had ruled slowly came apart after 1200 B.C. as other strong civilizations rose to challenge Egypt's power. Shortly after Ramses died, the entire eastern Mediterranean suffered a wave of invasions.

Invasions by Land and Sea Both the Egyptian empire and the Hittite kingdom were attacked by invaders called the "Sea Peoples" in Egyptian texts. These invaders may have included the Philistines, who are often mentioned in the Bible. Whoever they were, the Sea Peoples caused great destruction.

The Egyptians faced other attacks. In the east, the tribes of Palestine often rebelled against their Egyptian overlords. In the west, the vast desert no longer served as a barrier against Libyan raids on Egyptian villages.

Egypt's Empire Fades After these invasions, Egypt never recovered its previous power. The Egyptian empire broke apart into regional units, and numerous small kingdoms arose. Each was eager to protect its independence.

Almost powerless, Egypt soon fell to its neighbors' invasions. Libyans crossed the desert to the Nile Delta. There they established independent dynasties. From around 950 to 730 B.C., Libyan pharaohs ruled Egypt and erected cities. But instead of imposing their own culture, the Libyans adopted the Egyptian way of life. When the Nubians came north to seize power, they too adopted Egyptian culture.

The Kushites Conquer the Nile Region

For centuries, Egypt dominated Nubia and the Nubian kingdom of **Kush**, which lasted for about a thousand years, between 2000 and 1000 B.C. During this time, Egyptian armies raided and even occupied Kush for a brief period. But as Egypt fell into decline during the Hyksos period, Kush began to emerge as a regional power. Nubia now established its own Kushite dynasty on the throne of Egypt.

The People of Nubia Nubia lay south of Egypt between the first cataract of the Nile, an area of churning rapids, and the division of the river into the Blue Nile and the White Nile. Despite several cataracts around which boats had to be carried, the Nile provided the best north-south trade route. Several Nubian kingdoms, including Kush, served as a trade corridor. They linked Egypt and the Mediterranean world to the interior of Africa and to the Red Sea. Goods and ideas flowed back and forth along the river for centuries. The first Nubian kingdom, Kerma, arose shortly after 2000 B.C.

The Interaction of Egypt and Nubia With Egypt's revival during the New Kingdom, pharaohs forced Egyptian rule on Kush. Egyptian governors, priests, soldiers, and artists strongly influenced the Nubians. Indeed, Kush's capital, Napata, became the center for the spread of Egyptian culture to Kush's other African trading partners.

History *in* Depth

Egyptian Influence on Nubian Culture

Nubia was heavily influenced by Egypt. This influence is particularly apparent in Nubian religious practices and burial traditions. But even though the Nubians adopted Egyptian ways, they didn't abandon their cultural identity. In many of these religious and funeral practices, the Nubians blended Egyptian customs with their own traditions.

Temples This stone ram, representing the Egyptian god Amen, lay at the entrance to a Nubian temple dedicated to that god. Although the Nubians worshiped many Egyptian gods, Amen's temple was located near another dedicated to Apedemak, a Nubian god.

Pyramids Unlike the Egyptian pyramids, the pyramids of Nubia had steeply sloping sides and were probably designed with a flat top.

Kushite princes went to Egypt. They learned the Egyptian language and worshiped Egyptian gods. They adopted the customs and clothing styles of the Egyptian upper class. When they returned home, the Kushite nobles brought back royal rituals and hieroglyphic writing.

With Egypt's decline, beginning about 1200 B.C., Kush regained its independence. The Kushites viewed themselves as more suitable guardians of Egyptian values than the Libyans. They sought to guard these values by conquering Egypt and ousting its Libyan rulers. **B**

MAIN IDEA

Making Inferences

B Why might the Kushites have viewed themselves as guardians of Egyptian values?

Piankhi Captures the Egyptian Throne In 751 B.C., a Kushite king named **Piankhi** overthrew the Libyan dynasty that had ruled Egypt for over 200 years. He united the entire Nile Valley from the delta in the north to Napata in the south. Piankhi and his descendants became Egypt's 25th Dynasty. After his victory, Piankhi erected a monument in his homeland of Kush. On the monument, he had words inscribed that celebrated his victory. The inscription provided a catalog of the riches of the north:

PRIMARY SOURCE

Then the ships were laden with silver, gold, copper, clothing, and everything of the Northland, every product of Syria and all sweet woods of God's-Land. His Majesty sailed upstream [south], with glad heart, the shores on his either side were jubilating. West and east were jubilating in the presence of His Majesty.

PIANKHI, monument in Cairo Museum

Statues These figurines represented Nubian slaves. They were buried with Nubian kings and meant to serve them in death. The figurines reflect traditional Egyptian style. The human faces, however, reveal Nubian features.

SKILLBUILDER: Interpreting Visual Sources

Forming Opinions *Why did the Nubians combine Egyptian culture with elements of their own culture?*

However, Piankhi's dynasty proved short-lived. In 671 B.C., the Assyrians, a warlike people from Southwest Asia, conquered Egypt. The Kushites fought bravely, but they were forced to retreat south along the Nile. There the Kushites would experience a golden age, despite their loss of Egypt.

▼ This ring, bearing the head of a Kushite guardian god, was found inside a Meroë queen's pyramid. It dates from the late first century B.C.

The Golden Age of Meroë

After their defeat by the Assyrians, the Kushite royal family eventually moved south to **Meroë** (MEHR•oh•EE). Meroë lay closer to the Red Sea than Napata did, and so became active in the flourishing trade among Africa, Arabia, and India. (See the map on page 93.)

The Wealth of Kush Kush used the natural resources around Meroë and thrived for several hundred years. Unlike Egyptian cities along the Nile, Meroë enjoyed significant rainfall. And, unlike Egypt, Meroë boasted abundant supplies of iron ore. As a result, Meroë became a major center for the manufacture of iron weapons and tools.

In Meroë, ambitious merchants loaded iron bars, tools, and spearheads onto their donkeys. They then transported the goods to the Red Sea, where they exchanged these goods for jewelry, fine cotton cloth, silver lamps, and glass bottles. As the mineral wealth of the central Nile Valley flowed out of Meroë, luxury goods from India and Arabia flowed in.

The Decline of Meroë After four centuries of prosperity, from about 250 B.C. to A.D. 150, Meroë began to decline. Aksum, another kingdom located 400 miles to the southeast, contributed to Meroë's fall. With a seaport on the Red Sea, Aksum came to dominate North African trade. Aksum defeated Meroë around A.D. 350.

Centuries earlier, around the time the Kushite pharaoh sat on the Egyptian throne, a new empire—Assyria—had risen in the north. Like Kush, Assyria came to dominate Egypt.

NEW YORK CORE CURRICULUM REVIEW

TERMS & NAMES **1.** For each term or name, write a sentence explaining its significance.

• Hyksos • New Kingdom • Hatshepsut • Thutmose III • Nubia • Ramses II • Kush • Piankhi • Meroë

USING YOUR NOTES

2. Which empire was invaded more often? Why?

1570 B.C. — A.D. 350

Egyptian New Kingdom established — Aksum defeats Meroë

MAIN IDEAS

3. How did the New Kingdom of Egypt become so powerful and wealthy?

4. What cultural aspects of Egyptian civilization did the Kushites adopt?

5. Why was Kush able to thrive after losing Egypt to the Assyrians?

CRITICAL THINKING & WRITING

6. DRAWING CONCLUSIONS What role did geography play in Egypt's rise and fall?

7. MAKING INFERENCES How did trade help both Egypt and Nubia maintain their dominance in the Nile region?

8. HYPOTHESIZING What might have happened if the Kushites had imposed their own culture on Egypt?

9. WRITING ACTIVITY CULTURAL INTERACTION How did Egypt and Nubia strengthen each other at various times in their histories? Support your ideas in a one-paragraph **analysis**.

CONNECT TO TODAY **CREATING A TIME LINE**

Research to learn about the collapse of the Soviet Union—a modern-day empire—in 1991. Create a **time line** of the events that led to the collapse.

The Assyrian Empire

CONNECT TO THE NEW YORK STATE CORE CURRICULUM

Unit 1.B.1.a. Human and physical geography of early river civilizations
Unit 1.B.1.e.4. Architecture

TERMS & NAMES

- Assyria
- Sennacherib
- Nineveh
- Ashurbanipal
- Medes
- Chaldeans
- Nebuchadnezzar

SETTING THE STAGE For more than two centuries, the Assyrian army advanced across Southwest Asia. It overwhelmed foes with its military strength. After the Assyrians seized control of Egypt, the Assyrian king Esarhaddon proclaimed, "I tore up the root of Kush, and not one therein escaped to submit to me." The last Kushite pharaoh retreated to Napata, Kush's capital city.

A Mighty Military Machine

Beginning around 850 B.C., **Assyria** (uh•SEER•ee•uh) acquired a large empire. It accomplished this by means of a highly advanced military organization and state-of-the-art weaponry. For a time, this campaign of conquest made Assyria the greatest power in Southwest Asia.

TAKING NOTES

Analyzing Causes Use a chart to identify the causes of the rise and decline of Assyrian power.

Assyrian Power

Causes for Rise	Causes for Decline
Need to defend against attacks	Hated by conquered people

The Rise of a Warrior People The Assyrians came from the northern part of Mesopotamia. (See the map on page 96.) Their flat, exposed land made them easy for other people to attack. Invaders frequently swept down into Assyria from the nearby mountains. The Assyrians may have developed their warlike behavior in response to these invasions. Through constant warfare, Assyrian kings eventually built an empire that stretched from east and north of the Tigris River all the way to central Egypt. One of these Assyrian kings, **Sennacherib** (sih•NAK•uhr•ihb), bragged that he had destroyed 89 cities and 820 villages, burned Babylon, and ordered most of its inhabitants killed.

Military Organization and Conquest Assyria was a society that glorified military strength. Its soldiers were well equipped for conquering an empire. Making use of the ironworking technology of the time, the soldiers covered themselves in stiff leather and metal armor. They wore copper or iron helmets, padded loincloths, and leather skirts layered with metal scales. Their weapons were iron swords and iron-pointed spears.

Advance planning and technical skill allowed the Assyrians to lay siege to enemy cities. When deep water blocked their passage, engineers would span the rivers with pontoons, or floating structures used to support a bridge. Before attacking, the Assyrians dug beneath the city's walls to weaken them. Then, with disciplined organization, foot soldiers marched shoulder to shoulder. The foot soldiers approached the city walls and shot wave upon wave of arrows. Meanwhile, another group of troops hammered the city's gates with massive, iron-tipped battering rams.

GEOGRAPHY SKILLBUILDER: Interpreting Maps

1. **Location** *What is the approximate distance between Nineveh and Thebes?*
2. **Location** *What is the southernmost part of the Assyrian Empire and to what other empire did it previously belong?*

When the city gates finally splintered, the Assyrians showed no mercy. They killed or enslaved their victims. To prevent their enemies from rebelling again, the Assyrians forced captives to settle far away in the empire's distant provinces and dependent states.

The Empire Expands

Between 850 and 650 B.C., the kings of Assyria defeated Syria, Palestine, and Babylonia. Eventually, the Assyrians ruled lands that extended far beyond the Fertile Crescent into Anatolia and Egypt.

Assyrian Rule At its peak around 650 B.C., the Assyrian Empire included almost all of the old centers of civilization and power in Southwest Asia. Assyrian officials governed lands closest to Assyria as provinces and made them dependent territories. Assyrian kings controlled these dependent regions by choosing their rulers or by supporting kings who aligned themselves with Assyria. The Assyrian system of having local governors report to a central authority became the fundamental model of administration, or system of government management.

In addition, the military campaigns added new territory to the empire. These additional lands brought taxes and tribute to the Assyrian treasury. If a conquered people refused to pay, the Assyrians destroyed their cities and sent the people into exile. Such methods enabled the Assyrians to effectively govern an extended empire.

Assyrian Culture Some of Assyria's most fearsome warriors earned reputations as great builders. For example, the same King Sennacherib who had burned Babylon also established Assyria's capital at **Nineveh** (NIHN•uh•vuh) along the Tigris River. This great walled city, about three miles long and a mile wide, was the largest city of its day. In the ruins of Nineveh and other Assyrian cities, archaeologists found finely carved sculptures. Two artistic subjects particularly fascinated the Assyrians: brutal military campaigns and the lion hunt.

Nineveh also held one of the ancient world's largest libraries. In this unique library, King **Ashurbanipal** (AH•shur•BAH•nuh•PAHL) collected more than 20,000 clay tablets from throughout the Fertile Crescent. The collection included the ancient Sumerian poem the *Epic of Gilgamesh* and provided historians with much information about the earliest civilizations in Southwest Asia. The library was the first to have many of the features of a modern library. For instance, the collection was organized into many rooms according to subject matter. The collection was also cataloged. Europeans would not use a library cataloging system for centuries.

Analyzing Primary Sources

INTERACTIVE

Assyrian Sculpture

This relief shows ferocious Assyrian warriors attacking a fortified city. A relief is a sculpture that has figures standing out from a flat background. The Assyrian war machine included a variety of weapons and methods of attack.

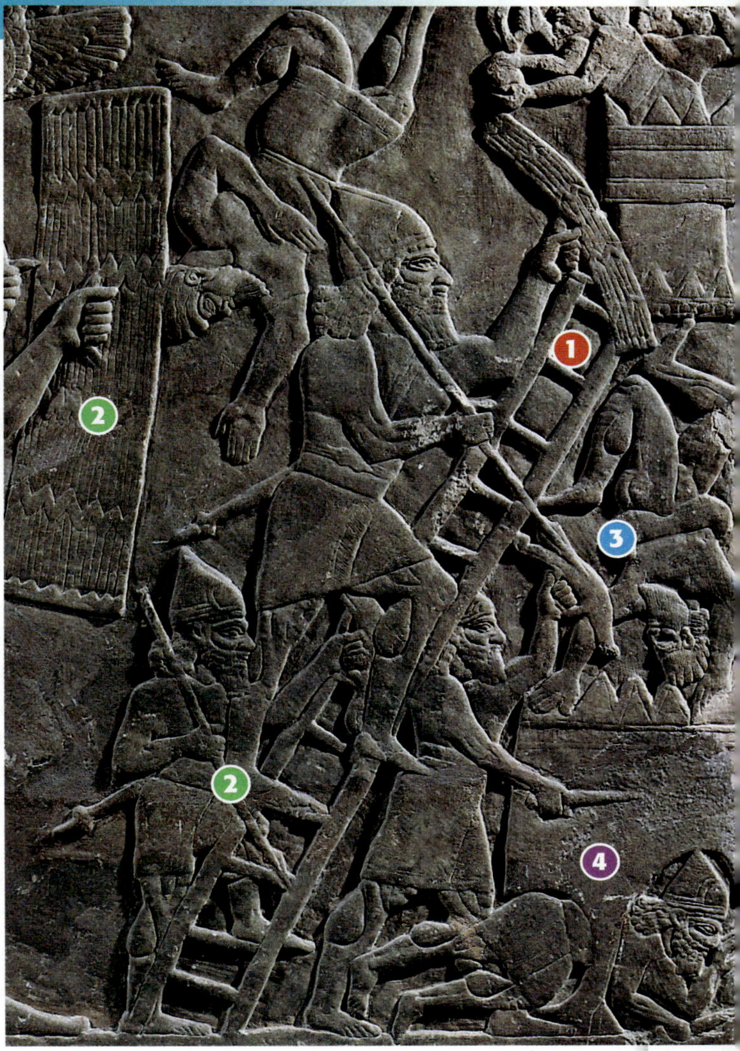

1 Ladders

Assyrian archers launched waves of arrows against opponents defending the city walls. Meanwhile, Assyrian troops threw their ladders up against the walls and began their climb into the enemy's stronghold.

2 Weapons

Troops were armed with the best weapons of the time, iron-tipped spears, as well as iron daggers and swords. They were also protected with armor and large shields.

3 Tactics

The Assyrians were savage in their treatment of defeated opponents. Those who were not slaughtered in the initial attack were often impaled or beheaded, while women and children were sometimes murdered or sold into slavery.

4 Tunnels

The Assyrian army used sappers—soldiers who dug tunnels to sap, or undermine, the foundations of the enemy's walls so that they would fall.

SKILLBUILDER: Interpreting Visual Sources

1. **Making Inferences** *What emotions might the relief have inspired in the Assyrian people?*
2. **Making Inferences** *How might the Assyrians' enemies have reacted to the sculpture?*

The Empire Crumbles

Ashurbanipal proved to be one of the last of the mighty Assyrian kings. Assyrian power had spread itself too thin. Also, the cruelty displayed by the Assyrians had earned them many enemies. Shortly after Ashurbanipal's death, Nineveh fell.

Decline and Fall In 612 B.C., a combined army of **Medes** (meedz), **Chaldeans** (kal•DEE•uhnz), and others burned and leveled Nineveh. However, because the clay writing tablets in Nineveh's library had been baked in a pottery oven, many survived the fire.

Most people in the region rejoiced at Nineveh's destruction. The Hebrew prophet Nahum (NAY•huhm) gave voice to the feelings of many:

MAIN IDEA

Analyzing Primary Sources

A What was Nahum's opinion on the collapse of the Assyrian Empire?

PRIMARY SOURCE A

And it shall come to pass, that all they that look upon thee shall flee from thee, and say, Nineveh is laid waste: who will bemoan her? Whence shall I seek comforters for thee? . . . Thy shepherds slumber, O king of Assyria: thy nobles shall dwell in the dust: thy people is scattered upon the mountains, and no man gathereth them.

NAHUM 3:7, 18 (Bible)

Rebirth of Babylon Under the Chaldeans After defeating the Assyrians, the Chaldeans made Babylon their capital. Around 600 B.C., Babylon became the center

▲ This is an artist's rendering of the legendary hanging gardens of Babylon. Slaves watered the plants by using hidden pumps that drew water from the Euphrates River.

of a new empire, more than 1,000 years after Hammurabi had ruled there. A Chaldean king named **Nebuchadnezzar** (NEHB•uh•kuhd•NEHZ•uhr) restored the city. Perhaps the most impressive part of the restoration was the famous hanging gardens. Greek scholars later listed them as one of the seven wonders of the ancient world. According to legend, one of Nebuchadnezzar's wives missed the flowering shrubs of her mountain homeland. To please her, he had fragrant trees and shrubs planted on terraces that rose 75 feet above Babylon's flat, dry plain.

Indeed, the entire city was a wonder. Its walls were so thick that, according to one report, a four-horse chariot could wheel around on top of them. To ensure that the world knew who ruled Babylon, the king had the bricks inscribed with the words, "I am Nebuchadnezzar, King of Babylon."

The highest building in Babylon was a great, seven-tiered ziggurat more than 300 feet high. It was visible for miles. At night, priests observed the stars from the top of this tower and others in the city. Chaldean astronomers kept detailed records of how the stars and planets seemed to change position in the night sky. They also concluded that the sun, moon, Earth, and five other planets belonged to the same solar system. The Chaldeans' observations formed the basis for both astronomy and astrology.

Nebuchadnezzar's empire fell shortly after his death. The Persians who next came to power adopted many Assyrian military, political, and artistic inventions. The Persians would use the organization the Assyrians had developed to stabilize the region.

NEW YORK CORE CURRICULUM REVIEW

TERMS & NAMES 1. For each term or name, write a sentence explaining its significance.

- Assyria
- Sennacherib
- Nineveh
- Ashurbanipal
- Medes
- Chaldeans
- Nebuchadnezzar

USING YOUR NOTES

2. Why did the Assyrians develop into a great military power? Why did their power decline?

Assyrian Power

Causes for Rise	Causes for Decline
Need to defend against attacks	Hated by conquered people

MAIN IDEAS

3. What methods did the Assyrians use when they attacked enemy cities?
4. What contributions to government administration and culture did the Assyrians make?
5. Why did the people in the region rejoice when the Assyrian Empire was defeated?

CRITICAL THINKING & WRITING

6. **FORMING OPINIONS** Do you think the Assyrians' almost exclusive reliance on military power was a good strategy for creating their empire? Why or why not?
7. **MAKING INFERENCES** Why might the Assyrian warrior kings have had such a great interest in writing and reading?
8. **COMPARING** In what ways were King Ashurbanipal and King Nebuchadnezzar similar?
9. **WRITING ACTIVITY** EMPIRE BUILDING Write a one-paragraph **essay** on how developments in technology influenced the rise and decline of the Assyrian Empire.

CONNECT TO TODAY **CREATING A POSTER**

Research an instance when a modern ruler used excessive force to govern or put down opposition. Create a **poster** that tells about and illustrates the ruler and the event.

The Persian Empire

CONNECT TO THE NEW YORK STATE CORE CURRICULUM

Unit 1.B.1.a. Human and physical geography of early river civilizations
Unit 1.B.1.c. Political systems

TERMS & NAMES

- Cyrus
- Cambyses
- Darius
- satrap
- Royal Road
- Zoroaster

SETTING THE STAGE The Medes, along with the Chaldeans and others, helped to overthrow the Assyrian Empire in 612 B.C. The Medes marched to Nineveh from their homeland in the area of present-day northern Iran. Meanwhile, the Medes' close neighbor to the south, Persia, began to expand its horizons and territorial ambitions.

The Rise of Persia

The Assyrians employed military force to control a vast empire. In contrast, the Persians based their empire on tolerance and diplomacy. They relied on a strong military to back up their policies. Ancient Persia included what today is Iran.

The Persian Homeland-Indo-Europeans first migrated from Central Europe and southern Russia to the mountains and plateaus east of the Fertile Crescent around 1000 B.C. This area extended from the Caspian Sea in the north to the Persian Gulf in the south. (See the map on page 101.) In addition to fertile farmland, ancient Iran boasted a wealth of minerals. These included copper, lead, gold, silver, and gleaming blue lapis lazuli. A thriving trade in these minerals put the settlers in contact with their neighbors to the east and the west.

At first, dozens of tiny kingdoms occupied the region. Eventually two major powers emerged: the Medes and the Persians. In time, a remarkable ruler would lead Persia to dominate the Medes and found a huge empire.

Cyrus the Great Founds an Empire The rest of the world paid little attention to the Persians until 550 B.C. In that year, **Cyrus** (SY•ruhs), Persia's king, began to conquer several neighboring kingdoms. Cyrus was a military genius, leading his army from victory to victory between 550 and 539 B.C. In time, Cyrus controlled an empire that spanned 2,000 miles, from the Indus River in the east to Anatolia in the west.

Even more than his military genius, though, Cyrus's most enduring legacy was his method of governing. His kindness toward conquered peoples revealed a wise and tolerant view of empire. For example, when Cyrus's army marched into a city, his generals prevented Persian soldiers from looting and burning. Unlike other conquerors, Cyrus believed in honoring local customs and religions. Instead of destroying the local temple, Cyrus would kneel there to pray.

TAKING NOTES

Comparing and Contrasting Use a diagram to identify the similarities and differences between Cyrus and Darius.

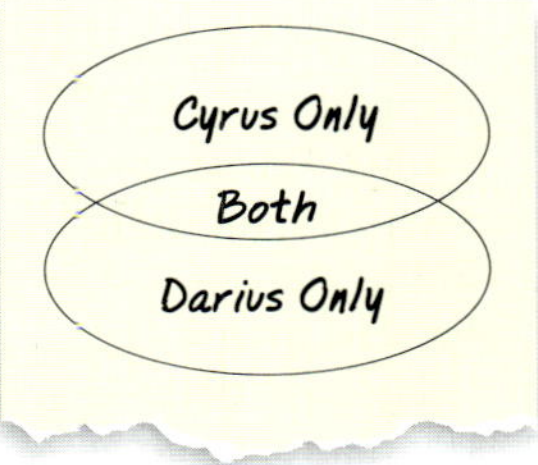

Cyrus also allowed the Jews, who had been driven from their homeland by the Babylonians, to return to Jerusalem in 538 B.C. Under Persian rule, the Jews rebuilt their city and temple. The Jews were forever grateful to Cyrus, whom they considered one of God's anointed ones. The Hebrew prophet Ezra tells of Cyrus's kindness:

PRIMARY SOURCE

This is the word of Cyrus king of Persia: The Lord the God of heaven has given me all the kingdoms of the earth, and he himself has charged me to build him a house at Jerusalem in Judah. To every man of his people now among you I say, God be with him, and let him go up to Jerusalem in Judah, and rebuild the house of the Lord the God of Israel, the God whose city is Jerusalem.

EZRA 1: 2–3 (Bible)

Cyrus was killed as he fought nomadic invaders on the eastern border of his empire. According to the Greek historian Arrian, his simple, house-shaped tomb bore these words: "O man, I am Cyrus the son of Cambyses. I established the Persian Empire and was king of Asia. Do not begrudge me my memorial." (A)

MAIN IDEA

Summarizing

(A) What are some examples of Cyrus's tolerant method of governing?

Persian Rule

The task of unifying conquered territories fell to rulers who followed Cyrus. They succeeded by combining Persian control with local self-government.

Cambyses and Darius Cyrus died in 530 B.C. His son **Cambyses** (kam•BY•seez), named after Cyrus's father, expanded the Persian Empire by conquering Egypt. However, the son neglected to follow his father's wise example. Cambyses scorned the Egyptian religion. He ordered the images of Egyptian gods to be burned. After ruling for only eight years, Cambyses died. Immediately, widespread rebellions broke out across the empire. Persian control had seemed strong a decade earlier. It now seemed surprisingly fragile.

Cambyses's successor, **Darius** (duh•RY•uhs), a noble of the ruling dynasty, had begun his career as a member of the king's bodyguard. An elite group of Persian soldiers, the Ten Thousand Immortals, helped Darius seize the throne around 522 B.C. Darius spent the first three years of his reign putting down revolts. He spent the next few years establishing a well-organized and efficient administration.

Having brought peace and stability to the empire, Darius turned his attention to conquest. He led his armies eastward into the mountains of present-day Afghanistan and then down into the river valleys of India. The immense Persian Empire now extended over 2,500 miles, embracing Egypt and Anatolia in the west, part of India in the east, and the Fertile Crescent in the center. Darius's only failure was his inability to conquer Greece.

▼ Sculpted figures bring gifts to Darius. The relief sculpture, located in the ancient Persian capital of Persepolis, dates from around the sixth century B.C.

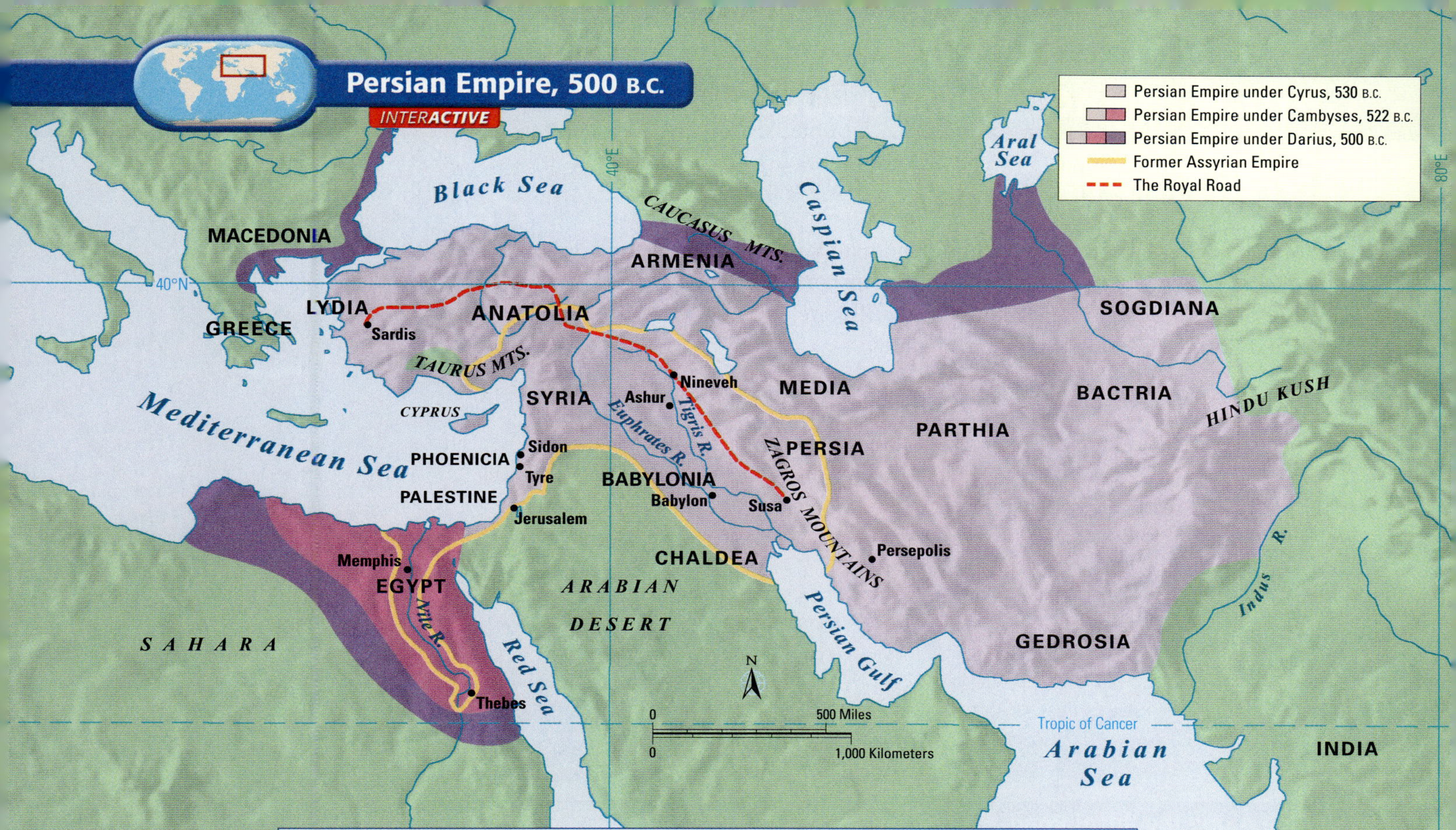

GEOGRAPHY SKILLBUILDER: Interpreting Maps

1. **Region** *What part of the ancient world did Cambyses add to the Persian Empire?*
2. **Region** *Compare the map of the Persian Empire with that of the Assyrian Empire on page 96. What areas did the Persians rule that the Assyrians did not?*

Provinces and Satraps Although Darius was a great warrior, his real genius lay in administration. To govern his sprawling empire, Darius divided it into 20 provinces. These provinces were roughly similar to the homelands of the different groups of people who lived within the Persian Empire. Under Persian rule, the people of each province still practiced their own religion. They also spoke their own language and followed many of their own laws. This administrative policy of many groups—sometimes called "nationalities"—living by their own laws within one empire was repeatedly practiced in Southwest Asia.

Although tolerant of the many groups within his empire, Darius still ruled with absolute power. In each province, Darius installed a governor called a **satrap** (SAY•TRAP), who ruled locally. Darius also appointed a military leader and a tax collector for each province. To ensure the loyalty of these officials, Darius sent out inspectors known as the "King's Eyes and Ears."

Two other tools helped Darius hold together his empire. An excellent system of roads allowed Darius to communicate quickly with the most distant parts of the empire. The famous **Royal Road**, for example, ran from Susa in Persia to Sardis in Anatolia, a distance of 1,677 miles. Darius borrowed the second tool, manufacturing metal coins, from the Lydians of Asia Minor. For the first time, coins of a standard value circulated throughout an extended empire. People no longer had to weigh and measure odd pieces of gold or silver to pay for what they bought. The network roads and the wide use of standardized coins promoted trade. Trade, in turn, helped to hold together the empire.

The Royal Road

One of the ways in which societies build and maintain empires is by establishing systems of communication and transportation. The Royal Road, built by the rulers of the Persian Empire, connected Susa in Persia to Sardis in Anatolia.

▶ This four-horse chariot dates from the 6th to 4th centuries B.C. It is the type of vehicle that would have traveled the Royal Road in the time of Darius. The studs on the wheels were designed to help prevent the chariot from slipping.

A Ride Along the Royal Road

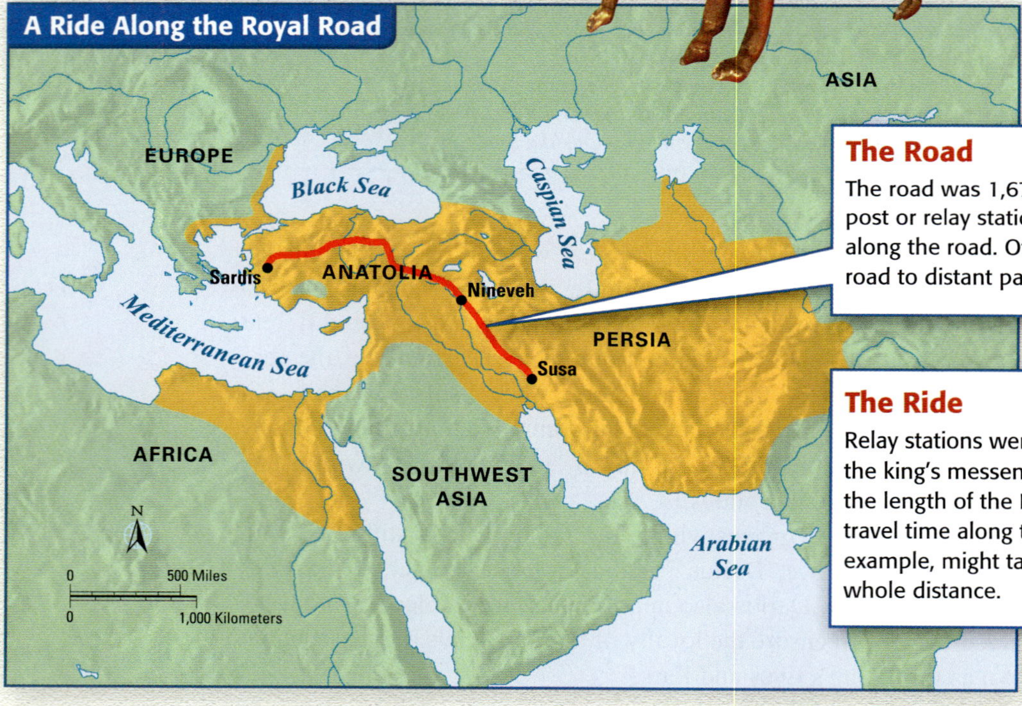

The Road

The road was 1,677 miles in length. There were 111 post or relay stations spaced about 15 miles apart along the road. Other roads branched off the main road to distant parts of the empire.

The Ride

Relay stations were equipped with fresh horses for the king's messengers. Royal messengers could cover the length of the Royal Road in seven days. Normal travel time along the road was longer. A caravan, for example, might take three months to travel the whole distance.

Patterns of Interaction

Building Empires: The Rise of the Persians and the Inca

Strong road networks like the Royal Road enabled empires to expand and maintain control over people and places. Like the Persians, the Inca of South America created a road system thousands of miles long. These roads allowed the Inca to extend their rule over as many as 16 million people. Empires throughout history have shared characteristics such as efficient communication systems, effective leaders, and powerful armies.

Connect *to* Today

1. **Recognizing Effects** How would the Royal Road enable a ruler to maintain power in the empire?
   See Skillbuilder Handbook, Page R6.
2. **Comparing** What systems of communication and transportation today might be compared to the Royal Road of the Persians?

The Persian Legacy

By the time of Darius's rule, about 2,500 years had passed since the first Sumerian city-states had been built. During those years, people of the Fertile Crescent had endured war, conquest, and famine. These events gave rise to a basic question: Why should so much suffering and chaos exist in the world? A Persian prophet named **Zoroaster** (ZAWR•oh•AS•tuhr), who lived around 600 B.C., offered an answer.

Zoroaster's Teachings Zoroaster taught that the earth is a battleground where a great struggle is fought between the spirit of good and the spirit of evil. Each person, Zoroaster preached, is expected to take part in this struggle. The Zoroastrian religion teaches a belief in one god, Ahura Mazda (ah•HUR•uh-MAZ•duh). At the end of time, Ahura Mazda will judge everyone according to how well he or she fought the battle for good. Traces of Zoroastrianism—such as the concept of Satan and a belief in angels—can be found in Judaism, Christianity, and Islam.

After the Muslim conquest of Persia in the A.D. 600s, the Zoroastrian religion declined. Some groups carried the faith eastward to India. Zoroastrianism also was an important influence in the development of Manichaeism (MAN•ih•KEE•IHZ•uhm), a religious system that competed with early Christianity for believers. The followers of Mithra, a Zoroastrian god, spread westward to become a popular religion among the military legions in the Roman Empire. Today, modern Zoroastrians continue to observe the religion's traditions in several countries including Iran and India, where its followers are called Parsis. **B**

MAIN IDEA

Comparing

B What ideas and world view did Zoroastrianism share with other religions?

Political Order-Through their tolerance and good government, the Persians brought political order to Southwest Asia. They preserved ideas from earlier civilizations and found new ways to live and rule. Their respect for other cultures helped to preserve those cultures for the future. The powerful dynasty Cyrus established in Persia lasted 200 years and grew into a huge empire. As you will learn in Section 4, great empires also arose in China and dominated that region.

NEW YORK CORE CURRICULUM REVIEW

TERMS & NAMES 1. For each term or name, write a sentence explaining its significance.

- Cyrus
- Cambyses
- Darius
- satrap
- Royal Road
- Zoroaster

USING YOUR NOTES

2. Which of the differences between Cyrus and Darius do you consider most important? Why?

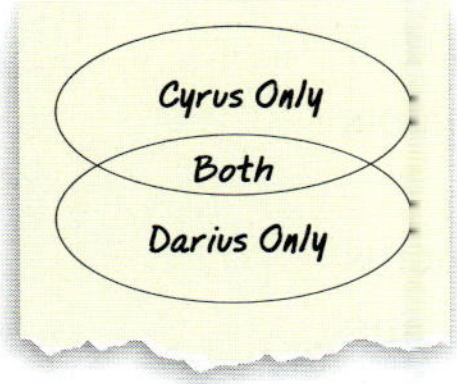

MAIN IDEAS

3. How did Cyrus treat the peoples he conquered?
4. What methods and tools did Darius use to hold together his empire?
5. What did Zoroaster teach?

CRITICAL THINKING & WRITING

6. **MAKING INFERENCES** What do the words that appeared on Cyrus's tomb suggest about his character?
7. **DRAWING CONCLUSIONS** How did the Royal Road help Darius maintain control over his people?
8. **DEVELOPING HISTORICAL PERSPECTIVE** What events led to the development of Zoroastrianism?
9. **WRITING ACTIVITY** EMPIRE BUILDING Write an **expository essay** explaining how Darius's methods of administration gave stability to the Persian Empire. In your essay, consider such topics as the structure of the empire, the policy of tolerance, and the role of the satrap.

INTEGRATED TECHNOLOGY **INTERNET ACTIVITY**

Use the Internet to find information on modern Zoroastrianism. Create a **chart** to present your findings.

INTERNET KEYWORD
Zoroastrianism

The Unification of China

CONNECT TO THE NEW YORK STATE CORE CURRICULUM

Unit 1.E.1.d. Chinese philosophies (Confucianism, Daoism)
Unit 1.E.1.h. Legalism

TERMS & NAMES

- Confucius
- filial piety
- bureaucracy
- Daoism
- Legalism
- *I Ching*
- yin and yang
- Qin Dynasty
- Shi Huangdi
- autocracy

SETTING THE STAGE The Zhou Dynasty, as you read in Chapter 2, lasted for at least eight centuries, from approximately 1027 to 256 B.C. For the first 300 years of their long reign, the Zhou kings controlled a large empire, including both eastern and western lands. Local rulers reported to the king, who had the ultimate power. By the latter years of the Zhou Dynasty, the lords of dependent territories began to think of themselves as independent kings. Their almost constant conflict, which is known as "the warring states period," led to the decline of the Zhou Dynasty.

TAKING NOTES
Recognizing Effects Use a web to indicate how the chaos of the warring states affected the philosophy, politics, and cities of China.

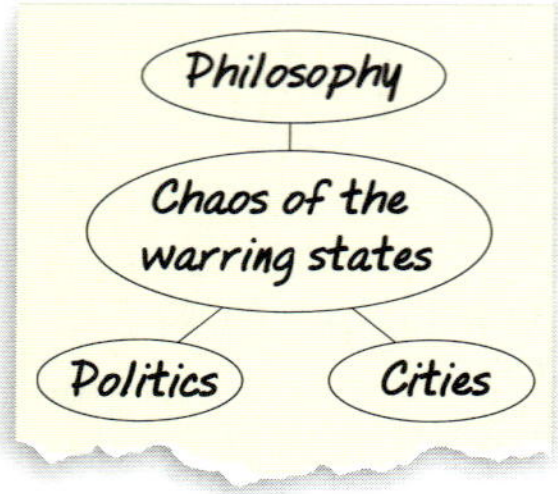

Confucius and the Social Order

Toward the end of the Zhou Dynasty, China moved away from its ancient values of social order, harmony, and respect for authority. Chinese scholars and philosophers developed different solutions to restore these values.

Confucius Urges Harmony China's most influential scholar was **Confucius** (kuhn•FYOO•shuhs). Born in 551 B.C., Confucius lived in a time when the Zhou Dynasty was in decline. He led a scholarly life, studying and teaching history, music, and moral character.

Confucius was born at a time of crisis and violence in China. He had a deep desire to restore the order and moral living of earlier times to his society. Confucius believed that social order, harmony, and good government could be restored in China if society were organized around five basic relationships. These were the relationships between: (1) ruler and subject, (2) father and son, (3) husband and wife, (4) older brother and younger brother, and (5) friend and friend. A code of proper conduct regulated each of these relationships. For example, rulers should practice kindness and virtuous living. In return, subjects should be loyal and law-abiding.

Three of Confucius's five relationships were based upon the family. Confucius stressed that children should practice **filial piety**, or respect for their parents and ancestors. Filial piety, according to Confucius, meant devoting oneself to one's parents during their lifetimes. It also required honoring their memories after death through the performance of certain rituals.

In the following passage, Confucius—the "Master"—expresses his thoughts on the concept:

PRIMARY SOURCE

Ziyou [a disciple of Confucius] asked about filial piety. The Master said: "Nowadays people think they are dutiful sons when they feed their parents. Yet they also feed their dogs and horses. Unless there is respect, where is the difference?"

CONFUCIUS, *Analects* 2.7

Confucius wanted to reform Chinese society by showing rulers how to govern wisely. Impressed by Confucius's wisdom, the duke of Lu appointed him minister of justice. According to legend, Confucius so overwhelmed people by his kindness and courtesy that almost overnight, crime vanished from Lu. When the duke's ways changed, however, Confucius became disillusioned and resigned.

Vocabulary
legend: a story handed down from earlier times, especially one believed to be historical

Confucius spent the remainder of his life teaching. His students later collected his words in a book called the *Analects.* A disciple named Mencius (MEHN•shee•uhs) also spread Confucius's ideas.

Confucian Ideas About Government Confucius said that education could transform a humbly born person into a gentleman. In saying this, he laid the groundwork for the creation of a **bureaucracy**, a trained civil service, or those who run the government. According to Confucius, a gentleman had four virtues: "In his private conduct he was courteous, in serving his master he was punctilious [precise], in providing for the needs of the people he gave them even more than their due; in exacting service from the people, he was just." Education became critically important to career advancement in the bureaucracy.

Confucianism was never a religion, but it was an ethical system, a system based on accepted principles of right and wrong. It became the foundation for Chinese government and social order. In addition, the ideas of Confucius spread beyond China and influenced civilizations throughout East Asia.

History Makers

Confucius
551–479 B.C.

Confucius was born to a poor family. As an adult, he earned his living as a teacher. But he longed to put his principles into action by advising political leaders. Finally, at around age 50, Confucius won a post as minister in his home state. According to legend, he set such a virtuous example that a purse lying in the middle of the street would be untouched for days.

After Confucius resigned his post as minister, he returned to teaching. He considered himself a failure because he had never held high office. Yet Confucius's ideas have molded Chinese thought for centuries.

Laozi
sixth century B.C.

Although a person named Laozi is credited with being the first philosopher of Daoism, no one knows for sure whether he really existed. Legend has it that Laozi's mother carried him in her womb for 62 years and that he was born with white hair and wrinkled skin. Laozi's followers claimed that he was a contemporary of Confucius.

Unlike Confucius, however, Laozi believed that government should do as little as possible and leave the people alone. Laozi thought that people could do little to influence the outcome of events. Daoism offered communion with nature as an alternative to political chaos.

INTEGRATED TECHNOLOGY

RESEARCH LINKS For more on Confucius and Laozi, go to **classzone.com**

Other Ethical Systems

In addition to Confucius, other Chinese scholars and philosophers developed ethical systems with very different philosophies. Some stressed the importance of nature, others, the power of government.

Daoists Seek Harmony For a Chinese thinker named Laozi (low•dzuh), who may have lived during the sixth century B.C., only the natural order was important. The natural order involves relations among all living things. His book *Dao De Jing* (*The Way of Virtue*) expressed Laozi's belief. He said that a universal force called the Dao (dow), meaning "the Way," guides all things. Of all the creatures of nature, according to Laozi, only humans fail to follow the Dao. They argue about questions of right and wrong, good manners or bad. According to Laozi, such arguments are pointless. In the following, he explains the wisdom of the Dao:

PRIMARY SOURCE **A**

The Dao never does anything,
yet through it all things are done.

If powerful men and women
could center themselves in it,
the whole world would be transformed
by itself, in its natural rhythms.
People would be content
with their simple, everyday lives, in harmony, and free of desire.

When there is no desire,
all things are at peace.

LAOZI, *Dao De Jing,* Passage 37

MAIN IDEA

Analyzing Primary Sources

A What do you think is the Daoist attitude toward being a powerful person?

The philosophy of Laozi came to be known as **Daoism**. Its search for knowledge and understanding of nature led Daoism's followers to pursue scientific studies. Daoists made many important contributions to the sciences of alchemy, astronomy, and medicine.

Legalists Urge Harsh Rule In sharp contrast to the followers of Confucius and Laozi was a group of practical political thinkers called the Legalists. They believed that a highly efficient and powerful government was the key to restoring order in society. They got their name from their belief that government should use the law to end civil disorder and restore harmony. Hanfeizi and Li Si were among the founders of **Legalism**.

The Legalists taught that a ruler should provide rich rewards for people who carried out their duties well. Likewise, the disobedient should be harshly punished. In practice, the Legalists stressed punishment more than rewards. For example, anyone caught outside his own village without a travel permit should have his ears or nose chopped off.

The Legalists believed in controlling ideas as well as actions. They suggested that a ruler burn all writings that might encourage people to criticize government.

Chinese Ethical Systems

Confucianism	Daoism	Legalism
• Social order, harmony, and good government should be based on family relationships. • Respect for parents and elders is important to a well-ordered society. • Education is important both to the welfare of the individual and to society.	• The natural order is more important than the social order. • A universal force guides all things. • Human beings should live simply and in harmony with nature.	• A highly efficient and powerful government is the key to social order. • Punishments are useful to maintain social order. • Thinkers and their ideas should be strictly controlled by the government.

SKILLBUILDER: Interpreting Charts

1. **Comparing** *Which of these three systems stresses the importance of government and a well-ordered society?*
2. **Synthesizing** *Which of these systems seems to be most moderate and balanced? Explain.*

MAIN IDEA

Summarizing

B How did the Legalists think that a society could be made to run well?

After all, it was for the prince to govern and the people to obey. Eventually, Legalist ideas gained favor with a prince of a new dynasty that replaced the Zhou. That powerful ruler soon brought order to China. **B**

▲ Traditional yin-and-yang symbol

I Ching* and Yin and Yang** People with little interest in the philosophical debates of the Confucians, Daoists, and Legalists found answers to life's questions elsewhere. Some consulted a book of oracles called ***I Ching (also spelled *Yi Jing*) to solve ethical or practical problems. Readers used the book by throwing a set of coins, interpreting the results, and then reading the appropriate oracle, or prediction. The *I Ching* (*The Book of Changes*) helped people to lead a happy life by offering good advice and simple common sense.

Other people turned to the ideas of ancient thinkers, such as the concept of **yin and yang**—two powers that together represented the natural rhythms of life. Yin represents all that is cold, dark, soft, and mysterious. Yang is the opposite—warm, bright, hard, and clear. The symbol of yin and yang is a circle divided into halves, as shown in the emblem to the upper right. The circle represents the harmony of yin and yang. Both forces represent the rhythm of the universe and complement each other. Both the *I Ching* and yin and yang helped Chinese people understand how they fit into the world.

The Qin Dynasty Unifies China

In the third century B.C., the **Qin Dynasty** (chihn) replaced the Zhou Dynasty. It emerged from the western state of Qin. The ruler who founded the Qin Dynasty employed Legalist ideas to subdue the warring states and unify his country.

A New Emperor Takes Control In 221 B.C., after ruling for over 20 years, the Qin ruler assumed the name **Shi Huangdi** (shihr hwahng•dee), which means "First Emperor." The new emperor had begun his reign by halting the internal battles that had sapped China's strength. Next he turned his attention to defeating invaders and crushing resistance within China to his rule. Shi Huangdi's armies attacked the invaders north of the Huang He and south as far as what is now Vietnam. His victories doubled China's size. Shi Huangdi was determined to unify China.

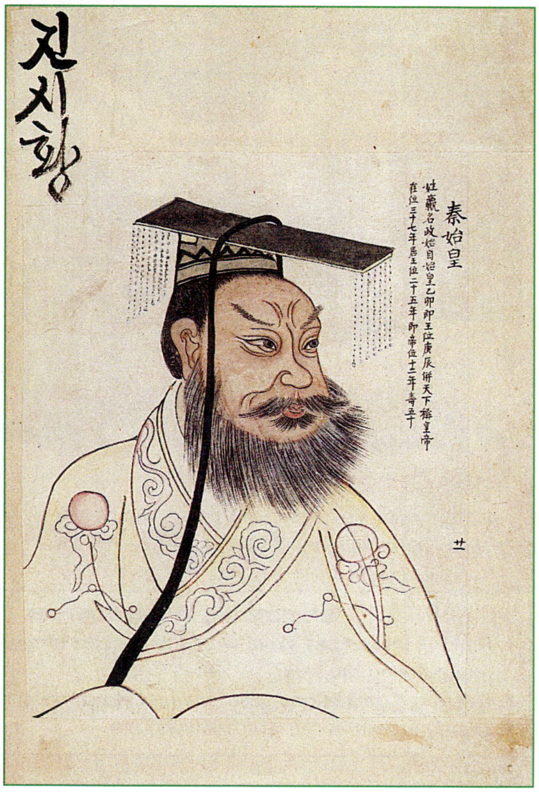

▼ Although a tyrant, Shi Huangdi is considered the founder of unified China. The word *Qin* is the origin of *China*.

Shi Huangdi acted decisively to crush political opposition at home. To destroy the power of rival warlords, he introduced a policy called "strengthening the trunk and weakening the branches." He commanded all the noble families to live in the capital city under his suspicious gaze. This policy, according to tradition, uprooted 120,000 noble families. Seizing their land, the emperor carved China into 36 administrative districts. He sent Qin officials to control them.

To prevent criticism, Shi Huangdi and his prime minister, the Legalist philosopher Li Su, murdered hundreds of Confucian scholars. They also ordered "useless" books burned. These books were the works of Confucian thinkers and poets who disagreed with the Legalists. Practical books about medicine and farming, however, were spared. Through measures

The Great Wall of China

From the Yellow Sea in the east to the Gobi Desert in the west, the Great Wall twisted like a dragon's tail for thousands of miles. Watch towers rose every 200 to 300 yards along the wall.

In the time of Shi Huangdi, hundreds of thousands of peasants collected, hauled, and dumped millions of tons of stone, dirt, and rubble to fill the core of the Great Wall.

Slabs of cut stone on the outside of the wall enclosed a heap of pebbles and rubble on the inside. Each section of the wall rose to a height of 20 to 25 feet.

Although Shi Huangdi built the earliest unified wall, the wall as it exists today dates from the later Ming Dynasty (1368–1644).

SKILLBUILDER: Interpreting Visual Sources

1. **Making Inferences** *What were the benefits of the watch towers along the wall?*
2. **Drawing Conclusions** *What modern structures serve the same purpose as the watch towers?*

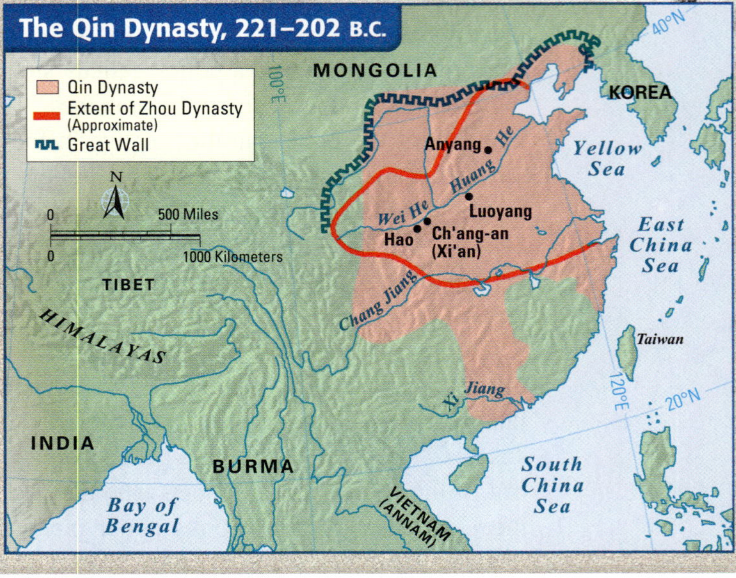

such as these, Shi Huangdi established an **autocracy**—a government that has unlimited power and uses it in an arbitrary manner.

A Program of Centralization Shi Huangdi's sweeping program of centralization included the building of a highway network of more than 4,000 miles. Also, he set the same standards throughout China for writing, law, currency, and weights and measures—even down to the length of cart axles. This last standard made sure that all vehicles could fit into the ruts of China's main roads.

Under Shi Huangdi's rule, irrigation projects increased farm production. Trade blossomed, thanks to the new road system. Trade pushed a new class of merchants into prominence. Despite these social advances, harsh taxes and repressive government made the Qin regime unpopular. Shi Huangdi had unified China at the expense of human freedom. (C)

MAIN IDEA

Recognizing Effects

(C) What were the positive and negative effects of Shi Huangdi's rule?

Great Wall of China Scholars hated Shi Huangdi for his book burning. Poor people hated him because they were forced to work on the building of a huge defensive wall. Earlier, Zhou rulers had erected smaller walls to discourage attacks by northern nomads. Shi Huangdi determined to close the gaps and extend the wall almost the length of the empire's border. Enemies would have to gallop halfway to Tibet to get around it.

The Great Wall of China arose on the backs of hundreds of thousands of peasants. The wall builders worked neither for wages nor for love of empire. They faced a terrible choice: work on the wall or die. Many of the laborers worked on the wall and died anyway, victims of the crushing labor or the harsh winter weather.

The Fall of the Qin The Qin Dynasty lasted only a short time. Though fully as cruel as his father, Shi Huangdi's son proved less able. Peasants rebelled just three years after the second Qin emperor took office. One of their leaders, a peasant from the land of Han, marched his troops into the capital city. By 202 B.C., the harsh Qin Dynasty gave way to the Han Dynasty, one of the longest in Chinese history.

While the Chinese explored the best ways to govern, ancient Greece also was experimenting with different forms of government, as you will read in Chapter 5.

NEW YORK CORE CURRICULUM REVIEW

TERMS & NAMES 1. For each term or name, write a sentence explaining its significance.

• Confucius • filial piety • bureaucracy • Daoism • Legalism • *I Ching* • yin and yang • Qin Dynasty • Shi Huangdi • autocracy

USING YOUR NOTES

2. Which aspect of Chinese life was most affected by the chaos created by the warring states?

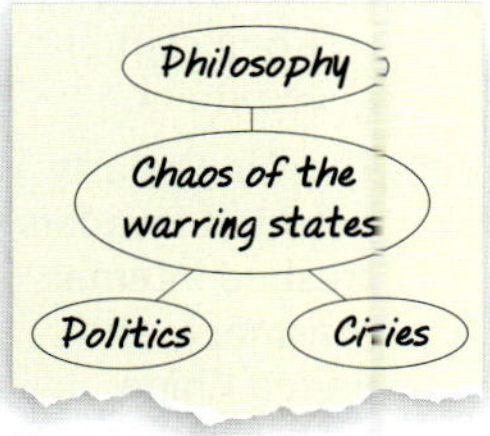

MAIN IDEAS

3. How did Confucius believe that social order, harmony, and good government could be restored in China?
4. What did the Legalists see as the key to restoring order?
5. What measures did Shi Huangdi take to crush political opposition at home?

CRITICAL THINKING & WRITING

6. **HYPOTHESIZING** How would followers of the three philosophical traditions in China react to the idea that "all men are created equal"?
7. **ANALYZING CAUSES** Why did Shi Huangdi have his critics murdered?
8. **MAKING INFERENCES** Would a ruler who followed Confucian or Daoist ideas have built the Great Wall? Why or why not?
9. **WRITING ACTIVITY** RELIGIOUS AND ETHICAL SYSTEMS Write a **comparison-contrast paragraph** in which you discuss the three Chinese ethical systems.

CONNECT TO TODAY **PREPARING AN ORAL REPORT**

Research to find out about the Great Wall today. Prepare an **oral report** in which you explain what the Great Wall looks like today and what it is used for.

Chapter 4 Assessment

TERMS & NAMES

For each term or name below, briefly explain its connection to the history of the first age of empires between 1570 and 200 B.C.

1. Ramses II
2. Kush
3. Assyria
4. Ashurbanipal
5. Cyrus
6. Royal Road
7. Zoroaster
8. Confucius
9. Daoism
10. Shi Huangdi

MAIN IDEAS

The Egyptian and Nubian Empires Section 1 (pages 89–94)

11. How did the Kushites treat Egyptian culture after they conquered Egypt?
12. When did Kush experience a golden age?

The Assyrian Empire Section 2 (pages 95–98)

13. How did Assyria acquire its empire?
14. What were the positive achievements of the Assyrian Empire?

The Persian Empire Section 3 (pages 99–103)

15. What is Cyrus's enduring legacy?
16. How far did Darius extend the Persian Empire?

The Unification of China Section 4 (pages 104–109)

17. Around what five basic relationships did Confucius believe society should be organized?
18. Why did Shi Huangdi have the Great Wall built?

CRITICAL THINKING

1. **USING YOUR NOTES**
   EMPIRE BUILDING Create a table and list the successes and failures of the leaders discussed in this chapter.

Leader	Successes	Failures
Thutmose III		
Sennacherib		
Cyrus		

2. **DRAWING CONCLUSIONS**
   RELIGIOUS AND ETHICAL SYSTEMS Religious and ethical systems in Persia and China arose in response to what similar conditions?

3. **DEVELOPING HISTORICAL PERSPECTIVE**
   How have Cyrus's and Sennacherib's contrasting ruling styles probably affected their legacies?

4. **RECOGNIZING EFFECTS**
   CULTURAL INTERACTION What positive results occur when cultures interact? What negative results might there be?

5. **SYNTHESIZING**
   What similar purpose was served by the Persians' Royal Road and by the Great Wall of China?

VISUAL SUMMARY

First Age of Empires

EMPIRE BUILDING

Egypt 1570–1075 B.C.
- Pharaohs set up a professional army.
- Pharaohs invaded territories in Africa and Southwest Asia.
- Egypt drew vast wealth from the lands it controlled.

Nubia 751 B.C.–A.D. 350
- Nubia and Egypt interacted and spread their culture through trade.
- The kings of Nubia conquered Egypt and maintained the Egyptian way of life.
- Nubia established trade among Africa, Arabia, and India.

Assyria 850–612 B.C.
- Assyria used a sophisticated military organization to conquer an empire.
- The empire engaged in brutal treatment of its conquered peoples.
- Kings used harsh taxes to control conquered peoples.

Persia 550–330 B.C.
- Persian kings were tolerant.
- Kings permitted a high degree of local self-government.
- The empire was divided into 20 provinces.

China 221–202 B.C.
- Ethical systems laid the groundwork for a strong central government.
- The Qin Dynasty defeated invaders, crushed internal resistance, and united China.
- China initiated a sweeping program of centralization.

NEW YORK STATE REGENTS EXAM PRACTICE

Use the quotation and your knowledge of world history to answer questions 1 and 2.
Additional Test Practice, pp. S1–S33

PRIMARY SOURCE

Guide the people with governmental measures and control or regulate them by the threat of punishment, and the people will try to keep out of jail, but will have no sense of honor or shame. Guide the people by virtue and control or regulate them by *li* [moral rules and customs], and the people will have a sense of honor and respect.

CONFUCIUS, *Analects 2.3*

1 Which phrase best describes Confucius's belief about human nature and lawful behavior?

(1) People are naturally moral and can control their behavior on their own.
(2) People are best controlled by fear.
(3) People learn good behavior by example.
(4) People cannot be controlled by any means.

2 Which of the following rulers might have held a similar belief?

(1) Shi Huangdi
(2) Cyrus
(3) King Ashurbanipal
(4) Ramses II

Use the relief below depicting King Ashurbanipal and his queen at a garden party and your knowledge of world history to answer question 3.

3 What characteristic of the Assyrians does this relief seem to reflect?

(1) their love of luxury
(2) their military might
(3) their administrative organization
(4) their love of learning

INTEGRATED TECHNOLOGY
TEST PRACTICE Go to **classzone.com**
- Diagnostic tests
- Tutorials
- Strategies
- Additional practice

ALTERNATIVE ASSESSMENT

1. Interact *with* History

Recall your discussion of the question on page 88: "How will the empire help you or harm you?" You thought about the advantages and disadvantages of empire before studying the rise of the first great empires. Now that you've read the chapter, rethink the advantages and disadvantages of empire. Discuss the following questions with a small group:

- Do empires benefit conquered peoples?
- Do empires impose penalties on those they conquer?
- Which outweighs the other—the benefits or the penalties?

2. WRITING ABOUT HISTORY

Study page 108, which deals with the Great Wall of China. Imagine that you are one of the workers who built the Great Wall. Write three **journal entries** describing the following:

- the work you carry out on the Great Wall
- your experiences
- your impressions

INTEGRATED TECHNOLOGY

Creating a Web Site

Create a Web site on the first empires for a museum exhibit. Choose one of these empires to research: Assyria, Kush, Persia, or Qin. Consider including:

- art, artifacts, and maps
- a description of the empire with dates, location, and rulers
- information on major events and conflicts
- the rise and fall of the empire
- a discussion of the empire's legacy
- a list of Web sites used in your research

The Rise of Civilizations

Thousands of years ago, several societies in different parts of the world changed from hunting and gathering to farming. Some began to produce surpluses of food. Those surpluses helped bring about the world's first civilizations.

In Unit 1, you learned that most historians define civilization as a complex culture with these five characteristics: (1) advanced cities, (2) specialized workers, (3) complex institutions, (4) record keeping and writing, and (5) advanced technology. You also learned about several early civilizations. In the next six pages, you will explore what those ancient civilizations had in common and how they differed.

Ancient Civilizations over Time

Some of these ancient civilizations lasted only a few hundred years, but others lasted more than 3,000 years. Earlier civilizations often had influence on later ones that shared the same area. The civilizations shown here did not all develop in isolation of each other. Trade linked some. Some fought wars against each other.

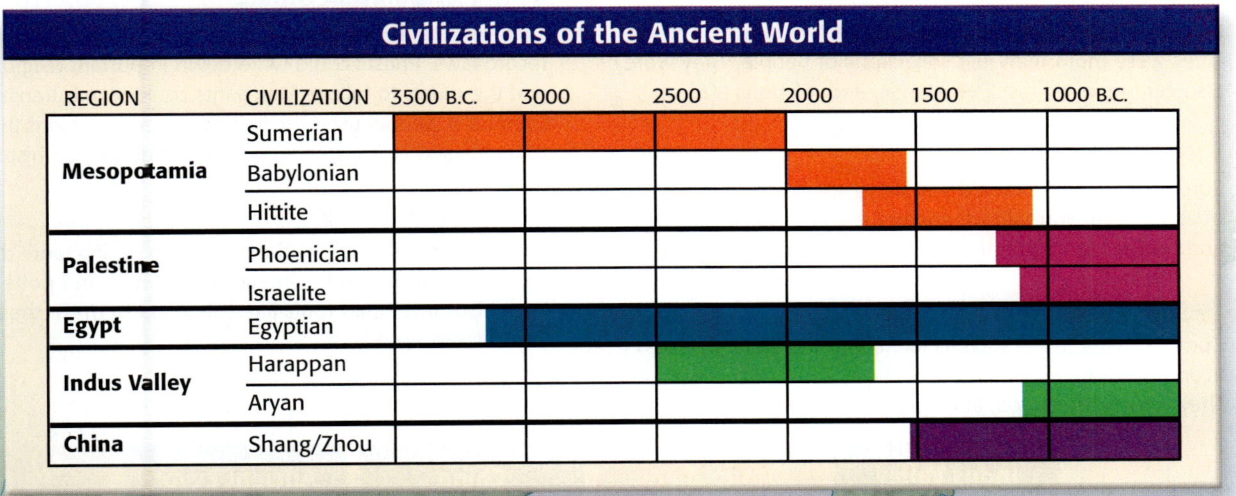

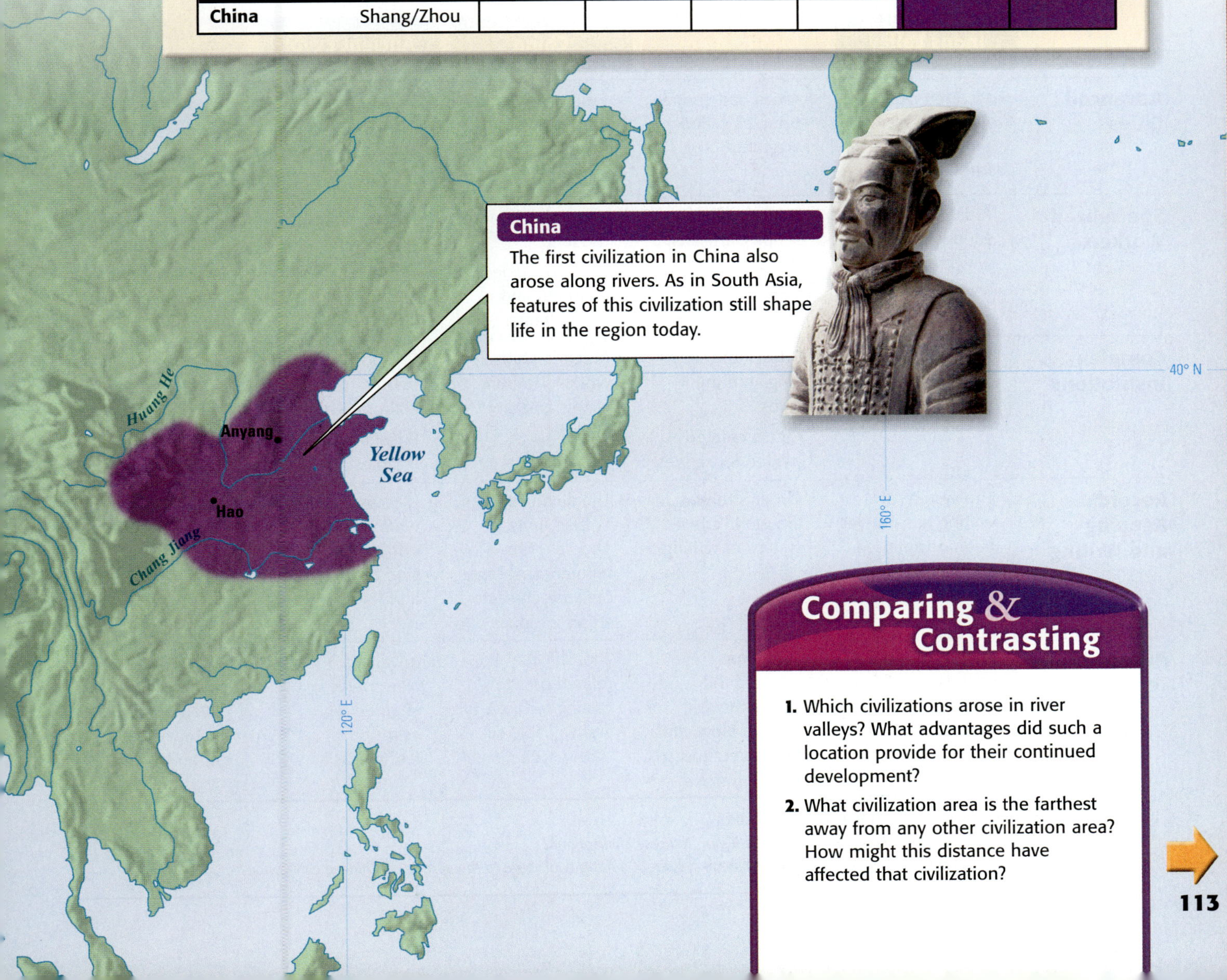

China

The first civilization in China also arose along rivers. As in South Asia, features of this civilization still shape life in the region today.

Comparing & Contrasting

1. Which civilizations arose in river valleys? What advantages did such a location provide for their continued development?
2. What civilization area is the farthest away from any other civilization area? How might this distance have affected that civilization?

Characteristics of Civilizations

The civilizations you studied in Unit 1 each demonstrated the five characteristics that historians use to define a civilization.

Advanced Cities

Cities were key features of the ancient civilizations. These cities were more than just collections of people. They were also centers of political, economic, and religious life.

Specialized Workers

Surpluses of food allowed people to specialize in jobs outside of agriculture. Specialized workers such as artisans, traders, and soldiers strengthened and expanded civilization.

Complex Institutions

Complex institutions such as law codes, religion, and an economy were another characteristic of ancient civilizations. They organized, united, and helped civilizations to prosper.

Record Keeping and Writing

Each civilization developed a system of writing. Rulers could record laws. Priests could write down important religious dates and the rituals to follow. Merchants could record transactions. Eventually, people used the writing system to record their thoughts and ideas, creating literature and written history.

Advanced Technology

The civilizations developed new ways of doing work and new materials to work with, such as metals and pottery. They also developed tools like calendars to make their world more orderly.

	Indus Valley	Mesopotamia	China	Ancient Egypt	Palestine
Advanced Cities	• Planned cities had neatly laid-out streets and fortified areas.	• Cities had central temples called ziggurats.	• Cities had massive earthen walls for protection.	• Cities had power over the surrounding lands.	• Phoenician cities were busy ports. • Jerusalem had a large temple.
Specialized Workers	• Artisans made various goods, which traders exchanged with other peoples.	• Priests, warriors, scribes, artisans, and farmers all had special tasks.	• Warriors defended the land. • Artisans made beautiful and useful items.	• Rulers, officials, priests, and wealthy land-owners led society.	• Phoenician sailors carried goods. • Israelite religious leaders had great influence.
Complex Institutions	• Rulers organized the work of laying out the cities.	• Priests and then kings ran the cities. • Rulers created written law codes.	• Rulers organized workers to build canals and city walls.	• Pharaohs ordered people to build elaborate tombs. • Priests ran large temples.	• Israelites developed the belief in one god. They saw the law as a gift from God.
Record Keeping and Writing	• The system of writing has not yet been deciphered.	• Cuneiform was the world's first system of writing.	• The writing system helped unify peoples with different languages because characters stood for ideas.	• Hieroglyphic writing had symbols that stood for ideas and for sounds.	• The Phoenician alphabet became the basis of many alphabets.
Advanced Technology	• Engineers made sophisticated buildings and plumbing systems.	• Sumerians invented the wheel, the sail, and the plow, and discovered how to make bronze.	• The Chinese refined bronze casting technology and valuable silk cloth production.	• Advances were made in engineering, astronomy, and medicine.	• Phoenicians built ships with advances such as the steering oar and the sail.

SKILLBUILDER: Interpreting Charts

1. **Synthesizing** *How important was religion to these civilizations?*
2. **Analyzing Motives** *How did the Chinese system of writing contribute to the spread of Chinese civilization?*

Development of Law

Laws are a complex institution of civilizations. They are designed to do many things—settle conflicts between individuals, provide citizens with guidance on proper behavior, and outline an individual's relationship with the government. Thus, laws are important for building stable civilizations.

PRIMARY SOURCE

INTERACTIVE

Hammurabi's Code

If a son has struck his father, they shall cut off his hand.

If a [noble] has destroyed the eye of a [noble], they shall destroy his eye.

If he has broken another [noble's] bone, they shall break his bone.

If he has destroyed the eye of a commoner or broken the bone of a commoner, he shall pay one mina of silver.

If he has destroyed the eye of a [noble's] slave or broken the bone of a [noble's] slave, he shall pay one-half [the slave's] value.

If a [noble] has knocked out the tooth of a [noble], they shall knock out his tooth.

If he has knocked out a commoner's tooth, he shall pay one-third mina of silver.

DOCUMENT-BASED QUESTION

Is the Code applied equally to all people? Explain your answer.

PRIMARY SOURCE

INTERACTIVE

Old Testament

Whoever strikes a man so that he dies shall be put to death. But if he did not lie in wait for him, but God let him fall into his hand, then I will appoint for you a place to which he may flee. . . .

Whoever strikes his father or his mother shall be put to death. . . .

Whoever curses his father or his mother shall be put to death.

When men quarrel and one strikes the other with a stone or with his fist and the man does not die but keeps his bed, then if the man rises again and walks abroad with his staff, he that struck him shall be clear; only he shall pay for the loss of his time. . . .

When a man strikes his slave, male or female, with a rod and the slave dies under his hand, he shall be punished. . . .

When a man strikes the eye of his slave, male or female, and destroys it, he shall let the slave go free for the eye's sake. If he knocks out the tooth of his slave, male or female, he shall let the slave go free for the tooth's sake.

DOCUMENT-BASED QUESTION

What principle underlies these laws? How would you describe the punishments in these laws?

PRIMARY SOURCE

INTERACTIVE

Confucius

The Master said, "A young man's duty is to behave well to his parents at home and to his elders abroad, to be cautious in giving promises and punctual in keeping them, to have kindly feelings towards everyone, but seek the intimacy of the Good."

The Master said, "Govern the people by regulations, keep order among them by chastisements, and they will flee from you, and lose all self-respect. Govern them by moral force, keep order among them by ritual, and they will keep their self-respect and come to you of their own accord."

DOCUMENT-BASED QUESTION

What behavior does Confucius expect of ordinary people and of rulers?

Comparing & Contrasting

1. How is the treatment of slaves in Hammurabi's Code and the Old Testament laws similar? How is it different?
2. For which of the civilizations on the chart do you think laws were most important? Why?

Record Keeping and Writing

As institutions became more complex, people realized the need for record keeping. Officials tracked taxes and laws, priests recorded important rituals, and merchants totaled accounts. Record keeping provided stability for the complex institutions.

PRIMARY SOURCE

Indus Valley Seals

The system of writing used in the Indus Valley has not been deciphered. Scholars have identified about 400 symbols, but they do not know if these stand for ideas or sounds. Many of the examples are found on small seals. The seals might have been used to mark objects to show ownership. In that case, the symbols might give a person's name.

DOCUMENT-BASED QUESTION

Based on what you see on this seal, what are some possibilities for its translation?

PRIMARY SOURCE

Sumerian Cuneiform

Cuneiform originated in people's desire to keep track of goods they owned. By around 3000 B.C., Sumerians had more than 1,000 symbols. Each stood for an idea. Later, symbols stood for sounds. This system of writing was used in Mesopotamia for about 3,000 years. Different peoples adapted it for their own languages. At first, cuneiform was read from top to bottom. Later, it was read from left to right.

DOCUMENT-BASED QUESTION

What visual clue suggests that this cuneiform sample was read from left to right and not top to bottom?

PRIMARY SOURCE

Egyptian Hieroglyphics

Hieroglyphics were read in the direction that the human and animal heads faced. Usually this was from right to left. Sometimes, though, the direction could be changed to make a more pleasing appearance. Some symbols stood for ideas. Some stood for consonant sounds—vowels were not included. Some gave clues to how a word was used, such as whether a name referred to a person or a place.

DOCUMENT-BASED QUESTION

In the bottom row on the left, you can see an owl. What other symbols do you recognize?

PRIMARY SOURCE

Phoenician Alphabet

The alphabet used by the ancient Phoenicians had symbols for 22 consonants. This alphabet was adapted by the Greeks, and it became the basis for writing all European languages. The Phoenician alphabet also influenced how Hebrew and Arabic were written, and it was adapted to write the languages of India and Ethiopia.

DOCUMENT-BASED QUESTION

Do any of the letters in this Phoenician sample look similar to letters we use today? If so, which ones?

Advanced Technology

New technologies gave the ancient civilizations new ways of solving problems. Some solved age-old problems—for example, the plow made it easier to till the soil. Some solved new problems. Egyptians learned how to embalm the bodies of dead rulers as part of their complex beliefs about life after death.

PRIMARY SOURCE

Phoenician Sailing

The Phoenicians traded throughout the Mediterranean Sea and beyond. They were the most skilled sailors of their time. The first ships relied on rowers and did not have sails. They also lacked rudders for steering. By about 700 B.C., though, the Phoenicians had made advances. They added long steering oars in the back and a single sail, which could catch the wind and move the ship forward. Captains came to rely on the sails, though rowers had to work when the weather was calm or when the wind was not blowing from behind the ship.

DOCUMENT-BASED QUESTION
What is the advantage of having a sail on the ship?

PRIMARY SOURCE

Bronze from Shang China

During the Shang Dynasty, Chinese artisans grew highly skilled at making bronze. Bronze is a mixture of copper and tin. They made bronze weapons and vessels for religious ceremonies. Bronzes were made by creating pottery molds that were carved on the inside, in reverse, to leave the desired pattern on the final object. Hot liquid bronze was poured inside. When it had cooled, the pottery molds were broken.

DOCUMENT-BASED QUESTION
What does the intricate detail of this piece suggest about Shang society?

Comparing & Contrasting

1. How do the ancient systems of writing differ from the way words are written today?
2. What role did trade play in the development of writing?
3. Which technological advances do you think were more important–Chinese skill in making bronzes or Phoenician skill in sailing? Why?

EXTENSION ACTIVITY

Technological changes have continued throughout history. Choose one area of life, such as land transportation, communication, medicine, or raising food. Using this textbook or an encyclopedia, find out what technology one of these ancient civilizations had in that area. Then identify technological changes in that area over the centuries. Create an illustrated time line to show how that technology has changed.

UNIT 2

New Directions in Government and Society

2000 B.C. – A.D. 700

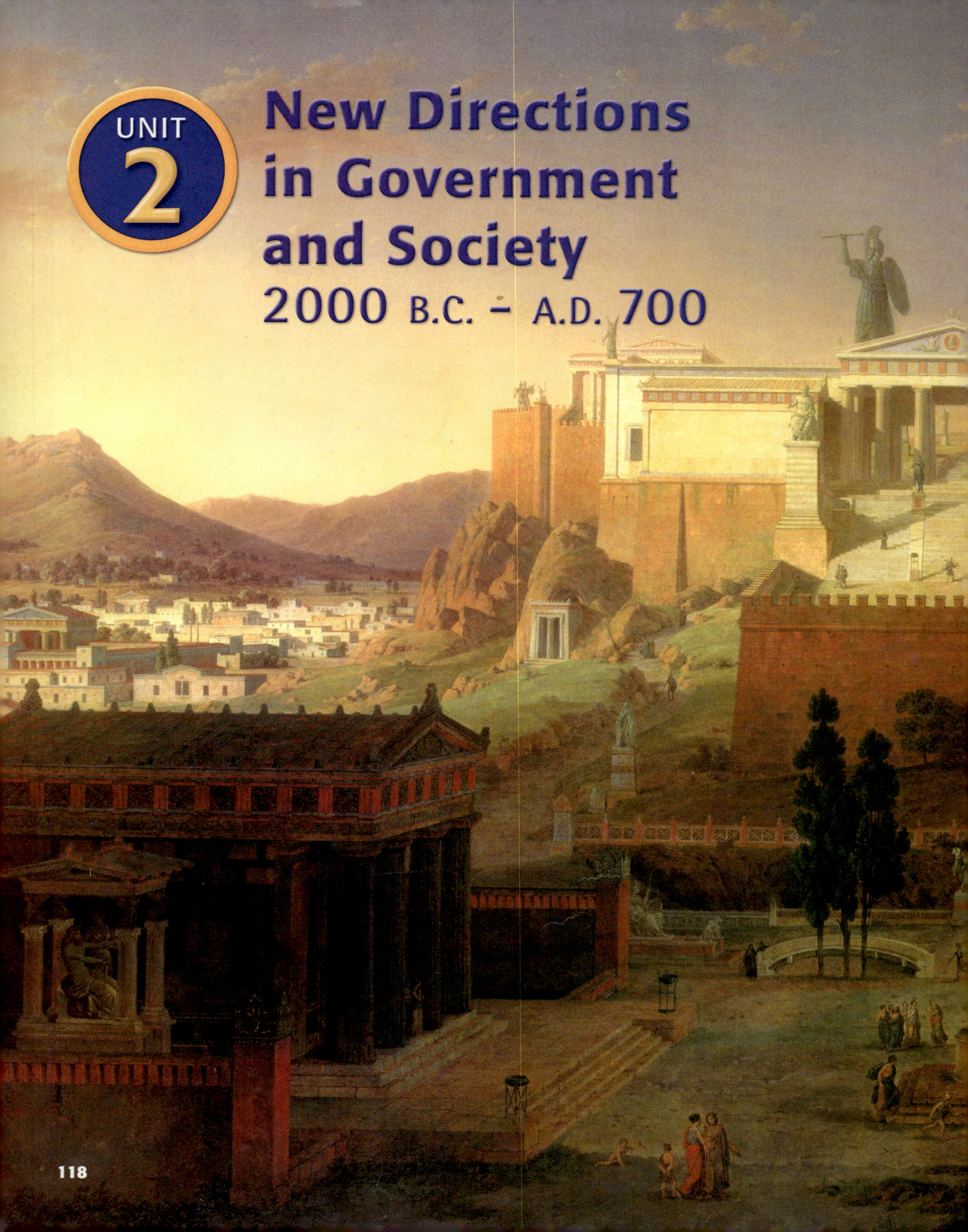

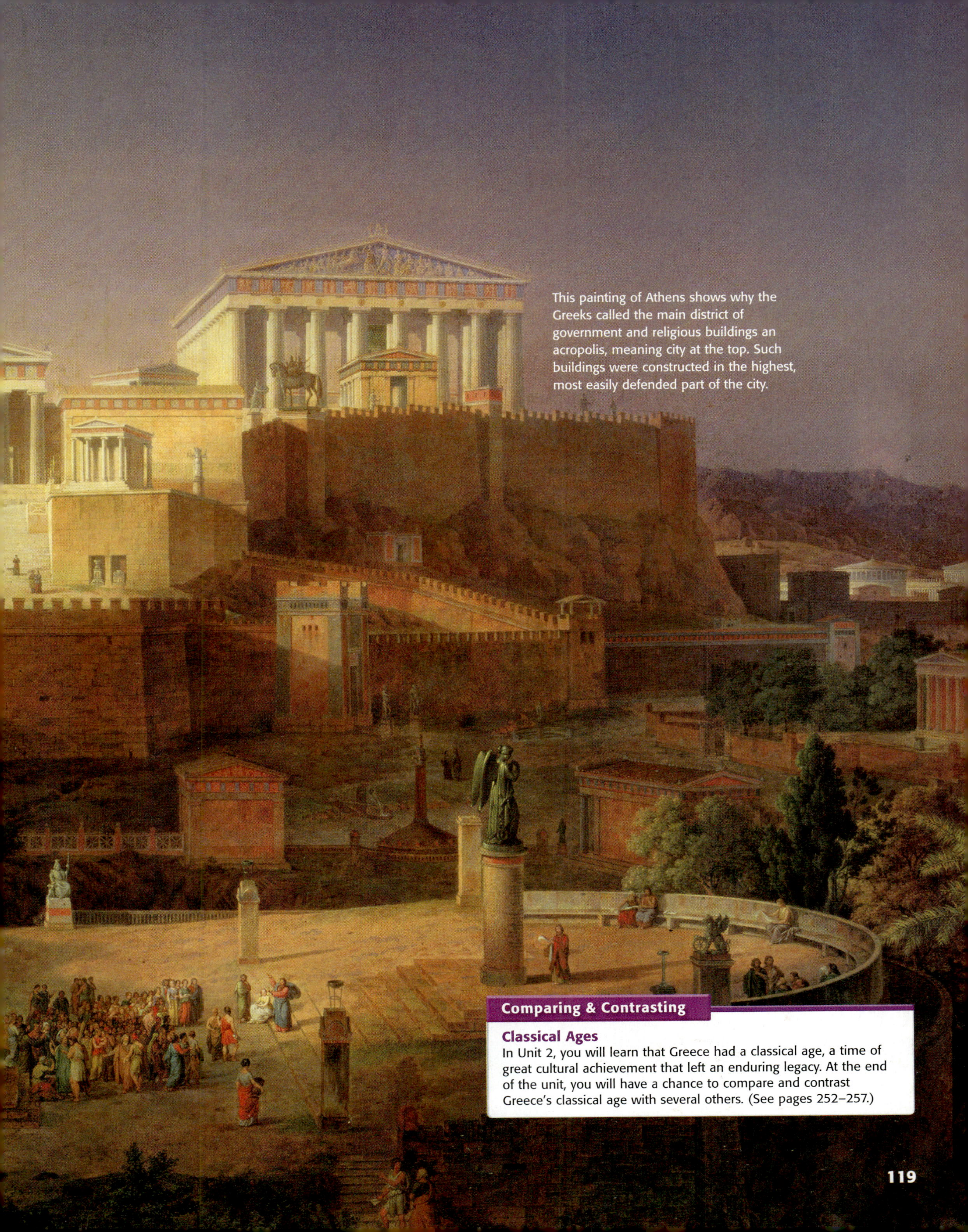

This painting of Athens shows why the Greeks called the main district of government and religious buildings an acropolis, meaning city at the top. Such buildings were constructed in the highest, most easily defended part of the city.

Comparing & Contrasting

Classical Ages

In Unit 2, you will learn that Greece had a classical age, a time of great cultural achievement that left an enduring legacy. At the end of the unit, you will have a chance to compare and contrast Greece's classical age with several others. (See pages 252–257.)

CHAPTER 5

Classical Greece, 2000 B.C.–300 B.C.

Previewing Main Ideas

POWER AND AUTHORITY In the Greek city-state of Athens, a new form of government developed—democracy—in which citizens exercised power.

Geography *What geographic factors might have confined democracy largely to Athens?*

CULTURAL INTERACTION Alexander the Great spread Greek culture throughout much of Asia. Greek, Egyptian, and Asian cultures then blended to create Hellenistic culture.

Geography *Why might the sea have been important to the spread of Greek culture?*

EMPIRE BUILDING Athens assumed control of a defense league and eventually built it into an empire. Later, Alexander conquered the Persian Empire and beyond to create a vast new empire of his own.

Geography *What geographic features might have strengthened the Macedonian desire to build an empire to the south and east?*

NEW YORK CORE CURRICULUM FOCUS

- Athens developed a democracy, while Sparta built a military state.
- Art, architecture, and philosophy flourished during Greece's golden age.

INTEGRATED TECHNOLOGY

eEdition
- Interactive Maps
- Interactive Visuals
- Interactive Primary Sources

INTERNET RESOURCES

Go to **classzone.com** for:
- Research Links
- Internet Activities
- Primary Sources
- Chapter Quiz
- Maps
- Test Practice
- Current Events

GREECE

2000 B.C. Minoan civilization prospers on Crete. (Minoan vase) ▶

1500 B.C. Mycenaean culture thrives on Greek mainland.

2000 B.C. **1500 B.C.**

WORLD

1780 B.C. Hammurabi issues code of laws.

1472 B.C. Hatshepsut, woman pharoah, begins her reign. (Head from statue of Hatshepsut) ▶

1200 B.C. Trojan war takes place.

750 B.C. Greek city-states flourish.

479 B.C. Greece triumphs in Persian Wars.

334 B.C. Alexander starts to build his empire.

1000 B.C.

300 B.C.

1027 B.C. ◀ Zhou Dynasty begins in China. (Zhou animal mask)

850 B.C. Assyrians expand their empire.

500 B.C. ◀ Zapotec of Mexico build Monte Albán. (Zapotec shield)

321 B.C. Chandragupta founds Mauryan Empire in India.

Interact *with* History

What does this art tell you about Greek culture?

When you think of ancient Greece, what is the first thing that comes to mind? You can learn a lot about a culture from its works of art and literature, as well as from the statements of its leaders, philosophers, and historians. Look at these Greek works of art and read the quotations.

▲ This stone relief panel of Democracy crowning Athens was placed in the marketplace, where citizens could see it daily.

"Our constitution is called a democracy because power is in the hands not of a minority but of the whole people."

PERICLES, an Athenian statesman

"As an oak tree falls on the hillside crushing all that lies beneath, so Theseus. He presses out the life, the brute's savage life, and now it lies dead."

EDITH HAMILTON, "Theseus," *Mythology*

▼ This plate shows Theseus, the greatest hero of Athens, killing the mythological beast the Minotaur.

▲ The Greeks often adorned their public buildings with graceful sculptures of gods and goddesses.

"For we are lovers of the beautiful in our tastes."

THUCYDIDES, a historian

EXAMINING *the* ISSUES

- **What does the relief panel suggest about the role of democracy in Greek society?**
- **Why might the Greeks decorate pottery with a heroic scene?**
- **Why might the Greeks place graceful statues in and around their public buildings?**

Break into small groups and discuss what these artworks suggest about ancient Greek culture. Also discuss what the quotations tell you about the culture and its ideals. As you read about ancient Greece, think about how its culture influenced later civilizations.

Cultures of the Mountains and the Sea

CONNECT TO THE NEW YORK STATE CORE CURRICULUM

Unit 1.C.2.a. Human and physical geography
Unit 1.C.2.c. Contributions: art, architecture, philosophy, science

TERMS & NAMES

- Mycenaean
- Trojan War
- Dorian
- Homer
- epic
- myth

SETTING THE STAGE In ancient times, Greece was not a united country. It was a collection of separate lands where Greek-speaking people lived. By 3000 B.C., the Minoans lived on the large Greek island of Crete. The Minoans created an elegant civilization that had great power in the Mediterranean world. At the same time, people from the plains along the Black Sea and Anatolia migrated and settled in mainland Greece.

Geography Shapes Greek Life

Ancient Greece consisted mainly of a mountainous peninsula jutting out into the Mediterranean Sea. It also included about 2,000 islands in the Aegean (ih•JEE•uhn) and Ionian (eye•OH•nee•uhn) seas. Lands on the eastern edge of the Aegean were also part of ancient Greece. (See the map on page 121.) The region's physical geography directly shaped Greek traditions and customs.

TAKING NOTES
Categorizing Use a chart to organize information about the roots of Greek culture.

Culture	Contribution
Minoan	Writing System: pottery designs
Mycenaean	
Dorian	

The Sea The sea shaped Greek civilization just as rivers shaped the ancient civilizations of Egypt, the Fertile Crescent, India, and China. In one sense, the Greeks did not live *on* a land but *around* a sea. Greeks rarely had to travel more than 85 miles to reach the coastline. The Aegean Sea, the Ionian Sea, and the neighboring Black Sea were important transportation routes for the Greek people. These seaways linked most parts of Greece. As the Greeks became skilled sailors, sea travel connected Greece with other societies. Sea travel and trade were also important because Greece lacked natural resources, such as timber, precious metals, and usable farmland.

The Land Rugged mountains covered about three-fourths of ancient Greece. The mountain chains ran mainly from northwest to southeast along the Balkan Peninsula. Mountains divided the land into a number of different regions. This significantly influenced Greek political life. Instead of a single government, the Greeks developed small, independent communities within each little valley and its surrounding mountains. Most Greeks gave their loyalty to these local communities.

In ancient times, the uneven terrain also made land transportation difficult. Of the few roads that existed, most were little more than dirt paths. It often took travelers several days to complete a journey that might take a few hours today.

Much of the land itself was stony, and only a small part of it was arable, or suitable for farming. Tiny but fertile valleys covered about one-fourth of Greece.

The small streams that watered these valleys were not suitable for large-scale irrigation projects. With so little fertile farmland or fresh water for irrigation, Greece was never able to support a large population. Historians estimate that no more than a few million people lived in ancient Greece at any given time. Even this small population could not expect the land to support a life of luxury. A desire for more living space, grassland for raising livestock, and adequate farmland may have been factors that motivated the Greeks to seek new sites for colonies. **A**

MAIN IDEA

Analyzing Causes

A In what ways did Greece's location by the sea and its mountainous land affect its development?

The Climate Climate was the third important environmental influence on Greek civilization. Greece has a varied climate, with temperatures averaging 48 degrees Fahrenheit in the winter and 80 degrees Fahrenheit in the summer. In ancient times, these moderate temperatures supported an outdoor life for many Greek citizens. Men spent much of their leisure time at outdoor public events. They met often to discuss public issues, exchange news, and take an active part in civic life.

Mycenaean Civilization Develops

As Chapter 3 explained, a large wave of Indo-Europeans migrated from the Eurasian steppes to Europe, India, and Southwest Asia. Some of the people who settled on the Greek mainland around 2000 B.C. were later known as **Mycenaeans**. The name came from their leading city, Mycenae (my•SEE•nee).

Mycenae was located in southern Greece on a steep, rocky ridge and surrounded by a protective wall more than 20 feet thick. The fortified city of Mycenae could withstand almost any attack. From Mycenae, a warrior-king ruled the surrounding villages and farms. Strong rulers controlled the areas around other Mycenaean cities, such as Tiryns and Athens. These kings dominated Greece from about 1600 to 1100 B.C.

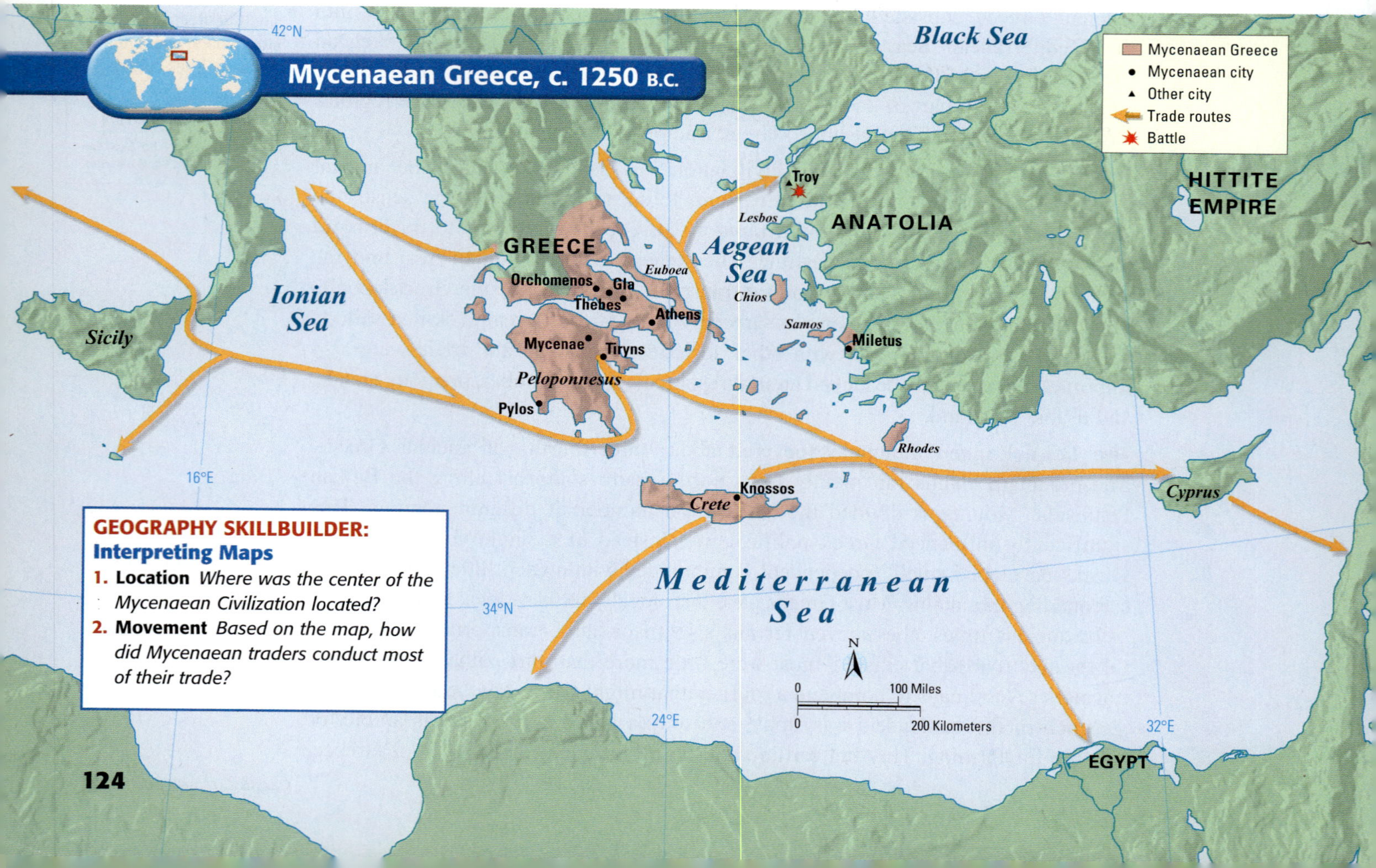

GEOGRAPHY SKILLBUILDER: Interpreting Maps

1. **Location** *Where was the center of the Mycenaean Civilization located?*
2. **Movement** *Based on the map, how did Mycenaean traders conduct most of their trade?*

Contact with Minoans Sometime after 1500 B.C., through either trade or war, the Mycenaeans came into contact with the Minoan civilization. From their contact with the Minoans, the Mycenaeans saw the value of seaborne trade. Mycenaean traders soon sailed throughout the eastern Mediterranean, making stops at Aegean islands, coastal towns in Anatolia, and ports in Syria, Egypt, Italy, and Crete.

The Minoans also influenced the Mycenaeans in other ways. The Mycenaeans adapted the Minoan writing system to the Greek language and decorated vases with Minoan designs. The Minoan-influenced culture of Mycenae formed the core of Greek religious practice, art, politics, and literature. Indeed, Western civilization has its roots in these two early Mediterranean civilizations. **B**

MAIN IDEA

Recognizing Effects

B How did contact with the Minoans affect Mycenaean culture?

▲ Greek stories tell of their army's capture of the legendary city of Troy by hiding soldiers in a hollow wooden horse.

The Trojan War During the 1200s B.C., the Mycenaeans fought a ten-year war against Troy, an independent trading city located in Anatolia. According to legend, a Greek army besieged and destroyed Troy because a Trojan prince had kidnapped Helen, the beautiful wife of a Greek king.

For many years, historians thought that the legendary stories told of the **Trojan War** were totally fictional. However, excavations conducted in northwestern Turkey during the 1870s by German archaeologist Heinrich Schliemann suggested that the stories of the Trojan War might have been based on real cities, people, and events. Further archaeological studies conducted in the 20th century support Schliemann's findings. Although the exact nature of the Trojan War remains unclear, this attack on Troy was almost certainly one of the last Mycenaean battle campaigns.

Greek Culture Declines Under the Dorians

Not long after the Trojan War, Mycenaean civilization collapsed. Around 1200 B.C., sea raiders attacked and burned many Mycenaean cities. According to tradition, a new group of people, the **Dorians** (DAWR•ee•uhnz), moved into the war-torn countryside. The Dorians spoke a dialect of Greek and may have been distant relatives of the Bronze Age Greeks.

The Dorians were far less advanced than the Mycenaeans. The economy collapsed and trade eventually came to a standstill soon after their arrival. Most important to historians, Greeks appear to have temporarily lost the art of writing during the Dorian Age. No written record exists from the 400-year period between 1150 and 750 B.C. As a result, little is known about this period of Greek history.

Epics of Homer Lacking writing, the Greeks of this time learned about their history through the spoken word. According to tradition, the greatest storyteller was a blind man named **Homer**. Little is known of his personal life. Some historians believe that Homer composed his **epics**, narrative poems celebrating heroic deeds, sometime between 750 and 700 B.C. The Trojan War forms the backdrop for one of Homer's great epic poems, the *Iliad*.

The heroes of the *Iliad* are warriors: the fierce Greek Achilles (uh•KIHL•eez) and the courageous and noble Hector of Troy. In the following dramatic excerpt, Hector's wife begs him not to fight Achilles:

▲ This is a marble sculpture of Polyphemus—a cyclops, or one-eyed monster—who appears in another of Homer's epics, the *Odyssey.*

PRIMARY SOURCE

"My dear husband, your warlike spirit will be your death. You've no compassion for your infant child, for me, your sad wife, who before long will be your widow. . . . As for me, it would be better, if I'm to lose you, to be buried in the ground. . . ."

Great Hector . . . replied, "Wife, all this concerns me, too. But I'd be disgraced, dreadfully shamed . . . , if I should slink away from war, like a coward. [F]or I have learned always to be brave, to fight alongside Trojans at the front, striving to win great fame for my father, for myself."

HOMER, the *Iliad* (translated by Ian Johnston)

Hector's response to his wife gives insight into the Greek heroic ideal of *aretē* (ar•uh•TAY), meaning virtue and excellence. A Greek could display this ideal on the battlefield in combat or in athletic contests on the playing field.

Greeks Create Myths The Greeks developed a rich set of **myths**, or traditional stories, about their gods. The works of Homer and another epic, *Theogony* by Hesiod, are the source of much of Greek mythology. Through the myths, the Greeks sought to understand the mysteries of nature and the power of human passions. Myths explained the changing of the seasons, for example.

Greeks attributed human qualities, such as love, hate, and jealousy, to their gods. The gods quarreled and competed with each other constantly. However, unlike humans, the gods lived forever. Zeus, the ruler of the gods, lived on Mount Olympus with his wife, Hera. Hera was often jealous of Zeus' relationships with other women. Athena, goddess of wisdom, was Zeus' daughter and his favorite child. The Greeks thought of Athena as the guardian of cities, especially of Athens, which was named in her honor. You will learn about Athens and other cities in Section 2.

NEW YORK CORE CURRICULUM REVIEW

TERMS & NAMES 1. For each term or name, write a sentence explaining its significance.

- Mycenaean
- Trojan War
- Dorian
- Homer
- epic
- myth

USING YOUR NOTES

2. Which of the cultures on your chart do you think contributed the most to Greek culture? Explain.

Culture	Contribution
Minoan	Writing System: pottery designs
Mycenaean	
Dorian	

MAIN IDEAS

3. What impact did nearness to the sea have on the development of Greece?
4. What aspects of culture did the Mycenaeans adopt from the Minoans?
5. Why were the epics of importance to the Greeks of the Dorian period?

CRITICAL THINKING & WRITING

6. **DRAWING CONCLUSIONS** How did the physical geography of Greece cause Greek-speaking peoples to develop separate, isolated communities?
7. **ANALYZING CAUSES** Other than the explanation offered in the legend, why do you think the Greeks went to war with Troy?
8. **MAKING INFERENCES** The Dorian period is often called Greece's Dark Age. Why do you think this is so?
9. **WRITING ACTIVITY** CULTURAL INTERACTION Write an expository **essay** explaining why the Greek epics and myths are so well known and studied in today's society.

CONNECT TO TODAY **WRITING EXPLANATIONS**

Many names and phrases from this period of Greek history have been absorbed into the English language. Use library resources to find examples, such as *Achilles heel, Homeric,* and *Trojan horse.* Write a brief **explanation** of each example.

Warring City-States

CONNECT TO THE NEW YORK STATE CORE CURRICULUM

Unit 1.C.2.b. The rise of city-states,–Athens/Sparta
Unit 1.C.2.d. Growth of democracy in Athens versus the Spartan political system

TERMS & NAMES

- polis
- acropolis
- monarchy
- aristocracy
- oligarchy
- tyrant
- democracy
- helot
- phalanx
- Persian Wars

SETTING THE STAGE During the Dorian period, Greek civilization experienced decline. However, two things changed life in Greece. First, Dorians and Mycenaeans alike began to identify less with the culture of their ancestors and more with the local area where they lived. Second, by the end of this period, the method of governing areas had changed from tribal or clan control to more formal governments—the city-states.

Rule and Order in Greek City-States

By 750 B.C., the city-state, or **polis**, was the fundamental political unit in ancient Greece. A polis was made up of a city and its surrounding countryside, which included numerous villages. Most city-states controlled between 50 and 500 square miles of territory. They were often home to fewer than 10,000 residents. At the agora, or marketplace, or on a fortified hilltop called an **acropolis** (uh•KRAHP•uh•lihs), citizens gathered to discuss city government.

TAKING NOTES

Following Chronological Order

On a double time line, note the important events in the development of Athens and Sparta.

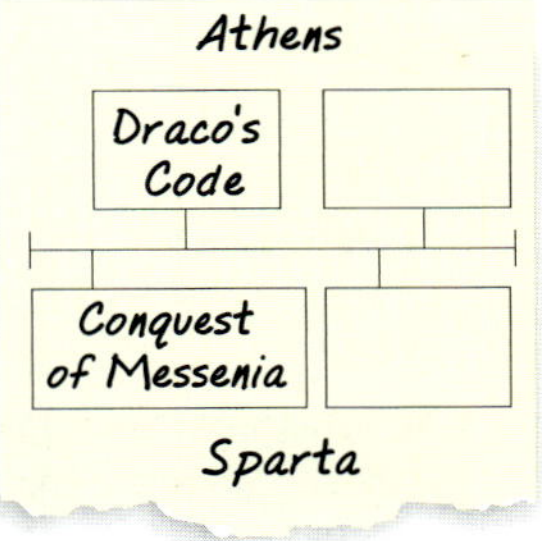

Greek Political Structures Greek city-states had many different forms of government. (See the chart on page 128.) In some, a single person, called a king, ruled in a government called a **monarchy**. Others adopted an **aristocracy** (AR•ih•STAHK•ruh•see), a government ruled by a small group of noble, landowning families. These very rich families often gained political power after serving in a king's military cavalry. Later, as trade expanded, a new class of wealthy merchants and artisans emerged in some cities. When these groups became dissatisfied with aristocratic rule, they sometimes took power or shared it with the nobility. They formed an **oligarchy**, a government ruled by a few powerful people.

Tyrants Seize Power In many city-states, repeated clashes occurred between rulers and the common people. Powerful individuals, usually nobles or other wealthy citizens, sometimes seized control of the government by appealing to the common people for support. These rulers were called **tyrants**. Unlike today, tyrants generally were not considered harsh and cruel. Rather, they were looked upon as leaders who would work for the interests of the ordinary people. Once in power, for example, tyrants often set up building programs to provide jobs and housing for their supporters.

Athens Builds a Limited Democracy

The idea of representative government also began to take root in some city-states, particularly Athens. Like other city-states, Athens went through power struggles between rich and poor. However, Athenians avoided major political upheavals by making timely reforms. Athenian reformers moved toward **democracy**, rule by the people. In Athens, citizens participated directly in political decision making.

Building Democracy The first step toward democracy came when a nobleman named Draco took power. In 621 B.C., Draco developed a legal code based on the idea that all Athenians, rich and poor, were equal under the law. Draco's code dealt very harshly with criminals, making death the punishment for practically every crime. It also upheld such practices as debt slavery, in which debtors worked as slaves to repay their debts.

Vocabulary
The legal code prepared by Draco was so harsh that the word *draconian* has come to mean "extreme cruelty or severity."

More far-reaching democratic reforms were introduced by Solon (SO•luhn), who came to power in 594 B.C. Stating that no citizen should own another citizen, Solon outlawed debt slavery. He organized all Athenian citizens into four social classes according to wealth. Only members of the top three classes could hold political office. However, all citizens, regardless of class, could participate in the Athenian assembly. Solon also introduced the legal concept that any citizen could bring charges against wrongdoers.

Around 500 B.C., the Athenian leader Cleisthenes (KLYS•thuh•NEEZ) introduced further reforms. He broke up the power of the nobility by organizing citizens into ten groups based on where they lived rather than on their wealth. He also increased the power of the assembly by allowing all citizens to submit laws for debate and passage. Cleisthenes then created the Council of Five Hundred. This body proposed laws and counseled the assembly. Council members were chosen by lot, or at random.

The reforms of Cleisthenes allowed Athenian citizens to participate in a limited democracy. However, citizenship was restricted to a relatively small number of Athenians. Only free adult male property owners born in Athens were considered citizens. Women, slaves, and foreigners were excluded from citizenship and had few rights. (A)

MAIN IDEA
Contrasting
(A) How is Athenian democracy different from modern American democracy?

Athenian Education For the most part, only the sons of wealthy families received formal education. Schooling began around the age of seven and largely prepared boys to be good citizens. They studied reading, grammar, poetry, history, mathematics, and music. Because citizens were expected to debate issues in the assembly, boys also received training in logic and public speaking. And since the Greeks believed that it was important to train and develop the body, part of each day

Forms of Government

Monarchy	Aristocracy	Oligarchy	Direct Democracy
• State ruled by a king • Rule is hereditary • Some rulers claim divine right • Practiced in Mycenae by 2000 B.C.	• State ruled by nobility • Rule is hereditary and based on family ties, social rank, wealth • Social status and wealth support rulers' authority • Practiced in Athens prior to 594 B.C.	• State ruled by a small group of citizens • Rule is based on wealth or ability • Ruling group controls military • Practiced in Sparta by 500 B.C.	• State ruled by its citizens • Rule is based on citizenship • Majority rule decides vote • Practiced in Athens by about 500 B.C.

SKILLBUILDER: Interpreting Charts
1. **Summarizing** *Which forms of government feature rule based on wealth or property ownership?*
2. **Clarifying** *In which form of government do citizens have the most power?*

Analyzing Primary Sources

A Husband's Advice

In this excerpt from *The Economist*, the Greek historian Xenophon describes how a husband might respond to his wife's question about how she could remain attractive:

PRIMARY SOURCE

I counseled her to oversee the baking woman as she made the bread; to stand beside the housekeeper as she measured out her stores; to go on tours of inspection to see if all things were in order as they should be. For, as it seemed to me, this would at once be walking exercise and supervision. And, as an excellent gymnastic, I recommended her to knead the dough and roll the paste; to shake the coverlets and make the beds; adding, if she trained herself in exercise of this sort she would enjoy her food, grow vigorous in health, and her complexion would in very truth be lovelier. The very look and aspect of the wife.

XENOPHON, *The Economist,* Book 10 (Translated by H. G. Dakyns)

DOCUMENT-BASED QUESTIONS

1. **Making Inferences** *What is the husband suggesting in his advice to his wife?*
2. **Synthesizing** *How is the husband's advice representative of Athenian attitudes toward women?*

was spent in athletic activities. When they got older, boys went to military school to help them prepare for another important duty of citizenship—defending Athens.

Athenian girls did not attend school. Rather, they were educated at home by their mothers and other female members of the household. They learned about child-rearing, weaving cloth, preparing meals, managing the household, and other skills that helped them become good wives and mothers. Some women were able to take their education farther and learned to read and write. A few even became accomplished writers. Even so, most women had very little to do with Athenian life outside the boundaries of family and home.

Sparta Builds a Military State

Located in the southern part of Greece known as the Peloponnesus (PEHL•uh•puh•NEE•sus), Sparta was nearly cut off from the rest of Greece by the Gulf of Corinth. (See the map on page 121.) In outlook and values, Sparta contrasted sharply with the other city-states, Athens in particular. Instead of a democracy, Sparta built a military state.

Sparta Dominates Messenians Around 725 B.C., Sparta conquered the neighboring region of Messenia and took over the land. The Messenians became **helots** (HEHL•uhts), peasants forced to stay on the land they worked. Each year, the Spartans demanded half of the helots' crops. In about 650 B.C., the Messenians, resentful of the Spartans' harsh rule, revolted. The Spartans, who were outnumbered eight to one, just barely put down the revolt. Shocked at their vulnerability, they dedicated themselves to making Sparta a strong city-state.

Festivals and Sports

The ancient Greeks believed that strong healthy citizens helped strengthen the city-state. They often included sporting events in the festivals they held to honor their gods. The most famous sports festival was the Olympic games, held every four years. Records of Olympics winners started in 776 B.C. At first, the festival lasted only one day and had only one contest, a race called the stade. Later, many other events were added, including a long-distance race, wrestling, the long jump, the javelin, and the discus throw. The Olympics was expanded to five days in 472 B.C.

Women's Sports ►

Women had their own sports festival in ancient Greece. It was the festival devoted to Hera, the wife of Zeus. Like the Olympics, the Hera festival was held every four years. One of the main events was a foot race for unmarried women.

◄ Discus Thrower

Ancient athletes, such as this discus thrower, would be considered amateurs today because they received no pay for competing. However, they trained rigorously for months at a time. Victors were given lavish gifts and were hailed as heroes. Many athletes competed full-time.

▼ Mount Olympus

The ancient Olympics honored Zeus, the father of all Greek gods and goddesses. According to legend, Zeus hurled a thunderbolt from Mount Olympus at a spot in rural Greece. An altar for Zeus was built on that spot. Eventually, many buildings were erected around the altar. This area was called Olympia and became the site for the Olympic games.

SKILLBUILDER: Interpreting Visual Sources

1. **Evaluating Decisions** *Do you think it was a good decision for the Greeks to add more sporting events to the Olympics? Explain.*
2. **Comparing and Contrasting** *How are today's Olympics similar to and different from the Olympics in ancient Greece?*

Sparta's Government and Society Spartan government had several branches. An assembly, which was composed of all Spartan citizens, elected officials and voted on major issues. The Council of Elders, made up of 30 older citizens, proposed laws on which the assembly voted. Five elected officials carried out the laws passed by the assembly. These men also controlled education and prosecuted court cases. In addition, two kings ruled over Sparta's military forces.

The Spartan social order consisted of several groups. The first were citizens descended from the original inhabitants of the region. This group included the ruling families who owned the land. A second group, noncitizens who were free, worked in commerce and industry. The helots, at the bottom of Spartan society, were little better than slaves. They worked in the fields or as house servants.

Spartan Daily Life From around 600 until 371 B.C., Sparta had the most powerful army in Greece. However, the Spartan people paid a high price for their military supremacy. All forms of individual expression were discouraged. As a result, Spartans did not value the arts, literature, or other artistic and intellectual pursuits. Spartans valued duty, strength, and discipline over freedom, individuality, beauty, and learning. **B**

MAIN IDEA

Comparing

B How would you compare the ideals of Spartan and Athenian societies?

Since men were expected to serve in the army until the age of 60, their daily life centered on military training. Boys left home when they were 7 and moved into army barracks, where they stayed until they reached the age of 30. They spent their days marching, exercising, and fighting. They undertook these activities in all weathers, wearing only light tunics and no shoes. At night, they slept without blankets on hard benches. Their daily diet consisted of little more than a bowl of coarse black porridge. Those who were not satisfied were encouraged to steal food. Such training produced tough, resourceful soldiers.

Spartan girls also led hardy lives. They received some military training, and they also ran, wrestled, and played sports. Like boys, girls were taught to put service to Sparta above everything—even love of family. A legend says that Spartan women told husbands and sons going to war to "come back *with* your shield or *on* it." As adults, Spartan women had considerable freedom, especially in running the family estates when their husbands were on active military service. Such freedom surprised men from other Greek city-states. This was particularly true of Athens, where women were expected to remain out of sight and quietly raise children.

The Persian Wars

Danger of a helot revolt led Sparta to become a military state. Struggles between rich and poor led Athens to become a democracy. The greatest danger of all—invasion by Persian armies—moved Sparta and Athens alike to their greatest glory.

A New Kind of Army Emerges During the Dorian Age, only the rich could afford bronze spears, shields, breastplates, and chariots. Thus, only the rich served in armies. Iron later replaced bronze in the manufacture of weapons. Harder than bronze, iron was more common and therefore cheaper. Soon, ordinary citizens could afford to arm and defend themselves. The shift from bronze to iron weapons made possible a new kind of army composed not only of the rich but also of merchants, artisans, and small landowners. The foot soldiers of this army, called hoplites, stood side by side, each holding a spear in one hand and a shield in the other. This fearsome formation, or **phalanx** (FAY•LANGKS), became the most powerful fighting force in the ancient world.

Battle at Marathon The **Persian Wars**, between Greece and the Persian Empire, began in Ionia on the coast of Anatolia. (See the map on page 132.) Greeks had long been settled there, but around 546 B.C., the Persians conquered the area. When

Ionian Greeks revolted, Athens sent ships and soldiers to their aid. The Persian king Darius the Great defeated the rebels and then vowed to destroy Athens in revenge.

In 490 B.C., a Persian fleet carried 25,000 men across the Aegean Sea and landed northeast of Athens on a plain called Marathon. There, 10,000 Athenians, neatly arranged in phalanxes, waited for them. Vastly outnumbered, the Greek soldiers charged. The Persians, who wore light armor and lacked training in this kind of land combat, were no match for the disciplined Greek phalanx. After several hours, the Persians fled the battlefield. The Persians lost more than 6,000 men. In contrast, Athenian casualties numbered fewer than 200.

Pheidippides Brings News Though the Athenians won the battle, their city now stood defenseless. According to tradition, army leaders chose a young runner named Pheidippides (fy•DIP•uh•DEEZ) to race back to Athens. He brought news of the Persian defeat so that Athenians would not give up the city without a fight. Dashing the 26 miles from Marathon to Athens, Pheidippides delivered his message, "Rejoice, we conquer." He then collapsed and died. Moving rapidly from Marathon, the Greek army arrived in Athens not long after. When the Persians sailed into the harbor, they found the city heavily defended. They quickly put to sea in retreat.

Thermopylae and Salamis Ten years later, in 480 B.C., Darius the Great's son and successor, Xerxes (ZURK•seez), assembled an enormous invasion force to crush Athens. The Greeks were badly divided. Some city-states agreed to fight the Persians. Others thought it wiser to let Xerxes destroy Athens and return home. Some Greeks even fought on the Persian side. Consequently, Xerxes' army met no resistance as it marched down the eastern coast of Greece.

When Xerxes came to a narrow mountain pass at Thermopylae (thur•MAHP•uh•lee), 7,000 Greeks, including 300 Spartans, blocked his way. Xerxes assumed that his troops would easily push the Greeks aside. However, he underestimated their fighting ability. The Greeks stopped the Persian advance for three days. Only a traitor's informing the Persians about a secret path around the pass ended their brave stand. Fearing defeat, the Spartans held the Persians back while the other Greek forces retreated. The Spartans' valiant sacrifice—all were killed—made a great impression on all Greeks.

Meanwhile, the Athenians debated how best to defend their city. Themistocles, an Athenian leader, convinced them to evacuate the city and fight at sea. They positioned their fleet in a narrow channel near the island of Salamis (SAL•uh•mihs), a few miles southwest of Athens. After setting fire to Athens, Xerxes sent his warships to

GEOGRAPHY SKILLBUILDER: Interpreting Maps

1. **Movement** *By what routes did the Persians choose to attack Greece? Explain why.*
2. **Location** *Where did most of the battles of the Persian Wars occur? How might their citizens have been affected?*

block both ends of the channel. However, the channel was very narrow, and the Persian ships had difficulty turning. Smaller Greek ships armed with battering rams attacked, puncturing the hulls of many Persian warships. Xerxes watched in horror as more than one-third of his fleet sank. He faced another defeat in 479 B.C., when the Greeks crushed the Persian army at the Battle of Plataea (pluh•TEE•uh). After this major setback, the Persians were always on the defensive.

The following year, several Greek city-states formed an alliance called the Delian (DEE•lee•uhn) League. (The alliance took its name from Delos, the island in the Aegean Sea where it had its headquarters.) League members continued to press the war against the Persians for several more years. In time, they drove the Persians from the territories surrounding Greece and ended the threat of future attacks.

Consequences of the Persian Wars-With the Persian threat ended, all the Greek city-states felt a new sense of confidence and freedom. Athens, in particular, basked in the glory of the Persian defeat. During the 470s, Athens emerged as the leader of the Delian League, which had grown to some 200 city-states. Soon thereafter, Athens began to use its power to control the other league members. It moved the league headquarters to Athens, and used military force against members that challenged its authority. In time, these city-states became little more than provinces of a vast Athenian empire. The prestige of victory over the Persians and the wealth of the Athenian empire set the stage for a dazzling burst of creativity in Athens. The city was entering its brief golden age. C

MAIN IDEA

Recognizing Effects

C How did the Persian Wars affect the Greek people, especially the Athenians?

Connect to Today

Modern Marathons

Pheidippides' heroic act in the Persian Wars inspired officials at the first modern Olympic Games—held in Athens in 1896—to add a 26-mile race to their competition. The course of the race ran from Marathon to the Olympic Stadium in Athens.

Today, most of the world's major cities stage marathons every year. Many, like the one held in Boston, attract wheelchair competitors.

INTEGRATED TECHNOLOGY

INTERNET ACTIVITY Create an illustrated history of the marathon. Go to **classzone.com** for your research.

NEW YORK CORE CURRICULUM REVIEW

TERMS & NAMES 1. For each term or name, write a sentence explaining its significance.

- polis
- acropolis
- monarchy
- aristocracy
- oligarchy
- tyrant
- democracy
- helot
- phalanx
- Persian Wars

USING YOUR NOTES

2. Which of the events on your time line do you think was the most important for life today? Explain.

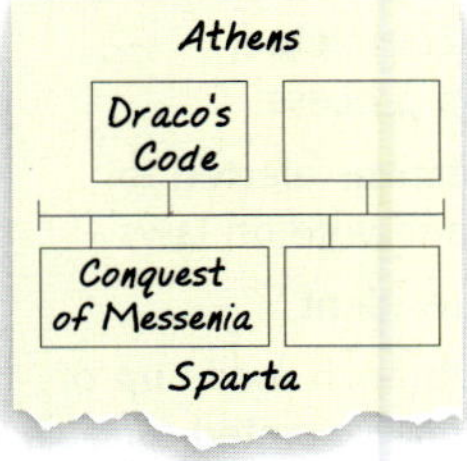

MAIN IDEAS

3. How does an aristocracy differ from an oligarchy?
4. What contributions did Solon and Cleisthenes make to the development of Athenian democracy?
5. How did Athens benefit from victory in the Persian Wars?

CRITICAL THINKING & WRITING

6. **CONTRASTING** How was living in Athens different from living in Sparta?
7. **MAKING INFERENCES** The introduction of cheap iron weapons meant that ordinary Greek citizens could arm themselves. How might the ability to own weapons change the outlook of ordinary citizens?
8. **ANALYZING MOTIVES** Why were the Spartan soldiers willing to sacrifice themselves at Thermopylae?
9. **WRITING ACTIVITY** POWER AND AUTHORITY Write a brief political **monologue** about democracy from an Athenian slave's point of view.

INTEGRATED TECHNOLOGY **INTERNET ACTIVITY**

New England town meetings are similar to the kind of democracy practiced in Ancient Greece. Use the Internet to find information on the town meeting. Present your findings to the class in a brief **oral report.**

INTERNET KEYWORD
town meeting

3

Democracy and Greece's Golden Age

CONNECT TO THE NEW YORK STATE CORE CURRICULUM

Unit 1.C.2.d. Growth of democracy in Athens versus the Spartan political system
Unit 1.C.2.c. Contributions: art, architecture, philosophy, science–Plato, Socrates, Aristotle

TERMS & NAMES

- direct democracy
- classical art
- tragedy
- comedy
- Peloponnesian War
- philosopher
- Socrates
- Plato
- Aristotle

SETTING THE STAGE For close to 50 years (from 477 to 431 B.C.), Athens experienced a growth in intellectual and artistic learning. This period is often called the Golden Age of Athens. During this golden age, drama, sculpture, poetry, philosophy, architecture, and science all reached new heights. The artistic and literary legacies of the time continue to inspire and instruct people around the world.

TAKING NOTES
Recognizing Effects Use a web diagram to organize information about Pericles' goals for Athens.

Pericles' Plan for Athens

A wise and able statesman named Pericles led Athens during much of its golden age. Honest and fair, Pericles held onto popular support for 32 years. He was a skillful politician, an inspiring speaker, and a respected general. He so dominated the life of Athens from 461 to 429 B.C. that this period often is called the Age of Pericles. He had three goals: (1) to strengthen Athenian democracy, (2) to hold and strengthen the empire, and (3) to glorify Athens.

Stronger Democracy To strengthen democracy, Pericles increased the number of public officials who were paid salaries. Earlier in Athens, most positions in public office were unpaid. Thus, only wealthier Athenian citizens could afford to

Athenian and United States Democracy

Athenian Democracy

- Citizens: male; 18 years old; born of citizen parents
- Laws voted on and proposed directly by assembly of all citizens
- Leader chosen by lot
- Executive branch composed of a council of 500 men
- Juries varied in size
- No attorneys; no appeals; one-day trials

Both

- Political power exercised by citizens
- Three branches of government
- Legislative branch passes laws
- Executive branch carries out laws
- Judicial branch conducts trials with paid jurors

U.S. Democracy

- Citizens: born in United States or completed citizenship process
- Representatives elected to propose and vote on laws
- Elected president
- Executive branch made up of elected and appointed officials
- Juries composed of 12 jurors
- Defendants and plaintiffs have attorneys; long appeals process

hold public office. Now even the poorest citizen could serve if elected or chosen by lot. Consequently, Athens had more citizens engaged in self-government than any other city-state in Greece. This reform made Athens one of the most democratic governments in history.

The introduction of **direct democracy**, a form of government in which citizens rule directly and not through representatives, was an important legacy of Periclean Athens. Few other city-states practiced this style of government. In Athens, male citizens who served in the assembly established all the important government policies that affected the polis. In a speech honoring the Athenian war dead, Pericles expressed his great pride in Athenian democracy:

MAIN IDEA

Analyzing Primary Sources

A How accurate do you consider Pericles' statement that Athenian democracy was in the hands of "the whole people"?

PRIMARY SOURCE A

Our constitution is called a democracy because power is in the hands not of a minority but of the whole people. When it is a question of settling private disputes, everyone is equal before the law; when it is a question of putting one person before another in positions of public responsibility, what counts is not membership in a particular class, but the actual ability which the man possesses. No one, so long as he has it in him to be of service to the state, is kept in political obscurity because of poverty.

PERICLES, "The Funeral Oration," from Thucydides, *The Peloponnesian War*

Athenian Empire After the defeat of the Persians, Athens helped organize the Delian League. In time, Athens took over leadership of the league and dominated all the city-states in it. Pericles used the money from the league's treasury to make the Athenian navy the strongest in the Mediterranean. A strong navy was important because it helped Athens strengthen the safety of its empire. Prosperity depended on gaining access to the surrounding waterways. Athens needed overseas trade to obtain supplies of grain and other raw materials.

Athenian military might allowed Pericles to treat other members of the Delian League as part of the empire. Some cities in the Peloponnesus, however, resisted Athens and formed their own alliances. As you will read later in this section, Sparta in particular was at odds with Athens.

Glorifying Athens Pericles also used money from the Delian League to beautify Athens. Without the league's approval, he persuaded the Athenian assembly to vote huge sums of the league's money to buy gold, ivory, and marble. Still more money went to pay the artists, architects, and workers who used these materials.

Glorious Art and Architecture

Pericles' goal was to have the greatest Greek artists and architects create magnificent sculptures and buildings to glorify Athens. At the center of his plan was one of architecture's noblest works—the Parthenon.

Architecture and Sculpture The Parthenon, a masterpiece of architectural design and craftsmanship, was not unique in style. Rather, Greek architects constructed the 23,000-square-foot building in the traditional style that had been used to create Greek temples for 200 years. This temple,

History Makers

Pericles 495–429 B.C.

Pericles came from a rich and high-ranking noble family. His aristocratic father had led the Athenian assembly and fought at the Battle of Salamis in the Persian Wars. His mother was the niece of Cleisthenes, the Athenian noble who had introduced important democratic reforms.

Pericles was well known for his political achievements as leader of Athens. Pericles the man, however, was harder to know. One historian wrote: "[He] no doubt, was a lonely man. . . . He had no friend . . . [and] he only went out [of his home] for official business."

INTEGRATED TECHNOLOGY

RESEARCH LINKS For more on Pericles, go to **classzone.com**

built to honor Athena, the goddess of wisdom and the protector of Athens, contained examples of Greek art that set standards for future generations of artists around the world. Pericles entrusted much of the work on the Parthenon to the sculptor Phidias (FIDH•ee•uhs). Within the temple, Phidias crafted a giant statue of Athena that not only contained such precious materials as gold and ivory, but also stood over 30 feet tall.

Phidias and other sculptors during this golden age aimed to create figures that were graceful, strong, and perfectly formed. Their faces showed neither joy nor anger, only serenity. Greek sculptors also tried to capture the grace of the idealized human body in motion. They wanted to portray ideal beauty, not realism. Their values of harmony, order, balance, and proportion became the standard of what is called **classical art**.

Drama and History

The Greeks invented drama as an art form and built the first theaters in the West. Theatrical productions in Athens were both an expression of civic pride and a tribute to the gods. As part of their civic duty, wealthy citizens bore the cost of producing the plays. Actors used colorful costumes, masks, and sets to dramatize stories. The plays were about leadership, justice, and the duties owed to the gods. They often included a chorus that danced, sang, and recited poetry.

▼ This poster promotes an 1898 production of Euripides' *Medea,* starring the great French actress Sarah Bernhardt.

Tragedy and Comedy The Greeks wrote two kinds of drama—tragedy and comedy. A **tragedy** was a serious drama about common themes such as love, hate, war, or betrayal. These dramas featured a main character, or tragic hero. The hero usually was an important person and often gifted with extraordinary abilities. A tragic flaw usually caused the hero's downfall. Often this flaw was hubris, or excessive pride.

In ancient times, Greece had three notable dramatists who wrote tragedies. Aeschylus (EHS•kuh•luhs) wrote more than 80 plays. His most famous work is the trilogy—a three-play series—*Oresteia* (ohr•res•TEE•uh). It is based on the family of Agamemnon, the Mycenaean king who commanded the Greeks at Troy. The plays examine the idea of justice. Sophocles (SAHF•uh•kleez) wrote more than 100 plays, including the tragedies *Oedipus the King* and *Antigone*. Euripides (yoo•RIP•uh•DEEZ), author of the play *Medea*, often featured strong women in his works.

In contrast to Greek tragedies, a **comedy** contained scenes filled with slapstick situations and crude humor. Playwrights often made fun of politics and respected people and ideas of the time. Aristophanes (AR•ih•STAHF•uh•neez) wrote the first great comedies for the stage, including *The Birds* and *Lysistrata*. *Lysistrata* portrayed the women of Athens forcing their husbands to end the Peloponnesian War. The fact that Athenians could listen to criticism of themselves showed the freedom and openness of public discussion that existed in democratic Athens. **B**

MAIN IDEA

Contrasting

B How did tragedy differ from comedy?

History As you learned earlier in this chapter, there are no written records from the Dorian period. The epic poems of Homer recount stories, but are not accurate recordings of what took place. Herodotus, a Greek who lived in Athens for a time, pioneered the accurate reporting of events. His book on the Persian Wars is considered the first work of history. However, the greatest historian of the classical age was the Athenian Thucydides (thoo•SID•ih•DEEZ). He believed that certain types of events and political situations recur over time. Studying those events and situations, he felt, would aid in understanding the present. The approaches Thucydides used in his work still guide historians today.

Athenians and Spartans Go to War

As Athens grew in wealth, prestige, and power, other city-states began to view it with hostility. Ill will was especially strong between Sparta and Athens. Many people thought that war between the two was inevitable. Instead of trying to avoid conflict, leaders in Athens and Sparta pressed for a war to begin, as both groups of leaders believed their own city had the advantage. Eventually, Sparta declared war on Athens in 431 B.C.

Peloponnesian War When the **Peloponnesian War** between the two city-states began, Athens had the stronger navy. Sparta had the stronger army, and its location inland meant that it could not easily be attacked by sea. Pericles' strategy was to avoid land battles with the Spartan army and wait for an opportunity to strike Sparta and its allies from the sea. C

MAIN IDEA

Analyzing Motives

C What might have been Pericles' goals in the Peloponnesian War?

Eventually, the Spartans marched into Athenian territory. They swept over the countryside, burning the Athenian food supply. Pericles responded by bringing residents from the surrounding region inside the city walls. The city was safe from hunger as long as ships could sail into port with supplies from Athenian colonies and foreign states.

In the second year of the war, however, disaster struck Athens. A frightful plague swept through the city, killing perhaps one-third of the population, including Pericles. Although weakened, Athens continued to fight for several years. Then, in 421 B.C., the two sides, worn down by the war, signed a truce.

Sparta Gains Victory The peace did not last long. In 415 B.C., the Athenians sent a huge fleet carrying more than 20,000 soldiers to the island of Sicily. Their plan was to destroy the city-state of Syracuse, one of Sparta's wealthiest allies. The expedition ended with a crushing defeat in 413 B.C. In his study of the Peloponnesian War, Thucydides recalled: "[The Athenians] were destroyed with a total

GEOGRAPHY SKILLBUILDER: Interpreting Maps

1. **Location** *Where were most of the allies of Athens located?*
2. **Movement** *Why was the sea important to Athens during the Peloponnesian War?*

destruction—their fleet, their army—there was nothing that was not destroyed, and few out of many returned home." Somehow, a terribly weakened Athens fended off Spartan attacks for another nine years. Finally, in 404 B.C., the Athenians and their allies surrendered. Athens had lost its empire, power, and wealth.

Philosophers Search for Truth

After the war, many Athenians lost confidence in democratic government and began to question their values. In this time of uncertainty, several great thinkers appeared. They were determined to seek the truth, no matter where the search led them. The Greeks called such thinkers **philosophers**, meaning "lovers of wisdom." These Greek thinkers based their philosophy on the following two assumptions:

- The universe (land, sky, and sea) is put together in an orderly way, and subject to absolute and unchanging laws.
- People can understand these laws through logic and reason.

One group of philosophers, the Sophists, questioned people's unexamined beliefs and ideas about justice and other traditional values. One of the most famous Sophists was Protagoras, who questioned the existence of the traditional Greek gods. He also argued that there was no universal standard of truth, saying "Man [the individual] is the measure of all things." These were radical and dangerous ideas to many Athenians. D

MAIN IDEA

Making Inferences

D Why would philosophers start questioning traditional beliefs at this particular time in Athenian history?

Socrates One critic of the Sophists was **Socrates** (SAHK•ruh•TEEZ). Unlike the Sophists, he believed that absolute standards did exist for truth and justice. However, he encouraged Greeks to go farther and question themselves and their moral character. Historians believe that it was Socrates who once said, "The unexamined life is not worth living." Socrates was admired by many who understood his ideas. However, others were puzzled by this man's viewpoints.

In 399 B.C., when Socrates was about 70 years old, he was brought to trial for "corrupting the youth of Athens" and "neglecting the city's gods." In his own defense, Socrates said that his teachings were good for Athens because they forced people to think about their values and actions. The jury disagreed and condemned him to death. He died by drinking hemlock, a slow-acting poison.

▼ Surrounded by supporters, Socrates prepares to drink poison.

Plato A student of Socrates, **Plato** (PLAY•toh), was in his late 20s when his teacher died. Later, Plato wrote down the conversations of Socrates "as a means of philosophical investigation." Sometime in the 370s B.C., Plato wrote his most famous work, *The Republic*. In it, he set forth his vision of a perfectly governed society. It was not a democracy. In his ideal society, all citizens would fall naturally into three groups: farmers and artisans, warriors, and the ruling class. The person with the greatest insight and intellect from the ruling class would be chosen philosopher-king. Plato's writings dominated philosophic thought in Europe for nearly 1,500

History Makers

Socrates 470–399 B.C.

Socrates encouraged his students to examine their beliefs. He asked them a series of leading questions to show that people hold many contradictory opinions. This question-and-answer approach to teaching is known as the Socratic method. Socrates devoted his life to gaining self-knowledge and once said, "There is only one good, knowledge, and one evil, ignorance."

Plato 427–347 B.C.

Born into a wealthy Athenian family, Plato had careers as a wrestler and a poet before he became a philosopher. After Socrates, his teacher, died, Plato left Greece. He later returned to Athens and founded a school called the Academy in 387 B.C. The school lasted for approximately 900 years. It was Plato who once stated, "Philosophy begins in wonder."

Aristotle 384–322 B.C.

Aristotle, the son of a physician, was one of the brightest students at Plato's Academy. He came there as a young man and stayed for 20 years until Plato's death. In 335 B.C., Aristotle opened his own school in Athens called the Lyceum. The school eventually rivaled the Academy. Aristotle once argued, "He who studies how things originated . . . will achieve the clearest view of them."

years. His only rivals in importance were his teacher, Socrates, and his own pupil, Aristotle (AR•ih•STAHT•uhl).

Aristotle The philosopher **Aristotle** questioned the nature of the world and of human belief, thought, and knowledge. Aristotle came close to summarizing all the knowledge up to his time. He invented a method for arguing according to rules of logic. He later applied his method to problems in the fields of psychology, physics, and biology. His work provides the basis of the scientific method used today.

One of Aristotle's most famous pupils was Alexander, son of King Philip II of Macedonia. Around 343 B.C., Aristotle accepted the king's invitation to tutor the 13-year-old prince. Alexander's status as a student abruptly ended three years later, when his father called him back to Macedonia. You will learn more about Alexander in Section 4.

NEW YORK CORE CURRICULUM REVIEW

TERMS & NAMES 1. For each term or name, write a sentence explaining its significance.

• direct democracy • classical art • tragedy • comedy • Peloponnesian War • philosopher • Socrates • Plato • Aristotle

USING YOUR NOTES

2. Which of Pericles' goals do you think had the greatest impact on the modern world? Explain your choice.

MAIN IDEAS

3. What steps did Pericles take to strengthen democracy in Athens?
4. What were the battle strategies of Athens and Sparta in the Peloponnesian War?
5. Why do you think some Athenians found the ideas of Socrates so disturbing?

CRITICAL THINKING & WRITING

6. **MAKING INFERENCES** How does the concept of hubris from Greek tragedy apply to the Peloponnesian War?
7. **DRAWING CONCLUSIONS** Was the rule of Pericles a "golden age" for Athens? Explain.
8. **FORMING AND SUPPORTING OPINIONS** Do you agree with Socrates that there are absolute standards for truth and justice? Why or why not?
9. **WRITING ACTIVITY** POWER AND AUTHORITY Write a two- or three-paragraph **essay** comparing the system of direct democracy adopted by Athens and the system of government Plato described in *The Republic.*

CONNECT TO TODAY **CREATING AN ILLUSTRATED REPORT**

One of Pericles' goals was to create magnificent sculptures and buildings to glorify Athens. Identify local buildings or works of art that were created to honor your community, state, or the United States. Write a brief **illustrated report** on these buildings.

Greek Art and Architecture

During ancient times, the Greeks established artistic standards that strongly influenced the later art of the Western world. The aim of Greek art was to express true ideals. To do this, the Greeks used balance, harmony, and symmetry in their art.

A major branch of Greek art was sculpture. Greek sculptors did not create realistic works, but instead made statues that reflected what they considered ideal beauty. Greek art also included pottery.

In Greek architecture, the most important type of building was the temple. The walled rooms in the center of the temple held sculptures of gods and goddesses and lavish gifts to these deities.

INTEGRATED TECHNOLOGY

RESEARCH LINKS For more on Greek art and architecture, go to **classzone.com**

Nike of Samothrace ►

Discovered in 1863, the Nike (or Winged Victory) of Samothrace was probably created around 203 B.C. to honor a sea battle. Through its exaggerated features and artful portrayal of flowing drapery, the Nike conveys a sense of action and triumph. Currently, it is displayed at the Louvre Museum in Paris.

◄ Red and Black Pottery

Greek art also included pottery, which is known for its beauty of form and decoration. The two major types of Greek pottery are black-figure pottery (shown on the vessel) and red-figure pottery (shown on the plate). The vessel shows a scene from Greek mythology. The god Zeus, disguised as a bull, carries off a young woman named Europa. The figures on the plate demonstrate the importance of the sea and seafood in Greek culture.

The Parthenon ▲

Built between 447 and 432 B.C., the Parthenon was a Greek temple dedicated to Athena. It serves as an excellent example of the Greek expression of harmony, symmetry, and balance. Just as Greek philosophers tried to understand the basic laws of nature, so Greek architects looked to nature for guidance. They discovered a ratio in nature that they believed created pleasing proportions and used that ratio to design the rectangles in the Parthenon.

◄ Dramatic Masks and Theater

In the 6th century B.C., the Greeks became the first people to use theater for its own sake and not for religious rituals. They wrote two types of plays, comedy and tragedy. For both forms, actors wore theatrical masks that exaggerated human expressions. The plays were performed in outdoor theaters. The stage or dancing floor was partially surrounded by a semicircular seating area fitted into a hillside, such as the one shown here.

Connect *to* Today

1. **Drawing Conclusions** How does the Parthenon display the Greek preference for symmetry and balance?

   See Skillbuilder Handbook, Page R11.

2. **Hypothesizing** On what does our culture today base its standards of beauty? Give examples to support your hypothesis.

Alexander's Empire

CONNECT TO THE NEW YORK STATE CORE CURRICULUM

Unit 1.C.2.e. Alexander the Great and Hellenistic culture–cultural diffusion
Unit 1.C.2.a. Human and physical geography

TERMS & NAMES

- Philip II
- Macedonia
- Alexander the Great
- Darius III

SETTING THE STAGE-The Peloponnesian War severely weakened several Greek city-states. This caused a rapid decline in their military and economic power. In the nearby kingdom of Macedonia, King **Philip II** took note. Philip dreamed of taking control of Greece and then moving against Persia to seize its vast wealth. Philip also hoped to avenge the Persian invasion of Greece in 480 B.C.

TAKING NOTES
Outlining Use an outline to organize main ideas about the growth of Alexander's empire.

Alexander's Empire
I. Philip Builds Macedonian Power
A.
B.
II. Alexander Conquers Persia

Philip Builds Macedonian Power

The kingdom of **Macedonia**, located just north of Greece, had rough terrain and a cold climate. The Macedonians were a hardy people who lived in mountain villages rather than city-states. Most Macedonian nobles thought of themselves as Greeks. The Greeks, however, looked down on the Macedonians as uncivilized foreigners who had no great philosophers, sculptors, or writers. The Macedonians did have one very important resource—their shrewd and fearless kings.

Philip's Army In 359 B.C., Philip II became king of Macedonia. Though only 23 years old, he quickly proved to be a brilliant general and a ruthless politician. Philip transformed the rugged peasants under his command into a well-trained professional army. He organized his troops into phalanxes of 16 men across and 16 deep, each one armed with an 18-foot pike. Philip used this heavy phalanx formation to break through enemy lines. Then he used fast-moving cavalry to crush his disorganized opponents. After he employed these tactics successfully against northern opponents, Philip began to prepare an invasion of Greece.

Conquest of Greece Demosthenes (dee•MAHS•thuh•NEEZ), the Athenian orator, tried to warn the Greeks of the threat Philip and his army posed. He urged them to unite against Philip. However, the Greek city-states could not agree on any single policy. Finally, in 338 B.C., Athens and Thebes—a city-state in central Greece—joined forces to fight Philip. By then, however, it was too late. The Macedonians soundly defeated the Greeks at the battle of Chaeronea (KAIR•uh•NEE•uh). This defeat ended Greek independence. The city-states retained self-government in local affairs. However, Greece itself remained firmly under the control of a succession of foreign powers—the first of which was Philip's Macedonia.

MAIN IDEA

Analyzing Causes

A How did the Peloponnesian War pave the way for Philip's conquest of Greece?

Although Philip planned to invade Persia next, he never got the chance. At his daughter's wedding in 336 B.C., he was stabbed to death by a former guardsman. Philip's son Alexander immediately proclaimed himself king of Macedonia. Because of his accomplishments over the next 13 years, he became known as **Alexander the Great**. **A**

Alexander Defeats Persia

Although Alexander was only 20 years old when he became king, he was well prepared to lead. Under Aristotle's teaching, Alexander had learned science, geography, and literature. Alexander especially enjoyed Homer's description of the heroic deeds performed by Achilles during the Trojan War. To inspire himself, he kept a copy of the *Iliad* under his pillow.

As a young boy, Alexander learned to ride a horse, use weapons, and command troops. Once he became king, Alexander promptly demonstrated that his military training had not been wasted. When the people of Thebes rebelled, he destroyed the city. About 6,000 Thebans were killed. The survivors were sold into slavery. Frightened by his cruelty, the other Greek city-states quickly gave up any idea of rebellion.

Invasion of Persia With Greece now secure, Alexander felt free to carry out his father's plan to invade and conquer Persia. In 334 B.C., he led 35,000 soldiers across the Hellespont into Anatolia. (See the map on page 144.) Persian messengers raced along the Royal Road to spread news of the invasion. An army of about 40,000 men rushed to defend Persia. The two forces met at the Granicus River. Instead of waiting for the Persians to make the first move, Alexander ordered his cavalry to attack. Leading his troops into battle, Alexander smashed the Persian defenses.

Vocabulary

The Hellespont is the ancient name for the Dardanelles, the narrow straits that separate Europe from Asia Minor.

Alexander's victory at Granicus alarmed the Persian king, **Darius III**. Vowing to crush the invaders, he raised a huge army of between 50,000 and 75,000 men to face the Macedonians near Issus. Realizing that he was outnumbered, Alexander surprised his enemies. He ordered his finest troops to break through a weak point in the Persian lines. The army then charged straight at Darius. To avoid capture, the frightened king fled, followed by his panicked army. This victory gave Alexander control over Anatolia.

History Makers

Alexander 356–323 B.C.

When Alexander was only eight or nine years old, he tamed a wild horse that none of his father's grooms could manage. Alexander calmed the horse, whose name was Bucephalus, by speaking gently. Seeing the control that Alexander had over the horse, Philip II said: "You'll have to find another kingdom; Macedonia isn't going to be big enough for you."

Alexander took his father's advice. Riding Bucephalus at the head of a great army, he conquered the lands from Greece to the Indus Valley. When the horse died in what is now Pakistan, Alexander named the city of Bucephala after it. Maybe he was tired of the name Alexandria. By that time, he had already named at least a dozen cities after himself!

Conquering the Persian Empire Shaken by his defeat, Darius tried to negotiate a peace settlement. He offered Alexander all of his lands west of the Euphrates River. Alexander's advisers urged him to accept. However, the rapid collapse of Persian resistance fired Alexander's ambition. He rejected Darius's offer and confidently announced his plan to conquer the entire Persian Empire.

Alexander marched into Egypt, a Persian territory, in 332 B.C. The Egyptians welcomed Alexander as a liberator. They crowned him pharaoh—or god-king. During his time in Egypt, Alexander founded the city of Alexandria at the mouth of the Nile. After leaving Egypt, Alexander moved east into Mesopotamia to confront Darius. The desperate Persian king assembled a force of some 250,000 men. The two armies met at Gaugamela (GAW•guh•MEE•luh), a small village near the ruins of ancient Nineveh. Alexander launched a massive phalanx attack followed by a cavalry charge. As the Persian lines crumbled, Darius again panicked and fled. Alexander's victory at Gaugamela ended Persia's power.

Within a short time, Alexander's army occupied Babylon, Susa, and Persepolis. These cities yielded a huge treasure, which Alexander distributed among his army. A few months after it was occupied, Persepolis, Persia's royal capital, burned to the ground. Some people said Alexander left the city in ashes to signal the total destruction of the Persian Empire. The Greek historian Arrian, writing about 500 years after Alexander's time, suggested that the fire was set in revenge for the Persian burning of Athens. However, the cause of the fire remains a mystery.

Alexander's Other Conquests

Alexander now reigned as the unchallenged ruler of southwest Asia. But he was more interested in expanding his empire than in governing it. He left the ruined Persepolis to pursue Darius and conquer Persia's remote Asian provinces. Darius's trail led Alexander to a deserted spot south of the Caspian Sea. There he found Darius already dead, murdered by one of his provincial governors. Rather than return to Babylon, Alexander continued east. During the next three years, his army fought its way across the desert wastes and mountains of Central Asia. He pushed on, hoping to reach the farthest edge of the continent. **B**

MAIN IDEA

Analyzing Motives

B Why did Alexander continue his conquests after Darius was dead?

Alexander in India In 326 B.C., Alexander and his army reached the Indus Valley. At the Hydaspes River, a powerful Indian army blocked their path. After winning a fierce battle, Alexander's soldiers marched some 200 miles farther, but their morale was low. They had been fighting for 11 years and had marched more than 11,000 miles. They had endured both scorching deserts and drenching monsoon rains. The exhausted soldiers yearned to go home. Bitterly disappointed, Alexander agreed to turn back.

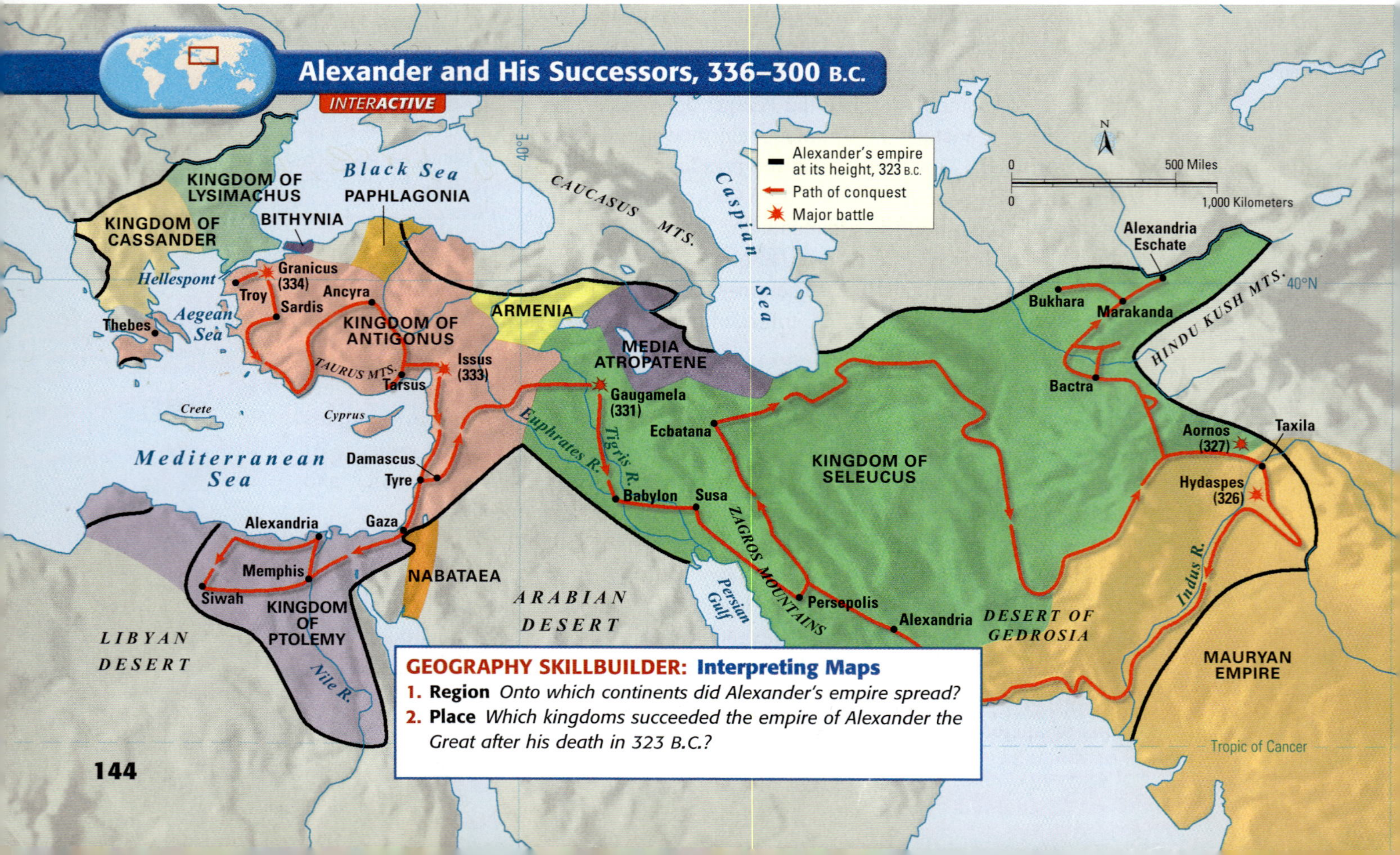

GEOGRAPHY SKILLBUILDER: Interpreting Maps

1. **Region** *Onto which continents did Alexander's empire spread?*
2. **Place** *Which kingdoms succeeded the empire of Alexander the Great after his death in 323 B.C.?*

Alexander's Empire and Its Legacy, 336–306 B.C.

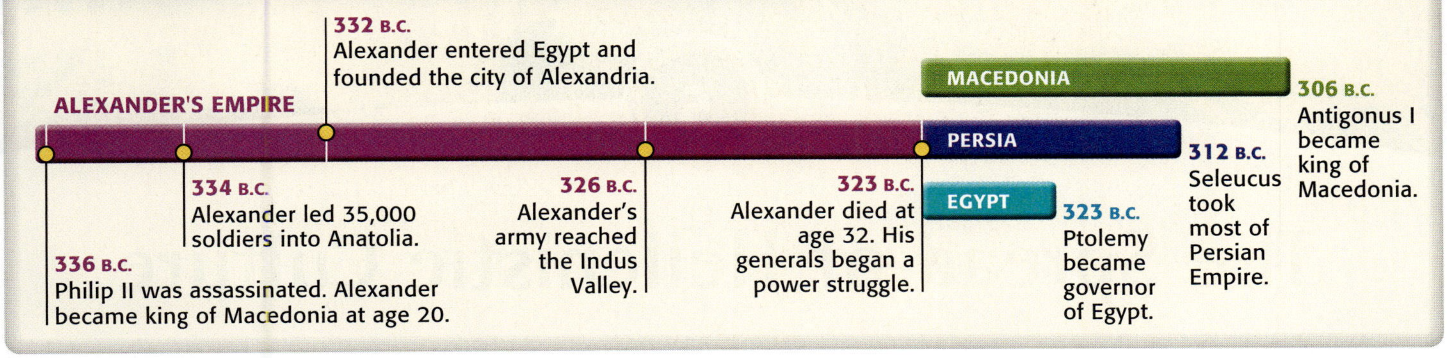

By the spring of 323 B.C., Alexander and his army had reached Babylon. Restless as always, Alexander announced plans to organize and unify his empire. He would construct new cities, roads, and harbors and conquer Arabia. However, Alexander never carried out his plans. He became seriously ill with a fever and died a few days later. He was just 32 years old.

Alexander's Legacy After Alexander died, his Macedonian generals fought among themselves for control of his empire. Eventually, three ambitious leaders won out. Antigonus (an•TIG•uh•nuhs) became king of Macedonia and took control of the Greek city-states. Ptolemy (TAHL•uh•mee) seized Egypt, took the title of pharaoh, and established a dynasty. Seleucus (sih•LOO•kuhs) took most of the old Persian Empire, which became known as the Seleucid kingdom. Ignoring the democratic traditions of the Greek polis, these rulers and their descendants governed with complete power over their subjects. **C**

> **MAIN IDEA**
> **Hypothesizing**
> **C** Was the power struggle that followed Alexander's death inevitable?

Alexander's conquests had an interesting cultural impact. Alexander himself adopted Persian dress and customs and married a Persian woman. He included Persians and people from other lands in his army. As time passed, Greek settlers throughout the empire also adopted new ways. A vibrant new culture emerged from the blend of Greek and Eastern customs.

TERMS & NAMES 1. For each term or name, write a sentence explaining its significance.

- Philip II
- Macedonia
- Alexander the Great
- Darius III

USING YOUR NOTES

2. Which of Alexander's conquests do you think was the most significant? Why?

Alexander's Empire
I. Philip Builds Macedonian Power
A.
B.
II. Alexander Conquers Persia

MAIN IDEAS

3. How was Philip II able to conquer Greece?
4. Philip II's goal was to conquer Persia. Why did Alexander continue his campaign of conquest after this goal had been achieved?
5. What happened to Alexander's empire after his death?

CRITICAL THINKING & WRITING

6. **FORMING AND SUPPORTING OPINIONS** Do you think that Alexander was worthy of the title "Great"? Explain.
7. **HYPOTHESIZING** If Alexander had lived, do you think he would have been as successful in ruling his empire as he was in building it? Explain.
8. **MAKING INFERENCES** Why do you think Alexander adopted Persian customs and included Persians in his army?
9. **WRITING ACTIVITY** EMPIRE BUILDING In small groups, create **storyboards** for a video presentation on the growth of Alexander's empire.

CONNECT TO TODAY **CREATING A MAP**

Use atlases to find the modern countries that occupy the lands included in Alexander's empire. Create a **map** that shows the boundaries and names of these countries. Compare your map to the map of Alexander's empire on page 144.

The Spread of Hellenistic Culture

CONNECT TO THE NEW YORK STATE CORE CURRICULUM

Unit 1.C.2.e. Alexander the Great and Hellenistic culture–cultural diffusion
Unit 1.C.2.c. Contributions: art, architecture, philosophy, science

TERMS & NAMES

- Hellenistic
- Alexandria
- Euclid
- Archimedes
- Colossus of Rhodes

SETTING THE STAGE Alexander's ambitions were cultural as well as military and political. During his wars of conquest, he actively sought to meld the conquered culture with that of the Greeks. He started new cities as administrative centers and outposts of Greek culture. These cities, from Egyptian Alexandria in the south to the Asian Alexandrias in the east, adopted many Greek patterns and customs. After Alexander's death, trade, a shared Greek culture, and a common language continued to link the cities together. But each region had its own traditional ways of life, religion, and government that no ruler could afford to overlook.

TAKING NOTES
Categorizing Use a chart to list Hellenistic achievements in various categories.

Category	Achievements
astronomy	
geometry	
philosophy	
art	

Hellenistic Culture in Alexandria

As a result of Alexander's policies, a vibrant new culture emerged. Greek (also known as Hellenic) culture blended with Egyptian, Persian, and Indian influences. This blending became known as **Hellenistic** culture. Koine (koy•NAY), the popular spoken language used in Hellenistic cities, was the direct result of cultural blending. The word *koine* came from the Greek word for "common." The language was a dialect of Greek. This language enabled educated people and traders from diverse backgrounds to communicate in cities throughout the Hellenistic world.

Trade and Cultural Diversity-Among the many cities of the Hellenistic world, the Egyptian city of **Alexandria** became the foremost center of commerce and Hellenistic civilization. Alexandria occupied a strategic site on the western edge of the Nile delta. Trade ships from all around the Mediterranean docked in its spacious harbor. Alexandria's thriving commerce enabled it to grow and prosper. By the third century B.C., Alexandria had become an international community, with a rich mixture of customs and traditions from Egypt and from the Aegean. Its diverse population exceeded half a million people.

Alexandria's Attractions-Both residents and visitors admired Alexandria's great beauty. Broad avenues lined with statues of Greek gods divided the city into blocks. Rulers built magnificent royal palaces overlooking the harbor. A much visited tomb contained Alexander's elaborate glass coffin. Soaring more than 350 feet over the harbor stood an enormous stone lighthouse called the Pharos. This lighthouse contained a polished bronze mirror that, at night, reflected the

Vocabulary
Museum means "house of the muses."

light from a blazing fire. Alexandria's greatest attractions were its famous museum and library. The museum was a temple dedicated to the Muses, the Greek goddesses of arts and sciences. It contained art galleries, a zoo, botanical gardens, and even a dining hall. The museum was an institute of advanced study.

The Alexandrian Library stood nearby. Its collection of half a million papyrus scrolls included many of the masterpieces of ancient literature. As the first true research library in the world, it helped promote the work of a gifted group of scholars. These scholars greatly respected the earlier works of classical literature and learning. They produced commentaries that explained these works.

Science and Technology

Hellenistic scholars, particularly those in Alexandria, preserved Greek and Egyptian learning in the sciences. Until the scientific advances of the 16th and 17th centuries, Alexandrian scholars provided most of the scientific knowledge available to the West.

Astronomy Alexandria's museum contained a small observatory in which astronomers could study the planets and stars. One astronomer, Aristarchus (AR•ih•STAHR•kuhs) of Samos, reached two significant scientific conclusions. In one, he estimated that the Sun was at least 300 times larger than Earth. Although he greatly underestimated the Sun's true size, Aristarchus disproved the widely held belief that the Sun was smaller than Greece. In another conclusion, he proposed that Earth and the other planets revolve around the Sun. Unfortunately for science, other astronomers refused to support Aristarchus' theory. In the second century A.D., Alexandria's last renowned astronomer, Ptolemy, incorrectly placed Earth at the center of the solar system. Astronomers accepted this view for the next 14 centuries.

Eratosthenes (EHR•uh•TAHS•thuh•NEEZ), the director of the Alexandrian Library, tried to calculate Earth's true size. Using geometry, he computed Earth's circumference at between 28,000 and 29,000 miles. Modern measurements put the circumference at 24,860 miles. As well as a highly regarded astronomer and mathematician, Eratosthenes also was a poet and historian.

Mathematics and Physics In their work, Eratosthenes and Aristarchus used a geometry text compiled by **Euclid** (YOO•klihd). Euclid was a highly regarded

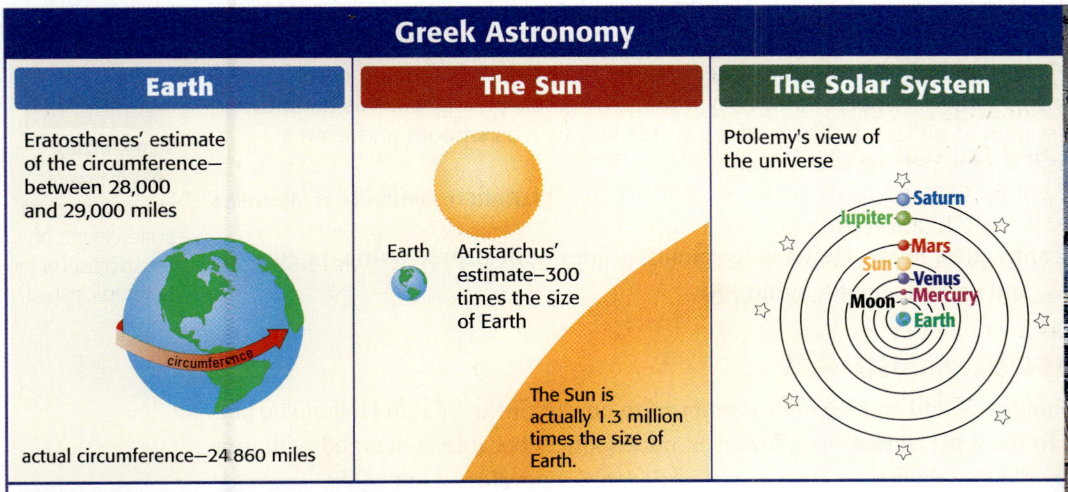

SKILLBUILDER: Interpreting Charts

1. **Comparing** *Where were Greek astronomers' ideas most incorrect compared with modern concepts?*
2. **Clarifying** *Which estimate is closest to modern measurements? How could the Hellenists be so accurate?*

▼ Hipparchus, who lived in Alexandria for a time, charted the position of 850 stars.

Global Patterns

Pythagorean Theorem

Geometry students remember Pythagoras for his theorem on the triangle, but its principles were known earlier. This formula states that the square of a right triangle's hypotenuse equals the sum of the squared lengths of the two remaining sides. Chinese mathematicians knew this theory perhaps as early as 1100 B.C. Egyptian surveyors put it to practical use even earlier.

However, the work of the school that Pythagoras founded caught the interest of later mathematicians. Shown are Euclid's proof in Greek along with a Chinese and an Arabic translation. The Arabs who conquered much of Alexander's empire spread Greek mathematical learning to the West. The formula became known as the Pythagorean theorem throughout the world.

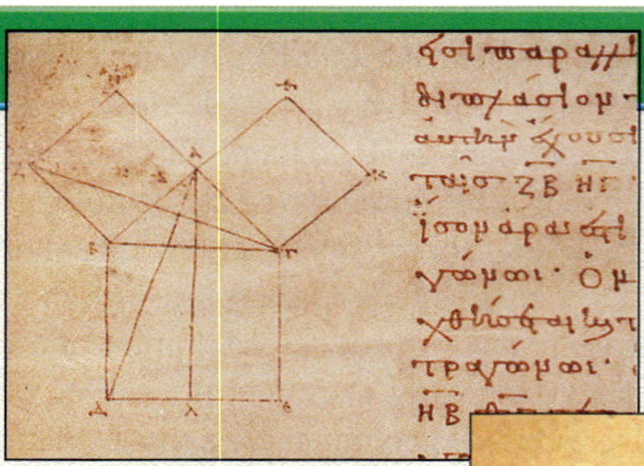

Greek, A.D. 800

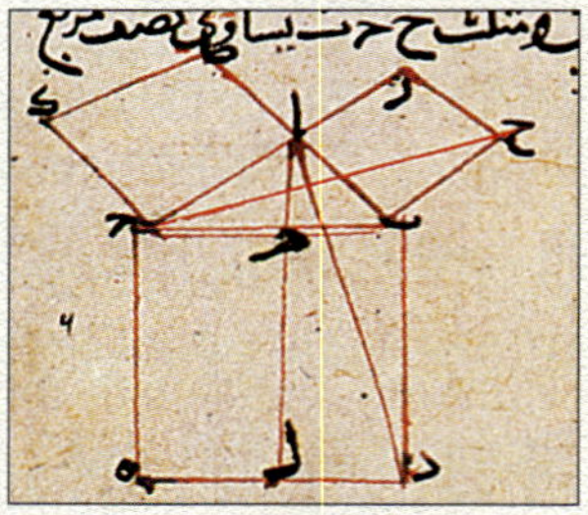

Arabic, A.D. 1250

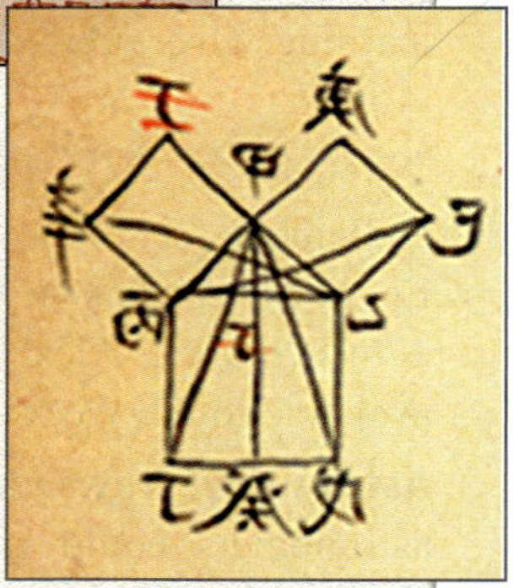

Chinese, A.D. 1607

mathematician who taught in Alexandria. His best-known book, *Elements,* contained 465 carefully presented geometry propositions and proofs. Euclid's work is still the basis for courses in geometry.

Another important Hellenistic scientist, **Archimedes** (AHR•kuh•MEE•deez) of Syracuse, studied at Alexandria. He accurately estimated the value of pi (π)—the ratio of the circumference of a circle to its diameter. In addition, Archimedes explained the law of the lever.

Gifted in both geometry and physics, Archimedes also put his genius to practical use. He invented the Archimedes screw, a device that raised water from the ground, and the compound pulley to lift heavy objects. The writer Plutarch described how Archimedes demonstrated to an audience of curious onlookers how something heavy can be moved by a small force:

PRIMARY SOURCE

Archimedes took a . . . ship . . . which had just been dragged up on land with great labor and many men; in this he placed her usual complement of men and cargo, and then sitting at some distance, without any trouble, by gently pulling with his hand the end of a system of pulleys, he dragged it towards him with as smooth and even a motion as if it were passing over the sea.

PLUTARCH, *Parallel Lives: Marcellus*

Using Archimedes' ideas, Hellenistic scientists later built a force pump, pneumatic machines, and even a steam engine. (A)

MAIN IDEA

Summarizing

(A) What were some of the main achievements of the scientists of the Hellenistic period?

Philosophy and Art

The teachings of Plato and Aristotle continued to be very influential in Hellenistic philosophy. In the third century B.C., however, philosophers became concerned with how people should live their lives. Two major philosophies developed out of this concern.

Stoicism and Epicureanism A Greek philosopher named Zeno (335–263 B.C.) founded the school of philosophy called Stoicism (STOH•ih•SIHZ•uhm). Stoics proposed that people should live virtuous lives in harmony with the will of god or the natural laws that God established to run the universe. They also preached that human desires, power, and wealth were dangerous distractions that should be checked. Stoicism promoted social unity and encouraged its followers to focus on what they could control.

Epicurus (EHP•uh•KYUR•uhs) founded the school of thought called Epicureanism. He taught that gods who had no interest in humans ruled the universe. Epicurus believed that the only real objects were those that the five senses perceived. He taught that the greatest good and the highest pleasure came from virtuous conduct and the absence of pain. Epicureans proposed that the main goal of humans was to achieve harmony of body and mind. Today, the word *epicurean* means a person devoted to pursuing human pleasures, especially the enjoyment of good food. However, during his lifetime, Epicurus advocated moderation in all things. B

MAIN IDEA

Drawing Conclusions

B What was the main concern of the Stoic and Epicurean schools of philosophy?

Realism in Sculpture-Like science, sculpture flourished during the Hellenistic age. Rulers, wealthy merchants, and cities all purchased statues to honor gods, commemorate heroes, and portray ordinary people in everyday situations. The largest known Hellenistic statue was created on the island of Rhodes. Known as the **Colossus of Rhodes**, this bronze statue stood more than 100 feet high. One of the seven wonders of the ancient world, this huge sculpture was toppled by an earthquake in about 225 B.C. Later, the bronze was sold for scrap. Another magnificent Hellenistic sculpture found on Rhodes was the Nike (or Winged Victory) of Samothrace. It was created around 203 B.C. to commemorate a Greek naval victory.

Hellenistic sculpture moved away from the harmonic balance and idealized forms of the classical age. Instead of the serene face and perfect body of an idealized man or woman, Hellenistic sculptors created more natural works. They felt free to explore new subjects, carving ordinary people such as an old, wrinkled peasant woman.

By 150 B.C., the Hellenistic world was in decline. A new city, Rome, was growing and gaining strength. Through Rome, Greek-style drama, architecture, sculpture, and philosophy were preserved and eventually became the core of Western civilization.

NEW YORK CORE CURRICULUM REVIEW

TERMS & NAMES 1. For each term or name, write a sentence explaining its significance.

- Hellenistic
- Alexandria
- Euclid
- Archimedes
- Colossus of Rhodes

USING YOUR NOTES

2. Which Hellenistic achievement had the greatest impact? Why?

Category	Achievements
astronomy	
geometry	
philosophy	
art	

MAIN IDEAS

3. How did trade contribute to cultural diversity in the Hellenistic city of Alexandria?
4. How did Euclid influence some of the developments in astronomy during the Hellenistic period?
5. What did Stoicism and Epicureanism have in common?

CRITICAL THINKING & WRITING

6. **SYNTHESIZING** Describe how the growth of Alexander's empire spread Greek culture.
7. **MAKING INFERENCES** What do you think was the greatest scientific advance of the Hellenistic period? Why?
8. **COMPARING** How was the purpose served by architecture and sculpture in the Hellenistic period similar to the purpose served by these arts in the Golden Age of Athens?
9. **WRITING ACTIVITY** CULTURAL INTERACTION -The Hellenistic culture brought together Egyptian, Greek, Persian, and Indian influences. Write a brief **essay** showing how American culture is a combination of different influences.

CONNECT TO TODAY **CREATING A COLLAGE**

Archimedes developed, or provided the ideas for, many practical devices—the lever, for example. Consider some of the everyday implements that are related to these devices. Create a **collage** of pictures of these implements. Accompany each visual with a brief annotation.

Chapter 5 Assessment

TERMS & NAMES

For each term or name below, briefly explain its connection to Classical Greece.

1. Trojan War
2. Homer
3. polis
4. democracy
5. classical art
6. Aristotle
7. Alexander the Great
8. Hellenistic

MAIN IDEAS

Cultures of the Mountains and the Sea
Section 1 (pages 123–126)

9. Why was sea travel important to early Greece?
10. Why did the Greeks develop myths?

Warring City-States Section 2 (pages 127–133)

11. What were the two most powerful city-states in early Greece?
12. What were the consequences of the Persian Wars?

Democracy and Greece's Golden Age
Section 3 (pages 134–141)

13. What were Pericles' three goals for Athens?
14. Who were the three renowned philosophers of the golden age?

Alexander's Empire Section 4 (pages 142–145)

15. Why was Greece so easily conquered by Macedonia?
16. What was the full extent of Alexander's empire before his death?

The Spread of Hellenistic Culture
Section 5 (pages 146–149)

17. What four influences blended to form Hellenistic culture?
18. What are some of the scientific achievements of the Hellenistic period?

CRITICAL THINKING

1. USING YOUR NOTES

In a diagram like the one below, show the development of direct democracy in Athens.

2. DRAWING CONCLUSIONS

POWER AND AUTHORITY "Years of uncertainty and insecurity have changed the country. It once was Athens, but now it has become Sparta." What do you think this statement means? Use information from the chapter to illustrate your answer.

3. ANALYZING ISSUES

CULTURAL INTERACTION Based on the Visual Summary below and your review of the chapter, how do you think Classical Greece has influenced the United States? Support your answer with examples.

4. MAKING INFERENCES

EMPIRE BUILDING Consider Pericles and Alexander the Great. What qualifications or characteristics do you think are needed for a leader to build an empire? Why?

VISUAL SUMMARY

NEW YORK STATE REGENTS EXAM PRACTICE

Use the quotation and your knowledge of world history to answer questions 1 and 2.
Additional Test Practice, pp. S1–S33

PRIMARY SOURCE

Where ought the sovereign power of the state to reside?-.-.-. The state aims to consist as far as possible of those who are alike and equal, a condition found chiefly among the middle section. . . . The middle class is also the steadiest element, the least eager for change. They neither covet, like the poor the possessions of others, nor do others covet theirs, as the poor covet those of the rich. . . . Tyranny often emerges from an over-enthusiastic democracy or from an oligarchy, but much more rarely from middle class constitutions.

ARISTOTLE, *Politics*

1 Why does Aristotle support the middle class as the location of power?

(1) He finds poor people too backward to rule.
(2) He thinks the rich are too greedy.
(3) The middle class is very enthusiastic about democracy.
(4) The middle class is steady and is less eager for change.

2 According to Aristotle, what often emerges from an "over-enthusiastic democracy"?

(1) tyranny
(2) oligarchy
(3) monarchy
(4) aristocracy

Use this scene pictured on a piece of Greek pottery and your knowledge of world history to answer question 3.

3 This scene shows a battle formation used by the Greeks. What is the formation called?

(1) shield and spear
(2) massed formation
(3) phalanx
(4) acropolis

INTEGRATED TECHNOLOGY

TEST PRACTICE Go to **classzone.com**

- Diagnostic tests
- Tutorials
- Strategies
- Additional practice

ALTERNATIVE ASSESSMENT

1. Interact *with* History

On page 122, you drew certain conclusions about Greek culture and values without knowing details of Greek history. Now that you have read the chapter, reexamine the artworks and reread the Greeks' words. Conduct a class debate about how the art and ideals of Greece have influenced modern society.

2. WRITING ABOUT HISTORY

Write an **epic poem** (between two and three pages long) about an event or an individual that you read about in Chapter 5. Possible subjects you might select include the Trojan War, the Persian Wars, the Peloponnesian War, Hector, Pericles, and Alexander. In writing your poem, try to imitate the style of the *Iliad* or the *Odyssey*.

INTEGRATED TECHNOLOGY

NetExplorations: The Parthenon

Go to *NetExplorations* at **classzone.com** to learn more about the Parthenon. Search the Internet for additional information on the Parthenon and the sculptor Phidias, who oversaw its construction. Use the information you gather to record a mock radio or television interview with Phidias, and play it in class. Have Phidias answer questions about

- his designs for the statues and carvings that adorned the Parthenon.
- the significance of the Parthenon for his fellow Athenians.
- other works of art he created.

CHAPTER 6

Ancient Rome and Early Christianity, 500 B.C.–A.D. 500

Previewing Main Ideas

POWER AND AUTHORITY Rome began as a republic, a government in which elected officials represent the people. Eventually, absolute rulers called emperors seized power and expanded the empire.

Geography *About how many miles did the Roman Empire stretch from east to west?*

EMPIRE BUILDING At its height, the Roman Empire touched three continents—Europe, Asia, and Africa. For several centuries, Rome brought peace and prosperity to its empire before its eventual collapse.

Geography *Why was the Mediterranean Sea important to the Roman Empire?*

RELIGIOUS AND ETHICAL SYSTEMS Out of Judea rose a monotheistic, or single-god, religion known as Christianity. Based on the teachings of Jesus of Nazareth, it soon spread throughout Rome and beyond.

Geography *What geographic features might have helped or hindered the spread of Christianity throughout the Roman Empire?*

NEW YORK CORE CURRICULUM FOCUS

- Ancient Rome began as a republic, in which elected officials represented the people.
- Rome's Twelve Tables established the idea that the law should protect all free citizens.

INTEGRATED TECHNOLOGY

eEdition
- Interactive Maps
- Interactive Visuals
- Interactive Primary Sources

INTERNET RESOURCES

Go to **classzone.com** for:
- Research Links
- Internet Activities
- Primary Sources
- Chapter Quiz
- Maps
- Test Practice
- Current Events

ROME

509 B.C. Rome becomes a republic.

264 B.C. First Punic War begins.

218 B.C. In the Second Punic War, Hannibal invades Italy.

500 B.C. | 300 B.C. | 100 B.C.

WORLD

321 B.C. Chandragupta Maurya founds Mauryan Empire in India.

202 B.C. ◀ Han Dynasty takes power in China. (sculpted figure from Han period)

The Roman World, 265 B.C.–A.D. 117

31 B.C.
Octavian defeats the forces of Antony and Cleopatra. (bust of Cleopatra) ▶

A.D. 284
Diocletian becomes emperor of Rome.

A.D. 476
▲ Western Roman Empire falls. (Roman horseman)

A.D. 100 — A.D. 300 — A.D. 500

A.D. 100
Moche culture arises in South America. (gold toucan from Moche era) ▶

A.D. 300
Aksum kingdom emerges in east Africa.

Interact *with* History

What makes a successful leader?

You are a member of the senate in ancient Rome. Soon you must decide whether to support or oppose a powerful leader who wants to become ruler. Many consider him a military genius for having gained vast territory and wealth for Rome. Others point out that he disobeyed orders and is both ruthless and devious. You wonder whether his ambition would lead to greater prosperity and order in the empire or to injustice and unrest.

▲ This 19th-century painting by Italian artist Cesare Maccari shows Cicero, one of ancient Rome's greatest public speakers, addressing fellow members of the Roman Senate.

EXAMINING *the* ISSUES

- **Which is more important in measuring leadership—results or integrity?**
- **Does a leader have to be likable in order to succeed?**

As a class, discuss these questions. Based on your discussion, think about what you have learned about other leaders in history, such as Alexander the Great and Darius of Persia. What qualities helped them to be successful or caused them to fail? As you read about Rome, see how the qualities of its leaders helped or hindered its development.

The Roman Republic

CONNECT TO THE NEW YORK STATE CORE CURRICULUM

Unit 1.C.3.a. Human and physical geography
Unit 1.C.3.b. Contributions–law (Twelve Tables), architecture, literature, roads, bridges

TERMS & NAMES

- republic
- patrician
- plebeian
- tribune
- consul
- senate
- dictator
- legion
- Punic Wars
- Hannibal

SETTING THE STAGE While the great civilization of Greece was in decline, a new city to the west was developing and increasing its power. Rome grew from a small settlement to a mighty civilization that eventually conquered the Mediterranean world. In time, the Romans would build one of the most famous and influential empires in history.

The Origins of Rome

According to legend, the city of Rome was founded in 753 B.C. by Romulus and Remus, twin sons of the god Mars and a Latin princess. The twins were abandoned on the Tiber River as infants and raised by a she-wolf. The twins decided to build a city near the spot. In reality, it was men not immortals who built the city, and they chose the spot largely for its strategic location and fertile soil.

Rome's Geography Rome was built on seven rolling hills at a curve on the Tiber River, near the center of the Italian peninsula. It was midway between the Alps and Italy's southern tip. Rome also was near the midpoint of the Mediterranean Sea. The historian Livy wrote about the city's site:

PRIMARY SOURCE

Not without reason did gods and men choose this spot for the site of our city—the [salubrious] hills, the river to bring us produce from the inland regions and sea-borne commerce from abroad, the sea itself, near enough for convenience yet not so near as to bring danger from foreign fleets, our situation in the very heart of Italy—all these advantages make it of all places in the world the best for a city destined to grow great.

LIVY, *The Early History of Rome*

TAKING NOTES

Outlining Use an outline to organize the main ideas and details.

I. The Origins of Rome
 A.
 B.
II. The Early Republic
 A.
 B.
III. Rome Spreads Its Power
 A.
 B.

The First Romans The earliest settlers on the Italian peninsula arrived in prehistoric times. From about 1000 to 500 B.C., three groups inhabited the region and eventually battled for control. They were the Latins, the Greeks, and the Etruscans. The Latins built the original settlement at Rome, a cluster of wooden huts atop one of its seven hills, Palatine Hill. These settlers were considered to be the first Romans.

Between 750 and 600 B.C., the Greeks established colonies along southern Italy and Sicily. The cities became prosperous and commercially active. They brought all of Italy, including Rome, into closer contact with Greek civilization.

The Etruscans were native to northern Italy. They were skilled metalworkers and engineers. The Etruscans strongly influenced the development of Roman civilization. They boasted a system of writing, for example, and the Romans adopted their alphabet. They also influenced Rome's architecture, especially the use of the arch.

The Early Republic

Around 600 B.C., an Etruscan became king of Rome. In the decades that followed, Rome grew from a collection of hilltop villages to a city that covered nearly 500 square miles. Various kings ordered the construction of Rome's first temples and public centers—the most famous of which was the Forum, the heart of Roman political life.

The last king of Rome was Tarquin the Proud. A harsh tyrant, he was driven from power in 509 B.C. The Romans declared they would never again be ruled by a king. Instead, they established a republic, from the Latin phrase *res publica,* which means "public affairs." A **republic** is a form of government in which power rests with citizens who have the right to vote for their leaders. In Rome, citizenship with voting rights was granted only to free-born male citizens.

Patricians and Plebeians In the early republic, different groups of Romans struggled for power. One group was the **patricians**, the wealthy landowners who held most of the power. The other important group was the **plebeians**, the common farmers, artisans, and merchants who made up the majority of the population.

The patricians inherited their power and social status. They claimed that their ancestry gave them the authority to make laws for Rome. The plebeians were citizens of Rome with the right to vote. However, they were barred by law from holding most important government positions. In time, Rome's leaders allowed the plebeians to form their own assembly and elect representatives called **tribunes**. Tribunes protected the rights of the plebeians from unfair acts of patrician officials. (A)

MAIN IDEA

Making Inferences

(A) Why did patricians want to prevent plebeians from holding important positions?

Twelve Tables An important victory for the plebeians was to force the creation of a written law code. With laws unwritten, patrician officials often interpreted the law to suit themselves. In 451 B.C., a group of ten officials began writing down Rome's laws. The laws were carved on twelve tablets, or tables, and hung in the Forum. They became the basis for later Roman law. The Twelve Tables established the idea that all free citizens had a right to the protection of the law.

▶ Ruins of the Forum, the political center of the Roman Empire, still stand in present-day Rome.

Comparing Republican Governments	Rome	United States of America
Executive	• Two consuls, elected by the assembly for one year—chief executives of the government and commanders-in-chief of the army.	• A president, elected by the people for four years—chief executive of the government and commander-in-chief of the army.
Legislative	• Senate of 300 members, chosen from aristocracy for life—controls foreign and financial policies, advises consuls. • Centuriate Assembly, all citizen-soldiers are members for life—selects consuls, makes laws. • Tribal Assembly, citizens grouped according to where they live are members for life—elects tribunes and makes laws.	• Senate of 100 members, elected by the people for six-year terms—makes laws, advises president on foreign policy. • House of Representatives of 435 members, elected by the people for two years—makes laws, originates revenue bills.
Judicial	• Praetors, eight judges chosen for one year by Centuriate Assembly—two oversee civil and criminal courts (the others govern provinces).	• Supreme Court, nine justices appointed for life by president—highest court, hears civil and criminal appeals cases.
Legal code	• Twelve Tables—a list of rules that was the basis of Roman legal system	• U.S. Constitution—basic law of the United States
Citizenship	• All adult male landowners	• All native-born or naturalized adults

SKILLBUILDER: Interpreting Charts

1. **Comparing** *What similarities do you see in the governments of the Roman Republic and the United States?*
2. **Drawing Conclusions** *Which government seems more democratic? Why?*

Government Under the Republic In the first century B.C., Roman writers boasted that Rome had achieved a balanced government. What they meant was that their government had taken the best features of a monarchy (government by a king), an aristocracy (government by nobles), and a democracy (government by the people—see the comparison above of Rome to the United States). Rome had two officials called **consuls**. Like kings, they commanded the army and directed the government. However, their power was limited. A consul's term was only one year long. The same person could not be elected consul again for ten years. Also, one consul could always overrule, or veto, the other's decisions.

Vocabulary
The word *veto* comes from the Latin for "I forbid."

The **senate** was the aristocratic branch of Rome's government. It had both legislative and administrative functions in the republic. Its 300 members were chosen from the upper class of Roman society. Later, plebeians were allowed in the senate. The senate exercised great influence over both foreign and domestic policy.

The assemblies represented the more democratic side of the government. For example, an assembly organized by the plebeians, the Tribal Assembly, elected the tribunes and made laws for the common people—and later for the republic itself.

In times of crisis, the republic could appoint a **dictator**—a leader who had absolute power to make laws and command the army. A dictator's power lasted for only six months. Dictators were chosen by the consuls and then elected by the senate.

The Roman Army In addition to their government, the Romans placed great value on their military. All citizens who owned land were required to serve in the army. Seekers of certain public offices had to perform ten years of military service. Roman soldiers were organized into large military units called **legions**. The Roman legion was made up of some 5,000 heavily armed foot soldiers (infantry). A group of soldiers on horseback (cavalry) supported each legion. Legions were divided into smaller groups of 80 men, each of which was called a century. The military organization and fighting skill of the Roman army were key factors in Rome's rise to greatness.

Vocabulary
The term *legion* also means a multitude.

Rome Spreads Its Power

For hundreds of years after the founding of the republic, Rome sought to expand its territories through trade and conquest.

Rome Conquers Italy Roman power grew slowly but steadily as the legions battled for control of the Italian peninsula. By the fourth century B.C., the Romans dominated central Italy. Eventually, they defeated the Etruscans to the north and the Greek city-states to the south. By 265 B.C., the Romans were masters of nearly all Italy.

Rome had different laws and treatment for different parts of its conquered territory. The neighboring Latins on the Tiber became full citizens of Rome. In territories farther from Rome, conquered peoples enjoyed all the rights of Roman citizenship except the vote. All other conquered groups fell into a third category, allies of Rome. Rome did not interfere with its allies, as long as they supplied troops for the Roman army and did not make treaties of friendship with any other state. The new citizens and allies became partners in Rome's growth. This lenient policy toward defeated enemies helped Rome to succeed in building a long-lasting empire. For more than two centuries after 265 B.C., Roman power spread far beyond Italy. **B**

MAIN IDEA

Analyzing Issues

B How did its treatment of conquered people affect Rome's expansion?

History Makers

Hannibal 247–183 B.C.

When Hannibal was only a boy of nine, his father, Hamilcar Barca, a general in Carthage's army, made him swear that he would always hate Rome and seek to destroy it.

After his defeat at the battle of Zama and Carthage's loss in the Second Punic War, Hannibal took refuge among Rome's enemies. He fought against Roman forces as an ally of the kings of Syria and Bithynia. When Roman agents came for him in Bithynia on the Black Sea in Anatolia in 183 B.C., he committed suicide rather than submit to Rome.

INTEGRATED TECHNOLOGY

INTERNET ACTIVITY Create an annotated map of Hannibal's journey through the Alps. Go to **classzone.com** for your research.

Rome's Commercial Network Rome's location gave it easy access to the riches of the lands ringing the Mediterranean Sea. Roman merchants moved by land and sea. They traded Roman wine and olive oil for a variety of foods, raw materials, and manufactured goods from other lands. However, other large and powerful cities interfered with Roman access to the Mediterranean. One such city was Carthage. Once a colony of Phoenicia, Carthage was located on a peninsula on the North African coast. Its rise to power soon put it in direct opposition with Rome.

War with Carthage In 264 B.C., Rome and Carthage went to war. This was the beginning of the long struggle known as the **Punic Wars**. Between 264 and 146 B.C., Rome and Carthage fought three wars. The first, for control of Sicily and the western Mediterranean, lasted 23 years (264–241 B.C.). It ended in the defeat of Carthage. The Second Punic War began in 218 B.C. The mastermind behind the war was a 29-year-old Carthaginian general named **Hannibal**. Hannibal was a brilliant military strategist who wanted to avenge Carthage's earlier defeat.

Vocabulary

The term *Punic* comes from the Latin word for Phoenician.

Hannibal assembled an army of 50,000 infantry, 9,000 cavalry, and 60 elephants with the intent of capturing Rome. Instead of a head-on attack, however, Hannibal sought to surprise the Romans with a most daring and risky move. He led his army on a long trek from Spain across France and through the Alps. Despite losing more than half his men and most of his elephants, the general's move initially worked. For more than a decade, he marched his forces up and down the Italian peninsula at will. Hannibal won his greatest victory at Cannae, in 216 B.C. There his army inflicted enormous losses on the Romans. However, the Romans regrouped and with the aid of many allies stood firm. They prevented Hannibal from capturing Rome.

GEOGRAPHY SKILLBUILDER: Interpreting Maps

1. **Movement** *How many miles did Hannibal's forces march to reach Cannae?*
2. **Region** *What territory did Rome add between 264 B.C. and 146 B.C.?*

Rome Triumphs Finally, the Romans found a daring military leader to match Hannibal's boldness. A general named Scipio (SIHP•ee•oh) devised a plan to attack Carthage. This strategy forced Hannibal to return to defend his native city. In 202 B.C., at Zama near Carthage, the Romans finally defeated Hannibal.

During the Third Punic War (149–146 B.C.), Rome laid siege to Carthage. In 146 B.C., the city was set afire and its 50,000 inhabitants sold into slavery. Its territory was made a Roman province.

Rome's victories in the Punic Wars gave it dominance over the western Mediterranean. The Romans then went on to conquer the eastern half. By about 70 B.C., Rome's Mediterranean empire stretched from Anatolia in the east to Spain in the west. As you will read in Section 2, however, such growth and power brought with it a new set of difficulties. C

MAIN IDEA

Drawing Conclusions

C Why were the Punic Wars important?

NEW YORK CORE CURRICULUM REVIEW

TERMS & NAMES 1. For each term or name, write a sentence explaining its significance.

• republic • patrician • plebeian • tribune • consul • senate • dictator • legion • Punic Wars • Hannibal

USING YOUR NOTES

2. What do you consider to be the key characteristic of the early Roman Republic? Why?

I. The Origins of Rome
A.
B.
II. The Early Republic
A.
B.
III. Rome Spreads Its Power
A.
B.

MAIN IDEAS

3. What limits were there on the power of the Roman consuls?
4. What was the significance of the Twelve Tables?
5. How was Hannibal's attack on Rome daring and different?

CRITICAL THINKING & WRITING

6. **FORMING OPINIONS** Do you think the Roman Republic owed its success more to its form of government or its army? Why?
7. **ANALYZING ISSUES** Do you agree with claims that early Rome had achieved a "balanced" government? Explain.
8. **CLARIFYING** How did Rome expand its territory and maintain control over it?
9. **WRITING ACTIVITY** POWER AND AUTHORITY Write a brief **essay** explaining what problems might arise from appointing a dictator during times of crisis.

CONNECT TO TODAY **PREPARING AN ORAL REPORT**

Use the library and other resources to locate any monuments built to either Hannibal or the Punic Wars. Then present what you found and the circumstances surrounding the monument's creation in an **oral report.**

The Roman Empire

CONNECT TO THE NEW YORK STATE CORE CURRICULUM

Unit 1.D.2.a. Human and physical geography
Unit 1.D.2.f. Pax Romana

TERMS & NAMES

- civil war
- Julius Caesar
- triumvirate
- Augustus
- *Pax Romana*

SETTING THE STAGE As Rome enlarged its territory, its republican form of government grew increasingly unstable. Eventually, the Roman Republic gave way to the formation of a mighty dictator-ruled empire that continued to spread Rome's influence far and wide.

TAKING NOTES
Clarifying Make a bulleted chart showing how Rome changed as it became an empire.

Changes in Rome
• Dictator claims sole power • •

The Republic Collapses

Rome's increasing wealth and expanding boundaries brought many problems. The most serious were growing discontent among the lower classes of society and a breakdown in military order. These problems led to a shakeup of the republic—and the emergence of a new political system.

Economic Turmoil As Rome grew, the gap between rich and poor grew wider. Many of Rome's rich landowners lived on huge estates. Thousands of enslaved persons—many of whom had been captured peoples in various wars—were forced to work on these estates. By 100 B.C., enslaved persons formed perhaps one-third of Rome's population.

Small farmers found it difficult to compete with the large estates run by the labor of enslaved people. Many of these farmers were former soldiers. A large number of them sold their lands to wealthy landowners and became homeless and jobless. Most stayed in the countryside and worked as seasonal migrant laborers. Some headed to Rome and other cities looking for work. They joined the ranks of the urban poor, a group that totaled about one-fourth of Roman society.

Two brothers, Tiberius and Gaius (GUY•us) Gracchus (GRAK•us), attempted to help Rome's poor. As tribunes, they proposed such reforms as limiting the size of estates and giving land to the poor. Tiberius spoke eloquently about the plight of the landless former soldiers:

PRIMARY SOURCE
The savage beasts have their . . . dens, . . . but the men who bear arms and expose their lives for the safety of their country, enjoy . . . nothing more in it but the air and light . . . and wander from place to place with their wives and children.
TIBERIUS GRACCHUS quoted in Plutarch, *The Lives of Noble Greeks and Romans*

The brothers made enemies of numerous senators, who felt threatened by their ideas. Both met violent deaths—Tiberius in 133 B.C. and Gaius in 121 B.C.

A period of **civil war**, or conflict between groups within the same country, followed their deaths.

Military Upheaval Adding to the growing turmoil within the republic was a breakdown of the once-loyal military. As the republic grew more unstable, generals began seizing greater power for themselves. They recruited soldiers from the landless poor by promising them land. These soldiers fought for pay and owed allegiance only to their commander. They replaced the citizen-soldiers whose loyalty had been to the republic. It now was possible for a military leader supported by his own troops to take over by force. Eventually, one would do just that.

Julius Caesar Takes Control In 60 B.C., a military leader named **Julius Caesar** joined forces with Crassus, a wealthy Roman, and Pompey, a popular general. With their help, Caesar was elected consul in 59 B.C. For the next ten years, these men dominated Rome as a **triumvirate**, a group of three rulers.

Caesar was a strong leader and a genius at military strategy. Following tradition, he served only one year as consul. He then appointed himself governor of Gaul (now France). During 58–50 B.C., Caesar led his legions in a grueling but successful campaign to conquer all of Gaul. Because he shared fully in the hardships of war, he won his men's loyalty and devotion.

The reports of Caesar's successes in Gaul made him very popular with the people of Rome. Pompey, who had become his political rival, feared Caesar's ambitions. In 50 B.C., the senate, at Pompey's urgings, ordered Caesar to disband his legions and return home.

Caesar defied the senate's order. On the night of January 10, 49 B.C., he took his army across the Rubicon River in Italy, the southern limit of the area he commanded. He marched his army swiftly toward Rome, and Pompey fled. Caesar's troops defeated Pompey's armies in Greece, Asia, Spain, and Egypt. In 46 B.C., Caesar returned to Rome, where he had the support of the army and the masses. That same year, the senate appointed him dictator. In 44 B.C., he was named dictator for life.

Caesar's Reforms Caesar governed as an absolute ruler, one who has total power. However, he started a number of reforms. He granted Roman citizenship to many people in the provinces. He expanded the senate, adding friends and supporters from Italy and other regions. Caesar also helped

History Makers

Julius Caesar
100–44 B.C.

In 44 B.C., on March 15, Caesar prepared to go to speak to the Senate, unaware that important senators plotted his death. According to legend, his wife, Calpurnia, begged him not to go. She said she had seen him in a dream dying in her arms of stab wounds.

When Caesar arrived at the Senate chamber, he sat in his chair. Soon the plotters encircled him, took knives hidden in their togas, and stabbed him 23 times, as depicted in the painting below. They were led by Gaius Cassius and Caesar's friend Marcus Brutus. Caesar's last words were "Et tu, Brute?" ("You, too, Brutus?")

INTEGRATED TECHNOLOGY
RESEARCH LINKS For more on Julius Caesar, go to **classzone.com**

the poor by creating jobs, especially through the construction of new public buildings. He started colonies where people without land could own property, and he increased pay for soldiers.

Many nobles and senators expressed concern over Caesar's growing power, success, and popularity. Some feared losing their influence. Others considered him a tyrant. A number of important senators, led by Marcus Brutus and Gaius Cassius, plotted his assassination. On March 15, 44 B.C., they stabbed him to death in the senate chamber. **A**

MAIN IDEA

Analyzing Motives

A Why did Caesar's rivals feel they had to kill him?

Beginning of the Empire After Caesar's death, civil war broke out again and destroyed what was left of the Roman Republic. Three of Caesar's supporters banded together to crush the assassins. Caesar's 18-year-old grandnephew and adopted son Octavian (ahk•TAY•vee•uhn) joined with an experienced general named Mark Antony and a powerful politician named Lepidus. In 43 B.C., they took control of Rome and ruled for ten years as the Second Triumvirate.

Their alliance, however, ended in jealousy and violence. Octavian forced Lepidus to retire. He and Mark Antony then became rivals. While leading troops against Rome's enemies in Anatolia, Mark Antony met Queen Cleopatra of Egypt. He fell in love with her and followed her to Egypt. Octavian accused Antony of plotting to rule Rome from Egypt, and another civil war erupted. Octavian defeated the combined forces of Antony and Cleopatra at the naval battle of Actium in 31 B.C. Later, Antony and Cleopatra committed suicide.

While he restored some aspects of the republic, Octavian became the unchallenged ruler of Rome. Eventually he accepted the title of **Augustus** (aw•GUHS•tuhs), or "exalted one." He also kept the title *imperator,* or "supreme military commander," a term from which *emperor* is derived. Rome was now an empire ruled by one man.

History Makers

Augustus
63 B.C.–A.D. 14

Augustus was the most powerful ruler of the mightiest empire of the ancient world. Yet, amid the pomp of Rome, he lived a simple and frugal life. His home was modest by Roman standards. His favorite meal consisted of coarse bread, a few sardines, and a piece of cheese—the usual food of a common laborer.

Augustus was also a very religious and family-oriented man. He held to a strict moral code. He had his only child, Julia, exiled from Rome for not being faithful in her marriage.

INTEGRATED TECHNOLOGY

RESEARCH LINKS For more on Augustus, go to **classzone.com**

A Vast and Powerful Empire

Rome was at the peak of its power from the beginning of Augustus's rule in 27 B.C. to A.D. 180. For 207 years, peace reigned throughout the empire, except for some fighting with tribes along the borders. This period of peace and prosperity is known as the ***Pax Romana***— "Roman peace." **B**

MAIN IDEA

Summarizing

B To what does the term *Pax Romana* refer?

During this time, the Roman Empire included more than 3 million square miles. Its population numbered between 60 and 80 million people. About 1 million people lived in the city of Rome itself.

A Sound Government The Romans held their vast empire together in part through efficient government and able rulers. Augustus was Rome's ablest emperor. He stabilized the frontier, glorified Rome with splendid public buildings, and created a system of government that survived for centuries. He set up a civil service. That is, he paid workers to manage the affairs of government, such as the grain supply, tax collection, and the postal system. Although the senate still functioned, civil servants drawn from plebeians and even former slaves actually administered the empire.

Vocabulary

The term *civil service* refers to persons employed in the civil administration of government.

After Augustus died in A.D. 14, the system of government that he established maintained the empire's stability. This

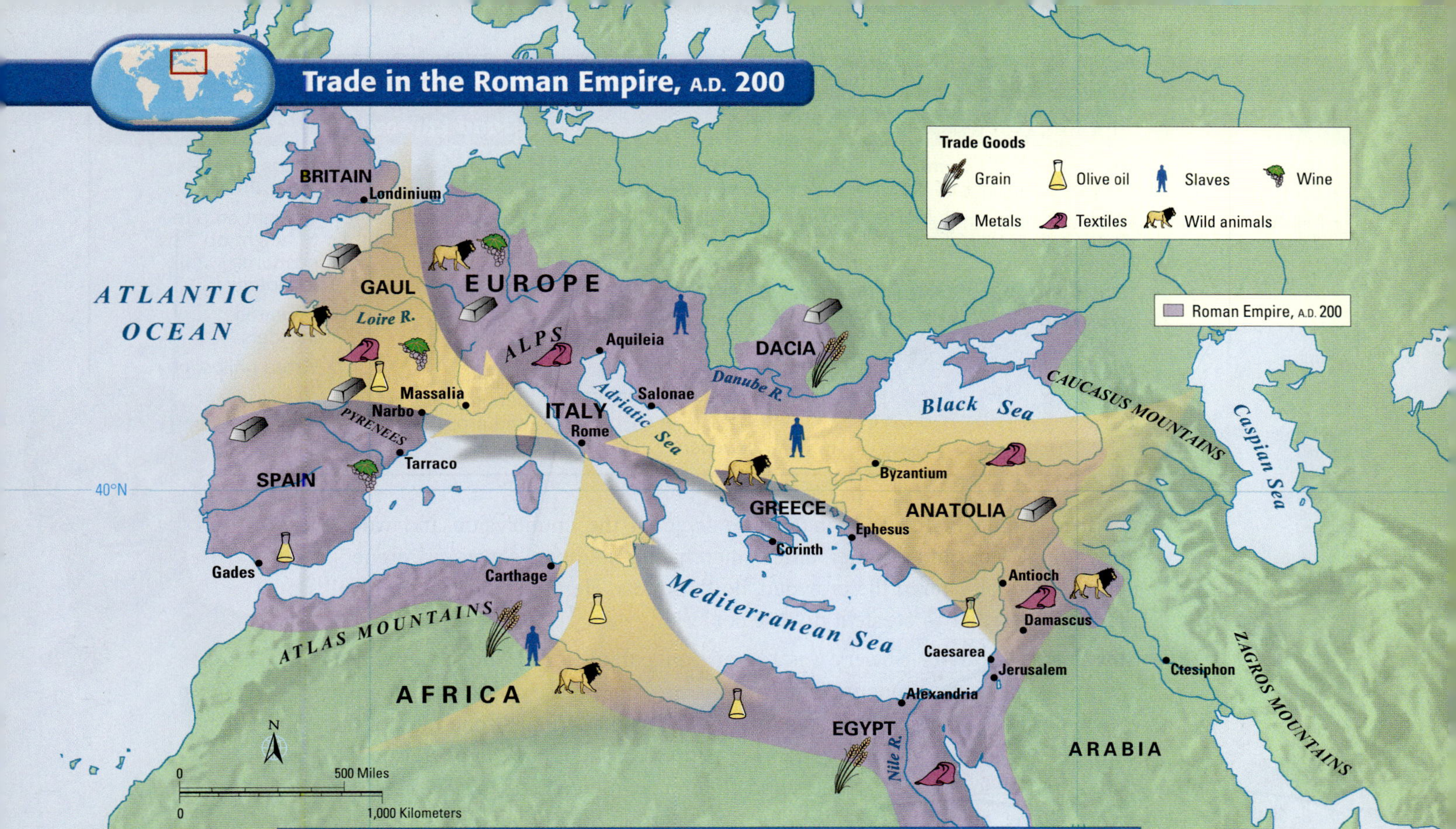

GEOGRAPHY SKILLBUILDER: Interpreting Maps

1. **Movement** *From what three continents did trade goods come to Rome?*
2. **Location** *Which goods were supplied by all three areas?*

was due mainly to the effectiveness of the civil service in carrying out day-to-day operations. The Romans managed to control an empire that by the second century A.D. reached from Spain to Mesopotamia, from North Africa to Britain. Included in its provinces were people of many languages, cultures, and customs.

Agriculture and Trade Agriculture was the most important industry in the empire. All else depended on it. About 90 percent of the people were engaged in farming. Most Romans survived on the produce from their local area. Additional food (when needed) and luxury items for the rich were obtained through trade. In Augustus's time, a silver coin called a denarius was in use throughout the empire. Having common coinage made trade between different parts of the empire much easier.

Rome had a vast trading network. Ships from the east traveled the Mediterranean protected by the Roman navy. Cities such as Corinth in Greece, Ephesus in Anatolia, and Antioch on the eastern coast of the Mediterranean grew wealthy. Rome also traded with China and India.

A complex network of roads linked the empire to such far-flung places as Persia and southern Russia. These roads were originally built by the Roman army for military purposes. Trade also brought Roman ways to the provinces and beyond.

The Roman World

Throughout its history, Rome emphasized the values of discipline, strength, and loyalty. A person with these qualities was said to have the important virtue of *gravitas.* The Romans were a practical people. They honored strength more than beauty, power more than grace, and usefulness more than elegance.

Roman Emperors, A.D. 37–A.D. 180

Group	Emperor	Reign	Notes
Bad Emperors	Caligula	37–41	Mentally disturbed
Bad Emperors	Nero	54–68	Good administrator but vicious; Murdered many; Persecuted Christians
Bad Emperors	Domitian	81–96	Ruled dictatorially; Feared treason everywhere and executed many
Good Emperors	Nerva	96–98	Began custom of adopting heir
Good Emperors	Trajan	98–117	Empire reached its greatest extent; Undertook vast building program; Enlarged social welfare
Good Emperors	Hadrian	117–138	Consolidated earlier conquests; Reorganized the bureaucracy
Good Emperors	Antoninus Pius	138–161	Reign largely a period of peace and prosperity
Good Emperors	Marcus Aurelias	161–180	Brought empire to height of economic prosperity; Defeated invaders; Wrote philosophy

Caligula

Trajan

Most people in the Roman Empire lived in the countryside and worked on farms. In Rome and smaller cities, merchants, soldiers, slaves, foreigners, and philosophers all shared the crowded, noisy streets. Here, people from all walks of life came together to create a diverse society.

Slaves and Captivity Slavery was a significant part of Roman life. It was widespread and important to the economy. The Romans made more use of slaves than any previous civilization. Numbers of slaves may have reached as high as one-third of the total population. Most slaves were conquered peoples brought back by victorious Roman armies and included men, women, and children. Children born to slaves also became slaves. Slaves could be bought and sold. According to Roman law, slaves were the property of their owners. They could be punished, rewarded, set free, or put to death as their masters saw fit.

Slaves worked both in the city and on the farm. Many were treated cruelly and worked at hard labor all day long. Some—strong, healthy males—were forced to become gladiators, or professional fighters, who fought to the death in public contests. Other slaves, particularly those who worked in wealthy households, were better treated. Occasionally, slaves would rebel. None of the slave revolts succeeded. More than a million slaves lost their lives attempting to gain their freedom.

Gods and Goddesses The earliest Romans worshiped powerful spirits or divine forces, called *numina,* that they thought resided in everything around them. Closely related to these spirits were the Lares (LAIR-eez), who were the guardian spirits of each family. They gave names to these powerful gods and goddesses and honored them through various rituals, hoping to gain favor and avoid misfortune.

In Rome, government and religion were linked. The deities were symbols of the state. Romans were expected to honor them not only in private rituals at shrines in their homes but also in public worship ceremonies conducted by priests in temples. Among the most important Roman gods and goddesses were Jupiter, father of the gods; Juno, his wife, who watched over women; and Minerva, goddess of wisdom and of the arts and crafts. During the empire, worship of the emperor also became part of the official religion of Rome.

Society and Culture By the time of the empire, wealth and social status made huge differences in how people lived. Classes had little in common. The rich lived extravagantly. They spent large sums of money on homes, gardens, slaves, and luxuries. They gave banquets that lasted for many hours and included foods that were rare and costly, such as boiled ostrich and parrot-tongue pie.

However, most people in Rome barely had the necessities of life. During the time of the empire, much of the city's population was unemployed. The government supported these people with daily rations of grain. In the shadow of Rome's

History *in* Depth

Gladiator Games

Thumbs up or thumbs down—that is how a match often ended for a gladiator (shown in this mosaic battling a tiger). When one of the combatants fell, the organizer of the games usually determined his fate. A thumbs up sign from him meant that the fighter would live. Thumbs down meant his death.

The crowd usually played a key role in these life-and-death decisions. If the masses liked the fallen gladiator, he most likely would live to fight another day. If not, he was doomed.

great temples and public buildings, poor people crowded into rickety, sprawling tenements. Fire was a constant danger.

To distract and control the masses of Romans, the government provided free games, races, mock battles, and gladiator contests. By A.D. 250, there were 150 holidays a year. On these days of celebration, the Colosseum, a huge arena that could hold 50,000, would fill with the rich and the poor alike. The spectacles they watched combined bravery and cruelty, honor and violence. In the animal shows, wild creatures brought from distant lands, such as tigers, lions, and bears, fought to the death. In other contests, gladiators engaged in combat with animals or with each other, often until one of them was killed.

During this time of *Pax Romana,* another activity slowly emerged in the Roman Empire—the practice of a new religion known as Christianity. The early followers of this new faith would meet with much brutality and hardship for their beliefs. But their religion would endure and spread throughout the empire, and eventually become one of the dominant faiths of the world.

NEW YORK CORE CURRICULUM REVIEW

TERMS & NAMES 1. For each term or name, write a sentence explaining its significance.

- civil war
- Julius Caesar
- triumvirate
- Augustus
- *Pax Romana*

USING YOUR NOTES

2. What changes do you consider negative? Why?

Changes in Rome
• Dictator claims sole power
•
•

MAIN IDEAS

3. What factors contributed to the fall of the Roman Republic?
4. What were the main reasons for the Romans' success in controlling such a large empire?
5. What measures did the government take to distract and control the masses of Rome?

CRITICAL THINKING & WRITING

6. **ANALYZING CAUSES** What role did Julius Caesar play in the decline of the republic and the rise of the empire?
7. **ANALYZING ISSUES** What aspects of Roman society remained similar from republic to empire?
8. **RECOGNIZING EFFECTS** What was Augustus's greatest contribution to Roman society? Why?
9. **WRITING ACTIVITY** EMPIRE BUILDING Write a brief **dialogue** in which various members of society comment on conditions in the Roman Empire during the *Pax Romana.* Participants might include a senator, a civil servant, a slave, a merchant, and a former soldier.

CONNECT TO TODAY CREATING A POSTER

Create a **poster** depicting the sporting events and other forms of entertainment that you enjoy watching. Include an introductory paragraph that explains what about them appeals to you.

Life in a Roman Villa

Much of what we know about Roman homes comes from archaeological excavations of the ancient cities of Pompeii and Herculaneum. In A.D. 79, Pompeii and Herculaneum were buried in volcanic ash by a tremendous eruption of Mount Vesuvius. The illustration you see here is modeled after a home in Pompeii. Notice the rich artwork and refined architecture of this home.

INTEGRATED TECHNOLOGY

RESEARCH LINKS For more on life in a Roman villa, go to **classzone.com**

▼ The Villa

Very few Romans could afford to live in such luxury, but those who could left a legacy that still inspires wonder.

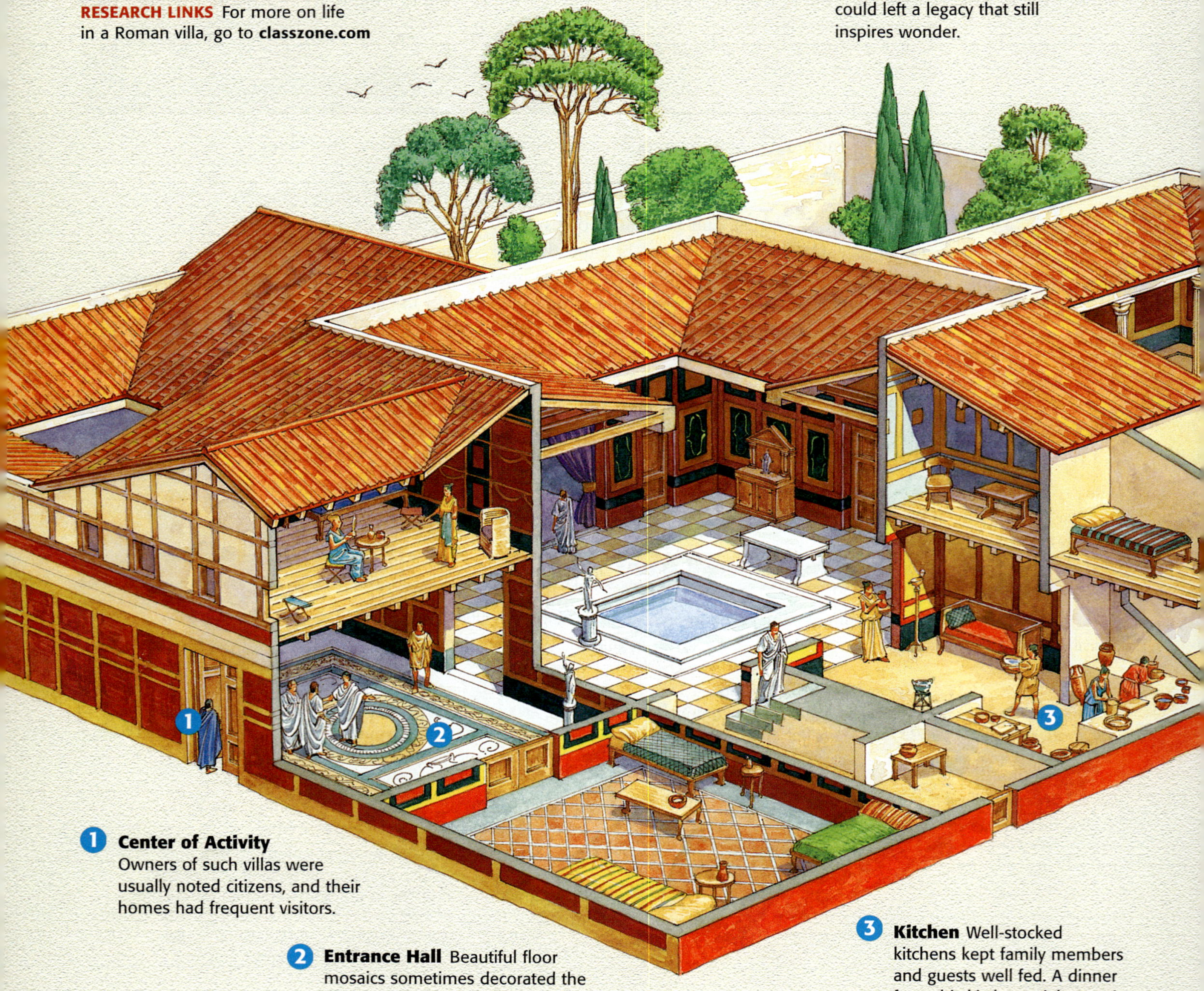

1 Center of Activity Owners of such villas were usually noted citizens, and their homes had frequent visitors.

2 Entrance Hall Beautiful floor mosaics sometimes decorated the villa's entrance. Skilled artisans created the intricate designs like the one shown in the entry of this home.

3 Kitchen Well-stocked kitchens kept family members and guests well fed. A dinner from this kitchen might consist of eggs, vegetables, shellfish, meat, cakes, and fruit.

▲ Frescoes

A fresco is a painting made on damp plaster. Roman artists used this technique to brighten the walls of Roman homes. This fresco from the ruins of Pompeii reflects a couple's pride at being able to read and write—she holds tools for writing and he a scroll.

4 Gardens Wealthy Romans maintained gardens decorated with fountains, sculptures, and frescoes.

► Archaeological Excavation

When Mount Vesuvius erupted, ash rained down, covered everything, and hardened. Bread (shown above) carbonized in the bakeries. Bodies decayed under the ash leaving hollow spaces. An archaeologist developed the technique of pouring plaster into the spaces and then removing the ash. The result was a cast of the body where it fell.

> DATA FILE

Pompeii

- Of the 10,000 to 20,000 people who lived in Pompeii, only 2,000 bodies have been uncovered.
- About three-fourths of the city has been excavated.

Mount Vesuvius

- Scientists believe there may be a reservoir of magma 400 kilometers (about 249 miles) wide sitting below Mount Vesuvius.
- Today, in the first 15 minutes of a medium-to-large-scale eruption, an area within a 4-mile radius of the volcano could be destroyed—about 1 million people live and work in this area.

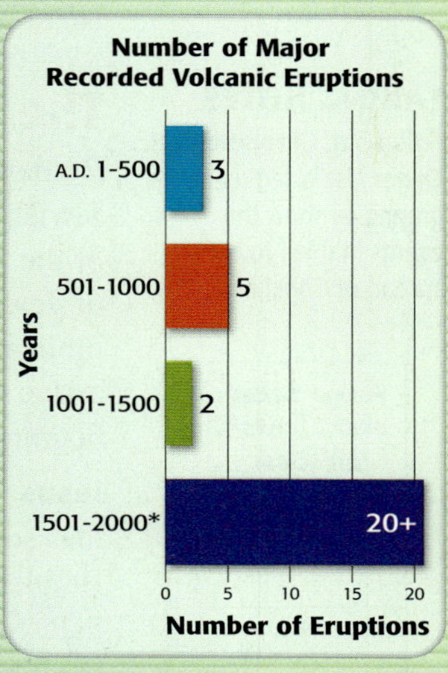

* The last eruption occurred in 1944.
Source: *Encyclopaedia Britannica*

Connect *to* Today

1. **Making Inferences** What other types of rooms or activities can you identify in the illustration?
   See Skillbuilder Handbook, page R10.
2. **Comparing and Contrasting** How are homes today similar to a Roman villa? How are they different?

The Rise of Christianity

CONNECT TO THE NEW YORK STATE CORE CURRICULUM

Unit 1.E.1.f. Christianity
Unit 1.E.2. Expansion of Christianity, Islam, Confucianism, and Buddhism

TERMS & NAMES

- Jesus
- apostle
- Paul
- Diaspora
- Constantine
- bishop
- Peter
- pope

SETTING THE STAGE While religion played an important role in Roman society, the worship of Roman gods was impersonal and often practiced without a great deal of emotion. As the empire grew, so, too, did a new religion called Christianity. Born as a movement within Judaism, it emphasized a more personal relationship between God and people—and attracted many Romans.

TAKING NOTES
Following Chronological Order Use a sequence graphic to show the events that led to the spread of Christianity .

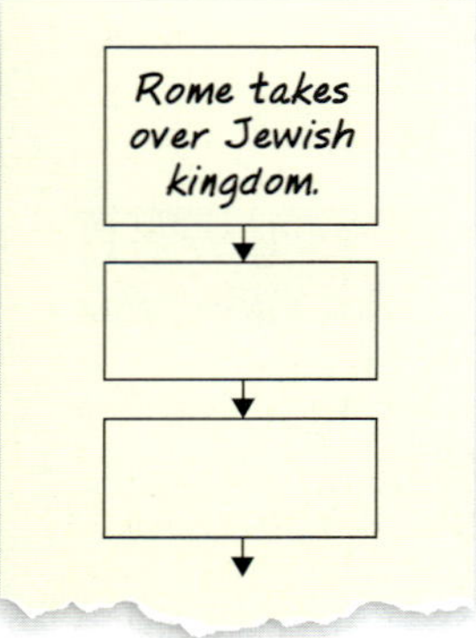

The Life and Teachings of Jesus

Roman power spread to Judea, the home of the Jews, around 63 B.C. At first the Jewish kingdom remained independent, at least in name. Rome then took control of the Jewish kingdom in A.D. 6 and made it a province of the empire. A number of Jews, however, believed that they would once again be free. According to biblical tradition, God had promised that a savior known as the Messiah would arrive and restore the kingdom of the Jews. Roughly two decades after the beginning of Roman rule, many believed that such a savior had arrived.

Jesus of Nazareth Although the exact date is uncertain, historians believe that sometime around 6 to 4 B.C., a Jew named **Jesus** was born in the town of Bethlehem in Judea. Jesus was raised in the village of Nazareth in northern Palestine. He was baptized by a prophet known as John the Baptist. As a young man, he took up the trade of carpentry.

At the age of 30, Jesus began his public ministry. For the next three years, he preached, taught, did good works, and reportedly performed miracles. His teachings contained many ideas from Jewish tradition, such as monotheism, or belief in only one god, and the principles of the Ten Commandments. Jesus emphasized God's personal relationship to each human being. He stressed the importance of people's love for God, their neighbors, their enemies, and even themselves. He also taught that God would end wickedness in the world and would establish an eternal kingdom after death for people who sincerely repented their sins. (Refer to pages 286–287 for more about Christianity.)

A Growing Movement Historical records of the time mention very little about Jesus. The main source of information about his teachings are the Gospels, the first four books of the New Testament of the Bible. Some of the Gospels are thought to have been written by one or more of Jesus' disciples, or pupils. These 12 men later came to be called **apostles**.

As Jesus preached from town to town, his fame grew. He attracted large crowds, and many people were touched by his message. Because Jesus ignored wealth and status, his message had special appeal to the poor. "Blessed are the meek, for they shall inherit the earth," he said. His words, as related in the Gospels, were simple and direct:

PRIMARY SOURCE

Love your enemies, do good to those who hate you, bless those who curse you, and pray for those who mistreat you. If anyone hits you on the cheek, let him hit the other one too; if someone takes your coat, let him have your shirt as well. Give to everyone who asks you for something, and when someone takes what is yours, do not ask for it back. Do for others just what you want them to do for you.

Luke 6:27–31

Jesus' Death Jesus' growing popularity concerned both Roman and Jewish leaders. When Jesus visited Jerusalem about A.D. 29, enthusiastic crowds greeted him as the Messiah, or king—the one whom the Bible had said would come to rescue the Jews. The chief priests of the Jews, however, denied that Jesus was the Messiah. They said his teachings were blasphemy, or contempt for God. The Roman governor Pontius Pilate accused Jesus of defying the authority of Rome. Pilate arrested Jesus and sentenced him to be crucified, or nailed to a large wooden cross to die.

After Jesus' death, his body was placed in a tomb. According to the Gospels, three days later his body was gone, and a living Jesus began appearing to his followers. The Gospels go on to say that then he ascended into heaven. The apostles were more convinced than ever that Jesus was the Messiah. It was from this belief that Jesus came to be referred to as Jesus Christ. *Christos* is a Greek word meaning "messiah" or "savior." The name *Christianity* was derived from "Christ." (A)

MAIN IDEA

Hypothesizing

(A) Why did the followers of Jesus think he was the Messiah?

Christianity Spreads Through the Empire

Strengthened by their conviction that he had triumphed over death, the followers of Jesus continued to spread his ideas. Jesus' teachings did not contradict Jewish law, and his first followers were Jews. Soon, however, these followers began to create a new religion based on his messages. Despite political and religious opposition, the new religion of Christianity spread slowly but steadily throughout the Roman Empire.

▼ *Christ's Charge to Saint Peter* by Renaissance artist Raphael depicts Jesus calling the apostle Peter to duty as the other apostles look on.

Paul's Mission One man, the apostle **Paul**, had enormous influence on Christianity's development. Paul was a Jew who had never met Jesus and at first was an enemy of Christianity. While traveling to Damascus in Syria, he reportedly had a vision of Jesus. He spent the rest of his life spreading and interpreting Jesus' teachings.

The *Pax Romana,* which made travel and the exchange of ideas fairly safe, provided the ideal conditions for Christianity to spread. Common languages—Latin and Greek—allowed the message to be easily understood. Paul wrote influential letters, called Epistles, to groups of believers. In his teaching, Paul stressed that Jesus was the son of God who died for people's sins. He also declared that Christianity should welcome all converts, Jew or Gentile (non-Jew). It was this universality that enabled Christianity to become more than just a local religion.

Jewish Rebellion During the early years of Christianity, much Roman attention was focused on the land of Jesus' birth and on the Jews. In A.D. 66, a band of Jews rebelled against Rome. In A.D. 70, the Romans stormed Jerusalem and destroyed the Temple complex. All that remained was a western portion of the wall, which today is the holiest Jewish shrine. The Jewish fortress near Masada (see map at right) held out until A.D. 73. About a half million Jews were killed in the course of this rebellion.

The Jews made another attempt to break free of the Romans in A.D. 132. Another half-million Jews died in three years of fighting. Although the Jewish religion survived, the Jewish political state ceased to exist for more than 1,800 years. Most Jews were driven from their homeland into exile. The dispersal of the Jews is called the **Diaspora**.

Global Impact

The Jewish Diaspora

Centuries of Jewish exile followed the destruction of their temple and the fall of Jerusalem in A.D. 70. This period is called the Diaspora, from the Greek word for "dispersal." Jews fled to many parts of the world, including Europe.

In the 1100s, many European Jews were expelled from their homes. Some moved to Turkey, Palestine, and Syria. Others went to Poland and neighboring areas.

The statelessness of the Jews did not end until the creation of Israel in 1948.

Persecution of the Christians Christians also posed a problem for Roman rulers. The main reason was that they refused to worship Roman gods. This refusal was seen as opposition to Roman rule. Some Roman rulers also used Christians as scapegoats for political and economic troubles.

Vocabulary
Scapegoats are groups or individuals that innocently bear the blame for others.

By the second century, as the *Pax Romana* began to crumble, persecution of the Christians intensified. Romans exiled, imprisoned, or executed Christians for refusing to worship Roman deities. Thousands were crucified, burned, or killed by wild animals in the circus arenas. Other Christians and even some non-Christians regarded persecuted Christians as martyrs. Martyrs were people willing to sacrifice their lives for the sake of a belief or a cause.

A World Religion

Despite persecution of its followers, Christianity became a powerful force. By the late third century A.D., there were millions of Christians in the Roman Empire and beyond. The widespread appeal of Christianity was due to a variety of reasons. Christianity grew because it

- embraced all people—men and women, enslaved persons, the poor, and nobles;
- gave hope to the powerless;
- appealed to those who were repelled by the extravagances of imperial Rome;
- offered a personal relationship with a loving God;
- promised eternal life after death. **B**

MAIN IDEA
Making Inferences
B Why were the citizens of the Roman Empire so drawn to Christianity?

GEOGRAPHY SKILLBUILDER: Interpreting Maps

1. **Location** *Where was Christianity most widespread in A.D. 325?*
2. **Region** *What was the extent (north to south, east to west) of Christianity's spread by A.D. 500?*

Constantine Accepts Christianity A critical moment in Christianity occurred in A.D. 312, when the Roman emperor **Constantine** was fighting three rivals for leadership of Rome. He had marched to the Tiber River at Rome to battle his chief rival. On the day before the battle at Milvian Bridge, Constantine prayed for divine help. He reported that he then saw an image of a cross—a symbol of Christianity. He ordered artisans to put the Christian symbol on his soldiers' shields. Constantine and his troops were victorious in battle. He credited his success to the help of the Christian God.

In the next year, A.D. 313, Constantine announced an end to the persecution of Christians. In the Edict of Milan, he declared Christianity to be one of the religions approved by the emperor. Christianity continued to gain strength. In 380, the emperor Theodosius made it the empire's official religion.

Vocabulary
A *hierarchy* is a group of persons organized in order of ranks, with each level subject to the authority of the one above.

Early Christian Church By this time, Christians had given their religion a structure, much as the Roman Empire had a hierarchy. At the local level, a priest led each small group of Christians. A **bishop**, who was also a priest, supervised several local churches. The apostle **Peter** had traveled to Rome from Jerusalem and became the first bishop there. According to tradition, Jesus referred to Peter as the "rock" on which the Christian Church would be built. As a result, all priests and bishops traced their authority to him.

Eventually, every major city had its own bishop. However, later bishops of Rome claimed to be the heirs of Peter. These bishops said that Peter was the first **pope**, the father or head of the Christian Church. They said that whoever was bishop of Rome was also the leader of the whole Church. Also, as Rome was the capital of the empire, it seemed the logical choice to be the center of the Church.

A Single Voice As Christianity grew, disagreements about beliefs developed among its followers. Church leaders called any belief that appeared to contradict the basic teachings a heresy. Dispute over beliefs became intense. In an attempt to end conflicts, Church leaders tried to set a single, official standard of belief. These beliefs were compiled in the New Testament, which contained the four Gospels, the Epistles of Paul, and other documents. The New Testament was added to the Hebrew Bible, which Christians called the Old Testament. In A.D. 325, Constantine moved to solidify further the teachings of Christianity. He called Church leaders to Nicaea in Anatolia. There they wrote the Nicene Creed, which defined the basic beliefs of the Church.

The Fathers of the Church-Also influential in defining Church teachings were several early writers and scholars who have been called the Fathers of the Church. One of the most important was Augustine, who became bishop of the city of Hippo in North Africa in 396. Augustine taught that humans needed the grace of God to be saved. He further taught that people could not receive God's grace unless they belonged to the Church and received the sacraments.

One of Augustine's most famous books is *The City of God*. It was written after Rome was plundered in the fifth century. Augustine wrote that the fate of cities such as Rome was not important because the heavenly city, the city of God, could never be destroyed:

PRIMARY SOURCE (C)

The one consists of those who live by human standards, the other of those who live according to God's will. . . . By two cities I mean two societies of human beings, one of which is predestined to reign with God for all eternity, the other is doomed to undergo eternal punishment with the Devil.

ST. AUGUSTINE, *The City of God*

MAIN IDEA

Analyzing Primary Sources

(C) Why would St. Augustine write his book after Rome had been attacked?

While Christianity continued its slow but steady rise, the Roman Empire itself was gradually weakening. Under the weight of an increasing number of both foreign and domestic problems, the mighty Roman Empire eventually began to crumble.

NEW YORK CORE CURRICULUM REVIEW

TERMS & NAMES 1. For each term or name, write a sentence explaining its significance.

- Jesus
- apostle
- Paul
- Diaspora
- Constantine
- bishop
- Peter
- pope

USING YOUR NOTES

2. What event do you think had the biggest impact? Explain.

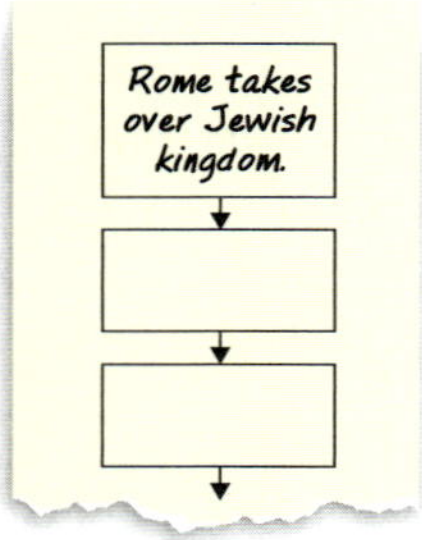

MAIN IDEAS

3. What did Jesus emphasize in his early teachings?
4. Why did the early Christians face persecution from the Romans?
5. What was the importance of the Nicene Creed?

CRITICAL THINKING & WRITING

6. **HYPOTHESIZING** Do you think Christianity would have developed in the same way if it had arisen in an area outside the Roman Empire? Explain.
7. **FORMING AND SUPPORTING OPINIONS** Who did more to spread Christianity—Paul or Constantine? Why?
8. **ANALYZING ISSUES** Why do you think Roman leaders so opposed the rise of a new religion among their subjects?
9. **WRITING ACTIVITY** RELIGIOUS AND ETHICAL SYSTEMS Imagine you are a resident of Judea during the time of Jesus. Write a **letter** to a friend in Rome describing Jesus and his teachings.

CONNECT TO TODAY **OUTLINING A SPEECH**

Locate a recent speech by the pope or the leader of another Christian church and **outline** its main ideas. Then read some of the speech to the class and discuss its main points.

The Fall of the Roman Empire

CONNECT TO THE NEW YORK STATE CORE CURRICULUM

Unit 1.D.2.d. Causes of decline
Unit 1.D.2.e. Role of migrating nomadic groups from Central Asia

TERMS & NAMES

- inflation
- mercenary
- Diocletian
- Constantinople
- Attila

SETTING THE STAGE In the third century A.D., Rome faced many problems. They came both from within the empire and from outside. Only drastic economic, military, and political reforms, it seemed, could hold off collapse.

A Century of Crisis

Historians generally agree that the end of the reign of the emperor Marcus Aurelius (A.D. 161–180) marked the end of two centuries of peace and prosperity known as the *Pax Romana*. The rulers that followed in the next century had little or no idea of how to deal with the giant empire and its growing problems. As a result, Rome began to decline.

Rome's Economy Weakens During the third century A.D., several factors prompted the weakening of Rome's economy. Hostile tribes outside the boundaries of the empire and pirates on the Mediterranean Sea disrupted trade. Having reached their limit of expansion, the Romans lacked new sources of gold and silver. Desperate for revenue, the government raised taxes. It also started minting coins that contained less and less silver. It hoped to create more money with the same amount of precious metal. However, the economy soon suffered from **inflation**, a drastic drop in the value of money coupled with a rise in prices.

Agriculture faced equally serious problems. Harvests in Italy and western Europe became increasingly meager because overworked soil had lost its fertility. What's more, years of war had destroyed much farmland. Eventually, serious food shortages and disease spread, and the population declined.

Military and Political Turmoil By the third century A.D., the Roman military was also in disarray. Over time, Roman soldiers in general had become less disciplined and loyal. They gave their allegiance not to Rome but to their commanders, who fought among themselves for the throne. To defend against the increasing threats to the empire, the government began to recruit **mercenaries**, foreign soldiers who fought for money. While mercenaries would accept lower pay than Romans, they felt little sense of loyalty to the empire.

Feelings of loyalty eventually weakened among average citizens as well. In the past, Romans cared so deeply about their republic that they willingly sacrificed their lives for it. Conditions in the later centuries of the empire caused citizens to lose their sense of patriotism. They became indifferent to the empire's fate.

TAKING NOTES

Analyzing Causes and Recognizing Effects Identify the main causes of the effects listed below.

Causes	Effects
	Inflation
	Untrustworthy army
	Political Instability

Emperors Attempt Reform

Remarkably, Rome survived intact for another 200 years. This was due largely to reform-minded emperors and the empire's division into two parts.

Diocletian Reforms the Empire In A.D. 284, **Diocletian**, a strong-willed army leader, became the new emperor. He ruled with an iron fist and severely limited personal freedoms. Nonetheless, he restored order to the empire and increased its strength. Diocletian doubled the size of the Roman army and sought to control inflation by setting fixed prices for goods. To restore the prestige of the office of emperor, he claimed descent from the ancient Roman gods and created elaborate ceremonies to present himself in a godlike aura.

Diocletian believed that the empire had grown too large and too complex for one ruler. In perhaps his most significant reform, he divided the empire into the Greek-speaking East (Greece, Anatolia, Syria, and Egypt) and the Latin-speaking West (Italy, Gaul, Britain, and Spain). He took the eastern half for himself and appointed a co-ruler for the West. While Diocletian shared authority, he kept overall control. His half of the empire, the East, included most of the empire's great cities and trade centers and was far wealthier than the West.

Because of ill health, Diocletian retired in A.D. 305. However, his plans for orderly succession failed. Civil war broke out immediately. By 311, four rivals were competing for power. Among them was an ambitious young commander named Constantine, the same Constantine who would later end the persecution of Christians.

Constantine Moves the Capital Constantine gained control of the western part of the empire in A.D. 312 and continued many of the social and economic policies

Multiple Causes: Fall of the Western Roman Empire

Contributing Factors

Political
- Political office seen as burden, not reward
- Military interference in politics
- Civil war and unrest
- Division of empire
- Moving of capital to Byzantium

Social
- Decline in interest in public affairs
- Low confidence in empire
- Disloyalty, lack of patriotism, corruption
- Contrast between rich and poor
- Decline in population due to disease and food shortage

Economic
- Poor harvests
- Disruption of trade
- No more war plunder
- Gold and silver drain
- Inflation
- Crushing tax burden
- Widening gap between rich and poor and increasingly impoverished Western Empire

Military
- Threat from northern European tribes
- Low funds for defense
- Problems recruiting Roman citizens; recruiting of non-Romans
- Decline of patriotism and loyalty among soldiers

Immediate Cause

Invasion by Germanic tribes and by Huns

FALL OF ROMAN EMPIRE

SKILLBUILDER: Interpreting Charts

1. **Analyzing Issues** *Could changes in any contributing factors have reversed the decline of the empire? Why or why not?*
2. **Analyzing Causes** *Which contributing factors—political, social, economic, or military—were the most significant in the fall of the Western Roman Empire?*

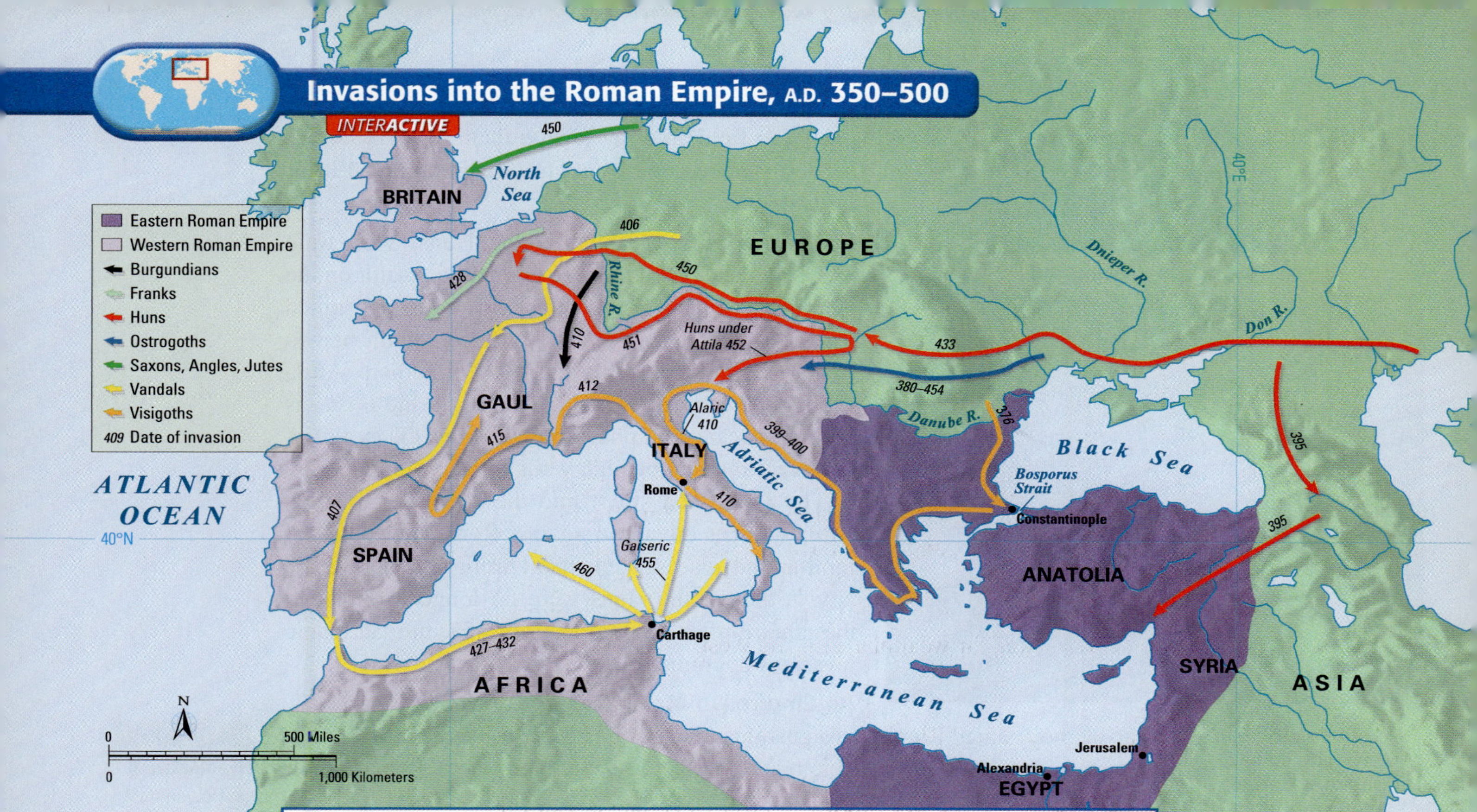

Invasions into the Roman Empire, A.D. 350–500

GEOGRAPHY SKILLBUILDER: Interpreting Maps

1. **Movement** *What group of invaders came the greatest distance?*
2. **Location** *What areas of the empire were not threatened by invasion?*

of Diocletian. In 324 Constantine also secured control of the East, thus restoring the concept of a single ruler.

In A.D. 330, Constantine took a step that would have great consequence for the empire. He moved the capital from Rome to the Greek city of Byzantium (bih•ZAN•tshee•uhm), in what is now Turkey. The new capital stood on the Bosporus Strait, strategically located for trade and defense purposes on a crossroads between West and East. (A)

MAIN IDEA

Analyzing Motives

(A) Why did Constantine choose the location of Byzantium for his new capital?

With Byzantium as its capital, the center of power in the empire shifted from Rome to the east. Soon the new capital stood protected by massive walls and filled with imperial buildings modeled after those in Rome. The city eventually took a new name—**Constantinople** (KAHN•stan•tuhn•OH•puhl), or the city of Constantine. After Constantine's death, the empire would again be divided. The East would survive; the West would fall.

The Western Empire Crumbles

The decline of the Western Roman Empire took place over many years. Its final collapse was the result of worsening internal problems, the separation of the Western Empire from the wealthier Eastern part, and outside invasions.

Germanic Invasions Since the days of Julius Caesar, Germanic peoples had gathered on the northern borders of the empire and coexisted in relative peace with Rome. Around A.D. 370, all that changed when a fierce group of Mongol nomads from central Asia, the Huns, moved into the region and began destroying all in their path.

In an effort to flee from the Huns, the various Germanic people pushed into Roman lands. (Romans called all invaders "barbarians," a term that they used to refer to non-Romans.) They kept moving through the Roman provinces of Gaul,

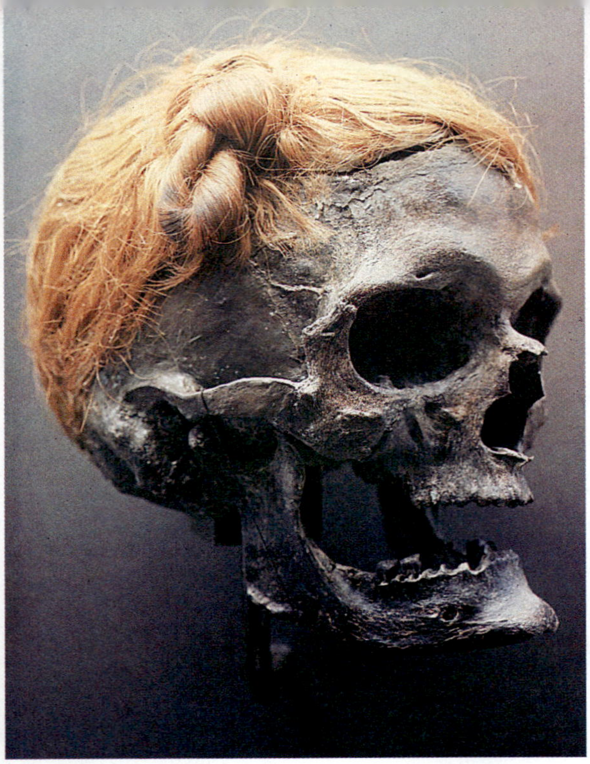

▲ This skull, still retaining its hair, shows a kind of topknot in the hair that some Germanic peoples wore to identify themselves.

Spain, and North Africa. The Western Empire was unable to field an army to stop them. In 410, hordes of Germans overran Rome itself and plundered it for three days.

Attila the Hun Meanwhile, the Huns, who were indirectly responsible for the Germanic assault on the empire, became a direct threat. In 444, they united for the first time under a powerful chieftain named **Attila** (AT•uhl•uh). With his 100,000 soldiers, Attila terrorized both halves of the empire. In the East, his armies attacked and plundered 70 cities. (They failed, however, to scale the high walls of Constantinople.)

The Huns then swept into the West. In A.D. 452, Attila's forces advanced against Rome, but bouts of famine and disease kept them from conquering the city. Although the Huns were no longer a threat to the empire after Attila's death in 453, the Germanic invasions continued.

An Empire No More The last Roman emperor, a 14-year-old boy named Romulus Augustulus, was ousted by German forces in 476. After that, no emperor even pretended to rule Rome and its western provinces. Roman power in the western half of the empire had disappeared. **B**

The eastern half of the empire, which came to be called the Byzantine Empire, not only survived but flourished. It preserved the great heritage of Greek and Roman culture for another 1,000 years. (See Chapter 11.) The Byzantine emperors ruled from Constantinople and saw themselves as heirs to the power of Augustus Caesar. The empire endured until 1453, when it fell to the Ottoman Turks.

Even though Rome's political power in the West ended, its cultural influence did not. Its ideas, customs, and institutions influenced the development of Western civilization—and still do so today.

MAIN IDEA

Hypothesizing

B Do you think Rome would have fallen to invaders if the Huns had not moved into the west? Explain.

NEW YORK CORE CURRICULUM REVIEW

TERMS & NAMES 1. For each term or name, write a sentence explaining its significance.

• inflation • mercenary • Diocletian • Constantinople • Attila

USING YOUR NOTES

2. How did these problems open the empire to invading peoples?

Causes	Effects
	Inflation
	Untrustworthy army
	Political Instability

MAIN IDEAS

3. What were the main internal causes of the empire's decline?
4. How did Diocletian succeed in preserving the empire?
5. Why did so many Germanic tribes begin invading the Roman Empire?

CRITICAL THINKING & WRITING

6. **DRAWING CONCLUSIONS** How do you think the splitting of the empire into two parts helped it survive for another 200 years?
7. **IDENTIFYING PROBLEMS** Which of Rome's internal problems do you think were the most serious? Why?
8. **ANALYZING ISSUES** Why do you think the eastern half of the empire survived?
9. **WRITING ACTIVITY** EMPIRE BUILDING Imagine you are a journalist in the Roman Empire. Write an **editorial** in which you comment—favorably or unfavorably—on Constantine's decision to move the capital of the empire.

INTEGRATED TECHNOLOGY **INTERNET ACTIVITY**

Use the Internet to gather information and create a **travel brochure** about modern-day Constantinople, now known as Istanbul. Include an introductory paragraph about the city and any facts you think a traveler might want to know.

INTERNET KEYWORD
Istanbul tourism

INTERACTIVE

The Fall of the Roman Empire

Since the fifth century, historians and others have argued over the empire's fall. They have attributed it to a variety of causes, coming both from within and outside the empire. The following excerpts are examples of the differing opinions.

A SECONDARY SOURCE

Edward Gibbon

In the 1780s Gibbon published *The History of the Decline and Fall of the Roman Empire.* In this passage, Gibbon explains that a major cause of the collapse was that the empire was simply just too large.

The decline of Rome was the natural and inevitable effect of immoderate greatness. Prosperity ripened the principle of decay; the causes of destruction multiplied with the extent of conquest; and, as soon as time or accident had removed the artificial supports, the stupendous fabric yielded to the pressure of its own weight. The story of its ruin is simple and obvious; and instead of inquiring why the Roman Empire was destroyed, we should rather be surprised that it had subsisted so long.

B SECONDARY SOURCE

Arther Ferrill

In his book *The Fall of the Roman Empire* (1986), Arther Ferrill argues that the fall of Rome was a military collapse.

In fact the Roman Empire of the West did fall. Not every aspect of the life of Roman subjects was changed by that, but the fall of Rome as a political entity was one of the major events of the history of Western man. It will simply not do to call that fall a myth or to ignore its historical significance merely by focusing on those aspects of Roman life that survived the fall in one form or another. At the opening of the fifth century a massive army, perhaps more than 200,000 strong, stood at the service of the Western emperor and his generals. The destruction of Roman military power in the fifth century was the obvious cause of the collapse of Roman government in the West.

C SECONDARY SOURCE

Finley Hooper

In this passage from his *Roman Realities* (1967), Hooper argues against the idea of a "fall."

The year was 476. For those who demand to know the date Rome fell, that is it. Others will realize that the fall of Rome was not an event but a process. Or, to put it another way, there was no fall at all—ancient Roman civilization simply became something else, which is called medieval. [It evolved into another civilization, the civilization of the Middle Ages.]

D PRIMARY SOURCE

St. Jerome

This early Church leader did not live to see the empire's end, but he vividly describes his feelings after a major event in Rome's decline—the attack and plunder of the city by Visigoths in 410.

It is the end of the world . . . Words fail me. My sobs break in . . . The city which took captive the whole world has itself been captured.

Document-Based QUESTIONS

1. Compare the reasons for the fall of Rome given in Sources A and B. How might they be considered similar?
2. What became of Rome according to Source C? Do you agree or disagree with that conclusion?
3. Source D is different from the other sources. How?

5

Rome and the Roots of Western Civilization

CONNECT TO THE NEW YORK STATE CORE CURRICULUM

Unit 1.D.2.c. Contributions
Unit 1.D.2.b. Factors leading to growth (engineering, empire building, trade)

TERMS & NAMES

- Greco-Roman culture
- Pompeii
- Virgil
- Tacitus
- aqueduct

SETTING THE STAGE Romans borrowed and adapted cultural elements freely, especially from the Greek and Hellenistic cultures. However, the Romans created a great civilization in their own right, whose art and architecture, language and literature, engineering, and law became its legacy to the world.

TAKING NOTES
Summarizing Use a chart to list the accomplishments of Roman civilization.

Fine Arts	Literature
Law	Engineering

The Legacy of Greco-Roman Civilization

Under the Roman Empire, hundreds of territories were knitted into a single state. Each Roman province and city was governed in the same way. The Romans were proud of their unique ability to rule, but they acknowledged Greek leadership in the fields of art, architecture, literature, and philosophy.

By the second century B.C., Romans had conquered Greece and had come to greatly admire Greek culture. Educated Romans learned the Greek language. As Horace, a Roman poet, said, "Greece, once overcome, overcame her wild conqueror." The mixing of elements of Greek, Hellenistic, and Roman culture produced a new culture, called **Greco-Roman culture**. This is also often called classical civilization.

Roman artists, philosophers, and writers did not merely copy their Greek and Hellenistic models. They adapted them for their own purposes and created a style of their own. Roman art and literature came to convey the Roman ideals of strength, permanence, and solidity.

Roman Fine Arts Romans learned the art of sculpture from the Greeks. However, while the Greeks were known for the beauty and idealization of their sculpture, Roman sculptors created realistic portraits in stone. Much Roman art was practical in purpose, intended for public education.

The reign of Augustus was a period of great artistic achievement. At that time the Romans further developed a type of sculpture called bas-relief. In bas-relief, or low-relief, images project from a flat background. Roman sculptors used bas-relief to tell stories and to represent crowds of people, soldiers in battle, and landscapes.

Roman artists also were particularly skilled in creating mosaics. Mosaics were pictures or designs made by setting small pieces of stone, glass, or tile onto a surface. Most Roman villas, the country houses of the wealthy, had at least one colorful mosaic. (See the Social History feature on pages 166–167.)

In addition, Romans excelled at the art of painting. Most wealthy Romans had bright, large murals, called frescoes, painted directly on their walls. Few have survived. The best examples of Roman painting are found in the Roman town of **Pompeii** and date from as early as the second century B.C. In A.D. 79, nearby Mount Vesuvius erupted, covering Pompeii in a thick layer of ash and killing about 2,000 residents. The ash acted to preserve many buildings and works of art.

Learning and Literature Romans borrowed much of their philosophy from the Greeks. Stoicism, the philosophy of the Greek teacher Zeno, was especially influential. Stoicism encouraged virtue, duty, moderation, and endurance.

In literature, as in philosophy, the Romans found inspiration in the works of their Greek neighbors. While often following Greek forms and models, Roman writers promoted their own themes and ideas. The poet **Virgil** spent ten years writing the most famous work of Latin literature, the *Aeneid* (ih•NEE•ihd), the epic of the legendary Aeneas. Virgil modeled the *Aeneid*, written in praise of Rome and Roman virtues, after the Greek epics of Homer. Here he speaks of government as being Rome's most important contribution to civilization:

PRIMARY SOURCE

Romans, never forget that government is your medium! Be this your art:—to practice men in habit of peace, Generosity to the conquered, and firmness against aggressors.

VIRGIL, *Aeneid*

While Virgil's writing carries all the weight and seriousness of the Roman character, the poet Ovid wrote light, witty poetry for enjoyment. In *Amores,* Ovid relates that he can only compose when he is in love: "When I was from Cupid's passions free, my Muse was mute and wrote no elegy."

Global Patterns

The Epic

While many know the epics of Virgil and the Greek poet Homer, other cultures throughout history have created their own narrative poems about heroic figures. India's *Mahabharata* tells the story of a battle for control of a mighty kingdom, while the Spanish epic *El Cid* celebrates a hero of the wars against the Moors. And while it is not a poem, *The Lord of the Rings,* the fantasy trilogy by English writer J.R.R. Tolkien, is considered to contain many aspects of the epic.

Most epics follow a pattern derived from the works of Homer. However, the emergence of epics around the world was not so much the result of one writer but the common desire among civilizations to promote their values and ideals through stories.

▶ Depictions of scenes from *The Lord of the Rings* (left), *El Cid* (top right), and *Mahabharata* (bottom right)

Analyzing Key Concepts

Western Civilization

Western civilization is generally seen as the heritage of ideas that spread to Europe and America from ancient Greece and Rome. Some historians observe, however, that Western civilization does not belong to any particular place—that it is the result of cultures coming together, interacting, and changing. Still, the legacy of Greece and Rome can be seen today.

The diagram below shows how ancient Greek and Roman ideas of government, philosophy, and literature can be traced across time. As with many cultural interactions, the links between the examples are not necessarily direct. Instead, the chart traces the evolution of an idea or theme over time.

Influence of Greek and Roman Ideas

Government	Philosophy	Literature
509 B.C. Rome developed a form of representative government.	**300s B.C.** Aristotle developed his philosophical theories.	**ABOUT 800 B.C.** Homer wrote the *Odyssey*.
400s B.C. Greece implemented a direct democracy.	**A.D. 1200s** Thomas Aquinas attempted to prove the existence of a single god using Aristotelian ideas.	**19 B.C.** Virgil used the *Odyssey* to guide his *Aeneid*.
1600s England became a constitutional monarchy.	**1781** Philosopher Immanuel Kant wrote that Aristotle's theories on logic were still valid.	**1922** James Joyce patterned his epic, *Ulysses*, after Homer's work.
1776 The United States declared independence from England and began building the republican democracy we know today.	**Present** Scholars still hold conferences focusing on questions Aristotle raised.	**2000** The Coen brothers' film *O Brother, Where Art Thou?* brought a very different adaptation of the *Odyssey* to the big screen.

INTEGRATED TECHNOLOGY

RESEARCH LINKS For more on Western civilization, go to **classzone.com**

DATA FILE

DEMOCRACY

- Theoretically, 40,000 people could attend the Greek Assembly—in practice, about 6,000 people attended.
- In 1215, King John of England granted the Magna Carta, which largely influenced subsequent democratic thought.
- In the 1970s, there were 40 democratic governments worldwide.
- In 2002, over 120 established and emerging democracies met to discuss their common issues.

Current Forms of World Governments

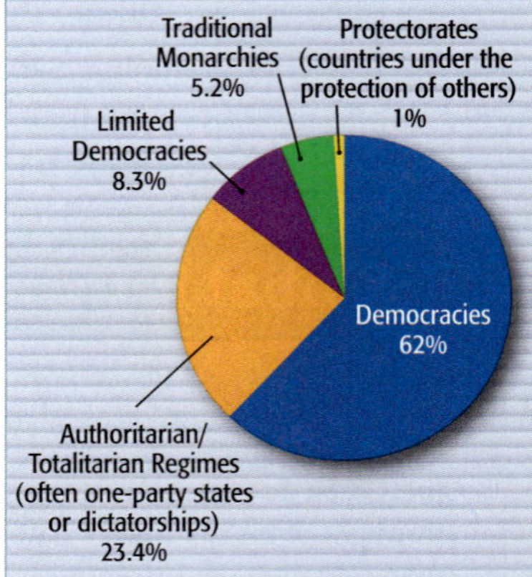

Source: adapted from *Democracy's Century*, Freedom House online (2003)

Connect *to* Today

1. **Hypothesizing** Why do you think ancient Greek and Roman cultures have had such a lasting influence on Western civilization?

   See Skillbuilder Handbook, page R15.

2. **Comparing and Contrasting** From what you know of ancient Greece and Rome, what is another element of either culture that can still be seen today? Provide an example.

▲ This Roman aqueduct in modern France has survived the centuries. The cross section indicates how the water moved within the aqueduct.

The Romans also wrote excellent prose, especially history. Livy compiled a multivolume history of Rome from its origins to 9 B.C. He used legends freely, creating more of a national myth of Rome than a true history. **Tacitus** (TAS•ih•tuhs), another Roman historian, is notable among ancient historians because he presented the facts accurately. He also was concerned about the Romans' lack of morality. In his *Annals* and *Histories*, he wrote about the good and bad of imperial Rome.

Here, Tacitus shows his disgust with the actions of the Emperor Nero, who many consider to be one of Rome's cruelest rulers.

PRIMARY SOURCE

While Nero was frequently visiting the show, even amid his pleasures there was no cessation to his crimes. For during the very same period Torquatus Silanus was forced to die, because over and above his illustrious rank as one of the Junian family he claimed to be the great grandson of Augustus. Accusers were ordered to charge him with prodigality [wastefulness] in lavishing gifts, and with having no hope but in revolution. . . . Then the most intimate of his freedmen were put in chains and torn from him, till, knowing the doom which impended, Torquatus divided the arteries in his arms. A speech from Nero followed, as usual, which stated that though he was guilty and with good reason distrusted his defense, he would have lived, had he awaited the clemency of the judge.

TACITUS, *Annals*

The Legacy of Rome

The presence of Rome is still felt daily in the languages, the institutions, and the thought of the Western world.

The Latin Language Latin, the language of the Romans, remained the language of learning in the West long after the fall of Rome. It was the official language of the Roman Catholic Church into the 20th century.

Latin was adopted by different peoples and developed into French, Spanish, Portuguese, Italian, and Romanian. These languages are called Romance languages because of their common Roman heritage. Latin also influenced other languages. For example, more than half the words in English have a basis in Latin. (A)

MAIN IDEA
Clarifying
(A) What impact did the Romans have on our English language?

Master Builders Visitors from all over the empire marveled at the architecture of Rome. The arch, the dome, and concrete were combined to build spectacular structures, such as the Colosseum.

Arches also supported bridges and **aqueducts**. Aqueducts were designed by Roman engineers to bring water into cities and towns. When the water channel spanned a river or ravine, the aqueduct was lifted high up on arches.

INTERACTIVE

The Colosseum

The Colosseum was one of the greatest feats of Roman engineering and a model for the ages. The name comes from the Latin word *colossus*, meaning "gigantic." Its construction was started by the Emperor Vespasian and was completed by his sons, emperors Titus and Domitian. For centuries after its opening in A.D. 80, spectators, both rich and poor, cheered a variety of free, bloody spectacles—from gladiator fights to animal hunts.

▲ The Colosseum in Rome as it appears today

INTEGRATED TECHNOLOGY

RESEARCH LINKS For more information on the Colosseum, go to **classzone.com**

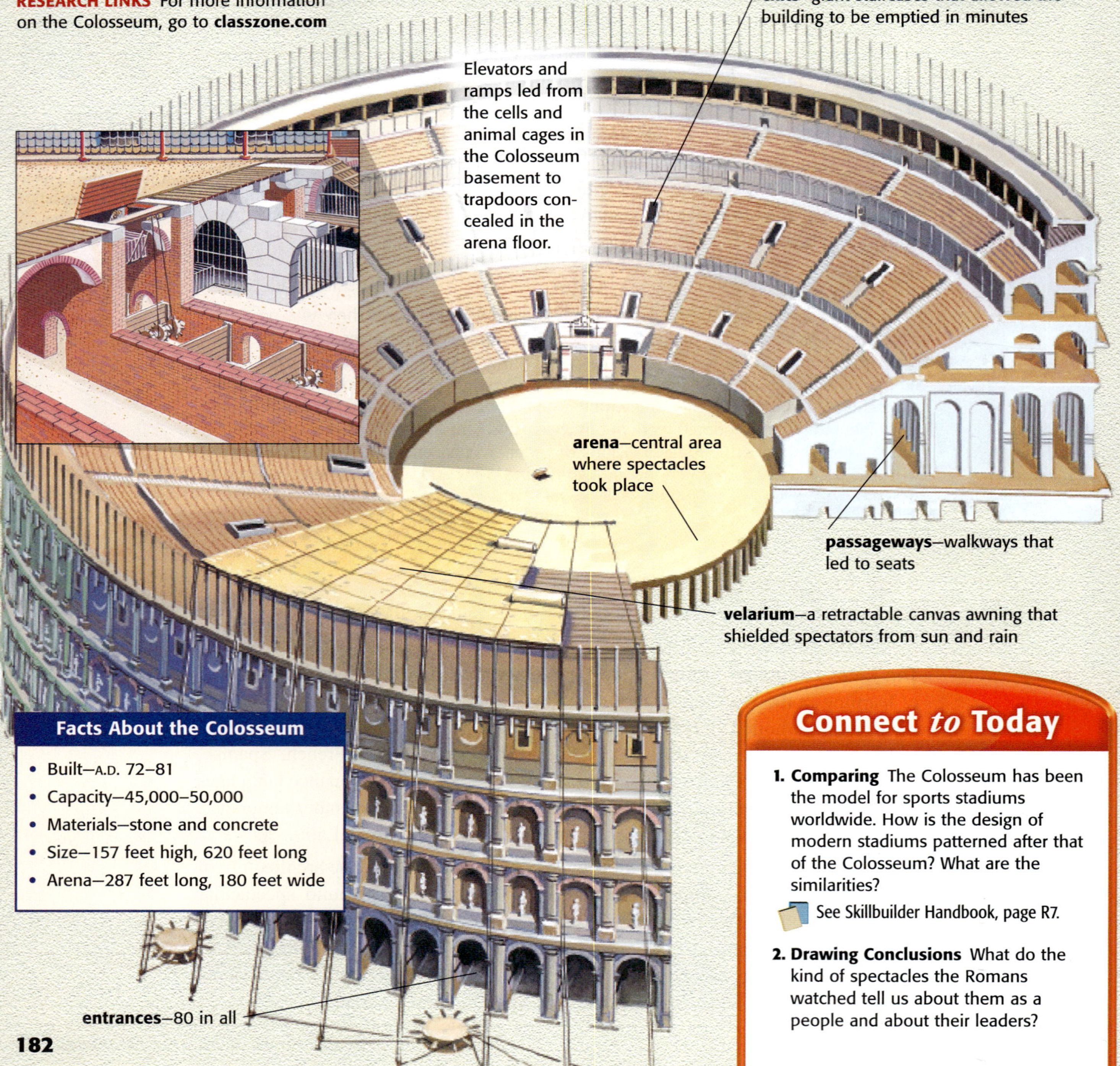

Facts About the Colosseum

- Built—A.D. 72–81
- Capacity—45,000–50,000
- Materials—stone and concrete
- Size—157 feet high, 620 feet long
- Arena—287 feet long, 180 feet wide

Connect *to* Today

1. **Comparing** The Colosseum has been the model for sports stadiums worldwide. How is the design of modern stadiums patterned after that of the Colosseum? What are the similarities?

   See Skillbuilder Handbook, page R7.

2. **Drawing Conclusions** What do the kind of spectacles the Romans watched tell us about them as a people and about their leaders?

Because Roman architectural forms were so practical, they have remained popular. Thomas Jefferson began a Roman revival in the United States in the 18th century. Many large public buildings, such as the U.S. Capitol and numerous state capitols, include Roman features.

Roman roads were also technological marvels. The army built a vast network of roads constructed of stone, concrete, and sand that connected Rome to all parts of the empire. Many lasted into the Middle Ages; some are still used.

Roman System of Law Rome's most lasting and widespread contribution was its law. Early Roman law dealt mostly with strengthening the rights of Roman citizens. As the empire grew, however, the Romans came to believe that laws should be fair and apply equally to all people, rich and poor. Slowly, judges began to recognize certain standards of justice. These standards were influenced largely by the teachings of Stoic philosophers and were based on common sense and practical ideas. Some of the most important principles of Roman law were:

- All persons had the right to equal treatment under the law.
- A person was considered innocent until proven guilty.
- The burden of proof rested with the accuser rather than the accused.
- A person should be punished only for actions, not thoughts.
- Any law that seemed unreasonable or grossly unfair could be set aside.

The principles of Roman law endured to form the basis of legal systems in many European countries and of places influenced by Europe, including the United States of America. **B**

MAIN IDEA

Analyzing Issues

B How did Roman law protect those accused of crimes?

Rome's Enduring Influence By preserving and adding to Greek civilization, Rome strengthened the Western cultural tradition. The world would be a very different place had Rome not existed. Historian R. H. Barrow has stated that Rome never fell because it turned into something even greater—an idea—and achieved immortality.

As mighty as the Roman Empire had been, however, it was not the only great civilization of its time. Around the same period that Rome was developing its enduring culture, different but equally complex empires were emerging farther east. In India, the Mauryan and Gupta empires dominated the land, while the Han Empire ruled over China.

NEW YORK CORE CURRICULUM REVIEW

TERMS & NAMES 1. For each term or name, write a sentence explaining its significance.

- Greco-Roman culture
- Pompeii
- Virgil
- Tacitus
- aqueduct

USING YOUR NOTES

2. Which accomplishment do you consider most important? Why?

Fine Arts	Literature
Law	Engineering

MAIN IDEAS

3. What is Greco-Roman culture?
4. In what way did Roman art differ from Greek art?
5. What influence did Latin have on the development of Western languages?

CRITICAL THINKING & WRITING

6. **DRAWING CONCLUSIONS** Which principle of law do you think has been Rome's greatest contribution to modern legal systems?
7. **FORMING AND SUPPORTING OPINIONS** Do you agree with Horace's claim on page 178 that when it came to culture, Greece in essence conquered Rome? Explain.
8. **HYPOTHESIZING** Describe how the world might be different if Rome had not existed.
9. **WRITING ACTIVITY** POWER AND AUTHORITY Imagine you are a historian. Write an **expository essay** describing the importance of Rome's legacy.

CONNECT TO TODAY **PRESENTING A REPORT**

Locate several Latin phrases still in use today. Use the necessary materials to help translate those phrases, and then explain in a brief **report** the meaning and intent of those phrases.

Chapter 6 Assessment

VISUAL SUMMARY

Ancient Rome and Early Christianity

Early Rome

1000 B.C. Latins enter region
753 B.C. Rome founded

Roman Republic

509 B.C. Republic created
451 B.C. Twelve Tables written
405–265 B.C. Italy conquered
264–146 B.C. Punic Wars fought
44 B.C. Julius Caesar assassinated

Roman Empire

27 B.C. Empire and *Pax Romana* begin with reign of Augustus
A.D. 29 Jesus crucified
A.D. 64 Christian persecution begins
A.D. 79 Pompeii destroyed
A.D. 180 *Pax Romana* ends
A.D. 253 Germanic tribes enter frontier regions
A.D. 285 Diocletian divides empire into East and West
A.D. 313 Christianity given recognition
A.D. 324 Constantine reunites empire
A.D. 370 Huns invade frontier
A.D. 380 Christianity made official religion
A.D. 395 Empire permanently split
A.D. 476 Last emperor deposed

TERMS & NAMES

For each term below, briefly explain its connection to ancient Rome or the rise of Christianity.

1. republic
2. senate
3. Julius Caesar
4. Augustus
5. Jesus
6. Constantine
7. inflation
8. Greco-Roman culture

MAIN IDEAS

The Roman Republic Section 1 (pages 155–159)

9. Name the three main parts of government under the Roman republic.
10. How did Rome treat different sections of its conquered territory?

The Roman Empire Section 2 (pages 160–167)

11. How did Augustus change Roman government?
12. How did Rome's population fare during the golden age of the *Pax Romana*?

The Rise of Christianity Section 3 (pages 168–172)

13. How did the apostle Paul encourage the spread of Christianity?
14. Why did the Roman emperors persecute Christians?

The Fall of the Roman Empire Section 4 (pages 173–177)

15. What was the most significant reform that the Emperor Diocletian made?
16. How did the Western Roman Empire fall?

Rome and the Roots of Western Civilization
Section 5 (pages 178–183)

17. Why did so much of Roman culture have a Greek flavor?
18. What aspects of Roman culture influenced future civilizations?

CRITICAL THINKING

1. USING YOUR NOTES
In a diagram, compare the Roman Republic with the Roman Empire when both were at the peak of their power.

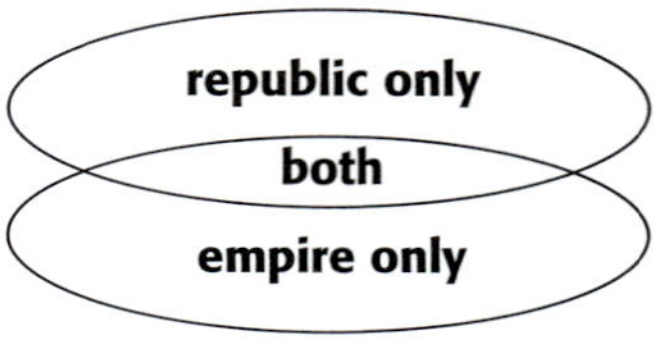

2. ANALYZING ISSUES
RELIGIOUS AND ETHICAL SYSTEMS What type of person do you think became a martyr? Consider the personal characteristics of individuals who refused to renounce their faith even in the face of death.

3. EVALUATING DECISIONS AND COURSES OF ACTION
POWER AND AUTHORITY What do you think of Diocletian's decision to divide the Roman Empire into two parts? Was it wise? Consider Diocletian's possible motives and the results of his actions.

4. CLARIFYING
EMPIRE BUILDING Explain more fully what the historian R. H. Barrow meant when he said on page 183 that Rome never really fell but instead achieved immortality.

NEW YORK STATE REGENTS EXAM PRACTICE

Use the quotation and your knowledge of world history to answer questions 1 and 2.
Additional Test Practice, pp. S1–S33

PRIMARY SOURCE

Whereas the divine providence that guides our life has displayed its zeal and benevolence by ordaining for our life the most perfect good, bringing to us Augustus, whom it has filled with virtue for the benefit of mankind, employing him as a saviour for us and our descendants, him who has put an end to wars and adorned peace; . . . and the birthday of the god [Augustus] is the beginning of all the good tidings brought by him to the world.

Decree from the Roman Province of Asia

1 Based on the passage, the author of the decree
(1) greatly approved of the rule of Augustus
(2) feared the amount of power Augustus had
(3) considered Augustus's birthday a national holiday
(4) thought Augustus should grant Asia its independence

2 During which period in Roman history was this passage most likely written?
(1) the Punic Wars
(2) the *Pax Romana*
(3) the founding of the republic
(4) the fall of the Western Empire

Use this scene depicted on a Roman monument to answer question 3.

3 What aspect of society does the image show the Romans celebrating?
(1) education
(2) commerce
(3) government
(4) military strength

INTEGRATED TECHNOLOGY

TEST PRACTICE Go to **classzone.com**
- Diagnostic tests
- Tutorials
- Strategies
- Additional practice

ALTERNATIVE ASSESSMENT

1. Interact *with* History

On page 154, you considered the qualities that made a successful leader before knowing what the Romans thought about leadership. Now that you have read the chapter, reevaluate your decision. What qualities were needed for Roman leaders to be effective? What qualities hindered their success? How would you rate the overall leadership of the Roman Empire? Discuss your opinions in small groups.

2. WRITING ABOUT HISTORY

Study the information about Rome's impact on the development of Western civilization in the Key Concepts feature on Western Civilization on page 180. Write an **essay** of several paragraphs summarizing the empire's impact on the Western world that developed after it. Provide the following:
- how the empire influenced later governments
- what influence the empire had on philosophy
- what impact the empire had on literature
- why you think Roman culture has been so enduring

INTEGRATED TECHNOLOGY

Creating a Virtual Field Trip

Plan a two-week virtual trip through the Roman Empire. After selecting and researching the sites you'd like to visit, use the historical maps from this chapter and contemporary maps of the region to determine your itinerary. Consider visiting the following places: Rome, Carthage, Pompeii, Hadrian's Wall, the Appian Way, Bath, Lepcis Magna, Horace's Villa, the Pont du Gard, and the Roman theater at Orange. You may want to include the following:
- maps of the Roman Empire
- pictures of the major sites on the field trip
- audio clips describing the sites or events that took place there
- reasons each site is an important destination

CHAPTER 7

India and China Establish Empires, 400 B.C.–A.D. 550

Previewing Main Ideas

POWER AND AUTHORITY In both India and China in the 200s B.C., military leaders seized power and used their authority to strengthen the government.

Geography *Study the map. What geographic factors might have made further expansion difficult for both empires?*

CULTURAL INTERACTION From the time of the Aryan nomads, Indian civilization was a product of interacting cultures. In China, the government pressured conquered people to adopt Chinese culture.

Geography *What geographic feature was the main connection between the empires of India and China?*

RELIGIOUS AND ETHICAL SYSTEMS Hinduism and Buddhism were India's main religions by 250 B.C. The ethical teachings of Confucius played an important role in Chinese life. Buddhism also took root in China.

Geography *What dates on the time line are associated with religious changes in China and India?*

NEW YORK CORE CURRICULUM FOCUS

- India experienced great achievement in science, the arts, and religious thought during the Gupta Empire.
- The Han Dynasty in China created a strong centralized government.

INTEGRATED TECHNOLOGY

eEdition
- Interactive Maps
- Interactive Visuals
- Interactive Primary Sources

VIDEO *Patterns of Interaction: Silk Roads and the Pacific Rim*

INTERNET RESOURCES

Go to **classzone.com** for:
- Research Links
- Internet Activities
- Primary Sources
- Chapter Quiz
- Maps
- Test Practice
- Current Events

INDIA AND CHINA

321 B.C. Chandragupta Maurya founds Mauryan Empire.

202 B.C. Liu Bang establishes China's Han Dynasty. (Han Dynasty bronze horse) ▶

400 B.C. — **200 B.C.**

WORLD

264 B.C. Punic wars between Rome and Carthage begin.

200 B.C. Nazca culture emerges in Peru.

A.D. 65 Buddhism takes root in China. ▶

A.D. 105 Chinese invent paper.

A.D. 220 Han Dynasty falls.

A.D. 320 Gupta Empire forms in India and encourages a renewal of Hindu faith. (Hindu god Shiva) ▶

A.D. 200 A.D. 400 A.D. 500

A.D. 29 Jesus is crucified in Jerusalem.

A.D. 100 Bantu speakers begin massive migrations throughout Africa. (Bantu mask) ▶

A.D. 476 Western Roman Empire falls.

Interact *with* History

Would you spy for your government?

You are a merchant selling cloth out of your shop when a stranger enters. You fear it is one of the emperor's inspectors, coming to check the quality of your cloth. The man eyes you sternly and then, in a whisper, asks if you will spy on other weavers. You would be paid four years' earnings. But you might have to turn in a friend if you suspect he is not paying enough taxes to the government.

1. This person comments to his friend on something he sees in the street.
2. This soldier's job is to check that everyone pays taxes. He seems suspicious of the man carrying bananas.
3. This man, who stands behind a wall watching, may be a spy.

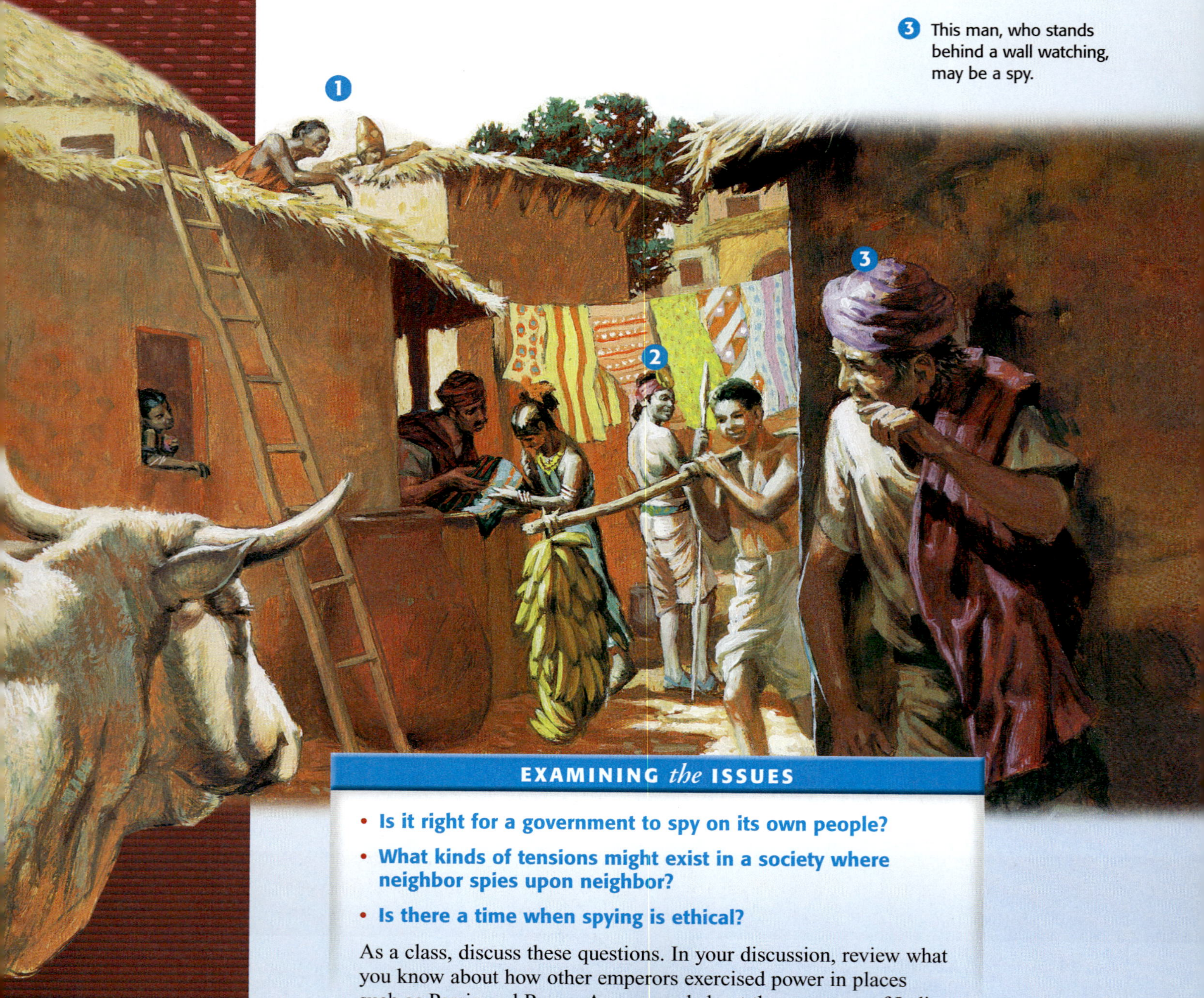

EXAMINING *the* ISSUES

- **Is it right for a government to spy on its own people?**
- **What kinds of tensions might exist in a society where neighbor spies upon neighbor?**
- **Is there a time when spying is ethical?**

As a class, discuss these questions. In your discussion, review what you know about how other emperors exercised power in places such as Persia and Rome. As you read about the emperors of India and China, notice how they try to control their subjects' lives.

India's First Empires

CONNECT TO THE NEW YORK STATE CORE CURRICULUM

Unit 1.C.4.b. Contributions–government system
Unit 2.A.4. Organizational structure

TERMS & NAMES

- Mauryan Empire
- Asoka
- religious toleration
- Tamil
- Gupta Empire
- patriarchal
- matriarchal

SETTING THE STAGE By 600 B.C., almost 1,000 years after the Aryan migrations, many small kingdoms were scattered throughout India. In 326 B.C., Alexander the Great brought the Indus Valley in the northwest under Macedonian control—but left almost immediately. Soon after, a great Indian military leader, Chandragupta Maurya (chuhn•druh•GUP•tuh-MAH•oor•yuh), seized power.

The Mauryan Empire Is Established

Chandragupta Maurya may have been born in the powerful kingdom of Magadha. Centered on the lower Ganges River, the kingdom was ruled by the Nanda family. Chandragupta gathered an army, killed the unpopular Nanda king, and in about 321 B.C. claimed the throne. This began the **Mauryan Empire**.

TAKING NOTES

Comparing Use a chart to compare the Mauryan and Gupta empires.

Mauryan	Gupta
1.	1.
2	2
3	3

Chandragupta Maurya Unifies North India Chandragupta moved northwest, seizing all the land from Magadha to the Indus. Around 305 B.C., Chandragupta began to battle Seleucus I, one of Alexander the Great's generals. Seleucus had inherited part of Alexander's empire. He wanted to reestablish Macedonian control over the Indus Valley. After several years of fighting, however, Chandragupta defeated Seleucus. By 303 B.C., the Mauryan Empire stretched more than 2,000 miles, uniting north India politically for the first time. (See map on page 191.)

To win his wars of conquest, Chandragupta raised a vast army: 600,000 soldiers on foot, 30,000 soldiers on horseback, and 9,000 elephants. To clothe, feed, and pay these troops, the government levied high taxes. For example, farmers had to pay up to one-half the value of their crops to the king.

Running the Empire Chandragupta relied on an adviser named Kautilya (kow•TIHL•yuh), a member of the priestly caste. Kautilya wrote a ruler's handbook called the *Arthasastra* (AHR•thuh• SHAHS•truh). This book proposed tough-minded policies to hold an empire together, including spying on the people and employing political assassination. Following Kautilya's advice, Chandragupta created a highly bureaucratic government. He divided the empire into four provinces, each headed by a royal prince. Each province was then divided into local districts, whose officials assessed taxes and enforced the law.

Life in the City and the Country Eager to stay at peace with the Indian emperor, Seleucus sent an ambassador, Megasthenes (muh•GAS•thuh•neez), to

Chandragupta's capital. Megasthenes wrote glowing descriptions of Chandragupta's palace, with its gold-covered pillars, many fountains, and imposing thrones. The capital city featured beautiful parks and bustling markets. Megasthenes also described the countryside and how farmers lived:

▲ This pillar, on which Asoka's edicts are written, is located at Vaishali.

PRIMARY SOURCE Ⓐ

[Farmers] are exempted from military service and cultivate their lands undisturbed by fear. They do not go to cities, either on business or to take part in their tumults. It therefore frequently happens that at the same time, and in the same part of the country, men may be seen marshaled for battle and risking their lives against the enemy, while other men are ploughing or digging in perfect security under the protection of these soldiers.

MEGASTHENES, in *Geography* by Strabo

MAIN IDEA

Analyzing Primary Sources

Ⓐ What information in this quotation indicates that Mauryan India valued agriculture?

In 301 B.C., Chandragupta's son assumed the throne. He ruled for 32 years. Then Chandragupta's grandson, **Asoka** (uh•SOH•kuh), brought the Mauryan Empire to its greatest heights.

Asoka Promotes Buddhism Asoka became king of the Mauryan Empire in 269 B.C. At first, he followed in Chandragupta's footsteps, waging war to expand his empire. During a bloody war against the neighboring state of Kalinga, 100,000 soldiers were slain, and even more civilians perished.

Although victorious, Asoka felt sorrow over the slaughter at Kalinga. As a result, he studied Buddhism and decided to rule by the Buddha's teaching of "peace to all beings." Throughout the empire, Asoka erected huge stone pillars inscribed with his new policies. Some edicts guaranteed that Asoka would treat his subjects fairly and humanely. Others preached nonviolence. Still others urged **religious toleration**—acceptance of people who held different religious beliefs.

Vocabulary
Edicts are official, public announcements of policy.

Asoka had extensive roads built so that he could visit the far corners of India. He also improved conditions along these roads to make travel easier for his

History Makers

Chandragupta Maurya
?–298 B.C.

Chandragupta feared being assassinated—maybe because he had killed a king to get his throne. To avoid being poisoned, he made servants taste all his food. To avoid being murdered in bed, he slept in a different room every night.

Although Chandragupta was a fierce warrior, in 301 B.C., he gave up his throne and converted to Jainism. Jains taught nonviolence and respect for all life. With a group of monks, Chandragupta traveled to southern India. There he followed the Jainist custom of fasting until he starved to death.

▲ This grouping of Asoka's lions is used as a symbol of India.

Asoka
?–232 B.C.

One of Asoka's edicts states,

> *If one hundredth part or one thousandth of those who died in Kalinga . . . should now suffer similar fate, [that] would be a matter of pain to His Majesty.*

Even though Asoka wanted to be a loving, peaceful ruler, he had to control a huge empire. He had to balance Kautilya's methods of keeping power and Buddha's urgings to be unselfish.

Asoka softened Chandragupta's harsher policies. Instead of spies, he employed officials to look out for his subjects' welfare. He kept his army but sought to rule humanely. In addition, Asoka sent missionaries to Southeast Asia to spread Buddhism.

INTEGRATED TECHNOLOGY

RESEARCH LINKS For more on Chandragupta Maurya and Asoka, go to **classzone.com**

officials and to improve communication in the vast empire. For example, every nine miles he had wells dug and rest houses built. This allowed travelers to stop and refresh themselves. Such actions demonstrated Asoka's concern for his subjects' well-being. Noble as his policies of toleration and nonviolence were, they failed to hold the empire together after Asoka died in 232 B.C. **B**

MAIN IDEA

Clarifying

B Which of Asoka's actions show the influence of Buddha's teaching of "peace to all beings"?

A Period of Turmoil

Asoka's death left a power vacuum. In northern and central India, regional kings challenged the imperial government. The kingdoms of central India, which had only been loosely held in the Mauryan Empire, soon regained their independence. The Andhra (AHN•druh) Dynasty arose and dominated the region for hundreds of years. Because of their central position, the Andhras profited from the extensive trade between north and south India and also with Rome, Sri Lanka, and Southeast Asia.

At the same time, northern India had to absorb a flood of new people fleeing political instability in other parts of Asia. For 500 years, beginning about 185 B.C., wave after wave of Greeks, Persians, and Central Asians poured into northern India. These invaders disrupted Indian society. But they also introduced new languages and customs that added to the already-rich blend of Indian culture.

Southern India also experienced turmoil. It was home to three kingdoms that had never been conquered by the Mauryans. The people who lived in this region spoke the **Tamil** (TAM•uhl) language and are called the Tamil people. These three kingdoms often were at war with one another and with other states.

GEOGRAPHY SKILLBUILDER: Interpreting Maps

1. **Region** *Compare the region occupied by the Gupta Empire to that occupied by the Mauryan Empire. Discuss size, location, and physical characteristics.*
2. **Place** *Why did neither the Mauryan nor the Gupta Empire expand to the northeast?*

The Gupta Empire Is Established

After 500 years of invasion and turmoil, a strong leader again arose in the northern state of Magadha. His name was Chandra Gupta (GUP•tuh), but he was no relation to India's first emperor, Chandragupta Maurya. India's second empire, the **Gupta Empire**, oversaw a great flowering of Indian civilization, especially Hindu culture.

Chandra Gupta Builds an Empire The first Gupta emperor came to power not through battle but by marrying a daughter of an influential royal family. After his marriage, Chandra Gupta I took the title "Great King of Kings" in A.D. 320. His empire included Magadha and the area north of it, with his power base along the Ganges River. His son, Samudra (suh•MU•druh) Gupta, became king in A.D. 335. Although a lover of the arts, Samudra had a warlike side. He expanded the empire through 40 years of conquest.

▲ This terra-cotta tile, showing a musician playing a stringed instrument, is from a Hindu temple of the Gupta period.

Daily Life in India The Gupta era is the first period for which historians have much information about daily life in India. Most Indians lived in small villages. The majority were farmers, who walked daily from their homes to outlying fields. Craftspeople and merchants clustered in specific districts in the towns. They had shops on the street level and lived in the rooms above.

Most Indian families were **patriarchal**, headed by the eldest male. Parents, grandparents, uncles, aunts, and children all worked together to raise their crops. Because drought was common, farmers often had to irrigate their crops. There was a tax on water, and every month, people had to give a day's worth of labor to maintain wells, irrigation ditches, reservoirs, and dams. As in Mauryan times, farmers owed a large part of their earnings to the king.

Southern India followed a different cultural pattern. Some Tamil groups were **matriarchal**, headed by the mother rather than the father. Property, and sometimes the throne, was passed through the female line. C

MAIN IDEA

Contrasting

C How were the family systems of north and south India different?

Height of the Gupta Empire While village life followed unchanging traditional patterns, the royal court of the third Gupta emperor was a place of excitement and growth. Indians revered Chandra Gupta II for his heroic qualities. He defeated the Shakas—enemies to the west—and added their coastal territory to his empire. This allowed the Guptas to engage in profitable trade with the Mediterranean world. Chandra Gupta II also strengthened his empire through peaceful means by negotiating diplomatic and marriage alliances. He ruled from A.D. 375 to 415.

During the reign of the first three Guptas, India experienced a period of great achievement in the arts, religious thought, and science. These will be discussed in Section 2. After Chandra Gupta II died, new invaders threatened northern India. These fierce fighters, called the Hunas, were related to the Huns who invaded the Roman Empire. Over the next 100 years, the Gupta Empire broke into small kingdoms. Many were overrun by the Hunas or other Central Asian nomads. The Empire ended about 535.

NEW YORK CORE CURRICULUM REVIEW

TERMS & NAMES 1. For each term or name, write a sentence explaining its significance.

• Mauryan Empire • Asoka • religious toleration • Tamil • Gupta Empire • patriarchal • matriarchal

USING YOUR NOTES

2. Which similarity of the empires do you consider the most significant? Explain.

Mauryan	Gupta
1.	1.
2	2
3	3

MAIN IDEAS

3. Why was Asoka's first military campaign also his last campaign?
4. Who were the Tamil people?
5. What caused the fall of the Gupta Empire?

CRITICAL THINKING & WRITING

6. **SUPPORTING OPINIONS** Which Indian ruler described in this section would you rather live under? Explain.
7. **DRAWING CONCLUSIONS** What impact did the Greeks, Persians, and Central Asians have on Indian life between the Mauryan and Gupta empires?
8. **ANALYZING ISSUES** Which empire, Mauryan or Gupta, had a more significant impact on Indian history? Explain.
9. **WRITING ACTIVITY** POWER AND AUTHORITY For three of the rulers in this section, choose an object or image that symbolizes how that ruler exercised power. Write **captions** explaining why the symbols are appropriate.

CONNECT TO TODAY **CREATING A PIE GRAPH**

Use the Internet or library sources to create a **pie graph** showing the percentage of the population in India today that is Hindu, Buddhist, or a follower of other religions.

2

Trade Spreads Indian Religions and Culture

CONNECT TO THE NEW YORK STATE CORE CURRICULUM

Unit 1.E.2. Expansion of Christianity, Islam, Confucianism, and Buddhism
Unit 2.A.2. Artistic, scientific, and mathematical contributions

TERMS & NAMES

- Mahayana
- Theravada
- stupa
- Brahma
- Vishnu
- Shiva
- Kalidasa
- Silk Roads

SETTING THE STAGE The 500 years between the Mauryan and Gupta empires was a time of upheaval. Invaders poured into India, bringing new ideas and customs. In response, Indians began to change their own culture.

Buddhism and Hinduism Change

By 250 B.C., Hinduism and Buddhism were India's two main faiths. (See Chapter 3.) Hinduism is a complex polytheistic religion that blended Aryan beliefs with the many gods and cults of the diverse peoples who preceded them. Buddhism teaches that desire causes suffering and that humans should overcome desire by following the Eightfold Path. Over the centuries, both religions had become increasingly removed from the people. Hinduism became dominated by priests, while the Buddhist ideal of self-denial proved difficult for many to follow.

TAKING NOTES
Categorizing Use a chart to list one or more specific developments of Indian culture.

Religion	
Arts	
Science/ Math	
Trade	

A More Popular Form of Buddhism The Buddha had stressed that each person could reach a state of peace called nirvana. Nirvana was achieved by rejecting the sensory world and embracing spiritual discipline. After the Buddha died, his followers developed many different interpretations of his teachings.

Although the Buddha had forbidden people to worship him, some began to teach that he was a god. Some Buddhists also began to believe that many people could become Buddhas. These potential Buddhas, called bodhisattvas (BOH•dih•SUHT•vuhz), could choose to give up nirvana and work to save humanity through good works and self-sacrifice. The new ideas changed Buddhism from a religion that emphasized individual discipline to a mass religion that offered salvation to all and allowed popular worship.

By the first century A.D., Buddhists had divided over the new doctrines. Those who accepted them belonged to the **Mahayana** (MAH•huh•YAH•nuh) sect. Those who held to the Buddha's stricter, original teachings belonged to the **Theravada** (THEHR•uh•VAH•duh) sect. This is also called the Hinayana (HEE•nuh•YAH•nuh) sect, but Theravada is preferred.

These new trends in Buddhism inspired Indian art. For example, artists carved huge statues of the Buddha for people to worship. Wealthy Buddhist merchants who were eager to do good deeds paid for the construction of **stupas**—mounded stone structures built over holy relics. Buddhists walked the paths circling the stupas as a part of their meditation. Merchants also commissioned the carving of cave temples out of solid rock. Artists then adorned these temples with beautiful sculptures and paintings.

A Hindu Rebirth Like Buddhism, Hinduism had become remote from the people. By the time of the Mauryan Empire, Hinduism had developed a complex set of sacrifices that could be performed only by the priests. People who weren't priests had less and less direct connection with the religion.

Gradually, through exposure to other cultures and in response to the popularity of Buddhism, Hinduism changed. Although the religion continued to embrace hundreds of gods, a trend toward monotheism was growing. Many people began to believe that there was only one divine force in the universe. The various gods represented parts of that force. The three most important Hindu gods were **Brahma** (BRAH•muh), creator of the world; **Vishnu** (VIHSH•noo), preserver of the world; and **Shiva** (SHEE•vuh), destroyer of the world. Of the three, Vishnu and Shiva were by far the favorites. Many Indians began to devote themselves to these two gods. As Hinduism evolved into a more personal religion, its popular appeal grew. (A)

MAIN IDEA

Drawing Conclusions

(A) Why did the changes in Buddhism and Hinduism make these religions more popular?

▲ This Buddha is carved in the Gandharan artistic style, a blend of Greco-Roman and Indian styles.

Achievements of Indian Culture

Just as Hinduism and Buddhism underwent changes, so did Indian culture and learning. India entered a highly productive period in literature, art, science, and mathematics that continued until roughly A.D. 500.

Literature and the Performing Arts One of India's greatest writers was **Kalidasa** (KAH•lee•DAH•suh). He may have been the court poet for Chandra Gupta II. Kalidasa's most famous play is *Shakuntala.* It tells the story of a beautiful girl who falls in love with and marries a middle-aged king. After Shakuntala and her husband are separated, they suffer tragically because of a curse that prevents the king from recognizing his wife when they meet again. Generations of Indians have continued to admire Kalidasa's plays because they are skillfully written and emotionally stirring.

Southern India also has a rich literary tradition. In the second century A.D., the city of Madurai in southern India became a site of writing academies. More than 2,000 Tamil poems from this period still exist. In the following excerpt from a third-century poem, a young man describes his sweetheart cooking him a meal:

PRIMARY SOURCE

There dwells my sweetheart, curving and lovely,
languid of gaze, with big round earrings,
and little rings on her tiny fingers.
She has cut the leaves of the garden plantain
and split them in pieces down the stalk
to serve as platters for the meal.
Her eyes are filled with the smoke of cooking.
Her brow, as fair as the crescent moon,
is covered now with drops of sweat.
She wipes it away with the hem of her garment
and stands in the kitchen, and thinks of me.

ANONYMOUS TAMIL POET, quoted in *The Wonder That Was India*

In addition to literature, drama was very popular. In southern India, traveling troupes of actors put on performances in cities across the region. Women as well as men took part in these shows, which combined drama and dance. Many of the classical dance forms in India today are based on techniques explained in a book written between the first century B.C. and the first century A.D.

Connect *to* Today

Entertainment in India: Bollywood

Today, drama remains hugely popular in India. India has the largest movie industry in the world. About twice as many full-length feature films are released yearly in India as in the United States. India produces both popular and serious films. Indian popular films, such as *Monsoon Wedding,* are often love stories that blend music, dance, and drama. India's serious films have received worldwide critical praise. In 1992, the Indian director Satyajit Ray received a lifetime-achievement Academy Award for making artistic films. His films brought Indian culture to a global audience.

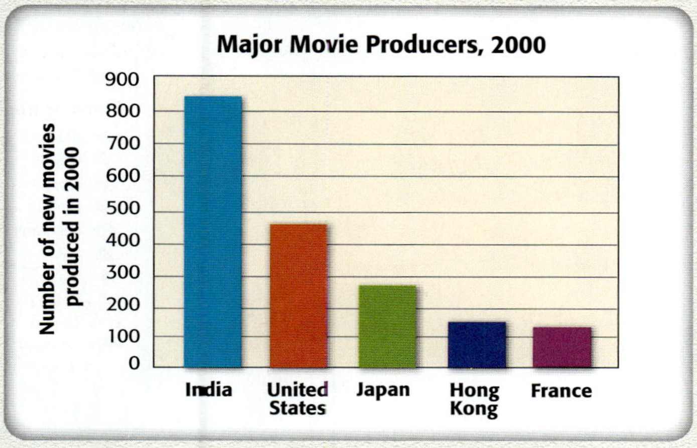

Source: *Focus 2002: World Film Market Trends*

Astronomy, Mathematics, and Medicine The expansion of trade spurred the advance of science. Because sailors on trading ships used the stars to help them figure their position at sea, knowledge of astronomy increased. From Greek invaders, Indians adapted Western methods of keeping time. They began to use a calendar based on the cycles of the sun rather than the moon. They also adopted a seven-day week and divided each day into hours.

During the Gupta Empire (A.D. 320 to about 500), knowledge of astronomy increased further. Almost 1,000 years before Columbus, Indian astronomers proved that the earth was round by observing a lunar eclipse. During the eclipse, the earth's shadow fell across the face of the moon. The astronomers noted that the earth's shadow was curved, indicating that the earth itself was round.

Indian mathematics was among the most advanced in the world. Modern numerals, the zero, and the decimal system were invented in India. Around A.D. 500, an Indian named Aryabhata (AHR•yuh•BUHT•uh) calculated the value of pi (π) to four decimal places. He also calculated the length of the solar year as 365.3586805 days. This is very close to modern calculations made with an atomic clock. In medicine, two important medical guides were compiled. They described more than 1,000 diseases and more than 500 medicinal plants. Hindu physicians performed surgery—including plastic surgery—and possibly gave injections. **B**

MAIN IDEA

Drawing Conclusions

B What achievements by Indian mathematicians are used today?

The Spread of Indian Trade

In addition to knowledge, India has always been rich in precious resources. Spices, diamonds, sapphires, gold, pearls, and beautiful woods—including ebony, teak, and fragrant sandalwood—have been valuable items of exchange. Trade between

Asian Trade Routes, A.D. 400

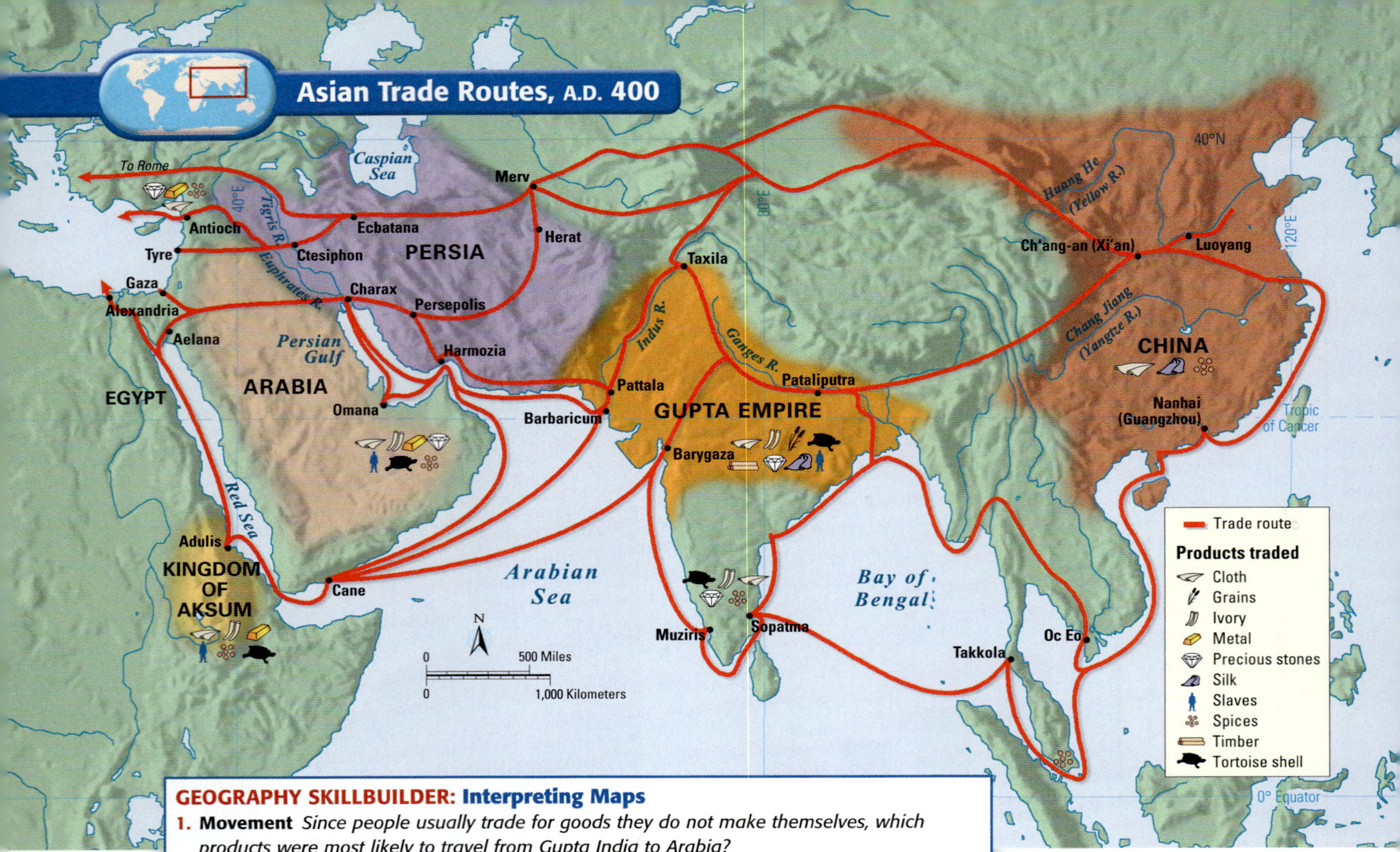

GEOGRAPHY SKILLBUILDER: Interpreting Maps

1. **Movement** *Since people usually trade for goods they do not make themselves, which products were most likely to travel from Gupta India to Arabia?*
2. **Movement** *How far did trade goods travel to get from Luoyang in China to Alexandria in Egypt?*

India and regions as distant as Africa and Sumeria began more than 4,000 years ago. Trade expanded even after the Mauryan Empire ended around 185 B.C.

Overland Trade, East and West Groups who invaded India after Mauryan rule ended helped to expand India's trade to new regions. For example, Central Asian nomads told Indians about a vast network of caravan routes known as Silk Roads. These routes were called the **Silk Roads** because traders used them to bring silk from China to western Asia and then on to Rome.

Once Indians learned of the Silk Roads, they realized that they could make great profits by acting as middlemen. Middlemen are go-betweens in business transactions. For example, Indian traders would buy Chinese goods and sell them to traders traveling to Rome. To aid their role as middlemen, Indians built trading stations along the Silk Roads. They were located at oases, which are fertile spots in desert areas. C

MAIN IDEA

Hypothesizing

C How might the Asian trade routes have spread Indian sciences and math to other civilizations?

Sea Trade, East and West Sea trade also increased. Traders used coastal routes around the rim of the Arabian Sea and up the Persian Gulf to bring goods from India to Rome. In addition, traders from southern India would sail to Southeast Asia to collect spices. They brought the spices back to India and sold them to merchants from Rome. Archaeologists have found hoards of Roman gold coins in southern India. Records show that some Romans were upset about the amount of gold their countrymen spent on Indian luxuries. They believed that to foster a healthy economy, a state must collect gold rather than spend it.

Rome was not India's only sea-trading partner. India imported African ivory and gold, and exported cotton cloth. Rice and wheat went to Arabia in exchange for dates and horses. After trade with Rome declined around the third century A.D., India's sea trade with China and the islands of southeast Asia increased. The Chinese, for example, imported Indian cotton cloth, monkeys, parrots, and elephants and sent India silk.

Effects of Indian Trade-Increased trade led to the rise of banking in India. Commerce was quite profitable. Bankers were willing to lend money to merchants and charge them interest on the loans. Interest rates varied, depending on how risky business was. During Mauryan times, the annual interest rate on loans used for overseas trade was 240 percent! During the Gupta Empire, bankers no longer considered sea trade so dangerous, so they charged only 15 to 20 percent interest a year. **D**

MAIN IDEA

Analyzing Causes-

D Why would dangerous conditions make bankers charge higher interest on loans for trade?

A number of Indian merchants went to live abroad and brought Indian culture with them. As a result, people throughout Asia picked up and adapted a variety of Indian traditions. For example, Indian culture affected styles in art, architecture, and dance throughout South and Southeast Asia. Indian influence was especially strong in Thailand, Cambodia, and on the Indonesian island of Java.

Traders also brought Indian religions to new regions. Hinduism spread northeast to Nepal and southeast to Sri Lanka and Borneo. Buddhism spread because of traveling Buddhist merchants and monks. In time, Buddhism even influenced China, as discussed in Section 3.

Global Impact

INTERACTIVE

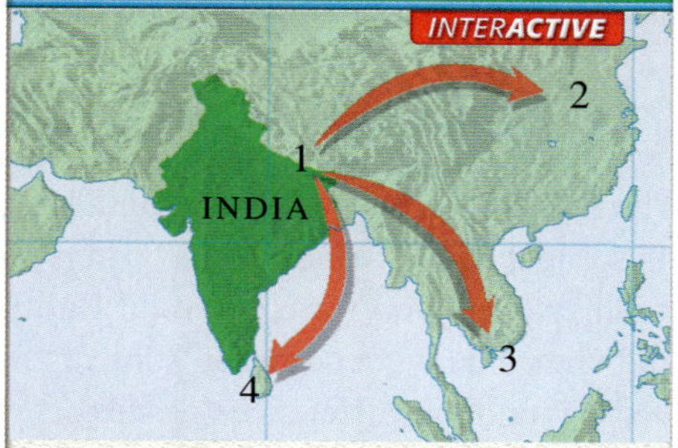

The Spread of Buddhism

Buddhism became a missionary religion during Asoka's reign. From his capital city (1), Asoka sent out Buddhist missionaries. After Indians began trading along the Silk Roads, Buddhist monks traveled the roads and converted people along the way.

Buddhist monks from India established their first monastery in China (2) in A.D. 65, and many Chinese became Buddhists. From China, Buddhism reached Korea in the fourth century and Japan in the sixth century.

Today, Buddhism is a major religion in East and Southeast Asia. The Theravada school is strong in Myanmar, Cambodia (3), Sri Lanka (4), and Thailand. The Mahayana school is strong in Japan and Korea.

NEW YORK CORE CURRICULUM REVIEW

TERMS & NAMES 1. For each term or name, write a sentence explaining its significance.

- Mahayana
- Theravada
- stupa
- Brahma
- Vishnu
- Shiva
- Kalidasa
- Silk Roads

USING YOUR NOTES

2. Which of the developments listed had the most lasting impact?

Religion	
Arts	
Science/ Math	
Trade	

MAIN IDEA

3. How did Buddhism change after the Buddha's death?
4. What were India's main trade goods in the fifth century?
5. What were some of India's contributions to science during the Gupta period?

CRITICAL THINKING & WRITING

6. **RECOGNIZING EFFECTS** What do you think was the most significant effect of the changes in Buddhism and Hinduism during this period? Explain.
7. **MAKING INFERENCES** Why did Indian culture flourish during the Gupta Empire?
8. **FORMING AND SUPPORTING OPINIONS** Which do you think was more important to India's economy, overland trade or sea trade? Provide details to support your answer.
9. **WRITING ACTIVITY** CULTURAL INTERACTION -Cite three of the cultures that interacted with India. Explain in a brief **expository essay** the result of each cultural interaction.

INTEGRATED TECHNOLOGY **INTERNET ACTIVITY**

Use the Internet to research Indian trade today. Then prepare a **chart** listing the type of goods bought and sold and the trading partner for each type.

INTERNET KEYWORD
India trade

Hindu and Buddhist Art

The main difference between Buddhist art and Hindu art in India was its subject matter. Buddhist art often portrayed the Buddha or bodhisattvas, who were potential Buddhas. Hindu gods, such as Vishnu and Ganesha, were common subjects in Hindu art.

Beyond the differences in subject, Hindu and Buddhist beliefs had little influence on Indian artistic styles. For example, a Hindu sculpture and a Buddhist sculpture created at the same place and time were stylistically the same. In fact, the same artisans often created both Hindu and Buddhist art.

INTEGRATED TECHNOLOGY

RESEARCH LINKS For more on Hindu and Buddhist art, go to **classzone.com**

▼ Buddha

This bronze Buddha was made in India during the sixth century. Each detail of a Buddhist sculpture has meaning. For example, the headpiece and long earlobes shown here are lakshana, traditional bodily signs of the Buddha. The upraised hand is a gesture that means "Have no fear."

▼ The Great Stupa

Built during the third to first centuries B.C., the Great Stupa is a famous Buddhist monument in Sanchi, India. This stone structure is 120 feet across and 54 feet high; it has a staircase leading to a walkway that encircles the stupa. Stupas serve as memorials and often contain sacred relics. During Buddhist New Year festivals, worshipers hold images of the Buddha and move in processions around the circular walkway.

▲ **Devi Jagadambi Temple in Khajuraho**

Hardly any Hindu temples from the Gupta period remain. This temple, built in the 11th century, shows architectural trends begun in Gupta times. These include building with stone rather than wood; erecting a high, pyramidal roof instead of a flat roof; and sculpting elaborate decorations on the walls.

▲ **Ganesha**

Carved in the fifth century B.C., this stone sculpture represents the elephant-headed god Ganesha. According to Hindu beliefs, Ganesha is the god of success, education, wisdom, and wealth. He also is worshiped as the lifter of obstacles. The smaller picture is a recent image of Ganesha, who has gained great popularity during modern times.

Connect *to* Today

1. **Contrasting** How do the Buddhist stupa and the Hindu temple differ? According to the information on page 198, what might be the reason for those differences?
   See Skillbuilder Handbook, Page R7.

2. **Making Inferences** Why do you think Ganesha is a popular god among Hindus today? Explain.

Han Emperors in China

CONNECT TO THE NEW YORK STATE CORE CURRICULUM

Unit 1.D.1.b. Factors leading to growth
Unit 1.D.1.c. Contributions

TERMS & NAMES

- Han Dynasty
- centralized government
- civil service
- monopoly
- assimilation

SETTING THE STAGE Under Shi Huangdi, the Qin Dynasty had unified China. Shi Huangdi established a strong government by conquering the rival kings who ruled small states throughout China. After Shi Huangdi died in 210 B.C., his son proved to be a weak, ineffective leader. China's government fell apart.

TAKING NOTES

Outlining Use an outline to organize main ideas and details.

Han China
I. The Han Restore Unity to China
A.
B.
C.
II. A Highly Structured Society
III. Han Technology, Commerce, and Culture

The Han Restore Unity to China

Rumblings of discontent during the Qin Dynasty grew to roars in the years after Shi Huangdi's death. Peasants were bitter over years of high taxes, harsh labor quotas, and a severe penal system. They rebelled. Rival kings were eager to regain control of the regions they had held before Shi Huangdi. They raised armies and fought over territory.

Liu Bang Founds the Han Dynasty During the civil war that followed, two powerful leaders emerged. Xiang Yu (shee•ANG-yoo) was an aristocratic general who was willing to allow the warlords to keep their territories if they would acknowledge him as their feudal lord. Liu Bang (LEE•oo-bahng) was one of Xiang Yu's generals.

Eventually, Liu Bang turned against Xiang Yu. The two fought their final battle in 202 B.C. Liu Bang won and declared himself the first emperor of the Han Dynasty. The **Han Dynasty**, which ruled China for more than 400 years, is divided into two periods. The Former Han ruled for about two centuries, until A.D. 9. After a brief period when the Han were out of power, the Later Han ruled for almost another two centuries. The Han Dynasty so influenced China that even today many Chinese call themselves "people of the Han."

▼ Emperor Liu Bang

Liu Bang's first goal was to destroy the rival kings' power. He followed Shi Huangdi's policy of establishing **centralized government**, in which a central authority controls the running of a state. Reporting to Liu Bang's central government were hundreds of local provincials called commanderies.

To win popular support, Liu Bang departed from Shi Huangdi's strict legalism. He lowered taxes and softened harsh punishments. People throughout the empire appreciated the peace and stability that Liu Bang brought to China.

The Empress Lü When Liu Bang died in 195 B.C., his son became emperor, but in name only. The real ruler was his mother, Empress Lü. Although Lü had not been Liu Bang's only wife, she had powerful friends at court who helped her seize power. The empress outlived her son and retained control of the throne by naming first one infant and then another as emperor. Because the infants were too young to rule, she remained in control. When Empress Lü died in 180 B.C., people who remained loyal to Liu Bang's family, rather than to Lü's family, came back into power. They rid the palace of the old empress's relatives by executing them.

Such palace plots occurred often throughout the Han Dynasty. Traditionally, the emperor chose the favorite among his wives as the empress and appointed one of her sons as successor. Because of this, the palace women and their families competed fiercely for the emperor's notice. The families would make alliances with influential people in the court. The resulting power plays distracted the emperor and his officials so much that they sometimes could not govern efficiently.

Vocabulary
Martial means warlike.

The Martial Emperor When Liu Bang's great-grandson took the throne, he continued Liu Bang's centralizing policies. Wudi (woo•dee), who reigned from 141 to 87 B.C., held the throne longer than any other Han emperor. He is called the "Martial Emperor" because he adopted the policy of expanding the Chinese empire through war.

Wudi's first set of enemies were the Xiongnu (shee•UNG•noo), fierce nomads known for their deadly archery skills from horseback. The Xiongnu roamed the steppes to the north and west of China. They made raids into China's settled farmland. There they took hostages and stole grain, livestock, and other valuable items. The early Han emperors tried to buy off the Xiongnu by sending them thousands of pounds of silk, rice, alcohol, and money. Usually, the Xiongnu just accepted these gifts and continued their raids.

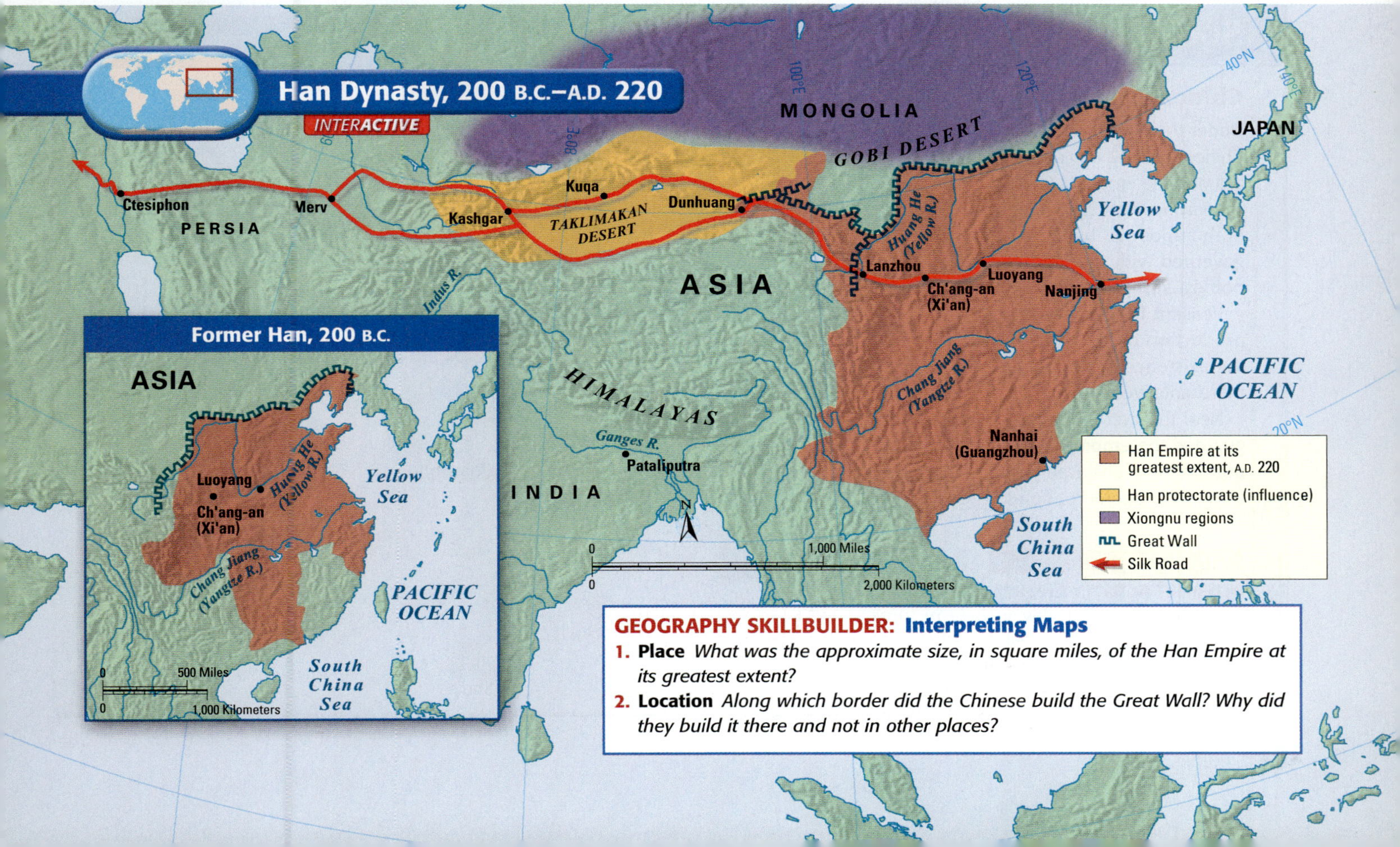

GEOGRAPHY SKILLBUILDER: Interpreting Maps

1. **Place** *What was the approximate size, in square miles, of the Han Empire at its greatest extent?*
2. **Location** *Along which border did the Chinese build the Great Wall? Why did they build it there and not in other places?*

When Wudi realized that the bribes were simply making the Xiongnu stronger, he sent more than 100,000 soldiers to fight them. To help defeat the Xiongnu, Wudi also made allies of their enemies:

PRIMARY SOURCE

The Xiongnu had defeated the king of the Yuezhi people and had made his skull into a drinking vessel. As a result the Yuezhi . . . bore a constant grudge against the Xiongnu, though as yet they had been unable to find anyone to join them in an attack on their enemy. . . . When the emperor [Wudi] heard this, he decided to try to send an envoy to establish relations with the Yuezhi.

SIMA QIAN, *Records of the Grand Historian*

After his army forced the nomads to retreat into Central Asia, Wudi attempted to make his northwest border safe by settling his troops on the Xiongnu's former pastures. Although this tactic succeeded for a time, nomadic raiders continued to cause problems during much of China's later history.

Wudi also colonized areas to the northeast, now known as Manchuria and Korea. He sent his armies south, where they conquered mountain tribes and set up Chinese colonies all the way into what is now Vietnam. By the end of Wudi's reign, the empire had expanded nearly to the bounds of present-day China.

A Highly Structured Society

Chinese society under the Han Dynasty was highly structured. (See Social History below.) Just as Han emperors tried to control the people they conquered, they exerted vast control over the Chinese themselves. Because the Chinese believed their emperor to have divine authority, they accepted his exercise of power. He was the link between heaven and earth. If the emperor did his job well, China had peace

Social History

Chinese Society

Under the Han Dynasty, the structure of Chinese society was clearly defined. At the top was the emperor, who was considered semidivine. Next came kings and governors, both appointed by the emperor. They governed with the help of state officials, nobles, and scholars.

Peasant farmers came next. Their production of food was considered vital to the existence of the empire. Artisans and merchants were below them.

Near the bottom were the soldiers, who guarded the empire's frontiers. At the bottom were enslaved persons, who were usually conquered peoples.

INTEGRATED TECHNOLOGY

INTERNET ACTIVITY Create a photo exhibit on Chinese society today. Include pictures of people from various walks of life. Go to **classzone.com** for your research.

and prosperity. If he failed, the heavens showed their displeasure with earthquakes, floods, and famines. However, the emperor did not rule alone.

Structures of Han Government The Chinese emperor relied on a complex bureaucracy to help him rule. Running the bureaucracy and maintaining the imperial army were expensive. To raise money, the government levied taxes. Like the farmers in India, Chinese peasants owed part of their yearly crops to the government. Merchants also paid taxes.

Besides taxes, the peasants owed the government a month's worth of labor or military service every year. With this source of labor, the Han emperors built roads and dug canals and irrigation ditches. The emperors also filled the ranks of China's vast armies and expanded the Great Wall, which stretched across the northern frontier.

Confucianism, the Road to Success Wudi's government employed more than 130,000 people. The bureaucracy included 18 different ranks of **civil service** jobs, which were government jobs that civilians obtained by taking examinations. At times, Chinese emperors rewarded loyal followers with government posts. However, another way to fill government posts evolved under the Han. This method involved testing applicants' knowledge of Confucianism—the teachings of Confucius, who had lived 400 years before.

The early Han emperors had employed some Confucian scholars as court advisers, but it was Wudi who began actively to favor them. Confucius had taught that gentlemen should practice "reverence [respect], generosity, truthfulness, diligence [industriousness], and kindness." Because these were exactly the qualities he wanted his government officials to have, Wudi set up a school where hopeful job applicants from all over China could come to study Confucius's works. (A)

MAIN IDEA

Making Inferences

(A) Why would Wudi want his officials to have qualities such as diligence?

After their studies, job applicants took formal examinations in history, law, literature, and Confucianism. In theory, anyone could take the exams. In practice, few peasants could afford to educate their sons. So only sons of wealthy landowners had a chance at a government career. In spite of this flaw, the civil service system begun by Wudi worked so efficiently that it continued in China until 1912.

Han Technology, Commerce, and Culture

The 400 years of Han rule saw not only improvements in education but also great advances in Chinese technology and culture. In addition, the centralized government began to exert more control over commerce and manufacturing.

Vocabulary

Commerce is the buying and selling of goods.

Technology Revolutionizes Chinese Life Advances in technology influenced all aspects of Chinese life. Paper was invented in A.D. 105. Before that, books were usually written on silk. But paper was cheaper, so books became more readily available. This helped spread education in China. The invention of paper also affected Chinese government. Formerly, all government documents had been recorded on strips of wood. Paper was much more convenient to use for record keeping, so Chinese bureaucracy expanded.

Another technological advance was the collar harness for horses. This invention allowed horses to pull much heavier loads than did the harness being used in Europe at the time.

Global Impact

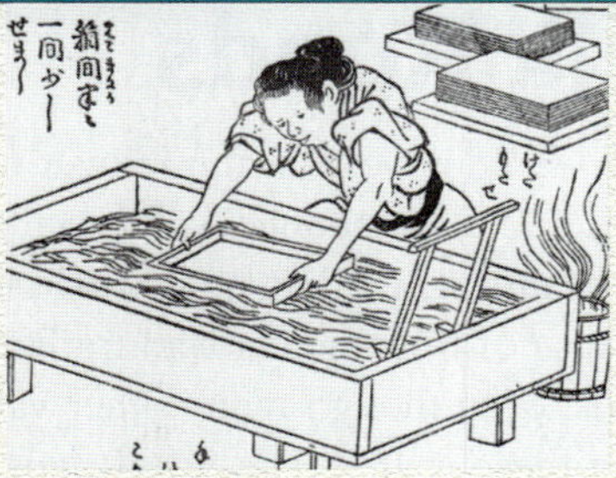

Papermaking

People in ancient China wrote on pottery, bones, stone, silk, wood, and bamboo. Then, about 2,000 or more years ago, the Chinese invented paper. They began to use plants, such as hemp, to make thin paper. In A.D. 105, Ts'ai Lun, a Han official, produced a stronger paper by mixing mulberry bark and old rags with hemp fiber.

The art of papermaking slowly spread to the rest of the world. First, it moved east to Korea and Japan. Then, it spread westward to the Arab world in the 700s, and from there to Europe.

The Chinese perfected a plow that was more efficient because it had two blades. They also improved iron tools, invented the wheelbarrow, and began to use water mills to grind grain. **B**

MAIN IDEA

Making Inferences

B Which of these inventions helped to feed China's huge population?

Agriculture Versus Commerce During the Han Dynasty, the population of China swelled to 60 million. Because there were so many people to feed, Confucian scholars and ordinary Chinese people considered agriculture the most important and honored occupation. An imperial edict written in 167 B.C. stated this philosophy quite plainly:

PRIMARY SOURCE

Agriculture is the foundation of the world. No duty is greater. Now if [anyone] personally follows this pursuit diligently, he has yet [to pay] the impositions of the land tax and tax on produce. . . . Let there be abolished the land tax and the tax on produce levied upon the cultivated fields.

BAN GU and **BAN ZHAO** in *History of the Former Han Dynasty*

Although the same decree dismissed commerce as the least important occupation, manufacturing and commerce were actually very important to the Han Empire. The government established monopolies on the mining of salt, the forging of iron, the minting of coins, and the brewing of alcohol. A **monopoly** occurs when a group has exclusive control over the production and distribution of certain goods.

For a time, the government also ran huge silk mills—competing with private silk weavers in making this luxurious cloth. As contact with people from other lands increased, the Chinese realized how valuable their silk was as an item of trade.

Global Impact: Trade Networks

INTERACTIVE

Silk Roads

Why would anyone struggle over mountains and across deserts to buy fabric? Ancient peoples valued silk because it was strong, lightweight, and beautiful. Traders made fortunes carrying Chinese silk to the West. Because of this, the caravan trails that crossed Asia were called Silk Roads, even though many other valuable trade goods were also carried along these routes. The Silk Roads also encouraged cultural diffusion.

Camel Caravans ►

No trader traveled the whole length of the Silk Roads. Mediterranean merchants went partway, then traded with Central Asian nomads—who went east until they met Chinese traders near India. Many traders traveled in camel caravans.

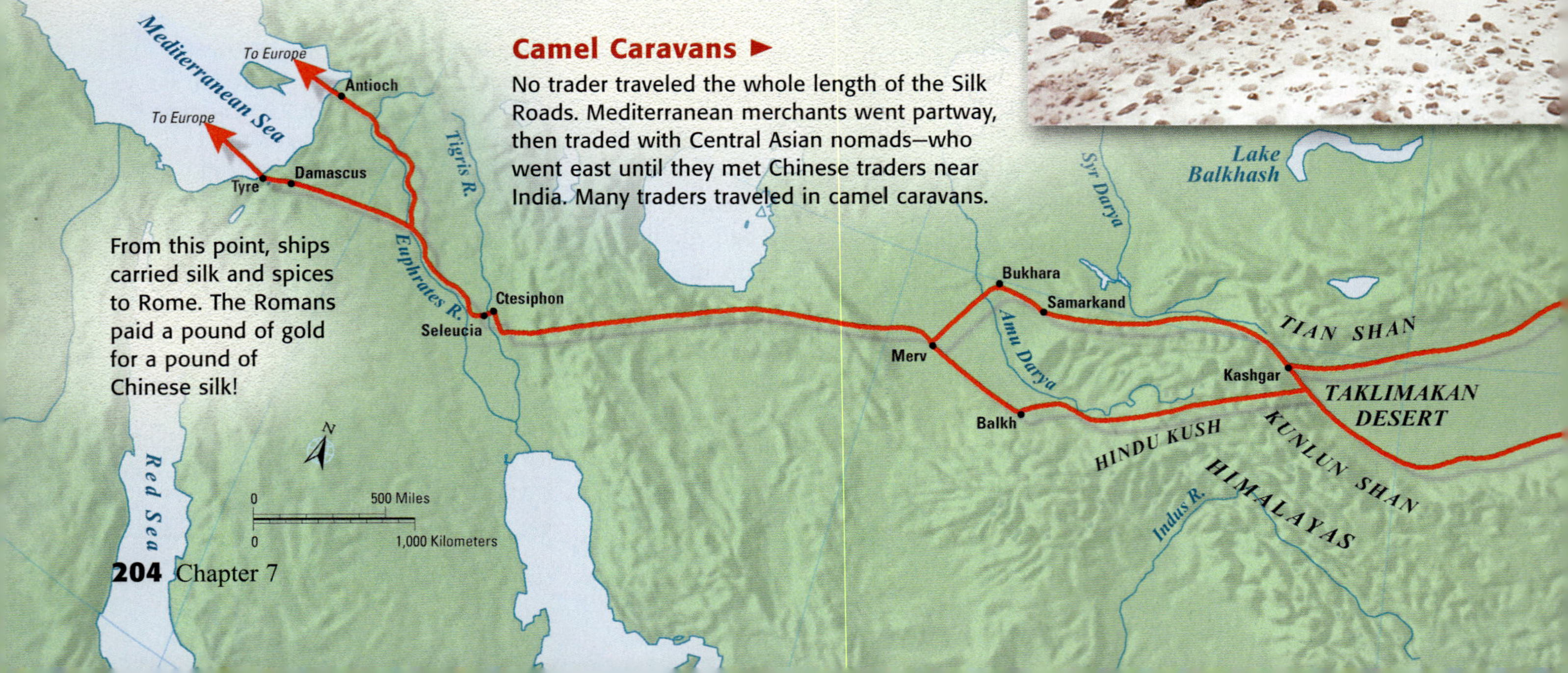

From this point, ships carried silk and spices to Rome. The Romans paid a pound of gold for a pound of Chinese silk!

Because of this, the techniques of silk production became a closely guarded state secret. Spurred by the worldwide demand for silk, Chinese commerce expanded along the Silk Roads to most of Asia and, through India, all the way to Rome.

The Han Unifies Chinese Culture

As the Han empire expanded its trade networks, the Chinese began to learn about the foods and fashions common in foreign lands. Similarly, expanding the empire through conquest brought people of different cultures under Chinese rule.

Unification Under Chinese Rule To unify the empire, the Chinese government encouraged **assimilation**, the process of making conquered peoples part of Chinese culture. To promote assimilation, the government sent Chinese farmers to settle newly colonized areas. It also encouraged them to intermarry with local peoples. Government officials set up schools to train local people in the Confucian philosophy and then appointed local scholars to government posts.

Several writers also helped to unify Chinese culture by recording China's history. Sima Qian (SU•MAH chee•YEHN), who lived from 145 to 85 B.C., is called the Grand Historian for his work in compiling a history of China from the ancient dynasties to Wudi. To write accurately, Sima Qian visited historical sites, interviewed eyewitnesses, researched official records, and examined artifacts. His book is called *Records of the Grand Historian*. Another famous book was the *History of the Former Han Dynasty*. Ban Biao (BAHN bee•OW), who lived from A.D. 3 to 54, started the project. After his death, his son Ban Gu (bahn goo) and later his daughter Ban Zhao

Traded Gold ►

Gold was an important trade good. The object to the right is a Chinese gold dagger handle from the Zhou Dynasty. Many artifacts found along the Silk Roads show a mix of Greek, Central Asian, and Indian styles. This indicates that ideas traveled as well as objects.

Patterns of Interaction

Trade Connects the World: Silk Roads and the Pacific Rim

Throughout history, the desire for material goods led to the development of long-distance trade routes such as the Silk Roads. In turn, trade caused cultural diffusion. Similarly today, trade in the Pacific Rim has helped spread many products across the globe.

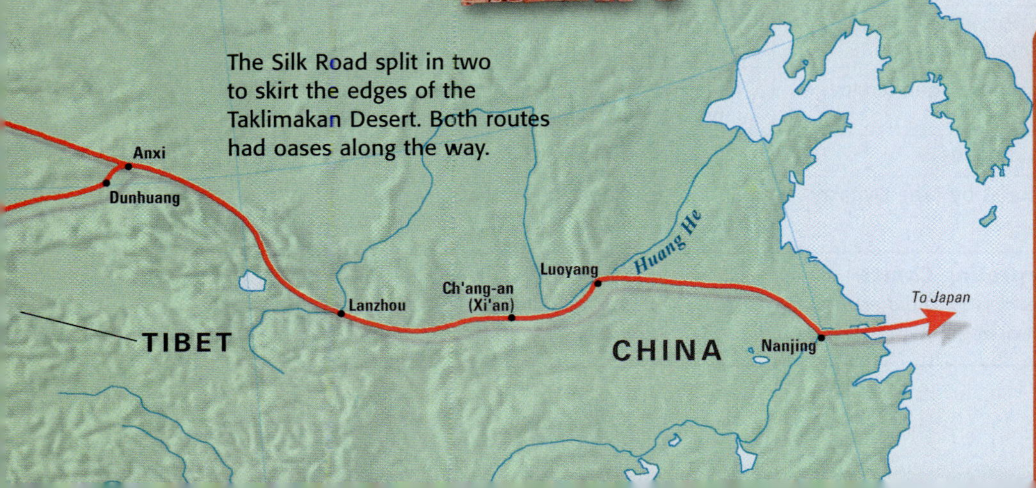

The Silk Road split in two to skirt the edges of the Taklimakan Desert. Both routes had oases along the way.

Connect *to* Today

1. **Hypothesizing** How might patterns of trade and cultural diffusion have differed if Rome, not China, had learned the secret of making silk?
See Skillbuilder Handbook, Page R11.
2. **Comparing** What are China's top three exports today, and which countries buy those products?

(bahn jow) worked on it. Ban Zhao also wrote a guide called *Lessons for Women*, which called upon women to be humble and obedient but also industrious.

Women's Roles—Wives, Nuns, and Scholars Although Ban Zhao gained fame as a historian, most women during the Han Dynasty led quiet lives at home. Confucian teachings had dictated that women were to devote themselves to their families. However, women made important contributions to their family's economic life through duties in the home and work in the fields of the family farm.

Some upper-class women lived much different lives. As explained earlier, a few empresses wielded great power. Daoist—and later, Buddhist—nuns were able to gain an education and lead lives apart from their families. Women in aristocratic and landowning families also sometimes pursued education and culture. Some women ran small shops; still others practiced medicine.

The Fall of the Han and Their Return

In spite of economic and cultural advances, the Han emperors faced grave problems. One of the main problems was an economic imbalance caused by customs that allowed the rich to gain more wealth at the expense of the poor.

The Rich Take Advantage of the Poor According to custom, a family's land was divided equally among all of the father's male heirs. Unless a farmer could afford to buy more land during his lifetime, each generation inherited smaller plots. With such small plots of land, farmers had a hard time raising enough food to sell or even to feed the family. Because of this, small farmers often went into debt and had to borrow money from large landowners, who charged very high interest rates. If the farmer couldn't pay back the debt, the landowner took possession of the farmer's land.

Large landowners were not required to pay taxes, so when their land holdings increased, the amount of land that was left for the government to tax decreased. With less money coming in, the government pressed harder to collect money from the small farmers. As a result, the gap between rich and poor increased.

Wang Mang Overthrows the Han During this time of economic change, political instability grew. At the palace, court advisers, palace servants, and rival influential families wove complex plots to influence the emperor's choice of who would

▲ Chinese warrior

Comparing Two Great Empires: Han China and Rome

Han Dynasty—202 B.C. to A.D. 220	Roman Empire—27 B.C. to A.D. 476
Empire replaced rival kingdoms	Empire replaced republic
Centralized, bureaucratic government	Centralized, bureaucratic government
Built roads and defensive walls	Built roads and defensive walls
Conquered many diverse peoples in regions bordering China	Conquered many diverse peoples in regions of three continents
At its height—area of 1.5 million square miles and a population of 60 million	At its height—area of 3.4 million square miles and a population of 55 million
Chinese became common written language throughout empire	Latin did not replace other written languages in empire
Ongoing conflict with nomads	Ongoing conflict with nomads
Empire fell apart; restored by Tang Dynasty in 618	Empire fell apart; never restored

▲ Roman soldier

SKILLBUILDER: Interpreting Charts

1. **Drawing Conclusions** *How long did each empire last? When did they both exist?*
2. **Comparing and Contrasting** *How were Han China and the Roman Empire similar? Different?*

succeed him as ruler. From about 32 B.C. until A.D. 9, one inexperienced emperor replaced another. Chaos reigned in the palace, and with peasant revolts, unrest spread across the land as well.

Finally, Wang Mang (wahng-mahng), a Confucian scholar and member of the court, decided that a strong ruler was needed to restore order. For six years, he had been acting as regent for the infant who had been crowned emperor. In A.D. 9, Wang Mang took the imperial title for himself and overthrew the Han, thus ending the Former Han, the first half of the Han Dynasty.

Vocabulary
A *regent* is a person who rules temporarily while a monarch is too young.

Wang Mang tried to bring the country under control. He minted new money to relieve the treasury's shortage and set up public granaries to help feed China's poor. Wang Mang also took away large landholdings from the rich and planned to redistribute the land to farmers who had lost their land. But this plan angered powerful landholders. Wang Mang's larger supply of money disrupted the economy, because it allowed people to increase their spending, which encouraged merchants to raise prices.

Then, in A.D. 11, a great flood left thousands dead and millions homeless. The public granaries did not hold enough to feed the displaced, starving people. Huge peasant revolts rocked the land. The wealthy, opposed to Wang Mang's land policies, joined in the rebellion. The rebels assassinated Wang Mang in A.D. 23. Within two years, a member of the old imperial family took the throne and began the second period of Han rule—called the Later Han. **C**

MAIN IDEA

Recognizing Effects

C How did Wang Mang's policies help cause his own downfall?

The Later Han Years-With peace restored to China, the first decades of the Later Han Dynasty were quite prosperous. The government sent soldiers and merchants westward to regain control of posts along the Silk Roads. But this expansion could not make up for social, political, and economic weaknesses within the empire itself. Within a century, China suffered from the same economic imbalances, political intrigues, and social unrest that had toppled the Former Han. By 220, the Later Han Dynasty had disintegrated into three rival kingdoms.

In the next chapter, you will learn about the early civilizations and kingdoms that developed in Africa.

▲ Silk was the trade good that linked the Han and Roman empires. This fragment of silk was found along the Silk Roads.

NEW YORK CORE CURRICULUM REVIEW

TERMS & NAMES 1. For each term or name, write a sentence explaining its significance.

- Han Dynasty
- centralized government
- civil service
- monopoly
- assimilation

USING YOUR NOTES

2. What was the most lasting development of the Han Empire? Explain.

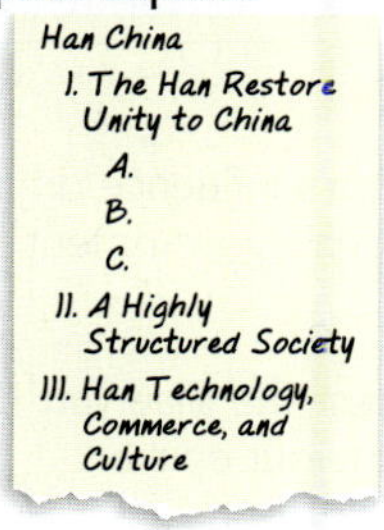

MAIN IDEAS

3. How did Wudi encourage learning?
4. What role did women play in Han society?
5. How did the Han Chinese attempt to assimilate conquered peoples?

CRITICAL THINKING & WRITING

6. **IDENTIFYING PROBLEMS** What problem do you think was most responsible for weakening the Han Dynasty? Explain.
7. **ANALYZING CAUSES** How important were Confucian teachings in the lives of people of the Han Empire? Provide details to support your answer.
8. **DRAWING CONCLUSIONS** Why was agriculture considered the most important and honored occupation in Han China?
9. **WRITING ACTIVITY** RELIGIOUS AND ETHICAL SYSTEMS -Review the five qualities Confucius said gentlemen should have. Write one **sentence** for each describing the action a government official could take to demonstrate the quality.

CONNECT TO TODAY **CREATING AN ORGANIZATIONAL CHART**

Research information about the current government of the People's Republic of China. Then create an **organizational chart** showing its structure.

Chapter 7 Assessment

VISUAL SUMMARY

India and China Establish Empires

300 B.C. — 100 B.C. — A.D. 100 — A.D. 300 — A.D. 500

Mauryan Empire

321 B.C. **Chandragupta Maurya** seized throne and began Mauryan Empire.

269 B.C. **Asoka** began rule; conquered Kalinga; regretted slaughter and converted to Buddhism; sent out missionaries.

232 B.C. **Asoka** died; empire started to break apart.

185 B.C. Greeks invaded India, beginning five centuries of turmoil.

Han Dynasty

202 B.C. **Liu Bang** started Han Dynasty; strengthened central government.

141 B.C. **Wudi** began reign; conquered neighboring regions; started civil service.

A.D. 9 **Wang Mang** temporarily overthrew the Han.

- 1st century A.D. Later Han rulers encouraged Silk Road trade with West.
- Chinese invented paper, collar harness, water mill.

Gupta Empire

A.D. 320 **Chandra Gupta I** began empire.

A.D. 375 **Chandra Gupta II** started reign. Indian art, literature, and dance flowered.

A.D. 500 Indian astronomers realized Earth was round; mathematician calculated value of pi and length of solar year.

- Buddhism and Hinduism developed more popular forms.
- Trade spread Indian culture, Hinduism, and Buddhism.

TERMS & NAMES

For each term or name below, briefly explain its connection to the empires in India and China between 321 B.C. and A.D. 550.

1. Mauryan Empire
2. Asoka
3. religious toleration
4. Gupta Empire
5. Kalidasa
6. Silk Roads
7. Han Dynasty
8. centralized government
9. civil service
10. assimilation

MAIN IDEAS

India's First Empires Section 1 (pages 189–192)

11. What were three significant accomplishments of the Mauryan rulers?
12. How did India change during the 500 years between the decline of the Mauryan Empire and the rise of the Gupta Empire?
13. How did the southern tip of India differ from the rest of India?

Trade Spreads Indian Religions and Culture Section 2 (pages 193–199)

14. How did changes in Buddhism influence art in India?
15. What advances in science and mathematics had been made in India by about 500?
16. What were the economic and cultural links between India and Southeast Asia?

Han Emperors in China Section 3 (pages 200–207)

17. Why was Wudi one of China's most significant rulers? Explain.
18. Under the Chinese civil-service system, who could become government officials?
19. How did silk influence China's government, economy, and culture during the Han period?
20. How did economic problems lead to the decline of the Han?

CRITICAL THINKING

1. USING YOUR NOTES

In a diagram like the one to the right, fill in the information comparing the Mauryan, Gupta, and Han empires.

Empire	Period of Influence	Key Leaders	Significant Achievements
Mauryan			
Gupta			
Han			

2. CONTRASTING

RELIGIOUS AND ETHICAL SYSTEMS Contrast Buddhism's influence on India's government with Confucianism's influence on China's government.

3. EVALUATING

POWER AND AUTHORITY Which of the three empires—the Mauryan, Gupta, or Han—was most successful? Explain and support your opinion.

4. DRAWING CONCLUSIONS

CULTURAL INTERACTION How significant were the Silk Roads to the economy of India? Defend your viewpoint with text references.

5. DEVELOPING HISTORICAL PERSPECTIVE

What was the importance of the Chinese invention of paper?

NEW YORK STATE REGENTS EXAM PRACTICE

Use the quotation and your knowledge of world history to answer questions 1 and 2.
Additional Test Practice, pp. S1–S33

PRIMARY SOURCE

Kalinga was conquered by his Sacred and Gracious Majesty when he had been consecrated eight years. 150,000 persons were thence carried away captive, 100,000 were slain, and many times that number died. . . . Thus arose his Sacred Majesty's remorse for having conquered the Kalingas, because the conquest of a country previously unconquered involves the slaughter, death, and carrying away captive of the people.

ASOKA in *A History of Modern India* by Percival Spear

1 Why was Asoka remorseful about the campaign against Kalinga?

(1) His army was not victorious.
(2) The battle took too long to fight.
(3) Many people were killed or made captives.
(4) He was not able to play a more active role in the battle.

2 What did the conquest of Kalinga cause Asoka to realize about the nature of war?

(1) War leads to the deaths of innocent people.
(2) War is the best means possible to expand an empire.
(3) War cannot be avoided.
(4) War is very expensive to fight.

Use the photograph of this 16-inch, bronze sculpture from Han China and your knowledge of world history to answer question 3.

3 What does this sculpture reveal about life in Han China?

(1) that the Chinese invented the wheel
(2) that the Chinese used chariots in warfare
(3) that only privileged classes used this form of transportation
(4) that the Chinese were skilled in the use of bronze

INTEGRATED TECHNOLOGY

TEST PRACTICE Go to **classzone.com**

- Diagnostic tests
- Tutorials
- Strategies
- Additional practice

ALTERNATIVE ASSESSMENT

1. Interact *with* History

On page 188, you looked at a situation in which a government hired people to spy on each other. Now that you have read the chapter, reevaluate your decision about being a spy. What do you think are the best methods for a government to use to control large numbers of people? Consider the methods used by Chandragupta, Asoka, and the Han emperors.

2. WRITING ABOUT HISTORY

Write a newspaper **editorial** either praising or criticizing Asoka and his methods of governing.

- In the first paragraph, introduce your opinion.
- In the middle paragraphs, give reasons and historical evidence to support your opinion.
- In the concluding paragraph, restate your opinion in a forceful way.

INTEGRATED TECHNOLOGY

Creating a Virtual Field Trip

Plan a two-week virtual field trip through China and India. Decide which cities you would visit from the Mauryan and Gupta empires in India and the Han Empire in China. Make sure also to include sites along the Silk Roads. Create an online or classroom presentation that includes the following:

- maps showing the route of your trip
- images of the major historic sites you would visit and why each site is historically significant
- images of the commercial goods and art objects you might see along the way

CHAPTER

8

African Civilizations,

1500 B.C.–A.D. 700

Previewing Main Ideas

INTERACTION WITH ENVIRONMENT The varied climates and natural resources of Africa offered opportunities for developing different lifestyles. By 500 B.C., the Nok people of West Africa had pioneered iron-making technology.

Geography *Look at the location of ironworking sites on the map. What might explain why ironworking took place at these sites?*

CULTURAL INTERACTION Massive migrations of Bantu-speaking people changed the culture of eastern and southern Africa. The migrating people brought new skills and ideas about society to people in the south and east.

Geography *Study the time line and the map. Where did ironworking spread from Nok, and which group probably brought the skills?*

POWER AND AUTHORITY The kingdom of Aksum became a major trading center for Indian Ocean and Arabian trade. It also became the center of Christianity in East Africa.

Geography *Why was Aksum better suited for trade than Nok or Djenné-Djeno?*

NEW YORK CORE CURRICULUM FOCUS

- Early African cultures practiced animism, a religion based on spirits.
- The Bantu migrations spread African culture and populated the southern third of the continent.

INTEGRATED TECHNOLOGY

eEdition

- Interactive Maps
- Interactive Visuals
- Interactive Primary Sources

INTERNET RESOURCES

Go to **classzone.com** for:

- Research Links
- Internet Activities
- Primary Sources
- Chapter Quiz
- Maps
- Test Practice
- Current Events

AFRICA

1500s B.C.
Africans south of the Sahara live in scattered farming communities, as pastoralists or hunter-gatherers.

751 B.C.
Kushite king, Pianki, conquers Memphis in Egypt.

1500 B.C. — **1000 B.C.**

WORLD

1200 B.C.
◀ Olmec culture rises in southern Mexico. (stone Olmec head)

461 B.C.
◀ Age of Pericles in Greece.

Spread of Ironworking, 500 B.C.– A.D. 700

500 B.C.
Nok people make iron tools. (Nok sculpture) ▶

250 B.C.
Djenné-Djeno established in West Africa.

A.D. 100s
Bantu migrations under way.

A.D. 320
◀ King Ezana rules Aksum. (crown from Aksum)

500 B.C. — **500 A.D.**

27 B.C.
◀ Pax Romana begins. (Roman soldier statue)

105 A.D.
Chinese invent paper.

Interact *with* History

How can newcomers change a community?

The year is 100 B.C., and you've spent most of the day gathering berries. The hunters have brought back some small game to add to the simmering pot. Just then you see something out of the ordinary. A stranger is approaching. He is carrying a spear and leading cows—a type of animal that none of you has ever seen. Your first reaction is fear. But you are also curious. Who is he? What does he want? Where has he come from? The communal elders have similar concerns, yet they cautiously go forward to greet him.

1 The hunter-gatherer community is small and tightly knit. There is, however, room to accommodate newcomers.

2 Having traveled long distances, this stranger might have valuable survival skills to share.

3 His spears could indicate that he is a good hunter or that his group may be hostile invaders—or both.

EXAMINING *the* ISSUES

- **How might both native people and newcomers benefit from their interaction?**
- **How would such interaction change everyone involved?**

Discuss these questions as a class. In your discussion, remember what you've learned about other peoples who dealt with foreigners, such as the Indo-European invaders of Asia and India. As you read about the early African civilizations in this chapter, notice how African peoples interacted with each other.

Diverse Societies in Africa

CONNECT TO THE NEW YORK STATE CORE CURRICULUM

Unit 1.B.2.a. Human and physical geography
Unit 1.E.1.a. Animism–African

TERMS & NAMES

- Sahara
- Sahel
- savanna
- animism
- griot
- Nok
- Djenné-Djeno

SETTING THE STAGE Africa spreads across the equator. It includes a broad range of Earth's environments—from steamy coastal plains to snow-capped mountain peaks. Some parts of Africa suffer from constant drought, while others receive over 200 inches of rain a year. Vegetation varies from sand dunes and rocky wastes to dense green rain forests. Interaction with the African environment has created unique cultures and societies. Each group found ways to adapt to the land and the resources it offers.

TAKING NOTES

Outlining Organize ideas and details about Africa.

Africa
I. A Land of Geographic Contrasts
A.
B.
II. Early Humans Adapt to Their Environments

A Land of Geographic Contrasts

Africa is the second largest continent in the world. It stretches 4,600 miles from east to west and 5,000 miles from north to south. With a total of 11.7 million square miles, it occupies about one-fifth of Earth's land surface. Narrow coastlines (50 to 100 miles) lie on either side of a central plateau. Waterfalls and rapids often form as rivers drop down to the coast from the plateau, making navigation impossible to or from the coast. Africa's coastline has few harbors, ports, or inlets. Because of this, the coastline is actually shorter than that of Europe, a land one-third Africa's size.

Challenging Environments Each African environment offers its own challenges. The deserts are largely unsuitable for human life and also hamper people's movement to more welcoming climates. The largest deserts are the **Sahara** in the north and the Kalahari (kahl•uh•HAHR•ee) in the south.

Stretching from the Atlantic Ocean to the Red Sea, the Sahara covers an area roughly the size of the United States. Only a small part of the Sahara consists of sand dunes. The rest is mostly a flat, gray wasteland of scattered rocks and gravel. Each year the desert takes over more and more of the land at the southern edge of the Sahara Desert, the **Sahel** (suh•HAYL).

Another very different—but also partly uninhabitable—African environment is the rain forest. Sometimes called "nature's greenhouse," it produces mahogany and teak trees up to 150 feet tall. Their leaves and branches form a dense canopy that keeps sunlight from reaching the forest floor. The tsetse (TSET•see) fly is found in the rain forest. Its presence prevented Africans from using cattle, donkeys, and horses to farm near the rain forests. This deadly insect also prevented invaders—especially Europeans—from colonizing fly-infested territories.

Vegetation Regions of Africa

1 The deadliest creature lurking in rain forests is a small fly called the tsetse fly. Tsetse flies carry a disease that is deadly to livestock and can cause fatal sleeping sickness in humans.

2 Sahel means "coastline" in Arabic. African people may have named it this because the Sahara seemed like a vast ocean of sand.

4 The dense trees and lack of edible vegetation in the humid rain forest make it an unwelcoming environment for most people.

3 The savannas are home to herds of animals such as giraffes, wildebeest, and antelope. They also support grain crops of millet, wheat, and maize (corn).

GEOGRAPHY SKILLBUILDER: Interpreting Maps

1. **Place** *About what percent of Africa is desert? savanna?*
2. **Region** *If you were to fold a map of Africa in half along the equator, what do you notice about the similar vegetation zones above and below the fold?*

Welcoming Lands The northern coast and the southern tip of Africa have welcoming Mediterranean-type climates and fertile soil. Because these coastal areas are so fertile, they are densely populated with farmers and herders.

Most people in Africa live on the **savannas**, or grassy plains. Africa's savannas are not just endless plains. They include mountainous highlands and swampy tropical stretches. Covered with tall grasses and dotted with trees, the savannas cover over 40 percent of the continent. Dry seasons alternate with rainy seasons—often, two of each a year. Unfortunately, the topsoil throughout Africa is thin, and heavy rains strip away minerals. In most years, however, the savannas support abundant agricultural production.

Early Humans Adapt to Their Environments

The first humans appeared in the Great Rift Valley, a deep gash in Earth's crust that runs through the floor of the Red Sea and across eastern Africa. As you learned earlier, people moved outward from this area in the world's first migration. They developed technologies that helped them survive in—and then alter—their surroundings.

Nomadic Lifestyle Africa's earliest peoples were nomadic hunter-gatherers. Today, some of the San of the Kalahari Desert and the BaMbuti (bah•uhm•BOO•tee) of the rain forests of Congo are still hunter-gatherers. The San, for example, travel in small bands of a few related families. The men hunt with spears and bows and arrows, and the women and children gather roots and berries.

Other early Africans eventually learned to domesticate and raise a variety of animals for food. Called herders, or pastoralists, these people kept cattle, goats, or sheep. They were nomads who drove their animals to find water and good pastures for grazing during the dry season. Millions of modern Africans are pastoral herders as well. The Masai (mah•SEYE) of Tanzania and southern Kenya, for example, still measure their wealth by the size of their herds. A

MAIN IDEA

Making Inferences

A Why might Africans continue living in a nomadic lifestyle?

Transition to a Settled Lifestyle Experts believe that agriculture in Africa probably began by 6000 B.C. Between 8000 and 6000 B.C., the Sahara received increased rainfall and turned into a savanna. But about 6000 B.C., the Sahara began to dry up again. To survive, many early farmers moved east into the Nile Valley and south into West Africa. Some settled on the savannas, which had the best agricultural land. Grain grew well in the savannas. In addition to growing grain, Africans began to raise cattle. In areas where the tsetse fly was found, it was not possible to keep cattle. However, south and east of the rain forests, cattle raising became an important part of agricultural life. Other Africans learned to farm in the rain forest, where they planted root crops, such as yams, that needed little sun.

Agriculture drastically changed the way Africans lived. Growing their own food enabled them to build permanent shelters in one location. Settlements expanded because reliable food supplies led to longer, healthier lives and an increased birthrate. The increased food supply also freed

Social History

Collecting Water

Finding and collecting water traditionally has been the job of women, whether they have a settled lifestyle or a nomadic one.

Each day they set out to find clean water for their families. Drought in Africa, which has lasted for many years, has increased the difficulty of finding clean water. In the past, it was estimated that women spent about nine minutes a day collecting water. In 2003, that time increased to 21 minutes, and women had to walk as far as six miles (about 10 kilometers) to find the water.

Obtaining clean water will continue to be a challenging daily task, even for people who have made the transition to a settled lifestyle on small plots of land.

INTEGRATED TECHNOLOGY

INTERNET ACTIVITY Create a photographic report outlining African clean water problems and solutions. Go to **classzone.com** for your research.

▲ This rock painting in northwestern Africa shows a line of calves tied to a rope in a pastoralist camp.

some members of the community to practice activities such as working metal, making pottery, and crafting jewelry.

These increasingly complex settlements of people required more organization than smaller communities. Various types of governing bodies developed to fill this need. Some governments consisted of a village chief and a council of the leaders of individual family groups. As strong groups moved to extend their land and conquered weaker settlements, they centralized their power and their governments. Some of these societies eventually developed into great kingdoms.

Early Societies in Africa

The societies south of the Sahara—like all human cultures—shared common elements. One of these elements was the importance of the basic social unit, the family. Besides parents and children, this primary group often included grandparents, aunts, uncles, and cousins in an extended family. Families that shared common ancestors sometimes formed groups known as clans.

Local Religions African peoples organized themselves into family groups. They also developed belief systems that helped them understand and organize information about their world. Nearly all of these local religions involved a belief in one creator, or god. They generally also included elements of **animism**, a religion in which spirits play an important role in regulating daily life. Animists believe that spirits are present in animals, plants, and other natural forces, and also take the form of the souls of their ancestors.

Keeping a History Few African societies had written languages. Instead, storytellers shared orally the history and literature of a culture. In West Africa, for example, these storytellers, or **griots** (gree•OHZ), kept this history alive, passing it from parent to child:

PRIMARY SOURCE **B**

I am a griot . . . master in the art of eloquence. . . . We are vessels of speech, we are the repositories [storehouses] which harbor secrets many centuries old. . . . Without us the names of kings would vanish. . . . We are the memory of mankind; by the spoken word we bring to life the deeds . . . of kings for younger generations. . . . For the world is old, but the future springs from the past.

DJELI MAMOUDOU KOUYATE, from *Sundiata, an Epic of Old Mali*

MAIN IDEA

Analyzing Primary Sources

B Why were griots important to African societies?

Vocabulary
desertification: the steady process of drying of the soil

Recent discoveries in West Africa have proved how old and extensive the history of this part of Africa is. Archaeologists believe that early peoples from the north moved into West Africa as desertification forced them south to find better farmland. Discoveries in the areas of modern Mali and Nigeria reveal that West Africans developed advanced societies and cities long before outsiders came to the continent.

West African Iron Age

Archaeologists' main source of information about early West African cultures has been from artifacts such as pottery, charcoal, and slag—a waste product of iron smelting. By dating these artifacts, scientists can piece together a picture of life in West Africa as early as 500 B.C.

Unlike cultures to the north, the peoples of Africa south of the Sahara seem to have skipped the Copper and Bronze Ages and moved directly into the Iron Age. Evidence of iron production dating to around 500 B.C. has been found in the area just north of the Niger and Benue rivers. The ability to smelt iron was a major technological achievement of the ancient Nok of sub-Saharan Africa.

The Nok Culture West Africa's earliest known culture was that of the **Nok** (nahk) people. They lived in what is now Nigeria between 500 B.C. and A.D. 200. Their name came from the village where the first artifacts from their culture were discovered. Nok artifacts have been found in an area stretching for 300 miles between the Niger and Benue rivers. They were the first West African people known to smelt iron. The iron was fashioned into tools for farming and weapons for hunting. Some of the tools and weapons made their way into overland trade routes.

> Analyzing Art

Nok Sculpture

Nok artifacts show evidence of a sophisticated culture. Their sculptures are made of terra cotta, a reddish-brown baked clay. Sculptures include animals as well as people. This Nok figure features a classical look called "elongated" style.

Most Nok figurines have these characteristics:

- distinctive features such as bulging eyes, flaring nostrils, and protruding lips
- an elongated style, especially used for the head
- the hand or chin on the knee in some figures
- hairstyle still common in Nigeria

SKILLBUILDER: Interpreting Visual Sources
Formulating Historical Questions *What questions would you ask if you could speak with the creator of this sculpture?*

African Ironworking

Refining metal was an important technological advance in every civilization. Africa was no exception. Iron tools were stronger than copper or bronze tools, so iron tools and the technology to produce them were very valuable.

Producing iron began by mining the iron ore. The iron itself was bound up with other minerals in rocks. The trick was separating the iron from the unwanted minerals. That was the function of the furnace shown below. This process is known as smelting.

INTEGRATED TECHNOLOGY

RESEARCH LINKS For more information on ironworking, go to **classzone.com**

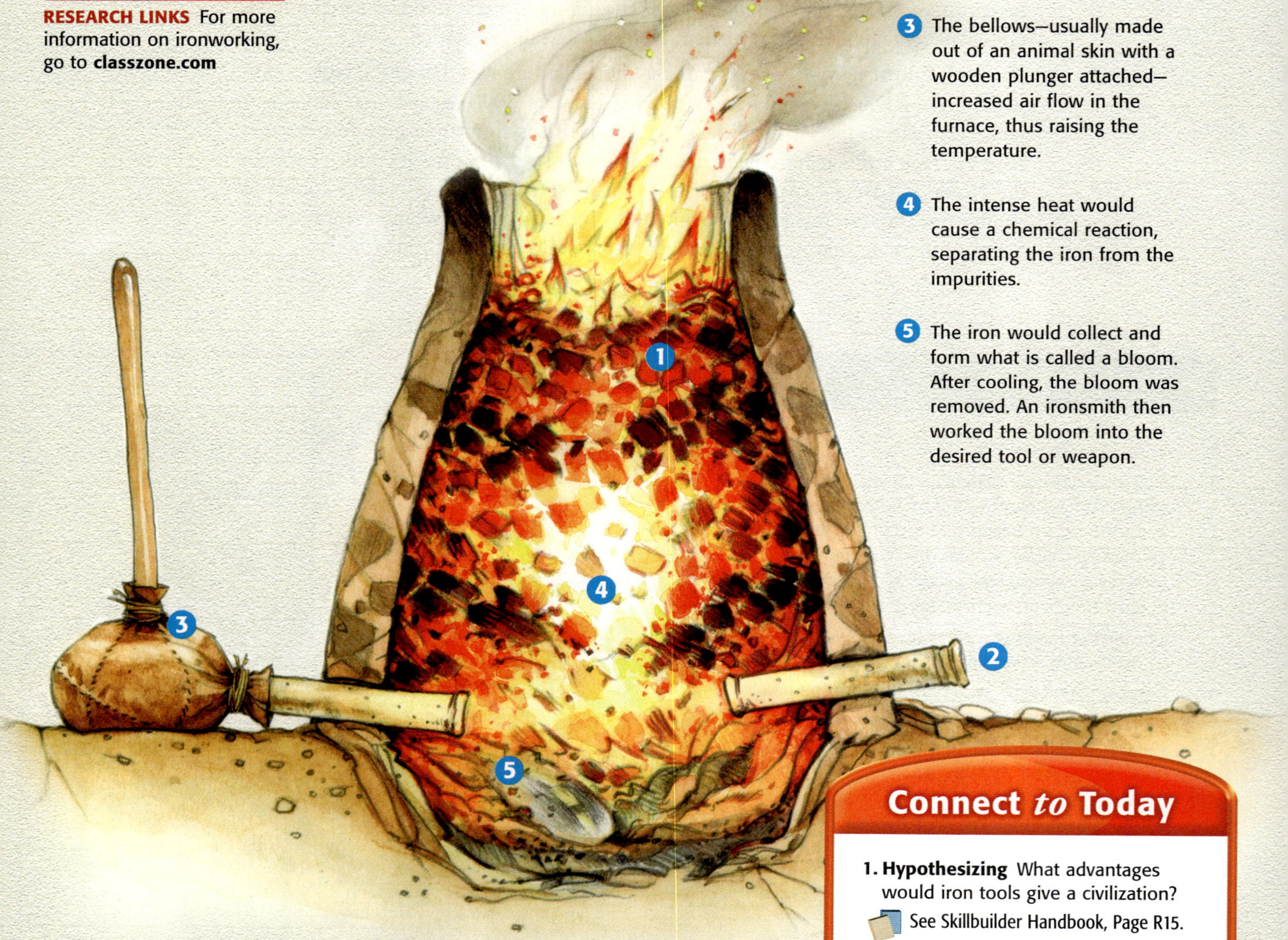

1. Layers of iron ore were alternated with layers of charcoal fuel inside the furnace. Temperatures inside the furnace would reach about 2000° F.
2. A tuyère (twee•YAIR) was a clay pipe that allowed air to flow through the furnace.
3. The bellows—usually made out of an animal skin with a wooden plunger attached—increased air flow in the furnace, thus raising the temperature.
4. The intense heat would cause a chemical reaction, separating the iron from the impurities.
5. The iron would collect and form what is called a bloom. After cooling, the bloom was removed. An ironsmith then worked the bloom into the desired tool or weapon.

Connect *to* Today

1. **Hypothesizing** What advantages would iron tools give a civilization?
   See Skillbuilder Handbook, Page R15.
2. **Comparing and Contrasting** Use the Internet to research the history of modern ironworking techniques. What improvements have been made, and how do they benefit our life today?

Djenné-Djeno In the region south of the Sahel, most Africans lived in small villages. However, cities began to develop sometime between 600 B.C. and 200 B.C. Usually they were in areas along rivers or at an oasis. One of these cities was Djenné-Djeno.

Djenné-Djeno (jeh•NAY-jeh•NOH), or ancient Djenné, was uncovered by archaeologists in 1977. Djenné-Djeno is located on a tributary of the Niger River in West Africa. There, scientists discovered hundreds of thousands of artifacts. These objects included pottery, copper hair ornaments, clay toys, glass beads, stone bracelets, and iron knives.

The oldest objects found there dated from 250 B.C., making Djenné-Djeno the oldest known city in Africa south of the Sahara. The city was abandoned sometime after A.D. 1400.

▲ A modern artist, Charles Santore, has pictured life in Djenné-Djeno around A.D. 1000.

At its height, Djenné-Djeno had some 50,000 residents. They lived in round reed huts plastered with mud. Later, they built enclosed houses made of mud bricks. They fished in the Niger River, herded cattle, and raised rice on the river's fertile floodplains. By the third century B.C., they had learned how to smelt iron. They exchanged their rice, fish, and pottery for copper, gold, and salt from other peoples who lived along the river. Djenné-Djeno became a bustling trading center linked to other towns not only by the Niger, but also by overland camel routes. (C)

MAIN IDEA

Comparing-
(C) In what ways were the cultures of Djenné-Djeno and the Nok alike?

The early inhabitants of West Africa were developing cities, cultures, and technologies that would make their mark on history. Meanwhile, other groups in West Africa were beginning to make an historic move out of West Africa. The Bantu-speaking people would take their culture and ironworking techniques with them to parts of eastern and southern Africa.

NEW YORK CORE CURRICULUM REVIEW

TERMS & NAMES 1. For each term or name, write a sentence explaining its significance.
- Sahara
- Sahel
- savanna
- animism
- griot
- Nok
- Djenné-Djeno

USING YOUR NOTES
2. How were history and culture preserved in African societies?

Africa
I. A Land of Geographic Contrasts
A.
B.
II. Early Humans Adapt to Their Environments

MAIN IDEAS
3. What are four general vegetation types found in Africa?
4. What is the main source of information about early African cultures?
5. How is the African Iron Age different from that in other regions?

CRITICAL THINKING & WRITING
6. **ANALYZING CAUSES** Why did diverse cultures develop in Africa?
7. **RECOGNIZING EFFECTS** How did agriculture change the way Africans lived?
8. **DRAWING CONCLUSIONS** What evidence shows that Djenné-Djeno was a major trading city in West Africa?
9. **WRITING ACTIVITY** INTERACTION WITH ENVIRONMENT Choose one of the climate or vegetation zones of Africa. Write a **poem** from the perspective of a person living in the zone and interacting with the environment.

CONNECT TO TODAY **CREATING A MAP**
Create a three-dimensional **map** of Africa that illustrates both vegetation zones and geographic features. Use your map to demonstrate the geographic challenges to people living on the continent.

2

Migration

CASE STUDY: Bantu-Speaking Peoples

CONNECT TO THE NEW YORK STATE CORE CURRICULUM

Unit 1.B.2.b. Causes of migration
Unit 1.B.2.c. Impact on other areas of Africa

TERMS & NAMES

- migration
- push-pull factors
- Bantu-speaking peoples

SETTING THE STAGE Human history is a constantly recurring set of movement, collision, settlement, and more movement. Throughout history, people have chosen to uproot themselves and move to explore their world. Sometimes they migrate in search of new opportunities. Other times, migration is a desperate attempt to find a place to survive or to live in peace.

TAKING NOTES
Analyzing Causes and Recognizing Effects Identify causes and effects of specific events related to Bantu migration.

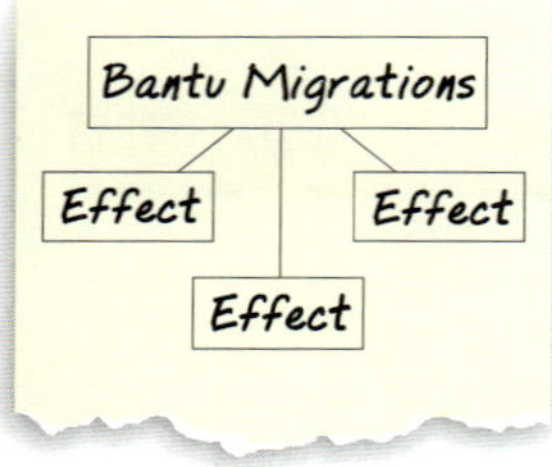

People on the Move

As an important pattern in human culture, migrations have influenced world history from its outset. **Migration** is a permanent move from one country or region to another.

Causes of Migration Aside from the general human desire for change, the causes of migrations fall into three categories: environmental, economic, and political. In the early history of human life, environmental factors were most likely the strongest. Later, economic and political causes played a greater role. For example, in the 15th century, the Ottomans' drive for power pushed them to move all over the ancient world to create a massive empire. As the world became more industrialized, more people moved to cities where work in factories was available. Elsewhere, religious or ethnic persecution supported by governments often drove groups of people to flee in order to survive. Seventeenth-century European settlers were pulled to America by the hope of religious tolerance, land for farming, or better economic conditions.

When looking at migration, historians and geographers speak of **push-pull factors**. These factors can either push people out of an area or pull them into an area. An example of an environmental pull factor might be abundant land that attracts people. On the other hand, the depletion of natural resources forces people away from a location—a push factor. Employment or the lack of it is an economic push or pull factor. Political conditions such as freedom or persecution can encourage people to move or to stay where they are. Urbanization also causes migration because job opportunities and other

▼ A mask of the Kuba, a Bantu-speaking people, from Congo and Zaire

Migration: Push-Pull Factors

Push Examples	Migration Factors	Pull Examples
Climate changes, exhausted resources, earthquakes, volcanoes, drought/famine	Environmental	Abundant land, new resources, good climate
Unemployment, slavery	Economic	Employment opportunities
Religious, ethnic, or political persecution, war	Political	Political and/or religious freedom

SKILLBUILDER: Interpreting Charts

1. **Developing Historical Perspective** *Are environmental factors still a cause of migration in the modern world? Explain.*
2. **Analyzing Causes** *Which cause do you think is most important in modern migrations? Why?*

benefits attract people. The chart above shows how causes of migration are related to push-pull factors.

Effects of Migration Life in a newly populated area changes because of the influx of new people. The results of migration may be positive or negative.

- Redistribution of the population may change population density.
- Cultural blending of languages or ways of life may occur.
- Ideas and technologies may be shared.
- People's quality of life may be improved as a result of moving.
- Clashes between groups may create unrest, persecution, or even war.
- Environmental conditions may change, causing famine or depleted natural resources.
- Employment opportunities may dry up, creating unemployment and poverty.

Migration changes the lives of those who migrate and also of the people in communities where they settle. Both groups may need to make adjustments in the way they live. Some adjustments may be relatively easy to make. For example, more advanced technology may improve living conditions. Other adjustments may be more difficult and may occur over a longer period of time. One of these adjustments may include language. (A)

MAIN IDEA

Forming Opinions

(A) Which of the effects of migration do you think are most negative? Explain.

Tracing Migration Through Language One way experts can trace the patterns of movement of people over time is by studying the spread of languages. People bring their languages with them when they move to new places. And languages, like the people who speak them, are living things that evolve and change in predictable ways. If two languages have similar words for a particular object or idea, for example, it is likely that the people who spoke those languages probably had close contact at one time.

Experts have studied languages in Africa. One group of African languages, the Niger-Congo, includes over 900 individual languages. A family of languages in this group developed from a single parent tongue, Proto-Bantu. Many anthropologists believe that the language spread across Africa as a result of migration. Today in Africa, Bantu speakers live in a region from south of the Sahara to the tip of Africa. A Bantu language is the first language of nearly one-third of all Africans.

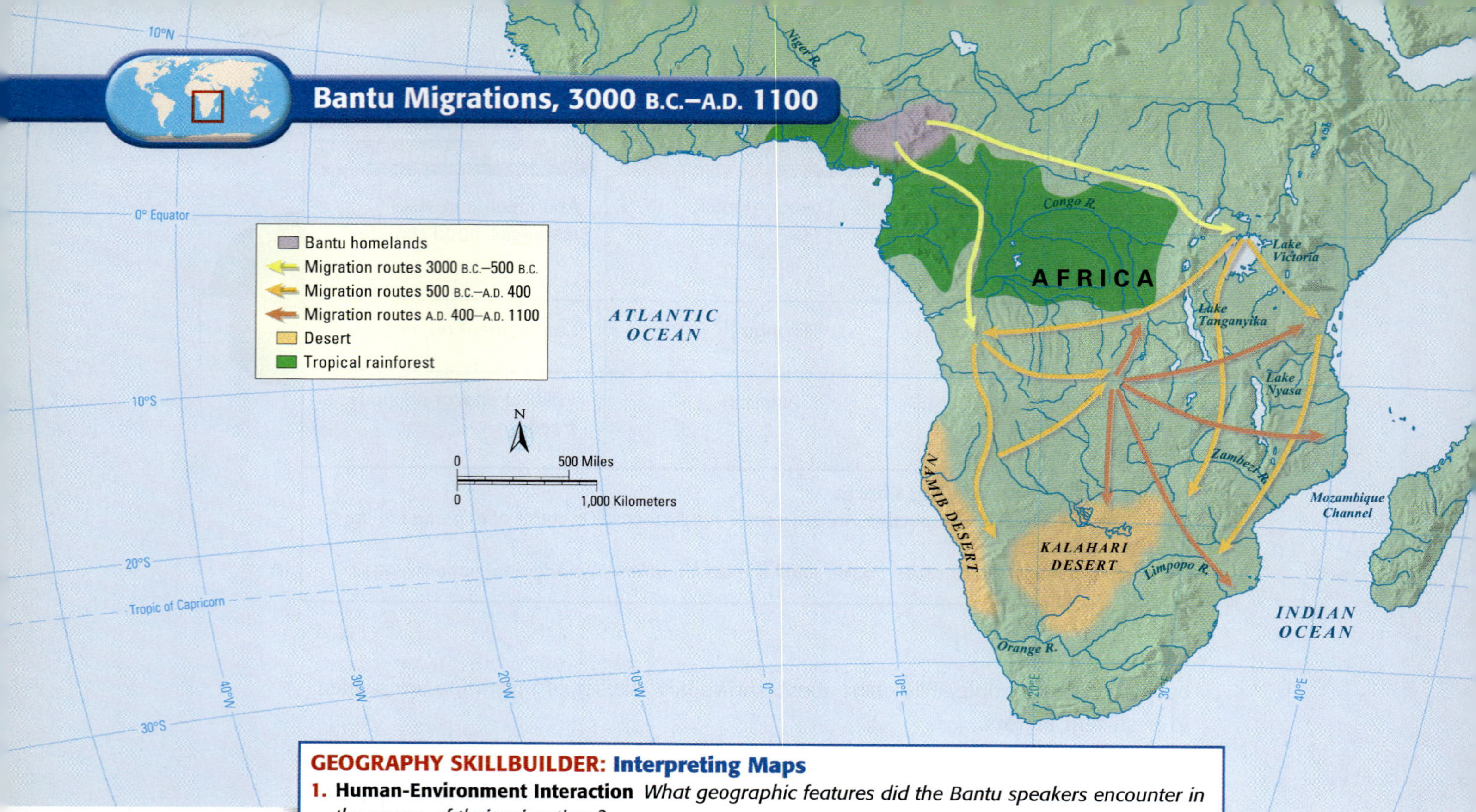

GEOGRAPHY SKILLBUILDER: Interpreting Maps

1. **Human-Environment Interaction** *What geographic features did the Bantu speakers encounter in the course of their migrations?*
2. **Movement** *Why didn't the Bantu speakers migrate northward?*

CASE STUDY: Bantu-speaking Peoples

Massive Migrations

Early Africans made some of the greatest migrations in history. When the migrations were over they or their descendants populated the southern third of the continent. Starting in the first few centuries A.D. and continuing over 1,500 years, small groups moved southward throughout Africa, spreading their language and culture. Historians refer to these people as the **Bantu-speaking peoples**. (The word Bantu itself means "the people.") The Bantu-speaking peoples originally lived in the savanna south of the Sahara, in the area that is now southeastern Nigeria.

Migration Begins Bantu speakers were not one people, but rather a group of peoples who shared certain cultural characteristics. They were farmers and nomadic herders who developed and passed along the skill of ironworking. Many experts believe they were related to the Nok peoples.

Beginning at least 2,000 years ago or earlier, small groups of Bantu speakers began moving to the south and east. The farming techniques used by these people forced them to move every few years. The technique is called slash and burn. A patch of the forest is cut down and burned. The ashes are mixed into the soil creating a fertile garden area. However, the land loses its fertility quickly and is abandoned for another plot in a new location. When they moved, the Bantu speakers shared their skills with the people they met, adapted their methods to suit each new environment, and learned new customs. They followed the Congo River through the rain forests. There they farmed the riverbanks—the only place that received enough sunlight to support agriculture.

As they moved eastward into the savannas, they adapted their techniques for herding goats and sheep to raising cattle. Passing through what is now Kenya and

Tanzania, they learned to cultivate new crops. One such crop was the banana, which came from Southeast Asia via Indonesian travelers.

Causes of Migration Although it is impossible to know exactly what caused the Bantu-speaking peoples to migrate, anthropologists have proposed a logical explanation. These experts suggest that once these peoples developed agriculture, they were able to produce more food than they could obtain by hunting and gathering. As a result, the population of West Africa increased. Because this enlarged population required more food, the earliest Bantu speakers planted more land. Soon there wasn't enough land to go around. They couldn't go north in search of land, because the area was densely populated. The areas that once had been savanna were becoming more desertlike. The Sahara was slowly advancing toward them. So the people moved southward.

The Bantu people probably brought with them the technology of iron smelting. As they moved southward, they were searching for locations with iron ore resources and hardwood forests. They needed the hardwood to make charcoal to fuel the smelting furnaces. (See the Science & Technology feature on page 218.)

As you can see from the map, the migrations split into eastern and western streams. Eventually, the Bantu speakers worked their way around the geographical barriers of the Kalahari and Namib deserts. Within 1,500 years or so—a short time in the span of history—they reached the southern tip of Africa. The Bantu speakers now populated much of the southern half of Africa. **B**

MAIN IDEA

Clarifying

B How did the Bantu deal with the problems they encountered in their migrations?

Effects of the Migration When the Bantu speakers settled into an area, changes occurred. The lands they occupied were not always unpopulated. Some areas into

Connect *to* Today

Bantu Languages: Swahili

An estimated 240 million people in Africa speak one of the Bantu languages as their first language. Of that number, about 50 million people in central and east Africa speak Swahili (also known as Kiswahili). The word swahili means "the coast." Swahili is widely used on the east coast of Africa, but is found elsewhere, too. It is the official language of Kenya and Tanzania.

In fact, after Arabic, Swahili is the most commonly spoken language in Africa. Swahili uses Bantu basics along with Arabic and Persian words. It probably developed as people of East Africa interacted with traders from the Indian Ocean trade networks and with Arabic traders.

The greeting *"Jambo. U mzima?"* (Hello. How are you?) and the answer *"U hali gani"* (The health is good.) can be understood by modern-day Swahili speakers from East Africa.

▲ This Kuba mask represents the sister of the founding ancestor of the Kuba culture group, a Bantu-speaking people.

which the Bantu moved were sparsely populated with peoples like the BaMbuti and the San. These Africans were not Bantu speakers. They were not engaged in agriculture but were instead hunter-gatherers. They had to find ways to get along with the Bantu, get out of their way, or defend their lands and way of life.

As the Bantu speakers spread south into hunter-gatherers' lands, territorial wars often broke out. Fighting with iron-tipped spears, the newcomers easily drove off the BaMbuti and the San, who were armed only with stone weapons. Today, the BaMbuti are confined to a corner of the Congo Basin. The San live only around the Kalahari Desert in northwestern South Africa, Namibia, and Botswana. Both groups live a very simple life. They do not speak a Bantu language, and their culture does not reflect the influence of the Bantu-speaking peoples.

The Bantu speakers exchanged ideas and intermarried with the people they joined. This intermingling created new cultures with unique customs and traditions. The Bantu speakers brought new techniques of agriculture to the lands they occupied. They passed on the technology of ironworking to forge tools and weapons from copper, bronze, and iron. They also shared ideas about social and political organization. Some of these ideas still influence the political scene in eastern and southern Africa. Although the Bantu migrations produced a great diversity of cultures, language had a unifying influence on the continent. **C**

In the next section, you will see how cultures on the east coast of Africa experienced growth and change. These changes came about as a result of human migrations from Arabia and cultural interaction with traders from North Africa and the Indian Ocean trade routes.

MAIN IDEA

Analyzing Effects

C How did the Bantu migrations change the history of Africa?

NEW YORK CORE CURRICULUM REVIEW

TERMS & NAMES 1. For each term or name, write a sentence explaining its significance.

- migration
- push-pull factors
- Bantu-speaking peoples

USING YOUR NOTES

2. Which effects of the Bantu-speaking migrations do you think had the most long-term impact? Explain.

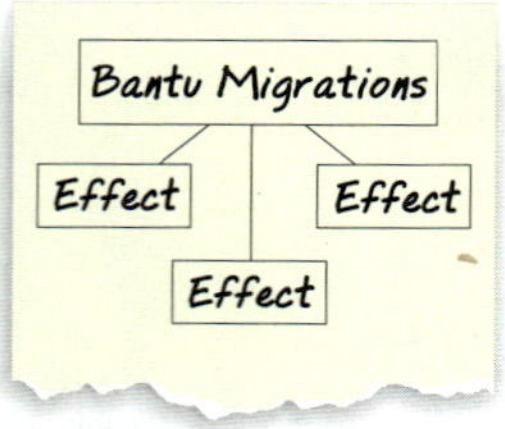

MAIN IDEAS

3. What are push-pull factors in migration?
4. What are three effects of migration?
5. Into which regions of Africa did the Bantu-speaking migration move?

CRITICAL THINKING & WRITING

6. **MAKING INFERENCES** How can the effects of one migration become a cause of another migration?
7. **RECOGNIZING EFFECTS** How does migration shape the modern world?
8. **HYPOTHESIZING** How might the population of Africa be different today if the Bantu-speaking migrations had not taken place?
9. **WRITING ACTIVITY** CULTURAL INTERACTION Write a **compare-and-contrast essay** addressing how migrating Bantu speakers and the peoples they encountered may have reacted to each other.

CONNECT TO TODAY **CREATING A DATABASE**

Use online or library resources to find information on Bantu languages and the countries in which they are spoken. Build a **database** using the information.

The Kingdom of Aksum

CONNECT TO THE NEW YORK STATE CORE CURRICULUM

Unit 1.C.7.c.1. Linking Africa and Eurasia
Unit 1.E.2. Expansion of Christianity, Islam, Confucianism, and Buddhism

TERMS & NAMES

- Aksum
- Adulis
- Ezana
- terraces

SETTING THE STAGE While migrations were taking place in the southern half of Africa, they were also taking place along the east coast. Arab peoples crossed the Red Sea into Africa perhaps as early as 1000 B.C. There they intermarried with Kushite herders and farmers and passed along their written language, Ge'ez (GEE•ehz). The Arabs also shared their skills of working stone and building dams and aqueducts. This blended group of Africans and Arabs would form the basis of a new and powerful trading kingdom.

The Rise of the Kingdom of Aksum

TAKING NOTES
Summarizing List the achievements of Aksum.

You learned in Chapter 4 that the East African kingdom of Kush became powerful enough to push north and conquer Egypt. During the next century, fierce Assyrians swept into Egypt and drove the Kushite pharaohs south. However, Kush remained a powerful kingdom for over 1,000 years. Finally, a more powerful kingdom arose and conquered Kush. That kingdom was **Aksum** (AHK•soom). It was located south of Kush on a rugged plateau on the Red Sea, in what are now the countries of Eritrea and Ethiopia. (See map on page 226.)

In this area of Africa, sometimes called the Horn of Africa, Arab traders from across the Red Sea established trading settlements. These traders were seeking ivory to trade in Persia and farther east in the Indian Ocean trade. They brought silks, textiles, and spices from eastern trade routes. Eventually, the trading settlements became colonies of farmers and traders. Trade with Mediterranean countries also flowed into seaports located here.

The Origins of Aksum A legend traces the founding of the kingdom of Aksum and the Ethiopian royal dynasty to the son of King Solomon (of ancient Israel) and of the Queen of Sheba, (a country in southern Arabia). That dynasty lasted into the 20th century, until the last ruler, Haile Selassie, died in 1975.

The first mention of Aksum was in a Greek guidebook written around A.D. 100, *Periplus of the Erythraean Sea*. It describes Zoskales (ZAHS•kuh•leez), thought to be the first king of Aksum. He was "a stickler about his possessions and always [greedy] for getting more, but in other respects a fine person and well versed in reading and writing Greek." Under Zoskales and other rulers, Aksum seized areas along the Red Sea and the Blue Nile in Africa. The rulers also

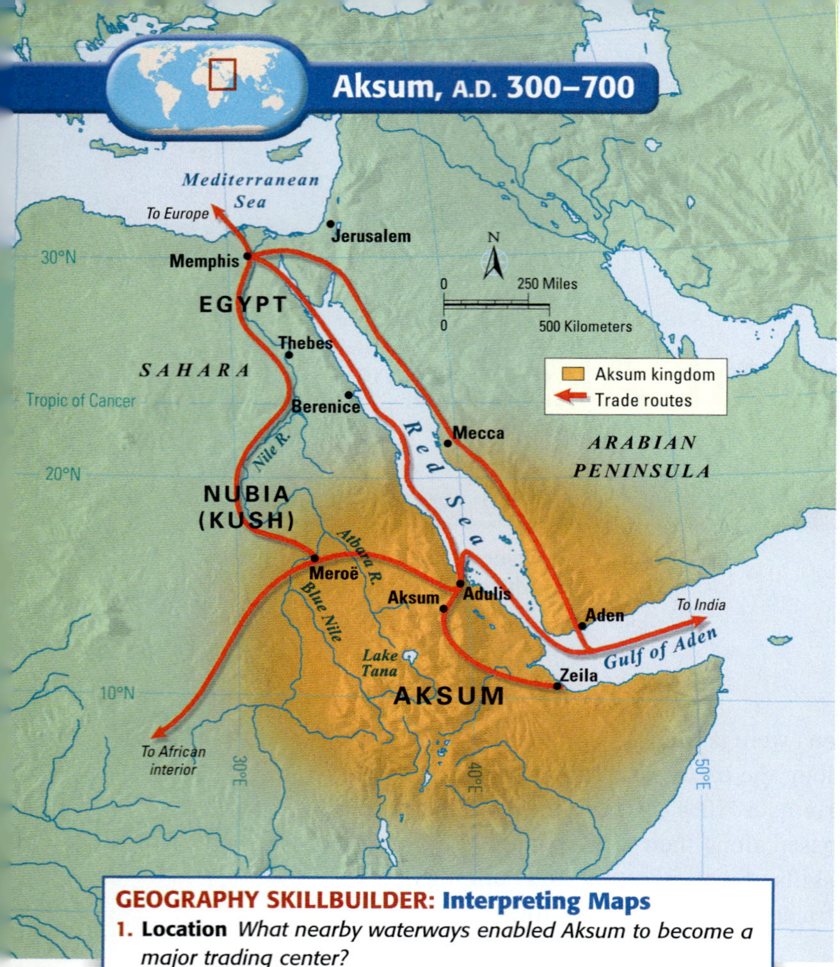

GEOGRAPHY SKILLBUILDER: Interpreting Maps

1. **Location** *What nearby waterways enabled Aksum to become a major trading center?*
2. **Movement** *To which continents or countries did Aksum's trade routes give it access?*

crossed the Red Sea and took control of lands on the southwestern Arabian Peninsula.

Aksum Controls International Trade Aksum's location and expansion made it a hub for caravan routes to Egypt and Meroë. Access to sea trade on the Mediterranean Sea and Indian Ocean helped Aksum become an international trading power. Traders from Egypt, Arabia, Persia, India, and the Roman Empire crowded Aksum's chief seaport, **Adulis** (AHD•uh•luhs), near present-day Massawa. (A)

MAIN IDEA

Recognizing Effects

(A) How did Aksum's location and interactions with other regions affect its development?

Aksumite merchants traded necessities such as salt and luxuries such as rhinoceros horns, tortoise shells, ivory, emeralds, and gold. In return, they chose from items such as imported cloth, glass, olive oil, wine, brass, iron, and copper. Around A.D. 550, an Egyptian merchant named Cosmas described how Aksumite agents bargained for gold from the people in southern Ethiopia:

PRIMARY SOURCE (B)

They take along with them to the mining district oxen, lumps of salt, and iron, and when they reach its neighborhood they . . . halt . . . and form an encampment, which they fence round with a great hedge of thorns. Within this they live, and having slaughtered the oxen, cut them in pieces and lay the pieces on top of the thorns along with the lumps of salt and the iron. Then come the natives bringing gold in nuggets like peas . . . and lay one or two or more of these upon what pleases them. . . . Then the owner of the meat approaches, and if he is satisfied he takes the gold away, and upon seeing this its owner comes and takes the flesh or the salt or the iron.

COSMAS quoted in *Travellers in Ethiopia*

MAIN IDEA

Analyzing Primary Sources

(B) Why don't the traders speak to each other instead of laying down goods or gold?

A Strong Ruler Expands the Kingdom The kingdom of Aksum reached its height between A.D. 325 and 360, when an exceptionally strong ruler, **Ezana** (AY•zah•nah), occupied the throne. Determined to establish and expand his authority, Ezana first conquered the part of the Arabian peninsula that is now Yemen. Then, in 330, Ezana turned his attention to Kush, which already had begun to decline. In 350, he conquered the Kushites and burned Meroë to the ground:

PRIMARY SOURCE

I carried war against [them] when they had rebelled. . . . I burnt their towns of stone and their towns of straw. At the same time, my men plundered [stole] their grain, their bronze, their iron and their copper, destroyed the idols in their homes, their stocks of corn and of cotton; and they threw themselves into the river.

KING EZANA OF AKSUM, quoted in *Africa: Past and Present*

An International Culture Develops

From the beginning, Aksumites had a diverse cultural heritage. This blend included traditions of the Arab peoples who crossed the Red Sea into Africa and those of the Kushite peoples they settled among. As the kingdom expanded and became a powerful trading center, it attracted people from all over the ancient world.

The port city of Adulis was particularly cosmopolitan. It included people from Aksum's widespread trading partners, such as Egypt, Arabia, Greece, Rome, Persia, India, and even Byzantium. In the babble of tongues heard in Aksum, Greek stood out as the international language of the time, much as English does in the world today.

Aksumite Religion The Aksumites, like other ancient Africans, traditionally believed in one god. They called their god Mahrem and believed that their king was directly descended from him. They were also animists, however, and worshiped the spirits of nature and honored their dead ancestors. They offered sacrifices—often as many as a dozen oxen at a time—to those spirits, to Mahrem, and often to the Greek god of war, Ares.

Merchants exchanged more than raw materials and finished goods in Aksum. They shared ideas as well. One of these ideas was a new religion, Christianity, which you learned about in Chapter 6. Based on the teachings of Jesus and a belief in one God—monotheism—Christianity began in Palestine about A.D. 30. It spread throughout the Roman Empire and then to Africa, and eventually to Aksum.

Aksum Becomes Christian Ezana succeeded to the throne as an infant after the death of his father. While his mother ruled the kingdom, a young Christian man from Syria who had been captured and taken into the court educated him.

Global Impact

A Road Paved with Gold: Aksum to Rome

The kingdom of Aksum had a tremendous impact on the ancient Mediterranean world. It particularly influenced one of the most important powers of the time, the Roman Empire. Roman ships came to Adulis weekly to trade with the Aksumites. Many Roman merchants lived in Adulis and in the capital city, Aksum.

One of the chief commodities that linked the two powers was gold. The Aksumites had access to it from inland gold mines, and the Romans needed it to support the monetary system of their growing empire. Rome and Aksum were linked not only by gold, however. They also shared a spiritual link in their commitment to Christianity.

▼ This mural depicting Bible stories is located on the wall of one of the oldest Christian churches in Aksum.

When Ezana finally became ruler of Aksum, he converted to Christianity and established it as the kingdom's official religion. He vowed, "I will rule the people with righteousness and justice and will not oppress them, and may they preserve this Throne which I have set up for the Lord of Heaven." King Ezana's conversion and his devout practice of Christianity strengthened its hold in Aksum. The establishment of Christianity was the longest lasting achievement of the Aksumites. Today, the land of Ethiopia, where Aksum was located, is home to millions of Christians. (C)

MAIN IDEA

Analyzing Causes

(C) What conditions led to Aksum's becoming Christian?

Aksumite Innovations The inscription on Ezana's stele is written in Ge'ez, the language brought to Aksum by its early Arab inhabitants. Aside from Egypt and Meroë, Aksum was the only ancient African kingdom known to have developed a written language. It was also the first state south of the Sahara to mint its own coins. Made of bronze, silver, and gold, these coins were imprinted with the saying, "May the country be satisfied." Ezana apparently hoped that this inscription would make him popular with the people. Every time they used a coin, it would remind them that he had their interests at heart.

In addition to these cultural achievements, the Aksumites adapted creatively to their rugged, hilly environment. They created a new method of agriculture, terrace farming. This enabled them to greatly increase the productivity of their land. **Terraces**, or steplike ridges constructed on mountain slopes, helped the soil retain water and prevented its being washed downhill in heavy rains. The Aksumites dug canals to channel water from mountain streams into the fields. They also built dams and cisterns, or holding tanks, to store water.

> Analyzing Architecture

Pillars of Aksum

Aksumites developed a unique architecture. They put no mortar on the stones used to construct vast royal palaces and public buildings. Instead, they carved stones to fit together tightly. Huge stone pillars were erected as monuments or tomb markers. The carvings on the pillars are representations of the architecture of the time.

To the left, the towering stone pillar, or stele, was built to celebrate Aksum's achievements. Still standing today, its size and elaborate inscriptions make it an achievement in its own right. It has many unique features:

- False doors, windows, and timber beams are carved into the stone.
- Typically, the top of the pillar is a rounded peak.
- The tallest stele was about 100 feet high. Of those steles left standing, one is 60 feet tall and is among the largest structures in the ancient world.
- The stone for the pillar was quarried and carved two to three miles away and then brought to the site.
- Ezana dedicated one soaring stone pillar to the Christian God, "the Lord of heaven, who in heaven and upon earth is mightier than everything that exists."

SKILLBUILDER: Interpreting Visual Sources

Comparing *How would constructing these pillars be similar to constructing the pyramids in Egypt?*

The Fall of Aksum

Aksum's cultural and technological achievements enabled it to last for 800 years. The kingdom finally declined, however, under invaders who practiced the religion called Islam (ihs•LAHM). Its founder was the prophet Muhammad; by his death in 632, his followers had conquered all of Arabia. In Chapter 10, you will learn more about Islam and Muhammad. This territory included Aksum's lands on the Arabian coast of the Red Sea.

Islamic Invaders Between 632 and 750 Islamic invaders conquered vast territories in the Mediterranean world, spreading their religion as they went. (See the map on page 261.) Aksum protected Muhammad's family and followers during their rise to power. As a result, initially they did not invade Aksum's territories on the African coast of the Red Sea. Retaining control of that coastline enabled Aksum to remain a trading power.

Before long, though, the invaders seized footholds on the African coast as well. In 710 they destroyed Adulis. This conquest cut Aksum off from the major ports along both the Red Sea and the Mediterranean. As a result, the kingdom declined as an international trading power. But it was not only Aksum's political power that weakened. Its spiritual identity and environment were also endangered.

MAIN IDEA

Recognizing Effects

D How did the Muslim conquest of Africa affect the kingdom of Aksum?

Aksum Isolated As the invaders spread Islam to the lands they conquered, Aksum became isolated from other Christian settlements. To escape the advancing wave of Islam, Aksum's rulers moved their capital over the mountains into what is now northern Ethiopia. Aksum's new geographic isolation—along with depletion of the forests and soil erosion—led to its decline as a world power. **D**

Although the kingdom of Aksum reached tremendous heights and left a lasting legacy in its religion, architecture, and agriculture, it never expanded outside a fairly small area. This is a pattern found in other cultures, both in Africa and around the world. In the next chapter, you will study the pattern as it played out among the native peoples of North and South America.

NEW YORK CORE CURRICULUM REVIEW

TERMS & NAMES 1. For each term or name, write a sentence explaining its significance.

- Aksum
- Adulis
- Ezana
- terraces

USING YOUR NOTES

2. Which of Aksum's achievements has continued into modern times?

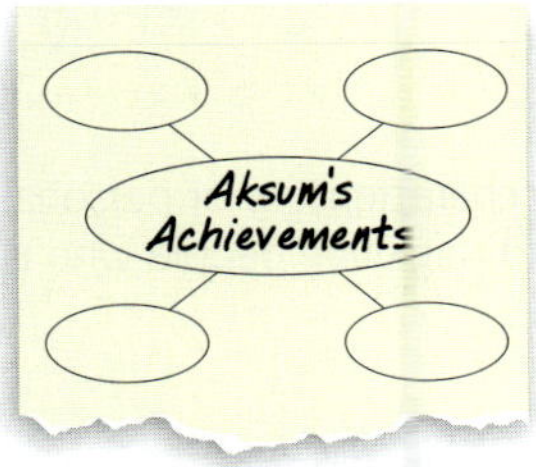

MAIN IDEAS

3. How did Aksum's location help make it a trade city?
4. Why did the people of Aksum become Christians?
5. Why did Aksum's leaders move their capital?

CRITICAL THINKING & WRITING

6. **DRAWING CONCLUSIONS** How did Aksum's location and interaction with other regions affect its development?
7. **ANALYZING CAUSES** Why did the kingdom of Aksum decline?
8. **EVALUATING DECISIONS** What impact did Ezana's decision to become a Christian have on the kingdom of Aksum?
9. **WRITING ACTIVITY** POWER AND AUTHORITY Write an **opinion paper** on the following statement: The kingdom of Aksum would have reached the same heights even if Ezana had not become king.

INTEGRATED TECHNOLOGY **INTERNET ACTIVITY**

Use the Internet to trace the beginnings of the Ethiopian dynasties to the Aksum kings. Then create an Ethiopian dynasty **family tree** showing the dynasty in power until late in the 20th century.

INTERNET KEYWORD
Ethiopian dynasty

Chapter 8 Assessment

VISUAL SUMMARY

African Civilizations

1. Diverse Societies in Africa

- Savanna and Mediterranean areas are most hospitable.
- Nomadic lifestyles are replaced with settled life.
- Djenné-Djeno becomes a major trade center.
- Nok people develop ironworking.

2. Migration

- Environmental, economic, or political reasons cause migration.
- Push-pull factors influence migration.
- Bantu-speaker migrations influence most of Africa south of the Sahara.

3. The Kingdom of Aksum

- Aksum is a major trade center on the Indian Ocean trade routes.
- King Ezana converts to Christianity.
- Islamic invaders isolate Aksum.

TERMS & NAMES

Briefly explain the importance of each of the following to African civilizations in the period from 1500 B.C. to A.D. 700.

1. Sahara
2. animism
3. griot
4. Nok
5. Djenné-Djeno
6. push-pull factors
7. Bantu-speaking peoples
8. Aksum

MAIN IDEAS

Diverse Societies in Africa Section 1 (pages 213–219)

9. How did geographic features affect the settlement of Africa?
10. What technology did the Nok introduce to West Africa?
11. What circumstances enabled Djenné-Djeno to become a bustling trade center?

Case Study: Migration Section 2 (pages 220–224)

12. What are three general causes of migration?
13. How are push-pull factors related to migration?
14. What caused the Bantu-speaking peoples to migrate?
15. Why were the migrations of Bantu speakers so extensive and successful?

The Kingdom of Aksum Section 3 (pages 225–229)

16. Why was Aksum able to control international trade?
17. In what ways did Ezana contribute to the rise of his kingdom?
18. Why did Aksum fall?

CRITICAL THINKING

1. USING YOUR NOTES
INTERACTION WITH ENVIRONMENT Use a flow chart to trace the main events that followed the development of agriculture on the African savannas.

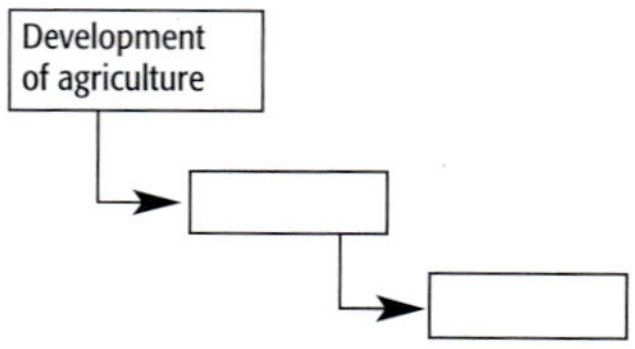

2. MAKING INFERENCES
How are the spread of ironmaking technology to east and south Africa and the Bantu migrations related?

3. EVALUATING DECISIONS
POWER AND AUTHORITY What were some of Ezana's most crucial leadership decisions?

4. FORMING OPINIONS
CULTURAL INTERACTION Do you think cultural characteristics or personal qualities determine how individuals act toward migrating people who settle among them? Explain.

5. COMPARING AND CONTRASTING
What are some positive and negative effects of migration?

Use the quotation about trade goods coming to Aksum and your knowledge of world history to answer questions 1 and 2.

Additional Test Practice pp. S1–S3

PRIMARY SOURCE

Small axes are imported, and adzes and swords; copper drinking-cups, round and large; a little coin for those coming to the market; wine of Laodicea [on the Syrian coast] and Italy, not much; olive oil, not much; . . . there are imported Indian cloth called monaché [fine quality cotton] and that called sagmotogene [probably tree cotton].

Adapted from *Travellers in Ethiopia* edited by
RICHARD PANKHURST

1 According to this passage, trade goods came to Aksum from which continents?

(1) Africa, Asia, and South America
(2) Asia and Europe
(3) Europe and Africa
(4) Africa, Asia, and Europe

2 What reason might be cited for the importing of cotton cloth?

(1) Cotton cloth was cheap and plentiful.
(2) Cotton cloth was popular with Aksumites.
(3) There was little or no cotton production in the country of Aksum.
(4) It is not possible to determine a reason from the passage.

Use the diagram and your knowledge of world history to answer question 3.

3 Based on the diagram above, what conclusions can you draw about the land area of the continent of Africa?

(1) It is the largest continent on Earth.
(2) It is smaller than India.
(3) It is smaller than Europe.
(4) The Sahara is larger than the United States.

INTEGRATED TECHNOLOGY

TEST PRACTICE Go to **classzone.com**

- Diagnostic tests
- Tutorials
- Strategies
- Additional practice

ALTERNATIVE ASSESSMENT

1. Interact *with* History

On page 212, you considered the effects newcomers would have on a community. Now that you've read the chapter and learned about people's interactions with their environments and with other cultures, how would you modify your answer? Discuss your ideas with a small group.

2. WRITING ABOUT HISTORY

Look at the causes for migration shown in the chart on page 221. Think about which of the causes might have an impact on you personally. Write a **paragraph** describing a cause that would force you to migrate to another part of the country or the world. Be sure to identify either the push or pull factor that might influence your decision. Consider the following:

- environmental conditions in the area in which you live
- economic or political factors that might have a direct effect on your life

INTEGRATED TECHNOLOGY

Creating a Documentary Film Script

Create a documentary film script on a current African ethnic group or country struggling to survive in its environment. Consider the following:

- current locations of drought, desertification, or overuse of land
- how the people are trying to deal with the problem
- what actions are needed to prevent a recurrence of the problem
- images, sounds, and interviews to tell the story

CHAPTER 9

The Americas: A Separate World, 40,000 B.C.–A.D. 700

NEW YORK CORE CURRICULUM FOCUS

- The Olmec created the first civilization in the Americas.
- Olmec art styles and urban design influenced later civilizations, such as the Maya.

Previewing Main Ideas

POWER AND AUTHORITY The first civilizations in the Americas arose as people came together to create more powerful and structured societies.

Geography *What geographical feature do most of these early American civilizations share?*

CULTURAL INTERACTION From their art to their technology, the early Mesoamerican and South American civilizations influenced the better-known empires that followed them.

Geography *Why is it likely that the Nazca and Moche civilizations were aware of each other?*

INTERACTION WITH ENVIRONMENT The Olmec in Mesoamerica took advantage of their surroundings, while the groups in South America carved societies out of rough terrain.

Geography *How were geographic conditions different for the Olmec and Chavín peoples?*

INTEGRATED TECHNOLOGY

eEdition
- Interactive Maps
- Interactive Visuals
- Interactive Primary Sources

INTERNET RESOURCES
Go to **classzone.com** for:
- Research Links
- Internet Activities
- Primary Sources
- Chapter Quiz
- Maps
- Test Practice
- Current Events

AMERICAS

10,000 B.C.

10,000 B.C. Last Ice Age ends; land bridge to Asia disappears.

7000 B.C. Agriculture begins in central Mexico.

1200 B.C. Olmec civilization emerges in southeast Mexico. (figure of Olmec wrestler or ball player) ▶

1200 B.C.

WORLD

1200 B.C. ◀ Egyptian Empire begins to decline. (Egyptian sphinx and pyramid)

American Civilizations, 1200 B.C.–A.D. 700

900 B.C.
Chavín culture arises in Peru.

500 B.C.
Zapotecs build Monte Albán.

200 B.C.
Nazca civilization arises in southern Peru.

A.D. 100
Moche culture emerges. (Moche gold monkey head bead)▶

250 B.C.

A.D. 700

480 B.C.
Golden Age of Greece begins.

202 B.C.
Han Dynasty begins in China.

A.D. 120
Roman Empire reaches its height. (marble bust of Emperor Hadrian)▶

Interact *with* History

How can killing a mammoth help you survive?

You are a hunter living in ancient North America. Along with several other hunters, you have been tracking the mammoth for days. This giant beast is a challenging prey. Close to 14 feet high at the shoulders, it can easily crush a human. Its curved tusks, measuring more than 15 feet in length, are sharp and therefore dangerous. Yet the rewards of killing the huge animal are worth the risks for you, your fellow hunters, and your families.

Suddenly you spot the massive creature. Aside from spears, your only weapons are some simple tools and your superior intelligence.

EXAMINING *the* ISSUES

- **What uses might hunters and their families make of the slain mammoth?**
- **What roles might strategy and cooperation play in the hunt?**

As a class, discuss these questions. In your discussion, consider how this situation speaks to the difficulties of life in a hunter-gatherer society. As you read about the growth of civilization in the Americas, notice how the old hunting and gathering way of life dramatically changed with the development of agriculture.

The Earliest Americans

CONNECT TO THE NEW YORK STATE CORE CURRICULUM

Unit 1.A.2. Hunters and gatherers–nomadic groups
Unit 2.A.5.c. Role of maize

TERMS & NAMES

- Beringia
- Ice Age
- maize

SETTING THE STAGE While civilizations were developing in Africa, Asia, and Europe, they were also emerging in the Americas. Human settlement in the Americas is relatively recent compared to that in other parts of the world. However, it followed a similar pattern. At first the ancient people of the Americas survived mainly by hunting. Over time, they developed farming methods that ensured a more reliable supply of food. This in turn led to the growth of the first civilizations in the Americas.

A Land Bridge

The American continents include North and South America. They are connected and span two hemispheres, from the frigid Arctic Circle in the north to the icy waters around Antarctica in the south. Although this land mass narrows greatly around modern-day Panama, it stretches unbroken for about 9,000 miles. This large and rugged land is isolated from the rest of the world by vast oceans. Yet, thousands of years ago, the Americas were connected by a land bridge to Asia. Most experts believe that some of the first people came to the Americas from Asia over this land bridge. The land bridge is known as **Beringia**. Other people may have arrived by boat.

TAKING NOTES
Analyzing Causes and Recognizing Effects
Use a chart to list causes and effects of the development of the Americas.

Cause	Effect
1.	1.
2.	2.

Peopling the Americas The first Americans arrived sometime toward the end of the last **Ice Age**, which lasted from roughly 1.9 million to about 10,000 B.C. Huge sheets of moving ice, called glaciers, spread southward from the Arctic Circle. They covered large portions of North America. The buildup of glaciers locked up huge amounts of the earth's water. It lowered sea levels and created a land corridor between Asia and Alaska across what is now the Bering Strait.

Herds of wild animals from Siberia, including the mammoth, migrated across the plains of the Beringia land bridge. Gradually, Siberian hunters followed these animals into North America. They most likely were unaware that they were entering a new continent. These migrants became the first Americans.

Thomas Canby, a writer for *National Geographic* magazine, spent a year with archaeologists as they searched for ancient burial sites throughout the Americas. From his experience, Canby described the type of world that might have greeted these hunters and migrants as they entered the Americas:

PRIMARY SOURCE **A**

What a wild world it was! To see it properly, we must board a time machine and travel back into the Ice Age. The northern half of North America has vanished, buried beneath ice sheets two miles thick. Stretching south to Kentucky, they buckle the earth's crust with their weight. . . . Animals grow oversize. . . . Elephant-eating jaguars stand tall as lions, beavers grow as big as bears, South American sloths as tall as giraffes. With arctic cold pushing so far southward, walrus bask on Virginia beaches, and musk-oxen graze from Maryland to California.

THOMAS CANBY, "The Search for the First Americans," *National Geographic*

MAIN IDEA

Analyzing Primary Sources

A What might account for the abundance of animal life that Canby describes?

No one knows for sure when the first Americans arrived. Some scholars contend that the migration across the land bridge began as early as 40,000 B.C. Others argue it occurred as late as 10,000 B.C. For years, many researchers have regarded the discovery of spearheads dating back to 9500 B.C. near Clovis, New Mexico, to be the earliest evidence of humankind in the Americas.

However, recent discoveries of possible pre-Clovis sites have challenged this theory. One such discovery was made at Monte Verde, Chile, near the southern tip of the Americas. Researchers there have found evidence of human life dating back to 10,500 B.C. Underneath this site—a sandy bank near a creek—archaeologists discovered pieces of animal hide and various tools. They also found a preserved chunk of meat and a child's single footprint. The evidence at Monte Verde suggests that the first Americans arrived well before the Clovis era. To reach southern Chile at such an early date, some experts believe, humans would have had to cross the land bridge at least 20,000 years ago.

Most experts believe the earliest Americans traveled by foot across the land bridge. However, some scholars think they also may have paddled from Asia to the Pacific Coast in small boats. A skull discovered near Mexico City has recently been dated to about 11,000 B.C., making it the oldest skull ever found in the Americas. Some scientists studying the skull believe that it is related to the Ainu people of Japan and that these descendants of the Ainu reached the Americas by island-hopping on boats.

Hunters and Gatherers

Questions remain about how and when the first Americans arrived. What appears more certain—from the discovery of chiseled spearheads and charred bones at ancient sites—is that the earliest Americans lived as hunters. Perhaps their most challenging and rewarding prey was the mammoth. Weighing more than seven tons, this animal provided meat, hide, and bones for food, clothing, shelters, and tools.

Following the Game Eventually, large animals like the mammoth were overhunted and became extinct. Hunters soon turned to smaller prey, such as deer and rabbits, for their survival. They also fished and gathered edible plants and fruits. Because they were hunters, the earliest Americans found it necessary to move regularly in search of food. Whenever they did settle in one place for a short time, prehistoric Americans lived in caves or temporary shelters in the open air. **B**

MAIN IDEA

Recognizing Effects

B How did the earliest Americans adapt to the loss of large animals?

With the end of the Ice Age, around 12,000 to 10,000 years ago, came the end of land travel across Beringia. As the great glaciers melted, sea levels rose. The ancient land bridge disappeared under the Bering Strait. By this time, however, humans inhabited most regions of the Americas. Wherever they roamed, from the grassy plains of the modern-day United States to the steamy tropical forests of Central America, the first Americans adapted to the variety of environments they inhabited. In doing so, they carved out unique ways of life.

Migration Routes, 40,000–10,000 B.C.

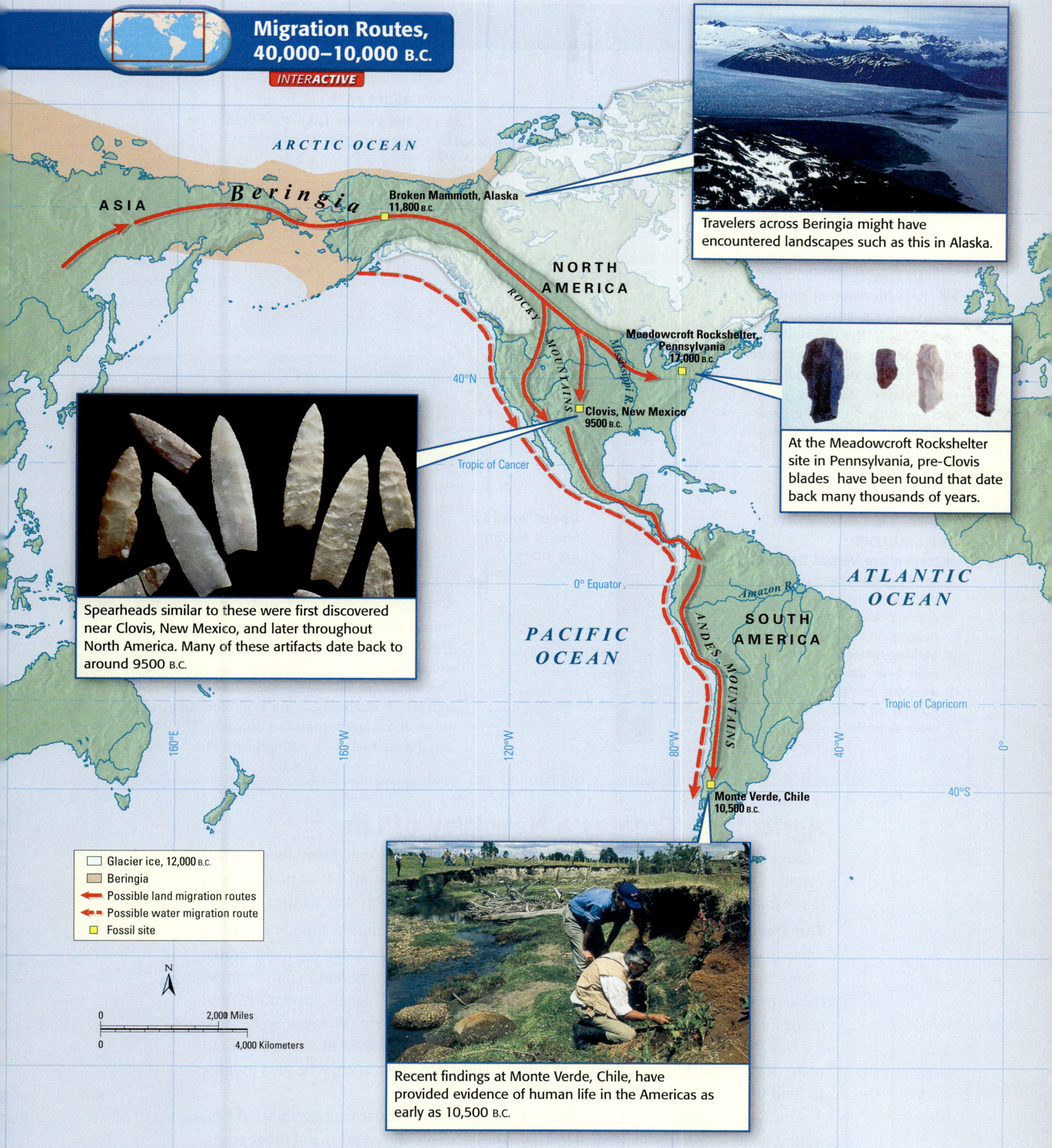

Travelers across Beringia might have encountered landscapes such as this in Alaska.

At the Meadowcroft Rockshelter site in Pennsylvania, pre-Clovis blades have been found that date back many thousands of years.

Spearheads similar to these were first discovered near Clovis, New Mexico, and later throughout North America. Many of these artifacts date back to around 9500 B.C.

Recent findings at Monte Verde, Chile, have provided evidence of human life in the Americas as early as 10,500 B.C.

GEOGRAPHY SKILLBUILDER: Interpreting Maps

1. **Location** *What two continents does the Beringia land bridge connect?*
2. **Movement** *From where do scholars believe the first Americans came? How did they come?*

Analyzing Artifacts

INTERACTIVE

A Bison Kill Site

The first hunters roaming North America hunted mammoths, deer, and bison. Researchers found the bones of bison at a kill site near Calgary, Alberta, in Canada. This kill site is believed to have been in use for more than 8,000 years.

Different layers of remains and artifacts have been found at the kill site, with different kinds of points—spears, arrows, knives, and so forth. The different styles of points can tell archaeologists about the age of a site and its various layers. Weapons and tools such as those shown here were used to kill and butcher animals for the hunters and their families to consume.

About A.D. 1
The Pelican Lake style points are the youngest or most recent. They are about 2,000 years old.

About 2500 B.C.
The McKean style points are in the middle range. They are about 4,500 years old.

About 4300 B.C.
Mount Mazama explodes

About 6000 B.C.
Other points, buried beneath a layer of volcanic ash, are the oldest of all. They are about 8,000 years old. The ash arrived in the Calgary area about 6,300 years ago when Mount Mazama exploded. Deposits beneath this ash are older than the eruption. The bones above are the remains of a young bison butchered at the site.

SKILLBUILDER:
Interpreting Visual Sources

1. **Drawing Conclusions** *What resources besides food might animals have provided to early hunters and their families?*
2. **Making Inferences** *What might have been the effect of the weapons and tools of early hunters on the big-game animals of the Americas?*

Agriculture Creates a New Way of Life

Gradually, the earliest Americans became more familiar with plant foods. They began to experiment with simple methods of farming. Their efforts at planting and harvesting led to agriculture. This dramatically changed their way of life.

The Development of Farming Around 7000 B.C., a revolution quietly began in what is now central Mexico. There, people began to rely more on wild edible plants, raising some of them from seeds. By 5000 B.C., many had begun to grow these preferred plants. They included squashes, gourds, beans, avocados, and chilies. By 3400 B.C., these early farmers grew **maize**, or corn. Maize soon became the most important crop. This highly nourishing crop flourished in the tropical climate of Mexico. There, a family of three could raise enough corn in four months to feed themselves for a long time.

Gradually, people settled in permanent villages in the Tehuacan (TAY•wuh•KAHN) Valley, south of present-day Mexico City. These people raised corn and other crops. The techniques of agriculture spread over North and South America. However, it is believed that people in some areas, such as Peru and eastern North America, may have discovered the secrets of cultivating local edible plants independently.

The Effects of Agriculture

Before Agriculture	After Agriculture
• People hunted or gathered what they ate. • Families continually moved in search of big game. • Groups remained small due to the scarcity of reliable sources of food. • Humans devoted much of their time to obtaining food.	• People enjoyed a more reliable and steady source of food. • Families settled down and formed larger communities. • Humans concentrated on new skills: arts and crafts, architecture, social organization. • Complex societies eventually arose.

SKILLBUILDER: Interpreting Charts

1. **Recognizing Effects** *How did life change after the development of agriculture?*
2. **Making Inferences** *How might the establishment of agriculture have helped humans to develop new skills and interests?*

Over the next several centuries, farming methods became more advanced. In central Mexico native farmers created small islands in swamps and shallow lakes by stacking layers of vegetation, dirt, and mud. They then planted crops on top of the island soil. The surrounding water provided irrigation. These floating gardens were very productive, yielding up to three harvests a year.

MAIN IDEA

Making Inferences

C Why might the development of agriculture be characterized by some as a turning point in human history?

Farming Brings Great Change In the Americas, as in other regions of the world, agriculture brought great and lasting change to people's way of life. The cultivation of corn and other crops provided a more reliable and expanding food supply. This encouraged population growth and the establishment of large, settled communities. As the population grew, and as farming became more efficient and productive, more people turned their attention to nonagricultural pursuits. They developed specialized skills in arts and crafts, building trades, and other fields. Differences between social classes—between rich and poor, ruler and subject—began to emerge. With the development of agriculture, society became more complex. The stage was set for the rise of more advanced civilizations. C

NEW YORK CORE CURRICULUM REVIEW

TERMS & NAMES 1. For each term or name, write a sentence explaining its significance.

- Beringia
- Ice Age
- maize

USING YOUR NOTES

2. Which effect do you think had the most significant impact on the Americas? Explain.

Cause	Effect
1.	1.
2.	2.

MAIN IDEAS

3. How did human beings come to the Americas?
4. How did humans get food before the development of farming?
5. What sorts of changes did farming bring?

CRITICAL THINKING & WRITING

6. **FORMING OPINIONS** Why do you think early Americans, isolated from the rest of the world, developed in ways similar to other early humans?
7. **HYPOTHESIZING** What sailing routes might early humans have traveled to the Americas?
8. **COMPARING** What sorts of problems might the earliest Americans have encountered in their travels?
9. **WRITING ACTIVITY** POWER AND AUTHORITY What type of person might hold power in a hunter-gatherer society? in a settled, agricultural society? Support your opinions in a two-paragraph **essay.**

INTEGRATED TECHNOLOGY **INTERNET ACTIVITY**

Use the Internet to find information on early archaeological sites in the Americas. Locate these sites on an **outline map** and show the dates that scientists have assigned to these sites.

INTERNET KEYWORD
Clovis, Meadowcroft Rockshelter

Early Mesoamerican Civilizations

CONNECT TO THE NEW YORK STATE CORE CURRICULUM

Unit 2.A.5.a. Human and physical geography
Unit 2.A.5.b. Contributions (mathematics, astronomy, science, arts, architecture, and technology)

TERMS & NAMES

- Mesoamerica
- Olmec
- Zapotec
- Monte Albán

SETTING THE STAGE The story of developed civilizations in the Americas begins in a region called **Mesoamerica**. (See map on opposite page.) This area stretches south from central Mexico to northern Honduras. It was here, more than 3,000 years ago, that the first complex societies in the Americas arose.

TAKING NOTES

Comparing Use a Venn diagram to compare Olmec and Zapotec cultures.

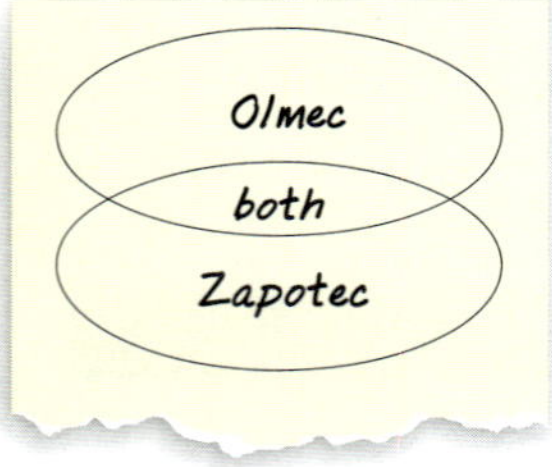

The Olmec

Mesoamerica's first known civilization builders were a people known as the **Olmec**. They began carving out a society around 1200 B.C. in the jungles of southern Mexico. The Olmec influenced neighboring groups, as well as the later civilizations of the region. They often are called Mesoamerica's "mother culture."

The Rise of Olmec Civilization Around 1860, a worker clearing a field in the hot coastal plain of southeastern Mexico uncovered an extraordinary stone sculpture. It stood five feet tall and weighed an estimated eight tons. The sculpture was of an enormous head, wearing a headpiece. (See History Through Art, pages-244–245.) The head was carved in a strikingly realistic style, with thick lips, a flat nose, and large oval eyes. Archaeologists had never seen anything like it in the Americas.

This head, along with others that were discovered later, was a remnant of the Olmec civilization. The Olmec emerged about 1200 B.C. and thrived from approximately 800–400 B.C. They lived along the Gulf Coast of Mexico, in the modern-day Mexican states of Veracruz and Tabasco.

Gulf Coast Geography On the surface, the Gulf Coast seemed an unlikely site for a high culture to take root. The region was hot and humid and covered with swamps and jungle. In some places, giant trees formed a thick cover that prevented most sunlight from reaching the ground. Up to 100 inches of rain fell every year. The rainfall swelled rivers and caused severe flooding.

However, the region also had certain advantages. There were abundant deposits of salt and tar, as well as fine clay used in making pottery. There was also wood and rubber from the rain forest. The hills to the north provided hard stone from which the Olmec could make tools and monuments. The rivers that laced the region provided a means of transport. Most important, the flood plains of these rivers provided fertile land for farming.

The Olmec used their resources to build thriving communities. The oldest site, San Lorenzo, dates back to around 1150 B.C. Here archaeologists uncovered important clues that offered a glimpse into the Olmec world. **A**

MAIN IDEA

Making Inferences

A In what ways did the Olmec's environment help in the creation of its civilization?

Olmec Society At San Lorenzo archaeologists discovered earthen mounds, courtyards, and pyramids. Set among these earthworks were large stone monuments. They included columns, altars, and more colossal, sculpted heads, which may have represented particular Olmec rulers. These giant monuments weigh as much as 44 tons. Some scholars think that Olmec workers may have moved these sculptures over land on rolling logs to the river banks. From there, they may have rafted the monuments along waterways to various sites.

GEOGRAPHY SKILLBUILDER: Interpreting Maps

1. **Movement** *Judging from the map, what was one way in which the Olmec spread their influence?*
2. **Movement** *What difficulties might the Olmec have encountered in developing their trade routes?*

To the east of San Lorenzo, another significant Olmec site, La Venta, rose around 900 B.C. Here, researchers discovered a 100-foot-high mound of earth and clay. This structure may have served as the tomb of a great Olmec ruler. Known as the Great Pyramid, the mound also may have been the center of the Olmec religion. Experts believe the Olmec prayed to a variety of nature gods.

Most of all, they probably worshiped the jaguar spirit. Numerous Olmec sculptures and carvings depict a half-human, half-jaguar creature. Some scholars believe that the jaguar represented a powerful rain god. Others contend that there were several jaguar gods, representing the earth, fertility, and maize.

Trade and Commerce Archaeologists once believed that sites such as La Venta were ceremonial centers where important rituals were performed but few people lived. In recent years, however, experts have begun to revise that view. The Olmec appear to have been a prosperous people who directed a large trading network throughout Mesoamerica. Olmec goods traveled as far as Mexico City to the north and Honduras to the south. In addition, raw materials—including iron ore and various stones—reached San Lorenzo from faraway regions. This trade network helped boost the Olmec economy and spread Olmec influence.

MAIN IDEA

Hypothesizing

B What might lead to the disappearance of an entire civilization?

Decline of the Olmec For reasons that are not fully understood, Olmec civilization eventually collapsed. Scholars believe San Lorenzo was destroyed around 900 B.C. La Venta may have fallen sometime around 400 B.C. Some experts speculate that outside invaders caused the destruction. Others believe the Olmec may have destroyed their own monuments upon the death of their rulers. **B**

Zapotec Civilization Arises

By the time Olmec civilization had collapsed, another people—the **Zapotec**—were developing an advanced society to the southwest, in what is now the Mexican state of Oaxaca (wuh•HAH•kah). Though they showed traces of Olmec influence, the Zapotec built a unique civilization.

Peoples of the Oaxaca Valley Oaxaca is a rugged region of mountains and valleys in southern Mexico. In the center of the state, three valleys meet to form a large open area known as the Oaxaca Valley. This valley has fertile soil, a mild climate, and enough rainfall to support agriculture. As a result, various peoples have made the Oaxaca Valley their home, including the ancient Zapotec.

For centuries the Zapotec lived in scattered villages throughout the valley. By 1000 B.C., however, one site—San José Mogote—was emerging as the main power in the region. At this site, the Zapotec constructed stone platforms. They also built temples and began work on monumental sculptures. By 500 B.C. they had developed early forms of writing and a calendar system.

The Zapotec Flourish at Monte Albán Around 500 B.C., Zapotec civilization took a major leap forward. High atop a mountain at the center of the Oaxaca Valley, the Zapotec built the first real urban center in the Americas, **Monte Albán**. This city, with its commanding view of the entire valley, grew and prospered over the next several centuries. By 200 B.C., Monte Albán was home to around 15,000 people. The city eventually would reach a peak population of almost 25,000. (C)

From A.D. 250 to A.D. 700, Monte Albán was truly impressive. At the heart of the city was a giant plaza paved with stones. Towering pyramids, temples, and

MAIN IDEA

Comparing

(C) How does Monte Albán's population compare to the populations of today's major cities?

Global Patterns

Pyramids

A number of ancient peoples used pyramids for temples, tombs, and observatories. The Egyptians built pyramids as tombs. Their pyramids had smooth sides and came to a point. In contrast, the pyramids built by the Zapotec at Monte Albán (shown below) have stepped sides, with flat tops that served as platforms for temples.

INTEGRATED TECHNOLOGY

INTERNET ACTIVITY Make a poster about the different kinds of pyramids in Egypt and Mesoamerica. Go to **classzone.com** for your research.

palaces, all made out of stone, surrounded this plaza. There was even an observatory for observing the stars to establish a calendar. Nearby was a series of stone carvings of corpses. Their facial features show an Olmec influence.

For more than a thousand years the Zapotec controlled the Oaxaca Valley and the surrounding region. Sometime after A.D. 600, the Zapotec began to decline. Some scholars believe they may have suffered a loss of trade or other economic difficulties. As with the Olmec, the fall of Zapotec civilization remains a puzzle.

The Early Mesoamericans' Legacy

Although both the Zapotec and Olmec civilizations eventually collapsed, each culture influenced the Mesoamerican civilizations that followed.

The Olmec Leave Their Mark The Olmec contributed much to later Mesoamerican civilizations. They influenced the powerful Maya, who will be discussed in Chapter 16. Olmec art styles, especially the use of the jaguar motif, can be seen in the pottery and sculpture of later peoples in the region. In addition, future Mesoamerican societies copied the Olmec pattern of urban design.

The Olmec also left behind the notions of planned ceremonial centers, ritual ball games, and an elite ruling class. And while there is no clear evidence that the Olmec used a written language, their descendants or a related people carved out stone symbols that may have influenced later glyph writing. D

MAIN IDEA

Forming Opinions

D What do you consider to be the Olmec's most important contributions to later cultures?

Zapotec Contributions-The Zapotec left behind their own legacy. It included a hieroglyphic writing system and a calendar system based on the movement of the sun. In addition, the Zapotec are noted as the Americas' first city builders. Monte Albán combined ceremonial grandeur with residential living space. This style influenced the development of future urban centers and became a hallmark of Mesoamerican civilizations.

As the Zapotec and Olmec flourished and then declined, civilizations were also taking shape in South America. Along the rough and mountainous terrain in what is now Peru, ancient peoples came together. There, they created more advanced and complex societies.

NEW YORK CORE CURRICULUM REVIEW

TERMS & NAMES 1. For each term or name, write a sentence explaining its significance.

- Mesoamerica
- Olmec
- Zapotec
- Monte Albán

USING YOUR NOTES

2. What was one characteristic unique to Olmec culture?

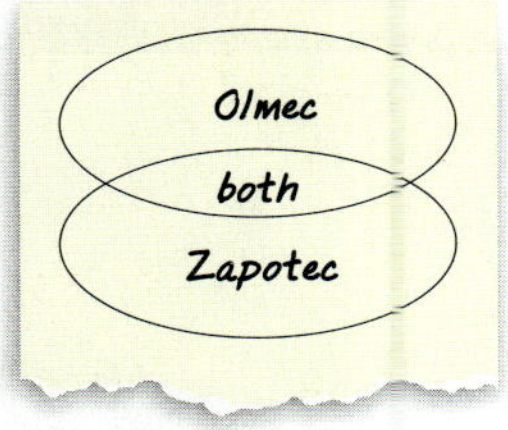

MAIN IDEAS

3. Why did Olmec civilization collapse?
4. What was the role of trade in Olmec civilization?
5. What were some important Zapotec contributions to later cultures?

CRITICAL THINKING & WRITING

6. **DRAWING CONCLUSIONS** Why do you think the Olmec are called Mesoamerica's "mother culture"?
7. **ANALYZING CAUSES** What factors made the Oaxaca Valley a likely place for civilization to develop?
8. **COMPARING** What were some similarities between the Olmec and Zapotec cultures?
9. **WRITING ACTIVITY** CULTURAL INTERACTION As a trader from a small Mesoamerican village, you have just returned from your first visit to the Olmec site at La Venta. Write a **description** of what you might tell your family about the things you saw at the site.

CONNECT TO TODAY **DRAWING A MASK**

What are some events or holidays in North America where participants wear masks? Draw a picture of a jaguar **mask** that you would like to wear for such a festival.

History *through* Art

Olmec Sculpture

Around 1200 B.C., the Olmec civilization appeared in southeastern Mexico. Over the next several hundred years, its culture spread into the Valley of Mexico and into parts of Central America. The Olmec are especially known for their huge sculptures of heads and their small, finely crafted stone carvings. Much of their art reflects a fascination with the jaguar.

INTEGRATED TECHNOLOGY

RESEARCH LINKS For more on Olmec art, go to **classzone.com**

Olmec Head ►

The Olmec Center at San Lorenzo, Honduras, contains several huge carved heads. Some of them are 9 feet high and weigh about 40 tons. The heads may be portraits of Olmec leaders or of players in a sacred ball game. The stone used for the sculptures came from a site more than 250 miles away. The Olmec transported this stone over mountain ranges, rivers, and swamps.

◄ Jaguar Figure

The Olmec created many carvings of beings that were part human, part jaguar. Peter Furst, in "New Light on the Olmec" in *National Geographic,* explains why: "You can almost call the Olmec the people of the jaguar. In tropical America, jaguars were the shamans [medicine men] of the animal world, the alter ego [other identity] of the shaman." Olmec jaguar art greatly influenced later Mesoamerican cultures.

▲ Olmec Altar
This Olmec altar has a carved figure at the base situated at the mouth of a cave. This figure's elaborate headdress shows that he is a ruler. The ruler holds a rope that winds around the base of the altar and binds a carved figure at the back. Scholars believe that the altar was used as a throne.

▲ Jade Figure
Many Olmec figurines, such as this adult holding a baby, are made of this beautiful blue-green stone, a fact that puzzled scientists for decades because they believed that no jade deposits existed in the Americas. However, in May 2002, a scientist discovered what he believes to be an ancient Olmec jade mine in Guatemala.

Connect *to* Today

1. **Hypothesizing** The Olmec probably did not use the wheel. How do you think the Olmec transported the stone for the huge head sculptures?
See Skillbuilder Handbook, Page R15.

2. **Comparing and Contrasting** Mount Rushmore in the United States also shows giant stone heads of leaders. Find out how it was made by using an encyclopedia or the Internet. What are similarities and differences between the way Mount Rushmore was made and the way the Olmec heads were made?

3

Early Civilizations of the Andes

CONNECT TO THE NEW YORK STATE CORE CURRICULUM

Unit 2.A.5.a. Human and physical geography
Unit 2.A.5.b. Contributions (mathematics, astronomy, science, arts, architecture, and technology)

TERMS & NAMES

- Chavín
- Nazca
- Moche

SETTING THE STAGE While civilizations were emerging in Mesoamerica, advanced societies were independently developing in South America. The early cultures of South America arose in a difficult environment, the rugged terrain of the Andes Mountains.

TAKING NOTES
Determining Main Ideas Use a chart to record important information about early Andean civilizations.

Culture	Time Span	Location	Achievements
Chavín			
Nazca			
Moche			

Societies Arise in the Andes

The Andes Mountains stretch about 4,500 miles down the western edge of South America, from Colombia in the north to Chile in the south. After the Himalayas in southern Asia, the Andes is the next highest mountain range in the world. The Andes has a number of peaks over 20,000 feet in elevation. South America's first civilizations emerged in the northern Andes region, in Peru.

Settlements on the Coastal Plain Peru was a harsh place to develop a civilization. The Andes are steep and rocky, with generally poor soil. Ice and snow cover the highest elevations year-round. Overland travel often is difficult. The climate is also severe: hot and dry during the day, and often freezing at night.

Between the mountains and the Pacific Ocean lies a narrow coastal plain. Most of this plain is harsh desert where rain seldom falls. In some places, however, rivers cross the desert on their path from the mountains to the sea. It was in these river valleys that the first settlements occurred.

Between 3600 and 2500 B.C., people began to establish villages along the Pacific coast. These first inhabitants were hunter-gatherers who relied on seafood and small game for their survival. Around 3000 B.C., these people began to farm. By 1800 B.C., a number of thriving communities existed along the coast.

The Chavín Period The first influential civilization in South America arose not on the coast, however, but in the mountains. This culture, known as the **Chavín** (chah•VEEN), flourished from around 900 B.C. to 200 B.C. Archaeologists named the culture after a major ruin, Chavín de Huántar, in the northern highlands of Peru. This site features pyramids, plazas, and massive earthen mounds.

Chavín culture spread quickly across much of northern and central Peru. Archaeologists have found no evidence of political or economic organization within the culture. Thus, they conclude that the Chavín were primarily a religious civilization. Nevertheless, the spread of Chavín art styles and religious images—as seen in stone carving, pottery, and textiles—shows the powerful influence of this culture. Ancient Peruvians may have visited Chavín temples to pay their respects. They then carried ideas back to their communities. The Chavín are believed to have established certain patterns that helped unify Andean culture and lay the foundation for later civilizations in Peru. Thus, like the Olmec in Mesoamerica, the Chavín may have acted as a "mother culture" in South America.

Other Andean Civilizations Flourish

Around the time Chavín culture declined, other civilizations were emerging in Peru. First the Nazca and then the Moche (MOH•chay) built societies that flourished in the Andes.

Nazca Achievements The **Nazca** culture flourished along the southern coast of Peru from around 200 B.C. to A.D. 600. This area is extremely dry. The Nazca developed extensive irrigation systems, including underground canals, that allowed them to farm the land. The Nazca are known for their beautiful textiles and pottery. Both feature images of animals and mythological beings. They are even more famous, however, for an extraordinary but puzzling set of creations known as the Nazca Lines. (See History in Depth on the next page.) A

Moche Culture Meanwhile, on the northern coast of Peru, another civilization was reaching great heights. This was the **Moche** culture, which lasted from about A.D. 100 to A.D. 700.

MAIN IDEA

Contrasting

A How did the environment of the Andes region differ from that of much of Mesoamerica?

History *in* Depth

Headhunters

The striking images on their pottery indicate that the Nazca may have been headhunters. In numerous ceramic and textile designs, Nazca artisans depict the taking of human heads, probably from enemies in combat. Shown above is a shrunken head. Taking and displaying the head of an enemy was considered a way of increasing the strength and well-being of a community.

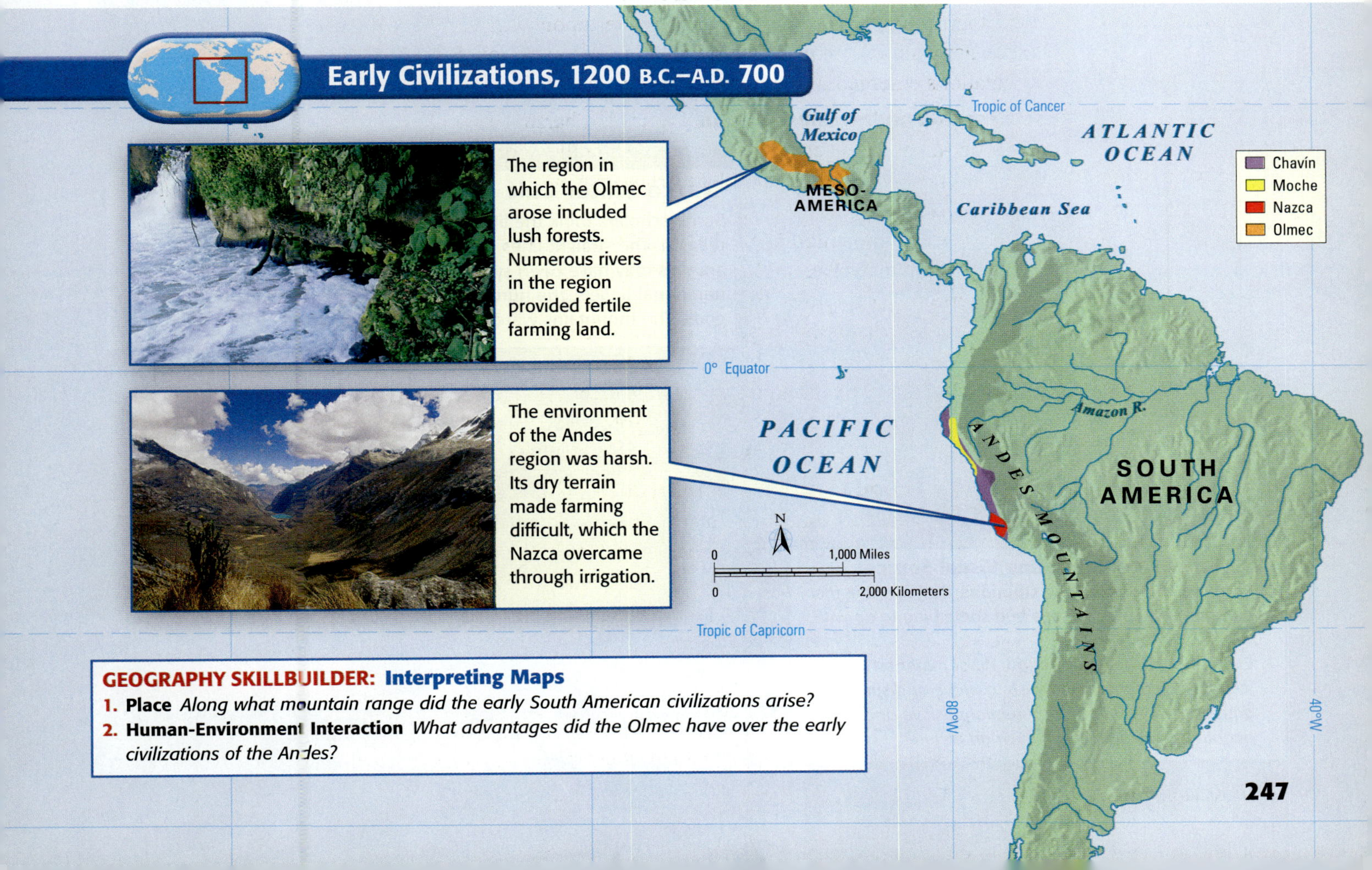

GEOGRAPHY SKILLBUILDER: Interpreting Maps

1. **Place** *Along what mountain range did the early South American civilizations arise?*
2. **Human-Environment Interaction** *What advantages did the Olmec have over the early civilizations of the Andes?*

Nazca Lines

Etched on the plains of southeastern Peru are more than 1,000 drawings of animals, plants, humans, and geometric shapes. Most of them are so large that they can be recognized only from the air. Scientists believe that the Nazca people made the drawings between 200 B.C. and A.D. 600. Since the lines were discovered in 1927, people have proposed many theories about their purpose, including the following:

- The Nazca people worshiped mountain or sky gods and created the drawings to please them.
- The lines indicated where surface water entered the plain and marked elevated land between ancient riverbeds.
- The lines are a huge map that marks the course of underground aquifers, or water sources. (This is the most recent theory.)

Durability of the Nazca Lines

This spider was created more than 1,000 years ago. It survived because the region has little erosion. The plains are one of the driest regions on earth with only 20 minutes of rain a year. Also, the ground is flat and stony, so wind rarely carries away the soil.

Size of the Nazca Lines

Many of the Nazca drawings are huge. Some of the wedges (below) are more than 2,500 feet long. The hummingbird (right) is 165 feet long. The Nazca people probably created small model drawings and used math to reproduce them at such a vast scale.

Nazca Water Cult

Some scholars think the lines were linked to a Nazca water cult, or religion. The straight lines may have led to ceremonial sites. The animals may have been symbols. For example, according to traditional beliefs, the hummingbird (above) represents the mountain gods. The mountains were a main source of water.

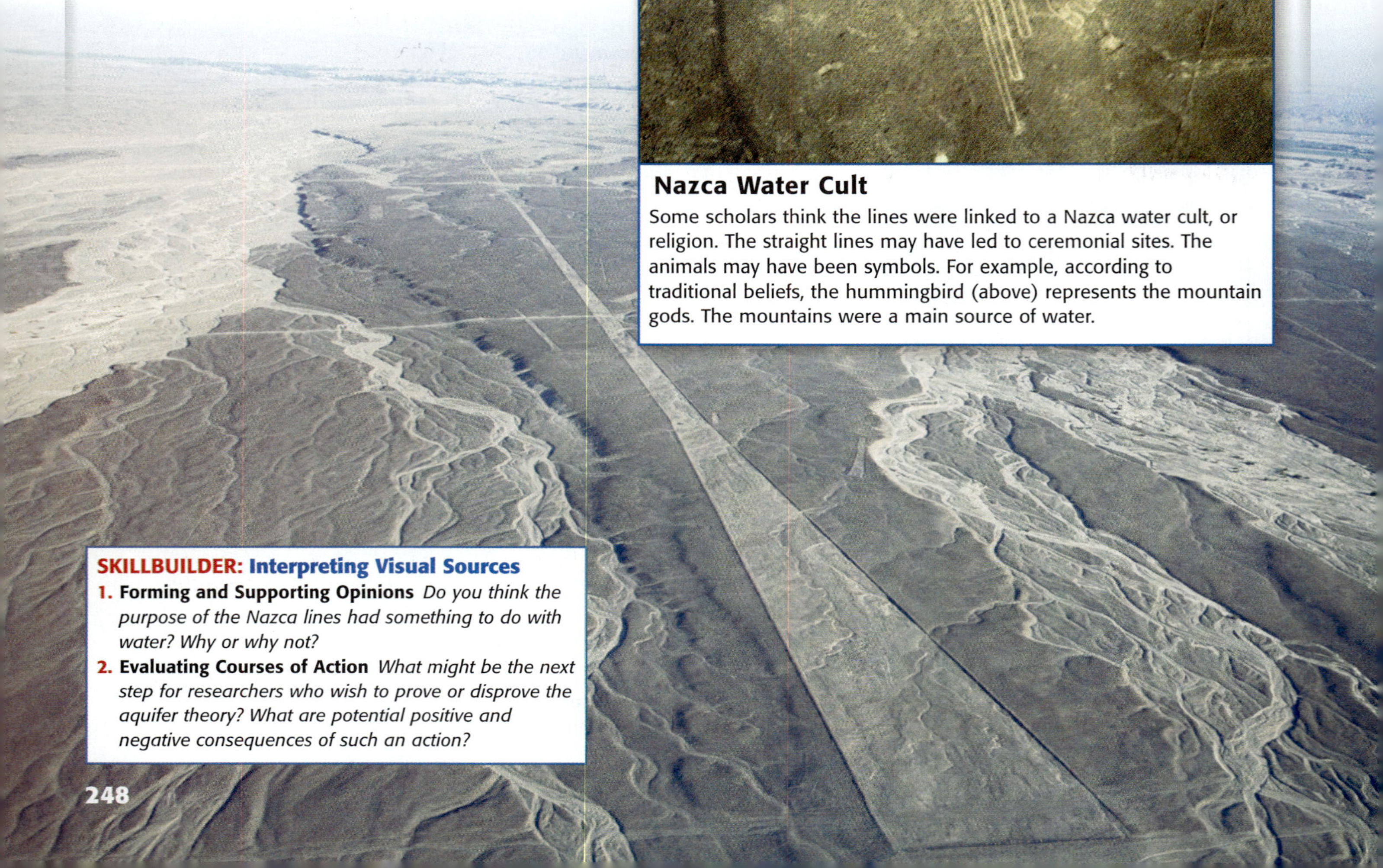

SKILLBUILDER: Interpreting Visual Sources

1. **Forming and Supporting Opinions** *Do you think the purpose of the Nazca lines had something to do with water? Why or why not?*
2. **Evaluating Courses of Action** *What might be the next step for researchers who wish to prove or disprove the aquifer theory? What are potential positive and negative consequences of such an action?*

The Moche took advantage of the rivers that flowed from the Andes Mountains. They built impressive irrigation systems to water their wide range of crops, which included corn, beans, potatoes, squash, and peanuts. According to Peruvian archaeologist Walter Alva, the Moche enjoyed a variety of foods. These included both fish and game:

PRIMARY SOURCE

The Moche enjoyed a diet rich in protein and probably better balanced than that of many modern Peruvians. Fish from the nearby Pacific were eaten fresh or sun dried. They ate Muscovy ducks and guinea pigs. To drink, there was potent *chicha,* a cloudy beverage fermented from corn that had been ground and boiled. Deer, now rare, were abundant. . . . Crayfish in irrigation ditches supplemented seafood from the coast.

WALTER ALVA, "Richest Unlooted Tomb of a Moche Lord," *National Geographic*

Moche tombs uncovered in the recent past have revealed a civilization with enormous wealth. Archaeologists have found beautiful jewelry crafted from gold, silver, and semiprecious stones. The Moche were also brilliant ceramic artists. They created pottery that depicted scenes from everyday life. Moche pots show doctors healing patients, women weaving cloth, and musicians playing instruments. They also show fierce soldiers armed with spears, leading enemy captives. Although the Moche never developed a written language, their pottery provides a wealth of detail about Moche life. **B**

MAIN IDEA

Analyzing Issues

B How were archaeologists able to gain so much information about the Moche without the help of a written language?

Nevertheless, many questions about the Moche remain. Experts still do not fully understand Moche religious beliefs. Nor do they know why the Moche fell. Like many early cultures of the Americas, the Moche remain something of a mystery awaiting further archaeological discoveries.

Unlike the lands you will read about in the next chapter—which were unified by the spread of Islam—the Americas would remain a patchwork of separate civilizations until the early 16th century. Around that time, as you will read in Chapter 20, the Europeans would begin to arrive and bring dramatic and lasting changes to the American continents.

NEW YORK CORE CURRICULUM REVIEW

TERMS & NAMES 1. For each term or name, write a sentence explaining its significance.

- Chavín
- Nazca
- Moche

USING YOUR NOTES

2. What achievements, if any, did all three cultures share? Explain.

Culture	Time Span	Location	Achievements
Chavín			
Nazca			
Moche			

MAIN IDEAS

3. Why was Peru a difficult place for a civilization to develop?
4. How was the Chavín culture like the Olmec culture?
5. How did the Nazca deal with their dry environment?

CRITICAL THINKING & WRITING

6. **HYPOTHESIZING** Would the Chavín culture have been more influential if it had arisen along the Peruvian coast?
7. **COMPARING** In which civilization did religion seem to play the most central role? Explain.
8. **DRAWING CONCLUSIONS** How did the Nazca and the Moche adapt to their environment in order to build flourishing societies? Give evidence.
9. **WRITING ACTIVITY** INTERACTION WITH ENVIRONMENT How did the Nazca change their environment to make it suitable for agriculture? Write an **expository essay** explaining their methods.

CONNECT TO TODAY **MAKING A POSTER**

Research recent findings on one of the three Andean cultures discussed in this section: Chavín, Nazca, or Moche. Then present your findings in a **poster** that will be displayed in the classroom.

Chapter 9 Assessment

TERMS & NAMES

For each term or name below, briefly explain its connection to the early peoples and civilizations of the Americas.

1. Beringia
2. maize
3. Olmec
4. Zapotec
5. Monte Albán
6. Chavín
7. Nazca
8. Moche

MAIN IDEAS

The Earliest Americans Section 1 (pages 235–239)

9. How do scientists know the first Americans were hunters?
10. Why was corn an important crop to early peoples?
11. What were the main differences between hunter-gatherer societies and those based primarily on agriculture?

Early Mesoamerican Civilizations Section 2 (pages 240–245)

12. Where did the Olmec arise?
13. How did the Olmec's location contribute to the development of their civilization?
14. How did the Olmec influence the Zapotec civilization?
15. How do archaeologists know that the Zapotec city of Monte Albán was more than just a ceremonial center?

Early Civilizations of the Andes Section 3 (pages 246–249)

16. In what ways did the Chavín influence other peoples?
17. What do scholars believe the Nazca lines represent?
18. How did the Nazca and Moche develop rich farmland?

CRITICAL THINKING

1. USING YOUR NOTES
In a sequence diagram, show how the early Americans' way of life developed through several stages.

Hunting → [ ] → [ ]

2. SUMMARIZING
INTERACTION WITH ENVIRONMENT What environmental challenges did the first Americans face?

3. SUPPORTING OPINIONS
Would you rather have lived in a hunting or farming society?

4. DRAWING CONCLUSIONS
POWER AND AUTHORITY Why do you think the Olmec or Zapotec civilizations might have declined?

5. MAKING INFERENCES
CULTURAL INTERACTION What geographic factors would have made interactions between early Mesoamerican and Andean civilizations difficult?

VISUAL SUMMARY

The Americas: A Separate World

The Earliest Americans

- Hunted big game and later fished and gathered berries and plants
- Lived in small groups, as they had to move continually in search of food
- Eventually developed farming and settled down into large communities
- Developed various new skills, including arts and crafts, architecture, and social and political organization
- Gradually forged more complex societies

Early South American Societies

The Chavín

- Established powerful religious worship centers
- Created influential artistic styles

The Nazca and Moche

- Developed extensive irrigation systems for farming
- Crafted intricate ceramics and textiles and other decorative art

Early Mesoamerican Societies

The Olmec

- Designed and built pyramids, plazas, and monumental sculptures
- Developed ceremonial centers, ritual ball games, and a ruling class
- Directed a large trade network throughout Mesoamerica

The Zapotec

- Built a magnificent urban center at Monte Albán
- Developed early forms of hieroglyphic writing and a calendar system

NEW YORK STATE REGENTS EXAM PRACTICE

Use the quotation and your knowledge of world history to answer questions 1 and 2 about a Chavín shrine.
Additional Test Practice, pp. S1–S33

PRIMARY SOURCE

Its U-shaped temple opens east toward the nearby Mosna River and the rising sun. The sacred precinct faces away from the nearby prehistoric settlement, presenting a high, almost menacing, wall to the outside world. The entire effect is one of mystery and hidden power. . . . Worshippers entered the sacred precincts by a roundabout route, passing along the temple pyramid to the river, then up some low terraces that led into the heart of the shrine. Here they found themselves in a sacred landscape set against a backdrop of mountains. Ahead of them lay the hidden place where the axis of the world passed from the sky into the underworld, an oracle famous for miles around.

BRIAN FAGAN, *quoted in* The Peru Reader

1 How might visitors have felt upon entering this shrine for the first time?

(1) amused
(2) awestruck
(3) arrogant
(4) angry

2 What effect might this shrine have had on the influence of the Chavín culture in the region?

(1) helped spread culture's influence
(2) limited its influence
(3) shrine had no effect on spread of culture
(4) undermined importance of the culture

Use the map and your knowledge of world history to answer question 3.

Early America, 1200 B.C.–A.D. 700

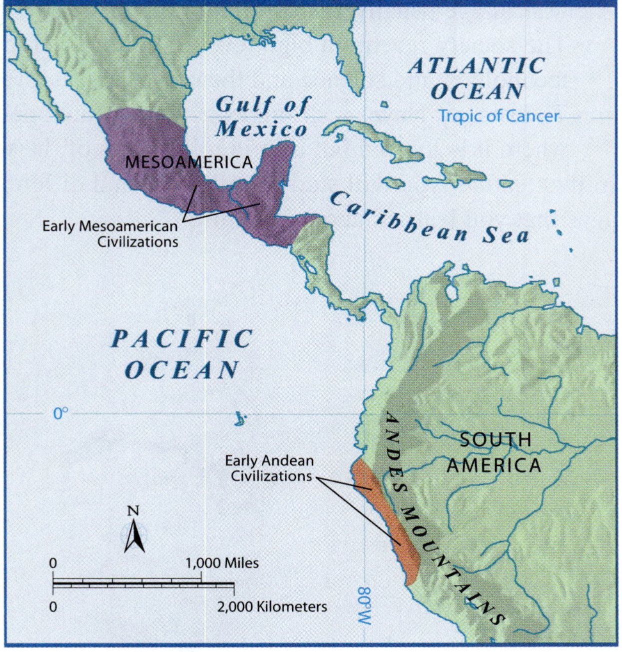

3 About how many miles apart by land do the early Mesoamerican and Andean civilizations appear to be?

(1) 1,500
(2) 2,500
(3) 3,500
(4) 4,500

INTEGRATED TECHNOLOGY

TEST PRACTICE Go to **classzone.com**

- Diagnostic tests
- Tutorials
- Strategies
- Additional practice

ALTERNATIVE ASSESSMENT

1. Interact *with* History

On page 234 you examined how killing a mammoth would help you survive and discussed the difficulties of living in a hunter-gatherer society. Now that you have read the chapter, discuss why the early Americans moved from a hunting to a farming existence. In what ways was food gathering easier in an agricultural society?

2. WRITING ABOUT HISTORY

Write a two-paragraph **essay** explaining why it might have taken many years to travel from the land bridge in upper North America to the southern tip of South America.

As you plan your essay, consider the following:

- means of transportation
- distances traveled
- nature of the terrain

INTEGRATED TECHNOLOGY

Writing a Documentary Film Script

Write a documentary film script on the spread of American culture. Contrast the spread of culture today with the modes of transmission among the earliest known inhabitants of the Americas. Consider the role, then and now, of factors such as climate change, war, trade, and technology. Provide a definition of culture in your script, and include examples of the following:

- ways in which culture was spread among the earliest peoples of the Americas
- agents and barriers to the spread of culture
- the role of trade in spreading culture today

Lasting Achievements

A classical age usually has two important characteristics:

- The society reaches a high level of cultural achievement, with advances in technology and science and the creation of impressive works of art.
- The society leaves a strong legacy for future ages, not only in the region where it is located but also in other parts of the world.

In this feature, you will study similarities and differences among five classical ages that you learned about in Unit 2.

◄ Greece
Pericles, shown at left, led the city-state of Athens during its golden age. The ancient Greeks of Athens and other cities created art, literature, philosophy, and political institutions that have influenced the world for thousands of years.

Greece 750–300 B.C.

Rome 500 B.C.–A.D 476

1200 B.C. | 1000 | 800 | 600 | 400 | 200

Olmec 1200–400 B.C.

Han China 202 B.C.–A.D. 220

Olmec ►
Some scholars theorize that the sculpture at right shows the face of an **Olmec ruler**. The Olmec people left no written records. Even so, their civilization influenced the art, religion, architecture, and political structure of peoples who followed them in Mesoamerica.

Han China ►
Liu Bang, shown at right, seized control of China and founded the Han Dynasty. He and his successors ruled a vast empire, which saw the growth and spread of Chinese culture. Even today, many Chinese call themselves "the people of Han," a tribute to the lasting cultural impact of this period.

◄ Rome

The emperor **Augustus,** whose statue is shown at left, ruled for about 40 years during Rome's 200-year golden age. First a republic and then an empire, Rome controlled the Mediterranean region and a large part of Europe. Roman government, law, society, art, literature, and language still influence much of the world, as does the Christian religion Rome eventually adopted.

A.D. 200 400 600

Gupta India
A.D. 320–535

◄ Gupta India

Chandragupta II, shown on this coin, was one of the rulers of India's Gupta Empire. They oversaw an age of peace, prosperity, and artistic creativity. During this time, Hinduism and Buddhism took full form in India and spread through trade to other regions.

Comparing & Contrasting

1. Which of these societies controlled the most territory? the least? Explain how the size of a society's territory might affect its ability to leave a legacy.
2. Which classical ages had religion as an important part of their legacy? Why does religion have such an impact on societies?

Cultural Achievements

These five classical ages had impressive cultural achievements. Their beliefs are still studied—and in some cases followed—today. Their art and architecture are counted among the world's treasures. Their advances in science and technology paved the way for later discoveries.

	Greece	Rome	Gupta India
Beliefs	• The Greeks worshiped many gods who behaved in very human ways. • Philosophers used reason to understand the world.	• Rome adopted many of the Greek gods, but usually changed and added to them. • Later, Rome adopted Christianity and helped spread it.	• Hinduism became a more personal religion and gained followers. • A more popular form of Buddhism developed and spread.
Art	• Sculpture portrayed ideal beauty, and at a later period, moved toward realism—as shown by this Roman copy of a later Greek statue. 	• Romans modeled sculpture after Greek statues and developed more realistic sculpture. They also made beautiful mosaics. 	• Gupta statues were of Hindu gods and the Buddha, such as this figure. 
Science and Technology	• Scientists made advances in astronomy and mathematics.	• Engineers developed domes and arches and built superb roads.	• Scholars made discoveries in astronomy, mathematics, and medicine.
Architecture	• Greek buildings show balance and symmetry; columns and pedestals were often used. 	• Roman advances include domes and arches, such as those in the Colosseum. 	• Hindu temples like this temple of Vishnu at Deogarh began to have pyramidal roofs. 

Han China	Olmec
• The Han adopted the ethical system of Confucius as the basis for government.	• The Olmec worshiped a jaguar spirit. • They built religious centers with pyramids.
• The Han made intricate bronzes like this figure of a galloping horse. 	• The Olmec carved giant stone heads and small figurines like this ceremonial object. 
• The Han invented paper, various farming tools, and watermills.	• The Olmec moved heavy stone for monuments without use of the wheel.
• Han buildings were wooden and none survive. This ceramic model of a three-story wooden tower shows Han styles. 	• This step pyramid at the Zapotec site in Monte Albán reflects Olmec architectural influence. 

SKILLBUILDER: Interpreting Charts

1. **Drawing Conclusions** *Which of the art pieces shown here are religious in subject and which are not?*
2. **Contrasting** *How were the beliefs of Han China different from the other societies that had classical ages?*

". . . to the glory that was Greece and the grandeur that was Rome"

Edgar Allan Poe, from "To Helen"

"The inhabitants [of the Gupta Empire] are rich and prosperous, and vie with one another in the practice of benevolence and righteousness."

Fa Xian, from *The Travels of Fa Xian*

Comparing & Contrasting

1. Which of the societies seemed to be more interested in mathematical and scientific theories? Which seemed to be more interested in practical technology?
2. What functions did monumental buildings fill for these societies? Explain whether the functions were similar or different.

Legacy of Classical Ages

The societies of the classical ages lasted for many centuries. In the end, though, they faded from the world scene. Still, some of their achievements have had an enduring impact on later societies.

Architecture

The Smolny Institute (below left) built in the early 1800s in St. Petersburg, Russia, reflects Greek and Roman architectural ideas. A modern hotel in South Africa (below right) recalls Olmec style.

DOCUMENT-BASED QUESTION

Compare these buildings to the Greek, Roman, and Olmec structures on pages 254–255. What similarities do you see?

Religion

Buddhism and Roman Catholicism are still widely practiced today, with millions of followers in countries far from the lands where the religions originated. The Buddhist monks (below left) are praying in Seoul, South Korea. Pope John Paul II (below right), head of the Catholic Church, greets nuns and other believers who visit Rome from around the world.

DOCUMENT-BASED QUESTION

What similarity do you see in the religious legacies of Rome and Gupta India?

Government

The classical ages studied in Unit 2 laid foundations for government that influenced later times—even today. Read about three examples of their contributions.

PRIMARY SOURCE

INTERACTIVE

Pericles

In a famous speech known as the Funeral Oration, the Athenian leader Pericles described the advantages of democracy.

[Our government] favors the many instead of the few; this is why it is called a democracy. If we look to the laws, they afford equal justice to all; . . . if no social standing, advancement in public life falls to reputation for capacity [ability], class considerations not being allowed to interfere with merit; nor again does poverty bar the way, if a man is able to serve the state, he is not hindered by the obscurity of his condition.

DOCUMENT-BASED QUESTION

According to Pericles, what values did Athens stand for?

SECONDARY SOURCE

INTERACTIVE

Rhoads Murphey

In this passage from *A History of Asia,* historian Rhoads Murphey examines the lasting impact of the government of Han China.

Confucianism was more firmly established as the official orthodoxy and state ideology, and the famous Chinese imperial civil service system recruited men of talent, schooled in classical Confucian learning, to hold office through competitive examination regardless of their birth. . . . In China, the original Han ideal endured through the rise and fall of successive dynasties and, with all its imperfections, built a long and proud tradition of power combined with service that is still very much alive in China.

DOCUMENT-BASED QUESTION

What qualities of Han government still influence China today?

SECONDARY SOURCE

INTERACTIVE

Henry C. Boren

In this excerpt from his book *Roman Society,* historian Henry C. Boren discusses the permanent legacy of Roman law.

The most imitated and studied code of law in history is the formulation by a group of lawyers . . . under the eastern Roman emperor Justinian. . . . This code served as a model for many of the nations of western Europe in the modern age and also for South Africa, Japan, and portions of Canada and the United States. Indirectly the principles of the Roman law, though perhaps not the procedures, have also strongly affected the development of the Anglo-Saxon common law, which is the basis of the legal systems in most English-speaking nations.

DOCUMENT-BASED QUESTION

According to this historian, how has Roman law affected the world?

Comparing & Contrasting

1. How did the idea of merit play a part in the governments of both Athens and Han China?
2. How is the U.S. government similar to each of the governments described in the excerpts?
3. What were some of the different forces that spread the ideas of these classical ages to many regions of the world?

EXTENSION ACTIVITY

Another Mesoamerican society that had a classical age was the Maya, which you will study in Chapter 16. Read about the Classic Age of the Maya either in this textbook or an encyclopedia. Then create a chart or a poster listing Maya beliefs and their achievements in the arts, science, technology, and architecture.

UNIT 3

An Age of Exchange and Encounter 500–1500

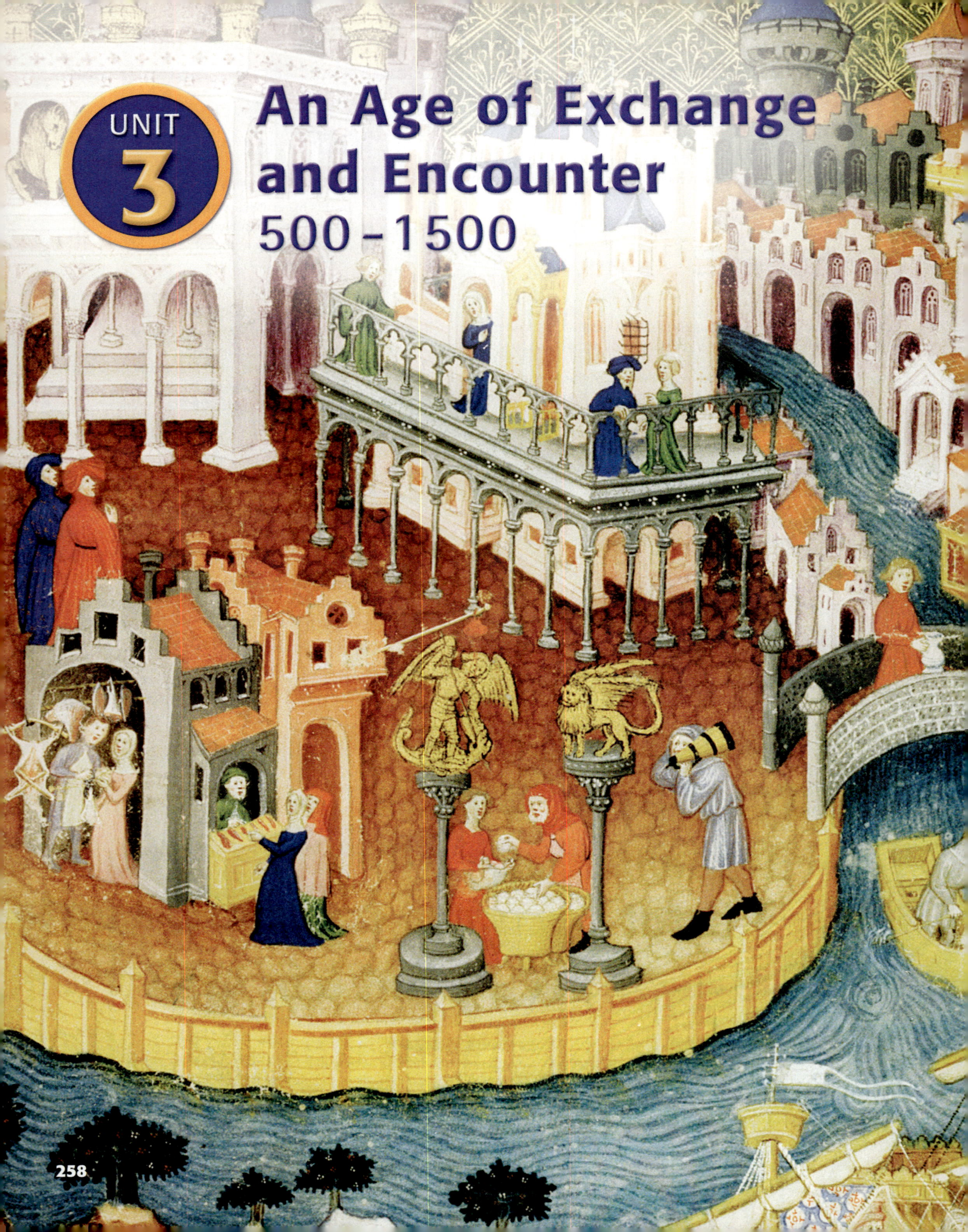

Venice at the time of Marco Polo was a vibrant, bustling city. This depiction of the city comes from the *Romance of Alexander*, a 14th-century illuminated manuscript that included a French account of Polo's travels.

Comparing & Contrasting

Trade Networks

In Unit 3, you will learn how trade began to connect regions of the world and how it made the exchange of goods and ideas easier. At the end of the unit, you will have a chance to compare and contrast five different trade networks. (See pages 430–435.)

CHAPTER 10

The Muslim World, 600–1250

Previewing Main Ideas

RELIGIOUS AND ETHICAL SYSTEMS Islam, a monotheistic religion begun by Muhammad, developed during the 600s. Its followers, called Muslims, spread Islam through Southwest and Central Asia, parts of Africa, and Europe.

Geography *Study the time line and the map. What were some of the major cities of the Muslim world? Locate them on the map.*

EMPIRE BUILDING The leaders following Muhammad built a huge empire that by A.D. 750 included millions of people from diverse ethnic, language, and religious groups.

Geography *How did the location of the Arabian Peninsula—the origin of the Muslim world—promote empire building?*

CULTURAL INTERACTION Tolerance of conquered peoples and an emphasis on learning helped to blend the cultural traits of people under Muslim rule.

Geography *How far might cultural interaction have spread if the Muslims had won a key battle at Tours in 732?*

NEW YORK CORE CURRICULUM FOCUS

- Muslims spread Islam through Southwest and Central Asia, Africa, and Europe.
- Islamists assembled a body of laws called the shari'a to guide moral conduct and daily life.

INTEGRATED TECHNOLOGY

eEdition
- Interactive Maps
- Interactive Visuals
- Interactive Primary Sources

INTERNET RESOURCES
Go to **classzone.com** for:
- Research Links
- Internet Activities
- Primary Sources
- Chapter Quiz
- Maps
- Test Practice
- Current Events

MUSLIM WORLD

630 Muhammad returns to Mecca after making the Hijrah to Medina.

732 ◀ Charles Martel defeats the Muslims at Tours.

800s Al-Khwarizmi writes the first algebra textbook.

600 — **800**

WORLD

800 ◀ Pope crowns Charlemagne (shown) emperor of the Romans.

850 Chinese invent gunpowder.

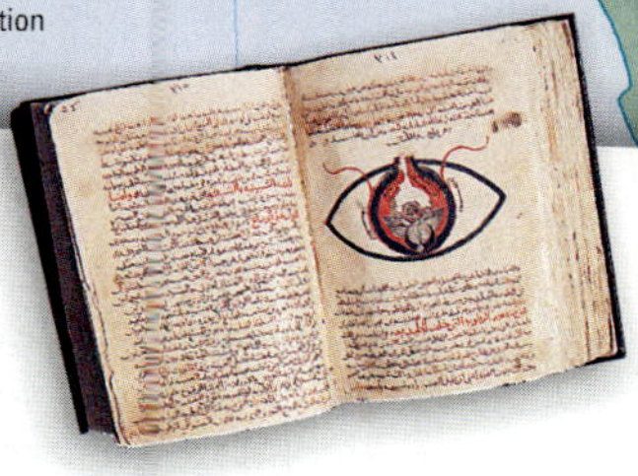

1000s
◀ Muslim scholars, who preserved Greek medical works, share them with Europeans.

1100s
Muslim literature flourishes.

1000 — **1250**

960
Song Dynasty is established in China.

1054
Christian Church divides.

1209
◀ Genghis Khan begins the Mongol conquest.

Interact *with* History

How does a culture bloom in the desert?

In 642, Alexandria and the rest of Egypt fell to the Muslim army. Alexandria had been part of the Byzantine Empire. By 646, however, the city was firmly under Muslim rule.

You are a Muslim trader from Mecca. You admire Alexandria (shown below), with its cultural blend of ancient Egypt, Greece, and Rome. Now, as Islam spreads, the Muslim Empire is borrowing from conquered cultures and enriching its desert culture. As you look around Alexandria, you consider the cultural elements you might bring to your desert home in Mecca.

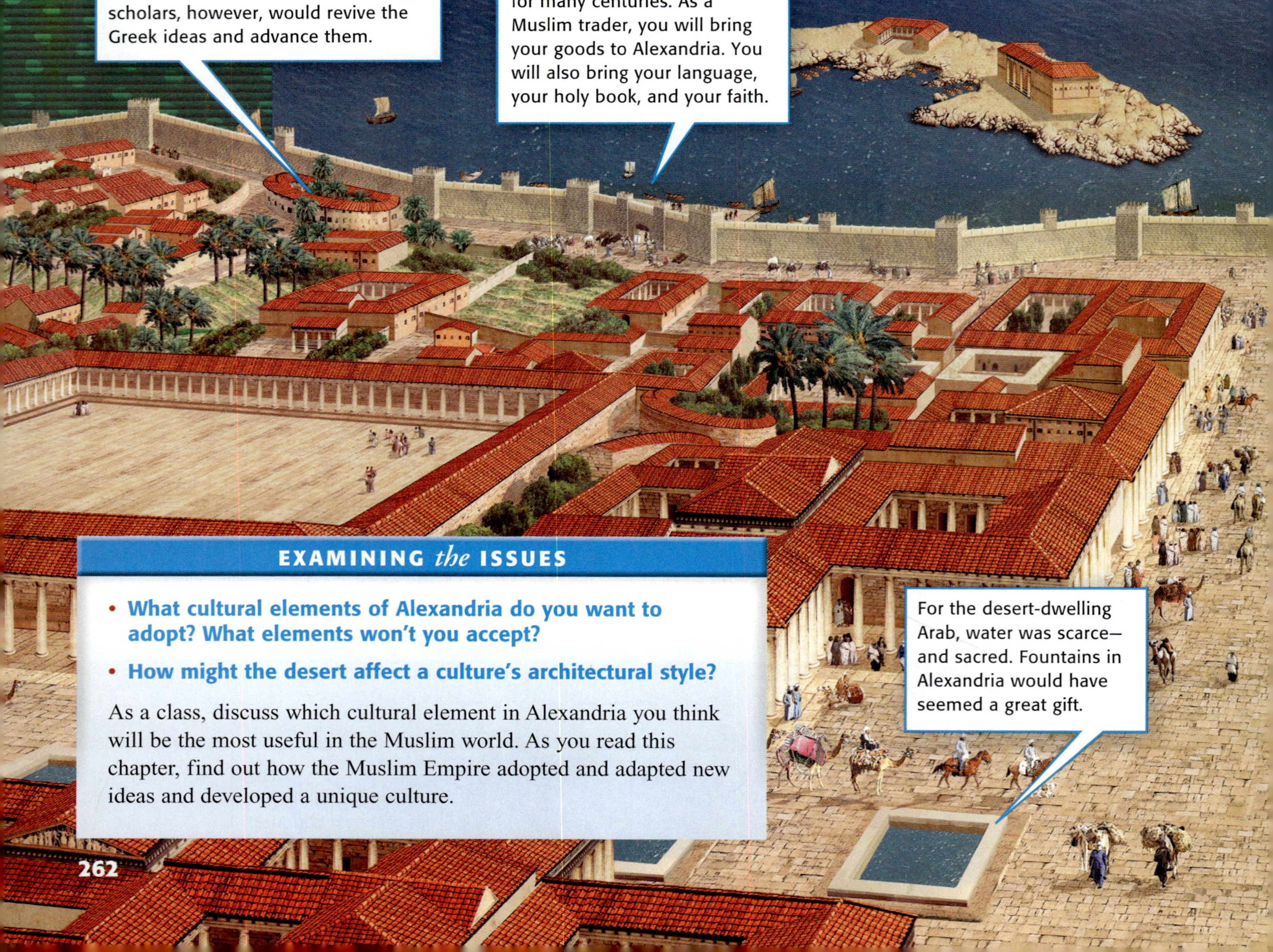

EXAMINING *the* ISSUES

- **What cultural elements of Alexandria do you want to adopt? What elements won't you accept?**
- **How might the desert affect a culture's architectural style?**

As a class, discuss which cultural element in Alexandria you think will be the most useful in the Muslim world. As you read this chapter, find out how the Muslim Empire adopted and adapted new ideas and developed a unique culture.

The Rise of Islam

CONNECT TO THE NEW YORK STATE CORE CURRICULUM

Unit 1.E.1.g. Islam
Unit 2.E.3. The development of Islamic law and its impact

TERMS & NAMES

- Allah
- Muhammad
- Islam
- Muslim
- Hijrah
- mosque
- hajj
- Qur'an
- Sunna
- shari'a

SETTING THE STAGE The cultures of the Arabian Peninsula were in constant contact with one another for centuries. Southwest Asia (often referred to as the Middle East) was a bridge between Africa, Asia, and Europe, where goods were traded and new ideas were shared. One set of shared ideas would become a powerful force for change in the world—the religion of Islam.

TAKING NOTES
Synthesizing Use a diagram to list important aspects of Islam.

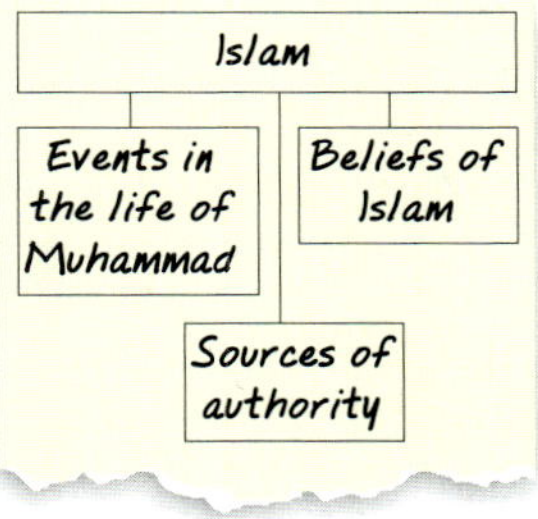

Deserts, Towns, and Trade Routes

The Arabian Peninsula is a crossroads of three continents—Africa, Europe, and Asia. At its longest and widest points, the peninsula is about 1,200 miles from north to south and 1,300 miles from east to west. Only a tiny strip of fertile land in south Arabia and Oman and a few oases can support agriculture. The remainder of the land is desert, which in the past was inhabited by nomadic Arab herders.

Desert and Town Life On this desert, the Arab nomads, called Bedóuins (BEHD•oo•ihnz), were organized into tribes and groups called clans. These clans provided security and support for a life made difficult by the extreme conditions of the desert. The Bedouin ideals of courage and loyalty to family, along with their warrior skills, would become part of the Islamic way of life.

The areas with more fertile soil and the larger oases had enough water to support farming communities. By the early 600s, many Arabs had chosen to settle in an oasis or in a market town. Larger towns near the western coast of Arabia became market towns for local, regional, and long-distance trade goods.

Crossroads of Trade and Ideas By the early 600s, trade routes connected Arabia to the major ocean and land trade routes, as you can see on the map on the next page. Trade routes through Arabia ran from the extreme south of the peninsula to the Byzantine and Sassanid (Persian) empires to the north. Merchants from these two empires moved along the caravan routes, trading for goods from the Silk Roads of the east. They transported spices and incense from Yemen and other products to the west. They also carried information and ideas from the world outside Arabia.

Mecca During certain holy months, caravans stopped in Mecca, a city in western Arabia. They brought religious pilgrims who came to worship at an ancient shrine in the city called the Ka'aba (KAH•buh). The Arabs associated this house

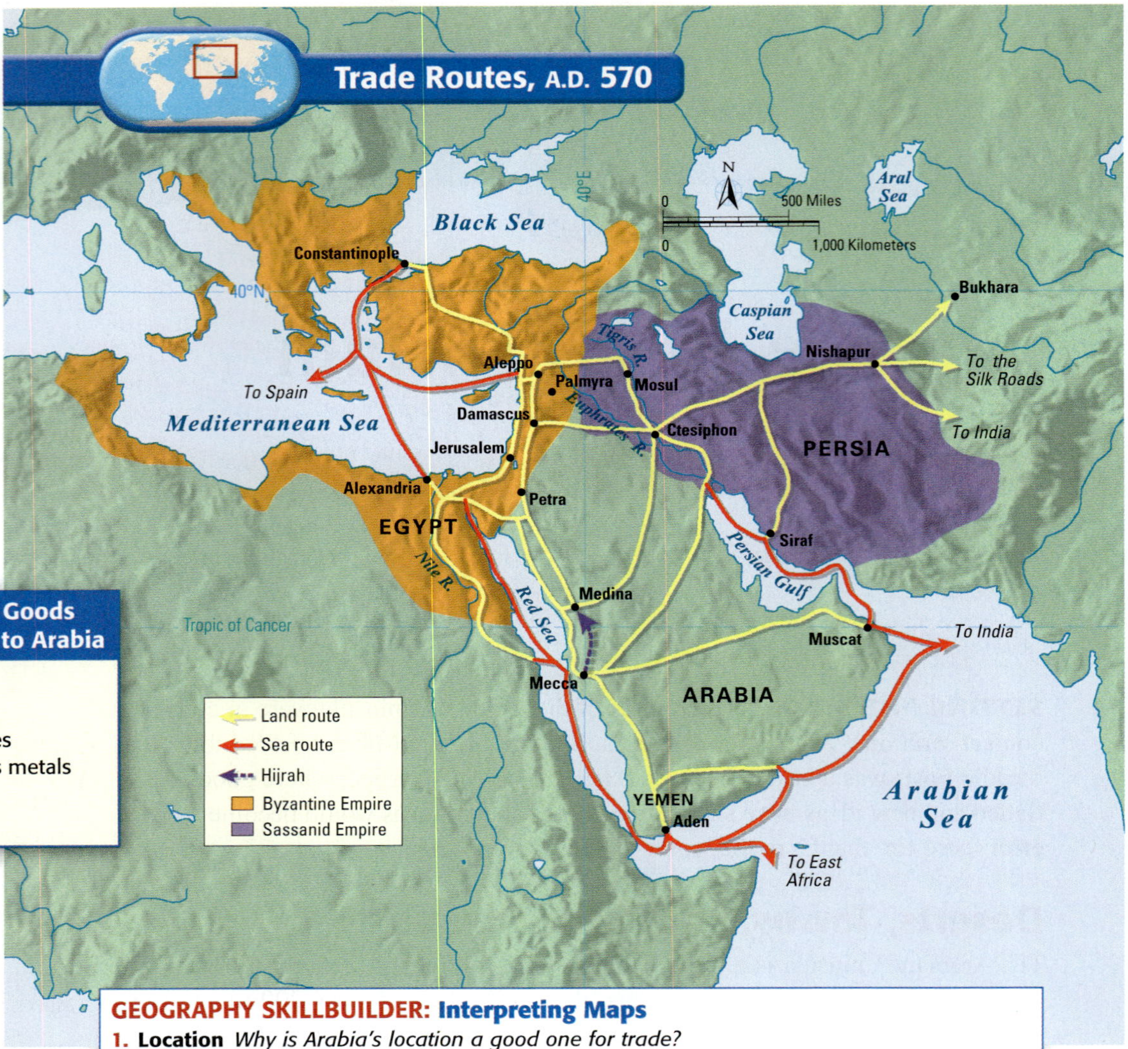

Trade Goods Brought to Arabia

- spices
- incense
- perfumes
- precious metals
- ivory
- silk

GEOGRAPHY SKILLBUILDER: Interpreting Maps

1. **Location** *Why is Arabia's location a good one for trade?*
2. **Movement** *Why was the location of Mecca ideal for the spread of ideas?*

of worship with Abraham, a Hebrew prophet and a believer in one God. Over the years, they had introduced the worship of many gods and spirits to the place. The Ka'aba contained over 360 idols brought by many tribes.

The concept of belief in one God, called **Allah** (AL•uh) in Arabic, was known on the Arabian Peninsula. Many Christians and Jews lived there and practiced monotheism. Into this mixed religious environment of Mecca, around A.D. 570, Muhammad was born.

The Prophet Muhammad

Muhammad (mu•HAM•id) was born into the clan of a powerful Meccan family. Orphaned at the age of six, Muhammad was raised by his grandfather and uncle. He received little schooling and began working in the caravan trade as a very young man. At the age of 25, Muhammad became a trader and business manager for Khadijah (kah•DEE•juh), a wealthy businesswoman of about 40. Later, Muhammad and Khadijah married. Theirs was both a good marriage and a good business partnership.

Revelations Muhammad took great interest in religion and often spent time alone in prayer and meditation. At about the age of 40, Muhammad's life was changed overnight when a voice called to him while he meditated in a cave outside Mecca. According to Muslim belief, the voice was that of the angel Gabriel, who told

Muhammad that he was a messenger of Allah. "What shall I proclaim?" asked Muhammad. The voice answered:

MAIN IDEA

Analyzing Primary Sources

A What kind of teaching does the phrase "the use of the pen" refer to?

PRIMARY SOURCE **A**

Proclaim! In the name of thy Lord and Cherisher, who created man out of a (mere) clot of congealed blood. Proclaim! And thy Lord is most bountiful. He who taught (the use of) the pen taught man that which he knew not.

QUR'AN, sura 96:1–5

After much soul-searching, Muhammad came to believe that the Lord who spoke to him through Gabriel was Allah. Muhammad became convinced that he was the last of the prophets. He began to teach that Allah was the one and only God and that all other gods must be abandoned. People who agreed to this basic principle of Islam were called Muslims. In Arabic, **Islam** (ihs•LAHM) means "submission to the will of Allah." **Muslim** (MUHZ•lihm) means "one who has submitted." Muhammad's wife, Khadijah, and several close friends and relatives were his first followers.

By 613, Muhammad had begun to preach publicly in Mecca, but he met with some hostility. Many Meccans believed his revolutionary ideas would lead to neglect of the traditional Arab gods. They feared that Mecca would lose its position as a pilgrimage center if people accepted Muhammad's monotheistic beliefs.

The Hijrah After some of his followers had been attacked, Muhammad decided to leave Mecca in 622. Following a small band of supporters he sent ahead, Muhammad moved to the town of Yathrib, over 200 miles to the north of Mecca. This migration became known as the **Hijrah** (HIHJ•ruh). The Hijrah to Yathrib marked a turning point for Muhammad. He attracted many devoted followers. Later, Yathrib was renamed Medina.

In Medina, Muhammad displayed impressive leadership skills. He fashioned an agreement that joined his own people with the Arabs and Jews of Medina as a single community. These groups accepted Muhammad as a political leader. As a religious leader, he drew many more converts who found his message appealing. Finally, Muhammad also became a military leader in the growing hostilities between Mecca and Medina.

Returning to Mecca In 630, the Prophet and 10,000 of his followers marched to the outskirts of Mecca. Facing sure defeat, Mecca's leaders surrendered. The Prophet entered the city in triumph. He destroyed the idols in the Ka'aba and had the call to prayer made from its roof.

Most Meccans pledged their loyalty to Muhammad, and many converted to Islam. By doing so, they joined the *umma,* or Muslim religious community. Muhammad died two years later, at about the age of 62. However, he had taken great strides toward unifying the entire Arabian Peninsula under Islam.

▼ The Abyssinian army set out to destroy the Ka'aba. Their elephants, however, refused to attack.

> Analyzing Architecture

The Dome of the Rock

The Dome of the Rock, located in Jerusalem, is the earliest surviving Islamic monument. It was completed in 691 and is part of a larger complex, which is the third most holy place in Islam. It is situated on Mount Moriah, the site of the Jewish temple destroyed by Romans in A.D. 70.

The rock on the site is the spot from which Muslims say Muhammad ascended to heaven to learn of Allah's will. With Allah's blessing, Muhammad returned to earth to bring God's message to all people. Jews identify the same rock as the site where Abraham was prepared to sacrifice his son Isaac.

▼ This model displays the interior of the building. The dome is about 100 feet tall and 60 feet in diameter. It rests on 16 pillars and columns and is surrounded by an octagonal colonnade of 24 pillars and columns. The exterior walls are about 60 feet long, 36 feet tall, and also form an octagon.

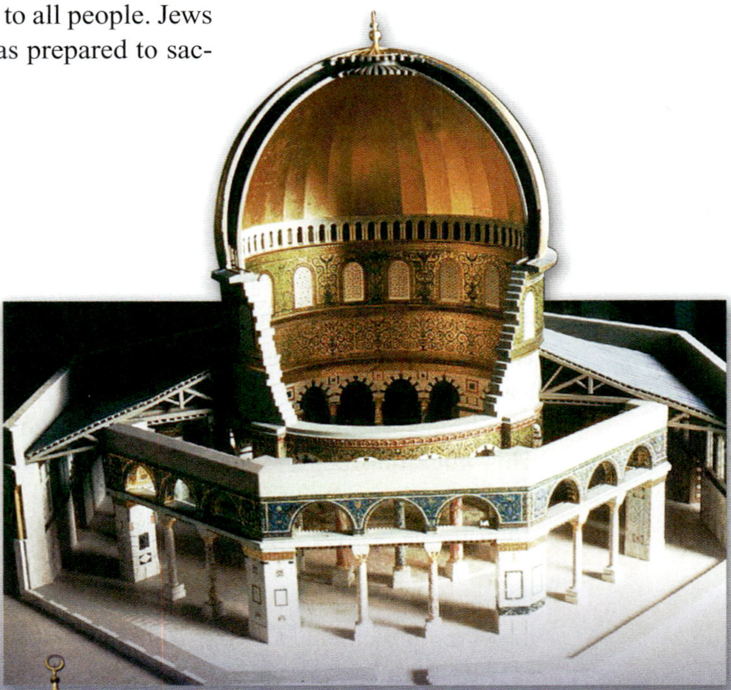

▼ The ornate decorations of the exterior are also found on the interior of the building. Notice the geometric designs that appear in everything from the tile to the carpet. This is a feature often found in Muslim art.

SKILLBUILDER: Interpreting Visual Sources

1. **Making Inferences** *If you knew nothing about this building, what elements of the building might give you the impression that it is a religious structure?*
2. **Comparing and Contrasting** *How is the Dome of the Rock similar to or different from other religious buildings you have seen?*

Beliefs and Practices of Islam

The main teaching of Islam is that there is only one God, Allah. All other beliefs and practices follow from this teaching. Islam teaches that there is good and evil, and that each individual is responsible for the actions of his or her life.

The Five Pillars To be a Muslim, all believers have to carry out five duties. These duties are known as the Five Pillars of Islam.

- **Faith** To become a Muslim, a person has to testify to the following statement of faith: "There is no God but Allah, and Muhammad is the Messenger of Allah." This simple statement is heard again and again in Islamic rituals and in Muslim daily life.
- **Prayer** Five times a day, Muslims face toward Mecca to pray. They may assemble at a **mosque** (mahsk), an Islamic house of worship, or wherever they find themselves.
- **Alms** Muhammad taught that all Muslims have a responsibility to support the less fortunate. Muslims meet that social responsibility by giving alms, or money for the poor, through a special religious tax.
- **Fasting** During the Islamic holy month of Ramadan, Muslims fast between dawn and sunset. A simple meal is eaten at the end of the day. Fasting serves to remind Muslims that their spiritual needs are greater than their physical needs.
- **Pilgrimage** All Muslims who are physically and financially able perform the **hajj** (haj), or pilgrimage to Mecca, at least once. Pilgrims wear identical garments so that all stand as equals before Allah.

A Way of Life Carrying out the Five Pillars of Islam ensures that Muslims live their religion while serving in their community. Along with the Five Pillars, there are other customs, morals, and laws for Islamic society that affect Muslims' daily lives. Believers are forbidden to eat pork or to drink intoxicating beverages. Friday afternoons are set aside for communal worship. Unlike many other religions, Islam has no priests or central religious authority. Every Muslim is expected to worship Allah directly. Islam does, however, have a scholar class called the *ulama*. The *ulama* includes religious teachers who apply the words and deeds of Muhammad to everyday life.

Sources of Authority The original source of authority for Muslims is Allah. According to Islamic belief, Allah expressed his will through the angel Gabriel, who revealed it to Muhammad. While Muhammad lived, his followers memorized and recited the revelations he received from Gabriel. Soon after the Prophet's death, it was suggested that the revelations be collected in a book. This book is the **Qur'an** (kuh•RAN), the holy book of the Muslims.

The Qur'an is written in Arabic, and Muslims consider only the Arabic version to be the true word of Allah. Only Arabic can be used in worship. Wherever Muslims carried the Qur'an, Arabic became the language of worshipers and scholars. Thus, the

▼ Artists decorate the Qur'an as a holy act. The geometric design often repeats to show the infinite quality of Allah.

Social History

Muslim Prayer

Five times a day—dawn, noon, mid-afternoon, sunset, and evening—Muslims face toward Mecca to pray. Worshipers are called to prayer by a *muezzin*. The call to prayer sometimes is given from a minaret and even over public address systems or the radio in large cities.

Because they believe that standing before Allah places them on holy ground, Muslims perform a ritual cleansing before praying. They also remove their shoes.

INTEGRATED TECHNOLOGY

INTERNET ACTIVITY Create a chart in which you identify and explain the meaning of Muslim prayer rituals. Go to **classzone.com** for your research.

Arabic language helped unite conquered peoples as Muslim control expanded.

Muslims believe that Muhammad's mission as a prophet was to receive the Qur'an and to demonstrate how to apply it in life. To them, the **Sunna** (SOON•uh), or Muhammad's example, is the best model for proper living. The guidance of the Qur'an and Sunna was assembled in a body of law known as **shari'a** (shah•REE•ah). This system of law regulates the family life, moral conduct, and business and community life of Muslims. **B**

MAIN IDEA

Clarifying

B What are the sources of authority for Muslims?

Links to Judaism and Christianity To Muslims, Allah is the same God that is worshiped in Christianity and Judaism. However, Muslims view Jesus as a prophet, not as the Son of God. They regard the Qur'an as the word of Allah as revealed to Muhammad, in the same way that Jews and Christians believe the Torah and the Gospels were revealed to Moses and the New Testament writers. Muslims believe that the Qur'an perfects the earlier revelations. To them, it is the final book, and Muhammad was the final prophet. All three religions believe in heaven and hell and a day of judgment. The Muslims trace their ancestry to Abraham, as do the Jews and Christians.

Muslims refer to Christians and Jews as "people of the book" because each religion has a holy book with teachings similar to those of the Qur'an. Shari'a law requires Muslim leaders to extend religious tolerance to Christians and Jews. A huge Muslim empire, as you will learn in Section 2, grew to include people of many different cultures and religions.

NEW YORK CORE CURRICULUM REVIEW

TERMS & NAMES **1.** For each term or name, write a sentence explaining its significance.

• Allah • Muhammad • Islam • Muslim • Hijrah • mosque • hajj • Qur'an • Sunna • shari'a

USING YOUR NOTES

2. What event in the life of Muhammad signaled the beginning of Islam?

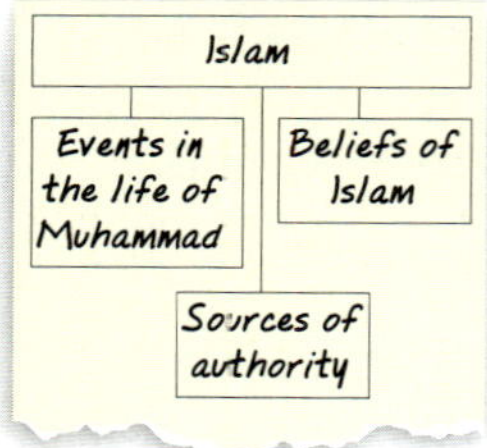

MAIN IDEAS

3. Why was Mecca an important city in western Arabia?

4. What are the Five Pillars of Islam?

5. Why did Muslims consider Christians and Jews "people of the book"?

CRITICAL THINKING & WRITING

6. RECOGNIZING EFFECTS How did the beliefs and practices of Islam create unity and strength among Muslims in the 600s?

7. COMPARING In what ways are the teachings of the Muslims similar to those of Christians and Jews?

8. DRAWING CONCLUSIONS How did Islam help spread Arabic culture?

9. WRITING ACTIVITY RELIGIOUS AND ETHICAL SYSTEMS Write a **letter** to Muhammad, describing his legacy and that of Islam today.

CONNECT TO TODAY **PREPARING AN ORAL REPORT**

Today, tensions run high between Muslims and Jews in the Middle East. Research to find out the causes of this tension. Present your findings in an **oral report.**

Islam Expands

CONNECT TO THE NEW YORK STATE CORE CURRICULUM

Unit 1.E.2. Expansion of Christianity, Islam, Confucianism, and Buddhism
Unit 2.E.2. Organizational structure

TERMS & NAMES

- caliph
- Umayyads
- Shi'a
- Sunni
- Sufi
- Abbasids
- al-Andalus
- Fatimid

SETTING THE STAGE When Muhammad died in 632, the community faced a crisis. Muslims, inspired by the message of Allah, believed they had a duty to carry his word to the world. However, they lacked a clear way to choose a new leader. Eventually, the issue of leadership would divide the Muslim world.

Muhammad's Successors Spread Islam

Muhammad had not named a successor or instructed his followers how to choose one. Relying on ancient tribal custom, the Muslim community elected as their leader Abu-Bakr, a loyal friend of Muhammad. In 632, Abu-Bakr became the first **caliph** (KAY•lihf), a title that means "successor" or "deputy."

"Rightly Guided" Caliphs Abu-Bakr and the next three elected caliphs—Umar, Uthman, and Ali—all had known Muhammad. They used the Qur'an and Muhammad's actions as guides to leadership. For this, they are known as the "rightly guided" caliphs. Their rule was called a caliphate (KAY•lih•FAYT).

Abu-Bakr had promised the Muslim community he would uphold what Muhammad stood for. Shortly after the Prophet's death, some tribes on the Arabian Peninsula abandoned Islam. Others refused to pay taxes, and a few individuals even declared themselves prophets. For the sake of Islam, Abu-Bakr invoked *jihad.* The word *jihad* means "striving" and can refer to the inner struggle against evil. However, the word is also used in the Qur'an to mean an armed struggle against unbelievers. For the next two years, Abu-Bakr applied this meaning of *jihad* to encourage and justify the expansion of Islam.

When Abu-Bakr died in 634, the Muslim state controlled all of Arabia. Under Umar, the second caliph, Muslim armies conquered Syria and lower Egypt, which were part of the Byzantine Empire. They also took parts of the Sassanid Empire. The next two caliphs, Uthman and Ali, continued to expand Muslim territory. By 750, the Muslim Empire stretched 6,000 miles from the Atlantic Ocean to the Indus River. (See the map on page 261.)

Reasons for Success The four "rightly guided" caliphs made great progress in their quest to spread Islam. Before his death, Muhammad had expressed a desire to spread the faith to the peoples of the north. Muslims of the day saw their victories as a sign of Allah's support and drew energy and inspiration from their faith. They fought to defend Islam and were willing to struggle to extend its word.

TAKING NOTES

Summarizing Use a table to summarize developments that occurred in Islam during each ruler's period in power.

Rulers	Period of Rule	Developments in Islam
Rightly guided caliphs		
Umayyads		
Abbasids		

▲ From 632 to 750, highly mobile troops mounted on camels were successful in conquering lands in the name of Allah.

The Muslim armies were well disciplined and expertly commanded. However, the success of the armies was also due to weakness in the two empires north of Arabia. The Byzantine and Sassanid empires had been in conflict for a long period of time and were exhausted militarily.

Another reason for Muslim success was the persecution suffered by people under Byzantine or Sassanid rule because they did not support the official state religions, Christianity or Zoroastrianism. The persecuted people often welcomed the invaders and their cause and chose to accept Islam. They were attracted by the appeal of the message of Islam, which offered equality and hope in this world. They were also attracted by the economic benefit for Muslims of not having to pay a poll tax. (A)

MAIN IDEA

Analyzing Causes

(A) Why were Muslims successful conquerers?

Treatment of Conquered Peoples Because the Qur'an forbade forced conversion, Muslims allowed conquered peoples to follow their own religion. Christians and Jews, as "people of the book," received special consideration. They paid a poll tax each year in exchange for exemption from military duties. However, they were also subject to various restrictions on their lives. Before entering the newly conquered city of Damascus in the northern Arabian province of Syria, Khalid ibn al-Walid, one of Abu-Bakr's chief generals, detailed the terms of surrender:

PRIMARY SOURCE

In the name of Allah, the compassionate, the merciful, this is what Khalid ibn al-Walid would grant to the inhabitants of Damascus. . . . He promises to give them security for their lives, property and churches. Their city wall shall not be demolished, neither shall any Muslim be quartered in their houses. Thereunto we give to them the pact of Allah and the protection of His Prophet, the Caliphs and the believers. So long as they pay the tax, nothing but good shall befall them.

KHALID IBN AL-WALID, quoted in *Early Islam*

Tolerance like this continued after the Muslim state was established. Though Christians and Jews were not allowed to spread their religion, they could be officials, scholars, and bureaucrats.

Internal Conflict Creates a Crisis

Despite spectacular gains on the battlefield, the Muslim community had difficulty maintaining a unified rule. In 656, Uthman was murdered, starting a civil war in which various groups struggled for power. Ali, as Muhammad's cousin and son-in-law, was the natural choice as a successor to Uthman. However, his right to rule was challenged by Muawiya, a governor of Syria. Then, in 661, Ali, too, was assassinated. The elective system of choosing a caliph died with him.

A family known as the **Umayyads** (oo•MY•adz) then came to power. The Umayyads moved the Muslim capital to Damascus. This location, away from Mecca, made controlling conquered territories easier. However, the Arab Muslims felt it was too far away from their lands. In addition, the Umayyads abandoned the simple life of previous caliphs and began to surround themselves with wealth and ceremony similar to that of non-Muslim rulers. These actions, along with the leadership issue, gave rise to a fundamental division in the Muslim community.

Sunni–Shi'a Split In the interest of peace, the majority of Muslims accepted the Umayyads' rule. However, a minority continued to resist. This group developed an alternate view of the office of caliph. In this view, the caliph needed to be a descendant of the Prophet. This group was called **Shi'a**, meaning the "party" of Ali. Members of this group are called Shi'ites. Those who did not outwardly resist the rule of the Umayyads later became known as **Sunni**, meaning followers of Muhammad's example. Another group, the **Sufi** (SOO•fee), rejected the luxurious life of the Umayyads. They pursued a life of poverty and devotion to a spiritual path.

Basic Differences Between Sunni and Shi'a Muslims

Sunni	Shi'a
• Believe that the first four caliphs were "rightly guided"	• Believe that Ali, the Prophet's son-in-law, should have succeeded Muhammad
• Believe that Muslim rulers should follow the Sunna, or Muhammad's example	• Believe that all Muslim rulers should be descended from Muhammad; do not recognize the authority of the Sunna
• Claim that the Shi'a have distorted the meaning of various passages in the Qur'an	• Claim that the Sunni have distorted the meaning of various passages in the Qur'an

Percentage Today of Sunni and Shi'a Muslims Worldwide

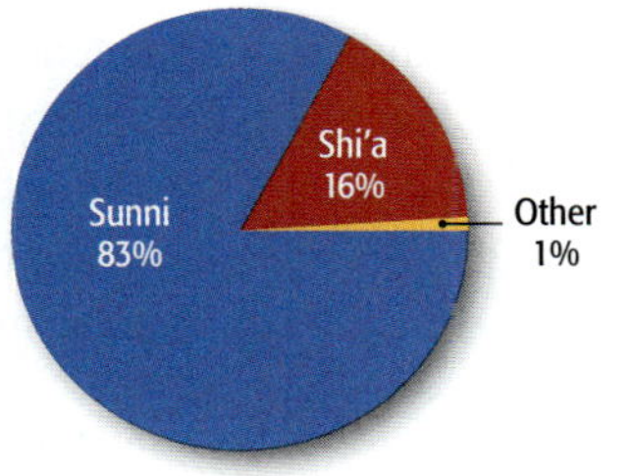

Vigorous religious and political opposition to the Umayyad caliphate led to its downfall. Rebel groups overthrew the Umayyads in the year 750. The most powerful of those groups, the **Abbasids** (uh•BAS•IHDZ), took control of the empire. **B**

MAIN IDEA
Summarizing
B What are three groups within Islam and how do they differ?

Control Extends Over Three Continents

When the Abbasids came to power in 750, they ruthlessly murdered the remaining members of the Umayyad family. One prince named Abd al-Rahman escaped the slaughter and fled to Spain. There he set up an Umayyad caliphate. Spain had already been conquered and settled by Muslims from North Africa, who were known as Berbers. The Berber armies advanced north to within 200 miles of Paris before being halted at the Battle of Tours in 732. They then settled in southern Spain, where they helped form an extraordinary Muslim state in **al-Andalus** (al•AN•duh•LUS).

Abbasids Consolidate Power To solidify power, the Abbasids moved the capital of the empire in 762 to a newly created city, Baghdad, in central Iraq. The location on key trade routes gave the caliph access to trade goods, gold, and information about the far-flung empire.

The Abbasids developed a strong bureaucracy to conduct the huge empire's affairs. A treasury kept track of the money flow. A special department managed the business of the army. Diplomats from the empire were sent to courts in Europe,

Africa, and Asia to conduct imperial business. To support this bureaucracy, the Abbasids taxed land, imports and exports, and non-Muslims' wealth.

Rival Groups Divide Muslim Lands The Abbasid caliphate lasted from 750 to 1258. During that time, the Abbasids increased their authority by consulting religious leaders. But they failed to keep complete political control of the immense territory. Independent Muslim states sprang up, and local leaders dominated many smaller regions. The **Fatimid** (FAT•uh•MIHD) caliphate was formed by Shi'a Muslims who claimed descent from Muhammad's daughter Fatima. The caliphate began in North Africa and spread across the Red Sea to western Arabia and Syria. However, the Fatimids and other smaller states were still connected to the Abbasid caliphate through religion, language, trade, and the economy.

▼ This 13th-century miniature shows Arab traders navigating the Indian Ocean.

Muslim Trade Network At this time, two major sea-trading networks existed—the Mediterranean Sea and the Indian Ocean. Through these networks, the Muslim Empire could engage in sea trade with the rest of the world. The land network connected the Silk Roads of China and India with Europe and Africa. Muslim merchants needed only a single language, Arabic, and a single currency, the Abbasid dinar, to travel in the empire. C

MAIN IDEA

Recognizing Effects

C Why would a single language and a single currency be such an advantage to a trader?

To encourage the flow of trade, Muslim money changers set up banks in cities throughout the empire. Banks offered letters of credit, called *sakks,* to merchants. A merchant with a *sakk* from a bank in Baghdad could exchange it for cash at a bank in any other city in the empire. In Europe, *sakk* was pronounced "check." Thus, using checks dates back to the Muslim Empire.

At one end of the Muslim Empire was the city of Córdoba in al-Andalus. In the tenth century, this city had a population of 200,000; Paris, in contrast, had 38,000. The city attracted poets, philosophers, and scientists. Many non-Muslims adopted Muslim customs, and Córdoba became a dazzling center of Muslim culture.

In Córdoba, Damascus, Cairo, and Baghdad, a cultural blending of people fueled a period of immense achievements in the arts and the sciences.

NEW YORK CORE CURRICULUM REVIEW

TERMS & NAMES **1.** For each term or name, write a sentence explaining its significance.

- caliph
- Umayyads
- Shi'a
- Sunni
- Sufi
- Abbasids
- al-Andalus
- Fatimid

USING YOUR NOTES

2. Which period of rule do you think was most effective?

Rulers	Period of Rule	Developments in Islam
Rightly guided caliphs		
Umayyads		
Abbasids		

MAIN IDEAS

3. How did Muslims under the "rightly guided" caliphs treat conquered peoples?

4. Why did the Shi'a oppose the rule of the Umayyads?

5. What tied the Abbasid caliphate and the independent Muslim states together?

CRITICAL THINKING & WRITING

6. EVALUATING COURSES OF ACTION Do you think Muhammad should have appointed a successor? Why or why not?

7. DRAWING CONCLUSIONS What attracted non-Muslims to Islam and Islamic culture?

8. MAKING INFERENCES What does opposition to the luxurious life of the Umayyads suggest about what is important to most Muslims?

9. WRITING ACTIVITY EMPIRE BUILDING Write a one-paragraph **summary** in which you determine whether or not the Muslim Empire was well run.

INTEGRATED TECHNOLOGY **INTERNET ACTIVITY**

Use the Internet to find out the number of Sunni and Shi'a Muslims today in Iran, Iraq, Saudi Arabia, and Syria. Create a **pie chart** showing the results of your research.

INTERNET KEYWORD
country studies, Sunni, Shi'a

Muslim Culture

CONNECT TO THE NEW YORK STATE CORE CURRICULUM

Unit 2.E.6.a. Contributions to mathematics, science, medicine, art, architecture, and literature
Unit 2.E.4. Social class: women and slavery in Muslim society

TERMS & NAMES

- House of Wisdom
- calligraphy

SETTING THE STAGE The Abbasids governed during a prosperous period of Muslim history. Riches flowed into the empire from all over Europe, Asia, and Africa. Rulers could afford to build luxurious cities. They supported the scientists, mathematicians, and philosophers that those cities attracted. In the special atmosphere created by Islam, the scholars preserved existing knowledge and produced an enormous body of original learning.

TAKING NOTES
Clarifying Use a web diagram to show the key elements of Muslim culture.

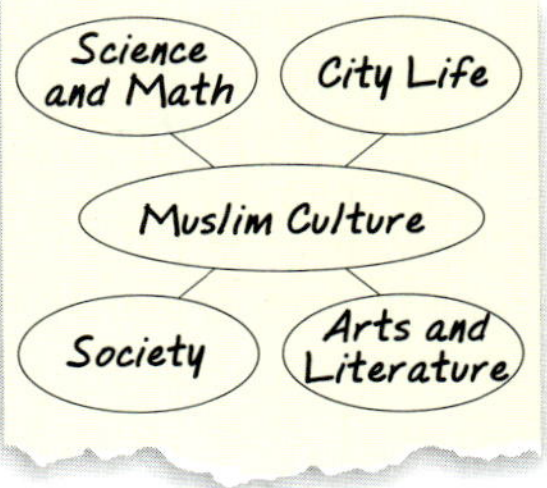

Muslim Society

Over time, the influence of Muslims grew as the empire attracted people from a variety of lands. The many cultural traditions combined with the Arabic culture to create an international flavor. Muslim society had a sophistication matched at that time only by the Tang Empire of China. That cosmopolitan character was most evident in urban centers.

The Rise of Muslim Cities Until the construction of Baghdad, Damascus was the leading city. It was also the cultural center of Islamic learning. Other cities grew up around power centers, such as Córdoba (the Umayyad capital), Cairo (the Fatimid capital), and Jerusalem. (See the map on page 261.) Cities, which symbolized the strength of the caliphate, were very impressive.

Cities, A.D. 900

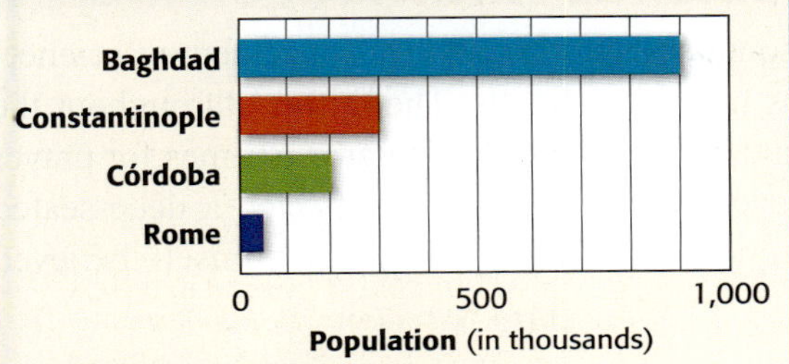

Source: Tertius Chandler and Gerald Fox, *3,000 Years of Urban Growth.*

SKILLBUILDER: Interpreting Graphs
Comparing *How much larger in population was Baghdad than Córdoba?*

The Abbasid capital city, Baghdad, impressed all who saw it. Caliph al-Mansur chose the site for his capital on the west bank of the Tigris River in 762. Extensive planning went into the city's distinctive circular design, formed by three circular protective walls. The caliph's palace of marble and stone sat in the innermost circle, along with the grand mosque. Originally, the main streets between the middle wall and

▲ In a miniature painting from Persia, women are shown having a picnic in a garden. Gardens were seen as earthly representations of paradise.

the palace were lined with shops. Later, the marketplace moved to a district outside the walls. Baghdad's population approached one million at its peak.

Four Social Classes Baghdad's population, made up of different cultures and social classes, was typical for a large Muslim city in the eighth and ninth centuries. Muslim society was made up of four classes. The upper class included those who were Muslims at birth. Converts to Islam were in the second class. The third class consisted of the "protected people" and included Christians, Jews, and Zoroastrians. The lowest class was composed of slaves. Many slaves were prisoners of war, and all were non-Muslim. Slaves most frequently performed household work or fought in the military.

Role of Women The Qur'an says, "Men are the managers of the affairs of women," and "Righteous women are therefore obedient." However, the Qur'an also declares that men and women, as believers, are equal. The shari'a gave Muslim women specific legal rights concerning marriage, family, and property. Thus, Muslim women had more economic and property rights than European, Indian, and Chinese women of the same time period. Nonetheless, Muslim women were still expected to submit to men. When a husband wanted to divorce his wife, all he had to do was repeat three times, "I dismiss thee." The divorce became final in three months.

Responsibilities of Muslim women varied with the income of their husbands. The wife of a poor man would often work in the fields with her husband. Wealthier women supervised the household and its servants. They had access to education, and among them were poets and scholars. Rich or poor, women were responsible for the raising of the children. In the early days of Islam, women could also participate in public life and gain an education. However, over time, Muslim women were forced to live increasingly isolated lives. When they did go out in public, they were expected to be veiled.

Muslim Scholarship Extends Knowledge

Muslims had several practical reasons for supporting the advancement of science. Rulers wanted qualified physicians treating their ills. The faithful throughout the empire relied on mathematicians and astronomers to calculate the times for prayer and the direction of Mecca. However, their attitude also reflected a deep-seated curiosity about the world and a quest for truth. Muhammad himself believed strongly in the power of learning:

PRIMARY SOURCE (A)

Acquire knowledge. It enableth its possessor to distinguish right from wrong; it lighteth the way to Heaven; it is our friend in the desert, our society in solitude, our companion when friendless; it guideth us to happiness; it sustaineth us in misery; it is an ornament amongst friends, and an armour against enemies.

MUHAMMAD, quoted in *The Sayings of Muhammad*

MAIN IDEA

Analyzing Primary Sources

(A) According to Muhammad, what are the nine valuable results of knowledge?

Astronomy

Muslim interest in astronomy developed from the need to fulfill three of the Five Pillars of Islam—fasting during Ramadan, performing the hajj, and praying toward Mecca. A correct lunar calendar was needed to mark religious periods such as the month of Ramadan and the month of the hajj. Studying the skies helped fix the locations of cities so that worshipers could face toward Mecca as they prayed. Extensive knowledge of the stars also helped guide Muslim traders to the many trading cities of the ancient world.

INTEGRATED TECHNOLOGY

RESEARCH LINKS For more on astronomy, go to **classzone.com**

The device shown here is called an **armillary sphere.** The man standing in the center is aligning the sphere, while the seated man records the observations. Astronomers calculated the time of day or year by aligning the rings with various stars. This helped Muslims set their religious calendar.

Muslim observatories were great centers of learning. This scene depicts astronomers working at the observatory in Istanbul. They are using many instruments including an astrolabe like the one shown on this page.

The astrolabe was an early scientific instrument. It had a fixed "plate" and a rotating "rete." The plate was a map of the sky and the rete simulated the daily movement of the earth in relation to the stars. Using this tool, one could calculate time, celestial events, and relative position. For Muslims, the astrolabe helped determine where they were in relation to Mecca.

This is the plate. The plate was etched with a map of the sky for a certain latitude.

This is the rete—it rotated over the plate. The rete was mostly cut away so the map beneath was visible.

These pointers on the rete represented different stars. At night, observers could look at the sky, position the pointers, and make their calculations.

Connect *to* Today

1. **Recognizing Effects** How did fulfilling religious duties lead Muslims to astronomy and a better understanding of the physical world?

   See Skillbuilder Handbook, page R6.

2. **Comparing and Contrasting** Muslim astronomers developed instruments to improve their observations of the sky. We do the same thing today. Research how modern astronomers make their observations and compare their methods with early Muslim astronomers. Write two paragraphs on how their methods are similar to and different from each other.

The Prophet's emphasis on study and scholarship led to strong support of places of learning by Muslim leaders. After the fall of Rome in A.D. 476, Europe entered a period of upheaval and chaos, an era in which scholarship suffered. The scientific knowledge gained up to that time might have been lost. However, Muslim leaders and scholars preserved and expanded much of that knowledge. Both Umayyads and Abbasids encouraged scholars to collect and translate scientific and philosophical texts. In the early 800s, Caliph al-Ma'mun opened in Baghdad a combination library, academy, and translation center called the **House of Wisdom**. There, scholars of different cultures and beliefs worked side by side translating texts from Greece, India, Persia, and elsewhere into Arabic.

Art and Sciences Flourish

Scholars at the House of Wisdom included researchers, editors, linguists, and technical advisers. These scholars developed standards and techniques for research that are a part of the basic methods of today's research. Some Muslim scholars used Greek ideas in fresh new ways. Others created original work of the highest quality. In these ways, Muslims in the Abbasid lands, especially in Córdoba and Baghdad, set the stage for a later revival of European learning.

Muslim Literature Literature had been a strong tradition in Arabia even before Islam. Bedouin poets, reflecting the spirit of desert life, composed poems celebrating ideals such as bravery, love, generosity, and hospitality. Those themes continued to appear in poetry written after the rise of Islam.

The Qur'an is the standard for all Arabic literature and poetry. Early Muslim poets sang the praises of the Prophet and of Islam and, later, of the caliphs and other patrons who supported them. During the age of the Abbasid caliphate, literary tastes expanded to include poems about nature and the pleasures of life and love.

Popular literature included *The Thousand and One Nights,* a collection of fairy tales, parables, and legends. The core of the collection has been linked to India and Persia, but peoples of the Muslim Empire added stories and arranged them, beginning around the tenth century.

Muslim Art and Architecture As the Muslim Empire expanded, the Arabs entered regions that had rich artistic traditions. Muslims continued these traditions but often adapted them to suit Islamic beliefs and practices. For example, since Muslims believed that only Allah can create life, images of living beings were discouraged. Thus, many artists turned to **calligraphy**, or the art of beautiful handwriting. Others expressed themselves through the decorative arts, such as woodwork, glass, ceramics, and textiles.

It is in architecture that the greatest cultural blending of the Muslim world can be seen. To some extent, a building reflected the culture of people of the area. For example, the Great Mosque of Damascus was built on the site of a Christian church. In many ways, the huge dome and vaulted ceiling of the mosque blended Byzantine architecture with Muslim ideas. In Syrian areas, the architecture included features that were very Roman, including baths using Roman heating systems. In Córdoba, the Great

Global Impact

The Thousand and One Nights

The Thousand and One Nights is a collection of stories tied together using a frame story. The frame story tells of King Shahryar, who marries a new wife each day and has her killed the next. When Scheherezade marries the king, however, she tells him fascinating tales for a thousand and one nights, until the king realizes that he loves her.

The tradition of using a frame story dates back to at least 200 B.C., when the ancient Indian fables of the *Panchatantra* were collected. Italian writer Giovanni Boccaccio also set his great work, *The Decameron,* within a frame story in 1335.

Analyzing Art

Muslim Art

Muslim art is intricate and colorful but often does not contain images of living beings. Muslim leaders feared that people might worship the images rather than Allah. Thus, Muslim artists found different ways to express their creativity, as shown on this page.

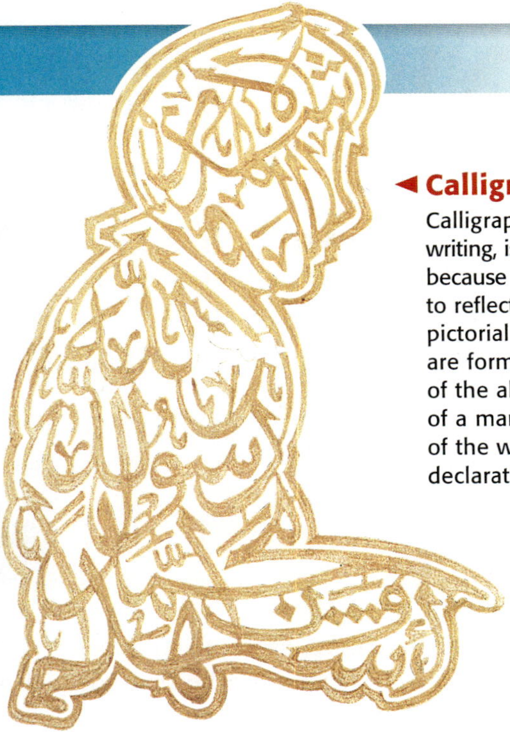

◄ Calligraphy

Calligraphy, or ornamental writing, is important to Muslims because it is considered a way to reflect the glory of Allah. In pictorial calligraphy, pictures are formed using the letters of the alphabet. This picture of a man praying is made up of the words of the Muslim declaration of faith.

▲ Arabesque

Arabesque decoration is a complex, ornate design. It usually incorporates flowers, leaves, and geometric patterns. These arabesque tiles are from the Jami Masjid Mosque. Arabesque designs are also found in Muslim mosaics, textiles, and sculptures.

◄ Geometric Patterns

Muslim artwork sometimes focuses on strictly geometric patterns. Geometric designs can be found in everything from pottery to architecture. This mosaic is from the Jami Masjid Mosque in India (shown below) and uses intricate patterns radiating out from the central shape.

SKILLBUILDER: Interpreting Visual Sources

Drawing Conclusions *What do these three artistic techniques suggest about Muslim art?*

▲ This interior view of the Great Mosque of Córdoba showed a new architectural style. Two tiers of arches support the ceiling.

Mosque used two levels of arches in a style unknown before. The style was based on principles used in earlier mosques. These blended styles appeared in all the lands occupied by the Muslims.

Medical Advances Muslim contributions in the sciences were most recognizable in medicine, mathematics, and astronomy. A Persian scholar named al-Razi (Rhazes, according to the European pronunciation) was the greatest physician of the Muslim world and, more than likely, of world civilization between A.D. 500 and 1500. He wrote an encyclopedia called the *Comprehensive Book* that drew on knowledge from Greek, Syrian, Arabic, and Indian sources as well as on his own experience. Al-Razi also wrote *Treatise on Smallpox and Measles,* which was translated into several languages. He believed patients would recover more quickly if they breathed cleaner air.

Math and Science Stretch Horizons Among the ideas that Muslim scholars introduced to modern math and science, two especially stand out. They are the reliance on scientific observation and experimentation, and the ability to find mathematical solutions to old problems. As for science, Muslims translated and studied Greek texts. But they did not follow the Greek method of solving problems. Aristotle, Pythagoras, and other Greek thinkers preferred logical reasoning over uncovering facts through observation. Muslim scientists preferred to solve problems by conducting experiments in laboratory settings.

Muslim scholars believed that mathematics was the basis of all knowledge. Al-Khwarizmi, a mathematician born in Baghdad in the late 700s, studied Indian rather than Greek sources. He wrote a textbook in the 800s explaining "the art of bringing together unknowns to match a known quantity." He called this technique *al-jabr*—today called algebra.

Many of the advances in mathematics were related to the study of astronomy. Muslim observatories charted stars, comets, and planets. Ibn al-Haytham (Alhazen), a brilliant mathematician, produced a book called *Optics* that revolutionized ideas about vision. He showed that people see objects because rays pass from the objects to the eyes, not from the eyes to the objects as was commonly believed. His studies about optics were used in developing lenses for telescopes and microscopes.

Philosophy and Religion Blend Views

In addition to scientific works, scholars at the House of Wisdom in Baghdad translated works of Greek philosophers like Aristotle and Plato into Arabic. In the 1100s, Muslim philosopher Ibn Rushd (also known as Averroës), who lived in

Córdoba, was criticized for trying to blend Aristotle's and Plato's views with those of Islam. However, Ibn Rushd argued that Greek philosophy and Islam both had the same goal: to find the truth.

Moses Ben Maimon (Maimonides), a Jewish physician and philosopher, was born in Córdoba and lived in Egypt. Like Ibn Rushd, he faced strong opposition for his ideas, but he came to be recognized as the greatest Jewish philosopher in history. Writing during the same time as Ibn Rushd, Maimonides produced a book, *The Guide for the Perplexed,* that blended philosophy, religion, and science.

The "Ideal Man" The values of many cultures were recognized by the Muslims. A ninth-century Muslim philosophical society showed that it recognized the empire's diverse nature when it described its "ideal man":

PRIMARY SOURCE

The ideal and morally perfect man should be of East Persian derivation, Arabic in faith, of Iraqi education, a Hebrew in astuteness, a disciple of Christ in conduct, as pious as a Greek monk, a Greek in the individual sciences, an Indian in the interpretation of all mysteries, but lastly and especially a Sufi in his whole spiritual life.

IKHWAN AS-SAFA, quoted in *The World of Islam*

Though the unified Muslim state broke up, Muslim culture continued. Three Muslim empires—the Ottoman, the Safavid, and the Mughal—would emerge that would reflect the blended nature of the culture of this time. The knowledge developed and preserved by the Muslim scholars would be drawn upon by European scholars in the Renaissance, beginning in the 14th century. **B**

MAIN IDEA

Drawing Conclusions

B What is the advantage of blending various traditions within a culture?

History Makers

Ibn Rushd
1126–1198

Today Ibn Rushd is considered by many to be the most important of all-Muslim philosophers. Yet his views were so offensive to Islamic conservatives that he was once stoned in the Great Mosque of Córdoba. In 1184, the philosopher began serving as physician to Caliph al-Mansur in Marrakech. Under pressure by conservatives, however, the caliph accused Ibn Rushd of heresy and ordered some of his books to be burned.

Fortunately, all of his work was not lost. Ibn Rushd's writings had a great impact on Europe in the 13th century and played a major role in the revival of Christian scholarship. In the 16th century, Italian painter Raphael placed Ibn Rushd among the ancient Greek philosophers in *School of Athens.*

INTEGRATED TECHNOLOGY

RESEARCH LINKS For more on Ibn Rushd, go to **classzone.com**

NEW YORK CORE CURRICULUM REVIEW

TERMS & NAMES 1. For each term or name, write a sentence explaining its significance.

- House of Wisdom
- calligraphy

USING YOUR NOTES

2. Which of these elements most strengthened the Abbasid rule? Explain.

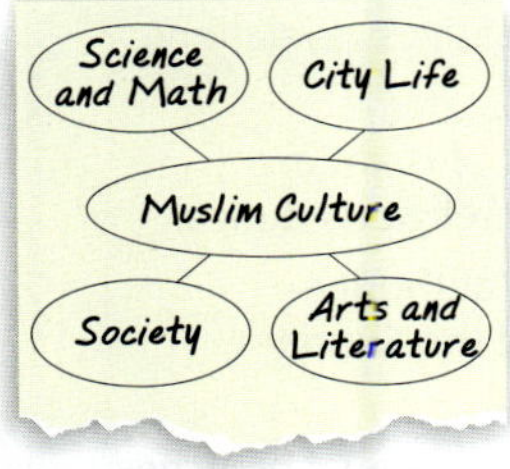

MAIN IDEAS

3. What was the role of women in Muslim society?
4. How did Muslim scholars help preserve the knowledge of the ancient Greeks and Romans?
5. What were some of the Muslim contributions in medicine, mathematics, and astronomy?

CRITICAL THINKING & WRITING

6. **EVALUATING** What do you consider to be the five most significant developments in scholarship and the arts during the reign of the Abbasids?
7. **MAKING INFERENCES** What united the scholars of different cultures who worked in the House of Wisdom?
8. **SYNTHESIZING** What role did cities play in the advancement of Muslim culture?
9. **WRITING ACTIVITY** CULTURAL INTERACTION Write a one-paragraph **analysis** explaining how the primary source quotation on this page reflects the Muslim Empire's diversity.

CONNECT TO TODAY **CREATING A POSTER**

Research to find out how the discoveries of Muslim physician al-Razi have influenced medicine today. Present your findings in a **poster.**

Chapter 10 Assessment

TERMS & NAMES

For each term or name below, briefly explain its connection to the Muslim world between 600 and 1250.

1. Allah
2. Muhammad
3. Islam
4. Hijrah
5. hajj
6. Shi'a
7. Sufi
8. House of Wisdom

MAIN IDEAS

The Rise of Islam Section 1 (pages 263–268)

9. Describe the religious environment into which Muhammad was born.
10. Why did many people in Mecca reject Muhammad's ideas at first?
11. How did early Muslims view and treat Jews and Christians?

Islam Expands Section 2 (pages 269–272)

12. Why were the "rightly guided" caliphs so successful in spreading Islam?
13. What were the main reasons for the split between the Sunni and the Shi'a?
14. Why did trade flourish under the Abbasids?

Muslim Culture Section 3 (pages 273–279)

15. How was Muslim society structured?
16. What were some of the practical reasons Muslims had for supporting the advancement of science?
17. In which fields of learning did Muslims excel?
18. How did the art and architecture of the Muslims reflect cultural blending?

CRITICAL THINKING

1. USING YOUR NOTES

In a time line, list the five most important events in the development and expansion of Islam between 550 and 1250.

550 650 750 850 950 1050 1150 1250

2. SYNTHESIZING

CULTURAL INTERACTION How did the development of Islam influence the blending of cultures in the region where Europe, Africa, and Asia come together?

3. MAKING INFERENCES

RELIGIOUS AND ETHICAL SYSTEMS In what ways did the religious duties of Islam affect the everyday lives of Muslims?

4. SUMMARIZING

EMPIRE BUILDING How did the Abbasids keep the affairs of their empire under control?

5. DEVELOPING HISTORICAL PERSPECTIVE

What rebirth of learning might not have taken place in Europe if Muhammad had not encouraged the pursuit of knowledge?

VISUAL SUMMARY

The Muslim World

ISLAM

Empire Building

Four major Muslim caliphates build empires on parts of three continents.

- 661–750: Umayyad caliphate
- 750–1258: Abbasid caliphate
- 756–976: Umayyads of al-Andalus (Spain)
- 909–1171: Fatimid caliphate (North Africa, Egypt, Western Arabia, and Syria)

Culture

Muslim scholars preserve, blend, and expand knowledge, especially in mathematics, astronomy, architecture, and medical science.

Religion

- Muhammad receives revelations from Allah.
- The Five Pillars of Islam are Muslims' basic religious duties.
- The sources of authority—the Qur'an and the Sunna—guide daily life.
- Islam divides into several branches, including Sunni and Shi'a.

NEW YORK STATE REGENTS EXAM PRACTICE

Use the quotation and your knowledge of world history to answer questions 1 and 2.
Additional Test Practice, pp. S1–S33

PRIMARY SOURCE

One should read histories, study biographies and the experiences of nations. By doing this, it will be as though, in his short life space, he lived contemporaneously with peoples of the past, was on intimate terms with them, and knew the good and the bad among them. . . . You should model your conduct on that of the early Muslims. Therefore, read the biography of the Prophet, study his deeds and concerns, follow in his footsteps, and try your utmost to imitate him.

ABD AL-LATIF quoted in *A History of the Arab Peoples*

1 Why does al-Latif advocate studying history?
(1) because history repeats itself
(2) because history provides insight into the lives of past peoples
(3) because studying history is a good intellectual exercise
(4) because studying history is required of all Muslims

2 Why does he want people to study the life of Muhammad?
(1) because Muhammad is a great historical figure
(2) because Muslim law requires it
(3) to learn to be like the Prophet
(4) to learn about cultural blending

Use the chart and your knowledge of world history to answer question 3.

Muslim Population, 1990s

Country	Population	% of Total Population
Albania	2,275,000	70.0
Argentina	370,000	1.1
Brazil	500,000	0.3
Bulgaria	1,200,000	13.0
Canada	350,000	1.3
France	3,500,000	6.1
Germany	1,700,000	2.1
Guyana	130,000	13.0
Spain	300,000	0.8
Surinam	150,000	30.0
United Kingdom	1,500,000	2.7
United States	6,000,000	2.4

Source: *The Cambridge Illustrated History of the Islamic World*

3 Which nations have a population of Muslims that is similar to that of the United States in terms of percentage?
(1) Canada and France
(2) Germany and Argentina
(3) United Kingdom and France
(4) Germany and United Kingdom

INTEGRATED TECHNOLOGY
TEST PRACTICE Go to **classzone.com**
- Diagnostic tests
- Tutorials
- Strategies
- Additional practice

ALTERNATIVE ASSESSMENT

1. Interact *with* History

In this chapter, you learned that a culture blooms by spreading ideas through trade, war and conquest, and through scholarly exchange. With a partner, make a list of at least five ways to spread an idea in today's world—ways that were not available to Muslims in A.D. 600–1250.

2. WRITING ABOUT HISTORY

Imagine that you are a newspaper reporter investigating the newly opened House of Wisdom. Write a brief **newspaper article** about the new center in Baghdad and the work being undertaken there. In the article, be sure to
- describe the center and the scholars who work there
- include quotations from the scholars
- summarize some of the center's accomplishments and goals

INTEGRATED TECHNOLOGY

Creating a Multimedia Presentation

Use the Internet, books, and other reference sources to create a multimedia presentation on the rise, growth, and culture of Islam. Write brief summaries on each topic. Use maps, pictures, and quotations to accompany your text and illustrate and enhance your presentation. Be sure to include information on the following:
- the life of Muhammad
- a time line of major events in the development of Islam
- the key beliefs and practices of Islam
- the impact of the Muslim Empire on other cultures
- the impact of Muslim learning in science and the arts

A Global View

Religion is defined as an organized system of beliefs, ceremonies, practices, and worship that centers on one or more gods. As many chapters in this book explain, religion has had a significant impact on world history. Throughout the centuries, religion has guided the beliefs and actions of millions around the globe. It has brought people together. But it has also torn them apart.

Religion continues to be a dominant force throughout the world, affecting everything from what people wear to how they behave. There are thousands of religions in the world. The following pages concentrate on five major religions and on Confucianism, an ethical system. They examine some of the characteristics and rituals that make these religions and systems similar as well as unique. They also present some of each religion's sects and denominations.

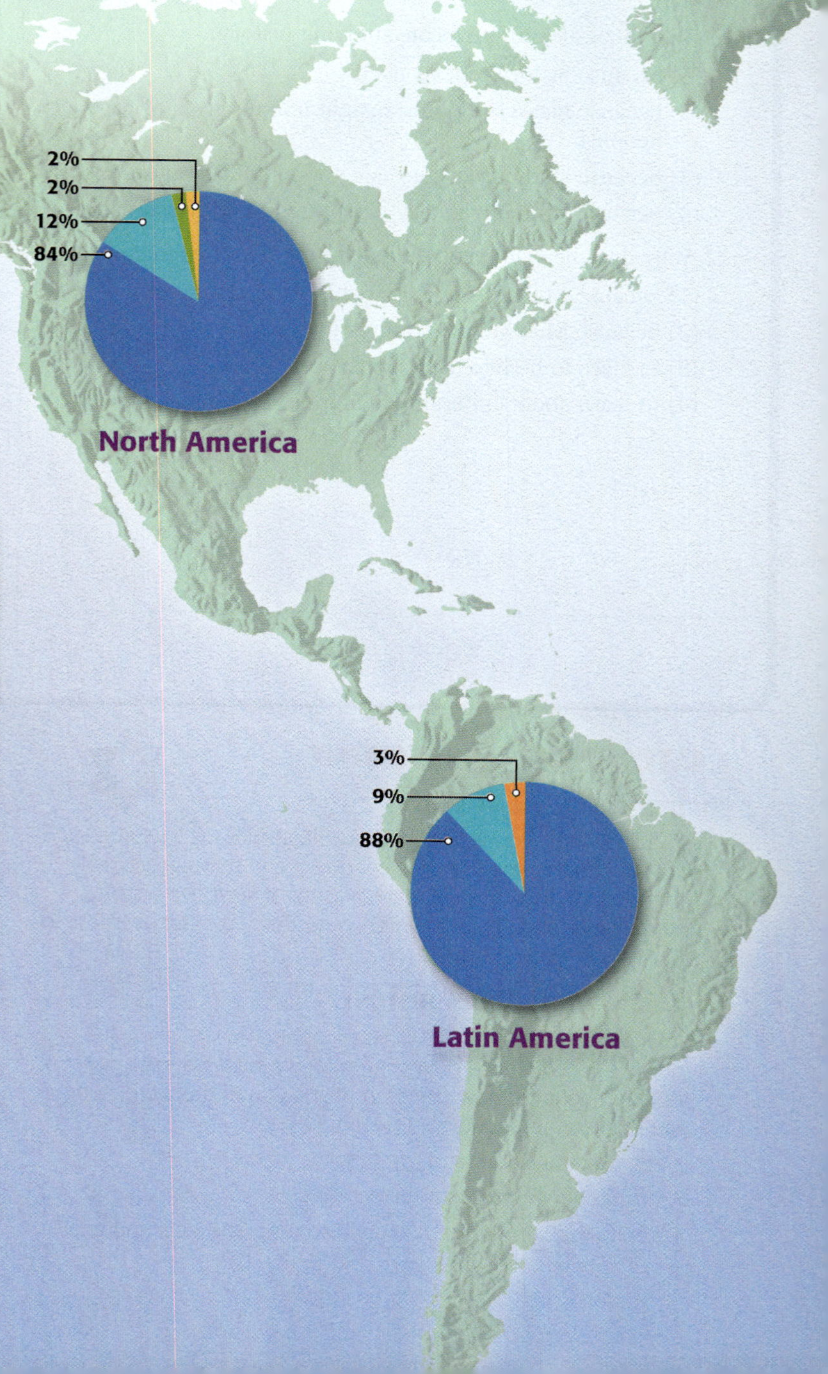

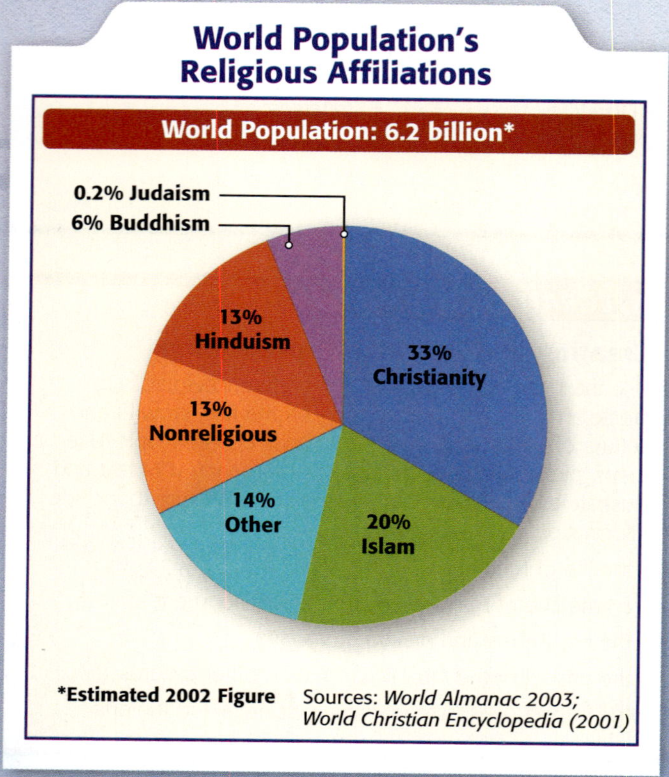

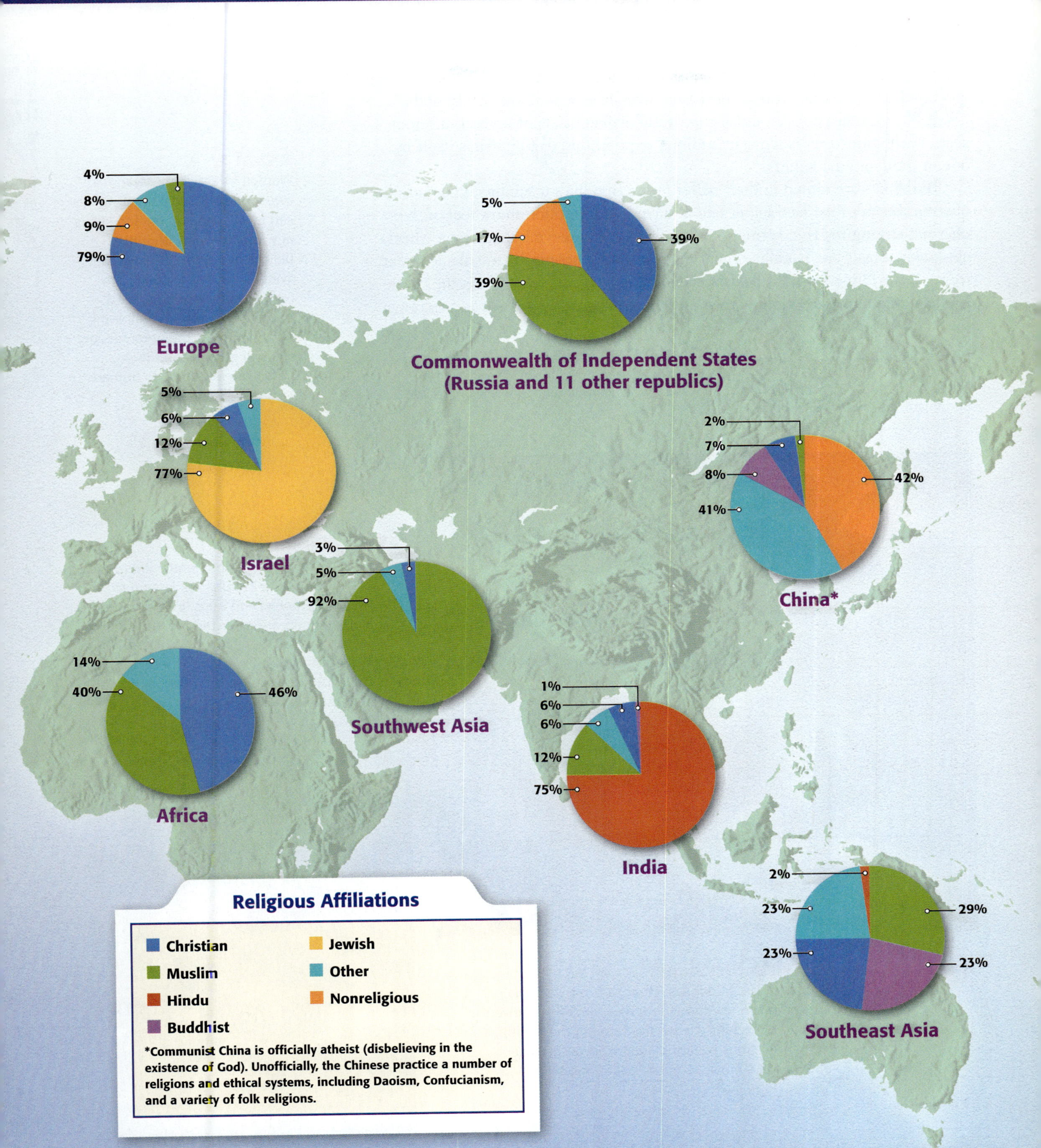
Europe
4%
8%
9%
79%
Commonwealth of Independent States
(Russia and 11 other republics)
5%
17%
39%
39%
Israel
5%
6%
12%
77%
China*
2%
7%
8%
41%
42%
Southwest Asia
3%
5%
92%
Africa
14%
40%
46%
India
1%
6%
6%
12%
75%
Southeast Asia
2%
23%
23%
29%
23%
Religious Affiliations
Christian
Muslim
Hindu
Buddhist
Jewish
Other
Nonreligious
*Communist China is officially atheist (disbelieving in the existence of God). Unofficially, the Chinese practice a number of religions and ethical systems, including Daoism, Confucianism, and a variety of folk religions.

Buddhism

Buddhism has influenced Asian religion, society, and culture for over 2,500 years. Today, most Buddhists live in Sri Lanka, East and Southeast Asia, and Japan. Buddhism consists of several different sects. A religious sect is a group within a religion that distinguishes itself by one or more unique beliefs.

Buddhists are united in their belief in the Buddha's teachings, known as the dharma. Because the Buddha is said to have "set in motion the wheel of the dharma" during his first sermon, his teaching is often symbolized by a wheel, as shown above. The Buddha taught that the key to happiness was detachment from all worldly goods and desires. This was achieved by following the Noble Eightfold Path, or the Middle Way, a life between earthly desires and extreme forms of self-denial.

INTEGRATED TECHNOLOGY

RESEARCH LINKS For more on Buddhism, go to **classzone.com**

Ritual ►

Women in Rangoon, Myanmar, sweep the ground so that monks can avoid stepping on and killing any insects. Many Buddhists believe in rebirth, the idea that living beings, after death, are reborn and continue to exist. Buddhists believe that all living beings possess the potential for spiritual growth—and the possibility of rebirth as humans.

▲ Worship Practices

Statues of the Buddha, such as this one in China, appear in shrines throughout Asia. Buddhists strive to follow the Buddha's teachings through meditation, a form of religious contemplation. They also make offerings at shrines, temples, and monasteries.

▼ Leadership

Those who dedicate their entire life to the teachings of the Buddha are known as Buddhist monks and nuns. In many Buddhist sects, monks are expected to lead a life of poverty, meditation, and study. Here, Buddhist monks file past shrines in Thailand. To learn humility, monks must beg for food and money.

Learn More About Buddhism

Major Buddhist Sects

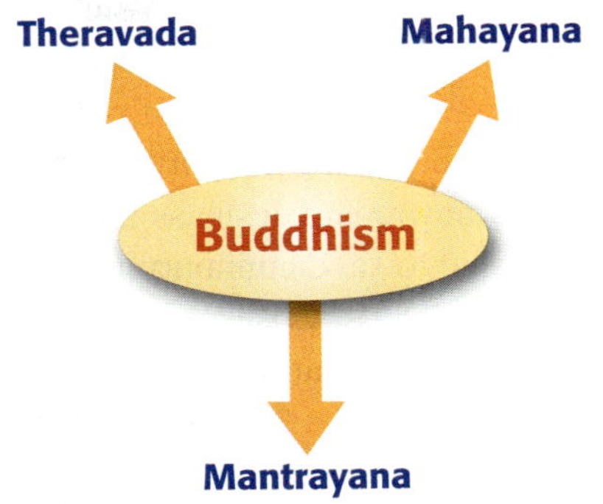

The Three Cardinal Faults

This image depicts what Buddhists consider the three cardinal faults of humanity: greed (the pig); hatred (the snake); and delusion (the rooster).

Dhammapada

PRIMARY SOURCE

One of the most well-known Buddhist scriptures is the *Dhammapada*, or *Verses of Righteousness.* The book is a collection of sayings on Buddhist practices. In this verse, Buddhists are instructed to avoid envying others:

> *Let him not despise what he has received, nor should he live envying the gains of others. The disciple who envies the gains of others does not attain concentration.*
>
> *Dhammapada* 365

Chapter Connection
For a more in-depth examination of Buddhism, see pages 68–71 of Chapter 3, and page 193 of Chapter 7.

Christianity

Christianity is the largest religion in the world, with about 2 billion followers. It is based on the life and teachings of Jesus Christ. Most Christians are members of one of three major groups: Roman Catholic, Protestant, or Eastern Orthodox. Christianity teaches the existence of only one God. Christians regard Jesus as the son of God. They believe that Jesus entered the world and died to save humanity from sin. The cross shown above, a symbol of the crucifixion of Jesus Christ, represents Jesus' love for humanity by dying for its sins. Christians believe that they reach salvation by following the teachings of Jesus Christ.

INTEGRATED TECHNOLOGY

RESEARCH LINKS For more on Christianity, go to **classzone.com**

Ritual ►

Each year, hundreds of thousands of Christians from all over the world visit the Basilica of Guadalupe in northern Mexico City. The church is considered the holiest in Mexico. It is near the site where the Virgin Mary, the mother of Jesus Christ, is said to have appeared twice in 1531. Out of deep respect for Mary, some pilgrims approach the holy cathedral on their knees.

Worship Practices ►

Worshiping as a group is an important part of Christian life. Most Protestant services include praying, singing, and a sermon. Some services include baptism and communion, in which bread and wine are consumed in remembrance of Jesus' death.

Communion celebrates the last meal Jesus took with his disciples, as illustrated here in the *Last Supper* by Leonardo da Vinci.

▲ Leadership

In some Christian churches, the person who performs services in the local church is known as a priest. Shown here is a priest of the Ethiopian Orthodox Church. These priests, like the ministers and clergy in other Christian sects, conduct worship services and preside over marriages and funerals. Monks and nuns also provide leadership and guidance in the Christian church.

Learn More About Christianity

Major Christian Sects

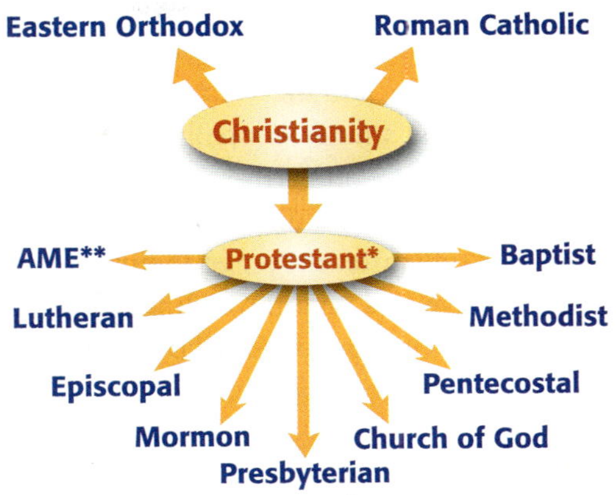

*In the United States alone, there are 30 Protestant denominations with over 400,000 members in each.
**African Methodist Episcopal

Fish Symbol

The fish is an early symbol of Christianity. There are many theories about the origin of the symbol, but some Christians believe that it derives from the fact that Jesus called his disciples, or followers, "fishers of men."

The Bible

PRIMARY SOURCE

The Bible is the most sacred book of the Christian religion. It is divided into two major parts: the Old Testament, which focuses on Jewish history, and the New Testament, which describes the teachings of Jesus Christ. The following verse from the New Testament reveals the fundamental teaching of Jesus:

> *"Men, what must I do to be saved?" And they said, "Believe in the Lord Jesus, and you will be saved, you and your household."*
>
> Acts 16:30–31

Chapter Connection
For more about Christianity, see pages 168–172 of Chapter 6. To learn about the Protestant and Catholic Reformations, see sections 3 and 4 of Chapter 17.

Hinduism

Hinduism, one of the world's oldest surviving religions, is the major religion of India. It also has followers in Indonesia, as well as in parts of Africa, Europe, and the Western Hemisphere. Hinduism is a collection of religious beliefs that developed over thousands of years. Hindus worship several gods, which represent different forms of Brahman. Brahman is the most divine spirit in the Hindu religion. Hinduism, like Buddhism, stresses that persons reach true enlightenment and happiness only after they free themselves from their earthly desires. Followers of Hinduism achieve this goal through worship, the attainment of knowledge, and a lifetime of virtuous acts. The sound "Om," or "Aum," shown above, is the most sacred syllable for Hindus. It often is used in prayers.

INTEGRATED TECHNOLOGY

RESEARCH LINKS For more on Hinduism, go to **classzone.com**

▼ Ritual

Each year, thousands of Hindus make a pilgrimage to India's Ganges River. The Ganges is considered a sacred site in the Hindu religion. Most Hindus come to bathe in the water, an act they believe will cleanse and purify them. The sick and disabled come in the belief that the holy water might cure their ailments.

Learn More About Hinduism

▲ Leadership

Gurus, or spiritual teachers, play a major role in spreading Hindu beliefs. These holy men are believed to have had the gods' words revealed to them. Brahmin priests, like the one shown here, are also religious leaders. They take care of the divine images in the temples and read from the sacred books.

▲ Celebration

Each spring, Hindus in India celebrate the festival of Holi. Originally a harvest festival, Holi also symbolizes the triumph of good over evil. The festival recalls the story of Prince Prahlada, who faced death rather than cease worshiping Vishnu. During this joyous celebration, people dance in the streets and shower each other with colored powder and dyed water.

Major Hindu Sects

Three Main Gods

This statue represents Brahma, creator of the universe. Brahma, Vishnu, and Shiva are the three main gods of Hinduism. Vishnu is the preserver of the universe, while Shiva is its destroyer.

Rig Veda

PRIMARY SOURCE

The Vedas are the oldest Hindu scriptures—and they are older than the sacred writings of any other major religion. The following is a verse from the Rig Veda, the oldest of the four Vedas:

> *He who gives liberally goes straight to the gods; on the high ridge of heaven he stands exalted.*
>
> Rig Veda 1.125.5

Chapter Connection

For a closer look at the origins and beliefs of Hinduism, see pages 66–67 of Chapter 3, and pages 193–194 of Chapter 7.

Islam

Islam is a religion based on the teachings of the prophet Muhammad. Followers of Islam, known as Muslims, believe that God revealed these teachings to Muhammad through the angel Gabriel. Muslims are concentrated from southwest to central Asia and parts of Africa. Islam also has many followers in Southeast Asia. Sunni Muslims believe that their leaders should follow Muhammad's example. Shi'a Muslims believe that their leaders should be Muhammad's descendants.

Islam teaches the existence of only one God, called Allah in the Arabic language. Muslims believe in all prophets of Judaism and Christianity. They show their devotion by performing lifelong acts of worship known as the Five Pillars of Islam. These include faith, prayer, almsgiving (charity), fasting, and a pilgrimage to Mecca. The crescent moon (shown above) has become a familiar symbol for Islam. It may be related to the new moon that begins each month in the Islamic lunar calendar, which orders religious life for Muslims. The five points of the star may represent the Five Pillars of Islam.

INTEGRATED TECHNOLOGY

RESEARCH LINKS For more on Islam, go to **classzone.com**

▼ Ritual

At least once in their lifetime, all Muslims who are physically and financially able go on hajj, or pilgrimage, to the holy city of Mecca in Saudi Arabia. There, pilgrims perform several rites, or acts of worship. One rite, shown here, is walking seven times around the Ka'aba—the house of worship that Muslims face in prayer.

▲ Celebration

During the sacred month known as Ramadan, Muslims fast, or abstain from food and drink, from dawn to sunset. The family shown here is ending their fast. The most important night of Ramadan is called the Night of Power. This is believed to be the night the angel Gabriel first spoke to Muhammad.

▲ Worship Practices

Five times a day Muslims throughout the world face Mecca and pray to Allah. Pictured here are Muslims praying at a mosque in Turkey.

There are no priests or other clergy in Islam. However, a Muslim community leader known as the imam conducts the prayers in a mosque. Islam also has a scholar class called the ulama, which includes religious teachers.

Learn More About Islam

Major Islamic Sects

Sunni

Islam

Shi'a

Prayer Rug

Muslims often pray by kneeling on a rug. The design of the rug includes a pointed or arch-shaped pattern. The rug must be placed so that the arch points toward Mecca.

The Qur'an

PRIMARY SOURCE

The Qur'an, the sacred book of Muslims, consists of verses grouped into 114 chapters, or suras. The book is the spiritual guide on matters of Muslim faith. It also contains teachings for Muslim daily life. In the following verse, Muslims are instructed to appreciate the world's physical and spiritual riches:

> *Do you not see that God has*
> *subjected to your use all things*
> *in the heavens and on earth,*
> *and has made His bounties flow*
> *to you in exceeding measure,*
> *both seen and unseen?*
>
> Qur'an, sura 31:20

Chapter Connection

For a closer look at Islam, including the rise and spread of Islam and Muslim culture, see Chapter 10.

Judaism

Judaism is the religion of the more than 14 million Jews throughout the world. Judaism was the first major religion to teach the existence of only one god. The basic laws and teachings of Judaism come from the Torah, the first five books of the Hebrew Bible. Judaism teaches that a person serves God by studying the Torah and living by its teachings. Orthodox Jews obey the Torah without question. Conservative and Reform Jews interpret the Torah to make its teachings relevant to today's world. The Star of David (shown above), also called the Shield of David, is the universal symbol of Judaism. The emblem refers to King David, who ruled the kingdom of Israel from about 1000–962 B.C.

INTEGRATED TECHNOLOGY

RESEARCH LINKS For more on Judaism, go to **classzone.com**

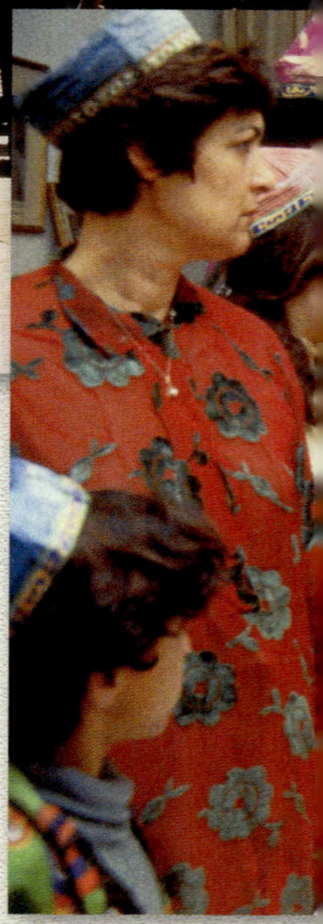

Ritual ►
Major events in a Jew's life are marked by special rites and ceremonies. When Jewish children reach the age of 13, for example, they enter the adult religious community. The event is marked in the synagogue with a ceremony called a bar mitzvah for a boy and a bat mitzvah for a girl, shown here.

▲ Worship Practices
The synagogue is the Jewish house of worship and the center of Jewish community life. Services in the synagogue are usually conducted by a rabbi, the congregation's spiritual leader. Many Jews make the pilgrimage to the Western Wall, shown here. The sacred structure, built in the second century B.C., formed the western wall of the courtyard of the Second Temple of Jerusalem. The Romans destroyed the temple in A.D. 70.

▼ Celebration

Jews celebrate a number of holidays that honor their history as well as their God. Pictured here are Jews celebrating the holiday of Purim. Purim is a festival honoring the survival of the Jews who, in the fifth century B.C., were marked for death by their Persian rulers.

Jews celebrate Purim by sending food and gifts. They also dress in costumes and hold carnivals and dances.

Learn More About Judaism

Major Jewish Sects

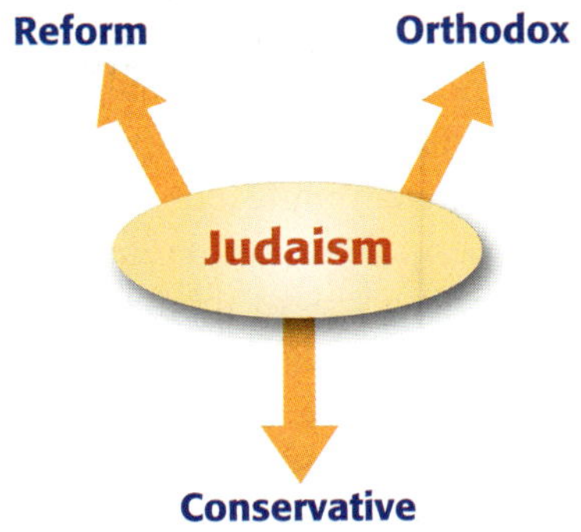

Yarmulke

Out of respect for God, Jewish men are not supposed to leave their head uncovered. Therefore, many Orthodox and Conservative Jews wear a skullcap known as a yarmulke, or kippah.

The Torah

PRIMARY SOURCE

During a synagogue service, the Torah scroll is lifted, while the congregation declares: "This is the Law which Moses set before the children of Israel." The following verse from the Torah makes clear Moses's law regarding belief in one God:

> *Hear O Israel: the Lord our God, the Lord is One.*

Deuteronomy 6:4

Chapter Connection

For a historical examination of Judaism, as well as the development of the Kingdom of Israel, see pages 77–80 of Chapter 3.

Confucianism

With no clergy and with no gods to worship, Confucianism is not a religion in the traditional sense. Rather, it is an ethical system that provides direction for personal behavior and good government. However, this ancient philosophy guides the actions and beliefs of millions of Chinese and other peoples of the East. Thus, many view it as a religion.

Confucianism is a way of life based on the teachings of the Chinese scholar Confucius. It stresses social and civic responsibility. Over the centuries, however, Confucianism has greatly influenced people's spiritual beliefs as well. While East Asians declare themselves to follow any one of a number of religions, many also claim to be Confucian. The yin and yang symbol shown above represents opposite forces in the world working together. It symbolizes the social order and harmony that Confucianism stresses.

INTEGRATED TECHNOLOGY

RESEARCH LINKS For more on Confucianism, go to **classzone.com**

▼ Celebration

While scholars remain uncertain of Confucius's date of birth, people throughout East Asia celebrate it on September 28. In Taiwan, it is an official holiday, known as Teachers' Day. The holiday also pays tribute to teachers. Confucius himself was a teacher, and he believed that education was an important part of a fulfilled life. Here, dancers take part in a ceremony honoring Confucius.

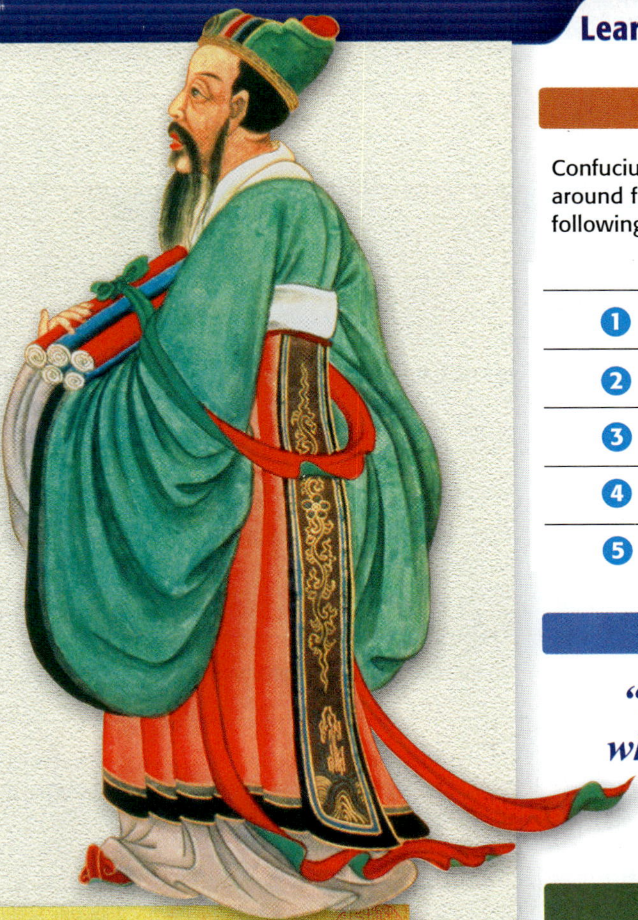

Leadership ►

Confucius was born at a time of crisis and violence in China. He hoped his ideas and teachings would restore the order of earlier times to his society. But although he was active in politics, he never had enough political power to put his ideas into practice. Nonetheless, his ideas would become the foundation of Chinese thought for more than 2,000 years.

▲ Ritual

A key aspect of Confucianism is filial piety, the respect children owe their parents. Traditionally, filial piety meant complete obedience to one's parents during their lifetime. It also required the performance of certain rituals after their death. In this 12th-century Chinese painting, a sage instructs a pupil on the virtue of filial piety.

Learn More About Confucianism

The Five Relationships

Confucius believed society should be organized around five basic relationships between the following:

1	ruler ⟷	subject
2	father ⟷	son
3	husband ⟷	wife
4	older brother ⟷	younger brother
5	friend ⟷	friend

Confucius's Golden Rule

"Do not do unto others what you would not want others to do unto you."

The *Analects*

PRIMARY SOURCE

The earliest and most authentic record of Confucius's ideas was collected by his students. Around 400 B.C., they compiled Confucius's thoughts in a book called the *Analects*. In the following selection from the *Analects*, Confucius (the Master) advises people to avoid judging others:

> *The Master said: "Don't worry if people don't recognize your merits; worry that you may not recognize theirs."*
>
> *Analects* 1.16

Chapter Connection

For a closer look at the life and teachings of Confucius, see pages 104–105 of Chapter 4.

World Religions *and* Ethical Systems

A Comparison

	Buddhism	Christianity	Hinduism	Islam	Judaism	Confucianism
Followers Worldwide (estimated 2001 figures)	362 million	2 billion	820 million	1.2 billion	14.5 million	6.3 million
Name of Deity	The Buddha did not teach a personal deity.	God	Three main gods: Brahma, Vishnu, Shiva	God (Allah)	God (Yahweh)	Confucius (viewed by many as a god)
Founder	The Buddha	Jesus Christ	No one founder	Muhammad	Abraham	Confucius
Holy Book	No one book—sacred texts, including the *Dhammapada*	Bible	No one book—sacred texts, including the Vedas, the Puranas	Qur'an	Hebrew Bible, including the Torah	the *Analects*, the Five Classics
Leadership	Buddhist monks and nuns	Priests, ministers, monks, and nuns	Guru, holy man, Brahmin priest	No clergy but a scholar class called the ulama and the imam, who may lead prayers	Rabbis	No clergy
Basic Beliefs	• Persons achieve complete peace and happiness (nirvana) by eliminating their attachment to worldly things. • Nirvana is reached by following the Noble Eightfold Path: Right views; Right resolve; Right speech; Right conduct; Right livelihood; Right effort; Right mindfulness; Right concentration.	• There is only one God, who watches over and cares for his people. • Jesus Christ was the son of God. He died to save humanity from sin. His death and resurrection made eternal life possible for others.	• The soul never dies, but is continually reborn. • Persons achieve happiness and enlightenment after they free themselves from their earthly desires. • Freedom from earthly desires comes from a lifetime of worship, knowledge, and virtuous acts.	• Persons achieve salvation by following the Five Pillars of Islam and living a just life. These pillars are: faith; prayer; almsgiving, or charity to the poor; fasting, which Muslims perform during Ramadan; pilgrimage to Mecca.	• There is only one God, who watches over and cares for his people. • God loves and protects his people, but also holds people accountable for their sins and shortcomings. • Persons serve God by studying the Torah and living by its teachings.	• Social order, harmony, and good government should be based on strong family relationships. • Respect for parents and elders is important to a well-ordered society. • Education is important both to the welfare of the individual and to society.

Assessment

MAIN IDEAS

Buddhism (pages 284–285)

1. According to the Buddha, how does one achieve happiness and fulfillment?
2. Why do Buddhists take special care to avoid killing any living being?

Christianity (pages 286–287)

3. Why is Jesus Christ central to the Christian religion?
4. What do Christians hope to achieve by following the teachings of Jesus Christ?

Hinduism (pages 288–289)

5. What is the importance of the Ganges River in Hinduism?
6. Who are the three main gods of Hinduism?

Islam (pages 290–291)

7. What is the most important night of Ramadan? Why?
8. What are the Five Pillars of Islam?

Judaism (pages 292–293)

9. Why do Jews consider the Western Wall to be sacred?
10. What is the role of the rabbi in the Jewish tradition?

Confucianism (pages 294–295)

11. Around what five relationships did Confucius believe society should be organized?
12. According to tradition, what does filial piety require of children?

CRITICAL THINKING

1. **COMPARING AND CONTRASTING**
Using information from the text and chart at left, choose two religions and identify their similarities and differences in a Venn diagram.

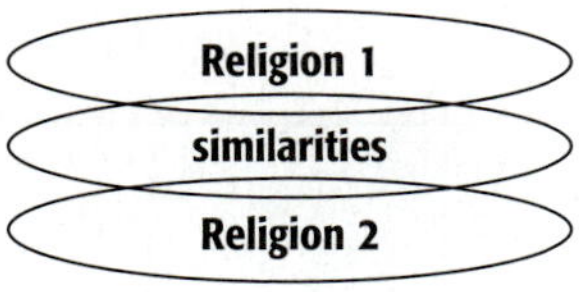

2. **SYNTHESIZING**
What basic principles do all of the religions have in common?

3. **DRAWING CONCLUSIONS**
What role does religion play in people's everyday lives?

4. **MAKING INFERENCES**
Why do you think ritual and celebrations are an important part of all religions?

5. **FORMING OPINIONS**
What do you think people hope to gain from their religion?

STANDARDS-BASED ASSESSMENT

Use the quotation and your knowledge of world history to answer questions 1 and 2.
Additional Test Practice, pp. S1–S33

PRIMARY SOURCE

Human beings are spiritual animals. Indeed, there is a case for arguing that *Homo sapiens* is also *Homo religiosus*. Men and women started to worship gods as soon as they became recognizably human; they created religions at the same time they created works of art. . . . These early faiths expressed the wonder and mystery that seem always to have been an essential component of the human experience of this beautiful yet terrifying world. Like art, religion has been an attempt to find meaning and value in life, despite the suffering that flesh is heir to.

KAREN ARMSTRONG, *A History of God*

1. With which of the following opinions would Armstrong probably agree?
   A. People are naturally religious.
   B. People have no need of religion.
   C. People only believe in what they can see.
   D. People created religion out of fear.

2. According to Armstrong, what is the main similarity between art and religion?
   A. They both express the suffering human beings must endure.
   B. They first appeared at around the same time.
   C. They both place value on beauty.
   D. They are both used to find life's meaning.

INTEGRATED TECHNOLOGY

TEST PRACTICE Go to **classzone.com**

- Diagnostic tests
- Tutorials
- Strategies
- Additional practice

ALTERNATIVE ASSESSMENT

1. **Interact *with* History**
Imagine that you could meet one of the founders listed in the chart on page 296. What questions would you ask about his life and beliefs? What views of your own would you share? Take turns role-playing your conversation with a partner.

2. **WRITING ABOUT HISTORY**
Research to learn more about one of the celebrations you read about in this section. Then write a three-paragraph **essay** about its origins. Discuss the celebration's history, symbolism, and meaning.

CHAPTER 11

Byzantines, Russians, and Turks Interact, 500–1500

Previewing Main Ideas

RELIGIOUS AND ETHICAL SYSTEMS Two world religions, Islam and Christianity, met head-to-head as Arabs and Turks battled Byzantines and then Crusaders. At the same time, disputes over doctrine split Christianity into competing branches.

Geography *What land did the Seljuk Turks occupy?*

CULTURAL INTERACTION Byzantine influence inspired the growth of a unique Russian culture. The Turks meanwhile adopted Islam and sponsored a rebirth of Persian ways to create a dynamic cultural blend.

Geography *Why might the Dnieper River have been important to Kievan Russia?*

EMPIRE BUILDING The Byzantines, Slavs, Arabs, Turks, and Mongols waged bloody wars to expand their territories. However, each empire also brought together people of diverse traditions.

Geography *How does the map indicate that there was probably conflict between the Byzantine and Seljuk empires?*

NEW YORK CORE CURRICULUM FOCUS

- The Byzantine Empire created the Justinian Code to regulate Byzantine life.
- Christianity split into the Roman Catholic Church in the West and the Orthodox Church in the East.

INTEGRATED TECHNOLOGY

eEdition

- Interactive Maps
- Interactive Visuals
- Interactive Primary Sources

INTERNET RESOURCES

Go to **classzone.com** for:

- Research Links
- Internet Activities
- Primary Sources
- Chapter Quiz
- Maps
- Test Practice
- Current Events

CENTRAL ASIA

527 Justinian becomes ruler of Byzantine Empire. ▶

850s Byzantine culture spreads to Russia.

500 — 700 — 900

WORLD

690 Empress Wu Zhao assumes throne in China.

771 Charlemagne becomes ruler of Frankish Kingdom in Europe.

Three Empires: Byzantine, Russian, Seljuk, c. 1100

1240
◀ Mongols destroy Kiev. (Mongolian archer on horseback)

1453
◀ Constantinople falls to Ottoman Turks.

1100 **1300** **1500**

1095
◀ Pope Urban II (shown addressing the bishops of France) launches the first Crusade.

1347
Bubonic plague devastates Europe.

1502
Montezuma II takes charge of the Aztec Empire in modern-day Mexico.

Interact *with* History

How will you expand your empire?

You are the new ruler of the Byzantine Empire. Through expansion, you hope to make the empire even greater. Military conquest is an option, as shown here in a painting of a Turkish invasion of India. Your diplomats might persuade other groups to join you. You also know that rulers of several countries outside your empire would like to see their sons or daughters marry into your family. Now you must consider the best way to enlarge your empire.

EXAMINING *the* ISSUES

- **What are the benefits and drawbacks of a military conquest?**
- **Why might you choose diplomacy, or intermarriage with an outside ruling family?**

As a class, discuss the various ways to expand an empire. What option or options will you choose? Explain your decision. As you read the chapter, think about how empires expand.

1 The Byzantine Empire

CONNECT TO THE NEW YORK STATE CORE CURRICULUM

Unit 2.C.2. Achievements (law–Justinian Code, engineering, art, and commerce)
Unit 2.C.3. The Orthodox Christian Church

TERMS & NAMES

- Justinian
- Justinian Code
- Hagia Sophia
- patriarch
- icon
- excommunication
- Cyrillic alphabet

SETTING THE STAGE As you learned in Chapter 6, the Western Roman Empire crumbled in the fifth century as it was overrun by invading Germanic tribes. By this time, however, the once great empire had already undergone significant changes. It had been divided into western and eastern empires, and its capital had moved east from Rome to the Greek city of Byzantium. The city would become known as Constantinople after the emperor Constantine, who made it the new capital in A.D.-330. (Byzantium would remain as the name of the entire Eastern Empire.) For nearly a thousand years after the collapse of the Western Empire, Byzantium and its flourishing capital would carry on the glory of Rome.

A New Rome in a New Setting

TAKING NOTES

Clarifying Use a cluster diagram to show Justinian's accomplishments as emperor of the New Rome.

Roman leaders had divided the empire in 395, largely due to difficulties in communications between the eastern and the troubled western parts of the empire. Still, rulers in the East continued to see themselves as emperors for all of Rome.

In 527, a high-ranking Byzantine nobleman named **Justinian** succeeded his uncle to the throne of the Eastern Empire. In an effort to regain Rome's fading glory, Justinian in 533 sent his best general, Belisarius (behl•uh•SAIR•ee•uhs), to recover North Africa from the invading Germanic tribes. Belisarius and his forces quickly succeeded.

Two years later, Belisarius attacked Rome and seized it from a group known as the Ostrogoths. But the city faced repeated attacks by other Germanic tribes. Over the next 16 years, Rome changed hands six times. After numerous campaigns, Justinian's armies won nearly all of Italy and parts of Spain. Justinian now ruled almost all the territory that Rome had ever ruled. He could honestly call himself a new Caesar.

Like the last of the old Caesars, the Byzantine emperors ruled with absolute power. They headed not just the state but the church as well. They appointed and dismissed bishops at will. Their politics were brutal—and often deadly. Emperors lived under constant risk of assassination. Of the 88 Byzantine emperors, 29 died violently, and 13 abandoned the throne to live in monasteries.

▼ A glittering cross from the 11th century, Byzantine Empire

Life in the New Rome

A separate government and difficult communications with the West gave the Byzantine Empire its own character, different from that of the Western Empire. The citizens thought of themselves as sharing in the Roman tradition, but few spoke Latin anymore. Most Byzantines spoke Greek.

Having unified the two empires, Justinian set up a panel of legal experts to regulate Byzantium's increasingly complex society. The panel combed through 400 years of Roman law. It found a number of laws that were outdated and contradictory. The panel created a single, uniform code known as the **Justinian Code**. After its completion, the code consisted of four works.

1. The *Code* contained nearly 5,000 Roman laws that were still considered useful for the Byzantine Empire.
2. The *Digest* quoted and summarized the opinions of Rome's greatest legal thinkers about the laws. This massive work ran to a total of 50 volumes.
3. The *Institutes* was a textbook that told law students how to use the laws.
4. The *Novellae* (New Laws) presented legislation passed after 534.

Vocabulary
A *code* is a general system of laws, and it stems from the Latin word *codex,* meaning "book."

The Justinian Code decided legal questions that regulated whole areas of Byzantine life. Marriage, slavery, property, inheritance, women's rights, and criminal justice were just some of those areas. Although Justinian himself died in 565, his code served the Byzantine Empire for 900 years.

Creating the Imperial Capital While his scholars were creating the legal code, Justinian launched the most ambitious public building program ever seen in the Roman world. He rebuilt the crumbling fortifications of Constantinople, as workers constructed a 14-mile stone wall along the city's coastline and repaired the massive fortifications along its western land border.

GEOGRAPHY SKILLBUILDER: Interpreting Maps
Human-Environment Interaction *What aspects of Constantinople might slow an invasion from the west?*

▲ The Ortakoy Mosque towers above modern-day Constantinople, now called Istanbul.

Church building, however, was the emperor's greatest passion. Justinian viewed churches as the most visible sign of the close connection between church and state in his empire. The crowning glory of his reign was **Hagia Sophia** (HAY•ee•uh soh•FEE•uh), which means "Holy Wisdom" in Greek. A church of the same name had been destroyed in riots that swept Constantinople in 532. When Justinian rebuilt Hagia Sophia, many visitors hailed it as the most splendid church in the Christian world. (A)

MAIN IDEA

Analyzing Motives

(A) Why do you think governments so often build magnificent buildings like Hagia Sophia?

As part of his building program, Justinian enlarged his palace into a vast complex. He also built baths, aqueducts, law courts, schools, and hospitals. By the time the emperor was finished, the city teemed with an almost visible excitement.

Beneath such excitement, a less obvious but vitally important activity took place: the preservation of Greco-Roman culture. Byzantine families valued education—specifically classical learning. Basic courses for Byzantine students focused on Greek and Latin grammar, and philosophy. The classics of Greek and Roman literature served as textbooks. Students memorized Homer. They learned geometry from Euclid, history from Herodotus, and medicine from Galen. The modern world owes Byzantine scholars a huge debt for preserving many of the great works of Greece and Rome.

Constantinople's Hectic Pace The main street running through Constantinople was the Mese (MEHS•ee), or "Middle Way." Merchant stalls lined the main street and filled the side streets. Products from the most distant corners of Asia, Africa, and Europe passed through these stalls. Everywhere, food stands filled the air with the smell of their delicacies, while acrobats and street musicians performed.

Meanwhile, citizens could enjoy free entertainment at the Hippodrome, which offered wild chariot races and performance acts. The Hippodrome (from Greek words meaning "horse" and "racecourse") held 60,000 spectators. Fans of the different teams formed rowdy gangs named for the colors worn by their heroes.

In 532, two such fan groups sparked citywide riots called the Nika Rebellion (because the mob cried "Nika!" or "Victory!"). Both sides were angry with the government. They felt that city officials had been too severe in putting down a previous riot of Hippodrome fans. They packed the Hippodrome and demanded the overthrow of Justinian. Belisarius, however, broke in with his troops and slaughtered about 30,000 rebels.

Justinian had considered fleeing during the Nika Rebellion, but his wife, Theodora, urged him to stay. As her husband's steely adviser, Theodora had immense power. She rallied Justinian to remain in the capital with a fiery speech:

PRIMARY SOURCE

My opinion is that now is a poor time for flight, even though it bring safety. For any man who has seen the light of day will also die, but one who has been an emperor cannot endure to be a fugitive. If now you wish to go, Emperor, nothing prevents you. There is the sea, there are the steps to the boats. But take care that after you are safe, you do not find that you would gladly exchange that safety for death.

THEODORA, quoted by Procopius in *History of the Wars*

History Makers

Empress Theodora
500–548

The most powerful woman in Byzantine history rose from deep poverty. Early in life, Theodora was an actress. Eventually, she met Justinian, and in 525, they married.

As empress, Theodora met with foreign envoys, wrote to foreign leaders, passed laws, and built churches. During one political crisis, Theodora even confiscated the property of the general Belisarius. After she died in 548, Justinian was so depressed that he passed no major laws for the rest of his reign.

INTEGRATED TECHNOLOGY

RESEARCH LINKS For more on Empress Theodora, go to **classzone.com**

The Empire Falls

After Justinian's death in 565, the empire suffered countless setbacks. There were street riots, religious quarrels, palace intrigues, and foreign dangers. Each time the empire moved to the edge of collapse, it found some way to revive—only to face another crisis.

The Plague of Justinian The first crisis actually began before Justinian's death. It was a disease that resembled what we now know as the bubonic plague. This horrifying illness hit Constantinople in the later years of Justinian's reign. The plague probably arrived from India on ships infested with rats. Historians estimate that in 542, the worst year of the plague, 10,000 people were dying every day. The illness broke out repeatedly until around 700, when it finally faded. By that time, it had destroyed a huge percentage of the Byzantine population. **B**

MAIN IDEA

Making Inferences

B How might the plague have helped make Byzantium more vulnerable to foreign attack?

Attacks from East and West From the very start of its rise to power, Byzantium faced constant challenges from foreign enemies. Lombards overran Justinian's conquests in the west. Avars, Slavs, and Bulgars made frequent raids on the northern borders. The powerful Sassanid Persians attacked relentlessly in the east. The Persians and Avars struck against Constantinople itself in 626. With the rise of Islam, Arab armies attacked the city in 674 and once again in 717. Russians attempted invasions of the city three times between 860 and 1043. In the 11th century, the Turks took over the Muslim world and fought their way slowly into Byzantine territory.

The Byzantines used bribes, diplomacy, political marriages, and military power to keep their enemies at bay. In the seventh century, Emperor Heraclius reorganized the empire along military lines. Provinces became themes, or military districts. Each theme was run by a general who reported directly to the emperor. These strategies, however, could not work forever. Slowly, the Byzantine Empire shrank under the impact of foreign attacks. By 1350, it was reduced to the tip of Anatolia and a strip of the Balkans. Yet thanks to its walls, its fleet, and its strategic location, Constantinople held out for another 100 years. Finally, the city fell to the Ottoman Turks in 1453.

The Church Divides

During the Byzantine Empire, Christianity underwent a dramatic development. Christianity had begun to develop differently in the Western and Eastern Roman Empires, due largely to the distance and lack of contact between the two regions. As the Eastern Empire became Byzantium and flourished, those differences grew and ultimately split apart the Church.

A Religious Split Eastern Christianity built its heritage on the works of early Church fathers. One was Saint Basil, who, around 357, wrote rules for the life of monks. Here, Saint Basil describes how monks and Christians should behave:

▼ Saint Basil

PRIMARY SOURCE **C**

The Christian should not be ostentatious [showy] in clothing or sandals, for all this is idle boasting. He should wear cheap clothes according to the need of the body. He should consume nothing beyond what is necessary or which tends to extravagance, for all this is abuse. He should not strive for honour nor always seek the first place. Each one should hold all men above himself. He should not be disobedient. . . . He should not be desirous of money, nor treasure up unnecessary things to no avail. He who approaches God ought to embrace poverty in all things, and be pierced with the fear of God.

SAINT BASIL, quoted in *The Letters*

MAIN IDEA

Analyzing Primary Sources

C How might Saint Basil view a lavish and extravagant lifestyle?

Analyzing Key Concepts

Roman Catholicism and Eastern Orthodoxy

Originally, Christianity had one church. Because of political conflicts and differences in belief, the western and eastern parts of the Christian Church split apart in 1054. The western church became the Roman Catholic Church, and the eastern church became the Eastern Orthodox Church.

Both churches believe in the gospel of Jesus and in the Bible as interpreted by their church. They also believe that God uses sacraments to convey his love to humans. Sacraments are visible signs of something sacred; for instance, the water used in baptism is a sign of God's power to cleanse people of sin. The Venn diagram below shows other similarities and differences.

The 11th Century: Comparing Two Churches

Roman Catholic

Services are conducted in Latin.

The pope has authority over all other bishops.

The pope claims authority over all kings and emperors.

Priests may not marry.

Divorce is not permitted.

Similarities

They base their faith on the gospel of Jesus and the Bible.

They use sacraments such as baptism.

Their religious leaders are priests and bishops.

They seek to convert people.

Eastern Orthodox

Services are conducted in Greek or local languages.

The patriarch and other bishops head the Church as a group.

The emperor claims authority over the patriarch and other bishops of the empire.

Priests may be married.

Divorce is allowed under certain conditions.

Leaders of the Two Churches

Pope Benedict XVI (right) is the supreme head of the Roman Catholic Church. Ecumenical Patriarch Bartholomew (left) holds a slightly different position in the Orthodox Church. Eastern Orthodox churches pay him their highest honors because he heads the ancient Church of Constantinople, but they do not consider him their supreme authority.

INTEGRATED TECHNOLOGY

RESEARCH LINKS For more on Roman Catholicism and Eastern Orthodoxy, go to **classzone.com**

DATA FILE

ROMAN CATHOLIC AND EASTERN ORTHODOX DATA

- U.S. state with highest percentage of Roman Catholics: Rhode Island, 51 percent.
  2001 American Religious Identification Survey by Graduate Center of City University of New York
- U.S. states with highest percentage of Eastern Orthodox: New Hampshire and New Jersey, 0.90 percent each.
  1990 National Survey of Religious Identification
- Vatican City is an independent state located in Rome, Italy. The Roman Catholic Church claims more than a billion members worldwide.
  Concise Columbia Encyclopedia, third edition; www.adherents.com
- The largest of the Eastern Orthodox churches is the Russian Orthodox Church. It claims 90 million members worldwide.
  www.adherents.com
- In 2003, the world region with the largest population of Roman Catholics: Latin America, 473,000,000
  Encyclopaedia Britannica Book of the Year 2004
- In 2003, the world region with the largest population of Eastern Orthodox members: Europe, 158,450,000
  Encyclopaedia Britannica Book of the Year 2004

Connect *to* Today

1. **Forming and Supporting Opinions** What do you think was the most important issue dividing the two churches? Explain your answer.
   See Skillbuilder Handbook, page R20.
2. **Making Predictions** Do you think the schism between the Roman Catholic Church and the Eastern Orthodox Church will ever be healed and the two churches reunited? Why or why not?

Another significant figure was Saint John Chrysostom (KRIHS•uhs•tuhm). As bishop of Constantinople from 398 to 404, Chrysostom was the **patriarch** (PAY•tree•AHRK), or leading bishop of the East. But even the patriarch bowed to the emperor.

A controversy that tested the emperor's authority over religious matters broke out in the eighth century. In 730, Emperor Leo III banned the use of **icons**, religious images used by Eastern Christians to aid their devotions. The emperor viewed the use of icons as idol worship. People responded with riots, and the clergy rebelled.

In the West, the pope became involved in this eastern dispute and supported the use of icons. One pope even ordered the **excommunication** of a Byzantine emperor—that is, he declared the emperor to be an outcast from the Church. In 843, more than 100 years after the controversy began, Empress Theodora restored icons to Eastern churches.

▲ (top) An 11th-century silver chalice displays the Cyrillic alphabet. (bottom) A closeup of the alphabet reveals its likeness to English.

Differences between the Eastern and Western churches, continued to grow. In 1054, matters came to a head when the pope and the patriarch excommunicated each other in a dispute over religious doctrine. Shortly afterward, Christianity officially split between the Roman Catholic Church in the West and the Orthodox Church in the East.

Byzantine Missionaries Convert the Slavs As West and East grew apart, the two traditions of Christianity competed for converts. Missionaries from the Orthodox Church, for example, took their form of Christianity to the Slavs, groups that inhabited the forests north of the Black Sea. Two of the most successful Eastern missionaries, Saint Methodius and Saint Cyril (SEER•uhl), worked among the Slavs in the ninth century. Cyril and Methodius invented an alphabet for the Slavic languages. With an alphabet, Slavs would be able to read the Bible in their own tongues. Many Slavic languages, including Russian, are now written in what is called the **Cyrillic** (suh•RIHL•ihk) **alphabet**.

As these missionaries carried out their work, the Slavs themselves were creating a culture that would form one of history's most influential countries: Russia.

NEW YORK CORE CURRICULUM REVIEW

TERMS & NAMES 1. For each term or name, write a sentence explaining its significance.

- Justinian
- Justinian Code
- Hagia Sophia
- patriarch
- icon
- excommunication
- Cyrillic alphabet

USING YOUR NOTES

2. In your opinion, was Justinian a great leader? Why or why not?

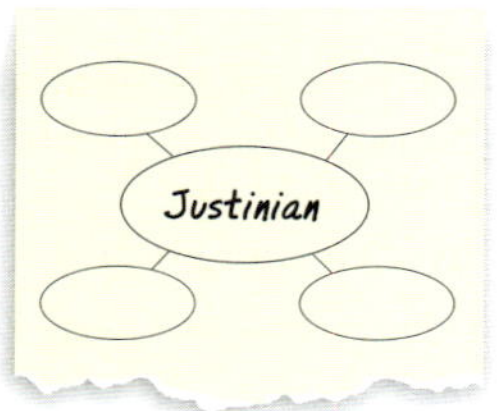

MAIN IDEAS

3. How did the Byzantines help to preserve Greco-Roman culture?
4. What various methods did the Byzantines use to hold off their enemies?
5. Why did Eastern Christians rebel against Emperor Leo III in 730?

CRITICAL THINKING & WRITING

6. **FORMING AND SUPPORTING OPINIONS** Do you agree or disagree with the characterization of Justinian as a new Caesar? Why?
7. **ANALYZING MOTIVES** Why do you think Justinian decided the time had come to reform Roman law?
8. **DRAWING CONCLUSIONS** Why do you think the Justinian Code lasted so long?
9. **WRITING ACTIVITY** RELIGIOUS AND ETHICAL SYSTEMS Imagine you are a Byzantine missionary attempting to convert a group of Slavs. Write a **speech** that you would give to the group in order to sway them.

CONNECT TO TODAY **CREATING A LIST**

Locate the Cyrillic alphabet and make a **list** of what, if any, letters resemble their English counterparts. Discuss with the class why this might be.

The Russian Empire

CONNECT TO THE NEW YORK STATE CORE CURRICULUM

Unit 2.D.3. Kiev
Unit 2.C.4. Russian Orthodox Church

TERMS & NAMES

- Slavs
- Vladimir
- Yaroslav the Wise
- Alexander Nevsky
- Ivan III
- czar

SETTING THE STAGE In addition to sending its missionaries to the land of the **Slavs** during the ninth century, Byzantium actively traded with its neighbors to the north. Because of this increased interaction, the Slavs began absorbing many Greek Byzantine ways. It was this blending of Slavic and Greek traditions that eventually produced Russian culture.

Russia's Birth

Russia's first unified territory originated west of the Ural Mountains in the region that runs from the Black Sea to the Baltic Sea. Hilly grasslands are found in the extreme south of that area. The north, however, is densely forested, flat, and swampy. Slow-moving, interconnecting rivers allow boat travel across these plains in almost any direction. Three great rivers, the Dnieper (NEE•puhr), the Don, and the Volga, run from the heart of the forests to the Black Sea or the Caspian Sea. (See the map on page 308.)

In the early days of the Byzantine Empire, these forests were inhabited by tribes of Slavic farmers and traders. They spoke similar languages but had no political unity. Sometime in the 800s, small bands of adventurers came down among them from the north. These Varangians, or Rus as they were also called, were most likely Vikings. (The name "Russia" is taken from this group.) Eventually, these Vikings built forts along the rivers and settled among the Slavs.

Slavs and Vikings Russian legends say the Slavs invited the Viking chief Rurik to be their king. So in 862, he founded Novgorod (NAHV•guh•rahd), Russia's first important city. That account is given in *The Primary Chronicle,* a history of Russia written by monks in the early 1100s. Around 880, a nobleman from Novgorod named Oleg moved south to Kiev (KEE•ehf), a city on the Dnieper River. From Kiev, the Vikings could sail by river and sea to Constantinople. There they could trade for products from distant lands.

Kiev grew into a principality, a small state ruled by a prince. As it did, the Viking nobles intermarried with their Slavic subjects and adopted many aspects of Slavic culture. Gradually, the line between Slavs and Vikings vanished.

Kiev Becomes Orthodox In 957, a member of the Kievan nobility, Princess Olga, paid a visit to Constantinople and publicly converted to Christianity. From 945 to 964, she governed Kiev until her son was old enough to rule. Her son

TAKING NOTES
Recognizing Effects Use a chart to show how Mongol rule affected different parts of Russian society.

Nobles	Church
People	**Moscow Princes**

The Viking Invasions of Eastern Europe, 820-941

GEOGRAPHY SKILLBUILDER: Interpreting Maps

1. **Human-Environment Interaction** *Which geographical feature of Russia did Vikings use to further their invasions?*
2. **Human-Environment Interaction** *Besides east, what was the other basic direction taken by Vikings in their Eastern European invasions? Why do you think they chose to invade in that direction?*

resisted Christianity. However, soon after Olga's grandson **Vladimir** (VLAD•uh•meer) came to the throne about 980, he considered conversion to Christianity. *The Primary Chronicle* reports that Vladimir sent out teams to observe the major religions of the times. Three of the teams returned with lukewarm accounts of Islam, Judaism, and Western Christianity. But the team from Byzantium told quite a different story:

PRIMARY SOURCE

The Greeks led us to the [buildings] where they worship their God, and we knew not whether we were in heaven or on earth. For on earth there is no such splendor or such beauty, and we are at a loss how to describe it. We only know that God dwells there among men, and . . . we cannot forget that beauty.

from *The Primary Chronicle*

This report convinced Vladimir to convert to Byzantine Christianity and to make all his subjects convert, too. In 989, a baptism of all the citizens of Kiev was held in the Dnieper River. Kiev, already linked to Byzantium by trade, now looked to the empire for religious guidance. Vladimir imported teachers to instruct the people in the new faith. All the beliefs and traditions of Orthodox Christianity flourished in Kiev. Vladimir appreciated the Byzantine idea of the emperor as supreme ruler of the Church. So the close link between Church and state took root in Russia as well. **A**

MAIN IDEA

Analyzing Motives

A Why might Vladimir think it important that all his subjects become Christian?

Kiev's Power and Decline

Thanks to its Byzantine ties, Kiev grew from a cluster of crude wooden forts to the glittering capital of a prosperous and educated people. The rise of Kiev marked the appearance of Russia's first important unified territory.

Kievan Russia Vladimir led the way in establishing Kiev's power. He expanded his state west into Poland and north almost to the Baltic Sea. He also fought off troublesome nomads from the steppes to the south.

In 1019, Vladimir's son **Yaroslav the Wise** came to the throne and led Kiev to even greater glory. Like the rulers of Byzantium, Yaroslav skillfully married off his daughters and sisters to the kings and princes of Western Europe. Those marriages helped him to forge important trading alliances. At the same time, he created a legal code tailored to Kiev's commercial culture. Many of its rules dealt with crimes against property. Yaroslav also built the first library in Kiev. Under his rule, Christianity prospered. By the 12th century, Kiev was home to some 400 churches.

Kiev's Decline The decline of the Kievan state started with the death of Yaroslav in 1054. During his reign, Yaroslav had made what turned out to be a crucial error. He had divided his realm among his sons, instead of following the custom of passing on the throne to the eldest son. Upon their father's death, the sons tore the state apart fighting for the choicest territories. And because this system of dividing the kingdom among sons continued, each generation saw new struggles. The Crusades—the numerous clashes between Christians and Muslims for control of the Holy Lands of the Middle East that began in 1095—added to Kiev's troubles by disrupting trade. Then, just when it seemed that things could not get worse, a new threat emerged.

The Mongol Invasions

In the middle 1200s, a ferocious group of horsemen from central Asia slashed their way into Russia. These nomads were the Mongols. (See Chapter 12.) They had exploded onto the world scene at the beginning of the 1200s under Genghis Khan (JEHNG•gihs KAHN), one of the most feared warriors of all time.

Vocabulary
Khan is the Mongol word for "ruler."

The Mongols may have been forced to move out by economic or military pressures. They may have been lured by the wealth of cities to the west. Whatever their reasons for leaving, they rode their swift horses across the steppes of Asia and on into Europe. Their savage killing and burning won them a reputation for ruthless brutality. When Genghis Khan died in 1227, his successors continued the conquering that he had begun. At its fullest extent, the Mongol Empire stretched from the Yellow Sea to the Baltic Sea and from the Himalayas to northern Russia.

In 1240, the Mongols attacked and demolished Kiev. They rode under the leadership of Batu Khan, Genghis's grandson. So many inhabitants were slaughtered, a Russian historian reported, that "no eye remained to weep." A Roman Catholic bishop traveling through Kiev five years later wrote, "When we passed through that land, we found lying in the field countless heads and bones of dead people." After the fall of Kiev, Mongols ruled all of southern Russia for 200 years. The empire's official name was the "Khanate of the Golden Horde": *Khanate,* from the Mongol word for "kingdom"; *Golden,* because gold was the royal color of the Mongols; and *Horde,* from the Mongol word for "camp."

Mongol Rule in Russia Under Mongol rule, the Russians could follow all their usual customs, as long as they made no attempts to rebel. As fierce as they were, the Mongols tolerated all the religions in their realms. The Church, in fact, often acted as a mediator between the Russian people and their Mongol rulers.

GEOGRAPHY SKILLBUILDER: Interpreting Maps

1. **Location** *About how many miles did the Khanate of the Golden Horde stretch from east to west?*
2. **Region** *What role might geography have played in the Delhi Sultanate's escape from Mongol rule?*

Analyzing Primary Sources

Resisting Mongol Rule

Although Russians by and large obeyed their Mongol rulers, pockets of resistance existed, shown by this 1259 diary entry of a resident of Novgorod.

PRIMARY SOURCE

The same winter the accursed raw-eating Tartars [Mongols], Berkai and Kasachik, came with their wives, and many others, and there was great tumult in Novgorod, and they did much evil in the province, taking contribution for the accursed Tartars. And the accursed ones began to fear death; they said to [Prince] Alexander: 'Give us guards, lest they kill us.' And the Knayz ordered the son of Posadnik and all the sons of the Boyars to protect them by night. The Tartars said: 'Give us your numbers for tribute or we will run away and return in greater strength.' And the common people would not give their numbers for tribute but said: 'Let us die honourably for St. Sophia and for the angelic houses.'

Resident of Novgorod, from *Medieval Russia*

Rebelling Against the Mongols

Resistance against Mongol rule occasionally broke out into open rebellion, as this account from an anti-Mongol uprising in Tver in 1327 indicates.

PRIMARY SOURCE

The lawless Shevkal, the destroyer of Christianity, . . . came to Tver, drove the Grand Prince from his court and entrenched himself there with great haughtiness and violence. . . . The entire city assembled and the uprising was in the making. The Tverians cried out and began to kill the Tartars wherever they found them until they killed Shevkal and the rest [of his men]. They missed killing the messengers who were with the horses that grazed in the meadow [outside the city]. They [the messengers] saddled their best horses and swiftly galloped to Moscow and from there to the [Golden] Horde, where they brought the news of the death of Shevkal.

Tver Eyewitness Account, from *Medieval Russia*

DOCUMENT-BASED QUESTIONS

1. **Comparing** *In what way did the reasons for the uprisings in Novgorod and Tver differ?*
2. **Making Predictions** *Based on what you have read about the Mongols, what do you think their response was to the above events of resistance and rebellion?*

The Mongols demanded just two things from Russians: absolute obedience and massive amounts of tribute, or payments. By and large, the Russian nobles agreed. Novgorod's prince and military hero **Alexander Nevsky**, for example, advised his fellow princes to cooperate with the Mongols. The Russian nobles often crushed revolts against the Mongols and collected oppressive taxes for the foreign rulers.

Mongol rule isolated the Russians more than ever from their neighbors in Western Europe. This meant that among other things, the Russians had little access to many new ideas and inventions. During this period, however, forces were at work that eventually would lead to the rise of a new center of power in the country, and to Russia's liberation.

Russia Breaks Free

The city of Moscow was first founded in the 1100s. By 1156, it was a crude village protected by a log wall. Nonetheless, it was located near three major rivers: the Volga, Dnieper, and Don. From that strategic position, a prince of Moscow who could gain control of the three rivers could control nearly all of European Russia—and perhaps successfully challenge the Mongols. **B**

MAIN IDEA

Analyzing Issues

B What about Moscow's location was significant?

Moscow's Powerful Princes A line of Russian princes eventually emerged on the scene who would do just that. During the late 1320s, Moscow's Prince Ivan I had earned the gratitude of the Mongols by helping to crush a Russian revolt against Mongol rule. For his services, the Mongols appointed Ivan I as tax collector of all the Slavic lands they had conquered. They also gave him the title of "Grand Prince." Ivan had now become without any doubt the most powerful of all Russian princes. He also became the wealthiest and was known as "Ivan Moneybag."

Ivan convinced the Patriarch of Kiev, the leading bishop of Eastern Europe, to move to Moscow. The move improved the city's prestige and gave Moscow's princes a powerful ally: the Church. Ivan I and his successors used numerous strategies to enlarge their territory: land purchases, wars, trickery, and shrewd marriages. From generation to generation, they schemed to gain greater control over the small states around Moscow.

An Empire Emerges-The Russian state would become a genuine empire during the long, 43-year reign of **Ivan III**. Upon becoming the prince of Moscow, Ivan openly challenged Mongol rule. He took the name **czar** (zahr), the Russian version of Caesar, and publicly claimed his intent to make Russia the "Third Rome." (The title "czar" became official only during the reign of Ivan IV.)

In 1480, Ivan made a final break with the Mongols. After he refused to pay his rulers further tribute, Russian and Mongol armies faced each other at the Ugra River, about 150 miles southwest of Moscow. However, neither side advanced to fight. So, after a time, both armies turned around and marched home. Russians have traditionally marked this bloodless standoff as their liberation from Mongol rule. After this liberation, the czars could openly pursue an empire.

Such a defeat for the Mongols would have seemed impossible nearly two centuries earlier, as they pushed west from present-day China and crushed nearly everything in their path. One of the peoples whom they conquered back then was a new group that had risen to power in Central Asia—the Turks.

History Makers

Ivan III
1440–1505

Those around him often viewed Ivan as cold, calculating, and ruthless. This may have been due in part to a difficult upbringing. Ivan came of age during a time of great civil strife in Russia. His father, Grand Prince Vasali II, was at one point imprisoned and blinded by opposition forces.

Ivan's cautious and calculating style drew criticism from Russians eager for more bold and swift action against the Mongols. Even a close aide questioned his tactics. "Would you surrender Russia to fire and sword?" he asked the prince. After Russian forces won the standoff at the Ugra River, however, such criticism turned to praise.

NEW YORK CORE CURRICULUM REVIEW

TERMS & NAMES 1. For each term or name, write a sentence explaining its significance.

- Slavs
- Vladimir
- Yaroslav the Wise
- Alexander Nevsky
- Ivan III
- czar

USING YOUR NOTES

2. Which group fared the worst under Mongol rule?

Nobles	Church
People	**Moscow Princes**

MAIN IDEAS

3. How did Yaroslav's decision to divide his realm among his sons help cause Kiev's decline?
4. What main demands did the Mongols make on their Russian subjects?
5. How did Ivan III lead the Russians to their independence from the Mongols?

CRITICAL THINKING & WRITING

6. **RECOGNIZING EFFECTS** How did Vladimir's conversion to Christianity affect Kiev?
7. **FORMING AND SUPPORTING OPINIONS** Do you approve of Nevsky's cooperation with the Mongols? Was his policy practical or cowardly? Explain.
8. **ANALYZING ISSUES** How was Ivan I both friend and foe to the Mongol rulers?
9. **WRITING ACTIVITY** EMPIRE BUILDING Imagine you are a reporter for a major Russian newspaper. Write a **headline** and lead **paragraph** about Ivan III's standoff with Mongol forces at the Ugra River and its aftermath.

INTEGRATED TECHNOLOGY **INTERNET ACTIVITY**

Use the Internet to create a **photo gallery** of modern-day Moscow. Possible subjects include the city's architecture, street scenes, and people.

INTERNET KEYWORD
Moscow photos

Russian Religious Art and Architecture

Russian religious art follows an ancient tradition dating back to the early Church. At first, Christians feared that artwork showing people might lead to idol worship. Gradually, however, the Church came to accept the use of icons, or depictions of holy people. In the West, other types of art eventually replaced the icon, but the Eastern Orthodox Church still uses icons today.

Icons are painted according to strict rules. This approach also shaped other religious art in Russia. To construct a church or create a religious artifact was a sacred task, performed according to rigid guidelines. Art was not a form of self-expression.

INTEGRATED TECHNOLOGY

RESEARCH LINKS For more on religious art, go to **classzone.com**

Icon ►

This 12th-century Russian icon is of the Archangel Gabriel. According to the Bible, Gabriel was the messenger who told the Virgin Mary that she would give birth to Jesus. In Orthodox churches, artists must follow certain rules when making icons. For example, icons are always two-dimensional because they are seen as windows through which worshipers can view heaven.

▲ Cross and Illuminated Manuscript ►

The cross above was carved from ivory and shows the Archangel Michael. In Christian belief, Michael is the leader of the heavenly hosts and a spiritual warrior who helped the Israelites. That is why he is often shown with a sword, as he is here.

The illuminated manuscript was made during the 15th century and shows a scribe writing out the Gospel. Illuminated manuscripts were handwritten books decorated with gold or silver, vivid colors, elaborate designs, and small pictures. The word *illumination* originally referred to the gold or silver decoration, which made the pages seem as if light were shining on them.

▲ Reliquary

This elaborately decorated silver chest is a Russian cathedral reliquary. Reliquaries are containers that hold sacred relics, such as the bones of a saint. Most reliquaries are portable, allowing them to be carried in processions.

◄ Wooden Churches

Located in Varzuga, Russia, the Church of the Dormition was built in 1674. It is just one of many churches in Russia made out of wood. These churches were often built on a hilltop overlooking forests and villages. Roughly cut logs were used for the walls. However, the designs of the ceilings were complex and included the use of onion domes, as shown here. In the Russian Orthodox Church, onion domes represent heaven.

Connect *to* Today

1. **Making Inferences** Why do you think the archangels Michael and Gabriel were popular subjects for Russian religious art?

See Skillbuilder Handbook, Page R10.

2. **Comparing and Contrasting** What types of religious art are common in our society today? How are they similar to or different from the art on these two pages?

▲ This drawing from an early 13th-century manuscript illustrates the Turkish siege of a city.

Seljuks Confront Crusaders and Mongols

Malik Shah ruled as the last of the strong Seljuk leaders. After his unexpected death in 1092, no capable shah appeared to replace him. So, the Seljuk Empire quickly disintegrated into a loose collection of minor kingdoms. Just at that point, the West launched a counterattack against the Turks and other Muslims for control of the Holy Land of the Middle East. This series of military campaigns was known as the Crusades.

The Seljuks and the Crusaders Pope Urban II launched the First Crusade in 1095. He called on Christians to drive the Turks out of Anatolia and recover Jerusalem from Muslim rule. Armies from Western Europe soon poured through Constantinople and proceeded on to Palestine. In 1099, the Crusaders captured Jerusalem and massacred its Jewish and Muslim inhabitants. They established a Latin Christian kingdom that lasted about a century. **B**

MAIN IDEA

Summarizing

B Why did the Crusades take place?

Eventually, a fragment of the former Seljuk Empire gathered enough strength to fight back. Under their famous Kurdish captain Saladin, the Muslims recovered Jerusalem in 1187. Eventually, Saladin and his Western opponent King Richard I of England signed a truce. Their agreement gave Jerusalem to the Muslims but granted Western pilgrims access to Christian holy places.

Subsequent popes called for further Crusades. But each new military expedition proved weaker than the last. By the 13th century, the Western powers seemed to pose little problem for the Turks. It was around this time, however, that a new threat emerged from the east—the mighty and brutal Mongols.

Seljuks Face the Mongols As you have read previously, the Mongols were a group of nomadic clans along the Asian steppes. In the early 1200s, they grew into a unified force under the ruler Genghis Khan and swiftly conquered China.

The Mongol armies eventually turned to the west and leveled any cities that dared to resist them. They slaughtered whole populations. In 1258, Genghis's grandson Hulagu led his troops to the outskirts of Baghdad, which by this time was surrounded by a defensive wall. The account of what followed by Persian historian

Wassaf speaks to the Mongols' fierce and overwhelming fighting methods:

PRIMARY SOURCE

The arrows and bolts, the lances and spears, the stones from the slings and catapults of both sides shot swiftly up to heaven, like the messengers of the prayers of the just, then fell as swiftly, like the judgements of fate. . . . In this way, Baghdad was besieged and terrorized for fifty days. But since the city still held out the order was given for baked bricks lying outside the walls to be collected, and with them high towers were built in every direction, overlooking the streets and alleys of Baghdad. On top of these they set up the catapults. Now the city was filled with the thunder and lightning of striking stones and flaring naphtha pots. A dew of arrows rained from a cloud of bows and the population was trampled underfoot. . . . The cry went up, 'Today we have no strength against Goliath and his army!'

WASSAF, quoted in *The Mongol Empire*

When Hulagu finally took Baghdad, he burned down the caliph's palace and had tens of thousands of people killed. Mongol belief forbade the spilling of sacred blood. So Hulagu executed the last Abbasid caliph by having him wrapped in a carpet and trampled to death by horses.

With untold brutality, Genghis Khan and his successors shaped the biggest land empire in history. (See Chapter 12 for more about the Mongol Empire.) The warrior Mongols, however, knew little about administering their territory. As a result, their vast empire crumbled in just a few generations. And out of the rubble of the Mongol Empire rose another group of Turks—the Ottomans. They would build an empire that lasted into the 20th century. You will learn more about the Ottoman Empire in Chapter 18.

Connect *to* Today

Turkey

Today, Turkey is a nation located between Europe and Asia just north of the Mediterranean Sea. About 80 percent of its residents are descendants of the Seljuks and other Turkish groups.

Turkey became a republic in 1923. Many of today's Turks, like their ancestors, practice Islam, as evidenced by the nation's flag (shown above). It depicts the crescent and the five-pointed star, the symbols of the Islamic faith.

INTEGRATED TECHNOLOGY

INTERNET ACTIVITY Write about a cultural practice in Turkey. Go to **classzone.com** for your research.

NEW YORK CORE CURRICULUM REVIEW

TERMS & NAMES 1. For each term or name, write a sentence explaining its significance.

- Seljuks
- vizier
- Malik Shah

USING YOUR NOTES

2. Which occupier proved to be the worst for Baghdad?

Occupiers	Events
Abbasids	
Persians	
Seljuks	
Mongols	

MAIN IDEAS

3. Why did the Seljuks need to seek religious guidance from the Persian peoples they had conquered?
4. How did the death of Malik Shah affect the Seljuk Empire?
5. What agreement did Saladin and England's King Richard I reach about Jerusalem?

CRITICAL THINKING & WRITING

6. **ANALYZING ISSUES** In what ways would it be accurate to say that the Persians actually won over the Turks?
7. **FORMING AND SUPPORTING OPINIONS** Do you think it is wise for rulers to place members of conquered peoples in positions of government? Why or why not?
8. **MAKING INFERENCES** Based on the observations by the Persian historian Wassaf, why do you think the Mongols were such successful conquerors?
9. **WRITING ACTIVITY** CULTURAL INTERACTION Write several **paragraphs** comparing the ways in which the different groups in this section interacted.

CONNECT TO TODAY **CREATING A SUMMARY**

Identify a modern-day Arab poet. Then analyze one of his or her works and write a brief **summary** that expresses its main idea.

Chapter 11 Assessment

TERMS & NAMES

For each term or name below, briefly explain its connection to the Byzantine, Russian, and Turkish empires between 500 and 1500.

1. Justinian Code
2. Hagia Sophia
3. patriarch
4. icon
5. Slavs
6. Alexander Nevsky
7. Seljuks
8. Malik Shah

MAIN IDEAS

The Byzantine Empire Section 1 (pages 301–306)

9. What were the names and characteristics of the four parts of the Justinian Code?
10. What were some important features of life in Constantinople?
11. Which peoples attacked the Byzantine Empire? What part of the empire did they invade?
12. What two main religions emerged out of the split in the Christian Church?

The Russian Empire Section 2 (pages 307–313)

13. What does *The Primary Chronicle* say about Rurik and the origin of Novgorod?
14. According to *The Primary Chronicle,* how did Vladimir choose Byzantine Christianity?
15. How did Moscow's location contribute to its growth?
16. What event marked Russia's liberation from Mongol rule?

Turkish Empires Rise in Anatolia Section 3 (pages 314–317)

17. In what ways did the Turks show respect for their Persian subjects?
18. What group eventually conquered the empire established by the Seljuk Turks?

CRITICAL THINKING

1. USING YOUR NOTES

On a chart, describe several key characteristics about the Vikings, Turks, and Mongols—all of whom moved into foreign lands.

	Where from?	Where settled?	Interactions with people
Vikings			
Turks			
Mongols			

2. ANALYZING ISSUES

EMPIRE BUILDING What were Justinian's goals in creating his law code? Why might a leader want to organize the laws?

3. FOLLOWING CHRONOLOGICAL ORDER

Examine the time lines on this page. How many years did the Byzantine Empire last? How long did it take the Seljuk Empire to decline after the Seljuks took Baghdad?

4. COMPARING AND CONTRASTING

CULTURAL INTERACTION What was different about the way in which the Seljuk Turks and Mongols interacted with their subjects?

VISUAL SUMMARY

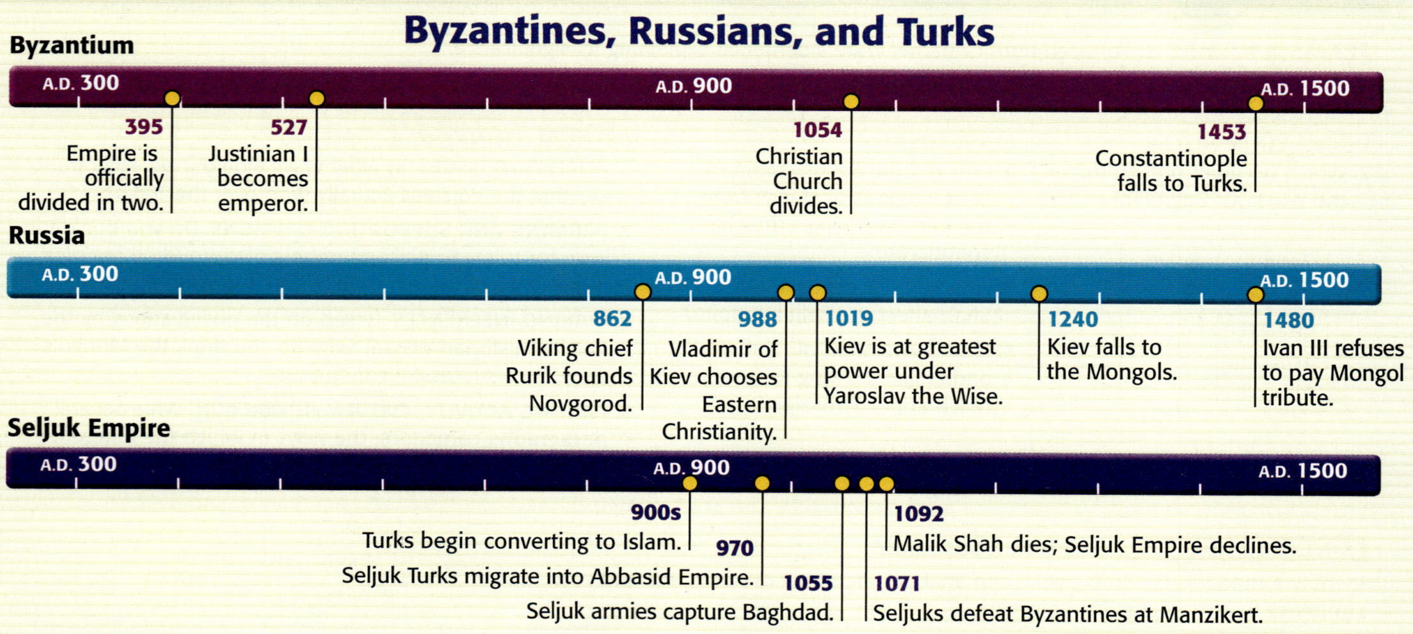

NEW YORK STATE REGENTS EXAM PRACTICE

Use this comparison chart of various empires and your knowledge of world history to answer questions 1 and 2.
Additional Test Practice, pp. S1–S33

Five Empires

	Dates	Greatest Territory*	Greatest Population**
Persian	550 B.C.–330 B.C.	2.0	14.0
Roman	27 B.C.–A.D. 476	3.4	54.8
Byzantine	A.D. 395–A.D.1453	1.4	30.0
Mongol	A.D. 1206–A.D. 1380	11.7	125.0
Aztec	A.D. 1325–A.D. 1521	0.2	6.0

* Estimated in millions of square miles
** Estimated in millions of people

1 Which of the empires shown here lasted the longest?
(1) Mongol
(2) Roman
(3) Persian
(4) Byzantine

2 The population of Byzantium was five times the size of which empire?
(1) Aztec
(2) Persian
(3) Roman
(4) Mongol

Use the quotation and your knowledge of world history to answer question 3.

PRIMARY SOURCE

On the dawn of the sixth day the pagan warriors began to storm the city. . . . And the Tartars [Mongols] cut down many people, including women and children. Still others were drowned in the river. And they killed without exception all monks and priests. And they burned this holy city with all its beauty and wealth. . . . And churches of God were destroyed, and much blood was spilled on the holy altars. And not one man remained alive in the city. All were dead. . . . And this happened for our sins.

ZENKOVSKY, *Medieval Russia's Epics, Chronicles, and Tales*

3 According to the author, why did the Mongols destroy the city?
(1) It was located along a strategic river.
(2) The Mongols wanted to make it their new capital.
(3) The city's residents had to be punished for their sins.
(4) The Mongols sought to wipe out all who opposed their religion.

INTEGRATED TECHNOLOGY
TEST PRACTICE Go to **classzone.com**
- Diagnostic tests
- Strategies
- Tutorials
- Additional practice

ALTERNATIVE ASSESSMENT

1. Interact *with* History

On page 300, you considered ways of expanding the Byzantine Empire. Which approach did you choose and why? Now that you've read about the Byzantine Empire, do you think that you chose the right strategy? Discuss your present ideas on enlarging an empire.

2. WRITING ABOUT HISTORY

RELIGIOUS AND ETHICAL SYSTEMS Find a photograph of a holy place connected with the Byzantine, Russian, or Turkish empire. Write a two-minute **documentary script** about the site. Record your documentary on audio- or videocassette and present it to the class. Provide the following:
- the meaning or importance of the site
- a brief history of the site
- the beliefs associated with the site

INTEGRATED TECHNOLOGY

Writing an Internet-based Research Paper

Go to the *Web Research Guide* at **classzone.com** to learn about conducting research on the Internet. Then, working with a partner, use the Internet to find examples of how two peoples today have influenced each other. Focus on such characteristics as language, food, clothing, music, social customs, religion, and systems of government. Present the results of your research in a well-organized paper. Be sure to:
- apply a search strategy when using directories and search engines to locate Web resources
- judge the usefulness and reliability of each Web site
- correctly cite your Web sources
- peer edit for organization and correct use of language

Interact *with* History

Which Chinese invention would be most useful to your society?

Imagine yourself in the year 1292. You have spent the last 17 years traveling in China—the world's most advanced country. Your own civilization is on the other side of the world. It, too, is very sophisticated, but it lacks many of the innovations you have seen on your travels.

During your stay in China, you were of great assistance to the emperor. As a going-away present, he asks you to choose one of the inventions shown here to take back to your own society. He also will provide you with the knowledge of how to create the invention of your choice.

Silk makes a luxurious cloth—soft to the touch but also amazingly strong and warm.

The magnetic compass can help sailors navigate the open sea.

Gunpowder can be used for fireworks or made into explosive weapons.

Paper is a relatively inexpensive and easy-to-produce surface for writing and printing.

EXAMINING *the* ISSUES

- **Which invention would most improve the quality of life?**
- **Which might be the most profitable?**
- **What benefits and drawbacks might there be to introducing the item into your society?**

Discuss these questions with your classmates. In your discussion, remember what you have learned about the spread of new ideas. As you read about China in this chapter, see how its ideas spread from the East to the West.

NEW YORK STATE REGENTS EXAM PRACTICE

Use this comparison chart of various empires and your knowledge of world history to answer questions 1 and 2.
Additional Test Practice, pp. S1–S33

Five Empires

	Dates	Greatest Territory*	Greatest Population**
Persian	550 B.C.–330 B.C.	2.0	14.0
Roman	27 B.C.–A.D. 476	3.4	54.8
Byzantine	A.D. 395–A.D.1453	1.4	30.0
Mongol	A.D. 1206–A.D. 1380	11.7	125.0
Aztec	A.D. 1325–A.D. 1521	0.2	6.0

* Estimated in millions of square miles
** Estimated in millions of people

1 Which of the empires shown here lasted the longest?

(1) Mongol
(2) Roman
(3) Persian
(4) Byzantine

2 The population of Byzantium was five times the size of which empire?

(1) Aztec
(2) Persian
(3) Roman
(4) Mongol

Use the quotation and your knowledge of world history to answer question 3.

PRIMARY SOURCE

On the dawn of the sixth day the pagan warriors began to storm the city. . . . And the Tartars [Mongols] cut down many people, including women and children. Still others were drowned in the river. And they killed without exception all monks and priests. And they burned this holy city with all its beauty and wealth. . . . And churches of God were destroyed, and much blood was spilled on the holy altars. And not one man remained alive in the city. All were dead. . . . And this happened for our sins.

ZENKOVSKY, *Medieval Russia's Epics, Chronicles, and Tales*

3 According to the author, why did the Mongols destroy the city?

(1) It was located along a strategic river.
(2) The Mongols wanted to make it their new capital.
(3) The city's residents had to be punished for their sins.
(4) The Mongols sought to wipe out all who opposed their religion.

INTEGRATED TECHNOLOGY

TEST PRACTICE Go to **classzone.com**

- Diagnostic tests
- Tutorials
- Strategies
- Additional practice

ALTERNATIVE ASSESSMENT

1. Interact *with* History

On page 300, you considered ways of expanding the Byzantine Empire. Which approach did you choose and why? Now that you've read about the Byzantine Empire, do you think that you chose the right strategy? Discuss your present ideas on enlarging an empire.

2. WRITING ABOUT HISTORY

RELIGIOUS AND ETHICAL SYSTEMS Find a photograph of a holy place connected with the Byzantine, Russian, or Turkish empire. Write a two-minute **documentary script** about the site. Record your documentary on audio- or videocassette and present it to the class. Provide the following:

- the meaning or importance of the site
- a brief history of the site
- the beliefs associated with the site

INTEGRATED TECHNOLOGY

Writing an Internet-based Research Paper

Go to the *Web Research Guide* at **classzone.com** to learn about conducting research on the Internet. Then, working with a partner, use the Internet to find examples of how two peoples today have influenced each other. Focus on such characteristics as language, food, clothing, music, social customs, religion, and systems of government. Present the results of your research in a well-organized paper. Be sure to:

- apply a search strategy when using directories and search engines to locate Web resources
- judge the usefulness and reliability of each Web site
- correctly cite your Web sources
- peer edit for organization and correct use of language

CHAPTER 12

Empires in East Asia, 600–1350

Previewing Main Ideas

RELIGIOUS AND ETHICAL SYSTEMS Buddhism, which had reached China from India, spread from China to Japan. Both Hindu and Buddhist missionaries from India spread their religions across Southeast Asia.

Geography *Why might the Khmer Empire, rather than Korea or Japan, be more open to influence from India?*

EMPIRE BUILDING The Tang Dynasty built China into the most powerful and advanced empire in the world. Later, China fell to another group of empire builders, the Mongols.

Geography *Locate the Great Wall on the map. Why do you think the Chinese constructed the wall along their northern border?*

CULTURAL INTERACTION Chinese culture spread across East Asia, influencing Korea, Japan, and much of mainland Southeast Asia. The Mongol conquests led to interaction between settled and nomadic peoples across Asia.

Geography *Why would China tend to exert a strong influence over other parts of East Asia?*

NEW YORK CORE CURRICULUM FOCUS

- During the Tang and Song dynasties, the Chinese invented movable type, gunpowder, and the magnetic compass.
- The Mongols created a vast empire across much of Asia.

INTEGRATED TECHNOLOGY

eEdition
- Interactive Maps
- Interactive Visuals
- Interactive Primary Sources

INTERNET RESOURCES
Go to **classzone.com** for:
- Research Links
- Internet Activities
- Primary Sources
- Chapter Quiz
- Maps
- Test Practice
- Current Events

EAST AND SOUTHEAST ASIA

618 Tang Dynasty begins 289-year rule in China. (Tang statuette) ▶

794 Heian period begins in Japan.

935 Koryu Dynasty controls Korea.

600 — 800

WORLD

630s Muhammad unifies Arabian Peninsula under Islam.

800 Charlemagne crowned Holy Roman Emperor by pope.

900s ◀ Maya civilization goes into decline. (Maya stone sculpture)

East and Southeast Asia, 900–1200

960
Song Dynasty established in China.

1192
Kamakura Shogunate rules Japan. (Kamakura period painting) ▶

1279
Kublai Khan conquers China.

1000 1200 1400

1054
◀ The pope expels the patriarch of Constantinople, splitting Christianity into Roman Catholic and Orthodox branches.

1324
Mali king Mansa Musa makes hajj to Mecca.

1347
Bubonic plague strikes Europe.

Interact *with* History

Which Chinese invention would be most useful to your society?

Imagine yourself in the year 1292. You have spent the last 17 years traveling in China—the world's most advanced country. Your own civilization is on the other side of the world. It, too, is very sophisticated, but it lacks many of the innovations you have seen on your travels.

During your stay in China, you were of great assistance to the emperor. As a going-away present, he asks you to choose one of the inventions shown here to take back to your own society. He also will provide you with the knowledge of how to create the invention of your choice.

Silk makes a luxurious cloth—soft to the touch but also amazingly strong and warm.

The magnetic compass can help sailors navigate the open sea.

Gunpowder can be used for fireworks or made into explosive weapons.

Paper is a relatively inexpensive and easy-to-produce surface for writing and printing.

EXAMINING *the* ISSUES

- **Which invention would most improve the quality of life?**
- **Which might be the most profitable?**
- **What benefits and drawbacks might there be to introducing the item into your society?**

Discuss these questions with your classmates. In your discussion, remember what you have learned about the spread of new ideas. As you read about China in this chapter, see how its ideas spread from the East to the West.

Tang and Song China

CONNECT TO THE NEW YORK STATE CORE CURRICULUM

Unit 2.B.2. Contributions
Unit 2.B.4. Cultural Flowering

TERMS & NAMES

- Tang Taizong
- Wu Zhao
- movable type
- gentry

SETTING THE STAGE After the Han Dynasty collapsed in A.D. 220, no emperor was strong enough to hold China together. Over the next 350 years, more than 30 local dynasties rose and fell. Finally, by 589, an emperor named Wendi had united northern and southern China once again. He restored a strong central government. Under the next two dynasties, the Tang and the Song, China experienced a prolonged golden age. It became the richest, most powerful, and most advanced country in the world.

The Tang Dynasty Expands China

Wendi declared himself the first emperor of the Sui (sway) Dynasty. The dynasty lasted through only two emperors, from 581 to 618. The Sui emperors' greatest accomplishment was the completion of the Grand Canal. This waterway connected the Huang He and the Chang Jiang. The canal provided a vital route for trade between the northern cities and the southern rice-producing region of the Chang delta.

TAKING NOTES
Comparing and Contrasting Use a Venn diagram to note the similarities and differences between the Tang and Song dynasties.

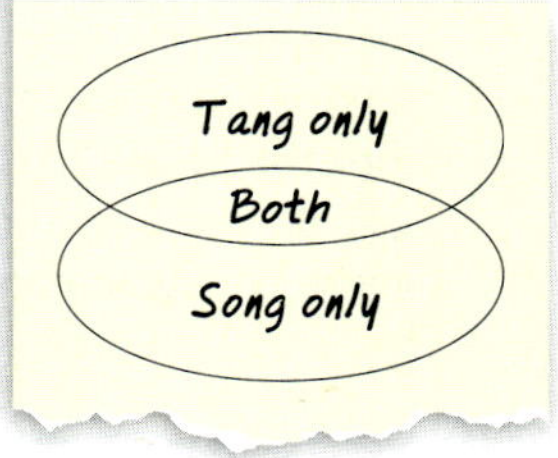

About a million peasant men and women toiled five years to dig the more than 1,000-mile waterway. Perhaps as many as half of the workers died on this project. Thousands more toiled and died rebuilding the Great Wall. The endless labor on state projects turned the people against the Sui Dynasty. Overworked and overtaxed, they finally revolted. In 618, a member of the imperial court assassinated the second Sui emperor.

Tang Rulers Create a Powerful Empire While short-lived, the Sui Dynasty built a strong foundation for the great achievements of the next dynasty, the Tang (tahng). The Tang Dynasty ruled for nearly 300 years (618–907). The Tang emperor who began these achievements was **Tang Taizong**. His brilliant reign lasted from 626 to 649.

Under the Tang rulers, the empire expanded. Taizong's armies reconquered the northern and western lands that China had lost since the decline of the Han Dynasty. By 668, China had extended its influence over Korea as well. The ruler during the campaign in Korea was the empress **Wu Zhao** (woo-jow). From about 660 on, she held the real power while weak emperors sat on the throne. Finally, in 690, Empress Wu assumed the title of emperor for herself—the only woman ever to do so in China.

History Makers

Tang Taizong 600–649

The man who restored China to its glory was a distinguished general named Li Shimin. He seized the imperial throne in 626 after killing his brothers and forcing his father, the first Tang emperor, to step aside. As emperor, Li Shimin took the title Taizong, meaning "Great Ancestor."

Taizong's military campaigns extended China's borders north to Manchuria, south to Vietnam, and west to the Aral Sea. At home, aided by his gifted advisers, Taizong reformed the government organization and law code. These became models for all of East Asia.

Wu Zhao 625–705

At the age of 13, the beautiful Wu Zhao arrived at the court of Tang Taizong to become one of the emperor's secondary wives. After Taizong's death, she became a favored wife of his son and successor. Wu Zhao soon rose above rival wives and became the emperor's chief wife, or empress.

For many years, Empress Wu virtually ruled China on behalf of her sickly husband. After his death, two of their sons briefly held the throne. Frustrated by their lack of ability, she took the throne herself at the age of 65. She was 80 when she finally lost power. A strong leader, Wu Zhao continued the work begun by Taizong to build and expand China.

Tang rulers further strengthened the central government of China. They expanded the network of roads and canals begun by the Sui. This helped to pull the empire together. They also promoted foreign trade and improvements in agriculture.

Scholar-Officials To manage their large empire, the Tang rulers needed to restore China's vast bureaucracy. They did this by reviving and expanding the civil service examination system begun by the Han Dynasty. The relatively few candidates who passed the tough exams became part of an elite group of scholar-officials.

In theory, the exams were open to all men, even commoners. However, only the wealthy could afford the necessary years of education. Also, men with political connections could obtain high positions without taking the exams. Despite these flaws, the system created a remarkably intelligent and capable governing class in China. Before the Tang Dynasty, a few noble families dominated the country. As the examination system grew in importance, talent and education became more important than noble birth in winning power. As a result, many moderately wealthy families shared in China's government. **A**

MAIN IDEA

Recognizing Effects

A What resulted from the revival and expansion of the civil service system?

The Tang Lose Power To meet the rising costs of government, Tang rulers imposed crushing taxes in the mid-700s. These brought hardship to the people but failed to cover the costs of military expansion and new building programs.

Moreover, the Tang struggled to control the vast empire they had built. In 751, Muslim armies soundly defeated the Chinese at the Battle of Talas. As a result, Central Asia passed out of Chinese control and into foreign hands. After this time, border attacks and internal rebellions steadily chipped away at the power of the imperial government. Finally, in 907, Chinese rebels sacked and burned the Tang capital at Ch'ang-an and murdered the last Tang emperor, a child.

The Song Dynasty Restores China

After the fall of the Tang Dynasty, rival warlords divided China into separate kingdoms. Then, in 960, an able general named Taizu reunited China and proclaimed himself the first Song (sung) emperor. The Song Dynasty, like the Tang, lasted about three centuries (960–1279). Although the Song ruled a smaller empire than either the Han or the Tang, China remained stable, powerful, and prosperous.

Song armies never regained the western lands lost after 751. Nor did they regain northern lands that had been lost to nomadic tribes during the Tang decline. For a time, Song emperors tried to buy peace with their northern enemies. They paid hefty annual tributes of silver, silk, and tea. This policy, however, ultimately failed to stop the threat from the north. In the early 1100s, a Manchurian people called the Jurchen conquered northern China and established the Jin Empire. The Jurchen forced the Song to retreat south across the Huang He. After 1127, the Song emperors ruled only southern China.

The Song rulers established a grand new capital at Hangzhou, a coastal city south of the Chang Jiang. Despite its military troubles, the dynasty of the Southern Song (1127–1279) saw rapid economic growth. The south had become the economic heartland of China. Merchants in southern cities grew rich from trade with Chinese in the north, nomads of Central Asia, and people of western Asia and Europe.

An Era of Prosperity and Innovation

During the Tang and Song dynasties, China's population nearly doubled, soaring to 100 million. By the Song era, China had at least ten cities with a population of 1 million each. China had become the most populous country in the world. It also had become the most advanced.

Science and Technology Artisans and scholars made important technological advances during the Tang and Song eras. Among the most important inventions were movable type and gunpowder. With **movable type**, a printer could arrange blocks of individual characters in a frame to make up a page for printing. Previously, printers had carved the words of a whole page into one large block. The development of gunpowder, in time, led to the creation of explosive weapons such as bombs, grenades, small rockets, and cannons. Other important inventions of this period include porcelain, the mechanical clock, paper money, and the use of the magnetic compass for sailing. (See the Social History feature on pages 328–329.)

The 1000s to the 1200s was a rich period for Chinese mathematics. The Chinese made advances in arithmetic and algebra. Many mathematical ideas, such as using negative numbers, spread from China southward and westward. B

MAIN IDEA

Making Inferences

B How might the spread of mathematical ideas from China affect other countries?

Agriculture The rapid growth of China resulted in part from advances in farming. Farmers especially improved the cultivation of rice. In about the year 1000, China imported a new variety of fast-ripening rice from Vietnam. This allowed the farmers to harvest two rice crops each year rather than one. To make sure that farmers knew about this improved variety, Chinese officials distributed seedlings throughout the country. The agricultural improvements enabled China's farmers to produce more food. This was necessary to feed the rapidly expanding population in the cities.

Trade and Foreign Contacts Under the Tang and Song emperors, foreign trade flourished. Tang imperial armies guarded the great Silk Roads, which linked China to the West. Eventually, however, China lost control over these routes during the long Tang decline. After this time, Chinese merchants relied increasingly on ocean trade. Chinese advances in sailing technology, including use of the magnetic compass, made it possible for sea trade to expand. Up and down China's long coastline, the largest port cities in the

Connect *to* Today

INTERACTIVE

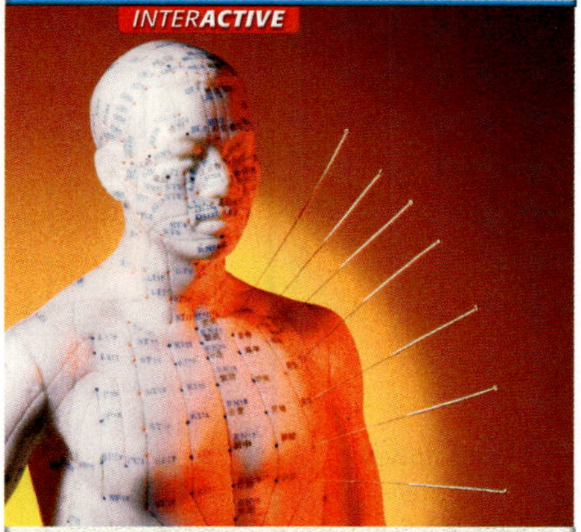

Acupuncture

During the Song Dynasty, the Chinese carefully studied human anatomy and created charts and models of the body. These helped to improve the practice of acupuncture, a system of treatment that involves inserting slender needles into the body at specific points, depending on the nature of the problem.

In recent years, this ancient practice has gained some acceptance in mainstream Western medicine. More and more practicing doctors are seeking training in acupuncture methods. And mainstream doctors are increasing their referrals to acupuncture specialists. In 2001 alone, Americans made about 20 million visits to acupuncturists, seeking treatment for everything from migraine headaches to drug dependency.

world bustled with international trade. Merchant ships carried trade goods to Korea and Japan. They sailed across the Indian Ocean to India, the Persian Gulf, and even the coast of Africa. Chinese merchants established trading colonies around Southeast Asia. Many foreign traders, mostly Arabs, resided in Chinese cities. Through trade and travel, Chinese culture spread throughout East Asia. One major cultural export was Buddhism. This religion spread from China to Vietnam, Korea, and Japan. The exchange of goods and ideas was two-way. For example, foreign religions, including Islam and some Eastern sects of Christianity, spread to China and won followers.

A Golden Age of Poetry and Art The prosperity of the Tang and Song dynasties nourished an age of artistic brilliance. The Tang period produced great poetry. Two of its most celebrated poets were Li Bo, who wrote about life's pleasures, and Tu Fu, who praised orderliness and Confucian virtues. Tu Fu also wrote critically about war and the hardships of soldiers. Once he himself was captured by rebels and taken to Ch'ang-an, the capital city. He had sent his family to the village of Fuzhou for safety. Here he describes their separation:

PRIMARY SOURCE C

The same moon is above Fuzhou tonight;
From the open window she will be watching it alone,
The poor children are too little to be able to remember Ch'ang-an.
Her perfumed hair will be dampened by the dew, the air may be too chilly on her delicate arms.
When can we both lean by the wind-blown curtains and see the tears dry on each other's face?

TU FU, "Moonlight Night"

MAIN IDEA

Analyzing Primary Sources

C What themes does Tu Fu explore in this poem?

Chinese painting reached new heights of beauty during the Song Dynasty. Painting of this era shows Daoist influence. Artists emphasized the beauty of natural landscapes and objects such as a single branch or flower. The artists did not use bright colors. Black ink was their favorite paint. Said one Song artist, "Black is ten colors."

Birds and flowers were favorite subjects for Song painters. ▼

Changes in Chinese Society

China's prosperity produced many social changes during the Tang and Song periods. Chinese society became increasingly mobile. People moved to the cities in growing numbers. The Chinese also experienced greater social mobility than ever before. The most important avenue for social advancement was the civil service system.

Levels of Society During Tang and Song times, the power of the old aristocratic families began to fade. A new, much larger upper class emerged, made up of scholar-officials and their families. Such a class of powerful, well-to-do people is called the **gentry**. The gentry attained their status through education and civil service positions rather than through land ownership. Below the gentry was an urban middle class. It included merchants, shopkeepers, skilled artisans, minor officials, and others. At the bottom of urban society were laborers, soldiers, and servants. In the countryside lived the largest class by far, the peasants. They toiled for wealthy landowners as they had for centuries.

The Status of Women Women had always been subservient to men in Chinese society. Their status further declined during the Tang and Song periods. This was especially true among the upper classes in cities. There a woman's work was deemed less important to the family's prosperity and status. Changing attitudes affected peasant families less, however. Peasant women worked in the fields and helped produce their family's food and income.

One sign of the changing status of women was the new custom of binding the feet of upper-class girls. When a girl was very young, her feet were bound tightly with cloth, which eventually broke the arch and curled all but the big toe under. This produced what was admiringly called a "lily-foot." Women with bound feet were crippled for life. To others in society, such a woman reflected the wealth and prestige of her husband, who could afford such a beautiful but impractical wife. D

MAIN IDEA

Making Inferences

D How did the practice of foot binding reflect the changing status of Chinese women?

The social, economic, and technological transformations of the Tang and Song periods permanently shaped Chinese civilization. They endured even as China fell to a group of nomadic outsiders, the Mongols, whom you will learn about in Section 2.

NEW YORK CORE CURRICULUM REVIEW

TERMS & NAMES 1. For each term or name, write a sentence explaining its significance.

- Tang Taizong
- Wu Zhao
- movable type
- gentry

USING YOUR NOTES

2. How are the accomplishments of the two dynasties similar?

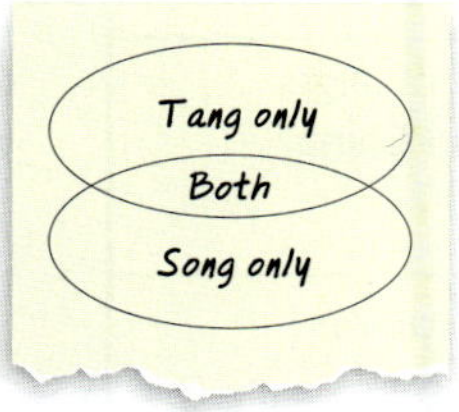

MAIN IDEAS

3. How did the Tang Dynasty benefit from the accomplishments of the Sui?
4. What steps did the Tang take to restore China's bureaucracy?
5. Describe the urban social classes that emerged during the Tang and Song periods.

CRITICAL THINKING & WRITING

6. **RECOGNIZING EFFECTS** What impact did improvements in transportation have on Tang and Song China?
7. **FORMING AND SUPPORTING OPINIONS** "Gaining power depends on merit, not birth." Do you agree with this view of China under the Tang and Song? Explain.
8. **PRIMARY SOURCES** How do the feelings expressed in Tu Fu's poem on page 326 still relate to life today?
9. **WRITING ACTIVITY** EMPIRE BUILDING Write two short **paragraphs,** one discussing how Tang and Song emperors strengthened China's empire, and the other discussing how they weakened it.

CONNECT TO TODAY **CREATING A LIST**

Gunpowder is used in the making of fireworks. Conduct research to find interesting facts about fireworks in the United States—the number produced in a year, the amount of gunpowder in a typical firework, and so on. Present your findings in a **list** titled "Fun Facts About Fireworks."

Tang and Song China: People and Technology

The Tang and Song dynasties were eras of major technological advancement in China. The technologies improved China as a country and, in turn, helped people conduct their daily business.

Much of China's technology spread to other parts of the world where it improved the lives of the people living there. The table on this page identifies some of that movement.

INTEGRATED TECHNOLOGY

RESEARCH LINKS For more on Tang and Song China, go to **classzone.com**

Porcelain ►

Marco Polo was the first to describe the pottery found in China as porcelain. The plain piece shown here is an early example of porcelain work from the Song Dynasty. A piece like this might be used daily. Later porcelain work, such as the distinctive blue and white porcelain of the Ming Dynasty, became more decorative. Porcelain, however, was a luxury reserved for the middle and upper classes of Chinese society.

Inventions of Tang and Song China

	Description	Impact
Porcelain Late 700s	Bone-hard, white ceramic made of a special clay and a mineral found only in China	Became a valuable export—so associated with Chinese culture that it is now called china; technology remained a Chinese secret for centuries
Mechanical clock 700s	Clock in which machinery (driven by running water) regulated the movements	Early Chinese clocks short-lived; idea for mechanical clock carried by traders to medieval Europe
Printing Block printing: 700s Movable type: 1040	Block printing: one block on which a whole page is cut; movable type: individual characters arranged in frames, used over and over	Printing technology spread to Korea and Japan; movable type also developed later in Europe
Explosive powder 800s	Made from mixture of saltpeter, sulfur, and charcoal	First used for fireworks, then weapons; technology spread west within 300 years
Paper money 1020s	Paper currency issued by Song government to replace cumbersome strings of metal cash used by merchants	Contributed to development of large-scale commercial economy in China
Magnetic compass (for navigation) 1100s	Floating magnetized needle that always points north-south; device had existed in China for centuries before it was adapted by sailors for use at sea	Helped China become a sea power; technology quickly spread west

SKILLBUILDER: Interpreting Charts

1. **Making Inferences** *Which inventions eventually affected warfare and exploration?*
2. **Forming and Supporting Opinions** *Which of these inventions do you think had the greatest impact on history? Why?*

Movable Type ▼

Traditionally, an entire page of characters was carved into a block of wood from which prints were made. Pi Sheng, a Chinese alchemist, came up with the idea of creating individual characters that could be reused whenever needed. Later, a government official created rotating storage trays for the characters.

As you have read, Tang rulers restored China's system of scholar-officials. Thus, education and printed materials became important to a larger part of Chinese society.

The trays allowed the typesetter to quickly find the characters. The typesetter would then order the characters in a tray that would be used to produce the printed pages. The two wheels held about 60,000 characters.

Explosive Powder ►

Around A.D. 900, Chinese alchemists first discovered that the right mixture of saltpeter, sulfur, and charcoal could be explosive. The Chinese initially used the powder for fireworks, then for military applications. It is now commonly referred to as gunpowder.

The device shown here is a modern reproduction of an ancient rocket launcher. The Chinese tied gunpowder charges to arrows, balanced them, and placed them in a holder. The holder helped aim the rockets, and its flared shape spread the rockets over a large area.

> DATA FILE

LEGACY OF TANG AND SONG CHINA

Printing

- U.S. publishers produced 122,108 books in 2000.
- The Library of Congress, the largest library in the world, has over 18 million books.
- The world's best-selling book is the Bible. Since 1815, around 2.5 billion copies of the Bible have been sold.

Porcelain

- The United States imported 423,041 one-piece toilet bowls and tanks in 2002. Of those, 302,489 came from China.
- In 2001, a Chinese newspaper reported the production of possibly the world's largest porcelain kettle—just under 10 feet tall, about 6 feet in diameter, and weighing 1.5 tons.

Explosive Powder

- In 2002, the United States imported over 90 percent of its fireworks from China.
- The largest single firework was used at a Japanese festival in 1988. It weighed over 1,000 pounds, and its burst was over half a mile wide.

Connect *to* Today

1. **Forming and Supporting Opinions** Of all the inventions listed on these pages, which do you think had the most lasting impact? Why?
   See Skillbuilder Handbook, page R20.
2. **Hypothesizing** What are some modern inventions that you believe will still have an impact 1,000 years from now?

The Mongol Conquests

CONNECT TO THE NEW YORK STATE CORE CURRICULUM

Unit 3.B.1. Human and physical geography
Unit 3.B.4. Extent of empire under Ghengis Khan and Kublai Khan

TERMS & NAMES

- pastoralist
- clan
- Genghis Khan
- Pax Mongolica

SETTING THE STAGE While the Chinese prospered during the Song Dynasty, a great people far to the north were also gaining strength. The Mongols of the Asian steppe lived their lives on the move. They prided themselves on their skill on horseback, their discipline, their ruthlessness, and their courage in battle. They also wanted the wealth and glory that came with conquering mighty empires. This desire soon exploded into violent conflict that transformed Asia and Europe forever.

TAKING NOTES
Following Chronological Order Use a chart to list the series of events leading to the creation of the Mongol Empire.

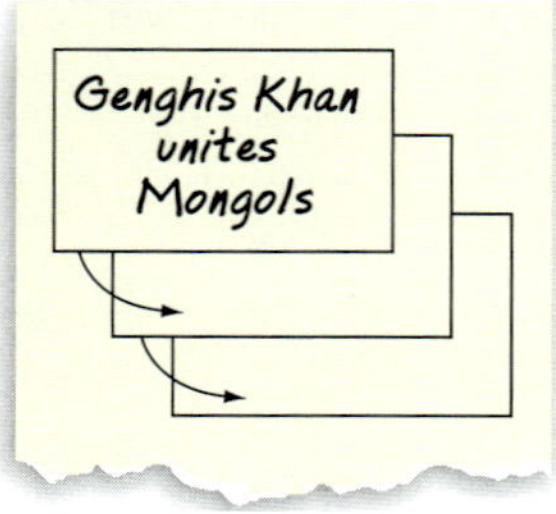

Nomads of the Asian Steppe

A vast belt of dry grassland, called the steppe, stretches across the landmass of Eurasia. The significance of the steppe to neighboring civilizations was twofold. First, it served as a land trade route connecting the East and the West. Second, it was home to nomadic peoples who frequently swept down on their neighbors to plunder, loot, and conquer.

Geography of the Steppe There are two main expanses of the Eurasian steppe. The western steppe runs from Central Asia to eastern Europe. It was the original home of some of the ancient invaders you have read about, including the Hittites. The eastern steppe, covering the area of present-day Mongolia, was the first home of the Huns, the Turks, and the Mongols.

Very little rain falls on the steppe, but the dry, windswept plain supports short, hardy grasses. Seasonal temperature changes can be dramatic. Temperatures in Mongolia, for example, range from –57°F in winter to 96°F in the summer. Rainfall is somewhat more plentiful and the climate milder in the west than in the east. For this reason, movements of people have historically tended to be toward the west and the south.

The Nomadic Way of Life Nomadic peoples were **pastoralists**—that is, they herded domesticated animals. They were constantly on the move, searching for good pasture to feed their herds. But they did not wander. Rather, they followed a familiar seasonal pattern and returned on a regular basis to the same campsites. Keeping claim to land that was not permanently occupied was difficult. Battles frequently arose among nomadic groups over grassland and water rights.

Asian nomads practically lived on horseback as they followed their huge herds over the steppe. They depended on their animals for food, clothing, and housing. Their diet consisted of meat and mare's milk. They wore clothing made of skins and wool, and they lived in portable felt tents called yurts.

Steppe nomads traveled together in kinship groups called **clans**. The members of each clan claimed to be descended from a common ancestor. Different clans sometimes came together when they needed a large force to attack a common enemy or raid their settled neighbors.

Steppe Nomads and Settled Societies The differing ways of life of nomadic and settled peoples resulted in constant interaction between them. Often, they engaged in peaceful trade. The nomads exchanged horses, for example, for basic items they lacked, such as grain, metal, cloth, and tea. Nomads were accustomed to scarcity and hardship. They prided themselves on their toughness. However, they were sometimes tempted by the rich land and relative wealth of townspeople and took what they wanted by force. As a result, settled peoples lived in constant fear of raids.

Time and again in history, nomadic peoples rode out of the steppe to invade border towns and villages. When a state or empire was strong and organized, it could protect its frontier. If the state or empire became divided and weak, the nomads could increase their attacks and gain more plunder. Occasionally, a powerful nomadic group was able to conquer a whole empire and become its rulers. Over generations, these nomadic rulers often became part of the civilization they conquered. (A)

MAIN IDEA

Making Inferences

(A) How might a strong, organized empire defend its frontier?

The Rise of the Mongols

For centuries, the Mongol people had roamed the eastern steppe in loosely organized clans. It took a military and political genius to unite the Mongols into a force with a single purpose—conquest.

Genghis Khan Unites the Mongols Around 1200, a Mongol clan leader named Temujin sought to unify the Mongols under his leadership. He fought and defeated his rivals one by one. In 1206, Temujin accepted the title **Genghis Khan**, or "universal ruler" of the Mongol clans.

Over the next 21 years, Genghis led the Mongols in conquering much of Asia. His first goal was China. After invading the northern Jin Empire in 1211, however, his attention turned to the Islamic region west of Mongolia. Angered by the murder of Mongol traders and an ambassador at the hands of the Muslims, Genghis launched a campaign of terror across Central Asia. The Mongols destroyed one city after another—Utrar, Samarkand, Bukhara—and slaughtered many inhabitants. By 1225, Central Asia was under Mongol control.

History Makers

Genghis Khan 1162?–1227

Temujin, according to legend, was born with a blood clot in his fist. In his lifetime, his hands were often covered with the blood of others.

When Temujin was about nine, the Tatars, a rival people, poisoned his father. For a time, he and his family lived in extreme poverty, abandoned by their clan. When in manhood he fought and defeated the Tatars, he slaughtered every male taller than a cart axle.

While driven by revenge, Genghis also loved conquest. He once remarked to his personal historian:

> *Man's greatest good fortune is to chase and defeat his enemy, seize his total possessions, leave his married women weeping and wailing, [and] ride his [horse].*

INTEGRATED TECHNOLOGY

RESEARCH LINKS For more on Genghis Khan, go to **classzone.com**

Genghis the Conqueror Several characteristics lay behind Genghis Khan's stunning success as a conqueror. First, he was a brilliant organizer. He assembled his Mongol warriors into a mighty fighting force (see below). Following the model of the Chinese military, Genghis grouped his warriors in armies of 10,000. These in turn were organized into 1,000-man brigades, 100-man companies, and 10-man squads. He put his most battle-proven and loyal men in command of these units.

Second, Genghis was a gifted strategist. He used various tricks to confuse his enemy. Sometimes, a small Mongol cavalry unit would attack, then pretend to gallop away in flight. The enemy usually gave chase. Then the rest of the Mongol army would appear suddenly and slaughter the surprised enemy forces.

Finally, Genghis Khan used cruelty as a weapon. He believed in terrifying his enemies into surrender. If a city refused to open its gates to him, he might kill the entire population when he finally captured the place. The terror the Mongols inspired spread ahead of their armies, which led many towns to surrender without a fight. As one Arab historian wrote, "In the countries that have not yet been overrun by them, everyone spends the night afraid that they may appear there too." B

MAIN IDEA

Summarizing

B What were some of the tactics Genghis Khan used in war?

The Mongol Empire

Genghis Khan died in 1227—not from violence, but from illness. His successors continued to expand his empire. In less than 50 years, the Mongols conquered territory from China to Poland. In so doing, they created the largest unified land empire in history. (See the map on page 334.)

History *in* Depth

INTERACTIVE

A Mighty Fighting Force

Mongol soldiers were superb horsemen, having spent all their lives in the saddle. Annual game roundups gave young men the chance to practice skills they would use in battle and gave their leaders the opportunity to spot promising warriors. When on the move, each soldier was accompanied by three extra horses. By changing mounts, soldiers could stay in the saddle for up to ten days and nights at a time. When charging toward a target, they covered as much as 120 miles a day. If food was scarce, a Mongol soldier might make a small gash in the neck of one of his horses and sustain himself by drinking the blood.

A key to Mongol horsemanship was the stirrup, which was invented on the steppe in the second century B.C. Stirrups enabled a mounted warrior to stand, turn, and shoot arrows behind him.

The Khanates After Genghis's death, his sons and grandsons continued the campaign of conquest. Armies under their leadership drove south, east, and west out of inner Asia. They completed their conquest of northern China and invaded Korea. They leveled the Russian city of Kiev and reached the banks of the Adriatic Sea. The cities of Venice and Vienna were within their grasp. However, in the 1250s the Mongols halted their westward campaign and turned their attention to Persia. By 1260, the Mongols had divided their huge empire into four regions, or khanates. (See the map on page 334.) These were the Khanate of the Great Khan (Mongolia and China), the Khanate of Chagatai (Central Asia), the Ilkhanate (Persia), and the Khanate of the Golden Horde (Russia). A descendant of Genghis ruled each khanate.

The Mongols as Rulers Many of the areas invaded by the Mongols never recovered. The populations of some cities were wiped out. In addition, the Mongols destroyed ancient irrigation systems in areas such as the Tigris and Euphrates valleys. Thus, the land could no longer support resettlement. While ferocious in war, the Mongols were quite tolerant in peace. They rarely imposed their beliefs or way of life on those they conquered. Over time, some Mongol rulers even adopted aspects of the culture of the people they ruled. The Ilkhans and the Golden Horde, for example, became Muslims. Growing cultural differences among the khanates contributed to the eventual splitting up of the empire.

The Mongol Peace From the mid-1200s to the mid-1300s, the Mongols imposed stability and law and order across much of Eurasia. This period is sometimes called the **Pax Mongolica**, or Mongol Peace. The Mongols guaranteed safe passage for trade caravans, travelers, and missionaries from one end of the empire to another.

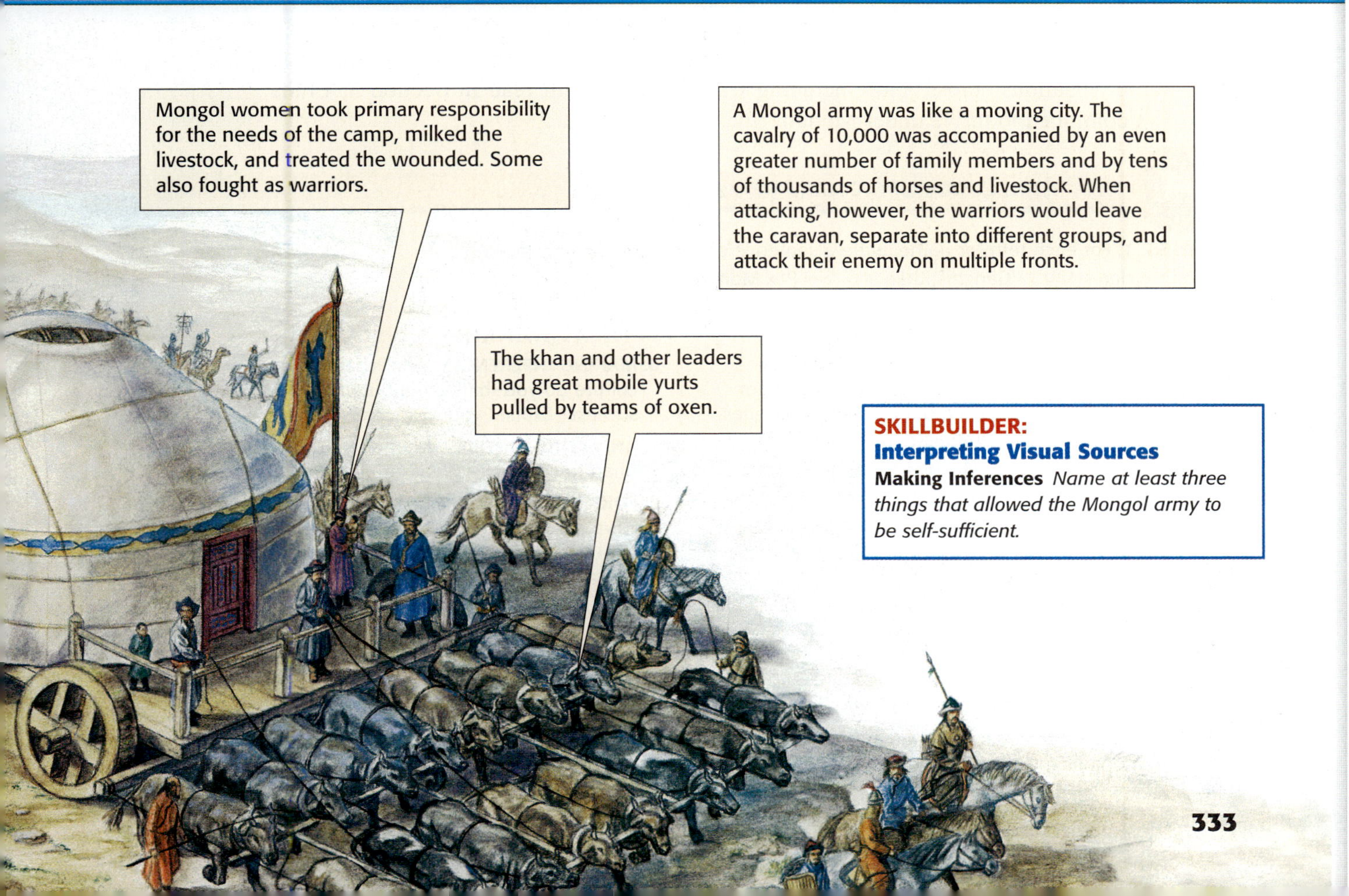

SKILLBUILDER:
Interpreting Visual Sources
Making Inferences *Name at least three things that allowed the Mongol army to be self-sufficient.*

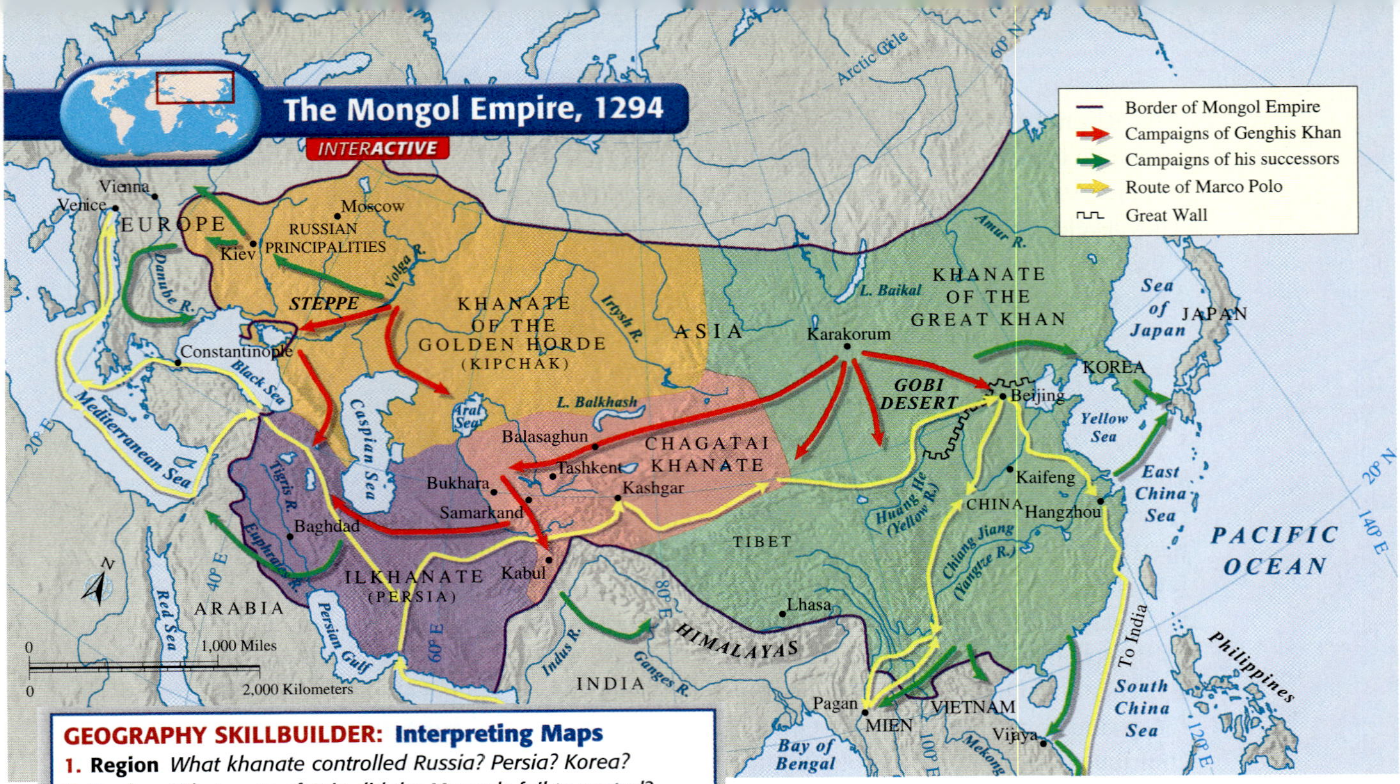

GEOGRAPHY SKILLBUILDER: Interpreting Maps

1. **Region** *What khanate controlled Russia? Persia? Korea?*
2. **Region** *What parts of Asia did the Mongols fail to control?*

Trade between Europe and Asia had never been more active. Ideas and inventions traveled along with the trade goods. Many Chinese innovations, such as gunpowder, reached Europe during this period.

Other things spread along with the goods and the ideas. Some historians speculate that the epidemic of bubonic plague that devastated Europe during the 1300s was first spread by the Mongols. (See Chapter 14.) The disease might have traveled along trade routes or have been passed to others by infected Mongol troops.

For a brief period of history, the nomadic Mongols were the lords of city-based civilizations across Asia, including China. As you will read in Section 3, China continued to thrive under Mongol rule.

NEW YORK CORE CURRICULUM REVIEW

TERMS & NAMES 1. For each term or name, write a sentence explaining its significance.

- pastoralist
- clan
- Genghis Khan
- Pax Mongolica

USING YOUR NOTES

2. Which of the listed events do you think is the most important? Why?

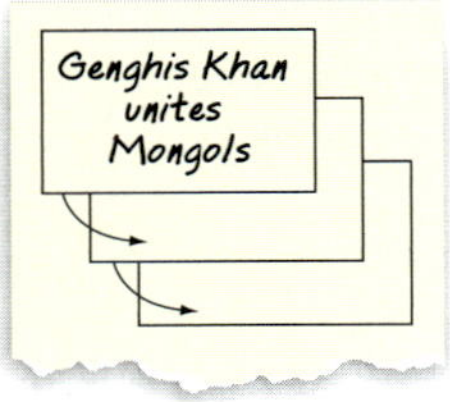

MAIN IDEAS

3. In what ways did steppe nomads and the people of neighboring settled societies interact?
4. Why was terror an important weapon for Genghis Khan?
5. What happened to the Mongol Empire in the years after Genghis Khan's death?

CRITICAL THINKING & WRITING

6. **MAKING INFERENCES** What characteristics of their culture do you think contributed to the Mongols' military success? Explain your response.
7. **ANALYZING MOTIVES** What do you think drove Genghis Khan to conquer a great empire? Explain your answer.
8. **FORMING AND SUPPORTING OPINIONS** "The Mongols were great conquerors but poor rulers." Do you agree with this statement? Why or why not?
9. **WRITING ACTIVITY** CULTURAL INTERACTION Write a brief **essay** discussing the impact of interaction between the Mongols and the various cultures that they conquered.

INTEGRATED TECHNOLOGY **INTERNET ACTIVITY**

Today, most Mongols live in the country of Mongolia. Use the Internet to find information on Mongolian ways of life. Then create an **illustrated report** comparing ways of life today and in Genghis Khan's time.

INTERNET KEYWORD
Mongolia

3 The Mongol Empire

CONNECT TO THE NEW YORK STATE CORE CURRICULUM

Unit 3.B.3. The Yuan Dynasty: a foreign non-Chinese dynasty
Unit 3.B.7. Interaction with the West and global trade, Pax Mongolia (e.g., Marco Polo)

TERMS & NAMES

- Kublai Khan
- Marco Polo

SETTING THE STAGE **Kublai Khan**, the grandson of Genghis Khan, assumed the title Great Khan in 1260. In theory, the Great Khan ruled the entire Mongol Empire. In reality, the empire had split into four khanates. Other descendants of Genghis ruled Central Asia, Persia, and Russia as semi-independent states. So, Kublai focused instead on extending the power and range of his own khanate, which already included Mongolia, Korea, Tibet, and northern China. To begin, however, he had to fulfill the goal of his grandfather to conquer all of China.

Kublai Khan Becomes Emperor

The Chinese held off Kublai's attacks for several years. However, his armies finally overwhelmed them in 1279. Throughout China's long history, the Chinese feared and fought off invasions by northern nomads. China sometimes lost territory to nomadic groups, but no foreigner had ever ruled the whole country. With Kublai's victory, that changed.

TAKING NOTES
Recognizing Effects Use a web diagram to show the impact of Kublai Khan on East Asia.

Beginning a New Dynasty As China's new emperor, Kublai Khan founded a new dynasty called the Yuan (yoo•AHN) Dynasty. It lasted less than a century, until 1368, when it was overthrown. However, the Yuan era was an important period in Chinese history for several reasons. First, Kublai Khan united China for the first time in more than 300 years. For this he is considered one of China's great emperors. Second, the control imposed by the Mongols across all of Asia opened China to greater foreign contacts and trade. Finally, Kublai and his successors tolerated Chinese culture and made few changes to the system of government.

Unlike his Mongol ancestors, Kublai abandoned the Mongolian steppes for China. He did not share his ancestors' dislike of the settled life. On the contrary, he rather enjoyed living in the luxurious manner of a Chinese emperor. He maintained a beautiful summer palace at Shangdu, on the border between Mongolia and China. He also built a new square-walled capital at the site of modern Beijing. Kublai built this palace to enhance his prestige, but his new capital meant something more. Previously, the Great Khans had ruled their empire from Mongolia. Moving the capital from Mongolia to China was a sign that Kublai intended to make his mark as emperor of China.

Failure to Conquer Japan After conquering China, Kublai Khan tried to extend his rule to Japan. In 1274 and again in 1281, the Great Khan sent huge fleets

▲ This detail from a 13th-century Japanese scroll depicts Japanese warriors fighting off a Mongol warship.

against Japan. The Mongols forced Koreans to build, sail, and provide provisions for the boats, a costly task that almost ruined Korea. Both times the Japanese turned back the Mongol fleets.

The second fleet carried 150,000 Mongol, Chinese, and Korean warriors—the largest seaborne invasion force in history until World War II. After 53 days, Japanese warriors had fought the invaders to a standstill. Then, on the following day, the sky darkened and a typhoon swept furiously across the Sea of Japan. Mongol ships were upended, swamped, and dashed to bits against the rocky shore, despite their sailors' attempts to escape onto the open sea. For centuries afterward, the Japanese spoke reverently of the *kamikaze,* or "divine wind," that had saved Japan.

Mongol Rule in China

Early in Kublai Khan's reign, one of his Chinese advisers told him, "I have heard that one can conquer the empire on horseback, but one cannot govern it on horseback." This advice illustrates the problems Kublai faced as emperor. Mongol ways would not work in a sophisticated civilization like China's. Besides, the number of Mongols in China was few compared to the huge native population. Kublai would need to make use of non-Mongol officials to help him rule successfully.

The Mongols and the Chinese The Mongol rulers had little in common with their Chinese subjects. Because of their differences, the Mongols kept their separate identity. Mongols lived apart from the Chinese and obeyed different laws. They kept the Chinese out of high government offices, although they retained as many Chinese officials as possible to serve on the local level. Most of the highest government posts went to Mongols or to foreigners. The Mongols believed that foreigners were more trustworthy since they had no local loyalties. (A)

MAIN IDEA

Making Inferences

(A) How might the Chinese have felt about their lack of power in Kublai's government?

Despite his differences with the Chinese, Kublai Khan was an able leader. He restored the Grand Canal and extended it 135 miles north to Beijing. Along its banks he built a paved highway that ran some 1,100 miles, from Hangzhou to Beijing. These land and water routes ensured the north a steady supply of grain and other goods from the southern heartland.

Foreign Trade Foreign trade increased under Kublai Khan. This was largely due to the Mongol Peace, which made the caravan routes across Central Asia safe for trade and travel. Traders transported Chinese silk and porcelain, which were greatly valued in Europe and western Asia, over the Silk Roads and other routes. These traders also carried with them such Chinese products and inventions as printing, gunpowder, the compass, paper currency, and playing cards.

Kublai further encouraged trade by inviting foreign merchants to visit China. Most of them were Muslims from India, Central Asia, and Persia. Many European traders and travelers, including Christian missionaries, also reached China.

Marco Polo at the Mongol Court The most famous European to visit China in these years was a young Venetian trader, **Marco Polo**. He traveled by caravan on the Silk Roads with his father and uncle, arriving at Kublai Khan's court around 1275. Polo had learned several Asian languages in his travels, and Kublai Khan sent him to various Chinese cities on government missions. Polo served the Great Khan well for 17 years. In 1292, the Polos left China and made the long journey back to Venice. B

MAIN IDEA

Analyzing Motives

B Why do you think Kublai Khan employed Marco Polo?

Later, during a war against Venice's rival city, Genoa, Marco Polo was captured and imprisoned. In prison he had time to tell the full story of his travels and adventures. To his awed listeners, he spoke of China's fabulous cities, its fantastic wealth, and the strange things he had seen there. He mentioned the burning of "black stones" (coal) in Chinese homes. (Coal as a fuel was little known in Europe.) He also recorded the practical workings of Kublai's government and aspects of Chinese life. Here is his description of trade in Beijing:

PRIMARY SOURCE

[M]ore precious and costly wares are imported into Khan-balik [Beijing] than into any other city in the world. . . . All the treasures that come from India—precious stones, pearls, and other rarities—are brought here. So too are the choicest and costliest products of Cathay [China] itself and every other province.

MARCO POLO, *The Travels of Marco Polo*

A fellow prisoner gathered Polo's stories into a book. It was an instant success in Europe, but most readers did not believe a word of it. They thought Polo's account was a marvelous collection of tall tales. It was clear to Marco Polo, however, that the civilization he had visited was the greatest in the world.

History Makers

Kublai Khan 1215–1294

As ruler of both China and the Mongol Empire, Kublai Khan straddled two worlds. He built luxurious palaces, dressed as a Chinese emperor, and supported the work of Chinese artists. However, he remained a Mongol warrior at heart. The Great Khan is said to have planted a plot of grass from the steppe in the gardens at Beijing to remind himself of his home. He also loved to hunt and enclosed a large hunting ground at his palace at Shangdu.

Marco Polo 1254?–1324

The man who described Kublai Khan to Europeans left behind very little information about himself. According to Polo, Kublai recognized his "merit and worth" and sent him on special missions around the empire. His impressions of China became the basis of his book, but he described few actual events about his life.

Since his book first appeared, people have debated whether Polo even visited China. He is not mentioned in Chinese accounts of this time. His tales also fail to mention such common features of China as tea, acupuncture, or foot binding. On his deathbed, Polo was asked if his travel stories were true. He replied that he had told barely half of what he had seen.

INTEGRATED TECHNOLOGY

RESEARCH LINKS For more on Kublai Khan and Marco Polo, go to **classzone.com**

The End of Mongol Rule

During the last years of Kublai Khan's reign, weaknesses began to appear in Mongol rule. In an attempt to further expand his empire, Kublai sent several expeditions into Southeast Asia. His armies and navies suffered many humiliating defeats at a huge expense of lives and equipment. Heavy spending on fruitless wars, on public works, and on the luxuries of the Yuan court burdened the treasury and created resentment among the overtaxed Chinese. This presented problems that Kublai's less able successors could not resolve.

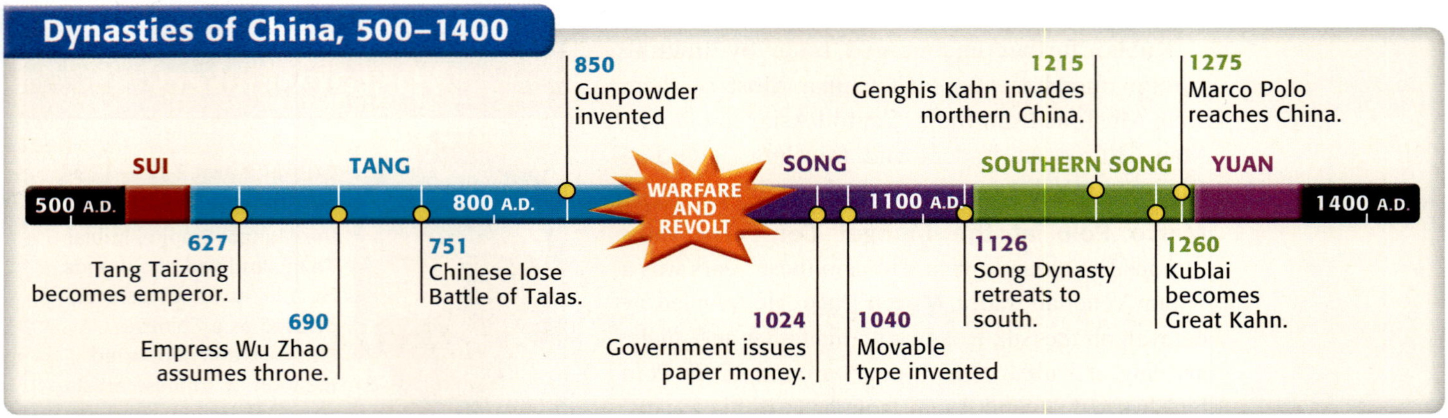

Yuan Dynasty Overthrown Kublai Khan died in 1294. After his death, the Yuan Dynasty began to fade. Family members continually argued over who would rule. In one eight-year period, four different khans took the throne.

Rebellions broke out in many parts of China in the 1300s. The Chinese had long resented their Mongol rulers, and the Mongol humiliation of the Chinese only increased under Kublai Khan's successors. The rebellions were also fueled by years of famine, flood, and disease, along with growing economic problems and official corruption. In 1368, Chinese rebels finally overthrew the Mongols. The rebel leader founded a new dynasty, the Ming, which you will read about in Chapter 19. (C)

MAIN IDEA

Analyzing Causes

(C) What factors contributed to the decline and fall of the Yuan Dynasty?

Decline of the Mongol Empire By the time of the collapse of the Yuan Dynasty, the entire Mongol Empire had disintegrated. The government of the Ilkhanate in Persia fell apart in the 1330s. The Chagatai khans ruled Central Asia until the 1370s. Only the Golden Horde in Russia stayed in power. The Golden Horde ruled Russia for 250 years. As you read in Chapter 11, Ivan III finally led Russia to independence from Mongol rule in 1480.

The rise and fall of Mongol rule affected civilizations from eastern Europe to China. Kublai Khan had tried to extend this influence to Japan but had failed. However, several centuries earlier, the Japanese had embraced the influence of an outside culture—China. This development is described in Section 4.

NEW YORK CORE CURRICULUM REVIEW

TERMS & NAMES 1. For each term or name, write a sentence explaining its significance.

- Kublai Khan
- Marco Polo

USING YOUR NOTES

2. Select one of the entries. Did this event make China stronger or weaker?

MAIN IDEAS

3. Why did the Mongols employ foreigners rather than Chinese in high government offices?
4. How did Europeans view Marco Polo's account of his time in China?
5. What happened to the Yuan Dynasty after Kublai Khan's death?

CRITICAL THINKING & WRITING

6. **EVALUATING DECISIONS** Judging from the events of the Yuan Dynasty, do you think the Mongol policies toward the Chinese were effective? Explain your answer.
7. **RECOGNIZING EFFECTS** What impact did the Mongol Peace have on interaction between East and West?
8. **FORMING AND SUPPORTING OPINIONS** Do you think that Kublai Khan was a successful ruler? Why or why not?
9. **WRITING ACTIVITY** CULTURAL INTERACTION Adopt the role of a traveler in Mongol China. Write a **letter** to friends explaining how the Chinese way of life has influenced the Mongol conquerors.

CONNECT TO TODAY **WRITING A SUMMARY**

Some people consider Marco Polo to be the first travel writer. Locate modern travel writing on China. Select and read descriptions of major cities, such as Beijing. Using photographs and sketches, create an **illustrated summary** of the main points included in the descriptions.

Feudal Powers in Japan

CONNECT TO THE NEW YORK STATE CORE CURRICULUM

Unit 3.A.1. Human and physical geography
Unit 3.A.3. Ties with China and Korea: cultural diffusion, Buddhism, and Confucianism

TERMS & NAMES

- Shinto
- samurai
- Bushido
- shogun

SETTING THE STAGE Japan lies east of China, in the direction of the sunrise. In fact, the name Japan comes from the Chinese word *ri-ben,* which means "origin of the sun" or "land of the rising sun." From ancient times, Japan had borrowed ideas, institutions, and culture from the Chinese people. Japan's genius was its ability to take in new ideas and make them uniquely its own.

The Growth of Japanese Civilization

TAKING NOTES
Following Chronological Order Use a time line to record the main periods and events in Japanese history from 300 to 1300.

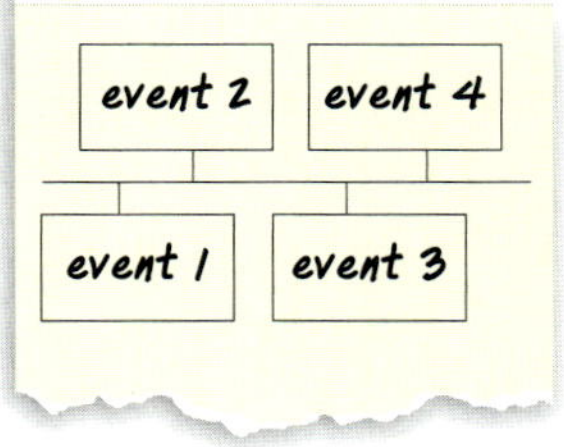

Japan's island location shaped the growth of its civilization. About 120 miles of water separates Japan from its closest neighbor, Korea, and 500 miles of water separates Japan from China. The Japanese were close enough to feel the civilizing effect of China. Yet they were far enough away to be reasonably safe from invasion.

The Geography of Japan About 4,000 islands make up the Japanese archipelago (AHR•kuh•PEHL•uh•GOH), or island group, that extends in an arc more than 1,200 miles long. Historically, most Japanese people have lived on the four largest islands: Hokkaido (hah•KY•doh), Honshu (HAHN•shoo), Shikoku (shee•KAW•koo), and Kyushu (kee•OO•shoo).

Japan's geography has both advantages and disadvantages. Southern Japan enjoys a mild climate with plenty of rainfall. The country is so mountainous, however, that only about 12 percent of the land is suitable for farming. Natural resources such as coal, oil, and iron are in short supply. During the late summer and early fall, strong tropical storms called typhoons occur. Earthquakes and tidal waves are also threats.

Early Japan The first historic mention of Japan comes from Chinese writings of the first century B.C. Japan at this time was not a united country. Instead, hundreds of clans controlled their own territories. Each clan worshiped its own nature gods and goddesses. In different parts of Japan, people honored thousands of local gods. Their varied customs and beliefs eventually combined to form Japan's earliest religion. In later times, this religion was called **Shinto** (SHIHN•toh), meaning "way of the gods."

Shinto was based on respect for the forces of nature and on the worship of ancestors. Shinto worshipers believed in *kami,* divine spirits that dwelled in nature. Any unusual or especially beautiful tree, rock, waterfall, or mountain was considered the home of a *kami.*

GEOGRAPHY SKILLBUILDER: Interpreting Maps

1. **Location** *How far is the southern end of the Japanese island of Kyushu from China?*
2. **Location** *On what island did Japan's major cities develop?*

The Yamato Emperors By the A.D. 400s, the Yamato clan had established itself as the leading clan. The Yamato claimed to be descended from the sun goddess Amaterasu. By the seventh century, the Yamato chiefs called themselves the emperors of Japan. The early emperors did not control the entire country, or even much of it, but the Japanese gradually accepted the idea of an emperor.

Although many of the Yamato rulers lacked real power, the dynasty was never overthrown. When rival clans fought for power, the winning clan claimed control of the emperor and then ruled in the emperor's name. Japan had both an emperor who served as a figurehead and a ruling power who reigned behind the throne. This dual structure became an enduring characteristic of Japanese government.

Japanese Culture

During the 400s, the Japanese began to have more and more contact with mainland Asia. They soon came under the influence of Chinese ideas and customs, which they first learned about from Korean travelers.

Buddhism in Japan One of the most important influences brought by Korean travelers was Buddhism. In the mid-700s, the Japanese imperial court officially accepted Buddhism in Japan. By the eighth or ninth century, Buddhist ideas and worship had spread through Japanese society. The Japanese, however, did not give up their Shinto beliefs. Some Buddhist rituals became Shinto rituals, and some Shinto gods and goddesses were worshiped in Buddhist temples.

Cultural Borrowing from China Interest in Buddhist ideas at the Japanese court soon grew into an enthusiasm for all things Chinese. The most influential convert to Buddhism was Prince Shotoku (shoh•toh•ku), who served as regent for his aunt, the empress Suiko. (A regent is someone who rules when a monarch is absent, ill, or too young to rule.) In 607, Prince Shotoku sent the first of three missions to China. His people studied Chinese civilization firsthand. Over the next 200 years, the Japanese sent many such groups to learn about Chinese ways. (A)

MAIN IDEA
Synthesizing
(A) How did Chinese culture spread to Japan?

The Japanese adopted the Chinese system of writing. Japanese artists painted landscapes in the Chinese manner. The Japanese also followed Chinese styles in the simple arts of everyday living, such as cooking, gardening, drinking tea, and hairdressing. For a time, Japan even modeled its government on China's. Prince Shotoku planned a strong central government like that of the Tang rulers. He also tried to introduce China's civil-service system. However, this attempt failed. In Japan, noble birth remained the key to winning a powerful position. Unlike China, Japan continued to be a country where a few great families held power.

The Japanese adapted Chinese ways to suit their own needs. While they learned much, they still retained their own traditions. Eventually, the Japanese imperial court decided it had learned enough from Tang China. In the late ninth century, it ended formal missions to the Tang Empire, which had fallen into decline. Although Chinese cultural influence would remain strong in Japan, Japan's own culture was about to bloom.

Life in the Heian Period

In the late 700s, the imperial court moved its capital from Nara to Heian (HAY•ahn), the modern Kyoto (kee•OH•toh). Many of Japan's noble families also moved to Heian. Among the upper class in Heian, a highly refined court society arose. This era in Japanese history, from 794 to 1185, is called the Heian period.

Gentlemen and ladies of the court filled their days with elaborate ritual and artistic pursuits. Rules dictated every aspect of court life—the length of swords, the color of official robes, forms of address, even the number of skirts a woman wore. Etiquette was also extremely important. Laughing aloud in public, for example, was frowned upon. And everyone at court was expected to write poetry and to paint.

Vocabulary
etiquette: the code governing correct behavior and appearance

The best accounts of Heian society come from the diaries, essays, and novels written by the women of the court. One of the finest writers of the period was Lady Murasaki Shikibu. Lady Murasaki's 11th-century masterpiece, *The Tale of Genji,* is an account of the life of a prince in the imperial court. This long prose narrative is considered the world's first novel.

Feudalism Erodes Imperial Authority

During the Heian period, Japan's central government was relatively strong. However, this strength was soon to be challenged by great landowners and clan chiefs who acted more and more as independent local rulers.

Decline of Central Power For most of the Heian period, the rich Fujiwara family held the real power in Japan. By about the middle of the 11th century, however, the power of the central government and the Fujiwaras began to slip.

Large landowners living away from the capital set up private armies. The countryside became lawless and dangerous. Armed soldiers on horseback preyed on farmers and travelers, and pirates took control of the seas. For safety, farmers and

> Analyzing Art

Women of the Heian Court

The Tale of Genji picture scroll—an illustrated version of the story—provides insights into the life of women at the Heian court. Since servants did almost all domestic chores, upper class women had much leisure time. How did they spend this time?

1. Because women were expected to look attractive, they spent time on personal grooming, such as hair care.
2. Women spent much time reading, usually the *monogatari,* or prose fiction, popular at the time. As the prince notes in *The Tale of Genji,* "Without these monogatari how on earth would [women entertain themselves] during these tedious hours?"

SKILLBUILDER: Interpreting Visual Sources

1. **Drawing Conclusions** *From what you have read about Heian court life, why do you think women spent so much time in personal grooming?*
2. **Making Inferences** *Based on what you have read, in what other ways might the women of the Heian court have spent their time?*

Japanese Samurai

Samurai were members of Japan's warrior class. Early samurai protected local aristocratic landowners. In the late 1100s, however, the warrior class secured national power and dominated Japanese government until 1868.

Samurai warriors followed an unwritten code that emphasized honor, bravery, and loyalty. This code came to be known as Bushido. Their reputation as fearsome warriors has become legendary.

▲ **Female Samurai**

Samurai were not always men. Here, Lady Tomoe Gozen, a famous female warrior of the 1180s, enters bravely into battle.

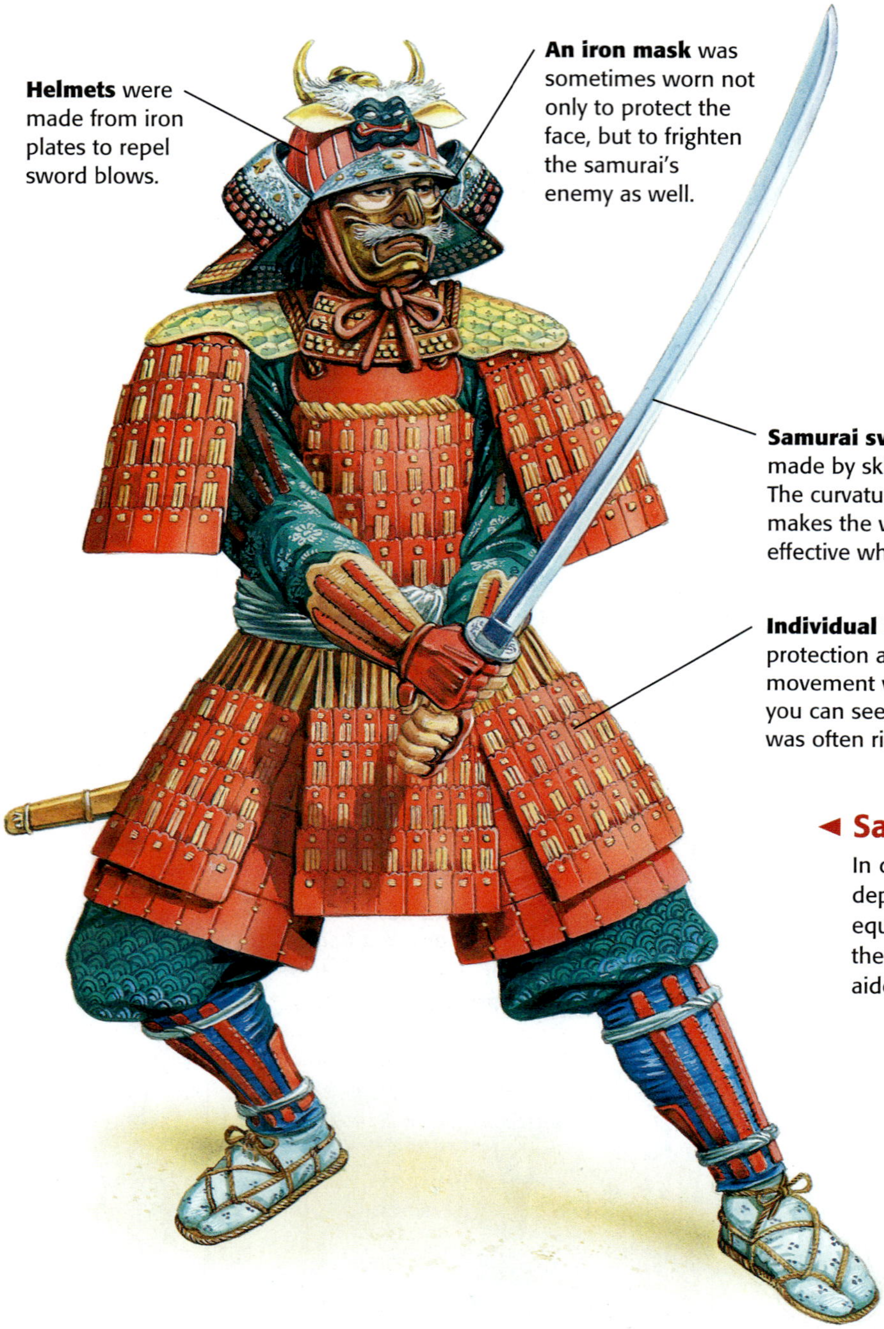

◄ **Samurai Warrior**

In combat, a samurai's life depended on his skill and his equipment. Here you can see how the samurai's weapons and armor aided him or her in battle.

SKILLBUILDER:
Interpreting Visual Sources

1. **Comparing and Contrasting** *What are some similarities or differences between Japanese samurai and European knights?*
2. **Hypothesizing** *How might the code of the Samurai help them in battle?*

small landowners traded parts of their land to strong warlords in exchange for protection. With more land, the lords gained more power. This marked the beginning of a feudal system of localized rule like that of ancient China and medieval Europe.

Samurai Warriors Since wars between rival lords were commonplace, each lord surrounded himself with a bodyguard of loyal warriors called **samurai** (SAM•uh•RY). (*Samurai* means "one who serves.") Samurai lived according to a demanding code of behavior called **Bushido** (BUSH•ih•DOH), or "the way of the warrior." A samurai was expected to show reckless courage, reverence for the gods, fairness, and generosity toward those weaker than himself. Dying an honorable death was judged more important than living a long life.

The Kamakura Shogunate During the late 1100s, Japan's two most powerful clans fought for power. After almost 30 years of war, the Minamoto family emerged victorious. In 1192, the emperor gave a Minamoto leader named Yoritomo the title of **shogun**, or "supreme general of the emperor's army." In effect, the shogun had the powers of a military dictator.

Following tradition, the emperor still reigned from Kyoto. (Kyoto was rebuilt on the ruins of Heian, which had been destroyed in war.) However, the real center of power was at the shogun's military headquarters at Kamakura (KAHM•uh•KUR•uh). The 1200s are known in Japanese history as the Kamakura shogunate. The pattern of government in which shoguns ruled through puppet emperors lasted in Japan until 1868. **B**

MAIN IDEA

Drawing Conclusions

B What advantages were there to preserving the imperial dynasty, even if it lacked real power?

The Kamakura shoguns were strong enough to turn back the two naval invasions sent by the great Mongol ruler Kublai Khan in 1274 and 1281. However, the Japanese victory over the Mongols drained the shoguns' treasury. Loyal samurai were bitter when the government failed to pay them. The Kamakura shoguns lost prestige and power. Samurai attached themselves more closely to their local lords, who soon fought one another as fiercely as they had fought the Mongols.

Although feudal Japan no longer courted contact with China, it would continue to absorb Chinese ideas and shape them into the Japanese way. As you will read in Section 5, China's culture also influenced Korea and kingdoms of Southeast Asia.

NEW YORK CORE CURRICULUM REVIEW

TERMS & NAMES 1. For each term or name, write a sentence explaining its significance.

- Shinto
- samurai
- Bushido
- shogun

USING YOUR NOTES

2. What event would you consider the most important turning point in Japan's early history? Why?

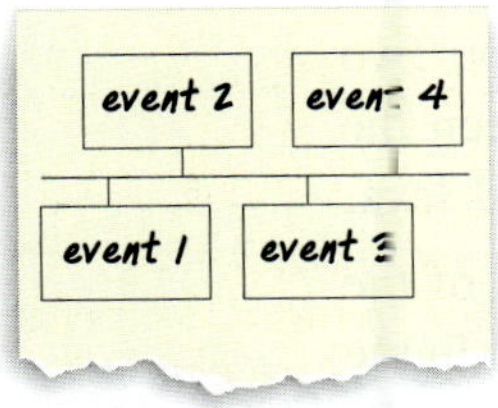

MAIN IDEAS

3. Why were Japanese missions to Tang China so important?
4. What was life like in the Heian court?
5. What purpose did the samurai serve?

CRITICAL THINKING & WRITING

6. **FORMING AND SUPPORTING OPINIONS** "The Japanese selectively borrowed from Chinese culture." Use information from the text to support this statement.
7. **EVALUATING COURSES OF ACTION** Why do you think the shoguns chose to rule through puppet emperors rather than simply seizing the imperial throne themselves?
8. **DRAWING CONCLUSIONS** Was the rise of the shogun beneficial for Japan overall? Explain.
9. **WRITING ACTIVITY** RELIGIOUS AND ETHICAL SYSTEMS -Write a **dialogue** between two members of a Japanese family on why they have decided to convert to Buddhism.

CONNECT TO TODAY **PREPARING AN ORAL REPORT**

After World War II, the Japanese adopted aspects of American culture such as baseball. Find information about baseball in Japan, noting how the Japanese have adapted the game to suit their own traditions. Present your findings in a brief **oral report.**

Kingdoms of Southeast Asia and Korea

CONNECT TO THE NEW YORK STATE CORE CURRICULUM

Unit 3.A.3. Ties with China and Korea: cultural diffusion, Buddhism, and Confucianism
Unit 2.B.3. Chinese influence on Korea and Japan

TERMS & NAMES

- Khmer Empire
- Angkor Wat
- Koryu Dynasty

SETTING THE STAGE To the south of China lies the region called Southeast Asia. It includes the modern countries of Myanmar (Burma), Laos, Cambodia, Vietnam, Malaysia, Indonesia, Thailand, Singapore, Brunei, and the Philippines. Thousands of miles from this region, to China's northeast, lies the Korean peninsula. This peninsula is currently divided between North Korea and South Korea. In the shadow of powerful China, many small but prosperous kingdoms rose and fell in Southeast Asia and Korea.

TAKING NOTES
Categorizing Use a chart to note important information on the kingdoms discussed in this section.

Kingdom	Notes
Khmer	
Dai Viet	
Korea	
Sailendra	
Srivijaya	

Kingdoms of Southeast Asia

In Southeast Asia's river valleys and deltas and on its islands, many kingdoms had centuries of glory and left monuments of lasting beauty.

Geography of Southeast Asia Southeast Asia lies between the Indian and Pacific oceans and stretches from Asia almost to Australia. It consists of two main parts: (1) Indochina, the mainland peninsula that borders China to the north and India to the west, and (2) the islands, the largest of which include Sumatra, Borneo, and Java. All of Southeast Asia lies within the warm, humid tropics. Monsoon winds bring the region heavy seasonal rains.

Seas and straits separate the islands of Southeast Asia. On the mainland, five great rivers flow from the north and cut valleys to the sea. Between the valleys rise hills and mountains, making travel and communication difficult. Over time, many different peoples settled the region, so it was home to many cultures.

Throughout Southeast Asia's history, the key to political power often has been control of trade routes and harbors. This is because Southeast Asia lies on the most direct sea route between the Indian Ocean and the South China Sea. Two important waterways connect the two seas: the Strait of Malacca, between the Malay Peninsula and Sumatra, and the Sunda Strait, between Sumatra and Java.

Influence of India and China Indian merchant ships, taking advantage of the monsoon winds, began arriving in Southeast Asia by the first century A.D. In the period that followed, Hindu and Buddhist missionaries spread their faiths to the region. In time, kingdoms arose that followed these religions and were modeled on Indian political ideas. Gradually, Indian influence shaped many aspects of the region's culture. This early Indian influence on Southeast Asia is evident today in the region's religions, languages, and art forms.

Chinese ideas and culture spread southward in the region through migration and trade. At different times, the Chinese also exerted political influence over parts of mainland Southeast Asia, either through direct rule or by demanding tribute from local rulers.

The Khmer Empire The **Khmer** (kmair) **Empire**, in what is now Cambodia, was for centuries the main power on the Southeast Asian mainland. By the 800s, the Khmer had conquered neighboring kingdoms and created an empire. This empire reached the peak of its power around 1200.

Improved rice cultivation helped the Khmer become prosperous. The Khmer built elaborate irrigation systems and waterways. These advances made it possible to grow three or four crops of rice a year in an area that had previously produced only one.

At their capital, Angkor, Khmer rulers built extensive city-and-temple complexes. One of these, called **Angkor Wat**, is one of the world's greatest architectural achievements. The complex, which covers nearly a square mile, was built as a symbolic mountain dedicated to the Hindu god Vishnu. The Khmer also used it as an observatory. (A)

MAIN IDEA

Making Inferences

(A) What does the size and splendor of Angkor Wat suggest about the empire that constructed it?

Island Trading Kingdoms Powerful kingdoms also developed on Southeast Asia's islands. For example, a dynasty called Sailendra ruled an agricultural kingdom on the island of Java. The Sailendra kings left behind another of the world's great architectural monuments, the Buddhist temple at Borobudur. Built around 800, this temple—like Angkor Wat—reflects strong Indian influence. The massive complex has nine terraced levels like a stepped pyramid.

The Sailendra Dynasty eventually fell under the domination of the powerful island empire of Srivijaya. At its height from the 7th to the 13th centuries, Srivijaya ruled the Strait of Malacca and other waters around the islands of Sumatra, Borneo, and Java. It grew wealthy by taxing the trade that passed through its waters. The

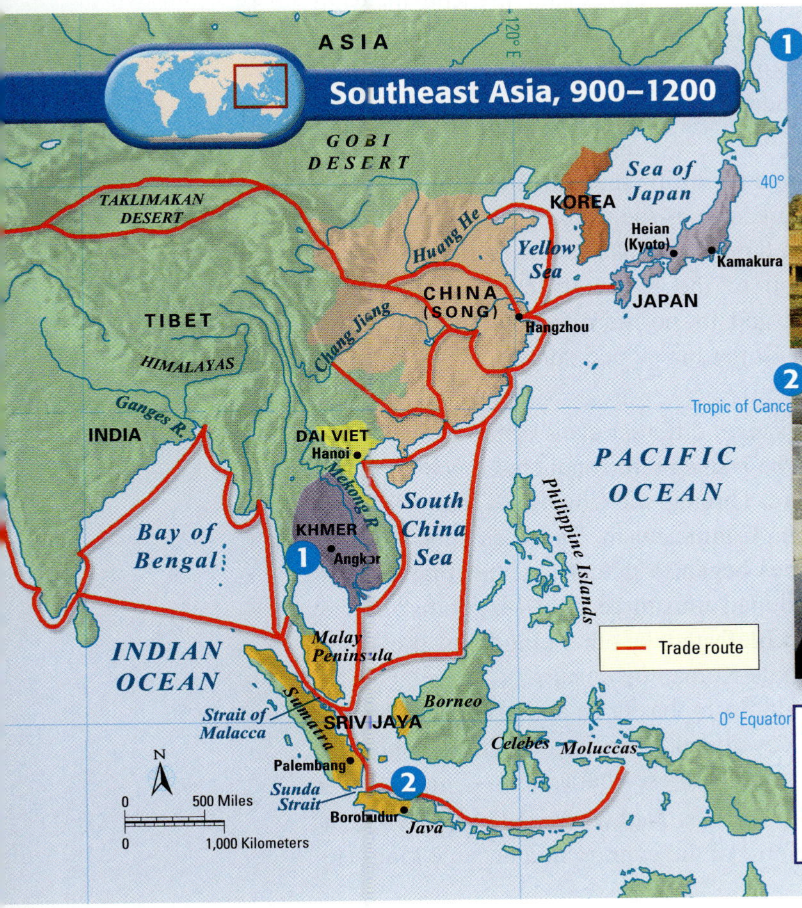

▲ Built in the 1100s, Angkor Wat is the world's largest religious structure.

◄ The temple at Borobudur has 92 statues of Buddha on its top level.

GEOGRAPHY SKILLBUILDER: Interpreting Maps

1. **Location** *Where is the Strait of Malacca and why was it important to trade?*
2. **Movement** *Name one way Chinese culture might have spread around Southeast Asia.*

▲ An uprising against the Chinese in A.D. 40 was led by Vietnamese women.

Srivijayas established their capital, Palembang, on Sumatra. Palembang became a great center of Buddhist learning, where Chinese monks could study instead of traveling to India.

Dai Viet The people of Southeast Asia least influenced by India were the Vietnamese. Located in the coastal region just south of China, Vietnam fell under Chinese domination. Around 100 B.C., during the mighty Han Dynasty, China took northern Vietnam. When China's Tang Dynasty weakened in the early A.D. 900s, Vietnam managed to break away. It became an independent kingdom, known as Dai Viet, in 939.

The Vietnamese absorbed many Chinese cultural influences, including Buddhism and ideas about government. However, they also preserved a strong spirit of independence and kept their own cultural identity. Vietnamese women, for example, traditionally had more freedom and influence than their Chinese counterparts. B

MAIN IDEA

Comparing

B How was Vietnam's culture influenced by Chinese culture?

Rulers of the Ly Dynasty (1009–1225) located their capital at Hanoi, on the Red River delta. They established a strong central government, encouraged agriculture and trade, and greatly improved road and river transportation. The changes made by the Ly continued to influence life in Vietnam long after they fell from power.

Korean Dynasties

According to a Korean legend, the first Korean state was founded by the hero Tan'gun, whose father was a god and whose mother was a bear. Another legend relates that it was founded by a royal descendant of the Chinese Shang Dynasty. These legends reflect two sides of Korean culture. On one hand, the Koreans were a distinct people who developed their own native traditions. On the other hand, their culture was shaped by Chinese influences from early dynastic times. However, like the Japanese, the Koreans adapted borrowed culture to fit their own needs and maintained a distinct way of life.

Geography of Korea Korea is located on a peninsula that juts out from the Asian mainland toward Japan. It is about the same size as the state of Utah. Korea's climate is hot in the summer and very cold in the winter. Like Japan, Korea is a mountainous land, and only a limited portion of the peninsula can be farmed. A mountainous barrier lies between Korea and its northern neighbor, Manchuria. Because of the mountains and the seas, Korea developed somewhat in isolation from its neighbors.

Early History In early Korea, as in early Japan, different clans or tribes controlled different parts of the country. In 108 B.C., the Han empire conquered much of Korea and established a military government there. Through the Chinese, Koreans learned about such ideas as centralized government, Confucianism, Buddhism, and writing. During Han rule, the various Korean tribes began to gather together into federations. Eventually, these federations developed into three rival kingdoms. In the mid-600s, one of these kingdoms, the Silla, defeated the other kingdoms, drove out the Chinese, and gained control of the whole Korean peninsula.

Under Silla rule, the Koreans built Buddhist monasteries and produced elegant stone and bronze sculptures. They also developed a writing system suitable for writing Korean phonetically though still using Chinese characters.

The Koryu Dynasty By the tenth century, Silla rule had weakened. Around 935, a rebel officer named Wang Kon gained control of the country and became king. He named his new dynasty Koryu. The **Koryu Dynasty** lasted four and a half centuries, from 935 to 1392.

The Koryu Dynasty modeled its central government after China's. It also established a civil service system. However, this system did not provide the social mobility for Koreans that it did for the Chinese. Koryu society was sharply divided between a landed aristocracy and the rest of the population, including the military, commoners, and slaves. Despite the examination system, the sons of nobles received the best positions, and these positions became hereditary. C

MAIN IDEA

Comparing

C How did the Koryu government compare with the early imperial government of Japan (page 340)?

The Koryu Dynasty faced a major threat in 1231, when the Mongols swept into Korea. They demanded a crushing tribute including 20,000 horses, clothing for 1 million soldiers, and many children and artisans, who were to be taken away as slaves. The harsh period of Mongol occupation lasted until the 1360s, when the Mongol Empire collapsed.

In 1392, a group of scholar-officials and military leaders overthrew the Koryu Dynasty and instituted land reforms. They established a new dynasty, called the Choson (or Yi) Dynasty, which would rule for 518 years.

Koryu Culture The Koryu period produced great achievements in Korean culture. Inspired by Song porcelain artists, Korean potters produced the much-admired celadon pottery, famous for its milky green glaze. Korean artisans produced one of the great treasures of the Buddhist world—many thousands of large wooden blocks for printing all the Buddhist scriptures. This set of blocks was destroyed by the Mongols, but the disaster sparked a national effort to re-create them. The more than 80,000 blocks in the new set remain in Korea today.

Connect *to* Today

Two Koreas

Since the end of World War II, Korea has been arbitrarily divided into two countries—communist North Korea and democratic South Korea. For years, many Koreans longed for their country to be reunited. Hopes for such a day rose in 2000 when the presidents of the two nations sat down to discuss reunification. In 2002, however, North Korea announced that it was developing nuclear weapons and would use them against South Korea if necessary. This greatly dimmed people's hopes for one Korea.

INTEGRATED TECHNOLOGY

INTERNET ACTIVITY Write a news story outlining the latest developments in relations between the two Koreas. Go to **classzone.com** for your research.

NEW YORK CORE CURRICULUM REVIEW

TERMS & NAMES 1. For each term or name, write a sentence explaining its significance.

- Khmer Empire
- Angkor Wat
- Koryu Dynasty

USING YOUR NOTES

2. What common themes do you notice about the mainland kingdoms? about the island kingdoms?

Kingdom	Notes
Khmer	
Dai Viet	
Korea	
Sailendra	
Srivijaya	

MAIN IDEAS

3. On what was Khmer prosperity based?
4. How did Srivijaya become wealthy and powerful?
5. Why are there two sides to the development of Korean culture?

CRITICAL THINKING & WRITING

6. **RECOGNIZING EFFECTS** How did geography influence the history and culture of Southeast Asia and of Korea? Illustrate your answer with examples.
7. **COMPARING** In what ways did the cultural development of Vietnam resemble that of Korea?
8. **DRAWING CONCLUSIONS** Why do you think that of all the cultures of Southeast Asia, Vietnam was the least influenced by India?
9. **WRITING ACTIVITY** RELIGIOUS AND ETHICAL SYSTEMS Create an **annotated map** showing how Hinduism and Buddhism entered Southeast Asia from China and India.

CONNECT TO TODAY **CREATING A TRAVEL BROCHURE**

Conduct research to find information about Angkor Wat or the Buddhist temple at Borobudur. Use your findings to create a one-page **illustrated travel brochure.**

Chapter 12 Assessment

TERMS & NAMES

For each term or name below, briefly explain its connection to East Asia between 600 and 1350.

1. Tang Taizong
2. Wu Zhao
3. Genghis Khan
4. Kublai Khan
5. Marco Polo
6. Shinto
7. Angkor Wat
8. Koryu Dynasty

MAIN IDEAS

Tang and Song China Section 1 (pages 323–329)

9. Why was the reform of the civil service under the Tang so significant?
10. How did changes in agriculture support other developments during the Song Dynasty?

The Mongol Conquests Section 2 (pages 330–334)

11. Why were nomads and settled peoples sometimes in conflict?
12. What were the most important accomplishments of the Mongol Empire?

The Mongol Empire Section 3 (pages 335–338)

13. Explain how Kublai Khan treated his Chinese subjects.
14. How did Kublai Khan encourage trade?

Feudal Powers in Japan Section 4 (pages 339–343)

15. Describe the impact of Chinese culture on Japan.
16. How did feudalism develop in Japan?

Kingdoms of Southeast Asia and Korea Section 5 (pages 344–347)

17. Describe the two sources of prosperity for Southeast Asian empires.
18. What were the major accomplishments of the Koryu Dynasty?

CRITICAL THINKING

1. USING YOUR NOTES

Create diagrams to identify two results from these developments: (a) completion of the Grand Canal under the Sui, and (b) the use of compass at sea.

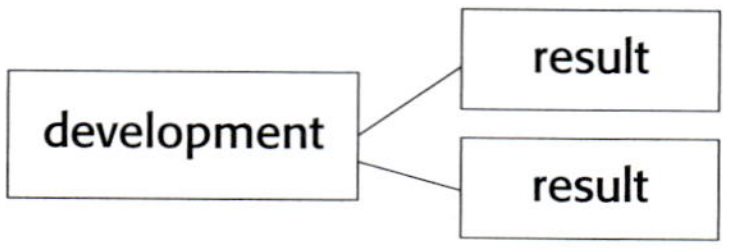

2. HYPOTHESIZING

EMPIRE BUILDING How might history have been different if the Mongols had conquered all or most of Europe? Discuss the possible immediate and long-term consequences for Europe and the rest of the Mongol Empire.

3. IDENTIFYING PROBLEMS AND SOLUTIONS

This chapter describes the rise and fall of three Chinese dynasties. What recurring patterns appear in the decline of these dynasties? What advice, based on those patterns, might you give a Chinese emperor?

4. DRAWING CONCLUSIONS

CULTURAL INTERACTION How does Japanese adaptation of Buddhism illustrate the process of selective cultural borrowing?

VISUAL SUMMARY

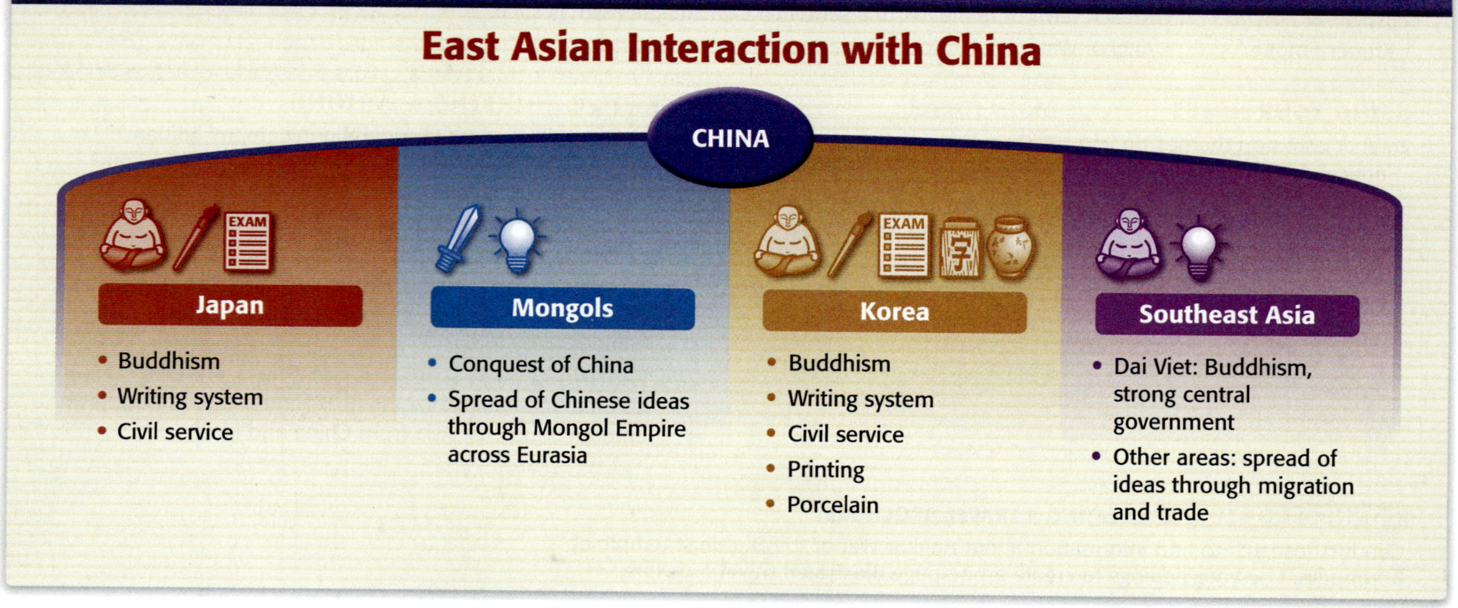

Use the quotation—part of a message sent by Kublai Khan to Japan's imperial court—and your knowledge of world history to answer questions 1 and 2.
Additional Test Practice, pp. S1–S33.

PRIMARY SOURCE

The Emperor of the Great Mongols addresses the King of Japan as follows: . . . I am sending you my envoys bearing my personal message. It is my hope that the communication between our two countries be opened and maintained and that our mutual friendship be established. A sage regards the whole world as one family; how can different countries be considered one family if there is not friendly communication between them? Is force really necessary to establish friendly relations? I hope that you will give this matter your most careful attention.

SUNG LIEN, quoted in *The Essence of Chinese Civilization*

1 What is Kublai Khan asking of the Japanese?
(1) to surrender without a fight
(2) to exchange prisoners of war
(3) to establish diplomatic relations with the Mongols
(4) to join the Mongols in a war against Europe

2 Which of the following best describes the tone of the message?
(1) mildly threatening
(2) funny
(3) extremely violent
(4) pleading

Use the map and your knowledge of world history to answer question 3.

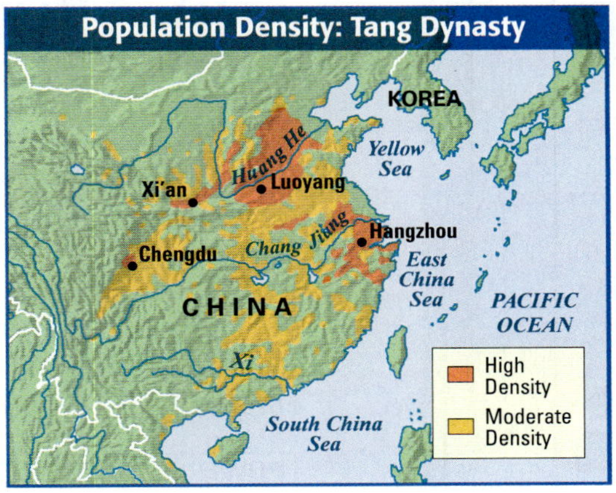

3 During the Tang Dynasty, which areas of China were most densely populated?
(1) east and north
(2) west and south
(3) central China
(4) far west

INTEGRATED TECHNOLOGY

TEST PRACTICE Go to **classzone.com**
- Diagnostic tests
- Tutorials
- Strategies
- Additional practice

ALTERNATIVE ASSESSMENT

1. Interact *with* History

Through the activity on page 322, you looked at the importance of Chinese inventions in world history. (After reading the chapter, you may have recognized that this imaginary situation was inspired by the travels of Marco Polo.) Now that you have read the chapter, consider the impact of Chinese inventions and how they spread. Would you now choose a different invention? Is there any other invention you would choose instead of those on page 322? Discuss these questions with a small group.

2. WRITING ABOUT HISTORY

RELIGIOUS AND ETHICAL SYSTEMS Write a **report** on the Japanese religion of Shinto. Illustrate your report with photographs and sketches. In your report, consider the following:
- essential Shinto beliefs
- development of Shinto, especially the influence of Buddhism and Confucianism
- Shinto rituals and shrines

INTEGRATED TECHNOLOGY

NetExplorations: Chinese Healing Arts

Go to *NetExplorations* at **classzone.com** to learn more about Chinese healing arts. Use the Internet to learn how Chinese and Western doctors treat a variety of common illnesses and how long these treatments have been common practice. You may want to include the following illnesses in your research:
- the common cold
- influenza
- asthma
- arthritis

Create a table comparing Chinese and Western treatments for these illnesses. Display the table online or in the classroom.

CHAPTER 13

European Middle Ages, 500–1200

Previewing Main Ideas

EMPIRE BUILDING In western Europe, the Roman Empire had broken into many small kingdoms. During the Middle Ages, Charlemagne and Otto the Great tried to revive the idea of empire. Both allied with the Church.

Geography *Study the maps. What were the six major kingdoms in western Europe about A.D. 500?*

POWER AND AUTHORITY Weak rulers and the decline of central authority led to a feudal system in which local lords with large estates assumed power. This led to struggles over power with the Church.

Geography *Study the time line and the map. The ruler of what kingdom was crowned emperor by Pope Leo III?*

RELIGIOUS AND ETHICAL SYSTEMS During the Middle Ages, the Church was a unifying force. It shaped people's beliefs and guided their daily lives. Most Europeans at this time shared a common bond of faith.

Geography *Find Rome, the seat of the Roman Catholic Church, on the map. In what kingdom was it located after the fall of the Roman Empire in A.D. 476?*

NEW YORK CORE CURRICULUM FOCUS

- Charlemagne created the Frankish Empire by uniting many Germanic kingdoms.
- Feudalism established a social structure based on rights and obligations.

INTEGRATED TECHNOLOGY

eEdition
- Interactive Maps
- Interactive Visuals
- Interactive Primary Sources

INTERNET RESOURCES
Go to **classzone.com** for:
- Research Links
- Internet Activities
- Primary Sources
- Chapter Quiz
- Maps
- Test Practice
- Current Events

EUROPE

511 Clovis unites Franks under Christian rule.

732 ◀ Charles Martel stops Muslim invasion. (Charles Martel and advisers)

800 Pope Leo III crowns the Frankish king Charlemagne emperor.

500 — 700

WORLD

527 Justinian becomes Byzantine emperor.

750 Abbasids in Persia take control of the Muslim Empire.

800 Empire of Ghana thrives in West Africa.

843
Treaty of Verdun divides Charlemagne's empire.

900s
Outside invasions spur growth of feudalism. (Viking helmet) ▶

962
Otto the Great becomes emperor.

1190
◀ Holy Roman Empire weakens.

900 **1100**

900
Classic period of Mayan civilization in Central America ends.

960
Song Dynasty begins in China. (poem on silk) ▶

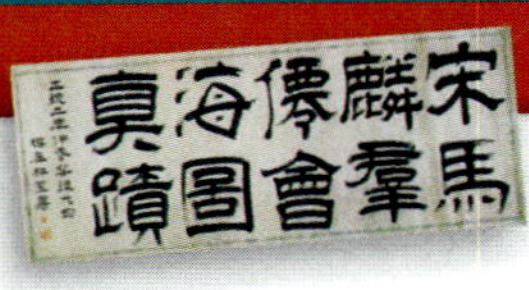

1185
Kamakura Shogunate rules Japan.

Interact *with* History

What freedoms would you give up for protection?

You are living in the countryside of western Europe during the 1100s. Like about 90 percent of the population, you are a peasant working the land. Your family's hut is located in a small village on your lord's estate. The lord provides all your basic needs, including housing, food, and protection. Especially important is his protection from invaders who repeatedly strike Europe.

1. For safety, peasants retreat behind the castle walls during attacks.
2. Peasants owe their lord two or three days' labor every week farming his land.
3. This peasant feels that the right to stay on his lord's land is more important than his freedom to leave.
4. Peasants cannot marry without their lord's consent.

EXAMINING *the* ISSUES

- **What is secure about your world?**
- **How is your life limited?**

As a class, discuss these questions. In your discussion, think about other people who have limited power over their lives. As you read about the lot of European peasants in this chapter, see how their living arrangements determine their role in society and shape their beliefs.

Charlemagne Unites Germanic Kingdoms

CONNECT TO THE NEW YORK STATE CORE CURRICULUM

Unit 2.F.1. Human and physical geography
Unit 2.F.2. Frankish Empire–Charlemagne

TERMS & NAMES

- Middle Ages
- Franks
- monastery
- secular
- Carolingian Dynasty
- Charlemagne

SETTING THE STAGE The gradual decline of the Roman Empire ushered in an era of European history called the **Middle Ages**, or the medieval period. It spanned the years from about 500 to 1500. During these centuries, a new society slowly emerged. It had roots in: (1) the classical heritage of Rome, (2) the beliefs of the Roman Catholic Church, and (3) the customs of various Germanic tribes.

TAKING NOTES
Following Chronological Order Note important events in the unification of the Germanic kingdoms.

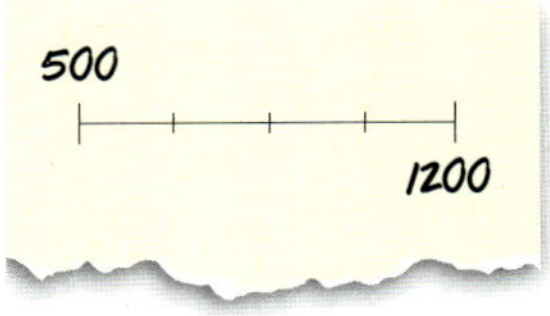

Invasions of Western Europe

In the fifth century, Germanic invaders overran the western half of the Roman Empire (see map on page 351). Repeated invasions and constant warfare caused a series of changes that altered the economy, government, and culture:

- **Disruption of Trade** Merchants faced invasions from both land and sea. Their businesses collapsed. The breakdown of trade destroyed Europe's cities as economic centers. Money became scarce.
- **Downfall of Cities** With the fall of the Roman Empire, cities were abandoned as centers of administration.
- **Population Shifts** As Roman centers of trade and government collapsed, nobles retreated to the rural areas. Roman cities were left without strong leadership. Other city dwellers also fled to the countryside, where they grew their own food. The population of western Europe became mostly rural.

The Decline of Learning The Germanic invaders who stormed Rome could not read or write. Among Romans themselves, the level of learning sank sharply as more and more families left for rural areas. Few people except priests and other church officials were literate. Knowledge of Greek, long important in Roman culture, was almost lost. Few people could read Greek works of literature, science, and philosophy. The Germanic tribes, though, had a rich oral tradition of songs and legends. But they had no written language.

Loss of a Common Language As German-speaking peoples mixed with the Roman population, Latin changed. While it was still an official language, it was no longer understood. Different dialects developed as new words and phrases became part of everyday speech. By the 800s, French, Spanish, and other Roman-based languages had evolved from Latin. The development of various languages mirrored the continued breakup of a once-unified empire.

Germanic Kingdoms Emerge

In the years of upheaval between 400 and 600, small Germanic kingdoms replaced Roman provinces. The borders of those kingdoms changed constantly with the fortunes of war. But the Church as an institution survived the fall of the Roman Empire. During this time of political chaos, the Church provided order and security.

The Concept of Government Changes Along with shifting boundaries, the entire concept of government changed. Loyalty to public government and written law had unified Roman society. Family ties and personal loyalty, rather than citizenship in a public state, held Germanic society together. Unlike Romans, Germanic peoples lived in small communities that were governed by unwritten rules and traditions.

Every Germanic chief led a band of warriors who had pledged their loyalty to him. In peacetime, these followers lived in their lord's hall. He gave them food, weapons, and treasure. In battle, warriors fought to the death at their lord's side. They considered it a disgrace to outlive him. But Germanic warriors felt no obligation to obey a king they did not even know. Nor would they obey an official sent to collect taxes or administer justice in the name of an emperor they had never met. The Germanic stress on personal ties made it impossible to establish orderly government for large territories.

Clovis Rules the Franks In the Roman province of Gaul (mainly what is now France and Switzerland), a Germanic people called the **Franks** held power. Their leader was Clovis (KLOH•vihs). He would bring Christianity to the region. According to legend, his wife, Clothilde, had urged him to convert to her faith, Christianity. In 496, Clovis led his warriors against another Germanic army. Fearing defeat, he appealed to the Christian God. "For I have called on my gods," he prayed, "but I find they are far from my aid. . . . Now I call on Thee. I long to believe in Thee. Only, please deliver me from my enemies." The tide of the battle shifted and the Franks won. Afterward, Clovis and 3,000 of his warriors asked a bishop to baptize them.

The Church in Rome welcomed Clovis's conversion and supported his military campaigns against other Germanic peoples. By 511, Clovis had united the Franks into one kingdom. The strategic alliance between Clovis's Frankish kingdom and the Church marked the start of a partnership between two powerful forces.

▼ Illuminated manuscripts, such as the one below, were usually the work of monks.

Germans Adopt Christianity

Politics played a key role in spreading Christianity. By 600, the Church, with the help of Frankish rulers, had converted many Germanic peoples. These new converts had settled in Rome's former lands. Missionaries also spread Christianity. These religious travelers often risked their lives to bring religious beliefs to other lands. During the 300s and 400s, they worked among the Germanic and Celtic groups that bordered the Roman Empire. In southern Europe, the fear of coastal attacks by Muslims also spurred many people to become Christians in the 600s.

Monasteries, Convents, and Manuscripts To adapt to rural conditions, the Church built religious communities called **monasteries**. There, Christian men called monks gave up their private possessions and devoted their lives to serving God. Women who followed this way of life were called nuns and lived in convents.

History Makers

Benedict
480?–543

At 15, Benedict left school and hiked up to the Sabine Hills, where he lived in a cave as a hermit. After learning about Benedict's deep religious conviction, a group of monks persuaded him to lead their monastery. Benedict declared:

> *We must prepare our hearts and bodies for combat under holy obedience to the divine commandments. . . . We are therefore going to establish a school in which one may learn the service of the Lord.*

In his book describing the rules for monastic life, Benedict emphasized a balance between work and study. Such guidelines turned monasteries into centers of stability and learning.

Scholastica
480?–543

Scholastica is thought to be the twin sister of Benedict. She was born into a wealthy Italian family in the late Roman Empire. Little is known of her early life, except that she and Benedict were inseparable.

Like her brother, Scholastica devoted her life to the Church. She is thought to have been the abbess of a convent near the monastery founded by Benedict and is considered the first nun of the Benedictine order. She was a strong influence on her brother as he developed rules that guide Benedictine monasteries to this day. They died in the same year and are buried in one grave.

INTEGRATED TECHNOLOGY

RESEARCH LINKS For more on Benedict and Scholastica, go to **classzone.com**

Around 520, an Italian monk named Benedict began writing a book describing a strict yet practical set of rules for monasteries. Benedict's sister, Scholastica (skuh•LAS•tik•uh), headed a convent and adapted the same rules for women. These guidelines became a model for many other religious communities in western Europe. Monks and nuns devoted their lives to prayer and good works.

Monasteries also became Europe's best-educated communities. Monks opened schools, maintained libraries, and copied books. In 731, the Venerable Bede, an English monk, wrote a history of England. Scholars still consider it the best historical work of the early Middle Ages. In the 600s and 700s, monks made beautiful copies of religious writings, decorated with ornate letters and brilliant pictures. These illuminated manuscripts preserved at least part of Rome's intellectual heritage. (A)

MAIN IDEA

Making Inferences

(A) What role did monasteries play during this time of chaos?

Papal Power Expands Under Gregory I In 590, Gregory I, also called Gregory the Great, became pope. As head of the Church in Rome, Gregory broadened the authority of the papacy, or pope's office, beyond its spiritual role. Under Gregory, the papacy also became a **secular**, or worldly, power involved in politics. The pope's palace was the center of Roman government. Gregory used church revenues to raise armies, repair roads, and help the poor. He also negotiated peace treaties with invaders such as the Lombards.

According to Gregory, the region from Italy to England and from Spain to Germany fell under his responsibility. Gregory strengthened the vision of Christendom. It was a spiritual kingdom fanning out from Rome to the most distant churches. This idea of a churchly kingdom, ruled by a pope, would be a central theme of the Middle Ages. Meanwhile, secular rulers expanded their political kingdoms.

An Empire Evolves

After the Roman Empire dissolved, small kingdoms sprang up all over Europe. For example, England splintered into seven tiny kingdoms. Some of them were no

GEOGRAPHY SKILLBUILDER: Interpreting Maps

1. **Region** *By 814, what was the extent of Charlemagne's empire (north to south, east to west)?*
2. **Region** *Based on the map, why did the Treaty of Verdun signal the decline of Charlemagne's empire?*

larger than the state of Connecticut. The Franks controlled the largest and strongest of Europe's kingdoms, the area that was formerly the Roman province of Gaul. When the Franks' first Christian king, Clovis, died in 511, he had extended Frankish rule over most of what is now France.

Charles Martel Emerges By 700, an official known as the *major domo,* or mayor of the palace, had become the most powerful person in the Frankish kingdom. Officially, he had charge of the royal household and estates. Unofficially, he led armies and made policy. In effect, he ruled the kingdom.

The mayor of the palace in 719, Charles Martel (Charles the Hammer), held more power than the king. Charles Martel extended the Franks' reign to the north, south, and east. He also defeated Muslim raiders from Spain at the Battle of Tours in 732. This battle was highly significant for Christian Europeans. If the Muslims had won, western Europe might have become part of the Muslim Empire. Charles Martel's victory at Tours made him a Christian hero.

At his death, Charles Martel passed on his power to his son, Pepin the Short. Pepin wanted to be king. He shrewdly cooperated with the pope. On behalf of the Church, Pepin agreed to fight the Lombards, who had invaded central Italy and threatened Rome. In exchange, the pope anointed Pepin "king by the grace of God." Thus began the **Carolingian** (KAR•uh•LIHN•juhn) **Dynasty**, the family that would rule the Franks from 751 to 987.

Charlemagne Becomes Emperor

Pepin the Short died in 768. He left a greatly strengthened Frankish kingdom to his two sons, Carloman and Charles. After Carloman's death in 771, Charles, who was known as **Charlemagne** (SHAHR•luh•MAYN), or Charles the Great, ruled the kingdom. An imposing figure, he stood six feet four inches tall. His admiring secretary, a monk named Einhard, described Charlemagne's achievements:

PRIMARY SOURCE

[Charlemagne] was the most potent prince with the greatest skill and success in different countries during the forty-seven years of his reign. Great and powerful as was the realm of Franks, Karl [Charlemagne] received from his father Pippin, he nevertheless so splendidly enlarged it . . . that he almost doubled it.

EINHARD, *Life of Charlemagne*

Charlemagne Extends Frankish Rule Charlemagne built an empire greater than any known since ancient Rome. Each summer he led his armies against enemies that surrounded his kingdom. He fought Muslims in Spain and tribes from other

Germanic kingdoms. He conquered new lands to both the south and the east. Through these conquests, Charlemagne spread Christianity. He reunited western Europe for the first time since the Roman Empire. By 800, Charlemagne's empire was larger than the Byzantine Empire. He had become the most powerful king in western Europe.

In 800, Charlemagne traveled to Rome to crush an unruly mob that had attacked the pope. In gratitude, Pope Leo III crowned him emperor. The coronation was historic. A pope had claimed the political right to confer the title "Roman Emperor" on a European king. This event signaled the joining of Germanic power, the Church, and the heritage of the Roman Empire.

▲ Emperor Charlemagne

Charlemagne Leads a Revival Charlemagne strengthened his royal power by limiting the authority of the nobles. To govern his empire, he sent out royal agents. They made sure that the powerful landholders, called counts, governed their counties justly. Charlemagne regularly visited every part of his kingdom. He also kept a close watch on the management of his huge estates—the source of Carolingian wealth and power. One of his greatest accomplishments was the encouragement of learning. He surrounded himself with English, German, Italian, and Spanish scholars. For his many sons and daughters and other children at the court, Charlemagne opened a palace school. He also ordered monasteries to open schools to train future monks and priests. **B**

MAIN IDEA

Drawing Conclusions

B What were Charlemagne's most notable achievements?

Charlemagne's Heirs A year before Charlemagne died in 814, he crowned his only surviving son, Louis the Pious, as emperor. Louis was a devoutly religious man but an ineffective ruler. He left three sons: Lothair (loh•THAIR), Charles the Bald, and Louis the German. They fought one another for control of the Empire. In 843, the brothers signed the Treaty of Verdun, dividing the empire into three kingdoms. As a result, Carolingian kings lost power and central authority broke down. The lack of strong rulers led to a new system of governing and landholding—feudalism.

NEW YORK CORE CURRICULUM REVIEW

TERMS & NAMES 1. For each term or name, write a sentence explaining its significance.

- Middle Ages
- Franks
- monastery
- secular
- Carolingian Dynasty
- Charlemagne

USING YOUR NOTES

2. What was the most important event in the unification of the Germanic kingdoms? Why?

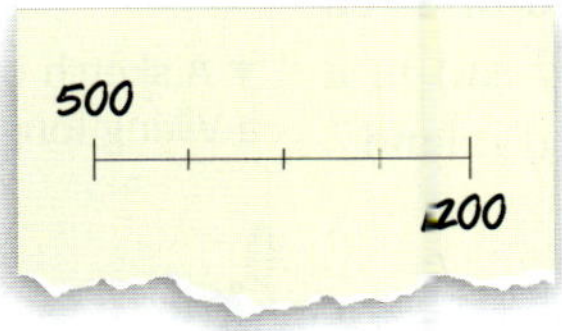

MAIN IDEAS

3. What were three roots of medieval culture in western Europe?
4. What are three ways that civilization in western Europe declined after the Roman Empire fell?
5. What was the most important achievement of Pope Gregory I?

CRITICAL THINKING & WRITING

6. **DRAWING CONCLUSIONS** How was the relationship between a Frankish king and the pope beneficial to both?
7. **RECOGNIZING EFFECTS** Why was Charles Martel's victory at the Battle of Tours so important for Christianity?
8. **EVALUATING** What was Charlemagne's greatest achievement? Give reasons for your answer.
9. **WRITING ACTIVITY** EMPIRE BUILDING How does Charlemagne's empire in medieval Europe compare with the Roman Empire? Support your opinions in a three-paragraph **expository essay**.

INTEGRATED TECHNOLOGY **INTERNET ACTIVITY**

Use the Internet to locate a medieval monastery that remains today in western Europe. Write a two-paragraph **history** of the monastery and include an illustration.

INTERNET KEYWORD
Medieval monasteries

2

Feudalism in Europe

CONNECT TO THE NEW YORK STATE CORE CURRICULUM

Unit 2.F.3. Manorialism
Unit 2.F.4.a. Social hierarchy and stratification

TERMS & NAMES

- lord
- fief
- vassal
- knight
- serf
- manor
- tithe

SETTING THE STAGE After the Treaty of Verdun, Charlemagne's three feuding grandsons broke up the kingdom even further. Part of this territory also became a battleground as new waves of invaders attacked Europe. The political turmoil and constant warfare led to the rise of European feudalism, which, as you read in Chapter 2, is a political and economic system based on land ownership and personal loyalty.

TAKING NOTES
Analyzing Causes and Recognizing Effects Use a web diagram to show the causes and effects of feudalism.

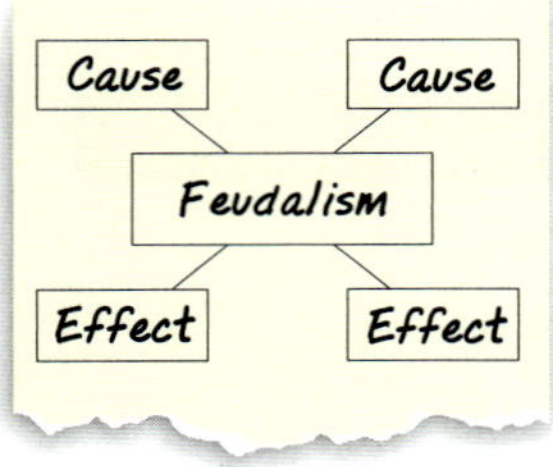

Invaders Attack Western Europe

From about 800 to 1000, invasions destroyed the Carolingian Empire. Muslim invaders from the south seized Sicily and raided Italy. In 846, they sacked Rome. Magyar invaders struck from the east. Like the earlier Huns and Avars, they terrorized Germany and Italy. And from the north came the fearsome Vikings.

The Vikings Invade from the North The Vikings set sail from Scandinavia (SKAN•duh•NAY•vee•uh), a wintry, wooded region in Northern Europe. (The region is now the countries of Denmark, Norway, and Sweden.) The Vikings, also called Northmen or Norsemen, were a Germanic people. They worshiped warlike gods and took pride in nicknames like Eric Bloodaxe and Thorfinn Skullsplitter.

The Vikings carried out their raids with terrifying speed. Clutching swords and heavy wooden shields, these helmeted seafarers beached their ships, struck quickly, and then moved out to sea again. They were gone before locals could mount a defense. Viking warships were awe-inspiring. The largest of these long ships held 300 warriors, who took turns rowing the ship's 72 oars. The prow of each ship swept grandly upward, often ending with the carved head of a sea monster. A ship might weigh 20 tons when fully loaded. Yet, it could sail in a mere three feet of water. Rowing up shallow creeks, the Vikings looted inland villages and monasteries.

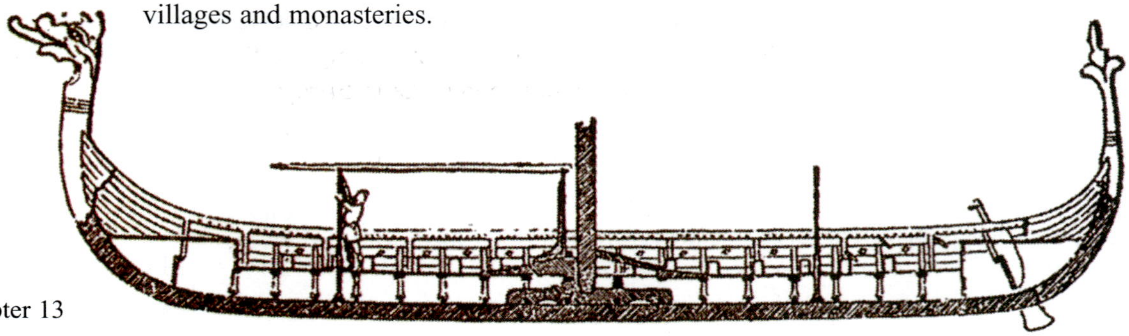

▼ A sketch of a Viking longboat

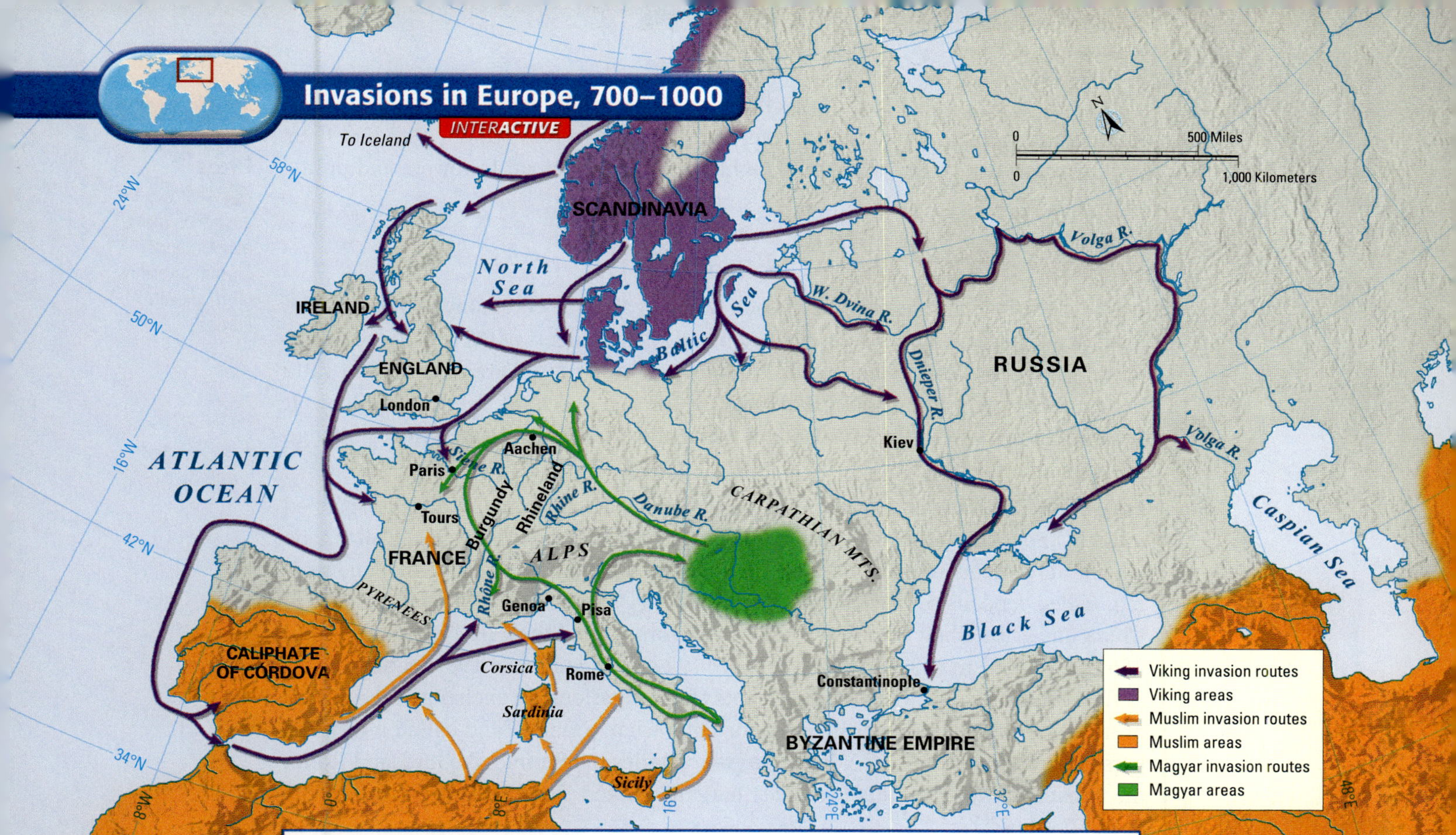

GEOGRAPHY SKILLBUILDER: Interpreting Maps

1. **Location** *What lands did the Vikings raid?*
2. **Movement** *Why were the Viking, Magyar, and Muslim invasions so threatening to Europe?*

The Vikings were not only warriors but also traders, farmers, and explorers. They ventured far beyond western Europe. Vikings journeyed down rivers into the heart of Russia, to Constantinople, and even across the icy waters of the North Atlantic. A Viking explorer named Leif (leef) Ericson reached North America around 1000, almost 500 years before Columbus. About the same time, the Viking reign of terror in Europe faded away. As Vikings gradually accepted Christianity, they stopped raiding monasteries. Also, a warming trend in Europe's climate made farming easier in Scandinavia. As a result, fewer Scandinavians adopted the seafaring life of Viking warriors.

Magyars and Muslims Attack from the East and South As Viking invasions declined, Europe became the target of new assaults. The Magyars, a group of nomadic people, attacked from the east, from what is now Hungary. Superb horsemen, the Magyars swept across the plains of the Danube River and invaded western Europe in the late 800s. They attacked isolated villages and monasteries. They overran northern Italy and reached as far west as the Rhineland and Burgundy. The Magyars did not settle conquered land. Instead, they took captives to sell as slaves.

The Muslims struck from the south. They began their encroachments from their strongholds in North Africa, invading through what are now Italy and Spain. In the 600s and 700s, the Muslim plan was to conquer and settle in Europe. By the 800s and 900s, their goal was also to plunder. Because the Muslims were expert seafarers, they were able to attack settlements on the Atlantic and Mediterranean coasts. They also struck as far inland as Switzerland.

The invasions by Vikings, Magyars, and Muslims caused widespread disorder and suffering. Most western Europeans lived in constant danger. Kings could not effectively defend their lands from invasion. As a result, people no longer looked to a central ruler for security. Instead, many turned to local rulers who had their own armies. Any leader who could fight the invaders gained followers and political strength. (A)

MAIN IDEA

Recognizing Effects

(A) What was the impact of Viking, Magyar, and Muslim invasions on medieval Europe?

A New Social Order: Feudalism

In 911, two former enemies faced each other in a peace ceremony. Rollo was the head of a Viking army. Rollo and his men had been plundering the rich Seine (sayn) River valley for years. Charles the Simple was the king of France but held little power. Charles granted the Viking leader a huge piece of French territory. It became known as Northmen's land, or Normandy. In return, Rollo swore a pledge of loyalty to the king.

Feudalism Structures Society The worst years of the invaders' attacks spanned roughly 850 to 950. During this time, rulers and warriors like Charles and Rollo made similar agreements in many parts of Europe. The system of governing and landholding, called feudalism, had emerged in Europe. A similar feudal system existed in China under the Zhou Dynasty, which ruled from around the 11th century B.C. until 256 B.C. Feudalism in Japan began in A.D. 1192 and ended in the 19th century.

The feudal system was based on rights and obligations. In exchange for military protection and other services, a **lord**, or landowner, granted land called a **fief**. The person receiving a fief was called a **vassal**. Charles the Simple, the lord, and Rollo, the vassal, showed how this two-sided bargain worked. Feudalism depended on the control of land.

The Feudal Pyramid The structure of feudal society was much like a pyramid. At the peak reigned the king. Next came the most powerful vassals—wealthy landowners such as nobles and bishops. Serving beneath these vassals were knights. **Knights** were mounted horsemen who pledged to defend their lords' lands in exchange for fiefs. At the base of the pyramid were landless peasants who toiled in the fields. (See Analyzing Key Concepts on next page.)

Vocabulary
Status is social ranking.

Social Classes Are Well Defined In the feudal system, status determined a person's prestige and power. Medieval writers classified people into three groups: those who fought (nobles and knights), those who prayed (men and women of the Church), and those who worked (the peasants). Social class was usually inherited.

In Europe in the Middle Ages, the vast majority of people were peasants. Most peasants were serfs. **Serfs** were people who could not lawfully leave the place where they were born. Though bound to the land, serfs were not slaves. Their lords could not sell or buy them. But what their labor produced belonged to the lord.

Manors: The Economic Side of Feudalism

The **manor** was the lord's estate. During the Middle Ages, the manor system was the basic economic arrangement. The manor system rested on a set of rights and obligations between a lord and his serfs. The lord provided the serfs with housing, farmland, and protection from bandits. In return, serfs tended the lord's lands, cared for his animals, and performed other tasks to maintain the estate. Peasant women shared in the farm work with their husbands. All peasants, whether free or serf, owed the lord certain duties. These included at least a few days of labor each week and a certain portion of their grain.

A Self-Contained World Peasants rarely traveled more than 25 miles from their own manor. By standing in the center of a plowed field, they could see their entire world at a glance. A manor usually covered only a few square miles of land. It

> Analyzing Key Concepts

Feudalism

Feudalism was a political system in which nobles were granted the use of land that legally belonged to the king. In return, the nobles agreed to give their loyalty and military services to the king. Feudalism developed not only in Europe but also in countries like Japan.

European Feudalism

Japanese Feudalism

INTEGRATED TECHNOLOGY

RESEARCH LINKS For more on feudalism, go to **classzone.com**

> DATA FILE

FEUDAL FACTS AND FIGURES

- In the 14th century, before the bubonic plague struck, the population of France was probably between 10 and 21 million people.
- In feudal times, the building of a cathedral took between 50 to 150 years.
- In feudal times, dukedoms were large estates ruled by a duke. In 1216, the Duke of Anjou had 34 knights, the Duke of Brittany had 36 knights, and the Count of Flanders had 47 knights.
- In the 14th century, the nobility in France made up about 1 percent of the population.
- The word *feudalism* comes from the Latin word *feudum*, meaning *fief.*
- The Japanese word *daimyo* comes from the words *dai*, meaning "large," and *myo* (shorten from myoden), meaning "name-land" or "private land."

* *SOURCES: A Distant Mirror* by Barbara Tuchman; *Encyclopaedia Britannica*

Connect *to* Today

1. **Comparing** What are the similarities between feudalism in Europe and feudalism in Japan?

   See Skillbuilder Handbook, Page R7.

2. **Forming and Supporting Opinions** Today, does the United States have a system of social classes? Support your answer with evidence.

History *in* Depth

The Medieval Manor

The medieval manor varied in size. The illustration to the right is a plan of a typical English manor.

1. **Manor House**
   The dwelling place of the lord and his family and their servants
2. **Village Church**
   Site of both religious services and public meetings
3. **Peasant Cottages**
   Where the peasants lived
4. **Lord's Demesne**
   Fields owned by the lord and worked by the peasants
5. **Peasant Crofts**
   Gardens that belonged to the peasants
6. **Mill**
   Water-powered mill for grinding grain
7. **Common Pasture**
   Common area for grazing animals
8. **Woodland**
   Forests provided wood for fuel.

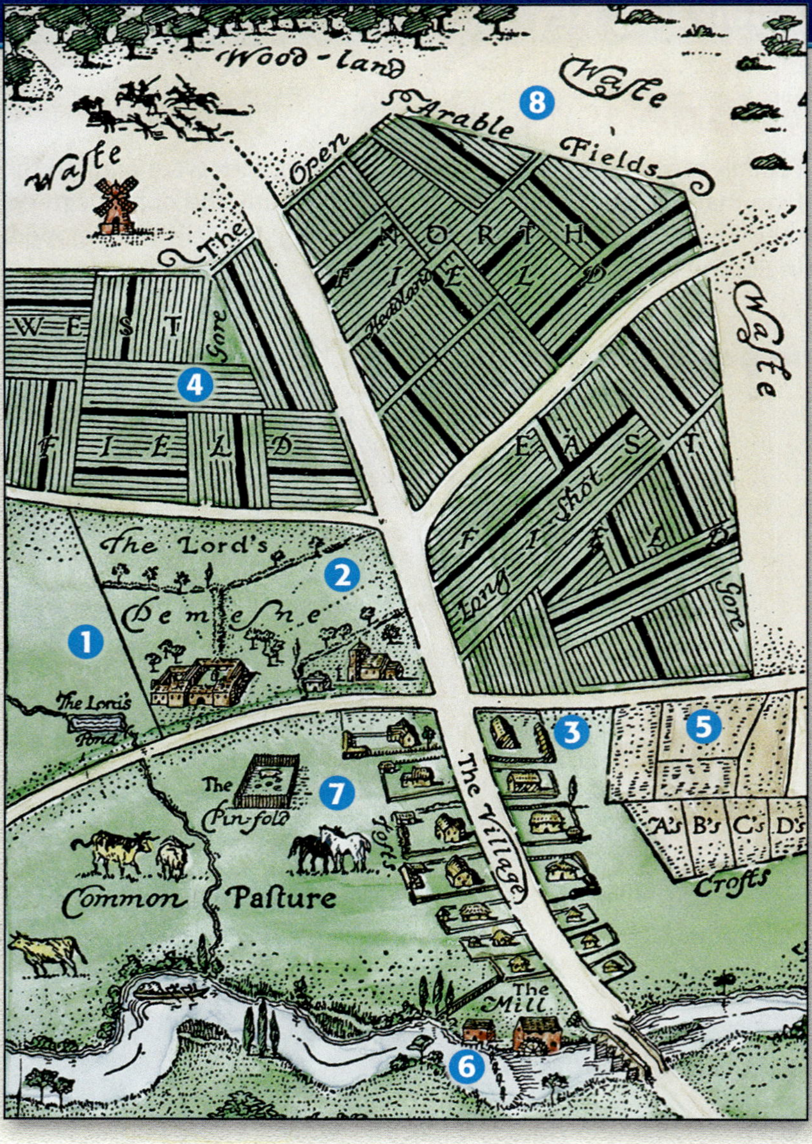

typically consisted of the lord's manor house, a church, and workshops. Generally, 15 to 30 families lived in the village on a manor. Fields, pastures, and woodlands surrounded the village. Sometimes a stream wound through the manor. Streams and ponds provided fish, which served as an important source of food. The mill for grinding the grain was often located on the stream.

The manor was largely a self-sufficient community. The serfs and peasants raised or produced nearly everything that they and their lord needed for daily life—crops, milk and cheese, fuel, cloth, leather goods, and lumber. The only outside purchases were salt, iron, and a few unusual objects such as millstones. These were huge stones used to grind flour. Crops grown on the manor usually included grains, such as wheat, rye, barley, and oats, and vegetables, such as peas, beans, onions, and beets. **B**

MAIN IDEA

Analyzing Causes

B How might the decline of trade during the early Middle Ages have contributed to the self-sufficiency of the manor system?

The Harshness of Manor Life For the privilege of living on the lord's land, peasants paid a high price. They paid a tax on all grain ground in the lord's mill. Any attempt to avoid taxes by baking bread elsewhere was treated as a crime. Peasants also paid a tax on marriage. Weddings could take place only with the lord's consent. After all these payments to the lord, peasant families owed the village priest a **tithe**, or church tax. A tithe represented one-tenth of their income.

Serfs lived in crowded cottages, close to their neighbors. The cottages had only one or two rooms. If there were two rooms, the main room was used for cooking, eating, and household activities. The second was the family bedroom. Peasants warmed their dirt-floor houses by bringing pigs inside. At night, the family huddled on a pile of straw that often crawled with insects. Peasants' simple diet consisted mainly of vegetables, coarse brown bread, grain, cheese, and soup.

Piers Plowman, written by William Langland in 1362, reveals the hard life of English peasants:

MAIN IDEA

Analyzing Primary Sources

C What problems did peasant families face?

PRIMARY SOURCE **C**

What by spinning they save, they spend it in house-hire,
Both in milk and in meal to make a mess of porridge,
To cheer up their children who chafe for their food,
And they themselves suffer surely much hunger
And woe in the winter, with waking at nights
And rising to rock an oft restless cradle.

WILLIAM LANGLAND, *Piers Plowman*

For most serfs, both men and women, life was work and more work. Their days revolved around raising crops and livestock and taking care of home and family. As soon as children were old enough, they were put to work in the fields or in the home. Many children did not survive to adulthood. Illness and malnutrition were constant afflictions for medieval peasants. Average life expectancy was about 35 years. And during that short lifetime, most peasants never traveled more than 25 miles from their homes.

Yet, despite the hardships they endured, serfs accepted their lot in life as part of the Church's teachings. They, like most Christians during medieval times, believed that God determined a person's place in society.

NEW YORK CORE CURRICULUM REVIEW

TERMS & NAMES **1.** For each term or name, write a sentence explaining its significance.

- lord
- fief
- vassal
- knight
- serf
- manor
- tithe

USING YOUR NOTES

2. What is the main reason feudalism developed? Explain.

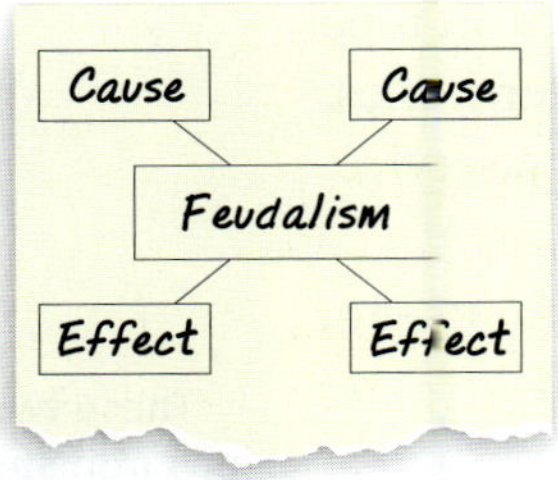

MAIN IDEAS

3. What groups invaded Europe in the 800s?

4. What obligations did a peasant have to the lord of the manor?

5. What were the three social classes of the feudal system?

CRITICAL THINKING & WRITING

6. COMPARING How were the Vikings different from earlier Germanic groups that invaded Europe?

7. MAKING INFERENCES How was a manor largely self-sufficient both militarily and economically during the early Middle Ages?

8. DRAWING CONCLUSIONS What benefits do you think a medieval manor provided to the serfs who lived there?

9. WRITING ACTIVITY POWER AND AUTHORITY Draw up a **contract** between a lord and a vassal, such as a knight, or between the lord of a manor and a serf. Include the responsibilities, obligations, and rights of each party.

CONNECT TO TODAY **WRITING A NEWS ARTICLE**

Research modern marauders, who, like the Vikings of history, are involved in piracy on the seas. Write a brief **news article** describing their activities.

The Age of Chivalry

CONNECT TO THE NEW YORK STATE CORE CURRICULUM

Unit 2.F.4.a. Social hierarchy and stratification
Unit 2.F.4.b. Role of men and women

TERMS & NAMES

- chivalry
- tournament
- troubadour

SETTING THE STAGE During the Middle Ages, nobles constantly fought one another. Their feuding kept Europe in a fragmented state for centuries. Through warfare, feudal lords defended their estates, seized new territories, and increased their wealth. Lords and their armies lived in a violent society that prized combat skills. By the 1100s, though, a code of behavior began to arise. High ideals guided warriors' actions and glorified their roles.

TAKING NOTES
Summarizing Identify the ideas associated with chivalry.

Knights: Warriors on Horseback

Soldiers mounted on horseback became valuable in combat during the reign of Charlemagne's grandfather, Charles Martel, in the 700s. Charles Martel had observed that the Muslim cavalry often turned the tide of battles. As a result, he organized Frankish troops of armored horsemen, or knights.

The Technology of Warfare Changes Leather saddles and stirrups changed the way warfare was conducted in Europe during the 700s. Both had been developed in Asia around 200 B.C.

The saddle kept a warrior firmly seated on a moving horse. Stirrups enabled him to ride and handle heavier weapons. Without stirrups to brace him, a charging warrior was likely to topple off his own horse. Frankish knights, galloping full tilt, could knock over enemy foot soldiers and riders on horseback. Gradually, mounted knights became the most important part of an army. Their warhorses played a key military role.

The Warrior's Role in Feudal Society By the 11th century, western Europe was a battleground of warring nobles vying for power. To defend their territories, feudal lords raised private armies of knights. In exchange for military service,

These two-inch iron spikes, called caltrops, were strewn on a battlefield to maim warhorses or enemy foot soldiers.

feudal lords used their most abundant resource—land. They rewarded knights, their most skilled warriors, with fiefs from their sprawling estates. Wealth from these fiefs allowed knights to devote their lives to war. Knights could afford to pay for costly weapons, armor, and warhorses.

As the lord's vassal, a knight's main obligation was to serve in battle. From his knights, a lord typically demanded about 40 days of combat a year. Knights' pastimes also often revolved around training for war. Wrestling and hunting helped them gain strength and practice the skills they would need on the battlefield.

Knighthood and the Code of Chivalry

Knights were expected to display courage in battle and loyalty to their lord. By the 1100s, the code of **chivalry** (SHIHV•uhl•ree), a complex set of ideals, demanded that a knight fight bravely in defense of three masters. He devoted himself to his earthly feudal lord, his heavenly Lord, and his chosen lady. The chivalrous knight also protected the weak and the poor. The ideal knight was loyal, brave, and courteous. Most knights, though, failed to meet all of these high standards. For example, they treated the lower classes brutally.

A Knight's Training Sons of nobles began training for knighthood at an early age and learned the code of chivalry. At age 7, a boy would be sent off to the castle of another lord. As a page, he waited on his hosts and began to practice fighting skills. At around age 14, the page reached the rank of squire. A squire acted as a servant to a knight. At around age 21, a squire became a full-fledged knight.

Analyzing Art

Chivalry

The Italian painter Paolo Uccello captures the spirit of the age of chivalry in this painting, *St. George and the Dragon* (c. 1455–1460). According to myth, St. George rescues a captive princess by killing her captor, a dragon.

- **The Knight** St. George, mounted on a horse and dressed in armor, uses his lance to attack the dragon.
- **The Dragon** The fierce-looking dragon represents evil.
- **The Princess** The princess remains out of the action as her knight fights the dragon on her behalf.

SKILLBUILDER:
Interpreting Visual Sources
In what way does this painting show the knight's code of chivalry?

INTERACTIVE

Castles and Siege Weapons

Attacking armies carefully planned how to capture a castle. Engineers would inspect the castle walls for weak points in the stone. Then, enemy soldiers would try to ram the walls, causing them to collapse. At the battle site, attackers often constructed the heavy and clumsy weapons shown here.

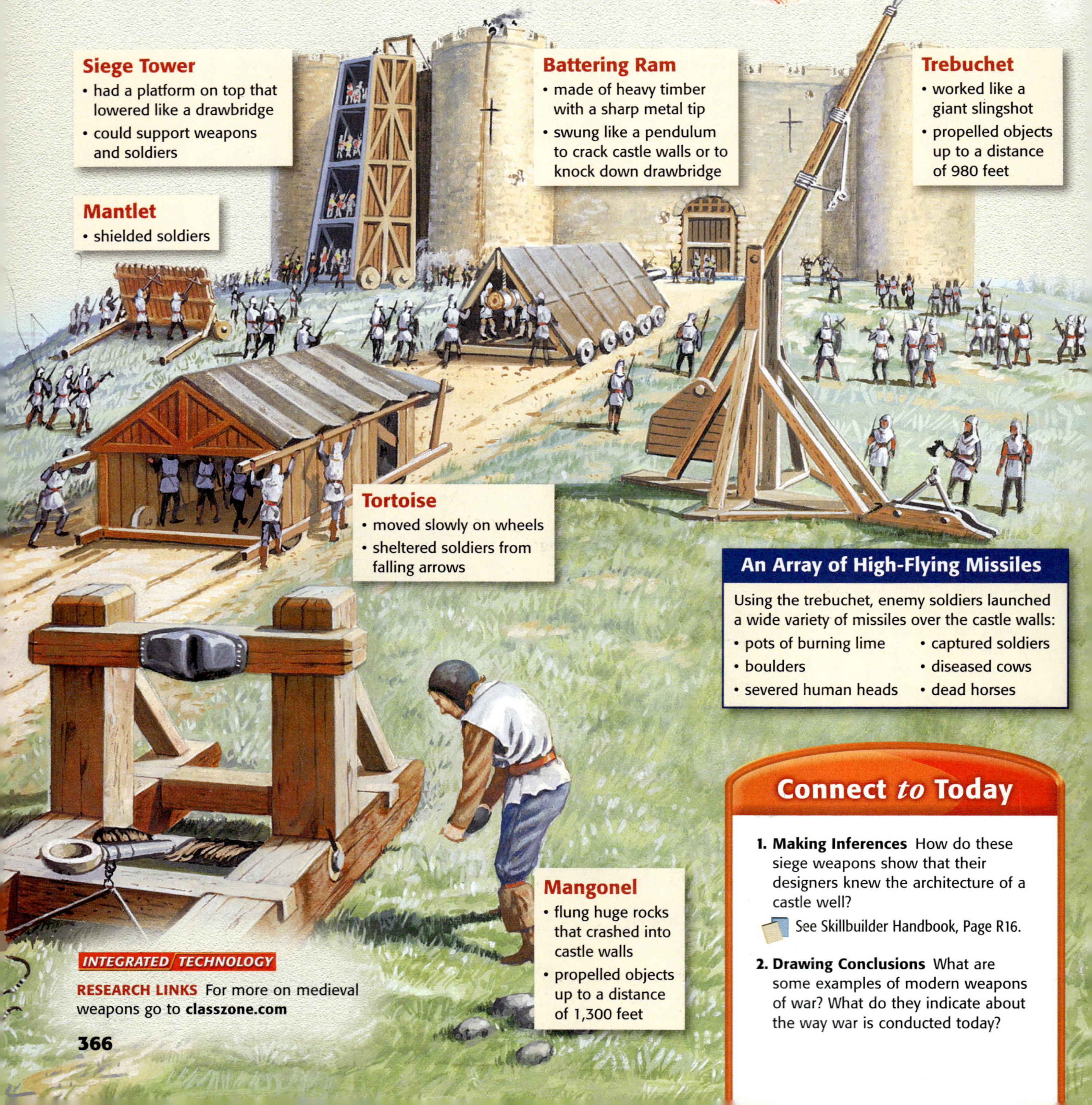

Siege Tower
- had a platform on top that lowered like a drawbridge
- could support weapons and soldiers

Mantlet
- shielded soldiers

Battering Ram
- made of heavy timber with a sharp metal tip
- swung like a pendulum to crack castle walls or to knock down drawbridge

Trebuchet
- worked like a giant slingshot
- propelled objects up to a distance of 980 feet

Tortoise
- moved slowly on wheels
- sheltered soldiers from falling arrows

Mangonel
- flung huge rocks that crashed into castle walls
- propelled objects up to a distance of 1,300 feet

An Array of High-Flying Missiles

Using the trebuchet, enemy soldiers launched a wide variety of missiles over the castle walls:
- pots of burning lime
- boulders
- severed human heads
- captured soldiers
- diseased cows
- dead horses

Connect *to* Today

1. **Making Inferences** How do these siege weapons show that their designers knew the architecture of a castle well?
   See Skillbuilder Handbook, Page R16.
2. **Drawing Conclusions** What are some examples of modern weapons of war? What do they indicate about the way war is conducted today?

INTEGRATED TECHNOLOGY

RESEARCH LINKS For more on medieval weapons go to **classzone.com**

After being dubbed a knight, most young men traveled for a year or two. The young knights gained experience fighting in local wars. Some took part in mock battles called **tournaments**. Tournaments combined recreation with combat training. Two armies of knights charged each other. Trumpets blared, and lords and ladies cheered. Like real battles, tournaments were fierce and bloody competitions. Winners could usually demand large ransoms from defeated knights. (A)

MAIN IDEA

Comparing

(A) How are tournaments like modern sports competitions?

Brutal Reality of Warfare The small-scale violence of tournaments did not match the bloodshed of actual battles, especially those fought at castles. By the 1100s, massive walls and guard towers encircled stone castles. These castles dominated much of the countryside in western Europe. Lord and lady, their family, knights and other men-at-arms, and servants made their home in the castle. The castle also was a fortress, designed for defense.

Vocabulary

A *siege* is a military blockade staged by enemy armies trying to capture a fortress.

A castle under siege was a gory sight. Attacking armies used a wide range of strategies and weapons to force castle residents to surrender. Defenders of a castle poured boiling water, hot oil, or molten lead on enemy soldiers. Expert archers were stationed on the roof of the castle. Armed with crossbows, they fired deadly bolts that could pierce full armor.

The Literature of Chivalry

In the 1100s, the themes of medieval literature downplayed the brutality of knighthood and feudal warfare. Many stories idealized castle life. They glorified knighthood and chivalry, tournaments and real battles. Songs and poems about a knight's undying love for a lady were also very popular.

Epic Poetry Feudal lords and their ladies enjoyed listening to epic poems. These poems recounted a hero's deeds and adventures. Many epics retold stories about legendary heroes such as King Arthur and Charlemagne.

The Song of Roland is one of the earliest and most famous medieval epic poems. It praises a band of French soldiers who perished in battle during Charlemagne's reign. The poem transforms the event into a struggle. A few brave French knights led by Roland battle an overwhelming army of Muslims from Spain. Roland's friend, Turpin the Archbishop, stands as a shining example of medieval ideals. Turpin represents courage, faith, and chivalry:

PRIMARY SOURCE

And now there comes the Archbishop.
He spurs his horse, goes up into a mountain,
summons the French; and he preached them a sermon:
"Barons, my lords, [Charlemagne] left us in this place.
We know our duty: to die like good men for our King.
Fight to defend the holy Christian faith."

from *The Song of Roland*

Love Poems and Songs Under the code of chivalry, a knight's duty to his lady became as important as his duty to his lord. In many medieval poems, the hero's difficulties resulted from a conflict between those two obligations.

Troubadours were traveling poet-musicians at the castles and courts of Europe. They composed short verses and

Connect *to* Today

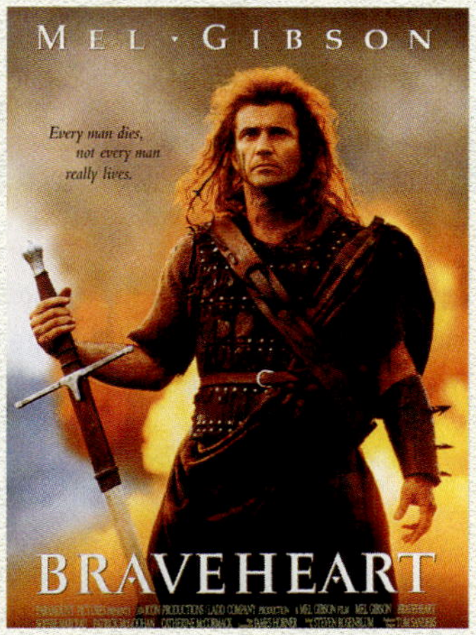

Epic Films

The long, narrative epic poem has given way in modern times to the epic film. Epic films feature larger-than-life characters in powerful stories that deal with mythic and timeless themes. These films take their stories from history, legend, and fantasy. The first epic film was *Birth of a Nation*, released in 1915.

Some modern epic films are *Braveheart* (1995), pictured above; *Gladiator* (2000); and the *Star Wars* saga (six films, 1977–2005).

INTEGRATED TECHNOLOGY

INTERNET ACTIVITY Research five epic films. Write a one-sentence description of the historical content for each. Go to **classzone.com** for your research.

songs about the joys and sorrows of romantic love. Sometimes troubadours sang their own verses in the castles of their lady. They also sent roving minstrels to carry their songs to courts.

A troubadour might sing about love's disappointments: "My loving heart, my faithfulness, myself, my world she deigns to take. Then leave me bare and comfortless to longing thoughts that ever wake."

Other songs told of lovesick knights who adored ladies they would probably never win: "Love of a far-off land/For you my heart is aching/And I can find no relief." The code of chivalry promoted a false image of knights, making them seem more romantic than brutal. In turn, these love songs created an artificial image of women. In the troubadour's eyes, noblewomen were always beautiful and pure.

The most celebrated woman of the age was Eleanor of Aquitaine (1122–1204). Troubadours flocked to her court in the French duchy of Aquitaine. Later, as queen of England, Eleanor was the mother of two kings, Richard the Lion-Hearted and John. Richard himself composed romantic songs and poems.

Women's Role in Feudal Society

Most women in feudal society were powerless, just as most men were. But women had the added burden of being thought inferior to men. This was the view of the Church and was generally accepted in feudal society. Nonetheless, women

> Analyzing Primary Sources

Daily Life of a Noblewoman

This excerpt describes the daily life of an English noblewoman of the Middle Ages, Cicely Neville, Duchess of York. A typical noblewoman is pictured below.

PRIMARY SOURCE

She gets up at 7a.m., and her chaplain is waiting to say morning prayers . . . and when she has washed and dressed . . . she has breakfast, then she goes to the chapel, for another service, then has dinner. . . . After dinner, she discusses business . . . then has a short sleep, then drinks ale or wine. Then . . . she goes to the chapel for evening service, and has supper. After supper, she relaxes with her women attendants. . . . After that, she goes to her private room, and says nighttime prayers. By 8 p.m. she is in bed.

DAILY ROUTINE OF CICELY, DUCHESS OF YORK, quoted in *Women in Medieval Times* by Fiona Macdonald

Daily Life of a Peasant Woman

This excerpt describes the daily life of a typical medieval peasant woman as pictured below.

PRIMARY SOURCE

I get up early . . . milk our cows and turn them into the field. . . . Then I make butter. . . . Afterward I make cheese. . . . Then the children need looking after. . . . I give the chickens food . . . and look after the young geese. . . . I bake, I brew. . . . I twist rope. . . . I tease out wool, and card it, and spin it on a wheel. . . . I organize food for the cattle, and for ourselves. . . . I look after all the household.

FROM A BALLAD FIRST WRITTEN DOWN IN ABOUT 1500, quoted in *Women in Medieval Times* by Fiona Macdonald

DOCUMENT-BASED QUESTIONS

1. **Drawing Conclusions** *What seem to be the major concerns in the noblewoman's life? How do they compare with those of the peasant woman?*
2. **Making Inferences** *What qualities would you associate with the peasant woman and the life she lived?*

played important roles in the lives of both noble and peasant families.

Noblewomen Under the feudal system, a noblewoman could inherit an estate from her husband. Upon her lord's request, she could also send his knights to war. When her husband was off fighting, the lady of a medieval castle might act as military commander and a warrior. At times, noblewomen played a key role in defending castles. They hurled rocks and fired arrows at attackers. (See the illustration to the right.)

▲ The noblewomen depicted in this manuscript show their courage and combat skills in defending a castle against enemies.

In reality, however, the lives of most noblewomen were limited. Whether young or old, females in noble families generally were confined to activities in the home or the convent. Also, noblewomen held little property because lords passed down their fiefs to sons and not to daughters. **B**

MAIN IDEA

Summarizing

B What privileges did a noblewoman have in medieval society?

Peasant Women For the vast majority of women of the lower classes, life had remained unchanged for centuries. Peasant women performed endless labor around the home and often in the fields, bore children, and took care of their families. Young peasant girls learned practical household skills from their mother at an early age, unlike daughters in rich households who were educated by tutors. Females in peasant families were poor and powerless. Yet, the economic contribution they made was essential to the survival of the peasant household.

As you have read in this section, the Church significantly influenced the status of medieval women. In Section 4, you will read just how far-reaching was the influence of the Church in the Middle Ages.

NEW YORK CORE CURRICULUM REVIEW

TERMS & NAMES 1. For each term or name, write a sentence explaining its significance.

- chivalry
- tournament
- troubadour

USING YOUR NOTES

2. Which ideas associated with chivalry have remnants in today's society? Explain.

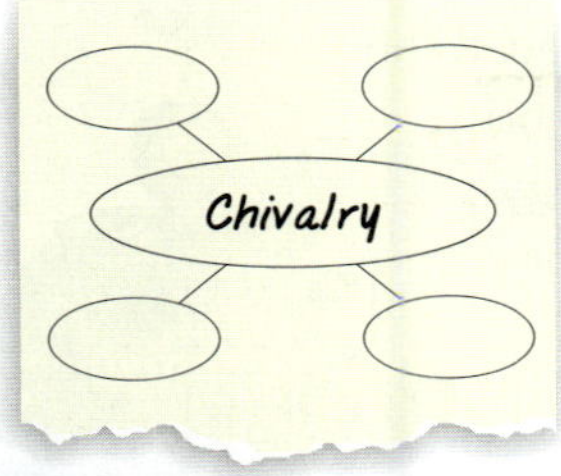

MAIN IDEAS

3. What were two inventions from Asia that changed the technology of warfare in western Europe?
4. Who were the occupants of a castle?
5. What were some of the themes of medieval literature?

CRITICAL THINKING & WRITING

6. **DEVELOPING HISTORICAL PERSPECTIVE** How important a role did knights play in the feudal system?
7. **MAKING INFERENCES** How was the code of chivalry like the idea of romantic love?
8. **COMPARING AND CONTRASTING** In what ways were the lives of a noblewoman and a peasant woman the same? different?
9. **WRITING ACTIVITY** RELIGIOUS AND ETHICAL SYSTEMS -Write a **persuasive essay** in support of the adoption of a code of chivalry, listing the positive effects it might have on feudal society.

CONNECT TO TODAY **WRITING AN ADVERTISEMENT**

Conduct research to learn more about tournaments. Then, write a 50-word **advertisement** promoting a tournament to be held at a modern re-creation of a medieval fair.

The Power of the Church

CONNECT TO THE NEW YORK STATE CORE CURRICULUM

Methodology.A.5. Roles and contributions of individuals and groups
Unit 2.F.5. Spiritual and secular role of the Church

TERMS & NAMES

- clergy
- sacrament
- canon law
- Holy Roman Empire
- lay investiture

SETTING THE STAGE Amid the weak central governments in feudal Europe, the Church emerged as a powerful institution. It shaped the lives of people from all social classes. As the Church expanded its political role, strong rulers began to question the pope's authority. Dramatic power struggles unfolded in the Holy Roman Empire, the scene of mounting tensions between popes and emperors.

TAKING NOTES
Following Chronological Order List the significant dates and events for the Holy Roman Empire.

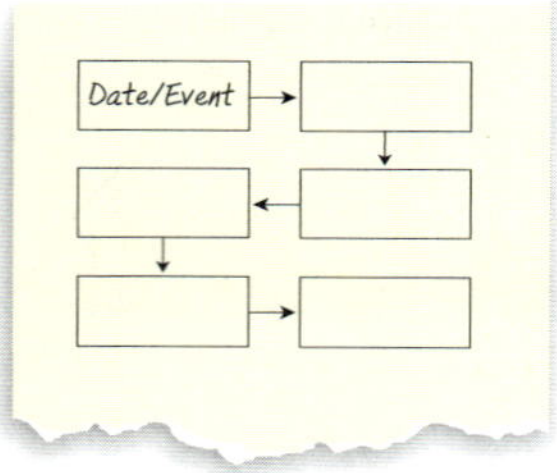

The Far-Reaching Authority of the Church

In crowning Charlemagne as the Roman Emperor in 800, the Church sought to influence both spiritual and political matters. Three hundred years earlier, Pope Gelasius I recognized the conflicts that could arise between the two great forces—the Church and the state. He wrote, "There are two powers by which this world is chiefly ruled: the sacred authority of the priesthood and the authority of kings."

Gelasius suggested an analogy to solve such conflicts. God had created two symbolic swords. One sword was religious. The other was political. The pope held a spiritual sword. The emperor wielded a political one. Gelasius thought that the pope should bow to the emperor in political matters. In turn, the emperor should bow to the pope in religious matters. If each ruler kept the authority in his own realm, Gelasius suggested, the two leaders could share power in harmony. In reality, though, they disagreed on the boundaries of either realm. Throughout the Middle Ages, the Church and various European rulers competed for power.

The Structure of the Church Like the system of feudalism, the Church had its own organization. Power was based on status. Church structure consisted of different ranks of clergy, or religious officials. The pope in Rome headed the Church. All **clergy**, including bishops and priests, fell under his authority. Bishops supervised priests, the lowest ranking members of the clergy. Bishops also settled disputes over Church teachings and practices. For most people, local priests served as the main contact with the Church.

Religion as a Unifying Force Feudalism and the manor system created divisions among people. But the shared beliefs in the teachings of the Church bonded people together. The church was a stable force during an era of constant warfare and political turmoil. It provided Christians with a sense of security and of belonging to a religious community. In the Middle Ages, religion occupied center stage.

▼ A pope's tiara symbolized his power.

Medieval Christians' everyday lives were harsh. Still, they could all follow the same path to salvation—everlasting life in heaven. Priests and other clergy administered the **sacraments**, or important religious ceremonies. These rites paved the way for achieving salvation. For example, through the sacrament of baptism, people became part of the Christian community.

At the local level, the village church was a unifying force in the lives of most people. It served as a religious and social center. People worshiped together at the church. They also met with other villagers. Religious holidays, especially Christmas and Easter, were occasions for festive celebrations. (A)

MAIN IDEA

Analyzing Motives

(A) Why did medieval peasants support the Church?

The Law of the Church The Church's authority was both religious and political. It provided a unifying set of spiritual beliefs and rituals. The Church also created a system of justice to guide people's conduct. All medieval Christians, kings and peasants alike, were subject to **canon law**, or Church law, in matters such as marriage and religious practices. The Church also established courts to try people accused of violating canon law. Two of the harshest punishments that offenders faced were excommunication and interdict.

Popes used the threat of excommunication, or banishment from the Church, to wield power over political rulers. For example, a disobedient king's quarrel with a pope might result in excommunication. This meant the king would be denied salvation. Excommunication also freed all the king's vassals from their duties to him. If an excommunicated king continued to disobey the pope, the pope, in turn, could use an even more frightening weapon, the interdict.

Under an interdict, many sacraments and religious services could not be performed in the king's lands. As Christians, the king's subjects believed that without such sacraments they might be doomed to hell. In the 11th century, excommunication and the possible threat of an interdict would force a German emperor to submit to the pope's commands.

Social History

An Age of Superstition

Lacking knowledge of the laws of nature, many people during the Middle Ages were led to irrational beliefs. They expected the dead to reappear as ghosts. A friendly goblin might do a person a good deed, but an evil witch might cause great harm. Medieval people thought an evil witch had the power to exchange a healthy child for a sickly one.

The medieval Church frowned upon superstitions such as these:

- preparing a table with three knives to please good fairies
- making a vow by a tree, a pond, or any place but a church
- believing that a person could change into the shape of a wolf
- believing that the croak of a raven or meeting a priest would bring a person good or bad luck

The Church and the Holy Roman Empire

When Pope Leo III crowned Charlemagne emperor in 800, he unknowingly set the stage for future conflicts between popes and emperors. These clashes would go on for centuries.

Otto I Allies with the Church The most effective ruler of medieval Germany was Otto I, known as Otto the Great. Otto, crowned king in 936, followed the policies of his hero, Charlemagne. Otto formed a close alliance with the Church. To limit the nobles' strength, he sought help from the clergy. He built up his power base by gaining the support of the bishops and abbots, the heads of monasteries. He dominated the Church in Germany. He also used his power to defeat German princes. Following in Charlemagne's footsteps, Otto also invaded Italy on the pope's behalf. In 962, the pope rewarded Otto by crowning him emperor.

Signs of Future Conflicts The German-Italian empire Otto created was first called the Roman Empire of the German Nation. It later became the **Holy Roman Empire**. It remained the strongest state in Europe until about 1100. However,

Otto's attempt to revive Charlemagne's empire caused trouble for future German leaders. Popes and Italian nobles, too, resented German power over Italy.

The Emperor Clashes with the Pope

The Church was not happy that kings, such as Otto, had control over clergy and their offices. It especially resented the practice of **lay investiture**, a ceremony in which kings and nobles appointed church officials. Whoever controlled lay investiture held the real power in naming bishops, who were very influential clergy that kings sought to control. Church reformers felt that kings should not have that power. In 1075, Pope Gregory VII banned lay investiture.

The furious young German emperor, Henry IV, immediately called a meeting of the German bishops he had appointed. With their approval, the emperor ordered Gregory to step down from the papacy. Gregory then excommunicated Henry. Afterward, German bishops and princes sided with the pope. To save his throne, Henry tried to win the pope's forgiveness.

Showdown at Canossa In January 1077, Henry crossed the snowy Alps to the Italian town of Canossa (kuh•NAHS•uh). He approached the castle where Gregory was a guest. Gregory later described the scene:

PRIMARY SOURCE

There, having laid aside all the belongings of royalty, wretchedly, with bare feet and clad in wool, he [Henry IV] continued for three days to stand before the gate of the castle. Nor did he desist from imploring with many tears the aid and consolation of the apostolic mercy until he had moved all of those who were present there.

POPE GREGORY, in *Basic Documents in Medieval History*

GEOGRAPHY SKILLBUILDER: Interpreting Maps

1. **Region** *How many states made up the Holy Roman Empire? What does this suggest about ruling it as an empire?*
2. **Location** *How did the location of the Papal States make them an easy target for frequent invasions by Germanic rulers?*

The Pope was obligated to forgive any sinner who begged so humbly. Still, Gregory kept Henry waiting in the snow for three days before ending his excommunication. Their meeting actually solved nothing. The pope had humiliated Henry, the proudest ruler in Europe. Yet, Henry felt triumphant and rushed home to punish rebellious nobles. **B**

MAIN IDEA

Making Inferences

B Why was Henry's journey to Canossa a political act?

Concordat of Worms The successors of Gregory and Henry continued to fight over lay investiture until 1122. That year, representatives of the Church and the emperor met in the German city of Worms (wurms). They reached a compromise known as the Concordat of Worms. By its terms, the Church alone could appoint a bishop, but the emperor could veto the appointment. During Henry's struggle, German princes regained power lost under Otto. But a later king, Frederick I, would resume the battle to build royal authority.

Disorder in the Empire

Vocabulary
Barbarossa means "red beard" in Italian.

By 1152, the seven princes who elected the German king realized that Germany needed a strong ruler to keep the peace. They chose Frederick I, nicknamed "Barbarossa" for his red beard.

▲ This manuscript shows Frederick I at the height of his imperial power.

The Reign of Frederick I Frederick I was the first ruler to call his lands the Holy Roman Empire. However, this region was actually a patchwork of feudal territories. His forceful personality and military skills enabled him to dominate the German princes. Yet, whenever he left the country, disorder returned. Following Otto's example, Frederick repeatedly invaded the rich cities of Italy. His brutal tactics spurred Italian merchants to unite against him. He also angered the pope, who joined the merchants in an alliance called the Lombard League.

In 1176, the foot soldiers of the Lombard League faced Frederick's army of mounted knights at the Battle of Legnano (lay•NYAHN•oh). In an astonishing victory, the Italian foot soldiers used crossbows to defeat feudal knights for the first time in history. In 1177, Frederick made peace with the pope and returned to Germany. His defeat, though, had undermined his authority with the German princes. After he drowned in 1190, his empire fell to pieces.

MAIN IDEA
Analyzing Causes
C What political trend kept German states separate during the Middle Ages?

German States Remain Separate German kings after Frederick, including his grandson Frederick II, continued their attempts to revive Charlemagne's empire and his alliance with the Church. This policy led to wars with Italian cities and to further clashes with the pope. These conflicts were one reason why the feudal states of Germany did not unify during the Middle Ages. Another reason was that the system of German princes electing the king weakened royal authority. German rulers controlled fewer royal lands to use as a base of power than French and English kings of the same period, who, as you will learn in Chapter 14, were establishing strong central authority. **C**

NEW YORK CORE CURRICULUM REVIEW

TERMS & NAMES 1. For each term or name, write a sentence explaining its significance.

- clergy
- sacrament
- canon law
- Holy Roman Empire
- lay investiture

USING YOUR NOTES

2. Which of the events were power struggles between the Church and rulers? Explain.

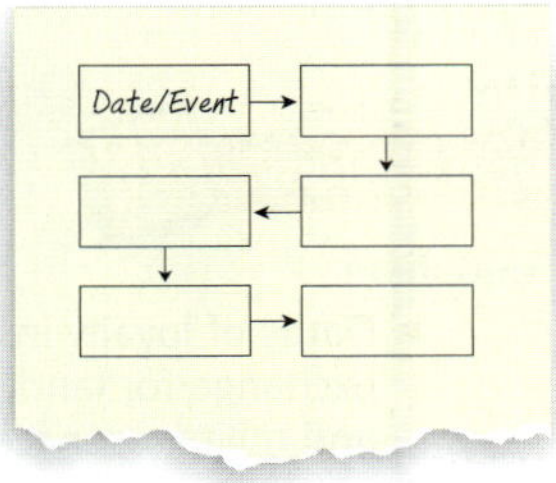

MAIN IDEAS

3. What were some of the matters covered by canon law?
4. How did Otto the Great make the crown stronger than the German nobles?
5. Why did lay investiture cause a struggle between kings and popes?

CRITICAL THINKING & WRITING

6. **COMPARING** How was the structure of the Church like that of the feudal system?
7. **EVALUATING DECISIONS** Was the Concordat of Worms a fair compromise for both the emperor and the Church? Why or why not?
8. **DRAWING CONCLUSIONS** Why did German kings fail to unite their lands?
9. **WRITING ACTIVITY** POWER AND AUTHORITY Why did Henry IV go to Canossa to confront Pope Gregory VII? Write a brief **dialogue** that might have taken place between them at their first meeting.

CONNECT TO TODAY **CREATING A CHART**

Research the ruling structure of the modern Roman Catholic Church and then create a **chart** showing the structure or hierarchy.

Chapter 13 Assessment

TERMS & NAMES

For each term or name below, briefly explain its connection to the Middle Ages from 500 to 1200.

1. monastery
2. Charlemagne
3. vassal
4. serf
5. manor
6. chivalry
7. clergy
8. Holy Roman Empire

MAIN IDEAS

Charlemagne Unites Germanic Kingdoms Section 1 (pages 353–357)

9. How did Gregory I increase the political power of the pope?
10. What was the outcome of the Battle of Tours?
11. What was the significance of the pope's declaring Charlemagne emperor?

Feudalism in Europe Section 2 (pages 358–363)

12. Which invading peoples caused turmoil in Europe during the 800s?
13. What exchange took place between lords and vassals under feudalism?
14. What duties did the lord of a manor and his serfs owe one another?

The Age of Chivalry Section 3 (pages 364–369)

15. What were the stages of becoming a knight?
16. What were common subjects of troubadours' songs?
17. What role did women play under feudalism?

The Power of the Church Section 4 (pages 370–373)

18. What was Gelasius's two-swords theory?
19. Why was Otto I the most effective ruler of Medieval Germany?
20. How was the conflict between Pope Gregory VII and Henry IV resolved?

CRITICAL THINKING

1. USING YOUR NOTES

In a chart, compare medieval Europe to an earlier civilization, such as Rome or Greece. Consider government, religion, and social roles.

Medieval Europe	
government	
religion	
social roles	

2. COMPARING AND CONTRASTING

EMPIRE BUILDING How did Otto I and Frederick I try to imitate Charlemagne's approach to empire building?

3. DRAWING CONCLUSIONS

POWER AND AUTHORITY Why do you think the ownership of land became an increasing source of power for feudal lords?

4. ANALYZING ISSUES

Why did the appointment of bishops become the issue in a struggle between kings and popes?

5. SYNTHESIZING

RELIGIOUS AND ETHICAL SYSTEMS What generalizations could you make about the relationship between politics and religion in the Middle Ages?

VISUAL SUMMARY

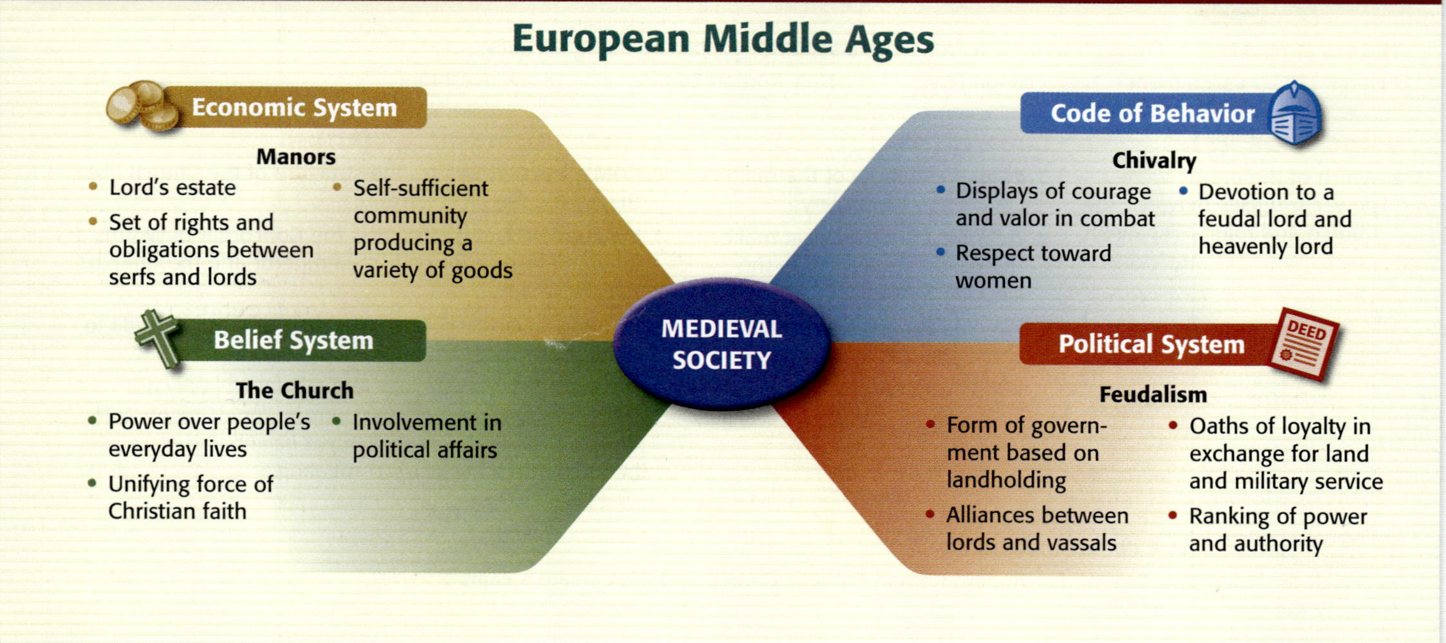

Use the quotation and your knowledge of world history to answer questions 1 and 2.
Additional Test Practice, pp. S1–S33

PRIMARY SOURCE

There was a knight, a most distinguished man,
Who from the day on which he first began
To ride abroad had followed chivalry,
Truth, honor, generous, and courtesy.
He had done nobly in sovereign's war
And ridden in battle, no man more,
As well as Christian in heathen places
And ever honored for his noble graces.

GEOFFREY CHAUCER, *The Canterbury Tales*

1 Which of these phrases best characterizes the knight Chaucer describes?
(1) inexperienced in battle
(2) a heathen
(3) a young man
(4) a well-traveled warrior

2 What qualities of knighthood do you think are missing from Chaucer's description?
(1) that a knight was of noble birth
(2) that a knight was a skilled warrior
(3) that a knight adored his chosen lady
(4) that a knight devoted himself to his heavenly Lord

Use the bar graph and your knowledge of world history to answer question 3.

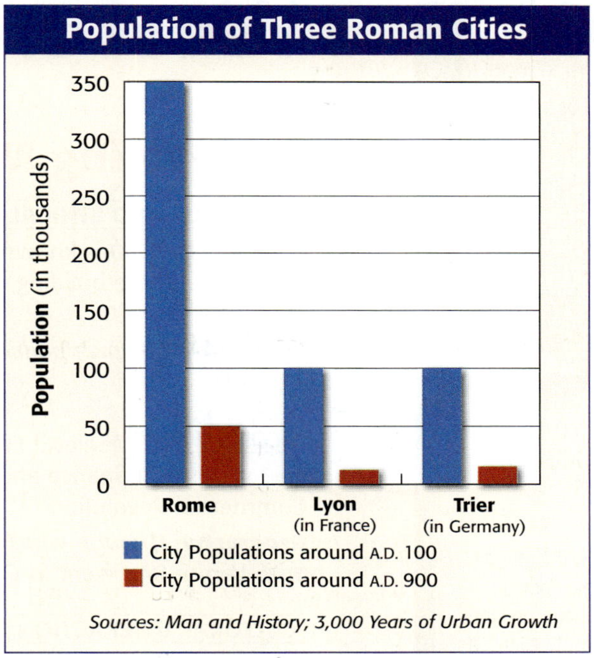

3 What is the most important point this chart is making?
(1) Trier and Lyon were not as large as Rome.
(2) Rome was the most populous city in the Roman Empire.
(3) All three cities lost significant population after the fall of the Roman Empire.
(4) Rome lost about 300,000 people from A.D. 100 to A.D. 200.

INTEGRATED TECHNOLOGY

TEST PRACTICE Go to **classzone.com**
- Diagnostic tests
- Tutorials
- Strategies
- Additional practice

ALTERNATIVE ASSESSMENT

1. Interact *with* History

On page 352, you considered the issue of what freedoms you would give up for protection. Now that you have read the chapter, reconsider your answer. How important was security? Was it worth not having certain basic freedoms? Discuss your ideas in a small group.

2. WRITING ABOUT HISTORY

Refer to the text, and then write a three-paragraph **character sketch** of a religious or political figure described in this chapter. Consider the following:
- why the figure was important
- how the figure performed his or her role

INTEGRATED TECHNOLOGY

Designing a Video Game

Use the Internet, books, and other reference materials to find out more about medieval tournaments. Then create a video game that imitates a medieval tournament between knights. Describe your ideas in a proposal that you might send to a video game company.

Think about video games that are based on contests. You might adapt some of the rules to your game. Consider the following:
- the rules of the game
- the system of keeping score of wins and losses
- weapons that should be used

CHAPTER 14

The Formation of Western Europe, 800–1500

Previewing Main Ideas

RELIGIOUS AND ETHICAL SYSTEMS In Western Europe the time period from 800 to 1500 is known as the Age of Faith. Christian beliefs inspired the Crusades and the building of great cathedrals, and guided the development of universities.

Geography *In which political unit was the capital of Christianity, Rome, located?*

ECONOMICS Medieval Europeans developed new methods of trade and new systems of finance and commerce. The changes are known as the Commercial Revolution.

Geography *Through which political units would a trader pass if he left from Venice and went to Calais using a land route?*

CULTURAL INTERACTION Although destructive in many ways, the Crusades resulted in a great deal of cultural exchange. Medieval Christian Europe learned and adopted much from the Muslim world.

Geography *A stopping place for Crusaders on their way to the Holy Land was the city of Constantinople. In what political unit is Constantinople located?*

NEW YORK CORE CURRICULUM FOCUS

- During the Middle Ages, the Catholic Church launched the Crusades to gain control of the Holy Land.
- For Muslims, the Crusades left behind a legacy of bitterness and hatred.

INTEGRATED TECHNOLOGY

eEdition
- Interactive Maps
- Interactive Visuals
- Interactive Primary Sources

VIDEO *Patterns of Interaction: Bubonic Plague and Smallpox*

INTERNET RESOURCES

Go to **classzone.com** for:
- Research Links
- Internet Activities
- Primary Sources
- Chapter Quiz
- Maps
- Test Practice
- Current Events

EUROPE

800 — 1000

987 Capetian dynasty begins in France.

1066 Norman invasion of England

1095 First Crusade begins. ▶

WORLD

980 ◀ Toltec Empire at its peak. (a Toltec warrior figurine)

1041 Movable type invented in China.

1215 King John approves Magna Carta.

1347 ◀ Bubonic plague strikes Europe.

1429 Joan of Arc leads the French to victory over the English at Orleans.

1453 Hundred Years' War ends with French victory.

1200

1500

1206 ◀ Genghis Khan unites Mongols and is proclaimed the Great Khan.

1325 The Aztec establish Tenochtitlán.

Interact *with* History

What are the dangers and rewards of going on a Crusade?

You are a squire in England. The knight you serve has decided to join a Christian Crusade (a holy war) to capture the city of Jerusalem from the Muslims. He has given you the choice of joining or staying home to look after his family and manor. On an earlier Crusade, the knight and his friends looted towns and manors, taking jewels and precious objects. But some of the knights were also held for ransom, robbed, and murdered. You are torn between the desire for adventure and possible riches that you might find on the Crusade, and fear of the hazards that await you on such a dangerous journey.

1 Richard the Lion-Hearted leads a group of Crusaders on the Third Crusade to regain Jerusalem from the Muslims.

2 Servants and women sometimes accompanied the Crusaders as they made their way toward the Holy Land.

EXAMINING *the* ISSUES

- **What reasons might an individual have to join a Crusade?**
- **What might be the advantages and disadvantages of staying home to defend the knight's family and estate?**

As a class, discuss these questions. In your discussion, remember what you've learned about the power of religious beliefs to move people to action. As you read about the Crusades in this chapter, see how events turned out for the Crusaders.

Church Reform and the Crusades

CONNECT TO THE NEW YORK STATE CORE CURRICULUM

Unit 2.G.2. Impacts on Southwest Asia, Byzantium, and Europe
Unit 2.G.4. Key individuals-Urban II, Saladin, and Richard the Lion–Hearted

TERMS & NAMES

- simony
- Gothic
- Urban II
- Crusade
- Saladin
- Richard the Lion-Hearted
- Reconquista
- Inquisition

SETTING THE STAGE Some historians have called the period in Western Europe between 500 and 1000 a "dark age." Magyars seeking plunder pushed up from the Danube River region. Vikings raided western European church monasteries. These groups destroyed many of these centers of learning. Around the 900s, however, a new spirit invaded the church and brought about a spiritual revival in the clergy. Filled with new energy, the church began restructuring itself and started massive building programs to create new places of worship.

TAKING NOTES
Following Chronological Order Use a time line to note important events in the Age of Faith.

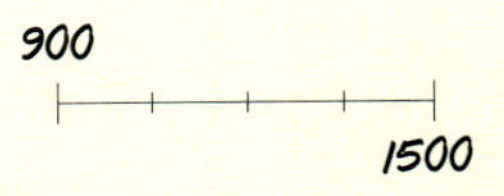

The Age of Faith

Monasteries led the spiritual revival. The monastery founded at Cluny in France in 910 was especially important. The reformers there wanted to return to the basic principles of the Christian religion. To do so, they established new religious orders. Influenced by the religious devotion and reverence for God shown by the new monasteries, the popes began to reform the Church. They restored and expanded its power and authority. A new age of religious feeling was born—the Age of Faith. Still, many problems troubled the Church.

Problems in the Church Some priests were nearly illiterate and could barely read their prayers. Some of the popes were men of questionable morals. Many bishops and abbots cared more about their positions as feudal lords than about their duties as spiritual leaders. Reformers were most distressed by three main issues.

- Many village priests married and had families. Such marriages were against Church rulings.
- Bishops sold positions in the Church, a practice called **simony** (SY•muh•nee).
- Using the practice of lay investiture, kings appointed church bishops. Church reformers believed the Church alone should appoint bishops.

Reform and Church Organization Pope Leo IX and Pope Gregory VII enforced Church laws against simony and the marriage of priests. The popes who followed Leo and Gregory reorganized the Church to continue the policy of reform. In the 1100s and 1200s, the Church was restructured to resemble a kingdom, with the pope at its head. The pope's group of advisers was called the papal Curia. The Curia also acted as a court. It developed canon law (the law of the Church) on matters such as marriage, divorce, and inheritance. The Curia also decided cases based on these laws. Diplomats for the pope traveled through Europe dealing with bishops and kings. In this way the popes established their authority throughout Europe.

The Church collected taxes in the form of tithes. These consumed one-tenth the yearly income from every Christian family. The Church used some of the money to perform social services such as caring for the sick and the poor. In fact, the Church operated most hospitals in medieval Europe. (A)

MAIN IDEA

Evaluating Courses of Action

(A) How did the popes increase their power and authority?

New Religious Orders In the early 1200s, wandering friars traveled from place to place preaching and spreading the Church's ideas. Like monks, friars took vows of chastity, poverty, and obedience. Unlike monks, friars did not live apart from the world in monasteries. Instead, they preached to the poor throughout Europe's towns and cities. Friars owned nothing and lived by begging.

Dominic, a Spanish priest, founded the Dominicans, one of the earliest orders of friars. Because Dominic emphasized the importance of study, many Dominicans were scholars. Francis of Assisi (uh•SEE•zee), an Italian, founded another order of friars, the Franciscans. Francis treated all creatures, including animals, as if they were his spiritual brothers and sisters.

Women played an important role in the spiritual revival. Women joined the Dominicans, Benedictines, and Franciscans. In 1212, a woman named Clare and her friend Francis of Assisi founded the Franciscan order for women. It was known as the Poor Clares. In Germany, Hildegard of Bingen, a mystic and musician, founded a Benedictine convent in 1147. Like friars, these women lived in poverty and worked to help the poor and sick. Unlike the friars, however, women were not allowed to travel from place to place as preachers.

Cathedrals—Cities of God

During the medieval period most people worshiped in small churches near their homes. Larger churches called cathedrals were built in city areas. The cathedral was viewed as the representation of the City of God. As such, it was decorated with all the richness that Christians could offer. Between about 800 and 1100, churches were built in the Romanesque (ROH•muh•NEHSK) style. The churches had round arches and a heavy roof held up by thick walls and pillars. The thick walls had tiny windows that let in little light.

A New Style of Church Architecture A new spirit in the church and access to more money from the growing wealth of towns and from trade helped fuel the building of churches in several European countries. In the early 1100s, a new style of architecture, known as **Gothic**, evolved throughout medieval Europe. The term *Gothic* comes from a Germanic tribe named the Goths. Unlike the heavy, gloomy Romanesque buildings, Gothic cathedrals thrust upward as if reaching toward heaven. Light streamed in through huge stained glass windows. Other arts of the medieval world were evident around or in the Gothic cathedral—sculpture, woodcarvings, and stained glass windows. All of these elements were meant to inspire the worshiper with the magnificence of God. See the diagram on the next page to learn more about Gothic cathedrals.

Soon Gothic cathedrals were built in many towns of France. In Paris, the vaulted ceiling of the Cathedral of Notre Dame (NOH•truh DAHM) eventually rose to more than 100 feet. Then Chartres, Reims, Amiens, and Beauvais built even taller cathedrals. In all, nearly 500 Gothic churches were built between 1170 and 1270.

INTERACTIVE

Gothic Architecture

The master builders in France, where the Gothic style originated, developed techniques of structural engineering that were key to Gothic architecture: ❶ ribbed vaults that supported the roof's weight, ❷ flying buttresses that transferred weight to thick, exterior walls, ❸ pointed arches that framed huge stained glass windows, and ❹ tall spires that seemed to be pointing to heaven.

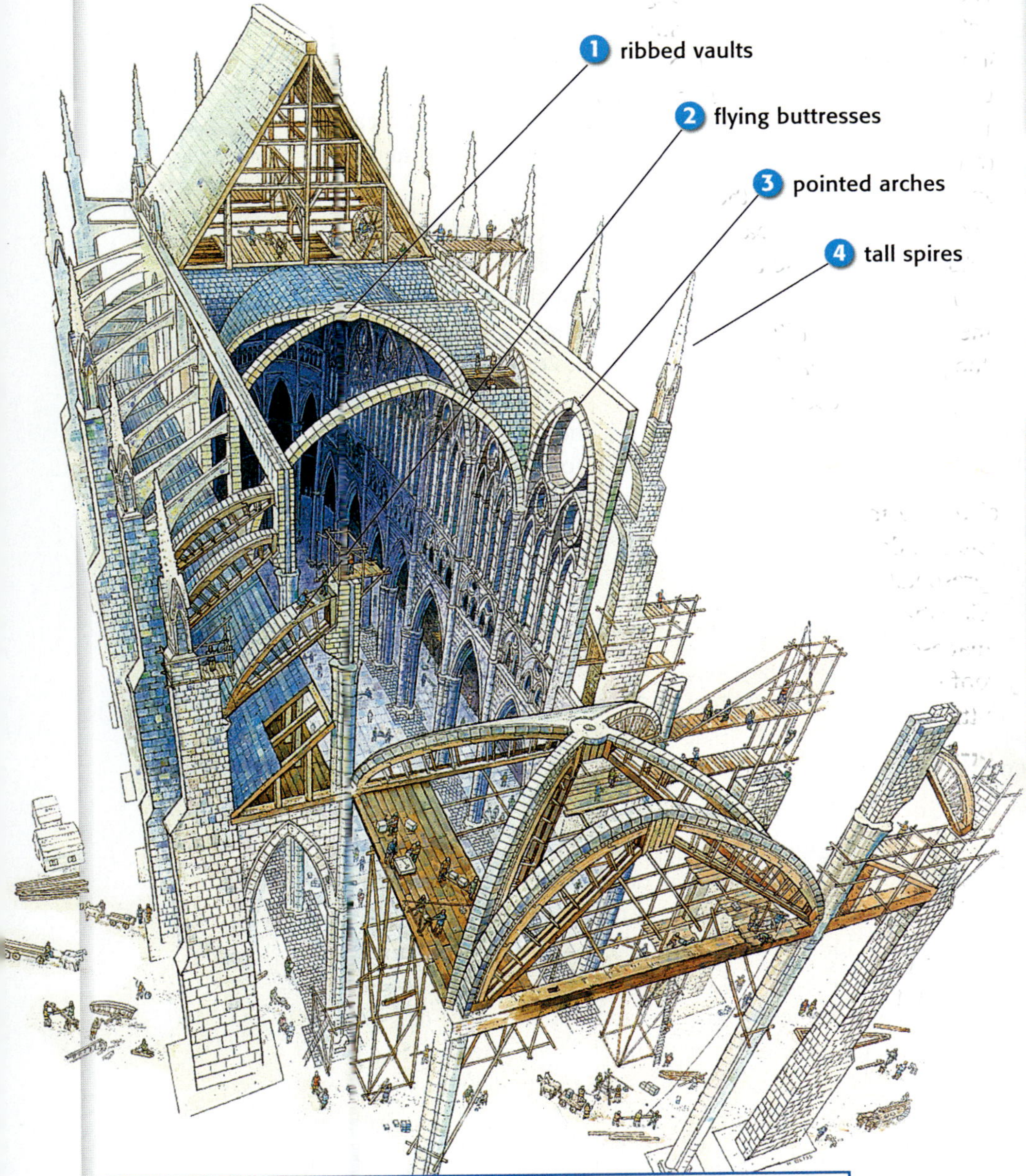

▲ Chartres Cathedral

The cathedral of Chartres (shahrt) is a masterpiece of Gothic architecture. The cathedral has hundreds of sculptures. The stone carvings that frame every door illustrate Bible stories. In this photograph, you can see the cathedral has not one, but two bell towers.

▲ Stained Glass

In addition to its sculpture and soaring towers, Chartres Cathedral has some of the most beautiful stained glass windows of any Gothic cathedral in Europe. The windows illustrate stories from the Bible. As illiterate peasants walked past the 176 windows, they could view those stories. The window above depicts the parable of the Good Samaritan.

SKILLBUILDER: Interpreting Visual Sources

1. **Drawing Conclusions** *Pose and answer three questions about elements in the style of Gothic architecture that might affect the sense of height and light inside.*
2. **Comparing and Contrasting** *Think about stained glass windows you have seen. Do they tell a story? What figures or events do they illustrate?*

The Crusades

The Age of Faith also inspired wars of conquest. In 1093, the Byzantine emperor Alexius Comnenus sent an appeal to Robert, Count of Flanders. The emperor asked for help against the Muslim Turks. They were threatening to conquer his capital, Constantinople:

PRIMARY SOURCE

Come then, with all your people and give battle with all your strength, so that all this treasure shall not fall into the hands of the Turks. . . . Therefore act while there is still time lest the kingdom of the Christians shall vanish from your sight and, what is more important, the Holy Sepulchre [the tomb where Jesus was buried] shall vanish. And in your coming you will find your reward in heaven, and if you do not come, God will condemn you.

EMPEROR ALEXIUS COMNENUS, quoted in *The Dream and the Tomb* by Robert Payne

Pope **Urban II** also read that letter. Shortly after this appeal, he issued a call for what he termed a "holy war," a **Crusade**, to gain control of the Holy Land. Over the next 300 years, a number of such Crusades were launched.

Vocabulary
Holy Land: Palestine; the area where Jesus lived and preached

Goals of the Crusades The Crusades had economic, social, and political goals as well as religious motives. Muslims controlled Palestine (the Holy Land) and threatened Constantinople. The Byzantine emperor in Constantinople appealed to Christians to stop Muslim attacks. In addition, the pope wanted to reclaim Palestine and reunite Christendom, which had split into Eastern and Western branches in 1054.

In addition, kings and the Church both saw the Crusades as an opportunity to get rid of quarrelsome knights who fought each other. These knights threatened the peace of the kingdoms, as well as Church property.

Others who participated in the Crusades were younger sons who, unlike eldest sons, did not stand to inherit their father's property. They were looking for land and a position in society, or for adventure.

In the later Crusades, merchants profited by making cash loans to finance the journey. They also leased their ships for a hefty fee to transport armies over the Mediterranean Sea. In addition, the merchants of Pisa, Genoa, and Venice hoped to win control of key trade routes to India, Southeast Asia, and China from Muslim traders.

▼ The red cross on his tunic identifies this knight as a crusader.

The First and Second Crusades Pope Urban's call brought a tremendous outpouring of religious feeling and support for the Crusade. According to the pope, those who died on Crusade were assured of a place in heaven. With red crosses sewn on tunics worn over their armor and the battle cry of "God wills it!" on their lips, knights and commoners were fired by religious zeal and became Crusaders.

By early 1097, three armies of knights and people of all classes had gathered outside Constantinople. Most of the Crusaders were French, but Bohemians, Germans, Englishmen, Scots, Italians, and Spaniards came as well. The Crusaders were ill-prepared for war in this First Crusade. Many knew nothing of the geography, climate, or culture of the Holy Land. They had no grand strategy to capture Jerusalem. The nobles argued among themselves and couldn't agree on a leader. Finally an army of 12,000 (less than one-fourth of the original army) approached Jerusalem. The Crusaders besieged the city for over a month. On July 15, 1099, they captured the city.

The Crusades, 1096–1204

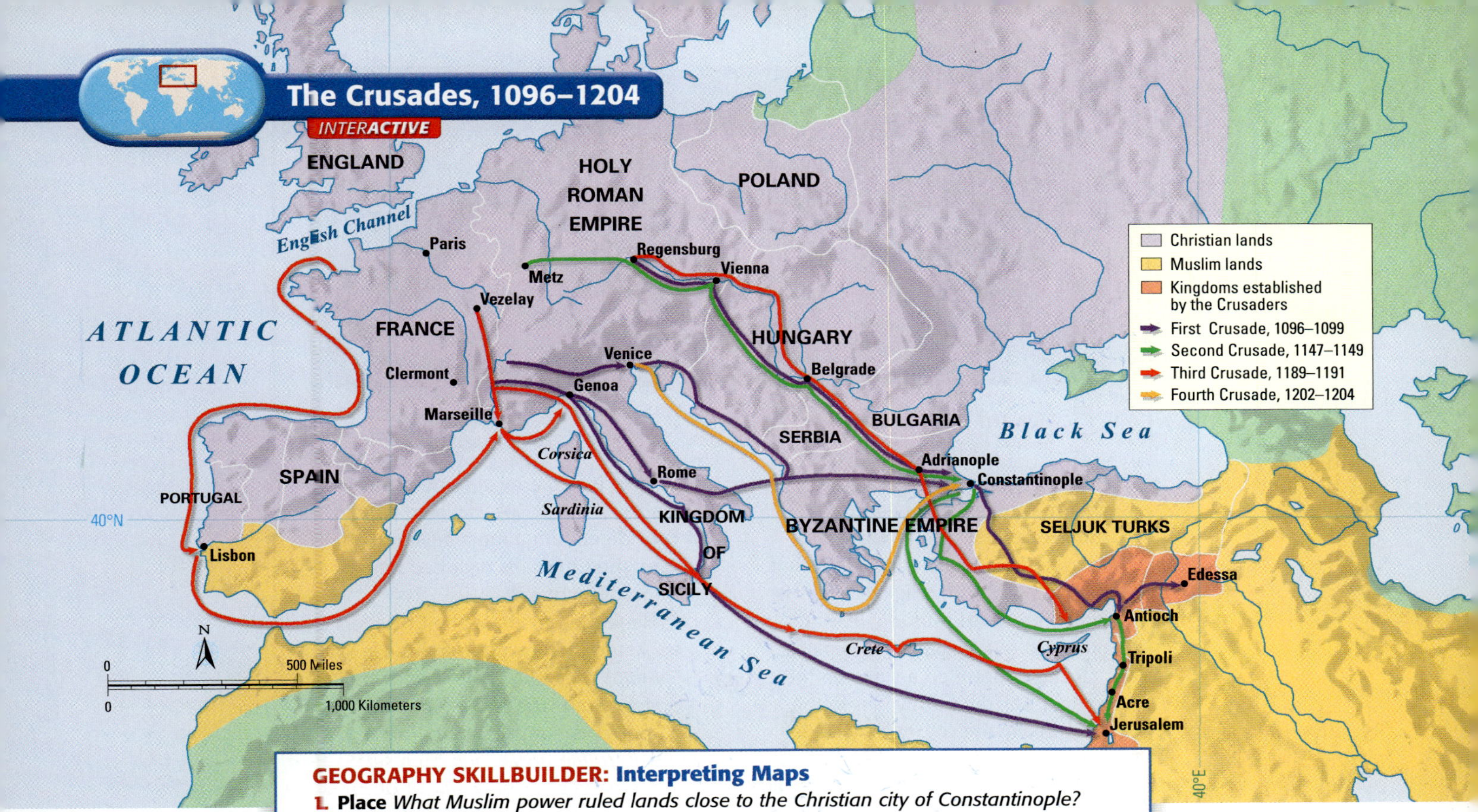

GEOGRAPHY SKILLBUILDER: Interpreting Maps

1. **Place** *What Muslim power ruled lands close to the Christian city of Constantinople?*
2. **Movement** *Which Crusade did not make it to Jerusalem? Where did this Crusade end?*

All in all, the Crusaders had won a narrow strip of land. It stretched about 650 miles from Edessa in the north to Jerusalem in the south. Four feudal Crusader states were carved out of this territory, each ruled by a European noble.

The Crusaders' states were extremely vulnerable to Muslim counterattack. In 1144, Edessa was reconquered by the Turks. The Second Crusade was organized to recapture the city. But its armies straggled home in defeat. In 1187, Europeans were shocked to learn that Jerusalem itself had fallen to a Kurdish warrior and Muslim leader **Saladin** (SAL•uh•dihn). **B**

MAIN IDEA

Summarizing

B What, if anything, had the Crusaders gained by the end of the Second Crusade?

The Third Crusade The Third Crusade to recapture Jerusalem was led by three of Europe's most powerful monarchs. They were Philip II (Augustus) of France, German emperor Frederick I (Barbarossa), and the English king, **Richard the Lion-Hearted**. Philip argued with Richard and went home. Barbarossa drowned on the journey. So, Richard was left to lead the Crusaders in an attempt to regain the Holy Land from Saladin. Both Richard and Saladin were brilliant warriors. After many battles, the two agreed to a truce in 1192. Jerusalem remained under Muslim control. In return, Saladin promised that unarmed Christian pilgrims could freely visit the city's holy places.

The Crusading Spirit Dwindles

In 1204, the Fourth Crusade to capture Jerusalem failed. The knights did not reach the Holy Land. Instead, they ended up looting the city of Constantinople. In the 1200s, four more Crusades to free the holy land were also unsuccessful. The religious spirit of the First Crusade faded, and the search for personal gain grew. In two later Crusades, armies marched not to the Holy Land but to Egypt. The Crusaders intended to weaken Muslim forces there before going to the Holy Land. But none of these attempts conquered much land.

History Makers

Richard the Lion-Hearted
1157–1199

Richard was noted for his good looks, charm, courage, grace—and ruthlessness. When he heard that Jerusalem had fallen to the Muslims, he was filled with religious zeal. He joined the Third Crusade, leaving others to rule England in his place.

Richard mounted a siege on the city of Acre. Saladin's army was in the hills overlooking the city, but it was not strong enough to defeat the Crusaders. When finally the city fell, Richard had the Muslim survivors—some 3,000 men, women, and children—slaughtered. The Muslim army watched helplessly from the hills.

Saladin
1138–1193

Saladin was the most famous Muslim leader of the 1100s. His own people considered him a most devout man. Even the Christians regarded him as honest and brave.

He wished to chase the Crusaders back into their own territories. He said:

> *I think that when God grants me victory over the rest of Palestine, I shall divide my territories, make a will stating my wishes, then set sail on this sea for their far-off lands and pursue the Franks there, so as to free the earth from anyone who does not believe in Allah, or die in the attempt.*

The Children's Crusade The Children's Crusade took place in 1212. In two different movements, thousands of children set out to conquer Jerusalem. One group in France was led by 12-year-old Stephen of Cloyes. An estimated 30,000 children under 18 joined him. They were armed only with the belief that God would give them Jerusalem. On their march south to the Mediterranean, many died from cold and starvation. The rest drowned at sea or were sold into slavery.

In Germany, Nicholas of Cologne gathered about 20,000 children and young adults. They began marching toward Rome. Thousands died in the cold and treacherous crossing of the Alps. Those who survived the trip to Italy finally did meet the pope. He told them to go home and wait until they were older. About 2,000 survived the return trip to Germany. A few boarded a ship for the Holy Land and were never heard of again. **C**

MAIN IDEA
Making Inferences
C How does the Children's Crusade illustrate the power of the Church?

A Spanish Crusade In Spain, Muslims (called Moors) controlled most of the country until the 1100s. The **Reconquista** (reh•kawn•KEES•tah) was a long effort by the Spanish to drive the Muslims out of Spain. By the late 1400s, the Muslims held only the tiny kingdom of Granada. In 1492, Granada finally fell to the Christian army of Ferdinand and Isabella, the Spanish monarchs.

To unify their country under Christianity and to increase their power, Isabella and Ferdinand made use of the **Inquisition**. This was a court held by the Church to suppress heresy. Heretics were people whose religious beliefs differed from the teachings of the Church. Many Jews and Muslims in Spain converted to Christianity during the late 1400s. Even so, the inquisitors suspected these Jewish and Muslim converts of heresy. A person suspected of heresy might be questioned for weeks and even tortured. Once suspects confessed, they were often burned at the stake. In 1492, the monarchs expelled all practicing Jews and Muslims from Spain.

The Effects of the Crusades

The Crusades are a forceful example of the power of the Church during the medieval period. The call to go to the Holy Land encouraged thousands to leave their homes and travel to faraway lands. For those who stayed home, especially women, it meant a chance to manage affairs on the estates or to operate shops and inns.

European merchants who lived and traded in the Crusader states expanded trade between Europe and Southwest Asia. The goods imported from Southwest Asia included spices, fruits, and cloth. This trade with the West benefited both Christians and Muslims.

However, the failure of later Crusades also lessened the power of the pope. The Crusades weakened the feudal nobility and increased the power of kings. Thousands of knights and other participants lost their lives and fortunes. The fall of Constantinople weakened the Byzantine Empire.

▲ This scene reveals torture used in the Inquisition.

For Muslims, the intolerance and prejudice displayed by Christians in the Holy Land left behind a legacy of bitterness and hatred. This legacy continues to the present. For Christians and Jews who remained in the Muslim controlled region after the fall of the Crusader states, relations with the Muslim leadership worsened. For Jews in Europe, the Crusades were a time of increased persecution.

The Crusades grew out of religious fervor, feudalism, and chivalry, which came together with explosive energy. This same energy led to the growth of trade, towns, and universities in medieval Europe.

NEW YORK CORE CURRICULUM REVIEW

TERMS & NAMES 1. For each term or name, write a sentence explaining its significance.
• simony • Gothic • Urban II • Crusade • Saladin • Richard the Lion-Hearted • Reconquista • Inquisition

USING YOUR NOTES

2. Which of the events of the Age of Faith do you think was most important to the Church? Explain.

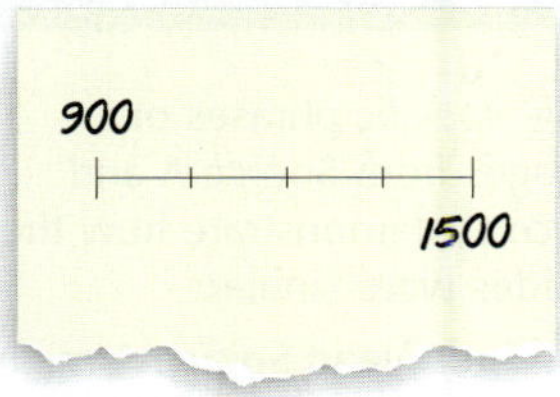

MAIN IDEAS

3. What were three main causes of the need to reform the Church?
4. Which Crusade was the only successful one?
5. How did the goals of the Crusades change over the years?

CRITICAL THINKING & WRITING

6. **FORMING AND SUPPORTING OPINIONS** Which of the following do you think best represents the spirit of the Age of Faith—Church reform, the Crusades, or the Gothic cathedrals? Explain.
7. **MAKING INFERENCES** What evidence supports the idea that the Church functioned like a kingdom?
8. **RECOGNIZING EFFECTS** How did the Crusades change the history of Europe? Give reasons for your answer.
9. **WRITING ACTIVITY** CULTURAL INTERACTION Write a **script** about an encounter between a Crusader and a Muslim defender of Jerusalem.

INTEGRATED TECHNOLOGY **INTERNET ACTIVITY**

Review the information on page 381. Use the Internet to research the Washington National Cathedral. Prepare a **multimedia presentation** showing the Gothic characteristics of the Washington National Cathedral.

INTERNET KEYWORD
Washington National Cathedral

INTERACTIVE

The Crusades

In the Crusades, both Christians and Muslims believed that God was on their side. They both felt justified in using violence to win or to keep the Holy Land. The following excerpts show their belief in the rightness of their deeds.

A PRIMARY SOURCE

Pope Urban II

In 1095, Pope Urban II issued a plea that resulted in the First Crusade. The pope assured his listeners that God was on their side.

Let the holy sepulcher of our Lord and Saviour, which is possessed by the unclean nations, especially arouse you. . . . This royal city [Jerusalem], situated at the center of the earth, is now held captive by the enemies of Christ and is subjected, by those who do not know God, to the worship of the heathen. Accordingly, undertake this journey eagerly for the remission of your sins, with the assurance of the reward of imperishable glory in the kingdom of heaven.

B PRIMARY SOURCE

William of Tyre

A Christian bishop, William of Tyre, drew upon eyewitness accounts of the capture of Jerusalem by Crusaders.

It was impossible to look upon the vast numbers of the slain without horror; everywhere lay fragments of human bodies, and the very ground was covered with the blood of the slain. It was not alone the spectacle of headless bodies and mutilated limbs strewn in all directions that roused horror in all who looked upon them. Still more dreadful was it to gaze upon the victors themselves, dripping with blood from head to foot, an ominous sight which brought terror to all who met them. It is reported that within the Temple enclosure alone about ten thousand infidels perished, in addition to those who lay slain everywhere throughout the city in the streets and squares, the number of whom was estimated as no less.

C PRIMARY SOURCE

Saladin

This is an excerpt of Saladin's reply to a letter from Frederick I (Barbarossa) threatening Saladin. Saladin wrote the letter after he recaptured Jerusalem.

Whenever your armies are assembled . . . we will meet you in the power of God. We will not be satisfied with the land on the seacoast, but we will cross over with God's good pleasure and take from you all your lands in the strength of the Lord. . . . And when the Lord, by His power, shall have given us victory over you, nothing will remain for us to do but freely to take your lands by His power and with His good pleasure. . . . By the virtue and power of God we have taken possession of Jerusalem and its territories; and of the three cities that still remain in the hands of the Christians . . . we shall occupy them also.

D PRIMARY SOURCE

Luttrell Psalter

The illustration below from a Latin text shows Richard the Lion-Hearted (left) unhorsing Saladin during the Third Crusade. However, the two men never actually met in personal combat.

Document-Based QUESTIONS

1. Using specific phrases or passages from Source A and Source C, demonstrate how their attitudes were similar.
2. What directive in Source A might have been at the root of the action described in Source B?
3. What evidence in Source D reveals the artist's bias about the confrontation between Islam and Christianity?

Changes in Medieval Society

CONNECT TO THE NEW YORK STATE CORE CURRICULUM

Unit 3.A.1.c. Medieval guilds
Unit 3.A.1.b. Trade fairs and towns

TERMS & NAMES

- three-field system
- guild
- Commercial Revolution
- burgher
- vernacular
- Thomas Aquinas
- scholastics

SETTING THE STAGE While Church reform, cathedral building, and the Crusades were taking place, other important changes were occurring in medieval society. Between 1000 and 1300, agriculture, trade, and finance made significant advances. Towns and cities grew. This was in part due to the growing population and to territorial expansion of western Europe. Cultural interaction with the Muslim and Byzantine worlds sparked the growth of learning and the birth of an institution new to Europe—the university.

A Growing Food Supply

Europe's great revival would have been impossible without better ways of farming. Expanding civilization required an increased food supply. A warmer climate, which lasted from about 800 to 1200, brought improved farm production. Farmers began to cultivate lands in regions once too cold to grow crops. They also developed new methods to take advantage of more available land.

TAKING NOTES
Determining Main Ideas Use a diagram to identify changes in medieval society.

Switch to Horsepower For hundreds of years, peasants had depended on oxen to pull their plows. Oxen lived on the poorest straw and stubble, so they were easy to keep. Horses needed better food, but a team of horses could plow three times as much land in a day as a team of oxen.

Before farmers could use horses, however, a better harness was needed. Sometime before 900, farmers in Europe began using a harness that fitted across the horse's chest, enabling it to pull a plow. As a result, horses gradually replaced oxen for plowing and for pulling wagons. All over Europe, axes rang as the great forests were cleared for new fields.

The Three-Field System Around A.D. 800, some villages began to organize their lands into three fields instead of two. Two of the fields were planted and the other lay fallow (resting) for a year. Under this new **three-field system**, farmers could grow crops on two-thirds of their land each year, not just on half of it. As a result, food production increased. Villagers had more to eat. Well-fed people, especially children, could better resist disease and live longer, and as a result the European population grew dramatically.

Social History

Surnames

Many people can trace their last names, or surnames, back to a medieval occupation in Europe. The name Smith, for example, refers to someone who "smites," or works, metal. The surname Silversmith would belong to a person who works silver. In German-speaking areas, a smith was named Schmidt.

Someone who made goods out of wood was often surnamed Carpenter. In French-speaking areas, a carpenter was called Charpentier, while in German areas, the same person would be called Zimmerman.

The last name of Boulanger indicated a baker in France. A baker in Germany often had the surname Becker.

The Guilds

A second change in the European economy was the development of the guild. A **guild** was an organization of individuals in the same business or occupation working to improve the economic and social conditions of its members. The first guilds were merchant guilds. Merchants banded together to control the number of goods being traded and to keep prices up. They also provided security in trading and reduced losses.

About the same time, skilled artisans, such as wheelwrights, glassmakers, winemakers, tailors, and druggists, began craft guilds. In most crafts, both husband and wife worked at the family trade. In a few crafts, especially for cloth making, women formed the majority. The guilds set standards for quality of work, wages, and working conditions. For example, bakers were required to sell loaves of bread of a standard size and weight. The guilds also created plans for supervised training of new workers.

By the 1000s, artisans and craftspeople were manufacturing goods by hand for local and long-distance trade. More and better products were now available to buyers in small towns, in bigger cities, and at trade fairs. Guilds became powerful forces in the medieval economy. The wealth they accumulated helped them establish influence over the government and the economy of towns and cities. (A)

MAIN IDEA

Summarizing

(A) How did guilds change the way business was conducted and products made?

History *in* Depth

Craft Guilds

Craft guilds formed an important part of town life during the medieval period. They trained young people in a skilled job, regulated the quality of goods sold, and were major forces in community life.

Guild Services	
To members:	**To the community:**
• Set working conditions	• Built almshouses for victims of misfortune
• Covered members with a type of health insurance	• Guaranteed quality work
• Provided funeral expenses	• Took turns policing the streets
• Provided dowries for poor girls	• Donated windows to the Church

Apprentice
- Parents paid for training
- Lived with a master and his family
- Required to obey the master
- Trained 2–7 years
- Was not allowed to marry during training
- When trained progressed to journeyman

Journeyman
(Day Worker)
- Worked for a master to earn a salary
- Worked 6 days a week
- Needed to produce a masterpiece (his finest work) to become a master
- Had to be accepted by the guild to become a master

Master
- Owned his own shop
- Worked with other masters to protect their trade
- Sometimes served in civic government

Commercial Revolution

Just as agriculture was expanding and craftsmanship changing, so were trade and finance. Increased availability of trade goods and new ways of doing business changed life in Europe. Taken together, this expansion of trade and business is called the **Commercial Revolution**.

Fairs and Trade Most trade took place in towns. Peasants from nearby manors traveled to town on fair days, hauling items to trade. Great fairs were held several times a year, usually during religious festivals, when many people would be in town. People visited the stalls set up by merchants from all parts of Europe.

Cloth was the most common trade item. Other items included bacon, salt, honey, cheese, wine, leather, dyes, knives, and ropes. Such local markets met all the needs of daily life for a small community. No longer was everything produced on a self-sufficient manor.

More goods from foreign lands became available. Trade routes spread across Europe from Flanders to Italy. Italian merchant ships traveled the Mediterranean to ports in Byzantium such as Constantinople. They also traveled to Muslim ports along the North African coast. Trade routes were opened to Asia, in part by the Crusades.

Increased business at markets and fairs made merchants willing to take chances on buying merchandise that they could sell at a profit. Merchants then reinvested the profits in more goods.

Vocabulary
Letters of credit: A letter issued by a bank allowing the bearer to withdraw a specific amount of money from the bank or its branches.

Business and Banking As traders moved from fair to fair, they needed large amounts of cash or credit and ways to exchange many types of currencies. Enterprising merchants found ways to solve these problems. For example, bills of exchange established exchange rates between different coinage systems. Letters of credit between merchants eliminated the need to carry large amounts of cash and made trading easier. Trading firms and associations formed to offer these services to their groups.

▼ This fish market expanded the variety of food available in a medieval town.

The Commercial Revolution

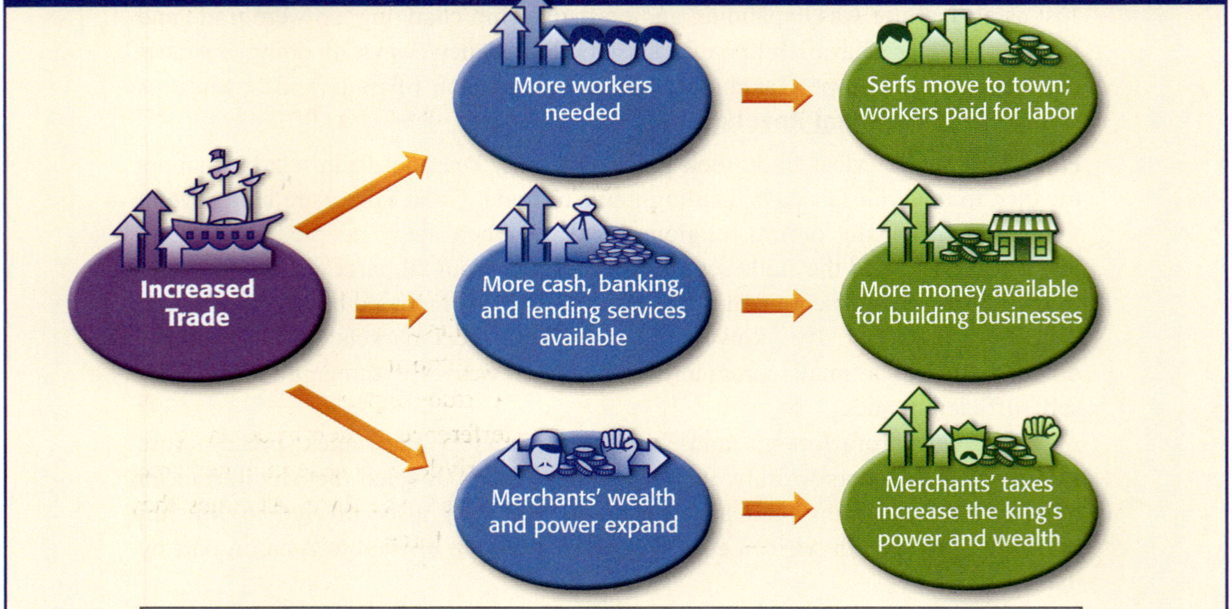

SKILLBUILDER: Interpreting Graphics

1. **Drawing Conclusions** *How did increased trade increase the power of the king?*
2. **Making Inferences** *Why would workers now have to be paid?*

Merchants looked for new markets and opportunities to make a profit. Merchants first had to purchase goods from distant places. To do so they had to borrow money, but the Church forbade Christians from lending money at interest, a sin called usury. Over time, the Church relaxed its rule on usury and Christians entered the banking business. Banking became an important business, especially in Italy. **B**

MAIN IDEA

Drawing Conclusions

B Why were changes in financial services necessary to expand trade?

Society Changes The changes brought about by the Commercial Revolution were slow, yet they had a major effect on the lives of Europeans. As you can see in the diagram shown above, increased trade brought many changes to aspects of society. Two of the most important changes involved what people did to earn a living and where they lived. As towns attracted workers, the towns grew into cities. Life in the cities was different from life in the sleepy villages or on manors.

Urban Life Flourishes

Scholars estimate that between 1000 and 1150, the population of western Europe rose from around 30 million to about 42 million. Towns grew and flourished. Compared to great cities like Constantinople, European towns were unsophisticated and tiny. Europe's largest city, Paris, probably had no more than 60,000 people by the year 1200. A typical town in medieval Europe had only about 1,500 to 2,500 people. Even so, these small communities became a powerful force for change in Europe.

Trade and Towns Grow Together By the later Middle Ages, trade was the very lifeblood of the new towns, which sprung up at ports and crossroads, on hilltops, and along rivers. As trade grew, towns all over Europe swelled with people. The excitement and bustle of towns drew many people. But there were some drawbacks to living in a medieval town. Streets were narrow, filled with animals and their waste. With no sewers, most people dumped household and human waste into the street in front of the house. Most people never bathed, and their houses lacked fresh air, light, and clean water. Because houses were built of wood with thatched roofs, they were a constant fire hazard. Nonetheless, many people chose to move to towns to pursue the economic and social opportunities they offered.

People were no longer content with their old feudal existence on manors or in tiny villages. Even though legally bound to their lord's manor, many serfs ran away. According to custom, a serf could now become free by living within a town for a year and a day. A saying of the time went, "Town air makes you free." Many of these runaway serfs, now free people, made better lives for themselves in towns.

Merchant Class Shifts the Social Order The merchants and craftspeople of medieval towns did not fit into the traditional medieval social order of noble, clergy, and peasant. At first, towns came under the authority of feudal lords, who used their authority to levy fees, taxes, and rents. As trade expanded, the **burghers**, or merchant-class town dwellers, resented this interference in their trade and commerce. They organized themselves and demanded privileges. These included freedom from certain kinds of tolls and the right to govern the town. At times they fought against their landlords and won these rights by force.

The Revival of Learning

During the Crusades, European contact with Muslims and Byzantines greatly expanded. This contact brought a new interest in learning, especially in the works of Greek philosophers. The Muslim and Byzantine libraries housed copies of these writings. Most had disappeared during the centuries following the fall of Rome and the invasions of western Europe. C

MAIN IDEA

Recognizing Effects

C How did the Crusades contribute to the expansion of trade and learning?

The Muslim Connection In the 1100s, Christian scholars from Europe began visiting Muslim libraries in Spain. Few Western scholars knew Greek but most did know Latin. So Jewish scholars living in Spain translated the Arabic versions of works by Aristotle and other Greek writers into Latin. All at once, Europeans acquired a huge new body of knowledge. This included science, philosophy, law, mathematics, and other fields. In addition, the Crusaders brought back to Europe superior Muslim technology in ships, navigation, and weapons.

Scholars and the University At the center of the growth of learning stood a new European institution—the university. The word *university* originally referred to a group of scholars meeting wherever they could. People, not buildings, made up the medieval university. Universities arose at Paris and at Bologna, Italy, by the end of the 1100s. Others followed at the English town of Oxford and at Salerno, Italy. Most students were the sons of burghers or well-to-do artisans. For most students, the goal was a job in government or the Church. Earning a bachelor's degree in theology might take five to seven years in school; becoming a master of theology took at least 12 years of study.

New ideas and forms of expression began to flow out of the universities. At a time when serious scholars and writers were writing in Latin, a few remarkable poets began using a lively **vernacular**, or the everyday language of their homeland. Some of these writers wrote masterpieces that are still

History *in* Depth

Muslim Scholars

A number of Islamic scholars had a great influence on European thought. The image above shows Ibn Sina, known in the West as Avicenna. He was a Persian philosopher, astronomer, poet, and physician. His book, *The Cure*, an interpretation of Aristotle's philosophy, greatly affected Western thought. This work, translated into Latin, influenced the scholastics.

INTEGRATED TECHNOLOGY

INTERNET ACTIVITY Create a documentary film script on Muslim scholars. Go to **classzone.com** for your research.

▲ Thomas Aquinas's writings focused on questions of faith versus reason and logic.

read today. Dante Alighieri wrote *The Divine Comedy* (1308–1314) in Italian. Geoffrey Chaucer wrote *The Canterbury Tales* (about 1386–1400) in English. Christine de Pisan wrote *The Book of The City of Ladies* (1405) in French. Since most people couldn't read or understand Latin, these works written in the vernacular brought literature to many people.

Aquinas and Medieval Philosophy Christian scholars were excited by the ideas of Greek philosophers. They wondered if a Christian scholar could use Aristotle's logical approach to truth and still keep faith with the Bible.

In the mid-1200s, the scholar **Thomas Aquinas** (uh•KWY•nuhs) argued that the most basic religious truths could be proved by logical argument. Between 1267 and 1273, Aquinas wrote the *Summa Theologicae.* Aquinas's great work, influenced by Aristotle, combined ancient Greek thought with the Christian thought of his time. Aquinas and his fellow scholars who met at the great universities were known as schoolmen, or **scholastics**. The scholastics used their knowledge of Aristotle to debate many issues of their time. Their teachings on law and government influenced the thinking of western Europeans, particularly the English and French. Accordingly, they began to develop democratic institutions and traditions.

NEW YORK CORE CURRICULUM REVIEW

TERMS & NAMES 1. For each term or name, write a sentence explaining its significance.

• three-field system • guild • Commercial Revolution • burgher • vernacular • Thomas Aquinas • scholastics

USING YOUR NOTES

2. How did medieval society change between 1000 and 1500?

MAIN IDEAS

3. How did guilds influence business practices in medieval towns?
4. How were Muslim scholars linked to the revival of learning in Europe?
5. In what ways did burghers expand their freedom from landlords?

CRITICAL THINKING & WRITING

6. **RECOGNIZING EFFECTS** What was the effect of the development of towns on the feudal system?
7. **ANALYZING MOTIVES** Why would writers choose to produce works in the vernacular instead of in Latin?
8. **RECOGNIZING EFFECTS** How did the Commercial Revolution lay the foundation for the economy of modern Europe?
9. **WRITING ACTIVITY** ECONOMICS Write a brief **news article** on the value of letters of credit and how they have changed commercial trade activities.

CONNECT TO TODAY **WRITING AN INVESTIGATIVE REPORT**

Contact a local bank and find out what services are available to its commercial clients. Write a brief **report** on the banking services. Identify which services seem to have had their beginnings in the late medieval period and which ones are modern.

England and France Develop

CONNECT TO THE NEW YORK STATE CORE CURRICULUM

Unit 3.H.a. Forces moving toward centralization
Unit 4.G.1. Background–Magna Carta

TERMS & NAMES

- William the Conqueror
- Henry II
- common law
- Magna Carta
- parliament
- Hugh Capet
- Philip II
- Estates-General

SETTING THE STAGE By the early 800s, small Anglo-Saxon kingdoms covered the former Roman province of Britain. In Europe, the decline of the Carolingian Empire in the 900s left a patchwork of feudal states controlled by local lords. Gradually, the growth of towns and villages, and the breakup of the feudal system were leading to more centralized government and the development of nations. The earliest nations in Europe to develop a strong unified government were England and France. Both would take similar paths.

England Absorbs Waves of Invaders

For centuries, invaders from various regions in Europe landed on English shores. The Angles and the Saxons stayed, bringing their own ways and creating an Anglo-Saxon culture.

Early Invasions In the 800s, Britain was battered by fierce raids of Danish Vikings. These invaders were so feared that a special prayer was said in churches: "God, deliver us from the fury of the Northmen." Only Alfred the Great, Anglo-Saxon king from 871 to 899, managed to turn back the Viking invaders. Gradually he and his successors united the kingdom under one rule, calling it England, "land of the Angles." The Angles were one of the Germanic tribes that had invaded the island of Britain.

In 1016, the Danish king Canute (kuh•NOOT) conquered England, molding Anglo-Saxons and Vikings into one people. In 1042, King Edward the Confessor, a descendant of Alfred the Great, took the throne. Edward died in January 1066 without an heir. A great struggle for the throne erupted, leading to one last invasion.

The Norman Conquest The invader was William, duke of Normandy, who became known as **William the Conqueror**. Normandy is a region in the north of France that had been conquered by the Vikings. Its name comes from the French term for the Vikings—North men, or Norman. The Normans were descended from the Vikings, but they were French in language and in culture. As King Edward's cousin, William claimed the English crown and invaded England with a Norman army.

William's rival was Harold Godwinson, the Anglo-Saxon who claimed the throne. Harold was equally ambitious. On October 14, 1066, Normans and

TAKING NOTES

Clarifying Identify major steps toward democratic government.

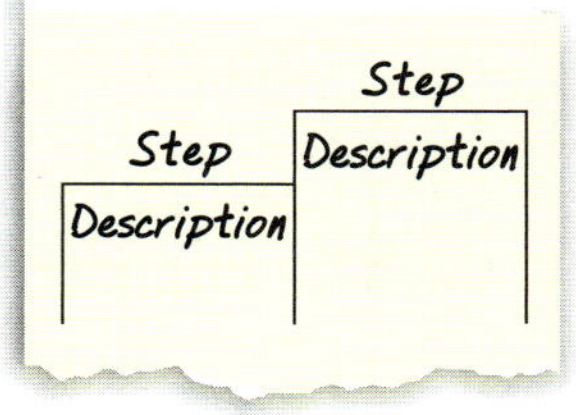

History Makers

Eleanor of Aquitaine
1122–1204

Eleanor of Aquitaine was one of the most remarkable women in history. She was wife to two kings and mother to two kings. She married Louis VII of France when the Second Crusade began. In 1147, she accompanied him to the Holy Land. Shortly afterward their marriage was annulled. Eleanor then married Henry Plantagenet, who was to become Henry II of England. Their marriage produced eight children. Two became English kings, Richard the Lion-Hearted and John.

INTEGRATED TECHNOLOGY

RESEARCH LINKS For more on Eleanor of Aquitaine, go to **classzone.com**

Anglo-Saxons fought the battle that changed the course of English history—the Battle of Hastings. After Harold was killed by an arrow that pierced his eye, the Normans won a decisive victory.

After his victory, William declared all England his personal property. William kept about one-fifth of England for himself. The English lords who supported Harold lost their lands. William then granted their lands to about 200 Norman lords who swore oaths of loyalty to him personally. By doing this, William unified control of the lands and laid the foundation for centralized government in England.

England's Evolving Government

Over the next centuries, English kings tried to achieve two goals. First, they wanted to hold and add to their French lands. Second, they wanted to strengthen their own power over the nobles and the Church.

William the Conqueror's descendants owned land both in Normandy and in England. The English king **Henry II** added to these holdings by marrying Eleanor of Aquitaine from France.

The marriage brought Henry a large territory in France called Aquitaine. He added Aquitaine to the lands in Normandy he had already inherited from William the Conqueror. Because Henry held lands in France, he was a vassal to the French king. But he was also a king in his own right.

Juries and Common Law Henry ruled England from 1154 to 1189. He strengthened the royal courts of justice by sending royal judges to every part of England at least once a year. They collected taxes, settled lawsuits, and punished crimes. Henry also introduced the use of the jury in English courts. A jury in medieval England was a group of loyal people—usually 12 neighbors of the accused—who answered a royal judge's questions about the facts of a case. Jury trials became a popular means of settling disputes. Only the king's courts were allowed to conduct them.

Over the centuries, case by case, the rulings of England's royal judges formed a unified body of law that became known as **common law**. Today the principles of English common law are the basis for law in many English-speaking countries, including the United States. (A)

MAIN IDEA

Recognizing Effects

(A) What impact did the English common law have on the United States?

The Magna Carta Henry was succeeded first by his son Richard the Lion-Hearted, hero of the Third Crusade. When Richard died, his younger brother John took the throne. John ruled from 1199 to 1216. He failed as a military leader, earning the nickname John Softsword. John lost Normandy and all his lands in northern France to the French under Philip Augustus. This loss forced a confrontation with his own nobles.

Some of John's problems stemmed from his own personality. He was cruel to his subjects and tried to squeeze money out of them. He alienated the Church and threatened to take away town charters guaranteeing self-government. John raised taxes to an all-time high to finance his wars. His nobles revolted. On June 15, 1215, they forced John to agree to the most celebrated document in English history, the **Magna Carta** (Great Charter). This document, drawn up by English nobles and reluctantly approved by King John, guaranteed certain basic political rights. The nobles wanted to safeguard their own feudal rights and limit the king's powers. In later years, however, English people of all classes argued that certain clauses in the Magna Carta applied to every citizen. Guaranteed rights included no taxation without representation, a jury trial, and the protection of the law. The Magna Carta guaranteed what are now considered basic legal rights both in England and in the United States. **B**

MAIN IDEA

Summarizing

B What is the significance of the Magna Carta?

Vocabulary

borough: a self-governing town

The Model Parliament Another important step toward democratic government came during the rule of the next English king, Edward I. Edward needed to raise taxes for a war against the French, the Welsh, and the Scots. In 1295, Edward summoned two burgesses (citizens of wealth and property) from every borough and two knights from every county to serve as a **parliament**, or legislative group. In November 1295, knights, burgesses, bishops, and lords met together at Westminster in London. This is now called the Model Parliament because its new makeup (commoners, or non-nobles, as well as lords) served as a model for later kings.

Over the next century, from 1300 to 1400, the king called the knights and burgesses whenever a new tax was needed. In Parliament, these two groups gradually formed an assembly of their own called the House of Commons. Nobles and bishops met separately as the House of Lords. Under Edward I, Parliament was in part a royal tool that weakened the great lords. As time went by, Parliament became strong. Like the Magna Carta, it provided a check on royal power.

> Analyzing Primary Sources

The Magna Carta

The Magna Carta is considered one of the cornerstones of democratic government. The underlying principle of the document is the idea that all must obey the law, even the king. Its guaranteed rights are an important part of modern liberties and justice.

PRIMARY SOURCE

38. No bailiff [officer of the court] for the future shall, upon his own unsupported complaint, put anyone to his "law," without credible witnesses brought for this purposes.

39. No freeman shall be taken or imprisoned . . . or exiled or in any way destroyed, nor will we [the king] go upon him nor send upon him, except by the lawful judgement of his peers or by the law of the land.

40. To no one will we sell, to no one will we refuse or delay, right or justice.

45. We will appoint as justices, constables, sheriffs, or bailiffs only such as know the law of the realm and mean to observe it well.

DOCUMENT-BASED QUESTIONS

1. **Analyzing Motives** *Why might the English nobles have insisted on the right listed in number 45?*
2. **Making Inferences** *Which of the statements is a forerunner to the right to a speedy public trial guaranteed in the Sixth Amendment of the U.S. Constitution?*

▲ The coronation of Philip II in Reims Cathedral

Capetian Dynasty Rules France

The kings of France, like those of England, looked for ways to increase their power. After the breakup of Charlemagne's empire, French counts and dukes ruled their lands independently under the feudal system. By the year 1000, France was divided into about 47 feudal territories. In 987, the last member of the Carolingian family—Louis the Sluggard—died. **Hugh Capet** (kuh•PAY), an undistinguished duke from the middle of France, succeeded him. The Capet family ruled only a small territory, but at its heart stood Paris. Hugh Capet began the Capetian dynasty of French kings that ruled France from 987 to 1328.

France Becomes a Separate Kingdom Hugh Capet, his son, and his grandson all were weak rulers, but time and geography favored the Capetians. Their territory, though small, sat astride important trade routes in northern France. For 300 years, Capetian kings tightened their grip on this strategic area. The power of the king gradually spread outward from Paris. Eventually, the growth of royal power would unite France.

Philip II Expands His Power One of the most powerful Capetians was **Philip II**, called Philip Augustus, who ruled from 1180 to 1223. As a child, Philip had watched his father lose land to King Henry II of England. When Philip became king at the age of 15, he set out to weaken the power of the English kings in France. Philip was crafty, unprincipled, and willing to do whatever was necessary to achieve his goals.

Philip had little success against Henry II or Henry's son, Richard the Lion-Hearted. However, when King John, Richard's brother, gained the English throne, it was another matter. Philip earned the name Augustus (from the Latin word meaning "majestic"), probably because he greatly increased the territory of France. He seized Normandy from King John in 1204 and within two years had gained other territory. By the end of Philip's reign, he had tripled the lands under his direct control. For the first time, a French king had become more powerful than any of his vassals.

Philip II not only wanted more land, he also wanted a stronger central government. He established royal officials called bailiffs. They were sent from Paris to every district in the kingdom to preside over the king's courts and to collect the king's taxes.

Philip II's Heirs France's central government became even stronger during the reign of Philip's grandson, Louis IX, who ruled from 1226 to 1270. Unlike his grandfather, Louis was pious and saintly. He was known as the ideal king. After his death, he was made a saint by the Catholic Church. Louis created a French appeals court, which could overturn the decisions of local courts. These royal courts of France strengthened the monarchy while weakening feudal ties.

In 1302, Philip IV, who ruled France from 1285 to 1314, was involved in a quarrel with the pope. The pope refused to allow priests to pay taxes to the king. Philip disputed the right of the pope to control Church affairs in his kingdom. As in England, the French king usually called a meeting of his lords and bishops when he needed support for his policies. To win wider support against the pope, Philip IV decided to include commoners in the meeting.

The Development of England and France

England	France
• William the Conqueror invades England in 1066. • Henry II (1154–1189) introduces use of the jury in English courts. • John (1199–1216) agrees to the Magna Carta in 1215. • Edward I (1272–1307) calls the Model Parliament in 1295.	• Hugh Capet increases the territory of France. • Philip II (1180–1223) established bailiffs to preside over courts and collect taxes. • Louis IX (1226–1270) creates a French appeals court. • Philip IV (1285–1314) adds Third Estate to the Estates-General.

SKILLBUILDER: Interpreting Charts

1. **Clarifying** *What aspects of courts were developed during the rule of Henry II and Philip II?*
2. **Developing Historical Perspective** *Which aspect of centralized government developed about the same time in both England and France?*

Estates-General In France, the Church leaders were known as the First Estate, and the great lords as the Second Estate. The commoners, wealthy landholders or merchants, that Philip invited to participate in the council became known as the Third Estate. The whole meeting was called the **Estates-General**. C

MAIN IDEA

Summarizing

C What three estates made up the Estates-General?

Like the English Parliament in its early years, the Estates-General helped to increase royal power against the nobility. Unlike Parliament, however, the Estates-General never became an independent force that limited the king's power. However, centuries later, the Third Estate would play a key role in overthrowing the French monarchy during the French Revolution.

Beginnings of Democracy England and France were just beginning to establish a democratic tradition. This tradition rested on setting up a centralized government that would be able to govern widespread lands. The creation of common law and court systems was a first step toward increased central government power. Including commoners in the decision-making process of government was also an important step in the direction of democratic rule. Before England and France could move forward in this direction, however, they had to contend with a century of turmoil that included religious disputes, plague, and war.

NEW YORK CORE CURRICULUM REVIEW

TERMS & NAMES 1. For each term or name, write a sentence explaining its significance.

• William the Conqueror • Henry II • common law • Magna Carta • parliament • Hugh Capet • Philip II • Estates-General

USING YOUR NOTES

2. Which of the steps toward democratic government are similar to U.S. practices? Explain.

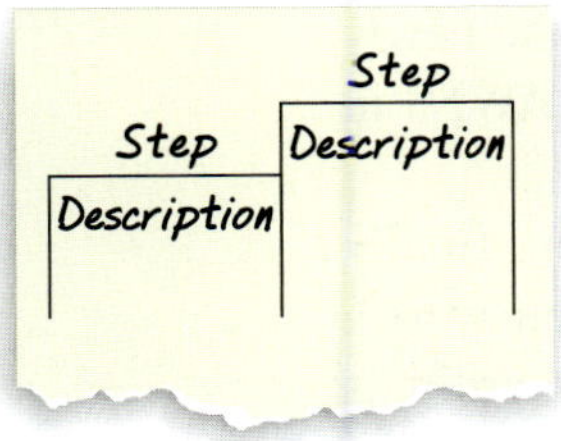

MAIN IDEAS

3. What two legal practices date back to Henry II?
4. What are some basic rights guaranteed by the Magna Carta?
5. Why did Philip II call the Estates-General together?

CRITICAL THINKING & WRITING

6. **COMPARING** Compare the way in which England and France began developing as nations.
7. **RECOGNIZING EFFECTS** Which of the changes in English government is reflected in the government of the United States today?
8. **EVALUATING COURSES OF ACTION** What steps were necessary to centralize governments in England and France?
9. **WRITING ACTIVITY** POWER AND AUTHORITY Imagine that you are an adviser to the English or French king. Write him a **letter** to argue for or against including commoners in the Parliament or Estates-General.

CONNECT TO TODAY **COMPARING HISTORICAL DOCUMENTS**

Find a copy of the Magna Carta and a copy of the Bill of Rights of the United States Constitution. Study both documents and create a **table** showing where the Constitution reflects the ideas of the Magna Carta.

4

The Hundred Years' War and the Plague

CONNECT TO THE NEW YORK STATE CORE CURRICULUM

Unit 3.E. Social, economic, and political impacts of the plague on Eurasia and Africa
Unit 3.H.b. Role of nationalism

TERMS & NAMES

- Avignon
- Great Schism
- John Wycliffe
- Jan Hus
- bubonic plague
- Hundred Years' War
- Joan of Arc

SETTING THE STAGE The 1300s were filled with disasters, both natural and human-made. The Church seemed to be thriving but soon would face a huge division. A deadly epidemic claimed millions of lives. So many people died in the epidemic that the structure of the economy changed. Claims to thrones in France and England led to wars in those lands. The wars would result in changes in the governments of both France and England. By the end of the century, the medieval way of life was beginning to disappear.

TAKING NOTES

Analyzing Causes and Recognizing Effects Use the chart to identify causes and effects of major events at the end of the Middle Ages.

	Cause & Effect
Split in Church	
Plague	
100 Years' War	

A Church Divided

At the beginning of the 1300s, the Age of Faith still seemed strong. Soon, however, both the pope and the Church were in desperate trouble.

Pope and King Collide In 1300, Pope Boniface VIII attempted to enforce papal authority on kings as previous popes had. When King Philip IV of France asserted his authority over French bishops, Boniface responded with an official document. It stated that kings must always obey popes.

Philip merely sneered at this statement. In fact, one of Philip's ministers is said to have remarked that "my master's sword is made of steel, the pope's is made of [words]." Instead of obeying the pope, Philip had him held prisoner in September 1303. The king planned to bring him to France for trial. The pope was rescued, but the elderly Boniface died a month later. Never again would a pope be able to force monarchs to obey him.

Avignon and the Great Schism In 1305, Philip IV persuaded the College of Cardinals to choose a French archbishop as the new pope. Clement V, the newly selected pope, moved from Rome to the city of **Avignon** (av•vee•NYAWN) in France. Popes would live there for the next 69 years.

The move to Avignon badly weakened the Church. When reformers finally tried to move the papacy back to Rome, however, the result was even worse. In 1378, Pope Gregory XI died while visiting Rome. The College of Cardinals then met in Rome to choose a successor. As they deliberated, they could hear a mob outside screaming, "A Roman, a Roman, we want a Roman for pope, or at least an Italian!" Finally, the cardinals announced to the crowd that an Italian had been chosen: Pope Urban VI. Many cardinals regretted their choice almost immediately. Urban VI's passion for reform and his arrogant personality caused the cardinals to elect a second pope a few months later. They chose Robert of Geneva, who spoke French. He took the name Clement VII.

Now there were two popes. Each declared the other to be a false pope, excommunicating his rival. The French pope lived in Avignon, while the Italian pope lived in Rome. This began the split in the Church known as the **Great Schism** (SIHZ•uhm), or division.

In 1414, the Council of Constance attempted to end the Great Schism by choosing a single pope. By now, there were a total of three popes: the Avignon pope, the Roman pope, and a third pope elected by an earlier council at Pisa. With the help of the Holy Roman Emperor, the council forced all three popes to resign. In 1417, the Council chose a new pope, Martin V, ending the Great Schism but leaving the papacy greatly weakened.

Scholars Challenge Church Authority The papacy was further challenged by an Englishman named **John Wycliffe** (WIHK•lihf). He preached that Jesus Christ, not the pope, was the true head of the Church. He was much offended by the worldliness and wealth many clergy displayed. Wycliffe believed that the clergy should own no land or wealth. Wycliffe also taught that the Bible alone—not the pope—was the final authority for Christian life. He helped spread this idea by inspiring an English translation of the New Testament of the Bible.

MAIN IDEA

Contrasting

A According to the different beliefs of the time, what was the true source of religious authority?

Influenced by Wycliffe's writings, **Jan Hus**, a professor in Bohemia (now part of the Czech Republic), taught that the authority of the Bible was higher than that of the pope. Hus was excommunicated in 1412. In 1414, he was seized by Church leaders, tried as a heretic, and then burned at the stake in 1415. **A**

The Bubonic Plague Strikes

During the 1300s an epidemic struck parts of Asia, North Africa, and Europe. Approximately one-third of the population of Europe died of the deadly disease known as the **bubonic plague**. Unlike catastrophes that pull communities together, this epidemic was so terrifying that it ripped apart the very fabric of society. Giovanni Boccaccio, an Italian writer of the time, described its effect:

▼ This painting, titled *The Triumph of Death,* depicts the effect of the plague.

PRIMARY SOURCE

This scourge had implanted so great a terror in the hearts of men and women that brothers abandoned brothers, uncles their nephews, sisters their brothers, and in many cases wives deserted their husbands. But even worse, . . . fathers and mothers refused to nurse and assist their own children.

GIOVANNI BOCCACCIO, *The Decameron*

Origins and Impact of the Plague The plague began in Asia. Traveling trade routes, it infected parts of Asia, the Muslim world, and Europe. In 1347, a fleet of Genoese merchant ships arrived in Sicily carrying bubonic plague, also known as the Black Death. It got the name because of the purplish or blackish spots it produced on the skin. The disease swept through Italy. From there it followed trade routes to Spain, France, Germany, England, and other parts of Europe and North Africa.

INTERACTIVE

The Bubonic Plague

The bubonic plague, or Black Death, was a killer disease that swept repeatedly through many areas of the world. It wiped out two-thirds of the population in some areas of China, destroyed populations of Muslim towns in Southwest Asia, and then decimated one-third of the European population.

Route of the Plague

1. The horse-riding Mongols likely carried infected fleas and rats in their food supplies as they swooped into China.
2. The disease came with merchants along the trade routes of Asia to southern Asia, southwest Asia, and Africa.
3. In 1345–1346, a Mongol army besieged Kaffa. A year later, Italian merchants returned to Italy, unknowingly bringing the plague with them.

Disease Spreads

Black rats carried fleas that were infested with a bacillus called *Yersinia pestis*. Because people did not bathe, almost all had fleas and lice. In addition, medieval people threw their garbage and sewage into the streets. These unsanitary streets became breeding grounds for more rats. The fleas carried by rats leapt from person to person, thus spreading the bubonic plague with incredible speed.

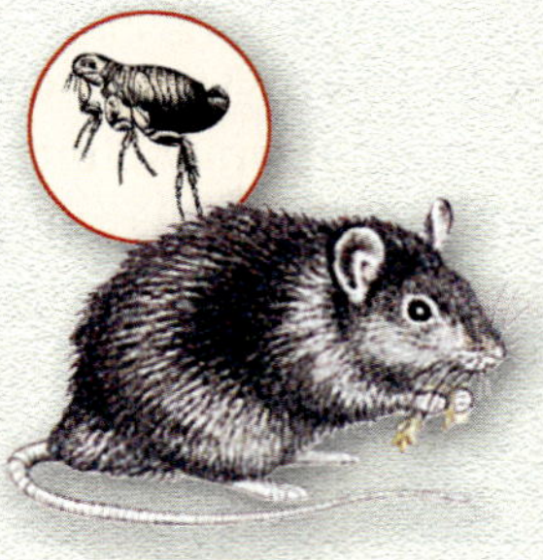

Symptoms of the Bubonic Plague

- Painful swellings called buboes (BOO•bohz) in the lymph nodes, particularly those in the armpits and groin
- Sometimes purplish or blackish spots on the skin
- Extremely high fever, chills, delirium, and in most cases, death

Death Tolls, 1300s

Western Europe	☠☠☠☠☠☠	20–25 million
China, India, other Asians	☠☠☠☠☠☠	25 million
	☠ = 4 million	

Patterns of Interaction

The Spread of Epidemic Disease: Bubonic Plague and Smallpox

The spread of disease has been a very tragic result of cultures interacting with one another across place and time. Such diseases as smallpox and influenza have killed millions of people, sometimes—as with the Aztecs—virtually destroying civilizations.

Connect *to* Today

1. **Hypothesizing** Had people known the cause of the bubonic plague, what might they have done to slow its spread?

   See Skillbuilder Handbook, page R15.

2. **Comparing** What diseases of today might be compared to the bubonic plague? Why?

The bubonic plague took about four years to reach almost every corner of Europe. Some communities escaped unharmed, but in others, approximately two-thirds to three-quarters of those who caught the disease died. Before the bubonic plague ran its course, it killed almost 25 million Europeans and many more millions in Asia and North Africa.

The plague returned every few years, though it never struck as severely as in the first outbreak. However, the periodic attacks further reduced the population.

Effects of the Plague The economic and social effects of the plague were enormous. The old manorial system began to crumble. Some of the changes that occurred included these:

- Town populations fell.
- Trade declined. Prices rose.
- The serfs left the manor in search of better wages.
- Nobles fiercely resisted peasant demands for higher wages, causing peasant revolts in England, France, Italy, and Belgium.
- Jews were blamed for bringing on the plague. All over Europe, Jews were driven from their homes or, worse, massacred.
- The Church suffered a loss of prestige when its prayers failed to stop the onslaught of the bubonic plague and priests abandoned their duties. **B**

MAIN IDEA

Recognizing Effects

B Which of the effects of the plague do you think most changed life in the medieval period?

If the Plague Struck America Today

The bubonic plague reportedly wiped out about one-third of Europe's population in the 1300s. In the United States today, a one-third death toll would equal over 96 million people, or the number living in the states represented by the color ■.

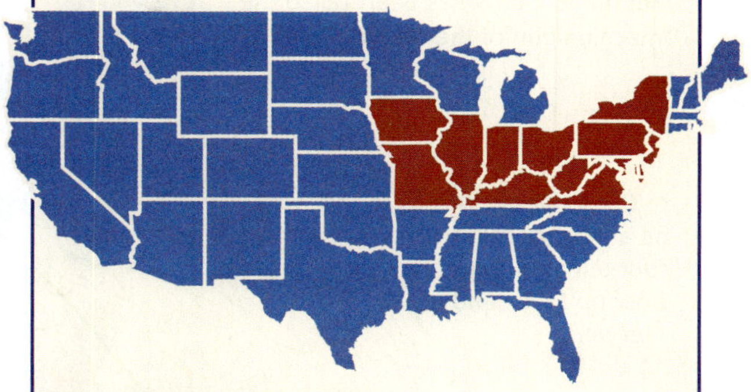

Source: U.S. Bureau of the Census

SKILLBUILDER: Interpreting Charts

1. **Clarifying** *How many states on the chart would have lost their entire population to the plague?*
2. **Drawing Conclusions** *How might the chart help explain why many Europeans thought the world was ending?*

The bubonic plague and its aftermath disrupted medieval society, hastening changes that were already in the making. The society of the Middle Ages was collapsing. The century of war between England and France was that society's final death struggle.

The Hundred Years' War

Not only did the people in Europe during the 1300s have to deal with epidemic disease, but they also had to deal with war. England and France battled with each other on French soil for just over a century. The century of war between England and France marked the end of medieval Europe's society.

When the last Capetian king died without a successor, England's Edward III, as grandson of Philip IV, claimed the right to the French throne. The war that Edward III launched for that throne continued on and off from 1337 to 1453. It became known as the **Hundred Years' War**. Victory passed back and forth between the two countries. Finally, between 1421 and 1453, the French rallied and drove the English out of France entirely, except for the port city of Calais.

The Hundred Years' War brought a change in the style of warfare in Europe. At this time some combatants were still operating under medieval ideals of chivalry. They looked with contempt on the common foot soldiers and archers who fought alongside them. This contempt would change as the longbow changed warfare.

History *in* Depth

The Longbow

The longbow was cheap, easy to carry, and deadly. It was powerful enough to penetrate armor, thus reducing the impact of mounted cavalry. Bowmen could fire so fast that the longbow has been called the "machine gun of the Middle Ages."

▶ The longbow was as tall as a man, or taller. A six-foot-tall man might have a bow up to six and a half feet tall.

▶ English archers usually carried a case with extra bowstrings and a sheaf of 24 arrows. The arrows were about 27 inches long and balanced in flight by feathers.

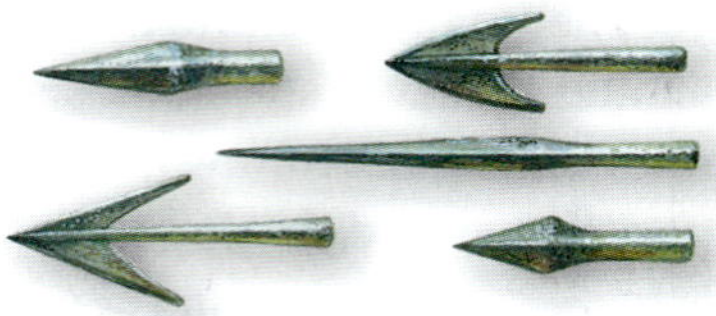

▲ The arrows were absolutely fatal when shot within 100 yards. The average archer could fire 12 to 15 arrows per minute and hit a man at 200 yards away.

The Longbow Changes Warfare The English introduced the longbow and demonstrated its power in three significant battles: Crécy, Poitiers, and Agincourt. The first and most spectacular battle was the Battle of Crécy (KREHS•ee) on August 26, 1346. The English army, including longbowmen, was outnumbered by a French army three times its size. The French army included knights and archers with crossbows. French knights believed themselves invincible and attacked.

English longbowmen let fly thousands of arrows at the oncoming French. The crossbowmen, peppered with English arrows, retreated in panic. The knights trampled their own archers in an effort to cut a path through them. English longbowmen sent volley after volley of deadly arrows. They unhorsed knights who then lay helplessly on the ground in their heavy armor. Then, using long knives, the English foot soldiers attacked, slaughtering the French. At the end of the day, more than a third of the French force lay dead. Among them were some of the most honored in chivalry. The longbow, not chivalry, had won the day. The mounted, heavily armored medieval knight was soon to become extinct.

The English repeated their victory ten years later at the Battle of Poitiers (pwah•TYAY). The third English victory, the Battle of Agincourt (AJ•ihn•KAWRT), took place in 1415. The success of the longbow in these battles spelled doom for chivalric warfare.

Joan of Arc In 1420, the French and English signed a treaty stating that Henry V would inherit the French crown upon the death of the French king Charles VI. Then, in 1429, a teenage French peasant girl named **Joan of Arc** felt moved by God to rescue France from its English conquerors. When Joan was just 13 she began to have visions and hear what she believed were voices of the saints. They urged her to drive the English from France and give the French crown to France's true king, Charles VII, son of Charles VI.

On May 7, 1429, Joan led the French army into battle at a fort city near Orléans. The fort blocked the road to Orléans. It was a hard-fought battle for both sides. The French finally retreated in despair. Suddenly, Joan and a few soldiers charged back toward the fort. The entire French army stormed after her. The siege of Orléans was broken. Joan of Arc guided the French onto the path of victory.

After that victory, Joan persuaded Charles to go with her to Reims. There he was crowned king on July 17, 1429. In 1430, the Burgundians, England's allies, captured Joan in battle. They turned her over to the English. The English, in turn, handed her over to Church authorities to stand trial. Although the French king Charles VII owed his crown to Joan, he did nothing to rescue her. Condemned as a witch and a heretic because of her claim to hear voices, Joan was burned at the stake on May 30, 1431.

The Impact of the Hundred Years' War The long, exhausting war finally ended in 1453. Each side experienced major changes.

- A feeling of nationalism emerged in England and France. Now people thought of the king as a national leader, fighting for the glory of the country, not simply a feudal lord.
- The power and prestige of the French monarch increased.
- The English suffered a period of internal turmoil known as the War of the Roses, in which two noble houses fought for the throne. (C)

Some historians consider the end of the Hundred Years' War in 1453 as the end of the Middle Ages. The twin pillars of the medieval world, religious devotion and the code of chivalry, both crumbled. The Age of Faith died a slow death. This death was caused by the Great Schism, the scandalous display of wealth by the Church, and the discrediting of the Church during the bubonic plague. The Age of Chivalry died on the battlefields of Crécy, Poitiers, and Agincourt.

MAIN IDEA

Drawing Conclusions

(C) How did the Hundred Years' War change the perception of people toward their king?

History Makers

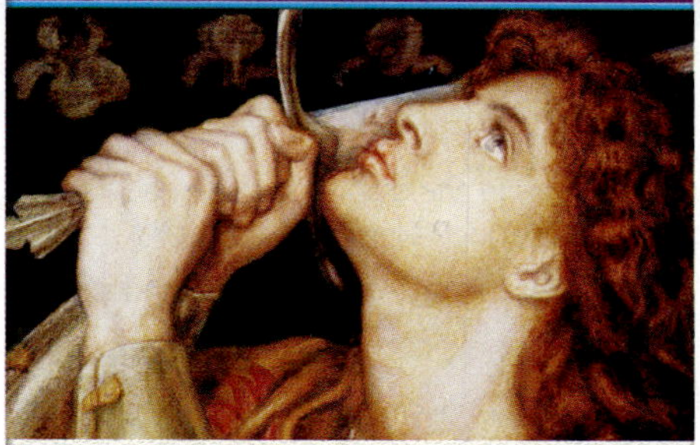

Joan of Arc
1412?–1431

In the 1420s, rumors circulated among the French that a young woman would save France from the English. So when Joan arrived on the scene she was considered the fulfillment of that prophecy. Joan cut her hair short and wore a suit of armor and carried a sword.

Her unusual appearance and extraordinary confidence inspired French troops. Eventually she was given command of troops that broke the siege of Orléans. In 1430, she was turned over to a Church court for trial. In truth, her trial was more political than religious. The English were determined to prove her a fake and to weaken her image.

INTEGRATED TECHNOLOGY

RESEARCH LINKS For more on Joan of Arc, go to **classzone.com**

NEW YORK CORE CURRICULUM REVIEW

TERMS & NAMES 1. For each term or name, write a sentence explaining its significance.

• Avignon • Great Schism • John Wycliffe • Jan Hus • bubonic plague • Hundred Years' War • Joan of Arc

USING YOUR NOTES

2. Which event had some economic effects? Explain.

	Cause & Effect
Split in Church	
Plague	
100 Years' War	

MAIN IDEAS

3. What was the Great Schism?
4. What were three effects of the bubonic plague?
5. What impact did Joan of Arc have on the Hundred Years' War?

CRITICAL THINKING & WRITING

6. **RECOGNIZING EFFECTS** Which event do you think diminished the power of the Church more—the Great Schism or the bubonic plague?
7. **IDENTIFYING PROBLEMS** What problems did survivors face after the bubonic plague swept through their town?
8. **RECOGNIZING EFFECTS** How did the Hundred Years' War encourage a feeling of nationalism in both France and England?
9. **WRITING ACTIVITY** RELIGIOUS AND ETHICAL SYSTEMS Write a **persuasive essay** supporting the right of the pope to appoint French bishops.

CONNECT TO TODAY **MAPPING AN EPIDEMIC**

Research the number of AIDS victims in countries throughout the world. Then, create an annotated **world map** showing the numbers in each country. Be sure to list your sources.

Chapter 14 Assessment

TERMS & NAMES

Briefly explain the importance of each of the following to western Europe during the medieval period.

1. Crusade
2. Reconquista
3. Commercial Revolution
4. Magna Carta
5. parliament
6. Great Schism
7. bubonic plague
8. Hundred Years' War

MAIN IDEAS

Church Reform and the Crusades Section 1 (pages 379–386)

9. Explain the three main abuses that most distressed Church reformers.
10. What were the effects of the Crusades?

Changes in Medieval Society Section 2 (pages 387–392)

11. How did trade and finance change in the period from 1000 to 1500?
12. How did the growth of towns hurt the feudal system?
13. What role did Muslims play in Europe's revival of learning?

England and France Develop Section 3 (pages 393–397)

14. How did English kings increase their power and reduce the power of the nobles?
15. Why was Philip II called Augustus?

The Hundred Years' War and the Plague Section 4 (pages 398–403)

16. Summarize the main ideas of John Wycliffe.
17. Why did the bubonic plague cause people to turn away from the Church?
18. How did the Hundred Years' War change warfare in Europe?

CRITICAL THINKING

1. USING YOUR NOTES

In a diagram, show how governments became more centralized in France and in England.

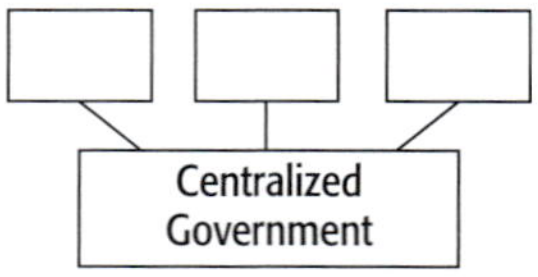

2. SUMMARIZING

CULTURAL INTERACTION What role did Jews and Muslims play in Christian Europe's financial revolution?

3. ANALYZING CAUSES

RELIGIOUS AND ETHICAL SYSTEMS Identify and discuss the events that led to the decline of the power of the Church in the period from 1000 to 1500.

4. CLARIFYING

ECONOMICS In what ways did the guilds change business and employment practices?

5. HYPOTHESIZING

Using the visual summary and your notes, suggest how the history of Western Europe would have been different if one of the events shown on the visual summary had not occurred.

VISUAL SUMMARY

Europe in the Middle Ages

Economics	Politics/Government	Religion	Society
• Better farming methods increased food production. • Trade expanded. • Guilds formed for both merchants and artisans.	• England and France developed strong central governments. • Parliament and the Estates-General bring representation to commoners. • The Hundred Years' War further weakened feudal power.	• Kings and popes engaged in power struggles. • The Great Schism weakened the Church. • The First Crusade captured Jerusalem. • Later Crusades accomplished little.	• Population increased in the Middle Ages. • The bubonic plague killed millions and weakened the manorial economy. • Europe's first universities developed.

Use the quotation and your knowledge of world history to answer questions 1 and 2.
Additional Test Practice, pp. S1–S33

PRIMARY SOURCE

The king to the sheriff of Northampton, greeting. Whereas we wish to have a conference and discussion with the earls, barons, and other nobles of our realm concerning the provision of remedies for the dangers that in these days threaten the same kingdom . . . we command and firmly enjoin you that without delay you cause two knights, of the more discreet and more capable of labor, to be elected from the aforesaid county, and two citizens from each city of the aforesaid county, and two burgesses from each borough, and that you have them come to us . . . to do whatever in the aforesaid matters may be ordained by common counsel.

KING EDWARD I in a letter to sheriffs in England

1 Why is the king calling a meeting of Parliament?
(1) He wants to raise taxes.
(2) He wants to select new knights.
(3) He wants to discuss threats to the kingdom.
(4) He wants to give advice to the leaders.

2 How will the representatives be chosen?
(1) They will be selected by the sheriff.
(2) They will be elected by the people.
(3) They will be selected by the lords.
(4) They will be elected by the knights.

Use the chart and your knowledge of world history to answer question 3.

Population in Europe, 1000–1340

Area	Population Estimates in Millions, 1000	Population Estimates in Millions, 1340
Mediterranean	17	25
Western and Central Europe	12	35.5
Eastern Europe	9.5	13
Total	38.5	73.5

Source: J.C. Russell, *The Control of Late Ancient and Medieval Population*

3 What reason can be suggested for the dramatic increase in Western and Central Europe's population?
(1) Invading peoples settled in the area.
(2) Technical developments allowed people to live longer.
(3) Agricultural production increased.
(4) Trade expanded in Europe.

INTEGRATED TECHNOLOGY
TEST PRACTICE Go to **classzone.com**
- Diagnostic tests
- Strategies
- Tutorials
- Additional practice

ALTERNATIVE ASSESSMENT

1. Interact *with* History

On page 378, you thought about whether or not you would join a Crusade before completely understanding what the Crusades were and what sort of rewards and dangers they entailed. Now that you've read the chapter, reexamine whether or not you would join a Crusade. What might a Crusader bring home from his travels? What problems might a Crusader encounter on his adventures? Discuss your opinions with a small group.

2. WRITING ABOUT HISTORY

Study the information on Joan of Arc in the chapter. Write a brief **biography** about her. Be sure to include information on her influence on Charles and on the nation of France.

Consider the following:
- What are the major events in her life?
- Why did Charles value her advice?
- How is she viewed in France today?

INTEGRATED TECHNOLOGY

Writing an Internet-Based Research Paper

Go to the *Web Research Guide* at **classzone.com** to learn about conducting research on the Internet. Then, working with a partner, use the Internet to find examples of the impact of the bubonic plague and the Hundred Years' War on the economy of medieval Europe. Consider changes in population, working conditions, and the volume of trade. Present the results of your research in a well-organized paper. Be sure to
- apply a search strategy when using directories and search engines to locate Web resources
- judge the usefulness and reliability of each Web site
- correctly cite your Web sources
- peer-edit for organization and correct use of language

CHAPTER 15

Societies and Empires of Africa, 800–1500

Previewing Main Ideas

RELIGIOUS AND ETHICAL SYSTEMS Beginning about 640, Islam created two North African empires. Merchants and traders spread Islam into both West and East Africa, where it influenced rulers.

Geography *What empires developed in West Africa during this period?*

INTERACTION WITH ENVIRONMENT In parts of Africa, hunter-gatherers used up an area's food supply and then moved on. In some Saharan villages, workers built houses of salt. The location of gold determined trade routes.

Geography *What factors might have caused three empires to arise in the same area?*

ECONOMICS Trade networks developed in Africa because different regions had items that other regions wanted. African city-states and empires that were able to control and tax such trade became wealthy and powerful.

Geography *How were the locations of Timbuktu and Kilwa different and how might that have influenced trade?*

NEW YORK CORE CURRICULUM FOCUS

- Merchants and traders spread Islam to East and West Africa.
- Ghana, Mali, and Songhai grew into powerful trading empires in West Africa.

INTEGRATED TECHNOLOGY

eEdition
- Interactive Maps
- Interactive Visuals
- Interactive Primary Sources

INTERNET RESOURCES

Go to **classzone.com** for:
- Research Links
- Internet Activities
- Primary Sources
- Chapter Quiz
- Maps
- Test Practice
- Current Events

AFRICA

800 Empire of Ghana thrives on trade.

1000 ◀ Hausa city-states begin to emerge. (bronze head)

1100 Yoruba kingdom of Ife is established.

800 — 1000

WORLD

850s Byzantine culture spreads to Russia.

1095 ◀ First Crusade begins. (battle between Muslims and Crusaders)

Africa, 800–1500

1235
Sundiata founds Mali Empire.

1324
◀ Mali king Mansa Musa goes on hajj to Mecca. (mapmaker's depiction of Mansa Musa)

1464
Sunni Ali begins Songhai Empire.

1200 1400 1500

1279
Kublai Khan conquers China.

1347
Bubonic plague devastates ▶ Europe. (illustration of Death strangling a victim of the plague)

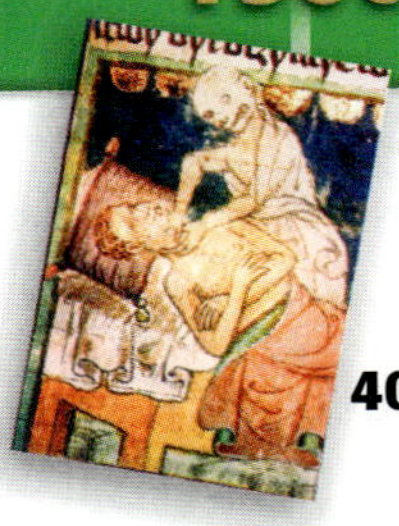

Interact *with* History

How might trade benefit both sides?

You are crossing the Sahara with goods to trade. Your destination is Timbuktu, the great trading center of Africa. There you will meet with other traders, especially those from the gold-mining regions to the south. You hope to make the journey worthwhile by trading salt and manufactured goods for as much gold as possible. The gold traders will want to receive as much of your salt and manufactured goods as they can in exchange. Together you must come to an agreement on what your trade items are worth.

EXAMINING *the* ISSUES

- **What elements are necessary for a mutually successful trade?**
- **How do scarcity and abundance affect trade?**

As you discuss these questions in class, think about what you have learned about other trading peoples, such as the Phoenicians and the Europeans. As you read about trade in the various regions of Africa, notice what steps rulers took to control trade moving through their territory.

North and Central African Societies

CONNECT TO THE NEW YORK STATE CORE CURRICULUM

Unit 2.E.1. Human and physical geography
Unit 1.A.5.1.b. Decision making

TERMS & NAMES

- lineage
- stateless societies
- patrilineal
- matrilineal
- Maghrib
- Almoravids
- Almohads

SETTING THE STAGE Throughout history, different groups of Africans have found different ways to organize themselves to meet their political, economic, and social needs. In the varied regions of Africa, climate and topography, or landforms, influenced how each community developed.

TAKING NOTES

Summarizing Use a web diagram to list characteristics of stateless societies.

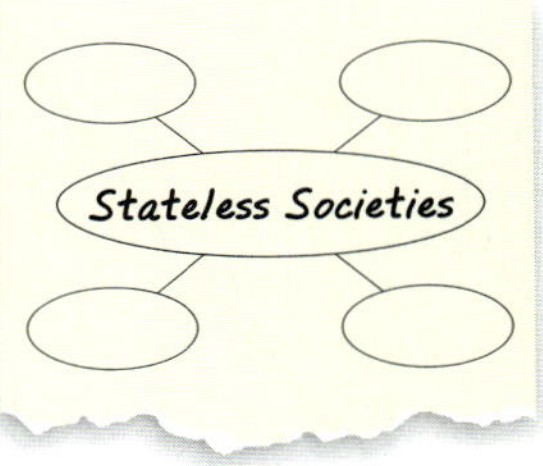

Hunting-Gathering Societies

Hunting-gathering societies—the oldest form of social organization in the world—began in Africa. Hunting-gathering societies still exist in Africa today, though they form an extremely small percentage of the population. Scattered throughout Africa, these groups speak their own languages and often use their own hunting techniques. By studying these groups, scholars learn clues about how hunter-gatherers may have lived in the past.

Forest Dwellers The Efe (AY•fay) are just one of several hunting-gathering societies in Africa. They make their home in the Ituri Forest in the Democratic Republic of Congo (formerly Zaire). Like their ancestors, the modern-day Efe live in small groups of between 10 and 100 members, all of whom are related. Each family occupies its own grass-and-brush shelter within a camp, but their homes are rarely permanent. Their search for food causes them to be somewhat nomadic. As a result, the Efe collect few possessions and move to new camps as they use up the resources in the surrounding area.

In the Efe society, women are the gatherers. They walk through the forest searching for roots, yams, mushrooms, and wild seeds. Efe men and older boys do all the hunting. Sometimes they gather in groups to hunt small antelope called duikers. At other times, hunters go solo and use poison-tipped arrows to kill mammals such as monkeys. The Efe add to their diet by trading honey, wild game, and other forest products for crops grown by farmers in nearby villages.

Social Structure A respected older male, such as a father, uncle, or father-in-law, typically serves as group leader. Although members of the group listen to and value this man's opinion, he does not give orders or act as chief. Each family within the band makes its own decisions and is free to come and go. Group members settle arguments through long discussions. If conflicts cannot be settled by talking, a group member may decide to move to a different hunting band. Daily life for the Efe is not governed by formal written laws.

Stateless Societies

As in other parts of the world, family organization is central to African society. In many African societies, families are organized in groups called lineages. The members of a **lineage** (LIHN•ee•ihj) believe they are descendants of a common ancestor. Besides its living members, a lineage includes past generations (spirits of ancestors) and future generations (children not yet born). Within a lineage, members feel strong loyalties to one another.

South of the Sahara, many African groups developed systems of governing based on lineages. In some African societies, lineage groups took the place of rulers. These societies, known as **stateless societies**, did not have a centralized system of power. Instead, authority in a stateless society was balanced among lineages of equal power so that no one family had too much control. The Igbo (IHG•boh) people—also called Ibo—of southern Nigeria lived in a stateless society as early as the ninth century. (Although the Igbo lived in West Africa, their political structure was similar to stateless societies found in central Africa.) If a dispute arose within an Igbo village, respected elders from different lineages settled the problem. Igbos later encountered challenges from 19th-century European colonizers who expected one single leader to rule over society.

Tracing Family Descent In African societies, the way a society traces lineage determines how possessions and property are passed on and what groups individuals belong to. Members of a **patrilineal** society trace their ancestors through their fathers. Inheritance passes from father to son. When a son marries, he, his wife, and their children remain part of his father's extended family.

In a **matrilineal** society, children trace their ancestors through their mothers. Young men from a matrilineal culture inherit land and wealth from their mother's family. However, even in a matrilineal society, men usually hold the positions of authority.

Age-Set System In many African societies, young people form close ties to individuals outside their lineage through the age-set system. An age set consists of young people within a region who are born during a certain time period. Each age set passes together through clearly identified life stages, such as warrior or elder. Ceremonies mark the passage to each new stage.

Men and women have different life stages, and each stage has its own duties and importance. Societies like the Igbo use the age-set system to teach discipline, community service, and leadership skills to their young. (A)

MAIN IDEA

Making Inferences

(A) What advantages might an age-set system have for a society?

Social History

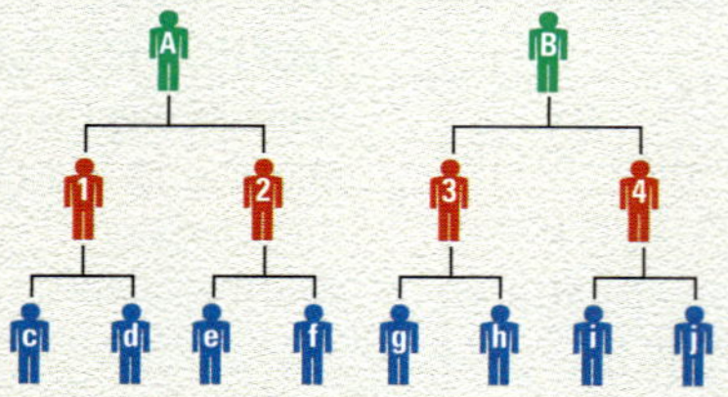

Negotiating Conflict in Stateless Societies

In a stateless society, the power to negotiate conflicts shifts from generation to generation as circumstances demand.

Look at the diagram of two lineages above. If **d** is in conflict with **f**, then **c** will side with his brother **d**, and **e** will side with his brother **f**. Therefore, the parents—**1** and **2**—will meet to negotiate.

If **f** is in conflict with **g**, both entire lineages will take sides in the dispute. Therefore, the members of the oldest surviving generation—**A** and **B**—must meet to negotiate.

INTEGRATED TECHNOLOGY

INTERNET ACTIVITY Use the Internet to prepare a poster on methods of conflict resolution. Go to **classzone.com** for your research.

Muslim States

While stateless societies developed south of the Sahara, Islam played a vital role in North Africa. After Muhammad's death in 632, Muslims swept across the northwest part of the continent. They converted many by the sword of conquest and others peacefully. By 670, Muslims ruled Egypt and had entered the **Maghrib**, the part of North Africa that is today the Mediterranean coast of Libya, Tunisia, Algeria, and Morocco.

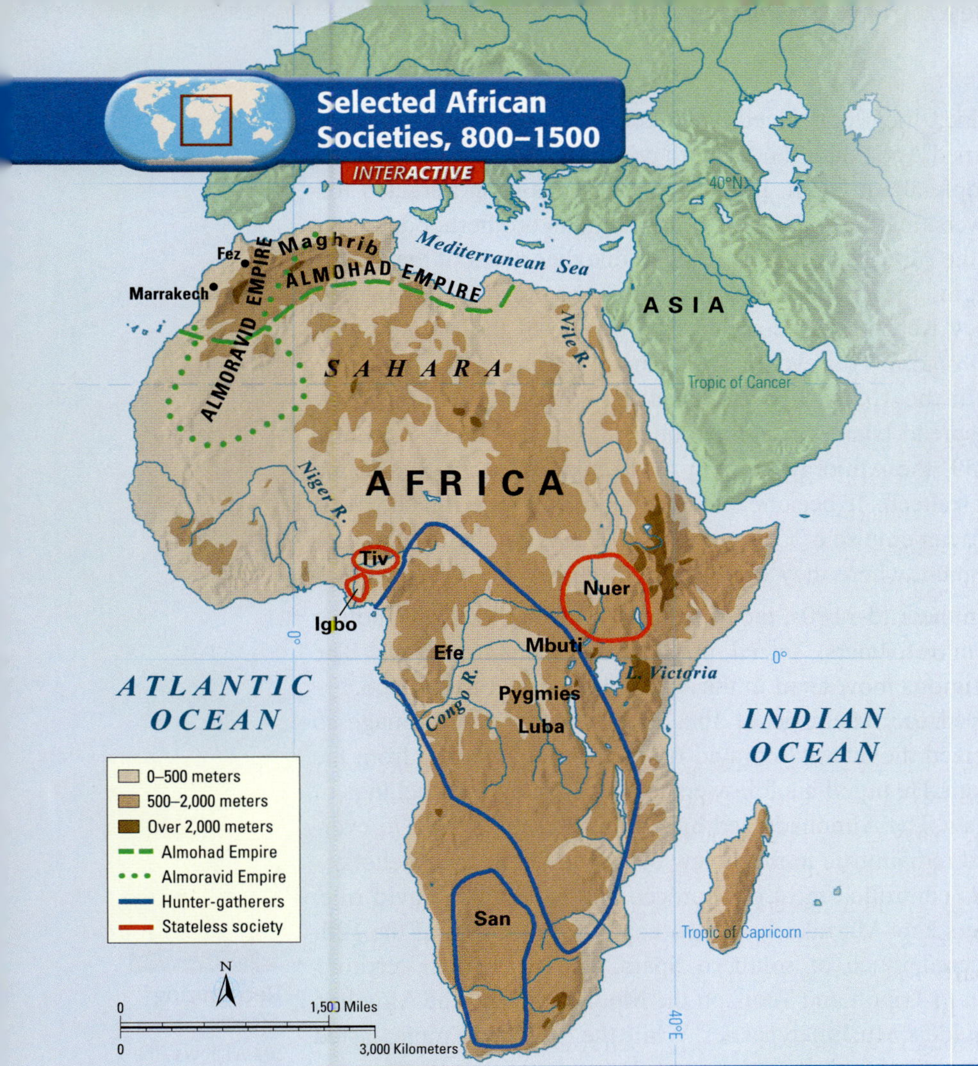

Societies

Hunter-Gatherers

The seminomadic hunter-gatherers lived by gathering wild foods and hunting animals.

- The Efe were hunter-gatherers who traded with farming villages.
- The San (also called the Bushmen) lived in southern Africa and part of East Africa.

Stateless Societies

Stateless societies did not have centralized power. Instead, power was balanced among lineage groups, usually within villages.

- The Tiv had no formal government.
- The Igbo resolved disputes by having elders from different lineages meet.
- The Nuer organized over 250,000 people without an official ruler.

Muslim States

In North Africa, two groups of Muslim reformers founded empires.

- In the 11th century, the Almoravid Empire controlled Mauritania, Morocco, Algeria, and part of Spain.
- Beginning in the mid-1100s, the Almohad Empire controlled Morocco, much of the Maghrib, and part of Spain.

GEOGRAPHY SKILLBUILDER: Interpreting Maps

1. **Location** *Where were the Muslim states located?*
2. **Region** *Why would hunter-gatherers be spread across such a large region?*

As Islam spread, some African rulers converted to Islam. These African Muslim rulers then based their government upon Islamic law. Muslims believe that God's law is a higher authority than any human law. Therefore, Muslim rulers often relied on religious scholars as government advisers. (See World Religions, pages 290–291.)

Islamic Law In Islam, following the law is a religious obligation. Muslims do not separate their personal life from their religious life, and Islamic law regulates almost all areas of human life. Islamic law helped to bring order to Muslim states.

However, various Muslim states had ethnic and cultural differences. Further, these states sometimes had differing interpretations, and schools, of Islamic law. Nonetheless, Islamic law has been such a significant force in history that some states, especially in North Africa, are still influenced by it today.

Among those who converted to Islam were the Berbers. Fiercely independent desert and mountain dwellers, the Berbers were the original inhabitants of North Africa. While they accepted Islam as their faith, many maintained their Berber identities and loyalties. Two Berber groups, the Almoravids and the Almohads, founded empires that united the Maghrib under Muslim rule.

Almoravid Reformers In the 11th century, Muslim reformers founded the Almoravid (al•muh•RAHV•uhd) Empire. Its members came from a Berber group living in the western Sahara in what is today Mauritania. The movement began after devout Berber Muslims made a hajj, or pilgrimage, to Mecca. On their journey

▲ Carpets for sale in Marrakech, Morocco

home, they convinced a Muslim scholar from Morocco named Abd Allah Ibn Yasin to return with them to teach their people about Islam. Ibn Yasin's teachings soon attracted followers, and he founded a strict religious brotherhood, known as the **Almoravids**. According to one theory about the name's origin, the group lived in a *ribat,* or fortified monastery. They were therefore called the "people of the *ribat,*" or *al-Murabitun.* This eventually became "Almoravid."

In the 1050s, Ibn Yasin led the Almoravids in an effort to spread Islam through conquest. After Ibn Yasin's death in 1059, the Almoravids went on to take Morocco and found Marrakech. It became their capital. They overran the West African empire of Ghana by 1076. The Almoravids also captured parts of southern Spain, where they were called Moors.

Almohads Take Over In the mid-1100s, the **Almohads** (AL•moh•HADZ), another group of Berber Muslim reformers, seized power from the Almoravids. The Almohads began as a religious movement in the Atlas Mountains of Morocco.

The Almohads followed the teachings of Ibn Tumart. After a pilgrimage to Mecca, Ibn Tumart criticized the later Almoravid rulers for moving away from the traditional practice of Islam. He urged his followers to strictly obey the teachings of the Qur'an and Islamic law. The Almohads, led by Abd al-Mumin, fought to overthrow the Almoravids and remain true to their view of traditional Islamic beliefs.

By 1148 the Almohads controlled most of Morocco and ended Almoravid rule. The new Muslim reformers kept Marrakech as their capital. By the end of the 12th century, they had conquered much of southern Spain. In Africa, their territory stretched from Marrakech to Tripoli and Tunis on the Mediterranean. The Almohad Empire broke up into individual Muslim dynasties. While the Almohad Empire lasted just over 100 years, it united the Maghrib under one rule for the first time. **B**

Stronger empires were about to emerge. Societies in West Africa created empires that boasted economic and political power and strong links to trade routes.

MAIN IDEA

Recognizing Effects

B What was the main effect of Almohad rule on the Maghrib?

NEW YORK CORE CURRICULUM REVIEW

TERMS & NAMES **1.** For each term or name, write a sentence explaining its significance.

• lineage • stateless societies • patrilineal • matrilineal • Maghrib • Almoravids • Almohads

USING YOUR NOTES

2. How might these characteristics have helped stateless societies to endure for many centuries? Explain.

MAIN IDEAS

3. What sorts of food do the Efe hunt and gather in the Ituri Forest?

4. What different purposes does the age-set system serve in African societies?

5. What role did Islam play in the political history of North Africa?

CRITICAL THINKING & WRITING

6. ANALYZING ISSUES What was the main disagreement that the Almohads had with the Almoravids?

7. DRAWING CONCLUSIONS How did the law help to unify Muslim society?

8. COMPARING In what ways are hunting-gathering societies and stateless societies similar?

9. WRITING ACTIVITY RELIGIOUS AND ETHICAL SYSTEMS
Working with a partner, prepare a **time line** showing the impact of Islam on North Africa. Include significant events for the period described in this section. Display your time line in the classroom.

CONNECT TO TODAY **MAKING A CHART**

Research hunting-gathering societies in Africa today. Find out their numbers and where they live and present your findings in a **chart.**

West African Civilizations

CONNECT TO THE NEW YORK STATE CORE CURRICULUM

Unit 3.D.3. Contributions
Unit 3.D.5. Spread and impact of Islam–Mansa Musa

TERMS & NAMES

- Ghana
- Mali
- Sundiata
- Mansa Musa
- Ibn Battuta
- Songhai
- Hausa
- Yoruba
- Benin

SETTING THE STAGE While the Almohads and Almoravids were building empires in North Africa, three powerful empires flourished in West Africa. These ancient African empires arose in the Sahel, the savanna region just south of the Sahara. They grew strong by controlling trade. In this section you will learn about the West African empires of Ghana, Mali, and Songhai.

TAKING NOTES
Comparing and Contrasting Use a Venn diagram to compare and contrast information about the Mali and Songhai empires.

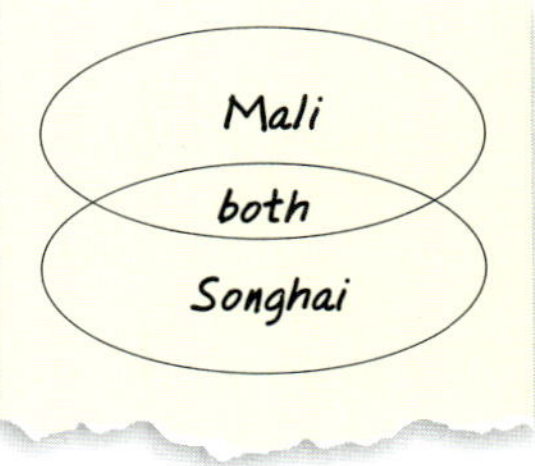

Empire of Ghana

By A.D. 200, trade across the Sahara had existed for centuries. However, this trade remained infrequent and irregular because of the harsh desert conditions. Most pack animals—oxen, donkeys, and horses—could not travel very far in the hot, dry Sahara without rest or water. Then, in the third century A.D., Berber nomads began using camels. The camel could plod steadily over much longer distances, covering as much as 60 miles in a day. In addition, it could travel more than ten days without water, twice as long as most pack animals. With the camel, nomads blazed new routes across the desert and trade increased.

The trade routes crossed the savanna through the region farmed by the Soninke (soh•NIHN•keh) people. The Soninke people called their ruler *ghana,* or war chief. Muslim traders began to use the word to refer to the Soninke region. By the 700s, **Ghana** was a kingdom, and its rulers were growing rich by taxing the goods that traders carried through their territory.

Gold-Salt Trade The two most important trade items were gold and salt. Gold came from a forest region south of the savanna between the Niger (NY•juhr) and Senegal (SEHN•ih•GAWL) rivers. Miners dug gold from shafts as deep as 100 feet or sifted it from fast-moving streams. Some sources estimate that until about 1350, at least two-thirds of the world's supply of gold came from West Africa. Although rich in gold, West Africa's savanna and forests lacked salt, a material essential to human life. The Sahara contained deposits of salt. In fact, in the Saharan village of Taghaza, workers built their houses from salt blocks because it was the only material available.

Arab and Berber traders crossed the desert with camel caravans loaded down with salt. They also carried cloth, weapons, and manufactured goods from ports on the Mediterranean. After a long journey, they reached the market towns of the savanna. Meanwhile, African traders brought gold north from the forest regions.

West African Empires, 1000–1500

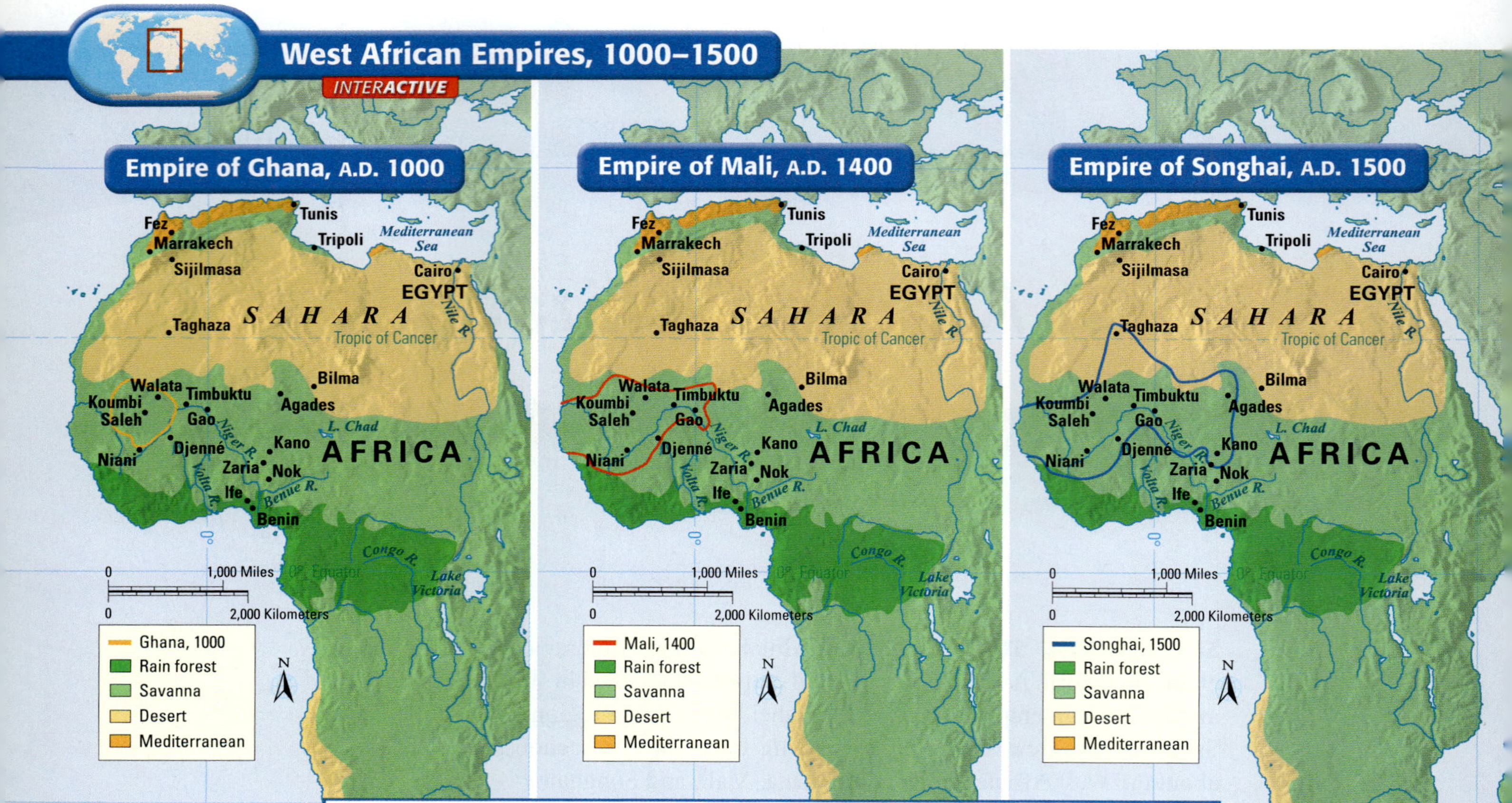

GEOGRAPHY SKILLBUILDER: Interpreting Maps

1. **Region** *Compare the regions occupied by the Ghana, Mali, and Songhai empires in terms of size and location.*
2. **Human-Environment Interaction** *How did the environment both contribute resources to and cause problems for traders?*

Merchants met in trading cities, where they exchanged goods under the watchful eye of the king's tax collector. In addition to taxing trade, royal officials made sure that all traders weighed goods fairly and did business according to law. Royal guards also provided protection from bandits.

Land of Gold By the year 800, Ghana had become an empire. Because Ghana's king controlled trade and commanded a large army, he could demand taxes and gifts from the chiefs of surrounding lands. As long as the chiefs made their payments, the king left them in peace to rule their own people.

In his royal palace, the king stored gold nuggets and slabs of salt (collected as taxes). Only the king had the right to own gold nuggets, although gold dust freely circulated in the marketplace. By this means, the king limited the supply of gold and kept its price from falling. Ghana's African ruler acted as a religious leader, chief judge, and military commander. He headed a large bureaucracy and could call up a huge army. In 1067, a Muslim geographer and scholar named al-Bakri wrote a description of Ghana's royal court:

PRIMARY SOURCE

The king adorns himself . . . wearing necklaces and bracelets. . . . The court of appeal is held in a domed pavilion around which stand ten horses with gold embroidered trappings. Behind the king stand ten pages holding shields and swords decorated with gold, and on his right are the sons of the subordinate [lower] kings of his country, all wearing splendid garments and with their hair mixed with gold.

AL-BAKRI, quoted in *Africa in the Days of Exploration*

Islamic Influences While Islam spread through North Africa by conquest, south of the Sahara, Islam spread through trade. Muslim merchants and teachers settled in the states south of the Sahara and introduced their faith there.

Eventually, Ghana's rulers converted to Islam. By the end of the 11th century, Muslim advisers were helping the king run his kingdom. While Ghana's African rulers accepted Islam, many people in the empire clung to their animistic beliefs and practices. Animism is the belief that spirits living in animals, plants, and natural forces play an important role in daily life. Much of the population never converted. Those who did kept many of their former beliefs, which they observed along with Islam. Among the upper class, Islam's growth encouraged the spread of literacy. To study the Qur'an, converts to Islam had to learn Arabic.

In 1076 the Muslim Almoravids of North Africa completed their conquest of Ghana. Although the Almoravids eventually withdrew from Ghana, the war had badly disrupted the gold-salt trade. As a result, Ghana never regained its power. (A)

MAIN IDEA

Analyzing Causes

(A) Why would the disruption of trade destroy Ghana's power?

Empire of Mali

By 1235 the kingdom of **Mali** had emerged. Its founders were Mande-speaking people, who lived south of Ghana. Mali's wealth, like Ghana's, was built on gold. As Ghana remained weak, people who had been under its control began to act independently. In addition, miners found new gold deposits farther east. This caused the most important trade routes to shift eastward, which made a new group of people—the people of Mali—wealthy. It also enabled them to seize power.

Sundiata Conquers an Empire Mali's first great leader, **Sundiata** (sun•JAHT•ah), came to power by crushing a cruel, unpopular leader. Then, in the words of a Mande oral tradition, "the world knew no other master but Sundiata." Sundiata became Mali's *mansa,* or emperor. Through a series of military victories, he took over the kingdom of Ghana and the trading cities of Kumbi and Walata. A period of peace and prosperity followed.

Sundiata proved to be as great a leader in peace as he had been in war. He put able administrators in charge of Mali's finances, defense, and foreign affairs. From his new capital at Niani, he promoted agriculture and reestablished the gold-salt trade. Niani became an important center of commerce and trade. People began to call Sundiata's empire Mali, meaning "where the king lives."

Mansa Musa Expands Mali Sundiata died in 1255. Some of Mali's next rulers became Muslims. These African Muslim rulers built mosques, attended public prayers, and supported the preaching of Muslim holy men. The most famous of them was **Mansa Musa** (MAHN•sah moo•SAH), who may have been Sundiata's grandnephew. Mansa Musa ruled from about 1312 to 1332.

History Makers

Sundiata
?–1255

Sundiata came from the kingdom of Kangaba near the present-day Mali-Guinea border. According to tradition, he was one of 12 brothers who were heirs to the throne of Kangaba.

When Sumanguru, ruler of a neighboring state, overran Kangaba in the early 1200s, he wanted to eliminate rivals, so he murdered all of Sundiata's brothers. He spared Sundiata, who was sickly and seemed unlikely to survive.

However, as Sundiata grew up, he gained strength and became a popular leader of many warriors. In 1235, Sundiata's army defeated Sumanguru and his troops.

Mansa Musa
?–1332?

Mansa Musa, the strongest of Sundiata's successors, was a devout Muslim. On his hajj, Mansa Musa stopped in Cairo, Egypt. Five hundred slaves, each carrying a staff of gold, arrived first. They were followed by 80 camels, each carrying 300 pounds of gold dust. Hundreds of other camels brought supplies. Thousands of servants and officials completed the procession.

Mansa Musa gave away so much gold in Cairo that the value of this precious metal declined in Egypt for 12 years.

INTEGRATED TECHNOLOGY

RESEARCH LINKS For more on Sundiata and Mansa Musa, go to **classzone.com**

Analyzing Primary Sources

Mansa Musa's Kingdom

In 1324, Mansa Musa left Mali for the hajj to Mecca. On the trip, he gave away enormous amounts of gold. Because of this, Europeans learned of Mali's wealth. In 1375, a Spanish mapmaker created an illustrated map showing Mansa Musa's kingdom in western Africa. Drawn on the map is Mansa Musa holding a gold nugget.

At the top of the map is Spain. At the bottom of Spain, the Mediterranean meets the Atlantic Ocean at the Strait of Gibraltar. South of Gibraltar is Africa. Filling most of the map is North Africa, with the Mediterranean extending east and the Atlantic west of Gibraltar.

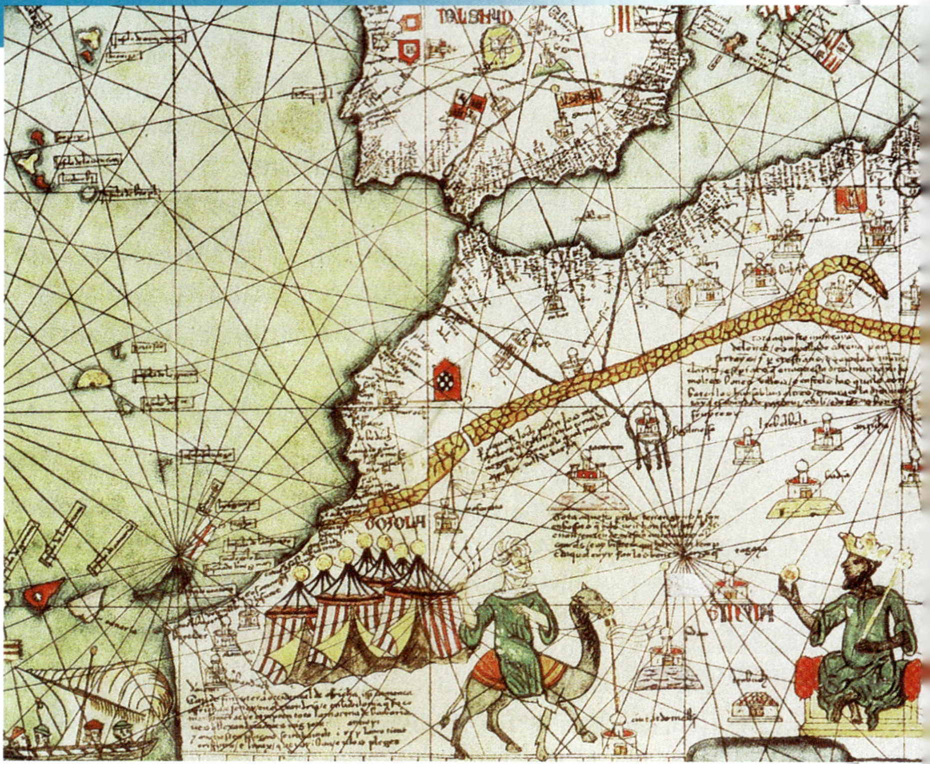

DOCUMENT-BASED QUESTIONS

1. **Determining Main Ideas** *What was a major source of wealth for the Empire of Mali?*
2. **Making Inferences** *How might Mali's (and Africa's) wealth have influenced interactions between Africans and Europeans?*

Between the reigns of Sundiata and Mansa Musa, Mali experienced turmoil. There had been seven different rulers in approximately 50 years. Like Sundiata, Mansa Musa was a skilled military leader who exercised royal control over the gold-salt trade and put down every rebellion. His 100,000-man army kept order and protected Mali from attack. Under Mansa Musa, the empire expanded to roughly twice the size of the empire of Ghana. To govern his far-reaching empire, Mansa Musa divided it into provinces and appointed governors, who ruled fairly and efficiently.

A devout Muslim, Mansa Musa went on a hajj to Mecca from 1324 to 1325. When he returned, he ordered the building of new mosques at the trading cities of Timbuktu (TIHM•buhk•TOO) and Gao. Timbuktu became one of the most important cities of the empire. It attracted Muslim judges, doctors, religious leaders, and scholars from far and wide. They attended Timbuktu's outstanding mosques and universities.

Travels of Ibn Battuta In 1352, one of Mansa Musa's successors prepared to receive a traveler and historian named **Ibn Battuta** (IHB•uhn ba•TOO•tah). A native of Tangier in North Africa, Ibn Battuta had traveled for 27 years, visiting most of the countries in the Islamic world.

After leaving the royal palace, Ibn Battuta visited Timbuktu and other cities in Mali. He found he could travel without fear of crime. As a devout Muslim, he praised the people for their study of the Qur'an. However, he also criticized them for not strictly practicing Islam's moral code. Even so, Mali's justice system greatly impressed him:

PRIMARY SOURCE

They are seldom unjust, and have a greater abhorrence of injustice than any other people. Their sultan shows no mercy to anyone who is guilty of the least act of it. There is complete security in their country. Neither traveler nor inhabitant in it has anything to fear from robbers.

IBN BATTUTA, quoted in *Africa in the Days of Exploration*

Ibn Battuta left Mali in 1353. Within 50 years, the once-powerful empire began to weaken. Most of Mansa Musa's successors lacked his ability to govern well. In addition, the gold trade that had been the basis of Mali's wealth shifted eastward as new goldfields were developed elsewhere.

Empire of Songhai

As Mali declined in the 1400s, people who had been under its control began to break away. Among them were the **Songhai** (SAWNG•HY) people to the east. They built up an army and extended their territory to the large bend in the Niger River near Gao. They gained control of the all-important trade routes. Gao was the capital of their empire. B

MAIN IDEA

Making Inferences

B Why might the people who had been conquered by Mali want to break away?

Sunni Ali, a Conquering Hero The Songhai had two extraordinary rulers, both of whom were Muslims. One was Sunni Ali, who built a vast empire by military conquest. Sunni Ali's rule began in 1464 and lasted almost 30 years.

Sunni Ali built a professional army that had a riverboat fleet of war canoes and a mobile fighting force on horseback. He expanded Songhai into an empire through his skill as a military commander and his aggressive leadership. In 1468, Sunni Ali achieved his first major military triumph. He captured the city of Timbuktu, which had been an important part of Mali's empire.

Five years later, he took Djenné, also a trade city that had a university. To take Djenné, Sunni Ali surrounded the city with his army for seven years before it fell in 1473. Sunni Ali completed the takeover of Djenné by marrying its queen.

Askia Muhammad Governs Well After Sunni Ali's death in 1492, his son succeeded him as ruler. Almost at once, the son faced a major revolt by Muslims who were angry that he did not practice their religion faithfully. The leader of the revolt was a devout Muslim named Askia Muhammad. He drove Sunni Ali's son from power and replaced him.

During his 37-year rule, Askia Muhammad proved to be an excellent administrator. He set up an efficient tax system and chose able officials. Adding to the centralized government created by Sunni Ali, he appointed officials to serve as ministers of the treasury, army, navy, and agriculture. Under his rule, the well-governed empire thrived.

Despite its wealth and learning, the Songhai Empire lacked modern weapons. The Chinese had invented gunpowder in the ninth century. About 1304, Arabs developed the first gun, which shot arrows. In 1591, a Moroccan fighting force of several thousand men equipped with gunpowder and cannons crossed the Sahara and invaded Songhai. The Moroccan troops quickly defeated the Songhai warriors, who were armed only with swords and spears. The collapse of the Songhai Empire ended a 1,000-year period in which powerful kingdoms and empires ruled the central region of West Africa.

Social History

Islam in West Africa

South of the Sahara, many converts to Islam also kept their African beliefs. They found ways to include their traditional rituals and customs in their new religion.

The status of women in West African societies demonstrates how local custom altered Muslim practice. In many 15th-century Muslim societies, women seldom left their homes. When they did, they veiled their faces. Muslim women in West Africa, however, did not wear veils. They also mingled freely with men in public, which shocked visiting Muslim religious leaders.

Other Peoples of West Africa

While empires rose and fell, city-states developed in other parts of West Africa. As in Ghana, Mali, and Songhai, Muslim traditions influenced some of these city-states. Other city-states held to their traditional African beliefs.

Hausa City-States Compete The **Hausa** (HOW•suh) were a group of people named after the language they spoke. The

History *in* Depth

Queen Amina's Reign

In the 1500s, the Hausa city-state of Zazzau (later called Zaria) was governed by Queen Amina. She was remembered as the "headdress among the turbans." Her rule was distinguished for its military conquests.

The *Kano Chronicle,* a history of the city-state of Kano, records:

> *At this time Zaria, under Queen Amina, conquered all the towns as far as Kawarajara and Nupe. Every town paid tribute to her. . . . Her conquests extended over 34 years.*

Queen Amina's commitment to her Muslim faith also led her to encourage Muslim scholars, judges, and religious leaders from religious centers at Kano and Timbuktu to come to Zazzau.

city-states of the Hausa people first emerged between the years 1000 and 1200 in the savanna area east of Mali and Songhai in what is today northern Nigeria. Songhai briefly ruled the Hausa city-states, but they soon regained their independence. In such city-states as Kano, Katsina, and Zazzau (later Zaria), local rulers built walled cities for their capitals. From their capitals, Hausa rulers governed the farming villages outside the city walls.

Each ruler depended on the crops of the farmers and on a thriving trade in salt, grain, and cotton cloth made by urban weavers. Because they were located on trade routes that linked other West African states with the Mediterranean, Kano and Katsina became major trading states. They profited greatly from supplying the needs of caravans. Kano was noted for its woven and dyed cloth and for its leather goods.

Zazzau, the southernmost state, conducted a vigorous trade in enslaved persons. Zazzau's traders raided an area south of the city and sold their captives to traders in other Hausa states. These traders sold them to other North or West African societies in exchange for horses, harnesses, and guns. The Hausa kept some slaves to build and repair city walls and grow food for the cities.

All the Hausa city-states had similar forms of government. Rulers held great power over their subjects, but ministers and other officials acted to check this power. For protection, each city-state raised an army of mounted horsemen. Although rulers often schemed and fought to gain control over their neighbors, none succeeded for long. The constant fighting among city-states prevented any one of them from building a Hausa empire. **C**

MAIN IDEA

Analyzing Causes

C What was the main reason that the Hausa did not develop an empire?

▼ This Yoruba crown made of glass beads and grass cloth stands about 20 inches high.

Yoruba Kings and Artists Like the Hausa, the **Yoruba** (YAWR•uh•buh) people all spoke a common language. Originally the Yoruba-speaking people belonged to a number of small city-states in the forests on the southern edge of the savanna in what is today Benin and southwestern Nigeria. In these communities most people farmed. Over time, some of these smaller communities joined together under strong leaders. This led to the formation of several Yoruba kingdoms.

Considered divine, Yoruba kings served as the most important religious and political leaders in their kingdoms. All Yoruba chiefs traced their descent from the first ruler of Ife (EE•fay). According to legend, the creator sent this first ruler down to earth at Ife, where he founded the first Yoruba state. His many sons became the heads of other Yoruba kingdoms. All Yoruba chiefs regarded the king of Ife as their highest spiritual authority. A secret society of religious and political leaders limited the king's rule by reviewing the decisions he made.

Ife and Oyo were the two largest Yoruba kingdoms. Ife, developed by 1100, was the most powerful Yoruba kingdom until the late 1600s, when Oyo became more prosperous. As large urban centers, both Ife and Oyo had high walls surrounding them. Most rural farms in the surrounding areas produced surplus food, which was sent to the cities. This enabled city dwellers to become both traders and craftspeople.

Vocabulary
terra cotta: a reddish-brown clay, hard ceramic

The Ife were gifted artists who carved in wood and ivory. They produced terra cotta sculptures and cast in metal. Some scholars believe that the rulers supported artists. Many clay and metal casts portray Ife rulers in an idealistic way.

Kingdom of Benin To the south and west of Ife, near the delta of the Niger River, lay the kingdom of **Benin** (buh•NIHN). Like the Yoruba people of Ife and Oyo, the people of Benin made their homes in the forest. The first kings of Benin date from the 1200s. Like the Yoruba kings, the oba, or ruler, of Benin based his right to rule on claims of descent from the first king of Ife.

▲ This ivory mask is one of four taken from the king of Benin in 1897. It was worn on the belt of a ceremonial costume.

In the 1400s, the oba named Ewuare made Benin into a major West African state. He did so by building a powerful army. He used it to control an area that by 1500 stretched from the Niger River delta in the east to what is today Lagos, Nigeria. Ewuare also strengthened Benin City by building walls around it. Inside the city, broad streets were lined by neat rows of houses.

The huge palace contained many courtyards and works of art. Artists working for the oba created magnificent brass heads of the royal family and copper figurines. Brass plaques on the walls and columns of the royal palace of the oba showed legends, historical scenes, and the deeds of the oba and his nobles. According to tradition, Benin artists learned their craft from an Ife artist brought to Benin by the oba to teach them.

In the 1480s, Portuguese trading ships began to sail into Benin's port at Gwatto. The Portuguese traded with Benin merchants for pepper, leopard skins, ivory, and enslaved persons. This began several centuries of European interference in Africa, during which they enslaved Africans and seized African territories for colonies. Meanwhile, East Africans—discussed in Section 3—prospered from trade and developed thriving cities and empires.

NEW YORK CORE CURRICULUM REVIEW

TERMS & NAMES 1. For each term or name, write a sentence explaining its significance.

- Ghana
- Mali
- Sundiata
- Mansa Musa
- Ibn Battuta
- Songhai
- Hausa
- Yoruba
- Benin

USING YOUR NOTES

2. What are some similarities between the two empires? Explain.

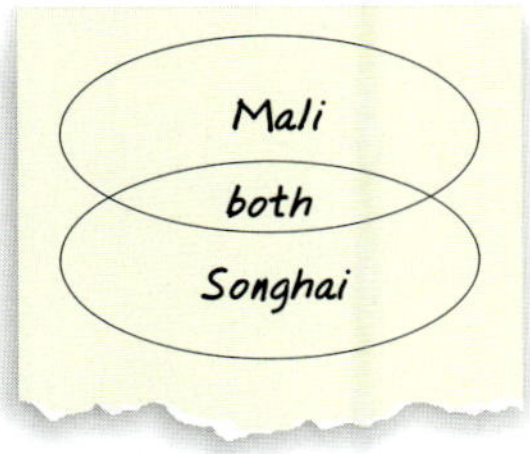

MAIN IDEAS

3. How did Ghana's gold-salt trade work?
4. How did Sunni Ali build an empire?
5. What form of government was typical of Hausa city-states?

CRITICAL THINKING & WRITING

6. **DRAWING CONCLUSIONS** Which of the two—the Yoruba or the people of Benin—had more influence on the other?
7. **COMPARING** What are some of the similarities between the Hausa city-states and other city-states you have read about?
8. **COMPARING** What are some of the similarities between Sundiata and Mansa Musa?
9. **WRITING ACTIVITY** ECONOMICS What do you think was the most effective method Ghana used to regulate its economy? Explain your answer in a short **paragraph** in which you touch upon trade routes, gold, and taxes.

CONNECT TO TODAY **CREATING A POSTER**
Learn more about the mining and production of salt today. Present your findings in a **poster**, with illustrations and captions.

History *through* Art

Benin Bronzes

Benin is famous for its bronze and brass sculptures. Benin sculpture was made by guilds controlled by the king. One of the main functions of Benin art was to please the ruler by recording his history or by displaying his power. For instance, brass plaques commemorating the ruler's great achievements adorned the palace walls. Busts of the ruler and his family showed them as idealized figures.

INTEGRATED TECHNOLOGY

RESEARCH LINKS For more on Benin art, go to **classzone.com**

Queen Mother ►

Perhaps the most widely known type of Benin sculpture was the royal head, such as this one. In Benin, the Queen Mother held a lot of power. To symbolize that power, she wore a woven crown called a "chicken's beak."

◄ Plaque

Plaques such as this decorated the palace of the Oba, or ruler, of Benin

The Lost-Wax Process

Many of the Benin sculptures were made using the lost-wax process.

1. The artist forms a core of clay that is roughly the shape of the planned sculpture.

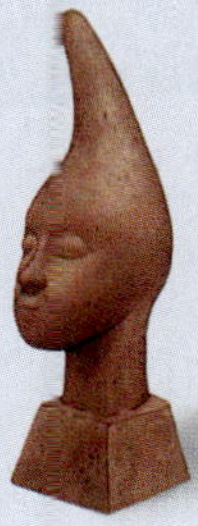

2. The artist applies a layer of wax over the core, then carves fine details into the surface of the wax.

3. A layer of fine clay is spread over the wax surface. This creates a smooth finish and captures the small details.

4. Several layers of coarse clay are applied to create the mold.

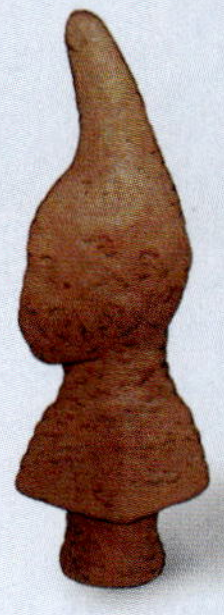

5. The entire object is fired in a kiln (oven). The clay hardens, and the wax melts away, leaving a clay mold. (The melted wax is the origin of the name "lost-wax.")

6. Melted bronze is poured into the mold and left to harden.

7. The clay mold is broken off, revealing the finished bronze sculpture.

Leopard ►
Admired for its power, fierceness, and intelligence, the leopard was depicted on many royal objects. This snarling leopard is a symbol of the king's power. It is also a water vessel that was used on ceremonial occasions.

◄ Musician
This figure was probably made in the late 16th or early 17th century. It shows an attendant of the king blowing a horn or flute. This type of figure was often found on altars.

Connect *to* Today

1. **Making Inferences** Why do you think the figure of a servant blowing a horn was found on an altar?
   See Skillbuilder Handbook, Page R10.
2. **Comparing and Contrasting** Use library resources to identify a sculpture of a U.S. leader. What quality about that leader does the sculpture portray? How is it similar to or different from Benin's royal sculptures?

3

Eastern City-States and Southern Empires

CONNECT TO THE NEW YORK STATE CORE CURRICULUM

Unit 3.D.4. Roles in global trade routes
Unit 2.E.4. Social class: women and slavery in Muslim society

TERMS & NAMES

- Swahili
- Great Zimbabwe
- Mutapa

SETTING THE STAGE As early as the third century A.D., the kingdom of Aksum had taken part in an extensive trade network. From its Red Sea port, Aksum traded with Arabia, Persia, India, and Rome. In the 600s, Muslim forces gained control of Arabia, the Red Sea, and North Africa. The Muslims cut off the Aksumites from their port. The Aksumites moved their capital south from Aksum to Roha (later called Lalibela) shortly before 1100. In the meantime, other cities on the east coast were thriving because of Indian Ocean trade. In this section, you will learn about East African trade, Islamic influences in East Africa, and the peoples of southern Africa.

TAKING NOTES

Analyzing Causes Use a chart to explain one example of cultural interaction resulting from trade.

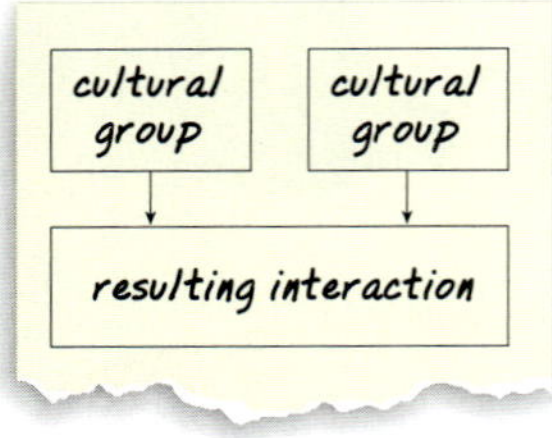

East Coast Trade Cities

Villages along the east coast began to develop into important trade cities. By 1100, waves of Bantu-speaking people had migrated across central Africa to the east coast. There they established farming and fishing villages. Slowly, the existing coastal villages grew into bustling seaports, built on trade between East African merchants and traders from Arabia, Persia, and India. As trade increased, many Muslim Arab and Persian traders settled in these port cities. Arabic blended with the Bantu language to create the **Swahili** (swah•HEE•lee) language.

Persian traders moved south from the Horn of Africa, a triangular peninsula near Arabia. They brought Asian manufactured goods to Africa and African raw materials to Asia. In the coastal markets, Arab traders sold porcelain bowls from China and jewels and cotton cloth from India. They bought African ivory, gold, tortoiseshell, ambergris, leopard skins, and rhinoceros horns to carry to Arabia.

By 1300, more than 35 trading cities dotted the coast from Mogadishu in the north to Kilwa and Sofala in the south. Like the empires of West Africa, these seaports grew wealthy by controlling all incoming and outgoing trade. Some cities also manufactured trade goods for export. For example, weavers in Mogadishu and Sofala made cloth. Workers in Mombasa and Malindi made iron tools.

The City-State of Kilwa In 1331, Ibn Battuta visited Kilwa. He admired the way that its Muslim rulers and merchants lived. Rich families lived in fine houses of coral and stone. They slept in beds inlaid with ivory and their meals were served on porcelain. Wealthy Muslim women wore silk robes and gold and silver bracelets.

East African Trade, 1000

Trade Goods

Origin	Raw Materials	Products Made
Savanna region	leopard skins	saddles
Coastal region	tortoiseshells	combs
Southern African	gold from mines	coins, jewelry
Savanna region	ivory from elephants	chess pieces, sword hilts

GEOGRAPHY SKILLBUILDER: Interpreting Maps

1. **Movement** *How far did a trader have to travel to make a round trip from Calicut in India to Kilwa in Africa and back again?*
2. **Human-Environment Interaction** *Which monsoon would a trader rely on to sail from India to Africa?*
3. **Region** *Which raw materials came from the savanna region?*

Kilwa grew rich because it was as far south on the coast as a ship from India could sail in one monsoon season. Therefore, trade goods from southerly regions had to funnel into Kilwa, so Asian merchants could buy them.

In addition, in the late 1200s Kilwa had seized the port of Sofala, which was a trading center for gold mined inland. By controlling Sofala, Kilwa was able to control the overseas trade of gold from southern Africa. As a result, Kilwa became the wealthiest, most powerful coastal city-state. (A)

MAIN IDEA

Analyzing Causes

(A) What were the two main reasons Kilwa became so wealthy?

Portuguese Conquest In 1488, the first Portuguese ships rounded the southern tip of Africa and sailed north, looking for a sea route to India. They wanted to gain profits from the Asian trade in spices, perfumes, and silks. When the Portuguese saw the wealth of the East African city-states, they decided to conquer those cities and take over the trade themselves.

Using their shipboard cannon, the Portuguese took Sofala, Kilwa, and Mombasa. They burned parts of Kilwa and built forts on the sites of Kilwa and Mombasa. The Portuguese kept their ports and cities on the East African coast for the next two centuries.

Islamic Influences

Muslim traders introduced Islam to the East African coast, and the growth of commerce caused the religion to spread. Even the smallest towns had a mosque for the faithful. A Muslim sultan, or ruler, governed most cities. In addition, most government officials and wealthy merchants were Muslims. However, the vast majority of people along the East African coast held on to their traditional religious beliefs.

> Analyzing Primary Sources

Islamic Law in Mogadishu

In 1331, Ibn Battuta, traveling by caravan similar to the one at right, visited the African city of Mogadishu. He described how Muslim officials decided legal matters.

PRIMARY SOURCE

The Shaikh [sultan] takes his place in his hall of audience and sends for the Qadi [judge]. He takes his place on the Shaikh's left and then the lawyers come in and the chief of them sit in front of the Shaikh. . . . Then food is brought and . . . those who are in the audience chamber eat in the presence of the Shaikh. . . . After this the Shaikh retires to his private apartments and the Qadi, the wazirs [government ministers] . . . and . . . chief amirs [military commanders] sit to hear causes and complaints. Questions of religious law are decided by the Qadi, other cases are judged by the . . . wazirs and amirs. If a case requires the views of the [Shaikh], it is put in writing for him. He sends back an immediate reply.

IBN BATTUTA, *Travels of Ibn Battuta*

DOCUMENT-BASED QUESTIONS

1. **Summarizing** *Who were the four types of people who decided legal matters?*
2. **Clarifying** *What types of cases did they judge?*

This was also true of the people who lived in inland villages.

Enslavement of Africans Along with luxury goods, Arab Muslim traders exported enslaved persons from the East African coast. Traders sent Africans acquired through kidnapping to markets in Arabia, Persia, and Iraq. Wealthy people in these countries often bought slaves to do domestic tasks. Muslim traders shipped enslaved Africans across the Indian Ocean to India, where Indian rulers employed them as soldiers. Enslaved Africans also worked on docks and ships at Muslim-controlled ports and as household servants in China.

▲ An Arab slave market in Yemen, A.D. 1237

Although Muslim traders had been enslaving East Africans and selling them overseas since about the ninth century, the numbers remained small—perhaps about 1,000 a year. The trade in slaves did not increase dramatically until the 1700s. At that time, Europeans started to buy captured Africans for their colonial plantations. **B**

MAIN IDEA

Summarizing

B How extensive was the trade in enslaved persons from East Africa before 1700?

Southern Africa and Great Zimbabwe

The gold and ivory that helped the coastal city-states grow rich came from the interior of southern Africa. In southeastern Africa the Shona people established a city called **Great Zimbabwe** (zihm•BAHB•way), which grew into an empire built on the gold trade.

Great Zimbabwe By 1000, the Shona people had settled the fertile, well-watered plateau between the Zambezi and Limpopo rivers in modern Zimbabwe. The area was well suited to farming and cattle raising. Its location also had economic advantages. The city of Great Zimbabwe stood near an important trade route linking the goldfields with the coastal trading city of Sofala. Sometime after 1000, Great Zimbabwe gained control of these trade routes. From the 1200s through the 1400s, it became the capital of a thriving state. Its leaders taxed the traders who traveled these routes. They also demanded payments from less powerful chiefs. Because of this growing wealth, Great Zimbabwe became the economic, political, and religious center of its empire.

But by 1450, Great Zimbabwe was abandoned. No one knows for sure why it happened. According to one theory, cattle grazing had worn out the grasslands. In addition, farming had worn out the soil, and people had used up the salt and timber. The area could no longer support a large population.

Almost everything that is known about Great Zimbabwe comes from its impressive ruins. Portuguese explorers knew about the site in the 1500s. Karl Mauch, a German explorer, was one of the first Europeans to discover the remains of these stone dwellings in 1871.

> Analyzing Architecture

INTERACTIVE

Great Zimbabwe

Great Zimbabwe was an important city in southern Africa. The word *zimbabwe* comes from a Shona phrase meaning "stone houses." The ruins consist of two complexes of stone buildings that once housed the royal palace of Great Zimbabwe's rulers. There are great curving walls around the ruins. Because there was no way for soldiers to climb to the top of the walls, archaeologists theorize that they were not used primarily as defenses.

The massive walls were probably built to impress visitors with the strength of Zimbabwe and its ruler. Inside the walls stands a cone-shaped tower. Among the ruins were found tall figures of birds, carved from soapstone. Archaeologists believe the construction of Great Zimbabwe may have taken about 400 years.

City of Great Zimbabwe

The Shona people built this impressive city as the center of their empire.

- It covered many acres.
- Its population was more than 10,000.
- The walls contain approximately 900,000 stone blocks. They were so well built that the blocks hold together without mortar.
- The Great Enclosure is a curving wall up to 36 feet high and 15 feet thick.

This photograph shows part of the Great Enclosure.

This picture of two girls standing next to a wall shows how very high the enclosing walls are.

SKILLBUILDER: Interpreting Visual Sources

1. **Drawing Conclusions** *If the walls were not built for defense, what does this suggest about the safety and security of Great Zimbabwe?*
2. **Making Inferences** *If military assault did not account for the fall of Zimbabwe, what other factors might have played a part?*

The Mutapa Empire

According to Shona oral tradition, a man named Mutota left Great Zimbabwe about 1420 to find a new source of salt. Traveling north, he settled in a valley with fertile soil, good rainfall, and ample wood. There he founded a new state to replace Great Zimbabwe. As the state grew, its leader Mutota used his army to dominate the northern Shona people living in the area. He forced them to make payments to support him and his army.

Mutapa Rulers These conquered people called Mutota and his successors *mwene mutapa,* meaning "conqueror" or "master pillager." The Portuguese who arrived on the East African coast in the early 1500s believed *mwene mutapa* to be a title of respect for the ruler. The term is also the origin of the name of the **Mutapa** Empire. By the time of Mutota's death, the Mutapa Empire had conquered all of what is now Zimbabwe except the eastern portion. By 1480 Mutota's son Matope claimed control of the area along the Zambezi River to the Indian Ocean coast.

The Mutapa Empire was able to mine gold deposited in nearby rivers and streams. In addition, Mutapa rulers forced people in conquered areas to mine gold for them. The rulers sent gold to the coastal city-states in exchange for luxuries. Even before the death of Matope, the southern part of his empire broke away. However, the Mutapa Dynasty remained in control of the smaller empire.

In the 1500s, the Portuguese tried to conquer the empire. When they failed to do so, they resorted to interfering in Mutapa politics. They helped to overthrow one ruler and replace him with one they could control. This signaled increasing European interference in Africa in centuries to come. C

MAIN IDEA

Making Inferences
C Why do you think the Portuguese wanted to conquer the Mutapa Empire?

Global Impact

Swahili

Over the centuries, contacts between two peoples—Bantu speakers and Arabs—led to the creation of a new people and a new language. Many Arab traders married African women. People of mixed Arab and African ancestry came to be called Swahili. The word comes from an Arabic term meaning "people of the coast" and refers to the East African coast.

Although Swahili peoples do not share a single culture, they do speak a common language. Swahili is a Bantu language with many words borrowed from Arabic. The Swahili peoples traded the gold and ivory of Africa for goods from India and China. During the 1500s and 1600s, the Portuguese looted Swahili cities and damaged Swahili trade.

NEW YORK CORE CURRICULUM REVIEW

TERMS & NAMES 1. For each term or name, write a sentence explaining its significance.
- Swahili
- Great Zimbabwe
- Mutapa

USING YOUR NOTES

2. Do you think this interaction had a positive or negative effect? Explain.

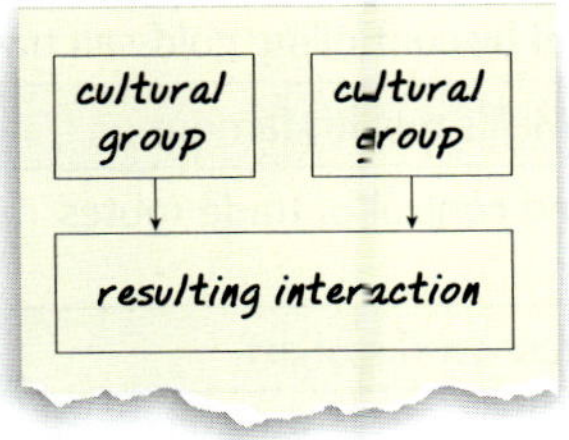

MAIN IDEAS

3. How did the Swahili language develop?
4. How was Islam introduced to East Africa?
5. How did the people of Great Zimbabwe positively interact with their environment?

CRITICAL THINKING & WRITING

6. **COMPARING** Compare the Portuguese who arrived in East Africa with the rulers of the Mutapa Empire.
7. **SYNTHESIZING** What were some of the effects of East African trade on different cultural groups?
8. **DRAWING CONCLUSIONS** How is Swahili an example of cultural interaction?
9. **WRITING ACTIVITY** INTERACTION WITH ENVIRONMENT How did the people of Great Zimbabwe negatively interact with their environment? Write a one-paragraph **essay** explaining your answer.

INTEGRATED TECHNOLOGY **INTERNET ACTIVITY**

Use the Internet to research the modern African country of Zimbabwe. Find out where it is located in Africa, its capital, and other information. Enter your findings on an **outline map** of Africa.

INTERNET KEYWORD
Zimbabwe

Chapter 15 Assessment

TERMS & NAMES

For each term or name below, briefly explain its connection to African history from 800 to 1500.

1. lineage
2. stateless society
3. matrilineal
4. Ghana
5. Mali
6. Songhai
7. Swahili
8. Great Zimbabwe

MAIN IDEAS

North and Central African Societies
Section 1 (pages 409–412)

9. How is a dispute settled in Efe society?
10. What is an age-set system?
11. How were the beginnings of the Almoravid and Almohad empires similar?

West African Civilizations
Section 2 (pages 413–421)

12. What accounted for Ghana's financial success?
13. What were two ways that Islam spread through Africa?
14. What was the economy of the Hausa city-states like?

Eastern City-States and Southern Empires
Section 3 (pages 422–427)

15. How did the Swahili language evolve?
16. Why was it important for Kilwa to control Sofala?
17. Who was most affected by the introduction of Islam to East Africa?
18. What was the relationship of Great Zimbabwe to the Mutapa Empire?

CRITICAL THINKING

1. USING YOUR NOTES
In a chart like the one shown, list for each leader what group of people he led and one of his achievements.

Leader	Group	Achievement
Ibn Yasin		
Askia Muhammad		
Ewuare		

2. RECOGNIZING EFFECTS
RELIGIOUS AND ETHICAL SYSTEMS In what way did Islam encourage the spread of literacy?

3. RECOGNIZING EFFECTS
INTERACTION WITH ENVIRONMENT How did people adapt to the harsh conditions of the Sahara? Discuss traders who crossed the Sahara and people who lived in the Saharan village of Taghaza.

4. SUMMARIZING
How are group membership, inheritance rights, and positions of authority usually decided in a matrilineal society?

5. CLARIFYING
Why was the location of Great Zimbabwe advantageous?

VISUAL SUMMARY

Societies and Empires of Africa

	Organization & Time Period	Important Facts
Igbo People	Existed as a stateless society from **9th to 19th centuries**	Elders resolved conflicts
Almoravids	Muslim state from **mid-1000s to mid-1100s**	Founded city of Marrakech
Almohads	Muslim state from **mid-1100s to mid-1200s**	Unified the Maghrib under one authority for first time in history
Ghana	West African empire from **700s to 1076**	Grew wealthy and powerful by controlling gold-salt trade
Mali	West African empire from **1235 to 1400s**	Mansa Musa's hajj made Mali's wealth famous
Songhai	West African empire that flourished in the **1400s and 1500s**	Conquered Mali and gained control of trade routes
Benin	West African trading kingdom strong in **1400s and 1500s**	Famous for bronze and brass works of art
Kilwa	East African city-state flourished from **1200s to 1400s**	Grew wealthy from trade
Great Zimbabwe	Capital of trade-based empire from **1200s until about 1450**	City abandoned, perhaps because natural resources were used up
Mutapa Empire	Founded about **1420** by man from Great Zimbabwe	Remained independent in spite of Portuguese attempts

Use the map and your knowledge of world history to answer the questions.
Additional Test Practice, pp. S1–S33

1 Which is the most widespread ethnic group?
(1) Soninke
(2) Berbers
(3) Hausa
(4) Igbo

2 Which group lives in modern Mauritania?
(1) Hausa
(2) Igbo
(3) Berbers
(4) Soninke

3 Which modern Africa country has the most ethnic groups?
(1) Nigeria
(2) Mali
(3) Cameroon
(4) Libya

4 What geographical feature might explain why there are no ethnic groups shown in the center of the map?
(1) Atlantic Ocean
(2) equator
(3) the Sahara
(4) Tropic of Cancer

INTEGRATED TECHNOLOGY
TEST PRACTICE Go to **classzone.com**
- Diagnostic tests
- Tutorials
- Strategies
- Additional practice

ALTERNATIVE ASSESSMENT

1. Interact *with* History

Recall your discussion of the question on page 408: How might trade benefit both sides? Now that you've read the chapter, reevaluate what makes trade beneficial. How did environmental conditions affect what items had value in Africa? Did government policies have any effect on value? Consider what you learned about trading states in both West and East Africa.

2. WRITING ABOUT HISTORY

ECONOMICS Do you think Africa was connected to most of the world through trade, or was it relatively isolated from the rest of the world? Write an **essay** in which you support your answer with evidence from the chapter.

Consider the following:
- Muslim states of North Africa
- gold-salt trade
- empires and kingdoms of West Africa
- east coast trade cities

INTEGRATED TECHNOLOGY

Participating in a WebQuest

Introduction Today, much of eastern Africa still relies heavily on trade. With a group of students, have each member choose one East African country to research in terms of its trade and culture. Issues to investigate might include what goods present-day East African nations trade and who their trading partners are.

Task Create an electronic presentation of information on exports and imports, quantities shipped, where the goods are going, and how they are being transported.

Process and Resources Have each member of the group bring his or her information on East African trade and culture to the group to create a presentation. Use this chapter and the Internet as resources for your research.

Evaluation and Conclusion East African trade has been important to the economies of the region. How did this project contribute to your understanding of the interrelationship between prosperity and trade?

Trade Creates Links

A trade network exists when a group of people or countries buys from or sells to each other on a regular basis. Historically, trade networks arose as merchants traded local products for those from other places—often very distant places. Trade is a good way to spread products that are in high demand. Unit 3 discussed trade networks in the Arabian Peninsula, Asia, the Mediterranean Sea, the Sahara, and the Indian Ocean. In the next six pages, you will see how these networks worked.

Components of Trade Networks

Trading Partners

Merchants could grow rich selling highly desired goods that were not produced locally. To obtain such goods, merchants traded with people in other regions. When two regions trade regularly, they become trading partners.

Trade Goods

Products become trade goods when one region lacks them and another has a surplus to sell. Trade goods may be valuable because they are rare (such as ivory), useful (such as salt to preserve meat), or beautiful (such as silk).

Modes of Transport

Caravans of camels, mules, or other animals carried trade goods over land. Vessels that relied on wind power (such as the dhow) or the strength of human rowers shipped trade goods across the seas.

Currency

Merchants do not always exchange one product directly for another. They may buy goods with money. Currency is any item that is accepted as money in a region. Besides paper money, cowrie shells, salt, and metals served as currency.

Middlemen

Because some trade goods traveled very long distances, merchants did not always buy products directly from their places of origin. Middlemen acted as go-betweens, buying goods from merchants in one region to sell to merchants in another.

Types of Trade Networks

Trade networks frequently include more than two partners. Merchants from one area might sell their goods to several different regions. Middlemen might also do business with various different partners. The diagrams below show three basic types of trade networks.

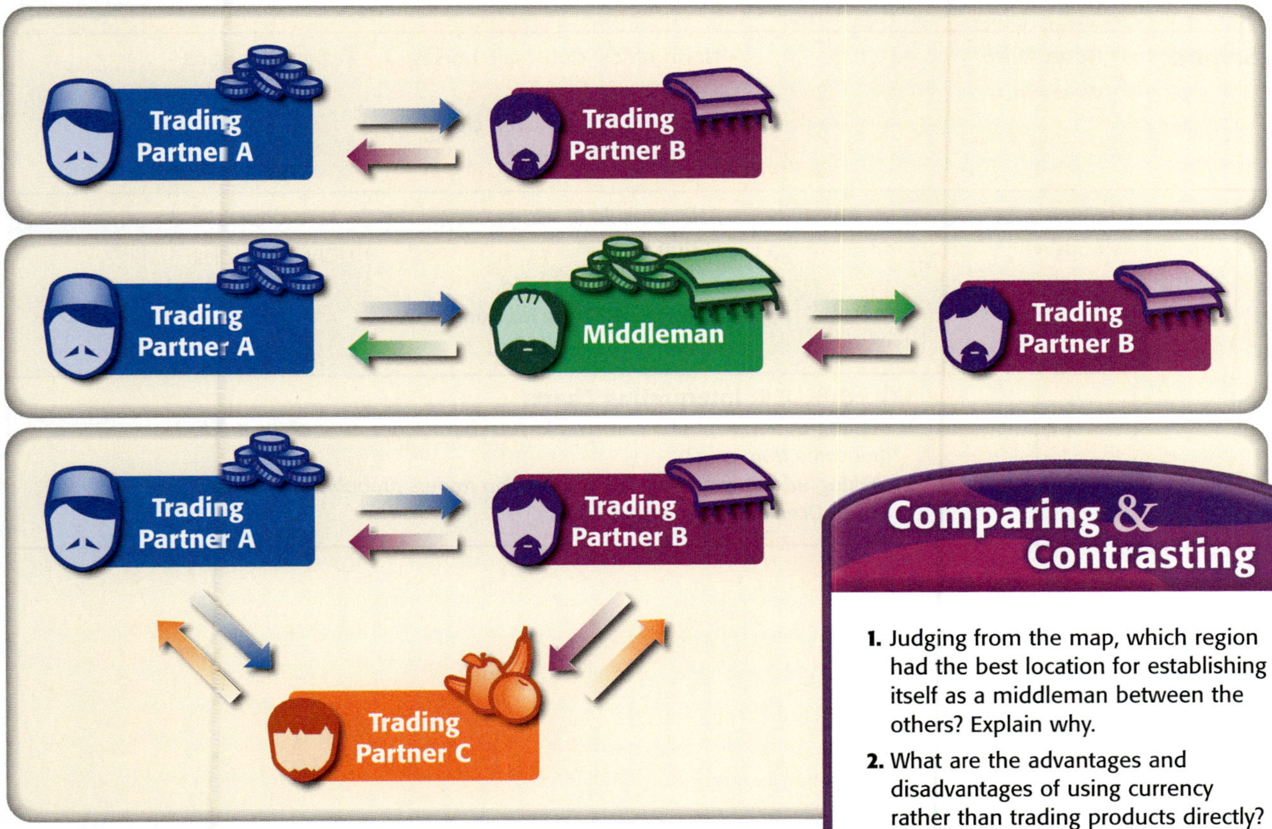

Comparing & Contrasting

1. Judging from the map, which region had the best location for establishing itself as a middleman between the others? Explain why.
2. What are the advantages and disadvantages of using currency rather than trading products directly?

Major Trade Networks

The five major trade networks that you studied in Unit 3 are listed on the chart. Notice who the different trading partners were in each network and the products that they sold each other. Consider why the dhow and the camel described on the next page were particularly useful as modes of transport.

	Trading Partners	Trade Goods	Modes of Transport
Trans-Arabia	• Sassanid Empire • Arabia • Byzantine Empire	• East Asia: silk, gems, dyes, cotton cloth • Arabia: incense, spices • Southwest Asia: wool, gold, silver	• camel caravans
Silk Roads	• China • India • Persia and Central Asia • Europe	• Asia: silk, porcelain, spices, precious woods, gems • Europe: wool cloth, gold, silver	• caravans of camels and other pack animals
Mediterranean	• Europe • North Africa • Southwest Asia	• Europe: wool and linen cloth, wine, metal • North Africa: wool • Asia: spices, fruit, cloth	• by sea, galleys with numerous rowers • overland, caravans of pack animals
Trans-Sahara	• North Africa • West Africa	• North Africa: cloth, salt, horses, guns • West Africa: gold, dyed cloth, leather goods, slaves	• camel caravans
Indian Ocean	• China • India • Arabia • East Africa	• Asia: porcelain, silk, jewelry, cotton • East Africa: ivory, gold, tortoiseshell, leopard skins, slaves	• Arab dhows • Chinese junks

SKILLBUILDER: Interpreting Charts

1. **Making Generalizations** *How would you characterize most of the products that came from Asia?*
2. **Making Inferences** *What role did Arabian traders probably play in the Indian Ocean trade network? Explain.*

By Land or by Sea?

The different modes of transport used were well suited to their environments.

Advantages of Dhow Ocean Travel

- Stern rudders made dhows (shown in photograph) easy to maneuver.
- Lateen, or triangular, sails enabled sailors to sail against the wind.

Advantages of Land Travel by Camel

- Camels can carry heavy burdens over long distances.
- Fat reserves in their humps enable them to go without food or water for many days.
- Double sets of eyelashes, hairy ears, and nostrils that close protect camels from sand.
- Soft feet that stretch out make camels sure-footed on sand or snow.

Astrolabe ►
Sailors used astrolabes to measure the height of the sun or a star above the horizon. With that information, they could determine both the time of day and the latitude where they were located.

◄ Chinese Compass
Although the floating compass needle actually points to magnetic north, sailors could calculate true north and use that information to navigate. Knowing which way was north also enabled them to figure out in what direction the wind was blowing their ship.

Comparing & Contrasting

1. Read the information about the camel above. Then notice which trade networks on the chart on page 432 relied on camel caravans. What geographic information can you infer about those trade routes?
2. Which of the two navigation instruments do you think would be most useful for land travelers, such as those who traveled the Silk Roads or the trans-Saharan routes? Why?

Trade Goods

As trade networks developed, trading partners began to manufacture goods specifically for sale in other places. The more they learned about other cultures, the better they were able to design products that would suit foreign tastes. Consider how the items below were appropriate for sale in foreign places.

PRIMARY SOURCE

Moon Flask

This porcelain object is known as a moon flask for its round shape. During the Yuan Dynasty (1279–1368), China produced delicate porcelains with elaborate painted decorations such as this. Like silk, porcelain originated in China. It was several centuries before Europe learned how to produce porcelain of such a high quality.

DOCUMENT-BASED QUESTION

A trade good may be valued for its usefulness, rarity, or beauty. For which of those reasons do you think people wanted this porcelain flask? Explain.

PRIMARY SOURCE

African Ivory Spoon

Ivory, which usually comes from elephant tusks, was one of Africa's most common trade goods. Frequently, it was carved into utensils or decorative objects. This carved spoon came from Benin.

DOCUMENT-BASED QUESTION

Why would people in Europe or China need to trade to obtain ivory?

PRIMARY SOURCE

Silk Cloth

The Chinese began manufacturing silk by about 2500 B.C. and trading it to foreign lands by the time of the Han Dynasty (202 B.C. to A.D. 220). Many people desired silk because it was shiny and could be dyed many beautiful colors. It was also extremely strong yet lightweight.

DOCUMENT-BASED QUESTION

What class of people do you think were most likely to wear clothes made of silk?

Trade Narratives

The following excerpts describe life in towns and countries along the different trade routes that merchants traveled.

PRIMARY SOURCE

INTERACTIVE

Francesco Balducci Pegolotti

An Italian commercial agent, Pegolotti wrote a guidebook around 1340 for European merchants traveling overland to China.

Whatever silver the merchants may carry with them as far as Cathay [China] the lord of Cathay will take from them and put into his treasury. And to merchants who thus bring silver they give that paper money of theirs in exchange . . . With this money you can readily buy silk and other [merchandise] . . . And all the people of the country are bound to receive it. And yet you shall not pay a higher price for your goods because your money is of paper.

DOCUMENT-BASED QUESTION
Judging from this excerpt, were Pegolotti's European readers familiar with paper money? How can you tell?

PRIMARY SOURCE

INTERACTIVE

Ibn Battuta

The following excerpt was written by the Muslim traveler Ibn Battuta. In it, he describes the West African city of Takadda (also spelled Takedda).

The people of Takadda carry on no business but trading. Every year they travel to Egypt and bring from there everything there is in the country by way of fine cloths and other things. . . .

There is a copper mine outside Takadda. The people . . . make [the copper] into rods: . . . some are of fine gauge and some thick . . . It is their means of exchange. They buy meat and firewood with the fine rods: they buy male and female slaves, millet, ghee [a butter product], and wheat with the thick.

DOCUMENT-BASED QUESTION
Why did the people of Takadda need to produce copper rods?

PRIMARY SOURCE

INTERACTIVE

Fernão Lopes de Castanheda

The following description of the goods available in Calicut is from *History of the Discovery and Conquest of India,* published in 1552.

[Calicut is] the richest mart [market] of all India; in which is to be found all the spices, drugs, nutmegs, . . . pearls and seed-pearls, musk, sanders [sandalwood], fine dishes of earthenware, lacquer, gilded coffers, and all the fine things of China, gold, amber, wax, ivory, fine and coarse cotton goods, both white and dyed of many colours, much raw and twisted silk, . . . cloth of gold, cloth of tissue, grain, scarlets, silk carpets, copper, . . . and all kinds of conserves.

DOCUMENT-BASED QUESTION
How does Lopes de Castanheda support his point that Calicut is the richest market in India?

Comparing & Contrasting

1. Judging from the information in the sources, why did Takadda and Cathay use such different types of currency?
2. Which of the trade goods shown on the opposite page are mentioned in the description of Calicut? What does this tell you about the reason for Calicut's riches?

EXTENSION ACTIVITY

Go to a supermarket or produce store and write down what fruits and vegetables are being sold that are out of season or not native to your area. Then find out where they come from. Start by looking at signs and boxes where foods are packed. Interview the produce manager to find out what countries supplied the produce. Then create a chart or map that conveys the information you have learned.

UNIT 4

Connecting Hemispheres
500–1800

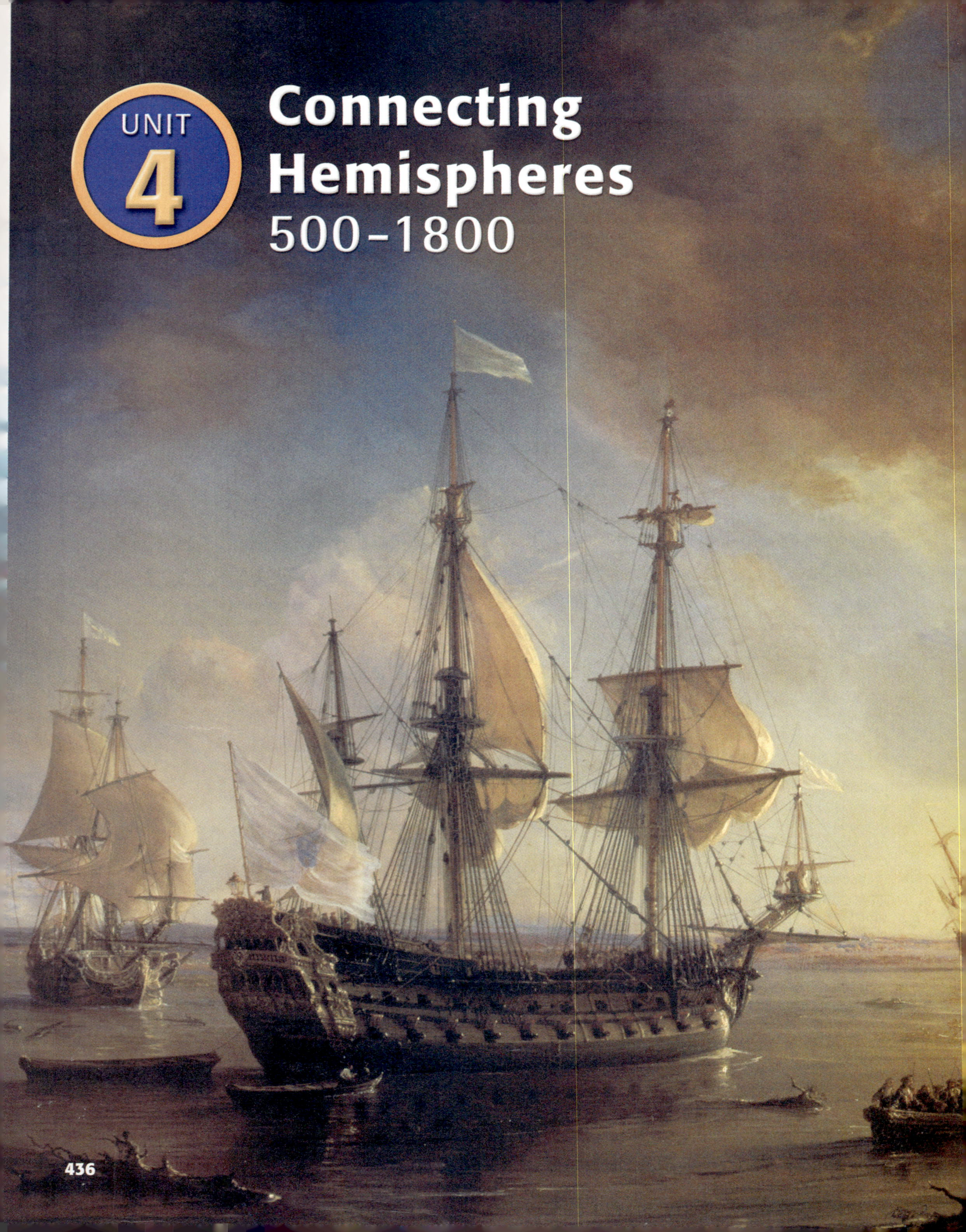

Seeking new land and new markets, European explorers sailed around the world. This painting by Theodore Gudin depicts French explorer La Salle's Louisiana expedition of 1684.

Comparing & Contrasting

Methods of Government

In Unit 4, you will learn about different methods of ruling a nation or empire. At the end of the unit, you will have a chance to compare and contrast the governments you have studied. (See pages 578–583.)

CHAPTER 16

People and Empires in the Americas, 500–1500

Previewing Main Ideas

CULTURAL INTERACTION Cultures in the Americas had frequent contact across distance and time. Both conquest and trade brought different cultures together.

Geography *In which part of the Americas do you think the greatest cultural interaction occurred? Why?*

POWER AND AUTHORITY Societies in the Americas ranged from small tribal bands to immense empires. Warrior-kings or priest-kings ruled most of these empires.

Geography *Which empire covered the greatest geographic area?*

RELIGIOUS AND ETHICAL SYSTEMS Religion was a powerful force in the Americas. Many societies combined religious and state rule. Much of their art and architecture concerned the gods and the need to please them.

Geography *The Aztecs adopted the gods of other Mesoamerican cultures. Why do you think this happened?*

NEW YORK CORE CURRICULUM FOCUS

- The Maya created a vast empire based on city-states in Mesoamerica.
- The Maya developed a calendar and made important contributions to mathematics and astronomy.

INTEGRATED TECHNOLOGY

eEdition
- Interactive Maps
- Interactive Visuals
- Interactive Primary Sources

INTERNET RESOURCES
Go to **classzone.com** for:
- Research Links
- Internet Activities
- Primary Sources
- Chapter Quiz
- Maps
- Test Practice
- Current Events

THE AMERICAS

500s Teotihuacán reaches population peak in central Mexico. (mask from Teotihuacán) ▶

800 Anasazi culture develops in the Southwest.

900 Classic period of Maya civilization ends.

500 — 750

WORLD

618 Tang Dynasty begins 289-year rule in China.

800 Charlemagne crowned Holy Roman Emperor by the pope. (crown of the Holy Roman Empire) ▶

The Americas, 800 B.C.–A.D. 1535

1000 **1250** **1500**

1066 Normans invade England.

1100 Mississippian culture thrives at Cahokia.

1300 ◀ Renaissance begins in Italy. (Michelangelo's *David*)

1324 Mansa Musa, king of Mali, goes on hajj to Mecca.

1325 ◀ Aztecs build Tenochtitlán. (figure of an Aztec goddess)

1438 Pachacuti becomes Incan emperor.

1492 Columbus makes first voyage to the Americas.

1502 Montezuma II crowned Aztec emperor.

Interact *with* History

What does this headdress tell you about the people who made it?

You are preparing an exhibit for your local history museum on an early Native American society—one with no written language. In many ways, you must act like a detective. You sift through the evidence for clues and then draw conclusions based on your findings. Imagine you want to include this headdress in the exhibit. Study the headdress carefully to see how much you can learn about the Kwakiutl, the people who made it.

▲ This headdress was used by the Kwakiutl in religious ceremonies. Carved of red cedar and painted, it shows a thunderbird, the highest of the spirits in the Kwakiutl religion. Like a huge eagle, the thunderbird flew high in the sky. When it was hungry, it swooped down to catch and eat killer whales.

EXAMINING *the* ISSUES

- **What does the figure represented by the headdress and the materials used to make it tell you about Kwakiutl culture?**
- **How else might you find out information about this culture?**

Discuss these questions with your classmates. Think about the kinds of information you have learned about other cultures that did not have a written language. As you read this chapter, examine the symbolic objects made by different peoples of the Americas. Think about what these objects reveal about the various cultures.

North American Societies

CONNECT TO THE NEW YORK STATE CORE CURRICULUM

Unit 1.A.1. Human and physical geography
Unit 1.A.3. Relationship to the environment

TERMS & NAMES

- potlatch
- Anasazi
- pueblo
- Mississippian
- Iroquois
- totem

SETTING THE STAGE Between 40,000 and 12,000 years ago, hunter-gatherers migrated across the Bering Strait land bridge from Asia and began to populate the Americas. Migrating southward, those first Americans reached the southern tip of South America by somewhere between 12,000 and 7000 B.C. At the same time, they began to spread out east and west across North America. Over the centuries, the early North American peoples adapted to their environment, creating a very diverse set of cultures.

Complex Societies in the West

In some ways, the early North American cultures were less developed than those of South America and Mesoamerica. The North American groups created no great empires. They left few ruins as spectacular as those of ancient Mexico or Peru. Nevertheless, the first peoples of North America did create complex societies. These societies were able to conduct long-distance trade and construct magnificent buildings.

TAKING NOTES

Comparing and Contrasting Use a Venn diagram to compare and contrast the Native Americans of the Northwest and the Southwest.

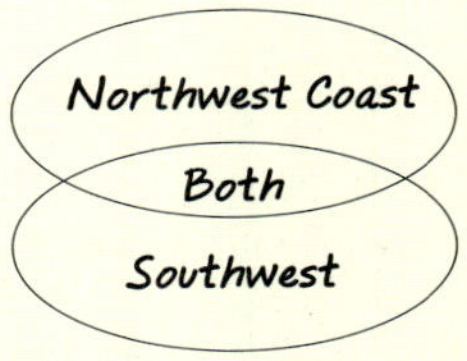

Cultures of Abundance The Pacific Northwest—from Oregon to Alaska—was rich in resources and supported a sizable population. To the Kwakiutl, Nootka, and Haida peoples, the most important resource was the sea. (See the map on page 442.) They hunted whales in canoes. Some canoes were large enough to carry at least 15 people. In addition to the many resources of the sea, the coastal forest provided plentiful food. In this abundant environment, the Northwest Coast tribes developed societies in which differences in wealth created social classes. Families displayed their rank and prosperity in an elaborate ceremony called the **potlatch** (PAHT•LACH). In this ceremony, they gave food, drink, and gifts to the community.

Accomplished Builders The dry, desert lands of the Southwest were a much harsher environment than the temperate Pacific coastlands. However, as early as 1500 B.C., the peoples of the Southwest were beginning to farm the land. Among the most successful of these early farmers were the Hohokam (huh•HOH•kuhm) of central Arizona. (See the map on page 439.) They used irrigation to produce harvests of corn, beans, and squash. Their use of pottery rather than baskets, as well as certain religious rituals, showed contact with Mesoamerican peoples to the south.

North American Culture Areas, c. 1400

GEOGRAPHY SKILLBUILDER: Interpreting Maps

1. **Region** *Which Native American culture groups had the largest number of tribes?*
2. **Human-Environment Interaction** *In which culture areas would movement of trade goods be made easier by river and lake connections?*

A people to the north—the **Anasazi** (AH•nuh•SAH•zee)—also influenced the Hohokam. They lived in the Four Corners region, where the present-day states of Utah, Arizona, Colorado, and New Mexico meet. The Anasazi built impressive cliff dwellings, such as the ones at Mesa Verde, Colorado. These large houses were built on top of mesas—flat-topped hills—or in shallow caves in the sheer walls of deep canyons. By the A.D. 900s, the Anasazi were living in **pueblos** (PWEHB•lohs), villages of large, apartment-style compounds made of stone and adobe, or sun-baked clay.

▲ Cliff Palace, Mesa Verde, had 217 rooms and 23 kivas.

The largest Anasazi pueblo, begun around A.D. 900, was Pueblo Bonito, a Spanish name meaning "beautiful village." Its construction required a high degree of social organization and inventiveness. The Anasazi relied on human labor to quarry sandstone from the canyon walls and move it to the site. Skilled builders then used a mudlike mortar to construct walls up to five stories high. Windows were small to keep out the burning sun. When completed, Pueblo Bonito probably housed about 1,000 people and contained more than 600 rooms. In addition, a number of underground or partly underground ceremonial chambers called kivas (KEE•vuhs) were used for a variety of religious practices.

Many Anasazi pueblos were abandoned around 1200, possibly because of a prolonged drought. The descendants of the Anasazi, the Pueblo peoples, continued many of their customs. Pueblo groups like the Hopi and Zuni used kivas for religious ceremonies. They also created beautiful pottery and woven blankets. They traded these, along with corn and other farm products, with Plains Indians to the east, who supplied bison meat and hides. These nomadic Plains tribes eventually became known by such names as the Comanche, Kiowa, and Apache.

Mound Builders and Other Woodland Cultures

Beyond the Great Plains, in the woodlands east of the Mississippi River, other ancient peoples—the Mound Builders—were creating their own unique traditions. (See the map on page 439.) Beginning around 700 B.C., a culture known as the Adena began to build huge earthen mounds in which they buried their dead. Mounds that held the bodies of tribal leaders often were filled with gifts, such as finely crafted copper and stone objects.

Some 500 years later, the Hopewell culture also began building burial mounds. Their mounds were much larger and more plentiful than those of the Adena. Some of the Hopewell mounds may have been used for purposes other than burials. For example, the Great Serpent Mound, near Hillsboro, Ohio, may have played a part in Hopewell religious ceremonies.

The last Mound Builder culture, the **Mississippian**, lasted from around A.D. 800 until the arrival of Europeans in the 1500s. These people created thriving villages based on farming and trade. Between 1000 and 1200, perhaps as many as 30,000

▲ Great Serpent Mound runs some 1,300 feet along its coils and is between 4 and 5 feet high.

people lived at Cahokia (kuh•HOH•kee•uh), the leading site of Mississippian culture. Cahokia was led by priest-rulers, who regulated farming activities. The heart of the community was a 100-foot-high, flat-topped earthen pyramid, which was crowned by a wooden temple.

These Mississippian lands were located in a crossroads region between east and west. They enjoyed easy transportation on the Mississippi and Ohio rivers. Items found in burial mounds show that the Mississippians had traded with peoples in the West and, possibly, Mesoamerica. Similar evidence shows that they also came into contact with peoples from the Northeast.

Northeastern Tribes Build Alliances The northeastern woodlands tribes developed a variety of cultures. The woodlands peoples often clashed with each other over land. In some areas, tribes formed political alliances to ensure protection of tribal lands. The best example of a political alliance was the **Iroquois** (IHR•uh•KWOY), a group of tribes speaking related languages living in the eastern Great Lakes region. In the late 1500s, five of these tribes in upper New York—the Mohawk, Oneida, Onondaga, Cayuga, and Seneca—formed the Iroquois League. According to legend, Chief Hiawatha helped to create this league. His goal was to promote joint defense and cooperation among the tribes. **A**

MAIN IDEA

Drawing Conclusions

A Of what value would a political alliance be to an individual tribe?

Cultural Connections

The Iroquois alliance was a notable example of a political link among early North American peoples. For the most part, however, the connections between native North Americans were economic and cultural. They traded, had similar religious beliefs, and shared social patterns.

Trading Networks Tie Tribes Together Trade was a major factor linking the peoples of North America. Along the Columbia River in Oregon, the Chinook people established a lively marketplace that brought together trade goods from all over the West. And the Mississippian trade network stretched from the Rocky Mountains to the Atlantic coast and from the Great Lakes to the Gulf of Mexico.

Religion Shapes Views of Life Another feature that linked early Americans was their religious beliefs. Nearly all native North Americans believed that the world around them was filled with nature spirits. Most Native Americans recognized a number of sacred spirits. Some groups held up one supreme being, or Great Spirit, above all others. North American peoples believed that the spirits gave them rituals and customs to guide them in their lives and to satisfy their basic needs. If people practiced these rituals, they would live in peace and harmony.

Native American religious beliefs also included great respect for the land as the source of life. Native Americans used the land but tried to alter it as little as possible. The land was sacred, not something that could be bought and sold. Later, when Europeans claimed land in North America, the issue of land ownership created conflict.

Shared Social Patterns The family was the basis for social organization for Native Americans. Generally, the family unit was the extended family, including parents, children, grandparents, and other close relatives. Some tribes further organized families into clans, groups of families descended from a common ancestor. In some tribes, clan members lived together in large houses or groups of houses.

Common among Native American clans was the use of **totems** (TOH•tuhmz). The term refers to a natural object with which an individual, clan, or group identifies itself. The totem was used as a symbol of the unity of a group or clan. It also helped define certain behaviors and the social relationships of a group. The term comes from an Ojibwa word, but refers to a cultural practice found throughout the Americas. For example, Northwestern peoples displayed totem symbols on masks, boats, and huge poles set in front of their houses. Others used totem symbols in rituals or dances associated with important group events such as marriages, the naming of children, or the planting or harvesting of crops. **B**

There were hundreds of different patterns of Native American life in North America. Some societies were small and dealt with life in a limited region of the vast North American continent. Other groups were much larger, and were linked by trade and culture to other groups in North America and Mesoamerica. As you will learn in Section 2, peoples in Mesoamerica and South America also lived in societies that varied from simple to complex. Three of these cultures—the Maya, the Aztec, and the Incan—would develop very sophisticated ways of life.

Social History

Iroquois Women

Iroquois society was matrilineal. This means that all Iroquois traced their descent through their female ancestors. Clans of the mother controlled property, held ceremonies, and determined official titles.

The ability to grant titles to men was handed down from mother to daughter. The most important title given to men was that of "sachem," the peace, or civil, chief.

A council of sachems met once a year to decide on war and peace and other important matters. Since sachems could not go to war, they appointed warriors to lead a war party. Thus, in a way women had a say in warfare in the Iroquois tribes.

MAIN IDEA

Making Inferences

B What artificial symbols are used by nations or organizations in a way similar to totems?

NEW YORK CORE CURRICULUM REVIEW

TERMS & NAMES 1. For each term or name, write a sentence explaining its significance.

- potlatch
- Anasazi
- pueblo
- Mississippian
- Iroquois
- totem

USING YOUR NOTES

2. How did environment affect the development of the cultures of the Northwest Coast and the Southwest?

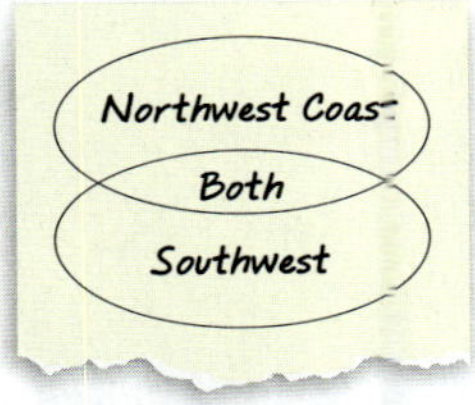

MAIN IDEAS

3. What was the most important resource for the peoples of the Northwest? Why?
4. For what purpose did the Mound Builder cultures use earthen mounds?
5. Why did the tribes of upper New York form a political alliance?

CRITICAL THINKING & WRITING

6. **ANALYZING MOTIVES** Why might the people of the Northwest consider the potlatch to be a good way to signal social standing and wealth?
7. **ANALYZING CAUSES** Why might location have been important to the power and wealth of the Mississippian culture?
8. **COMPARING** In what ways did the peoples of North America share similar cultural patterns?
9. **WRITING ACTIVITY** CULTURAL INTERACTION Write a brief **essay** detailing the evidence that shows how societies in North America interacted with each other.

INTEGRATED TECHNOLOGY **INTERNET ACTIVITY**

Use the Internet to research one of the Native American groups discussed in this section. Use your findings to write an **illustrated report.** Focus your report on how the group lives today.

INTERNET KEYWORD
Native American Nations

Maya Kings and Cities

CONNECT TO THE NEW YORK STATE CORE CURRICULUM

Unit 1.C.5.b. Contributions (mathematics, astronomy, science, arts, architecture, and technology)
Unit 1.C.5.d. Religion

TERMS & NAMES

- Tikal
- glyph
- codex
- *Popol Vuh*

SETTING THE STAGE In the early centuries A.D., most North American peoples were beginning to develop complex societies. Further south, the peoples of Mexico and Central America were entering into the full flower of civilization. A prime example of this cultural flowering were the Maya, who built an extraordinary civilization in the heart of Mesoamerica.

TAKING NOTES
Summarizing Use a graphic organizer to note the major features of the Maya civilization.

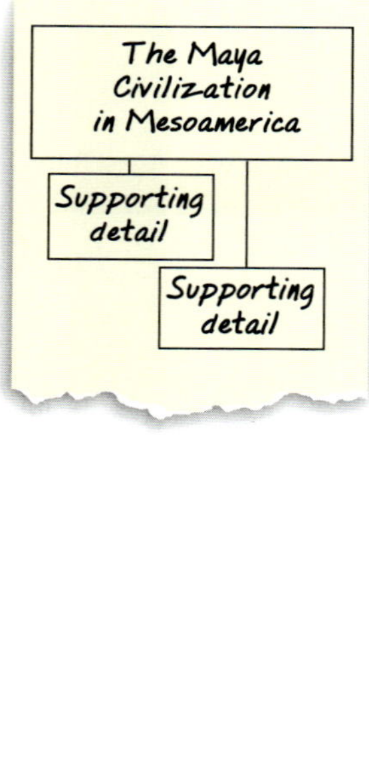

Maya Create City-States

The homeland of the Maya stretched from southern Mexico into northern Central America. This area includes a highland region and a lowland region. The lowlands lie to the north. They include the dry scrub forest of the Yucatán (YOO•kuh•TAN) Peninsula and the dense, steamy jungles of southeastern Mexico and northern Guatemala. The highlands are further south—a range of cool, cloud-wreathed mountains that stretch from southern Mexico to El Salvador.

While the Olmec were building their civilization along the Gulf Coast in the period from 1200 B.C. to 400 B.C., the Maya were also evolving. (See Chapter 9.) They took on Olmec influences, blending these with local customs. By A.D. 250, Maya culture had burst forth in a flourishing civilization.

Urban Centers The period from A.D. 250 to 900 is known as the Classic Period of Maya civilization. During this time, the Maya built spectacular cities such as **Tikal** (tee•KAHL), a major center in northern Guatemala. Other important sites included Copán, Palenque, Uxmal, and Chichén Itzá (chee•CHEHN-ee•TSAH). (See the map on page 447.) Each of these was an independent city-state, ruled by a god-king and serving as a center for religious ceremonies and trade. Maya cities featured giant pyramids, temples, palaces, and elaborate stone carvings dedicated to the gods and to important rulers. Tens of thousands of people lived in residential areas surrounding the city center, which bustled with activity.

Archaeologists have identified at least 50 major Maya sites, all with monumental architecture. For example, Temple IV pyramid at Tikal stretched 212 feet into the jungle sky. In addition to temples and pyramids, each

▼ Maya jade death mask, seventh century A.D.

Maya city featured a ball court. In this stone-sided playing field, the Maya played a game that had religious and political significance. The Maya believed the playing of this game would maintain the cycles of the sun and moon and bring life-giving rains. **A**

MAIN IDEA

Drawing Conclusions

A What does the ability to construct complex buildings reveal about a society?

GEOGRAPHY SKILLBUILDER: Interpreting Maps

1. **Region** *Which civilization occupied the Yucatán Peninsula?*
2. **Region** *What other civilization areas were eventually incorporated into the Aztec area?*

Agriculture and Trade Support Cities Although the Maya city-states were independent of each other, they were linked through alliances and trade. Cities exchanged their local products such as salt, flint, feathers, shells, and honey. They also traded craft goods like cotton textiles and jade ornaments. While the Maya did not have a uniform currency, cacao (chocolate) beans sometimes served as one.

As in the rest of Mesoamerica, agriculture—particularly the growing of maize, beans, and squash—provided the basis for Maya life. For years, experts assumed that the Maya practiced slash-and-burn agriculture. This method involves farmers clearing the land by burning existing vegetation and planting crops in the ashes. Evidence now shows, however, that the Maya also developed more sophisticated methods, including planting on raised beds above swamps and on hillside terraces.

Kingdoms Built on Dynasties Successful farming methods led to the accumulation of wealth and the development of social classes. The noble class, which included priests and the leading warriors, occupied the top rung of Maya society. Below them came merchants and those with specialized knowledge, such as skilled artisans. Finally, at the bottom, came the peasant majority.

The Maya king sat at the top of this class structure. He was regarded as a holy figure, and his position was hereditary. When he died, he passed the throne on to his eldest son. Other sons of the ruler might expect to join the priesthood.

Religion Shapes Maya Life

Religion influenced most aspects of Maya life. The Maya believed in many gods. There were gods of corn, of death, of rain, and of war. Gods could be good or evil, and sometimes both. Gods also were associated with the four directions and with different colors: white for north, black for west, yellow for south, red for east, and green in the center. The Maya believed that each day was a living god whose behavior could be predicted with the help of a system of calendars.

Religious Practices The Maya worshiped their gods in various ways. They prayed and made offerings of food, flowers, and incense. They also pierced and cut their bodies and offered their blood, believing that this would nourish the gods. Sometimes the Maya even carried out human sacrifice, usually of captured enemies. At Chichén Itzá, they threw captives into a deep sinkhole lake, called a *cenote* (say•NO•tay), along with gold, jade, and other offerings. The Maya believed that human sacrifice pleased the gods and kept the world in balance. Nevertheless, the Maya's use of sacrifice never reached the extremes of some other Mesoamerican peoples.

Math and Religion Maya religious beliefs also led to the development of the calendar, mathematics, and astronomy. The Maya believed that time was a burden carried on the back of a god. At the end of a day, month, or year, one god would lay the burden down and another would pick it up. A day would be lucky or unlucky, depending on the nature of the god. So it was very important to have an accurate calendar to know which god was in charge of the day.

The Maya developed a 260-day religious calendar, which consisted of thirteen 20-day months. A second 365-day solar calendar consisted of eighteen 20-day months, with a separate period of 5 days at the end. The two calendars were linked together like meshed gears so that any given day could be identified in both cycles. The calendar helped identify the best times to plant crops, attack enemies, and crown new rulers.

The Maya based their calendar on careful observation of the planets, sun, and moon. Highly skilled Maya astronomers and mathematicians calculated the solar year at 365.2420 days. This is only .0002 of a day short of the figure generally accepted today! The Maya astronomers were able to attain such great precision by using a math system that included the concept of zero. The Maya used a shell symbol for zero, dots for the numbers one to four, and a bar for five. The Maya number system was a base-20 system. They used the numerical system primarily for calendar and astronomical work. **B**

MAIN IDEA

Making Inferences

B How are math, astronomy, and calendars related?

Written Language Preserves History The Maya also developed the most advanced writing system in the ancient Americas. Maya writing consisted of about 800 hieroglyphic symbols, or **glyphs** (glihfs). Some of these glyphs stood for whole words, and others represented syllables. The Maya used their writing system to record important historical events, carving their glyphs in stone or recording them in a bark-paper book known as a **codex** (KOH•DEHKS). Only three of these ancient books have survived.

Other original books telling of Maya history and customs do exist, however. Maya peoples wrote down their history after the arrival of the Spanish. The most famous of these books, the ***Popol Vuh*** (POH•pohl VOO), recounts the Highland Maya's version of the story of creation. "Before the world was created, Calm and Silence were the great kings that ruled," reads the first sentence in the book. "Nothing existed, there was nothing."

PRIMARY SOURCE

Then let the emptiness fill! they said. Let the water weave its way downward so the earth can show its face! Let the light break on the ridges, let the sky fill up with the yellow light of dawn! Let our glory be a man walking on a path through the trees! "Earth!" the Creators called. They called only once, and it was there, from a mist, from a cloud of dust, the mountains appeared instantly.

From the *Popol Vuh*

▼ A detail from the Maya *Codex Troano*

Rise and Fall of the Maya		
Traits of Civilization	**Strength Leading to Power**	**Weakness Leading to Decline**
• Religious beliefs and theocracy • Independent city-states • Intensive agriculture	• United culture • Loyalty to the king • Wealthy and prosperous culture • Production of more food feeds a larger population	• Many physical and human resources funneled into religious activities • Frequent warfare occurs between kingdoms • Population growth creates need for more land

SKILLBUILDER: Interpreting Charts

1. **Recognizing Effects** *Which trait aids in building a sense of loyalty to the ruler?*
2. **Drawing Conclusions** *How can intensive agriculture be both a strength and a weakness?*

Mysterious Maya Decline

The remarkable history of the Maya ended in mystery. In the late 800s, the Maya suddenly abandoned many of their cities. Invaders from the north, the Toltec, moved into the lands occupied by the Maya. These warlike peoples from central Mexico changed the culture. The high civilization of Maya cities like Tikal and Copán disappeared.

No one knows exactly why this happened, though experts offer several overlapping theories. By the 700s, warfare had broken out among the various Maya city-states. Increased warfare disrupted trade and produced economic hardship. In addition, population growth and over-farming may have damaged the environment, and this led to food shortages, famine, and disease. By the time the Spanish arrived in the early 1500s, the Maya were divided into small, weak city-states that gave little hint of their former glory. C

MAIN IDEA

Analyzing Causes

C Why did the Maya civilization go into decline?

As the Maya civilization faded, other peoples of Mesoamerica were growing in strength and sophistication. Like the Maya, these peoples would trace some of their ancestry to the Olmec. Eventually, these people would dominate the Valley of Mexico and lands beyond it, as you will learn in Section 3.

NEW YORK CORE CURRICULUM REVIEW

TERMS & NAMES 1. For each term or name, write a sentence explaining its significance.

• Tikal • glyph • codex • *Popol Vuh*

USING YOUR NOTES

2. How do the characteristics of Maya civilization compare with the characteristics of a typical civilization?

MAIN IDEAS

3. What was the basis of Maya life?
4. Why was the calendar important for the Maya religion?
5. What three explanations have been given for the collapse of the Maya civilization?

CRITICAL THINKING & WRITING

6. **RECOGNIZING EFFECTS** Why was trade important to the Maya civilization?
7. **DRAWING CONCLUSIONS** How important do you think the development of advanced mathematics was in the creation of the Maya calendar?
8. **ANALYZING CAUSES** Which of the causes for the fall of the Maya do you think was most important? Explain.
9. **WRITING ACTIVITY** RELIGIOUS AND ETHICAL SYSTEMS Imagine that you are a reporter visiting Maya city-states. Write a one-page **news article** that describes various aspects of the Maya religion.

CONNECT TO TODAY **CREATING A MAP**

Conduct research to discover the countries in which the modern Maya live. Use your findings to create a **map** showing the areas within these countries occupied by the Maya.

History *through* Art

Maya Architecture

Maya architects created beautiful and monumental structures. The buildings are artistic in structure, as well as in ornamentation. The style and complexity of the ornamentation varies by region, but narrative, ceremonial, and celestial themes are common. Archaeologists and tourists alike are still awed by Maya architecture.

These large structures seem to be designed for ceremonial or religious purposes and dominate the landscapes of the cities. The most recognizable structures are the pyramids, but there is much more to the artful Maya architecture.

INTEGRATED TECHNOLOGY

RESEARCH LINKS For more on Maya architecture, go to **classzone.com**

▲ **Detailing**

One characteristic of Maya architecture is the exterior and interior ornamental detailing. This two-headed jaguar throne was found at Uxmal. It represents the jaguar god of the underworld, one of the many Maya gods. An ancient Maya manuscript lists over 160 gods.

◄ **Stele**

A stele (STEE•lee) is an inscribed or carved marker that is often used to mark special dates or as a building marker. This stele is in the Maya city of Copán and is part of a series of finely carved commemorative steles in the great plaza. The 13th king is represented on most of the steles in ceremonial clothing.

▲ Ball Court

Ball courts were a feature of ancient Maya cities. The games held deep religious significance, and the same artistic detail is found in the ball courts as in other religious structures. The court shown here is at Chichén Itzá in modern Mexico. It is 545 feet long and 223 feet wide, and is the largest in the Americas. The ornate hoop (above left) is 20 feet off the ground.

The exact rules and method of scoring the game are unknown. However, inscriptions indicate that players could not use their hands or feet to move a solid rubber ball, and that members of the losing team might be sacrificed by beheading.

◄ Pyramid

Archaeologists have found pyramids at many Maya cities. Pyramids were religious structures and, as in Egypt, could be used as tombs. The pyramid shown here is known as Temple I in the Maya city of Tikal. It is the tomb of Ha Sawa Chaan K'awil, a Tikal ruler. The pyramid is about 160 feet tall. Another pyramid in the city is 212 feet tall. In fact, the Tikal pyramids were the tallest structures in the Americas until 1903, when the Flatiron Building was built in New York City.

Connect *to* Today

1. **Making Inferences** What does the size and ornamentation of Maya architecture indicate about their society?

   See Skillbuilder Handbook, Page R10.

2. **Comparing and Contrasting** What are some examples of large-scale architecture in the United States? What do they indicate about our culture?

The Aztecs Control Central Mexico

CONNECT TO THE NEW YORK STATE CORE CURRICULUM

Unit 4.D.2. Organizational structure
Unit 4.D.4. Trade

TERMS & NAMES

- obsidian
- Quetzalcoatl
- Triple Alliance
- Montezuma II

SETTING THE STAGE While the Maya were developing their civilization to the south, other high cultures were evolving in central Mexico. Some of the most important developments took place in and around the Valley of Mexico. This valley, where modern Mexico City is located, eventually became the site of the greatest empire of Mesoamerica, the Aztec. The Aztecs were preceded by two other important civilizations that traced their ancestry to the Olmec and Zapotec. You learned about the Olmec and Zapotec in Chapter 9.

TAKING NOTES

Following Chronological Order Use a "chain of events" diagram to list events in the establishment and growth of the Aztec Empire.

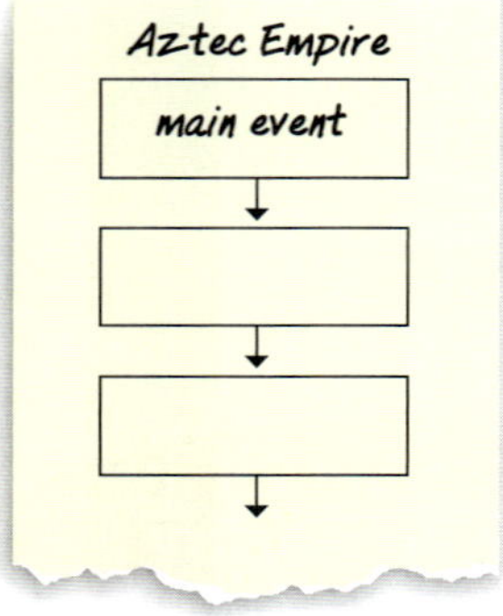

The Valley of Mexico

The Valley of Mexico, a mountain basin about 7,500 feet above sea level, served as the home base of several powerful cultures. The valley had several large, shallow lakes at its center, accessible resources, and fertile soil. These advantages attracted the people of Teotihuacán (TAY•oh•TEE•wah•KAHN) and the Toltecs. They settled in the valley and developed advanced civilizations that controlled much of the area. (See the map on page 447.)

An Early City-State The first major civilization of central Mexico was Teotihuacán, a city-state whose ruins lie just outside Mexico City. In the first century A.D., villagers at this site began to plan and construct a monumental city, even larger than Monte Albán, in Oaxaca.

At its peak in the sixth century, Teotihuacán had a population of between 150,000 and 200,000 people, making it one of the largest cities in the world at the time. The heart of the city was a central avenue lined with more than 20 pyramids dedicated to various gods. The biggest of these was the giant Pyramid of the Sun. This imposing building stood more than 200 feet tall and measured close to 3,000 feet around its base. The people of Teotihuacán lived in apartment-block buildings in the area around the central avenue.

Teotihuacán became the center of a thriving trade network that extended far into Central America. The

▼ Quetzalcoatl was a god for many ancient Mexican civilizations.

▲ The Pyramid of the Sun (left background) dominates Teotihuacán's main highway, the Avenue of the Dead.

city's most valuable trade item was **obsidian** (ahb•SIHD•ee•uhn), a green or black volcanic glass found in the Valley of Mexico and used to make razor-sharp weapons. There is no evidence that Teotihuacán conquered its neighbors or tried to create an empire. However, evidence of art styles and religious beliefs from Teotihuacán have been found throughout Mesoamerica.

After centuries of growth, the city abruptly declined. Historians believe this decline was due either to an invasion by outside forces or conflict among the city's ruling classes. Regardless of the causes, the city was virtually abandoned by 750. The vast ruins astonished later settlers in the area, who named the site Teotihuacán, which means "City of the Gods."

Toltecs Take Over After the fall of Teotihuacán, no single culture dominated central Mexico for decades. Then around 900, a new people—the Toltecs—rose to power. For the next three centuries, the Toltecs ruled over the heart of Mexico from their capital at Tula. (See the map on page 447.) Like other Mesoamericans, they built pyramids and temples. They also carved tall pillars in the shape of armed warriors.

In fact, the Toltecs were an extremely warlike people whose empire was based on conquest. They worshiped a fierce war god who demanded blood and human sacrifice from his followers. Sometime after 1000, a Toltec ruler named Topiltzin (toh•PEELT•zeen) tried to change the Toltec religion. He called on the Toltec people to end the practice of human sacrifice. He also encouraged them to worship a different god, **Quetzalcoatl** (keht•SAHL•koh•AHT•uhl), or the Feathered Serpent. Followers of the war god rebelled, however, forcing Topiltzin and his followers into exile on the Yucatán Peninsula. There, they greatly influenced late-Mayan culture. After Topiltzin's exile, Toltec power began to decline. By the early 1200s, their reign over the Valley of Mexico had ended. (A)

MAIN IDEA

Making Inferences

(A) Why might the followers of the war god rebel against Topiltzin?

In time, Topiltzin and Quetzalcoatl became one in the legends of the people of the Valley of Mexico. According to these legends, after his exile from Tula, the god traveled east, crossing the sea on a raft of snakes. He would return one day, bringing a new reign of light and peace. The story of Quetzalcoatl would come back to haunt the greatest empire of Mexico, the Aztecs.

The Aztec Empire

The Aztecs arrived in the Valley of Mexico around A.D. 1200. The valley contained a number of small city-states that had survived the collapse of Toltec rule. The Aztecs, who were then called the Mexica, were a poor, nomadic people from the harsh deserts of northern Mexico. Fierce and ambitious, they soon adapted to local ways, finding work as soldiers-for-hire to local rulers.

According to one of the Aztec legends, the god of the sun and warfare, Huitzilopochtli (wee•tsee•loh•POHCH•tlee), told them to found a city of their own. He said to look for a place where an eagle perched on a cactus, holding a snake in its mouth. These words capture part of the legend:

PRIMARY SOURCE

The place where the eagle screams,
where he spreads his wings;
the place where he feeds,
where the fish jump,
where the serpents
coil up and hiss!
This shall be Mexico Tenochtitlán
and many things shall happen!

Crónica Mexicayotl

They found such a place on a small island in Lake Texcoco, at the center of the valley. There, in 1325, they founded their city, which they named Tenochtitlán (teh•NOCH•tee•TLAHN).

Aztecs Grow Stronger Over the years, the Aztecs gradually increased in strength and number. In 1428, they joined with two other city-states—Texcoco and Tlacopan—to form the **Triple Alliance**. This alliance became the leading power in the Valley of Mexico and soon gained control over neighboring regions. By the early 1500s, they controlled a vast empire that covered some 80,000 square miles stretching from central Mexico to the Atlantic and Pacific coasts and south into Oaxaca. This empire was divided into 38 provinces. It had an estimated population of between 5 and 15 million people.

The Aztecs based their power on military conquest and the tribute they gained from their conquered subjects. The Aztecs generally exercised loose control over the empire, often letting local rulers govern their own regions. The Aztecs did demand tribute, however, in the form of gold, maize, cacao beans, cotton, jade, and other products. If local rulers failed to pay tribute, or offered any other kind of resistance, the Aztecs responded brutally. They destroyed the rebellious villages and captured or slaughtered the inhabitants. **B**

MAIN IDEA

Comparing

B How were the Aztecs' methods of controlling the empire like those of other empires you have read about?

Nobles Rule Aztec Society At the height of the Aztec Empire, military leaders held great power in Aztec society. Along with government officials and priests, these military leaders made up the noble class. Many nobles owned vast estates, which they ruled over like lords, living a life of great wealth and luxury.

There were two other broad classes in Aztec society, commoners and enslaved persons. Commoners included merchants, artisans, soldiers, and farmers who owned their own land. The merchants formed a special type of elite. They often traveled widely, acting as spies for the emperor and gaining great wealth for themselves. The lowest class, enslaved persons, were captives who did many different jobs.

The emperor sat atop the Aztec social pyramid. Although he sometimes consulted with top generals or officials, his power was absolute. The emperor lived in a magnificent

Global Patterns

Warriors and Animal Symbols

Some of the highest-ranking Aztec leaders were eagle warriors. (A statue of an eagle warrior is shown above.) In battle, they wore eagle costumes in honor of the sun god, Huitzilopochtli, who often took the form of an eagle.

The use of animal symbols by warriors was a widespread practice in ancient times. The eagle was a favorite among Roman soldiers because they thought it symbolized victory. In many cultures, warriors adopted an animal so that they would inherit the animal's qualities. Celtic fighters, for example, wore boars' heads on their helmets so that they, like the boar, would be strong and fearless. Similarly, many African warriors adopted the lion for its fighting ferocity.

INTEGRATED TECHNOLOGY

INTERNET ACTIVITY Plan a Web page that identifies and explains some animal symbols used by ancient warriors. Go to **classzone.com** for your research.

palace, surrounded by servants and his wives. Visitors—even nobles—entered his presence in bare feet and cast their eyes down so as not to look at him.

Tenochtitlán: A Planned City

By the early 1500s, Tenochtitlán had become an extraordinary urban center. With a population of between 200,000 and 400,000 people, it was larger than London or any other European capital of the time. Tenochtitlán remained on its original island site. To connect the island to the mainland, Aztec engineers built three raised roads, called causeways, over the water and marshland. Other smaller cities ringed the lake, creating a dense concentration of people in the Valley of Mexico.

Streets and broad avenues connected the city center with outlying residential districts. The canals that intersected with these roadways allowed canoes to bring people directly into the city center. Canoes also brought goods from the farthest reaches of the empire to the economic heart of the city, the huge market of Tlatelolco (TLAH•tehl•AWL•koh). Visitors to the market also found a great deal of local agricultural produce on display, including avocados, beans, chili peppers, corn, squash, and tomatoes. Most of the fruits and vegetables sold at the market were grown on *chinampas,* farm plots built on the marshy fringes of the lake. These plots, sometimes called "floating gardens," were extremely productive, providing the food needed for a huge urban population.

At the center of the city was a massive, walled complex, filled with palaces, temples, and government buildings. The main structure in the complex was the Great Temple. This giant pyramid with twin temples at the top, one dedicated to the sun god and the other to the rain god, served as the center of Aztec religious life.

Analyzing Primary Sources

The Market at Tlatelolco

Hernando Cortés, the Spanish conqueror of Mexico, noted that the market at Tlatelolco was twice the size of the market at Salamanca, the Spanish city where he had attended university.

PRIMARY SOURCE

Day after day 60,000 people congregate here to buy and sell. Every imaginable kind of merchandise is available from all parts of the Empire, foodstuffs and dress, . . . gold, silver, copper, . . . precious stones, leather, bone, mussels, coral, cotton, feathers. . . . Everything is sold by the piece or by measurement, never by weight. In the main market there is a law court in which there are always ten or twelve judges performing their office and taking decisions on all marketing controversies.

HERNANDO CORTÉS, *Letters of Information*

Tenochtitlán—A Bustling City

Bernal Díaz, one of Cortés's soldiers, was amazed to find a bustling urban center in the heart of Mexico.

PRIMARY SOURCE

When we saw all those cities and villages built in the water, and other great towns on dry land, and that straight and level causeway leading to Mexico, we were astounded. These great towns and cues [pyramids] and buildings rising from the water, all made of stone, seemed like an enchanted vision. . . . Indeed, some of our soldiers asked whether it was not all a dream.

BERNAL DÍAZ, *The Conquest of New Spain*

DOCUMENT-BASED QUESTIONS

1. **Contrasting** *How do the descriptions of Cortés and Díaz differ?*
2. **Making Inferences** *How do you think Cortés and Díaz feel about Aztec accomplishments?*

Religion Rules Aztec Life

Religion played a major role in Aztec society. Tenochtitlán contained hundreds of temples and religious structures dedicated to the approximately 1,000 gods that the Aztecs worshiped. The Aztecs adopted many of these gods, and religious practices related to them, from other Mesoamerican peoples. For example, the Aztecs worshiped the Toltec god Quetzalcoatl in many forms. They saw him as the god of learning and books, the god of the wind, and a symbol of death and rebirth. The Aztecs pictured Quetzalcoatl not only as a feathered serpent, but also as a pale-skinned man with a beard.

▲ This mural, in the National Palace in Mexico City, shows Quetzalcoatl in many forms.

Religious Practices Aztec religious practices centered on elaborate public ceremonies designed to communicate with the gods and win their favor. At these ceremonies, priests made offerings to the gods and presented ritual dramas, songs, and dances featuring masked performers. The Aztec ceremonial calendar was full of religious festivals, which varied according to the god being honored.

Sacrifices for the Sun God The most important rituals involved a sun god, Huitzilopochtli. According to Aztec belief, Huitzilopochtli made the sun rise every day. When the sun set, he had to battle the forces of evil to get to the next day. To make sure that he was strong enough for this ordeal, he needed the nourishment of human blood. Without regular offerings of human blood, Huitzilopochtli would be too weak to fight. The sun would not rise, the world would be plunged into darkness, and all life would perish. For this reason, Aztec priests practiced human sacrifice on a massive scale. Each year, thousands of victims were led to the altar atop the Great Temple, where priests carved out their hearts using obsidian knives.

Sacrificial victims included enslaved persons, criminals, and people offered as tribute by conquered provinces. Prisoners of war, however, were the preferred victims. As a result, the priests required a steady supply of war captives. This in turn pushed the Aztec military to carry out new conquests. In fact, the Aztecs often went to war not to conquer new lands, but simply to capture prisoners for sacrifice. They even adapted their battle tactics to ensure that they took their opponents alive. **C**

MAIN IDEA
Clarifying
C Why did the Aztecs take so many war captives?

Problems in the Aztec Empire

In 1502, a new ruler, **Montezuma II** (MAHN•tih•ZOO•muh), was crowned emperor. Under Montezuma, the Aztec Empire began to weaken. For nearly a century, the Aztecs had been demanding tribute and sacrificial victims from the provinces under their control. Now, with the population of Tenochtitlán growing ever greater, Montezuma called for even more tribute and sacrifice. A number of provinces rose

History *in* Depth

INTERACTIVE

The Aztec Calendar

The Aztec system of tracking the days was very intricate. Archaeologists believe that the Aztec calendar system was derived from the Maya system. The Aztecs followed two main calendars: a sacred one with 13 months of 20 days and an agricultural or solar one with 18 months of 20 days. (Notice that this comes to 360 days. The Aztecs then had an unlucky five-day period known as *nemontemi*, making their solar calendar 365 days long.) Every 52 years, the two calendars would start on the same day, and a great ceremony of fire marked the occasion.

▲ Aztec Gods

The Aztecs worshiped many different gods. They were a vital part of the Aztec calendar and daily life. The Aztecs paid tribute to different gods depending, in part, on the day, week, month, year, and religious cycle of the Aztec calendars. The god shown here is a sun god, Tonatiuh.

◄ Aztec Sunstone

Originally located in the main ceremonial plaza of Tenochtitlán, the Aztec calendar stone measures 13 feet in diameter and weighs 24 tons. It was uncovered in Mexico City in 1790. The Sunstone, as it is called, contains a wealth of information about the days that began and ended the Aztec months, the gods associated with the days, and many other details.

This is an artist's rendition of the inner circle of the Sunstone. In the center is the god Tonatiuh.

The four squares that surround Tonatiuh are glyphs or symbols of the four ages preceding the time of the Aztecs: Tiger, Water, Wind, and Rain.

In the ring just outside the symbols of the previous ages, 20 segments represent the 20 days that made up an Aztec month. Each day had its own symbol and a god who watched over the day. The symbol pointed to here is Ocelotl, the jaguar.

SKILLBUILDER: Interpreting Visual Sources

1. **Hypothesizing** *Why do you think the Aztecs put Tonatiuh, a sun god, in the center of the Sunstone? Explain your reasons.*
2. **Comparing and Contrasting** *How is the Aztec calendar different from the calendar we use today? How is it similar?*

Rise and Fall of the Aztecs		
Traits of Civilization	**Strength Leading to Power**	**Weakness Leading to Decline**
• Religious beliefs and theocracy • Powerful army • Empire of tribute states	• United culture • Loyalty to the emperor • Adds land, power, and prisoners for religious sacrifice • Provides wealth and power and prisoners for religious sacrifice	• Many physical and human resources funneled into religious activities • Need for prisoners changes warfare style to less deadly and less aggressive • Tribute states are rebellious and need to be controlled

SKILLBUILDER: Interpreting Charts

1. **Drawing Conclusions** *How was the tribute system both a strength and a weakness?*
2. **Clarifying** *How are the army and religious beliefs linked in the Aztec Empire?*

up against Aztec oppression. This began a period of unrest and rebellion, which the military struggled to put down.

Over time, Montezuma tried to lessen the pressure on the provinces. For example, he reduced the demand for tribute payment by cutting the number of officials in the Aztec government. But resentment continued to grow. Many Aztecs began to predict that terrible things were about to happen. They saw bad omens in every unusual occurrence—lightning striking a temple in Tenochtitlán, or a partial eclipse of the sun, for example. The most worrying event, however, was the arrival of the Spanish. For many Aztecs, these fair-skinned, bearded strangers from across the sea brought to mind the legend of the return of Quetzalcoatl. **D**

Further south in the high mountain valleys of the Andes, another empire was developing, one that would transcend the Aztec Empire in land area, power, and wealth. Like the Aztecs, the people of this Andean empire worshiped the sun and had large armies. However, the society they built was much different from that of the Aztecs, as you will see in Section 4.

MAIN IDEA

Making Inferences

D Why would cutting the number of government officials reduce the need for tribute money?

NEW YORK CORE CURRICULUM REVIEW

TERMS & NAMES 1. For each term or name, write a sentence explaining its significance.

• obsidian • Quetzalcoatl • Triple Alliance • Montezuma II

USING YOUR NOTES

2. How do you think the Aztecs were able to establish an extensive empire in such a relatively short period of time?

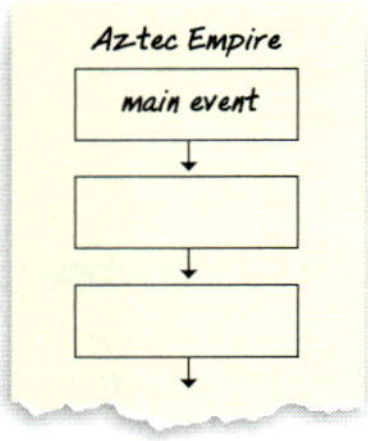

MAIN IDEA

3. On what was Teotihuacán's power and wealth based?
4. How did the Aztecs rule their empire?
5. Why did the Aztecs think it was necessary to make blood sacrifices to the sun god, Huitzilopochtli?

CRITICAL THINKING & WRITING

6. **IDENTIFYING SOLUTIONS** How were the Aztecs able to overcome the problems associated with Tenochtitlán's island location?
7. **ANALYZING MOTIVES** Why do you think the Aztecs allowed some conquered peoples to govern themselves with relatively little interference?
8. **RECOGNIZING EFFECTS** How did the Aztec need for victims for sacrifice lead to problems controlling the empire?
9. **WRITING ACTIVITY** POWER AND AUTHORITY Write a short **play** in which Montezuma discusses with his advisers how to gain control of the empire's rebellious provinces.

CONNECT TO TODAY CREATING A MENU

Many of the foods eaten by Mexicans today date back to Aztec times. Conduct research to discover more about the Aztec origins of Mexican food. Use your findings to create a **menu** for a modern "Aztec" meal.

4

The Inca Create a Mountain Empire

CONNECT TO THE NEW YORK STATE CORE CURRICULUM

Unit 4.D.2. Organizational structure
Unit 4.D.3. Contributions

TERMS & NAMES

- Pachacuti
- ayllu
- mita
- quipu

SETTING THE STAGE While the Aztecs ruled in the Valley of Mexico, another people—the Inca—created an equally powerful state in South America. From Cuzco, their capital in southern Peru, the Inca spread outward in all directions. They brought various Andean peoples under their control and built an empire that stretched from Ecuador in the north to Chile in the south. It was the largest empire ever seen in the Americas.

TAKING NOTES

Categorizing Use a web diagram to identify the methods the Inca used to build their vast, unified empire.

The Inca Build an Empire

Like the Aztecs, the Inca built their empire on cultural foundations thousands of years old. (See Chapter 9.) Ancient civilizations such as Chavín, Moche, and Nazca had already established a tradition of high culture in Peru. They were followed by the Huari and Tiahuanaco cultures of southern Peru and Bolivia. The Chimú, an impressive civilization of the 1300s based in the northern coastal region once controlled by the Moche, came next. The Inca would create an even more powerful state, however, extending their rule over the entire Andean region.

Incan Beginnings The Inca originally lived in a high plateau of the Andes. After wandering the highlands for years, the Inca finally settled on fertile lands in the Valley of Cuzco. By the 1200s, they had established their own small kingdom in the valley.

During this early period, the Inca developed traditions and beliefs that helped launch and unify their empire. One of these traditions was the belief that the Incan ruler was descended from the sun god, Inti, who would bring prosperity and greatness to the Incan state. Only men from one of 11 noble lineages believed to be descendants of the sun god could be selected as Incan leaders.

Pachacuti Builds an Empire At first the Incan kingdom grew slowly. In 1438, however, a powerful and ambitious ruler, **Pachacuti** (PAH•chah•KOO•tee), took the throne. Under his leadership, the Inca conquered all of Peru and then moved into neighboring lands. By 1500, the Inca ruled an empire that stretched 2,500 miles along the western coast of South America. (See the map on page 461.) The Inca called this empire "Land of the Four Quarters." It included about 80 provinces and was home to as many as 16 million people.

Pachacuti and his successors accomplished this feat of conquest through a combination of diplomacy and military force. The Inca had a powerful military

History Makers

Pachacuti
c. 1391–c. 1473

As the second son of the Incan ruler Viracocha, Pachacuti did not expect to succeed to the throne. However, when Cuzco was attacked in 1438, Viracocha and Pachacuti's older brother fled the city. Pachacuti stayed and drove off the attackers. He then proclaimed himself the new Incan ruler.

Pachacuti, whose name means "World Transformer" or "Earthshaker," ruled for 33 years. During that time, he drew up the plans for the rebuilding of Cuzco and established the Incan system of government.

INTEGRATED TECHNOLOGY

RESEARCH LINKS For more on Pachacuti and other Incan rulers, go to **classzone.com**

but used force only when necessary. They were also clever diplomats. Before attacking, they typically offered enemy states an honorable surrender. They would allow them to keep their own customs and rulers in exchange for loyalty to the Incan state. Because of this treatment, many states gave up without resisting. Even when force was used, the Inca took a similar approach. Once an area was defeated, they made every effort to gain the loyalty of the newly conquered people.

Incan Government Creates Unity

To control the huge empire, the rulers divided their territory and its people into manageable units, governed by a central bureaucracy. The Inca created an efficient economic system to support the empire and an extensive road system to tie it together. They also imposed a single official language, Quechua (KEHCH•wuh), and founded schools to teach Incan ways. Certain social groups were identified by officially dictated patterns on clothing. All of these actions were calculated to unify the variety of people controlled by the Inca. **A**

MAIN IDEA

Forming Opinions

A Of all of the methods used to create unity, which do you think would be most successful? Why?

Incan Cities Show Government Presence To exercise control over their empire, the Inca built many cities in conquered areas. The architecture of government buildings was the same all over the empire, making the presence of the government apparent. As in Rome, all roads led to the capital, Cuzco. The heart of the Incan empire, Cuzco was a splendid city of temples, plazas, and palaces. "Cuzco was grand and stately," wrote Cieza de León. "It had fine streets, . . . and the houses were built of solid stones, beautifully joined." Like the Romans, the Inca were masterful engineers and stonemasons. Though they had no iron tools and did not use the wheel, Incan builders carved and transported huge blocks of stone, fitting them together perfectly without mortar. Many Incan walls still stand in Cuzco today, undisturbed by the region's frequent earthquakes.

Incan Government The Incan state exercised almost total control over economic and social life. It controlled most economic activity, regulating the production and distribution of goods. Unlike the Maya and the Aztecs, the Inca allowed little private commerce or trade.

The Incan social system was based on an age-old form of community cooperation—the ayllu (EYE•loo). The **ayllu**, or extended family group, undertook tasks too big for a single family. These tasks included building irrigation canals or cutting agricultural terraces into steep hillsides. The ayllu also stored food and other supplies to distribute among members during hard times.

The Inca incorporated the ayllu structure into a governing system based on the decimal system. They divided families into groups of 10, 100, 1,000, and 10,000. A chief led each group. He was part of a chain of command. That chain stretched from the community and regional levels all the way to Cuzco, where the Incan ruler and his council of state held court. In general, local administration was left in the hands of local rulers, and villages were allowed to continue their traditional ways. If a community resisted Incan control, however, the Inca might relocate the whole group

MAIN IDEA

Identifying Solutions

B How would relocating troublesome people help government control of an area?

to a different territory. The resisters would be placed under the control of rulers appointed by the government in Cuzco. **B**

The main demand the Incan state placed on its subjects was for tribute, usually in the form of labor. The labor tribute was known as **mita** (MEE•tuh). It required all able-bodied citizens to work for the state a certain number of days every year. Mita workers might labor on state farmlands, produce craft goods for state warehouses, or help with public works projects.

Historians have compared the Incan system to a type of socialism or a modern welfare state. Citizens were expected to work for the state and were cared for in return. For example, the aged and disabled were often supported by the state. The state also made sure that the people did not go hungry when there were bad harvests. Freeze-dried potatoes, called *chuño,* were stored in huge government warehouses for distribution in times of food shortages.

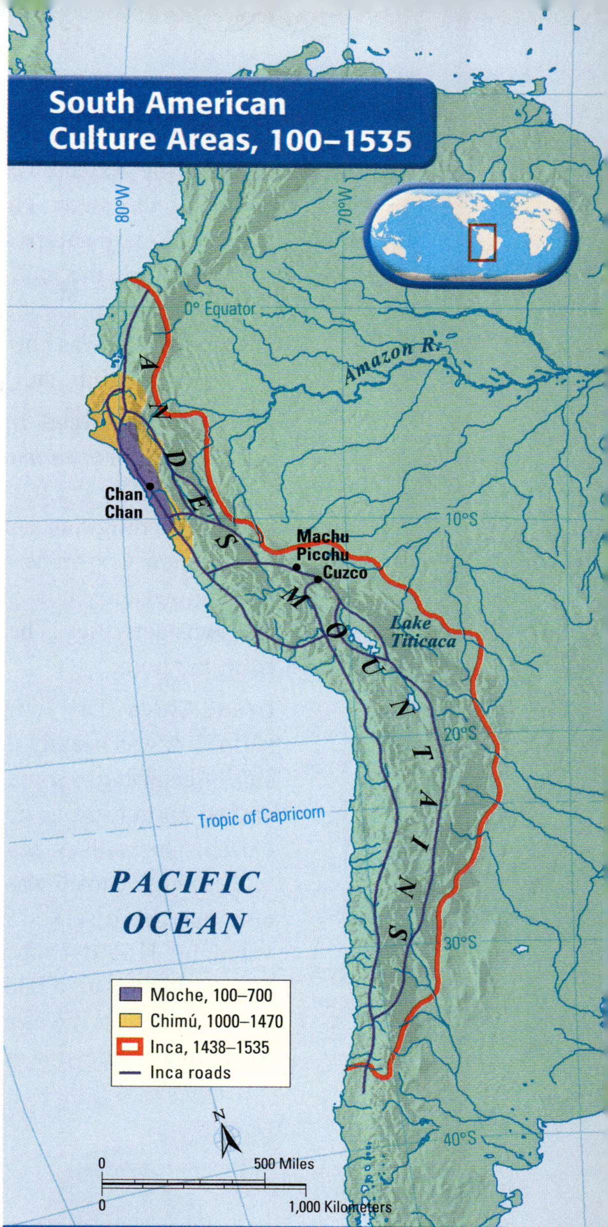

South American Culture Areas, 100–1535

GEOGRAPHY SKILLBUILDER: Interpreting Maps

1. **Place** *The lands of which earlier South American cultures were included in the Incan Empire?*
2. **Human-Environment Interaction** *Look at the shape and terrain of the Incan Empire. What problems related to geography might occur in controlling the land?*

Public Works Projects The Inca had an ambitious public works program. The most spectacular project was the Incan road system. A marvel of engineering, this road system symbolized the power of the Incan state. The 14,000-mile-long network of roads and bridges spanned the empire, traversing rugged mountains and harsh deserts. The roads ranged from paved stone to simple paths. Along the roads, the Inca built guesthouses to provide shelter for weary travelers. A system of runners, known as *chasquis* (SHAH•skeys), traveled these roads as a kind of postal service, carrying messages from one end of the empire to the other. The road system also allowed the easy movement of troops to bring control to areas of the empire where trouble might be brewing.

Government Record-Keeping Despite the sophistication of many aspects of Incan life, the Inca never developed a writing system. History and literature were memorized as part of an oral tradition. For numerical information, the Inca created an accounting device known as the **quipu**, a set of knotted strings that could be used to record data. (See the Global Patterns feature on page 20.) The knots and their position on the string indicated numbers. Additionally, the colors of the strings represented different categories of information important to the government. For example, red strings were used to count warriors; yellow strings were used to count gold. However, the meanings of the colors changed depending on the general purpose of the quipu. **C**

MAIN IDEA

Recognizing Effects

C How might the Incan system of record-keeping help support a strong government?

Some historians believe that the Inca also developed an elaborate calendar system with two types of calendars, one for night and one for day. They were used primarily for religious purposes. Like the calendars of the Maya and the Aztecs, the two calendars provided information about the gods whom the Inca believed ruled the day and time.

Religion Supports the State

As with the Aztecs, religion was important to the Inca and helped reinforce the power of the state. The Inca worshiped fewer gods than the Aztecs. The Inca focused on key nature spirits such as the moon, the stars, and thunder. In the balance of nature, the Inca saw patterns for the way humans should relate to each other and to the earth. The primary Incan god was a creator god called Viracocha. Next in importance was the sun god, Inti. Because the Incan ruler was considered a descendant of Inti, sun worship amounted to worship of the king.

Religious Practices Incan priests led the sun-worship services, assisted by young women known as *mamakuna,* or "virgins of the sun." These women, all unmarried, were drafted by the Inca for a lifetime of religious service. The young women were trained in religious activities, as teachers, spinners, weavers, and beer makers. Young men, known as *yamacuna,* also served as full-time workers for the state and in religious activities. Sacrifice of llamas and exchange of goods were a part of the religious activities. The goods were distributed by the priests to the people as gifts from the gods.

Great Cities The Temple of the Sun in Cuzco was the most sacred of all Incan shrines. It was heavily decorated in gold, a metal the Inca referred to as "sweat of the sun." According to some sources, the temple even had a garden with plants and animals crafted entirely from gold and silver. In fact, gold was a common sight throughout Cuzco. The walls of several buildings had a covering of thin gold sheeting.

Although Cuzco was the religious capital of the Incan Empire, other Incan cities also may have served a ceremonial purpose. For example, Machu Picchu, excavated by Hiram Bingham in 1912, was isolated and mysterious. Like Cuzco, Machu Picchu also had a sun temple, public buildings, and a central plaza. Some sources suggest it was a religious center. Others think it was an estate of Pachacuti. Still others believe it was a retreat for Incan rulers or the nobility.

▼ Machu Picchu lies some 8,000 feet above sea level on a ridge between two mountain peaks.

Rise and Fall of the Inca		
Traits of Civilization	**Strength Leading to Power**	**Weakness Leading to Decline**
• Religious beliefs and theocracy • Major road systems • Type of welfare state with huge bureaucracy	• United culture • Loyalty to the emperor • Connected entire empire and aided control • Care for entire population during good and bad times	• Many physical and human resources funneled into religious activities • Enemy could also use roads to move troops • People struggled to care for themselves with the elimination of the welfare state

SKILLBUILDER: Interpreting Charts

1. **Forming and Supporting Opinions** *In your opinion, which of the three traits leading to power was the most valuable? Briefly discuss your reasons.*
2. **Comparing** *Which trait did you find repeated in the Maya and Aztec empires?*

Discord in the Empire

The Incan Empire reached the height of its glory in the early 1500s during the reign of Huayna Capac. Trouble was brewing, however. In the 1520s, Huayna Capac undertook a tour of Ecuador, a newly conquered area of the empire. In the city of Quito, he received a gift box. When he opened it, out flew butterflies and moths, considered an evil omen. A few weeks later, while still in Quito, Huayna Capac died of disease—probably smallpox.

After his death, the empire was split between his sons, Atahualpa (ah•tah•WAHL•pah) and Huascar (WAHS•kahr). Atahualpa received Ecuador, about one-fifth of the empire. The rest went to Huascar. At first, this system of dual emperors worked. Soon, however, Atahualpa laid claim to the whole of the empire. A bitter civil war followed. Atahualpa eventually won, but the war tore apart the empire. As you will learn in Chapter 20, the Spanish arrived in the last days of this war. Taking advantage of Incan weakness, they would soon divide and conquer the empire.

NEW YORK CORE CURRICULUM REVIEW

TERMS & NAMES 1. For each term or name, write a sentence explaining its significance.

• Pachacuti • ayllu • mita • quipu

USING YOUR NOTES

2. Which of these methods for unification were acceptable to the conquered people? Explain.

MAIN IDEAS

3. How were the Inca able to conquer such a vast empire?
4. What methods did the Inca use to create unity among the diverse peoples in their empire?
5. What role did the mita play in building the Incan Empire?

CRITICAL THINKING & WRITING

6. **IDENTIFYING SOLUTIONS** How did the Inca overcome geographical obstacles in building and ruling their empire?
7. **ANALYZING MOTIVES** Why do you think the Inca used the ayllu system as the basis for governing in the empire?
8. **COMPARING AND CONTRASTING** How were Incan and Aztec religious practices similar? How were they different?
9. **WRITING ACTIVITY** POWER AND AUTHORITY -Write a short **description** of one of the great public works projects completed by the Inca.

CONNECT TO TODAY **CREATING AN ORAL REPORT**

The Incan Empire has been compared to a modern welfare state. Study the government of one such state—Sweden, for example. In an **oral report,** compare the Incan government with the government of the country you studied.

Incan Mummies

For the Inca, death was an important part of life. The Inca worshiped the spirits and the bodies of their ancestors. They believed in an afterlife, and tombs and the mummies they held were considered holy.

Like the Egyptians, the Inca embalmed their dead to preserve the body. The mummies were bundled with offerings of food, tools, and precious items to help them in the afterlife. These "mummy bundles" were then buried or put in an aboveground tomb to be worshiped. Mummies have been found from many different social classes, and, as you will read, not all of them died natural deaths.

INTEGRATED TECHNOLOGY

RESEARCH LINKS For more on mummies, go to **classzone.com**

► Royal Treatment

The mummies of Incan rulers were among the holiest objects of Incan religion. The mummies were actually treated as if they were still alive. They had servants, maintained ownership of their property, were consulted as oracles, and were taken to major festivals or to visit other mummies. The mummy shown at right in a 16th-century Spanish codex is being transported in the same manner as the living royalty.

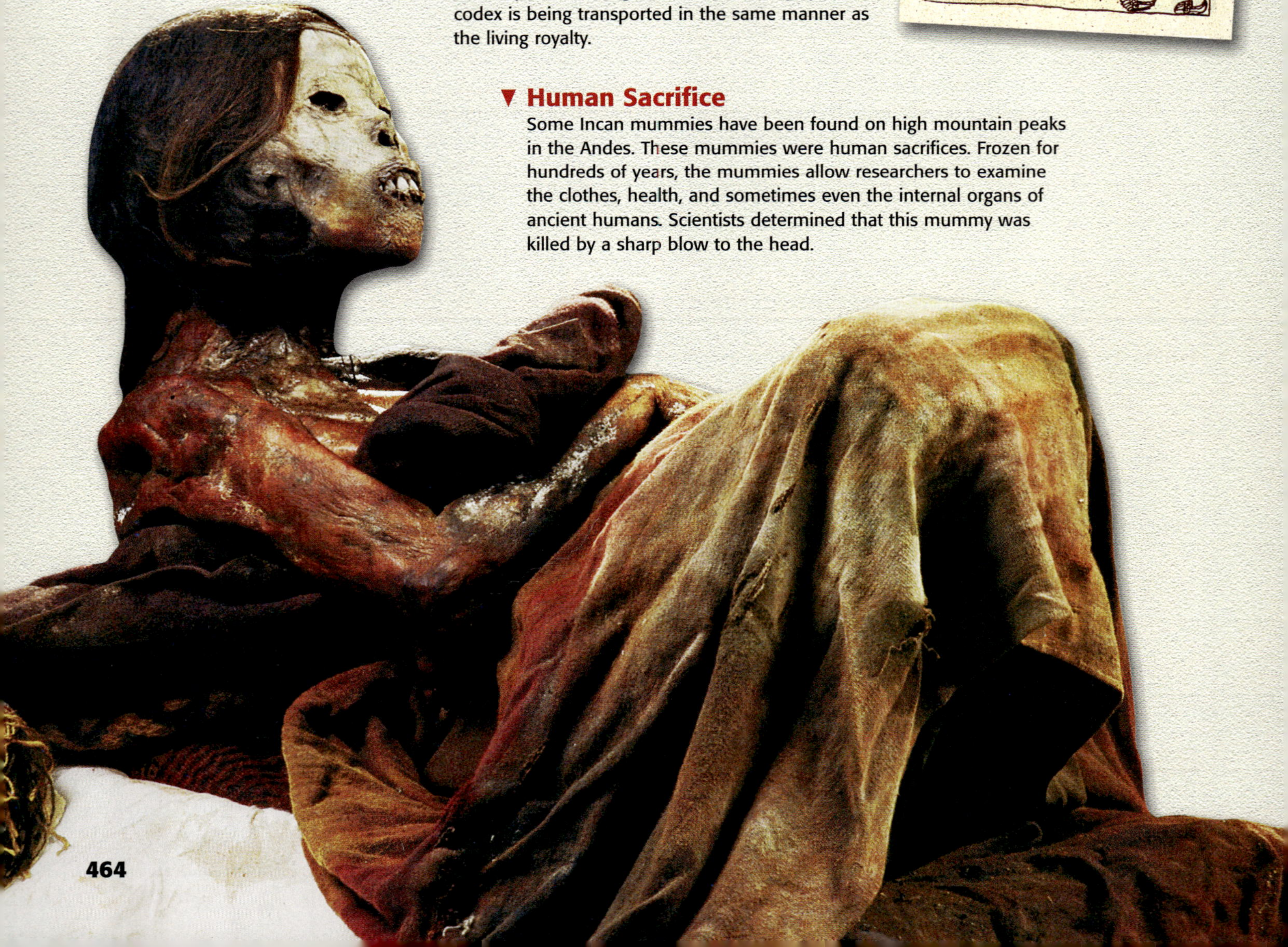

▼ Human Sacrifice

Some Incan mummies have been found on high mountain peaks in the Andes. These mummies were human sacrifices. Frozen for hundreds of years, the mummies allow researchers to examine the clothes, health, and sometimes even the internal organs of ancient humans. Scientists determined that this mummy was killed by a sharp blow to the head.

► Mummy Bundles

At a site known as Puruchuco, just outside of Lima, Peru, archaeologists discovered a huge Incan cemetery. Some of the mummies unearthed were wrapped in layers of cotton. The outside of the bundle might have a false head made of cloth like the one shown on the right. Inside the bundle were the mummy, religious offerings, and personal items. The illustration shown below re-creates the inside of an actual bundle that archaeologists unwrapped.

Corn, or maize, was the Inca's most important crop and is often found in Incan burials.

This man wears a feathered headdress that indicates high social standing.

The Inca used gourds as bowls and containers. The gourds found in this bundle held food and cotton.

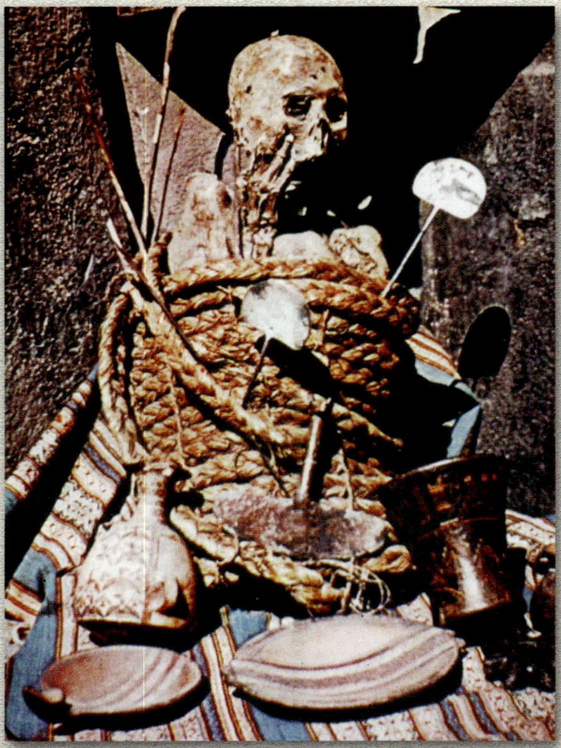

◄ Gifts for the Dead

The Inca sometimes placed mummies in aboveground tombs called *chullpas*. Descendants of the mummy would bring offerings of food and precious goods to honor their ancestor. This mummy is shown as it might have appeared in its tomb.

> DATA FILE

AN INCAN GRAVEYARD

The Puruchuco graveyard lies beneath a shantytown in Peru called Tupac Amaru. In 1999, when archaeologists discovered the extent of the site, it was about to be bulldozed. Archaeologists began an emergency recovery effort.

- The remains of over 2,000 men, women, and children were recovered.
- The site may contain as many as 10,000 individuals.
- Some bundles contained up to seven bodies and weighed as much as 400 pounds.
- Between 50,000 and 60,000 artifacts were recovered.
- One of the mummy bundles became known as the "Cotton King." The mummy was wrapped in about 300 pounds of raw cotton.
- The Cotton King's bundle contained 70 artifacts, including food, pottery, animal skins, and sandals. Footwear was not common among the Inca, and sandals were a status symbol.

Connect *to* Today

1. **Making Inferences** What do Incan mummification practices suggest about Incan culture?

   See Skillbuilder Handbook, page R10.

2. **Forming and Supporting Opinions** Why do you think mummification is not a common practice in the United States today?

Chapter 16 Assessment

VISUAL SUMMARY

People and Empires in the Americas

North America: 600–late 1500s

- Government by a variety of small tribes to very complex societies
- Similar religious beliefs in the Great Spirit
- Economy influenced by the environment
- Trade links to other groups

Mesoamerica: Maya 250–900

- Government by city-state kings
- Religion plays a major role in society and rule
- Trade links between city-states and other Mesoamerican groups
- Math and astronomy develop to support religious beliefs
- Pyramid builders
- Written language using hieroglyphs

Mesoamerica: Aztec 1200–1521

- Government by warrior-kings
- Religion plays a major role in society and rule
- Trade links between tribute states and other Mesoamerican groups
- Human sacrifice practiced for religious offerings
- Pyramid builders
- Pictorial written language

South America: Inca 1400–1532

- Government by theocracy—sun-god king
- Religion plays a major role in society and rule
- Social welfare state cares for all people
- Extensive road system links the country together

TERMS & NAMES

For each term or name below, briefly explain its connection to the development of Native American cultures in North America, Mesoamerica, or South America.

1. pueblo
2. Mississippian
3. Iroquois
4. Tikal
5. glyph
6. Quetzalcoatl
7. Triple Alliance
8. Montezuma II
9. Pachacuti
10. mita

MAIN IDEAS

North American Societies Section 1 (pages 441–445)

11. Why were Native American societies in North America so diverse?

12. What were the three things that most Native Americans in North America had in common?

Maya Kings and Cities Section 2 (pages 446–451)

13. What role did religion play in Maya life?

14. What were three major achievements of the Maya civilization?

The Aztecs Control Central Mexico Section 3 (pages 452–458)

15. How did the Aztecs build and control their empire?

16. Why did the Aztecs sacrifice human beings to their gods?

The Inca Create a Mountain Empire Section 4 (pages 459–465)

17. List three ways in which the Incan government involved itself in people's lives.

18. How did Incan religion reinforce the power of the state?

CRITICAL THINKING

1. USING YOUR NOTES

On a double time line, place two dates for each of the major culture groups that controlled the Valley of Mexico from the beginning of the first century A.D. Write a brief description of the importance of each date.

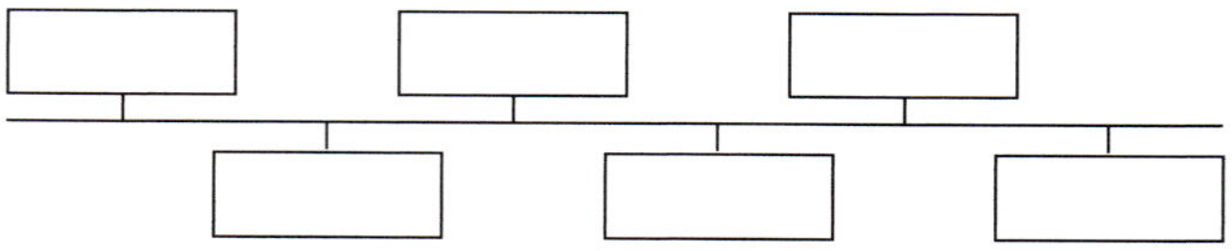

2. FORMULATING HISTORICAL QUESTIONS

Study the information on the Mound Builders again. What questions might you ask to gain a better understanding of these cultures?

3. COMPARING AND CONTRASTING

RELIGIOUS AND ETHICAL SYSTEMS Compare the religious beliefs of the Maya, the Aztecs, and the Inca. How were they similar? How were they different?

4. MAKING INFERENCES

POWER AND AUTHORITY What can you infer about the values of the Inca from the fact that the government provided care for citizens who were aged or unable to care for themselves?

5. FORMING AND SUPPORTING OPINIONS

The Maya was the most advanced of the early American civilizations. Do you agree or disagree with this statement? Give reasons for your answer.

Use the excerpt and your knowledge of world history to answer questions 1 and 2.
Additional Test Practice, pp. S1–S33

PRIMARY SOURCE

> We return thanks to our mother, the earth, which sustains us. We return thanks to the rivers and streams, which supply us with water. . . . We return thanks to the corn, and to her sisters, the beans and squashes, which give us life. . . . We return thanks to the sun, that he has looked upon the earth with a beneficent eye. . . . We return thanks to the Great Spirit . . . who directs all things for the good of his children.
>
> Quoted in *In the Trail of the Wind*

1 How did the Iroquois feel about nature?
(1) They felt angry at nature.
(2) They felt grateful to nature.
(3) Nature was seen as a mere tool to the Iroquois.
(4) Nature played little part in the lives of the Iroquois.

2 Which statement best sums up the overall role that the Great Spirit played in Iroquois life?
(1) The Great Spirit ruled over all for the good of all.
(2) The Great Spirit provided food for the Iroquois.
(3) The Great Spirit ruled over the earth and the sun.
(4) The Great Spirit provided the Iroquois with water.

Use this map, which provides a bird's-eye view of the island city of Tenochtitlán, and your knowledge of world history to answer question 3.

3 What appears to be in the center of the city?
(1) an enormous lake
(2) a small harbor
(3) a temple complex
(4) an empty square

INTEGRATED TECHNOLOGY

TEST PRACTICE Go to **classzone.com**
- Diagnostic tests
- Tutorials
- Strategies
- Additional practice

ALTERNATIVE ASSESSMENT

1. Interact *with* History

From the headdress clues and detective thinking, you should have determined that Kwakiutl lived in the forests by the Pacific Ocean. They probably used the headdress in a ceremony asking the gods to protect them. Using the guide questions on page 440, look back in the chapter at other artifacts in each section to see what you can determine about other cultures.

2. WRITING ABOUT HISTORY

CULTURAL INTERACTION In recent years, Aztec cultural ruins have been excavated in Mexico City. Using the Internet and library resources, conduct research into some of these archaeological finds, such as the Plaza of Three Cultures and the Great Temple. Then write an illustrated **magazine article** that describes these places and shows the heritage of the Mexican people.

INTEGRATED TECHNOLOGY

NetExplorations: Counting Calendars and Cords

Go to *NetExplorations* at **classzone.com** to learn more about the Aztec and Maya calendars. Use the Internet to learn about the calendars of other civilizations during the same period. Find out:
- how various calendars were organized
- what names were given to the various time periods on each calendar (for example, agricultural names or names of important gods)
- which calendars were most accurate
- how long each calendar was in use

Use the information and images you find to create a virtual museum where viewers can compare and contrast civilizations, their notions of time, and the calendars they used.

CHAPTER 17

European Renaissance and Reformation, 1300–1600

Previewing Main Ideas

CULTURAL INTERACTION Trade with the East and the rediscovery of ancient manuscripts caused Europeans to develop new ideas about culture and art. This period was called the "Renaissance," which means rebirth.

Geography *Study the time line and the map. In which countries did the Renaissance begin?*

RELIGIOUS AND ETHICAL SYSTEMS Martin Luther began a movement to reform practices in the Catholic Church that he believed were wrong. That movement, the Reformation, led to the founding of non-Catholic churches.

Geography *Locate Wittenberg, the city where the Reformation began. What geographical features helped the Reformation spread from there?*

REVOLUTION The invention of the printing press allowed books and pamphlets to be made faster and more cheaply. This new technology helped spread the revolutionary ideas of the Renaissance and Reformation.

Geography *Printing spread from Mainz to other parts of Europe. How might the location of Mainz have helped the spread of printing?*

NEW YORK CORE CURRICULUM FOCUS

- Europeans experienced a rebirth in learning and interest in art during the Renaissance.
- Martin Luther's 95 Theses led to the Reformation and the Counter Reformation.

INTEGRATED TECHNOLOGY

eEdition
- Interactive Maps
- Interactive Visuals
- Interactive Primary Sources

INTERNET RESOURCES

Go to **classzone.com** for:
- Research Links
- Internet Activities
- Primary Sources
- Chapter Quiz
- Maps
- Test Practice
- Current Events

EUROPE

1300
In the 1300s the Renaissance begins in Italian city-states such as Florence, Milan, and Mantua.

1434
◀ Medici family takes control of Florence. (bust of Lorenzo Medici)

1300 **1400**

WORLD

1324
Mali king Mansa Musa makes a pilgrimage to Mecca.

1368
◀ Hongwu founds Ming Dynasty in China. (vase from that period)

1405
Chinese explorer Zheng He begins exploration of Asia and Africa.

1455
Gutenberg Bible printed in Mainz. ▶

1517
Martin Luther begins the Reformation in Wittenberg.

1534
English king Henry VIII starts the Church of England.

1563
Council of Trent mandates reforms in Catholic Church.

1500

1600

1453
Ottoman Turks capture Constantinople.

1492
Columbus reaches the Americas.

1526
Babur establishes Mughal Empire in India. (Mughal noble) ▶

Interact *with* History

What can you learn from art?

You work at a museum that is considering buying this painting by Jan van Eyck. It is a portrait of Chancellor Rolin, a powerful government official in Burgundy (later part of France). Before deciding, the museum director wants to know what this painting can teach the public about the Renaissance.

INTERACTIVE

1 **Classical Art** Renaissance artists admired classical art. The columns show classical style.

2 **Perspective** Van Eyck used the technique of perspective, which shows distant objects as smaller than close ones. He also used oil paints, a new invention.

3 **Religion** This painting portrays the infant Jesus and his mother Mary in 15th-century Europe. Such a depiction shows the continuing importance of religion during the Renaissance.

4 **The Individual** Renaissance artists portrayed the importance of individuals. Chancellor Rolin is wearing a fur-trimmed robe that shows his high status.

5 **Beauty** Van Eyck included many details simply to add beauty. These include the design on the floor, the folds of Mary's cloak, and the scenery outside.

▲ *The Madonna of Chancellor Rolin* (about 1435), Jan van Eyck

EXAMINING *the* ISSUES

- **What can you infer about the setting of the painting?**
- **What details in the painting give you an idea of the role of religion in society?**

As a class, discuss these questions to see what you can learn about this art. Also recall what you know about art in such places as Egypt and India. As you read about the Renaissance, notice what the art of that time reveals about European society.

1 Italy: Birthplace of the Renaissance

CONNECT TO THE NEW YORK STATE CORE CURRICULUM

Unit 3.F.4. Art and architecture (e.g., da Vinci and Michelangelo)
Unit 3.F.6. Political science (e.g., Machiavelli)

TERMS & NAMES

- Renaissance
- humanism
- secular
- patron
- perspective
- vernacular

SETTING THE STAGE During the late Middle Ages, Europe suffered from both war and plague. Those who survived wanted to celebrate life and the human spirit. They began to question institutions of the Middle Ages, which had been unable to prevent war or to relieve suffering brought by the plague. Some people questioned the Church, which taught Christians to endure suffering while they awaited their rewards in heaven. In northern Italy, writers and artists began to express this new spirit and to experiment with different styles. These men and women would greatly change how Europeans saw themselves and their world.

Italy's Advantages

This movement that started in Italy caused an explosion of creativity in art, writing, and thought that lasted approximately from 1300 to 1600. Historians call this period the **Renaissance** (REHN•ih•SAHNS). The term means rebirth, and in this context, it refers to a revival of art and learning. The educated men and women of Italy hoped to bring back to life the culture of classical Greece and Rome. Yet in striving to revive the past, the people of the Renaissance created something new. The contributions made during this period led to innovative styles of art and literature. They also led to new values, such as the importance of the individual.

The Renaissance eventually spread from northern Italy to the rest of Europe. Italy had three advantages that made it the birthplace of the Renaissance: thriving cities, a wealthy merchant class, and the classical heritage of Greece and Rome.

TAKING NOTES

Outlining Use an outline to organize main ideas and details.

Italian Renaissance
I. Italy's advantages
A.
B.
II. Classical and worldly values

City-States Overseas trade, spurred by the Crusades, had led to the growth of large city-states in northern Italy. The region also had many sizable towns. Thus, northern Italy was urban while the rest of Europe was still mostly rural. Since cities are often places where people exchange ideas, they were an ideal breeding ground for an intellectual revolution.

In the 1300s, the bubonic plague struck these cities hard, killing up to 60 percent of the population. This brought economic changes. Because there were fewer laborers, survivors could demand higher wages. With few opportunities to expand business, merchants began to pursue other interests, such as art.

Merchants and the Medici A wealthy merchant class developed in each Italian city-state. Because city-states like Milan and Florence were relatively small, a high percentage of citizens could be intensely involved in political life.

History Makers

Medici Family

A rival family grew so jealous of the Medici that they plotted to kill Lorenzo (above) and his brother Giuliano. As the Medici attended Mass, assassins murdered Giuliano at the altar. Drawing his sword, Lorenzo escaped to a small room and held off his attackers until help arrived. Later, he had the killers brutally, publicly executed.

More positively, Lorenzo was a generous patron of the arts who collected many rare manuscripts. Eventually the Medici family made their library available to the public.

Merchants dominated politics. Unlike nobles, merchants did not inherit social rank. To succeed in business, they used their wits. As a result, many successful merchants believed they deserved power and wealth because of their individual merit. This belief in individual achievement became important during the Renaissance.

Since the late 1200s, the city-state of Florence had a republican form of government. But during the Renaissance, Florence came under the rule of one powerful banking family, the Medici (MEHD•ih•chee). The Medici family bank had branch offices throughout Italy and in the major cities of Europe. Cosimo de Medici was the wealthiest European of his time. In 1434, he won control of Florence's government. He did not seek political office for himself, but influenced members of the ruling council by giving them loans. For 30 years, he was dictator of Florence.

Cosimo de Medici died in 1464, but his family continued to control Florence. His grandson, Lorenzo de Medici, came to power in 1469. Known as Lorenzo the Magnificent, he ruled as a dictator yet kept up the appearance of having an elected government.

Looking to Greece and Rome Renaissance scholars looked down on the art and literature of the Middle Ages. Instead, they wanted to return to the learning of the Greeks and Romans. They achieved this in several ways. First, the artists and scholars of Italy drew inspiration from the ruins of Rome that surrounded them. Second, Western scholars studied ancient Latin manuscripts that had been preserved in monasteries. Third, Christian scholars in Constantinople fled to Rome with Greek manuscripts when the Turks conquered Constantinople in 1453. (A)

MAIN IDEA

Analyzing Causes

(A) What three advantages fostered the Renaissance in Italy?

Classical and Worldly Values

As scholars studied these manuscripts, they became more influenced by classical ideas. These ideas helped them to develop a new outlook on life and art.

Classics Lead to Humanism The study of classical texts led to **humanism**, an intellectual movement that focused on human potential and achievements. Instead of trying to make classical texts agree with Christian teaching as medieval scholars had, humanists studied them to understand ancient Greek values. Humanists influenced artists and architects to carry on classical traditions. Also, humanists popularized the study of subjects common to classical education, such as history, literature, and philosophy. These subjects are called the humanities.

Vocabulary

The words *humanist* and *humanities* come from the Latin word *humanitas,* which refers to the literary culture that every educated person should possess.

Worldly Pleasures In the Middle Ages, some people had demonstrated their piety by wearing rough clothing and eating plain foods. However, humanists suggested that a person might enjoy life without offending God. In Renaissance Italy, the wealthy enjoyed material luxuries, good music, and fine foods.

Most people remained devout Catholics. However, the basic spirit of Renaissance society was **secular**—worldly rather than spiritual and concerned with the here and now. Even church leaders became more worldly. Some lived in beautiful mansions, threw lavish banquets, and wore expensive clothes.

Patrons of the Arts Church leaders during the Renaissance beautified Rome and other cities by spending huge amounts of money for art. They became **patrons** of the arts by financially supporting artists. Renaissance merchants and wealthy families also were patrons of the arts. By having their portraits painted or by donating art to the city to place in public squares, the wealthy demonstrated their own importance.

The Renaissance Man Renaissance writers introduced the idea that all educated people were expected to create art. In fact, the ideal individual strove to master almost every area of study. A man who excelled in many fields was praised as a "universal man." Later ages called such people "Renaissance men."

Baldassare Castiglione (KAHS•teel•YOH•nay) wrote a book called *The Courtier* (1528) that taught how to become such a person. A young man should be charming, witty, and well educated in the classics. He should dance, sing, play music, and write poetry. In addition, he should be a skilled rider, wrestler, and swordsman.

The Renaissance Woman According to *The Courtier,* upper-class women also should know the classics and be charming. Yet they were not expected to seek fame. They were expected to inspire art but rarely to create it. Upper-class Renaissance women were better educated than medieval women. However, most Renaissance women had little influence in politics.

A few women, such as Isabella d'Este, did exercise power. Born into the ruling family of the city-state of Ferrara, she married the ruler of another city-state, Mantua. She brought many Renaissance artists to her court and built a famous art collection. She was also skilled in politics. When her husband was taken captive in war, she defended Mantua and won his release. **B**

MAIN IDEA

Comparing

B How were expectations for Renaissance men and Renaissance women similar?

Analyzing Primary Sources

The Renaissance Man

In *The Courtier,* Baldassare Castiglione described the type of accomplished person who later came to be called the Renaissance man.

PRIMARY SOURCE

Let the man we are seeking be very bold, stern, and always among the first, where the enemy are to be seen; and in every other place, gentle, modest, reserved, above all things avoiding ostentation [showiness] and that impudent [bold] self-praise by which men ever excite hatred and disgust in all who hear them. . . .

I would have him more than passably accomplished in letters, at least in those studies that are called the humanities, and conversant not only with the Latin language but with Greek, for the sake of the many different things that have been admirably written therein. Let him be well versed in the poets, and not less in the orators and historians, and also proficient in writing verse and prose.

BALDASSARE CASTIGLIONE, *The Courtier*

The Renaissance Woman

Although Renaissance women were not expected to create art, wealthy women often were patrons of artists, as this letter by Isabella d'Este demonstrates.

PRIMARY SOURCE

To Master Leonardo da Vinci, the painter: Hearing that you are settled at Florence, we have begun to hope that our cherished desire to obtain a work by your hand might be at length realized. When you were in this city and drew our portrait in carbon, you promised us that you would some day paint it in colors. But because this would be almost impossible, since you are unable to come here, we beg you to keep your promise by converting our portrait into another figure, which would be still more acceptable to us; that is to say, a youthful Christ of about twelve years . . . executed with all that sweetness and charm of atmosphere which is the peculiar excellence of your art.

Mantua, May 14, 1504

ISABELLA D'ESTE, *Letters*

DOCUMENT-BASED QUESTIONS

1. **Drawing Conclusions** *Do the qualities called for in the ideal Renaissance man and woman seem to emphasize the individual or the group?*
2. **Making Inferences** *Isabella d'Este's portrait was painted by Titian, and Castiglione's by Raphael, two famous painters. What does this tell you about the subjects' social status?*

The Renaissance Revolutionizes Art

Supported by patrons like Isabella d'Este, dozens of artists worked in northern Italy. As the Renaissance advanced, artistic styles changed. Medieval artists had used religious subjects to convey a spiritual ideal. Renaissance artists often portrayed religious subjects, but they used a realistic style copied from classical models. Greek and Roman subjects also became popular. Renaissance painters used the technique of **perspective**, which shows three dimensions on a flat surface.

Realistic Painting and Sculpture Following the new emphasis on individuals, painters began to paint prominent citizens. These realistic portraits revealed what was distinctive about each person. In addition, artists such as the sculptor, poet, architect, and painter Michelangelo (MY•kuhl•AN•juh•LOH) Buonarroti used a realistic style when depicting the human body. (C)

MAIN IDEA

Synthesizing

(C) What major change did a belief in individual merit bring about in art?

Donatello (DAHN•uh•TEHL•oh) also made sculpture more realistic by carving natural postures and expressions that reveal personality. He revived a classical form in his statue of David, a boy who, according to the Bible, became a great king. Donatello's statue was created in the late 1460s. It was the first European sculpture of a large, free-standing nude since ancient times. For sculptors of the period, including Michelangelo, David (page 478) was a favorite subject.

Analyzing Art

Perspective

Perspective creates the appearance of three dimensions. Classical artists had used perspective, but medieval artists abandoned the technique. In the 1400s, Italian artists rediscovered it.

Perspective is based on an optical illusion. As parallel lines stretch away from a viewer, they seem to draw together, until they meet at a spot on the horizon called the vanishing point. The use of perspective was a feature of most Western painting for the next 450 years.

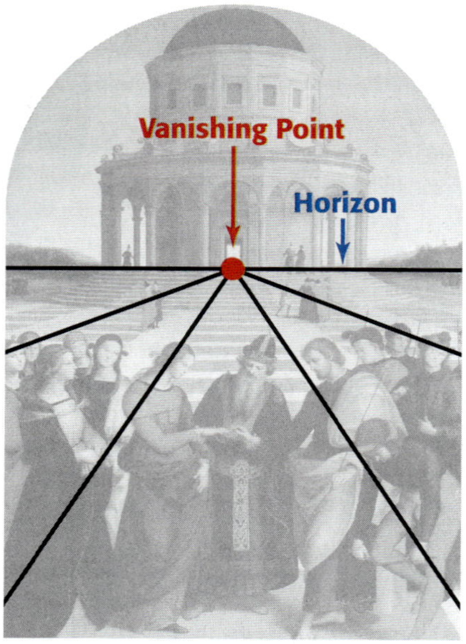

Marriage of the Virgin (1504), Raphael

SKILLBUILDER: Interpreting Visual Sources

Contrasting *What is the major difference between the figures in the background of the painting and the figures in the foreground? What is the effect of this difference?*

Leonardo, Renaissance Man Leonardo da Vinci (LAY•uh•NAHR•doh duh•VIHN•chee) was a painter, sculptor, inventor, and scientist. A true "Renaissance man," he was interested in how things worked. He studied how a muscle moves and how veins are arranged in a leaf. He filled his notebooks with observations and sketches. Then he incorporated his findings in his art.

Among his many masterpieces, Leonardo painted one of the best-known portraits in the world, the *Mona Lisa* (page 478). The woman in the portrait seems so real that many writers have tried to explain the thoughts behind her smile. Leonardo also produced a famous religious painting, *The Last Supper.* It shows the personalities of Jesus' disciples through facial expressions.

Raphael Advances Realism Raphael (RAHF•ee•uhl) Sanzio was younger than Michelangelo and Leonardo. He learned from studying their works. One of Raphael's favorite subjects was the Madonna and child. Raphael often portrayed their expressions as gentle and calm. He was famous for his use of perspective.

In his greatest achievement, Raphael filled the walls of Pope Julius II's library with paintings. One of these, *School of Athens* (page 479), conveys the classical influence on the Renaissance. Raphael painted famous Renaissance figures, such as Michelangelo, Leonardo, and himself, as classical philosophers and their students.

Anguissola and Gentileschi Renaissance society generally restricted women's roles. However, a few Italian women became notable painters. Sofonisba Anguissola (ahng•GWEES•soh•lah) was the first woman artist to gain an international reputation. She is known for her portraits of her sisters and of prominent people such as King Philip II of Spain. Artemisia Gentileschi (JAYN•tee•LEHS•kee) was another accomplished artist. She trained with her painter father and helped with his work. In her own paintings, Gentileschi painted pictures of strong, heroic women.

History Makers

Leonardo da Vinci
1452–1519

Leonardo da Vinci's notebooks—and life—are mysterious. Some 3,500 pages closely covered with writings and drawings survive. His writing is clear and easy to read, but only if you look at it in a mirror. No one knows why he wrote backwards.

Leonardo planned scholarly works and great feats of engineering that were never completed. Only 17 of his paintings survive. And yet the work that Leonardo did produce is so amazing that it confirms his genius.

Michelangelo Buonarroti
1475–1564

Like Leonardo, Michelangelo was a Renaissance man. He excelled as a painter, sculptor, architect, and poet.

Michelangelo is most famous for the way he portrayed the human body in painting and sculpture. Influenced by classical art, he created figures that are forceful and show heroic grandeur.

Among his achievements are the dome of St. Peter's, the paintings on the ceiling of the Sistine Chapel, and the statue of David.

INTEGRATED TECHNOLOGY

INTERNET ACTIVITY Plan a Web site on Renaissance leaders that showcases these two artists. Go to **classzone.com** for your research.

Renaissance Writers Change Literature

Renaissance writers produced works that reflected their time, but they also used techniques that writers rely on today. Some followed the example of the medieval writer Dante. He wrote in the **vernacular**, his native language, instead of Latin. Dante's native language was Italian. In addition, Renaissance writers wrote either for self-expression or to portray the individuality of their subjects. In these ways, writers of the Renaissance began trends that modern writers still follow.

Petrarch and Boccaccio Francesco Petrarch (PEE•trahrk) was one of the earliest and most influential humanists. Some have called him the father of Renaissance humanism. He was also a great poet. Petrarch wrote both in Italian and in Latin. In

Italian, he wrote sonnets—14-line poems. They were about a mysterious woman named Laura, who was his ideal. (Little is known of Laura except that she died of the plague in 1348.) In classical Latin, he wrote letters to many important friends.

The Italian writer Giovanni Boccaccio (boh•KAH•chee•oh) is best known for the *Decameron,* a series of realistic, sometimes off-color stories. The stories are supposedly told by a group of worldly young people waiting in a rural villa to avoid the plague sweeping through Florence:

PRIMARY SOURCE

In the year of Our Lord 1348 the deadly plague broke out in the great city of Florence, most beautiful of Italian cities. Whether through the operation of the heavenly bodies or because of our own iniquities [sins] which the just wrath of God sought to correct, the plague had arisen in the East some years before, causing the death of countless human beings. It spread without stop from one place to another, until, unfortunately, it swept over the West. Neither knowledge nor human foresight availed against it, though the city was cleansed of much filth by chosen officers in charge and sick persons were forbidden to enter it, while advice was broadcast for the preservation of health.

GIOVANNI BOCCACCIO, Preface, *Decameron*

The *Decameron* presents both tragic and comic views of life. In its stories, the author uses cutting humor to illustrate the human condition. Boccaccio presents his characters in all of their individuality and all their folly.

Machiavelli Advises Rulers *The Prince* (1513) by Niccolò Machiavelli (MAK•ee•uh•VEHL•ee) also examines the imperfect conduct of human beings. It does so by taking the form of a political guidebook. In *The Prince,* Machiavelli examines how a ruler can gain power and keep it in spite of his enemies. In answering this question, he began with the idea that most people are selfish, fickle, and corrupt.

To succeed in such a wicked world, Machiavelli said, a prince must be strong as a lion and shrewd as a fox. He might have to trick his enemies and even his own people for the good of the state. In *The Prince,* Machiavelli was not concerned with what was morally right, but with what was politically effective.

He pointed out that most people think it is praiseworthy in a prince to keep his word and live with integrity. Nevertheless, Machiavelli argued that in the real world of power and politics a prince must sometimes mislead the people and lie to his opponents. As a historian and political thinker, Machiavelli suggested that in order for a prince to accomplish great things, he must be crafty enough to not only overcome the suspicions but also gain the trust of others:

PRIMARY SOURCE D

From this arises the question whether it is better to be loved more than feared, or feared more than loved. The reply is, that one ought to be both feared and loved, but as it is difficult for the two to go together, it is much safer to be feared than loved, if one of the two has to be wanting. For it may be said of men in general that they are ungrateful, voluble [changeable], dissemblers [liars], anxious to avoid danger, and covetous of gain; as long as you benefit them, they are entirely yours; they offer you their blood, their goods, their life, and their children, as I have before said, when the necessity is remote; but when it approaches, they revolt. And the prince who has relied solely on their words, without making preparations, is ruined.

NICCOLÒ MACHIAVELLI, *The Prince*

MAIN IDEA

Analyzing Primary Sources

D Does Machiavelli think that a prince should prefer to be loved or feared? Why?

Vittoria Colonna The women writers who gained fame during the Renaissance usually wrote about personal subjects, not politics. Yet, some of them had great influence. Vittoria Colonna (1492–1547) was born of a noble family. In 1509, she married the Marquis of Pescara. He spent most of his life away from home on military campaigns.

Vittoria Colonna exchanged sonnets with Michelangelo and helped Castiglione publish *The Courtier.* Her own poems express personal emotions. When her husband was away at the Battle of Ravenna in 1512, she wrote to him:

PRIMARY SOURCE

But now in this perilous assault,
in this horrible, pitiless battle
that has so hardened my mind and heart,
your great valor has shown you an equal
to Hector and Achilles. But what good is
this to me, sorrowful, abandoned? . . .
Your uncertain enterprises do not hurt you;
but we who wait, mournfully grieving,
are wounded by doubt and fear.
You men, driven by rage, considering nothing
but your honor, commonly go off, shouting,
with great fury, to confront danger.
We remain, with fear in our heart and
grief on our brow for you; sister longs for
brother, wife for husband, mother for son.

VITTORIA COLONNA, *Poems*

Toward the end of the 15th century, Renaissance ideas began to spread north from Italy. As you will read in Section 2, northern artists and thinkers adapted Renaissance ideals in their own ways.

Global Patterns

Other Renaissances

In addition to the Italian Renaissance, there have been rebirths and revivals in other places around the world. For example, the Tang (618–907) and Song (960–1279) dynasties in China saw periods of great artistic and technological advances.

Like the Italian Renaissance, the achievements of the Tang and the Song had roots in an earlier time, the Han Dynasty (202 B.C. to A.D. 220). After the Han collapsed, China experienced turmoil.

When order was restored, Chinese culture flourished. The Chinese invented gunpowder and printing. Chinese poets wrote literary masterpieces. Breakthroughs were made in architecture, painting, and pottery. The Song painting above, *Waiting for Guests by Lamplight,* was done with ink and color on silk.

NEW YORK CORE CURRICULUM REVIEW

TERMS & NAMES 1. For each term or name, write a sentence explaining its significance.

• Renaissance • humanism • secular • patron • perspective • vernacular

USING YOUR NOTES

2. Which of Italy's advantages was most important? Why?

MAIN IDEAS

3. What are some of the characteristics of the "Renaissance man" and "Renaissance woman"?
4. How did Italy's cities help to make it the birthplace of the Renaissance?
5. What was the attitude of Church leaders and the wealthy toward the arts? Why?

CRITICAL THINKING & WRITING

6. **DRAWING CONCLUSIONS** How did study of the classics influence branches of learning such as history, literature, and philosophy?
7. **MAKING INFERENCES** How is the humanism of the Renaissance reflected in its art? Explain with examples.
8. **COMPARING** What were the differences between the Middle Ages and the Renaissance in the attitude toward worldly pleasures?
9. **WRITING ACTIVITY** REVOLUTION How did the Renaissance revolutionize European art and thought? Support your opinions in a three-paragraph **essay.**

CONNECT TO TODAY **WRITING A DESCRIPTION**

In a book on modern art, find an artist who worked in more than one medium, such as painting and sculpture. Write a **description** of one of the artist's works in each medium.

Renaissance Ideas Influence Renaissance Art

The Renaissance in Italy produced extraordinary achievements in many different forms of art, including painting, architecture, sculpture, and drawing. These art forms were used by talented artists to express important ideas and attitudes of the age.

The value of humanism is shown in Raphael's *School of Athens,* a depiction of the greatest Greek philosophers. The realism of Renaissance art is seen in a portrait such as the *Mona Lisa,* which is an expression of the subject's unique features and personality. And Michelangelo's *David* shares stylistic qualities with ancient Greek and Roman sculpture.

INTEGRATED TECHNOLOGY

RESEARCH LINKS For more on Renaissance art, go to **classzone.com**

▲ Portraying Individuals

Da Vinci The *Mona Lisa* (c. 1504–1506) is thought to be a portrait of Lisa Gherardini, who, at 16, married Francesco del Giocondo, a wealthy merchant of Florence who commissioned the portrait. Mona Lisa is a shortened form of Madonna Lisa (Madam, or My Lady, Lisa). Renaissance artists showed individuals as they really looked.

▼ Classical and Renaissance Sculpture

Michelangelo Influenced by classical statues, Michelangelo sculpted *David* from 1501 to 1504. Michelangelo portrayed the biblical hero in the moments just before battle. David's posture is graceful, yet his figure also displays strength. The statue, which is 18 feet tall, towers over the viewer.

▲ **The Importance of Ancient Greece**

Raphael The painting *School of Athens* (1508) for the pope's apartments in the Vatican shows that the scholars of ancient Greece were highly honored. Under the center arch stand Plato and Aristotle. To their right, Socrates argues with several young men. Toward the front, Pythagoras draws a lesson on a slate and Ptolemy holds a globe.

▲ **Renaissance Science and Technology**

Da Vinci Leonardo da Vinci filled his notebooks with observations and sketches of new inventions. This drawing from his notebooks shows a design for a spiral screw to achieve vertical flight. Leonardo's drawing anticipated the helicopter.

Connect *to* Today

1. **Clarifying** How do the works of Renaissance artists and architects reflect Renaissance ideas? Explain.

   See Skillbuilder Handbook, page R4.

2. **Synthesizing** Look through books on architecture to find examples of American architects who were influenced by the architects and buildings of the Italian Renaissance. Share your findings with the class.

The Northern Renaissance

CONNECT TO THE NEW YORK STATE CORE CURRICULUM

Unit 3.F.5. Literature (e.g., Dante, Cervantes, Shakespeare)
Unit 3.F.7. New scientific and technological innovations (Gutenberg's moveable type printing press, cartography, naval engineering, and navigational and nautical devices)

TERMS & NAMES

- utopia
- William Shakespeare
- Johann Gutenberg

SETTING THE STAGE The work of such artists as Leonardo da Vinci, Michelangelo, and Raphael showed the Renaissance spirit. All three artists demonstrated an interest in classical culture, a curiosity about the world, and a belief in human potential. Humanist writers expanded ideas about individuality. These ideas impressed scholars, students, and merchants who visited Italy. By the late 1400s, Renaissance ideas had spread to Northern Europe—especially England, France, Germany, and Flanders (now part of France and the Netherlands).

TAKING NOTES
Following Chronological Order On a time line, note important events of the Northern Renaissance.

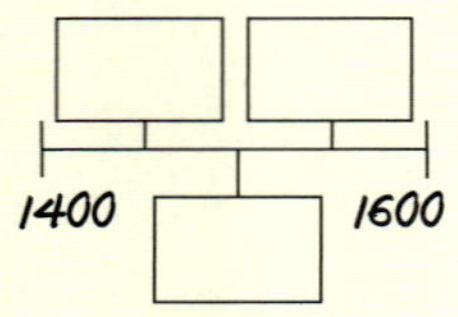

The Northern Renaissance Begins

By 1450 the population of northern Europe, which had declined due to bubonic plague, was beginning to grow again. When the destructive Hundred Years' War between France and England ended in 1453, many cities grew rapidly. Urban merchants became wealthy enough to sponsor artists. This happened first in Flanders, which was rich from long-distance trade and the cloth industry. Then, as wealth increased in other parts of Northern Europe, patronage of artists increased as well.

As Section 1 explained, Italy was divided into city-states. In-contrast, England and France were unified under strong monarchs. These rulers often sponsored the arts by purchasing paintings and by supporting artists and writers. For example, Francis I of France invited Leonardo da Vinci to retire in France, and hired Italian artists and architects to rebuild and decorate his castle at Fontainebleau (FAHN•tihn•BLOH). The castle became a showcase for Renaissance art.

As Renaissance ideas spread out of Italy, they mingled with northern traditions. As a result, the northern Renaissance developed its own character. For example, the artists were especially interested in realism. The Renaissance ideal of human dignity inspired some northern humanists to develop plans for social reform based on Judeo-Christian values.

Artistic Ideas Spread

In 1494, a French king claimed the throne of Naples in southern Italy and launched an invasion through northern Italy. As the war dragged on, many Italian artists and writers left for a safer life in Northern Europe. They brought with them the styles and techniques of the Italian Renaissance. In addition, Northern European artists who studied in Italy carried Renaissance ideas back to their homelands.

German Painters Perhaps the most famous person to do this was the German artist Albrecht Dürer (DYUR•uhr). He traveled to Italy to study in 1494. After returning to Germany, Dürer produced woodcuts and engravings. Many of his prints portray religious subjects. Others portray classical myths or realistic landscapes. The popularity of Dürer's work helped to spread Renaissance styles.

Dürer's emphasis upon realism influenced the work of another German artist, Hans Holbein (HOHL•byn) the Younger. Holbein specialized in painting portraits that are almost photographic in detail. He emigrated to England where he painted portraits of King Henry VIII and other members of the English royal family.

Flemish Painters The support of wealthy merchant families in Flanders helped to make Flanders the artistic center of northern Europe. The first great Flemish Renaissance painter was Jan van Eyck (yahn van YK). Van Eyck used recently developed oil-based paints to develop techniques that painters still use. By applying layer upon layer of paint, van Eyck was able to create a variety of subtle colors in clothing and jewels. Oil painting became popular and spread to Italy.

In addition to new techniques, van Eyck's paintings display unusually realistic details and reveal the personality of their subjects. His work influenced later artists in Northern Europe.

Flemish painting reached its peak after 1550 with the work of Pieter Bruegel (BROY•guhl) the Elder. Bruegel was also interested in realistic details and individual people. He was very skillful in portraying large numbers of people. He captured scenes from everyday peasant life such as weddings, dances, and harvests. Bruegel's rich colors, vivid details, and balanced use of space give a sense of life and feeling. (A)

MAIN IDEA

Summarizing

(A) What techniques does Bruegel use to give life to his paintings?

> Analyzing Art

Peasant Life

The Flemish painter Pieter Bruegel's paintings provide information about peasant life in the 1500s. *Peasant Wedding* (1568) portrays a wedding feast.

- **The Bride** The bride sits under the paper crown hanging on the green cloth.
- **The Servers** Men who may be her brothers are passing out plates.
- **The Guests** Several children have come to the party.
- **The Musicians** They are carrying bagpipes. One glances hungrily at the food.

SKILLBUILDER:
Interpreting Visual Sources
Forming Generalizations
In what ways does this painting present a snapshot of peasant life?

Northern Writers Try to Reform Society

Italian humanists were very interested in reviving classical languages and classical texts. When the Italian humanist ideas reached the north, people used them to examine the traditional teachings of the Church. The northern humanists were critical of the failure of the Christian Church to inspire people to live a Christian life. This criticism produced a new movement known as Christian humanism. The focus of Christian humanism was the reform of society. Of particular importance to humanists was education. The humanists promoted the education of women and founded schools attended by both boys and girls.

Christian Humanists The best known of the Christian humanists were Desiderius Erasmus (DEHZ•ih•DEER•ee•uhs ih•RAZ•muhs) of Holland and Thomas More of England. The two were close friends.

In 1509, Erasmus wrote his most famous work, *The Praise of Folly.* This book poked fun at greedy merchants, heartsick lovers, quarrelsome scholars, and pompous priests. Erasmus believed in a Christianity of the heart, not one of ceremonies or rules. He thought that in order to improve society, all people should study the Bible.

Thomas More tried to show a better model of society. In 1516, he wrote the book *Utopia.* In Greek, **utopia** means "no place." In English it has come to mean an ideal place as depicted in More's book. The book is about an imaginary land where greed, corruption, and war have been weeded out. In Utopia, because there was little greed, Utopians had little use for money:

▼ Christian humanist Thomas More

PRIMARY SOURCE

Gold and silver, of which money is made, are so treated . . . that no one values them more highly than their true nature deserves. Who does not see that they are far inferior to iron in usefulness since without iron mortals cannot live any more than without fire and water?

THOMAS MORE, *Utopia*

More wrote in Latin. As his work became popular, More's works were translated into a variety of languages including French, German, English, Spanish, and Italian.

Women's Reforms During this period the vast majority of Europeans were unable to read or write. Those families who could afford formal schooling usually sent only their sons. One woman spoke out against this practice. Christine de Pizan was highly educated for the time and was one of the first women to earn a living as a writer. Writing in French, she produced many books, including short stories, biographies, novels, and manuals on military techniques. She frequently wrote about the objections men had to educating women. In one book, *The Book of The City of Ladies,* she wrote:

▼ Christine de Pizan is best known for her works defending women.

PRIMARY SOURCE **B**

I am amazed by the opinion of some men who claim that they do not want their daughters, wives, or kinswomen to be educated because their mores [morals] would be ruined as a result. . . . Here you can clearly see that not all opinions of men are based on reason and that these men are wrong.

CHRISTINE DE PIZAN, *The Book of The City of Ladies*

MAIN IDEA

Analyzing Primary Sources

B What does de Pizan argue for in this passage?

Christine de Pizan was one of the first European writers to question different treatment of boys and girls. However, her goal of formal education for children of both sexes would not be achieved for several centuries.

The Elizabethan Age

The Renaissance spread to England in the mid-1500s. The period was known as the Elizabethan Age, after Queen Elizabeth I. Elizabeth reigned from 1558 to 1603. She was well educated and spoke French, Italian, Latin, and Greek. She also wrote poetry and music. As queen she did much to support the development of English art and literature.

William Shakespeare The most famous writer of the Elizabethan Age was **William Shakespeare**. Many people regard him as the greatest playwright of all time. Shakespeare was born in 1564 in Stratford-upon-Avon, a small town about 90 miles northwest of London. By 1592 he was living in London and writing poems and plays, and soon he would be performing at the Globe Theater.

Like many Renaissance writers, Shakespeare revered the classics and drew on them for inspiration and plots. His works display a masterful command of the English language and a deep understanding of human beings. He revealed the souls of men and women through scenes of dramatic conflict. Many of these plays examine human flaws. However, Shakespeare also had one of his characters deliver a speech that expresses the Renaissance's high view of human nature:

PRIMARY SOURCE

What a piece of work is a man, how noble in reason, how infinite in faculties, in form and moving, how express and admirable; in action how like an angel, in apprehension [understanding] how like a god: the beauty of the world, the paragon of animals.

WILLIAM SHAKESPEARE, *Hamlet (Act 2, Scene 2)*

MAIN IDEA

Summarizing

(C) What are two ways in which Shakespeare's work showed Renaissance influences?

Shakespeare's most famous plays include the tragedies *Macbeth, Hamlet, Othello, Romeo and Juliet,* and *King Lear,* and the comedies *A Midsummer Night's Dream* and *The Taming of the Shrew.* (C)

Connect *to* Today

Shakespeare's Popularity

Even though he has been dead for about 400 years, Shakespeare is one of the favorite writers of filmmakers. His works are produced both in period costumes and in modern attire. The themes or dialogue have been adapted for many films, including some in foreign languages. The posters at the right illustrate *Othello* (done in period costume); *Romeo and Juliet* in a modern setting; a Japanese film, *Ran,* an adaptation of *King Lear;*. and *10 Things I Hate About You,* an adaptation of *The Taming of the Shrew.*

Printing Spreads Renaissance Ideas

The Chinese invented block printing, in which a printer carved words or letters on a wooden block, inked the block, and then used it to print on paper. Around 1045, Bi Sheng invented movable type, or a separate piece of type for each character in the language. The Chinese writing system contains thousands of different characters, so most Chinese printers found movable type impractical. However, the method would prove practical for Europeans because their languages have a very small number of letters in their alphabets.

Gutenberg Improves the Printing Process During the 13th century, block-printed items reached Europe from China. European printers began to use block printing to create whole pages to bind into books. However, this process was too slow to satisfy the Renaissance demand for knowledge, information, and books.

Around 1440 **Johann Gutenberg**, a craftsman from Mainz, Germany, developed a printing press that incorporated a number of technologies in a new way. The process made it possible to produce books quickly and cheaply. Using this improved process, Gutenberg printed a complete Bible, the Gutenberg Bible, in about 1455. It was the first full-sized book printed with movable type. **D**

The printing press enabled a printer to produce hundreds of copies of a single work. For the first time, books were cheap enough that many people could buy them. At first printers produced mainly religious works. Soon they began to provide books on other subjects such as travel guides and medical manuals.

MAIN IDEA

Recognizing Effects

D What were the major effects of the invention of the printing press?

Global Impact

The Printing Press

Many inventions are creative combinations of known technologies. In 1452, Johann Gutenberg combined known technologies from Europe and Asia with his idea for molding movable type to create a printing press that changed the world.

A copyist took five months to produce a single book.

One man and a printing press could produce 500 books in the same amount of time.

SKILLBUILDER: Interpreting Graphics

1. **Drawing Conclusions** *About how many books could a printing press produce in a month?*
2. **Making Inferences** *Which areas of the world contributed technologies to Gutenberg's printing press?*

The Legacy of the Renaissance

The European Renaissance was a period of great artistic and social change. It marked a break with the medieval-period ideals focused around the Church. The Renaissance belief in the dignity of the individual played a key role in the gradual rise of democratic ideas. Furthermore, the impact of the movable-type printing press was tremendous. Some historians have suggested that its effects were even more dramatic than the arrival of personal computers in the 20th century. Below is a summary of the changes that resulted from the Renaissance.

Changes in the Arts

- Art drew on techniques and styles of classical Greece and Rome.
- Paintings and sculptures portrayed individuals and nature in more realistic and lifelike ways.
- Artists created works that were secular as well as those that were religious.
- Writers began to use vernacular languages to express their ideas.
- The arts praised individual achievement.

Changes in Society

- Printing changed society by making more information available and inexpensive enough for society at large.
- A greater availability of books prompted an increased desire for learning and a rise in literacy throughout Europe.
- Published accounts of new discoveries, maps, and charts led to further discoveries in a variety of fields.
- Published legal proceedings made the laws clear so that people were more likely to understand their rights.
- Christian humanists' attempts to reform society changed views about how life should be lived.
- People began to question political structures and religious practices.

Renaissance ideas continued to influence European thought—including religious thought—as you will see in Section 3.

NEW YORK CORE CURRICULUM REVIEW

TERMS & NAMES 1. For each term or name, write a sentence explaining its significance.

- utopia
- William Shakespeare
- Johann Gutenberg

USING YOUR NOTES

2. Which of the events listed do you think was most important? Explain.

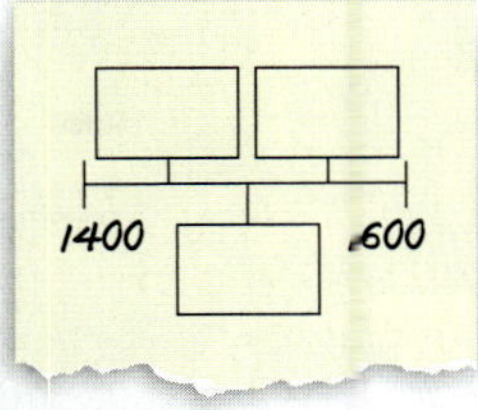

MAIN IDEAS

3. How did Albrecht Dürer's work reflect the influence of the Italian Renaissance?
4. What was one way the Renaissance changed society?
5. Why was the invention of the printing press so important?

CRITICAL THINKING & WRITING

6. **COMPARING** How were the works of German painters different from those of the Flemish painters? Give examples.
7. **ANALYZING MOTIVES** What reasons did humanists give for wanting to reform society? Explain.
8. **RECOGNIZING EFFECTS** How did the availability of cheap books spread learning?
9. **WRITING ACTIVITY** CULTURAL INTERACTION Reread the primary source quotation from Christine de Pizan on page 482. Write a one paragraph **opinion piece** about the ideas expressed there.

INTEGRATED TECHNOLOGY **INTERNET ACTIVITY**

Use the Internet to find information on the number of books published in print and those published electronically last year. Create a **pie graph** showing the results of your research.

INTERNET KEYWORD
book publishing statistics

Social History

City Life in Renaissance Europe

Throughout the 1500s, the vast majority of Europeans—more than 75 percent—lived in rural areas. However, the capital and port cities of most European countries experienced remarkable growth during this time. The population of London, for example, stood at about 200,000 in 1600, making it perhaps the largest city in Europe. In London, and in other large European cities, a distinctively urban way of life developed in the Renaissance era.

INTEGRATED TECHNOLOGY
RESEARCH LINKS For more on life in Renaissance Europe, go to **classzone.com**

▲ **Entertainment**
Performances at playhouses like the Globe often were wild affairs. If audiences did not like the play, they booed loudly, pelted the stage with garbage, and sometimes attacked the actors.

▼ **Joblessness**
Many newcomers to London struggled to find jobs and shelter. Some turned to crime to make a living. Others became beggars. However, it was illegal for able-bodied people to beg. To avoid a whipping or prison time, beggars had to be sick or disabled.

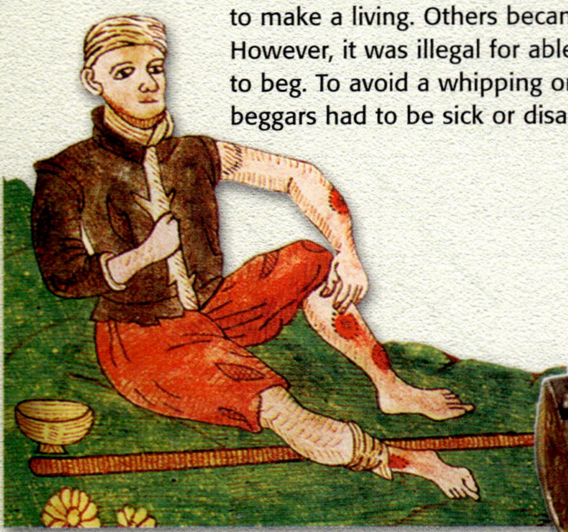

▼ **Sanitation**
This small pomander (POH•man•durh), a metal container filled with spices, was crafted in the shape of orange segments. Well-to-do Londoners held pomanders to their noses to shield themselves from the stench of the rotting garbage that littered the streets.

▼ Food

A typical meal for wealthy Londoners might include fish, several kinds of meat, bread, and a variety of vegetables, served on silver or pewter tableware. The diet of the poor was simpler. They rarely ate fish, meat, or cheese. Usually, their meals consisted of a pottage—a kind of soup—of vegetables. And the poor ate their meals from a trencher, a hollowed-out slab of stale bread or wood.

▼ Transportation

Many of London's streets were so narrow that walking was the only practical means of transportation. Often, however, the quickest way to get from here to there in the city was to take the river. Boat traffic was especially heavy when the playhouses were open. On those days, as many as 4,000 people crossed the Thames from the city to Southwark, where most of the theaters were located.

> DATA FILE

COST OF LIVING IN RENAISSANCE LONDON

These tables show what typical Londoners earned and spent in the late 1500s. The basic denominations in English currency at the time were the pound (£), the shilling, and the penny (12 pence equaled 1 shilling, and 20 shillings equaled 1 pound). The pound of the late 1500s is roughly equivalent to $400 in today's U.S. currency.

Typical Earnings

Merchant	£100 per year
Skilled Worker	£13 per year (about 5 shillings/week)
Unskilled Worker	£5 per year (about 4 pence/day)
Servant	£1 to £2 per year (plus food and lodging)

Typical Prices

Lodging	4 to 8 pence a week
Beef	3 pence per lb
Chickens	1 penny each
Eggs	2 pence per dozen
Apples	1 penny per dozen
Onions	1/2 penny a sack
Various Spices	10 to 11 shillings per lb

Connect *to* Today

1. **Making Inferences** Study the images and captions as well as the information in the Data File. What inferences about the standard of living of London's wealthy citizens can you make from this information? How did it compare to the standard of living of London's common people?

   See Skillbuilder Handbook, page R9.

2. **Comparing** How does diet in the United States today compare to the diet of Renaissance Europeans? Cite specific examples in your answer.

3

Luther Leads the Reformation

CONNECT TO THE NEW YORK STATE CORE CURRICULUM

Unit 3.G.2. Martin Luther's Ninety-Five Theses: the challenge to the power and authority of the Roman Catholic Church
Unit 3.G.4. Henry VIII and the English Reformation

TERMS & NAMES

- indulgence
- Reformation
- Lutheran
- Protestant
- Peace of Augsburg
- annul
- Anglican

SETTING THE STAGE By the tenth century, the Roman Catholic Church had come to dominate religious life in Northern and Western Europe. However, the Church had not won universal approval. Over the centuries, many people criticized its practices. They felt that Church leaders were too interested in worldly pursuits, such as gaining wealth and political power. Even though the Church made some reforms during the Middle Ages, people continued to criticize it. Prompted by the actions of one man, that criticism would lead to rebellion.

TAKING NOTES
Recognizing Effects Use a chart to identify the effects of Martin Luther's protests.

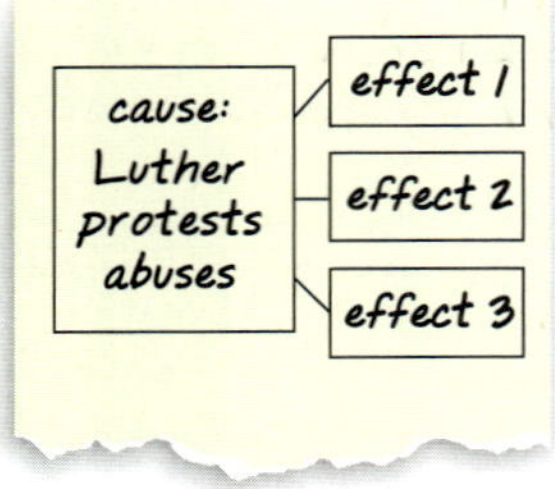

Causes of the Reformation

By 1500, additional forces weakened the Church. The Renaissance emphasis on the secular and the individual challenged Church authority. The printing press spread these secular ideas. In addition, some rulers began to challenge the Church's political power. In Germany, which was divided into many competing states, it was difficult for the pope or the emperor to impose central authority. Finally, northern merchants resented paying church taxes to Rome. Spurred by these social, political, and economic forces, a new movement for religious reform began in Germany. It then swept much of Europe.

Criticisms of the Catholic Church Critics of the Church claimed that its leaders were corrupt. The popes who ruled during the Renaissance patronized the arts, spent extravagantly on personal pleasure, and fought wars. Pope Alexander VI,

Causes of the Reformation

Social	Political	Economic	Religious
• The Renaissance values of humanism and secularism led people to question the Church. • The printing press helped to spread ideas critical of the Church.	• Powerful monarchs challenged the Church as the supreme power in Europe. • Many leaders viewed the pope as a foreign ruler and challenged his authority.	• European princes and kings were jealous of the Church's wealth. • Merchants and others resented having to pay taxes to the Church.	• Some Church leaders had become worldly and corrupt. • Many people found Church practices such as the sale of indulgences unacceptable.

for example, admitted that he had fathered several children. Many popes were too busy pursuing worldly affairs to have much time for spiritual duties.

The lower clergy had problems as well. Many priests and monks were so poorly educated that they could scarcely read, let alone teach people. Others broke their priestly vows by marrying, and some drank to excess or gambled.

Early Calls for Reform Influenced by reformers, people had come to expect higher standards of conduct from priests and church leaders. In the late 1300s and early 1400s, John Wycliffe of England and Jan Hus of Bohemia had advocated Church reform. They denied that the pope had the right to worldly power. They also taught that the Bible had more authority than Church leaders did. In the 1500s, Christian humanists like Desiderius Erasmus and Thomas More added their voices to the chorus of criticism. In addition, many Europeans were reading religious works and forming their own opinions about the Church. The atmosphere in Europe was ripe for reform by the early 1500s.

History Makers

Martin Luther
1483–1546

In one way, fear led Luther to become a monk. At the age of 21, Luther was caught in a terrible thunderstorm. Convinced he would die, he cried out, "Saint Anne, help me! I will become a monk."

Even after entering the monastery, Luther felt fearful, lost, sinful, and rejected by God. He confessed his sins regularly, fasted, and did penance. However, by studying the Bible, Luther came to the conclusion that faith alone was the key to salvation. Only then did he experience peace.

INTEGRATED TECHNOLOGY

RESEARCH LINKS For more on Martin Luther, go to **classzone.com**

Luther Challenges the Church

Martin Luther's parents wanted him to be a lawyer. Instead, he became a monk and a teacher. From 1512 until his death, he taught scripture at the University of Wittenberg in the German state of Saxony. All he wanted was to be a good Christian, not to lead a religious revolution.

The 95 Theses In 1517, Luther decided to take a public stand against the actions of a friar named Johann Tetzel. Tetzel was raising money to rebuild St. Peter's Cathedral in Rome. He did this by selling indulgences. An **indulgence** was a pardon. It released a sinner from performing the penalty that a priest imposed for sins. Indulgences were not supposed to affect God's right to judge. Unfortunately, Tetzel gave people the impression that by buying indulgences, they could buy their way into heaven.

Luther was troubled by Tetzel's tactics. In response, he wrote 95 Theses, or formal statements, attacking the "pardon-merchants." On October 31, 1517, he posted these statements on the door of the castle church in Wittenberg and invited other scholars to debate him. Someone copied Luther's words and took them to a printer. Quickly, Luther's name became known all over Germany. His actions began the **Reformation**, a movement for religious reform. It led to the founding of Christian churches that did not accept the pope's authority.

Luther's Teachings Soon Luther went beyond criticizing indulgences. He wanted full reform of the Church. His teachings rested on three main ideas:

- People could win salvation only by faith in God's gift of forgiveness. The Church taught that faith and "good works" were needed for salvation.
- All Church teachings should be clearly based on the words of the Bible. Both the pope and Church traditions were false authorities.
- All people with faith were equal. Therefore, people did not need priests to interpret the Bible for them. (A)

MAIN IDEA
Summarizing
(A) What were the main points of Luther's teachings?

The Response to Luther

Luther was astonished at how rapidly his ideas spread and attracted followers. Many people had been unhappy with the Church for political and economic reasons. They saw Luther's protests as a way to challenge Church control.

The Pope's Threat Initially, Church officials in Rome viewed Luther simply as a rebellious monk who needed to be punished by his superiors. However, as Luther's ideas became more popular, the pope realized that this monk was a serious threat. In one angry reply to Church criticism, Luther actually suggested that Christians drive the pope from the Church by force.

In 1520, Pope Leo X issued a decree threatening Luther with excommunication unless he took back his statements. Luther did not take back a word. Instead, his students at Wittenberg gathered around a bonfire and cheered as he threw the pope's decree into the flames. Leo excommunicated Luther.

Vocabulary
Excommunication is the taking away of a person's right to membership in the Church.

The Emperor's Opposition Holy Roman Emperor Charles V, a devout Catholic, also opposed Luther's teaching. Charles controlled a vast empire, including the German states. He summoned Luther to the town of Worms (vawrmz) in 1521 to stand trial. Told to recant, or take back his statements, Luther refused:

PRIMARY SOURCE

I am bound by the Scriptures I have quoted and my conscience is captive to the Word of God. I cannot and I will not retract anything, since it is neither safe nor right to go against conscience. I cannot do otherwise, here I stand, may God help me. Amen.

MARTIN LUTHER, quoted in *The Protestant Reformation* by Lewis W. Spitz

A month after Luther made that speech, Charles issued an imperial order, the Edict of Worms. It declared Luther an outlaw and a heretic. According to this edict, no one in the empire was to give Luther food or shelter. All his books were to be burned. However, Prince Frederick the Wise of Saxony disobeyed the emperor. For almost a year after the trial, he sheltered Luther in one of his castles. While there, Luther translated the New Testament into German.

Vocabulary
A *heretic* is a person who holds beliefs that differ from official Church teachings.

Luther returned to Wittenberg in 1522. There he discovered that many of his ideas were already being put into practice. Instead of continuing to seek reforms in the Catholic Church, Luther and his followers had become a separate religious group, called **Lutherans**.

The Peasants' Revolt Some people began to apply Luther's revolutionary ideas to society. In 1524, German peasants, excited by reformers' talk of Christian freedom, demanded an end to serfdom. Bands of angry peasants went about the countryside raiding monasteries, pillaging, and burning. The revolt horrified Luther. He wrote a pamphlet urging the German princes to show the peasants no mercy. The princes' armies crushed the revolt, killing as many as 100,000 people. Feeling betrayed, many peasants rejected Luther's religious leadership. **B**

MAIN IDEA

Analyzing Causes

B Why did Luther's ideas encourage the German peasants to revolt?

Germany at War In contrast to the bitter peasants, many northern German princes supported Lutheranism. While some princes genuinely shared Luther's beliefs, others liked Luther's ideas for selfish reasons. They saw his teachings as a good excuse to seize Church property and to assert their independence from Charles V.

In 1529, German princes who remained loyal to the pope agreed to join forces against Luther's ideas. Those princes who supported Luther signed a protest against that agreement. These protesting princes came to be known as Protestants. Eventually, the term **Protestant** was applied to Christians who belonged to non-Catholic churches.

Protestantism

Protestantism is a branch of Christianity. It developed out of the Reformation, the 16th-century protest in Europe against beliefs and practices of the Catholic Church. Three distinct branches of Protestantism emerged at first. They were Lutheranism, based on the teachings of Martin Luther in Germany; Calvinism, based on the teachings of John Calvin in Switzerland; and Anglicanism, which was established by King Henry VIII in England. Protestantism spread throughout Europe in the 16th century, and later, the world. As differences in beliefs developed, new denominations formed.

The Division of Christianity

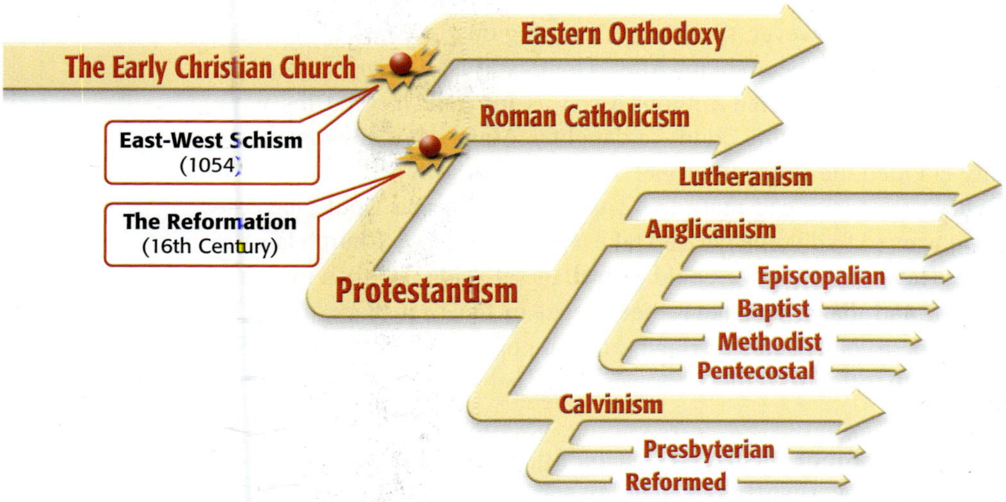

Religious Beliefs and Practices in the 16th Century

	Roman Catholicism	Lutheranism	Calvinism	Anglicanism
Leadership	Pope is head of the Church	Ministers lead congregations	Council of elders govern each church	English monarch is head of the Church
Salvation	Salvation by faith and good works	Salvation by faith alone	God has predetermined who will be saved	Salvation by faith alone
Bible	Church and Bible tradition are sources of revealed truth	Bible is sole source of revealed truth	Bible is sole source of revealed truth	Bible is sole source of revealed truth
Worship Service	Worship service based on ritual	Worship service focused on preaching and ritual	Worship service focused on preaching	Worship service based on ritual and preaching
Interpretation of Beliefs	Priests interpret Bible and Church teachings for believers	Believers interpret the Bible for themselves	Believers interpret the Bible for themselves	Believers interpret the Bible using tradition and reason

INTEGRATED TECHNOLOGY
RESEARCH LINKS For more on Protestantism, go to **classzone.com**

> DATA FILE

PROTESTANTISM TODAY

Membership:
- Nearly 400 million Protestants worldwide
- About 65 million Protestants in the United States

Branches:
- More than 465 major Protestant denominations worldwide
- Major denominational families worldwide: Anglican, Assemblies of God, Baptist, Methodist, Lutheran, and Presbyterian
- More than 250 denominations in the United States
- About 40 denominations with more than 400,000 members each in the United States

Religious Adherents in the United States:

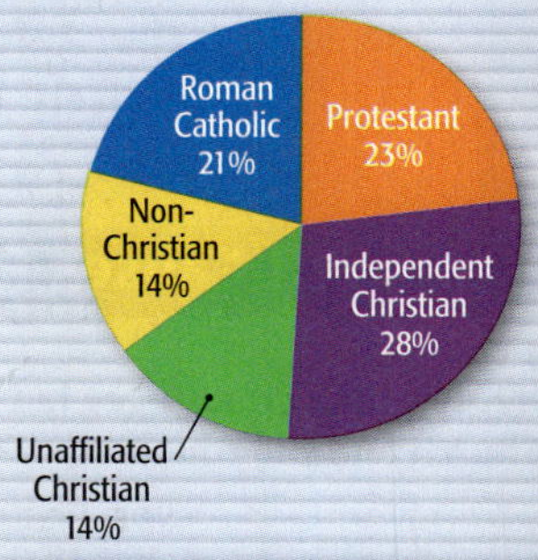

Sources: *Britannica Book of the Year 2003*

Connect *to* Today

1. **Comparing** Which of the branches on the chart at left are most different and which are most similar?
   See Skillbuilder Handbook, page R7.

2. **Developing Historical Perspective** Do research on Protestantism. Select a denomination not shown on this page and write a paragraph tracing its roots to Reformation Protestantism.

Still determined that his subjects should remain Catholic, Charles V went to war against the Protestant princes. Even though he defeated them in 1547, he failed to force them back into the Catholic Church. In 1555, Charles, weary of fighting, ordered all German princes, both Protestant and Catholic, to assemble in the city of Augsburg. There the princes agreed that each ruler would decide the religion of his state. This famous religious settlement was known as the **Peace of Augsburg**.

England Becomes Protestant

The Catholic Church soon faced another great challenge to its authority, this time in England. Unlike Luther, the man who broke England's ties to the Roman Catholic Church did so for political and personal, not religious, reasons.

Henry VIII Wants a Son When Henry VIII became king of England in 1509, he was a devout Catholic. Indeed, in 1521, Henry wrote a stinging attack on Luther's ideas. In recognition of Henry's support, the pope gave him the title "Defender of the Faith." Political needs, however, soon tested his religious loyalty. He needed a male heir. Henry's father had become king after a long civil war. Henry feared that a similar war would start if he died without a son as his heir. He and his wife, Catherine of Aragon, had one living child—a daughter, Mary—but no woman had ever successfully claimed the English throne.

By 1527, Henry was convinced that the 42-year-old Catherine would have no more children. He wanted to divorce her and take a younger queen. Church law did not allow divorce. However, the pope could **annul**, or set aside, Henry's marriage if proof could be found that it had never been legal in the first place. In 1527, Henry asked the pope to annul his marriage, but the pope turned him down. The pope did not want to offend Catherine's powerful nephew, the Holy Roman Emperor Charles V.

The Reformation Parliament Henry took steps to solve his marriage problem himself. In 1529, he called Parliament into session and asked it to pass a set of laws

Henry VIII Causes Religious Turmoil

Henry's many marriages led to conflict with the Catholic Church and the founding of the Church of England.

1510 — 1520 — 1530

1509 Henry VIII becomes king; marries Catherine of Aragon.

1516 Daughter Mary is born.

1527 Henry asks the pope to end his first marriage; the pope refuses.

1529 Henry summons the Reformation Parliament; dismantling of pope's power in England begins.

1531 Parliament recognizes Henry as head of the Church.

1533 Parliament places clergy under Henry's control; Henry divorces Catherine, marries Anne Boleyn (at left); daughter Elizabeth born.

1534 Act of Supremacy names Henry and his successors supreme head of the English Church.

that ended the pope's power in England. This Parliament is known as the Reformation Parliament.

In 1533, Henry secretly married Anne Boleyn (BUL•ihn), who was in her twenties. Shortly after, Parliament legalized Henry's divorce from Catherine. In 1534, Henry's break with the pope was completed when Parliament voted to approve the Act of Supremacy. This called on people to take an oath recognizing the divorce and accepting Henry, not the pope, as the official head of England's Church.

The Act of Supremacy met some opposition. Thomas More, even though he had strongly criticized the Church, remained a devout Catholic. His faith, he said, would not allow him to accept the terms of the act and he refused to take the oath. In response, Henry had him arrested and imprisoned in the Tower of London. In 1535, More was found guilty of high treason and executed.

Consequences of Henry's Changes Henry did not immediately get the male heir he sought. After Anne Boleyn gave birth to a daughter, Elizabeth, she fell out of Henry's favor. Eventually, she was charged with treason. Like Thomas More, she was imprisoned in the Tower of London. She was found guilty and beheaded in 1536. Almost at once, Henry took a third wife, Jane Seymour. In 1537, she gave him a son named Edward. Henry's happiness was tempered by his wife's death just two weeks later. Henry married three more times. None of these marriages, however, produced children.

After Henry's death in 1547, each of his three children ruled England in turn. This created religious turmoil. Henry's son, Edward, became king when he was just nine years old. Too young to rule alone, Edward VI was guided by adult advisers. These men were devout Protestants, and they introduced Protestant reforms to the English Church. Almost constantly in ill health, Edward reigned for just six years. Mary, the daughter of Catherine of Aragon, took the throne in 1553. She was a Catholic who returned the English Church to the rule of the pope. Her efforts met with considerable resistance, and she had many Protestants executed. When Mary died in 1558, Elizabeth, Anne Boleyn's daughter, inherited the throne.

1536
Anne Boleyn is beheaded.

1537
Henry's third wife, Jane Seymour, has son, Edward. She dies from complications.

1540-1542
Henry divorces Anne of Cleves, his fourth wife, and executes Catherine Howard (above), his fifth wife.

1547
Henry dies; Catherine Parr, his sixth wife, outlives him; Edward VI begins six-year rule; Protestants are strong.

1553
Mary I (at left) begins rule and restores the Catholic Church.

1558
Elizabeth I (at right) begins rule; she restores the Protestant Church.

1540 1550 1560

History Makers

Elizabeth I
1533–1603

Elizabeth I, like her father, had a robust nature and loved physical activity. She had a particular passion for dancing. Her fondness for exercise diminished little with age, and she showed amazing energy and strength well into her sixties.

Elizabeth also resembled her father in character and temperament. She was stubborn, strong-willed, and arrogant, and she expected to be obeyed without question. And Elizabeth had a fierce and unpredictable temper. To her subjects, Elizabeth was an object of both fear and love. She was their "most dread sovereign lady."

Elizabeth Restores Protestantism Elizabeth I was determined to return her kingdom to Protestantism. In 1559, Parliament followed Elizabeth's wishes and set up the Church of England, or **Anglican** Church, with Elizabeth as its head. This was to be the only legal church in England.

Elizabeth decided to establish a state church that moderate Catholics and moderate Protestants might both accept. To please Protestants, priests in the Church of England were allowed to marry. They could deliver sermons in English, not Latin. To please Catholics, the Church of England kept some of the trappings of the Catholic service such as rich robes. In addition, church services were revised to be somewhat more acceptable to Catholics. (C)

MAIN IDEA

Recognizing Effects

(C) How did Henry-VIII's marriages and divorces cause religious turmoil in England?

Elizabeth Faces Other Challenges By taking this moderate approach, Elizabeth brought a level of religious peace to England. Religion, however, remained a problem. Some Protestants pushed for Elizabeth to make more far-reaching church reforms. At the same time, some Catholics tried to overthrow Elizabeth and replace her with her cousin, the Catholic Mary Queen of Scots. Elizabeth also faced threats from Philip II, the Catholic king of Spain.

Elizabeth faced other difficulties. Money was one problem. In the late 1500s, the English began to think about building an American empire as a new source of income. While colonies strengthened England economically, they did not enrich the queen directly. Elizabeth's constant need for money would carry over into the next reign and lead to bitter conflict between the monarch and Parliament. You will read more about Elizabeth's reign in Chapter 21. In the meantime, the Reformation gained ground in other European countries.

NEW YORK CORE CURRICULUM REVIEW

TERMS & NAMES 1. For each term or name, write a sentence explaining its significance.
• indulgence • Reformation • Lutheran • Protestant • Peace of Augsburg • annul • Anglican

USING YOUR NOTES

2. Which effect do you think had the most permanent impact? Explain.

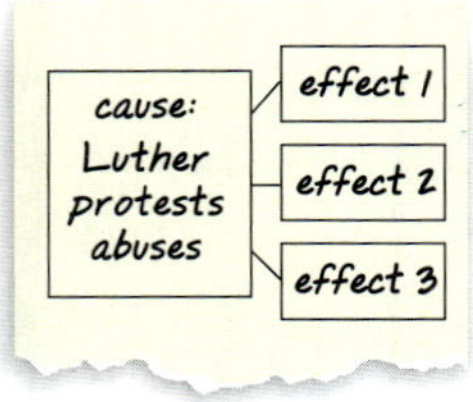

MAIN IDEAS

3. What political, economic, and social factors helped bring about the Reformation?
4. From where did the term *Protestantism* originate?
5. What impact did Henry VIII's actions have on England in the second half of the 1500s?

CRITICAL THINKING & WRITING

6. **DRAWING CONCLUSIONS** Explain how Elizabeth I was able to bring a level of religious peace to England.
7. **COMPARING** Do you think Luther or Henry VIII had a better reason to break with the Church? Provide details to support your answer.
8. **ANALYZING MOTIVES** How did the Catholic Church respond to Luther's teachings? Why do you think this was so?
9. **WRITING ACTIVITY** REVOLUTION Imagine Martin Luther and a leader of the Catholic Church are squaring off in a public debate. Write a brief **dialogue** between the two.

CONNECT TO TODAY **CREATING A GRAPHIC**
Use library resources to find information on the countries in which Protestantism is a major religion. Use your findings to create a **graphic** that makes a comparison among those countries.

The Reformation Continues

CONNECT TO THE NEW YORK STATE CORE CURRICULUM

Unit 3.G.5. Calvin and other reformers
Unit 3.G.6. Counter Reformation (Ignatius Loyola, Council of Trent)

TERMS & NAMES

- predestination
- Calvinism
- theocracy
- Presbyterian
- Anabaptist
- Catholic Reformation
- Jesuits
- Council of Trent

SETTING THE STAGE Under the leadership of Queen Elizabeth I, the Anglican Church, though Protestant, remained similar to the Catholic Church in many of its doctrines and ceremonies. Meanwhile, other forms of Protestantism were developing elsewhere in Europe. Martin Luther had launched the Reformation in northern Germany, but reformers were at work in other countries. In Switzerland, another major branch of Protestantism emerged. Based mainly on the teachings of John Calvin, a French follower of Luther, it promoted unique ideas about the relationship between people and God.

TAKING NOTES

Comparing Use a chart to compare the ideas of the reformers who came after Luther.

Reformers	Ideas
Zwingli	
Calvin	
Anabaptists	
Catholic Reformers	

Calvin Continues the Reformation

Religious reform in Switzerland was begun by Huldrych Zwingli (HUL•drykh ZWIHNG•lee), a Catholic priest in Zurich. He was influenced both by the Christian humanism of Erasmus and by the reforms of Luther. In 1520, Zwingli openly attacked abuses in the Catholic Church. He called for a return to the more personal faith of early Christianity. He also wanted believers to have more control over the Church.

Zwingli's reforms were adopted in Zurich and other cities. In 1531, a bitter war between Swiss Protestants and Catholics broke out. During the fighting, Zwingli met his death. Meanwhile, John Calvin, then a young law student in France with a growing interest in Church doctrine, was beginning to clarify his religious beliefs.

Calvin Formalizes Protestant Ideas When Martin Luther posted his 95 Theses in 1517, John Calvin had been only eight years old. But Calvin grew up to have as much influence in the spread of Protestantism as Luther did. He would give order to the faith Luther had begun.

In 1536, Calvin published *Institutes of the Christian Religion.* This book expressed ideas about God, salvation, and human nature. It was a summary of Protestant theology, or religious beliefs. Calvin wrote that men and women are sinful by nature. Taking Luther's idea that humans cannot earn salvation, Calvin went on to say that God chooses a very few people to save. Calvin called these few the "elect." He believed that God has known since the beginning of time who will be saved. This doctrine is called **predestination**. The religion based on Calvin's teachings is called **Calvinism**.

History Makers

John Calvin
1509–1564

A quiet boy, Calvin grew up to study law and philosophy at the University of Paris. In the 1530s, he was influenced by French followers of Luther. When King Francis I ordered Protestants arrested, Calvin fled. Eventually, he moved to Geneva.

Because Calvin and his followers rigidly regulated morality in Geneva, Calvinism is often described as strict and grim. But Calvin taught that people should enjoy God's gifts. He wrote that it should not be "forbidden to laugh, or to enjoy food, or to add new possessions to old."

Calvin Leads the Reformation in Switzerland Calvin believed that the ideal government was a **theocracy**, a government controlled by religious leaders. In 1541, Protestants in Geneva, Switzerland, asked Calvin to lead their city.

When Calvin arrived there in the 1540s, Geneva was a self-governing city of about 20,000 people. He and his followers ran the city according to strict rules. Everyone attended religion class. No one wore bright clothing or played card games. Authorities would imprison, excommunicate, or banish those who broke such rules. Anyone who preached different doctrines might be burned at the stake. Yet, to many Protestants, Calvin's Geneva was a model city of highly moral citizens.

Calvinism Spreads One admiring visitor to Geneva was a Scottish preacher named John Knox. When he returned to Scotland in 1559, Knox put Calvin's ideas to work. Each community church was governed by a group of laymen called elders or presbyters (PREHZ•buh•tuhrs). Followers of Knox became known as **Presbyterians**. In the 1560s, Protestant nobles led by Knox made Calvinism Scotland's official religion. They also deposed their Catholic ruler, Mary Queen of Scots, in favor of her infant son, James.

Elsewhere, Swiss, Dutch, and French reformers adopted the Calvinist form of church organization. One reason Calvin is considered so influential is that many Protestant churches today trace their roots to Calvin. Over the years, however, many of them have softened Calvin's strict teachings.

In France, Calvin's followers were called Huguenots. Hatred between Catholics and Huguenots frequently led to violence. The most violent clash occurred in Paris on August 24, 1572—the Catholic feast of St. Bartholomew's Day. At dawn, Catholic mobs began hunting for Protestants and murdering them. The massacres spread to other cities and lasted six months. Scholars believe that as many as 12,000 Huguenots were killed.

Other Protestant Reformers

Protestants taught that the Bible is the source of all religious truth and that people should read it to discover those truths. As Christians interpreted the Bible for themselves, new Protestant groups formed over differences in belief. (A)

MAIN IDEA
Analyzing Causes
(A) How did Protestant teaching lead to the forming of new groups?

The Anabaptists One such group baptized only those persons who were old enough to decide to be Christian. They said that persons who had been baptized as children should be rebaptized as adults. These believers were called **Anabaptists**, from a Greek word meaning "baptize again." The Anabaptists also taught that church and state should be separate, and they refused to fight in wars. They shared their possessions.

Viewing Anabaptists as radicals who threatened society, both Catholics and Protestants persecuted them. But the Anabaptists survived and became the forerunners of the Mennonites and the Amish. Their teaching influenced the later Quakers and Baptists, groups who split from the Anglican Church.

Women's Role in the Reformation Many women played prominent roles in the Reformation, especially during the early years. For example, the sister of King

GEOGRAPHY SKILLBUILDER: Interpreting Maps

1. **Region** *Which European countries became mostly Protestant and which remained mostly Roman Catholic?*
2. **Location** *Judging from the way the religions were distributed, where would you expect religious conflicts to take place? Explain.*

▲ Although Catholic, Marguerite of Navarre supported the call for reform in the Church.

Francis I, Marguerite of Navarre, protected John Calvin from being executed for his beliefs while he lived in France. Other noblewomen also protected reformers. The wives of some reformers, too, had influence. Katherina Zell, married to Matthew Zell of Strasbourg, once scolded a minister for speaking harshly of another reformer. The minister responded by saying that she had "disturbed the peace." She answered his criticism sharply:

PRIMARY SOURCE

Do you call this disturbing the peace that instead of spending my time in frivolous amusements I have visited the plague-infested and carried out the dead? I have visited those in prison and under sentence of death. Often for three days and three nights I have neither eaten nor slept. I have never mounted the pulpit, but I have done more than any minister in visiting those in misery.

KATHERINA ZELL, quoted in *Women of the Reformation*

Katherina von Bora played a more typical, behind-the-scenes role as Luther's wife. Katherina was sent to a convent at about age ten, and had become a nun. Inspired by Luther's teaching, she fled the convent. After marrying Luther, Katherina had six children. She also managed the family finances, fed all who visited their house, and supported her husband's work. She respected Luther's position but argued with him about woman's equal role in marriage.

As Protestant religions became more firmly established, their organization became more formal. Male religious leaders narrowly limited women's activities to the home and discouraged them from being leaders in the church. In fact, it was Luther who said, "God's highest gift on earth is a pious, cheerful, God-fearing, home-keeping wife." **B**

MAIN IDEA

Making Inferences

B Why was it easier for women to take part in the earlier stages of the Reformation than in the later stages?

The Catholic Reformation

While Protestant churches won many followers, millions remained true to Catholicism. Helping Catholics to remain loyal was a movement within the Catholic Church to reform itself. This movement is now known as the **Catholic Reformation**. Historians once referred to it as the Counter Reformation. Important leaders in this movement were reformers, such as Ignatius (ihg•NAY•shuhs) of Loyola, who founded new religious orders, and two popes—Paul III and Paul IV—who took actions to reform and renew the Church from within.

Ignatius of Loyola Ignatius grew up in his father's castle in Loyola, Spain. The great turning point in his life came in 1521 when he was injured in a war. While recovering, he thought about his past sins and about the life of Jesus. His daily devotions, he believed, cleansed his soul. In 1522, Ignatius began writing a book called *Spiritual Exercises* that laid out a day-by-day plan of meditation, prayer, and study. In it, he compared spiritual and physical exercise:

PRIMARY SOURCE

Just as walking, traveling, and running are bodily exercises, preparing the soul to remove ill-ordered affections, and after their removal seeking and finding the will of God with respect to the ordering of one's own life and the salvation of one's soul, are Spiritual Exercises.

IGNATIUS OF LOYOLA, *Spiritual Exercises*

▲ Church leaders consult on reforms at the Council of Trent in this 16th-century painting.

For the next 18 years, Ignatius gathered followers. In 1540, the pope created a religious order for his followers called the Society of Jesus. Members were called **Jesuits** (JEHZH•oo•ihts). The Jesuits focused on three activities. First, they founded schools throughout Europe. Jesuit teachers were well-trained in both classical studies and theology. The Jesuits' second mission was to convert non-Christians to Catholicism. So they sent out missionaries around the world. Their third goal was to stop the spread of Protestantism. The zeal of the Jesuits overcame the drift toward Protestantism in Poland and southern Germany.

Reforming Popes Two popes took the lead in reforming the Catholic Church. Paul III, pope from 1534 to 1549, took four important steps. First, he directed a council of cardinals to investigate indulgence selling and other abuses in the Church. Second, he approved the Jesuit order. Third, he used the Inquisition to seek out heresy in papal territory. Fourth, and most important, he called a council of Church leaders to meet in Trent, in northern Italy.

Vocabulary
The *Inquisition* was a papal judicial process established to try and punish those thought to be heretics.

From 1545 to 1563, at the **Council of Trent**, Catholic bishops and cardinals agreed on several doctrines:

- The Church's interpretation of the Bible was final. Any Christian who substituted his or her own interpretation was a heretic.
- Christians needed faith and good works for salvation. They were not saved by faith alone, as Luther argued.
- The Bible and Church tradition were equally powerful authorities for guiding Christian life.
- Indulgences were valid expressions of faith. But the false selling of indulgences was banned.

The next pope, Paul IV, vigorously carried out the council's decrees. In 1559, he had officials draw up a list of books considered dangerous to the Catholic faith. This list was known as the Index of Forbidden Books. Catholic bishops throughout Europe were ordered to gather up the offensive books (including Protestant Bibles) and burn them in bonfires. In Venice alone, followers burned 10,000 books in one day.

Global Impact

Jesuit Missionaries

The work of Jesuit missionaries has had a lasting impact around the globe. By the time Ignatius died in 1556, about a thousand Jesuits had brought his ministry to Europe, Africa, Asia, and the Americas. Two of the most famous Jesuit missionaries of the 1500s were Francis Xavier, who worked in India and Japan, and Matteo Ricci, who worked in China.

One reason the Jesuits had such an impact is that they founded schools throughout the world. For example, the Jesuits today run about 45 high schools and 28 colleges and universities in the United States. Four of these are Georgetown University (shown above), Boston College, Marquette University, and Loyola University of Chicago.

The Legacy of the Reformation

The Reformation had an enduring impact. Through its religious, social, and political effects, the Reformation set the stage for the modern world. It also ended the Christian unity of Europe and left it culturally divided.

Religious and Social Effects of the Reformation Despite religious wars and persecutions, Protestant churches flourished and new denominations developed. The Roman Catholic Church itself became more unified as a result of the reforms started at the Council of Trent. Both Catholics and Protestants gave more emphasis to the role of education in promoting their beliefs. This led to the founding of parish schools and new colleges and universities throughout Europe.

Some women reformers had hoped to see the status of women in the church and society improve as a result of the Reformation. But it remained much the same both under Protestantism and Roman Catholicism. Women were still mainly limited to the concerns of home and family.

Political Effects of the Reformation As the Catholic Church's moral and political authority declined, individual monarchs and states gained power. This led to the development of modern nation-states. In the 1600s, rulers of nation-states would seek more power for themselves and their countries through warfare, exploration, and expansion.

The Reformation's questioning of beliefs and authority also laid the groundwork for the Enlightenment. As you will read in Chapter 22, this intellectual movement would sweep Europe in the late 18th century. It led some to reject all religions and others to call for the overthrow of existing governments.

NEW YORK CORE CURRICULUM REVIEW

TERMS & NAMES 1. For each term or name, write a sentence explaining its significance.

• predestination • Calvinism • theocracy • Presbyterian • Anabaptist • Catholic Reformation • Jesuits • Council of Trent

USING YOUR NOTES

2. Which Catholic reform do you think had the most impact?

Reformers	Ideas
Zwingli	
Calvin	
Anabaptists	
Catholic Reformers	

MAIN IDEAS

3. What was Calvin's idea of the "elect" and their place in society?
4. What role did noblewomen play in the Reformation?
5. What were the goals of the Jesuits?

CRITICAL THINKING & WRITING

6. **DRAWING CONCLUSIONS** How did the Reformation set the stage for the modern world? Give examples.
7. **MAKING INFERENCES** Why do you think the Church wanted to forbid people to read certain books?
8. **COMPARING** How did steps taken by Paul III and Paul IV to reform the Catholic Church differ from Protestant reforms? Support your answer with details from the text.
9. **WRITING ACTIVITY** RELIGIOUS AND ETHICAL SYSTEMS Write a two-paragraph **essay** on whether church leaders should be political rulers.

CONNECT TO TODAY **PRESENTING AN ORAL REPORT**

Research the religious origins of a university in the United States. Then present your findings to the class in an **oral report.**

INTERACTIVE

The Reformation

Martin Luther's criticisms of the Catholic Church grew sharper over time. Some Catholics, in turn, responded with personal attacks on Luther. In recent times, historians have focused less on the theological and personal issues connected with the Reformation. Instead, many modern scholars analyze the political, social, and economic conditions that contributed to the Reformation.

A PRIMARY SOURCE

Martin Luther

In 1520, Martin Luther attacked the whole system of Church government and sent the pope the following criticism of the Church leaders who served under him in Rome.

The Roman Church has become the most licentious [sinful] den of thieves. . . . They err who ascribe to thee the right of interpreting Scripture, for under cover of thy name they seek to set up their own wickedness in the Church, and, alas, through them Satan has already made much headway under thy predecessors. In short, believe none who exalt thee, believe those who humble thee.

B SECONDARY SOURCE

Steven Ozment

In 1992, historian Steven Ozment published *Protestants: The Birth of a Revolution.* Here, he comments on some of the political aspects of the Reformation.

Beginning as a protest against arbitrary, self-aggrandizing, hierarchical authority in the person of the pope, the Reformation came to be closely identified in the minds of contemporaries with what we today might call states' rights or local control. To many townspeople and villagers, Luther seemed a godsend for their struggle to remain politically free and independent; they embraced his Reformation as a conserving political force, even though they knew it threatened to undo traditional religious beliefs and practices.

C SECONDARY SOURCE

G. R. Elton

In *Reformation Europe,* published in 1963, historian G. R. Elton notes the role of geography and trade in the spread of Reformation ideas.

Could the Reformation have spread so far and so fast if it had started anywhere but in Germany? The fact that it had its beginnings in the middle of Europe made possible a very rapid radiation in all directions. . . . Germany's position at the center of European trade also helped greatly. German merchants carried not only goods but Lutheran ideas and books to Venice and France; the north German Hanse [a trade league] transported the Reformation to the Scandinavian countries.

D PRIMARY SOURCE

Hans Brosamer

"Seven-Headed Martin Luther" (1529) The invention of the printing press enabled both Protestants and Catholics to engage in a war of words and images. This anti-Luther illustration by German painter Hans Brosamer depicted Martin Luther as a seven-headed monster—doctor, monk, infidel, preacher, fanatic swarmed by bees, self-appointed pope, and thief Barabbas from the Bible.

Document-Based QUESTIONS

1. In what way does Luther's letter (Source A) support the point of view of the historian in Source B?
2. Based on Source C, why was Germany's location important to the spread of Reformation ideas?
3. Why might Hans Brosamer's woodcut (Source D) be an effective propaganda weapon against Martin Luther?

Chapter 17 Assessment

VISUAL SUMMARY

European Renaissance and Reformation

The Renaissance and the Reformation bring dramatic changes to social and cultural life in Europe.

1. Italy: Birthplace of the Renaissance

- A period of intellectual and artistic creativity begins in Italy around the 1300s.
- Artists and writers revive techniques, styles, and subjects from classical Greece and Rome and celebrate human achievements.

2. The Northern Renaissance

- Renaissance ideas spread to Northern Europe, where German and Flemish artists create distinctive works of art.
- Thousands of books and pamphlets created on printing presses spread political, social, and artistic ideas.

3. Luther Leads the Reformation

- Martin Luther starts a movement for religious reform and challenges the authority of the Catholic Church.
- King Henry VIII breaks ties with the Catholic Church and starts the Church of England.

4. The Reformation Continues

- Protestant groups divide into several denominations, including the Calvinists and the Anabaptists.
- The Catholic Church introduces its own reforms.

TERMS & NAMES

For each term or name below, briefly explain its connection to European history from 1300 to 1600.

1. Renaissance
2. vernacular
3. utopia
4. Reformation
5. Protestant
6. Peace of Augsburg
7. Catholic Reformation
8. Council of Trent

MAIN IDEAS

Italy: Birthplace of the Renaissance Section 1 (pages 471–479)

9. How did the merchant class in northern Italy influence the Renaissance?
10. In what ways did literature and the arts change during the Renaissance?

The Northern Renaissance Section 2 (pages 480–487)

11. What did northern European rulers do to encourage the spread of Renaissance ideas?
12. How were the Christian humanists different from the humanists of the Italian Renaissance?

Luther Leads the Reformation Section 3 (pages 488–494)

13. On what three teachings did Martin Luther rest his Reformation movement?
14. Why did the Holy Roman emperor go to war against Protestant German princes?
15. Why did Henry VIII create his own church? Refer to the time line on pages 492–493.

The Reformation Continues Section 4 (pages 495–501)

16. In what ways was John Calvin's church different from the Lutheran Church?
17. What was the goal of the Catholic Reformation?
18. What are three legacies of the Reformation?

CRITICAL THINKING

1. USING YOUR NOTES

In a diagram, show how the Reformation led to great changes in European ideas and institutions.

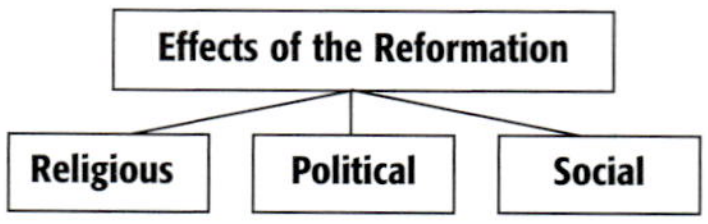

2. ANALYZING ISSUES

REVOLUTION What role did the printing press play in the spread of the Reformation and the spread of democracy?

3. RECOGNIZING EFFECTS

CULTURAL INTERACTION How did the Renaissance and Reformation expand cultural interaction both within Europe and outside of it?

4. DEVELOPING HISTORICAL PERSPECTIVE

What conditions needed to exist before the Renaissance could occur?

5. SYNTHESIZING

How did views of the role of women change in the Renaissance period?

NEW YORK STATE REGENTS EXAM PRACTICE

Use the quotation and your knowledge of world history to answer questions 1 and 2.
Additional Test Practice, pp. S1–S33

PRIMARY SOURCE

A prince must also show himself a lover of merit [excellence], give preferment [promotion] to the able, and honour those who excel in every art. Moreover he must encourage his citizens to follow their callings [professions] quietly, whether in commerce, or agriculture, or any other trade that men follow. . . . [The prince] should offer rewards to whoever does these things, and to whoever seeks in any way to improve his city or state.

NICCOLÒ MACHIAVELLI, *The Prince*

1 Which phrase best describes the advice given by Machiavelli?
(1) Rule with an iron hand in a velvet glove.
(2) Do not give your subjects any freedoms.
(3) Reward hard work and patriotism.
(4) To retain your rule, you must interfere in the lives of your subjects.

2 In his book *The Prince*, the writer of this advice also suggested
(1) the pope should listen to the calls for reform of the Church
(2) a prince might have to trick his people for the good of the state
(3) merchants should try to take control of the cities away from the prince
(4) the prince should reform society by establishing a utopia

Use this drawing of a machine from the notebooks of Leonardo da Vinci and your knowledge of world history to answer question 3.

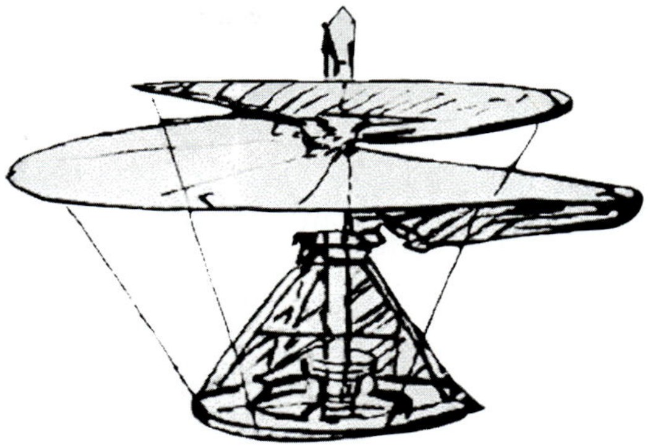

3 The principles upon which this machine is based evolved into what modern machine?
(1) food blender
(2) a fan
(3) a well-digging machine
(4) helicopter

INTEGRATED TECHNOLOGY
TEST PRACTICE Go to **classzone.com**
- Diagnostic tests
- Strategies
- Tutorials
- Additional practice

ALTERNATIVE ASSESSMENT

1. Interact *with* History

On page 470, you looked at a painting and discussed what you learned about Renaissance society from that painting. Now choose one other piece of art from the chapter. Explain what you can learn about Renaissance or Reformation society from that piece of art.

2. WRITING ABOUT HISTORY

RELIGIOUS AND ETHICAL SYSTEMS Study the information about Protestantism in the Analyzing Key Concepts on page 491. Write a three-paragraph **essay** analyzing the effects Protestantism had on the Christian Church.

- Examine its impact on the number of denominations.
- Explain the different beliefs and practices it promoted.

INTEGRATED TECHNOLOGY

Writing an Internet-based Research Paper

Go to the *Web Research Guide* at **classzone.com** to learn about conducting research on the Internet. Then, working with a partner, use the Internet to research major religious reforms of the 20th century. You might search for information on changes in the Catholic Church as a result of Vatican II, or major shifts in the practices or doctrines of a branch of Hinduism, Islam, Judaism, or Protestantism. Compare the 20th-century reforms with those of the Protestant Reformation. Present the results of your research in a well-organized paper. Be sure to

- apply a search strategy when using directories and search engines to locate Web resources.
- judge the usefulness and reliability of each Web site.
- correctly cite your Web sources.
- peer-edit for organization and correct use of language.

CHAPTER 18

The Muslim World Expands, 1300–1700

Previewing Main Ideas

EMPIRE BUILDING Three of the great empires of history—the Ottomans in Turkey, the Safavids in Persia, and the Mughals in India—emerged in the Muslim world between the 14th and the 18th centuries.

Geography *Locate the empires on the map. Which of the empires was the largest? Where was it located?*

CULTURAL INTERACTION As powerful societies moved to expand their empires, Turkish, Persian, Mongol, and Arab ways of life blended. The result was a flowering of Islamic culture that peaked in the 16th century.

Geography *The Ottoman Empire included cultures from which continents?*

POWER AND AUTHORITY The rulers of all three great Muslim empires of this era based their authority on Islam. They based their power on strong armies, advanced technology, and loyal administrative officers.

Geography *Study the time line and the map. When was the Mughal Empire founded? Where was Babur's empire located?*

NEW YORK CORE CURRICULUM FOCUS

- The Ottomans established a vast Muslim empire that lasted for more than 600 years.
- The Ottoman leader Suleyman was known as the Lawgiver because of the code of laws he developed.

INTEGRATED TECHNOLOGY

eEdition
- Interactive Maps
- Interactive Visuals
- Interactive Primary Sources

INTERNET RESOURCES
Go to **classzone.com** for:
- Research Links
- Internet Activities
- Primary Sources
- Chapter Quiz
- Maps
- Test Practice
- Current Events

MUSLIM WORLD

1300 Osman founds Ottoman state. ▶

1398 Timur the Lame destroys Delhi.

1453 Ottomans capture Constantinople.

1300 — 1400

WORLD

1325 Aztecs build Tenochtitlán. (ornament of an Aztec snake god) ▶

1455 ◀ Gutenberg prints the Bible.

1501 Safavids conquer Persia.

1526 Babur founds Mughal Empire.

1587 Shah Abbas I rules Safavid Empire.

1632 ◀ Shah Jahan orders construction of Taj Mahal at Agra.

1500 **1600** **1700**

1522 Magellan's crew sails around the world.

1603 Tokugawa regime begins in Japan.

1607 British settle in North America at Jamestown.

Interact *with* History

How do you govern a diverse empire?

Your father is a Safavid shah, the ruler of a growing empire. With a well-trained army and modern weapons, he has easily conquered most of the surrounding area. Because you are likely to become the next ruler, you are learning all you can about how to rule. You wonder what is best for the empire. Should conquered people be given the freedom to practice a religion that is different from your own and to follow their own traditions? Or would it be better to try and force them to accept your beliefs and way of life—or even to enslave them?

INTERACTIVE

1. The shah entertains the emperor of a neighboring land. Both lands have great diversity of people and cultures.
2. Distinctive headgear marks the status of military leaders and scholars gathered from all parts of the empire.
3. Clothing, music, dancing, and food reflect the customs of several groups within the empire.
4. People in the court, from the servants to the members of the court, mirror the empire's diversity.

EXAMINING *the* ISSUES

- **What problems might conquered people present for their conqueror?**
- **In what ways might a conqueror integrate conquered people into the society?**

As a class, discuss the ways other empires—such as those of Rome, Assyria, and Persia—treated their conquered peoples. As you read about the three empires featured in this chapter, notice how the rulers dealt with empires made up of different cultures.

The Ottomans Build a Vast Empire

CONNECT TO THE NEW YORK STATE CORE CURRICULUM

Unit 4.B.1. Human and physical geography
Unit 4.B.3. Suleyman I (the Magnificent, the Lawgiver)

TERMS & NAMES

- ghazi
- Ottoman
- sultan
- Timur the Lame
- Mehmed II
- Suleyman the Lawgiver
- *devshirme*
- janissary

SETTING THE STAGE By 1300, the Byzantine Empire was declining, and the Mongols had destroyed the Turkish Seljuk kingdom of Rum. Anatolia was inhabited mostly by the descendants of nomadic Turks. These militaristic people had a long history of invading other countries. Loyal to their own groups, they were not united by a strong central power. A small Turkish state occupied land between the Byzantine Empire and that of the Muslims. From this place, a strong leader would emerge to unite the Turks into what eventually would become an immense empire stretching across three continents.

Turks Move into Byzantium

Many Anatolian Turks saw themselves as **ghazis** (GAH•zees), or warriors for Islam. They formed military societies under the leadership of an emir, a chief commander, and followed a strict Islamic code of conduct. They raided the territories of people who lived on the frontiers of the Byzantine Empire.

Osman Establishes a State The most successful ghazi was Osman. People in the West called him Othman and named his followers **Ottomans**. Osman built a small Muslim state in Anatolia between 1300 and 1326. His successors expanded it by buying land, forming alliances with some emirs, and conquering others.

The Ottomans' military success was largely based on the use of gunpowder. They replaced their archers on horseback with musket-carrying foot soldiers. They also were among the first people to use cannons as weapons of attack. Even heavily walled cities fell to an all-out attack by the Turks.

The second Ottoman leader, Orkhan I, was Osman's son. He felt strong enough to declare himself **sultan**, meaning "overlord" or "one with power." And in 1361, the Ottomans captured Adrianople (ay•dree•uh•NOH•puhl), the second most important city in the Byzantine Empire. A new Turkish empire was on the rise.

The Ottomans acted wisely toward the people they conquered. They ruled through local officials appointed by the sultan and often improved the lives of the peasants. Most Muslims had to serve in Turkish armies and make contributions required by their faith. Non-Muslims did not have to serve in the army but had to pay for their exemption with a small tax.

TAKING NOTES

Comparing List the main rulers of the Ottoman Empire and their successes.

Rulers	Successes

Timur the Lame Halts Expansion The rise of the Ottoman Empire was briefly interrupted in the early 1400s by a rebellious warrior and conqueror from Samarkand in Central Asia. Permanently injured by an arrow in the leg, he was called Timur-i-Lang, or **Timur the Lame**. Europeans called him Tamerlane. Timur burned the powerful city of Baghdad in present-day Iraq to the ground. He crushed the Ottoman forces at the Battle of Ankara in 1402. This defeat halted the expansion of their empire.

Powerful Sultans Spur Dramatic Expansion

Soon Timur turned his attention to China. When he did, war broke out among the four sons of the Ottoman sultan. Mehmed I defeated his brothers and took the throne. His son, Murad II, defeated the Venetians, invaded Hungary, and overcame an army of Italian crusaders in the Balkans. He was the first of four powerful sultans who led the expansion of the Ottoman Empire through 1566.

Mehmed II Conquers Constantinople Murad's son **Mehmed II**, or Mehmed the Conqueror, achieved the most dramatic feat in Ottoman history. By the time Mehmed took power in 1451, the ancient city of Constantinople had shrunk from a population of a million to a mere 50,000. Although it controlled no territory outside its walls, it still dominated the Bosporus Strait. Controlling this waterway meant that it could choke off traffic between the Ottomans' territories in Asia and in the Balkans.

Mehmed II decided to face this situation head-on. "Give me Constantinople!" he thundered, shortly after taking power at age 21. Then, in 1453, he launched his attack.

GEOGRAPHY SKILLBUILDER: Interpreting Maps

1. **Location** *To which waterways did the Ottoman Empire have access?*
2. **Movement** *In which time period did the Ottoman Empire gain the most land?*

Analyzing Primary Sources

The Conquest of Constantinople

Kritovoulos, a Greek who served in the Ottoman administration, recorded the following about the Ottoman takeover of Constantinople. The second source, the French miniature at the right, shows a view of the siege of Constantinople.

PRIMARY SOURCE

After this the Sultan entered the City and looked about to see its great size, its situation, its grandeur and beauty, its teeming population, its loveliness, and the costliness of its churches and public buildings and of the private houses and community houses and those of the officials. . . .

When he saw what a large number had been killed and the ruin of the buildings, and the wholesale ruin and destruction of the City, he was filled with compassion and repented not a little at the destruction and plundering. Tears fell from his eyes as he groaned deeply and passionately: "What a city we have given over to plunder and destruction."

KRITOVOULOS, *History of Mehmed the Conqueror*

DOCUMENT-BASED QUESTIONS

1. **Comparing and Contrasting** *In what details do the two sources agree? disagree?*
2. **Making Inferences** *Why do you think the sultan wept over the destruction?*

Mehmed's Turkish forces began firing on the city walls with mighty cannons. One of these was a 26-foot gun that fired 1,200-pound boulders. A chain across the Golden Horn between the Bosporus Strait and the Sea of Marmara kept the Turkish fleet out of the city's harbor. Finally, one night Mehmed's army tried a daring tactic. They dragged 70 ships over a hill on greased runners from the Bosporus to the harbor. Now Mehmed's army was attacking Constantinople from two sides. The city held out for over seven weeks, but the Turks finally found a break in the wall and entered the city.

Mehmed the Conqueror, as he was now called, proved to be an able ruler as well as a magnificent warrior. He opened Constantinople to new citizens of many religions and backgrounds. Jews, Christians, and Muslims, Turks and non-Turks all flowed in. They helped rebuild the city, which was now called Istanbul. (A)

> **MAIN IDEA**
> **Analyzing Motives**
> (A) Why was taking Constantinople so important to Mehmed II?

Ottomans Take Islam's Holy Cities Mehmed's grandson, Selim the Grim, came to power in 1512. He was an effective sultan and a great general. In 1514, he defeated the Safavids (suh•FAH•vihdz) of Persia at the Battle of Chaldiran. Then he swept south through Syria and Palestine and into North Africa. At the same time that Cortez was toppling the Aztec Empire in the Americas, Selim's empire took responsibility for Mecca and Medina. Finally he took Cairo, the intellectual center of the Muslim world. The once-great civilization of Egypt had become just another province in the growing Ottoman Empire.

History Makers

Suleyman the Lawgiver
1494–1566

In the halls of the U.S. Congress are images of some of the greatest lawgivers of all time. Included in that group are such persons as Thomas Jefferson, Moses, and Suleyman.

Suleyman's law code prescribed penalties for various criminal acts and for bureaucratic and financial corruption. He also sought to reduce bribes, did not allow imprisonment without a trial, and rejected promotions that were not based on merit. He also introduced the idea of a balanced budget for governments.

INTEGRATED TECHNOLOGY

RESEARCH LINKS For more on Suleyman, go to **classzone.com**

Suleyman the Lawgiver

The Ottoman Empire didn't reach its peak size and grandeur until the reign of Selim's son, Suleyman I (SOO•lay•mahn). Suleyman came to the throne in 1520 and ruled for 46 years. His own people called him **Suleyman the Lawgiver**. He was known in the West, though, as Suleyman the Magnificent. This title was a tribute to the splendor of his court and to his cultural achievements.

The Empire Reaches Its Limits Suleyman was a superb military leader. He conquered the important European city of Belgrade in 1521. The next year, Turkish forces captured the island of Rhodes in the Mediterranean and now dominated the whole eastern Mediterranean.

Applying their immense naval power, the Ottomans captured Tripoli on the coast of North Africa. They continued conquering peoples along the North African coastline. Although the Ottomans occupied only the coastal cities of North Africa, they managed to control trade routes to the interior of the continent.

In 1526, Suleyman advanced into Hungary and Austria, throwing central Europe into a panic. Suleyman's armies then pushed to the outskirts of Vienna, Austria. Reigning from Istanbul, Suleyman had waged war with central Europeans, North Africans, and Central Asians. He had become the most powerful monarch on earth. Only Charles V, head of the Hapsburg Empire in Europe, came close to rivaling his power.

Highly Structured Social Organization Binding the Ottoman Empire together in a workable social structure was Suleyman's crowning achievement. The massive empire required an efficient government structure and social organization. Suleyman created a law code to handle both criminal and civil actions. He also simplified and limited taxes, and systematized and reduced government bureaucracy. These changes improved the lives of most citizens and helped earn Suleyman the title of Lawgiver.

The sultan's 20,000 personal slaves staffed the palace bureaucracy. The slaves were acquired as part of a policy called *devshirme* (dehv•SHEER•meh). Under the ***devshirme*** system, the sultan's army drafted boys from the peoples of conquered Christian territories. The army educated them, converted them to Islam, and trained them as soldiers. An elite force of 30,000 soldiers known as **janissaries** was trained to be loyal to the sultan only. Their superb discipline made them the heart of the Ottoman war machine. In fact, Christian families sometimes bribed officials to take their children into the sultan's service, because the brightest ones could rise to high government posts or military positions. B

MAIN IDEA

Making Inferences

B What were the advantages of the *devshirme* system to the sultan?

As a Muslim, Suleyman was required to follow Islamic law. In accordance with Islamic law, the Ottomans granted freedom of worship to other religious communities, particularly to Christians and Jews. They treated these communities as *millets,* or nations. They allowed each *millet* to follow its own religious laws and practices. The head of the *millets* reported to the sultan and his staff. This system kept conflict among people of the various religions to a minimum.

▲ Sinan's Mosque of Suleyman in Istanbul is the largest mosque in the Ottoman Empire.

Cultural Flowering Suleyman had broad interests, which contributed to the cultural achievements of the empire. He found time to study poetry, history, geography, astronomy, mathematics, and architecture. He employed one of the world's finest architects, Sinan, who was probably from Albania. Sinan's masterpiece, the Mosque of Suleyman, is an immense complex topped with domes and half domes. It includes four schools, a library, a bath, and a hospital.

Art and literature also flourished under Suleyman's rule. This creative period was similar to the European Renaissance. Painters and poets looked to Persia and Arabia for models. The works that they produced used these foreign influences to express original Ottoman ideas in the Turkish style. They are excellent examples of cultural blending. C

MAIN IDEA

Comparing

C Which cultural achievements of Suleyman's reign were similar to the European Renaissance?

The Empire Declines Slowly

Despite Suleyman's magnificent social and cultural achievements, the Ottoman Empire was losing ground. Suleyman killed his ablest son and drove another into exile. His third son, the incompetent Selim II, inherited the throne.

Suleyman set the pattern for later sultans to gain and hold power. It became customary for each new sultan to have his brothers strangled. The sultan would then keep his sons prisoner in the harem, cutting them off from education or contact with the world. This practice produced a long line of weak sultans who eventually brought ruin on the empire. However, the Ottoman Empire continued to influence the world into the early 20th century.

NEW YORK CORE CURRICULUM REVIEW

TERMS & NAMES 1. For each term or name, write a sentence explaining its significance.

• ghazi • Ottoman • sultan • Timur the Lame • Mehmed II • Suleyman the Lawgiver • *devshirme* • janissary

USING YOUR NOTES

2. Which do you consider more significant to the Ottoman Empire, the accomplishments of Mehmed II or those of Selim the Grim? Explain.

Rulers	Successes

MAIN IDEAS

3. By what means did the early Ottomans expand their empire?
4. Why was Suleyman called the Lawgiver?
5. How powerful was the Ottoman Empire compared to other empires of the time?

CRITICAL THINKING & WRITING

6. **EVALUATING DECISIONS** Do you think that the Ottomans were wise in staffing their military and government with slaves? Explain.
7. **EVALUATING COURSES OF ACTION** How did Suleyman's selection of a successor eventually spell disaster for the Ottoman Empire?
8. **ANALYZING MOTIVES** Do you think that Suleyman's religious tolerance helped or hurt the Ottoman Empire?
9. **WRITING ACTIVITY** EMPIRE BUILDING-Using the description of Mehmed II's forces taking Constantinople, write a **newspaper article** describing the action.

CONNECT TO TODAY **CREATING A TIME LINE**

Create a **time line** showing events in the decline of the Ottoman Empire and the creation of the modern nation of Turkey.

2

Cultural Blending

CASE STUDY: The Safavid Empire

CONNECT TO THE NEW YORK STATE CORE CURRICULUM

Methodology.A.2. Understand the concepts of change and continuity over time
Unit 2.E.1. Human and physical geography

TERMS & NAMES

- Safavid
- Isma'il
- shah
- Shah Abbas
- Esfahan

SETTING THE STAGE Throughout the course of world history, cultures have interacted with each other. Often such interaction has resulted in the mixing of different cultures in new and exciting ways. This process is referred to as cultural blending. The **Safavid** Empire, a Shi'ite Muslim dynasty that ruled in Persia between the 16th and 18th centuries, provides a striking example of how interaction among peoples can produce a blending of cultures. This culturally diverse empire drew from the traditions of Persians, Ottomans, and Arabs.

TAKING NOTES
Drawing Conclusions Identify examples of cultural blending in the Safavid Empire.

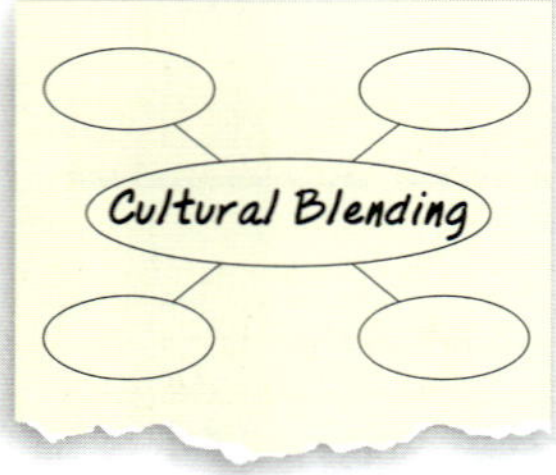

Patterns of Cultural Blending

Each time a culture interacts with another, it is exposed to ideas, technologies, foods, and ways of life not exactly like its own. Continental crossroads, trade routes, ports, and the borders of countries are places where cultural blending commonly begins. Societies that are able to benefit from cultural blending are those that are open to new ways and are willing to adapt and change. The blended ideas spread throughout the culture and produce a new pattern of behavior. Cultural blending has several basic causes.

Causes of Cultural Blending Cultural change is most often prompted by one or more of the following four activities:

- migration
- pursuit of religious freedom or conversion
- trade
- conquest

The blending that contributed to the culture of the Ottomans, which you just read about in Section 1, depended on some of these activities. Surrounded by the peoples of Byzantium, the Turks were motivated to win territory for their empire. The Ottoman Empire's location on a major trading route created many opportunities for contact with different cultures. Suleyman's interest in learning and culture prompted him to bring the best foreign artists and scholars to his court. They brought new ideas about art, literature, and learning to the empire.

Results of Cultural Blending Cultural blending may lead to changes in language, religion, styles of government, the use of technology, and military tactics.

Cultural Blending			
Location	**Interacting Cultures**	**Reason for Interaction**	**Some Results of Interaction**
India—1000 B.C.	Aryan and Dravidian Indian Arab, African, Indian	Migration	Vedic culture, forerunner of Hinduism
East Africa—A.D. 700	Islamic, Christian	Trade, religious conversion	New trade language, Swahili
Russia—A.D. 1000	Christian and Slavic	Religious conversion	Eastern Christianity, Russian identity
Mexico—A.D. 1500	Spanish and Aztec	Conquest	Mestizo culture, Mexican Catholicism
United States—A.D. 1900	European, Asian, Caribbean	Migration, religious freedom	Cultural diversity

SKILLBUILDER: Interpreting Charts
1. **Determining Main Ideas** *What are the reasons for interaction in the Americas?*
2. **Hypothesizing** *What are some aspects of cultural diversity?*

These changes often reflect unique aspects of several cultures. For example:

- **Language** Sometimes the written characters of one language are used in another, as in the case of written Chinese characters used in the Japanese language. In the Safavid Empire, the language spoken was Persian. But after the area converted to Islam, a significant number of Arabic words appeared in the Persian language.
- **Religion and ethical systems** Buddhism spread throughout Asia. Yet the Buddhism practiced by Tibetans is different from Japanese Zen Buddhism.
- **Styles of government** The concept of a democratic government spread to many areas of the globe. Although the basic principles are similar, it is not practiced exactly the same way in each country.
- **Racial or ethnic blending** One example is the mestizo, people of mixed European and Indian ancestry who live in Mexico.
- **Arts and architecture** Cultural styles may be incorporated or adapted into art or architecture. For example, Chinese artistic elements are found in Safavid Empire tiles and carpets as well as in European paintings.

The chart above shows other examples of cultural blending that have occurred over time in various areas of the world. (A)

MAIN IDEA
Recognizing Effects
(A) Which of the effects of cultural blending do you think is the most significant? Explain.

CASE STUDY: The Safavid Empire

The Safavids Build an Empire

Conquest and ongoing cultural interaction fueled the development of the Safavid Empire. Originally, the Safavids were members of an Islamic religious brotherhood named after their founder, Safi al-Din. In the 15th century, the Safavids aligned themselves with the Shi'a branch of Islam.

The Safavids were also squeezed geographically between the Ottomans and Uzbek tribespeople and the Mughal Empire. (See the map on page 514.) To protect themselves from these potential enemies, the Safavids concentrated on building a powerful army.

Isma'il Conquers Persia The Safavid military became a force to reckon with. In 1499, a 12-year-old named **Isma'il** (ihs•MAH•eel) began to seize most of what is now Iran. Two years later he completed the task.

▼ Grandson of Isma'il, Shah Abbas led the Safavid Empire during its Golden Age.

GEOGRAPHY SKILLBUILDER: Interpreting Maps

1. **Movement** *What waterways might have enabled the Safavids to interact with other cultures?*
2. **Location** *Why might the Safavids not have expanded further?*

To celebrate his achievement, he took the ancient Persian title of **shah**, or king. He also established Shi'a Islam as the state religion.

Isma'il became a religious tyrant. Any citizen who did not convert to Shi'ism was put to death. Isma'il destroyed the Sunni population of Baghdad in his confrontation with the Ottomans. Their leader, Selim the Grim, later ordered the execution of all Shi'a in the Ottoman Empire. As many as 40,000 died. Their final face-off took place at the Battle of Chaldiran in 1514. Using artillery, the Ottomans pounded the Safavids into defeat. Another outcome of the battle was to set the border between the two empires. It remains the border today between Iran and Iraq.

Isma'il's son Tahmasp learned from the Safavids' defeat at Chaldiran. He adopted the use of artillery with his military forces. He expanded the Safavid Empire up to the Caucasus Mountains, northeast of Turkey, and brought Christians under Safavid rule. Tahmasp laid the groundwork for the golden age of the Safavids. **B**

MAIN IDEA

Drawing Conclusions

B How did Tahmasp's cultural borrowing lead to the expansion of the Safavid Empire?

A Safavid Golden Age

Shah Abbas, or Abbas the Great, took the throne in 1587. He helped create a Safavid culture and golden age that drew from the best of the Ottoman, Persian, and Arab worlds.

Reforms Shah Abbas reformed aspects of both military and civilian life. He limited the power of the military and created two new armies that would be loyal to him alone. One of these was an army of Persians. The other was a force that Abbas recruited from the Christian north and modeled after the Ottoman janissaries. He equipped both of these armies with modern artillery.

Abbas also reformed his government. He punished corruption severely and promoted only officials who proved their competence and loyalty. He hired foreigners from neighboring countries to fill positions in the government.

To convince European merchants that his empire was tolerant of other religions, Abbas brought members of Christian religious orders into the empire. As a result, Europeans moved into the land. Then industry, trade, and art exchanges grew between the empire and European nations.

A New Capital The Shah built a new capital at **Esfahan**. With a design that covered four and a half miles, the city was considered one of the most beautiful in the world. It was a showplace for the many artisans, both foreign and Safavid, who worked on the buildings and the objects in them. For example, 300 Chinese potters produced glazed building tiles for the buildings in the city, and Armenians wove carpets.

Art Works Shah Abbas brought hundreds of Chinese artisans to Esfahan. Working with Safavid artists, they produced intricate metalwork, miniature paintings, calligraphy, glasswork, tile work, and pottery. This collaboration gave rise to artwork that blended Chinese and Persian ideas. These decorations beautified the many mosques, palaces, and marketplaces.

Carpets The most important result of Western influence on the Safavids, however, may have been the demand for Persian carpets. This demand helped change carpet weaving from a local craft to a national industry. In the beginning, the carpets reflected traditional Persian themes. As the empire became more culturally blended, the designs incorporated new themes. In the 16th century, Shah Abbas sent artists to Italy to study under the Renaissance artist Raphael. Rugs then began to reflect European designs. C

▲ The Masjid-e-Imam mosque in Esfahan is a beautiful example of the flowering of the arts in the Safavid Empire.

MAIN IDEA

Comparing

C In what ways were Shah Abbas and Suleyman the Lawgiver similar?

The Dynasty Declines Quickly

In finding a successor, Shah Abbas made the same mistake the Ottoman monarch Suleyman made. He killed or blinded his ablest sons. His incompetent grandson, Safi, succeeded Abbas. This pampered young prince led the Safavids down the same road to decline that the Ottomans had taken, only more quickly.

In 1736, however, Nadir Shah Afshar conquered land all the way to India and created an expanded empire. But Nadir Shah was so cruel that one of his own troops assassinated him. With Nadir Shah's death in 1747, the Safavid Empire fell apart.

At the same time that the Safavids flourished, cultural blending and conquest led to the growth of a new empire in India, as you will learn in Section 3.

NEW YORK CORE CURRICULUM REVIEW

TERMS & NAMES 1. For each term or name, write a sentence explaining its significance.

- Safavid
- Isma'il
- shah
- Shah Abbas
- Esfahan

USING YOUR NOTES

2. What are some examples of cultural blending in the Safavid Empire?

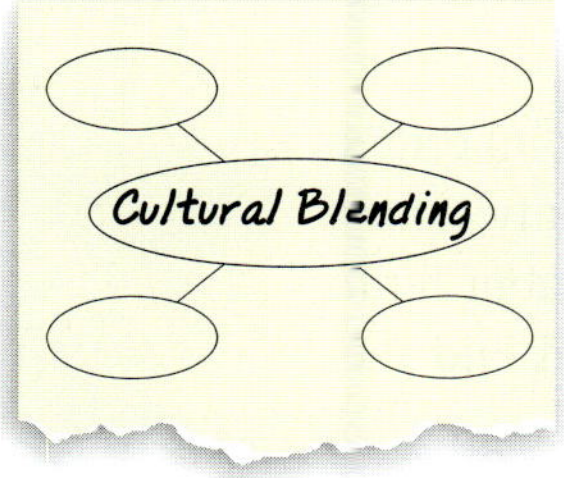

MAIN IDEAS

3. What are the four causes of cultural blending?
4. What reforms took place in the Safavid Empire under Shah Abbas?
5. Why did the Safavid Empire decline so quickly?

CRITICAL THINKING & WRITING

6. **FORMING OPINIONS** Which of the results of cultural blending do you think has the most lasting effect on a country? Explain.
7. **DRAWING CONCLUSIONS** How did the location of the Safavid Empire contribute to the cultural blending in the empire?
8. **ANALYZING MOTIVES** Why might Isma'il have become so intolerant of the Sunni Muslims?
9. **WRITING ACTIVITY** CULTURAL INTERACTION Write a **letter** from Shah Abbas to a Chinese artist persuading him to come teach and work in the Safavid Empire.

INTEGRATED TECHNOLOGY **INTERNET ACTIVITY**

Use the Internet to research the charge that Persian rugs are largely made by children under the age of 14. Write a television documentary **script** detailing your research results.

INTERNET KEYWORD
child labor rug making

The Mughal Empire in India

CONNECT TO THE NEW YORK STATE CORE CURRICULUM

Unit 2.E.1. Human and physical geography
Unit 4.F.4. Case studies: Akbar the Great, Suleyman the Magnificent, Philip II, Louis XIV, Ivan the Terrible, and Peter the Great

TERMS & NAMES

- Mughal
- Babur
- Akbar
- Sikh
- Shah Jahan
- Taj Mahal
- Aurangzeb

SETTING THE STAGE The Gupta Empire, which you read about in Chapter 7, crumbled in the late 400s. First, Huns from Central Asia invaded. Then, beginning in the 700's, warlike Muslim tribes from Central Asia carved northwestern India into many small kingdoms. The people who invaded descended from Muslim Turks and Afghans. Their leader was a descendant of Timur the Lame and of the Mongol conqueror Genghis Khan. They called themselves **Mughals**, which means "Mongols." The land they invaded had been through a long period of turmoil.

TAKING NOTES
Following Chronological Order Create a time line of the Mughal emperors and their successes.

1494
Babur

Early History of the Mughals

The 8th century began with a long clash between Hindus and Muslims in this land of many kingdoms. For almost 300 years, the Muslims were able to advance only as far as the Indus River valley. Starting around the year 1000, however, well-trained Turkish armies swept into India. Led by Sultan Mahmud (muh•MOOD) of Ghazni, they devastated Indian cities and temples in 17 brutal campaigns. These attacks left the region weakened and vulnerable to other conquerors. Delhi eventually became the capital of a loose empire of Turkish warlords called the Delhi Sultanate. These sultans treated the Hindus as conquered people.

Delhi Sultanate Between the 13th and 16th centuries, 33 different sultans ruled this divided territory from their seat in Delhi. In 1398, Timur the Lame destroyed Delhi. The city was so completely devastated that according to one witness, "for months, not a bird moved in the city." Delhi eventually was rebuilt. But it was not until the 16th century that a leader arose who would unify the empire.

Babur Founds an Empire In 1494, an 11-year-old boy named **Babur** inherited a kingdom in the area that is now Uzbekistan and Tajikistan. It was only a tiny kingdom, and his elders soon took it away and drove him south. But Babur built up an army. In the years that followed, he swept down into India and laid the foundation for the vast Mughal Empire.

Babur was a brilliant general. In 1526, for example, he led 12,000 troops to victory against an army of 100,000 commanded by a sultan of Delhi. A year later, Babur also defeated a massive rajput army. After Babur's death, his incompetent son, Humayun, lost most of the territory Babur had gained. Babur's 13-year-old grandson took over the throne after Humayun's death.

Akbar's Golden Age

Babur's grandson was called **Akbar**, which means "Great." Akbar certainly lived up to his name, ruling India with wisdom and tolerance from 1556 to 1605.

A Military Conqueror Akbar recognized military power as the root of his strength. In his opinion, a King must always be aggresive so that his neighbors will not try to conquer him.

Like the Safavids and the Ottomans, Akbar equipped his armies with heavy artillery. Cannons enabled him to break into walled cities and extend his rule into much of the Deccan plateau. In a brilliant move, he appointed some rajputs as officers. In this way he turned potential enemies into allies. This combination of military power and political wisdom enabled Akbar to unify a land of at least 100 million people—more than in all of Europe put together.

GEOGRAPHY SKILLBUILDER: Interpreting Maps

1. **Movement** *During which time period was the most territory added to the Mughal Empire?*
2. **Human-Environment Interaction** *What landform might have prevented the empire from expanding farther east?*

A Liberal Ruler Akbar was a genius at cultural blending. A Muslim, he continued the Islamic tradition of religious freedom. He permitted people of other religions to practice their faiths. He proved his tolerance by marrying Hindu princesses without forcing them to convert. He allowed his wives to practice their religious rituals in the palace. He proved his tolerance again by abolishing both the tax on Hindu pilgrims and the hated *jizya*, or tax on non-Muslims. He even appointed a Spanish Jesuit to tutor his second son.

Akbar governed through a bureaucracy of officials. Natives and foreigners, Hindus and Muslims, could all rise to high office. This approach contributed to the quality of his government. Akbar's chief finance minister, Todar Mal, a Hindu, created a clever—and effective—taxation policy. He levied a tax similar to the present-day U.S. graduated income tax, calculating it as a percentage of the value of the peasants' crops. Because this tax was fair and affordable, the number of peasants who paid it increased. This payment brought in much needed money for the empire. (A)

MAIN IDEA

Comparing

(A) In what ways were Akbar's attitudes toward religion similar to those of Suleyman the Lawgiver?

Akbar's land policies had more mixed results. He gave generous land grants to his bureaucrats. After they died, however, he reclaimed the lands and distributed them as he saw fit. On the positive side, this policy prevented the growth of feudal aristocracies. On the other hand, it did not encourage dedication and hard work by the Mughal officials. Their children would not inherit the land or benefit from their parents' work. So the officials apparently saw no point in devoting themselves to their property.

History Makers

Akbar
1542–1605

Akbar was brilliant and curious, especially about religion. He even invented a religion of his own—the "Divine Faith"—after learning about Hinduism, Jainism, Christianity, and Sufism. The religion attracted few followers, however, and offended Muslims so much that they attempted a brief revolt against Akbar in 1581. When he died, so did the "Divine Faith."

Surprisingly, despite his wisdom and his achievements, Akbar could not read. He hired others to read to him from his library of 24,000 books.

INTEGRATED TECHNOLOGY

RESEARCH LINKS For more on Akbar, go to **classzone.com**

Blended Cultures As Akbar extended the Mughal Empire, he welcomed influences from the many cultures in the empire. This cultural blending affected art, education, politics, and language. Persian was the language of Akbar's court and of high culture. The common people, however, spoke Hindi, a language derived from Sanskrit. Hindi remains one of the most widely spoken languages in India today. Out of the Mughal armies, where soldiers of many backgrounds rubbed shoulders, came yet another new language. This language was Urdu, which means "from the soldier's camp." A blend of Arabic, Persian, and Hindi, Urdu is today the official language of Pakistan.

The Arts and Literature The arts flourished at the Mughal court, especially in the form of book illustrations. These small, highly detailed, and colorful paintings were called miniatures. They were brought to a peak of perfection in the Safavid Empire. (See Section 2.) Babur's son, Humayun, brought two masters of this art to his court to teach it to the Mughals. Some of the most famous Mughal miniatures adorned the *Akbarnamah* ("Book of Akbar"), the story of the great emperor's campaigns and deeds. Indian art drew from traditions developed earlier in Rajput kingdoms.

Hindu literature also enjoyed a revival in Akbar's time. The poet Tulsi Das, for example, was a contemporary of Akbar's. He retold the epic love story of Rama and Sita from the fourth century B.C. Indian poem the *Ramayana* (rah•MAH•yuh•nuh) in Hindi. This retelling, the *Ramcaritmanas,* is now even more popular than the original.

Architecture Akbar devoted himself to architecture too. The style developed under his reign is still known as Akbar period architecture. Its massive but graceful structures are decorated with intricate stonework that portrays Hindu themes. The capital city of Fatehpur Sikri is one of the most important examples of this type of architecture. Akbar had this red-sandstone city built to thank a Sufi saint, Sheik Salim Chisti, who had predicted the birth of his first son. **B**

MAIN IDEA

Drawing Conclusions

B How was Akbar able to build such an immense empire?

Akbar's Successors

With Akbar's death in 1605, the Mughal court changed to deal with the changing times. The next three emperors each left his mark on the Mughal Empire.

Jahangir and Nur Jahan Akbar's son called himself Jahangir (juh•hahn•GEER), or "Grasper of the World." However, for most of his reign, he left the affairs of state to his wife, who ruled with an iron hand.

Jahangir's wife was the Persian princess Nur Jahan. She was a brilliant politician who perfectly understood the use of power. As the real ruler of India, she installed her father as prime minister in the Mughal court. She saw Jahangir's son Khusrau as her ticket to future power. But when Khusrau rebelled against his father, Nur Jahan removed him. She then shifted her favor to another son.

This rejection of Khusrau affected more than the political future of the empire. It was also the basis of a long and bitter religious conflict. Jahangir tried to promote Islam in the Mughal state, but was tolerant of other religions. When Khusrau

Connect *to* Today

Women Leaders of the Indian Subcontinent

Since World War II, the subcontinent of India has seen the rise of several powerful women. Unlike Nur Jahan, however, they achieved power on their own—not through their husbands.

Indira Gandhi headed the Congress Party and dominated Indian politics for almost 30 years. She was elected prime minister in 1966 and again in 1980. Gandhi was assassinated in 1984 by Sikh separatists.

Benazir Bhutto took charge of the Pakistan People's Party after her father was executed by his political enemies. She won election as her country's prime minister in 1988, the first woman to run a modern Muslim state. She was reelected in 1993.

Chandrika Bandaranaike Kumaratunga is the president of Sri Lanka. She was elected in 1994 with 62 percent of the votes cast. She survived an assassination attempt in 1999 and was reelected.

Khaleda Zia became Bangladesh's first woman prime minister in 1991. She was reelected several times, the last time in 2001. She has made progress in empowering women and girls in her nation.

Indira Gandhi

Benazir Bhutto

Chandrika Bandaranaike Kumaratunga

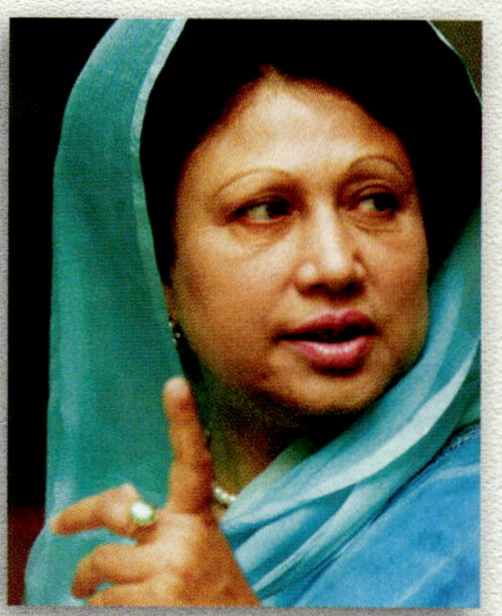
Khaleda Zia

MAIN IDEA
Analyzing Causes
C How did the Mughals' dislike of the Sikhs develop?

rebelled, he turned to the **Sikhs**. This was a nonviolent religious group whose doctrines contained elements similar to Hinduism and Sufism (Islamic mysticism). However, the Sikhs see themselves as an independent tradition and not an offshoot of another religion. Their leader, Guru Arjun, sheltered Khusrau and defended him. In response, the Mughal rulers had Arjun arrested and tortured to death. The Sikhs became the target of the Mughals' particular hatred. **C**

Shah Jahan Jahangir's son and successor, **Shah Jahan**, could not tolerate competition and secured his throne by assassinating all his possible rivals. He had a great passion for two things: beautiful buildings and his wife Mumtaz Mahal (moom•TAHZ mah•HAHL). Nur Jahan had arranged this marriage between Jahangir's son and her niece for political reasons. Shah Jahan, however, fell genuinely in love with his Persian princess.

In 1631, Mumtaz Mahal died at age 39 while giving birth to her 14th child. To enshrine his wife's memory, he ordered that a tomb be built "as beautiful as she was beautiful." Fine white marble and fabulous jewels were gathered from many parts of Asia. This memorial, the **Taj Mahal**, has been called one of the most beautiful buildings in the world. Its towering marble dome and slender minaret towers look like lace and seem to change color as the sun moves across the sky.

The People Suffer But while Shah Jahan was building gardens, monuments, and forts, his country was suffering. There was famine in the land. Furthermore, farmers needed tools, roads, and ways of irrigating their crops and dealing with India's harsh environment. What they got instead were taxes and more taxes to support the building of monuments, their rulers' extravagant living, and war.

▲ Mirrored in a reflecting pool is the Taj Mahal, a monument to love and the Mughal Empire.

History *in* Depth

Building the Taj Mahal

Some 20,000 workers labored for 22 years to build the famous tomb. It is made of white marble brought from 250 miles away. The minaret towers are about 130 feet high. The building itself is 186 feet square.

The design of the building is a blend of Hindu and Muslim styles. The pointed arches are of Muslim design, and the perforated marble windows and doors are typical of a style found in Hindu temples.

The inside of the building is a glittering garden of thousands of carved marble flowers inlaid with tiny precious stones. One tiny flower, one inch square, had 60 different inlays.

INTEGRATED TECHNOLOGY

INTERNET ACTIVITY Use the Internet to take a virtual trip to the Taj Mahal. Create a brochure about the building. Go to **classzone.com** for your research.

All was not well in the royal court either. When Shah Jahan became ill in 1657, his four sons scrambled for the throne. The third son, **Aurangzeb** (AWR•uhng•zehb), moved first and most decisively. In a bitter civil war, he executed his older brother, who was his most serious rival. Then he arrested his father and put him in prison, where he died several years later. After Shah Jahan's death, a mirror was found in his room, angled so that he could look out at the reflection of the Taj Mahal.

Aurangzeb's Reign A master at military strategy and an aggressive empire builder, Aurangzeb ruled from 1658 to 1707. He expanded the Mughal holdings to their greatest size. However, the power of the empire weakened during his reign.

This loss of power was due largely to Aurangzeb's oppression of the people. He rigidly enforced Islamic laws, outlawing drinking, gambling, and other activities viewed as vices. He appointed censors to police his subjects' morals and make sure they prayed at the appointed times. He also tried to erase all the gains Hindus had made under Akbar. For example, he brought back the hated tax on non-Muslims and dismissed Hindus from high positions in his government. He banned the construction of new temples and had Hindu monuments destroyed. Not surprisingly, these actions outraged the Hindus.

The Hindu rajputs, whom Akbar had converted from potential enemies to allies, rebelled. Aurangzeb defeated them repeatedly, but never completely. In the southwest, a Hindu warrior community called Marathas founded their own state. Aurangzeb captured their leader but could never conquer them. Meanwhile, the Sikhs transformed themselves into a brotherhood of warriors. They began building a state in the Punjab, an area in northwest India.

Aurangzeb levied oppressive taxes to pay for the wars against the increasing numbers of enemies. He had done away with all taxes not authorized by Islamic law, so he doubled the taxes on Hindu merchants. This increased tax burden deepened the Hindus' bitterness and led to further rebellion. As a result, Aurangzeb needed to raise more money to increase his army. The more territory he conquered, the more desperate his situation became. **D**

> **MAIN IDEA**
> **Recognizing Effects**
> **D** How did Aurangzeb's personal qualities and political policies affect the Mughal Empire?

The Empire's Decline and Decay

By the end of Aurangzeb's reign, he had drained the empire of its resources. Over 2 million people died in a famine while Aurangzeb was away waging war. Most of his subjects felt little or no loyalty to him.

As the power of the central state weakened, the power of local lords grew. After Aurangzeb's death, his sons fought a war of succession. In fact, three emperors reigned in the first 12 years after Aurangzeb died. By the end of this period, the Mughal emperor was nothing but a wealthy figurehead. He ruled not a united empire but a patchwork of independent states.

As the Mughal Empire rose and fell, Western traders slowly built their own power in the region. The Portuguese were the first Europeans to reach India. In fact, they arrived just before Babur did. Next came the Dutch, who in turn gave way to the French and the English. However, the great Mughal emperors did not feel threatened by the European traders. In 1661, Aurangzeb casually handed them the port of Bombay. Aurangzeb had no idea that he had given India's next conquerors their first foothold in a future empire.

NEW YORK CORE CURRICULUM REVIEW

TERMS & NAMES 1. For each term or name, write a sentence explaining its significance.

• Mughal • Babur • Akbar • Sikh • Shah Jahan • Taj Mahal • Aurangzeb

USING YOUR NOTES

2. Which of the Mughal emperors on your time line had a positive effect on the empire? Which had negative effects?

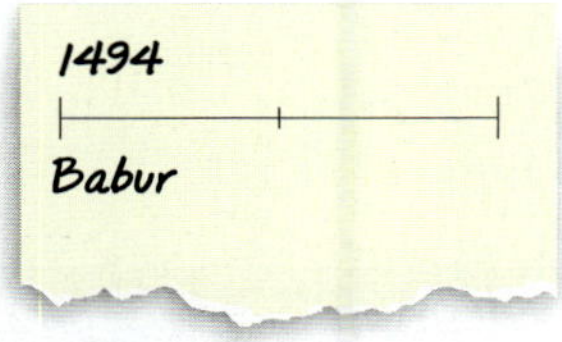

MAIN IDEAS

3. How did Akbar demonstrate tolerance in his empire?
4. What pattern is seen in the ways individuals came to power in the Mughal Empire?
5. Why did the empire weaken under the rule of Aurangzeb?

CRITICAL THINKING & WRITING

6. **CLARIFYING** Why were Akbar's tax policies so successful?
7. **MAKING INFERENCES** Why was Nur Jahan able to hold so much power in Jahangir's court?
8. **EVALUATING COURSES OF ACTION** Why were the policies of Aurangzeb so destructive to the Mughal Empire?
9. **WRITING ACTIVITY** POWER AND AUTHORITY Write a **compare-and-contrast essay** on the policies of Akbar and Aurangzeb. Use references from the text in your response.

CONNECT TO TODAY **CREATING A BIOGRAPHY**

Select one of the women leaders in Connect to Today on page 519. Research her life and write a short **biography** of her.

Cultural Blending in Mughal India

As you have read, Mughal India enjoyed a golden age under Akbar. Part of Akbar's success—indeed, the success of the Mughals—came from his religious tolerance. India's population was largely Hindu, and the incoming Mughal rulers were Muslim. The Mughal emperors encouraged the blending of cultures to create a united India.

This cultural integration can be seen in the art of Mughal India. Muslim artists focused heavily on art with ornate patterns of flowers and leaves, called arabesque or geometric patterns. Hindu artists created naturalistic and often ornate artworks. These two artistic traditions came together and created a style unique to Mughal India. As you can see, the artistic collaboration covered a wide range of art forms.

INTEGRATED TECHNOLOGY

RESEARCH LINKS For more on art in Mughal India, go to **classzone.com**

▼ Decorative Arts

Decorative work on items from dagger handles to pottery exhibits the same cultural blending as other Mughal art forms. This dagger handle shows some of the floral and geometric elements common in Muslim art, but the realistic depiction of the horse comes out of the Hindu tradition.

▼ Architecture

Mughal emperors brought to India a strong Muslim architectural tradition. Indian artisans were extremely talented with local building materials—specifically, marble and sandstone. Together, they created some of the most striking and enduring architecture in the world, like Humayun's Tomb shown here.

▼ Painting

Mughal painting was largely a product of the royal court. Persian artists brought to court by Mughal emperors had a strong influence, but Mughal artists quickly developed their own characteristics. The Mughal style kept aspects of the Persian influence—particularly the flat aerial perspective. But, as seen in this colorful painting, the Indian artists incorporated more naturalism and detail from the world around them.

▲ Fabrics

Mughal fabrics included geometric patterns found in Persian designs, but Mughal weavers, like other Mughal artisans, also produced original designs. Themes that were common in Mughal fabrics were landscapes, animal chases, floral latticeworks, and central flowering plants like the one on this tent hanging.

Connect *to* Today

1. **Clarifying** What does the art suggest about the culture of Mughal India?
   See Skillbuilder Handbook, page R4.

2. **Forming and Supporting Opinions** What are some modern examples of cultural blending in art? What elements of each culture are represented in the artwork? Consider other art forms, such as music and literature, as well.

Chapter 18 Assessment

TERMS & NAMES

Briefly explain the importance of each of the following to the Ottoman, Safavid, or Mughal empires.

1. Suleyman the Lawgiver
2. *devshirme*
3. janissary
4. shah
5. Shah Abbas
6. Akbar
7. Sikh
8. Taj Mahal

MAIN IDEAS

The Ottomans Build a Vast Empire
Section 1 (pages 507–511)

9. Why were the Ottomans such successful conquerors?
10. How did Mehmed the Conqueror show his tolerance of other cultures?
11. Why was Selim's capture of Mecca, Medina, and Cairo so significant?

Case Study: Cultural Blending Section 2 (pages 512–515)

12. What are some of the causes of cultural blending in the Safavid Empire?
13. In what ways did the Safavids weave foreign ideas into their culture?

The Mughal Empire in India Section 3 (pages 516–523)

14. In what ways did Akbar defend religious freedom during his reign?
15. How did Akbar's successors promote religious conflict in the empire?

CRITICAL THINKING

1. USING YOUR NOTES
In a chart, compare and contrast the Mughal Empire under Akbar, the Safavid Empire under Shah Abbas, and the Ottoman Empire under Suleyman I.

	Government Reforms	Cultural Blending
Akbar		
Abbas		
Suleyman		

2. EVALUATING COURSES OF ACTION
POWER AND AUTHORITY How did the use of artillery change the way empires in this chapter and lands that bordered them reacted to each other?

3. RECOGNIZING EFFECTS
CULTURAL INTERACTION What impact did religion have on governing each of the three empires in this chapter?

4. EVALUATING DECISIONS
EMPIRE BUILDING What was the value of treating conquered peoples in a way that did not oppress them?

5. MAKING INFERENCES
Why do you think the three empires in this chapter did not unite into one huge empire? Give reasons for your answer.

6. MAKING INFERENCES
Conquest of new territories contributed to the growth of the Muslim empires you read about in this chapter. How might it have also hindered this growth?

VISUAL SUMMARY

The Muslim World Expands

Muslims control Middle East, India, North Africa, and parts of Europe.

Ottoman Empire
- Move into Byzantium
- Take Constantinople
- Add Syria and Palestine
- Use janissaries and *devshirme* to control the empire

Safavid Empire
- Take old Persian Empire
- Expand to Caucasus Mountains
- Build a new capital
- Use janissary-style army to control the empire

Mughal Empire
- Delhi Sultanate loosely controls Indian subcontinent
- Babur lays groundwork for an empire
- Akbar controls most of subcontinent in empire
- Aurangzeb expands empire to its largest size

Use the graphs and your knowledge of world history to answer questions 1 and 2.

Additional Test Practice, pp. S1–S33

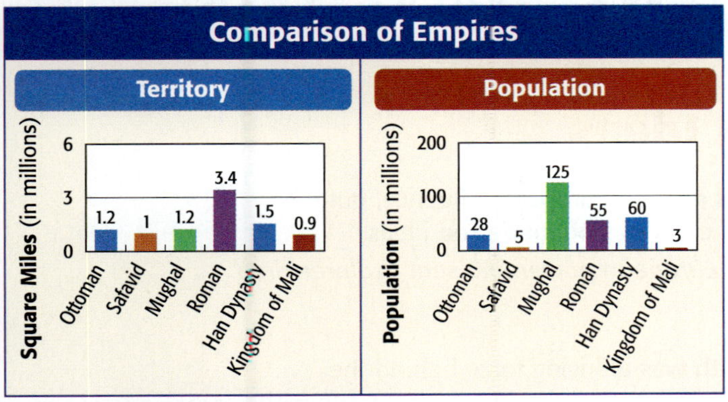

Source: Atlas of World Population History

1 Which empire was most densely populated?

(1) Han
(2) Roman
(3) Mughal
(4) Mali

2 Of the three Asian Muslim empires shown on the graph, which one had the smallest territory?

(1) Ottoman
(2) Safavid
(3) Mughal
(4) Mali

Use the quotation from Kritovoulos, a Greek historian and a governor in the court of Mehmed II, and your knowledge of world history to answer question 3.

PRIMARY SOURCE

When the Sultan [Mehmed] had captured the City of Constantinople, almost his very first care was to have the City repopulated. He also undertook the further care and repairs of it. He sent an order in the form of an imperial command to every part of his realm, that as many inhabitants as possible be transferred to the City, not only Christians but also his own people and many of the Hebrews.

KRITOVOULOS, *History of Mehmed the Conqueror*

3 What groups of people were to be sent to Constantinople?

(1) Hebrews and Christians
(2) Christians and Turks
(3) Christians, Hebrews, and Turkish Muslims
(4) Imperial armies

INTEGRATED TECHNOLOGY

TEST PRACTICE Go to **classzone.com**

- Diagnostic tests
- Strategies
- Tutorials
- Additional practice

ALTERNATIVE ASSESSMENT

1. Interact *with* History

On page 506, you considered how you might treat the people you conquered. Now that you have learned more about three Muslim empires, in what ways do you think you would change your policies? Discuss your thoughts with a small group of classmates.

2. WRITING ABOUT HISTORY

Think about the experience of being a janissary in the court of Suleyman the Lawgiver. Write a **journal entry** about your daily activities. Consider the following:

- how a janissary was recruited
- what jobs or activities a janissary may have done
- the grandeur of the court of Suleyman

INTEGRATED TECHNOLOGY

Creating a Database

The three empires discussed in this chapter governed many religious and ethnic groups. Gather information on the religious and ethnic makeup of the modern nations of the former Ottoman, Safavid, and Mughal empires. Organize the information in a population database.

- Create one table for each empire.
- Make row headings for each modern nation occupying the lands of that empire.
- Make column headings for each ethnic group and each religious group.
- Insert the most recent population figures or percentages for each group.
- Use the final column to record the population total for each modern nation.

CHAPTER 19

An Age of Explorations and Isolation, 1400–1800

Previewing Main Ideas

CULTURAL INTERACTION Asians resisted European influence, but this cultural interaction did produce an exchange of goods and ideas.

Geography *Study the map. What European power first sent explorers into the Indian Ocean?*

ECONOMICS The desire for wealth was a driving force behind the European exploration of the East. Europeans wanted to control trade with Asian countries.

Geography *How did the voyages of Bartolomeu Dias and Vasco da Gama compare in length?*

SCIENCE AND TECHNOLOGY Europeans were able to explore faraway lands after they improved their sailing technology.

Geography *Look at the map and time line. What country sent the first expedition to explore the Indian Ocean in the 15th century?*

NEW YORK CORE CURRICULUM FOCUS

- A desire for new sources of wealth led Europeans to seek new trade routes to Asia.
- During the Ming Dynasty, Chinese admiral Zheng He led voyages to distant lands to show Chinese superiority.

INTEGRATED TECHNOLOGY

eEdition
- Interactive Maps
- Interactive Visuals
- Interactive Primary Sources

INTERNET RESOURCES
Go to **classzone.com** for:
- Research Links
- Internet Activities
- Primary Sources
- Chapter Quiz
- Maps
- Test Practice
- Current Events

EUROPE AND ASIA

1405 Zheng He takes first voyage.

1419 Prince Henry ▶ founds navigation school.

1494 Spain and Portugal sign Treaty of Tordesillas.

1400 **1500**

WORLD

1453 ◀ Ottomans capture Constantinople.

1464 Songhai Empire begins in West Africa.

1511 First enslaved Africans arrive in the Americas.

1603
Tokugawa shoguns rule Japan.

1619
Dutch open trade with Java.

1644
Manchus establish Qing Dynasty in China.

1793
Britain seeks to trade with China.

1600 1700 1800

1608
◀ Samuel de Champlain founds Quebec. (French flag)

1776
◀ American colonies declare independence from Britain. (George Washington)

Interact *with* History

Would you sail into the unknown?

It is a gray morning in 1430. You are standing on a dock in the European country of Portugal, staring out at the mysterious Atlantic Ocean. You have been asked to go on a voyage of exploration. Yet, like most people at the time, you have no idea what lies beyond the horizon. The maps that have been drawn show some of the dangers you might face. And you've heard the terrifying stories of sea monsters and shipwrecks (see map below). You also have heard that riches await those who help explore and claim new lands. Now, you must decide whether to go.

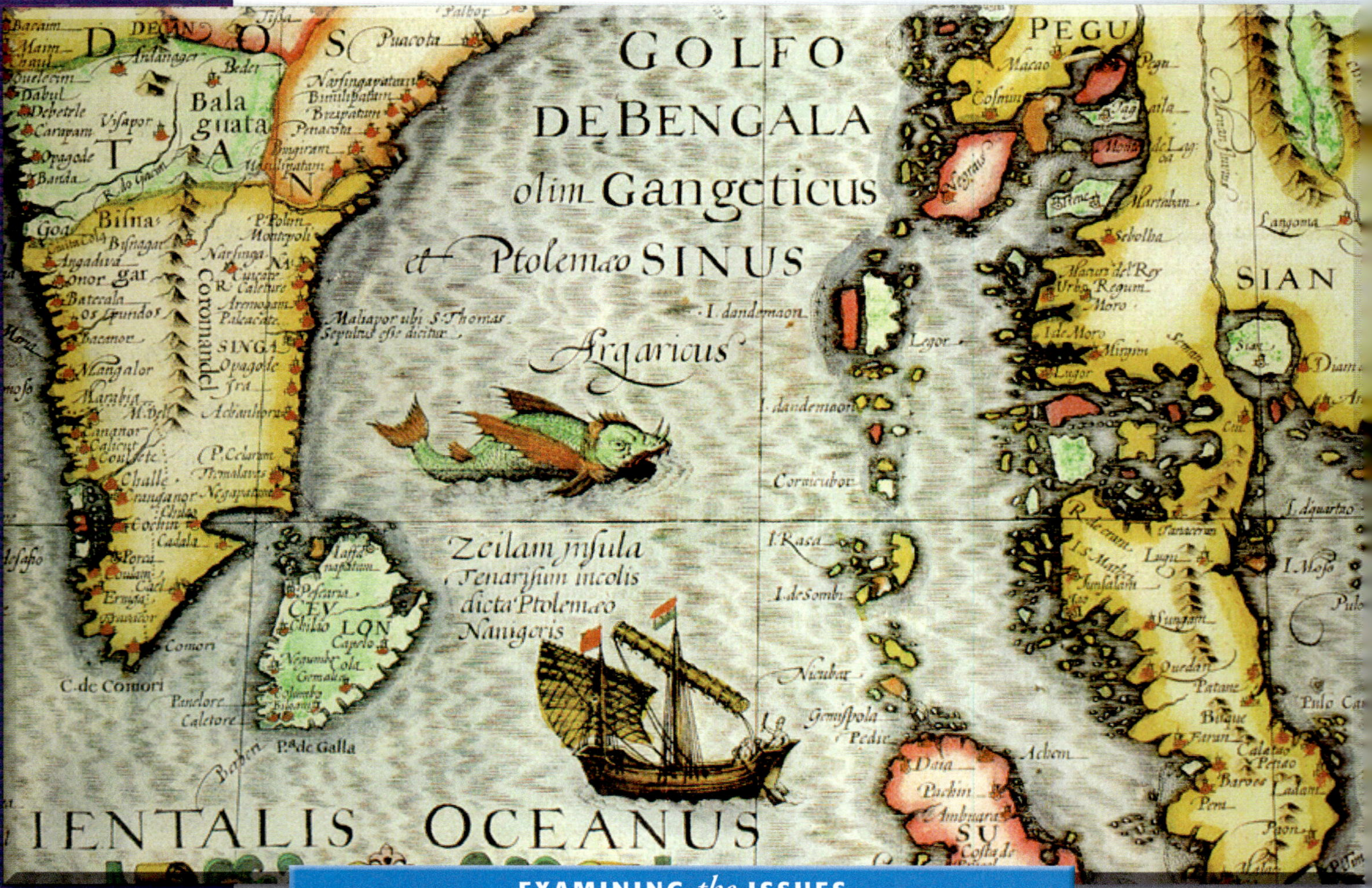

EXAMINING *the* ISSUES

- **What possible rewards might come from exploring the seas for new lands?**
- **What are the risks involved in embarking on a voyage into the unknown?**

Discuss these questions with your classmates. In your discussion, recall what you have learned about the lands beyond Europe and what they have to offer. As you read about the age of explorations and isolation, see why Europeans explored and what they achieved.

Europeans Explore the East

CONNECT TO THE NEW YORK STATE CORE CURRICULUM

Unit 3.F.7. New scientific and technological innovations (Gutenberg's moveable type printing press, cartography, naval engineering, and navigational and nautical devices)
Unit 4.C.1. Human and physical geography

TERMS & NAMES

- Bartolomeu Dias
- Prince Henry
- Vasco da Gama
- Treaty of Tordesillas
- Dutch East India Company

SETTING THE STAGE By the early 1400s, Europeans were ready to venture beyond their borders. As Chapter 17 explained, the Renaissance encouraged, among other things, a new spirit of adventure and curiosity. This spirit of adventure, along with several other important reasons, prompted Europeans to explore the world around them. This chapter and the next one describe how these explorations began a long process that would bring together the peoples of many different lands and permanently change the world.

TAKING NOTES

Following Chronological Order On a time line, note the important events in the European exploration of the East.

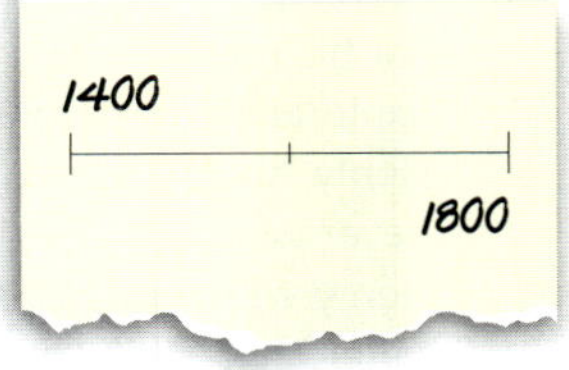

For "God, Glory, and Gold"

Europeans had not been completely isolated from the rest of the world before the 1400s. Beginning around 1100, European crusaders battled Muslims for control of the Holy Lands in Southwest Asia. In 1275, the Italian trader Marco Polo reached the court of Kublai Khan in China. For the most part, however, Europeans had neither the interest nor the ability to explore foreign lands. That changed by the early 1400s. The desire to grow rich and to spread Christianity, coupled with advances in sailing technology, spurred an age of European exploration.

Europeans Seek New Trade Routes The desire for new sources of wealth was the main reason for European exploration. Through overseas exploration, merchants and traders hoped ultimately to benefit from what had become a profitable business in Europe: the trade of spices and other luxury goods from Asia. The people of Europe had been introduced to these items during the Crusades, the wars fought between Christians and Muslims from 1096 to 1270 (see Chapter 14). After the Crusades ended, Europeans continued to demand such spices as nutmeg, ginger, cinnamon, and pepper, all of which added flavor to the bland foods of Europe. Because demand for these goods was greater than the supply, merchants could charge high prices and thus make great profits.

The Muslims and the Italians controlled the trade of goods from East to West. Muslims sold Asian goods to Italian merchants, who controlled trade across the land routes of the Mediterranean region. The Italian merchants resold the items at increased prices to merchants

▼ This early globe depicts the Europeans' view of Europe and Africa around 1492.

throughout Europe. Other European traders did not like this arrangement. Paying such high prices to the Italians severely cut into their own profits. By the 1400s, European merchants—as well as the new monarchs of England, Spain, Portugal, and France—sought to bypass the Italian merchants. This meant finding a sea route directly to Asia.

The Spread of Christianity The desire to spread Christianity also motivated Europeans to explore. The Crusades had left Europeans with a taste for spices, but more significantly with feelings of hostility between Christians and Muslims. European countries believed that they had a sacred duty not only to continue fighting Muslims, but also to convert non-Christians throughout the world.

Europeans hoped to obtain popular goods directly from the peoples of Asia. They also hoped to Christianize them. **Bartolomeu Dias**, an early Portuguese explorer, explained his motives: "To serve God and His Majesty, to give light to those who were in darkness and to grow rich as all men desire to do." (A)

MAIN IDEA

Summarizing

(A) How might the phrase "God, glory, and gold" summarize the Europeans' motives for exploration?

Technology Makes Exploration Possible While "God, glory, and gold" were the primary motives for exploration, advances in technology made the voyages of discovery possible. During the 1200s, it would have been nearly impossible for a European sea captain to cross 3,000 miles of ocean and return again. The main problem was that European ships could not sail against the wind. In the 1400s, shipbuilders designed a new vessel, the caravel. The caravel was sturdier than earlier vessels. In addition, triangular sails adopted from the Arabs allowed it to sail effectively against the wind.

Europeans also improved their navigational techniques. To better determine their location at sea, sailors used the astrolabe, which the Muslims had perfected. The astrolabe was a brass circle with carefully adjusted rings marked off in degrees. Using the rings to sight the stars, a sea captain could calculate latitude, or how far north or south of the equator the ship was. Explorers were also able to more accurately track direction by using a magnetic compass, a Chinese invention.

History Makers

Prince Henry
1394–1460

For his role in promoting Portuguese exploration, historians call Prince Henry "the Navigator." Although he never went on voyages of discovery, Henry was consumed by the quest to find new lands and to spread Christianity. A devout Catholic, he wanted "to make increase in the faith of our lord Jesus Christ and bring to him all the souls that should be saved."

To that end, Henry used his own fortune to organize more than 14 voyages along the western coast of Africa, which was previously unexplored by Europeans. As a result, Henry died in debt. The Portuguese crown spent more than 60 years paying off his debts.

INTEGRATED TECHNOLOGY

RESEARCH LINKS For more on Prince Henry, go to **classzone.com**

Portugal Leads the Way

The leader in developing and applying these sailing innovations was Portugal. Located on the Atlantic Ocean at the southwest corner of Europe, Portugal was the first European country to establish trading outposts along the west coast of Africa. Eventually, Portuguese explorers pushed farther east into the Indian Ocean.

The Portuguese Explore Africa Portugal took the lead in overseas exploration in part due to strong government support. The nation's most enthusiastic supporter of exploration was **Prince Henry**, the son of Portugal's king. Henry's dreams of overseas exploration began in 1415 when he helped conquer the Muslim city of Ceuta in North Africa. There, he had his first glimpse of the dazzling wealth that lay beyond Europe. In Ceuta, the Portuguese invaders found exotic stores filled with pepper, cinnamon, cloves, and other spices. In addition, they encountered large supplies of gold, silver, and jewels.

INTERACTIVE

The Tools of Exploration

Out on the open seas, winds easily blew ships off course. With only the sun, moon, and stars to guide them, few sailors willingly ventured beyond the sight of land. In order to travel to distant places, European inventors and sailors experimented with new tools for navigation and new designs for sailing ships, often borrowing from other cultures.

INTEGRATED TECHNOLOGY

RESEARCH LINKS For more on the tools of exploration, go to **classzone.com**

▲ Here, a French mariner uses an early navigation instrument that he has brought ashore to fix his ship's position. It was difficult to make accurate calculations aboard wave-tossed vessels.

1. The average caravel was 65 feet long. This versatile ship had triangular sails for maneuverability and square sails for power.
2. The large cargo area could hold the numerous supplies needed for long voyages.
3. Its shallow draft (depth of the ship's keel below the water) allowed it to explore close to the shore.

▲ This 17th-century compass is typical of those taken by navigators on voyages of exploration. The compass was invented by the Chinese.

◀ The sextant replaced the astrolabe in the mid-1700s as the instrument for measuring the height of the stars above the horizon—to determine latitude and longitude.

Connect *to* Today

1. **Analyzing Motives** Why did inventors and sailors develop better tools for navigation?
   See Skillbuilder Handbook, page R16.
2. **Summarizing** What types of navigational or other tools do sailors use today? Choose one type of tool and write a brief explanation of what it does.

History *in* Depth

A Ship's Rations

The captain of a 17th-century sailing vessel, with a crew of 190 sailors, would normally order the following food items for a three-month trip:

- 8,000 pounds of salt beef; 2,800 pounds of salt pork; 600 pounds of salt cod; a few beef tongues
- 15,000 brown biscuits; 5,000 white biscuits
- 30 bushels of oatmeal; 40 bushels of dried peas; 1 1/2 bushels of mustard seed
- 1 barrel of salt; 1 barrel of flour
- 11 small wooden casks of butter; 1 large cask of vinegar
- 10,500 gallons of beer; 3,500 gallons of water; 2 large casks of cider

INTEGRATED TECHNOLOGY

INTERNET ACTIVITY Research food services aboard a modern U.S. warship and prepare a menu for a typical meal. Go to **classzone.com** for your research.

Henry returned to Portugal determined to reach the source of these treasures in the East. The prince also wished to spread the Christian faith. In 1419, Henry founded a navigation school on the southwestern coast of Portugal. Mapmakers, instrument makers, shipbuilders, scientists, and sea captains gathered there to perfect their trade.

Within several years, Portuguese ships began sailing down the western coast of Africa. By the time Henry died in 1460, the Portuguese had established a series of trading posts along western Africa's shores. There, they traded with Africans for such profitable items as gold and ivory. Eventually, they traded for African captives to be used as slaves. Having established their presence along the African coast, Portuguese explorers plotted their next move. They would attempt to find a sea route to Asia.

Portuguese Sailors Reach Asia The Portuguese believed that to reach Asia by sea, they would have to sail around the southern tip of Africa. In 1488, Portuguese captain Bartolomeu Dias ventured far down the coast of Africa until he and his crew reached the tip. As they arrived, a huge storm rose and battered the fleet for days. When the storm ended, Dias realized his ships had been blown around the tip to the other side. Dias explored the southeast coast of Africa and then considered sailing to India. However, his crew was exhausted and food supplies were low. As a result, the captain returned home.

With the tip of Africa finally rounded, the Portuguese continued pushing east. In 1497, Portuguese explorer **Vasco da Gama** began exploring the east African coast. In 1498, he reached the port of Calicut, on the southwestern coast of India. Da Gama and his crew were amazed by the spices, rare silks, and precious gems that filled Calicut's shops. The Portuguese sailors filled their ships with such spices as pepper and cinnamon and returned to Portugal in 1499. Their cargo was worth 60 times the cost of the voyage. Da Gama's remarkable voyage of 27,000 miles had given Portugal a direct sea route to India.

Spain Also Makes Claims

As the Portuguese were establishing trading posts along the west coast of Africa, Spain watched with increasing envy. The Spanish monarchs also desired a direct sea route to Asia.

In 1492, an Italian sea captain, Christopher Columbus, convinced Spain to finance a bold plan: finding a route to Asia by sailing west across the Atlantic Ocean. In October of that year, Columbus reached an island in the Caribbean. He was mistaken in his thought that he had reached the East Indies. But his voyage would open the way for European colonization of the Americas—a process that would forever change the world. The immediate impact of Columbus's voyage, however, was to increase tensions between Spain and Portugal.

The Portuguese believed that Columbus had indeed reached Asia. Portugal suspected that Columbus had claimed for Spain lands that Portuguese sailors might have reached first. The rivalry between Spain and Portugal grew more tense. In 1493, Pope Alexander VI stepped in to keep peace between the two nations. He suggested an imaginary dividing line, drawn north to south, through the Atlantic Ocean. All lands to the west of the line, known as the Line of Demarcation, would be Spain's. These lands included most of the Americas. All lands to the east of the line would belong to Portugal.

MAIN IDEA

Analyzing Issues

B How did the Treaty of Tordesillas ease tensions between Spain and Portugal?

Portugal complained that the line gave too much to Spain. So it was moved farther west to include parts of modern-day Brazil for the Portuguese. In 1494, Spain and Portugal signed the **Treaty of Tordesillas**, in which they agreed to honor the line. The era of exploration and colonization was about to begin in earnest. **B**

Trading Empires in the Indian Ocean

With da Gama's voyage, Europeans had finally opened direct sea trade with Asia. They also opened an era of violent conflict in the East. European nations scrambled to establish profitable trading outposts along the shores of South and Southeast Asia. And all the while they battled the region's inhabitants, as well as each other.

Portugal's Trading Empire In the years following da Gama's voyage, Portugal built a bustling trading empire throughout the Indian Ocean. As the Portuguese moved into the region, they took control of the spice trade from Muslim merchants. In 1509, Portugal extended its control over the area when it defeated a Muslim fleet off the coast of India, a victory made possible by the cannons they had added aboard their ships.

Portugal strengthened its hold on the region by building a fort at Hormuz in 1514. It established control of the Straits of Hormuz, connecting the Persian Gulf and Arabian Sea, and helped stop Muslim traders from reaching India.

In 1510, the Portuguese captured Goa, a port city on India's west coast. They made it the capital of their trading empire. They then sailed farther east to Indonesia, also known as the East Indies. In 1511, a Portuguese fleet attacked the city of Malacca on the west coast of the Malay Peninsula. In capturing the town, the Portuguese seized control of the Strait of Malacca. Seizing this waterway gave them control of the Moluccas. These were islands so rich in spices that they became known as the Spice Islands.

In convincing his crew to attack Malacca, Portuguese sea captain Afonso de Albuquerque stressed his country's intense desire to crush the Muslim-Italian domination over Asian trade:

MAIN IDEA

Analyzing Primary Sources

C What did de Albuquerque see as the outcome of a Portuguese victory at Malacca?

PRIMARY SOURCE **C**

If we deprive them [Muslims] of this their ancient market there, there does not remain for them a single port in the whole of these parts, where they can carry on their trade in these things. . . . I hold it as very certain that if we take this trade of Malacca away out of their hands, Cairo and Mecca are entirely ruined, and to Venice will no spiceries . . . [be] . . . conveyed except that which her merchants go and buy in Portugal.

AFONSO DE ALBUQUERQUE, from *The Commentaries of the Great Afonso Dalbuquerque*

Portugal did break the old Muslim-Italian domination on trade from the East, much to the delight of European consumers. Portuguese merchants brought back goods from Asia at about one-fifth of what they cost when purchased through the Arabs and Italians. As a result, more Europeans could afford these items.

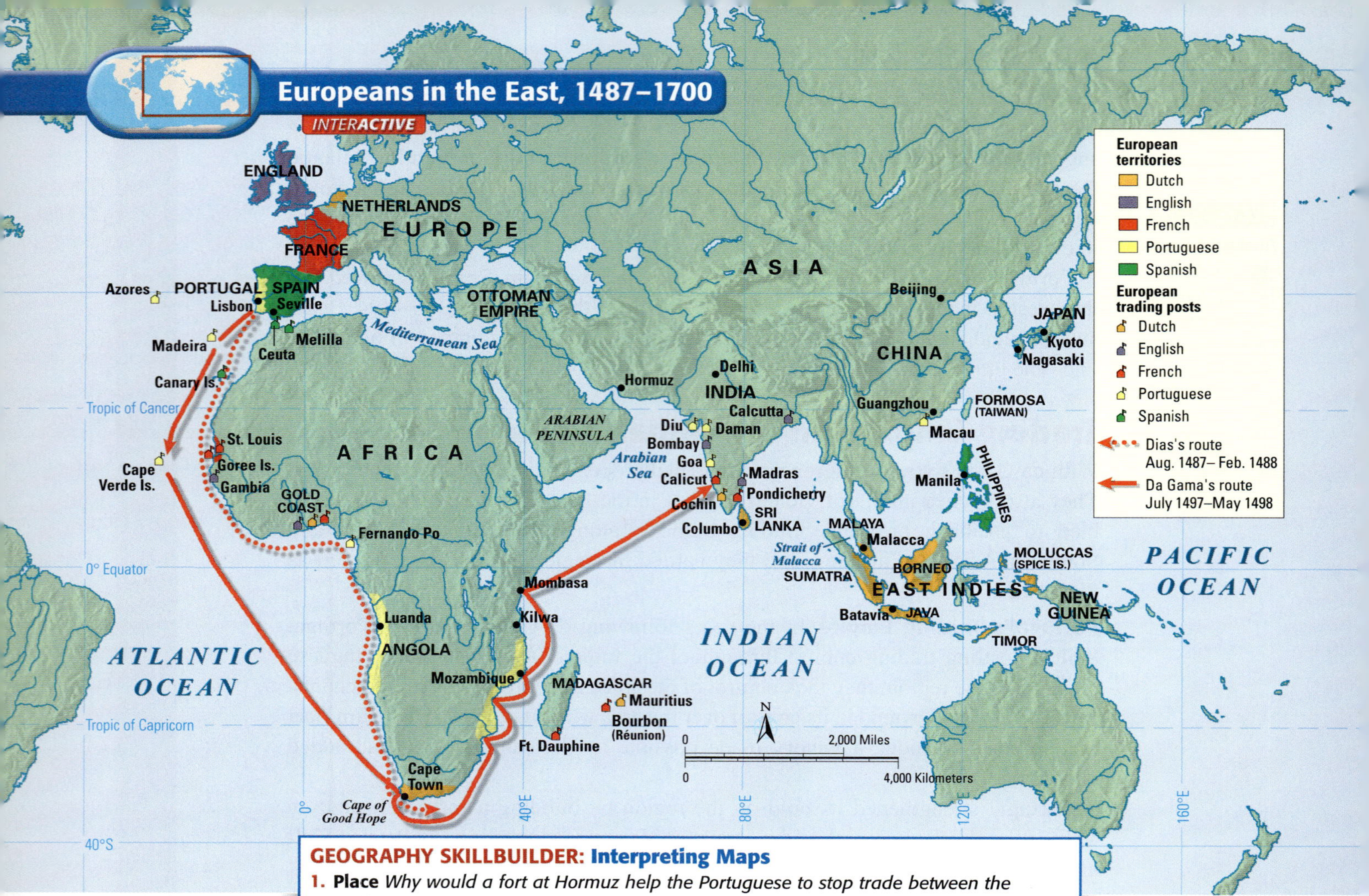

GEOGRAPHY SKILLBUILDER: Interpreting Maps

1. **Place** *Why would a fort at Hormuz help the Portuguese to stop trade between the Arabian Peninsula and India?*
2. **Region** *Where was the Dutch influence the greatest?*

In time, Portugal's success in Asia attracted the attention of other European nations. As early as 1521, a Spanish expedition led by Ferdinand Magellan arrived in the Philippines. Spain claimed the islands and began settling them in 1565. By the early 1600s, the rest of Europe had begun to descend upon Asia. They wanted to establish their own trade empires in the East.

Other Nations Challenge the Portuguese Beginning around 1600, the English and Dutch began to challenge Portugal's dominance over the Indian Ocean trade. The Dutch Republic, also known as the Netherlands, was a small country situated along the North Sea in northwestern Europe. Since the early 1500s, Spain had ruled the area. In 1581, the people of the region declared their independence from Spain and established the Dutch Republic.

In a short time, the Netherlands became a leading sea power. By 1600, the Dutch owned the largest fleet of ships in the world—20,000 vessels. Pressure from Dutch and also English fleets eroded Portuguese control of the Asian region. The Dutch and English then battled one another for dominance of the area.

Both countries had formed an East India Company to establish and direct trade throughout Asia. These companies had the power to mint money, make treaties, and even raise their own armies. The **Dutch East India Company** was richer and more powerful than England's company. As a result, the Dutch eventually drove out the English and established their dominance over the region. **D**

Dutch Trade Outposts In 1619, the Dutch established their trading headquarters at Batavia on the island of Java. From there, they expanded west to

MAIN IDEA

Analyzing Issues

D How were the Dutch able to dominate the Indian Ocean trade?

conquer several nearby islands. In addition, the Dutch seized both the port of Malacca and the valuable Spice Islands from Portugal. Throughout the 1600s, the Netherlands increased its control over the Indian Ocean trade. With so many goods from the East traveling to the Netherlands, the nation's capital, Amsterdam, became a leading commercial center. By 1700, the Dutch ruled much of Indonesia and had trading posts in several Asian countries. They also controlled the Cape of Good Hope on the southern tip of Africa, which was used as a resupply stop.

British and French Traders By 1700 also, Britain and France had gained a foothold in the region. Having failed to win control of the larger area, the English East India Company focused much of its energy on establishing outposts in India. There, the English developed a successful business trading Indian cloth in Europe. In 1664, France also entered the Asia trade with its own East India Company. It struggled at first, as it faced continual attacks by the Dutch. Eventually, the French company established an outpost in India in the 1720s. However, it never showed much of a profit.

As the Europeans battled for a share of the profitable Indian Ocean trade, their influence inland in Southeast Asia remained limited. European traders did take control of many port cities in the region. But their impact rarely spread beyond the ports. From 1500 to about 1800, when Europeans began to conquer much of the region, the peoples of Asia remained largely unaffected by European contact. As the next two sections explain, European traders who sailed farther east to seek riches in China and Japan had even less success in spreading Western culture. **E**

MAIN IDEA

Recognizing Effects

E How did the arrival of Europeans affect the peoples of the East in general?

Connect *to* Today

Trading Partners

Global trade is important to the economies of Asian countries now just as it was when the region first began to export spices, silks, and gems centuries ago. Today, a variety of products, including automobiles and electronic goods, as well as tea and textiles, are shipped around the world. (Hong Kong harbor is pictured.)

Regional trade organizations help to strengthen economic cooperation among Asian nations and promote international trade. They include the Association of Southeast Asian Nations (ASEAN) and the South Asian Association of Regional Co-operation (SAARC).

NEW YORK CORE CURRICULUM REVIEW

TERMS & NAMES 1. For each term or name, write a sentence explaining its significance.

- Bartolomeu Dias
- Prince Henry
- Vasco da Gama
- Treaty of Tordesillas
- Dutch East India Company

USING YOUR NOTES

2. Which event in the European exploration of the East is the most significant? Explain with references from the text.

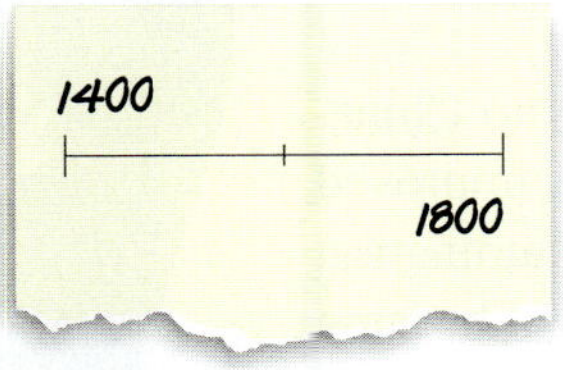

MAIN IDEAS

3. What role did the Renaissance play in launching an age of exploration?
4. What was Prince Henry's goal and who actually achieved it?
5. What European countries were competing for Asian trade during the age of exploration?

CRITICAL THINKING & WRITING

6. **MAKING INFERENCES** What did the Treaty of Tordesillas reveal about Europeans' attitudes toward non-European lands and peoples?
7. **ANALYZING MOTIVES** What were the motives behind European exploration in the 1400s? Explain.
8. **RECOGNIZING EFFECTS** In what ways did Europeans owe some of their sailing technology to other peoples?
9. **WRITING ACTIVITY** SCIENCE AND TECHNOLOGY Review "The Tools of Exploration" on page 531. Write a one-paragraph **opinion piece** on which technological advancement was the most important for European exploration.

CONNECT TO TODAY **WRITING A DESCRIPTION**

Research the Global Positioning System (GPS). Then write a brief **description** of this modern navigation system.

China Limits European Contacts

CONNECT TO THE NEW YORK STATE CORE CURRICULUM

Unit 4.A.4. China's relationship with the West
Unit 4.A.4.6. Expansion of trade (Zheng He, 1405–1433)

TERMS & NAMES

- Ming Dynasty
- Hongwu
- Yonglo
- Zheng He
- Manchus
- Qing Dynasty
- Kangxi

SETTING THE STAGE The European voyages of exploration had led to opportunities for trade. Europeans made healthy profits from trade in the Indian Ocean region. They began looking for additional sources of wealth. Soon, European countries were seeking trade relationships in East Asia, first with China and later with Japan. By the time Portuguese ships dropped anchor off the Chinese coast in 1514, the Chinese had driven out their Mongol rulers and had united under a new dynasty.

TAKING NOTES

Summarizing Use a chart to summarize relevant facts about each emperor.

Emperor	Facts
1.	1.
2.	2.
3.	3.

China Under the Powerful Ming Dynasty

China had become the dominant power in Asia under the **Ming Dynasty** (1368–1644). In recognition of China's power, vassal states from Korea to Southeast Asia paid their Ming overlords regular tribute, which is a payment by one country to another to acknowledge its submission. China expected Europeans to do the same. Ming rulers were not going to allow outsiders from distant lands to threaten the peace and prosperity the Ming had brought to China when they ended Mongol rule.

The Rise of the Ming-A peasant's son, **Hongwu**, commanded the rebel army that drove the Mongols out of China in 1368. That year, he became the first Ming emperor. Hongwu continued to rule from the former Yuan capital of Nanjing in the south. (See the map on page 527.) He began reforms designed to restore agricultural lands devastated by war, erase all traces of the Mongol past, and promote China's power and prosperity. Hongwu's agricultural reforms increased rice production and improved irrigation. He also encouraged fish farming and growing commercial crops, such as cotton and sugar cane.

Hongwu used respected traditions and institutions to bring stability to China. For example, he encouraged a return to Confucian moral standards. He improved imperial administration by restoring the merit-based civil service examination system. Later in his rule, however, when problems developed, Hongwu became a ruthless tyrant. Suspecting plots against his rule everywhere, he conducted purges of the government, killing thousands of officials.

Hongwu's death in 1398 led to a power struggle. His son **Yonglo** (yung•lu) emerged victorious. Yonglo continued many of his father's policies, although he moved the royal court to Beijing. (See the Forbidden City feature on page 538.)

▼ Porcelain vase from the Ming Dynasty

Zheng He's Treasure Ship

◄ Zheng He's treasure ship compared with Christopher Columbus's *Santa Maria*

Yonglo also had a far-ranging curiosity about the outside world. In 1405, before Europeans began to sail beyond their borders, he launched the first of seven voyages of exploration. He hoped they would impress the world with the power and splendor of Ming China. He also wanted to expand China's tribute system.

The Voyages of Zheng He A Chinese Muslim admiral named **Zheng He** (jung huh) led all of the seven voyages. His expeditions were remarkable for their size. Everything about them was large—distances traveled, fleet size, and ship measurements. The voyages ranged from Southeast Asia to eastern Africa. From 40 to 300 ships sailed in each expedition. Among them were fighting ships, storage vessels, and huge "treasure" ships measuring more than 400 feet long. The fleet's crews numbered over 27,000 on some voyages. They included sailors, soldiers, carpenters, interpreters, accountants, doctors, and religious leaders. Like a huge floating city, the fleet sailed from port to port along the Indian Ocean.

Everywhere Zheng He went, he distributed gifts including silver and silk to show Chinese superiority. As a result, more than 16 countries sent tribute to the Ming court. Even so, Chinese scholar-officials complained that the voyages wasted valuable resources that could be used to defend against barbarians' attacks on the northern frontier. After the seventh voyage, in 1433, China withdrew into isolation. (A)

MAIN IDEA

Making Inferences

(A) What do you think the people of other countries thought about China after one of Zheng He's visits?

Ming Relations with Foreign Countries China's official trade policies in the 1500s reflected its isolation. To keep the influence of outsiders to a minimum, only the government was to conduct foreign trade, and only through three coastal ports, Canton, Macao, and Ningbo. In reality, trade flourished up and down the coast. Profit-minded merchants smuggled cargoes of silk, porcelain, and other valuable goods out of the country into the eager hands of European merchants. Usually, Europeans paid for purchases with silver, much of it from mines in the Americas.

Demand for Chinese goods had a ripple effect on the economy. Industries such as silk-making and ceramics grew rapidly. Manufacturing and commerce increased. But China did not become highly industrialized for two main reasons. First, the idea of commerce offended China's Confucian beliefs. Merchants, it was said, made their money "supporting foreigners and robbery." Second, Chinese economic policies traditionally favored agriculture. Taxes on agriculture stayed low. Taxes on manufacturing and trade skyrocketed.

Christian missionaries accompanied European traders into China. They brought Christianity and knowledge of European science and technology, such as the clock. The first missionary to have an impact was an Italian Jesuit named Matteo Ricci. He

The Forbidden City

When Yonglo moved the Chinese capital to Beijing, he ordered the building of a great palace complex to symbolize his power and might. Construction took 14 years, from 1406 to 1420. Red walls 35 feet in height surrounded the complex, which had dozens of buildings, including palaces and temples. The complex became known as the Forbidden City because commoners and foreigners were not allowed to enter.

1

▲ Hall of Supreme Harmony
Taihe Hall, or the Hall of Supreme Harmony, is the largest building in the compound. It measures 201 by 122 feet and stands about 125 feet high. This hall was used for important ceremonies, such as those marking the emperor's birthday or the day the crown prince took the throne.

2

▲ Hall of Central Harmony
Zhonge Hall, or the Hall of Central Harmony, was a smaller square building between the two main halls. It was a sort of private office where the emperor could stop to rest on his way to ceremonies.

▼ Nine-Dragon Wall
This wall, or screen, of glazed tiles shows nine dragons playing with pearls against a background of sea and sky. From ancient times, the dragon was the symbol of the imperial family. This is the largest of three famous nine-dragon screens that exist in China.

3

SKILLBUILDER: Interpreting Visuals

1. **Analyzing Motives** *Why do you think the emperor wanted to keep common people out of the Forbidden City?*
2. **Drawing Conclusions** *What aspects of the Forbidden City helped to convey the power of the emperor?*

gained special favor at the Ming court through his intelligence and fluency in Chinese. Still, many educated Chinese opposed the European and Christian presence.

Manchus Found the Qing Dynasty

By 1600, the Ming had ruled for more than 200 years, and the dynasty was weakening. Its problems grew—ineffective rulers, corrupt officials, and a government that was out of money. Higher taxes and bad harvests pushed millions of peasants toward starvation. Civil strife and rebellion followed.

Northeast of the Great Wall lay Manchuria. In 1644, the **Manchus** (MAN•chooz), the people of that region, invaded China and the Ming Dynasty collapsed. The Manchus seized Beijing, and their leader became China's new emperor. As the Mongols had done in the 1300s, the Manchus took a Chinese name for their dynasty, the **Qing** (chihng) **Dynasty**. They would rule for more than 260 years and expand China's borders to include Taiwan, Chinese Central Asia, Mongolia, and Tibet.

China Under the Qing Many Chinese resisted rule by the non-Chinese Manchus. Rebellions flared up periodically for decades. The Manchus, however, slowly earned the people's respect. They upheld China's traditional Confucian beliefs and social structures. They made the country's frontiers safe and restored China's prosperity. Two powerful Manchu rulers contributed greatly to the acceptance of the new dynasty.

The first, **Kangxi** (kahng•shee), became emperor in 1661 and ruled for some 60 years. He reduced government expenses and lowered taxes. A scholar and patron of the arts, Kangxi gained the support of intellectuals by offering them government positions. He also enjoyed the company of the Jesuits at court. They told him about developments in science, medicine, and mathematics in Europe. Under his grandson Qian-long (chyahn•lung), who ruled from 1736 to 1795, China reached its greatest size and prosperity. An industrious emperor like his grandfather, Qian-long often rose at dawn to work on the empire's problems. These included armed nomads on its borders and the expanding presence of European missionaries and merchants in China.

History Makers

Kangxi
1654–1722

The emperor Kangxi had too much curiosity to remain isolated in the Forbidden City. To calm the Chinese in areas devastated by the Manchu conquest, Kangxi set out on a series of "tours."

> *On tours I learned about the common people's grievances by talking with them. . . . I asked peasants about their officials, looked at their houses, and discussed their crops.*

In 1696, with Mongols threatening the northern border, Kangxi exhibited leadership unheard of in later Ming times. Instead of waiting in the palace for reports, he personally led 80,000 troops to victory over the Mongols.

Manchus Continue Chinese Isolation To the Chinese, their country—called the Middle Kingdom—had been the cultural center of the universe for 2,000 years. If foreign states wished to trade with China, they would have to follow Chinese rules. These rules included trading only at special ports and paying tribute.

The Dutch were masters of the Indian Ocean trade by the time of Qian-long. They accepted China's restrictions. Their diplomats paid tribute to the emperor through gifts and by performing the required "kowtow" ritual. This ritual involved kneeling in front of the emperor and touching one's head to the ground nine times. As a result, the Chinese accepted the Dutch as trading partners. The Dutch returned home with traditional porcelains and silk, as well as a new trade item, tea. By 1800, tea would make up 80 percent of shipments to Europe. **B**

MAIN IDEA
Making Inferences
B Why do you think the kowtow ritual was so important to the Chinese emperor?

Great Britain also wanted to increase trade with China. But the British did not like China's trade restrictions. In 1793, Lord George Macartney delivered a letter from King George III to Qian-long. It asked for a better trade arrangement, including Chinese acceptance of British manufactured goods. Macartney refused to kowtow, and Qian-long denied Britain's request. As the emperor made clear in a letter to the king, China was self-sufficient and did not need the British:

PRIMARY SOURCE

There is nothing we lack, as your principal envoy and others have themselves observed. We have never set much store on strange or ingenious objects, nor do we need any more of your country's manufactures.

QIAN-LONG, from a letter to King George III of Great Britain

In the 1800s, the British, Dutch, and others would attempt to chip away at China's trade restrictions until the empire itself began to crack, as Chapter 28 will describe.

Korea Under the Manchus In 1636, even before they came to power in China, the Manchus conquered nearby Korea and made it a vassal state. Although Korea remained independent it existed in China's shadow. Koreans organized their government according to Confucian principles. They also adopted China's technology, its culture, and especially its policy of isolation.

When the Manchus established the Qing dynasty, Korea's political relationship with China did not change. But Korea's attitude did. The Manchu invasion, combined with a Japanese attack in the 1590s, provoked strong feelings of nationalism in the Korean people. This sentiment was most evident in their art. Instead of traditional Chinese subjects, many artists chose to show popular Korean scenes.

Social History

China's Population Boom

China's population grew dramatically from 1650 to 1900. General peace and increased agricultural productivity were the causes.

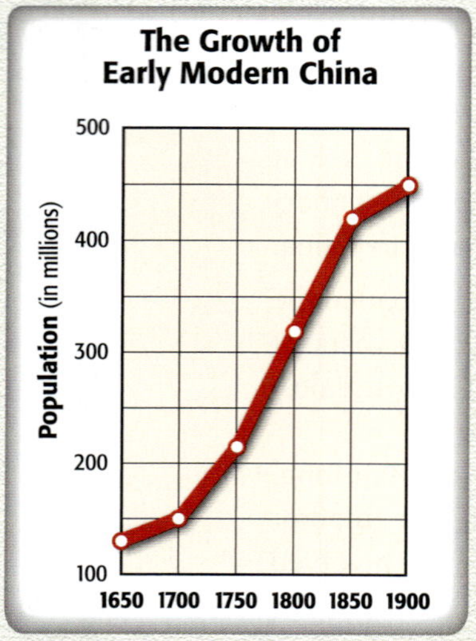

SKILLBUILDER: Interpreting Graphs

Comparing *By what percentage did China's population increase between 1650 and 1900?*

▲ A Chinese family prepares for a wedding in the 1800s.

Life in Ming and Qing China

In the 1600s and 1700s, there was general peace and prosperity in China. Life improved for most Chinese.

Families and the Role of Women Most Chinese families had farmed the land the same way their ancestors had. However, during the Qing Dynasty, irrigation and fertilizer use increased. Farmers grew rice and new crops, such as corn and sweet potatoes, brought by Europeans from the Americas. As food production increased, nutrition improved and families expanded. A population explosion followed.

These expanded Chinese families favored sons over daughters. Only a son was allowed to perform vital religious rituals. A son also would raise his own family under his parents' roof, assuring aging parents of help with the farming. As a result, females were not valued, and many female infants were killed. Although men dominated the household and their wives, women had significant responsibilities. Besides working in the fields, they supervised the children's education and managed the family's finances. While most women were forced to remain secluded in their homes, some found outside jobs such as working as midwives or textile workers.

▲ These 12th-century Chinese women work outside the home making silk.

Vocabulary
A *midwife* is a woman trained to assist women in childbirth.

Cultural Developments-The culture of early modern China was based mainly on traditional forms. The great masterpiece of traditional Chinese fiction was written during this period. *Dream of the Red Chamber* by Cao Zhan examines upper class Manchu society in the 1700s. Most artists of the time painted in traditional styles, which valued technique over creativity. In pottery, technical skill as well as experimentation led to the production of high-quality ceramics, including porcelain. Drama was a popular entertainment, especially in rural China where literacy rates were low. Plays that presented Chinese history and cultural heroes entertained and also helped unify Chinese society by creating a national culture. **C**

MAIN IDEA

Making Inferences
C What was the effect of the emphasis on tradition in early modern China?

While China preserved its traditions in isolation, another civilization that developed in seclusion—the Japanese—was in conflict, as you will read in Section 3.

NEW YORK CORE CURRICULUM REVIEW

TERMS & NAMES 1. For each term or name, write a sentence explaining its significance.

- Ming Dynasty
- Hongwu
- Yonglo
- Zheng He
- Manchus
- Qing Dynasty
- Kangxi

USING YOUR NOTES

2. Which of these emperors was most influential? Explain with text references.

Emperor	Facts
1.	1.
2.	2.
3.	3.

MAIN IDEAS

3. How did Beijing become the capital of China?
4. What evidence indicates that China lost interest in contacts abroad after 1433?
5. What did Christian missionaries bring to China?

CRITICAL THINKING & WRITING

6. **MAKING DECISIONS** Do you think Lord George Macartney should have kowtowed to Emperor Qian-long? Why?
7. **ANALYZING CAUSES** What factors, both within China and outside its borders, contributed to the downfall of the Ming Dynasty?
8. **DRAWING CONCLUSIONS** What was Korea's relationship with China under the Qing Dynasty?
9. **WRITING ACTIVITY** CULTURAL INTERACTION Choose one emperor of China and write a one-paragraph **biography** using the information you listed in your Taking Notes chart and from the text.

CONNECT TO TODAY **WRITING AN ESSAY**
Learn more about popular culture in China today. Then write a two-paragraph **expository essay** on some form of popular entertainment in the arts or sports.

Japan Returns to Isolation

CONNECT TO THE NEW YORK STATE CORE CURRICULUM

Unit 3.A.3. Ties with China and Korea: cultural diffusion, Buddhism, and Confucianism
Unit 3.A.4. Tokugawa Shogunate

TERMS & NAMES

- daimyo
- Oda Nobunaga
- Toyotomi Hideyoshi
- Tokugawa Shogunate
- haiku
- kabuki

SETTING THE STAGE In the 1300s, the unity that had been achieved in Japan in the previous century broke down. Shoguns, or military leaders, in the north and south fiercely fought one another for power. Although these two rival courts later came back together at the end of the century, a series of politically weak shoguns let control of the country slip from their grasp. The whole land was torn by factional strife and economic unrest. It would be centuries before Japan would again be unified.

TAKING NOTES
Comparing Use a chart to compare the achievements of the daimyos who unified Japan.

Daimyo	Achievements

A New Feudalism Under Strong Leaders

In 1467, civil war shattered Japan's old feudal system. The country collapsed into chaos. Centralized rule ended. Power drained away from the shogun to territorial lords in hundreds of separate domains.

Local Lords Rule A violent era of disorder followed. This time in Japanese history, which lasted from 1467 to 1568, is known as the Sengoku, or "Warring States," period. Powerful samurai seized control of old feudal estates. They offered peasants and others protection in return for their loyalty. These warrior-chieftains, called **daimyo** (DY•mee•OH), became lords in a new kind of Japanese feudalism. Daimyo meant "great name." Under this system, security came from this group of powerful warlords. The emperor at Kyoto became a figurehead, having a leadership title but no actual power.

The new Japanese feudalism resembled European feudalism in many ways. The daimyo built fortified castles and created small armies of samurai on horses. Later they added foot soldiers with muskets (guns) to their ranks. Rival daimyo often fought each other for territory. This led to disorder throughout the land.

New Leaders Restore Order A number of ambitious daimyo hoped to gather enough power to take control of the entire country. One, the brutal and ambitious **Oda Nobunaga** (oh•dah-noh•boo•nah•gah), defeated his rivals and seized the imperial capital Kyoto in 1568.

Following his own motto "Rule the empire by force," Nobunaga sought to eliminate his remaining enemies. These included rival daimyo as well as wealthy Buddhist monasteries aligned with them. In 1575, Nobunaga's 3,000 soldiers armed with muskets crushed an enemy force of samurai cavalry. This was the first time firearms had been used effectively in battle in Japan. However,

A samurai warrior ▼

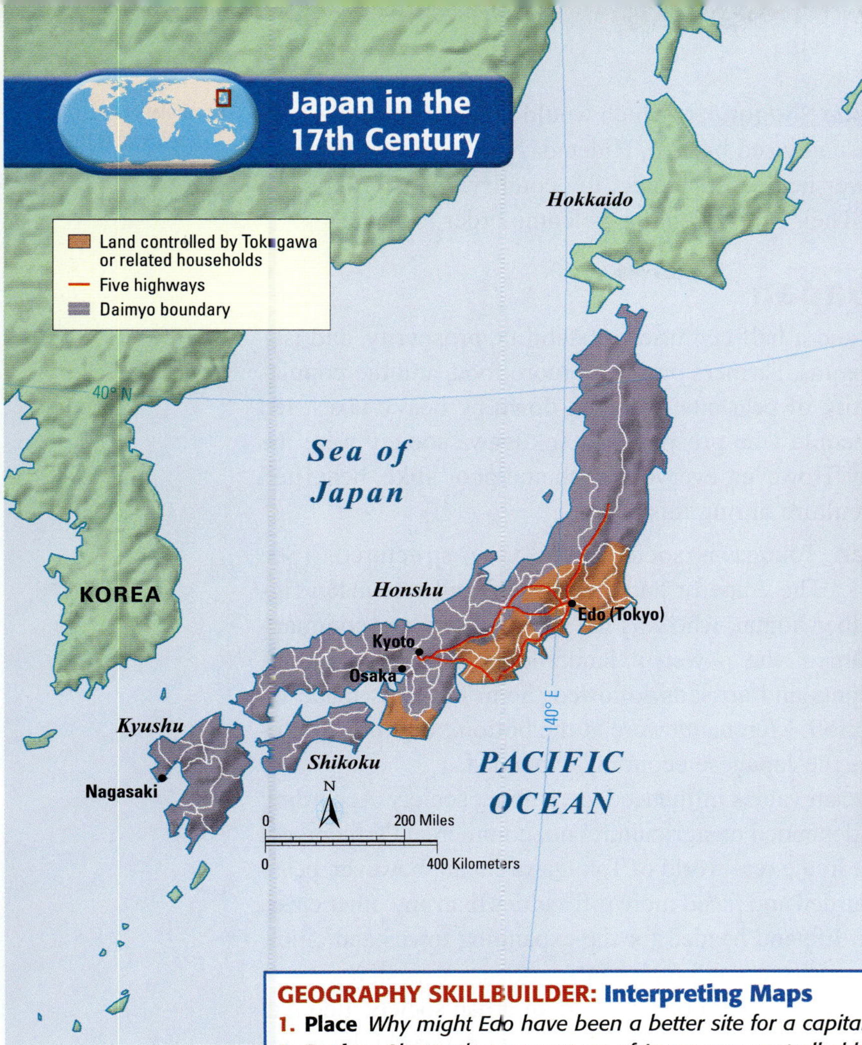

▲ Himeji Castle, completed in the 17th century, is near Kyoto.

GEOGRAPHY SKILLBUILDER: Interpreting Maps

1. **Place** *Why might Edo have been a better site for a capital in the 17th century than Kyoto?*
2. **Region** *About what percentage of Japan was controlled by Tokugawa or related households when Tokugawa Ieyasu took power in the early 1600s?*

Nobunaga was not able to unify Japan. He committed *seppuku,* the ritual suicide of a samurai, in 1582, when one of his own generals turned on him.

Nobunaga's best general, **Toyotomi Hideyoshi** (toh•you•toh•mee hee•deh•yoh•shee), continued his fallen leader's mission. Hideyoshi set out to destroy the daimyo that remained hostile. By 1590, by combining brute force with shrewd political alliances, he controlled most of the country. Hideyoshi did not stop with Japan. With the idea of eventually conquering China, he invaded Korea in 1592 and began a long campaign against the Koreans and their Ming Chinese allies. When Hideyoshi died in 1598, his troops withdrew from Korea.

Tokugawa Shogunate Unites Japan One of Hideyoshi's strongest daimyo allies, Tokugawa Ieyasu (toh•koo•gah•wah ee•yeh•yah•soo), completed the unification of Japan. In 1600, Ieyasu defeated his rivals at the Battle of Sekigahara. His victory earned him the loyalty of daimyo throughout Japan. Three years later, Ieyasu became the sole ruler, or shogun. He then moved Japan's capital to his power base at Edo, a small fishing village that would later become the city of Tokyo.

Japan was unified, but the daimyo still governed at the local level. To keep them from rebelling, Ieyasu required that they spend every other year in the capital. Even when they returned to their lands, they had to leave their families behind as hostages in Edo. Through this "alternate attendance policy" and other restrictions, Ieyasu tamed the daimyo. This was a major step toward restoring centralized government to Japan. As a result, the rule of law overcame the rule of the sword. **A**

MAIN IDEA

Drawing Conclusions

A How would the "alternate attendance policy" restrict the daimyo?

Ieyasu founded the **Tokugawa Shogunate**, which would hold power until 1867. On his deathbed in 1616, Ieyasu advised his son, Hidetada, "Take care of the people. Strive to be virtuous. Never neglect to protect the country." Most Tokugawa shoguns followed that advice. Their rule brought a welcome order to Japan.

Vocabulary
A *shogunate* is the administration or rule of a shogun.

Life in Tokugawa Japan

Japan enjoyed more than two and a half centuries of stability, prosperity, and isolation under the Tokugawa shoguns. Farmers produced more food, and the population rose. Still, the vast majority of peasants, weighed down by heavy taxes, led lives filled with misery. The people who prospered in Tokugawa society were the merchant class and the wealthy. However, everyone, rich and poor alike, benefited from a flowering of Japanese culture during this era.

Society in Tokugawa Japan Tokugawa society was very structured. (See Feudalism feature on page 361.) The emperor had the top rank but was just a figurehead. The actual ruler was the shogun, who was the supreme military commander. Below him were the daimyo, the powerful landholding samurai. Samurai warriors came next. The peasants and artisans followed them. Peasants made up about four-fifths of the population. Merchants were at the bottom, but they gradually became more important as the Japanese economy expanded.

In Japan, as in China, Confucian values influenced ideas about society. According to Confucius, the ideal society depended on agriculture, not commerce. Farmers, not merchants, made ideal citizens. In the real world of Tokugawa Japan, however, peasant farmers bore the main tax burden and faced more difficulties than any other class. Many of them abandoned farm life and headed for the expanding towns and cities. There, they mixed with samurai, artisans, and merchants.

By the mid-1700s, Japan began to shift from a rural to an urban society. Edo had grown from a small village in 1600 to perhaps the largest city in the world. Its population was more than 1 million. The rise of large commercial centers also increased employment opportunities for women. Women found jobs in entertainment, textile manufacturing, and publishing. Still, the majority of Japanese women led sheltered and restricted lives as peasant wives. They worked in the fields, managed the household, cared for the children, and each woman obeyed her husband without question.

Culture Under the Tokugawa Shogunate Traditional culture continued to thrive. Samurai attended ceremonial *noh* dramas, which were based on tragic themes. They read tales of ancient warriors and their courage in battle. In their homes, they hung paintings that showed scenes from classical literature. But traditional entertainment faced competition in the cities from new styles of literature, drama, and art.

Townspeople read a new type of fiction, realistic stories about self-made merchants or the hardships of life. The people also read **haiku** (HY•koo), 5-7-5-syllable, 3-line verse poetry. This poetry presents images rather than ideas. For example, Matsuo Basho, the greatest haiku poet, wrote before his death in 1694:

PRIMARY SOURCE (B)

On a journey, ailing—
My dreams roam about
Over a withered moor.

MATSUO BASHO, from *Matsuo Basho*

Tabi ni yande
Yume wa Kareno o
Kakemeguru

MATSUO BASHO, in Japanese

MAIN IDEA

Analyzing Primary Sources

(B) How is Matsuo Basho's haiku a poem about death?

Townspeople also attended **kabuki** theater. Actors in elaborate costumes, using music, dance, and mime, performed skits about modern life. The paintings the people enjoyed were often woodblock prints showing city life.

Connect *to* Today

Kabuki Theater

Kabuki is a traditional form of Japanese theater. It makes use of extravagant costumes, masklike makeup, and exaggerated postures and gestures. The illustrations to the right show a contemporary actor and a 19th-century performer playing warriors.

Although kabuki was created by a woman, all roles, both male and female, are performed by men. Kabuki plays are about grand historical events or the everyday life of people in Tokugawa Japan.

For 400 years, kabuki has provided entertainment for the Japanese people. And more recently, kabuki has been performed for audiences around the world, including the United States. Major centers for kabuki theater in Japan are Tokyo, Kyoto, and Osaka.

Contact Between Europe and Japan

Europeans began coming to Japan in the 16th century, during the Warring States period. Despite the severe disorder in the country, the Japanese welcomed traders and missionaries, from Portugal and, later, other European countries. These newcomers introduced fascinating new technologies and ideas. Within a century, however, the aggressive Europeans had worn out their welcome.

Portugal Sends Ships, Merchants, and Technology to Japan The Japanese first encountered Europeans in 1543, when shipwrecked Portuguese sailors washed up on the shores of southern Japan. Portuguese merchants soon followed. They hoped to involve themselves in Japan's trade with China and Southeast Asia. The Portuguese brought clocks, eyeglasses, tobacco, firearms, and other unfamiliar items from Europe. Japanese merchants, eager to expand their markets, were happy to receive the newcomers and their goods. C

MAIN IDEA

Analyzing Motives

C Why did Europeans want to open trade with Japan?

The daimyo, too, welcomed the strangers. They were particularly interested in the Portuguese muskets and cannons, because every daimyo sought an advantage over his rivals. One of these warlords listened intently to a Japanese observer's description of a musket:

PRIMARY SOURCE

In their hands they carried something two or three feet long, straight on the outside with a passage inside, and made of a heavy substance. . . . This thing with one blow can smash a mountain of silver and a wall of iron. If one sought to do mischief in another man's domain and he was touched by it, he would lose his life instantly.

ANONYMOUS JAPANESE WRITER, quoted in *Sources of Japanese Tradition* (1958)

The Japanese purchased weapons from the Portuguese and soon began their own production. Firearms forever changed the time-honored tradition of the Japanese warrior, whose principal weapon had been the sword. Some daimyo recruited and trained corps of peasants to use muskets. Many samurai, who retained the sword as their principal weapon, would lose their lives to musket fire in future combat.

The cannon also had a huge impact on warfare and life in Japan. Daimyo had to build fortified castles to withstand the destructive force of cannonballs. (See the photograph of Himeji Castle on page 543.) The castles attracted merchants, artisans, and others to surrounding lands. Many of these lands were to grow into the towns and cities of modern Japan, including Edo (Tokyo), Osaka, Himeji, and Nagoya.

Christian Missionaries in Japan In 1549, Christian missionaries began arriving in Japan. The Japanese accepted the missionaries in part because they associated them with the muskets and other European goods that they wanted to purchase. However, the religious orders of Jesuits, Franciscans, and Dominicans came to convert the Japanese.

Francis Xavier, a Jesuit, led the first mission to Japan. He wrote that the Japanese were "very sociable. . . and much concerned with their honor, which they prize above everything else." Francis Xavier baptized about a hundred converts before he left Japan. By the year 1600, other European missionaries had converted about 300,000 Japanese to Christianity.

The success of the missionaries upset Tokugawa Ieyasu. He found aspects of the Christian invasion troublesome. Missionaries, actively seeking converts, scorned traditional Japanese beliefs and sometimes involved themselves in local politics. At first, Ieyasu did not take any action. He feared driving off the Portuguese, English, Spanish, and Dutch traders who spurred Japan's economy. By 1612, however, the shogun had come to fear religious uprisings more. He banned Christianity and focused on ridding his country of all Christians.

Ieyasu died in 1616, but repression of Christianity continued off and on for the next two decades under his successors. In 1637, the issue came to a head. An uprising in southern Japan of some 30,000 peasants, led by dissatisfied samurai, shook the Tokugawa shogunate. Because so many of the rebels were Christian, the shogun decided that Christianity was at the root of the rebellion. After that, the shoguns ruthlessly persecuted Christians. European missionaries were killed or driven out of Japan. All Japanese were forced to demonstrate faithfulness to some branch of Buddhism. These policies eventually eliminated Christianity in Japan and led to the formation of an exclusion policy. D

MAIN IDEA

Comparing

D How was the treatment of Europeans different in Japan and China? How was it similar?

▼ Japanese merchants and Jesuit missionaries await the arrival of a Portuguese ship at Nagasaki in the 1500s in this painting on wood panels.

The Closed Country Policy

The persecution of Christians was part of an attempt to control foreign ideas. When Europeans first arrived, no central authority existed to contain them. The strong leaders who later took power did not like the introduction of European ideas and ways, but they valued European trade. As time passed, the Tokugawa shoguns realized that they could safely exclude both the missionaries and the merchants. By 1639, they had sealed Japan's borders and instituted a "closed country policy."

Japan in Isolation Most commercial contacts with Europeans ended. One port, Nagasaki, remained open to foreign traders. But only Dutch and Chinese merchants were allowed into the port. Earlier, the English had left Japan voluntarily; the Spanish and the Portuguese had been expelled. Since the Tokugawa shoguns controlled Nagasaki, they now had a monopoly on foreign trade, which continued to be profitable.

For more than 200 years, Japan remained basically closed to Europeans. In addition, the Japanese were forbidden to leave, so as not to bring back foreign ideas. Japan would continue to develop, but as a self-sufficient country, free from European attempts to colonize or to establish their presence.

Europeans had met with much resistance in their efforts to open the East to trade. But expansion to the West, in the Americas, as you will learn in Chapter 20, would prove much more successful for European traders, missionaries, and colonizers.

History *in* Depth

Zen Buddhism

The form of Buddhism that had the greatest impact on Japanese culture was Zen Buddhism. It especially influenced the samurai.

Zen Buddhists sought spiritual enlightenment through meditation. Strict discipline of mind and body was the Zen path to wisdom. Zen monks would sit in meditation for hours, as shown in the sculpture above. If they showed signs of losing concentration, a Zen master might shout at them or hit them with a stick.

NEW YORK CORE CURRICULUM REVIEW

TERMS & NAMES 1. For each term or name, write a sentence explaining its significance.

- daimyo
- Oda Nobunaga
- Toyotomi Hideyoshi
- Tokugawa Shogunate
- haiku
- kabuki

USING YOUR NOTES

2. Which contribution by a daimyo was the most significant? Why?

Daimyo	Achievements

MAIN IDEAS

3. What happened during the period of the "Warring States"?
4. What was the structure of society in Tokugawa Japan?
5. What were the new styles of drama, art, and literature in Tokugawa Japan?

CRITICAL THINKING & WRITING

6. **DRAWING CONCLUSIONS** Why do you think that the emperor had less power than a shogun?
7. **ANALYZING CAUSES** Why did the Japanese policy toward Christians change from acceptance to repression?
8. **FORMING OPINIONS** Do you think Japan's closed country policy effectively kept Western ideas and customs out of Japan?
9. **WRITING ACTIVITY** CULTURAL INTERACTION Write a two-paragraph **comparison** of the similarities and differences between the roles of women in China (discussed on page 541) and in Japan (page 544).

INTEGRATED TECHNOLOGY **INTERNET ACTIVITY**

Use the Internet to find information on the Japanese government today. Then create an **organizational chart** showing the structure of the government.

INTERNET KEYWORD
country profiles

Chapter 19 Assessment

VISUAL SUMMARY

An Age of Explorations and Isolation

Explorations

1405 **Zheng He of China** launches voyages of exploration to Southeast Asia, India, Arabia, and eastern Africa.

1500s **The Portuguese** establish trading outposts throughout Asia and gain control of the spice trade.

1600s **The Dutch** drive out the Portuguese and establish their own trading empire in the East. (Below, a Dutch ship is pictured on a plate made in China for European trade.)

Europeans sail farther east to China and Japan in search of more trade; both nations ultimately reject European advances.

Isolation

1433 **China** abandons its voyages of exploration.

1500s **The Chinese** severely restrict trade with foreigners.

1612 **Japan** outlaws Christianity and drives out Christian missionaries.

1630s **The Japanese** institute a "closed country policy" and remain isolated from Europe for 200 years.

TERMS & NAMES

For each term or name below, briefly explain its importance to European exploration and the development of China and Japan.

1. Bartolomeu Dias
2. Vasco da Gama
3. Treaty of Tordesillas
4. Dutch East India Company
5. Ming dynasty
6. Manchus
7. Qing dynasty
8. Oda Nobunaga
9. Toyotomi Hideyoshi
10. Tokugawa Shogunate

MAIN IDEAS

Europeans Explore the East Section 1 (pages 529–535)

11. What factors helped spur European exploration?
12. What role did Portugal's Prince Henry play in overseas exploration?
13. What was the significance of Dias's voyage? da Gama's voyage?
14. Why were the Dutch so successful in establishing a trading empire in the Indian Ocean?

China Limits European Contacts Section 2 (pages 536–541)

15. Why did China not undergo widespread industrialization?
16. What did Christian missionaries bring to China?
17. What are five reasons the Ming Dynasty fell to civil disorder?

Japan Returns to Isolation Section 3 (pages 542–547)

18. Why was the time between 1467 and 1568 called the period of the "Warring States"?
19. What was the difference between the Confucian ideal of society and the real society of Japan?
20. How did the Japanese express themselves culturally under the Tokugawa shoguns?

CRITICAL THINKING

1. USING YOUR NOTES
In a time line, trace the events that led to Japan's expulsion of European Christians.

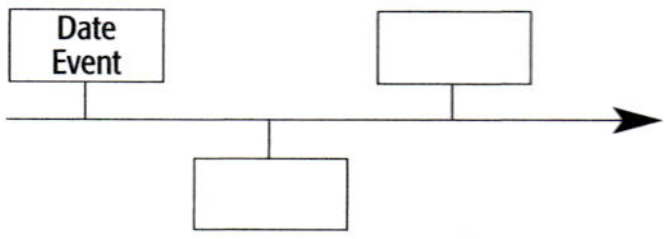

2. RECOGNIZING EFFECTS
How might a Chinese emperor's leadership be affected by living in the Forbidden City? Explain and support your opinion.

3. ANALYZING ISSUES
SCIENCE AND TECHNOLOGY Of the technological advances that helped spur European exploration, which do you think was the most important? Why?

4. ANALYZING CAUSES
CULTURAL INTERACTION What caused Japan to institute a policy of isolation? Defend your viewpoint with text references.

5. SUMMARIZING
ECONOMICS How did the Manchus earn the respect of the Chinese? Support your answer with details from the chapter.

Use the quotation and your knowledge of world history to answer questions 1 and 2.
Additional Test Practice, pp. S1–S33

PRIMARY SOURCE

But I was careful not to refer to these Westerners as "Great Officials," and corrected Governor Liu Yin-shu when he referred to the Jesuits Regis and Fridelli . . . as if they were honored imperial commissioners. For even though some of the Western methods are different from our own, and may even be an improvement, there is little about them that is new. The principles of mathematics all derive from the Book of Changes, and the Western methods are Chinese in origin: this algebra—"A-erh-chu-pa-erh"—springs from an Eastern word. And though it was indeed the Westerners who showed us something our ancient calendar experts did not know—namely how to calculate the angles of the northern pole—this but shows the truth of what Chu Hsi arrived at through his investigation of things: the earth is like the yolk within an egg.

KANGXI, quoted in *Emperor of China: Self-Portrait of K'Ang-Hsi*

1 Which phrase best describes Kangxi's thoughts about Europeans, or "Westerners"?
(1) Westerners use methods that are inferior to Chinese methods.
(2) Westerners would make good trading partners.
(3) Westerners use methods that are based on Chinese methods.
(4) There are too many Westerners in China.

2 What can be inferred about Kangxi's beliefs about China?
(1) China needs the assistance of Westerners.
(2) China is superior to countries of the West.
(3) China has many problems.
(4) China is destined to rule the world.

Use this map produced by German cartographer Henricus Martellus in about 1490 and your knowledge of world history to answer question 3.

3 Which of these statements about Martellus's map is accurate?
(1) Martellus shows North America and Africa.
(2) Martellus shows North America and Asia.
(3) Martellus shows Africa, Asia, and Europe.
(4) Martellus shows North America, Africa, and Europe.

INTEGRATED TECHNOLOGY

TEST PRACTICE Go to **classzone.com**

- Diagnostic tests
- Tutorials
- Strategies
- Additional practice

ALTERNATIVE ASSESSMENT

1. Interact *with* History

On page 528, you decided whether or not you would sail into the unknown. Now that you have read the chapter, reevaluate your decision. If you decided to go, did what you read reaffirm your decision? Why or why not? If you chose not to go, explain what your feelings are now. Discuss your answers within a small group.

2. WRITING ABOUT HISTORY

Imagine you are the Jesuit missionary Matteo Ricci. Write an **expository essay** describing your impressions of Chinese rule and culture. Consider the following in the essay:

- Matteo Ricci's values
- Chinese culture as compared with Western Christian culture

INTEGRATED TECHNOLOGY

Planning a Television Special

Use the Internet, books, and other reference materials to create a script for a television special "The Voyages of Zheng He." The script should address the historical context of Zheng He's voyages and their impact on China and the lands visited. The script should include narration, sound, re-creations, and locations. In researching, consider the following:

- biographical data on Zheng He
- information on the ships, crews, and cargo
- descriptions of the voyages
- music and visuals

CHAPTER 20

The Atlantic World, 1492–1800

Previewing Main Ideas

CULTURAL INTERACTION The voyages of Columbus prompted a worldwide exchange of everything from religious and political ideas to new foods and plants.

Geography *According to the map, what lands were included in the viceroyalty of New Spain in 1700?*

ECONOMICS The vast wealth to be had from colonizing the Americas sealed the fate of millions of Native Americans and Africans who were forced to work in mines and on plantations.

Geography *On which coast of the Americas would enslaved persons from Africa have arrived?*

EMPIRE BUILDING Over the span of several centuries, Europeans conquered the Americas' native inhabitants and built powerful American empires.

Geography *What two major Native American empires did the Spanish conquer in the sixteenth century?*

NEW YORK CORE CURRICULUM FOCUS

- Columbus's voyages led European nations to compete for colonies in the Americas.
- Europeans met their growing need for labor in the Americas through the slave trade.

INTEGRATED TECHNOLOGY

eEdition
- Interactive Maps
- Interactive Visuals
- Interactive Primary Sources

VIDEO *Patterns of Interaction: The Impact of Potatoes and Sugar*

INTERNET RESOURCES

Go to **classzone.com** for:
- Research Links
- Internet Activities
- Primary Sources
- Chapter Quiz
- Maps
- Test Practice
- Current Events

AMERICAS

1492 Columbus makes first voyage.

1521 Cortés conquers Aztec Empire. ▶

1533 Pizarro conquers Incan Empire.

1607 English found Jamestown.

1500 — **1600**

WORLD

1494 Spain and Portugal sign Treaty of Tordesillas.

1547 Ivan the Terrible assumes throne of Russia.

1603 ◀ Tokugawa shoguns rule Japan.

1608
Champlain claims Quebec for France. ▶

1754
French and Indian War begins.

1700

1800

1649
King Charles I of England is executed.

1789
◀ Storming of Bastille ignites French Revolution.

Interact *with* History

What might you gain or lose by joining the fight?

You are a Native American living in central Mexico in 1520. Suddenly you are faced with a decision that may change your life forever. Invaders, known as the Spanish, are engaged in a fierce battle with the nearby Aztecs, who are cruel and harsh rulers. Like many of your people, you hate the powerful Aztecs and hope for their defeat. The newcomers, however, are equally frightening. They ride on large beasts and fire loud, deadly weapons. You wonder whether you should follow the example of your friends and join the fight, or not fight at all.

▲ This 16th-century painting by an Indian artist depicts a battle on the left between the Aztecs and Spanish. The right side shows the Spanish with their main Indian allies, the Tlaxcalans.

EXAMINING *the* ISSUES

- **What are the advantages and disadvantages of not fighting?**
- **Which might be the lesser of two evils—supporting the Aztecs, whom you know as oppressors, or the fierce invaders, about whom you know almost nothing?**

Discuss these questions with your classmates. In your discussion, examine whether invading armies throughout history have made life better or worse for people in the areas they conquer. As you read about colonization in the Americas, learn the outcome of the battle between the Aztecs and the Spanish.

Spain Builds an American Empire

CONNECT TO THE NEW YORK STATE CORE CURRICULUM

Unit 4.C.4.a. Columbus
Unit 4.E.1. Human and physical geography

TERMS & NAMES

- Christopher Columbus
- colony
- Hernando Cortés
- conquistador
- Francisco Pizarro
- Atahualpa
- mestizo
- *encomienda*

SETTING THE STAGE Competition for wealth in Asia among European nations was fierce. This competition prompted a Genoese sea captain named **Christopher Columbus** to make a daring voyage from Spain in 1492. Instead of sailing south around Africa and then east, Columbus sailed west across the Atlantic in search of an alternate trade route to Asia and its riches. Columbus never reached Asia. Instead, he stepped onto an island in the Caribbean. That event would bring together the peoples of Europe, Africa, and the Americas.

TAKING NOTES

Following Chronological Order Use a diagram to trace the major events in the establishment of Spain's empire in the Americas.

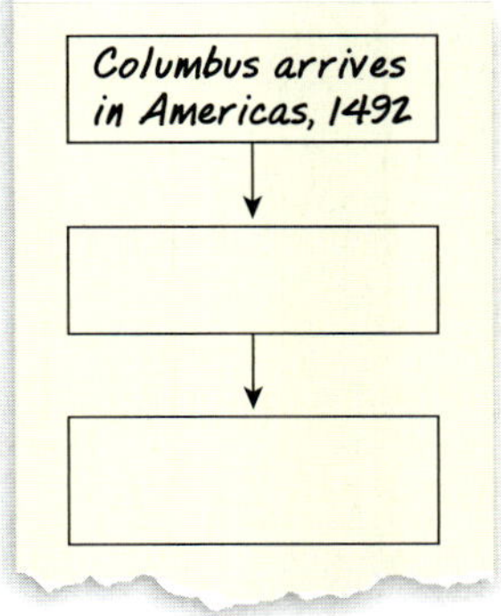

The Voyages of Columbus

The *Niña, Pinta,* and *Santa María* sailed out of a Spanish port around dawn on August 3, 1492. In a matter of months, Columbus's fleet would reach the shores of what Europeans saw as an astonishing new world.

First Encounters In the early hours of October 12, 1492, the long-awaited cry came. A lookout aboard the *Pinta* caught sight of a shoreline in the distance. *"Tierra! Tierra!"* he shouted. "Land! Land!" By dawn, Columbus and his crew were ashore. Thinking he had successfully reached the East Indies, Columbus called the surprised inhabitants who greeted him, *los indios*. The term translated into "Indian," a word mistakenly applied to all the native peoples of the Americas. In his journal, Columbus recounted his first meeting with the native peoples:

PRIMARY SOURCE

I presented them with some red caps, and strings of glass beads to wear upon the neck, and many other trifles of small value, wherewith they were much delighted, and became wonderfully attached to us. Afterwards they came swimming to the boats where we were, bringing parrots, balls of cotton thread, javelins, and many other things which they exchanged for articles we gave them . . . in fact they accepted anything and gave what they had with the utmost good will.

CHRISTOPHER COLUMBUS, *Journal of Columbus*

Columbus had miscalculated where he was. He had not reached the East Indies. Scholars believe he landed instead on an island in the Bahamas in the Caribbean Sea. The natives there were not Indians, but a group who called themselves the Taino. Nonetheless, Columbus claimed the island for Spain. He named it San Salvador, or "Holy Savior."

▲ *Portrait of a Man Called Christopher Columbus* (1519) by Sebastiano del Piombo

Columbus, like other explorers, was interested in gold. Finding none on San Salvador, he explored other islands, staking his claim to each one. "It was my wish to bypass no island without taking possession," he wrote.

In early 1493, Columbus returned to Spain. The reports he relayed about his journey delighted the Spanish monarchs. Spain's rulers, who had funded his first voyage, agreed to finance three more trips. Columbus embarked on his second voyage to the Americas in September of 1493. He journeyed no longer as an explorer, but as an empire builder. He commanded a fleet of some 17 ships that carried over 1,000 soldiers, crewmen, and colonists. The Spanish intended to transform the islands of the Caribbean into **colonies**, or lands that are controlled by another nation. Over the next two centuries, other European explorers began sailing across the Atlantic in search of new lands to claim.

Other Explorers Take to the Seas In 1500, the Portuguese explorer Pedro Álvares Cabral reached the shores of modern-day Brazil and claimed the land for his country. A year later, Amerigo Vespucci (vehs•POO•chee), an Italian in the service of Portugal, also traveled along the eastern coast of South America. Upon his return to Europe, he claimed that the land was not part of Asia, but a "new" world. In 1507, a German mapmaker named the new continent "America" in honor of Amerigo Vespucci.

In 1519, Portuguese explorer Ferdinand Magellan led the boldest exploration yet. Several years earlier, Spanish explorer Vasco Núñez de Balboa had marched through modern-day Panama and had become the first European to gaze upon the Pacific Ocean. Soon after, Magellan convinced the king of Spain to fund his voyage into the newly discovered ocean.

With about 250 men and five ships, Magellan sailed around the southern end of South America and into the waters of the Pacific. The fleet sailed for months without seeing land, except for some small islands. Food supplies soon ran out.

After exploring the island of Guam, Magellan and his crew eventually reached the Philippines. Unfortunately, Magellan became involved in a local war there and was killed. His crew, greatly reduced by disease and starvation, continued sailing west toward home. Out of Magellan's original crew, only 18 men and one ship arrived back in Spain in 1522, nearly three years after they had left. They were the first persons to circumnavigate, or sail around, the world. (A)

MAIN IDEA

Making Inferences

(A) What was the significance of Magellan's voyage?

Spanish Conquests in Mexico

In 1519, as Magellan embarked on his historic voyage, a Spaniard named **Hernando Cortés** landed on the shores of Mexico. After colonizing several Caribbean islands, the Spanish had turned their attention to the American mainland. Cortés marched inland, looking to claim new lands for Spain. Cortés and the many other Spanish explorers who followed him were known as **conquistadors** (conquerors). Lured by rumors of vast lands filled with gold and silver, conquistadors carved out colonies in regions that would become Mexico, South America, and the United States. The Spanish were the first European settlers in the Americas. As a result of their colonization, the Spanish greatly enriched their empire and left a mark on the cultures of North and South America that exists today.

GEOGRAPHY SKILLBUILDER: Interpreting Maps

1. **Movement** *How many different voyages did Columbus make to the Americas?*
2. **Region** *Which general region did the Spanish and Portuguese explore? Where did the English, Dutch, and French explore?*

Native Population of Central Mexico, 1500–1620

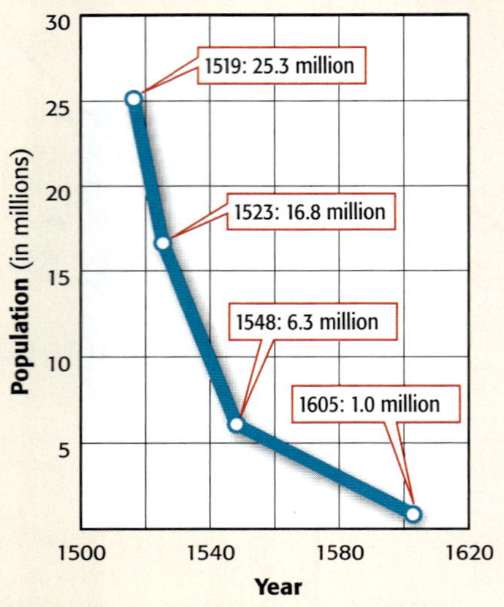

Source: *The Population of Latin America: A History*

SKILLBUILDER: Interpreting Graphs

1. **Drawing Conclusions** *By what percentage did the native population decrease between 1519 and 1605?*
2. **Making Inferences** *How did the sharp decline in the native population, due greatly to disease, affect the Spaniards' attempts to conquer the region?*

Cortés Conquers the Aztecs Soon after landing in Mexico, Cortés learned of the vast and wealthy Aztec Empire in the region's interior. (See Chapter 16.) After marching for weeks through difficult mountain passes, Cortés and his force of roughly 600 men finally reached the magnificent Aztec capital of Tenochtitlán (teh•NAWCH•tee•TLAHN). The Aztec emperor, Montezuma II, was convinced at first that Cortés was a god wearing armor. He agreed to give the Spanish explorer a share of the empire's existing gold supply. The conquistador was not satisfied. Cortés admitted that he and his comrades had a "disease of the heart that only gold can cure."

In the late spring of 1520, some of Cortés's men killed many Aztec warriors and chiefs while they were celebrating a religious festival. In June of 1520, the Aztecs rebelled against the Spanish intruders and drove out Cortés's forces.

The Spaniards, however, struck back. Despite being greatly outnumbered, Cortés and his men conquered the Aztecs in 1521. Several factors played a key role in the stunning victory. First, the Spanish had the advantage of superior weaponry. Aztec arrows were no match for the Spaniards' muskets and cannons.

Second, Cortés was able to enlist the help of various native groups. With the aid of a native woman translator named Malinche, Cortés learned that some natives resented the Aztecs. They hated their harsh practices, including human sacrifice. Through Malinche, Cortés convinced these natives to fight on his side.

Finally, and most important, the natives could do little to stop the invisible warrior that marched alongside the Spaniards—disease. Measles, mumps, smallpox, and typhus were just some of the diseases Europeans were to bring with them to the Americas. Native Americans had never been exposed to these diseases. Thus, they had developed no natural immunity to them. As a result, they died by the hundreds of thousands. By the time Cortés launched his counterattack, the Aztec population had been greatly reduced by smallpox and measles. In time, European disease would truly devastate the natives of central Mexico, killing millions of them. **B**

MAIN IDEA

Summarizing

B What factors enabled the Spanish to defeat the Aztecs?

Spanish Conquests in Peru

In 1532, another conquistador, **Francisco Pizarro**, marched a small force into South America. He conquered the Incan Empire, as you learned in Chapter 16.

Pizarro Subdues the Inca Pizarro and his army of about 200 met the Incan ruler, **Atahualpa** (AH•tuh•WAHL•puh), near the city of Cajamarca. Atahualpa, who commanded a force of about 30,000, brought several thousand mostly unarmed men for the meeting. The Spaniards waited in ambush, crushed the Incan force, and kidnapped Atahualpa.

Atahualpa offered to fill a room once with gold and twice with silver in exchange for his release. However, after receiving the ransom, the Spanish strangled the Incan king. Demoralized by their leader's death, the remaining Incan force retreated from Cajamarca. Pizarro then marched on the Incan capital, Cuzco. He captured it without a struggle in 1533.

As Cortés and Pizarro conquered the civilizations of the Americas, fellow conquistadors defeated other native peoples. Spanish explorers also conquered the Maya in Yucatan and Guatemala. By the middle of the 16th century, Spain had created an American empire. It included New Spain (Mexico and parts of Guatemala), as well as other lands in Central and South America and the Caribbean.

Spain's Pattern of Conquest In building their new American empire, the Spaniards drew from techniques used during the *reconquista* of Spain. When conquering the Muslims, the Spanish lived among them and imposed their Spanish culture upon them. The Spanish settlers to the Americas, known as *peninsulares,* were mostly men. As a result, relationships between Spanish settlers and native women were common. These relationships created a large **mestizo**—or mixed Spanish and Native American—population.

Although the Spanish conquerors lived among the native people, they also oppressed them. In their effort to exploit the land for its precious resources, the Spanish forced Native Americans to work within a system known as ***encomienda***. Under this system, natives farmed, ranched, or mined for Spanish landlords. These landlords had received the rights to the natives' labor from Spanish authorities. The holders of *encomiendas* promised the Spanish rulers that they would act fairly and respect the workers. However, many abused the natives and worked many laborers to death, especially inside dangerous mines.

The Portuguese in Brazil One area of South America that remained outside of Spanish control was Brazil. In 1500, Cabral claimed the land for Portugal. During the 1530s, colonists began settling Brazil's coastal region. Finding little gold or silver, the settlers began growing sugar. Clearing out huge swaths of forest land, the Portuguese built giant sugar plantations. The demand for sugar in Europe was great, and the colony soon enriched Portugal. In time, the colonists pushed farther west into Brazil. They settled even more land for the production of sugar.

History Makers

Francisco Pizarro 1475?–1541

Pizarro was the son of an infantry captain and a young peasant woman. His parents never married. Raised by his mother's poor family, he never learned to read. Ambitious, brave, and ruthless, he determined to make his fortune as an explorer and conqueror.

Embarked on a voyage of conquest down the west coast of South America, Pizarro was ordered by the governor of Panama to abandon the expedition to prevent the loss of lives. Pizarro took his sword and drew a line in the dust, inviting those of his followers who desired wealth and fame to cross the line and follow him. Thus began the conquest of Peru.

Pizarro founded the city of Lima, Peru's capital, in 1535. He became governor of Peru and encouraged settlers from Spain.

Atahualpa 1502?–1533

Atahualpa was the last ruler of the Incan empire in Peru. After Atahualpa was captured and held for ransom by the Spanish, the Incan people throughout the empire brought gold and silver that the Spanish then had melted down into bullion and ingots. They accumulated 24 tons of gold and silver, the richest ransom in history.

The Spanish executed Atahualpa despite the ransom paid by his people. As he was about to be burned at the stake, the Spanish offered him a more merciful death by strangulation if he agreed to convert to Christianity, which he did. Thus died the last emperor of the Inca.

INTEGRATED TECHNOLOGY

INTERNET ACTIVITY Create a poster about the ransom paid by the Incan people to rescue Atahualpa. Go to **classzone.com** for your research.

This U.S. postage ▶ stamp was issued in 1940 to celebrate the 400th anniversary of the Coronado expedition.

Spain's Influence Expands

Spain's American colonies helped make it the richest, most powerful nation in the world during much of the 16th century. Ships filled with treasures from the Americas continually sailed into Spanish harbors. This newfound wealth helped usher in a golden age of art and culture in Spain. (See Chapter 21.)

Throughout the 16th century, Spain also increased its military might. To protect its treasure-filled ships, Spain built a powerful navy. The Spanish also strengthened their other military forces, creating a skillful and determined army. For a century and a half, Spain's army seldom lost a battle. Meanwhile, Spain enlarged its American empire by settling in parts of what is now the United States.

Conquistadors Push North Dreams of new conquests prompted Spain to back a series of expeditions into the southwestern United States. The Spanish actually had settled in parts of the United States before they even dreamed of building an empire on the American mainland. In 1513, Spanish explorer Juan Ponce de León landed on the coast of modern-day Florida and claimed it for Spain.

By 1540, after building an empire that stretched from Mexico to Peru, the Spanish once again looked to the land that is now the United States. In 1540–1541, Francisco Vásquez de Coronado led an expedition throughout much of present-day Arizona, New Mexico, Texas, Oklahoma, and Kansas. He was searching for another wealthy empire to conquer. Coronado found little gold amidst the dry deserts of the Southwest. As a result, the Spanish monarchy assigned mostly priests to explore and colonize the future United States.

Catholic priests had accompanied conquistadors from the very beginning of American colonization. The conquistadors had come in search of wealth. The priests who accompanied them had come in search of converts. In the winter of 1609–1610, Pedro de Peralta, governor of Spain's northern holdings, called New Mexico, led settlers to a tributary on the upper Rio Grande. They built a capital called Santa Fe, or "Holy Faith." In the next two decades, a string of Christian missions arose among the Pueblo, the native inhabitants of the region. Scattered missions, forts, and small ranches dotted the lands of New Mexico. These became the headquarters for advancing the Catholic religion. C

MAIN IDEA

Contrasting

C How did Spain's colony in New Mexico differ from its colonies in New Spain?

Opposition to Spanish Rule

Spanish priests worked to spread Christianity in the Americas. They also pushed for better treatment of Native Americans. Priests spoke out against the cruel treatment of natives. In particular, they criticized the harsh pattern of labor that emerged under the *encomienda* system. "There is nothing more detestable or more cruel," Dominican monk Bartolomé de Las Casas wrote, "than the tyranny which the Spaniards use toward the Indians for the getting of pearl [riches]."

African Slavery and Native Resistance The Spanish government abolished the *encomienda* system in 1542. To meet the colonies' need for labor, Las Casas suggested Africans. "The labor of one . . . [African] . . . [is] more valuable than that of four Indians," he said. The priest later changed his view and denounced African slavery. However, others promoted it.

Opposition to the Spanish method of colonization came not only from Spanish priests, but also from the natives themselves. Resistance to Spain's attempt at domination began shortly after the Spanish arrived in the Caribbean. In November of 1493, Columbus encountered resistance in his attempt to conquer the present-day island of St. Croix. Before finally surrendering, the inhabitants defended themselves by firing poison arrows.

As late as the end of the 17th century, natives in New Mexico fought Spanish rule. Although they were not risking their lives in silver mines, the natives still felt the weight of Spanish force. In converting the natives, Spanish priests and soldiers burned their sacred objects and prohibited native rituals. The Spanish also forced natives to work for them and sometimes abused them physically.

In 1680, Popé, a Pueblo ruler, led a well-organized rebellion against the Spanish. The rebellion involved more than 8,000 warriors from villages all over New Mexico. The native fighters drove the Spanish back into New Spain. For the next 12 years, until the Spanish regained control of the area, the southwest region of the future United States once again belonged to its original inhabitants. **D**

By this time, however, the rulers of Spain had far greater concerns. The other nations of Europe had begun to establish their own colonies in the Americas.

MAIN IDEA

Analyzing Causes

D Why did the natives of New Mexico revolt against Spanish settlers?

NEW YORK CORE CURRICULUM REVIEW

TERMS & NAMES 1. For each term or name, write a sentence explaining its significance.

- Christopher Columbus
- colony
- Hernando Cortés
- conquistador
- Francisco Pizarro
- Atahualpa
- mestizo
- *encomienda*

USING YOUR NOTES

2. Which of these events do you think had the greatest impact?

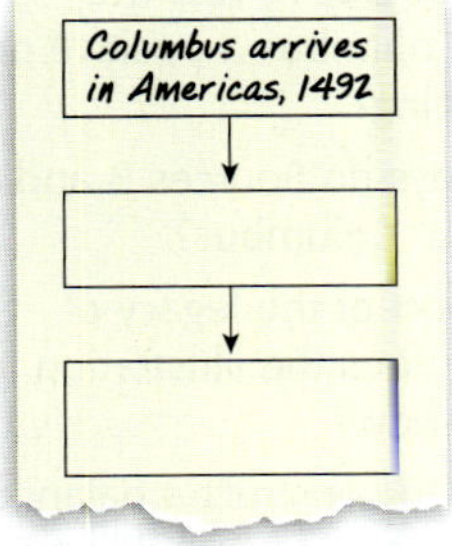

MAIN IDEAS

3. What process did Columbus and his followers begin?
4. Why were most of the Spanish explorers drawn to the Americas?
5. Which country was the richest and most powerful in the 16th century, and why?

CRITICAL THINKING & WRITING

6. **ANALYZING PRIMARY SOURCES** Reread the primary source on page 553. How might Columbus's view of the Taino have led the Spanish to think they could take advantage of and impose their will on the natives?
7. **COMPARING** What might have been some similarities in character between Cortés and Pizarro?
8. **CLARIFYING** Through what modern-day states did Coronado lead his expedition?
9. **WRITING ACTIVITY** EMPIRE BUILDING Write a **dialogue** in which a Native American and a conquistador debate the merits of Spain's colonization of the Americas.

CONNECT TO TODAY **MAKING A DATABASE**

Use library resources to compile a **database** of places and geographical features in the Americas named after Columbus. Display your list in the classroom.

INTERACTIVE

The Legacy of Columbus

In the years and centuries since Christopher Columbus's historic journeys, people still debate the legacy of his voyages. Some argue they were the heroic first steps in the creation of great and democratic societies. Others claim they were the beginnings of an era of widespread cruelty, bloodshed, and epidemic disease.

A SECONDARY SOURCE

Samuel Eliot Morison

Morison, a strong supporter of Columbus, laments that the sea captain died without realizing the true greatness of his deeds.

One only wishes that the Admiral might have been afforded the sense of fulfillment that would have come from foreseeing all that flowed from his discoveries; that would have turned all the sorrows of his last years to joy. The whole history of the Americas stems from the Four Voyages of Columbus; and as the Greek city-states looked back to the deathless gods as their founders, so today a score of independent nations and dominions unite in homage to Christopher, the stout-hearted son of Genoa, who carried Christian civilization across the Ocean Sea.

B PRIMARY SOURCE

Bartolomé de Las Casas

Las Casas was an early Spanish missionary who watched fellow Spaniards unleash attack dogs on Native Americans.

Their other frightening weapon after the horses: twenty hunting greyhounds. They were unleashed and fell on the Indians at the cry of *Tómalo!* ["Get them!"]. Within an hour they had preyed on one hundred of them. As the Indians were used to going completely naked, it is easy to imagine what the fierce greyhounds did, urged to bite naked bodies and skin much more delicate than that of the wild boars they were used to. . . . This tactic, begun here and invented by the devil, spread throughout these Indies and will end when there is no more land nor people to subjugate and destroy in this part of the world.

C SECONDARY SOURCE

Suzan Shown Harjo

Harjo, a Native American, disputes the benefits that resulted from Columbus's voyages and the European colonization of the Americas that followed.

Columbus Day, never on Native America's list of favorite holidays, became somewhat tolerable as its significance diminished to little more than a good shopping day. But this next long year [1992] of Columbus hoopla will be tough to take amid the spending sprees and horn blowing to tout a five-century feeding frenzy that has left Native people and this red quarter of Mother Earth in a state of emergency. For Native people, this half millennium of land grabs and one-cent treaty sales has been no bargain.

D PRIMARY SOURCE

Anonymous

Contemporary with the Spanish conquest of the Americas, this illustration depicts a medicine man tending to an Aztec suffering from smallpox, which killed millions of Native Americans.

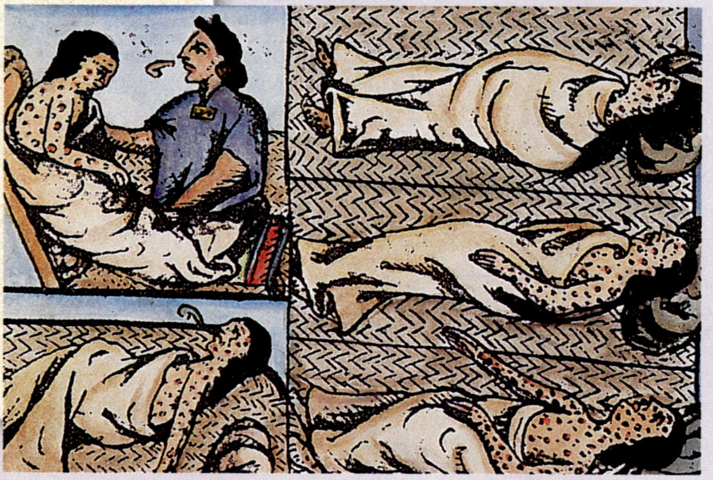

Document-Based QUESTIONS

1. Based on Source A, was the legacy of Columbus a positive or negative thing?
2. In what ways do Sources B and C agree about Columbus?
3. Which aspect of the legacy of Columbus does the illustration in Source D show?
4. If you had to construct a balance sheet on Columbus, would you come up with a positive or negative balance? On a poster board, make up a list of positive and negative elements, and display your chart in the classroom.

2

European Nations Settle North America

CONNECT TO THE NEW YORK STATE CORE CURRICULUM

Methodology.A.5. Roles and contributions of individuals and groups
Unit 4.E.2. European competition for colonies in the Americas, Africa, East Asia, and Southeast Asia–The "old imperialism"

TERMS & NAMES

- New France
- Jamestown
- Pilgrims
- Puritans
- New Netherland
- French and Indian War
- Metacom

SETTING THE STAGE Spain's successful colonization efforts in the Americas did not go unnoticed. Other European nations, such as England, France, and the Netherlands, soon became interested in obtaining their own valuable colonies. The Treaty of Tordesillas, signed in 1494, had divided the newly discovered lands between Spain and Portugal. However, other European countries ignored the treaty. They set out to build their own empires in the Americas. This resulted in a struggle for North America.

Competing Claims in North America

Magellan's voyage showed that ships could reach Asia by way of the Pacific Ocean. Spain claimed the route around the southern tip of South America. Other European countries hoped to find an easier and more direct route to the Pacific. If it existed, a northwest trade route through North America to Asia would become highly profitable. Not finding the route, the French, English, and Dutch instead established colonies in North America.

TAKING NOTES

Clarifying Use a chart to record information about early settlements.

Name of Settlement	General Location
New France	
New Netherland	
Massachusetts Bay	

Explorers Establish New France The early French explorers sailed west with dreams of reaching the East Indies. One explorer was Giovanni da Verrazzano (VEHR•uh•ZAHN•noh), an Italian in the service of France. In 1524, he sailed to North America in search of a sea route to the Pacific. While he did not find the route, Verrazzano did discover what is today New York harbor. Ten years later, the Frenchman Jacques Cartier (kahr•TYAY) reached a gulf off the eastern coast of Canada that led to a broad river. Cartier named it the St. Lawrence. He followed it inward until he reached a large island dominated by a mountain. He named the island Mont Real (Mount Royal), which later became known as Montreal. In 1608, another French explorer, Samuel de Champlain, sailed up the St. Lawrence with about 32 colonists. They founded Quebec, which became the base of France's colonial empire in North America, known as **New France**.

Then the French penetrated the North American continent. In 1673, French Jesuit priest Jacques Marquette and trader Louis Joliet explored the Great Lakes and the upper Mississippi River. Nearly 10 years later, Sieur de La Salle explored the lower Mississippi. He claimed the entire river valley for France. He named it Louisiana in honor of the French king, Louis XIV. By the early 1700s, New France covered much of what is now the midwestern United States and eastern Canada.

A Trading Empire France's North American empire was immense. But it was sparsely populated. By 1760, the European population of New France had grown to only about 65,000. A large number of French colonists had no desire to build towns or raise families. These settlers included Catholic priests who sought to convert Native Americans. They also included young, single men engaged in what had become New France's main economic activity, the fur trade. Unlike the English, the French were less interested in occupying territories than they were in making money off the land. (A)

MAIN IDEA

Summarizing

(A) Why were France's North American holdings so sparsely populated?

The English Arrive in North America

The explorations of the Spanish and French inspired the English. In 1606, a company of London investors received from King James a charter to found a colony in North America. In late 1606, the company's three ships, and more than 100 settlers, pushed out of an English harbor. About four months later, in 1607, they reached the coast of Virginia. The colonists claimed the land as theirs. They named the settlement **Jamestown** in honor of their king.

The Settlement at Jamestown The colony's start was disastrous. The settlers were more interested in finding gold than in planting crops. During the first few years, seven out of every ten people died of hunger, disease, or battles with the Native Americans.

Despite their nightmarish start, the colonists eventually gained a foothold in their new land. Jamestown became England's first permanent settlement in North America. The colony's outlook improved greatly after farmers there discovered tobacco. High demand in England for tobacco turned it into a profitable cash crop.

Puritans Create a "New England" In 1620, a group known as **Pilgrims** founded a second English colony, Plymouth, in Massachusetts. Persecuted for their religious beliefs in England, these colonists sought religious freedom. Ten years later, a group known as **Puritans** also sought religious freedom from England's Anglican Church. They established a larger colony at nearby Massachusetts Bay.

▼ Henry Hudson's ship arrives in the bay of New York on September 12, 1609.

The Puritans wanted to build a model community that would set an example for other Christians to follow. Although the colony experienced early difficulties, it gradually took hold. This was due in large part to the numerous families in the colony, unlike the mostly single, male population in Jamestown.

The Dutch Found New Netherland Following the English and French into North America were the Dutch. In 1609, Henry Hudson, an Englishman in the service of the Netherlands, sailed west. He was searching for a northwest sea route to Asia. Hudson did not find a route. He did, however, explore three waterways that were later named for him—the Hudson River, Hudson Bay, and Hudson Strait.

The Dutch claimed the region along these waterways. They established a fur trade with the Iroquois Indians. They built trading posts along the Hudson River at Fort Orange (now Albany) and on Manhattan Island. Dutch merchants formed the Dutch West India Company. In 1621, the Dutch government granted the company permission to colonize the region and expand the fur trade. The Dutch holdings in North America became known as **New Netherland**.

Although the Dutch company profited from its fur trade, it was slow to attract Dutch colonists. To encourage settlers, the colony opened its doors to a variety of peoples. Gradually more Dutch, as well as Germans, French, Scandinavians, and other Europeans, settled the area. (B)

MAIN IDEA
Contrasting
(B) How were the Dutch and French colonies different from the English colonies in North America?

Colonizing the Caribbean During the 1600s, the nations of Europe also colonized the Caribbean. The French seized control of present-day Haiti, Guadeloupe, and Martinique. The English settled Barbados and Jamaica. In 1634, the Dutch captured what are now the Netherlands Antilles and Aruba from Spain.

On these islands, the Europeans built huge cotton and sugar plantations. These products, although profitable, demanded a large and steady supply of labor. Enslaved Africans eventually would supply this labor.

The Struggle for North America

As they expanded their settlements in North America, the nations of France, England, and the Netherlands battled each other for colonial supremacy.

The English Oust the Dutch To the English, New Netherland separated their northern and southern colonies. In 1664, the English king, Charles II, granted his brother, the Duke of York, permission to drive out the Dutch. When the duke's fleet arrived at New Netherland, the Dutch surrendered without firing a shot. The Duke of York claimed the colony for England and renamed it New York.

With the Dutch gone, the English colonized the Atlantic coast of North America. By 1750, about 1.2 million English settlers lived in 13 colonies from Maine to Georgia.

England Battles France The English soon became hungry for more land for their colonial population. So they pushed farther west into the continent. By doing so, they collided with France's North American holdings. As their colonies expanded, France and England began to interfere with each other. It seemed that a major conflict was on the horizon.

In 1754 a dispute over land claims in the Ohio Valley led to a war between the British and French on the North

History *in* Depth

Pirates

The battle for colonial supremacy occurred not only on land, but also on the sea. Acting on behalf of their government, privately owned armed ships, known as privateers, attacked merchant ships of enemy nations and sank or robbed them.

Also patrolling the high seas were pirates. They attacked ships for their valuables and did not care what nation the vessels represented. One of the best-known pirates was Edward B. Teach, whose prominent beard earned him the nickname Blackbeard. According to one account, Blackbeard attempted to frighten his victims by sticking "lighted matches under his hat, which appeared on both sides of his face and eyes, naturally fierce and wild."

GEOGRAPHY SKILLBUILDER: Interpreting Maps

1. **Region** *Which nation claimed the largest area of the present-day United States in 1754?*
2. **Place** *How did Britain's North American empire change by 1763?*

American continent. The conflict became known as the **French and Indian War**. The war became part of a larger conflict known as the Seven Years' War. Britain and France, along with their European allies, also battled for supremacy in Europe, the West Indies, and India.

In North America, the British colonists, with the help of the British Army, defeated the French in 1763. The French surrendered their North American holdings. As a result of the war, the British seized control of the eastern half of North America.

Native Americans Respond

As in Mexico and South America, the arrival of Europeans in the present-day United States had a great impact on Native Americans. European colonization brought mostly disaster for the lands' original inhabitants.

A Strained Relationship French and Dutch settlers developed a mostly cooperative relationship with the Native Americans. This was due mainly to the mutual benefits of the fur trade. Native Americans did most of the trapping and then traded the furs to the French for such items as guns, hatchets, mirrors, and beads. The Dutch also cooperated with Native Americans in an effort to establish a fur-trading enterprise.

The groups did not live together in complete harmony. Dutch settlers fought with various Native American groups over land claims and trading rights. For the most part, however, the French and Dutch colonists lived together peacefully with their North American hosts. C

MAIN IDEA

Analyzing Issues

C Why were the Dutch and French able to coexist in relative peace with the Native Americans?

The same could not be said of the English. Early relations between English settlers and Native Americans were cooperative. However, they quickly worsened over the issues of land and religion. Unlike the French and Dutch, the English sought to populate their colonies in North America. This meant pushing the natives off their land. The English colonists seized more land for their population—and to grow tobacco.

Religious differences also heightened tensions. The English settlers considered Native Americans heathens, people without a faith. Over time, many Puritans viewed Native Americans as agents of the devil and as a threat to their godly society. Native Americans developed a similarly harsh view of the European invaders. D

MAIN IDEA

Identifying Problems-

D Why did the issues of land and religion cause strife between Native Americans and settlers?

Settlers and Native Americans Battle The hostility between the English settlers and Native Americans led to warfare. As early as 1622, the Powhatan tribe attacked colonial villages around Jamestown and killed about 350 settlers. During the next few years, the colonists struck back and massacred hundreds of Powhatan.

One of the bloodiest conflicts between colonists and Native Americans was known as King Philip's War. It began in 1675 when the Native American ruler **Metacom** (also known as King Philip) led an attack on colonial villages throughout Massachusetts. In the months that followed, both sides massacred hundreds of victims. After a year of fierce fighting, the colonists defeated the natives. During the 17th century, many skirmishes erupted throughout North America.

Natives Fall to Disease More destructive than the Europeans' weapons were their diseases. Like the Spanish in Central and South America, the Europeans who settled North America brought with them several diseases. The diseases devastated the native population in North America.

In 1616, for example, an epidemic of smallpox ravaged Native Americans living along the New England coast. The population of one tribe, the Massachusett, dropped from 24,000 to 750 by 1631. From South Carolina to Missouri, nearly whole tribes fell to smallpox, measles, and other diseases.

One of the effects of this loss was a severe shortage of labor in the colonies. In order to meet their growing labor needs, European colonists soon turned to another group: Africans, whom they would enslave by the million.

NEW YORK CORE CURRICULUM REVIEW

TERMS & NAMES 1. For each term or name, write a sentence explaining its significance.

- New France
- Jamestown
- Pilgrims
- Puritans
- New Netherland
- French and Indian War
- Metacom

USING YOUR NOTES

2. What did these settlements have in common?

Name of Settlement	General Location	Reasons Settled
New France		
New Netherland		
Massachusetts Bay		

MAIN IDEAS

3. What was a basic difference between French and English attitudes about the land they acquired in North America?
4. What was the main result of the French and Indian War?
5. What were some of the results for Native Americans of European colonization of North America?

CRITICAL THINKING & WRITING

6. **MAKING INFERENCES** What may have been one reason the English eventually beat the French in North America?
7. **DRAWING CONCLUSIONS** What need drove the English farther west into the North American continent?
8. **COMPARING** In what ways did the colonies at Jamestown and Massachusetts Bay differ?
9. **WRITING ACTIVITY** EMPIRE BUILDING What were some of the grievances of Native Americans toward English colonists? Make a bulleted **list** of Native American complaints to display in the classroom.

INTEGRATED TECHNOLOGY **INTERNET ACTIVITY**

Use the Internet to research French Cajun culture in Louisiana. Make a **poster** displaying your findings.

INTERNET KEYWORD
Cajun

The Atlantic Slave Trade

CONNECT TO THE NEW YORK STATE CORE CURRICULUM

Unit 4.E.3. Global demographic shifts case study: The triangular trade and slavery
Unit 4.E.4. The extent of European expansionism

TERMS & NAMES

- Atlantic slave trade
- triangular trade
- middle passage

SETTING THE STAGE Sugar plantations and tobacco farms required a large supply of workers to make them profitable for their owners. European owners had planned to use Native Americans as a source of cheap labor. But millions of Native Americans died from disease, warfare, and brutal treatment. Therefore, the Europeans in Brazil, the Caribbean, and the southern colonies of North America soon turned to Africa for workers. This demand for cheap labor resulted in the brutalities of the slave trade.

TAKING NOTES

Recognizing Effects Use a diagram like the one below to list effects of the Atlantic slave trade.

Consequences of the slave trade
I. in Africa
A.
B.
II. in the Americas
A.
B.

The Causes of African Slavery

Beginning around 1500, European colonists in the Americas who needed cheap labor began using enslaved Africans on plantations and farms.

Slavery in Africa Slavery had existed in Africa for centuries. In most regions, it was a relatively minor institution. The spread of Islam into Africa during the seventh century, however, ushered in an increase in slavery and the slave trade. Muslim rulers in Africa justified enslavement with the Muslim belief that non-Muslim prisoners of war could be bought and sold as slaves. As a result, between 650 and 1600, Muslims transported about 17 million Africans to the Muslim lands of North Africa and Southwest Asia.

In most African and Muslim societies, slaves had some legal rights and an opportunity for social mobility. In the Muslim world, a few slaves even occupied positions of influence and power. Some served as generals in the army. In African societies, slaves could escape their bondage in numerous ways, including marrying into the family they served.

The Demand for Africans The first Europeans to explore Africa were the Portuguese during the 1400s. Initially, Portuguese traders were more interested in trading for gold than for captured Africans. That changed with the colonization of the Americas, as natives began dying by the millions.

Europeans saw advantages in using Africans in the Americas. First, many Africans had been exposed to European diseases and had built up some immunity. Second, many Africans had experience in farming and could be taught plantation work. Third, Africans were less likely to escape because they did not know their way around the new land. Fourth, their skin color made it easier to catch them if they escaped and tried to live among others.

In time, the buying and selling of Africans for work in the Americas—known as the **Atlantic slave trade**—became a massive enterprise. Between 1500 and 1600, nearly 300,000 Africans were transported to the Americas. During the next century, that number climbed to almost 1.3 million. By the time the Atlantic slave trade ended around 1870, Europeans had imported about 9.5 million Africans to the Americas. **A**

MAIN IDEA
Analyzing Motives
A What advantages did Europeans see in enslaving Africans?

Spain and Portugal Lead the Way The Spanish took an early lead in importing Africans to the Americas. Spain moved on from the Caribbean and began to colonize the American mainland. As a result, the Spanish imported and enslaved thousands more Africans. By 1650, nearly 300,000 Africans labored throughout Spanish America on plantations and in gold and silver mines.

By this time, however, the Portuguese had surpassed the Spanish in the importation of Africans to the Americas. During the 1600s, Brazil dominated the European sugar market. As the colony's sugar industry grew, so too did European colonists' demand for cheap labor. During the 17th century, more than 40 percent of all Africans brought to the Americas went to Brazil.

Slavery Spreads Throughout the Americas

As the other European nations established colonies in the Americas, their demand for cheap labor grew. Thus, they also began to import large numbers of Africans.

England Dominates the Slave Trade As England's presence in the Americas grew, it came to dominate the Atlantic slave trade. From 1690 until England abolished the slave trade in 1807, it was the leading carrier of enslaved Africans. By the time the slave trade ended, the English had transported nearly 1.7 million Africans to their colonies in the West Indies.

African slaves were also brought to what is now the United States. In all, nearly 400,000 Africans were sold to Britain's North American colonies. Once in North America, however, the slave population steadily grew. By 1830, roughly 2 million slaves toiled in the United States.

History in Depth

Slavery

Slavery probably began with the development of farming about 10,000 years ago. Farmers used prisoners of war to work for them.

Slavery has existed in societies around the world. People were enslaved in civilizations from Egypt to China to India. The picture at the right shows slaves working in a Roman coal mine.

Race was not always a factor in slavery. Often, slaves were captured prisoners of war, or people of a different nationality or religion.

However, the slavery that developed in the Americas was based largely on race. Europeans viewed black people as naturally inferior. Because of this, slavery in the Americas was hereditary.

African Cooperation and Resistance Many African rulers and merchants played a willing role in the Atlantic slave trade. Most European traders, rather than travel inland, waited in ports along the coasts of Africa. African merchants, with the help of local rulers, captured Africans to be enslaved. They then delivered them to the Europeans in exchange for gold, guns, and other goods. **B**

As the slave trade grew, some African rulers voiced their opposition to the practice. Nonetheless, the slave trade steadily grew. Lured by its profits, many African rulers continued to participate. African merchants developed new trade routes to avoid rulers who refused to cooperate.

MAIN IDEA

Analyzing Issues

B Why did many African rulers participate in the Atlantic slave trade?

A Forced Journey

After being captured, African men and women were shipped to the Americas as part of a profitable trade network. Along the way, millions of Africans died.

The Triangular Trade Africans transported to the Americas were part of a transatlantic trading network known as the **triangular trade**. Over one trade route, Europeans transported manufactured goods to the west coast of Africa. There, traders exchanged these goods for captured Africans. The Africans were then transported across the Atlantic and sold in the West Indies. Merchants bought sugar, coffee, and tobacco in the West Indies and sailed to Europe with these products.

On another triangular route, merchants carried rum and other goods from the New England colonies to Africa. There they exchanged their merchandise for Africans. The traders transported the Africans to the West Indies and sold them for sugar and molasses. They then sold these goods to rum producers in New England.

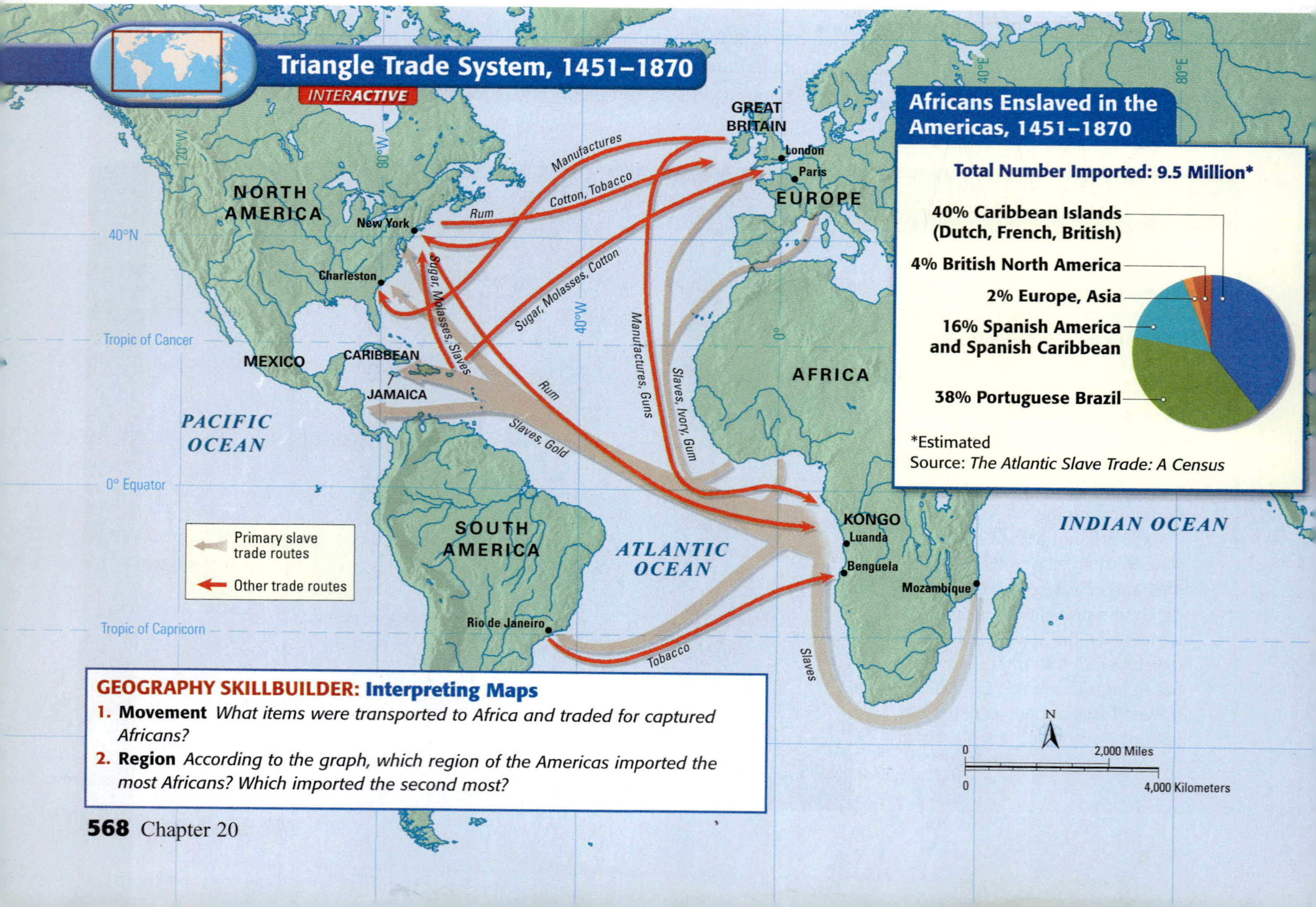

GEOGRAPHY SKILLBUILDER: Interpreting Maps

1. **Movement** *What items were transported to Africa and traded for captured Africans?*
2. **Region** *According to the graph, which region of the Americas imported the most Africans? Which imported the second most?*

Analyzing Primary Sources

The Horrors of the Middle Passage

One African, Olaudah Equiano, recalled the inhumane conditions on his trip from West Africa to the West Indies at age 12 in 1762.

PRIMARY SOURCE

I was soon put down under the decks, and there I received such a salutation [greeting] in my nostrils as I never experienced in my life; so that, with the loathsomeness of the stench, and crying together, I became so sick and low that I was not able to eat . . . but soon, to my grief, two of the white men offered me eatables; and on my refusing to eat, one of them held me fast by the hands, and laid me across . . . the windlass, while the other flogged me severely.

OLAUDAH EQUIANO, quoted in *Eyewitness: The Negro in American History*

This diagram of a British slave ship shows how slave traders packed Africans onto slave ships in the hold below decks for the brutal middle passage.

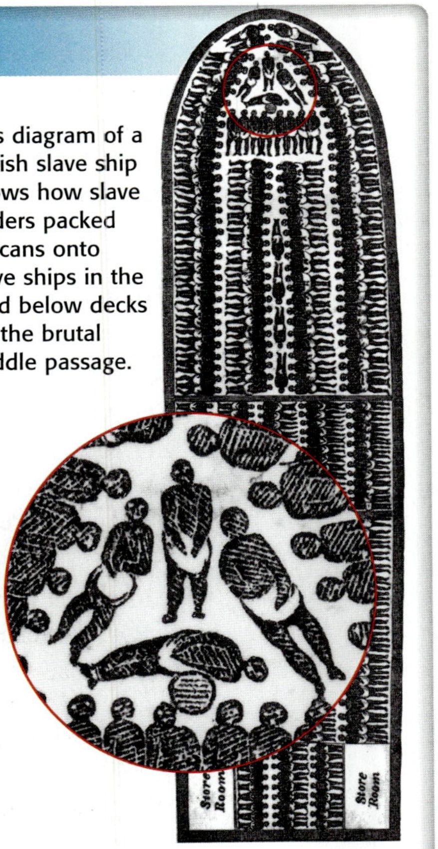

DOCUMENT-BASED QUESTIONS

1. **Making Inferences** *Why might the white men have forced Equiano to eat?*
2. **Drawing Conclusions** *What does the diagram of the slave ship suggest about conditions on board?*

Various other transatlantic routes existed. The "triangular" trade encompassed a network of trade routes crisscrossing the northern and southern colonies, the West Indies, England, Europe, and Africa. The network carried a variety of traded goods.

The Middle Passage The voyage that brought captured Africans to the West Indies and later to North and South America was known as the **middle passage**. It was considered the middle leg of the transatlantic trade triangle. Sickening cruelty characterized this journey. In African ports, European traders packed Africans into the dark holds of large ships. On board, Africans endured whippings and beatings from merchants, as well as diseases that swept through the vessel. Numerous Africans died from disease or physical abuse aboard the slave ships. Many others committed suicide by drowning. Scholars estimate that roughly 20 percent of the Africans aboard each slave ship perished during the brutal trip.

Slavery in the Americas

Africans who survived their ocean voyage faced a difficult life in the Americas. Forced to work in a strange land, enslaved Africans coped in a variety of ways.

A Harsh Life Upon arriving in the Americas, captured Africans usually were auctioned off to the highest bidder. After being sold, slaves worked in mines or fields or as domestic servants. Slaves lived a grueling existence. Many lived on little food in small, dreary huts. They worked long days and suffered beatings. In much of the Americas, slavery was a lifelong condition, as well as a hereditary one.

Resistance and Rebellion To cope with the horrors of slavery, Africans developed a way of life based on their cultural heritage. They kept alive such things as their musical traditions as well as the stories of their ancestors.

Slaves also found ways to resist. They made themselves less productive by breaking tools, uprooting plants, and working slowly. Thousands also ran away.

Some slaves pushed their resistance to open revolt. As early as 1522, about 20 slaves on Hispaniola attacked and killed several Spanish colonists. Larger revolts occurred throughout Spanish settlements during the 16th century.

Occasional uprisings also occurred in Brazil, the West Indies, and North America. In 1739, a group of slaves in South Carolina led an uprising known as the Stono Rebellion. Uprisings continued into the 1800s.

Consequences of the Slave Trade

The Atlantic slave trade had a profound impact on both Africa and the Americas. In Africa, numerous cultures lost generations of their fittest members—their young and able—to European traders and plantation owners. In addition, countless African families were torn apart. Many of them were never reunited. The slave trade devastated African societies in another way: by introducing guns into the continent.

While they were unwilling participants in the growth of the colonies, African slaves contributed greatly to the economic and cultural development of the Americas. Their greatest contribution was their labor. Without their back-breaking work, colonies such as those on Haiti and Barbados may not have survived. In addition to their muscle, enslaved Africans brought their expertise, especially in agriculture. They also brought their culture. Their art, music, religion, and food continue to influence American societies.

The influx of so many Africans to the Americas also has left its mark on the very population itself. From the United States to Brazil, many of the nations of the Western Hemisphere today have substantial African-American populations. Many Latin American countries have sizable mixed-race populations.

As the next section explains, Africans were not the only cargo transported across the Atlantic during the colonization of the Americas. The settlement of the Americas brought many different items from Europe, Asia, and Africa to North and South America. It also introduced items from the Americas to the rest of the world.

NEW YORK CORE CURRICULUM REVIEW

TERMS & NAMES 1. For each term or name, write a sentence explaining its significance.

- Atlantic slave trade
- triangular trade
- middle passage

USING YOUR NOTES

2. What seems to have been the most important consequence? Explain.

Consequences of the slave trade
I. in Africa
A.
B.
II. in the Americas
A.
B.

MAIN IDEAS

3. What effect did the spread of Islam have on the slave trade?
4. How did enslaved Africans resist their bondage?
5. How did African slaves contribute to the development of the Americas?

CRITICAL THINKING & WRITING

6. **COMPARING AND CONTRASTING** How was slavery in the Americas different from slavery in Africa?
7. **SYNTHESIZING** What does the percentage of enslaved Africans imported to the Caribbean Islands and Brazil suggest about the racial makeup of these areas?
8. **MAKING INFERENCES** Why do you think the slave trade flourished for so long?
9. **WRITING ACTIVITY** CULTURAL INTERACTION Imagine you are an African ruler. Write a **letter** to a European leader in which you try to convince him or her to stop participating in the slave trade.

CONNECT TO TODAY **MAKING A MAP**

Research which of the original 13 colonies had the greatest numbers of slaves in the late 18th century. Then make a **map** of the colonies in which you show the numbers for each state.

4

The Columbian Exchange and Global Trade

CONNECT TO THE NEW YORK STATE CORE CURRICULUM

Unit 4.E.5. European mercantilism
Unit 4.E.8. Exchange of food and disease

TERMS & NAMES

- Columbian Exchange
- capitalism
- joint-stock company
- mercantilism
- favorable balance of trade

SETTING THE STAGE The colonization of the Americas dramatically changed the world. It prompted both voluntary and forced migration of millions of people. It led to the establishment of new and powerful societies. Other effects of European settlement of the Americas were less noticeable but equally important. Colonization resulted in the exchange of new items that greatly influenced the lives of people throughout the world. The new wealth from the Americas resulted in new business and trade practices in Europe.

The Columbian Exchange

The global transfer of foods, plants, and animals during the colonization of the Americas is known as the **Columbian Exchange**. Ships from the Americas brought back a wide array of items that Europeans, Asians, and Africans had never before seen. They included such plants as tomatoes, squash, pineapples, tobacco, and cacao beans (for chocolate). And they included animals such as the turkey, which became a source of food in the Eastern Hemisphere.

Perhaps the most important items to travel from the Americas to the rest of the world were corn and potatoes. Both were inexpensive to grow and nutritious. Potatoes, especially, supplied many essential vitamins and minerals. Over time, both crops became an important and steady part of diets throughout the world. These foods helped people live longer. Thus they played a significant role in boosting the world's population. The planting of the first white potato in Ireland and the first sweet potato in China probably changed more lives than the deeds of 100 kings.

Traffic across the Atlantic did not flow in just one direction, however. Europeans introduced various livestock animals into the Americas. These included horses, cattle, sheep, and pigs. Foods from Africa (including some that originated in Asia) migrated west in European ships. They included bananas, black-eyed peas, and yams. Grains introduced to the Americas included wheat, rice, barley, and oats.

Some aspects of the Columbian Exchange had a tragic impact on many Native Americans. Disease was just as much a part of the Columbian Exchange as goods and food. The diseases Europeans brought with them, which included smallpox and measles, led to the deaths of millions of Native Americans.

TAKING NOTES

Recognizing Effects Use a chart to record information about the Columbian Exchange.

Food/ Livestock/ Disease	Place of Origin	Effect
Potato		
Horse		
Smallpox		

The Columbian Exchange

Few events transformed the world like the Columbian Exchange. This global transfer of plants, animals, disease, and especially food brought together the Eastern and Western hemispheres and touched, in some way, nearly all the peoples of the world.

"The culinary life we owe Columbus is a progressive dinner in which the whole human race takes part but no one need leave home to sample all the courses."

Raymond Sokolov

Frightening Foods

Several foods from the Americas that we now take for granted at first amazed and terrified Europeans. Early on, people thought the tomato was harmful to eat. One German official warned that the tomato "should not be taken internally." In 1619, officials in Burgundy, France, banned potatoes, explaining that "too frequent use of them caused the leprosy." In 1774, starving peasants in Prussia refused to eat the spud.

The Columbian Exchange

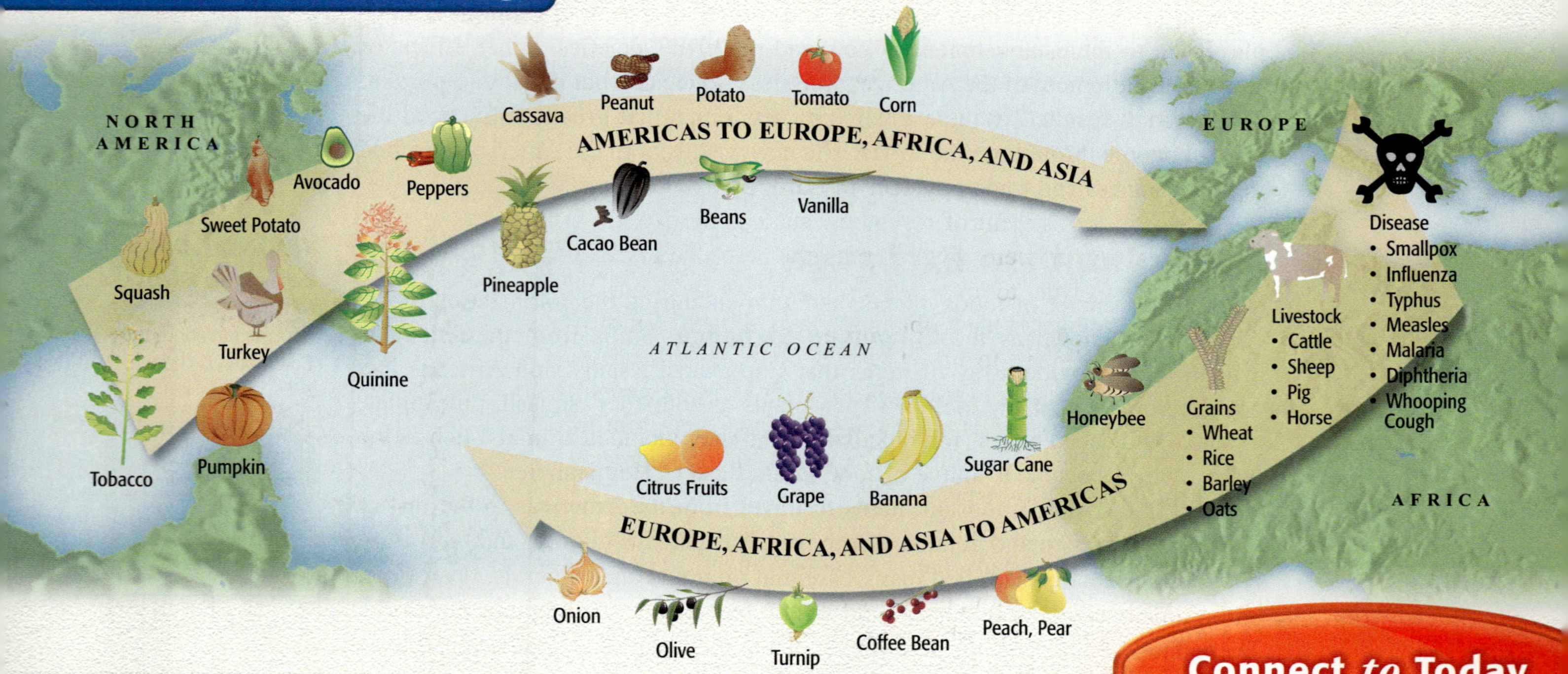

Patterns of Interaction

The Geography of Food: The Impact of Potatoes and Sugar

Think about your favorite foods. Chances are that at least one originated in a distant land. Throughout history, the introduction of new foods into a region has dramatically changed lives—for better and worse. Dependence on the potato, for example, led to a famine in Ireland. This prompted a massive migration of Irish people to other countries. In the Americas, the introduction of sugar led to riches for some and enslavement for many others.

Connect *to* Today

1. **Forming Opinions** Have students work in small groups to pose and answer questions about the beneficial and harmful aspects of the Columbian Exchange.
   See Skillbuilder Handbook, page R20.
2. **Comparing and Contrasting** Find out what major items are exchanged or traded between the United States and either Asia, Africa, or Europe. How do the items compare with those of the Columbian Exchange? Report your findings to the class.

A Spanish missionary in Mexico described the effects of smallpox on the Aztecs:

PRIMARY SOURCE

There was a great havoc. Very many died of it. They could not walk. . . . They could not move; they could not stir; they could not change position, nor lie on one side; nor face down, nor on their backs. And if they stirred, much did they cry out. Great was its destruction.

BERNARDINO DE SAHAGUN, quoted in *Seeds of Change*

MAIN IDEA

Making Inferences

A Why is the Columbian Exchange considered a significant event?

Other diseases Europeans brought with them included influenza, typhus, malaria, and diphtheria. **A**

Global Trade

The establishment of colonial empires in the Americas influenced the nations of Europe in still other ways. New wealth from the Americas was coupled with a dramatic growth in overseas trade. The two factors together prompted a wave of new business and trade practices in Europe during the 16th and 17th centuries. These practices, many of which served as the root of today's financial dealings, dramatically changed the economic atmosphere of Europe.

The Rise of Capitalism One aspect of the European economic revolution was the growth of **capitalism**. Capitalism is an economic system based on private ownership and the investment of resources, such as money, for profit. No longer were governments the sole owners of great wealth. Due to overseas colonization and trade, numerous merchants had obtained great wealth. These merchants continued to invest their money in trade and overseas exploration. Profits from these investments enabled merchants and traders to reinvest even more money in other enterprises. As a result, businesses across Europe grew and flourished.

The increase in economic activity in Europe led to an overall increase in many nations' money supply. This in turn brought on inflation, or the steady rise in the price of goods. Inflation occurs when people have more money to spend and thus demand more goods and services. Because the supply of goods is less than the demand for them, the goods become both scarce and more valuable. Prices then rise. At this time in Europe, the costs of many goods rose. Spain, for example, endured a crushing bout of inflation during the 1600s, as boatloads of gold and silver from the Americas greatly increased the nation's money supply.

Joint-Stock Companies Another business venture that developed during this period was known as the **joint-stock company**. The joint-stock company worked much like the modern-day corporation, with investors buying shares of stock in a company. It involved a number of people combining their wealth for a common purpose.

Three Worlds Meet, 1492–1700

1492 (Europeans)
Columbus embarks on voyage.

1511 (Africans)
Africans begin working as slaves in the Americas.

1521 (Americans)
The Aztec Empire in Mexico is conquered by Hernando Cortés.

1533 (Americans)
The Inca Empire in South America falls to Francisco Pizarro.

1630 (Europeans)
Puritans establish the Massachusetts Bay Colony in North America.

1650 (Africans)
The number of Africans toiling in Spanish America reaches 300,000.

1675 (Americans)
Native Americans battle colonists in King Philip's War.

1500 — 1550 — 1600 — 1650 — 1700

Analyzing Key Concepts

Mercantilism

As you have read, mercantilism was an economic theory practiced in Europe from the 16th to the 18th centuries. Economists of the period believed that a country's power came from its wealth. Thus, a country would do everything possible to acquire more gold, preferably at the expense of its rivals. A mercantilist country primarily sought gold in two ways: establishing and exploiting colonies, and establishing a favorable balance of trade with a rival country. In the example to the right, England is the home country, America is England's colony, and France is England's rival.

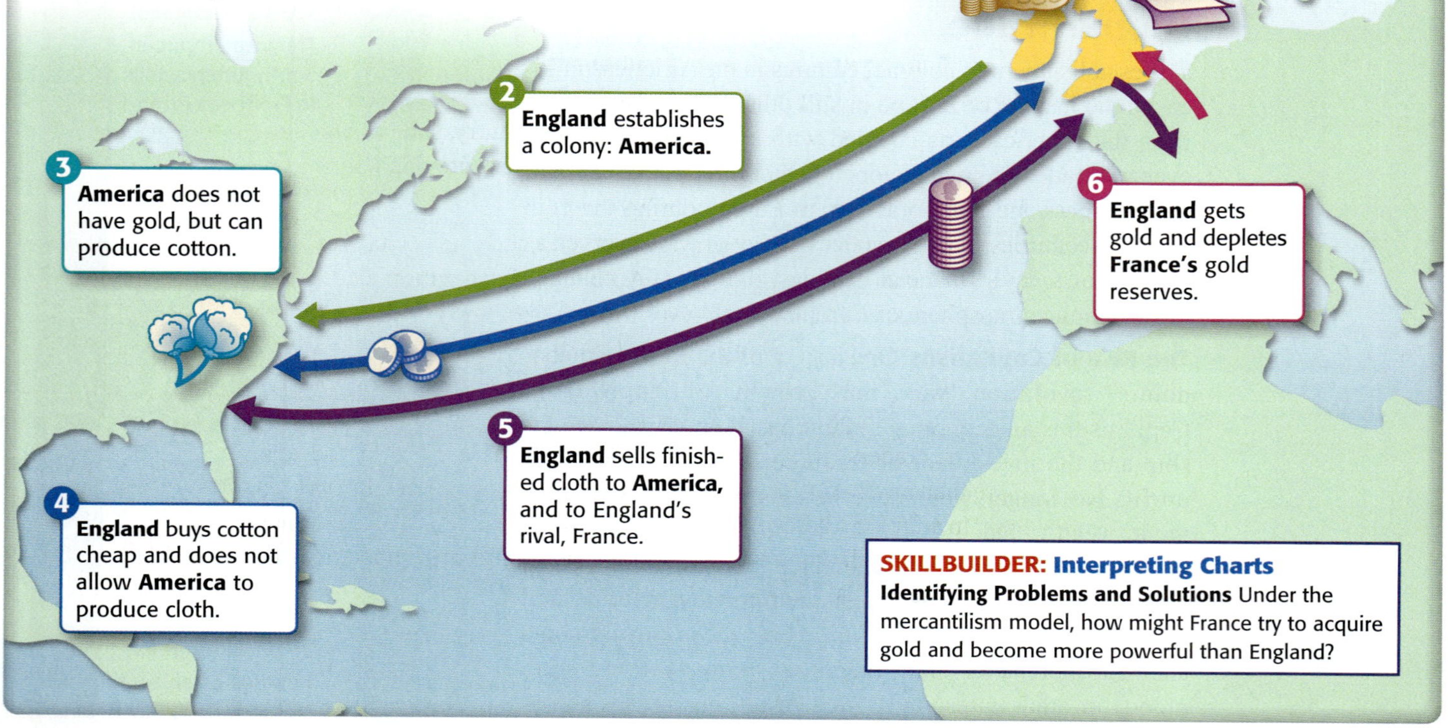

SKILLBUILDER: Interpreting Charts
Identifying Problems and Solutions Under the mercantilism model, how might France try to acquire gold and become more powerful than England?

In Europe during the 1500s and 1600s, that common purpose was American colonization. It took large amounts of money to establish overseas colonies. Moreover, while profits may have been great, so were risks. Many ships, for instance, never completed the long and dangerous ocean voyage. Because joint-stock companies involved numerous investors, the individual members paid only a fraction of the total colonization cost. If the colony failed, investors lost only their small share. If the colony thrived, the investors shared in the profits. It was a joint-stock company that was responsible for establishing Jamestown, England's first North American colony. B

MAIN IDEA
Making Inferences
B Why would a joint-stock company be popular with investors in overseas colonies?

The Growth of Mercantilism

During this time, the nations of Europe adopted a new economic policy known as **mercantilism**. The theory of mercantilism (shown above) held that a country's power depended mainly on its wealth. Wealth, after all, allowed nations to build strong navies and purchase vital goods. As a result, the goal of every nation became the attainment of as much wealth as possible.

Balance of Trade According to the theory of mercantilism, a nation could increase its wealth and power in two ways. First, it could obtain as much gold and silver as possible. Second, it could establish a **favorable balance of trade**, in which it sold more goods than it bought. A nation's ultimate goal under mercantilism was to become self-sufficient, not dependent on other countries for goods. An English author of the time wrote about the new economic idea of mercantilism:

PRIMARY SOURCE

Although a Kingdom may be enriched by gifts received, or by purchases taken from some other Nations . . . these are things uncertain and of small consideration when they happen. The ordinary means therefore to increase our wealth and treasure is by Foreign Trade, wherein we must ever observe this rule: to sell more to strangers yearly than we consume of theirs in value.

THOMAS MUN, quoted in *World Civilizations*

Mercantilism went hand in hand with colonization, for colonies played a vital role in this new economic practice. Aside from providing silver and gold, colonies provided raw materials that could not be found in the home country, such as wood or furs. In addition to playing the role of supplier, the colonies also provided a market. The home country could sell its goods to its colonies. (C)

MAIN IDEA

Summarizing-

(C) What role did colonies play in mercantilism?

Economic Revolution Changes European Society The economic changes that swept through much of Europe during the age of American colonization also led to changes in European society. The economic revolution spurred the growth of towns and the rise of a class of merchants who controlled great wealth.

The changes in European society, however, only went so far. While towns and cities grew in size, much of Europe's population continued to live in rural areas. And although merchants and traders enjoyed social mobility, the majority of Europeans remained poor. More than anything else, the economic revolution increased the wealth of European nations. In addition, mercantilism contributed to the creation of a national identity. Also, as Chapter 21 will describe, the new economic practices helped expand the power of European monarchs, who became powerful rulers.

NEW YORK CORE CURRICULUM REVIEW

TERMS & NAMES 1. For each term or name, write a sentence explaining its significance.

- Columbian Exchange
- capitalism
- joint-stock company
- mercantilism
- favorable balance of trade

USING YOUR NOTES

2. Which effect do you think had the greatest impact on history?

Food/ Livestock/ Disease	Place of Origin	Effect
Potato		
Horse		
Smallpox		

MAIN IDEAS

3. What were some of the food items that traveled from the Americas to the rest of the world?
4. What food and livestock from the rest of the world traveled to the Americas?
5. What were some of the effects on European society of the economic revolution that took place in the 16th and 17th centuries?

CRITICAL THINKING & WRITING

6. **MAKING INFERENCES** Why were colonies considered so important to the nations of Europe?
7. **DRAWING CONCLUSIONS** Why might establishing overseas colonies have justified high profits for those who financed the colonies?
8. **COMPARING** What were some of the positive and negative consequences of the Columbian Exchange?
9. **WRITING ACTIVITY** ECONOMICS Do you think the economic changes in Europe during the era of American colonization qualify as a revolution? Why or why not? Support your opinions in a two-paragraph **essay.**

CONNECT TO TODAY **MAKING A POSTER**

Research one crop that developed in the Americas (such as corn or potatoes) and its impact on the world today. Show your findings in a **poster.**

Chapter 20 Assessment

TERMS & NAMES

For each term or name below, briefly explain its connection to the Atlantic world from 1492 to 1800.

1. conquistador
2. *encomienda*
3. Jamestown
4. French and Indian War
5. Atlantic slave trade
6. triangular trade
7. Columbian Exchange
8. mercantilism

MAIN IDEAS

Spain Builds an American Empire Section 1 (pages 553–560)

9. Why did Columbus set sail westward?
10. What were three goals of the Spanish in the Americas?
11. Why did Popé lead a rebellion against the Spanish?

European Nations Settle North America Section 2 (pages 561–565)

12. What did the Europeans mostly grow in their Caribbean colonies?
13. What was the result of the French and Indian War?

The Atlantic Slave Trade Section 3 (pages 566–570)

14. What factors led European colonists to use Africans to resupply their labor force?
15. What were the conditions on board a slave ship?
16. What were several ways in which enslaved Africans resisted their treatment in the Americas?

The Columbian Exchange and Global Trade Section 4 (pages 571–575)

17. Why was the introduction of corn and potatoes to Europe and Asia so significant?
18. What was the economic policy of mercantilism?

CRITICAL THINKING

1. **USING YOUR NOTES**
Use the chart to identify which nation sponsored each explorer and the regions he explored.

Explorer	Nation	Regions
Cabral		
Magellan		
Cartier		

2. **DRAWING CONCLUSIONS**
EMPIRE BUILDING What factors helped the Europeans conquer the Americas? Which was the most important? Why?

3. **RECOGNIZING EFFECTS**
ECONOMICS Explain the statement, "Columbus's voyage began a process that changed the world forever." Consider all the peoples and places American colonization affected economically.

4. **COMPARING AND CONTRASTING**
CULTURAL INTERACTION What might have been some of the differences in the Europeans' and Native Americans' views of colonization?

5. **SYNTHESIZING**
How did enslaved Africans help create the societies in the New World?

VISUAL SUMMARY

The Atlantic World

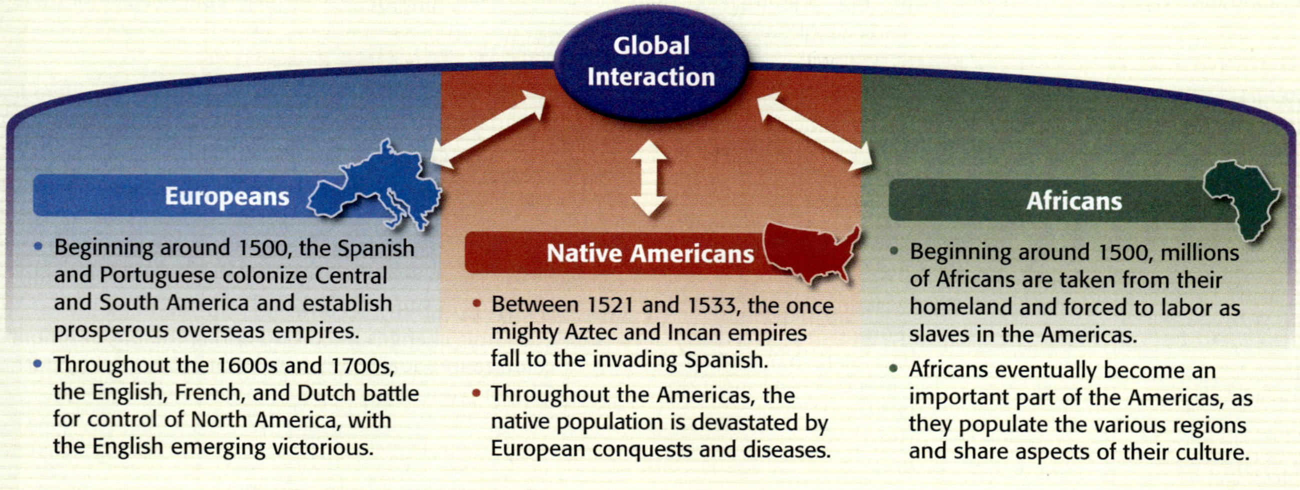

Use the quotation and your knowledge of world history to answer questions 1 and 2.
Additional Test Practice, pp. S1–S33

PRIMARY SOURCE

Where there is a vacant place, there is liberty for . . . [Christians] to come and inhabit, though they neither buy it nor ask their leaves. . . . Indeed, no nation is to drive out another without special commission from Heaven . . . unless the natives do unjustly wrong them, and will not recompense the wrongs done in a peaceable fort [way]. And then they may right themselves by lawful war and subdue the country unto themselves.

JOHN COTTON from "God's Promise to His Plantation"

1 What do you think Native Americans might have said about Cotton's statement that America was a "vacant place"?
(1) agreed that the continent was largely empty
(2) discussed development plans with him
(3) pointed out that they inhabited the land
(4) offered to sell the land to him

2 How might the last part of Cotton's statement have helped the Puritans justify taking land from the Native Americans?
(1) Puritans could claim natives had wronged them.
(2) Natives could claim Puritans had wronged them.
(3) Puritans believed war was wrong in all circumstances.
(4) Native Americans were willing to negotiate their grievances.

Use the Aztec drawing below and your knowledge of world history to answer question 3.

3 How does the artist depict the clash of Aztec and Spanish cultures?
(1) meeting to negotiate peace
(2) meeting as warriors
(3) engaging in a sports competition
(4) meeting as friends

INTEGRATED TECHNOLOGY
TEST PRACTICE Go to **classzone.com**
- Diagnostic tests
- Tutorials
- Strategies
- Additional practice

ALTERNATIVE ASSESSMENT

1. Interact *with* History

On page 552 you examined the choices some Native Americans faced during the invasion by Spanish conquistadors. Now that you have read the chapter, rethink the choice you made. If you chose to side with the Spaniards, would you now change your mind? Why? If you decided to fight with the Aztecs, what are your feelings now? Discuss your thoughts and opinions with a small group.

2. WRITING ABOUT HISTORY

An English colony would have looked strange and different to a Native American of the time. Write a **paragraph** describing an English colony of the 17th century. In your paragraph, provide details about the following:
- clothes
- food
- shelter
- weapons

INTEGRATED TECHNOLOGY

Participating in a WebQuest

Introduction The Columbian Exchange marked the beginning of worldwide trade. Imagine that you are an exporter of a product and want to know how tariffs will affect your sales in various countries.

Task Collect and organize data about a particular product, including how much of the product various countries import and the tariff each country imposes.

Process and Resources With a team of four other students, use the Internet to research your product. Internet keyword: *customs tariffs various countries.* Identify at least five countries that import the product. Organize your findings in a spreadsheet.

Evaluation and Conclusion How did this project contribute to your understanding of global trade? How do you think tariffs will affect demand for your product in each country?

Four Governments

In Unit 4, you studied how cultures around the world organized and governed themselves. The next six pages focus on four of those governments—the Incan Empire, Italian city-states, Tokugawa Japan, and the Ottoman Empire. How they functioned and the physical symbols they used to communicate their power are important themes. The chart below identifies some key characteristics of the four different governments, and the map locates them in time and place. Take notes on the similarities and differences between the four governments.

Key Characteristics

	Incan Empire	Italian City-States	Tokugawa Japan	Ottoman Empire
Title of Ruler	• Inca	• varied by city: some had title of nobility, others of an elected position	• Shogun; emperor was a figurehead only	• Sultan
Ruling Structure	• monarchical	• oligarchic	• militaristic	• bureaucratic
Basis of Authority	• ruler believed to be descendant of the Sun god	• inheritance or social status supported by financial influence	• absolute loyalty and devoted service of samurai to their daimyo	• military power
Distinctive Feature of Government	• Officials reported from the village level up to the king. • Members of an ethnic group, or *mitimas,* were moved from their homes to other areas to increase agricultural output or put down rebellions. • Children of Inca, local officials, and some others were taken to Cuzco for training.	• Power was in the hands of the ruling family or of a few wealthy families of bankers and merchants. • Many cities had constitutions and elected assemblies with little power.	• Daimyo were the shogun's vassals and local administrators. • Shogun controlled daimyo's marriage alliances and the number of samurai each had. • To ensure cooperation, daimyo's families were held hostage at court while daimyos administered their home regions.	• Sultan owned everything of value (such as land and labor); his bureaucracy was in charge of managing and protecting it. • Members of the bureaucracy derived status from the sultan but were his slaves along with their families. • Heads of *millets* governed locally.

SKILLBUILDER: Interpreting Charts
Drawing Conclusions *How did the rulers of most of these governments keep themselves in power?*

Monarchy in the Incan Empire, 1438–1535

The Incan monarchy was different from European monarchies. In the Incan Empire, all people worked for the state, either as farmers, or artisans making cloth, for example. Men also served as road builders, as messengers, or as soldiers. The state provided clothing, food, and any necessities in short supply. Every year, the amount of land every family had was reviewed to make sure it could produce enough food to live on.

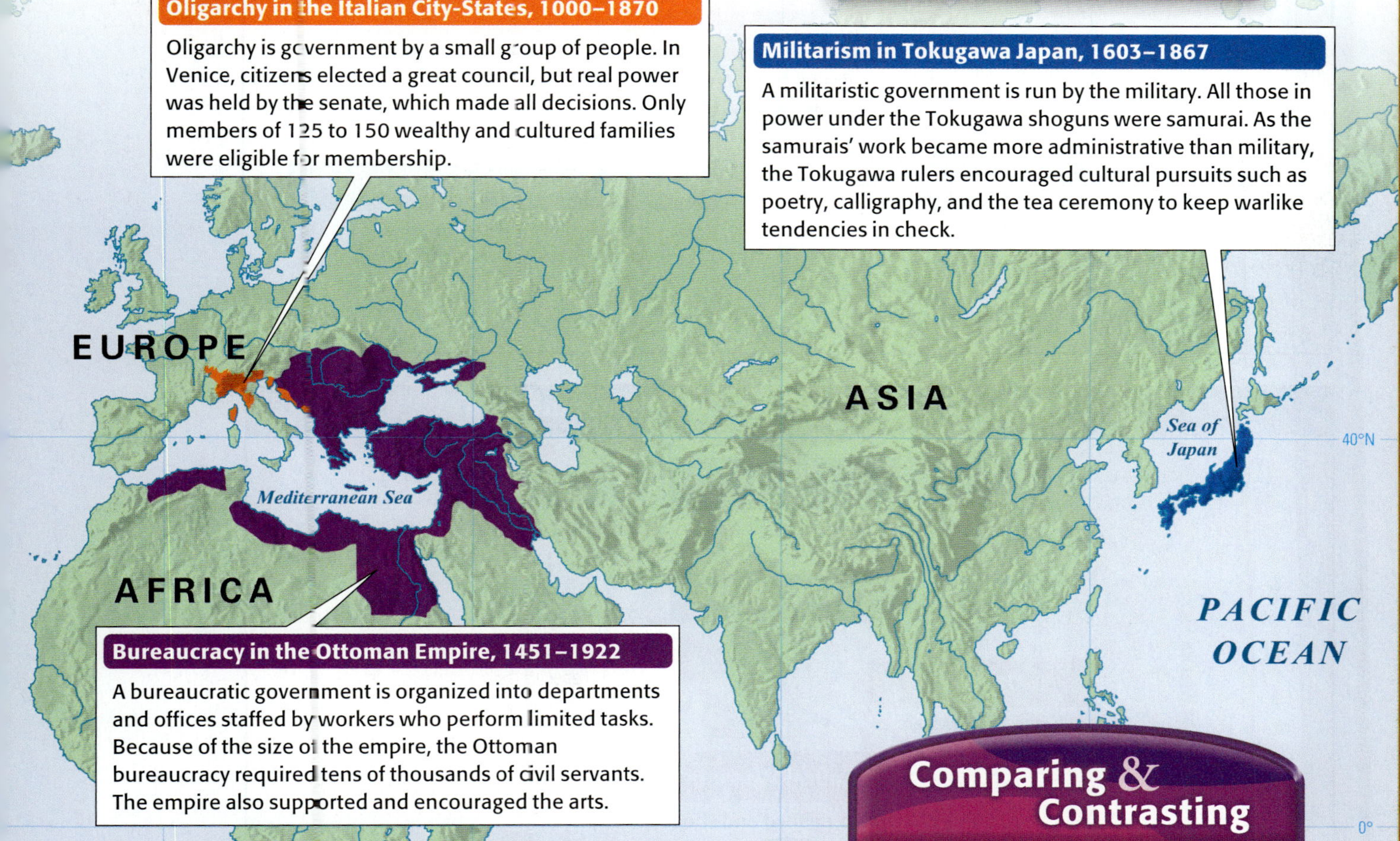

Oligarchy in the Italian City-States, 1000–1870

Oligarchy is government by a small group of people. In Venice, citizens elected a great council, but real power was held by the senate, which made all decisions. Only members of 125 to 150 wealthy and cultured families were eligible for membership.

Militarism in Tokugawa Japan, 1603–1867

A militaristic government is run by the military. All those in power under the Tokugawa shoguns were samurai. As the samurais' work became more administrative than military, the Tokugawa rulers encouraged cultural pursuits such as poetry, calligraphy, and the tea ceremony to keep warlike tendencies in check.

Bureaucracy in the Ottoman Empire, 1451–1922

A bureaucratic government is organized into departments and offices staffed by workers who perform limited tasks. Because of the size of the empire, the Ottoman bureaucracy required tens of thousands of civil servants. The empire also supported and encouraged the arts.

Comparing & Contrasting

1. In what ways did the Incan government resemble the Ottoman bureaucracy?
2. What similarities and differences were there in the way the sultans and shoguns controlled government officials?
3. What characteristic did the ruling class of the Italian city-states and Tokugawa Japan have in common?

Structures of Government

All of the governments have officials at different levels with varying degrees of power and responsibility. Compare the governmental structure of the Ottoman bureaucracy with that of Tokugawa Shogunate's militaristic government using the charts below.

Organization of the Ottoman Government

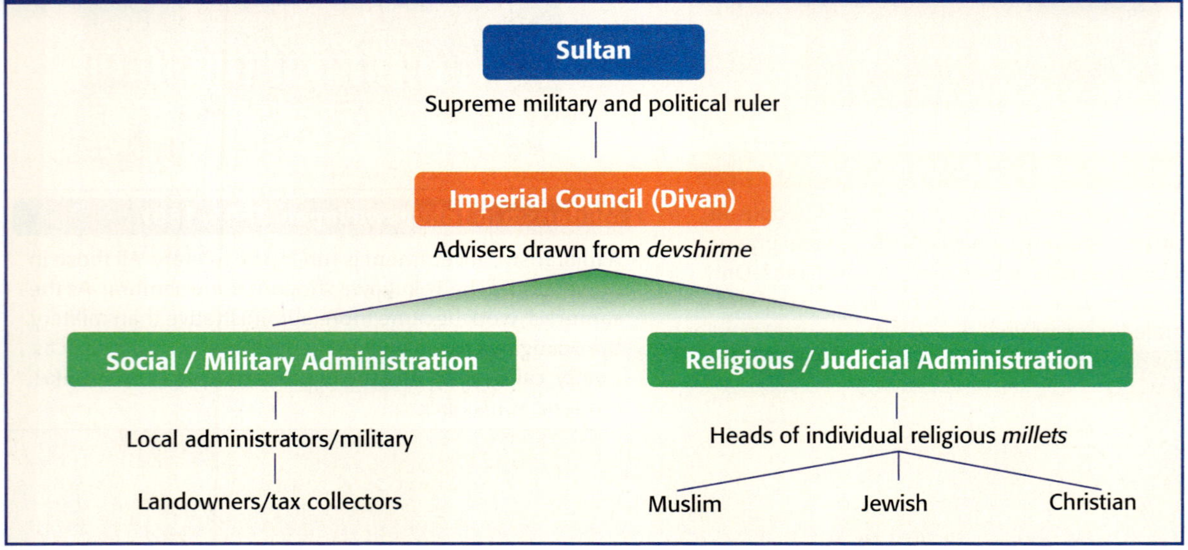

Organization of the Tokugawa Shogunate

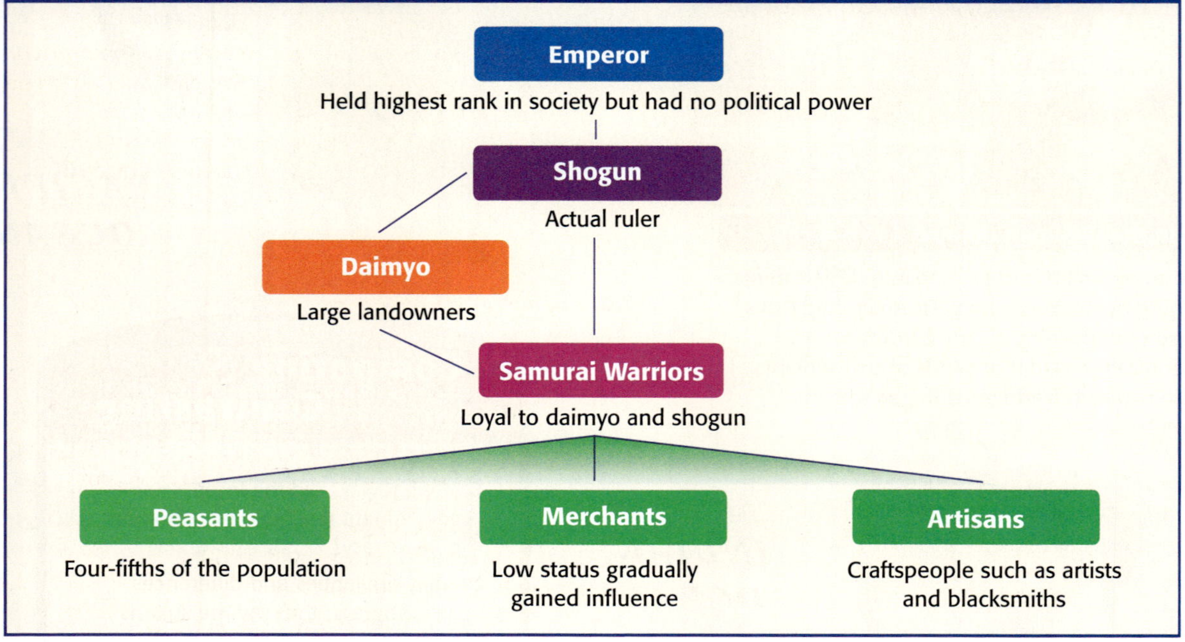

SKILLBUILDER: Interpreting Charts

1. **Clarifying** *To whom were the heads of the* millets *answerable?*
2. **Drawing Conclusions** *How might the samurai's loyalty to his daimyo conflict with his loyalty to the shogun?*

Artifacts of Power

The everyday objects used by members of government often serve a symbolic purpose. Note how the objects below communicated the rank and importance of the person who used them. Examine them and consider the effect they probably had on the people who saw them.

◄ Japanese Sword
Beautiful weapons and armor were symbols of status and power in Tokugawa Japan. Swords were the special weapons of the samurai, who were the only people allowed to carry arms. Daimyo had artisans make fine swords with expensively decorated hilts and scabbards for ceremonial occasions.

Italian Medici Pitcher ▲
As well as being great patrons of the fine arts, wealthy Italians surrounded themselves with luxurious practical objects. Even ordinary items, like a pitcher, were elaborately made of expensive materials.

◄ Incan Headdress
All of the people in the Incan Empire were required to wear the clothing of their particular ethnic group. The patterns on clothes and headdresses immediately identified a person's place of birth and social rank.

Comparing & Contrasting

1. How did the role of the sultan compare with the role of the Japanese emperor?
2. What message were expensive personal items meant to convey?
3. How does a household item like the pitcher differ from a sword or headdress as a symbol of power?

Architecture of Government

A ruler's castle or palace was a luxurious and safe home where he was surrounded by vassals who protected him. It was also a center of government where his administrators carried on their work under his supervision. Castles and palaces are a show of greatness. Large rooms that accommodate many guests demonstrate the ruler's authority over many people. Rich decorations display the ruler's wealth, refinement, and superior rank.

Japanese Palace ►
Osaka Castle was originally built by Toyotami Hideyoshi and has been rebuilt twice since then due to fire. It is surrounded by gardens, and the interior was known for its wall paintings and painted screens. During the Tokugawa period, the city of Osaka was a center of trade for agricultural and manufactured goods. The city was governed directly by the shoguns who owned the castle.

◄ Ottoman Palace
Topkapi Palace in modern Istanbul, Turkey, was the home of the Ottoman sultans. The buildings were built around several courtyards. Within the outer walls were gardens, a school for future officials, the treasury, and an arsenal. Elaborate paintings, woodwork, and tile designs decorated the walls and ceilings of rooms used by the sultan and his high officials.

Descriptions of Government

The following passages were written by writers who were reflecting not only on the past, but also on places and events they had personally witnessed.

PRIMARY SOURCE

INTERACTIVE

Machiavelli

In this excerpt from *The Discourses,* Italian writer Niccolò Machiavelli discusses six types of government—three good and three bad.

[T]he three bad ones result from the degradation of the other three. . . . Thus monarchy becomes tyranny; aristocracy degenerates into oligarchy; and the popular government lapses readily into licentiousness [lack of restraint].

[S]agacious legislators . . . have chosen one that should partake of all of them, judging that to be the most stable and solid. In fact, when there is combined under the same constitution a prince, a nobility, and the power of the people then these three powers will watch and keep each other reciprocally in check.

DOCUMENT-BASED QUESTION

Why does Machiavelli think a combined government is the best type of government?

PRIMARY SOURCE

INTERACTIVE

Garcilaso de la Vega

This description of government administration comes from Garcilaso's history of the Inca.

[Local administrators] were obliged each lunar month to furnish their superiors . . . with a record of the births and deaths that had occurred in the territory administered by them. . . .

[E]very two years . . . the wool from the royal herds was distributed in every village, in order that each person should be decently clothed during his entire life. It should be recalled that . . . the people . . . possessed only very few cattle, whereas the Inca's and the Sun's herds were . . . numerous. . . . Thus everyone was always provided with clothing, shoes, food, and all that is necessary in life.

DOCUMENT-BASED QUESTION

What and how did the Incan authorities provide for the common people's needs?

Comparing & Contrasting

1. How do Osaka Castle and Topkapi Palace project the importance of their owners? Explain.
2. Does Machiavelli favor a system of government that would provide directly for people's needs? Explain.

EXTENSION ACTIVITY

Use the library to get some additional information about the government structure of the Incan Empire and Renaissance Venice. Then draw an organizational chart for each of those governments like the charts on page 580.

UNIT 5

Absolutism to Revolution

1500–1900

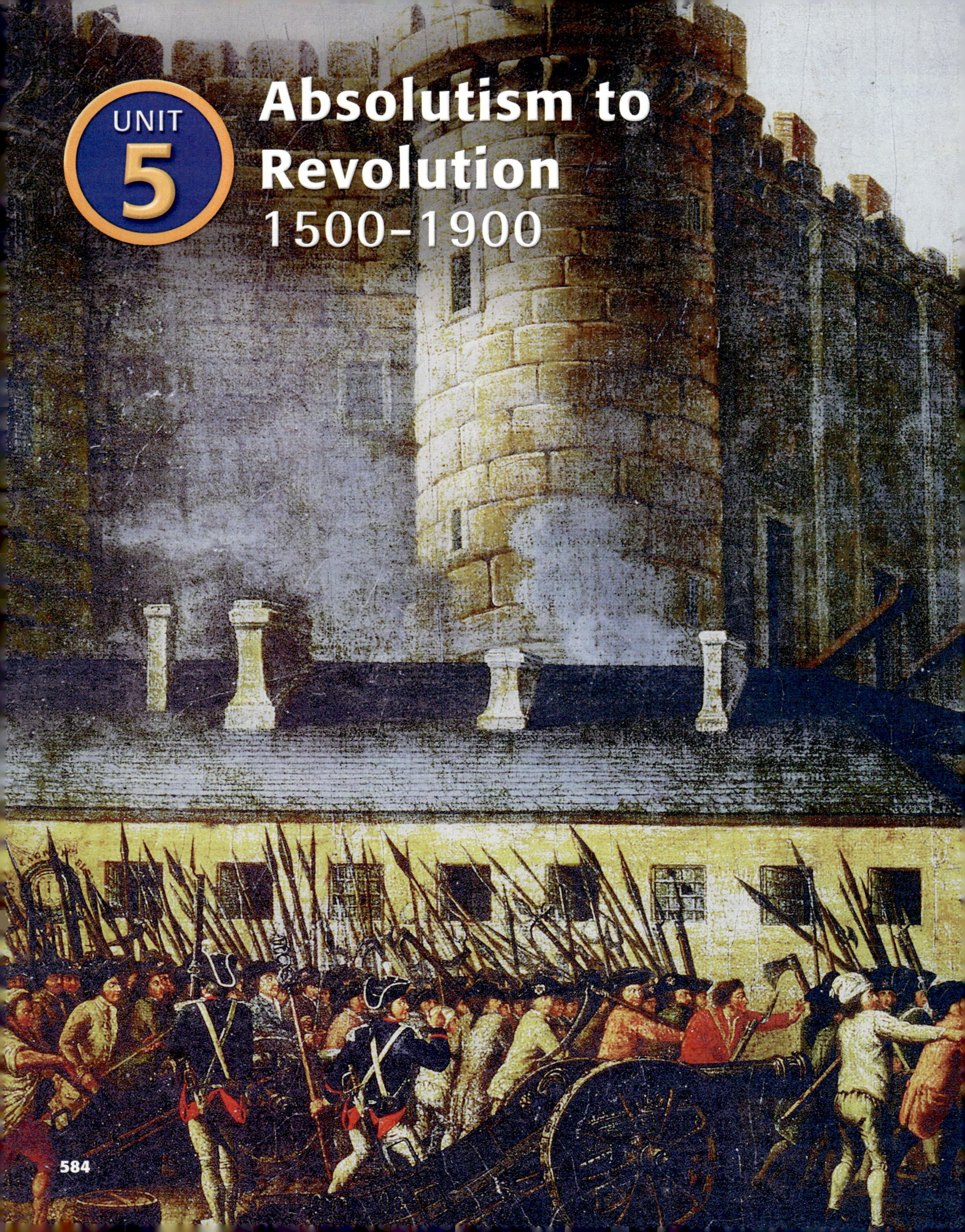

On July 14, 1789, an angry French mob attacked the Bastille, a state prison in Paris, because it was looking for arms and gunpowder. The capture of this prison is considered the beginning of the French Revolution.

Comparing & Contrasting

Political Revolutions

In Unit 5, you will learn that new ideas about human rights and government led to political revolutions in many countries during the late 1700s and the 1800s. At the end of the unit, you will have a chance to compare and contrast those revolutions. (See pages 706–711.)

CHAPTER 21

Absolute Monarchs in Europe, 1500–1800

Previewing Main Ideas

POWER AND AUTHORITY As feudalism declined, stronger national kingdoms in Spain, France, Austria, Prussia, and Russia emerged under the control of absolute rulers.

Geography *Study the map. What large empire was surrounded by many of these national kingdoms?*

ECONOMICS Absolute rulers wanted to control their countries' economies so that they could free themselves from limitations imposed by the nobility. In France, Louis XIV's unrestrained spending left his country with huge debts.

Geography *What other evidence of unrestrained spending by an absolute ruler does the time line suggest?*

REVOLUTION In Great Britain, Parliament and the British people challenged the monarch's authority. The overthrow of the king led to important political changes.

Geography *Study the map and the time line. Which British Stuart lands were most affected by the event occurring in 1649?*

NEW YORK CORE CURRICULUM FOCUS

- Absolute rulers believed in divine right, the idea that monarchs answered only to God.
- Philip II, Louis XIV, Ivan the Terrible, and Peter the Great were absolute rulers.

INTEGRATED TECHNOLOGY

eEdition
- Interactive Maps
- Interactive Visuals
- Interactive Primary Sources

INTERNET RESOURCES

Go to **classzone.com** for:
- Research Links
- Internet Activities
- Primary Sources
- Chapter Quiz
- Maps
- Test Practice
- Current Events

EUROPE

1588 British defeat Philip II's Spanish Armada.

1500 | **1600**

WORLD

1521 Cortés conquers Aztec Empire.

1533 Pizarro conquers Incan Empire.

1603 Tokugawa shoguns rule Japan.

1643
Louis XIV begins to rule France.

1649
Puritans under Oliver Cromwell (at right) execute English king.

1696
Peter the Great becomes sole czar of Russia.

1756
Prussian king Frederick the Great begins Seven Years' War against Austria.

1700

1800

1631
Shah Jahan orders construction of Taj Mahal.

1776
American colonists declare their independence from England.

Interact *with* History

What are the benefits and drawbacks of having an absolute ruler?

You live under the most powerful monarch in 17th-century Europe, Louis XIV of France, shown below. As Louis's subject, you feel proud and well protected because the French army is the strongest in Europe. But Louis's desire to gain lands for France and battle enemies has resulted in costly wars. And he expects you and his other subjects to pay for them.

INTERACTIVE

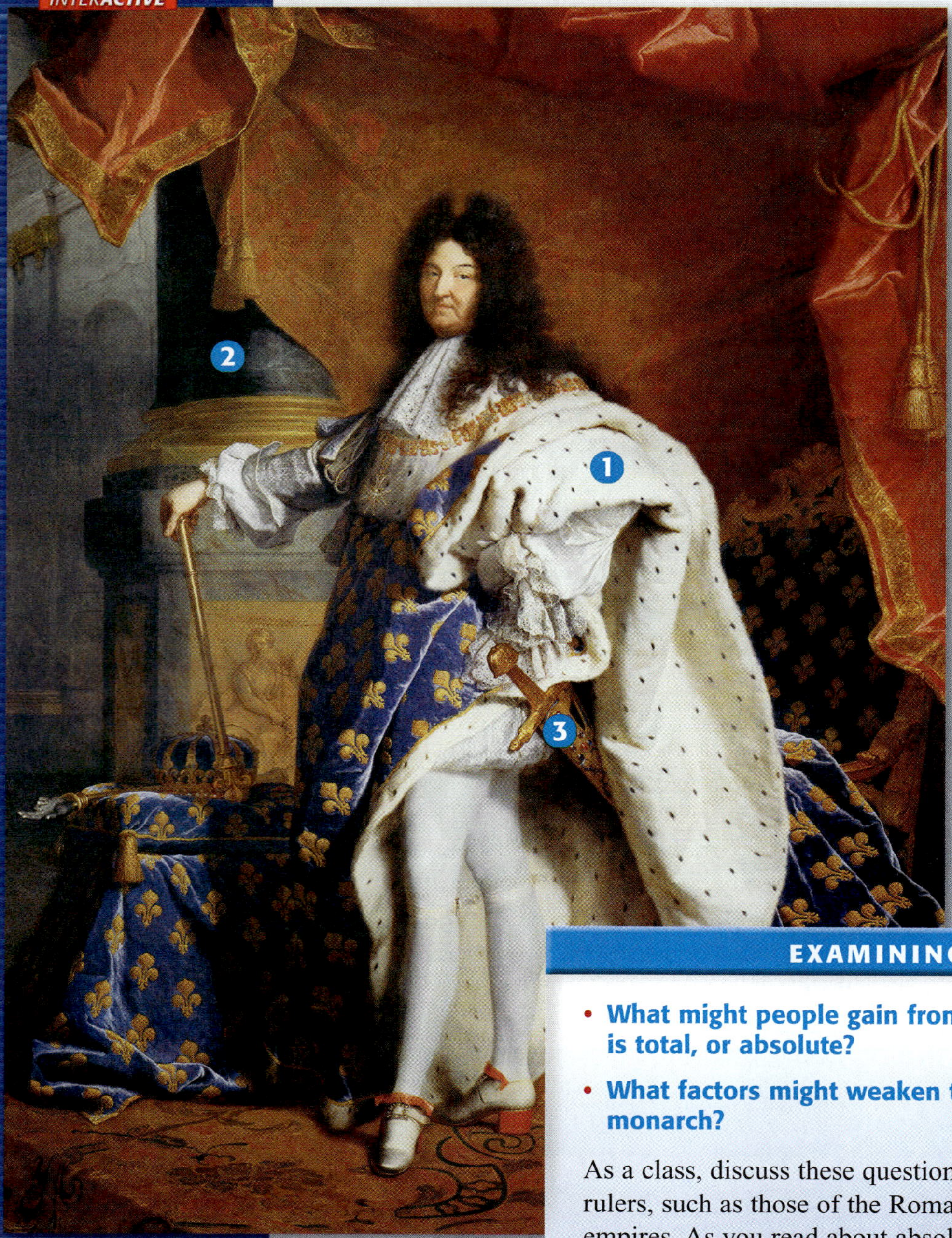

1 Louis XIV uses his clothing to demonstrate his power and status, as his portrait shows. The gold flower on his robe is the symbol of French kings.

2 Louis's love of finery is apparent not only in his clothing but also in the ornate setting for this painting. As absolute ruler, Louis imposes taxes to pay for the construction of a magnificent new palace and to finance wars.

3 The government of Louis XIV enforces laws and provides security. His sword, scepter, and crown symbolize the power he wields. Yet the French people have no say in what laws are passed or how they are enforced.

EXAMINING *the* ISSUES

- **What might people gain from having a ruler whose power is total, or absolute?**
- **What factors might weaken the power of an absolute monarch?**

As a class, discuss these questions. You may want to refer to earlier rulers, such as those of the Roman, Ottoman, and Carolingian empires. As you read about absolute monarchs in Europe, notice what strengthened and weakened their power.

Spain's Empire and European Absolutism

CONNECT TO THE NEW YORK STATE CORE CURRICULUM

Unit 4.F.1.1. Human and physical geography
Unit 4.F.4. Case studies: Akbar the Great, Suleyman the Magnificent, Philip II, Louis XIV, Ivan the Terrible, and Peter the Great

TERMS & NAMES

- Philip II
- absolute monarch
- divine right

SETTING THE STAGE As you learned in Chapter 18, from 1520 to 1566, Suleyman I exercised great power as sultan of the Ottoman Empire. A European monarch of the same period, Charles V, came close to matching Suleyman's power. As the Hapsburg king, Charles inherited Spain, Spain's American colonies, parts of Italy, and lands in Austria and the Netherlands. As the elected Holy Roman emperor, he ruled much of Germany. It was the first time since Charlemagne that a European ruler controlled so much territory.

A Powerful Spanish Empire

A devout Catholic, Charles not only fought Muslims but also opposed Lutherans. In 1555, he unwillingly agreed to the Peace of Augsburg, which allowed German princes to choose the religion for their territory. The following year, Charles V divided his immense empire and retired to a monastery. To his brother Ferdinand, he left Austria and the Holy Roman Empire. His son, **Philip II**, inherited Spain, the Spanish Netherlands, and the American colonies.

TAKING NOTES

Clarifying Use a chart to list the conditions that allowed European monarchs to gain power.

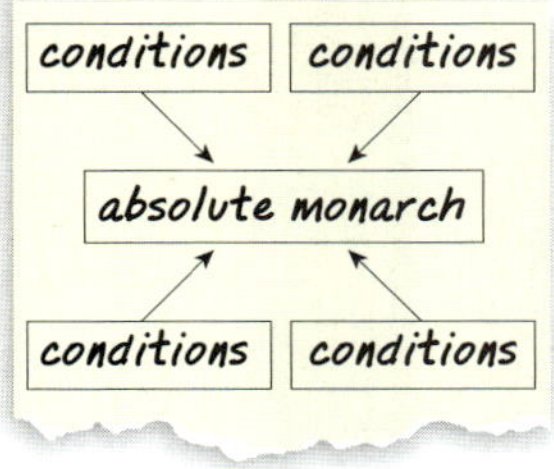

Philip II's Empire Philip was shy, serious, and—like his father—deeply religious. He was also very hard working. Yet Philip would not allow anyone to help him. Deeply suspicious, he trusted no one for long. As his own court historian wrote, "His smile and his dagger were very close."

Perhaps above all, Philip could be aggressive for the sake of his empire. In 1580, the king of Portugal died without an heir. Because Philip was the king's nephew, he seized the Portuguese kingdom. Counting Portuguese strongholds in Africa, India, and the East Indies, he now had an empire that circled the globe.

Philip's empire provided him with incredible wealth. By 1600, American mines had supplied Spain with an estimated 339,000 pounds of gold. Between 1550 and 1650, roughly 16,000 tons of silver bullion were unloaded from Spanish galleons, or ships. The king of Spain claimed between a fourth and a fifth of every shipload of treasure as his royal share. With this wealth, Spain was able to support a large standing army of about 50,000 soldiers.

Defender of Catholicism When Philip assumed the throne, Europe was experiencing religious wars caused by the Reformation. However, religious conflict was not new to Spain. The Reconquista, the campaign to drive Muslims from Spain, had been completed only 64 years before. In addition, Philip's great-grandparents

Defeat of the Spanish Armada, 1588

In the summer of 1588, Philip II sent about 130 ships carrying 19,000 soldiers to the English Channel. English warships, however, outmaneuvered the Spanish vessels and bombarded the Armada with their heavier long-range cannons.

GEOGRAPHY SKILLBUILDER: Interpreting Maps

1. **Location** *Off what English town did the first clash between the Spanish Armada and the English fleet take place?*
2. **Movement** *Why do you think the Spanish captains chose to sail north around Scotland rather than take the more direct route home back through the English Channel?*

Isabella and Ferdinand had used the Inquisition to investigate suspected heretics, or nonbelievers in Christianity.

Philip believed it was his duty to defend Catholicism against the Muslims of the Ottoman Empire and the Protestants of Europe. In 1571, the pope called on all Catholic princes to take up arms against the mounting power of the Ottoman Empire. Philip responded like a true crusader. More than 200 Spanish and Venetian ships defeated a large Ottoman fleet in a fierce battle near Lepanto. In 1588, Philip launched the Spanish Armada in an attempt to punish Protestant England and its queen, Elizabeth I. Elizabeth had supported Protestant subjects who had rebelled against Philip. However, his fleet was defeated. (See map opposite.)

MAIN IDEA

Making Inferences

A What did Philip want his palace to demonstrate about his monarchy?

Although this setback seriously weakened Spain, its wealth gave it the appearance of strength for a while longer. Philip's gray granite palace, the Escorial, had massive walls and huge gates that demonstrated his power. The Escorial also reflected Philip's faith. Within its walls stood a monastery as well as a palace. **A**

Golden Age of Spanish Art and Literature

Spain's great wealth did more than support navies and build palaces. It also allowed monarchs and nobles to become patrons of artists. During the 16th and 17th centuries, Spain experienced a golden age in the arts. The works of two great painters show both the faith and the pride of Spain during this period.

El Greco and Velázquez Born in Crete, El Greco (GREHK•oh) spent much of his adult life in Spain. His real name was Domenikos Theotokopoulos, but Spaniards called him El Greco, meaning "the Greek." El Greco's art often puzzled the people of his time. He chose brilliant, sometimes clashing colors, distorted the human figure, and expressed emotion symbolically in his paintings. Although unusual, El Greco's techniques showed the deep Catholic faith of Spain. He painted saints and martyrs as huge, long-limbed figures that have a supernatural air.

The paintings of Diego Velázquez (vuh•LAHS•kehs), on the other hand, reflected the pride of the Spanish monarchy. Velázquez, who painted 50 years after El Greco, was the court painter to Philip IV of Spain. He is best known for his portraits of the royal family and scenes of court life. Like El Greco, he was noted for using rich colors.

▼ In *Las Meninas (The Maids of Honor)*, Velázquez depicts King Philip IV's daughter and her attendants.

Don Quixote The publication of *Don Quixote de la Mancha* in 1605 is often called the birth of the modern European novel. In this book, Miguel de Cervantes (suhr•VAN•teez) wrote about a poor Spanish nobleman who went a little crazy after reading too many books about heroic knights.

Hoping to "right every manner of wrong," Don Quixote rode forth in a rusty suit of armor, mounted on a feeble horse. At one point, he mistook some windmills for giants:

PRIMARY SOURCE

He rushed with [his horse's] utmost speed upon the first windmill he could come at, and, running his lance into the sail, the wind whirled about with such swiftness, that the rapidity of the motion presently broke the lance into shivers, and hurled away both knight and horse along with it, till down he fell, rolling a good way off in the field.

MIGUEL DE CERVANTES, *Don Quixote de la Mancha*

Some critics believe that Cervantes was mocking chivalry, the knightly code of the Middle Ages. Others maintain that the book is about an idealistic person who longs for the romantic past because he is frustrated with his materialistic world.

The Spanish Empire Weakens

Certainly, the age in which Cervantes wrote was a materialistic one. The gold and silver coming from the Americas made Spain temporarily wealthy. However, such treasure helped to cause long-term economic problems.

Inflation and Taxes One of these problems was severe inflation, which is a decline in the value of money, accompanied by a rise in the prices of goods and services. Inflation in Spain had two main causes. First, Spain's population had been growing. As more people demanded food and other goods, merchants were able to raise prices. Second, as silver bullion flooded the market, its value dropped. People needed more and more amounts of silver to buy things.

Spain's economic decline also had other causes. When Spain expelled the Jews and Moors (Muslims) around 1500, it lost many valuable artisans and businesspeople. In addition, Spain's nobles did not have to pay taxes. The tax burden fell on the lower classes. That burden prevented them from accumulating enough wealth to start their own businesses. As a result, Spain never developed a middle class.

Making Spain's Enemies Rich Guilds that had emerged in the Middle Ages still dominated business in Spain. Such guilds used old-fashioned methods. This made Spanish cloth and manufactured goods more expensive than those made elsewhere. As a result, Spaniards bought much of what they needed from France, England, and the Netherlands. Spain's great wealth flowed into the pockets of foreigners, who were mostly Spain's enemies.

To finance their wars, Spanish kings borrowed money from German and Italian bankers. When shiploads of silver came in, the money was sent abroad to repay debts. The economy was so feeble that Philip had to declare the Spanish state bankrupt three times. **B**

The Dutch Revolt In the Spanish Netherlands, Philip had to maintain an army to keep his subjects under control. The Dutch had little in common with their Spanish rulers. While Spain was Catholic, the Netherlands had many Calvinist congregations. Also, Spain had a sluggish economy, while the Dutch had a prosperous middle class.

Philip raised taxes in the Netherlands and took steps to crush Protestantism. In response, in 1566, angry Protestant mobs swept through Catholic churches. Philip then sent an

Global Impact

Tulip Mania

Tulips came to Europe from Turkey around 1550. People went wild over the flowers and began to buy rare varieties. However, the supply of tulips could not meet the demand, and prices began to rise. Soon people were spending all their savings on bulbs and taking out loans so that they could buy more.

Tulip mania reached a peak between 1633 and 1637. Soon after, tulip prices sank rapidly. Many Dutch families lost property and were left with bulbs that were nearly worthless.

MAIN IDEA

Identifying Problems

B Why didn't Spain's economy benefit from the gold and silver from the Americas?

army under the Spanish duke of Alva to punish the rebels. On a single day in 1568, the duke executed 1,500 Protestants and suspected rebels.

The Dutch continued to fight the Spanish for another 11 years. Finally, in 1579, the seven northern provinces of the Netherlands, which were largely Protestant, united and declared their independence from Spain. They became the United Provinces of the Netherlands. The ten southern provinces (present-day Belgium) were Catholic and remained under Spanish control.

The Independent Dutch Prosper

The United Provinces of the Netherlands was different from other European states of the time. For one thing, the people there practiced religious toleration. In addition, the United Provinces was not a kingdom but a republic. Each province had an elected governor, whose power depended on the support of merchants and landholders.

Dutch Art During the 1600s, the Netherlands became what Florence had been during the 1400s. It boasted not only the best banks but also many of the best artists in Europe. As in Florence, wealthy merchants sponsored many of these artists.

Rembrandt van Rijn (REHM•BRANT vahn RYN) was the greatest Dutch artist of the period. Rembrandt painted portraits of wealthy middle-class merchants. He also produced group portraits. In *The Night Watch* (shown below), he portrayed a group of city guards. Rembrandt used sharp contrasts of light and shadow to draw attention to his focus.

Another artist fascinated with the effects of light and dark was Jan Vermeer (YAHN vuhr•MEER). Like many other Dutch artists, he chose domestic, indoor settings for his portraits. He often painted women doing such familiar activities as pouring milk from a jug or reading a letter. The work of both Rembrandt and Vermeer reveals how important merchants, civic leaders, and the middle class in general were in 17th-century Netherlands.

◀ In *The Night Watch,* Rembrandt showed the individuality of each man by capturing distinctive facial expressions and postures.

Dutch Trading Empire The stability of the government allowed the Dutch people to concentrate on economic growth. The merchants of Amsterdam bought surplus grain in Poland and crammed it into their warehouses. When they heard about poor harvests in southern Europe, they shipped the grain south while prices were highest. The Dutch had the largest fleet of ships in the world—perhaps 4,800 ships in 1636. This fleet helped the Dutch East India Company (a trading company controlled by the Dutch government) to dominate the Asian spice trade and the Indian Ocean trade. Gradually, the Dutch replaced the Italians as the bankers of Europe.

Absolutism in Europe

Even though Philip II lost his Dutch possessions, he was a forceful ruler in many ways. He tried to control every aspect of his empire's affairs. During the next few centuries, many European monarchs would also claim the authority to rule without limits on their power.

The Theory of Absolutism These rulers wanted to be **absolute monarchs**, kings or queens who held all of the power within their states' boundaries. Their goal was to control every aspect of society. Absolute monarchs believed in **divine right**, the idea that God created the monarchy and that the monarch acted as God's representative on Earth. An absolute monarch answered only to God, not to his or her subjects. C

MAIN IDEA

Drawing Conclusions

C How was Philip II typical of an absolute monarch?

Analyzing Key Concepts

Absolutism

Absolutism was the political belief that one ruler should hold all of the power within the boundaries of a country. Although practiced by several monarchs in Europe during the 16th through 18th centuries, absolutism has been used in many regions throughout history. In ancient times, Shi Huangdi in China, Darius in Persia, and the Roman caesars were all absolute rulers. (See Chapters 4, 5, and 6.)

Causes

- Religious and territorial conflicts created fear and uncertainty.
- The growth of armies to deal with conflicts caused rulers to raise taxes to pay troops.
- Heavy taxes led to additional unrest and peasant revolts.

ABSOLUTISM

Effects

- Rulers regulated religious worship and social gatherings to control the spread of ideas.
- Rulers increased the size of their courts to appear more powerful.
- Rulers created bureaucracies to control their countries' economies.

SKILLBUILDER: Interpreting Charts

1. **Making Inferences** *Why do you think absolute rulers controlled social gatherings?*
   See Skillbuilder Handbook, page R10.
2. **Hypothesizing** *Today several nations of the world (such as Saudi Arabia) have absolute rulers. Judging from what you know of past causes of absolutism, why do you think absolute rulers still exist today?*

Growing Power of Europe's Monarchs-As Europe emerged from the Middle Ages, monarchs grew increasingly powerful. The decline of feudalism, the rise of cities, and the growth of national kingdoms all helped to centralize authority. In addition, the growing middle class usually backed monarchs, because they promised a peaceful, supportive climate for business. Monarchs used the wealth of colonies to pay for their ambitions. Church authority also broke down during the late Middle Ages and the Reformation. That opened the way for monarchs to assume even greater control. In 1576, Jean Bodin, an influential French writer, defined absolute rule:

PRIMARY SOURCE

The first characteristic of the sovereign prince is the power to make general and special laws, but—and this qualification is important—without the consent of superiors, equals, or inferiors. If the prince requires the consent of superiors, then he is a subject himself; if that of equals, he shares his authority with others; if that of his subjects, senate or people, he is not sovereign.

JEAN BODIN, *Six Books on the State*

Crises Lead to Absolutism The 17th century was a period of great upheaval in Europe. Religious and territorial conflicts between states led to almost continuous warfare. This caused governments to build huge armies and to levy even heavier taxes on an already suffering population. These pressures in turn brought about widespread unrest. Sometimes peasants revolted.

In response to these crises, monarchs tried to impose order by increasing their own power. As absolute rulers, they regulated everything from religious worship to social gatherings. They created new government bureaucracies to control their countries' economic life. Their goal was to free themselves from the limitations imposed by the nobility and by representative bodies such as Parliament. Only with such freedom could they rule absolutely, as did the most famous monarch of his time, Louis XIV of France. You'll learn more about him in the next section.

NEW YORK CORE CURRICULUM REVIEW

TERMS & NAMES 1. For each term or name, write a sentence explaining its significance.
- Philip II
- absolute monarch
- divine right

USING YOUR NOTES

2. Which condition is probably most necessary for a monarch to gain power? Why?

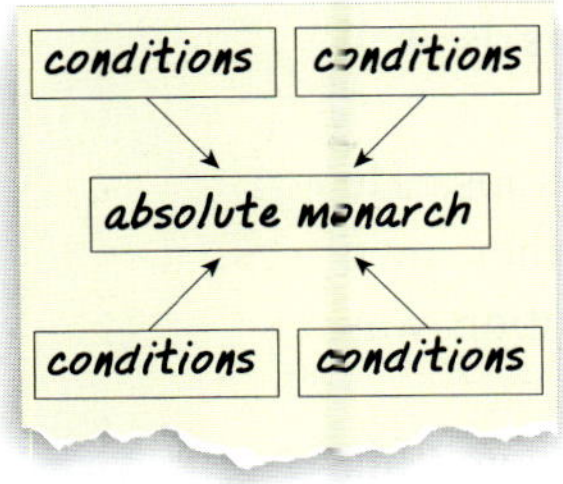

MAIN IDEAS

3. What is the significance of England's defeat of the Spanish Armada?
4. Why did the Dutch revolt against Spain?
5. Why did absolute monarchs believe that they were justified in exercising absolute power?

CRITICAL THINKING & WRITING

6. **DRAWING CONCLUSIONS** What does the art described in this section reveal about the cultures of Spain and the Netherlands?
7. **ANALYZING CAUSES** What role did religion play in the struggle between the Spanish and the Dutch?
8. **MAKING INFERENCES** How did the lack of a middle class contribute to the decline of Spain's economy?
9. **WRITING ACTIVITY** ECONOMICS Write a **comparison-contrast paragraph** on the economies of Spain and the Netherlands around 1600.

INTEGRATED TECHNOLOGY **INTERNET ACTIVITY**

Use the Internet to identify the religious affiliations of people in Spain and in the Netherlands today. Create a **graph** for each country showing the results of your research.

INTERNET KEYWORD
religion in Spain; religion in the Netherlands

The Reign of Louis XIV

CONNECT TO THE NEW YORK STATE CORE CURRICULUM

Unit 3.G.8. Religious wars in Europe: causes and impacts
Unit 4.F.4. Case studies: Akbar the Great, Suleyman the Magnificent, Philip II, Louis XIV, Ivan the Terrible, and Peter the Great

TERMS & NAMES

- Edict of Nantes
- Cardinal Richelieu
- skepticism
- Louis XIV
- intendant
- Jean Baptiste Colbert
- War of the Spanish Succession

SETTING THE STAGE In 1559, King Henry II of France died, leaving four young sons. Three of them ruled, one after the other, but all proved incompetent. The real power behind the throne during this period was their mother, Catherine de Médicis. Catherine tried to preserve royal authority, but growing conflicts between Catholics and Huguenots—French Protestants—rocked the country. Between 1562 and 1598, Huguenots and Catholics fought eight religious wars. Chaos spread through France.

TAKING NOTES
Following Chronological Order Use a time line to list the major events of Louis XIV's reign.

Religious Wars and Power Struggles

In 1572, the St. Bartholomew's Day Massacre in Paris sparked a six-week, nationwide slaughter of Huguenots. The massacre occurred when many Huguenot nobles were in Paris. They were attending the marriage of Catherine's daughter to a Huguenot prince, Henry of Navarre. Most of these nobles died, but Henry survived.

Henry of Navarre Descended from the popular medieval king Louis IX, Henry was robust, athletic, and handsome. In 1589, when both Catherine and her last son died, Prince Henry inherited the throne. He became Henry IV, the first king of the Bourbon dynasty in France. As king, he showed himself to be decisive, fearless in battle, and a clever politician.

Many Catholics, including the people of Paris, opposed Henry. For the sake of his war-weary country, Henry chose to give up Protestantism and become a Catholic. Explaining his conversion, Henry reportedly declared, "Paris is well worth a mass."

In 1598, Henry took another step toward healing France's wounds. He declared that the Huguenots could live in peace in France and set up their own houses of worship in some cities. This declaration of religious toleration was called the **Edict of Nantes**.

Aided by an adviser who enacted wise financial policies, Henry devoted his reign to rebuilding France and its prosperity. He restored the French monarchy to a strong position. After a generation of war, most French people welcomed peace. Some people, however, hated Henry for his religious compromises. In 1610, a fanatic leaped into the royal carriage and stabbed Henry to death.

Louis XIII and Cardinal Richelieu After Henry IV's death, his son Louis XIII reigned. Louis was a weak king, but in 1624, he appointed a strong minister who made up for all of Louis's weaknesses.

Cardinal Richelieu (RIHSH•uh•LOO) became, in effect, the ruler of France. For several years, he had been a hard-working leader of the Catholic church in France. Although he tried sincerely to lead according to moral principles, he was also ambitious and enjoyed exercising authority. As Louis XIII's minister, he was able to pursue his ambitions in the political arena.

Richelieu took two steps to increase the power of the Bourbon monarchy. First, he moved against Huguenots. He believed that Protestantism often served as an excuse for political conspiracies against the Catholic king. Although Richelieu did not take away the Huguenots' right to worship, he forbade Protestant cities to have walls. He did not want them to be able to defy the king and then withdraw behind strong defenses.

Second, he sought to weaken the nobles' power. Richelieu ordered nobles to take down their fortified castles. He increased the power of government agents who came from the middle class. The king relied on these agents, so there was less need to use noble officials.

▲ Cardinal Richelieu probably had himself portrayed in a standing position in this painting to underscore his role as ruler.

MAIN IDEA

Making Inferences

A How did Richelieu's actions toward Huguenots and the nobility strengthen the monarchy?

Richelieu also wanted to make France the strongest state in Europe. The greatest obstacle to this, he believed, was the Hapsburg rulers, whose lands surrounded France. The Hapsburgs ruled Spain, Austria, the Netherlands, and parts of the Holy Roman Empire. To limit Hapsburg power, Richelieu involved France in the Thirty Years' War. A

Writers Turn Toward Skepticism

As France regained political power, a new French intellectual movement developed. French thinkers had witnessed the religious wars with horror. What they saw turned them toward **skepticism**, the idea that nothing can ever be known for certain. These thinkers expressed an attitude of doubt toward churches that claimed to have the only correct set of doctrines. To doubt old ideas, skeptics thought, was the first step toward finding truth.

Montaigne and Descartes Michel de Montaigne lived during the worst years of the French religious wars. After the death of a dear friend, Montaigne thought deeply about life's meaning. To communicate his ideas, Montaigne developed a new form of literature, the essay. An essay is a brief work that expresses a person's thoughts and opinions.

In one essay, Montaigne pointed out that whenever a new belief arose, it replaced an old belief that people once accepted as truth. In the same way, he went on, the new belief would also probably be replaced by some different idea in the future. For these reasons, Montaigne believed that humans could never have absolute knowledge of what is true.

Another French writer of the time, René Descartes, was a brilliant thinker. In his *Meditations on First Philosophy,* Descartes examined the skeptical argument that one could never be certain of anything. Descartes used his observations and his reason to answer such arguments. In doing so, he created a philosophy that influenced modern thinkers and helped to develop the scientific method. Because of this, he became an important figure in the Enlightenment, which you will read about in Chapter 22.

History Makers

Louis XIV
1638–1715

Although Louis XIV stood only 5 feet 5 inches tall, his erect and dignified posture made him appear much taller. (It also helped that he wore high-heeled shoes.)

Louis had very strong likes and dislikes. He hated cities and loved to travel through France's countryside. The people who traveled with him were at his mercy, however, for he allowed no stopping except for his own comfort.

It is small wonder that the vain Louis XIV liked to be called the Sun King. He believed that, as with the sun, all power radiated from him.

INTEGRATED TECHNOLOGY

RESEARCH LINKS For more on Louis XIV, go to **classzone.com**

Louis XIV Comes to Power

The efforts of Henry IV and Richelieu to strengthen the French monarchy paved the way for the most powerful ruler in French history—**Louis XIV**. In Louis's view, he and the state were one and the same. He reportedly boasted, *"L'état, c'est moi,"* meaning "I am the state." Although Louis XIV became the strongest king of his time, he was only a four-year-old boy when he began his reign.

Louis, the Boy King When Louis became king in 1643 after the death of his father, Louis XIII, the true ruler of France was Richelieu's successor, Cardinal Mazarin (MAZ•uh•RAN). Mazarin's greatest triumph came in 1648, with the ending of the Thirty Years' War.

Many people in France, particularly the nobles, hated Mazarin because he increased taxes and strengthened the central government. From 1648 to 1653, violent anti-Mazarin riots tore France apart. At times, the nobles who led the riots threatened the young king's life. Even after the violence was over, Louis never forgot his fear or his anger at the nobility. He determined to become so strong that they could never threaten him again.

In the end, the nobles' rebellion failed for three reasons. Its leaders distrusted one another even more than they distrusted Mazarin. In addition, the government used violent repression. Finally, peasants and townspeople grew weary of disorder and fighting. For many years afterward, the people of France accepted the oppressive laws of an absolute king. They were convinced that the alternative—rebellion—was even worse. **B**

MAIN IDEA

Recognizing Effects

B What effects did the years of riots have on Louis XIV? on his subjects?

Louis Weakens the Nobles' Authority When Cardinal Mazarin died in 1661, the 22-year-old Louis took control of the government himself. He weakened the power of the nobles by excluding them from his councils. In contrast, he increased the power of the government agents called **intendants**, who collected taxes and administered justice. To keep power under central control, he made sure that local officials communicated regularly with him.

Economic Growth Louis devoted himself to helping France attain economic, political, and cultural brilliance. No one assisted him more in achieving these goals than his minister of finance, **Jean Baptiste Colbert** (kawl•BEHR). Colbert believed in the theory of mercantilism. To prevent wealth from leaving the country, Colbert tried to make France self-sufficient. He wanted it to be able to manufacture everything it needed instead of relying on imports.

Vocabulary

mercantilism: the economic theory that nations should protect their home industries and export more than they import

To expand manufacturing, Colbert gave government funds and tax benefits to French companies. To protect France's industries, he placed a high tariff on goods from other countries. Colbert also recognized the importance of colonies, which provided raw materials and a market for manufactured goods. The French government encouraged people to migrate to France's colony in Canada. There the fur trade added to French trade and wealth.

After Colbert's death, Louis announced a policy that slowed France's economic progress. In 1685, he canceled the Edict of Nantes, which protected the religious freedom of Huguenots. In response, thousands of Huguenot artisans and business people fled the country. Louis's policy thus robbed France of many skilled workers.

The Sun King's Grand Style

In his personal finances, Louis spent a fortune to surround himself with luxury. For example, each meal was a feast. An observer claimed that the king once devoured four plates of soup, a whole pheasant, a partridge in garlic sauce, two slices of ham, a salad, a plate of pastries, fruit, and hard-boiled eggs in a single sitting! Nearly 500 cooks, waiters, and other servants worked to satisfy his tastes.

Louis Controls the Nobility Every morning, the chief valet woke Louis at 8:30. Outside the curtains of Louis's canopy bed stood at least 100 of the most privileged nobles at court. They were waiting to help the great king dress. Only four would be allowed the honor of handing Louis his slippers or holding his sleeves for him.

Meanwhile, outside the bedchamber, lesser nobles waited in the palace halls and hoped Louis would notice them. A kingly nod, a glance of approval, a kind word—these marks of royal attention determined whether a noble succeeded or failed. A duke recorded how Louis turned against nobles who did not come to court to flatter him:

MAIN IDEA

Analyzing Primary Sources

C How did Louis's treatment of the nobles reflect his belief in his absolute authority?

PRIMARY SOURCE C

He looked to the right and to the left, not only upon rising but upon going to bed, at his meals, in passing through his apartments, or his gardens. . . . He marked well all absentees from the Court, found out the reason of their absence, and never lost an opportunity of acting toward them as the occasion might seem to justify. . . . When their names were in any way mentioned, "I do not know them," the King would reply haughtily.

DUKE OF SAINT-SIMON, *Memoirs of Louis XIV and the Regency*

▼ Though full of errors, Saint-Simon's memoirs provide valuable insight into Louis XIV's character and life at Versailles.

Having the nobles at the palace increased royal authority in two ways. It made the nobility totally dependent on Louis. It also took them from their homes, thereby giving more power to the intendants. Louis required hundreds of nobles to live with him at the splendid palace he built at Versailles, about 11 miles southwest of Paris.

As you can see from the pictures on the following page, everything about the Versailles palace was immense. It faced a huge royal courtyard dominated by a statue of Louis XIV. The palace itself stretched for a distance of about 500 yards. Because of its great size, Versailles was like a small royal city. Its rich decoration and furnishings clearly showed Louis's wealth and power to everyone who came to the palace.

Patronage of the Arts Versailles was a center of the arts during Louis's reign. Louis made opera and ballet more popular. He even danced the title role in the ballet *The Sun King*. One of his favorite writers was Molière (mohl•YAIR), who wrote some of the funniest plays in French literature. Molière's comedies include *Tartuffe,* which mocks religious hypocrisy.

Not since Augustus of Rome had there been a European monarch who supported the arts as much as Louis. Under Louis, the chief purpose of art was no longer to glorify God, as it had been in the Middle Ages. Nor was its purpose to glorify human potential, as it had been in the Renaissance. Now the purpose of art was to glorify the king and promote values that supported Louis's absolute rule.

INTERACTIVE

The Palace at Versailles

Louis XIV's palace at Versailles was proof of his absolute power. Only a ruler with total control over his country's economy could afford such a lavish palace. It cost an estimated $2.5 billion in 2003 dollars. Louis XIV was also able to force 36,000 laborers and 6,000 horses to work on the project.

Many people consider the Hall of Mirrors the most beautiful room in the palace. Along one wall are 17 tall mirrors. The opposite wall has 17 windows that open onto the gardens. The hall has gilded statues, crystal chandeliers, and a painted ceiling.

It took so much water to run all the fountains at once that it was done only for special events. On other days, when the king walked in the garden, servants would turn on fountains just before he reached them. The fountains were turned off after he walked away.

The gardens at Versailles remain beautiful today. Originally, Versailles was built with:

- 5,000 acres of gardens, lawns, and woods
- 1,400 fountains

SKILLBUILDER: Interpreting Visuals

1. **Analyzing Motives** *Why do you think Louis XIV believed he needed such a large and luxurious palace? Explain what practical and symbolic purposes Versailles might have served.*
2. **Developing Historical Perspective** *Consider the amount of money and effort that went into the construction of this extravagant palace. What does this reveal about the way 17th-century French society viewed its king?*

Louis Fights Disastrous Wars

Under Louis, France was the most powerful country in Europe. In 1660, France had about 20 million people. This was four times as many as England and ten times as many as the Dutch republic. The French army was far ahead of other states' armies in size, training, and weaponry.

Attempts to Expand France's Boundaries In 1667, just six years after Mazarin's death, Louis invaded the Spanish Netherlands in an effort to expand France's boundaries. Through this campaign, he gained 12 towns. Encouraged by his success, he personally led an army into the Dutch Netherlands in 1672. The Dutch saved their country by opening the dikes and flooding the countryside. This was the same tactic they had used in their revolt against Spain a century earlier. The war ended in 1678 with the Treaty of Nijmegen. France gained several towns and a region called Franche-Comté.

Louis decided to fight additional wars, but his luck had run out. By the end of the 1680s, a Europeanwide alliance had formed to stop France. By banding together, weaker countries could match France's strength. This defensive strategy was meant to achieve a balance of power, in which no single country or group of countries could dominate others.

In 1689, the Dutch prince William of Orange became the king of England. He joined the League of Augsburg, which consisted of the Austrian Hapsburg emperor, the kings of Sweden and Spain, and the leaders of several smaller European states. Together, these countries equaled France's strength.

MAIN IDEA

Recognizing Effects

D How did Louis's wars against weaker countries backfire?

France at this time had been weakened by a series of poor harvests. That, added to the constant warfare, brought great suffering to the French people. So, too, did new taxes, which Louis imposed to finance his wars. D

War of the Spanish Succession Tired of hardship, the French people longed for peace. What they got was another war. In 1700, the childless king of Spain, Charles II, died after promising his throne to Louis XIV's 16-year-old grandson, Philip of Anjou. The two greatest powers in Europe, enemies for so long, were now both ruled by the French Bourbons.

Other countries felt threatened by this increase in the Bourbon dynasty's power. In 1701, England, Austria, the Dutch Republic, Portugal, and several German and Italian states joined together to prevent the union of the French and Spanish thrones. The long struggle that followed is known as the **War of the Spanish Succession**.

The costly war dragged on until 1714. The Treaty of Utrecht was signed in that year. Under its terms, Louis's grandson was allowed to remain king of Spain so long as the thrones of France and Spain were not united.

The big winner in the war was Great Britain. From Spain, Britain took Gibraltar, a fortress that controlled the entrance to the Mediterranean. Spain also granted a British company an *asiento*, permission to send enslaved Africans to Spain's American colonies. This increased Britain's involvement in trading enslaved Africans.

▼ The painting below shows the Battle of Denain, one of the last battles fought during the War of the Spanish Succession.

Debt of the Royal Family, 1643–1715

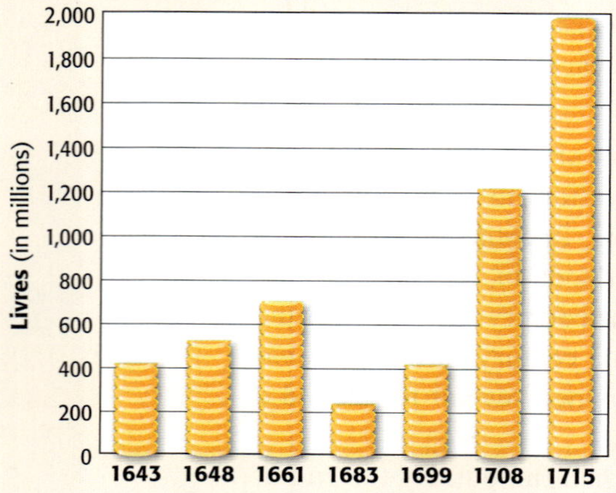

A livre is equal to approximately $10.50 in 1992 U.S. dollars.
Source: *Early Modern France 1560–1715*

SKILLBUILDER: Interpreting Charts

1. **Comparing** *How many times greater was the royal debt in 1715 than in 1643?*
2. **Synthesizing** *What was the royal debt of 1715 equal to in 1992 dollars?*

In addition, France gave Britain the North American territories of Nova Scotia and Newfoundland, and abandoned claims to the Hudson Bay region. The Austrian Hapsburgs took the Spanish Netherlands and other Spanish lands in Italy. Prussia and Savoy were recognized as kingdoms.

Louis's Death and Legacy Louis's last years were more sad than glorious. Realizing that his wars had ruined France, he regretted the suffering he had brought to his people. He died in bed in 1715. News of his death prompted rejoicing throughout France. The people had had enough of the Sun King.

Louis left a mixed legacy to his country. On the positive side, France was certainly a power to be reckoned with in Europe. France ranked above all other European nations in art, literature, and statesmanship during Louis's reign. In addition, France was considered the military leader of Europe. This military might allowed France to develop a strong empire of colonies, which provided resources and goods for trade.

On the negative side, constant warfare and the construction of the Palace of Versailles plunged France into staggering debt. Also, resentment over the tax burden imposed on the poor and Louis's abuse of power would plague his heirs—and eventually lead to revolution.

Absolute rule didn't die with Louis XIV. His enemies in Prussia and Austria had been experimenting with their own forms of absolute monarchy, as you will learn in Section 3.

NEW YORK CORE CURRICULUM REVIEW

TERMS & NAMES 1. For each term or name, write a sentence explaining its significance.

• Edict of Nantes • Cardinal Richelieu • skepticism • Louis XIV • intendant • Jean Baptiste Colbert • War of the Spanish Succession

USING YOUR NOTES

2. Which events on your time line strengthened the French monarchy? Which weakened it?

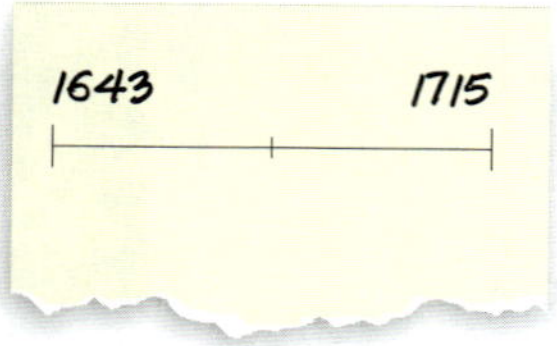

MAIN IDEAS

3. What impact did the French religious wars have on French thinkers?
4. How did Jean Baptiste Colbert intend to stimulate economic growth in France?
5. What was the result of the War of the Spanish Succession?

CRITICAL THINKING & WRITING

6. **SUPPORTING OPINIONS** Many historians think of Louis XIV as the perfect example of an absolute monarch. Do you agree? Explain why or why not.
7. **RECOGNIZING EFFECTS** How did the policies of Colbert and Louis XIV affect the French economy? Explain both positive and negative effects.
8. **SYNTHESIZING** To what extent did anti-Protestantism contribute to Louis's downfall?
9. **WRITING ACTIVITY** POWER AND AUTHORITY Write a **character sketch** of Louis XIV. Discuss his experiences and character traits.

CONNECT TO TODAY **CREATING AN ORAL PRESENTATION**

Research to find out what happened to Versailles after Louis's death and what its function is today. Then present your findings in an **oral presentation**.

Central European Monarchs Clash

CONNECT TO THE NEW YORK STATE CORE CURRICULUM

Unit 3.G.8. Religious wars in Europe: causes and impacts
Unit 5.B.3. The enligntened despots–Maria Theresa and Catherine the Great

TERMS & NAMES

- Thirty Years' War
- Maria Theresa
- Frederick the Great
- Seven Years' War

SETTING THE STAGE For a brief while, the German rulers appeared to have settled their religious differences through the Peace of Augsburg (1555). They had agreed that the faith of each prince would determine the religion of his subjects. Churches in Germany could be either Lutheran or Catholic, but not Calvinist. The peace was short-lived—soon to be replaced by a long war. After the Peace of Augsburg, the Catholic and Lutheran princes of Germany watched each other suspiciously.

TAKING NOTES

Comparing Use a chart to compare Maria Theresa with Frederick the Great. Compare their years of reign, foreign policy, and success in war.

Maria Theresa	Frederick the Great

The Thirty Years' War

Both the Lutheran and the Catholic princes tried to gain followers. In addition, both sides felt threatened by Calvinism, which was spreading in Germany and gaining many followers. As tension mounted, the Lutherans joined together in the Protestant Union in 1608. The following year, the Catholic princes formed the Catholic League. Now, it would take only a spark to set off a war.

Bohemian Protestants Revolt That spark came in 1618. The future Holy Roman emperor, Ferdinand II, was head of the Hapsburg family. As such, he ruled the Czech kingdom of Bohemia. The Protestants in Bohemia did not trust Ferdinand, who was a foreigner and a Catholic. When he closed some Protestant churches, the Protestants revolted. Ferdinand sent an army into Bohemia to crush the revolt. Several German Protestant princes took this chance to challenge their Catholic emperor.

Thus began the **Thirty Years' War**, a conflict over religion and territory and for power among European ruling families. The war can be divided into two main phases: the phase of Hapsburg triumphs and the phase of Hapsburg defeats.

Hapsburg Triumphs The Thirty Years' War lasted from 1618 to 1648. During the first 12 years, Hapsburg armies from Austria and Spain crushed the troops hired by the Protestant princes. They succeeded in putting down the Czech uprising. They also defeated the German Protestants who had supported the Czechs.

Ferdinand II paid his army of 125,000 men by allowing them to plunder, or rob, German villages. This huge army destroyed everything in its path.

Hapsburg Defeats The Protestant Gustavus Adolphus of Sweden and his disciplined army of 23,000 shifted the tide of war in 1630. They drove the Hapsburg armies out of northern Germany. However, Gustavus Adolphus was killed in battle in 1632.

Cardinal Richelieu and Cardinal Mazarin of France dominated the remaining years of the war. Although Catholic, these two cardinals feared the Hapsburgs more than the Protestants. They did not want other European rulers to have as much power as the French king. Therefore, in 1635, Richelieu sent French troops to join the German and Swedish Protestants in their struggle against the Hapsburg armies.

Peace of Westphalia The war did great damage to Germany. Its population dropped from 20 million to about 16 million. Both trade and agriculture were disrupted, and Germany's economy was ruined. Germany had a long, difficult recovery from this devastation. That is a major reason it did not become a unified state until the 1800s.

The Peace of Westphalia (1648) ended the war. The treaty had these important consequences:

- weakened the Hapsburg states of Spain and Austria;
- strengthened France by awarding it German territory;
- made German princes independent of the Holy Roman emperor;
- ended religious wars in Europe;
- introduced a new method of peace negotiation whereby all participants meet to settle the problems of a war and decide the terms of peace. This method is still used today. **A**

Beginning of Modern States The treaty thus abandoned the idea of a Catholic empire that would rule most of Europe. It recognized Europe as a group of equal, independent states. This marked the beginning of the modern state system and was the most important result of the Thirty Years' War.

MAIN IDEA

Drawing Conclusions

A Judging from their actions, do you think the two French cardinals were motivated more by religion or politics? Why?

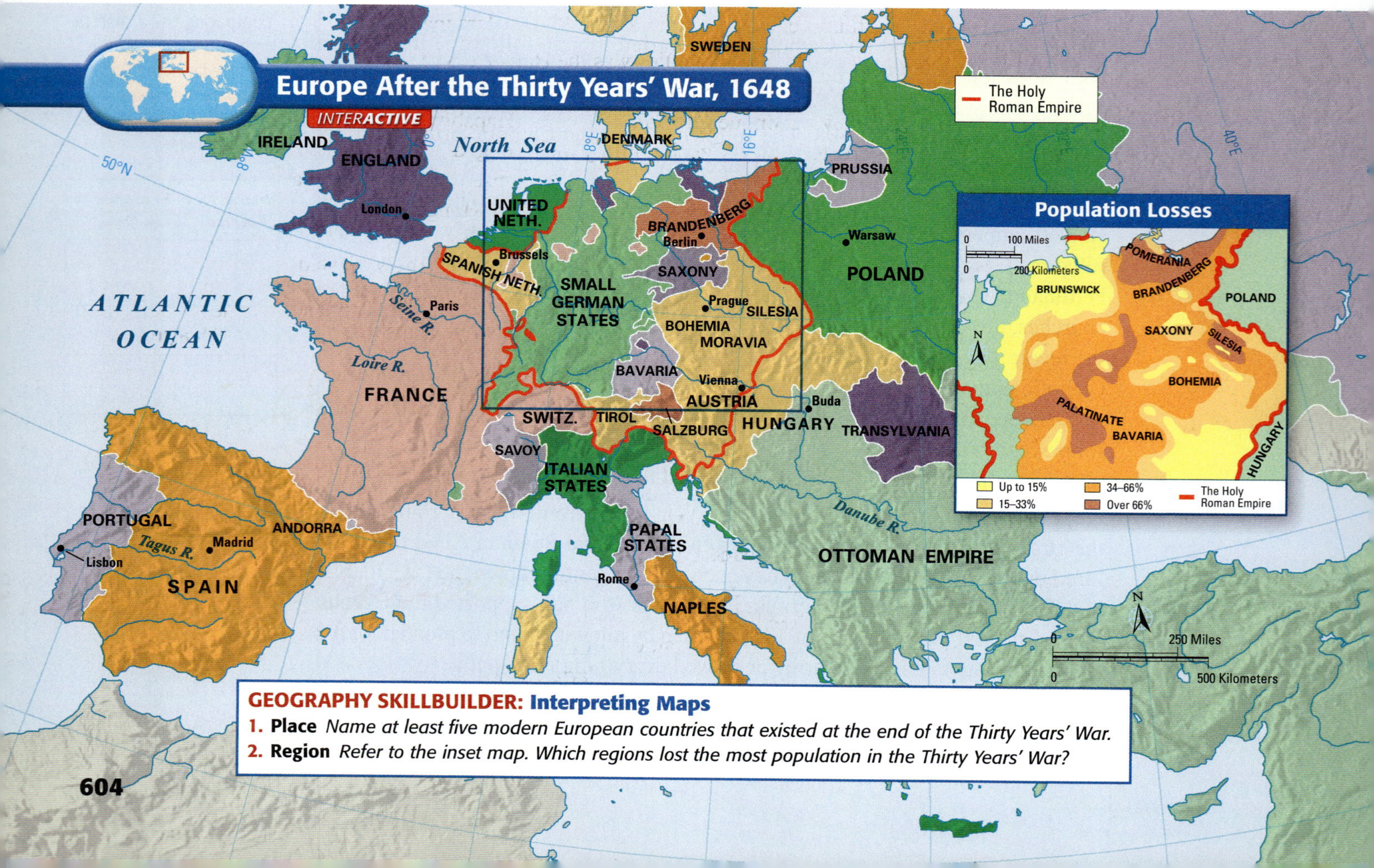

GEOGRAPHY SKILLBUILDER: Interpreting Maps

1. **Place** *Name at least five modern European countries that existed at the end of the Thirty Years' War.*
2. **Region** *Refer to the inset map. Which regions lost the most population in the Thirty Years' War?*

States Form in Central Europe

Strong states formed more slowly in central Europe than in western Europe. The major powers of this region were the kingdom of Poland, the Holy Roman Empire, and the Ottoman Empire. None of them was very strong in the mid-1600s.

Economic Contrasts with the West One reason for this is that the economy of central Europe developed differently from that of western Europe. During the late Middle Ages, serfs in western Europe slowly won freedom and moved to towns. There, they joined middle-class townspeople, who gained economic power because of the commercial revolution and the development of capitalism.

By contrast, the landowning aristocracy in central Europe passed laws restricting the ability of serfs to gain freedom and move to cities. These nobles wanted to keep the serfs on the land, where they could produce large harvests. The nobles could then sell the surplus crops to western European cities at great profit.

Several Weak Empires The landowning nobles in central Europe not only held down the serfs but also blocked the development of strong kings. For example, the Polish nobility elected the Polish king and sharply limited his power. They allowed the king little income, no law courts, and no standing army. As a result, there was not a strong ruler who could form a unified state.

The two empires of central Europe were also weak. Although Suleyman the Magnificent had conquered Hungary and threatened Vienna in 1529, the Ottoman Empire could not take its European conquest any farther. From then on, the Ottoman Empire declined from its peak of power.

In addition, the Holy Roman Empire was seriously weakened by the Thirty Years' War. No longer able to command the obedience of the German states, the Holy Roman Empire had no real power. These old, weakened empires and kingdoms left a power vacuum in central Europe. In the late 1600s, two German-speaking families decided to try to fill this vacuum by becoming absolute rulers themselves.

Austria Grows Stronger One of these families was the Hapsburgs of Austria. The Austrian Hapsburgs took several steps to become absolute monarchs. First, during the Thirty Years' War, they reconquered Bohemia. The Hapsburgs wiped out Protestantism there and created a new Czech nobility that pledged loyalty to them. Second, after the war, the Hapsburg ruler centralized the government and created a standing army. Third, by 1699, the Hapsburgs had retaken Hungary from the Ottoman Empire.

In 1711, Charles VI became the Hapsburg ruler. Charles's empire was a difficult one to rule. Within its borders lived a diverse assortment of people—Czechs, Hungarians, Italians, Croatians, and Germans. Only the fact that one Hapsburg ruler wore the Austrian, Hungarian, and Bohemian crowns kept the empire together.

Maria Theresa Inherits the Austrian Throne How could the Hapsburgs make sure that they continued to rule all those lands? Charles VI spent his entire reign working out an answer to this problem. With endless arm-twisting, he persuaded other leaders of Europe to sign an agreement that declared they would recognize Charles's eldest daughter as the heir to all his Hapsburg territories. That heir was a young woman named **Maria Theresa**. In theory, this agreement guaranteed Maria Theresa a peaceful reign. Instead, she faced years of war. Her main enemy was Prussia, a state to the north of Austria. (See map opposite.)

▼ The imperial crest of the Hapsburgs shows a double-headed eagle with a crown.

History Makers

Maria Theresa 1717–1780

An able ruler, Maria Theresa also devoted herself to her children, whom she continued to advise even after they were grown. Perhaps her most famous child was Marie Antoinette, wife of Louis XVI of France.

As the Austrian empress, Maria Theresa decreased the power of the nobility. She also limited the amount of labor that nobles could force peasants to do. She argued: "The peasantry must be able to sustain itself."

Frederick the Great 1712–1786

Although they reigned during the same time, Frederick the Great and Maria Theresa were very different. Where Maria was religious, Frederick was practical and atheistic. Maria Theresa had a happy home life and a huge family, while Frederick died without a son to succeed him.

An aggressor in foreign affairs, Frederick once wrote that "the fundamental role of governments is the principle of extending their territories." Frederick earned the title "the Great" by achieving his goals for Prussia.

INTEGRATED TECHNOLOGY

INTERNET ACTIVITY Create a family tree showing Maria Theresa's parents and children. Go to **classzone.com** for your research.

Prussia Challenges Austria

Like Austria, Prussia rose to power in the late 1600s. Like the Hapsburgs of Austria, Prussia's ruling family, the Hohenzollerns, also had ambitions. Those ambitions threatened to upset central Europe's delicate balance of power.

The Rise of Prussia The Hohenzollerns built up their state from a number of small holdings, beginning with the German states of Brandenburg and Prussia. In 1640, a 20-year-old Hohenzollern named Frederick William inherited the title of elector of Brandenburg. After seeing the destruction of the Thirty Years' War, Frederick William, later known as the Great Elector, decided that having a strong army was the only way to ensure safety.

To protect their lands, the Great Elector and his descendants moved toward absolute monarchy. They created a standing army, the best in Europe. They built it to a force of 80,000 men. To pay for the army, they introduced permanent taxation. Beginning with the Great Elector's son, they called themselves kings. They also weakened the representative assemblies of their territories.

Prussia's landowning nobility, the Junkers (YUNG•kuhrz), resisted the king's growing power. However, in the early 1700s, King Frederick William I bought their cooperation. He gave the Junkers the exclusive right to be officers in his army. As a result, Prussia became a rigidly controlled, highly militarized society. **B**

MAIN IDEA

Clarifying

B What steps did the Prussian monarchs take to become absolute monarchs?

Frederick the Great Frederick William worried that his son, Frederick, was not military enough to rule. The prince loved music, philosophy, and poetry. In 1730, when he and a friend tried to run away, they were caught. To punish Frederick, the king ordered him to witness his friend's beheading. Despite such bitter memories, Frederick II, known as **Frederick the Great**, followed his father's military policies when he came to power. However, he also softened some of his father's laws. With regard to domestic affairs, he encouraged religious toleration and legal reform. According to his theory of government, Frederick believed that a ruler should be like a father to his people:

PRIMARY SOURCE

A prince . . . is only the first servant of the state, who is obliged to act with probity [honesty] and prudence. . . . As the sovereign is properly the head of a family of citizens, the father of his people, he ought on all occasions to be the last refuge of the unfortunate.

FREDERICK II, *Essay on Forms of Government*

War of the Austrian Succession In 1740, Maria Theresa succeeded her father, just five months after Frederick II became king of Prussia. Frederick wanted the Austrian land of Silesia, which bordered Prussia. Silesia produced iron ore, textiles, and food products. Frederick underestimated Maria Theresa's strength. He assumed that because she was a woman, she would not be forceful enough to defend her lands. In 1740, he sent his army to occupy Silesia, beginning the War of the Austrian Succession. C

MAIN IDEA

Clarifying

C Why would iron ore, agricultural lands, and textiles be helpful acquisitions for Frederick the Great?

Even though Maria Theresa had recently given birth, she journeyed to Hungary. There she held her infant in her arms as she asked the Hungarian nobles for aid. Even though the nobles resented their Hapsburg rulers, they pledged to give Maria Theresa an army. Great Britain also joined Austria to fight its longtime enemy France, which was Prussia's ally. Although Maria Theresa did stop Prussia's aggression, she lost Silesia in the Treaty of Aix-la-Chapelle in 1748. With the acquisition of Silesia, Prussia became a major European power.

The Seven Years' War-Maria Theresa decided that the French kings were no longer Austria's chief enemies. She made an alliance with them. The result was a diplomatic revolution. When Frederick heard of her actions, he signed a treaty with Britain—Austria's former ally. Now, Austria, France, Russia, and others were allied against Britain and Prussia. Not only had Austria and Prussia switched allies, but for the first time, Russia was playing a role in European affairs.

In 1756, Frederick attacked Saxony, an Austrian ally. Soon every great European power was involved in the war. Fought in Europe, India, and North America, the war lasted until 1763. It was called the **Seven Years' War**. The war did not change the territorial situation in Europe.

It was a different story on other continents. Both France and Britain had colonies in North America and the West Indies. Both were competing economically in India. The British emerged as the real victors in the Seven Years' War. France lost its colonies in North America, and Britain gained sole economic domination of India. This set the stage for further British expansion in India in the 1800s, as you will see in Chapter 27.

NEW YORK CORE CURRICULUM REVIEW

TERMS & NAMES 1. For each term or name, write a sentence explaining its significance.

- Thirty Years' War
- Maria Theresa
- Frederick the Great
- Seven Years' War

USING YOUR NOTES

2. In what ways were the rulers similar?

Maria Theresa	Frederick the Great

MAIN IDEAS

3. What were the major conflicts in the Thirty Years' War?
4. What steps did the Austrian Hapsburgs take toward becoming absolute monarchs?
5. What countries were allies during the Seven Years' War?

CRITICAL THINKING & WRITING

6. **RECOGNIZING EFFECTS** How did the Peace of Westphalia lay the foundations of modern Europe?
7. **ANALYZING MOTIVES** Why did Maria Theresa make an alliance with the French kings, Austria's chief enemies?
8. **DRAWING CONCLUSIONS** Based on Frederick's assumption about Maria Theresa at the outset of the War of the Austrian Succession, what conclusions can you draw about how men viewed women in 1700s Europe?
9. **WRITING ACTIVITY** POWER AND AUTHORITY -Write an **outline** for a lecture on "How to Increase Royal Power and Become an Absolute Monarch."

CONNECT TO TODAY **CREATING A POSTER**

Today much of western Europe belongs to an organization called the European Union (EU). Find out which countries belong to the EU and how they are linked economically and politically. Present your findings—including maps, charts, and pictures—in a **poster.**

Absolute Rulers of Russia

CONNECT TO THE NEW YORK STATE CORE CURRICULUM

Methodology.A.3. The connections and interactions of people across time and space
Unit 4.F.4. Case studies: Akbar the Great, Suleyman the Magnificent, Philip II, Louis XIV, Ivan the Terrible, and Peter the Great

TERMS & NAMES

- Ivan the Terrible
- boyar
- Peter the Great
- westernization

SETTING THE STAGE Ivan III of Moscow, who ruled Russia from 1462 to 1505, accomplished several things. First, he conquered much of the territory around Moscow. Second, he liberated Russia from the Mongols. Third, he began to centralize the Russian government. Ivan III was succeeded by his son, Vasily, who ruled for 28 years. Vasily continued his father's work of adding territory to the growing Russian state. He also increased the power of the central government. This trend continued under his son, Ivan IV, who would become an absolute ruler.

TAKING NOTES
Summarizing Use a cluster diagram to list the important events of Peter the Great's reign.

The First Czar

Ivan IV, called **Ivan the Terrible**, came to the throne in 1533 when he was only three years old. His young life was disrupted by struggles for power among Russia's landowning nobles, known as **boyars**. The boyars fought to control young Ivan. When he was 16, Ivan seized power and had himself crowned czar. This title meant "caesar," and Ivan was the first Russian ruler to use it officially. He also married the beautiful Anastasia, related to an old boyar family, the Romanovs.

The years from 1547 to 1560 are often called Ivan's "good period." He won great victories, added lands to Russia, gave Russia a code of laws, and ruled justly.

Rule by Terror Ivan's "bad period" began in 1560 after Anastasia died. Accusing the boyars of poisoning his wife, Ivan turned against them. He organized his own police force, whose chief duty was to hunt down and murder people Ivan considered traitors. The members of this police force dressed in black and rode black horses.

Using these secret police, Ivan executed many boyars, their families, and the peasants who worked their lands. Thousands of people died. Ivan seized the boyars' estates and gave them to a new class of nobles, who had to remain loyal to him or lose their land.

Eventually, Ivan committed an act that was both a personal tragedy and a national disaster. In 1581, during a violent quarrel, he killed his oldest son and heir. When Ivan died three years later, only his weak second son was left to rule.

Rise of the Romanovs Ivan's son proved to be physically and mentally incapable of ruling. After he died without an heir, Russia experienced a period of

MAIN IDEA

Recognizing Effects

A What were the long-term effects of Ivan's murder of his oldest son?

turmoil known as the Time of Troubles. Boyars struggled for power, and heirs of czars died under mysterious conditions. Several impostors tried to claim the throne.

Finally, in 1613, representatives from many Russian cities met to choose the next czar. Their choice was Michael Romanov, grandnephew of Ivan the Terrible's wife, Anastasia. Thus began the Romanov dynasty, which ruled Russia for 300 years (1613–1917). **A**

Peter the Great Comes to Power

Over time, the Romanovs restored order to Russia. They strengthened government by passing a law code and putting down a revolt. This paved the way for the absolute rule of Czar Peter I. At first, Peter shared the throne with his half-brother. However, in 1696, Peter became sole ruler of Russia. He is known to history as **Peter the Great**, because he was one of Russia's greatest reformers. He also continued the trend of increasing the czar's power.

Russia Contrasts with Europe When Peter I came to power, Russia was still a land of boyars and serfs. Serfdom in Russia lasted into the mid-1800s, much longer than it did in western Europe. Russian landowners wanted serfs to stay on the land and produce large harvests. The landowners treated the serfs like property. When a Russian landowner sold a piece of land, he sold the serfs with it. Landowners could give away serfs as presents or to pay debts. It was also against the law for serfs to run away from their owners.

Most boyars knew little of western Europe. In the Middle Ages, Russia had looked to Constantinople, not to Rome, for leadership. Then Mongol rule had cut Russia off from the Renaissance and the Age of Exploration. Geographic barriers also isolated Russia. Its only seaport, Archangel in northern Russia, was choked with ice much of the year. The few travelers who reached Moscow were usually Dutch or German, and they had to stay in a separate part of the city.

Religious differences widened the gap between western Europe and Russia. The Russians had adopted the Eastern Orthodox branch of Christianity. Western Europeans were mostly Catholics or Protestants, and the Russians viewed them as heretics and avoided them. **B**

MAIN IDEA

Summarizing

B Why was Russia culturally different from western Europe?

Peter Visits the West In the 1680s, people in the German quarter of Moscow were accustomed to seeing the young Peter striding through their neighborhood on his long legs. (Peter was more than six and a half feet tall.) He was fascinated by the modern tools and machines in the foreigners' shops. Above all, he had a passion for ships and the sea. The young czar believed that Russia's future depended on having a warm-water port. Only then could Russia compete with the more modern states of western Europe.

Peter was 24 years old when he became the sole ruler of Russia. In 1697, just one year later, he embarked on the "Grand Embassy," a long visit to western Europe. One of Peter's goals was to learn about European customs and manufacturing techniques. Never before had a czar traveled among Western "heretics."

History Makers

Peter the Great
1672–1725

Peter the Great had the mind of a genius, the body of a giant, and the ferocious temper of a bear. He was so strong that he was known to take a heavy silver plate and roll it up as if it were a piece of paper. If someone annoyed him, he would knock the offender unconscious.

The painting above represents Peter as he looked when he traveled through western Europe. He dressed in the plain clothes of an ordinary worker to keep his identity a secret.

INTEGRATED TECHNOLOGY

RESEARCH LINKS For more on Peter the Great, go to **classzone.com**

Peter Rules Absolutely

Inspired by his trip to the West, Peter resolved that Russia would compete with Europe on both military and commercial terms. Peter's goal of **westernization**, of using western Europe as a model for change, was not an end in itself. Peter saw it as a way to make Russia stronger.

Peter's Reforms Although Peter believed Russia needed to change, he knew that many of his people disagreed. As he said to one official, "For you know yourself that, though a thing be good and necessary, our people will not do it unless forced to." To force change upon his state, Peter increased his powers as an absolute ruler. C

> MAIN IDEA
> **Analyzing Bias**
> C Judging from this remark, what was Peter's view of his people?

Peter brought the Russian Orthodox Church under state control. He abolished the office of patriarch, head of the Church. He set up a group called the Holy Synod to run the Church under his direction.

Like Ivan the Terrible, Peter reduced the power of the great landowners. He recruited men from lower-ranking families. He then promoted them to positions of authority and rewarded them with grants of land.

To modernize his army, Peter hired European officers, who drilled his soldiers in European tactics with European weapons. Being a soldier became a lifetime job. By the time of Peter's death, the Russian army numbered 200,000 men. To pay for this huge army, Peter imposed heavy taxes.

Westernizing Russia As part of his attempts to westernize Russia, Peter undertook the following:

- introduced potatoes, which became a staple of the Russian diet
- started Russia's first newspaper and edited its first issue himself
- raised women's status by having them attend social gatherings
- ordered the nobles to give up their traditional clothes for Western fashions
- advanced education by opening a school of navigation and introducing schools for the arts and sciences

The Expansion of Russia, 1500–1800

INTERACTIVE

GEOGRAPHY SKILLBUILDER: Interpreting Maps

1. **Location** *Locate the territories that Peter added to Russia during his reign, from 1682 to 1725. What bodies of water did Russia gain access to because of these acquisitions?*
2. **Region** *Who added a larger amount of territory to Russia—Ivan III, who ruled from 1462 to 1505, or Peter the Great?*

Peter believed that education was a key to Russia's progress. In former times, subjects were forbidden under pain of death to study the sciences in foreign lands. Now subjects were not only permitted to leave the country, many were forced to do it.

Establishing St. Petersburg To promote education and growth, Peter wanted a seaport that would make it easier to travel to the West. Therefore, Peter fought Sweden to gain a piece of the Baltic coast. After 21 long years of war, Russia finally won the "window on Europe" that Peter had so desperately wanted.

Actually, Peter had secured that window many years before Sweden officially surrendered it. In 1703, he began building a new city on Swedish lands occupied by Russian troops. Although the swampy site was unhealthful, it seemed ideal to Peter. Ships could sail down the Neva River into the Baltic Sea and on to western Europe. Peter called the city St. Petersburg, after his patron saint.

To build a city on a desolate swamp was no easy matter. Every summer, the army forced thousands of luckless serfs to leave home and work in St. Petersburg. An estimated 25,000 to 100,000 people died from the terrible working conditions and widespread diseases. When St. Petersburg was finished, Peter ordered many Russian nobles to leave the comforts of Moscow and settle in his new capital. In time, St. Petersburg became a busy port. D

For better or for worse, Peter the Great had tried to westernize and reform the culture and government of Russia. To an amazing extent he had succeeded. By the time of his death in 1725, Russia was a power to be reckoned with in Europe. Meanwhile, another great European power, England, had been developing a form of government that limited the power of absolute monarchs, as you will see in Section 5.

Global Patterns

East Meets West

In the East, Western influence would affect not only Russia. Other eastern nations would give way—not always willingly—to the West and Western culture. In 1854, Japan was forced to open its doors to the United States. By 1867, however, Japan had decided to embrace Western civilization. The Japanese modernized their military based on the German and British models. They also adopted the American system of public education. China and Korea, on the other hand, would resist foreign intervention well into the 1900s.

MAIN IDEA

Synthesizing

D Which of Peter's actions in building St. Petersburg show his power as an absolute monarch?

NEW YORK CORE CURRICULUM REVIEW

TERMS & NAMES 1. For each term or name, write a sentence explaining its significance.

- Ivan the Terrible
- boyar
- Peter the Great
- westernization

USING YOUR NOTES

2. Which event had the most impact on modern Russia? Why?

MAIN IDEAS

3. How did Ivan the Terrible deal with his enemies during his "bad period"?
4. Why did Peter the Great believe that Russia's future depended on having a warm-water port?
5. What were some of the ways Peter tried to westernize Russia?

CRITICAL THINKING & WRITING

6. **SUPPORTING OPINIONS** Who do you think was more of an absolute monarch: Ivan the Terrible or Peter the Great?
7. **DRAWING CONCLUSIONS** Which class of Russian society probably didn't benefit from Peter's reforms? Why?
8. **HYPOTHESIZING** How might Peter's attempts at westernization have affected his people's opinion of Christians in western Europe?
9. **WRITING ACTIVITY** POWER AND AUTHORITY Write a one-paragraph **expository essay** explaining which of Peter the Great's actions reveal that he saw himself as the highest authority in Russia.

CONNECT TO TODAY **STAGING A DEBATE**

Peter the Great's reforms were a first step toward Russia's westernization. Today the country continues the process by experimenting with democratization. Research to find out how Russia has fared as a democracy. Then stage a **debate** to argue whether the experiment is working.

Surviving the Russian Winter

Much of Russia has severe winters. In Moscow, snow usually begins to fall in mid-October and lasts until mid-April. Siberia has been known to have temperatures as low as -90°F. Back in the 18th century, Russians did not have down parkas or high-tech insulation for their homes. But they had other ways to cope with the climate.

For example, in the 18th century, Russian peasants added potatoes and corn to their diet. During the winter, these nutritious foods were used in soups and stews. Such dishes were warming and provided plenty of calories to help fight off the cold.

INTEGRATED TECHNOLOGY

RESEARCH LINKS For more on Russian winters, go to **classzone.com**

Silver Samovar ►

In the mid-18th century, samovars were invented in Russia. These large, often elaborately decorated urns were used to boil water for tea. Fire was kept burning in a tube running up the middle of the urn—keeping the water piping hot.

◄ Crimean Dress

These people are wearing the traditional dress of tribes from the Crimean Peninsula, a region that Russia took over in the 1700s. Notice the heavy hats, the fur trim on some of the robes, and the leggings worn by those with shorter robes. All these features help to conserve body heat.

▼ Troika

To travel in winter, the wealthy often used sleighs called troikas. *Troika* means "group of three"; the name comes from the three horses that draw this kind of sleigh. The middle horse trotted while the two outside horses galloped.

Winter Festival ►

Russians have never let their climate stop them from having fun outdoors. Here, they are shown enjoying a Shrovetide festival, which occurs near the end of winter. Vendors sold food such as blinis (pancakes with sour cream). Entertainments included ice skating, dancing bears, and magic shows.

The people in the foreground are wearing heavy fur coats. Otter fur was often used for winter clothing. This fur is extremely thick and has about one million hairs per square inch.

▼ Wooden House

Wooden houses, made of logs, were common in Russia during Peter the Great's time. To insulate the house from the wind, people stuffed moss between the logs. Russians used double panes of glass in their windows. For extra protection, many houses had shutters to cover the windows. The roofs were steep so snow would slide off.

> DATA FILE

FROSTY FACTS

- According to a 2001 estimate, Russian women spend about $500 million a year on fur coats and caps.
- The record low temperature in Asia of -90°F was reached twice, first in Verkhoyansk, Russia, in 1892 and then in Oimekon, Russia, in 1933.
- The record low temperature in Europe of -67°F was recorded in Ust'Shchugor, Russia.
- One reason for Russia's cold climate is that most of the country lies north of the 45° latitude line, closer to the North Pole than to the Equator.

Source: *Worldclimate.com*

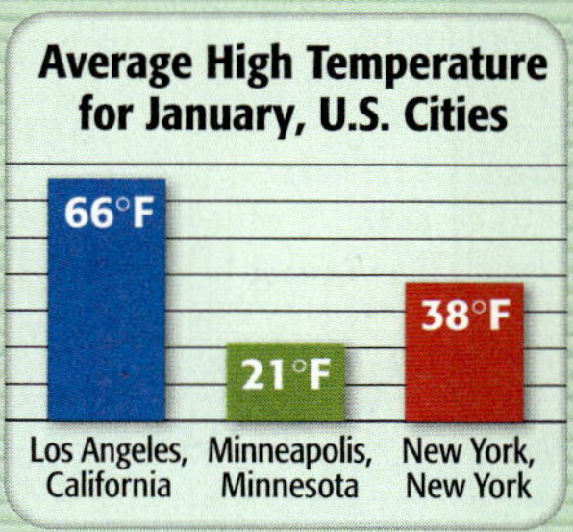

Source: *Worldclimate.com*

Connect *to* Today

1. **Making Inferences** In the 18th century, how did Russians use their natural resources to help them cope with the climate?

   See Skillbuilder Handbook, page R10.

2. **Comparing and Contrasting** How has coping with winter weather changed from 18th-century Russia to today's world? How has it stayed the same?

5

Parliament Limits the English Monarchy

CONNECT TO THE NEW YORK STATE CORE CURRICULUM

Unit 4.G.2. Divine Right of Monarchy–Stuart rule
Unit 4.G.3. Puritan Revolution–Oliver Cromwell

TERMS & NAMES

- Charles I
- English Civil War
- Oliver Cromwell
- Restoration
- *habeas corpus*
- Glorious Revolution
- constitutional monarchy
- cabinet

SETTING THE STAGE During her reign, Queen Elizabeth I of England had had frequent conflicts with Parliament. Many of the arguments were over money, because the treasury did not have enough funds to pay the queen's expenses. By the time Elizabeth died in 1603, she had left a huge debt for her successor to deal with. Parliament's financial power was one obstacle to English rulers' becoming absolute monarchs. The resulting struggle between Parliament and the monarchy would have serious consequences for England.

TAKING NOTES

Analyzing Causes Use a chart to list the causes of each monarch's conflicts with Parliament.

Monarch	Conflicts with Parliament
James I	
Charles I	
James II	

Monarchs Defy Parliament

Elizabeth had no child, and her nearest relative was her cousin, James Stuart. Already king of Scotland, James Stuart became King James I of England in 1603. Although England and Scotland were not united until 1707, they now shared a ruler.

James's Problems James inherited the unsettled issues of Elizabeth's reign. His worst struggles with Parliament were over money. In addition, James offended the Puritan members of Parliament. The Puritans hoped he would enact reforms to purify the English church of Catholic practices. Except for agreeing to a new translation of the Bible, however, he refused to make Puritan reforms.

Charles I Fights Parliament In 1625, James I died. **Charles I**, his son, took the throne. Charles always needed money, in part because he was at war with both Spain and France. Several times when Parliament refused to give him funds, he dissolved it.

By 1628, Charles was forced to call Parliament again. This time it refused to grant him any money until he signed a document that is known as the Petition of Right. In this petition, the king agreed to four points:

- He would not imprison subjects without due cause.
- He would not levy taxes without Parliament's consent.
- He would not house soldiers in private homes.
- He would not impose martial law in peacetime.

After agreeing to the petition, Charles ignored it. Even so, the petition was important. It set forth the idea that the law was higher than the king. This idea contradicted theories of absolute monarchy. In 1629, Charles dissolved Parliament and refused to call it back into session. To get money, he imposed all kinds of fees and fines on the English people. His popularity decreased year by year.

English Civil War

Charles offended Puritans by upholding the rituals of the Anglican Church. In addition, in 1637, Charles tried to force the Presbyterian Scots to accept a version of the Anglican prayer book. He wanted both his kingdoms to follow one religion. The Scots rebelled, assembled a huge army, and threatened to invade England. To meet this danger, Charles needed money—money he could get only by calling Parliament into session. This gave Parliament a chance to oppose him.

War Topples a King During the autumn of 1641, Parliament passed laws to limit royal power. Furious, Charles tried to arrest Parliament's leaders in January 1642, but they escaped. Equally furious, a mob of Londoners raged outside the palace. Charles fled London and raised an army in the north of England, where people were loyal to him.

From 1642 to 1649, supporters and opponents of King Charles fought the **English Civil War**. Those who remained loyal to Charles were called Royalists or Cavaliers. On the other side were Puritan supporters of Parliament. Because these men wore their hair short over their ears, Cavaliers called them Roundheads.

At first neither side could gain a lasting advantage. However, by 1644 the Puritans found a general who could win—**Oliver Cromwell**. In 1645, Cromwell's New Model Army began defeating the Cavaliers, and the tide turned toward the Puritans. In 1647, they held the king prisoner.

In 1649, Cromwell and the Puritans brought Charles to trial for treason against Parliament. They found him guilty and sentenced him to death. The execution of Charles was revolutionary. Kings had often been overthrown, killed in battle, or put to death in secret. Never before, however, had a reigning monarch faced a public trial and execution.

Cromwell's Rule Cromwell now held the reins of power. In 1649, he abolished the monarchy and the House of Lords. He established a commonwealth, a republican form of government. In 1653, Cromwell sent home the remaining members of Parliament. Cromwell's associate John Lambert drafted a constitution, the first written constitution of any modern European state. However, Cromwell eventually tore up the document and became a military dictator. (A)

MAIN IDEA

Comparing

(A) What did Cromwell's rule have in common with an absolute monarchy?

Cromwell almost immediately had to put down a rebellion in Ireland. English colonization of Ireland had begun in the 1100s under Henry II. Henry VIII and his children had brought the country firmly under English rule in the 1500s. In 1649, Cromwell landed on Irish shores with an army and crushed the uprising. He seized the lands and homes of the Irish and gave them to English soldiers. Fighting, plague, and famine killed hundreds of thousands.

▼ This engraving depicts the beheading of Charles I.

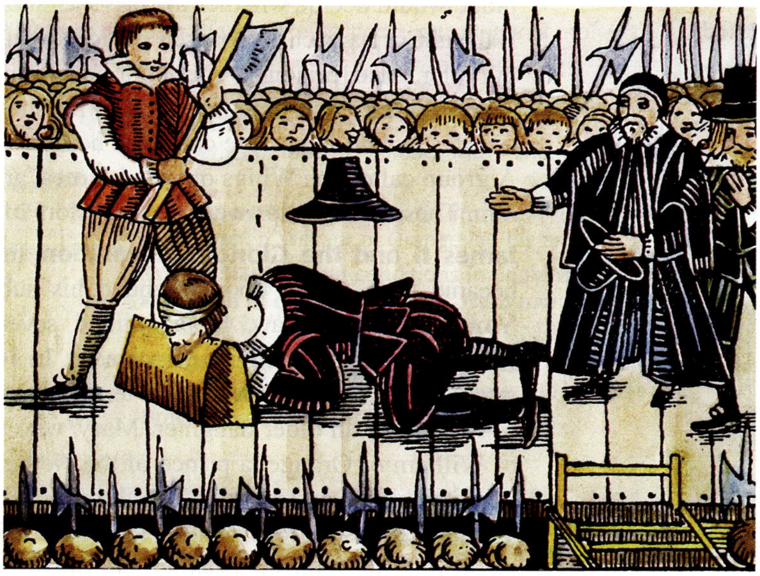

Puritan Morality In England, Cromwell and the Puritans sought to reform society. They made laws that promoted Puritan morality and abolished activities they found sinful, such as the theater, sporting events, and dancing. Although he was a strict

Chapter 21 Assessment

VISUAL SUMMARY

Absolute Monarchs in Europe

Long-Term Causes

- decline of feudalism
- rise of cities and support of middle class
- growth of national kingdoms
- loss of Church authority

Immediate Causes

- religious and territorial conflicts
- buildup of armies
- need for increased taxes
- revolts by peasants or nobles

European Monarchs Claim Divine Right to Rule Absolutely

Immediate Effects

- regulation of religion and society
- larger courts
- huge building projects
- new government bureaucracies appointed by the government
- loss of power by nobility and legislatures

Long-Term Effects

- revolution in France
- western European influence on Russia
- English political reforms that influence U.S. democracy

TERMS & NAMES

For each term or name below, briefly explain its connection to European history from 1500 to 1800.

1. absolute monarch
2. divine right
3. Louis XIV
4. War of the Spanish Succession
5. Thirty Years' War
6. Seven Years' War
7. Peter the Great
8. English Civil War
9. Glorious Revolution
10. constitutional monarchy

MAIN IDEAS

Spain's Empire and European Absolutism Section 1 (pages 589–595)

11. What three actions demonstrated that Philip II of Spain saw himself as a defender of Catholicism?
12. According to French writer Jean Bodin, should a prince share power with anyone else? Explain why or why not.

The Reign of Louis XIV Section 2 (pages 596–602)

13. What strategies did Louis XIV use to control the French nobility?
14. In what ways did Louis XIV cause suffering to the French people?

Central European Monarchs Clash Section 3 (pages 603–607)

15. What were six results of the Peace of Westphalia?
16. Why did Maria Theresa and Frederick the Great fight two wars against each other?

Absolute Rulers of Russia Section 4 (pages 608–613)

17. What were three differences between Russia and western Europe?
18. What was Peter the Great's primary goal for Russia?

Parliament Limits the English Monarchy Section 5 (pages 614–617)

19. List the causes, participants, and outcome of the English Civil War.
20. How did Parliament try to limit the power of the English monarchy?

CRITICAL THINKING

1. USING YOUR NOTES

POWER AND AUTHORITY In a chart, list actions that absolute monarchs took to increase their power. Then identify the monarchs who took these actions.

Actions of Absolute Rulers	Monarchs Who Took Them

2. DRAWING CONCLUSIONS

ECONOMICS What benefits might absolute monarchs hope to gain by increasing their countries' territory?

3. DEVELOPING HISTORICAL PERSPECTIVE

What conditions fostered the rise of absolute monarchs in Europe?

4. COMPARING AND CONTRASTING

Compare the reign of Louis XIV with that of Peter the Great. Which absolute ruler had a more lasting impact on his country? Explain why.

5. HYPOTHESIZING

Would Charles I have had a different fate if he had been king of another country in western or central Europe? Why or why not?

Use the excerpt from the English Bill of Rights passed in 1689 and your knowledge of world history to answer questions 1 and 2.

Additional Test Practice, pp. S1–S33.

PRIMARY SOURCE

That the pretended power of suspending [canceling] of laws or the execution [carrying out] of laws by regal authority without consent of Parliament is illegal; . . .

That it is the right of the subjects to petition [make requests of] the king, and all commitments [imprisonments] and prosecutions for such petitioning are illegal;

That the raising or keeping a standing army within the kingdom in time of peace, unless it be with consent of Parliament, is against the law; . . .

That election of members of Parliament ought to be free [not restricted].

English Bill of Rights

1 According to the excerpt, which of the following is illegal?
(1) the enactment of laws without Parliament's permission
(2) the unrestricted election of members of Parliament
(3) the right of subjects to make requests of the king
(4) keeping a standing army in time of peace with Parliament's consent

2 The English Bill of Rights was passed as a means to
(1) limit Parliament's power
(2) increase Parliament's power
(3) overthrow the monarch
(4) increase the monarch's power

Use the map and your knowledge of world history to answer question 3.

Modern European Monarchs, 2003

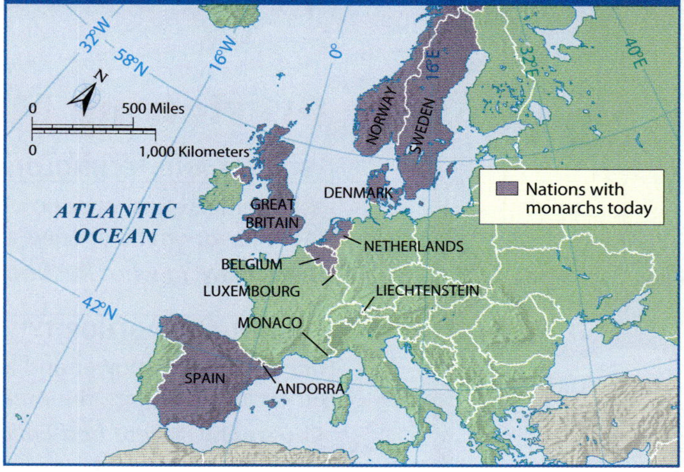

3 Of the countries that you studied in this chapter, which have monarchs today?
(1) Spain, Great Britain, the Netherlands
(2) Liechtenstein, Monaco
(3) Luxembourg, Andorra
(4) Great Britain, Norway, Sweden

INTEGRATED TECHNOLOGY

TEST PRACTICE Go to **classzone.com**
- Diagnostic tests
- Tutorials
- Strategies
- Additional practice

ALTERNATIVE ASSESSMENT

1. Interact *with* History

On page 588, you thought about the advantages and disadvantages of absolute power. Now that you have read the chapter, what do you consider to be the main advantage and the main disadvantage of being an absolute ruler?

2. WRITING ABOUT HISTORY

REVOLUTION Reread the information on Oliver Cromwell. Then write a **History Maker,** like the ones you've seen throughout this textbook, on Cromwell as a leader of a successful revolution. Be sure to

- include biographical information about Cromwell.
- discuss his effectiveness as a leader.
- use vivid language to hold your reader's attention.

INTEGRATED TECHNOLOGY

Creating a Television News Report

Use a video recorder to tape a television news report on the trial of Charles I. Role-play an announcer reporting a breaking news story. Relate the facts of the trial and interview key participants, including:

- a member of Parliament
- a Puritan
- a Royalist
- Charles I

CHAPTER 22

Enlightenment and Revolution, 1550–1789

Previewing Main Ideas

SCIENCE AND TECHNOLOGY The Scientific Revolution began when astronomers questioned how the universe operates. By shattering long-held views, these astronomers opened a new world of discovery.

Geography *In what Russian city did Enlightenment ideas bloom?*

POWER AND AUTHORITY The thinkers of the Enlightenment challenged old ideas about power and authority. Such new ways of thinking led to, among other things, the American Revolution.

Geography *Where had Enlightenment ideas spread outside Europe?*

REVOLUTION Between the 16th and 18th centuries, a series of revolutions helped to usher in the modern era in Western history. Revolutions in both thought and action forever changed European and American society.

Geography *What city in Brandenburg-Prussia was an Enlightenment center?*

NEW YORK CORE CURRICULUM FOCUS

- The scientific method and other products of the Scientific Revolution laid the foundation for modern science.
- Enlightenment ideas helped spur the American Revolution.

INTEGRATED TECHNOLOGY

eEdition

- Interactive Maps
- Interactive Visuals
- Interactive Primary Sources

INTERNET RESOURCES

Go to **classzone.com** for:

- Research Links
- Internet Activities
- Primary Sources
- Chapter Quiz
- Maps
- Test Practice
- Current Events

EUROPE AND NORTH AMERICA

1500

1543 Copernicus publishes heliocentric theory.

1609 Galileo observes heavens through a telescope similar to this one.

1600

WORLD

1556 Golden Age of Mughal Empire begins in India. (portrait of Mughal princess)

1603 Tokugawa Ieyasu becomes ruler of all Japan.

1687
Newton publishes treatise on law of gravity.

1776
◀ With Liberty Bell symbolizing their freedom, American colonies declare independence.

1789
Revolution erupts in France.

1700 **1800**

1644
Manchus invade China and establish Qing Dynasty. (Qing ruler Lohan) ▶

1722
Chinese emperor Kangxi dies after a 61-year reign.

1776
Tukolor Kingdom arises in the former Songhai region of West Africa.

Interact *with* History

How would you react to a revolutionary idea?

You are a university student during the late 1600s, and it seems that the world as you know it has turned upside down. An English scientist named Isaac Newton has just theorized that the universe is not a dark mystery but a system whose parts work together in ways that can be expressed mathematically. This is just the latest in a series of arguments that have challenged old ways of thinking in fields from astronomy to medicine. Many of these ideas promise to open the way for improving society. And yet they are such radical ideas that many people refuse to accept them.

▲ This painting by English artist Joseph Wright depicts adults and children gazing at a miniature planetarium and its new ideas about the universe.

EXAMINING *the* ISSUES

- **Why might people have difficulty accepting new ideas or ways of thinking?**
- **What are the risks of embracing a different idea? What are some risks of always refusing to do so?**

Meet in small groups and discuss these questions. As you discuss these and other issues, recall other times in history when people expressed ideas that were different from accepted ones. As you read this chapter, watch for the effects of revolutionary ideas, beliefs, and discoveries.

The Scientific Revolution

CONNECT TO THE NEW YORK STATE CORE CURRICULUM

Unit 5.A.1. The development of scientific methods
Unit 5.A.2. The work of Copernicus, Galileo, Newton, and Descartes

TERMS & NAMES

- geocentric theory
- Scientific Revolution
- heliocentric theory
- Galileo Galilei
- scientific method
- Isaac Newton

SETTING THE STAGE As you recall, the period between 1300 and 1600 was a time of great change in Europe. The Renaissance, a rebirth of learning and the arts, inspired a spirit of curiosity in many fields. Scholars began to question ideas that had been accepted for hundreds of years. Meanwhile, the religious movement known as the Reformation prompted followers to challenge accepted ways of thinking about God and salvation. While the Reformation was taking place, another revolution in European thought had begun, one that would permanently change how people viewed the physical world.

The Roots of Modern Science

Before 1500, scholars generally decided what was true or false by referring to an ancient Greek or Roman author or to the Bible. Few European scholars challenged the scientific ideas of the ancient thinkers or the church by carefully observing nature for themselves.

The Medieval View During the Middle Ages, most scholars believed that the earth was an immovable object located at the center of the universe. According to that belief, the moon, the sun, and the planets all moved in perfectly circular paths around the earth. Common sense seemed to support this view. After all, the sun appeared to be moving around the earth as it rose in the morning and set in the evening.

This earth-centered view of the universe was called the **geocentric theory**. The idea came from Aristotle, the Greek philosopher of the fourth century B.C. The Greek astronomer Ptolemy (TOL•a•mee) expanded the theory in the second century A.D. In addition, Christianity taught that God had deliberately placed the earth at the center of the universe. Earth was thus a special place on which the great drama of life unfolded.

A New Way of Thinking Beginning in the mid-1500s, a few scholars published works that challenged the ideas of the ancient thinkers and the church. As these scholars replaced old assumptions with new theories, they launched a change in European thought that historians call the **Scientific Revolution**. The Scientific Revolution was a new way of thinking about the natural world. That way was based upon careful observation and a willingness to question accepted beliefs.

TAKING NOTES

Analyzing Causes Use a diagram to list the events and circumstances that led to the Scientific Revolution.

A combination of discoveries and circumstances led to the Scientific Revolution and helped spread its impact. During the Renaissance, European explorers traveled to Africa, Asia, and the Americas. Such lands were inhabited by peoples and animals previously unknown in Europe. These discoveries opened Europeans to the possibility that there were new truths to be found. The invention of the printing press during this period helped spread challenging ideas—both old and new—more widely among Europe's thinkers.

The age of European exploration also fueled a great deal of scientific research, especially in astronomy and mathematics. Navigators needed better instruments and geographic measurements, for example, to determine their location in the open sea. As scientists began to look more closely at the world around them, they made observations that did not match the ancient beliefs. They found they had reached the limit of the classical world's knowledge. Yet, they still needed to know more.

A Revolutionary Model of the Universe

An early challenge to accepted scientific thinking came in the field of astronomy. It started when a small group of scholars began to question the geocentric theory.

The Heliocentric Theory Although backed by authority and common sense, the geocentric theory did not accurately explain the movements of the sun, moon, and planets. This problem troubled a Polish cleric and astronomer named Nicolaus Copernicus (koh•PUR•nuh•kuhs). In the early 1500s, Copernicus became interested in an old Greek idea that the sun stood at the center of the universe. After studying planetary movements for more than 25 years, Copernicus reasoned that indeed, the stars, the earth, and the other planets revolved around the sun.

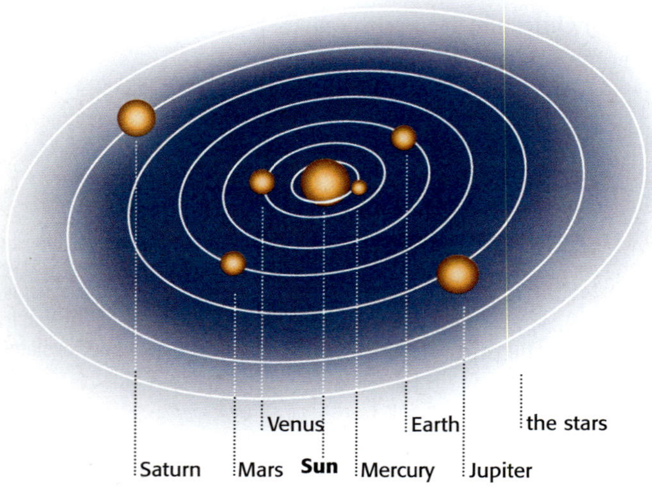

▲ This model shows how Copernicus saw the planets revolving around the sun.

Copernicus's **heliocentric**, or sun-centered, **theory** still did not completely explain why the planets orbited the way they did. He also knew that most scholars and clergy would reject his theory because it contradicted their religious views. Fearing ridicule or persecution, Copernicus did not publish his findings until 1543, the last year of his life. He received a copy of his book, *On the Revolutions of the Heavenly Bodies,* on his deathbed.

While revolutionary, Copernicus's book caused little stir at first. Over the next century and a half, other scientists built on the foundations he had laid. A Danish astronomer, Tycho Brahe (TEE•koh brah), carefully recorded the movements of the planets for many years. Brahe produced mountains of accurate data based on his observations. However, it was left to his followers to make mathematical sense of them.

After Brahe's death in 1601, his assistant, a brilliant mathematician named Johannes Kepler, continued his work. After studying Brahe's data, Kepler concluded that certain mathematical laws govern planetary motion. One of these laws showed that the planets revolve around the sun in elliptical orbits instead of circles, as was previously thought. Kepler's laws showed that Copernicus's basic ideas were true. They demonstrated mathematically that the planets revolve around the sun. (A)

MAIN IDEA

Recognizing Effects

(A) How did Kepler's findings support the heliocentric theory?

Galileo's Discoveries An Italian scientist named **Galileo Galilei** built on the new theories about astronomy. As a young man, Galileo learned that a Dutch lens maker had built an instrument that could enlarge far-off objects. Galileo built his own telescope and used it to study the heavens in 1609.

Then, in 1610, he published a small book called *Starry Messenger,* which described his astonishing observations. Galileo announced that Jupiter had four moons and that the sun had dark spots. He also noted that the earth's moon had a rough, uneven surface. This shattered Aristotle's theory that the moon and stars were made of a pure, perfect substance. Galileo's observations, as well as his laws of motion, also clearly supported the theories of Copernicus.

Conflict with the Church Galileo's findings frightened both Catholic and Protestant leaders because they went against church teaching and authority. If people believed the church could be wrong about this, they could question other church teachings as well.

In 1616, the Catholic Church warned Galileo not to defend the ideas of Copernicus. Although Galileo remained publicly silent, he continued his studies. Then, in 1632, he published *Dialogue Concerning the Two Chief World Systems.* This book presented the ideas of both Copernicus and Ptolemy, but it clearly showed that Galileo supported the Copernican theory. The pope angrily summoned Galileo to Rome to stand trial before the Inquisition.

Galileo stood before the court in 1633. Under the threat of torture, he knelt before the cardinals and read aloud a signed confession. In it, he agreed that the ideas of Copernicus were false.

MAIN IDEA

Analyzing Primary Sources

B In what two ways does Galileo seek to appease the Church?

PRIMARY SOURCE B

With sincere heart and unpretended faith I abjure, curse, and detest the aforesaid errors and heresies [of Copernicus] and also every other error . . . contrary to the Holy Church, and I swear that in the future I will never again say or assert . . . anything that might cause a similar suspicion toward me.

GALILEO GALILEI, quoted in *The Discoverers*

Galileo was never again a free man. He lived under house arrest and died in 1642 at his villa near Florence. However, his books and ideas still spread all over Europe. (In 1992, the Catholic Church officially acknowledged that Galileo had been right.)

▲ Galileo stands before the papal court.

The Scientific Method

The revolution in scientific thinking that Copernicus, Kepler, and Galileo began eventually developed into a new approach to science called the **scientific method**. The scientific method is a logical procedure for gathering and testing ideas. It begins with a problem or question arising from an observation. Scientists next form a hypothesis, or unproved assumption. The hypothesis is then tested in an experiment or on the basis of data. In the final step, scientists analyze and interpret their data to reach a new conclusion. That conclusion either confirms or disproves the hypothesis.

Major Steps in the Scientific Revolution

1520 — 1570 — 1620

1543 Copernicus publishes heliocentric theory.
Vesalius publishes human anatomy textbook.

1566 Marie de Coste Blanche publishes *The Nature of the Sun and Earth.*

1590 Janssen invents microscope.

1609 Kepler publishes first two laws of planetary motion.

1610 Galileo publishes *Starry Messenger.*

1620 Bacon's book *Novum Organum* (New Instrument) encourages experimental method.

▲ Nicolaus Copernicus began the Scientific Revolution with his heliocentric theory.

Bacon and Descartes The scientific method did not develop overnight. The work of two important thinkers of the 1600s, Francis Bacon and René Descartes (day•KAHRT), helped to advance the new approach.

Francis Bacon, an English statesman and writer, had a passionate interest in science. He believed that by better understanding the world, scientists would generate practical knowledge that would improve people's lives. In his writings, Bacon attacked medieval scholars for relying too heavily on the conclusions of Aristotle and other ancient thinkers. Instead of reasoning from abstract theories, he urged scientists to experiment and then draw conclusions. This approach is called empiricism, or the experimental method.

In France, René Descartes also took a keen interest in science. He developed analytical geometry, which linked algebra and geometry. This provided an important new tool for scientific research.

Like Bacon, Descartes believed that scientists needed to reject old assumptions and teachings. As a mathematician, however, he approached gaining knowledge differently than Bacon. Rather than using experimentation, Descartes relied on mathematics and logic. He believed that everything should be doubted until proved by reason. The only thing he knew for certain was that he existed—because, as he wrote, "I think, therefore I am." From this starting point, he followed a train of strict reasoning to arrive at other basic truths. (C)

MAIN IDEA
Contrasting
(C) How did Descartes's approach to science differ from Bacon's?

Modern scientific methods are based on the ideas of Bacon and Descartes. Scientists have shown that observation and experimentation, together with general laws that can be expressed mathematically, can lead people to a better understanding of the natural world.

Newton Explains the Law of Gravity

By the mid-1600s, the accomplishments of Copernicus, Kepler, and Galileo had shattered the old views of astronomy and physics. Later, the great English scientist **Isaac Newton** helped to bring together their breakthroughs under a single theory of motion.

Changing Idea: Scientific Method

Old Science	New Science
Scholars generally relied on ancient authorities, church teachings, common sense, and reasoning to explain the physical world.	In time, scholars began to use observation, experimentation, and scientific reasoning to gather knowledge and draw conclusions about the physical world.

- **1620**
- **1628** Harvey reveals how human heart functions.
- **1633** Galileo faces Inquisition for support of Copernicus's theory.
- **1637** Descartes's book *Discourse on Method* sets forth his scientific method of reasoning from the basis of doubt.
- **1643** Torricelli invents barometer.
- **1660** England establishes Royal Society to support scientific study.
- **1662** Boyle discovers mathematical relationship between the pressure and volume of gases, known as Boyle's law.
- **1666** France establishes Academy of Sciences.
- **1670**
- **1674** Leeuwenhoek observes bacteria through microscope.
- **1687** Newton publishes law of gravity.
- **1714** Fahrenheit invents mercury thermometer.
- **1720**

▲ Isaac Newton's law of gravity explained how the same physical laws governed motion both on earth and in the heavens.

Newton studied mathematics and physics at Cambridge University. By the time he was 26, Newton was certain that all physical objects were affected equally by the same forces. Newton's great discovery was that the same force ruled motion of the planets and all matter on earth and in space. The key idea that linked motion in the heavens with motion on the earth was the law of universal gravitation. According to this law, every object in the universe attracts every other object. The degree of attraction depends on the mass of the objects and the distance between them.

In 1687, Newton published his ideas in a work called *The Mathematical Principles of Natural Philosophy*. It was one of the most important scientific books ever written. The universe he described was like a giant clock. Its parts all worked together perfectly in ways that could be expressed mathematically. Newton believed that God was the creator of this orderly universe, the clockmaker who had set everything in motion. **D**

MAIN IDEA

Clarifying

D Why was the law of gravitation important?

The Scientific Revolution Spreads

As astronomers explored the secrets of the universe, other scientists began to study the secrets of nature on earth. Careful observation and the use of the scientific method eventually became important in many different fields.

Scientific Instruments Scientists developed new tools and instruments to make the precise observations that the scientific method demanded. The first microscope was invented by a Dutch maker of eyeglasses, Zacharias Janssen (YAHN•suhn), in 1590. In the 1670s, a Dutch drapery merchant and amateur scientist named Anton van Leeuwenhoek (LAY•vuhn•HUK) used a microscope to observe bacteria swimming in tooth scrapings. He also examined red blood cells for the first time.

In 1643, one of Galileo's students, Evangelista Torricelli (TAWR•uh•CHEHL•ee), developed the first mercury barometer, a tool for measuring atmospheric pressure and predicting weather. In 1714, the German physicist Gabriel Fahrenheit (FAR•uhn•HYT) made the first thermometer to use mercury in glass. Fahrenheit's thermometer showed water freezing at 32°. A Swedish astronomer, Anders Celsius (SEHL•see•uhs), created another scale for the mercury thermometer in 1742. Celsius's scale showed freezing at 0°.

Medicine and the Human Body During the Middle Ages, European doctors had accepted as fact the writings of an ancient Greek physician named Galen. However, Galen had never dissected the body of a human being. Instead, he had studied the anatomy of pigs and other animals. Galen assumed that human anatomy was much the same. A Flemish physician named Andreas Vesalius proved Galen's assumptions wrong. Vesalius dissected human corpses and published his observations. His

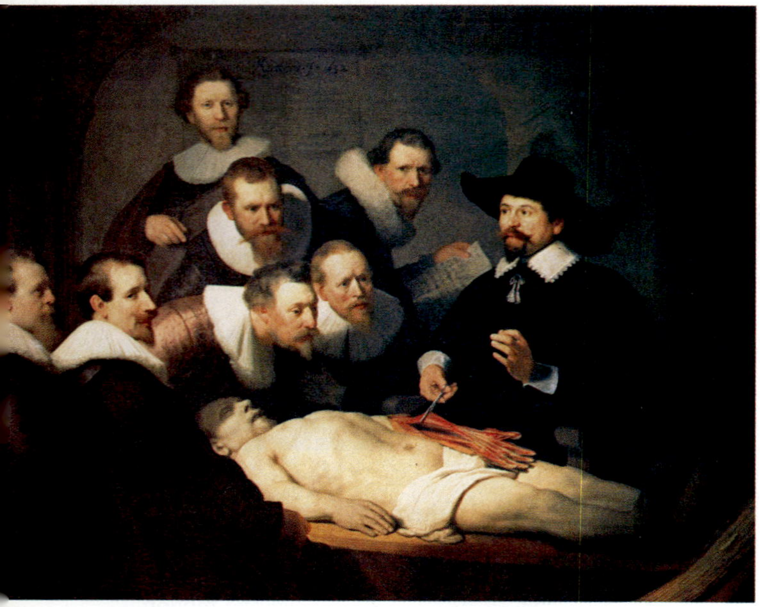

▲ The famous Dutch painter Rembrandt painted *Anatomy Lesson of Dr. Tulp* in 1632 from an actual anatomy lesson. The corpse was that of a criminal.

book, *On the Structure of the Human Body* (1543), was filled with detailed drawings of human organs, bones, and muscle.

In the late 1700s, British physician Edward Jenner introduced a vaccine to prevent smallpox. Inoculation using live smallpox germs had been practiced in Asia for centuries. While beneficial, this technique could also be dangerous. Jenner discovered that inoculation with germs from a cattle disease called cowpox gave permanent protection from smallpox for humans. Because cowpox was a much milder disease, the risks for this form of inoculation were much lower. Jenner used cowpox to produce the world's first vaccination.

Vocabulary
Inoculation is the act of injecting a germ into a person's body so as to create an immunity to the disease.

Discoveries in Chemistry Robert Boyle pioneered the use of the scientific method in chemistry. He is considered the founder of modern chemistry. In a book called *The Sceptical Chymist* (1661), Boyle challenged Aristotle's idea that the physical world consisted of four elements—earth, air, fire, and water. Instead, Boyle proposed that matter was made up of smaller primary particles that joined together in different ways. Boyle's most famous contribution to chemistry is Boyle's law. This law explains how the volume, temperature, and pressure of gas affect each other.

The notions of reason and order, which spurred so many breakthroughs in science, soon moved into other fields of life. Philosophers and scholars across Europe began to rethink long-held beliefs about the human condition, most notably the rights and liberties of ordinary citizens. These thinkers helped to usher in a movement that challenged the age-old relationship between a government and its people, and eventually changed forever the political landscape in numerous societies.

NEW YORK CORE CURRICULUM REVIEW

TERMS & NAMES 1. For each term or name, write a sentence explaining its significance.

- geocentric theory
- Scientific Revolution
- heliocentric theory
- Galileo Galilei
- scientific method
- Isaac Newton

USING YOUR NOTES

2. Which event or circumstance do you consider to be the most significant? Why?

MAIN IDEAS

3. Before the 1500s, who and what were the final authorities with regard to most knowledge?
4. How did the heliocentric theory of the universe differ from the geocentric theory?
5. What are the main steps of the scientific method?

CRITICAL THINKING & WRITING

6. **DRAWING CONCLUSIONS** "If I have seen farther than others," said Newton, "it is because I have stood on the shoulders of giants." Could this be said of most scientific accomplishments? Explain.
7. **ANALYZING MOTIVES** Why might institutions of authority tend to reject new ideas?
8. **FORMING AND SUPPORTING OPINIONS** Do you agree with Galileo's actions during his Inquisition? Explain.
9. **WRITING ACTIVITY** SCIENCE AND TECHNOLOGY Create a television **script** for a discovery of the Scientific Revolution. Include key people, ideas, and accomplishments.

CONNECT TO TODAY **CREATING A GRAPHIC**

Research a modern-day invention or new way of thinking and then describe it and its impact on society to the class in a **poster** or **annotated diagram.**

The Enlightenment in Europe

CONNECT TO THE NEW YORK STATE CORE CURRICULUM

Unit 5.B.1. The writings of Locke, Voltaire, Rousseau, and Montesquieu
Unit 5.B.2. The impact of the Enlightenment on nationalism and democracy

TERMS & NAMES

- Enlightenment
- social contract
- John Locke
- philosophe
- Voltaire
- Montesquieu
- Rousseau
- Mary Wollstonecraft

SETTING THE STAGE In the wake of the Scientific Revolution, and the new ways of thinking it prompted, scholars and philosophers began to reevaluate old notions about other aspects of society. They sought new insight into the underlying beliefs regarding government, religion, economics, and education. Their efforts spurred the **Enlightenment**, a new intellectual movement that stressed reason and thought and the power of individuals to solve problems. Known also as the Age of Reason, the movement reached its height in the mid-1700s and brought great change to many aspects of Western civilization.

TAKING NOTES

Outlining Use an outline to organize main ideas and details.

Enlightenment in Europe
I. Two Views on Government
A.
B.
II. The Philosophes Advocate Reason
A.
B.

Two Views on Government

The Enlightenment started from some key ideas put forth by two English political thinkers of the 1600s, Thomas Hobbes and John Locke. Both men experienced the political turmoil of England early in that century. However, they came to very different conclusions about government and human nature.

Hobbes's Social Contract Thomas Hobbes expressed his views in a work called *Leviathan* (1651). The horrors of the English Civil War convinced him that all humans were naturally selfish and wicked. Without governments to keep order, Hobbes said, there would be "war . . . of every man against every man," and life would be "solitary, poor, nasty, brutish, and short."

Hobbes argued that to escape such a bleak life, people had to hand over their rights to a strong ruler. In exchange, they gained law and order. Hobbes called this agreement by which people created a government the **social contract**. Because people acted in their own self-interest, Hobbes said, the ruler needed total power to keep citizens under control. The best government was one that had the awesome power of a leviathan (sea monster). In Hobbes's view, such a government was an absolute monarchy, which could impose order and demand obedience.

Changing Idea: The Right to Govern

Old Idea	New Idea
A monarch's rule is justified by divine right.	A government's power comes from the consent of the governed.

Locke's Natural Rights The philosopher **John Locke** held a different, more positive, view of human nature. He believed that people could learn from experience and improve themselves. As reasonable beings, they had the natural ability to govern their own affairs and to look after the welfare of society. Locke criticized absolute monarchy and favored the idea of self-government.

According to Locke, all people are born free and equal, with three natural rights—life, liberty, and property. The purpose of government, said Locke, is to protect these rights. If a government fails to do so, citizens have a right to overthrow it. Locke's theory had a deep influence on modern political thinking. His belief that a government's power comes from the consent of the people is the foundation of modern democracy. The ideas of government by popular consent and the right to rebel against unjust rulers helped inspire struggles for liberty in Europe and the Americas. (A)

MAIN IDEA

Contrasting

(A) How does Locke's view of human nature differ from that of Hobbes?

The Philosophes Advocate Reason

The Enlightenment reached its height in France in the mid-1700s. Paris became the meeting place for people who wanted to discuss politics and ideas. The social critics of this period in France were known as **philosophes** (FIHL•uh•SAHFS), the French word for philosophers. The philosophes believed that people could apply reason to all aspects of life, just as Isaac Newton had applied reason to science. Five concepts formed the core of their beliefs:

1. **Reason** Enlightened thinkers believed truth could be discovered through reason or logical thinking.
2. **Nature** The philosophes believed that what was natural was also good and reasonable.
3. **Happiness** The philosophes rejected the medieval notion that people should find joy in the hereafter and urged people to seek well-being on earth.
4. **Progress** The philosophes stressed that society and humankind could improve.
5. **Liberty** The philosophes called for the liberties that the English people had won in their Glorious Revolution and Bill of Rights.

Voltaire Combats Intolerance Probably the most brilliant and influential of the philosophes was François Marie Arouet. Using the pen name **Voltaire**, he published more than 70 books of political essays, philosophy, and drama.

Voltaire often used satire against his opponents. He made frequent targets of the clergy, the aristocracy, and the government. His sharp tongue made him enemies at the French court, and twice he was sent to prison. After his second jail term, Voltaire was exiled to England for more than two years.

Vocabulary

Satire is the use of irony, sarcasm, or wit to attack folly, vice, or stupidity.

Although he made powerful enemies, Voltaire never stopped fighting for tolerance, reason, freedom of religious belief, and freedom of speech. He used his quill pen as if it were a deadly weapon in a thinker's war against humanity's worst enemies—intolerance, prejudice, and superstition. He summed up his staunch defense of liberty in one of his most famous quotes: "I do not agree with a word you say but will defend to the death your right to say it."

History Makers

Voltaire
1694–1778

Voltaire befriended several European monarchs and nobles. Among them was the Prussian king Frederick II. The two men seemed like ideal companions. Both were witty and preferred to dress in shabby, rumpled clothes.

Their relationship eventually soured, however. Voltaire disliked editing Frederick's mediocre poetry, while Frederick suspected Voltaire of shady business dealings. Voltaire eventually described the Prussian king as "a nasty monkey, perfidious friend, [and] wretched poet." Frederick in turn called Voltaire a "miser, dirty rogue, [and] coward."

INTEGRATED TECHNOLOGY

RESEARCH LINKS For more on Voltaire, go to **classzone.com**

Montesquieu and the Separation of Powers Another influential French writer, the Baron de **Montesquieu** (MAHN•tuh•SKYOO), devoted himself to the study of political liberty. Montesquieu believed that Britain was the best-governed and most politically balanced country of his own day. The British king and his ministers held executive power. They carried out the laws of the state. The members of Parliament held legislative power. They made the laws. The judges of the English courts held judicial power. They interpreted the laws to see how each applied to a specific case. Montesquieu called this division of power among different branches separation of powers.

Montesquieu oversimplified the British system. It did not actually separate powers this way. His idea, however, became a part of his most famous book, *On the Spirit of Laws* (1748). In his book, Montesquieu proposed that separation of powers would keep any individual or group from gaining total control of the government. "Power," he wrote, "should be a check to power." This idea later would be called checks and balances.

MAIN IDEA

Analyzing Issues

B What advantages did Montesquieu see in the separation of powers?

Montesquieu's book was admired by political leaders in the British colonies of North America. His ideas about separation of powers and checks and balances became the basis for the United States Constitution. B

Rousseau: Champion of Freedom A third great philosophe, Jean Jacques **Rousseau** (roo•SOH), was passionately committed to individual freedom. The son of a poor Swiss watchmaker, Rousseau won recognition as a writer of essays. A strange, brilliant, and controversial figure, Rousseau strongly disagreed with other

Analyzing Primary Sources

Laws Protect Freedom

Both Montesquieu and Rousseau believed firmly that fair and just laws—not monarchs or unrestrained mobs—should govern society. Here, Rousseau argues that laws established by and for the people are the hallmark of a free society.

PRIMARY SOURCE

I . . . therefore give the name "Republic" to every state that is governed by laws, no matter what the form of its administration may be: for only in such a case does the public interest govern, and the *res republica* rank as a *reality*. . . . Laws are, properly speaking, only the conditions of civil association. The people, being subject to the laws, ought to be their author: the conditions of the society ought to be regulated . . . by those who come together to form it.

JEAN JACQUES ROUSSEAU, *The Social Contract*

Laws Ensure Security

While laws work to protect citizens from abusive rulers, Montesquieu argues that they also guard against anarchy and mob rule.

PRIMARY SOURCE

It is true that in democracies the people seem to act as they please; but political liberty does not consist in an unlimited freedom. . . . We must have continually present to our minds the difference between independence and liberty. Liberty is a right of doing whatever the laws permit, and if a citizen could do what they [the laws] forbid he would be no longer possessed of liberty, because all his fellow-citizens would have the same power.

BARON DE MONTESQUIEU, *The Spirit of Laws*

DOCUMENT-BASED QUESTIONS

1. **Analyzing Issues** *Why should citizens be the authors of society's laws, according to Rousseau?*
2. **Making Inferences** *Why does Montesquieu believe that disobeying laws leads to a loss of liberty?*

Enlightenment thinkers on many matters. Most philosophes believed that reason, science, and art would improve life for all people. Rousseau, however, argued that civilization corrupted people's natural goodness. "Man is born free, and everywhere he is in chains," he wrote.

Rousseau believed that the only good government was one that was freely formed by the people and guided by the "general will" of society—a direct democracy. Under such a government, people agree to give up some of their freedom in favor of the common good. In 1762, he explained his political philosophy in a book called *The Social Contract.*

Rousseau's view of the social contract differed greatly from that of Hobbes. For Hobbes, the social contract was an agreement between a society and its government. For Rousseau, it was an agreement among free individuals to create a society and a government.

Like Locke, Rousseau argued that legitimate government came from the consent of the governed. However, Rousseau believed in a much broader democracy than Locke had promoted. He argued that all people were equal and that titles of nobility should be abolished. Rousseau's ideas inspired many of the leaders of the French Revolution who overthrew the monarchy in 1789.

Beccaria Promotes Criminal Justice An Italian philosophe named Cesare Bonesana Beccaria (BAYK•uh•REE•ah) turned his thoughts to the justice system. He believed that laws existed to preserve social order, not to avenge crimes. Beccaria regularly criticized common abuses of justice. They included torturing of witnesses and suspects, irregular proceedings in trials, and punishments that were arbitrary or cruel. He argued that a person accused of a crime should receive a speedy trial, and that torture should never be used. Moreover, he said, the degree of punishment should be based on the seriousness of the crime. He also believed that capital punishment should be abolished.

Beccaria based his ideas about justice on the principle that governments should seek the greatest good for the greatest number of people. His ideas influenced criminal law reformers in Europe and North America.

Major Ideas of the Enlightenment

Idea	Thinker	Impact
Natural rights—life, liberty, property	Locke	Fundamental to U.S. Declaration of Independence
Separation of powers	Montesquieu	France, United States, and Latin American nations use separation of powers in new constitutions
Freedom of thought and expression	Voltaire	Guaranteed in U.S. Bill of Rights and French Declaration of the Rights of Man and Citizen; European monarchs reduce or eliminate censorship
Abolishment of torture	Beccaria	Guaranteed in U.S. Bill of Rights; torture outlawed or reduced in nations of Europe and the Americas
Religious freedom	Voltaire	Guaranteed in U.S. Bill of Rights and French Declaration of the Rights of Man and Citizen; European monarchs reduce persecution
Women's equality	Wollstonecraft	Women's rights groups form in Europe and North America

SKILLBUILDER: Interpreting Charts

1. **Analyzing Issues** *What important documents reflect the influence of Enlightenment ideas?*
2. **Forming Opinions** *Which are the two most important Enlightenment ideas? Support your answer with reasons.*

Women and the Enlightenment

The philosophes challenged many assumptions about government and society. But they often took a traditional view toward women. Rousseau, for example, developed many progressive ideas about education. However, he believed that a girl's education should mainly teach her how to be a helpful wife and mother. Other male social critics scolded women for reading novels because they thought it encouraged idleness and wickedness. Still, some male writers argued for more education for women and for women's equality in marriage.

Women writers also tried to improve the status of women. In 1694, the English writer Mary Astell published *A Serious Proposal to the Ladies*. Her book addressed the lack of educational opportunities for women. In later writings, she used Enlightenment arguments about government to criticize the unequal relationship between men and women in marriage. She wrote, "If absolute sovereignty be not necessary in a state, how comes it to be so in a family? . . . If all men are born free, how is it that all women are born slaves?"

During the 1700s, other women picked up these themes. Among the most persuasive was **Mary Wollstonecraft**, who published an essay called *A Vindication of the Rights of Woman* in 1792. In the essay, she disagreed with Rousseau that women's education should be secondary to men's. Rather, she argued that women, like men, need education to become virtuous and useful. Wollstonecraft also urged women to enter the male-dominated fields of medicine and politics. **C**

MAIN IDEA

Drawing Conclusions

C Why do you think the issue of education was important to both Astell and Wollstonecraft?

Women made important contributions to the Enlightenment in other ways. In Paris and other European cities, wealthy women helped spread Enlightenment ideas through social gatherings called salons, which you will read about later in this chapter.

One woman fortunate enough to receive an education in the sciences was Emilie du Châtelet (shah•tlay). Du Châtelet was an aristocrat trained as a mathematician and physicist. By translating Newton's work from Latin into French, she helped stimulate interest in science in France.

History Makers

Mary Wollstonecraft
1759–1797

A strong advocate of education for women, Wollstonecraft herself received little formal schooling. She and her two sisters taught themselves by studying books at home. With her sisters, she briefly ran a school. These experiences shaped much of her thoughts about education.

Wollstonecraft eventually took a job with a London publisher. There, she met many leading radicals of the day. One of them was her future husband, the writer William Godwin. Wollstonecraft died at age 38, after giving birth to their daughter, Mary. This child, whose married name was Mary Wollstonecraft Shelley, went on to write the classic novel *Frankenstein*.

INTEGRATED TECHNOLOGY

RESEARCH LINKS For more on Mary Wollstonecraft, go to **classzone.com**

Legacy of the Enlightenment

Over a span of a few decades, Enlightenment writers challenged long-held ideas about society. They examined such principles as the divine right of monarchs, the union of church and state, and the existence of unequal social classes. They held these beliefs up to the light of reason and found them in need of reform.

The philosophes mainly lived in the world of ideas. They formed and popularized new theories. Although they encouraged reform, they were not active revolutionaries. However, their theories eventually inspired the American and French revolutions and other revolutionary movements in the 1800s. Enlightenment thinking produced three other long-term effects that helped shape Western civilization.

Belief in Progress The first effect was a belief in progress. Pioneers such as Galileo and Newton had discovered the key for unlocking the mysteries of nature in the 1500s and 1600s. With the door thus opened, the growth of scientific knowledge seemed to quicken in the 1700s. Scientists made key new discoveries in chemistry, physics, biology, and mechanics. The successes of the Scientific Revolution gave people the confidence that human reason could solve social problems. Philosophes and reformers urged an end to the practice of slavery and argued for greater social equality, as well as a more democratic style of government.

A More Secular Outlook A second outcome was the rise of a more secular, or non-religious, outlook. During the Enlightenment, people began to question openly their religious beliefs and the teachings of the church. Before the Scientific Revolution, people accepted the mysteries of the universe as the workings of God. One by one, scientists discovered that these mysteries could be explained mathematically. Newton himself was a deeply religious man, and he sought to reveal God's majesty through his work. However, his findings often caused people to change the way they thought about God.

Meanwhile, Voltaire and other critics attacked some of the beliefs and practices of organized Christianity. They wanted to rid religious faith of superstition and fear and promote tolerance of all religions.

Importance of the Individual Faith in science and in progress produced a third outcome, the rise of individualism. As people began to turn away from the church and royalty for guidance, they looked to themselves instead.

The philosophes encouraged people to use their own ability to reason in order to judge what was right or wrong. They also emphasized the importance of the individual in society. Government, they argued, was formed by individuals to promote their welfare. The British thinker Adam Smith extended the emphasis on the individual to economic thinking. He believed that individuals acting in their own self-interest created economic progress. Smith's theory is discussed in detail in Chapter 25.

During the Enlightenment, reason took center stage. The greatest minds of Europe followed each other's work with interest and often met to discuss their ideas. Some of the kings and queens of Europe were also very interested. As you will learn in Section 3, they sought to apply some of the philosophes' ideas to create progress in their countries.

NEW YORK CORE CURRICULUM REVIEW

TERMS & NAMES 1. For each term or name, write a sentence explaining its significance.

- Enlightenment • social contract • John Locke • philosophe • Voltaire • Montesquieu • Rousseau • Mary Wollstonecraft

USING YOUR NOTES

2. Which impact of the Enlightenment do you consider most important? Why?

Enlightenment in Europe
I. Two Views on Government
A.
B.
II. The Philosophes Advocate Reason
A.
B.

MAIN IDEAS

3. What are the natural rights with which people are born, according to John Locke?
4. Who were the philosophes and what did they advocate?
5. What was the legacy of the Enlightenment?

CRITICAL THINKING & WRITING

6. **SYNTHESIZING** Explain how the following statement reflects Enlightenment ideas: "Power should be a check to power."
7. **ANALYZING ISSUES** Why might some women have been critical of the Enlightenment?
8. **DRAWING CONCLUSIONS** Do you think the philosophes were optimistic about the future of humankind? Explain.
9. **WRITING ACTIVITY** POWER AND AUTHORITY Compare the views of Hobbes, Locke, and Rousseau on government. Then write one **paragraph** about how their ideas reflect their understanding of human behavior.

CONNECT TO TODAY **PRESENTING AN ORAL REPORT**

Identify someone considered a modern-day social critic. Explore the person's beliefs and methods and present your findings to the class in a brief **oral report.**

INTERACTIVE

European Values During the Enlightenment

Writers and artists of the Enlightenment often used satire to comment on European values. Using wit and humor, they ridiculed various ideas and customs. Satire allowed artists to explore human faults in a way that is powerful but not preachy. In the two literary excerpts and the painting below, notice how the writer or artist makes his point.

A PRIMARY SOURCE

Voltaire

Voltaire wrote *Candide* (1759) to attack a philosophy called Optimism, which held that all is right with the world. The hero of the story, a young man named Candide, encounters the most awful disasters and human evils. In this passage, Candide meets a slave in South America, who explains why he is missing a leg and a hand.

"When we're working at the sugar mill and catch our finger in the grinding-wheel, they cut off our hand. When we try to run away, they cut off a leg. I have been in both of these situations. This is the price you pay for the sugar you eat in Europe. . . .

"The Dutch fetishes [i.e., missionaries] who converted me [to Christianity] tell me every Sunday that we are all the sons of Adam, Whites and Blacks alike. I'm no genealogist, but if these preachers are right, we are all cousins born of first cousins. Well, you will grant me that you can't treat a relative much worse than this."

B PRIMARY SOURCE

Jonathan Swift

The narrator of *Gulliver's Travels* (1726), an English doctor named Lemuel Gulliver, takes four disastrous voyages that leave him stranded in strange lands. In the following passage, Gulliver tries to win points with the king of Brobdingnag—a land of giants—by offering to show him how to make guns and cannons.

The king was struck with horror at the description I had given of those terrible engines. . . . He was amazed how so impotent and grovelling an insect as I (these were his expressions) could entertain such inhuman ideas, and in so familiar a manner as to appear wholly unmoved at all the scenes of blood and desolation, which I had painted as the common effects of those destructive machines; whereof, he said, some evil genius, enemy to mankind, must have been the first contriver [inventor].

C PRIMARY SOURCE

William Hogarth

The English artist William Hogarth often used satire in his paintings. In this painting, *Canvassing for Votes,* he comments on political corruption. While the candidate flirts with the ladies on the balcony, his supporters offer a man money for his vote.

Document-Based QUESTIONS

1. What is the main point that Voltaire is making in Source A? What technique does he use to reinforce his message?
2. What does the king's reaction in Source B say about Swift's view of Europe's military technology?
3. Why might Hogarth's painting in Source C be difficult for modern audiences to understand? Does this take away from his message?

The Enlightenment Spreads

CONNECT TO THE NEW YORK STATE CORE CURRICULUM

Unit 5.B.2. The impact of the Enlightenment on nationalism and democracy
Unit 5.B.3. The enlightened despots–Maria Theresa and Catherine the Great

TERMS & NAMES

- salon
- baroque
- neoclassical
- enlightened despot
- Catherine the Great

SETTING THE STAGE The philosophes' views about society often got them in trouble. In France it was illegal to criticize either the Catholic Church or the government. Many philosophes landed in jail or were exiled. Voltaire, for example, experienced both punishments. Nevertheless, the Enlightenment spread throughout Europe with the help of books, magazines, and word of mouth. In time, Enlightenment ideas influenced everything from the artistic world to the royal courts across the continent.

TAKING NOTES
Summarizing Use a web diagram to list examples of each concept related to the spread of ideas.

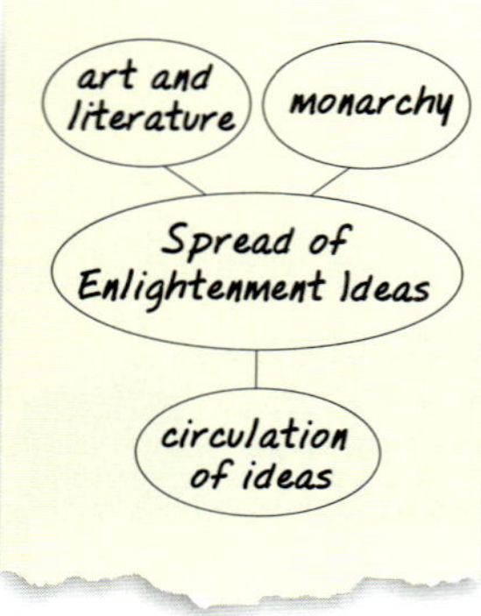

A World of Ideas

In the 1700s, Paris was the cultural and intellectual capital of Europe. Young people from around Europe—and also from the Americas—came to study, philosophize, and enjoy the culture of the bustling city. The brightest minds of the age gathered there. From their circles radiated the ideas of the Enlightenment.

The buzz of Enlightenment ideas was most intense in the mansions of several wealthy women of Paris. There, in their large drawing rooms, these hostesses held regular social gatherings called **salons**. At these events, philosophers, writers, artists, scientists, and other great intellects met to discuss ideas.

Diderot's *Encyclopedia* The most influential of the salon hostesses in Voltaire's time was Marie-Thérèse Geoffrin (zhuh•frehn). She helped finance the project of a leading philosophe named Denis Diderot (DEE•duh•ROH). Diderot created a large set of books to which many leading scholars of Europe contributed articles and essays. He called it *Encyclopedia* and began publishing the first volumes in 1751.

The Enlightenment views expressed in the articles soon angered both the French government and the Catholic Church. Their censors banned the work. They said it undermined royal authority, encouraged a spirit of revolt, and fostered "moral corruption, irreligion, and unbelief." Nonetheless, Diderot continued publishing his *Encyclopedia.*

The salons and the *Encyclopedia* helped spread Enlightenment ideas to educated people all over Europe. Enlightenment ideas also eventually spread through newspapers, pamphlets, and even political songs. Enlightenment ideas about government and equality attracted the attention of a growing literate middle class, which could afford to buy many books and support the work of artists.

Connect *to* Today

Cybercafés

These days, when people around the world gather to explore new ideas and discuss current events, many do so at Internet cafés. These are coffee shops or restaurants that also provide access to computers for a small fee.

While Internet cafés originated in the United States, they are thought to be on the decline in America as more people become able to afford their own computers.

Overseas, however, Internet cafés continue to boom. Observers estimate that some 200,000 operate in China. Most of them are illegal. China's Communist government has little desire to give so many of its citizens access to the kind of uncensored information that the Internet provides. As was the case with the Enlightenment, however, the spread of new ideas is often too powerful to stop.

New Artistic Styles

The Enlightenment ideals of order and reason were reflected in the arts—music, literature, painting, and architecture.

Neoclassical Style Emerges European art of the 1600s and early 1700s had been dominated by the style called **baroque**, which was characterized by a grand, ornate design. Baroque styles could be seen in elaborate palaces such as Versailles (see page 600) and in numerous paintings.

Under the influence of the Enlightenment, styles began to change. Artists and architects worked in a simple and elegant style that borrowed ideas and themes from classical Greece and Rome. The artistic style of the late 1700s is therefore called **neoclassical** ("new classical").

Changes in Music and Literature Music styles also changed to reflect Enlightenment ideals. The music scene in Europe had been dominated by such composers as Johann Sebastian Bach of Germany and George Friedrich Handel of England. These artists wrote dramatic organ and choral music. During the Enlightenment, a new, lighter, and more elegant style of music known as *classical* emerged. Three composers in Vienna, Austria, rank among the greatest figures of the classical period in music. They were Franz Joseph Haydn, Wolfgang Amadeus Mozart, and Ludwig van Beethoven.

Writers in the 18th century also developed new styles and forms of literature. A number of European authors began writing novels, which are lengthy works of prose fiction. Their works had carefully crafted plots, used suspense, and explored characters' thoughts and feelings. These books were popular with a wide middle-class audience, who liked the entertaining stories written in everyday language. Writers, including many women, turned out a flood of popular novels in the 1700s.

Samuel Richardson's *Pamela* is often considered the first true English novel. It tells the story of a young servant girl who refuses the advances of her master. Another English masterpiece, *Tom Jones,* by Henry Fielding, tells the story of an orphan who travels all over England to win the hand of his lady.

Enlightenment and Monarchy

From the salons, artists' studios, and concert halls of Europe, the Enlightenment spirit also swept through Europe's royal courts. Many philosophes, including Voltaire, believed that the best form of government was a monarchy in which the ruler respected the people's rights. The philosophes tried to convince monarchs to rule justly. Some monarchs embraced the new ideas and made reforms that reflected the Enlightenment spirit. They became known as **enlightened despots**. Despot means "absolute ruler."

The enlightened despots supported the philosophes' ideas. But they also had no intention of giving up any power. The changes they made were motivated by two desires: they wanted to make their countries stronger and their own rule more effective. The foremost of Europe's enlightened despots were Frederick II of Prussia, Holy Roman Emperor Joseph II of Austria, and Catherine the Great of Russia. (A)

MAIN IDEA

Analyzing Motives

(A) Why did the enlightened despots undertake reforms?

Frederick the Great Frederick II, the king of Prussia from 1740 to 1786, committed himself to reforming Prussia. He granted many religious freedoms, reduced censorship, and improved education. He also reformed the justice system and abolished the use of torture. However, Frederick's changes only went so far. For example, he believed that serfdom was wrong, but he did nothing to end it since he needed the support of wealthy landowners. As a result, he never tried to change the existing social order.

Vocabulary

Serfdom was a system in which peasants were forced to live and work on a landowner's estate.

Perhaps Frederick's most important contribution was his attitude toward being king. He called himself "the first servant of the state." From the beginning of his reign, he made it clear that his goal was to serve and strengthen his country. This attitude was clearly one that appealed to the philosophes.

▲ Joseph II

Joseph II The most radical royal reformer was Joseph II of Austria. The son and successor of Maria Theresa, Joseph II ruled Austria from 1780 to 1790. He introduced legal reforms and freedom of the press. He also supported freedom of worship, even for Protestants, Orthodox Christians, and Jews. In his most radical reform, Joseph abolished serfdom and ordered that peasants be paid for their labor with cash. Not surprisingly, the nobles firmly resisted this change. Like many of Joseph's reforms, it was undone after his death.

Catherine the Great The ruler most admired by the philosophes was Catherine II, known as **Catherine the Great**. She ruled Russia from 1762 to 1796. The well-educated empress read the works of philosophes, and she exchanged many letters with Voltaire. She ruled with absolute authority but also sought to reform Russia.

In 1767, Catherine formed a commission to review Russia's laws. She presented it with a brilliant proposal for reforms based on the ideas of Montesquieu and Beccaria. Among other changes, she recommended allowing religious toleration and abolishing torture and capital punishment. Her commission, however, accomplished none of these lofty goals.

Catherine eventually put in place limited reforms, but she did little to improve the life of the Russian peasants. Her views about enlightened ideas changed after a massive uprising of serfs in 1773. With great brutality, Catherine's army crushed the

Changing Idea: Relationship Between Ruler and State

Old Idea	New Idea
The state and its citizens exist to serve the monarch. As Louis XIV reportedly said, "I am the state."	The monarch exists to serve the state and support citizens' welfare. As Frederick the Great said, a ruler is only "the first servant of the state."

rebellion. Catherine had previously favored an end to serfdom. However, the revolt convinced her that she needed the nobles' support to keep her throne. Therefore, she gave the nobles absolute power over the serfs. As a result, Russian serfs lost their last traces of freedom. **B**

MAIN IDEA

Synthesizing

B How accurately does the term enlightened despot describe Catherine the Great? Explain.

Catherine Expands Russia Peter the Great, who ruled Russia in the early 1700s, had fought for years to win a port on the Baltic Sea. Likewise, Catherine sought access to the Black Sea. In two wars with the Ottoman Turks, her armies finally won control of the northern shore of the Black Sea. Russia also gained the right to send ships through Ottoman-controlled straits leading from the Black Sea to the Mediterranean Sea.

Catherine also expanded her empire westward into Poland. In Poland, the king was relatively weak, and independent nobles held the most power. The three neighboring powers—Russia, Prussia, and Austria—each tried to assert their influence over the country. In 1772, these land-hungry neighbors each took a piece of Poland in what is called the First Partition of Poland. In further partitions in 1793 and 1795, they grabbed up the rest of Poland's territory. With these partitions, Poland disappeared as an independent country for more than a century.

By the end of her remarkable reign, Catherine had vastly enlarged the Russian empire. Meanwhile, as Russia was becoming an international power, another great power, Britain, faced a challenge from its North American colonies. Inspired by Enlightenment ideas, colonial leaders decided to do the unthinkable: break away from their ruling country and found an independent republic.

History Makers

Catherine the Great
1729–1796

The daughter of a minor German prince, Catherine was 15 when she was handed over to marry the Grand Duke Peter, heir to the Russian throne.

Peter was mentally unstable. Catherine viewed her husband's weakness as her chance for power. She made important friends among Russia's army officers and became known as the most intelligent and best-informed person at court.

In 1762, only months after her husband became czar, Catherine had him arrested and confined. Soon afterward, Peter conveniently died, probably by murder.

NEW YORK CORE CURRICULUM REVIEW

TERMS & NAMES 1. For each term or name, write a sentence explaining its significance.

- salon
- baroque
- neoclassical
- enlightened despot
- Catherine the Great

USING YOUR NOTES

2. What are two generalizations you could make about the spread of Enlightenment ideas?

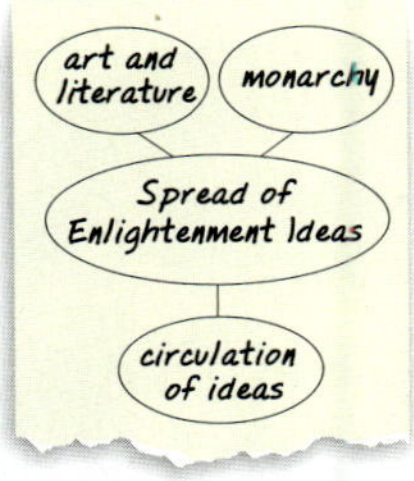

MAIN IDEAS

3. What were the defining aspects of neoclassical art?
4. What new form of literature emerged during the 18th century and what were its main characteristics?
5. Why were several rulers in 18th century Europe known as enlightened despots?

CRITICAL THINKING & WRITING

6. **DRAWING CONCLUSIONS** What advantages did salons have over earlier forms of communication in spreading ideas?
7. **ANALYZING ISSUES** In what way were the enlightened despots less than true reformers? Cite specific examples from the text.
8. **MAKING INFERENCES** How did the *Encyclopedia* project reflect the age of Enlightenment?
9. **WRITING ACTIVITY** POWER AND AUTHORITY -Imagine you are a public relations consultant for an enlightened despot. Write a **press release** explaining why your client is "Most Enlightened Despot of the 1700s."

INTEGRATED TECHNOLOGY **INTERNET ACTIVITY**

Use the Internet to find out more about a composer or writer mentioned in this section. Then write a brief **character sketch** on that artist, focusing on interesting pieces of information about his or her life.

INTERNET KEYWORDS
biography European Enlightenment

The American Revolution

CONNECT TO THE NEW YORK STATE CORE CURRICULUM

Unit 5.C.2.a. Impact of the Enlightenment on the American Revolution
Unit 5.C.2.b. Impact of the American Revolution on other revolutions

TERMS & NAMES

- Declaration of Independence
- Thomas Jefferson
- checks and balances
- federal system
- Bill of Rights

SETTING THE STAGE Philosophes such as Voltaire considered England's government the most progressive in Europe. The Glorious Revolution of 1688 had given England a constitutional monarchy. In essence, this meant that various laws limited the power of the English king. Despite the view of the philosophes, however, a growing number of England's colonists in North America accused England of tyrannical rule. Emboldened by Enlightenment ideas, they would attempt to overthrow what was then the mightiest power on earth and create their own nation.

TAKING NOTES
Identifying Problems and Solutions Use a chart to list the problems American colonists faced in shaping their republic and solutions they found.

Problem	Solution
1. 2. 3.	1. 2. 3.

Britain and Its American Colonies

Throughout the 1600s and 1700s, British colonists had formed a large and thriving settlement along the eastern shore of North America. When George III became king of Great Britain in 1760, his North American colonies were growing by leaps and bounds. Their combined population soared from about 250,000 in 1700 to 2,150,000 in 1770, a nearly ninefold increase. Economically, the colonies thrived on trade with the nations of Europe.

Along with increasing population and prosperity, a new sense of identity was growing in the colonists' minds. By the mid-1700s, colonists had been living in America for nearly 150 years. Each of the 13 colonies had its own government, and people were used to a great degree of independence. Colonists saw themselves less as British and more as Virginians or Pennsylvanians. However, they were still British subjects and were expected to obey British law.

In 1651, the British Parliament passed a trade law called the Navigation Act. This and subsequent trade laws prevented colonists from selling their most valuable products to any country except Britain. In addition, colonists had to pay high taxes on imported French and Dutch goods. Nonetheless, Britain's policies benefited both the colonies and the motherland. Britain bought American raw materials for low prices and sold manufactured goods to the colonists. And despite various British trade restrictions, colonial merchants also thrived. Such a spirit of relative harmony, however, soon would change.

▼ This French snuffbox pictures (left to right) Voltaire, Rousseau, and colonial statesman Benjamin Franklin.

Americans Win Independence

In 1754, war erupted on the North American continent between the English and the French. As you recall, the French had also colonized parts of North America throughout the 1600s and 1700s. The conflict was known as the French and Indian War. (The name stems from the fact that the French enlisted numerous Native American tribes to fight on their side.) The fighting lasted until 1763, when Britain and her colonists emerged victorious—and seized nearly all French land in North America.

The victory, however, only led to growing tensions between Britain and its colonists. In order to fight the war, Great Britain had run up a huge debt. Because American colonists benefited from Britain's victory, Britain expected the colonists to help pay the costs of the war. In 1765, Parliament passed the Stamp Act. According to this law, colonists had to pay a tax to have an official stamp put on wills, deeds, newspapers, and other printed material. **A**

MAIN IDEA
Analyzing Causes
A How did the French and Indian War lead to the Stamp Act?

American colonists were outraged. They had never paid taxes directly to the British government before. Colonial lawyers argued that the stamp tax violated colonists' natural rights, and they accused the government of "taxation without representation." In Britain, citizens consented to taxes through their representatives in Parliament. The colonists, however, had no representation in Parliament. Thus, they argued they could not be taxed.

Growing Hostility Leads to War Over the next decade, hostilities between the two sides increased. Some colonial leaders favored independence from Britain. In 1773, to protest an import tax on tea, a group of colonists dumped a large load of British tea into Boston Harbor. George III, infuriated by the "Boston Tea Party," as it was called, ordered the British navy to close the port of Boston.

Such harsh tactics by the British made enemies of many moderate colonists. In September 1774, representatives from every colony except Georgia gathered in Philadelphia to form the First Continental Congress. This group protested the treatment of Boston. When the king paid little attention to their complaints, the colonies decided to form the Second Continental Congress to debate their next move.

On April 19, 1775, British soldiers and American militiamen exchanged gunfire on the village green in Lexington, Massachusetts. The fighting spread to nearby Concord. The Second Continental Congress voted to raise an army and organize for battle under the command of a Virginian named George Washington. The American Revolution had begun.

The Influence of the Enlightenment Colonial leaders used Enlightenment ideas to justify independence. The colonists had asked for the same political rights as people in Britain, they said, but the king had stubbornly refused. Therefore, the colonists were justified in rebelling against a tyrant who had broken the social contract.

In July 1776, the Second Continental Congress issued the **Declaration of Independence**. This document, written by political leader **Thomas Jefferson**,

History Makers

Thomas Jefferson
1743–1826

The author of the Declaration of Independence, Thomas Jefferson of Virginia, was a true figure of the Enlightenment. As a writer and statesman, he supported free speech, religious freedom, and other civil liberties. At the same time, he was also a slave owner.

Jefferson was a man of many talents. He was an inventor as well as one of the great architects of early America. He designed the Virginia state capitol building in Richmond and many buildings for the University of Virginia. Of all his achievements, Jefferson wanted to be most remembered for three: author of the Declaration of Independence, author of the Statute of Virginia for Religious Freedom, and founder of the University of Virginia.

INTEGRATED TECHNOLOGY

INTERNET ACTIVITY Create a time line of Jefferson's major achievements. Go to **classzone.com** for your research.

Changing Idea: Colonial Attachment to Britain	
Old Idea	**New Idea**
American colonists considered themselves to be subjects of the British king.	After a long train of perceived abuses by the king, the colonists asserted their right to declare independence.

was firmly based on the ideas of John Locke and the Enlightenment. The Declaration reflected these ideas in its eloquent argument for natural rights. "We hold these truths to be self-evident," states the beginning of the Declaration, "that all men are created equal, that they are endowed by their Creator with certain unalienable rights, that among these are life, liberty, and the pursuit of happiness."

Since Locke had asserted that people had the right to rebel against an unjust ruler, the Declaration of Independence included a long list of George III's abuses. The document ended by declaring the colonies' separation from Britain. The colonies, the Declaration said, "are absolved from all allegiance to the British crown."

Success for the Colonists The British were not about to let their colonies leave without a fight. Shortly after the publication of the Declaration of Independence, the two sides went to war. At first glance, the colonists seemed destined to go down in quick defeat. Washington's ragtag, poorly trained army faced the well-trained forces of the most powerful country in the world. In the end, however, the Americans won their war for independence.

GEOGRAPHY SKILLBUILDER: Interpreting Maps

1. **Region** *What feature formed the western border of the United States?*
2. **Human-Environment Interaction** *What European countries had claims on the North American continent in 1783?*

Several reasons explain the colonists' success. First, the Americans' motivation for fighting was much stronger than that of the British, since their army was defending their homeland. Second, the overconfident British generals made several mistakes. Third, time itself was on the side of the Americans. The British could win battle after battle, as they did, and still lose the war. Fighting an overseas war, 3,000 miles from London, was terribly expensive. After a few years, tax-weary British citizens called for peace.

Finally, the Americans did not fight alone. Louis XVI of France had little sympathy for the ideals of the American Revolution. However, he was eager to weaken France's rival, Britain. French entry into the war in 1778 was decisive. In 1781, combined forces of about 9,500 Americans and 7,800 French trapped a British army commanded by Lord Cornwallis near Yorktown, Virginia. Unable to escape, Cornwallis eventually surrendered. The Americans had shocked the world and won their independence.

Democracy

Ancient Greece and Rome were strong influences on the framers of the U.S. system of government. Democracy as it is practiced today, however, is different from the Greek and Roman models.

The most famous democracy today is the United States. The type of government the United States uses is called a federal republic. "Federal" means power is divided between the national and state governments. In a republic, the people vote for their representatives. Two key components of democracy in the United States are the Constitution and voting.

Enlightenment Ideas and the U.S. Constitution

Many of the ideas contained in the Constitution are built on the ideas of Enlightenment thinkers.

Enlightenment Idea	U.S. Constitution
Locke A government's power comes from the consent of the people.	• Preamble begins "We the people of the United States" to establish legitimacy. • Creates representative government • Limits government powers
Montesquieu Separation of powers	• Federal system of government • Powers divided among three branches • System of checks and balances
Rousseau Direct democracy	• Public election of president and Congress
Voltaire Free speech, religious toleration	• Bill of Rights provides for freedom of speech and religion.
Beccaria Accused have rights, no torture	• Bill of Rights protects rights of accused and prohibits cruel and unusual punishment.

Who Votes?

Voting is an essential part of democracy. Universal suffrage means that all adult citizens can vote. Universal suffrage is part of democracy in the United States today, but that was not always the case. This chart shows how the United States gradually moved toward giving all citizens the right to vote.

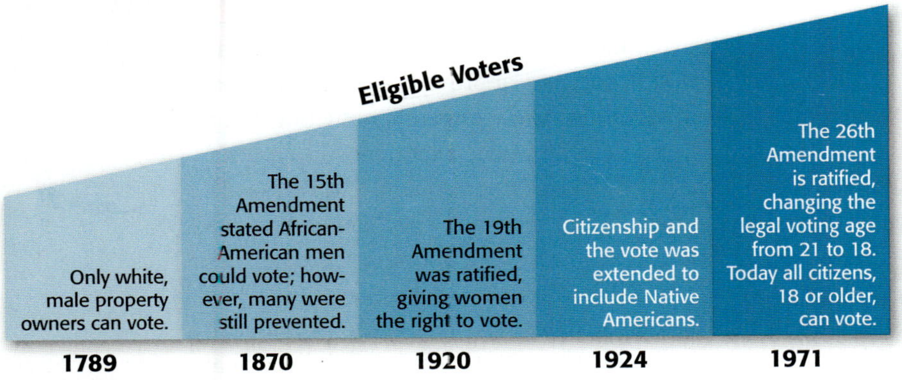

INTEGRATED TECHNOLOGY

RESEARCH LINKS For more on democracy, go to **classzone.com**

> DATA FILE

U.S. Constitution

- There have been 27 amendments to the Constitution since its creation.
- The U.S. Constitution has been used by many other countries as a model for their constitutions.
- In 2002, over 120 established and emerging democracies met to discuss their common issues.

Voting

- In the 2000 U.S. presidential election, only 36.1 percent of people between 18 and 24 years old voted.
- Some countries, such as Australia, fine citizens for not voting. Australia's voter turnout has been over 90 percent since 1925.

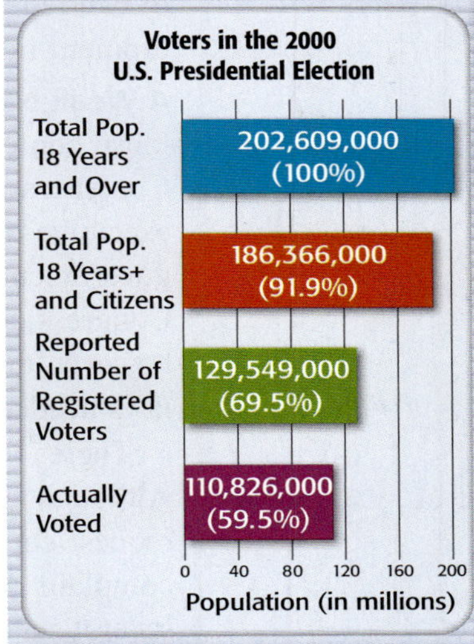

Source: U.S. Census Bureau, Current Population Survey, November 2000.

Connect *to* Today

1. **Synthesizing** If so much of the U.S. Constitution can be found in European ideas, why were the framers of the U.S. Constitution so important?
   See Skillbuilder Handbook, Page R21.
2. **Hypothesizing** Why is it important that every citizen has, and exercises, his or her right to vote?

Global Impact

The French Revolution

The American Revolution inspired the growing number of French people who sought reform in their own country. They saw the new government of the United States as the fulfillment of Enlightenment ideals, and longed for such a government in France.

The Declaration of Independence was widely circulated and admired in France. French officers like the Marquis de Lafayette (shown here), who fought for American independence, captivated his fellow citizens with accounts of the war. One Frenchman remarked about this time period, "We talked of nothing but America." Less than a decade after the American Revolution ended, an armed struggle to topple the government would begin in France.

Americans Create a Republic

Shortly after declaring their independence, the 13 individual states recognized the need for a national government. As victory became certain, all 13 states ratified a constitution in 1781. This plan of government was known as the Articles of Confederation. The Articles established the United States as a republic, a government in which citizens rule through elected representatives.

A Weak National Government To protect their authority, the 13 states created a loose confederation in which they held most of the power. Thus, the Articles of Confederation deliberately created a weak national government. There were no executive or judicial branches. Instead, the Articles established only one body of government, the Congress. Each state, regardless of size, had one vote in Congress. Congress could declare war, enter into treaties, and coin money. It had no power, however, to collect taxes or regulate trade. Passing new laws was difficult because laws needed the approval of 9 of the 13 states.

These limits on the national government soon produced many problems. Although the new national government needed money to operate, it could only request contributions from the states. Angry Revolutionary War veterans bitterly complained that Congress still owed them back pay for their services. Meanwhile, several states issued their own money. Some states even put tariffs on goods from neighboring states. **B**

MAIN IDEA
Making Inferences
B What was the main cause of the nation's problems under the Articles?

A New Constitution Colonial leaders eventually recognized the need for a strong national government. In February 1787, Congress approved a Constitutional Convention to revise the Articles of Confederation. The Constitutional Convention held its first session on May 25, 1787. The 55 delegates were experienced statesmen who were familiar with the political theories of Locke, Montesquieu, and Rousseau.

Although the delegates shared basic ideas on government, they sometimes disagreed on how to put them into practice. For almost four months the delegates argued over important questions. Who should be represented in Congress? How many representatives should each state have? The delegates' deliberations produced not only compromises but also new approaches to governing. Using the political ideas of the Enlightenment, the delegates created a new system of government.

The Federal System Like Montesquieu, the delegates distrusted a powerful central government controlled by one person or group. They therefore established three separate branches—legislative, executive, and judicial. This setup provided a built-in system of **checks and balances**, with each branch checking the actions of the other two. For example, the president received the power to veto legislation passed by Congress. However, the Congress could override a presidential veto with the approval of two-thirds of its members.

Although the Constitution created a strong central government, it did not eliminate local governments. Instead, the Constitution set up a **federal system** in which power was divided between national and state governments.

The Bill of Rights The delegates signed the new Constitution on September 17, 1787. In order to become law, however, the Constitution required approval by conventions in at least 9 of the 13 states. These conventions were marked by sharp debate. Supporters of the Constitution were called Federalists. They argued in their famous work, the *Federalist Papers*, that the new government would provide a better balance between national and state powers. Their opponents, the Antifederalists, feared that the Constitution gave the central government too much power. They also wanted a bill of rights to protect the rights of individual citizens. C

MAIN IDEA

Analyzing Issues

C What were the opposing views regarding ratification of the Constitution?

In order to gain support, the Federalists promised to add a bill of rights to the Constitution. This promise cleared the way for approval. Congress formally added to the Constitution the ten amendments known as the **Bill of Rights**. These amendments protected such basic rights as freedom of speech, press, assembly, and religion. Many of these rights had been advocated by Voltaire, Rousseau, and Locke.

The Constitution and Bill of Rights marked a turning point in people's ideas about government. Both documents put Enlightenment ideas into practice. They expressed an optimistic view that reason and reform could prevail and that progress was inevitable. Such optimism swept across the Atlantic. However, the monarchies and the privileged classes didn't give up power and position easily. As Chapter 23 explains, the struggle to attain the principles of the Enlightenment led to violent revolution in France.

▼ Early copy of the U.S. Constitution

NEW YORK CORE CURRICULUM REVIEW

TERMS & NAMES 1. For each term or name, write a sentence explaining its significance.

- Declaration of Independence
- Thomas Jefferson
- checks and balances
- federal system
- Bill of Rights

USING YOUR NOTES

2. Which of the solutions that you recorded represented a compromise?

Problem	Solution
1.	1.
2.	2.
3.	3.

MAIN IDEAS

3. Why did the colonists criticize the Stamp Act as "taxation without representation"?
4. How did John Locke's notion of the social contract influence the American colonists?
5. Why were the colonists able to achieve victory in the American Revolution?

CRITICAL THINKING & WRITING

6. **MAKING INFERENCES** Why might it be important to have a Bill of Rights that guarantees basic rights of citizens?
7. **FORMING AND SUPPORTING OPINIONS** Do you think the American Revolution would have happened if there had not been an Age of Enlightenment?
8. **ANALYZING CAUSES** Why do you think the colonists at first created such a weak central government?
9. **WRITING ACTIVITY** REVOLUTION Summarize in several **paragraphs** the ideas from the American Revolution concerning separation of powers, basic rights of freedom, and popular sovereignty.

CONNECT TO TODAY **CELEBRATING AMERICA'S BIRTHDAY**

Create a **birthday poster** to present to the United States this July 4th. The poster should include images or quotes that demonstrate the ideals upon which the nation was founded.

Chapter 22 Assessment

TERMS & NAMES

For each term or name below, briefly explain its connection to European history from 1550–1789.

1. heliocentric theory
2. Isaac Newton
3. social contract
4. philosophe
5. salon
6. enlightened despot
7. Declaration of Independence
8. federal system

MAIN IDEAS

The Scientific Revolution Section 1 (pages 623–628)

9. According to Ptolemy, what was the earth's position in the universe? How did Copernicus's view differ?
10. What are the four steps in the scientific method?
11. What four new instruments came into use during the Scientific Revolution? What was the purpose of each one?

The Enlightenment in Europe Section 2 (pages 629–635)

12. How did the ideas of Hobbes and Locke differ?
13. What did Montesquieu admire about the government of Britain?
14. How did the Enlightenment lead to a more secular outlook?

The Enlightenment Spreads Section 3 (pages 636–639)

15. What were three developments in the arts during the Enlightenment?
16. What sorts of reforms did the enlightened despots make?

The American Revolution Section 4 (pages 640–645)

17. Why did the Articles of Confederation result in a weak national government?
18. How did the writers of the U.S. Constitution put into practice the idea of separation of powers? A system of checks and balances?

CRITICAL THINKING

1. USING YOUR NOTES

List in a table important new ideas that arose during the Scientific Revolution and Enlightenment. In the right column, briefly explain why each idea was revolutionary.

New Idea	Why Revolutionary

2. RECOGNIZING EFFECTS

SCIENCE AND TECHNOLOGY What role did technology play in the Scientific Revolution?

3. ANALYZING ISSUES

POWER AND AUTHORITY How did the U.S. Constitution reflect the ideas of the Enlightenment? Refer to specific Enlightenment thinkers to support your answer.

4. CLARIFYING

How did the statement by Prussian ruler Frederick the Great that a ruler is only "the first servant of the state" highlight Enlightenment ideas about government?

VISUAL SUMMARY

Enlightenment and Revolution, 1550–1789

Scientific Revolution

- Heliocentric theory challenges geocentric theory.
- Mathematics and observation support heliocentric theory.
- Scientific method develops.
- Scientists make discoveries in many fields.

A new way of thinking about the world develops, based on observation and a willingness to question assumptions.

Enlightenment

- People try to apply the scientific approach to aspects of society.
- Political scientists propose new ideas about government.
- Philosophes advocate the use of reason to discover truths.
- Philosophes address social issues through reason.

Enlightenment writers challenge many accepted ideas about government and society.

Spread of Ideas

- Enlightenment ideas appeal to thinkers and artists across Europe.
- Salons help spread Enlightenment thinking.
- Ideas spread to literate middle class.
- Enlightened despots attempt reforms.

Enlightenment ideas sweep through European society and to colonial America.

American Revolution

- Enlightenment ideas influence colonists.
- Britain taxes colonists after French and Indian War.
- Colonists denounce taxation without representation.
- War begins in Lexington and Concord.

Colonists declare independence, defeat Britain, and establish republic.

Use the quotation and your knowledge of world history to answer questions 1 and 2.
Additional Test Practice, pp. S1–S33

PRIMARY SOURCE

We the People of the United States, in order to form a more perfect Union, establish Justice, insure domestic Tranquility, provide for the common defense, promote the general Welfare, and secure the Blessings of Liberty to ourselves and our Posterity, do ordain and establish this Constitution of the United States of America.

Preamble, *Constitution of the United States of America*

1 Which of the following are stated objectives of the Constution?
(1) justice and prosperity
(2) prosperity and liberty
(3) defense and prosperity
(4) liberty and justice

2 With whom does the ultimate power in society lie, according to the Constitution?
(1) the church
(2) the military
(3) the citizens
(4) the monarchy

Use this engraving, entitled *The Sleep of Reason Produces Monsters,* and your knowledge of world history to answer question 3.

3 Which of the following statements best summarizes the main idea of this Enlightenment engraving?
(1) Nothing good comes from relaxation or laziness.
(2) A lack of reason fosters superstition and irrational fears.
(3) Dreams are not restricted by the boundaries of reason.
(4) Rulers that let down their guard risk rebellion and overthrow.

INTEGRATED TECHNOLOGY
TEST PRACTICE Go to **classzone.com**
- Diagnostic tests
- Tutorials
- Strategies
- Additional practice

ALTERNATIVE ASSESSMENT

1. Interact *with* History

On page 622, you examined how you would react to a different or revolutionary idea or way of doing things. Now that you have read the chapter, consider how such breakthroughs impacted society. Discuss in a small group what you feel were the most significant new ideas or procedures and explain why.

2. WRITING ABOUT HISTORY

REVOLUTION Re-examine the material on the Scientific Revolution. Then write a three paragraph **essay** summarizing the difference in scientific understanding before and after the various scientific breakthroughs. Focus on
- the ultimate authority on many matters before the Scientific Revolution.
- how and why that changed after the Revolution.

INTEGRATED TECHNOLOGY

Writing an Internet-based Research Paper

Go to the *Web Research Guide* at **classzone.com** to learn about conducting research on the Internet. Use the Internet to explore a recent breakthrough in science or medicine. Look for information that will help you explain why the discovery is significant and how the new knowledge changes what scientists had thought about the topic.

In a well-organized paper, compare the significance of the discovery you are writing about with major scientific or medical discoveries of the Scientific Revolution. Be sure to
- apply a search strategy when using directories and search engines to locate Web resources.
- judge the usefulness of each Web site.
- correctly cite your Web resources.
- revise and edit for correct use of language.

CHAPTER 23

The French Revolution and Napoleon, 1789–1815

NEW YORK CORE CURRICULUM FOCUS

- Economic and social inequalities led to the French Revolution.
- Unrest in France enabled Napoleon Bonaparte to seize power and forge a short-lived empire.

Previewing Main Ideas

ECONOMICS The gap between rich and poor in France was vast. The inequalities of the economy of France were a major cause of the French Revolution.

Geography *Why do you think the royal palace at Versailles became a focal point for the anger of the poor people of Paris during the Revolution?*

REVOLUTION Driven by the example of the American Revolution and such Enlightenment ideas as liberty, equality, and democracy, the French ousted the government of Louis XVI and established a new political order.

Geography *Why do you think some historians cite the "wind from America" as a cause of the French Revolution?*

POWER AND AUTHORITY After seizing power in 1799, Napoleon conquered a huge empire that included much of Western Europe. His attempt to conquer Russia, however, led to his downfall.

Geography *What challenges and hazards of invading Russia might be inferred from the map?*

INTEGRATED TECHNOLOGY

eEdition
- Interactive Maps
- Interactive Visuals
- Interactive Primary Sources

INTERNET RESOURCES
Go to **classzone.com** for:
- Research Links
- Internet Activities
- Primary Sources
- Chapter Quiz
- Maps
- Test Practice
- Current Events

EUROPE

1789 Storming of the Bastille ignites the French Revolution.

1793 King Louis XVI is executed by guillotine; Reign of Terror begins. ▶

1796 Directory appoints Napoleon commander of French forces in Italy.

1789

WORLD

1789 George Washington is inaugurated as first U.S. president. ▶

1795 Great Britain seizes the Cape Colony in South Africa from the Dutch.

1799
Napoleon overthrows the Directory through a coup d'état.

1804
Napoleon crowns himself emperor, begins to create a vast European empire. ▶

1815
Napoleon is defeated at the Battle of Waterloo.

1800 — **1815**

1800
Opium trade begins in China.

1804
Saint Domingue gains independence. (Toussaint L'Ouverture) ▶

1810
Padre Hidalgo calls for Mexican independence.

1814
War of 1812 between Great Britain and the United States ends.

Interact *with* History

How would you change an unjust government?

You are living in France in the late 1700s. Your parents are merchants who earn a good living. However, after taxes they have hardly any money left. You know that other people, especially the peasants in the countryside, are even worse off than you. At the same time, the nobility lives in luxury and pays practically no taxes.

Many people in France are desperate for change. But they are uncertain how to bring about that change. Some think that representatives of the people should demand fair taxes and just laws. Others support violent revolution. In Paris, that revolution seems to have begun. An angry mob has attacked and taken over the Bastille, a royal prison. You wonder what will happen next.

1. One of the mob leaders triumphantly displays the keys to the Bastille.
2. Although they were in search of gunpowder and firearms, the conquerors of the Bastille took whatever they could find.
3. One man drags the royal standard behind him.

▲ The conquerors of the Bastille parade outside City Hall in Paris.

EXAMINING *the* ISSUES

- **How would you define an unjust government?**
- **What, if anything, would lead you to take part in a violent revolution?**

Discuss these questions with your classmates. In your discussion, remember what you've learned about the causes of revolutionary conflicts such as the American Revolution and the English Civil War. As you read about the French Revolution in this chapter, see what changes take place and how these changes came about.

The French Revolution Begins

CONNECT TO THE NEW YORK STATE CORE CURRICULUM

Unit 5.C.3.a. Causes
Unit 5.C.3.c. Impact on France and other nations

TERMS & NAMES

- Old Regime
- estate
- Louis XVI
- Marie Antoinette
- Estates-General
- National Assembly
- Tennis Court Oath
- Great Fear

SETTING THE STAGE In the 1700s, France was considered the most advanced country of Europe. It had a large population and a prosperous foreign trade. It was the center of the Enlightenment, and France's culture was widely praised and imitated by the rest of the world. However, the appearance of success was deceiving. There was great unrest in France, caused by bad harvests, high prices, high taxes, and disturbing questions raised by the Enlightenment ideas of Locke, Rousseau, and Voltaire.

The Old Order

In the 1770s, the social and political system of France—the **Old Regime**—remained in place. Under this system, the people of France were divided into three large social classes, or **estates**.

TAKING NOTES
Analyzing Causes Use a web diagram to identify the causes of the French Revolution.

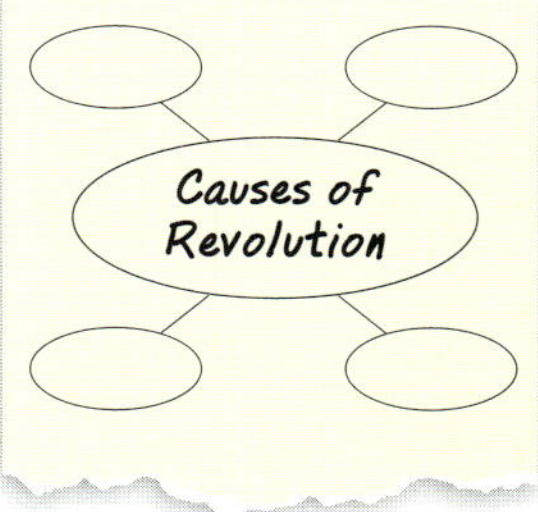

The Privileged Estates Two of the estates had privileges, including access to high offices and exemptions from paying taxes, that were not granted to the members of the third. The Roman Catholic Church, whose clergy formed the First Estate, owned 10 percent of the land in France. It provided education and relief services to the poor and contributed about 2 percent of its income to the government. The Second Estate was made up of rich nobles. Although they accounted for just 2 percent of the population, the nobles owned 20 percent of the land and paid almost no taxes. The majority of the clergy and the nobility scorned Enlightenment ideas as radical notions that threatened their status and power as privileged persons.

The Third Estate About 97 percent of the people belonged to the Third Estate. The three groups that made up this estate differed greatly in their economic conditions. The first group—the bourgeoisie (BUR•zhwah•ZEE), or middle class—were bankers, factory owners, merchants, professionals, and skilled artisans. Often, they were well educated and believed strongly in the Enlightenment ideals of liberty and equality. Although some of the bourgeoisie were as rich as nobles, they paid high taxes and, like the rest of the Third Estate, lacked privileges. Many felt that their wealth entitled them to a greater degree of social status and political power.

The workers of France's cities formed the second, and poorest, group within the Third Estate. These urban workers included tradespeople, apprentices, laborers, and domestic servants. Paid low wages and frequently out of work, they often

The Three Estates

A First Estate
- made up of clergy of Roman Catholic Church
- scorned Enlightenment ideas

B Second Estate
- made up of rich nobles
- held highest offices in government
- disagreed about Enlightenment ideas

C Third Estate
- included bourgeoisie, urban lower class, and peasant farmers
- had no power to influence government
- embraced Enlightenment ideas
- resented the wealthy First and Second Estates.

Population of France, 1787

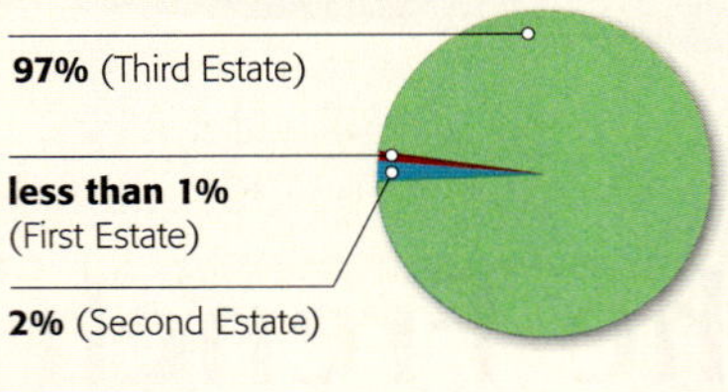

Percent of Income Paid in Taxes

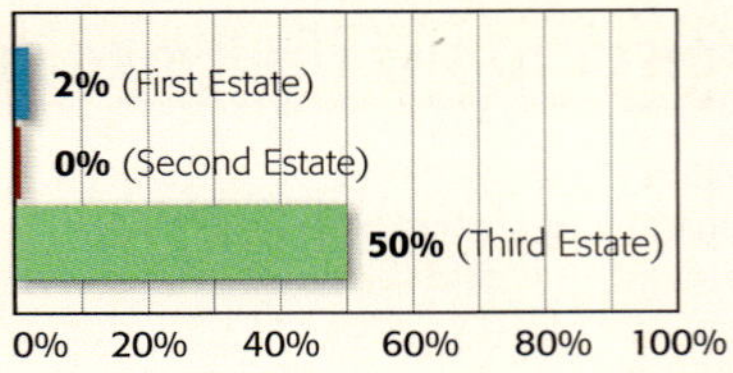

SKILLBUILDER: Interpreting Charts and Political Cartoons

1. **Drawing Conclusions** *How do the chart and the graphs help explain the political cartoon?*
2. **Making Inferences** *Why might the First and Second Estates be opposed to change?*

went hungry. If the cost of bread rose, mobs of these workers might attack grain carts and bread shops to steal what they needed.

Peasants formed the largest group within the Third Estate, more than 80 percent of France's 26 million people. Peasants paid about half their income in dues to nobles, tithes to the Church, and taxes to the king's agents. They even paid taxes on such basic staples as salt. Peasants and the urban poor resented the clergy and the nobles for their privileges and special treatment. The heavily taxed and discontented Third Estate was eager for change.

Vocabulary
tithe: a church tax, normally about one-tenth of a family's income

The Forces of Change

In addition to the growing resentment among the lower classes, other factors contributed to the revolutionary mood in France. New ideas about government, serious economic problems, and weak and indecisive leadership all helped to generate a desire for change.

Enlightenment Ideas New views about power and authority in government were spreading among the Third Estate. Members of the Third Estate were inspired by the success of the American Revolution. They began questioning long-standing notions about the structure of society. Quoting Rousseau and Voltaire, they began to demand equality, liberty, and democracy. The Comte D'Antraigues, a friend of Rousseau, best summed up their ideas on what government should be:

PRIMARY SOURCE

The Third Estate is the People and the People is the foundation of the State; it is in fact the State itself; the . . . People is everything. Everything should be subordinated to it. . . . It is in the People that all national power resides and for the People that all states exist.

COMTE D'ANTRAIGUES, quoted in *Citizens: A Chronicle of the French Revolution*

Economic Troubles By the 1780s, France's once prosperous economy was in decline. This caused alarm, particularly among the merchants, factory owners, and bankers of the Third Estate. On the surface, the economy appeared to be sound, because both production and trade were expanding rapidly. However, the heavy burden of taxes made it almost impossible to conduct business profitably within France. Further, the cost of living was rising sharply. In addition, bad weather in the 1780s caused widespread crop failures, resulting in a severe shortage of grain. The price of bread doubled in 1789, and many people faced starvation.

During the 1770s and 1780s, France's government sank deeply into debt. Part of the problem was the extravagant spending of **Louis XVI** and his queen, **Marie Antoinette**. Louis also inherited a considerable debt from previous kings. And he borrowed heavily in order to help the American revolutionaries in their war against Great Britain, France's chief rival. This nearly doubled the government's debt. In 1786, when bankers refused to lend the government any more money, Louis faced serious problems.

A Weak Leader Strong leadership might have solved these and other problems. Louis XVI, however, was indecisive and allowed matters to drift. He paid little attention to his government advisers, and had little patience for the details of governing. The queen only added to Louis's problems. She often interfered in the government, and frequently offered Louis poor advice. Further, since she was a member of the royal family of Austria, France's long-time enemy, Marie Antoinette had been unpopular from the moment she set foot in France. Her behavior only made the situation worse. As queen, she spent so much money on gowns, jewels, gambling, and gifts that she became known as "Madame Deficit."

Vocabulary
deficit: debt

Rather than cutting expenses, Louis put off dealing with the emergency until he practically had no money left. His solution was to impose taxes on the nobility. However, the Second Estate forced him to call a meeting of the **Estates-General**—an assembly of representatives from all three estates—to approve this new tax. The meeting, the first in 175 years, was held on May 5, 1789, at Versailles.

History Makers

Louis XVI
1754–1793

Louis XVI's tutors made little effort to prepare him for his role as king—and it showed. He was easily bored with affairs of state, and much preferred to spend his time in physical activities, particularly hunting. He also loved to work with his hands, and was skilled in several trades, including lock-making, metalworking, and bricklaying.

Despite these shortcomings, Louis was well intentioned and sincerely wanted to improve the lives of the common people. However, he lacked the ability to make decisions and the determination to see policies through. When he did take action, it often was based on poor advice from ill-informed members of his court. As one politician of the time noted, "His reign was a succession of feeble attempts at doing good, shows of weakness, and clear evidence of his inadequacy as a leader."

Marie Antoinette
1755–1793

Marie Antoinette was a pretty, lighthearted, charming woman. However, she was unpopular with the French because of her spending and her involvement in controversial court affairs. She referred to Louis as "the poor man" and sometimes set the clock forward an hour to be rid of his presence.

Marie Antoinette refused to wear the tight-fitting clothing styles of the day and introduced a loose cotton dress for women. The elderly, who viewed the dress as an undergarment, thought that her clothing was scandalous. The French silk industry was equally angry.

In constant need of entertainment, Marie Antoinette often spent hours playing cards. One year she lost the equivalent of $1.5 million by gambling in card games.

INTEGRATED TECHNOLOGY

RESEARCH LINKS For more on Louis XVI and Marie Antoinette, go to **classzone.com**

Dawn of the Revolution

The clergy and the nobles had dominated the Estates-General throughout the Middle Ages and expected to do so in the 1789 meeting. Under the assembly's medieval rules, each estate's delegates met in a separate hall to vote, and each estate had one vote. The two privileged estates could always outvote the Third Estate.

The National Assembly The Third Estate delegates, mostly members of the bourgeoisie whose views had been shaped by the Enlightenment, were eager to make changes in the government. They insisted that all three estates meet together and that each delegate have a vote. This would give the advantage to the Third Estate, which had as many delegates as the other two estates combined. (A)

MAIN IDEA

Analyzing Motives

(A) Why did the Third Estate propose a change in the Estates-General's voting rules?

Siding with the nobles, the king ordered the Estates-General to follow the medieval rules. The delegates of the Third Estate, however, became more and more determined to wield power. A leading spokesperson for their viewpoint was a clergyman sympathetic to their cause, Emmanuel-Joseph Sieyès (syay•YEHS). In a dramatic speech, Sieyès suggested that the Third Estate delegates name themselves the **National Assembly** and pass laws and reforms in the name of the French people.

After a long night of excited debate, the delegates of the Third Estate agreed to Sieyès's idea by an overwhelming majority. On June 17, 1789, they voted to establish the National Assembly, in effect proclaiming the end of absolute monarchy and the beginning of representative government. This vote was the first deliberate act of revolution.

Three days later, the Third Estate delegates found themselves locked out of their meeting room. They broke down a door to an indoor tennis court, pledging to stay until they had drawn up a new constitution. This pledge became known as the **Tennis Court Oath**. Soon after, nobles and members of the clergy who favored reform joined the Third Estate delegates. In response to these events, Louis stationed his mercenary army of Swiss guards around Versailles.

Vocabulary

mercenary army: a group of soldiers who will work for any country or employer that will pay them

Storming the Bastille In Paris, rumors flew. Some people suggested that Louis was intent on using military force to dismiss the National Assembly. Others charged that the foreign troops were coming to Paris to massacre French citizens.

▼ The attack on the Bastille claimed the lives of about 100 people.

People began to gather weapons in order to defend the city against attack. On July 14, a mob searching for gunpowder and arms stormed the Bastille, a Paris prison. The mob overwhelmed the guard and seized control of the building. The angry attackers hacked the prison commander and several guards to death, and then paraded around the streets with the dead men's heads on pikes.

The fall of the Bastille became a great symbolic act of revolution to the French people. Ever since, July 14—Bastille Day—has been a French national holiday, similar to the Fourth of July in the United States.

Social History

Bread

Bread was a staple of the diet of the common people of France. Most families consumed three or four 4-pound loaves a day. And the purchase of bread took about half of a worker's wages—when times were good. So, when the price of bread jumped dramatically, as it did in the fall of 1789, people faced a real threat of starvation.

On their march back from Versailles, the women of Paris happily sang that they were bringing "the baker, the baker's wife, and the baker's lad" with them. They expected the "baker"—Louis—to provide the cheap bread that they needed to live.

A Great Fear Sweeps France

Before long, rebellion spread from Paris into the countryside. From one village to the next, wild rumors circulated that the nobles were hiring outlaws to terrorize the peasants. A wave of senseless panic called the **Great Fear** rolled through France. The peasants soon became outlaws themselves. Armed with pitchforks and other farm tools, they broke into nobles' manor houses and destroyed the old legal papers that bound them to pay feudal dues. In some cases, the peasants simply burned down the manor houses.

In October 1789, thousands of Parisian women rioted over the rising price of bread. Brandishing knives, axes, and other weapons, the women marched on Versailles. First, they demanded that the National Assembly take action to provide bread. Then they turned their anger on the king and queen. They broke into the palace, killing some of the guards. The women demanded that Louis and Marie Antoinette return to Paris. After some time, Louis agreed.

A few hours later the king, his family, and servants left Versailles, never again to see the magnificent palace. Their exit signaled the change of power and radical reforms about to overtake France. **B**

MAIN IDEA

Recognizing Effects

B How did the women's march mark a turning point in the relationship between the king and the people?

NEW YORK CORE CURRICULUM REVIEW

TERMS & NAMES 1. For each term or name, write a sentence explaining its significance.

- Old Regime • estates • Louis XVI • Marie Antoinette • Estates-General • National Assembly • Tennis Court Oath • Great Fear

USING YOUR NOTES

2. Select one of the causes you listed and explain how it contributed to the French Revolution.

MAIN IDEAS

3. Why were members of the Third Estate dissatisfied with life under the Old Regime?
4. How did Louis XVI's weak leadership contribute to the growing crisis in France?
5. How did the purpose of the meeting of the Estates-General in 1789 change?

CRITICAL THINKING & WRITING

6. **FORMING AND SUPPORTING OPINIONS** Do you think that changes in the French government were inevitable? Explain.
7. **ANALYZING MOTIVES** Why do you think some members of the First and Second Estates joined the National Assembly and worked to reform the government?
8. **COMPARING AND CONTRASTING** How were the storming of the Bastille and the women's march on Versailles similar? How were they different?
9. **WRITING ACTIVITY** POWER AND AUTHORITY In the role of a member of the Third Estate, write a brief **speech** explaining why the French political system needs to change.

CONNECT TO TODAY **CREATING A COLLAGE**

Conduct research on how Bastille Day is celebrated in France today. Use your findings to create an **annotated collage** titled "Celebrating the Revolution."

Revolution Brings Reform and Terror

CONNECT TO THE NEW YORK STATE CORE CURRICULUM

Unit 5.C.3.b. Key individuals (Robespierre and Louis XVI)
Unit 5.C.3.c. Impact on France and other nations

TERMS & NAMES

- Legislative Assembly
- émigré
- sans-culotte
- Jacobin
- guillotine
- Maximilien Robespierre
- Reign of Terror

SETTING THE STAGE Peasants were not the only members of French society to feel the Great Fear. Nobles and officers of the Church were equally afraid. Throughout France, bands of angry peasants struck out against members of the upper classes, attacking and destroying many manor houses. In the summer of 1789, a few months before the women's march to Versailles, some nobles and members of clergy in the National Assembly responded to the uprisings in an emotional late-night meeting.

TAKING NOTES

Recognizing Effects Use a flow chart to identify the major events that followed the creation of the Constitution of 1791.

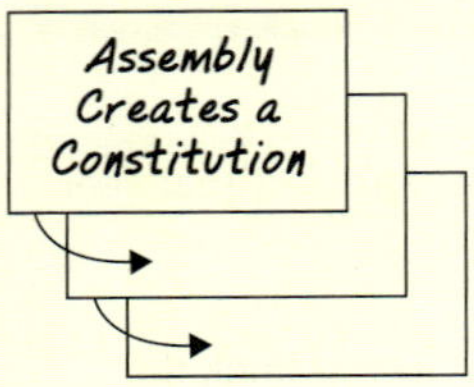

The Assembly Reforms France

Throughout the night of August 4, 1789, noblemen made grand speeches, declaring their love of liberty and equality. Motivated more by fear than by idealism, they joined other members of the National Assembly in sweeping away the feudal privileges of the First and Second Estates, thus making commoners equal to the nobles and the clergy. By morning, the Old Regime was dead.

The Rights of Man Three weeks later, the National Assembly adopted a statement of revolutionary ideals, the Declaration of the Rights of Man and of the Citizen. Reflecting the influence of the Declaration of Independence, the document stated that "men are born and remain free and equal in rights." These rights included "liberty, property, security, and resistance to oppression." The document also guaranteed citizens equal justice, freedom of speech, and freedom of religion.

In keeping with these principles, revolutionary leaders adopted the expression "Liberty, Equality, Fraternity" as their slogan. Such sentiments, however, did not apply to everyone. When writer Olympe de Gouges (aw•LIMP-duh-GOOZH) published a declaration of the rights of women, her ideas were rejected. Later, in 1793, she was declared an enemy of the Revolution and executed.

A State-Controlled Church Many of the National Assembly's early reforms focused on the Church. The assembly took over Church lands and declared that Church officials and priests were to be elected and paid as state officials. Thus, the Catholic Church lost both its lands and its political independence. The reasons for the assembly's actions were largely economic. Proceeds from the sale of Church lands helped pay off France's huge debt.

The assembly's actions alarmed millions of French peasants, who were devout Catholics. The effort to make the Church a part of the state offended them, even

◀ One of the people who stopped Louis from escaping said that he recognized the king from his portrait on a French bank note.

though it was in accord with Enlightenment philosophy. They believed that the pope should rule over a church independent of the state. From this time on, many peasants opposed the assembly's reforms.

Louis Tries to Escape As the National Assembly restructured the relationship between church and state, Louis XVI pondered his fate as a monarch. Some of his advisers warned him that he and his family were in danger. Many supporters of the monarchy thought France unsafe and left the country. Then, in June 1791, the royal family tried to escape from France to the Austrian Netherlands. As they neared the border, however, they were apprehended and returned to Paris under guard. Louis's attempted escape increased the influence of his radical enemies in the government and sealed his fate.

Divisions Develop

For two years, the National Assembly argued over a new constitution for France. By 1791, the delegates had made significant changes in France's government and society.

A Limited Monarchy In September 1791, the National Assembly completed the new constitution, which Louis reluctantly approved. The constitution created a limited constitutional monarchy. It stripped the king of much of his authority. It also created a new legislative body—the **Legislative Assembly**. This body had the power to create laws and to approve or reject declarations of war. However, the king still held the executive power to enforce laws.

Factions Split France Despite the new government, old problems, such as food shortages and government debt, remained. The question of how to handle these problems caused the Legislative Assembly to split into three general groups, each of which sat in a different part of the meeting hall. Radicals, who sat on the left side of the hall, opposed the idea of a monarchy and wanted sweeping changes in the way the government was run. Moderates sat in the center of the hall and wanted some changes in government, but not as many as the radicals. Conservatives sat on the right side of the hall. They upheld the idea of a limited monarchy and wanted few changes in government. (A)

MAIN IDEA

Recognizing Effects

(A) How did differences of opinion on how to handle such issues as food shortages and debt affect the Legislative Assembly?

Connect *to* Today

Left, Right, and Center

The terms we use today to describe where people stand politically derive from the factions that developed in the Legislative Assembly in 1791.

- People who want to radically change government are called left wing or are said to be on the left.
- People with moderate views often are called centrist or are said to be in the center.
- People who want few or no changes in government often are called right wing or are said to be on the right.

In addition, factions outside the Legislative Assembly wanted to influence the direction of the government too. **Émigrés** (EHM•ih•GRAYZ), nobles and others who had fled France, hoped to undo the Revolution and restore the Old Regime. In contrast, some Parisian workers and small shopkeepers wanted the Revolution to bring even greater changes to France. They were called **sans-culottes** (SANZ kyoo•LAHTS), or "those without knee breeches." Unlike the upper classes, who wore fancy knee-length pants, sans-culottes wore regular trousers. Although they did not have a role in the assembly, they soon discovered ways to exert their power on the streets of Paris.

War and Execution

Monarchs and nobles in many European countries watched the changes taking place in France with alarm. They feared that similar revolts might break out in their own countries. In fact, some radicals were keen to spread their revolutionary ideas across Europe. As a result, some countries took action. Austria and Prussia, for example, urged the French to restore Louis to his position as an absolute monarch. The Legislative Assembly responded by declaring war in April 1792.

History Makers

Jean-Paul Marat
1743–1793

Marat was a thin, high-strung, sickly man whose revolutionary writings stirred up the violent mood in Paris. Because he suffered from a painful skin disease, he often found comfort by relaxing in a cold bath—even arranging things so that he could work in his bathtub!

During the summer of 1793, Charlotte Corday, a supporter of a rival faction whose members had been jailed, gained an audience with Marat by pretending to have information about traitors. Once inside Marat's private chambers, she fatally stabbed him as he bathed. For her crime, Corday went to the guillotine.

France at War The war began badly for the French. By the summer of 1792, Prussian forces were advancing on Paris. The Prussian commander threatened to destroy Paris if the revolutionaries harmed any member of the royal family. This enraged the Parisians. On August 10, about 20,000 men and women invaded the Tuileries, the palace where the royal family was staying. The mob massacred the royal guards and imprisoned Louis, Marie Antoinette, and their children.

Shortly after, the French troops defending Paris were sent to reinforce the French army in the field. Rumors began to spread that supporters of the king held in Paris prisons planned to break out and seize control of the city. Angry and fearful citizens responded by taking the law into their own hands. For several days in early September, they raided the prisons and murdered over 1,000 prisoners. Many nobles, priests, and royalist sympathizers fell victim to the angry mobs in these September Massacres. (B)

MAIN IDEA

Analyzing Causes

(B) What did the September Massacres show about the mood of the people?

Under pressure from radicals in the streets and among its members, the Legislative Assembly set aside the Constitution of 1791. It declared the king deposed, dissolved the assembly, and called for the election of a new legislature. This new governing body, the National Convention, took office on September 21. It quickly abolished the monarchy and declared France a republic. Adult male citizens were granted the right to vote and hold office. Despite the important part they had already played in the Revolution, women were not given the vote.

Jacobins Take Control Most of the people involved in the governmental changes in September 1792 were members of a radical political organization, the Jacobin (JAK•uh•bihn) Club. One of the most prominent **Jacobins**, as club members were called, was Jean-Paul Marat (mah•RAH). During the Revolution, he edited a newspaper called *L'Ami du Peuple* (Friend of the People). In his fiery editorials, Marat called for

INTERACTIVE

The Guillotine

If you think the guillotine was a cruel form of capital punishment, think again. Dr. Joseph Ignace Guillotin proposed a machine that satisfied many needs—it was efficient, humane, and democratic. A physician and member of the National Assembly, Guillotin claimed that those executed with the device "wouldn't even feel the slightest pain."

Prior to the guillotine's introduction in 1792, many French criminals had suffered through horrible punishments in public places. Although public punishments continued to attract large crowds, not all spectators were pleased with the new machine. Some witnesses felt that death by the guillotine occurred much too quickly to be enjoyed by an audience.

INTEGRATED TECHNOLOGY

RESEARCH LINKS For more on the guillotine, go to **classzone.com**

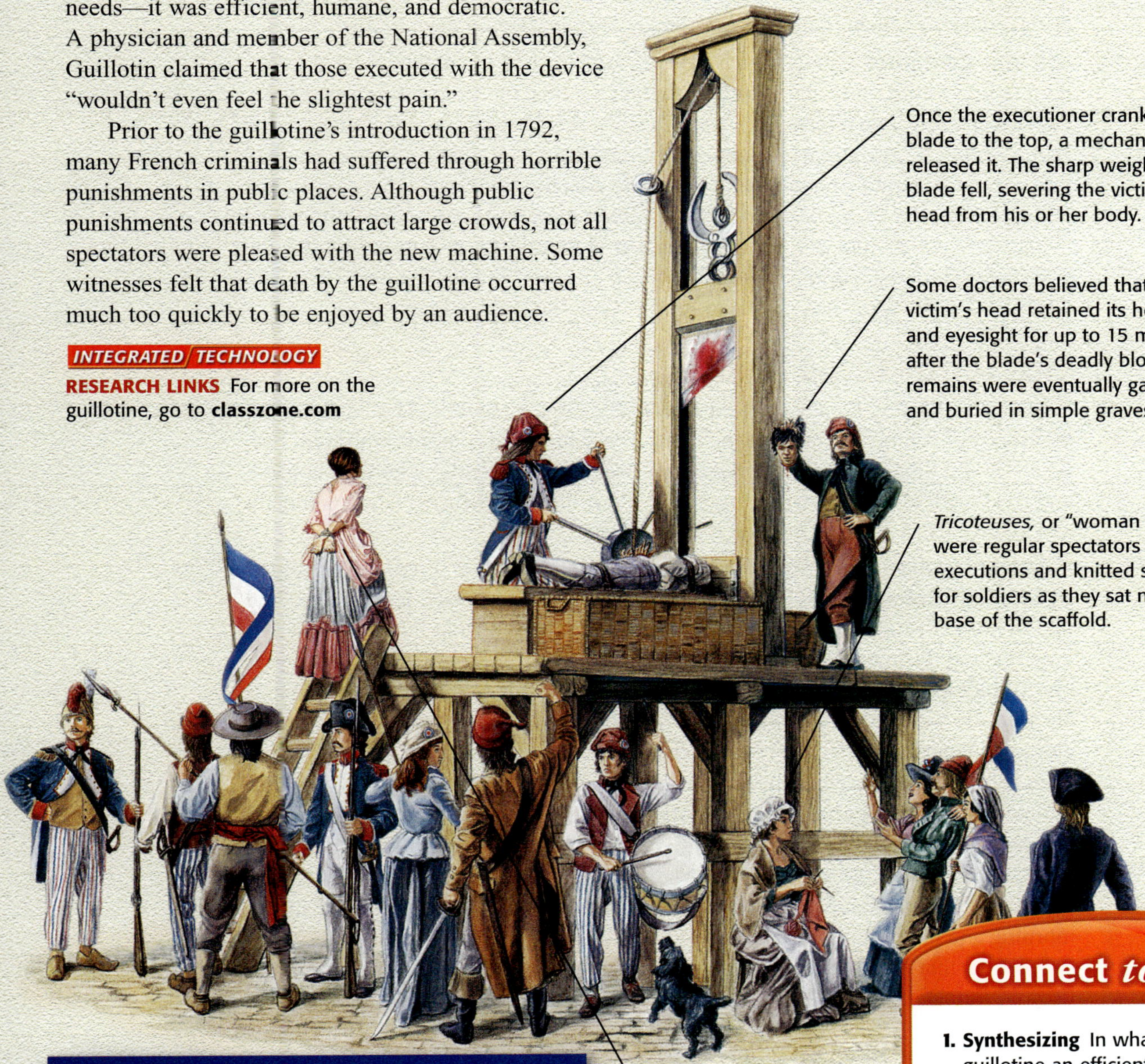

Once the executioner cranked the blade to the top, a mechanism released it. The sharp weighted blade fell, severing the victim's head from his or her body.

Some doctors believed that a victim's head retained its hearing and eyesight for up to 15 minutes after the blade's deadly blow. All remains were eventually gathered and buried in simple graves.

Tricoteuses, or "woman knitters," were regular spectators at executions and knitted stockings for soldiers as they sat near the base of the scaffold.

Before each execution, bound victims traveled from the prison to the scaffold in horse-drawn carts during a one and one-half hour procession through city streets.

Beheading by Class

More than 2,100 people were executed during the last 132 days of the Reign of Terror. The pie graph below displays the breakdown of beheadings by class.

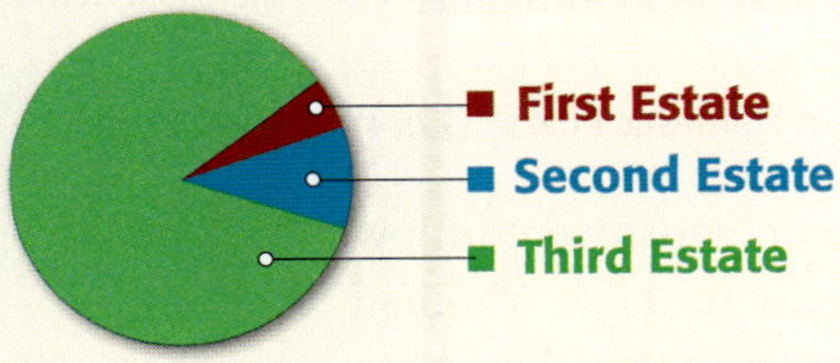

Connect *to* Today

1. **Synthesizing** In what ways was the guillotine an efficient means of execution?

   See Skillbuilder Handbook, page R21.

2. **Comparing** France continued to use the guillotine until 1977. Four years later, France abolished capital punishment. Conduct research to identify countries where capital punishment is still used. Use your findings to create a map titled "Countries Using Capital Punishment."

the death of all those who continued to support the king. Georges Danton (zhawrzh dahn•TAWN), a lawyer, was among the club's most talented and passionate speakers. He also was known for his devotion to the rights of Paris's poor people.

The National Convention had reduced Louis XVI's role from that of a king to that of a common citizen and prisoner. Now, guided by radical Jacobins, it tried Louis for treason. The Convention found him guilty, and, by a very close vote, sentenced him to death. On January 21, 1793, the former king walked with calm dignity up the steps of the scaffold to be beheaded by a machine called the **guillotine** (GIHL•uh•TEEN). (See the Science & Technology feature on page 659.)

The War Continues The National Convention also had to contend with the continuing war with Austria and Prussia. At about the time the Convention took office, the French army won a stunning victory against the Austrians and Prussians at the Battle of Valmy. Early in 1793, however, Great Britain, Holland, and Spain joined Prussia and Austria against France. Forced to contend with so many enemies, the French suffered a string of defeats. To reinforce the French army, Jacobin leaders in the Convention took an extreme step. At their urging, in February 1793 the Convention ordered a draft of 300,000 French citizens between the ages of 18 and 40. By 1794, the army had grown to 800,000 and included women.

The Terror Grips France

Foreign armies were not the only enemies of the French republic. The Jacobins had thousands of enemies within France itself. These included peasants who were horrified by the king's execution, priests who would not accept government control, and rival leaders who were stirring up rebellion in the provinces. How to contain and control these enemies became a central issue.

Robespierre Assumes Control In the early months of 1793, one Jacobin leader, **Maximilien Robespierre** (ROHBZ•peer), slowly gained power. Robespierre and his supporters set out to build a "republic of virtue" by wiping out every trace of France's past. Firm believers in reason, they changed the calendar, dividing the year into 12 months of 30 days and renaming each month. This calendar had no Sundays because the radicals considered religion old-fashioned and dangerous. They even closed all churches in Paris, and cities and towns all over France soon did the same.

In July 1793, Robespierre became leader of the Committee of Public Safety. For the next year, Robespierre governed France virtually as a dictator, and the period of his rule became known as the **Reign of Terror**. The Committee of Public Safety's chief task was to protect the Revolution from its enemies. Under Robespierre's leadership, the committee often had these "enemies" tried in the morning and guillotined in the afternoon. Robespierre justified his use of terror by suggesting that it enabled French citizens to remain true to the ideals of the Revolution. He also saw a connection between virtue and terror:

PRIMARY SOURCE C

The first maxim of our politics ought to be to lead the people by means of reason and the enemies of the people by terror. If the basis of popular government in time of peace is virtue, the basis of popular government in time of revolution is both virtue and terror: virtue without which terror is murderous, terror without which virtue is powerless. Terror is nothing else than swift, severe, indomitable justice; it flows, then, from virtue.

MAXIMILIEN ROBESPIERRE, "On the Morals and Political Principles of Domestic Policy" (1794)

MAIN IDEA

Analyzing Primary Sources

C How did Robespierre justify the use of terror?

The "enemies of the Revolution" who troubled Robespierre the most were fellow radicals who challenged his leadership. In 1793 and 1794, many of those who had led the Revolution received death sentences. Their only crime was that they were considered less radical than Robespierre. By early 1794, even Georges Danton found himself in danger. Danton's friends in the National Convention, afraid to defend him, joined in condemning him. On the scaffold, he told the executioner, "Don't forget to show my head to the people. It's well worth seeing."

The Terror claimed not only the famous, such as Danton and Marie Antoinette, the widowed queen. Thousands of unknown people also were sent to their deaths, often on the flimsiest of charges. For example, an 18-year-old youth was sentenced to die for cutting down a tree that had been planted as a symbol of liberty. Perhaps as many as 40,000 were executed during the Terror. About 85 percent were peasants or members of the urban poor or middle class—for whose benefit the Revolution had been launched.

▲ At his trial, Georges Danton defended himself so skillfully that the authorities eventually denied him the right to speak.

End of the Terror

In July 1794, fearing for their own safety, some members of the National Convention turned on Robespierre. They demanded his arrest and execution. The Reign of Terror, the radical phase of the French Revolution, ended on July 28, 1794, when Robespierre went to the guillotine.

French public opinion shifted dramatically after Robespierre's death. People of all classes had grown weary of the Terror. They were also tired of the skyrocketing prices for bread, salt, and other necessities of life. In 1795, moderate leaders in the National Convention drafted a new plan of government, the third since 1789. It placed power firmly in the hands of the upper middle class and called for a two-house legislature and an executive body of five men, known as the Directory. These five were moderates, not revolutionary idealists. Some of them were corrupt and made themselves rich at the country's expense. Even so, they gave their troubled country a period of order. They also found the right general to command France's armies—Napoleon Bonaparte.

NEW YORK CORE CURRICULUM REVIEW

TERMS & NAMES 1. For each term or name, write a sentence explaining its significance.

- Legislative Assembly
- émigré
- sans-culotte
- Jacobin
- guillotine
- Maximilien Robespierre
- Reign of Terror

USING YOUR NOTES

2. Do you think this chain of events could have been changed in any way? Explain.

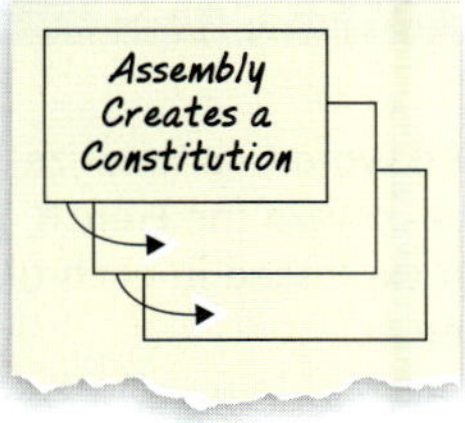

MAIN IDEAS

3. What major reforms did the National Assembly introduce?
4. What did the divisions in the Legislative Assembly say about the differences in French society?
5. How did the Reign of Terror come to an end?

CRITICAL THINKING & WRITING

6. **SYNTHESIZING** How did the slogan "Liberty, Equality, Fraternity" sum up the goals of the Revolution?
7. **COMPARING AND CONTRASTING** What similarities and differences do you see between the political factions in the Legislative Assembly and those in the U.S. government today?
8. **ANALYZING CAUSES** What factors led to Robespierre becoming a dictator?
9. **WRITING ACTIVITY** REVOLUTION Working in small teams, write short **biographies** of three revolutionary figures mentioned in this section.

INTEGRATED TECHNOLOGY **INTERNET ACTIVITY**

Use the Internet to conduct research on governments that use terrorism against their own people. Prepare an **oral report** on the methods these countries use.

INTERNET KEYWORD
human rights

INTERACTIVE

The French Revolution

Over time, people have expressed a wide variety of opinions about the causes and outcomes of the French Revolution. The following excerpts, dating from the 1790s to 1859, illustrate this diversity of opinion.

A SECONDARY SOURCE

Charles Dickens

In 1859, the English writer Dickens wrote *A Tale of Two Cities,* a novel about the French Revolution for which he did much research. In the following scene, Charles Darnay—an aristocrat who gave up his title because he hated the injustices done to the people—has returned to France and been put on trial.

His judges sat upon the bench in feathered hats; but the rough red cap and tricolored cockade was the headdress otherwise prevailing. Looking at the jury and the turbulent audience, he might have thought that the usual order of things was reversed, and that the felons were trying the honest men. The lowest, cruelest, and worst populace of a city, never without its quantity of low, cruel, and bad, were the directing spirits of the scene. . . .

Charles Evrémonde, called Darnay, was accused by the public prosecutor as an emigrant, whose life was forfeit to the Republic, under the decree which banished all emigrants on pain of Death. It was nothing that the decree bore date since his return to France. There he was, and there was the decree; he had been taken in France, and his head was demanded.

"Take off his head!" cried the audience. "An enemy to the Republic!"

▶ In this illustration from *A Tale of Two Cities*, Sidney Carton goes to the guillotine in Darnay's place.

B PRIMARY SOURCE

Edmund Burke

Burke, a British politician, was one of the earliest and most severe critics of the French Revolution. In 1790, he expressed this opinion.

[The French have rebelled] against a mild and lawful monarch, with more fury, outrage, and insult, than ever any people has been known to rise against the most illegal usurper, or the most [bloodthirsty] tyrant. . . .

They have found their punishment in their success. Laws overturned; tribunals subverted; . . . the people impoverished; a church pillaged, and . . . civil and military anarchy made the constitution of the kingdom. . . .

Were all these dreadful things necessary?

C PRIMARY SOURCE

Thomas Paine

In 1790, Paine—a strong supporter of the American Revolution—defended the French Revolution against Burke and other critics.

It is no longer the paltry cause of kings or of this or of that individual, that calls France and her armies into action. It is the great cause of all. It is the establishment of a new era, that shall blot despotism from the earth, and fix, on the lasting principles of peace and citizenship, the great Republic of Man.

The scene that now opens itself to France extends far beyond the boundaries of her own dominions. Every nation is becoming her ally, and every court has become her enemy. It is now the cause of all nations, against the cause of all courts.

Document-Based QUESTIONS

1. In your own words, summarize the attitude toward the French Revolution expressed in each of these excerpts.
2. Why might Edmund Burke (Source B) be so against the French Revolution?
3. In Source C, what is the distinction Thomas Paine is making between nations and courts?

Napoleon Forges an Empire

CONNECT TO THE NEW YORK STATE CORE CURRICULUM

Unit 5.C.3.d. Rise to power of Napoleon and his impact (Napoleonic Code)
Unit 5.C.3.c. Impact on France and other nations

TERMS & NAMES

- Napoleon Bonaparte
- coup d'état
- plebiscite
- lycée
- concordat
- Napoleonic Code
- Battle of Trafalgar

SETTING THE STAGE Napoleon Bonaparte was quite a short man—just five feet three inches tall. However, he cast a long shadow over the history of modern times. He would come to be recognized as one of the world's greatest military geniuses, along with Alexander the Great of Macedonia, Hannibal of Carthage, and Julius Caesar of Rome. In only four years, from 1795 to 1799, Napoleon rose from a relatively obscure position as an officer in the French army to become master of France.

TAKING NOTES

Following Chronological Order On a time line, note the events that led to Napoleon's crowning as emperor of France.

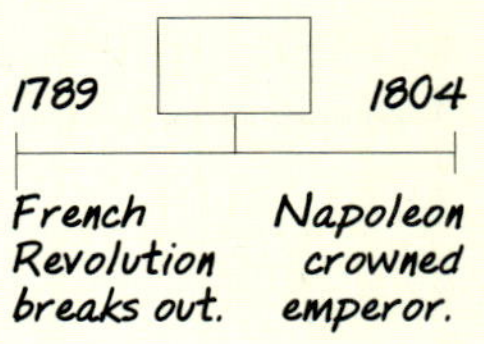

Napoleon Seizes Power

Napoleon Bonaparte was born in 1769 on the Mediterranean island of Corsica. When he was nine years old, his parents sent him to a military school. In 1785, at the age of 16, he finished school and became a lieutenant in the artillery. When the Revolution broke out, Napoleon joined the army of the new government.

Hero of the Hour In October 1795, fate handed the young officer a chance for glory. When royalist rebels marched on the National Convention, a government official told Napoleon to defend the delegates. Napoleon and his gunners greeted the thousands of royalists with a cannonade. Within minutes, the attackers fled in panic and confusion. Napoleon Bonaparte became the hero of the hour and was hailed throughout Paris as the savior of the French republic.

In 1796, the Directory appointed Napoleon to lead a French army against the forces of Austria and the Kingdom of Sardinia. Crossing the Alps, the young general swept into Italy and won a series of remarkable victories. Next, in an attempt to protect French trade interests and to disrupt British trade with India, Napoleon led an expedition to Egypt. But he was unable to repeat the successes he had achieved in Europe. His army was pinned down in Egypt, and the British admiral Horatio Nelson defeated his naval forces. However, Napoleon managed to keep stories about his setbacks out of the newspapers and thereby remained a great hero to the people of France.

Coup d'État By 1799, the Directory had lost control of the political situation and the confidence of the French people. When Napoleon returned from Egypt, his friends urged him to seize political power. Napoleon took action in early November 1799. Troops under his command surrounded the national legislature and drove out most of its members. The lawmakers who remained then voted to

History Makers

Napoleon Bonaparte
1769–1821

Because of his small stature and thick Corsican accent, Napoleon was mocked by his fellow students at military school. Haughty and proud, Napoleon refused to grace his tormentors' behavior with any kind of response. He simply ignored them, preferring to lose himself in his studies. He showed a particular passion for three subjects—classical history, geography, and mathematics.

In 1784, Napoleon was recommended for a career in the army and he transferred to the Ecole Militaire (the French equivalent of West Point) in Paris. There, he proved to be a fairly poor soldier, except when it came to artillery. His artillery instructor quickly noticed Napoleon's abilities: "He is most proud, ambitious, aspiring to everything. This young man merits our attention."

dissolve the Directory. In its place, they established a group of three consuls, one of whom was Napoleon. Napoleon quickly took the title of first consul and assumed the powers of a dictator. A sudden seizure of power like Napoleon's is known as a *coup*—from the French phrase **coup d'état** (KOO day•TAH), or "blow to the state." (A)

MAIN IDEA

Analyzing Causes

(A) How was Napoleon able to become a dictator?

At the time of Napoleon's coup, France was still at war. In 1799, Britain, Austria, and Russia joined forces with one goal in mind, to drive Napoleon from power. Once again, Napoleon rode from Paris at the head of his troops. Eventually, as a result of war and diplomacy, all three nations signed peace agreements with France. By 1802, Europe was at peace for the first time in ten years. Napoleon was free to focus his energies on restoring order in France.

Napoleon Rules France

At first, Napoleon pretended to be the constitutionally chosen leader of a free republic. In 1800, a **plebiscite** (PLEHB•ih•SYT), or vote of the people, was held to approve a new constitution. Desperate for strong leadership, the people voted overwhelmingly in favor of the constitution. This gave all real power to Napoleon as first consul.

Restoring Order at Home Napoleon did not try to return the nation to the days of Louis XVI. Rather, he kept many of the changes that had come with the Revolution. In general, he supported laws that would both strengthen the central government and achieve some of the goals of the Revolution.

His first task was to get the economy on a solid footing. Napoleon set up an efficient method of tax collection and established a national banking system. In addition to ensuring the government a steady supply of tax money, these actions promoted sound financial management and better control of the economy. Napoleon also took steps to end corruption and inefficiency in government. He dismissed corrupt officials and, in order to provide the government with trained officials, set up **lycées**, or government-run public schools. These lycées were open to male students of all backgrounds. Graduates were appointed to public office on the basis of merit rather than family connections.

One area where Napoleon disregarded changes introduced by the Revolution was religion. Both the clergy and many peasants wanted to restore the position of the Church in France. Responding to their wishes, Napoleon signed a **concordat**, or agreement, with Pope Pius VII. This established a new relationship between church and state. The government recognized the influence of the Church, but rejected Church control in national affairs. The concordat gained Napoleon the support of the organized Church as well as the majority of the French people.

Napoleon thought that his greatest work was his comprehensive system of laws, known as the **Napoleonic Code**. This gave the country a uniform set of laws and eliminated many injustices. However, it actually limited liberty and promoted order and authority over individual rights. For example, freedom of speech and of the press, established during the Revolution, were restricted under the code. The code also restored slavery in the French colonies of the Caribbean.

Napoleon Crowned as Emperor In 1804, Napoleon decided to make himself emperor, and the French voters supported him. On December 2, 1804, dressed in a splendid robe of purple velvet, Napoleon walked down the long aisle of Notre Dame Cathedral in Paris. The pope waited for him with a glittering crown. As thousands watched, the new emperor took the crown from the pope and placed it on his own head. With this gesture, Napoleon signaled that he was more powerful than the Church, which had traditionally crowned the rulers of France. **B**

MAIN IDEA
Analyzing Motives
B Why do you think Napoleon crowned himself emperor?

Napoleon Creates an Empire

Napoleon was not content simply to be master of France. He wanted to control the rest of Europe and to reassert French power in the Americas. He envisioned his western empire including Louisiana, Florida, French Guiana, and the French West Indies. He knew that the key to this area was the sugar-producing colony of Saint Domingue (now called Haiti) on the island of Hispaniola.

Loss of American Territories In 1789, when the ideas of the Revolution reached the planters in Saint Domingue, they demanded that the National Assembly give them the same privileges as the people of France. Eventually, enslaved Africans in the colony demanded their rights too—in other words, their freedom. A civil war erupted, and enslaved Africans under the leadership of Toussaint L'Ouverture seized control of the colony. In 1801, Napoleon decided to take back the colony and restore its productive sugar industry. However, the French forces were devastated by disease. And the rebels proved to be fierce fighters.

After the failure of the expedition to Saint Domingue, Napoleon decided to cut his losses in the Americas. He offered to sell all of the Louisiana Territory to the United States, and in 1803 President Jefferson's administration agreed to purchase the land for $15 million. Napoleon saw a twofold benefit to the sale. First, he would gain money to finance operations in Europe. Second, he would punish the British. "The sale assures forever the power of the United States," he observed, "and I have given England a rival who, sooner or later, will humble her pride." **C**

MAIN IDEA
Recognizing Effects
C What effects did Napoleon intend the sale of Louisiana to have on France? on the United States? on Britain?

Conquering Europe Having abandoned his imperial ambitions in the New World, Napoleon turned his attention to Europe. He had already annexed the Austrian Netherlands and parts of Italy to France and set up a puppet government in Switzerland. Now he looked to expand his influence further. Fearful of his ambitions, the British persuaded Russia, Austria, and Sweden to join them against France.

Napoleon met this challenge with his usual boldness. In a series of brilliant battles, he crushed the opposition. (See the map on page 666.) The commanders of the enemy armies could never predict his next move and often took heavy losses. After the Battle of Austerlitz in 1805, Napoleon issued a proclamation expressing his pride in his troops:

▼ This painting by Jacques Louis David shows Napoleon in a heroic pose.

PRIMARY SOURCE

Soldiers! I am pleased with you. On the day of Austerlitz, you justified everything that I was expecting of [you]. . . . In less than four hours, an army of 100,000 men, commanded by the emperors of Russia and Austria, was cut up and dispersed. . . . 120 pieces of artillery, 20 generals, and more than 30,000 men taken prisoner—such are the results of this day which will forever be famous. . . . And it will be enough for you to say, "I was at Austerlitz," to hear the reply: "There is a brave man!"

NAPOLEON, quoted in *Napoleon* by André Castelot

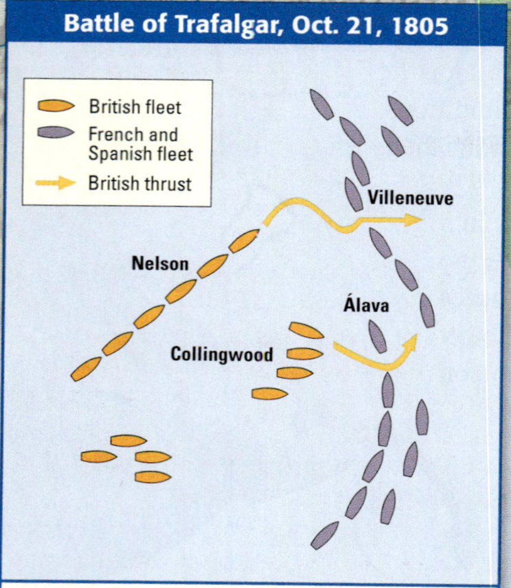

By dividing Villeneuve's formation, Admiral Nelson captured nearly two-thirds of the enemy fleet.

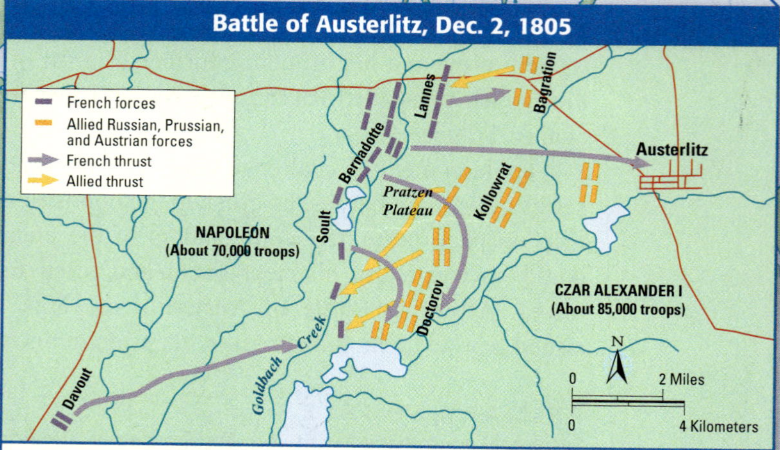

By drawing an Allied attack on his right flank, Napoleon was able to split the Allied line at its center.

GEOGRAPHY SKILLBUILDER: Interpreting Maps

1. **Region** *What was the extent of the lands under Napoleon's control?*
2. **Location** *Where was the Battle of Trafalgar fought? What tactic did Nelson use in the battle, and why was it successful?*

In time, Napoleon's battlefield successes forced the rulers of Austria, Prussia, and Russia to sign peace treaties. These successes also enabled him to build the largest European empire since that of the Romans. France's only major enemy left undefeated was the great naval power, Britain.

The Battle of Trafalgar In his drive for a European empire, Napoleon lost only one major battle, the **Battle of Trafalgar** (truh•FAL•guhr). This naval defeat, however, was more important than all of his victories on land. The battle took place in 1805 off the southwest coast of Spain. The British commander, Horatio Nelson, was as brilliant in warfare at sea as Napoleon was in warfare on land. In a bold maneuver, he split the larger French fleet, capturing many ships. (See the map inset on the opposite page.)

The destruction of the French fleet had two major results. First, it ensured the supremacy of the British navy for the next 100 years. Second, it forced Napoleon to give up his plans of invading Britain. He had to look for another way to control his powerful enemy across the English Channel. Eventually, Napoleon's extravagant efforts to crush Britain would lead to his own undoing.

The French Empire During the first decade of the 1800s, Napoleon's victories had given him mastery over most of Europe. By 1812, the only areas of Europe free from Napoleon's control were Britain, Portugal, Sweden, and the Ottoman Empire. In addition to the lands of the French Empire, Napoleon also controlled numerous supposedly independent countries. (See the map on the opposite page.) These included Spain, the Grand Duchy of Warsaw, and a number of German kingdoms in Central Europe. The rulers of these countries were Napoleon's puppets; some, in fact, were members of his family. Furthermore, the powerful countries of Russia, Prussia, and Austria were loosely attached to Napoleon's empire through alliances. Although not totally under Napoleon's control, they were easily manipulated by threats of military action. **D**

MAIN IDEA

Drawing Conclusions-

D By 1805, how successful had Napoleon been in his efforts to build an empire?

The French Empire was huge but unstable. Napoleon was able to maintain it at its greatest extent for only five years—from 1807 to 1812. Then it quickly fell to pieces. Its sudden collapse was caused in part by Napoleon's actions.

NEW YORK CORE CURRICULUM REVIEW

TERMS & NAMES 1. For each term or name, write a sentence explaining its significance.

- Napoleon Bonaparte
- coup d'état
- plebiscite
- lycée
- concordat
- Napoleonic Code
- Battle of Trafalgar

USING YOUR NOTES

2. Which of these events do you think had the greatest impact on Napoleon's rise to power?

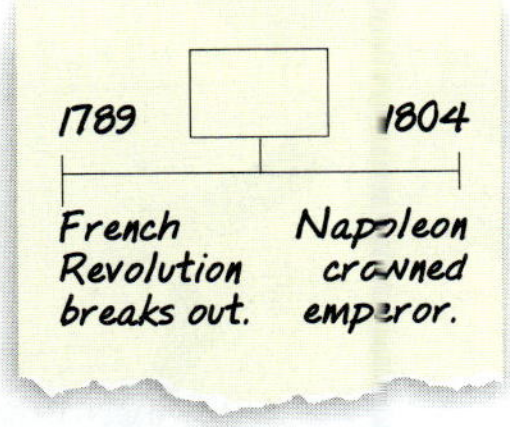

MAIN IDEAS

3. How did Napoleon become a hero in France?
4. What did Napoleon consider his greatest triumph in domestic policy?
5. How was Napoleon able to control the countries neighboring the French Empire?

CRITICAL THINKING & WRITING

6. **FORMING OPINIONS** In your opinion, was Napoleon the creator or the creation of his times?
7. **ANALYZING ISSUES** Napoleon had to deal with forces both inside and outside the French Empire. In your judgment, which area was more important to control?
8. **MAKING INFERENCES** If you had been a member of the bourgeoisie, would you have been satisfied with the results of Napoleon's actions? Explain.
9. **WRITING ACTIVITY** POWER AND AUTHORITY Look at the painting on page 665. Write a **paragraph** discussing why the painter portrayed Napoleon in this fashion.

CONNECT TO TODAY **CREATING A VENN DIAGRAM**

Identify and conduct research on a present-day world leader who has used dictatorial powers to rule his or her country. Use your findings to create a **Venn diagram** comparing this leader's use of power to Napoleon's use of power.

4

Napoleon's Empire Collapses

CONNECT TO THE NEW YORK STATE CORE CURRICULUM

Unit 5.C.3.d. Rise to power of Napoleon and his impact (Napoleonic Code)
Unit 5.D.4.a. Impact of the French Revolution and Napoleon

TERMS & NAMES

- blockade
- Continental System
- guerrilla
- Peninsular War
- scorched-earth policy
- Waterloo
- Hundred Days

SETTING THE STAGE Napoleon worried about what would happen to his vast empire after his death. He feared it would fall apart unless he had an heir whose right to succeed him was undisputed. His wife, Josephine, had failed to bear him a child. He, therefore, divorced her and formed an alliance with the Austrian royal family by marrying Marie Louise, the grandniece of Marie Antoinette. In 1811, Marie Louise gave birth to a son, Napoleon II, whom Napoleon named king of Rome.

TAKING NOTES
Recognizing Effects Use a chart to identify Napoleon's three mistakes and the impact they had on the French Empire.

Napoleon's Mistakes	Effect on Empire

Napoleon's Costly Mistakes

Napoleon's own personality proved to be the greatest danger to the future of his empire. His desire for power had raised him to great heights, and the same love of power led him to his doom. In his efforts to extend the French Empire and crush Great Britain, Napoleon made three disastrous mistakes.

The Continental System In November 1806, Napoleon set up a **blockade**—a forcible closing of ports—to prevent all trade and communication between Great Britain and other European nations. Napoleon called this policy the **Continental System** because it was supposed to make continental Europe more self-sufficient. Napoleon also intended it to destroy Great Britain's commercial and industrial economy.

Napoleon's blockade, however, was not nearly tight enough. Aided by the British, smugglers managed to bring cargo from Britain into Europe. At times, Napoleon's allies also disregarded the blockade. Even members of Napoleon's family defied the policy, including his brother, Louis, whom he had made king of Holland. While the blockade weakened British trade, it did not destroy it. In addition, Britain responded with its own blockade. And because the British had a stronger navy, they were better able than the French to make the blockade work.

To enforce the blockade, the British navy stopped neutral ships bound for the continent and forced them to sail to a British port to be searched and taxed. American ships were among those stopped by the British navy. Angered, the U.S.

▼ "Little Johnny Bull"—Great Britain—waves a sword at Napoleon as the emperor straddles the globe.

Congress declared war on Britain in 1812. Even though the War of 1812 lasted two years, it was only a minor inconvenience to Britain in its struggle with Napoleon.

The Peninsular War In 1808, Napoleon made a second costly mistake. In an effort to get Portugal to accept the Continental System, he sent an invasion force through Spain. The Spanish people protested this action. In response, Napoleon removed the Spanish king and put his own brother, Joseph, on the throne. This outraged the Spanish people and inflamed their nationalistic feelings. The Spanish, who were devoutly Catholic, also worried that Napoleon would attack the Church. They had seen how the French Revolution had weakened the Catholic Church in France, and they feared that the same thing would happen to the Church in Spain.

For six years, bands of Spanish peasant fighters, known as **guerrillas**, struck at French armies in Spain. The guerrillas were not an army that Napoleon could defeat in open battle. Rather, they worked in small groups that ambushed French troops and then fled into hiding. The British added to the French troubles by sending troops to aid the Spanish. Napoleon lost about 300,000 men during this **Peninsular War**—so called because Spain lies on the Iberian Peninsula. These losses weakened the French Empire.

In Spain and elsewhere, nationalism, or loyalty to one's own country, was becoming a powerful weapon against Napoleon. People who had at first welcomed the French as their liberators now felt abused by a foreign conqueror. Like the Spanish guerrillas, Germans and Italians and other conquered peoples turned against the French. (A)

MAIN IDEA

Recognizing Effects

(A) How could the growing feelings of nationalism in European countries hurt Napoleon?

The Invasion of Russia Napoleon's most disastrous mistake of all came in 1812. Even though Alexander I had become Napoleon's ally, the Russian czar refused to stop selling grain to Britain. In addition, the French and Russian rulers suspected each other of having competing designs on Poland. Because of this breakdown in their alliance, Napoleon decided to invade Russia.

In June 1812, Napoleon and his Grand Army of more than 420,000 soldiers marched into Russia. As Napoleon advanced, Alexander pulled back his troops, refusing to be lured into an unequal battle. On this retreat, the Russians practiced a **scorched-earth policy**. This involved burning grain fields and slaughtering livestock so as to leave nothing for the enemy to eat.

▼ Francisco Goya's painting *The Third of May, 1808* shows a French firing squad executing Spanish peasants suspected of being guerrillas.

GEOGRAPHY SKILLBUILDER: Interpreting Maps

1. **Movement** *How long did it take the Grand Army to cover the distance between the Russian border and Moscow?*
2. **Place** *Why was it a mistake for Napoleon to stay in Moscow until mid-October?*

On September 7, 1812, the two armies finally clashed in the Battle of Borodino. (See the map on this page.) After several hours of indecisive fighting, the Russians fell back, allowing Napoleon to move on Moscow. When Napoleon entered Moscow seven days later, the city was in flames. Rather than surrender Russia's "holy city" to the French, Alexander had destroyed it. Napoleon stayed in the ruined city until the middle of October, when he decided to turn back toward France.

As the snows—and the temperature—began to fall in early November, Russian raiders mercilessly attacked Napoleon's ragged, retreating army. Many soldiers were killed in these clashes or died of their wounds. Still more dropped in their tracks from exhaustion, hunger, and cold. Finally, in the middle of December, the last survivors straggled out of Russia. The retreat from Moscow had devastated the Grand Army—only 10,000 soldiers were left to fight.

Napoleon's Downfall

Napoleon's enemies were quick to take advantage of his weakness. Britain, Russia, Prussia, and Sweden joined forces against him. Austria also declared war on Napoleon, despite his marriage to Marie Louise. All of the main powers of Europe were now at war with France.

Napoleon Suffers Defeat In only a few months, Napoleon managed to raise another army. However, most of his troops were untrained and ill prepared for battle. He faced the allied armies of the European powers outside the German city of Leipzig (LYP•sihg) in October 1813. The allied forces easily defeated his inexperienced army and French resistance crumbled quickly. By January of 1814, the allied armies were pushing steadily toward Paris. Some two months later, King

Frederick William III of Prussia and Czar Alexander I of Russia led their troops in a triumphant parade through the French capital.

Napoleon wanted to fight on, but his generals refused. In April 1814, he accepted the terms of surrender and gave up his throne. The victors gave Napoleon a small pension and exiled, or banished, him to Elba, a tiny island off the Italian coast. The allies expected no further trouble from Napoleon, but they were wrong.

The Hundred Days Louis XVI's brother assumed the throne as Louis XVIII. (The executed king's son, Louis XVII, had died in prison in 1795.) However, the new king quickly became unpopular among his subjects, especially the peasants. They suspected him of wanting to undo the Revolution's land reforms.

The news of Louis's troubles was all the incentive Napoleon needed to try to regain power. He escaped from Elba and, on March 1, 1815, landed in France. Joyous crowds welcomed him on the march to Paris. And thousands of volunteers swelled the ranks of his army. Within days, Napoleon was again emperor of France. (B)

MAIN IDEA

Analyzing Motives

(B) Why do you think the French people welcomed back Napoleon so eagerly?

In response, the European allies quickly marshaled their armies. The British army, led by the Duke of Wellington, prepared for battle near the village of **Waterloo** in Belgium. On June 18, 1815, Napoleon attacked. The British army defended its ground all day. Late in the afternoon, the Prussian army arrived. Together, the British and the Prussian forces attacked the French. Two days later, Napoleon's exhausted troops gave way, and the British and Prussian forces chased them from the field.

▲ British soldiers who fought at the battle of Waterloo received this medal.

This defeat ended Napoleon's last bid for power, called the **Hundred Days**. Taking no chances this time, the British shipped Napoleon to St. Helena, a remote island in the South Atlantic. There, he lived in lonely exile for six years, writing his memoirs. He died in 1821 of a stomach ailment, perhaps cancer.

Without doubt, Napoleon was a military genius and a brilliant administrator. Yet all his victories and other achievements must be measured against the millions of lives that were lost in his wars. The French writer Alexis de Tocqueville summed up Napoleon's character by saying, "He was as great as a man can be without virtue." Napoleon's defeat opened the door for the freed European countries to establish a new order.

NEW YORK CORE CURRICULUM REVIEW

TERMS & NAMES 1. For each term or name, write a sentence explaining its significance.

- blockade
- Continental System
- guerrilla
- Peninsular War
- scorched-earth policy
- Waterloo
- Hundred Days

USING YOUR NOTES

2. Which of Napoleon's mistakes was the most serious? Why?

Napoleon's Mistakes	Effect on Empire

MAIN IDEAS

3. How did Great Britain combat Napoleon's naval blockade?
4. Why did Napoleon have trouble fighting the enemy forces in the Peninsular War?
5. Why was Napoleon's delay of the retreat from Moscow such a great blunder?

CRITICAL THINKING & WRITING

6. **ANALYZING MOTIVES** Why did people in other European countries resist Napoleon's efforts to build an empire?
7. **EVALUATING COURSES OF ACTION** Napoleon had no choice but to invade Russia. Do you agree with this statement? Why or why not?
8. **FORMING AND SUPPORTING OPINIONS** Do you think that Napoleon was a great leader? Explain.
9. **WRITING ACTIVITY** POWER AND AUTHORITY In the role of a volunteer in Napoleon's army during the Hundred Days, write a **letter** to a friend explaining why you are willing to fight for the emperor.

CONNECT TO TODAY **CREATING A MAP**

Conduct research on how nationalist feelings affect world affairs today. Create a **map** showing the areas of the world where nationalist movements are active. Annotate the map with explanations of the situation in each area.

The Congress of Vienna

CONNECT TO THE NEW YORK STATE CORE CURRICULUM

Unit 5.D.1. Human and physical geography
Unit 5.D.2. Balance of power politics and the Congress of Vienna (Klemens von Metternich)

TERMS & NAMES

- Congress of Vienna
- Klemens von Metternich
- balance of power
- legitimacy
- Holy Alliance
- Concert of Europe

SETTING THE STAGE European heads of government were looking to establish long-lasting peace and stability on the continent after the defeat of Napoleon. They had a goal of the new European order—one of collective security and stability for the entire continent. A series of meetings in Vienna, known as the **Congress of Vienna**, were called to set up policies to achieve this goal. Originally, the Congress of Vienna was scheduled to last for four weeks. Instead, it went on for eight months.

TAKING NOTES

Recognizing Effects Use a chart to show how the three goals of Metternich's plan at the Congress of Vienna solved a political problem.

Metternich's Plan	
Problem	Solution

Metternich's Plan for Europe

Most of the decisions made in Vienna during the winter of 1814–1815 were made in secret among representatives of the five "great powers"—Russia, Prussia, Austria, Great Britain, and France. By far the most influential of these representatives was the foreign minister of Austria, Prince **Klemens von Metternich** (MEHT•uhr•nihk).

Metternich distrusted the democratic ideals of the French Revolution. Like most other European aristocrats, he felt that Napoleon's behavior had been a natural outcome of experiments with democracy. Metternich wanted to keep things as they were and remarked, "The first and greatest concern for the immense majority of every nation is the stability of laws—never their change." Metternich had three goals at the Congress of Vienna. First, he wanted to prevent future French aggression by surrounding France with strong countries. Second, he wanted to restore a **balance of power**, so that no country would be a threat to others. Third, he wanted to restore Europe's royal families to the thrones they had held before Napoleon's conquests.

The Containment of France The Congress took the following steps to make the weak countries around France stronger:

- The former Austrian Netherlands and Dutch Republic were united to form the Kingdom of the Netherlands.
- A group of 39 German states were loosely joined as the newly created German Confederation, dominated by Austria.
- Switzerland was recognized as an independent nation.
- The Kingdom of Sardinia in Italy was strengthened by the addition of Genoa.

▲ Delegates at the Congress of Vienna study a map of Europe.

These changes enabled the countries of Europe to contain France and prevent it from overpowering weaker nations. (See the map on page 674.)

Balance of Power Although the leaders of Europe wanted to weaken France, they did not want to leave it powerless. If they severely punished France, they might encourage the French to take revenge. If they broke up France, then another country might become so strong that it would threaten them all. Thus, the victorious powers did not exact a great price from the defeated nation. As a result, France remained a major but diminished European power. Also, no country in Europe could easily overpower another.

Legitimacy The great powers affirmed the principle of **legitimacy**—agreeing that as many as possible of the rulers whom Napoleon had driven from their thrones be restored to power. The ruling families of France, Spain, and several states in Italy and Central Europe regained their thrones. The participants in the Congress of Vienna believed that the return of the former monarchs would stabilize political relations among the nations.

The Congress of Vienna was a political triumph in many ways. For the first time, the nations of an entire continent had cooperated to control political affairs. The settlements they agreed upon were fair enough that no country was left bearing a grudge. Therefore, the Congress did not sow the seeds of future wars. In that sense, it was more successful than many other peace meetings in history.

MAIN IDEA

Drawing Conclusions

(A) In what ways was the Congress of Vienna a success?

By agreeing to come to one another's aid in case of threats to peace, the European nations had temporarily ensured that there would be a balance of power on the continent. The Congress of Vienna, then, created a time of peace in Europe. It was a lasting peace. None of the five great powers waged war on one another for nearly 40 years, when Britain and France fought Russia in the Crimean War. (A)

Political Changes Beyond Vienna

The Congress of Vienna was a victory for conservatives. Kings and princes resumed power in country after country, in keeping with Metternich's goals. Nevertheless, there were important differences from one country to another. Britain and France now had constitutional monarchies. Generally speaking, however, the governments in Eastern and Central Europe were more conservative. The rulers of Russia, Prussia, and Austria were absolute monarchs.

GEOGRAPHY SKILLBUILDER: Interpreting Maps

1. **Region** *What parts of Napoleon's French Empire did France lose as a result of the Congress of Vienna?*
2. **Region** *In what sense did the territorial changes of 1815 reflect a restoration of order and balance?*

Conservative Europe The rulers of Europe were very nervous about the legacy of the French Revolution. They worried that the ideals of liberty, equality, and fraternity might encourage revolutions elsewhere. Late in 1815, Czar Alexander I, Emperor Francis I of Austria, and King Frederick William III of Prussia signed an agreement called the **Holy Alliance**. In it, they pledged to base their relations with other nations on Christian principles in order to combat the forces of revolution. Finally, a series of alliances devised by Metternich, called the **Concert of Europe**, ensured that nations would help one another if any revolutions broke out.

Across Europe, conservatives held firm control of the governments, but they could not contain the ideas that had emerged during the French Revolution. France after 1815 was deeply divided politically. Conservatives were happy with the monarchy of Louis XVIII and were determined to make it last. Liberals, however, wanted the king to share more power with the legislature. And many people in the lower classes remained committed to the ideals of liberty, equality, and fraternity. Similarly, in other countries there was an explosive mixture of ideas and factions that would contribute directly to revolutions in 1830 and 1848. **B**

> **MAIN IDEA**
> **Making Inferences**
> **B** What seeds of democracy had been sown by the French Revolution?

Despite their efforts to undo the French Revolution, the leaders at the Congress of Vienna could not turn back the clock. The Revolution had given Europe its first experiment in democratic government. Although the experiment had failed, it had set new political ideas in motion. The major political upheavals of the early 1800s had their roots in the French Revolution.

Revolution in Latin America The actions of the Congress of Vienna had consequences far beyond events in Europe. When Napoleon deposed the king of Spain during the Peninsular War, liberal Creoles (colonists born in Spanish America) seized control of many colonies in the Americas. When the Congress of Vienna restored the king to the Spanish throne, royalist *peninsulares* (colonists born in Spain) tried to regain control of these colonial governments. The Creoles, however, attempted to retain and expand their power. In response, the Spanish king took steps to tighten control over the American colonies.

This action angered the Mexicans, who rose in revolt and successfully threw off Spain's control. Other Spanish colonies in Latin America also claimed independence. At about the same time, Brazil declared independence from Portugal. (See Chapter 24.)

Long-Term Legacy The Congress of Vienna left a legacy that would influence world politics for the next 100 years. The continent-wide efforts to establish and maintain a balance of power diminished the size and the power of France. At the same time, the power of Britain and Prussia increased.

Nationalism began to spread in Italy, Germany, Greece, and to other areas that the Congress had put under foreign control. Eventually, the nationalistic feelings would explode into revolutions, and new nations would be formed. European colonies also responded to the power shift. Spanish colonies took advantage of the events in Europe to declare their independence and break away from Spain.

At the same time, ideas about the basis of power and authority had changed permanently as a result of the French Revolution. More and more, people saw democracy as the best way to ensure equality and justice for all. The French Revolution, then, changed the social attitudes and assumptions that had dominated Europe for centuries. A new era had begun. C

MAIN IDEA

Recognizing Effects

C How did the French Revolution affect not only Europe but also other areas of the world?

Connect *to* Today

Congress of Vienna and the United Nations

The Congress of Vienna and the Concert of Europe tried to keep the world safe from war. The modern equivalent of these agreements is the United Nations (UN), an international organization established in 1945 and continuing today, whose purpose is to promote world peace.

Like the Congress of Vienna, the United Nations was formed by major powers after a war—World War II. These powers agreed to cooperate to reduce tensions and bring greater harmony to international relations. Throughout its history, the United Nations has used diplomacy as its chief method of keeping the peace.

INTEGRATED TECHNOLOGY

INTERNET ACTIVITY Create a graphic organizer to show the major agencies and functions of the United Nations. Go to **classzone.com** for your research.

NEW YORK CORE CURRICULUM REVIEW

TERMS & NAMES 1. For each term or name, write a sentence explaining its significance.

- Congress of Vienna
- Klemens von Metternich
- balance of power
- legitimacy
- Holy Alliance
- Concert of Europe

USING YOUR NOTES

2. What was the overall effect of Metternich's plan on France?

Metternich's Plan	
Problem	Solution

MAIN IDEAS

3. What were the three points of Metternich's plan for Europe?
4. Why was the Congress of Vienna considered a success?
5. What was the long-term legacy of the Congress of Vienna?

CRITICAL THINKING & WRITING

6. **DRAWING CONCLUSIONS** From France's point of view, do you think the Congress of Vienna's decisions were fair?
7. **ANALYZING ISSUES** Why did liberals and conservatives differ over who should have power?
8. **MAKING INFERENCES** What do you think is meant by the statement that the French Revolution let the "genie out of the bottle"?
9. **WRITING ACTIVITY** -In the role of a newspaper editor in the early 1800s, write an **editorial**—pro or con—on the Congress of Vienna and its impact on politics in Europe.

CONNECT TO TODAY **CREATING A SCRAPBOOK**

Work in pairs to locate recent articles in newspapers and magazines on the peacekeeping efforts of the UN. Photocopy or clip the articles and use them to create a **scrapbook** titled "The UN as Peacekeeper."

Chapter 23 Assessment

VISUAL SUMMARY

The French Revolution and Napoleon

Long-Term Causes

- Social and economic injustices of the Old Regime
- Enlightenment ideas—liberty and equality
- Example furnished by the American Revolution

Immediate Causes

- Economic crisis—famine and government debt
- Weak leadership
- Discontent of the Third Estate

Revolution

- Fall of the Bastille
- National Assembly
- Declaration of the Rights of Man and of the Citizen and a new constitution

Immediate Effects

- End of the Old Regime
- Execution of monarch
- War with other European nations
- Reign of Terror
- Rise of Napoleon

Long-Term Effects

- Conservative reaction
- Decline in French power
- Spread of Enlightenment ideas
- Growth of nationalism
- Revolutions in Latin America

TERMS & NAMES

For each term or name below, briefly explain its connection to the French Revolution or the rise and fall of Napoleon.

1. estate
2. Great Fear
3. guillotine
4. Maximilien Robespierre
5. coup d'état
6. Napoleonic Code
7. Waterloo
8. Congress of Vienna

MAIN IDEAS

The French Revolution Begins Section 1 (pages 651–655)

9. Why were the members of the Third Estate dissatisfied with their way of life under the Old Regime?

10. Why was the fall of the Bastille important to the French people?

Revolution Brings Reform and Terror Section 2 (pages 656–662)

11. What political reforms resulted from the French Revolution?

12. What was the Reign of Terror, and how did it end?

Napoleon Forges an Empire Section 3 (pages 663–667)

13. What reforms did Napoleon introduce?

14. What steps did Napoleon take to create an empire in Europe?

Napoleon's Empire Collapses Section 4 (pages 668–671)

15. What factors led to Napoleon's defeat in Russia?

16. Why were the European allies able to defeat Napoleon in 1814 and again in 1815?

The Congress of Vienna Section 5 (pages 672–675)

17. What were Metternich's three goals at the Congress of Vienna?

18. How did the Congress of Vienna ensure peace in Europe?

CRITICAL THINKING

1. USING YOUR NOTES
Copy the chart of dates and events in Napoleon's career into your notebook. For each event, draw an arrow up or down to show whether Napoleon gained or lost power because of the event.

Defense of National Convention	Coup	Emperor	Winning battles	Trafalgar	Large empire	Russia	Elba	Waterloo
1795	1799	1804	1805	1805	1810	1812	1814	1815

2. COMPARING AND CONTRASTING
ECONOMICS How were the economic conditions in France and the American colonies before their revolutions similar? How were they different?

3. ANALYZING ISSUES
REVOLUTION There is a saying: "Revolutions devour their own children." What evidence from this chapter supports that statement?

4. RECOGNIZING EFFECTS
POWER AND AUTHORITY How did the Congress of Vienna affect power and authority in European countries after Napoleon's defeat? Consider who held power in the countries and the power of the countries themselves.

NEW YORK STATE REGENTS EXAM PRACTICE

Use the excerpt—from the South American liberator Simón Bolívar, whose country considered giving refuge to Napoleon after Waterloo—and your knowledge of world history to answer questions 1 and 2.
Additional Test Practice, pp. S1–S33

PRIMARY SOURCE

If South America is struck by the thunderbolt of Bonaparte's arrival, misfortune will ever be ours if our country accords him a friendly reception. His thirst for conquest is insatiable [cannot be satisfied]; he has mowed down the flower of European youth . . . in order to carry out his ambitious projects. The same designs will bring him to the New World.

SIMÓN BOLÍVAR

1 In Bolívar's opinion, if his country gave Napoleon a friendly reception it would
(1) be beset by misfortune
(2) become a great power in South America
(3) become a part of the French Empire
(4) be attacked by the United States

2 Which of the following gives Bolívar's view of Napoleon?
(1) His desire for power cannot be satisfied.
(2) He is not ambitious.
(3) He cares for the lives of others.
(4) He does not want to come to the New World.

Use the map, which shows Great Britain and the French Empire in 1810, and your knowledge of world history to answer question 3.

3 What geographical barrier helped to protect Britain from an invasion by Napoleon?
(1) Mediterranean Sea
(2) English Channel
(3) Alps
(4) Pyrenees

INTEGRATED TECHNOLOGY
TEST PRACTICE Go to **classzone.com**
- Diagnostic tests
- Tutorials
- Strategies
- Additional practice

ALTERNATIVE ASSESSMENT

1. Interact *with* History

On page 650, you considered how to bring about change in the French government in the late 1700s. Now that you have read the chapter, reevaluate your thoughts on how to change an unjust government. Was violent revolution justified? effective? Would you have advised different actions? Discuss your opinions with a small group.

2. WRITING ABOUT HISTORY

Imagine that you lived in Paris throughout the French Revolution. Write **journal entries** on several of the major events of the Revolution. Include the following events:

- the storming of the Bastille
- the women's march on Versailles
- the trial of Louis XVI
- the Reign of Terror
- the rise of Napoleon

INTEGRATED TECHNOLOGY

NetExplorations: The French Revolution

Go to *NetExplorations* at **classzone.com** to learn more about the French Revolution. Then plan a virtual field trip to sites in France related to the revolution. Be sure to include sites outside Paris. Begin your research by exploring the Web sites recommended at *NetExplorations*. Include the following in your field trip plan:

- a one-paragraph description of each site and the events that happened there
- specific buildings, statues, or other items to view at each site
- documents and other readings to help visitors prepare for each stop on the field trip
- topics to discuss at each site
- a list of Web sites used to create your virtual field trip

CHAPTER 24

Nationalist Revolutions Sweep the West, 1789–1900

Previewing Main Ideas

REVOLUTION Inspired by Enlightenment ideas, the people of Latin America rebelled against European rule in the early 19th century. Rebels in Europe responded to nationalistic calls for independence.

Geography *Study the time line. What were the first two countries in Latin America and the Caribbean to work toward independence?*

POWER AND AUTHORITY Challenges by nationalist groups created unrest in Europe. Strong leaders united Italian lands and German-speaking lands.

Geography *Based on the map, in which area of Europe did the greatest number of revolts occur?*

CULTURAL INTERACTION Artists and intellectuals created new schools of thought. Romanticism and realism changed the way the world was viewed.

Geography *Which event shown on the time line involves a realistic way to view the world?*

NEW YORK CORE CURRICULUM FOCUS

- Nationalism emerged in Europe as political groups struggle for power.
- Nationalism led to the formation of Germany and Italy and shook old empires like Russia.

INTEGRATED TECHNOLOGY

eEdition
- Interactive Maps
- Interactive Visuals
- Interactive Primary Sources

VIDEO *Patterns of Interaction: Revolutions in Latin America and South Africa*

INTERNET RESOURCES

Go to **classzone.com** for:
- Research Links
- Internet Activities
- Primary Sources
- Chapter Quiz
- Maps
- Test Practice
- Current Events

LATIN AMERICA AND EUROPE

1804 Haiti wins freedom from France.

1810 Padre Hidalgo calls for Mexican independence. ▶

1837 Louis Daguerre perfects a method for photography.

1800 **1825**

WORLD

1804 Napoleon crowned Emperor. ▶

1815 Napoleon defeated and exiled.

1848
Revolts shake Europe.

1861
Russia frees serfs.

1870
Italy unites.

1871
Wilhelm I crowned Kaiser of united Germany. ▶

1850 **1875** **1900**

1863
◀ Lincoln's Emancipation Proclamation frees enslaved persons in Confederate states.

1869
Suez Canal completed.

1884–1885
Berlin Conference divides Africa among European nations.

Interact *with* History

What symbolizes your country's values?

You are an artist in a nation that has just freed itself from foreign rule. The new government is asking you to design a symbol that will show what your country stands for. It's up to you to design the symbol that best suits the spirit and values of your people. Look at the symbols below. Will your symbol be peaceful or warlike, dignified or joyful? Or will it be a combination of these and other qualities?

Botswana
Industry and livestock are connected by water, the key to the country's prosperity. *Pula* in the Setswana language means "rain." But to a Setswana speaker, it is also a common greeting meaning luck, life, and prosperity.

Austria
The eagle was the symbol of the old Austrian Empire. The shield goes back to medieval times. The hammer and sickle symbolize agriculture and industry. The broken chains celebrate Austria's liberation from Germany at the end of World War II.

United States
The 13 original colonies are symbolized in the stars, stripes, leaves, and arrows. The Latin phrase *E pluribus unum* means "Out of many, one," expressing unity of the states. The American bald eagle holds an olive branch and arrows to symbolize a desire for peace but a readiness for war.

EXAMINING *the* ISSUES

- **What values and goals of your new country do you want to show?**
- **Will your symbols represent your country's past or future?**

As a class, discuss these questions. During the discussion, think of the role played by symbols in expressing a country's view of itself and the world. As you read about the rise of new nations in Latin America and Europe, think of how artists encourage national pride.

1 Latin American Peoples Win Independence

CONNECT TO THE NEW YORK STATE CORE CURRICULUM

Unit 5.C.4.a. Causes
Unit 5.E.2. Roles of social classes: land-holding elite, creoles, mestizos, native peoples, and slaves

TERMS & NAMES

- *peninsulare*
- creole
- mulatto
- Simón Bolívar
- José de San Martín
- Miguel Hidalgo
- José María Morelos

SETTING THE STAGE The successful American Revolution, the French Revolution, and the Enlightenment changed ideas about who should control government. Ideas of liberty, equality, and democratic rule found their way across the seas to European colonies. In Latin America, most of the population resented the domination of European colonial powers. The time seemed right for the people who lived there to sweep away old colonial masters and gain control of the land.

TAKING NOTES

Clarifying Identify details about Latin American independence movements.

Who	Where
When	Why

Colonial Society Divided

In Latin American colonial society, class dictated people's place in society and jobs. At the top of Spanish-American society were the ***peninsulares*** (peh•neen•soo•LAH•rehs), people who had been born in Spain, which is on the Iberian peninsula. They formed a tiny percentage of the population. Only *peninsulares* could hold high office in Spanish colonial government. **Creoles**, Spaniards born in Latin America, were below the *peninsulares* in rank. Creoles could not hold high-level political office, but they could rise as officers in

The Divisions in Spanish Colonial Society, 1789

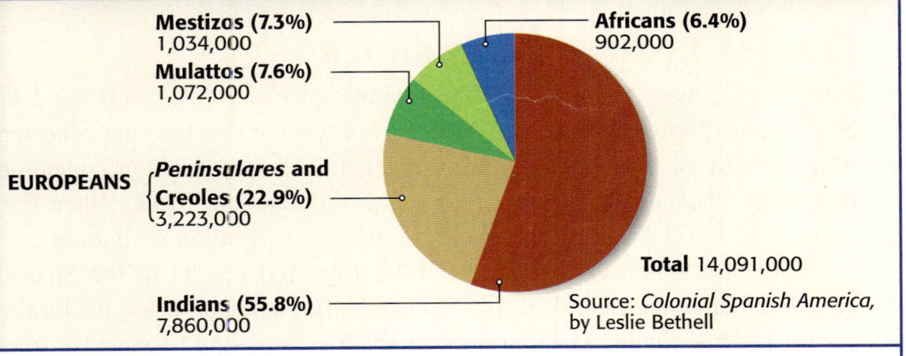

Source: *Colonial Spanish America*, by Leslie Bethell

SKILLBUILDER: Interpreting Graphs

1. **Clarifying** *Which two groups made up the vast majority of the population in Spanish America?*
2. **Making Inferences** *Of the Europeans, which group—*peninsulares *or* creoles*—probably made up a larger percentage?*

Spanish colonial armies. Together these two groups controlled land, wealth, and power in the Spanish colonies.

Below the *peninsulares* and creoles came the mestizos, persons of mixed European and Indian ancestry. Next were the **mulattos**, persons of mixed European and African ancestry, and enslaved Africans. Indians were at the bottom of the social ladder.

Revolutions in the Americas

By the late 1700s, colonists in Latin America, already aware of Enlightenment ideas, were electrified by the news of the American and French Revolutions. The success of the American Revolution encouraged them to try to gain freedom from their European masters.

Revolution in Haiti The French colony called Saint Domingue was the first Latin American territory to free itself from European rule. The colony, now known as Haiti, occupied the western third of the island of Hispaniola in the Caribbean Sea.

Nearly 500,000 enslaved Africans worked on French plantations, and they outnumbered their masters dramatically. White masters used brutal methods to terrorize them and keep them powerless.

While the French Revolution was taking place, oppressed people in the French colony of Haiti rose up against their French masters. In August 1791, 100,000 enslaved Africans rose in revolt. A leader soon emerged, Toussaint L'Ouverture (too•SAN loo•vair•TOOR). Formerly enslaved, Toussaint was unfamiliar with military and diplomatic matters. Even so, he rose to become a skilled general and diplomat. By 1801, Toussaint had taken control of the entire island and freed all the enslaved Africans.

▼ Toussaint L'Ouverture led enslaved Africans in a revolt against the French that ended slavery and resulted in the new nation of Haiti.

In January 1802, 30,000 French troops landed in Saint Domingue to remove Toussaint from power. In May, Toussaint agreed to halt the revolution if the French would end slavery. Despite the agreement, the French soon accused him of planning another uprising. They seized him and sent him to a prison in the French Alps, where he died in April 1803.

Haiti's Independence Toussaint's lieutenant, Jean-Jacques Dessalines (zhahn•ZHAHK day•sah•LEEN), took up the fight for freedom. On January 1, 1804, General Dessalines declared the colony an independent country. It was the first black colony to free itself from European control. Dessalines called the country Haiti, which in the language of the Arawak natives meant "mountainous land."

Creoles Lead Independence

Even though they could not hold high public office, creoles were the least oppressed of those born in Latin America. They were also the best educated. In fact, many wealthy young creoles traveled to Europe for their education. In Europe, they read about and adopted Enlightenment ideas. When they returned to Latin America, they brought ideas of revolution with them.

Napoleon's conquest of Spain in 1808 triggered revolts in the Spanish colonies. Removing Spain's King Ferdinand VII, Napoleon made his brother Joseph king of Spain. Many creoles might have supported a Spanish king. However, they felt no loyalty to a king imposed by the French. Creoles, recalling Locke's idea of the consent of the governed, argued that when the real king was removed, power shifted to the people. In 1810, rebellion broke out in several parts of Latin America. The drive toward independence had begun. (A)

MAIN IDEA

Recognizing Effects

(A) How did the French Revolution affect the colonists in the Americas?

History Makers

Simón Bolívar
1783–1830

Called *Libertador* (Liberator), Bolívar was a brilliant general, a visionary, a writer, and a fighter. He is called the "George Washington of South America." Bolívar planned to unite the Spanish colonies of South America into a single country called Gran Colombia. The area of upper Peru was renamed Bolivia in his honor.

Discouraged by political disputes that tore the new Latin American nations apart, he is reported to have said, "America is ungovernable. Those who have served the revolution have ploughed the sea."

José de San Martín
1778–1850

Unlike the dashing Bolívar, San Martín was a modest man. Though born in Argentina, he spent much of his youth in Spain as a career military officer. He fought with Spanish forces against Napoleon. He returned to Latin America to be a part of its liberation from Spain. Fighting for 10 years, he became the liberator of Argentina, Chile, and Peru.

Discouraged by political infighting, San Martín sailed for Europe. He died, almost forgotten, on French soil in 1850.

The South American wars of independence rested on the achievements of two brilliant creole generals. One was **Simón Bolívar** (see•MAWN boh•LEE•vahr), a wealthy Venezuelan creole. The other great liberator was **José de San Martín** (hoh•SAY day san mahr•TEEN), an Argentinian.

Bolívar's Route to Victory Simón Bolívar's native Venezuela declared its independence from Spain in 1811. But the struggle for independence had only begun. Bolívar's volunteer army of revolutionaries suffered numerous defeats. Twice Bolívar had to go into exile. A turning point came in August 1819. Bolívar led over 2,000 soldiers on a daring march through the Andes into what is now Colombia. (See the 1830 map on page 685.) Coming from this direction, he took the Spanish army in Bogotá completely by surprise and won a decisive victory.

By 1821, Bolívar had won Venezuela's independence. He then marched south into Ecuador. In Ecuador, Bolívar finally met José de San Martín. Together they would decide the future of the Latin American revolutionary movement.

San Martín Leads Southern Liberation Forces San Martín's Argentina had declared its independence in 1816. However, Spanish forces in nearby Chile and Peru still posed a threat. In 1817, San Martín led an army on a grueling march across the Andes to Chile. He was joined there by forces led by Bernardo O'Higgins, son of a former viceroy of Peru. With O'Higgins's help, San Martín finally freed Chile.

In 1821, San Martín planned to drive the remaining Spanish forces out of Lima, Peru. But to do so, he needed a much larger force. San Martín and Bolívar discussed this problem when they met at Guayaquil, Ecuador, in 1822.

No one knows how the two men reached an agreement. But San Martín left his army for Bolívar to command. With unified revolutionary forces, Bolívar's army went on to defeat the Spanish at the Battle of Ayacucho (Peru) on December 9, 1824. In this last major battle of the war for independence, the Spanish colonies in Latin America won their freedom. The future countries of Venezuela, Colombia, Panama, and Ecuador were united into a country called Gran Colombia.

Struggling Toward Democracy

Revolutions are as much a matter of ideas as they are of weapons. Simón Bolívar, the hero of Latin American independence, was both a thinker and a fighter. By 1800, Enlightenment ideas spread widely across the Latin American colonies. Bolívar combined Enlightenment political ideas, ideas from Greece and Rome, and his own original thinking. The result was a system of democratic ideas that would help spark revolutions throughout Latin America.

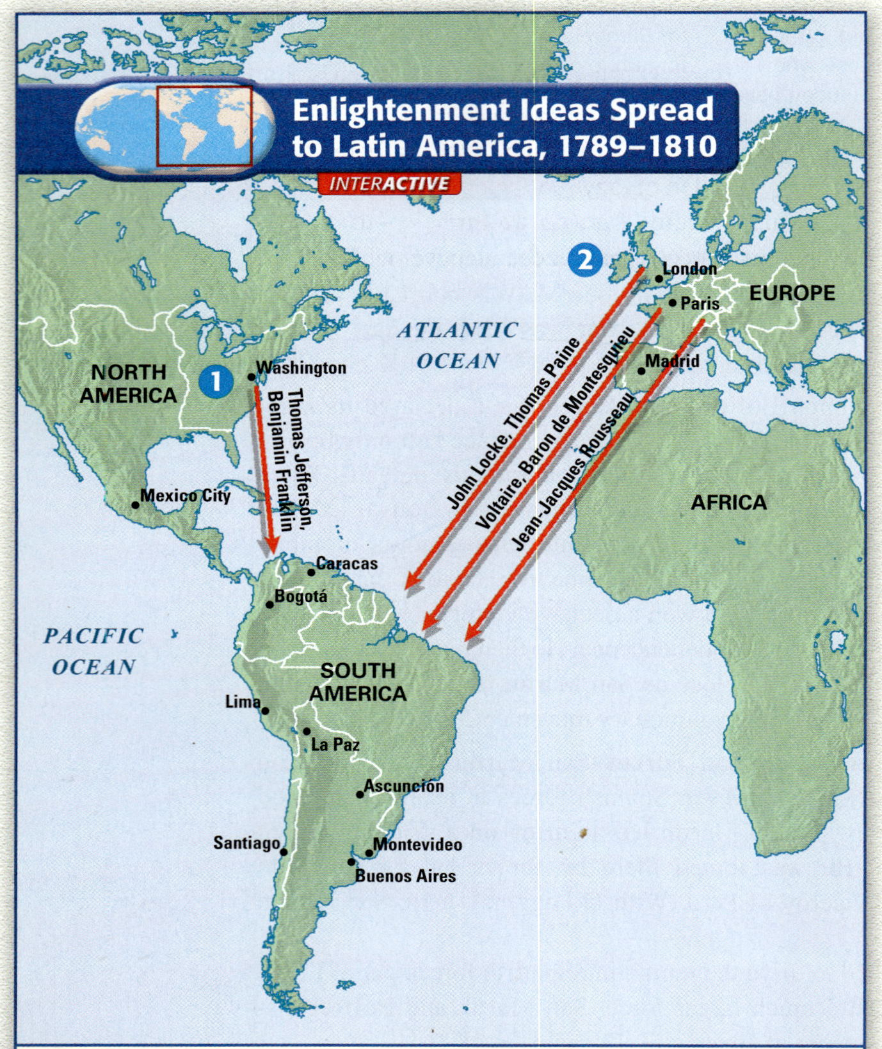

1. Bolívar's 1807 return from Europe by way of the United States allowed him to study the American system of government.

2. In 1810, Bolívar went to London to seek support for the revolution in Latin America. At the same time, he studied British institutions of government.

After winning South American independence, Simón Bolívar realized his dream of Gran Colombia, a sort of United States of South America.

Patterns of Interaction

Struggling Toward Democracy: Revolutions in Latin America and South Africa

The Latin American independence movement is one example of how the Enlightenment spread democratic ideals throughout the world. Democratic ideals continue to inspire people to struggle for political independence and to overthrow oppressive governments.

Connect *to* Today

1. **Making Inferences** How are Enlightenment thought and the successes of the American and French Revolutions reflected in Bolívar's thinking?

   See Skillbuilder Handbook, page R10.

2. **Comparing** What recent events in today's world are similar to Simón Bolívar's movement for Latin American independence?

Mexico Ends Spanish Rule

In most Latin American countries, creoles led the revolutionary movements. But in Mexico, ethnic and racial groups mixed more freely. There, Indians and mestizos played the leading role.

A Cry for Freedom In 1810, Padre **Miguel Hidalgo** (mee•GEHL ee•THAHL•goh), a priest in the small village of Dolores, took the first step toward independence. Hidalgo was a poor but well-educated man. He firmly believed in Enlightenment ideals. On September 16, 1810, he rang the bells of his village church. When the peasants gathered in the church, he issued a call for rebellion against the Spanish. Today, that call is known as the *grito de Dolores* (the cry of Dolores).

The very next day, Hidalgo's Indian and mestizo followers began a march toward Mexico City. This unruly army soon numbered 80,000 men. The uprising of the lower classes alarmed the Spanish army and creoles, who feared the loss of their property, control of the land, and their lives. The army defeated Hidalgo in 1811. The rebels then rallied around another strong leader, Padre **José María Morelos** (moh•RAY•lohs). Morelos led the revolution for four years. However, in 1815, a creole officer, Agustín de Iturbide (ah•goos•TEEN day ee•toor•BEE•day), defeated him.

Mexico's Independence Events in Mexico took yet another turn in 1820 when a revolution in Spain put a liberal group in power there. Mexico's creoles feared the loss of their privileges in the Spanish-controlled colony. So they united in support of Mexico's independence from Spain. Ironically, Agustín de Iturbide—the man who had defeated the rebel Padre Morelos—proclaimed independence in 1821.

GEOGRAPHY SKILLBUILDER: Interpreting Maps

1. **Region** *What two European countries held the largest colonial empires in Latin America in 1800?*
2. **Region** *Comparing the two maps, which independent countries had emerged by 1830 from Spanish territory in the Americas?*

Before the Mexican revolution, Central America was part of the viceroyalty of New Spain. It had been governed by the Spanish from the seat of colonial government in Mexico. In 1821, several Central American states declared their independence from Spain—and from Mexico as well. However, Iturbide (who had declared himself emperor), refused to recognize the declarations of independence. Iturbide was finally overthrown in 1823. Central America then declared its absolute independence from Mexico. It took the name the United Provinces of Central America. The future countries of Nicaragua, Guatemala, Honduras, El Salvador, and Costa Rica would develop in this region.

Brazil's Royal Liberator

Brazil's quest for independence was unique in this period of Latin American history because it occurred without violent upheavals or widespread bloodshed. In fact, a member of the Portuguese royal family actually played a key role in freeing Brazil from Portugal.

In 1807, Napoleon's armies invaded both Spain and Portugal. Napoleon's aim was to close the ports of these countries to British shipping. As French troops approached Lisbon, the Portuguese capital, Prince John (later King John VI) and the royal family boarded ships to escape capture. They took their court and royal treasury to Portugal's largest colony, Brazil. Rio de Janiero became the capital of the Portuguese empire. For 14 years, the Portuguese ran their empire from Brazil. After Napoleon's defeat in 1815, King John and the Portuguese government returned to Portugal six years later. Dom Pedro, King John's son, stayed behind in Brazil.

King John planned to make Brazil a colony again. However, many Brazilians could not accept a return to colonial status. In 1822, creoles demanded Brazil's independence from Portugal. Eight thousand Brazilians signed a petition asking Dom Pedro to rule. He agreed. On September 7, 1822, he officially declared Brazil's independence. Brazil had won its independence in a bloodless revolution. **B**

Meanwhile, the ideas of the French Revolution and the aftermath of the Napoleonic Wars were causing upheaval in Europe, as you will learn in Section 2.

MAIN IDEA

Making Inferences

B In what way did the presence of the royal family in Brazil help Portugal's largest colony?

NEW YORK CORE CURRICULUM REVIEW

TERMS & NAMES 1. For each term or name, write a sentence explaining its significance.

- *peninsulare*
- creole
- mulatto
- Simón Bolívar
- José de San Martín
- Miguel Hidalgo
- José María Morelos

USING YOUR NOTES

2. Which independence movement was led by Toussaint L'Ouverture?

Who	Where
When	Why

MAIN IDEAS

3. How was Spanish colonial society structured?
4. How was the Haitian Revolution different from revolutions in the rest of Latin America?
5. Which groups led the quest for Mexican independence?

CRITICAL THINKING & WRITING

6. **COMPARING AND CONTRASTING** Compare and contrast the leadership of the South American revolutions to the leadership of Mexico's revolution.
7. **FORMING AND SUPPORTING OPINIONS** Would creole revolutionaries tend to be democratic or authoritarian leaders? Explain.
8. **ANALYZING CAUSES** How were events in Europe related to the revolutions in Latin America?
9. **WRITING ACTIVITY** REVOLUTION Write a **response** to this statement: "Through its policies, Spain gave up its right to rule in South America."

INTEGRATED TECHNOLOGY **INTERNET ACTIVITY**

Use the Internet to find information on the Mexican Indian rebel group, the *Zapatistas*. Create a **multimedia presentation** describing the group and its goals.

INTERNET KEYWORD
Zapatistas

2 Europe Faces Revolutions

CONNECT TO THE NEW YORK STATE CORE CURRICULUM

Unit 5.D.3. Revolutions of 1848
Unit 5.D.4.b. 19th-century Russian serfdom

TERMS & NAMES

- conservative
- liberal
- radical
- nationalism
- nation-state
- the Balkans
- Louis-Napoleon
- Alexander II

SETTING THE STAGE As revolutions shook the colonies in Latin America, Europe was also undergoing dramatic changes. Under the leadership of Prince Metternich of Austria, the Congress of Vienna had tried to restore the old monarchies and territorial divisions that had existed before the French Revolution. (See Chapter 23.) On an international level, this attempt to turn back history succeeded. For the next century, European countries seldom turned to war to solve their differences. Within countries, however, the effort failed. Revolutions erupted across Europe between 1815 and 1848.

TAKING NOTES
Summarizing Identify major revolutions in Europe.

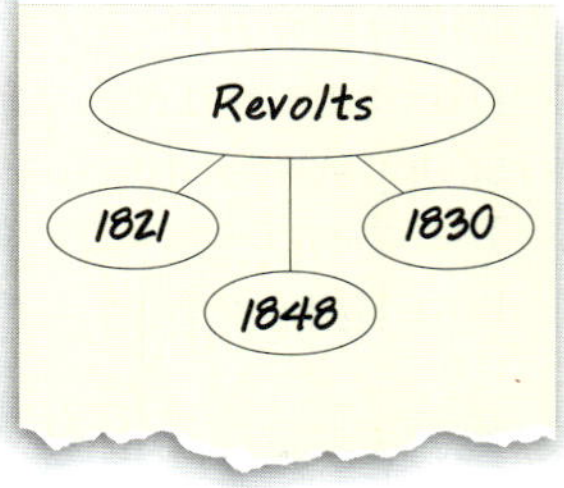

Clash of Philosophies

In the first half of the 1800s, three schools of political thought struggled for supremacy in European societies. Each believed that its style of government would best serve the people. Each attracted a different set of followers. The list below identifies the philosophies, goals, and followers.

- **Conservative**: usually wealthy property owners and nobility. They argued for protecting the traditional monarchies of Europe.
- **Liberal**: mostly middle-class business leaders and merchants. They wanted to give more power to elected parliaments, but only the educated and the landowners would vote.
- **Radical**: favored drastic change to extend democracy to all people. They believed that governments should practice the ideals of the French Revolution—liberty, equality, and brotherhood.

▼ Prince Clemens von Metternich shaped conservative control of Europe for almost 40 years.

Nationalism Develops

As conservatives, liberals, and radicals debated issues of government, a new movement called nationalism emerged. **Nationalism** is the belief that people's greatest loyalty should not be to a king or an empire but to a nation of people who share a common culture and history. The nationalist movement would blur the lines that separated the three political theories.

When a nation had its own independent government, it became a **nation-state**. A nation-state defends the nation's territory and way of life, and it represents the nation to the rest of the world. In Europe in 1815, only

Analyzing Key Concepts

Nationalism

Nationalism—the belief that people should be loyal to their nation—was not widespread until the 1800s. The rise of modern nationalism is tied to the spread of democratic ideas and the growth of an educated middle class. People wanted to decide how they were governed, instead of having monarchs impose government on them.

Bonds That Create a Nation-State

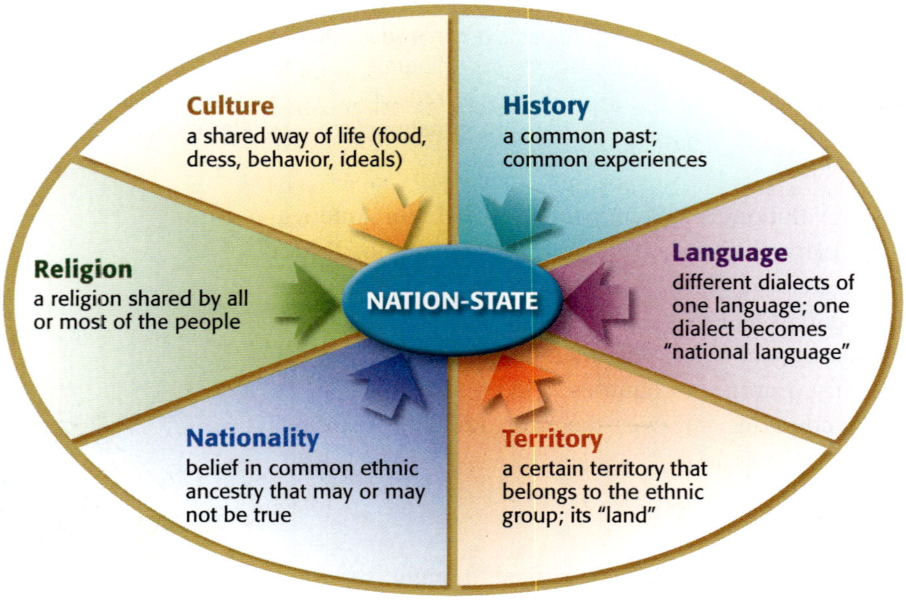

Positive and Negative Results of Nationalism

Nationalism has not always been a positive influence. For example, extremely strong nationalistic feelings sometimes lead a group to turn against outsiders. The chart below lists some positive and negative results of nationalism. Note how some results, such as competition, can be both positive and negative.

Positive Results	Negative Results
• People within a nation overcoming their differences for the common good • The overthrow of colonial rule	• Forced assimilation of minority cultures into a nation's majority culture • Ethnic cleansing, such as in Bosnia and Herzegovina in the 1990s
• Democratic governments in nations throughout the world • Competition among nations spurring scientific and technological advances	• The rise of extreme nationalistic movements, such as Nazism • Competition between nations leading to warfare

INTEGRATED TECHNOLOGY

RESEARCH LINKS For more on nationalism, go to **classzone.com**

DATA FILE

IMPACT OF NATIONALISM

- Between 1950 and 1980, 47 African countries overthrew colonial rulers and became independent nations.
- In the 1990s, the republics of Bosnia and Herzegovina, Croatia, Slovenia, and Macedonia broke away from Yugoslavia.
- In 2003, Yugoslavia changed its name to Serbia and Montenegro.
- Europe has 47 countries. (Some of those lie partially in Europe, partially in Asia.) About 50 languages are spoken in the region.
- In most of Latin America, Spanish or Portuguese is the official language. However, many native languages are still spoken. For example, Bolivia has three official languages: Spanish and the Indian languages of Aymara and Quechua.

Connect *to* Today

1. **Forming and Supporting Opinions** Do you think nationalism has had more of a positive or negative impact on the world? Support your opinion with evidence.

   See Skillbuilder Handbook, page R20.

2. **Comparing and Contrasting** Which of the bonds used to create nation-states are found in the United States?

France, England, and Spain could be called nation-states. But soon that would change as nationalist movements achieved success.

Most of the people who believed in nationalism were either liberals or radicals. In most cases, the liberal middle class—teachers, lawyers, and businesspeople—led the struggle for constitutional government and the formation of nation-states. In Germany, for example, liberals wanted to gather the many different German states into a single nation-state. Other liberals in large empires, such as the Hungarians in the Austrian Empire, wanted to split away and establish self-rule.

Nationalists Challenge Conservative Power

The first people to win self-rule during this period were the Greeks. For centuries, Greece had been part of the Ottoman Empire. The Ottomans controlled most of **the Balkans**. That region includes all or part of present-day Greece, Albania, Bulgaria, Romania, Turkey, and the former Yugoslavia. Greeks, however, had kept alive the memory of their ancient history and culture. Spurred on by the nationalist spirit, they demanded independence and rebelled against the Ottoman Turks in 1821.

Greeks Gain Independence The most powerful European governments opposed revolution. However, the cause of Greek independence was popular with people around the world. Russians, for example, felt a connection to Greek Orthodox Christians, who were ruled by the Muslim Ottomans. Educated Europeans and Americans loved and respected ancient Greek culture.

Eventually, as popular support for Greece grew, the powerful nations of Europe took the side of the Greeks. In 1827, a combined British, French, and Russian fleet destroyed the Ottoman fleet at the Battle of Navarino. In 1830, Britain, France, and Russia signed a treaty guaranteeing an independent kingdom of Greece. **A**

MAIN IDEA

Analyzing Motives

A Why would Europeans and Americans support the Greek revolutionary movement?

1830s Uprisings Crushed By the 1830s, the old order, carefully arranged at the Congress of Vienna, was breaking down. Revolutionary zeal swept across Europe. Liberals and nationalists throughout Europe were openly revolting against conservative governments.

Nationalist riots broke out against Dutch rule in the Belgian city of Brussels. In October 1830, the Belgians declared their independence from Dutch control. In Italy, nationalists worked to unite the many separate states on the Italian peninsula. Some were independent. Others were ruled by Austria, or by the pope. Eventually, Prince Metternich sent Austrian troops to restore order in Italy. The Poles living under the rule of Russia staged a revolt in Warsaw late in 1830. Russian armies took nearly an entire year to crush the Polish uprising. By the mid-1830s, the old order seemed to have reestablished itself. But the appearance of stability did not last long.

1848 Revolutions Fail to Unite In 1848, ethnic uprisings erupted throughout Europe. (See the map on page 679.) After an unruly mob in Vienna clashed with police, Metternich resigned and liberal uprisings broke out throughout the Austrian empire. In Budapest, nationalist leader Louis Kossuth called for a parliament and self-government

Social History

Nationalistic Music

As the force of nationalism began to rise in Europe, ethnic groups recognized their music as a unique element of their culture. Composers used folk melodies in their works. For example, Czech composer Antonin Dvořák (DVAWR•zhahk), pictured above, and the Norwegian composer Edvard Grieg incorporated popular melodies and legends into their works. These works became a source of pride and further encouraged the sense of nationalism. Richard Wagner created a cycle of four musical dramas called *Der Ring des Nibelungen*. His operas are considered the pinnacle of German nationalism.

▲ In *Combat Before the Hotel de Ville, July 28th, 1830,* Victor Schnetz portrays the riots in Paris that forced Charles X to flee to Great Britain.

for Hungary. Meanwhile in Prague, Czech liberals demanded Bohemian independence.

European politics continued to seesaw. Many liberal gains were lost to conservatives within a year. In one country after another, the revolutionaries failed to unite themselves or their nations. Conservatives regained their nerve and their power. By 1849, Europe had practically returned to the conservatism that had controlled governments before 1848. **B**

MAIN IDEA

Hypothesizing

B Why weren't the revolutions of 1830 and 1848 successful?

Radicals Change France

Radicals participated in many of the 1848 revolts. Only in France, however, was the radical demand for democratic government the main goal of revolution. In 1830, France's King Charles X tried to stage a return to absolute monarchy. The attempt sparked riots that forced Charles to flee to Great Britain. He was replaced by Louis-Philippe, who had long supported liberal reforms in France.

The Third Republic However, in 1848, after a reign of almost 18 years, Louis-Philippe fell from popular favor. Once again, a Paris mob overturned a monarchy and established a republic. The new republican government began to fall apart almost immediately. The radicals split into factions. One side wanted only political reform. The other side also wanted social and economic reform. The differences set off bloody battles in Parisian streets. The violence turned French citizens away from the radicals. As a result, a moderate constitution was drawn up later in 1848. It called for a parliament and a strong president to be elected by the people.

France Accepts a Strong Ruler In December 1848, **Louis-Napoleon**, the nephew of Napoleon Bonaparte, won the presidential election. Four years later, Louis-Napoleon Bonaparte took the title of Emperor Napoleon III. A majority of French voters accepted this action without complaint. The French were weary of instability. They welcomed a strong ruler who would bring peace to France. **C**

As France's emperor, Louis-Napoleon built railroads, encouraged industrialization, and promoted an ambitious program of public works. Gradually, because of Louis-Napoleon's policies, unemployment decreased in France, and the country experienced real prosperity.

MAIN IDEA

Summarizing

C How would you describe the political swings occurring in France between 1830 and 1852?

Reform in Russia

Unlike France, Russia in the 1800s had yet to leap into the modern industrialized world. Under Russia's feudal system, serfs were bound to the nobles whose land they worked. Nobles enjoyed almost unlimited power over them. By the 1820s, many Russians believed that serfdom must end. In their eyes, the system was morally wrong. It also prevented the empire from advancing economically. The czars, however, were reluctant to free the serfs. Freeing them would anger the landowners, whose support the czars needed to stay in power.

Defeat Brings Change Eventually, Russia's lack of development became obvious to Russians and to the whole world. In 1853, Czar Nicholas I threatened to take over part of the Ottoman Empire in the Crimean War. However, Russia's industries and transportation system failed to provide adequate supplies for the country's troops. As a result, in 1856, Russia lost the war against the combined forces of France, Great Britain, Sardinia, and the Ottoman Empire.

After the war, Nicholas's son, **Alexander II**, decided to move Russia toward modernization and social change. Alexander and his advisers believed that his reforms would allow Russia to compete with western Europe for world power.

Reform and Reaction The first and boldest of Alexander's reforms was a decree freeing the serfs in 1861. The abolition of serfdom, however, went only halfway. Peasant communities—rather than individual peasants—received about half the farmland in the country. Nobles kept the other half. The government paid the nobles for their land. Each peasant community, on the other hand, had 49 years to pay the government for the land it had received. So, while the serfs were legally free, the debt still tied them to the land.

Political and social reforms ground to a halt when terrorists assassinated Alexander II in 1881. His successor, Alexander III, tightened czarist control over the country. Alexander III and his ministers, however, encouraged industrial development to expand Russia's power. A major force behind Russia's drive toward industrial expansion was nationalism. Nationalism also stirred other ethnic groups. During the 1800s, such groups were uniting into nations and building industries to survive among other nation-states. **D**

MAIN IDEA

Analyzing Issues

D Why did czars push for industrialization?

History *in* Depth

Emancipation

In 1861, on the day before Abraham Lincoln became president of the United States, Czar Alexander II issued the Edict of Emancipation, freeing 20 million serfs. Less than two years later, President Lincoln issued the Emancipation Proclamation, freeing enslaved peoples living under the Confederacy.

The emancipation edicts did not entirely fulfill the hopes of Russian serfs or former slaves in the United States. Russian peasant communities, like the one pictured above, were still tied to the land. And Lincoln did not free enslaved people in the border states.

NEW YORK CORE CURRICULUM REVIEW

TERMS & NAMES 1. For each term or name, write a sentence explaining its significance.

- conservative
- liberal
- radical
- nationalism
- nation-state
- the Balkans
- Louis-Napoleon
- Alexander II

USING YOUR NOTES

2. Why did most of the revolts fail?

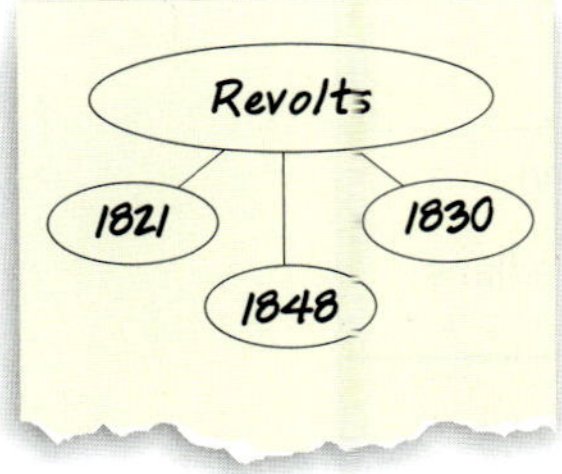

MAIN IDEAS

3. How were radicals different from liberals?
4. Why did France's Third Republic fail?
5. What was the driving force behind Russia's industrial expansion?

CRITICAL THINKING & WRITING

6. **MAKING INFERENCES** Why might liberals and radicals join together in a nationalist cause?
7. **DRAWING CONCLUSIONS** Why did some liberals disapprove of the way Louis-Napoleon ruled France after the uprisings of 1848?
8. **EVALUATING DECISIONS** What consequences did Alexander's reforms have on Russia?
9. **WRITING ACTIVITY** REVOLUTION Imagine you live in Europe in 1848. Write a **letter** to a friend, stating your political position—conservative, liberal, or radical. Express your feelings about the uprisings and the future of Europe.

CONNECT TO TODAY **WRITING A TV NEWS SCRIPT**

Early in the 21st century, hostility between Greeks and Turks on the island of Cyprus was reduced. Prepare a **TV news script** about the current status of governing the island.

3

Nationalism

CASE STUDY: Italy and Germany

CONNECT TO THE NEW YORK STATE CORE CURRICULUM

Unit 5.F.3.a. Unification of Italy and Germany (Camillo Cavour, Otto von Bismarck)
Unit 5.F.2. Role in political revolutions

TERMS & NAMES

- Russification
- Camillo di Cavour
- Giuseppe Garibaldi
- Junker
- Otto von Bismarck
- realpolitik
- kaiser

SETTING THE STAGE Nationalism was the most powerful idea of the 1800s. Its influence stretched throughout Europe and the Americas. It shaped countries by creating new ones or breaking up old ones. In Europe, it also upset the balance of power set up at the Congress of Vienna in 1815, affecting the lives of millions. Empires in Europe were made up of many different groups of people. Nationalism fed the desire of most of those groups to be free of the rule of empires and govern themselves in their traditional lands.

TAKING NOTES
Following Chronological Order List major events in the unification of Italy and of Germany.

1800 — 1900

Nationalism: A Force for Unity or Disunity

During the 1800s, nationalism fueled efforts to build nation-states. Nationalists were not loyal to kings, but to their people—to those who shared common bonds. Nationalists believed that people of a single "nationality," or ancestry, should unite under a single government. However, people who wanted to restore the old order from before the French Revolution saw nationalism as a force for disunity.

Gradually, authoritarian rulers began to see that nationalism could also unify masses of people. They soon began to use nationalist feelings for their own purposes. They built nation-states in areas where they remained firmly in control.

Types of Nationalist Movements

Type	Characteristics	Examples
Unification	• Mergers of politically divided but culturally similar lands	• 19th century Germany • 19th century Italy
Separation	• Culturally distinct group resists being added to a state or tries to break away	• Greeks in the Ottoman Empire • French-speaking Canadians
State-building	• Culturally distinct groups form into a new state by accepting a single culture	• The United States • Turkey

SKILLBUILDER: Interpreting Charts
1. **Categorizing** *What types of nationalist movements can evolve in lands with culturally distinct groups?*
2. **Drawing Conclusions** *What must be present for state-building to take place?*

In the chart on page 692, you can see the characteristics and examples of three types of nationalist movements. In today's world, groups still use the spirit of nationalism to unify, separate, or build up nation-states.

Nationalism Shakes Aging Empires

Three aging empires—the Austrian Empire of the Hapsburgs, the Russian Empire of the Romanovs, and the Ottoman Empire of the Turks—contained a mixture of ethnic groups. Control of land and ethnic groups moved back and forth between these empires, depending on victories or defeats in war and on royal marriages. When nationalism emerged in the 19th century, ethnic unrest threatened and eventually toppled these empires.

The Breakup of the Austrian Empire The Austrian Empire brought together Slovenes, Hungarians, Germans, Czechs, Slovaks, Croats, Poles, Serbs, and Italians. In 1866, Prussia defeated Austria in the Austro-Prussian War. With its victory, Prussia gained control of the newly organized North German Confederation, a union of Prussia and 21 smaller German political units. Then, pressured by the Hungarians, Emperor Francis Joseph of Austria split his empire in half, declaring Austria and Hungary independent states, with himself as ruler of both. The empire was now called Austria-Hungary or the Austro-Hungarian Empire. Nationalist disputes continued to weaken the empire for more than 40 years. Finally, after World War I, Austria-Hungary broke into several separate nation-states.

The Russian Empire Crumbles Nationalism also helped break up the 370-year-old empire of the czars in Russia. In addition to the Russians themselves, the czar ruled over 22 million Ukrainians, 8 million Poles, and smaller numbers of Lithuanians, Latvians, Estonians, Finns, Jews, Romanians, Georgians, Armenians, Turks, and others. Each group had its own culture.

The ruling Romanov dynasty of Russia was determined to maintain iron control over this diversity. They instituted a policy of **Russification**, forcing Russian culture on all the ethnic groups in the empire. This policy actually strengthened ethnic nationalist feelings and helped to disunify Russia. The weakened czarist empire finally could not withstand the double shock of World War I and the communist revolution. The last Romanov czar gave up his power in 1917. (A)

MAIN IDEA

Making Inferences

(A) Why might a policy like Russification produce results that are opposite those intended?

The Ottoman Empire Weakens The ruling Turks of the Ottoman Empire controlled Greeks, Slavs, Arabs, Bulgarians, and Armenians. In 1856, under pressure from the British and French, the Ottomans granted equal citizenship to all the people under their rule. That measure angered conservative Turks, who wanted no change in the situation, and caused tensions in the empire. For example, in response to nationalism in

◀ Driven from their homes, Armenians beg for bread at a refugee center.

Armenia, the Ottomans massacred and deported Armenians from 1894 to 1896 and again in 1915. Like Austria-Hungary, the Ottoman Empire broke apart soon after World War I.

CASE STUDY: ITALY

Cavour Unites Italy

While nationalism destroyed empires, it also built nations. Italy was one of the countries to form from the territory of crumbling empires. Between 1815 and 1848, fewer and fewer Italians were content to live under foreign rulers.

Cavour Leads Italian Unification Italian nationalists looked for leadership from the kingdom of Piedmont-Sardinia, the largest and most powerful of the Italian states. The kingdom had adopted a liberal constitution in 1848. So, to the liberal Italian middle classes, unification under Piedmont-Sardinia seemed a good plan.

In 1852, Sardinia's king, Victor Emmanuel II, named Count **Camillo di Cavour** (kuh•VOOR) as his prime minister. Cavour was a cunning statesman who worked tirelessly to expand Piedmont-Sardinia's power. Using skillful diplomacy and well-chosen alliances he set about gaining control of northern Italy for Sardinia.

Cavour realized that the greatest roadblock to annexing northern Italy was Austria. In 1858, the French emperor Napoleon III agreed to help drive Austria out of the northern Italian provinces. Cavour then provoked a war with the Austrians. A combined French-Sardinian army won two quick victories. Sardinia succeeded in taking all of northern Italy, except Venetia.

GEOGRAPHY SKILLBUILDER: Interpreting Maps

1. **Movement** *During what time period was the greatest share of territory unified in Italy?*
2. **Region** *Which territories did the Italians lose to France during their process of unification?*

Garibaldi Brings Unity As Cavour was uniting northern Italy, he secretly started helping nationalist rebels in southern Italy. In May 1860, a small army of Italian nationalists led by a bold and visionary soldier, **Giuseppe Garibaldi** (GAR•uh• BAWL•dee), captured Sicily. In battle, Garibaldi always wore a bright red shirt, as did his followers. As a result, they became known as the Red Shirts.

From Sicily, Garibaldi and his forces crossed to the Italian mainland and marched north. Eventually, Garibaldi agreed to unite the southern areas he had conquered with the kingdom of Piedmont-Sardinia. Cavour arranged for King Victor Emmanuel II to meet Garibaldi in Naples. "The Red One" willingly agreed to step aside and let the Sardinian king rule. **B**

MAIN IDEA

Hypothesizing

B What reasons might Garibaldi have had to step aside and let the Sardinian king rule?

In 1866, the Austrian province of Venetia, which included the city of Venice, became part of Italy. In 1870,

Analyzing Political Cartoons

"Right Leg in the Boot at Last"

In this 1860 British cartoon, the king of Sardinia is receiving control of lands taken by the nationalist Garibaldi. The act was one of the final steps in the unification of Italy.

SKILLBUILDER: Analyzing Political Cartoons

1. **Clarifying** *What symbol does the cartoonist use for the soon-to-be nation of Italy?*
2. **Making Inferences** *How is Garibaldi portrayed?*
3. **Analyzing Bias** *What does the title of the cartoon say about the cartoonist's view of Italian unification?*

See Skillbuilder Handbook, page R29

Italian forces took over the last part of a territory known as the Papal States. With this victory, the city of Rome came under Italian control. Soon after, Rome became the capital of the united kingdom of Italy. The pope, however, would continue to govern a section of Rome known as Vatican City.

CASE STUDY: GERMANY

Bismarck Unites Germany

Like Italy, Germany also achieved national unity in the mid-1800s. Beginning in 1815, 39 German states formed a loose grouping called the German Confederation. The Austrian Empire dominated the confederation. However, Prussia was ready to unify all the German states.

Prussia Leads German Unification Prussia enjoyed several advantages that would eventually help it forge a strong German state. First of all, unlike the Austro-Hungarian Empire, Prussia had a mainly German population. As a result, nationalism actually unified Prussia. In contrast, ethnic groups in Austria-Hungary tore the empire apart. Moreover, Prussia's army was by far the most powerful in central Europe. In 1848, Berlin rioters forced a constitutional convention to write up a liberal constitution for the kingdom, paving the way for unification.

Bismarck Takes Control In 1861, Wilhelm I succeeded Frederick William to the throne. The liberal parliament refused him money for reforms that would double the strength of the army. Wilhelm saw the parliament's refusal as a major challenge to his authority. He was supported in his view by the **Junkers** (YUNG•kuhrz), strongly conservative members of Prussia's wealthy landowning class. In 1862, Wilhelm chose a conservative Junker named **Otto von Bismarck** as his prime minister. Bismarck was a master of what came to be known as **realpolitik**. This

History Makers

Otto von Bismarck
1815–1898

To some Germans, Bismarck was the greatest and noblest of Germany's statesmen. They say he almost single-handedly unified the nation and raised it to greatness. To others, he was nothing but a devious politician who abused his powers and led Germany into dictatorship.

His speeches, letters, and memoirs show him to be both crafty and deeply religious. At one moment, he could declare, "It is the destiny of the weak to be devoured by the strong." At another moment he might claim, "We Germans shall never wage aggressive war, ambitious war, a war of conquest."

INTEGRATED TECHNOLOGY

INTERNET ACTIVITY Create an interactive time line of Bismarck's actions to unite Germany. Go to **classzone.com** for your research.

German term means "the politics of reality." The term is used to describe tough power politics with no room for idealism. With realpolitik as his style, Bismarck would become one of the commanding figures of German history.

With the king's approval, Bismarck declared that he would rule without the consent of parliament and without a legal budget. Those actions were in direct violation of the constitution. In his first speech as prime minister, he defiantly told members of the Prussian parliament, "It is not by means of speeches and majority resolutions that the great issues of the day will be decided—that was the great mistake of 1848 and 1849—but by blood and iron." **C**

MAIN IDEA

Hypothesizing

C Bismarck ignored both the parliament and the constitution. How do you think this action would affect Prussian government?

Prussia Expands In 1864, Bismarck took the first step toward molding an empire. Prussia and Austria formed an alliance and went to war against Denmark to win two border provinces, Schleswig and Holstein.

A quick victory increased national pride among Prussians. It also won new respect from other Germans and lent support for Prussia as head of a unified Germany. After the victory, Prussia governed Schleswig, while Austria controlled Holstein.

Seven Weeks' War Bismarck purposely stirred up border conflicts with Austria over Schleswig and Holstein. The tensions provoked Austria into declaring war on Prussia in 1866. This conflict was known as the Seven Weeks' War. The Prussians used their superior training and equipment to win a devastating victory. They humiliated Austria. The Austrians lost the region of Venetia, which was given to Italy. They had to accept Prussian annexation of more German territory.

With its victory in the Seven Weeks' War, Prussia took control of northern Germany. For the first time, the eastern and western parts of the Prussian kingdom were joined. In 1867, the remaining states of the north joined the North German Confederation, which Prussia dominated completely.

The Franco-Prussian War By 1867, a few southern German states remained independent of Prussian control. The majority of southern Germans were Catholics. Many in the region resisted domination by a Protestant Prussia. However, Bismarck felt he could win the support of southerners if they faced a threat from outside. He reasoned that a war with France would rally the south.

Bismarck was an expert at manufacturing "incidents" to gain his ends. For example, he created the impression that the French ambassador had insulted the Prussian king. The French reacted to Bismarck's deception by declaring war on Prussia on July 19, 1870.

The Prussian army immediately poured into northern France. In September 1870, the Prussian army surrounded the main French force at Sedan. Among the 83,000 French prisoners taken was Napoleon III himself. Parisians withstood a German siege until hunger forced them to surrender.

The Franco-Prussian War was the final stage in German unification. Now the nationalistic fever also seized people in southern Germany. They finally accepted Prussian leadership. On January 18, 1871, at the captured French palace of

Versailles, King Wilhelm I of Prussia was crowned **kaiser** (KY•zuhr), or emperor. Germans called their empire the Second Reich. (The Holy Roman Empire was the first.) Bismarck had achieved Prussian dominance over Germany and Europe "by blood and iron."

A Shift in Power

The 1815 Congress of Vienna had established five Great Powers in Europe—Britain, France, Austria, Prussia, and Russia. In 1815, the Great Powers were nearly equal in strength. The wars of the mid-1800s greatly strengthened one of the Great Powers, as Prussia joined with other German states to form Germany.

By 1871, Britain and Germany were clearly the most powerful, both militarily and economically. Austria and Russia lagged far behind. France struggled along somewhere in the middle. The European balance of power had broken down. This shift also found expression in the art of the period. In fact, during that century, artists, composers, and writers pointed to paths that they believed European society should follow.

GEOGRAPHY SKILLBUILDER: Interpreting Maps

1. **Location** *What was unusual about the territory of Prussia as it existed in 1865?*
2. **Movement** *After 1865, what year saw the biggest expansion of Prussian territory?*

NEW YORK CORE CURRICULUM REVIEW

TERMS & NAMES 1. For each term or name, write a sentence explaining its significance.

- Russification
- Camillo di Cavour
- Giuseppe Garibaldi
- Junker
- Otto von Bismarck
- realpolitik
- kaiser

USING YOUR NOTES

2. Identify an event that made the unification of Italy or Germany possible.

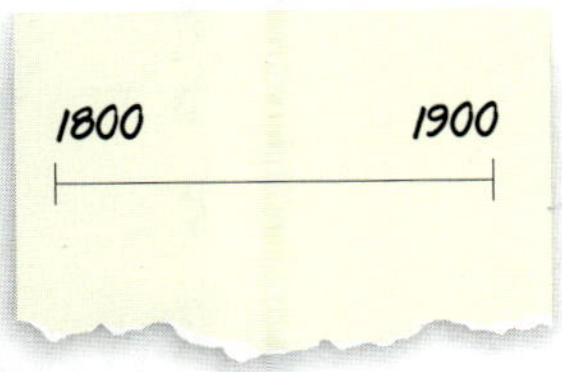

MAIN IDEAS

3. Which aging empires suffered from the forces of nationalism?
4. What role did Garibaldi play in the unification of Italy?
5. What advantages did Prussia have in leading the German states to unify?

CRITICAL THINKING & WRITING

6. **CLARIFYING** How can nationalism be both a unifying and a disunifying force?
7. **FORMING GENERALIZATIONS** Why did the Austrian, Russian, and Ottoman Empires face such great challenges to their control of land?
8. **EVALUATING COURSES OF ACTION** Many liberals wanted government by elected parliaments. How was Bismarck's approach to achieving his goals different?
9. **WRITING ACTIVITY** POWER AND AUTHORITY Write a one paragraph **biographical essay** on either Garibaldi or Cavour.

CONNECT TO TODAY **CREATING A MAP AND DATABASE**

Study the chart on page 692. Research the names of nations that have emerged in the last ten years. Categorize each nation's nationalist movement using the chart. Then create a **database** and **map** showing the location of the new nations and the category into which each new nation falls.

4

Revolutions in the Arts

CONNECT TO THE NEW YORK STATE CORE CURRICULUM

Methodology A.2. Understand the concepts of change and continuity over time
Methodology A.5. Roles and contributions of individuals and groups

TERMS & NAMES

- romanticism
- realism
- impressionism

SETTING THE STAGE During the first half of the 1800s, artists focused on ideas of freedom, the rights of individuals, and an idealistic view of history. After the great revolutions of 1848, political focus shifted to leaders who practiced realpolitik. Similarly, intellectuals and artists expressed a "realistic" view of the world. In this view, the rich pursued their selfish interests while ordinary people struggled and suffered. Newly invented photography became both a way to detail this struggle and a tool for scientific investigation.

TAKING NOTES

Outlining Organize ideas and details about movements in the arts.

I. The Romantic Movement
A.
B.
II. The Shift to Realism in the Arts

The Romantic Movement

At the end of the 18th century, the Enlightenment idea of reason gradually gave way to another major movement in art and ideas: **romanticism**. This movement reflected deep interest both in nature and in the thoughts and feelings of the individual. In many ways, romantic thinkers and writers reacted against the ideals of the Enlightenment. They turned from reason to emotion, from society to nature. Romantics rejected the rigidly ordered world of the middle class. Nationalism also fired the romantic imagination. For example, George Gordon, Lord Byron, one of the leading romantic poets of the time, fought for Greece's freedom.

The Ideas of Romanticism Emotion, sometimes wild emotion, was a key element of romanticism. However, romanticism went beyond feelings. Romantics expressed a wide range of ideas and attitudes. In general, romantic thinkers and artists shared these beliefs:

- emphasized inner feelings, emotions, and imagination
- focused on the mysterious, the supernatural, and the exotic, grotesque, or horrifying
- loved the beauties of untamed nature
- idealized the past as a simpler and nobler time
- glorified heroes and heroic actions
- cherished folk traditions, music, and stories
- valued the common people and the individual
- promoted radical change and democracy

Romanticism in Literature Poetry, music, and painting were the most influential arts because they were able to capture the emotion of romanticism. To romantics, poetry was the highest

▼ Romantic poet Lord Byron fought with Greek nationalists. He did not live to see their victory.

form of expression. The British romantic poets William Wordsworth and Samuel Taylor Coleridge both honored nature as the source of truth and beauty. Later English romantic poets, such as Lord Byron, Percy Bysshe Shelley, and John Keats, wrote poems celebrating rebellious heroes, passionate love, and the mystery and beauty of nature. Like many romantics, many of these British poets lived stormy lives and died young. Byron, for example, died at the age of 36, while Shelley died at 29.

Germany produced one of the earliest and greatest romantic writers. In 1774, Johann Wolfgang von Goethe (YO•hahn VUHLF•gahng fuhn GER•tuh) published *The Sorrows of Young Werther*. Goethe's novel told of a sensitive young man whose hopeless love for a virtuous married woman drives him to suicide. Also in Germany, the brothers Jakob and Wilhelm Grimm collected German fairy tales and created a dictionary and grammar of the German language. Both the tales and the dictionary celebrated the German spirit.

Victor Hugo led the French romantics. His works also reflect the romantic fascination with history and the individual. His novels *Les Misérables* and *The Hunchback of Notre Dame* show the struggles of individuals against a hostile society.

The Gothic Novel Gothic horror stories became hugely popular. These novels often took place in medieval Gothic castles. They were filled with fearful, violent, sometimes supernatural events. Mary Shelley, wife of the poet Percy Bysshe Shelley, wrote one of the earliest and most successful Gothic horror novels, *Frankenstein*. The novel told the story of a monster created from the body parts of dead human beings.

Composers Emphasize Emotion Emotion dominated the music produced by romantic composers. These composers moved away from the tightly controlled, formal compositions of the Enlightenment period. Instead, they celebrated heroism and national pride with a new power of expression.

As music became part of middle-class life, musicians and composers became popular heroes. Composer and pianist Franz Liszt (lihst), for example, achieved earnings and popularity comparable to those of today's rock stars.

One of the composers leading the way into the Romantic period was also its greatest: Ludwig van Beethoven (LOOD•vihg vahn BAY•toh•vuhn). His work evolved from the classical music of the Enlightenment into romantic compositions. His Ninth Symphony soars, celebrating freedom, dignity, and the triumph of the human spirit.

Later romantic composers also appealed to the hearts and souls of their listeners. Robert Schumann's compositions sparkle with merriment. Like many romantic composers, Felix Mendelssohn drew on literature, such as Shakespeare's A *Midsummer Night's Dream*, as the inspiration for his music. Polish composer and concert pianist Frederic Chopin (SHOH•pan) used Polish dance rhythms in his music. Guiseppe Verdi and Richard Wagner brought European opera to a dramatic and theatrical high point. (A)

MAIN IDEA

Summarizing

(A) What are some of the themes that are key to romantic literature and art?

History Makers

Ludwig van Beethoven
1770–1827

A genius of European music, Beethoven suffered the most tragic disability a composer can endure. At the age of 30, he began to go deaf. His deafness grew worse for 19 years. By 1819, it was total.

At first, Beethoven's handicap barely affected his career. By 1802, however, he knew that his hearing would only worsen. He suffered from bouts of depression. The depression would bring him to the brink of suicide. Nonetheless, he would rebound:

> *It seemed unthinkable for me to leave the world forever before I had produced all that I felt called upon to produce.*

INTEGRATED TECHNOLOGY

RESEARCH LINKS For more on Ludwig van Beethoven, go to **classzone.com**

The Shift to Realism in the Arts

By the middle of the 19th century, rapid industrialization deeply affected everyday life in Europe. The growing class of industrial workers lived grim lives in dirty, crowded cities. Industrialization began to make the dreams of the romantics seem pointless. In literature and the visual arts, **realism** tried to show life as it was, not as it should be. Realist painting reflected the increasing political importance of the working class in the 1850s. Along with paintings, novels proved especially suitable for describing workers' suffering.

Photographers Capture Reality As realist painters and writers detailed the lives of actual people, photographers could record an instant in time with scientific precision. The first practical photographs were called daguerreotypes (duh•GEHR•uh•TYPS). They were named after their French inventor, Louis Daguerre. The images in his daguerreotypes were startlingly real and won him worldwide fame.

British inventor William Talbot invented a light-sensitive paper that he used to produce photographic negatives. The advantage of paper was that many prints could be made from one negative. The Talbot process also allowed photos to be reproduced in books and newspapers. Mass distribution gained a wide audience for the realism of photography. With its scientific, mechanical, and mass-produced features, photography was the art of the new industrial age.

Writers Study Society Realism in literature flourished in France with writers such as Honoré de Balzac and Émile Zola. Balzac wrote a massive series of almost 100 novels entitled *The Human Comedy*. They describe in detail the brutal struggle for wealth and power among all levels of French society. Zola's novels exposed the

> Analyzing Photographs

Motion Studies

Eadweard Muybridge had a varied career as a photographer. He devoted part of his career to motion studies. These photographic studies froze the motion of an object at an instant in time. They allowed scientists to study motion and to better understand time. The equipment he built helped lead to the development of motion pictures.

This series of photographs taken in 1878, titled "The Horse in Motion," was designed to discover if all of a running horse's legs ever left the ground at the same time.

SKILLBUILDER: Interpreting Visual Sources

1. **Drawing Conclusions** *What do the series of photographs reveal about the question of whether all the legs of a horse ever left the ground at the same time?*
2. **Developing Historical Perspective** *What reaction do you think these pictures would have generated among the general public?*

See Skillbuilder Handbook, page R23.

MAIN IDEA

Forming Opinions

B Which do you think would be more effective in spurring reforms—photographs or a realist novel? Explain.

miseries of French workers in small shops, factories, and coal mines. His revelations shocked readers and spurred reforms of labor laws and working conditions in France. The famous English realist novelist Charles Dickens created unforgettable characters and scenes of London's working poor. Many of the scenes were humorous, but others showed the despair of London's poor. In his book *Little Dorrit*, Dickens described the life of a working-class person as sheer monotony set in a gloomy neighborhood. **B**

Impressionists React Against Realism

Beginning in the 1860s, a group of painters in Paris reacted against the realist style. Instead of showing life "as it really was," they tried to show their impression of a subject or a moment in time. For this reason, their style of art came to be known as **impressionism**. Fascinated by light, impressionist artists used pure, shimmering colors to capture a moment seen at a glance.

Life in the Moment Unlike the realists, impressionists showed a more positive view of the new urban society in western Europe. Instead of abused workers, they showed shop clerks and dock workers enjoying themselves in dance halls and cafés. They painted performers in theaters and circuses. And they glorified the delights of the life of the rising middle class. Claude Monet (moh•NAY), Edgar Degas (duh•GAH), and Pierre-Auguste Renoir (ruhn•WHAR) were leaders in the movement that became very popular.

Composers also created impressions of mood and atmosphere. By using different combinations of instruments, tone patterns, and music structures, they were able to create mental pictures of such things as flashing lights, the feel of a warm summer day, or the sight of the sea. French composers Maurice Ravel and Claude Debussy are the most notable members of the impressionist music movement.

Changes in political, social, artistic, and intellectual movements during the 19th century signaled important changes in daily life. One of the most significant causes of change was industrialization, which you will learn about in Chapter 25.

NEW YORK CORE CURRICULUM REVIEW

TERMS & NAMES 1. For each term or name, write a sentence explaining its significance.

- romanticism
- realism
- impressionism

USING YOUR NOTES

2. What was the goal of realist writers?

I. The Romantic Movement
  A.
  B.
II. The Shift to Realism in the Arts

MAIN IDEAS

3. What was the key element of romanticism?
4. What characteristics did photography have that made it the art of the industrial age?
5. What was the goal of impressionist painters?

CRITICAL THINKING & WRITING

6. **COMPARING AND CONTRASTING** How are the movements of romanticism and realism alike and different?
7. **ANALYZING CAUSES** How might a realist novel bring about changes in society? Describe the ways by which this might happen.
8. **SUMMARIZING** How did nationalism influence the artistic movements you read about?
9. **WRITING ACTIVITY** CULTURAL INTERACTION Listen to a piece of music by Beethoven, and then listen to a piece of contemporary music that you like. Write a **comparison-and-contrast essay** on the two pieces of music.

CONNECT TO TODAY **Creating an Arts Chart**

Look at newspaper listings for films being shown today. Make a **chart** showing which of them might be categorized as romantic and which might be categorized as realistic. Present reasons why each film fell into the designated category.

Revolutions in Painting

European painting underwent revolutionary changes during the 1800s. In the early years, romanticism—which stressed emotion above all else—was the dominant style. As revolutions swept Europe in the 1840s, some artists rejected romanticism in favor of realism. They portrayed common people and everyday life in a realistic manner. Toward the end of the century, art underwent another revolution, influenced by scientific discoveries about vision. Impressionist painters experimented with light and color to capture their impressions of a passing moment.

INTEGRATED TECHNOLOGY

RESEARCH LINKS For more on 19th-century painting go to **classzone.com**

▼ Romanticism

In their eagerness to explore emotion, romantic artists had certain favorite subjects: nature, love, religion, and nationalism. This painting, *The Lion Hunt* by Eugène Delacroix, shows that violence and exotic cultures were also popular themes. The swirling capes, snarling lions, and bold reds and yellows help convey the ferocity of the hunt.

▲ Realism

The Stone Breakers by Gustave Courbet shows that realist artists tried to portray everyday life just as it was, without making it pretty or trying to tell a moralistic story. Notice how the workers' clothes are torn and shabby. The boy rests the heavy basket of stones on his knee to ease his burden, while the man bends to his task. The colors are dull and gritty, just as the job itself is.

▼ Impressionism

The impressionists wanted to record the perceptions of the human eye rather than physical reality. To do this, they tried to portray the effect of light on landscapes and buildings. They combined short strokes of many colors to create a shimmering effect. They also used brighter, lighter colors than the artists before them had used. As the painting *Ducal Palace, Venice* by Claude Monet shows, the impressionists often painted water because of its reflective nature.

Connect *to* Today

1. **Developing Historical Perspective** If you were a political revolutionary of the 1800s, which of these artistic styles would you use for your propaganda posters? Why?
   See Skillbuilder Handbook, page R12.

2. **Drawing Conclusions** Impressionism remains extremely popular more than a century after it was first developed. What do you think accounts for its popularity today?

Chapter 24 Assessment

TERMS & NAMES

Briefly explain the importance of each of the following to the revolutions in Latin America or Europe.

1. conservative
2. liberal
3. nationalism
4. nation-state
5. realpolitik
6. romanticism
7. realism
8. impressionism

MAIN IDEAS

Latin American Peoples Win Independence
Section 1 (pages 681–686)

9. What caused the creoles in South America to rebel against Spain?
10. What role did Agustín de Iturbide play in the independence of Mexico?
11. Who was Dom Pedro, and what role did he play in Brazil's move to independence?

Europe Faces Revolutions Section 2 (pages 687–691)

12. How is a liberal different from a conservative?
13. How successful were the revolts of 1848? Explain.
14. Why did the French accept Louis-Napoleon as an emperor?

Case Study: Nationalism Section 3 (pages 692–697)

15. How did nationalism in the 1800s work as a force for both disunity and unity?
16. What approaches did Camillo di Cavour use to acquire more territory for Piedmont-Sardinia?
17. What strategy did Otto von Bismarck use to make Prussia the leader of a united Germany?

Revolutions in the Arts Section 4 (pages 698–703)

18. What are five elements of romanticism?
19. What are two ideas or attitudes of the romantic movement that reflect the ideals of nationalism?
20. What new conditions caused a change in the arts from romanticism to realism?

CRITICAL THINKING

1. USING YOUR NOTES
Using a chart, describe the nationalist movement in each of the countries listed and the results of each movement.

Country	Nationalism and Its Results
Mexico	
Greece	
Italy	
Germany	

2. EVALUATING DECISIONS
POWER AND AUTHORITY Why do you think Giuseppe Garibaldi stepped aside to let Victor Emmanuel II rule areas that Garibaldi had conquered in southern Italy?

3. ANALYZING MOTIVES
REVOLUTION How do you think nationalism might help revolutionaries overcome the disadvantages of old weapons and poor supplies to win a war for national independence? Explain.

4. MAKING INFERENCES
Do you believe the Latin American revolutions would have occurred without a push from European events? Explain.

5. SYNTHESIZING
CULTURAL INTERACTION How did artistic and intellectual movements reflect and fuel changes in Europe in the 1800s?

VISUAL SUMMARY

Nationalist Revolutions Sweep the West

NATIONALISM

Latin America
- Enlightenment ideas
- Haiti: slave-led
- South America: creole-led, especially Bolívar and San Martín
- Brazil: royalty-led

1830 & 1848 Revolutions
- Reactions against conservatives
- A few reforms
- Most failed

Unification Movements
- Garibaldi begins in Italy.
- Prime Minister Cavour completes the task.
- Prime Minister Bismarck leads the way in Germany.

The Arts
- Romantics inspired by emotion
- Dedication to common people or the group
- Realists see flaws and set new goals for nation.
- Impressionists capture the moment.

NEW YORK STATE REGENTS EXAM PRACTICE

Use the quotation and your knowledge of world history to answer questions 1 and 2.
Additional Test Practice, pp. S1–S33

PRIMARY SOURCE

> When I say that we must strive continually to be ready for all emergencies, I advance the proposition that, on account of our geographical position, we must make greater efforts than other powers would be obliged to make in view of the same ends. We lie in the middle of Europe. We have at least three fronts on which we can be attacked. France has only an eastern boundary; Russia only its western, exposed to assault. . . . So we are spurred forward on both sides to endeavors which perhaps we would not make otherwise.
>
> **OTTO VON BISMARCK,** *speech to the German parliament on February 6, 1888*

1 According to Bismarck, what key factor makes Germany a potential target for invasion?
   (1) dangerous neighbors
   (2) three borders to protect
   (3) location in the middle of Europe
   (4) massive supplies of coal and iron

2 Based on his remarks above, what actions might Bismarck take?
   (1) form alliances with other nations in Europe
   (2) make peace with France
   (3) make peace with England
   (4) expand industry

Use this 20th-century mural titled *Grito de Dolores* painted by Juan O'Gorman and your knowledge of world history to answer question 3.

3 Look at the people portrayed in the mural. What does the artist suggest about the Mexican revolt against the Spanish?
   (1) It was condemned by the Catholic Church.
   (2) Only the poor fought against Spanish rule.
   (3) People of all classes fought against Spanish rule.
   (4) Only Indians fought Spanish rule.

INTEGRATED TECHNOLOGY
TEST PRACTICE Go to **classzone.com**
- Diagnostic tests
- Tutorials
- Strategies
- Additional practice

ALTERNATIVE ASSESSMENT

1. Interact *with* History

On page 680, you were asked to create a symbol for your newly independent country. Show your symbol to the class. Explain the elements of your design and what they are intended to express. With your classmates' comments in mind, what might you change in your design?

2. WRITING ABOUT HISTORY

Write a **speech** that might have been delivered somewhere in Europe at a rally for Greek independence. Urge the country's leaders to help the Greeks in their struggle for independence from the Ottoman Empire. Consider the following:
- the connections of Greece to Europeans
- reasons to support Greek revolutionaries
- the cause of democracy

INTEGRATED TECHNOLOGY

Creating a Web Page

Use the Internet, newspapers, magazines, and your own experience to make a list of movies that portray social and political conditions. Then create a Web page that classifies each portrayal as either romantic or realistic. Remember to focus on the meanings of the terms romantic and realistic as they apply to the two movements in art and literature. You may want to include on your Web page:
- descriptions of movie plots or character portrayals
- still shots from movies that support your conclusions
- romantic or realistic quotations from movies

Revolutions Across Time

Revolution—which is a sudden or significant change in the old ways of doing things—can occur in many areas, such as government, technology, or art. In Unit 5, you studied political revolutions in Europe and the Americas, in which people rebelled against unjust rulers to gain more rights. Each revolution led to major changes in governmental, social, and economic structures. In these six pages, you will gain a better understanding of those revolutions by examining their similarities and differences.

English Civil War and Glorious Revolution ►

In 1642, civil war broke out between those who supported Parliament and those who supported the king. Parliament won and set up a commonwealth, led by Oliver Cromwell. In time, he became a dictator. After his death, the monarchy returned, but tensions built anew. In 1688, Parliament ousted King James II, shown at right, in the Glorious Revolution and invited William and Mary to rule.

1642 — 1776 — 1789

◄ American Revolution

After 1763, Americans began to resent British rule. Clashes such as the Boston Massacre, shown at left, took place. The colonies declared their independence **in 1776.** War ensued, and the United States won its freedom by defeating Britain.

▼ French Revolution

Beginning in 1789, the French people rose up to overthrow their king. The uprisings included the march by hungry women shown below. Differing goals soon split the revolutionaries. Several years of terror followed. Napoleon restored order and eventually made himself emperor of France.

1791

▲ Latin American Revolutions

From 1791 to 1824, revolutions took place in Haiti, Mexico, and the huge Spanish empire that spread across Central and South America. By the end of that period, nearly all of Latin America had gained its independence from European control. One of South America's great liberators was José de San Martín, shown in the painting above.

Model of a Revolution

From his study of the French Revolution, historian Crane Brinton developed a model of the stages that revolutions often go through. The model below is based on his work. Compare it with the revolutions you learned about in this unit.

STAGE 1 Fall of the Old Order

Revolutions usually cannot occur until a ruler becomes weak. Often this weakness results in problems such as starvation and unfair taxes. Anger builds until the ruler is overthrown.

STAGE 2 Rule by Moderates

The people relax because they think they have achieved their goal. A moderate group rules. But simply overthrowing the old order rarely solves the problems that led to the revolution.

STAGE 3 The Terror

When people realize that the old problems still exist, they look for someone to blame. Radicals take control, push for more extreme changes, and execute "enemies of the revolution."

STAGE 4 Turn from Radical Rule

In time, the violence sickens people, and the use of terror ends. The former radicals adopt a more gradual plan for effecting change.

STAGE 5 Military Rule

The terror often kills most of a country's leaders. Then the turn from radicalism makes people doubt revolutionary ideals. A military leader steps into the gap and becomes dictator.

STAGE 6 Restoration

When the dictatorship ends, through death or overthrow, a power vacuum results. The order that existed before the revolution is restored.

Comparing & Contrasting

1. Which of the revolutions on the time line, besides the French Revolution, is most like the model? Explain.
2. Which revolution is least like the model? Explain.

Causes of the Revolutions

Each of the revolutions you studied in this unit had political, economic, and social causes, as shown in the chart below. Some of the causes mentioned on the chart are the subjects of the primary sources located on the next page. Use the chart and the primary sources together to understand the causes of revolution more fully.

	England	North America	France	Latin America
Political	• King claimed divine right. • King dissolved Parliament. • Parliament sought guarantee of freedoms.	• Colonists accused British leaders of tyranny. • Colonists demanded the same rights as English citizens.	• Third Estate wanted greater representation. • Louis XVI was a weak ruler; his wife was unpopular. • American Revolution inspired political ideas.	• French Revolution inspired political ideas. • Royal officials committed injustices and repression. • Napoleon's conquest of Spain triggered revolts.
Economic	• King wanted money for wars. • King levied taxes and fines without Parliament's approval.	• Britain imposed mercantilism. • Britain expected colonies to pay for defense. • Colonists opposed taxation without representation.	• Wars and royal extravagance created debt. • Inflation and famine caused problems. • Peasants made little money but paid high taxes.	• Peninsulares and creoles controlled wealth. • Lower classes toiled as peasants with little income or as slaves.
Social	• Early Stuart kings refused to make Puritan reforms. • Parliament feared James II would restore Catholicism.	• Colonists began to identify as Americans. • Colonists were used to some independence. • Enlightenment ideas of equality and liberty spread.	• Third Estate resented the First and Second estates' privileges. • Enlightenment ideas of equality and liberty spread.	• Only peninsulares and creoles had power. • Mestizos, mulattos, Africans, and Indians had little status. • Educated creoles spread Enlightenment ideas.

SKILLBUILDER: Interpreting Charts

1. **Analyzing Causes** *What was the most frequent political cause of revolution? economic cause? social cause?*
2. **Contrasting** *How did the causes of the revolutions in Latin America differ from those of the other three revolutions?*

In the 1780s, many French peasants could not afford bread to feed their families. At the same time, Marie Antoinette spent so much money on clothes that her enemies called her Madame Deficit. The harsh contrast between starvation and luxury sparked the anger that led to the Revolution.

PRIMARY SOURCE

Political Cartoon, 1789

This French political cartoon portrayed the way the privileges of the First and Second estates affected the Third Estate.

DOCUMENT-BASED QUESTION

Do you think a member of the First, Second, or Third Estate created this cartoon? Interpret the cartoon and explain who was most likely to hold the viewpoint conveyed.

PRIMARY SOURCE

INTERACTIVE

The English Bill of Rights, 1689

This excerpt from the English Bill of Rights attempted to justify the Glorious Revolution by describing the injustices King James II committed.

The late King James the Second, by the assistance of diverse evil counselors, judges and ministers employed by him, did endeavor to subvert and extirpate [destroy] the Protestant religion and the laws and liberties of this kingdom;

By assuming and exercising a power of dispensing with and suspending of laws and the execution of laws without consent of Parliament; . . .

By levying money for and to the use of the Crown by pretense of prerogative [privilege] for other time and in other manner than the same was granted by Parliament;

By raising and keeping a standing army within this kingdom in time of peace without consent of Parliament; . . .

By violating the freedom of election of members to serve in Parliament; . . .

And excessive bail hath been required of persons committed in criminal cases to elude the benefit of the laws made for the liberty of the subjects;

And excessive fines have been imposed;

And illegal and cruel punishments inflicted.

DOCUMENT-BASED QUESTION

According to this document, how did King James II take away power from Parliament? How did he violate the rights of citizens?

PRIMARY SOURCE

Political Cartoon, 1765

This political cartoon expressed an opinion about the Stamp Act. The act was a British law that required all legal and commercial documents in the American colonies to carry a stamp showing that a tax had been paid.

DOCUMENT-BASED QUESTION

What opinion does this cartoon express about the effect of the Stamp Act on the American economy?

Comparing & Contrasting

1. How are the opinions expressed by the three primary sources similar?
2. Reread the excerpt from the English Bill of Rights. Based on this document, what causes could you add to the chart on page 708?

Effects of Revolutions

The chart below shows political, economic, and social effects of the various revolutions. The primary sources on these two pages describe the political outcomes that three different revolutionaries expected to achieve. Use the chart and the primary sources together to understand the effects of revolution more fully.

	England	North America	France	Latin America
Political	• A constitutional monarchy was established. • The Bill of Rights increased Parliament's power and guaranteed certain rights. • The overthrow of a monarch helped inspire American revolutionaries.	• The United States gained independence. • The Constitution set up a republican government. • Revolutionary ideals continued to inspire groups seeking political equality. • The American Revolution inspired later revolutions.	• The Revolution led to a succession of governments: a republic, a dictatorship, a restored monarchy. • It created expectations for equality and freedom that sparked later uprisings in France. • It inspired later revolutions.	• Nearly all colonial rule in Latin America ended. • New countries were established. • Representative government was slow to develop. The military or the wealthy controlled much of the region until the late 1900s.
Economic	• Because it was answerable to taxpayers, Parliament encouraged trade.	• The removal of Britain's mercantilist policies allowed free enterprise to develop.	• The Revolution and ensuing wars with Europe devastated France's economy.	• Upper classes kept control of wealth. • Many places kept the plantation system.
Social	• England remained Protestant.	• The ideals of the Revolution continued to inspire groups seeking social equality.	• The French feudal system was abolished.	• Much of Latin America continued to have a strong class system.

SKILLBUILDER: Interpreting Charts

1. **Contrasting** *Which revolutions had positive economic effects, and which had negative? Explain.*
2. **Recognizing Effects** *What common political effect did the revolutions in North America and Latin America achieve?*

PRIMARY SOURCE

INTERACTIVE

Thomas Paine

In this excerpt from the pamphlet *Common Sense,* Thomas Paine described the ideal government he wanted to see set up after the American Revolution.

But where, say some, is the king of America? I'll tell you, friend, he reigns above, and doth not make havoc of mankind like the Royal Brute of Great Britain. . . . Let a day be solemnly set apart for proclaiming the charter [constitution]; let it be brought forth placed on the divine law, the Word of God; let a crown be placed thereon, by which the world may know, that so far as we approve of monarchy, that in America THE LAW IS KING. For as in absolute governments the king is law, so in free countries the law *ought* to BE king, and there ought to be no other.

DOCUMENT-BASED QUESTION

What did Paine believe should be the highest power in a new American government?

PRIMARY SOURCE

INTERACTIVE

Simón Bolívar

"The Jamaica Letter" is one of Simón Bolívar's most important political documents. In this excerpt, he discussed his political goals for South America after the revolution—and his fear that South Americans were not ready to achieve those goals.

The role of the inhabitants of the American hemisphere has for centuries been purely passive. Politically they were non-existent. . . . We have been harassed by a conduct which has not only deprived us of our rights but has kept us in a sort of permanent infancy with regard to public affairs. . . . Americans today, and perhaps to a greater extent than ever before, who live within the Spanish system occupy a position in society no better than that of serfs destined for labor. . . . Although I seek perfection for the government of my country, I cannot persuade myself that the New World can, at the moment, be organized as a great republic.

DOCUMENT-BASED QUESTION

Why did Bolívar believe that South Americans were not ready for a republican form of government?

PRIMARY SOURCE

INTERACTIVE

Maximilien Robespierre

In a speech given on February 5, 1794, Robespierre described his goals for the French Revolution. In this excerpt, he explained his reasons for using terror.

It is necessary to annihilate both the internal and external enemies of the republic or perish with its fall. Now, in this situation your first political maxim should be that one guides the people by reason, and the enemies of the people by terror.

If the driving force of popular government in peacetime is virtue, that of popular government during a revolution is both virtue and terror: virtue, without which terror is destructive; terror, without which virtue is impotent. Terror is only justice that is prompt, severe, and inflexible; it is thus an emanation of virtue; it is less a distinct principle than a consequence of the general principle of democracy applied to the most pressing needs of the patrie [nation].

DOCUMENT-BASED QUESTION

Why did Robespierre believe the use of terror against his enemies was necessary?

Comparing & Contrasting

1. Judging from the information on the chart, which revolutions resulted in the establishment of representative government, and which resulted in a return to tyrannical rule?
2. How do the political goals of the revolutionary leaders quoted here differ?
3. Compare the types of government set up in the United States, France, and Latin America after their revolutions. Did Paine, Robespierre, and Bolívar achieve the political goals quoted? Explain.

EXTENSION ACTIVITY

Revolutionary activity continued after the period covered by this unit. Two major 20th-century revolutions were the Russian Revolution (see Chapter 30) and the Chinese revolution and civil war (see Chapter 30 and Chapter 33). Read about one of these revolutions either in this textbook or in an encyclopedia. Then create a chart comparing that revolution with either the American Revolution or the French Revolution.

UNIT 6 Industrialism and the Race for Empire 1700–1914

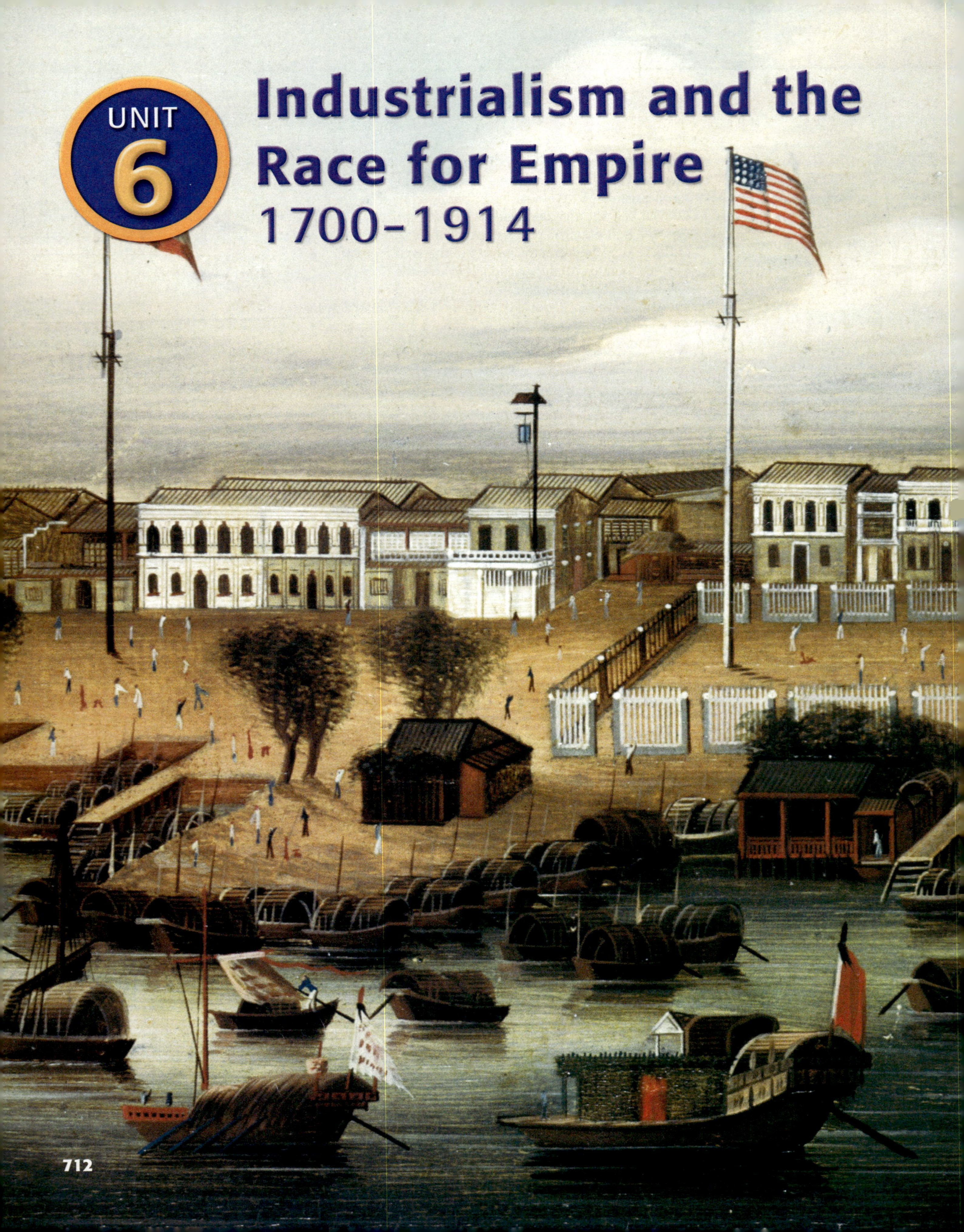

Although this painting shows Canton, China, the flags flying over the fenced-in areas near the shore are those of Spain, the United States, Great Britain, and the Netherlands. Canton was one of only two Chinese ports open to Westerners until 1842.

Comparing & Contrasting

Scientific and Technological Changes

In Unit 6, you will learn about scientific and technological changes that led to the Industrial Revolution and helped Western nations establish colonies around the world. At the end of the unit, you will have a chance to compare and contrast those changes. (See pages 830–835.)

CHAPTER 25

The Industrial Revolution, 1700–1900

Previewing Main Ideas

SCIENCE AND TECHNOLOGY From the spinning jenny to the locomotive train, there was an explosion of inventions and technological advances. These improvements paved the way for the Industrial Revolution.

Geography *What other European countries besides England had coal, iron, and textile industries in the 1800s?*

EMPIRE BUILDING The global power balance shifted after the Industrial Revolution. This shift occurred because industrialized nations dominated the rest of the world.

Geography *Study the map. Which country appears to be the most industrialized?*

ECONOMICS The Industrial Revolution transformed economic systems. In part, this was because nations dramatically changed the way they produced and distributed goods.

Geography *What geographic factors might have encouraged the development of industry in certain places?*

NEW YORK CORE CURRICULUM FOCUS

- The improved farming techniques of the agricultural revolution helped pave the way for the Industrial Revolution.
- The changes brought by industrialization led to calls for social reforms.

INTEGRATED TECHNOLOGY

eEdition
- Interactive Maps
- Interactive Visuals
- Interactive Primary Sources

VIDEO *Patterns of Interaction: The Industrial and Electronic Revolutions*

INTERNET RESOURCES
Go to **classzone.com** for:
- Research Links
- Internet Activities
- Primary Sources
- Chapter Quiz
- Maps
- Test Practice
- Current Events

EUROPE AND UNITED STATES

1701 Jethro Tull invents seed drill. ▶

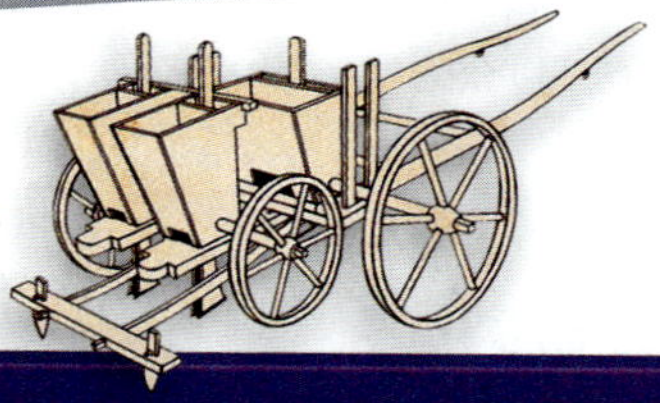

1765 James Watt builds steam engine.

1700

1750

WORLD

1736 Qian-long begins his reign as emperor of China. (Imperial Palace compound at Beijing) ▶

1793
Eli Whitney invents cotton gin. ▶

1848
Marx and Engels publish *The Communist Manifesto.* ▶

1875
British unions win right to strike.

1800 1850 1900

1804
Haiti wins freedom from France.

1867
Meiji era begins a period of modernization in Japan.

1869
Suez Canal opens in Africa.

Interact *with* History

What are fair working conditions?

You are a 15-year-old living in England where the Industrial Revolution has spurred the growth of thousands of factories. Cheap labor is in great demand. Like millions of other teenagers, you do not go to school. Instead, you work in a factory 6 days a week, 14 hours a day. The small pay you receive is needed to help support your family. You trudge to work before dawn every day and work until after sundown. Inside the workplace the air is hot and foul, and after sunset it is so dark it is hard to see. Minding the machines is exhausting, dirty, and dangerous.

1 **Long hours:** The sun may be shining through the windows as this child's day begins, but it will have disappeared by the time his day ends.

2 **Dangerous machines:** Children usually worked in bare feet with no safety equipment among machines with many moving parts.

3 **Hot temperatures and dust-filled air:** Dust particles from thousands of bobbins cling to the clothing and hang in air heated by the machinery.

EXAMINING *the* ISSUES

- **Would you attempt to change your working conditions in the factory?**
- **Would you join a union, go to school, or run away?**

In small groups, discuss these questions. Share your conclusions with your class. In your discussions, think about how children lived in preindustrial and industrial societies all over the world. As you read about the changes caused by industrialization, note how reform movements eventually improved conditions for most laborers.

The Beginnings of Industrialization

CONNECT TO THE NEW YORK STATE CORE CURRICULUM

Unit 5.G.1. Human and physical geography
Unit 5.G.2. Agrarian revolution

TERMS & NAMES

- Industrial Revolution
- enclosure
- crop rotation
- industrialization
- factors of production
- factory
- entrepreneur

SETTING THE STAGE-In the United States, France, and Latin America, political revolutions brought in new governments. A different type of revolution now transformed the way people worked. The **Industrial Revolution** refers to the greatly increased output of machine-made goods that began in England in the middle 1700s. Before the Industrial Revolution, people wove textiles by hand. Then, machines began to do this and other jobs. Soon the Industrial Revolution spread from England to Continental Europe and North America.

TAKING NOTES

Following Chronological Order On a time line, note important events in Britain's industrialization.

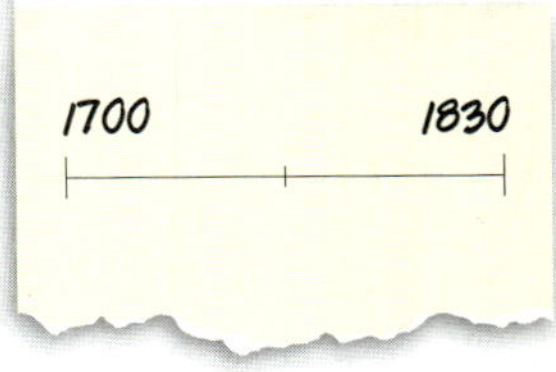

Industrial Revolution Begins in Britain

In 1700, small farms covered England's landscape. Wealthy landowners, however, began buying up much of the land that village farmers had once worked. The large landowners dramatically improved farming methods. These innovations amounted to an agricultural revolution.

The Agricultural Revolution-Paves the Way After buying up the land of village farmers, wealthy landowners enclosed their land with fences or hedges. The increase in their landholdings enabled them to cultivate larger fields. Within these larger fields, called **enclosures**, landowners experimented with more productive seeding and harvesting methods to boost crop yields. The enclosure movement had two important results. First, landowners tried new agricultural methods. Second, large landowners forced small farmers to become tenant farmers or to give up farming and move to the cities.

Jethro Tull was one of the first of these scientific farmers. He saw that the usual way of sowing seed by scattering it across the ground was wasteful. Many seeds failed to take root. He solved this problem with an invention called the seed drill in about 1701. It allowed farmers to sow seeds in well-spaced rows at specific depths. A larger share of the seeds took root, boosting crop yields.

Rotating Crops The process of **crop rotation** proved to be one of the best developments by the scientific farmers. The process improved upon older methods of crop rotation, such as the medieval three-field system discussed in Chapter 14. One year, for example, a farmer might plant a field with wheat, which exhausted soil nutrients. The next year he planted a root crop, such as turnips, to restore nutrients. This might be followed in turn by barley and then clover.

▸ An English farmer plants his fields in the early 1700s using a seed drill.

Livestock breeders improved their methods too. In the 1700s, for example, Robert Bakewell increased his mutton (sheep meat) output by allowing only his best sheep to breed. Other farmers followed Bakewell's lead. Between 1700 and 1786, the average weight for lambs climbed from 18 to 50 pounds. As food supplies increased and living conditions improved, England's population mushroomed. An increasing population boosted the demand for food and goods such as cloth. As farmers lost their land to large enclosed farms, many became factory workers. **A**

MAIN IDEA

Recognizing Effects

A How did population growth spur the Industrial Revolution?

Why the Industrial Revolution Began in England In addition to a large population of workers, the small island country had extensive natural resources. **Industrialization**, which is the process of developing machine production of goods, required such resources. These natural resources included

- water power and coal to fuel the new machines
- iron ore to construct machines, tools, and buildings
- rivers for inland transportation
- harbors from which merchant ships set sail

In addition to its natural resources, Britain had an expanding economy to support industrialization. Businesspeople invested in the manufacture of new inventions. Britain's highly developed banking system also contributed to the country's industrialization. People were encouraged by the availability of bank loans to invest in new machinery and expand their operations. Growing overseas trade, economic prosperity, and a climate of progress led to the increased demand for goods.

Britain's political stability gave the country a tremendous advantage over its neighbors. Though Britain took part in many wars during the 1700s, none occurred on British soil. Their military successes gave the British a positive attitude. Parliament also passed laws to help encourage and protect business ventures. Other countries had some of these advantages. But Britain had all the **factors of production**, the resources needed to produce goods and services that the Industrial Revolution required. They included land, labor, and capital (or wealth).

Inventions Spur Industrialization

In an explosion of creativity, inventions now revolutionized industry. Britain's textile industry clothed the world in wool, linen, and cotton. This industry was the first to be transformed. Cloth merchants boosted their profits by speeding up the process by which spinners and weavers made cloth.

Changes in the Textile Industry As you will learn in the feature on textile technology on page 719, by 1800, several major inventions had modernized the cotton industry. One invention led to another. In 1733, a machinist named John Kay made a shuttle that sped back and forth on wheels. This flying shuttle, a boat-shaped piece

Textiles Industrialize First

The Industrial Revolution that began in Britain was spurred by a revolution in technology. It started in the textile industry, where inventions in the late 1700s transformed the manufacture of cloth. The demand for clothing in Britain had greatly increased as a result of the population boom caused by the agricultural revolution. These developments, in turn, had an impact worldwide. For example, the consumption of cotton rose dramatically in Britain (see graph at right). This cotton came from plantations in the American South, where cotton production skyrocketed from 1820 to 1860 in response to demand from English textile mills.

British Cotton Consumption, 1800–1900

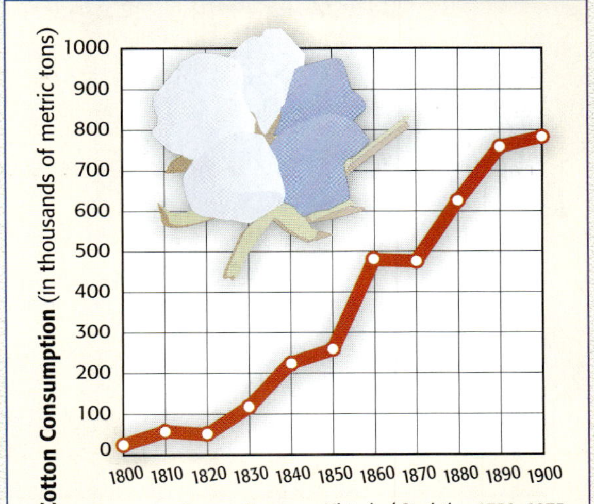

Source: *European Historical Statistics, 1750–1975*

▶ John Kay's flying shuttle (below) speedily carried threads of yarn back and forth when the weaver pulled a handle on the loom. The flying shuttle greatly increased the productivity of weavers.

▲ Flying shuttle

Patterns of Interaction

Technology Transforms an Age: The Industrial and Electronic Revolutions

Inventions in the textile industry started in Britain and brought about the Industrial Revolution. This revolution soon spread to other countries. The process of industrialization is still spreading around the world, especially in developing countries. A similar technological revolution is occurring in electronics today, transforming the distribution of information around the world.

Connect *to* Today

1. **Synthesizing** How might the technological innovation and industrialization that took place in the textile industry during the Industrial Revolution have provided a model for other industries?
   See Skillbuilder Handbook, Page R21.
2. **Recognizing Effects** Research the textile industry today to learn how it has been affected by new technology, including computerization. Prepare a two-paragraph summary on the effects of the new technology.

History *in* Depth

Inventions in America

In the United States, American inventors worked at making railroad travel more comfortable, inventing adjustable upholstered seats. They also revolutionized agriculture, manufacturing, and communications:

1831 Cyrus McCormick's reaper boosted American wheat production.

1837 Samuel F. B. Morse, a New England painter, first sent electrical signals over a telegraph.

1851 I. M. Singer improved the sewing machine by inventing a foot treadle (see photograph).

1876 Scottish-born inventor Alexander Graham Bell patented the telephone.

INTEGRATED TECHNOLOGY

INTERNET ACTIVITY Create a photo exhibit on American inventions of the 19th century. Include the name of the inventor and the date with each photograph. Go to **classzone.com** for your research.

of wood to which yarn was attached, doubled the work a weaver could do in a day. Because spinners could not keep up with these speedy weavers, a cash prize attracted contestants to produce a better spinning machine. Around 1764, a textile worker named James Hargreaves invented a spinning wheel he named after his daughter. His spinning jenny allowed one spinner to work eight threads at a time.

At first, textile workers operated the flying shuttle and the spinning jenny by hand. Then, Richard Arkwright invented the water frame in 1769. This machine used the waterpower from rapid streams to drive spinning wheels. In 1779, Samuel Crompton combined features of the spinning jenny and the water frame to produce the spinning mule. The spinning mule made thread that was stronger, finer, and more consistent than earlier spinning machines. Run by waterpower, Edmund Cartwright's power loom sped up weaving after its invention in 1787. **B**

MAIN IDEA

Summarizing

B What inventions transformed the textile industry?

The water frame, the spinning mule, and the power loom were bulky and expensive machines. They took the work of spinning and weaving out of the house. Wealthy textile merchants set up the machines in large buildings called **factories**. Factories needed waterpower, so the first ones were built near rivers and streams:

PRIMARY SOURCE

A great number of streams . . . furnish water-power adequate to turn many hundred mills: they afford the element of water, indispensable for scouring, bleaching, printing, dyeing, and other processes of manufacture: and when collected in their larger channels, or employed to feed canals, they supply a superior inland navigation, so important for the transit of raw materials and merchandise.

EDWARD BAINS, *The History of Cotton Manufacture in Great Britain* (1835)

England's cotton came from plantations in the American South in the 1790s. Removing seeds from the raw cotton by hand was hard work. In 1793, an American inventor named Eli Whitney invented a machine to speed the chore. His cotton gin multiplied the amount of cotton that could be cleaned. American cotton production skyrocketed from 1.5 million pounds in 1790 to 85 million pounds in 1810.

Improvements in Transportation

Progress in the textile industry spurred other industrial improvements. The first such development, the steam engine, stemmed from the search for a cheap, convenient source of power. As early as 1705, coal miners were using steam-powered pumps to remove water from deep mine shafts. But this early model of a steam engine gobbled great quantities of fuel, making it expensive to run.

Watt's Steam Engine James Watt, a mathematical instrument maker at the University of Glasgow in Scotland, thought about the problem for two years. In 1765, Watt figured out a way to make the steam engine work faster and more efficiently while burning less fuel. In 1774, Watt joined with a businessman named Matthew Boulton. Boulton was an **entrepreneur** (AHN•truh•pruh•NUR), a person who organizes, manages, and takes on the risks of a business. He paid Watt a salary and encouraged him to build better engines.

Water Transportation Steam could also propel boats. An American inventor named Robert Fulton ordered a steam engine from Boulton and Watt. He built a steamboat called the *Clermont*, which made its first successful trip in 1807. The *Clermont* later ferried passengers up and down New York's Hudson River.

In England, water transportation improved with the creation of a network of canals, or human-made waterways. By the mid-1800s, 4,250 miles of inland channels slashed the cost of transporting both raw materials and finished goods.

Road Transportation British roads improved, too, thanks largely to the efforts of John McAdam, a Scottish engineer. Working in the early 1800s, McAdam equipped road beds with a layer of large stones for drainage. On top, he placed a carefully smoothed layer of crushed rock. Even in rainy weather heavy wagons could travel over the new "macadam" roads without sinking in mud.

Private investors formed companies that built roads and then operated them for profit. People called the new roads turnpikes because travelers had to stop at tollgates (turnstiles or turnpikes) to pay tolls before traveling farther.

The Railway Age Begins

Steam-driven machinery powered English factories in the late 1700s. A steam engine on wheels—the railroad locomotive—drove English industry after 1820.

Steam-Driven Locomotives In 1804, an English engineer named Richard Trevithick won a bet of several thousand dollars. He did this by hauling ten tons of iron over nearly ten miles of track in a steam-driven locomotive. Other British engineers soon built improved versions of Trevithick's locomotive. One of these early

▼ First-class passengers on the Liverpool-Manchester Railway in the 1830s rode in covered cars; all others, in open cars.

▲ George Stephenson's *Rocket*

railroad engineers was George Stephenson. He had gained a solid reputation by building some 20 engines for mine operators in northern England. In 1821, Stephenson began work on the world's first railroad line. It was to run 27 miles from the Yorkshire coal fields to the port of Stockton on the North Sea. In 1825, the railroad opened. It used four locomotives that Stephenson had designed and built.

The Liverpool-Manchester Railroad News of this success quickly spread throughout Britain. The entrepreneurs of northern England wanted a railroad line to connect the port of Liverpool with the inland city of Manchester. The track was laid. In 1829, trials were held to choose the best locomotive for use on the new line. Five engines entered the competition. None could compare with the *Rocket*, designed by Stephenson and his son.

Smoke poured from the *Rocket*'s tall smokestack, and its two pistons pumped to and fro as they drove the front wheels. The locomotive hauled a 13-ton load at an unheard-of speed—more than 24 miles per hour. The Liverpool-Manchester Railway opened officially in 1830. It was an immediate success.

Railroads Revolutionize Life in Britain The invention and perfection of the locomotive had at least four major effects. First, railroads spurred industrial growth by giving manufacturers a cheap way to transport materials and finished products. Second, the railroad boom created hundreds of thousands of new jobs for both railroad workers and miners. These miners provided iron for the tracks and coal for the steam engines. Third, the railroads boosted England's agricultural and fishing industries, which could transport their products to distant cities.

Finally, by making travel easier, railroads encouraged country people to take distant city jobs. Also, railroads lured city dwellers to resorts in the countryside. Like a locomotive racing across the country, the Industrial Revolution brought rapid and unsettling changes to people's lives. C

MAIN IDEA

Synthesizing

C How did improvements in transportation promote industrialization in Britain?

NEW YORK CORE CURRICULUM REVIEW

TERMS & NAMES 1. For each term or name, write a sentence explaining its significance.

- Industrial Revolution • enclosure • crop rotation • industrialization • factors of production • factory • entrepreneur

USING YOUR NOTES

2. Which of the events listed do you think was the most important? Explain.

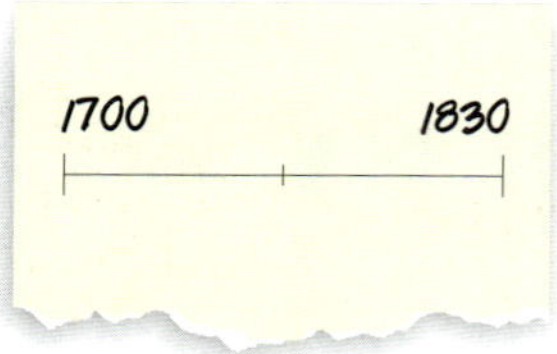

MAIN IDEAS

3. What were four factors that contributed to industrialization in Britain?
4. How did rising population help the Industrial Revolution?
5. What American invention aided the British textile industry?

CRITICAL THINKING & WRITING

6. **EVALUATING** Was the revolution in agriculture necessary to the Industrial Revolution? Explain.
7. **MAKING INFERENCES** What effect did entrepreneurs have upon the Industrial Revolution?
8. **FORMING AND SUPPORTING OPINIONS** Do you agree or disagree with the statement that the steam engine was the greatest invention of the Industrial Revolution? Why?
9. **WRITING ACTIVITY** SCIENCE AND TECHNOLOGY Write a **letter,** as a British government official during the Industrial Revolution, to an official in a nonindustrial nation explaining how the railroad has changed Britain.

CONNECT TO TODAY **CREATING AN ILLUSTRATED NEWS ARTICLE**

Find information on a recent agricultural or technological invention or improvement. Write a two-paragraph **news article** about its economic effects and include an illustration, if possible.

Industrialization

CASE STUDY: Manchester

CONNECT TO THE NEW YORK STATE CORE CURRICULUM

Unit 5.G.2.b. Factory system
Unit 5.G.2.d. Changes in social classes

TERMS & NAMES

- urbanization
- middle class

SETTING THE STAGE The Industrial Revolution affected every part of life in Great Britain, but proved to be a mixed blessing. Eventually, industrialization led to a better quality of life for most people. But the change to machine production initially caused human suffering. Rapid industrialization brought plentiful jobs, but it also caused unhealthy working conditions, air and water pollution, and the ills of child labor. It also led to rising class tensions, especially between the working class and the middle class.

TAKING NOTES

Outlining Organize main ideas and details.

I. Industrialization Changes Life
A.
B.
II. Class Tensions Grow

Industrialization Changes Life

The pace of industrialization accelerated rapidly in Britain. By the 1800s, people could earn higher wages in factories than on farms. With this money, more people could afford to heat their homes with coal from Wales and dine on Scottish beef. They wore better clothing, too, woven on power looms in England's industrial cities. Cities swelled with waves of job seekers.

Industrial Cities Rise For centuries, most Europeans had lived in rural areas. After 1800, the balance shifted toward cities. This shift was caused by the growth of the factory system, where the manufacturing of goods was concentrated in a central location. Between 1800 and 1850, the number of European cities boasting more than 100,000 inhabitants rose from 22 to 47. Most of Europe's urban areas at least doubled in population; some even quadrupled. This period was one of **urbanization**—city building and the movement of people to cities.

As cities grew, people crowded into tenements and row houses such as these in London.

The Day of a Child Laborer, William Cooper

William Cooper began working in a textile factory at the age of ten. He had a sister who worked upstairs in the same factory. In 1832, Cooper was called to testify before a parliamentary committee about the conditions among child laborers in the textile industry. The following sketch of his day is based upon his testimony.

5 A.M. The workday began. Cooper and his sister rose as early as 4:00 or 4:30 in order to get to the factory by 5:00. Children usually ate their breakfast on the run.

12 NOON The children were given a 40-minute break for lunch. This was the only break they received all day.

Factories developed in clusters because entrepreneurs built them near sources of energy, such as water and coal. Major new industrial centers sprang up between the coal-rich area of southern Wales and the Clyde River valley in Scotland. But the biggest of these centers developed in England. (See map on page 715.)

Britain's capital, London, was the country's most important city. It had a population of about one million people by 1800. During the 1800s, its population exploded, providing a vast labor pool and market for new industry. London became Europe's largest city, with twice as many people as its closest rival (Paris). Newer cities challenged London's industrial leadership. Birmingham and Sheffield became iron-smelting centers. Leeds and Manchester dominated textile manufacturing. Along with the port of Liverpool, Manchester formed the center of Britain's bustling cotton industry. During the 1800s, Manchester experienced rapid growth from around 45,000 in 1760 to 300,000 by 1850.

Living Conditions Because England's cities grew rapidly, they had no development plans, sanitary codes, or building codes. Moreover, they lacked adequate housing, education, and police protection for the people who poured in from the countryside to seek jobs. Most of the unpaved streets had no drains, and garbage collected in heaps on them. Workers lived in dark, dirty shelters, with whole families crowding into one bedroom. Sickness was widespread. Epidemics of the deadly disease cholera regularly swept through the slums of Great Britain's industrial cities. In 1842, a British government study showed an average life span to be 17 years for working-class people in one large city, compared with 38 years in a nearby rural area.

Elizabeth Gaskell's *Mary Barton* (1848) is a work of fiction. But it presents a startlingly accurate portrayal of urban life experienced by many at the time. Gaskell provides a realistic description of the dank cellar dwelling of one family in a Manchester slum:

▼ Elizabeth Gaskell (1810–1865) was a British writer whose novels show a sympathy for the working class.

PRIMARY SOURCE Ⓐ

You went down one step even from the foul area into the cellar in which a family of human beings lived. It was very dark inside. The window-panes many of them were broken and stuffed with rags . . . . the smell was so fetid [foul] as almost to knock the two men down. . . . they began to penetrate the thick darkness of the place, and to see three or four little children rolling on the damp, nay wet brick floor, through which the stagnant, filthy moisture of the street oozed up.

ELIZABETH GASKELL, *Mary Barton*

MAIN IDEA

Analyzing Primary Sources

Ⓐ How does Gaskell indicate her sympathy for the working class in this passage?

But not everyone in urban areas lived miserably. Well-to-do merchants and factory owners often built luxurious homes in the suburbs.

3 P.M. The children often became drowsy during the afternoon or evening hours. In order to keep them awake, adult overseers sometimes whipped the children.

6 P.M. There was no break allowed for an evening meal. Children again ate on the run.

9 P.M. William Cooper's day ended after an exhausting 16-hour shift at work.

11 P.M. Cooper's sister worked another two hours even though she had to be back at work at 5:00 the next morning.

Working Conditions To increase production, factory owners wanted to keep their machines running as many hours as possible. As a result, the average worker spent 14 hours a day at the job, 6 days a week. Work did not change with the seasons, as it did on the farm. Instead, work remained the same week after week, year after year.

Industry also posed new dangers for workers. Factories were seldom well lit or clean. Machines injured workers. A boiler might explode or a drive belt might catch an arm. And there was no government program to provide aid in case of injury. The most dangerous conditions of all were found in coal mines. Frequent accidents, damp conditions, and the constant breathing of coal dust made the average miner's life span ten years shorter than that of other workers. Many women and children were employed in the mining industry because they were the cheapest source of labor.

Class Tensions Grow

Though poverty gripped Britain's working classes, the Industrial Revolution created enormous amounts of wealth in the nation. Most of this new money belonged to factory owners, shippers, and merchants. These people were part of a growing **middle class**, a social class made up of skilled workers, professionals, businesspeople, and wealthy farmers.

The Middle Class The new middle class transformed the social structure of Great Britain. In the past, landowners and aristocrats had occupied the top position in British society. With most of the wealth, they wielded the social and political power. Now some factory owners, merchants, and bankers grew wealthier than the landowners and aristocrats. Yet important social distinctions divided the two wealthy classes. Landowners looked down on those who had made their fortunes in the "vulgar" business world. Not until late in the 1800s were rich entrepreneurs considered the social equals of the lords of the countryside.

Gradually, a larger middle class—neither rich nor poor—emerged. The upper middle class consisted of government employees, doctors, lawyers, and managers of factories, mines, and shops. The lower middle class included factory overseers and such skilled workers as toolmakers, mechanical drafters, and printers. These people enjoyed a comfortable standard of living. **B**

MAIN IDEA

Summarizing

B Describe the social classes in Britain.

The Working Class During the years 1800 to 1850, however, laborers, or the working class, saw little improvement in their living and working conditions. They watched their livelihoods disappear as machines replaced them. In frustration, some smashed the machines they thought were putting them out of work.

One group of such workers was called the Luddites. They were named after Ned Ludd. Ludd, probably a mythical English laborer, was said to have destroyed weaving machinery around 1779. The Luddites attacked whole factories in northern England beginning in 1811, destroying laborsaving machinery. Outside the factories, mobs of workers rioted, mainly because of poor living and working conditions.

Positive Effects of the Industrial Revolution

Despite the problems that followed industrialization, the Industrial Revolution had a number of positive effects. It created jobs for workers. It contributed to the wealth of the nation. It fostered technological progress and invention. It greatly increased the production of goods and raised the standard of living. Perhaps most important, it provided the hope of improvement in people's lives.

The Industrial Revolution produced a number of other benefits as well. These included healthier diets, better housing, and cheaper, mass-produced clothing. Because the Industrial Revolution created a demand for engineers as well as clerical and professional workers, it expanded educational opportunities.

The middle and upper classes prospered immediately from the Industrial Revolution. For the workers it took longer, but their lives gradually improved during the 1800s. Laborers eventually won higher wages, shorter hours, and better working conditions after they joined together to form labor unions.

Long-Term Effects The long-term effects of the Industrial Revolution are still evident. Most people today in industrialized countries can afford consumer goods that would have been considered luxuries 50 or 60 years ago. In addition, their living and working conditions are much improved over those of workers in the 19th century. Also, profits derived from industrialization produced tax revenues. These funds have allowed local, state, and federal governments to invest in urban improvements and raise the standard of living of most city dwellers.

The economic successes of the Industrial Revolution, and also the problems created by it, were clearly evident in one of Britain's new industrial cities in the 1800s—Manchester.

CASE STUDY: Manchester

The Mills of Manchester

Manchester's unique advantages made it a leading example of the new industrial city. This northern English town had ready access to waterpower. It also had available labor from the nearby countryside and an outlet to the sea at Liverpool.

"From this filthy sewer pure gold flows," wrote Alexis de Tocqueville (ah•lehk•SEE duh TOHK•vihl), the French writer, after he visited Manchester in 1835. Indeed, the industrial giant showed the best and worst of the Industrial Revolution. Manchester's rapid, unplanned growth made it an unhealthy place for the poor people who lived and worked there. But wealth flowed from its factories. It went first to the mill owners and the new middle class. Eventually, although not immediately, the working class saw their standard of living rise as well.

Manchester's business owners took pride in mastering each detail of the manufacturing process. They worked many hours and risked their own money. For their efforts, they were rewarded with high profits. Many erected gracious homes on the outskirts of town.

To provide the mill owners with high profits, workers labored under terrible conditions. Children as young as six joined their parents in the factories. There, for six days a week, they toiled from 6 A.M. to 7 or 8 P.M., with only half an hour for

Industrialization

Industrialization is the process of developing industries that use machines to produce goods. This process not only revolutionizes a country's economy, it also transforms social conditions and class structures.

Effects of Industrialization

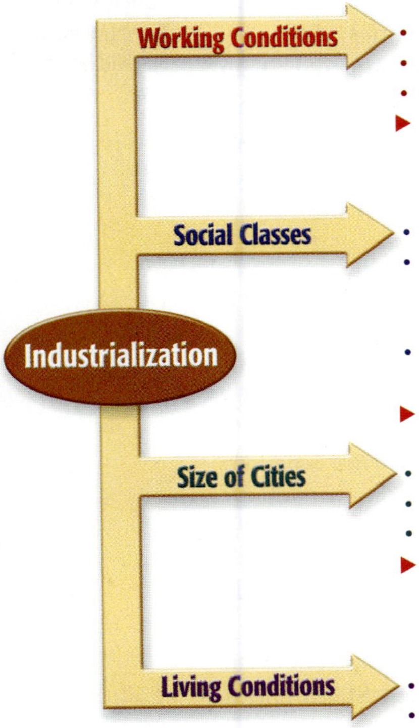

Working Conditions
- Industry created many new jobs.
- Factories were dirty, unsafe, and dangerous.
- Factory bosses exercised harsh discipline.
- ▶ **Long-Term Effect** Workers won higher wages, shorter hours, better conditions.

Social Classes
- Factory workers were overworked and underpaid.
- Overseers and skilled workers rose to lower middle class. Factory owners and merchants formed upper middle class.
- Upper class resented those in middle class who became wealthier than they were.
- ▶ **Long-Term Effect** Standard of living generally rose.

Size of Cities
- Factories brought job seekers to cities.
- Urban areas doubled, tripled, or quadrupled in size.
- Many cities specialized in certain industries.
- ▶ **Long-Term Effect** Suburbs grew as people fled crowded cities.

Living Conditions
- Cities lacked sanitary codes or building controls.
- Housing, water, and social services were scarce.
- Epidemics swept through the city.
- ▶ **Long-Term Effect** Housing, diet, and clothing improved.

▼ This engraving shows urban growth and industrial pollution in Manchester.

INTEGRATED TECHNOLOGY

RESEARCH LINKS For more on industrialization, go to **classzone.com**

> DATA FILE

GROWTH OF CITIES

MANCHESTER

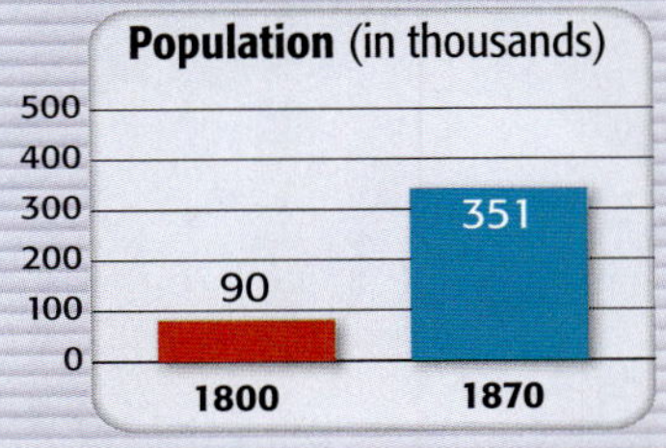

BIRMINGHAM

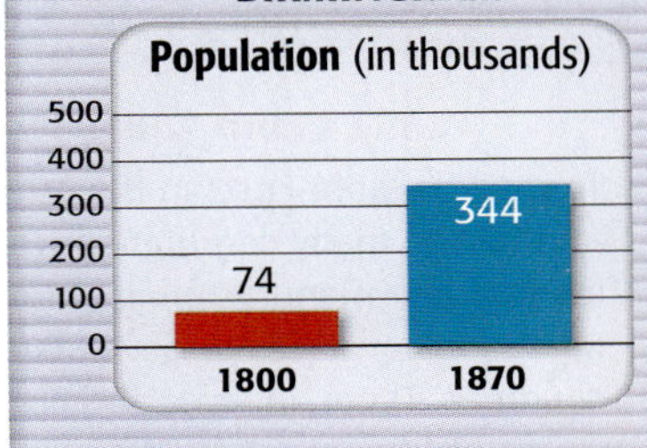

GLASGOW

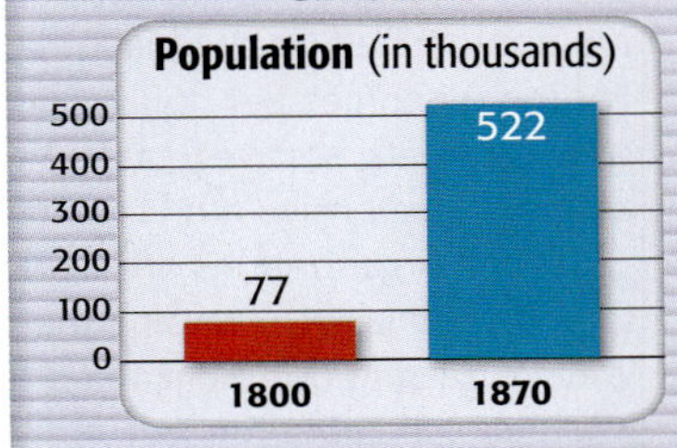

LONDON

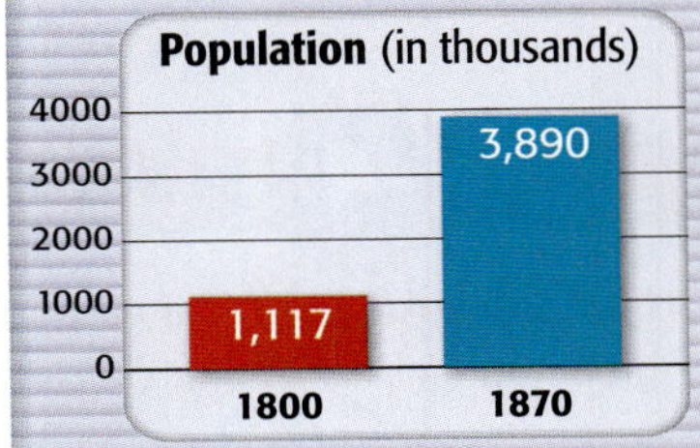

Source: European Historical Statistics, 1750–1975

Connect *to* Today

1. **Recognizing Effects** What were some advantages and disadvantages of industrialization?

   See Skillbuilder Handbook, page R6.

2. **Making Inferences** Many nations around the world today are trying to industrialize. What do you think they hope to gain from that process?

Connect *to* Today

Child Labor Today

To save on labor costs in the 1990s and 2000s, many corporations moved their manufacturing operations overseas to developing countries. There, in sweatshops, young children work long hours under wretched conditions. They are unprotected by child labor laws. For mere pennies per hour, children weave carpets, sort vegetables, or assemble expensive athletic shoes.

Several organizations are working to end child labor, including the Child Welfare League of America and the International Labor Rights Fund.

lunch and an hour for dinner. To keep the children awake, mill supervisors beat them. Tiny hands repaired broken threads in Manchester's spinning machines, replaced thread in the bobbins, or swept up cotton fluff. The dangerous machinery injured many children. The fluff filled their lungs and made them cough.

Until the first Factory Act passed in 1819, the British government exerted little control over child labor in Manchester and other factory cities. The act restricted working age and hours. For years after the act passed, young children still did heavy, dangerous work in Manchester's factories. **C**

MAIN IDEA

Drawing Conclusions

C Whose interests did child labor serve?

Putting so much industry into one place polluted the natural environment. The coal that powered factories and warmed houses blackened the air. Textile dyes and other wastes poisoned Manchester's Irwell River. An eyewitness observer wrote the following description of the river in 1862:

PRIMARY SOURCE

Steam boilers discharge into it their seething contents, and drains and sewers their fetid impurities; till at length it rolls on—here between tall dingy walls, there under precipices of red sandstone—considerably less a river than a flood of liquid manure.

HUGH MILLER, *"Old Red Sandstone"*

Like other new industrial cities of the 19th century, Manchester produced consumer goods and created wealth on a grand scale. Yet, it also stood as a reminder of the ills of rapid and unplanned industrialization.

As you will learn in Section 3, the industrialization that began in Great Britain spread to the United States and to continental Europe in the 1800s.

NEW YORK CORE CURRICULUM REVIEW

TERMS & NAMES 1. For each term or name, write a sentence explaining its significance.

- urbanization
- middle class

USING YOUR NOTES

2. Which change brought about by industrialization had the greatest impact?

I. Industrialization Changes Life
A.
B.
II. Class Tensions Grow

MAIN IDEAS

3. Why did people flock to British cities and towns during the Industrial Revolution?
4. What social class expanded as a result of industrialization?
5. What were some of the negative effects of the rapid growth of Manchester?

CRITICAL THINKING & WRITING

6. **SUMMARIZING** How did industrialization contribute to city growth?
7. **EVALUATING** How were class tensions affected by the Industrial Revolution?
8. **FORMING AND SUPPORTING OPINIONS** The Industrial Revolution has been described as a mixed blessing. Do you agree or disagree? Support your answer with text references.
9. **WRITING ACTIVITY** ECONOMICS -As a factory owner during the Industrial Revolution, write a **letter** to a newspaper justifying working conditions in your factory.

CONNECT TO TODAY **CREATING A COMPARISON CHART**

Make a **comparison chart** listing information on child labor in three developing nations—one each from Asia, Africa, and Latin America—and compare with data from the United States.

Industrialization Spreads

CONNECT TO THE NEW YORK STATE CORE CURRICULUM

Unit 5.G.1. Human and physical geography
Unit 5.G.3.g.8. Global migrations (19th century)

TERMS & NAMES

- stock
- corporation

SETTING THE STAGE Great Britain's favorable geography and its financial systems, political stability, and natural resources sparked industrialization. British merchants built the world's first factories. When these factories prospered, more laborsaving machines and factories were built. Eventually, the Industrial Revolution that had begun in Britain spread both to the United States and to continental Europe. Countries that had conditions similar to those in Britain were ripe for industrialization.

TAKING NOTES

Comparing Use a Venn diagram to compare industrialization in the United States and in Europe.

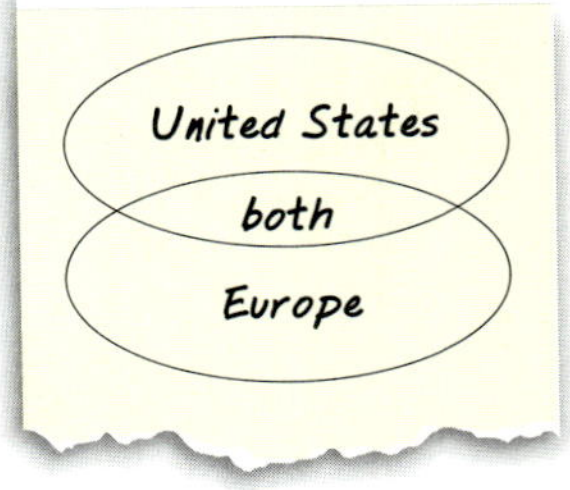

Industrial Development in the United States

The United States possessed the same resources that allowed Britain to mechanize its industries. America had fast-flowing rivers, rich deposits of coal and iron ore, and a supply of laborers made up of farm workers and immigrants. During the War of 1812, Britain blockaded the United States, trying to keep it from engaging in international trade. This blockade forced the young country to use its own resources to develop independent industries. Those industries would manufacture the goods the United States could no longer import.

Industrialization in the United States As in Britain, industrialization in the United States began in the textile industry. Eager to keep the secrets of industrialization to itself, Britain had forbidden engineers, mechanics, and toolmakers to leave the country. In 1789, however, a young British mill worker named Samuel Slater emigrated to the United States. There, Slater built a spinning machine from memory and a partial design. The following year, Moses Brown opened the first factory in the United States to house Slater's machines in Pawtucket, Rhode Island. But the Pawtucket factory mass-produced only one part of finished cloth, the thread.

▼ Teenage mill girls at a Georgia cotton mill

In 1813, Francis Cabot Lowell of Boston and four other investors revolutionized the American textile industry. They mechanized every stage in the manufacture of cloth. Their weaving factory in Waltham, Massachusetts, earned them enough money to fund a larger

The Growth of Railroads in the United States

Railroad System, 1840

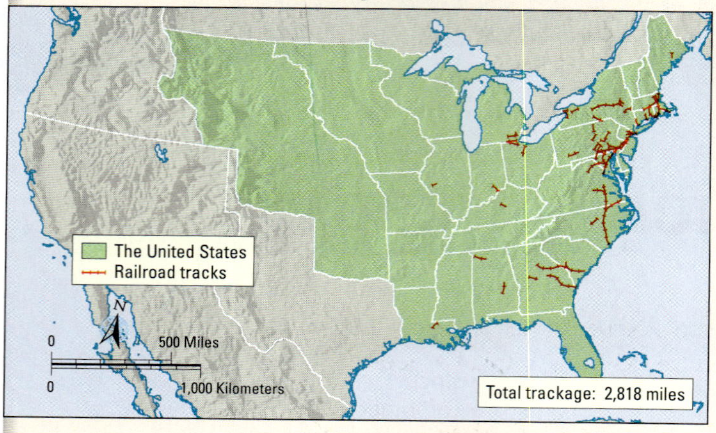

Railroad System, 1890

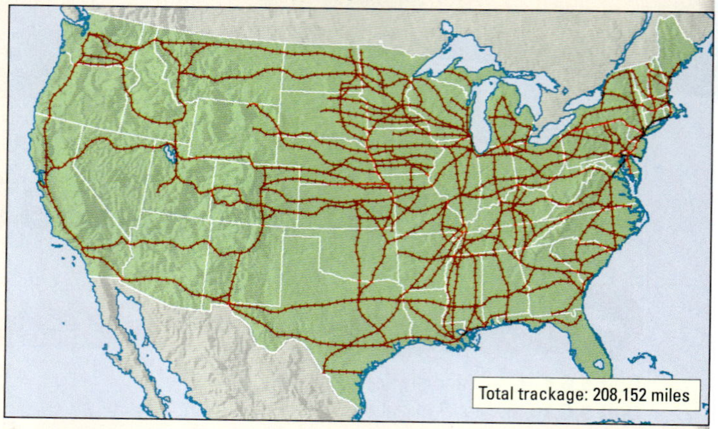

GEOGRAPHY SKILLBUILDER: Interpreting Maps

1. **Region** *In what part of the country were the first railroads built? By 1890, what other part of the country was densely covered by railroad tracks?*
2. **Movement** *In what direction did the railroads help people move across the country?*

operation in another Massachusetts town. When Lowell died, the remaining partners named the town after him. By the late 1820s, Lowell, Massachusetts, had become a booming manufacturing center and a model for other such towns.

Thousands of young single women flocked from their rural homes to work as mill girls in factory towns. There, they could make higher wages and have some independence. However, to ensure proper behavior, they were watched closely inside and outside the factory by their employers. The mill girls toiled more than 12 hours a day, 6 days a week, for decent wages. For some, the mill job was an alternative to being a servant and was often the only other job open to them:

PRIMARY SOURCE (A)

Country girls were naturally independent, and the feeling that at this new work the few hours they had of everyday leisure were entirely their own was a satisfaction to them. They preferred it to going out as "hired help." It was like a young man's pleasure in entering upon business for himself. Girls had never tried that experiment before, and they liked it.

LUCY LARCOM, *A New England Girlhood*

MAIN IDEA

Analyzing Primary Sources

(A) Why did Lucy Larcom think mill work benefited young women?

Textiles led the way, but clothing manufacture and shoemaking also underwent mechanization. Especially in the Northeast, skilled workers and farmers had formerly worked at home. Now they labored in factories in towns and cities such as Waltham, Lowell, and Lawrence, Massachusetts.

Later Expansion of U.S. Industry The Northeast experienced much industrial growth in the early 1800s. Nonetheless, the United States remained primarily agricultural until the Civil War ended in 1865. During the last third of the 1800s, the country experienced a technological boom. As in Britain, a number of causes contributed to this boom. These included a wealth of natural resources, among them oil, coal, and iron; a burst of inventions, such as the electric light bulb and the telephone; and a swelling urban population that consumed the new manufactured goods.

Also, as in Britain, railroads played a major role in America's industrialization. Cities like Chicago and Minneapolis expanded rapidly during the late 1800s. This was due to their location along the nation's expanding railroad lines. Chicago's stockyards and Minneapolis's grain industries prospered by selling products to the rest of the country. Indeed, the railroads themselves proved to be a profitable business. By the end of the 1800s, a limited number of large, powerful companies controlled more than two-thirds of the nation's railroad tracks. Businesses of all kinds began to merge as the railroads had. Smaller companies joined together to form a larger one.

The Rise of Corporations Building large businesses like railroads required a great deal of money. To raise the money, entrepreneurs sold shares of **stock**, or certain rights of ownership. Thus people who bought stock became part owners of these businesses, which were called corporations. A **corporation** is a business owned by stockholders who share in its profits but are not personally responsible for its debts. Corporations were able to raise the large amounts of capital needed to invest in industrial equipment.

In the late 1800s, large corporations such as Standard Oil (founded by John D. Rockefeller) and the Carnegie Steel Company (founded by Andrew Carnegie) sprang up. They sought to control every aspect of their own industries in order to make big profits. Big business—the giant corporations that controlled entire industries—also made big profits by reducing the cost of producing goods. In the United States as elsewhere, workers earned low wages for laboring long hours, while stockholders earned high profits and corporate leaders made fortunes.

Continental Europe Industrializes

European businesses yearned to adopt the "British miracle," the result of Britain's profitable new methods of manufacturing goods. But the troubles sparked by the French Revolution and the Napoleonic wars between 1789 and 1815 had halted trade, interrupted communication, and caused inflation in some parts of the continent. European countries watched the gap widen between themselves and Britain. Even so, industrialization eventually reached continental Europe.

▼ Danish workers labor in a steel mill in this 1885 painting by Peter Severin Kroyer.

Global Impact

Industrialization in Japan

With the beginning of the Meiji era in Japan in 1868, the central government began an ambitious program to transform the country into an industrialized state. It financed textile mills, coal mines, shipyards, and cement and other factories. It also asked private companies to invest in industry.

Some companies had been in business since the 1600s. But new companies sprang up too. Among them was the Mitsubishi company, founded in 1870 and still in business.

The industrializing of Japan produced sustained economic growth for the country. But it also led to strengthening the military and to Japanese imperialism in Asia.

Beginnings in Belgium Belgium led Europe in adopting Britain's new technology. It had rich deposits of iron ore and coal as well as fine waterways for transportation. As in the United States, British skilled workers played a key role in industrializing Belgium.

Samuel Slater had smuggled the design of a spinning machine to the United States. Much like him, a Lancashire carpenter named William Cockerill illegally made his way to Belgium in 1799. He carried secret plans for building spinning machinery. His son John eventually built an enormous industrial enterprise in eastern Belgium. It produced a variety of mechanical equipment, including steam engines and railway locomotives. Carrying the latest British advances, more British workers came to work with Cockerill. Several then founded their own companies in Europe.

Germany Industrializes Germany was politically divided in the early 1800s. Economic isolation and scattered resources hampered countrywide industrialization. Instead, pockets of industrialization appeared, as in the coal-rich Ruhr Valley of west central Germany. Beginning around 1835, Germany began to copy the British model. Germany imported British equipment and engineers. German manufacturers also sent their children to England to learn industrial management. **B**

MAIN IDEA

Analyzing Causes

B What factors slowed industrialization in Germany?

Most important, Germany built railroads that linked its growing manufacturing cities, such as Frankfurt, with the Ruhr Valley's coal and iron ore deposits. In 1858, a German economist wrote, "Railroads and machine shops, coal mines and iron foundries, spinneries and rolling mills seem to spring up out of the ground, and smokestacks sprout from the earth like mushrooms." Germany's economic strength spurred its ability to develop as a military power. By the late 1800s, a unified, imperial Germany had become both an industrial and a military giant.

Expansion Elsewhere in Europe In the rest of Europe, as in Germany, industrialization during the early 1800s proceeded by region rather than by country. Even in countries where agriculture dominated, pockets of industrialization arose. For example, Bohemia developed a spinning industry. Spain's Catalonia processed more cotton than Belgium. Northern Italy mechanized its textile production, specializing in silk spinning. Serf labor ran factories in regions around Moscow and St. Petersburg.

In France, sustained industrial growth occurred after 1830. French industrialization was more measured and controlled than in other countries because the agricultural economy remained strong. As a result, France avoided the great social and economic problems caused by industrialization. A thriving national market for new French products was created after 1850, when the government began railroad construction.

For a variety of reasons, many European countries did not industrialize. In some nations, the social structure delayed the adoption of new methods of production. The accidents of geography held back others. In Austria-Hungary and Spain, transportation posed great obstacles. Austria-Hungary's mountains defeated railroad builders. Spain lacked both good roads and waterways for canals.

The Impact of Industrialization

The Industrial Revolution shifted the world balance of power. It increased competition between industrialized nations and poverty in less-developed nations.

▲ The Crystal Palace Exposition in London in 1851 (shown above) celebrated the "works of industry of all nations."

Rise of Global Inequality Industrialization widened the wealth gap between industrialized and nonindustrialized countries, even while it strengthened their economic ties. To keep factories running and workers fed, industrialized countries required a steady supply of raw materials from less-developed lands. In turn, industrialized countries viewed poor countries as markets for their manufactured products.

Britain led in exploiting its overseas colonies for resources and markets. Soon other European countries, the United States, Russia, and Japan followed Britain's lead, seizing colonies for their economic resources. Imperialism, the policy of extending one country's rule over many other lands, gave even more power and wealth to these already wealthy nations. Imperialism was born out of the cycle of industrialization, the need for resources to supply the factories of Europe, and the development of new markets around the world. (See Chapter 27.) (C)

MAIN IDEA

Clarifying

(C) Why did imperialism grow out of industrialization?

Transformation of Society Between 1700 and 1900, revolutions in agriculture, production, transportation, and communication changed the lives of people in Western Europe and the United States. Industrialization gave Europe tremendous economic power. In contrast, the economies of Asia and Africa were still based on agriculture and small workshops. Industrialization revolutionized every aspect of society, from daily life to life expectancy. Despite the hardships early urban workers suffered, population, health, and wealth eventually rose dramatically in all industrialized countries. The development of a middle class created great opportunities for education and democratic participation. Greater democratic participation, in turn, fueled a powerful movement for social reform.

NEW YORK CORE CURRICULUM REVIEW

TERMS & NAMES 1. For each term or name, write a sentence explaining its significance.

- stock
- corporation

USING YOUR NOTES

2. Which development had the most impact in the United States? in continental Europe?

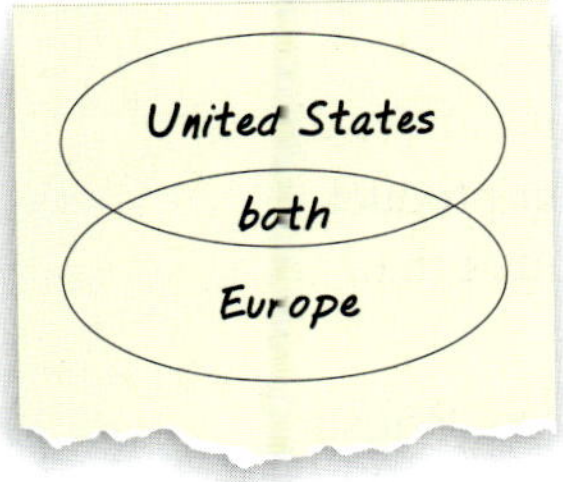

MAIN IDEAS

3. What early industries mechanized in the United States?
4. Why did Belgium lead Europe in adopting industrialization?
5. How did the Industrial Revolution shift the world balance of power?

CRITICAL THINKING & WRITING

6. **RECOGNIZING BIAS** Go back to the quote from Lucy Larcom on page 730. Do you think her feelings about working in the mill are typical? Why or why not?
7. **MAKING INFERENCES** Why was Britain unable to keep industrial secrets away from other nations?
8. **FORMING AND SUPPORTING OPINIONS** What was the most significant effect of the Industrial Revolution?
9. **WRITING ACTIVITY** EMPIRE BUILDING Draw a **political cartoon** that could have been used by the British government to show their sense of their own superiority over nonindustrialized nations that they planned to colonize.

INTEGRATED TECHNOLOGY **INTERNET ACTIVITY**

Use the Internet to research the economy of a less-developed nation in either Asia, Africa, or South America. Create a **database** of economic statistics for that country.

INTERNET KEYWORD
country profiles

Reforming the Industrial World

CONNECT TO THE NEW YORK STATE CORE CURRICULUM

Unit 5.G.3.g.2. Legislative reform
Unit 5.G.3.g.3. Role of unions

TERMS & NAMES

- laissez faire
- Adam Smith
- capitalism
- utilitarianism
- socialism
- Karl Marx
- communism
- union
- strike

SETTING THE STAGE In industrialized countries in the 19th century, the Industrial Revolution opened a wide gap between the rich and the poor. Business leaders believed that governments should stay out of business and economic affairs. Reformers, however, felt that governments needed to play an active role to improve conditions for the poor. Workers also demanded more rights and protection. They formed labor unions to increase their influence.

TAKING NOTES
Summarizing Use a chart to summarize the characteristics of capitalism and socialism.

Capitalism	Socialism
1.	1.
2.	2.
3.	3.

The Philosophers of Industrialization

The term **laissez faire** (LEHS•ay•FAIR) refers to the economic policy of letting owners of industry and business set working conditions without interference. This policy favors a free market unregulated by the government. The term is French for "let do," and by extension, "let people do as they please."

Laissez-faire Economics Laissez-faire economics stemmed from French economic philosophers of the Enlightenment. They criticized the idea that nations grow wealthy by placing heavy tariffs on foreign goods. In fact, they argued, government regulations only interfered with the production of wealth. These philosophers believed that if government allowed free trade—the flow of commerce in the world market without government regulation—the economy would prosper.

Adam Smith, a professor at the University of Glasgow, Scotland, defended the idea of a free economy, or free markets, in his 1776 book *The Wealth of Nations*. According to Smith, economic liberty guaranteed economic progress. As a result, government should not interfere. Smith's arguments rested on what he called the three natural laws of economics:

- the law of self-interest—People work for their own good.
- the law of competition—Competition forces people to make a better product.
- the law of supply and demand—Enough goods would be produced at the lowest possible price to meet demand in a market economy.

The Economists of Capitalism-Smith's basic ideas were supported by British economists Thomas Malthus and David Ricardo. Like Smith, they believed that natural laws governed economic life. Their important ideas were the foundation of laissez-faire capitalism. **Capitalism** is an economic system in which the factors of production are privately owned and money is invested in business ventures to make a profit. These ideas also helped bring about the Industrial Revolution.

In *An Essay on the Principle of Population*, written in 1798, Thomas Malthus argued that population tended to increase more rapidly than the food supply. Without wars and epidemics to kill off the extra people, most were destined to be poor and miserable. The predictions of Malthus seemed to be coming true in the 1840s.

David Ricardo, a wealthy stockbroker, took Malthus's theory one step further in his book, *Principles of Political Economy and Taxation* (1817). Like Malthus, Ricardo believed that a permanent underclass would always be poor. In a market system, if there are many workers and abundant resources, then labor and resources are cheap. If there are few workers and scarce resources, then they are expensive. Ricardo believed that wages would be forced down as population increased.

Laissez-faire thinkers such as Smith, Malthus, and Ricardo opposed government efforts to help poor workers. They thought that creating minimum wage laws and better working conditions would upset the free market system, lower profits, and undermine the production of wealth in society. (A)

MAIN IDEA

Summarizing

(A) What did Malthus and Ricardo say about the effects of population growth?

History Makers

Adam Smith
1723–1790

In his book *The Wealth of Nations*, Smith argued that if individuals freely followed their own self-interest, the world would be an orderly and progressive place. Social harmony would result without any government direction, "as if by an invisible hand."

Smith applied an invisible hand of his own. After his death, people discovered that he had secretly donated large sums of his income to charities.

INTEGRATED TECHNOLOGY

RESEARCH LINKS For more on Adam Smith, go to **classzone.com**

The Rise of Socialism

In contrast to laissez-faire philosophy, which advised governments to leave business alone, other theorists believed that governments should intervene. These thinkers believed that wealthy people or the government must take action to improve people's lives. The French writer Alexis de Tocqueville gave a warning:

PRIMARY SOURCE

Consider what is happening among the working classes. . . . Do you not see spreading among them, little by little, opinions and ideas that aim not to overturn such and such a ministry, or such laws, or such a government, but society itself, to shake it to the foundations upon which it now rests?

ALEXIS DE TOCQUEVILLE, 1848 speech

Utilitarianism English philosopher Jeremy Bentham modified the ideas of Adam Smith. In the late 1700s, Bentham introduced the philosoophy of **utilitarianism**. Bentham wrote his most influential works in the late 1700s. According to Bentham's theory, people should judge ideas, institutions, and actions on the basis of their utility, or usefulness. He argued that the government should try to promote the greatest good for the greatest number of people. A government policy was only useful if it promoted this goal. Bentham believed that in general the individual should be free to pursue his or her own advantage without interference from the state.

John Stuart Mill, a philosopher and economist, led the utilitarian movement in the 1800s. Mill came to question unregulated capitalism. He believed it was wrong that workers should lead deprived lives that sometimes bordered on starvation. Mill wished to help ordinary working people with policies that would lead to a more equal division of profits. He also favored a cooperative system of agriculture and women's rights, including the right to vote. Mill called for the government to do away with great differences in wealth. Utilitarians also pushed for reforms in the legal and prison systems and in education. (B)

MAIN IDEA

Clarifying

(B) How did Mill want to change the economic system?

Utopian Ideas Other reformers took an even more active approach. Shocked by the misery and poverty of the working class, a British factory owner named Robert Owen improved working conditions for his employees. Near his cotton mill in New Lanark, Scotland, Owen built houses, which he rented at low rates. He prohibited children under ten from working in the mills and provided free schooling.

Then, in 1824, he traveled to the United States. He founded a cooperative community called New Harmony in Indiana, in 1825. He intended this community to be a utopia, or perfect living place. New Harmony lasted only three years but inspired the founding of other communities.

Socialism French reformers such as Charles Fourier (FUR•ee•AY), Saint-Simon (san see•MOHN), and others sought to offset the ill effects of industrialization with a new economic system called socialism. In **socialism**, the factors of production are owned by the public and operate for the welfare of all.

Socialism grew out of an optimistic view of human nature, a belief in progress, and a concern for social justice. Socialists argued that the government should plan the economy rather than depend on free-market capitalism to do the job. They argued that government control of factories, mines, railroads, and other key industries would end poverty and promote equality. Public ownership, they believed, would help workers, who were at the mercy of their employers. Some socialists—such as Louis Blanc—advocated change through extension of the right to vote.

History Makers

Karl Marx
1818–1883

Karl Marx studied philosophy at the University of Berlin before he turned to journalism and economics. In 1849, Marx joined the flood of radicals who fled continental Europe for England. He had declared in *The Communist Manifesto* that "the working men have no country."

Marx's theories of socialism and the inevitable revolt of the working class made him little money. He earned a meager living as a journalist. His wealthy coauthor and fellow German, Friedrich Engels, gave Marx financial aid.

INTEGRATED TECHNOLOGY

RESEARCH LINKS For more on Karl Marx, go to **classzone.com**

Marxism: Radical Socialism

The writings of a German journalist named **Karl Marx** introduced the world to a radical type of socialism called Marxism. Marx and Friedrich Engels, a German whose father owned a textile mill in Manchester, outlined their ideas in a 23-page pamphlet called *The Communist Manifesto*.

The Communist Manifesto In their manifesto, Marx and Engels argued that human societies have always been divided into warring classes. In their own time, these were the middle class "haves" or employers, called the bourgeoisie (BUR•zhwah•ZEE), and the "have-nots" or workers, called the proletariat (PROH•lih•TAIR•ee•iht). While the wealthy controlled the means of producing goods, the poor performed backbreaking labor under terrible conditions. This situation resulted in conflict:

PRIMARY SOURCE

Freeman and slave, patrician and plebeian, lord and serf, guild-master and journeyman, in a word, oppressor and oppressed, stood in constant opposition to one another, carried on an uninterrupted, now hidden, now open fight, a fight that each time ended, either in a revolutionary reconstitution of society at large, or in the common ruin of the contending classes.

KARL MARX and **FRIEDRICH ENGELS**, *The Communist Manifesto* (1848)

According to Marx and Engels, the Industrial Revolution had enriched the wealthy and impoverished the poor. The two writers predicted that the workers would overthrow the owners: "The proletarians have nothing to lose but their chains. They have a world to win. Workingmen of all countries, unite." C

MAIN IDEA

Summarizing

C What were the ideas of Marx and Engels concerning relations between the owners and the working class?

> Analyzing Key Concepts

Capitalism vs. Socialism

The economic system called capitalism developed gradually over centuries, beginning in the late Middle Ages. Because of the ways industrialization changed society, some people began to think that capitalism led to certain problems, such as the abuse of workers. They responded by developing a new system of economic ideas called socialism.

Capitalism	Socialism
• Individuals and businesses own property and the means of production.	• The community or the state should own property and the means of production.
• Progress results when individuals follow their own self-interest.	• Progress results when a community of producers cooperate for the good of all.
• Businesses follow their own self-interest by competing for the consumer's money. Each business tries to produce goods or services that are better and less expensive than those of competitors.	• Socialists believe that capitalist employers take advantage of workers. The community or state must act to protect workers.
• Consumers compete to buy the best goods at the lowest prices. This competition shapes the market by affecting what businesses are able to sell.	• Capitalism creates unequal distribution of wealth and material goods. A better system is to distribute goods according to each person's need.
• Government should not interfere in the economy because competition creates efficiency in business.	• An unequal distribution of wealth and material goods is unfair. A better system is to distribute goods according to each person's need.

SKILLBUILDER: Interpreting Charts

1. **Developing Historical Perspective** *Consider the following people from 19th-century Britain: factory worker, shop owner, factory owner, unemployed artisan. Which of them would be most likely to prefer capitalism and which would prefer socialism? Why?*
2. **Forming and Supporting Opinions** *Which system of economic ideas seems most widespread today? Support your opinion.*

The Future According to Marx Marx believed that the capitalist system, which produced the Industrial Revolution, would eventually destroy itself in the following way. Factories would drive small artisans out of business, leaving a small number of manufacturers to control all the wealth. The large proletariat would revolt, seize the factories and mills from the capitalists, and produce what society needed. Workers, sharing in the profits, would bring about economic equality for all people. The workers would control the government in a "dictatorship of the proletariat." After a period of cooperative living and education, the state or government would wither away as a classless society developed.

Marx called this final phase pure communism. Marx described **communism** as a form of complete socialism in which the means of production—all land, mines, factories, railroads, and businesses—would be owned by the people. Private property would in effect cease to exist. All goods and services would be shared equally.

Published in 1848, *The Communist Manifesto* produced few short-term results. Though widespread revolts shook Europe during 1848 and 1849, Europe's leaders eventually put down the uprisings. Only after the turn of the century did the fiery Marxist pamphlet produce explosive results. In the 1900s, Marxism inspired revolutionaries such as Russia's Lenin, China's Mao Zedong, and Cuba's Fidel Castro. These leaders adapted Marx's beliefs to their own specific situations and needs.

Connect *to* Today

Communism Today

Communism expanded to all parts of the world during the Cold War that followed the end of World War II. (See map on page 963.) At the peak of Communist expansion in the 1980s, about 20 nations were Communist-controlled, including two of the world's largest—China and the Soviet Union. However, dissatisfaction with the theories of Karl Marx had been developing.

Eventually, most Communist governments were replaced. Today, there are only five Communist countries—China, North Korea, Vietnam, and Laos in Asia and Cuba in the Caribbean. (See map above.)

In *The Communist Manifesto*, Marx and Engels stated their belief that economic forces alone dominated society. Time has shown, however, that religion, nationalism, ethnic loyalties, and a desire for democratic reforms may be as strong influences on history as economic forces. In addition, the gap between the rich and the poor within the industrialized countries failed to widen in the way that Marx and Engels predicted, mostly because of the various reforms enacted by governments.

Labor Unions and Reform Laws

Factory workers faced long hours, dirty and dangerous working conditions, and the threat of being laid off. By the 1800s, working people became more active in politics. To press for reforms, workers joined together in voluntary labor associations called **unions**.

Unionization A union spoke for all the workers in a particular trade. Unions engaged in collective bargaining, negotiations between workers and their employers. They bargained for better working conditions and higher pay. If factory owners refused these demands, union members could **strike**, or refuse to work.

Skilled workers led the way in forming unions because their special skills gave them extra bargaining power. Management would have trouble replacing such skilled workers as carpenters, printers, and spinners. Thus, the earliest unions helped the lower middle class more than they helped the poorest workers.

The union movement underwent slow, painful growth in both Great Britain and the United States. For years, the British government denied workers the right to form unions. The government saw unions as a threat to social order and stability. Indeed, the Combination Acts of 1799 and 1800 outlawed unions and strikes. Ignoring the threat of jail or job loss, factory workers joined unions anyway. Parliament finally repealed the Combination Acts in 1824. After 1825, the British government unhappily tolerated unions.

British unions had shared goals of raising wages for their members and improving working conditions. By 1875, British trade unions had won the right to strike and picket peacefully. They had also built up a membership of about 1 million people.

In the United States, skilled workers had belonged to unions since the early 1800s. In 1886, several unions joined together to form the organization that would become the American Federation of Labor (AFL). A series of successful strikes won AFL members higher wages and shorter hours.

Reform Laws Eventually, reformers and unions forced political leaders to look into the abuses caused by industrialization. In both Great Britain and the United States, new laws reformed some of the worst abuses of industrialization. In the 1820s and 1830s, for example, Parliament began investigating child labor and working conditions in factories and mines. As a result of its findings, Parliament passed the Factory Act of 1833. The new law made it illegal to hire children under 9 years old. Children from the ages of 9 to 12 could not work more than 8 hours a day. Young people from 13 to 17 could not work more than 12 hours. In 1842, the Mines Act prevented women and children from working underground.

MAIN IDEA

D Summarizing

What were some of the important reform bills passed in Britain during this period?

In 1847, the Parliament passed a bill that helped working women as well as their children. The Ten Hours Act of 1847 limited the workday to ten hours for women and children who worked in factories. D

Reformers in the United States also passed laws to protect child workers. In 1904, a group of progressive reformers organized the National Child Labor Committee to end child labor. Arguing that child labor lowered wages for all workers, union members joined the reformers. Together they pressured national and state politicians to ban child labor and set maximum working hours.

In 1919, the U.S. Supreme Court objected to a federal child labor law, ruling that it interfered with states' rights to regulate labor. However, individual states were allowed to limit the working hours of women and, later, of men.

▲ Hungarian workers meet to plan their strategy before a strike.

The Reform Movement Spreads

Almost from the beginning, reform movements rose in response to the negative impact of industrialization. These reforms included improving the workplace and extending the right to vote to working-class men. The same impulse toward reform, along with the ideals of the French Revolution, also helped to end slavery and promote new rights for women and children.

The Abolition of Slavery William Wilberforce, a highly religious man, was a member of Parliament who led the fight for abolition—the end of the slave trade and slavery in the British Empire. Parliament passed a bill to end the slave trade in the British West Indies in 1807. After he retired from Parliament in 1825, Wilberforce continued his fight to free the slaves. Britain finally abolished slavery in its empire in 1833.

British antislavery activists had mixed motives. Some, such as the abolitionist Wilberforce, were morally against slavery. Others viewed slave labor as an economic threat. Furthermore, a new class of industrialists developed who supported cheap labor rather than slave labor. They soon gained power in Parliament.

In the United States the movement to fulfill the promise of the Declaration of Independence by ending slavery grew in the early 1800s. The enslavement of African people finally ended in the United States when the Union won the Civil War in 1865. Then, enslavement persisted in the Americas only in Puerto Rico, Cuba, and Brazil. In Puerto Rico, slavery was ended in 1873. Spain finally abolished slavery in its Cuban colony in 1886. Not until 1888 did Brazil's huge enslaved population win freedom.

The Fight for Women's Rights The Industrial Revolution proved a mixed blessing for women. On the one hand, factory work offered higher wages than work done at home. Women spinners in Manchester, for example, earned much more money than women who stayed home to spin cotton thread. On the other hand, women factory workers usually made only one-third as much money as men did.

Women led reform movements to address this and other pressing social issues. During the mid-1800s, for example, women formed unions in the trades where they dominated. In Britain, some women served as safety inspectors in factories where other women worked. In the United States, college-educated women like Jane Addams ran settlement houses. These community centers served the poor residents of slum neighborhoods.

History Makers

Jane Addams
1860–1935

After graduating from college, Jane Addams wondered what to do with her life.

> *I gradually became convinced that it would be a good thing to rent a house in a part of the city where many primitive and actual needs are found, in which young women who had been given over too exclusively to study, might . . . learn of life from life itself.*

Addams and her friend Ellen Starr set up Hull House in a working-class district in Chicago. Eventually the facilities included a nursery, a gym, a kitchen, and a boarding house for working women. Hull House not only served the immigrant population of the neighborhood, it also trained social workers.

In both the United States and Britain, women who had rallied for the abolition of slavery began to wonder why their own rights should be denied on the basis of gender. The movement for women's rights began in the United States as early as 1848. Women activists around the world joined to found the International Council for Women in 1888. Delegates and observers from 27 countries attended the council's 1899 meeting. **E**

MAIN IDEA

E Making Inferences- Why might women abolitionists have headed the movement for women's rights?

Reforms Spread to Many Areas of Life In the United States and Western Europe, reformers tried to correct the problems troubling the newly industrialized nations. Public education and prison reform ranked high on the reformers' lists.

One of the most prominent U.S. reformers, Horace Mann of Massachusetts, favored free public education for all children. Mann, who spent his own childhood working at hard labor, warned, "If we do not prepare children to become good citizens . . . if we do not enrich their minds with knowledge, then our republic must go down to destruction." By the 1850s, many states were starting public school systems. In Western Europe, free public schooling became available in the late 1800s.

In 1831, French writer Alexis de Tocqueville had contrasted the brutal conditions in American prisons to the "extended liberty" of American society. Those who sought to reform prisons emphasized the goal of providing prisoners with the means to lead to useful lives upon release.

During the 1800s, democracy grew in industrialized countries even as foreign expansion increased. The industrialized democracies faced new challenges both at home and abroad. You will learn about these challenges in Chapter 26.

NEW YORK CORE CURRICULUM REVIEW

TERMS & NAMES 1. For each term or name, write a sentence explaining its significance.

- laissez faire
- Adam Smith
- capitalism
- utilitarianism
- socialism
- Karl Marx
- communism
- union
- strike

USING YOUR NOTES

2. What characteristics do capitalism and socialism share?

Capitalism	Socialism
1.	1.
2.	2.
3.	3.

MAIN IDEAS

3. What were Adam Smith's three natural laws of economics?
4. What kind of society did early socialists want?
5. Why did workers join together in unions?

CRITICAL THINKING & WRITING

6. **IDENTIFYING PROBLEMS** What were the main problems faced by the unions during the 1800s and how did they overcome them?
7. **DRAWING CONCLUSIONS** Why do you think that Marx's "dictatorship of the proletariat" did not happen?
8. **MAKING INFERENCES** Why did the labor reform movement spread to other areas of life?
9. **WRITING ACTIVITY** ECONOMICS Write a two-paragraph **persuasive essay** on how important economic forces are in society. Support your opinion using evidence from this and previous chapters.

CONNECT TO TODAY **PREPARING AN ECONOMIC REPORT**

Research a present-day corporation. Prepare an **economic report** that includes the corporation's structure, products or services, number of employees, and any other relevant economic information you are able to find.

Different Perspectives: Using Primary and Secondary Sources

INTERACTIVE

Industrialization

Industrialization eventually raised the standard of living for many people in Europe and North America in the 1800s. Yet the process also brought suffering to countless workers who crowded into filthy cities to toil for starvation wages. The following excerpts reveal a variety of perspectives on this major historical event.

A PRIMARY SOURCE

Mary Paul

Mary Paul worked in a textile factory in Lowell, Massachusetts. In an 1846 letter to her father in New Hampshire, the 16-year-old expressed her satisfaction with her situation at Lowell.

I am at work in a spinning room tending four sides of warp which is one girl's work. The overseer tells me that he never had a girl get along better than I do. . . . I have a very good boarding place, have enough to eat. . . . The girls are all kind and obliging. . . . I think that the factory is the best place for me and if any girl wants employment, I advise them to come to Lowell.

B PRIMARY SOURCE

Andrew Carnegie

In his autobiography, published in 1920, the multimillionaire industrialist views with optimism the growth of American industry.

One great advantage which America will have in competing in the markets of the world is that her manufacturers will have the best home market. Upon this they can depend for a return upon capital, and the surplus product can be exported with advantage, even when the prices received for it do no more than cover actual cost, provided the exports be charged with their proportion of all expenses. The nation that has the best home market, especially if products are standardized, as ours are, can soon outsell the foreign producer.

C PRIMARY SOURCE

Friedrich Engels

Friedrich Engels, who coauthored *The Communist Manifesto* and also managed a textile factory in Manchester, England, spent his nights wandering the city's slums.

Nobody troubles about the poor as they struggle helplessly in the whirlpool of modern industrial life. The working man may be lucky enough to find employment, if by his labor he can enrich some member of the middle classes. But his wages are so low that they hardly keep body and soul together. If he cannot find work, he can steal, unless he is afraid of the police; or he can go hungry and then the police will see to it that he will die of hunger in such a way as not to disturb the equanimity of the middle classes.

D PRIMARY SOURCE

Walter Crane

This political cartoon was published in *Cartoons for the Cause* in Britain in 1886. It shows the vampire bat of Capitalism attacking a laborer. Socialism is pictured as an angel who is coming to the rescue.

Document-Based QUESTIONS

1. Why would Andrew Carnegie (Source B) and Friedrich Engels (Source C) disagree about the effects of industrialization?
2. What might be reasons for 16-year-old Mary Paul's (Source A) satisfaction with her job and life in Lowell?
3. Why might the political cartoon by Walter Crane (Source D) be useful in getting workers to rally to the cause of socialism?

Chapter 25 Assessment

VISUAL SUMMARY

The Industrial Revolution

Economic Effects

- New inventions and development of factories
- Rapidly growing industry in the 1800s
- Increased production and higher demand for raw materials
- Growth of worldwide trade
- Population explosion and expanding labor force
- Exploitation of mineral resources
- Highly developed banking and investment system
- Advances in transportation, agriculture, and communication

Social Effects

- Increase in population of cities
- Lack of city planning
- Loss of family stability
- Expansion of middle class
- Harsh conditions for laborers, including children
- Workers' progress versus laissez-faire economic attitudes
- Improved standard of living
- Creation of new jobs
- Encouragement of technological progress

Political Effects

- Child labor laws to end abuses
- Reformers urging equal distribution of wealth
- Trade unions formed
- Social reform movements, such as utilitarianism, utopianism, socialism, and Marxism
- Reform bills in Parliament and Congress

TERMS & NAMES

For each term or name below, briefly explain its connection to the Industrial Revolution.

1. Industrial Revolution
2. enclosure
3. factory
4. urbanization
5. middle class
6. corporation
7. laissez faire
8. socialism
9. Karl Marx
10. union

MAIN IDEAS

The Beginnings of Industrialization Section 1 (pages 717–722)

11. What were the four natural resources needed for British industrialization?
12. How did the enclosure movement change agriculture in England?
13. What were two important inventions created during the Industrial Revolution? Describe their impact.

Case Study: Industrialization Section 2 (pages 723–728)

14. What were the living conditions like in Britain during industrialization?
15. How did the new middle class transform the social structure of Great Britain during industrialization?
16. How did industrialization affect Manchester's natural environment?

Industrialization Spreads Section 3 (pages 729–733)

17. Why were other European countries slower to industrialize than Britain?
18. What might explain the rise of global inequality during the Industrial Revolution?

Reforming the Industrial World Section 4 (pages 734–741)

19. What were the two warring classes that Marx and Engels outlined in *The Communist Manifesto*?
20. How did women fight for change during the Industrial Revolution?

CRITICAL THINKING

1. USING YOUR NOTES

In a chart, list some of the major technological advances and their effects on society.

Technological Advance	Effect(s)

2. EVALUATING

SCIENCE AND TECHNOLOGY How significant were the changes that the Industrial Revolution brought to the world? Explain your conclusion.

3. ANALYZING CAUSES AND RECOGNIZING EFFECTS

ECONOMICS How important were labor unions in increasing the power of workers? Give reasons for your opinion.

4. DRAWING CONCLUSIONS

How did the Industrial Revolution help to increase Germany's military power? Support your answer with information from the chapter.

5. DEVELOPING HISTORICAL PERSPECTIVE

EMPIRE BUILDING Would a nonindustrialized or an industrialized nation more likely be an empire builder? Why?

Use the quotation about industrialization and your knowledge of world history to answer questions 1 and 2.
Additional Test Practice, pp. S1–S33

PRIMARY SOURCE

It was a town of red brick, or of brick that would have been red if the smoke and ashes had allowed it. . . . It was a town of machinery and tall chimneys, out of which interminable [endless] serpents of smoke trailed themselves for ever and ever. . . . It contained several large streets all very like one another, and many small streets still more like one another, inhabited by people equally like one another, who all went in and out at the same hours, with the same sound upon the same pavements, to do the same work, and to whom every day was the same as yesterday and tomorrow, and every year the counterpart of the last and the next.

CHARLES DICKENS, *Hard Times*

1 In this passage, the writer is trying to describe how
 (1) people came from the countryside to the city to work in industry
 (2) entrepreneurs built factories
 (3) capitalism works
 (4) difficult life is for workers in industrial cities

2 What is Dickens's view of industrialization?
 (1) that it is good for factory owners
 (2) that it brings progress to a nation
 (3) that it pollutes the air and exploits the workers
 (4) that it causes population growth

Use the graph below and your knowledge of world history to answer question 3.

The Growth of Cities, 1700–1900

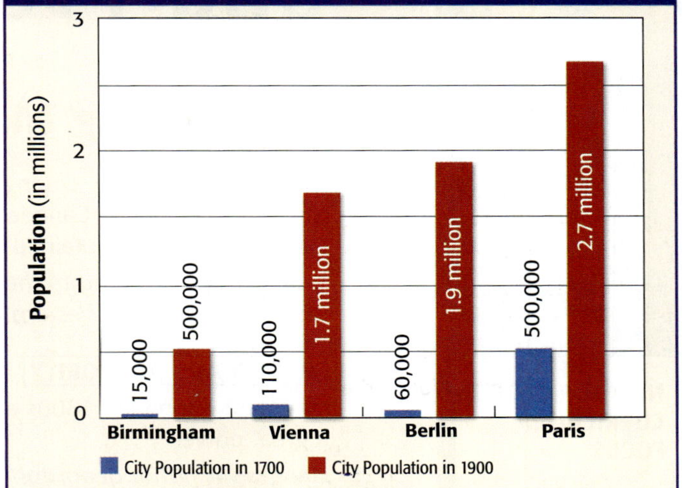

Sources: *European Historical Statistics*, 1750–1975; Eric Hopkins, *The Rise of the Manufacturing Town*

3 The graph above shows population growth in four European cities from 1700 to 1900, that is, before and after the Industrial Revolution. Which statement best describes the information in the chart?
 (1) All of the cities grew at the same rate.
 (2) The increase in population for each city was less than 2 million people.
 (3) Paris was the most populous city both before and after the Industrial Revolution.
 (4) Berlin's population in 1900 was four times its size in 1700.

INTEGRATED TECHNOLOGY

TEST PRACTICE Go to **classzone.com**
- Diagnostic tests
- Tutorials
- Strategies
- Additional practice

ALTERNATIVE ASSESSMENT

1. Interact *with* History

On page 716, you looked at working conditions in an English factory in the 19th century. Now that you have read the chapter about the Industrial Revolution, rethink your decision about what you would do to change your situation. What working conditions would you like to see change? What benefits might a union bring? What disadvantages might result if workers organize? Discuss your opinions with a small group.

2. WRITING ABOUT HISTORY

The Industrial Revolution's impact varied according to social class. Write a three-paragraph **expository essay** indicating how these people would view the changes in industry: an inventor, an entrepreneur, a skilled worker, and a hand weaver.

INTEGRATED TECHNOLOGY

Using Graphics Software

Make a list of five major inventions or innovations of the Industrial Revolution. Research each to learn about the scientific, economic, and social changes that contributed to its development and the effects that it caused. Use the Internet, books, and other resources to conduct your research. Then use graphics software to create a chart, graph, or diagram depicting the relationship between the inventions and innovations, the changes, and the effects.

You may include some of the following:
- the plow
- the power loom
- the sewing machine
- the cotton gin
- the telegraph

CHAPTER 26

An Age of Democracy and Progress, 1815–1914

NEW YORK CORE CURRICULUM FOCUS

- The changes brought by industrialization and urbanization led to calls for democratic reform.
- A great famine in Ireland led millions of people to flee the country.

Previewing Main Ideas

EMPIRE BUILDING During the 1800s, Great Britain gradually allowed three of its colonies—Canada, Australia, and New Zealand—greater self-rule. However, Britain maintained tight control over Ireland.

Geography *According to the map, what Western democracies existed in North America and Western Europe in 1900?*

POWER AND AUTHORITY The United States expanded across the continent during the 1800s and added new states to its territory to become a great power.

Geography *What geographical factors might have helped to make the United States a great power?*

SCIENCE AND TECHNOLOGY The transcontinental railroad helped to link the United States from the Atlantic Ocean to the Pacific Ocean. It was a triumph of 19th-century technology.

Geography *How might a technological achievement such as the transcontinental railroad have contributed to American prosperity?*

INTEGRATED TECHNOLOGY

eEdition
- Interactive Maps
- Interactive Visuals
- Interactive Primary Sources

INTERNET RESOURCES
Go to **classzone.com** for:
- Research Links
- Internet Activities
- Primary Sources
- Chapter Quiz
- Maps
- Test Practice
- Current Events

EUROPE

1837 ◀ Queen Victoria comes to power in Great Britain.

1845 Ireland is struck by famine.

1859 Darwin publishes theory of evolution.

1815 **1850**

WORLD

1821 Mexico wins independence from Spain.

1857 ◀ Sepoy Mutiny challenges British rule in India. (native troops in Britain's East India Company)

Western Democracies, 1900

1867 Dominion of Canada is formed.

1869 Suez Canal opens.

1871 Franco-Prussian War ends.

1880

1889 Eiffel Tower is completed in Paris. ▶

1893 New Zealand becomes first nation to allow women to vote.

1914 ◀ Panama Canal opens.

1915

Interact *with* History

What ideals might be worth fighting and dying for?

You are living in Paris in 1871. France is in a state of political upheaval following the Franco-Prussian War. When workers in Paris set up their own government, called the Paris Commune, French soldiers quickly stamp out the movement. Most of the Communards (the supporters of the Commune) are either killed or imprisoned. When your good friend Philippe dies in the fighting, you wonder whether self-government is worth dying for.

▲ Communards lie massacred in this painting titled *A Street in Paris in May 1871,* by Maximilien Luce.

EXAMINING *the* ISSUES

- **What might lead you to join a group seeking self-government?**
- **What ideals would you choose to help shape a new government?**

As a class, discuss these questions. During the discussion, think about some of the ideals that inspired American and French revolutionaries. As you read this chapter, consider the ideals that moved people to action. Also consider how people tried to change government to better reflect their ideals.

Democratic Reform and Activism

CONNECT TO THE NEW YORK STATE CORE CURRICULUM

Unit 5.G.3.g.6. Parliamentary reforms–expansion of suffrage
Unit 6.C.4. Women's suffrage movement

TERMS & NAMES

- suffrage
- Chartist movement
- Queen Victoria
- Third Republic
- Dreyfus affair
- anti-Semitism
- Zionism

SETTING THE STAGE Urbanization and industrialization brought sweeping changes to Western nations. People looking for solutions to the problems created by these developments began to demand reforms. They wanted to improve conditions for workers and the poor. Many people also began to call for political reforms. They demanded that more people be given a greater voice in government. Many different groups, including the middle class, workers, and women, argued that the right to vote be extended to groups that were excluded.

Britain Enacts Reforms

As Chapter 21 explained, Britain became a constitutional monarchy in the late 1600s. Under this system of government, the monarch serves as the head of state, but Parliament holds the real power. The British Parliament consists of a House of Lords and a House of Commons. Traditionally, members of the House of Lords either inherited their seats or were appointed. However, this changed in 1999, when legislation was passed that abolished the right of hereditary peers to inherit a seat in the House of Lords. Members of the House of Commons are elected by the British people.

In the early 1800s, the method of selecting the British government was not a true democracy. Only about five percent of the population had the right to elect the members of the House of Commons. Voting was limited to men who owned a substantial amount of land. Women could not vote at all. As a result, the upper classes ran the government.

The Reform Bill of 1832 The first group to demand a greater voice in politics was the wealthy middle class—factory owners, bankers, and merchants. Beginning in 1830, protests took place around England in favor of a bill in Parliament that would extend **suffrage**, or the right to vote. The Revolution of 1830 in France frightened parliamentary leaders. They feared that revolutionary violence would spread to Britain. Thus, Parliament passed the Reform Bill of 1832. This law eased the property requirements so that well-to-do men in the middle class could vote. The Reform Bill also modernized the districts for electing members of Parliament and gave the thriving new industrial cities more representation.

Chartist Movement Although the Reform Bill increased the number of British voters, only a small percentage of men were eligible to vote. A popular movement

TAKING NOTES

Evaluating Courses of Action Use a chart to list and evaluate events in this section according to whether they expanded (+) or impeded (-) democracy.

Event	Evaluation

Expansion of Suffrage in Britain

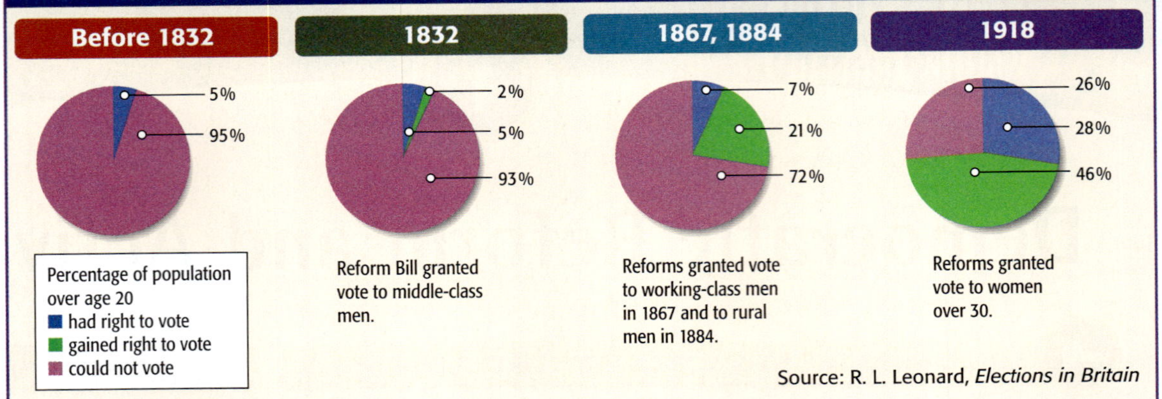

Source: R. L. Leonard, *Elections in Britain*

SKILLBUILDER: Interpreting Graphs

1. **Clarifying** *What percentage of the adults in Britain could vote in 1832?*
2. **Comparing** *By how much did the percentage of voters increase after the reforms of 1867 and 1884?*

arose among the workers and other groups who still could not vote to press for more rights. It was called the **Chartist movement** because the group first presented its demands to Parliament in a petition called The People's Charter of 1838.

The People's Charter called for suffrage for all men and annual Parliamentary elections. It also proposed to reform Parliament in other ways. In Britain at the time, eligible men voted openly. Since their vote was not secret, they could feel pressure to vote in a certain way. Members of Parliament had to own land and received no salary, so they needed to be wealthy. The Chartists wanted to make Parliament responsive to the lower classes. To do this, they demanded a secret ballot, an end to property requirements for serving in Parliament, and pay for members of Parliament.

Parliament rejected the Chartists' demands. However, their protests convinced many people that the workers had valid complaints. Over the years, workers continued to press for political reform, and Parliament responded. It gave the vote to working-class men in 1867 and to male rural workers in 1884. After 1884, most adult males in Britain had the right to vote. By the early 1900s, all the demands of the Chartists, except for annual elections, became law. (A)

The Victorian Age The figure who presided over all this historic change was **Queen Victoria**. Victoria came to the throne in 1837 at the age of 18. She was queen for nearly 64 years. During the Victorian Age, the British Empire reached the height of its wealth and power. Victoria was popular with her subjects, and she performed her duties capably. However, she was forced to accept a less powerful role for the monarchy.

The kings who preceded Victoria in the 1700s and 1800s had exercised great influence over Parliament. The spread of democracy in the 1800s shifted political power almost completely to Parliament, and especially to the elected House of Commons. Now the government was completely run by the prime minister and the cabinet.

History Makers

Queen Victoria and Prince Albert

About two years after her coronation, Queen Victoria (1819–1901) fell in love with her cousin Albert (1819–1861), a German prince. She proposed to him and they were married in 1840. Together they had nine children. Prince Albert established a tone of politeness and correct behavior at court, and the royal couple presented a picture of loving family life that became a British ideal.

After Albert died in 1861, the queen wore black silk for the rest of her life in mourning. She once said of Albert, "Without him everything loses its interest."

MAIN IDEA

Making Inferences

(A) Why do you think the Chartists demanded a secret ballot rather than public voting?

Women Get the Vote

By 1890, several industrial countries had universal male suffrage (the right of all men to vote). No country, however, allowed women to vote. As more men gained suffrage, more women demanded the same.

Organization and Resistance During the 1800s, women in both Great Britain and the United States worked to gain the right to vote. British women organized reform societies and protested unfair laws and customs. As women became more vocal, however, resistance to their demands grew. Many people, both men and women, thought that woman suffrage was too radical a break with tradition. Some claimed that women lacked the ability to take part in politics.

Militant Protests After decades of peaceful efforts to win the right to vote, some women took more drastic steps. In Britain, Emmeline Pankhurst formed the Women's Social and Political Union (WSPU) in 1903. The WSPU became the most militant organization for women's rights. Its goal was to draw attention to the cause of woman suffrage. When asked about why her group chose militant means to gain women's rights, Pankhurst replied:

PRIMARY SOURCE

I want to say here and now that the only justification for violence, the only justification for damage to property, the only justification for risk to the comfort of other human beings is the fact that you have tried all other available means and have failed to secure justice.

EMMELINE PANKHURST, *Why We Are Militant*

Global Impact

The Women's Movement

By the 1880s, women were working internationally to win more rights. In 1888, women activists from the United States, Canada, and Europe met in Washington, D.C., for the International Council of Women. In 1893, delegates and observers from many countries attended a large congress of women in Chicago. They came from lands as far apart as New Zealand, Argentina, Iceland, Persia, and China.

The first countries to grant suffrage to women were New Zealand (1893) and Australia (1902). Only in two European countries—Finland (1906, then part of the Russian Empire) and Norway (1913)—did women gain voting rights before World War I. In the United States, the territory of Wyoming allowed women to vote in 1869. Several other Western states followed suit.

Emmeline Pankhurst, her daughters Christabel and Sylvia, and other WSPU members were arrested and imprisoned many times. When they were jailed, the Pankhursts led hunger strikes to keep their cause in the public eye. British officials force-fed Sylvia and other activists to keep them alive.

Though the woman suffrage movement gained attention between 1880 and 1914, its successes were gradual. Women did not gain the right to vote in national elections in Great Britain and the United States until after World War I. **B**

MAIN IDEA

Analyzing Motives

B Was the use of militant action effective in achieving the goal of woman suffrage? Explain.

France and Democracy

While Great Britain moved toward greater democracy in the late 1800s, democracy finally took hold in France.

The Third Republic In the aftermath of the Franco-Prussian War, France went through a series of crises. Between 1871 and 1914, France averaged a change of government almost yearly. A dozen political parties competed for power. Not until 1875 could the National Assembly agree on a new government. Eventually, the members voted to set up a republic. The **Third Republic** lasted over 60 years. However, France remained divided.

The Dreyfus Affair During the 1880s and 1890s, the Third Republic was threatened by monarchists, aristocrats, clergy, and army leaders. These groups wanted a monarchy or military rule. A controversy known as the **Dreyfus affair** became a battleground for these opposing forces. Widespread feelings of **anti-Semitism**, or prejudice against Jews, also played a role in this scandal.

▲ *Zola Under Attack,* painted in 1898 by Henry de Groux, shows Émile Zola surrounded by an anti-Semitic mob.

In 1894, Captain Alfred Dreyfus, one of the few Jewish officers in the French army, was accused of selling military secrets to Germany. A court found him guilty, based on false evidence, and sentenced him to life in prison. In a few years, new evidence showed that Dreyfus had been framed by other army officers.

Public opinion was sharply divided over the scandal. Many army leaders, nationalists, leaders in the clergy, and anti-Jewish groups refused to let the case be reopened. They feared sudden action would cast doubt on the honor of the army. Dreyfus's defenders insisted that justice was more important. In 1898, the writer Émile Zola published an open letter titled *J'accuse!* (I accuse) in a popular French newspaper. In the letter, Zola denounced the army for covering up a scandal. Zola was sentenced to a year in prison for his views, but his letter gave strength to Dreyfus's cause. Eventually, the French government declared his innocence.

The Rise of Zionism The Dreyfus case showed the strength of anti-Semitism in France and other parts of Western Europe. However, persecution of Jews was even more severe in Eastern Europe. Russian officials permitted pogroms (puh•GRAHMS), organized campaigns of violence against Jews. From the late 1880s on, thousands of Jews fled Eastern Europe. Many headed for the United States.

For many Jews, the long history of exile and persecution convinced them to work for a homeland in Palestine. In the 1890s, a movement known as **Zionism** developed to pursue this goal. Its leader was Theodor Herzl (HEHRT•suhl), a writer in Vienna. It took many years, however, before the state of Israel was established.

NEW YORK CORE CURRICULUM REVIEW

TERMS & NAMES 1. For each term or name, write a sentence explaining its significance.

- suffrage • Chartist movement • Queen Victoria • Third Republic • Dreyfus affair • anti-Semitism • Zionism

USING YOUR NOTES

2. Which of these events most expanded democracy, and why?

Event	Evaluation

MAIN IDEAS

3. What were some effects of the Reform Bill of 1832?
4. What was the goal of the WSPU in Britain?
5. What was the Dreyfus affair?

CRITICAL THINKING & WRITING

6. **COMPARING** Why was the road to democracy more difficult for France than for England?
7. **SYNTHESIZING** Look again at the primary source on page 749. What is Pankhurst demanding?
8. **RECOGNIZING EFFECTS** What was the connection between anti-Semitism and Zionism?
9. **WRITING ACTIVITY** POWER AND AUTHORITY Among the Chartists' demands was pay for members of Parliament. Write a **letter to the editor** that supports or criticizes a pay raise for your legislators.

CONNECT TO TODAY **CREATING A POSTER**

Find information on issues in today's world that involve a call for social justice. Then make a **poster** in which you illustrate what you regard as the most compelling example of a current social injustice.

Self-Rule for British Colonies

CONNECT TO THE NEW YORK STATE CORE CURRICULUM

Unit 5.G.4.a. Growth of Irish nationalism
Unit 4.E.2. European competition for colonies in the Americas, Africa, East Asia, and Southeast Asia–The "old imperialism"

TERMS & NAMES

- dominion
- Maori
- Aborigine
- penal colony
- home rule
- Irish Republican Army

SETTING THE STAGE By 1800, Great Britain had colonies around the world. These included outposts in Africa and Asia. In these areas, the British managed trade with the local peoples, but they had little influence over the population at large. In the colonies of Canada, Australia, and New Zealand, on the other hand, European colonists dominated the native populations. As Britain industrialized and prospered in the 1800s, so did these colonies. Some were becoming strong enough to stand on their own.

TAKING NOTES

Comparing Use a chart to compare progress toward self-rule by recording significant events.

Country	Political Events
Canada	
Australia	
New Zealand	
Ireland	

Canada Struggles for Self-Rule

Canada was originally home to many Native American peoples. The first European country to colonize Canada was France. The earliest French colonists, in the 1600s and 1700s, had included many fur trappers and missionaries. They tended to live among the Native Americans. Some French intermarried with Native Americans.

Great Britain took possession of the country in 1763 after it defeated France in the French and Indian War. The French who remained lived mostly in the lower St. Lawrence Valley. Many English-speaking colonists arrived in Canada after it came under British rule. Some came from Great Britain, and others were Americans who had stayed loyal to Britain after the American Revolution. They settled separately from the French along the Atlantic seaboard and the Great Lakes.

French and English Canada Religious and cultural differences between the mostly Roman Catholic French and the mainly Protestant English-speaking colonists caused conflict in Canada. Both groups pressed Britain for a greater voice in governing their own affairs. In 1791 the British Parliament tried to resolve both issues by creating two new Canadian provinces. Upper Canada (now Ontario) had an English-speaking majority. Lower Canada (now Quebec) had a French-speaking majority. Each province had its own elected assembly.

The Durham Report-The division of Upper and Lower Canada temporarily eased tensions. In both colonies, the royal governor and a small group of wealthy British held most of the power. But during the early 1800s, middle-class professionals in both colonies began to demand political and economic reforms. In Lower Canada, these demands were also fueled by French resentment toward British rule. In the late 1830s, rebellions broke out in both Upper and Lower

History *in* Depth

Acadians to Cajuns

Colonists from France founded the colony of Acadia on the eastern coast of what is now Canada in 1604. Tensions flared between these settlers and later arrivals from England and Scotland.

In 1713, the British gained control of Acadia and renamed it Nova Scotia (New Scotland). They expelled thousands of descendants of the original Acadians. Many eventually settled in southern Louisiana. Today, their culture still thrives in the Mississippi Delta area, where the people are called Cajuns (an alteration of Acadian).

Canada. The British Parliament sent a reform-minded statesman, Lord Durham, to investigate.

In 1839, Durham sent a report to Parliament that urged two major reforms. First, Upper and Lower Canada should be reunited as the Province of Canada, and British immigration should be encouraged. In this way, the French would slowly become part of the dominant English culture. Second, colonists in the provinces of Canada should be allowed to govern themselves in domestic matters. (A)

MAIN IDEA

Recognizing Effects

(A) How do you think Durham's report affected French-speaking Canadians?

The Dominion of Canada By the mid-1800s, many Canadians believed that Canada needed a central government. A central government would be better able to protect the interests of Canadians against the United States, whose territory now extended from the Atlantic to the Pacific oceans. In 1867, Nova Scotia and New Brunswick joined the Province of Canada to form the Dominion of Canada. As a **dominion**, Canada was self-governing in domestic affairs but remained part of the British Empire.

Canada's Westward Expansion Canada's first prime minister, John MacDonald, expanded Canada westward by purchasing lands and persuading frontier territories to join the union. Canada stretched to the Pacific Ocean by 1871. MacDonald began the construction of a transcontinental railroad, completed in 1885.

Australia and New Zealand

The British sea captain James Cook claimed New Zealand in 1769 and part of Australia in 1770 for Great Britain. Both lands were already inhabited. In New Zealand, Cook was greeted by the **Maori**, a Polynesian people who had settled in New Zealand around A.D. 800. Maori culture was based on farming, hunting, and fishing.

When Cook reached Australia, he considered the land uninhabited. In fact, Australia was sparsely populated by **Aborigines**, as Europeans later called the native peoples. Aborigines are the longest ongoing culture in the world. These nomadic peoples fished, hunted, and gathered food.

Britain's Penal Colony Britain began colonizing Australia in 1788 with convicted criminals. The prisons in England were severely overcrowded. To solve this problem, the British government established a penal colony in Australia. A **penal colony** was a place where convicts were sent to serve their sentences. Many European nations used penal colonies as a way to prevent overcrowding of prisons. After their release, the newly freed prisoners could buy land and settle.

Free Settlers Arrive Free British settlers eventually joined the former convicts in both Australia and New Zealand. In the early 1800s, an Australian settler experimented with breeds of sheep until he found one that produced high quality wool and thrived in the country's warm, dry weather. Although sheep are not native to Australia, the raising and exporting of wool became its biggest business.

To encourage immigration, the government offered settlers cheap land. The population grew steadily in the early 1800s and then skyrocketed after a gold rush in 1851. The scattered settlements on Australia's east coast grew into separate colonies. Meanwhile, a few pioneers pushed westward across the vast dry interior and established outposts in western Australia.

GEOGRAPHY SKILLBUILDER: Interpreting Maps

1. **Region** *What sort of climate region is found along the eastern coast of Australia?*
2. **Region** *What regions of Australia and New Zealand were most densely inhabited by native peoples?*

Settling New Zealand European settlement of New Zealand grew more slowly. This was because Britain did not claim ownership of New Zealand, as it did Australia. Rather, it recognized the land rights of the Maori. In 1814, missionary groups began arriving from Australia seeking to convert the Maori to Christianity.

The arrival of more foreigners stirred conflicts between the Maori and the European settlers over land. Responding to the settlers' pleas, the British decided to annex New Zealand in 1839 and appointed a governor to negotiate with the Maori. In a treaty signed in 1840, the Maori accepted British rule in exchange for recognition of their land rights.

Self-Government Like Canadians, the colonists of Australia and New Zealand wanted to rule themselves yet remain in the British Empire. During the 1850s, the colonies in both Australia and New Zealand became self-governing and created parliamentary forms of government. In 1901, the Australian colonies were united under a federal constitution as the Commonwealth of Australia. During the early 1900s, both Australia and New Zealand became dominions.

The people of Australia and New Zealand pioneered a number of political reforms. For example, the secret ballot, sometimes called the Australian ballot, was first used in Australia in the 1850s. In 1893, New Zealand became the first nation in the world to give full voting rights to women. However, only white women gained these rights.

▼ This photograph shows a Maori warrior with traditional dress and face markings.

Status of Native Peoples Native peoples and other non-Europeans were excluded from democracy and prosperity. Diseases brought by the Europeans killed Aborigines and Maori. As Australian settlement grew, the colonists displaced or killed many Aborigines.

In New Zealand, tensions between settlers and Maori continued to grow after it became a British colony. Between 1845 and 1872, the colonial government fought the Maori in a series of wars. Reduced by disease and outgunned by British weapons, the Maori were finally driven into a remote part of the country. **B**

MAIN IDEA

Contrasting

B How did the colonial settlement of Australia and New Zealand differ?

The Irish Win Home Rule

English expansion into Ireland had begun in the 1100s, when the pope granted control of Ireland to the English king. English knights invaded Ireland, and many settled there to form a new aristocracy. The Irish, who had their own ancestry, culture, and language, bitterly resented the English presence. Laws imposed by the English in the 1500s and 1600s limited the rights of Catholics and favored the Protestant religion and the English language.

Over the years, the British government was determined to maintain its control over Ireland. It formally joined Ireland to Britain in 1801. Though a setback for Irish nationalism, this move gave Ireland representation in the British Parliament. Irish leader Daniel O'Connell persuaded Parliament to pass the Catholic Emancipation Act in 1829. This law restored many rights to Catholics.

The Great Famine In the 1840s, Ireland experienced one of the worst famines of modern history. For many years, Irish peasants had depended on potatoes as virtually their sole source of food. From 1845 to 1848, a plant fungus ruined nearly all of Ireland's potato crop. Out of a population of 8 million, about a million people died from starvation and disease over the next few years.

During the famine years, about a million and a half people fled from Ireland. Most went to the United States; others went to Britain, Canada, and Australia. At home, in Ireland, the British government enforced the demands of the English landowners that the Irish peasants pay their rent. Many Irish lost their land and fell hopelessly in debt, while large landowners profited from higher food prices.

Demands for Home Rule During the second half of the 1800s, opposition to British rule over Ireland took two forms. Some Irish wanted independence for Ireland. A greater number of Irish preferred **home rule**, local control over internal

Analyzing Primary Sources

Starvation in Ireland

A traveler described what he saw on a journey through Ireland in 1847:

PRIMARY SOURCE

We entered a cabin. Stretched in one dark corner, scarcely visible, from the smoke and rags that covered them, were three children huddled together, lying there because they were too weak to rise, pale and ghastly, their little limbs—on removing a portion of the filthy covering—perfectly emaciated, eyes sunk, voice gone, and evidently in the last stage of actual starvation.

WILLIAM BENNETT, quoted in *Narrative of a Recent Journey of Six Weeks in Ireland*

DOCUMENT-BASED QUESTIONS

1. **Determining Main Ideas** *What was the effect of the destruction of Ireland's potato crop on the population of Ireland?*
2. **Clarifying** *How did 18 percent of the population deal with the famine?*
3. **Comparing** *Which country received the most Irish emigrants?*

The Great Famine, 1845–1851

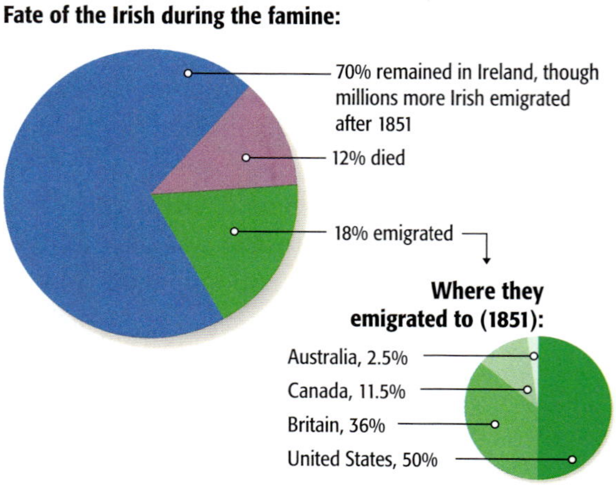

Sources: R. F. Foster, *Modern Ireland, 1600–1972;* D. Fitzpatrick, *Irish Emigration, 1804–1921*

matters only. The British, fearful of Irish moves toward independence, refused to consider either option.

One reason for Britain's opposition to home rule was concern for Ireland's Protestants. They feared being a minority in a country dominated by Catholics. Most Protestants lived in the northern part of Ireland, known as Ulster. Finally, in 1914, Parliament enacted a home rule bill for southern Ireland. Just one month before the plan was to take effect, World War I broke out in Europe. Irish home rule was put on hold.

Rebellion and Division Frustrated over the delay in gaining independence, a small group of Irish nationalists rebelled in Dublin during Easter week, 1916. British troops put down the Easter Rising and executed its leaders. Their fate, however, aroused wider popular support for the nationalist movement.

After World War I, the Irish nationalists won a victory in the elections for the British Parliament. To protest delays in home rule, the nationalist members decided not to attend Parliament. Instead, they formed an underground Irish government and declared themselves independent. The **Irish Republican Army** (IRA), an unofficial military force seeking independence for Ireland, staged a series of attacks against British officials in Ireland. The attacks sparked war between the nationalists and the British government.

In 1921, Britain divided Ireland and granted home rule to southern Ireland. Ulster, or Northern Ireland, remained a part of Great Britain. The south became a dominion called the Irish Free State. However, many Irish nationalists, led by Eamon De Valera, continued to seek total independence from Britain. In 1949, the Irish Free State declared itself the independent Republic of Ireland. C

MAIN IDEA

Evaluating Decisions

C Was Britain's policy in dividing Ireland successful? Why or why not?

Connect *to* Today

Northern Ireland Today

When Northern Ireland decided to stay united with Great Britain, many Catholics there refused to accept the partition, or division. In the late 1960s, Catholic groups began to demonstrate for more civil rights.

Their protests touched off fighting between Catholics and Protestants. Militant groups on both sides engaged in terrorism. This violent period, called the "troubles," continued into the 1990s.

In 1999, with a peace accord, Catholics and Protestants began sharing power in a new home-rule government. Nonetheless, tensions between the two sides remain.

INTEGRATED TECHNOLOGY

INTERNET ACTIVITY Design a Web page about the peace process in Northern Ireland today. Include key figures in the peace process, especially Gerry Adams and David Trimble. Go to **classzone.com** for your research.

NEW YORK CORE CURRICULUM REVIEW

TERMS & NAMES 1. For each term or name, write a sentence explaining its significance.

- dominion
- Maori
- Aborigine
- penal colony
- home rule
- Irish Republican Army

USING YOUR NOTES

2. In what ways was Ireland different from the other three colonies?

Country	Political Events
Canada	
Australia	
New Zealand	

MAIN IDEAS

3. What were the two major reforms urged by the Durham report?
4. What was unusual about the first European settlers in Australia?
5. What are the main countries to which the Irish emigrated during the famine?

CRITICAL THINKING & WRITING

6. **COMPARING** How was Britain's policy toward Canada beginning in the late 1700s similar to its policy toward Ireland in the 1900s?
7. **DRAWING CONCLUSIONS** What impact did the Great Famine have on the population of Ireland?
8. **CLARIFYING** Why did Britain create Upper Canada and Lower Canada, and who lived in each colony?
9. **WRITING ACTIVITY** EMPIRE BUILDING Britain encouraged emigration to each of the colonies covered in this section. What effects did this policy have on these areas? Write a **paragraph** in which you provide an explanation.

INTEGRATED TECHNOLOGY **INTERNET ACTIVITY**

Use the Internet to find information on Irish emigration to the United States. Create a **bar graph** showing the years when the largest numbers of Irish came to the United States.

INTERNET KEYWORD
Irish immigration

Life in Early Australia

European explorers located Australia long after they had begun colonizing other lands. Dutch explorers were probably the first Europeans to reach Australia around 1605. Australia was not claimed by a European power, however, until the British did so in 1770.

Early Australia had many groups of people with diverse interests, including a native population that had lived on the island for at least 40,000 years. On these pages you will discover the occupations, motivations, and interests of some Australians in the 17th and 18th centuries.

INTEGRATED TECHNOLOGY

RESEARCH LINKS For more on early Australia, go to **classzone.com**

▼ Original Australians

Aboriginal society developed in close harmony with nature. There were between 200 and 300 Aboriginal languages, and most people were bilingual or multilingual. By 1900, half of Australia's original inhabitants had died fighting the British or from disease. The engraving below depicts an Aboriginal man with ceremonial face paint and scars. The other image below is an ancient Aboriginal rock painting.

▼ Gold Miners

In 1851, lured by the potential of striking it rich, thousands of people began prospecting for gold in Australia. Sometimes whole families moved to the gold fields, but life in the gold camps was hard and very few people struck it rich. Searching for gold was hard and dirty work, as this painting illustrates.

▲ Farmers and Ranchers

Free settlers made the journey to Australia willingly. Many went into farming and ranching. Farms provided much-needed food, and sheep ranching provided wool as a valuable export. Convicts were hired out to farmers and ranchers as cheap labor. Sheep ranching, shown in the picture above, remains an important part of Australia's economy.

▼ Convicts

Beginning in 1788, England sent both male and female prisoners to Australia—sometimes with their children. Convicts built public buildings, roads, and bridges. England stopped sending convicts to Australia in 1868. The prison ship shown here housed prisoners before they went to Australia.

> DATA FILE

Australia Today

- Australia still mines gold, but it also produces 95 percent of the world's precious opals and 99 percent of black opals.
- Australia has 24 million head of cattle and is the world's largest exporter of beef.
- Australians had 8.6 million cell phones in 2000.

Australia's Population

- In 2001, there was an average of 6.5 people per square mile in Australia. That same year in the United States there were 77.8 people per square mile.
- In Australia's 2001 census, 410,003 people identified themselves as being of indigenous origin.

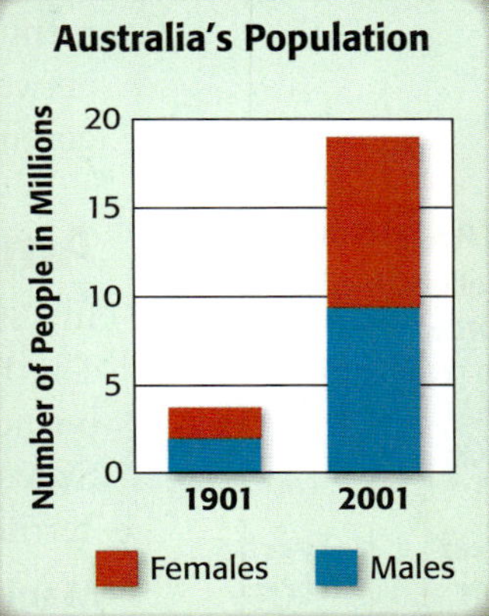

Connect *to* Today

1. **Forming and Supporting Opinions** Of the groups represented on this page, which do you believe had highest quality of living? Why?

   See Skillbuilder Handbook, page R20.

2. **Comparing and Contrasting** Use the Internet to research the issues that Australian Aborigines and Native Americans in the United States face today and compare them. How are they similar? How are they different?

3

War and Expansion in the United States

CONNECT TO THE NEW YORK STATE CORE CURRICULUM

Unit 4.E.3. Global demographic shifts Case study: The triangular trade and slavery
Unit 5.G.3.g.8. Global migrations (19th century)

TERMS & NAMES

- manifest destiny
- Abraham Lincoln
- secede
- U.S. Civil War
- Emancipation Proclamation
- segregation

SETTING THE STAGE The United States won its independence from Britain in 1783. At the end of the Revolutionary War, the Mississippi River marked the western boundary of the new republic. As the original United States filled with settlers, land-hungry newcomers pushed beyond the Mississippi. The government helped them by acquiring new territory for settlement. Meanwhile, tensions between northern and southern states over the issues of states' rights and slavery continued to grow and threatened to reach a boiling point.

TAKING NOTES

Following Chronological Order Create a time line to record major events of the United States in the 19th century.

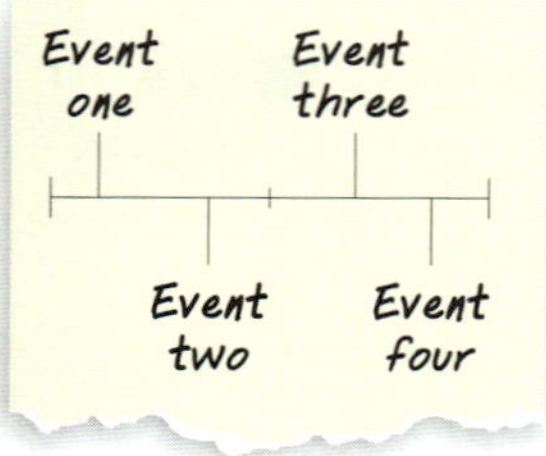

Americans Move West

In 1803, President Thomas Jefferson bought the Louisiana Territory from France. The Louisiana Purchase doubled the size of the new republic and extended its boundary to the Rocky Mountains. In 1819, Spain gave up Florida to the United States. In 1846, a treaty with Great Britain gave the United States part of the Oregon Territory. The nation now stretched from the Atlantic to the Pacific oceans.

Manifest Destiny Many Americans believed in **manifest destiny**, the idea that the United States had the right and duty to rule North America from the Atlantic Ocean to the Pacific Ocean. Government leaders used manifest destiny to justify evicting Native Americans from their tribal lands.

The Indian Removal Act of 1830 made such actions official policy. This law enabled the federal government to force Native Americans living in the East to move to the West. Georgia's Cherokee tribe challenged the law before the Supreme Court. The Court, however, ruled that the suit was not valid. The Cherokees had to move. Most of them traveled 800 miles to Oklahoma, mainly on foot, on a journey later called the Trail of Tears. About a quarter of the Cherokees died on the trip. A survivor recalled how the journey began:

PRIMARY SOURCE

The day was bright and beautiful, but a gloomy thoughtfulness was depicted in the lineaments of every face. . . . At this very moment a low sound of distant thunder fell on my ear . . . and sent forth a murmur, I almost thought a voice of divine indignation for the wrong of my poor and unhappy countrymen, driven by brutal power from all they loved and cherished in the land of their fathers.

WILLIAM SHOREY COODEY, quoted in *The Trail of Tears*

When the Cherokees reached their destination, they ended up on land inferior to that which they had left. As white settlers moved west during the 19th century, the government continued to push Native Americans off their land.

Texas Joins the United States When Mexico had gained its independence from Spain in 1821, its territory included the lands west of the Louisiana Purchase. With Mexico's permission, American settlers moved into the Mexican territory of Texas. However, settlers were unhappy with Mexico's rule.

In 1836, Texans revolted against Mexican rule and won their independence. Then, in 1845, the United States annexed Texas. Since Mexico still claimed Texas, it viewed this annexation as an act of war.

War with Mexico Between May 1846 and February 1848, war raged between the two countries. Finally, Mexico surrendered. As part of the settlement of the Mexican-American War, Mexico ceded territory to the United States. The Mexican Cession included California and a huge area in the Southwest. In 1853, the Gadsden Purchase from Mexico brought the lower continental United States to its present boundaries.

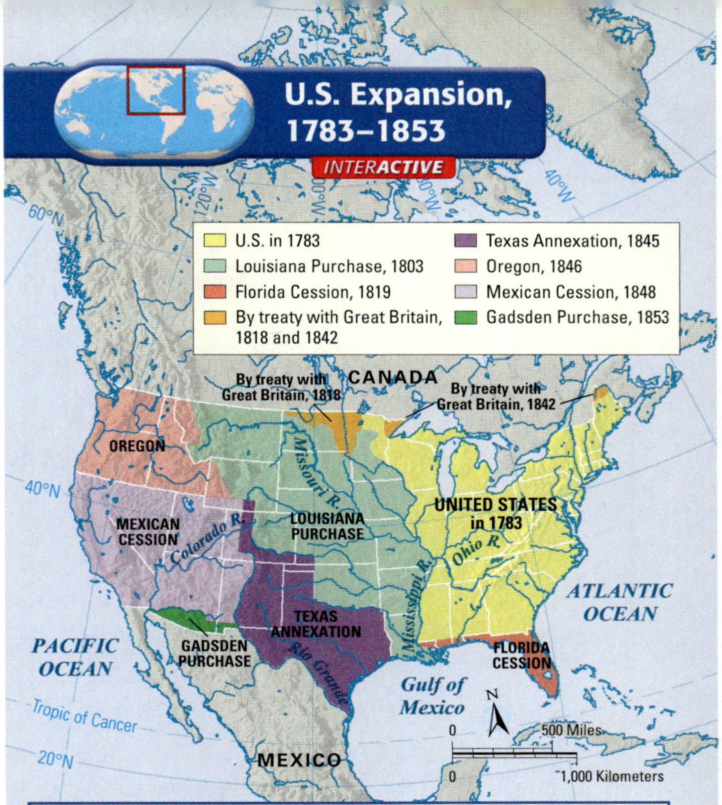

GEOGRAPHY SKILLBUILDER: Interpreting Maps

1. **Movement** *What was the first territory to be added to the United States after 1783?*
2. **Region** *What present-day states were part of the Mexican Cession?*

Civil War Tests Democracy

America's westward expansion raised questions about what laws and customs should be followed in the West. Since the nation's early days, the northern and southern parts of the United States had followed different ways of life. Each section wanted to extend its own way of life to the new territories and states in the West.

MAIN IDEA

Contrasting

A What were the main economic differences between the Northern and Southern states?

North and South The North had a diversified economy, with both farms and industry. For both its factories and farms, the North depended on free workers. The South's economy, on the other hand, was based on just a few cash crops, mainly cotton. Southern planters relied on slave labor. **A**

The economic differences between the two regions led to a conflict over slavery. Many Northerners considered slavery morally wrong. They wanted to outlaw slavery in the new western states. Most white Southerners believed slavery was necessary for their economy. They wanted laws to protect slavery in the West so that they could continue to raise cotton on the fertile soil there.

The disagreement over slavery fueled a debate about the rights of the individual states against those of the federal government. Southern politicians argued that the states had freely joined the Union, and so they could freely leave. Most Northerners felt that the Constitution had established the Union once and for all.

Civil War Breaks Out Conflict between the North and South reached a climax in 1860, when **Abraham Lincoln** was elected president. Southerners fiercely

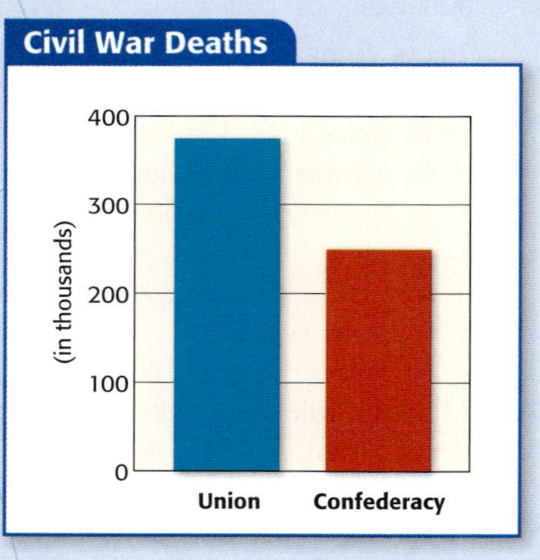

GEOGRAPHY SKILLBUILDER: Interpreting Maps

1. **Movement** *What can you tell about the strategy of the North to defeat the South?*
2. **Human-Environment Interaction** *Which side do you think suffered the most devastation? Why?*

opposed Lincoln, who had promised to stop the spread of slavery. One by one, Southern states began to **secede**, or withdraw, from the Union. These states came together as the Confederate States of America.

On April 12, 1861, Confederate forces fired on Fort Sumter, a federal fort in Charleston, South Carolina. Lincoln ordered the army to bring the rebel states back into the Union. The **U.S. Civil War** had begun. Four years of fighting followed, most of it in the South. Although the South had superior military leadership, the North had a larger population, better transportation, greater resources, and more factories. These advantages proved too much, and in April 1865, the South surrendered.

Abolition of Slavery Lincoln declared that the war was being fought to save the Union and not to end slavery. He eventually decided that ending slavery would help to save the Union. Early in 1863, he issued the **Emancipation Proclamation**, declaring that all slaves in the Confederate states were free. B

At first, the proclamation freed no slaves, because the Confederate states did not accept it as law. As Union armies advanced into the South, however, they freed slaves in the areas they conquered. The Emancipation Proclamation also showed European nations that the war was being fought against slavery. As a result, these nations did not send the money and supplies that the South had hoped they would.

In the aftermath of the war, the U.S. Congress passed the Thirteenth Amendment to the Constitution, which abolished slavery in the United States. The Fourteenth and Fifteenth Amendments extended the rights of citizenship to all Americans and guaranteed former slaves the right to vote.

Reconstruction From 1865 to 1877, Union troops occupied the South and enforced the constitutional protections. This period is called Reconstruction. After federal troops left the South, white Southerners passed laws that limited African

MAIN IDEA

Analyzing Issues

B Did the Emancipation Proclamation reflect a change in Lincoln's main goal for the war?

Americans' rights and made it difficult for them to vote. Such laws also encouraged **segregation**, or separation, of blacks and whites in the South. African Americans continued to face discrimination in the North as well.

The Postwar Economy

The need for mass production and distribution of goods during the Civil War speeded industrialization. After the war, the United States experienced industrial expansion unmatched in history. By 1914, it was a leading industrial power.

Immigration Industrialization could not have occurred so rapidly without immigrants. During the 1870s, immigrants arrived at a rate of nearly 2,000 a day. By 1914, more than 20 million people had moved to the United States from Europe and Asia. Many settled in the cities of the Northeast and Midwest. Others settled in the open spaces of the West.

The Railroads As settlers moved west, so did the nation's rail system. In 1862, Congress had authorized money to build a transcontinental railroad. For seven years, immigrants and other workers dug tunnels, built bridges, and laid track. When the railroad was completed in 1869, railroads linked California with the eastern United States. C

MAIN IDEA

Recognizing Effects

C How did railroads affect the growth of the United States?

By 1900, nearly 200,000 miles of track crossed the nation. This system linked farm to city and boosted trade and industry. The railroads bought huge quantities of steel. Also, trains brought materials such as coal and iron ore to factories and moved the finished goods to market. They carried corn, wheat, and cattle from the Great Plains to processing plants in St. Louis, Chicago, and Minneapolis. These developments helped to make the United States a world leader.

History Makers

Abraham Lincoln
1809–1865

Lincoln passionately believed in preserving the Union. His upbringing might help explain why. The son of rural, illiterate parents, he educated himself. After working as rail splitter, boatman, storekeeper, and surveyor, he taught himself to be a lawyer. This career path led eventually to the White House.

In Europe, people stayed at the level of society into which they had been born. Yet the United States had been founded on the belief that all men were created equal. Small wonder that Lincoln fought to preserve the democracy he described as the "last best hope of earth."

NEW YORK CORE CURRICULUM REVIEW

TERMS & NAMES 1. For each term or name, write a sentence explaining its significance.

- manifest destiny
- Abraham Lincoln
- secede
- U.S. Civil War
- Emancipation Proclamation
- segregation

USING YOUR NOTES

2. Which events contributed to U.S. expansion?

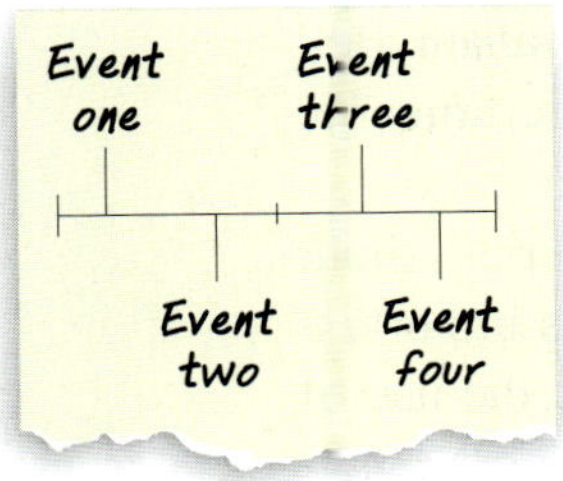

MAIN IDEAS

3. What territory did the Mexican-American War open up to American settlers?
4. What were some of the economic differences between the North and the South before the Civil War?
5. How did the Civil War speed up America's industrialization?

CRITICAL THINKING & WRITING

6. **DISTINGUISHING FACT FROM OPINION** Reread the quotation from William Shorey Coodey on page 758. What facts are conveyed in his statement? What opinions does he express about the Trail of Tears?
7. **COMPARING** What were the relative resources of the North and South in the U.S. Civil War?
8. **MAKING INFERENCES** How might the Mexican Cession (see map, page 759) have consequences today?
9. **WRITING ACTIVITY** POWER AND AUTHORITY Imagine that you are making the westward journey by wagon train. Write a number of **journal entries** describing your experience.

CONNECT TO TODAY **MAKING A TABLE**

Find information on countries today that are experiencing civil wars or conflicts. Make a **table** that includes the name of each country, the continent it is located on, and the dates of the conflict.

Nineteenth-Century Progress

CONNECT TO THE NEW YORK STATE CORE CURRICULUM

Unit 5.H.1. Reasons for imperialism–nationalistic, political, economic, "The White Man's Burden", Social Darwinism
Unit 5.A.1. The development of scientific methods

TERMS & NAMES

- assembly line
- Charles Darwin
- theory of evolution
- radioactivity
- psychology
- mass culture

SETTING THE STAGE The Industrial Revolution happened because of inventions such as the spinning jenny and the steam engine. By the late 1800s, advances in both industry and technology were occurring faster than ever before. In turn, the demands of growing industries spurred even greater advances in technology. A surge of scientific discovery pushed the frontiers of knowledge forward. At the same time, in industrialized countries, economic growth produced many social changes.

TAKING NOTES
Summarizing Use a web diagram to connect people with their ideas and inventions.

Inventions Make Life Easier

In the early 1800s, coal and steam drove the machines of industry. By the late 1800s, new kinds of energy were coming into use. One was gasoline (made from oil), which powered the internal combustion engine. This engine would make the automobile possible. Another kind of energy was electricity. In the 1870s, the electric generator was developed, which produced a current that could power machines.

Edison the Inventor During his career, Thomas Edison patented more than 1,000 inventions, including the light bulb and the phonograph. Early in his career, Edison started a research laboratory in Menlo Park, New Jersey. Most of his important inventions were developed there, with help from the researchers he employed, such as Lewis H. Latimer, an African-American inventor. Indeed, the idea of a research laboratory may have been Edison's most important invention.

Bell and Marconi Revolutionize Communication Other inventors helped harness electricity to transmit sounds over great distances. Alexander Graham Bell was a teacher of deaf students who invented the telephone in his spare time. He displayed his device at the Philadelphia Centennial Exposition of 1876.

The Italian inventor Guglielmo Marconi used theoretical discoveries about electromagnetic waves to create the first radio in 1895. This device was important because it sent messages (using Morse Code) through the air, without the use of wires. Primitive radios soon became standard equipment for ships at sea.

Ford Sparks the Automobile Industry In the 1880s, German inventors used a gasoline engine to power a vehicle—the automobile. Automobile technology developed quickly, but since early cars were built by hand, they were expensive.

An American mechanic named Henry Ford decided to make cars that were affordable for most people. Ford used standardized, interchangeable parts. He

Edison's Inventions

Thomas Alva Edison was one of the greatest inventors in history. He held thousands of patents for his inventions in over 30 countries. The United States Patent Office alone issued Edison 1,093 patents. Among his inventions was an electric light bulb, the phonograph, and motion pictures, all shown on this page.

Some scientists and historians, however, believe that Edison's greatest achievement was his development of the research laboratory. Edison worked with a team of different specialists to produce his creations. His precise manner is illustrated by his famous quote: "Genius is 1 percent inspiration and 99 percent perspiration."

▲ Thomas Edison in his West Orange, New Jersey, laboratory, 1915

INTEGRATED TECHNOLOGY

RESEARCH LINKS For more on Thomas Alva Edison, go to **classzone.com**

▼ **Phonograph** Commonplace today, a device for recording sound did not exist until Thomas Edison invented it. He first demonstrated his phonograph in 1877.

▼ **Motion pictures** The idea of "moving pictures" was not Edison's, but his "Kinetoscope," shown below, made movies practical.

6 THE MOVING PICTURE NEWS

THE EDISON KINETOSCOPE
Underwriters' Type "B"

WHY isn't your motion picture show making you the great big money you read about? How is it that the man in the next block can show the same pictures you do—and take the crowds away from you? We'll tell you. It's all in the machine—you need an

EDISON KINETOSCOPE

The Edison wins the crowd because it projects clear, flickerless pictures that don't tire the eyes and are a real pleasure to look at. There are no discouraging "intermissions for repairs". And the Edison Kinetoscope saves the extra money it makes, because it runs the longest time with the least upkeep expense. Get Posted. Send for Catalog 500 and a copy of the Edison Kinetogram.

Price, with Rheostat, 110 volts, 24-40 amperes - $225.00
Price, " 110 volt, 60 Cycle Transformer - - 245.00

THOMAS A. EDISON, Inc., 274 Lakeside Avenue, Orange, N. J.

In writing to advertisers please mention "MOVING PICTURE NEWS"

▲ **Light bulb** Edison and his team are working on an electric light bulb in this painting. Edison's inventions often developed from existing technologies. Many people were working on an electric light bulb, but Edison made it practical.

Connect *to* Today

1. **Clarifying** What did Edison mean when he said, "Genius is 1 percent inspiration and 99 percent perspiration"?
   See Skillbuilder Handbook, page R4.
2. **Forming and Supporting Opinions** Which of Edison's inventions shown on this page do you think has had the most influence?

An Age of Inventions

▲ **Telephone**
Alexander Graham Bell demonstrated the first telephone in 1876. It quickly became an essential of modern life. By 1900, there were 1.4 million telephones in the United States. By 1912, there were 8.7 million.

◀ **Automobile Assembly Line**
Ford's major innovation was to improve efficiency in his factory. By introducing the assembly line, he reduced the time it took to build a car from 12.5 to 1.5 worker-hours.

▲ **Airplane**
Through trial and error, the Wright brothers designed wings that provided lift and balance in flight. Their design is based on principles that are still used in every aircraft.

also built them on an **assembly line**, a line of workers who each put a single piece on unfinished cars as they passed on a moving belt.

Assembly line workers could put together an entire Model T Ford in less than two hours. When Ford introduced this plain, black, reliable car in 1908, it sold for $850. As his production costs fell, Ford lowered the price. Eventually it dropped to less than $300. Other factories adopted Ford's ideas. By 1916, more than 3.5 million cars were traveling around on America's roads. (A)

MAIN IDEA

Making Inferences

(A) Why do you think Ford reduced the price of the Model T?

The Wright Brothers Fly Two bicycle mechanics from Dayton, Ohio, named Wilbur and Orville Wright, solved the age-old riddle of flight. On December 17, 1903, they flew a gasoline-powered flying machine at Kitty Hawk, North Carolina. The longest flight lasted only 59 seconds, but it started the aircraft industry.

New Ideas in Medicine

As you learned in Chapter 22, earlier centuries had established the scientific method. Now this method brought new insights into nature as well as practical results.

The Germ Theory of Disease An important breakthrough in the history of medicine was the germ theory of disease. It was developed by French chemist Louis Pasteur in the mid-1800s. While examining the fermentation process of alcohol, Pasteur discovered that it was caused by microscopic organisms he called bacteria. He also learned that heat killed bacteria. This led him to develop the process of pasteurization to kill germs in liquids such as milk. Soon, it became clear to Pasteur and others that bacteria also caused diseases.

Joseph Lister, a British surgeon, read about Pasteur's work. He thought germs might explain why half of surgical patients died of infections. In 1865, he ordered that his surgical wards be kept spotlessly clean. He insisted that wounds be washed in antiseptics, or germ-killing liquids. As a result, 85 percent of Lister's patients survived. Other hospitals adopted Lister's methods.

Public officials, too, began to understand that cleanliness helped prevent the spread of disease. Cities built plumbing and sewer systems and took other steps to improve public health. Meanwhile, medical researchers developed vaccines or cures for such deadly diseases as typhus, typhoid fever, diphtheria, and yellow fever. These advances helped people live longer, healthier lives.

New Ideas in Science

No scientific idea of modern times aroused more controversy than the work of English naturalist **Charles Darwin**. The cause of the controversy was Darwin's answer to the question that faced biologists: How can we explain the tremendous variety of plants and animals on earth? A widely accepted answer in the 1800s was the idea of special creation—every kind of plant and animal had been created by God at the beginning of the world and had remained the same since then.

Darwin's Theory of Evolution Darwin challenged the idea of special creation. Based on his research as a naturalist on the voyage of the *H.M.S. Beagle,* he developed a theory that all forms of life, including human beings, evolved from earlier living forms that had existed millions of years ago.

In 1859, Darwin published his thinking in a book titled *On the Origin of Species by Means of Natural Selection.* According to the idea of natural selection, populations tend to grow faster than the food supply and so must compete for food. The members of a species that survive are those that are fittest, or best adapted to their environment. These surviving members of a species produce offspring that share their advantages. Gradually, over many generations, the species may change. In this way, new species evolve. Darwin's idea of change through natural selection came to be called the **theory of evolution**. B

MAIN IDEA

Clarifying

B According to Darwin, how does natural selection affect evolution?

Mendel and Genetics Although Darwin said that living things passed on their variations from one generation to the next, he did not know how they did so. In the 1850s and 1860s, an Austrian monk named Gregor Mendel discovered that there is a pattern to the way that certain traits are inherited. Although his work was not widely known until 1900, Mendel's work began the science of genetics.

Advances in Chemistry and Physics In 1803, the British chemist John Dalton theorized that all matter is made of tiny particles called atoms. Dalton showed that elements contain only one kind of atom, which has a specific weight. Compounds, on the other hand, contain more than one kind of atom.

In 1869, Dmitri Mendeleev (MEHN•duh•LAY•uhf), a Russian chemist, organized a chart on which all the known elements were arranged in order of weight, from lightest to heaviest. He left gaps where he predicted that new elements would be discovered. Later, his predictions proved correct. Mendeleev's chart, the Periodic Table, is still used today.

A husband and wife team working in Paris, Marie and Pierre Curie, discovered two of the missing elements, which they named radium and polonium. The elements were found in a mineral called pitchblende that released a powerful form of energy. In 1898, Marie Curie gave this energy the name **radioactivity**. In 1903, the Curies shared the Nobel Prize for physics for their work on radioactivity. In 1911, Marie Curie won the Nobel Prize for chemistry for the discovery of radium and polonium.

Physicists around 1900 continued to unravel the secrets of the atom. Earlier scientists believed that the atom was the smallest particle that existed. A British physicist named

History Makers

Marie Curie
1867–1934

Marie Curie's original name was Marya Sklodowska. Born in Warsaw, Poland, she emigrated to Paris to study, where she changed her name to Marie.

She achieved a number of firsts in her career. She was the first woman to teach in the Sorbonne, a world-famous college that was part of the University of Paris. She was the first woman to win a Nobel Prize—two, in fact.

In 1911, she won the Nobel prize for chemistry. In 1921, she made a journey to the U.S. In 1934, she died from leukemia caused by the radiation she had been exposed to in her work.

INTEGRATED TECHNOLOGY

RESEARCH LINKS For more on Marie Curie, go to **classzone.com.**

History *in* Depth

Social Darwinism

Charles Darwin (above) was a naturalist, but a number of 19th-century thinkers tried to apply his ideas to economics and politics. The leader in this movement was Herbert Spencer, an English philosopher.

Free economic competition, Spencer argued, was natural selection in action. The best companies make profits, while inefficient ones go bankrupt. Spencer applied the same rules to individuals. Those who were fittest for survival enjoyed wealth and success, while the poor remained poor because they were unfit. This idea became known as Social Darwinism. It also provided a rationalization for imperialism and colonialism.

Ernest Rutherford suggested that atoms were made up of yet smaller particles. Each atom, he said, had a nucleus surrounded by one or more particles called electrons. Soon other physicists such as Max Planck, Neils Bohr, and Albert Einstein were studying the structure and energy of atoms.

Social Sciences Explore Behavior

The scientific theories of the 1800s prompted scholars to study human society and behavior in a scientific way. Interest in these fields grew enormously during that century, as global expeditions produced a flood of new discoveries about ancient civilizations and world cultures. This led to the development of modern social sciences such as archaeology, anthropology, and sociology.

An important new social science was **psychology**, the study of the human mind and behavior. The Russian physiologist Ivan Pavlov believed that human actions were often unconscious reactions to experiences and could be changed by training.

Another pioneer in psychology, the Austrian doctor Sigmund Freud, also believed that the unconscious mind drives how people think and act. In Freud's view, unconscious forces such as suppressed memories, desires, and impulses shape behavior. He founded a type of therapy called psychoanalysis to deal with psychological conflicts created by these forces.

Freud's theories became very influential. However, his idea that the mind was beyond conscious control also shocked many people. The theories of Freud and Pavlov challenged the fundamental idea of the Enlightenment—that reason was supreme. The new ideas about psychology began to shake the 19th-century faith that humans could perfect themselves and society through reason. C

MAIN IDEA

Clarifying

C Why was the work of Pavlov and Freud groundbreaking?

The Rise of Mass Culture

In earlier periods, art, music, and theater were enjoyed by the wealthy. This group had the money, leisure time, and education to appreciate high culture. It was not until about 1900 that people could speak of **mass culture**—the appeal of art, writing, music, and other forms of entertainment to a larger audience.

Changes Produce Mass Culture There were several causes for the rise of mass culture. Their effects changed life in Europe and North America. Notice in the chart on the next page how working class people's lives were changed by mass culture. The demand for leisure activities resulted in a variety of new pursuits for people to enjoy. People went to music performances, movies, and sporting events.

Music Halls, Vaudeville, and Movies A popular leisure activity was a trip to the local music hall. On a typical evening, a music hall might offer a dozen or more different acts. It might feature singers, dancers, comedians, jugglers, magicians, and acrobats. In the United States, musical variety shows were called vaudeville. Vaudeville acts traveled from town to town, appearing at theaters.

During the 1880s, several inventors worked at trying to project moving images. One successful design came from France. Another came from Thomas Edison's laboratory. The earliest motion pictures were black and white and lasted less than a minute.

Rise of Mass Culture		
Cause	**Effect/Cause**	**Effect**
• Public education	• Increase in literacy	• Mass market for books and newspapers
• Improvement in communications	• Publications cheaper and more accessible	• Mass market for books and newspapers
• Invention of phonograph and records	• More music directly in people's homes	• Greater demand for musical entertainment
• Shorter workday— 10 hours shorter workweek— 5-1/2 days	• More leisure time	• Greater demand for mass entertainment activities

SKILLBUILDER: Interpreting Charts

1. **Analyzing Causes** *What was the immediate cause for the increased demand for mass entertainment activities?*
2. **Recognizing Effects** *What was the ultimate effect of public education and improved communications?*

By the early 1900s, filmmakers were producing the first feature films. Movies quickly became big business. By 1910, five million Americans attended some 10,000 theaters each day. The European movie industry experienced similar growth.

Sports Entertain Millions With time at their disposal, more people began to enjoy sports and outdoor activities. Spectator sports now became entertainment. In the United States, football and baseball soared in popularity. In Europe, the first professional soccer clubs formed and drew big crowds. Favorite English sports such as cricket spread to the British colonies of Australia, India, and South Africa.

As a result of the growing interest in sports, the International Olympic Games began in 1896. They revived the ancient Greek tradition of holding an athletic competition every four years. Fittingly, the first modern Olympics took place in Athens, Greece, the country where the games had originated.

NEW YORK CORE CURRICULUM REVIEW

TERMS & NAMES 1. For each term or name, write a sentence explaining its significance.

- assembly line
- Charles Darwin
- theory of evolution
- radioactivity
- psychology
- mass culture

USING YOUR NOTES

2. Which breakthrough helped people the most? Why?

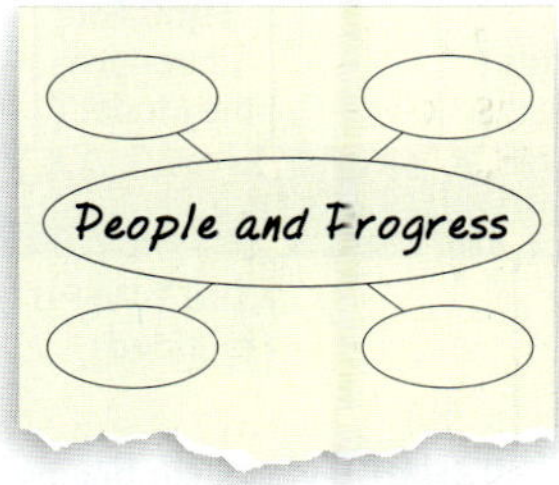

MAIN IDEAS

3. What effect did the assembly line have on production costs?
4. How did Joseph Lister improve the survival rate of his patients?
5. What effect did the spread of public education have on culture?

CRITICAL THINKING & WRITING

6. **COMPARING AND CONTRASTING** How is the mass culture that rose at the end of the 19th century similar to mass culture today? How is it different? Explain your response.
7. **RECOGNIZING EFFECTS** How did the germ theory change living conditions in Europe and the United States?
8. **ANALYZING CAUSES** What changes led to the rise of mass culture around 1900?
9. **WRITING ACTIVITY** SCIENCE AND TECHNOLOGY Write a two-paragraph **expository essay** in which you discuss whether advances in science and technology have had a largely positive or negative impact on society.

CONNECT TO TODAY **MAKING A POSTER**

Find information on the current state of medicines such as antibiotics and problems with their use and overuse. Create a **poster** that shows examples of current antibiotics, their benefits, and their potential negative long-term impact.

Chapter 26 Assessment

TERMS & NAMES

For each term or name below, briefly explain its connection to the reforms, crises, or advances of Western nations from 1815 to 1914.

1. suffrage
2. anti-Semitism
3. dominion
4. home rule
5. manifest destiny
6. Emancipation Proclamation
7. assembly line
8. theory of evolution

MAIN IDEAS

Democratic Reform and Activism Section 1 (pages 747–750)

9. What political reforms expanded democracy for men in Britain?
10. Why did the woman suffrage movement in Great Britain become more militant?

Self-Rule for British Colonies Section 2 (pages 751–757)

11. What cultural conflict caused problems for Canada?
12. How did Australia's early history differ from that of other British colonies?
13. Why did the British pass a home rule bill for southern Ireland only?

War and Expansion in the United States Section 3 (pages 758–761)

14. In what ways did the United States gain territory in the 1800s?
15. Why was the issue of slavery in the United States so divisive?

Nineteenth-Century Progress Section 4 (pages 762–767)

16. What was Darwin's principle of natural selection?
17. What prompted the growth of the social sciences?
18. What were some of the effects of increased leisure time?

CRITICAL THINKING

1. USING YOUR NOTES
Create a web diagram of the major political, economic, social and cultural, and scientific and technological changes of the 1800s and early 1900s.

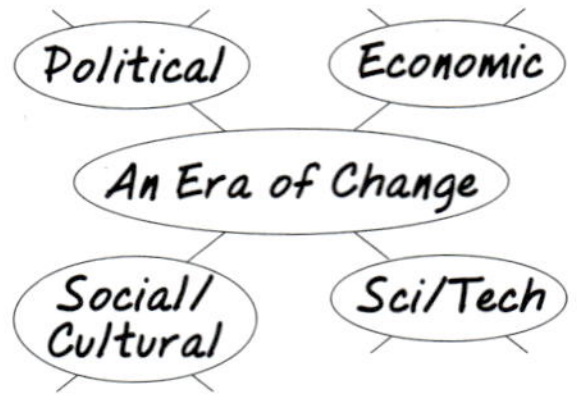

2. RECOGNIZING EFFECTS
SCIENCE AND TECHNOLOGY For a worker, what might be the advantages and disadvantages of an assembly line?

3. ANALYZING MOTIVES
POWER AND AUTHORITY What effect did the call for home rule in British colonies have on Ireland's desire for independence?

4. HYPOTHESIZING
Imagine that circumstances had forced the North to surrender to the South in the Civil War, causing two countries to share the region now occupied by the United States. What economic effects might this have had on the North? the South? the region as a whole?

5. DRAWING CONCLUSIONS
How did manifest destiny help shape the U.S. government's policies of land acquisition?

VISUAL SUMMARY

An Age of Democracy and Progress

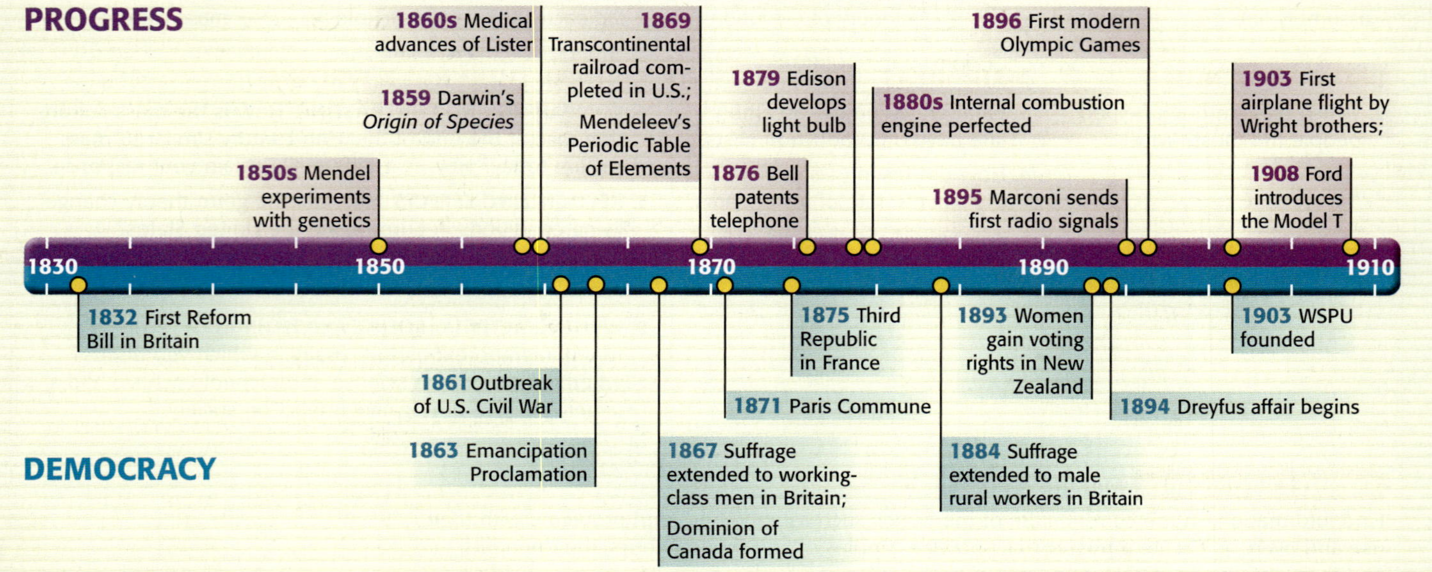

Use the declaration from the Seneca Falls convention (held in New York) and your knowledge of world history to answer questions 1 and 2.

Additional Test Practice, pp. S1–S33

PRIMARY SOURCE

The history of mankind is a history of repeated injuries and usurpations on the part of man toward woman, having in direct object the establishment of an absolute tyranny over her. To prove this, let facts be submitted to a candid world.

He has never permitted her to exercise her inalienable right to the elective franchise.

He has compelled her to submit to laws, in the formation of which she had no voice.

THE SENECA FALLS CONVENTION, *"Declaration of Sentiments"*

1 The purpose of the Seneca Falls convention was to
  (1) call for an end to slavery
  (2) call for the South to secede from the Union
  (3) call for women's rights
  (4) call for the release of Emmeline Pankhurst

2 The style of this primary source is based on
  (1) the U.S. Constitution
  (2) the U.S. Declaration of Independence
  (3) the Reform Bill of 1832
  (4) Émile Zola's *J'accuse!*

Use this cartoon (*A Court for King Cholera*) and your knowledge of world history to answer question 3.

3 Cholera is an infectious disease that has claimed many lives. What details does the artist show about what causes epidemic disease?
  (1) open windows and signs for travelers
  (2) children playing with a rat and a woman digging in trash
  (3) clothing hanging over the street
  (4) crowded street scene

INTEGRATED TECHNOLOGY

TEST PRACTICE Go to **classzone.com**

- Diagnostic tests
- Tutorials
- Strategies
- Additional practice

ALTERNATIVE ASSESSMENT

1. Interact *with* History

On page 746, you considered what political ideals might be worth fighting and possibly even dying for. Now that you have read the chapter, reexamine your conclusions both in terms of the content of the chapter and your knowledge of events in the world today. Discuss your opinions with a small group. Consider:

- political ideals
- religious ideals
- family values

2. WRITING ABOUT HISTORY

EMPIRE BUILDING Write an **editorial** that might have appeared in a newspaper in 19th-century New Zealand. In the editorial, address the issue of British settlers' taking land from the Maori, and the Maori response.

Consider the following:

- the original inhabitants of New Zealand
- means for negotiating land disputes
- balancing the rights of native peoples and new settlers

INTEGRATED TECHNOLOGY

Net Explorations: Mass Entertainment

Go to *NetExplorations* at **classzone.com** to learn more about the rise of mass culture and mass entertainment. Then use the Internet and the material at *NetExplorations* to research and write a newspaper article about spectators at one of the new forms of mass entertainment. Include in your article quotes from fictional visitors and their reactions to actual events and spectacles. You may want to mention one or more of the following:

- the Boston Pilgrims' victory over the Pittsburgh Pirates in baseball's first World Series
- the "Luna" ride at Coney Island
- a late 19th-century European appearance of Barnum & Bailey's circus
- a visit to the Palace of Electricity at the 1904 World's Fair in St. Louis

CHAPTER 27

The Age of Imperialism, 1850–1914

Previewing Main Ideas

EMPIRE BUILDING During the 19th and early 20th centuries, Western powers divided Africa and colonized large areas of Asia.

Geography *Study the map and time line. How many countries colonized Africa? Which country controlled India? the Philippines?*

POWER AND AUTHORITY At the Berlin Conference in 1884–1885, European nations established rules for the division of Africa with little concern about how their actions would affect the African people.

Geography *Which two countries claimed most of Africa?*

ECONOMICS Industrialization increased the need for raw materials and new markets. Western imperialists were driven by this need as they looked for colonies to acquire.

Geography *Compare the size of the Western countries with the areas they colonized. Why were these Western powers interested in lands in Africa and Asia?*

NEW YORK CORE CURRICULUM FOCUS

- The need for raw materials and new markets helped launch the age of imperialism.
- British control of India led to the Sepoy Mutiny and the growth of Indian nationalism.

INTEGRATED TECHNOLOGY

eEdition
- Interactive Maps
- Interactive Visuals
- Interactive Primary Sources

INTERNET RESOURCES

Go to **classzone.com** for:
- Research Links
- Internet Activities
- Primary Sources
- Chapter Quiz
- Maps
- Test Practice
- Current Events

AFRICA AND ASIA

1850 European trading with Africa becomes well established. (Asante brass sculpture) ▶

1869 Suez Canal opens.

1884–1885 Berlin Conference sets rules for African colonization.

1850 — 1875

WORLD

1852 Napoleon III proclaims himself emperor of France. ▶

1871 Bismarck completes unification of German Empire.

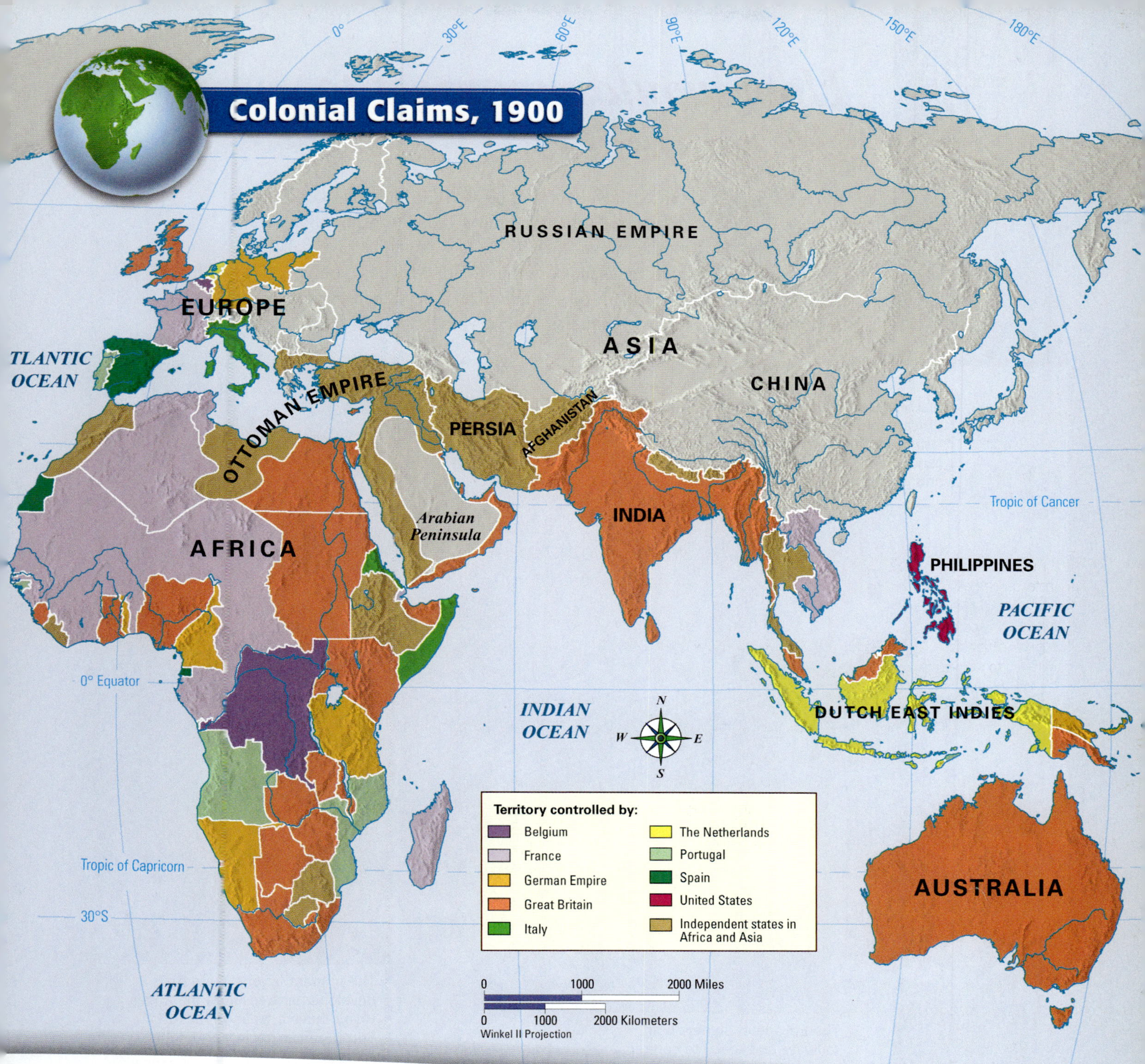

1898
United States acquires Philippines, annexes Hawaii.

1899
Boer War begins in South Africa. ▶

1914
Most of Africa is under European control.

1900 — **1925**

1898
United States wins Spanish-American War.

1910
◀ Mexican Revolution begins.

1914
World War I begins.

1918
World War I ends.

Interact *with* History

How would you react to the colonizers?

You are a young South African living in the 1880s. Gold and diamonds have recently been discovered in your country. The European colonizers need laborers to work the mines, such as the one shown below in an 1888 photograph. Along with thousands of other South Africans, you've left your farm and rural village to work for the colonizers. Separated from your family and living in a city for the first time, you don't know what to expect.

Many Africans, such as these in a South African gold mine, left their farms and families behind to work in the mining centers. As a result, new towns developed and existing ones greatly expanded.

The European owners built railways and roads to connect the mining centers, bridging the huge distances between villages and towns in South Africa.

The migrant labor system that developed as a result of the mines would have a great impact on South African society and culture.

EXAMINING *the* ISSUES

- **What advantages and disadvantages might colonizers bring?**
- **What does the photograph suggest about colonization?**

Discuss these questions with your classmates. In your discussion, remember what you have already learned about conquests and cultural interaction. As you read about imperialism in this chapter, look for its effects on both the colonizers and the colonized.

The Scramble for Africa

CONNECT TO THE NEW YORK STATE CORE CURRICULUM

Unit 5.H.1. Reasons for imperialism–nationalistic, political, economic, "The White Man's Burden", Social Darwinism
Unit 5.H.4.a. Scramble for Africa

TERMS & NAMES

- imperialism
- racism
- Social Darwinism
- Berlin Conference
- Shaka
- Boer
- Boer War

SETTING THE STAGE Industrialization stirred ambitions in many European nations. They wanted more resources to fuel their industrial production. They competed for new markets for their goods. Many nations looked to Africa as a source of raw materials and as a market for industrial products. As a result, colonial powers seized vast areas of Africa during the 19th and early 20th centuries. This seizure of a country or territory by a stronger country is called **imperialism**. As occurred throughout most of Africa, stronger countries dominated the political, economic, and social life of the weaker countries.

Africa Before European Domination

In the mid-1800s, on the eve of the European domination of Africa, African peoples were divided into hundreds of ethnic and linguistic groups. Most continued to follow traditional beliefs, while others converted to Islam or Christianity. These groups spoke more than 1,000 different languages. Politically, they ranged from large empires that united many ethnic groups to independent villages.

Europeans had established contacts with sub-Saharan Africans as early as the 1450s. However, powerful African armies were able to keep the Europeans out of most of Africa for 400 years. In fact, as late as 1880, Europeans controlled only 10 percent of the continent's land, mainly on the coast.

Furthermore, European travel into the interior on a large-scale basis was virtually impossible. Europeans could not navigate African rivers, which had many rapids, cataracts, and changing flows.The introduction of steam-powered riverboats in the early 1800s allowed Europeans to conduct major expeditions into the interior of Africa. Disease also discouraged European exploration.

Finally, Africans controlled their own trade networks and provided the trade items. These networks were specialized. The Chokwe, for example, devoted themselves to collecting ivory and beeswax in the Angolan highlands.

Nations Compete for Overseas Empires Those Europeans who did penetrate the interior of Africa were explorers, missionaries, or humanitarians who opposed the European and American slave trade. Europeans and Americans learned about Africa through travel books and newspapers. These publications competed for readers by hiring reporters to search the globe for stories of adventure, mystery, or excitement.

TAKING NOTES

Outlining Use an outline to list the forces and events surrounding imperialism in Africa.

The Scramble for Africa
I. Africa Before European Domination
A.
B.
II. Forces Driving Imperialism

▲ This stamp celebrates the centenary (100th) anniversary of Stanley and Livingstone's meeting in 1871.

The Congo Sparks Interest In the late 1860s, David Livingstone, a missionary from Scotland, traveled with a group of Africans deep into central Africa to promote Christianity. When several years passed with no word from him or his party, many people feared he was dead. An American newspaper hired reporter Henry Stanley to find Livingstone. In 1871, he found Dr. Livingstone on the shores of Lake Tanganyika. Stanley's famous greeting—"Dr. Livingstone, I presume?"—made headlines around the world.

Stanley set out to explore Africa himself and trace the course of the Congo River. His explorations sparked the interest of King Leopold II of Belgium, who commissioned Stanley to help him obtain land in the Congo. Between 1879 and 1882, Stanley signed treaties with local chiefs of the Congo River valley. The treaties gave King Leopold II of Belgium control of these lands.

Leopold claimed that his primary motive in establishing the colony was to abolish the slave trade and promote Christianity. However, he licensed companies that brutally exploited Africans by forcing them to collect sap from rubber plants. At least 10 million Congolese died due to the abuses inflicted during Leopold's rule. As a result of his cruelty, humanitarians around the world demanded changes. In 1908, the Belgian government took control of the colony away from Leopold. The Belgian Congo, as the colony later became known, was 80 times larger than Belgium. The Belgian government's seizure of the Congo alarmed France. Earlier, in 1882, the French had approved a treaty that gave France the north bank of the Congo River. Soon Britain, Germany, Italy, Portugal, and Spain were also claiming parts of Africa.

Forces Driving Imperialism

The motives that drove colonization in Africa were also at work in other lands. Similar economic, political, and social forces accelerated the drive to take over land in all parts of the globe. The Industrial Revolution in particular provided European countries with a reason to add lands to their control. As European nations industrialized, they searched for new markets and raw materials to improve their economies.

Belief in European Superiority The race for colonies also grew out of a strong sense of national pride. Europeans viewed an empire as a measure of national greatness. As the competition for colonies intensified, each country was determined to plant its flag on as much of the world as possible.

Many Europeans believed that they were better than other peoples. The belief that one race is superior to others is called **racism**. The attitude was a reflection of **Social Darwinism**, a social theory of the time. In this theory, Charles Darwin's ideas about evolution and natural selection were applied to human society. Those who were fittest for survival enjoyed wealth and success and were considered superior to others. According to the theory, non-Europeans were considered to be on a lower scale of cultural and physical development because they had not made the scientific and technological progress that Europeans had. Europeans believed that they had the right and the duty to bring the results of their progress to other countries. Cecil Rhodes, a successful businessman and a major supporter of British expansion, clearly stated this position:

MAIN IDEA

Analyzing Primary Sources

A What attitude about the British does Rhodes's statement display?

PRIMARY SOURCE **A**

I contend that we [Britons] are the first race in the world, and the more of the world we inhabit, the better it is for the human race. . . . It is our duty to seize every opportunity of acquiring more territory and we should keep this one idea steadily before our eyes that more territory simply means more of the Anglo-Saxon race, more of the best, the most human, most honourable race the world possesses.

CECIL RHODES, *Confession of Faith,* 1877

▲ Rhodes's De Beers Consolidated Mines is the biggest diamond company in the world today.

The push for expansion also came from missionaries who worked to convert the peoples of Asia, Africa, and the Pacific Islands to Christianity. Many missionaries believed that European rule was the best way to end evil practices such as the slave trade. They also wanted to "civilize," that is, to "Westernize," the peoples of the foreign land.

Factors Promoting Imperialism in Africa Several factors contributed to the Europeans' conquest of Africa. One overwhelming advantage was the Europeans' technological superiority. The Maxim gun, invented in 1884, was the world's first automatic machine gun. European countries quickly acquired the Maxim, while the resisting Africans were forced to rely on outdated weapons.

European countries also had the means to control their empire. The invention of the steam engine allowed Europeans to easily travel on rivers to establish bases of control deep in the African continent. Railroads, cables, and steamships allowed close communications within a colony and between the colony and its controlling nation.

Even with superior arms and steam engines to transport them, another factor might have kept Europeans confined to the coast. They were highly susceptible to malaria, a disease carried by the dense swarms of mosquitoes in Africa's interior. The perfection of the drug quinine in 1829 eventually protected Europeans from becoming infected with this disease.

Factors within Africa also made the continent easier for Europeans to colonize. Africans' huge variety of languages and cultures discouraged unity among them. Wars fought between ethnic groups over land, water, and trade rights also prevented a unified stand. Europeans soon learned to play rival groups against each other.

The Division of Africa

Vocabulary

scramble: a frantic struggle to obtain something. The word is frequently used to describe the competition for African land.

The scramble for African territory had begun in earnest about 1880. At that time, the French began to expand from the West African coast toward western Sudan. The discoveries of diamonds in 1867 and gold in 1886 in South Africa increased European interest in colonizing the continent. No European power wanted to be left out of the race.

Berlin Conference Divides Africa The competition was so fierce that European countries feared war among themselves. To prevent conflict, 14 European nations met at the **Berlin Conference** in 1884–85 to lay down rules for the division of Africa. They agreed that any European country could claim land in Africa by notifying other nations of its claims and showing it could control the area. The European nations divided the continent with little thought about how African ethnic or linguistic groups were distributed. No African ruler was invited to attend these meetings, yet the conference sealed Africa's fate. By 1914, only Liberia and Ethiopia remained free from European control. B

MAIN IDEA

Clarifying

B What was the purpose of the Berlin Conference?

Demand for Raw Materials Shapes Colonies When European countries began colonizing, many believed that Africans would soon be buying European goods in great quantities. They were wrong; few Africans bought European goods. However, European businesses still needed raw materials from Africa. The major source of great wealth in Africa proved to be the continent's rich mineral resources. The Belgian Congo contained untold wealth in copper and tin. Even these riches seemed small compared with the gold and diamonds in South Africa.

Businesses eventually developed cash-crop plantations to grow peanuts, palm oil, cocoa, and rubber. These products displaced the food crops grown by farmers to feed their families.

Three Groups Clash over South Africa

South Africa demonstrated the impact that Europeans had on African peoples. The history of South Africa is a history of Africans, Dutch, and British clashing over land and resources. Although the African lands seemed empty to the Europeans, various ethnic groups had competing claims over huge areas. The local control of these lands, especially in the east, had been in dispute for about 100 years.

Zulus Fight the British From the late 1700s to the late 1800s, a series of local wars shook southern Africa. Around 1816, a Zulu chief, **Shaka**, used highly disciplined warriors and good military organization to create a large centralized state.

▼ Reinstated as ruler over part of his former nation, King Cetshwayo was soon driven away and died in exile in 1884.

Shaka's successors, however, were unable to keep the kingdom together against the superior arms of the British invaders. In 1879, after Zulu king Cetshwayo refused to dismiss his army and accept British rule, the British invaded the Zulu nation. Although the Zulus used spears and shields against British guns, they nearly defeated the great European army. In July 1879, however, the Zulus lost the Battle of Ulundi and their kingdom. The Zulu nation fell to British control in 1887.

Boers and British Settle in the Cape The first Europeans to settle in South Africa had been the Dutch. The Dutch came to the Cape of Good Hope in 1652 to establish a way station for their ships sailing between the Dutch East Indies and the Netherlands. Dutch settlers known as **Boers** (Dutch for "farmers") gradually took Africans' land and established large farms. (The Boers are also known as Afrikaners.) When the British took over the Cape Colony permanently in the early 1800s, they and the Boers clashed over British policy regarding land and slaves.

GEOGRAPHY SKILLBUILDER: Interpreting Maps

1. **Region** *How does imperialism in Africa in 1878 compare with that in 1913?*
2. **Region** *What does the map of ethnic boundaries suggest about the number of ethnic groups in Africa in 1913?*

History *in* Depth

Winston Churchill and the Boer War

Winston Churchill, who served as the British prime minister during World War II, first came to public attention during the Boer War.

A war correspondent, Churchill was traveling with British soldiers when their train was ambushed by the Boers. Churchill pulled some of the wounded men to safety. When he returned to help the others, however, he was arrested by a Boer soldier. (The soldier, Louis Botha, would later become the prime minister of the Union of South Africa and Churchill's close friend.)

Churchill managed to escape from-the South African prison. When he returned to Britain, Churchill was hailed as a national hero at the age of-26.

In the 1830s, to escape the British, several thousand Boers began to move north. This movement has become known as the Great Trek. The Boers soon found themselves fighting fiercely with Zulu and other African groups whose land they were taking.

The Boer War Diamonds and gold were discovered in southern Africa in the 1860s and 1880s. Suddenly, adventurers from all parts of the world rushed in to make their fortunes. The Boers tried to keep these "outsiders" from gaining political rights. An attempt to start a rebellion against the Boers failed. The Boers blamed the British and, in 1899, took up arms against them.

In many ways, the **Boer War** (also known as the South African War) between the British and the Boers was the first modern "total" war. The Boers launched commando raids and used guerrilla tactics against the British. The British countered by burning Boer farms and imprisoning women and children in disease-ridden concentration camps.

Black South Africans were also involved in the war. Some fought; others served as scouts, guards, drivers, and workers. Many black South Africans were captured by the British and placed in concentration camps, where over 14,000 died.

Britain finally won the war. In 1910, the Boer republics were joined into a self-governing Union of South Africa, which was controlled by the British. (C)

The establishing of colonies signaled a change in the way of life of the Africans. The Europeans made efforts to change the political, social, and economic lives of the peoples they conquered. You will learn about these changes in Section 2.

MAIN IDEA

Contrasting

(C) How was the struggle for land in the Boer War different from other takeovers in Africa?

NEW YORK CORE CURRICULUM REVIEW

TERMS & NAMES **1.** For each term or name, write a sentence explaining its significance.

- imperialism
- racism
- Social Darwinism
- Berlin Conference
- Shaka
- Boer
- Boer War

USING YOUR NOTES

2. How did Europeans use Social Darwinism to justify empire building?

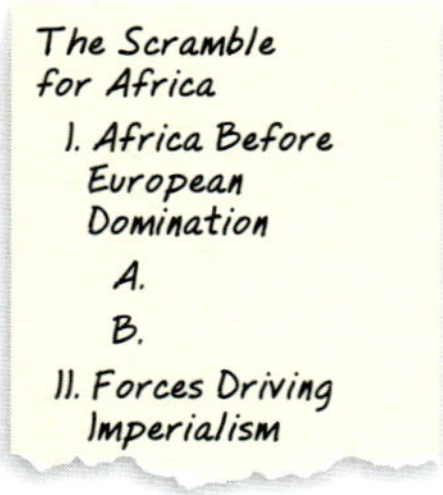

MAIN IDEAS

3. Why did the Europeans control such a small portion of Africa in the 1800s?

4. What were some of the internal factors that contributed to imperialism in Africa?

5. Why did the Boers and the British fight over southern Africa?

CRITICAL THINKING & WRITING

6. MAKING INFERENCES What can you infer about the Europeans' attitude toward Africans from the Berlin Conference?

7. FORMING OPINIONS Why do you think Africans weren't interested in buying European products?

8. DEVELOPING HISTORICAL PERSPECTIVE What sort of problems might result from combining or splitting groups of people without regard for ethnic or linguistic traditions?

9. WRITING ACTIVITY EMPIRE BUILDING Write an **expository essay** explaining which European motive behind imperialism in Africa was the most powerful.

INTEGRATED TECHNOLOGY **INTERNET ACTIVITY**

Use the Internet to find out about the population and status of Afrikaners, or Boers, in South Africa today. Present your findings in an **oral report.**

INTERNET KEYWORD

Afrikaners in South Africa

2

Imperialism

Case Study: Nigeria

CONNECT TO THE NEW YORK STATE CORE CURRICULUM

Unit 5.H.2. Spatial characteristics–"new imperialism"
Unit 5.H.6.a. Immediate/long-term changes made under European rule

TERMS & NAMES

- paternalism
- assimilation
- Menelik II

SETTING THE STAGE The Berlin Conference of 1884–85 was a European conference. And, although black South Africans participated in it, the Boer War was largely a European war. Europeans argued and fought-among themselves over the lands of Africa. In carving up the continent, the-European countries paid little or no attention to historical political divisions or to the many ethnic and language groupings in Africa. Uppermost in the minds of the Europeans was the ability to control Africa's land, its people, and its resources.

A New Period of Imperialism

The imperialism of the 18th and 19th centuries was conducted differently from the explorations of the 15th and 16th centuries. In the earlier period, imperial powers often did not penetrate far into the conquered areas in Asia and Africa. Nor did they always have a substantial influence on the lives of the people. During this new period of imperialism, the Europeans demanded more influence over the economic, political, and social lives of the people. They were determined to shape the economies of the lands to benefit European economies. They also wanted the people to adopt European customs.

TAKING NOTES
Summarizing Use a web to record the forms and methods of European imperialism in Africa, the resistance it met with, and its impact.

Forms of Control Each European nation had certain policies and goals for establishing colonies. To establish control of an area, Europeans used different techniques. Over time, four forms of colonial control emerged: colony, protectorate, sphere of influence, and economic imperialism. These terms are defined and discussed in the chart on page 780. In practice, gaining control of an area might involve the use of several of these forms.

Methods of Management European rulers also developed methods of day-to-day management of the colony. Two basic methods emerged. Britain and other nations—such as the United States in its Pacific Island colonies—preferred indirect control. France and most other European nations wielded a more direct control. Later, when colonies gained independence, the management method used had an influence on the type of government chosen in the new nation.

Indirect Control-Indirect control relied on existing political rulers. In some areas, the British asked a local ruler to accept British authority to rule. These local officials handled much of the daily management of the colony. In addition,

> Analyzing Key Concepts

Imperialism

Imperialism is a policy in which one country seeks to extend its authority by conquering other countries or by establishing economic and political dominance over other countries. The first chart below discusses the four forms of imperialist authority. The second chart shows the two management methods that can be used to control an area.

Forms of Imperialism

Form	Definition	Example
Colony	A country or a territory governed internally by a foreign power	Somaliland in East Africa was a French colony.
Protectorate	A country or a territory with its own internal government but under the control of an outside power	Britain established a protectorate over the Niger River delta.
Sphere of Influence	An area in which an outside power claims exclusive investment or trading privileges	Liberia was under the sphere of influence of the United States.
Economic Imperialism	An independent but less-developed country controlled by private business interests rather than other governments	The Dole Fruit company controlled pineapple trade in Hawaii.

Imperial Management Methods

Indirect Control	Direct Control
• Local government officials used • Limited self-rule • Goal: to develop future leaders • Government institutions are based on European styles but may have local rules.	• Foreign officials brought in to rule • No self-rule • Goal: assimilation • Government institutions are based only on European styles.
Examples: • British colonies such as Nigeria, India, Burma • U.S. colonies on Pacific Islands	Examples: • French colonies such as Somaliland, Vietnam • German colonies such as German East Africa • Portuguese colonies such as Angola

INTEGRATED TECHNOLOGY

RESEARCH LINKS For more on imperialism, go to **classzone.com**

> DATA FILE

In 1905, the British Empire

- was the largest and most powerful in the world's history.
- covered about 11 million square miles.
- had about 400 million inhabitants.

Today, the United Kingdom has 13 small dependent territories and is the head of a voluntary association of 54 independent states.

African Colonization and Independence

- In 1884, Western leaders met to divide Africa into colonial holdings.
- By 1914, nearly all of Africa had been distributed among European powers.
- European imperial powers set national borders in Africa without regard for local ethnic or political divisions. This continues to be a problem for African nations today.

Independent African Countries

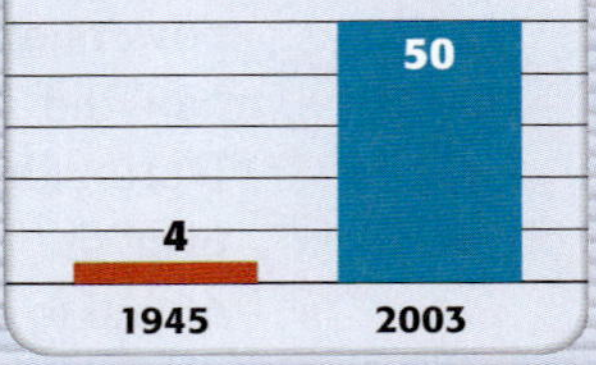

Connect *to* Today

1. **Forming and Supporting Opinions** Which form of managing imperial interests do you think would be most effective and why?

   See Skillbuilder Handbook, page R20.

2. **Recognizing Effects** Use the Internet or library resources to research the problems many African nations are facing today as a result of imperialism. Report your findings to the class.

each colony had a legislative council that included colonial officials as well as local merchants and professionals nominated by the colonial governor.

The assumption was that the councils would train local leaders in the British method of government and that a time would come when the local population would govern itself. This had happened earlier in the British colonies of Australia and Canada. In the 1890s, the United States began to colonize. It chose the indirect method of control for the Philippines.

Direct Control The French and other European powers preferred more direct control of their colonies. They viewed the Africans as unable to handle the complex business of running a country. Based on this attitude, the Europeans developed a policy called **paternalism**. Using that policy, Europeans governed people in a parental way by providing for their needs but not giving them rights. To accomplish this, the Europeans brought in their own bureaucrats and did not train local people in European methods of governing.

The French also supported a policy of **assimilation**. That policy was based on the idea that in time, the local populations would adopt French culture and become like the French. To aid in the transition, all local schools, courts, and businesses were patterned after French institutions. In practice, the French abandoned the ideal of assimilation for all but a few places and settled for a policy of "association," which was similar to indirect control. They recognized African institutions and culture but regarded them as inferior to French culture.

CASE STUDY: Nigeria

A British Colony

A close look at Britain's rule of Nigeria illustrates the forms of imperialism used by European powers to gain control of an area. It also shows management methods used to continue the control of the economic and political life of the area.

Gaining Control Britain gained control of southern Nigeria through both diplomatic and military means. Some local rulers agreed to sign treaties of protection with Britain and accepted British residents. However, others opposed the foreign intervention and rebelled against it. The British used force to put down and defeat these rebellions.

British conquest of northern Nigeria was accomplished by the Royal Niger Company. The company gained control of the palm-oil trade along the Niger River after the Berlin Conference gave Britain a protectorate over the Niger River delta. In 1914, the British claimed the entire area of Nigeria as a colony.

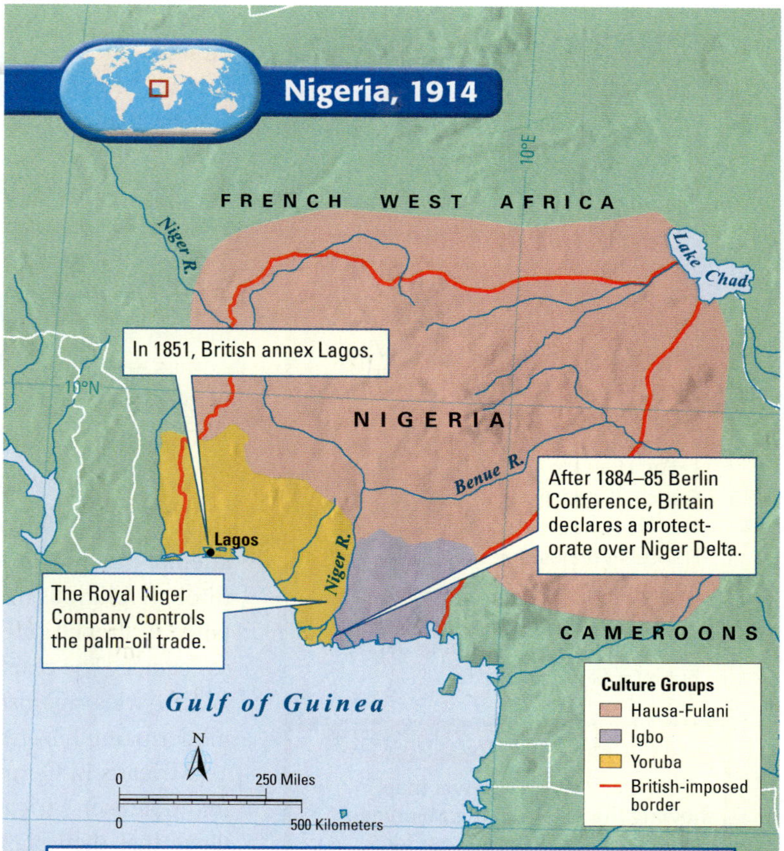

GEOGRAPHY SKILLBUILDER: Interpreting Maps

1. **Region** *How many major culture regions are found within the colony of Nigeria? What sort of problems might result from combining or splitting groups of people?*
2. **Movement** *Why might the British want to be able to control the Niger River?*

Managing the Colony In this new age of imperialism, it was necessary not only to claim a territory but also to govern the people living there. However, managing Nigeria would not prove to be easy. It was one of the most culturally diverse areas in Africa. (A)

MAIN IDEA

Summarizing

(A) Which forms of imperialistic control did Britain use in Nigeria?

About 250 different ethnic groups lived there. The three largest groups were the Hausa-Fulani in the north, the Yoruba in the southwest, and the Igbo in the southeast. These groups were different from one another in many ways, including language, culture, and religion. The Hausa-Fulani people were Muslim and had a strong central government. The Igbo and Yoruba peoples followed traditional religions and relied on local chiefs for control.

Britain did not have enough troops to govern such a complex area. As a result, the British turned to indirect rule of the land. Ruling indirectly through local officials worked well with the Hausa-Fulani. However, this management method did not work as well with the Igbo and Yoruba peoples. Their local chiefs resented having their power limited by the British.

African Resistance

As in Nigeria, Africans across the continent resisted European attempts to colonize their lands. However, the contest between African states and European powers was never equal because of the Europeans' superior arms. Africans resisted the Europeans with whatever forces they could raise and often surprised the Europeans with their military ability. With the single exception of Ethiopia, though, all these attempts at resistance ultimately failed. Edward Morel, a British journalist who lived for a time in the Congo, made an observation about the Africans' dilemma:

PRIMARY SOURCE

Nor is violent physical opposition to abuse and injustice henceforth possible for the African in any part of Africa. His chances of effective resistance have been steadily dwindling with the increasing perfectibility in the killing power of modern armament.

Thus the African is really helpless against the material gods of the white man, as embodied in the trinity of imperialism, capitalistic exploitation, and militarism.

EDWARD MOREL, *The Black Man's Burden*

Unsuccessful Movements The unsuccessful resistance attempts included active military resistance and resistance through religious movements. Algeria's almost 50-year resistance to French rule was one outstanding example of active resistance. The resistance movement led by Samori Touré in West Africa against the French is another example. After modernizing his army, Touré fought the French for 16 years.

Africans in German East Africa put their faith in a spiritual defense. African villagers resisted the Germans' insistence that they plant cotton, a cash crop for export, rather than attend to their own food crops. In 1905, the belief suddenly arose that a magic water (*maji-maji*) sprinkled on their bodies would turn the Germans' bullets into water. The uprising became known as the Maji Maji rebellion. Over 20 different ethnic groups united to fight for their freedom. The fighters believed that their war had been ordained by God and that their ancestors would return to life and assist their struggle.

History Makers

Samori Touré
about 1830–1900

Samori Touré is a hero of the Mandingo people. His empire is often compared to the great Mali Empire of the 1300s.

Touré was a nationalist who built a powerful Mandingo kingdom by conquering neighboring states. His kingdom became the third largest empire in West Africa.

For 16 years, Touré opposed the French imperialists in West Africa. The well-armed Mandingo were France's greatest foe in West Africa, and the two armies clashed several times. The Mandingo Empire was finally brought down, not in battle, but by a famine.

INTEGRATED TECHNOLOGY

INTERNET ACTIVITY Draw a map showing the extent of the Mandingo Empire. Go to **classzone.com** for your research.

However, when resistance fighters armed with spears and protected by the magic water attacked a German machine-gun post, they were mowed down by the thousands. Officially, Germans recorded 75,000 resisters dead. But more than twice that number perished in the famine that followed. The Germans were shaken by the rebellion and its outcome. As a result, they made some government reforms in an effort to make colonialism more acceptable to the Africans.

Ethiopia: A Successful Resistance Ethiopia was the only African nation that successfully resisted the Europeans. Its victory was due to one man—**Menelik II**. He became emperor of Ethiopia in 1889. He successfully played Italians, French, and British against each other, all of whom were striving to bring Ethiopia into their spheres of influence. In the meantime, he built up a large arsenal of modern weapons purchased from France and Russia. In 1889, shortly after Menelik had signed a treaty with Italy, he discovered differences between the wording of the treaty in the Ethiopian language and in Italian. Menelik believed he was giving up a tiny portion of Ethiopia. However, the Italians claimed all of Ethiopia as a protectorate. Meanwhile, Italian forces were advancing into northern Ethiopia. Menelik declared war. In 1896, in one of the greatest battles in the history of Africa—the Battle of Adowa—Ethiopian forces successfully defeated the Italians and kept their nation independent. After the battle, Menelik continued to stockpile rifles and other modern weapons in case another foreign power challenged Ethiopia's liberty.

▼ After defeating Italy, Menelik II modernized Ethiopia by constructing a railroad and weakening the power of the nobility.

GEOGRAPHY SKILLBUILDER: Interpreting Maps

1. **Region** *Which region had the largest area affected by resistance?*
2. **Region** *Was any region unaffected by resistance movements?*

The Legacy of Colonial Rule

European colonial rule forever altered Africans' lives. In some cases, the Europeans brought benefits, but for the most part, the effects were negative.

Negative Effects On the negative side, Africans lost control of their land and their independence. Many died of new diseases such as smallpox. They also lost thousands of their people in resisting the Europeans. Famines resulted from the change to cash crops in place of subsistence agriculture.

Africans also suffered from a breakdown of their traditional cultures. Traditional authority figures were replaced. Homes and property were transferred with little regard to their importance to the people. Men were forced to leave villages to find ways to support themselves and their families. Contempt for the traditional culture and admiration of European life undermined stable societies and caused identity problems for Africans.

The most harmful political legacy from the colonial period was the division of the African continent. Long-term rival chiefdoms were sometimes united, while at other times, kinship groups were split between colonies. The artificial boundaries combined or unnaturally divided groups, creating problems that plagued African colonies during European occupation. These boundaries continue to create problems for the nations that evolved from the former colonies.

Positive Effects On the positive side, colonialism reduced local warfare. Humanitarian efforts in some colonies improved sanitation and provided hospitals and schools. As a result, lifespans increased and literacy rates improved. Also positive was the economic expansion. African products came to be valued on the international market. To aid the economic growth, railroads, dams, and telephone and telegraph lines were built in African colonies. But for the most part, these benefited only European business interests, not Africans' lives.

The patterns of behavior of imperialist powers were similar, no matter where their colonies were located. Dealing with local traditions and peoples continued to cause problems in other areas of the world dominated by Europeans. Resistance to the European imperialists also continued, as you will see in Section 3. **B**

MAIN IDEA

Drawing Conclusions

B Why might the problems caused by artificial boundaries continue after the Europeans left?

NEW YORK CORE CURRICULUM REVIEW

TERMS & NAMES 1. For each term or name, write a sentence explaining its significance.

- paternalism
- assimilation
- Menelik II

USING YOUR NOTES

2. Do you think the positive effects of imperialism outweighed the negative impact? Why or why not?

MAIN IDEAS

3. What idea is the policy of assimilation based on?
4. Why were African resistance movements usually unsuccessful?
5. How did colonial rule cause a breakdown in traditional African culture?

CRITICAL THINKING & WRITING

6. **FORMING OPINIONS** Do you think Europeans could have conquered Africa if the Industrial Revolution had never occurred? Explain your answer.
7. **COMPARING** How was the policy of paternalism like Social Darwinism?
8. **ANALYZING CAUSES** Why would the French and Russians sell arms to Ethiopia?
9. **WRITING ACTIVITY** POWER AND AUTHORITY Write a **speech** that you might deliver to colonial rulers, expressing your views on European imperialism in Africa.

CONNECT TO TODAY **CREATING A POSTER**

After gaining its independence from Portugal in 1975, Angola was plagued by civil war for 27 years. Research to learn what role the legacy of colonialism played in Angola's conflict. Summarize your findings on a **poster** using text, pictures, maps, and charts.

Different Perspectives: Using Primary and Secondary Sources

INTERACTIVE

Views of Imperialism

European imperialism extended to the continents beyond Africa. As imperialism spread, the colonizer and the colonized viewed the experience of imperialism in very different ways. Some Europeans were outspoken about the superiority they felt toward the peoples they conquered. Others thought imperialism was very wrong. Even the conquered had mixed feelings about their encounter with the Europeans.

A PRIMARY SOURCE

J. A. Hobson

Hobson's 1902 book, *Imperialism,* made a great impression on his fellow Britons.

For Europe to rule Asia by force for purposes of gain, and to justify that rule by the pretence that she is civilizing Asia and raising her to a higher level of spiritual life, will be adjudged by history, perhaps, to be the crowning wrong and folly of Imperialism. What Asia has to give, her priceless stores of wisdom garnered from her experience of ages, we refuse to take; the much or little which we could give we spoil by the brutal manner of our giving. This is what Imperialism has done, and is doing, for Asia.

B PRIMARY SOURCE

Dadabhai Naoroji

Dadabhai Naoroji was the first Indian elected to the British Parliament. In 1871, he delivered a speech about the impact of Great Britain on India.

To sum up the whole, the British rule has been—morally, a great blessing; politically peace and order on one hand, blunders on the other, materially, impoverishment. . . . The natives call the British system "Sakar ki Churi," the knife of sugar. That is to say there is no oppression, it is all smooth and sweet, but it is the knife, notwithstanding. I mention this that you should know these feelings. Our great misfortune is that you do not know our wants. When you will know our real wishes, I have not the least doubt that you would do justice. The genius and spirit of the British people is fair play and justice.

C PRIMARY SOURCE

Jules Ferry

The following is from a speech Ferry delivered before the French National Assembly on July 28,1883.

Nations are great in our times only by means of the activities which they develop; it is not simply 'by the peaceful shining forth of institutions . . .' that they are great at this hour. . . . Something else is needed for France: . . . that she must also be a great country exercising all of her rightful influence over the destiny of Europe, that she ought to propagate this influence throughout the world and carry everywhere that she can her language, her customs, her flag, her arms, and her genius.

D PRIMARY SOURCE

This 1882 American political cartoon, titled "The Devilfish in Egyptian Waters," depicts England as an octopus. Notice that Egypt is not yet one of the areas controlled by the British.

THE DEVILFISH IN EGYPTIAN WATERS.

Document-Based QUESTIONS

1. According to Hobson (Source A), what mistake did European imperialists make in Asia?
2. What position on imperialism does Jules Ferry take in Source C?
3. In Source D, what does the representation of England suggest about the cartoonist's view of British imperialism?
4. In what way does the view of imperialism in Source B contrast with that in Source D?

Europeans Claim Muslim Lands

CONNECT TO THE NEW YORK STATE CORE CURRICULUM

Unit 5.H.1. Reasons for imperialism –nationalistic, political, economic, "The White Man's Burden", Social Darwinism
Unit 5.H.2. Spatial characteristics–"new imperialism"

TERMS & NAMES

- geopolitics
- Crimean War
- Suez Canal

SETTING THE STAGE-The European powers who carved up Africa also looked elsewhere for other lands to control. The Muslim lands that rimmed the Mediterranean had largely been claimed as a result of Arab and Ottoman conquests. As you learned in Chapter 18, the Ottoman Empire at its peak stretched from Hungary in the north, around the Black Sea, and across Egypt all the way west to the borders of Morocco. (See map opposite.) But during the empire's last 300 years, it had steadily declined in power. Europeans competed with each other to gain control of this strategically important area.

TAKING NOTES
Determining Main Ideas Use a diagram to fill in three details that support the main idea.

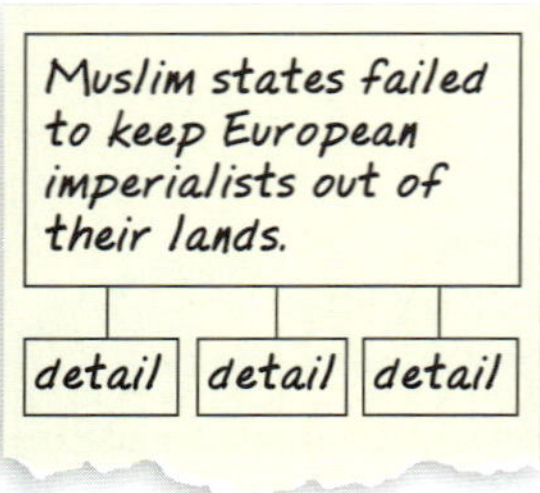

Ottoman Empire Loses Power

The declining Ottoman Empire had difficulties trying to fit into the modern world. However, the Ottomans made attempts to change before they finally were unable to hold back the European imperialist powers.

Reforms Fail When Suleyman I, the last great Ottoman sultan, died in 1566, he was followed by a succession of weak sultans. The palace government broke up into a number of quarreling, often corrupt factions. Weakening power brought other problems. Corruption and theft had caused financial losses. Coinage was devalued, causing inflation. Once the Ottoman Empire had embraced modern technologies, but now it fell further and further behind Europe.

When Selim III came into power in 1789, he attempted to modernize the army. However, the older janissary corps resisted his efforts. Selim III was overthrown, and reform movements were temporarily abandoned. Meanwhile, nationalist feelings began to stir among the Ottomans' subject peoples. In 1830, Greece gained its independence, and Serbia gained self-rule. The Ottomans' weakness was becoming apparent to European powers, who were expanding their territories. They began to look for ways to take the lands away from the Ottomans.

Europeans Grab Territory

Geopolitics, an interest in or taking of land for its strategic location or products, played an important role in the fate of the Ottoman Empire. World powers were attracted to its strategic location. The Ottomans controlled access to the Mediterranean and the Atlantic sea trade. Merchants in landlocked countries that lay beyond the Black Sea had to go through Ottoman lands. Russia, for example, desperately wanted passage for its grain exports across the Black Sea and into the Mediterranean Sea. This desire strongly influenced Russia's relations with the Ottoman Empire. Russia attempted to win Ottoman favor, formed alliances with Ottoman enemies, and finally waged war against the Ottomans. Discovery of oil in Persia around 1900 and in the Arabian Peninsula after World War I focused even more attention on the area.

Russia and the Crimean War Each generation of Russian czars launched a war on the Ottomans to try to gain land on the Black Sea. The purpose was to give Russia a warm-weather port. In 1853, war broke out between the Russians and the Ottomans. The war was called the **Crimean War**, after a peninsula in the Black Sea where most of the war was fought. Britain and France wanted to prevent the Russians from gaining control of additional Ottoman lands. So they entered the war on the side of the Ottoman Empire. The combined forces of the Ottoman Empire, Britain, and France defeated Russia. The Crimean War was the first war in which women, led by Florence Nightingale, established their position as army nurses. It was also the first war to be covered by newspaper correspondents.

MAIN IDEA

Making Inferences

A How did the Crimean War help lead to the decline of the Ottoman Empire?

The Crimean War revealed the Ottoman Empire's military weakness. Despite the help of Britain and France, the Ottoman Empire continued to lose lands. The Russians came to the aid of Slavic people in the Balkans who rebelled against the Ottomans. The Ottomans lost control of Romania, Montenegro, Cyprus, Bosnia, Herzegovina, and an area that became Bulgaria. The Ottomans lost land in Africa too. By the beginning of World War I, the Ottoman Empire was reduced in size and in deep decline. **A**

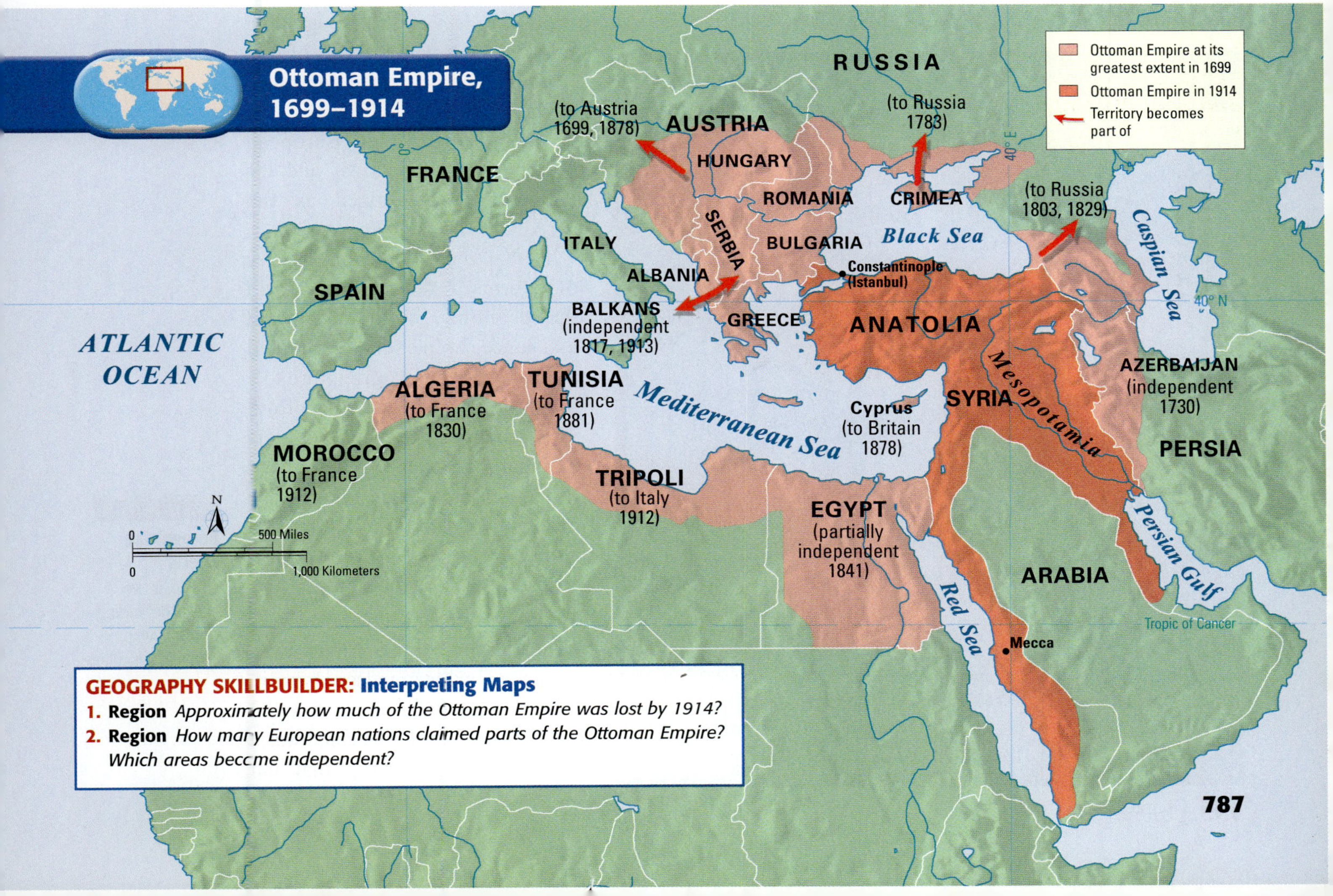

GEOGRAPHY SKILLBUILDER: Interpreting Maps

1. **Region** *Approximately how much of the Ottoman Empire was lost by 1914?*
2. **Region** *How many European nations claimed parts of the Ottoman Empire? Which areas become independent?*

The Great Game For much of the 19th century, Great Britain and Russia engaged in yet another geopolitical struggle, this time over Muslim lands in Central Asia. Known as the "Great Game," the war was waged over India, one of Britain's most profitable colonies. Russia sought to extend its empire and gain access to India's riches. Britain defended its colony and also attempted to spread its empire beyond India's borders. Afghanistan, which lay between the Russian and British empires, became the center of their struggle. (See the map on page 771.)

In the 1800s, Afghanistan was an independent Muslim kingdom. Its dry, mountainous terrain and determined people continually frustrated the invading imperial powers. After decades of fighting, Great Britain finally withdrew from Afghanistan in 1881. In 1921, Britain formally agreed that its empire would not extend beyond the Khyber Pass, which borders eastern Afghanistan. The newly formed Soviet Union, meanwhile, signed a nonaggression pact with Afghanistan. That agreement was honored until 1979, when the Soviet Union invaded Afghanistan.

Egypt Initiates Reforms

Observing the slow decline of the Ottoman Empire, some Muslim leaders decided that their countries would either have to adjust to the modern world or be consumed by it. Egypt initiated political and social reforms, in part to block European domination of its land.

▼ Muhammad Ali was a common soldier who rose to leadership as a result of his military skill and political shrewdness.

Military and Economic Reforms Modernization came to Egypt as a result of the interest in the area created by the French occupation. Egypt's strategic location at the head of the Red Sea appeared valuable to France and Britain. After Napoleon failed to win Egypt, a new leader emerged: Muhammad Ali. The Ottomans sent him as part of an expeditionary force to govern Egypt, but he soon broke away from Ottoman control. Beginning in 1831, he fought a series of battles in which he gained control of Syria and Arabia. Through the combined efforts of European powers, Muhammad Ali and his heirs were recognized as the hereditary rulers of Egypt.

Muhammad Ali began a series of reforms in the military and in the economy. Without foreign assistance, he personally directed a shift of Egyptian agriculture to a plantation cash crop—cotton. This brought Egypt into the international marketplace but at a cost to the peasants. They lost the use of lands they traditionally farmed and were forced to grow cash crops in place of food crops. **B**

MAIN IDEA

Recognizing Effects

B What two effects did raising cotton have on Egyptian agriculture?

The Suez Canal Muhammad Ali's efforts to modernize Egypt were continued by his grandson, Isma'il. Isma'il supported the construction of the **Suez Canal**. The canal was a human-made waterway that cut

History *in* Depth

Suez Canal

The Suez Canal was viewed as the "Lifeline of the Empire" because it allowed Britain quicker access to its colonies in Asia and Africa. In a speech to Parliament, Joseph Chamberlain explained that he believed Britain should continue its occupation of Egypt because of "the necessity for using every legitimate opportunity to extend our influence and control in that great African continent which is now being opened up to civilization and to commerce."

This painting represents the opening celebration of the canal on November 17, 1869.

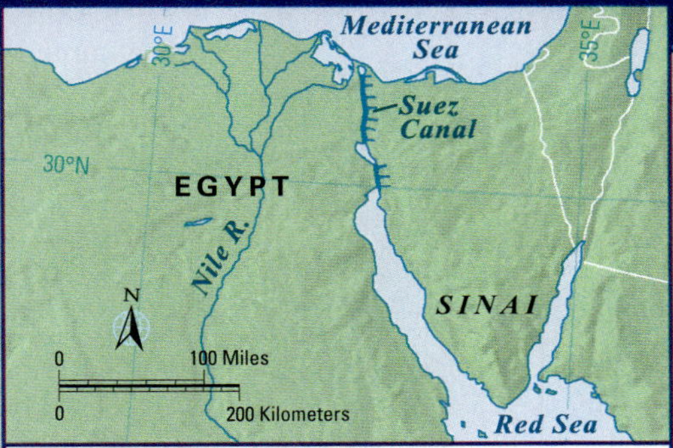

GEOGRAPHY SKILLBUILDER: Interpreting Maps
Place *Approximately how long is the Suez Canal?*

through the Isthmus of Suez. It connected the Red Sea to the Mediterranean. It was built mainly with French money from private interest groups, using Egyptian labor. The Suez Canal opened in 1869 with a huge international celebration. However, Isma'il's modernization efforts, such as irrigation projects and communication networks, were enormously expensive. Egypt soon found that it could not pay its European bankers even the interest on its $450 million debt. The British insisted on overseeing financial control of the canal, and in 1882 the British occupied Egypt.

Persia Pressured to Change

Elsewhere in southwest Asia, Russia and Britain competed to exploit Persia commercially and to bring that country under their own spheres of influence. (See map on page 787.) Russia was especially interested in gaining access to the Persian Gulf and the Indian Ocean. Twice Persia gave up territories to Russia, after military defeats in 1813 and 1828. Britain was interested in using Afghanistan as a buffer between India and Russia. In 1857, Persia resisted British demands but was forced to give up all claims to Afghanistan. Britain's interest in Persia increased greatly after the discovery of oil there in 1908.

Persia lacked the capital to develop its own resources. To raise money and to gain economic prestige, the Persian ruler began granting concessions to Western businesses. These concessions allowed businesses to buy the right to operate in a certain area or develop a certain product. For example, a British corporation, the Anglo-Persian Oil Company, began to develop Persia's rich oil fields in the early 1900s.

▲ Nasir al-Din was killed by one of al-Afghani's followers a few years after the boycott.

Battle over Tobacco Tension arose between the often corrupt rulers, who wanted to sell concessions to Europeans, and the people. The people were often backed by religious leaders who feared change or disliked Western influence in their nation. In 1890, Persian ruler Nasir al-Din sold a concession to a British company to export Persian tobacco. This action outraged Jamal al-Din al-Afghani, a leader who supported the modernization of Persia. He helped set up a tobacco boycott by the heavy-smoking Persians. In the following quote, he expresses his contempt for the Persian ruler:

PRIMARY SOURCE C

He has sold to the foes of our Faith the greater part of the Persian lands and the profits derived from them, for example . . . tobacco, with the chief centers of its cultivation, the lands on which it is grown and the warehouses, carriers, and sellers, wherever these are found. . . .

In short, this criminal has offered the provinces of Persia to auction among the Powers, and is selling the realms of Islam and the abodes of Muhammad and his household to foreigners.

JAMAL AL-DIN AL-AFGHANI, in a letter to Hasan Shirazi, April 1891

MAIN IDEA

Analyzing Primary Sources

C Why did al-Afghani condemn the actions of the Persian ruler?

The tobacco boycott worked. Riots broke out, and the ruler was forced to cancel the concession. As unrest continued in Persia, however, the government was unable to control the situation. In 1906, a group of revolutionaries forced the ruler to establish a constitution. In 1907, Russia and Britain took over the country and divided it into spheres of influence. They exercised economic control over Persia.

In the Muslim lands, many European imperialists gained control by using economic imperialism and creating spheres of influence. Although some governments made attempts to modernize their nations, in most cases it was too little too late. In other areas of the globe, imperialists provided the modernization. India, for example, became a colony that experienced enormous change as a result of the occupation of the imperialist British. You will learn about India in Section 4.

NEW YORK CORE CURRICULUM REVIEW

TERMS & NAMES 1. For each term or name, write a sentence explaining its significance.

- geopolitics
- Crimean War
- Suez Canal

USING YOUR NOTES

2. What imperialistic forms of control did the Europeans use to govern these lands?

Muslim states failed to keep European imperialists out of their lands.

detail | *detail* | *detail*

MAIN IDEAS

3. What is geopolitics?
4. Why did Great Britain want to control the Suez Canal?
5. Why did the Persian people oppose their ruler's policy of selling business concessions to Europeans?

CRITICAL THINKING & WRITING

6. **COMPARING AND CONTRASTING** How were the reactions of African and Muslim rulers to imperialism similar? How were they different?
7. **MAKING PREDICTIONS** What do you think happened as a result of Muhammad Ali's agriculture reform?
8. **ANALYZING BIAS** What does the quotation in the History in Depth on page 789 suggest about Joseph Chamberlain's view of British imperialism in Africa?
9. **WRITING ACTIVITY** EMPIRE BUILDING Write a **cause-and-effect paragraph** about reform efforts undertaken in Muslim lands.

CONNECT TO TODAY **CREATING A TIME LINE**

Iran (formerly Persia) has undergone many changes since the late 1800s. Create a **time line** of important events in Iran's modern history. Include photographs that illustrate the events.

British Imperialism in India

CONNECT TO THE NEW YORK STATE CORE CURRICULUM

Unit 5.H.3.a. British East India Company
Unit 5.H.3.b. Sepoy Mutiny

TERMS & NAMES

- sepoy
- "jewel in the crown"
- Sepoy Mutiny
- Raj

SETTING THE STAGE British economic interest in India began in the 1600s, when the British East India Company set up trading posts at Bombay, Madras, and Calcutta. At first, India's ruling Mughal Dynasty kept European traders under control. By 1707, however, the Mughal Empire was collapsing. Dozens of small states, each headed by a ruler or maharajah, broke away from Mughal control. In 1757, Robert Clive led East India Company troops in a decisive victory over Indian forces allied with the French at the Battle of Plassey. From that time until 1858, the East India Company was the leading power in India.

British Expand Control over India

The area controlled by the East India Company grew over time. Eventually, it governed directly or indirectly an area that included modern Bangladesh, most of southern India, and nearly all the territory along the Ganges River in the north.

TAKING NOTES

Recognizing Effects Use a diagram to identify the effects of the three causes listed.

Cause	Effect
1. Decline of the Mughal Empire	
2. Colonial policies	
3. Sepoy Mutiny	

East India Company Dominates Officially, the British government regulated the East India Company's efforts both in London and in India. Until the beginning of the 19th century, the company ruled India with little interference from the British government. The company even had its own army, led by British officers and staffed by **sepoys**, or Indian soldiers. The governor of Bombay, Mountstuart Elphinstone, referred to the sepoy army as "a delicate and dangerous machine, which a little mismanagement may easily turn against us."

Britain's "Jewel in the Crown"-At first, the British treasured India more for its potential than its actual profit. The Industrial Revolution had turned Britain into the world's workshop, and India was a major supplier of raw materials for that workshop. Its 300 million people were also a large potential market for British-made goods. It is not surprising, then, that the British considered India the brightest **"jewel in the crown,"** the most valuable of all of Britain's colonies.

The British set up restrictions that prevented the Indian economy from operating on its own. British policies called for India to produce raw materials for British manufacturing and to buy British goods. In addition, Indian competition with British goods was prohibited. For example, India's own handloom textile industry was almost put out of business by imported British textiles. Cheap cloth from England flooded the Indian market and undercut local producers.

▼ A sepoy in uniform

British Transport Trade Goods India became increasingly valuable to the British after they established a railroad network there. Railroads transported raw products from the interior to the ports and manufactured goods back again. Most of the raw materials were agricultural products produced on plantations. Plantation crops included tea, indigo, coffee, cotton, and jute. Another crop was opium. The British shipped opium to China and exchanged it for tea, which they then sold in England.

Trade in these crops was closely tied to international events. For example, the Crimean War in the 1850s cut off the supply of Russian jute to Scottish jute mills. This boosted the export of raw jute from Bengal, a province in India. Likewise, cotton production in India increased when the Civil War in the United States cut off supplies of cotton for British textile mills. **A**

Vocabulary
jute: a fiber used for sacks and cord

MAIN IDEA
Summarizing
A On which continents were Indian goods being traded?

Impact of Colonialism India both benefited from and was harmed by British colonialism. On the negative side, the British held much of the political and economic power. The British restricted Indian-owned industries such as cotton textiles. The emphasis on cash crops resulted in a loss of self-sufficiency for many villagers. The conversion to cash crops reduced food production, causing famines in the late 1800s. The British officially adopted a hands-off policy regarding Indian religious and social customs. Even so, the increased presence of missionaries and the racist attitude of most British officials threatened traditional Indian life.

On the positive side, the laying of the world's third largest railroad network was a major British achievement. When completed, the railroads enabled India to develop a modern economy and brought unity to the connected regions. Along with the railroads, a modern road network, telephone and telegraph lines, dams, bridges, and irrigation canals enabled India to modernize. Sanitation and public health improved. Schools and colleges were founded, and literacy increased. Also, British troops cleared central India of bandits and put an end to local warfare among competing local rulers.

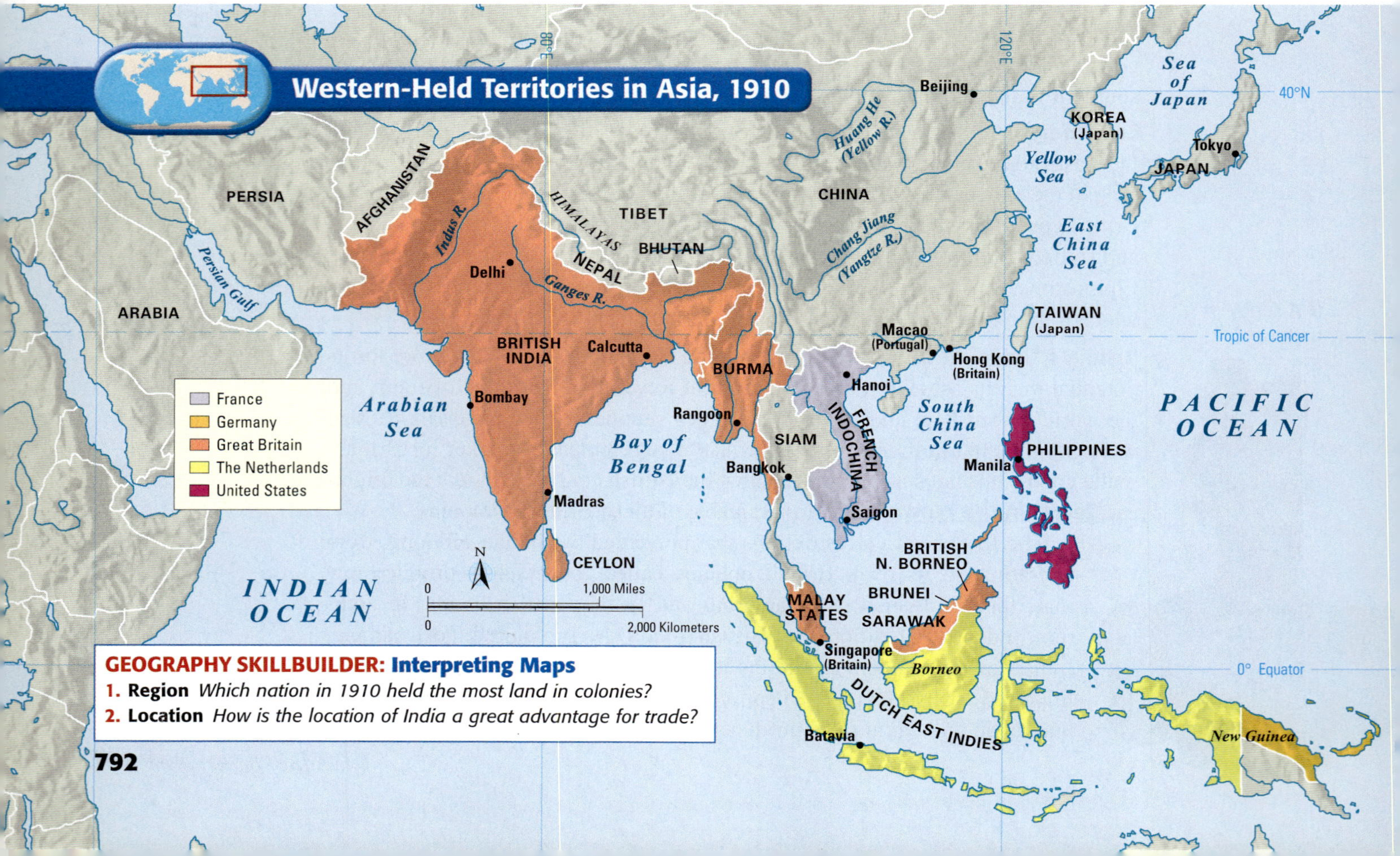

GEOGRAPHY SKILLBUILDER: Interpreting Maps
1. **Region** *Which nation in 1910 held the most land in colonies?*
2. **Location** *How is the location of India a great advantage for trade?*

Social History

Social Class in India

In the photograph at right, a British officer is waited on by Indian servants. This reflects the class system in India.

British Army

Social class determined the way of life for the British Army in India. Upper-class men served as officers. Lower-class British served at lesser rank and did not advance past the rank of sergeant. Only men with the rank of sergeant and above were allowed to bring their wives to India.

Each English officer's wife attempted to re-create England in the home setting. Like a general, she directed an army of 20 to 30 servants.

Indian Servants

Caste determined Indian occupations. Castes were divided into four broad categories called varna. Indian civil servants were of the third varna. House and personal servants were of the fourth varna.

Even within the varna, jobs were strictly regulated, which is why such large servant staffs were required. For example, in the picture here, both servants were of the same varna. Although the two servants were from the same varna, they had different jobs.

The Sepoy Mutiny

By 1850, the British controlled most of the Indian subcontinent. However, there were many pockets of discontent. Many Indians believed that in addition to controlling their land, the British were trying to convert them to Christianity. The Indian people also resented the constant racism that the British expressed toward them.

Indians Rebel As economic problems increased for Indians, so did their feelings of resentment and nationalism. In 1857, gossip spread among the sepoys, the Indian soldiers, that the cartridges of their new Enfield rifles were greased with beef and pork fat. To use the cartridges, soldiers had to bite off the ends. Both Hindus, who consider the cow sacred, and Muslims, who do not eat pork, were outraged by the news.

A garrison commander was shocked when 85 of the 90 sepoys refused to accept the cartridges. The British handled the crisis badly. The soldiers who had disobeyed were jailed. The next day, on May 10, 1857, the sepoys rebelled. They marched to Delhi, where they were joined by Indian soldiers stationed there. They captured the city of Delhi. From Delhi, the rebellion spread to northern and central India.

Some historians have called this outbreak the **Sepoy Mutiny**. The uprising spread over much of northern India. Fierce fighting took place. Both British and sepoys tried to slaughter each other's armies. The East India Company took more than a year to regain control of the country. The British government sent troops to help them. (B)

MAIN IDEA

Recognizing Effects

(B) Look back at Elphinstone's comment on page 791. Did the Sepoy Mutiny prove him correct?

The Indians could not unite against the British due to weak leadership and serious splits between Hindus and Muslims. Hindus did not want the Muslim Mughal Empire restored. Indeed, many Hindus preferred British rule to Muslim rule. Most of the princes and maharajahs who had made alliances with the East India

Company did not take part in the rebellion. The Sikhs, a religious group that had been hostile to the Mughals, also remained loyal to the British. Indeed, from then on, the bearded and turbaned Sikhs became the mainstay of Britain's army in India.

Turning Point The mutiny marked a turning point in Indian history. As a result of the mutiny, in 1858 the British government took direct command of India. The term **Raj** refers to British rule after India came under the British crown during the reign of Queen Victoria. A cabinet minister in London directed policy, and a British governor-general in India carried out the government's orders. After 1877, this official held the title of viceroy.

To reward the many princes who had remained loyal to Britain, the British promised to respect all treaties the East India Company had made with them. They also promised that the Indian states that were still free would remain independent. Unofficially, however, Britain won greater and greater control of those states.

The Sepoy Mutiny fueled the racist attitudes of the British. The British attitude is illustrated in the following quote by Lord Kitchener, British commander in chief of the army in India:

PRIMARY SOURCE

It is this consciousness of the inherent superiority of the European which has won for us India. However well educated and clever a native may be, and however brave he may prove himself, I believe that no rank we can bestow on him would cause him to be considered an equal of the British officer.

LORD KITCHENER, quoted in K. M. Panikkar, *Asia and Western Dominance*

The mutiny increased distrust between the British and the Indians. A political pamphlet suggested that both Hindus and Muslims "are being ruined under the tyranny and oppression of the . . . treacherous English." (C)

MAIN IDEA

Recognizing Effects

(C) In what ways did the Sepoy Mutiny change the political climate of India?

▼ This engraving shows sepoys attacking the British infantry at the Battle of Cawnpore in 1857.

Nationalism Surfaces in India

In the early 1800s, some Indians began demanding more modernization and a greater role in governing themselves. Ram Mohun Roy, a modern-thinking, well-educated Indian, began a campaign to move India away from traditional practices and ideas. Ram Mohun Roy saw arranged child marriages and the rigid caste separation as parts of Indian life that needed to be changed. He believed that if the practices were not changed, India would continue to be controlled by outsiders. Roy's writings inspired other Indian reformers to call for adoption of Western ways. Roy also founded a social reform movement that worked for change in India.

Besides modernization and Westernization, nationalist feelings started to surface in India. Indians hated a system that made them second-class citizens in their own country. They were barred from top posts in the Indian Civil Service. Those who managed to get middle-level jobs were paid less than Europeans. A British engineer on the East India Railway, for example, made nearly 20 times as much money as an Indian engineer.

Nationalist Groups Form This growing nationalism led to the founding of two nationalist groups, the Indian National Congress in 1885 and the Muslim League in 1906. At first, such groups concentrated on specific concerns for Indians. By the early 1900s, however, they were calling for self-government.

The nationalists were further inflamed in 1905 by the partition of Bengal. The province was too large for administrative purposes, so the British divided it into a Hindu section and a Muslim section. Keeping the two religious groups apart made it difficult for them to unite in calling for independence. In 1911, the British took back the order and divided the province in a different way. **D**

Conflict over the control of India continued to develop between the Indians and the British in the following years. Elsewhere in Southeast Asia, the same struggles for control of land took place between local groups and the major European powers that dominated them. You will learn about them in Section 5.

MAIN IDEA

Analyzing Motives

D Why would the British think that dividing the Hindus and Muslims into separate sections would be good?

NEW YORK CORE CURRICULUM REVIEW

TERMS & NAMES 1. For each term or name, write a sentence explaining its significance.

- sepoy
- "jewel in the crown"
- Sepoy Mutiny
- Raj

USING YOUR NOTES

2. Which of the effects you listed later became causes?

Cause	Effect
1. Decline of the Mughal Empire	
2. Colonial policies	
3. Sepoy Mutiny	

MAIN IDEAS

3. Why did Britain consider India its "jewel in the crown"?
4. Why didn't Indians unite against the British in the Sepoy Mutiny?
5. What form did British rule take under the Raj?

CRITICAL THINKING & WRITING

6. **MAKING INFERENCES**-How did economic imperialism lead to India's becoming a British colony?
7. **EVALUATING DECISIONS** What might the decision to grease the sepoys' cartridges with beef and pork fat reveal about the British attitude toward Indians?
8. **SYNTHESIZING** How did imperialism contribute to unity and to the growth of nationalism in India?
9. **WRITING ACTIVITY** EMPIRE BUILDING Write an **editorial** to an underground Indian newspaper, detailing grievances against the British and calling for self-government.

CONNECT TO TODAY **CREATING A POLITICAL CARTOON**

In 1947, India was divided into two countries: mostly Hindu India and mostly Muslim Pakistan. However, the two countries maintain a tense relationship today. Research to learn about the cause of this tension and illustrate it in a **political cartoon.**

Imperialism in Southeast Asia

CONNECT TO THE NEW YORK STATE CORE CURRICULUM

Unit 5.H.2. Spatial characteristics –"new imperialism"
Unit 5.H.6.a. Immediate/long-term changes made under European rule

TERMS & NAMES

- Pacific Rim
- King Mongkut
- Emilio Aguinaldo
- annexation
- Queen Liliuokalani

SETTING THE STAGE Just as the European powers rushed to divide Africa, they also competed to carve up the lands of Southeast Asia. These lands form part of the **Pacific Rim**, the countries that border the Pacific Ocean. Western nations desired the Pacific Rim lands for their strategic location along the sea route to China. Westerners also recognized the value of the Pacific colonies as sources of tropical agriculture, minerals, and oil. As the European powers began to appreciate the value of the area, they challenged each other for their own parts of the prize.

TAKING NOTES

Clarifying Use a spider map to identify a Western power and the areas it controlled.

European Powers Invade the Pacific Rim

Early in the 18th century, the Dutch East India Company established control over most of the 3,000-mile-long chain of Indonesian islands. The British established a major trading port at Singapore. The French took over Indochina on the Southeast Asian mainland. The Germans claimed the Marshall Islands and parts of New Guinea and the Solomon islands.

The lands of Southeast Asia were perfect for plantation agriculture. The major focus was on sugar cane, coffee, cocoa, rubber, coconuts, bananas, and pineapple. As these products became more important in the world trade markets, European powers raced each other to claim lands.

Dutch Expand Control The Dutch East India Company, chartered in 1602, actively sought lands in Southeast Asia. It seized Malacca from the Portuguese and fought the British and Javanese for control of Java. The discovery of oil and tin on the islands and the desire for more rubber plantations prompted the Dutch to gradually expand their control over Sumatra, part of Borneo, Celebes, the Moluccas, and Bali. Finally the Dutch ruled the whole island chain of Indonesia, then called the Dutch East Indies. (See map opposite.)

Management of plantations and trade brought a large Dutch population to the islands. In contrast to the British, who lived temporarily in India but retired in Britain, the Dutch thought of Indonesia as their home. They moved to Indonesia and created a rigid social class system there. The Dutch were on top, wealthy and educated Indonesians came next, and plantation workers were at the bottom. The Dutch also forced farmers to plant one-fifth of their land in specified export crops.

British Take the Malayan Peninsula To compete with the Dutch, the British sought a trading base that would serve as a stop for their ships that traveled the India-China sea routes. They found a large, sheltered harbor on Singapore, an island just off the tip of the Malay Peninsula. The opening of the Suez Canal and the increased demand for tin and rubber combined to make Singapore one of the world's busiest ports.

Britain also gained colonies in Malaysia and in Burma (modern Myanmar). Malaysia had large deposits of tin and became the world's leading rubber exporter. Needing workers to mine the tin and tap the rubber trees, Britain encouraged Chinese to immigrate to Malaysia. Chinese flocked to the area. As a result of such immigration, the Malays soon became a minority in their own country. Conflict between the resident Chinese and the native Malays remains unresolved today. (A)

MAIN IDEA

Analyzing Motives

(A) Why do you think so many Chinese moved to Malaysia?

GEOGRAPHY SKILLBUILDER: Interpreting Maps

1. **Location** *What was Siam's location relative to the nearest European colonies?*
2. **Region** *Which European country could access both the Indian and the Pacific oceans from its colony?*

French Control Indochina The French had been active in Southeast Asia since the 17th century. They even helped the Nguyen (nuh•WIN) dynasty rise to power in Vietnam. In the 1840s, during the rule of an anti-Christian Vietnamese emperor, seven French missionaries were killed. Church leaders and capitalists who wanted a larger share of the overseas market demanded military intervention. Emperor Napoleon III ordered the French army to invade southern Vietnam. Later, the French added Laos, Cambodia, and northern Vietnam to the territory. The combined states would eventually be called French Indochina.

Using direct colonial management, the French themselves filled all important positions in the government bureaucracy. They did not encourage local industry. Four times as much land was devoted to rice production. However, the peasants' consumption of rice decreased because much of the rice was exported. Anger over this reduction set the stage for Vietnamese resistance against the French.

Colonial Impact In Southeast Asia, colonization brought mixed results. Economies grew based on cash crops or goods that could be sold on the world market. Roads, harbors, and rail systems improved communication and transportation but mostly benefited European business. However, education, health, and sanitation did improve.

Unlike other colonial areas, millions of people from other areas of Asia and the world migrated to work on plantations and in the mines in Southeast Asia. The region became a melting pot of Hindus, Muslims, Christians, and Buddhists. The resulting cultural changes often led to racial and religious clashes that are still seen today.

Siam Remains Independent

While its neighbors on all sides fell under the control of imperialists, Siam (present-day Thailand) maintained its independence throughout the colonial period. Siam lay between British-controlled Burma and French Indochina. (See map above.) France and Britain each aimed to prevent the other from gaining control of Siam. Knowing this, Siamese kings skillfully promoted Siam as a neutral zone between the two powers.

Siam modernized itself under the guidance of **King Mongkut** and his son Chulalongkorn. In a royal proclamation, King Chulalongkorn showed his understanding of the importance of progress:

PRIMARY SOURCE

As the times and the course of things in our country have changed, it is essential to promote the advancement of all our academic and technical knowledge and to prevent it from succumbing [giving in] to competition from the outside. In order to achieve this, it is imperative to make haste in education so that knowledge and ability will increase.

KING CHULALONGKORN, "Royal Proclamation in Education"

To accomplish the changes, Siam started schools, reformed the legal system, and reorganized the government. The government built its own railroads and telegraph systems and ended slavery. Because the changes came from their own government, the Siamese people escaped the social turmoil, racist treatment, and economic exploitation that occurred in other countries controlled by foreigners.

U.S. Imperialism in the Pacific Islands

Because Americans had fought for their independence from Britain, most of them disliked the idea of colonizing other nations. However, two groups of Americans were outspoken in their support of imperialism. One group of ambitious empire builders felt the United States should fulfill its destiny as a world power, colonizing like the Europeans. The other group, composed of business interests, welcomed the opening of new markets and trade possibilities.

The Philippines Change Hands The United States acquired the Philippine Islands, Puerto Rico, and Guam as a result of the Spanish-American War in 1898. Gaining the Philippines touched off a debate in the United States over imperialism. President McKinley's views swayed many to his side. He told a group of Methodist ministers his intention to "educate Filipinos, and uplift and Christianize them."

Vocabulary
Filipino: an inhabitant of the Philippine Islands

Filipino nationalists were not happy to trade one colonizer—the Spanish—for another, the Americans. **Emilio Aguinaldo** (eh•MEE•lyoh AH•gee•NAHL•doh), leader of the Filipino nationalists, claimed that the United States had promised immediate independence after the Spanish-American War ended. The nationalists declared independence and established the Philippine Republic.

▼ This photograph shows American soldiers fighting the Filipino nationalists in the early years of the war.

The United States plunged into a fierce struggle with the Filipino nationalists in 1899 and defeated them in 1902. The United States promised the Philippine people that it would prepare them for self-rule. To achieve this goal, the United States built roads, railroads, and hospitals, and set up school systems. However, as with other Southeast Asian areas, businessmen encouraged growing cash crops such as sugar at the expense of basic food crops. This led to food shortages for the Filipinos.

Hawaii Becomes a Republic U.S. interest in Hawaii began around the 1790s when Hawaii was a port on the way to China and East India. Beginning about the 1820s, sugar trade began to change the Hawaiian economy. Americans established sugar-cane plantations and became highly successful. By the mid-19th century, American sugar plantations accounted for 75 percent of Hawaii's wealth. At the same time, American sugar planters also gained great political power in Hawaii.

Then in 1890, the McKinley Tariff Act passed by the U.S. government set off a crisis in the islands. The act eliminated the tariffs on all sugar entering the United States. Now, sugar from Hawaii was no longer cheaper than sugar produced elsewhere. That change cut into the sugar producers' profits. Some U.S. business leaders pushed for **annexation** of Hawaii, or the adding of the territory to the United States. Making Hawaii a part of the United States meant that Hawaiian sugar could be sold for greater profits because American producers got an extra two cents a pound from the U.S. government.

About the same time, the new Hawaiian ruler, **Queen Liliuokalani** (luh•LEE•uh•oh•kuh•LAH•nee), took the throne. In 1893, she called for a new constitution that would increase her power. It would also restore the political power of Hawaiians at the expense of wealthy planters. To prevent this from happening, a group of American businessmen hatched a plot to overthrow the Hawaiian monarchy. In 1893, Queen Liliuokalani was removed from power.

In 1894, Sanford B. Dole, a wealthy plantation owner and politician, was named president of the new Republic of Hawaii. The president of the new republic asked the United States to annex it. At first, President Cleveland refused. In 1898, however, the Republic of Hawaii was annexed by the United States.

The period of imperialism was a time of great power and domination of others by mostly European powers. As the 19th century closed, the lands of the world were all claimed. The European powers now faced each other with competing claims. Their battles would become the focus of the 20th century.

History Makers

Queen Liliuokalani
1838–1917

Liliuokalani was Hawaii's only queen and the last monarch of Hawaii. She bitterly regretted her brother's loss of power to American planters and worked to regain power for the Hawaiian monarchy. As queen, she refused to renew a treaty signed by her brother that would have given commercial privileges to foreign businessmen. It was a decision that would cost her the crown.

INTEGRATED TECHNOLOGY

RESEARCH LINKS For more on Queen Liliuokalani, go to **classzone.com**

NEW YORK CORE CURRICULUM REVIEW

TERMS & NAMES 1. For each term or name, write a sentence explaining its significance.

- Pacific Rim
- King Mongkut
- Emilio Aguinaldo
- annexation
- Queen Liliuokalani

USING YOUR NOTES

2. Which Western power do you think had the most negative impact on its colonies?

MAIN IDEAS

3. How were the Dutch East India Trading Company and the British East India Company similar?
4. What changes took place in Southeast Asia as a result of colonial control?
5. Why did some groups believe that the United States should colonize like the Europeans?

CRITICAL THINKING & WRITING

6. **DRAWING CONCLUSIONS** How did the reforms of the Siamese kings help Siam remain independent?
7. **ANALYZING BIAS** What does President McKinley's desire to "uplift and Christianize" the Filipinos suggest about his perception of the people?
8. **ANALYZING MOTIVES** Why do you think Sanford Dole wanted the United States to annex Hawaii?
9. **WRITING ACTIVITY** ECONOMICS Compose a **letter to the editor** expressing a Hawaiian's view on the U.S. businessmen who pushed for the annexation of Hawaii for economic gain.

CONNECT TO TODAY **DRAWING A BAR GRAPH**

Research to find out about the economic situation of Southeast Asian countries today. Rank the economies and present your findings in a **bar graph.**

Chapter 27 Assessment

TERMS & NAMES

For each term or name below, briefly explain its connection to the imperialism of 1850–1914.

1. imperialism
2. racism
3. Berlin Conference
4. Menelik II
5. geopolitics
6. Suez Canal
7. Raj
8. Queen Liliuokalani

MAIN IDEAS

The Scramble for Africa Section 1 (pages 773–778)

9. What motivated the nations of Europe to engage in imperialist activities?
10. What effect did the Boer War have on Africans?

Case Study: Imperialism Section 2 (pages 779–785)

11. What are the forms of imperial rule?
12. How did Ethiopia successfully resist European rule?

Europeans Claim Muslim Lands Section 3 (pages 786–790)

13. Why were the European nations interested in controlling the Muslim lands?
14. What methods did the Muslim leaders use to try to prevent European imperialism?

British Imperialism in India Section 4 (pages 791–795)

15. How was the economy of India transformed by the British?
16. What caused the Sepoy Mutiny?

Imperialism in Southeast Asia Section 5 (pages 796–799)

17. How did Siam manage to remain independent while other countries in the area were being colonized?
18. Describe American attitudes toward colonizing other lands.

CRITICAL THINKING

1. USING YOUR NOTES
In a chart, tell how the local people resisted the demands of the Europeans.

Africa	Muslim lands	India	Southeast Asia

2. RECOGNIZING EFFECTS
ECONOMICS What effects did imperialism have on the economic life of the lands and people colonized by the European imperialists?

3. DRAWING CONCLUSIONS
Why do you think the British viewed the Suez Canal as the lifeline of their empire?

4. SYNTHESIZING
What positive and negative impact did inventions such as the railroad and the steamship have on the land and people conquered by the imperialists?

5. DEVELOPING HISTORICAL PERSPECTIVE
EMPIRE BUILDING What economic, political, and social conditions encouraged the growth of imperialism in Africa and Asia?

VISUAL SUMMARY

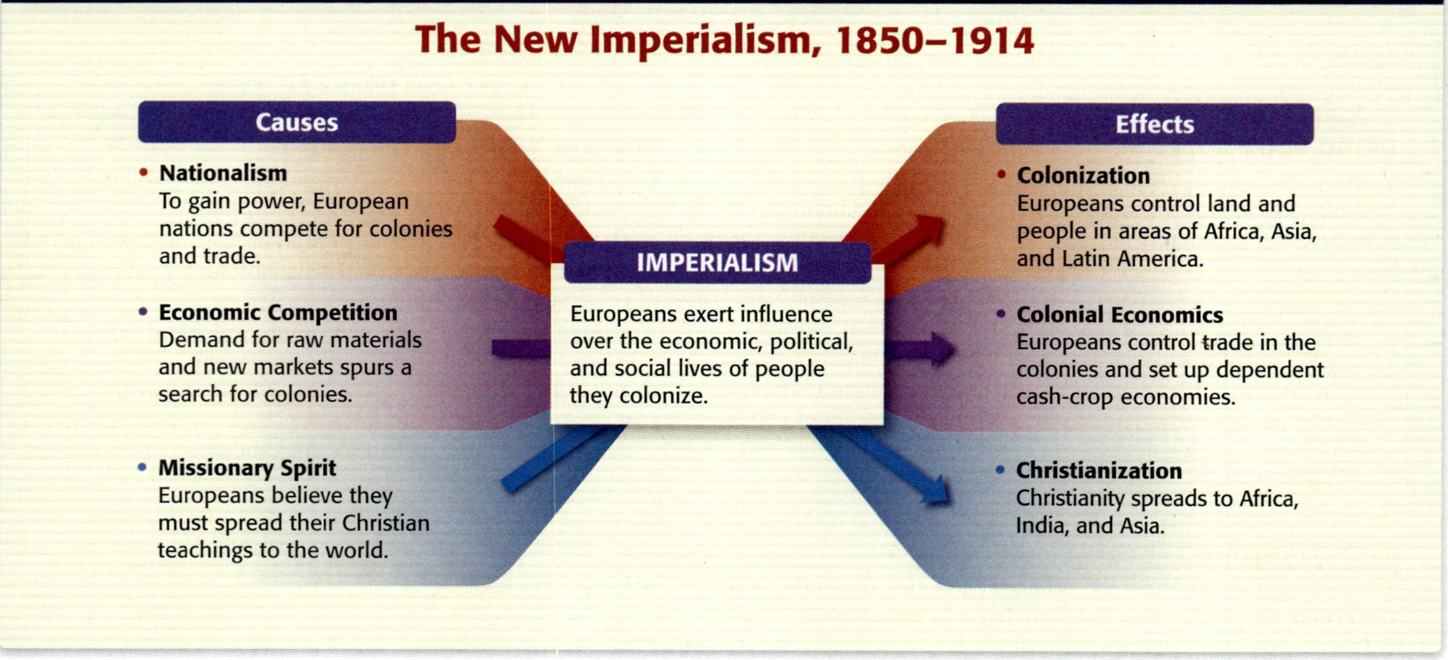

Use the quotation from the king of the Asante people and your knowledge of world history to answer questions 1 and 2.

Additional Test Practice, pp. S1–S33

PRIMARY SOURCE

> The suggestion that Ashanti [Asante] in its present state should come and enjoy the protection of Her Majesty the Queen and Empress of India, I may say this is a matter of serious consideration, and which I am happy to say we have arrived at the conclusion, that my kingdom of Ashanti will never commit itself to any such conclusion, that Ashanti must-remain independent as of old, at the same time to remain friendly with all white men. I do not write this with a-boastful spirit, but in the clear sense of its meaning. Ashanti is an independent kingdom.
>
> **KWAKU DUA III** to Frederic M. Hodgson, December 27, 1889

1 What is Kwaku Dua III's answer to the queen?
- (1) He would enjoy the protection of the queen.
- (2) He cannot commit himself at this time.
- (3) He is offended by her offer.
- (4) He refuses her offer.

2 Why do you think Kwaku Dua III responded that he wanted to remain friendly to white men?
- (1) He wanted his country to be placed under the protection of white men.
- (2) He was trying to be diplomatic.
- (3) He wanted to adopt white men's culture.
- (4) He wanted the assistance of white men.

Use the map of the British Empire and your knowledge of world history to answer question 3.

The British Empire, 1900

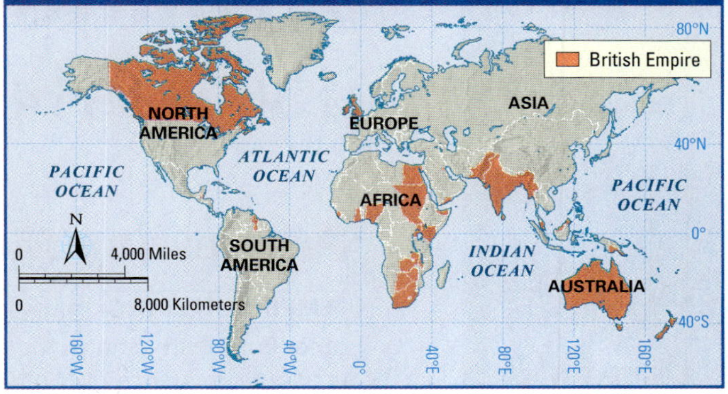

3 "The sun never sets on the British Empire" was a saying about the British Empire at the peak of its power. What do you think this saying meant?
- (1) The British Empire had colonies in every part of the world.
- (2) The British felt that the sun revolved around them.
- (3) The British Empire represented sunlight and hope to the rest of the world.
- (4) The British were hard working and never slept.

INTEGRATED TECHNOLOGY

TEST PRACTICE Go to **classzone.com**
- Diagnostic tests
- Tutorials
- Strategies
- Additional practice

ALTERNATIVE ASSESSMENT

1. Interact *with* History

On page 772, you considered the advantages and disadvantages of colonialism. Now, make a chart showing the advantages and disadvantages to a local person living in a place that became a European colony. Next, make a similar chart for a European living in a foreign place. How do they compare? Discuss with members of your class a way to decide whether the advantages outweigh the disadvantages for each group.

2. WRITING ABOUT HISTORY

POWER AND AUTHORITY Write a **news article** about the effects of colonization. Be sure to address the following points:
- Provide some background on the country you're writing about.
- Tell where the colonizers have come from.
- Describe how the colonizers treat the colonized people.
- Include quotations from both the colonizers and the colonized.
- Draw conclusions about each side's opinion of the other.

INTEGRATED TECHNOLOGY

Creating an Interactive Time Line

Use the Internet and your textbook to create a time line of the events covered in Chapter 27. The time line on pages 770–771 can serve as a guide. Use graphics software to add maps and pictures that illustrate the events. Be sure to include the following on your time line:
- important events in the colonization of Africa and Asia
- efforts on the part of the colonies to resist the imperialist powers
- people who played important roles in the events
- places where key events occurred
- visuals that illustrate the events

CHAPTER 28

Transformations Around the Globe, 1800–1914

NEW YORK CORE CURRICULUM FOCUS

- Western powers attempted to force China to open to foreign trade and influence.
- The United States exercised economic imperialism over Latin America in the 1800s.

Previewing Main Ideas

EMPIRE BUILDING During the 19th and early 20th centuries, Great Britain, other European nations, the United States, and Japan sought political and economic influence over other countries.

Geography *What foreign powers were involved in China in the late 1800s?*

CULTURAL INTERACTION Imperialism brought new religions, philosophies, and technological innovations to East Asia and Latin America. People in these areas resisted some Western ideas and adopted or adapted others.

Geography *What geographic factors might explain why certain parts of China were under Japanese, Russian, and French influence?*

REVOLUTION Both China and Japan struggled to deal with foreign influence and to modernize. Mexico underwent a revolution that brought political and economic reforms.

Geography *Japan built up its navy as a step toward modernization. Why do you think Japan wanted a strong navy?*

INTEGRATED TECHNOLOGY

eEdition
- Interactive Maps
- Interactive Visuals
- Interactive Primary Sources

INTERNET RESOURCES
Go to **classzone.com** for:
- Research Links
- Internet Activities
- Primary Sources
- Chapter Quiz
- Maps
- Test Practice
- Current Events

EAST ASIA AND LATIN AMERICA

1823 Monroe Doctrine reflects special U.S. interest in Americas.

1839 China and Britain clash in Opium War.

1853 ◄ Commodore Perry enters Tokyo harbor.

1800 — 1825 — 1850

WORLD

1815 Congress of Vienna creates a new balance of power in Europe.

1858 Great Britain establishes direct control of India.

Colonial Powers Carve Up China, 1850–1910

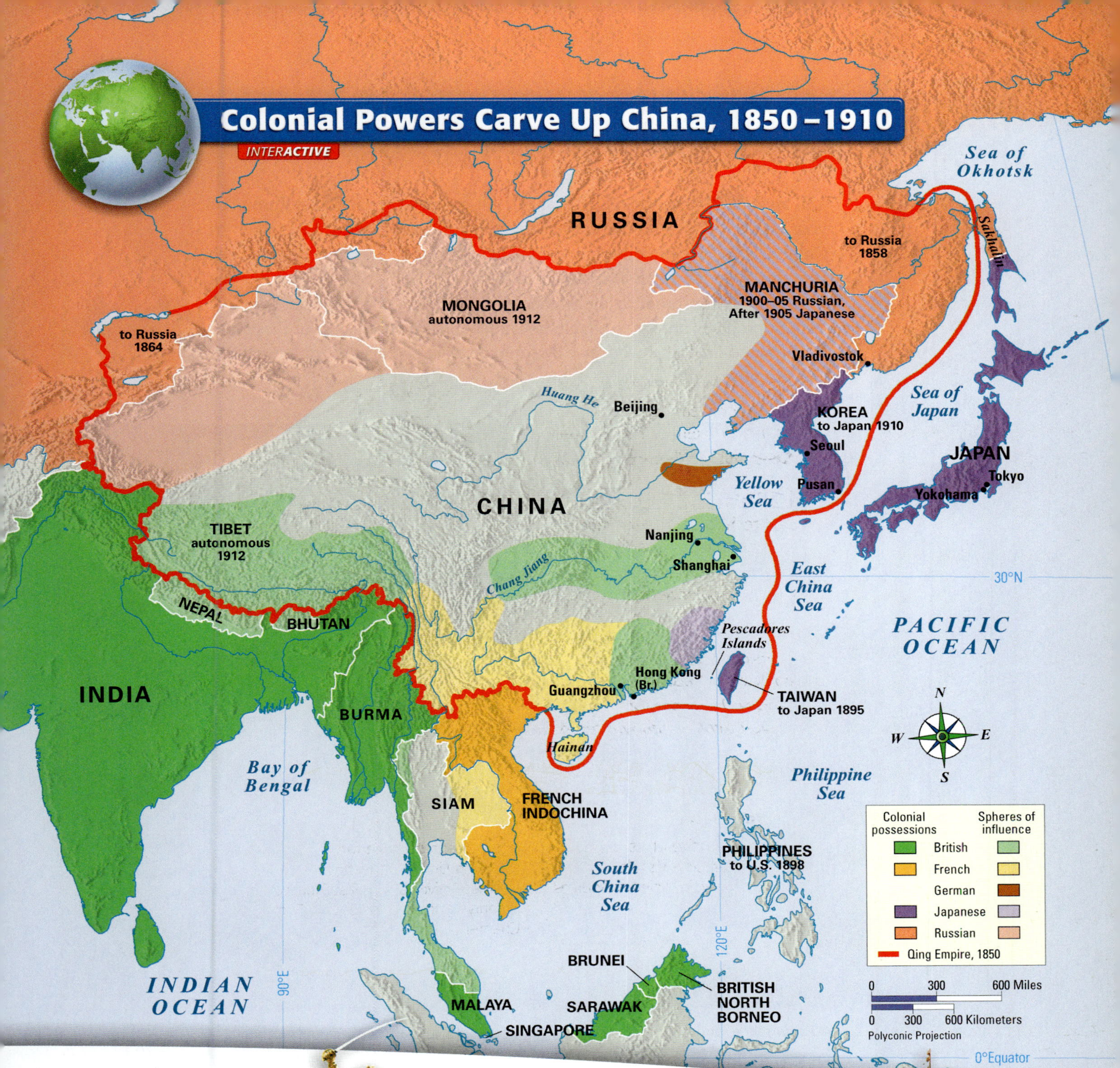

1898
United States wins Spanish-American War. (Teddy Roosevelt)

1910
Mexican Revolution begins.

1914
Panama Canal opens. ▶

1875 **1900** **1925**

1869
Suez Canal opens.

1901
◀ Australia becomes an independent nation. (British flag showing countries of the Empire)

1905
Russian soldiers open fire on protesting workers in St. Petersburg.

Interact *with* History

Why might you seek out or resist foreign influence?

You are a local government official in 19th-century China. You are proud of your country, which produces everything that its people need. Like other Chinese officials, you discourage contact with foreigners. Nevertheless, people from the West are eager to trade with China.

Most foreign products are inferior to Chinese goods. However, a few foreign products are not available in China. You are curious about these items. At the same time, you wonder why foreigners are so eager to trade with China and what they hope to gain.

▲ Finely made lanterns were among the Chinese goods favored by Western merchants.

EXAMINING *the* ISSUES

- **How might foreign products affect the quality of life in China both positively and negatively?**
- **What demands might foreigners make on countries they trade with?**

As a class, discuss these questions. Recall what happened in other parts of the world when different cultures came into contact for the first time. As you read this chapter, compare the decisions various governments made about foreign trade and the reasons they made those decisions.

China Resists Outside Influence

CONNECT TO THE NEW YORK STATE CORE CURRICULUM

Unit 5.H.5.a.1. Unequal treaties
Unit 5.H.5.b. Boxer Rebellion

TERMS & NAMES

- Opium War
- extraterritorial rights
- Taiping Rebellion
- sphere of influence
- Open Door Policy
- Boxer Rebellion

SETTING THE STAGE Out of pride in their ancient culture, the Chinese looked down on all foreigners. In 1793, however, the Qing emperor agreed to receive an ambassador from England. The Englishman brought gifts of the West's most advanced technology—clocks, globes, musical instruments, and even a hot-air balloon. The emperor was not impressed. In a letter to England's King George III, he stated that the Chinese already had everything they needed. They were not interested in the "strange objects" and gadgets that the West was offering them.

China and the West

China was able to reject these offers from the West because it was largely self-sufficient. The basis of this self-sufficiency was China's healthy agricultural economy. During the 11th century, China had acquired a quick-growing strain of rice from Southeast Asia. By the time of the Qing Dynasty, the rice was being grown throughout the southern part of the country. Around the same time, the 17th and 18th centuries, Spanish and Portuguese traders brought maize, sweet potatoes, and peanuts from the Americas. These crops helped China increase the productivity of its land and more effectively feed its huge population.

China also had extensive mining and manufacturing industries. Rich salt, tin, silver, and iron mines produced great quantities of ore. The mines provided work for tens of thousands of people. The Chinese also produced beautiful silks, high-quality cottons, and fine porcelain.

TAKING NOTES
Identifying Problems Use a chart to identify the internal and external problems faced by China in the 1800s and early 1900s.

China's Problems	
Internal	External

The Tea-Opium Connection Because of their self-sufficiency, the Chinese had little interest in trading with the West. For decades, the only place they would allow foreigners to do business was at the southern port of Guangzhou (gwahng•joh). And the balance of trade at Guangzhou was clearly in China's favor. This means that China earned much more for its exports than it spent on imports.

European merchants were determined to find a product the Chinese would buy in large quantities. Eventually they found one—opium. Opium is a habit-forming narcotic made from the poppy plant. Chinese doctors had been using it to relieve pain for hundreds of years. In the late 18th century, however, British merchants smuggled opium into China for nonmedical use. It took a few decades for opium smoking to catch on, but by 1835, as many as 12 million Chinese people were addicted to the drug.

War Breaks Out This growing supply of opium caused great problems for China. The Qing emperor was angry about the situation. In 1839, one of his highest advisers wrote a letter to England's Queen Victoria about the problem:

PRIMARY SOURCE

By what right do they [British merchants] . . . use the poisonous drug to injure the Chinese people? . . . I have heard that the smoking of opium is very strictly forbidden by your country; that is because the harm caused by opium is clearly understood. Since it is not permitted to do harm to your own country, then even less should you let it be passed on to the harm of other countries.

LIN ZEXU, quoted in *China's Response to the West*

The pleas went unanswered, and Britain refused to stop trading opium. The result was an open clash between the British and the Chinese—the **Opium War** of 1839. The battles took place mostly at sea. China's outdated ships were no match for Britain's steam-powered gunboats. As a result, the Chinese suffered a humiliating defeat. In 1842, they signed a peace treaty, the Treaty of Nanjing. **A**

MAIN IDEA

Analyzing Issues

A What conflicting British and Chinese positions led to the Opium War?

This treaty gave Britain the island of Hong Kong. After signing another treaty in 1844, U.S. and other foreign citizens also gained **extraterritorial rights**. Under these rights, foreigners were not subject to Chinese law at Guangzhou and four other Chinese ports. Many Chinese greatly resented the foreigners and the bustling trade in opium they conducted.

Growing Internal Problems

Foreigners were not the greatest of China's problems in the mid-19th century, however. The country's own population provided an overwhelming challenge. The number of Chinese grew to 430 million by 1850, a 30 percent gain in only 60 years. Yet, in the same period of time, food production barely increased. As a result, hunger was widespread, even in good years. Many people became discouraged, and opium addiction rose steadily. As their problems mounted, the Chinese began to rebel against the Qing Dynasty.

Connect *to* Today

Special Economic Zones

Today, as in the late 1800s, the Chinese government limits foreign economic activity to particular areas of the country. Most of these areas, called special economic zones (SEZs), are located on the coast and waterways of southeastern China. Established in the late 1970s, the SEZs are designed to attract, but also control, foreign investment.

One of the most successful SEZs is Shanghai (pictured at right). By the late 1990s, dozens of foreign companies—including IBM of the United States, Hitachi of Japan, Siemens of Germany, and Unilever of Great Britain—had invested about $21 billion in the building and operating of factories, stores, and other businesses. This investment had a huge impact on the economy of Shanghai. Throughout the 1990s, it grew by more than 10 percent each year.

The Taiping Rebellion During the late 1830s, Hong Xiuquan (hung shee•oo•choo•ahn), a young man from Guangdong province in southern China, began recruiting followers to help him build a "Heavenly Kingdom of Great Peace." In this kingdom, all Chinese people would share China's vast wealth and no one would live in poverty. Hong's movement was called the **Taiping Rebellion**, from the Chinese word *taiping,* meaning "great peace."

By the 1850s, Hong had organized a massive peasant army of some one million people. Over time, the Taiping army took control of large areas of southeastern China. Then, in 1853, Hong captured the city of Nanjing and declared it his capital. Hong soon withdrew from everyday life and left family members and his trusted lieutenants in charge of the government of his kingdom.

▲ A Taiping force surrounds and destroys an enemy village.

The leaders of the Taiping government, however, constantly feuded among themselves. Also, Qing imperial troops and British and French forces all launched attacks against the Taiping. By 1864, this combination of internal fighting and outside assaults had brought down the Taiping government. But China paid a terrible price. At least 20 million—and possibly twice that many—people died in the rebellion. B

MAIN IDEA
Recognizing Effects
B What were the results of the Taiping Rebellion?

Foreign Influence Grows

The Taiping Rebellion and several other smaller uprisings put tremendous internal pressure on the Chinese government. And, despite the Treaty of Nanjing, external pressure from foreign powers was increasing. At the Qing court, stormy debates raged about how best to deal with these issues. Some government leaders called for reforms patterned on Western ways. Others, however, clung to traditional ways and accepted change very reluctantly.

Resistance to Change During the last half of the 19th century, one person was in command at the Qing imperial palace. The Dowager Empress Cixi (tsoo•shee) held the reins of power in China from 1862 until 1908 with only one brief gap. Although she was committed to traditional values, the Dowager Empress did support certain reforms. In the 1860s, for example, she backed the self-strengthening movement. This program aimed to update China's educational system, diplomatic service, and military. Under this program, China set up factories to manufacture steam-powered gunboats, rifles, and ammunition. The self-strengthening movement had mixed results, however.

Vocabulary
A *dowager* is a widow who holds a title or property from her deceased husband.

Other Nations Step In Other countries were well aware of China's continuing problems. Throughout the late 19th century, many foreign nations took advantage of the situation and attacked China. Treaty negotiations after each conflict gave these nations increasing control over China's economy. Many of Europe's major powers and Japan gained a strong foothold in China. This foothold, or **sphere of influence**, was an area in which the foreign nation controlled trade and investment. (See the map on page 808.)

The United States was a long-time trading partner with China. Americans worried that other nations would soon divide China into formal colonies and shut out American traders. To prevent this occurrence, in 1899 the United States declared

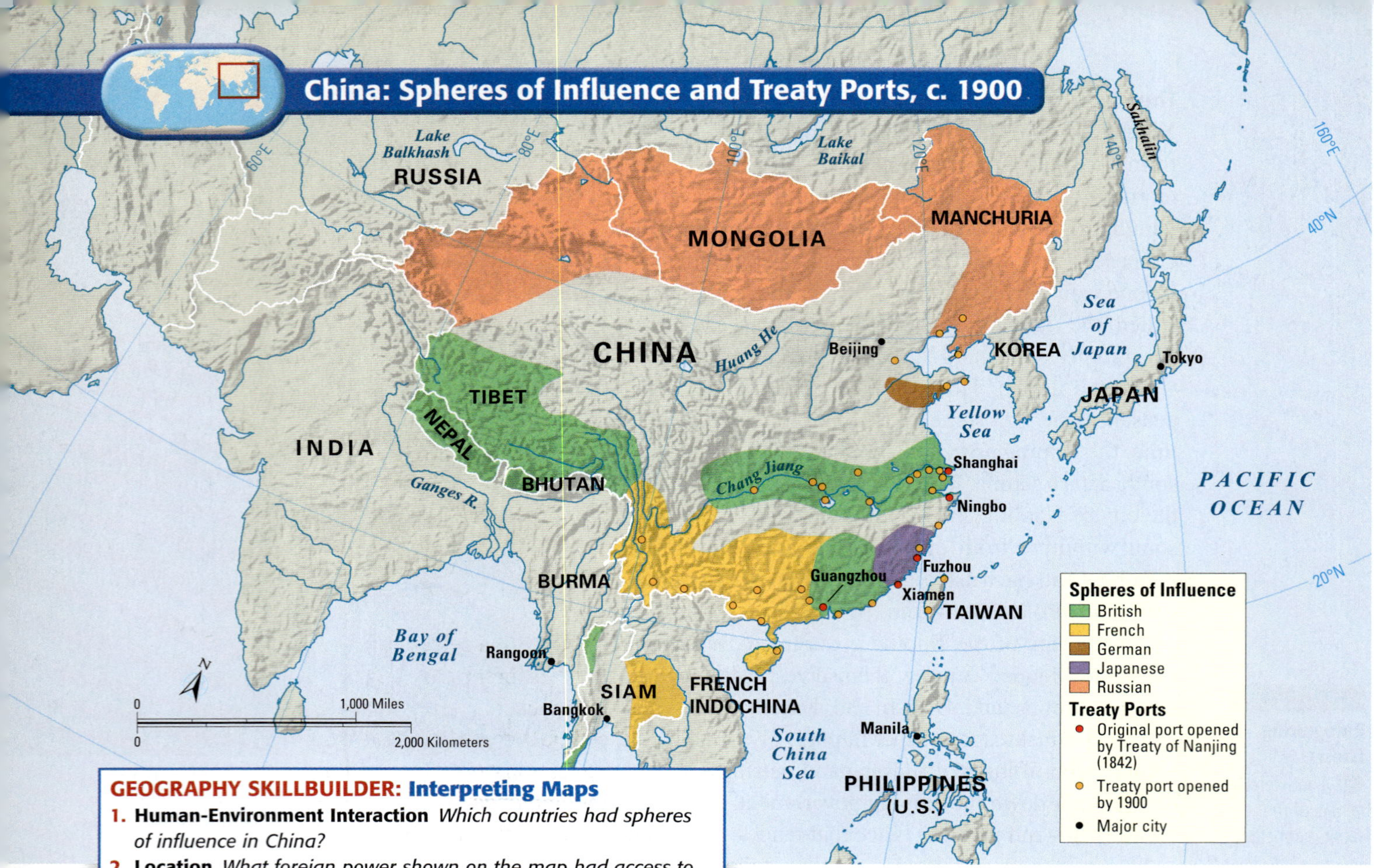

GEOGRAPHY SKILLBUILDER: Interpreting Maps

1. **Human-Environment Interaction** *Which countries had spheres of influence in China?*
2. **Location** *What foreign power shown on the map had access to inland China? What geographic feature made this possible?*

the **Open Door Policy**. This proposed that China's "doors" be open to merchants of all nations. Britain and the other European nations agreed. The policy thus protected both U.S. trading rights in China, and China's freedom from colonization. But the country was still at the mercy of foreign powers.

An Upsurge in Chinese Nationalism

Humiliated by their loss of power, many Chinese pressed for strong reforms. Among those demanding change was China's young emperor, Guangxu (gwahng•shoo). In June 1898, Guangxu introduced measures to modernize China. These measures called for reorganizing China's educational system, strengthening the economy, modernizing the military, and streamlining the government.

Most Qing officials saw these innovations as threats to their power. They reacted with alarm, calling the Dowager Empress back to the imperial court. On her return, she acted with great speed. She placed Guangxu under arrest and took control of the government. She then reversed his reforms. Guangxu's efforts brought about no change whatsoever. The Chinese people's frustration with their situation continued to grow.

The Boxer Rebellion This widespread frustration finally erupted into violence. Poor peasants and workers resented the special privileges granted to foreigners. They also resented Chinese Christians, who had adopted a foreign faith. To demonstrate their discontent, they formed a secret organization called the Society of Righteous and Harmonious Fists. They soon came to be known as the Boxers. Their campaign against the Dowager Empress's rule and foreigner privilege was called the **Boxer Rebellion**.

In the spring of 1900, the Boxers descended on Beijing. Shouting "Death to the foreign devils," the Boxers surrounded the European section of the city. They kept it under siege for several months. The Dowager Empress expressed support for the Boxers but did not back her words with military aid. In August, a multinational force of 19,000 troops marched on Beijing and quickly defeated the Boxers. C

MAIN IDEA

Analyzing Causes

C Why did the Boxer Rebellion fail?

▲ A gang of Boxers attacks Chinese Christians.

Despite the failure of the Boxer Rebellion, a strong sense of nationalism had emerged in China. The Chinese people realized that their country must resist more foreign intervention. Even more important, they felt that the government must become responsive to their needs.

The Beginnings of Reform At this point, even the Qing court realized that China needed to make profound changes to survive. In 1905, the Dowager Empress sent a select group of Chinese officials on a world tour to study the operation of different governments. The group traveled to Japan, the United States, Britain, France, Germany, Russia, and Italy. On their return in the spring of 1906, the officials recommended that China restructure its government. They based their suggestions on the constitutional monarchy of Japan. The empress accepted this recommendation and began making reforms. Although she convened a national assembly within a year, change was slow. In 1908, the court announced that it would establish a full constitutional government by 1917.

However, the turmoil in China did not end with these progressive steps. China experienced unrest for the next four decades as it continued to face internal and external threats. China's neighbor Japan also faced pressure from the West during this time. But it responded to this influence in a much different way.

NEW YORK CORE CURRICULUM REVIEW

TERMS & NAMES 1. For each term or name, write a sentence explaining its significance.

- Opium War
- extraterritorial rights
- Taiping Rebellion
- sphere of influence
- Open Door Policy
- Boxer Rebellion

USING YOUR NOTES

2. Which created the most trouble for China, internal problems or external problems? Why?

China's Problems	
Internal	External

MAIN IDEAS

3. Why did the Chinese have little interest in trading with the West?
4. What internal problems did China face prior to the Taiping Rebellion?
5. Why did Emperor Guangxu's efforts at reform and modernization fail?

CRITICAL THINKING & WRITING

6. **ANALYZING MOTIVES** Why do you think European powers established spheres of influence in China rather than colonies, as they did in Africa and other parts of Asia?
7. **MAKING INFERENCES** What importance did spheres of influence have for China?
8. **COMPARING AND CONTRASTING** What were the similarities and differences between the Taiping Rebellion and the Boxer Rebellion?
9. **WRITING ACTIVITY** CULTURAL INTERACTION -Write a **dialogue** between two of Dowager Empress Cixi's advisers—one arguing for continued isolation, the other for openness to foreign influence and trade.

INTEGRATED TECHNOLOGY **INTERNET ACTIVITY**

Use the Internet to find information on special economic zones in China. Use your findings to create an **annotated map** showing the location of these zones.

INTERNET KEYWORDS
special economic zones, SEZs

2

Modernization in Japan

CONNECT TO THE NEW YORK STATE CORE CURRICULUM

Unit 5.I.2.b. Impact upon Japan of Treaty of Kanagawa
Unit 5.I.3. Modernization, industrialization

TERMS & NAMES

- Treaty of Kanagawa
- Meiji era
- Russo-Japanese War
- annexation

SETTING THE STAGE In the early 17th century, Japan had shut itself off from almost all contact with other nations. Under the rule of the Tokugawa shoguns, Japanese society was very tightly ordered. The shogun parceled out land to the daimyo, or lords. The peasants worked for and lived under the protection of their daimyo and his small army of samurai, or warriors. This rigid feudal system managed to keep the country free of civil war. Peace and relative prosperity reigned in Japan for two centuries.

TAKING NOTES

Analyzing Causes List the steps that Japan took toward modernization and the events that contributed to its growth as an imperialistic power.

Modernization
Imperialism

Japan Ends Its Isolation

The Japanese had almost no contact with the industrialized world during this time of isolation. They continued, however, to trade with China and with Dutch merchants from Indonesia. They also had diplomatic contact with Korea. However, trade was growing in importance, both inside and outside Japan.

The Demand for Foreign Trade Beginning in the early 19th century, Westerners tried to convince the Japanese to open their ports to trade. British, French, Russian, and American officials occasionally anchored off the Japanese coast. Like China, however, Japan repeatedly refused to receive them. Then, in 1853, U.S. Commodore Matthew Perry took four ships into what is now Tokyo Harbor. These massive black wooden ships powered by steam astounded the Japanese. The ships' cannons also shocked them. The Tokugawa shogun realized he had no choice but to receive Perry and the letter Perry had brought from U.S. president Millard Fillmore.

Fillmore's letter politely asked the shogun to allow free trade between the United States and Japan. Perry delivered it with a threat, however. He would come back with a larger fleet in a year to receive Japan's reply. That reply was the **Treaty of Kanagawa** of 1854. Under its terms, Japan opened two ports at which U.S. ships could take on supplies. After the United States had pushed open the door, other Western powers soon followed. By 1860, Japan, like China, had granted foreigners permission to trade at several treaty ports. It had also extended extraterritorial rights to many foreign nations.

Meiji Reform and Modernization The Japanese were angry that the shogun had given in to the foreigners' demands. They turned to Japan's young emperor, Mutsuhito (moot•soo•HEE•toh), who seemed to symbolize the country's sense of pride and nationalism. In 1867, the Tokugawa shogun stepped down, ending the military dictatorships that had lasted since the 12th century. Mutsuhito took control of the government. He chose the name *Meiji* for his reign, which means "enlightened rule." Mutsuhito's reign, which lasted 45 years, is known as the **Meiji era**.

The Meiji emperor realized that the best way to counter Western influence was to modernize. He sent diplomats to Europe and North America to study Western ways. The Japanese then chose what they believed to be the best that Western civilization had to offer and adapted it to their own country. They admired Germany's strong centralized government, for example. And they used its constitution as a model for their own. The Japanese also admired the discipline of the German army and the skill of the British navy. They attempted to imitate these European powers as they modernized their military. Japan adopted the American system of universal public education and required that all Japanese children attend school. Their teachers often included foreign experts. Students could go abroad to study as well.

The emperor also energetically supported following the Western path of industrialization. By the early 20th century, the Japanese economy had become as modern as any in the world. The country built its first railroad line in 1872. The track connected Tokyo, the nation's capital, with the port of Yokohama, 20 miles to the south. By 1914, Japan had more than 7,000 miles of railroad. Coal production grew from half a million tons in 1875 to more than 21 million tons in 1913. Meanwhile, large, state-supported companies built thousands of factories. Traditional Japanese industries, such as tea processing and silk production, expanded to give the country unique products to trade. Developing modern industries, such as shipbuilding, made Japan competitive with the West.

Imperial Japan

Japan's race to modernize paid off. By 1890, the country had several dozen warships and 500,000 well-trained, well-armed soldiers. It had become the strongest military power in Asia.

Japan had gained military, political, and economic strength. It then sought to eliminate the extraterritorial rights of foreigners. The Japanese foreign minister assured foreigners that they could rely on fair treatment in Japan. This was because its constitution and legal codes were similar to those of European nations, he explained. His reasoning was convincing, and in 1894, foreign powers accepted the

China and Japan Confront the West

▲ The Dowager Empress Cixi (1862–1908)

China
- Remains committed to traditional values
- Loses numerous territorial conflicts
- Grants other nations spheres of influence within China
- Finally accepts necessity for reform

Both
- Have well-established traditional values
- Initially resist change
- Oppose Western imperialism

Japan
- Considers modernization to be necessary
- Borrows and adapts Western ways
- Strengthens its economic and military power
- Becomes an empire builder

▲ The Meiji Emperor Mutsuhito (1867–1912)

SKILLBUILDER: Interpreting Charts
1. **Contrasting** *According to the diagram, in what ways did China and Japan deal differently with Western influence?*
2. **Comparing** *What similar responses did each country share despite the different paths they followed?*

abolition of extraterritorial rights for their citizens living in Japan. Japan's feeling of strength and equality with the Western nations rose.

As Japan's sense of power grew, the nation also became more imperialistic. As in Europe, national pride played a large part in Japan's imperial plans. The Japanese were determined to show the world that they were a powerful nation. **A**

MAIN IDEA

Making Inferences

A Why did Japan become imperialistic?

Japan Attacks China The Japanese first turned their sights to their neighbor, Korea. In 1876, Japan forced Korea to open three ports to Japanese trade. But China also considered Korea to be important both as a trading partner and a military outpost. Recognizing their similar interests in Korea, Japan and China signed a hands-off agreement. In 1885, both countries pledged that they would not send their armies into Korea.

In June 1894, however, China broke that agreement. Rebellions had broken out against Korea's king. He asked China for military help in putting them down. Chinese troops marched into Korea. Japan protested and sent its troops to Korea to fight the Chinese. This Sino-Japanese War lasted just a few months. In that time, Japan drove the Chinese out of Korea, destroyed the Chinese navy, and gained a foothold in Manchuria. In 1895, China and Japan signed a peace treaty. This treaty gave Japan its first colonies, Taiwan and the neighboring Pescadores Islands. (See the map on page 803.)

Vocabulary
Sino: a prefix meaning "Chinese"

Russo-Japanese War Japan's victory over China changed the world's balance of power. Russia and Japan emerged as the major powers—and enemies—in East Asia. The two countries soon went to war over Manchuria. In 1903, Japan offered to recognize Russia's rights in Manchuria if the Russians would agree to stay out of Korea. But the Russians refused.

In February 1904, Japan launched a surprise attack on Russian ships anchored off the coast of Manchuria. In the resulting **Russo-Japanese War**, Japan drove

> Analyzing Political Cartoons

Warlike Japan

Cartoonists often use symbols to identify the countries, individuals, or even ideas featured in their cartoons. Russia has long been symbolized as a bear by cartoonists. Here, the cartoonist uses a polar bear.

Prior to the Meiji era, cartoonists usually pictured Japan as a fierce samurai. Later, however, Japan often was symbolized by a caricature of Emperor Mutsuhito. Here, the cartoonist has exaggerated the emperor's physical features to make him look like a bird of prey.

SKILLBUILDER:
Interpreting Political Cartoons

1. **Clarifying** *How does the cartoonist signify that Japan is warlike?*
2. **Making Inferences** *In their fight, Russia and Japan appear to be crushing someone. Who do you think this might be?*

Russian troops out of Korea and captured most of Russia's Pacific fleet. It also destroyed Russia's Baltic fleet, which had sailed all the way around Africa to participate in the war.

In 1905, Japan and Russia began peace negotiations. U.S. president Theodore Roosevelt helped draft the treaty, which the two nations signed on a ship off Portsmouth, New Hampshire. This agreement, the Treaty of Portsmouth, gave Japan the captured territories. It also forced Russia to withdraw from Manchuria and to stay out of Korea.

Global Impact

Western Views of the East

The Japanese victory over the Russians in 1905 exploded a strong Western myth. Many Westerners believed that white people were a superior race. The overwhelming success of European colonialism and imperialism in the Americas, Africa, and Asia had reinforced this belief. But the Japanese had shown Europeans that people of other races were their equals in modern warfare.

Unfortunately, Japan's military victory led to a different form of Western racism. Influenced by the ideas of Germany's Emperor Wilhelm II, the West imagined the Japanese uniting with the Chinese and conquering Europe. The resulting racist Western fear of what was called the *yellow peril* influenced world politics for many decades.

Vocabulary
protectorate:-a country under the partial control and protection of another nation

Japanese Occupation of Korea After defeating Russia, Japan attacked Korea with a vengeance. In 1905, it made Korea a protectorate. Japan sent in "advisers," who grabbed more and more power from the Korean government. The Korean king was unable to rally international support for his regime. In 1907, he gave up control of the country. Within two years the Korean Imperial Army was disbanded. In 1910, Japan officially imposed **annexation** on Korea, or brought that country under Japan's control.

The Japanese were harsh rulers. They shut down Korean newspapers and took over Korean schools. There they replaced the study of Korean language and history with Japanese subjects. They took land away from Korean farmers and gave it to Japanese settlers. They encouraged Japanese businessmen to start industries in Korea, but forbade Koreans from going into business. Resentment of Japan's repressive rule grew, helping to create a strong Korean nationalist movement. **B**

MAIN IDEA
Clarifying
B How did Japan treat the Koreans after it annexed the country?

The rest of the world clearly saw the brutal results of Japan's imperialism. Nevertheless, the United States and other European countries largely ignored what was happening in Korea. They were too busy with their own imperialistic aims, as you will learn in Section 3.

NEW YORK CORE CURRICULUM REVIEW

TERMS & NAMES 1. For each term or name, write a sentence explaining its significance.

- Treaty of Kanagawa
- Meiji era
- Russo-Japanese War
- annexation

USING YOUR NOTES

2. Do you think that Japan could have become an imperialistic power if it had not modernized? Why or why not?

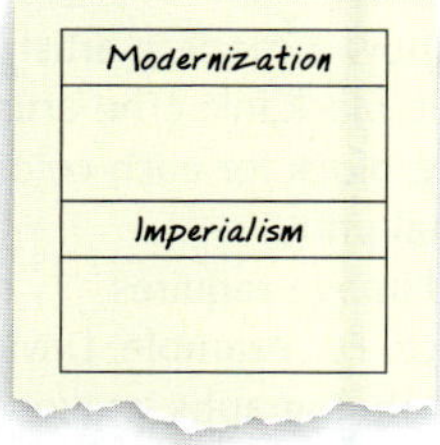

MAIN IDEAS

3. How was the Treaty of Kanagawa similar to the treaties that China signed with various European powers?
4. What steps did the Meiji emperor take to modernize Japan?
5. How did Japan begin its quest to build an empire?

CRITICAL THINKING & WRITING

6. **ANALYZING CAUSES** What influences do you think were most important in motivating Japan to build its empire?
7. **FORMING AND SUPPORTING OPINIONS** In your view, was Japan's aggressive imperialism justified? Support your answer with information from the text.
8. **ANALYZING BIAS** How did Japan's victory in the Russo-Japanese War both explode and create stereotypes?
9. **WRITING ACTIVITY** EMPIRE BUILDING -In the role of a Japanese official, write a **letter** to the government of a Western power explaining why you think it is necessary for your country to build an empire.

CONNECT TO TODAY **CREATING A SYMBOL**

Conduct research to discover the name that Akihito, the present emperor of Japan, chose for his reign. Then create a **symbol** that expresses the meaning of this name.

Japanese Woodblock Printing

Woodblock printing in Japan evolved from black-and-white prints created by Buddhists in the 700s. By the late 1700s, artists learned how to create multicolor prints.

Woodblock prints could be produced quickly and in large quantities, so they were cheaper than paintings. In the mid-1800s, a Japanese person could buy a woodblock print for about the same price as a bowl of noodles. As a result, woodblock prints like those shown here became a widespread art form. The most popular subjects included actors, beautiful women, urban life, and landscapes.

INTEGRATED TECHNOLOGY

RESEARCH LINKS For more on Japanese woodblock printing, go to **classzone.com**

▲ Naniwaya Okita

The artist Kitagawa Utamaro created many prints of attractive women. This print shows Naniwaya Okita, a famous beauty of the late 1700s. Her long face, elaborate hairstyle, and many-colored robes were all considered part of her beauty.

▲ Carving the Block

These photographs show a modern artist carving a block for the black ink. (The artist must carve a separate block for each color that will be in the final print.)

Carving the raised image requires precision and patience. For example, David Bull, the artist in the photographs, makes five cuts to create each strand of hair. One slip of the knife, and the block will be ruined.

▲ Under the Wave off Kanagawa

Katsushika Hokusai was one of the most famous of all Japanese printmakers. This scene is taken from his well-known series *Thirty-Six Views of Mount Fuji.* Mount Fuji, which many Japanese considered sacred, is the small peak in the background of this scene.

▲ Printing

After the carved block is inked, the artist presses paper on it, printing a partial image. He or she repeats this stage for each new color. The artist must ensure that every color ends up in exactly the right place, so that no blocks of color extend beyond the outlines or fall short of them.

Connect *to* Today

1. **Making Inferences** What personal qualities and skills would an artist need to be good at making woodblock prints?
   See Skillbuilder Handbook, page R10.
2. **Forming and Supporting Opinions** Hokusai's print of the wave, shown above, remains very popular today. Why do you think this image appeals to modern people?

U.S. Economic Imperialism

CONNECT TO THE NEW YORK STATE CORE CURRICULUM

Unit 5.E.1. Human and physical geography
Unit 5.E.4. Role of cash crop economies in a global market

TERMS & NAMES

- caudillo
- Monroe Doctrine
- José Martí
- Spanish-American War
- Panama Canal
- Roosevelt Corollary

SETTING THE STAGE Latin America's long struggle to gain independence from colonial domination between the late 18th and the mid-19th centuries left the new nations in shambles. Farm fields had been neglected and were overrun with weeds. Buildings in many cities bore the scars of battle. Some cities had been left in ruins. The new nations of Latin America faced a struggle for economic and political recovery that was every bit as difficult as their struggle for independence had been.

TAKING NOTES

Following Chronological Order Use a time line to list the major events in U.S. involvement in Latin America.

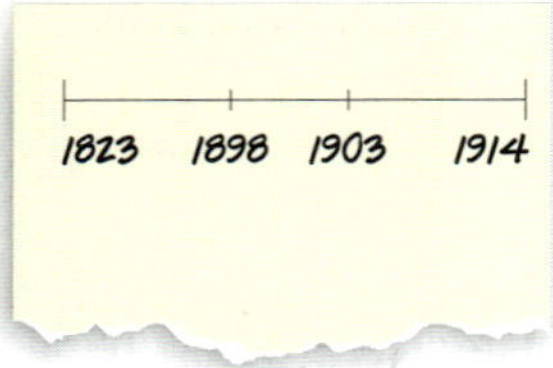

Latin America After Independence

Political independence meant little for most citizens of the new Latin American nations. The majority remained poor laborers caught up in a cycle of poverty.

Colonial Legacy Both before and after independence, most Latin Americans worked for large landowners. The employers paid their workers with vouchers that could be used only at their own supply stores. Since wages were low and prices were high, workers went into debt. Their debt accumulated and passed from one generation to the next. In this system known as peonage, "free" workers were little better than slaves.

Landowners, on the other hand, only got wealthier after independence. Many new Latin American governments took over the lands owned by native peoples and by the Catholic Church. Then they put those lands up for sale. Wealthy landowners were the only people who could afford to buy them, and they snapped them up. But as one Argentinean newspaper reported, "Their greed for land does not equal their ability to use it intelligently." The unequal distribution of land and the landowners' inability to use it effectively combined to prevent social and economic development in Latin America.

Political Instability Political instability was another widespread problem in 19th-century Latin America. Many Latin American army leaders had gained fame and power during their long struggle for independence. They often continued to assert their power. They controlled the new nations as military dictators, or **caudillos** (kaw•DEEL•yohz). They were able to hold on to power because they were backed by the military. By the mid-1800s, nearly all the countries of Latin America were ruled by caudillos. One typical caudillo was Juan Vicente Gómez.

He was a ruthless man who ruled Venezuela for nearly 30 years after seizing power in 1908. "All Venezuela is my cattle ranch," he once boasted.

There were some exceptions, however. Reform-minded presidents, such as Argentina's Domingo Sarmiento, made strong commitments to improving education. During Sarmiento's presidency, between 1868 and 1874, the number of students in Argentina doubled. But such reformers usually did not stay in office long. More often than not, a caudillo, supported by the army, seized control of the government.

▲ Argentine reformer Domingo Sarmiento

MAIN IDEA

Identifying Problems

A What difficulties did lower-class Latin Americans continue to face after independence?

The caudillos faced little opposition. The wealthy landowners usually supported them because they opposed giving power to the lower classes. In addition, Latin Americans had gained little experience with democracy under European colonial rule. So, the dictatorship of a caudillo did not seem unusual to them. But even when caudillos were not in power, most Latin Americans still lacked a voice in the government. Voting rights—and with them, political power—were restricted to the relatively few members of the upper and middle classes who owned property or could read. **A**

Economies Grow Under Foreign Influence

When colonial rule ended in Latin America in the early 1800s, the new nations were no longer restricted to trading with colonial powers. Britain and, later, the United States became Latin America's main trading partners.

Old Products and New Markets Latin America's economies continued to depend on exports, no matter whom they were trading with. As during the colonial era, each country concentrated on one or two products. With advances in technology, however, Latin America's exports grew. The development of the steamship and the building of railroads in the 19th century, for example, greatly increased Latin American trade. Toward the end of the century, the invention of refrigeration helped increase Latin America's exports. The sale of beef, fruits and vegetables, and other perishable goods soared.

But foreign nations benefited far more from the increased trade than Latin America did. In exchange for their exports, Latin Americans imported European and North American manufactured goods. As a result, they had little reason to develop their own manufacturing industries. And as long as Latin America remained unindustrialized, it could not play a leading role on the world economic stage.

▼ Workers unload coffee beans at a plantation in Brazil. Until recently, Brazil's economy depended heavily on the export of coffee.

Outside Investment and Interference Furthermore, Latin American countries used little of their export income to build roads, schools, or hospitals. Nor did they fund programs that would help them become self-sufficient. Instead, they often borrowed money at high interest rates to develop facilities for their export industries. Countries such as Britain, France, the United States, and Germany were willing lenders. The Latin American countries often were unable to pay back their loans, however. In response, foreign lenders sometimes threatened to collect the debt by force. At other times, they threatened to take over the facilities they had funded. In this way, foreign companies gained control of many Latin American industries. This began a new age of economic colonialism in Latin America.

History Makers

José Martí
1853–1895

José Martí was only 15 in 1868 when he first began speaking out for Cuban independence. In 1871, the Spanish colonial government punished Martí's open opposition with exile. Except for a brief return to his homeland in 1878, Martí remained in exile for about 20 years. For most of this time, he lived in New York City. There he continued his career as a writer and a revolutionary. "Life on earth is a hand-to-hand combat . . . between the law of love and the law of hate," he proclaimed.

While in New York, Martí helped raise an army to fight for Cuban independence. He died on the battlefield only a month after the war began. But Martí's cry for freedom echoes in his essays and poems and in folk songs about him that are still sung throughout the world.

INTEGRATED TECHNOLOGY

RESEARCH LINKS For more on José Martí, go to **classzone.com**

A Latin American Empire

Long before the United States had any economic interest in Latin American countries, it realized that it had strong links with its southern neighbors. Leaders of the United States were well aware that their country's security depended on the security of Latin America.

The Monroe Doctrine Most Latin American colonies had gained their independence by the early 1800s. But their position was not secure. Many Latin Americans feared that European countries would try to reconquer the new republics. The United States, a young nation itself, feared this too. So, in 1823, President James Monroe issued what came to be called the **Monroe Doctrine**. This document stated that "the American continents . . . are henceforth not to be considered as subjects for future colonization by any European powers." Until 1898, though, the United States did little to enforce the Monroe Doctrine. Cuba provided a real testing ground.

Cuba Declares Independence The Caribbean island of Cuba was one of Spain's last colonies in the Americas. In 1868, Cuba declared its independence and fought a ten-year war against Spain. In 1878, with the island in ruins, the Cubans gave up the fight. But some Cubans continued to seek independence from Spain. In 1895, **José Martí**, a writer who had been exiled from Cuba by the Spanish, returned to launch a second war for Cuban independence. Martí was killed early in the fighting, but the Cubans battled on.

By the mid-1890s, the United States had developed substantial business holdings in Cuba. Therefore it had an economic stake in the fate of the country. In addition, the Spanish had forced many Cuban civilians into concentration camps. Americans objected to the Spanish brutality. In 1898, the United States joined the Cuban war for independence. This conflict, which became known as the **Spanish-American War**, lasted about four months. U.S. forces launched their first attack not on Cuba but on the Philippine Islands, a Spanish colony thousands of miles away in the Pacific. Unprepared for a war on two fronts, the Spanish military quickly collapsed. (See the maps on the opposite page.) B

MAIN IDEA

Analyzing Motives

B Why did the United States join the Cuban war for independence?

GEOGRAPHY SKILLBUILDER: Interpreting Maps

1. **Location** *Where is Cuba located in relation to the United States?*
2. **Location** *In the war, the United States launched its first attack against the Philippine Islands. Why might this have surprised the Spanish?*

In 1901, Cuba became an independent nation, at least in name. However, the United States installed a military government and continued to exert control over Cuban affairs. This caused tremendous resentment among many Cubans, who had assumed that the United States' aim in intervening was to help Cuba become truly independent. The split that developed between the United States and Cuba at this time continues to keep these close neighbors miles apart more than a century later.

After its defeat in the Spanish-American War, Spain turned over the last of its colonies. Puerto Rico, Guam, and the Philippines became U.S. territories. Having become the dominant imperial power in Latin America, the United States next set its sights on Panama.

Vocabulary
A *colossus* is a huge statue that towers over the surrounding area.

Connecting the Oceans Latin Americans were beginning to regard the United States as the political and economic "Colossus of the North." The United States was a colossus in geographic terms too. By the 1870s, the transcontinental railroad connected its east and west coasts. But land travel still was time-consuming and difficult. And sea travel between the coasts involved a trip of about 13,000 miles around the tip of South America. If a canal could be dug across a narrow section of Central America, however, the coast-to-coast journey would be cut in half.

The United States had been thinking about such a project since the early 19th century. In the 1880s, a French company tried—but failed—to build a canal across Panama. Despite this failure, Americans remained enthusiastic about the canal. And no one was more enthusiastic than President Theodore Roosevelt, who led the nation from 1901 to 1909. In 1903, Panama was a province of Colombia. Roosevelt offered that country $10 million plus a yearly payment for the right to build a canal. When the Colombian government demanded more money, the United States

Science & Technology

INTERACTIVE

Panama Canal

The Panama Canal is considered one of the world's greatest engineering accomplishments. Its completion changed the course of history by opening a worldwide trade route between the Atlantic and Pacific oceans. As shown in the diagram below, on entering the canal, ships are raised about 85 feet in a series of three locks. On leaving the canal, ships are lowered to sea level by another series of three locks.

The canal also had a lasting effect on other technologies. Since the early 1900s, ships have been built to dimensions that will allow them to pass through the canal's locks.

INTEGRATED TECHNOLOGY

RESEARCH LINKS For more on the Panama Canal, go to **classzone.com**

▲ Ships passing through the Pedro Miguel Locks

Panama Canal Cross-section

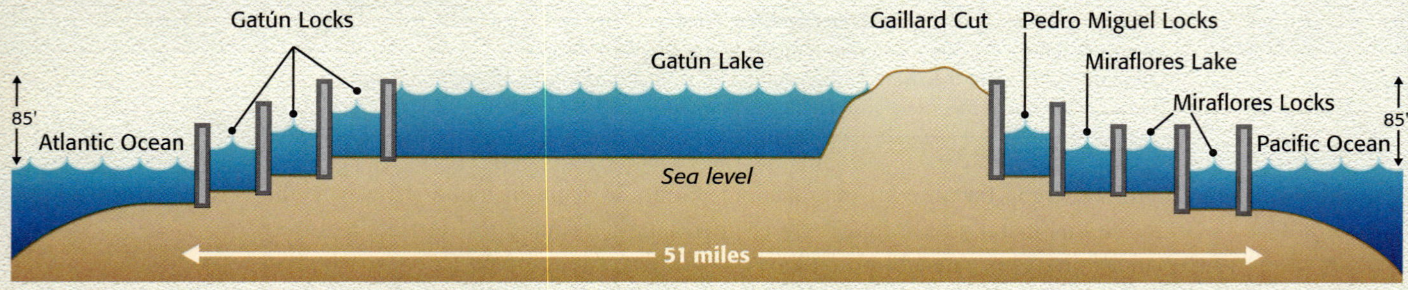

▲ This cross-section shows the different elevations and locks that a ship moves through on the trip through the canal.

Canal Facts

- The canal took ten years to build (1904–1914) and cost $380 million.
- During the construction of the canal, workers dug up more than 200 million cubic yards of earth.
- Thousands of workers died from diseases while building the canal.
- The trip from San Francisco to New York City via the Panama Canal is about 9,000 miles shorter than the trip around South America.
- The 51-mile trip through the canal takes 8 to 10 hours.
- The canal now handles more than 13,000 ships a year from around 70 nations carrying 192 million short tons of cargo.
- Panama took control of the canal on December 31, 1999.

Connect *to* Today

1. **Identifying Problems** What difficulties did workers face in constructing the canal?
   See Skillbuilder Handbook, page R5.
2. **Evaluating Decisions** In the more than 90 years since it was built, do you think that the benefits of the Panama Canal to world trade have outweighed the costs in time, money, and human life? Explain your answer.

responded by encouraging a revolution in Panama. The Panamanians had been trying to break away from Colombia for almost a century. In 1903, with help from the United States Navy, they won their country's independence. In gratitude, Panama gave the United States a ten-mile-wide zone in which to build a canal.

For the next decade, American engineers contended with floods and withering heat to build the massive waterway. However, their greatest challenge was the disease-carrying insects that infested the area. The United States began a campaign to destroy the mosquitoes that carried yellow fever and malaria, and the rats that carried bubonic plague. The effort to control these diseases was eventually successful. Even so, thousands of workers died during construction of the canal. The **Panama Canal** finally opened in 1914. Ships from around the world soon began to use it. Latin America had become a crossroads of world trade. And the United States controlled the tollgate. C

MAIN IDEA

Analyzing Motives

C Why was the United States so interested in building the Panama Canal?

The Roosevelt Corollary The building of the Panama Canal was only one way that the United States expanded its influence in Latin America in the early 20th century. Its presence in Cuba and its large investments in many Central and South American countries strengthened its foothold. To protect those economic interests, in 1904, President Roosevelt issued a corollary, or extension, to the Monroe Doctrine. The **Roosevelt Corollary** gave the United States the right to be "an international police power" in the Western Hemisphere.

The United States used the Roosevelt Corollary many times in the following years to justify U.S. intervention in Latin America. U.S. troops occupied some countries for decades. Many Latin Americans protested this intervention, but they were powerless to stop their giant neighbor to the north. The U.S. government simply turned a deaf ear to their protests. It could not ignore the rumblings of revolution just over its border with Mexico, however. You will learn about this revolution in Section 4.

▼ This cartoon suggests that the Roosevelt Corollary turned the Caribbean into a U.S. wading pool.

NEW YORK CORE CURRICULUM REVIEW

TERMS & NAMES 1. For each term or name, write a sentence explaining its significance.

- caudillo
- Monroe Doctrine
- José Martí
- Spanish-American War
- Panama Canal
- Roosevelt Corollary

USING YOUR NOTES

2. Which event do you think was most beneficial to Latin America? Why?

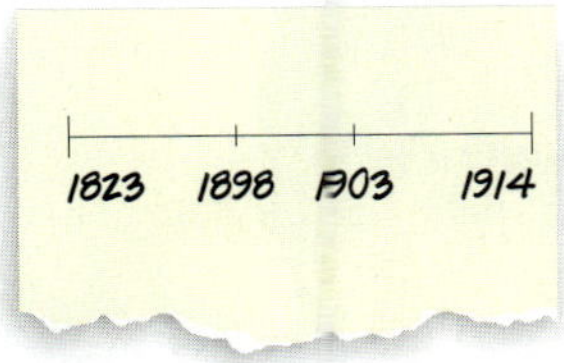

MAIN IDEAS

3. Why did the gap between rich and poor in Latin America grow after independence?
4. What economic gains and setbacks did Latin American countries experience after independence?
5. Why was the United States so interested in the security of Latin America?

CRITICAL THINKING & WRITING

6. **ANALYZING MOTIVES** Why do you think upper-class Latin Americans favored governments run by caudillos?
7. **FORMING OPINIONS** Do you think that U.S. imperialism was more beneficial or harmful to Latin American people? Explain.
8. **CONTRASTING** How was the principle of the Roosevelt Corollary different from that of the Monroe Doctrine?
9. **WRITING ACTIVITY** REVOLUTION -Assume the role of a Cuban fighting for independence from Spain. Design a political **poster** that shows your feelings about the United States joining the struggle for independence.

CONNECT TO TODAY **CREATING A DATAFILE**

Conduct research to find statistics on the ships and cargo that travel through the Panama Canal. Use your findings to create a **datafile** for usage of the canal in a recent year.

4

Turmoil and Change in Mexico

CONNECT TO THE NEW YORK STATE CORE CURRICULUM

Unit 5.E.5.b. Roles of Porfirio Diaz, Francisco "Pancho" Villa, and Emiliano Zapata
Unit 5.E.5.c. Economic and social nationalism

TERMS & NAMES

- Antonio López de Santa Anna
- Benito Juárez
- *La Reforma*
- Porfirio Díaz
- Francisco Madero
- "Pancho" Villa
- Emiliano Zapata

SETTING THE STAGE The legacy of Spanish colonialism and long-term political instability that plagued the newly emerging South American nations caused problems for Mexico as well. Mexico, however, had a further issue to contend with—a shared border with the United States. The "Colossus of the North," as the United States was known in Latin America, wanted to extend its territory all the way west to the Pacific Ocean. But most of the lands in the American Southwest belonged to Mexico.

TAKING NOTES

Comparing Use a chart to compare the major accomplishments of the Mexican leaders discussed in this section.

Leader	Major Accomplishment

Santa Anna and the Mexican War

During the early 19th century, no one dominated Mexican political life more than **Antonio López de Santa Anna**. Santa Anna played a leading role in Mexico's fight for independence from Spain in 1821. In 1829, he fought against Spain again as the European power tried to regain control of Mexico. Then, in 1833, Santa Anna became Mexico's president.

One of Latin America's most powerful caudillos, Santa Anna was a clever politician. He would support a measure one year and oppose it the next if he thought that would keep him in power. His policy seemed to work. Between 1833 and 1855, Santa Anna was Mexico's president four times. He gave up the presidency twice, however, to serve Mexico in a more urgent cause—leading the Mexican army in an effort to retain the territory of Texas.

The Texas Revolt In the 1820s, Mexico encouraged American citizens to move to the Mexican territory of Texas to help populate the country. Thousands of English-speaking colonists, or Anglos, answered the call. In return for inexpensive land, they pledged to follow the laws of Mexico. As the Anglo population grew, though, tensions developed between the colonists and Mexico over several issues, including slavery and religion. As a result, many Texas colonists wanted greater self-government. But when Mexico refused to grant this, Stephen Austin, a leading Anglo, encouraged a revolt against Mexico in 1835.

▼ Mexican leader Santa Anna

◀ Santa Anna's army met with strong resistance from the defenders of the Alamo.

Santa Anna led Mexican forces north to try to hold on to the rebellious territory. He won a few early battles, including a bitter fight at the Alamo, a mission in San Antonio. However, his fortunes changed at the Battle of San Jacinto. His troops were defeated and he was captured. Texan leader Sam Houston released Santa Anna after he promised to respect the independence of Texas. When Santa Anna returned to Mexico in 1836, he was quickly ousted from power.

War and the Fall of Santa Anna Santa Anna regained power, though, and fought against the United States again. In 1845, the United States annexed Texas. Outraged Mexicans considered this an act of aggression. In a dispute over the border, the United States invaded Mexico. Santa Anna's army fought valiantly, but U.S. troops defeated them after two years of war. In 1848, the two nations signed the Treaty of Guadalupe Hidalgo. The United States received the northern third of what was then Mexico, including California and the American Southwest. Santa Anna went into exile. He returned as dictator one final time, however, in 1853. After his final fall, in 1855, he remained in exile for almost 20 years. When he returned to Mexico in 1874, he was poor, blind, powerless, and essentially forgotten.

Juárez and *La Reforma*

During the mid-19th century, as Santa Anna's power rose and fell, a liberal reformer, **Benito Juárez** (HWAHR•ehz), strongly influenced the politics of Mexico. Juárez was Santa Anna's complete opposite in background as well as in goals. Santa Anna came from a well-off Creole family. Juárez was a poor Zapotec Indian who was orphaned at the age of three. While Santa Anna put his own personal power first, Juárez worked primarily to serve his country. (A)

MAIN IDEA

Contrasting

(A) In what ways did Benito Juárez differ from Santa Anna?

Juárez Rises to Power Ancestry and racial background were important elements of political power and economic success in 19th-century Mexico. For that reason, the rise of Benito Juárez was clearly due to his personal leadership qualities. Juárez was raised on a small farm in the Mexican state of Oaxaca. When he was 12, he moved to the city of Oaxaca. He started going to school at age 15, and in 1829, he entered a newly opened state-run university. He received a law degree in 1831.

Analyzing Art

Juárez: Symbol of Mexican Independence

In 1948, more than 75 years after Benito Juárez's death, Mexican mural painter José Clemente Orozco celebrated him in the fresco *Juárez, the Church and the Imperialists*. A portrait of Juárez, which accentuates his Indian features, dominates the work. The supporters of Emperor Maximilian, carrying his body, are shown below Juárez. To either side of Juárez, the soldiers of Mexican independence prepare to attack these representatives of imperialism. By constructing the fresco in this way, Orozco seemed to suggest that Juárez was both a symbol of hope and a rallying cry for Mexican independence.

SKILLBUILDER: Interpreting Visual Sources

1. **Contrasting** *How is Orozco's portrayal of the imperialists different from his portrayal of the forces of independence?*
2. **Drawing Conclusions** *Based on this fresco, how do you think Orozco felt about Benito Juárez?*

He then returned to the city of Oaxaca, where he opened a law office. Most of his clients were poor people who could not otherwise have afforded legal assistance. Juárez gained a reputation for honesty, integrity, hard work, and good judgment. He was elected to the city legislature and then rose steadily in power. Beginning in 1847, he served as governor of the state of Oaxaca.

Juárez Works for Reform Throughout the late 1840s and early 1850s, Juárez worked to start a liberal reform movement. He called this movement ***La Reforma***. Its major goals were redistribution of land, separation of church and state, and increased educational opportunities for the poor. In 1853, however, Santa Anna sent Juárez and other leaders of *La Reforma* into exile.

Just two years later, a rebellion against Santa Anna brought down his government. Juárez and other exiled liberal leaders returned to Mexico to deal with their country's tremendous problems. As in other Latin American nations, rich landowners kept most other Mexicans in a cycle of debt and poverty. Liberal leader Ponciano Arriaga described how these circumstances led to great problems for both poor farmers and the government:

PRIMARY SOURCE B

There are Mexican landowners who occupy . . . an extent of land greater than the areas of some of our sovereign states, greater even than that of one of several European states. In this vast area, much of which lies idle, deserted, abandoned . . . live four or five million Mexicans who know no other industry than agriculture, yet are without land or the means to work it, and who cannot emigrate in the hope of bettering their fortunes. . . . How can a hungry, naked, miserable people practice popular government? How can we proclaim the equal rights of men and leave the majority of the nation in [this condition]?

PONCIANO ARRIAGA, speech to the Constitutional Convention, 1856–1857

MAIN IDEA

Analyzing Primary Sources

B What does Ponciano Arriaga think is Mexico's greatest problem?

Not surprisingly, Arriaga's ideas and those of the other liberals in government threatened most conservative upper-class Mexicans. Many conservatives responded by launching a rebellion against the liberal government in 1858. They enjoyed some early successes in battle and seized control of Mexico City. The liberals kept up the fight from their headquarters in the city of Veracruz. Eventually the liberals gained the upper hand and, after three years of bitter civil war, they defeated the rebels. Juárez became president of the reunited country after his election in 1861.

The French Invade Mexico The end of the civil war did not bring an end to Mexico's troubles, though. Exiled conservatives plotted with some Europeans to reconquer Mexico. In 1862, French ruler Napoleon III responded by sending a large army to Mexico. Within 18 months, France had taken over the country. Napoleon appointed Austrian Archduke Maximilian to rule Mexico as emperor. Juárez and other Mexicans fought against French rule. After five years under siege, the French decided that the struggle was too costly. In 1867, Napoleon ordered the army to withdraw from Mexico. Maximilian was captured and executed.

Juárez was reelected president of Mexico in 1867. He returned to the reforms he had proposed more than ten years earlier. He began rebuilding the country, which had been shattered during years of war. He promoted trade with foreign countries, the opening of new roads, the building of railroads, and the establishment of a telegraph service. He set up a national education system separate from that run by the Catholic Church. In 1872, Juárez died of a heart attack. But after half a century of civil strife and chaos, he left his country a legacy of relative peace, progress, and reform.

Porfirio Díaz and "Order and Progress"

Juárez's era of reform did not last long, however. In the mid-1870s, a new caudillo, **Porfirio Díaz**, came to power. Like Juárez, Díaz was an Indian from Oaxaca. He rose through the army and became a noted general in the civil war and the fight against the French. Díaz expected to be rewarded with a government position for the part he played in the French defeat. Juárez refused his request, however. After this, Díaz opposed Juárez. In 1876, Díaz took control of Mexico by ousting the president. He had the support of the military, whose power had been reduced during and after the Juárez years. Indians and small landholders also supported him, because they thought he would work for more radical land reform.

During the Díaz years, elections became meaningless. Díaz offered land, power, or political favors to anyone who supported him. He terrorized many who refused to support him, ordering them to be beaten or put in jail. Using such strong-arm methods, Díaz managed to remain in power until 1911. Over the years, Díaz used a political slogan adapted from a rallying cry of the Juárez era. Juárez had called for "Liberty, Order, and Progress." Díaz, however, wanted merely "Order and Progress."

Díaz's use of dictatorial powers ensured that there was order in Mexico. But the country saw progress under Díaz too. Railroads expanded, banks were built, the currency stabilized, and foreign investment grew. Mexico seemed to be a stable, prospering country. Appearances were deceiving,

History Makers

Porfirio Díaz
1830–1915

To control all the various groups in Mexican society, Porfirio Díaz adopted an approach called *pan o palo*—"bread or the club." The "bread" he provided took many forms. To potential political opponents, he offered positions in his government. To business leaders, he gave huge subsidies or the chance to operate as monopolies in Mexico. And he won the support of the Church and wealthy landowners simply by promising not to meddle in their affairs. Those who turned down the offer of bread and continued to oppose Díaz soon felt the blow of the club. Thousands were killed, beaten, or thrown into jail.

His use of the club, Díaz admitted, was harsh and cruel—but also necessary if Mexico was to have peace. That peace, Díaz argued, enabled the country to progress economically. "If there was cruelty," he said, "results have justified it."

however. The wealthy acquired more and more land, which they did not put to good use. As a result, food costs rose steadily. Most Mexicans remained poor farmers and workers, and they continued to grow poorer. **C**

MAIN IDEA

Recognizing Effects

C What effects did Díaz's rule have on Mexico?

Revolution and Civil War

In the early 1900s, Mexicans from many walks of life began to protest Díaz's harsh rule. Idealistic liberals hungered for liberty. Farm laborers hungered for land. Workers hungered for fairer wages and better working conditions. Even some of Díaz's handpicked political allies spoke out for reform. A variety of political parties opposed to Díaz began to form. Among the most powerful was a party led by Francisco Madero.

Madero Begins the Revolution Born into one of Mexico's ten richest families, **Francisco Madero** was educated in the United States and France. He believed in democracy and wanted to strengthen its hold in Mexico. Madero announced his candidacy for president of Mexico early in 1910. Soon afterward, Díaz had him arrested. From exile in the United States, Madero called for an armed revolution against Díaz.

The Mexican Revolution began slowly. Leaders arose in different parts of Mexico and gathered their own armies. In the north, Francisco **"Pancho" Villa** became immensely popular. He had a bold Robin Hood policy of taking money from the rich and giving it to the poor. South of Mexico City, another strong, popular leader, **Emiliano Zapata**, raised a powerful revolutionary army. Like Villa, Zapata came from a poor family. He was determined to see that land was returned to peasants and small farmers. He wanted the laws reformed to protect their rights. *"Tierra y Libertad"* ("Land and Liberty") was his battle cry. Villa, Zapata, and other armed revolutionaries won important victories against Díaz's army. By the spring of 1911, Díaz agreed to step down. He called for new elections.

Mexican Leaders Struggle for Power Madero was elected president in November 1911. However, his policies were seen as too liberal by some and not revolutionary enough by others. Some of those who had supported Madero, including Villa and Zapata, took up arms against him. In 1913, realizing that he could not hold on to power, Madero resigned. The military leader General Victoriano Huerta then took over the presidency. Shortly after, Madero was assassinated, probably on Huerta's orders.

Huerta was unpopular with many people, including Villa and Zapata. These revolutionary leaders allied themselves with Venustiano Carranza, another politician who wanted to overthrow Huerta. Their three armies advanced, seizing the Mexican countryside from Huerta's forces and approaching the capital, Mexico City. They overthrew Huerta only 15 months after he took power.

Carranza took control of the government and then turned his army on his former revolutionary allies. Both Villa and Zapata continued to fight. In 1919, however, Carranza lured

History Makers

Emiliano Zapata 1879–1919

Shortly after Francisco Madero took office, he met with Emiliano Zapata, one of his leading supporters. Madero's reluctance to quickly enact real land reform angered Zapata. He left the meeting convinced that Madero was not the man to carry through the Mexican Revolution.

A few days later, Zapata issued the Plan of Ayala. This called for the removal of Madero and the appointment of a new president. The plan also demanded that the large landowners give up a third of their land for redistribution to the peasants. Zapata's rallying cry, "Land and Liberty," grew out of the Plan of Ayala.

When Venustiano Carranza ordered Zapata's assassination, he expected Zapata's revolutionary ideas on land reform to die with him. However, they lived on and were enacted by Alvaro Obregón, a follower of Zapata, who seized power from Carranza in 1920.

INTEGRATED TECHNOLOGY

INTERNET ACTIVITY Create a short biographical dictionary of leaders of the Mexican Revolution. Go to **classzone.com** for your research.

Reforms of Mexican Constitution of 1917

Land	Religion	Labor	Social Issues
• Breakup of large estates • Restrictions on foreign ownership of land • Government control of resources (oil)	• State takeover of land owned by the Church	• Minimum wage for workers • Right to strike • Institution of labor unions	• Equal pay for equal work • Limited legal rights for women (spending money and bringing lawsuits)

SKILLBUILDER: Interpreting Charts

1. **Making Inferences** *Which reforms do you think landowners resented?*
2. **Recognizing Effects** *Which reforms benefited workers?*

Zapata continued to fight. In 1919, however, Carranza lured Zapata into a trap and murdered him. With Zapata's death, the civil war also came to an end. More than a million Mexicans had lost their lives.

The New Mexican Constitution Carranza began a revision of Mexico's constitution. It was adopted in 1917. A revolutionary document, that constitution is still in effect today. As shown in the chart above, it promoted education, land reforms, and workers' rights. Carranza did not support the final version of the constitution, however, and in 1920, he was overthrown by one of his generals, Alvaro Obregón.

Although Obregón seized power violently, he did not remain a dictator. Instead, he supported the reforms the constitution called for, particularly land reform. He also promoted public education. Mexican public schools taught a common language—Spanish—and stressed nationalism. In this way, his policies helped unite the various regions and peoples of the country. Nevertheless, Obregón was assassinated in 1928. **D**

MAIN IDEA

Summarizing

D What were Obregón's accomplishments?

The next year, a new political party, the Institutional Revolutionary Party (PRI), arose. Although the PRI did not tolerate opposition, it initiated an ongoing period of peace and political stability in Mexico. While Mexico was struggling toward peace, however, the rest of the world was on the brink of war.

NEW YORK CORE CURRICULUM REVIEW

TERMS & NAMES 1. For each term or name, write a sentence explaining its significance.

• Antonio López de Santa Anna • Benito Juárez • *La Reforma* • Porfirio Díaz • Francisco Madero • "Pancho" Villa • Emiliano Zapata

USING YOUR NOTES

2. Which leader do you think benefited Mexico most? Why?

Leader	Major Accomplishment

MAIN IDEAS

3. In what ways was Santa Anna a typical caudillo?
4. How did Porfirio Díaz change the direction of government in Mexico?
5. How were "Pancho" Villa and Emiliano Zapata different from other Mexican revolutionary leaders?

CRITICAL THINKING & WRITING

6. **MAKING INFERENCES** Why might Benito Juárez's rise to power be considered surprising?
7. **ANALYZING CAUSES** Why did Villa and Zapata turn against Madero?
8. **SUPPORTING OPINIONS** The revision of Mexico's constitution is considered revolutionary. Do you agree with this characterization? Why or why not?
9. **WRITING ACTIVITY** REVOLUTION Juárez's motto was "Liberty, Order, and Progress." Díaz's slogan was "Order and Progress." Write an **expository essay** explaining what this difference in goals meant for the people of Mexico.

CONNECT TO TODAY **DESIGNING A CAMPAIGN POSTER**

Conduct research on the Institutional Revolutionary Party (PRI) today, particularly its political platform. Use your findings to design a **campaign poster** for the PRI in an upcoming election.

Chapter 28 Assessment

TERMS & NAMES

For each term or name below, briefly explain its connection to the changes in global power between 1800 and 1914.

1. Opium War
2. Boxer Rebellion
3. Meiji era
4. Russo-Japanese War
5. Monroe Doctrine
6. Spanish-American War
7. Benito Juárez
8. Porfirio Díaz

MAIN IDEAS

China Resists Outside Influence Section 1 (pages 805–809)

9. Why was China traditionally not interested in trading with the West?
10. Although Guangxu's effort at reform failed, what changes did it finally set in motion?

Modernization in Japan Section 2 (pages 810–815)

11. What events caused Japan to end its isolation and begin to westernize?
12. What were the results of Japan's growing imperialism at the end of the 19th century?

U.S. Economic Imperialism Section 3 (pages 816–821)

13. How were Latin American caudillos able to achieve power and hold on to it?
14. What effects did the Monroe Doctrine and the Roosevelt Corollary have on Latin America?

Turmoil and Change in Mexico Section 4 (pages 822–827)

15. What were the major causes of tension between the Mexicans and the American colonists who settled in Texas?
16. What roles did Francisco "Pancho" Villa and Emiliano Zapata play in the Mexican Revolution?

CRITICAL THINKING

1. USING YOUR NOTES

On a time line, indicate the major events of Santa Anna's military and political career in Mexico. Why do you think he was able to remain in power for so long?

Fights for independence from Spain

1820s

2. MAKING INFERENCES

Do you think that Emperor Guangxu would have been able to put his reforms into practice if the Dowager Empress Cixi had not intervened? Why or why not?

3. COMPARING

CULTURAL INTERACTION How do Japan's efforts at westernization in the late 1800s compare with Japan's cultural borrowing of earlier times?

4. EVALUATING COURSES OF ACTION

REVOLUTION Consider what you have learned in this and other chapters about Latin American colonial history and about how countries undergo change. What are the pros and cons of using both military strategies and peaceful political means to improve a country's economic, social, and political conditions?

VISUAL SUMMARY

Transformations Around the Globe

FOREIGN INFLUENCE

China

- Fails to prevent Britain from pursuing illegal opium trade
- Deals with internal unrest during almost two decades of Taiping Rebellion
- Attempts to build self-sufficiency during 1860s in self-strengthening movement
- Violently opposes foreigners in 1900 Boxer Rebellion
- Begins to establish constitutional government in 1908

Japan

- Signs 1854 Treaty of Kanagawa, opening Japanese ports to foreign trade
- Modernizes based on Western models during Meiji era (1867–1912)
- Fights 1894 Sino-Japanese War to control Korea
- Wages 1904 Russo-Japanese War to control Manchuria
- Annexes Korea in 1910

Latin America

- Depends on exports to fuel economy
- Receives much foreign investment
- Gains U.S. military support in 1898 Spanish-American War
- Becomes crossroads of world trade when U.S. completes Panama Canal in 1914

Mexico

- Fights to hold Texas territory from U.S. colonialism (1835–1845)
- Tries to establish a national identity in the early 1850s under Benito Juárez's *La Reforma*
- Overcomes French occupation in 1867
- Stages the Mexican Revolution in 1910

NEW YORK STATE REGENTS EXAM PRACTICE

Use the excerpt—which deals with changes made during the Meiji era in Japan—and your knowledge of world history to answer questions 1 and 2.

Additional Test Practice, pp. S1–S33

PRIMARY SOURCE

In the second and third years of Meiji, the demand for foreign goods remarkably increased. Those who formerly looked upon them with contempt changed their minds and even dressed in foreign clothes. Our males adopted the European style. They put on fine tall hats instead of wearing large [queues] on their heads, and took to carrying sticks after discarding their swords. They dressed in coats of the English fashion and trousers of the American. They would only eat from tables and nothing would satisfy them but French cookery.

Tokyo Times, 1877

1 According to the excerpt, what happened in the second and third years of Meiji?
 (1) The Japanese ate only English food.
 (2) The Japanese wore only Japanese clothes.
 (3) The demand for foreign goods increased.
 (4) The demand for Japanese goods decreased.

2 Which statement best sums up the way the writer feels about the Japanese adoption of foreign ways?
 (1) The writer expresses no opinion of the matter.
 (2) The writer chooses to reserve judgment until a later date.
 (3) The writer feels that it is a good thing for Japan.
 (4) The writer feels that it is a bad thing for Japan.

Use the graph and your knowledge of world history to answer question 3.

Tolls Collected on the Panama Canal, 1916–1920

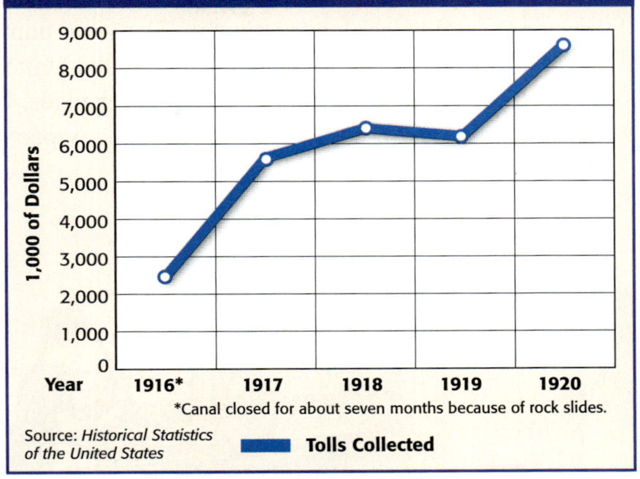

3 In which year did tolls collected on the Panama Canal first exceed $6 million?
 (1) 1917 (3) 1919
 (2) 1918 (4) 1920

INTEGRATED TECHNOLOGY

TEST PRACTICE Go to **classzone.com**
- Diagnostic tests
- Tutorials
- Strategies
- Additional practice

ALTERNATIVE ASSESSMENT

1. Interact *with* History

On page 804, you considered whether you would seek out or resist foreign influence. Now that you have learned how several countries dealt with foreign influence and what the results were, would you change your recommendation? Discuss your ideas in a small group.

2. WRITING ABOUT HISTORY

EMPIRE BUILDING Write a **dialogue** that might have taken place between a conservative member of the Dowager Empress Cixi's court and an official in Emperor Mutsuhito's Meiji government. In the dialogue, have the characters discuss
- the kinds of foreign intervention their countries faced
- the actions their leaders took to deal with this foreign intervention

INTEGRATED TECHNOLOGY

Planning a Television News Special

On May 5, 1862, badly outnumbered Mexican forces defeated the French at the Battle of Puebla. Mexicans still celebrate their country's triumph on the holiday Cinco de Mayo. Working in a group with two other students, plan a television news special on how Cinco de Mayo is celebrated by Mexicans today. Focus on celebrations in Mexico or in Mexican communities in cities in the United States. Consider including
- information on the Battle of Puebla
- an explanation of how and why Cinco de Mayo became a national holiday
- images of any special activities or traditions that have become part of the celebration
- interviews with participants discussing how they feel about Cinco de Mayo

A Period of Change

The period from 1700 to 1914 was a time of tremendous scientific and technological change. The great number of discoveries and inventions in Europe and the United States promoted economic, social, and cultural changes. Use the information on these six pages to study the impact of scientific and technological changes.

▲ Spinning Jenny
Using James Hargreaves's invention, a spinner could turn several spindles with one wheel and produce many threads. Machine-made thread was weak, so it was used only for the horizontal threads of fabric.

Theory of Atoms
John Dalton theorized that atoms are the basic parts of elements and that each type of atom has a specific weight. He was one of the founders of atomic chemistry.

▲ Steamboat
Robert Fulton held the first commercially successful steamboat run. One advantage of a steamboat was that it could travel against a river's current. These boats soon began to travel rivers around the world.

1733 — 1764 — 1785 — 1803 — 1807 — 1830

Flying Shuttle
A shuttle is a holder that carries horizontal threads back and forth between the vertical threads in weaving. John Kay's mechanical flying shuttle enabled one weaver to do the work of two.

Power Loom
Edmund Cartwright created the first water-powered loom. Others later improved on the speed and efficiency of looms and the quality of the fabrics.

▼ Steam Locomotive
In 1830, the first steam locomotive was put into operation in the United States. Besides passengers, locomotives could rapidly transport tons of raw materials from mines to factories, and manufactured goods from factories to consumers and ports.

Panama Canal
The Panama Canal shortened trips between the Atlantic and Pacific oceans by thousands of miles since ships no longer had to go around South America.

◄ Radioactivity
Marie Curie won the Nobel prize in chemistry for her (and her late husband's) discovery of the elements polonium and radium. Their work paved the way for later discoveries in nuclear physics and chemistry.

Antiseptics
Joseph Lister pioneered the use of carbolic acid to kill bacteria in operating rooms and later directly in wounds. The rate of death by infection after surgery dropped from about 50 to 15 percent.

Radio
Guglielmo Marconi's radio sent Morse code messages by electromagnetic waves that traveled through the air. It enabled rapid communication between distant places.

1865 1876 1879 1895 1903 1908 1911 1914

▼ Telephone
Alexander Graham Bell produced the first instrument that successfully carried the sounds of speech over electric wires. The telephone's design underwent a number of changes in its early years.

Airplane
The Wright brothers built the first machine-powered aircraft, which burned gasoline. The edge of the wing was adjusted during flight to steer.

Model T Ford
By using a moving assembly line, Henry Ford produced an automobile that working people could afford to buy.

Light Bulb
The light bulb that Thomas A. Edison and his staff made was first used in businesses and public buildings that installed small lighting plants. Cities slowly built the electrical systems needed to power lights.

Comparing & Contrasting

1. How were the steamboat and the locomotive similar in their impact?
2. How did the scientific theory of John Dalton differ from Joseph Lister's discovery in terms of its impact on daily life?

Impact of Technological Change

Use the charts below, and the documents and photograph on the next page, to learn about some of the great changes technology produced.

Technological Change

Industrialization

Economic Change

- Productivity increased, which led to an economic boom.
- Cheaper goods became available.
- A middle class emerged.
- Industries searched for overseas resources and markets, encouraging imperialism.
- Colonial economies were shaped to benefit Europe.

Social Change

- Cities grew at a rapid pace.
- Poor working and living conditions led to social unrest.
- Diseases spread in slums.
- Unions formed to protect workers.
- Laws were passed to improve working conditions.
- Immigration to North America increased.

Culture Change

- Businesses needed engineers, professionals, and clerical workers, so education was emphasized.
- The spread of public education increased literacy.
- The publishing industry grew; book and magazine sales boomed.
- Reform movements arose in response to unfair conditions.

Inventions/Progress

Economic Change

- Large machines led to the development of factories.
- Steamboats, canals, paved roads, and railroads opened travel to the interior of continents and reduced transportation costs.
- Investors formed corporations to undertake large projects.
- Superior arms and transport helped Europeans colonize.
- Inventions such as the telephone and electric light helped business grow.

Social Change

- Steamboats and railroads made travel cheaper and easier.
- The telegraph, telephone, and radio aided communication.
- Convenience products like canned food and ready-made clothes made daily life easier.
- The assembly line made products like cars affordable for many.
- Fewer workers were needed to produce the same amount of goods. Some workers lost jobs.

Culture Change

- People placed increasing emphasis on making homes more comfortable and convenient.
- Improvements in one aspect of agriculture and manufacturing promoted the creation of new inventions to improve other aspects.
- Mass culture grew through the availability of phonographs and movies, and an increase in leisure time.

SKILLBUILDER: Interpreting Charts

1. **Synthesizing** *How might limiting working hours for children promote literacy?*
2. **Analyzing Motives** *Why would Europeans build transportation and communication networks in their colonies?*

PRIMARY SOURCE

Child Workers in Textile Factory

Many jobs did not require skilled workers, so children were hired to do them because they could be paid lower wages than adults. Some industries also hired children because their small fingers could fit between the machinery or handle fine parts more easily than adult fingers could.

DOCUMENT-BASED QUESTION
Judging by the children's appearance, how generous were the wages they received? Explain your answer.

SECONDARY SOURCE

INTERACTIVE

How Technology Aided Imperialism

In this excerpt from the book *Guns, Germs, and Steel,* Jared Diamond related an incident to show how technology helped Europeans conquer other lands.

In 1808 a British sailor named Charlie Savage equipped with muskets and excellent aim arrived in the Fiji Islands. [He] proceeded single-handedly to upset Fiji's balance of power. Among his many exploits, he paddled his canoe up a river to the Fijian village of Kasavu, halted less than a pistol shot's length from the village fence, and fired away at the undefended inhabitants. His victims were so numerous that . . . the stream beside the village was red with blood. Such examples of the power of guns against native peoples lacking guns could be multiplied indefinitely.

DOCUMENT-BASED QUESTION
How did guns give Europeans an advantage over native peoples?

PRIMARY SOURCE

INTERACTIVE

Impact of the Telephone

In this excerpt from "Thirty Years of the Telephone," published in September 1906, John Vaughn discussed how Bell's invention affected life in the United States.

Various industries, unknown thirty years ago, but now sources of employment to many thousands of workers, depend entirely on the telephone for support. . . . The Bell Companies employ over 87,000 persons, and it may be added, pay them well. . . . These figures may be supplemented by the number of telephones in use (5,698,000), by the number of miles of wire (6,043,000) in the Bell lines, and by the number of conversations (4,479,500,000) electrically conveyed in 1905. The network of wire connects more than 33,000 cities, towns, villages, and hamlets.

DOCUMENT-BASED QUESTION
What were some of the effects of the invention of the telephone?

Comparing & Contrasting

1. Reread the passage by John Vaughn and then compare it with the information on the chart. What could you add to the chart based on this passage?
2. Does the photograph of factory workers confirm or contradict the information on the chart? Explain.

Impact of Scientific Change

Many scientific discoveries resulted in practical applications that affected daily life. Other discoveries increased our understanding of the way the universe works. Use the information on these two pages to explore the impact of scientific change.

Scientific Change

Economic Change

- Discovery of quinine as a malaria treatment helped people colonize tropical areas.
- Control of diseases like yellow fever and bubonic plague enabled the Panama Canal to be built.
- More accurate clocks and new astronomical discoveries led to safer navigation, which improved shipping.
- Study of electricity and magnetism led to the invention of the dynamo and motor, which aided industry.

Social Change

- Vulcanized rubber was used for raincoats and car tires.
- Discoveries about air, gases, and temperature resulted in better weather forecasting.
- Vaccines and treatments were found for illnesses like diphtheria and heart disease; X-rays and other new medical techniques were developed.
- Plumbing and sewers improved sanitation and public health.
- Psychiatry improved the treatment of mental illness.

Culture Change

- Many scientific and technical schools were founded; governments began funding scientific research.
- Psychological discoveries began to be applied to the social sciences, such as sociology and anthropology.
- Some painters and writers created work that reflected the new psychological ideas.
- Social Darwinism, the idea that some people were more "fit" than others, was used to justify racism.

SKILLBUILDER: Interpreting Charts

1. **Drawing Conclusions** *How do you think such advances in public health as vaccinations and sanitation services affected the lives of ordinary people?*
2. **Analyzing Bias** *Who would be more likely to accept the idea of social Darwinism–a European colonizer or an African in a colony? Why?*

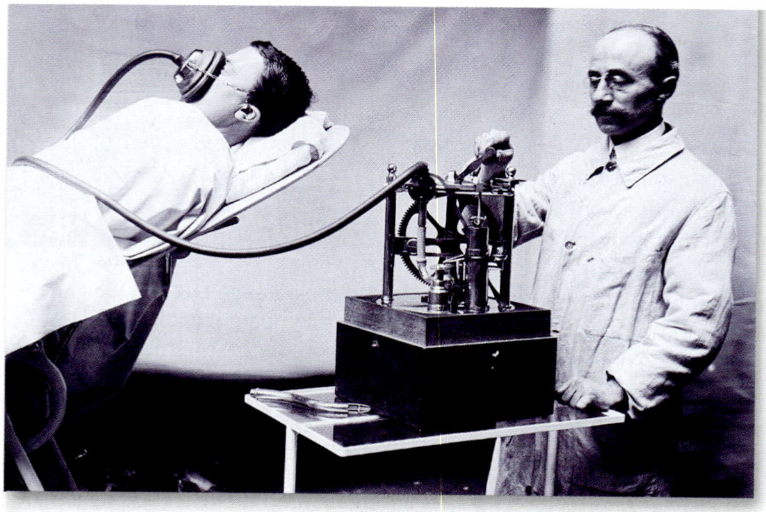

PRIMARY SOURCE

Chloroform Machine

The person with the mask is receiving the anesthetic chloroform. By removing pain, anesthetics enabled doctors to perform procedures—such as surgery—that would have been difficult for the patient to endure.

DOCUMENT-BASED QUESTION

How did practical inventions, like the chloroform machine, contribute to medicine and other sciences?

PRIMARY SOURCE

Smallpox Vaccination

This newspaper engraving shows a Board of Health doctor administering the smallpox vaccine to poor people at a police station in New York City.

DOCUMENT-BASED QUESTION

Why would public health officials especially want to carry out vaccination programs in poor neighborhoods?

SECONDARY SOURCE

INTERACTIVE

Impact of Scientific Research

This passage from *The Birth of the Modern* by Paul Johnson discusses the far-reaching results of Michael Faraday's experiments with electromagnetism in the 1820s.

[By 1831, Faraday] had not only the first electric motor, but, in essence, the first dynamo: He could generate power. . . . What was remarkable about his work between 1820 and 1831 was that by showing exactly how mechanical could be transformed into electrical power, he made the jump between theoretical research and its practical application a comparatively narrow one. The electrical industry was the direct result of his work, and its first product, the electric telegraph, was soon in use. The idea of cause and effect was of great importance, for both industry and governments now began to appreciate the value of fundamental research and to finance it.

DOCUMENT-BASED QUESTION

How did Faraday's work affect society in the long term?

Comparing & Contrasting

1. In your opinion, was there more economic progress or social progress during the period 1700 to 1914? Use information from the charts on pages 832 and 834 to support your answer.
2. Consider the impact of medical advances and the idea of Social Darwinism on imperialism. How were their impacts alike?

EXTENSION ACTIVITY

Research a more recent scientific or technological change, such as the development of computer chips, plastics, the Internet, or space travel. Make a chart like the one shown on page 834 listing the economic, social, and cultural changes that have resulted.

UNIT 7

The World at War 1900–1945

World War I was characterized by long, bloody battles. This painting by François Flameng shows one such engagement. French soldiers attempt to cross the River Yser in Belgium on pontoon bridges.

Comparing & Contrasting

The Changing Nature of Warfare

In Unit 7, you will learn about the changing nature of warfare in the 20th century. At the end of the unit, you will have a chance to compare and contrast different aspects of the wars you studied. (See pages 954–959.)

CHAPTER

29

The Great War, 1914–1918

Previewing Main Ideas

SCIENCE AND TECHNOLOGY Advances in weaponry, from improvements to the machine gun and airplane, to the invention of the tank, led to mass devastation during World War I.

Geography *Which Allied nation could the Central Powers invade only by airplane?*

ECONOMICS The war affected many European economies. Desperate for resources, the warring governments converted many industries to munitions factories. They also took greater control of the production of goods.

Geography *According to the map, why might Russia have struggled to obtain resources from its allies?*

POWER AND AUTHORITY The quest among European nations for greater power played a role in causing World War I. By the turn of the 20th century, relations among these countries had grown increasingly tense.

Geography *Which alliance may have had the greater challenge, given the geography of the conflict? Why?*

NEW YORK CORE CURRICULUM FOCUS

- New technologies and weapons of war made World War I the most destructive war the world had yet seen.
- World War I led to the collapse of the Ottoman Empire.

INTEGRATED TECHNOLOGY

eEdition

- Interactive Maps
- Interactive Visuals
- Interactive Primary Sources

INTERNET RESOURCES

Go to **classzone.com** for:

- Research Links
- Internet Activities
- Primary Sources
- Chapter Quiz
- Maps
- Test Practice
- Current Events

EUROPE

1914
World War I begins as Austria declares war on Serbia.

1915
◀ A World War I soldier readies for battle on the Western Front.

1914 — 1915

WORLD

1914
U.S.-built Panama Canal opens for operation.

May 1915
◀ German forces sink the British ship *Lusitania.*

1916
French and Germans engage in battle at Verdun.

1917
U.S. war poster encourages enlistment as America enters war. ▶

1918
Armistice signed as Allies defeat Central Powers.

1916 **1917** **1918**

1916
U.S. President Woodrow Wilson wins reelection. ▶

1917
Communists seize power in Russian Revolution.

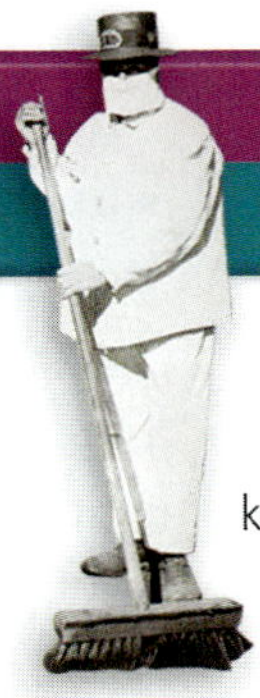

1918
◀ U.S. worker guards against deadly flu that kills millions worldwide.

Interact *with* History

Should you always support an ally?

World War I has begun. You are the leader of a European country and must decide what to do. Your nation is one of several that have agreed to support each other in the event of war. Some of your allies already have joined the fight. You oppose the thought of war and fear that joining will lead to even more lives lost. Yet, you believe in being loyal to your allies. You also worry that your rivals want to conquer all of Europe—and if you don't join the war now, your country may end up having to defend itself.

▲ A World War I poster urges nations to come to the aid of Serbia.

EXAMINING *the* ISSUES

- **Should you always support a friend, no matter what he or she does?**
- **What might be the long-term consequences of refusing to help an ally?**

As a class, discuss these questions. In your discussion, consider the various reasons countries go to war. As you read about World War I in this chapter, see what factors influenced the decisions of each nation.

Marching Toward War

CONNECT TO THE NEW YORK STATE CORE CURRICULUM

Unit 5.F.3.a. Balkans before World War I
Unit 6.A.2. Causes

TERMS & NAMES

- militarism
- Triple Alliance
- Kaiser Wilhelm II
- Triple Entente

SETTING THE STAGE At the turn of the 20th century, the nations of Europe had been largely at peace with one another for nearly 30 years. This was no accident. Efforts to outlaw war and achieve a permanent peace had been gaining momentum in Europe since the middle of the 19th century. By 1900, hundreds of peace organizations were active. In addition, peace congresses convened regularly between 1843 and 1907. Some Europeans believed that progress had made war a thing of the past. Yet in a little more than a decade, a massive war would engulf Europe and spread across the globe.

TAKING NOTES

Summarizing Create a time line of major events that led to the start of World War I.

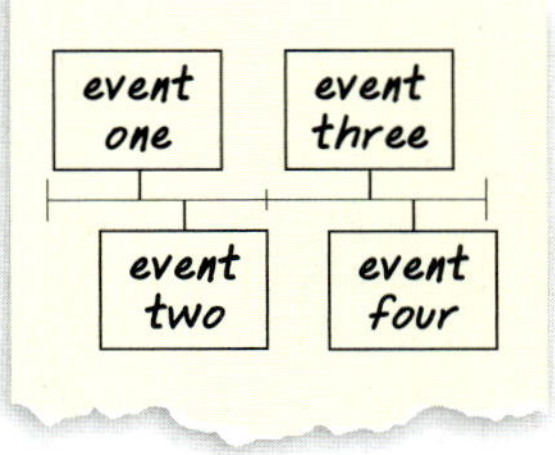

Rising Tensions in Europe

While peace and harmony characterized much of Europe at the beginning of the 1900s, there were less visible—and darker—forces at work as well. Below the surface of peace and goodwill, Europe witnessed several gradual developments that would ultimately help propel the continent into war.

The Rise of Nationalism One such development was the growth of nationalism, or a deep devotion to one's nation. Nationalism can serve as a unifying force within a country. However, it also can cause intense competition among nations, with each seeking to overpower the other. By the turn of the 20th century, a fierce rivalry indeed had developed among Europe's Great Powers. Those nations were Germany, Austria-Hungary, Great Britain, Russia, Italy, and France.

This increasing rivalry among European nations stemmed from several sources. Competition for materials and markets was one. Territorial disputes were another. France, for example, had never gotten over the loss of Alsace-Lorraine to Germany in the Franco-Prussian War (1870). Austria-Hungary and Russia both tried to dominate in the Balkans, a region in southeast Europe. Within the Balkans, the intense nationalism of Serbs, Bulgarians, Romanians, and other ethnic groups led to demands for independence.

Imperialism and Militarism Another force that helped set the stage for war in Europe was imperialism. As Chapter 27 explained, the nations of Europe competed fiercely for colonies in Africa and Asia. The quest for colonies sometimes pushed European nations to the brink of war. As European countries continued to compete for overseas empires, their sense of rivalry and mistrust of one another deepened.

Yet another troubling development throughout the early years of the 20th century was the rise of a dangerous European arms race. The nations of Europe believed that to be truly great, they needed to have a powerful military. By 1914, all the Great Powers except Britain had large standing armies. In addition, military experts stressed the importance of being able to quickly mobilize, or organize and move troops in case of a war. Generals in each country developed highly detailed plans for such a mobilization.

The policy of glorifying military power and keeping an army prepared for war was known as **militarism**. Having a large and strong standing army made citizens feel patriotic. However, it also frightened some people. As early as 1895, Frédéric Passy, a prominent peace activist, expressed a concern that many shared:

PRIMARY SOURCE

The entire able-bodied population are preparing to massacre one another; though no one, it is true, wants to attack, and everybody protests his love of peace and determination to maintain it, yet the whole world feels that it only requires some unforeseen incident, some unpreventable accident, for the spark to fall in a flash . . . and blow all Europe sky-high.

FRÉDÉRIC PASSY, quoted in *Nobel: The Man and His Prizes*

History Makers

Kaiser Wilhelm II
1859–1941

Wilhelm II was related to the leaders of two nations he eventually would engage in war. Wilhelm, George V of Great Britain, and Nicholas II of Russia were all cousins.

The kaiser thought a great deal of himself and his place in history. Once, when a doctor told him he had a small cold, Wilhelm reportedly responded, "No, it is a big cold. Everything about me must be big."

He also could be sly and deceitful. After forcing the popular Bismarck to resign, Wilhelm pretended to be upset. Most people, however, including Bismarck, were not fooled.

INTEGRATED TECHNOLOGY

RESEARCH LINKS For more on Wilhelm II, go to **classzone.com**

Tangled Alliances

Growing rivalries and mutual mistrust had led to the creation of several military alliances among the Great Powers as early as the 1870s. This alliance system had been designed to keep peace in Europe. But it would instead help push the continent into war.

Bismarck Forges Early Pacts Between 1864 and 1871, Prussia's blood-and-iron chancellor, Otto von Bismarck, freely used war to unify Germany. After 1871, however, Bismarck declared Germany to be a "satisfied power." He then turned his energies to maintaining peace in Europe.

Bismarck saw France as the greatest threat to peace. He believed that France still wanted revenge for its defeat in the Franco-Prussian War. Bismarck's first goal, therefore, was to isolate France. "As long as it is without allies," Bismarck stressed, "France poses no danger to us." In 1879, Bismarck formed the Dual Alliance between Germany and Austria-Hungary. Three years later, Italy joined the two countries, forming the **Triple Alliance**. In 1881, Bismarck took yet another possible ally away from France by making a treaty with Russia.

Shifting Alliances Threaten Peace In 1890, Germany's foreign policy changed dramatically. That year, **Kaiser Wilhelm II**—who two years earlier had become ruler of Germany—forced Bismarck to resign. A proud and stubborn man, Wilhelm II did not wish to share power with anyone. Besides wanting to assert his own power, the new kaiser was eager to show the world just how mighty Germany had become. The army was his greatest pride. "I and the army were born for one another," Wilhelm declared shortly after taking power.

Wilhelm let his nation's treaty with Russia lapse in 1890. Russia responded by forming a defensive military alliance with France in 1892 and 1894. Such an alliance had been Bismarck's fear. War with either Russia or France would make Germany the enemy of both. Germany would then be forced to fight a two-front war, or a war on both its eastern and western borders.

Next, Wilhelm began a tremendous shipbuilding program in an effort to make the German navy equal to that of the mighty British fleet. Alarmed, Great Britain formed an entente, or alliance, with France. In 1907, Britain made another entente, this time with both France and Russia. The **Triple Entente**, as it was called, did not bind Britain to fight with France and Russia. However, it did almost certainly ensure that Britain would not fight against them.

By 1907, two rival camps existed in Europe. On one side was the Triple Alliance—Germany, Austria-Hungary, and Italy. On the other side was the Triple Entente—Great Britain, France, and Russia. A dispute between two rival powers could draw all the nations of Europe into war.

Crisis in the Balkans

Nowhere was that dispute more likely to occur than on the Balkan Peninsula. This mountainous peninsula in the southeastern corner of Europe was home to an assortment of ethnic groups. With a long history of nationalist uprisings and ethnic clashes, the Balkans was known as the "powder keg" of Europe.

A Restless Region By the early 1900s, the Ottoman Empire, which included the Balkan region, was in rapid decline. While some Balkan groups struggled to free themselves from the Ottoman Turks, others already had succeeded in breaking away from their Turkish rulers. These peoples had formed new nations, including Bulgaria, Greece, Montenegro, Romania, and Serbia.

Nationalism was a powerful force in these countries. Each group longed to extend its borders. Serbia, for example, had a large Slavic population. It hoped to absorb all the Slavs on the Balkan Peninsula. Russia, itself a mostly Slavic nation, supported Serbian nationalism. However, Serbia's powerful northern neighbor, Austria-Hungary, opposed such an effort. Austria feared that efforts to create a Slavic state would stir rebellion among its Slavic population.

In 1908, Austria annexed, or took over, Bosnia and Herzegovina. These were two Balkan areas with large Slavic populations. Serbian leaders, who had sought to rule these provinces, were outraged. In the years that followed, tensions between Serbia and Austria steadily rose. The Serbs continually vowed to take Bosnia and Herzegovina away from Austria. In response, Austria-Hungary vowed to crush any Serbian effort to undermine its authority in the Balkans. (A)

MAIN IDEA

Analyzing Issues

(A) What were the reasons for the hostility between Austria-Hungary and Serbia?

GEOGRAPHY SKILLBUILDER: Interpreting Maps

1. **Place** *What region of the Austro-Hungarian Empire was located along the Adriatic Sea?*
2. **Location** *Based on the map, why might Serbia have staked a claim to Bosnia and Herzegovina?*

History *in* Depth

The Armenian Massacre

One group in southeastern Europe that suffered greatly for its independence efforts was the Armenians. By the 1880s, the roughly 2.5 million Armenians in the Ottoman Empire had begun to demand their freedom. As a result, relations between the group and its Turkish rulers grew strained.

Throughout the 1890s, Turkish troops killed tens of thousands of Armenians. When World War I erupted in 1914, the Armenians pledged their support to the Turks' enemies. In response, the Turkish government deported nearly 2 million Armenians. Along the way, more than 600,000 died of starvation or were killed by Turkish soldiers.

INTEGRATED TECHNOLOGY

INTERNET ACTIVITY Create a chart or graphic about any aspect of modern Armenian culture. Go to **classzone.com** for your research.

A Shot Rings Throughout Europe Into this poisoned atmosphere of mutual dislike and mistrust stepped the heir to the Austro-Hungarian throne, Archduke Franz Ferdinand, and his wife, Sophie. On June 28, 1914, the couple paid a state visit to Sarajevo, the capital of Bosnia. It would be their last. The royal pair was shot at point-blank range as they rode through the streets of Sarajevo in an open car. The killer was Gavrilo Princip, a 19-year-old Serbian and member of the Black Hand. The Black Hand was a secret society committed to ridding Bosnia of Austrian rule.

Because the assassin was a Serbian, Austria decided to use the murders as an excuse to punish Serbia. On July 23, Austria presented Serbia with an ultimatum containing numerous demands. Serbia knew that refusing the ultimatum would lead to war against the more powerful Austria. Therefore, Serbian leaders agreed to most of Austria's demands. They offered to have several others settled by an international conference.

Vocabulary
An *ultimatum* is a list of demands that, if not met, will lead to serious consequences.

Austria, however, was in no mood to negotiate. The nation's leaders, it seemed, had already settled on war. On July 28, Austria rejected Serbia's offer and declared war. That same day, Russia, an ally of Serbia with its largely Slavic population, took action. Russian leaders ordered the mobilization of troops toward the Austrian border.

Leaders all over Europe suddenly took notice. The fragile European stability seemed ready to collapse into armed conflict. The British foreign minister, the Italian government, and even Kaiser Wilhelm himself urged Austria and Russia to negotiate. But it was too late. The machinery of war had been set in motion.

NEW YORK CORE CURRICULUM REVIEW

TERMS & NAMES 1. For each term or name, write a sentence explaining its significance.

- militarism
- Triple Alliance
- Kaiser Wilhelm II
- Triple Entente

USING YOUR NOTES

2. Which event do you consider most significant? Why?

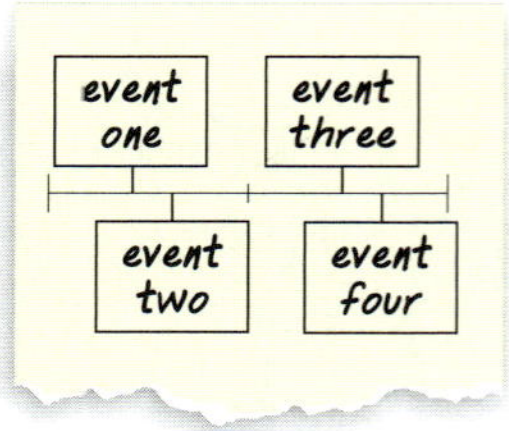

MAIN IDEAS

3. What were the three forces at work in Europe that helped set the stage for war?
4. Who were the members of the Triple Alliance? the Triple Entente?
5. What single event set in motion the start of World War I?

CRITICAL THINKING & WRITING

6. **ANALYZING CAUSES** Which of the forces at work in Europe played the greatest role in helping to prompt the outbreak of war?
7. **ANALYZING ISSUES** Was the description of the Balkans as the "powder keg" of Europe justified? Explain.
8. **FORMING AND SUPPORTING OPINIONS** Do you think World War I was avoidable? Use information from the text to support your answer.
9. **WRITING ACTIVITY** POWER AND AUTHORITY Write a brief **letter to the editor** of a European newspaper expressing what your views might have been about the coming war.

CONNECT TO TODAY **CREATING A TIME LINE**

Working with a partner, use the library and other resources to create a **time line** of key events in the Balkans from 1914 until today. Limit your time line to the six to eight events you consider most significant.

2

Europe Plunges into War

CONNECT TO THE NEW YORK STATE CORE CURRICULUM

Unit 6.A.1. Europe: the physical setting
Unit 6.A.4. Effects of scientific/technological advances on warfare

TERMS & NAMES

- Central Powers
- Allies
- Western Front
- Schlieffen Plan
- trench warfare
- Eastern Front

SETTING THE STAGE By 1914, Europe was divided into two rival camps. One alliance, the Triple Entente, included Great Britain, France, and Russia. The other, known as the Triple Alliance, included Germany, Austria-Hungary, and Italy. Austria-Hungary's declaration of war against Serbia set off a chain reaction within the alliance system. The countries of Europe followed through on their pledges to support one another. As a result, nearly all of Europe soon joined what would be the largest, most destructive war the world had yet seen.

The Great War Begins

In response to Austria's declaration of war, Russia, Serbia's ally, began moving its army toward the Russian-Austrian border. Expecting Germany to join Austria, Russia also mobilized along the German border. To Germany, Russia's mobilization amounted to a declaration of war. On August 1, the German government declared war on Russia.

Russia looked to its ally France for help. Germany, however, did not even wait for France to react. Two days after declaring war on Russia, Germany also declared war on France. Soon afterward, Great Britain declared war on Germany. Much of Europe was now locked in battle.

TAKING NOTES

Outlining Use an outline to organize main ideas and details.

I. The Great War Begins
A.
B.
II. A Bloody Stalemate

Nations Take Sides By mid-August 1914, the battle lines were clearly drawn. On one side were Germany and Austria-Hungary. They were known as the **Central Powers** because of their location in the heart of Europe. Bulgaria and the Ottoman Empire would later join the Central Powers in the hopes of regaining lost territories.

On the other side were Great Britain, France, and Russia. Together, they were known as the Allied Powers or the **Allies**. Japan joined the Allies within weeks. Italy joined later. Italy had been a member of the Triple Alliance with Germany and Austria-Hungary. However, the Italians joined the other side after accusing their former partners of unjustly starting the war.

In the late summer of 1914, millions of soldiers marched happily off to battle, convinced that the war would be short. Only a few people foresaw the horror ahead. One of them was Britain's foreign minister, Sir Edward Grey. Staring out over London at nightfall, Grey said sadly to a friend, "The lamps are going out all over Europe. We shall not see them lit again in our lifetime."

GEOGRAPHY SKILLBUILDER: Interpreting Maps

1. **Location** *In which country was almost all of the war in the West fought?*
2. **Location** *What geographic disadvantage did Germany and Austria-Hungary face in fighting the war? How might this have affected their war strategy?*

A Bloody Stalemate

It did not take long for Sir Edward Grey's prediction to ring true. As the summer of 1914 turned to fall, the war turned into a long and bloody stalemate, or deadlock, along the battlefields of France. This deadlocked region in northern France became known as the **Western Front**.

The Conflict Grinds Along Facing a war on two fronts, Germany had developed a battle strategy known as the **Schlieffen Plan**, named after its designer, General Alfred Graf von Schlieffen (SHLEE•fuhn). The plan called for attacking and defeating France in the west and then rushing east to fight Russia. The Germans felt they could carry out such a plan because Russia lagged behind the rest of Europe in its railroad system and thus would take longer to supply its front lines. Nonetheless, speed was vital to the Schlieffen Plan. German leaders knew they needed to win a quick victory over France.

Early on, it appeared that Germany would do just that. By early September, German forces had swept into France and reached the outskirts of Paris. A major German victory appeared just days away. On September 5, however, the Allies regrouped and attacked the Germans northeast of Paris, in the valley of the Marne River. Every available soldier was hurled into the struggle. When reinforcements were needed, more than 600 taxicabs rushed soldiers from Paris to the front. After four days of fighting, the German generals gave the order to retreat.

Although it was only the first major clash on the Western Front, the First Battle of the Marne was perhaps the single most important event of the war. The defeat of the Germans left the Schlieffen Plan in ruins. A quick victory in the west no longer seemed possible. In the east, Russian forces had already invaded Germany. Germany was going to have to fight a long war on two fronts. Realizing this, the German high command sent thousands of troops from France to aid its forces in the east. Meanwhile, the war on the Western Front settled into a stalemate. (A)

MAIN IDEA

Recognizing Effects

(A) Why was the Battle of the Marne so significant?

War in the Trenches By early 1915, opposing armies on the Western Front had dug miles of parallel trenches to protect themselves from enemy fire. This set the stage for what became known as **trench warfare**. In this type of warfare, soldiers fought each other from trenches. And armies traded huge losses of human life for pitifully small land gains.

Life in the trenches was pure misery. "The men slept in mud, washed in mud, ate mud, and dreamed mud," wrote one soldier. The trenches swarmed with rats. Fresh food was nonexistent. Sleep was nearly impossible.

The space between the opposing trenches won the grim name "no man's land." When the officers ordered an attack, their men went over the top of their trenches into this bombed-out landscape. There, they usually met murderous rounds of machine-gun fire. Staying put, however, did not ensure one's safety. Artillery fire brought death right into the trenches. "Shells of all calibers kept raining on our sector," wrote one French soldier. "The trenches disappeared, filled with earth . . . the air was unbreathable. Our blinded, wounded, crawling, and shouting soldiers kept falling on top of us and died splashing us with blood. It was living hell."

The Western Front had become a "terrain of death." It stretched nearly 500 miles from the North Sea to the Swiss border. A British officer described it in a letter:

PRIMARY SOURCE

Imagine a broad belt, ten miles or so in width, stretching from the Channel to the German frontier near Basle, which is positively littered with the bodies of men and scarified with their rude graves; in which farms, villages and cottages are shapeless heaps of blackened masonry; in which fields, roads and trees are pitted and torn and twisted by shells and disfigured by dead horses, cattle, sheep and goats, scattered in every attitude of repulsive distortion and dismemberment.

VALENTINE FLEMING, quoted in *The First World War*

▼ Allied troops crawl through a trench along the Western Front.

History *in* Depth

The New Weapons of War

Poison Gas

Soldiers wore masks like those shown at left to protect themselves from poison gas. Gas was introduced by the Germans but used by both sides. Some gases caused blindness or severe blisters, others death by choking.

Machine Gun

The machine gun, which fires ammunition automatically, was much improved by the time of World War I. The gun, shown to the left, could wipe out waves of attackers and thus made it difficult for forces to advance.

Tank

The tank, shown to the left, was an armored combat vehicle that moved on chain tracks—and thus could cross many types of terrain. It was introduced by the British in 1916 at the Battle of the Somme.

Submarine

In 1914, the Germans introduced the submarine as an effective warship. The submarine's primary weapon against ships was the torpedo, an underwater missile.

Military strategists were at a loss. New tools of war—machine guns, poison gas, armored tanks, larger artillery—had not delivered the fast-moving war they had expected. All this new technology did was kill greater numbers of people more effectively.

The slaughter reached a peak in 1916. In February, the Germans launched a massive attack against the French near Verdun. Each side lost more than 300,000 men. In July, the British army tried to relieve the pressure on the French. British forces attacked the Germans northwest of Verdun, in the valley of the Somme River. In the first day of battle alone, more than 20,000 British soldiers were killed. By the time the Battle of the Somme ended in November, each side had suffered more than half a million casualties.

Vocabulary
In war, a *casualty* is anyone killed, injured, captured, or considered missing in action.

What did the warring sides gain? Near Verdun, the Germans advanced about four miles. In the Somme valley, the British gained about five miles.

The Battle on the Eastern Front

Even as the war on the Western Front claimed thousands of lives, both sides were sending millions more men to fight on the **Eastern Front**. This area was a stretch of battlefield along the German and Russian border. Here, Russians and Serbs battled Germans and Austro-Hungarians. The war in the east was a more mobile war than that in the west. Here too, however, slaughter and stalemate were common.

Early Fighting At the beginning of the war, Russian forces had launched an attack into both Austria and Germany. At the end of August, Germany counterattacked near the town of Tannenberg. During the four-day battle, the Germans crushed the invading Russian army and drove it into full retreat. More than 30,000 Russian soldiers were killed.

Russia fared somewhat better against the Austrians. Russian forces defeated the Austrians twice in September 1914, driving deep into their country. Not until December of that year did the Austrian army manage to turn the tide. Austria defeated the Russians and eventually pushed them out of Austria-Hungary.

Russia Struggles By 1916, Russia's war effort was near collapse. Unlike the nations of western Europe, Russia had yet to become industrialized. As a result, the Russian army was continually short on food, guns, ammunition, clothes, boots, and blankets. Moreover, the Allied supply shipments to Russia were sharply limited by German control of the Baltic Sea, combined with Germany's relentless submarine campaign in the North Sea and beyond. In the south, the Ottomans still controlled the straits leading from the Mediterranean to the Black Sea.

The Russian army had only one asset—its numbers. Throughout the war the Russian army suffered a staggering number of battlefield losses. Yet the army continually rebuilt its ranks from the country's enormous population. For more than three years, the battered Russian army managed to tie up hundreds of thousands of German troops in the east. As a result, Germany could not hurl its full fighting force at the west. **B**

MAIN IDEA

Synthesizing

B Why was Russia's involvement in the war so important to the other Allies?

Germany and her allies, however, were concerned with more than just the Eastern or Western Front. As the war raged on, fighting spread beyond Europe to Africa, as well as to Southwest and Southeast Asia. In the years after it began, the massive European conflict indeed became a world war.

Social History

The Frozen Front

For soldiers on the Eastern Front, like those shown above, the overall misery of warfare was compounded by deadly winters. "Every day hundreds froze to death," noted one Austro-Hungarian officer during a particularly brutal spell.

Russian troops suffered too, mainly due to their lack of food and clothing. "I am at my post all the time—frozen [and] soaked . . . ," lamented one soldier. "We walk barefoot or in rope-soled shoes. It's incredible that soldiers of the Russian army are in rope-soled shoes!"

NEW YORK CORE CURRICULUM REVIEW

TERMS & NAMES 1. For each term or name, write a sentence explaining its significance.

- Central Powers
- Allies
- Western Front
- Schlieffen Plan
- trench warfare
- Eastern Front

USING YOUR NOTES

2. What were some of the conditions that soldiers on the front lines had to face?

I. The Great War Begins
  A.
  B.
II. A Bloody Stalemate

MAIN IDEAS

3. Which countries comprised the Central Powers? Which countries comprised the Allies?
4. What were the characteristics of trench warfare?
5. What factors contributed to Russia's war difficulties?

CRITICAL THINKING & WRITING

6. **COMPARING AND CONTRASTING** How was war on the Western and Eastern Fronts different? How was it the same?
7. **ANALYZING CAUSES** Why did the Schlieffen Plan ultimately collapse? Cite specific details from the text.
8. **MAKING INFERENCES** Why might it be fair to say that neither side won the battles of the Somme or Verdun?
9. **WRITING ACTIVITY** SCIENCE AND TECHNOLOGY In an **explanatory essay,** describe the effects of the new technology on warfare. Use examples from your reading.

CONNECT TO TODAY PRESENTING AN ORAL REPORT

Find an image of a World War I monument from any one of the combatant countries. In an **oral report**, present the image to the class and provide details about its origin and purpose.

Military Aviation

World War I introduced airplane warfare—and by doing so, ushered in an era of tremendous progress in the field of military aviation. Although the plane itself was relatively new and untested by 1914, the warring nations quickly recognized its potential as a powerful weapon. Throughout the conflict, countries on both sides built faster and stronger aircraft, and designed them to drop bombs and shoot at one another in the sky. Between the beginning and end of the war, the total number of planes in use by the major combatants soared from around 850 to nearly 10,000. After the war, countries continued to maintain a strong and advanced airforce, as they realized that supremacy of the air was a key to military victory.

▲ A World War I pilot shows off an early air-to-ground communication device.

INTEGRATED TECHNOLOGY

RESEARCH LINKS For more on military aviation go to **classzone.com**

1. Designers kept nearly all weight in the center, giving the planes tremendous maneuverability.
2. A timing device enabled machine guns to fire through the propeller.
3. Engines were continuously strengthened for greater speed and carrying capability.

Two Top Fighter Planes: A Comparison

	Fokker D VII (German)	Sopwith F1Camel (British)
Length	23 feet	18 feet 8 inches
Wingspan	29 feet 3 inches	28 feet
Maximum Speed	116 mph	122 mph
Maximum Height	22,900 feet	24,000 feet
Maximum Flight Time	1.5 hours	2.5 hours

Connect *to* Today

1. **Drawing Conclusions** Why would communication with someone outside the plane be important for pilots of World War I and today?

See Skillbuilder Handbook, Page R11.

2. **Comparing** Using the Internet and other resources, find out more about a recent innovation with regard to fighter planes and explain its significance.

A Global Conflict

CONNECT TO THE NEW YORK STATE CORE CURRICULUM

Unit 6.A.3. Impacts
Unit 6.A.7. The war as reflected in literature, art, and propaganda

TERMS & NAMES

- unrestricted submarine warfare
- total war
- rationing
- propaganda
- armistice

SETTING THE STAGE World War I was much more than a European conflict. Australia and Japan, for example, entered the war on the Allies' side, while India supplied troops to fight alongside their British rulers. Meanwhile, the Ottoman Turks and later Bulgaria allied themselves with Germany and the Central Powers. As the war promised to be a grim, drawn-out affair, all the Great Powers looked for other allies around the globe to tip the balance. They also sought new war fronts on which to achieve victory.

TAKING NOTES

Recognizing Effects Use a web diagram to show the effects of World War I.

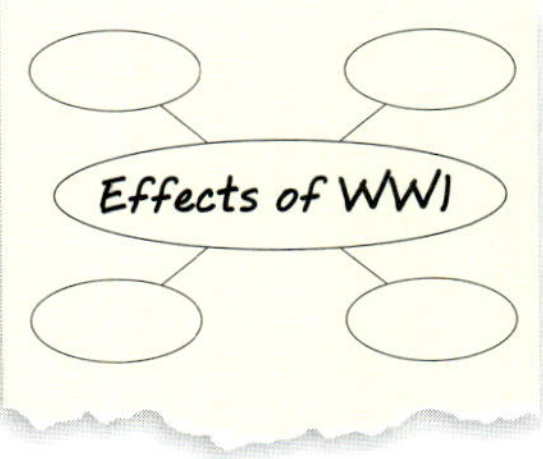

War Affects the World

As the war dragged on, the main combatants looked beyond Europe for a way to end the stalemate. However, none of the alliances they formed or new battlefronts they opened did much to end the slow and grinding conflict.

The Gallipoli Campaign A promising strategy for the Allies seemed to be to attack a region in the Ottoman Empire known as the Dardanelles. This narrow sea strait was the gateway to the Ottoman capital, Constantinople. By securing the Dardanelles, the Allies believed that they could take Constantinople, defeat the Turks, and establish a supply line to Russia.

Gallipoli Campaign

The effort to take the Dardanelles strait began in February 1915. It was known as the Gallipoli campaign. British, Australian, New Zealand, and French troops made repeated assaults on the Gallipoli Peninsula on the western side of the strait. Turkish troops, some commanded by German officers, vigorously defended the region. By May, Gallipoli had turned into another bloody stalemate. Both sides dug trenches, from which they battled for the rest of the year. In December, the Allies gave up the campaign and began to evacuate. They had suffered about 250,000 casualties.

Battles in Africa and Asia In various parts of Asia and Africa, Germany's colonial possessions came under assault. The Japanese quickly overran German outposts in

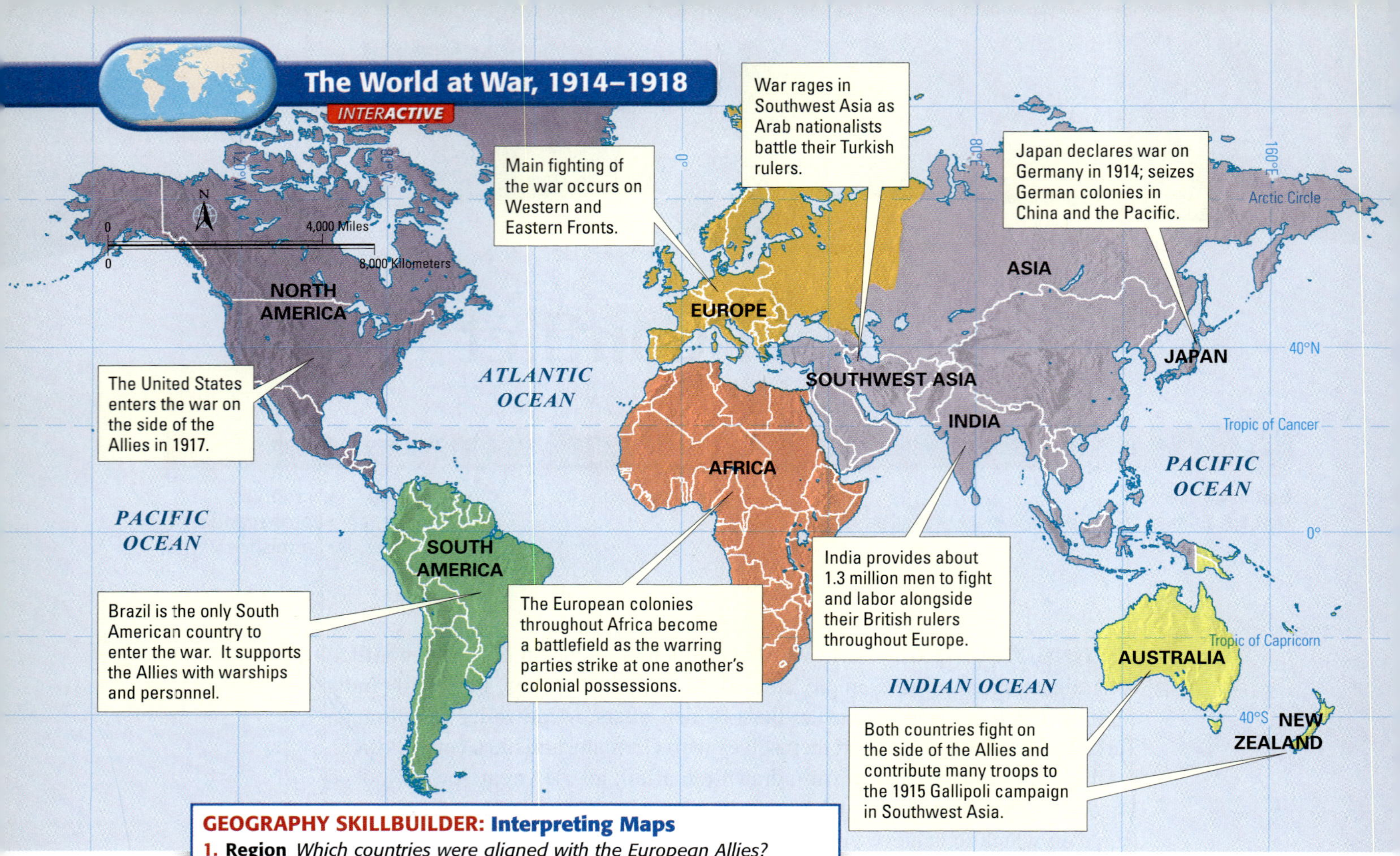

GEOGRAPHY SKILLBUILDER: Interpreting Maps

1. **Region** *Which countries were aligned with the European Allies?*
2. **Location** *Outside of Europe, where was World War I fought?*

China. They also captured Germany's Pacific island colonies. English and French troops attacked Germany's four African possessions. They seized control of three.

Elsewhere in Asia and Africa, the British and French recruited subjects in their colonies for the struggle. Fighting troops as well as laborers came from India, South Africa, Senegal, Egypt, Algeria, and Indochina. Many fought and died on the battlefield. Others worked to keep the front lines supplied. To be sure, some colonial subjects wanted nothing to do with their European rulers' conflicts. Others volunteered in the hope that service would lead to their independence. This was the view of Indian political leader Mohandas Gandhi, who supported Indian participation in the war. "If we would improve our status through the help and cooperation of the British," he wrote, "it was our duty to win their help by standing by them in their hour of need."

America Joins the Fight In 1917, the focus of the war shifted to the high seas. That year, the Germans intensified the submarine warfare that had raged in the Atlantic Ocean since shortly after the war began. In January 1917, the Germans announced that their submarines would sink without warning any ship in the waters around Britain. This policy was called **unrestricted submarine warfare**.

The Germans had tried this policy before. On May 7, 1915, a German submarine, or U-boat, had sunk the British passenger ship *Lusitania*. The attack left 1,198 people dead, including 128 U.S. citizens. Germany claimed that the ship had been carrying ammunition, which turned out to be true. Nevertheless, the American public was outraged. President Woodrow Wilson sent a strong protest to Germany. After two further attacks, the Germans finally agreed to stop attacking neutral and passenger ships.

Desperate for an advantage over the Allies, however, the Germans returned to unrestricted submarine warfare in 1917. They knew it might lead to war with the United States. They gambled that their naval blockade would starve Britain into defeat before the United States could mobilize. Ignoring warnings by President Wilson, German U-boats sank three American ships.

In February 1917, another German action pushed the United States closer to war. Officials intercepted a telegram written by Germany's foreign secretary, Arthur Zimmermann, stating that Germany would help Mexico "reconquer" the land it had lost to the United States if Mexico would ally itself with Germany.

The Zimmermann note simply proved to be the last straw. A large part of the American population already favored the Allies. In particular, America felt a bond with England. The two nations shared a common ancestry and language, as well as similar democratic institutions and legal systems. More important, America's economic ties with the Allies were far stronger than those with the Central Powers. On April 2, 1917, President Wilson asked Congress to declare war on Germany. The United States entered the war on the side of the Allies.

War Affects the Home Front

By the time the United States joined the Allies, the war had been raging for nearly three years. In those three years, Europe had lost more men in battle than in all the wars of the previous three centuries. The war had claimed the lives of millions and had changed countless lives forever. The Great War, as the conflict came to be known, affected everyone. It touched not only the soldiers in the trenches, but civilians as well.

Governments Wage Total War World War I soon became a **total war**. This meant that countries devoted all their resources to the war effort. In Britain, Germany, Austria, Russia, and France, the entire force of government was dedicated to winning the conflict. In each country, the wartime government took control of the economy. Governments told factories what to produce and how much.

Global Impact

The Influenza Epidemic

In the spring of 1918, a powerful new enemy emerged, threatening nations on each side of World War I. This "enemy" was a deadly strain of influenza. The Spanish flu, as it was popularly known, hit England and India in May. By the fall, it had spread through Europe, Russia, Asia, and to the United States.

The influenza epidemic killed soldiers and civilians alike. In India, at least 12 million people died of influenza. In Berlin, on a single day in October, 1,500 people died. In the end, this global epidemic was more destructive than the war itself, killing 20 million people worldwide.

▶ City officials and street cleaners in Chicago guard against the Spanish flu.

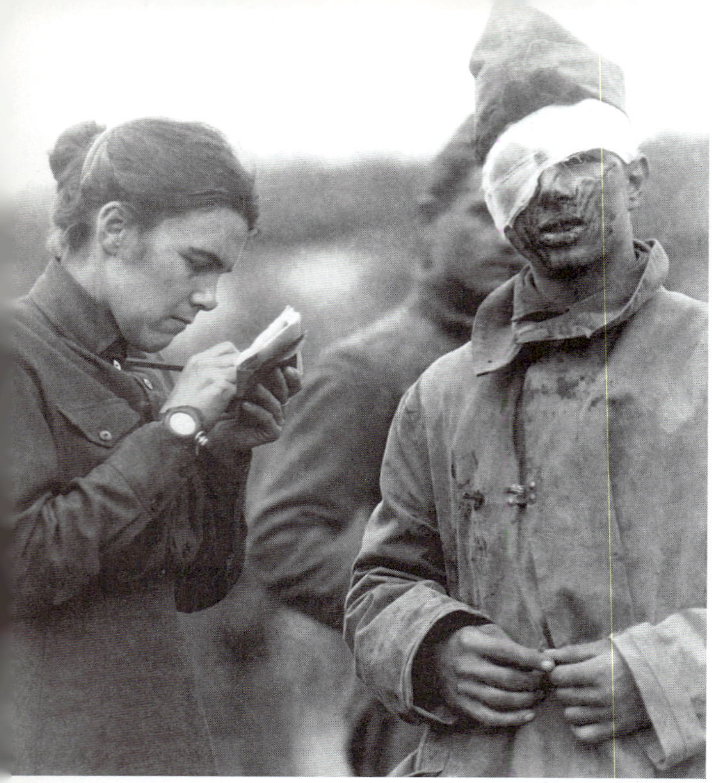

▲ A woman relief worker writes a letter home for a wounded soldier.

Numerous facilities were converted to munitions factories. Nearly every able-bodied civilian was put to work. Unemployment in many European countries all but disappeared.

So many goods were in short supply that governments turned to **rationing**. Under this system, people could buy only small amounts of those items that were also needed for the war effort. Eventually, rationing covered a wide range of goods, from butter to shoe leather.

Governments also suppressed antiwar activity, sometimes forcibly. In addition, they censored news about the war. Many leaders feared that honest reporting of the war would turn people against it. Governments also used **propaganda**, one-sided information designed to persuade, to keep up morale and support for the war. (A)

MAIN IDEA

Summarizing

(A) How did the governments of the warring nations fight a total war?

Women and the War Total war meant that governments turned to help from women as never before. Thousands of women replaced men in factories, offices, and shops. Women built tanks and munitions, plowed fields, paved streets, and ran hospitals. They also kept troops supplied with food, clothing, and weapons. Although most women left the work force when the war ended, they changed many people's views of what women were capable of doing.

Women also saw the horrors of war firsthand, working on or near the front lines as nurses. Here, American nurse Shirley Millard describes her experience with a soldier who had lost both eyes and feet:

A PRIMARY SOURCE

He moaned through the bandages that his head was splitting with pain. I gave him morphine. Suddenly aware of the fact that he had [numerous] wounds, he asked: "Sa-ay! What's the matter with my legs?" Reaching down to feel his legs before I could stop him, he uttered a heartbreaking scream. I held his hands firmly until the drug I had given him took effect.

SHIRLEY MILLARD, *I Saw Them Die*

The Allies Win the War

With the United States finally in the war, the balance, it seemed, was about to tip in the Allies' favor. Before that happened, however, events in Russia gave Germany a victory on the Eastern Front, and new hope for winning the conflict.

Russia Withdraws In March 1917, civil unrest in Russia—due in large part to war-related shortages of food and fuel—forced Czar Nicholas to step down. In his place a provisional government was established. The new government pledged to continue fighting the war. However, by 1917, nearly 5.5 million Russian soldiers had been wounded, killed, or taken prisoner. As a result, the war-weary Russian army refused to fight any longer.

Eight months after the new government took over, a revolution shook Russia (see Chapter 30). In November 1917, Communist leader Vladimir Ilyich Lenin seized power. Lenin insisted on ending his country's involvement in the war. One of his first acts was to offer Germany a truce. In March 1918, Germany and Russia signed the Treaty of Brest-Litovsk, which ended the war between them.

Analyzing Primary Sources

Allied View of Armistice

News of the armistice affected the Allied and Central powers differently. Here, a U.S. soldier named Harry Truman, who would go on to become president, recalls the day the fighting stopped.

PRIMARY SOURCE

Every single one of them [the French soldiers] had to march by my bed and salute and yell, "Vive President Wilson, Vive le capitaine d'artillerie américaine!" No sleep all night. The infantry fired Very pistols, sent up all the flares they could lay their hands on, fired rifles, pistols, whatever else would make noise, all night long.

HARRY TRUMAN, quoted in *The First World War*

German Reaction to Armistice

On the other side of the fighting line, German officer Herbert Sulzbach struggled to inform his troops of the war's end.

PRIMARY SOURCE

"Hostilities will cease as from 12 noon today." This was the order which I had to read out to my men. The war is over. . . . How we looked forward to *this* moment; how we used to picture it as the most splendid event of our lives; and here we are now, humbled, our souls torn and bleeding, and know that we've surrendered. Germany has surrendered to the Entente!

HERBERT SULZBACH, *With the German Guns*

DOCUMENT-BASED QUESTIONS

1. **Summarizing** *What is the main difference between these two excerpts?*
2. **Drawing Conclusions** *How did Herbert Sulzbach's vision of the armistice differ from what actually occurred?*

The Central Powers Collapse Russia's withdrawal from the war at last allowed Germany to send nearly all its forces to the Western Front. In March 1918, the Germans mounted one final, massive attack on the Allies in France. As in the opening weeks of the war, the German forces crushed everything in their path. By late May 1918, the Germans had again reached the Marne River. Paris was less than 40 miles away. Victory seemed within reach.

By this time, however, the German military had weakened. The effort to reach the Marne had exhausted men and supplies alike. Sensing this weakness, the Allies—with the aid of nearly 140,000 fresh U.S. troops—launched a counterattack. In July 1918, the Allies and Germans clashed at the Second Battle of the Marne. Leading the Allied attack were some 350 tanks that rumbled slowly forward, smashing through the German lines. With the arrival of 2 million more American troops, the Allied forces began to advance steadily toward Germany. **B**

MAIN IDEA

Comparing

B How was the Second Battle of the Marne similar to the first?

Soon, the Central Powers began to crumble. First the Bulgarians and then the Ottoman Turks surrendered. In October, revolution swept through Austria-Hungary. In Germany, soldiers mutinied, and the public turned on the kaiser.

On November 9, 1918, Kaiser Wilhelm II stepped down. Germany declared itself a republic. A representative of the new German government met with French Commander Marshal Foch in a railway car near Paris. The two signed an **armistice**, or an agreement to stop fighting. On November 11, World War I came to an end.

The Legacy of the War

World War I was, in many ways, a new kind of war. It involved the use of new technologies. It ushered in the notion of war on a grand and global scale. It also left behind a landscape of death and destruction such as was never before seen.

Both sides in World War I paid a tremendous price in terms of human life. About 8.5 million soldiers died as a result of the war. Another 21 million were wounded. In addition, the war led to the death of countless civilians by way of

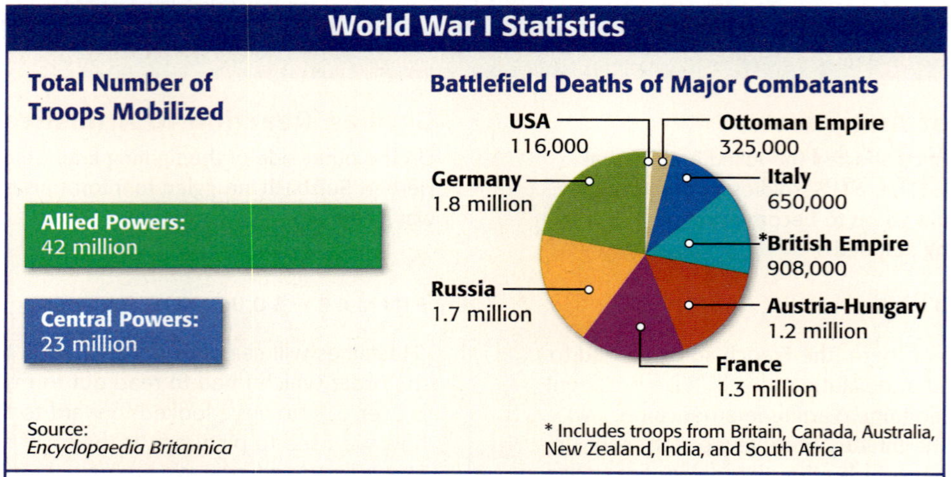

SKILLBUILDER: Interpreting Graphs

1. **Comparing** *Which Allied nation suffered the greatest number of battlefield deaths?*
2. **Analyzing Issues-***Which four nations accounted for about 75 percent of all battlefield deaths?*

starvation, disease, and slaughter. Taken together, these figures spelled tragedy—an entire generation of Europeans wiped out.

The war also had a devastating economic impact on Europe. The great conflict drained the treasuries of European countries. One account put the total cost of the war at $338 billion, a staggering amount for that time. The war also destroyed acres of farmland, as well as homes, villages, and towns.

The enormous suffering that resulted from the Great War left a deep mark on Western society as well. A sense of disillusionment settled over the survivors. The insecurity and despair that many people experienced are reflected in the art and literature of the time.

Another significant legacy of the war lay in its peace agreement. As you will read in the next section, the treaties to end World War I were forged after great debate and compromise. And while they sought to bring a new sense of security and peace to the world, they prompted mainly anger and resentment.

NEW YORK CORE CURRICULUM REVIEW

TERMS & NAMES 1. For each term or name, write a sentence explaining its significance.

- unrestricted submarine warfare
- total war
- rationing
- propaganda
- armistice

USING YOUR NOTES

2. Which effect do you think was most significant? Why?

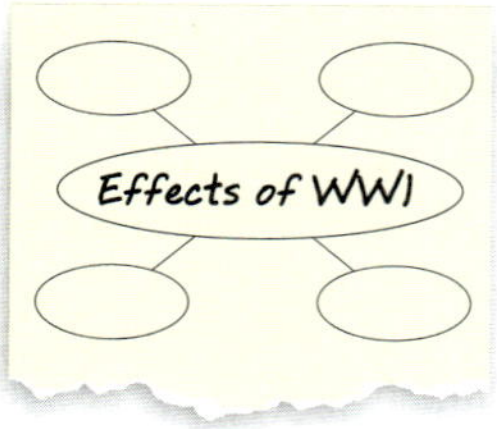

MAIN IDEAS

3. What factors helped prompt the United States to join the war for the Allies?
4. What role did women play in the war?
5. What was the significance of the Second Battle of the Marne?

CRITICAL THINKING & WRITING

6. **ANALYZING ISSUES** In what ways was World War I truly a global conflict?
7. **FORMING OPINIONS** Do you think governments are justified in censoring war news? Why or why not?
8. **DRAWING CONCLUSIONS** Which of the non-European countries had the greatest impact on the war effort? Explain.
9. **WRITING ACTIVITY** ECONOMICS Write a **paragraph** explaining how the concept of total war affected the warring nations' economies.

CONNECT TO TODAY CREATING A GRAPHIC

Using the library and other resources, compare the role of women in combat today in any two countries. Display your comparison in a **chart** or other type of **graphic**.

INTERACTIVE

Views of War

When World War I broke out, Europe had not experienced a war involving all the major powers for nearly a century, since Napoleon's defeat in 1815. As a result, people had an unrealistic view of warfare. Many expected the war to be short and romantic. Many men enlisted in the army because of patriotism or out of a desire to defend certain institutions. What the soldiers experienced changed their view of war forever.

A PRIMARY SOURCE

Woodrow Wilson

On April 2, 1917, President Wilson asked Congress to declare war so that the United States could enter World War I. This excerpt from his speech gives some of his reasons.

The world must be made safe for democracy. Its peace must be planted upon the tested foundations of political liberty. We have no selfish ends to serve. We desire no conquest, no dominion. We seek no indemnities for ourselves, no material compensation for the sacrifice we shall freely make. We are but one of the champions of the rights of mankind. We shall be satisfied when those rights have been made as secure as the faith and the freedom of nations can make them.

B FICTION

Erich Maria Remarque

In the German novel *All Quiet on the Western Front*, Erich Maria Remarque draws upon his own wartime experience of trench warfare.

No one would believe that in this howling waste there could still be men; but steel helmets now appear on all sides of the trench, and fifty yards from us a machine-gun is already in position and barking.

The wire entanglements are torn to pieces. Yet they offer some obstacle. We see the storm-troops coming. Our artillery opens fire. . . .

I see [a French soldier], his face upturned, fall into a wire cradle. His body collapses, his hands remain suspended as though he were praying. Then his body drops clean away and only his hands with the stumps of his arms, shot off, now hang in the wire.

C POETRY

Wilfred Owen

The English poet Wilfred Owen was killed in the trenches just one week before World War I ended. This excerpt from his poem "Dulce et Decorum Est" describes a gas attack.

Gas! GAS! Quick, boys!—An ecstasy of fumbling,
Fitting the clumsy helmets just in time;
But someone still was yelling out and stumbling,
And flound'ring like a man in fire or lime . . .
Dim, through the misty panes and thick green light,
As under a green sea, I saw him drowning.

In all my dreams, before my helpless sight,
He plunges at me, guttering, choking, drowning.

D PRIMARY SOURCE

Maurice Neumont

France, 1918

This French poster is titled, "They Shall Not Pass, 1914–1918." Translated into English, the text at the bottom reads, "Twice I have stood fast and conquered on the Marne, my brother civilian. A deceptive 'peace offensive' will attack you in your turn; like me you must stand firm and conquer. Be strong and shrewd—beware of Boche [German] hypocrisy."

Document-Based QUESTIONS

1. What reasons does Woodrow Wilson (Source A) give for entering the war?
2. What emotions does the French poster (Source D) try to arouse?
3. Judging from Sources B and C, what was it like for the average soldier in the trenches? Explain how you think such experiences affected the average soldier's view of war.

A Flawed Peace

CONNECT TO THE NEW YORK STATE CORE CURRICULUM

Unit 6.A.3. Impacts
Unit 6.C.2. Treaty of Versailles and the League of Nations

TERMS & NAMES

- Woodrow Wilson
- Georges Clemenceau
- Fourteen Points
- self-determination
- Treaty of Versailles
- League of Nations

SETTING THE STAGE World War I was over. The killing had stopped. The terms of peace, however, still had to be worked out. On January 18, 1919, a conference to establish those terms began at the Palace of Versailles, outside Paris. Attending the talks, known as the Paris Peace Conference, were delegates representing 32 countries. For one year, this conference would be the scene of vigorous, often bitter debate. The Allied powers struggled to solve their conflicting aims in various peace treaties.

TAKING NOTES
Clarifying Use a chart to record the reaction by various groups to the Treaty of Versailles.

Reaction to Treaty	
Germany	
Africans & Asians	
Italy & Japan	

The Allies Meet and Debate

Despite representatives from numerous countries, the meeting's major decisions were hammered out by a group known as the Big Four: **Woodrow Wilson** of the United States, **Georges Clemenceau** of France, David Lloyd George of Great Britain, and Vittorio Orlando of Italy. Russia, in the grip of civil war, was not represented. Neither were Germany and its allies.

Wilson's Plan for Peace In January 1918, while the war was still raging, President Wilson had drawn up a series of peace proposals. Known as the **Fourteen Points**, they outlined a plan for achieving a just and lasting peace.

The first four points included an end to secret treaties, freedom of the seas, free trade, and reduced national armies and navies. The fifth goal was the adjustment of colonial claims with fairness toward colonial peoples. The sixth through thirteenth points were specific suggestions for changing borders and creating new nations. The guiding idea behind these points was **self-determination**. This meant allowing people to decide for themselves under what government they wished to live.

Finally, the fourteenth point proposed a "general association of nations" that would protect "great and small states alike." This reflected Wilson's hope for an organization that could peacefully negotiate solutions to world conflicts.

The Versailles Treaty As the Paris Peace Conference opened, Britain and France showed little sign of agreeing to Wilson's vision of peace. Both nations were concerned with national security. They also wanted to strip Germany of its war-making power.

The differences in French, British, and U.S. aims led to heated arguments among the nations' leaders. Finally a compromise was reached. The **Treaty of Versailles** between Germany and the Allied powers was signed on June 28, 1919, five years to the day after Franz Ferdinand's assassination in Sarajevo. Adopting Wilson's fourteenth point, the treaty created a **League of Nations**. The league was to be an international association whose goal would be to keep peace among nations.

The treaty also punished Germany. The defeated nation lost substantial territory and had severe restrictions placed on its military operations. As tough as these provisions were, the harshest was Article 231. It was also known as the "war guilt" clause. It placed sole responsibility for the war on Germany's shoulders. As a result, Germany had to pay reparations to the Allies.

Vocabulary
Reparations is money paid by a defeated nation to compensate for damage or injury during a war.

All of Germany's territories in Africa and the Pacific were declared mandates, or territories to be administered by the League of Nations. Under the peace agreement, the Allies would govern the mandates until they were judged ready for independence.

A Troubled Treaty

The Versailles treaty was just one of five treaties negotiated by the Allies. In the end, these agreements created feelings of bitterness and betrayal—among the victors and the defeated.

The Creation of New Nations The Western powers signed separate peace treaties in 1919 and 1920 with each of the other defeated nations: Austria-Hungary, Bulgaria, and the Ottoman Empire. These treaties, too, led to huge land losses for the Central Powers. Several new countries were created out of the Austro-Hungarian Empire. Austria, Hungary, Czechoslovakia, and Yugoslavia were all recognized as independent nations.

The Ottoman Turks were forced to give up almost all of their former empire. They retained only the territory that is today the country of Turkey. The Allies carved up the lands that the Ottomans lost in Southwest Asia into mandates rather than independent nations. Palestine, Iraq, and Transjordan came under British control; Syria and Lebanon went to France.

Russia, which had left the war early, suffered land losses as well. Romania and Poland both gained Russian territory. Finland, Estonia, Latvia, and Lithuania, formerly part of Russia, became independent nations.

"A Peace Built on Quicksand" In the end, the Treaty of Versailles did little to build a lasting peace. For one thing, the United States—considered after the war to be the dominant nation in the world—ultimately rejected the treaty. Many Americans objected to the settlement and especially to President Wilson's League of Nations. Americans believed that the United States' best hope for peace was to stay out of European affairs. The United States worked out a separate treaty with Germany and its allies several years later.

History Makers

Woodrow Wilson
1856–1924

Wilson was tall and thin and often in poor health. He suffered from terrible indigestion and sometimes had to use a stomach pump on himself. A scholarly man, Wilson once served as president of Princeton University in New Jersey.

Passionate about international peace, he took on the U.S. Senate after it vowed to reject the Treaty of Versailles. During the political battle, he suffered a stroke that disabled him for the rest of his term.

Georges Clemenceau
1841–1929

The near opposite of Wilson, Clemenceau had a compact physique and a combative style that earned him the nickname "Tiger." He had worked as a physician and journalist before entering the political arena.

Determined to punish Germany, Clemenceau rarely agreed with Wilson and his larger quest for world peace. He once remarked of Wilson, "He thinks he is another Jesus Christ come upon earth to reform men."

INTEGRATED TECHNOLOGY

RESEARCH LINKS For more on Woodrow Wilson and Georges Clemenceau, go to **classzone.com**

Europe Pre-World War I

Europe Post-World War I

GEOGRAPHY SKILLBUILDER: Interpreting Maps

1. **Region** *Which Central Powers nation appears to have lost the most territory?*
2. **Location** *On which nation's former lands were most of the new countries created?*

The Treaty of Versailles: Major Provisions

League of Nations	Territorial Losses	Military Restrictions	War Guilt
• International peace organization; enemy and neutral nations initially excluded • Germany and Russia excluded	• Germany returns Alsace-Lorraine to France; French border extended to west bank of Rhine River • Germany surrenders all of its overseas colonies in Africa and the Pacific	• Limits set on the size of the German army • Germany prohibited from importing or manufacturing weapons or war material • Germany forbidden to build or buy submarines or have an air force	• Sole responsibility for the war placed on Germany's shoulders • Germany forced to pay the Allies $33 billion in reparations over 30 years

SKILLBUILDER: Interpreting Charts

1. **Analyzing Issues** *In what ways did the treaty punish Germany?*
2. **Clarifying** *What two provinces were returned to France as a result of the treaty?*

In addition, the treaty with Germany, in particular the war-guilt clause, left a legacy of bitterness and hatred in the hearts of the German people. Other countries felt cheated and betrayed by the peace settlements as well. Throughout Africa and Asia, people in the mandated territories were angry at the way the Allies disregarded their desire for independence. The European powers, it seemed to them, merely talked about the principle of national self-determination. European colonialism, disguised as the mandate system, continued in Asia and Africa. **A**

MAIN IDEA

Analyzing Issues

A What complaints did various mandated countries voice about the Treaty of Versailles?

Some Allied powers, too, were embittered by the outcome. Both Japan and Italy, which had entered the war to gain territory, had gained less than they wanted. Lacking the support of the United States, and later other world powers, the League of Nations was in no position to take action on these and other complaints. The settlements at Versailles represented, as one observer noted, "a peace built on quicksand." Indeed, that quicksand eventually would give way. In a little more than two decades, the treaties' legacy of bitterness would help plunge the world into another catastrophic war.

NEW YORK CORE CURRICULUM REVIEW

TERMS & NAMES 1. For each term or name, write a sentence explaining its significance.

• Woodrow Wilson • Georges Clemenceau • Fourteen Points • self-determination • Treaty of Versailles • League of Nations

USING YOUR NOTES

2. Which group was most justified in its reaction to the treaty? Why?

Reaction to Treaty	
Germany	
Africans & Asians	
Italy & Japan	

MAIN IDEAS

3. What was the goal of Woodrow Wilson's Fourteen Points?
4. What was the "war guilt" clause in the Treaty of Versailles?
5. Why did the United States reject the Treaty of Versailles?

CRITICAL THINKING & WRITING

6. **FORMING OPINIONS** Were the Versailles treaties fair? Consider all the nations affected.
7. **ANALYZING MOTIVES** Why might the European Allies have been more interested in punishing Germany than in creating a lasting peace?
8. **EVALUATING DECISIONS** Was the United States right to reject the Treaty of Versailles? Why or why not?
9. **WRITING ACTIVITY** POWER AND AUTHORITY -Create a list of five **interview questions** a reporter might ask Wilson or Clemenceau about the Paris Peace Conference. Then write the possible **answers** to those questions.

INTEGRATED TECHNOLOGY **INTERNET ACTIVITY**

Use the Internet to explore a recent achievement or activity by the United Nations, the modern-day equivalent of the League of Nations. Present your findings in a brief **oral report** to the class.

INTERNET KEYWORD
United Nations

Chapter 29 Assessment

VISUAL SUMMARY

The Great War

Long-Term Causes

- Nationalism spurs competition among European nations.
- Imperialism deepens national rivalries.
- Militarism leads to large standing armies.
- The alliance system divides Europe into two rival camps.

Immediate Causes

- The assassination of Archduke Franz Ferdinand in June 1914 prompts Austria to declare war on Serbia.
- The alliance system requires nations to support their allies.

Immediate Effects

- A generation of Europeans is killed or wounded.
- Dynasties fall in Germany, Austria-Hungary, and Russia.
- New countries are created.
- The League of Nations is established to help promote peace.

Long-Term Effects

- Many nations feel bitter and betrayed by the peace settlements.
- Forces that helped cause the war—nationalism, competition—remain.

TERMS & NAMES

For each term below, briefly explain its connection to World War I.

1. Triple Alliance
2. Triple Entente
3. Central Powers
4. Allies
5. total war
6. armistice
7. Fourteen Points
8. Treaty of Versailles

MAIN IDEAS

Marching Toward War Section 1 (pages 841–844)

9. How did nationalism, imperialism, and militarism help set the stage for World War I?
10. Why was the Balkans known as "the powder keg of Europe"?

Europe Plunges into War Section 2 (pages 845–850)

11. Why was the first Battle of the Marne considered so significant?
12. Where was the Western Front? the Eastern Front?
13. What were the characteristics of trench warfare?

A Global Conflict Section 3 (pages 851–857)

14. What was the purpose of the Gallipoli campaign?
15. What factors prompted the United States to enter the war?
16. In what ways was World War I a total war?

A Flawed Peace Section 4 (pages 858–861)

17. What was the purpose of the League of Nations?
18. What was the mandate system, and why did it leave many groups feeling betrayed?

CRITICAL THINKING

1. USING YOUR NOTES

Trace the formation of the two major alliance systems that dominated Europe on the eve of World War I by providing the event that corresponds with each date on the chart.

1879 — 1882 — 1887 — 1890 — 1892,1894 — 1907

2. EVALUATING DECISIONS

POWER AND AUTHORITY How did the Treaty of Versailles reflect the different personalities and agendas of the men in power at the end of World War I?

3. CLARIFYING

ECONOMICS How did the war have both a positive and negative impact on the economies of Europe?

4. ANALYZING ISSUES

One British official commented that the Allied victory in World War I had been "bought so dear [high in price] as to be indistinguishable from defeat." What did he mean by this statement? Use examples from the text to support your answer.

NEW YORK STATE REGENTS EXAM PRACTICE

Use the quotation about Germany's sinking of the British passenger ship *Lusitania* and your knowledge of world history to answer questions 1 and 2.
Additional Test Practice, pp. S1–S33.

PRIMARY SOURCE

The responsibility for the death of so many American citizens, which is deeply regretted by everyone in Germany, in a large measure falls upon the American government. It could not admit that Americans were being used as shields for English contraband [smuggled goods]. In this regard America had permitted herself to be misused in a disgraceful manner by England. And now, instead of calling England to account, she sends a note to the German government.

from *Vossische Zeitung,* May 18, 1915

1 Which of the following statements best describes the sentiments of the writer?
(1) The sinking of the Lusitania was a tragic mistake.
(2) America was right to blame Germany for the attack.
(3) The American government failed to protect its citizens.
(4) England should keep its vessels off the Atlantic Ocean.

2 The sinking of the Lusitania ultimately played a role in prompting Germany to
(1) abandon the Schlieffen Plan
(2) halt unrestricted submarine warfare
(3) declare war on the United States
(4) begin a widespread rationing program

Use this anti-German (Hun) World War I poster and your knowledge of world history to answer question 3.

3 Which of the following best describes the depiction of the German soldier in this poster?
(1) noble and courageous
(2) weak and disorganized
(3) cruel and barbaric
(4) dangerous and cunning

INTEGRATED TECHNOLOGY
TEST PRACTICE Go to **classzone.com**
- Diagnostic tests
- Strategies
- Tutorials
- Additional practice

ALTERNATIVE ASSESSMENT

1. Interact *with* History

On page 840, you examined whether it is always right to support an ally or friend. Now that you have read the chapter, reevaluate your decision. If you chose to follow your ally into World War I, do you still feel it was the right thing to do? Why or why not? If you decided to stay out of war, what are your feelings now? Discuss your opinions with a small group.

2. WRITING ABOUT HISTORY

SCIENCE AND TECHNOLOGY Explain in several **paragraphs** which one of the new or enhanced weapons of World War I you think had the greatest impact on the war and why. Consider the following:

- which weapon might have had the widest use
- which weapon might have inflicted the greatest damage on the enemy

INTEGRATED TECHNOLOGY

Conducting Internet Research

While World War I was extremely costly, staying prepared for the possibility of war today is also expensive. Work in groups of three or four to research the defense budgets of several of the world's nations. Have each group member be responsible for one country. Go to the *Web Research Guide* at **classzone.com** to learn about conducting research on the Internet. Use your research to

- examine how much money each country spends on defense, as well as what percentage of the overall budget such spending represents.
- create a large comparison chart of the countries' budgets.
- discuss with your classmates whether the amounts spent for military and defense are justified.

Present your research to the class. Include a list of your Web resources.

CHAPTER 30

Revolution and Nationalism, 1900–1939

Previewing Main Ideas

REVOLUTION Widespread social unrest troubled China and Russia during the late 1800s and early 1900s. Eventually revolutions erupted.

Geography *Study the time line. In what years did revolutions take place in China and in Russia?*

POWER AND AUTHORITY New nations appeared during the 1920s and 1930s in the former Ottoman Empire in Southwest Asia. These nations adopted a variety of government styles—from a republic to a monarchy.

Geography *According to the map, which new nations in Southwest Asia emerged from the former Ottoman Empire?*

EMPIRE BUILDING Nationalist movements in Southwest Asia, India, and China successfully challenged the British, Ottoman, and Chinese Empires.

Geography *According to the map, which European nations still control large areas of Southwest Asia?*

NEW YORK CORE CURRICULUM FOCUS

- Social unrest in Russia led to revolution in 1917 and the birth of the Soviet Union.
- Stalin established a totalitarian state in the Soviet Union when he came to power.

INTEGRATED TECHNOLOGY

eEdition
- Interactive Maps
- Interactive Visuals
- Interactive Primary Sources

INTERNET RESOURCES
Go to **classzone.com** for:
- Research Links
- Internet Activities
- Primary Sources
- Chapter Quiz
- Maps
- Test Practice
- Current Events

EUROPE AND ASIA

1905 Russian workers protest for better conditions.

1911 ◀ Chinese Nationalists oust the last Qing emperor. (Emperor P'u-i)

1917 Russian Bolsheviks rebel in October Revolution.

1900

1910

WORLD

1910 ◀ Mexican Revolution begins.

1914–1918 World War I

1920
Gandhi leads Indian campaign of civil disobedience. ▶

1923
Mustafa Kemal transforms Turkey into a republic.

1929
Stalin becomes dictator of Soviet Union.

1934
Mao Zedong heads Long March. ▶

1920 | 1930 | 1940

1922
Mussolini comes to power in Italy.

1929
U.S. stock market crashes.

1933
Hitler is named chancellor of Germany. ▶

Interact *with* History

How do you resist oppressive rule–with violent or nonviolent action?

You believe that the policies of your government are unjust and oppressive. The policies favor a small, wealthy class—but the vast majority of people are poor with few rights. The government has failed to tackle economic, social, and political problems. Many of your friends are joining revolutionary groups that plan to overthrow the government by force. Others support nonviolent methods of change, such as peaceful strikes, protests, and refusal to obey unjust laws. You wonder which course of action to choose.

▼ **Mao Zedong**, Communist leader, believed revolution would solve China's problems.

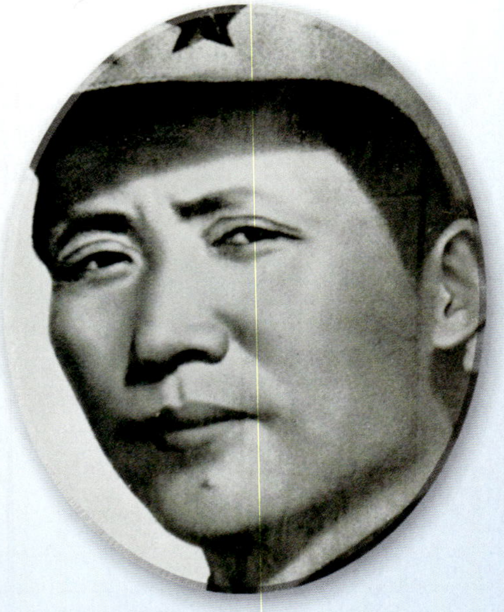

"Political power grows out of the barrel of a gun."

▼ **Mohandas K. Gandhi** became the leader of the independence movement to free India of British rule.

"Victory attained by violence is tantamount to a defeat, for it is momentary."

EXAMINING *the* ISSUES

- **How might armed and powerful opponents respond to groups committed to nonviolent action?**
- **Which strategy might prove more successful and bring more long-lasting consequences? Why?**

As a class, discuss these questions. In your discussion, consider what you have learned about the strategies revolutionaries use to accomplish change. As you read about the revolutions and independence movements, see which strategy was successful.

1

Revolutions in Russia

CONNECT TO THE NEW YORK STATE CORE CURRICULUM

Unit 6.B.3. March Revolution and provisional government
Unit 6.B.5. V.I. Lenin's rule in Russia

TERMS & NAMES

- proletariat
- Bolsheviks
- Lenin
- Rasputin
- provisional government
- soviet
- Communist Party
- Joseph Stalin

SETTING THE STAGE-The Russian Revolution was like a firecracker with a very long fuse. The explosion came in 1917, yet the fuse had been burning for nearly a century. The cruel, oppressive rule of most 19th-century czars caused widespread social unrest for decades. Army officers revolted in 1825. Secret revolutionary groups plotted to overthrow the government. In 1881, revolutionaries angry over the slow pace of political change assassinated the reform-minded czar, Alexander II. Russia was heading toward a full-scale revolution.

TAKING NOTES

Following Chronological Order Create a time line to show major events in the changing of Russian government.

1894 — 1922

Czars Resist Change

In 1881, Alexander III succeeded his father, Alexander II, and halted all reforms in Russia. Like his grandfather Nicholas I, Alexander III clung to the principles of autocracy, a form of government in which he had total power. Anyone who questioned the absolute authority of the czar, worshiped outside the Russian Orthodox Church, or spoke a language other than Russian was labeled dangerous.

Czars Continue Autocratic Rule To wipe out revolutionaries, Alexander III used harsh measures. He imposed strict censorship codes on published materials and written documents, including private letters. His secret police carefully watched both secondary schools and universities. Teachers had to send detailed reports on every student. Political prisoners were sent to Siberia, a remote region of eastern Russia.

To establish a uniform Russian culture, Alexander III oppressed other national groups within Russia. He made Russian the official language of the empire and forbade the use of minority languages, such as Polish, in schools. Alexander made Jews the target of persecution. A wave of pogroms—organized violence against Jews—broke out in many parts of Russia. Police and soldiers stood by and watched Russian citizens loot and destroy Jewish homes, stores, and synagogues.

When Nicholas II became czar in 1894, he continued the tradition of Russian autocracy. Unfortunately, it blinded him to the changing conditions of his times.

▼ Alexander III turned Russia into a police state, teeming with spies and informers.

Russia Industrializes

Rapid industrialization changed the face of the Russian economy. The number of factories more than doubled between 1863 and 1900. Still, Russia lagged behind the industrial nations of western Europe. In the 1890s, Nicholas's most capable minister launched a program to move the country forward. To finance the buildup of Russian industries, the government sought foreign investors and raised taxes. These steps boosted the growth of heavy industry, particularly steel. By around 1900, Russia had become the world's fourth-ranking producer of steel. Only the United States, Germany, and Great Britain produced more steel.

Vocabulary
minister: person in charge of an area of government, such as finance

With the help of British and French investors, work began on the world's longest continuous rail line—the Trans-Siberian Railway. Begun in 1891, the railway was not completed until 1916. It connected European Russia in the west with Russian ports on the Pacific Ocean in the east.

The Revolutionary Movement Grows Rapid industrialization stirred discontent among the people of Russia. The growth of factories brought new problems, such as grueling working conditions, miserably low wages, and child labor. The government outlawed trade unions. To try to improve their lives, workers unhappy with their low standard of living and lack of political power organized strikes. **A**

MAIN IDEA
Analyzing Causes
A Why did industrialization in Russia lead to unrest?

As a result of all of these factors, several revolutionary movements began to grow and compete for power. A group that followed the views of Karl Marx successfully established a following in Russia. The Marxist revolutionaries believed that the industrial class of workers would overthrow the czar. These workers would then form "a dictatorship of the proletariat." This meant that the **proletariat**—the workers—would rule the country.

In 1903, Russian Marxists split into two groups over revolutionary tactics. The more moderate Mensheviks (MEHN•shuh•vihks) wanted a broad base of popular support for the revolution. The more radical **Bolsheviks** (BOHL•shuh•vihks) supported a small number of committed revolutionaries willing to sacrifice everything for change.

The major leader of the Bolsheviks was Vladimir Ilyich Ulyanov (ool•YAH•nuhf). He adopted the name of **Lenin**. He had an engaging personality and was an excellent organizer. He was also ruthless. These traits would ultimately help him gain command of the Bolsheviks. In the early 1900s, Lenin fled to western Europe to avoid arrest by the czarist regime. From there he maintained contact with other Bolsheviks. Lenin then waited until he could safely return to Russia.

History Makers

V.I. Lenin
1870–1924

In 1887, when he was 17, Lenin's brother, Alexander, was hanged for plotting to kill the czar. Legend has it that this event turned Lenin into a revolutionary.

Though Alexander's execution influenced Lenin, he already harbored ill feelings against the government. By the early 1900s, he planned to overthrow the czar. After the revolution in 1917, Russians revered him as the "Father of the Revolution."

Following Lenin's death in 1924, the government placed his tomb in Red Square in Moscow. His preserved body, encased in a bulletproof, glass-topped coffin, is still on display. Many Russians today, though, favor moving Lenin's corpse away from public view.

INTEGRATED TECHNOLOGY
RESEARCH LINKS For more on V. I. Lenin, go to **classzone.com**

Crises at Home and Abroad

The revolutionaries would not have to wait long to realize their visions. Between 1904 and 1917, Russia faced a series of crises. These events showed the czar's weakness and paved the way for revolution.

The Russo-Japanese War In the late 1800s, Russia and Japan competed for control of Korea and Manchuria. The two nations signed a series of agreements over the territories, but Russia broke them. Japan retaliated by attacking the Russians at Port Arthur, Manchuria, in February 1904. News of repeated Russian losses sparked unrest at home and led to a revolt in the midst of the war.

▲ Soldiers fired on unarmed workers demonstrating at the czar's Winter Palace on "Bloody Sunday."

Bloody Sunday: The Revolution of 1905 On January 22, 1905, about 200,000 workers and their families approached the czar's Winter Palace in St. Petersburg. They carried a petition asking for better working conditions, more personal freedom, and an elected national legislature. Nicholas II's generals ordered soldiers to fire on the crowd. More than 1,000 were wounded and several hundred were killed. Russians quickly named the event "Bloody Sunday."

Bloody Sunday provoked a wave of strikes and violence that spread across the country. In October 1905, Nicholas reluctantly promised more freedom. He approved the creation of the Duma (DOO•muh)—Russia's first parliament. The first Duma met in May 1906. Its leaders were moderates who wanted Russia to become a constitutional monarchy similar to Britain. But because he was hesitant to share his power, the czar dissolved the Duma after ten weeks.

Vocabulary
constitutional monarchy: a form of government in which a single ruler heads the state and shares authority with elected lawmakers

World War I: The Final Blow In 1914, Nicholas II made the fateful decision to drag Russia into World War I. Russia was unprepared to handle the military and economic costs. Its weak generals and poorly equipped troops were no match for the German army. German machine guns mowed down advancing Russians by the thousands. Defeat followed defeat. Before a year had passed, more than 4 million Russian soldiers had been killed, wounded, or taken prisoner. As in the Russo-Japanese War, Russia's involvement in World War I revealed the weaknesses of czarist rule and military leadership.

In 1915, Nicholas moved his headquarters to the war front. From there, he hoped to rally his discouraged troops to victory. His wife, Czarina Alexandra, ran the government while he was away. She ignored the czar's chief advisers. Instead, she fell under the influence of the mysterious **Rasputin** (ras•PYOO•tihn). A self-described "holy man," he claimed to have magical healing powers.

Nicholas and Alexandra's son, Alexis, suffered from hemophilia, a life-threatening disease. Rasputin seemed to ease the boy's symptoms. To show her gratitude, Alexandra allowed Rasputin to make key political decisions. He opposed reform measures and obtained powerful positions for his friends. In 1916, a group of nobles murdered Rasputin. They feared his increasing role in government affairs.

Meanwhile, on the war front Russian soldiers mutinied, deserted, or ignored orders. On the home front, food and fuel supplies were dwindling. Prices were wildly inflated. People from all classes were clamoring for change and an end to the war. Neither Nicholas nor Alexandra proved capable of tackling these enormous problems.

The March Revolution

In March 1917, women textile workers in Petrograd led a citywide strike. In the next five days, riots flared up over shortages of bread and fuel. Nearly 200,000 workers swarmed the streets shouting, "Down with the autocracy!" and "Down with the war!" At first the soldiers obeyed orders to shoot the rioters but later sided with them.

The Czar Steps Down The local protest exploded into a general uprising—the March Revolution. It forced Czar Nicholas II to abdicate his throne. A year later revolutionaries executed Nicholas and his family. The three-century czarist rule of the Romanovs finally collapsed. The March Revolution succeeded in bringing down the czar. Yet it failed to set up a strong government to replace his regime.

Leaders of the Duma established a **provisional government**, or temporary government. Alexander Kerensky headed it. His decision to continue fighting in World War I cost him the support of both soldiers and civilians. As the war dragged on, conditions inside Russia worsened. Angry peasants demanded land. City workers grew more radical. Socialist revolutionaries, competing for power, formed soviets. **Soviets** were local councils consisting of workers, peasants, and soldiers. In many cities, the soviets had more influence than the provisional government. (B)

MAIN IDEA

Making Inferences

(B) Why did Kerensky's decision to continue fighting the war cost him the support of the Russian people?

Lenin Returns to Russia The Germans believed that Lenin and his Bolshevik supporters would stir unrest in Russia and hurt the Russian war effort against Germany. They arranged Lenin's return to Russia after many years of exile. Traveling in a sealed railway boxcar, Lenin reached Petrograd in April 1917.

The Bolshevik Revolution

Lenin and the Bolsheviks soon gained control of the Petrograd soviet, as well as the soviets in other major Russian cities. By the fall of 1917, people in the cities were rallying to the call, "All power to the soviets." Lenin's slogan—"Peace, Land, and Bread"—gained widespread appeal. Lenin decided to take action.

The Provisional Government Topples In November 1917, without warning, armed factory workers stormed the Winter Palace in Petrograd. Calling themselves

GEOGRAPHY SKILLBUILDER: Interpreting Maps

1. **Region** *What was the extent (north to south, east to west) of the Bolshevik territory in 1919?*
2. **Region** *Which European countries had territory that was no longer within Russian boundaries because of the Brest-Litovsk treaty?*

the Bolshevik Red Guards, they took over government offices and arrested the leaders of the provisional government. Kerensky and his colleagues disappeared almost as quickly as the czarist regime they had replaced.

Bolsheviks in Power Within days after the Bolshevik takeover, Lenin ordered that all farmland be distributed among the peasants. Lenin and the Bolsheviks gave control of factories to the workers. The Bolshevik government also signed a truce with Germany to stop all fighting and began peace talks.

In March 1918, Russia and Germany signed the Treaty of Brest-Litovsk. Russia surrendered a large part of its territory to Germany and its allies. The humiliating terms of this treaty triggered widespread anger among many Russians. They objected to the Bolsheviks and their policies and to the murder of the royal family.

▲ Red Army forces were victorious in the two-year civil war against the White Army.

Civil War Rages in Russia The Bolsheviks now faced a new challenge—stamping out their enemies at home. Their opponents formed the White Army. The White Army was made up of very different groups. There were those groups who supported the return to rule by the czar, others who wanted democratic government, and even socialists who opposed Lenin's style of socialism. Only the desire to defeat the Bolsheviks united the White Army. The groups barely cooperated with each other. At one point there were three White Armies fighting against the Bolsheviks' Red Army.

The revolutionary leader, Leon Trotsky, expertly commanded the Bolshevik Red Army. From 1918 to 1920, civil war raged in Russia. Several Western nations, including the United States, sent military aid and forces to Russia to help the White Army. However, they were of little help.

Causes and Effects of Two Russian Revolutions, 1917

Causes: Czarist Russia	**Effects/Causes:** March Revolution	**Effects:** Bolshevik Revolution
• Czar's leadership was weak.	• Czar abdicates.	• Provisional government is overthrown.
• Revolutionary agitation challenges the government.	• Provisional government takes over. • Lenin and soviets gain power.	• Bolsheviks take over.
• Widespread discontent found among all classes.	• Russia stays in World War I.	• Bolsheviks sign peace treaty with Germany and leave World War I. • Civil war begins in Russia.

SKILLBUILDER: Interpreting Charts

1. **Analyzing Causes** *What role did World War I play in the two revolutions?*
2. **Recognizing Effects** *Why were the effects of the March Revolution also causes of the Bolshevik Revolution?*

Russia's civil war proved far more deadly than the earlier revolutions. Around 14 million Russians died in the three-year struggle and in the famine that followed. The destruction and loss of life from fighting, hunger, and a worldwide flu epidemic left Russia in chaos. In the end, the Red Army crushed all opposition. The victory showed that the Bolsheviks were able both to seize power and to maintain it. (C)

MAIN IDEA

Identifying Problems

(C) What problems did Lenin and the Bolsheviks face after the revolution?

Comparing World Revolutions In its immediate and long-term effects, the Russian Revolution was more like the French Revolution than the American Revolution. The American Revolution expanded English political ideas into a constitutional government that built on many existing structures. In contrast, both the French and Russian revolutions attempted to destroy existing social and political structures. Revolutionaries in France and Russia used violence and terror to control people. France became a constitutional monarchy for a time, but the Russian Revolution established a state-controlled society that lasted for decades.

Lenin Restores Order

War and revolution destroyed the Russian economy. Trade was at a standstill. Industrial production dropped, and many skilled workers fled to other countries. Lenin turned to reviving the economy and restructuring the government.

New Economic Policy In March 1921, Lenin temporarily put aside his plan for a state-controlled economy. Instead, he resorted to a small-scale version of capitalism called the New Economic Policy (NEP). The reforms under the NEP allowed peasants to sell their surplus crops instead of turning them over to the government. The government kept control of major industries, banks, and means of communication, but it let some small factories, businesses, and farms operate under private ownership. The government also encouraged foreign investment.

> Analyzing Key Concepts

Communism

Communism is a political and economic system of organization. In theory, property is owned by the community and all citizens share in the common wealth according to their need. In practice, this was difficult to achieve.

German philosopher Karl Marx saw communism as the end result of an essential historical process. Russian revolutionary Vladimir Lenin built on Marx's theories and sought ways of applying those theories. Ultimately, however, Lenin's communist state—the Union of Soviet Socialist Republics (USSR)—became a one-party, totalitarian system. This chart compares how Marx and Lenin viewed communism.

SKILLBUILDER: Interpreting Charts

Comparing and Contrasting *How did Lenin's ideas about communism differ from those of Marx?*

Evolution of Communist Thought

Marx	Lenin
• History was the story of class struggle.	• History was the story of class struggle.
• The struggle Marx saw was between capitalists and the proletariat, or the workers.	• The struggle Lenin saw was capitalists against the proletariat and the peasants.
• The proletariat's numbers would become so great and their condition so poor that a spontaneous revolution would occur.	• The proletariat and the peasants were not capable of leading a revolution and needed the guidance of professional revolutionaries.
• The revolution would end with a "dictatorship of the proletariat"—the communal ownership of wealth. 	• After the revolution, the state needed to be run by a single party with disciplined, centrally directed administrators in order to ensure its goals. 

Thanks partly to the new policies and to the peace that followed the civil war, the country slowly recovered. By 1928, Russia's farms and factories were producing as much as they had before World War I.

Political Reforms Bolshevik leaders saw nationalism as a threat to unity and party loyalty. To keep nationalism in check, Lenin organized Russia into several self-governing republics under the central government. In 1922, the country was named the Union of Soviet Socialist Republics (USSR), in honor of the councils that helped launch the Bolshevik Revolution. **D**

MAIN IDEA

Summarizing

D How did the Communist government prevent nationalism from threatening the new state created by the revolution?

The Bolsheviks renamed their party the **Communist Party**. The name came from the writings of Karl Marx. He used the word *communism* to describe the classless society that would exist after workers had seized power. In 1924, the Communists created a constitution based on socialist and democratic principles. In reality, the Communist Party held all the power. Lenin had established a dictatorship of the Communist Party, not "a dictatorship of the proletariat," as Marx had promoted.

Stalin Becomes Dictator

Lenin suffered a stroke in 1922. He survived, but the incident set in motion competition for heading up the Communist Party. Two of the most notable men were Leon Trotsky and **Joseph Stalin**. Stalin was cold, hard, and impersonal. During his early days as a Bolshevik, he changed his name to Stalin, which means "man of steel" in Russian. The name fit well.

Stalin began his ruthless climb to the head of the government between 1922 and 1927. In 1922, as general secretary of the Communist Party, he worked behind the scenes to move his supporters into positions of power. Lenin believed that Stalin was a dangerous man. Shortly before he died in 1924, Lenin wrote, "Comrade Stalin . . . has concentrated enormous power in his hands, and I am not sure that he always knows how to use that power with sufficient caution." By 1928, Stalin was in total command of the Communist Party. Trotsky, forced into exile in 1929, was no longer a threat. Stalin now stood poised to wield absolute power as a dictator.

NEW YORK CORE CURRICULUM REVIEW

TERMS & NAMES 1. For each term or name, write a sentence explaining its significance.

- proletariat
- Bolsheviks
- Lenin
- Rasputin
- provisional government
- soviet
- Communist Party
- Joseph Stalin

USING YOUR NOTES

2. Which event on your time line caused the deaths of 14 million Russians?

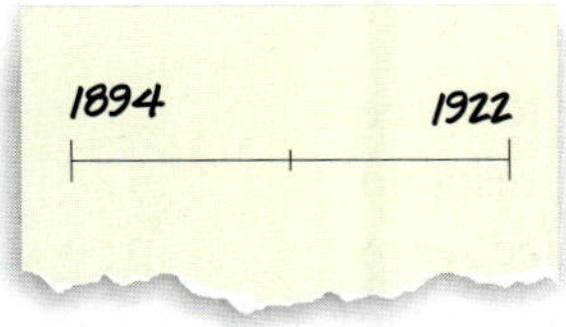

MAIN IDEAS

3. How did World War I help to bring about the Russian Revolution?
4. What groups made up the Red Army and the White Army?
5. Why did the Bolsheviks rename their party the Communist Party?

CRITICAL THINKING & WRITING

6. **DRAWING CONCLUSIONS** How did the czar's autocratic policies toward the people lead to social unrest?
7. **EVALUATING DECISIONS** What do you think were Czar Nicholas II's worst errors in judgment during his rule?
8. **FORMING OPINIONS** Which of the events during the last phase of czarist rule do you think was most responsible for the fall of the czar?
9. **WRITING ACTIVITY** REVOLUTION-Write a paragraph **analysis** of Lenin's leadership in the success of the Bolshevik Revolution.

INTEGRATED TECHNOLOGY **INTERNET ACTIVITY**

Use the Internet to visit Lenin's Tomb in Red Square in Moscow. Write an **evaluation** of the Web site.

INTERNET KEYWORD
Lenin's mausoleum

2

Totalitarianism

CASE STUDY: Stalinist Russia

CONNECT TO THE NEW YORK STATE CORE CURRICULUM

Unit 6.B.6. Stalin and the rise of a modern totalitarian state: industrialization, command economy, collectivization
Unit 6.B.9. Reign of Terror

TERMS & NAMES

- totalitarianism
- Great Purge
- command economy
- Five-Year Plan
- collective farm

SETTING THE STAGE Stalin, Lenin's successor, dramatically transformed the government of the Soviet Union. Stalin was determined that the Soviet Union should find its place both politically and economically among the most powerful of nations in the world. Using tactics designed to rid himself of opposition, Stalin worked to establish total control of all aspects of life in the Soviet Union. He controlled not only the government, but also the economy and many aspects of citizens' private lives.

TAKING NOTES

Categorizing Create a chart listing examples of methods of control used in the Soviet Union.

Methods of control	Example
1.	
2.	
3.	
4.	

A Government of Total Control

The term **totalitarianism** describes a government that takes total, centralized, state control over every aspect of public and private life. Totalitarian leaders appear to provide a sense of security and to give a direction for the future. In the 20th century, the widespread use of mass communication made it possible to reach into all aspects of citizens' lives.

A dynamic leader who can build support for his policies and justify his actions heads most totalitarian governments. Often the leader utilizes secret police to crush opposition and create a sense of fear among the people. No one is exempt from suspicion or accusations that he or she is an enemy of the state.

Totalitarianism challenges the highest values prized by Western democracies—reason, freedom, human dignity, and the worth of the individual. As the chart on the next page shows, all totalitarian states share basic characteristics.

To dominate an entire nation, totalitarian leaders devised methods of control and persuasion. These included the use of terror, indoctrination, propaganda, censorship, and religious or ethnic persecution.

Police Terror Dictators of totalitarian states use terror and violence to force obedience and to crush opposition. Normally, the police are expected to respond to criminal activity and protect the citizens. In a totalitarian state, the police serve to enforce the central government's policies. They may do this by spying on the citizens or by intimidating them. Sometimes they use brutal force and even murder to achieve their goals.

Indoctrination Totalitarian states rely on indoctrination—instruction in the government's beliefs—to mold people's minds. Control of education is absolutely essential to glorify the leader and his policies and to convince all citizens that their

Analyzing Key Concepts

Totalitarianism

Totalitarianism is a form of government in which the national government takes control of all aspects of both public and private life. Thus, totalitarianism seeks to erase the line between government and society. It has an ideology, or set of beliefs, that all citizens are expected to approve. It is often led by a dynamic leader and a single political party.

Mass communication technology helps a totalitarian government spread its aims and support its policies. Also, surveillance technology makes it possible to keep track of the activities of many people. Finally, violence, such as police terror, discourages those who disagree with the goals of the government.

Key Traits of Totalitarianism

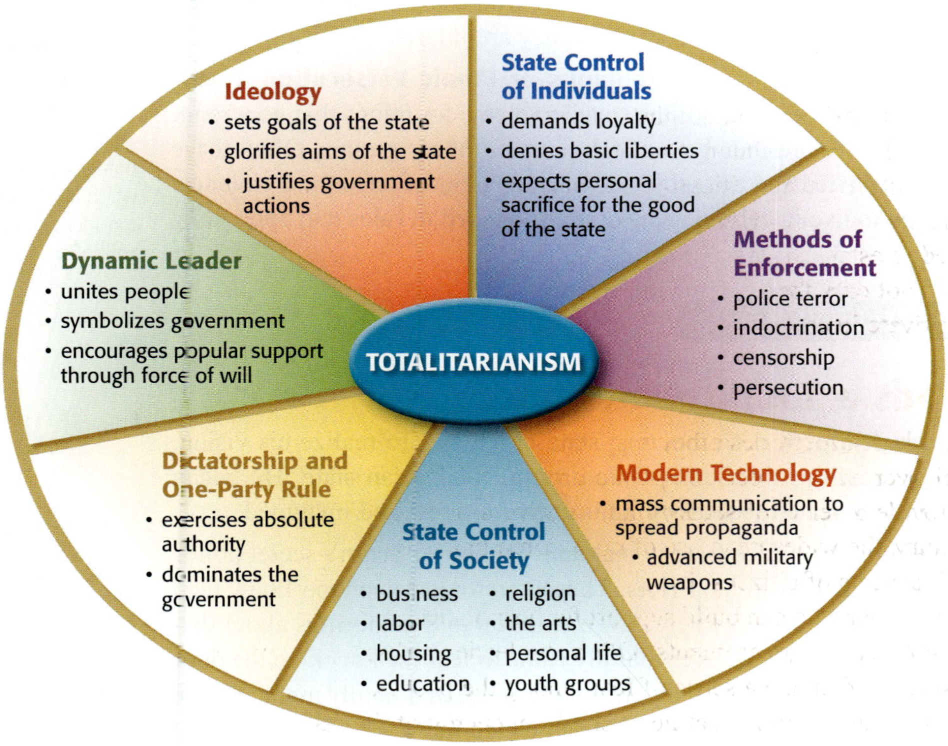

Fear of Totalitarianism

George Orwell illustrated the horrors of a totalitarian government in his novel, *1984*. The novel depicts a world in which personal freedom and privacy have vanished. It is a world made possible through modern technology. Even citizens' homes have television cameras that constantly survey their behavior.

INTEGRATED TECHNOLOGY

RESEARCH LINKS For more on totalitarianism, go to **classzone.com**

DATA FILE

Totalitarian leaders in the 20th century

- Adolf Hitler (Germany) 1933–1945
- Benito Mussolini (Italy) 1925–1943
- Joseph Stalin (Soviet Union) 1929–1953
- Kim IL Sung (North Korea) 1948–1994
- Saddam Hussein (Iraq) 1979–2003

State Terror

- The two most infamous examples of state terror in the 20th century were in Nazi Germany and Stalinist Russia.
- An estimated12.5–20 million people were killed in Nazi Germany.
- An estimated 8–20 million people were killed in Stalinist Russia.

Totalitarianism Today

- There are many authoritarian regimes in the world, but there are very few actual totalitarian governments. In 2000, one monitoring agency identified five totalitarian regimes—Afghanistan, Cuba, North Korea, Laos, and Vietnam.

Connect *to* Today

1. **Synthesizing** How does a totalitarian state attempt to make citizens obey its rules?
   See Skillbuilder Handbook, page R21.
2. **Hypothesizing** How would your life change if you lived in a totalitarian state?

▲ Members of a Russian youth group called Young Communists line up for a parade. Notice the picture of Stalin in the background.

unconditional loyalty and support are required. Indoctrination begins with very young children, is encouraged by youth groups, and is strongly enforced by schools.

Propaganda and Censorship Totalitarian states spread propaganda, biased or incomplete information used to sway people to accept certain beliefs or actions. Control of all mass media allows this to happen. No publication, film, art, or music is allowed to exist without the permission of the state. Citizens are surrounded with false information that appears to be true. Suggesting that the information is incorrect is considered an act of treason and severely punished. Individuals who dissent must retract their work or they are imprisoned or killed.

Religious or Ethnic Persecution Totalitarian leaders often create "enemies of the state" to blame for things that go wrong. Frequently these enemies are members of religious or ethnic groups. Often these groups are easily identified and are subjected to campaigns of terror and violence. They may be forced to live in certain areas or are subjected to rules that apply only to them. **A**

MAIN IDEA

Evaluating Courses of Action

A Of the weapons of totalitarianism, which allows the most long-term control?

CASE STUDY: Stalinist Russia

Stalin Builds a Totalitarian State

Stalin aimed to create a perfect Communist state in Russia. To realize his vision, Stalin planned to transform the Soviet Union into a totalitarian state. He began building his totalitarian state by destroying his enemies—real and imagined.

Police State Stalin built a police state to maintain his power. Stalin's secret police used tanks and armored cars to stop riots. They monitored telephone lines, read mail, and planted informers everywhere. Even children told authorities about disloyal remarks they heard at home. Every family came to fear the knock on the door in the early morning hours, which usually meant the arrest of a family member. The secret police arrested and executed millions of so-called traitors.

In 1934, Stalin turned against members of the Communist Party. In 1937, he launched the **Great Purge**, a campaign of terror directed at eliminating anyone who threatened his power. Thousands of old Bolsheviks who helped stage the Revolution in 1917 stood trial. They were executed or sent to labor camps for "crimes against the Soviet state." When the Great Purge ended in 1938, Stalin had gained total control of the Soviet government and the Communist Party. Historians estimate that during this time he was responsible for 8 million to 13 million deaths. **B**

MAIN IDEA

Recognizing Effects

B How would the actions of the Great Purge increase Stalin's power?

Russian Propaganda and Censorship Stalin's government controlled all newspapers, motion pictures, radio, and other sources of information. Many Soviet writers, composers, and other artists also fell victim to official censorship. Stalin would not tolerate individual creativity that did not conform to the views of the state. Soviet newspapers and radio broadcasts glorified the achievements of communism, Stalin, and his economic programs.

Under Stalin, the arts also were used for propaganda. In 1930, an editorial in the Communist Party newspaper *Pravda* explained the purpose of art: "Literature, the cinema, the arts are levers in the hands of the proletariat which must be used to show the masses positive models of initiative and heroic labor."

Education and Indoctrination Under Stalin, the government controlled all education from nursery schools through the universities. Schoolchildren learned the virtues of the Communist Party. College professors and students who questioned the Communist Party's interpretations of history or science risked losing their jobs or faced imprisonment. Party leaders in the Soviet Union lectured workers and peasants on the ideals of communism. They also stressed the importance of sacrifice and hard work to build the Communist state. State-supported youth groups trained future party members.

Religious Persecution Communists aimed to replace religious teachings with the ideals of communism. Under Stalin, the government and the League of the Militant Godless, an officially sponsored group of atheists, spread propaganda attacking religion. "Museums of atheism" displayed exhibits to show that religious beliefs were mere superstitions. Yet many people in the Soviet Union still clung to their faiths.

Vocabulary
atheists: people who do not think there is a god

The Russian Orthodox Church was the main target of persecution. Other religious groups also suffered greatly. The police destroyed magnificent churches and synagogues, and many religious leaders were killed or sent to labor camps.

Achieving the perfect Communist state came at a tremendous cost to Soviet citizens. Stalin's total control of society eliminated personal rights and freedoms in favor of the power of the state.

History Makers

Joseph Stalin
1879–1953

Stalin was born in bitter poverty in Georgia, a region in southern Russia. Unlike the well-educated and cultured Lenin, Stalin was rough and crude.

Stalin tried to create a myth that he was the country's father and savior. Stalin glorified himself as the symbol of the nation. He encouraged people to think of him as "The Greatest Genius of All Times and Peoples."

Many towns, factories, and streets in the Soviet Union were named for Stalin. A new metal was called Stalinite. An orchid was named Stalinchid. Children standing before their desks every morning said, "Thank Comrade Stalin for this happy life."

INTEGRATED TECHNOLOGY

INTERNET ACTIVITY Create a Web page on Joseph Stalin. Include pictures and a time line of his rule in the USSR. Go to **classzone.com** for your research.

Stalin Seizes Control of the Economy

As Stalin began to gain complete control of society, he was setting plans in motion to overhaul the economy. He announced, "We are fifty or a hundred years behind the advanced countries. We must make good this distance in ten years." In 1928 Stalin's plans called for a **command economy**, a system in which the government made all economic decisions. Under this system, political leaders identify the country's economic needs and determine how to fulfill them.

An Industrial Revolution Stalin outlined the first of several **Five-Year Plans** for the development of the Soviet Union's economy. The Five-Year Plans set impossibly high quotas, or numerical goals, to increase the output of steel, coal, oil, and electricity. To reach these targets, the government limited production of consumer goods. As a result, people faced severe shortages of housing, food, clothing, and other necessary goods.

Stalin's tough methods produced impressive economic results. Although most of the targets of the first Five-Year Plan fell short, the Soviets made substantial gains. (See the graphs on page 878 for coal and steel production.) A second plan, launched in 1933, proved equally successful. From 1928 to 1937, industrial production of steel increased more than 25 percent.

An Agricultural Revolution In 1928, the government began to seize over 25 million privately owned farms in the USSR. It combined them into large, government-owned farms, called **collective farms**. Hundreds of families worked on these farms, called collectives, producing food for the state. The government expected that the modern machinery on the collective farms would boost food production and reduce the number of workers. Resistance was especially strong among kulaks, a class of wealthy peasants. The Soviet government decided to eliminate them.

Peasants actively fought the government's attempt to take their land. Many killed livestock and destroyed crops in protest. Soviet secret police herded peasants onto collective farms at the point of a bayonet. Between 5 million and 10 million peasants died as a direct result of Stalin's agricultural revolution. By 1938, more than 90 percent of all peasants lived on collective farms. As you see in the charts below, agricultural production was on the upswing. That year the country produced almost twice the wheat than it had in 1928 before collective farming. C

In areas where farming was more difficult, the government set up state farms. These state farms operated like factories. The workers received wages instead of a share of the profits. These farms were much larger than collectives and mostly produced wheat.

MAIN IDEA

Clarifying

C What methods did Stalin use to bring agriculture under state control?

Daily Life Under Stalin

Stalin's totalitarian rule revolutionized Soviet society. Women's roles greatly expanded. People became better educated and mastered new technical skills. The dramatic changes in people's lives, came at great cost. Soviet citizens found their personal freedoms limited, consumer goods in short supply, and dissent prohibited.

Stalin's economic plans created a high demand for many skilled workers. University and technical training became the key to a better life. As one young man explained, "If a person does not want to become a collective farmer or just a cleaning woman, the only means you have to get something is through education."

Women Gain Rights The Bolshevik Revolution of 1917 declared men and women equal. Laws were passed to grant women equal rights. After Stalin became dictator, women helped the state-controlled economy prosper. Under his Five-Year

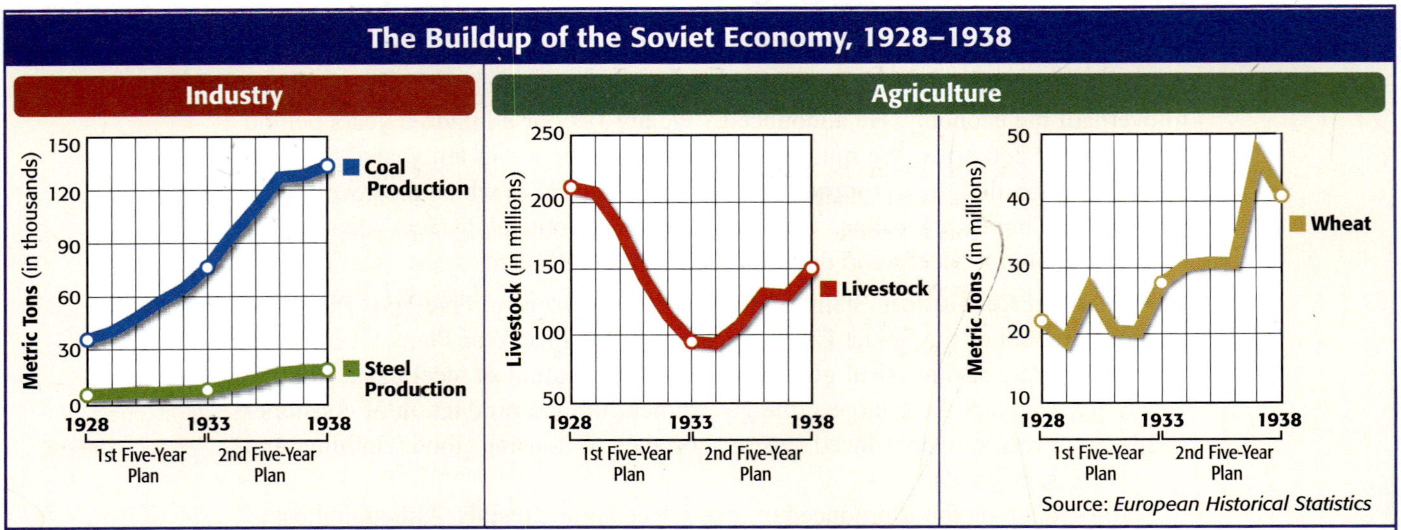

SKILLBUILDER: Interpreting Graphs

1. **Clarifying** *How many more metric tons of coal were produced in 1938 than in 1928?*
2. **Drawing Conclusions** *What do the graphs show about the contrast between the progress of industry and agriculture production under Stalin's first Five-Year Plan?*

Plans, they had no choice but to join the labor force. The state provided child care for all working mothers. Some young women performed the same jobs as men. Millions of women worked in factories and in construction. However, men continued to hold the best jobs.

Given new educational opportunities, women prepared for careers in engineering and science. Medicine, in particular, attracted many women. By 1950, they made up 75 percent of Soviet doctors.

Soviet women paid a heavy price for their rising status in society. Besides having full-time jobs, they were responsible for housework and child care. Motherhood is considered a patriotic duty in totalitarian regimes. Soviet women were expected to provide the state with future generations of loyal, obedient citizens. D

MAIN IDEA

Summarizing

D How did daily life under Stalin's rule change the lives of women in the Soviet Union?

Total Control Achieved

By the mid-1930s, Stalin had forcibly transformed the Soviet Union into a totalitarian regime and an industrial and political power. He stood unopposed as dictator and maintained his authority over the Communist Party. Stalin would not tolerate individual creativity. He saw it as a threat to the conformity and obedience required of citizens in a totalitarian state. He ushered in a period of total social control and rule by terror, rather than constitutional government.

Like Russia, China would fall under the influence of Karl Marx's theories and Communist beliefs. The dynamic leader Mao Zedong would pave the way for transforming China into a totalitarian Communist state, as you will read in Section 3.

Social History

Ukrainian Kulaks

The kulaks in Ukraine (shown above) fiercely resisted collectivization. They murdered officials, torched the property of the collectives, and burned their own crops and grain in protest.

Recognizing the threat kulaks posed to his policies, Stalin declared that they should "liquidate kulaks as a class." The state took control of kulak land and equipment, and confiscated stores of food and grain. More than 3 million Ukrainians were shot, exiled, or imprisoned. Some 6 million people died in the government-engineered famine that resulted from the destruction of crops and animals. By 1935, the kulaks had been eliminated.

NEW YORK CORE CURRICULUM REVIEW

TERMS & NAMES 1. For each term or name, write a sentence explaining its significance.

- totalitarianism
- Great Purge
- command economy
- Five-Year Plans
- collective farm

USING YOUR NOTES

2. Which of the methods of control do you think was most influential in maintaining Stalin's power? Why?

Methods of control	Example
1.	
2.	
3.	
4.	

MAIN IDEAS

3. What are the key traits of a totalitarian state?
4. What are some ways totalitarian rulers keep their power?
5. How did the Soviet economy change under the direction of Stalin?

CRITICAL THINKING & WRITING

6. **CONTRASTING** How do totalitarian states and constitutional governments differ?
7. **SUMMARIZING** Summarize Joseph Stalin's rise to power and how his control expanded.
8. **EVALUATING COURSES OF ACTION** Were the Five-Year plans the best way to move the Soviet economy forward? Explain.
9. **WRITING ACTIVITY** POWER AND AUTHORITY As an industrial worker, a female doctor, a Russian Orthodox priest, or a Communist Party member, write a **journal entry** about your life under Stalin.

CONNECT TO TODAY **Graphing Russia's Economy**

Research Russia's industrial and agricultural production in the last 10 years. Create a series of **graphs** similar to those found on page 878.

Propaganda

You have read how a totalitarian government can use propaganda to support its goals. These pages show three examples of visual propaganda from the Soviet Union—low-cost posters, traditional painting, and altered photographs.

Posters were mass produced and placed in very visible areas. They were constant reminders of Communist policy and guides for proper thought. Artists were required to paint scenes that supported and glorified the Communist Party. Even photographs were altered if they contained individuals who had fallen out of favor with the party leadership.

INTEGRATED TECHNOLOGY

RESEARCH LINKS For more on propaganda, go to **classzone.com**

◄ Factory Poster

"Help build the gigantic factories." This poster advertises a state loan for the building of large factories. Developing heavy industry was an important goal in the early days of the Soviet Union.

Woman Worker Poster ▲

A translation of this poster says, "What the October Revolution has given to working and peasant women." The woman is pointing to buildings such as a library, a worker's club, and a school for adults.

▼ Painting

In this painting the central figure, Communist leader Joseph Stalin, is greeted enthusiastically. The expressions of the diverse and happy crowd imply not only that Stalin has broad support, but that he is worshiped as well.

▼ Altered Photographs

Stalin attempted to enhance his legacy and erase his rivals from history by extensively altering photographs as this series shows.

1. The original photograph was taken in 1926 and showed, from left to right, Nikolai Antipov, Stalin, Sergei Kirov, and Nikolai Shvernik.

2. This altered image appeared in a 1949 biography of Stalin. Why Shvernik was removed is unclear—he was head of the Central Committee of the Communist Party until Stalin's death in 1954. Antipov, however, was arrested during Stalin's purge and executed in 1941.

3. This heroic oil painting by Isaak Brodsky is based on the original photograph, but only Stalin is left. Kirov was assassinated in 1934 by a student, but the official investigation report has never been released. Stalin did fear Kirov's popularity and considered him a threat to his leadership.

Connect *to* Today

1. **Forming and Supporting Opinions** Of the examples on this page, which do you think would have been most effective as propaganda? Why?
   See Skillbuilder Handbook, page R20.

2. **Comparing and Contrasting** What are the similarities and differences between propaganda and modern advertising campaigns? Support your answer with examples.

3

Imperial China Collapses

CONNECT TO THE NEW YORK STATE CORE CURRICULUM

Unit 5.H.5.c. Sun Yat-sen (Sun Yixian) and the Chinese Revolution (1910–1911)
Unit 6.D.8. War in China–Long March

TERMS & NAMES

- Kuomintang
- Sun Yixian
- May Fourth Movement
- Mao Zedong
- Jiang Jieshi
- Long March

SETTING THE STAGE In the early 1900s, China was ripe for revolution. China had faced years of humiliation at the hands of outsiders. Foreign countries controlled its trade and economic resources. Many Chinese believed that modernization and nationalism held the country's keys for survival. They wanted to build up the army and navy, to construct modern factories, and to reform education. Yet others feared change. They believed that China's greatness lay in its traditional ways.

TAKING NOTES

Comparing and Contrasting Make a chart to compare and contrast the actions of Jiang Jieshi and Mao Zedong in controlling China.

Jiang	Mao
1. 2. 3.	1. 2. 3.

Nationalists Overthrow Qing Dynasty

Among the groups pushing for modernization and nationalization was the **Kuomintang** (KWOH•mihn•TANG), or the Nationalist Party. Its first great leader was **Sun Yixian** (soon-yee•shyahn). In 1911, the Revolutionary Alliance, a forerunner of the Kuomintang, succeeded in overthrowing the last emperor of the Qing dynasty. The Qing had ruled China since 1644.

Shaky Start for the New Republic In 1912, Sun became president of the new Republic of China. Sun hoped to establish a modern government based on the "Three Principles of the People": (1) nationalism—an end to foreign control, (2) people's rights—democracy, and (3) people's livelihood—economic security for all Chinese. Sun Yixian considered nationalism vital. He said, "The Chinese people . . . do not have national spirit. Therefore even though we have four hundred million people gathered together in one China, in reality, they are just a heap of loose sand." Despite his lasting influence as a revolutionary leader, Sun lacked the authority and military support to secure national unity.

Sun turned over the presidency to a powerful general, Yuan Shikai, who quickly betrayed the democratic ideals of the revolution. His actions sparked local revolts. After the general died in 1916, civil war broke out. Real authority fell into the hands of provincial warlords or powerful military leaders. They ruled territories as large as their armies could conquer.

▼ Sun Yixian led the overthrow of the last Chinese emperor.

World War I Spells More Problems In 1917, the government in Beijing, hoping for an Allied victory, declared war against Germany. Some leaders mistakenly believed that for China's participation the thankful Allies would return control of Chinese territories that had previously belonged to Germany. However, under the Treaty of Versailles, the Allied leaders gave Japan those territories.

When news of the Treaty of Versailles reached China, outrage swept the country. On May 4, 1919, over 3,000 angry students gathered in the center of Beijing. The demonstrations spread to other cities and exploded into a national movement. It was called the **May Fourth Movement**. Workers, shopkeepers, and professionals joined the cause. Though not officially a revolution, these demonstrations showed the Chinese people's commitment to the goal of establishing a strong, modern nation. Sun Yixian and members of the Kuomintang also shared the aims of the movement. But they could not strengthen central rule on their own. Many young Chinese intellectuals turned against Sun Yixian's belief in Western democracy in favor of Lenin's brand of Soviet communism. (A)

MAIN IDEA

Identifying Problems

(A) What problems did the new Republic of China face?

The Communist Party in China

In 1921, a group met in Shanghai to organize the Chinese Communist Party. **Mao Zedong** (MOW dzuh•dahng), an assistant librarian at Beijing University, was among its founders. Later he would become China's greatest revolutionary leader.

Mao Zedong had already begun to develop his own brand of communism. Lenin had based his Marxist revolution on his organization in Russia's cities. Mao envisioned a different setting. He believed he could bring revolution to a rural country

Connect *to* Today

Tiananmen Square

In Tiananmen Square, the Gate of Heavenly Peace was the site of many political activities during the 20th century. Early in the century, May 4, 1919, thousands of students gathered there to protest the terms of the Versailles Treaty. (upper right). The May Fourth Movement was born that day. The movement marks the beginning of Chinese nationalism.

Seventy years later, in 1989, students once again gathered at the square to demand political reforms. Shortly after the anniversary of the May 4 event, thousands—and perhaps a million people—gathered at the square. On June 3, 1989, the Chinese army was ordered to clear the square of all protesters. Thousands were killed or injured.

where the peasants could be the true revolutionaries. He argued his point passionately in 1927:

PRIMARY SOURCE **B**

The force of the peasantry is like that of the raging winds and driving rain. It is rapidly increasing in violence. No force can stand in its way. The peasantry will tear apart all nets which bind it and hasten along the road to liberation. They will bury beneath them all forces of imperialism, militarism, corrupt officialdom, village bosses and evil gentry.

MAO ZEDONG, quoted in *Chinese Communism and the Rise of Mao*

MAIN IDEA

Analyzing Primary Sources

B What forces does Mao identify as those that the peasants will overcome?

Lenin Befriends China While the Chinese Communist Party was forming, Sun Yixian and his Nationalist Party set up a government in south China. Like the Communists, Sun became disillusioned with the Western democracies that refused to support his struggling government. Sun decided to ally the Kuomintang with the newly formed Communist Party. He hoped to unite all the revolutionary groups for common action.

Lenin seized the opportunity to help China's Nationalist government. In 1923, he sent military advisers and equipment to the Nationalists in return for allowing the Chinese Communists to join the Kuomintang.

▲ Jiang Jieshi and the Nationalist forces united China under one government in 1928.

Peasants Align with the Communists After Sun Yixian died in 1925, **Jiang Jieshi** (jee•ahng jee•shee), formerly called Chiang Kai-shek, headed the Kuomintang. Jiang was the son of a middle-class merchant. Many of Jiang's followers were bankers and businesspeople. Like Jiang, they feared the Communists' goal of creating a socialist economy modeled after the Soviet Union's.

Jiang had promised democracy and political rights to all Chinese. Yet his government became steadily less democratic and more corrupt. Most peasants believed that Jiang was doing little to improve their lives. As a result, many peasants threw their support to the Chinese Communist Party. To enlist the support of the peasants, Mao divided land that the Communists won among the local farmers.

Nationalists and Communists Clash At first, Jiang put aside his differences with the Communists. Together Jiang's Nationalist forces and the Communists successfully fought the warlords. Soon afterward, though, he turned against the Communists.

In April 1927, Nationalist troops and armed gangs moved into Shanghai. They killed many Communist leaders and trade union members in the city streets. Similar killings took place in other cities. The Nationalists nearly wiped out the Chinese Communist Party.

In 1928, Jiang became president of the Nationalist Republic of China. Great Britain and the United States both formally recognized the new government. Because of the slaughter of Communists at Shanghai, the Soviet Union did not. Jiang's treachery also had long-term effects. The Communists' deep-seated rage over the massacre erupted in a civil war that would last until 1949.

Civil War Rages in China

By 1930, Nationalists and Communists were fighting a bloody civil war. Mao and other Communist leaders established themselves in the hills of south-central China. Mao referred to this tactic of taking his revolution to the countryside as "swimming in the peasant sea." He recruited the peasants to join his Red Army. He then trained them in guerrilla warfare. Nationalists attacked the Communists repeatedly but failed to drive them out.

The Long March In 1933, Jiang gathered an army of at least 700,000 men. Jiang's army then surrounded the Communists' mountain stronghold. Outnumbered, the

The Long March

The Long March of the Chinese Communists from the south of China to the caves of Shaanxi [shahn•shee] in the north is a remarkable story. The march covered 6,000 miles, about the distance from New York to San Francisco and back again. They crossed miles of swampland. They slept sitting up, leaning back-to-back in pairs, to keep from sinking into the mud and drowning. In total, the Communists crossed 18 mountain ranges and 24 rivers in their yearlong flight from the Nationalist forces.

GEOGRAPHY SKILLBUILDER: Interpreting Maps

1. **Movement** *What was the course of the Long March, in terms of direction, beginning in Ruijin and ending near Yan'an?*
2. **Movement** *Why didn't Mao's forces move west or south?*

▼ In one of the more daring and difficult acts of the march, the Red Army crossed a bridge of iron chains whose planks had been removed.

▼ The Red Army had to cross the Snowy Mountains, some of the highest in the world. Every man carried enough food and fuel to last for ten days. They marched six to seven hours a day.

◀ After finally arriving at the caves in Shaanxi, Mao declared, "If we can survive all this, we can survive everything. This is but the first stage of our Long March. The final stage leads to Peking [Beijing]!"

▲ A Japanese landing party approaches the Chinese mainland. The invasion forced Mao and Jiang to join forces to fight the Japanese.

Communist Party leaders realized that they faced defeat. In a daring move, 100,000 Communist forces fled. They began a hazardous, 6,000-mile-long journey called the **Long March**. Between 1934 and 1935, the Communists kept only a step ahead of Jiang's forces. Thousands died from hunger, cold, exposure, and battle wounds.

Finally, after a little more than a year, Mao and the seven or eight thousand Communist survivors settled in caves in northwestern China. There they gained new followers. Meanwhile, as civil war between Nationalists and Communists raged, Japan invaded China. C

MAIN IDEA

Recognizing Effects

C What were the results of the Long March?

Civil War-Suspended In 1931, as Chinese fought Chinese, the Japanese watched the power struggles with rising interest. Japanese forces took advantage of China's weakening situation. They invaded Manchuria, an industrialized province in the northeast part of China.

In 1937, the Japanese launched an all-out invasion of China. Massive bombings of villages and cities killed thousands of Chinese. The destruction of farms caused many more to die of starvation. By 1938, Japan held control of a large part of China.

The Japanese threat forced an uneasy truce between Jiang's and Mao's forces. The civil war gradually ground to a halt as Nationalists and Communists temporarily united to fight the Japanese. The National Assembly further agreed to promote changes outlined in Sun Yixian's "Three Principles of the People"—nationalism, democracy, and people's livelihood. As you will learn in Section 4, similar principles were also serving as a guiding force in India and Southwest Asia.

NEW YORK CORE CURRICULUM REVIEW

TERMS & NAMES 1. For each term or name, write a sentence explaining its significance.

• Kuomintang • Sun Yixian • May Fourth Movement • Mao Zedong • Jiang Jieshi • Long March

USING YOUR NOTES

2. Whose reforms had a greater appeal to the peasants? Why?

Jiang	Mao
1.	1.
2.	2.
3.	3.

MAIN IDEAS

3. How did the Treaty of Versailles trigger the May Fourth Movement?
4. How was Mao's vision of communism different from that of Lenin?
5. What started the civil war in China?

CRITICAL THINKING & WRITING

6. **RECOGNIZING EFFECTS** What influence did foreign nations have on China from 1912 to 1938?
7. **ANALYZING CAUSES** What caused the Communist revolutionary movement in China to gain strength?
8. **HYPOTHESIZING** If the Long March had failed, do you think the Nationalist party would have been successful in uniting the Chinese? Why or why not?
9. **WRITING ACTIVITY** REVOLUTION Write a series of **interview questions** you would pose to Sun Yixian, Mao Zedong, and Jiang Jieshi.

CONNECT TO TODAY **REPORTING ON CURRENT EVENTS**

Research the selection of the newest Communist Party leader of China. Write a brief **report** identifying that person and explaining how this new leader got into office.

4

Nationalism in India and Southwest Asia

CONNECT TO THE NEW YORK STATE CORE CURRICULUM

Unit 6.C.9. Colonial response to European imperialism . . . .
Unit 6.C.3. Modernization and westernization of a secular Turkey–Kemal Atatürk

TERMS & NAMES

- Rowlatt Acts
- Amritsar Massacre
- Mohandas K. Gandhi
- civil disobedience
- Salt March
- Mustafa Kemal

SETTING THE STAGE As you learned in Chapter 29, the end of World War I broke up the Ottoman Empire. The British Empire, which controlled India, began to show signs of cracking. The weakening of these empires stirred nationalist activity in India, Turkey, and some Southwest Asian countries. Indian nationalism had been growing since the mid-1800s. Many upper-class Indians who attended British schools learned European views of nationalism and democracy. They began to apply these political ideas to their own country.

TAKING NOTES
Categorizing Create a web diagram identifying the styles of government adopted by nations in this section.

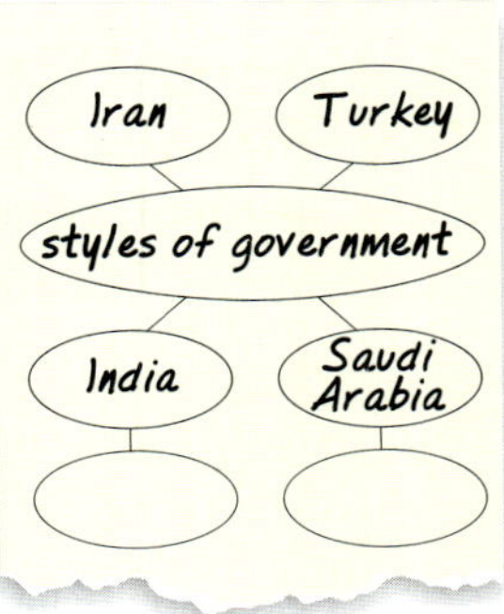

Indian Nationalism Grows

Two groups formed to rid India of foreign rule: the primarily Hindu Indian National Congress, or Congress Party, in 1885, and the Muslim League in 1906. Though deep divisions existed between Hindus and Muslims, they found common ground. They shared the heritage of British rule and an understanding of democratic ideals. These two groups both worked toward the goal of independence from the British.

World War I Increases Nationalist Activity Until World War I, the vast majority of Indians had little interest in nationalism. The situation changed as over a million Indians enlisted in the British army. In return for their service, the British government promised reforms that would eventually lead to self-government.

▼ Ali Jinnah, leader of the Muslim League of India, fought for Indian independence from Great Britain.

In 1918, Indian troops returned home from the war. They expected Britain to fulfill its promise. Instead, they were once again treated as second-class citizens. Radical nationalists carried out acts of violence to show their hatred of British rule. To curb dissent, in 1919 the British passed the **Rowlatt Acts**. These laws allowed the government to jail protesters without trial for as long as two years. To Western-educated Indians, denial of a trial by jury violated their individual rights.

Amritsar Massacre To protest the Rowlatt Acts, around 10,000 Hindus and Muslims flocked to Amritsar, a major city in the Punjab, in the spring of 1919. At a huge festival in an enclosed square, they intended to fast and pray and to listen to political speeches. The demonstration, viewed as a nationalist outburst, alarmed the British. They were especially concerned about the alliance of Hindus and Muslims.

Most people at the gathering were unaware that the British government had banned public meetings. However, the British commander at Amritsar believed they were openly defying the ban. He ordered his troops to fire on the crowd without warning. The shooting in the enclosed courtyard continued for ten minutes. Official reports showed nearly 400 Indians died and about 1,200 were wounded. Others estimate the numbers were higher.

News of the slaughter, called the **Amritsar Massacre**, sparked an explosion of anger across India. Almost overnight, millions of Indians changed from loyal British subjects into nationalists. These Indians demanded independence. (A)

MAIN IDEA

Recognizing Effects

(A) What changes resulted from the Amritsar massacre?

Gandhi's Tactics of Nonviolence

The massacre at Amritsar set the stage for **Mohandas K. Gandhi** (GAHN•dee) to emerge as the leader of the independence movement. Gandhi's strategy for battling injustice evolved from his deeply religious approach to political activity. His teachings blended ideas from all of the major world religions, including Hinduism, Jainism, Buddhism, Islam, and Christianity. Gandhi attracted millions of followers. Soon they began calling him the Mahatma (muh•HAHT•muh), meaning "great soul."

Noncooperation When the British failed to punish the officers responsible for the Amritsar massacre, Gandhi urged the Indian National Congress to follow a policy of noncooperation with the British government. In 1920, the Congress Party endorsed **civil disobedience**, the deliberate and public refusal to obey an unjust

Analyzing Primary Sources

Satyagraha

A central element of Gandhi's philosophy of nonviolence was called *satyagraha*, often translated as "soul-force" or "truth-force."

PRIMARY SOURCE

Passive resistance is a method of securing rights by personal suffering; it is the reverse of resistance by arms. When I refuse to do a thing that is repugnant to my conscience, I use soul-force. For instance, the government of the day has passed a law which is applicable to me: I do not like it, if, by using violence, I force the government to repeal the law, I am employing what may be termed body-force. If I do not obey the law and accept the penalty for its breach, I use soul-force. It involves sacrifice of self.

GANDHI Chapter XVII, *Hind Swaraj*

Nonviolence

In *The Origin of Nonviolence*, Gandhi offered a warning to those who were contemplating joining the struggle for independence.

PRIMARY SOURCE

[I]t is not at all impossible that we might have to endure every hardship that we can imagine, and wisdom lies in pledging ourselves on the understanding that we shall have to suffer all that and worse. If some one asks me when and how the struggle may end, I may say that if the entire community manfully stands the test, the end will be near. If many of us fall back under storm and stress, the struggle will be prolonged. But I can boldly declare, and with certainty, that so long as there is even a handful of men true to their pledge, there can only be one end to the struggle, and that is victory.

GANDHI *The Origin of Nonviolence*

DOCUMENT-BASED QUESTIONS

1. **Comparing** *How is soul-force different from body-force?*
2. **Making Inferences** *What do Gandhi's writings suggest about his view of suffering? Give examples from each document.*

law, and nonviolence as the means to achieve independence. Gandhi then launched his campaign of civil disobedience to weaken the British government's authority and economic power over India.

▲ Gandhi adopted the spinning wheel as a symbol of Indian resistance to British rule. The wheel was featured on the Indian National Congress flag, a forerunner of India's national flag.

Boycotts Gandhi called on Indians to refuse to buy British goods, attend government schools, pay British taxes, or vote in elections. Gandhi staged a successful boycott of British cloth, a source of wealth for the British. He urged all Indians to weave their own cloth. Gandhi himself devoted two hours each day to spinning his own yarn on a simple handwheel. He wore only homespun cloth and encouraged Indians to follow his example. As a result of the boycott, the sale of British cloth in India dropped sharply.

Strikes and Demonstrations Gandhi's weapon of civil disobedience took an economic toll on the British. They struggled to keep trains running, factories operating, and overcrowded jails from bursting. Throughout 1920, the British arrested thousands of Indians who had participated in strikes and demonstrations. But despite Gandhi's pleas for nonviolence, protests often led to riots.

The Salt March In 1930, Gandhi organized a demonstration to defy the hated Salt Acts. According to these British laws, Indians could buy salt from no other source but the government. They also had to pay sales tax on salt. To show their opposition, Gandhi and his followers walked about 240 miles to the seacoast. There they began to make their own salt by collecting seawater and letting it evaporate. This peaceful protest was called the **Salt March**.

Soon afterward, some demonstrators planned a march to a site where the British government processed salt. They intended to shut this saltworks down. Police officers with steel-tipped clubs attacked the demonstrators. An American journalist was an eyewitness to the event. He described the "sickening whacks of clubs on unprotected skulls" and people "writhing in pain with fractured skulls or broken shoulders." Still the people continued to march peacefully, refusing to defend themselves against their attackers. Newspapers across the globe carried the journalist's story, which won worldwide support for Gandhi's independence movement.

More demonstrations against the salt tax took place throughout India. Eventually, about 60,000 people, including Gandhi, were arrested. **B**

MAIN IDEA

Making Inferences

B How did the Salt March represent Gandhi's methods for change?

Britain Grants Limited Self-Rule

Gandhi and his followers gradually reaped the rewards of their civil disobedience campaigns and gained greater political power for the Indian people. In 1935, the British Parliament passed the Government of India Act. It provided local self-government and limited democratic elections, but not total independence.

However, the Government of India Act also fueled mounting tensions between Muslims and Hindus. These two groups had conflicting visions of India's future as an independent nation. Indian Muslims, outnumbered by Hindus, feared that Hindus would control India if it won independence. In Chapter 34, you will read about the outcome of India's bid for independence.

History Makers

Mustafa Kemal
1881–1938

As president of Turkey, Mustafa Kemal campaigned vigorously to mold the new republic into a modern nation. His models were the United States and other European countries.

Kemal believed that even the clothing of the Turks should be changed to reflect a civilized, international dress. To reach this goal, Kemal set rules for clothing. He required government workers to wear Western-style business suits and banned the fez, a brimless red felt hat that was part of traditional Turkish clothing.

Nationalism in Southwest Asia

The breakup of the Ottoman Empire and growing Western political and economic interest in Southwest Asia spurred the rise of nationalism in this region. Just as the people of India fought to have their own nation after World War I, the people of Southwest Asia also launched independence movements to rid themselves of imperial rulers.

Turkey Becomes a Republic At the end of World War I, the Ottoman Empire was forced to give up all its territories except Turkey. Turkish lands included the old Turkish homeland of Anatolia and a small strip of land around Istanbul.

In 1919, Greek soldiers invaded Turkey and threatened to conquer it. The Turkish sultan was powerless to stop the Greeks. However, in 1922, a brilliant commander, **Mustafa Kemal** (keh•MAHL), successfully led Turkish nationalists in fighting back the Greeks and their British backers. After winning a peace, the nationalists overthrew the last Ottoman sultan.

In 1923, Kemal became the president of the new Republic of Turkey, the first republic in Southwest Asia. To achieve his goal of transforming Turkey into a modern nation, he ushered in these sweeping reforms:

- separated the laws of Islam from the laws of the nation
- abolished religious courts and created a new legal system based on European law
- granted women the right to vote and to hold public office
- launched government-funded programs to industrialize Turkey and to spur economic growth

Kemal died in 1938. From his leadership, Turkey gained a new sense of its national identity. His influence was so strong that the Turkish people gave him the name Ataturk—"father of the Turks."

Persia Becomes Iran Before World War I, both Great Britain and Russia had established spheres of influence in the ancient country of Persia. After the war, when Russia was still reeling from the Bolshevik Revolution, the British tried to take over all of Persia. This maneuver triggered a nationalist revolt in Persia. In 1921, a Persian army officer seized power. In 1925 he deposed the ruling shah.

Persia's new leader, Reza Shah Pahlavi (PAL•uh•vee), like Kemal in Turkey, set out to modernize his country. He established public schools, built roads and railroads, promoted industrial growth, and extended women's rights. Unlike Kemal, Reza Shah Pahlavi kept all power in his own hands. In 1935, he changed the name of the country from the Greek name Persia to the traditional name Iran. (C)

MAIN IDEA

Comparing

(C) How were Kemal's leadership and Reza Shah Pahlavi's leadership similar?

Saudi Arabia Keeps Islamic Traditions While Turkey broke with many Islamic traditions, another new country held strictly to Islamic law. In 1902, Abd al-Aziz Ibn Saud (sah•OOD), a member of a once-powerful Arabian family, began a successful campaign to unify Arabia. In 1932, he renamed the new kingdom Saudi Arabia after his family.

Ibn Saud carried on Arab and Islamic traditions. Loyalty to the Saudi government was based on custom, religion, and family ties. Like Kemal and Reza Shah, Ibn Saud brought some modern technology, such as telephones and radios, to his country. However, modernization in Saudi Arabia was limited to religiously acceptable areas. There also were no efforts to begin to practice democracy.

Oil Drives Development While nationalism steadily emerged as a major force in Southwest Asia, the region's economy was also taking a new direction. The rising demand for petroleum products in industrialized countries brought new oil explorations to Southwest Asia. During the 1920s and 1930s, European and American companies discovered enormous oil deposits in Iran, Iraq, Saudi Arabia, and Kuwait. Foreign businesses invested huge sums of money to develop these oil fields. For example, the Anglo-Persian Oil Company, a British company, started developing the oil fields of Iran. Geologists later learned that the land around the Persian Gulf has nearly two-thirds of the world's known supply of oil.

This important resource led to rapid and dramatic economic changes and development. Because oil brought huge profits, Western nations tried to dominate this region. Meanwhile, these same Western nations were about to face a more immediate crisis as power-hungry leaders seized control in Italy and Germany.

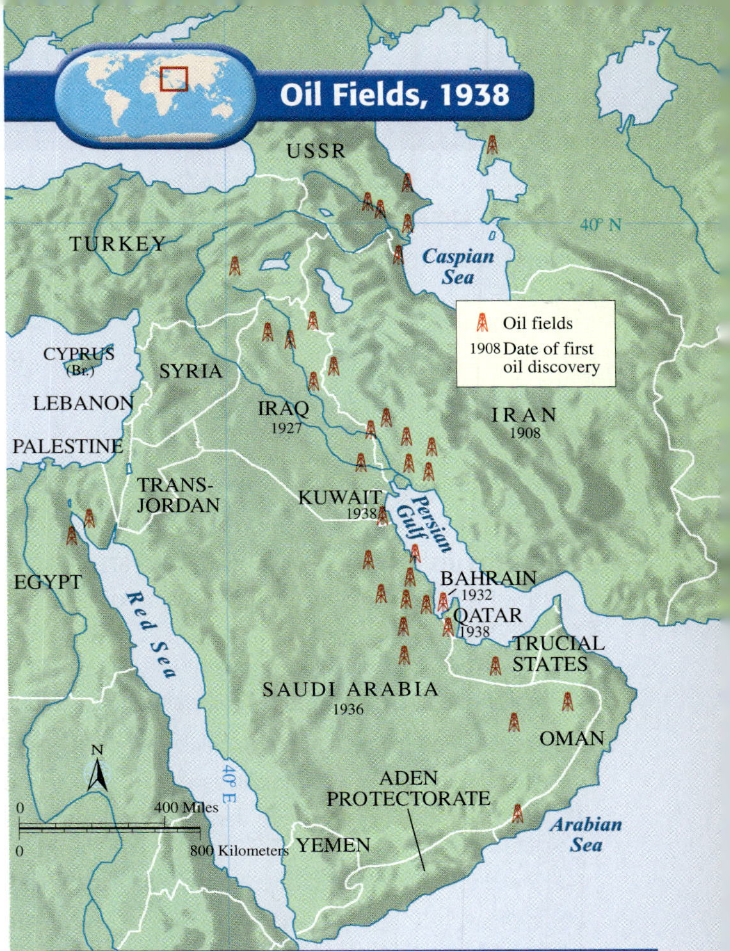

GEOGRAPHY SKILLBUILDER: Interpreting Maps

1. **Location**-*Along what geographical feature are most of the oil-producing regions located?*
2. **Movement**-*How will water transportation routes be changed by the discovery of oil in the region?*

NEW YORK CORE CURRICULUM REVIEW

TERMS & NAMES 1. For each term or name, write a sentence explaining its significance.

- Rowlatt Acts
- Amritsar Massacre
- Mohandas K. Gandhi
- civil disobedience
- Salt March
- Mustafa Kemal

USING YOUR NOTES

2. Why do you think the nations in this section adopted different styles of government?

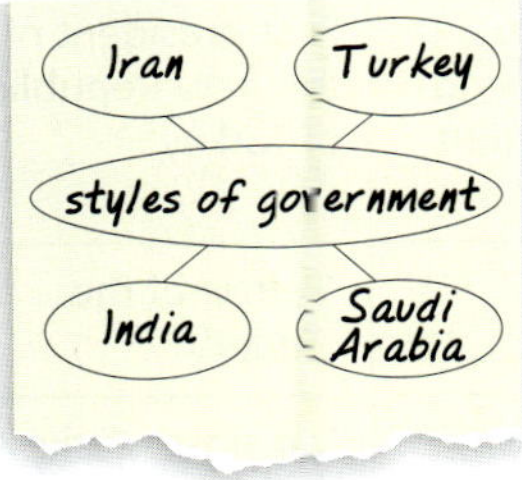

MAIN IDEAS

3. How did Gandhi's tactics of civil disobedience affect the British?
4. How did Southwest Asia change as a result of nationalism?
5. How did newly found petroleum supplies change the new nations in Southwest Asia?

CRITICAL THINKING & WRITING

6. **HYPOTHESIZING** What do you think a nation might gain and lose by modernizing?
7. **RECOGNIZING EFFECTS** How did World War I create an atmosphere for political change in both India and Southwest Asia?
8. **COMPARING AND CONTRASTING** Compare and contrast the different forms of government adopted by the four nations in this section.
9. **WRITING ACTIVITY** POWER AND AUTHORITY Write a **persuasive essay** supporting the use of nonviolent resistance.

CONNECT TO TODAY **GRAPHING OIL EXPORTS**

Do research to find out how many barrels of oil have been exported each year for the last ten years from Iran, Iraq, and Saudi Arabia. Create a **graph** showing your results.

Chapter 30 Assessment

TERMS & NAMES

Briefly explain the importance of each of the following in Russia, China, or India.

1. Bolsheviks
2. Lenin
3. soviet
4. Joseph Stalin
5. totalitarianism
6. Mao Zedong
7. Mohandas K. Gandhi
8. civil disobedience

MAIN IDEAS

Revolutions in Russia Section 1 (pages 867–873)

9. How did World War I lead to the downfall of Czar Nicholas II?
10. Why did the provisional government fail?
11. Explain the causes of Russia's civil war and its outcome.

Case Study: Totalitarianism Section 2 (pages 874–881)

12. What are the key traits of totalitarianism?
13. What individual freedoms are denied in a totalitarian state?
14. How did Joseph Stalin create a totalitarian state in the Soviet Union?

Imperial China Collapses Section 3 (pages 882–886)

15. Why did the peasants align themselves with the Chinese Communists?
16. Why did Mao Zedong undertake the Long March?

Nationalism in India and Southwest Asia Section 4 (pages 887–891)

17. What are some examples of civil disobedience led by Mohandas Gandhi?
18. What steps did Kemal take to modernize Turkey?

CRITICAL THINKING

1. USING YOUR NOTES
In a diagram show the causes of changes in government in the countries listed.

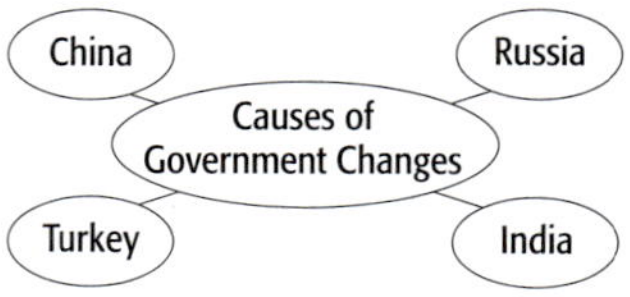

2. FORMING AND SUPPORTING OPINIONS
Which of the weapons of totalitarian governments do you think is most effective in maintaining control of a country? Explain.

3. ANALYZING CAUSES
REVOLUTION What role did World War I play in the revolutions and nationalistic uprisings discussed in this chapter?

4. HYPOTHESIZING
EMPIRE BUILDING Why were the empires discussed in this chapter unable to remain in control of all of their lands?

5. RECOGNIZING EFFECTS
POWER AND AUTHORITY How did women's roles change under Stalin in Russia and Kemal in Turkey?

VISUAL SUMMARY

Revolutionary Leaders: 1900–1939

	Lenin	Stalin	Sun Yixian	Mao Zedong	Gandhi	Kemal
Country	Russia	Russia	China	China	India	Turkey
Career	late 1890s–1924	early 1900s–1953	late 1890s–1925	early 1900s–1976	late 1800s–1948	early 1900s–1938
Key Role	Bolshevik revolutionary and first ruler of Communist Russia	Dictator	First president of the new Republic of China	Leader of the Chinese Communist Party	Leader of the Indian independence movement	First president of the new Republic of Turkey
Popular Name	"Father of the Revolution"	"Man of Steel"	"Father of Modern China"	"The Great Helmsman"	"Great Soul"	"Father of the Turks"
Goal	Promote a worldwide Communist revolution led by workers	Perfect a Communist state in Russia through totalitarian rule	Establish a modern government based on nationalism, democracy, and economic security	Stage a Communist revolution in China led by peasants	Achieve Indian self-rule through campaigns of civil disobedience	Transform Turkey into a modern nation

Use the quotation and your knowledge of world history to answers questions 1 and 2
Additional Test Practice, pp. S1–S33

PRIMARY SOURCE

India does not need to be industrialized in the modern sense of the term. It has 7,500,000 villages scattered over a vast area 1,900 miles long, 1,500 broad. The people are rooted to the soil, and the vast majority are living a hand-to-mouth life. . . . Agriculture does not need revolutionary changes. The Indian peasant requires a supplementary industry. The most natural is the introduction of the spinning-wheel.

MOHANDAS K. GANDHI, Letter to Sir Daniel Hamilton

1 What picture does Gandhi present of India and its people?
(1) India is adequately industrialized.
(2) India is dominated by the British.
(3) India is primarily an agricultural nation.
(4) Indians are well-off and do not need additional industries.

2 What did Gandhi believe about the spinning wheel?
(1) Gandhi believed that the spinning wheel would make Indians less dependent on the British economy.
(2) Gandhi believed that the spinning wheel was a threat to the Indian economy.
(3) Gandhi believed the main economic industry in India should be spinning cloth.
(4) Gandhi believed the spinning wheel was not necessary to the Indian economy.

Use the graph and your knowledge of world history to answer question 3.

Oil Output, 1910–1940

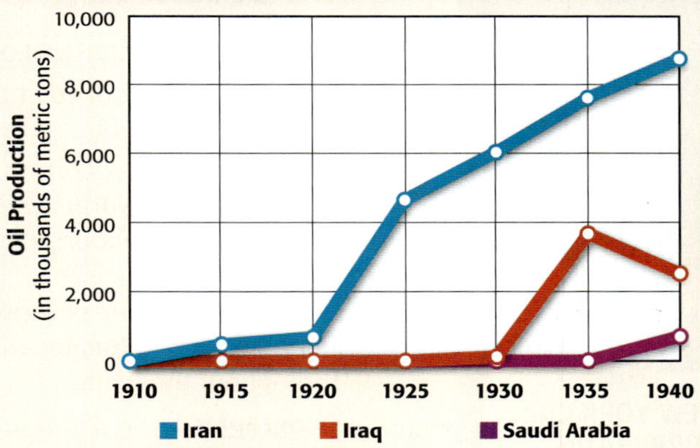

Source: *International Historical Statistics*

3 Between which years did Iran show a dramatic increase in oil production?
(1) 1910–1920
(2) 1920–1925
(3) 1930–1935
(4) 1935–1940

INTEGRATED TECHNOLOGY
TEST PRACTICE Go to **classzone.com**
- Diagnostic tests
- Tutorials
- Strategies
- Additional practice

ALTERNATIVE ASSESSMENT

1. Interact *with* History

On page 866, you played the role of a citizen whose country was brimming with revolutionary activity. You evaluated two tactics for change—violence and nonviolence. Now that you have read the chapter, how would you assess the pros and cons of Mao's and Gandhi's strategies? What role did violence play in the Russian and Chinese revolutions? How successful were Gandhi's nonviolent methods in India? Discuss your opinions in a small group.

2. WRITING ABOUT HISTORY

Write a **science fiction story** about a totalitarian state that uses modern technology to spread propaganda and control people. Refer to the case study on totalitarianism for ideas. Consider the following:
- the need to control information
- methods to control the actions of people
- reasons people oppose totalitarian control of a country

INTEGRATED TECHNOLOGY

Writing a Documentary Film Script

Write a documentary film script profiling a country where nationalistic revolutionary movements are currently active. Consider the following:
- What type of government is currently in power? (constitutional monarchy, single-party dictatorship, theocracy, republic) How long has it been in power?
- Who are the top political leaders, and how are they viewed inside and outside the country?
- Do citizens have complaints about their government? What are they?
- What nationalist revolutionary groups are active? What are their goals and strategies?

The script should also include narration, locations, sound, and visuals.

CHAPTER 31

Years of Crisis, 1919–1939

Previewing Main Ideas

SCIENCE AND TECHNOLOGY In the 1920s, new scientific ideas changed the way people looked at the world. New inventions improved transportation and communication.

Geography *Innovations in transportation allowed pilot Charles Lindbergh to fly solo from North America across the Atlantic Ocean. Toward what continent did Lindbergh fly?*

ECONOMICS The collapse of the American economy in 1929 triggered a depression that threatened the economic and political systems of countries throughout the world.

Geography *Study the map and time line. What events occurred after the economic crisis that changed the balance of world power?*

POWER AND AUTHORITY In the 1930s, several countries—including Japan, Germany, and Italy—adopted aggressive, militaristic policies.

Geography *What land did Germany invade in 1939?*

NEW YORK CORE CURRICULUM FOCUS

- Following World War I, women won the right to vote in many countries, including the United States and Great Britain.
- Economic and political turmoil led to the rise of fascism in Italy and Germany.

INTEGRATED TECHNOLOGY

eEdition
- Interactive Maps
- Interactive Visuals
- Interactive Primary Sources

INTERNET RESOURCES

Go to **classzone.com** for:
- Research Links
- Internet Activities
- Primary Sources
- Chapter Quiz
- Maps
- Test Practice
- Current Events

EUROPE

1919 Weimar Republic is established in Germany.

1921 Albert Einstein receives the Nobel Prize. ▶

1928 Kellogg-Briand peace pact is signed by almost every country in the world.

1920 — 1925

WORLD

1927 ◀ American pilot Charles Lindbergh crosses Atlantic.

1929 U.S. stock market crashes; Great Depression begins.

Expansion in Europe, 1931–1939

1933
Hitler is named German chancellor.

1936
◀ Spanish Civil War begins.

1939
Germany and Soviet Union sign nonaggression pact.

1930 **1935** **1940**

1931
Hirohito's Japan seizes Manchuria. ▶

1935
Ethiopia is invaded by Italian forces.

Interact *with* History

Which candidate will you choose?

On a spring evening in the early 1930s during the Great Depression, you are one of thousands of Germans gathered at an outdoor stadium in Munich. You are unemployed; your country is suffering. Like everyone else, you have come to this mass meeting to hear two politicians campaigning for office. Huge speakers blare out patriotic music, while you and the rest of the crowd wait impatiently for the speeches to begin.

Before long you will have to cast your ballot.

First candidate's platform

- Remember Germany's long and glorious past
- Replace our present indecisive leadership with a strong, effective leader
- Rebuild the army to protect against enemies
- Regain the lands taken unfairly from us
- Make sacrifices to return to economic health
- Put the welfare of the state above all, and our country will be a great power again

Second candidate's platform

- Realize that there are no simple or quick solutions to problems
- Put people back to work, but economic recovery will be slow
- Provide for the poor, elderly, and sick
- Avoid reckless military spending
- Act responsibly to safeguard democracy
- Be a good neighbor country; honor our debts and treaty commitments

EXAMINING *the* ISSUES

- **What strategy does each candidate have for solving the nation's problems?**
- **Which candidate makes the stronger appeal to the listener's emotions?**

As a class, discuss these questions. In your discussion, remember what you have read about the defeated nations' bitterness toward the Versailles Treaty following World War I. As you read this chapter, notice that dictators were voted into power as people lost faith in democratic government in the 1920s and 1930s.

Postwar Uncertainty

CONNECT TO THE NEW YORK STATE CORE CURRICULUM

Unit 6.C.1. Human and physical geography
Unit 6.C.4. Women's suffrage movement

TERMS & NAMES

- Albert Einstein
- theory of relativity
- Sigmund Freud
- existentialism
- Friedrich Nietzsche
- surrealism
- jazz
- Charles Lindbergh

SETTING THE STAGE The horrors of World War I shattered the Enlightenment belief that progress would continue and reason would prevail. In the postwar period, people began questioning traditional beliefs. Some found answers in new scientific developments, which challenged the way people looked at the world. Many enjoyed the convenience of technological improvements in transportation and communication. As society became more open, women demanded more rights, and young people adopted new values. Meanwhile, unconventional styles and ideas in literature, philosophy, and music reflected the uncertain times.

TAKING NOTES

Summarizing Use a chart to identify two people who contributed to each field.

Field	Contributors
science	
literature and philosophy	
art and music	
technology	

A New Revolution in Science

The ideas of Albert Einstein and Sigmund Freud had an enormous impact on the 20th century. These thinkers were part of a scientific revolution as important as that brought about centuries earlier by Copernicus and Galileo.

Impact of Einstein's Theory of Relativity-German-born physicist **Albert Einstein** offered startling new ideas on space, time, energy, and matter. Scientists had found that light travels at exactly the same speed no matter what direction it moves in relation to earth. In 1905, Einstein theorized that while the speed of light is constant, other things that seem constant, such as space and time, are not. Space and time can change when measured relative to an object moving near the speed of light—about 186,000 miles per second. Since relative motion is the key to Einstein's idea, it is called the **theory of relativity**. Einstein's ideas had implications not only for science but also for how people viewed the world. Now uncertainty and relativity replaced Isaac Newton's comforting belief of a world operating according to absolute laws of motion and gravity.

Influence of Freudian Psychology The ideas of Austrian physician **Sigmund Freud** were as revolutionary as Einstein's. Freud treated patients with psychological problems. From his experiences, he constructed a theory about the human mind. He believed that much of human behavior is irrational, or beyond reason. He called the irrational part of the mind the unconscious. In the unconscious, a number of drives existed, especially pleasure-seeking drives, of which the conscious mind was unaware. Freud's ideas weakened faith in reason. Even so, by the 1920s, Freud's theories had developed widespread influence.

Literature in the 1920s

The brutality of World War I caused philosophers and writers to question accepted ideas about reason and progress. Disillusioned by the war, many people also feared the future and expressed doubts about traditional religious beliefs. Some writers and thinkers expressed their anxieties by creating disturbing visions of the present and the future.

In 1922, T. S. Eliot, an American poet living in England, wrote that Western society had lost its spiritual values. He described the postwar world as a barren "wasteland," drained of hope and faith. In 1921, the Irish poet William Butler Yeats conveyed a sense of dark times ahead in the poem "The Second Coming": "Things fall apart; the centre cannot hold; / Mere anarchy is loosed upon the world."

Writers Reflect Society's Concerns The horror of war made a deep impression on many writers. The Czech-born author Franz Kafka wrote eerie novels such as *The Trial* (1925) and *The Castle* (1926). His books feature people caught in threatening situations they can neither understand nor escape. The books struck a chord among readers in the uneasy postwar years.

Many novels showed the influence of Freud's theories on the unconscious. The Irish-born author James Joyce gained widespread attention with his stream-of-consciousness novel *Ulysses* (1922). This book focuses on a single day in the lives of three people in Dublin, Ireland. Joyce broke with normal sentence structure and vocabulary in a bold attempt to mirror the workings of the human mind.

Vocabulary
stream of consciousness: a literary technique used to present a character's thoughts and feelings as they develop

Thinkers React to Uncertainties In their search for meaning in an uncertain world, some thinkers turned to the philosophy known as **existentialism**. A major leader of this movement was the philosopher Jean Paul Sartre (SAHR•truh) of France. Existentialists believed that there is no universal meaning to life. Each person creates his or her own meaning in life through choices made and actions taken.

Analyzing Primary Sources

Writers of the "Lost Generation"

During the 1920s, many American writers, musicians, and painters left the United States to live in Europe. These expatriates, people who left their native country to live elsewhere, often settled in Paris. American writer Gertrude Stein called them the "Lost Generation." They moved frantically from one European city to another, trying to find meaning in life. Life empty of meaning is the theme of F. Scott Fitzgerald's *The Great Gatsby* (1925).

PRIMARY SOURCE

And as I sat there brooding on the old, unknown world, I thought of Gatsby's wonder when he first picked out the green light at the end of Daisy's dock. He had come a long way to this blue lawn, and his dream must have seemed so close that he could hardly fail to grasp it. He did not know that it was already behind him, somewhere back in that vast obscurity beyond the city, where the dark fields of the republic rolled on under the night.

Gatsby believed in the green light, the . . . future that year by year recedes before us. It eluded us then, but that's no matter—tomorrow we will run faster, stretch out our arms farther. . . . And one fine morning—

So we beat on, boats against the current, borne back ceaselessly into the past.

F. SCOTT FITZGERALD, *The Great Gatsby*

A 1920s photo of F. Scott Fitzgerald

DOCUMENT-BASED QUESTIONS

1. **Making Inferences** *What seems to be the narrator's attitude toward the future?*
2. **Drawing Conclusions** *How would you describe the overall mood of the excerpt?*

The existentialists were influenced by the German philosopher **Friedrich Nietzsche** (NEE•chuh). In the 1880s, Nietzsche wrote that Western ideas such as reason, democracy, and progress had stifled people's creativity and actions. Nietzsche urged a return to the ancient heroic values of pride, assertiveness, and strength. His ideas attracted growing attention in the 20th century and had a great impact on politics in Italy and Germany in the 1920s and 1930s.

Revolution in the Arts

Although many of the new directions in painting and music began in the prewar period, they evolved after the war.

Artists Rebel Against Tradition Artists rebelled against earlier realistic styles of painting. They wanted to depict the inner world of emotion and imagination rather than show realistic representations of objects. Expressionist painters like Paul Klee and Wassily Kandinsky used bold colors and distorted or exaggerated forms.

Inspired by traditional African art, Georges Braque of France and Pablo Picasso of Spain founded Cubism in 1907. Cubism transformed natural shapes into geometric forms. Objects were broken down into different parts with sharp angles and edges. Often several views were depicted at the same time.

Surrealism, an art movement that sought to link the world of dreams with real life, was inspired by Freud's ideas. The term *surreal* means "beyond or above reality." Surrealists tried to call on the unconscious part of their minds. Many of their paintings have an eerie, dreamlike quality and depict objects in unrealistic ways. (A)

MAIN IDEA

Making Inferences

(A) What was the major trend in postwar art?

Composers Try New Styles In both classical and popular music, composers moved away from traditional styles. In his ballet masterpiece, *The Rite of Spring,* the Russian composer Igor Stravinsky used irregular rhythms and dissonances, or harsh combinations of sound. The Austrian composer Arnold Schoenberg rejected traditional harmonies and musical scales.

A new popular musical style called **jazz** emerged in the United States. It was developed by musicians, mainly African Americans, in New Orleans, Memphis, and Chicago. It swept the United States and Europe. The lively, loose beat of jazz seemed to capture the new freedom of the age.

◀ *The Persistence of Memory* (1931), a surrealist work by Spanish artist Salvador Dali, shows watches melting in a desert.

▲ Women like these marching in a 1912 suffrage parade in New York City helped gain American women's right to vote in 1920.

Society Challenges Convention

World War I had disrupted traditional social patterns. New ideas and ways of life led to a new kind of individual freedom during the 1920s. Young people especially were willing to break with the past and experiment with modern values.

Women's Roles Change The independent spirit of the times showed clearly in the changes women were making in their lives. The war had allowed women to take on new roles. Their work in the war effort was decisive in helping them win the right to vote. After the war, women's suffrage became law in many countries, including the United States, Britain, Germany, Sweden, and Austria.

Women abandoned restrictive clothing and hairstyles. They wore shorter, looser garments and had their hair "bobbed," or cut short. They also wore makeup, drove cars, and drank and smoked in public. Although most women still followed traditional paths of marriage and family, a growing number spoke out for greater freedom in their lives. Margaret Sanger and Emma Goldman risked arrest by speaking in favor of birth control. As women sought new careers, the numbers of women in medicine, education, journalism, and other professions increased. B

MAIN IDEA

Summarizing

B How did the changes of the postwar years affect women?

Technological Advances Improve Life

During World War I, scientists developed new drugs and medical treatments that helped millions of people in the postwar years. The war's technological advances were put to use to improve transportation and communication after the war.

The Automobile Alters Society The automobile benefited from a host of wartime innovations and improvements—electric starters, air-filled tires, and more powerful engines. Cars were now sleek and brightly polished, complete with headlights and chrome-plated bumpers. In prewar Britain, autos were owned exclusively by the rich. British factories produced 34,000 autos in 1913. After the war, prices dropped, and the middle class could afford cars. By 1937, the British were producing 511,000 autos a year.

Increased auto use by the average family led to lifestyle changes. More people traveled for pleasure. In Europe and the United States, new businesses opened to serve the mobile tourist. The auto also affected where people lived and worked. People moved to suburbs and commuted to work in the cities.

Airplanes Transform Travel International air travel became an objective after the war. In 1919, two British pilots made the first successful flight across the Atlantic, from Newfoundland to Ireland. In 1927, an American pilot named **Charles Lindbergh** captured world attention with a 33-hour solo flight from New York to Paris. Most of the world's major passenger airlines were established during the 1920s. At first only the rich were able to afford air travel. Still, everyone enjoyed the exploits of the aviation pioneers, including those of Amelia Earhart. She was an American who, in 1932, became the first woman to fly solo across the Atlantic.

Radio and Movies Dominate Popular Entertainment Guglielmo Marconi conducted his first successful experiments with radio in 1895. However, the real push for radio development came during World War I.

In 1920, the world's first commercial radio station—KDKA in Pittsburgh, Pennsylvania—began broadcasting. Almost overnight, radio mania swept the United States. Every major city had stations broadcasting news, plays, and even live sporting events. Soon most families owned a radio. C

MAIN IDEA

Recognizing Effects

C What were the results of the peacetime adaptations of the technology of war?

Motion pictures were also a major industry in the 1920s. Many countries, from Cuba to Japan, produced movies. In Europe, film was a serious art form. However, in the Hollywood district of Los Angeles, where 90 percent of all films were made, movies were entertainment.

The king of Hollywood's silent screen was the English-born Charlie Chaplin, a comic genius best known for his portrayal of the lonely little tramp bewildered by life. In the late 1920s, the addition of sound transformed movies.

The advances in transportation and communication that followed the war had brought the world in closer touch. Global prosperity came to depend on the economic well-being of all major nations, especially the United States.

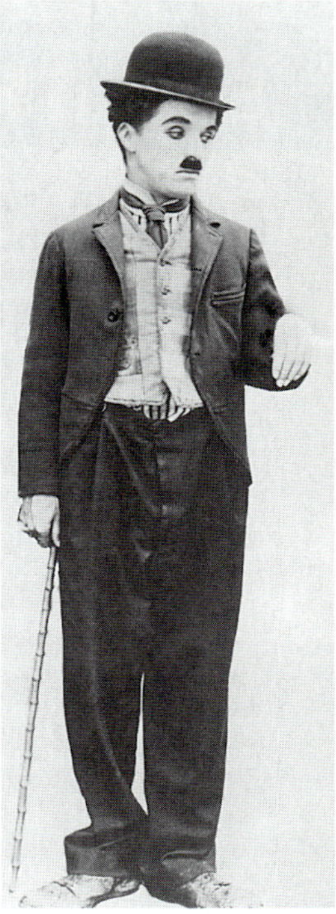

▲ Dressed in a ragged suit and oversize shoes, Charlie Chaplin's little tramp used gentle humor to get himself out of difficult situations.

NEW YORK CORE CURRICULUM REVIEW

TERMS & NAMES 1. For each term or name, write a sentence explaining its significance.

• Albert Einstein • theory of relativity • Sigmund Freud • existentialism • Friedrich Nietzsche • surrealism • jazz • Charles Lindbergh

USING YOUR NOTES

2. In your opinion, whose contribution has had the most lasting impact?

Field	Contributors
science	
literature and philosophy	

MAIN IDEAS

3. Why were the ideas of Einstein and Freud revolutionary?
4. How did literature in the 1920s reflect the uncertainty of the period?
5. What impact did the increased use of the automobile have on average people?

CRITICAL THINKING & WRITING

6. **HYPOTHESIZING** Why do you think writers and artists began exploring the unconscious?
7. **DEVELOPING HISTORICAL PERSPECTIVE** Why did some women begin demanding more political and social freedom?
8. **MAKING INFERENCES** Why were new medical treatments and inventions developed during World War I?
9. **WRITING ACTIVITY** SCIENCE AND TECHNOLOGY Write an **advertisement** that might have appeared in a 1920s newspaper or magazine for one of the technological innovations discussed in this section.

CONNECT TO TODAY **PREPARING AN ORAL REPORT**

Movies in the 1920s reflected the era. What do films made today say about our age? Review some recent, representative films and present your ideas in an **oral report.**

Labor-Saving Devices in the United States

Several changes that took place during the 1920s made the use of electrical household appliances more widespread.

- Wiring for electricity became common. In 1917, only 24 percent of U.S. homes had electricity; by 1930, that figure was almost 70 percent.
- Merchants offered the installment plan, which allowed buyers to make payments over time. That way, people could purchase appliances even if they didn't have the whole price.
- The use of advertising grew. Ads praised appliances, claiming that they would shorten tasks and give women more free time.

Ironically, the new labor-saving devices generally did not decrease the amount of time women spent doing housework. Because the tasks became less physically difficult, many families stopped hiring servants to do the work and relied on the wife to do all the jobs herself.

INTEGRATED TECHNOLOGY

RESEARCH LINKS For more on daily life in the 1920s, go to **classzone.com**

▼ Refrigerator

People used to keep perishable food in iceboxes cooled by large chunks of ice that gradually melted and had to be replaced. Electric refrigerators, like the one in this 1929 advertisement, kept the food at a fairly constant temperature, which reduced spoilage. Because food kept longer, housewives could shop less frequently.

▼ Washing Machine

To do laundry manually, women had to carry and heat about 50 gallons of water for each load. They rubbed the clothes on ridged washboards, rinsed them in tubs, and wrung them out by hand.

This early electric washing machine, photographed in 1933, made the job less strenuous. The casters on the legs made it easier to move tubs of water. The two rollers at the top of the machine squeezed water from clothes. That innovation alone saved women's wrists from constant strain.

▲ Iron

Before electrical appliances, women heated irons on a stove. The irons cooled quickly, and as they did so, women had to push down harder to press out wrinkles. Early electric irons also had inconsistent heat. This 1926 ad offered an electric iron that stayed evenly hot, so women didn't have to put so much force into their ironing. Therefore, they could iron sitting down.

Coffee Pot ►

The electric coffee pot shown in this 1933 photograph was a vacuum pot. The water in the bottom chamber would come to a boil and bubble up into the top chamber, where the grounds were. The resulting vacuum in the lower chamber pulled the liquid back through the grounds and into the lower chamber.

◄ Vacuum Cleaner

This 1920 ad promised "Twice as many rooms cleaned. . . . twice as much leisure left for you to enjoy." However, women rarely experienced that benefit. Because the new appliances made housework easier, people began to expect homes to be cleaner. As a result, many women vacuumed more often and generally used their newfound "leisure" time to do even more household chores than before.

> DATA FILE

APPLIANCES IN THE HOME

- In 1929, a survey of 100 Ford employees showed that 98 of them had electric irons in their homes.
- The same survey showed that 49 of the 100 had washing machines at home.

Source: *Historical Statistics of the United States*

Source: *Historical Statistics of the United States*

Connect *to* Today

1. **Analyzing Issues** What benefits did advertisers promise that the new electrical appliances would provide for women? Explain whether women actually received those benefits.

   See Skillbuilder Handbook, page R17.

2. **Comparing and Contrasting** Ask two or three adults about the way that technology has affected their work life and whether modern technologies are "labor-saving devices." How do your findings compare to the effect of electrical appliances in the 1920s?

A Worldwide Depression

CONNECT TO THE NEW YORK STATE CORE CURRICULUM

Unit 6.C.5. Great Depression–causes and impacts
Unit 6.C.6. Weimar Republic and the rise of fascism as an aftermath of World War I

TERMS & NAMES

- coalition government
- Weimar Republic
- Great Depression
- Franklin D. Roosevelt
- New Deal

SETTING THE STAGE By the late 1920s, European nations were rebuilding war-torn economies. They were aided by loans from the more prosperous United States. Only the United States and Japan came out of the war in better financial shape than before. In the United States, Americans seemed confident that the country would continue on the road to even greater economic prosperity. One sign of this was the booming stock market. Yet the American economy had serious weaknesses that were soon to bring about the most severe economic downturn the world had yet known.

TAKING NOTES

Recognizing Effects Use a diagram to show the effects of the Great Depression in the United States.

Postwar Europe

In both human suffering and economic terms, the cost of World War I was immense. The Great War left every major European country nearly bankrupt. In addition, Europe's domination in world affairs declined after the war.

Unstable New Democracies War's end saw the sudden rise of new democracies. From 1914 to 1918, Europe's last absolute rulers had been overthrown. The first of the new governments was formed in Russia in 1917. The Provisional Government, as it was called, hoped to establish constitutional and democratic rule. However, within months it had fallen to a Communist dictatorship. Even so, for the first time, most European nations had democratic governments.

Many citizens of the new democracies had little experience with representative government. For generations, kings and emperors had ruled Germany and the new nations formed from Austria-Hungary. Even in France and Italy, whose parliaments had existed before World War I, the large number of political parties made effective government difficult. Some countries had a dozen or more political groups. In these countries, it was almost impossible for one party to win enough support to govern effectively. When no single party won a majority, a **coalition government**, or temporary alliance of several parties, was needed to form a parliamentary majority. Because the parties disagreed on so many policies, coalitions seldom lasted very long.

Frequent changes in government made it hard for democratic countries to develop strong leadership and move toward long-term goals. The weaknesses of a coalition government became a major problem in times of crisis. Voters in several countries were then willing to sacrifice democratic government for strong, authoritarian leadership.

The Weimar Republic

Germany's new democratic government was set up in 1919. Known as the **Weimar** (WY•MAHR) **Republic**, it was named after the city where the national assembly met. The Weimar Republic had serious weaknesses from the start. First, Germany lacked a strong democratic tradition. Furthermore, postwar Germany had several major political parties and many minor ones. Worst of all, millions of Germans blamed the Weimar government, not their wartime leaders, for the country's defeat and postwar humiliation caused by the Versailles Treaty. (A)

MAIN IDEA

Identifying Problems

(A) What political problems did the Weimar Republic face?

Inflation Causes Crisis in Germany Germany also faced enormous economic problems that had begun during the war. Unlike Britain and France, Germany had not greatly increased its wartime taxes. To pay the expenses of the war, the Germans had simply printed money. After Germany's defeat, this paper money steadily lost its value. Burdened with heavy reparations payments to the Allies and with other economic problems, Germany printed even more money. As a result, the value of the mark, as Germany's currency was called, fell sharply. Severe inflation set in. Germans needed more and more money to buy even the most basic goods. For example, in Berlin a loaf of bread cost less than a mark in 1918, more than 160 marks in 1922, and some 200 billion marks by late 1923. People took wheelbarrows full of money to buy food. As a result, many Germans questioned the value of their new democratic government.

▼ German children use stacks of money as building blocks during the 1923 inflation.

Attempts at Economic Stability Germany recovered from the 1923 inflation thanks largely to the work of an international committee. The committee was headed by Charles Dawes, an American banker. The Dawes Plan provided for a $200 million loan from American banks to stabilize German currency and strengthen its economy. The plan also set a more realistic schedule for Germany's reparations payments.

Put into effect in 1924, the Dawes Plan helped slow inflation. As the German economy began to recover, it attracted more loans and investments from the United States. By 1929, German factories were producing as much as they had before the war.

Efforts at a Lasting Peace As prosperity returned, Germany's foreign minister, Gustav Stresemann (STRAY•zuh•MAHN), and France's foreign minister, Aristide Briand (bree•AHND), tried to improve relations between their countries. In 1925, the two ministers met in Locarno, Switzerland, with officials from Belgium, Italy, and Britain. They signed a treaty promising that France and Germany would never again make war against each other. Germany also agreed to respect the existing borders of France and Belgium. It then was admitted to the League of Nations.

In 1928, the hopes raised by the "spirit of Locarno" led to the Kellogg-Briand peace pact. Frank Kellogg, the U.S. Secretary of State, arranged this agreement with France's Briand. Almost every country in the world, including the Soviet Union, signed. They pledged "to renounce war as an instrument of national policy."

Unfortunately, the treaty had no means to enforce its provisions. The League of Nations, the obvious choice as enforcer, had no armed forces. The refusal of the United States to join the League also weakened it. Nonetheless, the peace agreements seemed a good start.

Financial Collapse

In the late 1920s, American economic prosperity largely sustained the world economy. If the U.S. economy weakened, the whole world's economic system might collapse. In 1929, it did.

A Flawed U.S. Economy Despite prosperity, several weaknesses in the U.S. economy caused serious problems. These included uneven distribution of wealth, overproduction by business and agriculture, and the fact that many Americans were buying less.

By 1929, American factories were turning out nearly half of the world's industrial goods. The rising productivity led to enormous profits. However, this new wealth was not evenly distributed. The richest 5 percent of the population received 33 percent of all personal income in 1929. Yet 60 percent of all American families earned less than $2,000 a year. Thus, most families were too poor to buy the goods being produced. Unable to sell all their goods, store owners eventually cut back their orders from factories. Factories in turn reduced production and laid off workers. A downward economic spiral began. As more workers lost their jobs, families bought even fewer goods. In turn, factories made further cuts in production and laid off more workers.

During the 1920s, overproduction affected American farmers as well. Scientific farming methods and new farm machinery had dramatically increased crop yields. American farmers were producing more food. Meanwhile, they faced new competition from farmers in Australia, Latin America, and Europe. As a result, a worldwide surplus of agricultural products drove prices and profits down.

Unable to sell their crops at a profit, many farmers could not pay off the bank loans that kept them in business. Their unpaid debts weakened banks and forced some to close. The danger signs of overproduction by factories and farms should have warned people against gambling on the stock market. Yet no one heeded the warning. **B**

The Stock Market Crashes In 1929, New York City's Wall Street was the financial capital of the world. Banks and investment companies lined its sidewalks. At Wall Street's New York Stock Exchange, optimism about the booming U.S. economy showed in soaring prices for stocks. To get in on the boom, many middle-income people began buying

History *in* Depth

Investing in Stocks

Stocks are shares of ownership in a company. Businesses get money to operate by selling "shares" of stock to investors, or buyers. Companies pay interest on the invested money in the form of dividends to the shareholders. Dividends rise or fall depending on a company's profits.

Investors do not buy stocks directly from the company; instead, stockbrokers transact the business of buying and selling.

Investors hope to make more money on stocks than if they put their money elsewhere, such as in a savings account with a fixed rate of interest. However, if the stock price goes down, investors lose money when they sell their stock at a lower price than when they bought it.

Stock Prices, 1925–1933

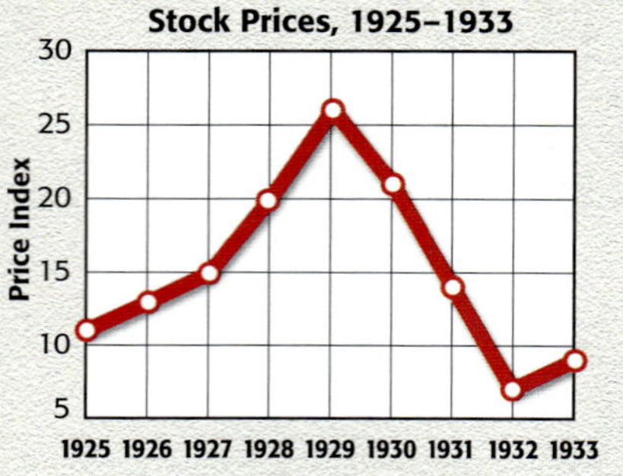

Source: *Historical Statistics of the United States*

MAIN IDEA

Identifying Problems

B What major weaknesses had appeared in the American economy by 1929?

Social History

Life in the Depression

During the Great Depression of 1929 to 1939, millions of people worldwide lost their jobs or their farms. At first the unemployed had to depend on the charity of others for food, clothing, and shelter. Many, like the men in this photo taken in New York City, made their home in makeshift shacks. Local governments and charities opened soup kitchens to provide free food. There were long lines of applicants for what work was available, and these jobs usually paid low wages.

INTEGRATED TECHNOLOGY

INTERNET ACTIVITY Create a photo-essay on the Great Depression in the United States. Go to **classzone.com** for your research.

stocks on margin. This meant that they paid a small percentage of a stock's price as a down payment and borrowed the rest from a stockbroker. The system worked well as long as stock prices were rising. However, if they fell, investors had no money to pay off the loan.

In September 1929, some investors began to think that stock prices were unnaturally high. They started selling their stocks, believing the prices would soon go down. By Thursday, October 24, the gradual lowering of stock prices had become an all-out slide downward. A panic resulted. Everyone wanted to sell stocks, and no one wanted to buy. Prices plunged to a new low on Tuesday, October 29. A record 16 million stocks were sold. Then the market collapsed.

The Great Depression

People could not pay the money they owed on margin purchases. Stocks they had bought at high prices were now worthless. Within months of the crash, unemployment rates began to rise as industrial production, prices, and wages declined. A long business slump, which would come to be called the **Great Depression**, followed. The stock market crash alone did not cause the Great Depression, but it quickened the collapse of the economy and made the Depression more difficult. By 1932, factory production had been cut in half. Thousands of businesses failed, and banks closed. Around 9 million people lost the money in their savings accounts when banks had no money to pay them. Many farmers lost their lands when they could not make mortgage payments. By 1933, one-fourth of all American workers had no jobs.

A Global Depression The collapse of the American economy sent shock waves around the world. Worried American bankers demanded repayment of their overseas loans, and American investors withdrew their money from Europe. The American market for European goods dropped sharply as the U.S. Congress placed high tariffs on imported goods so that American dollars would stay in the United States and pay for American goods. This policy backfired. Conditions worsened for the United

Vocabulary
tariffs: taxes charged by a government on imported or exported goods

Unemployment Rate, 1928–1938

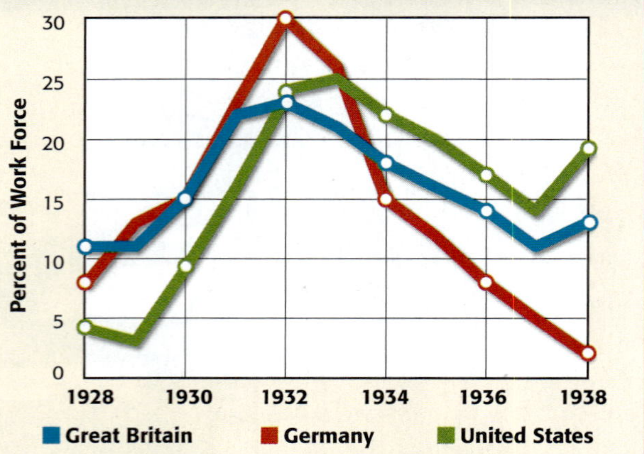

Sources: *European Historical Statistics: 1750–1970; Historical Statistics of the United States: Colonial Times to 1970.*

World Trade, 1929–1933

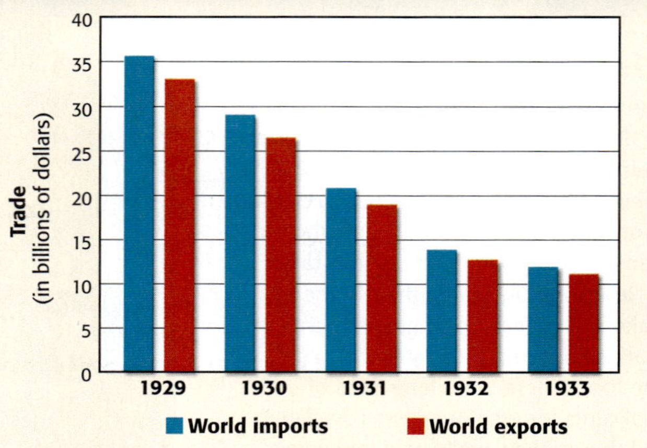

Source: Kenneth Oye, *Economic Discrimination and Political Exchange*

SKILLBUILDER: Interpreting Graphs

1. **Comparing** *What nation had the highest rate of unemployment? How high did it reach?*
2. **Clarifying** *Between 1929 and 1933, how much did world exports drop? What about world imports?*

States. Many countries that depended on exporting goods to the United States also suffered. Moreover, when the United States raised tariffs, it set off a chain reaction. Other nations imposed their own higher tariffs. World trade dropped by 65 percent. This contributed further to the economic downturn. Unemployment rates soared.

Effects Throughout the World Because of war debts and dependence on American loans and investments, Germany and Austria were particularly hard hit. In 1931, Austria's largest bank failed. In Asia, both farmers and urban workers suffered as the value of exports fell by half between 1929 and 1931. The crash was felt heavily in Latin America as well. As European and U.S. demand for such Latin American products as sugar, beef, and copper dropped, prices collapsed.

The World Confronts the Crisis

The Depression confronted democracies with a serious challenge to their economic and political systems. Each country met the crisis in its own way.

Britain Takes Steps to Improve Its Economy The Depression hit Britain severely. To meet the emergency, British voters elected a multiparty coalition known as the National Government. It passed high protective tariffs, increased taxes, and regulated the currency. It also lowered interest rates to encourage industrial growth. These measures brought about a slow but steady recovery. By 1937, unemployment had been cut in half, and production had risen above 1929 levels. Britain avoided political extremes and preserved democracy.

France Responds to Economic Crisis Unlike Britain, France had a more self-sufficient economy. In 1930, it was still heavily agricultural and less dependent on foreign trade. Nevertheless, by 1935, one million French workers were unemployed.

The economic crisis contributed to political instability. In 1933, five coalition governments formed and fell. Many political leaders were frightened by the growth of antidemocratic forces both in France and in other parts of Europe. So in 1936, moderates, Socialists, and Communists formed a coalition. The Popular Front, as it was called, passed a series of reforms to help the workers. Unfortunately, price increases quickly offset wage gains. Unemployment remained high. Yet France also preserved democratic government.

Socialist Governments Find Solutions The Socialist governments in the Scandinavian countries of Denmark, Sweden, and Norway also met the challenge of economic crisis successfully. They built their recovery programs on an existing tradition of cooperative community action. In Sweden, the government sponsored massive public works projects that kept people employed and producing. All the Scandinavian countries raised pensions for the elderly and increased unemployment insurance, subsidies for housing, and other welfare benefits. To pay for these benefits, the governments taxed all citizens. Democracy remained intact.

Recovery in the United States In 1932, in the first presidential election after the Depression had begun, U.S. voters elected **Franklin D. Roosevelt**. His confident manner appealed to millions of Americans who felt bewildered by the Depression. On March 4, 1933, the new president sought to restore Americans' faith in their nation.

MAIN IDEA

Analyzing Primary Sources

C What effect do you think Roosevelt's speech had on the American people?

PRIMARY SOURCE C

This great Nation will endure as it has endured, will revive and will prosper. . . . let me assert my firm belief that the only thing we have to fear is fear itself—nameless, unreasoning, unjustified terror which paralyzes needed efforts to convert retreat into advance.

FRANKLIN ROOSEVELT, First Inaugural Address

▲ Stricken with polio in 1921, Roosevelt vowed he would not allow bodily disability to defeat his will.

Roosevelt immediately began a program of government reform that he called the **New Deal**. Large public works projects helped to provide jobs for the unemployed. New government agencies gave financial help to businesses and farms. Large amounts of public money were spent on welfare and relief programs. Roosevelt and his advisers believed that government spending would create jobs and start a recovery. Regulations were imposed to reform the stock market and the banking system.

The New Deal did eventually reform the American economic system. Roosevelt's leadership preserved the country's faith in its democratic political system. It also established him as a leader of democracy in a world threatened by ruthless dictators, as you will read about in Section 3.

NEW YORK CORE CURRICULUM REVIEW

TERMS & NAMES 1. For each term or name, write a sentence explaining its significance.

- coalition government
- Weimar Republic
- Great Depression
- Franklin D. Roosevelt
- New Deal

USING YOUR NOTES

2. What did President Roosevelt do to try to counter the effects of the Great Depression?

MAIN IDEAS

3. How did World War I change the balance of economic power in the world?
4. What problems did the collapse of the American economy cause in other countries?
5. How did Europe respond to the economic crisis?

CRITICAL THINKING & WRITING

6. **MAKING PREDICTIONS** What did the weakness of the League of Nations in 1928 suggest about its future effectiveness?
7. **ANALYZING CAUSES** List one cause for each of the following effects: American market for European goods dropped; unemployment rates soared; European banks and businesses closed.
8. **EVALUATING COURSES OF ACTION** Why do you think Roosevelt immediately established the New Deal?
9. **WRITING ACTIVITY** ECONOMICS Write **headlines** on the stock market crash and the world's response to it.

INTEGRATED TECHNOLOGY **INTERNET ACTIVITY**

Use the Internet to follow the ups and downs of the stock market for a week. Chart the stock market's course in a **line graph**.

INTERNET KEYWORD
stock market

3

Fascism Rises in Europe

CONNECT TO THE NEW YORK STATE CORE CURRICULUM

Unit 6.C.6. Weimar Republic and the rise of fascism as an aftermath of World War I
Unit 6.D.3. Key individuals–Hitler, Mussolini, Stalin, Churchill, and Roosevelt

TERMS & NAMES

- fascism
- Benito Mussolini
- Adolf Hitler
- Nazism
- *Mein Kampf*
- *lebensraum*

SETTING THE STAGE Many democracies, including the United States, Britain, and France, remained strong despite the economic crisis caused by the Great Depression. However, millions of people lost faith in democratic government. In response, they turned to an extreme system of government called fascism. Fascists promised to revive the economy, punish those responsible for hard times, and restore order and national pride. Their message attracted many people who felt frustrated and angered by the peace treaties that followed World War I and by the Great Depression.

TAKING NOTES
Comparing and Contrasting Use a chart to compare Mussolini's rise to power and his goals with Hitler's.

Hitler	*Mussolini*
Rise:	*Rise:*
Goals:	*Goals:*

Fascism's Rise in Italy

Fascism (FASH•IHZ•uhm) was a new, militant political movement that emphasized loyalty to the state and obedience to its leader. Unlike communism, fascism had no clearly defined theory or program. Nevertheless, most Fascists shared several ideas. They preached an extreme form of nationalism, or loyalty to one's country. Fascists believed that nations must struggle—peaceful states were doomed to be conquered. They pledged loyalty to an authoritarian leader who guided and brought order to the state. In each nation, Fascists wore uniforms of a certain color, used special salutes, and held mass rallies.

In some ways, fascism was similar to communism. Both systems were ruled by dictators who allowed only their own political party (one-party rule). Both denied individual rights. In both, the state was supreme. Neither practiced any kind of democracy. However, unlike Communists, Fascists did not seek a classless society. Rather, they believed that each class had its place and function. In most cases, Fascist parties were made up of aristocrats and industrialists, war veterans, and the lower middle class. Also, Fascists were nationalists, and Communists were internationalists, hoping to unite workers worldwide.

Mussolini Takes Control Fascism's rise in Italy was fueled by bitter disappointment over the failure to win large territorial gains at the 1919 Paris Peace Conference. Rising inflation and unemployment also contributed to widespread social unrest. To growing numbers of Italians, their democratic government seemed helpless to deal with the country's problems. They wanted a leader who would take action.

Analyzing Key Concepts

Fascism

Fascism is a political movement that promotes an extreme form of nationalism and militarism. It also includes a denial of individual rights and dictatorial one-party rule. Nazism was the Fascist movement that developed in Germany in the 1920s and the 1930s; it included a belief in the racial superiority of the German people. The Fascists in Italy were led by Benito Mussolini, shown in the chart at right.

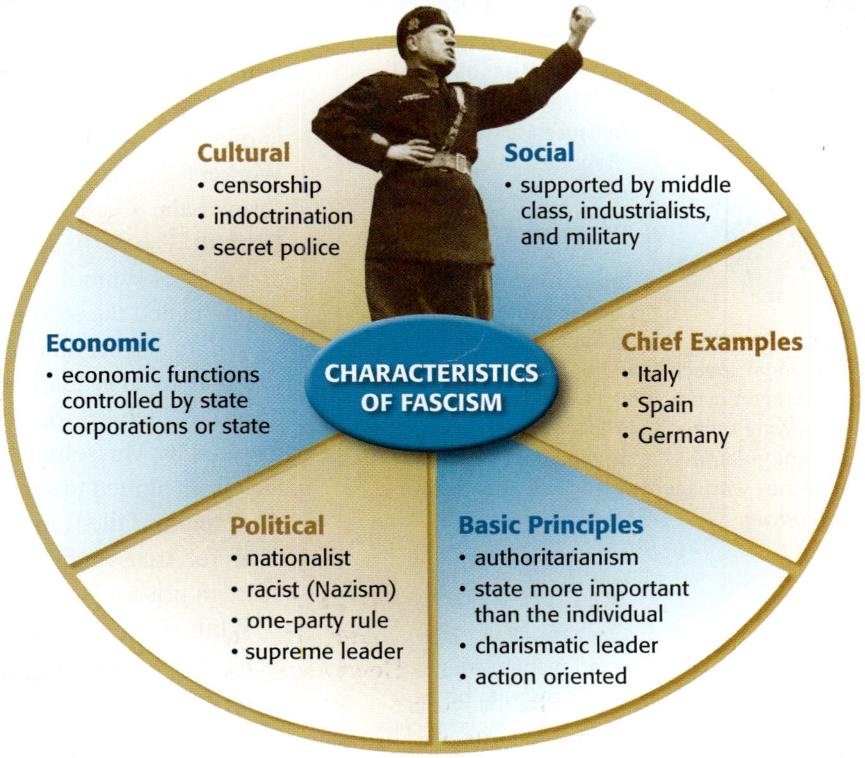

SKILLBUILDER: Interpreting Charts

1. **Synthesizing** *Which political, cultural, and economic characteristics helped make fascism an authoritarian system?*
2. **Making Inferences** *What characteristics of fascism might make it attractive to people during times of crisis such as the Great Depression?*

A newspaper editor and politician named **Benito Mussolini** boldly promised to rescue Italy by reviving its economy and rebuilding its armed forces. He vowed to give Italy strong leadership. Mussolini had founded the Fascist Party in 1919. As economic conditions worsened, his popularity rapidly increased. Finally, Mussolini publicly criticized Italy's government. Groups of Fascists wearing black shirts attacked Communists and Socialists on the streets. Because Mussolini played on the fear of a workers' revolt, he began to win support from the middle classes, the aristocracy, and industrial leaders.

In October 1922, about 30,000 Fascists marched on Rome. They demanded that King Victor Emmanuel III put Mussolini in charge of the government. The king decided that Mussolini was the best hope for his dynasty to survive. After widespread violence and a threatened uprising, Mussolini took power "legally." **A**

MAIN IDEA
Clarifying
A What promises did Mussolini make to the Italian people?

Il Duce's Leadership Mussolini was now Il Duce (ihl DOO•chay), or the leader. He abolished democracy and outlawed all political parties except the Fascists. Secret police jailed his opponents. Government censors forced radio stations and publications to broadcast or publish only Fascist doctrines. Mussolini outlawed strikes. He sought to control the economy by allying the Fascists with the industrialists and large landowners. However, Mussolini never had the total control achieved by Joseph Stalin in the Soviet Union or Adolf Hitler in Germany.

Hitler Rises to Power in Germany

When Mussolini became dictator of Italy in the mid-1920s, **Adolf Hitler** was a little-known political leader whose early life had been marked by disappointment. When World War I broke out, Hitler found a new beginning. He volunteered for the German army and was twice awarded the Iron Cross, a medal for bravery.

History Makers

Benito Mussolini
1883–1945

Because Mussolini was of modest height, he usually chose a location for his speeches where he towered above the crowds—often a balcony high above a public square. He then roused audiences with his emotional speeches and theatrical gestures and body movements.

Vowing to lead Italy "back to her ways of ancient greatness," Mussolini peppered his speeches with aggressive words such as *war* and *power.*

Adolf Hitler
1889–1945

Like Mussolini, Hitler could manipulate huge audiences with his fiery oratory. Making speeches was crucial to Hitler. He believed: "All great world-shaking events have been brought about . . . by the spoken word!"

Because he appeared awkward and unimposing, Hitler rehearsed his speeches. Usually he began a speech in a normal voice. Suddenly, he spoke louder as his anger grew. His voice rose to a screech, and his hands flailed the air. Then he would stop, smooth his hair, and look quite calm.

INTEGRATED TECHNOLOGY

RESEARCH LINKS For more on Benito Mussolini and Adolf Hitler, go to **classzone.com**

The Rise of the Nazis At the end of the war, Hitler settled in Munich. In 1919, he joined a tiny right-wing political group. This group shared his belief that Germany had to overturn the Treaty of Versailles and combat communism. The group later named itself the National Socialist German Workers' Party, called Nazi for short. Its policies formed the German brand of fascism known as **Nazism**. The party adopted the swastika, or hooked cross, as its symbol. The Nazis also set up a private militia called the storm troopers or Brown Shirts.

Within a short time, Hitler's success as an organizer and speaker led him to be chosen *der Führer* (duhr FYUR•uhr), or the leader, of the Nazi party. Inspired by Mussolini's march on Rome, Hitler and the Nazis plotted to seize power in Munich in 1923. The attempt failed, and Hitler was arrested. He was tried for treason but was sentenced to only five years in prison. He served less than nine months.

While in jail, Hitler wrote ***Mein Kampf*** (*My Struggle*). This book set forth his beliefs and his goals for Germany. Hitler asserted that the Germans, whom he incorrectly called "Aryans," were a "master race." He declared that non-Aryan "races," such as Jews, Slavs, and Gypsies, were inferior. He called the Versailles Treaty an outrage and vowed to regain German lands. Hitler also declared that Germany was overcrowded and needed more ***lebensraum***, or living space. He promised to get that space by conquering eastern Europe and Russia.

After leaving prison in 1924, Hitler revived the Nazi Party. Most Germans ignored him and his angry message until the Great Depression ended the nation's brief postwar recovery. When American loans stopped, the German economy collapsed. Civil unrest broke out. Frightened and confused, Germans now turned to Hitler, hoping for security and firm leadership.

Hitler Becomes Chancellor

The Nazis had become the largest political party by 1932. Conservative leaders mistakenly believed they could control Hitler and use him for their purposes. In January 1933, they advised President Paul von Hindenburg to name Hitler chancellor. Thus Hitler came to power legally. Soon after, General Erich Ludendorff, a former Hitler ally, wrote to Hindenburg:

Vocabulary
chancellor: the prime minister or president in certain countries

PRIMARY SOURCE

By naming Hitler as Reichschancellor, you have delivered up our holy Fatherland to one of the greatest [rabblerousers] of all time. I solemnly [predict] that this accursed man will plunge our Reich into the abyss and bring our nation into inconceivable misery.

ERICH LUDENDORFF, letter to President Hindenburg, February 1, 1933

Once in office, Hitler called for new elections, hoping to win a parliamentary majority. Six days before the election, a fire destroyed the Reichstag building, where the parliament met. The Nazis blamed the Communists. By stirring up fear of the Communists, the Nazis and their allies won by a slim majority.

Hitler used his new power to turn Germany into a totalitarian state. He banned all other political parties and had opponents arrested. Meanwhile, an elite, black-uniformed unit called the SS (*Schutzstaffel,* or protection squad) was created. It was loyal only to Hitler. In 1934, the SS arrested and murdered hundreds of Hitler's enemies. This brutal action and the terror applied by the Gestapo, the Nazi secret police, shocked most Germans into total obedience.

The Nazis quickly took command of the economy. New laws banned strikes, dissolved independent labor unions, and gave the government authority over business and labor. Hitler put millions of Germans to work. They constructed factories, built highways, manufactured weapons, and served in the military. As a result, the number of unemployed dropped from about 6 million to 1.5 million in 1936. B

MAIN IDEA

Making Inferences

B Why did Germans at first support Hitler?

The Führer Is Supreme Hitler wanted more than just economic and political power—he wanted control over every aspect of German life. To shape public opinion and to win praise for his leadership, Hitler turned the press, radio, literature, painting, and film into propaganda tools. Books that did not conform to Nazi beliefs were burned in huge bonfires. Churches were forbidden to criticize the Nazis or the government. Schoolchildren had to join the Hitler Youth (for boys) or the League of German Girls. Hitler believed that continuous struggle brought victory to the strong. He twisted the philosophy of Friedrich Nietzsche to support his use of brute force.

Hitler Makes War on the Jews Hatred of Jews, or anti-Semitism, was a key part of Nazi ideology. Although Jews were less than 1 percent of the population, the Nazis used them as scapegoats for all Germany's troubles since the war. This led to a wave of anti-Semitism across Germany. Beginning in 1933, the Nazis passed laws depriving Jews of most of their rights. Violence against Jews mounted. On the

▼ At a 1933 rally in Nuremberg, Germany, storm troopers carried flags bearing the swastika.

Global Impact

Fascism in Argentina

Juan Perón served as Argentina's president from 1946 to 1955 and again in 1973 and 1974. The two years he spent in Europe before World War II greatly influenced his strong-man rule.

A career army officer, Perón went to Italy in 1939 for military training. He then served at the Argentine embassy in Rome. A visit to Berlin gave Perón a chance to see Nazi Germany. The ability of Hitler and Mussolini to manipulate their citizens impressed Perón.

When Perón himself gained power, he patterned his military dictatorship on that of the European Fascists.

night of November 9, 1938, Nazi mobs attacked Jews in their homes and on the streets and destroyed thousands of Jewish-owned buildings. This rampage, called *Kristallnacht* (Night of the Broken Glass), signaled the real start of the process of eliminating the Jews from German life. You'll learn more about this in Chapter 32.

Other Countries Fall to Dictators

While Fascists took power in Italy and Germany, the nations formed in eastern Europe after World War I also were falling to dictators. In Hungary in 1919, after a brief Communist regime, military forces and wealthy landowners joined to make Admiral Miklós Horthy the first European postwar dictator. In Poland, Marshal Jozef Pilsudski (pihl•SOOT•skee) seized power in 1926. In Yugoslavia, Albania, Bulgaria, and Romania, kings turned to strong-man rule. They suspended constitutions and silenced foes. In 1935, only one democracy, Czechoslovakia, remained in eastern Europe.

Only in European nations with strong democratic traditions—Britain, France, and the Scandinavian countries—did democracy survive. With no democratic experience and severe economic problems, many Europeans saw dictatorship as the only way to prevent instability.

By the mid-1930s, the powerful nations of the world were split into two antagonistic camps—democratic and totalitarian. And to gain their ends, the Fascist dictatorships had indicated a willingness to use military aggression. Although all of these dictatorships restricted civil rights, none asserted control with the brutality of the Russian Communists or the Nazis.

NEW YORK CORE CURRICULUM REVIEW

TERMS & NAMES 1. For each term or name, write a sentence explaining its significance.

- fascism
- Benito Mussolini
- Adolf Hitler
- Nazism
- *Mein Kampf*
- *lebensraum*

USING YOUR NOTES

2. Do you think Hitler and Mussolini were more alike or different? Explain why.

Hitler	*Mussolini*
Rise:	*Rise:*
Goals:	*Goals:*

MAIN IDEAS

3. What factors led to the rise of fascism in Italy?
4. How did Hitler maintain power?
5. Why did the leadership of many eastern European nations fall to dictators?

CRITICAL THINKING & WRITING

6. **DRAWING CONCLUSIONS** Why did a movement like fascism and leaders like Mussolini and Hitler come to power during a period of crisis?
7. **ANALYZING MOTIVES** Why do you think Hitler had German children join Nazi organizations?
8. **SYNTHESIZING** What emotions did both Hitler and Mussolini stir in their followers?
9. **WRITING ACTIVITY** POWER AND AUTHORITY Reread the History Makers on Mussolini and Hitler on page 912. Then write a **description** of the techniques the two leaders used to appear powerful to their listeners.

CONNECT TO TODAY **PRESENTING AN ORAL REPORT**

Some modern rulers have invaded other countries for political and economic gain. Research to learn about a recent invasion and discuss your findings in an **oral report.**

Aggressors Invade Nations

CONNECT TO THE NEW YORK STATE CORE CURRICULUM

Unit 6.C.7.a. Manchuria, 1931
Unit 6.C.8. Policy of appeasement–Munich Pact

TERMS & NAMES

- appeasement
- Axis Powers
- Francisco Franco
- isolationism
- Third Reich
- Munich Conference

SETTING THE STAGE By the mid-1930s, Germany and Italy seemed bent on military conquest. The major democracies—Britain, France, and the United States—were distracted by economic problems at home and longed to remain at peace. With the world moving toward war, many nations pinned their hopes for peace on the League of Nations. As fascism spread in Europe, however, a powerful nation in Asia moved toward a similar system. Following a period of reform and progress in the 1920s, Japan fell under military rule.

Japan Seeks an Empire

During the 1920s, the Japanese government became more democratic. In 1922, Japan signed an international treaty agreeing to respect China's borders. In 1928, it signed the Kellogg-Briand Pact renouncing war. Japan's parliamentary system had several weaknesses, however. Its constitution put strict limits on the powers of the prime minister and the cabinet. Most importantly, civilian leaders had little control over the armed forces. Military leaders reported only to the emperor.

TAKING NOTES

Following Chronological Order Use a time line to trace the movement of Japan from democratic reform to military aggression.

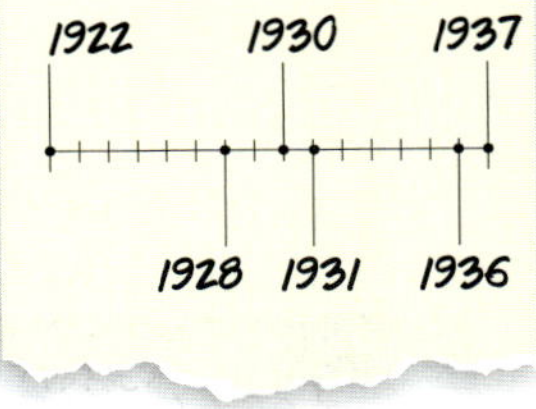

Militarists Take Control of Japan As long as Japan remained prosperous, the civilian government kept power. But when the Great Depression struck in 1929, many Japanese blamed the government. Military leaders gained support and soon won control of the country. Unlike the Fascists in Europe, the militarists did not try to establish a new system of government. They wanted to restore traditional control of the government to the military. Instead of a forceful leader like Mussolini or Hitler, the militarists made the emperor the symbol of state power.

Keeping Emperor Hirohito as head of state won popular support for the army leaders who ruled in his name. Like Hitler and Mussolini, Japan's militarists were extreme nationalists. They wanted to solve the country's economic problems through foreign expansion. They planned a Pacific empire that included a conquered China. The empire would provide Japan with raw materials and markets for its goods. It would also give Japan room for its rising population.

Japan Invades Manchuria Japanese businesses had invested heavily in China's northeast province, Manchuria. It was an area rich in iron and coal. In 1931, the Japanese army seized Manchuria, despite objections from the Japanese parliament. The army then set up a puppet government. Japanese engineers and technicians began arriving in large numbers to build mines and factories.

The Japanese attack on Manchuria was the first direct challenge to the League of Nations. In the early 1930s, the League's members included all major democracies except the United States. The League also included the three countries that posed the greatest threat to peace—Germany, Japan, and Italy. When Japan seized Manchuria, many League members vigorously protested. Japan ignored the protests and withdrew from the League in 1933. **A**

MAIN IDEA

Making Inferences

A What was the major weakness of the League of Nations?

Japan Invades China Four years later, a border incident touched off a full-scale war between Japan and China. Japanese forces swept into northern China. Despite having a million soldiers, China's army led by Jiang Jieshi was no match for the better equipped and trained Japanese.

Beijing and other northern cities as well as the capital, Nanjing, fell to the Japanese in 1937. Japanese troops killed tens of thousands of captured soldiers and civilians in Nanjing. Forced to retreat westward, Jiang Jieshi set up a new capital at Chongqing. At the same time, Chinese guerrillas led by China's Communist leader, Mao Zedong, continued to fight the Japanese in the conquered area.

European Aggressors on the March

The League's failure to stop the Japanese encouraged European Fascists to plan aggression of their own. The Italian leader Mussolini dreamed of building a colonial empire in Africa like those of Britain and France.

Mussolini Attacks Ethiopia Ethiopia was one of Africa's three independent nations. The Ethiopians had successfully resisted an Italian attempt at conquest during the 1890s. To avenge that defeat, Mussolini ordered a massive invasion of Ethiopia in October 1935. The spears and swords of the Ethiopians were no match for Italian airplanes, tanks, guns, and poison gas.

The Ethiopian emperor, Haile Selassie, urgently appealed to the League for help. Although the League condemned the attack, its members did nothing. Britain continued to let Italian troops and supplies pass through the British-controlled Suez Canal on their way to Ethiopia. By giving in to Mussolini in Africa, Britain and France hoped to keep peace in Europe.

Hitler Defies Versailles Treaty Hitler had long pledged to undo the Versailles Treaty. Among its provisions, the treaty limited the size of Germany's army. In March 1935, the Führer announced that Germany would not obey these restrictions. The League issued only a mild condemnation.

The League's failure to stop Germany from rearming convinced Hitler to take even greater risks. The treaty had forbidden German troops to enter a 30-mile-wide zone on either side of the Rhine River. Known as the Rhineland, the zone formed

Aggression in Europe, Asia, and Africa, 1931–1939

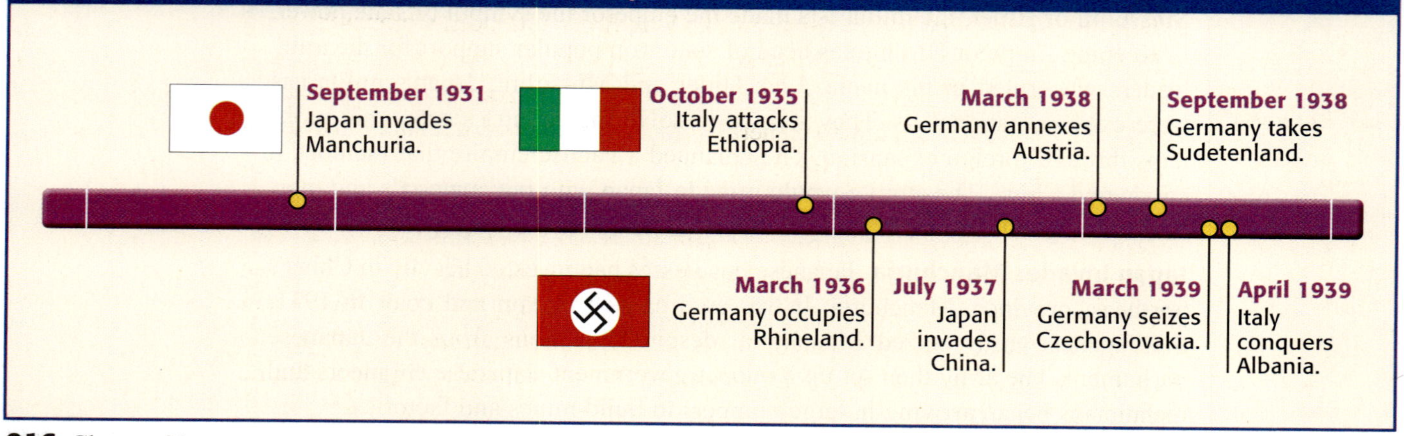

GEOGRAPHY SKILLBUILDER: Interpreting Maps

1. **Location** *On these maps, which countries are the aggressors?*
2. **Movement** *On what two continents did the aggression occur?*

a buffer between Germany and France. It was also an important industrial area. On March 7, 1936, German troops moved into the Rhineland. Stunned, the French were unwilling to risk war. The British urged **appeasement**, giving in to an aggressor to keep peace.

Hitler later admitted that he would have backed down if the French and British had challenged him. The German reoccupation of the Rhineland marked a turning point in the march toward war. First, it strengthened Hitler's power and prestige within Germany. Second, the balance of power changed in Germany's favor. France and Belgium were now open to attack from German troops. Finally, the weak response by France and Britain encouraged Hitler to speed up his expansion.

Hitler's growing strength convinced Mussolini that he should seek an alliance with Germany. In October 1936, the two dictators reached an agreement that became known as the Rome-Berlin Axis. A month later, Germany also made an agreement with Japan. Germany, Italy, and Japan came to be called the **Axis Powers**.

Vocabulary
axis: a straight line around which an object rotates. Hitler and Mussolini expected their alliance to become the axis around which Europe would rotate.

Civil War Erupts in Spain Hitler and Mussolini again tested the will of the democracies of Europe in the Spanish Civil War. Spain had been a monarchy until 1931, when a republic was declared. The government, run by liberals and Socialists, held office amid many crises. In July 1936, army leaders, favoring a Fascist-style government, joined General **Francisco Franco** in a revolt. Thus began a civil war that dragged on for three years.

Hitler and Mussolini sent troops, tanks, and airplanes to help Franco's forces, which were called the Nationalists. The armed forces of the Republicans, as supporters of Spain's elected government were known, received little help from abroad. The Western democracies remained neutral. Only the Soviet Union sent equipment and advisers. An international brigade of volunteers fought on the Republican side. Early in 1939, Republican resistance collapsed. Franco became Spain's Fascist dictator.

Analyzing Art

Guernica

On April 26, 1937, Franco's German allies bombed the ancient Basque city of Guernica in Spain. The photograph (above) shows the city reduced to rubble by the bombing. However, Spanish artist Pablo Picasso's painting, called *Guernica* (below), captures the human horror of the event.

Using the geometric forms of Cubism, Picasso shows a city and people that have been torn to pieces. Unnatural angles and overlapping images of people, severed limbs, and animals reflect the suffering and chaos caused by the attack. At left, a mother cries over her dead child. In the center, a horse screams and a soldier lies dead. At right, a woman falls from a burning house.

SKILLBUILDER:
Interpreting Visual Sources

1. **Analyzing Motives** *What were Picasso's probable motives for painting* Guernica?
2. **Hypothesizing** *What feelings do you think* Guernica *stirred in the public in the late 1930s?*

Democratic Nations Try to Preserve Peace

Instead of taking a stand against Fascist aggression in the 1930s, Britain and France repeatedly made concessions, hoping to keep peace. Both nations were dealing with serious economic problems as a result of the Great Depression. In addition, the horrors of World War I had created a deep desire to avoid war.

United States Follows an Isolationist Policy Many Americans supported **isolationism**, the belief that political ties to other countries should be avoided. Isolationists argued that entry into World War I had been a costly error. Beginning in 1935, Congress passed three Neutrality Acts. These laws banned loans and the sale of arms to nations at war.

The German Reich Expands On November 5, 1937, Hitler announced to his advisers his plans to absorb Austria and Czechoslovakia into the **Third Reich** (ryk), or German Empire. The Treaty of Versailles prohibited *Anschluss* (AHN•SHLUS), or a union between Austria and Germany. However, many Austrians supported unity with Germany. In March 1938, Hitler sent his army into Austria and annexed it. France and Britain ignored their pledge to protect Austrian independence.

Hitler next turned to Czechoslovakia. About three million German-speaking people lived in the western border regions of Czechoslovakia called the Sudetenland. (See map, page 895.) This heavily fortified area formed the Czechs' main defense against Germany. The Anschluss raised pro-Nazi feelings among Sudeten Germans. In September 1938, Hitler demanded that the Sudetenland be given to Germany. The Czechs refused and asked France for help.

Britain and France Again Choose Appeasement France and Britain were preparing for war when Mussolini proposed a meeting of Germany, France, Britain, and Italy in Munich, Germany. The **Munich Conference** was held on September 29, 1938. The Czechs were not invited. British prime minister Neville Chamberlain believed that he could preserve peace by giving in to Hitler's demand. Britain and France agreed that Hitler could take the Sudetenland. In exchange, Hitler pledged to respect Czechoslovakia's new borders.

When Chamberlain returned to London, he told cheering crowds, "I believe it is peace for our time." Winston Churchill, then a member of the British Parliament, strongly disagreed. He opposed the appeasement policy and gloomily warned of its consequences:

▲ Chamberlain waves the statement he read following the Munich Conference.

MAIN IDEA

Analyzing Primary Sources

B Why did Churchill believe that Chamberlain's policy of appeasement was a defeat for the British?

PRIMARY SOURCE B

We are in the presence of a disaster of the first magnitude. . . . we have sustained a defeat without a war. . . . And do not suppose that this is the end. . . . This is only the first sip, the first foretaste of a bitter cup which will be proffered to us year by year unless, by a supreme recovery of moral health and martial vigor, we arise again and take our stand for freedom as in the olden time.

WINSTON CHURCHILL, speech before the House of Commons, October 5, 1938

Less than six months after the Munich meeting, Hitler took Czechoslovakia. Soon after, Mussolini seized Albania. Then Hitler demanded that Poland return the former German port of Danzig. The Poles refused and turned to Britain and France for aid. But appeasement had convinced Hitler that neither nation would risk war.

Nazis and Soviets Sign Nonaggression Pact Britain and France asked the Soviet Union to join them in stopping Hitler's aggression. As Stalin talked with Britain and France, he also bargained with Hitler. The two dictators reached an agreement. Once bitter enemies, Fascist Germany and Communist Russia now publicly pledged never to attack one another. On August 23, 1939, their leaders signed a nonaggression pact. As the Axis Powers moved unchecked at the end of the decade, war appeared inevitable.

NEW YORK CORE CURRICULUM REVIEW

TERMS & NAMES 1. For each term or name, write a sentence explaining its significance.

- appeasement
- Axis Powers
- Francisco Franco
- isolationism
- Third Reich
- Munich Conference

USING YOUR NOTES

2. What event was the most significant? Why?

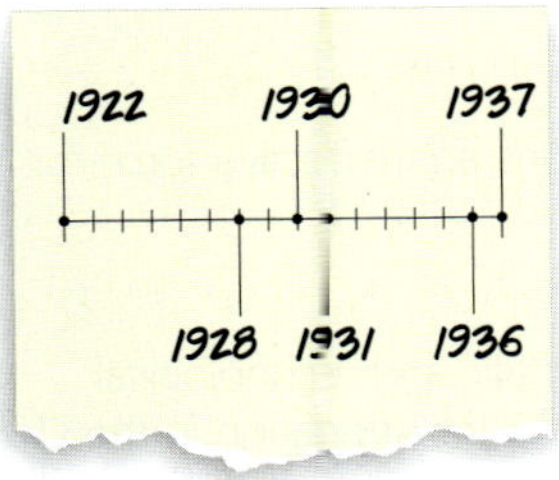

MAIN IDEAS

3. Compare the militarists in Japan with the European Fascists.
4. Which countries formed the Axis Powers?
5. What were the effects of isolationism and appeasement?

CRITICAL THINKING & WRITING

6. **SYNTHESIZING** What similar goals did Hitler, Mussolini, and Hirohito share?
7. **FORMING OPINIONS** Do you think the Fascist nations of the Axis Powers could have been stopped? Explain.
8. **EVALUATING DECISIONS** Why weren't the Czechs invited to take part in the Munich Conference?
9. **WRITING ACTIVITY** POWER AND AUTHORITY Write a **letter to the editor** in which you voice your opinion about the U.S. policy of isolationism during the 1930s.

CONNECT TO TODAY **STAGING A DEBATE**

Established in 1945, the United Nations was intended to be an improvement on the League of Nations. Research to learn about the recent successes and failures of the UN. Then hold a **debate** in which you argue whether the institution should be preserved.

Chapter 31 Assessment

VISUAL SUMMARY

The Great Depression

Long-Term Causes

- World economies are connected.
- Some countries have huge war debts from World War I.
- Europe relies on American loans and investments.
- Prosperity is built on borrowed money.
- Wealth is unequally distributed.

Immediate Causes

- U.S. stock market crashes.
- Banks demand repayment of loans.
- Farms fail and factories close.
- Americans reduce foreign trade to protect economy.
- Americans stop loans to foreign countries.
- American banking system collapses.

WORLDWIDE ECONOMIC DEPRESSION

Immediate Effects

- Millions become unemployed worldwide.
- Businesses go bankrupt.
- Governments take emergency measures to protect economies.
- Citizens lose faith in capitalism and democracy.
- Nations turn toward authoritarian leaders.

Long-Term Effects

- Nazis take control in Germany.
- Fascists come to power in other countries.
- Democracies try social welfare programs.
- Japan expands in East Asia.
- World War II breaks out.

TERMS & NAMES

For each term or name below, briefly explain its connection to world history from 1919 to 1939.

1. Albert Einstein
2. Sigmund Freud
3. Weimar Republic
4. New Deal
5. fascism
6. Benito Mussolini
7. Adolf Hitler
8. appeasement
9. Francisco Franco
10. Munich Conference

MAIN IDEAS

Postwar Uncertainty Section 1 (pages 897–903)

11. What effect did Einstein's theory of relativity and Freud's theory of the unconscious have on the public?
12. What advances were made in transportation and communication in the 1920s and 1930s?

A Worldwide Depression Section 2 (pages 904–909)

13. Why was the Weimar Republic considered weak?
14. What caused the stock market crash of 1929?

Fascism Rises in Europe Section 3 (pages 910–914)

15. For what political and economic reasons did the Italians turn to Mussolini?
16. What beliefs and goals did Hitler express in *Mein Kampf?*

Aggressors Invade Nations Section 4 (pages 915–919)

17. How did Japan plan to solve its economic problems?
18. Why was Germany's reoccupation of the Rhineland a significant turning point toward war?

CRITICAL THINKING

1. **USING YOUR NOTES**
   ECONOMICS Use a sequence graphic to identify the events that led to the stock market collapse.

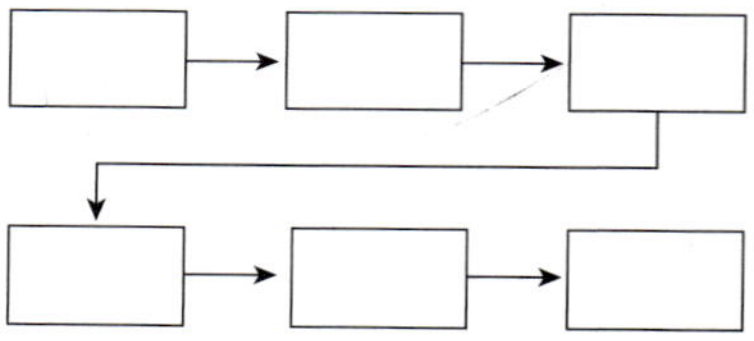

2. **MAKING INFERENCES**
   POWER AND AUTHORITY What were the advantages and disadvantages of being under Fascist rule?
3. **DRAWING CONCLUSIONS**
   What weaknesses made the League of Nations an ineffective force for peace in the 1920s and 1930s?
4. **SYNTHESIZING**
   SCIENCE AND TECHNOLOGY How did the scientific and technological revolutions of the 1920s help set the stage for transportation in the United States today?
5. **HYPOTHESIZING**
   What might have been the outcome if Great Britain, France, and other European nations had not chosen to appease German, Italian, and Japanese aggression?

NEW YORK STATE REGENTS EXAM PRACTICE

Use the quotation from a live radio report during the Munich Conference and your knowledge of world history to answer questions 1 and 2.
Additional Test Practice, pp. S1–S33

PRIMARY SOURCE

It took the Big Four [France, Britain, Italy, and Germany] just five hours and twenty-five minutes here in Munich today to dispel the clouds of war and come to an agreement over the partition of Czechoslovakia. There is to be no European war. . . the price of that peace is, roughly, the ceding by Czechoslovakia of the Sudeten territory to Herr Hitler's Germany. The German Führer gets what he wanted, only he has to wait a little longer for it.

WILLIAM SHIRER, quoted in *The Strenuous Decade*

1 Why did France, Britain, and Italy agree to give the Sudeten territory to Germany?
(1) to provoke war
(2) to avoid war
(3) to make Czechoslovakia happy
(4) to make Czechoslovakia unhappy

2 How were the expectations expressed in the radio report overturned by reality?
(1) Czechoslovakia refused to give the Sudeten territory to Hitler.
(2) Hitler did not get what he wanted.
(3) The Big Four didn't come to an agreement over Czechoslovakia.
(4) Europe was not saved from war.

Use the photograph of Adolf Hitler and your knowledge of world history to answer question 3.

3 Why do you think Hitler had his photograph taken with this little girl?
(1) to demonstrate his power
(2) to frighten his enemies
(3) to make him appear more human
(4) to demonstrate his hatred of Jews

INTEGRATED TECHNOLOGY
TEST PRACTICE Go to **classzone.com**
- Diagnostic tests
- Tutorials
- Strategies
- Additional practice

ALTERNATIVE ASSESSMENT

1. Interact *with* History

On page 896, you chose a candidate to support in German elections in the early 1930s. Now that you have read the chapter, did what you read confirm your decision? Why or why not? Would the candidate you selected have a good or bad effect on the rest of the world? Discuss your opinions with a small group.

2. WRITING ABOUT HISTORY

Write a **radio script** for a report on a speech given by Hitler or Mussolini. Imagine that you have just seen the dictator deliver the speech and you want to share your impressions with the public in your broadcast. Be sure to
- summarize the main ideas of the speech.
- describe the speaker's gestures and facial expressions.
- provide phrases that demonstrate the emotional power of the speech.
- convey the public's response to the speech.
- offer your opinion of the speech and speaker.

INTEGRATED TECHNOLOGY

NetExplorations: Life in the 1920s

Go to *NetExplorations* at **classzone.com** to learn more about life in the 1920s. Use your research to create a Web page on films from that era. Consider including
- reviews of the films, including a positive or negative recommendation.
- background information about silent films.
- biographical information about the stars and directors of the films.
- stills and clips from the films.
- a comparison between films of the 1920s and modern films.

CHAPTER 32

World War II, 1939–1945

Previewing Main Ideas

EMPIRE BUILDING Germany, Italy, and Japan tried to build empires. They began their expansion by conquering other nations and dominating them politically and economically.

Geography *What areas did the Axis powers control at the height of their power?*

SCIENCE AND TECHNOLOGY Far-reaching developments in science and technology changed the course of World War II. Improvements in aircraft, tanks, and submarines and the development of radar and the atomic bomb drastically altered the way wars were fought.

Geography *Why might submarines have been a key weapon for the Axis powers in their fight against Great Britain?*

ECONOMICS Fighting the Axis terror weakened the economies of Great Britain, the Soviet Union, and other European countries. In contrast, when the United States entered the war, its economy grew sharply. The strength of the American economy bolstered the Allied war effort.

Geography *In terms of location, why was the American economy able to function at a high level while the European economies struggled?*

NEW YORK CORE CURRICULUM FOCUS

- Japanese aggression in Asia and the bombing of Pearl Harbor led the Allies to war with Japan.
- The Holocaust resulted in the death of six million Jews and five million other "non-Aryans."

INTEGRATED TECHNOLOGY

eEdition

- Interactive Maps
- Interactive Visuals
- Interactive Primary Sources

VIDEO *Patterns of Interaction: Modern and Medieval Weapons*

INTERNET RESOURCES

Go to **classzone.com** for:

- Research Links
- Internet Activities
- Primary Sources
- Chapter Quiz
- Maps
- Test Practice
- Current Events

EUROPE AND THE MEDITERRANEAN

PACIFIC

1939

Sept. 1939
Germany invades Poland; France and Great Britain declare war on Germany. (political cartoon) ▼

1940

June 1940
France surrenders to Germany; Battle of Britain begins.

1941

June 1941
Germans invade Soviet Union.

Dec. 1941
◀ Japan attacks Pearl Harbor.

European and African Battles, 1939–1945

Nov. 1942
Allies invade North Africa.

Feb. 1943
Germans surrender at Stalingrad.

June 1944
◀ D-Day invasion takes place.

May 1945
Germany surrenders.

1942 **1943** **1944** **1945**

June 1942
Allies defeat Japan at Battle of Midway.

Feb. 1943
Allies defeat Japan at Guadalcanal.

Oct. 1944
Japanese suffer devastating defeat at the Battle of Leyte Gulf.

Aug.–Sept. 1945
Allies use atomic bombs; Japan surrenders.

Interact *with* History

Under what circumstances is war justified?

Every day your newspaper carries stories of the latest bombing raids on London and other British cities. The photographs of the devastation are shocking. As you read the stories and view the photographs, you wonder what the United States should do to help Great Britain, its longtime ally. The editorial pages of the newspapers ask the same question. Should the United States stand aside and let the European nations settle the issues themselves? Should it offer help to Great Britain in the form of arms and other supplies? Or should the United States join Britain in its struggle against the Axis powers?

▲ A German bombing raid on London during the Battle of Britain

EXAMINING *the* ISSUES

- **What circumstances would lead you to support or oppose your country's participation in a war?**
- **How are civilians sometimes as much a part of a war effort as soldiers?**

As a class, discuss these questions. In your discussion, weigh the arguments for and against fighting. As you read about World War II, think about the role that civilians play in a situation of total war. Think also about the hard moral choices that people often face in times of war.

Hitler's Lightning War

CONNECT TO THE NEW YORK STATE CORE CURRICULUM

Unit 6.D.3. Key individuals–Hitler, Mussolini, Stalin, Churchill, and Roosevelt
Unit 6.D.4. Key events–Dunkirk, the Blitz, D-Day, Hitler's second front, the war in the Pacific

TERMS & NAMES

- nonaggression pact
- blitzkrieg
- Charles de Gaulle
- Winston Churchill
- Battle of Britain
- Erwin Rommel
- Atlantic Charter

SETTING THE STAGE During the 1930s, Hitler played on the hopes and fears of the Western democracies. Each time the Nazi dictator grabbed new territory, he would declare an end to his demands. Peace seemed guaranteed—until Hitler moved again. After his moves into the Rhineland, Austria, and Czechoslovakia, Hitler turned his eyes to Poland. After World War I, the Allies had cut out the Polish Corridor from German territory to give Poland access to the sea. In 1939, Hitler demanded that the Polish Corridor be returned to Germany.

TAKING NOTES

Recognizing Effects Use a chart to identify the effects of some of the early events of World War II.

Cause	Effect
First blitzkrieg	
Allies stranded at Dunkirk	
Lend-Lease Act	

Germany Sparks a New War in Europe

At this point, as you recall from Chapter 31, Soviet dictator Joseph Stalin signed a ten-year **nonaggression pact** with Hitler. After being excluded from the Munich Conference, Stalin was not eager to join with the West. Also, Hitler had promised him territory. In a secret part of the pact, Germany and the Soviet Union agreed to divide Poland between them. They also agreed that the USSR could take over Finland and the Baltic countries of Lithuania, Latvia, and Estonia.

Germany's Lightning Attack After signing this nonaggression pact, Hitler quickly moved ahead with plans to conquer Poland. His surprise attack took place at dawn on September 1, 1939. German tanks and troop trucks rumbled across the Polish border. At the same time, German aircraft and artillery began a merciless bombing of Poland's capital, Warsaw.

France and Great Britain declared war on Germany on September 3. But Poland fell some time before those nations could make any military response. After his victory, Hitler annexed the western half of Poland. That region had a large German population.

The German invasion of Poland was the first test of Germany's newest military strategy—the **blitzkrieg** (BLIHTS•kreeg), or "lightning war." It involved using fast-moving airplanes and tanks, followed by massive infantry forces, to take enemy defenders by surprise and quickly overwhelm them. In the case of Poland, the strategy worked.

The Soviets Make Their Move On September 17, Stalin sent Soviet troops to occupy the eastern half of Poland. Stalin then moved to annex countries to the north of Poland. Lithuania, Latvia, and Estonia fell without a struggle, but Finland resisted. In November, Stalin sent nearly one million Soviet troops into

Finland. The Soviets expected to win a quick victory, so they were not prepared for winter fighting. This was a crucial mistake.

The Finns were outnumbered and outgunned, but they fiercely defended their country. In the freezing winter weather, soldiers on skis swiftly attacked Soviet positions. In contrast, the Soviets struggled to make progress through the deep snow. The Soviets suffered heavy losses, but they finally won through sheer force of numbers. By March 1940, Stalin had forced the Finns to accept his surrender terms. (A)

MAIN IDEA

Analyzing Motives

(A) What were Stalin's goals in Europe at the beginning of World War II?

The Phony War After they declared war on Germany, the French and British had mobilized their armies. They stationed their troops along the Maginot (MAZH•uh•NOH) Line, a system of fortifications along France's border with Germany. There they waited for the Germans to attack—but nothing happened. With little to do, the bored Allied soldiers stared eastward toward the enemy. Equally bored, German soldiers stared back from their Siegfried Line a few miles away. Germans jokingly called it the *sitzkrieg,* or "sitting war." Some newspapers referred to it simply as "the phony war."

Suddenly, on April 9, 1940, the calm ended. Hitler launched a surprise invasion of Denmark and Norway. In just four hours after the attack, Denmark fell. Two months later, Norway surrendered as well. The Germans then began to build bases along the Norwegian and Danish coasts from which they could launch strikes on Great Britain.

The Fall of France

In May of 1940, Hitler began a dramatic sweep through the Netherlands, Belgium, and Luxembourg. This was part of a strategy to strike at France. Keeping the Allies' attention on those countries, Hitler then sent an even larger force of tanks

SKILLBUILDER: Interpreting Maps

1. **Region** *Which countries did Germany invade?*
2. **Location** *In what way was Germany's geographic location an advantage when it was on the offensive in the war?*

and troops to slice through the Ardennes (ahr•DEHN). This was a heavily wooded area in northern France, Luxembourg, and Belgium. Moving through the forest, the Germans "squeezed between" the Maginot Line. From there, they moved across France and reached the country's northern coast in ten days.

Rescue at Dunkirk After reaching the French coast, the German forces swung north again and joined with German troops in Belgium. By the end of May 1940, the Germans had trapped the Allied forces around the northern French city of Lille (leel). Outnumbered, outgunned, and pounded from the air, the Allies retreated to the beaches of Dunkirk, a French port city near the Belgian border. They were trapped with their backs to the sea.

In one of the most heroic acts of the war, Great Britain set out to rescue the army. It sent a fleet of about 850 ships across the English Channel to Dunkirk. Along with Royal Navy ships, civilian craft—yachts, lifeboats, motorboats, paddle steamers, and fishing boats—joined the rescue effort. From May 26 to June 4, this amateur armada, under heavy fire from German bombers, sailed back and forth from Britain to Dunkirk. The boats carried some 338,000 battle-weary soldiers to safety.

France Falls Following Dunkirk, resistance in France began to crumble. By June 14, the Germans had taken Paris. Accepting the inevitable, French leaders surrendered on June 22, 1940. The Germans took control of the northern part of the country. They left the southern part to a puppet government headed by Marshal Philippe Pétain (pay•TAN), a French hero from World War I. The headquarters of this government was in the city of Vichy (VEESH•ee).

After France fell, **Charles de Gaulle** (duh GOHL), a French general, set up a government-in-exile in London. He committed all his energy to reconquering France. In a radio broadcast from England, de Gaulle called on the people of France to join him in resisting the Germans:

PRIMARY SOURCE

It is the bounden [obligatory] duty of all Frenchmen who still bear arms to continue the struggle. For them to lay down their arms, to evacuate any position of military importance, or agree to hand over any part of French territory, however small, to enemy control would be a crime against our country.

GENERAL CHARLES DE GAULLE, quoted in
Charles de Gaulle: A Biography

De Gaulle went on to organize the Free French military forces that battled the Nazis until France was liberated in 1944.

The Battle of Britain

With the fall of France, Great Britain stood alone against the Nazis. **Winston Churchill**, the new British prime minister, had already declared that his nation would never give in. In a rousing speech, he proclaimed, "We shall fight on the beaches, we shall fight on the landing grounds, we shall fight in the fields and in the streets . . . we shall never surrender."

Hitler now turned his mind to an invasion of Great Britain. His plan was first to knock out the Royal Air Force (RAF) and then to land more than 250,000 soldiers on England's shores.

History Makers

Winston Churchill
1874–1965

Possibly the most powerful weapon the British had as they stood alone against Hitler's Germany was the nation's prime minister—Winston Churchill. "Big Winnie," Londoners boasted, "was the lad for us."

Although Churchill had a speech defect as a youngster, he grew to become one of the greatest orators of all time. He used all his gifts as a speaker to rally the people behind the effort to crush Germany. In one famous speech he promised that Britain would

. . . wage war, by sea, land and air, with all our might and with all the strength that God can give us . . . against a monstrous tyranny.

INTEGRATED TECHNOLOGY

RESEARCH LINKS For more on Winston Churchill, go to **classzone.com**

▲ A London bus is submerged in a bomb crater after a German air raid.

In the summer of 1940, the Luftwaffe (LOOFT•VAHF•uh), Germany's air force, began bombing Great Britain. At first, the Germans targeted British airfields and aircraft factories. Then, on September 7, 1940, they began focusing on the cities, especially London, to break British morale. Despite the destruction and loss of life, the British did not waver.

Vocabulary
Luftwaffe is the German word for "air weapon."

The RAF, although badly outnumbered, began to hit back hard. Two technological devices helped turn the tide in the RAF's favor. One was an electronic tracking system known as radar. Developed in the late 1930s, radar could tell the number, speed, and direction of incoming warplanes. The other device was a German code-making machine named Enigma. A complete Enigma machine had been smuggled into Great Britain in the late 1930s. Enigma enabled the British to decode German secret messages. With information gathered by these devices, RAF fliers could quickly launch attacks on the enemy.

To avoid the RAF's attacks, the Germans gave up daylight raids in October 1940 in favor of night bombing. At sunset, the wail of sirens filled the air as Londoners flocked to the subways, which served as air-raid shelters. Some rode out the bombing raids at home in smaller air-raid shelters or basements. This **Battle of Britain** continued until May 10, 1941. Stunned by British resistance, Hitler decided to call off his attacks. Instead, he focused on the Mediterranean and Eastern Europe. The Battle of Britain taught the Allies a crucial lesson. Hitler's attacks could be blocked. B

MAIN IDEA
Recognizing Effects
B Why was the outcome of the Battle of Britain important for the Allies?

The Mediterranean and the Eastern Front

The stubborn resistance of the British in the Battle of Britain caused a shift in Hitler's strategy in Europe. He decided to deal with Great Britain later. He then turned his attention east to the Mediterranean area and the Balkans—and to the ultimate prize, the Soviet Union.

Axis Forces Attack North Africa Germany's first objective in the Mediterranean region was North Africa, mainly because of Hitler's partner, Mussolini. Despite its alliance with Germany, Italy had remained neutral at the beginning of the war. With Hitler's conquest of France, however, Mussolini knew he had to take action. After declaring war on France and Great Britain, Mussolini moved into France.

Mussolini took his next step in North Africa in September 1940. While the Battle of Britain was raging, he ordered his army to attack British-controlled Egypt. Egypt's Suez Canal was key to reaching the oil fields of the Middle East. Within a week, Italian troops had pushed 60 miles inside Egypt, forcing British units back. Then both sides dug in and waited.

Vocabulary
The *Middle East* includes the countries of Southwest Asia and northeast Africa.

Britain Strikes Back Finally, in December, the British struck back. The result was a disaster for the Italians. By February 1941, the British had swept 500 miles across North Africa and had taken 130,000 Italian prisoners. Hitler had to step in to save his Axis partner. To reinforce the Italians, Hitler sent a crack German tank force, the Afrika Korps, under the command of General **Erwin Rommel**. In late March 1941, Rommel's Afrika Korps attacked. Caught by surprise, British forces retreated east to Tobruk, Libya. (See the map on page 923.)

After fierce fighting for Tobruk, the British began to drive Rommel back. By mid-January 1942, Rommel had retreated to where he had started. By June 1942, the tide of battle turned again. Rommel regrouped, pushed the British back across the desert, and seized Tobruk—a shattering loss for the Allies. Rommel's successes in North Africa earned him the nickname "Desert Fox."

The War in the Balkans While Rommel campaigned in North Africa, other German generals were active in the Balkans. Hitler had begun planning to attack his ally, the USSR, as early as the summer of 1940. The Balkan countries of southeastern Europe were key to Hitler's invasion plan. Hitler wanted to build bases in southeastern Europe for the attack on the Soviet Union. He also wanted to make sure that the British did not interfere.

To prepare for his invasion, Hitler moved to expand his influence in the Balkans. By early 1941, through the threat of force, he had persuaded Bulgaria, Romania, and Hungary to join the Axis powers. Yugoslavia and Greece, which had pro-British governments, resisted. In early April 1941, Hitler invaded both countries. Yugoslavia fell in 11 days. Greece surrendered in 17. In Athens, the Nazis celebrated their victory by raising swastikas on the Acropolis.

Hitler Invades the Soviet Union With the Balkans firmly in control, Hitler could move ahead with Operation Barbarossa, his plan to invade the Soviet Union. Early in the morning of June 22, 1941, the roar of German tanks and aircraft announced the beginning of the invasion. The Soviet Union was not prepared for this attack. Although it had the largest army in the world, its troops were neither well equipped nor well trained.

The invasion rolled on week after week until the Germans had pushed 500 miles inside the Soviet Union. As the Soviet troops retreated, they burned and destroyed everything in the enemy's path. The Russians had used this scorched-earth strategy against Napoleon.

On September 8, German forces put Leningrad under siege. By early November, the city was completely cut off from the rest of the Soviet Union. To force a surrender, Hitler was ready to starve the city's more than 2.5 million inhabitants. German bombs destroyed warehouses where food was stored. Desperately hungry, people began eating cattle and horse feed, as well as cats and dogs and, finally, crows and rats. Nearly one million people died in Leningrad during the winter of 1941–1942. Yet the city refused to fall.

▼ Russian soldiers prepare to attack German lines outside Leningrad.

Impatient with the progress in Leningrad, Hitler looked to Moscow, the capital and heart of the Soviet Union. A Nazi drive on the capital began on October 2, 1941. By December, the Germans had advanced to the outskirts of Moscow. Soviet General Georgi Zhukov (ZHOO•kuhf) counterattacked. As temperatures fell, the Germans, in summer uniforms, retreated. Ignoring Napoleon's winter defeat 130 years before, Hitler sent his generals a stunning order: "No retreat!" German troops dug in about 125 miles west of Moscow. They held the line against the Soviets until March 1943. Hitler's advance on the Soviet Union gained nothing but cost the Germans 500,000 lives. C

MAIN IDEA

Making Inferences

C What does the fact that German armies were not prepared for the Russian winter indicate about Hitler's expectations for the Soviet campaign?

The United States Aids Its Allies

Most Americans felt that the United States should not get involved in the war. Between 1935 and 1937, Congress passed a series of Neutrality Acts. The laws made it illegal to sell arms or lend money to nations at war. But President Roosevelt knew that if the Allies fell, the United States would be drawn into the war. In September 1939, he asked Congress to allow the Allies to buy American arms. The Allies would pay cash and then carry the goods on their own ships.

Under the Lend-Lease Act, passed in March 1941, the president could lend or lease arms and other supplies to any country vital to the United States. By the summer of 1941, the U.S. Navy was escorting British ships carrying U.S. arms. In response, Hitler ordered his submarines to sink any cargo ships they met.

Although the United States had not yet entered the war, Roosevelt and Churchill met secretly and issued a joint declaration called the **Atlantic Charter**. It upheld free trade among nations and the right of people to choose their own government. The charter later served as the Allies' peace plan at the end of World War II.

On September 4, a German U-boat fired on a U.S. destroyer in the Atlantic. In response, Roosevelt ordered navy commanders to shoot German submarines on sight. The United States was now involved in an undeclared naval war with Hitler. To almost everyone's surprise, however, the attack that actually drew the United States into the war did not come from Germany. It came from Japan.

NEW YORK CORE CURRICULUM REVIEW

TERMS & NAMES 1. For each term or name, write a sentence explaining its significance.

• nonaggression pact • blitzkrieg • Charles de Gaulle • Winston Churchill • Battle of Britain • Erwin Rommel • Atlantic Charter

USING YOUR NOTES

2. Which of the listed events might be considered a turning point for the Allies? Why?

Cause	Effect
First blitzkrieg	
Allies stranded at Dunkirk	
Lend-Lease Act	

MAIN IDEAS

3. Why were the early months of World War II referred to as the "phony war"?
4. Why was Egypt of strategic importance in World War II?
5. Why did President Franklin Roosevelt want to offer help to the Allies?

CRITICAL THINKING & WRITING

6. **CLARIFYING** What do you think is meant by the statement that Winston Churchill possibly was Britain's most powerful weapon against Hitler's Germany?
7. **MAKING INFERENCES** What factors do you think a country's leaders consider when deciding whether to surrender or fight?
8. **COMPARING** How were Napoleon's invasion of Russia and Hitler's invasion of the Soviet Union similar?
9. **WRITING ACTIVITY** EMPIRE BUILDING Write a **magazine article** on German conquests in Europe through 1942.

CONNECT TO TODAY **PREPARING AN ORAL REPORT**

Conduct research into "stealth" technology, which is designed to evade radar. Use your findings to prepare a brief **oral report** titled "How Stealth Technology Works."

Japan's Pacific Campaign

CONNECT TO THE NEW YORK STATE CORE CURRICULUM

Unit 6.D.1. Human and physical geography
Unit 6.D.4. Key events–Dunkirk, the Blitz, D-Day, Hitler's second front, the war in the Pacific

TERMS & NAMES

- Isoroku Yamamoto
- Pearl Harbor
- Battle of Midway
- Douglas MacArthur
- Battle of Guadalcanal

SETTING THE STAGE Like Hitler, Japan's military leaders also had dreams of empire. Japan's expansion had begun in 1931. That year, Japanese troops took over Manchuria in northeastern China. Six years later, Japanese armies swept into the heartland of China. They expected quick victory. Chinese resistance, however, caused the war to drag on. This placed a strain on Japan's economy. To increase their resources, Japanese leaders looked toward the rich European colonies of Southeast Asia.

TAKING NOTES
Recognizing Effects Use a chart to identify the effects of four major events of the war in the Pacific between 1941 and 1943.

Event	Effect

Surprise Attack on Pearl Harbor

By October 1940, Americans had cracked one of the codes that the Japanese used in sending secret messages. Therefore, they were well aware of Japanese plans for Southeast Asia. If Japan conquered European colonies there, it could also threaten the American-controlled Philippine Islands and Guam. To stop the Japanese advance, the U.S. government sent aid to strengthen Chinese resistance. And when the Japanese overran French Indochina—Vietnam, Cambodia, and Laos—in July 1941, Roosevelt cut off oil shipments to Japan.

Despite an oil shortage, the Japanese continued their conquests. They hoped to catch the European colonial powers and the United States by surprise. So they planned massive attacks on British and Dutch colonies in Southeast Asia and on American outposts in the Pacific—at the same time. Admiral **Isoroku Yamamoto** (ih•soh•ROO•koo-YAH•muh•MOH•toh), Japan's greatest naval strategist, also called for an attack on the U.S. fleet in Hawaii. It was, he said, "a dagger pointed at [Japan's] throat" and must be destroyed.

Day of Infamy Early in the morning of December 7, 1941, American sailors at **Pearl Harbor** in Hawaii awoke to the roar of explosives. A Japanese attack was underway! U.S. military leaders had known from a coded Japanese message that an attack might come. But they did not know when or where it would occur. Within two hours, the Japanese had sunk or damaged 19 ships, including 8 battleships, moored in Pearl Harbor. More than 2,300 Americans were killed—with over 1,100 wounded. News of the attack stunned the American people. The next day, President Roosevelt addressed Congress. December 7, 1941, he declared, was "a date which will live in infamy." Congress quickly accepted his request for a declaration of war on Japan and its allies.

▲ The *U.S.S. West Virginia* is engulfed by flames after taking a direct hit during the Japanese attack on Pearl Harbor.

Almost at the same time of the Pearl Harbor attack, the Japanese launched bombing raids on the British colony of Hong Kong and American-controlled Guam and Wake Island. (See the map on the opposite page.) They also landed an invasion force in Thailand. The Japanese drive for a Pacific empire was under way.

Japanese Victories

Lightly defended, Guam and Wake Island quickly fell to Japanese forces. The Japanese then turned their attention to the Philippines. In January 1942, they marched into the Philippine capital of Manila. American and Filipino forces took up a defensive position on the Bataan (buh•TAN) Peninsula on the northwestern edge of Manila Bay. At the same time, the Philippine government moved to the island of Corregidor just to the south of Bataan. After about three months of tough fighting, the Japanese took the Bataan Peninsula in April. Corregidor fell the following month.

The Japanese also continued their strikes against British possessions in Asia. After seizing Hong Kong, they invaded Malaya from the sea and overland from Thailand. By February 1942, the Japanese had reached Singapore, strategically located at the southern tip of the Malay Peninsula. After a fierce pounding, the colony surrendered. Within a month, the Japanese had conquered the resource-rich Dutch East Indies (now Indonesia), including the islands of Java, Sumatra, Borneo, and Celebes (SEHL•uh•BEEZ). The Japanese also moved westward, taking Burma. From there, they planned to launch a strike against India, the largest of Great Britain's colonies.

By the time Burma fell, Japan had taken control of more than 1 million square miles of Asian land. About 150 million people lived in this vast area. Before these conquests, the Japanese had tried to win the support of Asians with the anticolonialist idea of "East Asia for the Asiatics." After victory, however, the Japanese quickly made it clear that they had come as conquerors. They often treated the people of their new colonies with extreme cruelty.

However, the Japanese reserved the most brutal treatment for Allied prisoners of war. The Japanese considered it dishonorable to surrender, and they had contempt for the prisoners of war in their charge. On the Bataan Death March—a forced march of more than 50 miles up the peninsula—the Japanese subjected their captives to terrible cruelties. One Allied prisoner of war reported:

PRIMARY SOURCE

I was questioned by a Japanese officer, who found out that I had been in a Philippine Scout Battalion. The [Japanese] hated the Scouts. . . . Anyway, they took me outside and I was forced to watch as they buried six of my Scouts alive. They made the men dig their own graves, and then had them kneel down in a pit. The guards hit them over the head with shovels to stun them and piled earth on top.

LIEUTENANT JOHN SPAINHOWER, quoted in *War Diary 1939–1945*

Of the approximately 70,000 prisoners who started the Bataan Death March, only 54,000 survived.

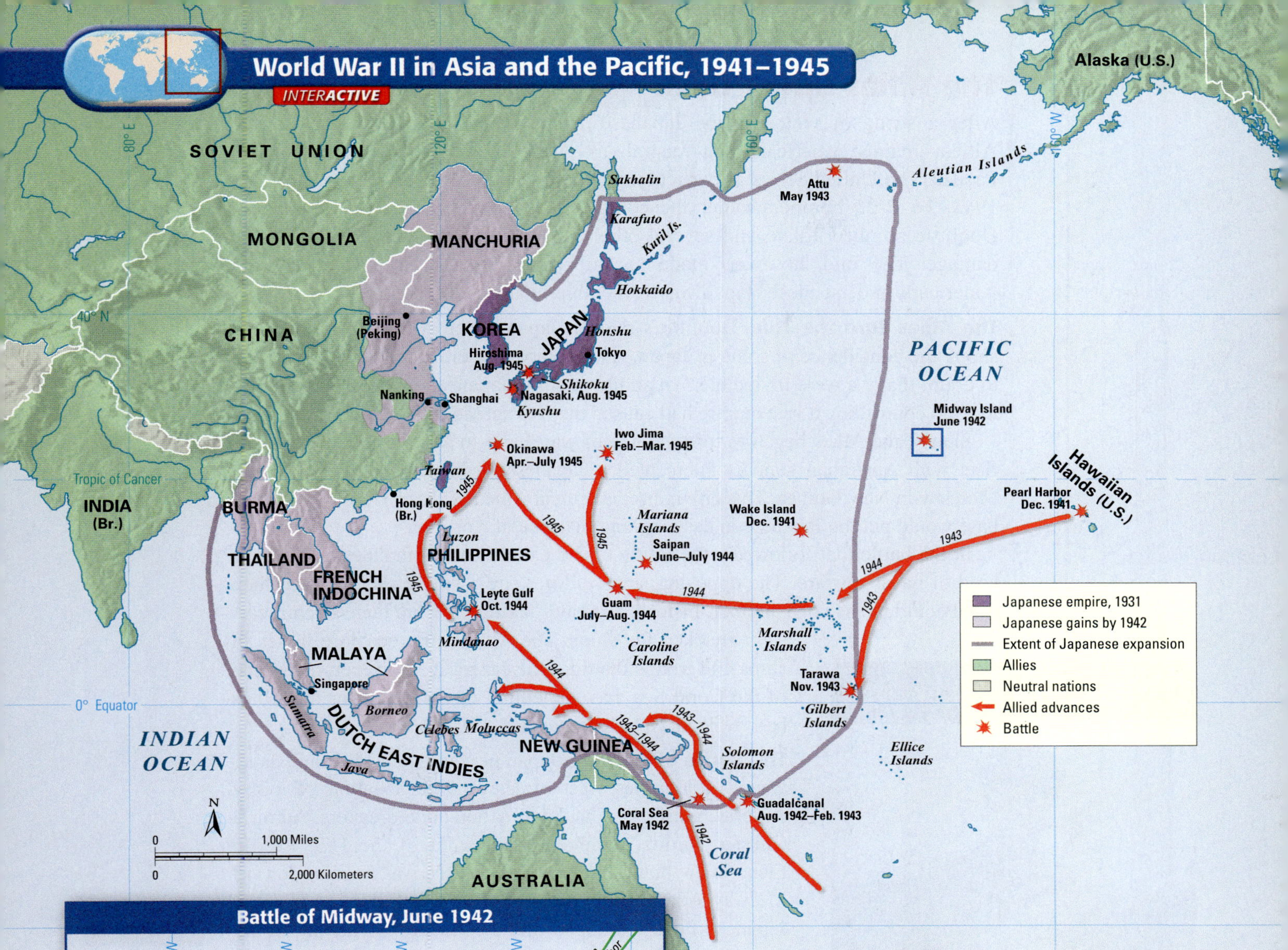

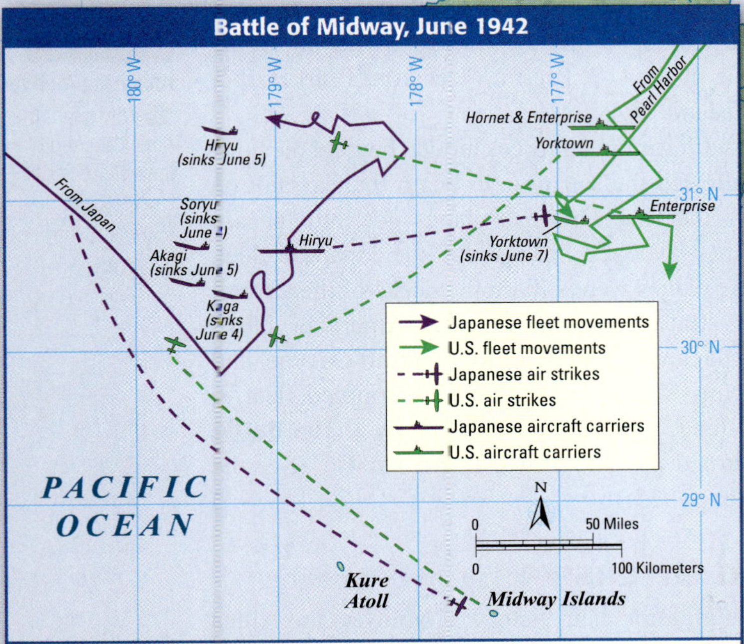

Some Japanese search aircraft were late getting into the air. As a result, the Japanese were completely unaware that U.S. ships were nearby.

The Japanese warship *Mikuma* lists and begins to sink after being struck by bombs from American aircraft during the Battle of Midway.

GEOGRAPHY SKILLBUILDER: Interpreting Maps

1. **Location** *Which battle was fought in the most northern region?*
2. **Movement** *From what two general directions did Allied forces move in on Japan?*

The Allies Strike Back

After a string of victories, the Japanese seemed unbeatable. Nonetheless, the Allies—mainly Americans and Australians—were anxious to strike back in the Pacific. The United States in particular wanted revenge for Pearl Harbor. In April 1942, 16 B-25 bombers under the command of Lieutenant Colonel James H. Doolittle bombed Tokyo and several other Japanese cities. The bombs did little damage. The raid, however, made an important psychological point to both Americans and Japanese: Japan was vulnerable to attack.

The Allies Turn the Tide Doolittle's raid on Japan raised American morale and shook the confidence of some in Japan. As one Japanese citizen noted, "We started to doubt that we were invincible." In addition, some Japanese worried that defending and controlling a vast empire had caused them to spread their resources too thin.

Vocabulary
invincible: unconquerable

Slowly, the Allies began to turn the tide of war. Early in May 1942, an American fleet with Australian support intercepted a Japanese strike force headed for Port Moresby in New Guinea. This city housed a critical Allied air base. Control of the air base would put the Japanese in easy striking distance of Australia.

In the battle that followed—the Battle of the Coral Sea—both sides used a new kind of naval warfare. The opposing ships did not fire a single shot. In fact, they often could not see one another. Instead, airplanes taking off from huge aircraft carriers attacked the ships. The Allies suffered more losses in ships and troops than did the Japanese. However, the Battle of the Coral Sea was something of a victory, for the Allies had stopped Japan's southward advance.

The Battle of Midway Japan next targeted Midway Island, some 1,500 miles west of Hawaii, the location of a key American airfield. Thanks to Allied code breakers, Admiral Chester Nimitz, commander in chief of the U.S. Pacific Fleet, knew that a huge Japanese force was heading toward Midway. Admiral Yamamoto himself was in command of the Japanese fleet. He hoped that the attack on Midway would draw the whole of the U.S. Pacific Fleet from Pearl Harbor to defend the island. (A)

MAIN IDEA
Analyzing Motives
(A) Why might the Americans send their entire Pacific Fleet to defend Midway Island?

On June 4, with American forces hidden beyond the horizon, Nimitz allowed the Japanese to begin their assault on the island. As the first Japanese planes got into the air, American planes swooped in to attack the Japanese fleet. Many Japanese planes were still on the decks of the aircraft carriers. The strategy was a success. American pilots destroyed 332 Japanese planes, all four aircraft carriers, and one support ship. Yamamoto ordered his crippled fleet to withdraw. By June 7, 1942, the battle was over. The **Battle of Midway** turned the tide of war in the Pacific. (See the inset map on page 933.)

History Makers

General Douglas MacArthur
1880–1964

Douglas MacArthur's qualities as a leader and a fighting soldier emerged in France during World War I. Showing incredible dash and courage on the battlefield, he received several decorations for bravery. And he won promotion from the rank of major to brigadier general.

After serving in several positions in the United States, MacArthur received a posting to the Philippines in 1935. He remained there until shortly before the islands fell in 1941. But he left very reluctantly. In a message to the troops who remained behind, he vowed, "I shall return." As you will read later in the chapter, MacArthur kept his promise.

An Allied Offensive

With morale high after their victory at Midway, the Allies took the offensive. The war in the Pacific involved vast distances. Japanese troops had dug in on hundreds of islands across the ocean. General **Douglas MacArthur**, the commander of the Allied land forces in the Pacific, developed a plan to handle this problem.

MAIN IDEA

Identifying Problems

B If the vast distances of the Pacific caused problems for the Allies, how might they have also caused problems for the Japanese?

MacArthur believed that storming each island would be a long, costly effort. Instead, he wanted to "island-hop" past Japanese strongholds. He would then seize islands that were not well defended but were closer to Japan. **B**

MacArthur's first target soon presented itself. U.S. military leaders had learned that the Japanese were building a huge air base on the island of Guadalcanal in the Solomon Islands. The Allies had to strike fast before the base was completed and became another Japanese stronghold. At dawn on August 7, 1942, several thousand U.S. Marines, with Australian support, landed on Guadalcanal and the neighboring island of Tulagi.

The marines had little trouble seizing Guadalcanal's airfield. But the battle for control of the island turned into a savage struggle as both sides poured in fresh troops. In February 1943, after six months of fighting on land and at sea, the **Battle of Guadalcanal** finally ended. After losing more than 24,000 of a force of 36,000 soldiers, the Japanese abandoned what they came to call "the Island of Death."

To American war correspondent Ralph Martin and the U.S. soldiers who fought there, Guadalcanal was simply "hell":

▲ U.S. Marines storm ashore at Guadalcanal.

PRIMARY SOURCE

Hell was red furry spiders as big as your fist, . . . enormous rats and bats everywhere, and rivers with waiting crocodiles. Hell was the sour, foul smell of the squishy jungle, humidity that rotted a body within hours. . . . Hell was an enemy . . . so fanatic that it used its own dead as booby traps.

RALPH G. MARTIN, *The GI War*

As Japan worked to establish a new order in Southeast Asia and the Pacific, the Nazis moved ahead with Hitler's design for a new order in Europe. This design included plans for dealing with those Hitler considered unfit for the Third Reich. You will learn about these plans in Section 3.

NEW YORK CORE CURRICULUM REVIEW

TERMS & NAMES 1. For each term or name, write a sentence explaining its significance.

• Isoroku Yamamoto • Pearl Harbor • Battle of Midway • Douglas MacArthur • Battle of Guadalcanal

USING YOUR NOTES

2. Which event was most important in turning the tide of the war in the Pacific against the Japanese? Why?

Event	Effect

MAIN IDEAS

3. How did the Japanese plan to catch the European colonial powers and the United States by surprise?
4. In what way was the Battle of the Coral Sea a new kind of naval warfare?
5. What was General Douglas MacArthur's island-hopping strategy?

CRITICAL THINKING & WRITING

6. **EVALUATING DECISIONS** Did Admiral Yamamoto make a wise decision in bombing Pearl Harbor? Why or why not?
7. **ANALYZING MOTIVES** Why do you think the Japanese changed their approach from trying to win the support of the colonized peoples to acting as conquerors?
8. **IDENTIFYING PROBLEMS** What problems did Japan face in building an empire in the Pacific?
9. **WRITING ACTIVITY** EMPIRE BUILDING Imagine you are a foreign diplomat living in Asia during World War II. Write **journal entries** describing the Japanese advance across Asia and the Pacific during 1941 and 1942.

INTEGRATED TECHNOLOGY **INTERNET ACTIVITY**

Use the Internet to research the Pearl Harbor Memorial in Hawaii. Create a **Web page** that describes the memorial and provides background information on the attack.

INTERNET KEYWORD
Pearl Harbor

3

The Holocaust

CONNECT TO THE NEW YORK STATE CORE CURRICULUM

Unit 6.D.5. The Nazi Holocaust: the extermination of Jews, Poles, other Slavs, Gypsies, disabled, and others
Unit 6.D.6. Resistance

TERMS & NAMES

- Aryan
- Holocaust
- *Kristallnacht*
- ghetto
- "Final Solution"
- genocide

SETTING THE STAGE As part of their vision for Europe, the Nazis proposed a new racial order. They proclaimed that the Germanic peoples, or **Aryans**, were a "master race." (This was a misuse of the term *Aryan*. The term actually refers to the Indo-European peoples who began to migrate into the Indian subcontinent around 1500 B.C.) The Nazis claimed that all non-Aryan peoples, particularly Jewish people, were inferior. This racist message would eventually lead to the **Holocaust**, the systematic mass slaughter of Jews and other groups judged inferior by the Nazis.

TAKING NOTES
Analyzing Bias Use a web diagram to identify examples of Nazi persecution.

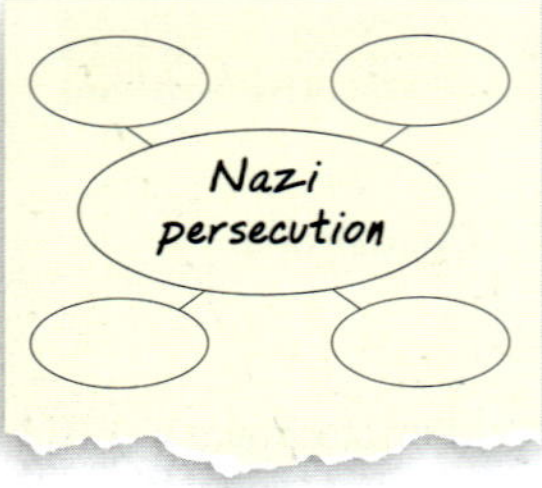

The Holocaust Begins

To gain support for his racist ideas, Hitler knowingly tapped into a hatred for Jews that had deep roots in European history. For generations, many Germans, along with other Europeans, had targeted Jews as the cause of their failures. Some Germans even blamed Jews for their country's defeat in World War I and for its economic problems after that war.

In time, the Nazis made the targeting of Jews a government policy. The Nuremberg Laws, passed in 1935, deprived Jews of their rights to German citizenship and forbade marriages between Jews and non-Jews. Laws passed later also limited the kinds of work that Jews could do.

"Night of Broken Glass" Worse was yet to come. Early in November 1938, 17-year-old Herschel Grynszpan (GRIHN•shpahn), a Jewish youth from Germany, was visiting an uncle in Paris. While Grynszpan was there, he received a postcard. It said that after living in Germany for 27 years, his father had been deported to Poland. On November 7, wishing to avenge his father's deportation, Grynszpan shot a German diplomat living in Paris.

When Nazi leaders heard the news, they launched a violent attack on the Jewish community. On November 9, Nazi storm troopers attacked Jewish homes, businesses, and synagogues across Germany and murdered close to 100 Jews. An American in Leipzig wrote. "Jewish shop windows by the hundreds were systematically . . . smashed. . . . The main streets of the city were a positive litter of shattered plate glass." It is for this reason that the night of November 9 became known as ***Kristallnacht*** (krih•STAHL•NAHKT), or "Night of Broken Glass." A 14-year-old boy described his memory of that awful night:

PRIMARY SOURCE

All the things for which my parents had worked for eighteen long years were destroyed in less than ten minutes. Piles of valuable glasses, expensive furniture, linens—in short, everything was destroyed. . . . The Nazis left us, yelling, "Don't try to leave this house! We'll soon be back again and take you to a concentration camp to be shot."

M. I. LIBAU, quoted in *Never to Forget: The Jews of the Holocaust*

Kristallnacht marked a major step-up in the Nazi policy of Jewish persecution. The future for Jews in Germany looked truly grim.

A Flood of Refugees After *Kristallnacht*, some Jews realized that violence against them was bound to increase. By the end of 1939, a number of German Jews had fled to other countries. Many however, remained in Germany. Later, Hitler conquered territories in which millions more Jews lived.

At first, Hitler favored emigration as a solution to what he called "the Jewish problem." Getting other countries to continue admitting Germany's Jews became an issue, however. After admitting tens of thousands of Jewish refugees, such countries as France, Britain, and the United States abruptly closed their doors to further immigration. Germany's foreign minister observed, "We all want to get rid of our Jews. The difficulty is that no country wishes to receive them."

▲ After 1941, all Jews in German-controlled areas had to wear a yellow Star of David patch.

MAIN IDEA

Recognizing Effects

Ⓐ What steps did Hitler take to rid Germany of Jews?

Isolating the Jews When Hitler found that he could not get rid of Jews through emigration, he put another plan into effect. He ordered Jews in all countries under his control to be moved to designated cities. In those cities, the Nazis herded the Jews into dismal, overcrowded **ghettos**, or segregated Jewish areas. The Nazis then sealed off the ghettos with barbed wire and stone walls. They hoped that the Jews inside would starve to death or die from disease. Ⓐ

Even under these horrible conditions, the Jews hung on. Some, particularly the Jews in Warsaw, Poland, formed resistance organizations within the ghettos. They also struggled to keep their traditions. Ghetto theaters produced plays and concerts. Teachers taught lessons in secret schools. Scholars kept records so that one day people would find out the truth.

The "Final Solution"

Hitler soon grew impatient waiting for Jews to die from starvation or disease. He decided to take more direct action. His plan was called the "**Final Solution**." It was actually a program of **genocide**, the systematic killing of an entire people.

▼ German soldiers round up Jews in the Warsaw ghetto.

Hitler believed that his plan of conquest depended on the purity of the Aryan race. To protect racial purity, the Nazis had to eliminate other races, nationalities, or groups they viewed as inferior—as "subhumans." They included Roma (gypsies), Poles, Russians, homosexuals, the insane, the disabled, and the incurably ill. But the Nazis focused especially on the Jews. **B**

MAIN IDEA

Analyzing Bias

B How was the "Final Solution" a natural outcome of Nazi racial theory?

The Killings Begin As Nazi troops swept across Eastern Europe and the Soviet Union, the killings began. Units from the SS (Hitler's elite security force) moved from town to town to hunt down Jews. The SS and their collaborators rounded up men, women, children, and even babies and took them to isolated spots. They then shot their prisoners in pits that became the prisoners' graves.

Jews in communities not reached by the killing squads were rounded up and taken to concentration camps, or slave-labor prisons. These camps were located mainly in Germany and Poland. Hitler hoped that the horrible conditions in the camps would speed the total elimination of the Jews.

The prisoners worked seven days a week as slaves for the SS or for German businesses. Guards severely beat or killed their prisoners for not working fast enough. With meals of thin soup, a scrap of bread, and potato peelings, most prisoners lost 50 pounds in the first few months. Hunger was so intense, recalled one survivor, "that if a bit of soup spilled over, prisoners would . . . dig their spoons into the mud and stuff the mess in their mouths."

The Final Stage Hitler's war on the Jews turned toward the "Final Solution" in 1942. The Nazis built extermination camps equipped with huge gas chambers that could kill as many as 6,000 human beings in a day. (See the map on page 953.)

When prisoners arrived at Auschwitz (OUSH•vihts), the largest of the extermination camps, they paraded before a committee of SS doctors. With a wave of the hand, these doctors separated the strong—mostly men—from the weak—mostly women, young children, the elderly, and the sick. Those labeled as weak would die that day. They were told to undress for a shower and then led into a chamber with

History *in* Depth

Jewish Resistance

Even in the extermination camps, Jews rose up and fought against the Nazis. At Treblinka in August 1943, and at Sobibor in October 1943, small groups of Jews revolted. They killed guards, stormed the camp armories and stole guns and grenades, and then broke out. In both uprisings, about 300 prisoners escaped. Most were killed soon after. Of those who survived, many joined up with partisan groups and continued to fight until the end of the war.

Late in 1944, prisoners at Auschwitz revolted, too. Like the escapees at Treblinka and Sobibor, most were caught and killed. Young women like Ella Gartner and Roza Robota made the Auschwitz uprising possible. Gartner smuggled gunpowder into the camp from the munitions factory where she worked. Robota helped organize resistance in the camp. Gartner and Robota were executed on January 6, 1945. Less than a month later, Auschwitz was liberated.

▲ Ella Gartner

▶ Roza Robota

Jews Killed Under Nazi Rule*			
	Original Jewish Population	Jews Killed	Percent Surviving
Poland	3,300,000	2,800,000	15%
Soviet Union (area occupied by Germans)	2,100,000	1,500,000	29%
Hungary	404,000	200,000	49%
Romania	850,000	425,000	50%
Germany/Austria	270,000	210,000	22%

*Estimates — Source: Hannah Vogt, *The Burden of Guilt*

fake showerheads. After the doors were closed, cyanide gas poured from the showerheads. All inside were killed in a matter of minutes. Later, the Nazis installed crematoriums, or ovens, to burn the bodies.

The Survivors Some six million European Jews died in these death camps and in Nazi massacres. Fewer than four million survived. Some escaped the horrors of the death camps with help from non-Jewish people. These rescuers, at great risk to their own lives, hid Jews in their homes or helped them escape to neutral countries.

Those who survived the camps were changed forever by what they had experienced. As Elie Wiesel, nearly 15 years old when he entered Auschwitz, noted:

PRIMARY SOURCE

Never shall I forget the little faces of the children, whose bodies I saw turned into wreaths of smoke beneath a silent blue sky. Never shall I forget those flames which consumed my faith forever. . . . Never shall I forget those moments which murdered my God and my soul and turned my dreams to dust. . . . Never.

ELIE WIESEL, quoted in *Night*

NEW YORK CORE CURRICULUM REVIEW

TERMS & NAMES 1. For each term or name, write a sentence explaining its significance.

- Aryan
- Holocaust
- *Kristallnacht*
- ghetto
- "Final Solution"
- genocide

USING YOUR NOTES

2. What Nazi actions were part of the "Final Solution"?

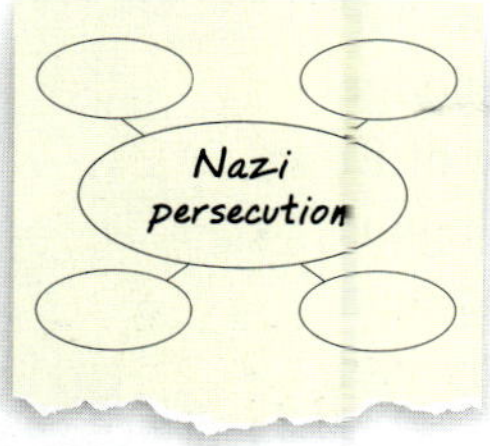

MAIN IDEAS

3. What was the new racial order proposed by the Nazis?
4. What Nazi action marked the final stage of the "Final Solution"?
5. How did some non-Jews oppose Hitler's "Final Solution"?

CRITICAL THINKING & WRITING

6. **ANALYZING MOTIVES** Why might people want to blame a minority group for most of their country's problems?
7. **MAKING INFERENCES** Why do you think the German people went along with the Nazi policy of persecution of the Jews?
8. **RECOGNIZING EFFECTS** What impact did the Holocaust have on the Jewish population of Europe?
9. **WRITING ACTIVITY** SCIENCE AND TECHNOLOGY -Write a **persuasive essay** discussing how German scientists, engineers, and doctors asked to participate in the Holocaust might have opposed Hitler's policy.

CONNECT TO TODAY **CREATING A MAP**

Find information on instances of genocide and ethnic cleansing in the last 20 years. Use the information to create an **annotated map** titled "Genocide in the Late 20th Century."

The Allied Victory

CONNECT TO THE NEW YORK STATE CORE CURRICULUM

Unit 6.D.4. Key events–Dunkirk, the Blitz, D-Day, Hitler's second front, the war in the Pacific
Unit 6.D.10. Hiroshima and Nagasaki

TERMS & NAMES

- Dwight D. Eisenhower
- Battle of Stalingrad
- D-Day
- Battle of the Bulge
- kamikaze

SETTING THE STAGE On December 22, 1941, just after Pearl Harbor, Winston Churchill and President Roosevelt met at the White House to develop a joint war policy. Stalin had asked his allies to relieve German pressure on his armies in the east. He wanted them to open a second front in the west. This would split the Germans' strength by forcing them to fight major battles in two regions instead of one. Churchill agreed with Stalin's strategy. The Allies would weaken Germany on two fronts before dealing a deathblow. At first, Roosevelt was torn, but ultimately he agreed.

TAKING NOTES
Recognizing Effects Use a chart to identify the outcomes of several major World War II battles.

Battle	Outcome
Battle of El Alamein	
Battle of Stalingrad	
D-Day Invasion	

The Tide Turns on Two Fronts

Churchill wanted Britain and the United States to strike first at North Africa and southern Europe. The strategy angered Stalin. He wanted the Allies to open the second front in France. The Soviet Union, therefore, had to hold out on its own against the Germans. All Britain and the United States could offer in the way of help was supplies. Nevertheless, late in 1942, the Allies began to turn the tide of war both in the Mediterranean and on the Eastern Front.

The North African Campaign As you recall from Section 1, General Erwin Rommel took the key Libyan port city of Tobruk in June 1942. With Tobruk's fall, London sent General Bernard Montgomery—"Monty" to his troops—to take control of British forces in North Africa. By the time Montgomery arrived, however, the Germans had advanced to an Egyptian village called El Alamein (AL•uh•MAYN), west of Alexandria. (See the map on page 942.) They were dug in so well that British forces could not go around them. The only way to dislodge them, Montgomery decided, was with a massive frontal attack. The Battle of El Alamein began on the night of October 23. The roar of about 1,000 British guns took the Axis soldiers totally by surprise. They fought back fiercely and held their ground for several days. By November 4, however, Rommel's army had been beaten. He and his forces fell back.

As Rommel retreated west, the Allies launched Operation Torch. On November 8, an Allied force of more than 100,000 troops—mostly Americans—landed in Morocco and Algeria. American general **Dwight D. Eisenhower** led this force. Caught between Montgomery's and Eisenhower's armies, Rommel's Afrika Korps was finally crushed in May 1943.

The Battle for Stalingrad As Rommel suffered defeats in North Africa, German armies also met their match in the Soviet Union. The German advance had stalled at Leningrad and Moscow late in 1941. And the bitter winter made the situation worse. When the summer of 1942 arrived, however, Hitler sent his Sixth Army, under the command of General Friedrich Paulus, to seize the oil fields in the Caucasus Mountains. The army was also to capture Stalingrad (now Volgograd), a major industrial center on the Volga River. (See the map on page 942.)

The **Battle of Stalingrad** began on August 23, 1942. The Luftwaffe went on nightly bombing raids that set much of the city ablaze and reduced the rest to rubble. The situation looked desperate. Nonetheless, Stalin had already told his commanders to defend the city named after him to the death.

▲ Soviet troops launch an attack during the battle for Stalingrad.

By early November 1942, Germans controlled 90 percent of the ruined city. Then another Russian winter set in. On November 19, Soviet troops outside the city launched a counterattack. Closing in around Stalingrad, they trapped the Germans inside and cut off their supplies. General Paulus begged Hitler to order a retreat. But Hitler refused, saying the city was "to be held at all costs." (A)

MAIN IDEA

Making Inferences

(A) What advantages might a weaker army fighting on its home soil have over a stronger invading army?

On February 2, 1943, some 90,000 frostbitten, half-starved German troops surrendered to the Soviets. These pitiful survivors were all that remained of an army of 330,000. Stalingrad's defense had cost the Soviets over one million soldiers. The city was 99 percent destroyed. However, the Germans were now on the defensive, with the Soviets pushing them steadily westward.

The Invasion of Italy As the Battle of Stalingrad raged, Stalin continued to urge the British and Americans to invade France. However, Roosevelt and Churchill decided to attack Italy first. On July 10, 1943, Allied forces landed on Sicily and captured it from Italian and German troops about a month later.

The conquest of Sicily toppled Mussolini from power. On July 25, King Victor Emmanuel III had the dictator arrested. On September 3, Italy surrendered. But the Germans seized control of northern Italy and put Mussolini back in charge. Finally, the Germans retreated northward, and the victorious Allies entered Rome on June 4, 1944. Fighting in Italy, however, continued until Germany fell in May 1945. On April 27, 1945, Italian resistance fighters ambushed some German trucks near the northern Italian city of Milan. Inside one of the trucks, they found Mussolini disguised as a German soldier. They shot him the next day and later hung his body in downtown Milan for all to see.

The Allied Home Fronts

Wherever Allied forces fought, people on the home fronts rallied to support them. In war-torn countries like the Soviet Union and Great Britain, civilians endured extreme hardships. Many lost their lives. Except for a few of its territories, such as Hawaii, the United States did not suffer invasion or bombing. Nonetheless, Americans at home made a crucial contribution to the Allied war effort. Americans produced the weapons and equipment that would help win the war.

GEOGRAPHY SKILLBUILDER: Interpreting Maps

1. **Region** *Which European countries remained neutral during World War II?*
2. **Movement** *What seems to be the destination for most of the Allied advances that took place in Europe during 1943–1944?*

Mobilizing for War Defeating the Axis powers required mobilizing for total war. In the United States, factories converted their peacetime operations to wartime production and made everything from machine guns to boots. Automobile factories produced tanks. A typewriter company made armor-piercing shells. By 1944, between 17 and 18 million U.S. workers—many of them women—had jobs in war industries.

With factories turning out products for the war, a shortage of consumer goods hit the United States. From meat and sugar to tires and gasoline, from nylon stockings to laundry soap, the American government rationed scarce items. Setting the speed limit at 35 miles per hour also helped to save gasoline and rubber. In European countries directly affected by the war, rationing was even more drastic.

Vocabulary
rationed: distributed in limited amounts

To inspire their people to greater efforts, Allied governments conducted highly effective propaganda campaigns. In the Soviet Union, a Moscow youngster collected enough scrap metal to produce 14,000 artillery shells. And a Russian family used its life savings to buy a tank for the Red Army. In the United States, youngsters saved their pennies and bought government war stamps and bonds to help finance the war.

▲ American schoolchildren helped the war effort by recycling scrap metal and rubber and by buying war bonds.

War Limits Civil Rights Government propaganda also had a negative effect. After Pearl Harbor, a wave of prejudice arose in the United States against Japanese Americans. Most lived in Hawaii and on the West Coast. The bombing of Pearl Harbor frightened Americans. This fear, encouraged by government propaganda, was turned against Japanese Americans. They were suddenly seen as "the enemy." On February 19, 1942, President Roosevelt issued an executive order calling for the internment of Japanese Americans because they were considered a threat to the country. **B**

MAIN IDEA
Analyzing Motives
B Why did U.S. government propaganda try to portray the Japanese as sinister?

In March, the military began rounding up "aliens" and shipping them to relocation camps. The camps were restricted military areas located far away from the coast. Such locations, it was thought, would prevent these "enemy aliens" from assisting a Japanese invasion. However, two-thirds of those interned were Nisei, native-born American citizens whose parents were Japanese. Many of them volunteered for military service and fought bravely for the United States, even though their families remained in the camps.

Victory in Europe

While the Allies were dealing with issues on the home front, they also were preparing to push toward victory in Europe. In 1943, the Allies began secretly building an invasion force in Great Britain. Their plan was to launch an attack on German-held France across the English Channel.

The D-Day Invasion By May 1944, the invasion force was ready. Thousands of planes, ships, tanks, and landing craft and more than three million troops awaited the order to attack. General Dwight D. Eisenhower, the commander of this enormous force, planned to strike on the coast of Normandy, in northwestern France. The Germans knew that an attack was coming. But they did not know where it would be launched. To keep Hitler guessing, the Allies set up a huge dummy army with its own headquarters and equipment. This make-believe army appeared to be preparing to attack the French seaport of Calais (ka•LAY).

The D-Day Invasion, June 6, 1944

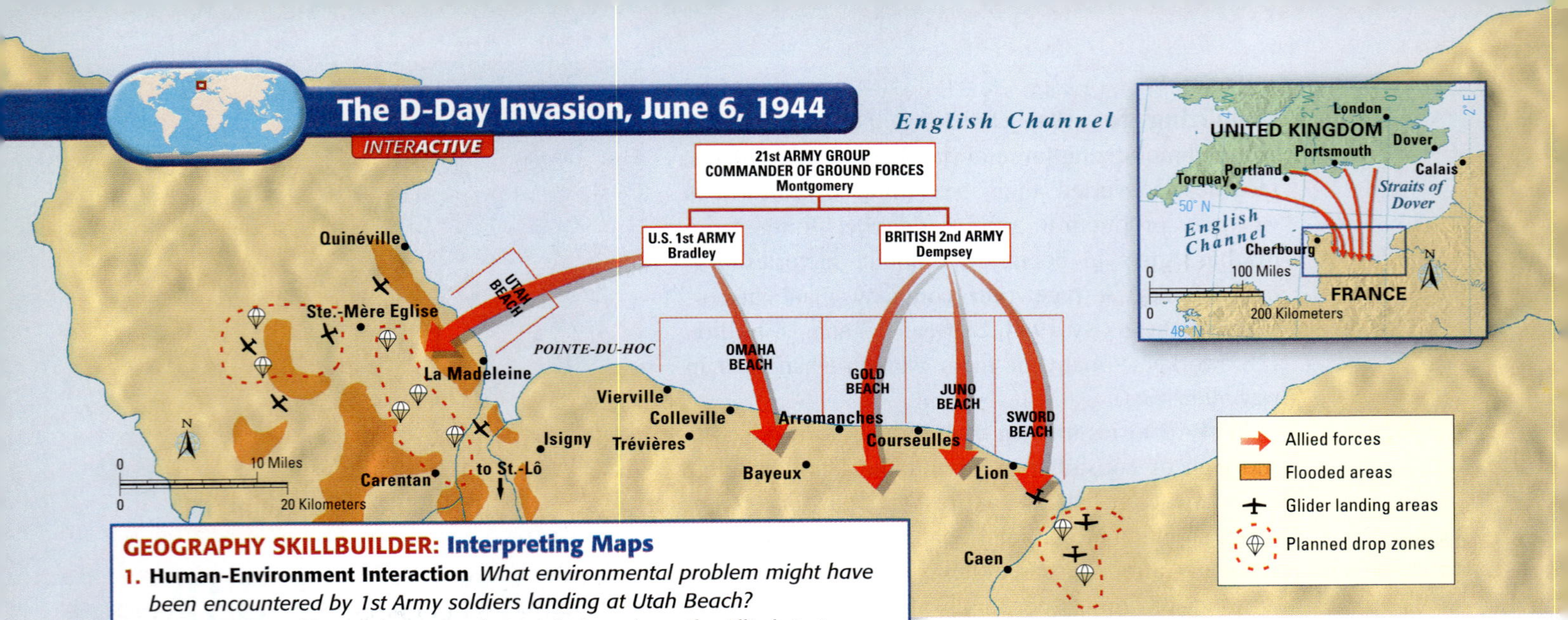

GEOGRAPHY SKILLBUILDER: Interpreting Maps

1. **Human-Environment Interaction** *What environmental problem might have been encountered by 1st Army soldiers landing at Utah Beach?*
2. **Movement** *Looking at the map, what might have been the Allied strategy behind parachuting troops into France?*

History Makers

General Dwight D. Eisenhower
1890–1969

In his career, U.S. General Dwight Eisenhower had shown an uncommon ability to work with all kinds of people—even competitive Allies. His chief of staff said of Eisenhower, "The sun rises and sets on him for me." He was also wildly popular with the troops, who affectionately called him "Uncle Ike."

So it was not a surprise when, in December 1943, U.S. Army Chief of Staff George Marshall named Eisenhower as supreme commander of the Allied forces in Europe. The new commander's "people skills" enabled him to join American and British forces together to put a permanent end to Nazi aggression.

INTEGRATED TECHNOLOGY

INTERNET ACTIVITY Create an illustrated report on Eisenhower's military career. Go to **classzone.com** for your research.

Code-named Operation Overlord, the invasion of Normandy was the largest land and sea attack in history. The invasion began on June 6, 1944—known as **D-Day**. At dawn on that day, British, American, French, and Canadian troops fought their way onto a 60-mile stretch of beach in Normandy. (See the map on this page.) The Germans had dug in with machine guns, rocket launchers, and cannons. They sheltered behind concrete walls three feet thick. Not surprisingly, the Allies took heavy casualties. Among the American forces alone, more than 2,700 men died on the beaches that day.

Despite heavy losses, the Allies held the beachheads. Within a month of D-Day, more than one million additional troops had landed. Then, on July 25, the Allies punched a hole in the German defenses near Saint-Lô (san•LOH), and the United States Third Army, led by General George Patton, broke out. A month later, the Allies marched triumphantly into Paris. By September, they had liberated France, Belgium, and Luxembourg. They then set their sights on Germany.

Vocabulary
beachheads: enemy shoreline captured just before invading forces move inland

The Battle of the Bulge As Allied forces moved toward Germany from the west, the Soviet army was advancing toward Germany from the east. Hitler now faced a war on two fronts. In a desperate gamble, he decided to counterattack in the west. Hitler hoped a victory would split American and British forces and break up Allied supply lines. Explaining the reasoning behind his plan, Hitler said, "This battle is to decide whether we shall live or die. . . . All resistance must be broken in a wave of terror."

On December 16, German tanks broke through weak American defenses along a 75-mile front in the Ardennes. The push into Allied lines gave the campaign its name—the **Battle of the Bulge**. Although caught off guard, the Allies eventually pushed the Germans back. The Germans had little choice but to retreat, since there were no reinforcements available.

Germany's Unconditional Surrender After the Battle of the Bulge, the war in Europe rapidly drew to a close. In late March 1945, the Allies rolled across the Rhine River into Germany. By the middle of April, a noose was closing around Berlin. About three million Allied soldiers approached Berlin from the southwest. Another six million Soviet troops approached from the east. By April 25, 1945, the Soviets had surrounded the capital and were pounding the city with artillery fire.

While Soviet shells burst over Berlin, Hitler prepared for his end in an underground headquarters beneath the crumbling city. On April 29, he married his longtime companion, Eva Braun. The next day, Hitler and Eva Braun committed suicide. Their bodies were then carried outside and burned.

On May 7, 1945, General Eisenhower accepted the unconditional surrender of the Third Reich from the German military. President Roosevelt, however, did not live to witness the long-awaited victory. He had died suddenly on April 12, as Allied armies were advancing toward Berlin. Roosevelt's successor, Harry Truman, received the news of the Nazi surrender. On May 9, the surrender was officially signed in Berlin. The United States and other Allied powers celebrated V-E Day—Victory in Europe Day. After nearly six years of fighting, the war in Europe had ended.

Victory in the Pacific

Although the war in Europe was over, the Allies were still fighting the Japanese in the Pacific. With the Allied victory at Guadalcanal, however, the Japanese advances in the Pacific had been stopped. For the rest of the war, the Japanese retreated before the counterattack of the Allied powers.

The Japanese in Retreat By the fall of 1944, the Allies were moving in on Japan. In October, Allied forces landed on the island of Leyte (LAY•tee) in the Philippines. General Douglas MacArthur, who had been ordered to leave the islands before their surrender in May 1942, waded ashore at Leyte with his troops. On reaching the beach, he declared, "People of the Philippines, I have returned."

▼ U.S. marines raise the Stars and Stripes after their victory at Iwo Jima.

Actually, the takeover would not be quite that easy. The Japanese had devised a bold plan to halt the Allied advance. They would destroy the American fleet, thus preventing the Allies from resupplying their ground troops. This plan, however, required risking almost the entire Japanese fleet. They took this gamble on October 23, in the Battle of Leyte Gulf. Within four days, the Japanese navy had lost disastrously—eliminating it as a fighting force in the war. Now, only the Japanese army and the feared kamikaze stood between the Allies and Japan. The **kamikazes** were Japanese suicide pilots. They would sink Allied ships by crash-diving their bomb-filled planes into them.

Vocabulary
These pilots took their name from the *kamikaze,* or "divine wind," that saved Japan from a Mongol invasion in 1281.

In March 1945, after a month of bitter fighting and heavy losses, American Marines took Iwo Jima (EE•wuh JEE•muh), an island 760 miles from Tokyo. On April 1, U.S. troops moved onto the island of Okinawa, only about 350 miles from southern Japan. The Japanese put up a desperate fight. Nevertheless, on June 21, one of the bloodiest land battles of the war ended. The Japanese lost over 100,000 troops, and the Americans 12,000.

The Atomic Bomb

On the eve of World War II, scientists in Germany succeeded in splitting the nucleus of a uranium atom, releasing a huge amount of energy. Albert Einstein wrote to President Franklin Roosevelt and warned him that Nazi Germany might be working to develop atomic weapons. Roosevelt responded by giving his approval for an American program, later code-named the Manhattan Project, to develop an atomic bomb. Roosevelt's decision set off a race to ensure that the United States would be the first to develop the bomb.

▶ At precisely 8:16 A.M., the atomic bomb exploded above Hiroshima, a city on the Japanese island of Honshu.

▼ On the morning of August 6, 1945, the B-29 bomber *Enola Gay,* flown by Colonel Paul W. Tibbets, Jr., took off from Tinian Island in the Mariana Islands.

Hiroshima: Day of Fire	
Impact of the Bombing	
Ground temperatures	7,000°F
Hurricane force winds	980 miles per hour
Energy released	20,000 tons of TNT
Buildings destroyed	62,000 buildings
Killed immediately	70,000 people
Dead by the end of 1945	140,000 people
Total deaths related to A-bomb	210,000 people

The overwhelming destructive power of the Hiroshima bomb, and of the bomb dropped on Nagasaki three days later, changed the nature of war forever. Nuclear destruction also led to questions about the ethics of scientists and politicians who chose to develop and use the bomb.

Patterns of Interaction

Arming for War: Modern and Medieval Weapons

Just as in World War I, the conflicts of World War II spurred the development of ever more powerful weapons. Mightier tanks, more elusive submarines, faster fighter planes—all emerged from this period. From ancient times to the present day, the pattern remains the same: Every new weapon causes other countries to develop weapons of similar or greater force. This pattern results in a deadly race for an ultimate weapon: for example, the atomic bomb.

▼ Nagasaki citizens trudge through the still smoldering ruins of their city in this photograph by Yosuke Yamahata.

Connect *to* Today

1. **Making Inferences** What advantages did the United States have over Germany in the race to develop the atomic bomb?
   See Skillbuilder Handbook, page R10.
2. **Comparing and Contrasting** If you were to design a memorial to the victims of the Hiroshima and Nagasaki bombings, what symbol would you use? Make a sketch of your memorial.

The Japanese Surrender After Okinawa, the next stop for the Allies had to be Japan. President Truman's advisers had informed him that an invasion of the Japanese homeland might cost the Allies half a million lives. Truman had to make a decision whether to use a powerful new weapon called the atomic bomb, or A-bomb. Most of his advisers felt that using it would bring the war to the quickest possible end. The bomb had been developed by the top-secret Manhattan Project, headed by General Leslie Groves and chief scientist J. Robert Oppenheimer. Truman first learned of the new bomb's existence when he became president.

The first atomic bomb was exploded in a desert in New Mexico on July 16, 1945. President Truman then warned the Japanese. He told them that unless they surrendered, they could expect a "rain of ruin from the air." The Japanese did not reply. So, on August 6, 1945, the United States dropped an atomic bomb on Hiroshima, a Japanese city of nearly 350,000 people. Between 70,000 and 80,000 people died in the attack. Three days later, on August 9, a second bomb was dropped on Nagasaki, a city of 270,000. More than 70,000 people were killed immediately. Radiation fallout from the two explosions killed many more.

The Japanese finally surrendered to General Douglas MacArthur on September 2. The ceremony took place aboard the United States battleship *Missouri* in Tokyo Bay. With Japan's surrender, the war had ended. Now, countries faced the task of rebuilding a war-torn world.

▲ J. Robert Oppenheimer (left) and General Leslie Groves inspect the site of the first atomic bomb test near Alamogordo, New Mexico.

NEW YORK CORE CURRICULUM REVIEW

TERMS & NAMES **1.** For each term or name, write a sentence explaining its significance.

- Dwight D. Eisenhower
- Battle of Stalingrad
- D-Day
- Battle of the Bulge
- kamikaze

USING YOUR NOTES

2. Which battle do you think was most important in turning the war in favor of the Allies? Why?

Battle	Outcome
Battle of El Alamein	
Battle of Stalingrad	
D-Day Invasion	

MAIN IDEAS

3. Why did Stalin want the United States and Britain to launch a second front in the west?

4. How did the Allies try to conceal the true location for the D-Day landings?

5. What brought about the Japanese surrender?

CRITICAL THINKING & WRITING

6. CLARIFYING How do governments gather support for a war effort on the home front?

7. ANALYZING ISSUES Should governments have the power to limit the rights of their citizens during wartime? Explain your answer.

8. FORMING AND SUPPORTING OPINIONS Did President Truman make the correct decision in using the atomic bomb? Why or why not?

9. WRITING ACTIVITY SCIENCE AND TECHNOLOGY Write a **research report** on the work of the Manhattan Project in developing the atomic bomb.

CONNECT TO TODAY **CREATING A POSTER**

During World War II, the U.S. government used propaganda posters to encourage citizens to support the war effort. Create a similar kind of **poster** to encourage support for a war on litter in your neighborhood.

Europe and Japan in Ruins

CONNECT TO THE NEW YORK STATE CORE CURRICULUM

Unit 6.D.1. Human and physical geography
Unit 6.D.2. The Nazi and Japanese states

TERMS & NAMES

- Nuremberg Trials
- demilitarization
- democratization

SETTING THE STAGE After six long years of war, the Allies finally were victorious. However, their victory had been achieved at a very high price. World War II had caused more death and destruction than any other conflict in history. It left 60 million dead. About one-third of these deaths occurred in one country, the Soviet Union. Another 50 million people had been uprooted from their homes and wandered the countryside in search of somewhere to live. Property damage ran into billions of U.S. dollars.

TAKING NOTES

Comparing and Contrasting Use a Venn diagram to compare and contrast the aftermath of World War II in Europe and Japan.

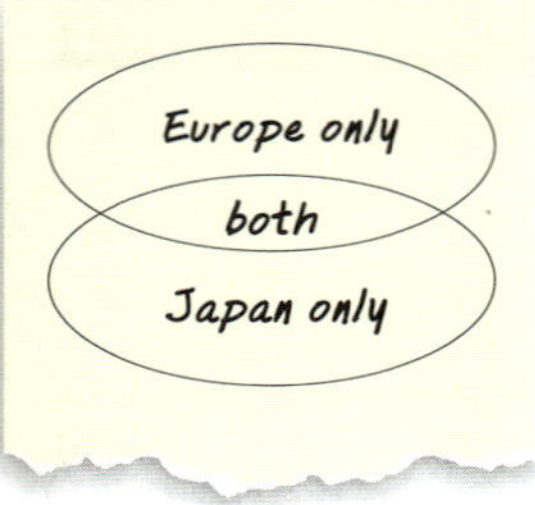

Devastation in Europe

By the end of World War II, Europe lay in ruins. Close to 40 million Europeans had died, two-thirds of them civilians. Constant bombing and shelling had reduced hundreds of cities to rubble. The ground war had destroyed much of the countryside. Displaced persons from many nations were left homeless.

A Harvest of Destruction A few of the great cities of Europe—Paris, Rome, and Brussels—remained largely undamaged by war. Many, however, had suffered terrible destruction. The Battle of Britain left huge areas of London little more than blackened ruins. Warsaw, the capital of Poland, was almost completely destroyed. In 1939, Warsaw had a population of nearly 1.3 million. When Soviet soldiers entered the city in January 1945, only 153,000 people remained. Thousands of tons of Allied bombs had demolished 95 percent of the central area of Berlin. One U.S. officer stationed in the German capital reported, "Wherever we looked we saw desolation. It was like a city of the dead."

After the bombings, many civilians stayed where they were and tried to get on with their lives. Some lived in partially destroyed homes or apartments. Others huddled in cellars or caves made from rubble. They had no water, no electricity, and very little food.

A large number of people did not stay where they were. Rather, they took to the roads. These displaced persons included the survivors of concentration camps, prisoners of war, and refugees who found themselves in the wrong country when postwar treaties changed national borders. They wandered across Europe, hoping to find their families or to find a safe place to live.

Simon Weisenthal, a prisoner at Auschwitz, described the search made by Holocaust survivors:

Costs of World War II: Allies and Axis			
	Direct War Costs	**Military Killed/Missing**	**Civilians Killed**
United States	$288.0 billion*	292,131**	–
Great Britain	$117.0 billion	272,311	60,595
France	$111.3 billion	205,707***	173,260†
USSR	$93.0 billion	13,600,000	7,720,000
Germany	$212.3 billion	3,300,000	2,893,000††
Japan	$41.3 billion	1,140,429	953,000

* In 1994 dollars.
** An additional 115,187 servicemen died from non-battle causes.
*** Before surrender to Nazis.
† Includes 65,000 murdered Jews.
†† Includes about 170,000 murdered Jews and 56,000 foreign civilians in Germany.

SKILLBUILDER: Interpreting Charts

1. **Drawing Conclusions** *Which of the nations listed in the chart suffered the greatest human costs?*
2. **Comparing** *How does U.S. spending on the war compare with the spending of Germany and Japan?*

PRIMARY SOURCE

Across Europe a wild tide of frantic survivors was flowing. . . . Many of them didn't really know where to go. . . . And yet the survivors continued their pilgrimage of despair. . . . "Perhaps someone is still alive. . . ." Someone might tell where to find a wife, a mother, children, a brother—or whether they were dead. . . . The desire to find one's people was stronger than hunger, thirst, fatigue.

SIMON WEISENTHAL, quoted in *Never to Forget: The Jews of the Holocaust*

Misery Continues After the War The misery in Europe continued for years after the war. The fighting had ravaged Europe's countryside, and agriculture had been completely disrupted. Most able-bodied men had served in the military, and the women had worked in war production. Few remained to plant the fields. With the transportation system destroyed, the meager harvests often did not reach the cities. Thousands died as famine and disease spread through the bombed-out cities. The first postwar winter brought more suffering as people went without shoes and coats.

Postwar Governments and Politics

Despairing Europeans often blamed their leaders for the war and its aftermath. Once the Germans had lost, some prewar governments—like those in Belgium, Holland, Denmark, and Norway—returned quickly. In countries like Germany, Italy, and France, however, a return to the old leadership was not desirable. Hitler's Nazi government had brought Germany to ruins. Mussolini had led Italy to defeat. The Vichy government had collaborated with the Nazis. Much of the old leadership was in disgrace. Also, in Italy and France, many resistance fighters were communists. **A**

MAIN IDEA

Identifying Problems

A Why might it have been difficult to find democratic government leaders in post-Nazi Germany?

After the war, the Communist Party promised change, and millions were ready to listen. In both France and Italy, Communist Party membership skyrocketed. The communists made huge gains in the first postwar elections. Anxious to speed up a political takeover, the communists staged a series of violent strikes. Alarmed French and Italians reacted by voting for anticommunist parties. Communist Party membership and influence began to decline. And they declined even more as the economies of France and Italy began to recover.

Connect to Today

A New War Crimes Tribunal

In 1993, the UN established the International Criminal Tribunal for the Former Yugoslavia (ICTY) to prosecute war crimes committed in the Balkan conflicts of the 1990s. (See Chapter 35.) This was the first international war crimes court since those held in Nuremberg and Tokyo after World War II.

The ICTY issued its first indictment in 1994 and began trial proceedings in 1996. By mid-2003, more than 30 defendants had been tried and found guilty. They received sentences of 5 to 48 years in jail. Another 25 were on trial or awaiting trial. The most prominent of these defendants was Slobadan Milosevic, the former president of Yugoslavia. He was charged with 66 counts of genocide, crimes against humanity, and other war crimes.

The Nuremberg Trials While nations were struggling to recover politically and economically, they also tried to deal with the issue of war crimes. During 1945 and 1946, an International Military Tribunal representing 23 nations put Nazi war criminals on trial in Nuremberg, Germany. In the first of these **Nuremberg Trials**, 22 Nazi leaders were charged with waging a war of aggression. They were also accused of committing "crimes against humanity"—the murder of 11 million people.

Adolf Hitler, SS chief Heinrich Himmler, and Minister of Propaganda Joseph Goebbels had committed suicide long before the trials began. However, Hermann Göring, the commander of the Luftwaffe; Rudolf Hess, Hitler's former deputy; and other high-ranking Nazi leaders remained to face the charges.

Hess was found guilty and was sentenced to life in prison. Göring received a death sentence, but cheated the executioner by committing suicide. Ten other Nazi leaders were hanged on October 16, 1946. Hans Frank, the "Slayer of Poles," was the only convicted Nazi to express remorse: "A thousand years will pass," he said, "and still this guilt of Germany will not have been erased." The bodies of those executed were burned at the concentration camp of Dachau (DAHK•ow). They were cremated in the same ovens that had burned so many of their victims.

Postwar Japan

The defeat suffered by Japan in World War II left the country in ruins. Two million lives had been lost. The country's major cities, including the capital, Tokyo, had been largely destroyed by bombing raids. The atomic bomb had turned Hiroshima and Nagasaki into blackened wastelands. The Allies had stripped Japan of its colonial empire.

Occupied Japan General Douglas MacArthur, who had accepted the Japanese surrender, took charge of the U.S. occupation of Japan. MacArthur was determined to be fair and not to plant the seeds of a future war. Nevertheless, to ensure that peace would prevail, he began a process of **demilitarization**, or disbanding the Japanese armed forces. He achieved this quickly, leaving the Japanese with only a small police force. MacArthur also began bringing war criminals to trial. Out of 25 surviving defendants, former Premier Hideki Tojo and six others were condemned to hang.

MacArthur then turned his attention to **democratization**, the process of creating a government elected by the people. In February 1946, he and his American political advisers drew up a new constitution. It changed the empire into a constitutional monarchy like that of Great Britain. The Japanese accepted the constitution. It went into effect on May 3, 1947.

MacArthur was not told to revive the Japanese economy. However, he was instructed to broaden land ownership and increase the participation of workers and farmers in the new democracy. To this end, MacArthur put forward a plan that required absentee landlords with huge estates to sell land to the government. The government then sold the land to tenant farmers at reasonable prices. Other reforms pushed by MacArthur gave workers the right to create independent labor unions. **B**

MAIN IDEA

Making Inferences

B How would demilitarization and a revived economy help Japan achieve democracy?

Occupation Brings Deep Changes

▲ Emperor Hirohito and U.S. General Douglas MacArthur look distant and uncomfortable as they pose here.

The new constitution was the most important achievement of the occupation. It brought deep changes to Japanese society. A long Japanese tradition had viewed the emperor as divine. He was also an absolute ruler whose will was law. The emperor now had to declare that he was not divine. That admission was as shocking to the Japanese as defeat. His power was also dramatically reduced. Like the ruler of Great Britain, the emperor became largely a figurehead—a symbol of Japan. **C**

MAIN IDEA

Analyzing Causes

C Why did the Americans choose the British system of government for the Japanese, instead of the American system?

The new constitution guaranteed that real political power in Japan rested with the people. The people elected a two-house parliament, called the Diet. All citizens over the age of 20, including women, had the right to vote. The government was led by a prime minister chosen by a majority of the Diet. A constitutional bill of rights protected basic freedoms. One more key provision of the constitution—Article 9—stated that the Japanese could no longer make war. They could fight only if attacked.

In September 1951, the United States and 47 other nations signed a formal peace treaty with Japan. The treaty officially ended the war. Some six months later, the U.S. occupation of Japan was over. However, with no armed forces, the Japanese agreed to a continuing U.S. military presence to protect their country. The United States and Japan, once bitter enemies, were now allies.

In the postwar world, enemies not only became allies. Sometimes, allies became enemies. World War II had changed the political landscape of Europe. The Soviet Union and the United States emerged from the war as the world's two major powers. They also ended the war as allies. However, it soon became clear that their postwar goals were very different. This difference stirred up conflicts that would shape the modern world for decades.

NEW YORK CORE CURRICULUM REVIEW

TERMS & NAMES 1. For each term or name, write a sentence explaining its significance.

- Nuremberg Trials
- demilitarization
- democratization

USING YOUR NOTES

2. How did the aftermath of the war in Europe differ from the aftermath of the war in Japan?

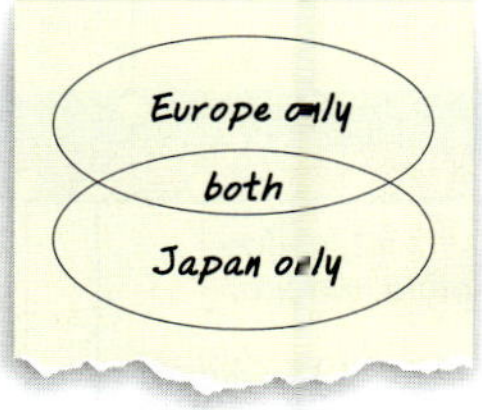

MAIN IDEAS

3. Why did so many Europeans take to the roads and wander the countryside after the war?
4. How did the Allies deal with the issue of war crimes in Europe?
5. What three programs did General Douglas MacArthur introduce during the U.S. occupation of Japan?

CRITICAL THINKING & WRITING

6. **ANALYZING CAUSES** Why do you think that many Europeans favored communism after World War II?
7. **FORMING AND SUPPORTING OPINIONS** Do you think it was right for the Allies to try only Nazi and Japanese leaders for war crimes? Why or why not?
8. **MAKING INFERENCES** Why was demilitarization such an important part of the postwar program for Japan?
9. **WRITING ACTIVITY** ECONOMICS In the role of an observer for the United States government, write a **report** on the economic situation in Europe after World War II. Illustrate your report with appropriate charts and graphs.

CONNECT TO TODAY **CREATING A RADIO NEWS REPORT**

Conduct research on a recent trial at the International War Crimes Tribunal in The Hague. Use your findings to create a two-minute radio **news report** on the trial.

Chapter 32 Assessment

TERMS & NAMES

For each term or name below, briefly explain its connection to World War II.

1. blitzkrieg
2. Atlantic Charter
3. Battle of Midway
4. Holocaust
5. genocide
6. D-Day
7. Nuremberg Trials
8. demilitarization

MAIN IDEAS

Hitler's Lightning War Section 1 (pages 925–930)

9. What event finally unleashed World War II?
10. Why was capturing Egypt's Suez Canal so important to the Axis powers?

Japan's Pacific Campaign Section 2 (pages 931–935)

11. What was Yamamoto's objective at Pearl Harbor?
12. How did Japan try to win support from other Asian countries?

The Holocaust Section 3 (pages 936–939)

13. Name two tactics that Hitler used to rid Germany of Jews before creating his "Final Solution."
14. What tactics did Hitler use during the "Final Solution"?

The Allied Victory Section 4 (pages 940–947)

15. Why were consumer goods rationed during the war?
16. What was Operation Overlord?

Europe and Japan in Ruins Section 5 (pages 948–951)

17. Why did Europeans leave their homes following the war?
18. What were two of the most important steps that MacArthur took in Japan following the war?

CRITICAL THINKING

1. USING YOUR NOTES

Copy the chart into your notebook and specify for each listed battle or conflict whether the Axis powers or the Allied powers gained an advantage.

Battle/Conflict	Allied or Axis Powers?
Battle of Britain	
War in the Balkans	
Pearl Harbor	
Battle of the Coral Sea	
Battle of Midway	

2. DRAWING CONCLUSIONS

Consider the personalities, tactics, and policies of Hitler, Rommel, MacArthur, and Churchill. What qualities make a good war leader?

3. COMPARING AND CONTRASTING

EMPIRE BUILDING Compare and contrast Japan's and Germany's goals in World War II.

4. EVALUATING COURSES OF ACTION

ECONOMICS Why do you think the governments of the United States and other countries encouraged people on the home front to organize programs for such activities as scrap collection and Victory gardens?

VISUAL SUMMARY

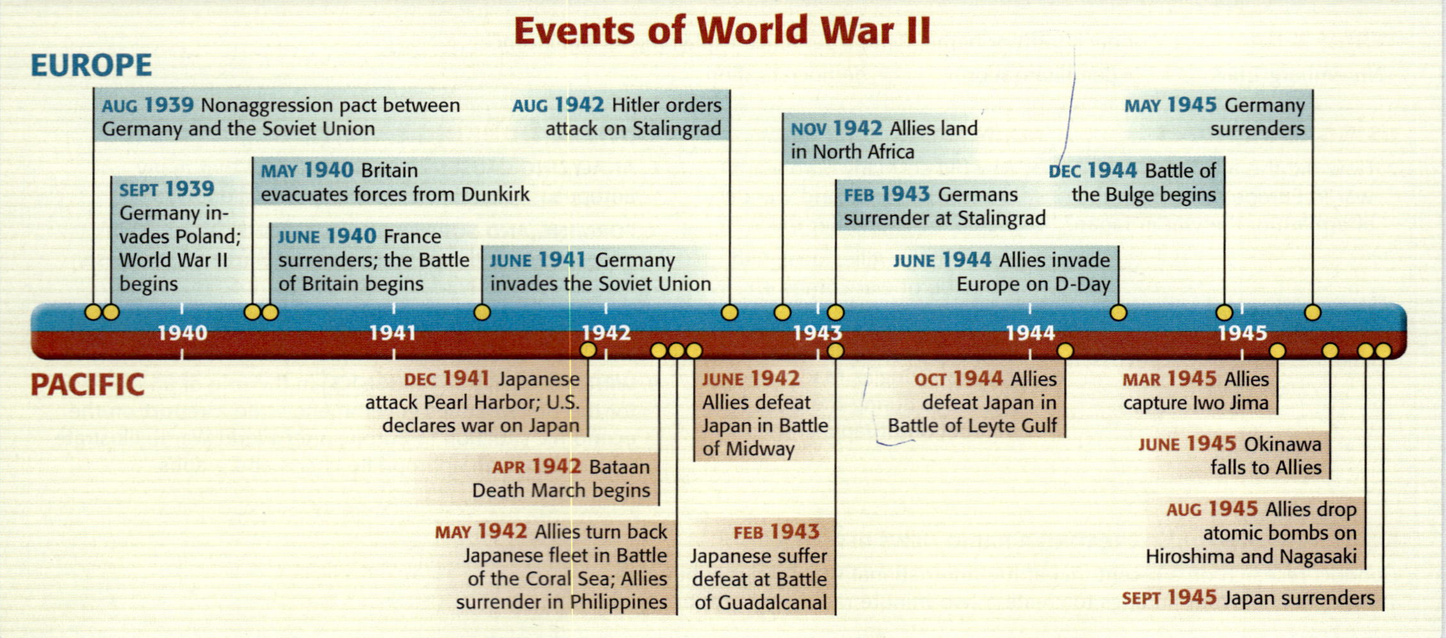

Use the excerpt and your knowledge of world history to answer question 1.
Additional Test Practice, pp. S1–S33

PRIMARY SOURCE

But there was no military advantage in hurling the bomb upon Japan without warning. The least we might have done was to announce to our foe that we possessed the atomic bomb; that its destructive power was beyond anything known in warfare; and that its terrible effectiveness had been experimentally demonstrated in this country. . . . If [Japan] doubted the good faith of our representations, it would have been a simple matter to select a demonstration target in the enemy's own country at a place where the loss of human life would be at a minimum. If, despite such warning, Japan had still held out, we would have been in a far less questionable position had we then dropped the bombs on Hiroshima and Nagasaki.

The Christian Century, August 29, 1945

1 According to the writer, what is the least the Allies might have done with reference to using the atomic bomb?

(1) tell Japan that they possessed the atomic bomb, a weapon with incredible destructive power

(2) demonstrate it on a selected target in the United States where loss of life would be limited

(3) invite Japanese leaders to a demonstration explosion of the bomb in the United States

(4) drop the bomb on cities in Germany as well as on Japanese cities

Use the map and your knowledge of world history to answer question 2.

2 In which country were most death camps located?

(1) Austria
(2) Germany
(3) Poland
(4) Yugoslavia

INTEGRATED TECHNOLOGY

TEST PRACTICE Go to **classzone.com**

- Diagnostic tests
- Tutorials
- Strategies
- Additional practice

ALTERNATIVE ASSESSMENT

1. Interact *with* History

On page 924, you had to decide under what circumstances war is justified. Now that you have read the chapter, do you think that Germany and Japan were justified in waging war? Were the Allies justified in declaring war on Germany and Japan? As you think about these questions, consider the moral issues that confront world leaders when they contemplate war as an option.

2. WRITING ABOUT HISTORY

SCIENCE AND TECHNOLOGY Conduct research on the scientific and technological developments used in the Allied war effort. Use your findings to create several **information cards** for a card series titled "Science and Technology During World War II." Organize the information on your cards in the following categories:

- name of invention or development
- country
- year
- use in the war
- use today

INTEGRATED TECHNOLOGY

Writing an Internet-Based Research Paper

During World War II, many consumer-goods manufacturers switched to the production of military goods. Many of these companies still exist. Working with a partner, use the Internet to research one such company. Find out what products the company made before and during the war, and how the company's wartime role affected its reputation. Go to the *Web Research Guide* at **classzone.com** to learn about conducting research on the Internet.

Present the results of your research in a well-organized paper. Be sure to

- apply a search strategy check when using directories and search engines to locate Web resources
- judge the usefulness and reliability of each Web site
- correctly cite your Web sources
- edit for organization and correct use of language

Technology of War

In Unit 7, you studied the economic and political upheavals that led to two world wars. For the first time, war involved not only the interested countries, but also their allies near and far and their colonies in far-flung places. In the next six pages, you will analyze the widespread use of machines and other technologies as tools for fighting and the increasingly involved role of civilians in war.

Maxim Machine Gun ▲
Hiram Maxim (above) invented the first portable, automatic machine gun. Machine guns fired hundreds of rounds per minute and were used by all the combatants in World War I.

Tanks ▲
Tanks, like the early British model shown above, enabled armies to travel over uneven ground and barbed wire. Although too slow to be used to full advantage at first, they were devastating against soldiers in trenches.

1884 — 1909 — 1915 — 1916

▼ First Military Plane
The earliest military planes were used for reconnaissance of enemy positions. A passenger could drop bombs (below) and, in later World War I models, operate a machine gun.

Poison Gas ▼
Poison gases were introduced to help break the stalemate of trench warfare. They caused suffocation, blistered skin, or blindness (below) to those exposed.

Blitzkrieg ▲
The Germans used blitzkrieg or "lightning war" to invade Poland. They employed air strikes, fast tanks, and artillery, followed by soldiers sped into battle on trucks (shown above). They swiftly overwhelmed Poland and disrupted its command and communications.

Atomic Bomb ►
The United States dropped two atomic bombs on Japan and became the first nation to use nuclear weapons. An atomic bomb (right) creates an explosion that causes massive damage. The radioactive particles released are carried by winds for weeks.

1939 | 1944 | 1945

▼ German Me 262
Military jet planes were first used by the Germans in 1944. These planes added speed to fire power. The Me 262 (below) was the only jet to be used extensively in World War II.

Comparing & Contrasting

1. How did technology change the nature of war in the 20th century?
2. Compared with earlier guns, what made machine guns so effective?
3. How did airplanes change the way war was carried out?

Expansion of Warfare

World War I and World War II both began as localized wars. As the allies of the opposing combatants became involved in the wars, combat spread to distant parts of the world. Countries attacked each other's colonies, attempted to gain territory for themselves, dedicated massive amounts of physical and human resources, and sometimes sought to kill entire populations.

Total War

A feature of warfare in the 20th century was how entire national economies were directed toward the war effort. As a result, civilians were not only potential victims of combat, but they also became actual targets themselves. Civilians also became active participants, producing arms, food, vehicles, and other goods needed for war. Many factories stopped producing consumer goods and began making products needed by the military.

London ►
The photograph shows a section of London destroyed by bombs in the Battle of Britain during World War II.

DOCUMENT-BASED QUESTION
What effect do you think the kind of destruction shown in the photograph had on the residents of London?

"All the News That's Fit to Print."

The New York Times.

EXTRA 5:30 A. M.

NEW YORK, SATURDAY, MAY 8, 1915.—TWENTY-FOUR PAGES. ONE CENT

LUSITANIA SUNK BY A SUBMARINE, PROBABLY 1,260 DEAD; TWICE TORPEDOED OFF IRISH COAST; SINKS IN 15 MINUTES; CAPT. TURNER SAVED, FROHMAN AND VANDERBILT MISSING; WASHINGTON BELIEVES THAT A GRAVE CRISIS IS AT HAND

SHOCKS THE PRESIDENT

Washington Deeply Stirred by the Loss of American Lives.

BULLETINS AT WHITE HOUSE

Wilson Reads Them Closely, but Is Silent on the Nation's Course.

HINTS OF CONGRESS CALL

Loss of Lusitania Recalls Firm Tone of Our First Warning to Germany.

CAPITAL FULL OF RUMORS

Reports That Liner Was to be Sunk Were Heard Before Actual News Came.

The Lost Cunard Steamship Lusitania

SOME DEAD TAKEN ASHORE

Several Hundred Survivors at Queenstown and Kinsale.

STEWARD TELLS OF DISASTER

Cunard Office Here Besieged for News; Fate of 1,918 on Lusitania Long in Doubt

Nothing Heard from the Well-Known Passengers on Board—Story of Disaster Long Unconfirmed While Anxious Crowds Seek Details.

List of Saved Includes Capt. Turner; Vanderbilt and Frohman Reported Lost

Saw the Submarine 100 Y... and Watched Torpedo as...

Ernest Cowper, a Toronto Newspa... Attack, Seen from Ship's Rai... Used in Torpedoes, Say Othe...

Queenstown, Saturday, May 8, 3:18 A. M.

ADVERTISEMENT.

NOTICE!

TRAVELLERS intending to embark on the Atlantic voyage are reminded that a state of war exists between Germany and her allies and Great Britain and her allies; that the zone of war includes the waters adjacent to the British Isles; that, in accordance with formal notice given by the Imperial German Government, vessels flying the flag of Great Britain, or of any of her allies, are liable to destruction in those waters and that travellers sailing in the war zone on ships of Great Britain or her allies do so at their own risk.

IMPERIAL GERMAN EMBASSY
WASHINGTON, D. C., APRIL 22, 1915.

◄ *Lusitania*
This newspaper shows the headline and various articles about the sinking of the British passenger ship *Lusitania* during World War I. Note also the announcement from the German embassy warning civilians not to travel to Great Britain because Germany considered it a war zone.

DOCUMENT-BASED QUESTION
What effect would the headline and photograph have on the American public?

Genocide

Genocide is the calculated and methodical destruction of a national, religious, ethnic, or racial group. The perpetrators consider their victims inferior or wish to take over their lands and property, or both. The mass killing of Armenians by Ottoman Turks beginning in 1915 is considered the first genocide of the 20th century. During the Holocaust, the Nazis killed more than 6 million people. As a result, in 1948 the United Nations approved an international convention to prevent and punish genocide.

PRIMARY SOURCE

INTERACTIVE

Genocide in WWI

The following excerpts are from telegrams sent to the secretary of state by the U.S. embassy in the Ottoman Empire. They concern the situation of Armenians in Turkey. The first passage was written by the American Consul General at Beirut and describes the deportation of villagers from the Zeitoon region, and the second calls attention to the killing of people in eastern Turkey.

July 20, 1915:
Whole villages were deported at an hours notice, with no opportunity to prepare for the journey, not even in some cases to gather together the scattered members of the family, so that little children were left behind. . . .

In many cases the men were (those of military age were nearly all in the army) bound tightly together with ropes or chains. Women with little children in their arms, or in the last days of pregnancy were driven along under the whip like cattle. Three different cases came under my knowledge where the woman was delivered on the road, and because her brutal driver hurried her along she died. . . .

These people are being scattered in small units, three or four families in a place, among a population of different race and religion, and speaking a different language. I speak of them as being composed of families, but four fifths of them are women and children.

July 31, 1915:
[The president of a charitable organization] has information from [a] reliable source that Armenians, mostly women and children, deported from the Erzerum district, have been massacred near Kemakh. . . . Similar reports comes from other sources showing that but few of these unfortunate people will ever reach their stated destination.

DOCUMENT-BASED QUESTION
What would be the result of scattering Armenian villagers in unfamiliar places under such terrible conditions?

PRIMARY SOURCE

INTERACTIVE

Genocide in WWII

Primo Levi describes how prisoners at the Nazi concentration camp of Auschwitz were selected for death.

Each one of us, as he comes naked out of the Tagesraum [common room] into the cold October air, has to run the few steps between the two doors, give the card to the SS man [the Nazi guard] and enter the dormitory door. The SS man, in the fraction of a second between two successive crossings, with a glance at one's back and front, judges everyone's fate, and in turn gives the card to the man on his right or his left, and this is the life or death of each of us. In three or four minutes a hut of 200 men is 'done', as is the whole camp of twelve thousand men in the course of the afternoon.

Jammed in the charnel-house [a place of great suffering] of the Tagesraum, I gradually felt the human pressure around me slacken, and in a short time it was my turn. Like everyone, I passed by with a brisk and elastic step, trying to hold my head high, my chest forward and my muscles contracted and conspicuous. With the corner of my eye I tried to look behind my shoulders, and my card seemed to end on the right.

DOCUMENT-BASED QUESTION
What was the Nazis' attitude toward selecting prisoners to be killed?

Comparing & Contrasting

1. Judging from the examples on these two pages, in what ways did warfare expand to include civilians?
2. If civilians manufacture materials for the war effort, should they be military targets? Why or why not?
3. How did modern weaponry contribute to both the sinking of the *Lusitania* and the bombing of London?

The Human Cost of War

The global nature of World Wars I and II wreaked a level of destruction unknown before. National economies were exhausted; farmland, towns, and villages were destroyed. More soldiers died in World War I than in all the conflicts of the previous three centuries, and millions more died in World War II. Civilians died by the millions as a result of military operations, concentration camps, the bombing of towns and cities, and starvation and disease.

Military Cost

Both sides in the two world wars suffered tremendous military casualties, including dead, wounded, and missing in action. About 8.5 million soldiers died in World War I and 19.4 million in World War II. The excerpts show how weapons and tactics contributed to the large number of casualties.

PRIMARY SOURCE

INTERACTIVE

Trench Warfare

British sergeant major Ernest Shephard remembers the first day of the Battle of the Somme in his diary.

A lovely day, intensely hot. Lots of casualties in my trench. The enemy are enfilading us with heavy shell, dropping straight on us. A complete trench mortar battery of men killed by one shell, scores of dead and badly wounded in trench . . . Every move we make brings intense fire, as trenches so badly battered the enemy can see all our movements. Lot of wounded [from the front] . . . several were hit again and killed in trench. We put as many wounded as possible in best spots in trench and I sent a lot down, but I had so many of my own men killed and wounded that after a time I could not do this. . . .

[L]iterally we were blown from place to place. Men very badly shaken. As far as possible we cleared trenches of debris and dead. These we piled in heaps, enemy shells pitching on them made matters worse.

DOCUMENT-BASED QUESTION
Judging from the quotation, what was Shephard's attitude toward the battle?

PRIMARY SOURCE

INTERACTIVE

Iwo Jima

Japan lost 21,000 soldiers and the United States 6,800 in the Battle of Iwo Jima. A U.S. Marines correspondent described part of the fighting below.

Behind a rolling artillery barrage and with fixed bayonets, the unit leaped forward in . . . [a] charge and advanced to the very mouths of the fixed [Japanese] defenses. . . . [T]he men flung themselves at the tiny flaming holes, throwing grenades and jabbing with bayonets. Comrades went past, hurdled the defenses and rushed across Airfield no. 2. . . . Men died at every step. That was how we broke their line. . . .

Across the field we attacked a ridge. The enemy rose up out of holes to hurl our assault back. The squads re-formed and went up again. At the crest they plunged on the [Japanese] with bayonets. . . . The [Japanese] on the ridge were annihilated.

DOCUMENT-BASED QUESTION
What attitude do you think the soldiers on both sides had to adopt to fight in such a bloody conflict as this?

Military Casualties, World War I and World War II

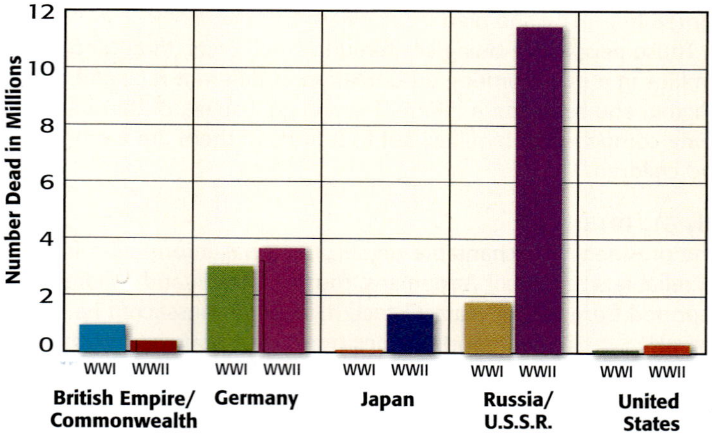

Source: Encyclopaedia Britannica

SKILLBUILDER: Interpreting Graphs
What factors may have contributed to the increased number of deaths in World War II over World War I?

Civilian Cost

Civilians suffered not only as the direct victims of war, but also from the loss of their homes, the workplaces that gave them an income and produced useful goods, and the farms that supplied food. They also experienced the unsanitary conditions that resulted from bombing.

PRIMARY SOURCE

INTERACTIVE

Displaced Persons

Laura de Gozdawa Turczynowicz, an American married to a Polish nobleman, described fleeing the advance of the German army into Suwalki, Poland.

At the [Vilno] station were crowds of Suwalki people. One man of our acquaintance had brought with him only his walking stick! Another man had become separated from his young son, fourteen, and daughter, sixteen, . . . and the poor father was on the verge of losing his reason. . . .

Such a lot of people came for help that my money melted like snow in the sunshine. I took just as many as could be packed in our [hotel] rooms. . . .

The next day dragged wearily along, everybody waiting, living only to hear better news. The city was rapidly filling with refugees. In one place, an old convent, they were given a roof to sleep under, and hot tea.

DOCUMENT-BASED QUESTION

Under what conditions did the Polish refugees flee from the Germans?

PRIMARY SOURCE

INTERACTIVE

Atomic Bomb

In this excerpt, Dr. Tatsuichiro Akizuki describes the people who began arriving at his hospital in Nagasaki the day the bomb was dropped.

It was all he could do to keep standing. Yet it didn't occur to me that he had been seriously injured. . . .

As time passed, more and more people in a similar plight came up to the hospital . . . All were of the same appearance, sounded the same. "I'm hurt, *hurt!* I'm burning! Water!" They all moaned the same lament. . . .[T]hey walked with strange, slow steps, groaning from deep inside themselves as if they had travelled from the depths of hell. They looked whitish; their faces were like masks.

DOCUMENT-BASED QUESTION

Why did the doctor not recognize his patients' symptoms?

PRIMARY SOURCE

Internment Camps

After Pearl Harbor, thousands of Japanese Americans were sent to internment camps mainly located in the western United States.

DOCUMENT-BASED QUESTION

Judging from the photograph, what was the government's attitude toward Japanese Americans?

Comparing & Contrasting

1. Given the conditions described during trench warfare and on Iwo Jima, why would soldiers continue to fight?
2. How were the human costs of war, military and civilian, similar to each other? How were they different?
3. Given what you have read on these pages, if another world war broke out, would you prefer to be in the military or to be a civilian? Why?

EXTENSION ACTIVITY

Look up the numbers of civilian casualties suffered in different countries during World War II in an encyclopedia or other reference source. Use the graph on page 958 as a model. Be sure to include the countries with the most significant figures in different parts of the world. Write a paragraph explaining why these countries had the greatest number of casualties.

UNIT 8

Perspectives On the Present
1945–present

On November 10, 1989, all borders between East and West Germany were opened. Here, people celebrate in front of the Brandenburg Gate, one of the former border crossings between East and West.

Comparing & Contrasting

Nation Building

In Unit 8, you will learn about the emergence or growth of several different nations. At the end of the unit, you will have a chance to compare and contrast the nations you have studied. (See pages 1100–1105.)

CHAPTER 33

Restructuring the Postwar World, 1945–Present

NEW YORK CORE CURRICULUM FOCUS

- After World War II, the U.S. and the Soviet Union launched the Cold War.
- Rather than fight each other, the superpowers supported conflicts in Asia, Latin America, and the Middle East.

Previewing Main Ideas

ECONOMICS Two conflicting economic systems, capitalism and communism, competed for influence and power after World War II. The superpowers in this struggle were the United States and the Soviet Union.

Geography *Study the map and the key. What does the map show about the state of the world in 1949?*

REVOLUTION In Asia, the Americas, and Eastern Europe, people revolted against repressive governments or rule by foreign powers. These revolutions often became the areas for conflict between the two superpowers.

Geography *Look at the map. Which of the three areas mentioned was not Communist in 1949?*

EMPIRE BUILDING The United States and the Soviet Union used military, economic, and humanitarian aid to extend their control over other countries. Each also tried to prevent the other superpower from gaining influence.

Geography *Why might the clear-cut division shown on this map be misleading?*

INTEGRATED TECHNOLOGY

eEdition
- Interactive Maps
- Interactive Visuals
- Interactive Primary Sources

INTERNET RESOURCES

Go to **classzone.com** for:
- Research Links
- Internet Activities
- Primary Sources
- Chapter Quiz
- Maps
- Test Practice
- Current Events

WORLD 1945 – 1965

1945 ◀ United Nations formed.

1947 Independent India partitioned into India and Pakistan.

1949 Communists take control of China.

1957 Soviets launch *Sputnik.*

1957 Ghana achieves independence from Great Britain. ▶

1959 Cuba becomes Communist. (Fidel Castro) ▶

Cold War Enemies, 1949

1969
U.S. lands astronauts on the moon. ▶

1973
Arab forces attack Israel in the Yom Kippur War.

1975
Vietnam War ends.

1985

1989
◀ Berlin Wall is knocked down in Germany.

1990
Communists voted out of power in Nicaragua.

1994
First all-race election in South Africa is held. (Nelson Mandela) ▶

2000
South Korea and North Korea meet to improve relations.

2003

Interact *with* History

If you were president, what policies would you follow to gain allies?

World War II has ended. You are the leader of a great superpower—one of two in the world. To keep the balance of power in your nation's favor, you want to gain as many allies as possible. You are particularly interested in gaining the support of nations in Africa, Asia, and Central and South America who do not yet favor either superpower.

You call your advisers together to develop policies for making uncommitted nations your allies.

EXAMINING *the* ISSUES

- **How might the actions taken affect your country? the other superpower?**
- **How might being caught in a struggle between superpowers affect a developing nation?**

As a class, discuss how the conflict between the superpowers affects the rest of the world. As you read about how the superpowers tried to gain allies, notice the part weaker countries played in their conflict.

Cold War: Superpowers Face Off

CONNECT TO THE NEW YORK STATE CORE CURRICULUM

Unit 7.A.1. Human and physical geography
Unit 7.A.4. Emergence of the superpowers

TERMS & NAMES

- United Nations
- iron curtain
- containment
- Truman Doctrine
- Marshall Plan
- Cold War
- NATO
- Warsaw Pact
- brinkmanship

SETTING THE STAGE During World War II, the United States and the Soviet Union had joined forces to fight against the Germans. The Soviet army marched west; the Americans marched east. When the Allied soldiers met at the Elbe River in Germany in 1945, they embraced each other warmly because they had defeated the Nazis. Their leaders, however, regarded each other much more coolly. This animosity caused by competing political philosophies would lead to a nearly half-century of conflict called the Cold War.

Allies Become Enemies

Even before World War II ended, the U.S. alliance with the Soviet Union had begun to unravel. The United States was upset that Joseph Stalin, the Soviet leader, had signed a nonaggression pact with Germany in 1939. Later, Stalin blamed the Allies for not invading German-occupied Europe earlier than 1944. Driven by these and other disagreements, the two allies began to pursue opposing goals.

Yalta Conference: A Postwar Plan The war was not yet over in February 1945. But the leaders of the United States, Britain, and the Soviet Union met at the Soviet Black Sea resort of Yalta. There, they agreed to divide Germany into zones of occupation controlled by the Allied military forces. Germany also would have

TAKING NOTES

Following Chronological Order Organize important early Cold War events in a time line.

1945 — 1960

Yalta conference — U-2 incident

▶ Winston Churchill Franklin D. Roosevelt, and Joseph Stalin meet at Yalta in 1945.

to pay the Soviet Union to compensate for its loss of life and property. Stalin agreed to join the war against Japan. He also promised that Eastern Europeans would have free elections. A skeptical Winston Churchill predicted that Stalin would keep his pledge only if the Eastern Europeans followed "a policy friendly to Russia."

Creation of the United Nations In June 1945, the United States and the Soviet Union temporarily set aside their differences. They joined 48 other countries in forming the **United Nations** (UN). This international organization was intended to protect the members against aggression. It was to be based in New York.

The charter for the new peacekeeping organization established a large body called the General Assembly. There, each UN member nation could cast its vote on a broad range of issues. An 11-member body called the Security Council had the real power to investigate and settle disputes, though. Its five permanent members were Britain, China, France, the United States, and the Soviet Union. Each could veto any Security Council action. This provision was intended to prevent any members of the Council from voting as a bloc to override the others.

Differing U.S. and Soviet Goals Despite agreement at Yalta and their presence on the Security Council, the United States and the Soviet Union split sharply after the war. The war had affected them very differently. The United States, the world's richest and most powerful country, suffered 400,000 deaths. But its cities and factories remained intact. The Soviet Union had at least 50 times as many fatalities. One in four Soviets was wounded or killed. Also, many Soviet cities were demolished. These contrasting situations, as well as political and economic differences, affected the two countries' postwar goals. (See chart below.) (A)

MAIN IDEA

Summarizing

(A) Why did the United States and the Soviet Union split after the war?

Superpower Aims in Europe

INTERACTIVE

United States

- Encourage democracy in other countries to help prevent the rise of Communist governments
- Gain access to raw materials and markets to fuel booming industries
- Rebuild European governments to promote stability and create new markets for U.S. goods
- Reunite Germany to stabilize it and increase the security of Europe

Soviet Union

- Encourage communism in other countries as part of a worldwide workers' revolution
- Rebuild its war-ravaged economy using Eastern Europe's industrial equipment and raw materials
- Control Eastern Europe to protect Soviet borders and balance the U.S. influence in Western Europe
- Keep Germany divided to prevent its waging war again

SKILLBUILDER: Interpreting Maps and Charts

1. **Drawing Conclusions** *Which countries separated the Soviet Union from Western Europe?*
2. **Comparing** *Which U.S. and Soviet aims in Europe conflicted?*

Eastern Europe's Iron Curtain

A major goal of the Soviet Union was to shield itself from another invasion from the west. Centuries of history had taught the Soviets to fear invasion. Because it lacked natural western borders, Russia fell victim to each of its neighbors in turn. In the 17th century, the Poles captured the Kremlin. During the next century, the Swedes attacked. Napoleon overran Moscow in 1812. The Germans invaded Russia during World Wars I and II.

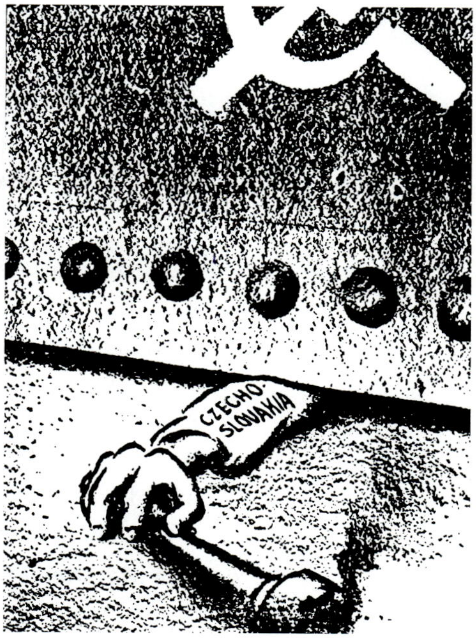

▲ The Iron Curtain is shown dropping on Czechoslovakia in this 1948 political cartoon.

Soviets Build a Buffer As World War II drew to a close, the Soviet troops pushed the Nazis back across Eastern Europe. At war's end, these troops occupied a strip of countries along the Soviet Union's own western border. Stalin regarded these countries as a necessary buffer, or wall of protection. He ignored the Yalta agreement and installed or secured Communist governments in Albania, Bulgaria, Hungary, Czechoslovakia, Romania, Poland, and Yugoslavia.

The Soviet leader's American partner at Yalta, Franklin D. Roosevelt, had died on April 12, 1945. To Roosevelt's successor, Harry S. Truman, Stalin's reluctance to allow free elections in Eastern European nations was a clear violation of those countries' rights. Truman, Stalin, and Churchill met at Potsdam, Germany, in July 1945. There, Truman pressed Stalin to permit free elections in Eastern Europe. The Soviet leader refused. In a speech in early 1946, Stalin declared that communism and capitalism could not exist in the same world.

An Iron Curtain Divides East and West Europe now lay divided between East and West. Germany had been split into two sections. The Soviets controlled the eastern part, including half of the capital, Berlin. Under a Communist government, East Germany was named the German Democratic Republic. The western zones became the Federal Republic of Germany in 1949. Winston Churchill described the division of Europe:

MAIN IDEA

Analyzing Primary Sources

B Why might Winston Churchill use "iron curtain" to refer to the division between Western and Eastern Europe?

PRIMARY SOURCE B

From Stettin in the Baltic to Trieste in the Adriatic, an iron curtain has descended across the continent. Behind that line lie all the capitals of the ancient states of Central and Eastern Europe. . . . All these famous cities and the populations around them lie in the Soviet sphere and all are subject in one form or another, not only to Soviet influence but to a very high and increasing measure of control from Moscow.

WINSTON CHURCHILL, "Iron Curtain" speech, March 5, 1946

Churchill's phrase "**iron curtain**" came to represent Europe's division into mostly democratic Western Europe and Communist Eastern Europe.

United States Tries to Contain Soviets

U.S.-Soviet relations continued to worsen in 1946 and 1947. An increasingly worried United States tried to offset the growing Soviet threat to Eastern Europe. President Truman adopted a foreign policy called **containment**. It was a policy directed at blocking Soviet influence and stopping the expansion of communism. Containment policies included forming alliances and helping weak countries resist Soviet advances.

The Truman Doctrine In a speech asking Congress for foreign aid for Turkey and Greece, Truman contrasted democracy with communism:

PRIMARY SOURCE

One way of life is based upon the will of the majority, and is distinguished by free institutions . . . free elections . . . and freedom from political oppression. The second way of life is based upon the will of a minority forcibly imposed upon the majority. It relies upon terror and oppression . . . fixed elections, and the suppression of personal freedoms. I believe it must be the policy of the United States to support free people . . . resisting attempted subjugation [control] by armed minorities or by outside pressures.

PRESIDENT HARRY S. TRUMAN, speech to Congress, March 12, 1947

Truman's support for countries that rejected communism was called the **Truman Doctrine**. It caused great controversy. Some opponents objected to American interference in other nations' affairs. Others argued that the United States could not afford to carry on a global crusade against communism. Congress, however, immediately authorized more than $400 million in aid to Turkey and Greece.

The Marshall Plan Much of Western Europe lay in ruins after the war. There was also economic turmoil—a scarcity of jobs and food. In 1947, U.S. Secretary of State George Marshall proposed that the United States give aid to needy European countries. This assistance program, called the **Marshall Plan**, would provide food, machinery, and other materials to rebuild Western Europe. (See chart.) As Congress debated the $12.5 billion program in 1948, the Communists seized power in Czechoslovakia. Congress immediately voted approval. The plan was a spectacular success. Even Communist Yugoslavia received aid after it broke away from Soviet domination. **C**

MAIN IDEA

Making Inferences

C What was Truman's major reason for offering aid to other countries?

Countries Aided by the Marshall Plan, 1948–1951

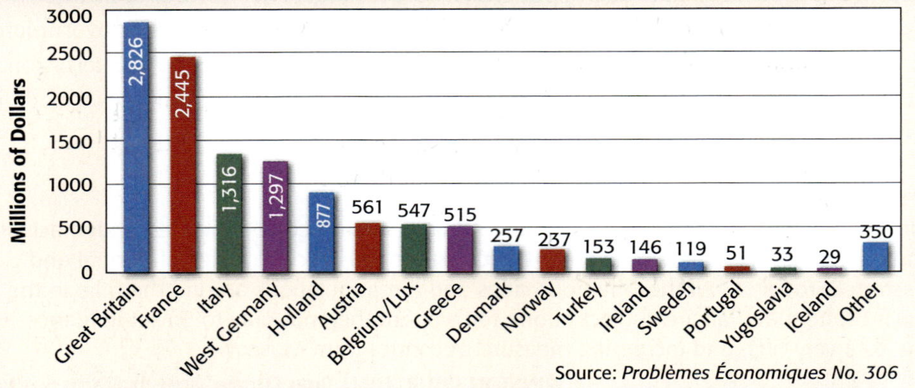

Source: *Problèmes Économiques No. 306*

SKILLBUILDER: Interpreting Charts

1. **Drawing Conclusions** *Which country received the most aid from the United States?*
2. **Making Inferences** *Why do you think Great Britain and France received so much aid?*

The Berlin Airlift While Europe began rebuilding, the United States and its allies clashed with the Soviet Union over Germany. The Soviets wanted to keep their former enemy weak and divided. But in 1948, France, Britain, and the United States decided to withdraw their forces from Germany and allow their occupation zones to form one nation. The Soviet Union responded by holding West Berlin hostage.

Although Berlin lay well within the Soviet occupation zone of Germany, it too had been divided into four zones. (See map on next page.) The Soviet Union cut off highway, water, and rail traffic into Berlin's western zones. The city faced starvation. Stalin gambled that the Allies would surrender West Berlin or give up

History in Depth

The Berlin Airlift

From June 1948 to May 1949, Allied planes took off and landed every three minutes in West Berlin. On 278,000 flights, pilots brought in 2.3 million tons of food, fuel, medicine, and even Christmas gifts to West Berliners.

Divided Germany, 1948–1949

MAIN IDEA

Summarizing

D What Soviet actions led to the Berlin airlift?

their idea of reunifying Germany. But American and British officials flew food and supplies into West Berlin for nearly 11 months. In May 1949, the Soviet Union admitted defeat and lifted the blockade. **D**

The Cold War Divides the World

These conflicts marked the start of the **Cold War** between the United States and the Soviet Union. A cold war is a struggle over political differences carried on by means short of military action or war. Beginning in 1949, the superpowers used spying, propaganda, diplomacy, and secret operations in their dealings with each other. Much of the world allied with one side or the other. In fact, until the Soviet Union finally broke up in 1991, the Cold War dictated not only U.S. and Soviet foreign policy, but influenced world alliances as well.

Superpowers Form Rival Alliances The Berlin blockade heightened Western Europe's fears of Soviet aggression. As a result, in 1949, ten western European nations joined with the United States and Canada to form a defensive military alliance. It was called the North Atlantic Treaty Organization (**NATO**). An attack on any NATO member would be met with armed force by all member nations.

The Soviet Union saw NATO as a threat and formed it's own alliance in 1955. It was called the **Warsaw Pact** and included the Soviet Union, East Germany, Czechoslovakia, Poland, Hungary, Romania, Bulgaria, and Albania. In 1961, the East Germans built a wall to separate East and West Berlin. The Berlin Wall symbolized a world divided into rival camps. However, not every country joined the new alliances. Some, like India, chose not to align with either side. And China, the largest Communist country, came to distrust the Soviet Union. It remained nonaligned.

The Threat of Nuclear War As these alliances were forming, the Cold War threatened to heat up enough to destroy the world. The United States already had atomic bombs. In 1949, the Soviet Union exploded its own atomic weapon. President Truman was determined to develop a more deadly weapon before the Soviets did. He authorized work on a thermonuclear weapon in 1950.

The hydrogen or H-bomb would be thousands of times more powerful than the A-bomb. Its power came from the fusion, or joining together, of atoms, rather than the splitting of atoms, as in the A-bomb. In 1952, the United States tested the first H-bomb. The Soviets exploded their own in 1953.

Dwight D. Eisenhower became the U.S. president in 1953. He appointed the firmly anti-Communist John Foster Dulles as his secretary of state. If the Soviet Union or its supporters attacked U.S. interests, Dulles threatened, the United States would "retaliate instantly, by means and at places of our own choosing." This willingness to go to the brink, or edge, of war became known as **brinkmanship**. Brinkmanship required a reliable source of nuclear weapons and airplanes to deliver them. So, the United States strengthened its air force and began producing stockpiles of nuclear weapons. The Soviet Union responded with its own military buildup, beginning an arms race that would go on for four decades. **E**

MAIN IDEA

Recognizing Effects

E How did the U.S. policy of brinkmanship contribute to the arms race?

The Cold War in the Skies The Cold War also affected the science and education programs of the two countries. In August 1957, the Soviets announced the development of a rocket that could travel great distances—an intercontinental ballistic missile, or ICBM. On October 4, the Soviets used an ICBM to push *Sputnik,* the first unmanned satellite, above the earth's atmosphere. Americans felt they had fallen behind in science and technology, and the government poured money into science education. In 1958, the United States launched its own satellite.

In 1960, the skies again provided the arena for a superpower conflict. Five years earlier, Eisenhower had proposed that the United States and the Soviet Union be able to fly over each other's territory to guard against surprise nuclear attacks. The Soviet Union said no. In response, the U.S. Central Intelligence Agency (CIA) started secret high-altitude spy flights over Soviet territory in planes called U-2s. In May 1960, the Soviets shot down a U-2 plane, and its pilot, Francis Gary Powers, was captured. This U-2 incident heightened Cold War tensions.

While Soviet Communists were squaring off against the United States, Communists in China were fighting a civil war for control of that country.

NEW YORK CORE CURRICULUM REVIEW

TERMS & NAMES 1. For each term or name, write a sentence explaining its significance.

• United Nations • iron curtain • containment • Truman Doctrine • Marshall Plan • Cold War • NATO • Warsaw Pact • brinkmanship

USING YOUR NOTES

2. Which effect of the Cold War was the most significant? Explain.

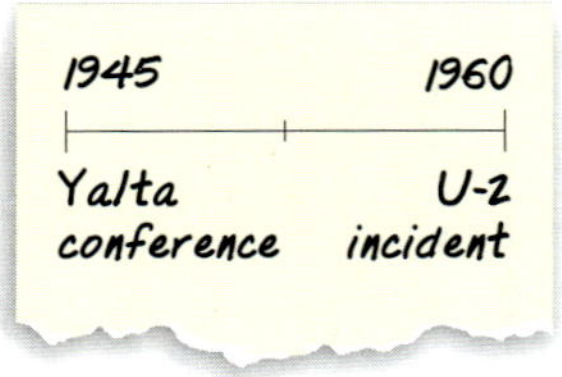

MAIN IDEAS

3. What was the purpose in forming the United Nations?
4. What was the goal of the Marshall Plan?
5. What were the goals of NATO and the Warsaw Pact?

CRITICAL THINKING & WRITING

6. **COMPARING AND CONTRASTING** What factors help to explain why the United States and the Soviet Union became rivals instead of allies?
7. **ANALYZING MOTIVES** What were Stalin's objectives in supporting Communist governments in Eastern Europe?
8. **ANALYZING ISSUES** Why might Berlin be a likely spot for trouble to develop during the Cold War?
9. **WRITING ACTIVITY** ECONOMICS Draw a **political cartoon** that shows either capitalism from the Soviet point of view or communism from the U.S. point of view.

INTEGRATED TECHNOLOGY **INTERNET ACTIVITY**

Use the Internet to research NATO today. Prepare a **chart** listing members today and the date they joined. Then compare it with a list of the founding members.

INTERNET KEYWORD
North Atlantic Treaty Organization

The Space Race

Beginning in the late 1950s, the United States and the Soviet Union competed for influence not only among the nations of the world, but in the skies as well. Once the superpowers had ICBMs (intercontinental ballistic missiles) to deliver nuclear warheads and aircraft for spying missions, they both began to develop technology that could be used to explore—and ultimately control—space. However, after nearly two decades of costly competition, the two superpowers began to cooperate in space exploration.

INTEGRATED TECHNOLOGY

RESEARCH LINKS For more on the space race, go to **classzone.com**

▲ In a major technological triumph, the United States put human beings on the moon on July 20, 1969. Astronaut Buzz Aldrin is shown on the lunar surface with the lunar lander spacecraft.

UNITED STATES

- **1958** U.S. launches an artificial satellite (*Explorer I*)
- **1961** First American in space (Alan Shepard)
- **1962** First American orbits Earth (John Glenn, Jr.); *Mariner 2* flies past Venus
- **1965** *Mariner 4* space probe flies past Mars
- **1969** *Apollo 11* first manned moon landing (Neil Armstrong, Buzz Aldrin, Michael Collins)
- **1973** *Pioneer 7* sent toward Jupiter

1975 U.S. and Soviet Union launch first joint space mission

SOVIET UNION

- **1957** Soviet Union launches *Sputnik*
- **1959** *Luna 2* probe reaches the moon
- **1961** First human orbits Earth (Yuri Gagarin)
- **1963** First woman in space (Valentina Tereshkova)
- **1970** *Venera 7* lands on Venus
- **1971** First manned space station; *Mars 3* drops capsule on Mars

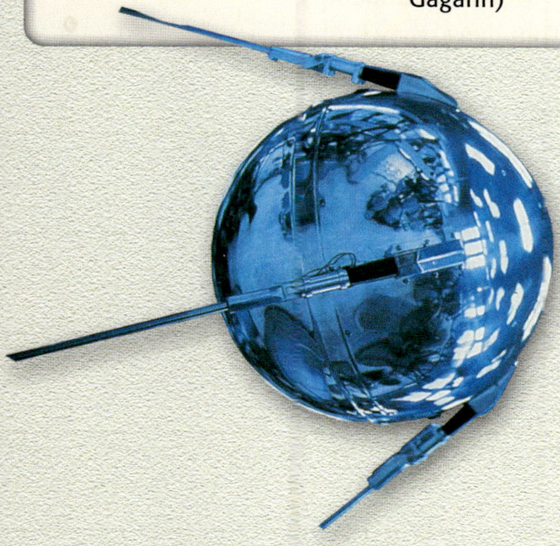

▲ The Soviet Union launched *Sputnik*, the first successful artificial space satellite, on October 4, 1957. As it circled the earth every 96 minutes, Premier Nikita Khrushchev boasted that his country would soon be "turning out long-range missiles like sausages." The United States accelerated its space program. After early failures, a U.S. satellite was launched in 1958.

◀ The joint *Apollo* and *Soyuz* mission ushered in an era of U.S.-Soviet cooperation in space.

Connect *to* Today

1. **Comparing** Which destinations in space did both the United States and the Soviet Union explore?
   See Skillbuilder Handbook, page R7.
2. **Making Inferences** What role might space continue to play in achieving world peace?

Communists Take Power in China

CONNECT TO THE NEW YORK STATE CORE CURRICULUM

Unit 7.D.2. Communist rise to power (1936–1949); Jiang Jieshi (Chiang Kai-shek), Mao Zedong
Unit 7.D.3.a. Great Leap Forward

TERMS & NAMES

- Mao Zedong
- Jiang Jieshi
- commune
- Red Guards
- Cultural Revolution

SETTING THE STAGE In World War II, China fought on the side of the victorious Allies. But the victory proved to be a hollow one for China. During the war, Japan's armies had occupied and devastated most of China's cities. China's civilian death toll alone was estimated between 10 to 22 million persons. This vast country suffered casualties second only to those of the Soviet Union. However, conflict did not end with the defeat of the Japanese. In 1945, opposing Chinese armies faced one another.

TAKING NOTES

Recognizing Effects Use a chart to identify the causes and effects of the Communist Revolution in China.

Cause	Effect
1.	1.
2.	2.
3.	3.

Communists vs. Nationalists

As you read in Chapter 30, a bitter civil war was raging between the Nationalists and the Communists when the Japanese invaded China in 1937. During World War II, the political opponents temporarily united to fight the Japanese. But they continued to jockey for position within China.

World War II in China Under their leader, **Mao Zedong** (MOW-dzuh•dahng), the Communists had a stronghold in northwestern China. From there, they mobilized peasants for guerrilla war against the Japanese in the northeast. Thanks to their efforts to promote literacy and improve food production, the Communists won the peasants' loyalty. By 1945, they controlled much of northern China.

Meanwhile, the Nationalist forces under **Jiang Jieshi** (jee•ahng-jee•shee) dominated southwestern China. Protected from the Japanese by rugged mountain ranges, Jiang gathered an army of 2.5 million men. From 1942 to 1945, the United States sent the Nationalists at least $1.5 billion in aid to fight the Japanese. Instead of benefiting the army, however, these supplies and money often ended up in the hands of a few corrupt officers. Jiang's army actually fought few battles against the Japanese. Instead, the Nationalist army saved its strength for the coming battle against Mao's Red Army. After Japan surrendered, the Nationalists and Communists resumed fighting.

Civil War Resumes The renewed civil war lasted from 1946 to 1949. At first, the Nationalists had the advantage. Their army outnumbered the Communists' army by as much as three to one. And the United States continued its support by providing nearly $2 billion in aid. The Nationalist forces, however, did little to win popular support. With China's economy collapsing, thousands of Nationalist soldiers deserted to the Communists. In spring 1949, China's major cities fell to

Chinese Political Opponents, 1945

Nationalists		Communists
Jiang Jieshi	**Leader**	Mao Zedong
Southern China	**Area Ruled**	Northern China
United States	**Foreign Support**	Soviet Union
Defeat of Communists	**Domestic Policy**	National liberation
Weak due to inflation and failing economy	**Public Support**	Strong due to promised land reform for peasants
Ineffective, corrupt leadership and poor morale	**Military Organization**	Experienced, motivated guerrilla army

SKILLBUILDER: Interpreting Charts

1. **Drawing Conclusions** *Which party's domestic policy might appeal more to Chinese peasants?*
2. **Forming and Supporting Opinions** *Which aspect of the Communist approach do you think was most responsible for Mao's victory? Explain.*

the well-trained Red forces. Mao's troops were also enthusiastic about his promise to return land to the peasants. The remnants of Jiang's shattered army fled south. In October 1949, Mao Zedong gained control of the country. He proclaimed it the People's Republic of China. Jiang and other Nationalist leaders retreated to the island of Taiwan, which Westerners called Formosa.

MAIN IDEA

Recognizing Effects

A How did the outcome of the Chinese civil war contribute to Cold War tensions?

Mao Zedong's victory fueled U.S. anti-Communist feelings. Those feelings only grew after the Chinese and Soviets signed a treaty of friendship in 1950. Many people in the United States viewed the takeover of China as another step in a Communist campaign to conquer the world. **A**

The Two Chinas Affect the Cold War

China had split into two nations. One was the island of Taiwan, or Nationalist China, with an area of 13,000 square miles. The mainland, or People's Republic of China, had an area of more than 3.5 million square miles. The existence of two Chinas, and the conflicting international loyalties they inspired, intensified the Cold War.

The Superpowers React After Jiang Jieshi fled to Taiwan, the United States helped him set up a Nationalist government on that small island. It was called the Republic of China. The Soviets gave financial, military, and technical aid to Communist China. In addition, the Chinese and the Soviets pledged to come to each other's defense if either was attacked. The United States tried to halt Soviet expansion in Asia. For example, when Soviet forces occupied the northern half of Korea after World War II and set up a Communist government, the United States supported a separate state in the south.

China Expands under the Communists In the early years of Mao's reign, Chinese troops expanded into Tibet, India, and southern, or Inner, Mongolia. Northern, or Outer, Mongolia, which bordered the Soviet Union, remained in the Soviet sphere.

In a brutal assault in 1950 and 1951, China took control of Tibet. The Chinese promised autonomy to Tibetans, who followed their religious leader, the Dalai Lama. When China's control over Tibet tightened in the late 1950s, the Dalai Lama fled to India. India welcomed many Tibetan refugees after a failed revolt in Tibet in

1959. As a result, resentment between India and China grew. In 1962, they clashed briefly over the two countries' unclear border. The fighting stopped but resentment continued.

The Communists Transform China

For decades, China had been in turmoil, engaged in civil war or fighting with Japan. So, when the Communists took power, they moved rapidly to strengthen their rule over China's 550 million people. They also aimed to restore China as a powerful nation.

Communists Claim a New "Mandate of Heaven" After taking control of China, the Communists began to tighten their hold. The party's 4.5 million members made up just 1 percent of the population. But they were a disciplined group. Like the Soviets, the Chinese Communists set up two parallel organizations, the Communist party and the national government. Mao headed both until 1959.

Mao's Brand of Marxist Socialism Mao was determined to reshape China's economy based on Marxist socialism. Eighty percent of the people lived in rural areas, but most owned no land. Instead, 10 percent of the rural population controlled 70 percent of the farmland. Under the Agrarian Reform Law of 1950, Mao seized the holdings of these landlords. His forces killed more than a million landlords who resisted. He then divided the land among the peasants. Later, to further Mao's socialist principles, the government forced peasants to join collective farms. Each of these farms was comprised of 200 to 300 households.

Mao's changes also transformed industry and business. Gradually, private companies were nationalized, or brought under government ownership. In 1953, Mao launched a five-year plan that set high production goals for industry. By 1957, China's output of coal, cement, steel, and electricity had increased dramatically. (B)

History Makers

Mao Zedong
1893–1976

Born into a peasant family, Mao embraced Marxist socialism as a young man. Though he began as an urban labor organizer, Mao quickly realized the revolutionary potential of China's peasants. In 1927, Mao predicted:

> *The force of the peasantry is like that of the raging winds and driving rain. . . . They will bury beneath them all forces of imperialism, militarism, corrupt officialdom, village bosses and evil gentry.*

Mao's first attempt to lead the peasants in revolt failed in 1927. But during the Japanese occupation, Mao and his followers won widespread peasant support by reducing rents and promising to redistribute land.

INTEGRATED TECHNOLOGY

RESEARCH LINKS For more on Mao Zedong, go to **classzone.com**

MAIN IDEA

Analyzing Issues

(B) What aspects of Marxist socialism did Mao try to bring to China?

"The Great Leap Forward" To expand the success of the first Five-Year Plan, Mao proclaimed the "Great Leap Forward" in early 1958. This plan called for still larger collective farms, or **communes**. By the end of 1958, about 26,000 communes had been created. The average commune sprawled over 15,000 acres and supported over 25,000 people. In the strictly controlled life of the communes, peasants worked the land together. They ate in communal dining rooms, slept in communal dormitories, and raised children in communal nurseries. And they owned nothing. The peasants had no incentive to work hard when only the state profited from their labor.

The Great Leap Forward was a giant step backward. Poor planning and inefficient "backyard," or home, industries hampered growth. The program was ended in 1961 after crop failures caused a famine that killed about 20 million people.

New Policies and Mao's Response China was facing external problems as well as internal ones in the late 1950s. The spirit of cooperation that had bound the Soviet Union and China began to fade. Each sought to lead the worldwide Communist movement. As they also shared the longest border in the world, they faced numerous territorial disputes.

After the failure of the Great Leap Forward and the split with the Soviet Union, Mao reduced his role in government. Other leaders moved away from Mao's strict socialist ideas. For example, farm families could live in their own homes and could sell crops they grew on small private plots. Factory workers could compete for wage increases and promotions.

Mao thought China's new economic policies weakened the Communist goal of social equality. He was determined to revive the revolution. In 1966, he urged China's young people to "learn revolution by making revolution." Millions of high school and college students responded. They left their classrooms and formed militia units called **Red Guards**.

The Cultural Revolution The Red Guards led a major uprising known as the **Cultural Revolution**. Its goal was to establish a society of peasants and workers in which all were equal. The new hero was the peasant who worked with his hands. The life of the mind—intellectual and artistic activity—was considered useless and dangerous. To stamp out this threat, the Red Guards shut down colleges and schools. They targeted anyone who resisted the regime. Intellectuals had to "purify" themselves by doing hard labor in remote villages. Thousands were executed or imprisoned.

Chaos threatened farm production and closed down factories. Civil war seemed possible. By 1968, even Mao admitted that the Cultural Revolution had to stop. The army was ordered to put down the Red Guards. Zhou Enlai (joh ehn•leye), Chinese Communist party founder and premier since 1949, began to restore order. While China was struggling to become stable, the Cold War continued to rage. Two full-scale wars were fought—in Korea and in Vietnam. C

MAIN IDEA

Drawing Conclusions

C Why did the Cultural Revolution fail?

History in Depth

The Red Guards

The Red Guards were students, mainly teenagers. They pledged their devotion to Chairman Mao and the Cultural Revolution. From 1966 to 1968, 20 to 30 million Red Guards roamed China's cities and countryside causing widespread chaos. To smash the old, non-Maoist way of life, they destroyed buildings and beat and even killed Mao's alleged enemies. They lashed out at professors, government officials, factory managers, and even parents.

Eventually, even Mao turned on them. Most were exiled to the countryside. Others were arrested and some executed.

NEW YORK CORE CURRICULUM REVIEW

TERMS & NAMES 1. For each term or name, write a sentence explaining its significance.

- Mao Zedong
- Jiang Jieshi
- commune
- Red Guards
- Cultural Revolution

USING YOUR NOTES

2. Which effect of the Communist Revolution in China do you think had the most permanent impact? Explain.

Cause	Effect
1.	1.
2.	2.
3.	3.

MAIN IDEAS

3. How did the Chinese Communists increase their power during World War II?
4. What actions did the Nationalists take during World War II?
5. What was the goal of the Cultural Revolution?

CRITICAL THINKING & WRITING

6. **MAKING INFERENCES** Why did the United States support the Nationalists in the civil war in China?
7. **ANALYZING ISSUES** What policies or actions enabled the Communists to defeat the Nationalists in their long civil war?
8. **IDENTIFYING PROBLEMS** What circumstances prevented Mao's Great Leap Forward from bringing economic prosperity to China?
9. **WRITING ACTIVITY** REVOLUTION Write **summaries** of the reforms Mao Zedong proposed for China that could be placed on a propaganda poster.

CONNECT TO TODAY **CREATING A COMPARISON CHART**

Find political, economic, and demographic information on the People's Republic of China and Taiwan, and make a **comparison chart**.

Wars in Korea and Vietnam

CONNECT TO THE NEW YORK STATE CORE CURRICULUM

Unit 7.A.6.c. Conduct of the war
Unit 7.E.4.a. Vietnam/Ho Chi Minh

TERMS & NAMES

- 38th parallel
- Douglas MacArthur
- Ho Chi Minh
- domino theory
- Ngo Dinh Diem
- Vietcong
- Vietnamization
- Khmer Rouge

SETTING THE STAGE When World War II ended, Korea became a divided nation. North of the **38th parallel**, a line that crosses Korea at 38 degrees north latitude, Japanese troops surrendered to Soviet forces. South of this line, the Japanese surrendered to American troops. As in Germany, two nations developed. (See map on next page.) One was the Communist industrial north, whose government had been set up by the Soviets. The other was the non-Communist rural south, supported by the Western powers.

TAKING NOTES

Comparing and Contrasting Use a diagram to compare and contrast the Korean and Vietnam Wars.

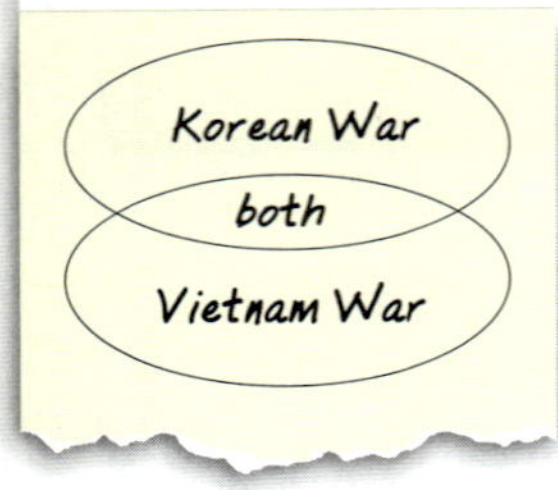

War in Korea

By 1949, both the United States and the Soviet Union had withdrawn most of their troops from Korea. The Soviets gambled that the United States would not defend South Korea. So they supplied North Korea with tanks, airplanes, and money in an attempt to take over the peninsula.

Standoff at the 38th Parallel On June 25, 1950, North Koreans swept across the 38th parallel in a surprise attack on South Korea. Within days, North Korean troops had penetrated deep into the south. President Truman was convinced that the North Korean aggressors were repeating what Hitler, Mussolini, and the Japanese had done in the 1930s. Truman's policy of containment was being put to the test. And Truman resolved to help South Korea resist communism.

South Korea also asked the United Nations to intervene. When the matter came to a vote in the Security Council, the Soviets were absent. They had refused to take part in the Council to protest admission of Nationalist China (Taiwan), rather than

▼ UN forces landing at Inchon in South Korea in 1950

Communist China, into the UN. As a result, the Soviet Union could not veto the UN's plan to send an international force to Korea to stop the invasion. A total of 15 nations, including the United States and Britain, participated under the command of General **Douglas MacArthur**.

Meanwhile, the North Koreans continued to advance. By September 1950, they controlled the entire Korean peninsula except for a tiny area around Pusan in the far southeast. That month, however, MacArthur launched a surprise attack. Troops moving north from Pusan met with forces that had made an amphibious landing at Inchon. Caught in this "pincer action," about half of the North Koreans surrendered. The rest retreated.

GEOGRAPHY SKILLBUILDER: Interpreting Maps

1. **Movement** *What was the northernmost Korean city UN troops had reached by November 1950?*
2. **Movement** *Did North or South Korean forces advance farther into the other's territory?*

The Fighting Continues The UN troops pursued the retreating North Koreans across the 38th parallel into North Korea. They pushed them almost to the Yalu River at the Chinese border. The UN forces were mostly from the United States. The Chinese felt threatened by these troops and by an American fleet off their coast. In October 1950, they sent 300,000 troops into North Korea.

The Chinese greatly outnumbered the UN forces. By January 1951, they had pushed UN and South Korean troops out of North Korea. The Chinese then moved into South Korea and captured the capital of Seoul. "We face an entirely new war," declared MacArthur. He called for a nuclear attack against China. Truman viewed MacArthur's proposals as reckless. "We are trying to prevent a world war, not start one," he said. MacArthur tried to go over the President's head by taking his case to Congress and the press. In response, Truman removed him.

Over the next two years, UN forces fought to drive the Chinese and North Koreans back. By 1952, UN troops had regained control of South Korea. Finally, in July 1953, the UN forces and North Korea signed a cease-fire agreement. The border between the two Koreas was set near the 38th parallel, almost where it had been before the war. In the meantime, 4 million soldiers and civilians had died. (A)

MAIN IDEA

Recognizing Effects

(A) What effects did the Korean war have on the Korean people and nation?

Aftermath of the War After the war, Korea remained divided. A demilitarized zone, which still exists, separated the two countries. In North Korea, the Communist dictator Kim Il Sung established collective farms, developed heavy industry, and built up the military. At Kim's death in 1994, his son Kim Jong Il took power. Under his rule, Communist North Korea developed nuclear weapons but had serious economic problems. On the other hand, South Korea prospered, thanks partly to massive aid from the United States and other countries. In the 1960s, South

Korea concentrated on developing its industry and expanding foreign trade. A succession of dictatorships ruled the rapidly developing country. With the 1987 adoption of a democratic constitution, however, South Korea established free elections. During the 1980s and 1990s, South Korea had one of the highest economic growth rates in the world.

Political differences have kept the two Koreas apart, despite periodic discussions of reuniting the country. North Korea's possession of nuclear weapons is a major obstacle. The United States still keeps troops in South Korea.

War Breaks Out in Vietnam

Much like its involvement in the Korean War, the involvement of the United States in Vietnam stemmed from its Cold War containment policy. After World War II, stopping the spread of communism was the principal goal of U.S. foreign policy.

The Road to War In the early 1900s, France controlled most of resource-rich Southeast Asia. (French Indochina included what are now Vietnam, Laos, and Cambodia.) But nationalist independence movements had begun to develop. A young Vietnamese nationalist, **Ho Chi Minh**, turned to the Communists for help in his struggle. During the 1930s, Ho's Indochinese Communist party led revolts and strikes against the French.

The French responded by jailing Vietnamese protesters. They also sentenced Ho to death. He fled into exile, but returned to Vietnam in 1941, a year after the Japanese seized control of his country during World War II. Ho and other nationalists founded the Vietminh (Independence) League. The Japanese were forced out of Vietnam after their defeat in 1945. Ho Chi Minh believed that independence would follow, but France intended to regain its colony.

The Fighting Begins Vietnamese Nationalists and Communists joined to fight the French armies. The French held most major cities, but the Vietminh had widespread support in the countryside. The Vietminh used hit-and-run tactics to confine the French to the cities. In France the people began to doubt that their colony was worth the lives and money the struggle cost. In 1954, the French suffered a major military defeat at Dien Bien Phu. They surrendered to Ho.

The United States had supported France in Vietnam. With the defeat of the French, the United States saw a rising threat to the rest of Asia. President Eisenhower described this threat in terms of the **domino theory**. The Southeast Asian nations were like a row of dominos, he said. The fall of one to communism would lead to the fall of its neighbors. This theory became a major justification for U.S. foreign policy during the Cold War era. **B**

Vietnam—A Divided Country After France's defeat, an international peace conference met in Geneva to discuss the future of Indochina. Based on these talks, Vietnam was divided at 17° north latitude. North of that line, Ho Chi Minh's Communist forces governed. To the south, the United States and France set up an anti-Communist government under the leadership of **Ngo Dinh Diem** (NOH dihn D'YEM).

History Makers

Ho Chi Minh
1890–1969

When he was young, the poor Vietnamese Nguyen That (uhng•wihn thaht) Thanh worked as a cook on a French steamship. In visiting U.S. cities where the boat docked, he learned about American culture and ideals. He later took a new name—Ho Chi Minh, meaning "He who enlightens." Though a Communist, in proclaiming Vietnam's independence from France in 1945, he declared, "All men are created equal."

His people revered him, calling him Uncle Ho. However, Ho Chi Minh did not put his democratic ideals into practice. He ruled North Vietnam by crushing all opposition.

MAIN IDEA

Making Inferences

B What actions might the United States have justified by the domino theory?

War in Vietnam, 1957–1973

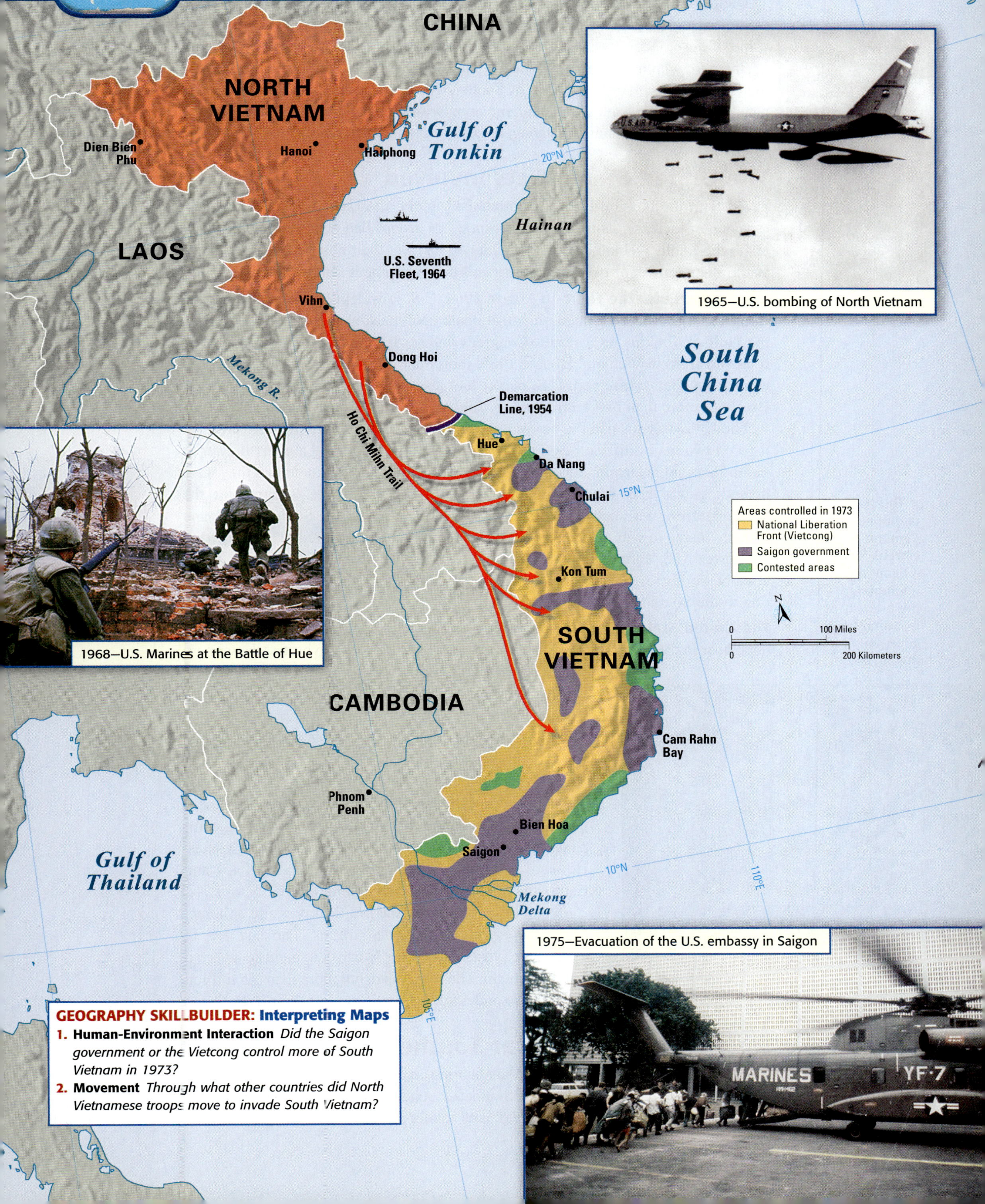

1965—U.S. bombing of North Vietnam

1968—U.S. Marines at the Battle of Hue

1975—Evacuation of the U.S. embassy in Saigon

GEOGRAPHY SKILLBUILDER: Interpreting Maps

1. **Human-Environment Interaction** *Did the Saigon government or the Vietcong control more of South Vietnam in 1973?*
2. **Movement** *Through what other countries did North Vietnamese troops move to invade South Vietnam?*

Diem ruled the south as a dictator. Opposition to his government grew. Communist guerrillas, called **Vietcong**, began to gain strength in the south. While some of the Vietcong were trained soldiers from North Vietnam, most were South Vietnamese who hated Diem. Gradually, the Vietcong won control of large areas of the countryside. In 1963, a group of South Vietnamese generals had Diem assassinated. But the new leaders were no more popular than he had been. It appeared that a takeover by the Communist Vietcong, backed by North Vietnam, was inevitable.

The United States Gets Involved

Faced with the possibility of a Communist victory, the United States decided to escalate, or increase, its involvement. Some U.S. troops had been serving as advisers to the South Vietnamese since the late 1950s. But their numbers steadily grew, as did the numbers of planes and other military equipment sent to South Vietnam.

U.S. Troops Enter the Fight In August 1964, U.S. President Lyndon Johnson told Congress that North Vietnamese patrol boats had attacked two U.S. destroyers in the Gulf of Tonkin. As a result, Congress authorized the president to send U.S. troops to fight in Vietnam. By late 1965, more than 185,000 U.S. soldiers were in combat on Vietnamese soil. U.S. planes had also begun to bomb North Vietnam. By 1968, more than half a million U.S. soldiers were in combat there.

The United States had the best-equipped, most advanced army in the world. Yet it faced two major difficulties. First, U.S. soldiers were fighting a guerrilla war in unfamiliar jungle terrain. Second, the South Vietnamese government that they were defending was becoming more unpopular. At the same time, support for the Vietcong grew, with help and supplies from Ho Chi Minh, the Soviet Union, and China. Unable to win a decisive victory on the ground, the United States turned to air power. U.S. forces bombed millions of acres of farmland and forest in an attempt to destroy enemy hideouts. This bombing strengthened peasants' opposition to the South Vietnamese government.

The United States Withdraws During the late 1960s, the war grew increasingly unpopular in the United States. Dissatisfied young people began to protest the tremendous loss of life in a conflict on the other side of the world. Bowing to intense public pressure, President Richard Nixon began withdrawing U.S. troops from Vietnam in 1969.

▼ The skulls and bones of Cambodian citizens form a haunting memorial to the brutality of its Communist government in the 1970s.

Nixon had a plan called **Vietnamization**. It allowed for U.S. troops to gradually pull out, while the South Vietnamese increased their combat role. To pursue Vietnamization while preserving the South Vietnamese government, Nixon authorized a massive bombing campaign against North Vietnamese bases and supply routes. He also authorized bombings in neighboring Laos and Cambodia to destroy Vietcong hiding places.

In response to protests and political pressure at home, Nixon kept withdrawing U.S. troops. The last left in 1973. Two years later, the North Vietnamese overran South Vietnam. The war ended, but more than 1.5 million Vietnamese and 58,000 Americans lost their lives.

Postwar Southeast Asia

War's end did not bring an immediate halt to bloodshed and chaos in Southeast Asia. Cambodia (also known as Kampuchea) was under siege by Communist rebels.

During the war, it had suffered U.S. bombing when it was used as a sanctuary by North Vietnamese and Vietcong troops.

Cambodia in Turmoil In 1975, Communist rebels known as the **Khmer Rouge** set up a brutal Communist government under the leadership of Pol Pot. In a ruthless attempt to transform Cambodia into a Communist society, Pol Pot's followers slaughtered 2 million people. This was almost one quarter of the nation's population. The Vietnamese invaded in 1978. They overthrew the Khmer Rouge and installed a less repressive government. But fighting continued. The Vietnamese withdrew in 1989. In 1993, under the supervision of UN peacekeepers, Cambodia adopted a democratic constitution and held free elections. (C)

MAIN IDEA

Recognizing Effects

(C) What was one of the effects of Pol Pot's efforts to turn Cambodia into a rural society?

Vietnam-after the War After 1975, the victorious North Vietnamese imposed tight controls over the South. Officials sent thousands of people to "reeducation camps" for training in Communist thought. They nationalized industries and strictly controlled businesses. They also renamed Saigon, the South's former capital, Ho Chi Minh City. Communist oppression caused 1.5 million people to flee Vietnam. Most escaped in dangerously overcrowded ships. More than 200,000 "boat people" died at sea. The survivors often spent months in refugee camps in Southeast Asia. About 70,000 eventually settled in the United States or Canada. Although Communists still govern Vietnam, the country now welcomes foreign investment. The United States normalized relations with Vietnam in 1995.

While the superpowers were struggling for advantage during the Korean and Vietnam wars, they also were seeking influence in other parts of the world.

Connect *to* Today

Vietnam Today

Vietnam remains a Communist country. But, like China, it has introduced elements of capitalism into its economy. In 1997, a travel magazine claimed that Hanoi, the capital of Vietnam, "jumps with vitality, its streets and shops jammed with locals and handfuls of Western tourists and businesspeople." Above, two executives tour the city.

Along Hanoi's shaded boulevards, billboards advertise U.S. and Japanese copiers, motorcycles, video recorders, and soft drinks. On the streets, enterprising Vietnamese businesspeople offer more traditional services. These include bicycle repair, a haircut, a shave, or a tasty snack.

NEW YORK CORE CURRICULUM REVIEW

TERMS & NAMES 1. For each term or name, write a sentence explaining its significance.

• 38th parallel • Douglas MacArthur • Ho Chi Minh • domino theory • Ngo Dinh Diem • Vietcong • Vietnamization • Khmer Rouge

USING YOUR NOTES

2. In what ways were the causes and effects of the wars in Korea and Vietnam similar?

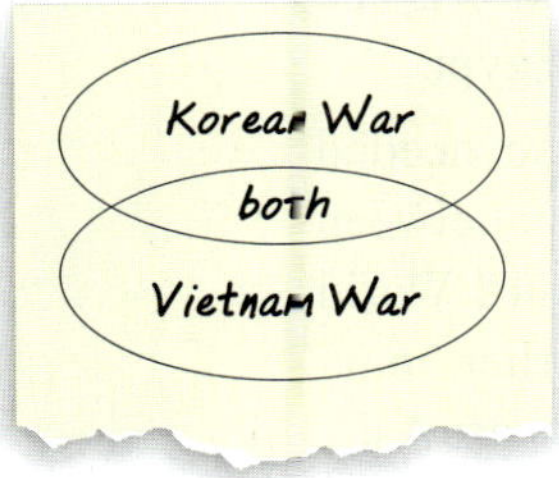

MAIN IDEAS

3. What role did the United Nations play in the Korean War?
4. How did Vietnam become divided?
5. What was the Khmer Rouge's plan for Cambodia?

CRITICAL THINKING & WRITING

6. **ANALYZING MOTIVES** What role did the policy of containment play in the involvement of the United States in wars in Korea and Vietnam?
7. **IDENTIFYING CAUSES** How might imperialism be one of the causes of the Vietnam War?
8. **FORMING OPINIONS** Do you think U.S. involvement in Vietnam was justified? Why or why not?
9. **WRITING ACTIVITY** EMPIRE BUILDING Write a two-paragraph **expository essay** for either the United States or the Soviet Union supporting its involvement in Asia.

CONNECT TO TODAY **WRITING A BIOGRAPHY**

Research the present-day leader of one of the countries discussed in this section. Then write a three-paragraph **biography**.

The Cold War Divides the World

CONNECT TO THE NEW YORK STATE CORE CURRICULUM

Unit 7.A.5.i. Role of nonaligned nations
Unit 7.H.3. Fidel Castro's Cuban Revolution–causes and impact

TERMS & NAMES

- Third World
- nonaligned nations
- Fidel Castro
- Anastasio Somoza
- Daniel Ortega
- Ayatollah Ruholla Khomeini

SETTING THE STAGE Following World War II, the world's nations were grouped politically into three "worlds." The first was the industrialized capitalist nations, including the United States and its allies. The second was the Communist nations led by the Soviet Union. The **Third World** consisted of developing nations, often newly independent, who were not aligned with either superpower. These nonaligned countries provided yet another arena for competition between the Cold War superpowers.

TAKING NOTES

Determining Main Ideas Use a chart to list main points about Third World confrontations.

Country	Conflict
Cuba	
Nicaragua	
Iran	

Fighting for the Third World

The Third World nations were located in Latin America, Asia, and Africa. They were economically poor and politically unstable. This was largely due to a long history of colonialism. They also suffered from ethnic conflicts and lack of technology and education. Each needed a political and economic system around which to build its society. Soviet-style communism and U.S.-style free-market democracy were the main choices.

Cold War Strategies The United States, the Soviet Union, and, in some cases, China, used a variety of techniques to gain influence in the Third World. (See feature on next page.) They backed wars of revolution, liberation, or counterrevolution. The U.S. and Soviet intelligence agencies—the CIA and the KGB—engaged in various covert, or secret, activities, ranging from spying to assassination attempts. The United States also gave military aid, built schools, set up programs to combat poverty, and sent volunteer workers to many developing nations. The Soviets offered military and technical assistance, mainly to India and Egypt.

Association of Nonaligned Nations Other developing nations also needed assistance. They became important players in the Cold War competition between the United States, the Soviet Union, and later, China. But not all Third World countries wished to play a role in the Cold War. As mentioned earlier India vowed to remain neutral. Indonesia, a populous island nation in Southeast Asia, also struggled to stay uninvolved. In 1955, it hosted many leaders from Asia and Africa at the Bandung Conference. They met to form what they called a "third force" of independent countries, or **nonaligned nations**. Some nations, such as India and Indonesia, were able to maintain their neutrality. But others took sides with the superpowers or played competing sides against each other.

How the Cold War Was Fought

During the Cold War, the United States and the Soviet Union both believed that they needed to stop the other side from extending its power. What differentiated the Cold War from other 20th century conflicts was that the two enemies did not engage in a shooting war. Instead, they pursued their rivalry by using the strategies shown below.

Egypt built the Aswan Dam with Soviet aid.

Major Strategies of the Cold War

Foreign Aid	Espionage	Multinational Alliances
The two superpowers tried to win allies by giving financial aid to other nations. For instance, Egypt took aid from the Soviet Union to build the Aswan High Dam (see photograph above).	Fearing the enemy might be gaining the advantage, each side spied on the other. One famous incident was the Soviet downing of a U.S. U-2 spy plane in 1960.	To gain the support of other nations, both the Soviet Union and the United States entered into alliances. Two examples of this were NATO and the Warsaw Pact (shown on map above).
Propaganda	**Brinkmanship**	**Surrogate Wars**
Both superpowers used propaganda to try to win support overseas. For example, Radio Free Europe broadcast radio programs about the rest of the world into Eastern Europe.	The policy of brinkmanship meant going to the brink of war to make the other side back down. One example was the Cuban Missile Crisis.	The word surrogate means substitute. Although the United States and the Soviet Union did not fight each other directly, they fought indirectly by backing opposing sides in many smaller conflicts.

SKILLBUILDER: Interpreting Visuals

1. **Generalizing** *Judging from the map, how would you describe the effect on Europe of multinational alliances?*
2. **Analyzing Motives** *What motive did the two superpowers have for fighting surrogate wars?*

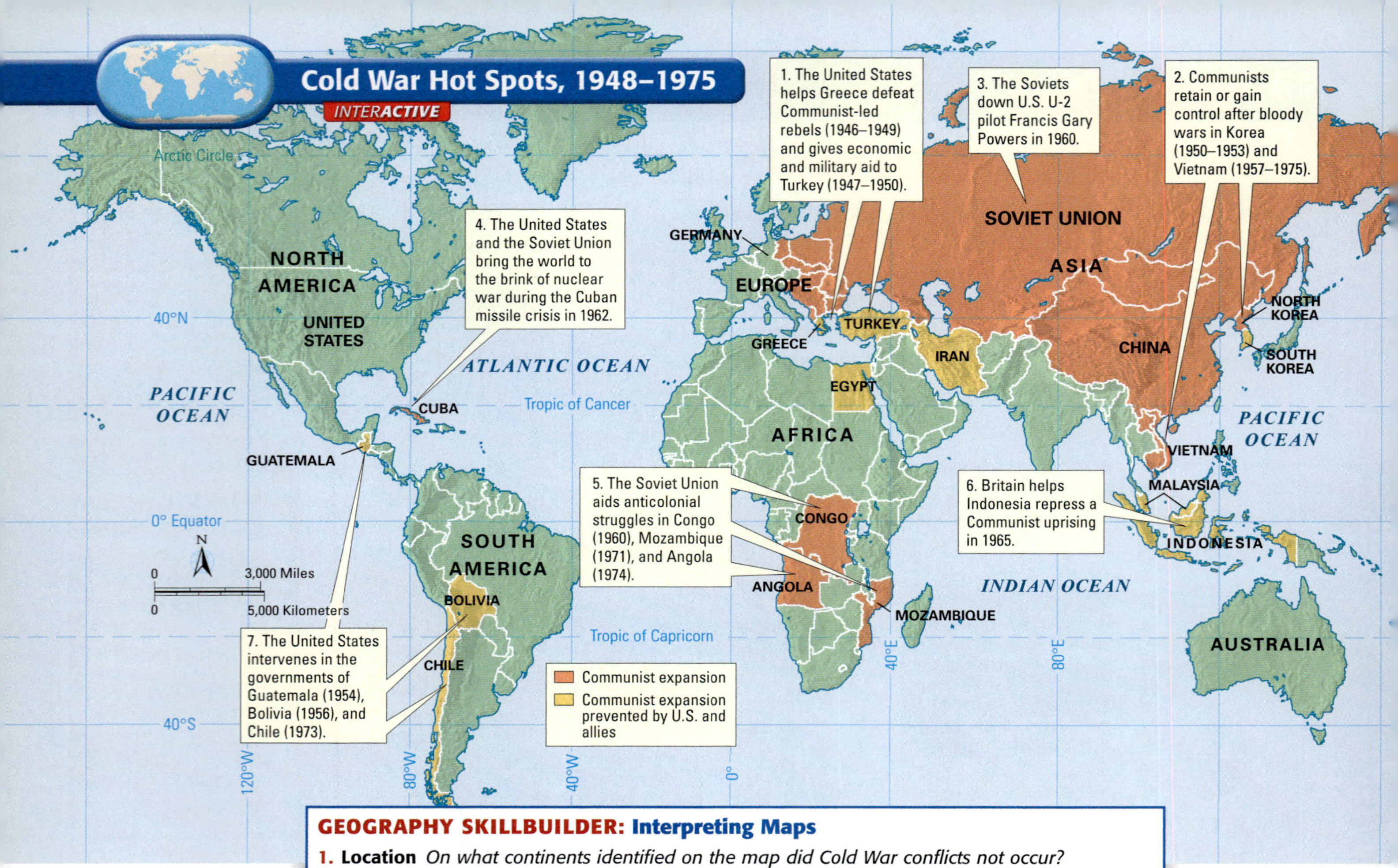

GEOGRAPHY SKILLBUILDER: Interpreting Maps

1. **Location** *On what continents identified on the map did Cold War conflicts not occur?*
2. **Region** *About what fraction of the globe did Communists control by 1975?*

Confrontations in Latin America

After World War II, rapid industrialization, population growth, and a lingering gap between the rich and the poor led Latin American nations to seek aid from both superpowers. At the same time, many of these countries alternated between short-lived democracy and harsh military rule. As described in Chapter 28, U.S. involvement in Latin America began long before World War II. American businesses backed leaders who protected U.S. interests but who also often oppressed their people. After the war, communism and nationalistic feelings inspired revolutionary movements. These found enthusiastic Soviet support. In response, the United States provided military and economic assistance to anti-Communist dictators.

Fidel Castro and the Cuban Revolution In the 1950s, Cuba was ruled by an unpopular dictator, Fulgencio Batista, who had U.S. support. Cuban resentment led to a popular revolution, which overthrew Batista in January 1959. A young lawyer named **Fidel Castro** led that revolution. At first, many people praised Castro for bringing social reforms to Cuba and improving the economy. Yet Castro was a harsh dictator. He suspended elections, jailed or executed his opponents, and tightly controlled the press.

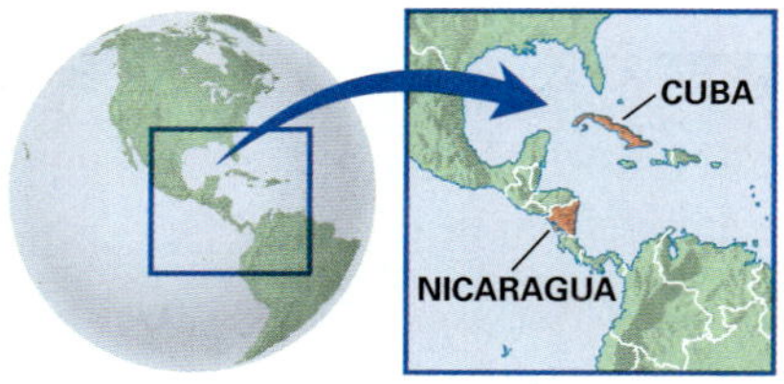

When Castro nationalized the Cuban economy, he took over U.S.-owned sugar mills and refineries. In response, Eisenhower ordered an embargo on all trade with Cuba. Castro then turned to the Soviets for economic and military aid.

In 1960, the CIA began to train anti-Castro Cuban exiles. In April 1961, they invaded Cuba, landing at the Bay of Pigs. However, the United States did not provide the hoped for air support. Castro's forces easily defeated the invaders, humiliating the United States.

Nuclear Face-off: the Cuban Missile Crisis The failed Bay of Pigs invasion convinced Soviet leader Nikita Khrushchev that the United States would not resist Soviet expansion in Latin America. So, in July 1962, Khrushchev secretly began to build 42 missile sites in Cuba. In October, an American spy plane discovered the sites. President John F. Kennedy declared that missiles so close to the U.S. mainland were a threat. He demanded their removal and also announced a naval blockade of Cuba to prevent the Soviets from installing more missiles.

Castro protested his country's being used as a pawn in the Cold War:

PRIMARY SOURCE

Cuba did not and does not intend to be in the middle of a conflict between the East and the West. Our problem is above all one of national sovereignty. Cuba does not mean to get involved in the Cold War.

FIDEL CASTRO, quoted in an interview October 27, 1962

But Castro and Cuba were deeply involved. Kennedy's demand for the removal of Soviet missiles put the United States and the Soviet Union on a collision course. People around the world feared nuclear war. Fortunately, Khrushchev agreed to remove the missiles in return for a U.S. promise not to invade Cuba. **A**

The resolution of the Cuban Missile Crisis left Castro completely dependent on Soviet support. In exchange for this support, Castro backed Communist revolutions in Latin America and Africa. Soviet aid to Cuba, however, ended abruptly with the breakup of the Soviet Union in 1991. This loss dealt a crippling blow to the Cuban economy. Eventually, Castro loosened state control of Cuba's economy and sought better relations with other countries.

MAIN IDEA

Contrasting

A What differing U.S. and Soviet aims led to the Cuban missile crisis?

History Makers

Fidel Castro
1926–

The son of a wealthy Spanish-Cuban farmer, Fidel Castro became involved in politics at the University of Havana. He first tried to overthrow the Cuban dictator, Batista, in 1953. He was imprisoned, but vowed to continue the struggle for independence:

Personally, I am not interested in power nor do I envisage assuming it at any time. All that I will do is to make sure that the sacrifices of so many compatriots should not be in vain.

Despite this declaration, Castro has ruled Cuba as a dictator for more than 40 years.

INTEGRATED TECHNOLOGY

INTERNET ACTIVITY Create a time line of the important events in Castro's rule of Cuba. Go to **classzone.com** for your research.

Civil War in Nicaragua Just as the United States had supported Batista in Cuba, it had funded the Nicaraguan dictatorship of **Anastasio Somoza** and his family since 1933. In 1979, Communist Sandinista rebels toppled Somoza's son. Both the United States and the Soviet Union initially gave aid to the Sandinistas and their leader, **Daniel Ortega** (awr•TAY•guh). The Sandinistas, however, gave assistance to other Marxist rebels in nearby El Salvador. To help the El Salvadoran government fight those rebels, the United States supported Nicaraguan anti-Communist forces called the Contras or *contrarevolucionarios*. **B**

MAIN IDEA

Analyzing Motives

B Why did the U.S. switch its support from the Sandinistas to the Contras?

The civil war in Nicaragua lasted more than a decade and seriously weakened the country's economy. In 1990, President Ortega agreed to hold free elections, the first in the nation's history. Violeta Chamorro, a reform candidate, defeated him. The Sandinistas were also defeated in elections in 1996 and 2001.

Confrontations in the Middle East

As the map on page 984 shows, Cold War confrontations continued to erupt around the globe. The oil-rich Middle East attracted both superpowers.

Religious and Secular Values Clash in Iran Throughout the Middle East, oil industry wealth fueled a growing clash between traditional Islamic values and modern Western materialism. In no country was this cultural conflict more dramatically shown than in Iran (Persia before 1935). After World War II, Iran's leader, Shah Mohammed Reza Pahlavi (pah•luh•vee), embraced Western governments and wealthy Western oil companies. Iranian nationalists resented these foreign alliances and united under Prime Minister Muhammed Mossadeq (moh•sah•DEHK). They nationalized a British-owned oil company and, in 1953, forced the shah to flee. Fearing Iran might turn to the Soviets for support, the United States helped restore the shah to power. C

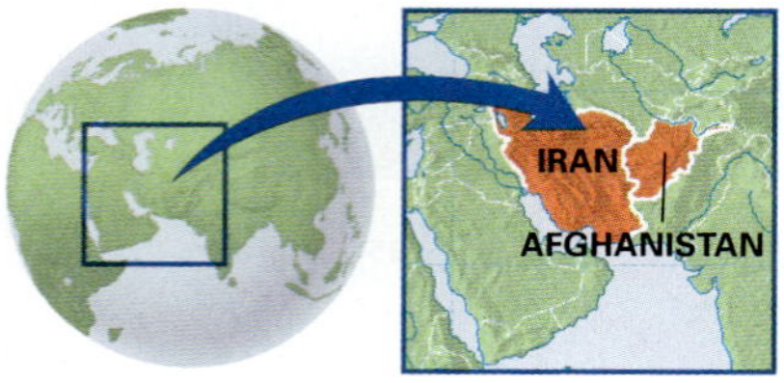

MAIN IDEA

Analyzing Motives

C Why did the United States support the shah of Iran?

The United States Supports Secular Rule With U.S. support, the shah westernized his country. By the end of the 1950s, Iran's capital, Tehran, featured gleaming skyscrapers, foreign banks, and modern factories. Millions of Iranians, however, still lived in extreme poverty. The shah tried to weaken the political influence of Iran's conservative Muslim leaders, known as ayatollahs (eye•uh• TOH•luhz), who opposed Western influences. The leader of this religious opposition, **Ayatollah Ruholla Khomeini** (koh• MAY•nee), was living in exile. Spurred by his tape-recorded messages, Iranians rioted in every major city in late 1978. Faced with overwhelming opposition, the shah fled Iran in 1979. A triumphant Khomeini returned to establish an Islamic state and to export Iran's militant form of Islam.

Khomeini's Anti-U.S. Policies Strict adherence to Islam ruled Khomeini's domestic policies. But hatred of the United States, because of U.S. support for the shah, was at the heart of his foreign policy. In 1979, with the ayatollah's blessing, young Islamic revolutionaries seized the U.S. embassy in Tehran. They took more than 60 Americans hostage and demanded the United States force the shah to face trial. Most hostages remained prisoners for 444 days before being released in 1981.

Khomeini encouraged Muslim radicals elsewhere to overthrow their secular governments. Intended to unify Muslims, this policy heightened tensions between Iran and its neighbor and territorial rival, Iraq. A military leader, Saddam Hussein (hoo•SAYN), governed Iraq as a secular state.

▼ Ayatollah Khomeini (inset) supported the taking of U.S. hostages by Islamic militants in Tehran in 1979.

War broke out between Iran and Iraq in 1980. The United States secretly gave aid to both sides because it did not want the balance of power in the region to change. The Soviet Union, on the other hand, had long been a supporter of Iraq. A million Iranians and Iraqis died in the war before the UN negotiated a ceasefire in 1988.

The Superpowers Face Off in Afghanistan For several years following World War II, Afghanistan maintained its independence from both the neighboring Soviet Union and the United States. In the 1950s, however, Soviet influence in the country began to increase. In the late 1970s, a Muslim revolt threatened to topple Afghanistan's Communist regime. This revolt led to a Soviet invasion in 1979.

The Soviets expected to prop up the Afghan Communists and quickly withdraw. Instead, just like the United States in Vietnam, the Soviets found themselves stuck. And like the Vietcong in Vietnam, rebel forces outmaneuvered a military superpower. Supplied with American weapons, the Afgan rebels, called mujahideen, or holy warriors, fought on. **D**

MAIN IDEA

Comparing

D In what ways were U.S. involvement in Vietnam and Soviet involvement in Afghanistan similar?

The United States had armed the rebels because they considered the Soviet invasion a threat to Middle Eastern oil supplies. President Jimmy Carter warned the Soviets against any attempt to gain control of the Persian Gulf. To protest the invasion, he stopped U.S. grain shipments to the Soviet Union and ordered a U.S. boycott of the 1980 Moscow Olympics. In the 1980s, a new Soviet president, Mikhail Gorbachev, acknowledged the war's devastating costs. He withdrew all Soviet troops by 1989. By then, internal unrest and economic problems were tearing apart the Soviet Union itself.

Connect *to* Today

The Taliban

Islamic religious students, or taliban, were among the *mujahideen* rebels who fought the Soviet occupation of Afghanistan. Various groups of students loosely organized themselves during a civil war among *mujahideen* factions that followed the Soviet withdrawal in 1989.

In 1996, one of these groups, called the Taliban, seized power and established an Islamic government. At first, they were popular among many Afghans. But they imposed a repressive rule especially harsh on women, and failed to improve the lives of the people. They also gave sanctuary to international Islamic terrorists. In 2001, an anti-terrorist coalition led by the United States drove them from power.

NEW YORK CORE CURRICULUM REVIEW

TERMS & NAMES 1. For each term or name, write a sentence explaining its significance.

- Third World
- nonaligned nations
- Fidel Castro
- Anastasio Somoza
- Daniel Ortega
- Ayatollah Ruholla Khomeini

USING YOUR NOTES

2. Which confrontation had the most lasting significance?

Country	Conflict
Cuba	
Nicaragua	
Iran	

MAIN IDEAS

3. How was the Cuban Missile Crisis resolved?
4. What was significant about the 1990 elections in Nicaragua?
5. Why did the Soviet Union invade Afghanistan?

CRITICAL THINKING & WRITING

6. **MAKING INFERENCES** What advantages and disadvantages might being nonaligned have offered a developing nation during the Cold War?
7. **COMPARING** What similarities do you see among U.S. actions in Nicaragua, Cuba, and Iran?
8. **ANALYZING CAUSES** What were the reasons that Islamic fundamentalists took control of Iran?
9. **WRITING ACTIVITY** REVOLUTION For either Cuba, Nicaragua, or Iran, write an annotated **time line** of events discussed in this section.

CONNECT TO TODAY WRITING AN OPINION PAPER

Research the effects of the U.S. trade embargo on Cuba. Write a two-paragraph **opinion paper** on whether it would be in the best interests of the United States to lift that embargo.

The Cold War Thaws

CONNECT TO THE NEW YORK STATE CORE CURRICULUM

Unit 7.A.5.e. Hungarian Revolt
Unit 7.A.5.f. Soviet invasion of Czechoslovakia

TERMS & NAMES

- Nikita Khrushchev
- Leonid Brezhnev
- John F. Kennedy
- Lyndon Johnson
- détente
- Richard M. Nixon
- SALT
- Ronald Reagan

SETTING THE STAGE In the postwar years, the Soviet Union kept a firm grip on its satellite countries in Eastern Europe. These countries were Poland, Czechoslovakia, Hungary, Romania, Bulgaria, Albania, and East Germany. (Yugoslavia had broken away from Soviet control in 1948, although it remained Communist.) The Soviet Union did not allow them to direct and develop their own economies. Instead, it insisted that they develop industries to meet Soviet needs. These policies greatly hampered Eastern Europe's economic recovery.

TAKING NOTES

Outlining Organize main ideas and details about the Cold War thaw.

I. Soviet Policy in Eastern Europe and China
  A.
  B.
II. From Brinkmanship to Détente

Soviet Policy in Eastern Europe and China

More moderate Soviet leaders came to power after Stalin's death. They allowed satellite countries somewhat more independence, as long as they remained allied with the Soviet Union. During the 1950s and 1960s, however, growing protest movements in Eastern Europe threatened the Soviet grip on the region. Increasing tensions with China also diverted Soviet attention and forces.

Destalinization and Rumblings of Protest After Stalin died in 1953, **Nikita Khrushchev** became the dominant Soviet leader. In 1956, the shrewd, tough Khrushchev denounced Stalin for jailing and killing loyal Soviet citizens. His speech signaled the start of a policy called destalinization, or purging the country of Stalin's memory. Workers destroyed monuments of the former dictator. Khrushchev called for "peaceful competition" with capitalist states.

But this new Soviet outlook did not change life in satellite countries. Their resentment at times turned to active protest. In October 1956, for example, the Hungarian army joined protesters to overthrow Hungary's Soviet-controlled government. Storming through the capital, Budapest, mobs waved Hungarian flags with the Communist hammer-and-sickle emblem cut out. "From the youngest child to the oldest man," one protester declared, "no one wants communism."

A popular and liberal Hungarian Communist leader named Imre Nagy (IHM•ray-nahj) formed a new government. Nagy promised free elections and demanded Soviet troops leave. In response, Soviet tanks and infantry entered Budapest in November. Thousands of Hungarian freedom fighters armed themselves with pistols and bottles, but were overwhelmed. A pro-Soviet government was installed, and Nagy was eventually executed.

History Makers

Imre Nagy (1896–1958)

Imre Nagy was born into a peasant family in Hungary. During World War I, he was captured by the Soviets and recruited into their army. He then became a Communist.

Nagy held several posts in his country's Communist government, but his loyalty remained with the peasants. Because of his independent approach, he fell in and out of favor with the Soviet Union. In October 1956, he led an anti-Soviet revolt. After the Soviets forcefully put down the uprising, they tried and executed him.

In 1989, after Communists lost control of Hungary's government, Nagy was reburied with official honors.

▲ Czech demonstrators fight Soviet tanks in 1968.

Alexander Dubček (1921–1992)

Alexander Dubček was the son of a Czech Communist Party member. He moved rapidly up through its ranks, becoming party leader in 1968.

Responding to the spirit of change in the 1960s, Dubček instituted broad reforms during the so-called Prague Spring of 1968. The Soviet Union reacted by sending tanks into Prague to suppress a feared revolt. The Soviets expelled Dubček from the party. He regained political prominence in 1989, when the Communists agreed to share power in a coalition government. When Czechoslovakia split into two nations in 1992, Dubček became head of the Social Democratic Party in Slovakia.

The Revolt in Czechoslovakia Despite the show of force in Hungary, Khrushchev lost prestige in his country as a result of the Cuban Missile Crisis in 1962. In 1964, party leaders voted to remove him from power. His replacement, **Leonid Brezhnev**, quickly adopted repressive domestic policies. The party enforced laws to limit such basic human rights as freedom of speech and worship. Government censors controlled what writers could publish. Brezhnev clamped down on those who dared to protest his policies. For example, the secret police arrested many dissidents, including Aleksandr Solzhenitsyn, winner of the 1970 Nobel Prize for literature. They then expelled him from the Soviet Union. (A)

MAIN IDEA

Analyzing Issues

(A) Why was Nikita Khruschev removed from power in 1964?

Brezhnev made clear that he would not tolerate dissent in Eastern Europe either. His policy was put to the test in early 1968. At that time, Czech Communist leader Alexander Dubček (DOOB•chehk) loosened controls on censorship to offer his country socialism with "a human face." This period of reform, when Czechoslovakia's capital bloomed with new ideas, became known as Prague Spring. However, it did not survive the summer. On August 20, armed forces from the Warsaw Pact nations invaded Czechoslovakia. Brezhnev justified this invasion by claiming the Soviet Union had the right to prevent its satellites from rejecting communism, a policy known as the Brezhnev Doctrine.

The Soviet-Chinese Split While many satellite countries resisted Communist rule, China was committed to communism. In fact, to cement the ties between Communist powers, Mao and Stalin had signed a 30-year treaty of friendship in 1950. Their spirit of cooperation, however, ran out before the treaty did.

The Soviets assumed the Chinese would follow Soviet leadership in world affairs. As the Chinese grew more confident, however, they resented being in Moscow's shadow. They began to spread their own brand of communism in Africa and other parts of Asia. In 1959, Khrushchev punished the Chinese by refusing to share nuclear secrets. The following year, the Soviets ended technical economic aid. The Soviet-Chinese split grew so wide that fighting broke out along their common border. After repeated incidents, the two neighbors maintained a fragile peace.

From Brinkmanship to Détente

In the 1970s, the United States and the Soviet Union finally backed away from the aggressive policies of brinkmanship that they had followed during the early postwar years. The superpowers slowly moved to lower tensions.

Brinkmanship Breaks Down The brinkmanship policy followed during the presidencies of Eisenhower, Kennedy, and Johnson led to one terrifying crisis after another. Though these crises erupted all over the world, they were united by a common fear. Nuclear war seemed possible.

In 1960, the U-2 incident prevented a meeting between the United States and the Soviet Union to discuss the buildup of arms on both sides. Then, during the administration of **John F. Kennedy** in the early 1960s, the Cuban Missile Crisis made the superpowers' use of nuclear weapons a real possibility. (See page 985.) The crisis ended when Soviet ships turned back to avoid a confrontation at sea. "We're eyeball to eyeball," the relieved U.S. Secretary of State Dean Rusk said, "and I think the other fellow just blinked." But Kennedy's secretary of defense, Robert McNamara, admitted how close the world had come to disaster:

PRIMARY SOURCE B

In the face of an air attack [on Cuba] and in the face of the probability of a ground attack, it was certainly possible, and I would say probable, that a Cuban sergeant or Soviet officer in a missile silo, without authority from Moscow, would have launched one or more of those intermediate-range missiles, equipped with a nuclear warhead, against one or more of the cities on the East Coast of the United States.

ROBERT MCNAMARA, quoted in *Inside the Cold War*

MAIN IDEA

Analyzing Primary Sources

B Do you think that Robert McNamara's view of the Soviet threat in Cuba was justified? Explain.

Tensions remained high. After the assassination of Kennedy in 1963, **Lyndon Johnson** assumed the presidency. Committed to stopping the spread of communism, President Johnson escalated U.S. involvement in the war in Vietnam.

The United States Turns to Détente Widespread popular protests wracked the United States during the Vietnam War. And the turmoil did not end with U.S. withdrawal. As it tried to heal its internal wounds, the United States backed away from its policy of direct confrontation with the Soviet Union. **Détente**, a policy of lessening Cold War tensions, replaced brinkmanship under **Richard M. Nixon**.

Vocabulary
Détente is a French word meaning "a loosening."

▼ U.S. president Nixon visits China in 1972, accompanied by Chinese premier Zhou Enlai (left).

President Nixon's move toward détente grew out of a philosophy known as realpolitik. This term comes from the German word meaning "realistic politics." In practice, realpolitik meant dealing with other nations in a practical and flexible manner. While the United States continued to try to contain the spread of communism, the two superpowers agreed to pursue détente and to reduce tensions.

Nixon Visits Communist Powers Nixon's new policy represented a personal reversal as well as a political shift for the country. His rise in politics in the 1950s was largely due to his strong anti-Communist position. Twenty years later, he became the first U.S. president to visit Communist China. The visit made sense in a world in which three, not just two, superpowers eyed each other suspiciously. "We want the Chinese with us when we sit down and negotiate with the Russians," Nixon explained.

Three months after visiting Beijing in February 1972, Nixon visited the Soviet Union. After a series of meetings called the Strategic Arms Limitation Talks (**SALT**), Nixon and Brezhnev signed the SALT I Treaty. This five-year agreement, limited to 1972 levels the number of intercontinental ballistic and submarine-launched missiles each country could have. In 1975, 33 nations joined the United States and the Soviet Union in signing a commitment to détente and cooperation, the Helsinki Accords.

▲ Ronald Reagan's 1980 political button highlights the strong patriotic theme of his campaign.

The Collapse of Détente

Under presidents Nixon and Gerald Ford, the United States improved relations with China and the Soviet Union. In the late 1970s, however, President Jimmy Carter was concerned over harsh treatment of protesters in the Soviet Union. This threatened to prevent a second round of SALT negotiations. In 1979, Carter and Brezhnev finally signed the SALT II agreement. When the Soviets invaded Afghanistan later that year, however, the U.S. Congress refused to ratify SALT II. Concerns mounted as more nations, including China and India, began building nuclear arsenals.

Reagan Takes an Anti-Communist Stance A fiercely anti-Communist U.S. president, **Ronald Reagan**, took office in 1981. He continued to move away from détente. He increased defense spending, putting both economic and military pressure on the Soviets. In 1983, Reagan also announced the Strategic Defense Initiative (SDI), a program to protect against enemy missiles. It was not put into effect but remained a symbol of U.S. anti-Communist sentiment. (C)

MAIN IDEA

Contrasting

(C) In what ways did Nixon's and Reagan's policies toward the Soviet Union differ?

Tensions increased as U.S. activities such as arming Nicaragua's Contras pushed the United States and Soviet Union further from détente. However, a change in Soviet leadership in 1985 brought a new policy toward the United States and the beginnings of a final thaw in the Cold War. Meanwhile, as you will learn in the next chapter, developing countries continued their own struggles for independence.

NEW YORK CORE CURRICULUM REVIEW

TERMS & NAMES 1. For each term or name, write a sentence explaining its significance.

• Nikita Khrushchev • Leonid Brezhnev • John F. Kennedy • Lyndon Johnson • détente • Richard M. Nixon • SALT • Ronald Reagan

USING YOUR NOTES

2. What do you consider the most significant reason for the collapse of détente?

I. Soviet Policy in Eastern Europe and China
A.
B.
II. From Brinkmanship to Détente

MAIN IDEAS

3. What effects did destalinization have on Soviet satellite countries?
4. What changes did Alexander Dubček seek to make in Czechoslovakia in 1968, and what happened?
5. Why was the policy of brinkmanship replaced?

CRITICAL THINKING & WRITING

6. **DEVELOPING HISTORICAL PERSPECTIVE** In view of Soviet policies toward Eastern Europe in the postwar era, what reasons did people in Eastern Europe have for resistance?
7. **EVALUATING DECISIONS** Do you think it was a wise political move for Nixon to visit Communist China and the Soviet Union? Why or why not?
8. **RECOGNIZING EFFECTS** What was the result of Reagan's move away from détente?
9. **WRITING ACTIVITY** REVOLUTION-Write a short **poem** or **song lyrics** expressing protest against Communist rule by a citizen of a country behind the Iron Curtain.

CONNECT TO TODAY **WRITING A SUMMARY**

Look through a major newspaper or newsmagazine for articles on Eastern European countries. Then, write a brief **summary** of recent developments there.

Chapter 33 Assessment

TERMS & NAMES

For each term or name below, briefly explain its connection to the restructuring of the postwar world since 1945.

1. containment
2. Cold War
3. Mao Zedong
4. Cultural Revolution
5. 38th parallel
6. Vietnamization
7. Fidel Castro
8. Nikita Khrushchev
9. détente
10. SALT

MAIN IDEAS

Cold War: Superpowers Face Off
Section 1 (pages 965–971)

11. Why did some Americans oppose the Truman Doctrine?
12. How did the Soviet Union respond to the U.S. policy of brinkmanship?

Communists Take Power in China
Section 2 (pages 972–975)

13. Who did the superpowers support in the Chinese civil war?
14. What were the results of Mao Zedong's Great Leap Forward and Cultural Revolution?

Wars in Korea and Vietnam Section 3 (pages 976–981)

15. What effects did the Korean War have on Korea's land and its people?
16. What difficulties did the U.S. Army face fighting the war in Vietnam?

The Cold War Divides the World
Section 4 (pages 982–987)

17. Why did developing nations often align themselves with one or the other superpower?
18. How did the Soviet Union respond to the Bay of Pigs?

The Cold War Thaws Section 5 (pages 988–991)

19. In what ways did Soviet actions hamper Eastern Europe's economic recovery after World War II?
20. What policies characterized realpolitik?

CRITICAL THINKING

1. USING YOUR NOTES
Use a diagram to show superpower Cold War tactics.

2. COMPARING
EMPIRE BUILDING In what ways were the United States and the Soviet Union more similar than different?

3. HYPOTHESIZING
ECONOMICS How might the Cold War have proceeded if the United States had been economically and physically damaged in World War II?

4. DRAWING CONCLUSIONS
REVOLUTION Which two Cold War events do you think had the greatest impact on the U.S. decision to pursue détente?

5. MAKING INFERENCES
Why do you think the United States and the Soviet Union chose cooperation in space after years of competition?

VISUAL SUMMARY

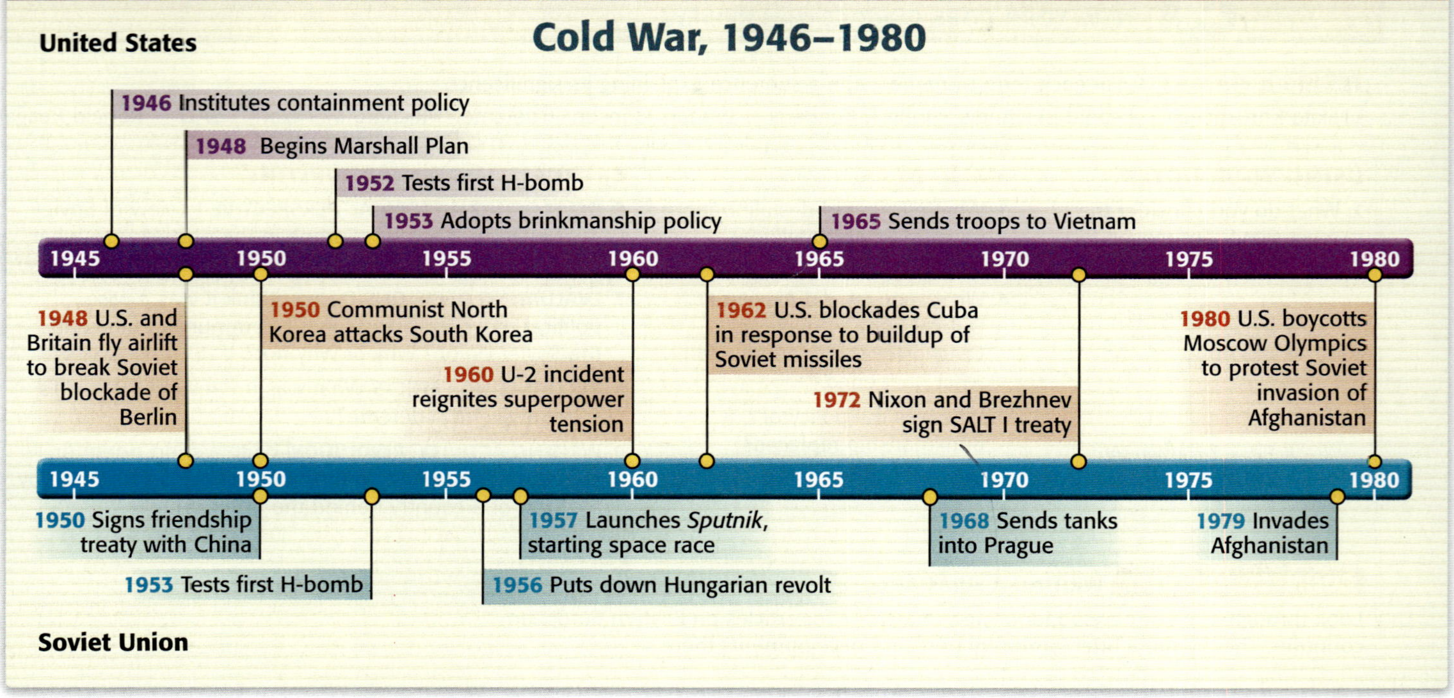

Use the quotation and your knowledge of world history to answer questions 1 and 2.

Additional Test Practice, pp. S1–S33

The following poem by Ho Chi Minh was broadcast over Hanoi Radio on January 1, 1968.

PRIMARY SOURCE

This Spring far outshines the previous Springs,
Of victories throughout the land come happy tidings.
South and North, rushing heroically together, shall
smite the American invaders!
Go Forward!
Total victory shall be ours.

HO CHI MINH, quoted in *America and Vietnam*

1 In Ho's opinion, who was the enemy in the Vietnam War?

(1) the South Vietnamese
(2) the changing seasons
(3) the United States
(4) the French

2 What purpose might the North Vietnamese have had in broadcasting this poem?

(1) to show that their political leader was also a poet
(2) to warn the United States that it would be defeated
(3) to single out the North Vietnamese people for special attention
(4) to be used as propaganda to show that North and South were fighting together

Use the chart and your knowledge of world history to answer question 3.

U.S.–Soviet Military Power, 1986–1987

U.S.		Soviet
1,010	Intercontinental ballistic missiles	1,398
640	Submarine-launched missiles	983
260	Long-range bombers	160
24,700	Nuclear warheads	36,800
0	Antiballistic missile launchers	100
14	Aircraft carriers	5
2,143,955	Armed forces personnel	5,130,000

Sources: The Military Balance 1986–1987; Nuclear Weapons Databook, Vol. IV, Soviet Nuclear Weapons

3 The chart clearly shows that

(1) the United States had more troops than the Soviet Union
(2) the Soviet Union had clear superiority in the number of ballistic missiles
(3) the United States and the Soviet Union were equal in nuclear warheads
(4) the Soviet Union had more aircraft carriers

INTEGRATED TECHNOLOGY

TEST PRACTICE Go to **classzone.com**

- Diagnostic tests
- Tutorials
- Strategies
- Additional practice

ALTERNATIVE ASSESSMENT

1. Interact *with* History

On page 964, you considered what policies a nation might follow to gain allies. Now that you have learned more about the Cold War, would your decision change? Discuss your ideas with a small group.

2. WRITING ABOUT HISTORY

Study the information in the infographic on how the Cold War was fought on page 983. Write a two-paragraph **persuasive essay** on which means was the most successful for the United States and which was most successful for the Soviet Union.

Consider the following:

- who received foreign aid
- whether propaganda was successful
- how strong the military alliances were
- what was gained in surrogate wars

INTEGRATED TECHNOLOGY

Creating an Interactive Time Line

In October 1962, President John F. Kennedy and his advisers had to defuse a potentially devastating nuclear standoff with the Soviet Union. Using books, the Internet, and other resources, create an interactive time line of the crisis. Use graphics software to add maps and photographs. In addition to noting key dates, use the time line to address some of the following:

- Who were members of Kennedy's inner circle during the crisis?
- What did Kennedy say about the events in his first public address to the nation?
- How did Soviet premier Nikita Krushchev approach the crisis in Cuba?
- What details did Americans learn only after the crisis had been resolved?

CHAPTER 34

The Colonies Become New Nations, 1945–Present

Previewing Main Ideas

REVOLUTION Independence movements swept Africa and Asia as World War II ended. Through both nonviolent and violent means, revolutionaries overthrew existing political systems to create their own nations.

Geography *Which continent witnessed the greatest number of its countries gain independence?*

POWER AND AUTHORITY Systems of government shifted for one billion people when colonies in Africa and Asia gained their freedom. New nations struggled to unify their diverse populations. In many cases, authoritarian rule and military dictatorships emerged.

Geography *According to the time line, which southeast Asian country dealt with dictatorship in the years following independence?*

ECONOMICS The emergence of new nations from European- and U.S.-ruled colonies brought a change in ownership of vital resources. In many cases, however, new nations struggled to create thriving economies.

Geography *Which colonial power had enjoyed the resources from the greatest number of regions of the world?*

NEW YORK CORE CURRICULUM FOCUS

- India achieved independence from Great Britain following World War II.
- In 1947, the United Nations partitioned Palestine into a Palestinian state and a Jewish state, which became Israel.

INTEGRATED TECHNOLOGY

eEdition
- Interactive Maps
- Interactive Visuals
- Interactive Primary Sources

INTERNET RESOURCES
Go to **classzone.com** for:
- Research Links
- Internet Activities
- Primary Sources
- Chapter Quiz
- Maps
- Test Practice
- Current Events

COLONIES

1945 Sukarno proclaims Indonesian independence.

1947 India gains independence from Britain.

1957 Ghana wins independence. (first prime minister Kwame Nkrumah) ▶

1945 — 1965

WORLD

1948 South Africa establishes apartheid system. ("whites only" sign) ▶

1966 Mao Zedong launches Cultural Revolution in China.

1986
◀ Election of Corazón Aquino ends Marcos dictatorship in Philippines.

1997
Mobutu dictatorship in Zaire falls.

1985 **2003**

1975
Communist North Vietnam conquers South Vietnam.

1982
Britain defeats Argent na in war over Falkland Islands.

1991
Soviet Union breaks up into 15 republics.

2003
United States drives Saddam Hussein from power in Iraq.

Interact *with* History

How would you build a new nation?

As a political leader of a former colony, you watch with pride as your country becomes independent. However, you know that difficult days lay ahead. You want peace and prosperity for your nation. To accomplish this, however, you need to create a sound government and a strong economy. In addition, food and adequate health care are scarce and many people receive little education. These and other challenges await your immediate attention.

▼ Agriculture

▼ Health Care

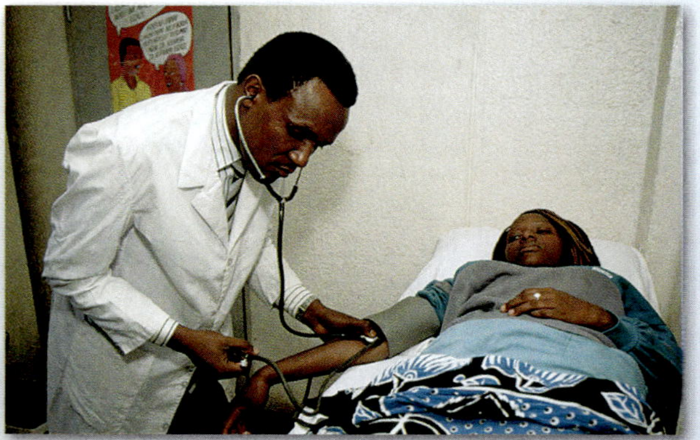

▲ Education

▲ Employment

▲ Voting Rights

EXAMINING *the* ISSUES

- **What are the first steps you would take? Why?**
- **What might be the most difficult challenge to overcome?**

As a class, discuss these questions. Remember what you have learned about what makes a stable and unified nation. As you read about the emergence of new nations around the world, note what setbacks and achievements they make in their effort to build a promising future.

1 The Indian Subcontinent Achieves Freedom

CONNECT TO THE NEW YORK STATE CORE CURRICULUM

Unit 7.E.2.b. Muslim/Hindu conflicts
Unit 7.E.2.d. Roles of Mohandas Gandhi and Jawaharlal Nehru

TERMS & NAMES

- Congress Party
- Muslim League
- Muhammad Ali Jinnah
- partition
- Jawaharlal Nehru
- Indira Gandhi
- Benazir Bhutto

SETTING THE STAGE After World War II, dramatic political changes began to take place across the world. This was especially the case with regard to the policy of colonialism. Countries that held colonies began to question the practice. After the world struggle against dictatorship, many leaders argued that no country should control another nation. Others questioned the high cost and commitment of holding colonies. Meanwhile, the people of colonized regions continued to press even harder for their freedom. All of this led to independence for one of the largest and most populous colonies in the world: British-held India.

TAKING NOTES

Following Chronological Order Create a time line of prominent Indian prime ministers from independence through the current day.

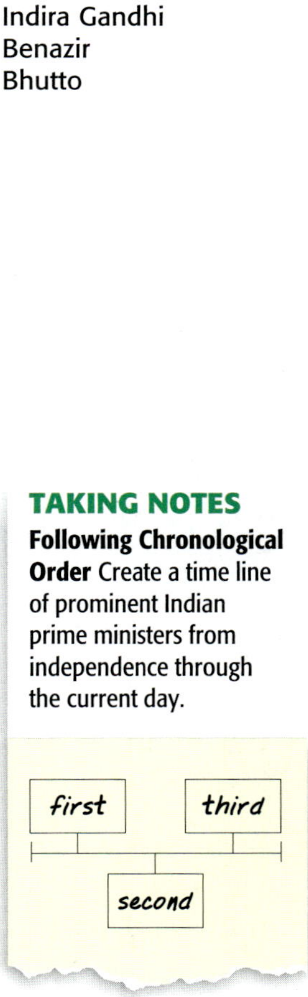

A Movement Toward Independence

The British had ruled India for almost two centuries. Indian resistance to Britain, which had existed from the beginning, intensified in 1939, when Britain committed India's armed forces to World War II without first consulting the colony's elected representatives. The move left Indian nationalists stunned and humiliated. Indian leader Mohandas Gandhi launched a nonviolent campaign of noncooperation with the British. Officials imprisoned numerous nationalists for this action. In 1942, the British tried to gain the support of the nationalists by promising governmental changes after the war. But the offer did not include Indian independence.

As they intensified their struggle against the British, Indians also struggled with each other. India has long been home to two main religious groups. In the 1940s, India had approximately 350 million Hindus and about 100 million Muslims. The Indian National Congress, or the **Congress Party**, was India's national political party. Most members of the Congress Party were Hindus, but the party at times had many Muslim members.

In competition with the Congress Party was the **Muslim League**, an organization founded in 1906 in India to protect Muslim interests. Members of the league felt that the mainly Hindu Congress Party looked out primarily for Hindu interests. The leader of the Muslim League, **Muhammad Ali Jinnah** (mu•HAM•ihd-ah•LEE-JINH•uh), insisted that all Muslims resign from the Congress Party. The Muslim League stated that it would never accept Indian independence if it meant rule by the Hindu-dominated Congress Party. Jinnah stated, "The only thing the Muslim has in common with the Hindu is his slavery to the British."

Freedom Brings Turmoil

When World War II ended, Britain found itself faced with enormous war debts. As a result, British leaders began to rethink the expense of maintaining and governing distant colonies. With India continuing to push for independence, the stage was set for the British to hand over power. However, a key problem emerged: Who should receive the power—Hindus or Muslims?

Partition and Bloodshed Muslims resisted attempts to include them in an Indian government dominated by Hindus. Rioting between the two groups broke out in several Indian cities. In August 1946, four days of clashes in Calcutta left more than 5,000 people dead and more than 15,000 hurt.

British officials soon became convinced that partition, an idea first proposed by India's Muslims, would be the only way to ensure a safe and secure region. **Partition** was the term given to the division of India into separate Hindu and Muslim nations. The northwest and eastern regions of India, where most Muslims lived, would become the new nation of Pakistan. (Pakistan, as the map shows, comprised two separate states in 1947: West Pakistan and East Pakistan.)

The British House of Commons passed an act on July 16, 1947, that granted two nations, India and Pakistan, independence in one month's time. In that short period, more than 500 independent native princes had to decide which nation they would join. The administration of the courts, the military, the railways, and the police—the whole of the civil service—had to be divided down to the last paper clip. Most difficult of all, millions of Indian citizens—Hindus, Muslims, and yet another significant religious group, the Sikhs—had to decide where to go.

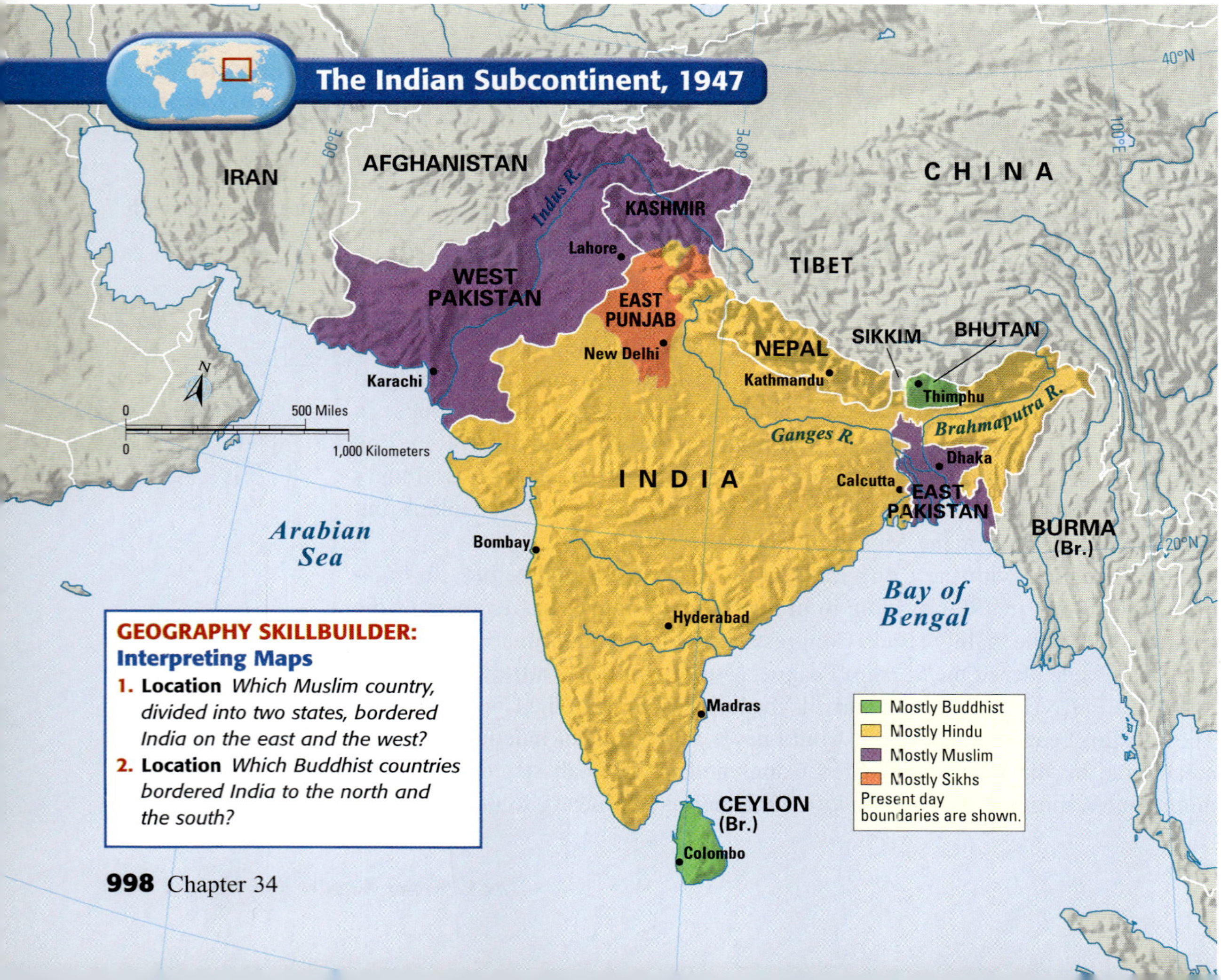

GEOGRAPHY SKILLBUILDER: Interpreting Maps

1. **Location** *Which Muslim country, divided into two states, bordered India on the east and the west?*
2. **Location** *Which Buddhist countries bordered India to the north and the south?*

During the summer of 1947, 10 million people were on the move in the Indian subcontinent. As people scrambled to relocate, violence among the different religious groups erupted. Muslims killed Sikhs who were moving into India. Hindus and Sikhs killed Muslims who were headed into Pakistan. The following passage is representative of the experiences of people in both the Hindu and Muslim communities:

PRIMARY SOURCE

All passengers were forced into compartments like sheep and goats. Because of which the heat and suffocating atmosphere was intensified and it was very hard to breathe. In the ladies compartment women and children were in a terrible condition. Women tried in vain to calm down and comfort their children. If you looked out the window you could see dead bodies lying in the distance. At many places you could see corpses piled on top of each other and no one seemed to have any concern. . . . These were the scenes that made your heart bleed and everybody loudly repented their sins and recited verses asking God's forgiveness. Every moment seemed to be the most terrifying and agonizing.

ZAHIDA AMJAD ALI, quoted in *Freedom, Trauma, Continuities*

In all, an estimated 1 million died. "What is there to celebrate?" Gandhi mourned. "I see nothing but rivers of blood." Gandhi personally went to the Indian capital of Delhi to plead for fair treatment of Muslim refugees. While there, he himself became a victim of the nation's violence. A Hindu extremist who thought Gandhi too protective of Muslims shot and killed him on January 30, 1948.

The Battle for Kashmir As if partition itself didn't result in enough bloodshed between India's Muslims and Hindus, the two groups quickly squared off over the small region of Kashmir. Kashmir lay at the northern point of India next to Pakistan. Although its ruler was Hindu, Kashmir had a majority Muslim population. Shortly after independence, India and Pakistan began battling each other for control of the region. The fighting continued until the United Nations arranged a cease-fire in 1949. The cease-fire left a third of Kashmir under Pakistani control and the rest under Indian control. The two countries continue to fight over the region today. (A)

MAIN IDEA

Analyzing Causes

(A) What was the cause of the conflict between India and Pakistan over Kashmir?

Connect *to* Today

The Coldest War

No part of Kashmir is beyond a fight for India and Pakistan—including the giant Siachen glacier high above the region. The dividing line established by the 1949 cease-fire did not extend to the glacier because officials figured neither side would try to occupy such a barren and frigid strip of land.

They figured wrong. In 1984, both sides sent troops to take the glacier, and they have been dug in ever since. At altitudes nearing 21,000 feet, Indian and Pakistani soldiers shoot at each other from trenches in temperatures that reach 70 degrees below zero. While it is believed that more soldiers have died from the cold than from enemy bullets, neither side will budge.

Modern India

With the granting of its independence on August 15, 1947, India became the world's largest democracy. As the long-awaited hour of India's freedom approached, **Jawaharlal Nehru**, the independent nation's first prime minister, addressed the country's political leaders:

PRIMARY SOURCE

Long years ago, we made a tryst [appointment] with destiny, and now the time comes when we shall redeem our pledge, not wholly or in full measure, but very substantially. At the stroke of the midnight hour, when the world sleeps, India will wake to life and freedom.

JAWAHARLAL NEHRU, speech before the Constituent Assembly, August 14, 1947

History Makers

Jawaharlal Nehru
1889–1964

Nehru's father was an influential attorney, and so the first prime minister of India grew up amid great wealth. As a young man, he lived and studied in England. "In my likes and dislikes I was perhaps more an Englishman than an Indian," he once remarked.

Upon returning to India, however, he became moved by the horrible state in which many of his fellow Indians lived. "A new picture of India seemed to rise before me," he recalled, "naked, starving, crushed, and utterly miserable." From then on, he devoted his life to improving conditions in his country.

INTEGRATED TECHNOLOGY

RESEARCH LINKS For more on Jawaharlal Nehru, go to **classzone.com**

Nehru Leads India Nehru served as India's leader for its first 17 years of independence. He had been one of Gandhi's most devoted followers. Educated in Britain, Nehru won popularity among all groups in India. He emphasized democracy, unity, and economic modernization.

Nehru used his leadership to move India forward. He led other newly independent nations of the world in forming an alliance of countries that were neutral in the Cold War conflicts between the United States and the Soviet Union. On the home front, Nehru called for a reorganization of the states by language. He also pushed for industrialization and sponsored social reforms. He tried to elevate the status of the lower castes, or those at the bottom of society, and help women gain the rights promised by the constitution.

Troubled Times Nehru died in 1964. His death left the Congress Party with no leader strong enough to hold together the many political factions that had emerged with India's independence. Then, in 1966, Nehru's daughter, **Indira Gandhi**, was chosen prime minister. After a short spell out of office, she was reelected in 1980.

Although she ruled capably, Gandhi faced many challenges, including the growing threat from Sikh extremists who themselves wanted an independent state. The Golden Temple at Amritsar stood as the religious center for the Sikhs. From there, Sikh nationalists ventured out to attack symbols of Indian authority. In June 1984, Indian army troops overran the Golden Temple. They killed about 500 Sikhs and destroyed sacred property. In retaliation, Sikh bodyguards assigned to Indira Gandhi gunned her down. This violent act set off another murderous frenzy, causing the deaths of thousands of Sikhs.

In the wake of the murder of Indira Gandhi, her son, Rajiv (rah•JEEV) Gandhi, took over as prime minister. His party, however, lost its power in 1989 because of accusations of widespread corruption. In 1991, while campaigning again for prime minister near the town of Madras, Rajiv was killed by a bomb. Members of a group opposed to his policies claimed responsibility.

Twenty-First Century Challenges Since winning election as prime minister in 1998, Atal Bihari Vajpayee, leader of the Hindu nationalist party, has ruled over a vibrant but often unstable nation. He faces challenges brought on by an increasing population that is expected to push India past China as the world's most populous nation by 2035. In addition, the country is racked with social inequality and constantly threatened by religious strife.

Even more troubling are India's tense relations with its neighbor Pakistan, and the fact that both have become nuclear powers. In 1974, India exploded a "peaceful" nuclear device. For the next 24 years, the nation quietly worked on building up its nuclear capability. In 1998, Indian officials conducted five underground nuclear tests. Meanwhile, the Pakistanis had been building their own nuclear program. Shortly after India conducted its nuclear tests, Pakistan demonstrated that it, too, had nuclear weapons. The presence of these weapons in the hands of such bitter enemies and neighbors has become a matter of great international concern, especially in light of their continuing struggle over Kashmir:

PRIMARY SOURCE

Now that India and Pakistan have tested nuclear weapons, the dispute over their border region of lush valleys and jagged Himalayan peaks has become a matter of urgent concern. . . . [There is] fear that a remote but savage ethnic and religious conflict could deteriorate into a nuclear exchange with global consequences. India and Pakistan must learn to talk to each other and move toward a more trusting relationship.

The *New York Times,* June 28, 1998

Pakistan Copes with Freedom

The history of Pakistan since independence has been no less turbulent than that of India. Pakistan actually began as two separate and divided states, East Pakistan and West Pakistan. East Pakistan lay to the east of India, West Pakistan to the northwest. These regions were separated by more than 1,000 miles of Indian territory. In culture, language, history, geography, economics, and ethnic background, the two regions were very different. Only the Islamic religion united them.

Civil War From the beginning, the two regions of Pakistan experienced strained relations. While East Pakistan had the larger population, it was often ignored by West Pakistan, home to the central government. In 1970, a giant cyclone and tidal wave struck East Pakistan and killed an estimated 266,000 residents. While international aid poured into Pakistan, the government in West Pakistan did not quickly transfer that aid to East Pakistan. Demonstrations broke out in East Pakistan, and protesters called for an end to all ties with West Pakistan.

On March 26, 1971, East Pakistan declared itself an independent nation called Bangladesh. A civil war followed between Bangladesh and Pakistan. Eventually,

A Turbulent History

Pakistan

1977
Ali Bhutto
Prime Minister Ali Bhutto of Pakistan is deposed in a coup led by General Zia. Bhutto is later hanged for having ordered the assassination of a political opponent.

1988
General Zia
General Zia, president of Pakistan, dies in a mysterious plane crash.

1950 | 1960 | 1970 | 1980 | 1990

India

1948
Mohandas Gandhi
Gandhi is shot to death by a Hindu extremist. The assassin opposes Gandhi's efforts to achieve equal treatment for all Indians, including Muslims.

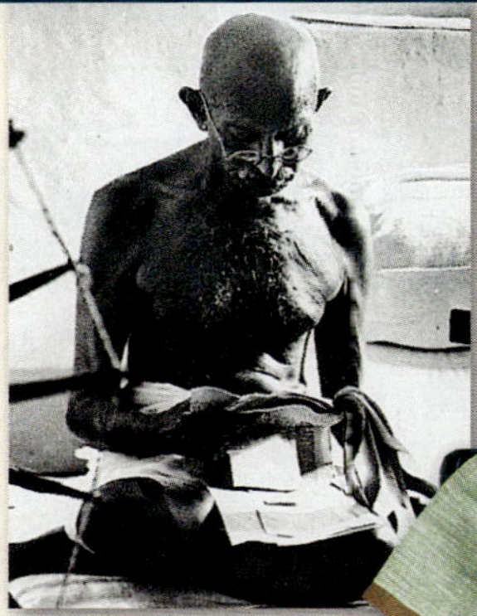

1984
Indira Gandhi
Indira Gandhi is gunned down by two of her Sikh bodyguards. Her murder is in retaliation for an attack she ordered on a Sikh temple.

1991
Rajiv Gandhi
Rajiv Gandhi is killed by a bomb while campaigning. The bomb is carried by a woman opposed to Gandhi's policies.

Indian forces stepped in and sided with Bangladesh. About two weeks after the arrival of Indian troops, Pakistan forces surrendered. More than 1 million people died in the war. Pakistan lost about one-seventh of its area and about one-half of its population to Bangladesh. **B**

MAIN IDEA

Comparing

B How does the history of Pakistan in 1971 parallel the history of India in 1947?

A Pattern of Instability Pakistan, however, could ill afford to dwell on its lost territory, for there were many problems at home. Muhammad Ali Jinnah, the first governor-general of Pakistan, died shortly after independence. This left the nation without strong leadership. As a result, Pakistan went through a series of military coups, the first in 1958. Ali Bhutto took control of the country following the civil war. A military coup in 1977 led by General Zia removed Bhutto, who was later executed for crimes allegedly committed while in office.

After Zia's death, Bhutto's daughter, **Benazir Bhutto**, was twice elected prime minister. After months of disorder, she was removed from office in 1996. Nawaz Sharif became prime minister after the 1997 elections. In 1999, army leaders ousted Sharif in yet another coup and imposed military rule over Pakistan. The nation continues to struggle with challenges from Muslim militants and ongoing disputes with India, especially over the territory of Kashmir.

Bangladesh and Sri Lanka Struggle

Meanwhile, the newly created nations of Bangladesh and Sri Lanka struggled with enormous problems of their own in the decades following independence.

Bangladesh Faces Many Problems The war with Pakistan had ruined the economy of Bangladesh and fractured its communications system. Rebuilding the shattered country seemed like an overwhelming task. Sheik Mujibur Rahman became the nation's first prime minister. He appeared more interested in strengthening his own power than in rebuilding his nation. He soon took over all authority and declared Bangladesh a one-party state. In August 1975, military leaders assassinated him.

Over the years Bangladesh has attempted with great difficulty to create a more democratic form of government. Charges of election fraud and government corruption are common. In recent years, however, the government has become more stable. The latest elections were held in October of 2001, and Begum Khaleda Zia took over as the nation's prime minister.

In the years following its independence, Bangladesh also has had to cope with crippling natural disasters. Bangladesh is a low-lying nation that is subject to many cyclones and tidal waves. Massive storms regularly flood the land, ruin crops and

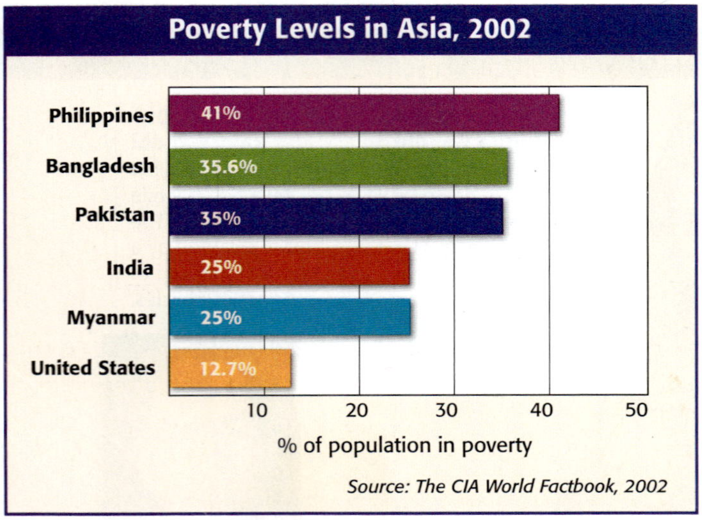

▼ Overcrowded and poor villages are a common sight throughout Bangladesh.

homes, and take lives. A particularly powerful cyclone hit in 1991 and killed approximately 139,000 people. Such catastrophes, along with a rapidly growing population, have put much stress on the country's economy. Bangladesh is one of the poorest nations in the world. The per capita income there is about $360 per year.

Civil Strife Grips Sri Lanka Another newly freed and deeply troubled country on the Indian subcontinent is Sri Lanka, a small, teardrop-shaped island nation just off the southeast coast of India. Formerly known as Ceylon, Sri Lanka gained its independence from Britain in February of 1948. Two main ethnic groups dominate the nation. Three-quarters of the population are Sinhalese, who are Buddhists. A fifth are Tamils, a Hindu people of southern India and northern Sri Lanka.

▲ This emblem of the separatist group Liberation Tigers of Tamil Eelam represents the struggle for independence of the Tamils.

Sri Lanka's recent history has also been one of turmoil. A militant group of Tamils has long fought an armed struggle for a separate Tamil nation. Since 1981, thousands of lives have been lost. In an effort to end the violence, Rajiv Gandhi and the Sri Lankan president tried to reach an accord in 1987. The agreement called for Indian troops to enter Sri Lanka and help disarm Tamil rebels. This effort was not successful, and the Indian troops left in 1990. A civil war between Tamils and other Sri Lankans continues today.

As difficult as post-independence has been for the countries of the Indian subcontinent, the same can be said for former colonies elsewhere. As you will read in the next section, a number of formerly held territories in Southeast Asia faced challenges as they became independent nations.

NEW YORK CORE CURRICULUM REVIEW

TERMS & NAMES 1. For each term or name, write a sentence explaining its significance.

• Congress Party • Muslim League • Muhammad Ali Jinnah • partition • Jawaharlal Nehru • Indira Gandhi • Benazir Bhutto

USING YOUR NOTES

2. What tragic connection did many of the leaders share?

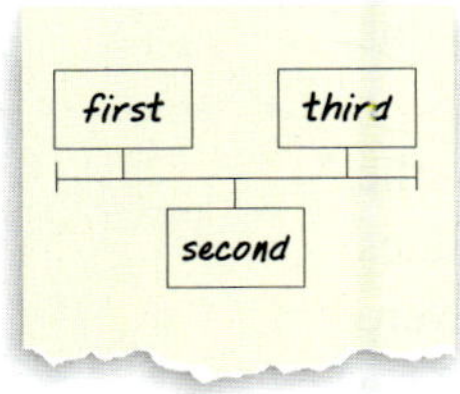

MAIN IDEAS

3. Why did British officials partition India into India and Pakistan?
4. In what way did Pakistan also undergo a partition?
5. What is the main cause today of civil strife in Sri Lanka?

CRITICAL THINKING & WRITING

6. **SYNTHESIZING** Why might India's political and economic success be so crucial to the future of democracy in Asia?
7. **ANALYZING ISSUES** How did religious and cultural differences create problems for newly emerging nations?
8. **DRAWING CONCLUSIONS** Why has the conflict between India and Pakistan over Kashmir become such a concern to the world today?
9. **WRITING ACTIVITY** POWER AND AUTHORITY Write several **paragraphs** detailing the problems shared by leaders of India and Pakistan.

CONNECT TO TODAY **CREATING A GRAPHIC**

Research the current percentages of religions in India, Pakistan, Bangladesh, or Sri Lanka. Create a **graphic** of your choosing to illustrate your findings.

Southeast Asian Nations Gain Independence

CONNECT TO THE NEW YORK STATE CORE CURRICULUM

Unit 7.E.4.c. Aung San Suu Kyi–Myanmar
Unit 8.B.4.d. Indonesian Christians

TERMS & NAMES

- Ferdinand Marcos
- Corazón Aquino
- Aung San Suu Kyi
- Sukarno
- Suharto

SETTING THE STAGE World War II had a significant impact on the colonized groups of Southeast Asia. During the war, the Japanese seized much of Southeast Asia from the European nations that had controlled the region for many years. The Japanese conquest helped the people of Southeast Asia see that the Europeans were far from invincible. When the war ended, and the Japanese themselves had been forced out, many Southeast Asians refused to live again under European rule. They called for and won their independence, and a series of new nations emerged.

TAKING NOTES
Summarizing Use a chart to summarize the major challenges that Southeast Asian countries faced after independence.

Nation	Challenges Following Independence
The Philippines	
Burma	
Indonesia	

The Philippines Achieves Independence

The Philippines became the first of the world's colonies to achieve independence following World War II. The United States granted the Philippines independence in 1946, on the anniversary of its own Declaration of Independence, the Fourth of July.

The United States and the Philippines The Filipinos' immediate goals were to rebuild the economy and to restore the capital of Manila. The city had been badly damaged in World War II. The United States had promised the Philippines $620 million in war damages. However, the U.S. government insisted that Filipinos approve the Bell Act in order to get the money. This act would establish free trade between the United States and the Philippines for eight years, to be followed by gradually increasing tariffs. Filipinos were worried that American businesses would exploit the resources and environment of the Philippines. In spite of this concern, Filipinos approved the Bell Act and received their money.

The United States also wanted to maintain its military presence in the Philippines. With the onset of the Cold War (see Chapter 33), the United States needed to protect its interests in Asia. Both China and the Soviet Union were rivals of the United States at the time. Both were Pacific powers with bases close to allies of the United States and to resources vital to U.S. interests. Therefore, the United States demanded a 99-year lease on its military and naval bases in the Philippines. The bases, Clark Air Force Base and Subic Bay Naval Base near Manila, proved to be critical to the United States later in the staging of the Korean and Vietnam wars.

GEOGRAPHY SKILLBUILDER: Interpreting Maps

1. **Location** *Which former Dutch colony is made up of a series of islands spread out from the Indian Ocean to the Pacific Ocean?*
2. **Region** *From what European country did the most colonies shown above gain their independence?*

MAIN IDEA

Making Inferences

A Why might the United States have been interested in maintaining military bases in the Philippines?

These military bases also became the single greatest source of conflict between the United States and the Philippines. Many Filipinos regarded the bases as proof of American imperialism. Later agreements shortened the terms of the lease, and the United States gave up both bases in 1992. **A**

After World War II, the Philippine government was still almost completely dependent on the United States economically and politically. The Philippine government looked for ways to lessen this dependency. It welcomed Japanese investments. It also broadened its contacts with Southeast Asian neighbors and with nonaligned nations.

From Marcos to Ramos **Ferdinand Marcos** was elected president of the Philippines in 1965. The country suffered under his rule from 1966 to 1986. Marcos imposed an authoritarian regime and stole millions of dollars from the public treasury. Although the constitution limited Marcos to eight years in office, he got around this restriction by imposing martial law from 1972 to 1981. Two years later, his chief opponent, Benigno Aquino, Jr., was assassinated as he returned from the United States to the Philippines, lured by the promise of coming elections.

In the elections of 1986, Aquino's widow, **Corazón Aquino**, challenged Marcos. Aquino won decisively, but Marcos refused to acknowledge her victory. When he declared himself the official winner, a public outcry resulted. He was forced into exile in Hawaii, where he later died. In 1995, the Philippines succeeded in recovering $475 million Marcos had stolen from his country and deposited in Swiss banks.

As she took the oath of office, Aquino promised to usher in a more open and democratic form of government.

PRIMARY SOURCE

I pledge a government dedicated to upholding truth and justice, morality and decency in government, freedom and democracy. I ask our people not to relax, but to maintain more vigilance in this, our moment of triumph. The Motherland can't thank them enough, yet we all realize that more is required of each of us to achieve a truly just society for our people. This is just the beginning.

CORAZÓN AQUINO, inaugural speech, Feb. 24, 1986

During Aquino's presidency, the Philippine government ratified a new constitution. It also negotiated successfully with the United States to end the lease on the U.S. military bases. In 1992, Fidel V. Ramos succeeded Aquino as president. Ramos was restricted by the constitution to a single six-year term. The single-term limit is intended to prevent the abuse of power that occurred during Marcos's 20-year rule.

The Government Battles Rebels Since gaining its independence, the Philippines has had to battle its own separatist group. For centuries, the southern part of the country has been a stronghold of Muslims known as the Moros. In the early 1970s, a group of Moros formed the Moro National Liberation Front (MNLF). They began an armed struggle for independence from Philippine rule.

In 1996, the government and rebels agreed to a cease-fire, and the Moros were granted an autonomous region in the southern Philippines. The agreement, however, did not satisfy a splinter group of the MNLF called Abu Sayyaf. These rebels have continued fighting the government, often using terror tactics to try to achieve their goals. In 2000, they kidnapped 21 people including foreign tourists. While the group eventually was freed, subsequent kidnappings by Abu Sayyaf have resulted in the death of several hostages. The current Philippines president, Gloria Macapagal Arroyo, has launched an all-out military response to this group. The United States has provided military assistance to the government's efforts.

History Makers

Aung San Suu Kyi
1945–

Aung San Suu Kyi won the Nobel Peace Prize in 1991 for her efforts to establish democracy in Myanmar. She could not accept the award in person, however, because she was still under house arrest.

The Nobel Prize committee said that in awarding her the peace prize, it intended:

> *to show its support for the many people throughout the world who are striving to attain democracy, human rights, and ethnic conciliation by peaceful means. Suu Kyi's struggle is one of the most extraordinary examples of civil courage in Asia in recent decades.*

British Colonies Gain Independence

Britain's timetable for granting independence to its Southeast Asian colonies depended on local circumstances. Burma had been pressing for independence from Britain for decades. It became a sovereign republic in 1948. In 1989, Burma was officially named Myanmar (myahn•MAH), its name in the Burmese language.

Burma Experiences Turmoil After gaining freedom, Burma suffered one political upheaval after another. Its people struggled between repressive military governments and pro-democracy forces. Conflict among Communists and ethnic minorities also disrupted the nation. In 1962, General Ne Win set up a military government, with the goal of making Burma a socialist state. Although Ne Win stepped down in 1988, the military continued to rule repressively.

In 1988, **Aung San Suu Kyi** (owng sahn soo chee) returned to Burma after many years abroad. She is the

Vocabulary
House arrest is confinement to one's quarters, or house, rather than to prison.

daughter of Aung San, a leader of the Burmese nationalists' army killed years before by political rivals. Aung San Suu Kyi became active in the newly formed National League for Democracy. For her pro-democracy activities, she was placed under house arrest for six years by the government. In the 1990 election—the country's first multiparty election in 30 years—the National League for Democracy won 80 percent of the seats. The military government refused to recognize the election, and it kept Aung San Suu Kyi under house arrest. She was finally released in 1995, only to be placed under house arrest again in 2000. Freed in 2002, she was detained again in 2003, leaving many residents to doubt whether Burma will embrace democracy anytime soon.

Malaysia and Singapore During World War II, the Japanese conquered the Malay Peninsula, formerly ruled by the British. The British returned to the peninsula after the Japanese defeat in 1945. They tried, unsuccessfully, to organize the different peoples of Malaya into one state. They also struggled to put down a Communist uprising. Ethnic groups resisted British efforts to unite their colonies on the peninsula and in the northern part of the island of Borneo. Malays were a slight majority on the peninsula, while Chinese were the largest group on the southern tip, the island of Singapore.

In 1957, officials created the Federation of Malaya from Singapore, Malaya, Sarawak, and Sabah. The two regions—on the Malay Peninsula and on northern Borneo—were separated by 400 miles of ocean. In 1965, Singapore separated from the federation and became an independent city-state. The federation, consisting of Malaya, Sarawak, and Sabah, became known as Malaysia. A coalition of many ethnic groups maintained steady economic progress in Malaysia.

MAIN IDEA
Making Inferences
B What do the top economies listed by the Geneva World Economic Forum have in common?

Singapore, which has one of the busiest ports in the world, has become an extremely prosperous nation. Lee Kuan Yew ruled Singapore as prime minister from 1959 to 1990. Under his guidance, Singapore emerged as a banking center as well as a center of trade. It had a standard of living far higher than any of its Southeast Asian neighbors. In 1997, the Geneva World Economic Forum listed the world's strongest economies. Singapore topped the list. It was followed, in order, by Hong Kong, the United States, Canada, New Zealand, Switzerland, and Great Britain. **B**

▼ A glittering skyline rises above the bustling harbor of Singapore.

Indonesia Gains Independence from the Dutch

Like members of other European nations, the Dutch, who ruled the area of Southeast Asia known as Indonesia, saw their colonial empire crumble with the onset of World War II. The Japanese conquered the region and destroyed the Dutch colonial order. When the war ended and the defeated Japanese were forced to leave, the people of Indonesia moved to establish a free nation.

Sukarno Leads the Independence Movement Leading the effort to establish an independent Indonesia was **Sukarno** (soo•KAHR•noh), known only by his one name. In August 1945, two days after the Japanese surrendered, Sukarno proclaimed Indonesia's independence and named himself president. A guerrilla army backed him. The Dutch, supported initially by Britain and the United States, attempted to regain control of Indonesia. But after losing the support of the United Nations and the United States, the Dutch agreed to grant Indonesia its independence in 1949.

The new Indonesia became the world's fourth most populous nation. It consisted of more than 13,600 islands, with 300 different ethnic groups, 250 languages, and most of the world's major religions. It contained the world's largest Islamic population. Sukarno, who took the official title of "life-time president," attempted to guide this diverse nation in a parliamentary democracy.

Instability and Turmoil Sukarno's efforts to build a stable democratic nation were unsuccessful. He was not able to manage Indonesia's economy, and the country slid downhill rapidly. Foreign banks refused to lend money to Indonesia and inflation occasionally soared as high as one thousand percent. In 1965, a group of junior army officers attempted a coup. A general named **Suharto** (suh•HAHR•toh) put down the rebellion. He then seized power for himself and began a bloodbath in which 500,000 to 1 million Indonesians were killed.

Vocabulary
A *coup* is the sudden overthrow of a government by a small group of people.

Suharto, officially named president in 1967, turned Indonesia into a police state and imposed frequent periods of martial law. Outside observers heavily criticized him for his annexation of nearby East Timor in 1976 and for human rights violations there. (See the map on page 1005.) Suharto's government also showed little tolerance for religious freedoms.

Bribery and corruption became commonplace. The economy improved under Suharto for a while but from 1997 through 1998 the nation suffered one of the worst financial crises in its history. Growing unrest over both government repression and a crippling economic crisis prompted Suharto to step down in 1998. While turmoil continued to grip the country, it moved slowly toward democracy. The daughter of Sukarno, Megawati Sukarnoputri, was elected to the presidency in 2001.

Upon taking office, the new president hailed the virtues of democracy and urged her fellow Indonesians to do what they could to maintain such a form of government:

PRIMARY SOURCE C

Democracy requires sincerity and respect for the rules of the game. Beginning my duty, I urge all groups to sincerely and openly accept the outcome of the democratic process . . . . In my opinion, respect for the people's voice, sincerity in accepting it, and respect for the rules of game are the main pillars of democracy which we will further develop. I urge all Indonesians to look forward to the future and unite to improve the life and our dignity as a nation.

MEGAWATI SUKARNOPUTRI, July 23, 2001

MAIN IDEA

Analyzing Primary Sources

C What are the cornerstones of democracy, according to Sukarnoputri?

Sukarnoputri faces enormous challenges, including a still-fragile economy, ethnic strife, security problems, and a government still hobbled by corruption.

East Timor Wins Independence As Indonesia worked to overcome its numerous obstacles, it lost control of East Timor. Indonesian forces had ruled the land with brutal force since Suharto seized it in the 1970s. The East Timorese, however, never stopped pushing to regain their freedom. Jose Ramos Horta, an East Timorese independence campaigner, won the 1996 Nobel Peace Prize (along with East Timor's Roman Catholic bishop) for his efforts to gain independence for the region without violence.

In a United Nations-sponsored referendum held in August 1999, the East Timorese voted overwhelmingly for independence. The election angered pro-Indonesian forces in the region. They ignored the referendum results and went on a bloody rampage. They killed hundreds and forced thousands into refugee camps in West Timor, which is a part of Indonesia. UN intervention forces eventually brought peace to the area. In 2002 East Timor celebrated independence.

As on the Indian subcontinent, violence and struggle were part of the transition in Southeast Asia from colonies to free nations. The same would be true in Africa, where numerous former colonies shed European rule and created independent countries in the wake of World War II.

▲ An earthquake off the coast of Indonesia on December 26, 2004, triggered a devastating tsunami. The tidal waves and floods killed more than 150,000 people.

NEW YORK CORE CURRICULUM REVIEW

TERMS & NAMES 1. For each term or name, write a sentence explaining its significance.

- Ferdinand Marcos
- Corazón Aquino
- Aung San Suu Kyi
- Sukarno
- Suharto

USING YOUR NOTES

2. Which nation faced the greatest challenges? Why?

Nation	Challenges Following Independence
The Philippines	
Burma	
Indonesia	

MAIN IDEAS

3. Why did the retention of U.S. military bases in the Philippines so anger Filipinos?
4. What was the outcome of the 1990 Myanmar election? How did the government respond?
5. How did Suharto come to power in Indonesia?

CRITICAL THINKING & WRITING

6. **CLARIFYING** How did World War II play a role in the eventual decolonization of Southeast Asia?
7. **MAKING INFERENCES** Why do you think that the United States demanded a 99-year lease on military and naval bases in the Philippines?
8. **COMPARING AND CONTRASTING** What was similar and different about the elections that brought defeat to the ruling governments in the Philippines and in Burma?
9. **WRITING ACTIVITY** ECONOMICS Write a two-paragraph **expository essay** contrasting Singapore's economy with others in Southeast Asia.

CONNECT TO TODAY **CREATING A TELEVISION NEWS SCRIPT**

Locate several of the most recent news articles about one of the countries discussed in this section. Combine the stories into a brief television **news script** and present it to the class.

Social History

Changing Times in Southeast Asia

As you have read, many countries in Southeast Asia have undergone revolutionary changes in their political and social organization. The region continues to struggle with its past and to face new challenges, but democratic reforms are becoming more common.

The past and present exist side by side throughout much of Southeast Asia. For an increasing number of Southeast Asians, housing, transportation, even purchasing food are a mixture of old and new. These images explore the differences between traditional and modern, rich and poor, past and present.

INTEGRATED TECHNOLOGY

RESEARCH LINKS For more on life in Southeast Asia, go to **classzone.com**

▲▼ Transportation

The water buffalo-drawn cart (shown above) is a common sight in rural Thailand. It is a mode of transport that reaches deep into the past.

In Bangkok, Thailand (shown below)—with its cars, motorcycles, and public buses—transportation is a very different thing. These distinctly past and present modes of transportation symbolize the changes many Southeast Asian countries are facing.

◄ Housing

The luxury apartment building (background) in Jakarta, Indonesia, towers over the shabby and polluted slum of Muarabaru (foreground). Indonesia declared its independence in 1945, but was not recognized by the United Nations until 1950. Since independence, Indonesians have enjoyed relative economic prosperity, but bridging the gap between rich and poor is an issue that faces Indonesia and much of Southeast Asia.

▲▼ Markets
As the post-colonial economies of Southeast Asia grow, traditional markets, like the floating market in Thailand (shown below), give way to the modern convenience of stores with prepackaged foods, like this street-side store (above) in Vietnam.

DATA FILE

SOUTHEAST ASIA

Geography

- Eleven countries are generally referred to as Southeast Asia: Brunei, Cambodia, East Timor, Indonesia, Laos, Malaysia, Myanmar, the Philippines, Singapore, Thailand, and Vietnam.

Population

- About 8 percent of the world's population lives in Southeast Asia.
- Indonesia is the world's fourth most populous country, behind China, India, and the United States.

Economics

- Ten Southeast Asian nations—Indonesia, Malaysia, the Philippines, Singapore, Brunei, Cambodia, Laos, Vietnam, Myanmar, and Thailand—make up a trading alliance known as the Association of South-East Asian Nations (ASEAN)

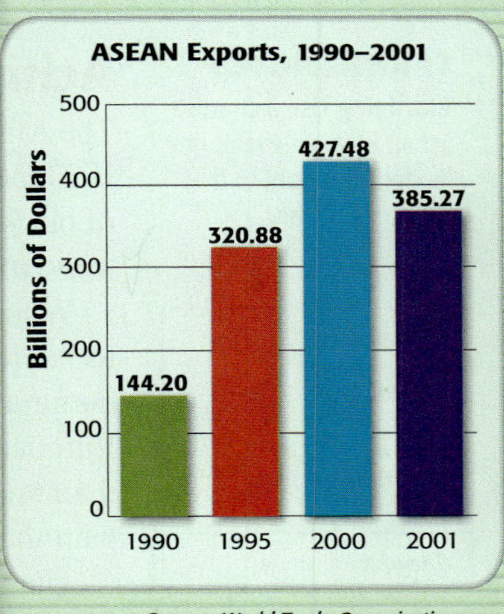

Source: World Trade Organization

Connect *to* Today

1. **Drawing Conclusions** Why might some countries in Southeast Asia have more successful economies than others?
   See Skillbuilder Handbook, page R10.
2. **Forming and Supporting Opinions** Are the issues facing Southeast Asians discussed here also a concern for Americans? Why or why not?

3

New Nations in Africa

CONNECT TO THE NEW YORK STATE CORE CURRICULUM

Unit 7.E.3.a. Changing political boundaries in Africa (Nigeria, Ghana, and Kenya)
Unit 7.E.3.f. Political and economic instability–Congo (Zaire) or any other examples

TERMS & NAMES

- Negritude movement
- Kwame Nkrumah
- Jomo Kenyatta
- Ahmed Ben Bella
- Mobutu Sese Seko

SETTING THE STAGE Throughout the first half of the 20th century, Africa resembled little more than a European outpost. As you recall, the nations of Europe had marched in during the late 1800s and colonized much of the continent. Like the diverse groups living in Asia, however, the many different peoples of Africa were unwilling to return to colonial domination after World War II. And so, in the decades following the great global conflict, they, too, won their independence from foreign rule and went to work building new nations.

TAKING NOTES
Clarifying Use a chart to list an idea, an event, or a leader important to that country's history.

Ghana	
Kenya	
Zaire	
Algeria	
Angola	

Achieving Independence

The African push for independence actually began in the decades before World War II. French-speaking Africans and West Indians began to express their growing sense of black consciousness and pride in traditional Africa. They formed the **Negritude movement**, a movement to celebrate African culture, heritage, and values.

When World War II erupted, African soldiers fought alongside Europeans to "defend freedom." This experience made them unwilling to accept colonial domination when they returned home. The war had changed the thinking of Europeans too. Many began to question the cost, as well as the morality, of maintaining colonies abroad. These and other factors helped African colonies gain their freedom throughout the 1950s and 1960s.

The ways in which African nations achieved independence, however, differed across the continent. In Chapter 27, you learned that European nations employed two basic styles of government in colonial Africa—direct and indirect. Under indirect rule, local officials did much of the governing and colonists enjoyed limited self-rule. As a result, these colonies generally experienced an easier transition to independence. For colonies under direct rule, in which foreigners governed at all levels and no self-rule existed, independence came with more difficulty. Some colonies even had to fight wars of liberation, as European settlers refused to surrender power to African nationalist groups.

No matter how they gained their freedom, however, most new African nations found the road to a strong and stable nation to be difficult. They had to deal with everything from creating a new government to establishing a postcolonial economy. Many new countries were also plagued by great ethnic strife. In colonizing Africa, the Europeans had created artificial borders that had little to do with the areas where ethnic groups actually lived. While national borders separated people with similar cultures, they also enclosed traditional enemies who began fighting each other soon after the Europeans left. For many African nations, all of this led to instability, violence, and an overall struggle to deal with their newly gained independence.

Ghana Leads the Way

The British colony of the Gold Coast became the first African colony south of the Sahara to achieve independence. Following World War II, the British in the Gold Coast began making preparations. For example, they allowed more Africans to be nominated to the Legislative Council. However, the Africans wanted full freedom. The leader of their largely nonviolent movement was **Kwame Nkrumah** (KWAH•mee uhn•KROO•muh). Starting in 1947, he worked to liberate the Gold Coast from the British. Nkrumah organized strikes and boycotts and was often imprisoned by the British government. Ultimately, his efforts were successful.

On receiving its independence in 1957, the Gold Coast took the name Ghana. This name honored a famous West African kingdom of the past. Nkrumah became Ghana's first prime minister and later its president-for-life. Nkrumah pushed through new roads, new schools, and expanded health facilities. These costly projects soon crippled the country. His programs for industrialization, health and welfare, and expanded educational facilities showed good intentions. However, the expense of the programs undermined the economy and strengthened his opposition.

Vocabulary
Pan-African refers to a vision of strengthening all of Africa, not just a single country.

In addition, Nkrumah was often criticized for spending too much time on Pan-African efforts and neglecting economic problems in his own country. He dreamed of a "United States of Africa." In 1966, while Nkrumah was in China, the army and police in Ghana seized power. Since then, the country has shifted back and forth between civilian and military rule and has struggled for economic stability. In 2000, Ghana held its first open elections.

Fighting for Freedom

In contrast to Ghana, nations such as Kenya and Algeria had to take up arms against their European rulers in order to ultimately win their freedom.

Kenya Claims Independence The British ruled Kenya, and many British settlers resisted Kenyan independence—especially those who had taken over prize farmland in the northern highlands of the country. They were forced to accept African self-government as a result of two developments. One was the strong leadership of Kenyan nationalist **Jomo Kenyatta**. The second was the rise of a group known as the Mau Mau (MOW mow). This was a secret society made up mostly of native Kenyan farmers forced out of the highlands by the British. **A**

MAIN IDEA
Contrasting
A How did the granting of independence to the British colonies of Ghana and Kenya differ?

Using guerrilla war tactics, the Mau Mau sought to push the white farmers into leaving the highlands. Kenyatta claimed to have no connection to the Mau Mau. However, he refused to condemn the organization. As a result, the

History Makers

Jomo Kenyatta
1891–1978

A man willing to spend years in jail for his beliefs, Kenyatta viewed independence as the only option for Africans.

> *The African can only advance to a "higher level" if he is free to express himself, to organize economically, politically and socially, and to take part in the government of his own country.*

On the official day that freedom finally came to Kenya, December 12, 1963, Kenyatta recalls watching with overwhelming delight as the British flag came down and the new flag of Kenya rose up. He called it "the greatest day in Kenya's history and the happiest day in my life."

INTEGRATED TECHNOLOGY
RESEARCH LINKS For more on Jomo Kenyatta, go to **classzone.com**

Africa, 1955

INTERACTIVE

Africa, 1975

INTERACTIVE

GEOGRAPHY SKILLBUILDER: Interpreting Maps

1. **Place** *Which countries in Africa were already independent in 1955?*
2. **Location** *In what decade did most of the African nations gain their independence?*

British imprisoned him for nearly a decade. By the time the British granted Kenya independence in 1963, more than 10,000 Africans and 100 settlers had been killed.

Kenyatta became president of the new nation. He worked hard to unite the country's various ethnic and language groups. Kenyatta died in 1978. His successor, Daniel arap Moi, was less successful in governing the country. Moi faced increasing opposition to his one-party rule. Adding to the nation's woes were corruption in Moi's government and ethnic conflicts that killed hundreds and left thousands homeless. Moi stepped down in 2002, and a new party gained power through free elections.

Algeria Struggles with Independence France's principal overseas colony, Algeria, had a population of one million French colonists and nine million Arabs and Berber Muslims. After World War II, the French colonists refused to share political power with the native Algerians. In 1954, the Algerian National Liberation Front, or FLN, announced its intention to fight for independence. The French sent about half a million troops into Algeria to fight the FLN. Both sides committed atrocities. The FLN prevailed, and Algeria gained its independence in July 1962.

The leader of the FLN, **Ahmed Ben Bella**, became first president of the newly independent Algeria. He attempted to make Algeria a socialist state, but was overthrown in 1965 by his army commander. From 1965 until 1988, Algerians tried unsuccessfully to modernize and industrialize the nation. Unemployment and dissatisfaction with the government contributed to the rise of religious fundamentalists who wanted to make Algeria an Islamic state. The chief Islamic party, the Islamic Salvation Front (FIS), won local and parliamentary elections in 1990 and 1991. However, the ruling government and army refused to accept the election results. As a result, a civil war broke out between Islamic militants and the government. The war continues, on and off, to this day.

Civil War in Congo and Angola

Civil war also plagued the new nations of Congo and Angola. Congo's problems lay in its corrupt dictatorship and hostile ethnic groups. Meanwhile, Angola's difficulties stemmed from intense political differences.

Freedom and Turmoil for Congo Of all the European possessions in Africa, one of the most exploited was the Belgian Congo. Belgium had ruthlessly plundered the colony's rich resources of rubber and copper. In addition, Belgian officials ruled with a harsh hand and provided the population with no social services. They also had made no attempt to prepare the people for independence. Not surprisingly, Belgium's granting of independence in 1960 to the Congo (known as Zaire from 1971 to 1997) resulted in upheaval. **B**

MAIN IDEA

Recognizing Effects

B Why was the Congo vulnerable to turmoil after independence?

▲ Mobuto Sese Seko

After years of civil war, an army officer, Colonel Joseph Mobutu, later known as **Mobutu Sese Seko** (moh•BOO•too SAY•say SAY•koh), seized power in 1965. For 32 years, Mobutu ruled the country that he renamed Zaire. He maintained control though a combination of force, one-party rule, and gifts to supporters. Mobutu successfully withstood several armed rebellions. He was finally overthrown in 1997 by rebel leader Laurent Kabila after months of civil war. Shortly thereafter, the country was renamed the Democratic Republic of the Congo.

On becoming president, Kabila promised a transition to democracy and free elections by April 1999. Such elections never came. By 2000 the nation endured another round of civil war, as three separate rebel groups sought to overthrow Kabila's autocratic rule. In January 2001, a bodyguard assassinated Kabila.

History *in* Depth

Genocide in Rwanda

Of all the African nations that have struggled with ethnic violence, perhaps none has seen more blood spilled than Rwanda. The tiny nation in East Africa gained its independence in 1962. Over the next 30 years, its main ethnic groups, Hutus and Tutsis, often clashed.

In the spring of 1994, the Rwandan president, a Hutu, died in a suspicious plane crash. In the months that followed, Hutus slaughtered about 1 million Tutsis before Tutsi rebels put an end to the killings. The United Nations set up a tribunal to punish those responsible for the worst acts of genocide.

His son, Joseph Kabila, took power and began a quest for peace. In July of 2002, some of the rebel forces agreed to a cease-fire, offering hope that a larger peace might one day become a reality.

War Tears at Angola To the southwest of Congo lies Angola, a country that not only had to fight to gain its freedom but to hold itself together after independence. The Portuguese had long ruled Angola and had no desire to stop. When an independence movement broke out in the colony, Portugal sent in 50,000 troops. The cost of the conflict amounted to almost half of Portugal's national budget. The heavy cost of fighting, as well as growing opposition at home to the war, prompted the Portuguese to withdraw from Angola in 1975.

Almost immediately, the Communist-leaning MPLA (Popular Movement for the Liberation of Angola) declared itself the new nation's rightful government. This led to a prolonged civil war, as various rebel groups fought the government and each other for power. Each group received help from outside sources. The MPLA was assisted by some 50,000 Cuban troops and by the Soviet Union. The major opposition to the MPLA was UNITA (National Union for the Total Independence of Angola), to which South Africa and the United States lent support. For decades, the two sides agreed to and then abandoned various cease-fire agreements. In 2002, the warring sides agreed to a peace accord, and the long civil war came to an end.

As the colonies of Africa worked to become stable nations, the new nation of Israel was emerging in the Middle East. Its growth, as you will read in the next section, upset many in the surrounding Arab world and prompted one of the longest-running conflicts in modern history.

NEW YORK CORE CURRICULUM REVIEW

TERMS & NAMES 1. For each term or name, write a sentence explaining its significance.
- Negritude movement
- Kwame Nkrumah
- Jomo Kenyatta
- Ahmed Ben Bella
- Mobutu Sese Seko

USING YOUR NOTES

2. Which item had the greatest impact on its country? Why?

Ghana	
Kenya	
Zaire	
Algeria	
Angola	

MAIN IDEAS

3. Who were the Mau Mau of Kenya? What was their goal?
4. What sparked the present-day civil struggle in Algeria?
5. What prompted Portugal to eventually grant Angola its freedom?

CRITICAL THINKING & WRITING

6. **DRAWING CONCLUSIONS** How did the way in which European colonialists carved up Africa in the 1800s lead to civil strife in many new African nations?
7. **ANALYZING MOTIVES** Why do you think the United States and the Soviet Union participated in Angola's civil war?
8. **ANALYZING ISSUES** Why do you think revolution swept so many African nations following their independence from European rule?
9. **WRITING ACTIVITY** REVOLUTION Imagine you are a reporter covering a revolution in one of the African nations. Write a **headline** and **article** describing it.

INTEGRATED TECHNOLOGY **INTERNET ACTIVITY**

Use the Internet to examine the current status of two countries discussed in this section. Choose from various economic, governmental, and social statistics and display your information in a **comparison chart**.

INTERNET KEYWORD
country profiles

Conflicts in the Middle East

CONNECT TO THE NEW YORK STATE CORE CURRICULUM

Unit 7.F.2. The creation of the State of Israel, Arab Palestinians, and Israel's Arab neighbors
Unit 7.F.4. Role of terrorism

TERMS & NAMES

- Anwar Sadat
- Golda Meir
- PLO
- Yasir Arafat
- Camp David Accords
- intifada
- Oslo Peace Accords

SETTING THE STAGE In the years following World War II, the Jewish people won what for so long had eluded them: their own state. The gaining of their homeland along the eastern coast of the Mediterranean Sea, however, came at a heavy price. A Jewish state was unwelcome in this mostly Arab region, and the resulting hostility led to a series of wars. Perhaps no Arab people, however, have been more opposed to a Jewish state than the Palestinians, who claim that much of the Jewish land belongs to them. These two groups have waged a bloody battle that goes on today.

Israel Becomes a State

The land called Palestine now consists of Israel, the West Bank, and the Gaza Strip. To Jews, their claim to the land dates back 3,000 years, when Jewish kings ruled the region from Jerusalem. To Palestinians (both Muslim and Christian), the land has belonged to them since the Jews were driven out around A.D. 135. To Arabs, the land has belonged to them since their conquest of the area in the 7th century.

After being forced out of Palestine during the second century, the Jewish people were not able to establish their own state and lived in different countries throughout the world. The global dispersal of the Jews is known as the Diaspora. During the late 19th and early 20th centuries, a group of Jews began returning to the region their ancestors had fled so long ago. They were known as Zionists, people who favored a Jewish national homeland in Palestine. At this time, Palestine was still part of the Ottoman Empire, ruled by Islamic Turks. After the defeat of the Ottomans in World War I, the League of Nations asked Britain to oversee Palestine until it was ready for independence.

By this time, the Jews had become a growing presence in Palestine, and were already pressing for their own nation in the territory. The Palestinians living in the region strongly opposed such a move. In a 1917 letter to Zionist leaders, British Foreign Secretary Sir Arthur Balfour promoted the idea of creating a Jewish homeland in Palestine while protecting the "rights of existing non-Jewish communities." Despite the Balfour Declaration, however, efforts to create a Jewish state failed—and hostility between Palestinians and Jews continued to grow.

TAKING NOTES

Following Chronological Order Use a graphic to fill in some important political and military events that occurred following the Suez Crisis.

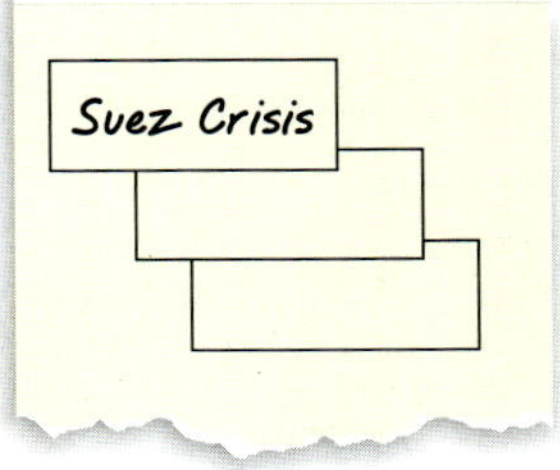

a Jewish state. Jerusalem was to be an international city owned by neither side. The terms of the partition gave Jews 55 percent of the area even though they made up only 34 percent of the population. In the wake of the war and the Holocaust, the United States and many European nations felt great sympathy for the Jews.

All of the Islamic countries voted against partition, and the Palestinians rejected it outright. They argued that the UN did not have the right to partition a country without considering the wishes of the majority of its people. Finally, the date was set for Israel's formation. On May 14, 1948, that date, David Ben Gurion, long-time leader of the Jews in Palestine, announced the creation of an independent Israel. **A**

MAIN IDEA

Summarizing

A What recommendations did the UN make for Palestine?

Israel and Arab States in Conflict

The new nation of Israel got a hostile greeting from its neighbors. The day after it proclaimed itself a state, six Islamic states—Egypt, Iraq, Jordan, Lebanon, Saudi Arabia, and Syria—invaded Israel. The first of many Arab-Israeli wars, this one ended within months in a victory for Israel. Full-scale war broke out again in 1956, 1967, and 1973. Because of Arab-Israeli tensions, several hundred thousand Jesus living in Arab lands moved to Israel.

Largely as a result of this fighting, the state that the UN had set aside for Palestinians never came into being. Israel seized half the land in the 1948–1949 fighting. While the fighting raged, at least 600,000 Palestinians fled, migrating from the areas under Israeli control. They settled in UN-sponsored refugee camps that ringed the borders of their former homeland. Meanwhile, various Arab nations seized other Palestinian lands. Egypt took control of the Gaza Strip, while Jordan annexed the West Bank of the Jordan River. (See the map at left.)

GEOGRAPHY SKILLBUILDER: Interpreting Maps

1. **Location** *What was the southernmost point in Israel in 1947 and what might have been its strategic value?*
2. **Region** *What country lies due north of Israel? east? northeast?*

The 1956 Suez Crisis The second Arab-Israeli war followed in 1956. That year, Egypt seized control of the Suez Canal, which ran along Egypt's eastern border between the Gulf of Suez and the Mediterranean Sea. Egyptian president Gamal Abdel Nasser sent in troops to take the canal, which was controlled by British interests. The military action was prompted in large part by Nasser's anger over the loss of U.S. and British financial support for the building of Egypt's Aswan Dam.

Outraged, the British made an agreement with France and Israel to retake the canal. With air support provided by their European allies, the Israelis marched on the Suez Canal and quickly defeated the Egyptians. However, pressure from the world community, including the United States and the Soviet Union, forced Israel and the Europeans to withdraw from Egypt. This left Egypt in charge of the canal and thus ended the Suez Crisis.

Arab-Israeli Wars Continue Tensions between Israel and the Arab states began to build again in the years following the resolution of the Suez Crisis. By early 1967, Nasser and his Arab allies, equipped with Soviet tanks and aircraft, felt ready to confront Israel. "We are eager for battle in order to force the enemy to awake from his dreams," Nasser announced, "and meet Arab reality face to face." He moved to close off the Gulf of Aqaba, Israel's outlet to the Red Sea.

Convinced that the Arabs were about to attack, the Israelis struck airfields in Egypt, Iraq, Jordan, and Syria. Safe from air attack, Israeli ground forces struck like lightning on three fronts. Israel defeated the Arab states in what became known as the Six-Day War, because it was over in six days. Israel lost 800 troops in the fighting, while Arab losses exceeded 15,000.

As a consequence of the Six-Day War, Israel gained control of the old city of Jerusalem, the Sinai Peninsula, the Golan Heights, and the West Bank. Israelis saw these new holdings along their southern, eastern, and western borders as a key buffer zone against further Arab attacks. Palestinians who lived in Jerusalem were given the choice of Israeli or Jordanian citizenship. Most chose the latter. Palestinians who lived in the other areas were not offered Israeli citizenship and simply came under Jewish control.

A fourth Arab-Israeli conflict erupted in October 1973. Nasser's successor, Egyptian president **Anwar Sadat** (AHN•wahr suh•DAT), planned a joint Arab attack on the date of Yom Kippur, the holiest of Jewish holidays. This time the Israelis were caught by surprise. Arab forces inflicted heavy casualties and recaptured some of the territory lost in 1967. The Israelis, under their prime minister, **Golda Meir** (MY•uhr), launched a counterattack and regained most of the lost territory. Both sides agreed to a truce after several weeks of fighting, and the Yom Kippur war came to an end. **B**

MAIN IDEA

Recognizing Effects

B What were some of the effects of the Arab-Israeli conflicts?

The Palestine Liberation Organization As Israel and its Arab neighbors battled each other, the Palestinians struggled for recognition. While the United Nations had granted the Palestinians their own homeland, the Israelis had seized much of that land, including the West Bank and Gaza Strip, during various wars. Israel insisted that such a move was vital to its national security.

In 1964, Palestinian officials formed the Palestine Liberation Organization (**PLO**) to push for the formation of a Palestinian state. Originally, the PLO was an umbrella organization made up of different groups—laborers, teachers, lawyers, and guerrilla fighters. Soon, guerrilla groups came to dominate the organization and insisted that the only way to achieve their goal was through armed struggle. In 1969 **Yasir Arafat** (YAH•sur AR•uh•FAT) became chairman of the PLO. Throughout the 1960s and 1970s the group carried out numerous attacks against Israel. Some of Israel's Arab neighbors supported the organization's goals by allowing the PLO to operate from their lands.

History Makers

Golda Meir
1898–1978

Meir was born in Kiev, Russia, but grew up in the American Heartland. Although a skilled carpenter, Meir's father could not find enough work in Kiev. So he sold his tools and other belongings and moved his family to Milwaukee, Wisconsin. Meir would spend more than a decade in the United States before moving to Palestine.

The future Israeli prime minister exhibited strong leadership qualities early on. When she learned that many of her fellow fourth grade classmates could not afford textbooks, she created the American Young Sisters Society, an organization that succeeded in raising the necessary funds.

Analyzing Primary Sources

The Palestinian View

Writer Fawaz Turki articulates the view held by many of his fellow Palestinians—that the Israelis are illegal occupiers of Palestinian land.

PRIMARY SOURCE

These people have walked off with our home and homeland, with our movable and immovable property, with our land, our farms, our shops, our public buildings, our paved roads, our cars, our theaters, our clubs, our parks, our furniture, our tricycles. They hounded us out of ancestral patrimony [land] and shoved us in refugee camps. . . . Now they were astride the whole of historic Palestine and then some, jubilant at the new role as latter day colonial overlords.

FAWAZ TURKI, quoted in *The Arab-Israeli Conflict*

The Israeli View

Many Israelis, including former Israeli General Abraham Tamir, feel that controlling Palestinian lands is vital to their security.

PRIMARY SOURCE

Since the establishment of the State of Israel, its national security policy has been designed to defend its existence, integrity and security, and not for expansionist territorial aspirations. Hence, if Arab confrontation states did not initiate wars against Israel or pose threats to its existence, then Israel would not start a war . . . to extend its territories . . . Our national security policy created from its very beginning the linkage between Israel's political willingness for peace and Israel's military capability to repel aggression of any kind and scale.

ABRAHAM TAMIR, quoted in *From War to Peace*

DOCUMENT-BASED QUESTIONS

1. **Analyzing Issues** *Why does Fawaz Turki refer to the Israelis as colonizers?*
2. **Drawing Conclusions** *What might be the best way for the Palestinians to regain control of their land, according to Abraham Tamir?*

Efforts at Peace

In November 1977, just four years after the Yom Kippur war, Anwar Sadat stunned the world by extending a hand to Israel. No Arab country up to this point had recognized Israel's right to exist. In a dramatic gesture, Sadat went before the Knesset, the Israeli parliament, and invited his one-time enemies to join him in a quest for peace.

PRIMARY SOURCE

Today, through my visit to you, I ask you why don't we stretch our hands with faith and sincerity and so that together we might . . . remove all suspicion of fear, betrayal, and bad intention? Why don't we stand together with the courage of men and the boldness of heroes who dedicate themselves to a sublime [supreme] aim? Why don't we stand together with the same courage and daring to erect a huge edifice [building] of peace? An edifice that . . . serves as a beacon for generations to come with the human message for construction, development, and the dignity of man.

ANWAR SADAT, Knesset speech, November 20, 1977

Sadat emphasized that in exchange for peace Israel would have to recognize the rights of Palestinians. Furthermore, it would have to withdraw from territory seized in 1967 from Egypt, Jordan, and Syria.

U.S. president Jimmy Carter recognized that Sadat had created a historic opportunity for peace. In 1978, Carter invited Sadat and Israeli prime minister Menachem Begin (mehn•AHK•hehm BAY•gihn) to Camp David, the presidential retreat in rural Maryland. Isolated from the press and from domestic political pressures, Sadat and Begin worked to reach an agreement. After 13 days of negotiations, Carter triumphantly announced that Egypt recognized Israel as a legitimate state. In exchange, Israel agreed to return the Sinai Peninsula to Egypt. Signed in 1979, the **Camp David Accords** ended 30 years of hostilities between Egypt and Israel and became the first signed agreement between Israel and an Arab country.

MAIN IDEA

Clarifying

C What was the significance of the Camp David Accords?

While world leaders praised Sadat, his peace initiative enraged many Arab countries. In 1981, a group of Muslim extremists assassinated him. However, Egypt's new leader, Hosni Mubarak (HAHS•nee moo•BAHR•uhk), has worked to maintain peace with Israel. **C**

Israeli-Palestinian Tensions Increase One Arab group that continued to clash with the Israelis was the Palestinians, a large number of whom lived in the West Bank and Gaza Strip—lands occupied by Israel. During the 1970s and 1980s, the military wing of the PLO intensified its armed struggle against Israel. Israel responded forcefully, bombing suspected rebel bases in Palestinian towns. In 1982, the Israeli army went as far as invading the neighboring country of Lebanon in an attempt to destroy Palestinian strongholds. The Israelis soon became involved in Lebanon's civil war and were forced to withdraw.

In 1987, Palestinians began to express their frustrations in a widespread campaign of civil disobedience called the **intifada**, or "uprising." The intifada took the form of boycotts, demonstrations, attacks on Israeli soldiers, and rock throwing by unarmed teenagers. The intifada continued into the 1990s, with little progress made toward a solution. However, the civil disobedience affected world opinion, which, in turn, put pressure on Israel to seek negotiations with the Palestinians. Finally, in October 1991, Israeli and Palestinian delegates met for a series of peace talks.

The Oslo Peace Accords Negotiations between the two sides made little progress, as the status of the Palestinian territories occupied by Israel proved to be a bitterly divisive issue. In 1993, however, secret talks held in Oslo, Norway, produced a surprise agreement: a document called the Declaration of Principles, also known as the **Oslo Peace Accords**. Israel, under the leadership of Prime Minister Yitzhak Rabin (YIHTS•hahk rah•BEEN), agreed to grant the Palestinians self-rule in the Gaza Strip and the West Bank, beginning with the town of Jericho. Rabin and Arafat signed the agreement on September 13, 1993.

The difficulty of making the agreement work was demonstrated by the assassination of Rabin in 1995. He was killed by a right-wing Jewish extremist who opposed concessions to the Palestinians. Rabin was succeeded as prime minister by Benjamin Netanyahu (neh•tan•YAH•hoo), who had opposed the Oslo Accords. Still, Netanyahu made efforts to keep to the agreement. In January 1997, Netanyahu met with Arafat to work out plans for a partial Israeli withdrawal from the West Bank.

The Israeli–Palestinian Struggle

1947 UN votes to partition Palestine into Jewish and Palestinian states.

1949 Israel repels attack by Arab states and takes more land than originally assigned.

1967 Israel wins Six-Day War and seizes more Palestinian land for what it calls security purposes.

1987 Palestinians intensify their resistance with start of intifada movement (see below).

1993 Israel agrees to withdraw from several Palestinian regions in historic Oslo Peace Accords.

2000 Visit by Israeli leader Ariel Sharon to holy Arab site launches second intifada and years of violence.

1950 | 1960 | 1970 | 1980 | 1990 | 2000

History *in* Depth

Signs of Hope

Amid the cycle of violence and disagreement in the Middle East, there are small but inspiring efforts to bring together Israelis and Palestinians. One is Seeds of Peace, a summer camp that hosts teenagers from opposing sides of world conflicts in the hopes of creating lasting friendships. Another is the West-Eastern Divan, an orchestra made up of Jewish and Arab musicians—the creation of famous Jewish conductor Daniel Barenboim and prominent Palestinian writer Edward Said.

▲ Edward Said (left) and Daniel Barenboim talk about their orchestra, shown above.

▲ Palestinian and Israeli campers bond at Seeds of Peace, located in Maine.

Peace Slips Away

In 1999, the slow and difficult peace negotiations between Israel and the Palestinians seemed to get a boost. Ehud Barak won election as Israeli prime minister. Many observers viewed him as a much stronger supporter of the peace plan than Netanyahu had been. The world community, led by the United States, was determined to take advantage of such a development.

In July of 2000, U.S. president Bill Clinton hosted a 15-day summit meeting at Camp David between Ehud Barak and Yasir Arafat. The two men, however, could not reach a compromise, and the peace plan once again stalled. Just two months later an Israeli political leader, Ariel Sharon, visited a Jewish holy place, the Temple Mount in Jerusalem. The Temple Mount is also the location of one of the most holy places for Muslims, The Dome of the Rock. Sharon's visit to the vicinity of such a revered Muslim site outraged Palestinians. A day later, riots broke out and a second intifada was launched.

The Conflict Intensifies The second intifada began much like the first with demonstrations, attacks on Israeli soldiers, and rock throwing by unarmed teenagers. But this time the Palestinian militant groups increasingly used suicide bombers. Their attacks on Jewish settlements in occupied territories and on civilian locations throughout Israel significantly raised the level of bloodshed. In the first 17 months of the uprising, one Israeli died for every three Palestinians, a rate much higher than during the first intifada.

In response to the uprising, Israeli forces moved into Palestinian refugee camps and clamped down on militants. Troops destroyed buildings in which they suspected extremists were hiding and bulldozed entire areas of Palestinian towns and camps. The Israeli army even bombed Arafat's headquarters, trapping him inside his compound for many days.

In recent years, peace between these two bitter enemies has seemed farther away than ever. In 2001, Ariel Sharon was elected Israeli prime minister. A former military leader, Sharon refused to negotiate with the Palestinians until attacks on Israelis stopped. Meanwhile, relations between Yasir Arafat and Israeli leaders grew so strained that Israeli officials declared they no longer would meet with the long-time leader of the PLO.

▲ A U.S. magazine cover highlights America's involvement in the Middle East crisis.

Working Toward a Solution Despite all this, peace efforts continue. Under intense pressure from the world community, Arafat agreed to take a less prominent role in peace talks with Israel. In early 2003, Palestinian leaders appointed their first-ever prime minister, high-ranking PLO official, Mahmoud Abbas. In his new position, Abbas became the main negotiator for the Palestinian side. Shortly afterward, U.S. president George W. Bush brought together Sharon and Abbas to begin working on a new peace plan known as the "road map."

The two men appeared committed to reaching an agreement. Abbas declared, "Our goal is two states, Israel and Palestine, living side by side in peace and security." Meanwhile, Sharon expressed his desire to see Palestinians "govern themselves in their own state." To be sure, many divisive issues remain between the two groups. With leaders from both sides willing to work together, however, hope remains that harmony will one day come to this region.

NEW YORK CORE CURRICULUM REVIEW

TERMS & NAMES 1. For each term or name, write a sentence explaining its significance.

- Anwar Sadat
- Golda Meir
- PLO
- Yasir Arafat
- Camp David Accords
- intifada
- Oslo Peace Accords

USING NOTES

2. Which event was most important? Why?

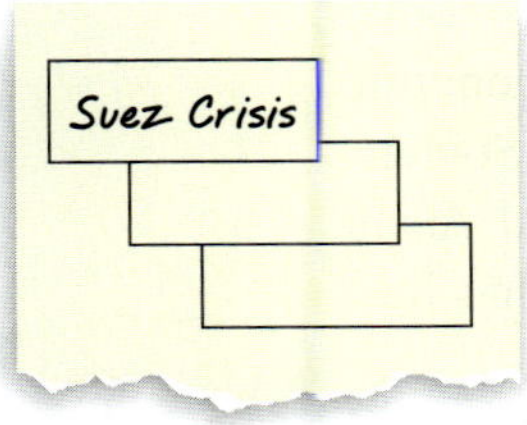

MAIN IDEAS

3. What historic claim do both Palestinians and Jews make to the land of Palestine?
4. What land did Israel gain from the wars against its Arab neighbors?
5. What were the terms of the Oslo Accords?

CRITICAL THINKING & WRITING

6. **COMPARING** How was the creation of Israel similar to the establishment of an independent India?
7. **DRAWING CONCLUSIONS** Why do you think all the Israeli-Palestinian accords ultimately have failed?
8. **ANALYZING ISSUES** Some have said that the Palestinian-Israeli conflict represents the struggle of right against right. Explain why you agree or disagree.
9. **WRITING ACTIVITY** POWER AND AUTHORITY In groups of three or four, create a list of ten **interview questions** for Gamal Abdel Nasser, Anwar Sadat, Yasir Arafat, Yitzhak Rabin, or a current leader of either Israel or Palestine.

CONNECT TO TODAY

DRAWING A POLITICAL CARTOON

Draw a **political cartoon** or other type of image that conveys your thoughts about the stalled peace effort today between Palestinians and Israelis.

Central Asia Struggles

CONNECT TO THE NEW YORK STATE CORE CURRICULUM

Unit 7.F.9. Islamic fundamentalism (Iran, Libya, Afghanistan, Algeria, Turkey)
Unit 8.A.4.b. Middle East (Saudi Arabia, Egypt, Afghanistan, and Algeria)

TERMS & NAMES

- Transcaucasian Republics
- Central Asian Republics
- mujahideen
- Taliban

SETTING THE STAGE For thousands of years, the different peoples of Central Asia suffered invasions and domination by powerful groups such as the Mongols, Byzantines, Ottomans, and finally the Communist rulers of the Soviet Union. While such occupation brought many changes to this region, its various ethnic groups worked to keep alive much of their culture. They also longed to create nations of their own, a dream they realized in the early 1990s with the collapse of the Soviet Union. In the decade since then, however, these groups have come to know the challenges of building strong and stable independent nations.

TAKING NOTES
Outlining Use an outline to organize main ideas and details.

Freedom Brings New Challenges
A.
B.
Afghanistan and the World
A.
B.

Freedom Brings New Challenges

In 1991 the Soviet Union collapsed, and the republics that it had conquered emerged as 15 independent nations. Among them were those that had made up the Soviet empire's southern borders. Geographers often group these new nations into two geographic areas.

Armenia, Azerbaijan, and Georgia make up the **Transcaucasian Republics**. These three nations lie in the Caucasus Mountains between the Black and Caspian seas. East of the Caspian Sea and extending to the Tian Shan and Pamir mountains lie the five nations known as the **Central Asian Republics**. They are Uzbekistan, Turkmenistan, Tajikistan, Kazakhstan, and Kyrgyzstan.

Economic Struggles Since gaining independence, these nations have struggled economically and are today some of the poorest countries in the world. Much of the problem stems from their heavy reliance on the Soviet Union for economic help. As a result, they have had a difficult time standing on their own. Economic practices during the Soviet era have created additional problems. The Soviets, for example, converted much of the available farmland in the Central Asian Republics to grow "white gold"—cotton. Dependence on a single crop has hurt the development of a balanced economy in these nations.

Azerbaijan, which is located among the oil fields of the Caspian Sea, has the best chance to build a solid economy based on the income from oil and oil products. Meanwhile, Kazakhstan and Turkmenistan are working hard to tap their large reserves of oil and natural gas.

Ethnic and Religious Strife Fighting among various ethnic and religious groups has created another obstacle to stability for many of the newly independent countries of Central Asia. The region is home to a number of different peoples, including some with long histories of hostility toward each other. With their iron-fisted rule, the Soviets kept a lid on these hostilities and largely prevented any serious ethnic clashes. After the breakup of the Soviet Union, however, long-simmering ethnic rivalries erupted into fighting. Some even became small regional wars.

Such was the case in Azerbaijan. Within this mostly Muslim country lies Nagorno-Karabakh, a small region of mainly Armenian Christians. In the wake of the Soviet Union's collapse, the people of this area declared their independence. Azerbaijan had no intention of letting go of this land, and fighting quickly broke out. Neighboring Armenia rushed to aid the Armenian people in the district. The war raged from 1991 through 1994, when the two sides agreed to a cease-fire. The status of Nagorno-Karabakh remains unresolved. **A**

MAIN IDEA

Clarifying

A Why was there little ethnic or religious strife in Central Asia during Soviet rule?

Afghanistan and the World

Just to the south of the Central Asian Republics lies one of the region's more prominent nations. Afghanistan is a small nation with both mountainous and desert terrain. It is one of the least-developed countries in the world, as most of its inhabitants are farmers or herders. And yet, over the past several decades, this mostly Muslim nation has grabbed the world's attention with two high-profile wars—one against the Soviet Union and the other against the United States.

Struggle for Freedom Afghanistan has endured a long history of struggle. During the 1800s, both Russia and Britain competed for control of its land. Russia wanted access to the Indian Ocean through Afghanistan, while Britain wanted control of the land in order to protect the northern borders of its Indian Empire. Britain fought three separate wars with the Afghanis before eventually leaving in 1919.

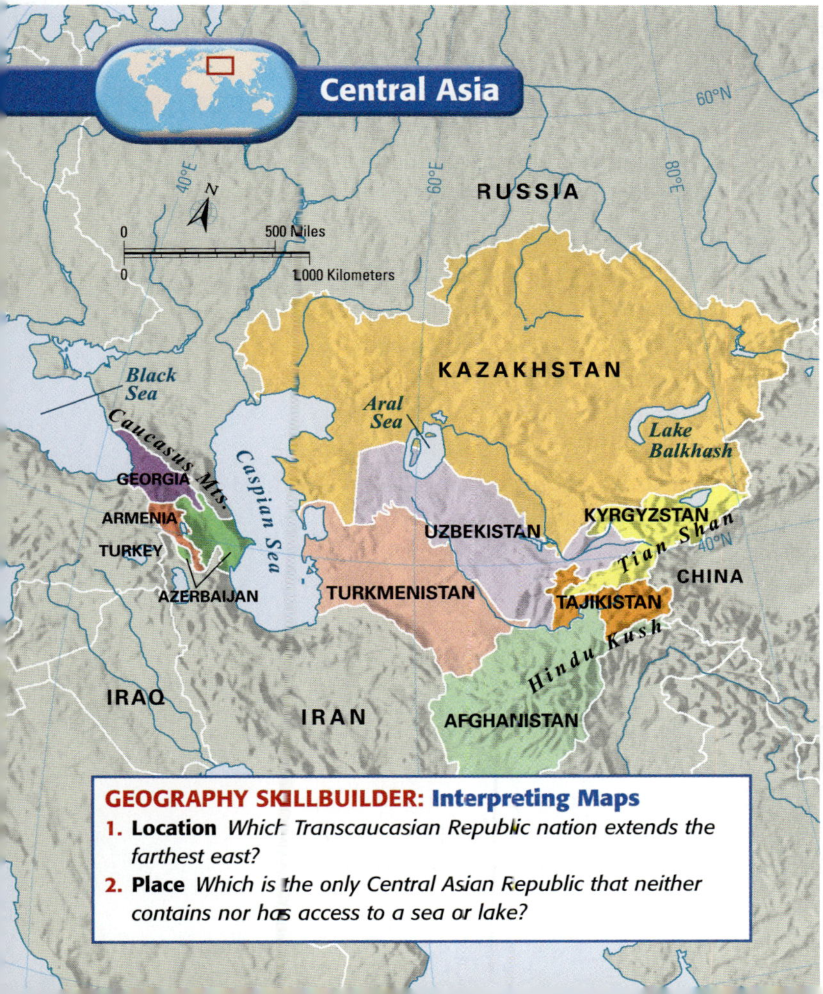

GEOGRAPHY SKILLBUILDER: Interpreting Maps

1. **Location** *Which Transcaucasian Republic nation extends the farthest east?*
2. **Place** *Which is the only Central Asian Republic that neither contains nor has access to a sea or lake?*

▼ The terrain of Central Asia varies widely, from mountains to plains.

That year, Afghanistan declared itself an independent nation and established a monarchy. The government implemented various reforms and tried to modernize the country. In 1964, the country devised a constitution that sought to establish a more democratic style of government. However, officials could not agree on a reform program and most people showed little interest in the effort to transform the government. As a result, a democratic system failed to develop.

Pushing Back the Soviets Nonetheless, Afghanistan had grown stable enough to establish good relations with many Western European nations and to hold its own on the world stage. When the Cold War conflict between the United States and Soviet Union broke out, Afghanistan chose to remain neutral. However, over the years, it received aid from both of the opposing superpowers.

Situated so close to the Soviet Union, however, Afghanistan could not hold out against the force of communism forever. In 1973, military leaders overthrew the government. Five years later, in 1978, a rival group with strong ties to the Soviet Union seized control of the country. Much of the population opposed the group and its strong association with communism. Many Afghanis felt that Communist policies conflicted with the teachings of Islam.

The opposition forces banded together to form a group known as the **mujahideen** (moo•JAH•heh•DEEN), or holy warriors. These rebels took up arms and fought fiercely against the Soviet-supported government. The rebellion soon prompted the Soviet Union to step in. In 1979 and 1980, Soviet troops rolled into Afghanistan to conquer the country and add it to their Communist empire.

With the Soviets' superior military force and advanced weaponry, the war had all the makings of a quick and lopsided affair. But the Afghan rebels used the land and guerrilla tactics to their advantage. In addition, the United States provided financial and military assistance. After nearly 10 years of bloody and fruitless fighting, the Soviet Union withdrew its troops. The Afghanis had taken on the world's Communist superpower and won. B

Rise and Fall of the Taliban With the Soviets gone, various Afghan rebel groups began battling each other for control of the country. A conservative Islamic group known as the **Taliban** emerged as the victor. By 1998, it controlled 90 percent of the country. Another rebel group, the Northern Alliance, held the northwest corner of the country. Observers initially viewed the Taliban as a positive force, as it brought order to the war-torn nation, rooted out corruption, and promoted the growth of business.

However, the group followed an extreme interpretation of Islamic law and applied it to nearly every aspect of Afghan society. Taliban leaders restricted women's lives by forbidding them to go to school or hold jobs. They banned everything from television and movies to modern music. Punishment for violating the rules included severe beatings, amputation, and even execution.

Even more troubling to the world community was the Taliban's role in the growing problem of world terrorism, which you will read more about in Chapter 36. Western

MAIN IDEA

Drawing Conclusions

B Why do you think the Soviets finally decided to leave Afghanistan?

History *in* Depth

Destroying the Past

Among the Taliban's extreme policies that stemmed from their interpretation of Islam, one in particular shocked and angered historians around the world. In the years after gaining power, Taliban leaders destroyed some of Afghanistan's most prized artifacts—two centuries-old Buddhas carved out of cliffs.

The Taliban deemed the giant statues offensive to Islam. Ignoring pleas from scholars and museums, they demolished the ancient figures with dynamite and bombs. One of the two statues was thought to have dated back to the third century A.D.

INTEGRATED TECHNOLOGY

INTERNET ACTIVITY Choose a country and highlight its top archaeological treasures. Go to **classzone.com** for your research.

leaders accused the Taliban of allowing terrorist groups to train in Afghanistan. The Taliban also provided refuge for terrorist leaders, including Osama bin Laden, whose al-Qaeda organization is thought to be responsible for numerous attacks on the West—including the attacks on the World Trade Center in New York and the Pentagon in Washington, D.C., on September 11, 2001.

In the wake of the September 11 attacks, the U.S. government demanded that the Taliban turn over bin Laden. After its leaders refused, the United States took military action. In October 2001, U.S. forces began bombing Taliban air defense, airfields, and command centers, as well as al-Qaeda training camps. On the ground, the United States provided assistance to anti-Taliban forces, such as the Northern Alliance. By December, the United States had driven the Taliban from power.

▲ In the Afghanistan elections, the ballot included photographs of the candidates and symbols for each party to help voters who could not read.

Challenges Ahead With the Taliban defeated, Afghan officials selected a new government under the leadership of Hamid Karzai. Later, in 2004, he was elected president for a five-year term. His government faces the task of rebuilding a country that has endured more than two decades of warfare. What's more, Afghanistan remains a country of roughly a dozen ethnic groups with distinct language and cultural patterns, all of which makes the job of creating a unified nation a difficult one.

The challenge before Afghanistan, however, is neither unique nor new. As you will read in the next chapter, over the past 50 years countries around the world have attempted to shed their old and often repressive forms of rule and implement a more democratic style of government.

NEW YORK CORE CURRICULUM REVIEW

TERMS & NAMES 1. For each term or name, write a sentence explaining its significance.

- Transcaucasian Republics
- Central Asian Republics
- mujahideen
- Taliban

USING YOUR NOTES

2. Which challenge for the Central Asian nations is most difficult to overcome?

Freedom Brings New Challenges
A.
B.
Afghanistan and the World
A.
B.

MAIN IDEA

3. What countries make up the Transcaucasian Republics? the Central Asian Republics?
4. Why did Afghanis oppose the notion of Communist rule?
5. Why did the United States take military action against the Taliban?

CRITICAL THINKING & WRITING

6. **MAKING INFERENCES** Some historians call the Soviet-Afghan war the Soviet Union's "Vietnam." What do they mean by this reference? Do you agree with it?
7. **DRAWING CONCLUSIONS** Why might Afghanis have been willing to accept Taliban rule by 1998?
8. **IDENTIFYING PROBLEMS** Why did the new nations of Central Asia experience such economic difficulties?
9. **WRITING ACTIVITY** POWER AND AUTHORITY Imagine you are a speechwriter for Hamid Karzai. Write what you feel would be an appropriate **first paragraph** for his initial speech upon taking power.

CONNECT TO TODAY **CREATING A TIME LINE**

Choose one of the countries discussed in this section and create a **time line** of the eight to ten most significant events in its history over the last 50 years.

Chapter 34 Assessment

VISUAL SUMMARY

The Struggle for Independence

The time line shows the dates on which various countries in Asia and Africa achieved their independence after World War II. It also shows (in parentheses) the countries from which they achieved independence.

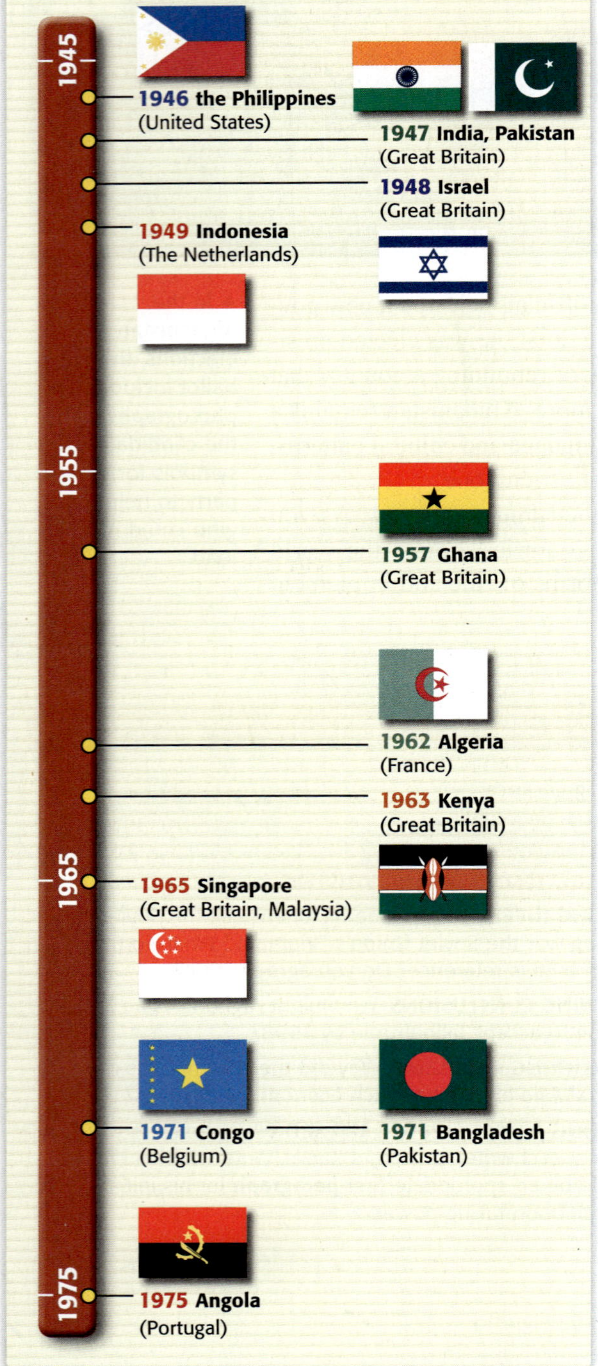

TERMS & NAMES

For each term or name below, briefly explain its connection to colonial independence around the world after World War II.

1. partition
2. Jawaharlal Nehru
3. Indira Gandhi
4. Corazón Aquino
5. Jomo Kenyatta
6. Anwar Sadat
7. PLO
8. mujahideen

MAIN IDEAS

The Indian Subcontinent Achieves Freedom
Section 1 (pages 997–1003)

9. What two nations emerged from the British colony of India in 1947?
10. Briefly explain the reason for the civil disorder in Sri Lanka.

Southeast Asian Nations Gain Independence
Section 2 (pages 1004–1011)

11. What were some concerns the Filipinos had regarding the Bell Act?
12. Who was Sukarno?

New Nations in Africa Section 3 (pages 1012–1016)

13. Why were Kwame Nkrumah's politics criticized?
14. Why did Zaire face such difficulty upon gaining independence?

Conflicts in the Middle East Section 4 (pages 1017–1023)

15. What was the Suez Crisis?
16. What were the Camp David Accords?

Central Asia Struggles Section 5 (pages 1024–1027)

17. Which nations comprise the Transcaucasian Republics?
18. What was the Taliban?

CRITICAL THINKING

1. USING YOUR NOTES

Use a web diagram to show some of the challenges that newly independent nations have faced.

2. FORMING AND SUPPORTING OPINIONS

REVOLUTION Do you think there should be a limit to the methods revolutionaries use? Explain your opinion.

3. ANALYZING ISSUES

ECONOMICS Why have so many of the new nations that emerged over the past half-century struggled economically?

4. DRAWING CONCLUSIONS

In your view, was religion a unifying or destructive force as colonies around the world became new nations? Support your answer with specific examples from the text.

Use the following excerpt from the Balfour Declaration and your knowledge of world history to answer questions 1 and 2.

Additional Test Practice, pp. S1–S33

PRIMARY SOURCE

His Majesty's Government view with favour the establishment in Palestine of a national home for the Jewish people, and will use their best endeavours to facilitate the achievement of this object, it being clearly understood that nothing shall be done which may prejudice the civil and religious rights of existing non-Jewish communities in Palestine, or the rights and political status enjoyed by Jews in any other country.

ARTHUR JAMES BALFOUR, in a letter to Lord Rothschild, November 2, 1917

1 The intent of the British government was to

(1) give all of Palestine to the Jewish people
(2) leave Palestine in the hands of the Arabs
(3) divide Palestine between Jews and Arabs
(4) ensure justice for Jews around the world

2 The group most likely to have opposed the Balfour Declaration was the

(1) Arabs
(2) Jews
(3) French
(4) Americans

Use the political cartoon about Corazón Aquino's election victory and your knowledge of world history to answer question 3.

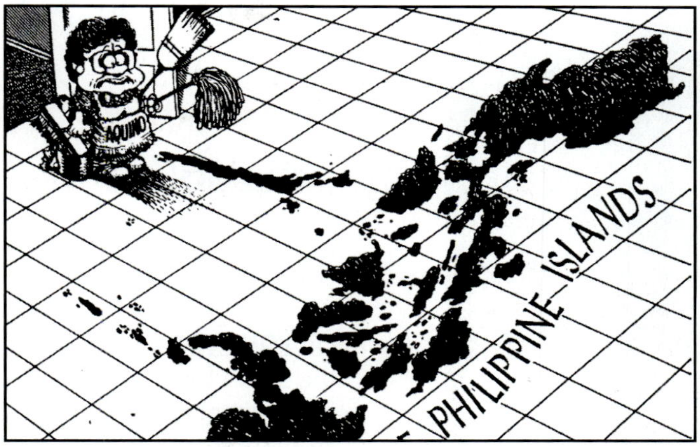

3 Aquino was expected by many to "clean up" the Philippines by ending years of

(1) slavery
(2) dictatorship
(3) business corruption
(4) unchecked pollution

INTEGRATED TECHNOLOGY

TEST PRACTICE Go to **classzone.com**

- Diagnostic tests
- Tutorials
- Strategies
- Additional practice

ALTERNATIVE ASSESSMENT

1. Interact *with* History

On page 996, you discussed the most important areas to address in building a new nation. Now that you have read about the efforts by so many former colonies to forge new countries, do you think that you focused on the right areas? Work as a class to identify the main factors that determine whether a new nation struggles or thrives. Be sure to cite specific examples from the text.

2. WRITING ABOUT HISTORY

POWER AND AUTHORITY Select one of the leaders discussed in this chapter. Review the decisions the leader made while in power. Write an evaluation of the leader's decisions and his or her impact on the country. Consider the following

- the leader's views on government and democracy
- the leader's handling of the economy
- the leader's accomplishments and failures

INTEGRATED TECHNOLOGY

Creating a Database

Use the Internet, library, and other reference materials to create a database showing the economic growth of any four countries discussed in this chapter. Create one table for each country, with column headings for each measure of economic growth you chose to record and row headings for each 10-year period. Then insert the most current data you can find. Consider the following questions to get started.

- What statistics will be most useful in making comparisons between nations?
- Which nations have capitalist economies? What other types of economies did you discover?
- Which nations have "one crop" economies?

CHAPTER **35**

Struggles for Democracy, 1945–Present

NEW YORK CORE CURRICULUM FOCUS

- Nations in Latin America and Africa have faced many challenges in establishing stable democracies.
- Democratic and economic reforms led to the collapse of the Soviet Union in 1991.

Previewing Main Ideas

ECONOMICS Many nations, such as Brazil, Poland, Russia, and China, discovered that economic stability is important for democratic progress.

Geography *Which type of government seems to predominate in the Western Hemisphere?*

REVOLUTION In 1989, revolutions overthrew Communist governments in the Soviet Union and Central and Eastern Europe. In China, the Communist government and the army put down a student protest calling for democracy.

Geography *Which two countries in the Eastern Hemisphere are still Communist?*

CULTURAL INTERACTION Chinese students imported democratic ideas from the West. Democratic reforms spread across Central and Eastern Europe, causing Communist governments to fall.

Geography *Which type of government predominates in the labeled countries of Europe?*

INTEGRATED TECHNOLOGY

eEdition
- Interactive Maps
- Interactive Visuals
- Interactive Primary Sources

INTERNET RESOURCES

Go to **classzone.com** for:
- Research Links
- Internet Activities
- Primary Sources
- Chapter Quiz
- Maps
- Test Practice
- Current Events

WORLD

1948 South Africa imposes apartheid policy of racial discrimination.

1959 ◀ Fidel Castro seizes power in Cuba.

1967 Nigerian civil war begins.

1945 **1965**

USA

1948 Harry Truman wins second term as president. ▶

1964 Congress authorizes President Johnson to send troops to Vietnam.

1969 Neil Armstrong wal on the moon in firs lunar landing.

Types of Government, 2003

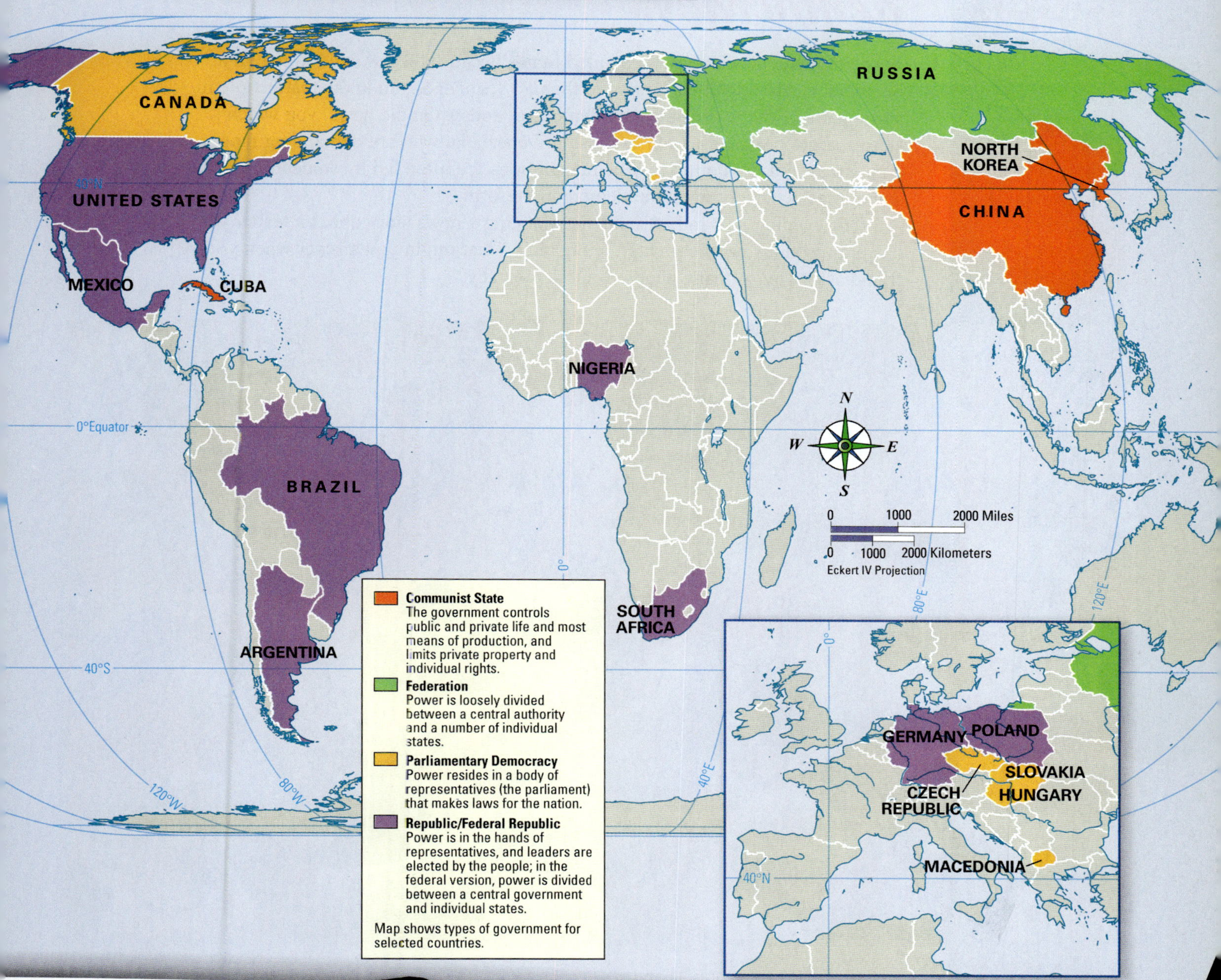

1978
Deng Xiaoping begins economic reforms in China. ▶

1989
Berlin Wall comes down.

1994
South Africa holds its first multiracial election.

1985

200

1980
◀ Ronald Reagan elected president.

1988
George Bush elected president.

1992
Bill Clinton elected president.

2000
George W. Bush elected president.

Interact *with* History

Why do so many people want democracy?

Your grandparents came to the United States because they wanted to live in a democracy. Although that was more than 50 years ago, you know that people in many parts of the world still seek democracy today. On the news, you watch stories about protesters, such as those in Venezuela, who are demanding more democracy and freedom. Their demonstrations are often led by students and sometimes help to bring about democratic reform.

One evening you and a friend are watching a news story about a leader who has promised his people greater democracy. What might you answer when your friend asks why so many people want democracy?

Protesters march in Caracas, Venezuela, in opposition to the policies of President Hugo Chávez.

EXAMINING *the* ISSUES

- **What rights and institutions are necessary for a government to be democratic?**
- **How do citizens participate in a democracy? How can participation be encouraged?**

Discuss these questions in class and list important points on the board. For your discussion, consider what you know about democracy in ancient Greece and in the United States. As you read this chapter, think about the challenges many countries face in trying to develop democratic systems.

1

Democracy

Case Study: Latin American Democracies

CONNECT TO THE NEW YORK STATE CORE CURRICULUM

Unit 8.A.4.d. Latin America
Unit 8.B.1.b. Latin America

TERMS & NAMES

- Brasília
- land reform
- standard of living
- recession
- PRI

SETTING THE STAGE By definition, democracy is government by the people. Direct democracy, in which all citizens meet to pass laws, is not practical for nations. Therefore, democratic nations developed indirect democracies, or republics, in which citizens elect representatives to make laws for them. For example, the United States is a republic. But democracy is more than a form of government. It is also a way of life and an ideal goal. A democratic way of life includes practices such as free and open elections.

TAKING NOTES

Summarizing Use a chart to sum up the steps Brazil, Mexico, and Argentina have taken toward democracy.

Nation	Steps toward democracy
Brazil	
Mexico	
Argentina	

Democracy As a Goal

The chart below lists four practices in a democracy, together with conditions that help these democratic practices succeed. Many nations follow these practices to a large degree. However, establishing democracy is a process that takes years.

Even in the United States, the establishment of democracy has taken time. Although the principle of equality is part of the Constitution, many Americans have struggled for equal rights. To cite one example, women did not receive the right to vote until 1920. Democracy is always a "work in progress."

Making Democracy Work

Common Practices	Conditions That Foster Those Practices
• Free elections	• Having more than one political party • Universal suffrage—all adult citizens can vote
• Citizen participation	• High levels of education and literacy • Economic security • Freedoms of speech, press, and assembly
• Majority rule, minority rights	• All citizens equal before the law • Shared national identity • Protection of such individual rights as freedom of religion • Representatives elected by citizens to carry out their will
• Constitutional government	• Clear body of traditions and laws on which government is-based • Widespread education about how government works • National acceptance of majority decisions • Shared belief that no one is above the law

Democratic institutions may not ensure stable, civilian government if other conditions are not present. The participation of a nation's citizens in government is essential to democracy. Education and literacy—the ability to read and write—give citizens the tools they need to make political decisions. Also, a stable economy with a strong middle class and opportunities for advancement helps democracy. It does so by giving citizens a stake in the future of their nation. **A**

MAIN IDEA

Making Inferences

A Why would democracy suffer if citizens didn't participate?

Other conditions advance democracy. First, a firm belief in the rights of the individual promotes the fair and equal treatment of citizens. Second, rule by law helps prevent leaders from abusing power without fear of punishment. Third, a sense of national identity helps encourage citizens to work together for the good of the nation.

The struggle to establish democracy continued into the 21st century as many nations abandoned authoritarian rule for democratic institutions. However, a United Nations study released in July 2002 warned that the spread of democracy around the world could be derailed if free elections in poor countries are not followed by economic growth. The UN Development Program's annual report warned particularly about Latin America.

CASE STUDY: Brazil

Dictators and Democracy

Many Latin American nations won their independence from Spain and Portugal in the early 1800s. However, three centuries of colonial rule left many problems. These included powerful militaries, economies that were too dependent on a single crop, and large gaps between rich and poor. These patterns persisted in the modern era.

After gaining independence from Portugal in 1822, Brazil became a monarchy. This lasted until 1889, when Brazilians established a republican government, which a wealthy elite controlled. Then, in the 1930s, Getulio Vargas became dictator. Vargas suppressed political opposition. At the same time, however, he promoted economic growth and helped turn Brazil into a modern industrial nation.

Kubitschek's Ambitious Program After Vargas, three popularly elected presidents tried to steer Brazil toward democracy. Juscelino Kubitschek (zhoo•suh•LEE•nuh KOO•bih•chehk), who governed from 1956 to 1961, continued to develop Brazil's economy. Kubitschek encouraged foreign investment to help pay for development projects. He built a new capital city, **Brasília** (bruh•ZIHL•yuh), in the country's interior. Kubitschek's dream proved expensive. The nation's foreign debt soared and inflation shot up.

Kubitschek's successors proposed reforms to ease economic and social problems. Conservatives resisted this strongly. They especially opposed the plan for **land reform**—breaking up large estates and distributing that land to peasants. In 1964, with the blessing of wealthy Brazilians, the army seized power in a military coup. **B**

MAIN IDEA

Analyzing Motives

B Why might the wealthy have preferred military rule to land reform?

Military Dictators For two decades military dictators ruled Brazil. Emphasizing economic growth, the generals fostered foreign investment. They began huge development projects in the Amazon jungle. The economy boomed.

The boom had a downside, though. The government froze wages and cut back on social programs. This caused a decline in the **standard of living**, or level of material comfort, which is judged by the amount of goods people have. When Brazilians protested, the government imposed censorship. It also jailed, tortured, and sometimes killed government critics. Nevertheless, opposition to military rule continued to grow.

The Road to Democracy By the early 1980s, a **recession**, or slowdown in the economy, gripped Brazil. At that point, the generals decided to open up the political system. They allowed direct elections of local, state, and national officials.

GEOGRAPHY SKILLBUILDER: Interpreting Maps

1. **Location** *Which country—Argentina, Brazil, or Mexico—spans the equator?*
2. **Region** *Which one of the three countries has a coast on the Caribbean Sea?*

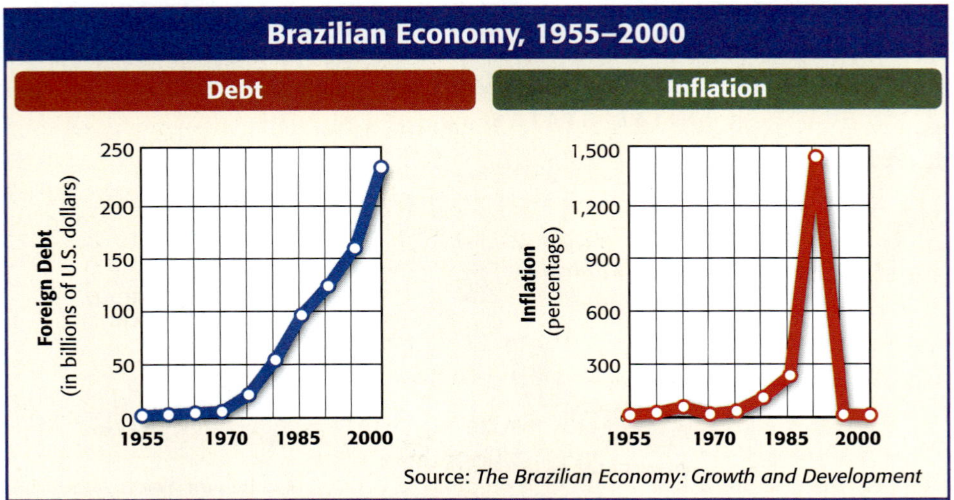

SKILLBUILDER: Interpreting Graphs

1. **Clarifying** *By how much did Brazil's foreign debt increase from 1955 to 2000?*
2. **Comparing** *Of the years shown on the line graph, which was the worst year for inflation?*

In 1985, a new civilian president, José Sarney (zhoh•ZAY SAHR•nay), took office. Sarney inherited a country in crisis because of foreign debt and inflation. He proved unable to solve the country's problems and lost support. The next elected president fared even worse. He resigned because of corruption charges. **C**

In 1994 and again in 1998, Brazilians elected Fernando Henrique Cardoso, who achieved some success in tackling the nation's economic and political problems. Although trained as a Marxist scholar, Cardoso became a strong advocate of free markets. One of his main concerns was the widening income gap in Brazil. He embarked on a program to promote economic reform.

MAIN IDEA

Analyzing Issues

C In your opinion, which of the problems faced by Sarney was worse? Explain.

The 2002 Presidential Election In the presidential election of October 2002, Cardoso's handpicked successor to lead his centrist coalition was José Serra. Serra faced two candidates who proposed a sharp break with Cardoso's pro-business policies. These candidates included Luiz Inácio Lula da Silva, a candidate of the leftist Workers Party.

An economic crisis hit many countries in South America, including Brazil, in 2002. Because of stalled economic growth, rising unemployment, and poverty, there was a backlash against free-market economic policies. This made the election of 2002 a close contest. Da Silva, the leftist candidate, won the hotly disputed election, defeating the ruling party candidate, Serra. Da Silva has proved a more moderate president than his supporters and opponents had expected. Although Brazil faces many challenges, it continues on the path of democracy.

CASE STUDY: Mexico

One-Party Rule

Unlike Brazil, Mexico enjoyed relative political stability for most of the 20th century. Following the Mexican Revolution, the government passed the Constitution of 1917. The new constitution outlined a democracy and promised reforms.

Beginnings of One-Party Domination From 1920 to 1934, Mexico elected several generals as president. However, these men did not rule as military dictators. They did create a ruling party—the National Revolutionary Party, which dominated Mexico under various names for the rest of the 20th century.

From 1934 to 1940, President Lázaro Cárdenas (KAHR•day•nahs) tried to improve life for peasants and workers. He carried out land reform and promoted labor rights. He nationalized the Mexican oil industry, kicking out foreign oil companies and creating a state-run oil industry. After Cárdenas, however, a series of more conservative presidents turned away from reform.

The Party Becomes the PRI In 1946, the main political party changed its name to the Institutional Revolutionary Party, or **PRI**. In the half-century that followed, the PRI became the main force for political stability in Mexico.

Although stable, the government was an imperfect democracy. The PRI controlled the congress and won every presidential election. The government allowed opposition parties to compete, but fraud and corruption tainted the elections.

Even as the Mexican economy rapidly developed, Mexico continued to suffer severe economic problems. Lacking land and jobs, millions of Mexicans struggled for survival. In addition, a huge foreign debt forced the government to spend money on interest payments. Two episodes highlighted Mexico's growing difficulties. In the late 1960s, students and workers began calling for economic and political change. On October 2, 1968, protesters gathered at the site of an ancient Aztec market in Mexico City. Soldiers hidden in the ruins opened fire on the protesters. The massacre claimed several hundred lives.

MAIN IDEA

Recognizing Effects

D Why does overreliance on one product weaken an economy?

A second critical episode occurred during the early 1980s. By that time, huge new oil and natural gas reserves had been discovered in Mexico. The economy had become dependent on oil and gas exports. In 1981, world oil prices fell, cutting Mexico's oil and gas revenues in half. Mexico went into an economic decline. **D**

Economic and Political Crises The 1980s and 1990s saw Mexico facing various crises. In 1988, opposition parties challenged the PRI in national elections. The PRI candidate, Carlos Salinas, won the presidency. Even so, opposition parties won seats in the congress and began to force a gradual opening of the political system.

> Analyzing Political Cartoons

Military Rule and Democracy

Throughout the 20th century, many Latin American countries were ruled by military dictators or political bosses. Most typically, the dictator's support came from the wealthy and the military. But sometimes the dictator's support came from the people.

"My goodness, if I'd known how badly you wanted democracy I'd have given it to you ages ago."

SKILLBUILDER:
Interpreting Visual Sources

1. **Drawing Conclusions** *Do dictators typically take into account the opinions of the people they rule?*
2. **Making Inferences** *What does this cartoon suggest about the dictator's attitude toward the opinion of the people he rules?*

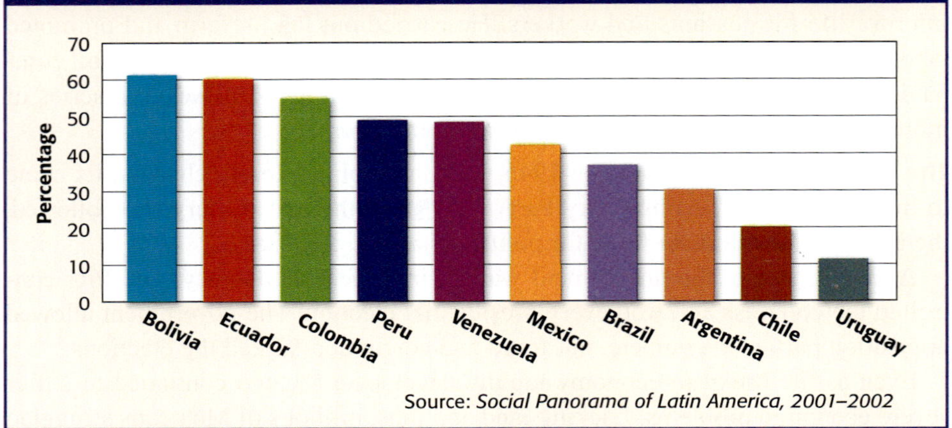

SKILLBUILDER: Interpreting Graphs

1. **Comparing** *In which three countries of Latin America is the percentage of people living in poverty the lowest?*
2. **Comparing** *In which three countries is the poverty rate highest?*

During his presidency, Salinas signed NAFTA, the North American Free Trade Agreement. NAFTA removed trade barriers between Mexico, the United States, and Canada. In early 1994, peasant rebels in the southern Mexican state of Chiapas (chee•AH•pahs) staged a major uprising. Shortly afterward, a gunman assassinated Luis Donaldo Colosio, the PRI presidential candidate for the upcoming election.

The PRI Loses Control After these events, Mexicans grew increasingly concerned about the prospects for democratic stability. Nevertheless, the elections of 1994 went ahead. The new PRI candidate, Ernesto Zedillo (zuh•DEE•yoh), won. Opposition parties continued to challenge the PRI.

In 1997, two opposition parties each won a large number of congressional seats, denying the PRI control of congress. Then, in 2000, Mexican voters ended 71 years of PRI rule by electing center-right candidate Vicente Fox as president.

▲ President Vicente Fox of Mexico

New Policies and Programs Fox's agenda was very ambitious. He advocated reforming the police, rooting out political corruption, ending the rebellion in Chiapas, and opening up Mexico's economy to free-market forces.

Fox also argued that the United States should legalize the status of millions of illegal Mexican immigrant workers. Fox hoped that a negotiated agreement between the United States and Mexico would provide amnesty for these undocumented Mexican workers in the United States. In the wake of the terrorist attacks of September 11, 2001, any such agreement appeared remote. However, in 2002, Fox created a cabinet-level agency to lobby for the interests of Mexico's 22 million citizens who lived abroad, a great many of whom lived in the United States. In the meantime, Mexico's democracy continued to strengthen.

CASE STUDY: Argentina

Political and Economic Disorder

Mexico and Brazil were not the only Latin American countries where democracy had made progress. By the late 1990s, most of Latin America was under democratic rule.

Perón Rules Argentina Argentina had struggled to establish democracy. It was a major exporter of grain and beef. It was also an industrial nation with a large working class. In 1946, Argentine workers supported an army officer, Juan Perón, who won the presidency and then established a dictatorship.

Vocabulary
welfare state: a government that tries to provide for all its citizens' needs–including health, education, and employment

Perón did not rule alone. He received critical support from his wife, Eva—known as Evita to the millions of Argentines who idolized her. Together, the Peróns created a welfare state. The state offered social programs with broad popular appeal but limited freedoms. After Eva's death in 1952, Perón's popularity declined and his enemies—the military and the Catholic Church—moved against him. In 1955, the military ousted Perón and drove him into exile.

▲ Eva Perón

Repression in Argentina-For many years, the military essentially controlled Argentine politics. Perón returned to power once more, in 1973, but ruled for only a year before dying in office. By the mid-1970s, Argentina was in chaos.

In 1976, the generals seized power again. They established a brutal dictatorship and hunted down political opponents. For several years, torture and murder were everyday events. By the early 1980s, several thousand Argentines had simply disappeared, kidnapped by their own government.

MAIN IDEA
Analyzing Causes
E What finally caused military rule to end in Argentina?

Democracy and the Economy In 1982, the military government went to war with Britain over the nearby Falkland Islands and suffered a defeat. Disgraced, the generals agreed to step down. In 1983, Argentines elected Raúl Alfonsín (ahl•fohn•SEEN) president in the country's first free election in 37 years. E

During the 1980s, Alfonsín worked to rebuild democracy and the economy. Carlos Menem gained the presidency in 1989 and continued the process. He attempted to stabilize the currency and privatize industry. By the late 1990s, however, economic problems intensified as the country lived beyond its means.

A Growing Crisis In December 2001, the International Monetary Fund (IMF) refused to provide financial aid to Argentina. Then President Fernando de la Rua resigned in the face of protests over the economy. He was succeeded by Eduardo Duhalde, who tried to deal with the economic and social crisis. In 2002, Argentina had an unemployment rate of about 24 percent. The country defaulted on $132 billion in debt, the largest debt default in history, and devalued its currency. In 2003, Argentina struggled to regain its political and economic footing. In elections that year, Nestor Kirchner became the new president of Argentina.

NEW YORK CORE CURRICULUM REVIEW

TERMS & NAMES 1. For each term or name, write a sentence explaining its significance.
- Brasília
- land reform
- standard of living
- recession
- PRI

USING YOUR NOTES

2. Which country do you think has made the most progress? Explain.

Nation	Steps toward democracy
Brazil	
Mexico	
Argentina	

MAIN IDEAS

3. What role did the military play in shaping the economy of Brazil?
4. What were some of the positive benefits of one-party rule in Mexico?
5. What effect did the Falklands war have on the military government in Argentina?

CRITICAL THINKING & WRITING

6. **COMPARING AND CONTRASTING** Compare and contrast the roles of the military in the governments of Brazil, Mexico, and Argentina.
7. **SYNTHESIZING** What have been some of the obstacles to democracy in Latin America?
8. **DEVELOPING HISTORICAL PERSPECTIVE** What are some of the attributes of democracy?
9. **WRITING ACTIVITY** ECONOMICS What might be the effect of a welfare state (such as that created in Argentina by the Peróns) on a nation's economy? Support your opinions in a two-paragraph **essay.**

CONNECT TO TODAY **MAKING A GRAPH**
Research the economies of Mexico, Brazil, and Argentina to determine which is doing the best. Present your findings in a **graph.**

2

The Challenge of Democracy in Africa

CONNECT TO THE NEW YORK STATE CORE CURRICULUM

Unit 7.E.3.d. Ethnic tensions versus nationalism: Nigeria and civil war
Unit 7.E.3.e.3. Leadership–Nelson Mandela, Desmond Tutu, F.W. de Klerk

TERMS & NAMES

- federal system
- martial law
- dissident
- apartheid
- Nelson Mandela

SETTING THE STAGE-Beginning in the late 1950s, dozens of European colonies in Africa gained their independence and became nations. As in Latin America, the establishment of democracy in Africa proved difficult. In many cases, the newly independent nations faced a host of problems that slowed their progress toward democracy. The main reason for Africa's difficulties was the negative impact of colonial rule. European powers had done little to prepare their African colonies for independence.

TAKING NOTES

Comparing Use a Venn diagram to compare political events in Nigeria and South Africa.

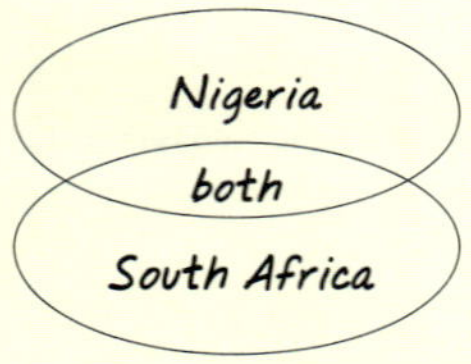

Colonial Rule Limits Democracy

The lingering effects of colonialism undermined efforts to build stable, democratic economies and states. This can be seen throughout Africa.

European Policies Cause Problems When the Europeans established colonial boundaries, they ignored existing ethnic or cultural divisions. New borders divided peoples of the same background or threw different—often rival—groups together. Because of this, a sense of national identity was difficult to develop. After independence, the old colonial boundaries became the borders of the newly independent states. As a result, ethnic and cultural conflicts remained.

Other problems had an economic basis. European powers had viewed colonies as sources of wealth for the home country. The colonial powers encouraged the export of one or two cash crops, such as coffee or rubber, rather than the production of a range of products to serve local needs. Europeans developed plantations and mines but few factories. Manufactured goods were imported from European countries. These policies left new African nations with unbalanced economies and a small middle class. Such economic problems lessened their chances to create democratic stability.

European rule also disrupted African family and community life. In some cases, colonial powers moved Africans far from their families and villages to work in mines or on plantations. In addition, most newly independent nations still lacked a skilled, literate work force that could take on the task of building a new nation.

Short-Lived Democracies When Britain and France gave up their colonies, they left fragile democratic governments in place. Soon problems threatened those governments. Rival ethnic groups often fought for power. Strong militaries became tools for ambitious leaders. In many cases, a military dictatorship replaced democracy.

GEOGRAPHY SKILLBUILDER: Interpreting Maps

1. **Region** *Describe the Eastern Region, which seceded as Biafra. Describe its size and location compared to the rest of Nigeria.*
2. **Location** *In which region is Lagos, Nigeria's capital in 1967?*

Civil War in Nigeria

Nigeria, a former British colony, won its independence peacefully in 1960. Nigeria is Africa's most populous country and one of its richest. However, the country was ethnically divided. This soon created problems that led to war.

A Land of Many Peoples Three major ethnic groups live within Nigeria's borders. In the north are the Hausa-Fulani, who are mostly Muslim. In the south are the Yoruba and the Igbo (also called Ibo), who are mostly Christians, Muslims, or animists, who believe that spirits are present in animals, plants, and natural objects. The Yoruba, a farming people with a tradition of kings, live to the west. The Igbo, a farming people who have a democratic tradition, live to the east.

After independence, Nigeria adopted a **federal system**. In a federal system, power is shared between state governments and a central authority. The Nigerians set up three states, one for each region and ethnic group, with a political party in each.

War with Biafra Although one group dominated each state, the states also had ethnic minorities. In the Western Region, non-Yoruba minorities began to resent Yoruba control. In 1963, they tried to break away and form their own region. This led to fighting. In January 1966, a group of army officers, most of them Igbo, seized power in the capital city of Lagos. These officers abolished the regional governments and declared **martial law**, or temporary military rule.

The Hausa-Fulani, who did not trust the Igbo, launched an attack from the north. They persecuted and killed many Igbo. The survivors fled east. In 1967, the Eastern Region seceded from Nigeria, declaring itself the new nation of Biafra (bee•AF•ruh).

The Nigerian government then went to war to reunite the country. The Igbo were badly outnumbered and outgunned. In 1970, Biafra surrendered. Nigeria was reunited, but perhaps more than a million Igbo died, most from starvation. A

MAIN IDEA

Recognizing Effects

A What was the effect of the war on the Igbo?

Nigeria's Nation-Building

After the war, Nigerians returned to the process of nation-building. "When the war ended," noted one officer, "it was like a referee blowing a whistle in a football game. People just put down their guns and went back to the business of living." The Nigerian government did not punish the Igbo. It used federal money to rebuild the Igbo region.

Federal Government Restored The military governed Nigeria for most of the 1970s. During this time, Nigerian leaders tried to create a more stable federal system, with a strong central government and a number of regional units. The government also tried to build a more modern economy, based on oil income.

In 1979, the military handed power back to civilian rulers. Nigerians were cheered by the return to democracy. Some people, however, remained concerned about ethnic divisions in the nation. Nigerian democracy was short-lived. In 1983, the military overthrew the civilian government, charging it with corruption. A new military regime, dominated by the Hausa-Fulani, took charge.

A Return to Civilian Rule In the years that followed, the military governed Nigeria, while promising to bring back civilian rule. The army held elections in 1993, which resulted in the victory of popular leader Moshood Abiola. However, officers declared the results invalid, and a dictator, General Sani Abacha, took control.

General Abacha banned political activity and jailed **dissidents**, or government opponents. Upon Abacha's death in 1998, General Abdulsalami Abubakar seized power and promised to end military rule. He kept his word. In 1999, Nigerians elected their first civilian president, Olusegun Obasanjo, in nearly 20 years. In 2003, Obasanjo was reelected.

Analyzing Primary Sources

Ken Saro-Wiwa

On November 10, 1995, Nigeria hanged nine political prisoners—all critics of the military government. Many around the world believed the nine were convicted on false charges to silence them. One of the nine was Ken Saro-Wiwa, a noted writer and activist. Shortly before his death, Saro-Wiwa smuggled several manuscripts out of prison.

DOCUMENT-BASED QUESTIONS

1. **Drawing Conclusions** *What do Saro-Wiwa's imprisonment and execution suggest about the government of the military dictator, General Sani Abacha?*
2. **Making Inferences** *What seems to be Saro-Wiwa's attitude toward his persecutors?*

PRIMARY SOURCE

Injustice stalks the land like a tiger on the prowl. To be at the mercy of buffoons [fools] is the ultimate insult. To find the instruments of state power reducing you to dust is the injury. . . .

It is also very important that we have chosen the path of non-violent struggle. Our opponents are given to violence and we cannot meet them on their turf, even if we wanted to. Non-violent struggle offers weak people the strength which they otherwise would not have. The spirit becomes important, and no gun can silence that. I am aware, though, that non-violent struggle occasions more death than armed struggle. And that remains a cause for worry at all times. Whether the Ogoni people will be able to withstand the rigors of the struggle is yet to be seen. Again, their ability to do so will point the way of peaceful struggle to other peoples on the African continent. It is therefore not to be underrated.

KEN SARO-WIWA, *A Month and a Day: A Detention Diary*

President Obasanjo Obasanjo was an ethnic Yoruba from southwest Nigeria. As a critic of Nigerian military regimes, he had spent three years in jail (1995–1998) under Sani Abacha. As a former general, Obasanjo had the support of the military.

Obasanjo worked for a strong, unified Nigeria. He made some progress in his battle against corruption. He also attempted to draw the attention of the world to the need for debt relief for Nigeria. In May 2001, he called on President George W. Bush to support the canceling of Nigeria's $30 billion debt to the international community. Obasanjo saw debt relief as essential to the relief of hunger and the future of democracy in Nigeria and the rest of Africa.

Despite Obasanjo's efforts, Nigeria was still beset by a variety of problems. These included war, violence, corruption, poverty, and hunger. Nonetheless, Nigeria was increasing its oil exports and experiencing economic growth.

South Africa Under Apartheid

In South Africa, racial conflict was the result of colonial rule. From its beginnings under Dutch and British control, South Africa was racially divided. A small white minority ruled a large black majority. In 1910, South Africa gained self-rule as a dominion of the British Empire. In 1931, it became an independent member of the British Commonwealth. Although South Africa had a constitutional government, the constitution gave whites power and denied the black majority its rights.

Apartheid Segregates Society In 1948, the National Party came to power in South Africa. This party promoted Afrikaner, or Dutch South African, nationalism. It also instituted a policy of **apartheid**, complete separation of the races. The minority government banned social contacts between whites and blacks. It established segregated schools, hospitals, and neighborhoods.

In 1959, the minority government set up reserves, called homelands, for the country's major black groups. Blacks were forbidden to live in white areas unless they worked as servants or laborers for whites. The homelands policy was totally unbalanced. Although blacks made up about 75 percent of the population, the government set aside only 13 percent of the land for them. Whites kept the best land. B

MAIN IDEA

Making Inferences

B How did the policy of apartheid strengthen whites' hold on power?

Blacks Protest The blacks of South Africa resisted the controls imposed by the white minority. In 1912, they formed the African National Congress (ANC) to fight for their rights. The ANC organized strikes and boycotts to protest racist policies. The government banned the ANC and imprisoned many of its members. One was ANC leader **Nelson Mandela** (man•DEHL•uh).

The troubles continued. In 1976, riots over school policies broke out in the black township of Soweto, leaving about 600 students dead. In 1977, police beat popular protest leader Stephen Biko to death while he was in custody. As protests mounted, the government declared a nationwide state of emergency in 1986.

▼ A young South African poll worker helps an elderly man to vote in the first election open to citizens of all races.

Struggle for Democracy

By the late 1980s, South Africa was under great pressure to change. For years, a black South African bishop, Desmond Tutu, had led an economic campaign against apartheid. He asked foreign nations not to do business with South Africa. In response, many nations imposed trade restrictions. They also isolated South Africa in other ways, for example, by banning South Africa from the Olympic Games. (In 1984, Tutu won the Nobel Peace Prize for his nonviolent methods.) C

MAIN IDEA

Recognizing Effects

C How did Desmond Tutu help force South Africa to end apartheid?

The First Steps In 1989, white South Africans elected a new president, F. W. de Klerk. His goal was to transform South Africa and end its isolation. In February 1990, he legalized the ANC and also released Nelson Mandela from prison.

These dramatic actions marked the beginning of a new era in South Africa. Over the next 18 months, the South African parliament repealed apartheid laws that had segregated public facilities and restricted land ownership by blacks. World leaders welcomed these changes and began to ease restrictions on South Africa.

Although some legal barriers had fallen, others would remain until a new constitution was in place. First, the country needed to form a multiracial government. After lengthy negotiations, President de Klerk agreed to hold South Africa's first universal elections, in which people of all races could vote, in April 1994.

Majority Rule Among the candidates for president were F. W. de Klerk and Nelson Mandela. During the campaign, the Inkatha Freedom Party—a rival party to the ANC—threatened to disrupt the process. Nevertheless, the vote went smoothly. South Africans of all races peacefully waited at the polls in long lines. To no one's surprise, the ANC won 63 percent of the vote. They won 252 of 400 seats in the National Assembly (the larger of the two houses in Parliament). Mandela was elected president. Mandela stepped down in 1999, but the nation's democratic government continued.

A New Constitution In 1996, after much debate, South African lawmakers passed a new, more democratic constitution. It guaranteed equal rights for all citizens. The constitution included a bill of rights modeled on the U.S. Bill of Rights. The political changes that South Africa had achieved gave other peoples around the world great hope for the future of democracy.

South Africa Today In 1999, ANC official Thabo Mbeki won election as president in a peaceful transition of power. As Mbeki assumed office, he faced a number of serious challenges. These included high crime rates—South Africa's

History Makers

Nelson Mandela
1918–

Nelson Mandela has said that he first grew interested in politics when he heard elders in his village describe how freely his people lived before whites came. Inspired to help his people regain that freedom, Mandela trained as a lawyer and became a top official in the ANC. Convinced that apartheid would never end peacefully, he joined the armed struggle against white rule. For this, he was imprisoned for 27 years.

After his presidential victory, Mandela continued to work to heal his country.

F. W. de Klerk
1936–

Like Mandela, Frederik W. de Klerk also trained as a lawyer. Born to an Afrikaner family with close links to the National Party, de Klerk was elected to Parliament in 1972.

A firm party loyalist, de Klerk backed apartheid but was also open to reform. Friends say that his flexibility on racial issues stemmed from his relatively liberal religious background.

In 1993, de Klerk and Mandela were jointly awarded the Nobel Peace Prize for their efforts to bring democracy to South Africa.

INTEGRATED TECHNOLOGY

RESEARCH LINKS For more on Nelson Mandela and F. W. de Klerk, go to **classzone.com**

South Africa, 1948–2000

- **1948** National Party comes to power, passes apartheid laws
- **1959** Black homelands established
- **1960** Sharpeville Massacre, 69 protesters killed
- **1962** Nelson Mandela jailed
- **1976** 600 black students killed during Soweto protest
- **1977** Stephen Biko killed in police custody
- **1989** F. W. de Klerk elected president
- **1990** ANC legalized and Mandela released
- **1994** ANC wins 63% of the vote; Mandela elected president
- **1996** New constitution adopted
- **1999** ANC candidate Thabo Mbeki elected president

▲ This was South Africa's flag from 1927 to 1994.

▲ South Africa adopted this flag in 1994.

rape and murder rates were among the highest in the world. Unemployment stood at about 40 percent among South Africa's blacks, and about 60 percent lived below the poverty level. In addition, an economic downturn discouraged foreign investment.

Mbeki promoted a free-market economic policy to repair South Africa's infrastructure and to encourage foreign investors. In 2002, South Africa was engaged in negotiations to establish free-trade agreements with a number of countries around the world, including those of the European Union as well as Japan, Canada, and the United States. This was an attempt at opening the South African economy to foreign competition and investment, and promoting growth and employment.

One of the biggest problems facing South Africa was the AIDS epidemic. Some estimates concluded that 6 million South Africans were likely to die of AIDS by 2010. Mbeki disputed that AIDS was caused by HIV (human immunodeficiency virus). His opinion put South Africa at odds with the scientific consensus throughout the world. The *New York Times* stated that Mbeki was in danger of undermining "all his good work with his stance on AIDS."

In Section 3, you will read how democratic ideas changed another part of the world, the Communist Soviet Union.

NEW YORK CORE CURRICULUM REVIEW

TERMS & NAMES 1. For each term or name, write a sentence explaining its significance.

- federal system
- martial law
- dissident
- apartheid
- Nelson Mandela

USING YOUR NOTES

2. Which country is more democratic? Explain.

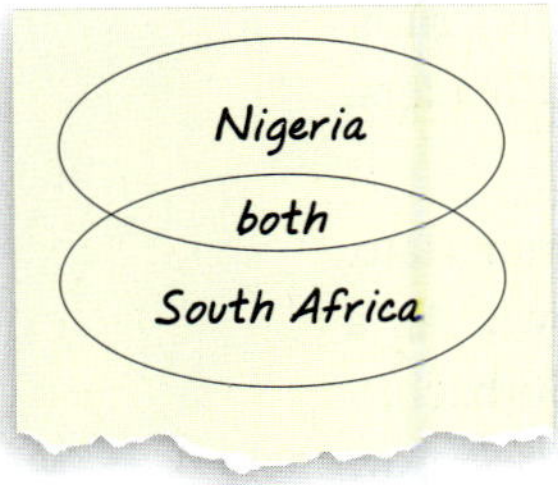

MAIN IDEAS

3. What effect did old colonial boundaries have on newly independent African states?
4. What was the outcome of the war between Nigeria and Biafra?
5. What were the homelands in South Africa?

CRITICAL THINKING & WRITING

6. **IDENTIFYING PROBLEMS** What do you think is the main problem that Nigeria must overcome before it can establish a democratic government?
7. **ANALYZING ISSUES** What are some of the important issues facing South Africa today?
8. **RECOGNIZING EFFECTS** What were the main negative effects of the economic policies of European colonizers?
9. **WRITING ACTIVITY** REVOLUTION Working in small teams, write **biographies** of South African leaders who were instrumental in the revolutionary overturn of apartheid. Include pictures if possible.

CONNECT TO TODAY **MAKING AN ORAL REPORT**

Do research on the current policy of Thabo Mbeki and the South African government on HIV and AIDS in South Africa. Report your findings in an **oral report** to the class.

3

The Collapse of the Soviet Union

CONNECT TO THE NEW YORK STATE CORE CURRICULUM

Unit 7.G.4. Mikhail Gorbachev (perestroika and glasnost)
Unit 7.G.8. Challenges faced by post-communist Russia–the world of Boris Yeltsin

TERMS & NAMES

- Politburo
- Mikhail Gorbachev
- glasnost
- perestroika
- Boris Yeltsin
- CIS
- "shock therapy"

SETTING THE STAGE After World War II, the Soviet Union and the United States engaged in a Cold War, which you read about in Chapter 33. Each tried to increase its worldwide influence. The Soviet Union extended its power over much of Eastern Europe. By the 1960s, it appeared that communism was permanently established in the region. During the 1960s and 1970s, the Soviet Union's Communist leadership kept tight control over the Soviet people. But big changes, including democratic reforms, were on the horizon.

TAKING NOTES

Following Chronological Order Use a time line to record significant events in the Soviet Union and Russia.

1985 — 2002

Gorbachev Moves Toward Democracy

Soviet premier Leonid Brezhnev and the **Politburo**—the ruling committee of the Communist Party—crushed all political disagreement. Censors decided what writers could publish. The Communist Party also restricted freedom of speech and worship. After Brezhnev's death in 1982, the aging leadership of the Soviet Union tried to hold on to power. However, each of Brezhnev's two successors died after only about a year in office. Who would succeed them?

A Younger Leader To answer that question, the Politburo debated between two men. One was **Mikhail Gorbachev** (mih•KYL-GAWR•buh•chawf). Gorbachev's supporters praised his youth, energy, and political skills. With their backing, Gorbachev became the party's new general secretary. In choosing him, Politburo members did not realize they were unleashing another Russian Revolution.

The Soviet people welcomed Gorbachev's election. At 54, he was the youngest Soviet leader since Stalin. Gorbachev was only a child during Stalin's ruthless purge of independent-minded party members. Unlike other Soviet leaders, Gorbachev decided to pursue new ideas.

Glasnost Promotes Openness-Past Soviet leaders had created a totalitarian state. It rewarded silence and discouraged individuals from acting on their own. As a result, Soviet society rarely changed, and the Soviet economy stagnated. Gorbachev realized that economic and social reforms could not occur without a free flow of ideas and information. In 1985, he announced a policy known as **glasnost** (GLAHS•nuhst), or openness.

Glasnost brought remarkable changes. The government allowed churches to open. It released dissidents from prison and allowed the publication of books by previously banned authors. Reporters investigated problems and criticized officials.

> Analyzing Political Cartoons

Glasnost

Mikhail Gorbachev's policies of glasnost and perestroika shook up the traditional way of doing things in the Soviet economy and in the society at large.

JEFF STAHLER
Courtesy Cincinnati Post

SKILLBUILDER:
Interpreting Visual Sources

1. **Making Inferences** *One arrow points down the road toward stagnation. Where is the other arrow, pointing in the opposite direction, likely to lead?*
2. **Drawing Conclusions** *Why might the Soviet Union look different to the figure in the cartoon?*

Reforming the Economy and Politics

The new openness allowed Soviet citizens to complain about economic problems. Consumers protested that they had to stand in lines to buy food and other basics.

Economic Restructuring Gorbachev blamed these problems on the Soviet Union's inefficient system of central planning. Under central planning, party officials told farm and factory managers how much to produce. They also told them what wages to pay and what prices to charge. Because individuals could not increase their pay by producing more, they had little motive to improve efficiency. (A)

MAIN IDEA
Making Inferences
(A) Why would it be inefficient for the central government to decide what should be produced all over the country?

In 1985, Gorbachev introduced the idea of **perestroika** (PEHR•ih•STROY•kuh), or economic restructuring. In 1986, he made changes to revive the Soviet economy. Local managers gained greater authority over their farms and factories, and people were allowed to open small private businesses. Gorbachev's goal was not to throw out communism, but to make the economic system more efficient and productive.

Democratization Opens the Political System Gorbachev also knew that for the economy to improve, the Communist Party would have to loosen its grip on Soviet society and politics. In 1987, he unveiled a third new policy, called democratization. This would be a gradual opening of the political system.

The plan called for the election of a new legislative body. In the past, voters had merely approved candidates who were handpicked by the Communist Party. Now, voters could choose from a list of candidates for each office. The election produced many surprises. In several places, voters chose lesser-known candidates and reformers over powerful party bosses.

Foreign Policy Soviet foreign policy also changed. To compete militarily with the Soviet Union, President Ronald Reagan had begun the most expensive military buildup in peacetime history, costing more than $2 trillion. Under pressure from U.S. military spending, Gorbachev realized that the Soviet economy could not afford the costly arms race. Arms control became one of Gorbachev's top priorities. In December 1987, he and Reagan signed the Intermediate-Range Nuclear Forces (INF) Treaty. This treaty banned nuclear missiles with ranges of 300 to 3,400 miles.

The Soviet Union Faces Turmoil

Gorbachev's new thinking led him to support movements for change in both the economic and political systems within the Soviet Union. Powerful forces for democracy were building in the country, and Gorbachev decided not to oppose reform. Glasnost, perestroika, and democratization were all means to reform the system. However, the move to reform the Soviet Union ultimately led to its breakup.

Various nationalities in the Soviet Union began to call for their freedom. More than 100 ethnic groups lived in the Soviet Union. Russians were the largest, most powerful group. However, non-Russians formed a majority in the 14 Soviet republics other than Russia.

Ethnic tensions brewed beneath the surface of Soviet society. As reforms loosened central controls, unrest spread across the country. Nationalist groups in Georgia, Ukraine, and Moldavia (now Moldova) demanded self-rule. The Muslim peoples of Soviet Central Asia called for religious freedom.

Lithuania Defies Gorbachev The first challenge came from the Baltic nations of Lithuania, Estonia, and Latvia. These republics had been independent states between the two world wars, until the Soviets annexed them in 1940. Fifty years later, in March 1990, Lithuania declared its independence. To try to force it back into the Soviet Union, Gorbachev ordered an economic blockade of the republic.

Although Gorbachev was reluctant to use stronger measures, he feared that Lithuania's example might encourage other republics to secede. In January 1991, Soviet troops attacked unarmed civilians in Lithuania's capital. The army killed 14 and wounded hundreds.

Yeltsin Denounces Gorbachev The assault in Lithuania and the lack of economic progress damaged Gorbachev's popularity. People looked for leadership to **Boris Yeltsin**. He was a member of parliament and former mayor of Moscow. Yeltsin criticized the crackdown in Lithuania and the slow pace of reforms. In June 1991, voters chose Yeltsin to become the Russian Federation's first directly elected president.

In spite of their rivalry, Yeltsin and Gorbachev faced a common enemy in the old guard of Communist officials. Hard-liners—conservatives who opposed reform—were furious that Gorbachev had given up the Soviet Union's role as the dominant force in Eastern Europe. They also feared losing their power and privileges. These officials vowed to overthrow Gorbachev and undo his reforms.

History Makers

Mikhail Gorbachev
1931–

Mikhail Gorbachev's background shaped the role he would play in history. Both of his grandfathers were arrested during Stalin's purges. Both were eventually freed. However, Gorbachev never forgot his grandfathers' stories.

After working on a state farm, Gorbachev studied law in Moscow and joined the Communist Party. As an official in a farming region, Gorbachev learned much about the Soviet system and its problems.

He advanced quickly in the party. When he became general secretary in 1985, he was the youngest Politburo member and a man who wanted to bring change. He succeeded. Although he pursued reform to save the Soviet Union, ultimately he triggered its breakup.

Boris Yeltsin
1931–

Boris Yeltsin was raised in poverty. For 10 years, his family lived in a single room.

As a youth, Yeltsin earned good grades but behaved badly. Mikhail Gorbachev named him party boss and mayor of Moscow in 1985. Yeltsin's outspokenness got him into trouble. At one meeting, he launched into a bitter speech criticizing conservatives for working against perestroika. Gorbachev fired him for the sake of party unity.

Yeltsin made a dramatic comeback and won a seat in parliament in 1989. Parliament elected him president of Russia in 1990, and voters reelected him in 1991. Due at least in part to his failing health (heart problems), Yeltsin resigned in 1999.

The Breakup of the Soviet Union, 1991

GEOGRAPHY SKILLBUILDER: Interpreting Maps

1. **Place** *What are the 15 republics of the former Soviet Union?*
2. **Region** *Which republic received the largest percentage of the former Soviet Union's territory?*

The August Coup On August 18, 1991, the hardliners detained Gorbachev at his vacation home on the Black Sea. They demanded his resignation as Soviet president. Early the next day, hundreds of tanks and armored vehicles rolled into Moscow. However, the Soviet people had lost their fear of the party. They were willing to defend their freedoms. Protesters gathered at the Russian parliament building, where Yeltsin had his office.

Around midday, Yeltsin emerged and climbed atop one of the tanks. As his supporters cheered, Yeltsin declared, "We proclaim all decisions and decrees of this committee to be illegal. . . . We appeal to the citizens of Russia to . . . demand a return of the country to normal constitutional developments."

On August 20, the hardliners ordered troops to attack the parliament building, but they refused. Their refusal turned the tide. On August 21, the military withdrew its forces from Moscow. That night, Gorbachev returned to Moscow. **B**

MAIN IDEA

Analyzing Motives

B Why do you think the Soviet troops refused the order to attack the parliament building?

End of the Soviet Union The coup attempt sparked anger against the Communist Party. Gorbachev resigned as general secretary of the party. The Soviet parliament voted to stop all party activities. Having first seized power in 1917 in a coup that succeeded, the Communist Party now collapsed because of a coup that failed.

The coup also played a decisive role in accelerating the breakup of the Soviet Union. Estonia and Latvia quickly declared their independence. Other republics soon followed. Although Gorbachev pleaded for unity, no one was listening. By early December, all 15 republics had declared independence.

Yeltsin met with the leaders of other republics to chart a new course. They agreed to form the Commonwealth of Independent States, or **CIS**, a loose federation of former Soviet territories. Only the Baltic republics and Georgia declined to join. The formation of the CIS meant the death of the Soviet Union. On Christmas Day 1991, Gorbachev announced his resignation as president of the Soviet Union, a country that ceased to exist.

Russia Under Boris Yeltsin

As president of the large Russian Federation, Boris Yeltsin was now the most powerful figure in the CIS. He would face many problems, including an ailing economy, tough political opposition, and an unpopular war.

Yeltsin Faces Problems One of Yeltsin's goals was to reform the Russian economy. He adopted a bold plan known as **"shock therapy,"** an abrupt shift to free-market economics. Yeltsin lowered trade barriers, removed price controls, and ended subsidies to state-owned industries.

Vocabulary
subsidies: government funds given in support of industries

Initially, the plan produced more shock than therapy. Prices soared; from 1992 to 1994, the inflation rate averaged 800 percent. Many factories dependent on government money had to cut production or shut down entirely. This forced thousands of people out of work. By 1993, most Russians were suffering economic hardship:

PRIMARY SOURCE

A visitor to Moscow cannot escape the feeling of a society in collapse. Child beggars accost foreigners on the street. . . . Children ask why they should stay in school when educated professionals do not make enough money to survive. . . . A garment worker complains that now her wages do not cover even the food bills, while fear of growing crime makes her dread leaving home.

DAVID M. KOTZ, "The Cure That Could Kill"

Economic problems fueled a political crisis. In October 1993, legislators opposed to Yeltsin's policies shut themselves inside the parliament building. Yeltsin ordered troops to bombard the building, forcing hundreds of rebel legislators to surrender. Many were killed. Opponents accused Yeltsin of acting like a dictator. C

MAIN IDEA
Evaluating Decisions
C Compare Yeltsin's action here to his actions during the August Coup. Which were more supportive of democracy?

Chechnya Rebels Yeltsin's troubles included war in Chechnya (CHEHCH•nee•uh), a largely Muslim area in southwestern Russia. In 1991, Chechnya declared its independence, but Yeltsin denied the region's right to secede. In 1994, he ordered 40,000 Russian troops into the breakaway republic. Russian forces reduced the capital city of Grozny (GROHZ•nee) to rubble. News of the death and destruction sparked anger throughout Russia.

With an election coming, Yeltsin sought to end the war. In August 1996, the two sides signed a cease-fire. That year, Yeltsin won reelection. War soon broke out again between Russia and Chechnya, however. In 1999, as the fighting raged, Yeltsin resigned and named Vladimir Putin as acting president.

▼ A Russian soldier throws away a spent shell case near the Chechnyan capital of Grozny.

Russia Under Vladimir Putin

Putin forcefully dealt with the rebellion in Chechnya—a popular move that helped him win the presidential election in 2000. Nonetheless, the fighting in the region dragged on for years.

Troubles Continue in Chechnya In 2002, Russia said that the war in Chechnya was nearing an end. In July 2002, the Kremlin said it would begin pulling some of its 80,000 troops out of Chechnya, but Russia had made and broken such a promise before. Then, in October 2002, Chechen rebels seized a theater in Moscow, and more than 150 people died in the rescue attempt by Russian forces.

Economic, Political, and Social Problems The nation's economic problems continued, and some observers wondered whether Russian democracy could survive. A decade of change and reform between 1992 and 2002 caused enormous social upheaval in Russia. Experts estimated that there were between 30,000 and 50,000 homeless children on the streets of Moscow. About half of these children were younger than 13. Other indications of a society experiencing severe stress included high rates of domestic violence and unemployment, a steep population decline, and declines in the standard of living and the average life expectancy.

Nonetheless, there were some signs of improvement under Putin. He stated that he favored a market economy, but one adapted to Russia's special circumstances. Unrest in the Soviet Union had an enormous impact on Central and Eastern Europe, as you will read in the next section.

History Makers

Vladimir Putin
1952–

Vladimir Putin worked for 15 years as an intelligence officer in the KGB (Committee for State Security). Six of those years were spent in East Germany. In 1990, at the age of 38, he retired from the KGB with the rank of lieutenant colonel.

Putin became first deputy mayor of Leningrad. In 1996, he moved to Moscow, where he joined the presidential staff. Eventually, Boris Yeltsin appointed Putin prime minister. When Yeltsin resigned at the end of 1999, he appointed Putin acting president. In March 2000, Putin won election as president.

INTEGRATED TECHNOLOGY
RESEARCH LINKS For more on Vladimir Putin, go to **classzone.com**

NEW YORK CORE CURRICULUM REVIEW

TERMS & NAMES 1. For each term or name, write a sentence explaining its significance.
- Politburo
- Mikhail Gorbachev
- glasnost
- perestroika
- Boris Yeltsin
- CIS
- "shock therapy"

USING YOUR NOTES

2. In what year did the Soviet Union break apart?

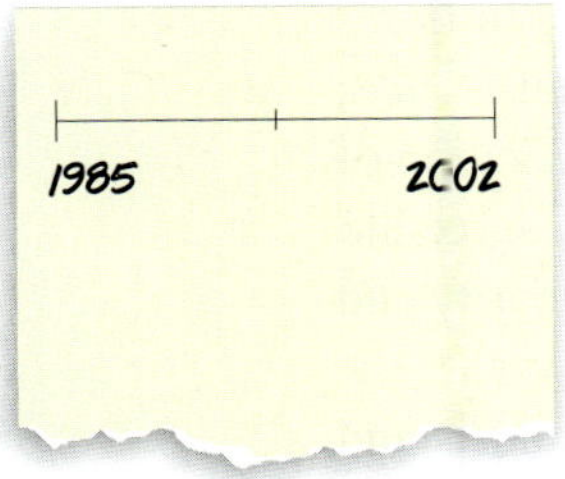

MAIN IDEAS

3. What are some of the changes that Gorbachev made to the Soviet economy?
4. After the breakup of the Soviet Union, what problems did Yeltsin face as the president of the Russian Federation?
5. How did Putin deal with Chechnya?

CRITICAL THINKING & WRITING

6. **SYNTHESIZING** How did Gorbachev's reforms help to move the Soviet Union toward democracy?
7. **ANALYZING ISSUES** What are some of the problems that faced President Vladimir Putin in Russia?
8. **COMPARING** In what ways were the policies of Gorbachev, Yeltsin, and Putin similar?
9. **WRITING ACTIVITY** REVOLUTION It has been said that Gorbachev's reforms led to another Russian Revolution. In your opinion, what did this revolution overthrow? Support your opinion in a two-paragraph **essay.**

INTEGRATED TECHNOLOGY **INTERNET ACTIVITY**

Use the Internet to research the situation in Chechnya today. Make a **poster** that includes a time line of the conflict, the leaders of the two sides, and war images.

INTERNET KEYWORD
Chechnya

4

Changes in Central and Eastern Europe

CONNECT TO THE NEW YORK STATE CORE CURRICULUM

Unit 7.G.5. Fall of the Berlin Wall and the reunification of Germany–causes and impacts
Unit 7.G.6. Ethnic conflict in former satellite states, e.g., Kosovo, Bosnia

TERMS & NAMES

- Solidarity
- Lech Walesa
- reunification
- ethnic cleansing

SETTING THE STAGE The Soviet reforms of the late 1980s brought high hopes to the people of Central and Eastern Europe. For the first time in decades, they were free to make choices about the economic and political systems governing their lives. However, they soon discovered that increased freedom sometimes challenges the social order. Mikhail Gorbachev's new thinking in the Soviet Union led him to urge Central and Eastern European leaders to open up their economic and political systems.

TAKING NOTES

Analyzing Causes Use a chart to record reasons that nations in Central and Eastern Europe broke apart.

Former nations	Reasons for breakup
Yugoslavia	
Czecho-slovakia	

Poland and Hungary Reform

The aging Communist rulers of Europe resisted reform. However, powerful forces for democracy were building in their countries. In the past, the threat of Soviet intervention had kept such forces in check. Now, Gorbachev was saying that the Soviet Union would not oppose reform.

Poland and Hungary were among the first countries in Eastern Europe to embrace the spirit of change. In 1980, Polish workers at the Gdansk shipyard went on strike, demanding government recognition of their union, **Solidarity**. When millions of Poles supported the action, the government gave in to the union's demands. Union leader **Lech Walesa** (lehk-vah•WEHN•sah) became a national hero.

Solidarity Defeats Communists The next year, however, the Polish government banned Solidarity again and declared martial law. The Communist Party discovered that military rule could not revive Poland's failing economy. In the 1980s, industrial production declined, while foreign debt rose to more than $40 billion.

Public discontent deepened as the economic crisis worsened. In August 1988, defiant workers walked off their jobs. They demanded raises and the legalization of Solidarity. The military leader, General Jaruzelski (YAH•roo•ZEHL•skee), agreed to hold talks with Solidarity leaders. In April 1989, Jaruzelski legalized Solidarity and agreed to hold Poland's first free election since the Communists took power.

In elections during 1989 and 1990, Polish voters voted against Communists and overwhelmingly chose Solidarity candidates. They elected Lech Walesa president.

Poland Votes Out Walesa After becoming president in 1990, Lech Walesa tried to revive Poland's bankrupt economy. Like Boris Yeltsin, he adopted a strategy of shock therapy to move Poland toward a free-market economy. As in Russia, inflation and unemployment shot up. By the mid-1990s, the economy was improving.

Nevertheless, many Poles remained unhappy with the pace of economic progress. In the elections of 1995, they turned Walesa out of office in favor of a former Communist, Aleksander Kwasniewski (kfahs•N'YEHF•skee).

Poland Under Kwasniewski President Kwasniewski led Poland in its drive to become part of a broader European community. In 1999, Poland became a full member of NATO. As a NATO member, Poland provided strong support in the war against terrorism after the attack on the World Trade Center in New York on September 11, 2001. In appreciation of Poland's support, President Bush invited Kwasniewski to Washington for a formal state visit in July 2002.

Kwasniewski continued the efforts of previous leaders to establish a strong market economy in Poland. Although unemployment and poverty continued to be deep-rooted problems, Kwasniewski pushed for democracy and free markets.

Hungarian Communists Disband Inspired by the changes in Poland, Hungarian leaders launched a sweeping reform program. To stimulate economic growth, reformers encouraged private enterprise and allowed a small stock market to operate. A new constitution permitted a multiparty system with free elections.

Vocabulary
deposed: removed from power

The pace of change grew faster when radical reformers took over a Communist Party congress in October 1989. The radicals deposed the party's leaders and then dissolved the party itself. Here was another first: a European Communist Party had voted itself out of existence. A year later, in national elections, the nation's voters put a non-Communist government in power.

In 1994, a socialist party—largely made up of former Communists—won a majority of seats in Hungary's parliament. The socialist party and a democratic party formed a coalition, or alliance, to rule.

In parliamentary elections in 1998, a liberal party won the most seats in the National Assembly. In 1999, Hungary joined the North Atlantic Treaty Organization as a full member. In the year 2001, there was a general economic downtown in Hungary. This was due to weak exports, decline in foreign investment, and excessive spending on state pensions and increased minimum wages.

Germany Reunifies

While Poland and Hungary were moving toward reform, East Germany's 77-year-old party boss, Erich Honecker, dismissed reforms as unnecessary. Then, in 1989, Hungary allowed vacationing East German tourists to cross the border into Austria. From there they could travel to West Germany. Thousands of East Germans took this new escape route to the west. (A)

MAIN IDEA
Analyzing Causes
(A) How did the fall of communism in Hungary contribute to turmoil in East Germany?

Fall of the Berlin Wall In response, the East German government closed its borders entirely. By October 1989, huge demonstrations had broken out

▼ The fall of the Berlin Wall, November 10, 1989

in cities across East Germany. The protesters demanded the right to travel freely, and later added the demand for free elections. Honecker lost his authority with the party and resigned on October 18.

In June 1987, President Reagan had stood before the Berlin Wall and demanded: "Mr. Gorbachev, tear down this wall!" Two years later, the wall was indeed about to come down. The new East German leader, Egon Krenz, boldly gambled that he could restore stability by allowing people to leave East Germany. On November 9, 1989, he opened the Berlin Wall. The long-divided city of Berlin erupted in joyous celebration. Krenz's dramatic gamble to save communism did not work. By the end of 1989, the East German Communist Party had ceased to exist.

Reunification With the fall of Communism in East Germany, many Germans began to speak of **reunification**—the merging of the two Germanys. However, the movement for reunification worried many people, who feared a united Germany.

The West German chancellor, Helmut Kohl, assured world leaders that Germans had learned from the past. They were now committed to democracy and human rights. Kohl's assurances helped persuade other European nations to accept German reunification. Germany was officially reunited on October 3, 1990. **B**

MAIN IDEA

Clarifying

B Why would Europeans fear the reunification of Germany?

Germany's Challenges The newly united Germany faced serious problems. More than 40 years of Communist rule had left eastern Germany in ruins. Its railroads, highways, and telephone system had not been modernized since World War II. East German industries produced goods that could not compete in the global market.

Rebuilding eastern Germany's bankrupt economy was going to be a difficult, costly process. To pay these costs, Kohl raised taxes. As taxpayers tightened their belts, workers in eastern Germany faced a second problem—unemployment. Inefficient factories closed, depriving millions of workers of their jobs.

GEOGRAPHY SKILLBUILDER: Interpreting Maps

1. **Location** *What is the relative location of business centers? Give possible reasons.*
2. **Movement** *Why might Hamburg and Kiel be shipbuilding centers, and what does this suggest about the movement of goods?*

A New Chancellor In 1998, voters turned Kohl out of office and elected a new chancellor, Gerhard Schroeder, of the Socialist Democratic Party. Schroeder started out as a market reformer, but the slow growth of the German economy made the task of reform difficult. Although Germany had the world's third largest economy, it was the slowest-growing economy in Europe in the early years of the 21st century. Germany's unemployment rate was among the highest in Europe, and rising inflation was also a continuing problem. Nonetheless, Schroeder won reelection in 2002.

Reunification forced Germany to rethink its role in international affairs. As Central Europe's largest country, Germany gained global responsibilities. Schroeder and his foreign minister took an active role in European affairs.

Democracy Spreads in Czechoslovakia

Changes in East Germany affected other European countries, including Czechoslovakia and Romania.

Czechoslovakia Reforms While huge crowds were demanding democracy in East Germany, neighboring Czechoslovakia remained quiet. A conservative government led by Milos Jakes resisted all change. In 1989, the police arrested several dissidents. Among these was the Czech playwright Václav Havel (VAH•tslahv HAH•vehl), a popular critic of the government.

On October 28, 1989, about 10,000 people gathered in Wenceslas Square in the center of Prague. They demanded democracy and freedom. Hundreds were arrested. Three weeks later, about 25,000 students inspired by the fall of the Berlin Wall gathered in Prague to demand reform. Following orders from the government, the police brutally attacked the demonstrators and injured hundreds.

The government crackdown angered the Czech people. Huge crowds gathered in Wenceslas Square. They demanded an end to Communist rule. On November 25, about 500,000 protesters crowded into downtown Prague. Within hours, Milos Jakes and his entire Politburo resigned. One month later, a new parliament elected Václav Havel president of Czechoslovakia.

Czechoslovakia Breaks Up In Czechoslovakia, reformers also launched an economic program based on "shock therapy." The program caused a sharp rise in unemployment. It especially hurt Slovakia, the republic occupying the eastern third of Czechoslovakia.

Unable to agree on economic policy, the country's two parts—Slovakia and the Czech Republic—drifted apart. In spite of President Václav Havel's pleas for unity, a movement to split the nation gained support among the people. Havel resigned because of this. Czechoslovakia split into two countries on January 1, 1993.

Havel was elected president of the Czech Republic. He won reelection in 1998. Then, in 2003, Havel stepped down as president, in part because of ill health. The Czech parliament chose Václav Klaus, a right-wing economist and former prime minister, to succeed him. The economy of the Czech Republic slowly improved in the face of some serious problems. The Czech Republic pushed to become a full member of the European Union (EU) by 2004.

Slovakia, too, proceeded on a reformist, pro-Western path. It experienced one of the highest economic growth rates in the region in 2002. It hoped to join both NATO and the EU in the near future.

Overthrow in Romania

By late 1989, only Romania seemed unmoved by the calls for reform. Romania's ruthless Communist dictator Nicolae Ceausescu (chow•SHES•koo) maintained a firm grip on power. His secret police enforced his orders brutally. Nevertheless, Romanians were aware of the reforms in other countries. They began a protest movement of their own.

A Popular Uprising In December, Ceausescu ordered the army to fire on demonstrators in the city of Timisoara

Social History

The Romanian Language

The Romanians are the only people in Eastern Europe whose ancestry and language go back to the ancient Romans. Romanian is the only Eastern European language that developed from Latin. For this reason, Romanian is very different from the other languages spoken in the region.

Today's Romanians are descended from the Dacians (the original people in the region), the Romans, and tribes that arrived later, such as the Goths, Huns, and Slavs.

Romanian remains the official language today. Minority groups within Romania (such as Hungarians, Germans, Gypsies, Jews, Turks, and Ukrainians) sometimes speak their own ethnic languages among themselves. Nonetheless, almost all the people speak Romanian as well.

INTEGRATED TECHNOLOGY

INTERNET ACTIVITY Create a poster on all the Romance languages, which developed from Latin. Go to **classzone.com** for your research.

(tee•mee•SHWAH•rah). The army killed and wounded hundreds of people. The massacre in Timisoara ignited a popular uprising against Ceausescu. Within days, the army joined the people. Shocked by the collapse of his power, Ceausescu and his wife attempted to flee. They were captured, however, and then tried and executed on Christmas Day, 1989. Romania held general elections in 1990, 1992, and 1996. In the 2000 elections, Ion Iliescu was elected to a third term as president. C

MAIN IDEA

Contrasting

C Contrast the democratic revolutions in Czechoslovakia and Romania.

The Romanian Economy Throughout the 1990s, Romania struggled with corruption and crime as it tried to salvage its economy. In 2001, overall production was still only 75 percent of what it had been in 1989, the year of Ceausescu's overthrow. In the first years of the 21st century, two-thirds of the economy was still state owned.

However, the government made economic reforms to introduce elements of capitalism. The government also began to reduce the layers of bureaucracy in order to encourage foreign investors. Furthermore, in order to achieve membership in the European Union, the Romanian government began to move away from a state-controlled economy.

The Breakup of Yugoslavia

Ethnic conflict plagued Yugoslavia. This country, formed after World War I, had eight major ethnic groups—Serbs, Croats, Muslims, Slovenes, Macedonians, Albanians, Hungarians, and Montenegrins. Ethnic and religious differences dating back centuries caused these groups to view one another with suspicion. After World War II, Yugoslavia became a federation of six republics. Each republic had a mixed population.

A Bloody Breakup Josip Tito, who led Yugoslavia from 1945 to 1980, held the country together. After Tito's death, ethnic resentments boiled over. Serbian leader Slobodan Milosevic (mee•LOH•sheh•vihch) asserted leadership over Yugoslavia. Many Serbs opposed Milosevic and his policies and fled the country.

▼ A view of downtown Sarajevo through a bullet-shattered window

Two republics, Slovenia and Croatia, declared independence. In June 1991, the Serbian-led Yugoslav army invaded both republics. After months of bloody fighting, both republics freed themselves from Serbian rule. Early in 1992, Bosnia-Herzegovina joined Slovenia and Croatia in declaring independence. (In April, Serbia and Montenegro formed a new Yugoslavia.) Bosnia's population included Muslims (44 percent), Serbs (31 percent), and Croats (17 percent). While Bosnia's Muslims and Croats backed independence, Bosnian Serbs strongly opposed it. Supported by Serbia, the Bosnian Serbs launched a war in March 1992.

During the war, Serbian military forces used violence and forced emigration against Bosnian Muslims living in Serb-held lands. Called **ethnic cleansing**, this policy was intended to rid Bosnia of its Muslim population. By 1995, the Serbian military controlled 70 percent of Bosnia. In December of that year, leaders of the three factions involved in the war signed a UN- and U.S.-brokered peace treaty. In September 1996, Bosnians elected a three-person presidency, one leader from each ethnic group. By 2001, Bosnia and

Ethnic Groups in the Former Yugoslavia

Many ethnic and religious groups lived within Yugoslavia, which was a federation of six republics. The map shows how the ethnic groups were distributed. Some of those groups held ancient grudges against one another. The chart summarizes some of the cultural differences among the groups.

Differences Among the Ethnic Groups

Group	Language (slavic unless noted)	Religion
Albanians	Albanian (not Slavic)	mostly Muslim
Croats	dialect of Serbo-Croatian*	mostly Roman Catholic
Hungarians	Magyar (not Slavic)	many types of Christians
Macedonians	Macedonian	mostly Eastern Orthodox
Montenegrins	dialect of Serbo-Croatian*	mostly Eastern Orthodox
Muslims	dialect of Serbo-Croatian*	Muslim (converted under Ottoman rule)
Serbs	dialect of Serbo-Croatian*	mostly Eastern Orthodox
Slovenes	Slovenian	mostly Roman Catholic

*** Since Yugoslavia broke apart, many residents of the former republics have started to refer to their dialects as separate languages: Croatian for Croats, Bosnian for Muslims, Serbian for Serbs and Montenegrins.**

SKILLBUILDER: Interpreting Visuals

1. **Analyzing Issues** *Use the chart to find out information about the various groups that lived in Bosnia and Herzegovina (as shown on the map). What were some of the differences among those groups?*
2. **Contrasting** *Kosovo was a province within Serbia. What group was in the majority there, and how did it differ from Serbs?*

Herzegovina began to stand on its own without as much need for supervision by the international community. **D**

Rebellion in Kosovo The Balkan region descended into violence and bloodshed again in 1998, this time in Kosovo, a province in southern Serbia made up almost entirely of ethnic Albanians. As an independence movement in Kosovo grew increasingly violent, Serbian military forces invaded the province and fought back with a harsh hand. In response to growing reports of atrocities—and the failure of diplomacy to bring peace—NATO began a bombing campaign against Yugoslavia in the spring of 1999. After enduring more than two months of sustained bombing, Yugoslav leaders finally withdrew their troops from Kosovo.

The Region Faces Its Problems In the early years of the 21st century, there were conflicting signs in Yugoslavia. Slobodan Milosevic was extradited to stand trial for war crimes. A large portion of the country's foreign debt was erased. Despite an independence movement in Kosovo, parliamentary elections under UN supervision took place in November 2001 without violence.

And in Montenegro (which together with Serbia made up Yugoslavia), an independence movement seemed to lack support from the people as well as from the international community. Nonetheless, in February 2003, Yugoslavia's parliament voted to replace what remained of the federation with a loose union of Serbia and Montenegro. Outright independence for each could come as early as 2006. However, problems remained, as indicated by the assassination of the Serbian prime minister, Zoran Djindjic, in March 2003.

The nations of Central and Eastern Europe made many gains in the early years of the 21st century. Even so, they continued to face serious obstacles to democracy. Resolving ethnic conflicts remained crucial, as did economic progress. If the nations of Central and Eastern Europe and the former Soviet Union can improve their standard of living, democracy may have a better chance to grow. Meanwhile, economic reforms in Communist China sparked demands for political reforms, as you will read in the next section.

MAIN IDEA

Identifying Problems

D Why did Bosnia's mixed population cause a problem after Bosnia declared independence?

NEW YORK CORE CURRICULUM REVIEW

TERMS & NAMES 1. For each term or name, write a sentence explaining its significance.

- Solidarity
- Lech Walesa
- reunification
- ethnic cleansing

USING YOUR NOTES

2. Which nation seems to have done best since the breakup? Explain.

Former nations	Reasons for breakup
Yugoslavia	
Czecho-slovakia	

MAIN IDEAS

3. How did Solidarity affect Communist rule in Poland?
4. What effect did reunification have on Germany's international role?
5. What was the main cause of the breakup of Czechoslovakia?

CRITICAL THINKING & WRITING

6. **ANALYZING CAUSES** Why did ethnic tension become such a severe problem in the Soviet Union and Yugoslavia?
7. **DRAWING CONCLUSIONS** What are some of the problems faced in Central and Eastern Europe in the 21st century?
8. **RECOGNIZING EFFECTS** What effect did economic reform have on Slovakia?
9. **WRITING ACTIVITY** With a partner, create a **cause-and-effect diagram** to show how democratic reform spread through Central and Eastern Europe. The diagram should show the order in which reform happened and which countries influenced others.

CONNECT TO TODAY **MAKING A PIE GRAPH**

Research the size of the populations of Central and Eastern Europe countries mentioned in this section. Construct a **pie graph** showing the comparative sizes of the populations.

5

China: Reform and Reaction

CONNECT TO THE NEW YORK STATE CORE CURRICULUM

Unit 7.D.4.a.1. Limited privatization
Unit 7.D.4.b.2. Tiananmen Square

TERMS & NAMES

- Zhou Enlai
- Deng Xiaoping
- Four Modernizations
- Tiananmen Square
- Hong Kong

SETTING THE STAGE The trend toward democracy around the world also affected China to a limited degree. A political reform movement arose in the late 1980s. It built on economic reforms begun earlier in the decade. However, although the leadership of the Communist Party in China generally supported economic reform, it opposed political reform. China's Communist government clamped down on the political reformers. At the same time, it maintained a firm grip on power in the country.

TAKING NOTES

Following Chronological Order Use a diagram to show events leading up to the demonstration in Tiananmen Square.

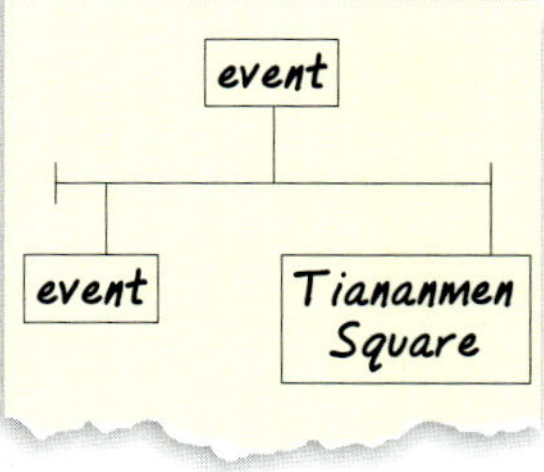

The Legacy of Mao

After the Communists came to power in China in 1949, Mao Zedong set out to transform China. Mao believed that peasant equality, revolutionary spirit, and hard work were all that was needed to improve the Chinese economy.

However, lack of modern technology damaged Chinese efforts to increase agricultural and industrial output. In addition, Mao's policies stifled economic growth. He eliminated incentives for higher production. He tried to replace family life with life in the communes. These policies took away the peasants' motive to work for the good of themselves and their families.

Facing economic disaster, some Chinese Communists talked of modernizing the economy. Accusing them of "taking the capitalist road," Mao began the Cultural Revolution in 1966 to cleanse China of antirevolutionary influences.

Mao's Attempts to Change China

Mao's Programs	Program Results
First Five-Year Plan 1953–1957	• Industry grew 15 percent a year. • Agricultural output grew very slowly.
Great Leap Forward 1958–1961	• China suffered economic disaster—industrial declines and food shortages. • Mao lost influence.
Cultural Revolution 1966–1976	• Mao regained influence by backing radicals. • Purges and conflicts among leaders created economic, social, and political chaos.

▲ Zhou Enlai, a translator, Mao Zedong, President Nixon, and Henry Kissinger meet in Beijing in 1972.

Instead of saving radical communism, however, the Cultural Revolution turned many people against it. In the early 1970s, China entered another moderate period under **Zhou Enlai** (joh ehn•ly). Zhou had been premier since 1949. During the Cultural Revolution, he had tried to restrain the radicals. (A)

MAIN IDEA

Recognizing Effects

(A) What was the ultimate result of Mao's radical Communist policies?

China and the West

Throughout the Cultural Revolution, China played almost no role in world affairs. In the early 1960s, China had split with the Soviet Union over the leadership of world communism. In addition, China displayed hostility toward the United States because of U.S. support for the government on Taiwan.

China Opened Its Doors China's isolation worried Zhou. He began to send out signals that he was willing to form ties to the West. In 1971, Zhou startled the world by inviting an American table-tennis team to tour China. It was the first visit by an American group to China since 1949.

The visit began a new era in Chinese-American relations. In 1971, the United States reversed its policy and endorsed UN membership for the People's Republic of China. The next year, President Nixon made a state visit to China. He met with Mao and Zhou. The three leaders agreed to begin cultural exchanges and a limited amount of trade. In 1979, the United States and China established diplomatic relations.

Economic Reform Both Mao and Zhou died in 1976. Shortly afterward, moderates took control of the Communist Party. They jailed several of the radicals who had led the Cultural Revolution. By 1980, **Deng Xiaoping** (duhng show•pihng) had emerged as the most powerful leader in China. He was the last of the "old revolutionaries" who had ruled China since 1949.

Although a lifelong Communist, Deng boldly supported moderate economic policies. Unlike Mao, he was willing to use capitalist ideas to help China's economy. He embraced a set of goals known as the **Four Modernizations**. These called for progress in agriculture, industry, defense, and science and technology. Deng launched an ambitious program of economic reforms.

First, Deng eliminated Mao's communes and leased the land to individual farmers. The farmers paid rent by delivering a fixed quota of food to the government. They could then grow crops and sell them for a profit. Under this system, food production increased by 50 percent in the years 1978 to 1984.

Deng extended his program to industry. The government permitted private businesses to operate. It gave the managers of state-owned industries more freedom to set production goals. Deng also welcomed foreign technology and investment.

Deng's economic policies produced striking changes in Chinese life. As incomes increased, people began to buy appliances and televisions. Chinese youths now wore stylish clothes and listened to Western music. Gleaming hotels filled with foreign tourists symbolized China's new policy of openness.

Massacre in Tiananmen Square

Deng's economic reforms produced a number of unexpected problems. As living standards improved, the gap between the rich and poor widened. Increasingly, the public believed that party officials profited from their positions.

Furthermore, the new policies admitted not only Western investments and tourists but also Western political ideas. Increasing numbers of Chinese students studied abroad and learned about the West. In Deng's view, the benefits of opening the economy exceeded the risks. Nevertheless, as Chinese students learned more about democracy, they began to question China's lack of political freedom. **B**

MAIN IDEA

Analyzing Causes

B How did economic reform introduce new political ideas to China?

Students Demand Democracy In 1989, students sparked a popular uprising that stunned China's leaders. Beginning in April of that year, more than 100,000 students occupied **Tiananmen** (tyahn•ahn•mehn) **Square**, a huge public space in the heart of Beijing. The students mounted a protest for democracy. (See photograph on page 1064.)

The student protest won widespread popular support. When thousands of students began a hunger strike to highlight their cause, people poured into Tiananmen Square to support them. Many students called for Deng Xiaoping to resign.

Deng Orders a Crackdown Instead of considering political reform, Deng declared martial law. He ordered about 100,000 troops to surround Beijing. Although many students left the square after martial law was declared, about 5,000 chose to remain and continue their protest. The students revived their spirits by defiantly erecting a 33-foot statue that they named the "Goddess of Democracy."

On June 4, 1989, the standoff came to an end. Thousands of heavily armed soldiers stormed Tiananmen Square. Tanks smashed through barricades and crushed the Goddess of Democracy. Soldiers sprayed gunfire into crowds of frightened students. They also attacked protesters elsewhere in Beijing. The assault killed hundreds and wounded thousands.

Analyzing Primary Sources

Training the Chinese Army

After the massacre in Tiananmen Square, Xiao Ye (a former Chinese soldier living in the United States) explained how Chinese soldiers are trained to obey orders without complaint.

PRIMARY SOURCE

We usually developed bleeding blisters on our feet after a few days of . . . hiking. Our feet were a mass of soggy peeling flesh and blood, and the pain was almost unbearable. . . . We considered the physical challenge a means of tempering [hardening] ourselves for the sake of the Party. . . . No one wanted to look bad. . . .

And during the days in Tiananmen, once again the soldiers did not complain. They obediently drove forward, aimed, and opened fire on command. In light of their training, how could it have been otherwise?

XIAO YE, "Tiananmen Square: A Soldier's Story"

DOCUMENT-BASED QUESTIONS

1. **Making Inferences** *For whom did the soldiers seem to believe they were making their physical sacrifices?*
2. **Drawing Conclusions** *What attitude toward obeying orders did their training seem to encourage in the soldiers?*

The attack on Tiananmen Square marked the beginning of a massive government campaign to stamp out protest. Police arrested thousands of people. The state used the media to announce that reports of a massacre were untrue. Officials claimed that a small group of criminals had plotted against the government. Television news, however, had already broadcast the truth to the world.

China Enters the New Millennium

The brutal repression of the prodemocracy movement left Deng firmly in control of China. During the final years of his life, Deng continued his program of economic reforms.

Although Deng moved out of the limelight in 1995, he remained China's leader. In February 1997, after a long illness, Deng died. Communist Party General Secretary Jiang Zemin (jee•ahng zeh•meen) assumed the presidency.

China Under Jiang Many questions arose after Deng's death. What kind of leader would Jiang be? Would he be able to hold on to power and ensure political stability? A highly intelligent and educated man, Jiang had served as mayor of Shanghai. He was considered skilled, flexible, and practical. However, he had no military experience. Therefore, Jiang had few allies among the generals. He also faced challenges from rivals, including hard-line officials who favored a shift away from Deng's economic policies.

Other questions following Deng's death had to do with China's poor human rights record, its occupation of Tibet, and relations with the United States. During the 1990s, the United States pressured China to release political prisoners and ensure basic rights for political opponents. China remained hostile to such pressure. Its government continued to repress the prodemocracy movement. Nevertheless, the desire for freedom still ran through Chinese society. If China remained economically open but politically closed, tensions seemed bound to surface.

In late 1997, Jiang paid a state visit to the United States. During his visit, U.S. protesters demanded more democracy in China. Jiang admitted that China had made some mistakes but refused to promise that China's policies would change.

President Jiang Zemin and Premier Zhu Rongji announced their retirement in late 2002. Jiang's successor was Hu Jintao. However, Jiang was expected to wield influence over his successor behind the scenes. Hu became president of the country and general secretary of the Communist Party. Jiang remained political leader of the military. Both supported China's move to a market economy.

Transfer of Hong Kong Another major issue for China was the status of **Hong Kong**. Hong Kong was a thriving business center and British colony on the southeastern coast of China. On July 1, 1997, Great Britain handed Hong Kong over to China, ending 155 years of colonial rule. As part of the transfer, China promised to respect Hong Kong's economic system and political liberties for 50 years.

Many of Hong Kong's citizens worried about Chinese rule and feared the loss of their freedoms. Others, however, saw the transfer as a way to reconnect with their Chinese

History Makers

Jiang Zemin
1926–

Jiang Zemin was trained as an engineer. After working as an engineer, heading several technological institutes, and serving as minister of the electronics industry, he moved up in politics.

In 1982, he joined the Central Committee of the Communist Party in China. He became mayor of Shanghai in 1985, in which post he proved to be an effective administrator. In 1989, he became general secretary of the Chinese Communist Party. This promotion was largely due to his support for the government's putdown of the prodemocracy demonstrations in that year. In 1993, he became president. In 2003, he stepped down and was replaced by Hu Jintao; however, Jiang retained power behind the scenes.

heritage. In the first four or five years after the transfer, the control of mainland China over Hong Kong tightened.

▲ People celebrate in Tiananmen Square after Beijing won the bid for the 2008 Olympic Games.

China Beyond 2000

The case of China demonstrates that the creation of democracy can be a slow, fitful, and incomplete process. Liberal reforms in one area, such as the economy, may not lead immediately to political reforms.

Economics and Politics In China, there has been a dramatic reduction in poverty. Some experts argue that China managed to reform its economy and reduce poverty because it adopted a gradual approach to selling off state industries and privatizing the economy rather than a more abrupt approach. At any rate, as the global economy slowed in the early years of the 21st century, China managed to maintain economic growth.

People in China and around the world have a desire for more political freedom. As economic and social conditions improve—for example, as the middle class expands and educational opportunities grow—the prospects for democracy also may improve. In addition, as countries are increasingly linked through technology and trade, they will have more opportunity to influence each other politically. In 2000, for example, the U.S. Congress voted to normalize trade with China. Supporters of such a move argue that the best way to prompt political change in China is through greater engagement rather than isolation. Another sign of China's increasing engagement with the world is its successful campaign to host the 2008 Summer Olympics in Beijing.

NEW YORK CORE CURRICULUM REVIEW

TERMS & NAMES 1. For each term or name, write a sentence explaining its significance.

- Zhou Enlai
- Deng Xiaoping
- Four Modernizations
- Tiananmen Square
- Hong Kong

USING YOUR NOTES

2. Other than the demonstration in Tiananmen Square, which of these events was most important? Explain.

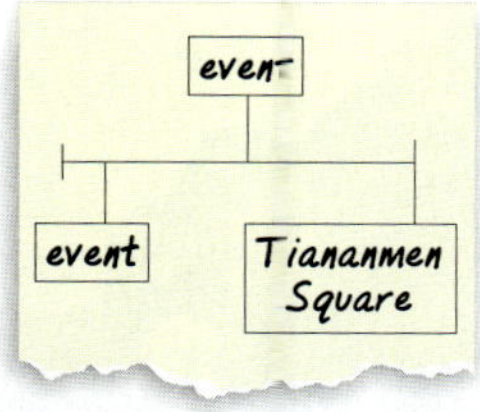

MAIN IDEAS

3. What effect did Mao's policies have on economic growth?
4. What were some of Deng Xiaoping's economic reforms?
5. How would you describe China's record on human rights?

CRITICAL THINKING & WRITING

6. **SUPPORTING OPINIONS** Judging from what you have read about the Chinese government, do you think Hong Kong will keep its freedoms under Chinese rule? Explain.
7. **FOLLOWING CHRONOLOGICAL ORDER** What were some of the events that followed the demonstration in Tiananmen Square?
8. **COMPARING AND CONTRASTING** Has there been greater progress in political or economic reform in China?
9. **WRITING ACTIVITY** CULTURAL INTERACTION Imagine that you are a Chinese student visiting the West. Write a **letter** home in which you explain what you have seen abroad.

CONNECT TO TODAY **MAKING A POSTER**

China will be hosting the 2008 Summer Olympics in Beijing. Research the efforts that China is making to prepare the city for the festivities and present your findings in a **poster.**

Photojournalism

From the earliest days of photography, magazines and newspapers have used photographs to convey the news. Photojournalists must respond quickly to recognize a history-making moment and to record that moment before it passes. As the photographs on this page demonstrate, photojournalists have captured many of the democratic struggles that have occurred in the last few decades. In some cases, news photographs have helped protesters or oppressed people gain the support of the world.

INTEGRATED TECHNOLOGY

RESEARCH LINKS For more on photojournalism, go to **classzone.com**

Flight from Srebrenica ►

During the conflicts in Bosnia and Herzegovina, the United Nations declared the city of Srebrenica a safe area. Even so, the Bosnian Serb army invaded in July 1995 and expelled more than 20,000 Muslims—nearly all of them women, children, or elderly people. In addition, the soldiers held more than 7,000 men and boys prisoner and over a five-day period massacred them.

▼ Man Defying Tanks

A single Chinese man blocked tanks on their way to crush prodemocracy protests in Tiananmen Square in June 1989. No one knows for sure what happened to the man afterward—or even who he was. Even so, this image has become one of the enduring photographs of the 20th century; it has come to stand for one man's courage in defying tyranny.

Abuelas de Plaza de Mayo ▲

From 1976 to 1983, the military government of Argentina tortured and killed thousands of political dissidents and sometimes stole their children. In this demonstration in December 1979, the *Abuelas de Plaza de Mayo* (Grandmothers of the Plaza de Mayo) demanded to know the fate of their relatives. The banner they carried reads "Disappeared Children."

Fall of the Wall ▼

When the East German government opened the Berlin Wall in November 1989, a huge celebration broke out. Some people began to use pickaxes to demolish the wall entirely. Others danced on top of the wall. (See also the image on page 1053.)

Voting Line

When South Africa held its first all-race election in April 1994, people were so eager to vote that they stood in lines that sometimes stretched nearly a kilometer (0.62 mile).

Connect *to* Today

1. **Forming and Supporting Opinions** Which of these photographs do you think has the greatest impact on the viewer? Explain why.

   See Skillbuilder Handbook, page R20.

2. **Forming and Supporting Opinions** Using Internet or library resources, find a news photograph that you think effectively shows a recent historic event. Bring a copy of the photograph to class, and explain orally or in writing what it conveys about the event.

Chapter 35 Assessment

TERMS & NAMES

For each term or name below, briefly explain its connection to the democratic movements that took place from 1945 to the present.

1. PRI
2. apartheid
3. Nelson Mandela
4. Mikhail Gorbachev
5. glasnost
6. Lech Walesa
7. Deng Xiaoping
8. Tiananmen Square

MAIN IDEAS

Case Study: Latin American Democracies Section 1 (pages 1033–1039)

9. What are four common democratic practices?
10. What group held up democratic progress in both Brazil and Argentina until the 1980s?

The Challenge of Democracy in Africa Section 2 (pages 1040–1045)

11. What brought about the civil war in Nigeria?
12. What were three significant steps toward democracy taken by South Africa in the 1990s?

The Collapse of the Soviet Union Section 3 (pages 1046–1051)

13. What were the main reforms promoted by Soviet leader Mikhail Gorbachev?
14. What was the August Coup and how did it end?

Changes in Central and Eastern Europe Section 4 (pages 1052–1058)

15. Which nations overthrew Communist governments in 1989?
16. What led to the breakup of Yugoslavia?

China: Reform and Reaction Section 5 (pages 1059–1065)

17. What changes took place in China during the 1970s?
18. How did the Chinese government react to demands for democratic reform?

CRITICAL THINKING

1. USING YOUR NOTES
List several leaders who helped their nations make democratic progress. For each, cite one positive action.

Leader	Nation	Positive Action

2. ANALYZING ISSUES
CULTURAL INTERACTION What are some examples from this chapter in which the negative impact of one culture on another blocked democratic progress?

3. SYNTHESIZING
Consider what conditions helped democratic movements succeed and what conditions caused difficulties for them. What do you think were their hardest challenges?

4. DRAWING CONCLUSIONS
ECONOMICS How does a nation's economy affect its democratic progress?

5. SUMMARIZING
What were Deng Xiaoping's economic reforms for China?

VISUAL SUMMARY

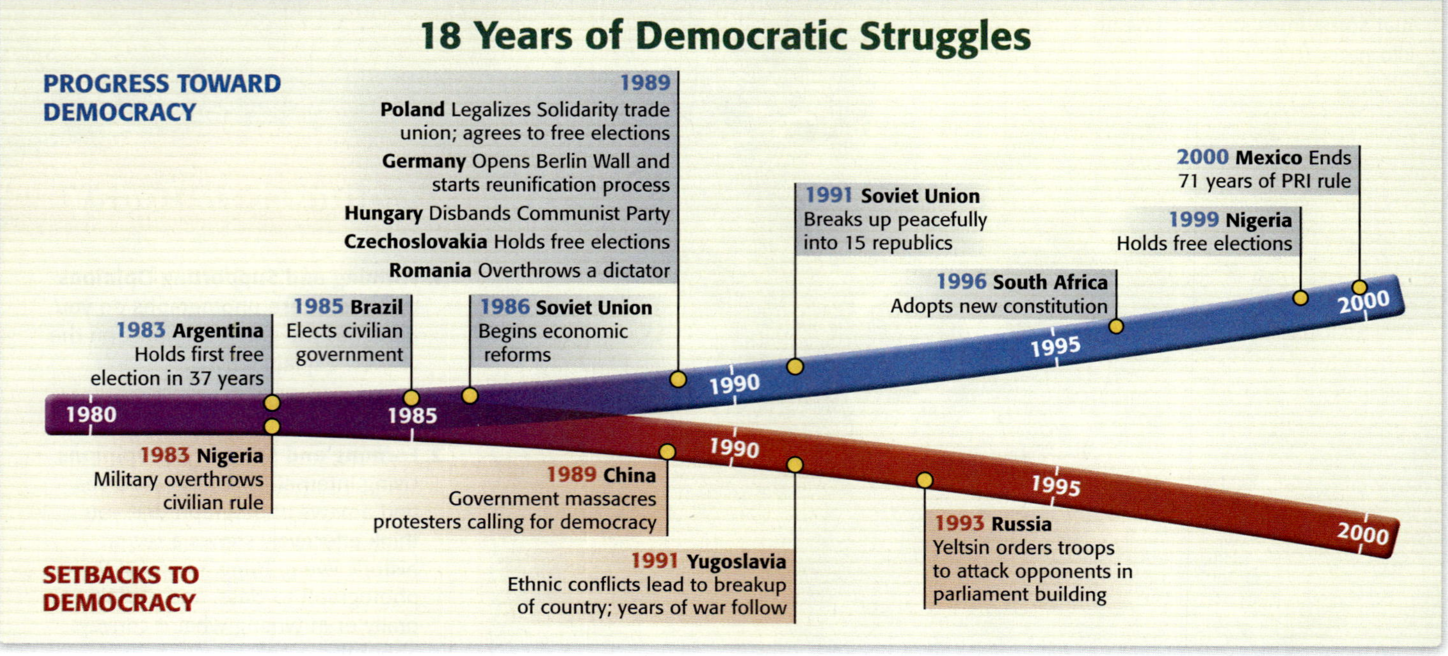

Use the quotation and your knowledge of world history to answer questions 1 and 2.
Additional Test Practice, pp. S1–S33

PRIMARY SOURCE

Whatever else you can say about the new Hong Kong, it will be more Chinese. Liu Heung-shing, the editor of the new Hong Kong magazine *The Chinese,* says that "for any meaningful art and culture to take off here, Hong Kong must find somewhere to anchor itself. To find that anchor, people will have to go north [to mainland China]." . . . Increasing numbers of Hong Kong's Cantonese speakers are studying mainland Mandarin. . . . At the same time that [Hong Kong] must resist China to retain Britain's legacy of rule of law, it knows that the most logical place for it to turn for commerce and culture is China.

ORVILLE SCHELL, "The Coming of Mao Zedong Chic"

1 What is the main change that is taking place in Hong Kong's culture?
(1) China is looking to Hong Kong for cultural inspiration.
(2) Hong Kong is turning to China for cultural inspiration.
(3) Hong Kong is turning to the West for cultural inspiration.
(4) Hong Kong is turning inward.

2 What point of view might a Hong Kong politician have about this change?
(1) may fear China will restrict the city's freedoms
(2) may welcome tighter controls from China
(3) may threaten military action against China
(4) may vow never to cooperate with mainland China

Use this political cartoon and your knowledge of world history to answer question 3.

3 What is the cartoon saying about the state of communism in Poland, China, and the Soviet Union?
(1) Communism is thriving.
(2) Communism is helping nations gain economic health.
(3) Communism is failing around the world.
(4) Communism is sick but will recover.

INTEGRATED TECHNOLOGY
TEST PRACTICE Go to **classzone.com**
- Diagnostic tests
- Tutorials
- Strategies
- Additional practice

ALTERNATIVE ASSESSMENT

1. Interact *with* History

REVOLUTION On page 1032, you considered why so many people want democracy. Now that you've read the chapter, have your explanations changed? Would you add anything to what you said before? Would you change anything you said before?

2. WRITING ABOUT HISTORY

A government official has asked you for suggestions on how to move a Communist economy to a free-market economy. Go through the chapter and compile a "Things to Do" **report** based on actions that other governments have taken. Consider the following issues:
- unemployment
- inflation
- political effects
- social upheaval

INTEGRATED TECHNOLOGY

Creating a Virtual Field Trip

With two other classmates, plan a two-week virtual field trip to explore the sights in China, including the Forbidden City and the sites of the 2008 Summer Olympics. After selecting and researching the sites you'd like to visit, use maps to determine your itinerary. Consider visiting these places and enjoying these excursions:
- Sites of the 2008 Summer Olympic games
- Sites around Beijing
- Great Wall
- A cruise along the Chang Jiang or Huang He rivers
- Three Gorges Dam
- Shanghai

For each place or excursion, give one reason why it is an important destination on a field trip to China. Include pictures and sound in your presentation.

CHAPTER 36

Global Interdependence, 1960–Present

Previewing Main Ideas

SCIENCE AND TECHNOLOGY Advances in science and technology have changed the lives of people around the globe. Improved communications and transportation have allowed goods, services, and ideas to move rapidly.

Geography *How does this map illustrate the idea of global interdependence?*

CULTURAL INTERACTION Inventions and innovations have brought the nations of the world closer and exposed people to other cultures. Cultures are now blending ideas and customs much faster than before.

Geography *Which countries in the Western Hemisphere are major destinations for immigrants?*

ECONOMICS Since World War II, nations have worked to expand trade and commerce in world markets. Changes in technology have blurred national boundaries and created a global market.

Geography *What do most countries with a net migration rate above 3.0 have in common economically?*

POWER AND AUTHORITY Since the end of World War II, nations have adopted collective efforts to ensure their security. One of the greatest challenges in maintaining global security is international terrorism.

Geography *What do most countries with a net migration rate above 3.0 have in common politically?*

NEW YORK CORE CURRICULUM FOCUS

- Globalization and free trade have made economies more interdependent.
- Religious and ethnic conflicts, human rights, health issues, and world hunger are some of the challenges facing the world today.

INTEGRATED TECHNOLOGY

eEdition
- Interactive Maps
- Interactive Visuals
- Interactive Primary Sources

VIDEO *Patterns of Interaction: The United States and the World*

INTERNET RESOURCES

Go to **classzone.com** for:
- Research Links
- Internet Activities
- Primary Sources
- Chapter Quiz
- Maps
- Test Practice
- Current Events

WORLD

1960

1968 ◀ Many nations sign the Nuclear Non-Proliferation Treaty. (atomic energy symbol)

1970

1972 U.S. and Soviet Union agree to joint space venture. Terrorists carry out attack at the Summer Olympic games in Munich. (masked terrorist in Munich) ▶

1975 Helsinki Accords support human rights.

World Migration, 2002

1980 **1990** **2000**

1981
U.S. carries out first space shuttle flight. ▶

1983
French research scientists isolate the AIDS virus.

1986
Accident takes place at Soviet nuclear power plant in Chernobyl.

1995
World Trade Organization is set up.

1998
Construction of the International Space Station begins.

2001
UN issues the Declaration of Commitment on HIV/AIDS. Terrorists launch attacks in New York and Washington, D.C.

2003
Human Genome Project is completed.

Interact *with* History

How do global events affect your daily life?

You have just seen a television program recapping some recent news events. You are surprised at the number of stories that involve the United States and other countries. You begin to think about how events in such distant places as China and Iraq can affect life in your own country.

▼ War in Iraq, 2003

▼ Mapping the Human Genome

▲ Homeland Security Alert

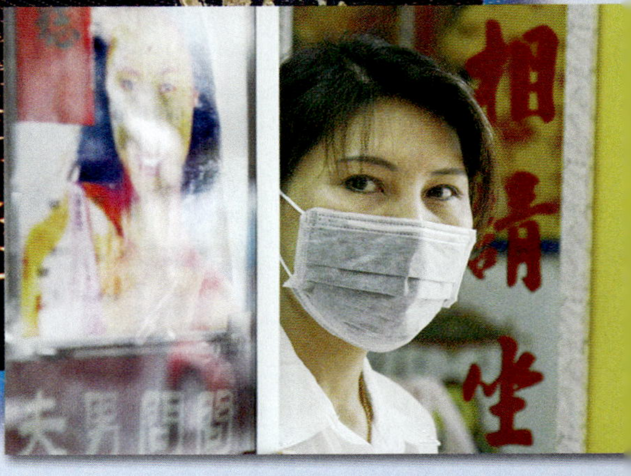

▲ Severe Acute Respiratory Syndrome in China

EXAMINING *the* ISSUES

- **How do the events shown in the photographs illustrate the political interdependence of different nations?**
- **What do these events tell you about scientific and cultural interdependence among nations?**

As a class, discuss these questions. Remember what you have learned about the recent history of nations in different regions of the world. Try to think of reasons that nations are becoming increasingly dependent on one another. As you read this chapter, look for examples of economic, political, and cultural interdependence among the nations of the world.

1 The Impact of Science and Technology

CONNECT TO THE NEW YORK STATE CORE CURRICULUM

Unit 8.D.1. Information age/Computer Revolution/Internet
Unit 8.D.6. Medical breakthroughs–disease control/life expectancy/genetics

TERMS & NAMES

- International Space Station
- Internet
- genetic engineering
- cloning
- green revolution

SETTING THE STAGE Beginning in the late 1950s, the United States and the Soviet Union competed in the exploration of space. The Soviets launched Earth's first artificial satellite and put the first human in orbit around the planet. By the late 1960s, however, the United States had surpassed the Soviets. U.S. astronauts landed on the moon in 1969. The heavy emphasis on science and technology that the space race required led to the development of products that changed life for people across the globe.

TAKING NOTES

Recognizing Effects Use a chart to list the effects of scientific and technological developments.

Developments	Effects
Communications	
Health and Medicine	
Green Revolution	

Exploring the Solar System and Beyond

In its early years, competition between the United States and the Soviet Union in the space race was intense. Eventually, however, space exploration became one of the world's first and most successful arenas for cooperation between U.S. and Soviet scientists.

Cooperation in Space In 1972, years before the end of the Cold War, the United States and Soviet space programs began work on a cooperative project—the docking of U.S. and Soviet spacecraft in orbit. This goal was achieved on July 17, 1975, when spacecraft from the two countries docked some 140 miles above Earth. Television viewers across the globe watched as the hatch between the space vehicles opened and crews from Earth's fiercest rival countries greeted each other.

This first cooperative venture in space between the United States and the Soviet Union was an isolated event. People from different countries, however, continued to work together to explore space. The Soviets were the first to send an international crew into space. The crew of *Soyuz 28,* which orbited Earth in 1978, included a Czech cosmonaut. Since the mid-1980s, crews on United States space shuttle flights have included astronauts from Saudi Arabia, France, Germany, Canada, Italy, Japan, Israel, and Mexico. (Space shuttles are larger than other spacecraft and are reusable.) Shuttle missions put crews in orbit around Earth to accomplish a variety of scientific and technological tasks.

The space shuttle is being used in the most ambitious cooperative space venture. The project, sponsored by the United States, Russia, and 14 other nations, involves the building of the **International Space Station** (ISS). Since 1998, U.S. shuttles and Russian spacecraft have transported sections of the ISS to be assembled in space. By the time it is completed, the ISS will cover an area the size

▲ This view of the ISS was taken from the space shuttle *Endeavor.*

of a football field and house a crew of six. Since October 2000, smaller crews have been working aboard the ISS. By early 2003, they had conducted more than 100 experiments. However, the suspension of the shuttle program after the crash of the shuttle *Columbia* in February 2003 put the future of the ISS in question.

Exploring the Universe Unmanned space probes have been used to study the farther reaches of the solar system. The Soviet *Venera* spacecraft in the 1970s and the U.S. probe *Magellan* in 1990 provided in-depth information about Venus. On a 12-year journey that began in 1977, the U.S. *Voyager 2* sent dazzling pictures of Jupiter, Saturn, Uranus, and Neptune back to Earth. Both the United States and the Soviet Union have shown particular interest in the planet Mars. The United States probe *Pathfinder,* which landed on Mars in 1997, provided spectacular results.

In 1990, the U.S. space agency, NASA, and the European space agency, ESA, worked together to develop and launch the Hubble Space Telescope. This orbiting telescope continues to observe and send back images of objects in the most remote regions of the universe. (A)

MAIN IDEA

Hypothesizing

(A) Why might rival nations cooperate in space activities but not on Earth?

Expanding Global Communications

Since the 1960s, artificial satellites launched into orbit around Earth have aided worldwide communications. With satellite communication, the world has been gradually transformed into a global village. Today, political and cultural events occurring in one part of the world often are witnessed live by people thousands of miles away. This linking of the globe through worldwide communications is made possible by the miniaturization of the computer.

Smaller, More Powerful Computers In the 1940s, when computers first came into use, they took up a huge room. The computer required fans or an elaborate air-conditioning system to cool the vacuum tubes that powered its operations. In the years since then, however, the circuitry that runs the computer has been miniaturized and made more powerful. This change is due, in part, to the space program, for which equipment had to be downsized to fit into tiny space capsules. Silicon chips replaced the bulky vacuum tubes used earlier. Smaller than contact lenses, silicon chips hold millions of microscopic circuits.

▼ Some computers are so small that they can be held in the hand.

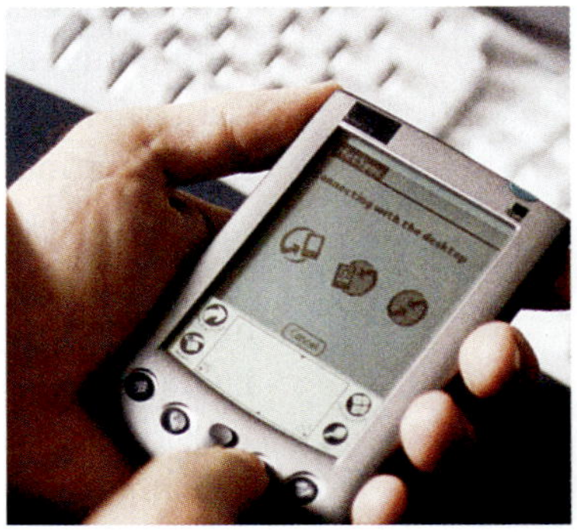

Following this development, industries began to use computers and silicon chips to run assembly lines. Today a variety of consumer products such as microwave ovens, telephones, keyboard instruments, and cars use computers and chips. Computers have become essential in most offices, and millions of people around the globe have computers in their homes.

Access to the Internet, 2002

Internet Users Worldwide

Africa	6.31 million
Asia and the Pacific	187.24 million
Europe	190.91 million
Middle East	5.12 million
Canada and U.S.	182.67 million
Latin America	33.35 million
Worldwide	**605.60 million**

Source: Nua Internet Surveys

Some Major Internet Nations (By Percentage of Population Online)

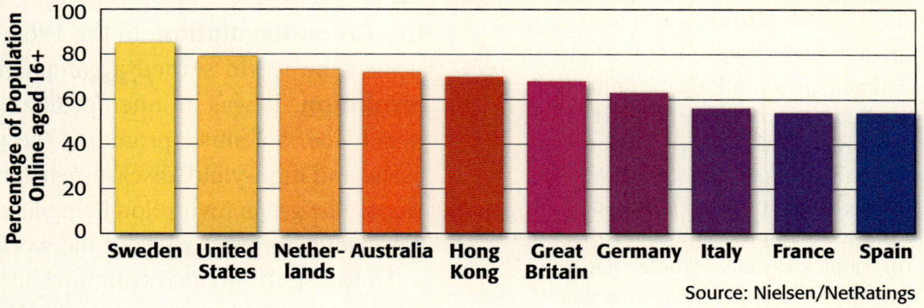

Source: Nielsen/NetRatings

SKILLBUILDER: Interpreting Charts and Graphs

1. **Comparing** *In which world region do most Internet users live?*
2. **Drawing Conclusions** *How would you describe most of the nations with large percentages of their populations online?*

Communications Networks Starting in the 1990s, businesses and individuals began using the **Internet**. The Internet is the voluntary linkage of computer networks around the world. It began in the late 1960s as a method of linking scientists so they could exchange information about research. Through telephone-line links, business and personal computers can be hooked up with computer networks. These networks allow users to communicate with people across the nation and around the world. Between 1995 and late 2002, the number of worldwide Internet users soared from 26 million to more than 600 million.

MAIN IDEA

Summarizing

B What types of technology have recently changed the workplace?

Conducting business on the Internet has become a way of life for many. The Internet, along with fax machines, transmits information electronically to remote locations. Both paved the way for home offices and telecommuting—working at home using a computer connected to a business network. Once again, as it has many times in the past, technology has changed how and where people work. **B**

Transforming Human Life

Advances with computers and communications networks have transformed not only the ways people work but lifestyles as well. Technological progress in the sciences, medicine, and agriculture has improved the quality of the lives of millions of people.

Health and Medicine Before World War II, surgeons seldom performed operations on sensitive areas such as the eye or the brain. However, in the 1960s and 1970s, new technologies, such as more powerful microscopes, the laser, and ultrasound, were developed. Many of these technologies advanced surgical techniques.

Advances in medical imaging also helped to improve health care. Using data provided by CAT scans and MRI techniques, doctors can build three-dimensional images of different organs or regions of the body. Doctors use these images to diagnose injuries, detect tumors, or collect other medical information.

In the 1980s, genetics, the study of heredity through research on genes, became a fast-growing field of science. Found in the cells of all organisms, genes are hereditary units that cause specific traits, such as eye color, in every living organism. Technology allowed scientists to isolate and examine individual genes that are responsible for different traits. Through **genetic engineering**, scientists were able to introduce new genes into an organism to give that organism new traits.

Another aspect of genetic engineering is **cloning**. This is the creation of identical copies of DNA, the chemical chains of genes that determine heredity. Cloning actually allows scientists to reproduce both plants and animals that are identical to

Social History

Molecular Medicine

In 2003, scientists employed on the Human Genome Project completed work on a map of the thousands of genes contained in DNA—human genetic material. The information provided by this map has helped in the development of a new field of medicine. Called "molecular medicine," it focuses on how genetic diseases develop and progress.

Researchers in molecular medicine are working to identify the genes that cause various diseases. This will help in detecting diseases in their early stages of development. Another area of interest to researchers is gene therapy. This involves replacing a patient's diseased genes with normal ones. The ultimate aim of workers in this field is to create "designer drugs" based on a person's genetic makeup.

existing plants and animals. The application of genetics research to everyday life has led to many breakthroughs, especially in agriculture.

The Green Revolution In the 1960s, agricultural scientists around the world started a campaign known as the **green revolution**. It was an attempt to increase food production worldwide. Scientists promoted the use of fertilizers, pesticides, and high-yield, disease-resistant strains of a variety of crops. The green revolution helped avert famine and increase crop yields in many parts of the world.

However, the green revolution had its negative side. Fertilizers and pesticides often contain dangerous chemicals that may cause cancer and pollute the environment. Also, the cost of the chemicals and the equipment to harvest more crops was far too expensive for an average peasant farmer. Consequently, owners of small farms received little benefit from the advances in agriculture. In some cases, farmers were forced off the land by larger agricultural businesses.

Advances in genetics research seem to be helping to fulfill some of the goals of the green revolution. In this new "gene revolution," resistance to pests is bred into plant strains, reducing the need for pesticides. Plants being bred to tolerate poor soil conditions also reduce the need for fertilizers. The gene revolution involves some risks, including the accidental creation of disease-causing organisms. However, the revolution holds great promise for increasing food production in a world with an expanding population. C

MAIN IDEA

Recognizing Effects

C What are some of the positive and negative effects of genetic engineering?

Science and technology have changed the lives of millions of people. What people produce and even their jobs have changed. These changes have altered the economies of nations. Not only have nations become linked through communications networks but they are also linked in a global economic network, as you will see in Section 2.

NEW YORK CORE CURRICULUM REVIEW

TERMS & NAMES 1. For each term or name, write a sentence explaining its significance.
- International Space Station
- Internet
- genetic engineering
- cloning
- green revolution

USING YOUR NOTES

2. Which of the three developments do you think has had the greatest global effect? Why?

Developments	Effects
Communications	
Health and Medicine	
Green Revolution	

MAIN IDEAS

3. How does the development of the International Space Station show that space exploration has become a cooperative endeavor?
4. How has the development of the computer and the Internet changed the way people work?
5. What areas of medicine have benefited from scientific and technological developments?

CRITICAL THINKING & WRITING

6. **MAKING INFERENCES** Why do you think that space exploration became an arena for cooperation between the Soviet Union and the United States?
7. **HYPOTHESIZING** How do you think the Internet will affect the world of work in the future?
8. **FORMING AND SUPPORTING OPINIONS** Is there a limit to how far cloning should go? Why or why not?
9. **WRITING ACTIVITY** SCIENCE AND TECHNOLOGY -Use encyclopedia yearbooks and science magazines to identify a technological advance made in the last year. Write a brief **report** on the impact this advance has had on daily life.

CONNECT TO TODAY **CREATING A GRAPH**

Conduct research into how people use the Internet. Use your findings to construct a **graph** showing the most common Internet activities.

Global Economic Development

CONNECT TO THE NEW YORK STATE CORE CURRICULUM

Unit 8.B.3. Economic interdependence
Unit 8.C.1. Pollution–air, water, toxic waste (Europe)

TERMS & NAMES

- developed nation
- emerging nation
- global economy
- free trade
- ozone layer
- sustainable growth

SETTING THE STAGE At the end of World War II, much of Europe and Asia lay in ruins, with many of the major cities leveled by bombing. The devastation of the war was immense. However, with aid from the United States, the economies of Western European nations and Japan began expanding rapidly within a decade. Their growth continued for half a century, long after the United States ceased supplying aid. Advances in science and technology contributed significantly to this ongoing economic growth.

Technology Revolutionizes the World's Economy

TAKING NOTES

Categorizing Use a web diagram to identify the forces that have shaped the global economy.

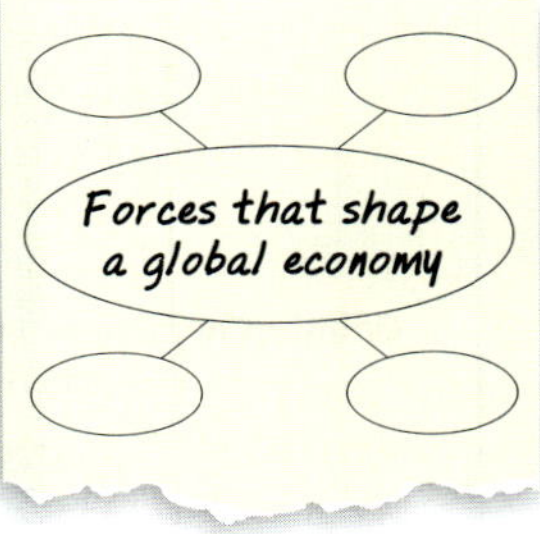

In both Asia and the Western world, an explosion in scientific knowledge prompted great progress that quickly led to new industries. A prime example was plastics. In the 1950s, a process to develop plastics from petroleum at low pressures and low temperatures was perfected. Within a few years, industries made a host of products easily and cheaply out of plastics. Other technological advances have also changed industrial processes, lowered costs, and increased the quality or the speed of production. For example, robotic arms on automobile assembly lines made possible the fast and safe manufacture of high-quality cars.

Information Industries Change Economies Technological advances in manufacturing reduced the need for factory workers. But in other areas of the economy, new demands were emerging. Computerization and communications advances changed the processing of information. By the 1980s, people could transmit information quickly and cheaply. Information industries such as financial services, insurance, market research, and communications services boomed. Those industries depended on "knowledge workers," or people whose jobs focus on working with information.

The Effects of New Economies In the postwar era, the expansion of the world's economies led to an increase in the production of goods and services so that many nations benefited. The economic base of some nations shifted. Manufacturing jobs began to move out of **developed nations**, those nations with the industrialization, transportation, and business facilities for advanced production of manufactured goods. The jobs moved to **emerging nations**, those in the process of becoming industrialized. Emerging nations became prime locations for new manufacturing operations. Some economists believe these areas were chosen because they had many eager workers whose skills fit manufacturing-type jobs. Also, these workers would work for less money than those in developed nations. On the other hand, information industries that required better-educated workers multiplied in the economies of developed nations. Thus the changes brought by technology then changed the workplace of both developed and emerging nations.

Economic Globalization

Economies in different parts of the world have been linked for centuries through trade and through national policies, such as colonialism. However, a true global economy did not begin to take shape until well into the second half of the 1800s. The **global economy** includes all the financial interactions—among people, businesses, and governments—that cross international borders. In recent decades, several factors hastened the process of globalization. Huge cargo ships could inexpensively carry enormous supplies of fuels and other goods from one part of the world to another. Telephone and computer linkages made global financial transactions quick and easy. In addition, multinational corporations developed around the world. (A)

MAIN IDEA

Analyzing Causes

(A) What elements helped to accelerate the process of globalization?

Multinational Corporations Companies that operate in a number of different countries are called multinational or transnational corporations. U.S. companies such as Exxon Mobil, General Motors, and Ford; European companies such as BP, DaimlerChrysler, and Royal Dutch/Shell; and Japanese companies such as Toyota, Mitsubishi, and Mitsui all became multinational giants.

All of these companies have established manufacturing plants, offices, or stores in many countries. For their manufacturing plants, they select spots where the raw materials or labor are cheapest. This enables them to produce components of their products on different continents. They ship the various components to another location to be assembled. This level of economic integration allows such companies to view the whole world as the market for their goods. Goods or services are distributed throughout the world as if there were no national boundaries.

Expanding Free Trade Opening up the world's markets to trade is a key aspect of globalization. In fact, a major goal of globalization is **free trade**, or the elimination of trade barriers, such as tariffs, among nations. This movement toward free trade is not new. As early as 1947, nations began discussing ways to open trade. The result of these discussions was the General Agreement on Tariffs and Trade (GATT). Over the years, several meetings among the nations that signed the GATT have brought about a general lowering of protective tariffs and considerable expansion of free trade. Since 1995, the World Trade Organization (WTO) has overseen the GATT to ensure that trade among nations flows as smoothly and freely as possible.

Vocabulary

tariff: a tax on goods imported from another country

Regional Trade Blocs A European organization set up in 1951 promoted tariff-free trade among member countries. This experiment in economic cooperation was so successful that six years later, a new organization, the European Economic Community (EEC), was formed. Over time,

Multinational Corporations, 2002

Based on a comparison of revenues with GDP, some of the top multinationals have economies bigger than those of several countries.

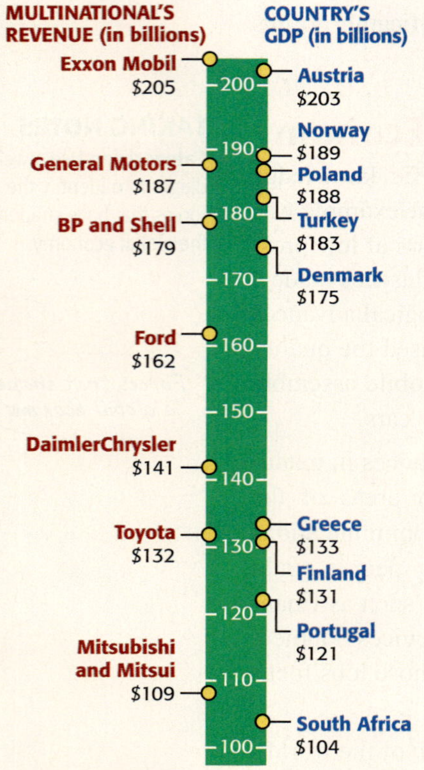

Source: *Forbes Magazine*/World Bank

SKILLBUILDER: Interpreting Graphs

1. **Comparing** *Which has the larger economy, Poland or Ford?*
2. **Clarifying** *Which multinationals have an economy greater than that of South Africa but smaller than that of Portugal?*

GEOGRAPHY SKILLBUILDER: Interpreting Maps

1. **Location** *Which countries in OPEC are located outside of Southwest Asia?*
2. **Location** *To which world trade organizations does the United States belong?*

most of the other Western European countries joined the organization, which has been known as the European Union (EU) since 1992. Several of the former Communist nations of Eastern Europe also have applied to become EU members.

Through this economic unification, Europe began to exert a major force in the world economy. The economic success of the EU inspired countries in other regions to make trade agreements with each other. The North American Free Trade Agreement (NAFTA), put into effect in 1994, called for the gradual elimination of tariffs and trade restrictions among Canada, the United States, and Mexico. Organizations in Asia, Africa, Latin America, and the South Pacific have also created regional trade policies.

Globalization—For and Against In recent years, there has been considerable debate on the impact of globalization. Supporters suggest that open, competitive markets and the free flow of goods, services, technology, and investments benefit all nations. Globalization, they argue, has resulted in a dramatic increase in the standard of living across the world. Even some opponents agree that practically all nations have seen some benefit from globalization. However, they note that the developed nations have benefited the most. Other opponents charge that globalization has been a disaster for the poorest countries. They suggest that many poor countries are worse off today than they were in the past. They argue that investment practices, trade agreements, and aid packages must be designed to protect the interests of the poorest nations.

> Analyzing Key Concepts

Globalization

Globalization can be described in broad terms as a process that makes something worldwide in its reach or operation. Currently, globalization is most often used in reference to the spread and diffusion of economic or cultural influences. The graphics below focus on economic globalization. The first shows a global corporation. The second lists some arguments for and against economic globalization.

Global Corporation

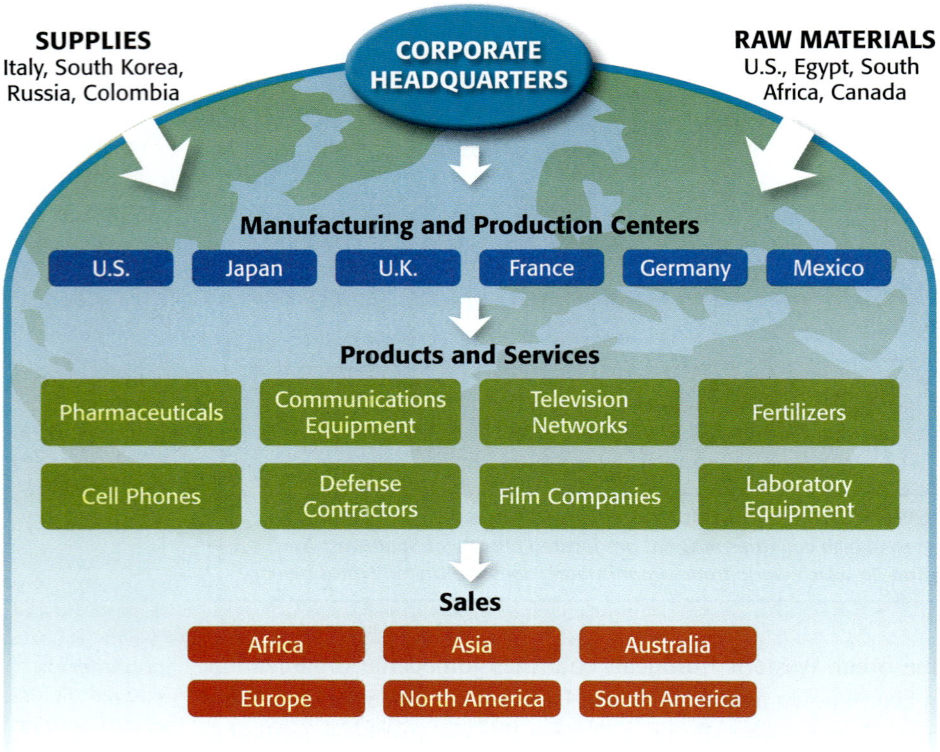

Arguments for and Against Economic Globalization

For	Against
• promotes peace through trade	• creates conflict because of an inherently unfair system
• raises the standard of living around the world	• benefits developed nations disproportionately
• creates jobs in emerging countries	• takes jobs from high-paid laborers in developed countries
• promotes investment in less developed countries	• benefits those who already have money
• creates a sense of world community	• erodes local cultures

INTEGRATED TECHNOLOGY
RESEARCH LINKS For more on globalization, go to **classzone.com**

> DATA FILE

INTERNATIONAL REGULATION

Many countries have joined international organizations to help regulate and stimulate the global economy. Such groups face the same criticisms against globalization in general.

World Trade Organization (WTO)

- Stated goal: "Help trade flow smoothly, freely, fairly, and predictably"
- 146 member nations; around 30 nations negotiating for admission (193 countries in the world)
- WTO members account for over 97 percent of world trade.

International Monetary Fund (IMF)

- Stated goal: "Promote international monetary cooperation; to foster economic growth and high levels of employment; and to provide temporary financial assistance to countries"
- 184 member countries
- In March 2003, IMF total resources were around $300 billion.

The World Bank Group

- Stated goal: "A world free of poverty"
- 184 member countries
- In 2002, this group provided $19.5 billion to emerging countries.

Connect *to* Today

1. **Making Inferences** How are money and culture related to each other when discussing globalization?
   See Skillbuilder Handbook, page R10.
2. **Making Predictions** Will globalization continue or will another process replace it? Why or why not?

Impact of Global Development

The development of the global economy has had a notable impact on the use of energy and other resources. Worldwide demand for these resources has led to both political and environmental problems.

Political Impacts Manufacturing requires the processing of raw materials. Trade requires the transport of finished goods. These activities, essential for development, require the use of much energy. For the past 50 years, one of the main sources of energy used by developed and emerging nations has been oil. For nations with little of this resource available in their own land, disruption of the distribution of oil causes economic and political problems.

On the other hand, nations possessing oil reserves have the power to affect economic and political situations in countries all over the world. For example, in the 1970s the Organization of Petroleum Exporting Countries (OPEC) declared an oil embargo—a restriction of trade. This contributed to a significant economic decline in many developed nations during that decade.

In 1990, Iraq invaded Kuwait and seized the Kuwaiti oil fields. Fears began to mount that Iraq would also invade Saudi Arabia, another major source of oil. This would have put most of the world's petroleum supplies under Iraqi control. Economic sanctions imposed by the UN failed to persuade Iraq to withdraw from Kuwait. Then, in early 1991, a coalition of some 39 nations declared war on Iraq. After several weeks of fighting, the Iraqis left Kuwait and accepted a cease-fire. This Persian Gulf War showed the extent to which the economies of nations are globally linked.

Environmental Impacts Economic development has had a major impact on the environment. The burning of coal and oil as an energy source releases carbon dioxide into the atmosphere, causing health-damaging air pollution and acid rain. Some scientists believe that the buildup of carbon dioxide in the atmosphere also has contributed to global warming.

The release of chemicals called chlorofluorocarbons (CFCs), used in refrigerators, air conditioners, and manufacturing processes, has destroyed ozone in Earth's upper atmosphere. The **ozone layer** is our main protection against the Sun's damaging ultraviolet rays. With the increase in ultraviolet radiation reaching Earth's surface, the incidence of skin cancer continues to rise in many parts of the world. Increased ultraviolet radiation also may result in damage to populations of plants and plankton at the bases of the food chains, which sustain all life on Earth.

▼ During the 1991 Persian Gulf War, the Iraqis set hundreds of Kuwaiti oil wells ablaze. Smoke from these fires clouded the skies more than 250 miles away.

Ozone Levels

A large area of the ozone layer has become much thinner in recent years.

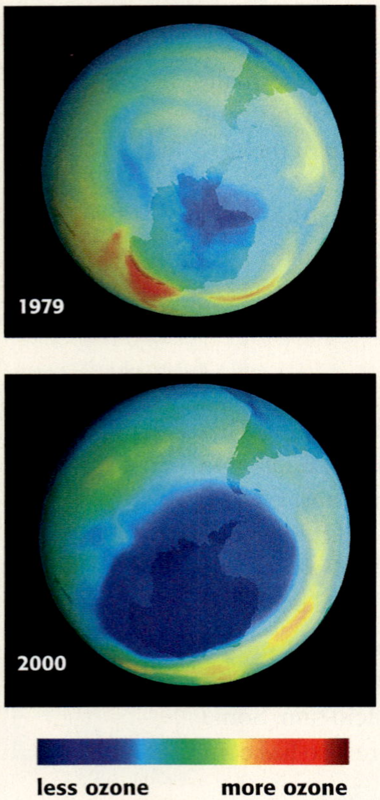

Economic development has also led to problems with the land. Large-scale soil erosion is a worldwide problem due to damaging farming techniques. The habitat destruction that comes from land development has also led to shrinking numbers of wildlife around the world. At present, the extinction rate of plants and animals is about a thousand times greater than it would naturally be, and appears to be increasing. This high extinction rate means that certain species can no longer serve as an economic resource. The resulting loss of wildlife could endanger complex and life-sustaining processes that keep Earth in balance.

"Sustainable Growth" Working together, economists and scientists are looking for ways to reduce the negative effect that development has on the environment. Their goal is to manage development so that growth can occur, but without destroying air, water, and land resources. The concept is sometimes called "green growth." Many people feel that the negative impact of economic growth on the environment will not be completely removed.

But "greener growth," also known as **sustainable growth**, is possible. This involves two goals: meeting current economic needs, while ensuring the preservation of the environment and the conservation of resources for future generations. Making such plans and putting them into practice have proved to be difficult. But many scientists believe that meeting both goals is essential for the health of the planet in the future. Because the economies of nations are tied to their political climates, such development plans will depend on the efforts of nations in both economic and political areas. **B**

MAIN IDEA

Clarifying

B What is meant by the term *sustainable growth*?

NEW YORK CORE CURRICULUM REVIEW

TERMS & NAMES 1. For each term or name, write a sentence explaining its significance.

- developed nation
- emerging nation
- global economy
- free trade
- ozone layer
- sustainable growth

USING YOUR NOTES

2. Which of these forces do you think has had the greatest impact on the development of a global economy?

MAIN IDEAS

3. Why are "knowledge workers" becoming more important in the developed nations?
4. What impact did the economic success of the EU have on other regions of the world?
5. How has global economic development affected the environment?

CRITICAL THINKING & WRITING

6. **RECOGNIZING EFFECTS** In what ways has technology changed the workplace of people across the world?
7. **ANALYZING MOTIVES** Why might some nations favor imposing tariffs on the imports of certain products?
8. **SUPPORTING OPINIONS** Do you think that sustainable growth is possible? Why or why not?
9. **WRITING ACTIVITY** ECONOMICS Make a survey of the labels on class members' clothing and shoes. List the countries in which these items were produced. Write a short **explanation** of how the list illustrates the global economy.

CONNECT TO TODAY **CREATING A POSTER**

Recycling is an important aspect of sustainable growth. Create a **poster** encouraging local businesses to recycle cans, paper products, and plastics.

Different **Perspectives:** **Using Primary and Secondary Sources**

INTERACTIVE

Economics and the Environment

Economists, politicians, and environmentalists came up with the concept of "sustainable growth"—both economic development and environmental protection are considered when producing a development plan for a nation. Some people see the relationship between economics and the environment as strained and getting worse. Others view policies protecting the environment as harmful to economies and ultimately harmful to the environment. The selections below examine these different perspectives.

A PRIMARY SOURCE

Lester R. Brown

Lester R. Brown is president of the Earth Policy Institute, which researches how to attain an environmentally sustainable economy and assesses current economic programs around the world.

Most decisions taken in economic policy are made by economic advisors. You can see this in the World Bank's annual development reports where they see the environment as a sub-sector of the economy. However, if you look at it as a natural scientist or ecologist, you have to conclude that the economy is a subset of the earth's ecosystem. . . .

Many of the problems that we face are the result of the incompatibility of the economy with the ecosystem. The relationship between the global economy, which has expanded sixfold over the last half century, and the earth's ecosystem is a very stressed one. The manifestations of this stress are collapsing fisheries, falling water tables, shrinking forests, expanding deserts, rising carbon dioxide levels, rising temperatures, melting ice, dying coral reefs, and so forth. Not only is this a stressed relationship but a deteriorating one.

B PRIMARY SOURCE

The Liberty Institute

The Liberty Institute is based in India and seeks to strengthen individual rights, rule of law, limited government, and free markets.

The market is the natural ally of the environment. Environmental resources, like other economic resources can be most efficiently allocated if these are brought under the discipline of the marketplace. It is ironic . . . [that] rather than creating a market for environmental resources, new restrictions are being imposed on the economy in the name of protecting the environment.

Environmental quality is like a value-added product that becomes economically affordable and technologically viable with economic growth. It is no paradox therefore that the environment is much cleaner and safer in industrially developed countries that adopted a more market-friendly approach. . . .

The market allows the consumer to register his price preference for a particular quality of product, including environmental quality.

C POLITICAL CARTOON

Chris Madden

Educating through humor, cartoonist Chris Madden illustrates the close connection between the environment and economics. A "ship of fools" is a metaphor for human weakness.

The ship of fools and the rocks of short-term economic planning

Document-Based QUESTIONS

1. Compare Sources A and B. Which perspective do you support? Why?
2. In your own words, describe the meaning of the cartoon in Source C.
3. Research an environmental issue facing your community and how economics is a part of the debate. Present your findings to the class.

Global Security Issues

CONNECT TO THE NEW YORK STATE CORE CURRICULUM

Unit 8.A.3.b. Global migration . . . .
Unit 8.D.1.7. Epidemics–AIDS

TERMS & NAMES

- proliferation
- Universal Declaration of Human Rights
- political dissent
- gender inequality
- AIDS
- refugee

SETTING THE STAGE World War II was one of history's most devastating conflicts. More than 55 million people died as a result of bombings, the Holocaust, combat, starvation, and disease. Near the end of the war, one of humankind's most destructive weapons, the atomic bomb, killed more than 100,000 people in Hiroshima and Nagasaki in a matter of minutes. Perhaps because of these horrors, world leaders look for ways to make the earth a safer, more secure place to live.

TAKING NOTES

Categorizing Use a chart to list collective methods employed by the world's nations to increase global security.

Method	*Examples*
Form military alliances	*NATO, SEATO, Warsaw Pact*

Issues of War and Peace

In the years after the end of World War II, the Cold War created new divisions and tensions among the world's nations. This uneasy situation potentially threatened the economic, environmental, and personal security of people across the world. So, nations began to work together to pursue collective security.

Nations Unite and Take Action Many nations consider that having a strong military is important to their security. After World War II, nations banded together to create military alliances. They formed the North Atlantic Treaty Organization (NATO), the Southeast Asia Treaty Organization (SEATO), the Warsaw Pact, and others. The member nations of each of these alliances generally pledged military aid for their common defense.

In addition to military alliances to increase their security, world leaders also took steps to reduce the threat of war. The United Nations (UN) works in a variety of ways toward increasing collective global security.

Peacekeeping Activities One of the major aims of the UN is to promote world peace. The UN provides a public forum, private meeting places, and skilled mediators to help nations try to resolve conflicts at any stage of their development. At the invitation of the warring parties, the UN also provides peacekeeping forces. These forces are made up of soldiers from different nations. They work to carry out peace agreements, monitor cease-fires, or put an end to fighting to allow peace negotiations to go forward.

As of the end of 2002, the UN had close to 40,000 soldiers and police in 13 peacekeeping forces around the world. Some forces, such as those in India and Pakistan, have been in place for decades. Others, such as those in East Timor, achieved their goals in only a few months.

Weapons of Mass Destruction Nations have not only worked to prevent and contain conflicts, they also have forged treaties to limit the manufacturing, testing, and trade of weapons. The weapons of most concern are those that cause mass destruction. These include nuclear, chemical, and biological weapons that can kill thousands, even millions of people.

▲ In central Baghdad, a U.S. Marine watches as a statue of Saddam Hussein is pulled down.

In 1968, many nations signed a Nuclear Non-Proliferation Treaty to help prevent the **proliferation**, or spread, of nuclear weapons to other nations. In the 1970s, the United States and the Soviet Union signed the Strategic Arms Limitation Treaties. In the 1980s, both countries talked about deactivating some of their nuclear weapons. Many nations also signed treaties promising not to produce biological or chemical weapons.

War in Iraq Other nations, however, have tried to develop weapons of mass destruction (WMD). Iraq, for example, used chemical weapons in conflicts during the 1980s. Many people suspected that the Iraqi leader, Saddam Hussein, had plans to develop biological and nuclear weapons too. As part of the cease-fire arrangements in the Persian Gulf War, Iraq agreed to destroy its weapons of mass destruction. UN inspectors were sent to monitor this disarmament process. However, in 1998, the Iraqis ordered the inspectors to leave.

In 2002, analysts once again suspected that Hussein might be developing WMD. UN weapons inspectors returned, but Hussein seemed reluctant to cooperate. U.S. President George Bush argued that Hussein might be close to building powerful weapons to use against the United States or its allies. In March 2003, Bush ordered American troops to invade Iraq. Troops from Great Britain and other countries supported the attack. After four weeks of fighting, Hussein's government fell.

However, violence in Iraq continued. Factions of Iraqis battled one another for power in the new government. Iraqis angered by the presence of foreign troops in their country fought American soldiers. By mid-2005, many thousands of Iraqis and over 1,800 Americans had been killed. No WMD had been found.

Ethnic and Religious Conflicts Some conflicts among people of different ethnic or religious groups have roots centuries old. Such conflicts include those between Protestants and Catholics in Ireland, between Palestinians and Israelis in the Middle East, and among Serbs, Bosnians, and Croats in southeastern Europe.

These conflicts have led to terrible violence. The Kurds of southwest Asia have also been the victims of such violence. For decades, Kurds have wanted their own country. But their traditional lands cross the borders of three countries—Turkey, Iran, and Iraq. In the past, the Turks responded to Kurdish nationalism by forbidding Kurds to speak their native language. The Iranians also persecuted the Kurds, attacking them over religious issues. In the late 1980s, the Iraqis dropped poison gas on the Kurds, killing 5,000. Several international organizations, including the UN, worked to end the human rights abuses inflicted upon the Kurds.

Human Rights Issues

In 1948, the UN issued the **Universal Declaration of Human Rights**, which set human rights standards for all nations. It stated that "All human beings are born free and equal in dignity and rights. . . . Everyone has the right to life, liberty, and security of person." The declaration further listed specific rights that all human beings should have. Later, in the Helsinki Accords of 1975, the UN addressed the issues of freedom of movement and freedom to publish and exchange information.

Both the declaration and the accords are nonbinding. However, the sentiments in these documents inspired many people around the world. They made a commitment to ensuring that basic human rights are respected. The UN and other international agencies, such as Amnesty International, identify and publicize human rights violations. They also encourage people to work toward a world in which liberty and justice are guaranteed for all.

Vocabulary
A *nonbinding* agreement means that a nation does not suffer a penalty if it does not meet the terms of the declaration.

Continuing Rights Violations Despite the best efforts of various human rights organizations, protecting human rights remains an uphill battle. Serious violations of fundamental rights continue to occur around the world.

One type of violation occurs when governments try to stamp out **political dissent**, or the difference of opinion over political issues. In many countries around the world, from Cuba to Iran to Myanmar, individuals and groups have been persecuted for holding political views that differ from those of the people in power. In some countries, ethnic or racial hatreds lead to human rights abuses. In Rwanda, for example, fighting between Hutus and Tutsis—the two main ethnic groups—led to horrendous rights violations. In 1994, Hutus massacred about 500,000 Tutsis in one of the worst cases of genocide. A

MAIN IDEA
Analyzing Issues
A What responsibilities do nations have for protecting human rights in other countries?

Women's Status Improves In the past, when women in Western nations entered the work force, they often faced discrimination in employment and salary. In non-Western countries, many women not only faced discrimination in jobs, they were denied access to education. In regions torn by war or ethnic conflict, they were often victims of violence and abuse. As women suffered, so too did their family members, especially children.

However, in the 1970s, a heightened awareness of human rights encouraged women in many countries to work to improve their lives. They pushed for new laws and government policies that gave them greater equality. In 1975, the UN held the first of several international conferences on women's status in the world. The fourth conference was held in Beijing, China, in 1995. It addressed such issues as preventing violence against women and empowering women to take leadership roles in politics and in business.

In 2000, the UN reviewed the status of women. Its report, titled *Progress of the World's Women 2000,* found that women had made notable gains during the 1990s, especially in the areas of education and work. Even so, the report concluded that **gender inequality**—the difference between men and women in terms of wealth and status—still very much existed.

History Makers

Mother Teresa 1910–1997

Mother Teresa was one of the great champions of human rights for all people. Born Agnes Gonxha Bojaxhiu in what today is Macedonia, Mother Teresa joined a convent in Ireland at the age of 18. A short time later, she headed to India to teach at a girls' school. Over time, she noticed many sick and homeless people in the streets. She soon vowed to devote her life to helping India's poor.

In 1948, she established the Order of the Missionaries of Charity in Calcutta, which committed itself to serving the sick, needy, and unfortunate. In recognition of her commitment to the downtrodden, Mother Teresa received the Nobel Peace Prize in 1979.

INTEGRATED TECHNOLOGY
RESEARCH LINKS For more on Mother Teresa, go to **classzone.com**

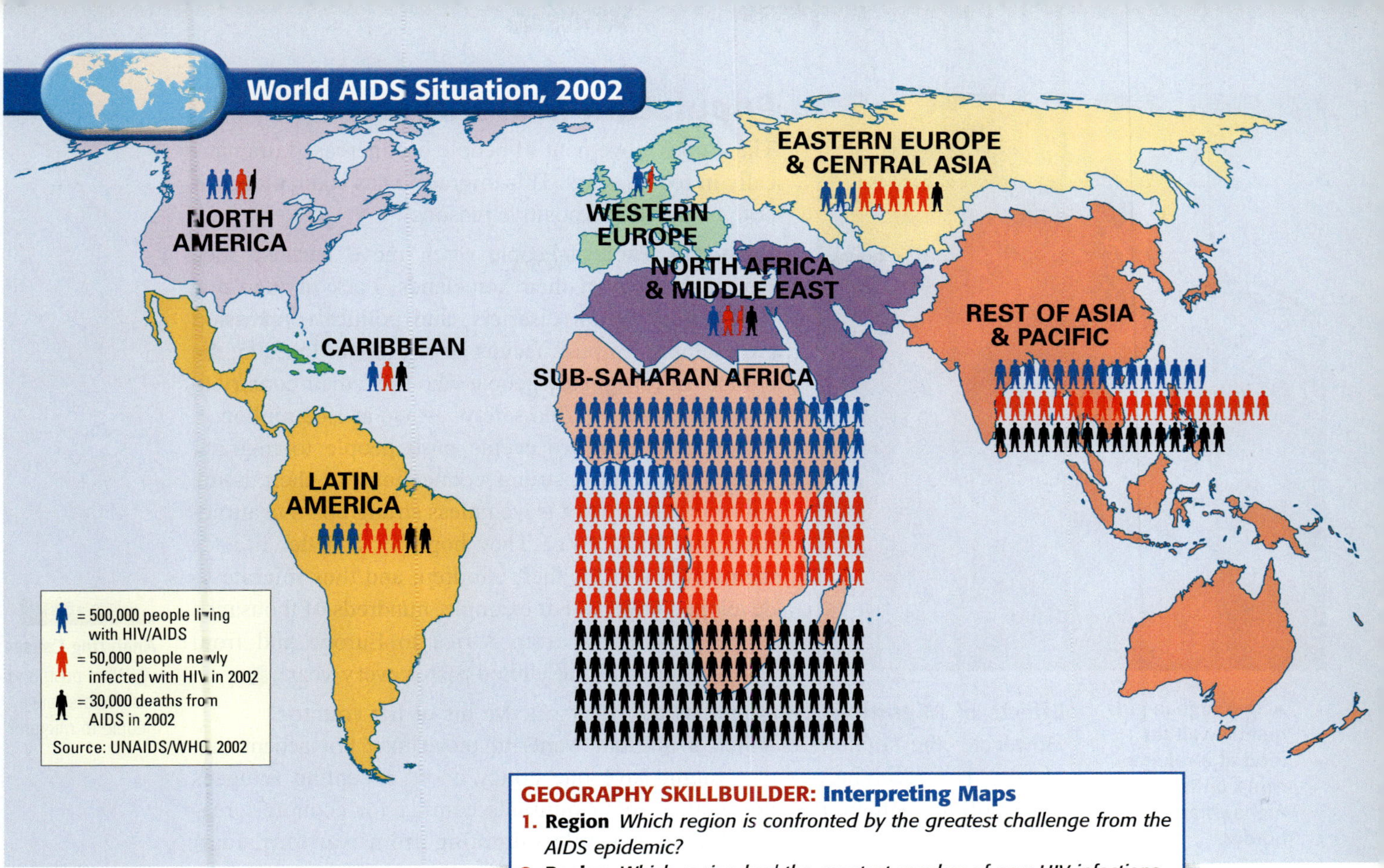

GEOGRAPHY SKILLBUILDER: Interpreting Maps

1. **Region** *Which region is confronted by the greatest challenge from the AIDS epidemic?*
2. **Region** *Which region had the greatest number of new HIV infections in 2002, Latin America or Eastern Europe and Central Asia?*

Health Issues

In recent decades, the enjoyment of a decent standard of health has become recognized as a basic human right. However, for many people across the world, poor health is still the norm. World health faced a major threat in 2003, with the outbreak of severe acute respiratory syndrome (SARS). This pneumonia-like disease emerged in China and rapidly spread to other Asian countries, Europe, and North America. Afraid of infection, many people canceled travel to Asia. The resulting loss of business hurt the economies of several Asian countries.

The AIDS Epidemic Perhaps the greatest global health issue is a disease known as **AIDS**, or acquired immune deficiency syndrome. It attacks the immune system, leaving sufferers open to deadly infections. The disease was first detected in the early 1980s. Since that time, AIDS has claimed the lives of nearly 25 million people worldwide. By the end of 2002, there were 42 million people across the world living with HIV (the virus that causes AIDS) or AIDS. And in 2002, 5 million people were newly infected with HIV.

While AIDS is a worldwide problem, Sub-Saharan Africa has suffered most from the epidemic. About 70 percent of the world's HIV and AIDS sufferers live in this region. And in 2002, on average more than 6,500 people died of AIDS each day. Most of the people dying are between the ages of 15 and 49—the years when people are at their most productive economically. AIDS, therefore, is reducing the number of people available as workers, managers, and entrepreneurs. As a result, economic growth is slowing in many countries in the region.

In response to the devastating impact of the disease, the UN issued the Declaration of Commitment on HIV/AIDS in 2001. This document set targets for halting the spread of AIDS and provided guidelines on how countries could pool their efforts.

▲ Two Afghan girls quietly wait for food at a refugee camp on the Afghanistan-Iran border.

Population Movement

The global movement of people has increased dramatically in recent years. This migration has taken place for both negative and positive reasons.

Push-Pull Factors People often move because they feel pushed out of their homelands. Lack of food due to drought, natural disasters, and political oppression are examples of push factors of migration. In 2005, the number of **refugees**—people who leave their country to move to another to find safety—stood at 19.2 million.

Not only negative events push people to migrate. Most people have strong connections to their home countries and do not leave unless strong positive attractions pull them away. They hope for a better life for themselves and for their children, and thus migrate to developed nations. For example, hundreds of thousands of people migrate from Africa to Europe and from Latin America to the United States every year. B

MAIN IDEA

Analyzing Causes

B What push and pull factors cause people to migrate?

Effects of Migration Everyone has the right to leave his or her country. However, the country to which a migrant wants to move may not accept that person. The receiving country might have one policy about accepting refugees from political situations, and another about migrants coming for economic reasons. Because of the huge volume of people migrating from war-torn, famine-stricken, and politically unstable regions, millions of immigrants have no place to go. Crowded into refugee camps, often under squalid conditions, these migrants face a very uncertain future.

On the positive side, immigrants often are a valuable addition to their new country. They help offset labor shortages in a variety of industries. They bring experiences and knowledge that can spur the economy. In addition, they contribute to the sharing, shaping, and blending of a newly enriched culture.

NEW YORK CORE CURRICULUM REVIEW

TERMS & NAMES 1. For each term or name, write a sentence explaining its significance.

- proliferation
- Universal Declaration of Human Rights
- political dissent
- gender inequality
- AIDS
- refugee

USING YOUR NOTES

2. What methods have resulted in the greatest contribution to global security? Why?

Method	Examples
Form military alliances	NATO, SEATO, Warsaw Pact

MAIN IDEAS

3. What steps have nations taken to control the proliferation of weapons of mass destruction?
4. How has AIDS affected the economy of Sub-Saharan Africa?
5. What positive effects does immigration have?

CRITICAL THINKING & WRITING

6. **MAKING INFERENCES** Why might nations want to retain or develop an arsenal of nuclear, biological, and chemical weapons?
7. **IDENTIFYING PROBLEMS** How are ethnic and religious conflicts related to problems of global security?
8. **RECOGNIZING EFFECTS** How can individuals affect social conditions around the world? Consider the example of Mother Teresa when writing your answer.
9. **WRITING ACTIVITY** SCIENCE AND TECHNOLOGY -Write a **paragraph** explaining how advances in science and technology have increased threats to global security.

CONNECT TO TODAY **CREATING A DATABASE**

Locate recent information on refugees around the world. Use your findings to create a **database** of charts and graphs titled "The Global Refugee Situation."

Terrorism

CASE STUDY: September 11, 2001

CONNECT TO THE NEW YORK STATE CORE CURRICULUM

Methodology.D.3. Political concepts of power, authority, governance,and law
Unit 7.F.4. Role of terrorism

TERMS & NAMES

- terrorism
- cyberterrorism
- Department of Homeland Security
- USA Patriot Act

SETTING THE STAGE Wars are not the only threat to international peace and security. **Terrorism**, the use of violence against people or property to force changes in societies or governments, strikes fear in the hearts of people everywhere. Recently, terrorist incidents have increased dramatically around the world. Because terrorists often cross national borders to commit their acts or to escape to countries friendly to their cause, most people consider terrorism an international problem.

TAKING NOTES

Categorizing Use a chart to note information about the September 11 terrorist attacks and other terrorist incidents around the world.

World Terrorist Incidents
September 11 Attacks

What Is Terrorism?

Terrorism is not new. Throughout history, individuals, small groups, and governments have used terror tactics to try to achieve political or social goals, whether to bring down a government, eliminate opponents, or promote a cause. In recent times, however, terrorism has changed.

Modern Terrorism Since the late 1960s, more than 14,000 terrorist attacks have occurred worldwide. International terrorist groups have carried out increasingly destructive, high-profile attacks to call attention to their goals and to gain major media coverage. Many countries also face domestic terrorists who oppose their governments' policies or have special interests to promote.

The reasons for modern terrorism are many. The traditional motives, such as gaining independence, expelling foreigners, or changing society, still drive various terrorist groups. These groups use violence to force concessions from their enemies, usually the governments in power. But other kinds of terrorists, driven by radical religious and cultural motives, began to emerge in the late 20th century.

The goal of these terrorists is the destruction of what they consider the forces of evil. This evil might be located in their own countries or in other parts of the world. These terrorists are ready to use any kind of weapon to kill their enemies. They are even willing to die to ensure the success of their attacks.

Terrorist Methods Terrorist acts involve violence. The weapons most frequently used by terrorists are the bomb and the bullet. The targets of terrorist attacks often are crowded places where people normally feel safe—subway stations, bus stops, restaurants, or shopping malls, for example. Or terrorists might target something that symbolizes what they are against, such as a government building

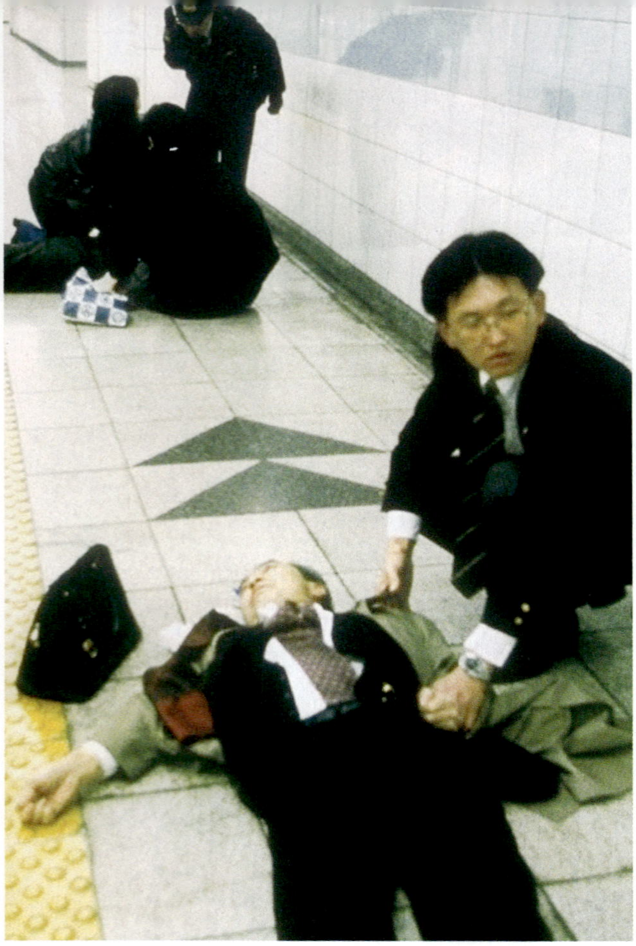

▲ The sarin gas attack in the Tokyo subway in 1995 is the most notorious act of biochemical terrorism.

or a religious site. Such targets are carefully chosen in order to gain the most attention and to achieve the highest level of intimidation. **A**

MAIN IDEA

Analyzing Motives

A Of what value would gaining public attention be to a terrorist group?

Recently, some terrorist groups have used biological and chemical agents in their attacks. These actions involved the release of bacteria or poisonous gases into the atmosphere. While both biological and chemical attacks can inflict terrible casualties, they are equally powerful in generating great fear among the public. This development in terrorism is particularly worrisome, because biochemical agents are relatively easy to acquire. Laboratories all over the world use bacteria and viruses in the development of new drugs. And the raw materials needed to make some deadly chemical agents can be purchased in many stores.

Cyberterrorism is another recent development. This involves politically motivated attacks on information systems, such as hacking into computer networks or spreading computer viruses. Experts suggest that as more governments and businesses switch to computers to store data and run operations, the threat of cyberterrorism will increase.

Responding to Terrorism Governments take various steps to stamp out terrorism. Most adopt a very aggressive approach in tracking down and punishing terrorist groups. This approach includes infiltrating the groups to gather information on membership and future plans. It also includes striking back harshly after a terrorist attack, even to the point of assassinating known terrorist leaders.

Another approach governments use is to make it more difficult for terrorists to act. This involves eliminating extremists' sources of funds and persuading governments not to protect or support terrorist groups. It also involves tightening security measures so as to reduce the targets vulnerable to attack.

Terrorism Around the World

The problem of modern international terrorism first came to world attention in a shocking way during the 1972 Summer Olympic Games in Munich, Germany (then West Germany). Members of a Palestinian terrorist group killed two Israeli athletes and took nine others hostage. Five of the terrorists, all the hostages, and a police officer were later killed in a bloody gun battle. Since then, few regions of the world have been spared from terrorist attacks.

The Middle East Many terrorist organizations have roots in the Israeli-Palestinian conflict over land in the Middle East. Groups such as the Palestine Islamic Jihad, Hamas, and Hizballah have sought to prevent a peace settlement between Israel and the Palestinians. They want a homeland for the Palestinians on their own terms, with the most extreme among them denying Israel's right to exist. In a continual cycle of violence, the Israelis retaliate after most terrorist attacks, and the terrorists strike again. Moderates in the region believe that the only long-term solution is a compromise between Israel and the Palestinians over the issue of land. However, the violence has continued with only an occasional break.

Europe Many countries in Europe have been targets of domestic terrorists who oppose government policies. For example, for decades the mostly Catholic Irish Republican Army (IRA) engaged in terrorist attacks against Britain because it opposed British control of Northern Ireland. Since 1998, however, the British, the IRA, and representatives of Northern Ireland's Protestants have been negotiating a peaceful solution to the situation. An agreement was reached in 2005.

Asia Afghanistan, in Southwest Asia, became a haven for international terrorists after the Taliban came to power in 1996. (See Chapter 34.) In that year, Osama bin Laden, a Saudi Arabian millionaire involved in terrorist activities, moved to Afghanistan. There he began using mountain hideouts as a base of operations for his global network of Muslim terrorists known as al-Qaeda.

Terrorist groups have arisen in East Asia, as well. One, known as Aum Shinrikyo ("Supreme Truth"), is a religious cult that wants to control Japan. In 1995, cult members released sarin, a deadly nerve gas, in subway stations in Tokyo. Twelve people were killed and more than 5,700 injured. This attack brought global attention to the threat of biological and chemical agents as terrorist weapons.

Africa Civil unrest and regional wars were the root causes of most terrorist activity in Africa at the end of the 20th century. But al-Qaeda cells operated in many African countries, and several major attacks against U.S. personnel and facilities in Africa were linked to al-Qaeda. In 1998, for example, bombings at the U.S. embassies in Kenya and Tanzania left over 200 dead and more than 5,000 people injured. The United States responded to these attacks with missile strikes on suspected terrorist facilities in Afghanistan and in Sudan, where bin Laden was based from 1991 to 1996.

Latin America Narcoterrorism, or terrorism linked to drug trafficking, is a major problem in Latin America, particularly in Colombia. The powerful groups that control that country's narcotics trade have frequently turned to violence. The Revolutionary Armed Forces of Colombia (FARC) is a left-wing guerrilla group that has links with these drug traffickers. The FARC has attacked Colombian political, military, and economic targets, as well as those with American ties. **B**

MAIN IDEA

Analyzing Causes

B What are some reasons for terrorism in various regions of the world?

International Terrorist Attacks

Total Attacks, 1982–2002

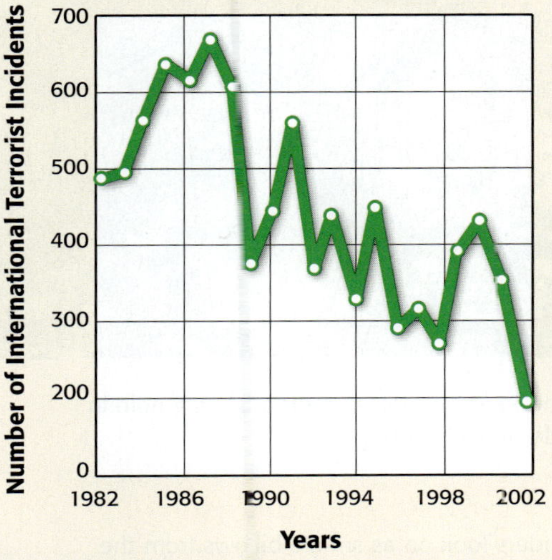

International Casualties of Terrorism, 1997–2002

	Africa	Asia	Eurasia	Latin America	Middle East	North America	Western Europe
1997	28	344	27	11	480	7	17
1998	5,379	635	12	195	68	0	405
1999	185	690	8	10	31	0	16
2000	102	904	103	20	78	0	4
2001	150	651	0	6	513	4,091	20
2002	12	1281	615	52	772	0	6
Total	5,856	4,505	765	294	1,942	4,098	468

Source: U.S. Department of State

SKILLBUILDER: Interpreting Charts and Graphs

1. **Comparing** *Which three areas suffered the greatest numbers of casualties of terrorism?*
2. **Drawing Conclusions** *How would you describe the overall trend in worldwide terrorist attacks since the mid-1980s?*

Case Study: September 11, 2001

Attack on the United States

On the morning of September 11, 2001, 19 Arab terrorists hijacked four airliners heading from East Coast airports to California. In a series of coordinated strikes, the hijackers crashed two of the jets into the twin towers of the World Trade Center in New York City and a third into the Pentagon outside Washington, D.C. The fourth plane crashed in an empty field in Pennsylvania. C

MAIN IDEA

Making Inferences

C Why were the specific targets of the September 11 attacks selected by the terrorists?

The Destruction The planes, loaded with fuel, became destructive missiles when they crashed into the World Trade Center and the Pentagon. The explosions and fires so weakened the damaged skyscrapers that they crumbled to the ground less than two hours after impact. The fire and raining debris caused nearby buildings to collapse as well. The damage at the Pentagon, though extensive, was confined to one section of the building.

The toll in human lives was great. About 3,000 people died in the attacks. All passengers on the four planes were killed, as well as workers and visitors in the World Trade Center and the Pentagon. The dead included more than 340 New York City firefighters and 60 police officers who rushed to the scene to help and were buried in the rubble when the skyscrapers collapsed.

The Impact of the Attack September 11 had a devastating impact on the way Americans looked at life. Many reported feeling that everything had changed—that life would never be the same. Before, Americans had viewed terrorism as something that happened in other countries. Now they felt vulnerable and afraid.

This sense of vulnerability was underscored just a few days after September 11, when terrorism struck the United States again. Letters containing spores of a bacterium that causes the disease anthrax were sent to people in the news media and to members of Congress in Washington, D.C. Anthrax bacteria, when inhaled, can

Destruction in New York City and the Pentagon

▲ The strike on the Pentagon left a charred, gaping hole in the southwest side of the building.

◄ Stunned bystanders look on as smoke billows from the twin towers of the World Trade Center.

▲ A hazardous materials team prepares to enter a congressional building during the anthrax scare.

damage the lungs and cause death. Five people who came in contact with spores from the tainted letters died of inhalation anthrax. Two were postal workers.

Investigators did not find a link between the September 11 attacks and the anthrax letters. Some of them believed that the letters might be the work of a lone terrorist rather than an organized group. Regardless of who was responsible for the anthrax scare, it caused incredible psychological damage. Many Americans were now fearful of an everyday part of life—the mail.

The United States Responds

Immediately after September 11, the United States called for an international effort to combat terrorist groups. President George W. Bush declared, "This battle will take time and resolve. But make no mistake about it: we will win."

As a first step in this battle, the U.S. government organized a massive effort to identify those responsible for the attacks. Officials concluded that Osama bin Laden directed the terrorists. The effort to bring him to justice led the United States to begin military action against Afghanistan in October, as you read in Chapter 34.

Antiterrorism Measures The federal government warned Americans that additional terrorist attacks were likely. It then took action to prevent such attacks. The **Department of Homeland Security** was created in 2002 to coordinate national efforts against terrorism. Antiterrorism measures included a search for terrorists in the United States and the passage of antiterrorism laws.

The al-Qaeda network was able to carry out its terrorist attacks partly through the use of "sleepers." These are agents who move to a country, blend into a community, and then, when directed, secretly prepare for and carry out terrorist acts. A search to find any al-Qaeda terrorists who remained in the United States was begun. Officials began detaining and questioning Arabs and other Muslims whose behavior was considered suspicious or who had violated immigration regulations.

Some critics charged that detaining these men was unfair to the innocent and violated their civil rights. However, the government held that the actions were justified because the hijackers had been Arabs. The government further argued that it was not unusual to curtail civil liberties during wartime in order to protect national security. This argument was also used to justify a proposal to try some terrorist suspects in military tribunals rather than in criminal courts. On October 26, 2001,

▲ Passengers wait to go through a security check at La Guardia Airport in New York.

President Bush signed an antiterrorism bill into law. The law, known as the **USA Patriot Act**, allowed the government to

- detain foreigners suspected of terrorism for seven days without charging them with a crime
- tap all phones used by suspects and monitor their e-mail and Internet use
- make search warrants valid across states
- order U.S. banks to investigate sources of large foreign accounts
- prosecute terrorist crimes without any time restrictions or limitations.

Again, critics warned that these measures allowed the government to infringe on people's civil rights.

Aviation Security The federal government also increased its involvement in aviation security. The Federal Aviation Administration (FAA) ordered airlines to install bars on cockpit doors to prevent passengers from gaining control of planes, as the hijackers had done. Sky marshals—trained security officers—were assigned to fly on planes, and National Guard troops began patrolling airports.

The Aviation and Transportation Security Act, which became law in November 2001, made airport security the responsibility of the federal government. Previously, individual airports had been responsible. The law provided for a federal security force that would inspect passengers and carry-on bags. It also required the screening of checked baggage.

Airline and government officials debated these and other measures for making air travel more secure. Major concerns were long delays at airports and respect for passengers' privacy. It has also become clear that public debate over security measures will continue as long as the United States fights terrorism and tries to balance national security with civil rights.

NEW YORK CORE CURRICULUM REVIEW

TERMS & NAMES **1.** For each term or name, write a sentence explaining its significance.

- terrorism
- cyberterrorism
- Department of Homeland Security
- USA Patriot Act

USING YOUR NOTES

2. How were the September 11 terrorist attacks unique? How were they similar to other terrorist incidents?

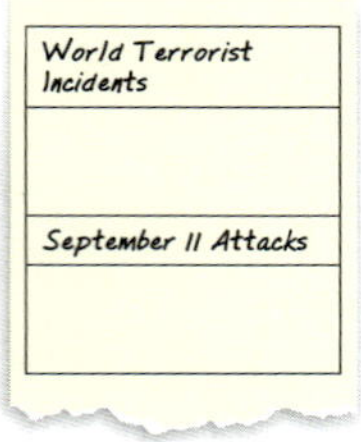

MAIN IDEAS

3. How has terrorism changed in recent years?

4. What methods do terrorists use?

5. What steps did the United States take in response to the terrorist attacks of September 11, 2001?

CRITICAL THINKING & WRITING

6. ANALYZING MOTIVES What might cause individuals to use terror tactics to bring about change?

7. FORMING AND SUPPORTING OPINIONS Is it important for the U.S. government to respect peoples' civil rights as it wages a war against terrorism? Why or why not?

8. DRAWING CONCLUSIONS What do you think has been the greatest impact of terrorism on American life?

9. WRITING ACTIVITY SCIENCE AND TECHNOLOGY Conduct research to find information on how science and technology are used to combat terrorism. Then write an **illustrated report** titled "Science and Counterterrorism."

INTEGRATED TECHNOLOGY **INTERNET ACTIVITY**

Use the Internet to research terrorist incidents since the end of 2001. Use your findings to create a **time line** titled "Recent Major Terrorist Attacks."

INTERNET KEYWORD
terrorism

Cultures Blend in a Global Age

CONNECT TO THE NEW YORK STATE CORE CURRICULUM

Unit 8.B.3. Economic interdependence
Unit 8.D.1. Information age/Computer Revolution/Internet

TERMS & NAMES

- popular culture
- materialism

SETTING THE STAGE Since the beginnings of civilization, people have blended ideas and ways of doing things from other cultures into their own culture. The same kind of cultural sharing and blending continues today. But, because of advances in technology, it occurs at a much more rapid pace and over much greater distances. Twenty-first-century technologies allow people from all over the world to have increasing interaction with one another. Such contacts promote widespread sharing of cultures.

TAKING NOTES

Categorizing Use a web diagram to identify areas of popular culture that have become international in scope.

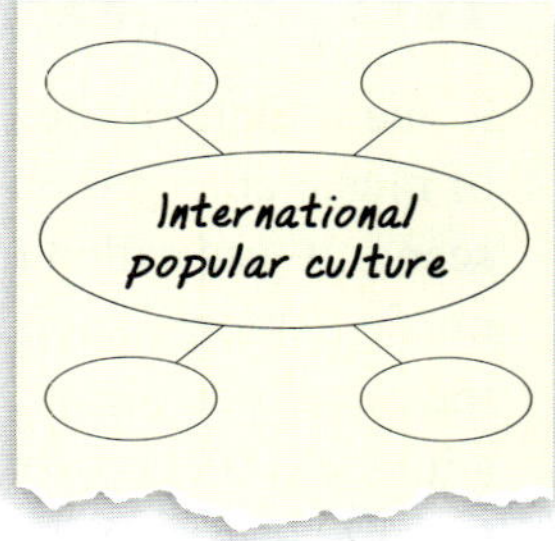

Cultural Exchange Accelerates

Cultural elements that reflect a group's common background and changing interests are called **popular culture**. Popular culture involves music, sports, movies, clothing fashions, foods, and hobbies or leisure activities. Popular culture around the world incorporates features from many different lands. Of all the technologies that contribute to such cultural sharing, television, movies, and other mass media have been the most powerful.

Mass Media More people in the United States have televisions than telephones. In fact, 98 percent of American households have at least one television set. Eighty-six percent of the homes have videocassette recorders (VCRs). In Western Europe, too, most households have one or more televisions. Access to television is not so widespread in the emerging nations, but it is growing. Recent estimates suggest that about half the population of the emerging world—some 2.5 billion people—have regular access to a television set.

Television provides a window to the world through daily newscasts and documentaries. The speed at which television can present information helps create an up-to-the-minute shared experience of global events. For example, in 2003, millions of television viewers across the world watched the war in Iraq. Wars, natural disasters, and political drama in faraway places have become a part of everyday life.

Television and other mass media, including radio and movies, are among the world's most popular forms of entertainment. Popular programs not only entertain but also show how people in other parts of the world live and what they value. Mass media is the major way popular culture spreads to all parts of the globe.

International Elements of Popular Culture The entertainment field, especially television, has a massive influence on popular culture. People from around

Global Patterns

International Baseball

The sport of baseball is an example of global popular culture. When American missionaries and teachers arrived in Japan in the 1870s, they introduced the game of baseball. Over the years the game gained popularity there. Today, some Major League teams have Japanese players and several American players play in the Japanese league.

Baseball spread to Mexico, Cuba, Puerto Rico, Panama, and the Dominican Republic in the late 19th and early 20th centuries. Today baseball is a popular game in these and other Latin American countries. And more than 25 percent of the players in Major League Baseball come from Latin America.

INTEGRATED TECHNOLOGY

INTERNET ACTIVITY Create a scrapbook of foreign players in Major League Baseball. Go to **classzone.com** for your research.

the world are avid viewers of American TV programs. For example, in Bhutan, a tiny country high in the Himalaya, ESPN, HBO, Cartoon Network, and CNN are among the most-watched channels. CNN truly is a global channel, since it reaches more than 200 million households in over 200 countries.

Television broadcasts of sporting events provide a front-row seat for sports fans all over the globe. Basketball and soccer are among the most popular televised sports. National Basketball Association (NBA) games are televised in over 200 countries. In China, for example, broadcasts of NBA games of the week regularly attract an audience in the millions. One of the most-watched international sporting events is the soccer World Cup. Nearly 63 million viewers worldwide watched the 2002 World Cup Final.

Music is another aspect of popular culture that has become international. As the equipment for listening to music has become more portable, there are only a few places in the world that do not have access to music from other cultures. People from around the world dance to reggae bands from the Caribbean, chant rap lyrics from the United States, play air guitar to rowdy European bands, and enjoy the fast drumming of Afropop tunes. And the performers who create this music often gain international fame. **A**

MAIN IDEA

Recognizing Effects

A What effects have television and mass media had on popular culture?

Global Impact: Cultural Crossroads

Rock 'n' Roll

In the middle of the 1950s, a new style of music emerged on the American scene. It was called rock 'n' roll. The music explored social and political themes. Rock music, which seemed to adults to reflect a youth rebellion, soon became the dominant popular music for young people across the world. As the influence of rock music spread, international artists added their own traditions, instruments, and musical styles to the mix called rock.

U2 ►

U2, led by singer Bono (right), is one of the world's most popular and influential rock bands. Over a career spanning more than 20 years, this Irish band has kept its music vibrant and fresh by absorbing and reworking all manner of musical styles. The band has drawn on the blues, gospel, 1950s rock 'n' roll, 1960s protest songs, and hip-hop to create a very distinctive kind of music.

"The King" ►

"Rock and roll music, if you like it and you feel it, you just can't help but move to it. That's what happens to me, I can't help it."—Elvis Presley, called the "King of rock 'n' roll" by many.

World Culture Blends Many Influences

Greater access to the ideas and customs of different cultures often results in cultural blending. As cultural ideas move with people among cultures, some beliefs and habits seem to have a greater effect than others. In the 20th century, ideas from the West have been very dominant in shaping cultures in many parts of the globe.

Westernizing Influences on Different Cultures Western domination of the worldwide mass media helps explain the huge influence the West has on many different cultures today. However, heavy Western influence on the rest of the world's cultures is actually rooted in the 19th century. Western domination of areas all over the globe left behind a legacy of Western customs and ideas. Western languages are spoken throughout the world, mainly because of Europe's history of colonization in the Americas, Asia, and Africa.

Over the past 50 years, English has emerged as the premier international language. English is spoken by about 500 million people as their first or second language. Although more people speak Mandarin Chinese than English, English speakers are more widely distributed. English is the most common language used on the Internet and at international conferences. The language is used by scientists, diplomats, doctors, and businesspeople around the world. The widespread use of English is responsible, in part, for the emergence of a dynamic global culture.

Western influence can be seen in other aspects of popular culture. For example, blue jeans are the clothes of choice of most of the world's youth. Western business suits are standard uniforms among many people. American-style hamburgers and soft drinks can be purchased in many countries of the world. Mickey Mouse and other Disney characters are almost universally recognized. Western influence also has an effect on ways of thinking in other parts of the world. For example, people

▲ **"World Pop"**

Youssou N'Dour, a singer from the West African country of Senegal, blends traditional African styles with American rock to create a new form that has been called "world-pop fusion."

Patterns of Interaction

Cultural Crossroads: The United States and the World

The spread of American culture, including sports, fashion, and fast food, has created an international culture recognizable in all corners of the globe. In some cases American culture is simply a powerful influence, as other societies blend American culture with local customs. Cultural blending is evident even in America's past. Symbols of American culture like baseball and hot dogs are themselves the result of cross-cultural influences.

Connect *to* Today

1. **Making Inferences** How have improvements in technology and global communications aided in the blending of musical styles?

See Skillbuilder Handbook, page R10.

2. **Creating Oral Presentations** Find out the global origins of such aspects of American culture as rock 'n' roll and baseball. Report your findings to the class in an oral presentation.

▲ Kenzaburo Oe of Japan was awarded the Nobel literature prize in 1994. Oe studied Western literature in college, and he has used Western literary styles to tell stories about his personal life and the myths and history of his country.

▲ South African writer Nadine Gordimer won the Nobel Prize for Literature in 1991. Many of her novels and stories published prior to 1991 focused on the evils of the apartheid system. As a result, much of her work was censored or banned by the South African government.

from many different cultures have adopted **materialism**, the Western mindset of placing a high value on acquiring material possessions.

Non-Western Influences Cultural ideas are not confined to moving only from the West to other lands. Non-Western cultures also influence people in Europe and the United States. From music and clothing styles to ideas about art and architecture, to religious and ethical systems, non-Western ideas are incorporated into Western life. And cultural blending of Western and non-Western elements opens communications channels for the further exchange of ideas throughout the globe.

The Arts Become International Modern art, like popular culture, has become increasingly international. Advances in transportation and technology have facilitated the sharing of ideas about art and the sharing of actual works of art. Shows and museums throughout the world exhibit art of different styles and from different places. It became possible to see art from other cultures that had not previously been available to the public.

Literature, too, has become internationally appreciated. Well-known writers routinely have their works translated into dozens of languages, resulting in truly international audiences. The list of Nobel Prize winners in literature over the last 20 years reflects a broad variety of nationalities, including Nigerian, Egyptian, Mexican, South African, West Indian, Japanese, Polish, Chinese, and Hungarian. B

MAIN IDEA

Summarizing

B Name three advances that allow a greater sharing of the arts.

Future Challenges and Hopes

Many people view with alarm the development of a global popular culture heavily influenced by Western, and particularly American, ways of life. They fear that this will result in the loss of their unique identity as a people or nation. As a result, many countries have adopted policies that reserve television broadcast time for national programming. For example, France requires that 40 percent of broadcast time be set aside for French-produced programs. And in South Korea, the government limits foreign programming to just 20 percent of broadcast time.

Some countries take a different approach to protecting cultural diversity in the media. Television programmers take American shows and rework them according to their own culture and traditions. As an Indian media researcher noted, "We really want to see things our own way." Other countries take more drastic steps to protect their cultural identity. They strictly censor the mass media to keep unwanted ideas from entering their nation.

Sometimes people respond to perceived threats to their culture by trying to return to traditional ways. Cultural practices and rites of passage may receive even more emphasis as a group tries to preserve its identity. In some countries, native groups take an active role in preserving the traditional ways of life. For example, the Maori in New Zealand have revived ancestral customs rather than face cultural extinction. Many Maori cultural activities are conducted in a way that preserves Maori ways of thinking and behaving. In 1987, the New Zealand government recognized the importance of this trend by making the Maori language one of the country's official languages. **C**

MAIN IDEA

Recognizing Effects

C How do people react against greater global interdependence?

Global Interdependence Despite the fear and uncertainty accompanying global interdependence, economic, political, and environmental issues do bring all nations closer together. Nations have begun to recognize that they are dependent on other nations and deeply affected by the actions of others far away. As elements of everyday life and expressions of culture become more international in scope, people across the world gain a sense of connectedness with people in other areas of the world. For example, the response to the events of September 11, 2001, was international in scope. People from around the world expressed their concern and support for the United States. It was as if this act of terrorism had struck their own countries.

Throughout history, human beings have faced challenges to survive and to live better. In the 21st century, these challenges will be faced by people who are in increasing contact with one another. They have a greater stake in learning to live in harmony together and with the physical planet. As Martin Luther King, Jr., stated, "Our loyalties must transcend our race, our tribe, our class, and our nation; and this means we must develop a world perspective."

NEW YORK CORE CURRICULUM REVIEW

TERMS & NAMES 1. For each term or name, write a sentence explaining its significance.

- popular culture
- materialism

USING YOUR NOTES

2. Which of the international popular culture aspects has the greatest effect on your life? Why?

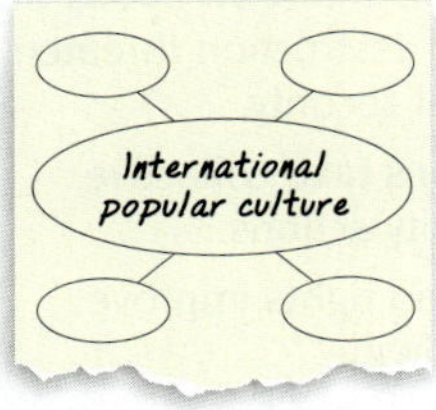

MAIN IDEAS

3. How do the mass media spread popular culture across the world?
4. Why do Western cultures tend to dominate other cultures?
5. What steps have governments and people taken to protect cultural diversity?

CRITICAL THINKING & WRITING

6. **CLARIFYING** Why are the mass media such an effective means of transmitting culture?
7. **RECOGNIZING EFFECTS** Do you think that limiting the amount of foreign television programming is an effective way to protect cultural diversity? Why or why not?
8. **FORMING AND SUPPORTING OPINIONS** "Ethnocentrism—the belief in the superiority of one's own ethnic group—has taken hold in the world." Do you agree or disagree? Explain.
9. **WRITING ACTIVITY** CULTURAL INTERACTION Write a **letter** to a friend in another country describing the elements of American popular culture they might appreciate.

CONNECT TO TODAY **CREATING A SCRAPBOOK**

Study current newspapers and magazines to find pictures that show cultural blending. Create a **scrapbook** of these pictures. Write captions explaining how each picture illustrates cultural blending.

Chapter 36 Assessment

TERMS & NAMES

For each term or name below, briefly explain its connection to global interdependence from 1960 to the present.

1. Internet
2. genetic engineering
3. global economy
4. free trade
5. political dissent
6. refugee
7. terrorism
8. USA Patriot Act
9. popular culture
10. materialism

MAIN IDEAS

The Impact of Science and Technology Section 1 (pages 1071–1074)

11. In what ways have science and technology changed the lives of people today?
12. What was the goal of the green revolution?

Global Economic Development Section 2 (pages 1075–1081)

13. How are a developed nation and an emerging nation different?
14. What is the function of the World Trade Organization?

Global Security Issues Section 3 (pages 1082–1086)

15. What methods has the world community used to resolve conflicts since World War II?
16. What efforts have been made to guarantee basic human rights?

Case Study: Terrorism Section 4 (pages 1087–1092)

17. What methods do terrorists employ?
18. How did the United States respond to the terrorist attacks of September 11, 2001?

Cultures Blend in a Global Age Section 5 (pages 1093–1097)

19. Which technologies have had the most powerful impact on cultural sharing?
20. Why have Western influences had a major impact all over the world?

CRITICAL THINKING

1. USING YOUR NOTES

SCIENCE AND TECHNOLOGY Use the diagram to show how advances in science and technology have changed lifestyles.

Cause	Effect
Miniaturization of computer parts →	
Expanded global communication →	
Genetic research →	

2. EVALUATING COURSES OF ACTION

POWER AND AUTHORITY How is the UN working to address the unresolved problems of the world?

3. IDENTIFYING SOLUTIONS

CULTURAL INTERACTION Imagine you are the culture minister of a small country. What steps would you take to ensure that your country's cultural identity is protected? Explain why you think these steps would be effective.

4. RECOGNIZING EFFECTS

ECONOMICS How are individuals affected by the global economy?

VISUAL SUMMARY

Global Interdependence

Economics

- Service industries grow in developed nations.
- Free trade expands world markets.
- Environmental challenges continue.

Culture

- Mass media spreads many cultures.
- Popular culture becomes more international.
- Global interdependence awareness develops.

Science and Technology

- Space cooperation stretches horizons.
- Advanced communications allow wider contact.
- Inventions improve life and health.

Politics

- Terrorism and weapons of mass destruction threaten global security.
- Nations take collective security actions.
- Human rights improve worldwide.
- Immigrants change cultures.

NEW YORK STATE REGENTS EXAM PRACTICE

Use the passage, which was written by a German journalist, and your knowledge of world history to answer questions 1 and 2.

Additional Test Practice, pp. S1–S33

PRIMARY SOURCE

Imagine a roomful of 14-year-olds—from Germany, Japan, Israel, Russia and Argentina. Obviously, they would all be wearing Levi's and baseball caps. But how would they relate to one another? They would communicate in English, though haltingly and with heavy accents. About what? . . . They would debate the merits of Nike versus Converse, of Chameleon versus Netscape. Sure, they would not discuss Herman Melville or George Gershwin, but neither would they compare notes on Dante or Thomas Mann. The point is that they would talk about icons and images "made in the U.S.A."

JOSEF JOFFE, from "America the Inescapable"

1 Which statement best describes the main idea of the excerpt?

(1) Many teenagers have little understanding of world literature.

(2) American popular culture plays a major role in teenagers' lives.

(3) All teenagers communicate in English.

(4) Most teenagers wear American-made clothes.

2 Which is the most likely way that teenagers in other countries learn about American popular culture?

(1) through the mass media

(2) through discussions with their parents

(3) through school textbooks

(4) through Internet bulletin boards

Use the graph and your knowledge of world history to answer question 3.

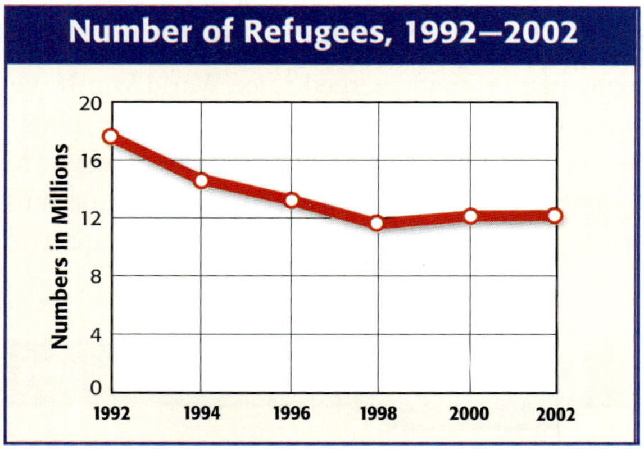

3 Which statement best describes the overall trend shown in this graph?

(1) There has been a steady rise in the number of refugees.

(2) The number of refugees has risen dramatically.

(3) There has been a steady fall in the number of refugees.

(4) The number of refugees has fallen dramatically.

INTEGRATED TECHNOLOGY

TEST PRACTICE Go to **classzone.com**

- Diagnostic tests
- Tutorials
- Strategies
- Additional practice

ALTERNATIVE ASSESSMENT

1. Interact *with* History

After reading Chapter 35, do you believe events in other nations affect your life? Which kinds of events are more likely to affect you in a very personal way? Create a survey about global interdependence to ask students in your class or school. Consider organizing your questions in four broad categories: science and technology, economics, security, and culture.

2. WRITING ABOUT HISTORY

Use the Internet and library resources to find information on SARS. Use your findings to write a brief **report.** Your report should cover the following topics:

- where and when the disease emerged.
- possible causes and methods of prevention.
- statistics on the disease.

INTEGRATED TECHNOLOGY

NetExplorations: The Environment

Go to *NetExplorations* at **classzone.com** to learn more about the environment and the dangers it faces. Working in a team with three other students, find information on a recent discovery concerning changes in the environment. Use your findings to create the script for a 10-minute television news segment on the discovery and its implications for everyday life. The script should include

- a description and explanation of the discovery
- interviews on the subject with scientists, government officials, and representatives of non-governmental organizations
- references to locations, sound, and visuals
- a concluding statement on the overall significance of the discovery and what, if anything, needs to be done about it

Five Developing Nations

Nation building is the creation of a state with a national identity. In Unit 8, you studied many nations that emerged since World War II. Forming a politically and economically stable country that safeguards basic human rights is a formidable task, especially in places where the people have different ethnic or religious backgrounds and different traditions and goals. To succeed, a new nation must forge a national identity. In the next six pages, you will see how five countries are working to become developed nations.

Israel

1945 1955 1965 1975

Six-Day War 1967
When the Egyptian military moved to strike Israel, Israeli forces attacked, destroying airfields in Syria, Jordan, Egypt, and Iraq. Israel won the war in six days.

India

1945 1975

Pakistan-India split 1947 ▲
After riots in 1946 killed thousands of Hindus and Muslims, the British agreed to partition India. About one million people were killed trying to move to one country or the other.

Mexico

1945 1955 1965 1975

The new party 1946
In 1946, the Mexican Revolutionary Party became the Institutional Revolutionary Party (PRI), which ruled for the next fifty years. Although the PRI promoted stability, it was politically corrupt.

Nigeria

1945 1965 1975

Independence 1960 ▲
Britain granted independence to Nigeria without military struggle.

War over Biafra 1967
The Ibos ethnic group tried to secede and form a new nation called Biafra. A bloody war ensued and the Ibos were defeated.

Philippines

1945 1955 1965 1975

Independence 1946
On July 4, the United States granted independence to the Philippines.

Marcos elected 1965
After being elected president, Ferdinand Marcos became an authoritarian ruler and stole money from the government. In 1972, he imposed martial law.

1985 1995 present

Camp David Accords 1979
Egypt and Israel signed the first treaty between Arabs and Israelis.

First intifada 1987 ►
The intifada was a widespread campaign of civil disobedience. Palestinians all over Israel participated in boycotts, demonstrations, rock throwing, and attacks on Israeli soldiers.

1985 1995 present

Indira Gandhi killed 1984
In October, prime minister Indira Gandhi was shot by two of her Sikh bodyguards in retaliation for an attack on a Sikh temple where terrorists were hiding.

Leadership changes 1998
The Congress Party had been in power in India since the country's creation in 1947, but in 1998 the Hindu nationalist party gained control.

1985 1995 present

Political opening 1988
In 1988, opposition parties were able to seriously challenge the ruling party for the first time.

Zapatista Uprising 1994 ►
Rebels seized control of several towns in the state of Chiapas, demanding more democracy and a better life for the native people.

1985 1995 present

Free election 1999
Nigeria held its first free election after almost 20 years of military dictators.

1985 1995 present

Fall of Marcos rule 1986 ▲
Marcos was forced into exile when he attempted to falsify the results of the 1986 election. Corazón Aquino became president.

Comparing & Contrasting

1. What are some problems that can arise in developing nations as a result of ethnic, religious, and economic problems?
2. How do Israel's religious problems differ from those of the other countries on the time line?

National Characteristics

Many developing nations are trying to bring together a patchwork of ethnic groups that historically competed or were hostile to each other. To complicate matters more, the groups often speak different languages. Choosing one group's language as the official language could earn government leaders the ill-will of the other groups. Moreover, the traditions of one group might be objectionable to another for moral or religious reasons. The chart below describes the current situation in the five sample countries.

	Political		Cultural	
	Government	**Flag**	**Language**	**Religion**
Israel	• Parliamentary democracy • Unicameral Knesset (parliament) • President elected for seven-year term by Knesset • Prime minister heads the largest party in the Knesset • Supreme Court appointed for life by president		• Hebrew (official) • Arabic (official for minority Arabs) • English (used commonly)	• Jewish, 80.1% • Muslim, 14.6% • Christian, 2.1%
India	• Federal Republic • Bicameral legislature elected by people and state assemblies • President chosen by electoral college; five-year term • Prime minister chosen by ruling party • Supreme Court appointed by president to serve until age 65		• Hindi (official and most common) • Over 200 languages spoken • English (used in education and government)	• Hindu, 81.3% • Muslim, 12% • Christian, 2.3% • Sikh, 1.9% • Buddhist, Jain, Parsi in small numbers
Mexico	• Federal Republic • Bicameral legislature, elected by popular vote or by party vote • President elected by popular vote for six-year term • Supreme Court appointed by president with consent of the Senate		• Spanish • Mayan, Nahuatl and other indigenous languages	• Roman Catholic, 89% • Protestant, 6%
Nigeria	• Republic • Bicameral legislature elected by popular vote • President elected by popular vote for one or two four-year terms • Supreme Court appointed by president		• English (official) • Hausa, Yoruba, Igbo, Fulani	• Muslim, 50% • Christian, 40% • Indigenous faiths, 10%
Philippines	• Republic • Bicameral legislature elected by popular vote • President elected by popular vote for six-year term • Supreme Court appointed by president to serve until age 70		• Filipino (official) • English (official) • Eight major dialects	• Roman Catholic, 83% • Protestant, 9% • Muslim, 5%

Economic	
Trading	**Main Export**
• Imports: crude oil, grains, military equipment, raw materials • Exports: fruits, vegetables, cut diamonds, high-technology equipment.	• cut diamonds 
• Imports: crude oil, machinery, fertilizer, chemicals, gems • Exports: software services, engineering products, gems, jewelry, textiles, chemicals, leather goods	• textiles and clothing 
• Imports: metalworking and agricultural machinery, electrical equipment, car parts for assembly and repair • Exports: petroleum products, silver, manufactured goods, cotton, coffee, fruits, and vegetables	• manufactured goods 
• Imports: machinery, chemicals, manufactured goods, food • Exports: petroleum and petroleum products, cocoa, rubber	• petroleum 
• Imports: fuels, consumer goods, raw materials, capital goods • Exports: coconut products, clothing, electronic products, machinery, and transport equipment	• electronics 

"How can [a people] think of themselves as a national people if they don't even have a single language unifying them? Language is one of the most important instruments of nation-building, a potentially powerful unifying force."

David Lamb, from *The Africans*

Comparing & Contrasting

1. What similarities are there among the governments of the countries listed on the chart?
2. Why does David Lamb think language is such an important part of nation building?

Important Trends

In their inaugural speeches, the following leaders outlined the principal problems they wished to address during their terms in office. Below are some highlights of what they said. Note that the problems they discuss are shared by many of the developing nations you studied in Unit 8.

PRIMARY SOURCE

INTERACTIVE

Israel

Prime Minister Ariel Sharon discusses the Israeli national identity.

I believe wholeheartedly that the State of Israel has no greater resource than themselves, the Jewish people. We shall strengthen the bond and connection with the Jews of the Diaspora and the Zionist education of our education system. We will work towards bringing masses of Jewish immigrants to Israel and their absorption in the country. We must educate our children towards values: to respect for others, to equality between people, to national pride and love of country.

DOCUMENT-BASED QUESTION

In Sharon's view, what should be the continuing objectives of Israel?

PRIMARY SOURCE

INTERACTIVE

India

President Abdul Kalam stresses the importance of keeping religion separate from government.

I wish to emphasize my unflinching commitment to the principle of secularism, which is the cornerstone of our nationhood and which is the key feature of our civilization strength. During the last one year I met a number of spiritual leaders of all religions. They all echoed one message, that is, unity of minds and hearts of our people will happen and we will see the golden age of our country, very soon. I would like to endeavor to work for bringing about unity of minds among the divergent traditions of our country.

DOCUMENT-BASED QUESTION

Why does Kalam think India needs a secular government?

PRIMARY SOURCE

INTERACTIVE

Mexico

Equal rights and economic opportunities are what the poor need in the view of President Vicente Fox.

I emphatically maintain that social justice is part of an efficient economy, not its adversary. It is time we recognized that everything cannot be solved by the State, nor can everything be solved by the market. I believe that the vote for democracy is inseparable from the vote for social equity.

Quality education, employment and regional development are the levers to remove, once and for all, the signs of poverty, which are inequity, injustice, discrimination and exclusion.

DOCUMENT-BASED QUESTION

According to Fox, what does Mexico have to provide its poor so they can obtain social equity?

PRIMARY SOURCE

INTERACTIVE

Nigeria

President Olusegun Obasanjo explains his plan to curb the military.

The incursion of the military into government has been a disaster for our country and for the military over the last thirty years. . . . [P]rofessionalism has been lost. Youths go into the military not to pursue a noble career but with the sole intention of taking part in coups and to be appointed as military administrators of states and chairmen of task forces. . . . A great deal of reorientation has to be undertaken and a re-definition of roles, re-training and re-education will have to be done to ensure that the military submits to civil authority and regains its pride, professionalism and traditions. We shall restore military cooperation and exchanges with our traditional friends.

DOCUMENT-BASED QUESTION

How does President Obasanjo propose to change the military culture in Nigeria?

PRIMARY SOURCE

INTERACTIVE

Philippines

President Gloria Macapagal Arroyo discusses the importance of the rule of law.

Politics and political power as traditionally practiced and used in the Philippines are among the roots of the social and economic inequities that characterize our national problems. Thus, to achieve true reforms, we need to outgrow our traditional brand of politics based on patronage and personality. Traditional politics is the politics of the status quo. It is a structural part of our problem.

We need to promote a new politics of true party programs and platforms, of an institutional process of dialogue with our citizenry. This new politics is the politics of genuine reform. It is a structural part of the solution.

DOCUMENT-BASED QUESTION

According to Macapagal Arroyo, how does traditional politics promote poverty and how does party politics promote social equity?

Comparing & Contrasting

1. How does Kalam's view of religion in national self-identity and government contrast with Sharon's?
2. How might party politics as described by Macapagal Arroyo help to achieve the solutions Fox considers essential?

EXTENSION ACTIVITY

Choose one of the countries studied in Unit 8 that became independent after World War II. Research on the Internet how that country has fared in recent times. Use the Web sites of major newspapers, magazines, and other news organizations to find information on how ethnic, religious, economic, and other relevant concerns are being handled. Organize this information into an oral presentation to explain how the country is or is not changing.

McDougal Littell

WORLD HISTORY

PATTERNS OF INTERACTION

Skillbuilder Handbook R1
Skills for reading, thinking, and researching

Primary Source Handbook R39
Historical documents from world history

Economics Handbook R64
Glossary of economic terms

Glossary R76
Important terms and definitions

Spanish Glossary R92
Important terms and definitions translated into Spanish

Index R107
Index of all topics in the textbook

Skillbuilder Handbook

Refer to the Skillbuilder Handbook when you need help in answering Main Idea questions or questions in Section Assessments and Chapter Assessments. In addition, the handbook will help you answer questions about maps, charts, and graphs.

SECTION 1: Reading Critically

1.1	Determining Main Ideas	**R2**
1.2	Following Chronological Order	**R3**
1.3	Clarifying; Summarizing	**R4**
1.4	Identifying Problems and Solutions	**R5**
1.5	Analyzing Causes and Recognizing Effects	**R6**
1.6	Comparing and Contrasting	**R7**
1.7	Distinguishing Fact from Opinion	**R8**

SECTION 2: Higher-Order Critical Thinking

2.1	Categorizing	**R9**
2.2	Making Inferences	**R10**
2.3	Drawing Conclusions	**R11**
2.4	Developing Historical Perspective	**R12**
2.5	Formulating Historical Questions	**R13**
2.6	Making Predictions	**R14**
2.7	Hypothesizing	**R15**
2.8	Analyzing Motives	**R16**
2.9	Analyzing Issues	**R17**
2.10	Analyzing Bias	**R18**
2.11	Evaluating Decisions and Courses of Action	**R19**
2.12	Forming and Supporting Opinions	**R20**
2.13	Synthesizing	**R21**

SECTION 3: Exploring Evidence: Print, Visual, Technology Sources

3.1	Analyzing Primary and Secondary Sources	**R22**
3.2	Visual, Audio, and Multimedia Sources	**R23**
3.3	Using the Internet	**R24**
3.4	Interpreting Maps	**R25**
3.5	Interpreting Charts	**R27**
3.6	Interpreting Graphs	**R28**
3.7	Analyzing Political Cartoons	**R29**

SECTION 4: Creating Presentations

4.1	Writing for Social Studies	**R30**
4.2	Creating a Map	**R31**
4.3	Creating Charts and Graphs	**R32**
4.4	Creating and Using a Database	**R33**
4.5	Creating a Model	**R34**
4.6	Creating/Interpreting a Research Outline	**R35**
4.7	Creating Oral Presentations	**R36**
4.8	Creating Written Presentations	**R37**

Section 1: *Reading Critically*

1.1 Determining Main Ideas

The **MAIN IDEA** is a statement that sums up the most important point of a paragraph, a passage, an article, or a speech. Determining the main idea will increase your understanding as you read about historic events, people, and places. Main ideas are supported by details and examples.

Understanding the Skill

STRATEGY: IDENTIFY THE TOPIC. To find the main idea of a passage, first identify the topic. Then, as you read, define the central idea about the topic that the many details explain or support. The following passage contains information about the Renaissance. The diagram organizes the information to help you determine the main idea.

1. **Identify the topic by first looking at the title or subtitle.** This title suggests a quick way to identify the topic by looking for the name of the Renaissance woman, Isabella d'Este.
2. **Look at the beginning and ending sentences of each paragraph for possible clues to the main idea.**
3. **Read the entire passage.** Look for details about the topic. What central idea do they explain or support?

1 A Renaissance Woman

Isabella d'Este was a woman who lived during the Renaissance. This historic period produced the ideal, or "universal," man—one who excelled in many fields. The concept of universal excellence applied almost exclusively to men. 2 Yet a few women managed to succeed in exercising power.

2 Isabella d'Este was one such woman. Born into the ruling family of the city-state of Ferrara, she married the ruler of Mantua, another city-state. Isabella brought many Renaissance artists to her court and acquired an art collection that was famous throughout Europe. She was also skilled in politics. When her husband was taken captive in war, Isabella defended Mantua and won his release. 3

STRATEGY: MAKE A DIAGRAM. State the topic and list the supporting details in a chart. Use the information you record to help you state the main idea.

Think how each detail supports the main idea.

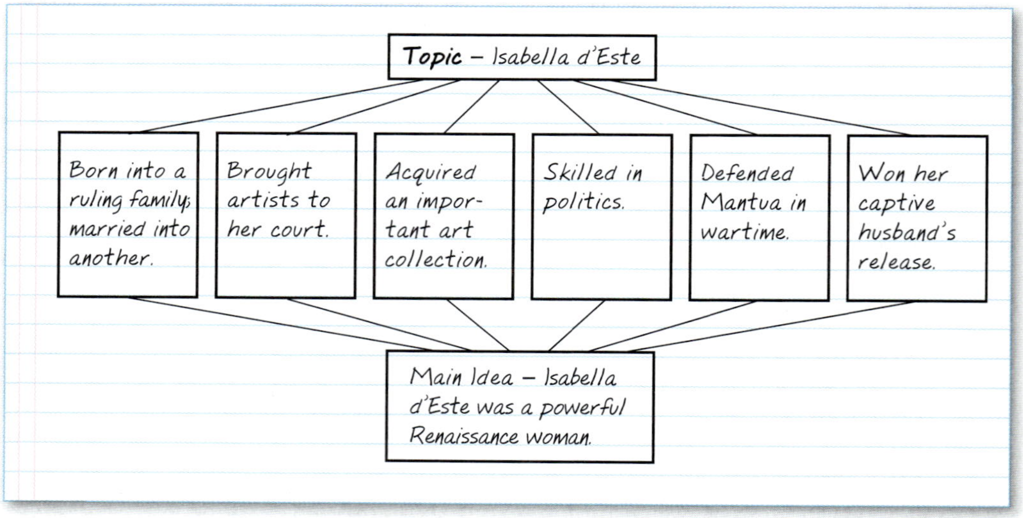

Applying the Skill

MAKE YOUR OWN DIAGRAM. Turn to Chapter 19, page 530. Read "Technology Makes Exploration Possible." Make a diagram, like the one above, to identify the topic, the most important details, and the main idea of the passage.

1.2 Following Chronological Order

CHRONOLOGICAL ORDER is the order in which events happen in time. Historians need to figure out the order in which things happened to get an accurate sense of the relationships among events. As you read history, figure out the sequence, or time order, of events.

Understanding the Skill

STRATEGY: LOOK FOR TIME CLUES. The following paragraph is about the rulers of England after the death of Henry VIII. Notice how the time line that follows puts the events in chronological order.

1. **Look for clue words about time.** These are words like *first, initial, next, then, before, after, followed, finally,* and *by that time.*
2. **Use specific dates provided in the text.**
3. **Watch for references to previous historical events that are included in the background.**

Henry's Children Rule England

(1) After the death of Henry VIII in (2) 1547, each of his three children eventually ruled. This created religious turmoil. Edward VI became king at age nine and ruled only six years. During his reign, the Protestants gained power. Edward's half-sister Mary (1) followed him to the throne. She was a Catholic who returned the English Church to the rule of the pope. Mary had many Protestants killed. England's (1) next ruler was Anne Boleyn's daughter, Elizabeth. After inheriting the throne in 1558, Elizabeth I returned her kingdom to Protestantism. In (2) 1559 Parliament followed Elizabeth's (3) request and set up a national church much like the one under Henry VIII.

STRATEGY: MAKE A TIME LINE.

If the events are complex, make a time line of them. Write the dates below the line and the events above the line.

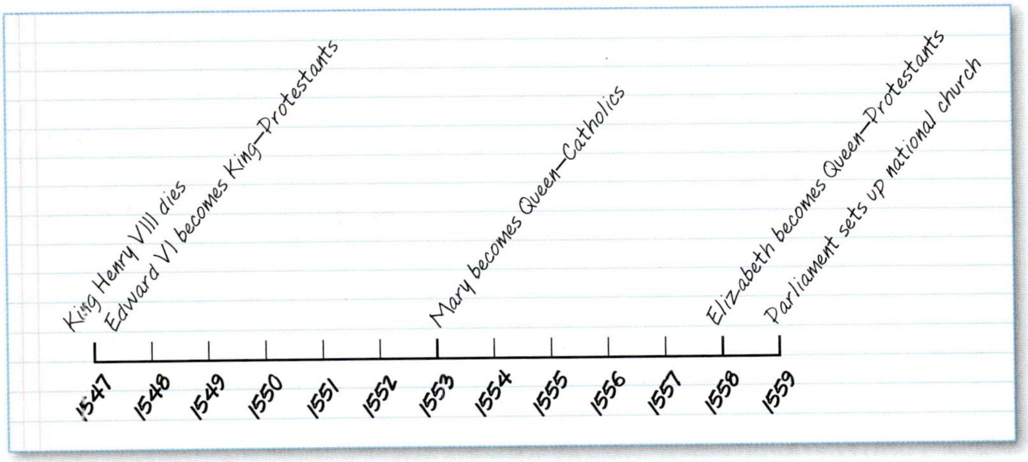

Applying the Skill

MAKE YOUR OWN TIME LINE. Skim Chapter 35, Section 4, "Changes in Central and Eastern Europe," to find out about the spread of democracy in parts of Europe controlled by the former Soviet Union. List the important dates and events. Start with the demonstrations in East Germany in October 1989, include events in Czechoslovakia and Romania and end with reunification of Germany in October of 1990. Decide on a scale for your time line. Show the important dates below the line and write what happened on each date above the line.

1.3 Clarifying; Summarizing

CLARIFYING means making clear and fully understanding what you read. One way to do this is by asking yourself questions about the material. In your answers, restate in your own words what you have read.

SUMMARIZING means condensing what you read into fewer words. You state only the main ideas and the most important details. In your own words, reduce the paragraph or section into a brief report of its general ideas.

Understanding the Skill

STRATEGY: UNDERSTAND AND CONDENSE THE TEXT. The passage below tells about trade in West Africa between 300 and 1600. Following the description is a summary that condenses and also clarifies the key information.

1. **Summarize: Look for topic sentences stating the main idea.** These are often at the beginning of a section or paragraph. Restate each main idea briefly.
2. **Clarify: Look up words or concepts you don't know.**
3. **Summarize: Include key facts and statistics.** Watch for numbers, dates, quantities, percentages, and facts.
4. **Clarify: Make sure you understand.** Ask yourself questions and answer them. For example, who's carrying what?

West African Trade

1 The wealth of the savanna empires was based on trade in two precious commodities, gold and salt. The gold came from a forest region south of the 2 savanna between the Niger and Senegal rivers. Working in utmost secrecy, miners dug gold from shafts as much as 100 feet deep or sifted it from fast-moving streams. 3 Until about 1350, at least two thirds of the world's supply of gold came from West Africa.

Although rich in gold, the savanna and forest areas lacked salt, a material essential to human life. In contrast, the 3 Sahara contained abundant deposits of salt. Arab traders, eager to obtain West African gold, carried salt across the Sahara by camel caravan. After a long journey, they reached the market towns of the savanna. 4 Meanwhile, the other traders brought gold north from the forest region. The two sets of merchants met in trading centers such as Timbuktu. Royal officials made sure that all traders weighed goods fairly and did business according to law.

STRATEGY: FIND AND CLEARLY RESTATE THE MAIN IDEA.

MAIN IDEA
Gold and salt were traded in West Africa.

STRATEGY: WRITE A SUMMARY.

Clarify and Summarize: Write a summary to clarify your understanding of the main ideas.

Summary
Trade in West Africa was based on gold from the south and salt from the north. Gold was mined in the forest regions. Two thirds of all the world's gold supply came from West Africa. Salt came from the desert. Arab traders met with African traders at trade centers such as Timbuktu.

Applying the Skill

CLARIFY AND WRITE YOUR OWN SUMMARY. Turn to Chapter 30, pages 874–876, and read "A Government of Total Control." Note the main ideas. Look up any words you don't recognize. Then write a summary of the section. Condense the section in your own words.

1.4 Identifying Problems and Solutions

IDENTIFYING PROBLEMS means finding and understanding the difficulties faced by a particular group of people at a certain time. Noticing how the people solved their problems is **IDENTIFYING SOLUTIONS.** Checking further to see how well those solutions worked is identifying outcomes.

Understanding the Skill

STRATEGY: LOOK FOR PROBLEMS AND SOLUTIONS. The passage below summarizes some economic problems facing Latin American nations during the early 20th century.

1. **Look for implied problems.** Problems may be suggested indirectly. This sentence suggests that a serious problem in Latin America was the uneven division of wealth.
2. **Look for problems people face.**
3. **Look for solutions people tried to deal with each problem.**
4. **Check outcomes to the solutions.** See how well the solutions worked. Sometimes the solution to one problem caused another problem.

Land Reform In Latin America

In Latin America, concentration of productive land in the hands of a (1) few created extremes of wealth and poverty. Poor peasants had no choice but to work large estates owned by a few wealthy families. Landlords had no reason to invest in expensive farm machinery when labor was so cheap. (2) Farming methods were inefficient and economic development was slow.

As Latin American nations began to modernize in the 20th century, land ownership became a political issue. In response, a handful of countries began land reform programs. These programs (3) divided large estates into smaller plots. Small plots of land were in turn distributed to farm families or granted to villages for communal farming. However, just turning over the land to the landless was not enough. (4) Peasant farmers needed instruction, seeds, equipment, and credit. If the land and the people were to be productive, governments would have to provide assistance to the peasants.

STRATEGY: MAKE A CHART.

Summarize the problems and solutions in a chart. Identify the problem or problems and the steps taken to solve them. Look for the short- and long-term effects of the solutions.

Problems	*Solutions*	*Outcomes*
A few wealthy people owned most of the land. *Inefficient farming resulted in slow economic development.*	*Land reform programs divided large estates into smaller plots.*	*Peasants were given land, and communal farms were set up.*
Peasants lacked equipment, resources, skills.	*Governments would have to assist with loans and instruction.*	*Not stated.*

Applying the Skill

MAKE YOUR OWN CHART. Turn to Chapter 31 and read "Postwar Europe" on page 904. Make a chart that lists the problems Germany faced after World War I. List the solutions that were tried and whatever outcomes are mentioned.

1.5 Analyzing Causes and Recognizing Effects

CAUSES are the events, conditions, and other reasons that lead to an event. Causes happen before the event in time; they explain why it happened. **EFFECTS** are the results or consequences of the event. One effect often becomes the cause of other effects, resulting in a chain of events. Causes and effects can be both short-term and long-term. Examining **CAUSE-AND-EFFECT RELATIONSHIPS** helps historians see how events are related and why they took place.

Understanding the Skill

STRATEGY: KEEP TRACK OF CAUSES AND EFFECTS AS YOU READ. The passage below describes events leading to the rise of feudalism in Japan. The diagram that follows summarizes the chain of causes and effects.

1. **Causes: Look for clue words that show cause.** These include *because, due to, since,* and *therefore.*
2. **Look for multiple causes and multiple effects.** The weakness of the central government caused the three effects (a,b,c) shown here.
3. **Effects: Look for results or consequences.** Sometimes these are indicated by clue words such as *brought about, led to, as a result,* and *consequently.*
4. **Notice that an effect may be the cause of another event.** This begins a chain of causes and effects.

Feudalism Comes to Japan

For most of the Heian period, the rich Fujiwara family held the real power in Japan. Members of this family held many influential posts. By about the middle of the 11th century, the power of the central government and the Fujiwaras began to slip. This was (1) due in part to court families' greater interest in luxury and artistic pursuits than in governing.

(2) Since the central government was weak, **(a)** large landowners living away from the capital set up private armies. (3) As a result, **(b)** the countryside became lawless and dangerous. Armed soldiers on horseback preyed on farmers and travelers, while pirates took control of the seas. **(c)** For safety, farmers and small landowners traded parts of their land to strong warlords in exchange for protection. (4) Because the lords had more land, the lords gained more power. This marked the beginning of a feudal system of localized rule like that of ancient China and medieval Europe.

STRATEGY: MAKE A CAUSE-AND-EFFECT DIAGRAM.

Summarize cause-and-effect relationships in a diagram. Starting with the first cause in a series, fill in the boxes until you reach the end result.

Cause →	Effect/Cause →	Effect/Cause →	Effect
Ruling families had little interest in governing.	Weak central government was unable to control the land.	• Landowners set up private armies. • Countryside became dangerous. • Farmers traded land for safety under warlords.	Feudalism was established in Japan.

Applying the Skill

MAKE YOUR OWN CAUSE-AND-EFFECT DIAGRAM. Turn to Chapter 28, pages 823–825. Read "Juárez and *La Reforma*" and make notes about the causes and effects of Juárez's reform movement in Mexico. Make a diagram, like the one shown above, to summarize the information you find.

1.6 Comparing and Contrasting

Historians compare and contrast events, personalities, ideas, behaviors, beliefs, and institutions in order to understand them thoroughly. **COMPARING** involves finding both similarities and differences between two or more things. **CONTRASTING** means examining only the differences between them.

Understanding the Skill

STRATEGY: LOOK FOR SIMILARITIES AND DIFFERENCES. The following passage describes life in the ancient Greek city-states of Sparta and Athens. The Venn diagram below shows some of the similarities and differences between the two city-states.

1 **Compare: Look for features that two subjects have in common.** Here you learn that both Athens and Sparta started out as farming communities.

2 **Compare: Look for clue words indicating that two things are alike.** Clue words include *all, both, like, as, likewise,* and *similarly.*

3 **Contrast: Look for clue words that show how two things differ.** Clue words include *unlike, by contrast, however, except, different,* and *on the other hand.*

4 **Contrast: Look for ways in which two things are different.** Here you learn that Athens and Sparta had different values.

Sparta and Athens

The Greek city-states developed separately but shared certain characteristics, (1) including language and religion. Economically, all began as farming economies, and all except Sparta eventually moved to trade. Politically, (2) all city-states, except for Sparta, evolved into early forms of democracies.

The leader in the movement to democracy was Athens. After a series of reforms, every Athenian citizen was considered equal before the law. However, as in the other Greek city-states, only about one fifth of the population were citizens. Slaves did much of the work, so Athenian citizens were free to create works of art, architecture, and literature, including drama.

(3) By contrast, Sparta lived in constant fear of revolts by *helots,* people who were held in slave-like conditions to work the land. The city was set up as a military dictatorship, and Spartan men dedicated their lives to the military. (4) In Sparta, duty, strength, and discipline were valued over beauty, individuality, and creativity. As a result, Spartans created little art, architecture, or literature.

STRATEGY: MAKE A VENN DIAGRAM.

Compare and Contrast: Summarize similarities and differences in a Venn diagram. In the overlapping area, list characteristics shared by both subjects. Then, in one oval list the characteristics of one subject not shared by the other. In the other oval, list unshared characteristics of the second subject.

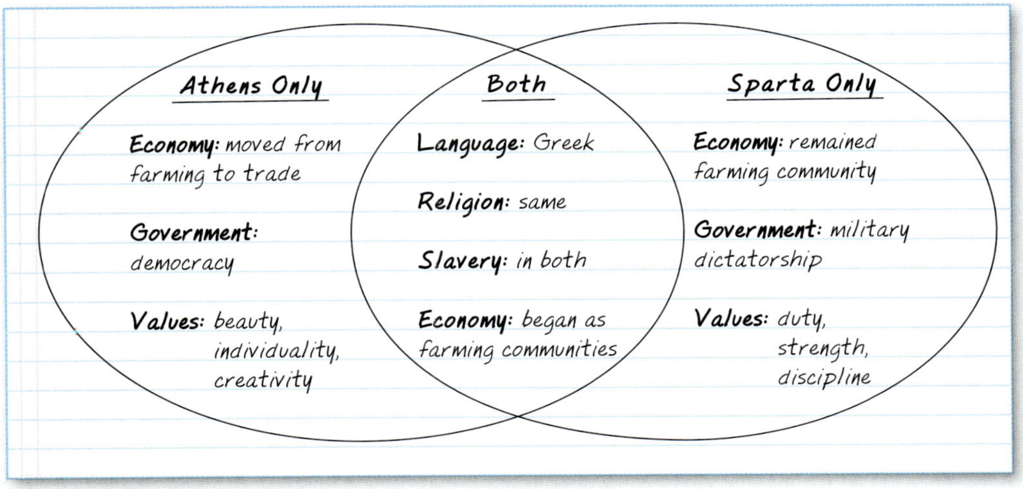

Applying the Skill

MAKE YOUR OWN VENN DIAGRAM. Turn to Chapter 20, pages 564–565, and read the section called "Native Americans Respond." Make a Venn diagram comparing and contrasting Dutch and English colonists' relations with Native Americans.

1.7 Distinguishing Fact from Opinion

FACTS are events, dates, statistics, or statements that can be proved to be true. Facts can be checked for accuracy. **OPINIONS** are judgments, beliefs, and feelings of the writer or speaker.

Understanding the Skill

STRATEGY: FIND CLUES IN THE TEXT. The following excerpt tells about the uprising of Jews in the Warsaw ghetto in 1943. The chart summarizes the facts and opinions.

1 **Facts: Look for specific names, dates, statistics, and statements that can be proved.** The first two paragraphs provide a factual account of the event.

2 **Opinion: Look for assertions, claims, hypotheses, and judgments.** Here Goebbels expresses his opinion of the uprising and of the Jews.

3 **Opinion: Look for judgment words that the writer uses to describe the people and events.** Judgment words are often adjectives that are used to arouse a reader's emotions.

The Warsaw Ghetto Uprising

With orders from Himmler to crush the Jews, 1 the Nazis attacked on April 19, 1943, at the start of the holiday of Passover. 1 Two thousand armed SS troops entered the ghetto, marching with tanks, rifles, machine guns, and trailers full of ammunition. The Jewish fighters were in position—in bunkers, in windows, on rooftops. 1 They had rifles and handguns, hand grenades and bombs that they had made. And they let fly. . . .

Unbelievably, the Jews won the battle that day. The Germans were forced to retreat. . . . 1 The Germans brought in more troops, and the fighting intensified. German pilots dropped bombs on the ghetto. . . .

2 On May 1, Goebbels [Nazi propaganda minister] wrote in his diary: "Of course this jest will probably not last long." He added a complaint. "But it shows what one can expect of the Jews if they have guns."

Goebbels' tone was mocking. But his forecast was inevitable—and correct. . . . Goebbels did not record in his diary, when the uprising was over, that the 3 starving Jews of the ghetto, with their 3 pathetic supply of arms, had held out against the German army for forty days, longer than Poland or France had held out.

Source: *A Nightmare in History*, by Miriam Chaikin. (New York: Clarion Books, 1987) pp. 77–78

STRATEGY: MAKE A CHART.

Divide facts and opinions in a chart. Summarize and separate the facts from the opinions expressed in a passage.

FACTS	OPINIONS
On April 19, 1943, 2,000 armed SS troops attacked the Warsaw ghetto. Jewish fighters held out for 40 days.	**Goebbels:** The uprising was a jest, but showed the danger of letting Jews get hold of guns. **Author:** It is difficult to believe that Warsaw Jews with their pathetic supply of arms were able to defeat the powerful Nazis.

Applying the Skill

MAKE YOUR OWN CHART. Turn to Chapter 26, page 769. Find the Primary Source from the Seneca Falls Convention. Make a chart in which you summarize the facts in your own words, and list the opinions and judgments stated. Look carefully at the language used in order to separate one from the other.

2.1 Categorizing

CATEGORIZING means organizing similar kinds of information into groups. Historians categorize information to help them identify and understand historical patterns.

Understanding the Skill

STRATEGY: DECIDE WHAT INFORMATION NEEDS TO BE CATEGORIZED. The following passage describes India's Taj Mahal, a memorial built by a Mughal ruler. As you read, look for facts and details that are closely related. Then choose appropriate categories.

1 Look at topic sentences for clues to defining categories.

2 Look at the type of information each paragraph contains. A paragraph often contains similar kinds of information.

Building the Taj Mahal

1 Some 20,000 workers labored for 22 years to build the famous tomb. It is made of white marble brought from 250 miles away. The minaret towers are about 130 feet high. The building itself is 186 feet square.

1 The design of the building is a blend of Hindu and Muslim styles. The pointed 2 arches are of Muslim design, and the perforated marble 2 windows and 2 doors are typical of a style found in Hindu temples.

The inside of the building is a glittering garden 2 thousands of carved marble flowers inlaid with tiny precious stones. One tiny flower, one inch square, had 60 different inlays.

STRATEGY: MAKE A CHART.

3 Add a title.

4 Sort information into the categories you have chosen.

5 Make one column for each category.

3 *THE TAJ MAHAL*

4 *Labor*	*Dimensions*	*Design features*
• *20,000 workers* • *22 years to complete*	• *Minaret towers: 130 feet high* • *Building: 186 feet*	• *Made of white marble* • *Pointed arches (Muslim influence)* • *Perforated marble windows and doors (Hindu influence)* • *Interior: thousands of carved marble flowers inlaid with precious stones*
5	5	5

Applying the Skill

MAKE YOUR OWN CHART. Turn to Chapter 22, page 637. Read "New Artistic Styles." Decide what categories you will use to organize the information. Then make a chart, like the one above, that organizes the information in the passage into the categories you have chosen.

2.2 Making Inferences

Inferences are ideas and meanings not stated in the material. **MAKING INFERENCES** means reading between the lines to extend the information provided. Your inferences are based on careful study of what is stated in the passage as well as your own common sense and previous knowledge.

Understanding the Skill

STRATEGY: DEVELOP INFERENCES FROM THE FACTS. This passage describes the Nok culture of West Africa. Following the passage is a diagram that organizes the facts and ideas that lead to inferences.

1. **Read the stated facts and ideas.**
2. **Use your knowledge, logic, and common sense to draw conclusions.** You could infer from these statements that the Nok were a settled people with advanced technology and a rich culture.
3. **Consider what you already know that could apply.** Your knowledge of history might lead you to infer the kinds of improvements in life brought about by better farming tools.
4. **Recognize inferences that are already made.** Phrases like "the evidence suggests" or "historians believe" indicate inferences and conclusions experts have made from historical records.

The Nok Culture

(1) The earliest known culture of West Africa was that of the Nok people. They lived in what is now Nigeria between 900 B.C. and A.D. 200. Their name came from the village where the first artifacts from their culture were discovered by archaeologists. The (2) Nok were farmers. They were also (2) the first West African people known to smelt iron. The Nok began making iron around 500 B.C., using it to make tools for farming and weapons for hunting. (3) These iron implements lasted longer than wood or stone and vastly improved the lives of the Nok.

Nok artifacts have been found in an area stretching for 300 miles between the Niger and Benue rivers. (2) Many are sculptures made of terra cotta, a reddish-brown clay. Carved in great artistic detail, some depict the heads of animals such as elephants and others depict human heads. The features of some of the heads reveal a great deal about their history. One of the human heads, for example, shows an elaborate hairdo arranged in six buns, a style that is still worn by some people in Nigeria today. (4) This similarity suggests that the Nok may have been the ancestors of modern-day Africans.

STRATEGY: MAKE A CHART.

Summarize the facts and inferences you make in a chart.

Stated Facts and Ideas	Inferences
• iron farming tools • iron harder than wood • tools improved life	iron tools improved agriculture and contributed to cultural development
• Nok artifacts found in 300-mile radius	Nok culture spread across this area
• heads carved in great artistic detail	Nok were skilled potters and sculptors
• sculptures included elephant heads	elephants played a role in people's lives

Applying the Skill

MAKE YOUR OWN CHART. Read the Tamil poem from ancient India quoted in Chapter 7 on page 194. Using a chart like the one above, make inferences from the poem about its author, its subject, and the culture it comes from.

2.3 Drawing Conclusions

DRAWING CONCLUSIONS means analyzing what you have read and forming an opinion about its meaning. To draw conclusions, you look closely at the facts, combine them with inferences you make, and then use your own common sense and experience to decide what the facts mean.

Understanding the Skill

STRATEGY: COMBINE INFORMATION TO DRAW CONCLUSIONS. The passage below presents information about the reunification of East and West Germany in 1990. The diagram that follows shows how to organize the information to draw conclusions.

1. **Read carefully to understand all the facts.** Fact: Reunification brought social and political freedoms to East Germans.
2. **Read between the lines to make inferences.** Inference: After a market economy was introduced, many industries in eastern Germany failed, which put people out of work.
3. **Use the facts to make an inference.** Inference: Reunification put a strain on government resources.
4. **Ask questions of the material.** What are the long-term economic prospects for eastern Germany? Conclusion: Although it faced challenges, it seemed to have a greater chance for success than other former Communist countries.

Germany is Reunified

On October 3, 1990, Germany once again became a single nation. (1) After more than 40 years of Communist rule, most East Germans celebrated their new political freedoms. Families that had been separated for years could now visit whenever they chose.

Economically, the newly united Germany faced serious problems. More than 40 years of Communist rule had left East Germany in ruins. Its transportation and telephone systems had not been modernized since World War II. State-run industries in East Germany had to be turned over to private control and operate under free-market rules. (2) However, many produced shoddy goods that could not compete in the global market.

Rebuilding eastern Germany's bankrupt economy was going to be a difficult, costly process. (3) Some experts estimated the price tag for reunification could reach $200 billion. In the short-term, the government had to provide (2) unemployment benefits to some 1.4 million workers from the east who found themselves out of work.

(4) In spite of these problems, Germans had reasons to be optimistic. Unlike other Eastern European countries, who had to transform their Communist economies by their own means, East Germany had the help of a strong West Germany. Many Germans may have shared the outlook expressed by one worker: "Maybe things won't be rosy at first, but the future will be better."

STRATEGY: MAKE A DIAGRAM.

Summarize the facts, inferences, and your conclusion in a diagram.

Facts →	Inferences →	Conclusion About Passage
East Germans gained freedoms.	East Germans welcomed the end of Communist rule.	Although eastern Germany was in bad shape at the time of reunification, it had the advantage of the strength of western Germany as it made the transition to democracy and capitalism.
Transportation and telephone systems were outmoded.	Rebuilding took time.	
State-run industries produced shoddy goods.	Industries couldn't compete in free-market economy.	
Unemployment skyrocketed.	Reunification put a great financial burden on Germany.	
Cost for reunification could be $200 billion.		

Applying the Skill

MAKE A DIAGRAM. Look at Chapter 6, pages 160–162, on the collapse of the Roman Republic. As you read, draw conclusions based on the facts. Use the diagram above as a model for organizing facts, inferences, and conclusions about the passage.

2.4 Developing Historical Perspective

DEVELOPING HISTORICAL PERSPECTIVE means understanding events and people in the context of their times. It means not judging the past by current values, but by taking into account the beliefs of the time.

Understanding the Skill

STRATEGY: LOOK FOR VALUES OF THE PAST. The following passage was written by Bartolomé de Las Casas, a Spanish missionary who defended the rights of Native Americans. It challenges an argument presented by a scholar named Sepúlveda, who held that the Spaniards had the right to enslave the Native Americans. Following the passage is a chart that summarizes the information from a historical perspective.

1 **Identify the historical figure, the occasion, and the date.**

2 **Look for clues to the attitudes, customs, and values of people living at the time.** As a Spanish missionary, Las Casas assumes that Europeans are more civilized than Native Americans and that Native Americans need to be converted to Catholicism.

3 **Explain how people's actions and words reflected the attitudes, values, and passions of the era.** Las Casas challenges prejudices about Native Americans that were widely held in Europe. His language emphasizes a favorable comparison between Native American and European societies.

4 **Notice words, phrases, and settings that reflect the period.** Las Casas speaks from a time when Europeans looked to classical Greece as a benchmark for civilization.

1 In Defense of the Indians (1550)
Bartolomé de Las Casas

Now if we shall have shown that among our Indians of the western and southern shores 2 (granting that we call them barbarians and that they are barbarians) there are important kingdoms, large numbers of people who live settled lives in a society, great cities, kings, judges and laws, persons who engage in commerce, buying, selling, lending, and the other contracts of the law of nations, will it not stand proved that the Reverend Doctor Sepúlveda has spoken wrongly and viciously against peoples like these?. . . From the fact that the Indians are barbarians it does not necessarily follow that they are incapable of government and have to be ruled by others, 2 except to be taught about the Catholic faith and to be admitted to the holy sacraments. 3 They are not ignorant, inhuman, or bestial. Rather, long before they had heard the word Spaniard they had 3 properly organized states, wisely ordered by excellent laws, religion, and custom. They cultivated friendship and, bound together in common fellowship, lived in populous cities in which they wisely administered the affairs of both peace and war justly and equitably, truly governed by laws that at very many points surpass ours, and could have won 4 the admiration of the sages of Athens. . . .

STRATEGY: WRITE A SUMMARY.

Use historical perspective to understand Las Casas's attitudes. In a chart, list key words, phrases, and details from the passage. In a short paragraph, summarize the basic values and attitudes of Las Casas.

Key Phrases	Las Casas's *In Defense of the Indians*
• barbarians • Catholic faith • not inhuman, ignorant, or bestial • properly organized states, wisely ordered • sages of Athens	Las Casas argues that Native Americans are not inhuman and do not deserve cruelty and slavery. Rather, they are fully capable of "coming up" to the level of Spanish civilization. Although he makes the statement that Native Americans are barbarians, his language and comparisons seem to suggest that he believes them to be highly civilized in many respects. At the same time, he believes in the importance of converting them to Catholicism.

Applying the Skill

WRITE YOUR OWN SUMMARY. Turn to Chapter 11, page 319, and read the excerpt from *Medieval Russia's Epics, Chronicles, and Tales*. Read the passage using historical perspective. Then summarize your ideas in a chart like the one above.

2.5 Formulating Historical Questions

FORMULATING HISTORICAL QUESTIONS is important as you examine primary sources—firsthand accounts, documents, letters, and other records of the past. As you analyze a source, ask questions about what it means and why it is significant. Then, when you are doing research, write questions that you want your research to answer. This step will help to guide your research and organize the information you collect.

Understanding the Skill

STRATEGY: QUESTION WHAT YOU READ. The Muslim scholar Ibn Battuta published an account of his journeys in Asia and Africa in the 1300s. The following passage is part of his description of China. After the passage is a web diagram that organizes historical questions about it.

1. **Ask about the historical record itself.** Who produced it? When was it produced?
2. **Ask about the facts presented.** Who were the main people? What did they do? What were they like?
3. **Ask about the person who created the record.** What judgments or opinions does the author express?
4. **Ask about the significance of the record.** How would you interpret the information presented? How does it fit in with the history of this time and place? What more do you need to know to answer these questions?

1 Ibn Battuta in China, Around 1345

2 The Chinese themselves are infidels, who worship idols and burn their dead like the Hindus. . . . In every Chinese city there is a quarter for Muslims in which they live by themselves, and in which they have mosques both for the Friday services and for other religious purposes. The Muslims are honored and respected. 3 The Chinese infidels eat the flesh of swine and dogs, and sell it in their markets. 2 They are wealthy folk and well-to-do, but they make no display either in their food or their clothes. You will see one of their principal merchants, a man so rich that his wealth cannot be counted, wearing a coarse cotton tunic. But there is one thing that the Chinese take a pride in, that is gold and silver plate. Every one of them carries a stick, on which they lean in walking, and which they call "the third leg." 4 Silk is very plentiful among them, because the silk-worm attaches itself to fruits and feeds on them without requiring much care. For that reason, it is so common as to be worn by even the very poorest there. Were it not for the merchants it would have no value at all, for a single piece of cotton cloth is sold in their country for the price of many pieces of silk.

STRATEGY: MAKE A WEB DIAGRAM.

Investigate a topic in more depth by asking questions. Ask a large question and then ask smaller questions that explore and develop from the larger question.

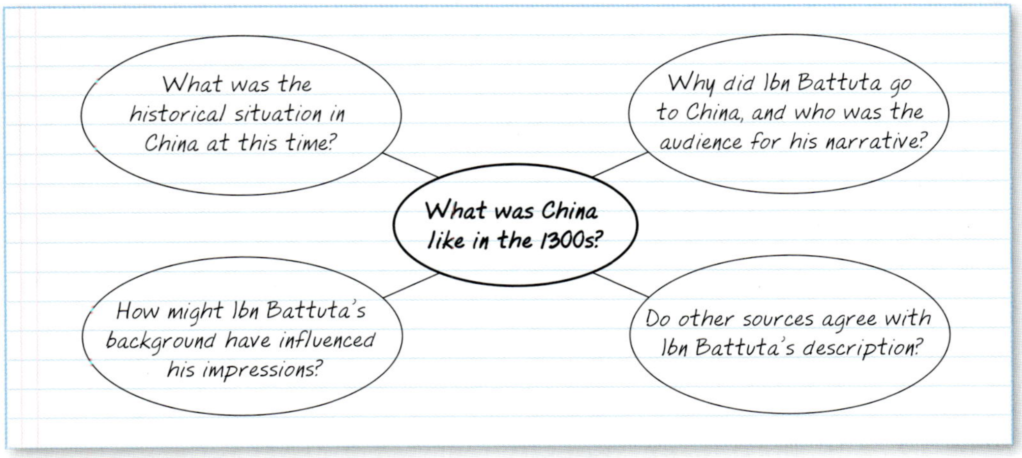

Applying the Skill

MAKE YOUR OWN WEB DIAGRAM. Turn to the quotation by Bernal Díaz in Chapter 16, page 455. Use a web diagram to write historical questions about the passage.

2.6 Making Predictions

MAKING PREDICTIONS means projecting the outcome of a situation that leaders or groups face or have faced in the past. Historians use their knowledge of past events and the decisions that led up to them to predict the outcome of current situations. Examining decisions and their alternatives will help you understand how events in the past shaped the future.

Understanding the Skill

STRATEGY: IDENTIFY DECISIONS. The following passage describes relations between Cuba and the United States following Fidel Castro's successful attempt to overthrow former Cuban dictator Fulgencio Batista. The chart lists decisions that affected U.S./Cuban relations, along with alternative decisions and predictions of their possible outcomes.

1. **To help you identify decisions, look for words such as *decide, decision,* and *chose.***
2. **Notice how one political decision often leads to another.**
3. **Notice both positive and negative decisions.**

U.S./Cuban Relations under Castro

During the 1950s, Cuban dictator Fidel Castro (1) chose to nationalize the Cuban economy, which resulted in the takeover of U.S.-owned sugar mills and refineries. (2) U.S. President Eisenhower responded by ordering an embargo on all trade with Cuba. As relations between the two countries deteriorated, Cuba became more dependent on the USSR for economic and military aid. In 1960, the CIA trained anti-Castro Cuban exiles to invade Cuba. (3) Although they landed at Cuba's Bay of Pigs, the United States (1) decided not to provide them with air support. Castro's forces defeated the exiles, which humiliated the United States.

STRATEGY: MAKE A CHART.

4. **Use a chart to record decisions.**
5. **Suggest alternative decisions.**
6. **Predict a possible outcome for each alternative decision.**

(4) Decisions	(5) Alternative Decisions	(6) Prediction of Outcome
Castro nationalized Cuban economy.	Castro did not nationalize Cuban economy.	There was no United States embargo of trade with Cuba.
The United States placed an embargo on trade with Cuba.	The United States continued to trade with Cuba.	Cuba continued to depend on the United States economically.
CIA trained Cuban exiles, who invaded Cuba.	The CIA did not train exiles to invade Cuba.	There was no invasion of Cuba.
The United States did not provide air support for the invasion.	The United States provided air support to the invaders.	The United States successfully invaded Cuba.

APPLYING THE SKILL

MAKE A CHART like the one above. Turn to Chapter 21, page 615, and read the first four paragraphs of the section "English Civil War." Identify three decisions of England's King Charles I. Record them on your chart, along with an alternative decision for each. Then predict a possible outcome for each alternative decision.

2.7 Hypothesizing

HYPOTHESIZING means developing a possible explanation for historical events. A hypothesis is an educated guess about what happened in the past or a prediction about what might happen in the future. A hypothesis takes available information, links it to previous experience and knowledge, and comes up with a possible explanation, conclusion, or prediction.

Understanding the Skill

STRATEGY: FIND CLUES IN THE READING. In studying the Indus Valley civilization, historians do not yet know exactly what caused that culture to decline. They have, however, developed hypotheses about what happened to it. Read this passage and look at the steps that are shown for building a hypothesis. Following the passage is a chart that organizes the information.

1. **Identify the event, pattern, or trend you want to explain.**
2. **Determine the facts you have about the situation.** These facts support various hypotheses about what happened to the Indus Valley civilization.
3. **Develop a hypothesis that might explain the event.** Historians hypothesize that a combination of ecological change and sudden catastrophe caused the Indus Valley civilization to collapse.
4. **Determine what additional information you need to test the hypothesis.** You might refer to a book about India, for example, to learn more about the impact of the Aryan invasions.

1 Mysterious End to Indus Valley Culture

2 Around 1750 B.C., the quality of building in the Indus Valley cities declined. Gradually, the great cities fell into decay. What happened? Some historians think that the Indus River changed course, as it tended to do, so that its floods no longer fertilized the fields near the cities. Other scholars suggest that people wore out the valley's land. They overgrazed it, overfarmed it, and overcut its trees, brush, and grass.

As the Indus Valley civilization neared its end, around 1500 B.C., a sudden catastrophe may have had a hand in the cities' downfall. 2 Archaeologists have found a half-dozen groups of skeletons in the ruins of Mohenjo-Daro, seemingly never buried. 3 Their presence suggests that the city, already weakened by its slow decline, may have been abandoned after a natural disaster or a devastating attack from human enemies. The Aryans, a nomadic people from north of the Hindu Kush mountains, swept into the Indus Valley at about this time. 4 Whether they caused the collapse of the Indus Valley civilization or followed in its wake is not known.

STRATEGY: MAKE A CHART.

Use a chart to summarize your hypothesis about events. Write down your hypothesis and the facts that support it. Then you can see what additional information you need to help prove or disprove it.

Hypothesis	*Facts that support the hypothesis*	*Additional information needed*
A combination of ecological change and sudden catastrophe caused the Indus Valley civilization to collapse	• *Building quality declined* • *Indus River tended to change course* • *Unburied skeletons were found at Mohenjo-Daro* • *Aryan invasions occurred around same time*	• *What was Indus Valley culture like?* • *What were the geographical characteristics of the region?* • *How did overfarming tend to affect the environment?* • *What factors affected the decline of other ancient civilizations?*

Applying the Skill

MAKE YOUR OWN CHART. Turn to Chapter 19, page 545, and read the Primary Source. Predict what impact the introduction of firearms might have had on Japan. Then read the surrounding text material. List facts that support your hypothesis and what additional information you might gather to help prove or disprove it.

2.8 Analyzing Motives

ANALYZING MOTIVES means examining the reasons why a person, group, or government takes a particular action. To understand those reasons, consider the needs, emotions, prior experiences, and goals of the person or group.

Understanding the Skill

STRATEGY: LOOK FOR REASONS WHY. On June 28, 1914, Serb terrorists assassinated Austria-Hungary's Archduke Franz Ferdinand and his wife when they visited Sarajevo, the capital of Bosnia. In the following passage, Borijove Jevtic, a Serb terrorist, explains why the assassination occurred. Before this passage, he explains that the terrorists had received a telegram stating that the Archduke would be visiting Sarajevo on June 28. The diagram that follows summarizes the motives of the terrorists for murdering the Archduke.

1 **Look for motives based on basic needs and human emotions.** Needs include food, shelter, safety, freedom. Emotions include fear, anger, pride, desire for revenge, and patriotism, for example.

2 **Look for motives based on past events or inspiring individuals.**

3 **Notice both positive and negative motives.**

The Assassination of the Archduke

How dared Franz Ferdinand, not only the representative of the oppressor but in his own person an 1 arrogant tyrant, enter Sarajevo on that day? Such an entry was a 1 studied insult.

2 28 June is a date engraved deeply in the heart of every Serb, so that the day has a name of its own. It is called the vidovnan. It is the day on which the old Serbian kingdom was conquered by the Turks at the battle of Amselfelde in 1389. It is also the day on which in the second Balkan War the Serbian arms took glorious revenge on the Turk for his old victory and for the years of enslavement.

3 That was no day for Franz Ferdinand, the new oppressor, to venture to the very doors of Serbia for a display of the force of arms which kept us beneath his heel.

Our decision was taken almost immediately. Death to the tyrant!

STRATEGY: MAKE A DIAGRAM.

Make a diagram that summarizes motives and actions. List the important action in the middle of the diagram. Then list motives in different categories around the action.

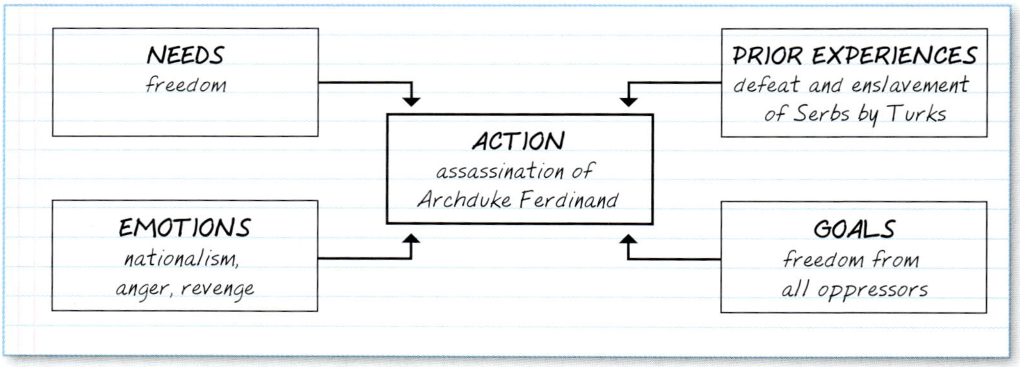

Applying the Skill

MAKE YOUR OWN DIAGRAM. Turn to Chapter 27, Section 1, "The Scramble for Africa." Read the section and look for motives of European nations in acquiring lands in other parts of the world. Make a diagram, like the one above, showing the European nations' motives for taking the land.

2.9 Analyzing Issues

An issue is a matter of public concern or debate. Issues in history are usually economic, social, political, or moral. Historical issues are often more complicated than they first appear. **ANALYZING AN ISSUE** means taking a controversy apart to find and describe the different points of view about the issue.

Understanding the Skill

STRATEGY: LOOK FOR DIFFERENT SIDES OF THE ISSUE. The following passage describes working conditions in English factories in the early 1800s. The cluster diagram that follows the passage helps you to analyze the issue of child labor.

1. **Look for a central problem with its causes and effects.**
2. **Look for facts and statistics.** Factual information helps you understand the issue and evaluate the different sides or arguments.
3. **Look for different sides to the issue.** You need to consider all sides of an issue before deciding your position.

Children at Work

(1) Child labor was one of the most serious problems of the early Industrial Revolution. Children as young as 6 years worked exhausting jobs in factories and mines. Because wages were very low, many families in cities could not survive unless all their members, including children, worked.

(2) In most factories, regular work hours were 6 in the morning to 6 in the evening, often with two "over-hours" until 8. It was common for 40 or more children to work together in one room—a room with little light or air. Those who lagged behind in their work were often beaten. Because safety was a low concern for many factory owners, accidents were common.

In 1831, Parliament set up a committee to investigate abuses of child labor. (2) Medical experts reported that long hours of factory work caused young children to become crippled or stunted in their growth. They recommended that children younger than age 14 should work no more than 8 hours. (3) Factory owners responded that they needed children to work longer hours in order to be profitable. As one owner testified, reduced working hours for children would "much reduce the value of my mill and machinery, and consequently of . . . my manufacture." As a result of the committee's findings, Parliament passed the Factory Act of 1833. The act made it illegal to hire children under 9 years old, and it limited the working hours of older children.

STRATEGY: MAKE A CLUSTER DIAGRAM.

If an issue is complex, make a cluster diagram. A cluster diagram can help you analyze an issue.

Issue: *Should Parliament restrict child labor?*

Facts:
- *Children as young as 6 years worked.*
- *Working hours were typically 12 hours a day, often with 2 hours overtime.*
- *Working conditions were dangerous, unhealthy, and inhumane.*
- *Factory work caused deformities in young children.*

In favor of child labor:	**Against child labor:**
Who: *factory owners, some parents*	**Who:** *medical examiners*
Reasons: *Shorter hours would reduce profits. Children's income essential for families.*	**Reasons:** *Children working in factories suffered permanent deformities.*

Applying the Skill

MAKE YOUR OWN CLUSTER DIAGRAM. Chapter 34, page 998, describes the partition of India. Make a cluster diagram to analyze the issue and the positions of the people involved.

2.10 Analyzing Bias

BIAS is a prejudiced point of view. Historical accounts that are biased tend to be one-sided and reflect the personal prejudices of the historian.

Understanding the Skill

STRATEGY: THINK ABOUT THE WRITER AS YOU READ. The European explorer Amerigo Vespucci reached the coast of Brazil in 1502, on his second voyage to the Americas. Below are his impressions of the people he met.

1. **Identify the author and information about him or her.** Does the author belong to a special-interest group, social class, political party, or movement that might promote a one-sided or slanted viewpoint on the subject?
2. **Search for clues.** Are there words, phrases, statements, or images that might convey a positive or negative slant? What might these clues reveal about the author's bias?
3. **Examine the evidence.** Is the information that the author presents consistent with other accounts? Is the behavior described consistent with human nature as you have observed it?

(1) Amerigo Vespucci Reports on the People of Brazil

For twenty-seven days I ate and slept among them, and what I learned about them is as follows.

Having no laws and no religious faith, they live according to nature. (2) They understand nothing of the immortality of the soul. There is no possession of private property among them, for everything is in common. They have no boundaries of kingdom or province. They have no king, nor do they obey anyone. Each one is his own master. (3) There is no administration of justice, which is unnecessary to them, because in their code no one rules…

They are also (2) a warlike people and very cruel to their own kind… That which made me… astonished at their wars and cruelty was that I could not understand from them why they made war upon each other, considering that they held no private property or sovereignty of empire and kingdoms and (3) did not know any such thing as lust for possession, that is pillaging or a desire to rule, which appear to me to be the causes of wars and every disorderly act. When we requested them to state the cause, they did not know how to give any other cause than that this curse upon them began in ancient times and they sought to avenge the deaths of their forefathers.

STRATEGY: MAKE A CHART.

Make a chart of your analysis. For each of the heads listed on the left side of the chart, summarize information presented in the passage.

Vespucci's impressions of the native peoples of Brazil

author, date	Amerigo Vespucci, 1502
occasion	exploration of coast of Brazil on second voyage to Americas
tone	judging, negative, superior
bias	Since the native people do not live in organized states and have no private property, they have no system of authority, laws, or moral principles. They have no apparent religious beliefs. They are warlike and cruel and seem to make war on one another for no reason. The author's comments about the soul seem to show a bias towards his own religious beliefs. He also reveals a prejudice that European customs and practices are superior to all others.

Applying the Skill

MAKE YOUR OWN CHART. Look at the quotation by the Qing emperor Kangxi in the Primary Source in Chapter 19, page 549. Summarize the underlying assumptions and biases using a chart like the one shown.

2.11 Evaluating Decisions and Courses of Action

EVALUATING DECISIONS means making judgments about the decisions that historical figures made. Historians evaluate decisions on the basis of their moral implications and their costs and benefits from different points of view.

EVALUATING VARIOUS COURSES OF ACTION means carefully judging the choices that historical figures had to make. By doing this, you can better understand why they made some of the decisions they did.

Understanding the Skill

STRATEGY: LOOK FOR CHOICES AND REASONS. The following passage describes the decisions U.S. President John Kennedy had to make when he learned of Soviet missile bases in Cuba. As you read it, think of the alternative responses he could have made at each turn of events. Following the passage is a chart that organizes information about the Cuban missile crisis.

1 **Look at decisions made by individuals or by groups.** Notice the decisions Kennedy made in response to Soviet actions.

2 **Look at the outcome of the decisions.**

3 **Analyze a decision in terms of the choices that were possible.** Both Kennedy and Khrushchev faced the same choice. Either could carry out the threat, or either could back down quietly and negotiate.

The Cuban Missile Crisis

During the summer of 1962, the flow of Soviet weapons into Cuba—including nuclear missiles—greatly increased. 1 President Kennedy responded cautiously at first, issuing a warning that the United States would not tolerate the presence of offensive nuclear weapons in Cuba. Then, on October 16, photographs taken by American U-2 planes showed the president that the Soviets were secretly building missile bases on Cuba. Some of the missiles, armed and ready to fire, could reach U.S. cities in minutes.

1 On the evening of October 22, the president made public the evidence of missiles and stated his ultimatum: any missile attack from Cuba would trigger an all-out attack on the Soviet Union. Soviet ships continued to head toward the island, while the U.S. navy prepared to stop them and U.S. invasion troops massed in Florida. To avoid confrontation, the Soviet ships suddenly halted. 2 Soviet Premier Nikita Khrushchev offered to remove the missiles from Cuba in exchange for a pledge not to invade the island. Kennedy agreed, and the crisis ended.

3 Some people criticized Kennedy for practicing brinkmanship, when private talks might have resolved the crisis without the threat of nuclear war. Others believed he had been too soft and had passed up a chance to invade Cuba and oust its Communist leader, Fidel Castro.

STRATEGY: MAKE A CHART.

Make a simple chart of your analysis. The problem was that Soviet nuclear missiles were being shipped to Cuba. The decision to be made was how the United States should respond.

Kennedy's Choices	Pros	Cons	My Evaluation
Publicly confront Khrushchev with navy and prepare for war.	Show Khrushchev and world the power and strong will of the U.S.; force him to back off.	Nuclear war could occur.	In your opinion, which was the better choice? Why?
Say nothing to U.S. public and negotiate quietly.	Avoid frightening U.S. citizens and avoid threat of nuclear war.	The U.S. would look weak publicly; Khrushchev could carry out plan.	

Applying the Skill

MAKE A CHART. Chapter 31, page 919, describes the decisions British and French leaders made when Hitler took over the Sudetenland in Czechoslovakia just before World War II. Make a chart, like the one shown, to summarize the pros and cons of their choice of appeasement and evaluate their decision yourself.

2.12 Forming and Supporting Opinions

Historians do more than reconstruct facts about the past. They also **FORM OPINIONS** about the information they encounter. Historians form opinions as they interpret the past and judge the significance of historical events and people. They **SUPPORT THEIR OPINIONS** with logical thinking, facts, examples, quotes, and references to events.

Understanding the Skill

STRATEGY: FIND ARGUMENTS TO SUPPORT YOUR OPINION. In the following passage, journalist Paul Gray summarizes differing opinions about the significance and impact of Columbus's voyages. As you read, develop your own opinion about the issue.

1 **Decide what you think about a subject after reading all the information available to you.** After reading this passage, you might decide that Columbus's legacy was primarily one of genocide, cruelty, and slavery. On the other hand, you might believe that, despite the negatives, his voyages produced many long-term benefits.

2 **Consider the opinions and interpretations of historians and other experts.** Weigh their arguments as you form your own opinion.

3 **Support your opinion with facts, quotes, and examples, including references to similar events from other historical eras.**

How Should History View the Legacy of Columbus?

In one version of the story, Columbus and the Europeans who followed him (1) brought civilization to two immense, sparsely populated continents, in the process fundamentally enriching and altering the Old World from which they had themselves come.

Among other things, Columbus' journey was the first step in a long process that eventually produced the United States of America, (2) a daring experiment in democracy that in turn became a symbol and a haven of individual liberty for people throughout the world. But the revolution that began with his voyages was far greater than that. It altered science, geography, philosophy, agriculture, law, religion, ethics, government—the sum, in other words, of what passed at the time as Western culture.

Increasingly, however, there is a counterchorus, an opposing rendition of the same events that deems Columbus' first footfall in the New World to be fatal to the world he invaded, and even to the rest of the globe. The indigenous peoples and their cultures were doomed by European (3) arrogance, (3) brutality, and (3) infectious diseases. Columbus' gift was (3) slavery to those who greeted him; (1) his arrival set in motion the ruthless destruction, continuing at this very moment, of the natural world he entered. Genocide, ecocide, exploitation... are deemed to be a form of Eurocentric theft of history from [the Native Americans].

STRATEGY: MAKE A CHART.

Summarize your opinion and supporting information in a chart. Write an opinion and then list facts, examples, interpretations, or other information that support it.

Opinion: Voyages of Columbus brought more bad than good to the Americas

Facts:	Historical interpretations:
• Europeans replaced existing cultures with their own. • European diseases killed many Native Americans. • Columbus enslaved Native Americans.	• Europeans were arrogant and brutal. • Columbus's arrival set in motion ruthless destruction of environment. • Through conquest and exploitation, Europeans "stole" Native Americans' history and culture.

Applying the Skill

MAKE YOUR OWN CHART. Look at the Different Perspectives on Economics and the Environment in Chapter 36, page 1081. Read the selections and form your own opinion about the concept of sustainable development. Summarize your supporting data in a chart like the one shown above.

2.13 Synthesizing

SYNTHESIZING is the skill historians use in developing interpretations of the past. Like detective work, synthesizing involves putting together clues, information, and ideas to form an overall picture of a historical event. A synthesis is often stated as a generalization, or broad summary statement.

Understanding the Skill

STRATEGY: BUILD AN INTERPRETATION AS YOU READ. The passage below describes the first settlement of the Americas. The highlighting indicates the different kinds of information that lead to a synthesis—an overall picture of Native American life.

1. **Read carefully to understand the facts.** Facts such as these enable you to base your interpretations on physical evidence.
2. **Look for explanations that link the facts together.** This statement is based on the evidence provided by baskets, bows and arrows, and nets, which are mentioned in the sentences that follow.
3. **Consider what you already know that could apply.** Your general knowledge will probably lead you to accept this statement as reasonable.
4. **Bring together the information you have about a subject.** This interpretation brings together different kinds of information to arrive at a new understanding of the subject.

The First Americans

(1) From the discovery of chiseled arrowheads and charred bones at ancient sites, it appears that the earliest Americans lived as big game hunters. The woolly mammoth, their largest prey, provided them with food, clothing, and bones for constructing tools and shelters. (2) People gradually shifted to hunting small game and gathering available plants. They created baskets to collect nuts, wild rice, chokeberries, gooseberries, and currants. Later they invented bows and arrows to hunt small game such as jackrabbits and deer. They wove nets to fish the streams and lakes.

Between 10,000 and 15,000 years ago, a revolution took place in what is now central Mexico. People began to raise plants as food. Maize may have been the first domesticated plant, with pumpkins, peppers, beans, and potatoes following. Agriculture spread to other regions.

(3) The rise of agriculture brought about tremendous changes to the Americas. Agriculture made it possible for people to remain in one place. It also enabled them to accumulate and store surplus food. As their surplus increased, people had the time to develop skills and more complex ideas about the world. (4) From this agricultural base rose larger, more stable societies and increasingly complex societies.

STRATEGY: MAKE A CLUSTER DIAGRAM.

Summarize your synthesis in a cluster diagram. Use a cluster diagram to organize the facts, opinions, examples, and interpretations that you have brought together to form a synthesis.

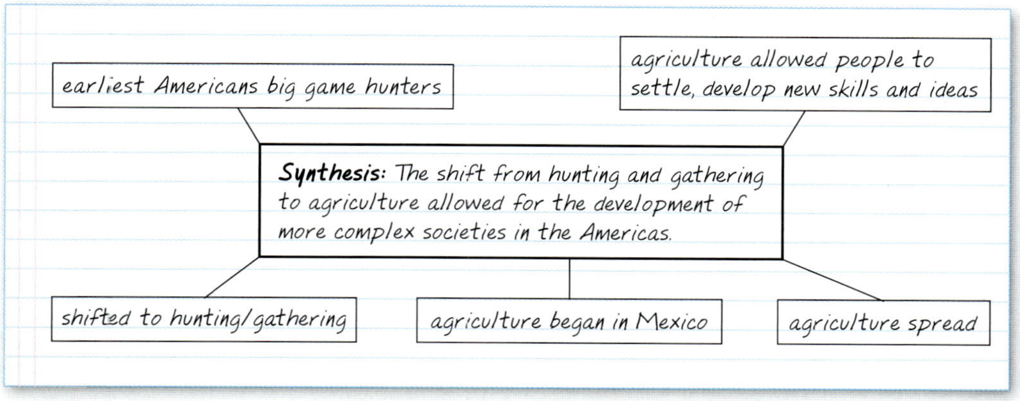

Applying the Skill

MAKE YOUR OWN CLUSTER DIAGRAM. In Chapter 17 on pages 488–489, the beginnings of the Protestant Reformation are discussed. Read the passage and look for information to support a synthesis about its fundamental causes. Summarize your synthesis in a cluster diagram.

3.1 Analyzing Primary and Secondary Sources

PRIMARY SOURCES are written or created by people who lived during a historical event. The writers might have been participants or observers. Primary sources include letters, diaries, journals, speeches, newspaper articles, magazine articles, eyewitness accounts, and autobiographies.

SECONDARY SOURCES are derived from primary sources by people who were not present at the original event. They are written after the event. They often combine information from a number of different accounts. Secondary sources include history books, historical essays, and biographies.

Understanding the Skill

STRATEGY: EVALUATE THE INFORMATION IN EACH TYPE OF SOURCE. This passage describes political reforms made by Pericles, who led Athens from 461 to 429 B.C. It is mainly a secondary source, but it includes a primary source in the form of a speech.

1. **Secondary Source: Look for information collected from several sources.** Here the writer presents an overall picture of the reforms made by Pericles and the reasons for them.
2. **Secondary Source: Look for analysis and interpretation.** A secondary source provides details and perspective that are missing in a primary source. It also provides context for the primary source.
3. **Primary Source: Identify the author and evaluate his or her credentials.** How is the speaker connected to the event? Here, this speaker is Pericles himself.
4. **Primary Source: Analyze the source using historical perspective.** Read the source for factual information while also noting the speaker's opinions, biases, assumptions, and point of view.

Stronger Democracy in Athens

(1) To strengthen democracy, Pericles increased the number of public officials who were paid salaries. Before, only wealthier citizens could afford to hold public office because most positions were unpaid. Now even the poorest could serve if elected or chosen by lot. (2) This reform made Athens one of the most democratic governments in history. However, political rights were still limited to those with citizenship status—a minority of Athens' total population.

The introduction of direct democracy was an important legacy of Periclean Athens. Few other city-states practiced this style of government. In Athens, male citizens who served in the assembly established all the important policies that affected the polis. In a famous "Funeral Oration" for soldiers killed in the Peloponnesian War, (3) Pericles expressed his great pride in Athenian democracy:

> (4) *Our constitution is called a democracy because power is in the hands not of a minority but of the whole people. When it is a question of settling private disputes, everyone is equal before the law; when it is a question of putting one person before another in positions of public responsibility, what counts is not membership of a particular class, but the actual ability which the man possesses. No one, as long as he has it in him to be of service to the state, is kept in political obscurity because of poverty.*

STRATEGY: MAKE A CHART.

Summarize information from primary and secondary sources on a chart.

Primary Source	Secondary Source
Author: Pericles **Qualifications:** main figure in the events described **Information:** describes his view of Athenian democracy—power in the hands of "the whole people"	**Author:** world history textbook **Qualifications:** had access to multiple accounts of event **Information:** puts events in historical perspective—Athens one of most democratic governments in history but limited rights to citizens

Applying the Skill

MAKE YOUR OWN CHART. Read the passage "Mehmed II Conquers Constantinople" in Chapter 18, pages 508–509, which includes a quote from the Greek historian Kritovoulos. Make a chart in which you summarize information from the primary and secondary sources.

3.2 Visual, Audio, and Multimedia Sources

In addition to written accounts, historians use many kinds of **VISUAL SOURCES.** These include paintings, photographs, political cartoons, and advertisements. Visual sources are rich with historical details and sometimes reflect the mood and trends of an era better than words can.

Spoken language has always been a primary means of passing on human history. **AUDIO SOURCES,** such as recorded speeches, interviews, press conferences, and radio programs, continue the oral tradition today.

Movies, CD-ROMs, television, and computer software are the newest kind of historical sources, called **MULTIMEDIA SOURCES.**

Understanding the Skill

STRATEGY: EXAMINE THE SOURCE CAREFULLY. Below are two portraits from the late 1700s, one of Marie Antoinette, the queen of France, and one of a woman who sells vegetables at the market. The chart that follows summarizes historical information gained from interpreting and comparing the two paintings.

1. **Identify the subject and source.**
2. **Identify important visual details.** Look at the faces, poses, clothing, hairstyles, and other elements.
3. **Make inferences from the visual details.** Marie Antoinette's rich clothing and her hand on the globe symbolize her wealth and power. The contrast between the common woman's ordinary clothing and her defiant pose suggests a different attitude about power.

Use comparisons, information from other sources, and your own knowledge to give support to your interpretation. Royalty usually had their portraits painted in heroic poses. Ordinary people were not usually the subjects of such portraits. David's choice of subject and pose suggests that he sees the common people as the true heroes of France.

A Woman of the Revolution [La maraîchère] (1795), Jacques Louis David 1

Marie Antoinette, Jacques Gautier d'Agoty 1

STRATEGY: MAKE A CHART.

Summarize your interpretation in a simple chart.

Subject	Visual Details	Inferences	Message
Common woman	Face is worn and clothing is plain, but her head is held high and she wears the red scarf of revolution	Has worked hard for little in life, but strong, proud, and defiant	Although the details are strikingly different, the two paintings convey similar characteristics about their subjects.
Marie Antoinette	Richly dressed and made up; strikes an imperial pose	Lives life of comfort and power; proud, strong, and defiant	

Applying the Skill

MAKE YOUR OWN CHART. Turn to the detail from a mural by Diego Rivera in Chapter 16, page 456. The painting shows the Aztec god Quetzalcoatl in many forms. Use a chart, like the one above, to analyze and interpret the painting.

3.3 Using the Internet

The **INTERNET** is a network of computers associated with universities, libraries, news organizations, government agencies, businesses, and private individuals worldwide. Each location on the Internet has a **HOME PAGE** with its own address, or **URL.**

With a computer connected to the Internet, you can reach the home pages of many organizations and services. You might view your library's home page to find the call number of a book or visit an online magazine to read an article. On some sites you can view documents, photographs, and even moving pictures with sound.

The international collection of home pages, known as the **WORLD WIDE WEB,** is a good source of up-to-the-minute information about current events as well as in-depth research on historical subjects. This textbook contains many suggestions for navigating the World Wide Web. Begin by entering **CLASSZONE.COM** to access the home page for McDougal Littell World History.

Understanding the Skill

STRATEGY: EXPLORE THE ELEMENTS ON THE SCREEN. The computer screen below shows the home page of the history area at PBS, the national public television service based in Washington, D.C.

1. **Go directly to a Web page.** If you know the address of a particular Web page, type the address in the box at the top of the screen and press ENTER (or RETURN). After a few seconds, the Web page will appear on your screen.
2. **Explore the links.** Click on any one of the images or topics to find out more about a specific subject. These links take you to another page at this Web site. Some pages include links to related information that can be found at other places on the Internet.
3. **Learn more about the page.** Scan the page to learn the types of information contained at this site. This site has information about PBS history programs as well as other historical information and special features.
4. **Explore the features of the page.** This page has a feature that lets you compare life today with life in the 1700s.

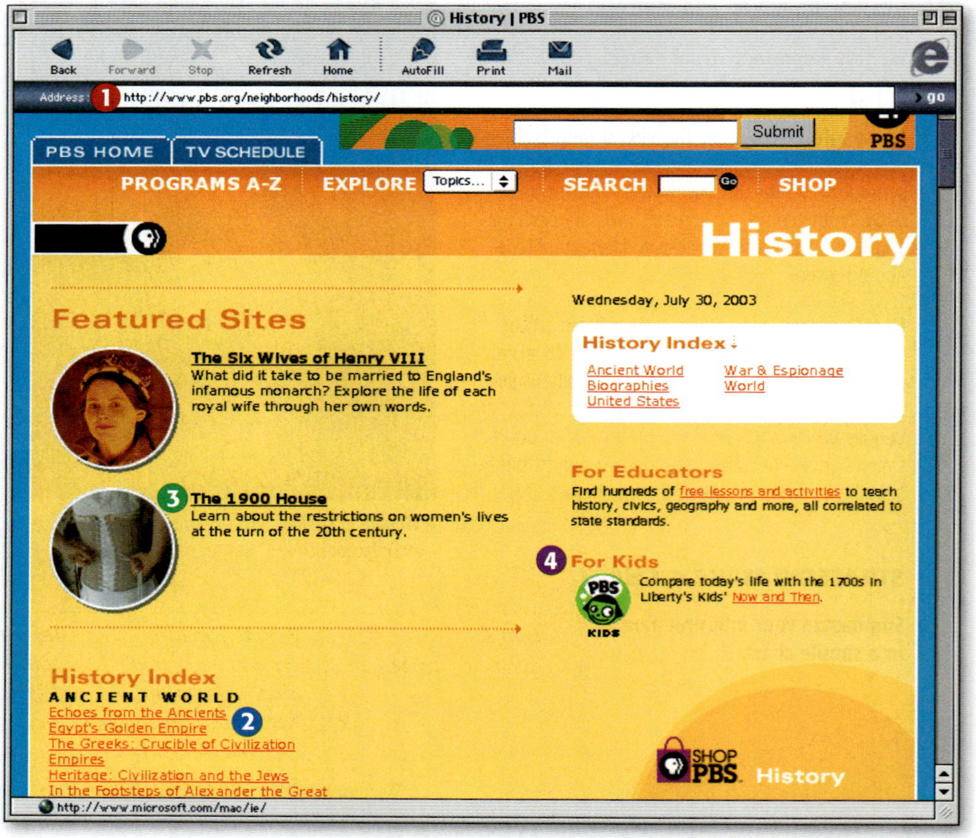

PBS History screen shot courtesy of PBS ONLINE®.

Applying the Skill

DO YOUR OWN INTERNET RESEARCH. Explore the web sites for Chapter 34 located at classzone.com. **PATH: CLASSZONE.COM** ➔ Social Studies ➔ World History ➔ Chapter 34 ➔ Research Links.

3.4 Interpreting Maps

MAPS are representations of features on the earth's surface. Historians use maps to locate historical events, to show how geography has influenced history, and to illustrate human interaction with the environment.

Different kinds of maps are used for specific purposes.

POLITICAL MAPS show political units, from countries, states, and provinces, to counties, districts, and towns. Each area is shaded a different color.

PHYSICAL MAPS show mountains, hills, plains, rivers, lakes, and oceans. They may use contour lines to indicate elevations on land and depths under water.

HISTORICAL MAPS illustrate such things as economic activity, political alliances, land claims, battles, population density, and changes over time.

1 Compass Rose The compass rose is a feature indicating the map's orientation on the globe. It may show all four cardinal directions (N, S, E, W) or just indicate north.

2 Locator A locator map shows which part of the world the map subject area covers.

3 Scale The scale shows the ratio between a unit of length on the map and a unit of distance on the earth. The maps in this book usually show the scale in miles and kilometers.

4 Lines Lines indicate rivers and other waterways, political boundaries, roads, and routes of exploration or migration.

5 Legend or Key The legend or key explains the symbols, lines, and special colors that appear on the map.

6 Symbols Locations of cities and towns often appear as dots. A capital city is often shown as a star or as a dot with a circle around it. Picture symbols might be used to indicate an area's products, resources, and special features.

7 Labels Key places such as cities, bodies of water, and landforms are labeled. Key dates, such as those for the founding of cities, may also be labeled.

8 Colors Maps use colors and shading for various purposes. On physical maps, color may be used to indicate different physical regions or altitudes. On political maps, color can distinguish different political units. On specialty maps, color can show variable features such as population density, languages, or cultural areas.

9 Inset An inset is a small map that appears within a larger map. It often shows an area of the larger map in greater detail. Inset maps may also show a different area that is in some way related to the area shown on the larger map.

10 Lines of Latitude and Longitude Lines of latitude and longitude appear on maps to indicate the absolute location of the area shown.

- Lines of latitude show distance measured in degrees north or south of the equator.
- Lines of longitude show distance measured in degrees east or west of the prime meridian, which runs through Greenwich, England.

3.4 (Continued)

Understanding the Skill

STRATEGY: READ ALL THE ELEMENTS OF THE MAP. The historical maps below show European landholdings in North America in 1754 and after 1763. Together they show changes over time.

1 Look at the map's title to learn the subject and purpose of the map. What area does the map cover? What does the map tell you about the area? Here the maps show North America in 1754 and after 1763 with the purpose of comparing European claims at two different times.

2 Look at the scale and compass. The scale shows you how many miles or kilometers are represented. Here the scale is 500 actual miles to approximately 5/8 inch on the map. The compass shows you which direction on the map is north.

3 Read the legend. The legend tells you what the symbols and colors on the map mean.

4 Find where the map area is located on the earth. These maps show a large area from the Arctic Circle to below latitude 20°N and 40° to 140°W.

STRATEGY: MAKE A CHART. Study the maps and pose questions about how the geographic patterns and distributions changed. Use the answers to create a chart.

Relate the map to the five geography themes by making a chart. The five themes are described on pages xxxii–xxxiii. Ask questions about the themes and record your answers on the chart.

What Was the Location? Large area from Arctic Circle to below 20° N, and 40° to 140° W

What Was the Place? North American continent

What Was the Region? Western Hemisphere

Was There Any Movement? Between 1754 and 1763, land claimed by France was taken over by the other two colonial powers. Spain expanded its territories northward, while Britain expanded westward.

How Did Humans Interact with the Environment? Europeans carved out political units in the continent, which already had inhabitants. They claimed vast areas, with waterways and large mountain ranges to cross.

Applying the Skill

MAKE YOUR OWN CHART. Turn to Chapter 12, page 334, and study the map titled "The Mongol Empire, 1294." Make a chart, like the one shown above, in which you summarize what the map tells you according to the five geography themes.

3.5 Interpreting Charts

CHARTS are visual presentations of materials. Historians use charts to organize, simplify, and summarize information in a way that makes it more meaningful or easier to remember. Several kinds of charts are commonly used.

SIMPLE CHARTS are used to summarize information or to make comparisons.

TABLES are used to organize statistics and other types of information into columns and rows for easy reference.

DIAGRAMS provide visual clues to the meaning of the information they contain. Venn diagrams are used for comparisons. Web diagrams are used to organize supporting information around a central topic. Illustrated diagrams or diagrams that combine different levels of information are sometimes called **INFOGRAPHICS.**

Understanding the Skill

STRATEGY: STUDY ALL THE ELEMENTS OF THE CHART. The infographic below conveys a great deal of information about the three estates, or classes, that existed in 18th-century France. The infographic visually combines a political cartoon, a bulleted chart, a pie graph, and a bar graph.

Read the title.

Identify the symbols and colors and what they represent. Here, three colors are used consistently in the infographic to represent the three estates.

Study each of the elements of the infographic. The political cartoon visually represents the power of the First and Second Estates over the Third Estate. The bulleted chart gives details about the estates. The two graphs give statistics.

Look for the main idea. Make connections among the types of information presented. What was the relationship among the three estates?

The Three Estates

A First Estate
- made up of clergy of Roman Catholic Church
- scorned Enlightenment ideas
- owned about 15% of the land

B Second Estate
- made up of rich nobles
- held highest offices in government
- disagreed about Enlightenment ideas
- owned about 20% of the land

C Third Estate
- included bourgeoisie, urban lower class, and peasant farmers
- had no power to influence government
- embraced Enlightenment ideas
- resented the wealthy First and Second Estates
- owned about 65% of the land

Population of France, 1787

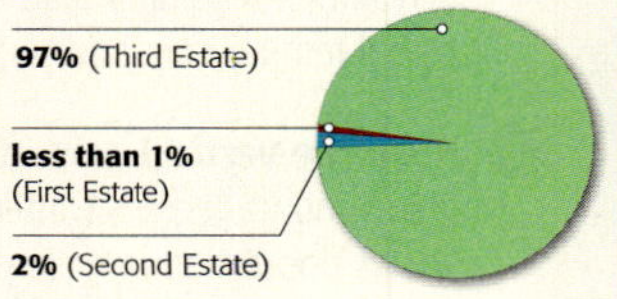

Percent of Income Paid in Taxes

Look for geographic patterns and distributions. Pose questions about the way land is distributed among the three estates. Include your answers in your summary paragraph.

STRATEGY: WRITE A SUMMARY.

Write a paragraph to summarize what you learned from the chart.

In 1787, French society was unevenly divided into three estates. Ninety-seven percent of the people belonged to the Third Estate. They had no political power, paid high taxes, and owned only 65 percent of the land. The First Estate, made up of the clergy, and the Second Estate, made up of rich nobles, held the power, the wealth, and more than their share of the land. Both opposed change and took advantage of the Third Estate.

Applying the Skill

WRITE YOUR OWN SUMMARY. Turn to Chapter 13, page 361, and look at the chart titled "Feudalism." Study the chart and write a paragraph in which you summarize what you learn from it.

3.6 Interpreting Graphs

GRAPHS show statistical information in a visual manner. Historians use graphs to show comparative amounts, ratios, economic trends, and changes over time.

LINE GRAPHS can show changes over time, or trends. Usually, the horizontal axis shows a unit of time, such as years, and the vertical axis shows quantities.

PIE GRAPHS are useful for showing relative proportions. The circle represents the whole, such as the entire population, and the slices represent the different groups that make up the whole.

BAR GRAPHS compare numbers or sets of numbers. The length of each bar indicates a quantity. With bar graphs, it is easy to see at a glance how different categories compare.

Understanding the Skill

STRATEGY: STUDY ALL THE ELEMENTS OF THE GRAPH. The line graphs below show average global temperatures and world population figures over a period of 25,000 years. Pose questions about geographic patterns and distributions shown on this graph; for example, when did worldwide temperature start to rise?

1. **Read the title to identify the main idea of the graph.** When two subjects are shown, look for a relationship between them. This set of graphs shows that the agricultural revolution had links to both global temperature and population.
2. **Read the vertical axis.** The temperature graph shows degrees Fahrenheit. The other shows population in millions, so that 125 indicates 125,000,000.
3. **Note any information that is highlighted in a box.**
4. **Read the horizontal axis.** Both graphs cover a period of time from 25,000 years ago to 0 (today).
5. **Look at the legend to understand what colors and certain marks stand for.**

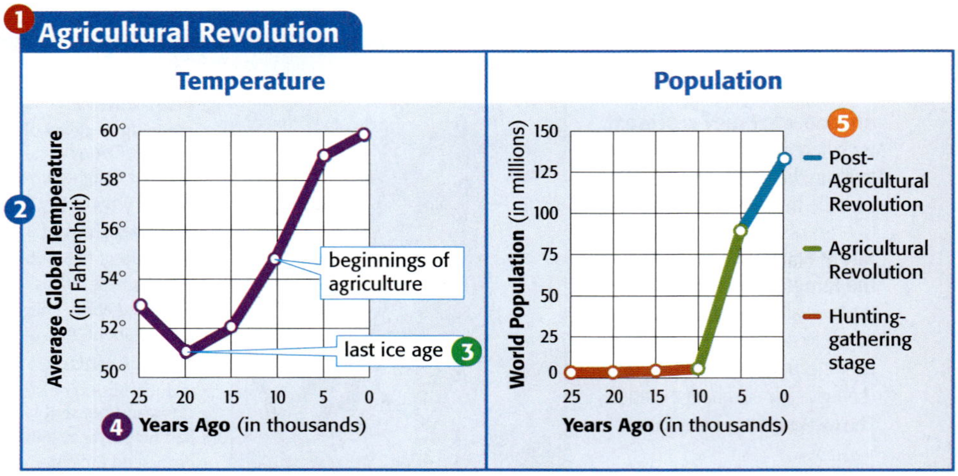

Summarize the information shown in each part of the graph. What trends or changes are shown in each line graph?

STRATEGY: WRITE A SUMMARY.

Use the answers to your questions about geographic patterns and distributions to write your summary paragraph.

Write a paragraph to summarize what you learned from the graphs.

Some 20,000 years ago, after the last Ice Age, temperatures started to rise worldwide. This steady rise in average temperature from 51° to 55° made possible the beginnings of agriculture. As a result of the agricultural revolution, world population grew from about 2 million to about 130 million over a period of 10,000 years.

Applying the Skill

WRITE YOUR OWN SUMMARY. Turn to Chapter 31, page 908, and look at the graph "World Trade, 1929–1933." Study the graph and write a paragraph in which you summarize what you learn from it.

3.7 Analyzing Political Cartoons

POLITICAL CARTOONS are drawings that express the artist's point of view about a local, national, or international situation or event. They may criticize, show approval, or draw attention to a particular issue, and may be either serious or humorous. Political cartoonists often use symbols as well as other visual clues to communicate their message.

Understanding the Skill

STRATEGY: EXAMINE THE CARTOON CAREFULLY. The cartoon below was drawn during the period of détente—a lessening of Cold War tensions between the United States and the Soviet Union.

1. **Look at the cartoon as a whole to determine the subject.**

2. **Look for symbols, which are especially effective in communicating ideas visually.** In this cartoon, Szabo uses symbols that stand for two nations. The stars and stripes stand for the United States. The hammer and sickle stand for the Soviet Union.

3. **Analyze the visual details, which help express the artist's point of view.** The lit fuse suggests that the world is in immediate danger. The United States and the Soviet Union are cooperating to reduce the danger by cutting the fuse.

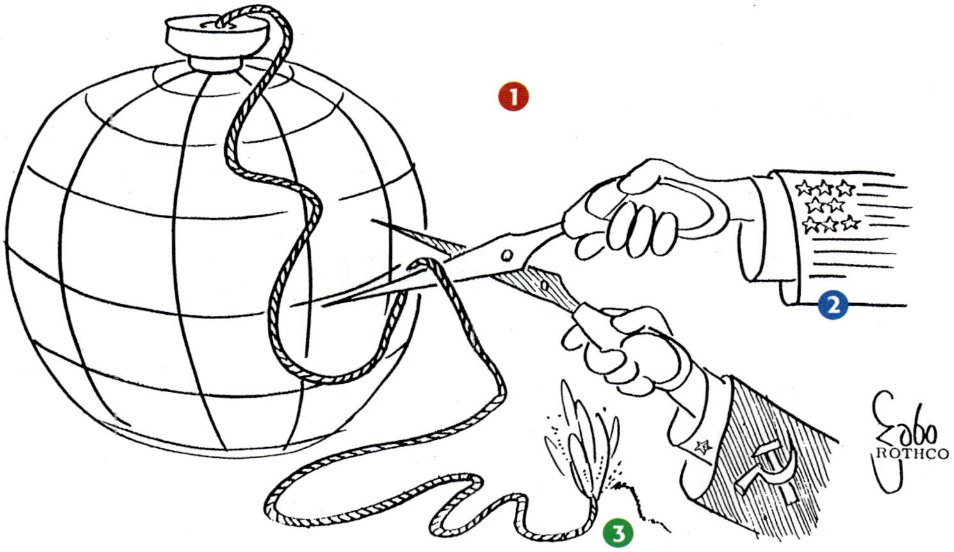

STRATEGY: MAKE A CHART.

Summarize your analysis in a chart. Look for details and analyze their significance. Then decide on the message of the cartoon.

Symbols and Visual Details	*Significance*	*Message*
• *Stars and stripes* • *Hammer and sickle* • *Lit fuse* • *Both nations hold the scissors*	• *United States* • *Soviet Union* • *Danger* • *Cooperation*	*The United States and the Soviet Union are trying to prevent their differences from destroying the world.*

Applying the Skill

MAKE YOUR OWN CHART. Turn to the political cartoon in Chapter 23, page 652. Read the information provided in the chart and graphs to help you understand the basis for the cartoon. Note the clothing and apparent attitudes of the figures in the drawing, as well as how they relate to one another. Then make a chart like the one above.

4.1 Writing for Social Studies

WRITING FOR SOCIAL STUDIES requires you to describe an idea, a situation, or an event. Often, you will be asked to take a stand on a particular issue or to make a specific point. To successfully describe an event or make a point, your writing needs to be clear, concise, and accurate. When you write reports or term papers, you will also need to create a bibliography of your sources; and you need to evaluate how reliable those sources are.

Understanding the Skill

STRATEGY: ORGANIZE INFORMATION AND WRITE CLEARLY. The following passage describes the rise and fall of Napoleon Bonaparte. Notice how the strategies below helped the writer explain the historical importance of Napoleon's power.

1. **Focus on your topic.** Be sure that you clearly state the main idea of your piece so that your readers know what you intend to say.

2. **Collect and organize your facts.** Collect accurate information about your topic to support the main idea you are trying to make. Use your information to build a logical case to prove your point

To express your ideas clearly, use standard grammar, spelling, sentence structure, and punctuation when writing for social studies. Proofread your work to make sure it is well organized and grammatically correct.

(1) The Rise and Fall of Napoleon, 1799–1814

The power that Napoleon used to bring order to France after the Revolution ultimately proved to be his undoing. Under his command, the troops drove out members of the legislature in 1799 and helped Napoleon seize control of France. (2) As emperor of France, he stabilized the country's economy. He even created a code of laws. However, Napoleon wanted to control all of Europe. But he made mistakes that cost him his empire. He established a blockade in 1806 to prevent trade between Great Britain and other Europeans nations. But smugglers, aided by the British, managed to get cargo through. He angered Spain by replacing the country's king with his own brother. In 1812, Napoleon also invaded Russia by using many troops who were not French and who felt little loyalty to him. Eventually, all the main powers of Europe joined forces and defeated Napoleon in the spring of 1814.

STRATEGY: USE STANDARD FORMATS WHEN MAKING CITATIONS. Use standard formats when citing books, magazines, newspapers, electronic media, and other sources. The following examples will help you to interpret and create bibliographies.

3. **Video**
4. **Newspaper**
5. **Magazine**
6. **Online database**
7. **Book**

(3) Fire and Ice. Prod. HistoryAlive Videocassette. BBC Video, 1998.

(4) Gutierrez, Andrew R. "Memorial for Scott at Antarctic." Los Angeles Times 8 January 2001: 14A.

(5) Hansen, Ron. "The Race for the South Pole." Smithsonian Institute 28 June 1999: 112.

(6) "Scott's Run for the South Pole." Facts on File. Online. Internet. 28 February 2000.

(7) Solomon, Susan. The Coldest March: Scott's Fatal Antarctic Expedition. New Haven, CT: Yale UP, 2001.

Applying the Skill

WRITE YOUR OWN RESPONSE. Turn to Chapter 23, Section 4, "Napoleon's Empire Collapses." Read the section and use the strategies above to write your answer to question 6 on page 671.

Find three or four different sources on the Internet or in the library relating to Napoleon's fall. Create a short bibliography and use standard formats for each type of source. Be sure to interpret, or evaluate, how reliable your sources are.

4.2 Creating a Map

CREATING A MAP can help you understand routes, regions, landforms, political boundaries, or other geographical information.

Understanding the Skill

STRATEGY: CREATE A MAP to clarify information and help you visualize what you read. Creating a map is similar to taking notes, except that you draw much of the information. After reading the passage below, a student sketched the map shown.

The French Explore North America

A number of Frenchmen were among the early explorers of North America. In 1534, Jacques Cartier sailed up a broad river that he named the St. Lawrence. When he came to a large island dominated by a mountain, he called the island Mont Real, which eventually became known as Montreal. In 1608, another French explorer, Samuel de Champlain, sailed further up the St. Lawrence and laid claim to a region he called Quebec. In 1673, Jacques Marquette and Louis Joliet explored the Great Lakes and the upper Mississippi River. Nearly 10 years later, Sieur de La Salle explored the lower Mississippi and claimed the entire river valley for France.

1. **Create a title that shows the purpose of the map**
2. **Consider the purpose of the map as you decide which features to include.** Because the main purpose of this sketch map is to show the routes of early explorers, it includes a scale of distance.
3. **Find one or more maps to use as a guide.** For this sketch map, the student consulted a historical map and a physical map.
4. **Create a legend to explain any colors or symbols used.**

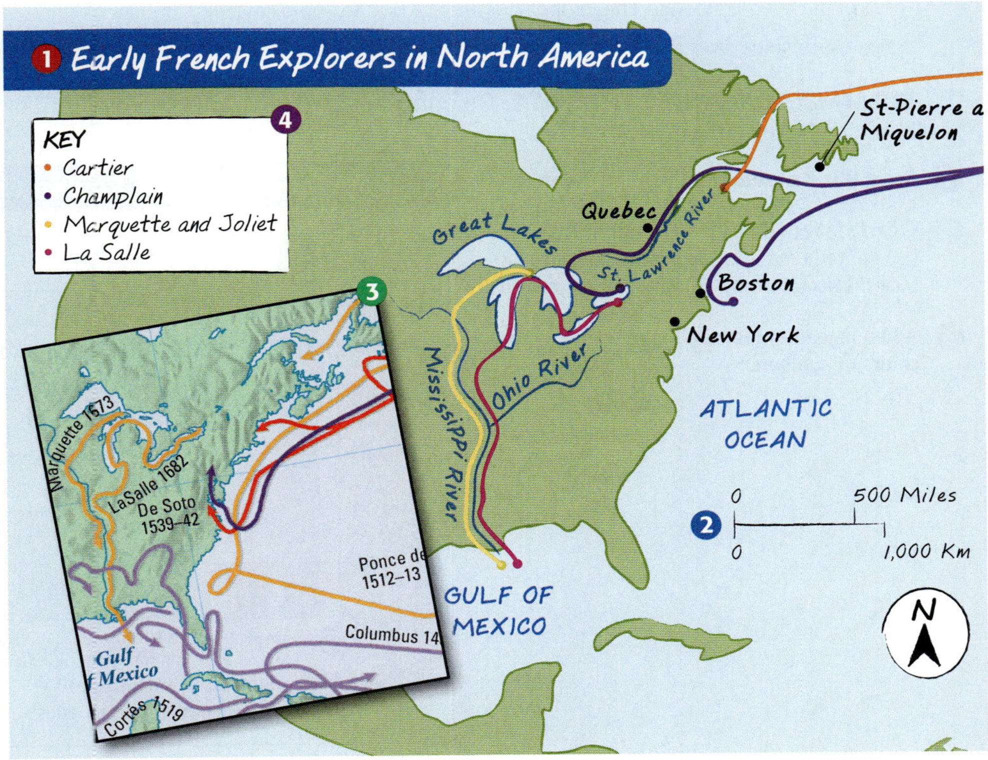

Applying the Skill

MAKE YOUR OWN SKETCH MAP. Turn to Chapter 20, page 556, and read the first three paragraphs of the section "Spanish Conquests in Peru." Create a sketch map showing the cities where Pizarro conquered the Inca. Use either a modern map of Peru or an historic map of the Incan Empire as a guide. (The conquered cities of the empire also belong to the modern nation of Peru.) Include a scale of miles to show the distance traveled by the Spanish to make their conquests. Add a legend to indicate which conquest involved a battle and which did not.

4.3 Creating Charts and Graphs

CHARTS and **GRAPHS** are visual representations of information. (See Skillbuilders 3.5, Interpreting Charts, and 3.6, Interpreting Graphs.) Three types of graphs are **BAR GRAPHS, LINE GRAPHS,** and **PIE GRAPHS.** Use a line graph to show changes over time, or trends. Use a pie graph to show relative proportions. Use a bar graph to display and compare information about quantities. Use a **CHART** to organize, simplify, and summarize information.

Understanding the Skill

STRATEGY: CREATE A BAR GRAPH. Choose the information that you wish to compare. After reading the following paragraph, a student created the bar graph below to compare population shifts in three European cities.

> Population Shifts
>
> The decline of the Roman Empire led to major population shifts. As Roman centers of trade and government collapsed, nobles retreated to the rural areas. Roman cities were left without strong leadership. The population of Rome dropped from 350,000 in A.D. 100 to 50,000 in A.D. 900. During the same period, other cities in the empire experienced similar declines. For example, the population of Trier, Germany, dropped from 100,000 to around 13,000. The population of Lyon, France, experienced an even greater decline, dropping from 100,000 to approximately 12,000.

STRATEGY: ORGANIZE THE DATA. Be consistent in how you present similar kinds of information.

1. **Use a title that sums up the information.**
2. **Clearly label vertical and horizontal axes.** Use the vertical axis to show increasing quantities. Label the horizontal axis with what is being compared.
3. **Add a legend to indicate the meaning of any colors or symbols.**

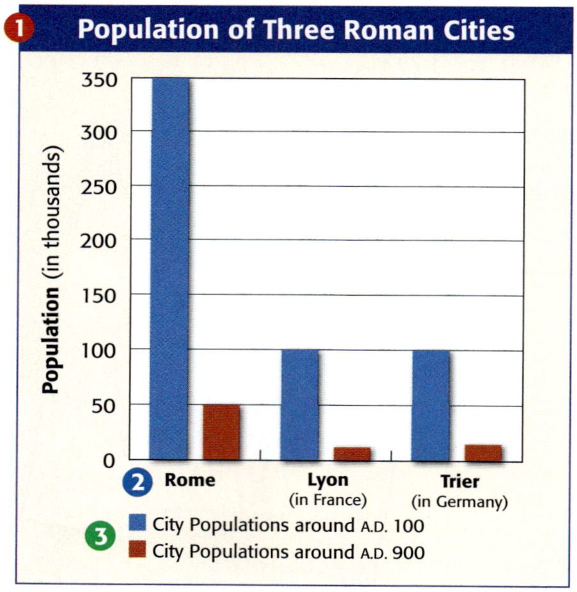

Applying the Skill

CREATE A BAR GRAPH. Turn to Chapter 23, page 670. Study the map "Napoleon's Russian Campaign, 1812." Use the information to create a bar graph showing the number of soldiers in Napoleon's army from June 1812 to December 6, 1812. Label the vertical axis Soldiers (in thousands) and show the grid in increments of 100, beginning with 0 and ending with 500. Provide a bar for each of the following dates: June 1812, September 7, 1812, November 1812, and December 6, 1812. Label each bar with the number of soldiers. Add a title. Be sure to read carefully the information in the boxes on the chart for each date you include in your graph.

4.4 Creating and Using a Database

A **DATABASE** is a collection of data, or information, that is organized so that you can find and retrieve information on a specific topic quickly and easily. Once a computerized database is set up, you can search it to find specific information without going through the entire database. The database will provide a list of all information in the database related to your topic. Learning how to use a database will help you learn how to create one.

Understanding the Skill

STRATEGY: CREATE THE DATABASE. First, identify the topic of the database. Both words in this title, "Five Empires," are important. These words were used to begin the research for this database.

1. **Determine the order of presentation of information.** For example, will you list items from largest to smallest? from oldest to newest? The five empires are listed in order of date, from earliest empire to latest.

2. **Identify the entries included under each heading.** Here, five empires from the text were chosen as topics for research.

3. **Ask yourself what kind of data to include.** For example, what geographic patterns and distributions will be shown? Your choice of data will provide the column headings. The key words *Dates, Greatest Territory,* and *Greatest Population* were chosen to focus the research.

Five Empires

	(1) Dates	Greatest Territory*	(3) Greatest Population**
(2) Persian	550 B.C.–330 B.C.	2.0	14.0
Roman	27 B.C.–A.D. 476	3.4	54.8
Byzantine	A.D. 395–A.D. 1453	1.4	30.0
Mongol	A.D. 1206–A.D. 1380	11.7	125.0
Aztec	A.D. 1325–A.D. 1521	0.2	6.0

(4) * Estimated in millions of square miles
** Estimated in millions of people

4. **Add labels or footnotes as necessary to clarify the nature of the data presented.** Are the figures shown in thousands? hundred of thousands? millions? Users of the database need to know what the figures represent.

STRATEGY: USE THE DATABASE. Use the database to help you find information quickly. For example, in this database you could search for "empires with populations of more than 10 million" and compile a list including the Persian, Roman, Byzantine, and Mongol empires.

Applying the Skill

CREATE A DATABASE for World War II that shows the dates and locations of important battles, estimated casualty figures, and the significance of the outcome for each battle. Use information presented in Chapter 32 to find the data. Follow a chart format similar to the one above for your database. Then use the database to list the three battles that resulted in the highest number of casualties.

4.5 Creating a Model

WHEN YOU CREATE A MODEL, you use information and ideas to show an event or a situation in a visual way. A model might be a poster or a diagram drawn to explain how something happened. Or, it might be a three-dimensional model, such as a diorama, that depicts an important scene or situation.

Understanding the Skill

STRATEGY: CREATE A MODEL. The poster below shows the hardships and dangers that children faced while working in the textile factories in the early 1800s. Use the strategies listed below to help you create your own model.

1. **Gather the information you need to understand the situation or event.** In this case, you need to be able to show the hardships and dangers of child labor.
2. **Visualize and sketch an idea for your model.** Once you have created a picture in your mind, make an actual sketch to plan how it might look.
3. **Think of symbols you may want to use.** Since the model should give information in a visual way, think about ways you can use color, pictures, or other visuals to tell the story.

Gather the supplies you will need and create the model. For example, you may need crayons and markers.

Child Labor in Britain in the Early 1800s

INDUSTRY COMES TO MANCHESTER, ENGLAND!

Applying the Skill

CREATE YOUR OWN MODEL. Read the Interact with History feature on page 716. Create a poster that shows how working conditions might be made more fair in England during the Industrial Revolution.

4.6 Creating/Interpreting a Research Outline

When you **CREATE A RESEARCH OUTLINE,** you arrange information you have gathered into an organized format. When you **INTERPRET A RESEARCH OUTLINE,** you use the outline's structure to guide you in writing a research report or paper that is clear and focused.

Understanding the Skill

STRATEGY: DECIDE HOW IDEAS ARE CONNECTED, THEN CREATE AN OUTLINE. As you research a topic, you are likely to gather names, dates, facts, and ideas. All of this information needs to be organized to show how the ideas connect to one another. To decide how the ideas connect, think about your purpose for writing the research report.

For example, suppose you are writing a report about Napoleon's retreat from Moscow. You might choose to create an outline using the sequence of events or using the causes and effects that led to the destruction of the Grand Army. Your outline would reflect your purpose.

1 An outline begins with a statement of purpose.

2 An outline is divided into two or more major sections, introduced by Roman numerals (I, II).

3 Each major section is divided into two or more subsections introduced by capital letters (A, B).

4 The subsections may be divided into sub-subsections introduced by Arabic numerals (1, 2).

Chronological outline

1 Purpose: Describe the events that led to Napoleon's defeat in Russia.

2 I. Napoleon's defeat in Russia
- A. June 1812
  - 1. march into Russia
  - 2. scorched-earth policy
- B. September 7, 1812
  - 1. Battle of Borodino
  - 2. narrow victory for the French
- C. September 14, 1812
  - 1. arrival in Moscow
  - 2. city in flames

2 II. Napoleon's defeat in Russia
- A. mid-October 1812
  - 1. waiting for offer of peace
  - 2. too late to advance
  - 3. begins retreat from Moscow
- B. early November 1812
  - 1. retreat in snow storm
  - 2. attack by Russians

Cause-and-effect outline

Purpose: Describe the reasons for Napoleon's defeat in Russia.

I. Napoleon's mistakes
- 3 A. troops not loyal to Napoleon
- B. waited too long to retreat
  - 4 1. starvation
  - 2. winter snows

II. Russian tactics
- A. scorched-earth policy
- B. no offer of peace from the czar
- C. attacks on the retreating army

STRATEGY: INTERPRET THE OUTLINE TO WRITE A RESEARCH REPORT.

Use the organization of the outline to choose signal words that match your purpose for writing.

Signal words to show time-order	*Signal words to show cause and effect*
dates: September 14, 1812	*because*
time frames: for five weeks	*so*
order: first, next, then, last	*as a result*

Applying the Skill

CREATE YOUR OWN OUTLINE. Read Chapter 29, "The Great War, 1914–1918." Create an outline that shows a sequence of events leading up to World War I or that shows the series of causes and effects that resulted in the war. Choose appropriate signal words to write a rough draft from your outline.

Skillbuilder Handbook

4.7 Creating Oral Presentations

When you **CREATE AN ORAL PRESENTATION,** you prepare a speech or a talk to give before an audience. The object of an oral presentation is to provide information about a particular topic or to persuade an audience to think or act in a particular way.

Understanding the Skill

STRATEGY: CHOOSE A TOPIC. The following is an excerpt from a student's speech in support of recycling.

1. **State your theme or point of view.**
2. **Include facts or arguments to support your theme.**
3. **Choose words and images that reflect the theme.** The comparison to Disneyland is a visual image that helps to communicate the amount of waste in the Fresh Kills Landfill.

(1) To help preserve the earth's dwindling natural resources, Americans need to get serious about recycling. At the moment, our track record is not very good. (2) Although people in the United States account for less than 5% of the world's population, they use 40% of the world's resources, and generate a huge amount of waste. The Fresh Kills Landfill, which serves New York City, is a prime example. It contains so much garbage that Fresh Kills Landfill is (3) four times the size of Disneyland. And that's just New York's garbage.

With so many people throwing so much away, is there any point in trying to change things? The answer is yes! Recyling one glass bottle saves enough energy to light a 100-watt light bulb for four hours. Twenty-five million trees could be saved every year by recycling just 10% of our newspapers. Making new aluminum products from recycled aluminum, rather than from bauxite, uses 95% less energy. By increasing the recycling of our bottles, jars, cans, and paper, we could dramatically reduce our demand for trees, fossil fuels, and other precious resources.

STRATEGY: USE THESE TIPS FOR SUCCESSFUL ORAL PRESENTATIONS.

- Maintain eye contact with your audience.
- Use gestures and body language to emphasize main points.
- Pace yourself. Speak slowly and distinctly.
- Vary your tone to help bring out the message you wish to make.

STRATEGY: PRACTICE THE PRESENTATION in front of a mirror or ask a friend or family member to listen to your presentation and give you feedback.

Applying the Skill

CREATE YOUR OWN ORAL PRESENTATION. Turn to Chapter 22. Choose a topic from the "New" section of one of the "Changing Idea" boxes on pages 626, 629, 638, or 642. Create an oral presentation in which you explain how the idea was new and why it was important. Use information from the chapter to support your chosen idea.

4.8 Creating Written Presentations

CREATING A WRITTEN PRESENTATION means writing an in-depth report on a topic in history. Your objective may be to inform or to support a particular point of view. To succeed, your writing must be clear and well organized. For additional information on creating a historical research paper, see Skillbuilder 4.1, Writing for Social Studies.

Understanding the Skill

STRATEGY: CREATE AN OUTLINE such as the one below. Use it as a guide to write your presentation.

1. **State the main idea.**
2. **Organize the information by category.**
3. **Add supporting facts and details.**

(1) **The Incan Empire**

I. The Inca created a large and highly developed empire.

(2) A. A Theocracy
1. Members of only 11 families could rule
2. Rulers believed to be descendants of the sun god
3. Religion supported the state; worship of the sun god, Inti, amounted to worship of the king

B. Expansion
1. Rulers conquered new territories to acquire wealth
2. Pachacuti created the largest empire in the Americas
3. Size by 1500: 2,500 miles along western coast, 16 million people

C. Unifying strategies
(3) 1. Rulers practiced diplomacy
2. Rulers imposed a single official language, Quechua
3. Schools taught conquered peoples the Incan ways
4. Extensive system of roads led to Cuzco, the capital

D. Early socialism
1. Supported aged and disabled
2. Rewarded citizens' labor with food and beer

E. Culturally advanced
1. Elaborate calendar system
2. Artisans created works in gold and silver
3. Exception: no writing system, but oral tradition

4.8 (Continued)

STRATEGY: EDIT AND REVISE YOUR PRESENTATION.

1. **Use punctuation marks for their correct purposes.** A comma follows a prepositional phrase at the beginning of a sentence.
2. **Capitalize all proper nouns.** Three lines under a letter means to capitalize.
3. **Check spelling with both an electronic spell checker and a dictionary.**
4. **Use consistent verb tense.** Use past tense for events in the past.
5. **Check for common agreement errors.** Subjects and verbs must agree in person and number.
6. **Use correct sentence structure.** Every sentence must have a subject and a verb.

The Incan Empire

The Inca created the largest empire ever seen in the Americas. Despite its size (1), the Incan Empire was highly unified. Its government was diplomatic, bureaucratic, and socialist in nature, and its ruler was believed to be a god-king.

The Incan ruler was selected from one of 11 noble families, who were believed to have descended from (2) inti, the sun god. Religion therefore supported the state, for worship of the sun god amounted to worship of the king. Thus, the empire was a theocracy, which is a state believed to be ruled directly by divine guidance.

The empire's expansion was largely the result of an important tradition: dead rulers retained the wealth they (3) acumulated [c] during their lives. To acquire wealth of their own, succeeding rulers often attempted to conquer new territories. One such ruler, Pachacuti, conquered all of Peru and many neighboring lands as well. By 1500, the Incan Empire extended 2,500 miles along the coast of western South America and included an estimated 16 million people.

Incan rulers used a number of strategies to achieve unification. They practiced diplomacy by allowing conquered peoples to retain their own customs as long as they were loyal to the state. The Inca imposed a single official language, Quechua, to be used throughout the empire. They founded schools to teach Incan ways. They (4) build [t] 14,000 miles of roads and bridges, which connected cities in conquered areas with Cuzco, the Incan capital.

The government's concern for the welfare of its citizens suggests an early form of socialism. Citizens worked for the state and, in turn, were taken care of. At public feasts, food and beer (5) ~~was~~ [were] distributed as a reward for labor. In addition, the aged and disabled often received state support.

Among the many cultural achievements of the Inca were the development of an elaborate calendar system and the creation of beautiful works in gold and silver. Surprisingly, (6) [the Inca had] no system of writing. They preserved their history and literature by means of an oral tradition.

Applying the Skill

CREATE A TWO-PAGE WRITTEN PRESENTATION on a topic of historical importance that interests you.

Primary Source Handbook

CONTENTS

Unit 1

Rig Veda, *Creation Hymn* (Chapter 3) R40
Bible, *Psalm 23* (Chapter 3) R41
Confucius, *Analects* (Chapter 4) R42

Unit 2

Thucydides, *History of the Peloponnesian War* (Chapter 5) R43
Plato, *The Apology* (Chapter 5) R44
Tacitus, *Annals* (Chapter 6) R45

Unit 3

Qur'an (Chapter 10) R46
Sei Shōnagon, *The Pillow Book* (Chapter 12) R47
Magna Carta (Chapter 14) R48

Unit 4

Popol Vuh (Chapter 16) R49
Niccolò Machiavelli, *The Prince* (Chapter 17) R50
Sir Thomas More, *Utopia* (Chapter 17) R51

Unit 5

James Madison, *The Federalist,* "Number 51" (Chapter 22) R52
Mary Wollstonecraft, *A Vindication of the Rights of Woman* (Chapter 22) R53
Élisabeth Vigée-Lebrun, *Memoirs of Madame Vigée-Lebrun* (Chapter 23) R54

Unit 6

Sadler Committee, *Report on Child Labor* (Chapter 25) R55
Abraham Lincoln, *Second Inaugural Address* (Chapter 26) R56
Elizabeth Cady Stanton, *The Natural Rights of Civilized Women* (Chapter 26) R57

Unit 7

Woodrow Wilson, *The Fourteen Points* (Chapter 29) R58
Elie Wiesel, *Night* (Chapter 32) R59
Jeanne Wakatsuki Houston, *Farewell to Manzanar* (Chapter 32) R60

Unit 8

Nelson Mandela, *Inaugural Address* (Chapter 35) R61
Martin Luther King, Jr., *I Have a Dream* (Chapter 36) R62
Cesar Chavez, *An Open Letter* (Chapter 36) R63

Primary Source Handbook

from the Rig Veda

SETTING THE STAGE The Rig Veda is one of the sacred scriptures of the Aryans, who invaded India around 1500 B.C. The oldest of four Vedas, or books of wisdom, it contains 1,028 hymns to Aryan gods. The "Creation Hymn" speculates about how the world was created.

PRIMARY SOURCE

There was neither non-existence nor existence then; there was neither the realm of space nor the sky which is beyond. What stirred? Where? In whose protection? Was there water, bottomlessly deep?

There was neither death nor immortality then. There was no distinguishing sign of night nor of day. That one breathed, windless, by its own impulse. Other than that there was nothing beyond.

Darkness was hidden by darkness in the beginning; with no distinguishing sign, all this was water. The life force that was covered with emptiness, that one arose through the power of heat.

Desire came upon that one in the beginning; that was the first seed of mind. Poets seeking in their heart with wisdom found the bond of existence in non-existence.

Their cord was extended across. Was there below? Was there above? There were seed-placers; there were powers. There was impulse beneath; there was giving-forth above.

Who really knows? Who will here proclaim it? Whence was it produced? Whence is this creation? The gods came afterwards, with the creation of this universe. Who then knows whence it has arisen?

Whence this creation has arisen—perhaps it formed itself, or perhaps it did not—the one who looks down on it, in the highest heaven, only he knows—or perhaps he does not know.

▲ Indra, the Aryan god of war, seated on an elephant

DOCUMENT-BASED QUESTIONS

1. *What is the basic two-part structure of the "Creation Hymn"?*
2. *Who knows how the universe was created, according to the "Creation Hymn"?*
3. *What questions does the hymn raise about how the universe was created? What answers does it give?*
4. *What are you told about "that one" who is mentioned in the hymn?*
5. *What might the following words mean: "The gods came afterwards, with the creation of this universe"?*

Primary Source Handbook

from the King James Bible, Psalm 23

SETTING THE STAGE The Book of Psalms is the hymnal of ancient Israel. Most of the psalms were written to be used during worship in the temple. Many have been traditionally attributed to King David, who ruled over Israel around 1000 B.C. The Book of Psalms contains 150 songs on a variety of topics. Psalm 23 focuses on the relationship between God and the individual.

PRIMARY SOURCE

The Lord is my shepherd;
I shall not want.
He maketh me to lie down in green pastures;
he leadeth me beside the still waters;

he restoreth my soul.
He leadeth me in the paths of righteousness
for his name's sake.

Yea, though I walk through the valley
of the shadow of death,

I will fear no evil: for thou art with me;
thy rod and thy staff they comfort me.

Thou preparest a table before me
in the presence of mine enemies:

Thou anointest my head with oil; my cup runneth over.

Surely goodness and mercy shall follow me
all the days of my life,

and I will dwell in the house of the Lord forever.

▲ David, the young shepherd, plays his pipe and a bell.

DOCUMENT-BASED QUESTIONS

1. *The rod and the staff are two tools of the shepherd. What does this suggest about the role of the Lord, "my shepherd"?*
2. *What kind of relationship does the person speaking have with the Lord?*
3. *In this psalm, the Lord is also presented as a generous host. What are some examples of this?*
4. *Why does the speaker expect goodness and mercy to follow him all the days of his life?*

from the Analects of Confucius

SETTING THE STAGE The *Analects (analect* means "a selection") is a short collection of about 500 sayings, dialogues, and brief stories, that was put together over a period of many years following Confucius' death. The *Analects* presents Confucius' teachings on how people should live to create an orderly and just society. Over time, Confucian thought became the basis for the Chinese system of government and remained a part of Chinese life into the 20th century.

PRIMARY SOURCE

The Master [Confucius] said: "Don't worry if people don't recognize your merits; worry that you may not recognize theirs." (1.16)

The Master said: "To study without thinking is futile [useless]. To think without studying is dangerous." (2.15)

Lord Ji Kang asked: "What should I do in order to make the people respectful, loyal, and zealous?" The Master said: "Approach them with dignity and they will be respectful. Be yourself a good son and a kind father, and they will be loyal. Raise the good and train the incompetent, and they will be zealous." (2.20)

The Master said: "Authority without generosity, ceremony without reverence, mourning without grief—these, I cannot bear to contemplate." (3.26)

The Master said: "Don't worry if you are without a position; worry lest you do not deserve a position. Do not worry if you are not famous; worry lest you do not deserve to be famous." (4.14)

The Master said: "Without ritual, courtesy is tiresome; without ritual, prudence is timid; without ritual, bravery is quarrelsome; without ritual, frankness is hurtful. When gentlemen treat their kin generously, common people are attracted to goodness; when old ties are not forgotten, common people are not fickle." (8.2)

Zingong asked: "Is there any single word that could guide one's entire life?" The master said: "Should it not be *reciprocity?* What you do not wish for yourself, do not do to others." (15.24)

▲ Confucius

DOCUMENT-BASED QUESTIONS

1. *What kinds of behavior does Confucius talk about in the* Analects?
2. *Do you think Confucius views human nature in an optimistic or a pessimistic way? Explain your opinion.*
3. *What does Confucius mean by* reciprocity?
4. *What kind of person does Confucius seem to be?*
5. *Are the teachings in the* Analects *surprising in any way? Explain.*
6. *Does Confucius seem more concerned with individual behavior or with behavior toward others?*

from History of the Peloponnesian War

by Thucydides

SETTING THE STAGE Thucydides was a Greek historian who wrote about the bitter 27-year-long Peloponnesian War between Athens and Sparta. As one of the ten military leaders of Athens, Thucydides was probably in attendance when Pericles, the greatest Athenian statesman of his time, gave a funeral oration. This speech honored the Athenian warriors who had been killed during the first year of the war. In the following excerpt, Pericles speaks of the distinctive qualities of Athens.

PRIMARY SOURCE

Our love of what is beautiful does not lead to extravagance; our love of the mind does not make us soft. We regard wealth as something to be properly used, rather than as something to boast about. As for poverty, no one need be ashamed to admit it: the real shame is in not taking practical measures to escape from it. Here each individual is interested not only in his own affairs but in the affairs of state as well: even those who are mostly occupied with their own business are extremely well-informed on general politics—this is a peculiarity of ours: we do not say that a man who takes no interest in politics is a man who minds his own business; we say that he has no business here at all. We Athenians, in our own persons, take our decisions on policy or submit them to proper discussions: for we do not think that there is an incompatibility between words and deeds; the worst thing is to rush into action before the consequences have been properly debated. And this is another point where we differ from other people. We are capable at the same time of taking risks and of estimating them beforehand. Others are brave out of ignorance; and, when they stop to think, they begin to fear. But the man who can most truly be accounted brave is he who best knows the meaning of what is sweet in life and of what is terrible, and then goes out undeterred to meet what is to come.

▲ Bust of Pericles; Roman copy of the Greek original

Primary Source Handbook

DOCUMENT-BASED QUESTIONS

1. *Why is it important to Pericles that all citizens participate in public life?*
2. *What seems to be the Athenians' attitude toward politics?*
3. *Why do the Athenians view public discussion as useful before taking action?*
4. *In what ways do Athenians lead a balanced life, according to Pericles?*
5. *What is Pericles's definition of courage?*
6. *According to Pericles, who has political power in Athens?*

from the Apology

by Plato

SETTING THE STAGE Socrates and Plato were two of the most important philosophers in history. Plato studied under Socrates in Athens. Though Socrates was popular with the young, some Athenians viewed him as a threat to Athenian traditions and ideals. In 399 B.C., a group of citizens came together to prosecute him, charging him with neglecting the gods of Athens and corrupting its youth. Socrates was brought to trial. A jury of 500 citizens heard the charges against him; then Socrates presented his own defense. By a majority of votes, Socrates was sentenced to death. Plato attended Socrates' trial and later based the *Apology* on his memory of what he had heard. In the following excerpt, Socrates addresses the jury.

PRIMARY SOURCE

Well, gentlemen, for the sake of a very small gain in time you are going to earn the reputation—and the blame from those who wish to disparage [belittle] our city—of having put Socrates to death, "that wise man"—because they will say I am wise even if I am not, these people who want to find fault with you. If you had waited just a little while, you would have had your way in the course of nature. You can see that I am well on in life and near to death. . . .

No doubt you think, gentlemen, that I have been condemned for lack of the arguments which I could have used if I had thought it right to leave nothing unsaid or undone to secure my acquittal. But that is very far from the truth. It is not a lack of arguments that has caused my condemnation, but a lack of effrontery [rude boldness] and impudence, and the fact that I have refused to address you in the way which would give you most pleasure. You would have liked to hear me weep and wail, doing and saying all sorts of things which I regard as unworthy of myself, but which you are used to hearing from other people. But I did not think then that I ought to stoop to servility [disgracefully humble behavior] because I was in danger, and I do not regret now the way in which I pleaded my case. I would much rather die as the result of this defense than live as the result of the other sort. In a court of law, just as in warfare, neither I nor any other ought to use his wits to escape death by any means. In battle it is often obvious that you could escape being killed by giving up your arms and throwing yourself upon the mercy of your pursuers, and in every kind of danger there are plenty of devices for avoiding death if you are unscrupulous enough to stick at nothing. But I suggest, gentlemen, that the difficulty is not so much to escape death; the real difficulty is to escape from doing wrong, which is far more fleet of foot.

▲ Roman fresco painting of Socrates

DOCUMENT-BASED QUESTIONS

1. *Socrates says that if his accusers would have waited, they could have had what they wanted. What do they want?*
2. *Socrates insists that he would rather die than have to defend himself in a different way. What would be so wrong if Socrates had defended himself in a different way?*
3. *What does Socrates mean when he says that evil is more of a threat to people than death?*
4. *Why doesn't Socrates tell the jury what it wants to hear?*
5. *What values do you think are most important to Socrates?*

from the Annals

by Tacitus

SETTING THE STAGE Tacitus was one of the greatest historians of ancient Rome. He lived in troubled times (A.D. 56–120) when plague and fire frequently ravaged Rome. The *Annals* deals with events from the death of Augustus in A.D. 14 to the death of Nero in A.D. 68. In the following excerpt, Tacitus tells about a terrible fire that swept through Rome in A.D. 64. The fire began near the Circus Maximus, an arena in which chariot races were held, and raged out of control for several days. At the time, Nero was emperor. Many Romans believed that Nero himself had set fire to the city in order to rebuild it according to his own designs.

PRIMARY SOURCE

Now started the most terrible and destructive fire which Rome had ever experienced. It began in the Circus, where it adjoins the . . . hills. Breaking out in shops selling inflammable goods, and fanned by the wind, the conflagration [large fire] instantly grew and swept the whole length of the Circus. There were no walled mansions or temples, or any other obstructions which could arrest it. First, the fire swept violently over the level spaces. Then it climbed the hills—but returned to ravage the lower ground again. It outstripped every countermeasure. The ancient city's narrow winding streets and irregular blocks encouraged its progress.

Terrified, shrieking women, helpless old and young, people intent on their own safety, people unselfishly supporting invalids or waiting for them, fugitives and lingerers alike—all heightened the confusion. When people looked back, menacing flames sprang up before them or outflanked them. When they escaped to a neighboring quarter, the fire followed—even districts believed remote proved to be involved. Finally, with no idea where or what to flee, they crowded on to the country roads, or lay in the fields. Some who had lost everything—even their food for the day—could have escaped, but preferred to die. So did others, who had failed to rescue their loved ones. Nobody dared fight the flames. Attempts to do so were prevented by menacing gangs. Torches, too, were openly thrown in, by men crying that they acted under orders. Perhaps they had received orders. Or they may just have wanted to plunder unhampered.

Nero was at Antium. He only returned to the city when the fire was approaching the mansion he had built to link the Gardens of Maecenas to the Palatine. The flames could not be prevented from overwhelming the whole of the Palatine, including his palace. Nevertheless, for the relief of the homeless, fugitive masses he threw open the Field of Mars, including Agrippa's public buildings, and even his own gardens. Nero also constructed emergency accommodation for the destitute [poor] multitude. Food was brought from Ostia and neighboring towns, and the price of corn was cut. . . . Yet these measures, for all their popular character, earned no gratitude. For a rumor had spread that, while the city was burning, Nero had gone to his private stage and, comparing modern calamities with ancient, had sung of the destruction of Troy. . . .

[P]eople believed that Nero was ambitious to found a new city to be called after himself.

DOCUMENT-BASED QUESTIONS

1. *Who might have ordered the menacing gangs to keep the fire burning?*
2. *What might have been Nero's motive if he indeed caused the fire to be started?*
3. *What actions of Nero suggest that he may not have ordered the burning of Rome?*
4. *What effect might a public calamity such as a fire or an earthquake have on political stability?*
5. *What different interpretations might the people of the time have given to such an event?*
6. *What might you have done to save yourself in the burning of Rome?*

Primary Source Handbook

from the Qur'an

SETTING THE STAGE In about A.D. 610, when the prophet Muhammad was 40 years old, he is said to have received his first visit from the archangel Gabriel. According to tradition, during this visit Gabriel revealed the Word of God to Muhammad. This revelation, or act of revealing, was the first of many experienced by Muhammad throughout his life. Together, these revelations formed the basis of the faith called Islam, which literally means "surrender to the will of Allah" (God). At first Muhammad reported God's revelations orally, and his followers memorized them and recited them in ritual prayers. Later the revelations were written down in a book called the Qur'an, which means "recitation."

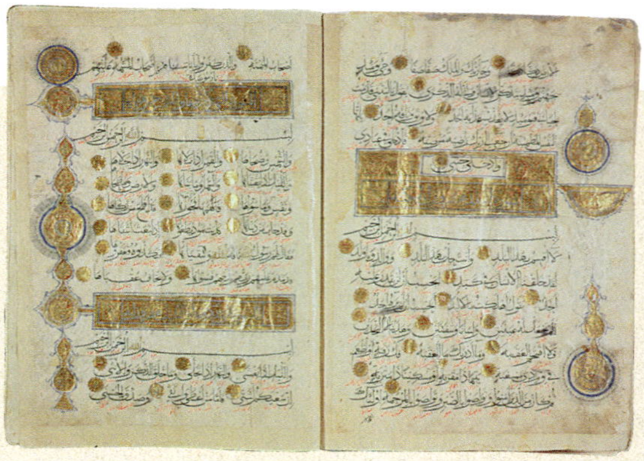

▲ Qur'an with colored inscriptions and decorative medallions from the 12th or 13th century

PRIMARY SOURCE

The Exordium

In the Name of God, the Compassionate, the Merciful
Praise be to God, Lord of the Universe,
The Compassionate, the Merciful,
Sovereign of the Day of Judgment!
You alone we worship, and to You alone we turn for help.
Guide us to the straight path,
The path of those whom You have favored,
Not of those who have incurred Your wrath,
Nor of those who have gone astray.

Faith in God

In the Name of God, the Compassionate, the Merciful
All that is in the heavens and the earth gives glory to God. He is the Mighty, the Wise One.

It is He that has sovereignty over the heavens and the earth. He ordains life and death, and has power over all things.

He is the First and the Last, the Visible and the Unseen. He has knowledge of all things.

It was He who created the heavens and the earth in six days, and then mounted the throne. He knows all that goes into the earth and all that emerges from it, all that comes down from heaven and all that ascends to it. He is with you wherever you are. God is cognizant [aware] of all your actions.

He has sovereignty over the heavens and the earth. To God shall all things return. He causes the night to pass into the day, and causes the day to pass into the night. He has knowledge of the inmost thoughts of men.

Have faith in God and His Apostle and give in alms of that which He has made your inheritance; for whoever of you believes and gives in alms shall be richly rewarded.

And what cause have you not to believe in God, when the Apostle calls on you to have faith in your Lord, who has made a covenant [agreement] with you, if you are true believers?

DOCUMENT-BASED QUESTIONS

1. Exordium *means a beginning or introduction. What qualities of God are emphasized in "The Exordium"?*
2. *What might be the purpose of the first five paragraphs in "Faith in God"?*
3. *What are some of the qualities and actions that make a person righteous?*
4. *How do these excerpts support the idea of "God, the Compassionate, the Merciful"?*
5. *How might the words of the Qur'an be applied to governments or social groups?*
6. *What kind of rules or guidelines for behavior do you think a person should follow in life? How do these compare with those in the Qur'an?*

from The Pillow Book

by Sei Shōnagon

SETTING THE STAGE Sei Shōnagon served as a lady in waiting to Empress Sadako during the last decade of the 900s. During this period, Shōnagon kept a diary recording many aspects of court life. This diary was published as *The Pillow Book,* a collection of character sketches, lists, anecdotes, and poems that provides a vivid glimpse into the lives of the Japanese nobility during the Heian period (794–1185). During this period, the capital was moved to Heian, the present-day city of Kyoto, and a highly refined court society arose among the upper class. The book reveals Shōnagon as an intelligent woman who enjoyed conversing and matching wits with men as equals. Scholar and translator Arthur Waley has called the collection of observations and anecdotes of Heian court life "the most important document of the period that we possess."

PRIMARY SOURCE

from "Hateful Things"

One is in a hurry to leave, but one's visitor keeps chattering away. If it is someone of no importance, one can get rid of him by saying, "You must tell me all about it next time"; but, should it be the sort of visitor whose presence commands one's best behavior, the situation is hateful indeed. . . .

A man who has nothing in particular to recommend him discusses all sorts of subjects at random as though he knew everything. . . .

To envy others and to complain about one's own lot; to speak badly about people; to be inquisitive about the most trivial matters and to resent and abuse people for not telling one, or, if one does manage to worm out some facts, to inform everyone in the most detailed fashion as if one had known all from the beginning—oh, how hateful!

One is just about to be told some interesting piece of news when a baby starts crying.

A flight of crows circle about with loud caws.

An admirer has come on a clandestine [secret] visit, but a dog catches sight of him and starts barking. One feels like killing the beast. . . .

One has gone to bed and is about to doze off when a mosquito appears, announcing himself in a reedy voice. One can actually feel the wind made by his wings and, slight though it is, one finds it hateful in the extreme.

A carriage passes with a nasty, creaking noise. Annoying to think that the passengers may not even be aware of this! If I am traveling in someone's carriage and I hear it creaking, I dislike not only the noise but also the owner of the carriage.

One is in the middle of a story when someone butts in and tries to show that he is the only clever person in the room. Such a person is hateful, and so, indeed, is anyone, child or adult, who tries to push himself forward.

One is telling a story about old times when someone breaks in with a little detail that he happens to know, implying that one's own version is inaccurate—disgusting behavior! . . .

A newcomer pushes ahead of the other members in a group; with a knowing look, this person starts laying down the law and forcing advice upon everyone—most hateful.

DOCUMENT-BASED QUESTIONS

1. *What sort of listing does this excerpt provide?*
2. *How would you describe the author, based on the things she finds hateful?*
3. *Murasaki Shikibu, a contemporary, described Shōnagon as self-satisfied. Do you agree or disagree?*
4. *What might Shōnagon's list of hateful things suggest about Heian court life?*
5. *Which item in Shōnagon's list do you find most hateful?*

from the **Magna Carta**

SETTING THE STAGE King John ruled England from 1199 to 1216. When he raised taxes to finance his wars, his nobles revolted. On June 15, 1215, they forced King John to agree to the Magna Carta (Great Charter). This document, drawn up by English nobles and reluctantly approved by the king, guaranteed certain basic political rights.

PRIMARY SOURCE

1. In the first place [I, John,] have granted to God and by this for our present Charter have confirmed, for us and our heirs . . . , that the English church shall be free, and shall have its rights undiminished and its liberties unimpaired. . . . We have also granted to all the free men of our realm for ourselves and our heirs for ever, all the liberties written below, to have and hold, them and their heirs from us and our heirs. . . .

12. No scutage [tax] or aid is to be levied in our realm except by the common counsel of our realm, unless it is for the ransom of our person, the knighting of our eldest son or the first marriage of our eldest daughter; and for these only a reasonable aid is to be levied. Aids from the city of London are to be treated likewise.

13. And the city of London is to have all its ancient liberties and free customs both by land and water. Furthermore, we will and grant that all other cities, boroughs, towns and ports shall have all their liberties and free customs.

20. A free man shall not be amerced [fined] for a trivial offense; and for a serious offense he shall be amerced according to its gravity, saving his livelihood; and a merchant likewise, saving his merchandise; in the same way a villein [serf] shall be amerced saving his wainage [farming tools]; if they fall into our mercy. And none of the aforesaid amercements shall be imposed except by the testimony of reputable men of the neighborhood.

▲ King John signs the Magna Carta.

21. Earls and barons shall not be amerced [fined] except by their peers and only in accordance with the nature of the offense. . . .

38. Henceforth no bailiff shall put anyone on trial by his own unsupported allegation, without bringing credible witnesses to the charge.

39. No free man shall be taken or imprisoned or disseised [dispossessed] or outlawed or exiled or in any way ruined, nor will we go or send against him, except by the lawful judgment of his peers or by the law of the land.

40. To no one will we sell, to no one will we deny or delay right or justice.

DOCUMENT-BASED QUESTIONS

1. *According to Article 1, to whom does the king grant the rights enumerated in the Magna Carta?*
2. *What are some of the liberties granted by the king to his subjects?*
3. *What do Articles 38 and 39 suggest about the fairness of arrests and trials in King John's England?*
4. *What does Article 40 suggest about the king's use of power?*
5. *What impact might the Magna Carta have had on developing ideas of representative government?*

from the Popol Vuh

SETTING THE STAGE The selection you are about to read is an excerpt from an important Maya work—the *Popol Vuh.* The *Popol Vuh,* or "Book of the Community," contains the Maya story of the creation of the world. It was written not long after the Spanish conquest by an anonymous Maya noble, who may have been trying to keep the work from becoming lost as a result of his people's defeat.

PRIMARY SOURCE

This is the beginning of the Ancient Word, here in this place called Quiché. Here we shall inscribe, we shall implant the Ancient Word, the potential and source for everything done in the citadel of Quiché, in the nation of Quiché people. . . .

This is the account, here it is:

Now it still ripples, now it still murmurs, ripples, it still sighs, still hums, and it is empty under the sky.

Here follow the first words, the first eloquence:

There is not yet one person, one animal, bird, fish, crab, tree, rock, hollow, canyon, meadow, forest. Only the sky alone is there; the face of the earth is not clear. Only the sea alone is pooled under all the sky; there is nothing whatever gathered together. It is at rest; not a single thing stirs. It is held back, kept at rest under the sky.

Whatever there is that might be is simply not there: only the pooled water, only the calm sea, only it alone is pooled.

Whatever might be is simply not there: only murmurs, ripples, in the dark, in the night. Only the Maker, Modeler alone, Sovereign Plumed Serpent, the Bearers, Begetters are in the water, a glittering light. They are there, they are enclosed in quetzal feathers, in blue-green.

Thus the name, "Plumed Serpent." They are great knowers, great thinkers in their very being.

And of course there is the sky, and there is also the Heart of Sky. This is the name of the god, as it is spoken.

And then came his word, he came here to the Sovereign Plumed Serpent, here in the blackness, in the early dawn. He spoke with the Sovereign Plumed Serpent, and they talked, then they thought, then they worried. They agreed with each other, they joined their words, their thoughts. Then it was clear, then they reached accord in the light, and then humanity was clear, when they conceived the growth, the generation of trees, of bushes, and the growth of life, of humankind, in the blackness, in the early dawn, all because of the Heart of Sky, named Hurricane. Thunderbolt Hurricane comes first, the second is Newborn Thunderbolt, and the third is Sudden Thunderbolt. So there were three of them, as Heart of Sky, who came to the Sovereign Plumed Serpent, when the dawn of life was conceived: "How should the sowing be, and the dawning? Who is to be the provider, nurturer?"

"Let it be this way, think about this: this water should be removed, emptied out for the formation of the earth's own plate and platform, then should come the sowing, the dawning of the sky-earth. But there will be no high days and no bright praise for our work, our design, until the rise of the human work, the human design," they said.

DOCUMENT-BASED QUESTIONS

1. *What are some of the names of the gods in this excerpt?*
2. *What are the gods thinking and talking about in this excerpt?*
3. *How do the gods seem to feel about their creation?*
4. *Why do the gods seem to think that humans are necessary to their creation?*
5. *What does this seem to imply about the relationship between gods and humans?*
6. *What surprised you most as you read this excerpt from the* Popol Vuh?

from The Prince
by Niccolò Machiavelli

SETTING THE STAGE Niccolò Machiavelli wrote a political guidebook for Renaissance rulers titled *The Prince* (1513). Machiavelli wrote the book to encourage Lorenzo de' Medici to expand his power in Florence. The book argues for a practical, realistic view of human nature and politics.

PRIMARY SOURCE

A prince should make himself feared in such a way that if he does not gain love, he at any rate avoids hatred; for fear and the absence of hatred may well go together, and will be always attained by one who abstains from interfering with the property of his citizens and subjects or with their women. And when he is obliged to take the life of any one, let him do so when there is a proper justification and manifest reason for it; but above all he must abstain from taking the property of others, for men forget more easily the death of their father than the loss of their patrimony. Then also pretexts for seizing property are never wanting, and one who begins to live by rapine will always find some reason for taking the goods of others, whereas causes for taking life are rarer and more fleeting.

But when the prince is with his army and has a large number of soldiers under his control, then it is extremely necessary that he should not mind being thought cruel; for without this reputation he could not keep an army united or disposed to any duty. Among the noteworthy actions of Hannibal is numbered this, that although he had an enormous army, composed of men of all nations and fighting in foreign countries, there never arose any dissension [disagreement] either among them or against the prince, either in good fortune or in bad. This could not be due to anything but his inhuman cruelty, which together with his infinite other virtues, made him always venerated and terrible in the sight of his soldiers, and without it his other virtues would not have sufficed to produce that effect. Thoughtless writers admire on the one hand his actions, and on the other blame the principal cause of them.

And that it is true that his other virtues would not have sufficed may be seen from the case of Scipio [a famous Roman general and opponent of Hannibal] . . . , whose armies rebelled against him in Spain, which arose from nothing but his excessive kindness, which allowed more license to the soldiers than was consonant with military discipline.

▲ Niccolò Machiavelli

DOCUMENT-BASED QUESTIONS

1. *What does Machiavelli believe is the relationship for a ruler and his people between fear on the one hand and love and hatred on the other?*
2. *Why does Machiavelli say that a ruler must show himself to be capable of cruelty to his army?*
3. *What does Machiavelli cite Hannibal as an example of? Explain.*
4. *How was the Roman general Scipio different from Hannibal?*
5. *Why does Machiavelli consider cruelty a virtue in a leader?*
6. *Are Machiavelli's thoughts on rulers still relevant today? Why or why not?*

from Utopia

by Sir Thomas More

SETTING THE STAGE Sir Thomas More's *Utopia* is a work of fiction devoted to the exploration of ideas. In 1516, when *Utopia* was published, English society was marked by great extremes in wealth, education, and status. In his book, More criticizes the evils of poverty and wealth that he sees in England. More describes a faraway land called Utopia that does not have the inequalities and injustices of England. Utopian society is governed according to principles of reason. As a result, everyone has work and everyone is educated. Since private property has been abolished there, the citizens have no need for money. Instead, all that is produced is shared equally.

PRIMARY SOURCE

Agriculture is the one pursuit which is common to all, both men and women, without exception. They are all instructed in it from childhood, partly by principles taught in school, partly by field trips to the farms closer to the city as if for recreation. Here they do not merely look on, but, as opportunity arises for bodily exercise, they do the actual work.

Besides agriculture (which is, as I said, common to all), each is taught one particular craft as his own. This is generally either wool-working or linen-making or masonry or metal-working or carpentry. There is no other pursuit which occupies any number worth mentioning. As for clothes, these are of one and the same pattern throughout the island and down the centuries, though there is a distinction between the sexes and between the single and the married. The garments are comely [pleasing] to the eye, convenient for bodily movement, and fit for wear in heat and cold. Each family, I say, does its own tailoring.

Of the other crafts, one is learned by each person, and not the men only, but the women too. The latter as the [women] have the lighter occupations and generally work wool and flax. To the men are committed the remaining more laborious crafts. For the most part, each is brought up in his father's craft, for which most have a natural inclination. But if anyone is attracted to another occupation, he is transferred by adoption to a family pursuing that craft for which he has a liking. Care is taken not only by his father but by the authorities, too, that he will be assigned to a [serious] and honorable householder. Moreover, if anyone after being thoroughly taught one craft desires another also, the same permission is given. Having acquired both, he practices his choice unless the city has more need of the one than of the other.

▲ Title page of a French edition of *Utopia*

DOCUMENT-BASED QUESTIONS

1. *How many occupations does each Utopian have? What are they?*
2. *Why might Utopians all wear clothes cut from the same pattern?*
3. *Most Utopian men learn their father's craft, and most workers follow the same schedules. What are the benefits and drawbacks of such a system?*
4. *What might be some of the advantages of living in Utopia?*
5. *What might be some of the disadvantages of living in Utopia?*
6. *What present-day societies do you think are most like Utopia? Explain.*

from The Federalist, "Number 51"

by James Madison

SETTING THE STAGE James Madison wrote 29 of the essays in *The Federalist* papers to argue in favor of ratifying the Constitution of the United States. In *The Federalist,* "Number 51," Madison explains how the government set up by the Constitution will protect the rights of the people by weakening the power of any interest, or group, to dominate the government.

PRIMARY SOURCE

It is of great importance in a republic not only to guard against the oppression of its rulers, but to guard one part of the society against the injustice of the other part. Different interests necessarily exist in different classes of citizens. If a majority be united by a common interest, the rights of the minority will be insecure. There are but two methods of providing against this evil: the one by creating a will in the community independent of the majority—that is, of the society itself; the other, by comprehending in the society so many separate descriptions of citizens as will render an unjust combination of a majority of the whole very improbable, if not impracticable. . . .

Whilst all authority in it will be derived from and dependent on the society, the society itself will be broken into so many parts, interests and classes of citizens, that the rights of individuals, or of the minority, will be in little danger from interested combinations of the majority. In a free government the security for civil rights must be the same as that for religious rights. It consists in the one case in the multiplicity of interests, and in the other in the multiplicity of sects. . . .

In the extended republic of the United States, and among the great variety of interests, parties, and sects which it embraces, a coalition of a majority of the whole society could seldom take place on any other principles than those of justice and the general good. . . .

It is no less certain that it is important . . . that the larger the society, provided it lie within a practicable sphere, the more duly capable it will be of self-government. And happily for the republican cause, the practicable sphere may be carried to a very great extent by a judicious modification and mixture of the *federal principle.*

▲ James Madison

DOCUMENT-BASED QUESTIONS

1. *Madison argues that society must be protected from abuses by rulers and by whom else?*
2. *What two methods does Madison suggest a society can use to protect minority rights?*
3. *Does Madison regard special interests in a society as a good thing or a bad? Explain.*
4. *Why does Madison believe that a large republic is likely to protect justice?*
5. *Why does Madison believe that a society broken into many parts will not endanger minority rights?*
6. *Does Madison think most people work for the common good or their own interests? Explain.*

from A Vindication of the Rights of Woman

by Mary Wollstonecraft

SETTING THE STAGE Although a number of 18th-century British writers discussed the role of women in society, none became as celebrated for her feminist views as Mary Wollstonecraft (1759–1797). Early in her life, Wollstonecraft learned the value of independence and became openly critical of a society that treated females as inferior creatures who were socially, financially, and legally dependent on men. In 1792, Wollstonecraft published *A Vindication of the Rights of Woman,* in which she called for an end to the prevailing injustices against females. Although her opinions on women's rights may seem conservative by modern standards, they were radical in 18th-century Britain.

PRIMARY SOURCE

My own sex, I hope, will excuse me if I treat them like rational creatures, instead of flattering their *fascinating* graces, and viewing them as if they were in a state of perpetual childhood, unable to stand alone. I earnestly wish to point out in what true dignity and human happiness consists—I wish to persuade women to endeavor to acquire strength, both of mind and body, and to convince them that the soft phrases, susceptibility of heart, delicacy of sentiment, and refinement of taste, are almost synonymous with epithets [terms] of weakness, and that those beings who are only the objects of pity and that kind of love, which has been termed its sister, will soon become objects of contempt. . . .

The education of women has, of late, been more attended to than formerly; yet they are still reckoned a frivolous sex, and ridiculed or pitied by the writers who endeavor by satire or instruction to improve them. It is acknowledged that they spend many of the first years of their lives in acquiring a smattering of accomplishments; meanwhile strength of body and mind are sacrificed to libertine [indecent] notions of beauty, to the desire of establishing themselves—the only way women can rise in the world—by marriage. And this desire making mere animals of them, when they marry they act as such children may be expected to act: they dress, they paint, and nickname God's creatures. Surely these weak beings are only fit for a seraglio [harem]! Can they be expected to govern a family with judgment, or take care of the poor babes whom they bring into the world?

▲ Mary Wollstonecraft

DOCUMENT-BASED QUESTIONS

1. *What is the subject and purpose of Wollstonecraft's essay?*
2. *According to Wollstonecraft, why isn't the system of marriage beneficial to women?*
3. *Would you like to hear Wollstonecraft speak on women's rights? Why or why not?*
4. *How does a woman's lack of education affect her husband and children?*
5. *Do you think that Wollstonecraft believes in the complete equality of men and women?*
6. *In your opinion, what social issues would concern Wollstonecraft today? Would she still feel a need to defend women's rights?*

from the Memoirs of Madame Vigée-Lebrun

by Élisabeth Vigée-Lebrun

SETTING THE STAGE Élisabeth Vigée-Lebrun was a gifted artist who painted portraits of the French nobility. In her memoirs she recalls events of her own life amidst the turmoil of the French Revolution, which began in 1789. She frequently painted Marie Antoinette, queen of France. Vigée-Lebrun became frightened by the increasingly aggressive harassment of the nobility by the revolutionaries and resolved to leave France. She and her daughter escaped at night by stagecoach.

PRIMARY SOURCE

I had my carriage loaded, and my passport ready, so that I might leave next day with my daughter and her governess, when a crowd of national guardsmen burst into my room with their muskets. Most of them were drunk and shabby, and had terrible faces. A few of them came up to me and told me in the coarsest language that I must not go, but that I must remain. I answered that since everybody had been called upon to enjoy his liberty, I intended to make use of mine. They would barely listen to me, and kept on repeating, "You will not go, citizeness; you will not go!" Finally they went away. I was plunged into a state of cruel anxiety when I saw two of them return. But they did not frighten me, although they belonged to the gang, so quickly did I recognize that they wished me no harm. "Madame," said one of them, "we are your neighbors, and we have come to advise you to leave, and as soon as possible. You cannot live here; you are changed so much that we feel sorry for you. But do not go in your carriage: go in the stage-coach; it is much safer." . . .

Opposite me in the coach was a very filthy man, who stunk like the plague, and told me quite simply that he had stolen watches and other things. . . . Not satisfied with relating his fine exploits to us, the thief talked incessantly of stringing up such and such people on lamp-posts, naming a number of my own acquaintances. My daughter thought this man very wicked. He frightened her, and this gave me the courage to say, "I beg you, sir, not to talk of killing before this child."

▲ *Self-Portrait in a Straw Hat* by Élisabeth Vigée-Lebrun

DOCUMENT-BASED QUESTIONS

1. *What does Vigée-Lebrun do to escape the Reign of Terror in France?*
2. *What details does Vigée-Lebrun use to create a vivid picture of the national guardsmen? What impression of them does the author convey?*
3. *What concerns does Vigée-Lebrun reveal in her account of her escape from Paris?*
4. *As you read, how did you feel about the situation Vigée-Lebrun finds herself in?*
5. *What seem to be Vigée-Lebrun's feelings about the French Revolution?*
6. *Do you find Vigée-Lebrun a sympathetic person? Why or why not?*

from the Report on Child Labor

by the Sadler Committee

SETTING THE STAGE In 1831 a parliamentary committee headed by Michael Thomas Sadler investigated child labor in British factories. The following testimony by Elizabeth Bentley, who worked as a child in a textile mill, is drawn from the records of the Sadler Committee. Michael Thomas Sadler is asking the questions.

PRIMARY SOURCE

What age are you?—Twenty-three. . . .

What time did you begin to work at a factory?—When I was six years old. . . .

What kind of mill is it?—Flax mill. . . .

What was your business in that mill?—I was a little doffer [cleaner of textile machines].

What were your hours of labor in that mill?—From 5 in the morning till 9 at night, when they were thronged [busy].

For how long a time together have you worked that excessive length of time?—For about half a year.

What were your usual hours of labor when you were not so thronged?—From 6 in the morning till 7 at night.

What time was allowed for your meals?—Forty minutes at noon.

Had you any time to get your breakfast or drinking?—No, we got it as we could.

And when your work was bad, you had hardly any time to eat it at all?—No; we were obliged to leave it or take it home, and when we did not take it, the overlooker [foreman] took it, and gave it to his pigs.

Do you consider doffing a laborious employment?—Yes.

Explain what it is you had to do.—When the frames are full, they have to stop the frames, and take the flyers off, and take the full bobbins off, and carry them to the roller; and then put empty ones on, and set the frames on again.

Does that keep you constantly on your feet?—Yes, there are so many frames and they run so quick.

Your labor is very excessive?—Yes; you have not time for any thing.

Suppose you flagged a little, or were too late, what would they do?—Strap [beat] us.

Are they in the habit of strapping those who are last in doffing?—Yes.

Constantly?—Yes.

Girls as well as boys?—Yes.

Have you ever been strapped?—Yes.

Severely?—Yes.

Could you eat your food well in that factory?—No, indeed, I had not much to eat, and the little I had I could not eat it, my appetite was so poor, and being covered with dust; and it was no use to take it home, I could not eat it, and the overlooker took it, and gave it to the pigs. . .

DOCUMENT-BASED QUESTIONS

1. *From the employers' and parents' point of view, what might have been some of the reasons for child labor?*
2. *What were some of the difficult working conditions faced by children in the factories?*
3. *How many hours per day did Elizabeth Bentley work when the factory was really busy, and when it was not so busy?*
4. *Do children work this hard today in factories in this country? What about in other parts of the world?*

from the Second Inaugural Address

by Abraham Lincoln

SETTING THE STAGE President Lincoln delivered his Second Inaugural Address on March 4, 1865, just before the end of the American Civil War. In this excerpt, he recalls the major cause of the war and vows to fight for the restoration of peace and unity.

PRIMARY SOURCE

One-eighth of the whole population were colored slaves. . . . These slaves constituted a peculiar and powerful interest. All knew that this interest was somehow the cause of the war. To strengthen, perpetuate, and extend this interest was the object for which the insurgents [rebels] would rend the Union even by war, while the Government claimed no right to do more than to restrict the territorial enlargement of it. Neither party expected for the war the magnitude or the duration which it has already attained. Neither anticipated that the cause of the conflict might cease with or even before the conflict itself should cease. Each looked for an easier triumph, and a result less fundamental and astounding. Both read the same Bible and pray to the same God, and each invokes His aid against the other. . . . Fondly do we hope, fervently do we pray, that this mighty scourge of war may speedily pass away. Yet, if God wills that it continue until all the wealth piled by the bondsman's [slave's] two hundred and fifty years of unrequited [unpaid for] toil shall be sunk, and until every drop of blood drawn with the lash shall be paid by another drawn with the sword, as was said three thousand years ago, so still it must be said "the judgments of the Lord are true and righteous altogether."

With malice toward none, with charity for all, with firmness in the right as God gives us to see the right, let us strive on to finish the work we are in, to bind up the nation's wounds, to care for him who shall have borne the battle and for his widow and his orphan, to do all which may achieve and cherish a just and lasting peace among ourselves and with all nations.

▲ Abraham Lincoln

DOCUMENT-BASED QUESTIONS

1. *According to Lincoln's Second Inaugural Address, why did the Confederacy go to war?*
2. *Why might Southerners have feared that prohibiting slavery in new territories would threaten slavery where it already existed?*
3. *Why do you think Lincoln believes it would be wiser for Americans not to blame one another?*
4. *In 1865, if the South had asked to rejoin the Union without ending slavery, do you think Lincoln would have agreed?*
5. *Reread the last sentence of Lincoln's speech. Do you think Americans are still working to reach the goals set by Lincoln?*

from The Natural Rights of Civilized Women

by Elizabeth Cady Stanton

SETTING THE STAGE Elizabeth Cady Stanton (1815–1902) led the fight for women's equality. Her first memory was the birth of a sister when she was four. So many people said, "What a pity it is she's a girl!" that Stanton felt sorry for the new baby. She later wrote, "I did not understand at that time that girls were considered an inferior order of beings." Stanton was determined to prove that girls were just as important as boys. The following excerpt comes from an address that Stanton gave to the New York state legislature in 1860 on a bill for woman suffrage that was before the state senate.

PRIMARY SOURCE

Now do not think, gentlemen, we wish you to do a great many troublesome things for us. We do not ask our legislators to spend a whole session in fixing up a code of laws to satisfy a class of most unreasonable women. We ask no more than the poor devils in the Scripture asked, "Let us alone." In mercy, let us take care of ourselves, our property, our children, and our homes. True, we are not so strong, so wise, so crafty as you are, but if any kind friend leaves us a little money, or we can by great industry earn fifty cents a day, we would rather buy bread and clothes for our children than cigars and champagne for our legal protectors.

There has been a great deal written and said about protection. We as a class are tired of one kind of protection, that which leaves us everything to do, to dare, and to suffer, and strips us of all means for its accomplishment. We would not tax man to take care of us. No, the Great Father has endowed all His creatures with necessary powers for self-support, self-defense, and protection. We do not ask man to represent us, it is hard enough in times like these to represent himself. So long as the mass of men spend most of their time on the fence, not knowing which way to jump, they are surely in no condition to tell us where we had better stand. In pity for man, we would no longer hang like a millstone round his neck. Undo what man did for us in the Dark Ages and strike out all special legislation for us; strike the words "white male" from all your constitutions and then, with fair sailing, let us sink or swim, live or die, survive or perish together.

▲ Elizabeth Cady Stanton

DOCUMENT-BASED QUESTIONS

1. *What basic right is Stanton asking for?*
2. *What sorts of special considerations and laws does Stanton think women are entitled to?*
3. *What group does Stanton think benefits unfairly from current laws and legislation?*
4. *According to Stanton, do women want special protection under the law? Explain.*
5. *What does Stanton mean by the "Dark Ages"?*
6. *What social issues do you think Stanton would address in today's world?*

The Fourteen Points

by Woodrow Wilson

SETTING THE STAGE Nine months after the United States entered World War I, President Wilson delivered to Congress a statement of war aims. This statement became known as the "Fourteen Points." In the speech, Wilson set forth 14 proposals for reducing the risk of war in the future. Numbers have been inserted to help identify the main points, as well as those omitted.

PRIMARY SOURCE

All the peoples of the world are in effect partners . . . , and for our own part we see very clearly that unless justice be done to others it will not be done to us. The program of the world's peace, therefore, is our program; and that program, . . . as we see it, is this:

[1] Open covenants [agreements] of peace, openly arrived at, after which there shall be no private international understandings of any kind but diplomacy shall proceed frankly and in the public view.

[2] Absolute freedom of navigation upon the seas . . . in peace and war. . . .

[3] The removal, so far as possible, of all economic barriers and the establishment of an equality of trade conditions among all the nations. . . .

[4] Adequate guarantees given and taken that national armaments [weapons and war supplies] will be reduced. . . .

[5] A free, open-minded, and absolutely impartial adjustment of all colonial claims, based upon . . . the principle that . . . the interests of the populations concerned must have equal weight with the . . . claims of the government whose title is to be determined.

[6–13: These eight points deal with specific boundary changes.]

[14] A general association of nations must be formed under specific covenants for the purpose of affording mutual guarantees of political independence and territorial integrity to great and small states alike.

▲ British Prime Minister David Lloyd George, French Premier Georges Clemenceau, and President Woodrow Wilson walk in Paris during negotiations for the Treaty of Versailles.

DOCUMENT-BASED QUESTIONS

1. *Why should diplomacy avoid private dealings and proceed in public view?*
2. *How might agreements arrived at in public prevent another world war?*
3. *How might equality of trade be important to keeping the peace?*
4. *What must nations join together to guarantee?*
5. *What might be unusual about a leader such as Wilson calling for an impartial adjustment of colonial claims?*
6. *How successful do you think Wilson's ideas have been in the 20th and 21st centuries?*

from Night

by Elie Wiesel

SETTING THE STAGE Elie Wiesel (EHL•ee vee•ZEHL) was a Jewish boy from Romania. In 1944, when Wiesel was just 15, the Nazis sent the Jews of his town to Auschwitz in Poland. Wiesel's mother and one of his sisters died there. Wiesel and his father were sent to the Buchenwald concentration camp, where Wiesel's father died just a few months before the camp was liberated. In this excerpt from *Night,* Wiesel describes the terror he experienced on his way to Auschwitz.

PRIMARY SOURCE

The train stopped at Kaschau, a little town on the Czechoslovak frontier. We realized then that we were not going to stay in Hungary. Our eyes were opened, but too late.

The door of the car slid open. A German officer, accompanied by a Hungarian lieutenant-interpreter, came up and introduced himself.

"From this moment, you come under the authority of the German army. Those of you who still have gold, silver, or watches in your possession must give them up now. Anyone who is later found to have kept anything will be shot on the spot. Secondly, anyone who feels ill may go to the hospital car. That's all."

The Hungarian lieutenant went among us with a basket and collected the last possessions from those who no longer wished to taste the bitterness of terror. "There are eighty of you in this wagon" added the German officer. "If anyone is missing, you'll all be shot, like dogs. . . ."

They disappeared. The doors were closed. We were caught in a trap, right up to our necks. The doors were nailed up; the way back was finally cut off. The world was a cattle wagon hermetically [completely] sealed.

▲ Elie Wiesel

Primary Source Handbook

DOCUMENT-BASED QUESTIONS

1. *What does the narrator mean when he says, "Our eyes were opened, but too late"?*
2. *What might be the effect on people of uprooting them from their homes?*
3. *What does the narrator mean when he describes "those who no longer wished to taste the bitterness of terror"?*
4. *What might be the effect of sealing people up in railway cars?*
5. *This excerpt is from a book called* Night. *What might be the meaning of the title?*
6. *What elements in this excerpt show the Germans treating the Jews as less than human?*

from Farewell to Manzanar

by Jeanne Wakatsuki Houston and James D. Houston

SETTING THE STAGE When Japan's attack on Pearl Harbor drew the United States into World War II, people on the west coast of the United States began to fear that those of Japanese descent living in their communities might secretly aid Japan. Despite the fact that there was no evidence of Japanese-American espionage or sabotage, President Franklin D. Roosevelt signed an order that cleared the way for the removal of Japanese people from their homes. Jeanne Wakatsuki was seven years old when her family was relocated. As this excerpt from her memoir opens, her family is living in Los Angeles after having been forced to move twice by the government, and is about to be moved a third time to Manzanar.

PRIMARY SOURCE

The American Friends Service helped us find a small house in Boyle Heights, another minority ghetto, in downtown Los Angeles, now inhabited briefly by a few hundred Terminal Island refugees. Executive Order 9066 had been signed by President Roosevelt, giving the War Department authority to define military areas in the western states and to exclude from them anyone who might threaten the war effort. There was a lot of talk about internment, or moving inland, or something like that in store for all Japanese Americans. I remember my brothers sitting around the table talking very intently about what we were going to do, how we would keep the family together. They had seen how quickly Papa was removed, and they knew now that he would not be back for quite a while. Just before leaving Terminal Island, Mama had received her first letter, from Bismarck, North Dakota. He had been imprisoned at Fort Lincoln, in an all-male camp for enemy aliens. . . .

The name Manzanar meant nothing to us when we left Boyle Heights. We didn't know where it was or what it was. We went because the government ordered us to. And in the case of my older brothers and sisters, we went with a certain amount of relief. They had all heard stories of Japanese homes being attacked, of beatings in the streets of California towns. . . .

The simple truth is the camp was no more ready for us when we got there than we were ready for it. We had only the dimmest ideas of what to expect. Most of the families, like us, had moved out from southern California with as much luggage as each person could carry. Some old men left Los Angeles wearing Hawaiian shirts and Panama hats and stepped off the bus at an altitude of 4,000 feet, with nothing available but sagebrush and tarpaper to stop the April winds pouring down off the back side of the Sierras.

▲ Camp boundary sign in California, 1943

DOCUMENT-BASED QUESTIONS

1. *In the foreword to* Farewell to Manzanar, *Jeanne Wakatsuki Houston says, "It has taken me 25 years to reach the point where I could talk openly about Manzanar." Why do you think it took so long for her to be able to talk about her experience?*
2. *Do you think that a forced internment, like that experienced by the Wakatsuki family, could happen in America today? Why or why not?*
3. *What is your impression of the Wakatsuki family?*
4. *How do you think you would have reacted if you had been brought to Manzanar?*

from the Inaugural Address
by Nelson Mandela

SETTING THE STAGE The son of a tribal chief, Nelson Mandela became a leader in the African National Congress (ANC), a political party that called for racial equality. In 1964, Mandela, who had advocated acts of sabotage against the government, was sentenced to life in prison, where he became an international symbol of South Africa's struggle against apartheid. After his release, Mandela agreed to work peacefully for racial justice. In 1993, Mandela was awarded a Nobel Prize, and the next year he became president of South Africa. The selection below comes from a speech he gave in 1994 when he was inaugurated as president of South Africa.

PRIMARY SOURCE

We are both humbled and elevated by the honor and privilege that you, the people of South Africa, have bestowed on us, as the first President of a united, democratic, nonracial, and nonsexist South Africa, to lead our country out of the valley of darkness.

We understand it still that there is no easy road to freedom.

We know it well that none of us acting alone can achieve success.

We must therefore act together as a united people, for national reconciliation, for nation building, for the birth of a new world.

Let there be justice for all.

Let there be peace for all.

Let there be work, bread, water and salt for all.

Let each know that for each the body, the mind, and the soul have been freed to fulfil themselves.

Never, never and never again shall it be that this beautiful land will again experience the oppression of one by another and suffer the indignity of being the skunk of the world.

Let freedom reign.

The sun shall never set on so glorious a human achievement!

God bless Africa!

▲ Nelson Mandela

Primary Source Handbook

DOCUMENT-BASED QUESTIONS

1. *What challenges do you think Mandela expects as the first black president of South Africa?*
2. *Do you think Mandela was speaking only to the audience gathered before him? Explain.*
3. *What does Mandela mean when he says that South Africa must never again be thought of as the "skunk of the world"?*
4. *What are some examples of Mandela's use of repetition in his speech?*

from I Have a Dream

by Martin Luther King, Jr.

SETTING THE STAGE On August 28, 1963, Martin Luther King, Jr., gave his most famous speech at the March on Washington. In it, he shared his dream of equality for all.

PRIMARY SOURCE

I say to you today, my friends, that even though we face the difficulties of today and tomorrow, I still have a dream. It is a dream deeply rooted in the American dream.

I have a dream that one day this nation will rise up and live out the true meaning of its creed—we hold these truths to be self-evident that all men are created equal.

I have a dream that my four little children will one day live in a nation where they will not be judged by the color of their skin but by the content of their character.

I have a dream today!

This is our hope. This is the faith that I will go back to the South with. . . . With this faith we will be able to work together, to pray together, to struggle together, to go to jail together, to stand up for freedom together, knowing that we will be free one day. This will be the day, this will be the day when all of God's children will be able to sing with new meaning "My country 'tis of thee, sweet land of liberty, of thee I sing. Land where my fathers died, land of the Pilgrim's pride, from every mountainside, let freedom ring!" And if America is to be a great nation, this must become true.

And when this happens, when we allow freedom to ring, when we let it ring from every tenement and every hamlet, from every state and every city, we will be able to speed up that day when all of God's children, black men and white men, Jews and Gentiles, Protestants and Catholics, will be able to join hands and sing in the words of the old Negro spiritual, "Free at last, free at last. Thank God Almighty, we are free at last."

▲ Martin Luther King, Jr., Washington, D.C., August 28, 1963

DOCUMENT-BASED QUESTIONS

1. *How do civil rights fit into the American dream?*
2. *Why do you think civil rights workers were willing to go to jail?*
3. *Why does King declare that the United States is not living up to its creed?*
4. *What does King say must happen before America can be considered a truly great nation?*

An Open Letter

by Cesar Chavez

SETTING THE STAGE In 1969, Cesar Chavez wrote a letter in which he denied accusations that he had used violence to win decent wages and better benefits for farm workers.

PRIMARY SOURCE

Today . . . we remember the life and sacrifice of Martin Luther King, Jr., who gave himself totally to the nonviolent struggle for peace and justice. In his letter from Birmingham jail, Dr. King describes better than I could our hopes for the strike and boycott: "Injustice must be exposed, with all the tension its exposure creates, to the light of human conscience and the air of public opinion before it can be cured." For our part, I admit that we have seized upon every tactic and strategy consistent with the morality of our cause to expose that injustice and thus to heighten the sensitivity of the American conscience so that farmworkers will have without bloodshed their own union and the dignity of bargaining with the agribusiness [large-scale farming] employers. . . .

Our strikers here in Delano and those who represent us throughout the world are well trained for this struggle. . . . They have been taught not to lie down and die or to flee in shame, but to resist with every ounce of human endurance and spirit. To resist not with retaliation in kind but to overcome with love and compassion, with ingenuity and creativity, with hard work and longer hours, with stamina and patient tenacity, with truth and public appeal, with friends and allies, with mobility and discipline, with politics and law, and with prayer and fasting. They were not trained in a month or even a year; after all, this new harvest season will mark our fourth full year of strike and even now we continue to plan and prepare for the years to come. . . .

We shall overcome and change if not by retaliation or bloodshed but by a determined nonviolent struggle carried on by those masses of farmworkers who intend to be free and human.

▲ Cesar Chavez, 1974

DOCUMENT-BASED QUESTIONS

1. *Why do you think farm workers wanted to organize a union?*
2. *Why might it be necessary to train for nonviolent protest?*
3. *Why do you think Chavez refers to Martin Luther King, Jr., in his speech?*
4. *In what ways were the problems faced by King and Chavez similar and different?*

NOTE: *Boldfaced words are terms that appear in this handbook.*

BOYCOTT

A refusal to have economic dealings with a person, a business, an organization, or a country.

The purpose of a boycott is to show disapproval of particular actions or to force changes in those actions. A boycott often involves an economic act, such as refusing to buy a company's goods or services.

Civil rights campaigners in the United States used boycotts to great effect during the 1950s and 1960s. For example, African Americans in Montgomery, Alabama, organized a bus boycott in 1955 to fight segregation on city buses. The boycotters kept many buses nearly empty for 381 days. The boycott ended when the Supreme Court outlawed bus segregation.

During the 1960s, groups in many countries launched boycotts against South African businesses to protest the policy of apartheid, or complete separation of the races. In the picture above, demonstrators march to protest a tour of Great Britain by the South African rugby team in 1969. Worldwide boycotts helped to bring about the end of apartheid in the 1990s. For information on the dismantling of the apartheid system, read page 1044.

In many countries, labor unions have used boycotts to win concessions for their members. Consumer groups, too, have organized boycotts to win changes in business practices.

BUSINESS CYCLE

A pattern of increases and decreases in economic activity.

A business cycle generally consists of four distinct phases—expansion, peak, contraction, and trough—as shown in the graph in the next column. An expansion is marked by increased business activity. The **unemployment rate** falls, businesses produce more, and consumers buy more goods and services. A peak is a transition period in which expansion slows. A contraction, or **recession,** occurs when business activity decreases. The unemployment rate rises, while both production and consumer spending fall. A deep and long-lasting contraction is called a **depression.** Business activity reaches its lowest point during a trough. After time, business activity starts to increase and a new cycle begins.

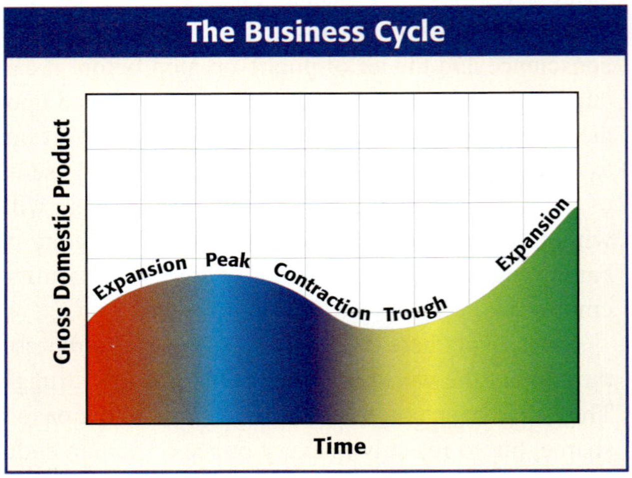

CAPITALISM

An economic system in which there is private ownership of natural resources and capital goods.

The basic idea of capitalism is that producers are driven by the desire to make a profit, the money left over after costs have been subtracted from revenues. This desire for profit motivates producers to provide consumers with the goods and services they desire. Prices and wages are determined by **supply and demand.**

Along with the opportunity to earn a profit there is a risk. Businesses tend to fail if they do not produce goods people want at prices they are willing to pay. Because anyone is free to start a business or enterprise, a capitalist system is also known as a **free enterprise** system.

Capitalism contrasts with **socialism,** an economic system in which the government owns and controls capital and sets prices and production levels. Critics of the capitalist system argue that it allows decisions that ought to be made democratically to be made instead by powerful business owners and that it allows too-great disparities in wealth and well-being between the poor and the rich. For a comparison of capitalism and socialism, read the Analyzing Key Concepts on page 737.

COMMUNISM

An economic system based on one-party rule, government ownership of the means of production, and decision making by centralized authorities.

Under communism there is little or no private ownership of property and little or no political freedom. Government planners make economic decisions, such as which and how many goods and services should be produced. Individuals have little say in a communist economy. Such a system, Communists believe, would end inequality. For more information on the ideas on which communism is based, read Chapter 25, Section 4.

During the 20th century, most communist economies failed to achieve their goals. Economic decisions frequently were made to benefit only Communist Party officials. Also, government economic planning was inefficient, often creating shortages of goods. Those goods that were available were often of poor quality.

People became discontented with the lack of prosperity and political freedom and began to call for change. These demands led in the late 1980s and early 1990s to the collapse of communist governments in the Soviet Union and Eastern Europe.

Even governments that clung to communism—China, for example—have introduced elements of **free enterprise.** The picture above shows people lining up at automated teller machines (ATMs) in Shanghai, one of China's largest free-enterprise zones. (For information on free enterprise in Shanghai, read the Connect to Today on page 806.) While China has allowed greater economic freedom for its citizens, it has not given them more political freedom.

CONSUMER PRICE INDEX (CPI)

A measure of the change in cost of the goods and services most commonly bought by consumers. In some countries, the CPI is called the retail price index.

The CPI is calculated by surveying the prices of a "basket" of goods and services bought by typical consumers. In Germany, the CPI follows the prices of more than 750 goods and services bought by average consumers on a regular basis. Items on which consumers spend a good deal of their income, such as food, are given more weight in the CPI than items on which consumers spend less.

Price changes are calculated by comparing current prices with prices at a set time in the past. In 2003, for example, the German CPI used the year 2000 as this base. Prices for this year are given a base value of 100. The prices for subsequent years are expressed as percentages of the base. Therefore, a CPI of 103 means that prices have risen by 3 percent since 2000. The graph below illustrates changes in the German CPI from 1992 to 2002.

Consumer Price Index in Germany, 1992–2002

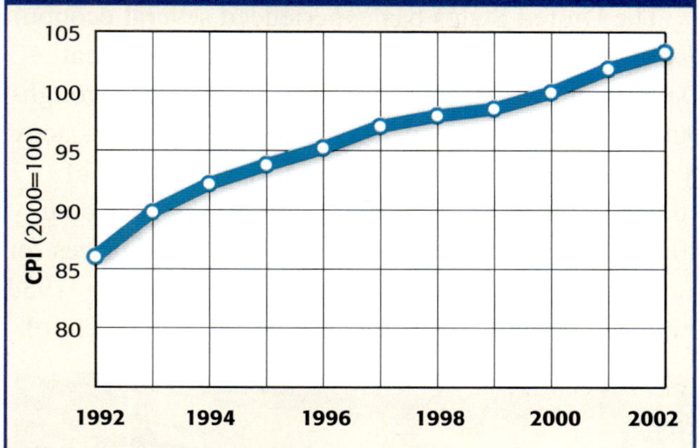

Source: Federal Statistical Office Germany

CORPORATION

A company owned by stockholders who have ownership rights to the company's profits.

Stockholders are issued stock, or shares of ownership in the corporation. A corporation sells stock to raise money to do business. Stockholders buy stock in the hope that the corporation will turn a profit. When a corporation does make a profit, stockholders often receive a dividend, a share of the corporation's income after taxes.

The corporation is a legal entity in itself and, therefore, is separate from its owners. As a result, business losses and debts are the responsibility of the corporation alone. Creditors cannot seek payment from the owners, whose liability is limited to the value of the stock they own.

DEFICIT SPENDING

A situation in which a government spends more money than it receives in revenues.

For the most part, the government engages in deficit spending when the economy is in a contraction phase of the **business cycle.** The government borrows or issues money to finance deficit spending.

In theory, the extra funds should stimulate business activity, pushing the economy into an expansion phase. As the economy recovers, revenues should increase, providing the government with a budget surplus. The government then can use the surplus to pay back the money it borrowed.

DEPRESSION

A very severe and prolonged contraction in economic activity.

During a depression, consumer spending, production levels, wages, prices, and profits fall sharply. Many businesses fail, and many workers lose their jobs.

The United States has experienced several economic depressions in its history. The worst was the Great Depression, which started in 1929 and lasted throughout the 1930s. Between 1929 and 1932, business activity in the United States decreased by an average of 10 percent each year. During the same period, some 40 percent of the country's banks failed, and prices for farm products dropped more than 50 percent. By 1933, the worst year of the Great Depression, 25 percent of American workers were unemployed. Americans in the thousands took to the roads and rail in search of gainful employment. The best job some could find was selling apples on street corners.

The situation in other countries was equally bad. In Great Britain, the unemployment rate averaged 14 percent throughout the Great Depression and hit a peak of 25 percent in early 1931. Unemployment was particularly problematic in such traditional industries as coal mining, shipbuilding, and textiles. The picture at the bottom of the previous column shows unemployed miners' families at a soup kitchen. For information about the global impact of the Great Depression and how the world responded to this economic crisis, read pages 907–909.

DEVELOPED NATION

A nation that has achieved industrialization, a market economy, widespread ownership of private property, and a relatively high standard of living.

Developed nations include the United States, Canada, most European countries, Japan, South Korea, Australia, and New Zealand. Although developed nations account for only one-quarter of the world's population, they produce more than three-quarters of the world's **gross domestic product (GDP).** Economists frequently use per capita GDP (GDP divided by the population) to establish a nation's level of economic development. Most developed nations have per capita GDPs in excess of $20,000.

E-COMMERCE

All forms of buying and selling goods and services electronically.

Short for "electronic commerce," e-commerce refers to business activity on the Internet and on private computer networks. There are two main types of e-commerce: business-to-consumer and business-to-business.

Consumer-related e-commerce includes sales to the public over the computer, usually through a seller's Web site. Many business transactions can be completed wholly electronically, such as sales of computer software, which can be paid for with a credit card number and delivered over the Internet directly to the buyer's computer. A growing proportion of financial transactions are also moving online, such as electronic banking and **stock market** trading, or e-trading. The convenience of online shopping has turned it into a booming enterprise. Between 1998 and 2002, for instance, U.S. consumer spending online grew from about $7.7 billion to more than $45 billion.

Business-to-business e-commerce is growing at an even greater rate, reaching around $700 billion in 2002. Much of that business includes Web-site design and servicing and online advertising. Businesses also use networked computers to purchase supplies and merchandise and to access information from subscription services.

For many businesses, e-commerce is not only convenient but also cost-effective. On average, corporations spend $100 on paperwork alone each time they make a purchase. Moving those transactions online could save companies millions of dollars annually.

EMBARGO

A government ban on trade with another nation, sometimes backed by military force.

In a civil embargo, the nation imposing an embargo prevents exports to or imports from the country against which it has declared the embargo. A hostile embargo involves seizing the goods of another nation.

The major purpose of an embargo is to show disapproval of a nation's actions. For example, in 1980 the United States imposed a civil embargo on grain sales to the Soviet Union to protest the December 1979 Soviet invasion of Afghanistan.

EMERGING NATION

A nation that has lower levels of agricultural and industrial production, lower savings and investment, fewer resources, and lower per capita ***gross domestic product (GDP)*** *than* ***developed nations.***

Emerging nations are sometimes called *developing nations* or *less-developed countries (LDCs).* Most countries in Africa, Asia, and Latin America and the Caribbean are considered emerging nations. Some three-quarters of the world's population lives in emerging nations, yet these nations produce less than one-quarter of the world's GDP. Therefore, emerging nations have low per capita GDPs; many have a per capita GDP of less than $1,000.

FREE ENTERPRISE

An economic system based on the private ownership of the means of production, free markets, and the right of individuals to make most economic decisions.

The free enterprise system is also called the free market system or **capitalism.** The United States has a free enterprise economic system. The diagram below illustrates how a free enterprise economy works.

A Free Market Economy

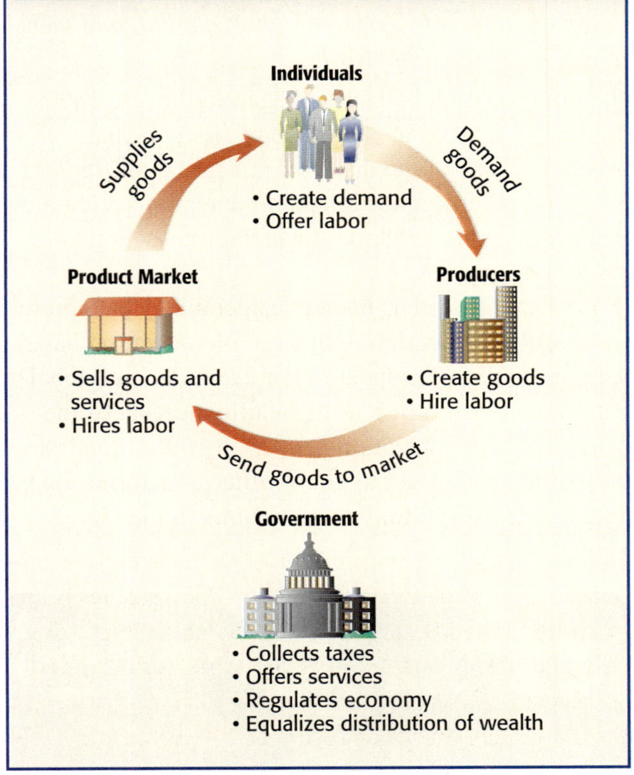

In a free enterprise system, producers and consumers are motivated by self-interest. To maximize their profits, producers try to make goods and services that consumers want. Producers also engage in competition through lowering prices, advertising their products, and improving product quality, to encourage consumers to buy their goods. Consumers serve their self-interest by purchasing the best goods and services for the lowest price.

Government plays a limited, but important, role in most free enterprise economies:

- It regulates economic activity to ensure there is fair competition, such as by preventing and prosecuting fraud and barring **monopolies.**

- It produces certain necessary goods and services that private producers consider unprofitable, such as roadways.
- It protects the public health and safety, such as through building codes, environmental protection laws, and labor laws.
- It provides economic stability, such as by regulating banks, coining money, and supervising unemployment insurance programs.

GLOBALIZATION

The process of rapid economic integration among countries. This integration involves the increased movement of goods, services, labor, capital, and technology throughout the world.

The process of globalization began in the late 1800s. However, its pace has increased in recent years largely because of the drive toward free trade and the introduction of new telecommunications technologies that have made global financial transactions quick and easy.

Recently, there has been considerable debate on the impact of globalization. Critics of globalization have been particularly outspoken. For example, antiglobalization demonstrations at the Seattle meeting of the World Trade Organization (WTO) in 1999 turned violent. Police were used to guard offices, factories, and stores of **multinational corporations** in the city (shown below).

For a review of the arguments for and against globalization, read the Analyzing Key Concepts on page 1078.

GOLD STANDARD

A monetary system in which a country's basic unit of currency is valued at, and can be exchanged for, a fixed amount of gold.

The gold standard tends to curb **inflation,** since a government cannot put more currency into circulation than it can back with its gold supplies. This gives people confidence in the currency.

This advantage is also a weakness of the gold standard. During times of **recession,** a government may want to increase the amount of money in circulation to encourage economic growth. Economic disruption during the Great Depression of the 1930s caused most nations to abandon the gold standard. The United States moved to a modified gold standard in 1934 and abandoned the gold standard completely in 1971.

GROSS DOMESTIC PRODUCT (GDP)

The market value of all the goods and services produced in a nation within a specific time period, such as a quarter (three months) or a year.

Gross domestic product is the standard measure of how a nation's economy is performing. If GDP is growing, the economy is probably in an expansion phase. If GDP is not increasing or is declining, the economy is probably in a contraction phase.

GDP is calculated by adding four components: spending by individual consumers on goods and services; investment in such items as new factories, new factory machinery, and houses; government spending on goods and services; and net exports—the value of exports less the value of imports. (See the diagram below.) GDP figures are presented in two ways. Nominal GDP is reported in current dollars. Real GDP is reported in constant dollars, or dollars adjusted for **inflation.**

INFLATION

A sustained rise in the average level of prices.

Since more money is required to make purchases when prices rise, inflation is sometimes defined as a decrease in the purchasing value of money. Economists measure price changes with various price indexes. The most widely used index in the United States is the **consumer price index (CPI).**

Inflation may result if the demand for goods increases without an increase in the production of goods. Inflation may also take place if the cost of producing goods increases. Producers pass on increased costs, such as higher wages and more expensive raw materials, by charging consumers higher prices.

INTEREST RATE

The cost of borrowing money.

Interest is calculated as a yearly percentage, or rate, of the money borrowed. A 10 percent interest rate, therefore, would require a borrower to pay $10 per year for every $100 borrowed.

When interest rates are low, people will borrow more, because the cost of borrowing is lower. However, they will save and invest less, because the return on their savings or investment is lower. With high interest rates, people save and invest more but borrow less. Because interest rates affect the economy, governments take steps to control them. The United States government does this through the Federal Reserve System, the nation's central banking system. The graph below shows the relationship between the rate of **inflation** and interest rates in the American economy over time.

Inflation and Interest Rates, 1980–2000

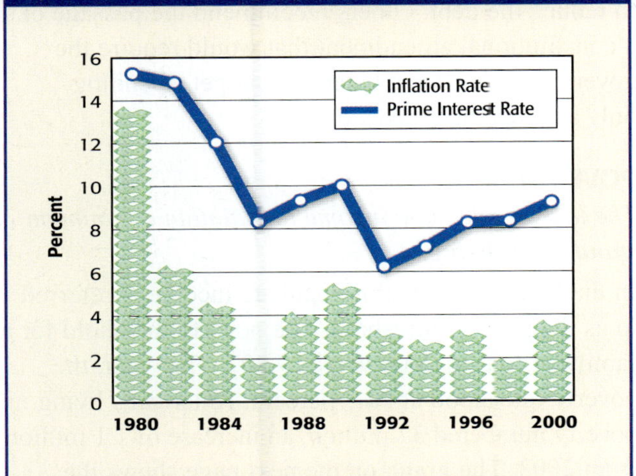

Source: Bureau of Labor Statistics; Federal Reserve System

KEYNESIAN ECONOMICS

The use of government spending to encourage economic activity by increasing the demand for goods.

This economic approach is based on the ideas of British economist John Maynard Keynes (shown below). In a 1936 study, Keynes pointed out that during economic downturns, more people are unemployed and have less income to spend. As a result, businesses cut production and lay off more workers.

Keynes's answer to this problem was for government to increase spending and reduce taxes. This would stimulate demand for goods and services by replacing the decline in consumer demand. Government would want goods and services for its new programs. More people would be working and earning an income and, therefore, would want to buy more goods and services. Businesses would increase production to meet this new demand. As a result, the economy would soon recover.

Critics maintain, however, that Keynesian economics has led to the growth of government and to high taxes, inflation, high unemployment, and greatly reduced economic growth.

MINIMUM WAGE

The minimum amount of money that employers may legally pay their employees for a set period of time worked.

Legislation sets the minimum wage at a fixed hourly, weekly, or monthly rate. In some countries, the minimum wage applies to all workers. In others, it applies only to workers in particular industries. Also, some countries set a different minimum wage for men, women, and young workers. The first country to pass minimum wage laws was New Zealand in 1894. Since that time, most industrialized countries have adopted such legislation. The graph on the next page shows estimates of minimum monthly wage rates in selected countries.

The first federal minimum wage law in the United States, the Fair Labor Standards Act of 1938, set the base wage at 25 cents an hour. Since then, amendments to the act have raised this hourly rate to $5.15, effective in 1997. The Fair Labor Standards Act applies to workers in most businesses involved in interstate commerce.

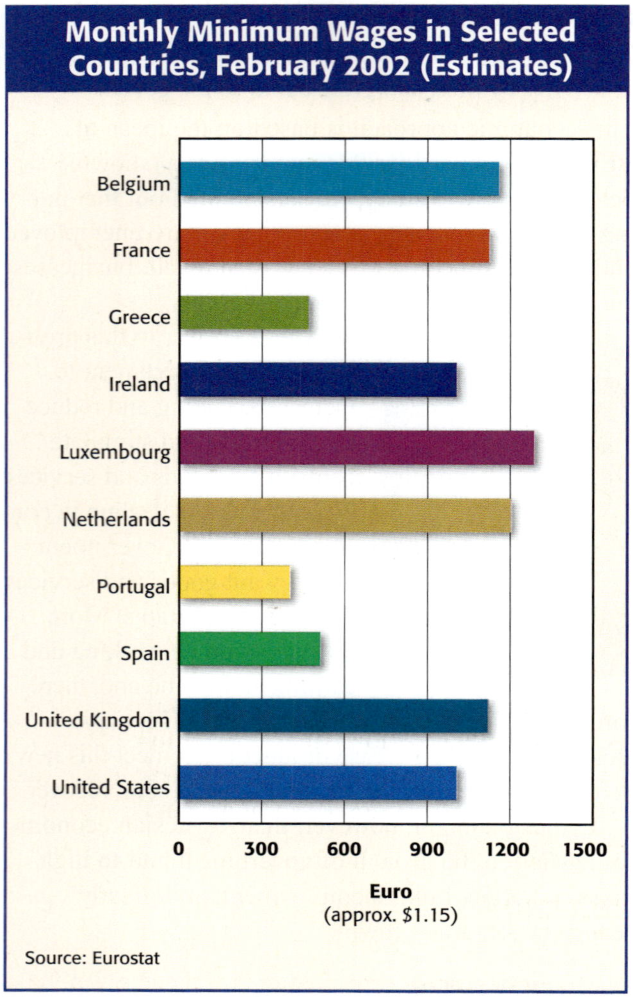

The original intent of minimum wage laws was to ensure that all workers earned enough to survive. However, some economists maintain that these laws may have reduced the chances for unskilled workers to get jobs. They argue that the minimum wage raises the **unemployment rate** because it increases labor costs for business.

MONOPOLY

A situation in which only one seller controls the production, supply, or pricing of a product for which there are no close substitutes.

In the United States, basic public services such as electrical power distributors and cable television suppliers operate as local monopolies. This way of providing utilities is economically more efficient than having several competing companies running electricity or cable lines in the same area.

Monopolies, however, can be harmful to the economy. Since it has no competition, a monopoly does not need to respond to the wants of consumers by improving product quality or by charging fair prices. The government counters the threat of monopoly either by breaking up or regulating the monopoly.

MULTINATIONAL CORPORATION

*A **corporation** that operates in more than one country.*

ExxonMobil (United States), DaimlerChrysler (Germany), Royal Dutch/Shell (Netherlands), BP (Great Britain), and Toyota (Japan) are examples of multinational corporations. A multinational corporation's foreign operations, including factories, offices, and stores, are usually wholly owned subsidiaries run by managers from the home country. Some multinationals, however, enter foreign markets by establishing joint ventures with foreign businesses. Others gain access to foreign markets by buying large amounts of stock in foreign companies.

Such tactics have allowed some multinationals to grow into economic giants with a truly global reach. For more information on the size of some top multinationals, see the graph on page 1076.

NATIONAL DEBT

The money owed by a national government.

During wartime, economic recession, or at other times, the government may employ **deficit spending.** However, the government may not pay back all the money it has borrowed to fund this policy. Each year's government budget deficit adds to the country's national debt. By August 2005, the national debt of the United States stood at $7.93 trillion, or about $26,900 for each citizen.

The rapid growth of the U.S. national debt since 1980 has prompted many Americans to call for changes in government economic policies. Some suggest that the government raise taxes and cut spending to reduce the debt. Others recommend the passage of a constitutional amendment that would require the government to have a balanced budget, spending only as much as it takes in.

POVERTY

*The lack of adequate income to maintain a minimum **standard of living.***

In the United States, this adequate income is referred to as the poverty threshold. The poverty threshold for a family of four in 2004 was $19,307. That year, the poverty rate stood at 12.7 percent. Americans living in poverty numbered 37 million, an increase of 1.1 million from 2003. The graph on the next page shows the changes in the poverty rate in the United States between 1981 and 2001.

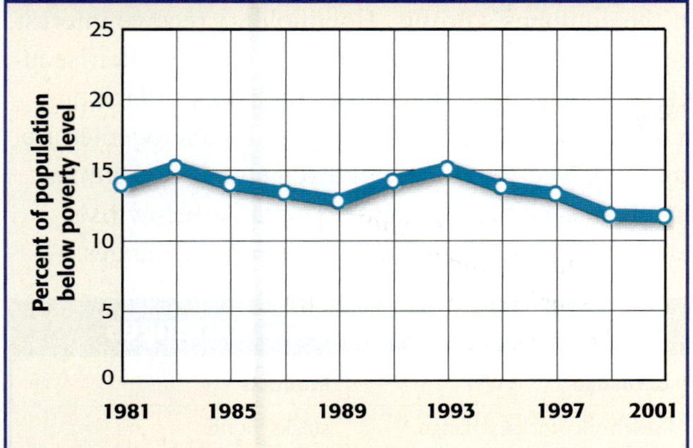

Poverty in the United States, 1981–2001

Source: U.S. Bureau of the Census

Because the factors used to determine poverty vary so much from country to country, world poverty figures are difficult to calculate. As a result, such international organizations as the World Bank and the United Nations view poverty differently. These organizations track extreme poverty, the threshold for which is less than $1 a day. In 2001, more than one billion people worldwide lived below this level. And according to World Bank estimates, another 2.7 billion lived on less than $2 a day.

PRODUCTIVITY

The relationship between the output of goods and services and the input of resources.

Productivity is the amount of goods or services that a person can produce at a given time. It is closely linked to economic growth, which is defined as an increase in a nation's real **gross domestic product (GDP)** from one year to the next. A substantial rise in productivity means the average worker is producing more, a key factor in spurring economic expansion. Between 1995 and the early 2000s, for example, worker productivity in the United States increased about 2.5 percent each year. This increase, along with other economic factors, helped the nation's real GDP grow an average of about 3.5 percent during those years.

A number of elements affect productivity, including available supplies of labor and raw materials, education and training, attitudes toward work, and technological innovations. Computer technology, for instance, is believed to have played a significant role in bolstering productivity during the 1990s by allowing workers to do their jobs more quickly and efficiently. Computer-operated robot arms (above, right) have greatly increased production in the automobile industry.

Conversely, a lack of adequate training and fewer technological innovations were thought to be behind the meager productivity growth rates of the 1970s and 1980s—when productivity rose at an annual rate of less than 1 percent.

RECESSION

A period of declining economic activity.

In economic terms, a recession takes place when the **gross domestic product (GDP)** falls for two quarters, or six months, in a row. The United States has experienced several of these **business-cycle** contractions in its history. On average, they have lasted about a year. If a recession persists and economic activity plunges, it is called a **depression.**

SOCIALISM

An economic system in which the government owns most of the means of production and distribution.

Like **communism,** the goal of socialism is to use the power of government to reduce inequality and meet people's needs. Under socialism, however, the government usually owns only major industries, such as coal, steel, and transportation. Other industries are privately owned but regulated by the government. Government and individuals, therefore, share economic decision-making. Also, under socialism, the government may provide such services as reasonably priced health care. The diagram on the next page shows the level of government involvement in various types of economic systems.

Economic Systems

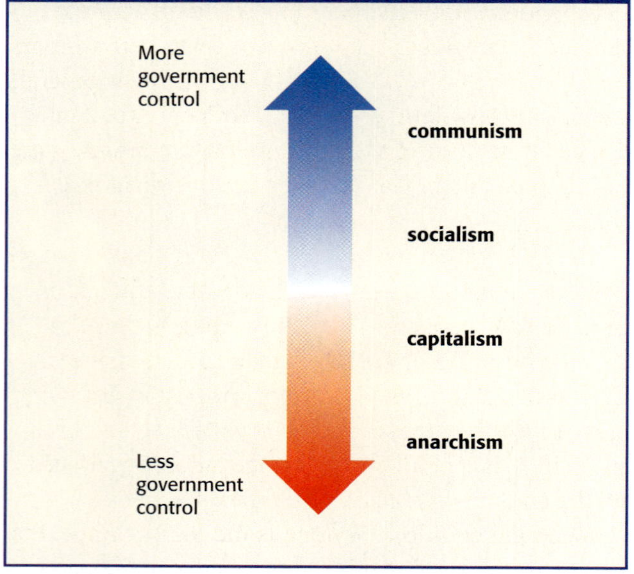

Some countries, such as Sweden, are called democratic socialist countries. In these nations there is less government ownership of property than in communist nations. These nations also have democratically elected governments.

Critics of socialism maintain that this system leads to less efficiency and higher taxes than does the **capitalist,** or **free enterprise,** system. For a comparison of socialism and capitalism, read the Analyzing Key Concepts on page 737.

STANDARD OF LIVING

The overall economic situation in which people live.

Economists differ on how best to measure the standard of living. Some suggest average personal income, while others propose per capita **gross domestic product**—the GDP divided by the population. Another possible measure is the value of the goods and services bought by consumers during a year. In general terms, the nation's standard of living rises as these measures rise. Some people argue that measuring the quality of life also requires consideration of noneconomic factors such as pollution, health, work hours, and even political freedom.

STOCK MARKET *or* STOCK EXCHANGE

A place where stocks and bonds are bought and sold.

Large companies often need extra money to fund expansion and to help cover operating costs. To raise money, they sell stocks, or shares of ownership, in their companies. They also may borrow by issuing bonds, or certificates of debt, promising to repay the money borrowed, plus interest.

Individuals invest in stocks and bonds to make a profit. Most stockholders receive dividends, or a share of the company's profits. Bondholders receive interest. Investors may also make a profit by selling their securities. This sale of stocks and bonds takes place on stock exchanges. Since stocks and bonds together are known as securities, a stock exchange is sometimes called a securities exchange. The table below lists some of the world's most active stock exchanges.

Selected World Stock Exchanges

Exchange	Products
New York Stock Exchange (NYSE)	stocks, bonds
American Stock Exchange (AMEX) (New York)	stocks, bonds, options
National Association of Securities Dealers Automated Quotations (NASDAQ)	over-the-counter stocks
London Stock Exchange	stocks
Tokyo Stock Exchange	stocks, bonds, futures, options
Hong Kong Exchanges	stocks, bonds, futures, options
German Stock Exchange (Frankfurt) (pictured below)	stocks

The largest and most important exchange in the United States is the New York Stock Exchange. Activity on this and other exchanges often signals how well the economy is doing. A bull market, when stock prices rise, usually indicates economic expansion. A bear market, when stock prices fall, usually indicates economic contraction.

A rapid fall in stock prices is called a crash. The worst stock market crash in the United States came in October 1929. To help protect against another drastic stock market crash, the federal government set up the Securities and Exchange Commission (SEC), which regulates the trading of securities. For more information on stocks and the stock market, read the History in Depth on page 906.

STRIKE

A work stoppage by employees to gain higher wages, better working conditions, or other benefits.

Strikes are also sometimes used as political protests. A strike is usually preceded by a failure in collective bargaining—the negotiation of contracts between labor unions and employers. Union members may decide to call a strike if they believe negotiations with the employer are deadlocked. In the United States, collective bargaining and strikes are regulated by the NLRA, or Wagner Act, of 1935, which is administered by the National Labor Relations Board (NLRB). There are also wildcat strikes, which are not authorized by unions.

Strikes often have a huge impact on everyday life, as the picture below illustrates. Commuters jam the platform of a subway station in Paris, France, during a one-day strike by transport workers in 2003. The strike, over pay and working conditions, shut down about half of the Paris subway network and severely disrupted traffic on the rest.

When strikes do occur, union representatives and employers try to negotiate a settlement. An outside party is sometimes asked to help work out an agreement.

SUPPLY AND DEMAND

The forces that determine prices of goods and services in a market economy.

Supply is the amount of a good or service that producers are willing and able to produce at a given price. Demand is the amount of a good or service consumers are willing and able to buy at a given price. In general, producers are willing to produce more of a good or service when prices are high; conversely, consumers are willing to buy more of a good or service when prices are low.

The table and graph below show supply and demand for a certain product. The line *S* shows the amount of the good that producers would be willing to make at various prices. The line *D* shows the amount that consumers would be willing to buy at various prices. Point *E*, where the two lines intersect, is called the equilibrium price. It is the price at which the amount produced and the amount demanded would be the same.

When the equilibrium price is the market price, the market operates efficiently. At prices above the equilibrium price, consumers will demand less than producers supply. Producers, therefore, will have to lower their prices to sell the surplus, or excess, products. At prices below equilibrium, consumers will demand more. Producers will be able to raise their prices because the product is scarce, or in short supply.

Supply and Demand

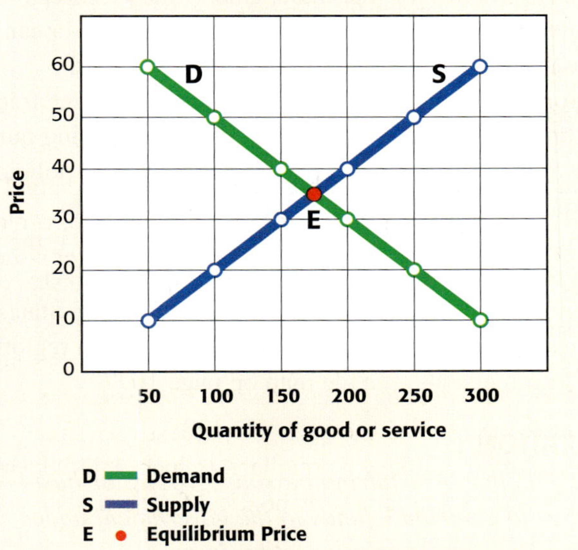

Supply and Demand Schedules

Supply	Price	Demand
50	10	300
100	20	250
150	30	200
200	40	150
250	50	100
300	60	50

SUPPLY-SIDE ECONOMICS

Government policies designed to stimulate the production of goods and services, or the supply side of the economy.

Supply-side economists developed these policies in opposition to **Keynesian economics.** Supply-side policies call for low tax rates particularly in income from investments. Lower taxes mean that people keep more of what they earn. Therefore, supply-side economists argue, people will work harder in order to earn more. They will then use their extra income to save and invest. This investment will fund the development of new businesses and, as a result, create more jobs.

TARIFF

A fee charged for goods brought into a state or country from another state or country.

Governments have collected tariffs since ancient times. Initially, tariffs were used to raise revenue. As time went on, however, governments used them as a way to control imports. In the United States, for example, Congress created tariffs in 1789 to raise revenue and to protect American products from foreign competition. Soon, however, special interest groups used tariffs to protect specific industries and increase profits.

After World War II, many governments moved away from tariffs toward free trade. One of the first steps came in the 1950s, with the creation of the European Economic Community (EEC), now known as the European Union. The EEC encouraged tariff-free trade among its members. In recent decades, a growing number of U.S. economists have favored free trade policies because they believe that such policies will help increase U.S. exports to other countries. In 1994, the North American Free Trade Agreement (NAFTA) established a free-trade zone among the United States, Canada, and Mexico. For more information on regional trade agreements, see the map on page 1077.

TAXATION

The practice of requiring persons, groups, or businesses to contribute funds to the government under which they reside or transact business.

In the United States, all levels of government—federal, state, and local—collect many kinds of taxes. Income taxes are the chief source of revenue for the federal government and an important revenue source for many states. Both corporations and individuals pay income tax, or taxes on earnings. Since its inception in 1913, the federal income tax has been a progressive tax, one that is graduated, or scaled, such that those with greater incomes are taxed at a greater rate. Sales taxes are another important source of income for state governments.

Property taxes are the main source of funds for local governments. Property tax is calculated as a percentage of the assessed value of real estate—land and improvements such as buildings.

TRADE

The exchange of goods and services between countries.

Almost all nations produce goods that other countries need, and they sell (export) those goods to buyers in other countries. At the same time, they buy (import) goods from other countries as well. For example, Americans sell goods such as wheat to people in Japan and buy Japanese goods such as automobiles in return.

The relationship between the value of a country's imports and the value of its exports is called the *balance of trade.* If a country exports more than it imports, it has a trade surplus. However, if the value of a country's imports exceeds the value of its exports, the country has a trade deficit. As the graph below shows, Japan maintained a trade surplus throughout the 1990s.

Japanese Foreign Trade, 1990–2000

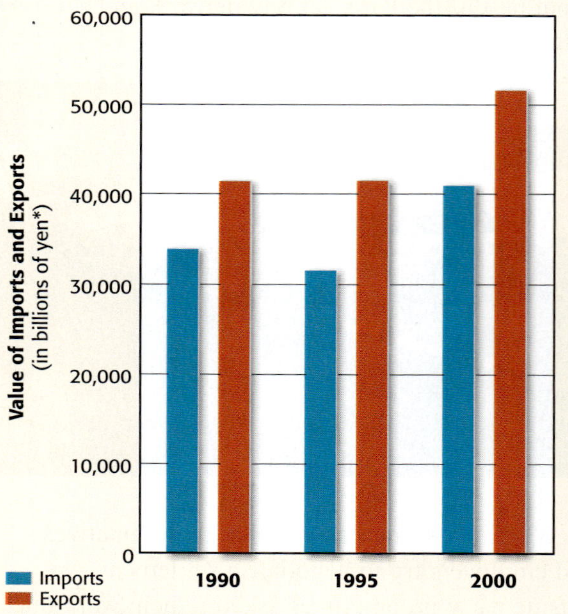

*$1 = approximately 120 yen

Source: Ministry of Finance, Government of Japan

Nations that trade with one another often become dependent on one another's products. Sometimes this brings nations closer together, as it did the United States, Great Britain, and France before World War I. At other times it causes tension among nations, such as that between the United States and Arab oil-producing countries in the 1970s. For an example of how trade influences foreign policy, see page 1079.

UNEMPLOYMENT RATE

The percentage of the labor force that is unemployed but actively looking for work.

The labor force consists of all civilians of working age, normally 15 to 16 years of age and older, who are employed or who are unemployed but actively looking and available for work. In the United States, the size of the labor force and the unemployment rate are determined by surveys conducted by the U.S. Bureau of the Census.

The unemployment rate provides an indicator of economic health. Rising unemployment rates signal a contraction in the economy, while falling rates indicate an economic expansion. The graphs below show two different methods of portraying unemployment in Canada.

Unemployment in Canada, 1992–2002

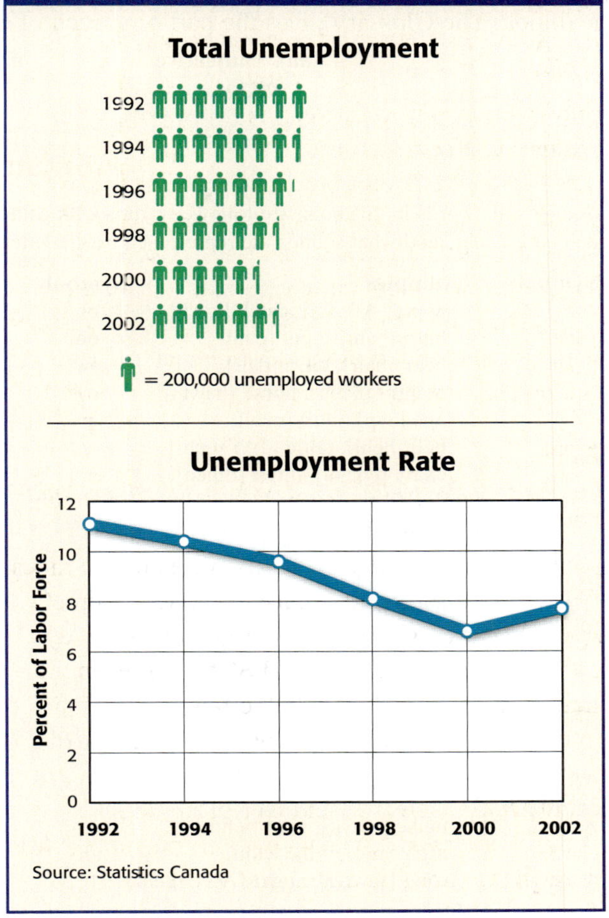

Glossary

The Glossary is an alphabetical listing of many of the key terms from the chapters, along with their meanings. The definitions listed in the Glossary are the ones that apply to the way the words are used in this textbook. The Glossary gives the part of speech of each word. The following abbreviations are used:

adj. **adjective** ***n.*** **noun** ***v.*** **verb**

Pronunciation Key

Some of the words in this book are followed by respellings that show how the words are pronounced. The following key will help you understand what sounds are represented by the letters used in the respellings.

Symbol	Examples	Symbol	Examples
a	**a**pple [AP•uhl], c**a**tch [kach]	oh	r**oa**d, [rohd], kn**ow** [noh]
ah	b**a**rn [bahrn], p**o**t [paht]	oo	sch**oo**l [skool], gl**ue** [gloo]
air	b**ear** [bair], d**are** [dair]	ow	**ou**t [owt], c**ow** [kow]
aw	b**ough**t [bawt], h**or**se [hawrs]	oy	c**oi**n [koyn], b**oy**s [boyz]
ay	**a**pe [ayp], m**ai**l [mayl]	p	**p**ig [pihg], to**p** [tahp]
b	**b**ell [behl], ta**b**le [TAY•buhl]	r	**r**ose [rohz], sta**r** [stahr]
ch	**ch**ain [chayn], di**tch** [dihch]	s	**s**oap [sohp], i**c**y [EYE•see]
d	**d**og [dawg], raine**d** [raynd]	sh	**sh**are [shair], na**ti**on [NAY•shuhn]
ee	**e**ven [EE•vuhn], m**ea**l [meel]	t	**t**ired [tyrd], boa**t** [boht]
eh	**e**gg [ehg], t**e**n [tehn]	th	**th**in [thihn], mo**th**er [MUH•thuhr]
eye	**i**ron [EYE•uhrn]	u	p**u**ll [pul], l**oo**k [luk]
f	**f**all [fawl], lau**gh** [laf]	uh	b**u**mp [buhmp], **a**wake [uh•WAYK],
g	**g**old [gohld], bi**g** [bihg]		happ**e**n [HAP•uhn], penc**i**l [PEHN•suhl],
h	**h**ot [haht], ex**h**ale [ehks•HAYL]		pil**o**t [PY•luht]
hw	**wh**ite [hwyt]	ur	**ear**th [urth], b**ir**d [burd], w**or**m [wurm]
ih	**i**nto [IHN•too], s**i**ck [sihk]	v	**v**ase [vays], lo**v**e [luhv]
j	**j**ar [jahr], ba**dge** [baj]	w	**w**eb [wehb], t**w**in [twihn]
k	**c**at [kat], lu**ck** [luhk]	y	As a consonant: **y**ard [yahrd], m**u**le [myool]
l	**l**oad [lohd], ba**ll** [bawl]		As a vowel: **i**ce [ys], tr**ie**d [tryd], s**igh** [sy]
m	**m**ake [mayk], ge**m** [jehm]	z	**z**one [zohn], rea**s**on [REE•zuhn]
n	**n**ight [nyt], wi**n** [wihn]	zh	trea**s**ure [TREHZH•uhr], gara**ge** [guh•RAHZH]
ng	so**ng** [sawng], a**n**ger [ANG•guhr]		

Syllables that are stressed when the words are spoken appear in CAPITAL LETTERS in the respellings. For example, the respelling of *patterns* (PAT•uhrnz) shows that the first syllable of the word is stressed.

Syllables that appear in SMALL CAPITAL LETTERS are also stressed, but not as strongly as those that appear in capital letters. For example, the respelling of *interaction* (IHN•tuhr•AK•shuhn) shows that the third syllable receives the main stress and the first syllable receives a secondary stress.

A

Abbasids [uh•BAS•IHDZ] *n.* a dynasty that ruled much of the Muslim Empire from A.D. 750 to 1258. (p. 271)

Aborigine [AB•uh•RIHJ•uh•nee] *n.* a member of any of the native peoples of Australia. (p. 752)

absolute monarch [MAHN•uhrk] *n.* a king or queen who has unlimited power and seeks to control all aspects of society. (p. 594)

acropolis [uh•KRAHP•uh•lihs] *n.* a fortified hilltop in an ancient Greek city. (p. 127)

Aksum [AHK•SOOM] *n.* an African kingdom, in what is now Ethiopia and Eritrea, that reached the height of its power in the fourth century A.D. (p. 225)

al-Andalus [al•AN•duh•LUS] *n.* a Muslim-ruled region in what is now Spain, established in the eighth century A.D. (p. 271)

Allah [AL•uh] *n.* God (an Arabic word, used mainly in Islam). (p. 264)

Allies [uh•LYZ] *n.* in World War I, the nations of Great Britain, France, and Russia, along with the other nations that fought on their side; also, the group of nations—including Great Britain, the Soviet Union, and the United States—that opposed the Axis Powers in World War II. (p. 845)

Almohads [AL•moh•HADZ] *n.* a group of Islamic reformers who overthrew the Almoravid dynasty and established an empire in North Africa and southern Spain in the 12th century A.D. (p. 412)

Almoravids [AL•muh•RAHV•uhdz] *n.* an Islamic religious brotherhood that established an empire in North Africa and southern Spain in the 11th century A.D. (p. 412)

Amritsar Massacre *n.* killing by British troops of nearly 400 Indians gathered at Amritsar to protest the Rowlatt Acts. (p. 888)

Anabaptist [AN•uh•BAP•tihst] *n.* in the Reformation, a member of a Protestant group that believed in baptizing only those persons who were old enough to decide to be Christian and believed in the separation of church and state. (p. 496)

Anasazi [AH•nuh•SAH•zee] *n.* an early Native American people who lived in the American Southwest. (p. 443)

Anatolia [AN•uh•TOH•lee•uh] *n.* the Southwest Asian peninsula now occupied by the Asian part of Turkey—also called Asia Minor. (p. 62)

Angkor Wat [ANG•kawr WAHT] *n.* a temple complex built in the Khmer Empire and dedicated to the Hindu god Vishnu. (p. 345)

Anglican [ANG•glih•kuhn] *adj.* relating to the Church of England. (p. 494)

animism [AN•uh•MIHZ•uhm] *n.* the belief that spirits are present in animals, plants, and other natural objects. (p. 216)

annexation [AN•ihk•SAY•shuhn] *n.* the adding of a region to the territory of an existing political unit. (pp. 799, 813)

annul [uh•NUHL] *v.* to cancel or set aside. (p. 492)

anti-Semitism [AN•tee•SEHM•ih•TIHZ•uhm] *n.* prejudice against Jews. (p. 749)

apartheid [uh•PAHRT•HYT] *n.* a South African policy of complete legal separation of the races, including the banning of all social contacts between blacks and whites. (p. 1043)

apostle [uh•PAHS•uhl] *n.* one of the followers of Jesus who preached and spread his teachings. (p. 168)

appeasement *n.* the making of concessions to an aggressor in order to avoid war. (p. 917)

aqueduct [AK•wih•DUHKT] *n.* a pipeline or channel built to carry water to populated areas. (p. 181)

aristocracy [AR•ih•STAHK•ruh•see] *n.* a government in which power is in the hands of a hereditary ruling class or nobility. (p. 127)

armistice [AHR•mih•stihs] *n.* an agreement to stop fighting. (p. 855)

artifact *n.* a human-made object, such as a tool, weapon, or piece of jewelry. (p. 5)

artisan [AHR•tih•zuhn] *n.* a skilled worker, such as a weaver or a potter, who makes goods by hand. (p. 20)

Aryans [AIR•ee•uhnz] *n.* **1.** an Indo-European people who, about 1500 B.C., began to migrate into the Indian subcontinent (p. 63). **2.** to the Nazis, the Germanic peoples who formed a "master race." (p. 936)

assembly line *n.* in a factory, an arrangement in which a product is moved from worker to worker, with each person performing a single task in its manufacture. (p. 764)

assimilation [uh•SIHM•uh•LAY•shuhn] *n.* **1.** the adoption of a conqueror's culture by a conquered people (p. 205). **2.** a policy in which a nation forces or encourages a subject people to adopt its institutions and customs. (p. 781)

Assyria [uh•SEER•ee•uh] *n.* a Southwest Asian kingdom that controlled a large empire from about 850 to 612 B.C. (p. 95)

Atlantic Charter *n.* a declaration of principles issued in August 1941 by British prime minister Winston Churchill and U.S. president Franklin Roosevelt, on which the Allied peace plan at the end of World War II was based. (p. 930)

Atlantic slave trade *n.* the buying, transporting, and selling of Africans for work in the Americas. (p. 567)

autocracy [aw•TAHK•ruh•see] *n.* a government in which the ruler has unlimited power and uses it in an arbitrary manner. (p. 109)

Axis Powers *n.* in World War II, the nations of Germany, Italy, and Japan, which had formed an alliance in 1936. (p. 917)

ayllu [EYE•loo] *n.* in Incan society, a small community or family group whose members worked together for the common good. (p. 460)

B

balance of power *n.* a political situation in which no one nation is powerful enough to pose a threat to others. (p. 672)

the Balkans [BAWL•kuhnz] *n.* the region of southeastern Europe now occupied by Greece, Albania, Bulgaria, Romania, the European part of Turkey, and the former republics of Yugoslavia. (p. 689)

Bantu-speaking peoples *n.* the speakers of a related group of languages who, beginning about 2,000 years ago, migrated from West Africa into most of the southern half of Africa. (p. 222)

baroque [buh•ROHK] *adj.* relating to a grand, ornate style that characterized European painting, music, and architecture in the 1600s and early 1700s. (p. 637)

barter *n.* a form of trade in which people exchange goods and services without the use of money. (p. 23)

Battle of Britain *n.* a series of battles between German and British air forces, fought over Britain in 1940–1941. (p. 928)

Battle of Guadalcanal [GWAHD•uhl•kuh•NAL] *n.* a 1942–1943 battle of World War II, in which Allied troops drove Japanese forces from the Pacific island of Guadalcanal. (p. 935)

Battle of Midway *n.* a 1942 sea and air battle of World War II, in which American forces defeated Japanese forces in the central Pacific. (p. 934)

Battle of Stalingrad [STAH•lihn•GRAD] *n.* a 1942–1943 battle of World War II, in which German forces were defeated in their attempt to capture the city of Stalingrad in the Soviet Union. (p. 941)

Battle of the Bulge *n.* a 1944–1945 battle in which Allied forces turned back the last major German offensive of World War II. (p. 944)

Battle of Trafalgar [truh•FAL•guhr] *n.* an 1805 naval battle in which Napoleon's forces were defeated by a British fleet under the command of Horatio Nelson. (p. 667)

Benin [buh•NIHN] *n.* a kingdom that arose near the Niger River delta in the 1300s and became a major West African state in the 1400s. (p. 419)

Beringia [buh•RIHN•jee•uh] *n.* an ancient land bridge over which the earliest Americans are believed to have migrated from Asia into the Americas. (p. 235)

Berlin Conference *n.* a meeting in 1884–1885 at which representatives of European nations agreed upon rules for the European colonization of Africa. (p. 776)

Bill of Rights *n.* the first ten amendments to the U.S. Constitution, which protect citizens' basic rights and freedoms. (p. 645)

Glossary

bishop *n.* a high-ranking Christian official who supervises a number of local churches. (p. 171)

blitzkrieg [BLIHTS•KREEG] *n.* "lightning war"—a form of warfare in which surprise attacks with fast-moving airplanes are followed by massive attacks with infantry forces. (p. 925)

blockade [blah•KAYD] *n.* the use of troops or ships to prevent commercial traffic from entering or leaving a city or region. (p. 668)

Boer [bohr] *n.* a Dutch colonist in South Africa. (p. 776)

Boer War *n.* a conflict, lasting from 1899 to 1902, in which the Boers and the British fought for control of territory in South Africa. (p. 778)

Bolsheviks [BOHL•shuh•VIHKS] *n.* a group of revolutionary Russian Marxists who took control of Russia's government in November 1917. (p. 868)

Boxer Rebellion *n.* a 1900 revolt in China, aimed at ending foreign influence in the country. (p. 808)

boyar [boh•YAHR] *n.* a landowning noble of Russia. (p. 608)

Brahma [BRAH•muh] *n.* a Hindu god considered the creator of the world. (p. 194)

Brahmin [BRAH•mihn] *n.* in Aryan society, a member of the social class made up of priests. (p. 63)

brinkmanship *n.* a policy of threatening to go to war in response to any enemy aggression. (p. 970)

Bronze Age *n.* a period in human history, beginning around 3000 B.C. in some areas, during which people began using bronze, rather than copper or stone, to fashion tools and weapons. (p. 21)

bubonic plague [boo•BAHN•ihk PLAYG] *n.* a deadly disease that spread across Asia and Europe in the mid-14th century, killing millions of people. (p. 399)

bureaucracy [byu•RAHK•ruh•see] *n.* a system of departments and agencies formed to carry out the work of government. (p. 105)

burgher [BUR•guhr] *n.* a medieval merchant-class town dweller. (p. 391)

Bushido [BUSH•ih•DOH] *n.* the strict code of behavior followed by samurai warriors in Japan. (p. 343)

C

cabinet *n.* a group of advisers or ministers chosen by the head of a country to help make government decisions. (p. 617)

caliph [KAY•lihf] *n.* a supreme political and religious leader in a Muslim government. (p. 269)

calligraphy [kuh•LIHG•ruh•fee] *n.* the art of beautiful handwriting. (p. 276)

Calvinism [KAL•vih•NIHZ•uhm] *n.* a body of religious teachings based on the ideas of the reformer John Calvin. (p. 495)

Camp David Accords *n.* the first signed agreement between Israel and an Arab country, in which Egyptian president Anwar Sadat recognized Israel as a legitimate state and Israeli prime minister Menachem Begin agreed to return the Sinai Peninsula to Egypt. (p. 1020)

canon law *n.* the body of laws governing the religious practices of a Christian church. (p. 371)

capitalism *n.* an economic system based on private ownership and on the investment of money in business ventures in order to make a profit. (pp. 573, 734)

Carolingian [KAR•uh•LIHN•juhn] **Dynasty** *n.* a dynasty of Frankish rulers, lasting from A.D. 751 to 987. (p. 356)

caste [kast] *n.* one of the four classes of people in the social system of the Aryans who settled in India—priests, warriors, peasants or traders, and non-Aryan laborers or craftsmen. (p. 64)

Catholic Reformation [REHF•uhr•MAY•shuhn] *n.* a 16th-century movement in which the Roman Catholic Church sought to make changes in response to the Protestant Reformation. (p. 498)

caudillo [kaw•DEEL•yoh] *n.* a military dictator of a Latin American country. (p. 816)

centralized government *n.* a government in which power is concentrated in a central authority to which local governments are subject. (p. 200)

Central Powers *n.* in World War I, the nations of Germany and Austria-Hungary, along with the other nations that fought on their side. (p. 845)

Chaldeans [kal•DEE•uhnz] *n.* a Southwest Asian people who helped to destroy the Assyrian Empire. (p. 97)

Chartist movement *n.* in 19th-century Britain, members of the working class demanded reforms in Parliament and in elections, including suffrage for all men. (p. 748)

Chavín [chah•VEEN] *n.* the first major South American civilization, which flourished in the highlands of what is now Peru from about 900 to 200 B.C. (p. 246)

checks and balances *n.* measures designed to prevent any one branch of government from dominating the others. (p. 645)

chivalry [SHIHV•uhl•ree] *n.* a code of behavior for knights in medieval Europe, stressing ideals such as courage, loyalty, and devotion. (p. 365)

CIS *n.* the Commonwealth of Independent States—a loose association of former Soviet republics that was formed after the breakup of the Soviet Union. (p. 1049)

city-state *n.* a city and its surrounding lands functioning as an independent political unit. (p. 31)

civil disobedience *n.* a deliberate and public refusal to obey a law considered unjust. (p. 888)

civilization *n.* a form of culture characterized by cities, specialized workers, complex institutions, record keeping, and advanced technology. (p. 20)

civil service *n.* the administrative departments of a government—especially those in which employees are hired on the basis of their scores on examinations. (p. 203)

civil war *n.* a conflict between two political groups within the same country. (p. 161)

clan *n.* a group of people descended from a common ancestor. (p. 331)

classical art *n.* the art of ancient Greece and Rome, in which harmony, order, and proportion were emphasized. (p. 136)

clergy [KLUR•jee] *n.* a body of officials who perform religious services—such as priests, ministers, or rabbis. (p. 370)

cloning [KLOH•nihng] *n.* the creation of plants or animals that are genetically identical to an existing plant or animal. (p. 1073)

coalition [KOH•uh•LIHSH•uhn] **government** *n.* a government controlled by a temporary alliance of several political parties. (p. 904)

codex [KOH•DEHKS] *n.* a book with pages that can be turned, like the one you are reading now. (p. 448)

Cold War *n.* the state of diplomatic hostility between the United States and the Soviet Union in the decades following World War II. (p. 969)

collective bargaining *n.* negotiations between workers and their employers. (p. 738)

collective farm *n.* a large government-controlled farm formed by combining many small farms. (p. 878)

colony *n.* a land controlled by another nation. (p. 554)

Colossus of Rhodes [kuh•LAHS•uhs uhv ROHDZ] *n.* an enormous Hellenistic statue that formerly stood near the harbor of Rhodes. (p. 149)

Columbian Exchange *n.* the global transfer of plants, animals, and diseases that occurred during the European colonization of the Americas. (p. 571)

comedy *n.* a humorous form of drama that often includes slapstick and satire. (p. 136)

command economy *n.* an economic system in which the government makes all economic decisions. (p. 877)

Commercial Revolution *n.* the expansion of trade and business that transformed European economies during the 16th and 17th centuries. (p. 389)

common law *n.* a unified body of law formed from rulings of England's royal judges that serves as the basis for law in many English-speaking countries today, including the United States. (p. 394)

commune [KAHM•YOON] *n.* in Communist China, a collective farm on which a great number of people work and live together. (p. 974)

Communist Party *n.* a political party practicing the ideas of Karl Marx and V.I. Lenin; originally the Russian Bolshevik Party. (p. 873)

communism *n.* an economic system in which all means of production—land, mines, factories, railroads, and businesses—are owned by the people, private property does not exist, and all goods and services are shared equally. (p. 737)

Concert [KAHN•SURT] **of Europe** *n.* a series of alliances among European nations in the 19th century, devised by Prince Klemens von Metternich to prevent the outbreak of revolutions. (p. 674)

concordat [kuhn•KAWR•DAT] *n.* a formal agreement—especially one between the pope and a government, dealing with the control of Church affairs. (p. 664)

Congress of Vienna [vee•EHN•uh] *n.* a series of meetings in 1814–1815, during which the European leaders sought to establish long-lasting peace and security after the defeat of Napoleon. (p. 672)

Congress Party *n.* a major national political party in India—also known as the Indian National Congress. (p. 997)

conquistadors [kahng•KEE•stuh•DAWRZ] *n.* the Spanish soldiers, explorers, and fortune hunters who took part in the conquest of the Americas in the 16th century. (p. 554)

conservative *n.* in the first half of the 19th century, a European—usually a wealthy landowner or noble—who wanted to preserve the traditional monarchies of Europe. (p. 687)

constitutional monarchy [MAHN•uhr•kee] *n.* a system of governing in which the ruler's power is limited by law. (p. 617)

consul [KAHN•suhl] *n.* in the Roman republic, one of the two powerful officials elected each year to command the army and direct the government. (p. 157)

containment *n.* a U.S. foreign policy adopted by President Harry Truman in the late 1940s, in which the United States tried to stop the spread of communism by creating alliances and helping weak countries to resist Soviet advances. (p. 967)

Continental System *n.* Napoleon's policy of preventing trade between Great Britain and continental Europe, intended to destroy Great Britain's economy. (p. 668)

corporation *n.* a business owned by stockholders who share in its profits but are not personally responsible for its debts. (p. 731)

Council of Trent *n.* a meeting of Roman Catholic leaders, called by Pope Paul III to rule on doctrines criticized by the Protestant reformers. (p. 499)

coup d'état [KOO day•TAH] *n.* a sudden seizure of political power in a nation. (p. 664)

covenant [KUHV•uh•nuhnt] *n.* a mutual promise or agreement—especially an agreement between God and the Hebrew people as recorded in the Bible. (p. 78)

creole [KREE•OHL] *n.* in Spanish colonial society, a colonist who was born in Latin America to Spanish parents. (p. 681)

Crimean [kry•MEE•uhn] **War** *n.* a conflict, lasting from 1853 to 1856, in which the Ottoman Empire, with the aid of Britain and France, halted Russian expansion in the region of the Black Sea. (p. 787)

crop rotation *n.* the system of growing a different crop in a field each year to preserve the fertility of the land. (p. 717)

Crusade *n.* one of the expeditions in which medieval Christian warriors sought to recover control of the Holy Land from the Muslims. (p. 382)

cultural diffusion *n.* the spreading of ideas or products from one culture to another. (p. 31)

Cultural Revolution *n.* a 1966–1976 uprising in China led by the Red Guards, with the goal of establishing a society of peasants and workers in which all were equal. (p. 975)

culture *n.* a people's unique way of life, as shown by its tools, customs, arts, and ideas. (p. 5)

cuneiform [KYOO•nee•uh•FAWRM] *n.* a system of writing with wedge-shaped symbols, invented by the Sumerians around 3000 B.C. (p. 20)

cyberterrorism *n.* politically motivated attacks on information systems. (p. 1088)

Cyrillic [suh•RIHL•ihk] **alphabet** *n.* an alphabet for the writing of Slavic languages, devised in the ninth century A.D. by Saints Cyril and Methodius. (p. 306)

czar [zahr] *n.* a Russian emperor (from the Roman title *Caesar*). (p. 311)

D

daimyo [DY•mee•OH] *n.* a Japanese feudal lord who commanded a private army of samurai. (p. 542)

Daoism [DOW•IHZ•uhm] *n.* a philosophy based on the ideas of the Chinese thinker Laozi, who taught that people should be guided by a universal force called the Dao (Way). (p. 106)

D-Day *n.* June 6, 1944—the day on which the Allies began their invasion of the European mainland during World War II. (p. 944)

Declaration of Independence *n.* a statement of the reasons for the American colonies' break with Britain, approved by the Second Continental Congress in 1776. (p. 641)

delta *n.* a marshy region formed by deposits of silt at the mouth of a river. (p. 36)

demilitarization [dee•MIHL•ih•tuhr•ih•ZAY•shuhn] *n.* a reduction in a country's ability to wage war, achieved by disbanding its armed forces and prohibiting it from acquiring weapons. (p. 950)

democracy *n.* a government controlled by its citizens, either directly or through representatives. (p. 128)

democratization *n.* the process of creating a government elected by the people. (p. 950)

Department of Homeland Security *n.* U.S. federal agency created in 2002 to coordinate national efforts against terrorism. (p. 1091)

détente [day•TAHNT] *n.* a policy of reducing Cold War tensions that was adopted by the United States during the presidency of Richard Nixon. (p. 990)

developed nation *n.* a nation with all the facilities needed for the advanced production of manufactured goods. (p. 1075)

devshirme [dehv•SHEER•meh] *n.* in the Ottoman Empire, the policy of taking boys from conquered Christian peoples to be trained as Muslim soldiers. (p. 510)

Diaspora [dy•AS•puhr•uh] *n.* the dispersal of the Jews from their homeland in Palestine—especially during the period of more than 1,800 years that followed the Romans' destruction of the Temple in Jerusalem in A.D. 70. (p. 170)

dictator *n.* in ancient Rome, a political leader given absolute power to make laws and command the army for a limited time. (p. 157)

direct democracy *n.* a government in which citizens rule directly rather than through representatives. (p. 135)

dissident [DIHS•ih•duhnt] *n.* an opponent of a government's policies or actions. (p. 1042)

divine right *n.* the idea that monarchs are God's representatives on earth and are therefore answerable only to God. (p. 594)

domestication *n.* the taming of animals for human use. (p. 16)

dominion *n.* in the British Empire, a nation (such as Canada) allowed to govern its own domestic affairs. (p. 752)

domino theory *n.* the idea that if a nation falls under Communist control, nearby nations will also fall under Communist control. (p. 978)

Dorians [DAWR•ee•uhnz] *n.* a Greek-speaking people that, according to tradition, migrated into mainland Greece after the destruction of the Mycenaean civilization. (p. 125)

Dreyfus [DRY•fuhs] **affair** *n.* a controversy in France in the 1890s, centering on the trial and imprisonment of a Jewish army officer, Captain Alfred Dreyfus, who had been falsely accused of selling military secrets to Germany. (p. 749)

Dutch East India Company *n.* a company founded by the Dutch in the early 17th century to establish and direct trade throughout Asia. (p. 534)

dynastic [dy•NAS•tihk] **cycle** *n.* the historical pattern of the rise, decline, and replacement of dynasties. (p. 54)

dynasty [DY•nuh•stee] *n.* a series of rulers from a single family. (p. 31)

E

Eastern Front *n.* in World War I, the region along the German-Russian border where Russians and Serbs battled Germans, Austrians, and Turks. (p. 848)

Edict of Nantes [EE•DIHKT uhv NAHNT] *n.* a 1598 declaration in which the French king Henry IV promised that Protestants could live in peace in France and could set up houses of worship in some French cities. (p. 596)

Emancipation Proclamation [ih•MAN•suh•PAY•shuhn PRAHK•luh•MAY•shuhn] *n.* a declaration issued by U.S. president Abraham Lincoln in 1863, stating that all slaves in the Confederate states were free. (p. 760)

emerging nation *n.* a nation in which the process of industrialization is not yet complete. (p. 1075)

émigré [EHM•ih•GRAY] *n.* a person who leaves their native country for political reasons, like the nobles and others who fled France during the peasant uprisings of the French Revolution. (p. 658)

empire *n.* a political unit in which a number of peoples or countries are controlled by a single ruler. (p. 33)

enclosure *n.* one of the fenced-in or hedged-in fields created by wealthy British landowners on land that was formerly worked by village farmers. (p. 717)

encomienda [ehng•kaw•MYEHN•dah] *n.* a grant of land made by Spain to a settler in the Americas, including the right to use Native Americans as laborers on it. (p. 557)

English Civil War *n.* a conflict, lasting from 1642 to 1649, in which Puritan supporters of Parliament battled supporters of England's monarchy. (p. 615)

enlightened despot [DEHS•puht] *n.* one of the 18th-century European monarchs who was inspired by Enlightenment ideas to rule justly and respect the rights of subjects. (p. 638)

enlightenment [ehn•LYT•uhn•muhnt] *n.* in Buddhism, a state of perfect wisdom in which one understands basic truths about the universe. (p. 68)

Enlightenment *n.* an 18th-century European movement in which thinkers attempted to apply the principles of reason and the scientific method to all aspects of society. (p. 629)

entrepreneur [AHN•truh•pruh•NUR] *n.* a person who organizes, manages, and takes on the risks of a business. (p. 721)

epic *n.* a long narrative poem celebrating the deeds of legendary or traditional heroes. (p. 125)

estate [ih•STAYT] *n.* one of the three social classes in France before the French Revolution—the First Estate consisting of the clergy; the Second Estate, of the nobility; and the Third Estate, of the rest of the population. (p. 651)

Estates-General [ih•STAYTS•JEHN•uhr•uhl] *n.* an assembly of representatives from all three of the estates, or social classes, in France. (pp. 397, 653)

ethnic cleansing *n.* a policy of murder and other acts of brutality by which Serbs hoped to eliminate Bosnia's Muslim population after the breakup of Yugoslavia. (p. 1056)

excommunication [EHKS•kuh•MYOO•nih•KAY•shuhn] *n.* the taking away of a person's right of membership in a Christian church. (p. 306)

existentialism [EHG•zih•STEHN•shuh•LIHZ•uhm] *n.* a philosophy based on the idea that people give meaning to their lives through their choices and actions. (p. 899)

extraterritorial [EHK•struh•TEHR•ih•TAWR•ee•uhl] **rights** *n.* an exemption of foreign residents from the laws of a country. (p. 806)

F

factors of production *n.* the resources—including land, labor, and capital—that are needed to produce goods and services. (p. 718)

factory *n.* a large building in which machinery is used to manufacture goods. (p. 720)

fascism [FASH•IHZ•uhm] *n.* a political movement that promotes an extreme form of nationalism, a denial of individual rights, and a dictatorial one-party rule. (p. 910)

Fatimid [FAT•uh•MIHD] *n.* a member of a Muslim dynasty that traced its ancestry to Muhammad's daughter Fatima and that built an empire in North Africa, Arabia, and Syria in the 10th–12th centuries. (p. 272)

favorable balance of trade *n.* an economic situation in which a country sells more goods abroad than it buys from abroad. (p. 575)

federal system *n.* a system of government in which power is divided between a central authority and a number of individual states. (pp. 645, 1041)

Fertile Crescent [FUHR•tuhl KREHS•uhnt] *n.* an arc of rich farmland in Southwest Asia, between the Persian Gulf and the Mediterranean Sea. (p. 29)

feudalism [FYOOD•uhl•IHZ•uhm] *n.* a political system in which nobles are granted the use of lands that legally belong to their king, in exchange for their loyalty, military service, and protection of the people who live on the land. (p. 54)

fief [feef] *n.* an estate granted to a vassal by a lord under the feudal system in medieval Europe. (p. 360)

filial piety [FIHL•ee•uhl PY•ih•tee] *n.* respect shown by children for their parents and elders. (p. 104)

"Final Solution" *n.* Hitler's program of systematically killing the entire Jewish people. (p. 937)

Five-Year Plans *n.* plans outlined by Joseph Stalin in 1928 for the development of the Soviet Union's economy. (p. 877)

Four Modernizations *n.* a set of goals adopted by the Chinese leader Deng Xiaoping in the late 20th century, involving progress in agriculture, industry, defense, and science and technology. (p. 1060)

Fourteen Points *n.* a series of proposals in which U.S. president Woodrow Wilson outlined a plan for achieving a lasting peace after World War I. (p. 858)

Franks *n.* a Germanic people who settled in the Roman province of Gaul (roughly the area now occupied by France) and established a great empire during the Middle Ages. (p. 354)

free trade *n.* commerce between nations without economic restrictions or barriers (such as tariffs). (p. 1076)

French and Indian War *n.* a conflict between Britain and France for control of territory in North America, lasting from 1754 to 1763. (p. 564)

G

gender inequality *n.* the difference between men and women in terms of wealth and status. (p. 1084)

genetic [juh•NEHT•ihk] **engineering** *n.* the transferring of genes from one living thing to another in order to produce an organism with new traits. (p. 1073)

genocide [JEHN•uh•SYD] *n.* the systematic killing of an entire people. (p. 937)

gentry *n.* a class of powerful, well-to-do people who enjoy a high social status. (p. 327)

geocentric theory *n.* in the Middle Ages, the earth-centered view of the universe in which scholars believed that the earth was an immovable object located at the center of the universe. (p. 623)

geopolitics [JEE•oh•PAHL•ih•tihks] *n.* a foreign policy based on a consideration of the strategic locations or products of other lands. (p. 786)

Ghana [GAH•nuh] *n.* a West African kingdom that grew rich from taxing and controlling trade and that established an empire in the 9th–11th centuries A.D. (p. 413)

ghazi [GAH•zee] *n.* a warrior for Islam. (p. 507)

ghettos [GEHT•ohz] *n.* city neighborhoods in which European Jews were forced to live. (p. 937)

glasnost [GLAHS•nuhst] *n.* a Soviet policy of openness to the free flow of ideas and information, introduced in 1985 by Mikhail Gorbachev. (p. 1046)

global economy *n.* all the financial interactions—involving people, businesses, and governments—that cross international boundaries. (p. 1076)

Glorious Revolution *n.* the bloodless overthrow of the English king James II and his replacement by William and Mary. (p. 616)

glyph [glihf] *n.* a symbolic picture—especially one used as part of a writing system for carving messages in stone. (p. 448)

Gothic [GAHTH•ihk] *adj.* relating to a style of church architecture that developed in medieval Europe, featuring ribbed vaults, stained glass windows, flying buttresses, pointed arches, and tall spires. (p. 380)

Great Depression *n.* the severe economic slump that followed the collapse of the U.S. stock market in 1929. (p. 907)

Great Fear *n.* a wave of senseless panic that spread through the French countryside after the storming of the Bastille in 1789. (p. 655)

Great Purge *n.* a campaign of terror in the Soviet Union during the 1930s, in which Joseph Stalin sought to eliminate all Communist Party members and other citizens who threatened his power. (p. 876)

Great Schism [SIHZ•uhm] *n.* a division in the medieval Roman Catholic Church, during which rival popes were established in Avignon and in Rome. (p. 399)

Greco-Roman culture *n.* an ancient culture that developed from a blending of Greek, Hellenistic, and Roman cultures. (p. 178)

green revolution *n.* a 20th-century attempt to increase food resources worldwide, involving the use of fertilizers and pesticides and the development of disease-resistant crops. (p. 1074)

griot [gree•OH] *n.* a West African storyteller. (p. 216)

guerrilla [guh•RIHL•uh] *n.* a member of a loosely organized fighting force that makes surprise attacks on enemy troops occupying his or her country. (p. 669)

guild [gihld] *n.* a medieval association of people working at the same occupation, which controlled its members' wages and prices. (p. 388)

guillotine [GIHL•uh•TEEN] *n.* a machine for beheading people, used as a means of execution during the French Revolution. (p. 660)

Gupta [GUP•tuh] **Empire** *n.* the second empire in India, founded by Chandra Gupta I in A.D. 320. (p. 191)

H

habeas corpus [HAY•bee•uhs KAWR•puhs] *n.* a document requiring that a prisoner be brought before a court or judge so that it can be decided whether his or her imprisonment is legal. (p. 616)

Hagia Sophia [HAY•ee•uh soh•FEE•uh] *n.* the Cathedral of Holy Wisdom in Constantinople, built by order of the Byzantine emperor Justinian. (p. 303)

haiku [HY•koo] *n.* a Japanese form of poetry, consisting of three unrhymed lines of five, seven, and five syllables. (p. 545)

hajj [haj] *n.* a pilgrimage to Mecca, performed as a duty by Muslims. (p. 267)

Han [hahn] **Dynasty** *n.* a Chinese dynasty that ruled from 202 B.C. to A.D. 9 and again from A.D. 23 to 220. (p. 200)

Harappan civilization *n.* another name for the Indus Valley civilization that arose along the Indus River, possibly as early as 7000 B.C.; characterized by sophisticated city planning. (p. 46)

Hausa [HOW•suh] *n.* a West African people who lived in several city-states in what is now northern Nigeria. (p. 417)

heliocentric [HEE•lee•oh•SEHN•trihk] **theory** *n.* the idea that the earth and the other planets revolve around the sun. (p. 624)

Hellenistic [HEHL•uh•NIHS•tihk] *adj.* relating to the civilization, language, art, science, and literature of the Greek world from the reign of Alexander the Great to the late second century B.C. (p. 146)

helot [HEHL•uht] *n.* in the society of ancient Sparta, a peasant bound to the land. (p. 129)

hieroglyphics [HY•uhr•uh•GLIHF•ihks] *n.* an ancient Egyptian writing system in which pictures were used to represent ideas and sounds. (p. 40)

Hijrah [HIHJ•ruh] *n.* Muhammad's migration from Mecca to Yathrib (Medina) in A.D. 622. (p. 265)

Hittites [HIHT•YTS] *n.* an Indo-European people who settled in Anatolia around 2000 B.C. (p. 62)

Holocaust [HAHL•uh•KAWST] *n.* a mass slaughter of Jews and other civilians, carried out by the Nazi government of Germany before and during World War II. (p. 936)

Holy Alliance *n.* a league of European nations formed by the leaders of Russia, Austria, and Prussia after the Congress of Vienna. (p. 674)

Holy Roman Empire *n.* an empire established in Europe in the 10th century A.D., originally consisting mainly of lands in what is now Germany and Italy. (p. 371)

home rule *n.* a control over internal matters granted to the residents of a region by a ruling government. (p. 754)

hominid [HAHM•uh•nihd] *n.* a member of a biological group including human beings and related species that walk upright. (p. 7)

Homo sapiens [HOH•moh SAY•pee•uhnz] *n.* the biological species to which modern human beings belong. (p. 8)

House of Wisdom *n.* a center of learning established in Baghdad in the 800s. (p. 276)

humanism [HYOO•muh•NIHZ•uhm] *n.* a Renaissance intellectual movement in which thinkers studied classical texts and focused on human potential and achievements. (p. 472)

Hundred Days *n.* the brief period during 1815 when Napoleon made his last bid for power, deposing the French king and again becoming emperor of France. (p. 671)

Hundred Years' War *n.* a conflict in which England and France battled on French soil on and off from 1337 to 1453. (p. 401)

hunter-gatherer *n.* a member of a nomadic group whose food supply depends on hunting animals and collecting plant foods. (p. 14)

Hyksos [HIHK•sohs] *n.* a group of nomadic invaders from Southwest Asia who ruled Egypt from 1640 to 1570 B.C. (p. 89)

I

Ice Age *n.* a cold period in which huge ice sheets spread outward from the polar regions, the last one of which lasted from about 1,900,000 to 10,000 B.C. (p. 235)

I Ching [ee jihng] *n.* a Chinese book of oracles, consulted to answer ethical and practical problems. (p. 107)

icon [EYE•KAHN] *n.* a religious image used by eastern Christians. (p. 306)

imperialism [ihm•FEER•ee•uh•LIHZ•uhm] *n.* a policy in which a strong nation seeks to dominate other countries politically, economically, or socially. (p. 773)

impressionism [ihm•PREHSH•uh•NIHZ•uhm] *n.* a movement in 19th-century painting, in which artists reacted against realism by seeking to convey their impressions of subjects or moments in time. (p. 701)

Indo-Europeans [IHN•doh•YUR•uh•PEE•uhnz] *n.* a group of seminomadic peoples who, about 1700 B.C., began to migrate from what is now southern Russia to the Indian subcontinent, Europe, and Southwest Asia. (p. 61)

indulgence [ihn•DUHL•juhns] *n.* a pardon releasing a person from punishments due for a sin. (p. 489)

industrialization [ihn•DUHS•tree•uh•lih•ZAY•shuhn] *n.* the development of industries for the machine production of goods. (p. 718)

Industrial Revolution *n.* the shift, beginning in England during the 18th century, from making goods by hand to making them by machine. (p. 717)

inflation *n.* a decline in the value of money, accompanied by a rise in the prices of goods and services. (p. 173)

Inquisition [IHN•kwih•ZIHSH•uhn] *n.* a Roman Catholic tribunal for investigating and prosecuting charges of heresy—especially the one active in Spain during the 1400s. (p. 384)

institution *n.* a long-lasting pattern of organization in a community. (p. 20)

intendant [ihn•TEHN•duhnt] *n.* a French government official appointed by the monarch to collect taxes and administer justice. (p. 598)

International Space Station *n.* cooperative venture sponsored by the United States, Russia, and 14 other nations to establish and maintain a working laboratory for scientific experimentation in space. (p. 1071)

Internet *n.* a linkage of computer networks that enables people around the world to exchange information and communicate with one another. (p. 1073)

intifada *n.* Palestinian campaign of civil disobedience against Israeli occupation of the West Bank and Gaza Strip, which continued into the 1990s. (p. 1021)

Irish Republican Army (IRA) *n.* an unofficial nationalist military force seeking independence for Ireland from Great Britain. (p. 755)

iron curtain *n.* during the Cold War, the boundary separating the Communist nations of Eastern Europe from the mostly democratic nations of Western Europe. (p. 967)

Iroquois [IHR•uh•KWOY] *n.* a group of Native American peoples who spoke related languages, lived in the eastern Great Lakes region of North America, and formed an alliance in the late 1500s. (p. 444)

Islam [ihs•LAHM] *n.* a monotheistic religion that developed in Arabia in the seventh century A.D. (p. 265)

isolationism *n.* a policy of avoiding political or military involvement with other countries. (p. 918)

Israel [IHZ•ree•uhl] *n.* a kingdom of the united Hebrews in Palestine, lasting from about 1020 to 922 B.C.; later, the northernmost of the two Hebrew kingdoms; now, the Jewish nation that was established in Palestine in 1948. (p. 81)

J

Jainism [JY•NIHZ•uhm] *n.* a religion founded in India in the sixth century B.C., whose members believe that everything in the universe has a soul and therefore should not be harmed. (p. 67)

janissary [JAN•ih•SEHR•ee] *n.* a member of an elite force of soldiers in the Ottoman Empire. (p. 510)

jazz *n.* a 20th-century style of popular music developed mainly by African-American musicians. (p. 899)

Jesuits [JEHZH•oo•ihts] *n.* members of the Society of Jesus, a Roman Catholic religious order founded by Ignatius of Loyola. (p. 499)

"jewel in the crown" *n.* the British colony of India—so called because of its importance in the British Empire, both as a supplier of raw materials and as a market for British trade goods. (p. 791)

joint-stock company *n.* a business in which investors pool their wealth for a common purpose, then share the profits. (p. 573)

Judah [JOO•duh] *n.* a Hebrew kingdom in Palestine, established around 922 B.C. (p. 81)

Justinian [juh•STIHN•ee•uhn] **Code** *n.* the body of Roman civil law collected and organized by order of the Byzantine emperor Justinian around A.D. 534. (p. 302)

K

kabuki [kuh•BOO•kee] *n.* a type of Japanese drama in which music, dance, and mime are used to present stories. (p. 545)

kaiser [KY•zuhr] *n.* a German emperor (from the Roman title *Caesar*). (p. 697)

kamikaze [KAH•mih•KAH•zee] *n.* during World War II, Japanese suicide pilots trained to sink Allied ships by crashing bomb-filled planes into them. (p. 945)

karma [KAHR•muh] *n.* in Hinduism and Buddhism, the totality of the good and bad deeds performed by a person, which is believed to determine his or her fate after rebirth. (p. 67)

Khmer [kmair] **Empire** *n.* a Southeast Asian empire, centered in what is now Cambodia, that reached its peak of power around A.D. 1200. (p. 345)

Khmer Rouge [roozh] *n.* a group of Communist rebels who seized power in Cambodia in 1975. (p. 981)

knight *n.* in medieval Europe, an armored warrior who fought on horseback. (p. 360)

Koryu [KAWR•yoo] **Dynasty** *n.* a dynasty that ruled Korea from A.D. 935 to 1392. (p. 347)

Kristallnacht [krih•STAHL•NAHKT] *n.* "Night of Broken Glass"—the night of November 9, 1938, on which Nazi storm troopers attacked Jewish homes, businesses, and synagogues throughout Germany. (p. 936)

Kuomintang [KWOH•mihn•TANG] *n.* the Chinese Nationalist Party, formed after the fall of the Qing Dynasty in 1912. (p. 882)

Kush [kuhsh] *n.* an ancient Nubian kingdom whose rulers controlled Egypt between 2000 and 1000 B.C. (p. 92)

L

laissez faire [LEHS•ay FAIR] *n.* the idea that government should not interfere with or regulate industries and businesses. (p. 734)

land reform *n.* a redistribution of farmland by breaking up large estates and giving the resulting smaller farms to peasants. (p. 1034)

La Reforma [lah reh•FAWR•mah] *n.* a liberal reform movement in 19th-century Mexico, led by Benito Juárez. (p. 824)

lay investiture [ihn•VEHS•tuh•chur] *n.* the appointment of religious officials by kings or nobles. (p. 372)

League of Nations *n.* an international association formed after World War I with the goal of keeping peace among nations. (p. 859)

lebensraum [LAY•buhns•ROWM] *n.* "living space"—the additional territory that, according to Adolf Hitler, Germany needed because it was overcrowded. (p. 912)

Legalism *n.* a Chinese political philosophy based on the idea that a highly efficient and powerful government is the key to social order. (p. 106)

legion *n.* a military unit of the ancient Roman army, made up of about 5,000 foot soldiers and a group of soldiers on horseback. (p. 157)

Legislative [LEHJ•ih•SLAY•tihv] **Assembly** *n.* a French congress with the power to create laws and approve declarations of war, established by the Constitution of 1791. (p. 657)

legitimacy [luh•JIHT•uh•muh•see] *n.* the hereditary right of a monarch to rule. (p. 673)

liberal *n.* in the first half of the 19th century, a European—usually a middle-class business leader or merchant—who wanted to give more political power to elected parliaments. (p. 687)

lineage [LIHN•ee•ihj] *n.* the people—living, dead, and unborn—who are descended from a common ancestor. (p. 410)

loess [LOH•uhs] *n.* a fertile deposit of windblown soil. (p. 50)

Long March *n.* a 6,000-mile journey made in 1934–1935 by Chinese Communists fleeing from Jiang Jieshi's Nationalist forces. (p. 886)

lord *n.* in feudal Europe, a person who controlled land and could therefore grant estates to vassals. (p. 360)

Lutheran [LOO•thuhr•uhn] *n.* a member of a Protestant church founded on the teachings of Martin Luther. (p. 490)

lycée [lee•SAY] *n.* a government-run public school in France. (p. 664)

M

Macedonia [MAS•ih•DOH•nee•uh] *n.* an ancient kingdom north of Greece, whose ruler Philip II conquered Greece in 338 B.C. (p. 142)

Maghrib [MUHG•ruhb] *n.* a region of western North Africa, consisting of the Mediterranean coastlands of what is now Morocco, Tunisia, and Algeria. (p. 410)

Magna Carta [MAG•nuh KAHR•tuh] *n.* "Great Charter"—a document guaranteeing basic political rights in England, drawn up by nobles and approved by King John in A.D. 1215. (p. 394)

Mahabharata [muh•huh•BAH•ruh•tuh] *n.* a great Indian epic poem, reflecting the struggles of the Aryans as they moved south into India. (p. 64)

Mahayana [MAH•huh•YAH•nuh] *n.* a sect of Buddhism that offers salvation to all and allows popular worship. (p. 193)

maize [mayz] *n.* a cultivated cereal grain that bears its kernels on large ears—usually called corn in the United States. (p. 238)

Mali [MAH•lee] *n.* a West African empire that flourished from 1235 to the 1400s and grew rich from trade. (p. 415)

Manchus [MAN•chooz] *n.* a people, native to Manchuria, who ruled China during the Qing Dynasty (1644–1912). (p. 539)

Mandate of Heaven *n.* in Chinese history, the divine approval thought to be the basis of royal authority. (p. 54)

manifest destiny *n.* the idea, popular among mid-19th-century Americans, that it was the right and the duty of the United States to rule North America from the Atlantic Ocean to the Pacific Ocean. (p. 758)

manor *n.* a lord's estate in feudal Europe. (p. 360)

Maori [MOW•ree] *n.* a member of a Polynesian people who settled in New Zealand around A.D. 800. (p. 752)

Marshall Plan *n.* a U.S. program of economic aid to European countries to help them rebuild after World War II. (p. 968)

martial [MAHR•shuhl] **law** *n.* a temporary rule by military authorities over a civilian population, usually imposed in times of war or civil unrest. (p. 1041)

mass culture *n.* the production of works of art and entertainment designed to appeal to a large audience. (p. 766)

materialism *n.* a placing of high value on acquiring material possessions. (p. 1096)

matriarchal [MAY•tree•AHR•kuhl] *adj.* relating to a social system in which the mother is head of the family. (p. 192)

matrilineal [MAT•ruh•LIHN•ee•uhl] adj. relating to a social system in which family descent and inheritance rights are traced through the mother. (p. 410)

Mauryan [MAH•ur•yuhn] **Empire** *n.* the first empire in India, founded by Chandragupta Maurya in 321 B.C. (p. 189)

May Fourth Movement *n.* a national protest in China in 1919, in which people demonstrated against the Treaty of Versailles and foreign interference. (p. 883)

Medes [meedz] *n.* a Southwest Asian people who helped to destroy the Assyrian Empire. (p. 97)

Meiji [MAY•JEE] **era** *n.* the period of Japanese history from 1867 to 1912, during which the country was ruled by Emperor Mutsuhito. (p. 811)

Mein Kampf [MYN KAHMPF] *n.* "My Struggle"—a book written by Adolf Hitler during his imprisonment in 1923–1924, in which he set forth his beliefs and his goals for Germany. (p. 912)

mercantilism [MUR•kuhn•tee•LIHZ•uhm] *n.* an economic policy under which nations sought to increase their wealth and power by obtaining large amounts of gold and silver and by selling more goods than they bought. (p. 574)

mercenary [MUR•suh•NEHR•ee] *n.* a soldier who is paid to fight in a foreign army. (p. 173)

Meroë [MEHR•oh•EE] *n.* center of the Kush dynasty from about 250 B.C. to A.D. 150; known for its manufacture of iron weapons and tools. (p. 94)

Mesoamerica [MEHZ•oh•uh•MEHR•ih•kuh] *n.* an area extending from central Mexico to Honduras, where several of the ancient complex societies of the Americas developed. (p. 240)

mestizo [mehs•TEE•zoh] *n.* a person of mixed Spanish and Native American ancestry. (p. 557)

Middle Ages *n.* the era in European history that followed the fall of the Roman Empire, lasting from about 500 to 1500—also called the medieval period. (p. 353)

middle class *n.* a social class made up of skilled workers, professionals, businesspeople, and wealthy farmers. (p. 725)

middle passage *n.* the voyage that brought captured Africans to the West Indies, and later to North and South America, to be sold as slaves—so called because it was considered the middle leg of the triangular trade. (p. 569)

migration *n.* the act of moving from one place to settle in another. (pp. 62, 220)

militarism [MIHL•ih•tuh•RIHZ•uhm] *n.* a policy of glorifying military power and keeping a standing army always prepared for war. (p. 842)

Ming Dynasty *n.* a Chinese dynasty that ruled from 1368 to 1644. (p. 530)

Minoans [mih•NOH•uhnz] *n.* a seafaring and trading people that lived on the island of Crete from about 2000 to 1400 B.C. (p. 72)

Mississippian [MIHS•ih•SIHP•ee•uhn] *adj.* relating to a Mound Builder culture that flourished in North America between A.D. 800 and 1500. (p. 443)

mita [MEE•tuh] *n.* in the Inca Empire, the requirement that all able-bodied subjects work for the state a certain number of days each year. (p. 461)

Moche [MOH•chay] *n.* a civilization that flourished on what is now the northern coast of Peru from about A.D. 100 to 700. (p. 247)

monarchy [MAHN•uhr•kee] *n.* a government in which power is in the hands of a single person. (p. 127)

monastery [MAHN•uh•STEHR•ee] *n.* a religious community of men (called monks) who have given up their possessions to devote themselves to a life of prayer and worship. (p. 354)

monopoly [muh•NAHP•uh•lee] *n.* a group's exclusive control over the production and distribution of certain goods. (p. 204)

monotheism [MAHN•uh•thee•IHZ•uhm] *n.* a belief in a single god. (p. 78)

Monroe Doctrine *n.* a U.S. policy of opposition to European interference in Latin America, announced by President James Monroe in 1823. (p. 818)

monsoon [mahn•SOON] *n.* a wind that shifts in direction at certain times of each year. (p. 45)

mosque [mahsk] *n.* an Islamic place of worship. (p. 267)

movable type *n.* blocks of metal or wood, each bearing a single character, that can be arranged to make up a page for printing. (p. 325)

Mughal [MOO•guhl] *n.* one of the nomads who invaded the Indian subcontinent in the 16th century and established a powerful empire there. (p. 516)

mujahideen [moo•JAH•heh•DEEN] *n.* in Afghanistan, holy warriors who banded together to fight the Soviet-supported government in the late 1970s. (p. 1026)

mulattos [mu•LAT•ohz] *n.* persons of mixed European and African ancestry. (p. 682)

mummification [MUHM•uh•fih•KAY•shuhn] *n.* a process of embalming and drying corpses to prevent them from decaying. (p. 38)

Munich [MYOO•nihk] **Conference** *n.* a 1938 meeting of representatives from Britain, France, Italy, and Germany, at which Britain and France agreed to allow Nazi Germany to annex part of Czechoslovakia in return for Adolf Hitler's pledge to respect Czechoslovakia's new borders. (p. 919)

Muslim [MUHZ•luhm] *n.* a follower of Islam. (p. 265)

Muslim League *n.* an organization formed in 1906 to protect the interests of India's Muslims, which later proposed that India be divided into separate Muslim and Hindu nations. (p. 997)

Mutapa [moo•TAHP•uh] *adj.* relating to a southern African empire established by Mutota in the 15th century A.D. (p. 427)

Mycenaean [MY•suh•NEE•uhn] *n.* an Indo-European person who settled on the Greek mainland around 2000 B.C. (p. 124)

myth *n.* a traditional story about gods, ancestors, or heroes, told to explain the natural world or the customs and beliefs of a society. (p. 126)

N

Napoleonic [nuh•POH•lee•AHN•ihk] **Code** *n.* a comprehensive and uniform system of laws established for France by Napoleon. (p. 664)

National Assembly *n.* a French congress established by representatives of the Third Estate on June 17, 1789, to enact laws and reforms in the name of the French people. (p. 654)

nationalism *n.* the belief that people should be loyal mainly to their nation—that is, to the people with whom they share a culture and history—rather than to a king or empire. (p. 687)

nation-state *n.* an independent geopolitical unit of people having a common culture and identity. (p. 687)

NATO [NAY•toh] *n.* the North Atlantic Treaty Organization—a defensive military alliance formed in 1949 by ten Western European nations, the United States, and Canada. (p. 969)

Nazca [NAHS•kah] *n.* a civilization that flourished on what is now the southern coast of Peru from about 200 B.C. to A.D. 600. (p. 247)

Nazism [NAHT•SIHZ•uhm] *n.* the fascist policies of the National Socialist German Workers' party, based on totalitarianism, a belief in racial superiority, and state control of industry. (p. 912)

Negritude [NEE•grih•TOOD] **movement** *n.* a movement in which French-speaking Africans and West Indians celebrated their heritage of traditional African culture and values. (p. 1012)

neoclassical [NEE•oh•KLAS•ih•kuhl] *adj.* relating to a simple, elegant style (based on ideas and themes from ancient Greece and Rome) that characterized the arts in Europe during the late 1700s. (p. 637)

Neolithic [NEE•uh•LIHTH•ihk] **Age** *n.* a prehistoric period that began about 8000 B.C. and in some areas ended as early as 3000 B.C., during which people learned to polish stone tools, make pottery, grow crops, and raise animals—also called the New Stone Age. (p. 7)

Neolithic Revolution *n.* the major change in human life caused by the beginnings of farming—that is, by people's shift from food gathering to food producing. (p. 15)

New Deal *n.* U.S. president Franklin Roosevelt's economic reform program designed to solve the problems created by the Great Depression. (p. 909)

New Kingdom *n.* the period of ancient Egyptian history that followed the overthrow of the Hyksos rulers, lasting from about 1570 to 1075 B.C. (p. 90)

nirvana [neer•VAH•nuh] *n.* in Buddhism, the release from pain and suffering achieved after enlightenment. (p. 69)

Nok [nahk] *n.* an African people who lived in what is now Nigeria between 500 B.C. and A.D. 200. (p. 217)

nomad *n.* a member of a group that has no permanent home, wandering from place to place in search of food and water. (p. 14)

nonaggression [NAHN•uh•GRESHS•uhn] **pact** *n.* an agreement in which nations promise not to attack one another. (p. 925)

nonaligned nations *n.* the independent countries that remained neutral in the Cold War competition between the United States and the Soviet Union. (p. 982)

Nuremberg [NUR•uhm•BURG] **Trials** *n.* a series of court proceedings held in Nuremberg, Germany, after World War II, in which Nazi leaders were tried for aggression, violations of the rules of war, and crimes against humanity. (p. 950)

O

obsidian [ahb•SIHD•ee•uhn] *n.* a hard, glassy volcanic rock used by early peoples to make sharp weapons. (p. 453)

Old Regime [ray•ZHEEM] *n.* the political and social system that existed in France before the French Revolution. (p. 651)

oligarchy [AHL•ih•GAHR•kee] *n.* a government in which power is in the hands of a few people—especially one in which rule is based upon wealth. (p. 127)

Olmec [AHL•mehk] *n.* the earliest-known Mesoamerican civilization, which flourished around 1200 B.C. and influenced later societies throughout the region. (p. 240)

Open Door Policy *n.* a policy, proposed by the United States in 1899, under which all nations would have equal opportunities to trade in China. (p. 808)

Opium War *n.* a conflict between Britain and China, lasting from 1839 to 1842, over Britain's opium trade in China. (p. 806)

oracle bone *n.* one of the animal bones or tortoise shells used by ancient Chinese priests to communicate with the gods. (p. 53)

Oslo Peace Accords *n.* an agreement in 1993 in which Israeli prime minister Rabin granted Palestinian self-rule in the Gaza Strip and the West Bank. (p. 1021)

ozone layer *n.* a layer of Earth's upper atmosphere, which protects living things from the sun's damaging ultraviolet rays. (p. 1079)

P

Pacific Rim *n.* the lands that border the Pacific Ocean—especially those in Asia. (p. 796)

Paleolithic [PAY•lee•uh•LIHTH•ihk] **Age** *n.* a prehistoric period that lasted from about 2,500,000 to 8000 B.C., during which people made use of crude stone tools and weapons—also called the Old Stone Age. (p. 7)

Panama Canal *n.* a human-made waterway connecting the Atlantic and Pacific oceans, built in Panama by the United States and opened in 1914. (p. 821)

papyrus [puh•PY•ruhs] *n.* a tall reed that grows in the Nile delta, used by the ancient Egyptians to make a paperlike material for writing on. (p. 40)

parliament [PAHR•luh•muhnt] *n.* a body of representatives that makes laws for a nation. (p. 395)

partition *n.* a division into parts, like the 1947 division of the British colony of India into the two nations of India and Pakistan. (p. 998)

pastoralist [PAS•tuhr•uh•lihst] *n.* a member of a nomadic group that herds domesticated animals. (p. 330)

paternalism [puh•TUR•nuh•LIHZ•uhm] *n.* a policy of treating subject people as if they were children, providing for their needs but not giving them rights. (p. 781)

patriarch [PAY•tree•AHRK] *n.* a principal bishop in the eastern branch of Christianity. (p. 306)

patriarchal [PAY•tree•AHR•kuhl] *adj.* relating to a social system in which the father is head of the family. (p. 192)

patrician [puh•TRIHSH•uhn] *n.* in ancient Rome, a member of the wealthy, privileged upper class. (p. 156)

patrilineal [PAT•ruh•LIHN•ee•uhl] *adj.* relating to a social system in which family descent and inheritance rights are traced through the father. (p. 410)

patron [PAY•truhn] *n.* a person who supports artists, especially financially. (p. 472)

Pax Mongolica [paks mahng•GAHL•ih-kuh] *n.* the "Mongol Peace"—the period from the mid-1200s to the mid-1300s when the Mongols imposed stability and law and order across much of Eurasia. (p. 333)

Pax Romana [PAHKS roh•MAH•nah] *n.* a period of peace and prosperity throughout the Roman Empire, lasting from 27 B.C. to A.D. 180. (p. 162)

Peace of Augsburg [AWGZ•BURG] *n.* a 1555 agreement declaring that the religion of each German state would be decided by its ruler. (p. 492)

Peloponnesian [PEHL•uh•puh•NEE•zhuhn] **War** *n.* a war, lasting from 431 to 404 B.C., in which Athens and its allies were defeated by Sparta and its allies. (p. 137)

penal [PEE•nuhl] **colony** *n.* a colony to which convicts are sent as an alternative to prison. (p. 752)

peninsulares [peh•neen•soo•LAH•rehs] *n.* in Spanish colonial society, colonists who were born in Spain. (p. 681)

Peninsular [puh•NIHN•syuh•luhr] **War** *n.* a conflict, lasting from 1808 to 1813, in which Spanish rebels, with the aid of British forces, fought to drive Napoleon's French troops out of Spain. (p. 669)

perestroika [PEHR•ih•STROY•kuh] *n.* a restructuring of the Soviet economy to permit more local decision making, begun by Mikhail Gorbachev in 1985. (p. 1047)

Persian Gulf War *n.* a 1991 conflict in which UN forces defeated Iraqi forces that had invaded Kuwait and threatened to invade Saudi Arabia. (p. 1079)

Persian Wars *n.* a series of wars in the fifth century B.C., in which Greek city-states battled the Persian Empire. (p. 131)

perspective [puhr•SPEHK•tihv] *n.* an artistic technique that creates the appearance of three dimensions on a flat surface. (p. 474)

phalanx [FAY•LANGKS] *n.* a military formation of foot soldiers armed with spears and shields. (p. 131)

pharaoh [FAIR•oh] *n.* a king of ancient Egypt, considered a god as well as a political and military leader. (p. 37)

philosophe [FIHL•uh•SAHF] *n.* one of a group of social thinkers in France during the Enlightenment. (p. 630)

philosopher *n.* a thinker who uses logic and reason to investigate the nature of the universe, human society, and morality. (p. 138)

Phoenicians [fih•NIHSH•uhnz] *n.* a seafaring people of Southwest Asia, who around 1100 B.C. began to trade and established colonies throughout the Mediterranean region. (p. 73)

Pilgrims *n.* a group of people who, in 1620, founded the colony of Plymouth in Massachusetts to escape religious persecution in England. (p. 562)

plebeian [plih•BEE•uhn] *n.* in ancient Rome, one of the common farmers, artisans, and merchants who made up most of the population. (p. 156)

plebiscite [PLEHB•ih•SYT] *n.* a direct vote in which a country's people have the opportunity to approve or reject a proposal. (p. 664)

PLO *n.* the Palestine Liberation Organization—an organization dedicated to the establishment of an independent state for Palestinians in the Middle East. (p. 1019)

polis [POH•lihs] *n.* a Greek city-state—the fundamental political unit of ancient Greece after about 750 B.C. (p. 127)

Politburo [PAHL•iht•BYOOR•oh] *n.* the ruling committee of the Communist Party in the Soviet Union. (p. 1046)

political dissent *n.* the difference of opinion over political issues. (p. 1084)

polytheism [PAHL•ee•thee•IHZ•uhm] *n.* a belief in many gods. (p. 31)

pope *n.* the bishop of Rome, head of the Roman Catholic Church. (p. 171)

Popol Vuh [POH•pohl VOO] *n.* a book containing a version of the Mayan story of creation. (p. 448)

popular culture *n.* the cultural elements—sports, music, movies, clothing, and so forth—that reflect a group's common background and changing interests. (p. 1093)

potlatch [PAHT•LACH] *n.* a ceremonial feast used to display rank and prosperity in some Northwest Coast tribes of Native Americans. (p. 441)

predestination [pree•DEHS•tuh•NAY•shuhn] *n.* the doctrine that God has decided all things beforehand, including which people will be eternally saved. (p. 495)

Presbyterian [PREHZ•bih•TEER•ee•uhn] *n.* a member of a Protestant church governed by presbyters (elders) and founded on the teachings of John Knox. (p. 496)

PRI *n.* the Institutional Revolutionary Party—the main political party of Mexico. (p. 1037)

proletariat [PROH•lih•TAIR•ee•iht] *n.* in Marxist theory, the group of workers who would overthrow the czar and come to rule Russia. (p. 868)

proliferation [pruh•LIHF•uh•RAY•shuhn] *n.* a growth or spread—especially the spread of nuclear weapons to nations that do not currently have them. (p. 1083)

propaganda [PRAHP•uh•GAN•duh] *n.* information or material spread to advance a cause or to damage an opponent's cause. (p. 854)

Protestant [PRAHT•ih•stuhnt] *n.* a member of a Christian church founded on the principles of the Reformation. (p. 490)

provisional government *n.* a temporary government. (p. 870)

psychology [sy•KAHL•uh•jee] *n.* the study of the human mind and human behavior. (p. 766)

pueblo [PWEHB•loh] *n.* a village of large apartment-like buildings made of clay and stone, built by the Anasazi and later peoples of the American Southwest. (p. 443)

Punic Wars *n.* a series of three wars between Rome and Carthage (264–146 B.C.); resulted in the destruction of Carthage and Rome's dominance over the western Mediterranean. (p. 158)

Puritans *n.* a group of people who sought freedom from religious persecution in England by founding a colony at Massachusetts Bay in the early 1600s. (p. 562)

push-pull factors *n.* conditions that draw people to another location (pull factors) or cause people to leave their homelands and migrate to another region (push factors). (p. 220)

pyramid [PIHR•uh•mihd] *n.* a massive structure with a rectangular base and four triangular sides, like those that were built in Egypt as burial places for Old Kingdom pharaohs. (p. 37)

Q

Qin [chihn] **Dynasty** *n.* a short-lived Chinese dynasty that replaced the Zhou Dynasty in the third century B.C. (p. 107)

Qing [chihng] **Dynasty** *n.* China's last dynasty, which ruled from 1644 to 1912. (p. 539)

Quetzalcoatl [keht•SAHL•koh•AHT•uhl] *n.* "the Feathered Serpent"—a god of the Toltecs and other Mesoamerican peoples. (p. 453)

quipu [KEE•poo] *n.* an arrangement of knotted strings on a cord, used by the Inca to record numerical information. (p. 461)

Qur'an [kuh•RAN] *n.* the holy book of Islam. (p. 267)

R

racism [RAY•SIHZ•uhm] *n.* the belief that one race is superior to others. (p. 775)

radical *n.* in the first half of the 19th century, a European who favored drastic change to extend democracy to all people. (p. 687)

radioactivity *n.* a form of energy released as atoms decay. (p. 765)

Raj [rahj] *n.* the British-controlled portions of India in the years 1757–1947. (p. 794)

rationing [RASH•uh•nihng] *n.* the limiting of the amounts of goods people can buy—often imposed by governments during wartime, when goods are in short supply. (p. 854)

realism *n.* a 19th-century artistic movement in which writers and painters sought to show life as it is rather than life as it should be. (p. 700)

realpolitik [ray•AHL•POH•lih•TEEK] *n.* "the politics of reality"—the practice of tough power politics without room for idealism. (p. 695)

recession *n.* a slowdown in a nation's economy. (p. 1034)

Reconquista [reh•kawn•KEES•tah] *n.* the effort by Christian leaders to drive the Muslims out of Spain, lasting from the 1100s until 1492. (p. 384)

Red Guards *n.* militia units formed by young Chinese people in 1966 in response to Mao Zedong's call for a social and cultural revolution. (p. 975)

Reformation [REHF•uhr•MAY•shuhn] *n.* a 16th-century movement for religious reform, leading to the founding of Christian churches that rejected the pope's authority. (p. 489)

refugee *n.* a person who leaves his or her country to move to another to find safety. (p. 1086)

Reign [rayn] **of Terror** *n.* the period, from mid-1793 to mid-1794, when Maximilien Robespierre ruled France nearly as a dictator and thousands of political figures and ordinary citizens were executed. (p. 660)

reincarnation [REE•ihn•kahr•NAY•shuhn] *n.* in Hinduism and Buddhism, the process by which a soul is reborn continuously until it achieves perfect understanding. (p. 67)

religious toleration *n.* a recognition of people's right to hold differing religious beliefs. (p. 190)

Renaissance [REHN•ih•SAHNS] *n.* a period of European history, lasting from about 1300 to 1600, during which renewed interest in classical culture led to far-reaching changes in art, learning, and views of the world. (p. 471)

republic *n.* a form of government in which power is in the hands of representatives and leaders are elected by citizens who have the right to vote. (p. 156)

Restoration [REHS•tuh•RAY•shuhn] *n.* the period of Charles II's rule over England, after the collapse of Oliver Cromwell's government. (p. 616)

reunification [ree•YOO•nuh•fih•KAY•shuhn] *n.* a bringing together again of things that have been separated, like the reuniting of East Germany and West Germany in 1990. (p. 1054)

romanticism [roh•MAN•tih•SIHZ•uhm] *n.* an early-19th-century movement in art and thought, which focused on emotion and nature rather than reason and society. (p. 698)

Roosevelt Corollary [ROH•zuh•VEHLT KAWR•uh•lehr•ee] *n.* President Theodore Roosevelt's 1904 extension of the Monroe Doctrine, in which he declared that the United States had the right to exercise "police power" throughout the Western Hemisphere. (p. 821)

Rowlatt Acts *n.* laws passed in 1919 that allowed the British government in India to jail anti-British protesters without trial for as long as two years. (p. 887)

Royal Road *n.* a road in the Persian Empire, stretching over 1,600 miles from Susa in Persia to Sardis in Anatolia. (p. 101)

Russification [RUHS•uh•fih•KAY•shuhn] *n.* the process of forcing Russian culture on all ethnic groups in the Russian Empire. (p. 693)

Russo-Japanese War *n.* a 1904–1905 conflict between Russia and Japan, sparked by the two countries' efforts to dominate Manchuria and Korea. (p. 812)

S

sacrament [SAK•ruh•muhnt] *n.* one of the Christian ceremonies in which God's grace is transmitted to people. (p. 371)

Safavid [suh•FAH•VIHD] *n.* a member of a Shi'a Muslim dynasty that built an empire in Persia in the 16th–18th centuries. (p. 512)

Sahel [suh•HAYL] *n.* the African region along the southern border of the Sahara. (p. 213)

salon [suh•LAHN] *n.* a social gathering of intellectuals and artists, like those held in the homes of wealthy women in Paris and other European cities during the Enlightenment. (p. 636)

SALT *n.* the Strategic Arms Limitation Talks—a series of meetings in the 1970s, in which leaders of the United States and the Soviet Union agreed to limit their nations' stocks of nuclear weapons. (p. 989)

Salt March *n.* a peaceful protest against the Salt Acts in 1930 in India in which Mohandas Gandhi led his followers on a 240-mile walk to the sea, where they made their own salt from evaporated seawater. (p. 889)

samurai [SAM•uh•RY] *n.* one of the professional warriors who served Japanese feudal lords. (p. 343)

sans-culottes [SANS•kyoo•LAHTS] *n.* in the French Revolution, a radical group made up of Parisian wage-earners and small shopkeepers who wanted a greater voice in government, lower prices, and an end to food shortages. (p. 658)

satrap [SAY•TRAP] *n.* a governor of a province in the Persian Empire. (p. 101)

savanna [suh•VAN•uh] *n.* a flat, grassy plain. (p. 215)

Schlieffen [SHLEE•fuhn] **Plan** *n.* Germany's military plan at the outbreak of World War I, according to which German troops would rapidly defeat France and then move east to attack Russia. (p. 846)

scholastics [skuh•LAS•tihks] *n.* scholars who gathered and taught at medieval European universities. (p. 392)

scientific method *n.* a logical procedure for gathering information about the natural world, in which experimentation and observation are used to test hypotheses. (p. 625)

Glossary

Scientific Revolution *n.* a major change in European thought, starting in the mid-1500s, in which the study of the natural world began to be characterized by careful observation and the questioning of accepted beliefs. (p. 623)

scorched-earth policy *n.* the practice of burning crops and killing livestock during wartime so that the enemy cannot live off the land. (p. 669)

scribe *n.* one of the professional record keepers in early civilizations. (p. 20)

secede [sih•SEED] *v.* to withdraw formally from an association or alliance. (p. 760)

secular [SEHK•yuh•luhr] *adj.* concerned with worldly rather than spiritual matters. (pp. 355, 472)

segregation [SEHG•rih•GAY•shuhn] *n.* the legal or social separation of people of different races. (p. 761)

self-determination [SEHLF•dih•TUR•muh•NAY•shuhn] *n.* the freedom of a people to decide under what form of government they wish to live. (p. 858)

Seljuks [SEHL•JOOKS] *n.* a Turkish group who migrated into the Abbasid Empire in the 10th century and established their own empire in the 11th century. (p. 315)

senate *n.* in ancient Rome, the supreme governing body, originally made up only of aristocrats. (p. 157)

sepoy [SEE•POY] *n.* an Indian soldier serving under British command. (p. 791)

Sepoy Mutiny [MYOOT•uh•nee] *n.* an 1857 rebellion of Hindu and Muslim soldiers against the British in India. (p. 793)

serf *n.* a medieval peasant legally bound to live on a lord's estate. (p. 360)

Seven Years' War *n.* a conflict in Europe, North America, and India, lasting from 1756 to 1763, in which the forces of Britain and Prussia battled those of Austria, France, Russia, and other countries. (p. 607)

shah [shah] *n.* hereditary monarch of Iran. (p. 513)

shari'a [shah•REE•ah] *n.* a body of law governing the lives of Muslims. (p. 268)

Shi'a [SHEE•uh] *n.* the branch of Islam whose members acknowledge Ali and his descendants as the rightful successors of Muhammad. (p. 271)

Shinto [SHIHN•toh] *n.* the native religion of Japan. (p. 339)

Shiva [SHEE•vuh] *n.* a Hindu god considered the destroyer of the world. (p. 194)

"shock therapy" *n.* an economic program implemented in Russia by Boris Yeltsin in the 1990s, involving an abrupt shift from a command economy to a free-market economy. (p. 1050)

shogun [SHOH•guhn] *n.* in feudal Japan, a supreme military commander who ruled in the name of the emperor. (p. 343)

Sikh [seek] *n.* a member of a nonviolent religious group whose beliefs blend elements of Buddhism, Hinduism, and Sufism. (p. 518)

Silk Roads *n.* a system of ancient caravan routes across Central Asia, along which traders carried silk and other trade goods. (p. 196)

simony [SY•muh•nee] *n.* the selling or buying of a position in a Christian church. (p. 379)

skepticism [SKEHP•tih•SIHZ•uhm] *n.* a philosophy based on the idea that nothing can be known for certain. (p. 597)

slash-and-burn farming *n.* a farming method in which people clear fields by cutting and burning trees and grasses, the ashes of which serve to fertilize the soil. (p. 15)

Slavs [slahvz] *n.* a people from the forests north of the Black Sea, ancestors of many peoples in Eastern Europe today. (p. 307)

social contract *n.* the agreement by which people define and limit their individual rights, thus creating an organized society or government. (p. 629)

Social Darwinism [DAHR•wih•NIHZ•uhm] *n.* the application of Charles Darwin's ideas about evolution and "survival of the fittest" to human societies—particularly as justification for imperialist expansion. (p. 775)

socialism *n.* an economic system in which the factors of production are owned by the public and operate for the welfare of all. (p. 736)

Solidarity [SAHL•ih•DAR•ih•tee] *n.* a Polish labor union that during the 1980s became the main force of opposition to Communist rule in Poland. (p. 1052)

Songhai [SAWNG•HY] *n.* a West African empire that conquered Mali and controlled trade from the 1400s to 1591. (p. 417)

soviet [SOH•vee•EHT] *n.* one of the local representative councils formed in Russia after the downfall of Czar Nicholas II. (p. 870)

Spanish-American War *n.* an 1898 conflict between the United States and Spain, in which the United States supported Cubans' fight for independence. (p. 818)

specialization *n.* the development of skills in a particular kind of work, such as trading or record keeping. (p. 20)

sphere of influence *n.* a foreign region in which a nation has control over trade and other economic activities. (p. 807)

standard of living *n.* the quality of life of a person or a population, as indicated by the goods, services, and luxuries available to the person or people. (p. 1034)

stateless societies *n.* cultural groups in which authority is shared by lineages of equal power instead of being exercised by a central government. (p. 410)

steppes [stehps] *n.* dry, grass-covered plains. (p. 61)

strike *v.* to refuse to work in order to force an employer to meet certain demands. (p. 738)

stupa [STOO-puh] *n.* mounded stone structures built over Buddhist holy relics. (p. 193)

subcontinent *n.* a large landmass that forms a distinct part of a continent. (p. 44)

Suez [soo•EHZ] **Canal** *n.* a human-made waterway, which was opened in 1869, connecting the Red Sea and the Mediterranean Sea. (p. 788)

suffrage [SUHF•rihj] *n.* the right to vote. (p. 747)

Sufi [SOO•fee] *n.* a Muslim who seeks to achieve direct contact with God through mystical means. (p. 271)

sultan *n.* "overlord," or "one with power"; title for Ottoman rulers during the rise of the Ottoman Empire. (p. 507)

Sunna [SOON•uh] *n.* an Islamic model for living, based on the life and teachings of Muhammad. (p. 268)

Sunni [SOON•ee] *n.* the branch of Islam whose members acknowledge the first four caliphs as the rightful successors of Muhammad. (p. 271)

surrealism [suh•REE•uh•LIHZ•uhm] *n.* a 20th-century artistic movement that focuses on the workings of the unconscious mind. (p. 899)

sustainable growth *n.* economic development that meets people's needs but preserves the environment and conserves resources for future generations. (p. 1080)

Swahili [swah•HEE•lee] *n.* an Arabic-influenced Bantu language that is spoken widely in eastern and central Africa. (p. 422)

T

Taiping [ty•pihng] **Rebellion** *n.* a mid-19th century rebellion against the Qing Dynasty in China, led by Hong Xiuquan. (p. 807)

Taj Mahal [TAHZH muh•HAHL] *n.* a beautiful tomb in Agra, India, built by the Mughal emperor Shah Jahan for his wife Mumtaz Mahal. (p. 519)

Taliban *n.* conservative Islamic group that took control of Afghanistan after the Soviet Union withdrew its troops; driven from power by U.S. forces in December, 2001, because of its harboring of suspected terrorists. (p. 1026)

Tamil [TAM•uhl] *n.* a language of southern India; also, the people who speak that language. (p. 191)

technology *n.* the ways in which people apply knowledge, tools, and inventions to meet their needs. (p. 8)

Tennis Court Oath *n.* a pledge made by the members of France's National Assembly in 1789, in which they vowed to continue meeting until they had drawn up a new constitution. (p. 654)

terraces *n.* a new form of agriculture in Aksum, in which stepped ridges constructed on mountain slopes help retain water and reduce erosion. (p. 228)

terrorism *n.* the use of force or threats to frighten people or governments to change their policies. (p. 1087)

theocracy [thee•AHK•ruh•see] *n.* **1.** a government in which the ruler is viewed as a divine figure. (p. 37) **2.** a government controlled by religious leaders. (p. 496)

theory of evolution *n.* the idea, proposed by Charles Darwin in 1859, that species of plants and animals arise by means of a process of natural selection. (p. 765)

theory of relativity [REHL•uh•TIHV•ih•tee] *n.* Albert Einstein's ideas about the interrelationships between time and space and between energy and matter. (p. 897)

Theravada [THEHR•uh•VAH•duh] *n.* a sect of Buddhism focusing on the strict spiritual discipline originally advocated by the Buddha. (p. 193)

Third Reich [ryk] *n.* the Third German Empire, established by Adolf Hitler in the 1930s. (p. 918)

Third Republic *n.* the republic that was established in France after the downfall of Napoleon III and ended with the German occupation of France during World War II. (p. 749)

Third World *n.* during the Cold War, the developing nations not allied with either the United States or the Soviet Union. (p. 982)

Thirty Years' War *n.* a European conflict over religion and territory and for power among ruling families, lasting from 1618 to 1648. (p. 603)

three-field system *n.* a system of farming developed in medieval Europe, in which farmland was divided into three fields of equal size and each of these was successively planted with a winter crop, planted with a spring crop, and left unplanted. (p. 387)

Tiananmen [tyahn•ahn•mehn] **Square** *n.* a huge public space in Beijing, China; in 1989, the site of a student uprising in support of democratic reforms. (p. 1061)

tithe [tyth] *n.* a family's payment of one-tenth of its income to a church. (p. 363)

Tokugawa Shogunate [TOH•koo•GAH•wah SHOH•guh•niht] *n.* a dynasty of shoguns that ruled a unified Japan from 1603 to 1867. (p. 544)

Torah [TAWR•uh] *n.* the first five books of the Hebrew Bible—the most sacred writings in the Jewish tradition. (p. 77)

totalitarianism [toh•TAL•ih•TAIR•ee•uh•NIHZ•uhm] *n.* government control over every aspect of public and private life. (p. 874)

total war *n.* a conflict in which the participating countries devote all their resources to the war effort. (p. 853)

totem [TOH•tuhm] *n.* an animal or other natural object that serves as a symbol of the unity of clans or other groups of people. (p. 445)

tournament *n.* a mock battle between groups of knights. (p. 367)

tragedy *n.* a serious form of drama dealing with the downfall of a heroic or noble character. (p. 136)

Treaty of Kanagawa [kah•NAH•gah•wah] *n.* an 1854 agreement between the United States and Japan, which opened two Japanese ports to U.S. ships and allowed the United States to set up an embassy in Japan. (p. 810)

Treaty of Tordesillas [TAWR•day•SEEL•yahs] *n.* a 1494 agreement between Portugal and Spain, declaring that newly discovered lands to the west of an imaginary line in the Atlantic Ocean would belong to Spain and newly discovered lands to the east of the line would belong to Portugal. (p. 533)

Treaty of Versailles [vuhr•SY] *n.* the peace treaty signed by Germany and the Allied powers after World War I. (p. 858)

trench warfare *n.* a form of warfare in which opposing armies fight each other from trenches dug in the battlefield. (p. 847)

triangular trade *n.* the transatlantic trading network along which slaves and other goods were carried between Africa, England, Europe, the West Indies, and the colonies in the Americas. (p. 568)

tribune [TRIHB•YOON] *n.* in ancient Rome, an official elected by the plebeians to protect their rights. (p. 156)

tribute *n.* a payment made by a weaker power to a stronger power to obtain an assurance of peace and security. (p. 82)

Triple Alliance *n.* **1.** an association of the city-states of Tenochtitlán, Texcoco, and Tlacopan, which led to the formation of the Aztec Empire (p. 454). **2.** a military alliance between Germany, Austria-Hungary, and Italy in the years preceding World War I. (p. 842)

Glossary

Triple Entente [ahn•TAHNT] *n.* a military alliance between Great Britain, France, and Russia in the years preceding World War I. (p. 843)

triumvirate [try•UHM•vuhr•iht] *n.* in ancient Rome, a group of three leaders sharing control of the government. (p. 161)

Trojan War *n.* a war, fought around 1200 B.C., in which an army led by Mycenaean kings attacked the independent trading city of Troy in Anatolia. (p. 125)

troubadour [TROO•buh•DAWR] *n.* a medieval poet and musician who traveled from place to place, entertaining people with songs of courtly love. (p. 367)

Truman Doctrine *n.* announced by President Harry Truman in 1947, a U.S. policy of giving economic and military aid to free nations threatened by internal or external opponents. (p. 968)

tyrant [TY•ruhnt] *n.* in ancient Greece, a powerful individual who gained control of a city-state's government by appealing to the poor for support. (p. 127)

UV

Umayyads [oo•MY•adz] *n.* a dynasty that ruled the Muslim Empire from A.D. 661 to 750 and later established a kingdom in al-Andalus. (p. 271)

union *n.* an association of workers, formed to bargain for better working conditions and higher wages. (p. 738)

United Nations *n.* an international peacekeeping organization founded in 1945 to provide security to the nations of the world. (p. 966)

Universal Declaration of Human Rights *n.* a 1948 statement in which the United Nations declared that all human beings have rights to life, liberty, and security. (p. 1084)

unrestricted submarine warfare *n.* the use of submarines to sink without warning any ship (including neutral ships and unarmed passenger liners) found in an enemy's waters. (p. 852)

urbanization [UR•buh•nih•ZAY•shuhn] *n.* the growth of cities and the migration of people into them. (p. 723)

U.S.A. Patriot Act *n.* an antiterrorism bill of 2001 that strengthened governmental rights to detain foreigners suspected of terrorism and prosecute terrorist crimes. (p. 1092)

U.S. Civil War *n.* a conflict between Northern and Southern states of the United States over the issue of slavery, lasting from 1861 to 1865. (p. 760)

utilitarianism [yoo•TIHL•ih•TAIR•ee•uh•NIHZ•uhm] *n.* the theory, proposed by Jeremy Bentham in the late 1700s, that government actions are useful only if they promote the greatest good for the greatest number of people. (p. 735)

utopia [yoo•TOH•pee•uh] *n.* an imaginary land described by Thomas More in his book *Utopia*—hence, an ideal place. (p. 482)

vassal [VAS•uhl] *n.* in feudal Europe, a person who received a grant of land from a lord in exchange for a pledge of loyalty and services. (p. 360)

Vedas [VAY•duhz] *n.* four collections of sacred writings produced by the Aryans during an early stage of their settlement in India. (p. 63)

vernacular [vuhr•NAK•yuh•luhr] *n.* the everyday language of people in a region or country. (pp. 391, 475)

Vietcong [vee•EHT•KAHNG] *n.* a group of Communist guerrillas who, with the help of North Vietnam, fought against the South Vietnamese government in the Vietnam War. (p. 980)

Vietnamization [vee•EHT•nuh•mih•ZAY•shuhn] *n.* President Richard Nixon's strategy for ending U.S. involvement in the Vietnam War, involving a gradual withdrawal of American troops and replacement of them with South Vietnamese forces. (p. 980)

Vishnu [VIHSH•noo] *n.* a Hindu god considered the preserver of the world. (p. 194)

vizier [vih•ZEER] *n.* a prime minister in a Muslim kingdom or empire. (p. 315)

W

War of the Spanish Succession *n.* a conflict, lasting from 1701 to 1713, in which a number of European states fought to prevent the Bourbon family from controlling Spain as well as France. (p. 601)

Warsaw Pact *n.* a military alliance formed in 1955 by the Soviet Union and seven Eastern European countries. (p. 969)

Weimar [WY•MAHR] **Republic** *n.* the republic that was established in Germany in 1919 and ended in 1933. (p. 905)

Western Front *n.* in World War I, the region of northern France where the forces of the Allies and the Central Powers battled each other. (p. 846)

westernization *n.* an adoption of the social, political, or economic institutions of Western—especially European or American—countries. (p. 610)

XYZ

yin and yang *n.* in Chinese thought, the two powers that govern the natural rhythms of life. (p. 107)

Yoruba [YAWR•uh•buh] *n.* a West African people who formed several kingdoms in what is now Benin and southern Nigeria. (p. 418)

Zapotec [ZAH•puh•TEHK] *n.* an early Mesoamerican civilization that was centered in the Oaxaca Valley of what is now Mexico. (p. 242)

ziggurat [ZIHG•uh•RAT] *n.* a tiered, pyramid-shaped structure that formed part of a Sumerian temple. (p. 23)

Zionism [ZY•uh•NIHZ•uhm] *n.* a movement founded in the 1890s to promote the establishment of a Jewish homeland in Palestine. (p. 750)

Spanish Glossary

A

Abbasids [abasidas] *s.* dinastía que gobernó gran parte del imperio musulmán entre 750 y 1258 d.C. (pág. 271)

Aborigine [aborigen] *s.* miembro de cualquiera de los pueblos nativos de Australia. (pág. 752)

absolute monarch [monarca absoluto] *s.* rey o reina que tiene poder ilimitado y que procura controlar todos los aspectos de la sociedad. (pág. 594)

acropolis [acrópolis] *s.* cima fortificada de las antiguas ciudades griegas. (pág. 127)

Aksum *s.* reino africano en lo que hoy es Etiopía y Eritrea, que alcanzó su mayor auge en el siglo 4. (pág. 225)

al-Andalus *s.* región gobernada por los musulmanes en lo que hoy es España, establecida en el siglo 8 d.C. (pág. 271)

Allah [Alah] *s.* Dios (palabra árabe usada en el islamismo). (pág. 264)

Allies [Aliados] *s.* durante la I Guerra Mundial, las naciones de Gran Bretaña, Francia y Rusia, junto con otras que lucharon a su lado; también, el grupo de naciones —entre ellas Gran Bretaña, la Unión Soviética y Estados Unidos— opuestas a las Potencias del Eje en la II Guerra Mundial. (pág. 845)

Almohads [almohades] *s.* grupo de reformadores islámicos que tumbaron la dinastía de los almorávides y que establecieron un imperio en el norte de África y en el sur de España en el siglo 12 d.C. (pág. 412)

Almoravids [almorávides] *s.* hermandad religiosa islámica que estableció un imperio en el norte de África y en el sur de España en el siglo 11 d.C. (pág. 412)

Amritsar Massacre [Masacre de Amritsar] *s.* matanza por tropas británicas de casi 400 indios, reunidos en Amritsar para protestar contra las Leyes Rowlatt. (pág. 888)

Anabaptist [anabaptista] *s.* en la Reforma, miembro de un grupo protestante que enseñaba que sólo los adultos podían ser bautizados, y que la Iglesia y el Estado debían estar separados. (pág. 496)

Anasazi [anasazi] *s.* grupo amerindio que se estableció en el Suroeste de Norteamérica. (pág. 443)

Anatolia *s.* península del suroeste de Asia actualmente ocupada por la parte asiática de Turquía; también llamada Asia Menor. (pág. 62)

Angkor Wat *s.* templo construido en el imperio Khmer y dedicado al dios hindú Visnú. (pág. 345)

Anglican [anglicano] *adj.* relacionado con la Iglesia de Inglaterra. (pág. 494)

animism [animismo] *s.* creencia de que en los animales, las plantas y otros objetos naturales habitan espíritus. (pág. 216)

annexation [anexión] *s.* añadir una región al territorio de una unidad política existente. (págs. 799, 813)

annul [anular] *v.* cancelar o suspender. (pág. 492)

anti-Semitism [antisemitismo] *s.*prejuicio contra los judíos. (pág. 749)

apartheid *s.* política de Sudáfrica de separación total y legalizada de las razas; prohibía todo contacto social entre negros y blancos. (pág. 1043)

apostle [apóstol] *s.* uno de los seguidores de Jesús que predicaba y difundía sus enseñanzas. (pág. 168)

appeasement [apaciguamiento] *s.* otorgar concesiones a un agresor a fin de evitar la guerra. (pág. 917)

aqueduct [acueducto] *s.* tubería o canal para llevar agua a zonas pobladas. (pág. 181)

aristocracy [aristocracia] *s.* gobierno en que el poder está en manos de una clase dominante hereditaria o nobleza. (pág. 127)

armistice [armisticio] *s.* acuerdo de suspender combates. (pág. 855)

artifact [artefacto] *s.* objeto hecho por el ser humano, como herramientas, armas o joyas. (pág. 5)

artisan [artesano] *s.* trabajador especializado, como hilandero o ceramista, que hace productos a mano. (pág. 20)

Aryans [arios] *s.* **1.** pueblo indoeuropeo que, hacia 1500 a.C., comenzó a emigrar al subcontinente de India. (pág. 63). **2.** para los nazis, los pueblos germanos que formaban una “raza maestra”. (pág. 936)

assembly line [línea de montaje] *s.* en una fábrica, correa que lleva un producto de un trabajador a otro, cada uno de los cuales desempeña una sola tarea. (pág. 764)

assimilation [asimilación] *s.* **1.** adopción de la cultura del conquistador por un pueblo conquistado. (pág. 205). **2.** política de una nación de obligar o alentar a un pueblo subyugado a adoptar sus instituciones y costumbres. (pág. 781)

Assyria [Asiria] *s.* reino del suroeste de Asia que controló un gran imperio de aproximadamente 850 a 612 a.C. (pág. 95)

Atlantic Charter [Carta del Atlántico] *s.* declaración de principios emitida en agosto de 1941 por el primer ministro británico Winston Churchill y el presidente de E.U.A. Franklin Roosevelt, en la cual se basó el plan de paz de los Aliados al final de la II Guerra Mundial. (pág. 930)

Atlantic slave trade [trata de esclavos del Atlántico] *s.* compra, transporte y venta de africanos para trabajar en las Américas. (pág. 567)

autocracy [autocracia] *s.* gobierno en el cual el gobernante tiene poder ilimitado y lo usa de forma arbitraria. (pág. 109)

Axis Powers [Potencias del Eje] *s.* en la II Guerra Mundial, las naciones de Alemania, Italia y Japón, que formaron una alianza en 1936. (pág. 917)

ayllu *s.* en la sociedad inca, pequeña comunidad o clan cuyos miembros trabajaban conjuntamente para el bien común. (pág. 460)

B

balance of power [equilibrio de poder] *s.* situación política en que ninguna nación tiene suficiente poder para ser una amenaza para las demás. (pág. 672)

the Balkans [Balcanes] *s.* región del sureste de Europa ocupada actualmente por Grecia, Albania, Bulgaria, Rumania, la parte eureopea de Turquía y las antiguas repúblicas de Yugoslavia. (pág. 689)

Bantu-speaking peoples [pueblos de habla bantú] *s.* hablantes de un grupo de lenguas relacionadas, que hace aproximadamente 2,000 años emigraron de África occidental a casi toda la mitad sur del continente. (pág. 222)

baroque [barroco] *s.* estilo grandioso y ornamentado del arte, la música y la arquitectura a fines del siglo 17 y principios del 18. (pág. 637)

barter [trueque] *s.* forma de comercio en la cual se intercambian productos y servicios sin dinero. (pág. 23)

Battle of Britain [Batalla Británica] *s.* batallas entre las fuerzas aéreas de Alemania y Gran Bretaña que se libraron sobre el territorio británico entre 1940–1941. (pág. 928)

Battle of Guadalcanal [Batalla de Guadalcanal] *s.* batalla de la II Guerra Mundial ocurrida en 1942–1943 en que las fuerzas aliadas expulsaron a las fuerzas japonesas de la isla de Guadalcanal en el Pacífico. (pág. 935)

Battle of Midway [Batalla del Midway] *s.* batalla aérea y naval de la II Guerra Mundial librada en 1941 en que las fuerzas estadounidenses derrotaron a las japonesas en el Pacífico central. (pág. 934)

Battle of Stalingrad [Batalla de Stalingrado] *s.* batalla de la II Guerra Mundial ocurrida en 1942–1943 en que las fuerzas alemanas perdieron y no lograron capturar la ciudad de Stalingrado en la Unión Soviética. (pág. 941)

Battle of the Bulge [Batalla del Bolsón] *s.* batalla de 1944–45 en que las fuerzas aliadas repulsaron la última ofensiva alemana de envergadura en la II Guerra Mundial. (pág. 944)

Battle of Trafalgar [Batalla de Trafalgar] *s.* batalla naval de 1805 en que las fuerzas de Napoleón fueron derrotadas por una flota inglesa al mando de Horacio Nelson. (pág. 667)

Benin *s.* reino que surgió en el siglo 14 cerca del delta del río Níger y llegó a ser un gran Estado de África occidental en el siglo 15. (pág. 419)

Beringia *s.* antiguo puente terrestre por el que se cree que los primeros habitantes de América migraron de Asia. (pág. 235)

Berlin Conference [Conferencia de Berlín] de 1884 *s.* reunión de 1884–1885 en la cual representantes de las naciones europeas acordaron reglas para la colonización europea de África. (pág. 776)

Bill of Rights [Carta de Derechos] *s.* primeras diez enmiendas a la Constitución de E.U.A., que protegen los derechos y libertades básicos de los ciudadanos. (pág. 645)

bishop [obispo] *s.* autoridad eclesiástica cristiana que supervisa varias iglesias. (pág. 171)

blitzkrieg *s.* "guerra relámpago"; táctica bélica de ataque sorpresa con aviones rápidos, seguidos de numerosas fuerzas de infantería. (pág. 925)

blockade [bloqueo] *s.* desplazamiento de tropas o barcos para impedir para evitar la entrada o salida de todo tráfico comercial a una ciudad o región. (pág. 668)

Boer [bóer] *s.* colono holandés que se estableció en Sudáfrica. (pág. 776)

Boer War [Guerra de los Bóers] *s.* conflicto de 1899 a 1902 entre los bóers y los británicos por el control de territorio en Sudáfrica. (pág. 778)

Bolsheviks [bolcheviques] *s.* grupo de marxistas revolucionarios rusos que tomó el control del gobierno ruso en noviembre de 1917. (pág. 868)

Boxer Rebellion [Rebelión de los Bóxers] *s.* rebelión de 1900 en China contra la influencia extranjera en el país. (pág. 808)

boyar [boyard] *s.* el noble terrateniente de Rusia. (pág. 608)

Brahma *s.* dios hindú considerado creador del mundo. (pág. 194)

Brahmin [brahamán] *s.* en la sociedad aria, miembro de la clase social formada por los sacerdotes. (pág. 63)

brinkmanship [política arriesgada] *s.* p
con lanzarse a la guerra en respuesta a
miga. (pág. 970)

Bronze Age [Edad del Bronce] *s.* período de
humana, que comenzó aproximadamente en 3
algunas partes, en el cual se comenzó a usar el
vez del cobre o la piedra, para elaborar herramien
armas. (pág. 21)

bubonic plague [peste bubónica] *s.* enfermedad mortal
que se extendió por Asia y Europa a mediados del siglo
14 y que cobró millones de víctimas. (pág. 399)

bureaucracy [burocracia] *s.* sistema de departamentos y dependencias formado para realizar las labores del gobierno. (pág. 105)

burgher [burgués] *s.* habitante de un pueblo medieval. (pág. 391)

Bushido *s.* estricto código de conducta de los guerreros samurai en Japón. (pág. 343)

C

cabinet [gabinete] *s.* grupo de asesores o ministros escogidos por el jefe de gobierno de un país para que participen en la toma de decisiones del gobierno. (pág. 617)

caliph [califa] *s.* líder político y religioso supremo de un gobierno musulmán. (pág. 269)

calligraphy [caligrafía] *s.* arte de escritura manuscrita. (pág. 276)

Calvinism [calvinismo] *s.* conjunto de enseñanzas religiosas basadas en las ideas del reformador Juan Calvino. (pág. 495)

Camp David Accords [Acuerdos de Camp David] *s.* primer tratado firmado entre Israel y un país árabe, en que el presidente Anwar Sadat de Egipto reconoció el derecho a existir de Israel y el primer ministro israelí Menachem Begin acordó devolver la península del Sinaí a Egipto. (pág. 1020)

canon law [derecho canónico] *s.* conjunto de leyes que gobierna una iglesia cristiana. (pág. 371)

capitalism [capitalismo] *s.* sistema económico basado en la propiedad privada y en la inversión de dinero en empresas comerciales con el objetivo de obtener ganancias. (págs. 573, 734)

Carolingian Dynasty [dinastía carolingia] *s.* dinastía de los reyes francos que abarcó del 751 al 887 d.C. (pág. 356)

caste [casta] *s.* una de las cuatro clases del sistema social de los arios que se establecieron en India: sacerdotes, guerreros, campesinos o comerciantes, y trabajadores o artesanos no arios. (pág. 64)

Catholic Reformation [Contrarreforma] *s.* movimiento del siglo 16 en el que la Iglesia Católica intentó reformarse en respuesta a la Reforma protestante. (pág. 498)

caudillo *s.* dictador militar de un país latinoamericano. (pág. 816)

centralized government [gobierno centralizado] *s.* gobierno en que el poder se concentra en una autoridad central a la cual se someten los gobiernos locales. (pág. 200)

Central Powers [Potencias Centrales] *s.* en la I Guerra Mundial, las naciones de Alemania y Austro-Hungría, y las demás que lucharon a su lado. (pág. 845)

Chaldeans [caldeos] *s.* pueblo del suroeste asiático que contribuyó a destruir el imperio asirio. (pág. 97)

artista] *s.* movimiento
ue miembros de la
en el Parlamento y
todos los hombres.

aciones de
ñas de lo que hoy
00 a.C. (pág. 246)

nsación de
rama del gobier-

de los caballeros
s como el valor,

de Estados Independientes: aso-
los antiguos territorios soviéticos formada cuando la Unión Soviética se desmembró. (pág. 1049)

city-state [ciudad Estado] *s.* ciudad y tierras de los alrededores que funcionaba como una unidad política independiente. (pág. 31)

civil disobedience [desobediencia civil] *s.* negativa pública y deliberada a obedecer una ley considerada injusta. (pág. 888)

civilization [civilización] *s.* forma de cultura que se caracteriza por tener ciudades, trabajadores especializados, instituciones complejas, un sistema de registro y tecnología avanzada. (pág. 20)

civil service [servicio público] *s.* departamentos administrativos del gobierno, especialmente los que requieren a los candidatos a empleo pasar ciertos exámenes. (pág. 203)

civil war [guerra civil] *s.* conflicto entre dos grupos políticos dentro de un mismo país. (pág. 161)

clan *s.* grupo de descendientes de un antepasado común. (pág. 331)

classical art [arte clásico] *s.* arte común de la antigua Grecia y Roma, que subraya la armonía, el orden y el equilibrio. (pág. 136)

clergy [clero] *s.* conjunto de eclesiásticos que celebran servicios religiosos, como sacerdotes, ministros o rabinos. (pág. 370)

cloning [clonación] *s.* creación de plantas o animales genéticamente idénticos a plantas o animales existentes. (pág. 1073)

coalition government [gobierno de coalición] *s.* gobierno controlado por una alianza temporal de varios partidos políticos. (pág. 904)

codex [códice] *s.* libro de páginas que se pueden pasar, como éste. (pág. 448)

Cold War [Guerra Fría] *s.* estado de hostilidad diplomática entre Estados Unidos y la Unión Soviética en las décadas siguientes a la II Guerra Mundial. (pág. 969)

collective bargaining [contrato colectivo] *s.* negociaciones entre trabajadores y patrones. (pág. 738)

collective farm [granja colectiva] *s.* granja controlada por el gobierno, formada mediante la unión de muchas pequeñas granjas. (pág. 878)

colony [colonia] *s.* tierra controlada por una nación distante. (pág. 554)

Colossus of Rhodes [Coloso de Rodas] *s.* enorme estatua helénica que se ubicaba cerca del puerto de Rodas. (pág. 149)

Columbian Exchange [trasferencia colombina] *s.* transferencia mundial de plantas, animales y enfermedades durante la colonización europea de América. (pág. 571)

comedy [comedia] *s.* forma humorística de drama con payasadas y sátira. (pág. 136)

command economy [economía de mando] *s.* sistema económico en el que el gobierno toma todas las decisiones económicas. (pág. 877)

Commercial Revolution [Revolución Comercial] *s.* expansión del comercio y los negocios que transformó las economías europeas en los siglos 16 y 17. (pág. 389)

common law [derecho consuetudinario] *s.* sistema de leyes desarrollado en Inglaterra, basado en costumbres y decisiones jurídicas anteriores. (pág. 394)

commune [comuna] *s.* en la China comunista, granja colectiva en la que mucha gente trabaja y vive junta. (pág. 974)

communism [comunismo] *s.* sistema económico en el que todos los medios de producción —tierras, minas, fábricas, ferrocarriles y negocios— son propiedad del pueblo, en que no existe la propiedad privada, y en que todos los productos y servicios se comparten por igual. (pág. 737)

Communist Party [Partido Comunista] *s.* partido político basado en las ideas de Karl Marx y V. I. Lenin; originalmente el Partido Bolchevique ruso. (pág. 873)

Concert of Europe [Concierto de Europa] *s.* serie de alianzas entre naciones europeas en el siglo 19, ideadas por el príncipe Klemens von Metternich para impedir revoluciones. (pág. 674)

concordat [concordato] *s.* acuerdo firmado entre Napoleón y el Papa para establecer una nueva relación entre la Iglesia y el Estado. (pág. 664)

Congress of Vienna [Congreso de Viena] *s.* serie de reuniones en 1814 y 1815 en las cuales los dirigentes europeos trataron de establecer una paz y seguridad duraderas tras la derrota de Napoleón. (pág. 672)

Congress Party [Partido del Congreso] *s.* importante partido político nacional de India; también se llama Congreso Nacional de India. (pág. 997)

conquistadors [conquistadores] *s.* soldados, exploradores y aventureros españoles que participaron en la conquista de América en el siglo 16. (pág. 554)

conservative [conservadore] *s.* en la primera mitad del siglo 19, el europeo—principalmente los terratenientes y nobles acaudalados—que querían preservar las monarquías tradicionales. (pág. 687)

constitutional monarchy [monarquía constitucional] *s.* monarquía en que el poder del gobernante está limitado por la ley. (pág. 617)

consul [cónsul] *s.* en la república romana, uno de los dos poderosos funcionarios elegidos cada año para comandar el ejército y dirigir el gobierno. (pág. 157)

containment [contención] *s.* política exterior estadounidense adoptada por el presidente Harry Truman a fines de la década de 1940 para impedir la expansión del comunismo creando alianzas con países débiles y ayudándolos a contener los avances soviéticos. (pág. 967)

Continental System [Sistema Continental] *s.* política de Napoleón de impedir el comercio de Gran Bretaña con la Europa continental para destruir la economía británica. (pág. 668)

corporation [corporación] *s.* empresa de accionistas que comparten las ganancias pero que no son personalmente responsables de sus deudas. (pág. 731)

Council of Trent [Concilio de Trento] *s.* reunión de líderes de la Iglesia Católica Romana, convocada por el papa Pablo III, para fallar sobre varias doctrinas criticadas por los reformadores protestantes. (pág. 499)

coup d'etat [golpe de Estado] *s.* toma repentina del poder político de una nación. (pág. 664)

covenant [pacto] *s.* promesa o acuerdo mutuo, especialmente un acuerdo entre Dios y el pueblo hebreo, como los que registra la Biblia. (pág. 78)

creole [criollo] *s.* en la sociedad española colonial, el colono nacido en Latinoamérica de padres españoles. (pág. 681)

Crimean War [Guerra de Crimea] *s.* conflicto de 1853 a 1856, en el cual el imperio otomano, con ayuda de Gran Bretaña y Francia, frenó la expansión rusa en la región del mar Negro. (pág. 787)

crop rotation [rotación de cultivos] *s.* sistema que cultiva distintos productos en un campo cada año para conservar la fertilidad de la tierra. (pág. 717)

Crusade [cruzada] *s.* una de las expediciones de guerreros cristianos medievales para quitarle Jerusalén y la Tierra Santa a los musulmanes. (pág. 382)

cultural diffusion [difusión cultural] *s.* proceso de difusión de ideas o productos de una cultura a otra. (pág. 31)

Cultural Revolution [Revolución Cultural] *s.* levantamiento de 1966–1976 en China, encabezado por los Guardias Rojos de Mao Tsetung, con el propósito de establecer una sociedad de campesinos y trabajadores donde todos fue-ran iguales. (pág. 975)

culture [cultura] *s.* forma distintiva de la vida de un pueblo, representada en sus herramientas, costumbres, artes y pensamiento. (pág. 5)

cuneiform [cuneiforme] *s.* sistema de escritura que usa símbolos en forma de cuña inventado por los sumerios hacia 3000 a.C. (pág. 20)

cyberterrorism [terrorismo cibernético] *s.* ataques por motivos políticos contra sistemas de tecnología informática. (pág. 1088)

Cyrillic alphabet [alfabeto cirílico] *s.* alfabeto inventado en el siglo 9 por los santos Cirilo y Metodio para la escritura de los idiomas eslavos. (pág. 306)

czar [zar] *s.* emperador ruso (de la palabra latina *Caesar*). (pág. 311)

D

daimyo *s.* señor feudal de Japón que comandaba un ejército privado de samurais. (pág. 542)

Daoism [taoísmo] *s.* filosofía basada en las ideas del pensador chino Laozi, quien enseñó a guiarse por una fuerza universal llamada Tao. (pág. 106)

D-Day [Día D] *s.* 6 de junio de 1944; día elegido para la invasión aliada de Europa continental durante la II Guerra Mundial. (pág. 944)

Declaration of Independence [Declaración de Independencia] *s.* declaración de las razones de la ruptura de las colonias americanas con Gran Bretaña, aprobada por el Segundo Congreso Continental. (pág. 641)

delta *s.* zona pantanosa que se forma con los depósitos de légamo en la desembocadura de un río. (pág. 36)

demilitarization [desmilitarización] *s.* reducción de la capacidad bélica de un país que se logra desbandando sus fuerzas armadas y prohibiéndole que adquiera armas. (pág. 950)

democracy [democracia] *s.* gobierno controlado por sus ciudadanos, bien sea directa o indirectamente, por medio de sus representantes. (pág. 128)

democratization [democratización] *s.* proceso de crear un gobierno elegido por el pueblo. (pág. 950)

Department of Homeland Security [Departamento de la Seguridad del Territorio Nacional] *s.* agencia federal estadounidense creada en 2002 para coordinar una estrategia nacional integral contra el terrorismo. (pág. 1091)

détente *s.* política de reducir las tensiones de la Guerra Fría, adoptada por Estados Unidos durante la presidencia de Richard Nixon. (pág. 990)

developed nation [país desarrollado] *s.* nación con las instalaciones necesarias para la producción avanzada de productos manufacturados. (pág. 1075)

devshirme *s.* en el imperio otomano, política de llevarse a los niños de los pueblos cristianos conquistados para entrenarlos como soldados musulmanes. (pág. 510)

Diaspora [diáspora] *s.* dispersión de los judíos fuera de Palestina, especialmente en los más de 1800 años que siguieron a la destrucción romana del Templo de Jerusalén en 70 d.C. (pág. 170)

dictator [dictador] *s.* en la antigua Roma, líder político con poder absoluto para decretar leyes y dirigir el ejército por un tiempo limitado. (pág. 157)

direct democracy [democracia directa] *s.* gobierno en el cual los ciudadanos gobiernan directamente, no a través de sus representantes. (pág. 135)

dissident [disidente] *s.* opositor a la política oficial de un gobierno. (pág. 1042)

divine right [derecho divino] *s.* noción de que los monarcas son representantes de Dios en la Tierra y, por lo tanto, sólo le deben responder a él. (pág. 594)

domestication [domesticación] *s.* entrenamiento de animales para beneficio humano. (pág. 16)

dominion [dominio] *s.* en el imperio británico, una nación (como Canadá) a la que se permitía gobernar sus asuntos internos. (pág. 752)

domino theory [teoría del dominó] *s.* noción de que si una nación cae bajo control comunista, los países vecinos también lo harán. (pág. 978)

Dorians [dorios] *s.* grupo de lengua griega que, según la tradición, emigró a Grecia después de la destrucción de la civilización micénica. (pág. 125)

Dreyfus affair [caso Dreyfus] *s.* controversia surgida en Francia en la década de 1890 por el juicio y encarcelamiento del capitán Alfred Dreyfus, oficial judío falsamente acusado de vender secretos militares a Alemania. (pág. 749)

Dutch East India Company [Compañía Holandesa de las Indias Orientales] *s.* empresa fundada por holandeses a principios del siglo 17 para establecer y dirigir comercio por todo Asia. (pág. 534)

dynastic cycle [ciclo dinástico] *s.* patrón histórico del surgimiento, caída y sustitución de dinastías. (pág. 54)

dynasty [dinastía] *s.* serie de gobernantes de una sola familia. (pág. 31)

E

Eastern Front [Frente Oriental] *s.* en la I Guerra Mundial, región a lo largo de la frontera ruso-alemana donde rusos y servios pelearon contra alemanes, austriacos y turcos. (pág. 848)

Edict of Nantes [Edicto de Nantes] *s.* declaración en que el rey francés Enrique IV prometió que los protestantes podían vivir en paz en Francia y tener centros de veneración en algunas ciudades. (pág. 596)

Emancipation Proclamation [Proclama de Emancipación] *s.* declaración emitida por el presidente Abraham Lincoln en 1862, asentando la libertad de todos los esclavos de los estados confederados. (pág. 760)

emerging nation [nación emergente] *s.* nación en proceso de industrialización cuyo desarrollo no ha terminado todavía. (pág. 1075)

émigré *s.* quien abandona su país de origen por razones políticas, como los nobles y otros que huyeron de Francia durante los levantamientos campesinos de la Revolución Francesa. (pág. 658)

empire [imperio] *s.* unidad política en que un solo gobernante controla varios pueblos o países. (pág. 33)

enclosure [cercado] *s.* uno de los campos rodeados de cercas o de arbustos que crearon terratenientes británicos ricos en tierras que antes trabajaban los campesinos. (pág. 717)

encomienda *s.* tierras otorgadas por España a un colonizador de América, con el derecho de hacer trabajar a los amerindios que vivían en ellas. (pág. 557)

English Civil War [Guerra Civil Inglesa] *s.* conflicto de 1642 a 1649 en que los seguidores puritanos del Parlamento lucharon contra los defensores de la monarquía de Inglaterra. (pág. 615)

enlightened despot [déspota ilustrado] *s.* uno de los monarcas europeos del siglo 18 inspirados por las ideas de la Ilustración a gobernar con justicia y respeto a los derechos de sus súbditos. (pág. 638)

enlightenment [iluminación] *s.* en budismo, estado de perfecta sabiduría en que se entienden las verdades básicas del universo. (pág. 68)

Enlightenment [Ilustración] *s.* movimiento del siglo 18 en Europa que trató de aplicar los principios de la razón y el método científico a todos los aspectos de la sociedad. (pág. 629)

entrepreneur [empresario] *s.* persona que organiza, administra y asume los riesgos de un negocio. (pág. 721)

epic [epopeya] *s.* la poema narrativo extenso que celebran las hazañas de héroes tradicionales o legendarios. (pág. 125)

estate [estado] *s.* una de las tres clases sociales existentes en Francia antes de la Revolución Francesa; el primer estado era el de la clerecía; el segundo era el de la nobleza; y el tercero era del resto de la población. (pág. 651)

Estates-General [Estados Generales] *s.* asamblea de representantes de los tres estados, o clases sociales, de Francia. (págs. 397, 653)

ethnic cleansing [limpia étnica] *s.* política de asesinatos y otros actos de brutalidad con que los servios quisieron eliminar la población musulmana de Bosnia después de la división de Yugoslavia. (pág. 1056)

excommunication [excomunión] *s.* expulsión de una iglesia cristiana. (pág. 306)

existentialism [existencialismo] *s.* filosofía basada en la idea de que el ser humano da significado a su vida con sus decisiones y acciones. (pág. 899)

extraterritorial rights [derechos extraterritoriales] *s.* exención a los extranjeros de las leyes de un país. (pág. 806)

F

factors of production [factores de producción] *s.* recursos —como tierra, mano de obra y capital— necesarios para producir bienes y servicios. (pág. 718)

factory [fábrica] *s.* construcción amplia en que se manufacturan productos con maquinaria. (pág. 720)

fascism [fascismo] *s.* movimiento político que postula una forma extrema de nacionalismo, la supresión de los derechos individuales y un régimen dictatorial de un solo partido. (pág. 910)

Fatimid [fatimitas] *s.* dinastía musulmana cuyos orígenes se remontan a Fátima, hija de Mahoma, y que construyó un imperio en África del Norte, Arabia y Siria en los siglos 9 a 12. (pág. 272)

favorable balance of trade [balanza comercial favorable] *s.* situación económica en la cual un país exporta más de lo que importa, es decir, que vende más productos de los que compra en el extranjero. (pág. 575)

federal system [sistema federal] *s.* sistema de gobierno en el que el poder se divide entre una autoridad central y varios estados. (págs. 645, 1041)

Fertile Crescent [Media Luna Fértil] *s.* arco de ricos terrenos de cultivo en el suroeste de Asia, entre el golfo Pérsico y el mar Mediterráneo. (pág. 29)

feudalism [feudalismo] *s.* sistema político en el cual a los nobles se les otorga el uso de tierras de propiedad del rey, a cambio de lealtad, servicio militar y protección de sus habitantes. (pág. 54)

fief [feudo] *s.* dominio concedido a un vasallo por un señor, conforme al sistema feudal de la Europa medieval. (pág. 360)

filial piety [amor filial] *s.* respeto de los hijos a los padres y a sus mayores. (pág. 104)

"Final Solution" [solución final] *s.* programa de Hitler de asesinar sistemáticamente a todo el pueblo judío. (pág. 937)

Five-Year Plans [Planes de Cinco Años] *s.* planes delineados por José Stalin en 1928 para desarrollar la economía de la Unión Soviética. (pág. 877)

Four Modernizations [cuatro modernizaciones] *s.* serie de objetivos adoptados por el líder chino Deng Xiaoping a finales del siglo 20 con miras al progreso en agricultura, industria, defensa, y ciencia y tecnología. (pág. 1060)

Fourteen Points [los catorce puntos] *s.* serie de propuestas en que el presidente estadounidense Woodrow Wilson esbozó un plan para alcanzar una paz duradera después de la I Guerra Mundial. (pág. 858)

Franks [francos] *s.* pueblo germano que se asentó en la provincia romana de Galia (a grandes rasgos, donde está hoy Francia) y que formó un gran imperio durante la Edad Media. (pág. 354)

free trade [libre comercio] *s.* comercio entre naciones sin restricciones o barreras económicas (tales como aranceles). (pág. 1076)

French and Indian War [Guerra contra Franceses e Indígenas] *s.* conflicto entre Gran Bretaña y Francia por control de territorio en Norteamérica, de 1754 a 1763. (pág. 564)

G

gender inequality [desigualdad de género] *s.* diferencia entre hombres y mujeres con respecto a riqueza y posición social. (pág. 1084)

genetic engineering [ingeniería genética] *s.* transferencia de genes de un organismo a otro para producir un organismo con nuevos rasgos. (pág. 1073)

genocide [genocidio] *s* .matanza sistemática de todo un pueblo. (pág. 937)

gentry [pequeña nobleza] *s.* clase de ricos y poderosos que gozan de alto nivel social. (pág. 327)

geocentric theory [teoría geocéntrica] *s.* teoría de la Edad Media en la que los eruditos creían que la Tierra era objeto fijo, localizado en el centro del universo. (pág. 623)

geopolitics [geopolítica] *s* .política exterior basada en una consideración de la ubicación estratégica o de los productos de otras tierras. (pág. 786)

Ghana *s.* reino de África occidental que se enriqueció debido a recaudación de impuestos y al control del comercio, y que estableció un imperio en los siglos 9 a 11. (pág. 413)

ghazi *s.* guerrero del islam. (pág. 507)

ghettos *s.* barrios en que tenían que vivir los judíos europeos. (pág. 937)

glasnost *s.* política soviética de "apertura" a la libre circulación de ideas e información introducida en 1985 por Mijail Gorbachev. (pág 1046)

global economy [economía global] *s.* todas las interacciones financieras —entre individuos, empresas y gobiernos— que rebasan fronteras internacionales. (pág. 1076)

Glorious Revolution [Revolución Gloriosa] *s.* derrocamiento incruento del rey Jacobo II de Inglaterra, quien fue reemplazado por Guillermo y María. (pág. 616)

glyph [glifo] *s.* dibujo simbólico, especialmente el usado como parte de un sistema de escritura para tallar mensajes en piedra. (pág. 448)

Gothic [gótico] *adj.* relacionado con un nuevo estilo de arquitectura religiosa surgido en la Europa medieval, caracterizado por bóvedas de nervadura, vitrales emplomados, contrafuertes volantes, arcos ojivales y altas agujas. (pág. 380)

Great Depression [Gran Depresión] *s.* crisis económica aguda que siguió a la caída del mercado de valores en 1929. (pág. 907)

Great Fear [Gran Miedo] *s.* ola de temor insensato que se extendió por las provincias francesas después de la toma de la Bastilla en 1789. (pág. 655)

Great Purge [Gran Purga] *s.* campaña de terror en la Unión Soviética durante la década de 1930, en la cual José Stalin trató de eliminar a todos los miembros del Partido Comunista y ciudadanos que amenazaban su poder. (pág. 876)

Great Schism [Gran Cisma] *s.* división de la Iglesia Católica Romana medieval, durante la cual había dos Papas rivales, uno en Avignon y el otro en Roma. (pág. 399)

Greco-Roman culture [cultura greco-romana] *s.* antigua cultura producto de la mezcla de la cultura griega, helénica y romana. (pág. 178)

green revolution [revolución verde] *s.* esfuerzo en el siglo 20 de aumentar los alimentos en el mundo entero, a través del uso de fertilizantes y pesticidas, y de la creación de cultivos resistentes a enfermedades. (pág. 1074)

griot *s.* narrador de África occidental. (pág. 216)

guerrilla [guerrillero] *s.* miembro de una unidad de combate informal que ataca por sorpresa las tropas enemigas que ocupan su país. (pág. 669)

guild [gremio] *s.* asociación medieval de personas que laboraban en lo mismo; controlaba salarios y precios. (pág. 388)

guillotine [guillotina] *s.* máquina para decapitar con que se hicieron ejecuciones durante la Revolución Francesa. (pág. 660)

Gupta Empire [imperio gupta] *s.* el segundo imperio en India, fundado por Chandra Gupta I en el 320 d.C. (pág. 191)

H

habeas corpus *s.* documento que requiere que un detenido comparezca ante un tribunal o juez para que se determine si su detención es legal. (pág. 616)

Hagia Sophia [Santa Sofía] *s.* catedral de la Santa Sabiduría en Constantinopla, construida por orden del emperador bizantino Justiniano. (pág. 303)

haiku *s.* poema japonés que tiene tres versos no rimados de cinco, siete y cinco sílabas. (pág. 545)

hajj *s.* peregrinación a la Meca realizada como deber por los musulmanes. (pág. 267)

Han Dynasty [dinastía Han] *s.* dinastía china que gobernó del 202 a.C. al 9 d.C. y nuevamente del 23 al 220 d.C. (pág. 200)

Harappan civilization [civilización harappa] *s.* nombre alternativo de la civilización del valle del Indo que surgió a lo largo del río Indo, posiblemente hacia 7000 a.C; caracterizada por planificación urbana avanzada. (pág. 46)

Hausa [hausa] *s.* pueblo de África occidental que vivía en varias ciudades Estado en el actual norte de Nigeria. (pág. 417)

heliocentric theory [teoría heliocéntrica] *s.* idea de que la Tierra y los otros planetas giran en torno al Sol. (pág. 624)

Hellenistic [helénico] *adj.* relacionado con la civilización, el idioma, el arte, la ciencia y la literatura del mundo griego a partir del reino de Alejandro el Magno hasta el siglo 2 a.C. (pág. 146)

helot [ilota] *s.* en la antigua Esparta, campesino atado a la tierra. (pág. 129)

hieroglyphics [jeroglíficos] *s.* antiguo sistema de escritura egipcia en el cual se usan imágenes para representar ideas y sonidos. (pág. 40)

Hijrah *s.* migración de Mahoma de la Meca a Yathrib (Medina) en el 622 d.C. (pág. 265)

Hittites [hititas] *s.* pueblo indoeuropeo que se estableció en Anatolia hacia 2000 a.C. (pág. 62)

Holocaust [Holocausto] *s.* matanza en masa de judíos y otros civiles, ejecutada por el gobierno de la Alemania nazi, antes y durante la II Guerra Mundial. (pág. 936)

Holy Alliance [Alianza Sagrada] *s.* liga de naciones europeas formada por los dirigentes de Rusia, Austria y Prusia después del Congreso de Viena. (pág. 674)

Holy Roman Empire [Sacro Imperio Romano] *s.* imperio establecido en Europa en el siglo 10, que inicialmente se formó con tierras de lo que hoy es Alemania e Italia. (pág. 371)

home rule [autogobierno] *s.* control sobre asuntos internos que da el gobierno a los residentes de una región. (pág. 754)

hominid [homínido] *s.* miembro del grupo biológico que abarca a los seres humanos y especies relacionadas que caminan erguidas. (pág. 7)

Homo sapiens *s.* especie biológica de los seres humanos modernos. (pág. 8)

House of Wisdom [Casa de la Sabiduría] *s.* centro de enseñanza en Bagdad en el siglo 9. (pág. 276)

humanism [humanismo] *s.* movimiento intelectual del Renacimiento que estudió los textos clásicos y se enfocó en el potencial y los logros humanos. (pág. 472)

Hundred Days [Cien Días] *s.* corto período de 1815 en que Napoleón hizo su último intento de recuperar el poder, depuso al rey francés y de nuevo se proclamó emperador de Francia. (pág. 671)

Hundred Years' War [Guerra de los Cien Años] *s.* conflicto en el cual Inglaterra y Francia lucharon en territorio francés de 1337 a 1453, con interrupciones. (pág. 401)

hunter-gatherer [cazador-recolector] *s.* miembro de un grupo nómada que se alimenta de la caza de animales y la recolección de frutos. (pág. 14)

Hyksos [hicsos] *s.* grupo nómada de invasores del suroeste de Asia que gobernó Egipto de 1640 a 1570 a.C. (pág. 89)

I

Ice Age [Edad de Hielo] *s.* período de fríos en que enormes capas de hielo se desplazan de las regiones polares; la última fue de aproximadamente 1,900,000 a 10,000 a.C. (pág. 235)

I Ching *s.* libro chino de oráculos consultado para solucionar problemas éticos y prácticos. (pág. 107)

icon [icono] *s.* imagen religiosa usada por los cristianos de Oriente. (pág. 306)

imperialism [imperialismo] *s.* política en que una nación fuerte buscar dominar la vida política, económica y social de otros países. (pág. 773)

impressionism [impresionismo] *s.* movimiento de la pintura del siglo 19 en reacción al realismo, que buscaba dar impresiones personales de sujetos o momentos. (pág. 701)

Indo-Europeans [indoeuropeos] *s.* grupo de pueblos seminómadas que, hacia 1700 a.C., comenzaron a emigrar de lo que es hoy el sur de Rusia al subcontinente hindú, Europa y el suroeste de Asia. (pág. 61)

indulgence [indulgencia] *s.* perdón que libera al pecador de la penitencia por un pecado. (pág. 489)

industrialization [industrialización] *s.* desarrollo de industrias para la producción con máquinas. (pág. 718)

Industrial Revolution [Revolución Industrial] *s.* cambio, que comenzó en Inglaterra durante el siglo 18, de la producción manual a la producción con máquinas. (pág. 717)

inflation [inflación] *s.* baja del valor de la moneda, acompañada de un alza de precios de bienes y servicios. (pág. 173)

Inquisition [Inquisición] *s.* tribunal de la Iglesia Católica para investigar y juzgar a los acusados de herejía, especialmente el establecido en España durante el siglo 15. (pág. 384)

institution [institución] *s.* patrón duradero de organización en una comunidad. (pág. 20)

intendant [intendente] *s.* funcionario del gobierno francés nombrado por el monarca para recaudar impuestos e impartir justicia. (pág. 598)

International Space Station [Estación Espacial Internacional] *s.* colaboración patrocinada por Estados Unidos, Rusia y otras 14 naciones para establecer y mantener un laboratorio activo para realizar experimentos científicos en el espacio. (pág. 1071)

Internet *s.* vinculación de redes de computadora que permite a gente de todo el mundo comunicarse e intercambiar información. (pág. 1073)

intifada [intifada] *s.* campaña palestina de desobediencia civil contra la ocupación israelí de Cisjordania y la Franja de Gaza, que continuó en la década de 1990. (pág. 1021)

Irish Republican Army (IRA) [Ejército Republicano Irlandés (el IRA)] *s.* fuerza paramilitar nacionalista que lucha porque Gran Bretaña dé la independencia la Irlanda del Norte. (pág. 755)

iron curtain [cortina de hierro] *s.* durante la Guerra Fría, división que separaba las naciones comunistas de Europa oriental de las naciones democráticas de Europa occidental. (pág. 967)

Iroquois [iroqueses] *s.* grupo de pueblos amerindios que hablaban lenguas relacionadas, vivían en la parte este de la región de los Grandes Lagos en Norteamérica y formaron una alianza a fines del siglo 16. (pág. 444)

Islam [islam] *s.* religión monoteísta que se desarrolló en Arabia en el siglo 7 d.C. (pág. 265)

isolationism [aislacionismo] *s.* política de evitar lazos políticos o militares con otros países. (pág. 918)

Israel *s.* reino de los hebreos unidos en Palestina, de aproximadamente 1020 a 922 a.C.; después, el reino norte de los dos reinos hebreos; actualmente, la nación judía establecida en Palestina en 1948. (pág. 81)

J

Jainism [jainismo] *s.* religión fundada en India durante el siglo 6, cuyos miembros creen que todo en el universo tiene alma y por lo tanto no debe ser lastimado. (pág. 67)

janissary [janísero] *s.* miembro de una fuerza élite de soldados del imperio otomano. (pág. 510)

jazz *s.* estilo de música popular del siglo 20 concebido principalmente por músicos afroamericanos. (pág. 899)

Jesuits [jesuitas] *s.* miembros de la Sociedad de Jesús, orden católica romana fundada por Ignacio de Loyola. (pág. 499)

"jewel in the crown" ["joya de la corona"] *s.* colonia británica de India, así llamada por su importancia para el imperio británico, tanto como proveedor de materia prima como mercado para sus productos. (pág. 791)

joint-stock company [sociedad de capitales] *s.* negocio en el que los inversionistas reúnen capital para un propósito común y después comparten las ganancias. (pág. 573)

Judah [Judea] *s.* reino hebreo establecido en Palestina alrededor del 922 a.C. (pág. 81)

Justinian Code [Código Justiniano] *s.* cuerpo del derecho civil romano recopilado y organizado por órdenes del emperador bizantino Justiniano hacia el 534 d.C. (pág. 293)

K

kabuki *s.* forma de teatro japonés en que se representa una historia con música, danza y mímica. (pág. 545)

kaiser *s.* emperador alemán (del título romano Caesar). (pág. 697)

kamikaze *s.* durante la II Guerra Mundial, pilotos suicidas japoneses entrenados para hundir barcos de los Aliados lanzándose sobre ellos con aviones llenos de bombas. (pág. 945)

karma *s.* en hinduismo y budismo, la totalidad de actos buenos y malos que comete una persona, que determinan su destino al renacer. (pág. 67)

Khmer Empire [imperio Khmer] *s.* imperio del sureste asiático, centrado en la actual Camboya, que alcanzó su mayor auge hacia 1200 d.C. (pág. 345)

Khmer Rouge *s.* grupo de rebeldes comunistas que tomaron el poder en Camboya en 1975. (pág. 981)

knight [caballero] *s.* en Europa medieval, guerrero con armadura y cabalgadura. (pág. 360)

Koryu Dynasty [dinastía koryu] *s.* dinastía coreana del 935 a 1392 d.C. (pág. 347)

Kristallnacht *s.* "Noche de cristales rotos": noche del 9 de noviembre de 1938, en que milicianos nazis atacaron hogares, negocios y sinagogas judíos en toda Alemania. (pág. 936)

Kuomintang *s.* Partido Nacionalista de China, formado después de la caída de la dinastía Qing en 1912. (pág. 882)

Kush *s.* antiguo reino nubio cuyos reyes gobernaron a Egipto del 751 a 671 a.C. (pág. 92)

L

laissez faire *s.* idea de que el gobierno no debe regular ni interferir en las industrias y empresas. (pág. 734)

land reform [reforma agraria] *s.* redistribución de tierras agrícolas con división de grandes latifundios y reparto de fincas a campesinos. (pág. 1034)

La Reforma *s.* movimiento de reforma liberal en el siglo 19 en México fundado por Benito Juárez. (pág. 824)

lay investiture [investidura seglar] *s.* nombramiento de funcionarios de la Iglesia por reyes y nobles. (pág. 372)

League of Nations [Liga de las Naciones] *s.* organización internacional formada después de la I Guerra Mundial cuyo propósito era mantener la paz entre las naciones. (pág. 859)

lebensraum *s.* "espacio vital": territorio adicional que, según Adolfo Hitler, Alemania necesitaba porque estaba sobrepoblada. (pág. 912)

Legalism [legalismo] *s.* filosofía política china basada en la idea de que un gobierno altamente eficiente y poderoso es la clave del orden social. (pág. 106)

legion [legión] *s.* unidad militar del ejército de la antigua Roma formada por aproximadamente 5,000 soldados de infantería y grupos de soldados de caballería (pág. 157)

Legislative Assembly [Asamblea Legislativa] *s.* congreso creado por la Constitución francesa de 1791, con poder para emitir leyes y aprobar declaraciones de guerra. (pág. 657)

legitimacy [legitimidad] *s.* derecho hereditario de un monarca a gobernar. (pág. 673)

liberal [liberale] *s.* en la primera mitad del siglo 19, europeo—principalmente empresarios y comerciantes de clase media— que deseaba darle más poder político a los parlamentos elegidos. (pág. 687)

lineage [linaje] *s.* individuos —vivos, muertos y sin nacer— que descienden de un antepasado común. (pág. 410)

loess [loes] *s.* depósito fértil de tierra traída por el viento. (pág. 50)

Long March [Larga Marcha] *s.* viaje de 6,000 millas que realizaron en 1934–35 las fuerzas comunistas de China para escapar de las fuerzas nacionalistas de Jiang Jieshi. (pág. 886)

lord [señor] *s.* en la Europa feudal, persona que controlaba tierras y por lo tanto podía dar feudos a vasallos. (pág. 360)

Lutheran [luterano] *s.* miembro de una iglesia protestante basada en las enseñanzas de Martín Lutero. (pág. 490)

lycée [liceo] *s.* escuela pública en Francia. (pág. 664)

M

Macedonia *s.* antiguo reino del norte de Grecia, cuyo rey Felipe II conquistó a Grecia en 338 a.C. (pág. 142)

Maghrib [Maghreb] *s.* región del norte de África que abarca la costa del Mediterráneo de lo que en la actualidad es Marruecos, Túnez y Argelia. (pág. 410)

Magna Carta [Carta Magna] *s.* "Gran Carta": documento de Inglaterra que garantiza derechos políticos elementales, elaborado por nobles ingleses y aprobado por el rey Juan en 1215 d.C. (pág. 394)

Mahabharata *s.* gran poema épico de India que relata las luchas arias durante su migración al sur de India. (pág. 64)

Mahayana *s.* secta del budismo que ofrece la salvación a todos y permite la veneración popular. (pág. 193)

maize [maíz] *s.* cereal cultivado cuyos granos se encuentran en grandes espigas, o mazorcas. (pág. 238)

Mali *s.* imperio de África occidental que floreció entre 1235 y el siglo 15, y se enriqueció con el comercio. (pág. 415)

Manchus [manchú] *s.* pueblo originario de Manchuria que gobernó en China durante la dinastía Qing (1644–1912). (pág. 539)

Mandate of Heaven [Mandato del Cielo] *s.* en China, creencia de que la autoridad real era producto de la aprobación divina. (pág. 54)

manifest destiny [destino manifiesto] *s.* idea popular en el siglo 19 en Estados Unidos de que era su derecho y obligación regir Norteamérica, desde el océano Atlántico hasta el Pacífico. (pág. 758)

manor [señorío] *s.* dominios de un señor en la Europa feudal. (pág. 360)

Maori [maorí] *s.* miembro de un pueblo polinesio establecido en Nueva Zelanda hacia 800 d.C. (pág. 752)

Marshall Plan [Plan Marshall] programa estadounidense de ayuda económica a países europeos para su reconstrucción después de la II Guerra Mundial. (pág. 968)

martial law [ley marcial] *s.* gobierno militar temporal impuesto a la población civil, normalmente en época de guerra o de trastornos civiles. (pág. 1041)

mass culture [cultura de masas] *s.* producción de obras de arte y diversión concebidas con el fin de atraer a un amplio público. (pág. 766)

materialism [materialismo] *s.* alto interés en la adquisición de posesiones materiales. (pág. 1096)

matriarchal [matriarcal] *adj.* relacionado con un sistema social en el que la madre es jefa de la familia. (pág. 192)

matrilineal *adj.* relacionado con un sistema social en el que la descendencia familiar y los derechos de herencia se trasmiten a través de la madre. (pág. 410)

Mauryan Empire [imperio maurio] *s.* primer imperio de India, fundado por Chandragupta Mauria en 321 a.C. (pág. 189)

May Fourth Movement [Movimiento del 4 de Mayo] *s.* protesta nacional china en 1919 con manifestaciones contra el Tratado de Versalles y la interferencia extranjera. (pág. 883)

Medes [medos] *s.* pueblo del suroeste asiático que contribuyó a derrotar al imperio asirio. (pág. 97)

Meiji era [era Meiji] *s.* período de la historia japonesa entre 1867 y 1912, cuando gobernó el emperador Mutshito. (pág. 811)

Mein Kampf *[Mi lucha]* *s.* libro escrito por Adolfo Hitler en prisión (1923–1924), en el cual expone sus creencias y sus ideales para Alemania. (pág. 912)

mercantilism [mercantilismo] *s.* política económica de aumentar la riqueza y poder de una nación obteniendo grandes cantidades de oro y plata, y vendiendo más bienes de los que se compran. (pág. 574)

mercenary [mercenario] *s.* soldado que recibe sueldo por pelear en un ejército extranjero. (pág. 173)

Meroë [Meroe] *s.* centro de la dinastía Kush de aproximadamente 250 a.C. a 150 d.C.; conocido por su manufactura de armas de hierro y herramientas. (pág. 94)

Mesoamerica [Mesoamérica] *s.* región que se extiende desde el centro de México hasta Honduras, donde se desarrollaron varias de las antiguas sociedades complejas de América. (pág. 240)

mestizo *s.* mezcla de español y amerindio. (pág. 557)

Middle Ages [Edad Media] *s.* era en la historia europea posterior a la caída del imperio romano, que abarca aproximadamente desde el 500 hasta 1500, también llamada época medieval. (pág. 353)

middle class [clase media] *s.* clase social formada por trabajadores especializados, profesionales, comerciantes y granjeros acaudalados. (pág. 725)

middle passage [travesía intermedia] *s.* viaje que trajo a africanos capturados al Caribe y, posteriormente, a América del Norte y del Sur, para venderlos como esclavos; recibió este nombre porque era considerada la porción media del triángulo comercial trasatlántico. (pág. 569)

migration [migración] *s.* acto de trasladarse de un lugar para establecerse en otro. (págs. 62, 220)

militarism [militarismo] *s.* política de glorificar el poder militar y de mantener un ejército permanente, siempre preparado para luchar. (pág. 842)

Ming Dynasty [dinastía Ming] *s.* dinastía que reinó en China desde 1368 hasta 1644. (pág. 536)

Minoans [minoicos] *s.* pueblo de navegantes y comerciantes que vivió en la isla de Creta de aproximadamente 2000 a 1400 a.C. (pág. 72)

Mississippian [misisipiense] *adj.* relacionado con una cultura constructora de túmulos que floreció en Norteamérica entre el 800 y 1500 d.C. (pág. 443)

mita *s.* en el imperio inca, obligación de todo súbdito de trabajar ciertos días al año para el Estado. (pág. 461)

Moche [moche] *s.* civilización que floreció en la actual costa norte de Perú de aproximadamente 100 a 700 d.C. (pág. 247)

monarchy [monarquía] *s.* gobierno en que el poder está en manos de una sola persona. (pág. 127)

monastery [monasterio] *s.* comunidad religiosa de hombres, llamados monjes, que ceden todas sus posesiones y se dedican a la oración y veneración. (pág. 354)

monopoly [monopolio] *s.* control exclusivo sobre la producción y distribución de ciertos bienes. (pág. 204)

monotheism [monoteísmo] *s.* creencia en un solo dios. (pág. 78)

Monroe Doctrine [doctrina Monroe] *s.* política estadounidense de oposición a la interferencia europea en Latinoamérica, anunciada por el presidente James Monroe en 1823. (pág. 818)

monsoon [monzón] *s.* viento que cambia de dirección en ciertas épocas del año. (pág. 45)

mosque [mezquita] *s.* lugar de veneración islámica. (pág. 267)

movable type [tipo móvil] *s.* bloques de metal o de madera, cada uno con caracteres individuales, que pueden distribuirse para formar una página de impresión. (pág. 325)

Mughal [mogol] *s.* uno de los nómadas que invadieron el subcontinente de India en el siglo 16 y establecieron un poderoso imperio. (pág. 516)

mujahideen [muyahidin] *s.* guerreros religiosos afganos que se unieron para luchar contra el gobierno apoyado por los soviéticos a fines de la década de 1970. (pág. 1026)

mulattos [mulatos] *s.* personas de ascendencia europea y africana. (pág. 682)

mummification [momificación] *s.* proceso de embalsamamiento y secado de cadáveres para evitar su descomposición. (pág. 38)

Munich Conference [Conferencia de Munich] *s.* reunión en 1938 de Inglaterra, Francia, Italia y Alemania, en la cual Gran Bretaña y Francia aceptaron que la Alemania nazi anexara parte de Checoslovaquia, a cambio de la promesa de Adolfo Hitler de respetar las nuevas fronteras checas. (pág. 919)

Muslim [musulmán] *s.* devoto del islam. (pág. 265)

Muslim League [Liga Musulmana] *s.* organización formada en 1906 para proteger los intereses de los musulmanes de India; después propuso la división del país en dos naciones: una musulmana y una hindú. (pág. 997)

Mutapa [mutapa] *adj.* con un imperio de África del sur establecido por Mutota en el siglo 15 a.D. (pág. 427)

Mycenaean [micénicos] *s.* el indoeuropeo que se estableció en Grecia hacia 2000 a.C. (pág. 124)

myth [mito] *s.* la narracion tradicional sobre dioses, antepasados o héroes, que explican el mundo natural o las costumbres y creencias de una sociedad. (pág. 126)

N

Napoleonic Code [código napoleónico] *s.* sistema extenso y uniforme de leyes establecido para Francia por Napoleón. (pág. 664)

National Assembly [Asamblea Nacional] *s.* congreso francés establecido el 17 de junio de 1789 por representantes del Tercer Estado para promulgar leyes y reformas en nombre del pueblo. (pág. 654)

nationalism [nacionalismo] *s.* creencia de que la principal lealtad del pueblo debe ser a su nación —es decir, a la gente con quien comparte historia y cultura— y no al rey o al imperio. (pág. 687)

nation-state [nación Estado] *s.* nación independiente de gente que tiene una cultura e identidad común. (pág. 687)

NATO [OTAN] *s.* Organización del Tratado del Atlántico Norte: alianza militar defensiva formada en 1949 por diez naciones de Europa occidental, Estados Unidos y Canadá. (pág. 969)

Nazca [nazca] *s.* civilización que floreció en la actual costa sur de Perú de 200 a.C. a 600 d.C. (pág. 247)

Nazism [nazismo] *s.* políticas fascistas del Partido Nacional socialista de los Trabajadores de Alemania, basadas en el totalitarismo, la creencia en superioridad racial y el control estatal de la industria. (pág. 912)

Negritude movement [movimiento de negritud] *s.* movimiento de africanos de lengua francesa que celebra el legado de la cultura tradicional africana y sus valores. (pág. 1012)

neoclassical [neoclásico] *adj.* relacionado con un estilo sencillo y elegante (inspirado en ideas y temas de la antigua Grecia y Roma) que caracterizó las artes en Europa a fines del siglo 18. (pág. 637)

Neolithic Age [Neolítico] *s.* período prehistórico que comenzó aproximadamente en 8000 a.C. y en algunas partes acabó desde 3000 a.C., durante el cual los grupos humanos aprendieron a pulir herramientas de piedra, hacer cerámica, cultivar alimentos y criar animales; también se llama Nueva Edad de Piedra. (pág. 7)

Neolithic Revolution [Revolución Neolítica] *s.* gran cambio en la vida humana causada por los comienzos de la agricultura; es decir, el cambio de recolectar a producir alimentos. (pág. 15)

New Deal *s.* programa de reformas económicas del presidente Franklin D. Roosevelt ideado para solucionar los problemas creados por la Gran Depresión. (pág. 909)

New Kingdom [Reino Nuevo] *s.* período de la historia del antiguo Egipto tras la caída de los gobernantes hicsos, desde 1570 hasta 1075 a.C. (pág. 90)

nirvana *s.* en budismo, la liberación del dolor y el sufrimiento alcanzada después de la iluminación. (pág. 69)

Nok [nok] *s.* pueblo africano que vivió en lo que es hoy Nigeria entre 500 a.C. y 200 d.C. (pág. 217)

nomad [nómada] *s.* miembro de un grupo que no tiene hogar permanente y que va de un lugar a otro en busca de agua y alimento. (pág. 14)

nonaggression pact [pacto de no agresión] *s.* acuerdo en que dos o más naciones prometen no atacarse. (pág. 925)

nonaligned nations [países no alineados] *s.* naciones independientes que permanecieron neutrales durante la Guerra Fría entre Estados Unidos y la Unión Soviética. (pág. 982)

Nuremberg Trials [juicios de Nuremberg] *s.* serie de juicios realizados en Nuremberg, Alemania, tras la II Guerra Mundial a líderes nazis por agresión, violación a las leyes de guerra y crímenes contra la humanidad. (pág. 950)

O

obsidian [obsidiana] *s.* roca volcánica dura y vítrea con que los primeros seres humanos elaboraban herramientas de piedra. (pág. 453)

Old Regime [antiguo régimen] *s.* sistema político y social que existía en Francia antes de la Revolución Francesa. (pág. 651)

oligarchy [oligarquía] *s.* gobierno en que el poder está en manos de pocas personas, particularmente un gobierno que se basa en la riqueza. (pág. 127)

Olmec [olmeca] *s.* civilización mesoamericana más antigua que se conoce, que floreció hacia 1200 a.C. e influyó sobre las posteriores sociedades de la región. (pág. 240)

Open Door Policy [política de puertas abiertas] *s.* política propuesta por E.U.A. en 1899, que postulaba que todas las naciones tuvieran las mismas oportunidades de comerciar con China. (pág. 808)

Opium War [Guerra del Opio] *s.* conflicto entre Inglaterra y China, de 1839 a 1842, por el comercio inglés de opio en China. (pág. 806)

oracle bone [hueso de oráculo] *s.* hueso de animal o caparazón de tortuga que usaban los antiguos sacerdotes chinos para comunicarse con los dioses. (pág. 53)

Oslo Peace Accords [Acuerdos de Paz de Oslo] *s.* acuerdos de 1993 cuando el primer ministro israelí, Rabin, otorgó autonomía a Palestina en la Franja de Gaza y Cisjordania. (pág. 1021)

ozone layer [capa de ozono] *s.* capa de la atmósfera superior de la Tierra que protege a los seres vivos de los rayos ultravioleta de la luz solar. (pág. 1079)

P

Pacific Rim [Cuenca del Pacífico] *s.* tierras que bordean el océano Pacífico, especialmente las de Asia. (pág. 796)

Paleolithic Age [Paleolítico] *s.* período prehistórico que abarcó aproximadamente desde 2.5 millones hasta 8000 a.C., durante el cual los seres humanos hicieron rudimentarias herramientas y armas de piedra; también se llama Antigua Edad de Piedra. (pág. 7)

Panama Canal [canal de Panamá] *s.* vía marítima que une al océano Atlántico con el Pacífico, construida en Panamá por Estados Unidos y terminada en 1914. (pág. 821)

papyrus [papiro] *s.* carrizo alto que crece en el delta del Nilo, usado por los antiguos egipcios para hacer hojas de escribir similares al papel. (pág. 40)

parliament [parlamento] *s.* cuerpo de representantes que promulga las leyes de una nación. (pág. 395)

partition [partición] *s.* división en partes, como la división en 1947 de la colonia británica de India en dos naciones: India y Paquistán. (pág. 998)

pastoralist [pastor] *s.* miembro de un grupo nómada que pastorea rebaños de animales domesticados. (pág. 330)

paternalism [paternalismo] *s.* política de tratar a los gobernados como si fueran niños, atendiendo a sus necesidades pero sin darles derechos. (pág. 781)

patriarch [patriarca] *s.* obispo principal de la rama oriental de la cristiandad. (pág. 306)

patriarchal [patriarcal] *adj.* relacionado con un sistema social en el que el padre es jefe de la familia. (pág. 192)

patrician [patricio] *s.* en la antigua Roma, miembro de la clase alta, privilegiada y rica. (pág. 156)

patrilineal [patrilineal] *adj.* relacionado con un sistema social en el que la descendencia y los derechos de herencia se trasmiten a través del padre. (pág. 410)

patron [mecenas] *s.* persona que apoya a los artistas, especialmente, en el aspecto financiero. (pág. 472)

Pax Mongolica [Paz Mongólica] *s.* período de mediados de 1200 a mediados de 1300 d.C., cuando los mongoles impusieron estabilidad y orden público en casi toda Eurasia. (pág. 333)

Pax Romana *s.* período de paz y prosperidad por todo el imperio romano, de 27 a.C. a 180 d.C. (pág. 162)

Spanish Glossary

Peace of Augsburg [Paz de Augsburgo] *s.* acuerdo realizado en 1555 que declaró que la religión de cada Estado alemán sería decidida por su gobernante. (pág. 492)

Peloponnesian War [Guerra del Peloponeso] *s.* guerra de 431 a 404 a.C., en la cual Atenas y sus aliados resultaron derrotados por Esparta y sus aliados. (pág. 137)

penal colony [colonia penal] *s.* colonia a donde se mandan convictos como alternativa a una prisión. (pág. 752)

peninsulares *s.* en la sociedad española colonial, colonos nacidos en España. (pág. 681)

Peninsular War [Guerra Peninsular] *s.* conflicto de 1808–1813 en que los rebeldes españoles lucharon con la ayuda de Gran Bretaña para expulsar de España las tropas de Napoleón. (pág. 669)

perestroika *s.* reestructuración de la economía soviética para permitir mayor poder de decisión local, iniciada por Mijail Gorbachev en 1985. (pág. 1047)

Persian Gulf War [Guerra del Golfo Pérsico] *s.* conflicto de 1991 en el que las fuerzas de la ONU derrotaron a fuerzas iraquíes que invadieron a Kuwait y amenazaban con invadir a Arabia Saudita. (pág. 1079)

Persian Wars [Guerras Pérsicas] *s.* guerras del siglo 5 a.C. entre las ciudades Estado de Grecia y el imperio persa. (pág. 131)

perspective [perspectiva] *s.* técnica artística que crea la apariencia de tres dimensiones en una superficie plana. (pág. 474)

phalanx [falange] *s.* formación militar de soldados de infantería armados con lanzas y escudos. (pág. 131)

pharaoh [faraón] *s.* rey del antiguo Egipto, considerado dios, así como líder político y militar. (pág. 37)

philosophe *s.* miembro de un grupo de pensadores sociales de la Ilustración en Francia. (pág. 630)

philosophers [filósofos] *s.* pensadores que investigan la naturaleza del universo, la sociedad humana y la moral a través de la lógica y la razón. (pág. 138)

Phoenicians [fenicios] *s.* pueblo de navegantes del suroeste de Asia, que aproximadamente en 1100 a.C. comenzó a comerciar y a fundar colonias en la región mediterránea. (pág. 73)

Pilgrims [peregrinos] *s.* grupo que en 1620 fundó la colonia de Plymouth en Massachusetts para escapar de persecución religiosa en Inglaterra. (pág. 562)

plebeian [plebeyo] *s.* en la antigua Roma, uno de los agricultores, artesanos o comerciantes comunes que conformaban la mayoría de la población. (pág. 156)

plebiscite [plebiscito] *s.* voto directo mediante el cual la población de un país tiene la oportunidad de aceptar o rechazar una propuesta. (pág. 664)

PLO [OLP] *s.* Organización de Liberación Palestina: organización dedicada a establecer un Estado independiente para los palestinos en el Medio Oriente. (pág. 1019)

polis *s.* ciudad Estado de Grecia; unidad política fundamental de la antigua Grecia a partir de 750 a.C. (pág. 127)

Politburo [Politburó] *s.* comité dirigente del Partido Comunista en la Unión Soviética. (pág. 1046)

political dissent [disidencia política] *s.* diferencia de opiniones sobre asuntos políticos. (pág. 1084)

polytheism [politeísmo] *s.* creencia en muchos dioses. (pág. 31)

pope [Papa] *s.* obispo de Roma y dirigente de la Iglesia Católica Romana. (pág. 171)

Popol Vuh *s.* libro que narra una versión de la historia maya de la creación. (pág. 448)

popular culture [cultura popular] *s.* elementos culturales—deportes, música, cine, ropa, etc.—que muestran los antecedentes comunes de un grupo y sus intereses cambiantes. (pág. 1093)

potlatch *s.* fiesta ceremonial celebrada para mostrar rango y prosperidad en varias tribus del Noroeste de Norteamérica. (pág. 441)

predestination [predestinación] *s.* doctrina que postula que Dios ha decidido todo de antemano, incluso quiénes obtendrán la salvación eterna. (pág. 495)

Presbyterian [presbiteriano] *s.* miembro de una iglesia protestante gobernada por presbíteros conforme a las enseñanzas de John Knox. (pág. 496)

PRI *s.* Partido Revolucionario Institucional: principal partido político en México. (pág. 1037)

proletariat [proletariado] *s.* según la teoría marxista, el grupo de trabajadores que derrocaría al zar y gobernaría a Rusia. (pág. 868)

proliferation [proliferación] *s.* crecimiento o expansión, especialmente la expansión de armas nucleares a naciones que actualmente no las tienen. (pág. 1083)

propaganda *s.* información o material distribuido para apoyar una causa o socavar una causa opuesta. (pág. 854)

Protestant [protestante] *s.* miembro de una iglesia cristiana fundada de acuerdo a los principios de la Reforma. (pág. 490)

provisional government [gobierno provisional] *s.* gobierno temporal. (pág. 870)

psychology [psicología] *s.* estudio de la mente y la conducta humanas. (pág. 766)

pueblos *s.* aldeas similares a complejos departamentales hechos de adobe, construidas por los anasazi y pueblos posteriores en el Suroeste de lo que hoy es Estados Unidos. (pág. 443)

Punic Wars [Guerras Púnicas] *s.* serie de tres guerras entre Roma y Cartago (264–146 a.C.); el resultado fue la destrucción de Cartago y la dominación romana de toda la región mediterránea occidental. (pág. 158)

Puritans [puritanos] *s.* grupo que, para liberarse de la persecución religiosa en Inglaterra, fundó una colonia en la bahía de Massachusetts a principios del siglo 17. (pág. 562)

push-pull factors [factores de empuje y de atracción] *s.* factores que hacen que la gente abandone sus hogares y emigre a otra región (factores de empuje); o factores que atraen a la gente a otros lugares (factores de atracción). (pág. 220)

pyramid [pirámide] *s.* enorme estructura de base rectangular y cuatro lados triangulares, como las que servían de tumba de los faraones del Reino Antiguo de Egipto. (pág. 37)

Q

Qin dynasty [dinastía Qin] *s.* dinastía china que reinó brevemente y sustituyó a la dinastía Zhou en el siglo 3 a.C. (pág. 107)

Qing dynasty [dinastía Qing] *s.* última dinastía china; reinó de 1644 a 1912. (pág. 539)

Quetzalcoatl [Quetzalcóatl] *s.* serpiente emplumada: dios de los toltecas y otros pueblos de Mesoamérica. (pág. 453)

quipu *s.* cuerda con nudos usadas para registrar información numérica por los incas. (pág. 461)

Qur'an [Corán] *s.* libro sagrado del islam. (pág. 267)

R

racism [racismo] *s.* creencia de que una raza es superior a otras. (pág. 775)

radical [radicale] *s.* en la primera mitad del siglo 19, el europeo a favor de cambios drásticos para extender la democracia a toda la población. (pág. 687)

radioactivity [radioactividad] *s.* forma de energía liberada mediante la descomposición de átomos. (pág. 765)

Raj *s.* la autoridad británica despues que India estaba bajo el dominio del la Corona británica durante el reino de la reina Victoria. (pág. 794)

rationing [racionamiento] *s.* limitación de la cantidad de bienes que la población puede comprar, generalmente impuesta por un gobierno durante una guerra debido a escasez. (pág. 854)

realism [realismo] *s.* movimiento artístico del siglo 19 en que los escritores y pintores trataron de mostrar la vida como es, no como debiera ser. (pág. 700)

realpolitik *s.* "política de la realidad"; posición política dura que no da lugar al idealismo. (pág. 695)

recession [recesión] *s.* descenso de la economía de una nación. (pág. 1034)

Reconquista *s.* campaña de líderes cristianos para expulsar a los musulmanes de España, que empezó en el siglo 12 y terminó en 1492. (pág. 384)

Red Guards [Guardias Rojos] *s.* unidades de milicianos formadas por jóvenes chinos en 1966 en respuesta al llamado de Mao Zedong a llevar a cabo una revolución social y cultural. (pág. 975)

Reformation [Reforma] *s.* movimiento del siglo 16 para realizar cambios religiosos que llevó a la fundación de iglesias cristianas que rechazaron la autoridad del Papa. (pág. 489)

refugee [refugiado] *s.* persona que sale de su país a otro país para buscar seguridad. (pág. 1086)

Reign of Terror [Régimen del Terror] *s.* período entre 1793–1794 en que Maximilien Robespierre gobernó a Francia casi como dictador, durante el cual fueron ejecutados miles de personajes políticos y de ciudadanos comunes. (pág. 660)

reincarnation [reencarnación] *s.* en hinduismo y budismo, creencia de que el alma renace una y otra vez hasta alcanzar un conocimiento perfecto. (pág. 67)

religious toleration [tolerancia religiosa] *s.* reconocimiento del derecho de otros a tener creencias religiosas diferentes. (pág. 190)

Renaissance [Renacimiento] *s.* período de la historia europea de aproximadamente 1300 a 1600, durante el cual renació un interés en la cultura clásica que generó importantes cambios en el arte, la educación y la visión del mundo. (pág. 471)

republic [república] *s.* forma de gobierno en que el poder está en manos de representantes y líderes elegidos por los ciudadanos. (pág. 156)

Restoration [Restauración] *s.* en Inglaterra, período del reinado de Carlos II, después del colapso del gobierno de Oliver Cromwell. (pág. 616)

reunification [reunificación] *s.* proceso de unir dos elementos que estaban separados, como la reunificación de Alemania oriental y Alemania occidental en 1990. (pág. 1054)

romanticism [romanticismo] *s.* movimiento de principios del siglo 19 en el arte y las ideas que recalca la emoción y la naturaleza, más que la razón y la sociedad. (pág. 698)

Roosevelt Corollary [corolario Roosevelt] *s.* ampliación de la doctrina Monroe, emitida por el presidente Theodore Roosevelt en 1904, en que declaró que Estados Unidos tenía el derecho de ejercer "poderes policiales" en el hemisferio occidental. (pág. 821)

Rowlatt Acts [Leyes Rowlatt] *s.* leyes, ratificadas en 1919, que los permitían al gobierno británico en India encarcelar a manifestantes por dos años sin juicio. (pág. 887)

Royal Road [Camino Real] *s.* carretera de más de 1,600 millas que cruzaba el imperio persa, desde Susa en Persia hasta Sardes en Anatolia. (pág. 101)

Russification [rusificación] *s.* proceso que obliga a todos los grupos étnicos a adoptar la cultura rusa en el imperio ruso. (pág. 693)

Russo-Japanese War [Guerra Ruso-Japonesa] *s.* conflicto de 1904–1905 entre Rusia y Japón, causada por el interés de los dos países de dominar Manchuria y Corea. (pág. 812)

S

sacrament [sacramento] *s.* una de las ceremonias cristianas en que se trasmite la gracia de Dios a los creyentes. (pág. 371)

Safavid [safávido] *s.* miembro de una dinastía musulmana shi'a que construyó un imperio en Persia del siglo 16 al 18. (pág. 512)

Sahel *s.* región africana a lo largo de la frontera sur del Sahara. (pág. 213)

salon [salón] *s.* reunión social de intelectuales y artistas, como las que celebraban en sus hogares señoras acaudaladas de París y otras ciudades europeas durante la Ilustración. (pág. 636)

SALT *s.* Conversaciones para la Limitación de Armas Estratégicas: serie de reuniones durante la década de 1970 en que líderes de Estados Unidos y la Unión Soviética acordaron limitar el número de armas nucleares de sus países. (pág. 989)

Salt March [Marcha de la Sal] *s.* manifestación pacífica en 1930 en India ocasionada por las Leyes de la Sal; Mohandas Gandhi condujo a sus seguidores, caminando 240 millas al mar, donde hicieron su propia sal del agua de mar evaporada. (pág. 889)

samurai *s.* guerrero profesional que servía a los nobles en el Japón feudal. (pág. 343)

sans-culottes *s.* en la Revolución Francesa, grupo político radical de parisienses asalariados y pequeños comerciantes que anhelaban más voz en el gobierno, bajas de precios y fin a la escasez de alimentos. (pág. 658)

satrap [sátrapa] *s.* gobernador de una provincia en el imperio persa. (pág. 101)

savanna [sabana] *s.* planicie con pastizales. (pág. 215)

Schlieffen Plan [Plan Schlieffen] *s.* plan militar alemán al comienzo de la I Guerra Mundial, que preveía que Alemania derrotaría rápidamente a Francia y después atacaría a Rusia en el este. (pág. 846)

scholastics [escolásticos] *s.* académicos que se reunían y enseñaban en las universidades medievales de Europa. (pág. 392)

scientific method [método científico] *s.* procedimiento lógico para reunir información sobre el mundo natural, en que se usa experimentación y observación para poner a prueba hipótesis. (pág. 625)

Scientific Revolution [Revolución Científica] *s.* profundo cambio en el pensamiento europeo que comenzó a mediados del siglo 16, en que el estudio del mundo natural se caracterizó por cuidadosa observación y cuestionamiento de teorías aceptadas. (pág. 623)

scorched-earth policy [política de arrasamiento de campos] *s.* práctica de quemar campos de cultivo y de matar ganado durante la guerra para que el enemigo no pueda vivir de las tierras. (pág. 669)

scribe [escriba] *s.* profesional especializado en llevar registros en las civilizaciones tempranas. (pág. 20)

secede [seceder] *v.* retirarse formalmente de una asociación o alianza. (pág. 760)

secular *adj.* relacionado con lo mundano más que con los asuntos espirituales. (págs. 355, 472)

segregation [segregación] *s.* separación legal o social de gente de diferentes razas. (pág. 761)

self-determination [autodeterminación] *s.* libertad de un pueblo para decidir libremente la forma de gobierno que desea. (pág. 858)

Seljuks [seljucs] *s.* grupo turco que emigró al imperio abasida en el siglo 10 y estableció su propio imperio en el siglo 11. (pág. 315)

senate [senado] *s.* en la antigua Roma, organismo supremo de gobierno formado inicialmente sólo por aristócratas. (pág. 157)

sepoy [cipayo] *s.* soldado hindú bajo el mando británico. (pág. 791)

Sepoy Mutiny [Motín de Cipayos] *s.* rebelión de 1857 de soldados hindúes y musulmanes contra los británicos en India. (pág. 793)

serf [siervo] *s.* campesino medieval legalmente obligado a vivir en los dominios de un señor. (pág. 360)

Seven Years' War [Guerra de los Siete Años] *s.* conflicto en Europa, Norteamérica e India de 1756 a 1763, en que las fuerzas de Inglaterra y Prusia lucharon con las de Austria, Francia, Rusia y otros países. (pág. 607)

shah [sha] *s.* monarca hereditario de Irán. (pág. 513)

shari'a *s.* conjunto de leyes que rigen la vida de los musulmanes. (pág. 268)

Shi'a [shi'a] *s.* rama del islam que reconoce a los primeros cuatro califas como legítimos sucesores de Mahoma. (pág. 271)

Shinto [shintoísmo] *s.* religión oriunda de Japón. (pág. 339)

Shiva *s.* dios hindú considerado destructor del mundo. (pág. 194)

"shock therapy" [terapia de shock] *s.* programa económico implementado en Rusia por Boris Yeltsin en la década de 1990, que implicó un cambio abrupto de una economía de mando a una economía de mercado libre. (pág. 1050)

shogun [shogún] *s.* en el Japón feudal, jefe militar supremo que regía en nombre del emperador. (pág. 343)

Sikh [sikh] *s.* miembro de un grupo religioso no violento cuyas creencias combinaban elementos del budismo, el hinduismo y el sufismo. (pág. 518)

Silk Roads [Ruta de la Seda] *s.* sistema de antiguas rutas de las caravanas por Asia central, por las que se transportaban seda y otros productos comerciales. (pág. 196)

simony [simonía] *s.* venta o compra de una posición en una iglesia cristiana. (pág. 379)

skepticism [escepticismo] *s.* filosofía basada en la noción de que nada puede saberse con certeza. (pág. 597)

slash-and-burn farming [agricultura de tala y quema] *s.* método agrícola de desbrozar terrenos talando y quemando árboles y pastos, cuyas cenizas sirven como fertilizante. (pág. 15)

Slavs [eslavos] *s.* pueblo de los bosques al norte del mar Negro, origen de muchos pueblos de la Europa oriental de nuestros días. (pág. 307)

social contract [contrato social] *s.* acuerdo mediante el cual el pueblo define y limita sus derechos individuales, creando así una sociedad o gobierno organizados. (pág. 629)

Social Darwinism [darvinismo social] *s.* aplicación de las teorías de Charles Darwin sobre la evolución y la "sobrevivencia del más apto" a las sociedades humanas, particularmente como justificación para la expansión imperialista. (pág. 775)

socialism [socialismo] *s.* sistema económico en el cual los factores de producción son propiedad del pueblo y se administran para el bienestar de todos. (pág. 736)

Solidarity [Solidaridad] *s.* sindicato polaco de trabajadores que presentó la principal fuerza de oposición al gobierno comunista en Polonia en la década de 1980. (pág. 1052)

Songhai *s.* imperio de África occidental que conquistó Malí y controló el comercio desde el siglo 15 hasta 1591. (pág. 417)

soviet *s.* consejo local de representantes formado en Rusia después de la caída del zar Nicolás II. (pág. 870)

Spanish-American War [Guerra Hispano-Americana] *s.* conflicto de 1898 entre Estados Unidos y España, en que Estados Unidos apoyó la lucha de independencia cubana. (pág. 818)

specialization [especialización] *s.* desarrollo de conocimientos para realizar determinado trabajo, como comerciar o llevar registros. (pág. 20)

sphere of influence [esfera de influencia] *s.* región extranjera en que una nación controla el comercio y otras actividades económicas. (pág. 807)

standard of living [nivel de vida] *s.* calidad de la vida de una persona o población que se mide conforme a los bienes, servicios y lujos que tiene a su disposición. (pág. 1034)

stateless societies [sociedades sin Estado] *s.* grupos culturales en los que la autoridad es compartida por linajes de igual poder, en vez de ser ejercida por un gobierno central. (pág. 410)

steppes [estepas] *s.* llanuras secas de pastizales. (pág. 61)

strike [huelga] *s.* paro de trabajo para obligar al patrón a acceder a ciertas demandas. (pág. 738)

stupa *s.* estructuras de piedra en forma de cúpula, construidas sobre reliquias budistas sagradas. (pág. 193)

subcontinent [subcontinente] *s.* gran masa que forma una parte claramente diferenciada de un continente. (pág. 44)

Suez Canal [canal de Suez] *s.* canal marítimo que une al mar Rojo y al golfo de Suez con el mar Mediterráneo, cuya construcción terminó en 1869. (pág. 788)

suffrage [sufragio] *s.* derecho al voto. (pág. 747)

Sufi [sufí] *s.* musulmán que busca contacto directo con Dios por medio del misticismo. (pág. 271)

sultan [sultán] *s.* "jefe supremo" o "el que tiene poder"; título de los gobernantes otomanos durante el auge del imperio otomano. (pág. 507)

Sunna [sunna] *s.* modelo islámico de vida que se basa en las enseñanzas y vida de Mahoma. (pág. 268)

Sunni [sunni] *s.* rama del islam que reconoce a Alí y a sus descendientes como sucesores legítimos de Mahoma. (pág. 271)

surrealism [surrealismo] *s.* movimiento artístico del siglo 20 que se concentra en el inconsciente. (pág. 899)

sustainable growth [crecimiento sostenido] *s.* desarrollo económico que satisface las necesidades de la población pero preserva el entorno y conserva recursos para futuras generaciones. (pág. 1080)

Swahili [suahili] *s.* lengua bantú con influencias árabes que se usa en África oriental y central. (pág. 422)

T

Taiping Rebellion [Rebelión Taiping] *s.* rebelión a mediados del siglo 19 contra la dinastía Qing en China, encabezada por Hong Xiuquan. (pág. 807)

Taj Mahal *s.* bella tumba en Agra, India, construida por el emperador mogol Shah Jahan para su esposa Mumtaz Mahal. (pág. 519)

Taliban [Talibán] *s.* grupo musulmán conservador que tomó el poder en Afganistán después de que la Unión Soviética retiró sus tropas; expulsado por el ejército estadounidense en diciembre de 2001 por darles amparo a sospechosos de terrorismo. (pág. 1026)

Tamil [tamil o tamul] *s.* idioma del sur de India; grupo que habla dicho idioma. (pág. 191)

technology [tecnología] *s.* formas de aplicar conocimientos, herramientas e inventos para satisfacer necesidades. (pág. 8)

Tennis Court Oath [Juramento de la Cancha de Tenis] *s.* promesa hecha por los miembros de la Asamblea Nacional de Francia en 1789 de permanecer reunidos hasta que elaboraran una nueva constitución. (pág. 654)

terraces [cultivos en andenes/cultivos en terrazas] *s.* en Aksum, una técnica nueva para cultivar la tierra, utilizando campos horizontales a manera de peldaños, cortados en laderas o pendientes de montañas, para retener agua y reducir la erosión. (pág. 228)

terrorism [terrorismo] *s.* uso de la fuerza o de amenazas para presionar a personas o gobiernos a que cambien sus políticas. (pág. 1087)

theocracy [teocracia] *s.* **1.** gobierno en el cual se ve al gobernante como una figura divina (pág. 37). **2.** gobierno controlado por líderes religiosos. (pág. 496)

theory of evolution [teoría de la evolución] *s.* concepto propuesto por Charles Darwin en 1859 de que las especies de plantas y animales surgen debido a un proceso de selección natural. (pág. 765)

theory of relativity [teoría de la relatividad] *s.* ideas de Albert Einstein acerca de la interrelación entre el tiempo y el espacio, y entre la energía y la materia. (pág. 897)

Theravada *s.* secta del budismo que se adhiere al énfasis original de Buda en la estricta disciplina espiritual. (pág. 193)

Third Reich [Tercer Reich] *s.* Tercer Imperio Alemán establecido por Adolfo Hitler en la década de 1930. (pág. 918)

Third Republic [Tercera República] *s.* república establecida en Francia después de la caída de Napoleón III; acabó con la ocupación alemana de Francia durante la II Guerra Mundial. (pág. 749)

Third World [Tercer Mundo] *s.* durante la Guerra Fría, naciones que no se aliaron ni con Estados Unidos ni con la Unión Soviética. (pág. 982).

Thirty Years' War [Guerra de los Treinta Años] *s.* conflicto europeo de 1618 a 1648 por cuestiones religiosas, territoriales y de poder entre familias reinantes. (pág. 603)

three-field system [sistema de tres campos] *s.* sistema agrícola de la Europa medieval en que las tierras de cultivo se dividían en tres campos de igual tamaño y cada uno se sembraba sucesivamente con un cultivo de invierno, un cultivo de primavera y el tercero se dejaba sin cultivar. (pág. 387)

Tiananmen Square [Plaza Tiananmen] *s.* plaza pública en Beijing, China; sede en 1989 de un enorme levantamiento estudiantil en favor de reformas democráticas. (pág. 1061)

tithe [diezmo] *s.* pago de una familia a la Iglesia de la décima parte de sus ingresos. (pág. 363)

Tokugawa Shogunate [shogunato Tokugawa] *s.* dinastía de shogúns que gobernó un Japón unificado de 1603 a 1867. (pág. 544)

Torah *s.* cinco primeros libros de la Biblia hebrea, los más sagrados de la tradición judía. (pág. 77)

totalitarianism [totalitarismo] *s.* gobierno que controla todo aspecto de la vida pública y privada. (pág. 874)

total war [guerra total] *s.* conflicto en el que los países participantes dedican todos sus recursos a la guerra. (pág. 853)

totem [tóteme] *s.* la animale u otro objeto natural que sirven de símbolo de unidad de clanes u otros grupos. (pág. 445)

tournament [torneo] *s.* justa deportiva entre grupos de caballeros. (pág. 367)

tragedy [tragedia] *s.* obra dramática seria profunda acerca de la caída de un personaje heroico o noble. (pág. 136)

Treaty of Kanagawa [Tratado de Kanagawa] *s.* acuerdo de 1854 entre Estados Unidos y Japón, que abrió dos puertos japoneses a los barcos de Estados Unidos y le permitió abrir una embajada en Japón. (pág. 810)

Treaty of Tordesillas [Tratado de Tordesillas] *s.* acuerdo de 1494 entre Portugal y España que estableció que las tierras descubiertas al oeste de una línea imaginaria en el océano Atlántico pertenecerían a España y las tierras al este pertenecerían a Portugal. (pág. 533)

Treaty of Versailles [Tratado de Versalles] *s.* acuerdo de paz firmado por Alemania y los Aliados después de la I Guerra Mundial. (pág. 858)

trench warfare [guerra de trincheras] *s.* forma de guerra en la que dos ejércitos contrincantes luchan detrás de trincheras cavadas en el campo de batalla. (pág. 847)

triangular trade [triángulo comercial] *s.* red comercial trasatlántica que transportaba esclavos y productos entre África, Inglaterra, Europa continental, el Caribe y las colonias de Norteamérica. (pág. 568)

tribune [tribuno] *s.* en la antigua Roma, funcionario elegido por los plebeyos para proteger sus derechos. (pág. 156)

tribute [tributo] *s.* pago de una potencia más débil a una potencia más fuerte para obtener una garantía de paz y seguridad. (pág. 82)

Triple Alliance [Triple Alianza] *s.* **1.** asociación de las ciudades Estado de Tenochtitlan, Texcoco y Tlacopan, que dio origen al imperio azteca (pág. 454). **2.** alianza militar establecida entre Alemania, Austro-Hungría e Italia antes de la I Guerra Mundial. (pág. 842)

Triple Entente [Triple Entente] *s.* alianza militar entre Gran Bretaña, Francia y Rusia establecida antes de la I Guerra Mundial. (pág. 843)

triumvirate [triunvirato] *s.* en la Roma antigua, grupo de tres líderes que compartían el control del gobierno. (pág. 161)

Trojan War [Guerra de Troya] *s.* guerra, aproximadamente en 1200 a.C., en que un ejército al mando de reyes micénicos atacó la ciudad comercial independiente de Troya, ubicada en Anatolia. (pág. 125)

troubadour [trovador] *s.* poeta y músico medieval que viajaba de un lugar a otro para divertir con sus cantos de amor cortesano. (pág. 367)

Truman Doctrine [Doctrina Truman] *s.* política estadounidense de dar ayuda económica y militar a las naciones libres amenazadas por oponentes internos o externos, anunciada por el presidente Harry Truman en 1947. (pág. 968)

tyrant [tirano] *s.* en la antigua Grecia, individuo poderoso que ganaba el control del gobierno de una ciudad Estado apelando al apoyo de los pobres. (pág. 127)

UV

Umayyads [omeyas] *s.* dinastía que gobernó el imperio musulmán del 661 al 750 d.C. y después estableció un reino en al-Andalus. (pág. 271)

union [sindicato] *s.* asociación de trabajadores formada para negociar mejores salarios y condiciones de trabajo. (pág. 738)

United Nations [Organización de las Naciones Unidas (ONU)] *s.* organización internacional fundada en 1945 con el propósito de ofrecer seguridad a las naciones del mundo. (pág. 966)

Universal Declaration of Human Rights [Declaración Universal de Derechos Humanos] *s.* declaración en que la ONU proclamó en 1948 que todos los seres humanos tienen derecho a la vida, la libertad y la seguridad. (pág. 1084)

unrestricted submarine warfare [guerra submarina irrestricta] *s.* uso de submarinos para hundir sin alerta previa cualquier barco (incluso barcos neutrales y de pasajeros sin armamento) que se encuentre en aguas enemigas. (pág. 852)

urbanization [urbanización] *s.* crecimiento de ciudades y migración hacia ellas. (pág. 723)

U.S.A. Patriot Act [Ley Patriota de E.U.A.] *s.* proyecto de ley antiterrorista de 2001 que hizo más fuerte los derechos gubernamentales para detener a extranjeros sospechosos de terrorismo y para procesar crímenes terroristas. (pág. 1092)

U.S. Civil War [Guerra Civil de E.U.A.] *s.* conflicto entre los estados del Norte y el Sur de Estados Unidos desde 1861 a 1865, sobre el asunto de la esclavitud. (pág. 760)

utilitarianism [utilitarismo] *s.* teoría, propuesta por Jeremy Bentham a fines del siglo 18, de que las acciones del gobierno sólo son útiles si promueven el mayor bien para el mayor número de personas. (pág. 735)

utopia [utopía] *s.* tierra imaginaria descrita por Tomás Moro en su libro del mismo nombre; lugar ideal. (pág. 482)

vassal [vasallo] *s.* en la Europa feudal, persona que recibía un dominio (tierras) de un señor a cambio de su promesa de lealtad y servicios. (pág. 360)

Vedas *s.* cuatro colecciones de escritos sagrados secretos, realizados durante la etapa temprana del asentamiento ario en India. (pág. 63)

vernacular *s.* lenguaje común y corriente de la gente de una región o país. (págs. 391, 475)

Vietcong *s.* grupo de guerrilleros comunistas que, con la ayuda de Vietnam del Norte, pelearon contra el gobierno de Vietnam del Sur durante la Guerra de Vietnam. (pág. 980)

Vietnamization [vietnamización] *s.* estrategia del presidente de E.U.A. Richard Nixon para terminar con la participación en la Guerra de Vietnam, mediante el retiro gradual de tropas estadounidenses y su reemplazo con fuerzas survietnamitas. (pág. 980)

Vishnu [Visnú] *s.* dios hindú considerado responsable de conservar al mundo. (pág. 194)

vizier [visir] *s.* primer ministro de un reino o imperio musulmán. (pág. 315)

W

War of the Spanish Succession [Guerra de Sucesión Española] *s.* conflicto de 1701 a 1713 en que varios Estados europeos lucharon para impedir que la familia Borbón controlara a España, como a Francia. (pág. 601)

Warsaw Pact [Pacto de Varsovia] *s.* alianza militar formada en 1955 por la Unión Soviética y siete países de Europa oriental. (pág. 969)

Weimar Republic [República de Weimar] *s.* república establecida en Alemania en 1919 que acabó en 1933. (pág. 905)

Western Front [Frente Occidental] *s.* en la I Guerra Mundial, región del norte de Francia donde peleaban las fuerzas de los Aliados y de las Potencias Centrales. (pág. 846)

westernization [occidentalización] *s.* adopción de las instituciones sociales, políticas o económicas del Occidente, especialmente de Europa o Estados Unidos. (pág. 610)

XYZ

yin and yang [yin y yang] *s.* en China, dos poderes que gobiernan los ritmos naturales de la vida; el yang representa las cualidades masculinas en el universo y el yin las femeninas. (pág. 107)

Yoruba [yoruba] *s.* pueblo del África occidental que formó varios reinos en lo que hoy es Benin y el sur de Nigeria. (pág. 418)

Zapotec [zapoteca] *s.* civilización mesoamericana centrada en el valle de Oaxaca de lo que hoy es México. (pág. 242)

ziggurat [zigurat] *s.* estructura de gradas en forma de pirámide, que formaba parte de un templo sumerio. (pág. 23)

Zionism [sionismo] *s.* movimiento fundado en la década de 1890 para promover el establecimiento de una patria judía en Palestina. (pág. 750)

Index

An *i* preceding an italic page reference indicates that there is an illustration, and usually text information as well, on that page. An *m* or a *c* preceding an italic page reference indicates a map or chart, as well as text information on that page.

A

Abbasid dynasty, 271–272, 273
Abbas the Great (Safavid Shah), 514–515
Abbas, Mahmoud, 1023
Aborigines, *i13*, 752–753, *i756*
absolute monarchs, 594–595, *c618. See also* monarchy.
absolute ruler, 161, 595
absolutism, 594–595, *c594*
Abraham, 77–78
Abubakar, Abdulsalami, 1042
Abu-Bakr (caliph), 269
acropolis, 127, 929
Addams, Jane, 739–740, *i740*
Adena and Hopewell, 443
Adolphus, Gustavus, 603–604
Adulis, 226–227, 229
Aegean Sea, 72, *m72*
Aeschylus, 136
***Aeneid* (Virgil),** 179
Afghanistan, 788, 987
 independence, 1026
 mujahideen, 1026
 Muslim terrorists and, *i987*, 1026–1027, 1089
 Soviet Union in, 987, 1026
 Taliban in, 1026–1027, *i1026–1027*
 U.S. military action in, *i987*, 1027, 1091
Africa, *m211. See also* East Africa; North Africa; South Africa; West Africa.
 age-set system, 410
 AIDS in, 1085
 Christianity in, 227–228, *c1102*
 civilizations of, 210–229, *c230*
 comparative size of, 213, *m231*
 cultural developments of, 224
 democracy in, 1040–1045
 desertification of, 217
 early art of, *i216*, *i217*
 early farming in, 16, 215
 economies of, 219, 413, 422
 empires of, 413–417, *m414*, 425–427, *c428*
 ethnic conflict in, 1012–1013
 family organization, 216, 410
 geographic contrasts, 213–215, *m214*
 griots, 216
 human origins in, 7–11, *m10*
 hunter-gatherers, *i212*, 224, 409, *c411*, *m411*
 imperialism in, 774–784
 independence of, 1012–1016
 lineage, 410
 maps
  800–1500, *m407*
  1955, *m1014*
  1975, *m1014*
  East African Trade, *m423*
  imperialism in, 1914, *m777*
  West African Empires, 1000–1500, *m414*
  Western Africa, 2003, *m429*
 Muslim states, 410–412
 nomads, 215, 222
 political developments in, 216
 Portuguese in, 424, 427, 530, 532, 1016
 religions in, 216, 229, 410, 415
 resistance movements in, 782–783, *m783*
 role of slavery in, 566
 Sahara, 213, *i214*, 215
 Sahel, 213, *i214*
 societies of, 409–410, *m411*, *c428*
 stateless societies, 215, 410, *c410*, *c411*, *m411*
 trade in, 226, *i408*, 413–414
 vegetation regions, 213–215, *m214*
 weaving in, 422
 in World War II, 928–929, 940
African National Congress (ANC), 1043–1044
Afrikaners, 776, 1043
afterlife. *See* burial rites.
Age of Faith, 379–386
Age of Reason, 629–635
Agricultural Revolution, 15, *c17*
agriculture. *See also* farming.
 in Africa, 16, 215, 222–223
 in the Americas, 16, 238–239
 in ancient China, 16, 50–51, 109
 beginnings, *c3*, 14–18, *m17*
 crops, 18, 571
 in Egypt, 35, 89
 as factor in social change, 18, *c239*
 of Han Dynasty, 204
 influence of Columbian Exchange on, 571, *i572*
 in Japan, 339
 Maya, 447
 modern advances in, 717
 revolution in, 15, *c17*
 in Roman Empire, 163, 173
 in Russia, 610
 slash-and-burn, 15, 222
 in Soviet Union, 878, *c878*
Aguinaldo, Emilio, 798
Ahhotep (Egyptian queen), 89
AIDS (acquired immune deficiency syndrome), 1045, 1085, *m1085*
Ainu people, 236
airplane
 Earhart, Amelia, 901
 hijacking of, 1090
 Lindbergh, Charles, 901
 as terrorist weapons, 1090
 in World War I, *i850*, *c954*
 in World War II, 927–928, 934, 945, *i955*
 Wright brothers, 764, *i764*, *c831*
Akbar, 517–518, *i518*
Akkad, 33
Aksum, 225–229, *m226*
Alamo, 823, *i823*
al-Andalus, 271–272
al-Din, Nasir (Persian ruler), 790, *i790*
Alexander the Great, 139, 143–145, *i143*
 cultural influence of, 145, 146–149
 empire of, *c87*, *c121*, 143–145, *m144*, *c145*
Alexander II (Russian czar), 691
Alexander III (Russian czar), 691, 867, *i867*
Alexandria, 143, 146–148, *i262*
Alfred the Great, 393
algebra. *See* mathematics.
Algeria
 FLN (Algerian National Liberation Front), 1015
 independence of, 1015
 resistance to French rule, 782, 1015
al-Khwarizimi, 278
Allah, 264–268
Allies
 World War I, 845, *m846*, 851
 World War II, 926–927, 930, 934, 940–947
Almohad dynasty, 412
Almoravid dynasty, 411–412
alphabet
 ancient and modern, *c74*
 Cyrillic, 306, *i306*
 Greek, 40, *c74*
 Phoenician, 74, *c74*, *i76*, *i116*
al-Qaeda, 1089
al-Razi, 278
"America." *See* Americas, the; United States.
American Revolution, 640–645, *c706*
 causes of, 640–641
 compared with Russian Revolution, 872
 effects of, 641–645
 Enlightenment, role of, 641–642, *c643*
 French influence on, 642, *c643*
Americas, the, *m233, c250. See also* Aztec civilization; Incan civilization; Maya civilization; North America.
 African influence on, 570
 agriculture's effect on, 238–239, *c239*
 ancient civilizations of, 20, *m233*, 240–251, *m241*, *m247*, *m251*
 astronomy in, 448
 colonization of, 554–558
 Columbian Exchange, 571–573, *i572*
 early Mesoamerican societies, 240–244
 early South American societies, 20
 economic developments of, 1077
 empires in, 446–449, 459–453
 European exploration of, 553–558, *m555*, 561–563
 maps
  800 B.C. to A.D. 1535, *m439*
  Europeans in, *m564*
Amina (Zazzau queen), 418, *i418*
Amnesty International, 1084
Amorites, 33
amphorae, *i75*
Amritsar Massacre, 887–888
Anabaptists, 496
***Analects* (Confucius),** 105, *i295*
Anasazi, 443
Anastasia, 608–609
Anatolia, *c58*, 62
ANC (African National Congress), 1043–1044

Ancient World, *m59*
Andean civilizations
Chavín period, *c59*, 246–247, *m247*
headhunters, *i247*
Moche culture, 247, 249
Nazca culture, 247, *i248*
religion, 246–249, *i248*
Andhra dynasty, 191
Angkor, 345
Angkor Wat, 70, 345, *i345*
Anglican Church, 494
Anglo-Saxons, 393–394
Angola, 773, 1016
animals
in agriculture, 21
in ancient China, 52
camels, *i433*
domestication of, 16, 18, 46, 215
in Egypt, 43
extinction of, 1080
horse, 364, 387
importance to nomads of, 331
in Indus Valley civilization, 48
livestock, 718
mammoth, *i234*, 235–236
in Minoan civilization, 73, *i73*
in prehistoric North America, 234–237, *i238*
Punic War elephants, 158
symbols of warriors, 454
animism, 216, 415
***Annals* (Tacitus),** 181
annexation, 799, 813
annul, 492
Anschluss, 918
anthrax
effects of, 1090–1091
September 11 terrorist attack and, 1090–1091
anthropologists, 5–6, *i7*, 221
anti-Semitism, 749–750, 913–914
Kristallnacht, 914, 936–937
antiseptics, *c831*
antiterrorism bill, 1091–1092
antiterrorism coalition
Great Britain and, 1083
apartheid, 1043–1044
apostles, 168, *i169*
appeasement, 917, 919
aqueducts, 47, 181, *i181*
Aquinas, Thomas, 392, *i392*
Aquino, Corazón, 1005–1006
Arab-Americans
civil rights of, 1091
Arabia. *See* Saudi Arabia.
Arabian Peninsula, *m261,* 263
Arab scholars, 391
Arafat, Yasir, 1019, 1023
arch, 181
archaeological dig, 5, 16, 42, 167
archaeological evidence
of Africa, *i426*
of ancient China, 52
of ancient Egypt, 42
of ancient Rome, 166–167, *i167*
of Aryan culture, 63
of Assyrian empire, 96
of Aztec civilization, *i457*
as clue to prehistory, 5
of Djenné-Djeno, 219, *i219*, *m219*
of Great Zimbabwe, *i426*
of Inca civilization, *i464–465*
of Indus civilization, *i27*, 46
at Jarmo, 16
of Maya society, 446, *i450*
of migration to the Americas, 235–237, *i237*
of Minoan culture, 72
at Monte Verde, 236, *i237*, *m237*
of Olmec culture, 240, *i244*
of Trojan War, 125
of Ur, 22–23
archaeologists, 5, 7–11, *m11*, 16, 18, 22
in the Americas, 236
in China, 52
archaeology, 5, 25
Archimedes, 148
architecture
Akbar period of, 518
Aksumite, *i228*
in Alexandria, 146–147, *i262*
in ancient Egypt, 37–38, *i39*, *i43*, 90–91, *i91*
of Angkor Wat, 345, *i345*
baroque, 637
Buddhist, *i198*
castle, *i366*, 367
cathedral, 380, *i381*
Chaldean, 98
church, 380, *i381*
Etruscan influence on Roman, 156
Gothic style, 380, *i381*
of government, *i582*
of Great Zimbabwe, *i426*
Greek, 135–135, 140, *i141*
Hindu, *i199*
Maya, 446–447, *i450–451*
Mesoamerican, 241, *i242*
Mughal Empire, 518–519, *i520*, *i522*
Muslim, *i266*, 276–278, *i276*, *i278*
neoclassical, 637
Parthenon, 135–136, *i141*
Persian, *i100*
pyramid, *i1*, 37–38, *i39*, *i92*, 444
Roman, 156, *i156*, 165, *i166–167*, 181, *i182*
Romanesque, 380
Sumerian, 22–23, 31, 32
Ziggurat, *i22*, 23, 31, 98
Argentina
democracy in, 1039
"Evita" (Eva Perōn), 1039
and Falkland Islands, 1039
fascism in, *i914*, 1039, *i1065*
independence of, 683
Perón, Juan, *i914*, 1038–1039
Aristarchus, 147
aristocracy, 127, *c128*
Aristophanes, 136
Aristotle, 139, *i139*, 151, 278–279, 623
arithmetic, 32
Armenian Massacre, 844
armistice (World War I), 855
armor
Assyrian, 95
Mongol, *i332*
samurai, *i342*
arms
control, 1047
race, 842, 1047
Arroyo, Gloria Macapagal, *i1105*
art. *See also* drama; painting; propaganda; sculpture.
African, 15, *i216*, *i217*, *i420–421*
Akkadian, *i26*
Andean, 246–247, *i248*, 249
Assyrian, *i97*
Australian, *i13*, 15, *i756*
Buddhist, *i198*
Buddhist influence on, 193
Catholic, 488, *i499*
cave painting, *i12–13*, 14
Chaldean, 98
Chavín, 246
Chinese, *i53*, *i209*, 326, *i326*
Christian, *i227*, *i286*, *i312–313*
civic duty to, 136
classical, 136, 178–179
Dutch, 593, *i593*
Egyptian, *i39*, *i42*, *i90*
Enlightenment values in, 637
Flemish, 481, *i481*
French, 701, *i703*
during French Revolution, *i665*
in global culture, 1096
Greek (ancient), 136, *i140–141*
Hindu, *i199*
Hittite, *i58*, *i63*
impressionism in, 701
international, 1096
Islamic beliefs in, *i267*, *i277*
Japanese woodblock printing, *i814–815*
jewelry, 216
magical qualities of, *i12*
Meroë, *i94*
Minoan, 72, *i73*
mosaic, *i165*, 178
Muslim, 276, *i277*
nationalism and, 698
Nok, *i217*
Northern Renaissance, 481, *i481*
Nubian, *i87, i92–93*
Olmec, *i58*, 240–241, 243, *i244*
oracle bones, *i53*
Ottoman Empire, 511
Paleolithic, 11, *i12–13*
Persian, *i100*, *i102*
perspective, 474, *i474*
Phoenician, 74
photography, 700, *i700*
political, *i857*, *i863*
post-World War I, 899, *i899*
potter's wheel, 21
pottery, 72, *i140*
prehistoric, 11, *i12–13*, 14–15
as propaganda, 876, *i876*
realism in, 700
religious, *i312–313*
religious beliefs in, *i32, i39*
Renaissance, *i470*, 474–475, *i478–479*
revolution in, 698–703
Roman, *i165*, *i167*, 178–179
Romantic movement, 698
Russian, *i312–313*
Safavid Empire, 515, *i515*
Shang Dynasty, *i53*, *i117*
Spanish, 591, *i591*
Spartan, 131
stone age, 11, *i12–13*
Sumerian, *i3*, *i32*
Surrealism, 899, *i899*
West African, *i418–421*
***Arthasastra* (Kautilya),** 189
artifacts, 5, 52, *i237, i581*
artisans, 20, 388
Aryans, 66
caste system, 63–64, *i64*
influence on Indian culture, 64–65, 193
invasions of India, *c58*, 63, *m65*
and Nazi philosophy, 936, 938
Vedas, 63
Asante, *i770*

Index

Ashurbanipal (Assyrian king), 96–97
Asia, *m321*
aggression in (1931–1937), *m917*, 932
"East Asia for the Asiatics," 932
imperialism in, 796–798, 805–808
independence, 1002–1003
poverty levels in 2002, *c1002*
Askia Muhammad (Muslim ruler of Songhai), 417
Asoka, 190–191, 209
assembly line, 764, *i764*
assimilation, 205, 781
Assyria, 82, 95
Nineveh, 96–97
Assyrian empire, *c87*, 95–97, *m96*, *c121*
culture, 34, 96
military power, 82, 94, 95–97, *i97*
astrolabe, *i275*, *i432*, 530
astrology, 98
astronomy
Aristarchus, 147, *c147*
Chaldean, 98
Daoist effect on, 106
Egyptian, 40–41
of Hellenistic period, 147, *i147*
Indian, 195
Maya, 448
Muslim, 274, *i275*, 278
Ptolemy, 147, *c147*, 623
and Scientific Revolution, 624–625
Atahualpa, 556, *i557*
Athena, 126, 136
Athens, 133, 134–138, 142
plague in, 137
war with Sparta, 137–138, *m137*
Atlantic Charter, 930
Atlantic slave trade, 566–570. *See also* slavery; slaves.
atomic bomb, *i955*
during Cold War, 969–970
effects of in World War II, *c946*
Hiroshima, *i946*, 947
Nagasaki, *i946*, 947, 959
atoms, theory of, *c830*
Attila the Hun, 176
Augustine, St., 172
Augustus (Roman emperor), 162, *i162*. *See also* Octavian.
Aum Shinrikyo, 1089
Aurangzeb, 520–521
Aurelius, Marcus, 173
Auschwitz, 938–939, 957
Australia
life in early, *i756–757*
geography of, *m753*
penal colony of, 752, *i757*
self-rule of, 753
australopithecines, *c2*, 7–8, *c8*, *m10*
Austria
Prussian control of, 607, 693
in World War I, 845, 848–849
Austria-Hungary, 693
Austro-Hungarian Empire, 693, 844
autocracy, 109, 867
automobiles, 762, 764, *i764*
Model T Ford, *c831*
post-World War I, 900–901
robot assembly of, 1075
aviation, *i850*
Avignon, 398
Axis Powers, 917–919
ayllu, 460
Azerbaijan, 1024–1025
Aztec civilization, 452–458
art of, *i457*
Cortés' conquest of, *i552*, 556
cultural developments of, 454–456
fall of, 458, *c458*
political developments of, 454–455
religious beliefs of, 456, *i457*
society, 454–455
trade in, 454–455
Triple Alliance, 454

B

Babur, 516
Babylon, 62, 97–98
hanging gardens of, 98, *i98*
Babylonian captivity, 82, 100
Babylonian empire, 28
Assyrian defeat of, 95
Persian rule of, 82
rebirth of, 97–98
reign of Hammurabi, 33–34
Bacon, Francis, 626
Baghdad, 273–274, 276
balance of power, 672
in 1800s, 672–673, 697
Balboa, Vasco Núñez de, 554
Balfour Declaration, 1017
Balkans
under Ottoman Empire, 508
in World War I, 841, 843
in World War II, 929
Baltic nations
in World War II, 925–926
Bangladesh, 1002–1003
Bantu-speaking peoples, 221–224
Ban Zhao, 204, 206
Barak, Ehud, 1022
barbarian, 175
barometer, 627
baroque style, 637
barter, 23
baseball, international, 1094
Basil, St., 304, *i304*
bas-relief, 178
Bastille, storming of, 654–655, *i654*
Bataan Death March, 932
Bathsheba, 81
battle
Adowa, 783
Agincourt, 402–403
Austerlitz, 665, *m666*
Britain, 928
the Bulge, 944–945
Chaldiran, 514
Crécy, 402–403
Guadalcanal, 935
Hastings, 394
Marne, 846
Midway, 934
Peninsular, 669
Poitiers, 402–403
Stalingrad, 941
Tours, 356
Trafalgar, *m666*, 667
Beccaria, Cesare Bonesana, 632
Bedouins, 263
Beethoven, Ludwig van, 637, 699, *i699*
Begin, Menachem, 1020
Belgium
Congo, colony of, 774, 1015
Industrial Revolution in, 732
in World War II, 926–927
Bell, Alexander Graham, 762
Bella, Ahmed Ben, 1015
Benedict (Italian monk), 355, *i355*
Benin, 419, *i420–421*
Bentham, Jeremy, 735
Berbers, 271, 411. *See also* Almohad dynasty; Almoravid dynasty.
Beringia, 235–237, *m237*
Bering Strait, 236
Berlin
airlift, 969, *i969*
Conference, 776
division, 968–969
Wall, 969, 1053–1054, *i1053*
Bhutto, Ali, *i1001*, 1002
Bhutto, Benazir, *i519*, 1002
Biafra, 1041–1042
Bible, 85, 100, *i227*. *See also* Torah.
as basis of truth, *i287*, *c491*
destruction of Nineveh in, 97
Gutenberg, 484
Hebrew, 77, *c80*, 172
King James, 614
Philistines of, 77
Protestant, *c491*
Roman Catholic, *c491*
Biko, Stephen, 1043
Bill of Rights
English, 617, 619, 709
South African, 1044
United States, 645, *i645*
bin Laden, Osama, 1091
as head of al-Qaeda, 1027, 1090
biological weapons. *See* weapons, of mass destruction.
bishop, 171
Bismarck, Otto von, 695–696, *i696*, 705, 842
Black Death. *See* bubonic plague.
blitzkrieg, 925, *i955*
blockade, 668
"Bloody Sunday," 869, *i869*
Boccaccio, Giovanni, 476
Boers, 776, 778
Boer War, 778
Bohemia, 603, 605
Bohr, Neils, 766
Boleyn, Anne, 493, *i493*
Bolívar, Simón, 677, 683, *i683*, *i684*, *i711*
Bolshevik Revolution, 870–871, *c871*
Bolsheviks, 868, 870–871, 873
Bonaparte, Napoleon. *See* Napoleon I.
Book of the Dead, 38
books
burning of, 107, 499, 913
history of making, 203, 484
Maya, 448, *i448*
in Middle Ages, *i354*, 355
Bosnia, 843–844, 1056, 1058, *i1064*
Bosnia-Herzegovina, 1056, 1058
"Boston Tea Party," 641
Bourbon dynasty, 596–597, 601
bourgeoisie, 651, 736
Boxer Rebellion, 808–809, *i809*
boyars, 608–609
Boyle, Robert, 628
Brahma, 67, 194
Brahmin, 63, *i64*, 67
Braidwood, Robert, 16
Braque, Georges, 899
Brasília, 1034
Brazil
da Silva, Luiz Inacio Lula, 1036
economy, *i816*, 1034, 1036, *c1036*

independence of, 675, 686, 1034
indians of, 566
land reform in, 1034
military dictatorship in, 1034
Portuguese in, 557, 567
Vargas, Getulio, 1034
in World War I, *m852*
Brezhnev, Leonid, 989
brinksmanship, 970, 990
Britain
American colonies of, 562–565, 640–641
Anglo-Saxons, 393–394
army, 848
Atlantic Charter, 930
colonies of, 562–565, 640, 751–753, 791–795, 797
development of, *c397*
East India Company, 535, 791, 793–794
English Civil War, 615, *m616*, *c706*
the Depression in, 908
and Hong Kong, transfer to China, 1062–1063
Hundred Years War, 401–403
in India, 791–795, 887–889
Industrial Revolution in, 717–722, 723–728
influence in East Asia, 535
invasions, 393
London, *i486–487*, 724
Manchester, 724, 726, 728
Magna Carta, 394–395, *i395*
North American colonies of, 562–563, 640
Parliament, 395, 492–493, 614–617, 747–748
population of, 724
revolutions in, 615–616, *c706*
role in slave trade, 567, 601
in Southeast Asia, 797, *m797*
territory of, 394, 601–602
World War II, 926–928, 930, 940–945
bronze, *c3, i3*, 22
first use of, 21, 32
sculpture, *i420–421*
in Shang dynasty, 52, *i117*
Bronze Age, 21
Bruegel, Pieter, 481, *i481*
Brutus, Marcus, 162
bubonic plague, 399–401
in Byzantine Empire, 304
death toll, *c400*, 401
economic effect of, 401
effects of, 401
Buddha, 68–69, *i69*, 193
Buddhism, 68–71, *c84*, *i284–285*, *c296*
central ideas of, 68–69, *c84*
enlightenment, 68
historical origins of, 68
in India, 70–71, 190–191
in Japan, 71, 340, *i547*
Mahayana, 193
nirvana, 69, 193
Siddhartha Gautama, 68, *i68*
spread of, 70–71, 190, *m197*
in Sri Lanka, 1003
Theravada, 193
in Vietnam, 346
in the West, 71
as world religion, 284–285
Zen, *i547*
bull leapers of Knossos, *i73*
bureaucracy
Abbasids, 271–272
Chinese, 203
Mauryan, 189
burghers, 391
Burke, Edmund, 662
Burma, 797, 1006–1007
burial rites
Egyptian, 38–39, *i39*, 91
Incan, *i464–465*
Native American, 444
Neanderthal, 9
Nubian, 92
reliquary, *i313*
Sumerian, 23, *i32*
Bush, George W.
anti-terrorism bill and, 1092
"road map" (Middle East peace plan), 1023
war against terrorism and, 1091
Bushido, 343
Byzantine Empire, 301–306, 382
in 1100, *m299*
Byzantium, 175, 301
education, 303
emperors, 302–304
fall of, 304
Greek and Roman influence on, 176, 301–303
Justinian (emperor), 303–304
Justinian Code of law, 302
Muslim defeat of, 270, 304
Turkish rule in, *i300*, 507

C

cabinet, 617
Caesar, Julius, 161–162, *i161*
Cahokia, 444
cajuns, *m752*
calendar
Aztec, *i457*
Egyptian, 40–41
Incan, 461
Indian, 195
Maya, 448
Muslim, *i275*
Paleolithic, *i2*
under Robespierre, 660
Zapotec, 243
Caligula, *c164*, *i164*
caliph, 269, 271–272
calligraphy
Islamic, 276, *i277*
Calvinism, 495–496
in Germany, *m497*
in Netherlands, 496, *m497*
Calvin, John, 495–496, *i496*
Cambodia
Khmer Rouge, *i980*, 981
Cambyses, 100
camel, *i433*
Camp David Accords, 1020
Canaan, 77–78, *m78*, 79, 80, 81
Canada, *m752*
Quebec, 561, 751
self-rule of, 751–752
trade and, 562
Canby, Thomas, 235–236, *i236*
cannons, 546, 556
canon law, 371
Canopic jars, *i39*
Canossa, 372
***Canterbury Tales, The* (Chaucer),** 375, 392
Canute (Danish king), 393
Capet, Hugh, 396
Capetian dynasty, 396
capitalism, 573, 734
compared to socialism, *c737*
roots of, *c737*
caravel, 530, *i531*
Cardoso, Fernando Henrique, 1036
Caribbean
colonization of, 563
Carnegie, Andrew, 731
Carolingian dynasty, 356–357
fall of, 357
Carter, Jimmy
boycott of 1980 Olympics, 987
and Camp David Accords, 1020
and SALT (Strategic Arms Limitation Talks) II, 991
Carthage, *c59*, 74, 76, 158–159
Cartier, Jacques, 561
Cassius, Gaius, 162
caste system, 69. *See also* social classes.
of India, 63–64, 67, *i793*
Castiglione, Baldassare, 473, *i473*
cast iron, 55
castles, *i366*, 367
Castro, Fidel, 984–985, *i985*
Catal Huyuk, 18
catapult, *i366*
cataract, 36
cathedrals, 380, *i381*
Catherine the Great (Russian empress), 638–639, *i639*
Catholicism. *See also* Inquisition.
in Spanish Empire, 589, 591
in Spanish Netherlands, 592–593
Catholic League, 603
Catholic Reformation, 498–499
Caucasus Mountains, 61
caudillos, 816–817
caveman. *See* Neanderthal.
cave painting, *i12–13*, 14
Cavour, Camillo di, 694
Ceausescu, Nicolae, 1055–1056
censorship
Nazi, 913
of Roman Catholic Church, 490
in Russia, 867
in Soviet Union, 876–877, 989, 1046
under Stalin, 876–877
Voltaire on, 630
Central America. *See also* Mesoamerican civilizations; Mexico.
United Provinces of, 686
Central Asia, *m1025*, *i1025*
economic struggles in, 1024
ethnic and religious strife, 1024–1025
Central Asian Republics, 1024–1025
Central Intelligence Agency (CIA), 982
centralized government, 200, 397
Central Powers, 845, 855
Cervantes, Miguel de, 591–592
Cetshwayo (Zulu king), 776, *i776*
Ceylon. *See* Sri Lanka.
CFCs (chlorofluorocarbons), 1079
Chaldeans, 97–98, 99
Chaldiran, Battle of, 514
Chamberlain, Neville, 919, *i919*
Champlain, Samuel de, 561
Champollion, Jean François, 40
Chandra Gupta (Indian king), 191–192
Chandra Gupta II (Indian emperor), 191–192
Chandragupta Maurya (Indian emperor), *c121*, 189–190
Chang Jiang. *See* Yangtze River.

Chaplin, Charlie, 901, *i901*
chariot(s), 52, 61, 89
charioteers, 63
four-horse, 98
in Hittite empire, 63, *i63*
racing in Rome, 165
two-wheeled, 90
Charlemagne (Holy Roman emperor), 356–357, *i357*
cultural revival, 357
division of kingdom by Treaty of
empire of, 356, m356
Verdun, 357
Charles I (English king), 614–615
Charles II (English king), 616
Charles V (Holy Roman emperor), 490, 492, 589
Charles VII (French king), 403
Charles X (French king), 690
Chartist movement, 747–748
Chartres Cathedral, 380, *i381*
Chaucer, Geoffrey, 375, 392
Chavín culture, *c59*, 246–247
Chechnya, 1050–1051
checks and balances, 631, 645. *See also* political ideas.
chemical weapons. *See* weapons, of mass destruction.
chemistry, 628, *c820*
Chiapas, 1038
Chichén Itzá, 446–447
child labor, *i716*, *c724–725*, 726, 728, *i728*, 738–739
in textile factories, *i833*
children
in African culture, 216
in Confucian thought, 104
in Crusades, 384
in Han dynasty
in Industrial Revolution, *i716, c724–725,* 726, 728, 738–739
slavery of, *i97*, 164
Children's Crusade, 384
China. *m51, m187. See also* names of dynasties.
in the 1990s, 1061–1062
acupuncture, *i325*
agriculture, 50, 204, 805
army, *i1061*
Boxer Rebellion, 808–809, *i809*
bureaucracy, 203
civil war in, 882, 884, 886, 972–973
coins, *i55*
and Cold War, 969, 973, 990–991
colonial powers carve up, *m803*
communes, 974
communism in, 883–884, 972–975, 1059–1060
cultural developments, 52, 541
Cultural Revolution, 975, 1059–1060
dynastic cycle in, *c54*
early cities, 52
early farming, 15
economic development, 1060, 1063
ethical systems, 105–107, *c106*
foot-binding, 327
Forbidden City, *i538*
geography of, 50–51, *m51*
"Great Leap Forward," 974–975
Great Wall of, *i108*, 109, 323
Han dynasty, 109, 200–207, *c208*, 252–257
and Hong Kong transfer to, 1062–1063
inventions, 204, *i322*, 325, *i328–329*
isolationism in, 805, 1060
Japanese invasion, 812, 886, *i886*, 916
last emperor, *i864*, 882
Long March, 884–886, *i885*
Mao Zedong, *i866*, 883–886, 972–975, *i974*, 1059–1060, *i1060*
May Fourth Movement, 883
Mongol rule, 336–338
nationalists in, 808–809, 882
Olympics in, 1063
Opium War, 806
peasants, 323, 884
People's Republic of China (mainland China), 973
political developments, 203, 323–324, 882–884, 1063
population, *c540*, 806
Qin dynasty, 107–109, *m108*, 200
Red Guards, 975, *i975*
reform in, 809, 1059–1060, 1063
religious beliefs, 54, 71
revolution in, 882
river dynasties of, 51–52, *i113*
Sima Qian ("Grand Historian"), 202, 205
social changes, 327, 1063
social values of ancient China, *c202*
Soviet split with, 974–975, 989–990, 1060
special economic zones (SEZs), *i806*
Taiwan, 973
Tiananmen Square, *i883*, 1061–1062, *i1064*
Tibet, 973
and World War I, 851–852, 883
and World War II, 931, 972
Wudi ("Martial Emperor"), 201–202
Chinese Heritage, The, 54
Chinese medicine, *i325*
chivalry
age of, 365, 367–368
decline of, 402–403
chlorofluorocarbons (CFCs), 1079
Christian humanists, 482
Christianity, 168–172, *i286–287*, *c296*. *See also* church; Crusades; Roman Catholic Church.
in Aksum, 227–228, *i227*
under Constantine, 171–172
and Enlightenment values, 634
Hagia Sophia and, 303
heresy, 172, 384
in Japan, 546
Jesus, 168–169, *i169*
politics and spread of, 171, 354
rise of, 168–172
in Roman Empire, 169–171, 172
schism, 399
and science, 625
sects, 490, 494–496
spread of, 169–171, *m171*, 354, 530
unifying force of, 170, 370–371
Viking conversion to, 359
widespread appeal of, 170
as world religion, 286–287
Christians
burial rites of, 169
martyrs, 170
missionaries, 354, 499, 546
in Muslim culture, 268
Roman persecution of, 170–171
church. *See also* Roman Catholic Church.
division of, 304, *c305*
Eastern Orthodox, 304–305, *c305*
Great Schism, 399
Hagia Sophia, 303
lay investiture, 372
Orthodox, 306
reform, 379–380, 398
Roman Catholic, 305–306, *c305*
Russian Orthodox, *c305*, *i313*, 610, 877
tithes, 363, 379
Churchill, Winston, 927, *i927*, 930, 940–941
on appeasement, 919
and Boer War, *i778*
"Iron Curtain" speech, 967
at Yalta Conference, *i965*, 966
CIA (Central Intelligence Agency), 982
CIS. *See* Commonwealth of Independent States.
citadel, 46
cities
and absolute monarchy, 595
of ancient China, 52
definition of, 20
early Mesoamerican, 242, *i242*
in early Middle Ages, 353
Forbidden, *i538*
growth of, 19, *c743*
Muslim, 273–274
planned, 46, 243, 455
rise of, 20, *c24*
Sumerian, *c3*, 20, 31
Ur, *c3*, 19–22
citizens
in ancient Greece, 127–128, 134–135
in ancient Rome, 156–157, *c157*, 158
in Inca civilization, 461
in limited democracy, 128
rights and responsibilities, 135
role in democracy, 128, 134, *c134*
in United States, *c134*
city-state(s)
African, 422–424
Athens as, 133, 134–138, 142
Carthage as, 76
East African, 422–424
Greek, *i87*, *c121*, *m121*, 127–133
Hausa, 417–418
Kilwa, 422, 424
Maya, 446–447
Northern Italian, *c578*
Phoenician, 73
Sparta as, 129, 131
Sumerian, *c3*, 30–31
Thebes as, 142
civic duty. *See* citizens.
civil disobedience, 888–889
in India, 889
in Israel, 1019, 1021–1022
civilization(s)
American (1200 B.C. to A.D. 700), *m233*
African, *c230*, 422–427
agriculture's effect on, 18, 19
ancient, 20–23, *c113*
characteristics of, 20–21, *c21*, *c114*
Confucian influence on, 105, 203
of Indus Valley, *c27*, 44–49, *i112*
prehistory to 2500 B.C., 5–23
rise of, *i112–113*
of river valleys (3500–500 B.C.), *c26–27*, *c56*
in Ur, 22–23, 31
civil rights
Arabs and, 1091
under dictatorship, *c875*
civil servants, 203

Index

civil service, 203
in Chinese empires, 203
in Korea, 347
in Tang dynasty, 324
civil war(s)
American, 759–760, *m760*
in Angola, 1016
in China, 882, 884, 886, 972–973
English, 615, *m616*
Incan, 463
in Japan, 542
in Lebanon, 1021
Muslim, 270–271
in Nicaragua, 985
in Nigeria, 1041–1042
Roman, 161, 162
Russian, 871–872, *c871*
Saint Domingue, 665, 682
Spanish, 917, *i918*
Cixi (Chinese Dowager Empress), 807–809
clan, 331
Clare, 380
classical ages
characteristics of, 252
cultural achievements of, *c254–255*
influence of, *i252–253*
legacy of, 256–257, *i256*
territory controlled by societies of, *m253*
time line, *c252–253*
classical art, 136, 178–179
Cleisthenes, 128, 135
Clemenceau, Georges, 858, *i859*
Cleopatra, 162
clergy, 370
climate
influence on Greek life of, 124
regions, world, *m57*
Clinton, Bill, 1022
clock
Chinese, 325, *c328*
mechanical, *c328*
cloning, 1073–1074
clothing, *i581*, 723, 1093, 1095
Clovis culture, 236, *i237*, *m237*
Clovis (Germanic king), 354, 356
Cluny, 379
coalition, 1083
coalition government, 904
coal mining, 725, 738
Code of Hammurabi. *See* Hammurabi's Code.
codex, 448, *i448*
coins
Aksumite, 228
first, 55, *i55*
Persian, 101
Roman, 163, 173, 196
Colbert, Jean Baptiste, 598–599
Cold War, 965–991, *m964*, *c992*
1946–1980, *c992*
in Angola, 1016
brinksmanship, 970, 990
China in, 973–974
détente, 990–991
end of, 991, 1046, 1054
enemies, *m963*
hot spots in, *m984*
NATO (North Atlantic Treaty Organization), 969, 1082
nonaligned nations, 982
nuclear threat, 969–970
revolutions during, 984–987
strategies, 969, 982, *c983*
and Third World, 982–987
time line, *c962–963*
U-2 incident, 970, 990
Warsaw Pact, 969,1082
collective bargaining, 738
collective farms, 878, 974
colonialism. *See also* colonies; imperialism.
British, 562–564, 776, 778, 781–782, 791–795, 797
and capitalism, 573
and democracy, 1040
economic, 817–818
effects of, 573–575, 784, 792
of France, 561–562, 682, 797, 1015
German, 782–783
impact on native Americans of, *c556*
in Latin America, 554–558, 675, 816
of Netherlands, 563
of Portugal, 427, 557
post-World War I, 887–889, 915–916
post-World War II, 982–987, 997–998, 1004, 1012
resistance to, 559, 782–783
and slavery, 559, 566–570
of Southeast Asia, 796–798
of Spain, 681–682
colonies, 554. *See also* colonialism.
in Africa and Asia, 887–889, 1015
of Belgian Congo, 774, 1015
British, 562–563, 565, 640, 751–753, 791–795, 887–889
Dutch, 563–564, 776, 796
French, 561–562, 564, 598, 682, 797, 1015
independence of British, 997–1003, 1013
revolt in French, 682
self-rule of, 751–753, 889
Colonna, Vittoria, 477
Colosseum, 165, 181, *i182*
Colossus of Rhodes, 149
Columbian Exchange, 571–573, *i572*
effect on food of, *i572*
Columbus, Christopher, 553–554, *i554*
legacy of, 560
native resistance to, 449
comedy, 136, *i141*
command economy, 877
Commercial Revolution, 389–390, *c390*
common law, 394
Commonwealth
of Australia, 753
Commonwealth of Independent States (CIS), 1049–1050
communes, 974
communications
global, 1072–1073
communism, 737, *c872*. *See also* Cold War.
in Cambodia, 980–981
in China, 883–886, 972–975, 989–990
and democratic reforms, 985
domino theory of, 978
in eastern Europe, 988–989, 1052
economic effects of, 737, 877–878, 974
evolution of communist thought, *c872*
fall of, 1049
and fascism, 910
historical origins of, 736–737, *c737*
in Latin America, 984–985
in Middle East, 986–987
Politburo of, 1046
post-World War II, 949
in Russia, *c872*, 873, 876–879
in Southeast Asia, 978, 981
spread of, 978
Communist Manifesto, The **(Marx and Engels),** 736–738
compass
magnetic, *i322*, 325, *i328–329*, *i433*
computers, 1072–1073
concordat, 664
Concordat of Worms, 372
Confucianism, *i294–295*, *c296*
and agriculture, 204
and commerce, 204
in China, 104–105, 203
five relationships, 104
and government, 105, 203
in Korea, 346
Legalists, 106–107, *c106*
social order, 104
values of, 104, *c106*
as world ethical system, 294–295
yin and yang, 107, *i107*, 109
Confucius, 104–105, *i105*, 115
Analects, 105, *i295*
Congo, 409, 774, 1015
Democratic Republic of, 1015
Congress of Vienna, 672–675
Congress Party, 997
conquistadors, 554–558
Conservatives, 657, 687, 690
Constantine (Roman emperor), 171–172, 174–175
conversion of, 171
Constantinople, *m302*
as capital, 175, 176, 301–304
fall of, 304, 383, 385
Hagia Sophia, 303
Hippodrome, 303
Nika Rebellion, 303
Ottoman defeat of, 304, 508–509, *i509*
Turkish threat to, 304, 315
constitution
first, 615
of Japan, post-World War II, 951
Korean, 978
Mexican, 827, *c827*
of the Philippines, 1006
South African, 1044
United States, *c643*, 644–645, 647
constitutional monarchy, 617, 657. *See also* monarchy.
consuls, 157
containment, 967
in South Korea, 976
in Vietnam, 978
Continental System, 668
Contras, 985, 991
convents, 354
Cook, James, 752
Copernicus, Nicolaus, 624–625
Coronado, Francisco Vásquez de, 558, *i558*
corporation, 731
Cortés, Hernando, 554, 556
cotton
consumption in Britain, *c719*
in India, 792
in United States, 720
cotton gin, 720
Council of Trent, 499
Counter Reformation. *See* Reformation, Catholic; Roman Catholic Church.
coup, 664
coup d'état, 664
covenant, 78
Hebrew, 78–80
Creoles, 674–675, 681–682, *c681*
Crete, 72, *m72*
criminal justice, 632
Croatia, 1056

Cro-Magnon, *c3, i3,* 9–10, *c9*
Cromwell, Oliver, 615–616
cross
as Christian symbol, 171, *i382*
crossbow, 402
Crusades, 382–386, *m383*
Children's, 383–384
economic impact of, 385
First Crusade, 382
in the Middle Ages, 382–386, *m383*
Muslim counterattacks, 316, 383
political impact of, 385
Second Crusade, 382
in Seljuk Empire, 316, 383
social impact of, *i378,* 385
Spanish, 384
Third Crusade, 383
Cry of Dolores. *See Grito de Dolores.*
Cuba
Batista, Fulgencio, 984
Bay of Pigs, 985
Castro, Fidel, 984–985, *i985*
independence of, 818–819
Revolution, 984
Cuban Missile Crisis, 985, 990
cultural blending, 63, 512–513, *c513. See also* global culture.
by Alexander the Great, 146
in Mughal India, *i522–523*
in Muslim Empire, 272, 273
of Nubia and Egypt, 92–93, *i92–93*
in Safavid Empire, 514–515
in world, 1095–1096
cultural diffusion, 31
cultural identity, 1097
Cultural Revolution (China), 975, 1059–1060
culture(s), 5–6. *See also* Africa; Americas, the; China; Hellinistic Culture; India; Japan; Roman Empire.
under Alexander the Great, 145, 146
components of, *c6*
mass, 766–767, *c767*
means of expanding, 76
and nationalism, 687, *c688*
popular, 1093–1095
cuneiform, 20, *i21,* 32, 40
Curie, Marie, 765, *i765, i831*
cybercafés, *i637*
cyberterrorism, 1088
cyclops, *i126*
Cyrillic alphabet. *See* alphabet, Cyrillic.
Cyrus the Great (Persian king), 82, 99–100, 103
czar(s). *See* individual names of czars.
Czechoslovakia
in 1990s, 1055
democracy in, 914, 1055
falls to Hitler, 919
reforms, 1055
resistance to communism in, 989

D

da Gama, Vasco, 532–533
daimyo, 542–546
Dai Viet, 346
Dalai Lama, 973
Dali, Salvador, *i899*
Dante Alighieri, 392
Danton, Georges, 660–661, *i661*
***Dao De Jing* (Laozi),** 105–106
Daoism, 105–106, *c106*
Laozi, 105–106, *105*
in Song Dynasty, 326
Darius (Persian king), 100–101, 132
Darius III (Persian king), 143–144
Darwin, Charles, 765, *i766*
da Silva, Luiz Inacio Lula, 1036
David (Israeli king), 81
da Vinci, Leonardo, *i286–287,* 475, *i475*
Dawes, Charles, 905
D-Day invasion (World War II), 943–944, *m944*
death rituals. *See* burial rites.
Deborah (Hebrew judge), 80
***Decameron* (Boccaccio),** 476
Deccan Plateau, 44
decimal system, 195
Declaration of Independence, 641–642
Locke's influence on, 630, 642
Declaration of Rights of Man, 656
de Gaulle, Charles, 927
de Klerk, F. W., 1044, *i1044*
Delhi, 516
Delhi Sultanate, 516
Delian League, 133, 135
delta, 36
demilitarization, 950
democracy, *c180. See also* democratic reforms; government, democratic and republican.
1945–present, *c1030–1031*
in Africa, 1013, 1015, 1040–1045
in ancient Greece, 128, 134–135, *c134*
in Cambodia, 978
in China, 1061–1063
and colonial rule, 1040
common practices of, *c1033*
Congress of Vienna and, 672
in Czechoslovakia, 1055
direct, 1033
and French Revolution, 652, 654, 656
in Great Britain, 747–748
in India, 999–1000
indirect, 1033
in industrialized countries, 740
in Japan, 950
in Latin America, 1033–1039
limited, 1040
loss of confidence in, 905, 910–914
monarchy and, 747
post-World War I, 904–906
role of photojournalism in, *i1064–1065*
in Russia, 1049–1051
in South Korea, 978
struggles, 1033–1065, *c1066*
time line of, *c1066*
in United States, 617, *c643*
Western, *c180, m745*
democratic reforms
in ancient Greece, 128, 135
in ancient Rome, 156–157
in England, 394–395, 617, 747–749
of French Revolution, 654, 656
in Industrial Revolution, 739–740
in Japan, 950–951
in Middle Ages, 394–397
in modern world, 1002
in revolutionary China, 882, 884
democratization, 950, 1047
Demosthenes, 142
Deng Xiaoping, 1060–1061
Four Modernizations, 1060
Department of Homeland Security, *i1070,* 1091
de Pizan, Christine, 482, *i482*
Depression, the, 904–909
causes of, 906–907, *c920*
effects of, 907–908, *c920*
and fascism, 910–912
global effects, 907–908
in Japan, 915
life in, *i907*
and Nazism, 912
recovery, 909
responses to, 908–909
Roosevelt, Franklin D., 909, *i909*
stock market, 906–907, *c906*
unemployment during, *c908*
in United States, 907, 909
Descartes, René, 626
desertification, 217
destalinization, 988
d'Este, Isabella, 473, *i473*
détente, 990–991
developed nations, 1075–1076
developing nations, *c1100–1101*
devshirme, 510
dharma, 70
Dias, Bartolomeu, 530, 532
Diaspora, 170, 1017
Díaz, Porfirio, 825–826, *i825*
dictators *See also* fascism; Nazism; individual names of dictators.
in Argentina, *i914,* 1038–1039
in Brazil, 1034
in Cuba, 984–985, *i985*
in France, 664–667
in Germany, 911–914
in Italy, 910–911
in Nicaragua, 985
in North Korea, 977
pre-World War II, 910–914
in Roman Republic, 157
in Russia, 873, 876–879
in Spain, 917
Diderot, Denis, 636
Diem, Ngo Dinh, 978, 980
Diocletian, 174–175
disease *See also* bubonic plague.
of Aborigines, 753
AIDS (acquired immune deficiency syndrome), 1045, 1085, *m1085*
in Central Mexico, impact of, *c556*
in Columbian Exchange, 571–573, *i573*
germ theory of, 764
during Industrial Revolution, 724
inoculation against, 628
of Maoris, 753
in North America, 556, *c556,* 565, 571–573
post-World War II, 949
SARS (Severe Acute Respiratory Syndrome), *i1070*
smallpox, 556, *i560,* 565, 571, 573, 628
vaccines, 764, 835
during World War I, *i853*
dissidents, 1042
***Divine Comedy, The* (Dante),** 392
divine right, 594
Djenné-Djeno, 219, *i219, m219*
DNA, 1073–1074
Dnieper River, 307, *m308,* 310
Dole, Sanford B., 799
Dome of the Rock, *i266*
domestication, 16, 18, 46, 215
dominion, 752
domino theory, 978
Domitian, *c164*

Index

Donatello, 474
Don Quixote de la Mancha **(Cervantes),** 591–592
Dorians, 125
drama. *See also* art.
Chinese, 541
Greek, 136, *i141*
Indian, 194, *i195*
Japanese, 544, *i545*
Dreyfus affair, 749–750
Dubček, Alexander, 989, *i989*
Duhalde, Eduardo, 1039
Duke of Shao, 54
Duma, 870
Dürer, Albrecht, 481
Durham, Lord, 752
Dutch. *See also* Netherlands.
colonies, 563–564, 776
East India Company, 534, 594, 796
in Southeast Asia, 534–535, 796, 1008
dye, 74, *i75*
dynastic cycle, 54, *c54*
dynasties, 31, 90. *See also* empire(s).
Abbasid, 271–272, 273
Almohad, 412
Almoravid, 411–412
Bourbon, 596–597, 601
Capetian, 396
Carolingian, 356–357
of China, *c338*
Egyptian, 37, 90–91
Fatimid, 272
Han, 200–207, 252–257
Korean, 346–347
Ming, 536–539
Muslim, 269–272
Qin, *c87,* 107–109, *m108,* 200
Qing, 539, 805, 882
Romanov, 609
Shang, 52
Song, 324–327
Tang, 323–327
Umayyad, 271–272
Xia, 51
Zhou, *c27*, 54–55, 104, *c121*

E

Earhart, Amelia, 901
Earth, planet, *c147*
time line, *i9*
East Africa, 422–425. *See also* Africa.
cultural blending in, 422
human origins in, 7–8, *m10*, 11
Islamic influences on, 424–425
slavery in, 425
trade in, 422, *m423*
East Asia. *m321. See also* empire(s).
foreign influence in, 805–813
growth in, 1007
Eastern Europe
in 1990s, 1052–1053, 1055–1058
invasion by Vikings of, *m308*
Eastern Front
in World War I, 848–849
in World War II, 928–930
Eastern Orthodox Church, 304–305, *c305*
East Germany. *See also* Germany.
Berlin Wall, 969, 1053–1054, *i1053*, *i1065*
East Timor, 1008–1009, *i1009*
economics
capitalism, 573, 734–735, *c737*
communism, 737, *c872*
effects of migration on, 221
environmental impact of, 1079–1080, 1081
factors of production, 718
gross domestic product, *c1076*
in Han Dynasty, 204–205, *m204–205*
of industrialization, 734–737
inflation, 573, 592, 905
laissez faire, 734–735
of manorialism, 360, 362–362
Marxism, 736–738, *c872*
in Middle Ages, 360, 362–363
socialism, 736–738, *c737*
economy *See also* economics.
command, 877
crisis in post-World-War-I Germany, 905
global, 1076, *c1078*
recession, 1034
reform of Russian, 872–873, 1051
Soviet, 877–878, *c878*, 1046
technology's effect on, 1075–1076
edict, 190
Edict of Milan, 171
Edict of Nantes, 596, 599
Edict of Worms, 490
Edison, Thomas, 762, *i763*, 766
education
in Byzantium, 303
under Charlemagne, 357
and colonial rule, 784, 792
in czarist Russia, 610–611
in democracy, 128
of girls, 129
lycées, 664
in Middle Ages, 391
in modern China, 1063
in Pacific Rim, 797
public, 740, 811
Spartan, 131
after *Sputnik*, 970
Sumerian, 32
in Tang Dynasty, 324, 327
in totalitarian states, 874, 876
Edward I (English king), 395, 405
Edward III (English king), 401
Edward VI (English king), 493
EEC (European Economic Community), 1076
Efe, 409
Egypt, 35–41
ancient, *c26,* 35–41, *c86*, 89–91, *i112*
Camp David Accords, 1020
Cleopatra, 162
cosmetics, *i43*
culture of, 38
divorce in, 40
dynasties of, 37, 90–91
geography of, 35, *m36*, *m91*
Hebrew migration from, 89
hierogylphics, 40, *i40*
invasion of ancient, 41, 89, 91
inventions, 40–41
kingdoms of, *c26*, 37, 90
mummification, 38–39, *i39*
Narmer, 37
Nile River, importance of, 16, 35
under Ottoman rule, 509
pets, 43
pharaohs of, 37, 39, 41, 90–91
pyramids, *i1*, 37–38, *i39*
reforms in, 788
relations with Israel, 1020–1021
religion of, 38–39
social classes in, 40
Suez Crisis, 1018–1019
Eightfold Path, 193
Einstein, Albert, 766, 897, *i946*
theory of relativity, 897
Eisenhower, Dwight D., 940, 943, *i944*
during Cold War, 970, 978
domino theory, 978
Eleanor of Aquitaine, 368, 394, *i394*
Elizabeth I (British queen), 483, 493–494, *i494*
Elizabethan Age
Renaissance in England, 483, *i486–487*
El Salvador, 686
Emancipation Proclamation, *i691*, 760
emerging nations, 1075–1076
émigrés, 658
emperor(s). *See also* individual names of rulers.
Byzantine, 301–304
China's last emperor, *i864*, 882
Chinese, 107, 109, 200–203, 539–541
Holy Roman, 370–373, *m372*
Japanese, 340
Roman, *c164*
empire(s), 33
Akkadian, 33
of Alexander the Great, *c87*, *c121*, 143–145, *m144*, *c145*
ancient, *m87*, 89–109
Assyrian, *c87*, 95–97, *m96*, *c121*
Austro-Hungarian, 844, 963
Aztec, 453–458, 556
Babylonian, *c27*, 28
British, *c780*, *m801*
Byzantine, 301–304
builders of first, 32–33, *c110*
characteristics of, 33, 90, *c110*
Chinese, 104–109, 200–207, 323–329, 536–541, 805–809
comparison of, *c319*, *c525*
East Asian, 330–343
Egyptian, 37–38, 89–91
First Age of Empires, 89–109
French, 667
of Ghana, 413–415, *m414*
Greek, 142–149
Gupta, 191–192, *c208*, 252–255
Han, 200–207
Hittite, 62–63
Holy Roman, 371–373, 605
Incan, 459–465
Indian, 189–192, 516–521
Khmer (Cambodia), 345
Kush, c87, 92–94, *m93*
Malian, 415–417, *m414*
Mauryan, *c121*, 189–191, *m191*, *c208*
Mongol, 309, *m309,* 332–334, *m334,* 335–338
Mughal, 516–523
Muslim, 269–272
Mutapa, 427
Napoleonic, *m649*, 665–671
nationalism's effect on, 687, *c688*
Nubian, *c87*, 92–94
Ottoman, 507–511, 605, 786–787
Persian, *c87*, 99–103, *m101*, 143
population of, *c319*
Qin, *c87*, 107–109, *m108*, 200
Roman, 160–165, 173–177, 252–257
Russian, 693
Safavid, 512–515, *m514*
Seljuk, 314–316
Songhai, 417, *m414*
southern African, 425–427

Spanish, 589–593
trading, 413–416
Turkish, 314–317
West African, 413–417, *m414*
Zhou, *c27*, 104, *c121*
empress. *See* individual names.
enclosures, 717
encomienda, 557, 559
Encyclopedia, 636
Engels, Friedrich, 736, 738
England. *See* Britain.
English Civil War. *See* civil war(s), Britain.
English language, 181, 1095
enlightened despot, 638
enlightenment, 68
Enlightenment, 623–645
and American Revolution, 641–642, *c643*
architecture of, *i600*, 637
centers of, *m621*, 630, 636
and French Revolution, 652
impact of, 633–634, 636–639
literature of, 633, 636, 637
music of, 637
Paris during, 630, 636
political ideas of, 629–632, *c632*
and revolution, *c646*, *m684*
values in, 639–635
women's contributions to, 633, 636
Enola Gay, *i946*
entrepreneur, 721
environmental influences. *See also* flooding.
in Africa, 213–216, 425
on agricultural revolution, 15, *c17*
in ancient China, 50–51, 207
in ancient Egypt, 35–36, 89
in ancient Greece, 123–124
in ancient Sumer, 29
in ancient trade, 76
on Andean cultures, 246
in Assyrian culture, 95
and decline of Aksum, 229
and decline of Mughal Empire, 521
of disease, 556
of economic development, 1079–1080
and end of Minoan culture, 73
on fall of Roman Empire, 173
of geopolitics, 786–787
on global community, 1079–1080
in Han dynasty, *m204–205*, 207
in India, 44–45, 195
of Industrial Revolution, 718, 732
in Indus Valley, 45
and isolationism, 339, 805
on Japan, 339
in Kush, 92, 94
in Mesopotamia, 29–30
on migrations, 215, 220, *c221*, 223
in native North America, 441, 443
in North American colonies, 562–563
in Olmec civilization, 240–241
on Peloponnesian War, 137
of the plague, 401
on the Renaissance, 471
on Southeast Asia, 344
of the tsetse fly, 213, *i214*, 215
on West African empires, 413, 415
on Zapotec society, 242
Epic of Gilgamesh, 32, 83, 96
epics, 125–126, 179, *i179*, 367, *i367*
Epicurianism, 149
Epicurus, 149
epidemics. *See also* bubonic plague, influenza; smallpox.
Erasmus, Desiderius, 482
Eratosthenes, 147
Ericson, Leif, 359
Esfahan, 514
estates (French social classes), 397, 651–652, *c652*
Estates-General, 397, 653–654
Este, Isabella d', 473, *i473*
Estonia, 925, 1049
ethical monotheism, 80
Ethiopia
Christianity in, 228
Haile Selassie, 225, 916
human origins in, *m10*
Mussolini, attacks by, 916
resistance movements in, 783
Ethiopian Orthodox Church, *i287*
ethnic cleansing. *See also* Hitler, Adolf.
in Bosnia, 1056, *i1064*
ethnic conflict, 1083
in Central Asia, 1024–1025
in post-colonial Africa, 1012–1013
Etruscans, 155–156
EU (European Union), 1077
Euclid, 147–148
Euphrates River, 22, 29
Euripides, 136
Europe. *See also* European exploration; Western Europe.
aggression in, 841–842, *c916*
in the East, 1487–1700, *m534*
invasions in, *m359*
and Japan, 545–547, 810–811
maps
500, *m351*
1500, *m469*
1650, *m587*
1805–1813, war in, *m666*
1810/1817, *m674*
1848, revolutions in, *m679*
1870, industry in, *i715*
1914, *m839*
1931–1939, expansion in, *c894–895*
in the Middle Ages, *m351*, 353–373, *m377*
post-Thirty Years' War, 604, *m604*
post-World War I, 897–891, 904–905
post-World War II, 948–950
religions in (1560), *m497*
during World War I, 845–854
European Economic Community (EEC), 1076
European exploration, *m527*, *c548*. *See also* colonialism; imperialism.
of the Americas, 1492–1682, *m555*
causes of, 529–530
cultural influence of, 558
effects of, *c556*
science and technology of, 530, *i531*
European Union (EU), 1077
evolution, 765
excavation, 5, 22, *i22*
excommunication, 306, 371
existentialism, 898–899
post-World War I, influence of, 899
Sartre, Jean Paul, 898
Exodus, 78
exploration, age of, 529–535, 553–558
extended family, 216
extraterritorial rights, 806, 810–812
Eyck, Jan van, *i470*, 481
Ezana (Aksumite king), 226–228
Ezekiel, 82

F

FAA (Federal Aviation Administration), 1092
factories, 720, 724, *c724–725*
Factory Act, 728
Falkland Islands, 1039
family
in African culture, 216, 410
in Confucian thought, 104–105
extended, 216
in Germanic society, 354
in Han dynasty, 206
lineage system, 410
matriarchal, 192
matrilineal, 410
in native America, 445
patriarchal, 192
patrilineal, 410
and slave trade, 570
famine
in China, 974
in Ireland, 754, *c754*
in Soviet Union, 872, *i879*
during World War I, 855–856
post-World War II, 949
farming. *See also* agriculture; Neolithic Revolution.
in the Americas, 16, 238–239, *c239*
change brought by, 16
crop rotation, 717
crops, 18, 42
early development of, 16, 18
floating gardens, 239, 455
of Indian empires, 190, 192
in the Middle Ages, 362, 387
role of slavery in, 164, 566
seed drill, 717, *i718*
soil erosion, 1080
terrace, 228
three-field system of, 387
fascism. *See also* World War II.
in Argentina, *i914*, 1039
in Italy, 910–911
in Spain, 917
Fatimid caliphate, 272
Federal Aviation Administration (FAA), 1092
Federal Government
aviation security and, 1092
federal system, 644–655
Ferrill, Arther, 177
Fertile Crescent, 29, 34, 88
in 2500 B.C., *m30*
Assyrian domination, 96
Persian empire in, 100–101, *m101*
feudalism, 54. *See also* feudal society.
Church authority, 363
cultural effect of, 363
decline of, 385
economics, 362–363
in Europe, *i361*, *c361*
in Japan, 341, 343, *i361*, *c361*, 542
manors, 360, 362, *i362*
Russian, 690–691, *i691*
feudal society. *See also* feudalism.
knights, 360, 364–365
samurai, *i342*, 343, 542, *i542*
women in, 368–369
fief, 360
filial piety, 104, 105
Filipino, 1004
"Final Solution," 937–939
fire, mastery over, 7–8
firearms, 545
First Reich, 697

Index

First World, 982
Fitzgerald, F. Scott, 898, *i898*
Five Pillars of Islam, 267, *i275*
Five-Year-Plans (Stalin), 877–878
FLN (Algerian National Liberation Front), 1015
Ahmed Ben Bella, 1015
flooding
in the Americas, 240
benefits of, 29
in China, 50, 207
control of, 51
of Fertile Crescent, 29
of Huang He, 50, *51*
of Indus River Valley, 44–45
of Nile, 35–36
flood story, 83, *i83*
Florida, 558
Forbidden City, *i538*
Ford, Gerald, 991
Ford, Henry, 762, 764, *c831*
forest dwellers, 409, *m411*
Formosa. *See* Taiwan.
Forum, Roman, 156, *i156*
fossil hunters, 5
fossils, 5
Four Modernizations, 1060
Four Noble Truths, *c69*
Fourteen Points, 858–859
Fox, Vicente, 1038, *i1038*, *i1104*
France, *m677*. *See also* French Revolution.
absolute monarchy in, 598–602
in American Revolution, 642, 653
art of prehistoric, *i13*
Capetian dynasty, 396
containment of, 672–673
de Gaulle, Charles, 927
democracy in, 397, 654, 656, 690, 749
the Depression in, 908
development of, *c397*
as empire, *m649*, 664–667
during Enlightenment, 630, 636
Estates-General, 397, 653–654
First, 397, 651, *c652*
Second, 397, 651, *c652*
Third, 651–652, *c652*
in Hundred Years' War, 401–403
in Indochina, 797, *m797*
influence in Southeast Asia, 797, 978
instability of, 652–653
Louis XIV of, *i588*, 598–602, *i598*
debt incurred by, *c602*
North American colonies of, 561–562, 564, 641, 682
Paris Commune, *i746*
reforms and revolution in, 651–661, 690
religions in, *m497*
as republic, 690
Third Republic, 690, 749
in Thirty Years' War, 604
in Vietnam, 797, 978
at war, 601, 658, 660
in World War I, 845–848, 855
in World War II, 926–927
Francis I (French king), 480
Francis of Assisi, St., 380
Franco, Francisco, 917
***Frankenstein* (Shelley),** 699
Franks. *See* Germanic empire.
Franz Ferdinand (Archduke of Austria), 844
Frederick I, "Barbarossa" (Holy Roman emperor), 373
Frederick William II, "Frederick the Great" (Prussian king), 606–607, *i606*, 638
free trade, 1076–1077
French Revolution, *c706*. *See also* Napoleon I.
Bastille, storming of, 654–655, *i654*
causes of, 652–654
compared with Russian Revolution, 872
democratic ideals of, 652–653
effects of, 655–661
Enlightenment ideas in, 652
estates, 651–652, *c652*, 654
Great Fear, 655
guillotine, *i659*, 660
influence of American Revolution on, *i644*, 652
Legislative Assembly, 657–658
National Assembly, 654, 656
Old Regime, 651, 658
opinions on, 662
reforms of, 656–657
Reign of Terror, 660–661
Robespierre, Maximilien, 660–661, *i660*, *i711*
social classes before, 651–652, *c652*
Tennis Court Oath, 654
war during, 658, 660
Freud, Sigmund, 766, 897, 898, 899
friars, 380
Fulton, Robert, 721
funeral rites. *See* burial rites.

G

Gadsden Purchase, 759, *m759*
Galilei, Galileo, 625, *i625*
Gallipoli campaign, 851, *m851*
Gandhi, Indira, *i519*, 1000, *i1001*
Gandhi, Mohandas K., 852, *i866*, 888–889, *i889*, 999
principles of nonviolence, 888–889, 997
Gandhi, Rajiv, 1000, *i1001*
Ganges River, 44
Garibaldi, Giuseppe, 694, *i694*
Gaskell, Elizabeth, 724, *i724*
GATT (General Agreement on Tariffs and Trade), 1076
Gaulle, Charles de, 927
GDP (gross domestic product), *c1076*
gender inequality, 1084
genetic engineering, 1073
genetics, 1073–1074
genocide, 937. *See also* Bosnia; Holocaust.
in Rwanda, *i1016*, 1084
in World War I, 957
gentry, 327
geocentric theory, 623–624
geographical isolation, 50
geography. *See also* environmental influences.
of Africa, 213–215, *m214*, *m429*
of Egypt, 35–36, *m36*
influence on Greek life, 123–124
influence on Indian culture, 197
geometry. *See* mathemetics, geometry.
geopolitics, 786
George III (English king), 539, 640
Germanic Empire. *See also* Prussia; reformation.
Christianity in, 354–357
Clovis, 354, 356
Franks, 354–356
Germany. *See also* Prussia; reformation.
allies with Soviets, 925
attacks North Africa, 928
Berlin Wall, 969, 1053–1054, *i1053*, *i1065*
the Depression in, 905
economic crisis in, 905
fall of Communism, 1054
Hitler, Adolf, 911–914, *i912*, 916–919, *i921*, 925–930
industrialization in, 732
inflation, 905, *i905*
major industries of, 2003, *m1054*
Nazism, 911–914
Neanderthals in, 9, *m10*
Renaissance in, 481–482
reunification of East and West Germany, 1054
in Russian Revolution, 870
splitting of, 967, *m969*
surrender in World War II, 945
Third Reich, 918, 945
Thirty Years' War in, 603–604
and Treaty of Versailles, 861, *c861*
unification of, 695–697, *m697*
Weimar Republic, 905
in World War I, 845–854
in World War II, 925–930, 936–945
Ghana
empire of, 413–415, *m414*
independence of, 1013
Islamic influences, 415
Soninke people, 413
ghazi, 507
ghettos, 938
Gibbon, Edward, 177
"gift of the Nile," 35
glaciers, 236, *i237*
gladiators, 164, 165, *i165*, *i182*
glasnost, 1046
global communications, 1072–1073
global culture
art of, 1096
English language, 1095
popular culture, 1093–1094
Western influences on, 1095–1096
global economy, 1076, *c1078*, 1079–1080
global interdependence, 1097, *c1098*
globalization, 1077–1079, *c1078*
global security, 1082–1083
and terrorism, 1088
Glorious Revolution, 616
glyphs. *See also* hieroglyphics.
Maya, 448
Gobi Desert, 50, *m51*
Goldman, Emma, 900
gold trade, 227, 413
Gorbachev, Mikhail
attempted coup of, 1049
glasnost, 1046
INF (Intermediate-Range Nuclear Forces) treaty, 1047
perestroika, 1047
Gospels (New Testament), 169
Gothic, 380, *i381*
Gouges, Olympe de, 656
government, *c180*. *See also* democracy; political systems.
of Africa, 216
of ancient China, 54, 203
architecture of, *i582*
aristocracy, 127, *c128*
of Assyrian empire, 96
of Athens, 128, 133, 134–135
under Augustus, 162, *i162*
autocratic, 867
beginnings of organized, 30–31
bureaucracy, 105, 203, *i579*
centralized, 200, 397

of China, 105, 200–203, 1059–1062
coalition, 904
commonwealth, 615
constitutional monarchy, 617
democracy, 123, *c128*, 157, *c180*
democratic, 128
descriptions of, 583
dictators in ancient Rome, 157
of Egypt, *c26*, 37, 41, 89–91
Incan, 460–461, *c578*
of Indus Valley civilization, 48
of Italian city-states, *c578*
in the Middle Ages, 354
military, 201–202, 1034
monarchy, 127, *c128*, *i578*, 594–595
natural rights in, 630, *c632*
oligarchy, 127, *c128*, *i579*
Ottoman, 510, *c578*
papal, 379
provisional, 870
representative, 128
republican, 157, c157, 644–645
responsibility of, 630
Roman influence of, 157
social contract in, 629
of Sparta, 131
structures of, *c580*
of Sumer, 32–34
of Tokugawa Japan, *c578*
types of in 2003, *m1031*
Goya, Francisco, *i669*
Gran Colombia, 683
***gravitas*,** 163
Gravity, Law of, 626–627
Great Britain. *See* Britain.
Great Depression. *See* Depression, the.
Great Famine, Irish (1845–1851), 754, *c754*
Great Fear, 655
***Great Gatsby, The* (Fitzgerald),** 898
Great Plains, 443
Great Purge, 876
Great Pyramid, 38, *i39*. *See also* pyramids.
Great Schism, 399
Great Trek, 778
Great Wall of China, *i108*, 109, 323
Great War. *See* World War I.
Great Zimbabwe, 425–427, *i426*
Greco, El, 591
Greco-Roman civilization, 178–183. *See also* Greece; Roman Empire.
Greco-Roman culture, 178
Greece. *See also* Hellenistic culture.
ancient, 122–126
architecture, 135–136, 140, *i141*
arts, *i122*, 136, *i140–141*, 178
city-states, *c87*, *c121*, *m121*, 127–133
classical age, 252–257
democracy in, *i122*, 128, 134–135
drama, 136, *i141*
economy of ancient, 123, 125, 135
environmental influences on, 123–124
geography of, 121, 123–124
independence of, 689, 786
legacy, 125, 134, *c150*
Macedonia's conquest of, 142
Minoan influence, 72, 123, 125
Mycenaeans, 124, *m124*
nationalism in, 689, 786
Parthenon, 135–136, *i141*
Peloponnesian War, 137–138, *m137*, 142
Pericles, 122, 134–135, *i135*, 136, *i252*, 257
philosophy, 148, 149
sculpture, *i122*, 136, *i140*, 149
Sparta, 129, 131, 137–138
sports in, 130
values, 135
war in, 131–133, 137–138
in World War II, 929
Green Revolution, 1074
griots, 216
***Grito de Dolores* (Cry of Dolores),** 685, *i705*
gross domestic product (GDP), *c1076*
Guam, 932, *m933*
***Guernica* (Picasso),** *i918*
guerrillas
in Peninsular War, 669
Vietcong, 980
guild, 388, *c388*
guillotine, *i659*, 660
Gulf War. *See* Persian Gulf War.
gunpowder, *i322*, 325, *i328–329*
Gupta Empire, 191–192, *c208*, 252–255
Gurion, David Ben, 1018
Gutenberg Bible, 484
Gutenberg, Johann, 484

H

***habeas corpus*,** 616
Hadrian, *c164*
Hagia Sophia, 303
haiku, 544
Haile Selassie (Ethiopian emperor), 225, 916
Hajj, 267
Hammurabi, 27, 33–34, *i34*
reign of, 33
Hammurabi's Code, 28, *i33*, 33–34, 115, *c120*
compared with Ten Commandments, 80
Han dynasty, 109, 200–207, *c208*
as classical age, 252–257
compared to Roman Empire, *c206*
Hannibal of Carthage, *i158*
Punic Wars, 158–159, *m159*
Rome's war with, 158–159, *m159*
and war elephants, 158
Hapsburgs, 597, 605
defeats, 603–604
triumphs, 603
Harappan civilization. *See* Indus Valley.
Hatshepsut (Egyptian pharaoh), 90, *i90*, *c120*
Hausa, 417–418
Hausa-Fulani, 782, 1041–1042
Havel, Vaclav, 1055
Hawaii, 798–799
Haydn, Joseph, 637
headhunters, *i247*
Hebrew Law, 169
Hebrews, 77–82. *See also* Jews; Judaism.
Abraham, 77–79
covenant, 78–80
Exodus, 78–79, 89
Israel, 81–82
judges, 80
kings, 81
monotheism, 78, 168
Moses, *i78*, 79
prophets, 80
Sumerian influence, 34
Ten Commandments, 79–80, *i79*, 168
Twelve Tribes, 80
heliocentric theory, 624–625
Hellenistic culture
in Alexandria, 146–147
arts, 149
Epicurianism, 149
library, 147
museum, 147
philosophy, 148–149, 179
science and technology in, 147–148
Stoicism, 148–149, 179
trade in, 146
helots, 129, 131
Helsinki Accords, 991
hemophilia, 869
Henry II (English king), 394
Henry IV (French king of Bourbon dynasty), 596
Henry IV (German emperor), 372
Henry VIII (English king), 492–493, *c492–493*
Henry of Navarre, 596
Henry the Navigator, 530, *i530*, 532
Henry, Prince. *See* Henry the Navigator.
Herculaneum, 166
heresy, 172, 384
Herodotus, 35, *i38*, 74, 136
Herzl, Theodor, 750
Hidalgo, Miguel, 685
hieroglyphics
Egyptian, 40, *i40*
Maya, 448
hijacking. *See* airplane, hijacking of.
Hijrah, 265
Hildegard of Bingen, 380
Himalayas, 44, *m45*, 50, *m51*
Hinduism, 66–67 *c84*, *i288–289*, *c296*
central ideas of, 66–67, 193, *c289*
gods of, 67, 194, *c289*
moksha, 66–67
origins of, 66
rebirth of, 194
in Southeast Asia, *m197*
sacred cows, 793
spread of, 197
in Sri Lanka, 1003
Upanishads, 66–67
Vedas, 63, 66, *i289*
as world religion, 288–289
Hindus
conflict with Muslims, 793, 998–999
Hippodrome, 303
Hirohito (Japanese emperor), 915, *i951*
Hiroshima, *i946*, 947
history
beginnings of written, 136
influence of migration on, 221–224
and nationalism, 687, *c688*
***History*, Book IV (Herodotus),** 74
***History of Herodotus*,** 38
Hitler, Adolf, *i912*, *i921*. *See also* World War II.
anti-Semitism, 913–914, 936
Czechoslovakia, 919
"Final Solution," 937–939
Mein Kampf, 912
and Munich Conference, 919
Poland, 925
Rhineland, 917
rise to power, 911–913
Scandinavia, 926
Soviet Union, 929–930
SS (*Schutzstaffell*), 913, 938
suicide of, 945

Hittites, *c58*, 62–63
Egyptians' battle with, 62, 90
Hobbes, Thomas, 629
Ho Chi Minh, 978, *i978*, 993
Hohenzollerns, 606
Hohokam, 441
Holocaust
Auschwitz, 938, 957
death camps, 938–939, *m953*
genocide, 937–939
Hitler's "Final Solution," 937
Jewish resistance, 937, *i938*
Kristallnacht, 914, 936–937
population killed during, *c939*
Holy Roman Empire, 371–373
in 1100, *m372*
Otto I, 371–372
weakening of, 373, 605
Homer, 125–126
home rule, 754
hominids, *i2*, 7–11, *c8–9*, *m10*, *i11*
development of, *c2–3*, 7–9
Homo erectus, *c2*, 8, *c9*, *m10*, 51
Homo habilis, 8, *c8*
Homo sapiens, 8–10
Hong Kong
under British control, 806
return to China, 1062–1063
Hongwu, 536
Hong Xiuquan, 807
Hooper, Finley, 177
Hopewell. *See* Adena and Hopewell.
hoplites, 131
Horta, Jose Ramos, 1009
Hormuz, Straits of. *See* Straits of Hormuz.
house arrest, 1007
House of Commons, 395, 747
House of Lords, 395, 747
House of Wisdom, 276
Huang He river, 16, 50, *i51*
Hubble Space Telescope, 1072
Huguenots, 496, 596–597, 599
Hu Jintao, 1062
Hulagu, 316–317
Hull House, *i740*
human genome project, *i1070*
humanists
Christian, 482
Petrarch, Francesco, 475–476
humanities, 472
Human Rights, Universal Declaration of, 1084
human rights violations, 1084. *See also* Holocaust; slavery.
in Argentina, 1039, *i1065*
Bataan Death March, 932
in Bosnia, 1056, *i1064*
of British, 778
in China, 1062
death and labor camps of Nazis, *m953*
in East Timor, 1008
in India, 887–888
in Iran, 986
of Japanese, 932
of Khmer Rouge, 981
in Nazi Germany, 936–939
in Nigeria, 1042, *i1042*
in Ottoman Empire, 694
in Romania, 1056
in Soviet Union, 876, *i979*
under Stalin, 876, *i879*
Hundred Days, 671
Hundred Years' War, 401–403
effect of, 403
Hungary
modern reforms in, 1053
resistance to Communism in, *i898,* 988
hunter-gatherers, 14, 16, 18, *c24*
of Africa, *i212,* 215, 224, 409, *c411, m411*
in the Americas, 236
modern, 215, 409
hunters, *i234*, 235–237, *m237*
Hus, Jan, 399
Hussein, Saddam, 986, 1083
Hyksos, 89–90
"Hymn to the Nile," 57

I

Ibn al-Haytham, 278
Ibn Battuta, 416, 422, 424
Ibn Rushd, 278–279
Ibn Saud, 890
Ibo. *See* Igbo.
Ice Age, 8–9, 236, *i237*
Ice Man, 4, *i15*
***I Ching* (Book of Changes),** 107
icons, 306, *i312*
Igbo (Ibo), 782
democratic tradition of, 410, 1041
stateless society of, 410
Ignatius of Loyola, 498–499
Iliad, 125–126
IMF (International Monetary Fund), *c1078*
immigration. *See* migration.
imperialism, *m771*, 773–799, 812–813
1850–1925, *c770–771*
American, 798–799, 818–821
British, 776, 778, 781–782, 788, 789–795
causes of, 774–776
economics of, 776, 817–818
economy, 774
effect of technology on, 833
forms of, 779–781, *c780*
and government, 779, 781
impact of, 784
and industrialization, 733, 774
Japanese, 812–813
management of, 779–781, *c780*
resistance to, 776, 782–783, 790
and Social Darwinism, *i766*, 775
in the Third World, 982–987
views of, 785
and World War I, 841
impressionism, 701
INC (Indian National Congress), 795, 887, 997
Inca civilization, *m439*, 459–465, *m461*
ayllu, 460–461
cultural developments of, 461–462
Cuzco, 462
economic developments of, 460
fall of, 463, *c463*
government of, 460–461, *c578*
Machu Picchu, 462, *i462*
mita, 461
mummies, *i464–465*
Pachacuti, 459–460, *i460*
Pizarro's conquest of, 556–557
political developments of, 461
quipu, *i20*, 461
religious beliefs of, 462
runner messengers, 461
trade in, 460
India
2500–1500 B.C., *m45*
321 B.C.–A.D. 9, *m187*
1947, *m998*
Alexander the Great's conquest of, 144, *m144*
Amritsar Massacre, 887–888
ancient (2500–1500 B.C.), *m45*
Aryan invasion of, *c58*, 64, *m65*
British imperialism in, 791–795, 887–889, 997, 999
Buddhism in, 70–71, 190–191, 193–194
caste system, 63–64, *i793*
Delhi Sultanate, 516
as developing nation, *c1100–1101*
during Cold War, 969, 974
Congress Party, 887, 997
economy of, *c1103*
empires, 189–192
flag of, *i1102*
Gandhi, Mohandas K., 852, *i866*, 888–889, *i889*, 997, 999
geography of, *m187*
government of, *c1102*
Government of India act, 889
Hinduism, 66–67, 71, 194
industry, 1000
Kalidasa, 194
Kashmir, 999, *i999*
languages of, *c1102*
lions as symbols of, *i190*
Mahabharata, 64–65
mathematics of, 195
modern leaders of, 999–1000, *c1001*
movie industry, *c195*
Mughal Empire, 516–523
nationalist movements, 795, 887–889
natural resources of, 195
nonviolence, 888–889, 997
partitioning of, 998–999
poverty in, *c1002*
religion, 997–999, *c1102*
Rowlatt Acts, 887
Salt March, 889
self-rule, 889
servants, *i793*
Silk Roads, 71, 196
social issues, 793, 1000
trade in, 195–197, *m196*
women leaders, *i519*, 1000
in World War I, 852
Indian culture
connection to Indus Valley, 49, 63
environmental influence on, 44–45, 61–62
Indian National Congress (INC), 795, 887, 997
Indian Removal Act, 758
Indians. *See* Native Americans; North America.
Indo-Europeans
language family, 61, *c61*
migrations of, 62, *m62*, 99, 124
Indonesia
during Cold War, 982
independence, 1008
indulgence, 489
Indus River Valley, 44–49, *m45*
centralized government in, 48
civilization, *c27*, 44–49, *i112*
geography of, 44, *m45*
religious artifacts, 48, *i49*
seals, *i48*, *i116*
industrialization, 718, 720. *See also* Industrial Revolution.
in Belgium, 732
in Britain, 717–722
effects of, *c727*

environmental effects of, 728
in Europe, *m715*
factors hindering, 732
in France, 690, 732
in Germany, 732
global effects of, 733
and imperialism, 733, 774
in Japan, 811
in Manchester (England), 724, 726, 728
philosophies of, 734–738
reform during, 738–740
reform laws, 738–739
in Russia, 868
social effects of, 725–726, 733, 739–740
in Soviet Union, 877–878, *c878*
in Third World, 984
in United States, 729–731
views of, 741
Industrial Revolution, 717–722. *See also* industrialization.
from 1700–1900, *c714–715*
causes of, 717–718, 720, 734–735
cultural effects of, 726
economic effects of, 733
effects of, *c742*
environmental effects of, 728
long-term effects of, 726
Marx and Engels on, 736
political effects of, 733
social effects of, 725–726, 733
technology of, 718–720, *i719*
inflation, 173, 573, 592
influenza epidemic, *i853*
information industry, 1075–1076
Inquisition
of Galileo, 625, *i625*
in Papal states, 384
Spanish, 384, *i385*
institution, 20
Institutional Revolutionary Party in Mexico (PRI), 827, 1037–1038
intendants, 598
interdict, 371
International Space Station (ISS), 1071–1072, *i1072*
International Monetary Fund (IMF), *c1078*
internet, 1073
access to, *c1073*
intifada, 1021–1023
invasions
of Britain, 393
Magyar, 359, *m359*
Muslim, 229, 269–270
Viking, *m308*, 358, *m359*
inventions. *See also* technology.
age of inventions, *c764*
airplane, 764, *i764*
of ancient China, 204, *i322*, 325, *i328–329*
automobile, 762, 764, *i764*, *c831*
caravel, 530, *i531*
cotton gin, 720
and democracy, *c769*
Egyptian, 40–41
gunpowder, *i322*, 325, *i328–329*
and imperialism, 775
of industrial revolution, 718–720, *i719*, *i720*
irrigation, 19, 22
light bulb, 762, *i763*, *c831*
magnetic compass, *i322*, 325, *i328–329*, *i433*
measurements of time, 325, *i328–329*
microscope, 627
movable type, 325, *i328–329*
movies, *i763*, 766–767
phonograph, 762, *i762*
photography, 700
printing, *i328–329*
printing press, 484, *i484*
radio, 762, *c831*
saddle, 364
sail, 19, 32
steam engine, 148, 721, 775
telephone, 762, *i764*, *c831*, *i831*, 833
time line of, *c830–831*
wheel, 19, 32
wheelbarrow, 204
Iran. *See also* Persia.
during Cold War, 986–987
as Islamic state, 986
Khomeini, Ayatollah Ruholla, 986, *i986*
natural resources of, 986
Pahlavi, Reza Shah, 890
Pahlavi, Shah Mohammed Reza, 986
secular rule in, 986
Shi'a Muslim sect, 271
siege of U.S. embassy in Tehran, 986, *i986*
war with Iraq, 987
Iraq
ancient, 20, 23
Baghdad, 23, *i1083*
as birthplace of agriculture, 16
invades Kuwait, 1079
Iraqi National Museum, 23
Persian Gulf War, 1079, *i1079*
Shanidar Cave, 9
Sunni Muslim sect, 271
2003 war, 1083
and UN weapons inspectors, 1083
war with Iran, 987
Ireland
home rule in, 754–755
Irish Republican Army (IRA), 755, 1089
Northern (Ulster), 755
rebellion in, 615
Irish Republican Army (IRA), 755, 1089
iron
in ancient Africa, 217–218, *i218*
cast, 55
importance of, 55, *i218*
of Meroë, 94
weapons, 55, 63, 94
of Assyrian empire, 95
of ancient Greece, 131
iron curtain, 967
ironworking, 63, 95, 217–218, *i218*
spread of, *m211*, 222–223
Iroquois League, 444, 445
irrigation
in ancient China, 51, 109
Incan, 460
invention of, 19, 22
Mongol destruction of, 333
of pueblos, 443
in Sumer 21, 29–30, 31
in Ur, 21
Isabella (Spanish queen), 384
Isfahan, 315
Islam, 229, *i290–291*, *c296*. *See also* Muslim world; Muslims.
in Algeria, 1015
Allah, 264–268
in Byzantium, 304
central ideas of, 267–268
Dome of the Rock, *i266*
in East Africa, 424–425
and ethical monotheism, 80
Five Pillars of Islam, 267, *i275*
hajj, 267
historical origins of, 263–265
influence of, 270, 424–425
in Iran, 986
Mecca, 263–265, 267
Muhammad, 264–268, 269, 274
political influences of, 267, 271–272
Qur'an, 265, 267–268, 276
Ramadan, 267, *i275*
rise of, 263–268
role in slavery, 425, 566
in Saudi Arabia, 890
shari'a, 268, 274
Shi'a Muslims, 271, *c271*, 272
spread of, 269–270, 410–411
Sufi sect, 271
Sunna, 268
Sunni Muslims, 271, *c271*
in West Africa, 417
as world religion, 290–291
Islamic law, 268, 411, *i424*, 510
Isma'il (Safavid ruler), 513–514, *i513*
isolationism
of China, 805, 1060
of Japan, 339, 547
of United States, 918
Israel, 1017–1018
Arab-Israeli wars, 1018–1019
birth of modern, 1017–1018
Camp David Accords, 1020
conflicts with Palestine, 1019–1023
Declaration of Principles, 1021
as developing nation, *c1100–1101*
economy of, *c1103*
flag of, *i1102*
government of, *c1102*
Kingdom of, 81
kings, 81
languages of, *c1102*
promised land, 81
relations with Palestine, 1021–1023
religions of, *c1102*
suicide bombers in, 1022
ISS (International Space Station), 1071–1072, *i1072*
Istanbul, 510–511, *i511*
Italy. *See also* Rome.
and Ethiopia, 783, 916
fascism in, 910–911
Florence, 472
and Holy Roman Empire, 373
under Mussolini, 910–911, 916, 941
nationalism in, 689, 694–695
and north Africa, 928
Renaissance in, 471–477
unification of, 694–695, *m694*
in World War I, 845
in World War II, 928, 941
Iturbide, Agustín de, 685–686
Ivan I (Moscow prince), 310
Ivan III (Russian czar), 311, *i311*
Ivan IV "Ivan the Terrible" (czar), 608
Iwo Jima, 945, *i945*, 958

Jacobin Club, 658, 660
Jahangir, 518–519

Index

Jainism, 67–68
Mahavira, 67
James I (English king), 614
James II (English king), 616
Jamestown, 562
janissaries, 510, 786
Japan
atomic bombing by United States, *i946*, 947, 959
Bataan Death March, 932
Buddhism in, 71, 340
Chinese influence on, 340
Christianity in, 546–547
"closed country policy," 547
contact with Europe, 545–547, 811
daimyo, 542–546
defeats Mongols, 336
demilitarization, 950
democracy in, 950
expansion, 811–813
feudalism in, 341–343, *c361*, *i361*, 542
flag of, *i886*
geography of, 339
Heian, 341
Heian period, 341
Hirohito, Emperor, 915, *i951*
imperialism of, 812–813, 886, 915–916
industrialization in, *i732*, 811
influence in East Asia, 812–813, 915–916
invades China, 886, *i886*, 916
invades Manchuria, 886, 915–916
isolationism in, 547, 810
Meiji Era, 810–811, 829
militarism in, *i579*, 915
Modernization of, 811
natural resources of, 339
Pearl Harbor, attack on, 931–932, *i932*
"rising sun," 339
samurai, *i342*, 343
Shinto, 339–340
social classes and values, 341, 343
"Warring States" period (Sengoku), 542
war with Russia, 812–813, 868–869
in World War I, 845, 851–852
in World War II, 931–935, 945–947
Japanese-American internment camps, 943, *i959*
Jarmo, 16
jazz, 899
Jefferson, Thomas, 641, *i641*, 665
Jenner, Edward, 628
Jerome, St., 177
Jerusalem, *c59*
Dome of the Rock, *i266*
Saladin's conquest of, 383
Western Wall (Wailing Wall), 170
Jesuits, 499, *i500*
Jesus of Nazareth, *i169*. *See also* Christianity.
apostles, 168
death, 169
disciples, 168
life and teachings, 168–169
"jewel in the crown," 791
Jews. *See also* Hebrews; Holocaust; Judaism.
anti-Semitism, 749–750, 913–914, 936
with Arabs of Medina, 265
under Cromwell's rule, 616
Diaspora, 170, 1017
Israel, 1017–1023
killed by Nazis, 937–939, *c939*
modern, i292–293
in Muslim culture, 268
Nazi rule, 936
persecution of, 384–385, 750, 867
pogroms, 750, 867
purim, *i293*
rebellion, 170
under Roman rule, 168, 170
sects, 292
in Spain, 384–385, 592
Star of David, *i292*, *i937*
Jiang Jieshi, 884, *i884*, 886, 972–973, *i973*
Jiang Zemin, 1062, *i1062*
Jinnah, Muhammad Ali, 997
Joan of Arc, 402–403, *i403*
Johanson, Donald, 7, *m10*
John (English king), 394–395
Johnson, Lyndon
and Vietnam, 980, 990
joint-stock companies, 573–574
Joseph II (Austrian king), 638
Joyce, James, 898
Juárez, Benito, 823–825, *i824*
Judah, 81–82
Judaism, *c84*, *i292–293*, *c296*. *See also* Jews.
central ideas of, 79–80, *c84*
civil and religious laws of, 81, 169
and ethical monotheism, 80
origin of, 77–82
spread of, 82
Star of David, *i937*
Ten Commandments, 79–80, *i79*
Torah, 77, *i79*, *c80*, 83
as world religion, 292–293
yarmulke, *i293*
Junkers, 606, 695
jury, 394–395
Justinian (Byzantine emperor), 301–304
Justinian Code, 302

K

Kabila, Joseph (Congolese president), 1016
Kabila, Laurent (Congolese president), 1015
Kabuki, 544, *i545*
Kafka, Franz, 898
kaiser, 697. *See also* Wilhelm I; Wilhelm II
Kai-shek, Chiang. *See* Jiang Jieshi.
Kalam, Abdul, *i1104*
Kalidasa, 194
Kamakura shogunate, 343
kamikaze, 945
Kamose (Egyptian pharaoh), 89
Kandinsky, Wassily, 899
Kangxi, 539, *i539*, 549
karma, 67
Karzai, Hamid, 1027
Kashmir, 999, *i999*
Kautilya, 189
Kellogg-Briand peace pact, 906
Kemal, Mustafa, 890, *i890*
Kennedy, John F.
in Cuban Missile Crisis, 985, 990
Kenya
independence of, 1013, 1015
and Mau Mau rebellion, 1013
nomads, 215
Kenyatta, Jomo, 1013, *i1013*, 1015
Kepler, Johannes, 624
KGB, 982
Khadija (wife of Muhammad), 264–265
Khan, Genghis, 309, 331–332, *i331*
"Khanate of the Golden Horde." *See* Mongols.
Khmer Empire (Cambodia), 345
Angkor Wat, 70, 345, *i345*
Khmer Rouge, 981
Khomeini, Ayatollah Ruholla, 986, *i986*
Khrushchev, Nikita
destalinization, 988
Kiev
Byzantine influence, 307–308
Eastern Orthodox Church, 308
Mongol rule, 309–310, *m309*, 333
Olga (princess), 307–308
Russian, 308–311
Vladimir, 308
Yaroslav the Wise, 308–309
King, Martin Luther, 1097
kingdom(s). *See also* dynasties.
Aksum, 225–229, *m226*
Aryan, 64
Benin, 419
of China, 51–55
of Egypt, *c26*, 37, 90
Germanic, 354–355
of Israel, 81
of the Jews, 81
of Judah, 81–82
of Kush, 92–94
matrilineal society, 410
Minoan, 72
patrilineal society, 410
Roman Catholic Church, 354–357
Seljuk, 315
of Southeast Asia, 344–347
West African, 413, 415
Yoruban, 418–419
Kim Il Sung, 977
king(s). *See also* czar(s); emperor(s); monarchy.
of Alexander the Great's empire, 143–144
of ancient Rome, 156
Etruscan, 156
Jewish, 81
Mycenaean, 124
Spartan, 131
warrior-kings,124
King James Bible, 614
Klee, Paul, 899
knights, 360, 367
education, 365, 367
Knossos, 72
knowledge worker, 1075
Knox, John, 496
Kohl, Helmut, 1054
Korea, *i347*. *See also* North Korea; South Korea.
38th parallel, 976–977
Choson dynasty, 347
dynasties, 346–347
geography, 346
Japanese invasion of, 812
under Japanese rule, 812
Koryu dynasty, 346–347
under Manchu rule, 540
war in, 976–977, *i976*, *m977*
Koryu dynasty, 346–347
Kosovo, 1058
Krishna, 65
kristallnacht, *914*, 936–937
Kublai Khan, 335–338, *i337*
kulaks, 878, *i879*
Kuomintang, 882, 884
Kurds, 1083
Kush empire, 93–94
Kushites, 93–94
Kuwait, 1079
Kwakiutl, *i440*
Kwasniewski, Aleksander, 1053

L

Lady Hao, 52
LAFTA (Latin American Free Trade Agreement), 1077
laissez faire, 734–735
land reform, 1034
language. *See also* writing.
of Aksum, 228
Arabic, 267–268, 276
Bantu, 221–224
Chinese, 53
and cultural unity, 1095
early spoken, 7–8, 10
effects of migration on, 61, 221, 223–224, *i223*
English, 181, 1095
French, 181
Ge'ez, 228
in global culture, 1095
Greek, 40, 125, 146
Hindi, 518
Indo-European, 61, *c61*
Latin, 181, 353
Maori, 1097
Maya glyphs, 448
and nationalism, *c688*
Niger-Congo, 221
Proto-Bantu, 221
Romance, 181
Romanian, 1055
Sanskrit, 61, *c61*
Slavic, 307
Swahili, *i223*, 422, 427
Tamil, 191
Urdu, 518
vernacular, 391–392, 475
of woodlands tribes, 444
Laozi, 105–106, *i105*
La Reforma, 824
Lascaux Cave, *i13*
Latimer, Lewis H., 762
Latin America
colonial legacy of, 681–682, 816
democracies in, 1033–1039
maps
in 1800 and 1830, *m685*
in 2003, *m1035*
percentage of population living in poverty, *c1038*
post-World War II, 984
revolutions in, 674–675, 681–686, *c707*
Latin American Free Trade Agreement (LAFTA), 1077
Latvia, 925, 1048, 1049
law(s), 28. *See also* constitution.
canon, 371, 379
common, 394
Draconian, 128
Greek, 134–135, *c134*
Hammurabi's Code, 33–34, 115
Hebrew, 169
Hittite, 63
Islamic, 268, 411, *i424*, 510
Justinian Code, 302
Magna Carta's influence on, 395, *i395*
martial, 1041
Napoleonic Code, 664
Petition of Right, 514
Roman, 156–157, *c157*, 183
rule by, 1034
of Suleyman, 510
unwritten Germanic, 354
written code of, 33–34, *i33*, 395
lay investiture, 372
League of Nations, 859–861, 906
Leakey, Louis, 7–8, 9
Leakey, Mary, 7–8, 9, *m10*
Leakey, Richard, 9, 25
Lebanon, 1018, 1021
lebensraum, 912
legalism, 106–107, *c106*
Legion (Roman), 157
Legislative Assembly, 657–658
legitimacy, 673
Lenin, Vladimir Ilyich, *i868*, 870–873
and China, 884
during World War I, 854, 870
Leningrad, 929–930
Leo III (Byzantine emperor), 306
Leopold II (Belgian king), 774
liberals, 687, 689–690
libraries
of Alexandria, 147, *i262*
of ancient world, 96
monasteries and, 355
Muslim, 276, 391
Libya
invasion of Egypt, 91–92
Lighthouse of Alexandria, 146–147, *i262*
Liliuokalani (Hawaiian queen), 799, *i799*
Lincoln, Abraham, 759–760, *i761*
Lindbergh, Charles, 901
lineage, 410
Lister, Joseph, 764
literature. *See also* writers.
of chivalry, 367–368
of early China, 105, 205–206
of the Enlightenment, 633, 637
epic, 32, 64, 83, 125–126, 179, *i179*
essay, 597
French, 597–598, 599
in global culture, 1096
Greek influence on, 135, 178
Hebrew, *c80*, 83
in Heian-period Japan, 341, *i341*
Hindu, 66–67, 518
Indian, 64, 83, 194
of Industrial Revolution, 724, 734–736
Japanese, 544
Mesopotamia, 32, 83, 96
Minoan influence on Greek, 125
Muslim, 276
Nazi, 913
novel, 637
in Ottoman Empire, 511
Persian, 315
realism in, 700–701
Renaissance, 475–477, 482–483
Roman influence on, *i179*, *c180*
Romanticism and, 698–699
Spanish, 591–592
Sumerian, 32
vernacular in, 392, 475
war's influence on, 856–857, 898
World War I's effect on, 898
Lithuania, 925, 1048, 1049
Liu Bang, 200–201, *i200*
Livingstone, David, 774, *i774*
Livy, 155
Lloyd George, David, 858
Locke, John, 629, 630, 642
locomotive, 721–722, *c830*, *i830*
loess, 50
Lombard League, 373
London, *i486–487*
German bombing of, *i924*, 928, *i956*
longbow, 402, *i402*
Long March, 884–886, *i885*
lord, 360
"Lost Generation," *i898*
Louis IX (French king), 396
Louis XIII (French king), 597
Louis XIV (French king), *i588*, 598–602, *i598*
Louis XVI (French king), 642, 653, *i653*, 657, 660
Louis XVIII (French king), 671
Louisiana
Purchase, 758–759, *m759*
Territory, 665, 758
L'Ouverture, Toussaint, 665, 682, *i682*
Lower Egypt, 36–37. *See also* Egypt.
Lü, Empress, 201
"Lucy," 7, *m10*
Luddites, 726
Ludendorff, Erich, 912
***Lusitania,* sinking of,** 852, 863, *i956*
Lutherans, 490
Luther, Martin, 489–490, *i489*. *See also* Reformation.
95 Theses, 489
excommunication, 490
lycées, 664

M

MacArthur, General Douglas, 934–935, *i934*, 945, 947, 950–951, *i951*, 977
Macedonia, 142–145, *m142*
Machiavelli, Niccolò, 476, *i476*, 503, *i583*
Machu Picchu, 462, *i462*
Madero, Francisco, 826
Magadha, 64
Magellan, Ferdinand, 534, 554
Maghrib, 410–411
Magna Carta, 394–395, *i395*
Magyars, 359, *m359*
Mahabarata, 64–65
Mahavira, 67
Mahayana sect, 193
Maimonides (Moses Ben Maimon), 279
maize, 238
Maji Maji Rebellion, 782–783
major domo, 356
Malaysia, 1007
Mali empire, 414–417, *m414*
Mansa Musa, 415–416, *m416*
Sundiata, 415
Malik Shah, 315–316
Malthus, Thomas, 734–735
mamelukes, 314
mammoth, 234–235, *i234*, *c238*
Manchester, 724, 726, 728
Manchuria, 539
invasion by Japan of, 886, 915–916
Manchus, 539–540
Mandate of Heaven, 54, *c54*
Mandela, Nelson, 1043–1044, *i1043*
Manicheanism, 103
manifest destiny, 758
Mann, Horace, 740
manor, 360, 362, *i362*
manorial system
Medieval, 360–363, *i362*
effect of plague on, 401
Mansa Musa, 415–417, *m416*
Maoris, 752–753, *i753*, 1097
Mao Zedong, *i866*, 883–886, 972–975, *i974*
Marxist socialism, 736–738, 974
reforms, 1059–1060, *c1059*, 974–975

maps
ancient empires, *m87*
prehistoric world, *m3*
Spanish, *m416*
Marat, Jean-Paul, 658, *i658*
Marathon (Greek city), 132
marathon (race), 133
Marconi, Guglielmo, 762
Marcos, Ferdinand, 1005–1006
Marcus Aurelius, 173
Marguerite of Navarre, 498, *i498*
Maria Theresa (Austrian empress), 605, *i606*, 607
Marie Antoinette (French queen), 653, *i653*
Mark Antony, 162
Marrakech, 412
Marshall Plan, 968, *c968*
Martel, Charles, 356
martial emperor, 201–202
martial law, 1041
Marti, José, 818, *i818*
Marxism, 736–738, *c872*, 873
Marx, Karl, 736–738, *i736*, 868, *c872*
Masai, 215
masks
Bantu, *i220, i224*
of Benin, *i419*
Maya, *i446*
Massacre at Amritsar, 887–888
mass culture, 766–767, *c767*
materialism, 1096
mathematics
algebra, 278
in ancient Egypt, 41, *i148*
in China, *i148,* 325
decimal system, 195
geometry, 32, 148, *i148*
of Hellenistic period, 147–148, *i148*
Indian, 195
Maya, 448
Muslim, *i148*, 278
pi, 148, 195
Pythagorean theorem, *i148*
in Scientific Revolution, 624, 626–627
in Sumer, 32
zero, 195
matriarchal, 192
matrilineal society, 410
Mau Mau rebellion, 1013
Mauryan Empire, *c121*, 189–191, *m191*, *c208*
Maya civilization, 446–450
calendar, 448
Classical Period, 446
cultural developments of, 447–448, *c449*
decline, 449, *c449*
economic developments, 447
hieroglyphs, 448
political developments of, 446–447
religious beliefs in, 447–448
science and technology, 448
Tikal, 446, *i450–451*
May Fourth Movement, 883
Mazarin, Cardinal, 598, 604
Mbeki, Thabo, 1044–1045
McAdam, John, 721
Mecca, 263–265, 267
Medes, 97, 99
Medici family, 472, *i472*, *i581*
medicine
acupuncture, *i325*
antiseptics, *c831*
Daoist effect on, 106
Egyptian, 41, 43
of Enlightenment, 627–628
genetics, 1073–1074
germ theory in, 764
heart function, 41
Indian, 195
Lister, Joseph, 764, *c831*
molecular medicine, 1074
Muslim, 274, 278
Pasteur, Louis, 764
quinine, 775
in Scientific Revolution, 627–628
Vesalius, Andreas, 627–628
Medieval period. *See* Middle Ages.
Medina, 265
Megasthenes, 189–190
Mehmed II, Mehmed the Conquerer (Ottoman emperor), 508–509
Meiji era, 810–811, 829
***Mein Kampf* (Hitler),** 912
Meir, Golda, 1019, *i1019*
Mendel, Gregor, 765
Menelik II (Ethiopian emperor), 783, *i783*
Menes (Egyptian king)
mercantilism, 574–575, *i574*
mercenary, 173
Meroë, 94
Mesoamerican civilizations, 240–244. *See also* Aztec, Maya, Olmec, and Zapotec civilizations.
cultural developments in, 241–242
economic developments in, 241
legacy of, 243
political developments of, 243
trade in, 241
Mesopotamia, *c3*, 20, 29–34, *m96*. *See also* Sumer; Sumerians.
city-states in, *c26*, 31–33, *i112*
kings of, 31–33
mestizo, 557, *c681*, 682
Metacom (King Philip), 565
Metternich, Klemens von, 672, 689
Mexico
Chiapas, 1038
civil war in, 826–827
cultural blending in, 685
democracy in, 1036–1038
as developing nation, *c1100–1101*
early farming in, 16, 238–239
economy of, *c1102*
flag of, *i1102*
government of, *c1102*
immigrant workers of, 1038
independence of, 675, 685, 822
languages of, *c1102*
oil in, 1037
political upheaval in, 826–827, 1037–1038
PRI (Institutional Reform Party), 827, 1037–1038
religions of, *c1102*
revolution in, 685–686, 826–827
Michelangelo, 474, *i475*
microscope, 278, 627
Middle Ages, 353
burghers, 391
castles, *i366*, 367
chivalry, 365, 367–368
church authorities, 370–371, 379, 398
cultural developments of, 364–368
economic developments of, 388–390
end of, 398–403
European, *m351*, 353–373
farming, 362
feudalism, 360–363, *c361*
guilds, 388, *c388*
Hundred Years' War, 401–403
monasteries, 354–355, 379, 380
political developments of, 354, *c361*, 394–397
population growth, 387, 390, *c405*
Roman Catholic church in, 354–355, 370–373, 379–385, 398–399
science and technology in, 623
towns, 390–391
trade in, 389–390, *c390*
weaponry, 364, *i366*, 402, *i402*
middle class
in 21st-century China, 1063
African, 1040
in Canadian colonies, 750–751
and capitalism, 736
in democracy, 1034
and democratic reforms, 747
during Enlightenment, 636
in French Revolution, 651–652, 654
during Industrial Revolution, 725, 736
Dutch, 593
Italian, 910–911
Marx and Engels on, 736
and monarchy, 595
rise of, 636, 725
role in government, 747, 1034
Middle East
1947–present, *m1018*
Israeli-Palestinian conflict in, 1019–1023
terrorism and, 1022,1088
Middle Kingdom, 52
middle passage, 569, *i569*
migration(s), 62, 220
from Asia to the Americas, 235–237, *m237*
of Bantu speakers, 220–224, *m222*
across Beringia, 235–237, *m237*
cultural influence of, 221
early human, 1,600,000–10,000 B.C., *m10*
effect of colonization on, 562
effects of large-scale, 221
global effects of, 1086
and Great Famine, 754, *c754*
the Hijrah, 265
historical influence of, 221
of *Homo erectus*, 8, *m10*
influence of, 221
of Indo-Europeans, 62, *m62*, 99, 124
of Jews to Palestine, 170, 1017
of Mesoamerican people, 453–454
migrants, 1086
political refugees, 1086
push-pull factors in, 220, *c221*, 1086
urbanization as factor in, 220
world, *m1069*
militarism
in World War I, 841–842
military power
Assyrian, 94, 95–97, *i97*
of Muslims, 270
of Persian empire, 99
of Roman legions, 157
Spartan, 131, 132
Mill, John Stuart, 735
Milosevic, Slobodan, 1056, 1058
Mines Act, 738
Ming Dynasty, 536–539
Minoan culture, 72–73
Minos (Minoan king), 72
Minotaur, 72
missionaries
Byzantine, 306
Christian, 354, 546

in colonies, 774–775
and imperialism, 775
Jesuit, 499, *i500*, 537, 546
Mississippian culture, 443–444
mita, 461
Mithra, 103
Mobutu, Colonel (later, Mobutu Sese Seko), 1015
Moche culture, 247, 249
moderates, 657
mohenjo-daro, *m46*
plumbing of, *i47*
Moi, Daniel arap, 1015
moksha, 66–67
Molière, 599
monarchs
absolute, 594–595, *c618*
European, 595
monarchy, 127, *c128*. *See also* kings.
clothing and, *i588*
constitutional, 617, 657, 747
divine origin of, 594
end of Roman, 156
and Enlightenment, 638–639
limited, 617
modern, 617
after Napoleon I, 673
in prehistory, *i578*
monasteries
under Charlemagne, 357
in Middle Ages, 354, 357, 379, 380
monastic revival, 380
as preservers of culture, 355
Monet, Claude, 701, *i703*
money, 163. *See also* coins.
paper, 325, *c328*
sakk, 272
Monghut (Siamese king), 798
Mongols
and bubonic plague, 334, *m400*
cavalry, *i332–333*
in China, 333–334
decline of, 337–338
defeat by Japan of, 335–336, *i336*
empire of Kublai Khan, 335–338
Genghis Khan, 309, 331–332, *i331*
Hulagu, 316–317
"Khanate of the Golden Horde," 309, *m309*, 333
in Korea, 347
overthrow of Seljuk Empire, 316–317
Pax Mongolica (Mongol Peace), 333
in Russia, 309–311
monopoly, 204
monotheism, 78, 227. *See also* ethical monotheism; polytheism.
in Aksum, 227–228
Hindu move towards, 194
of Muslims, Jews, and Christians, 268
in teachings of Jesus, 168
Monroe Doctrine, 818–821
monsoons
of India, 45, *m45*
monsoon winds, 76
Montaigne, Michel de, 597
Monte Albán, *c59*, *c121*, 242–243, *i242*
Montenegro, 1058
Montesquieu, Baron de, 631, *i631*
Montezuma II (Aztec emperor), 456, 458, 556
Montgomery, General Bernard, 940
More, Thomas, 482, *i482*
Morelos, Padre José Maria, 685
mosaics, *i165*, 178
Moscow, 310–311, 670. *See also* Russia.
mosque(s), 267, 273
of Córdoba, *i278*
of Damascus, 276
of Suleyman, *i511*
of Timbuktu, 416
mother goddess, 18
Mother Teresa, *i1084*
Mound Builders, 443–444, *i444*
Mount Vesuvius, 166–167, *c167*
movable type, 325, *i329*
movies, 766–767
Bollywood (India), *c195*, *i195*
Chaplin, Charlie, 901, *i901*
Hollywood, California, 901
Mozart, Wolfgang Amadeus, 637
Mubarak, Hosni, 1021
Mughal Empire
art of, *i522–523*
cultural developments of, 518, *i522–523*
decline of, 521
economic developments of, 517, 519
growth of, *m517*
political developments of, 517
Muhammad, 264–268, 268, 274
Hijrah, 265
Medina, 265
Muhammad Ali (Egyptian king), 788, *i788*
mujahideen, 987, 1026
mulattos, *c681*, 682
multinational corporations, 1076, *c1076*
mummification
Egyptian, 38–39
Incan, *i464–465*
Munich Conference, 919
Muses, 147
music
African, 570
in age of chivalry, 368
classical, 637, 899
in global culture, 1094
impressionistic, 701
jazz, 899
nationalistic, *i689*
neanderthal, 11
neoclassical, 637
post-World War I, 899
rock'n'roll, *i1094–1095*
Romanticism and, 699
Stravinsky, Igor, 899
of Ur, 22
vaudeville, 766
Muslim League, 795, 887, 997
Muslims
caliphs, 269, 271–272
conflict among, 270–271
conflict with Hindus, 516, 793, 998–999
and Crusades, 316, 383, 385
extremist groups, 1089, 1091
influence on sciences of, 274, 278
invasions of, 229, 359, *m359*
jihad, 269
Ka'aba, 263–265, *i265*
in Middle Ages, 263–279
Mongol conversion to, 333
in North Africa, 410–411
population, 1990s, *c281*
prayer, *i268*
and Reconquista, 384
scholars, *i391*
shari'a, 268, 274
under Soviet rule, 1050
Spanish defeat of, 384
United States' relations with, 1091
Muslim world, 263–279, *c280*, 507–523. *See also* Islam; Ottoman Empire.
in 1200, *m261*
al-Andalus, 271–272
art and architecture, *i266*, 276–278, *i277*, *i278*
civil war, 271–272
Córdoba, 272, *i278*
Damascus, 271, 276
Dynasties, 271–272
empires of, 507–521
House of Wisdom, 276
imperialism in, 271–272, 786–790
influence of, 273–279
mathematics in, 274, 278
population of, 272, *c273*, 274
religious tolerance in, 268, 270
science and technology in, 274, *i275*, 276, 278
slavery in, 274, 425, 566
social classes, 274
urban centers, 273–274
Mussolini, Benito, 910–911, *i911*, *i912*
defeat of, 941
and Munich Conference, 919
during World War II, 928, 941
Mutapa Empire, 427
Mutsuhito, 810–811, *i811*
Myanmar. *See* Burma.
Mycenaeans, 124–125, *m124*
myth(s)
Greek, 122, 126
of Minotaur, 72
of Quetzalcoatl, 453
Roman, 155

N

NAFTA (North American Free Trade Agreement), 1077
Nagasaki, Japan, *i946*, 947, 959
Nagy, Imre, 988, *i989*
Napoleon I, Napoleon Bonaparte (French emperor), 663–671
allies of, 667
exile, 671
nations controlled by, *m649*, 667
nations at war with, 665, *m666*, 667, 669
restoring order, 664
Russian campaign, 669–670, *m670*
at Waterloo, 671
Napoleon III, Louis-Napoleon (French emperor), 690, 825
Napoleonic Code, 664
Narmer, 37
National Assembly, 654, 656
National Convention, 658, 660
nationalism, 687, *c688*, 692
and art, 698
Asian, 808–811
Balkan, 689, 843
Chinese, 808–809, 882
in Europe, 687–691
under fascism, 910, *c911*
ideal of, 687–689
impact of, *c688*
and imperialism, 774
Indian, 795, 887–889
Korean, 813

Kurdish, 1083
against Napoleon I, 669
postive and negative results of, *c688*
and revolution, 682–686, 689–690
rise of, 687, 689
in Southwest Asia, 890–891
and World War I, 841
nationalist movements, *c692*
nation-state, 687, *c688*
Native Americans. *See also* North America, native.
burial rites of, 444
colonialism and, 564–565
slavery of, 557, 559
NATO (North Atlantic Treaty Organization), 969, 1082
natural order, 105–106
natural resources. *See also* environmental influences.
of Britain, 718
of Congo, 1015
natural rights, 630
Locke, John, 630, 642
nature. *See* environmental influences.
Nazca culture, 247, *i247*, *i248*
Nazca lines, *i248*
Nazis, 912–914, 936–939
Nazism, 912–913. *See also* Hitler, Adolf; World War II.
anti-Semitism, 913–914, 936–939
Neanderthals, 9–11, *c9*, *m10*
musical expression of, 11
Nebuchadnezzar (Chaldean king), 82, 98
Negritude movement, 1012
Nehru, Jawaharlal, 999–1000, *i1000*
neoclassical style, 637
Neolithic Age, *c3*, 7, 15–16, *i17*
Neolithic Revolution, 15
Nero, *c164*
Netanyahu, Benjamin, 1021
Netherlands, 534
Asian trade with, 534–535
French invasion of, 601
Japanese trade with, 547
republic of, 593
trade in, 535, 594
tulips of, *i592*
United provinces of, 592–593
Nevsky, Alexander, 310
New Deal, 909
New England, 562–563
New France, 561–562
New Kingdom of Egypt, *c86*, 90–91
New Netherland, 563
New Stone Age, 7, 15–16, *i17*
New Testament, 172
Newton, Isaac, 626–627, *i627*
New York City, 1090. *See also* September 11 terrorist attacks.
New Zealand, 752–753, 1097
Ngo Dinh Diem, 978
Nicaragua, 686, *m984*, 985, 991
Nicholas I (Russian czar), 691
Nicholas II (Russian czar), 867, 869–870
Nietzsche, Friedrich
and existentialists, 899
Hitler's use of, 913
Nigeria
in 1914, *m781*
civil war in, 1041–1042
under colonial rule, 781–782
democracy in, 1042–1043
as developing nation, *c1100–1101*
dissidents, 1042
economy of, *c1103*
flag of, *i1102*
government of, *c1102*
languages of, *c1102*
martial law, 1041
religions of, *c1102*
Niger River, 781, *m781*
Nightingale, Florence, 787
Nike of Samothrace, *i140*, 149
Nile River, 35–37, 92. *See also* pyramids.
9–11 terrorist attacks. *See* September 11 terrorist attacks.
***1984* (Orwell),** *i875*
Nineveh, 96–97
nirvana, 69
Nixon, Richard
in China, 990, *i990*, 1060, *i1060*
and détente, 990
in Soviet Union, 991
and Vietnam, 980
Nkrumah, Kwame, 1013
Noah's Ark, *i83*
Nobel Peace Prize, *i1006*, *i1044*, *i1084*
Nobunaga, Oda, 542–543
Nok, 217, *i217*, 222
nomads, 14. *See also* Mongols.
of Africa, 215
Aryan, 63
of Asian steppe, 330–331
Aztec, 453
Bantu, 222–224
Bedouins, 263
conflict of empires with, 89
Hyksos, 89
influence on Indian culture of, 63–65
in Iran, 99
Magyar, 359, *m359*
modern-day, 409
Mongol, 175, 309, 331
of North Africa, 409
of North America, 235–236, 441, 443
pastoral, 330–331
Seljuks, 314
on Silk Roads, 196, *m204–205*
transition of Jews from, 79
warriors, 33, 331
Xiongnu, 201–202
nonaggression pact, 919, 925
nonaligned nations, 982
nonviolence, 888–889
Normandy, Invasion of, 944
Normans, 393–394
North Africa
Islam, 410–412
Maghrib, 410–411
Muslim reformers, 411–412
in World War II, 928–929, 940
North America. *See also* North America, native.
in 1783, *m642*
colonization of, 554–558, 561–565
maps, *m439*, *m442*, *m564*
North America, native. *See also* North America; Native Americans.
colonization of, 554–558, 561–565
cultural developments of, 444–445
culture areas, c.1400, *m442*
early societies, 441–445
Iroquois League, 444, 445
Mound Builders, 443–444, *i444*
Pacific Northwest, *i440*, 441
political developments of, 441, 444
pueblo people of, 443
religion in, 444–445
trade in, 444
woodlands tribes of, 444–445
North American Free Trade Agreement (NAFTA), 1077
North Atlantic Treaty Organization (NATO), 969, 1082
Northern Alliance, 1026
as U.S. allies, 1027
Northern Ireland, 755, 1089
Northern Renaissance
art of, 480–481, *i481*
technology of, 484, *i484*
writers of, 482–483
North Korea, 976–978
Nubia, *m87*, 89–94, *m211*
Nuclear Non-Proliferation Treaty, 1083
nuclear weapons, *i946*
during Cold War, 969–970
in India and Pakistan, 1000
reduction of, 1083
in South Korea, 977
number systems, 41
base 60, 32
Nuremberg Trials, 950
Nur Jahan, 518

O

oases, 263
Obasanjo, Olusegun, 1042–1043, *i1105*
obsidian, 18, 453, 456
Octavian, 162, *i162*. *See also* Augustus.
Oda Nobunaga, 542–543
Odyssey, 126
Oedipus the King, 136
oil
in Central Asia, 1024
fields, 1938, *m891*
in Iran, 891, 986
in Mexico, 1037
in Middle East, 986
in Persia, 789–790
as political tool, 1079
in Southwest Asia, 891
supplies, 891
Old Regime, 651
Old Stone Age, 7–15
Old Testament, 77, 172. *See also* Bible.
Olduvai Gorge, 8, *m10*
oligarchy, 127, *c128*, *i579*
Olmec civilization, 240–241, *m241*, 243
as classical age, 252–255
decline of, 241
jaguar worship, 241, 243, *i244*
legacy, 243
sculpture, *i58*, 240–241, 243, *i244*
trade, 241
Olympic Games, 130
19th century, 767
boycott of 1980, 987
South Africa banned from, 1044
terrorist attack in 1972, 1088
OPEC (Organization of Petroleum Exporting Countries), 1079
Open Door Policy, 808
Opium War, 806
opposable thumb, 7
oppression. *See also* Holocaust; human rights violations; slavery.
during Cultural Revolution, 975, *i975*
industrialization and, 728, 738–739
and Nazi rule, 936–939
in post-war Vietnam, 981

in Russia, 867
in Soviet Union, 876–877, 879
oracle bones, *i53*
Oregon territory, *m759*
Organization of Petroleum Exporting Countries (OPEC), 1079
Ortega, Daniel, 985
Orthodox Church, 304–306, *c305*
Osama bin Laden. *See* bin Laden, Osama.
Osiris, 38
Oslo Peace Accords, 1021
Osman, 507
Otto I, Otto the Great (Holy Roman emperor), 371–372
Ottoman Empire, 507–511, 786–787
1451–1566, *m508*
1699–1914, *m787*
in the Balkans, 508, 843
cultural developments of, 511
decline of, 511, 605, 693–694, 786–787
government of, 510
nationalism weakens, 693–694, 786, 843
social organization, 510
sultan, 507
in World War I, 851, 855
Ovid, 179
Owen, Robert, 736
ozone layer, 1079–1080, *i1080*

P

Pachacuti (Inca ruler), 459–460, *i460*
Pacific Rim, 796
Pahlavi, Mohammed Reza (Iranian shah, post-World War II), 986
Pahlavi, Reza Shah (Iranian shah), 890
Paine, Thomas, 662, *i710*
painters. *See* names of individual artists and paintings.
painting. *See also* art.
African, *i216*
of Catal Huyuk, 18
cave, *i12–13,* 14
Chinese, *i107,* 326, *i326*
Dutch, 593, *i593*
Egyptian tomb, *i42*
of Enlightenment, 637
Flemish, 481, *i481*
French, 701
Guernica, *i918*
impressionism, 701, *i703*
Medieval, *i352*, *i357*
Nazi, 913
perspective in, 474, *i474*
realism in, *i703*
Renaissance, *i470*, 474–475, *i478–479*, 481, *i481*
of Richard the Lion-Hearted, *i384*
Roman, *i167*, 179
Romanticism and, *i702*
of Socrates, *i138*
of Song Dynasty, 326, *i326*
Spanish, 591, *i591*
Stone Age, *i12–13*, 14
of St. Petersburg, *i869*
of van Eyck, *i470*, 481
of Velázquez, 591, *i591*
Pakistan
civil war in, 1001–1002
independence of, 998, 1001
leaders of, 1002, *i1001*
modern leaders of, 1002
Palembang, *i345*, 346
Paleolithic Age, *c2*, 7–15
paleontologists, 5
Palestine, 77
British rule in, 1017
conflicts with Israel, 1019–1023, 1088
Declaration of Principles, 1021
independence, 1023
intifada, 1021–1023
Palestinian Liberation Organization (PLO), 1019, 1021, 1023
Panama Canal, 819–821, *i820*, *c829*, *c831*
Pankhurst, Emmeline, 749
papacy, 355
papal authority, 372
dispute over, 398
Papal States, 695
Inquisition in, 384
paper, 203, *i203*, *i322*
papyrus, 40, 43, 147
Paris Commune, *i746*
parliament
and absolute monarchs, 595
and Bill of Rights, 617
British, 395, 614–617, 747–748
democracy and, 395, 747–748
effect of democracy on, 748
and English monarchy, 395, 614–617, 747
French, 690
Reformation, 492–493
under William and Mary, 617
Parthenon, 135–136, *i141*
Partition of India, 998–999
Passover, 79
Pasteur, Louis, 764
pastoralists, 330–331
paternalism, 781
patriarch (leading bishop of East), 306
patriarchal, 192
patricians, 156
patrilineal society, 410
patriotism
lack of and fall of Roman Empire, 173, *c174*
during World War I, 857
patrons (of the arts), 472–473
Patton, General George, 944
Paul, the apostle, 170
Pavlov, Ivan, 766
Pax Mongolica, 333
Pax Romana, 162, 165, 170
Peace of Augsburg, 492
Peace of Westphalia, 604
Pearl Harbor, 931–932, *i932*
peasants revolt, 490
Peking man, 51
Peloponnesian War, 137–138, *m137*, 142
penal colony, 752, *i757*
peninsula, 681
peninsulares, 675, 681–682, *c681*
Pentagon
September 11 terrorist attack on, 1090
Pepin the Short, 356
perestroika, 1047
Pericles, 122, 134–135, *i135*, 137
Perón, Juan, *i914*, 1038–1039
Perry, Commodore Matthew, 810
Persia
becomes Iran, 986
carpets, 525
conquest of, 103
exploitation of, 789–790
rise of, 99
Persian empire, *c87*, 99–103, *m101*
Alexander the Great's conquest of, 143–144
Muslim defeat of, 103
Royal Road, 101, *i102*, *m102*
Zoroaster, 103
Persian Gulf, *m30*, 48
Persian Gulf War, 23, 1079, *i1079*
Persian Wars, 131–133, *m132*
perspective (in art), 474, *i474*
Peru, 16, 246–249, *m247*, 683
Peter, the apostle, *i169,* 171
Peter I, "Peter the Great" (Russian czar), 609–611, *i609*
Petrarch, Francesco, 475–476
phalanx, 131–132, 142
pharaoh(s)
Alexander the Great as, 143
Egyptian, 37, 39, 89–91
Hatshepsut, 90, *i90*, *c120*
Ramses II, 90–91, *i91*
Pharos, 146, *i262*
Pheidippides, 132, 133
Philip II (French king), 396
Philip II (Macedonian king), 142–143
Philip II (Spanish king), 589, 591–592
Philip IV (French king), 398
Philippine Islands
Bataan Death March, 932
as developing nation, *c1100–1101*
economy of, *c1103*
flag, *i1102*
government of, *c1102*
independence of, 1004–1005
languages of, *c1102*
Marcos regime, 1005–1006
religions of, *c1102*
as United States colony, 798
in World War II, 931–932, 945
Philistines, 77
philosopher-king, 138
philosophers, 138
Aristotle, 139, *i139*, 151, 278–279
Confucius, 104–105, *i105*, 115
Descartes, René, 626
Epicurus, 149
of industrialization, 734–739
Nietzsche, Friedrich, 899
Plato, 138–139, *i139*, 278–279
Rousseau, Jean Jacques, 631–632, *i631*
scholastics, 392
Socrates, 138, *i138*, *i139*
Zeno, 148
philosophes, 630–632, 638
philosophy
Chinese, 104–105
of Enlightenment, 630–632
existential, 898–899
Greek, 138–139, 148–149
Hellenistic, 148–149
Medieval, 392
Muslim, 278–279
Roman, 179
Social Darwinism, *i766*, 775
Phoenicia
alphabet, legacy of, 74, *c74*, *i76*
photojournalism, *i1064–1065*
physics
of Hellenistic period, 148
in Scientific Revolution, 626–627
pi, 148, 195
Piankhi (Kushite king), 93–94
Picasso, Pablo, 899, *i918*
pictographs, *i53*

***Piers Plowman* (Langland),** 363, *i363*
pilgrimages, 263, 267
pilgrims
religious, 263, 267, 562
Pilgrims, 562
pirates, *i563*
Pizarro, Francisco, 556–557, *i557*
plague. *See also* bubonic plague.
Black Death, 399
of Justinian, 304
in the Middle Ages, 399–401
in Peloponnesian War, 137
route of, *m400*
Planck, Max, 766
planned cities
of the Indus Valley, 46
Plato, 138–139, *i139*, 278–279
plebians, 156
plebiscite, 664
PLO (Palestinian Liberation Organization), 1019, 1021, 1023
plow, 19, 32, 204
plumbing
of ancient Rome, 47
of Mohenjo-Daro, 46, *i47*
Plutarch, 148
pogroms, 750, 867
Poland
in 1990s, 1052–1053
modern reforms in, 1052–1053
Solidarity, 1052
in World War II, 925
polis. *See* city-state.
Politburo, 1046
political cartoons, *i709*, *i1029*, *i1037*, *i1047*, *i1067*
political dissent, 1084
political ideas. *See also* political tolerance.
of American Revolution, *c643*, 644–645
balance of power, 672–673
checks and balances, 631, 645
civil disobedience, 888–889
direct democracy, 135
of English Civil War, 614–615
during Enlightenment, 629–632
equality before the law, 1034
of French Revolution, 652, 654
greatest good, 632
of Hammurabi's Code, 33–34, *i33*
importance of the individual, 634
in Kautilya's *Arthasastra*, 189
of Machiavelli, *i583*
monarchy, 127, *c128*, *i578*
natural rights, 630
progress, 630
of Russian Revolution, 868, *c872*
scholarly influence on, 629–634
secret ballot, 753
secularism, 634
separation of powers, 631, *c643*, 645
political persecution. *See* Holocaust.
political systems, *c180*. *See also* democracy; government.
absolute monarchy, 594–595
aristocracy, 127, *c128*
autocracy, 109, 867
direct democracy, 135
fascism, 910, *c911*
federal system, 644–645
feudalism, 54, 360
of hunter-gatherers, 410, *c410*
limited monarchy, 617
military state, 201–202, 1034
monarchy, 127, *c128*, *i578*
in Muslim states, 271–272
Nazism, 912–913
oligarchy, 127, *c128*, *i579*
representative government, 128, 156
republic, 156–157
republican government, 157, *c157*
socialism, 736
in stateless societies, 410
theocracy, 37, 496
totalitarianism, 874–879, *c875*
welfare state, 461, 1039
political tolerance. *See also* religious tolerance.
in ancient Persia, 99, 101
politics
global, 1097
Minoan influence on Greek, 125
and spread of Christianity, 171
Polo, Marco, *i258–259*, 337, *i337*
Pol Pot, 981
polytheism, 31, 38, 78. *See also* monotheism.
Pompeii, 166–167, *c167*, *i167*, 179
Pontius Pilate, 169
pope(s), 171
Benedict XVI, *i305*
Boniface VIII, 398
Byzantine, 306
Clement V, 398
Clement VII, 399
controversy over, 398–399
Council of Constance, 399
and Galileo, 625, *i625*
Gelasius I, 370
Great Schism, 399
Gregory the Great, 355
Gregory VII, 372, 379
and Holy Roman Empire, 372–373
Leo III, 357, 371
Leo IX, 379
Leo X, 490
Martin V, 399
Paul III, 499
Paul IV, 499
Urban II, 382, 386
Popol Vuh, 448
popular culture
movies, *c195*, *i195*, 766–767, 901
music, 1094, *i1094–1095*
sports, 767, 1094
television, 1093–1094
Western influence on, 1095–1096
population(s)
of Aztec civilization, *c319*, 454
of Byzantine Empire, *c319*
of China, *c540*, 806
of cities, A.D. 900, *c273*
during Agricultural Revolution, *c17*
economists on, 735
effect of farming on, *c17*, 387
effect of industrialization on, 723–724, *c727*
effect of trade on, 471
in empires, *c319*
in Europe, 1000–1340, *c405*
Israel's Jewish, *c1102*
of Mongol Empire, *c319*
of Monte Albán, 242
Muslim, 272, 274, *c281*
Persian, *c319*
religious affiliations of world's, *c282–283*
of Roman cities, 162
of Roman Empire, *c319*
porcelain, 325, *i328*, *c329*, *i536*
Portugal
Angolan colony of, 1016
Asian trade with, 532–533
colonies of, 557, 686
in European exploration, 530, 532, 554, 557
influence in Africa, 424, 427
Japanese trade with, 545
North American slaves, 567
rivalry with Spain, 533
slave trade of, 532, 566–567
trade with India, 521, 533
potlatch, 441
Pot, Pol, 981
poverty
in ancient Rome, 164–165
in Brazil, 1036
and Christianity, 170
predestination, 495
prehistoric civilizations
economic changes in, 31
social changes in, 32
prehistoric world
tools in, *i4*, 7–11, 14, *i15*
ways of investigating, 5, 22–23
Presbyterians, 496
PRI (Institutional Revolutionary Party in Mexico), 827, 1037–1038
priests
lack of, in Islam, 267
Roman, 164
Sumerian, 23, 31–32
prime minister, 617
***Prince, The* (Machiavelli),** 476, 503
printing
in China, 484
Gutenberg, 484, *i484*
Japanese woodblock, *i814–815*
and Renaissance ideas, 484
printing press, 484, *i484*
prison reform, 740
production, factors of, 718
proletariat, 736, 868, *c872*, 873
proliferation, 1083
Promised Land, 81
propaganda
Allied, *i857*, *i863*, 943, *i943*
totalitarian, *c875*, 876, *i921*
in World War I, 854, *i863*
in World War II, 943
prophets, 80, *c80*
Protagoras, 138
protectorate, 779, *c780*
Protestantism, *c491*
Calvin's influence on, 495–496
in Spanish Netherlands, 592–593
Protestants, 490, 596
Protestant Union, 603
provisional government, 870
Prussia
alliances of, 607
during the Enlightenment, 638
rise of, 606, 696
psychology
Freud, Sigmund, 766, 897, 898, 899
Pavlov, Ivan, 766
Ptolemy, 147, *c147*
public works projects
during the Depression, 909
of Incan civilization, 461
pyramids as, 38
pueblo, 443
pulley, 148
pump, 148
Punic Wars, 158–159, *m159*

purge, 876
Puritans
in English Civil War, 615
in "New England," 562–563
victory over Metacom, 565
Purusha, *i64*
Putin, Vladimir, 1050–1051, *i1051*
push-pull factors (in migration), 220, *c221*
pyramids
Aztec, 455
Egyptian, *i1*, 37–38, *i39*
Maya, 446, *i450*
in Mesoamerica, *i242*
of North America, 444
Nubian, *i92*
Pythagoras, *i148*
Pythagorean theorem, *i148*

Q

Qian-long, 539–540
Qin Dynasty, *c87*, 107–109, *m108*, 200
Qing Dynasty, 539, 805, 882
queens. *See* individual names.
Queen of Sheba, 225
Quetzalcoatl, *i452,* 453, 456, 458
quipu, *i20*, 461
quipucamayoc, 20
Qur'an, 265, 267–268, 276

R

Rabin, Yitzhak, 1021
racism
in India, 792, 794
and Social Darwinism, *i766*, 775
Western, 813
radar, 928
Radicals, 657, 687
radio, 762, *c831*
KDKA, 901
Nazi, 913
radioactivity, 765, *c831*
railroads
in England, 721–722, *i721–722*
and Indian economy, 792
in United States, 730–731, *i730,* 761
rain forest
African, 213, *i214*
Raj, 794
Ramses II (Egyptian pharaoh), 90–91, *i91*
Raphael, *i474*, 475
Rasputin, 869
rationing, 854, 943
Reagan, Ronald, *i991*
INF (Intermediate-Range Nuclear Forces) treaty, 1047
speech, Berlin Wall (1987), 1054
Strategic Defense Initiative, 991
realism, 700–701
realpolitik, 695–696, 990
recession, 1034
reconquista, 384, 557
Reconstruction, 760–761
record-keeping
"checks" in, 272
importance of paper to, 203
Incan, *i20*, 461
prehistoric, *i116*
Sumerian, 20–21, 32
Red Army, 871–872, *c871*
Red Guards, 870, 975, *i975*
Red Shirts, 694
Reformation, the, 488–501
and absolute monarchy, 493
Catholic, 498–499
causes of, 488–489, *c488*
characteristics of, 489
effects of, 490–494, 500
indulgences, 489
Luther, Martin, 489–490
peasant's revolt, 490
values in, 489
women in, 494, 496, 498
Reformation Parliament, 492–493
refugees, 1086
number of, 1992–2002, *c1099*
Reign of Terror, 660–661
reincarnation, 67
relativity, theory of, 897
religion. *See also* Buddhism; Christianity; Hinduism; Islam; Jainism; Judaism; Manicheanism; Zoroastrianism.
and death, 9, 38–39, 67
effect of printing press on, 485
in Europe (1560), *m497*
and nationalism, *c688*
in native North America, 444–445
Persian, 103
reformers, 489–490
Roman government and, 164, 170
spread of Indian, 197, *c197*
unifying force of, 371–372
and women, 67, 72
world, 282–296
religious affiliations, world's, *c282–283*
religious beliefs. *See also* religion; sacrifice.
of ancient China, 52–53
animism, 216, 415
in art, *i312*
Aztec, 456, *i457*
effects of science on, 625
empire worship, 164
ethical monotheism, 80
Incan, 462
jaguar worship, 241, *i244*
Maya, 447–448
Minoan influence on Greek, 72, 125
in native North America, 444–445
of Persia, 103
in prehistory, 9
Roman, 168, 174
sports in, 130
Sumerian, 23, 31–32
religious conflict, 1083
religious persecution. *See also* Christianity; Holocaust; Inquisition.
in Japan, 546
of Muslims, 1056
in Spanish colonies, 559
under Stalin, 877
religious rituals, 9. *See also* burial rites; sacrifice.
Sumerian, 23, 31–32
religious symbolism, *i287, c296*
cross as, *i312*
religious tolerance, 68
in Austria, 638
of Cyrus the Great, 99–100
in Edict of Nantes, 596
and French Revolution, 656
in Indian empires, 190
in Islamic law, 268
in Mughal Empire, 517
under Muslim rule, 270, 274
in Netherlands, 593
in Ottoman Empire, 510
reliquary, *i313*
Rembrandt (van Rijn), 593, *i593*, *i628*
Remus, 155
Renaissance. *See also* Northern Renaissance.
art, *i470*, 474, *i474*, *i478–479*, 481
British, 483
causes of, 471
characteristics of, 472–473, 475
Chinese, *i477*
da Vinci, Leonardo, 475, *i475*, *i478–479*
effects of, 485
European, 471–488
Flanders, 480–481
humanism, 472, 482
Italian, 471–477
literature, 475–477, 482–483
Michelangelo, 475, *i475*, *i478*
Muslim influence on, 279
Northern, 480–485
Petrarch, 475–476
Raphael, *i474*, 475, *i479*
themes of, 472
values of, 471–473, 480
women in, 473, *i473*, 477
"Renaissance men," 473, *i473*
"Renaissance women," 473, *i473*
republic
China, 882
French, 690
Roman, 155–159, *c157*
United States, *c157*, 644–645
Republic, The **(Plato),** 138
res publica, 156
Restoration, 616
reunification, 1054
revolution(s)
1848, *m679*
agricultural, 15, *c17*
American, 640–645, *c706*
Bolshevik, 870–871, *c871*
causes of, *c708*
Chinese, 882
Commercial, 389–390, *c390*
Cuban, 984
Cultural (Chinese), 975, 1059–1060
effects of, *c710*
English, 615–616, *c706*
and Enlightenment, 641–642, 652, *m684*
failed, 689–690
French, *i644*, 651–661, *c706*
Glorious, 616, *c706*
Green, 1074
in Haiti, 682
ideas and, 681, 684
Latin American, 682–686, *c707*
leaders of, *c892*
Mexican, 685–686, 826–827
model of, *c707*
nationalist, 682–686
role of Enlightenment in, 641–642, 652
Russian, 869–872
in Saint Domingue, 665, 682
Scientific, 623–628, *c626–627*
Southwest Asian, 890
in Soviet Union, 870–871, *c871*
time line of, *c706–707*
Rhodes, Cecil, 775, *i775*
Ricardo, David, 734–735
Ricci, Matteo, 537, 539

Index

Richardson, Samuel, 637
Richard the Lion-Hearted, *i378*, 383, *i384*
Richelieu, Cardinal, 597, *i597*, 604
Rig Veda, 63, *i289*
rights and responsibilities. *See also* Bill of Rights; constitution.
in Declaration of the Rights of Man, 656
in democracy, *c134*
of *habeas corpus*, 616
Locke's treatise on, 630
under Magna Carta, 394–395, *i395*
in Petition of Right, 614
religious freedom, 630. *c632*, 638
Universal Declaration of Human Rights, 1084
Rio de Janeiro, 686
roads. *See also* Royal Road; Silk Roads.
during industrial revolution, 721
Incan, 461
of Roman Empire, 163, 183
Robespierre, Maximilien, 660–661, *i660*, *i711*
Rockefeller, John D., 731
rock'n'roll, *i1094–1095*
Roman Catholic Church. *See also* church.
in the Americas, 558–559
authority of, 370–371, 399
canon law, 371, 379
division of, 398–399
during French Revolution, 656–657
effect of plague on, 401
in Enlightenment, 636
and fall of Roman Empire, 172
and Galileo, 625
and Holy Roman Empire, 371–372
and Huguenots, 496, 597
Inquisition in, 384, *i385*
and Medieval women, 354–355
in the Middle Ages, 354–355, 370–374, 379–385
problems in, 488–489
Reformation in, 498–499
reform of, 398, 489
structure of, 370
weakening of, 401
Roman Empire
ancient, 160
agriculture, 163, 164, 173
aqueducts, 47, 181, *i181*
army, 161, 173–174
art and architecture, *i166–167*, 178–179, 181, *i182*, 183
Augustus, 162, *i162*
beginnings, 160–161
Caesar, Julius, 161–162, *i161*
cities, 164, 165
civil wars, 161, 162, 174
as classical age, 252–257
Colosseum, 165, 181, *i182*
cultural influence of, 176, 178–181
decline of, 168, 172, 173–177, *c174*
economic developments of, 163
education, 179
emperors, 162, *c164*
family life in, 162
gladiators, 165, *i165*, *i182*
government of, 161–162, *c164*, 174
invasions into, 175–176, *m175*, 353
Latin language in, 170, 181
law in, 183
legacy of, 178–183
literature, 179, *c180*, 181
mercenaries, 173
Pax Romana, 162, 165, 170, 173
political developments of, 162
population of, 162, 164
reforms, 161–162, 174
religion in, 164, 168, 174
slavery in, 160, 162, 164
social classes, 164–165
social life, 164–165
triumvirate, 161–162
values, 163, 178
Romania, 1055–1056
fall of Communism, 1056
Romanovs, 608–609, 693
Roman Republic, *c87,* 155–160
army, 157–159
collapse of, 160–161
Etruscan influence on, 155–156
government, 157
compared with United States, *c157*
Greek influence on, 155
origins, 155–156
Punic Wars, 158–159, *m159*
Twelve Tables, 156
romanticism, 698–699
Rome. *See also* Roman Empire. Roman Republic.
Vatican City in, 695
Rommel, General Erwin, 928–929, 940
Romulus, 155
Roosevelt Corollary, 821
Roosevelt, Franklin D., *i909*, 931, 945, 967
and atomic weapons, *i946*
New Deal, 909
at Yalta Conference, *i965*
Roosevelt, Theodore, 819, 821, *i821*
Rosetta Stone, *i40*
Rousseau, Jean Jacques, 631–632, *i631*
Rowlatt Acts, 887
Roy, Ram Mohun, 795
Royal Road, 101, *i102*, *m102*
Rubicon River (Italy), 161
Russia. *See also* Russian empire; Russian Revolution; Soviet Union.
1905–1922, *m870*
Bolsheviks, 868, 870–873
boyars, 608–609
Chechnyan war, 1050–1051, *i1050*
civil war, *m870*, 871–872
and Crimean War, 787
democracy in, 1049–1051
expansion of 1500–1800, *m610*, 639
Japanese defeat of, 813
Lenin, Vladimir Ilyich, 854, 868, *i868*, 870–873
Napoleon I invades, 669–670, *m670*
nationalism in, 691,873
Nevsky, Alexander, 310
Novgorod, 307
Peter the Great, 609–611, *i609*
reform in, 690–691
religious art of, *i312–313*
revolution in, 869–872
serfs in, 690–691, *i691*
Slavic and Greek traditions in, 307
Stalin, Joseph, 873
and totalitarian state, 876–879
unified territory
winters of, *i612–613*
in World War I, 845, 848–849, 854–855, 869
Russian Empire
in 500–1500
under Catherine the Great, 638–639
fall of, 693
Russification, 693
Russian Revolution. *See also* Bolshevik Revolution.
"Bloody Sunday," 869, *i869*
causes of, 867–868
compared with American Revolution, 872
compared with French Revolution, 872
Duma, 870
effects of, 871–872, *c871*
Kerensky and provisional government, 870–871
March Revolution, 869–870
Rasputin, 869
Red Army, 871–872, *i871*
soviets, 870, 873
Treaty of Brest-Litvosk, 854, 871
Trotsky, Leon, 871, 873
Russification, 693
Rwanda, *i1016*, 1084

S

sacraments, 371
sacrifice
in Africa, 227
Aztec, 456
human, 73, 447–448, 456
Incan, 462, 464
Maya, 447–448
Minoan, 73
Sumerian, 23, 32
Sadat, Anwar, 1019–1021, *i1020*
Safavid Empire, 512–515, *m514*
Sahara, 213, *i214*, 215
salt trade of, 413
Sahel, 213, *i214*
sail, *i117*
sailing
in ancient Greece, 123
Phoenician, *i117*
Saint Domingue, 665, 682
St. Petersburg, 611, 869
Saladin, 383, *i384*, 386
Salamis, 132
salons, 636
salt, 413
Salt Acts (India), 889
Salt March, 889
trade, 413
SALT (Strategic Arms Limitation Talks) I, 991
SALT II, 991, 1083
samurai, *i342*, 343
Samyutta Nikaya, 69
Sandinistas, 985
Sanger, Margaret, 900
San Martín, José de, 683, *i683*
San people, 215, 224, *c411*, *m411*
sans-culottes, 658
Santa Anna, Antonio López de, 822–823, *i823*
Sargon of Akkad, 33
Saro-Wiwa, Ken, *i1042*
Satrap, 101
Saudi Arabia, 890–891
Saul (Israelite king), 81
savannas, *i214*, 215
Scandinavia, 926
Schlieffen Plan, 846–847
Schliemann, Heinrich, 125
Scholastica, 355, *i355*
scholastics, 392
Schroeder, Gerhard, 1054
science *See also* revolution, scientific; technology; tools.

chemistry, 628, *c830*
cloning, 1073–1074
of Egypt, 41
genetic engineering, 1073
genetics, 765, 1073–1074
global effect of, 1073
impact of changes in, *c834*
in Indus Valley, 46
in Muslim world, 274, *i275,* 278
physics, 626–627, 765–766
social, 766
space travel, 1071–1072
of sumer, 32
scientific method, 625–626
Bacon, Francis, 626
Descartes, René, 626
old science and new science, *c626*
Scientific Revolution, 623–628, *c626–627*
advances in medicine, 627–628, *i628*
advances in chemistry, 628, *c830*
tools and inventions, 627
Scipio, 159
scorched-earth policy, 669
Scorpion King, 37
scribes, 20–21
sculpture
Assyrian, 96, *i97*
Benin, *i419–421*
Buddhist, 193–194, *i194*, *i198*
Egyptian, *i90*
Greek, 136, *i140*, 178
Hellenistic, 149
Hittite, *i63*
Minoan, 72
Moche, 249
neoclassic, 637
Nok, *i217*
Nubian, *i92*, *i93*
Olmec, *i58*, 240–241, *i244*
Renaissance, 474, *i478–479*
Roman, 178
SEATO (Southeast Asia Treaty Organization), 1082
secede, 760
Second Reich, 697
Second World, 982
secular, 355, 472, 634
secular government, 986
segregation, 761
self-determination, 858
Selim the Grim, 509, 514
Selim II, 511
Selim III, 786
Seljuk Empire
c.1100, *m299*
Crusaders in, 316, 383
Malik Shah, 315–316
Mongol overthrow of, 316–317
Senate
Roman, *i154*, 157, *c157*
United States, *c157*
Seneca Falls Convention, 769
Sennacherib (Assyrian king), 95–96
separation of powers. *See* political ideas.
sepoy, 791, 793–794
Sepoy Mutiny, 793–794
September 11 terrorist attacks
anthrax and, 1090–1091
effect on air travel of, 1092
impact of, 1090–1091
international response to, 1097
rescue and recovery efforts, 1090
Serbia
in 1990s, 1056
Independence of, 1056
in World War I, 848
serfs, 360, 362–363, 605, 690–691, *i691*
Seven Wonders of the World, 98, 149
sextant, *i531*
Shah Jahan, 519–520
Shah, Malik, 315–316
shahs, 514
Shaka (Zulu chief), 776
Shakespeare, William, 483
Shang Di, 53
Shang dynasty, 52
artisans of, *i117*
social classes of, 52
Shanidar Cave, 9
Sharif, Nawaz, 1002
Sharon, Ariel, 1022–1023, *i1104*
shari'a, 268, 274
Shelley, Mary, 699
Shi'a Muslims, 271, *c271*, 272
Shi Huangdi, 107–109, *i107*, 200
Shinto, 339–340
shipbuilding, 74, *i75*
Shiva, 67, 194
"shock therapy" (Russian economic plan), 1050
shogun, 343
Siam, 797–798
Siddhartha Gautama, 68. *See also* Buddha; Buddhism.
siege, *i366*, 367
Sikhs, 519, 521, 998–999
in Sepoy Mutiny, 794
silk
importance to China, 204–205, *m204–205*
Silk Roads
in Arabian trade, 263
Chinese commerce along, 205, *m204–205*, *i207*
in Indian trade, 196
in Muslim trade, 272
trade networks on, 71, *i88*, *m204–205*
silt, 29, 35, 36, 44
Silva, Luiz Inacio Lula da, 1036
Sima Qian ("Grand Historian"), 202, 205
simony, 379
Singapore, 797, *i1008*
independence of, 1008
Sirius, 40
skepticism, 597
slash-and-burn farming, 15, 222
slavery, *i567*. *See also* slaves.
African, 418, 425, 566
in the Americas, 566–570
in Assyrian empire, 96
British role in, 567, 601
and colonialism, 566–570
effect of industrialization on, 739
in Egypt, 40, 89
Hebrews in, 78–79, 89
middle passage, 569, *i569*
under Napoleonic Code, 664
of Nazis, 938
Portugal's role in, 566–567
in the United States, 759–760
slaves. *See also* slavery.
African, 425, 566
in the Americas, 566–570
in ancient Rome, 159, 160, 164
of Athens, 128
Aztec, 454
Carthaginian, 159
children as, 164
in civil service, 510
in Egypt, 40, 89
as gladiators, 164
native American, 557, 559
Nubian, *i93*
in Ottoman Empire, 510
resistance of, 569–570
revolt in Saint Domingue, 665, 682
ships bearing, 569, *i569*
in Sumer, 32
Turkish military, 314
in the United States, 759–760
in West Africa, 418
Slavic speakers, 306, *c1057*
Slavs, 306–307
language of, 306
and Vikings, 307, *m308*
Slovenia, 1056
smallpox, 556, *i560*, 565, 571, 573, 628
Smith, Adam, 734–735, *i735*
social classes. *See also* middle class.
Aztec, 454–455
and Buddhism, 70
clothing of, 93
during Commercial Revolution, 390, *c390*
of Egypt, 40
under feudalism, 360, *i361*
of India, *i793*
of Indus Valley, 48
industrialization and, 725–726, 736
in Japan, 341, 343
Maya, 447
in Middle Ages, 390–391
in Muslim society, 274
Platonic ideal of, 138
of Rome, 156, 164–165
of Russian revolution, 868
of Shang dynasty, 52
of Sparta, 131
of Sumer, 32
in Tang and Song dynasties, 327
social contract, 629
in American Revolution, 641
Hobbes, Thomas, 629
Social Darwinism, *i766*, 775
socialism, 736–738
during the Depression, 909
Socrates, 138, *i138*, *i139*
soil erosion, 1080
solar system, *c147*
Solidarity, 1052
Solomon (Israelite king), 81, *i81*, 225
Solon, 128
Somoza, Anastasio, 985
Songhai, *m414*, 417
Askia Muhammad, 417
Sunni Ali, 417
Song dynasty
cultural advances in, 325–327
inventions of, 325, *i328–329*
population, 325
prosperity in, 325–326
renaissance of, 324–325
science and technology of, 325, *i328–329*
Sophists, 138
Sophocles, 136
South Africa
1948–2000, *c1045*
AIDS epidemic in, 1045
all-race election, 1044, *1065*
ANC (African National Congress), 1043–1045

Index

apartheid in, 1043–1044
constitution, 1044
Dutch in, 776, 1043
flags of, *i1045*
international boycott against, 1044
Mandela, Nelson, 1043–1044, *i1044*
Mbeki, Thabo, 1044–1045
resistance to imperialism in, 776
Southeast Asia Treaty Organization (SEATO), 1082
South America
cultures, *m247*, *m461*
empires, 459–463
Southeast Asia
900–1200, *m345*
1945–1975, *m1005*
colonies in, *m797*, 1004–1006, *m1005*
domino theory, 978
geography of, 344, *c1011*
housing, *i1010*
imperialism in, 796–797
independence of, 1004–1009
influences on, 344–345
Khmer Empire (Cambodia), 345
kingdoms of, 344–347
markets, *i1011*
population, *c1011*
post-World War II, 1004, 1006, 1008
trade of, *c1011*
transportation, *i1010*
South Korea, 976–978
Southwest Asia, *m865*, 890–891
soviets, 870, 873
Soviet Union. *See also* Commonwealth of Independent States (CIS); Russia; Stalin.
in Afghanistan, 788, 987, 1026
allies with Germany, 925
breakup of, 1024, 1049, *m1049*
and China, 884, 974–975, 989–990, 1060
during Cold War, 967–970, 973, 982–987, 990–991
détente, 990–991
in Eastern Europe, 988–989, 1052
economy, 877–878, *c878*
expansion of, 967–969
fall of, 1049
glasnost, 1046
modern reforms in, 1047–1048
and Nazis, 925, 929–930
perestroika, 1047
post-World War II goals, *c966*, 967
space race, 970–971
Sputnik, 970, *i971*
as superpower, *c966*, 969, *c993*
totalitarianism in, 873, 876–879
in World War II, 925, 929–930, 940–943
space race, 970–971
space shuttle, 1071–1072
Columbia, 1072
Spain
in the Americas, 554–559
civil war, 917, *i918*
conquest patterns of, 557
Native resistance to, 559
Crusades in, 384–385
fascism in, 917
Franco, Francisco, 917
in Latin America, 675, 681–686, 818
Napoleon's invasion of, 669
Nationalists, 917
North American colonies of, 554, 556–558, 682–686
persecution of Jews in, 384
reconquista, 384, 557
Republicans, 917
rivalry with Portugal, 533
slave trade of, 567
Spanish Armada
defeat of, *m590*, 591
Spanish Empire, 589–593
Sparta
military state of, 129, 131
war with Athens, 137–138, *m137*
special economic zones (SEZs), *i806*
specialization, 20
sphere of influence, 779, *c780*, 807
Spice Islands, 533, *m534*, 535
sports
19th century, 767
basketball, 1094
history of, 767
Maya ball game, 447, *i451*
Olmec, *i244*
Olympic games, 130, 133, 767
soccer, 1094
Sputnik, 970, *i971*
Sri Lanka, 1003
Srivijaya, 345–346, *m345*
Stalin, Joseph, 873, 876–879, *i877*
art as propaganda, 876, *i876*
denouncement of, 988
as dictator, 873, 876–879
exile of Trotsky, 873
Great Purge, 876
and Lenin, 873
occupation of Poland, 925
oppression of kulaks, 878, *i879*
post-World War II, 965–968
religious persecution, 877
Stalingrad, 941
standard of living, 1034
Stanley, Henry, 774, *i774*
"Star Wars" (missile defense), 991
stateless society, 410
steamboat, 721, *c830*, *i830*
steam engine, 148, 721, 775
steppes, 61, 330
stocks, 731, 906–907, *c906*
Stoicism, 148–149
Stone Age, Old and New. *See* Neolithic Age; Paleolithic Age.
Straits of Hormuz, 533
Strategic Arms Limitation Talks (SALT), 991, 1083
Stravinsky, Igor, 899
strike, 738
Stuart lands, *m587*
stupas, 193, *i198*
stylus, 21
subcontinent, 44
submarines, *i848*, 852–853
Sudetenland, 918
Suez Canal, *i789*, *m789*
Egyptian control of, 788–789
Suez crisis of, 1018–1019
in World War II
suffrage, 747
Sufi, 271
sugar
in New World territories, 557, 563, 567
and slavery, 563, 567
Suharto (Indonesian president), 1008
suicide bombers, 1022
Sukarno (Indonesian president), 1008
Sukarnoputri, Megawati (Indonesian president), 1008–1009, *i1008*
Suleyman the Lawgiver, 510–511, *i510*
sultan, 507
Sumer, *c3*, 20–23, 48. *See also* Sumerians.
architecture of, 22–23, 31, 32
city-states of, *c26*, 30–31, *i112*
environmental challenges in, 29–30
geography of, 29, *m30*
poetry, 32
Sumerians, 20–23. *See also* Sumer.
culture of, 22–23, 31–32
influence on Mesopotamia of, 20, 29–30
religion of, 23, 31–32
social classes of, 32
Sundiata, 415
Sunna, 268
Sunni, 271, *c271*
Sunni Ali (Songhai ruler), 417
Sun Yixian, 882, *i882*
superstition, age of, *i371*
supreme court, *c180*
surnames, 388
Surrealism, 899, *i899*
sustainable growth, 1080
Suu Kyi, Aung San, 1006–1007, *i1006*
Svetasvatara Upanishad, 67
Swahili, *i223*, 422, 427
swastika, 912
sweden, 358, *m610*, 611
symbols
alphabets, *c74*, *i116*
animal, 454
cuneiform, 20, *i21*, 32, 40, *i116*
glyphs, 448
hieroglyphs, 40, *i40*, 116
in language, *c74*
national, *i680*
pictographs, *i53*
in prehistoric art, 11, *i12–13*
in record keeping, 74, *i116*
religious, *i287*, *c296*
swastika, 912
of warriors, 454
writing, 53
yin and yang, 107, *i107*, 109
Syracuse, 137

T

Tacitus, 181
Taiping Rebellion, 807, *i807*
Taiwan
Nationalist China, 973
Republic of China, 973
Taj Mahal, 519, *i520*
Taliban, *i987*, 1089
destruction of artifacts by, *i1026*
rise and fall of, 1026–1027, *i1027*
Tamil, 191, 194
Eelam, *i1003*
Tammarlane. *See also* Timur the Lame.
Tang dynasty, 323–327
expansion of China under, 323–324
influence on Japan, 340
inventions of, *i322*, 325, *i328–329*
population of, 325
renaissance in, 325–326
science and technology, 325, *i328–329*
Tang Taizong, 323, *i324*
tariffs, 907–908, 1077
Tarquin the Proud, 156
technology, 8, 19, 21. *See also* inventions; science; weapons.
in 19th century, 762–764, *i954*
in 20th century, 764, *i902–903*, *i954–955*,

1072
of Africa, 217–218, *i218*
appliances, *c903*
of Bronze Age, 21
of China, 52, 55, 203–204
computers, 1072–1073
effect on imperialism, 833
of Egypt, 90
in European exploration, 530
global effect of, 1072–1073
of the harness, 203, 387
Hellenistic, 148
Hittite, 63
of *Homo erectus*, 8
horsepower, 387
impact of, *c832*
of Industrial Revolution, 718–722, *i719*
of Indus Valley, 46, *i47*
information industry, 1073, *c1073*
of Islam, *i275*, 278
labor-saving devices, *i902–903*
migration and, 221, 224
movies, *i763*, 766–767, 901
Muslim, *i275*, 278
of Northern Renaissance, 484
and popular culture, 1093
post-World War I, 900–903, *i902–903*
prehistoric, *i4*, 8, 14, *i15*
printing press, 484, *i484*
radio, 762, *c831*, 901
space travel, 1071–1072
of Sumer, 19, 21, 32
telephone, 762, *i764*
time line of changes in, *c830–831*
of war, 89, 402, *i954–955*
Tehuacan Valley, 238
telephone, 762, *i764*
telescope, 278
television
influence of, 1093–1094
news and, 1094
Ten Commandments, 79–80
as social code, 80
in teachings of Jesus, 168
Ten Hours Act, 739
Tennis Court Oath, 654
Tenochtitlán, 454–455, 458, *m467*
Teotihuacán, 452–453
terrorism. *See also* antiterrorism coalition; global security; terrorist groups; names of specific regions or countries.
definition of, 1087
domestic, 1090–1092
international, 1087
major centers of, 1088–1089
reasons for, 1087
tactics of, 1087–1088
terrorist attacks. *See also* September 11 terrorist attacks.
casualties of, *c1089*
international, *c1089*
in Kenya, 1013, 1089
in Tanzania, 1089
total attacks, *c1089*
in United States, 1090–1092
terrorist groups
in Africa, 1089
in Asia, 1089
Aum Shinrikyo, 1089
in Europe, 755, 1089
in Latin America, 1089
in Middle East, 1088
Texas Revolt, 759, 822–823
textile industry
in Britain, 718–720, *i719*, 791
in United States, 729–730
theater
comedy and tragedy, 136, *i141*
French, 599
Greek, 136, *i141*
Kabuki, 544, *i545*
Molière, 599
Shakespeare, 483, *i483*
theocracy, 37, 48, 496
Theodora (Byzantine empress), 303, *i303*, 306
theory of evolution, 765
theory of relativity, 897
Theravada sect, 193
thermometer, 627
Thermopylae, 132
Theseus, 122
Third Reich, 918, 945
Third Republic, 690, 749
Third World, 982–987
modern challenges of, 1033–1054
Thousand and One Nights, The, 276, *i276*
three cardinal faults, *i285*
three-field system, 387
Thucydides, 122, 135, 136–138
Thutmose III (Egyptian pharaoh), 90, 91
Tiananmen Square
in 1919, *i883*
in 1989, *i883*, 1061–1062, *i1064*
Tibet
Chinese takeover of, 973
Tiberius, 160
Tigris River, 29
Tikal, 446, *i450–451*
Timbuktu, 416
time
to Maya, 448
measuring, 325, *c328*
time lines
Africa
1500 B.C.–A.D. 500, *c210–211*
800–1500, *c406–407*
Africa and Asia, 1850–1925, *c770–771*
Africa, Southwest Asia, and China, 1570 B.C.–200 B.C., *c86–87*
Americas
10,000 B.C.–A.D. 700, *c232–233*
500–1500, *c438–439*
1500–1800, *c550–551*
Central Asia, 500–1500, *c298–299*
East and Southeast Asia, 600–1400, *c320-321*
East Asia and Latin America, 1800–1925, *c802–803*
Eastern Hemisphere/Western Hemisphere, 2000 B.C.–250 B.C., *c58–59*
Europe
500–1100, c350–351
800–1500, *c376–377*
1300–1600, *c468–469*
1500–1800, *c586–587*
1789–1815, *c648–649*
1815–1915, *c744–745*
1914–1918, *c838–839*
1920–1940, *c894–895*
Europe and Asia
1400–1800, *c526–527*
1900–1940, *c864–865*
Europe and North America, 1500–1800, *c620–621*
Europe and United States, 1700–1900, *c714–715*
Greece, 2000 B.C.–300 B.C., *c120–121*
India and China, 400 B.C.–A.D. 500, *c186–187*
Latin America and Europe, 1800–1900, *c678–679*
Muslim World
600–1250, *c260-261*
1300–1700, *c504–505*
Rome, 500 B.C.–A.D. 500, *c152–153*
World
4 million B.C.–2500 B.C., *c2–3*
3500 B.C.–500 B.C., *c26–27*
1945–2003, *c962–963*
1960–2003, *c1068–1069*
World Colonies Become New Nations, 1954–2000, *c994–995*
World Democracies, 1945–2005, *c1030–1031*
Timor. *See* East Timor.
Timur the Lame, 508
tithes, 363, 379
Tito, Joseph, 1056
tobacco, 790
Tocqueville, Alexis de, 671, 735, 740
toilet, flush, 47
Tokugawa Ieyasu, 543–544, 546
Tokugawa Shogunate, 544, 546, *c578*, *i581*, 810, 811
Toltecs, 453
tools, 19, 21. *See also* technology.
of exploration, *i531*
prehistoric, *i4*, 5, 7–11, 14, *i17*
Torah, 77, 79, *i79*, *c80*, 83
Tories, 616
totalitarianism. *See also* China; dictators; Nazism; Russia; Soviet Union.
key traits of, *c875*
life under, 874–876
in Stalinist Russia, 876–879
weapons of, 874
totalitarian state(s)
leaders of, in the 20th century, *c875*
total war, 853, 956
totems, 445
Toumai, 11
Touré, Samori, 782
tournaments, 367
Toyotomi Hideyoshi, 543
trade. *See also* slavery; trade networks.
African, 226 –227, *i406*, 422
apartheid, restrictions on, 1044
Arabian, 263, *m264*
Aztec, 454–455
balance of, 575
Buddhism and, 71, *m197*
Chinese, 197, *m204–205*, 325–326, 805, 807–808
colonial, 562–564
Columbian Exchange, 571–573, *i572*
and the Crusades, 385
Dutch, 534–535, 594
in the early Middle Ages, 353
East African, 422, *m423*
in Egypt, 37, 90, 92, 94
expansion of free, 1076–1077
French, 535, 562
Ghana, 413–414
global, 573–575
gold, 227
gold-salt, 413–414
goods, *i434*
Hellenistic, 146
Incan, 460

in India, 195–197, *m196*
and Industrial Revolution, 733, 734
in Indus Valley, 48
Japanese, 545, 810
under Kublai Khan, 336–337
in Mesoamerica, 241
in Middle Ages, 389–390
Minoan, 72, 125
Mongol effect on, 334, 336–337
Muslim, 272, 424
narratives, 435
native North American, 444
in Pacific Rim, 796–797
patterns of ancient, *m75*
Phoenician, *c59*, 73–76, *i75*
Portuguese, 424, 521, 533–534
regional trade blocs, 1076–1077
regional trading groups, 2003, *m1077*
in Roman Empire, 162, 163, *m163*, 164, 197
routes in Africa, Asia, Europe, *m430*
seafaring, 72–76, 163, 196–197
slave, 566–570
Triangular, 568–569, *m568*
in Ur, 23
Viking, 359
West African, 413–416
Zhou Dynasty, 55
trade networks
African, 773
components of, *c431*
Indian Ocean, *c432*
Mediterranean, *c432*
modes of transport, *i433*
Silk Roads, *c432*
Trans-Arabia, *c432*
Trans-Sahara, *c432*
types of, *c431*
tragedy, 136, *i141*
Trail of Tears, 758–759
Trajan, *c164*, *i164*
Transcaucasian Republics, 1024–1025
transportation, 721–722
Trans-Siberian Railway, 868
Treaty of Kanagawa, 810
Treaty of Tordesillas, 533
Treaty of Verdun, 357
Treaty of Versailles, 858–86, *c861*, 883
analysis, 859, 861
Hitler defies, 916–918
trench warfare, 847, *i847*, 958
triangular trade, 568–569, *m568*
tribunes, 156
tribute, 82
Triple Alliance (Aztec), 454
collapse of, 456, 458
Triple Alliance (European), 842–843
Triple Entente, 843
triumvirate, 161–162
Trojan horse, *i125*
Trojan War, *c121*, 125
Trotsky, Leon, 871, 873
troubadours, 367–368
love songs, 368
Troy, 125
Truman Doctrine, 968
Truman, Harry, 945, 947, 968, 976
tsetse fly, 213, *i214*, 215
Tull, Jethro, 717
Turkey, Republic of, *i317*, 890
Kemal, Mustafa, 890, *i890*
Turkish Empire, 314–317
Turks. *See also* Seljuk Empire.
in Christian Byzantium, 304
conflict with Greeks, 689, 693
migrations, 314
Seljuks, 314–316
in World War I, 851, 855
turnpike, 721
Tutankhamen (Egyptian pharaoh), *i39*
Tutu, Archbishop Desmond, 1044
Twelve Tables, 156, *c157*
tyrants, 127, 156, 514

U

Ukraine, *i879*
***Ulysses* (Joyce),** 898
Umayyad dynasty, 271
Umma, 265
unemployment, 907, *c907*
Union of Soviet Socialist Republics (USSR), 873. *See also* Russia; Soviet Union.
unionization, 738
unions, 738
United Kingdom, *c780*
United Nations
ceasefire, 1082
compared to Congress of Vienna, 675
creation of, 966
and human rights, 1084
peacekeepers, 1082
United States. *See also* Native Americans; North America.
Atlantic Charter, 930
Bill of Rights, 617, 645, *i645*
boycott of 1980 Olympics, 987
civil rights in World War II, 943
Civil War, 759–760, *m760*
during Cold War, 967–970, 973, 978, 982–987, 990–991
colonies of, 640–642, 798–799
Constitution, *c643*, 644–645, 647
and Cuba, 818–819, 984–985
Cuban Missile Crisis, 985, 990
culture, 1095–1097
democracy in, 617, *c643*
the Depression in, 906–907, 909
détente, 990–991
domino theory, 978
expansion (1783–1853), *m759*
government, *c643,* 644–645
immigrants to, 761
imperialism, 798–799, 818–821
industrialization, 729–731, 761
isolationism in, 918
in Korean War, 976–977
land acquisition in, 758–759
Lend-Lease Act, 930
Marshall Plan, 968, *c968*
and Middle East, 986–987, 1020, 1022–1023
Native Americans in, 758–759
occupation of Japan, 950–951
Pearl Harbor, 931–932, *i932*
and Philippines, 798, 932, 1004–1005
settlers in, 562–564
space race, 970–971
as superpower, *c966*, 969, *c993*
U-2 incident, 970, 990
war in Vietnam, 978–981, *m979*, *i979*
in World War I, 852–854
in World War II, 930, 940–947
Universal Declaration of Human Rights, 1084
university, 391
unrestricted submarine warfare, 852
untouchables, 64, *i64*
Upanishads, 66–67
Upper Egypt, 36–37. *See also* Egypt.
Ur, *c3*, 22–23
urban centers. *See also* cities.
Muslim, 273–274
Olmec design, 243
urbanization, 220, 723
Urdu, 518
USA Patriot Act, 1092
USSR (Union of Soviet Socialist Republics), 873. *See also* Russia; Soviet Union.
utilitarianism, 735
utopia, 482, 736
***Utopia* (More),** 482
U-2 incident, 970, 990

V

Vajpayee, Atal Bihari, 1000
Valley of the Kings, 91
Valley of Mexico, 452–453
values
in ancient Greece, 129, *i130*, 134–136
Chinese, 104–107
during Enlightenment, 630–632, 635
Medieval, 365
of Persian Empire, 99, 103
in Renaissance, 472–473, 480
return to traditional, 1097
of samurai, *i342*, 343
Spartan, 131
of Western culture, 1096
van Eyck, Jan, *i470*, 481
vassal, 360
Vedas, 63
Velázquez, Diego, 591, *i591*
Venezuela, 683, 817, *i1032*
Verdun, 848
Vermeer, Jan, 593
vernacular, 391–392, 475
Verrazzano, Giovanni da, 561
Versailles
Palace of, 47, 599, *i600*
Treaty of, 858–861, *c861*
Vesalius, Andreas, 627–628
Vespucci, Amerigo, 554
Vesuvius. *See* Mount Vesuvius.
Victor Emmanuel III (Italian king), 911, 941
Victoria (British queen), 748, *i748*
Victorian Age, 748–749
Vietcong, 980
Vietnam
"boat people," 981
capitalism in, *i981*
Dai Viet, 346
divided country, 978
domino theory, 978
and France, 797, 978
Ho Chi Minh, 978, *i978*, 993
Ngo Dinh Diem, 978, 980
and United States, 978–981
Vietnam War, 978–981, *i979*, *m979*
Vietnamization, 980
Vikings
Ericson, Leif, 359
invasions, *m308*, 358, *m359*, 393
longboats of, 358, *i358*
Rurik (Viking chief), 307
and Slavs, 307
villa (Roman), *i166–167*, 178
Villa, Francisco "Pancho," 826

villages
achievements of, 16, 18
becoming cities, 19–20
growth of, 16, *c24*
Virgil, 179
Vishnu, 67, 194
fish incarnation of, 83
vizier, 315
Vladimir, 308
volcanoes, 166–167, *c167*
Voltaire, 630, *i630*
voting. *See also* suffrage.
in ancient Rome, 156
in Britain, 747–748, *c748*
in United States, *c643*

W

Walesa, Lech, 1052–1053
Wang Mang, 206–207
war. *See also* civil war(s); empire(s); technology; war against terrorism.
of 1812, 729
American Revolutionary, 640–645
in ancient China, 55, 201–202
in ancient Sumer, 31, 32–33
Arab-Israeli, 1018–1019
of the Austrian Succession, 607
of Bantu-speaking peoples, 224
Boer, 778
in Bosnia, 1056, *i1064*
Chechnyan, 1050–1051
Cold, 967–970
Crimean, 787
elephants of, 158
English Civil, 615, *m616*
French and Indian, 564, 641
Franco-Prussian, 696
Hundred Years', 401–403
in Incan civilization, 459–460, 463
Korean, 976–977
Mexican-American, 759
in Nicaragua, 985
Opium, 806
Peloponnesian, 137–138, *m137*, 142
Peninsular, 669
Persian, 131–133, *m132*
Persian Gulf, 23, 1079, *i1079*
phalanx in, 131–132, 142
Punic, 158–159, *m159*
Roman civil, 161
of the Roses, 403
Russo-Japanese, 812–813, 868–869
Seven Weeks', 696
Seven Years', 607
Sino-Japanese, 812
Six-Day, 1019
slave trade in, 566
Spanish-American, 818–819, *m819*
of the Spanish Succession, 601
technology of, 63, 402, 542, *i848*, *i954–955*
Thirty Years', 603–604
total, 853, 956
in Vietnam, 978–981, *m979*
war against terrorism
in Afghanistan, *i987*, 1027, 1091
Bush administration and, 1091
in Iraq, 23, *i1070*
warriors, feudal, 364–365, 367, 542
Warsaw Pact, 969, 1082
Waterloo, 671
watermills, 720
water resources
in Industrial Revolution, 720
Watt, James, 721
weapons, 48. *See also* military power; technology.
Assyrian, 95, *i97*
Bronze, 22, 90
caltrops, *i364*
catapult, *i366*
of Cold War, 969–970
of Genghis Khan, 332, *i332*
iron, 55, 63, 94, 217
longbow, 402, *i402*
in mail, 1090–1091
of mass destruction, *i955*, 1083, 1088
Maxim gun, 775, *i954*
Mongol, *i332*
poison gas, *i954*
of samurai, *i342*
siege, *i366*, 366
tank, *i954*
of terrorism, 1087–1088
of totalitarianism, 874
Turkish, *i316*
of World War I, 848, *i848*, *i954*
of World War II, 947, *i955*, 959
Weimar Republic, 905
welfare state, 461, 1039
West Africa. *See also* Africa.
in 2003, *m429*
empires of, 413–417, *m414*
societies in, 418–419
Western civilization, *c180*. *See also* Greece; Roman Empire.
effect of Enlightenment on, 633–634
Greco-Roman influence on, 178–183
Greek influence on, 125, *c150*
influence on global culture, 1095–1096
Roman influence on, 181–183
and Russia, 610–611
values of, 183
Western Europe
A.D. 500, *m351*
in 14th century, *m377*
feudalism in, 360
formation of 800–1500, 379–403
invasions of, 353, 358–359, *m359*
Western Front
in World War I, 846–848
westernization, 610, 775
wheel, 38
wheelbarrow, 204
Whigs, 616
Whitney, Eli, 720
Wilhelm I (kaiser), 695, 697
Wilhelm II (kaiser), 842–843, *i842*
William the Conqueror (English king), 393–394
William of Orange (Dutch ruler), 616–617
Wilson, Woodrow, 852–853, 858–859, *i859*
Winged Victory, *i140*, 149
Wollstonecraft, Mary, 633, *i633*
women, 749. *See also* queens; writers, activists.
in agricultural revolution, 15
of ancient China, 52, 206, 327
in ancient Rome, 164
in ancient Sumer, 32
in Athens, 129, 131
in Buddhist society, 70
of China, 541
in Crimean War, 787
in czarist Russia, 610, 638–639
in Efe society, 409
in Egypt, 40, 89–90, *i90*
and the Enlightenment, 633
equality of, 749, 1084
under feudalism, 363, 368–369
during French Revolution, 655, 656, 660
in Greek drama, 136
in Han Dynasty, 201, 206
in Hebrew society, 80
of India, 194, *i519*
and industrial reform, 739–740
international conferences on status of, 1084
in Iran, 890
Iroquois, 445
of Japan, *i341*, 544
and labor laws, 738–740
in literature, 482
and manorialism, 363
in March Revolution, 869
and medicine, 879
in the Middle Ages, 354–355, 363, 368–369, *i368*
Minoan, 72
modern, 1084
Mongol, *i333*
in Muslim countries, 274
in New Zealand, 753
post-World War I, 900
of the Reformation, 494, 496, 498
religious orders of, 380
Renaissance, 473, *i473*, 477, 482
in science, 765, *i765*
Seneca Falls Convention, 769
slavery of, *i97*, 164
Soviet, 878–879
in Sparta, 131
suffrage of, 749
in Turkey, 890
Victorian, 749
of Vietnam, 346, *i346*
warrior-women, *i342*, *i346*
during World War I, 854, *i854*
during World War II, 943
WSPU (Women's Social and Political Union), 749
Woolley, Leonard, 22
World Bank Group, *c1078*
World Trade Center, 1090, *i1090*. *See also* September 11 terrorist attacks.
WTO (World Trade Organization), 1076, *c1078*
World War I, 841–861, *m860*
1914–1918, *c838–839*
alliances of, 843, 845
armistice, 855
aviation in, *i850*
battlefield deaths, 855–856, *c856*
casualties, *c958*
causes of, 841–844
and China, 851–852, 882
countries at war, 845
Eastern Front, 848–849
effect on Europe, 855–856
effects of, 855–856
in Europe, 845–854
Fourteen Points, 858–859
legacy of, 855–856
maps
in Europe, 1914–1918, *c846*
Europe on the eve of, 1914, *m843*
world at war, 1914–1918, m852
onset of, 845

peace treaties, 854
rationing, 854
and Russian Revolution, 854, 871
submarine warfare, *i848*, 852–853
technological effects of, 853–854
technology of war, 848, *i848*
time line, *c838–839*
Treaty of Versailles, 858–861, *c861*
trench warfare, 847, *i847*, 958
unemployment, 854
views of, 857
war aftermath, 856
Western Front, 846–848
Zimmermann note, 853
World War II, 925–951. *See also* communism; fascism; Hitler, Adolf; Holocaust; Nazism.
aggression, 925–926
alliances of, 925, 926, 928, 930, 935
Allied victory of, 945–947
in Asia and the Pacific, 931–935, *m933*
atomic bomb, *i946*, 947, *i955*, 959
Balkans, 929
Baltic states, 925
battles, 927–928, 934–935, 941
blitzkrieg, 925, *i955*
casualties, *c958*
causes of, 925–926
Churchill,Winston, 927, *i927*, 930, 940–941, *i965*
and Cold War, 965–967
costs of, *c949*, 958
D-Day invasion, 943–944, *m944*
death and labor camps, 938–939, *m953*
Eisenhower, Dwight D., 940, 943, *i944*
German advances, *m926*
Hitler, Adolf, 925–930, 936–938, 941, 944–945
Holocaust, 936–939
invasions, 919, 925, 926, 929–930
Japanese American internment, 943, *i959*
MacArthur, General Douglas, 934–935, *i934*, 945, 947, 950–951, *i951*
Montgomery, General Bernard, 940
Munich Conference, 919
Nazism, 936
nonaggression pact, 925
Nuremberg Trials, 950
Pearl Harbor, Japanese attack on, 931–932, *i932*
Rommel, General Erwin, 928–929, 940
and Soviet Union, 925–926, 929–930, 940–943
surrender, German, 945
surrender, Japanese, 947
technology of war, 928, 934, *i946*, 947, *i955*
time line, *c922–923*
V-E Day (Victory in Europe Day), 945
war aftermath, 948–951
weaponry, 934, *i946*, 947
Yalta Conference, 965–966
writers
Alighieri, Dante, 392
Aquinas, Thomas, 392, *i392*
Bacon, Francis, 626
Balzac, Honoré de, 700
Basho, Matsuo, 544, *i544*
Byron, Lord, 698, *i698*, 699
Cervantes, Miguel de, 591–592
Chaucer, Geoffrey, 375, 392
Colonna, Vittoria, 477
Dickens, Charles, 662, 701, 743
Eliot, T. S., 898
Fitzgerald, F. Scott, 898, *i898*
Gaskell, Elizabeth, 724, *i724*
Goethe, Johan Wolfgang von, 699
Gordimer, Nadine, *i1096*
Homer, 125–126
Hugo, Victor, 699
Joyce, James, 898
Kafka, Franz, 898
"Lost Generation," *i898*
Machiavelli, Niccolò, 476, *i476*, 503, *i583*
Marx, Karl, 736–738, *i736*, 868, *c872*
Nietzsche, Friedrich, 899
of Northern Renaissance, 482
Oe, Kenzaburo, *i1096*
Polo, Marco, 337, *i337*
of Renaissance, 475–477
Richardson, Samuel, 637
Sartre, Jean Paul, 898
Shakespeare, William, 483
Shelley, Mary, 699
Shelley, Percy Bysshe, 699
Shikibu, Lady Murasaki, 342
Solzhenitsyn, Aleksandr, 989
Tocqueville, Alexis de, 671, 735
Virgil, 179
Voltaire, 630, *i630*
Wiesel, Elie, 939
Wollstonecraft, Mary, 633, *i633*
Wordsworth, William, 699
Yeats, William Butler, 898
Zola, Émile, 700, 750
writing. *See also* writers.
in ancient Greece, 125
Chinese, 53
cunieform, 20, *i21*, 32, 40, *i116*
Etruscan influence on Roman, 156
hieroglyphics, 40, *i40*, *i116*
illuminated manuscripts, *i258–259*, *i312*
invention of, 20–21, *i21*
in Japan, 340
libraries, 96
of Alexandria, 147, *i262*
Maya, 448
Minoan, 72
Phoenician, 74, *c74*, *i76*, *i116*
pictographs, *i53*
record keeping, 20, 74, *i116*
in Roman Republic, 156
written records, 52, *i116*
writing systems
cuneiform, 20, *i21*, 32, 40, *i116*
hieroglyphics, 40, *i40*, *i116*
Wudi, 201–202
Wu Zhao (Chinese empress), 323, *i324*
Wycliffe, John, 399

X

Xenophon, 129
Xerxes, 132–133
Xia Dynasty, 51
Xiongxu, 201–202, *m201*

Y

Yahweh, 78–79
Yalta Conference, 965–966
Yamamoto, Admiral Isoruko, 931, 934
Yamato clan (Japanese rulers), 340
Yangtze River, 50
Yaroslav the Wise, 308–309
Yellow River. *See* Huang He river.
Yeltsin, Boris, 1048–1050, *i1048*
"shock therapy," 1050
Yemen, *i425*
yin and yang, 107, *i107*, 109
Yonglo, 536–537
Yoruba, 782, 1041
Ife, 418–419
Oyo, 418
Yu, 51
Yuan Dynasty, 335–338
Yucatan Peninsula, 446, *m447*
Yugoslavia
ethnic groups in former, *c1057*, *m1057*
independent republics of, 1056, 1058
post-World War II, 1056

Z

Zagros Mountains, 16, *m17*
early agriculture in, 16
Zaire, 1015. *See also* Congo, Democratic Republic of.
Zapata, Emiliano, 826–827, *i826*
Zapotec civilization, 242–243
Monte Albán, *c59*, *i59*, *c121*, 242–243, *i242*
Oaxaca, 242
San José Mogote, 242
Zell, Katherina, 498
Zemin, Jiang. *See* Jiang Zemin.
Zen Buddhism, *i547*
Zeno, 148, 179
zero, 195
Zeus, 126, 130
Zheng He, 537
Zhou Dynasty, *c27*, 54–55, 104, *c121*
feudalism in, 54
Zhou Enlai, 975,1060
Zia, Begum Khaleda, 1002
Zia, General, *i1001*, 1002
ziggurat, *i22*, 23, 31
of Babylon, 98
Zimbabwe, Great, 425–427, *i426*
Zimmermann, Arthur, 853
Zimmermann note, 853
Zionism
Herzl, Theodor, 750
in Middle East, 1017
Zola, Émile, 700, 750
Zoroaster, 103
Zoroastrianism
Ahura Mazda, 103
Mithra cult, 103
in Muslim culture, 274
Parsi sect, 103
in Persian culture, 103
Zoskales (Aksumite king), 225

Acknowledgments

Text Acknowledgments

Chapter 4, page 105: Excerpt from *The Analects of Confucius,* translated by Simon Leys. Copyright © 1997 by Pierre Ryckmans. Reprinted by permission of W. W. Norton & Company, Inc.

page 106: Excerpt from *Tao Te Ching: A New English Version with Foreword and Notes* by Stephen Mitchell. Translation copyright © 1988 by Stephen Mitchell. Reprinted by permission of HarperCollins Publishers Inc.

Chapter 5, page 126: Excerpt from the *Iliad* by Homer, translated by Ian Johnson, Malaspina University-College, Nanaimo, British Columbia.

Chapter 7, page 194: Excerpt from a Tamil poem from *The Wonder That Was India,* translated by A. L. Basham. Published by Sidgwick and Jackson. Reprinted by permission of Namita Catherine Basham.

Chapter 10, page 270: Excerpt from *Early Islam* by Desmond Stewart and The Editors of Time-Life Books. Copyright © 1967 by Time Inc. Reprinted by permission of Time Inc.

Chapter 11, page 280: Four lines from "Rumi Quatrain," from *Unseen Rain,* translated by John Moyne and Coleman Barks. Originally published by Threshold Books, 139 Main Street, Brattleboro, VT 05301. By permission of Threshold Books.

Chapter 12, page 290: "Moonlight Night," from *Tu Fu* by William Hung, Cambridge, Mass.: Harvard University Press. Copyright © 1952 by the President and Fellows of Harvard College.

Chapter 13, page 330: Seven lines from page 84 of *The Song of Roland* by Frederick Goldin, translator. Copyright © 1978 by W. W. Norton & Company, Inc. Reprinted by permission of W. W. Norton & Company, Inc.

page 337: Excerpt from "The Prologue," from *The Canterbury Tales* by Geoffrey Chaucer, translated by Nevill Coghill (Penguin Classics 1951) Copyright © 1951 by Nevill Coghill. Reprinted by permission of Penguin Books Ltd.

Chapter 18, page 509: Excerpt from *The Islamic World* by William H. McNeill and M.R. Waldham. Copyright © 1973 by The University of Chicago Press. Reprinted by permission of The University of Chicago Press.

Chapter 19, page 476: Haiku poem, from *Matsuo Basho,* translated by Makoto Veda. By permission of Makoto Veda.

Chapter 20, page 560: Excerpt from "I Won't Be Celebrating Columbus Day," by Suzan Shown Harjo. Copyright © 1991 by Suzan Shown Harjo. Reprinted by permission of Suzan Shown Harjo.

Chapter 29, page 857: Excerpt from *All Quiet on the Western Front* by Erich Maria Remarque. Copyright 1929, 1930 by Little, Brown and Company. Copyright renewed © 1957, 1958 by Erich Maria Remarque. "Im Westen Nichts Neues" by Erich Maria Remarque. Copyright 1928 by Ullstein A. G. Copyright renewed © 1956 by Erich Maria Remarque. All rights reserved. Used by permission of Pryor, Cashman, Sherman & Flynn on behalf of the Estate of Erich Maria Remarque.

Excerpt from "Dulce et Decorum Est," from *The Collected Poems of Wilfred Owen* by Wilfred Owen. Copyright © 1963 by Chatto & Windus, Ltd. Used by permission of New Directions Publishing Corp.

Chapter 30, page 888: Excerpt from *The Origin of Nonviolence* by M. K. Gandhi. Published by Cambridge University Press. Reprinted with the permission of Cambridge University Press.

Chapter 31, page 898: Excerpt from *The Great Gatsby* by F. Scott Fitzgerald. Copyright © 1925 by Charles Scribner's Sons. Copyright renewed 1953 by Frances Scott Fitzgerald Lanahan. Used by permission of Scribner, an imprint of Simon & Schuster Adult Publishing Group.

Chapter 35, page 1061: Excerpt from "Tienanmen Square: A Soldier's Story," by Xiao Ye from *Teenage Soldiers, Adult Wars.* Reprinted by permission of the Rosen Publishing Group.

page 1067: Excerpts from "The Coming of Mao Zedong Chic," from *Newsweek,* May 19, 1997, Newsweek, Inc. All rights reserved. Reprinted by permission.

Chapter 36, page 1081: Excerpt from "The Market is Green," by the Liberty Institute, New Delhi. Copyright © May 1999. Reprinted by permission of the Liberty Institute, New Delhi, India.

Excerpt from "Eco-Economy: Building an Economy for the Earth," by Lester Brown. Speech, Colloquium on Global Partnerships for Sustainable Development: Harnessing Action for the 21st Century; 24 March 2002 <http://www.earth-policy.org/Transcripts/TERI-4-02.htm>. Reprinted by permission of the Earth Policy Institute.

COMPARING & CONTRASTING FEATURES

Unit 1, Page 115: Excerpt from *The Analects of Confucius,* translated and annotated by Arthur Waley. Copyright © 1938 by George Allen & Unwin, copyright renewed 1966. Used with the permission of John Robinson, on behalf of the Arthur Waley Estate.

Unit 3, Page 435: Excerpt from *Ibn Battutta in Black Africa* by Said Hamdun and Noël King. Copyright © 1998 by Marcus Wiener Publishers. Reprinted by permission of Marcus Wiener Publishers.

World Religions, Page 711: Excerpt from *The French Revolution,* edited by Paul H. Beik. Copyright © 1971 by Paul H. Beik. Reprinted by permission of HarperCollins Publishers Inc.

Unit 6, Page 835: Excerpt from *The Birth of the Modern: World Society 1815–1830* by Paul Johnson. Copyright © 1991 by Paul Johnson. Reprinted by permission of HarperCollins Publishers Inc.

Unit 7, Page 957: Excerpt from *If This is a Man (Survival in Auschwitz)* by Primo Levi, translated by Stuart Woolf. Copyright © 1960 by Orion Press, Inc. Copyright © 1958 by Giulio Einaudi editore S.P.A. Reprinted by permission of Penguin Putnam, Inc., a division of Penguin Group (USA) Inc.

PRIMARY SOURCE HANDBOOK

Unit 1, Page R40: "Creation Hymn," from *The Rig Veda,* translated by Wendy Doniger O'Flaherty (Penguin Classics, 1981). Copyright © 1981 by Wendy Doniger O'Flaherty. Reproduced by permission of Penguin Books Ltd.

Page R42: Excerpt from *The Analects of Confucius,* translated by Simon Leys. Copyright © 1997 by Pierre Ryckmans. Reprinted by permission of W. W. Norton & Company, Inc.

Unit 2, Page R43: Excerpt from "Pericles' Funeral Oration," from *History of the Peloponnesian War* by Thucydides, translated by Rex Warner (Penguin Classics, 1954). Copyright © 1954 by Rex Warner. Reproduced by permission of Penguin Books Ltd.

Page R44: Excerpt from the *Apology* by Plato, translated by Hugh Tredennick, from *The Collected Dialogues of Plato,* edited by Edith Hamilton and Huntington Cairns. Copyright © 1961 by Princeton University Press. Reprinted by permission of Princeton University Press.

Page R45: Excerpt from "The Burning of Rome," from *The Annals of Imperial Rome* by Tacitus, translated by Michael Grant (Penguin Classics, 1956; sixth revised edition, 1989). Copyright © 1956, 1959, 1971, 1973, 1975, 1977, 1989, 1996 by Michael Grant Publications. Reprinted by permission of Penguin Books Ltd.

Unit 3, Page R46: Excerpt from *The Koran,* translated by N. J. Dawood (Penguin Classics, 1956; fifth revised edition, 1990). Copyright © 1956, 1959, 1966, 1968, 1974, 1990, 1995 by N. J. Dawood. Reprinted by permission of Penguin Books Ltd.

Page R47: Excerpt from *The Pillow Book of Sei Shōnagon,* translated and edited by Ivan Morris. Copyright © 1967 by Ivan Morris. Reprinted by permission of Columbia University Press.

Page R48: Excerpt from the *Magna Carta* by J. C. Holt. Copyright © 1965 by Cambridge University Press. Reprinted with permission of Cambridge University Press.

Unit 4, Page R49: Excerpt from *Popol Vuh: The Definitive Edition of the Mayan Book of The Dawn of Life and The Glories of Gods and Kings,* translated by Dennis Tedlock. Copyright © 1985 by Dennis Tedlock, 1996 (revised and additional material) by Dennis Tedlock. Reprinted with the permission of Simon & Schuster Adult Publishing Group.

Page R51: Excerpt from *Utopia* by St. Thomas More, edited by Edward Surtz, S.J. Copyright © 1964 by Yale University. Reproduced by permission of Yale University Press.

Unit 7, Page R59: Excerpt from *Night* by Elie Wiesel, translated by Stella Rodway. Copyright © 1960 by MacGibbon & Kee. Copyright renewed 1988 by the Collins Publishing Group. Reprinted by permission of Hill and Wang, a division of Farrar, Straus & Giroux, Inc.

Page R60: Excerpt from *Farewell to Manzanar* by James D. Houston and Jeanne Wakatsuki Houston. Copyright © 1973 by James D. Houston. Reprinted by permission of Houghton Mifflin Company. All rights reserved.

Unit 8, Page R61: Excerpt from "Glory and Hope" by Nelson Mandela, from *Vital Speeches of the Day,* Vol. LX, No. 16 (1 June 1994), page 486. Reprinted by permission of City News Publishing Company, Inc.

Page R62: Excerpt from "I Have A Dream" by Dr. Martin Luther King Jr. Copyright © 1963 by Dr. Martin Luther King Jr., copyright renewed 1991 by Coretta Scott King. Reprinted by arrangement with the Estate of Martin Luther King Jr., c/o Writers House as agent for the proprietor, New York, N.Y.

Page R63: Excerpt from "An Open Letter" by Cesar Chavez. Copyright © Cesar E. Chavez Foundation. Reprinted by permission of the Cesar E. Chavez Foundation.

McDougal Littell Inc. has made every effort to locate the copyright holders for selections used in this book and to make full acknowledgment for their use. Omissions brought to our attention will be corrected in a subsequent edition.

Art and Photography Credits

Maps supplied by Mapping Specialists

COVER

Taj Mahal © Brian A. Vikander/Corbis; *top sky* © Courtney Milne/Masterfile; *inset (left to right)* Queen Nefertiti. Photo by Margarete Buesing/Staatliche Museen zu Berlin/Aegyptisches Museum; Caesar coin © Richard T. Nowitz/Corbis; *Portrait of Queen Elizabeth I* (manner of Nicholas Hilliard). Philip Mould, Historical Portraits Ltd., London. Photo © The Bridgeman Art Library; Mayan sculpture © Craig Duncan/DDB Stock; Nelson Mandela © David Turnley/Corbis.

FRONT MATTER

i–ii Taj Mahal © Brian A. Vikander/Corbis; *top sky* © Courtney Milne/Masterfile; *inset (left to right)* Queen Nefertiti. Photo by Margarete Buesing/Staatliche Museen zu Berlin/Aegyptisches Museum; Caesar coin © Richard T. Nowitz/Corbis; *Portrait of Queen Elizabeth I* (manner of Nicholas Hilliard). Philip Mould, Historical Portraits Ltd., London. Photo © The Bridgeman Art Library; Mayan Sculpture © Craig Duncan/DDB Stock; Nelson Mandela © David Turnley/Corbis; **viii** *left (top to bottom)* Cave painting of Tassili n'Ajjer, (second millennium B.C.). Musée de l'Homme, Paris. Henri Lhote Collection. Photo © Erich Lessing/Art Resource, New York; Canopic sarcophagus containing the organs of Pharaoh Tutankhamen (18th dynasty), Egypt. Photo © Scala/Art Resource, New York; Noah's ark. Illumination from Add. MS 11639, f. 521r. By permission of The British Library; © Joseph McNally/Getty Images; *right* © Galen Rowell/Corbis; **ix** *left (top to bottom)* Asian & Nubian soldiers in the Egyptian army (2nd–1st millennium B.C.). Collection of Norbert Schimmel, New York. Photo © Erich Lessing/Art Resource, New York; © Mimmo Jodice/Corbis; Asoka Lions 3rd century B.C. Photo © Borromeo/Art Resource, New York; Ngady Amwaash, Kuba culture of Central Zaire. National Museum, Ghana. Photo © Werner Forman/Art Resource, New York; *top right* © Michele Burgess/SuperStock, Inc.; **x** *top left* © Stone/Getty Images; *top right* Steve Raymer/National Geographic Image Collection; *top left* © Buddy Mays; *center left* Greek cross (11th century), Byzantine. Photo © Dagli Orti/Museo della Civiltà Romana, Rome/The Art Archive; *bottom* Illustration by Peter Dennis; **xi** *top left* © Stone/Getty Images; *right (top to bottom)* Steve Raymer/National Geographic Image Collection; Golden Bull (about 1390). Illumination on parchment. Bildarchiv der Osterreichische Nationalbibliothek, Vienna, Austria; *Portrait of Charlemagne,* Albrecht Durer. © Germanisches Nationalmuseum, Nuremberg, Germany. Photo © Lauros-Giraudon, Paris/SuperStock Inc.; Benin, cast figure, bronze aquamanile. Photo © The British Museum; **xii** *left (top to bottom)* © Explorer, Paris/SuperStock, Inc.; *Elizabeth I* (1588), George Gower. Courtesy of The National Portrait Gallery, London; Shah Tahmasp I receiving the Moghul emperor Humayun. Period of Abbas II. Photo © Giraudon/Art Resource, New York; Globe by Martin Behaim (about 1492). Bibliothèque Nationale, Paris. Photo © Giraudon/Art Resource, New York; *top right* © Tim Hursley/SuperStock, Inc.; **xiii** *left* Detail of *Marriage of Louis XIV, King of France and Marie Therese of Austria* (17th century), unknown artist. Musée de Tesse, Le Mans. Photo © Dagli Orti/The Art Archive; *right (top to bottom)* © Todd A. Gipstein/Corbis; *Louis XIV, King of France* (1701), Hyacinthe Rigaud. Louvre, Paris. Photo © Erich Lessing/Art Resource, New York; Isaac Newton's reflecting telescope (1672). Photo by Eileen Tweedy/Royal Society/The Art Archive; *Combat Before the Hotel de Ville, July 28th 1830,* Victor Schnetz. Musée du Petit Palais, Paris. Photo by Bulloz © Réunion des Musées Nationaux/Art Resource, New York; **xiv** *left (top to bottom)* Aboriginal bark painting of abstract picture of body, Lipunja. Milingibi, Australia. Photo © Dagli Orti/Musée des Arts Africains et Oceaniens/The Art Archive; © Bettmann/Corbis; The Granger Collection, New York; *top right The Battle of Isandhlwana* (1879), Charles Fripp. National Army Museum, London. Photo © The Art Archive; **xv** *top left* Hulton/Archive/Getty Images; *right (top to bottom)* © KJ Historical/Corbis; Popperfoto; © Bettmann/Corbis; © UPI/Bettmann/Corbis; **xvi** *left (top to bottom)* © Steve Vidler/SuperStock, Inc.; Imperial War Museum, London. Photo © The Art Archive; © David Turnley/Corbis; © Corbis/Sygma; *top right* © SuperStock, Inc.; **xx** © John Heseltine/Corbis; **xxvi** Jeff Stahler/Courtesy *Cincinnati Post;* **xxvii** British Library/The Art Archive; **xxviii** Chateau de Malmaison, Rueil-Malmaison, France. Photo © Giraudon/Art Resource,

Art and Photography Credits (Cont.)

New York; **xxix** The Granger Collection, New York; **xxx** *top left Alexander the Great,* relief by Landolin Ohnmacht. Photo by AKG London; *bottom right Combat Before the Hotel de Ville, July 28th 1830,* Victor Schnetz. Musée du Petit Palais, Paris. Photo by Bulloz © Réunion des Musées Nationaux/Art Resource, New York; **xxxi** *top* © Chad Ehlers/Getty Images; *bottom* © Bettmann/Corbis; **xxxii–xxxiii** © Pacific Stock/Orion Press; **xxxiii** Travel Pix; **xxxvi** Stephen Alvarez/National Geographic Image Collection; **xxxvii** *top* © Kenneth Garrett; *center* Flying man, Leonardo da Vinci. Sketch from Codex Atlanticus. Biblioteca Ambrosiana, Milan, Italy/Art Resource, New York; *bottom* © Warren Morgan/Corbis.

UNIT ONE

0–1 spread © David Sutherland/Stone/Getty Images.

Chapter 1

2 *left* © John Reader/SPL/Photo Researchers; *right* Paleolithic engraving of a lunar calendar on a reindeer antler (38,000 B.C.), Dordogne, France. Photo © Réunion des Musées Nationaux/Art Resource, New York; **3** *left* © John Reader/SPL/Photo Researchers; *center* Knife, Bronze age. National Museum of Iran, Tehran, Iran. Photo © The Bridgeman Art Library; *right* Head of a bull. Musical instrument from Ur, Early dynastic (2450 B.C.) Photo © Scala/Art Resource, New York; **4** *top right, top left, center right* Photo Archives, South Tyrol Museum of Archaeology; *center left* Photo by Marco Sasadelli, South Tyrol Department of Archaeological Monuments; **5** *top left* Cave painting of Tassili n'Ajjer, (second millennium B.C.). Musée de l'Homme, Paris. Henri Lhote Collection. Photo © Erich Lessing/Art Resource, New York; *top right* © Galen Rowell/Corbis; **7** © Des Bartlett/Photo Researchers; **11** © AFP/Corbis; **12** *right* Cave painting of Tassili n'Ajjer, (second millennium B.C.). Musée de l'Homme, Paris. Henri Lhote Collection. Photo © Erich Lessing/Art Resource, New York; *bottom* Photograph by Alberto Gandsas. www.Agora-Gallery.com; **13** *top* © Sissie Brimberg/National Geographic Image Collection/Getty Images; *bottom* © Pam Gardner, Frank Lane Picture Agency/Corbis; **14** *top left* Cave painting of Tassili n'Ajjer, (second millennium B.C.). Musée de l'Homme, Paris. Henri Lhote Collection. Photo © Erich Lessing/Art Resource, New York; *top right* © Galen Rowell/Corbis; **15** *top* © Hanny Paul/Gamma-Liaison/Getty Images; *bottom* W. Neeb/Innsbruck University, Innsbruck, Austria; **16** University of Chicago News Office; **18** © Sonia Halliday Photographs; **20** © Werner Forman/Corbis; **21** Cuneiform. The British Museum, London. Photo © The Bridgeman Art Library; **22** *left* Courtesy of University of Pennsylvania Museum, Philadelphia (Neg.# S4-139540); *right* Ziggurat of Ur-Namu. Photo © The British Museum, London. **25** Bruce Coleman, Inc.

Chapter 2

26 *left* Bronze head of Akkadian ruler, from Nineveh (2350 B.C.). Iraq Museum, Baghdad, Iraq/Scala/Art Resource, New York; *right* Seated scribe, from Saqqara, Egypt (fifth dynasty). Painted limestone. Louvre, Paris. Photo © Giraudon/Art Resource, New York; **27** *left* Fragment of a vase depicting ibex, from Onengo-Daro. Indus Valley, Pakistan. National Museum of Karachi, Karachi, Pakistan. Photo © The Bridgeman Art Library; *right* Fandang (rectangular cooking vessel), Shang dynasty (1600–1100 B.C.). Bronze. From Ningxian, China. Photo © Giraudon/Art Resource, New York; **28** Illustration by Bill Cigliano; **29** *top left* © Jose Fuste Raga/Corbis; *top right* © Burstein Collection/Corbis; **31** Itur-Shamagen, king of Mari, in prayer. Early dynastic (Sumerian). National Museum, Damascus, Syria. Photo © Giraudon/Art Resource, New York; **32** © The British Museum; **33** © Gianni Dagli Orti/Corbis; **34** Hirmer Verlag GmbH, Munich, Germany; **35** *top left* © Jose Fuste Raga/Corbis; *top right* © Burstein Collection/Corbis; **36** Jacques Descloitres, MODIS Land Science Team/NASA; **38** Portrait bust of Herodotus, copy of Greek original (fourth century B.C.). Museo Archeologico Nazionale, Naples, Italy. Photo © The Bridgeman Art Library; **39** *top* © Bettmann/Corbis; *center left* © The British Museum; *center right* Canopic sarcophagus containing the organs of Pharoah Tutankhamen (18th dynasty). Egyptian Museum, Cairo, Egypt. Photo © Scala/Art Resource, New York; *bottom* © David Sutherland/Getty Images; **40** The Granger Collection, New York; **42–43** © Corbis; **42** *top center* Egyptian Museum, Cairo, Egypt/Scala/Art Resource, New York; *top right* © The British Museum; *left* Victor R. Boswell, Jr./National Geographic Image Collection; *bottom* © Archivo Iconografico, S.A./Corbis; **43** © The Image Works/Topham Picturepoint; **44** *top left* © Jose Fuste Raga/Corbis; *top right* © Burstein Collection/Corbis; **46** © 1994 West Publishing Company; **47** Illustration by Tom Jester; **48** *top* Seal depicting elephant and monograms, steatite, Indus civilization (2500–200 B.C.), from Mohenjo-Daro. National Museum, Karachi, Pakistan. Photo © Dagli Orti/The Art Archive; *center* Seal depicting armor-plated rhinoceros and monograms, steatite, Indus civilization (2500–200 B.C.), from Mohenjo-Daro. National Museum, Karachi, Pakistan. Photo © Dagli Orti/The Art Archive; *bottom* Seal depicting zebu and monograms, steatite, Indus Civilization (2500–200 B.C.), from Mohenjo-Daro. National Museum Karachi, Pakistan. Photo © Dagli Orti/The Art Archive; **49** © Archivo Iconografico, S.A./Corbis; **50** *top left* © Jose Fuste Raga/Corbis; *top right* © Burstein Collection/Corbis; **51** © Julia Waterlow/Eye Ubiquitous/Corbis; **53** © Royal Ontario Museum/Corbis; **55** © Lowell Georgia/Corbis.

Chapter 3

58 *top* Funerary stele of merchant holding weighing scales (eighth century B.C.), Hittite culture. Musée du Louvre, Paris. Photo © Dagli Orti/The Art Archive; *bottom* Colossal head no. 1, Olmec culture. Archaeological garden of La Venta in Villahermosa, Mexico. Photo © Dagli Orti/The Art Archive; **59** *left* Bearded head pendant (third century B.C.), Phoenician. National Museum of Carthage, Carthage, Tunisia. Photo © Erich Lessing/Art Resource, New York; *right* Jade mask of bat god (about 500 B.C.–A.D. 800), Zapotec culture. Museo Nacional de Antropologica, Mexico City. Photo © Michel Zabe/Art Resource, New York; **60** Illustration by Terence J. Gabbey; **61** *top left* Detail of Hindu god Krishna surrounded by his milk carriers, Rajasthan, India. Private collection, Paris. Photo © Dagli Orti/The Art Archive; *top right* Detail of zodiac mosaic (fourth century). Synagogue, Tiberias, Israel. Photo © Garo Nalbandian/Israelimages.com; **63** Archer on a chariot (ninth century B.C.), late Hittite. Museum of Oriental Antiquities, Istanbul, Turkey. Photo © Erich Lessing/Art Resource, New York; **64** Five-headed Brahma on his Vahana, the Cosmic Goose (19th century), Southern India. Photo © Victoria and Albert Museum, London/Art Resource, New York; **66** *top left* Detail of Hindu god Krishna surrounded by his milk carriers, Indian. Private collection, Paris. Photo © Dagli Orti/The Art Archive; *top right* Detail of mosaic (fourth century). Synagogue, Tiberias, Israel. Photo © Garo Nalbandian/Israelimages.com; **67** Vishnu Visvarrupa, preserver of the universe, represented as the whole world (early 19th century), Jaipur, India. Victoria and Albert Museum, London. Photo © Sally Chappell/The Art Archive; **68** © Ric Ergenbright/Corbis; **69** Reclining Buddha (14th–18th century A.D.), Ayuthaya school. National Museum, Bangkok, Thailand. Photo © Scala/Art Resource, New York; **70** © Glen Allison/Stone/Getty Images; **72** *left* Detail of Hindu god Krishna surrounded by his milk carriers, Rajasthan, India. Private collection, Paris. Photo © Dagli Orti/The Art Archive; *right* Detail of mosaic (fourth century). Synagogue, Tiberias, Israel. Photo © Garo Nalbandian/Israelimages.com; **73** Bull dancing (1700–1400 B.C.), Minoan fresco from Knossos, Crete. Heraklion (Crete) Museum. Photo © Dagli Orti/The Art Archive; **75** Illustration by Peter Dennis; **76** Detail of the inscription from the sarcophagus of Eshmunazar recounting how he and his mother Amashtarte, built temples to the gods of Sidon (3000–1200 B.C.), Phoenician. Louvre, Paris. Photo © Lauros-Giraudon/The Bridgeman Art Library; **77** *top left* Detail of Hindu god Krishna surrounded by his milk carriers, Rajasthan, India. Private collection, Paris. Photo © Dagli Orti/The Art Archive; *top right* Detail of Hindu god Krishna surrounded by his milk carriers, Rajasthan, India. Private collection, Paris. Photo © Dagli Orti/The Art Archive; **78** *Moses* (about 1520), Michaelangelo Buonarroti. Photo © Dagli Orti/The Art Archive; **79** © Zev Radovan, Jerusalem, Israel; **80** Mezuzah (mid–late 20th century), Bezalel school. The Jewish Museum, New York, gift of Mrs. William Minder. Photo by John Parnell/© The Jewish Museum of New York/Art Resource, New York; **81** King Solomon (15th century B.C.), Joos van Ghent. Galleria Nazionale delle Marche, Urbino, Italy. Photo © Alinari/Art Resource, New York; **83** Noah's ark. Illumination from Add. MS 11639, f. 521r. By permission of the British Library; **85** Gold pendant (17th century B.C.), Hittite, from Yozgat, near Bogzkoy, Turkey. Musée Louvre, Paris. Photo © Erich Lessing/Art Resource, New York.

Chapter 4

86 *left* Mask of Agamemnon, (16th century B.C.), Mycenaean. National Archaeological Museum, Athens, Greece. Photo © Dagli Orti/The Art Archive; *right* © Andrea Jemolo/Corbis; **87** *left* Ceramic jar from Grave 566, Meroitic period, Karanog, Nubia. Courtesy of University of Pennsylvania Museum, Philadelphia (Neg. #T4–55OC.2); *right* Alexander III, king of Macedonia (338 B.C.), Roman, copied from Greek statue by Eufranor. Staatliche Glypothek, Munich, Germany. Photo © Dagli Orti/The Art Archive; **88** Illustration by Peter Dennis; **89** *top left* Detail of procession road to the Ishtar gate (seventh century B.C.), Neo-Babylonian. Musée Louvre, Paris. Photo © Erich Lessing/Art Resource, New York; *top right* © Corbis; **90** Hatsheput enthroned, Egyptian. The Metropolitan Museum of Art, Rogers Fund and Contribution from Edward S. Harkness, 1929 (29.3.2). Photo © 1997 The Metropolitan Museum of Art; **91** Temple of Pharaoh Ramses II at Abu Simbel (1279–1213 B.C.). Photo © Dagli Orti /The Art Archive; **92–93** © Hugh Sitton/ImageState/PictureQuest; **92** *left* © Paul Almasy/Corbis; *right* Derek A. Welsby; **93** Shawabits of King Taharka (690–664 B.C.), Nubian, Napatan period. Museum of Fine Arts, Boston. Harvard University Museum-Museum of Fine Arts Expedition. Photo © 2003 Museum of Fine Arts, Boston; **94** Gold ring shield from Queen Amanishakheto's pyramid. Staatliche Museen zu Berlin, Preussischer Kulturbesitz, Aegyptisches Museum, Berlin. Photo by Margarete Busing; **95** *top left* Detail of procession road to the Ishtar Gate (seventh century B.C.), Neo-Babylonian. Musée Louvre, Paris. Photo © Erich Lessing/Art Resource, New York; *top right* © Corbis; **97** Warriors scaling walls with ladders fighting hand-to-hand, Ashurnazirpal's assault on a city, stone bas-relief from the palace of Ashurnazirpal II in Nimrud. The British Museum, London. Photo © Erich Lessing/Art Resource, New York; **98** © Bettmann/Corbis; **99** *top left* Detail of procession road to the Ishtar gate (seventh century B.C.), Neo-Babylonian. Musée Louvre, Paris. Photo © Erich Lessing/Art Resource, New York; *top right* © Corbis; **100** © Corbis; **102** © The British Museum; **104** *top left* Detail of procession road to the Ishtar Gate (seventh century B.C.), Neo-Babylonian. Musée Louvre, Paris. Photo © Erich Lessing/Art Resource, New York; *top right* © Corbis; **105** *top* China Pictorial News Service; *bottom* The Granger Collection, New York; **107** *top* © Photodisc/Getty Images; *bottom* By permission of the British Library; **108** *background* Illustration by Patrick Whelan; *inset* © Joseph McNally/Getty Images; **111** Ashurbanipal feasting, Assyrian relief. Photo © Michael Holford. **112** *top left* © The Boltin Picture Library; *top center* © The British Museum; *top right* Model of a cart pulled by two oxen, Harappan, Mohenjo-Daro, Indus Valley, Pakistan. National Museum of Karachi, Karachi, Pakistan. Photo © The Bridgeman Art Library; *bottom* © The British Museum; **113** © John Slater/Corbis; **115** Miniature Torah scroll, probably English (1765). Jewish Museum, London. Photo © The Bridgeman Art Library; **116** *top left* Man between tigers. Seal from Mohenjo-Daro. National Museum, New Delhi, India. Photo © Nimatallah/Art Resource, New York; *center right* © Diego Lezama Orezzoli/Corbis; *bottom left* Hieroglyphs (Middle Kingdom). Thebes. Photo © Erich Lessing/Art Resource, New York; *bottom right* Detail of the inscription from the sarcophagus of Eshmunazar recounting how he and his mother, Amashtarte, built temples to the gods of Sidon (3000–1200 B.C.), Phoenician. Louvre, Paris. Photo © Lauros-Giraudon/The Bridgeman Art Library; **117** *center right* Model of a Phoenician ship of 900 B.C. Museo della Scienza e della Tecnica, Milan, Italy. Photo © Scala/Art Resource, New York; *bottom* © Asian Art & Archaeology, Inc./Corbis.

UNIT TWO

118–119 The Athenian Acropolis (1846), Leo von Klenze. Neue Pinakothek, Munich. Photo © Joachim Blauel/Artothek.

Chapter 5

120 *left* Vase from Palaikastro, Minoan. Archaeological Museum, Heraklion, Crete. Photo © Nimatallah/Art Resource, New York; *right* Hatshepsut (18th dynasty), from the temple of Hatshepsut, Deir el Bahari, West Thebes. Egyptian Museum, Cairo, Egypt. Photo © Scala/Art Resource, New York; **121** *left* Animal mask (about 1100–771 B.C.), Chinese, Western Zhou dynasty. Musée des Arts Asiatiques-Guimet, Paris. Photo by Richard Lambert © Werner Forman/Art Resource, New York; *right* Breastplate, Mixtec, Postclassic Monte Alban V, Yanhuitlan, Oaxaca. Museo Nacional de Antropologia, Mexico City. Photo © Réunion des Musées Nationaux/Art Resource, New York; **122** *left* American School of Classical Studies at Athens, Greece, Angora excavations; *center* Red-figure dish depicting Theseus slaying the Minotaur (fifth century B.C.). The British Museum, London. Photo © The Bridgeman Art Library; *right Minerva with the Pectoral,* Pheidias. Musée Louvre, Paris. Photo by Herve Lewandowski © Réunion des Musées Nationaux/Art Resource, New York; **123** *top left* Young girl winning chariot race, Greek engraving from red-figure vase. Bibliothèque des Arts Décoratifs, Paris. Photo © Dagli Orti/The Art Archive; *top right* © Corbis; **125** © Bettmann/Corbis; **126** Head of Polyphemos (about 150 B.C. or later), Hellenistic or Roman period, Greece. Marble from Thasos, 15 1/8" (38.3 cm). Gift in Honor of Edward W. Forbes from his friends. Courtesy Museum of Fine Arts, Boston; **127** *top left* Young girl winning chariot race, Greek engraving from red-figure vase. Bibliothèque des Arts Décoratifs, Paris. Photo © Dagli Orti/The Art Archive; *top right* © Corbis; **129** Rijksmuseum van Oudheden, Leiden, The Netherlands; **130** *left Discobolos* [Discus thrower], Roman copy after Greek original by Myron of Athens (fifth century B.C.). Museo Nazionale Romano delle Terme, Rome. Photo © Scala/Art Resource, New York; *right* Black-figured hydria (sixth century), Painter of Micali. Museo Gregoriano Etrusco, Vatican Museums, Rome. Photo © Scala/Art Resource, New York; *background* © Vanni Archive/Corbis; **133** © AFP/Corbis; **134** *top left* Young girl winning chariot race, Greek engraving from red-figure vase. Bibliothèque des Arts Décoratifs, Paris. Photo © Dagli Orti/The Art Archive; *top right* © Corbis; **135** © Bettmann/Corbis; **136** © Christie's Images/Corbis; **138** *The Death of Socrates* (1780), Francois-Louis Joseph Watteau. Musée des Beaux-Arts, Lille, France. Photo by P. Bernard © Réunion des Musée Nationaux/Art Resource, New York; **139** *left* © Museo Capitolino, Rome/SuperStock, Inc.; *center* © Museo Capitolino, Rome/SuperStock, Inc.; *right* © SuperStock, Inc.; **140** *top right The Nike of Samothrace, goddess of Victory.* Louvre, Paris. Photo © Erich Lessing/Art Resource, New York; *bottom left Hydra with the Rape of Europa.* Muesu Nazionale di Villa Giulia/Photo © Scala/Art Resource, New York; *bottom right* Fish plate. Red figure vase painting (fourth century B.C.). Louvre, Paris/Photo © Réunion des Musées Nationaux/Art Resource, New York; **141** *top* Parthenon © Werner Forman/Art Resource, New York; *center left* © R. Sheridan/Ancient Art and Architecture; *center right* © The Lowe Art Museum, The University of Miami/Superstock; *bottom left* © Steve Vidler/Superstock; **142** *top left* Young girl winning chariot race, Greek engraving from red-figure vase. Bibliothèque des Arts Décoratifs, Paris. Photo © Dagli Orti/The Art Archive; *top right* © Corbis; **143** Detail of Alexander, from the Battle of Issus mosaic, House of the Faun, Pompei (about 80 B.C.). Museo Archeologico Nazionale, Naples, Italy. Photo © Scala/Art Resource, New York;**146** *top left* Young girl winning chariot race, Greek engraving from red-figure vase. Bibliothèque des Arts Décoratifs, Paris. Photo © Dagli Orti/The Art Archive; *top right* © Corbis; **147** The Granger Collection, New York; **148** *top* MS D'Orville 301 f. 31v. Photo © Bodleian Library, Oxford, United Kingdom.; *bottom left* The Granger Collection, New York; *bottom right* Smith Collection, Rare Book and Manuscript Library, Columbia University, New York; **150** © SuperStock, Inc.; **151** Detail of warriors on Chigi vase, Greek. Museo Nazionale di Villa Giulia, Rome, Italy. Photo © Scala/Art Resource, New York.

Art and Photography Credits (Cont.)

Chapter 6

152 Funerary figure (Han dynasty, 206 B.C.–A.D. 220). Private collection. Photo © Werner Forman/Art Resource, New York; **153** *left* © Ancient Art & Architecture Collection Ltd.; *center* Small gold figure studded with turquoises in the form of a toucan (about A.D. 1400–1534), Mochican. Private collection. Photo © Victoria and Albert Museum, London/Art Resource, New York; *right* Roman horseman (soldier). Musée des Antiquités Nationales, Saint Germain-en-Laye, France. Photo © Erich Lessing/Art Resource, New York; **154** *Cicero denouncing Catilina* (19th century), Cesare Maccari. Palazzo Madama, Rome, Italy. Photo © Scala/Art Resource, New York; **155** *top left* © Vanni Archive/Corbis; *top right* © Archivo Iconografico, S.A./Corbis; **156** Caesar's Forum and Temple of Venus Genetrix, Rome, Italy. Photo © Dagli Orti/The Art Archive; **158** *Hannibal* (about 1508–1513), Jacopo Ripanda. Museo Capitolino, Rome. Photo © Dagli Orti/The Art Archive; **160** *top left* © Vanni Archive/Corbis; *top right* © Archivo Iconografico, S.A./Corbis; **161** *The Death of Julius Caesar* (1793), Vincenzo Camuccini. Galleria d'Arte Moderna, Rome. Photo © Dagli Orti/The Art Archive; **162** Roman emperor Augustus with laurel wreath (about 1000), German, cameo from Lothair cross. Cathedral Treasury, Aachen, Germany, Photo © Dagli Orti/The Art Archive; **164** *left* © Charles & Josette Lenars/Corbis; *right* The Granger Collection, New York; **165** Gladiators fighting wild beasts (fourth century), Roman mosaic from Terranova, Italy. Galleria Borghese, Rome. Photo © Dagli Orti/The Art Archive; **166–167** Illustration by John James/Temple Rogers; **167** *top* © Mimmo Jodice/Corbis; *center* © Dorling Kindersley; *bottom* © Dorling Kindersley; **168** *top left* © Vanni Archive/Corbis; *top right* © Archivo Iconografico, S.A./Corbis; **169** *Christ's Charge to Saint Peter,* Raphael. Victoria and Albert Museum, London. Photo © Victoria and Albert Museum/Art Resource, New York; **172** *Saint Augustine of Hippo, Bishop and Doctor of the Church* (15th century), Swiss. Musée des Beaux Arts, Dijon, France. Photo © Dagli Orti/The Art Archive; **173** *top left* © Vanni Archive/Corbis; *top right* © Archivo Iconografico, S.A./Corbis; **176** © Stiftung Schleswig-Holsteinische Landesmuseen, Archaologisches Landesmuseum, Schloss Gottorf, Schleswing, Germany; **177** © Charles & Josette Lenars/Corbis; **178** *top left* © Vanni Archive/Corbis; *top right* © Archivo Iconografico, S.A./Corbis; **179** *Lord of the Rings,* 2001 poster. Photofest; *top right* El Cid in single combat with Martym Gomez at Callaforra (1344), from manuscript Chronicle of Spain. Science Academy, Lisbon, Portugal. Photo © Dagli Orti/The Art Archive; *bottom right* Illustration of the Mahabharata (19th century), Indian, Paithan school. Musée des Arts Asiatiques-Guimet, Paris. Photo by Richard Lambert © Réunion des Musées Nationaux/Art Resource, New York; **181** © Dennis Degnan/Corbis; **182** *top* © John Heseltine/Corbis; *bottom* Illustration by Phil Colprit/Wood Ronsaville Harlin, Inc.; **185** © Vittoriano Rastelli/Corbis.

Chapter 7

186 *Bronze Galloping Horse with One Hoof Resting on a Swallow* (second century, late Han dynasty), from the tomb at Wuwei, Chinese School. Photo © Giraudon/The Bridgeman Art Library; **187** *left* Buff sandstone head of the Buddha (fifth century), Samath. National Museum of India, New Delhi, India. Photo © The Bridgeman Art Library; *right* The Nelson-Atkins Museum of Art, Kansas City, Missouri (Purchase: Nelson Trust); *bottom* © Marc & Evelyn Bernheim/Woodfin Camp and Associates, Inc.; **188** Illustration by Shannon Stirnweis; **189** *top left* Brahma, stone relief from Aihole (sixth–seventh century A.D.) Gupta period. Prince of Wales Museum, Bombay, Maharashtra, India. Photo © Art Resource, New York; *top right* © The Image Bank/Getty Images; **190** *top* Column of Asoka (third century B.C.). Photo © Borromeo/Art Resource, New York; *bottom* Asoka Lions (3rd centtury B.C.) Photo © Borromeo/Art Resource, New York; **192** Terra cotta tile with a musician (fifth century A.D.), Gupta period, central India. Photo © The British Museum; **193** *top left* Brahma, stone relief from Aihole (sixth–seventh century A.D.), Gupta period. Prince of Wales Museum, Bombay, Maharashtra, India. Photo © Art Resource, New York; *top right* © The Image Bank/Getty Images; **194** National Museum, New Delhi, India/Scala/Art Resource, New York; **195** *Monsoon Wedding* movie still. Mirabai Films/Delhi Dot Com/The Kobal Collection; **198** *top* Buddha (sixth century), Gupta period, bronze. National Museum of India, New Delhi, India. Photo © The Bridgeman Art Library; *bottom* Stupa no. 3, Early Andhra dynasty, Sandhi, India. Photo © Scala/Art Resource, New York; **199** *top* © David Cumming/Eye Ubiquitous/Corbis; *center left* Ganesa (fifth century A.D.), Gupta dynasty, from Itar. Museum and Picture Library. Photo © Borromeo/Art Resource, New York; *center right* © Arvind Garg/Corbis; **200** *top left* Brahma, stone relief from Aihole (sixth–seventh century A.D.), Gupta period. Prince of Wales Museum, Bombay, Maharashtra, India. Photo © Art Resource, New York; *top right* The Image Bank/Getty Images; *bottom* British Library; **203** © Bettmann/Corbis; **204–205** *right inset* The Granger Collection, New York; **206** *left Striding Infantryman* (221–206 B.C.), Qin dynasty. Courtesy of the Cultural Relics Bureau, Beijing and The Metropolitan Museum of Art, New York; *bottom right* Bronze figurine of Roman legionnaire. Photo © The British Museum; **207** Robert Harding Picture Library; **209** Horse carriage with driver and attendant (second century A.D.), Eastern Han dynasty. National Museum, Beijing, China. Photo © Erich Lessing/Art Resource, New York.

Chapter 8

210 *left* Massive stone head, Olmec, Basalt. Anthropology Museum, Veracruz, Jalapa, Mexico. Photo © Werner Forman/Art Resource, New York; *right* Bust of Pericles (fifth century B.C.), Greek school. Vatican Museums and Galleries, Vatican City, Italy. Photo © Alinari/The Bridgeman Art Library; **211** *top left* Head (900 B.C.–A.D. 200), Nok. Nigeria. Entwistle Gallery, London. Photo © Werner Forman/Art Resource, New York; *bottom left* Bronze figurine of Roman legionnaire. Photo © The British Museum; *right* © Jane Taylor/Sonia Halliday Photographs; **212** *top* © David Turnley/Corbis; *center* © Paul Almasy/Corbis; **213** *top left* Asian and Nubian soldiers in the Egyptian army (second to first millennium B.C.). Collection of Norbert Schimmel, New York. Photo © Erich Lessing/Art Resource, New York; *top right* © Michele Burgess/SuperStock, Inc.; **214** © Martin Dohrn/Photo Researchers; *top right* © Photowood Inc./Corbis; *bottom left* © Michael Fogden/Bruce Coleman, Inc./PictureQuest; *bottom right inset* © Mary Ann McDonald/Corbis; **215** © Liba Taylor/Corbis; **216** Cave painting of Tassili n'Ajjer (second millennium B.C.). Musée de l'Homme, Paris. Henri Lhote Collection. Photo © Erich Lessing/Art Resource, New York; **217** Nok figure. Private collection. Photo by Joshua Nefsky, New York. Courtesy Entwistle, London; **218** Illustration by Terry Gabbey; **219** Charles Santore/National Geographic Image Collection; **220** Mask, Kuba culture, Zaire. Private collection. Photo © Aldo Tutino/Art Resource, New York; **223** *top left* © Joe McDonald/Corbis; *top right inset* © Photographers Library LTD/eStock Photography/PictureQuest; *bottom* © Staffan Widstrand/Corbis; **224** Ngady Amwaash Kuba Culture of Central Zaire. National Museum, Ghana. Photo © Werner Forman/Art Resource, New York; **225** *top left* Asian and Nubian soldiers in the Egyptian army (second–first millennium B.C.). Collection of Norbert Schimmel, New York. Photo © Erich Lessing/Art Resource, New York; *top right* © Michele Burgess/SuperStock, Inc.; **227** George Gerster/Rapho; **228** The tallest of the still erect stelas at Axum. Axum, Ethiopia. Photo © Werner Forman/Art Resource, New York; **230** *top* Charles Santore/National Geographic Image Collection; *center* © Photographers Library, Ltd./eStockPhotography/PictureQuest; *bottom* George Gerster/Rapho.

Chapter 9

232 *left* The Giza Sphinx with the pyramid of Chephren (Old Kingdom, Fourth dynasty). Pyramid of Chefren, Giza, Egypt. Photo © Werner Forman/Art Resource, New York; *right* © National Museum of Anthropology, Mexico/Explorer,

Paris/SuperStock, Inc.; **233** *top* Gold monkey-head bead (A.D. 100–600), Mochia, La Mina, Jequetepeque Valley, north coast of Peru. David Bernstein Fine Art. Photo © Werner Forman/Art Resource, New York; *bottom* Bust of emporer Hadrian (second century A.D.), Roman. Galleria degli Uffizi, Florence, Italy. Photo © Alinari/The Bridgeman Art Library; **234** © Chase Studio/Photo Researchers; **235** *top left* © Philip Beaurline/SuperStock, Inc.; *top right* © Mark Newman/SuperStock, Inc.; **236** Steve McCurry/Magnum Photos; **237** *top right* Kenneth Garrett/National Geographic Image Collection; *center left* © Warren Morgan/Corbis; *center right* J. M. Adovasio, Mercyhurst Archaeological Institute; *bottom* Kenneth Garrett/National Geographic Image Collection; **238** *top* Courtesy of Dale Walde/University of Calgary; *center* Courtesy of Dale Walde/University of Calgary; *bottom* Courtesy of Dale Walde/University of Calgary; **240** *top left* © Philip Beaurline/SuperStock, Inc.; *top right* © Mark Newman/SuperStock, Inc.; **242** © Robert Frerck/Odyssey/Chicago; **244** *top* Monolithic Olmec head found near La Venta, Mesoamerica, pre-Columbian. La Venta, Mexico. Photo © SEF/Art Resource, New York; *center* Colossal head, Olmec culture, Mesoamerica, pre-Columbian. La Venta, Mexico. Photo © Scala/Art Resource, New York; *bottom* Dumbarton Oaks, pre-Columbian Collection, Washington, D.C.; **245** *top* Altar no. 4 with Olmec lord in niche beneath jaguar pelt. Archaeological garden of La Venta in Villahermosa, Mexico. Photo © Dagli Orti/The Art Archive; *bottom* Standing figure holding a masked "baby" (800–500 B.C.), Olmec, Mexico. Jade, 8 5/8" x 3 3/16" x 1 5/8". On loan to the Brooklyn Museum of Art from the collection of Mr. Robin B. Martin; **246** *top left* © Philip Beaurline/SuperStock, Inc.; *top right* © Mark Newman/SuperStock, Inc.; **247** *top* © Julio Donoso/Corbis Sygma; *center* © Jonathan Blair/Corbis; *bottom* © SuperStock, Inc.; **248** *top* William Allard/National Geographic Image Collection; *center* © Philip Baird/ www.anthroarcheart.org; *bottom* © Yann Arthus-Bertrand/Corbis; **252** *top* Bust of Pericles (about 430 B.C.), Roman, copy of a Greek original. The British Museum, London. Photo © The Bridgeman Art Library; *bottom left* Seated ruler in ritual pose (about 900–500 B.C.), Highland Olmec culture, Mexico. Dallas Museum of Art, gift of Ms. Eugene McDermott, The Roberta Coke Camp Fund, and The Art Museum League Fund; *bottom right* Emperor Liu Ban (18th century), China. British Library. Photo © The Art Archive; **253** *top* Augustus, Roman emperor, marble bust. Musei Capitolini, Rome, Italy. Photo © SEF/Art Resource, New York; *bottom* Courtesy Stephen Album Rare Coins, Santa Rosa, California; **254** *top left* Pugilist resting (sixth–first century B.C.), Apollonios, or a Roman copy. Museo Nazionale Romano delle Terme, Rome, Italy. Photo © Erich Lessing/Art Resource, New York; *top center* © Archivo Iconografico, S.A./Corbis; *top right* Bronze figure of the seated Buddha (fifth century A.D.), Gupta period, from Danesar Khera, Central India. © The British Museum, London; *bottom left center* © John Heseltine/Corbis; *bottom right* Vishnu temple (fifth century A.D.), Gupta period. Photo © Borromeo/Art Resource, New York; **255** *top left* Flying horse, Eastern Han dynasty, China. National Museum, Beijing, China. Photo © Erich Lessing/Art Resource, New York; *top right* Jade ceremonial ax in form of feline monster, Olmec culture, Veracruz, Mexico. Museum of Mankind, London. Photo by Eileen Tweedy/The Art Archive; *bottom left* Green-glazed model of a tower in three detachable sections, Han dynasty. Private collection. Photo © The Bridgeman Art Library; *bottom right* © Bob Krist/Corbis; **256** *top left* © Paul Almasy/Corbis; *top right* © Lindsay Hebberd/Corbis; *bottom left* © Reuters NewMedia Inc./Corbis; *bottom right* © Vittoriano Rastelli/Corbis.

UNIT THREE

258–259 *Marco Polo Leaving Venice,* MS Bodl. 264, fol. 218r. Bodleian Library, University of Oxford.

Chapter 10

260 *top* © Bettman/Corbis; *bottom* Detail of scepter of King Charles V of France, surmounted by a statue of Charlemagne. Musée Louvre, Paris. Photo © Erich Lessing/Art Resource, New York; **261** *left* © A. Duncan/Middle East Archive/Peter Sanders; *right* © Stapleton Collection/Corbis; **262** Illustration by Yuan Lee; **263** *top left* © Stone/Getty Images; *top right* Steve Raymer/National Geographic Image Collection; **265** Abraham's elephants charging under the Ka'Bah (1368). From the Apostles Biography. Illuminated manuscript. Topkapi Museum, Istanbul, Turkey. Photo by Eileen Tweedy/The Art Archive; **266** *background* © Buddy Mays; *left inset* © Marvin Newman/Woodfin Camp; *right inset* Tower of David. Museum of History of Jerusalem; **267** Qu'ran Ju/XXVII, Mamluk (14th century), Arabic school. Private collection. Photo © Bonhams, London/The Bridgeman Art Library; **268** © Murat Ayranci/SuperStock, Inc.; **269** *top left* © Stone/Getty Images; *top right* Steve Raymer/National Geographic Image Collection; **270** *Battle of the Tribes.* Illumination from Add. Or 25900, f. 121v. By permission of the British Library; **272** Sonia Halliday Photographs; **273** *top left* © Stone/Getty Images; *top right* Steve Raymer/National Geographic Image Collection; **274** *Persian Garden Party.* MS Elliott 189, f. 192. Photo © Bodleian Library, Oxford, United Kingdom; **275** *top right* Istanbul University Library; *center left* The Granger Collection, New York; *bottom right* The Granger Collection, New York; **276** The Granger Collection, New York; **277** *left* © Arthur Thévenart/Corbis; *top right* © Peter Sanders; *center right* © Arthur Thévenart/Corbis; *bottom right* © Arthur Thévenart/Corbis; **278** © Brian Lawrence/ImageState-Pictor/PictureQuest.

World Religions

284–285 *top* © Luca I. Tettoni/Corbis; *bottom* The Hutchison Library; **284** Photo by Adrienne McGrath; **285** Thangka, depicting Wheel of Life turned by red Yama, Lord of Death, (19th–20th century), Tibetan. Oriental Museum, Durham University, England. Photo © The Bridgeman Art Library; *right* From *The Dhammapada,* translated by Eknath Easwaran, founder of the Blue Mountain Center of Meditation, © 1985, 1996; reprinted by permission of Nilgiri Press, P.O. Box 256, Tomales, California. For more information you may visit their website at www.nilgiri.org; **286–287** *The Last Supper* (1498), Leonardo da Vinci. S. Maria delle Grazie, Milan, Italy. Photo © Scala/Art Resource, New York; **286** Daniel Aguillar/Reuters News Picture Service; **287** *top left* © Haroldo de Faria Castro/International; *bottom left* © Photodisc/Getty Images; *right* The Granger Collection, New York; **288** © Gavin Hellier/Taxi/Getty Images; **289** *top left* © Ric Ergenbright/Corbis; *center right* Statue of Brahma. National Museum of India, New Delhi; *bottom left* © Lindsay Hebberd/Corbis; *bottom right* Courtesy Quest Books, www.questbooks.net; **290** © AFP/Corbis; **291** *top left* © Peter Sanders; *bottom left* James Stanfield/National Geographic Image Collection; *center right* From *Traditional Textiles of Central Asia* by Janet Harvey. Photo © 1996 Thames and Hudson Ltd., London. Reproduced by permission of the publishers; *bottom right* World Religions Photo Library; **292–293** *bottom* © Zev Radovan; *top* © Rose Eichenbaum/Corbis; **292** © Zbigniew Kosc/Circa Photo Library; **293** *center right* © Image Source/elektraVision/PictureQuest; *bottom right* The Granger Collection, New York; **294** New China Pictures/EastFoto; **295** *top* Confucius (17th century), from a Chinese scroll painting. Bibliothèque Nationale, Paris. Photo © Snark/Art Resource, New York; *bottom left* Chinese painting showing filial piety (12th century). Photo © The Art Archive; *bottom right* Cover from *The Analects* by Confucius, translated by Raymond Dawson. Used by permission of Oxford University Press.

Chapter 11

298 © Ancient Art & Architecture Collection Ltd.; **299** *top left Moorish Archer on Horseback,* Chinese, Ming dynasty. Photo © Victoria and Albert Museum/Art Resource, New York; *top right* Moorish forces surrounding Constantinople (13th century), folio 43V of Canticles of Saint Mary, manuscript by Alfonso X the Wise, king of Castile and Leon. Real Biblioteca de lo Escorial. Photo © Dagli Orti/The Art Archive; *bottom* Council of Clermont, arrival of Pope Urban II in France (1337), miniature from the Toman Godefroi de Bouillon. Bibliothèque Nationale, Paris. Photo © Giraudon/Art Resource, New York; **300** Timur's invasion of India. Victoria and Albert Museum, London. Photo by Eileen Tweedy/The Art Archive; **301** *top left* © Stone/Getty Images; *top right The Archangel Michael* (second half 14th century), Russian Byzantine icon. Tretyakov Gallery, Moscow. Photo © Scala/Art Resource, New York; *bottom* Greek cross (11th century), Byzantine. Museo della Civiltà Romana, Rome. Photo © Dagli Orti/The Art Archive; **302** © Sadik Demiroz/SuperStock, Inc.; **303** © R. Sheridan/Ancient Art & Architecture Collection Ltd.; **304** © Jonathan Blair/Corbis; **305** *left* © Mihai Barbu/Reuters/Corbis; *right* © Alessandro Bianchi/Reuters/Corbis; **306** Chalice (11th century), Basilica San Marco, Venice. Photo © Dagli Orti/The Art Archive; **307** *left* © Stone/Getty Images; *right The Archangel Michael* (second half 14th century), Russian Byzantine icon. Tretyakov Gallery, Moscow. Photo © Scala/Art Resource, New York; **311** © Archivo Iconografico, S.A./Corbis; 312–313 Church of the Assumption, Varzuga, Kola Peninsula, Russia. Photo © Vadim Gippenreiter/The Bridgeman Art Library; **312** *top* © Archivo Iconografico, S.A./Corbis; *center* © Massimo Listri/Corbis; *bottom* Scribe writing out the Gospel (late 15th century). Hermitage, St. Petersburg, Russia. Photo © The Bridgeman Art Library; **313** © Elio Ciol/Corbis; **314** *top left* © Stone/Getty Images; *top right The Archangel Michael* (second half 14th century), Russian Byzantine icon. Tretyakov Gallery, Moscow. Photo © Scala/Art Resource, New York; **315** © Jose Fuste Raga/Corbis; **316** Or. MS 20, f. 124v. By permission of the Edinburgh University Library; **317** © The Image Bank/Getty Images.

Chapter 12

320 *left* Horse, Tang dynasty. Musée des Arts Asiatiques-Guimet, Paris. Photo © Erich Lessing/Réunion des Musées Nationaux/Art Resource, New York; *right* Quetzalcoatl (post-classical period, 9th–13th century). Photo © Joseph Martin/The Art Archive; **321** *right* Ariwara-no-Narihara, Japanese poet (12th–13th century), Kamakura period, Silk painting, Paris. Photo © Dagli Orti/The Art Archive; *bottom* Pope Leo IX excommunicating Michael Keroularios (15th century), Greek manuscript. Biblioteca Nazionale, Palermo. Photo © Dagli Orti/The Art Archive; **322** *left* © Dorling Kindersley; *center* © Keren Su/Corbis; *right* Photo by Sharon Hoogstraten; **323** *top left* © Kelly-Mooney/Corbis; *top right* © Ernest Manewal/SuperStock, Inc.; **324** *top* Wan-go-Weng; *center* Empress Wu Zetian, Tang dynasty (18th century), Chinese. British Library. Photo © The Art Archive; **325** © William Whitehurst/Corbis; **326** *top* Tu Fu (18th century), Chinese. The British Museum, London. Photo © The Art Archive; *bottom* © Burstein Collection/Corbis; **328** *top* Flask, porcelain, Ming dynasty (early 15th century), China. Photo © Victoria and Albert Museum, London/Art Resource, New York; *inset* Small plate, Northern Sung dynasty, China. Musée des Arts Asiatiques-Guimet, Paris. Photo © Dagli Orti/The Art Archive; **329** *top* Illustration by Peter Dennis; *bottom* Ontario Science Center, Toronto, Canada; **330** *top left* © Kelly-Mooney/Corbis; *top right* © Ernest Manewal/SuperStock, Inc.; **331** James L. Stanfield/National Geographic Image Collection; **332–333** Illustration by Patrick Whelan; **335** *top left* © Kelly-Mooney/Corbis; *top right* © Ernest Manewal/SuperStock, Inc.; **336** © Imperial Collections, Sannomaru Shozo Kan. Photo courtesy of the International Society for Educational Information; **337** *top* William H. Boyd/National Geographic Image Collection; *bottom* © Biblioteca Nazionale, Turin, Italy/Silvio Fiore/SuperStock, Inc.; **339** *top left* © Kelly-Mooney/Corbis; *top right* © Ernest Manewal/SuperStock, Inc.; **341** © Laurie Platt Winfrey, Inc.; **342** *left* Illustration by Peter Dennis; *right* Tomoe, a brave woman of the Genji and Heishi period (about A.D. 900). Photo © The Art Archive; **344** *top left* © Kelly-Mooney/Corbis; *top right* © Ernest Manewal/SuperStock, Inc.; **345** *center right* © Corbis; *bottom right* © Steve Vidler/SuperStock, Inc.; **346** © Nguyen Dang Che.

Chapter 13

350 *Feats of the noble prince Charles Martel.* Musée Goya, Castres, France. Photo © Giraudon/Art Resource, New York; **351** *top left* Ove Holst © University Museum of Cultural Heritage-University of Oslo, Norway; *top right* Imperial orb (first half 11th century). Kunsthistorisches Museum, Vienna, Austria. Photo © Erich Lessing/Art Resource, New York; *bottom The Genies Gathering over the Sea,* poem by Ma Lin on silk (A.D. 960–1279), calligraphy, Chinese, Song dynasty. Musée des Arts Asiatiques-Guimet/ Paris. Inv.: EG 2146. Photo by Michel Urtado © Réunion des Musées Nationaux/Art Resource, New York; **352** Month of June from the Grimani Breviary (16th century). Biblioteca Marciana, Venice, Italy. Photo © Scala/Art Resource, New York; **353** *left* © Chris Bland/Eye Ubiquitous/Corbis; *right* The army leaves after sack of town (14th century manuscript). Biblioteca Nazionale Marciana, Venice, Italy. Photo © Dagli Orti/The Art Archive; **354** Golden Bull (about 1390), illumination on parchment. Bildarchiv der Osterreichische Nationalbibliothek, Vienna, Austria; **355** *left Saint Benedict,* Hans Memling. Uffizi, Florence, Italy. Photo © Scala/Art Resource, New York; *right* © National Gallery Collection; By kind permission of the trustees of the National Gallery, London/Corbis; **357** *Portrait of Charlemagne,* Albrecht Dürer. © Germanisches Nationalmuseum, Nuremberg, Germany. Photo © Lauros-Giraudon, Paris/SuperStock, Inc.; **358** *top left* © Chris Bland/Eye Ubiquitous/Corbis; *top right* The army leaves after sack of town (14th century). Manuscript. Biblioteca Nazionale Marciana, Venice, Italy. Photo © Dagli Orti/The Art Archive; *bottom* © DK Images; **361** Illustrations by Terry Gabbey; **362** © North Wind Picture Archives; **363** W. W. Norton & Company, Inc.; **364** *top left* © Chris Bland/Eye Ubiquitous/Corbis; *top right* The army leaves after sack of town (14th century). Manuscript. Biblioteca Nazionale Marciana, Venice, Italy. Photo © Dagli Orti/The Art Archive; *bottom* Royal Armouries; **365** *St. George and the Dragon* (about 1460), Paolo Uccello. National Gallery, London. Photo © The Bridgeman Art Library; **366** Illustration by Wood Ronsaville Harlin, Inc.; **367** *Braveheart* poster. Photofest; **368** *left* © Archivo Iconografico, S.A./Corbis; *right Peasant Woman With Scythe and Rake,* Alexei Venetsianov. Photo © The State Russian Museum/Corbis; **369** MS Bruxelles, B. R. 9961–9962, f.91v. Photo © Bibliothèque Royal Albert Ier, Brussels, Belgium; **370** *top left* © Chris Bland/Eye Ubiquitous/Corbis; *top right* The army leaves after sack of town (14th century). Manuscript. Biblioteca Nazionale Marciana, Venice, Italy. Photo © Dagli Orti/The Art Archive; *bottom* Museo Tesoro di San Pietro, Vatican State. Photo © Scala/Art Resource, New York; **371** © Aaron Horowitz/Corbis; **373** *Frederick Barbarossa and his Sons,* German school (12th century). Landesbibliothek, Fulda, Germany. Photo © Alinari/The Bridgeman Art Library.

Chapter 14

376 *left* © Gianni Dagli Orti/Corbis; *right* William the Conqueror (1289). Cloister of the Church of the Annunciation, Florence, Italy. Photo © Dagli Orti/The Art Archive; **377** *left* Portrait of Genghis Khan. National Palace Museum, Taipei, Taiwan. Photo © The Bridgeman Art Library; *right Hours of Marguerite de Coetivy: The Final Moments* (15th century), MS 74/1088 f. 90. Musée Condé, Chantilly, France. Photo © Bridgeman-Giraudon/Art Resource, New York; **378** *Richard Coeur de Lion on his way to Jerusalem,* James William Glass. Phillips, The International Fine Art Auctioneers, United Kingdom. Photo © The Bridgeman Art Library; **379** *top left* © Corbis; *top right* © Archivo Iconografico, S.A./Corbis; **381** *left* Harry Bliss/National Geographic Image Collection; *top right* © L. Salou/Explorer; *center right* Photo © Giraudon/Art Resource, New York; **382** Mary Evans Picture Library; **384** *left* © Bettmann/Corbis; *right* Portrait of Saladin, sultan of Egypt. Museo di Andrea del Castagno, Uffizi, Florence, Italy. Photo © SEF/Art Resource, New York; **385** *Scene at Court* (1710–1720), Alessandro Magnasco. Kunsthistorisches Museum, Vienna, Austria. Photo © Erich Lessing/Art Resource, New York; **386** By permission of the British Library; **387** *top left* © Corbis; *top right* © Archivo Iconografico, S.A./Corbis; **388** Illustration by Peter Dennis; **389** *Fish Market,* Joachim Beuklelaer. Museo

Nazionale de Capodimonte, Naples, Italy. Photo © Alinari/Art Resource, New York; **391** *Imaginary portrait of Avicenna,* Ibn Sina, French school. Bibliothèque de la Faculté de Medecine, Paris. Photo © Archives Charmet/The Bridgeman, Art Library; **392** St. Thomas Aquinas from the Demidoff altarpiece, Carlo Crivelli. Photo © National Gallery Collection/By kind permission of the Trustees of the National Gallery, London/Corbis; **393** *top left* © Corbis; *top right* © Archivo Iconografico, S.A./Corbis; **394** *Eleanor of Aquitaine* (19th century), French school. Bibliothèque Nationale, Paris. Photo © The Bridgeman Art Library; **395** National Archives; **396** MS français 6465, f. 212v. Bibliothèque Nationale, Paris. Photo by AKG London; **398** *top left* © Corbis; *top right* © Archivo Iconografico, S.A./Corbis; **399** *The Triumph of Death* (late 15th century), Flemish. Musée du Berry, Bourges, France. Photo © Giraudon/Art Resource, New York; **400** *center* Reader's Digest, London; *bottom* Private collection; **402** Illustration by Peter Dennis; **403** © Christie's Images/Corbis.

Chapter 15

406 *top* © Paul Almasy/Corbis; *bottom* © Bettmann/Corbis; **407** *left* The Granger Collection, New York; *right* Death strangling a victim of the plague (14th century), Czechoslovakia, from the Stiny Codex. University Library, Prague, Czech Republic. Photo © Werner Forman/Art Resource, New York; **408** Illustration by Yuan Lee; **409** *top left, top right* © Michele Burgess/SuperStock, Inc.; **412** © Richard Bickel/Corbis; **413** *top left, top right* © Michele Burgess/SuperStock, Inc.; **416** The Granger Collection, New York; **418** © North Carolina Museum of Art/Corbis; **419** © Seattle Art Museum/Corbis; **420** *foreground* Benin, queen mother's head. Photo © The British Museum; *background* © Catherine Secula/photolibrary/PictureQuest; **421** *top* Illustration by Yuan Lee; *bottom left* Bronze figure of a hornblower (late 16th–early 17th century A.D.), Edopeoples. Benin kingdom, Nigeria. Photo © The British Museum; *center right* Cast bronze figure, aquamanile, Benin kingdom, Nigeria. Photo © The British Museum; **422** *top left, top right* © Michele Burgess/SuperStock, Inc.; **424** The Granger Collection, New York; **425** The Granger Collection, New York; **426** © MIT Collection/Corbis; *left inset* © Colin Hoskins/Cordaiy Photo Library Ltd./Corbis; *right inset* © Robert Holmes/Corbis; **433** *top* © Nik Wheeler/Corbis; *center left* Camel (eighth century A.D.) from tomb of Cungpu, Shaanxi province, China. Genius of China Exhibition. Photo © The Art Archive; *center right* Astrolabe (ninth century), Ahmad Ibu Khalaf. Bibliothèque Nationale de Cartes et Plans. Paris. Photo © The Bridgeman Art Library; *bottom* © Science & Society Picture Library, London; **434** *top left* Chinese moon flask decorated in famille rose colours with birds and flowers (13th–14th century A.D.) Yuan dynasty, Percival David Foundation for Chinese Art/Harper Collins Publishers. Photo © The Art Archive; *top right* Spoon (16th–17th centuries), Edo peoples, Benin kingdom, Nigeria. Bequest of Mrs. Robert Woods Bliss. National Museum of African Art, Smithsonian Institution, Washington, D.C. Photo © Aldo Tutino/Art Resource, New York; *bottom* Photograph by Sharon Hoogstraten.

UNIT FOUR

436–437 *La Salle's Louisiana expedition in 1684,* J. A. Theodore Gudin. Photo © Réunion des Musées Nationaux/Art Resource, New York.

Chapter 16

438 *left* © Charles & Josette Lenars/Corbis; *right* Crown of the Holy Roman Empire (962?). Kunsthistorisches Museum, Vienna, Austria. Photo © Erich Lessing/Art Resource, New York; **439** *top* Fertility goddess (pre-Columbian), Aztec. The British Museum, London. Photo © Werner Forman/Art Resource, New York; *bottom* © David Lees/Corbis; **440** Thunderbird Hamatsa headdress (early 20th century), Native American, Kwakwaka'wakw. Seattle Art Museum, gift of John H. Hauberg. Photo © Paul Macapia; **441** *top left* © Explorer, Paris/SuperStock, Inc.; *top right* © Tim Hursley/SuperStock, Inc.; **443** © Corbis; **444** © Richard A. Cooke/Corbis; **446** *top left* © Explorer, Paris/SuperStock, Inc.; *top right* © Tim Hursley/SuperStock, Inc.; *bottom* Jade mask used in burial rituals (seventh century), Classic Maya, excavated from the Temple of Inscriptions at Palenque. Museo Nacional de Antropologia, Mexico City. Photo © Werner Forman/Art Resource, New York; **448** Detail of prisoners marching as a result of destruction of the land of Mu from Maya codex Troano or Tro-Cortesianus. Antochiw Collection, Mexico. Photo © Mireille Vautier/The Art Archive; **450–451** © Alison Wright/Corbis; **450** *bottom left* The Granger Collection, New York; *top right* Two-headed jaguar throne from Uxmal, Yucatan, Maya. Photo © Danielle Gustafson/Art Resource, New York; **451** *left* © Ludovic Maisant/Corbis; *right* Ball court at Chichen Itza, Maya, Yucatan, Mexico. Photo © Dagli Orti/The Art Archive; **452** *top left* © Explorer, Paris/SuperStock, Inc.; *top right* © Tim Hursley/SuperStock, Inc.; *bottom* Quetzalcoatl (tenth century), Toltec, western Yucatan, Mexico. Photo © Dagli Orti/The Art Archive; **453** © Angelo Hornak/Corbis; **454** Eagle warrior (pre-Columbian), Aztec. Museo del Templo Mayor, Mexico City. © Michel Zabe/Art Resource, New York; **456** Detail of *The Aztec World* (1929), Diego Rivera, mural. National Palace Museum, Mexico City. © Banco de Mexico trust. Photo © Schalkwijk/Art Resource, New York; **457** *right* Detail of Codex Vaticanus Mexico (before 1500), Aztec. Mexican National Library. Photo © Mireille Vautier/The Art Archive; *left* Disc with reliefs design representing a ball player, around the edge of the disc are a series of dates including day and 20-period signs (A.D. 590), Maya, from Chinkultic, Chiapas. Museo Nacional de Antropologia, Mexico City. Photo © Werner Forman/Art Resource, New York; *inset* Solar calendar (reconstruction), Aztec, Mexican culture. National Anthropological Museum, Mexico. Photo © Dagli Orti/The Art Archive; **459** *top left* © Explorer, Paris/SuperStock, Inc.; *top right* © Tim Hursley/SuperStock, Inc.; **460** Pachacutic Inca IX, detail from Geneaology (18th century), Cuzco school. Museo Pedro de Osma, Lima, Peru. Photo © Mireille Vautier/The Art Archive; **462** Machu Picchu, Peru, seen from royal quarters and House of the Inca. Photo © Dagli Orti/The Art Archive; **464** *top* Parading a sacred Inca mummy on a litter (1565), Felipe Guanman Poma de Ayala. From *El Primer Nueva Coronica y buen Gobierno,* Perus codex facsimile. Royal Library, Copenhagen, Denmark. Photo by Nick Saunders © Werner Forman/Art Resource, New York; *bottom* Stephen Alvarez/National Geographic Image Collection; **465** *top* © 2003 Ira Block; *center* Illustration by John Dawson/National Geographic Image Collection; *bottom* The Granger Collection, New York; **466** *top to bottom* © Corbis; Jade mask used in burial rituals (seventh century), Classic Maya. Excavated from the Temple of Inscriptions at Palenque. Museo Nacional de Antropologia, Mexico City. Photo © Werner Forman/Art Resource, New York; Quetzalcoatl (tenth century), Toltec, western Yucatan, Mexico. Photo © Dagli Orti/The Art Archive; Photo © Dagli Orti/The Art Archive; **467** Hernando Cortés, [Map of Tenochtitlan and the Gulf of Mexico], in his *Praeclara Ferinadi Cortesii de Nova maris Oceani Hyspania Narratio…* (Nuremberg: F. Peypus, 1524). Ayer *655.51 C8 1524D]. The Newberry Library, Chicago.

Chapter 17

468 *top* Bust of Lorenzo de Medici (15th or 16th century). Museo di Andrea del Castagno, Uffizi, Florence, Italy. Photo © Scala/Art Resource, New York; *bottom* Jar with dragon (1425–1435), Ming dynasty, reign of Xuande. Porcelain painted in underglaze blue; 19" high (48.3 cm). Gift of Robert E. Tod, 1937, The Metropolitan Museum of Art, New York. Photo © 2003 The Metropolitan Museum of Art; **469** *left Gutenberg Bible* (about 1455). Volume II, f. 45v-46. PML 818 ch1 ff1. The Pierpont Morgan Library, New York. Photo © The Pierpont Morgan Library/Art Resource, New York; *right* Detail of nobles entertained in garden by musicians and dancers (about 1590), Mughal. Photo © British Library/The Art Archive; **470** *The Madonna of Chancellor Rolin* (about 1434), Jan van Eyck. Louvre, Paris. Photo © Scala/Art Resource, New York; **471** *top* *left* © Photodisc/Getty Images; *top right* © Ulf E. Wallin/The Image Bank/Getty Images; **472** Detail of *Lorenzo de Medici 1449–1492 and the Arts in Florence* (about 1634–1636), Giovanni da Sangiovanni. Palazzo Pitti, Florence, Italy. Photo © Dagli Orti/The Art Archive; **473** *left Portrait of Baldassare Castilione,* Raphael. Louvre, Paris. © Scala/ Art Resource, New York; *right* The Granger Collection, New York; **474** *Marriage of the Virgin* (1504), Raphael. Brera, Milan, Italy. Photo © Scala/Art Resource, New York; **475** *top* © Stephano Bianchetti/Corbis; *bottom* The Granger Collection, New York; **476** *Portrait of Niccolo Machiavelli,* Santi di Tito. Palazzo Vecchio, Florence, Italy. Photo © Scala/Art Resource, New York; **477** The Granger Collection, New York; **478–479** © SuperStock, Inc.; **478** Mona Lisa (1503–1506), Leonardo da Vinci. Musée Louvre, Paris. Photo by R.G. Ojeda © Réunion des Musées Nationaux/Art Resource, New York; **479** *The School of Athens* (15th century), Raphael. Stanza della Segnatura, Vatican Palace, Vatican State. Photo © Scala/Art Resource, New York; *bottom* © Bettmann/Corbis; **480** *top left* © Photodisc/Getty Images; *top right* © Ulf E. Wallin/The Image Bank/Getty Images; **481** *Peasant Wedding* (1568), Peter Brueghel the Elder. Kunsthistorisches Museum, Vienna, Austria. Photo © Saskia Ltd./Art Resource, New York; **482** *left* Christine de Pizan teaches her son (about 1430). Harley MS 4431, f. 26 ff. The British Library, London. Photo by AKG London/British Library; *right Thomas More, Lord Chancellor* (late 15th century) Private Collection. Photo © The Stapleton Collection/The Bridgeman Art Library; **483** *left, Othello* movie still. Castle Rock/Dakota Films/The Kobal Collection; *center, 10 things I Hate About You* movie still. Touchstone/The Kobal Collection; *top right, Romeo & Juliet* movie still. Merrick Morton/20th Century Fox/The Kobal Collection; *bottom right, Ran* movie still. Herald Ace/Nippon Herald/Greenwich/The Kobal Collection; **484** Peter Dennis/Linda Rogers Associates; **486–487** MS Sloane 2596, f. 52. British Library. Photo by AKG London/British Library; **486** *top* Koninklijk Museum voor Schone Kunsten, Antwerpen, Belgium; *center left* By permission of the Folger Shakespeare Library, Washington, D.C.; *center* Musée de la parfumerie Fragonard, Paris. Photo © Dagli Orti/The Art Archive; **487** The Shakespeare Birthplace Trust; **488** *top left* © Photodisc/Getty Images; *top right* © Ulf E. Wallin/The Image Bank/Getty Images; **489** *Portrait of Martin Luther* (1529) Lucas Cranach the Elder. Museo Poldi Pezzoli, Milan, Italy. Photo © The Bridgeman Art Library; **492** *left Portrait of Henry VIII, King of England* (1540), Hans Holbein the Younger. Galleria Nazionale d'Arte Antica, Rome. Photo © Scala/Art Resource, New York; *right* Courtesy of the National Portrait Gallery, London; **493** *top left* © Stapleton Collection/Corbis; *bottom left Mary I Tudor, 1516–1558 Queen of England or Bloody Mary, Second Wife of King Philip II of Spain* (1554), Antonis Moro or Mor. Museo del Prado Madrid. Photo © Dagli Orti/The Art Archive; *right Elizabeth I, 1533–1603 Queen of England,* Federico Zuccari. Pinacoteca Nazionale di Siena. Photo © Dagli Orti/The Art Archive; **494** *Elizabeth I* (1588), George Gower. Courtesy of the National Portrait Gallery, London; **495** *left* © Photodisc/Getty Images; *right* © Ulf E. Wallin/The Image Bank/Getty Images; **496** *John Calvin as a young man,* Flemish School. Bibliothèque Publique et Universitaire, Geneva, Switzerland. Photo © Erich Lessing/Art Resource, New York; **498** Marguerite d'Angouleme, Queen of Navarre (16th century). Musée Condé, Chantilly, France/Photo © Bridgeman-Giraudon/Art Resource, New York; **499** *Pope Paul III Farnese at the Council of Trent* (1560–1566), Taddeo and Federico Zuccari. Farnese Palace Caprarola. Photo © Dagli Orti/The Art Archive; **500** © Richard T. Nowitz/Corbis; **501** Martin Luther, German priest and Protestant reformer, caricature as seven-headed monster. The British Library. Photo © British Library/The Art Archive; **502** *top to bottom* © SuperStock, Inc.; Peter Dennis/Linda Rogers Associates; *Portrait of Martin Luther* (1529) Lucas Cranach the Elder. Museo Poldi Pezzoli, Milan, Italy. Photo © The Bridgeman Art Library; Detail of *Pope Paul III Farnese at the Council of Trent* (1560–1566), Taddeo and Federico Zuccari. Farnese Palace Caprarola. Photo © Dagli Orti/The Art Archive; **503** © Bettmann/Corbis.

Chapter 18

504 *top* Topkapi Palace Museum, Istanbul, Turkey. Sonia Halliday and Laura Lushington; *bottom left* Pectoral ornament in the form of a double-headed serpent. Aztec. The British Museum, London. Photo © Werner Forman/Art Resource, New York; *bottom right* By permission of the British Library; **505** © Burstein Collection/Corbis; **506** Shah Tahmasp I receiving the Moghul Emperor Humayun (1660s). Period of Abbas II. Chihil Sutun, Isfahan, Iran. Photo © Giraudon/Art Resource, New York; **507** *top left* James L. Stanfield/National Geographic Image Collection; *top right* © SuperStock, Inc.; **509** Taking of Constantinople by the Turks, MS Fr. 9087 f. 207. *Voyage d'Outremer de Bertrand de la Broquiere,* Bibliothèque Nationale, Paris. Photo © Sonia Halliday Photographs; **510** *Suleiman the Magnificent.* Galleria degli Uffizi, Florence, Italy. Photo © Dagli Orti/The Art Archive; **511** Sonia Halliday Photographs; **513** Chihil Sutun, Isfahan, Iran. Photo © SEF/Art Resource, New York; **515** Dome of south Iwan (1611–1638). Safavid dynasty. Majid-i Shah, Isfahan, Iran. Photo © SEF/Art Resource, New York; **516** *top left* James L. Stanfield/National Geographic Image Collection; *top right* © SuperStock, Inc.; **518** Portrait of Akbar and Prince Salim (19th century). India, Mughal. Gift of Sally Sample Aal, 1997. The Newark Museum, Newark, New Jersey. Photo © The Newark Museum/Art Resource, New York; **519** *left* © Bettmann/Corbis; *left center* © Wally McNamee/Corbis; *right center, right* AP/Wide World Photos ; **520** © Brian A. Vikander/Corbis; **522** *top* Dagger handle in the form of a horse's head. Mughal. India. Victoria and Albert Museum, London. Photo © Victoria and Albert Museum, London/The Bridgeman Art Library; *bottom* © Abbie Enock/Travel Ink/Corbis; **523** *top* Tent hanging (early 18th century). Mughal dynasty. Victoria and Albert Museum, London. Photo © Victoria and Albert Museum, London/Art Resource, New York; *left* Akbar on the elephant Hawai pursuing the elephant rau Bagha (about 1590). Double page miniature from the Akbarnama. Mughal. Victoria and Albert Museum, London. Photo © Victoria and Albert Museum, London/Art Resource, New York.

Chapter 19

526 left Helmet (about 1500), Turkish. Victoria and Albert Museum, London. Photo © Victoria and Albert Museum, London/Art Resource, New York; *right* Detail of *St. Vincent Polyptych* (15th century), Nuno Goncalves. Museu Nacional de Arte Antiga, Lisbon, Portugal. Photo © Scala/Art Resource, New York; **527** *left* © The Flag Institute; *right Washington Crossing the Delaware,* Eastman Johnson. Copy after the Emmanuel Leutze painting in the Metropolitan Museum, New York. Private Collection. Photo © Art Resource, New York; **528** *India Orientalis* (1606), Gerard Mercator and Jodocus Hondius. *Atlas sive cosmographicae Meditationes.* Courtesy Sotheby's, London; **529** *top left* © Culver Pictures, Inc./SuperStock, Inc.; *top right* K'ossu (about 1600), Late Ming dynasty. China. Victoria and Albert Museum, London, UK. Photo © Sally Chappell/The Art Archive; *bottom* Globe by Martin Behaim (about 1492). Bibliothèque Nationale, Paris. Photo © Giraudon/Art Resource, New York; **530** Detail of *St. Vincent Polyptych* (15th century), Nuno Goncalves. Museu Nacional de Arte Antiga, Lisbon, Portugal. Photo © Scala/Art Resource, New York; **531** *top right inset* Courtesy of Bibliothèque Nationale, Paris; *bottom left inset* Compass with sextant and dial (1617), Elias Allen. Victoria and Albert Museum, London. Photo © Victoria and Albert Museum, London/Art Resource, New York; *bottom center* © DK Images; *background* © Bettmann/Corbis; **532** © Bettmann/Corbis; **533** © Stapleton Collection/Corbis; **535** Corbis; **536** *top left* © Culver Pictures, Inc./SuperStock, Inc.; *top right* K'ossu (about 1600) Late Ming dynasty. China. Victoria and Albert Museum, London, UK. Photo © Sally Chappell/The Art Archive; *bottom right* Ming vase. Chinese School. Musée des Arts Asiatiques-Guimet, Paris, France. Photo © The Bridgeman Art Library; **538** *top right* © John T. Young/Corbis; *center right* © Brian A. Vikander/Corbis; *bottom right* Harvey Lloyd/Taxi/Getty Images; **539** Palace Museum, Beijing, China; **540** Marriage ceremony (19th century), China.Victoria and Albert Museum, London. Photo by Eileen Tweedy/The Art Archive;

541 The Granger Collection, New York; **542** *top left* © Culver Pictures, Inc./SuperStock, Inc.; *top right* K'ossu (about 1600), Late Ming dynasty. China. Victoria and Albert Museum, London, UK. Photo © Sally Chappell/The Art Archive; *bottom* Rijksmuseum, Amsterdam, The Netherlands; **543** © B.S.P.I./Corbis; **544** © Asian Art & Archeology/Corbis **545** © Asian Art & Archaeology/Corbis; *inset* © Michael S. Yamashita/Corbis; **546** © 1995 Christie's Images Limited; **547** Monk Tokiyori. Musée des Arts Asiatiques-Guimet, Paris. Photo by Richard Lambert © Réunion des Musées Nationaux/Art Resource, New York; **548** Dutch Merchant ship plate (1756), Qing dynasty. China. Musée des Arts Asiatiques-Guimet, Paris. Photo © Réunion des Musées Nationaux/Art Resource, New York; **549** The Granger Collection, New York.

Chapter 20

550 *top* © Archivo Iconografico, S.A./Corbis; *bottom Portrait of Tokugawa Ieyasu* (17th century), Japanese. Private Collection. Photo © The Bridgeman Art Library; **551** *left* The Granger Collection, New York; *right The Taking of the Bastille, 14 July 1789* (18th century), French School. Musée de la Ville de Paris, Musée Carnevalet, Paris, France. Photo © The Bridgeman Art Library; **552** Lienzo de Tlaxcala Aniquendas Mexicana 16th century Battle for Tenochtitlan between Cortés and Spaniards and Aztecs. Antochiw Collection, Mexico. Photo © Mireille Vautier/The Art Archive; **553** *top left* © Bettmann/Corbis; top *right* Detail of letter from Christopher Columbus to his son Diego (5 February 1505). General Archive of the Indies, Seville, Spain. Photo © Dagli Orti/The Art Archive; **554** *Christopher Columbus* (15th century), Sebastiano del Piombo. Metropolitan Museum of Art, New York. Photo © The Bridgeman Art Library; **557** *left* The Granger Collection, New York; *right* South American Pictures; **558** The Granger Collection, New York; **560** The Granger Collection, New York; **561** *top left* Detail of letter from Christopher Columbus to his son Diego (5 February 1505). General Archive of the Indies, Seville, Spain. Photo © Dagli Orti/The Art Archive; *top right* © Bettmann/Corbis; **562** The Granger Collection, New York; **563** North Carolina Collection, University of North Carolina, Chapel Hill; **566** *top left* © Bettmann/Corbis; *top right* Detail of letter from Christopher Columbus to his son Diego (5 February 1505). General Archive of the Indies, Seville, Spain. Photo © Dagli Orti/The Art Archive; **567** The Granger Collection, New York; **569** *center* The Granger Collection, New York; *right* The Newberry Library, Chicago; **571** *top left* Detail of letter from Christopher Columbus to his son Diego (5 February 1505). General Archive of the Indies, Seville, Spain. Photo © Dagli Orti/The Art Archive; *top right* © Bettmann/Corbis; **573** The Granger Collection, New York; **577** The Granger Collection, New York; **578** Portrait of the last Inca Chief, Atahualpa. Private Collection. Photo © The Bridgeman Art Library; **579** *top left Cosimo de'Medici, the Elder,* Agnolo Bronzino. Museo Mediceo, Florence, Italy. Photo © Scala/Art Resource, New York; *top right* © Sakamoto Photo Research Laboratory/Corbis; *bottom* © Bettmann/Corbis; **581** *top* © Araldo de Luca/Corbis; *bottom left* Nautilus Pitcher (about 1570) Francesco de Medici Collection. Museo degli Argenti, Florence, Italy. Photo © Erich Lessing/Art Resource, New York; *bottom right* John Bigelow Taylor/American Museum of Natural History, No. 4959(2); **582** *top* © Yann Arthus-Bertrand/Corbis; bottom © Steve Vidler /SuperStock, Inc.; **583** © Archivo Iconografico, S.A./Corbis.

UNIT FIVE

584–585 *The Taking of the Bastille, July 14, 1789.* Anonymous French painter. Musée National du Chateau, Versailles, France. Photo © Erich Lessing/Art Resource, New York.

Chapter 21

586 *top Philip II, King of Spain and Portugal* (16th century), Alonso Sanchez Coello. Museo del Prado, Madrid, Spain. Photo © Erich Lessing/Art Resource, New York; *bottom Francisco Pizarro* (1835), Amable-Paul Coutan. Chateaux de Versailles et de Trianon, Versailles, France. Photo by Franck Raux © Réunion des Musées Nationaux/Art Resource, New York; **587** *top* The Granger Collection, New York; *bottom* © Pallava Bagla/Corbis; **588** *Louis XIV, King of France* (1701), Hyacinthe Rigaud. Louvre, Paris. Photo © Erich Lessing/Art Resource, New York; **589** *top left* Detail of *Marriage of Louis XIV, King of France and Marie Therese of Austria* (17th century), unknown artist. Musée de Tesse Le Mans. Photo © Dagli Orti/The Art Archive; *top right* © Todd A. Gipstein/Corbis; **590** The Granger Collection, New York; **591** *Las Meninas or The Family of Philip IV,* (about 1656), Diego Rodriguez de Silva y Velasquez. Prado, Madrid, Spain. Photo © The Bridgeman Art Library; **592** *Tulipa gesaeriana no. 1908* (late 16th–early 17th century), Jacopo Ligozzi. Gabinetto dei Disegni e delle Stampe. Ufizzi Florence, Italy. Photo © Scala/Art Resource, New York; **593** The Granger Collection, New York; **596** *top left* Detail of *Marriage of Louis XIV, King of France and Marie Therese of Austria* (17th century), unknown artist. Musée de Tesse Le Mans. Photo © Dagli Orti/The Art Archive; *top right* © Todd A. Gipstein/Corbis; **597** *Cardinal Richelieu* (1636), Phillippe de Champaigne. Musée Condé, Chantilly, France. Photo © Giraudon/Art Resource, New York; **598** Detail of *Colbert Presenting Louis XIV the Members of the Royal Academy of Sciences in 1667,* Henri Tetstelin. Photo © Gerard Blot/Réunion Musées Nationaux; **599** *Louis de Rouvroy, Duke of Saint-Simon* (1887), Viger du Vigneau. Chateaux de Versailles et de Trianon, Versailles, France. Photo © Réunion des Musées Nationaux/Art Resource, New York; **600** © Archivo Iconografico, S.A./Corbis; *left inset* © Archivo Iconografico, S.A./Corbis; *center inset* © Adam Woolfitt/Corbis; *right inset* © Ben Mangor/SuperStock, Inc.; **601** *Battle of Denain, 24th July 1712* (1839), Jean Alaux. Chateau de Versailles et de Trianon, France. Photo © Giraudon/The Bridgeman Art Library; **603** *top left* Detail of *Marriage of Louis XIV, King of France and Marie Therese of Austria* (17th century), unknown artist. Musée de Tesse Le Mans. Photo © Dagli Orti/The Art Archive; *top right* © Todd A. Gipstein/Corbis; **605** Flag of the Imperial Hapsburg dynasty (about 1700). Heeresgeschichtliches Museum, Vienna, Austria. © The Bridgeman Art Library; **606** *top* Detail of *Empress Maria Theresa of Austria.* Museum der Stadt Wien. Photo © Dagli Orti/The Art Archive; *center* Schloss Charlottenburg, Berlin/Bildarchiv Preussischer Kulturbesitz, Berlin; **608** *top left* Detail of *Marriage of Louis XIV, King of France and Marie Therese of Austria* (17th century), unknown artist. Musée de Tesse Le Mans. Photo © Dagli Orti/The Art Archive; *top right* © Todd A. Gipstein/Corbis; **609** The Granger Collection, New York; **612** *top right* © Dorling Kindersley; *center left* Costumes of Crimean tribes (1888), A. Racinet. From Historical Costumes vol, V. Musée des Arts Décoratifs, Paris.Photo © Dagli Orti/The Art Archive; *bottom* © Historical Picture Archive/Corbis; **613** *top Shrovetide* (1919), Boris Kustidiev. The I. Brodsky Museum, St. Petersburg, Russia. Photo courtesy of the Smithsonian Institution Traveling Exhibition Service; *bottom* © Scheufler Collection/Corbis; **614** *top left* Detail of *Marriage of Louis XIV, King of France and Marie Therese of Austria* (17th century), unknown artist. Musée de Tesse Le Mans. Photo © Dagli Orti/The Art Archive; *top right* © Todd A. Gipstein/Corbis; **615** The Granger Collection, New York.

Chapter 22

620 *left Portrait of a Princess Holding a Wine Cup* (17th–18th century), Mughal. India. The Newark Museum, Newark, New Jersey. Photo © The Newark Museum/Art Resource, New York; *right* Isaac Newton's reflecting telescope (1672), Royal Society. Photo by Eileen Tweedy/The Art Archive; **621** *left* Statuette of a Lohan, Ching dynasty. Musée des Arts Asiatiques-Guimet, Paris. Photo © Giraudon/Art Resource, New York; *right* © Leif Skoogfors/Corbis; **622** *A Philosopher Gives a Lecture on the Orrery* (1766), Joseph Wright of Derby. Canvas. Derby Museum and Art Gallery, Derby, Great Britain. Photo © Erich Lessing/Art Resource, New York; **623** *top left* Copernican Solar System (1661). From *Harmonia Macronici,* Andreae Cellarius. Page 30. Photo © Victoria and Albert Museum, London/Art Resource, New York; *top right* © Bettmann/Corbis; **625** *Galileo Before the Holy Office of the Vatican,* John Nicolas Robert-Fleury. Oil on canvas, Louvre, Paris. Photo by Gerard Blot © Réunion des Musées Nationaux /Art Resource, New York; **626** *left* © Bettmann/Corbis; *right* Isaac Newton's reflecting telescope (1672). Royal Society. Photo by Eileen Tweed/The Art Archive; **627** © Bettmann/Corbis; **628** *The Anatomy Lesson of Dr. Tulp,* Rembrandt van Rijn. Mauritshuis, The Hague, The Netherlands. Photo © Scala/Art Resource, New York; **629** *top left* Copernican Solar System (1661). From *Harmonia Macronici,* Andreae Cellarius. Page 30. Photo © Victoria and Albert Museum, London/Art Resource, New York; *top right* © Bettmann/Corbis; **630, 631** *left, right* The Granger Collection, New York; **633** Mary Evans Picture Library; **635** The Granger Collection, New York; **636** *top left* Copernican Solar System (1661). From *Harmonia Macronici,* Andreae Cellarius. Page 30. Photo © Victoria and Albert Museum, London/Art Resource, New York; *top right* © Bettmann/Corbis; **637** © Kevin Fleming/Corbis; **638** Joseph II, Emperor of Austria and of the Holy Roman Empire, King of Hungary and Bohemia (18th century), Austrian.Musée du Château de Versailles. Photo © Dagli Orti/The Art Archive; **639** © Anatoly Sapronenkov, Tomsk Regional Arts Museum/SuperStock, Inc.; **640** *top left* Copernican Solar System (1661). From *Harmonia Macronici,* Andreae Cellarius. Page 30. Photo © Victoria and Albert Museum, London/Art Resource, New York; *top right* © Bettmann/Corbis; *bottom* The Metropolitan Museum of Art, gift of William H. Huntington, 1883 (83.2.228); **641** Detail of *Thomas Jefferson* (about 1805), Rembrandt Peale. Oil on canvas. Photo © Collection of the New York Historical Society; **644** © Corbis; **645** © Jon Feingersh/Stock Boston, Inc./PictureQuest **647** **"***El sueño de la razón produce monstruos"* [The sleep of reason produces monsters] from *Los Caprichos* (1799) Francisco José de Goya y Lucientes. Etching and burnished aquatint, 21.5cm. x 15 cm. Bequest of William P. Babcock. Courtesy of Museum of Fine Arts, Boston.

Chapter 23

648 *right* Reduced model of a guillotine. Musée de la Ville de Paris, Musée Carnavalet, Paris. Photo © Giraudon/Art Resource, New York; *left George Washington,* George Healy. Musée du Château de Versailles. Photo © Dagli Orti/The Art Archive; **649** *top* detail of *Napoleon Bonaparte, Emperor of France.* Musée du Château de Versailles. Photo © Dagli Orti/The Art Archive; *bottom* The Granger Collection, New York; **650** *The Conquerors of the Bastille Before the Hotel de Ville* (1839), Paul Delaroche. Musée du Petit Palais, Paris. Photo © Erich Lessing/Art Resource, New York; **651** *top left* © SuperStock, Inc.; *top right* © Christie's Images/Corbis; **652** Detail of Caricature of the three estates: *"Il faut esperer que le jeu finira bientôt."* Color engraving, 18th century. Musée de la Ville de Paris, Musée Carnavalet, Paris. Photo by Bulloz © Réunion des Musées Nationaux /Art Resource, New York; **653** *left Louis XVI, King of France.* Musée de Château de Versailles. Photo © Dagli Orti/The Art Archive; *right Marie Antoinette, Queen of France* (replica of work painted in 1778). Musée du Château de Versailles. Photo © Dagli Orti/The Art Archive; **654** *The Storming of the Bastille,* Paris, France, July 14, 1789. Gouache. Musée Carnavalet, Paris. Photo © Dagli Orti/The Art Archive; **656** *left* © SuperStock, Inc.; *right* © Christie's Images/Corbis; **657** *Arrest of Louis XVI, King of France and his family attempting to flee the country at Varennes, France June 21–22, 1791.* Musée Carnavalet, Paris. Photo © Dagli Orti/The Art Archive; **658** Musées Royaux des Beaux-Arts, Brussels, Belgium. Photo © Giraudon/Art Resource, New York; **659** Illustration by Patrick Whelan; **660** *Portrait of Robespierre,* Louis L. Boilly. Musée des Beaux-Arts, Lille, France. Photo R.G. Ojeda © Réunion des Musées Nationaux/Art Resource, New York; **661** *Portrait of Danton* (18th century) Musée de la Ville de Paris, Musée Carnavalet, Paris, France. Photo © Giraudon/Art Resource, New York; **662** © Bettmann/Corbis; **663** *top left* © SuperStock, Inc.; *top right* © Christie's Images/Corbis; **664** *Portrait of Bonaparte, premier consul* (1803), Francois Gerard. Oil on canvas. Musée Condé, Chantilly, France. Photo by Harry Brejat © Réunion des Musées Nationaux/Art Resource, New York; **665** *Napoleon Bonaparte,* Jacques-Louis David. Chateau de Malmaison, Rueil-Malmaison, France. Photo © Giraudon/Art Resource, New York; **668** *top left* © SuperStock, Inc.; *top right* © Christie's Images/Corbis; *bottom* Fotomas Index; **669** © Archivo Iconografico, S.A./Corbis; **671** © Public Record Office/Topham-HIP/The Image Works; **672** *top left* © SuperStock, Inc.; *top right* © Christie's Images/Corbis; *673* © Christel Gerstenberg/Corbis; **676** *left* Parisian *sans culotte* (18th century), unknown artist. Musée de la Ville de Paris, Musée Carnavalet, Paris. Photo © Giraudon/Art Resource, New York; *right* Reduced model of a guillotine. Musée de la Ville de Paris, Musée Carnavalet, Paris. Photo © Giraudon/Art Resource, New York.

Chapter 24

678 *left Napoleon in his study at the Tuileries* (1812). Jacques-Louis David. Collection of Prince and Princess Napoleon, Paris. Photo © Giraudon/Art Resource, New York; *right* Miguel Hidalgo y Costilla (1895). From Mexican publication *Patria e Independencia, folleto illustrado.* Antiochiw Collection, Mexico. Photo © Mireille Vautier/The Art Archive; **679** *left* © Hulton-Deutsch Collection/Corbis; *right* © Francis G. Mayer/Corbis; **680** Courtesy of the Flag Institute; **681** *left* © Michael S. Lewis/Corbis; *right* © Archivo Iconografico, S.A./Corbis; **682** *Portrait of Francois-Dominique Toussaint, known as Toussaint L'Ouverture,* Anonymous. Musée des Arts d'Oceanie, Paris. Photo J.G. Berizzi © Réunion des Musées Nationaux/Art Resource, New York; **683** *left* © Christie's Images/Corbis; *right* The Granger Collection, New York; **684** © Bettmann/Corbis; **687** *top left* © Michael S. Lewis/Corbis; *top right* © Archivo Iconografico, S.A./Corbis; *bottom Klemens Metternich, Austrian prince and statesman.* Museo Glauco, Lombardi, Parma, Italy. Photo © Dagli Orti/The Art Archive; **689** © Archivo Iconografico, S.A./Corbis; **690** *Combat Before the Hotel de Ville, July 28th, 1830,* Victor Schnetz. Musée du Petit Palais, Paris. Photo by Bulloz © Réunion des Musées Nationaux/Art Resource, New York; **691** © Corbis; **695** The Granger Collection, New York; **696** © Bettmann/Corbis; **698** *top left* © Michael S. Lewis/Corbis; *top right* © Archivo Iconografico, S.A./Corbis; *bottom* © Bettmann/Corbis; **699** *Portrait of Ludwig von Beethoven,* Anonymous. Beethoven House, Bonn, Germany. Photo © Snark/Art Resource, New York; **700** © Hulton-Deutsch Collection/Corbis; **702** *Lion Hunt* (1860/1861) Eugène Delacroix, French 1798–1863. Potter Palmer Collection, 1922.404, Reproduction. The Art Institute of Chicago, Chicago, Illinois; **703** *top The Stone Breakers* (1849), Gustave Courbet. Gemäldegalerie, Dresden, Germany. Photo © The Bridgeman Art Library; *bottom* © Francis G. Mayer/Corbis; **705** The Granger Collection, New York; **706–707** *bottom* The Granger Collection, New York; **706** *left The Bloody Massacre perpetrated in...Boston on March 5th, 1770* (1770) Paul Revere. Colored engraving. The Gilder Collection GLC 1868. Photo by Joseph Zehavi © The Pierpont Morgan Library/Art Resource, New York; *right Portrait of James II* (about 1685), Benedetto Gennari the Younger. Phillip Mould, Historical Portraits Ltd, London. Photo © The Bridgeman Art Library; **707** The Granger Collection, New York; **708** *left* (detail of) *Marie-Antoinette Standing in her Court Robe with a Rose in her Hand* (1779) Louise Elizabeth Vigée-LeBrun. Châteaux de Versailles et de Trianon, Versailles, France. Photo © Réunion des Musées Nationaux/Art Resource, New York; *bottom right* © Photodisc/Getty Images; **709** *top "Il faut esperer que le jeu finira bientot"* [Peasant carrying a nobleman and a cleric] (1789). Musée de la Ville de Paris, Musée Carnavalet, Paris. Photo © Giraudon/Art Resource, New York; *bottom* The Granger Collection, New York; **710** The Granger Collection, New York; **711** *top* The Granger Collection, New York; *center Maximilien Robespierre* Musée Carnavalet, Paris. Photo © Dagli Orti/The Art Archive.

UNIT SIX

712–713 Martyn Gregory Gallery, London.

Chapter 25

714 *top* The Granger Collection, New York; *bottom* © Brian A. Vikander/Corbis; **715** *left* © Bettmann/Corbis; *right* Cover of *The Communist Manifesto* by Karl Marx and Friedrich Engels, edited by Martin Malia, © 1998 by Martin Malia. Used by permission of Signet, an imprint of Penguin Group USA; **716** © Corbis; **717** *top left* © Collin Garratt/Milepost 92 $^{1}/_{2}$/Corbis; *top right* © H. David Seawell/Corbis; **718** Hulton|Archive/Getty Images; **719** *center Blind man using a loom,* plate 17 from *Essai su l'Instruction des Aveugles* (1817), Dr. Sebastien Guillie. Colored engraving Julie Ribault. Bibliothèque de l'Institut d'Ophtalmologie, Paris, Archives Charmet. Photo © The Bridgeman Art Library; *left* © Michael St. Maur Sheil/Corbis; *bottom* Sheffield Galleries & Museum Trust; **720** © Bettmann/Corbis; **721** Liverpool and Manchester passenger train (about 1830). National Railway Museum, York, North Yorkshire, UK. Photo © The Bridgeman Art Library; **722** Hulton|Archive/Getty Images; **723** The Granger Collection, New York; **727** The Granger Collection, New York; **728** © Steve Raymer/Corbis; **729** *top left* © Collin Garratt/Milepost 92 $^{1}/_{2}$/Corbis; *top right* © H. David Seawell/Corbis; *bottom* © Corbis; **731** *The Steel Workers at Biermeister and Wain* (1885), Peter Severin Kroyer. Statens Museum for Kunst, Copenhagen, Denmark. Photo © Snark/Art Resource, New York; **733** Mary Evans Picture Library; **734** *top left* © Collin Garratt/Milepost 92 $^{1}/_{2}$/Corbis; *top right* © H. David Seawell/Corbis; **735** © Bettmann/Corbis; **736** © Archivo Iconografico, S.A./Corbis; **739** *Strike* (1895), Mihaly Munkacsy. Magyar Nemzeti Galeria, Budapest, Hungary. Photo © The Bridgeman Art Library; **740** *Jane Addams* (about 1920), George de Forest Brush. National Portrait Gallery, Smithsonian Institution, Washington, D.C. Photo © National Portrait Gallery, Smithsonian Institution/Art Resource, New York; **741** Woodcut, from *Cartoons for the Cause* (1886), Walter Crane.

Chapter 26

744 *top* Photograph of Queen Victoria (late 19th century). Victoria and Albert Museum, London. Photo © Victoria and Albert Museum, London/Art Resource, New York; *bottom* © The Stapleton Collection/Bridgeman Art Library; **745** *top* The Granger Collection, New York; *bottom* © Corbis; **746** *Une rue de Paris en mai 1871, ou La Commune* [A Paris street in May 1871; or, The commune] (1903–1905), Maximilien Luce. Oil on canvas. Musée D'Orsay, Paris. Photo © Erich Lessing/Art Resource, New York; **747** *top left* © Hulton-Deutsch Collection/Corbis; *top right* © Bettmann/Corbis; **748** © Bettmann/Corbis; **750** *Zola Under Attack* (1898), Henry de Groux. Photo by Musée Emile Zola, Médan, France; **751** *top left* © Hulton-Deutsch Collection/Corbis; *top right* © Bettmann/Corbis; **753** © Sean Sexton Collection/Corbis; **756** *center* Nouvelle-Hollande. Cour-Rou-Bari-Gal., Plate XVIII from *Atlas historique: du Voyage de decouvertes aux terres australes,* by Charles Alexandre Leseur and Nicolas-Martin Petit. State Library of South Australia; *center right* © Charles & Josette Lenars/Corbis; *bottom Australian Gold Diggings* (about 1855), Edwin Stocqueler. National Library of Australia, Canberra; **757** *top* © Graham Monro/photolibrary/PictureQuest; *bottom* The Granger Collection, New York; **758** *top left* © Hulton-Deutsch Collection/Corbis; *top right* © Bettmann/Corbis; **761** Library of Congress; **762** *top left* © Hulton-Deutsch Collection/Corbis; *top right* © Bettmann/Corbis; **763** *top right* The Granger Collection, New York; *center left* Institute of Experimental Physics/University of Innsbruck; *center right* Library of Congress; *bottom* The Granger Collection, New York; **764** *left* © Bettmann/Corbis; *center* © Bettmann/Corbis; *right* The Granger Collection, New York; **765** The Granger Collection, New York; **766** © Bettmann/Corbis; **769** By permission of the British Library.

Chapter 27

770 *top* © Werner Forman/Art Resource, New York; *bottom* The Bowes Museum, County Durham, Great Britain; **771** *top* © Bettmann/Corbis; *bottom* © Bettmann/Corbis; **772** Hulton|Archive/Getty Images; **773** *top left* Aboriginal Bark painting of abstract picture of body (19th–20th century), Lipunja. Musée des Arts Africains et Océaniens. Photo © Dagli Orti/The Art Archive; *top right The Battle of Isandhlwana* (19th century), Charles Fripp. National Army Museum, London. Photo © The Art Archive; **774** The Granger Collection, New York; **775** The Granger Collection, New York; **776** *Cetshwayo—King of the Zulus,* Carl Rudolph Sohn. The Royal Collection. Photo © 2003, Her Majesty Queen Elizabeth II; **778** © Hulton-Deutsch Collection/Corbis; **783** © Culver Pictures; **785** The Granger Collection, New York; **786** *top left* Aboriginal Bark painting of abstract picture of body, Lipunja. Musée des Arts Africains et Océaniens. Photo © Dagli Orti/The Art Archive; *top right The Battle of Isandhlwana* (19th century), Charles Fripp. National Army Museum, London. Photo © The Art Archive; **788** *Mehemet Ali, Viceroy of Egypt* (19th century), Louis Charles Auguste Couder. Chateau de Versailles, France. Photo © Lauros-Giraudon/The Bridgeman Art Library; **789** *Shipping on the Suez Canal* (1869), Edouard Riou. Chateau de Compiègne, Oise, France. Photo © Lauros-Giraudon/The Bridgeman Art Library; **790** Portrait of Nasir Al-Din Shah (19th century), unknown artist. Louvre, Paris. Photo © Réunion des Musées Nationaux/Art Resource, New York; **791** *top left* Aboriginal Bark painting of abstract picture of body, Lipunja. Musée des Arts Africains et Océaniens. Photo © Dagli Orti/The Art Archive; *top right The Battle of Isandhlwana* (19th century), Charles Fripp. National Army Museum, London. Photo © The Art Archive; *bottom A Sepoy (an Indian Soldier in the French Battalion) at Pondicherry* (19th century), Racinet. Photo © The Stapleton Collection/The Bridgeman Art Library; **793** Hulton|Archive/Getty Images; **794** The Granger Collection, New York; **796** *top left* Aboriginal Bark painting of abstract picture of body, Lipunja. Milingibi, Australia. Musée des Arts Africains et Oceaniens. Photo © Dagli Orti/The Art Archive; *top right The Battle of Isandhlwana* (19th century), Charles Fripp. National Army Museum, London. Photo © The Art Archive; **798** © Corbis; **799** The Granger Collection, New York.

Chapter 28

802 © Bettmann/Corbis; **803** *top left* © Corbis; *bottom left* Union Flag with portrait of Queen Victoria and British Colonies. The Bodleian Library, Oxford, England, John Johnson Collection (Printed Fabrics 1). Photo © The Bodleian Library/The Art Archive; *top right* © Corbis; **804** © Historical Picture Archive/Corbis; **805** *top left View of Landscape* (18th–19th century), Katsushika Hokusai. Oriental Art Museum, Genoa, Italy. Photo © Dagli Orti/The Art Archive; *top right* © Archivo Iconografico, S.A./Corbis; **806** © David Lawrence/Corbis; **807** The Granger Collection, New York; **809** © SuperStock, Inc.; **810** *top left View of Landscape* (18th–19th century), Katsushika Hokusai. Oriental Art Museum, Genoa, Italy. Photo © Dagli Orti/The Art Archive; *top right* © Archivo Iconografico, S.A./Corbis; **811** *left* The Granger Collection, New York; *right* © Bettmann/Corbis; **812** Mary Evans Picture Library; **814** *left* © Sakamoto Photo Research Laboratory/Corbis; *top right* Photo by Fumi Bull. Courtesy David Bull; *center right* Photo by Fumi Bull. Courtesy David Bull; *bottom right* Photo by Fumi Bull. Courtesy David Bull; **815** *top* © Historical Picture Archive/Corbis; *bottom* Photo by Fumi Bull. Courtesy David Bull; **816** *top left View of Landscape* (18th–19th century), Katsushika Hokusai. Oriental Art Museum, Genoa, Italy. Photo © Dagli Orti/The Art Archive; *top right* © Archivo Iconografico, S.A./Corbis; **817** *top* © Bettmann/Corbis; *bottom* © Underwood & Underwood/Corbis; **818** The Granger Collection, New York; **820** © Danny Lehman/Corbis; **821** The Granger Collection, New York; **822** *top left View of Landscape* (18th–19th century), Katsushika Hokusai. Oriental Art Museum, Genoa, Italy. Photo © Dagli Orti/The Art Archive; *top right* © Archivo Iconografico, S.A./Corbis; *bottom right* The Granger Collection, New York; **823** © Bettmann/Corbis; **824** The Granger Collection, New York; **825** *Portrait of Porfirio Diaz.* Antochiw Collection, Mexico. Photo © Mireille Vautier/The Art Archive; **826** *Emiliano Zapata* (19th–20th century), unknown artist. National History Museum, Mexico City. Photo © Dagli Orti/The Art Archive; **830** *top left, right* The Granger Collection, New York; *bottom* © Bettmann/Corbis; **831** *top, bottom* © Bettmann/Corbis; **833** © Corbis; **834** © Bettmann/Corbis; **835** The Granger Collection, New York.

Art and Photography Credits (Cont.)

UNIT SEVEN

836–837 On the River Yser. Belgium, French troops crossing over pontoon bridges. August, 1917. Musée de L'Armée, Paris. Photo © Dagli Orti/Art Archive.

Chapter 29

838 *top* © The Image Bank/Getty Images; *bottom* © Bettmann/Corbis; **839** *left* Mary Evans Picture Library; *center* © Bettmann/Corbis; *right* © Bettmann/Corbis; **840** Library of Congress; **841** *top left* © Bettmann/Corbis; *top right For King and Country* (20th century), E. F. Skinner. Royal Collection, United Kingdom. Photo by Eileen Tweedy/The Art Archive; **842** Mary Evans/Weimar Archive; **845** *top left* © Bettmann/Corbis; *top right For King and Country* (20th century), E. F. Skinner. Royal Collection, United Kingdom. Photo by Eileen Tweedy/The Art Archive; **847** © Corbis; **848** *top* © Popperfoto; *bottom* Hulton|Archive/Getty Images; **849** © Hulton-Deutsch Collection/Corbis; **850** top © Hulton-Deutsch Collection/Corbis; *bottom* © Fraser May; **851** *top left* © Bettmann/Corbis; *top right For King and Country* (20th century), E. F. Skinner. Royal Collection, United Kingdom. Photo by Eileen Tweedy/The Art Archive; **853** © Bettmann/Corbis; **854** © Corbis; **857** Library of Congress; **858** *top left* © Bettmann/Corbis; *top right For King and Country* (20th century), E. F. Skinner. Royal Collection, United Kingdom. Photo by Eileen Tweedy/The Art Archive; **859** *top Thomas Woodrow Wilson* (1921), Edmund Charles Tarbell. National Portrait Gallery, Smithsonian Institution. Photo © National Portrait Gallery, Smithsonian Institution/Art Resource, New York; *bottom Portrait of George Clemenceau* (1879–1880), Edouard Manet. Musée d'Orsay, Paris. Photo © Erich Lessing/Art Resource, New York; **863** Library of Congress.

Chapter 30

864 *top* © Bettmann/Corbis; *bottom* © The Flag Institute; **865** *left* © Elliott & Fry/Hulton-Deutsch Collection/Getty Images; *center* Hulton|Archive/Getty Images; *right* © AFP/Corbis; **866** *left* Hulton|Archive/Getty Images; *right* © Bettmann/Corbis; **867** *top left* © Swim Ink/Corbis; *top right* © Patrick Field/Eye Ubiquitous/Corbis; *bottom* © Archivo Iconografico, S.A./Corbis; **868** © Bettmann/Corbis; **869** © 2003 Tass/Sovfoto; **870** Mapping Specialists; **871** Itar-Tass/Sovfoto; **872** *left* © Archivo Iconografico, S.A./Corbis; *right* © Bettmann/Corbis; **876** © Bettmann/Corbis; **877** David King Collection, London; **879** Itar-Tass/Sovfoto; **880** *top left, top right* Collection of the International Institute of Social History, Amsterdam, Netherlands; *bottom* CTK/Eastfoto; **881** David King Collection, London; **882** *top left* © Swim Ink/Corbis; *top right* © Patrick Field/Eye Ubiquitous/Corbis; *bottom* Hulton|Archive/Getty Images; **883** *inset* Photo by Sidney D. Gamble; *bottom* © Peter Turnley/Corbis; **884** © Corbis; **885** *top right* From *Chinese Communist Sketches and Autobiographies of the Old Guard: Red Dust* by Nym Wales. June 1972. Greenwood Publishing Group; *bottom left* AP/Wide World Photos; *bottom right* © Rene Burri/Magnum Photos; **886** Hulton|Archive/Getty Images; **887** *top left* © Swim Ink/Corbis; *top left* © Patrick Field/Eye Ubiquitous/Corbis; *bottom* © Bettmann/Corbis; **889** *top* Margaret Bourke-White/Time Life Pictures/Getty Images; *inset* © The Flag Institute; **890** © Hulton-Deutsch Collection/Corbis; **892** *left to right* © Bettmann/Corbis; David King Collection, London; Hulton|Archive/Getty Images; Hulton|Archive/Getty Images; © Bettmann/Corbis; © Hulton-Deutsch Collection/Corbis.

Chapter 31

894 *top* Hulton|Archive/Getty Images; *bottom* Library of Congress; **895** *left* Roger-Viollet; *right* © Hulton-Deutsch Collection/Corbis; **896** © 1995 Chicago Historical Society; **897** *top left* Chicago Historical Society; *top right* *Life* cover (July 1, 1926) Fred Cooper; **898** AP/Wide World Photos; **899** *The Persistence of Memory* (1931), Salvador Dali. Oil on canvas, 9 1/2" x 13" (162.1934). The Museum of Modern Art, New York. Given anonymously. © 2003 Salvador Dali, Gala-Salvador Dali Foundation/Artists Rights Society (ARS), New York. Digital Image © The Museum of Modern Art/Licensed by Scala/Art Resource, New York; **900** The Granger Collection, New York; **901** © Bettmann/Corbis; **902** *left* The Granger Collection, New York; *right* © Schenectady Museum/ Hall of Electrical History Foundation/Corbis; **903** *top* The Granger Collection, New York; *center* © Schenectady Museum/ Hall of Electrical History Foundation/Corbis; *bottom* The Granger Collection, New York; **904** *top left* Chicago Historical Society; *top right Life* cover (July 1, 1926) Fred Cooper; **905** Hulton|Archive/Getty Images; **907** © Museum of the City of New York; **909** The Granger Collection, New York; **910** *top left* Chicago Historical Society; *top right Life* cover (July 1, 1926) Fred Cooper; **911** Hulton|Archive/Getty Images; **912** *top* Hulton|Archive/Getty Images; *bottom* Hulton|Archive/Getty Images; **913** © Getty Images; **914** © Bettmann/Corbis; **915** *top left* Chicago Historical Society; *top right Life* cover (July 1, 1926) Fred Cooper; **918** *top* © Corbis; *bottom* The Granger Collection, New York; **919** Hulton|Archive/Getty Images; **921** © Bettmann/Corbis.

Chapter 32

922 *left* The Granger Collection, New York; *right* © Museum of Flight/Corbis; **923** *top* © Bettmann/Corbis; *bottom* U.S. Air Force; **924** German planes bombing London, England (1940), *La Domenica del Corriere.* Photo © Dagli Orti/Art Archive; **925** *top left* Hulton|Archive/Getty Images; *top right* © KJ Historical/Corbis; **927** The Granger Collection, New York; **928** © William Vandivert/Getty Images; **929** Photo © The Art Archive; **931** *top left* Hulton|Archive/Getty Images; *top right* © KJ Historical/Corbis; **932** © UPI/Bettmann/Corbis; **933** The Granger Collection, New York; **934** © Bettmann/Corbis; **935** AP/Wide World Photos; **936** *top left* Hulton|Archive/Getty Images; *top right* © KJ Historical/Corbis; **937** *top* Courtesy of the Spertus Museum, Chicago; *bottom* © Hulton-Deutsch Collection/Corbis; **938** Courtesy of the United States Holocaust Memorial Museum Photo Archives; **940** *top left* Hulton|Archive/Getty Images; *top right* © KJ Historical/Corbis; **941** Hulton|Archive/Getty Images; **943** The Advertising Archive Ltd; **944** © Bettmann/Corbis; **945** Hulton|Archive/Getty Images; **946** *top left* © UPI/Bettmann/Corbis; *top right* U.S. Air Force; *bottom* Photo of aftermath of bombing of Nagasaki, August 10, 1945, by Yosuke Yamahata. Photo restoration by TX Unlimited, San Francisco; **947** © Bettmann/Corbis; **948** *top left* Hulton|Archive/Getty Images; *right* © KJ Historical/Corbis; **950** © AFP/Corbis; **951** AP/Wide World Photos. **954** *top left* © Bettmann/Corbis; *top right, bottom right* Hulton|Archive/Getty Images; *bottom left* © Corbis; **955** *top center right* © Corbis; *bottom* National Air and Space Museum/Smithsonian Institution; **956** *top* Williams Vandivert/Getty News Images; *bottom* © Bettmann/Corbis; **959** © Hulton-Deutsch Collection/Corbis.

UNIT 8

960–961 © Jacques Langevin/Corbis Sygma.

Chapter 33

962 *top* © Wally McNamee/Corbis; *bottom* © The Flag Institute; **963** *left* NASA; *center* © Peter Turnley/Corbis; *right* © David Turnley/Corbis; **964** *left* © Bettmann/Corbis; *right* © Geoffrey Clements/Corbis; **965** *top left* © Peter Turnley/Corbis; *top right* NASA; *bottom* Imperial War Museum. Photo © Art Archive; **967** Tom Little/Nashville Tennessean; **969** ©

UPI/Bettmann/Corbis; **971** *top, bottom center* NASA; *bottom left* Tass/Sovfoto; **972** *top left* © Peter Turnley/Corbis; *top right* NASA **973** *left* © Corbis; *right* © Roman Soumar/Corbis; **974** Hulton|Archive/Getty Images; **975** © Bettmann/Corbis; **976** *top left* © Peter Turnley/Corbis; *top right* NASA; *bottom* Hulton|Archive/Getty Images; **978** Hulton|Archive/Getty Images; **979** *top* USAF/TRH Pictures; *center* © Bettmann/Corbis; *bottom* Nik Wheeler/Black Star; **980** © Stone Les/Corbis Sygma; **981** © Catherine Karnow/Corbis; **982** *top left* © Peter Turnley/Corbis; *top right* NASA; **983** © Bettmann/Corbis; **985** © Wally McNamee/Corbis; **986** *right, left* © Alain Mingam/Getty News Services; **987** AP/Wide World Photos; **988** *top left* © Peter Turnley/Corbis; *top right* NASA; **989** *left* Sovfoto/PictureQuest; *center* AP/Wide World Photos; *right* © Peter Turnley/Corbis; **990** © Wally McNamee/Corbis; **991** Collection of David J. and Janice L. Frent.

Chapter 34

994 *left* AP/ Wide World Photos; *right* © Black Star; **995** AP/Wide World Photos; **996** *top left, bottom left, bottom right* AP/Wide World Photos; *bottom right* © Liba Taylor/Corbis; *center* © Gilbert Liz/Corbis Sygma; **997** *top left* © SuperStock, Inc.; *top right* © Steve Vidler/SuperStock, Inc.; **999** © AFP/Corbis; **1000** © Hulton-Deutsch Collection/Corbis; **1001** *top left* © 1979 Romano Cagnoni/Black Star; *top right* © Gamma; *bottom left* Margaret Bourke-White/Life Magazine©Time, Inc.; *bottom center* © 1968 Fred Mayer/Magnum Photos; *bottom right* © Gamma; **1002** © Nik Wheeler/Corbis; **1003** © Nokelsberg/Getty News Images; **1004** *top left* © SuperStock, Inc.; *top right* © Steve Vidler/SuperStock, Inc.; **1006** © Alison Wright/Corbis; **1007** © Paul Russell/Corbis; **1008** © AFP/Corbis; **1009** AP/Worldwide Photos; **1010** *top* © Jack Fields/Corbis; *bottom left* AP/Wide World Photos; *bottom right* © Jose Fuste Raga/Corbis; **1011** *top* © Steve Raymer/Corbis; *bottom* © ML Sinibaldi/Corbis; **1012** *top left* © SuperStock, Inc.; *top right* © Steve Vidler/SuperStock, Inc.; **1013** AP/Wide World Photos; **1015, 1016** © Reuters NewMedia Inc./Corbis; **1017** *top left* © SuperStock, Inc.; *top right* © Steve Vidler/SuperStock, Inc.; **1019, 1020** © Wally McNamee/Corbis; **1021** *left* © Peter Turnley/Corbis; *right* AP/Wide World Photos; **1022** AP/Wide World Photos; **1023** Time Inc./Time Life Pictures/Getty Images; **1024** *top left* © SuperStock, Inc.; *top right* © Steve Vidler/SuperStock, Inc.; **1025** *top* © Dean Conger/Corbis; *bottom* © Tiziana and Gianni Baldizzone/Corbis; **1026** © Reuters NewMedia Inc./Corbis; **1027** © Ahmad Masood/Reuters/Corbis; **1029** By permission of Bob Gorrell and Creators Syndicate, Inc.

Chapter 35

1030 *top* © Bettmann/Corbis; *bottom* Hulton|Archive/Getty Images; **1031** *left* © Wally McNamee/Corbis; *right* © Bettmann/Corbis; **1032** AP/Wide World Photos; **1037** © 2001 The New Yorker Collection from cartoonbank.com. All Rights Reserved; **1038** AP/Wide World Photos; **1039** © Bettmann/Corbis; **1040** *top left* © Owen Franken/Corbis; *top right* AP/Wide World Photos; **1042** © Greenpeace/Corbis Sygma; **1043** © David Turnley/Corbis; **1044** *top* © David Turnley/Corbis; *bottom* AP/Wide World Photos; **1046** *top left* © Owen Franken/Corbis; *top right* AP/Wide World Photos; **1047** Jeff Stahler. Reprinted by permission of Newspaper Enterprise Association, Inc.; **1048** *top* © Peter Turnley/Corbis; *bottom* © Peter Turnley/Corbis; **1050** AP/Wide World Photos; **1051** © Ron Sachs/Corbis; **1052** *top left* © Owen Franken/Corbis; *top right* AP/Wide World Photos; **1053** © Andreas Springer/Ullstein Bilderdienst, Berlin; **1056** © Chris Rainier/Corbis; **1059** *left* © Owen Franken/Corbis; *right* AP/Wide World Photos; **1060** © Bettmann/Corbis; **1061** AP/Wide World Photos; **1062** © Reuters NewMedia Inc./Corbis; **1063** AP/Wide World Photos; **1064** *top* Nick Sharp/Reuters Media; *bottom* AP/Wide World Photos; **1065** *top left* AP/Wide World Photos; *top right* © Gilles Peress/Magnum Photos; *bottom* © Peter Turnley/Corbis; **1067** © 1989 Tony Auth, *Philadelphia Inquirer*/Universal Press Syndicate.

Chapter 36

1068 *left* © Photodisc/Getty Images; *right* © Bettmann/Corbis; **1069** © AFP/Corbis; **1070** © Imtek Imagineering/Masterfile; *top left inset* AP/Wide World Photos; *bottom left inset* © AFP/Corbis; *top right inset* © Getty Images; *bottom right inset* © Reuters NewMedia Inc./Corbis; **1071** *top left* © Kelly Harriger/Corbis; *top right* © Stocktrek/Corbis; **1072** *top* © Corbis/Sygma; *bottom* © Peter Kornicker/Corbis; **1075** *top left* © Kelly Harriger/Corbis; *top right* © Stocktrek/Corbis; **1079** © Peter Turnley/Corbis; **1080** *top* NASA; *bottom* NASA; **1081** © Chris Madden; **1082** *top left* © Kelly Harriger/Corbis; *top right* © Stocktrek/Corbis; **1083** AP/Wide World Photos; **1084** AP/Wide World Photos; **1086** © Reuters NewMedia Inc./Corbis; **1087** *top left* © Kelly Harriger/Corbis; *top right* © Stocktrek/Corbis; **1088** © Tokyo Shimbum/Corbis Sygma; **1090** *left* AP/Wide World Photos; *right* © Reuters NewMedia Inc./Corbis; **1091** © AFP/Corbis; **1092** AP/Wide World Photos; **1093** *top left* © Kelly Harriger/Corbis; *top right* © Stocktrek/Corbis; **1094–1095** © John Marshall/Corbis Sygma; **1094** AP/Wide World Photos; **1095** AP/Wide World Photos; **1096** *right* © Reuters NewMedia Inc./Corbis; *left* AP/Wide World Photos. **1100** *top* AP/Wide World Photos; *bottom* © Bettmann/Corbis; **1101** *top* © AFP/Corbis; *center* © Keith Dannemiller/Corbis Saba; *bottom* AP/Wide World Photos; **1103** *top to bottom* © Rick Gayle/Corbis; © Michele Burgess/SuperStock,Inc.; Getty Images; Getty Images; © Firefly Productions/Corbis; **1104** *top left* Getty Images; *top right* © AFP/Corbis; *bottom* © Keith Dannemiller/Corbis; **1105** *top* © AFP/Corbis; *bottom* Photo by Mark Wilson/Getty Images.

End Matter

R23 *left La maraîchère* [Woman of the French Revolution]. Jacques Louis David. Musée de la Ville de Paris, Musée Carnavalet, Paris. Photo © Giraudon/Art Resource, New York; *right Marie Antoinette,* Jacques Gautier d'Agoty. Château, Versailles, France. Photo © Giraudon/Art Resource, New York; **R24** PBS History screen shot Courtesy of PBS ONLINE ® PBS has not authorized, sponsored, or endorsed, or approved this publication and it is not responsible for its content. All other product names and/or logos are trademarks of their respective owners. **R27** *"Il faut esperer que le jeu finira bientôt."* Color engraving, 18th century. Musée de la Ville de Paris, Musée Carnavalet, Paris. Photo by Bulloz © Réunion des Musées Nationaux /Art Resource, New York; **R29** © Szabo/Rothco; **R40** The Aryan God of War, Indra, seated on an elephant (about 1825). Probably Trichinopoly. Southern India. Victoria and Albert Museum, London. Photo © Victoria and Albert Museum, London/Art Resource, New York; **R41** The Granger Collection, New York; **R42** © Stapleton Collection/Corbis; **R43** Bust of Pericles (about 430 B.C.), Roman, copy of a Greek original. The British Museum, London. Photo © The Bridgeman Art Library; **R44** © Archivo Iconografico, S.A./Corbis; **R46** Seljuk-style Koran (12th–13th century), Islamic School. Museum of the Holy Ma'sumeh Shrine, Qom, Iran. Photo © The Bridgeman Art Library; **R48** © Bettmann/Corbis; **R50, R51** © Archivo Iconografico, S.A./Corbis; **R52** © Bettmann/Corbis; **R53** *Mary Wollstonecraft,* John Opie. Picture Library/National Portrait Gallery, London; **R54** *Self-Portrait in a Straw Hat,* Marie-Louise Elisabeth Vigée-Lebrun © National Gallery Collection; By kind permission of the Trustees of the National Gallery, London/Corbis; **R56** Library of Congress; **R57, R58** © Bettmann/Corbis; **R59** © Mitchell Gerber/Corbis; **R60** National Archives; **R61** © Jacques M. Chenet/Corbis; **R62** AP/Wide World Photos; **R63** © Hulton-Deutsch Collection/Corbis; **R64** Hulton|Archive/Getty Images; **R65** © Bohemian Nomad Picturemakers/Corbis; **R66** © Hulton-Deutsch Collection/Corbis; **R67** © Corbis; **R68** © Reuters NewMedia Inc./Corbis; **R69** © Bettmann/Corbis; **R71** © Ray Juno/Corbis; **R72** © Reuters NewMedia Inc./Corbis; **R73** © AFP/Corbis.

New York State Core Curriculum for Global History and Geography

Methodology of Global History and Geography
A. History
1. Skills of historical analysis
a. Investigate differing and competing interpretations of historical theories—multiple perspectives
b. Hypothesize about why interpretations change over time
c. Explain the importance of historical evidence
2. Understand the concepts of change and continuity over time
3. The connections and interactions of people across time and space
4. Time frames and periodization
5. Roles and contributions of individuals and groups
6. Oral histories
B. Geography
1. Elements of geography
a. Human geography
b. Physical geography
c. Political geography
d. Migration
e. Trade
f. Environment and society
g. The uses of geography
2. Critical thinking skills
a. Asking and answering geographic questions
b. Analyzing theories of geography
c. Acquiring, organizing, and analyzing geographic information
3. Identifying and defining world regions
C. Economics
1. Major economic concepts (scarcity, supply/demand, opportunity costs, production, resources)
2. Economic decision making
3. The interdependence of economics and economic systems throughout the world
4. Applying critical thinking skills in making informed and well-reasoned economic decisions
D. Political science
1. The purposes of government
2. Political systems around the world
3. Political concepts of power, authority, governance, and law
4. Rights and responsibilities of citizenship across time and space
5. Critical thinking skills

a. Probing ideas and assumptions
b. Posing and answering analytical questions
c. Assuming a skeptical attitude toward questionable political statements
d. Evaluating evidence and forming rational conclusions
e. Developing participatory skills
UNIT ONE: ANCIENT WORLD—CIVILIZATIONS AND RELIGIONS (4000 BC–500 AD)
A. Early peoples
1. Human and physical geography
2. Hunters and gatherers—nomadic groups
3. Relationship to the environment
4. Migration of early human populations
a. Out of Africa
b. Other theories
5. Early government
a. Purposes
b. Decision making
c. Move toward more complex government systems
B. Neolithic Revolution and early river civilizations
1. Compare and contrast (Mesopotamia, Egypt, the Indus Valley, and Yellow River civilizations)
a. Human and physical geography of early river civilizations
b. Traditional economies
c. Political systems
d. Social structures and urbanization
e. Contributions
1) Writing systems
2) Belief systems
3) Early technology—irrigation, tools, weapons
4) Architecture
5) Legal systems—Code of Hammurabi
2. Identify demographic patterns of early civilizations and movement of people—Bantu migration (500 BC–1500 AD)
a. Human and physical geography
b. Causes of migration
c. Impact on other areas of Africa
C. Classical civilizations
1. Chinese civilization
a. Human and physical geography
b. Chinese contributions (engineering, tools, writing, silk, bronzes, government system)
c. Dynastic cycles
d. Mandate of Heaven
2. Greek civilization
a. Human and physical geography

b.	The rise of city-states—Athens/Sparta
c.	Contributions: art, architecture, philosophy, science—Plato, Socrates, Aristotle
d.	Growth of democracy in Athens versus the Spartan political system
e.	Alexander the Great and Hellenistic culture—cultural diffusion
3.	**Roman Republic**
a.	Human and physical geography
b.	Contributions—law (Twelve Tables), architecture, literature, roads, bridges
4.	**Indian (Maurya) Empire**
a.	Human and physical geography (monsoons)
b.	Contributions—government system
5.	**Rise of agrarian civilizations in Mesoamerica—Mayan (200 BC–900 AD)**
a.	Human and physical geography
b.	Contributions (mathematics, astronomy, science, arts, architecture, and technology)
c.	Role of maize
d.	Religion
6.	**The status and role of women in classical civilizations**
7.	**The growth of global trade routes in classical civilizations**
a.	Phoenician trade routes
b.	Silk Road
c.	Maritime and overland trade routes
1)	Linking Africa and Eurasia
2)	Linking China, Korea, and Japan
D.	**The rise and fall of great empires**
1.	**Han Dynasty**
a.	Human and physical geography
b.	Factors leading to growth
c.	Contributions
d.	Causes of decline
e.	Role of migrating nomadic groups from Central Asia
2.	**Roman Empire**
a.	Human and physical geography
b.	Factors leading to growth (engineering, empire building, trade)
c.	Contributions
d.	Causes of decline
e.	Role of migrating nomadic groups from Central Asia
f.	Pax Romana
E.	**The emergence and spread of belief systems**
1.	**Place of origin and major beliefs**
a.	Animism—African
b.	Hinduism
c.	Buddhism

d. Chinese philosophies (Confucianism, Daoism)
e. Judaism
f. Christianity
g. Islam
h. Legalism
i. Shintoism
j. Jainism
2. Expansion of Christianity, Islam, Confucianism, and Buddhism
UNIT TWO: EXPANDING ZONES OF EXCHANGE AND ENCOUNTER (500–1200)
A. Gupta Empire (320–550 AD)
1. Human and physical geography
2. Artistic, scientific, and mathematical contributions
3. Ties to Hinduism
4. Organizational structure
B. Tang and Song Dynasty (618–1126 AD)
1. Human and physical geography
2. Contributions
3. Chinese influence on Korea and Japan
4. Cultural flowering
5. Growth of commerce and trade
C. Byzantine Empire (330–1453 AD)
1. Human and physical geography
2. Achievements (law–Justinian Code, engineering, art, and commerce)
3. The Orthodox Christian Church
4. Political structure and Justinian Code
5. Role in preserving and transmitting Greek and Roman cultures
6. Impact on Russia and Eastern Europe
D. Early Russia
1. Human and physical geography
2. Trade
3. Kiev
4. Russian Orthodox Church
E. The spread of Islam to Europe, Asia, and Africa
1. Human and physical geography
2. Organizational structure
3. The development of Islamic law and its impact
4. Social class: women and slavery in Muslim society
5. Position of "people of the book"
6. The golden age of Islam
a. Contributions to mathematics, science, medicine, art, architecture, and literature

b. Role in preserving Greek and Roman culture
c. Islamic Spain
7. Trade
F. Medieval Europe (500–1400)
1. Human and physical geography
2. Frankish Empire—Charlemagne
3. Manorialism
4. Feudalism
a. Social hierarchy and stratification
b. Role of men and women
5. Spiritual and secular role of the Church
6. Monastic centers of learning
7. Anti-Semitism
8. Art and architecture
G. Crusades
1. Causes
2. Impacts on Southwest Asia, Byzantium, and Europe
3. Perspectives
4. Key individuals—Urban II, Saladin, and Richard the Lion-Hearted
UNIT THREE: GLOBAL INTERACTIONS (1200–1650)
A. Early Japanese history and feudalism
1. Human and physical geography
2. Early traditions (Shintoism)
3. Ties with China and Korea: cultural diffusion, Buddhism, and Confucianism
4. Tokugawa Shogunate
5. Social hierarchy and stratification
6. Comparison to European feudalism
7. Zen Buddhism
B. The rise and fall of the Mongols and their impact on Eurasia
1. Human and physical geography
2. Origins—Central Asian nomadic tribes
3. The Yuan Dynasty: a foreign non-Chinese dynasty
4. Extent of empire under Ghengis Khan and Kublai Khan
5. Impact on Central Asia, China, Korea, Europe, India, Southwest Asia
6. Impact on the rise of Moscow
7. Interaction with the West and global trade, Pax Mongolia (e.g., Marco Polo)
8. Causes of decline
C. Global trade and interactions
1. Resurgence of Europe
a. Hanseatic League and Italian city-states

	b. Trade fairs and towns
	c. Medieval guilds
	d. Commercial revolution
	2. Major trading centers–Nanjing/Calicut/Mogadishu/Venice
	3. Ibn Battuta
	4. Expansion of the Portuguese spice trade to Southeast Asia and its impact on Asia and Europe
D.	**Rise and fall of African civilizations: Ghana, Mali, Axum, and Songhai empires**
	1. Human and physical geography
	2. Organizational structure
	3. Contributions
	4. Roles in global trade routes
	5. Spread and impact of Islam–Mansa Musa
	6. Timbuktu and African trade routes
E.	**Social, economic, and political impacts of the plague on Eurasia and Africa**
F.	**Renaissance and humanism**
	1. Human and physical geography
	2. Shift in worldview–otherworldly to secular
	3. Greco-Roman revival (interest in humanism)
	4. Art and architecture (e.g., da Vinci and Michelangelo)
	5. Literature (e.g., Dante, Cervantes, Shakespeare)
	6. Political science (e.g., Machiavelli)
	7. New scientific and technological innovations (Gutenberg's moveable type printing press, cartography, naval engineering, and navigational and nautical devices)
G.	**Reformation and Counter Reformation**
	1. Human and physical geography
	2. Martin Luther's *Ninety-Five Theses:* the challenge to the power and authority of the Roman Catholic Church
	3. Anti-Semitic laws and policies
	4. Henry VIII and the English Reformation
	5. Calvin and other reformers
	6. Counter Reformation (Ignatius Loyola, Council of Trent)
	7. Roles of men and women within the Christian churches
	8. Religious wars in Europe: causes and impacts
H.	**The rise and impact of European nation-states/decline of feudalism Case studies: England–Elizabeth I: France–Joan of Arc**
	a. Forces moving toward centralization
	b. Role of nationalism
UNIT FOUR: THE FIRST GLOBAL AGE (1450–1770)	
A.	**The Ming Dynasty (1368–1644)**
	1. Human and physical geography
	2. Restoration of Chinese rule, Chinese world vision
	3. The impact of China on East Asia and Southeast Asia

4. China's relationship with the West
5. Contributions
6. Expansion of trade (Zheng He, 1405–1433)
B. The impact of the Ottoman Empire on the Middle East and Europe
1. Human and physical geography
2. Contributions
3. Suleiman I (the Magnificent, the Lawgiver)
4. Disruption of established trade routes and European search for new ones
5. Limits of Ottoman Europe
C. Spain and Portugal on the eve of the encounter
1. Human and physical geography
2. Reconquista under Ferdinand and Isabella
3. Expulsion of Moors and Jews
4. Exploration and overseas expansion
a. Columbus
b. Magellan circumnavigates the globe
D. The rise of Mesoamerican empires: Aztec and Incan empires before 1500
1. Human and physical geography
2. Organizational structure
3. Contributions
4. Trade
E. The encounter between Europeans and the peoples of Africa, the Americas, and Asia Case study: The Columbian exchange
1. Human and physical geography
2. European competition for colonies in the Americas, Africa, East Asia, and Southeast Asia—The "old imperialism"
3. Global demographic shifts Case study: The triangular trade and slavery
4. The extent of European expansionism
5. European mercantilism
6. Spanish colonialism and the introduction of the Encomienda system to Latin America
7. Dutch colonization in East Asia (Japan and Indonesia)
8. Exchange of food and disease
F. Political ideologies: global absolutism
1. Human and physical geography
2. Thomas Hobbes, *The Leviathan*
3. Jacques-Benigne Bossuet: Absolutism and Divine right theory
4. Case studies: Akbar the Great, Suleiman the Magnificent, Philip II, Louis XIV, Ivan the Terrible, and Peter the Great
G. The response to absolutism: The rise of parliamentary democracy in England
1. Background—Magna Carta
2. Divine Right of Monarchy—Stuart rule

3. Puritan Revolution—Oliver Cromwell

4. Glorious Revolution—John Locke and the English Bill of Rights

UNIT FIVE: AN AGE OF REVOLUTION (1750–1914)

A. The Scientific Revolution

1. The development of scientific methods

2. The work of Copernicus, Galileo, Newton, and Descartes

B. The Enlightenment in Europe

1. The writings of Locke, Voltaire, Rousseau, and Montesquieu

2. The impact of the Enlightenment on nationalism and democracy

3. The enlightened despots—Maria Theresa and Catherine the Great

C. Political revolutions

1. Human and physical geography of revolutions

2. American Revolution

a. Impact of the Enlightenment on the American Revolution

b. Impact of the American Revolution on other revolutions

3. French Revolution

a. Causes

b. Key individuals (Robespierre and Louis XVI)

c. Impact on France and other nations

d. Rise to power of Napoleon and his impact (Napoleonic Code)

4. Independence movements in Latin America Case studies: Simon Bolivar, Toussaint L'Ouverture, José de San Martín

a. Causes

b. Impacts

D. The reaction against revolutionary ideas

1. Human and physical geography

2. Balance of power politics and the Congress of Vienna (Klemens von Metternich)

3. Revolutions of 1848

4. Russian absolutism: reforms and expansion

a. Impact of the French Revolution and Napoleon

b. 19th-century Russian serfdom

c. Expansion of Russia into Siberia

E. Latin America: The failure of democracy and the search for stability

1. Human and physical geography

2. Roles of social classes: land-holding elite, creoles, mestizos, native peoples, and slaves

3. Roles of the Church and military

4. Role of cash crop economies in a global market

5. The Mexican Revolution (1910–1930)

a. Cause and effect

b. Roles of Porfirio Diaz, Francisco "Pancho" Villa, and Emiliano Zapata

c. Economic and social nationalism

F. Global nationalism

- **1. Human and physical geography**
- **2. Role in political revolutions**
- **3. Force for unity and self-determination**
  - a. Unification of Italy and Germany (Camillo Cavour, Otto von Bismarck)
  - b. Asian and Middle Eastern nationalism
    - 1) India (Indian National Congress, Moslem League)
    - 2) Turkey—Young Turks
- **4. Zionism**
- **5. Force leading to conflicts**
  - a. Balkans before World War I
  - b. Ottoman Empire as the pawn of European powers

G. Economic and social revolutions

- **1. Human and physical geography**
- **2. Agrarian revolution**
- **3. The British Industrial Revolution**
  - a. Capitalism and a market economy
  - b. Factory system
  - c. Shift from mercantilism to laissez-faire economics—Adam Smith, *The Wealth of Nations*
  - d. Changes in social classes
  - e. Changing roles of men, women, and children
  - f. Urbanization
  - g. Responses to industrialization
    - 1) Utopian reform—Robert Owen
    - 2) Legislative reform
    - 3) Role of unions
    - 4) Karl Marx and Friedrich Engels and command economies
    - 5) Sadler Report and reform legislation
    - 6) Parliamentary reforms—expansion of suffrage
    - 7) Writers (Dickens and Zola)
    - 8) Global migrations (19th century)
    - 9) Writings of Thomas Malthus (*Essay on the Principles of Population*)
- **3. Mass starvation in Ireland (1845–1850)**
  - a. Growth of Irish nationalism
  - b. Global migration

H. Imperialism

- **1. Reasons for imperialism—nationalistic, political, economic, "The White Man's Burden", Social Darwinism**
- **2. Spatial characteristics—"new imperialism"**
- **3. British in India**
  - a. British East India Company
  - b. Sepoy Mutiny

4.	**British, French, Belgians, and Germans in Africa**
a.	Scramble for Africa
b.	The Congress of Berlin
c.	African resistance—Zulu Empire
d.	Boer War
e.	Cecil Rhodes
f.	19th-century anti-slave trade legislation
5.	**European spheres of influence in China**
a.	Opium Wars (1839–1842 and 1858–1860) and the Treaty of Nanjing
1)	Unequal treaties
2)	Extraterritoriality
b.	Boxer Rebellion
c.	Sun Yat-sen (Sun Yixian) and the Chinese Revolution (1910–1911)
6.	**Multiple perspectives toward imperialism**
a.	Immediate/long-term changes made under European rule
b.	Long-term effects in Europe and the rest of the world
I.	**Japan and the Meiji restoration**
1.	**Human and physical geography**
2.	**The opening of Japan**
a.	Commodore Matthew Perry
b.	Impact upon Japan of Treaty of Kanagawa
3.	**Modernization, industrialization**
4.	**Japan as an imperialist power**
a.	First Sino-Japanese War (1894–1895)
b.	Russo-Japanese War
c.	Annexation of Korea
d.	Dependence on world market
UNIT SIX: A HALF CENTURY OF CRISIS AND ACHIEVEMENT (1900–1945)	
A.	**World War I**
1.	**Europe: the physical setting**
2.	**Causes**
3.	**Impacts**
4.	**Effects of scientific/technological advances on warfare**
5.	**Armenian Massacre**
6.	**Collapse of the Ottoman Empire**
7.	**The war as reflected in literature, art, and propaganda**
B.	**Revolution and change in Russia—causes and impacts**
1.	**Czar Nicholas II**
2.	**The Revolution of 1905**
3.	**March Revolution and provisional government**

4. **Bolshevik Revolution**
5. **V.I. Lenin's rule in Russia**
6. **Stalin and the rise of a modern totalitarian state: industrialization, command economy, collectivization**
7. **Russification of ethnic republics**
8. **Forced famine in Ukraine**
9. **Reign of Terror**
C. Between the wars
1. **Human and physical geography**
2. **Treaty of Versailles and the League of Nations**
3. **Modernization and westernization of a secular Turkey—Kemal Atatürk**
4. **Women's suffrage movement**
5. **Great Depression—causes and impacts**
6. **Weimar Republic and the rise of fascism as an aftermath of World War I**
7. **Japanese militarism and imperialism**
a. Manchuria, 1931
b. Second Sino-Japanese War (1937-1945)
8. **Policy of appeasement—Munich Pact**
9. **Colonial response to European imperialism Case studies: Mohandas Gandhi, Reza Khan, Jiang Jieshi (Chiang Kaishek), Mao Zedong.; Zionism, Arab nationalism, the Amritsar massacre—Indian nationalism, Salt March, civil disobedience**
10. **Arabic and Zionist nationalism**
D. World War II—causes and impact
1. **Human and physical geography**
2. **The Nazi and Japanese states**
3. **Key individuals—Hitler, Mussolini, Stalin, Churchill, and Roosevelt**
4. **Key events—Dunkirk, the Blitz, D-Day, Hitler's second front, the war in the Pacific**
5. **The Nazi Holocaust: the extermination of Jews, Poles, other Slavs, Gypsies, disabled, and others**
6. **Resistance**
7. **Japan's role—Nanjing, Bataan, Pearl Harbor**
8. **War in China—Long March**
9. **Impacts of technology on total war**
10. **Hiroshima and Nagasaki**
11. **War crime trials**
12. **Global spatial arrangements—post-World War II world**
UNIT SEVEN: THE 20TH CENTURY SINCE 1945
A. Cold War balance of power
1. **Human and physical geography**
2. **The world in 1945: physical setting**
3. **United States occupation of Germany and Japan**
a. The adoption of democratic systems of government
b. Economic rebuilding of Germany and Japan

4. Emergence of the superpowers
5. Political climate of the Cold War
a. Marshall Plan
b. Truman Doctrine
c. Berlin airlift and a divided Germany
d. North Atlantic Treaty Organization (NATO)/Warsaw Pact–expanding membership and role of NATO
e. Hungarian Revolt
f. Soviet invasion of Czechoslovakia
g. Nuclear weapons and space
h. Surrogate superpower rivalries Case studies: (Egypt, Congo, Angola, Chile, Iran, Iraq, Vietnam, Guatemala)
i. Role of nonaligned nations
6. Korean War
a. United States role in the division of Korea
b. Comparison of Korea and Germany
c. Conduct of the war
B. Role of the United Nations
1. Peace keeping
2. Social and economic programs
3. Contemporary social conditions
C. Economic issues in the Cold War and Post-Cold War era
1. Human and physical geography
2. A comparison of market versus command economies (Western Europe versus Soviet Union)
3. Economic recovery in Europe and Japan
a. Western Germany becomes a major economic power
b. European economic community/Common Market/ European Union–steps toward European integration
c. Japan becomes an economic superpower
4. Organization of Petroleum Exporting Countries (OPEC): oil crisis in the 1970s
5. Pacific Rim economies/economic crisis
6. North America Free Trade Agreement (NAFTA), 1997
D. Chinese Communist Revolution
1. Human and physical geography
2. Communist rise to power (1936–1949); Jiang Jieshi (Chiang Kai-shek), Mao Zedong
3. Communism under Mao Zedong
a. Great Leap Forward
b. The Cultural Revolution and the Red Guard
4. Communism under Deng Xiaoping
a. Economic reforms–Four Modernizations
1) Limited privatization
2) Dismantling of Communes
3) Introduction of "responsibility system"
4) Foreign investment

b. Fifth modernization—democracy
1) April/May 1989
2) Tiananmen Square
5. Return of Hong Kong—July 1, 1997
6. The social system in communist China versus dynastic China
E. Collapse of European imperialism
1. Human and physical geography
2. India—independence and partition
a. Political system
b. Muslim/Hindu conflicts
c. Status of the caste system
d. Roles of Mohandas Gandhi and Jawaharlal Nehru
e. Nonalignment
f. Kashmir and Punjab
3. African independence movements and Pan Africanism
a. Changing political boundaries in Africa (Nigeria, Ghana, and Kenya
b. Roles of Jomo Kenyatta and Kwame Nkrumah
c. Continuance of economic linkages with former colonial powers
d. Ethnic tensions versus nationalism: Nigeria and civil war
e. Apartheid—policy of racial separation and segregation
1) Historical circumstances
2) African National Congress
3) Leadership—Nelson Mandela, Desmond Tutu, F. W. de Klerk
f. Political and economic instability—Congo (Zaire) or any other examples
g. Ethnic tensions: Rwanda—Hutu-Tutsi
4. Southeast Asia
a. Vietnam/Ho Chi Minh
b. Cambodia/Pol Pot/Khmer Rouge
c. Aung San Suu Kyi—Myanmar
F. Conflicts and change in the Middle East
1. Human and physical geography
2. The creation of the State of Israel, Arab Palestinians, and Israel's Arab neighbors
3. Roles of individuals—Golda Meir, Yasir Arafat, Anwar Sadat, King Hussein, Yitzhak Rabin, Palestine Liberation Organization (PLO)
a. Arab-Israeli wars
b. Peace treaties
4. Role of terrorism
5. Turkey and Iraq—Kurds
6. Migration of Jews from Europe, the United States, the Soviet Union, and Africa
7. The Iranian Revolution
a. Causes and impact

b. Ayatollah Ruhollah Khomeini versus Reza Pahlavi
8. Persian Gulf War–Saddam Hussein
9. Islamic fundamentalism (Iran, Libya, Afghanistan, Algeria, Turkey)
G. Collapse of communism and the breakup of the Soviet Union
1. Human and physical geography
2. Background events, 1970 to 1987
3. Poland's Solidarity and Lech Walesa
4. Mikhail Gorbachev (perestroika and glasnost)
5. Fall of the Berlin Wall and the reunification of Germany–causes and impacts
6. Ethnic conflict in former satellite states, e.g., Kosovo, Bosnia
7. Changing political boundaries
8. Challenges faced by post-communist Russia–the world of Boris Yeltsin
H. Political and economic change in Latin America
1. Latin America: physical setting
2. Argentina
a. Peron
b. The Mothers of the Plaza De Maya
3. Fidel Castro's Cuban Revolution–causes and impact
4. Nicaragua and the Sandinistas
5. Guatemala and the indigenous peoples
6. Changing role of the Roman Catholic Church in Latin America
7. Latin American immigration to the United States
8. Return of the Panama Canal
UNIT EIGHT: GLOBAL CONNECTIONS AND INTERACTIONS
A. Social and political patterns and change
1. Human and physical geography
2. Population pressures and poverty (China, India, Africa, and Latin America)
a. One-child policy–China
b. Family planning–India
c. Mother Theresa
d. Cycles of poverty and disease
3. Migration
a. Urbanization
b. Global migration Suggested case studies: Turkish, Italian, and Russian immigration to Germany, North African immigration to France, Latin American and Asian immigration to the United States, and Hutu and Tutsis immigration
4. Modernization/tradition–finding a balance
a. Japan
b. Middle East (Saudi Arabia Egypt, Afghanistan, and Algeria)
c. African
d. Latin America

5. Scientific and technological advances	
	a. Treatment of infectious diseases
	b. Improved standard of living
6. Urbanization–use and distribution of scarce resources (Africa, India, Latin America)	
7. Status of women and children	
	a. Economic issues, e.g., child labor
	b. Social issues, e.g., abuse and access to education
	c. Political issues, e.g., participation in the political process
8. Ethnic and religious tensions: an analysis of multiple perspectives	
	a. Northern Ireland
	b. Balkans: Serbs, Croats, and Muslims
	c. Sikhs and Tamils
	d. Indonesian Christians
	e. China–Tibet
	f. Indonesia–East Timor
B. Economic issues	
1. North/South dichotomy: issues of development (post-colonialism)	
	a. Africa
	b. Latin America
2. Korea's economic miracle	
3. Economic interdependence	
4. World hunger	
C. The environment and sustainability	
1. Pollution–air, water, toxic waste (Europe)	
2. Deforestation (Amazon Basin)	
3. Desertification (Sahel)	
4. Nuclear safety (Chernobyl)	
5. Endangered species (Africa)	
D. Science and technology	
1. Information age/Computer Revolution/Internet	
2. Impact of satellites	
3. Green Revolution	
4. Space exploration	
5. Literacy and education	
6. Medical breakthroughs–disease control/life expectancy/genetics	
7. Epidemics–AIDS	
8. Nuclear proliferation	